# THE WORLD FACTBOOK

## 2010
### (CIA's 2009 Edition)

Potomac Books, Inc.'s 2010 Edition (CIA's 2009 Edition)

In general, information available as of 1 January 2009 was used in the preparation of this edition.

*The World Factbook* is prepared by the Central Intelligence Agency for the use of US Government officials, and the style, format, coverage, and content are designed to meet their specific requirements. Information is provided by Antarctic Information Program (National Science Foundation), Armed Forces Medical Intelligence Center (Department of Defense), Bureau of the Census (Department of Commerce), Bureau of Labor Statistics (Department of Labor), Central Intelligence Agency, Council of Managers of National Antarctic Programs, Defense Intelligence Agency (Department of Defense), Department of State, Fish and Wildlife Service (Department of the Interior), Maritime Administration (Department of Transportation), National Geospatial-Intelligence Agency (Department of Defense), Naval Facilities Engineering Command (Department of Defense), Office of Insular Affairs (Department of the Interior), Office of Naval Intelligence (Department of Defense), US Board on Geographic Names (Department of the Interior), US Transportation Command (Department of Defense), Oil & Gas Journal, and other public and private sources.

Potomac Books publishes a commercial version of *The World Factbook* in order to extend the limited audience reached by the CIA's publication. This annual is a valuable primary source of information, and Potomac Books seeks to make it more readily available to bookstores and libraries so that the taxpayers who fund the US government can directly benefit from this excellent effort. Potomac Books makes no claim to copyright to this publication. Potomac Books's edition differs in two minor aspects from the CIA publication. This current Potomac Books edition is identified by the year 2010, following the pattern Potomac Books uses in other annual publications. The CIA completes its volume late each year, and Potomac Books republishes it the following year. Also, as a commercial publisher, Potomac Books does not include the simple but expensive four-color maps contained in the CIA publication. The cost to the consumer would be prohibitive, and these maps are not unique and are readily available elsewhere.

ISBN 978-1-59797-541-4 (alk. paper)

Printed in the United States of America on acid-free paper that meets the American National Standards Institute Z39-48 Standard.

Potomac Books, Inc.
22841 Quicksilver Drive
Dulles, Virginia 20166

First Edition

10 9 8 7 6 5 4 3 2 1

# THE WORLD FACTBOOK
## 2010
### (CIA's 2009 Edition)

Prepared by the Central Intelligence Agency

Potomac Books, Inc.
Washington, D.C.

# A Brief History of Basic Intelligence and
## *The World Factbook*

*The Intelligence Cycle is the process by which information is acquired, converted into intelligence, and made available to policymakers.* **Information** *is raw data from any source, data that may be fragmentary, contradictory, unreliable, ambiguous, deceptive, or wrong.* **Intelligence** *is information that has been collected, integrated, evaluated, analyzed, and interpreted.* **Finished intelligence** *is the final product of the Intelligence Cycle ready to be delivered to the policymaker.*

The three types of finished intelligence are: basic, current, and estimative. Basic intelligence provides the fundamental and factual reference material on a country or issue. Current intelligence reports on new developments. Estimative intelligence judges probable outcomes. The three are mutually supportive: basic intelligence is the foundation on which the other two are constructed; current intelligence continually updates the inventory of knowledge; and estimative intelligence revises overall interpretations of country and issue prospects for guidance of basic and current intelligence. *The World Factbook, The President's Daily Brief,* and the *National Intelligence Estimates* are examples of the three types of finished intelligence.

The United States has carried on foreign intelligence activities since the days of George Washington but only since World War II have they been coordinated on a government-wide basis. Three programs have highlighted the development of coordinated basic intelligence since that time: (1) *the Joint Army Navy Intelligence Studies* (JANIS), (2) *the National Intelligence Survey* (NIS), and (3) *The World Factbook*.

During World War II, intelligence consumers realized that the production of basic intelligence by different components of the US Government resulted in a great duplication of effort and conflicting information. The Japanese attack on Pearl Harbor in 1941 brought home to leaders in Congress and the executive branch the need for integrating departmental reports to national policymakers. Detailed and coordinated information was needed not only on such major powers as Germany and Japan, but also on places of little previous interest. In the Pacific Theater, for example, the Navy and Marines had to launch amphibious operations against many islands about which information was unconfirmed or nonexistent. Intelligence authorities resolved that the United States should never again be caught unprepared.

In 1943, Gen. George B. Strong (G-2), Adm. H. C. Train (Office of Naval Intelligence - ONI), and Gen. William J. Donovan (Director of the Office of Strategic Services - OSS) decided that a joint effort should be initiated. A steering committee was appointed on 27 April 1943 that recommended the formation of a Joint Intelligence Study Publishing Board to assemble, edit, coordinate, and publish the *Joint Army Navy Intelligence Studies* (JANIS). JANIS was the first interdepartmental basic intelligence program to fulfill the needs of the US Government for an authoritative and coordinated appraisal of strategic basic intelligence. Between April 1943 and July 1947, the board published 34 JANIS studies. JANIS performed well in the war effort, and numerous letters of commendation were received, including a statement from Adm. Forrest Sherman, Chief of Staff, Pacific Ocean Areas, which said, "JANIS has become the indispensable reference work for the shore-based planners."

The need for more comprehensive basic intelligence in the postwar world was well expressed in 1946 by George S. Pettee, a noted author on national security. He wrote in *The Future of American Secret Intelligence* (Infantry Journal Press, 1946, page 46) that world leadership in peace requires even more elaborate intelligence than in war. "The conduct of peace involves all countries, all human activities - not just the enemy and his war production."

The Central Intelligence Agency was established on 26 July 1947 and officially began operating on 18 September 1947. Effective 1 October 1947, the Director of Central Intelligence assumed operational responsibility for JANIS. On 13 January 1948, the National Security Council issued Intelligence Directive (NSCID) No. 3, which authorized the *National Intelligence Survey* (NIS) program as a peacetime replacement for the wartime JANIS program. Before adequate NIS country sections could be produced, government agencies had to develop more comprehensive gazetteers and better maps. The US Board on Geographic Names (BGN) compiled the names; the Department of the Interior produced the gazetteers; and CIA produced the maps.

The Hoover Commission's Clark Committee, set up in 1954 to study the structure and administration of the CIA, reported to Congress in 1955 that: "The National Intelligence Survey is an invaluable publication which provides the essential elements of basic intelligence on all areas of the world. There will always be a continuing requirement for keeping the Survey up-to-date." The *Factbook* was created as an annual summary and update to the encyclopedic NIS studies. The first classified *Factbook* was published in August 1962, and the first unclassified version was published in June 1971. The NIS program was terminated in 1973 except for the *Factbook*, map, and gazetteer components. The 1975 *Factbook* was the first to be made available to the public with sales through the US Government Printing Office (GPO). The *Factbook* was first made available on the Internet in June 1997. The year 2009 marks the 62nd anniversary of the establishment of the Central Intelligence Agency and the 66th year of continuous basic intelligence support to the US Government by *The World Factbook* and its two predecessor programs.

# The Evolution of
## *The World Factbook*

*National Basic Intelligence Factbook* produced semiannually until 1980. Country entries include sections on Land, Water, People, Government, Economy, Communications, and Defense Forces.

**1981** – Publication becomes an annual product and is renamed *The World Factbook*. A total of 165 nations are covered on 225 pages.

**1983** – Appendices (Conversion Factors, International Organizations) first introduced.

**1984** – Appendices expanded; now include: A. The United Nations, B. Selected United Nations Organizations, C. Selected International Organizations, D. Country Membership in Selected Organizations, E. Conversion Factors.

**1987** – A new Geography section replaces the former separate Land and Water sections. UN Organizations and Selected International Organizations appendices merged into a new International Organizations appendix. First multi-color-cover *Factbook*.

**1988** – More than 40 new geographic entities added to provide complete world coverage without overlap or omission. Among the new entities are Antarctica, oceans (Arctic, Atlantic, Indian, Pacific), and the World. The front-of-the-book explanatory introduction expanded and retitled to Notes, Definitions, and Abbreviations. Two new Appendices added: Weights and Measures (in place of Conversion Factors) and a Cross-Reference List of Geographic Names. *Factbook* size reaches 300 pages.

**1989** – Economy section completely revised and now includes an Overview briefly describing a country's economy. New entries added under People, Government, and Communications.

**1990** – The Government section revised and considerably expanded with new entries.

**1991** – A new International Organizations and Groups appendix added. *Factbook* size reaches 405 pages.

**1992** – Twenty new successor state entries replace those of the Soviet Union and Yugoslavia. New countries are respectively: Armenia, Azerbaijan, Belarus, Estonia, Georgia, Kazakhstan, Kyrgyzstan, Latvia, Lithuania, Moldova, Russia, Tajikistan, Turkmenistan, Ukraine, Uzbekistan; and Bosnia and Hercegovina, Croatia, Macedonia, Serbia and Montenegro, Slovenia. Number of nations in the *Factbook* rises to 188.

**1993** – Czechoslovakia's split necessitates new Czech Republic and Slovakia entries. New Eritrea entry added after it secedes from Ethiopia. Substantial enhancements made to Geography section.

**1994** – Two new appendices address Selected International Environmental Agreements. The gross domestic product (GDP) of most developing countries changed to a purchasing power parity (PPP) basis rather than an exchange rate basis. *Factbook* size up to 512 pages.

**1995** – The GDP of all countries now presented on a PPP basis. New appendix lists estimates of GDP on an exchange rate basis. Communications category split; Railroads, Highways, Inland waterways, Pipelines, Merchant marine, and Airports entries now make up a new Transportation category. *The World Factbook* is first produced on CD-ROM.

**1996** – Maps accompanying each entry now present more detail. Flags also introduced for nearly all entities. Various new entries appear under Geography and Communications. *Factbook* abbreviations consolidated into a new Appendix A. Two new appendices present a Cross-Reference List of Country Data Codes and a Cross-Reference List of Hydrogeographic Data Codes. Geographic coordinates added to Appendix H, Cross-Reference List of Geographic Names. *Factbook* size expands by 95 pages in one year to reach 652.

**1997** – A special edition for the CIA's 50th anniversary. A schema or Guide to Country Profiles introduced. New color maps and flags now accompany each country profile. Category headings distinguished by shaded backgrounds. Number of categories expanded to nine – the current number – with the addition of an Introduction (for only a few countries) and Transnational Issues (which includes Disputes-international and Illicit drugs). *The World Factbook* introduced onto the Internet.

**1998** – The Introduction category with two entries, Current issues and Historical perspective, expanded to more countries. Last year for the production of CD-ROM versions of the *Factbook*.

**1999** – Historical perspective and Current issues entries in the Introduction category combined into a new Background statement. Several new Economy entries introduced. A new physical map of the world added to the back-of-the-book reference maps.

**2000** – A new "country profile" added on the Southern Ocean. The Background statements dramatically expanded to over 200 countries and possessions. A number of new Communications entries added.

**2001** – Background entries completed for all 267 entities in the *Factbook*. Several new HIV/AIDS entries introduced under the People category. Revision begun on individual country maps to include elevation extremes and a partial geographic grid. Weights and Measures appendix deleted.

**2002** – New entry on Distribution of Family income – Gini index added. Revision of individual country maps continued (process still ongoing as of 2007).

**2003** – In the Economy category, petroleum entries added for oil production, consumption, exports, imports, and proved reserves, as well as natural gas proved reserves.

**2004** – Additional petroleum entries included for natural gas production, consumption, exports, and imports. In the Transportation category, under Merchant marine, subfields added for foreign-owned vessels and those registered in other countries. Descriptions of the many forms of government mentioned in the *Factbook* incorporated into the Notes and Definitions.

# The Evolution of
## *The World Factbook*

---

**2005** – In the People category, a Major infectious diseases field added for countries deemed to pose a higher risk for travelers. In the Economy category, entries included for Current account balance, Investment, Public debt, and Reserves of foreign exchange and gold. The Transnational issues category expanded to include Refugees and internally displaced persons. Category headings receive distinctive colored backgrounds. These distinguishing colors are used in both the printed and online versions of the *Factbook*. Size of the printed *Factbook* reaches 702 pages.

**2006** – In the Economy category, national GDP figures now presented at Official Exchange Rates (OER) in addition to GDP at purchasing power parity (PPP).

**2007** – In the Government category, the Capital entry significantly expanded with up to four subfields, including new information having to do with time. The subfields consist of the name of the capital itself, its geographic coordinates, the time difference at the capital from coordinated universal time (UTC), and, if applicable, information on daylight saving time (DST). Where appropriate, a special note is added to highlight those countries with multiple time zones. A Trafficking in persons entry added to the Transnational issues category. A new appendix, Weights and Measures, (re)introduced to the online version of the Factbook.

**2008** – In the Geography category, two fields focus on the vital resource of water: Total renewable water resources and Freshwater withdrawal. In the Economy category, three fields added for: Stock of direct foreign investment – at home, Stock of direct foreign investment – abroad, and Market value of publicly traded shares. Concise descriptions of all major religions included in the Notes and Definitions.

**2009** – In the People category, two new fields provide information on education in terms of opportunity and resources: School Life Expectancy and Education expenditures. Additionally, the Urbanization entry expanded to include all countries. In the Economy category, five additional fields introduced: Central bank discount rate, Commercial bank prime lending rate, Stock of money, Stock of quasi money, and Stock of domestic credit. Completely redesigned Web site launched on the World Wide Web.

# Contents

# Appendixes

# Definitions and Notes

---

**Abbreviations:** This information is included in Appendix **A: Abbreviations**, which includes all abbreviations and acronyms used in the *Factbook*, with their expansions.

**Acronyms:** An acronym is an abbreviation coined from the initial letter of each successive word in a term or phrase. In general, an acronym made up solely from the first letter of the major words in the expanded form is rendered in all capital letters (NATO from North Atlantic Treaty Organization; an exception would be ASEAN for Association of Southeast Asian Nations). In general, an acronym made up of more than the first letter of the major words in the expanded form is rendered with only an initial capital letter (Comsat from Communications Satellite Corporation; an exception would be NAM from Nonaligned Movement). Hybrid forms are sometimes used to distinguish between initially identical terms (ICC for International Chamber of Commerce and ICCt for International Criminal Court).

**Administrative divisions:** This entry generally gives the numbers, designatory terms, and first-order administrative divisions as approved by the US Board on Geographic Names (BGN). Changes that have been reported but not yet acted on by the BGN are noted.

**Age structure:** This entry provides the distribution of the population according to age. Information is included by sex and age group (*0-14 years, 15-64 years, 65 years and over*). The age structure of a population affects a nation's key socioeconomic issues. Countries with young populations (high percentage under age 15) need to invest more in schools, while countries with older populations (high percentage ages 65 and over) need to invest more in the health sector. The age structure can also be used to help predict potential political issues. For example, the rapid growth of a young adult population unable to find employment can lead to unrest.

**Agriculture - products:** This entry is an ordered listing of major crops and products starting with the most important.

**Airports:** This entry gives the total number of airports or airfields recognizable from the air. The runway(s) may be paved (concrete or asphalt surfaces) or unpaved (grass, earth, sand, or gravel surfaces) and may include closed or abandoned installations. Airports or airfields that are no longer recognizable (overgrown, no facilities, etc.) are not included. Note that not all airports have accommodations for refueling, maintenance, or air traffic control.

**Airports - with paved runways:** This entry gives the total number of airports with paved runways (concrete or asphalt surfaces) by length. For airports with more than one runway, only the longest runway is included according to the following five groups - (1) *over 3,047 m* (over 10,000 ft), (2) *2,438 to 3,047 m* (8,000 to 10,000 ft), (3) *1,524 to 2,437 m* (5,000 to 8,000 ft), (4) *914 to 1,523 m* (3,000 to 5,000 ft), and (5) *under 914 m* (under 3,000 ft). Only airports with usable runways are included in this listing. Not all airports have facilities for refueling, maintenance, or air traffic control. The type aircraft capable of operating from a runway of a given length is dependent upon a number of factors including elevation of the runway, runway gradient, average maximum daily temperature at the airport, engine types, flap settings, and take-off weight of the aircraft.

**Airports - with unpaved runways:** This entry gives the total number of airports with unpaved runways (grass, dirt, sand, or gravel surfaces) by length. For airports with more than one runway, only the longest runway is included according to the following five groups - (1) *over 3,047 m* (over 10,000 ft), (2) *2,438 to 3,047 m* (8,000 to 10,000 ft), (3) *1,524 to 2,437 m* (5,000 to 8,000 ft), (4) *914 to 1,523 m* (3,000 to 5,000 ft), and (5) *under 914 m* (under 3,000 ft). Only airports with usable runways are included in this listing. Not all airports have facilities for refueling, maintenance, or air traffic control. The type aircraft capable of operating from a runway of a given length is dependent upon a number of factors including elevation of the runway, runway gradient, average maximum daily temperature at the airport, engine types, flap settings, and take-off weight of the aircraft.

**Appendixes:** This section includes *Factbook*-related material by topic.

**Area:** This entry includes three subfields. *Total area* is the sum of all land and water areas delimited by international boundaries and/or coastlines. *Land area* is the aggregate of all surfaces delimited by international boundaries and/or coastlines, excluding inland water bodies (lakes, reservoirs, rivers). *Water area* is the sum of the surfaces of all inland water bodies, such as lakes, reservoirs, or rivers, as delimited by international boundaries and/or coastlines.

**Area - comparative:** This entry provides an area comparison based on total area equivalents. Most entities are compared with the entire US or one of the 50 states based on area measurements (1990 revised) provided by the US Bureau of the Census. The smaller entities are compared with Washington, DC (178 sq km, 69 sq mi) or The Mall in Washington, DC (0.59 sq km, 0.23 sq mi, 146 acres).

**Background:** This entry usually highlights major historic events and current issues and may include a statement about one or two key future trends.

**Birth rate:** This entry gives the average annual number of births during a year per 1,000 persons in the population at midyear; also known as crude birth rate. The birth rate is usually the dominant factor in determining the rate of population growth. It depends on both the level of fertility and the age structure of the population.

**Budget:** This entry includes *revenues*, *expenditures*, and capital expenditures. These figures are calculated on an exchange rate basis, i.e., not in purchasing power parity (PPP) terms.

**Capital:** This entry gives the *name* of the seat of government, its *geographic coordinates*, the *time difference* relative to **Coordinated Universal Time (UTC)** and the time observed in Washington, DC, and, if applicable, information on *daylight saving time* **(DST)**. Where appropriate, a special *note* has been added to highlight those countries that have multiple time zones.

**Central bank discount rate:** This entry provides the annualized interest rate a country's central bank charges commercial, depository banks for loans to meet temporary shortages of funds.

**Climate:** This entry includes a brief description of typical weather regimes throughout the year.

**Coastline:** This entry gives the total length of the boundary between the land area (including islands) and the sea.

**Commercial bank prime lending rate:** This entry provides a simple average of annualized interest rates commercial banks charge on new loans, denominated in the national currency, to their most credit-worthy customers.

**Communications:** This category deals with the means of exchanging information and includes the telephone, radio, television, and Internet host entries.

**Communications - note:** This entry includes miscellaneous communications information of significance not included elsewhere.

**Constitution:** This entry includes the dates of adoption, revisions, and major amendments.

**Coordinated Universal Time (UTC):** UTC is the international atomic time scale that serves as the basis of timekeeping for most of the world. The hours, minutes, and seconds expressed by UTC represent the time of day at the Prime Meridian (0º longitude) located near Greenwich, England as reckoned from midnight. UTC is calculated by the Bureau International des Poids et Measures (BIPM) in Sevres, France. The BIPM averages data collected from more than 200 atomic time and frequency standards located at about 50 laboratories worldwide. UTC is the basis for all civil time with the Earth divided into time zones expressed as positive or negative differences from UTC. UTC is also referred to as "Zulu time." See the Standard Time Zones of the World map included with the **Reference Maps**.

**Country data codes:** See **Data codes**.

**Country map:** Most versions of the *Factbook* provide a country map in color. The maps were produced from the best information available at the time of preparation. Names and/or boundaries may have changed subsequently.

**Country name:** This entry includes all forms of the country's name approved by the US Board on Geographic Names (Italy is used as an example): *conventional long form* (Italian Republic), *conventional short form* (Italy), *local long form* (Repubblica Italiana), *local short form* (Italia), *former* (Kingdom of Italy), as well as the *abbreviation*. Also see the **Terminology** note.

**Crude oil:** See entry for oil.

**Current account balance:** This entry records a country's net trade in goods and services, plus net earnings from rents, interest, profits, and dividends, and net transfer payments (such as pension funds and worker remittances) to and from the rest of the world during the period specified. These figures are calculated on an exchange rate basis, i.e., not in purchasing power parity (PPP) terms.

**Data codes:** This information is presented in **Appendix D: Cross-Reference List of Country Data Codes and Appendix E: Cross-Reference List of Hydrographic Data Codes.**

**Date of information:** In general, information available as of 1 January 2007 was used in the preparation of this edition.

**Daylight Saving Time (DST):** This entry is included for those entities that have adopted a policy of adjusting the official local time forward, usually one hour, from Standard Time during summer months. Such policies are most common in mid-latitude regions.

**Death rate:** This entry gives the average annual number of deaths during a year per 1,000 population at midyear; also known as crude death rate. The death rate, while only a rough indicator of the mortality situation in a country, accurately indicates the current mortality impact on population growth. This indicator is significantly affected by age distribution, and most countries will eventually show a rise in the overall death rate, in spite of continued decline in mortality at all ages, as declining fertility results in an aging population.

**Debt - external:** This entry gives the total public and private debt owed to nonresidents repayable in foreign currency, goods, or services. These figures are calculated on an exchange rate basis, i.e., not in purchasing power parity (PPP) terms.

**Dependency status:** This entry describes the formal relationship between a particular nonindependent entity and an independent state.

**Dependent areas:** This entry contains an alphabetical listing of all nonindependent entities associated in some way with a particular independent state.

**Diplomatic representation:** The US Government has diplomatic relations with 189 independent states, including 187 of the 192 UN members (excluded UN members are Bhutan, Cuba, Iran, North Korea, and the US itself). In addition, the US has diplomatic relations with 2 independent states that are not in the UN, the Holy See and Kosovo, as well as with the EU.

**Diplomatic representation from the US:** This entry includes the *chief of mission, embassy* address, *mailing address, telephone* number, *FAX* number, *branch office* locations, *consulate general* locations, and *consulate* locations.

**Diplomatic representation in the US:** This entry includes the *chief of mission, chancery, telephone, FAX, consulate general* locations, and *consulate* locations.

**Disputes - international:** This entry includes a wide variety of situations that range from traditional bilateral boundary disputes to unilateral claims of one sort or another. Information regarding disputes over international terrestrial and maritime boundaries has been reviewed by the US Department of State. References to other situations involving borders or frontiers may also be included, such as resource disputes, geopolitical questions, or irredentist issues; however, inclusion does not necessarily constitute official acceptance or recognition by the US Government.

**Distribution of family income - Gini index:** This index measures the degree of inequality in the distribution of family income in a country. The index is calculated from the Lorenz curve, in which cumulative family income is plotted against the number of families arranged from the poorest to the richest. The index is the ratio of (a) the area between a country's Lorenz curve and the 45 degree helping line to (b) the entire triangular area under the 45 degree line. The more nearly equal a country's income distribution, the closer its Lorenz curve to the 45 degree line and the lower its Gini index, e.g., a Scandinavian country with an index of 25. The more

## Definitions and Notes *(continued)*

unequal a country's income distribution, the farther its Lorenz curve from the 45 degree line and the higher its Gini index, e.g., a Sub-Saharan country with an index of 50. If income were distributed with perfect equality, the Lorenz curve would coincide with the 45 degree line and the index would be zero; if income were distributed with perfect inequality, the Lorenz curve would coincide with the horizontal axis and the right vertical axis and the index would be 100.

**Economy:** This category includes the entries dealing with the size, development, and management of productive resources, i.e., land, labor, and capital.

**Economy - overview:** This entry briefly describes the type of economy, including the degree of market orientation, the level of economic development, the most important natural resources, and the unique areas of specialization. It also characterizes major economic events and policy changes in the most recent 12 months and may include a statement about one or two key future macroeconomic trends.

**Education expenditures:** This entry provides the public expenditure on education as a percent of GDP.

**Electricity - consumption:** This entry consists of total electricity generated annually plus imports and minus exports, expressed in kilowatt-hours. The discrepancy between the amount of electricity generated and/or imported and the amount consumed and/or exported is accounted for as loss in transmission and distribution.

**Electricity - exports:** This entry is the total exported electricity in kilowatt-hours.

**Electricity - imports:** This entry is the total imported electricity in kilowatt-hours.

**Electricity - production:** This entry is the annual electricity generated expressed in kilowatt-hours. The discrepancy between the amount of electricity generated and/or imported and the amount consumed and/or exported is accounted for as loss in transmission and distribution.

**Elevation extremes:** This entry includes both the highest point and the lowest point.

**Entities:** Some of the independent states, dependencies, areas of special sovereignty, and governments included in this publication are not independent, and others are not officially recognized by the US Government. "Independent state" refers to a people politically organized into a sovereign state with a definite territory. "Dependencies" and "areas of special sovereignty" refer to a broad category of political entities that are associated in some way with an independent state. "Country" names used in the table of contents or for page headings are usually the short-form names as approved by the US Board on Geographic Names and may include independent states, dependencies, and areas of special sovereignty, or other geographic entities. There are a total of 266 separate geographic entities in *The World Factbook* that may be categorized as follows:

INDEPENDENT STATES

194    Afghanistan, Albania, Algeria, Andorra, Angola, Antigua and Barbuda, Argentina, Armenia, Australia, Austria, Azerbaijan, The Bahamas, Bahrain, Bangladesh, Barbados, Belarus, Belgium, Belize, Benin, Bhutan, Bolivia, Bosnia and Herzegovina, Botswana, Brazil, Brunei, Bulgaria, Burkina Faso, Burma, Burundi, Cambodia, Cameroon, Canada, Cape Verde, Central African Republic, Chad, Chile, China, Colombia, Comoros, Democratic Republic of the Congo, Republic of the Congo, Costa Rica, Cote d'Ivoire, Croatia, Cuba, Cyprus, Czech Republic, Denmark, Djibouti, Dominica, Dominican Republic, Ecuador, Egypt, El Salvador, Equatorial Guinea, Eritrea, Estonia, Ethiopia, Fiji, Finland, France, Gabon, The Gambia, Georgia, Germany, Ghana, Greece, Grenada, Guatemala, Guinea, Guinea-Bissau, Guyana, Haiti, Holy See, Honduras, Hungary, Iceland, India, Indonesia, Iran, Iraq, Ireland, Israel, Italy, Jamaica, Japan, Jordan, Kazakhstan, Kenya, Kiribati, North Korea, South Korea, Kosovo, Kuwait, Kyrgyzstan, Laos, Latvia, Lebanon, Lesotho, Liberia, Libya, Liechtenstein, Lithuania, Luxembourg, Macedonia, Madagascar, Malawi, Malaysia, Maldives, Mali, Malta, Marshall Islands, Mauritania, Mauritius, Mexico, Federated States of Micronesia, Moldova, Monaco, Mongolia, Montenegro, Morocco, Mozambique, Namibia, Nauru, Nepal, Netherlands, NZ, Nicaragua, Niger, Nigeria, Norway, Oman, Pakistan, Palau, Panama, Papua New Guinea, Paraguay, Peru, Philippines, Poland, Portugal, Qatar, Romania, Russia, Rwanda, Saint Kitts and Nevis, Saint Lucia, Saint Vincent and the Grenadines, Samoa, San Marino, Sao Tome and Principe, Saudi Arabia, Senegal, Serbia, Seychelles, Sierra Leone, Singapore, Slovakia, Slovenia, Solomon Islands, Somalia, South Africa, Spain, Sri Lanka, Sudan, Suriname, Swaziland, Sweden, Switzerland, Syria, Tajikistan, Tanzania, Thailand, Timor-Leste, Togo, Tonga, Trinidad and Tobago, Tunisia, Turkey, Turkmenistan, Tuvalu, Uganda, Ukraine, UAE, UK, US, Uruguay, Uzbekistan, Vanuatu, Venezuela, Vietnam, Yemen, Zambia, Zimbabwe

OTHER

2    Taiwan, European Union

DEPENDENCIES AND AREAS OF SPECIAL SOVEREIGNTY

6    Australia - Ashmore and Cartier Islands, Christmas Island, Cocos (Keeling) Islands, Coral Sea Islands, Heard Island and McDonald Islands, Norfolk Island

2    China - Hong Kong, Macau

2    Denmark - Faroe Islands, Greenland

9    France - Clipperton Island, French Polynesia, French Southern and Antarctic Lands, Mayotte, New Caledonia, Saint Barthelemy, Saint Martin, Saint Pierre and Miquelon, Wallis and Futuna

2    Netherlands - Aruba, Netherlands Antilles

3    New Zealand - Cook Islands, Niue, Tokelau

3    Norway - Bouvet Island, Jan Mayen, Svalbard

17    UK - Akrotiri, Anguilla, Bermuda, British Indian Ocean Territory, British Virgin Islands, Cayman Islands, Dhekelia, Falkland Islands, Gibraltar, Guernsey, Jersey, Isle of Man, Montserrat, Pitcairn Islands, Saint Helena, South Georgia and the South Sandwich Islands, Turks and Caicos Islands

14    US - American Samoa, Baker Island*, Guam, Howland Island*, Jarvis Island*, Johnston Atoll*, Kingman Reef*, Midway Islands*, Navassa Island, Northern Mariana Islands, Palmyra Atoll*, Puerto Rico, Virgin Islands, Wake Island (* consolidated in United States Pacific Island Wildlife Refuges entry)

MISCELLANEOUS
6   Antarctica, Gaza Strip, Paracel Islands, Spratly Islands, West Bank,
    Western Sahara

OTHER ENTITIES

5   oceans - Arctic Ocean, Atlantic Ocean, Indian Ocean, Pacific Ocean,
    Southern Ocean
1   World
___
266  total

**Environment - current issues:** This entry lists the most pressing and important environmental problems. The following terms and abbreviations are used throughout the entry:

Acidification - the lowering of soil and water pH due to acid precipitation and deposition usually through precipitation; this process disrupts ecosystem nutrient flows and may kill freshwater fish and plants dependent on more neutral or alkaline conditions (see acid rain).

Acid rain - characterized as containing harmful levels of sulfur dioxide or nitrogen oxide; acid rain is damaging and potentially deadly to the earth's fragile ecosystems; acidity is measured using the pH scale where 7 is neutral, values greater than 7 are considered alkaline, and values below 5.6 are considered acid precipitation; note - a pH of 2.4 (the acidity of vinegar) has been measured in rainfall in New England.

Aerosol - a collection of airborne particles dispersed in a gas, smoke, or fog.

Afforestation - converting a bare or agricultural space by planting trees and plants; reforestation involves replanting trees on areas that have been cut or destroyed by fire.

Asbestos - a naturally occurring soft fibrous mineral commonly used in fireproofing materials and considered to be highly carcinogenic in particulate form.

Biodiversity - also biological diversity; the relative number of species, diverse in form and function, at the genetic, organism, community, and ecosystem level; loss of biodiversity reduces an ecosystem's ability to recover from natural or man-induced disruption.

Bio-indicators - a plant or animal species whose presence, abundance, and health reveal the general condition of its habitat.

Biomass - the total weight or volume of living matter in a given area or volume.

Carbon cycle - the term used to describe the exchange of carbon (in various forms, e.g., as carbon dioxide) between the atmosphere, ocean, terrestrial biosphere, and geological deposits.

Catchments - assemblages used to capture and retain rainwater and runoff; an important water management technique in areas with limited freshwater resources, such as Gibraltar.

DDT (dichloro-diphenyl-trichloro-ethane) - a colorless, odorless insecticide that has toxic effects on most animals; the use of DDT was banned in the US in 1972.

Defoliants - chemicals which cause plants to lose their leaves artificially; often used in agricultural practices for weed control, and may have detrimental impacts on human and ecosystem health.

Deforestation - the destruction of vast areas of forest (e.g., unsustainable forestry practices, agricultural and range land clearing, and the over exploitation of wood products for use as fuel) without planting new growth.

Desertification - the spread of desert-like conditions in arid or semi-arid areas, due to overgrazing, loss of agriculturally productive soils, or climate change.

## Definitions and Notes *(continued)*

Dredging - the practice of deepening an existing waterway; also, a technique used for collecting bottom-dwelling marine organisms (e.g., shellfish) or harvesting coral, often causing significant destruction of reef and ocean-floor ecosystems.

Drift-net fishing - done with a net, miles in extent, that is generally anchored to a boat and left to float with the tide; often results in an over harvesting and waste of large populations of non-commercial marine species (by-catch) by its effect of "sweeping the ocean clean."

Ecosystems - ecological units comprised of complex communities of organisms and their specific environments.

Effluents - waste materials, such as smoke, sewage, or industrial waste which are released into the environment, subsequently polluting it.

Endangered species - a species that is threatened with extinction either by direct hunting or habitat destruction.

Freshwater - water with very low soluble mineral content; sources include lakes, streams, rivers, glaciers, and underground aquifers.

Greenhouse gas - a gas that "traps" infrared radiation in the lower atmosphere causing surface warming; water vapor, carbon dioxide, nitrous oxide, methane, hydrofluorocarbons, and ozone are the primary greenhouse gases in the Earth's atmosphere.

Groundwater - water sources found below the surface of the earth often in naturally occurring reservoirs in permeable rock strata; the source for wells and natural springs.

Highlands Water Project - a series of dams constructed jointly by Lesotho and South Africa to redirect Lesotho's abundant water supply into a rapidly growing area in South Africa; while it is the largest infrastructure project in southern Africa, it is also the most costly and controversial; objections to the project include claims that it forces people from their homes, submerges farmlands, and squanders economic resources.

Inuit Circumpolar Conference (ICC) - represents the 145,000 Inuits of Russia, Alaska, Canada, and Greenland in international environmental issues; a General Assembly convenes every three years to determine the focus of the ICC; the most current concerns are long-range transport of pollutants, sustainable development, and climate change.

Metallurgical plants - industries which specialize in the science, technology, and processing of metals; these plants produce highly concentrated and toxic wastes which can contribute to pollution of ground water and air when not properly disposed.

Noxious substances - injurious, very harmful to living beings.

Overgrazing - the grazing of animals on plant material faster than it can naturally regrow leading to the permanent loss of plant cover, a common effect of too many animals grazing limited range land.

Ozone shield - a layer of the atmosphere composed of ozone gas (O3) that resides approximately 25 miles above the Earth's surface and absorbs solar ultraviolet radiation that can be harmful to living organisms.

Poaching - the illegal killing of animals or fish, a great concern with respect to endangered or threatened species.

Pollution - the contamination of a healthy environment by man-made waste.

Potable water - water that is drinkable, safe to be consumed.

Salination - the process through which fresh (drinkable) water becomes salt (undrinkable) water; hence, desalination is the reverse process; also involves the accumulation of salts in topsoil caused by evaporation of excessive irrigation water, a process that can eventually render soil incapable of supporting crops.

Siltation - occurs when water channels and reservoirs become clotted with silt and mud, a side effect of deforestation and soil erosion.

Slash-and-burn agriculture - a rotating cultivation technique in which trees are cut down and burned in order to clear land for temporary agriculture; the land is used until its productivity declines at which point a new plot is selected and the process repeats; this practice is sustainable while population levels are low and time is permitted for regrowth of natural vegetation; conversely, where these conditions do not exist, the practice can have disastrous consequences for the environment.

Soil degradation - damage to the land's productive capacity because of poor agricultural practices such as the excessive use of pesticides or fertilizers, soil compaction from heavy equipment, or erosion of topsoil, eventually resulting in reduced ability to produce agricultural products.

Soil erosion - the removal of soil by the action of water or wind, compounded by poor agricultural practices, deforestation, overgrazing, and desertification.

Ultraviolet (UV) radiation - a portion of the electromagnetic energy emitted by the sun and naturally filtered in the upper atmosphere by the ozone layer; UV radiation can be harmful to living organisms and has been linked to increasing rates of skin cancer in humans.

Waterborne diseases - those in which bacteria survive in, and are transmitted through, water; always a serious threat in areas with an untreated water supply.

**Environment - international agreements:** This entry separates country participation in international environmental agreements into two levels - *party to* and *signed, but not ratified*. Agreements are listed in alphabetical order by the abbreviated form of the full name.

**Environmental agreements:** This information is presented in **Appendix C: Selected International Environmental Agreements**, which includes the name, abbreviation, date opened for signature, date entered into force, objective, and parties by category.

**Ethnic groups:** This entry provides an ordered listing of ethnic groups starting with the largest and normally includes the percent of total population.

**Exchange rates:** This entry provides the official value of a country's monetary unit at a given date or over a given period of time, as expressed in units of local currency per US dollar and as determined by international market forces or official fiat. The International Organization for Standardization (ISO) 4217 alphabetic currency code for the national medium of exchange is presented in parenthesis.

**Executive branch:** This entry includes several subfields. *Chief of state* includes the name and title of the titular leader of the country who represents the state at official and ceremonial functions but may not be involved with the day-to-day activities of the government. *Head of government* includes the name and title of the top administrative leader who is designated to manage the day-to-day activities of the government. For example, in the UK, the monarch is the chief of state, and the prime minister is the head of government. In the US, the president is both the chief of state and the head of government. *Cabinet* includes the official name for this body of high-ranking advisers and the method for selection of members. *Elections* includes the nature of election process or accession to power, date of the last election, and date of the next election. *Election results* includes the percent of vote for each candidate in the last election.

**Exports:** This entry provides the total US dollar amount of merchandise exports on an f.o.b. (free on board) basis. These figures are calculated on an exchange rate basis, i.e., not in purchasing power parity (PPP) terms.

**Exports - commodities:** This entry provides a listing of the highest-valued exported products; it sometimes includes the percent of total dollar value.

**Exports - partners:** This entry provides a rank ordering of trading partners starting with the most important; it sometimes includes the percent of total dollar value.

**Flag description:** This entry provides a written flag description produced from actual flags or the best information available at the time the entry was written. The flags of independent states are used by their dependencies unless there is an officially recognized local flag. Some disputed and other areas do not have flags.

**Flag graphic:** Color flag images may be found in the plates at the back of this volumet. The flag graphics were produced from actual flags or the best information available at the time of preparation. The flags of independent states are used by their dependencies unless there is an officially recognized local flag. Some disputed and other areas do not have flags.

**Freshwater withdrawal (domestic/industrial/agricultural):** This entry provides the annual quantity of water in cubic kilometers removed from available sources for use in any purpose. Water drawn-off is not necessarily entirely consumed and some portion may be returned for further use downstream. Domestic sector use refers to water supplied by public distribution systems. Note that some of this total may be used for small industrial and/or limited agricultural purposes. Industrial sector use is the quantity of water used by self-supplied industries not connected to a public distribution system. Agricultural sector use includes water used for irrigation and livestock watering, and does not account for agriculture directly dependent on rainfall. Included are figures for *total* annual water withdrawal and *per capita* water withdrawal.

**GDP (official exchange rate):** This entry gives the gross domestic product (GDP) or value of all final goods and services produced within a nation in a given year. A nation's GDP at official exchange rates (OER) is the home-currency-denominated annual GDP figure divided by the bilateral average US exchange rate with that country in that year. The measure is simple to compute and gives a precise measure of the value of output. Many economists prefer this measure when gauging the economic power an economy maintains vis-à-vis its neighbors, judging that an exchange rate captures the purchasing power a nation enjoys in the international marketplace. Official exchange rates, however, can be artificially fixed and/or subject to manipulation - resulting in claims of the country having an under- or over-valued currency - and are not necessarily the equivalent of a market-determined exchange rate. Moreover, even if the official exchange rate is market-determined, market exchange rates are frequently established by a relatively small set of goods and services (the ones the country trades) and may not capture the value of the larger set of goods the country produces. Furthermore, OER-converted GDP is not well suited to comparing domestic GDP over time, since appreciation/depreciation from one year to the next will make the OER GDP value rise/fall regardless of whether home-currency-denominated GDP changed.

**GDP (purchasing power parity):** This entry gives the gross domestic product (GDP) or value of all final goods and services produced within a nation in a given year. A nation's GDP at purchasing power parity (PPP) exchange rates is the sum value of all goods and services produced in the country valued at prices prevailing in the United States. This is the measure most economists prefer when looking at per-capita welfare and when comparing living conditions or use of resources across countries. The measure is difficult to compute, as a US dollar value has to be assigned to all goods and services in the country regardless of whether these goods and services have a direct equivalent in the United States (for example, the value of an ox-cart or non-US military equipment); as a result, PPP estimates for some countries are based on a small and sometimes different set of goods and services. In addition, many countries do not formally participate in the World Bank's PPP project that calculates these measures, so the resulting GDP estimates for these countries may lack precision. For many developing countries, PPP-based GDP measures are multiples of the official exchange rate (OER) measure. The differences between the OER- and PPP-denominated GDP values for most of the wealthy industrialized countries are generally much smaller.

**GDP - composition by sector:** This entry gives the percentage contribution of *agriculture*, *industry*, and *services* to total GDP. The distribution will total less than 100 percent if the data are incomplete.

**GDP - per capita (PPP):** This entry shows GDP on a purchasing power parity basis divided by population as of 1 July for the same year.

**GDP - real growth rate:** This entry gives GDP growth on an annual basis adjusted for inflation and expressed as a percent.

**GDP methodology:** In the **Economy** category, GDP dollar estimates for countries are reported both on an official exchange rate (OER) and a purchasing power parity (PPP) basis. Both measures contain information that is useful to the reader. The PPP method involves the use of standardized international dollar price weights, which are applied to the quantities of final goods and services produced in a given economy. The data derived from the PPP method probably provide the best available starting point for comparisons of economic strength and well-being between countries. In contrast, the currency exchange rate method involves a variety of international and domestic financial forces that may not capture the value of domestic output. Whereas PPP estimates for OECD countries are quite reliable, PPP estimates for developing countries are often rough approximations. In developing countries with weak currencies, the exchange rate estimate of GDP in dollars is typically one-fourth to one-half the PPP estimate. Most of the GDP estimates for developing countries are based on extrapolation of PPP numbers published by the UN International Comparison Program (UNICP) and by Professors Robert Summers and Alan Heston of the University of Pennsylvania and their colleagues. GDP derived using the OER method should be used for the purpose of calculating the share of items such as exports, imports, military expenditures, external debt, or the current account balance, because the dollar values presented in the *Factbook* for these items have been converted at official exchange rates, not at PPP. One should use the OER GDP figure to calculate the proportion of, say, Chinese defense expenditures in GDP, because that share will be the same as one calculated in local currency units. Comparison of OER GDP with PPP GDP may also indicate whether a currency is over- or under-valued. If OER GDP is smaller than PPP GDP, the official exchange rate may be undervalued, and vice versa. However, there is no strong historical evidence that market exchange rates move in the direction implied by the PPP rate, at least not in the short- or medium-term. Note: the numbers for GDP and other economic data should not be chained together from successive volumes of the *Factbook* because of changes in the US dollar measuring rod, revisions of data by statistical agencies, use of new or different sources of information, and changes in national statistical methods and practices.

## Definitions and Notes *(continued)*

**Geographic coordinates:** This entry includes rounded latitude and longitude figures for the purpose of finding the approximate geographic center of an entity and is based on the locations provided in the Geographic Names Server (GNS), maintained by the National Geospatial-Intelligence Agency on behalf of the US Board on Geographic Names.

**Geographic names:** This information is presented in **Appendix F: Cross Reference List of Geographic Names**. It includes a listing of various alternate names, former names, local names, and regional names referenced to one or more related *Factbook* entries. Spellings are normally, but not always, those approved by the US Board on Geographic Names (BGN). Alternate names and additional information are included in parentheses.

**Geography:** This category includes the entries dealing with the natural environment and the effects of human activity.

**Geography - note:** This entry includes miscellaneous geographic information of significance not included elsewhere.

**Gini index:** See entry for **Distribution of family income - Gini index**

**GNP:** Gross national product (GNP) is the value of all final goods and services produced within a nation in a given year, plus income earned by its citizens abroad, minus income earned by foreigners from domestic production. The *Factbook*, following current practice, uses GDP rather than GNP to measure national production. However, the user must realize that in certain countries net remittances from citizens working abroad may be important to national well-being.

**Government:** This category includes the entries dealing with the system for the adoption and administration of public policy.

**Government - note:** This entry includes miscellaneous government information of significance not included elsewhere.

**Government type:** This entry gives the basic form of government. Definitions of the major governmental terms are as follows. (Note that for some countries more than one definition applies.):

> Absolute monarchy - a form of government where the monarch rules unhindered, i.e., without any laws, constitution, or legally organized opposition.
> Anarchy - a condition of lawlessness or political disorder brought about by the absence of governmental authority.
> Authoritarian - a form of government in which state authority is imposed onto many aspects of citizens' lives.
> Commonwealth - a nation, state, or other political entity founded on law and united by a compact of the people for the common good.
> Communist - a system of government in which the state plans and controls the economy and a single - often authoritarian - party holds power; state controls are imposed with the elimination of private ownership of property or capital while claiming to make progress toward a higher social order in which all goods are equally shared by the people (i.e., a classless society).
> Confederacy (Confederation) - a union by compact or treaty between states, provinces, or territories, that creates a central government with limited powers; the constituent entities retain supreme authority over all matters except those delegated to the central government.

Constitutional - a government by or operating under an authoritative document (constitution) that sets forth the system of fundamental laws and principles that determines the nature, functions, and limits of that government.

Constitutional democracy - a form of government in which the sovereign power of the people is spelled out in a governing constitution.

Constitutional monarchy - a system of government in which a monarch is guided by a constitution whereby his/her rights, duties, and responsibilities are spelled out in written law or by custom.

Democracy - a form of government in which the supreme power is retained by the people, but which is usually exercised indirectly through a system of representation and delegated authority periodically renewed.

Democratic republic - a state in which the supreme power rests in the body of citizens entitled to vote for officers and representatives responsible to them.

Dictatorship - a form of government in which a ruler or small clique wield absolute power (not restricted by a constitution or laws).

Ecclesiastical - a government administrated by a church.

Emirate - similar to a monarchy or sultanate, but a government in which the supreme power is in the hands of an emir (the ruler of a Muslim state); the emir may be an absolute overlord or a sovereign with constitutionally limited authority.

Federal (Federation) - a form of government in which sovereign power is formally divided - usually by means of a constitution - between a central authority and a number of constituent regions (states, colonies, or provinces) so that each region retains some management of its internal affairs; differs from a confederacy in that the central government exerts influence directly upon both individuals as well as upon the regional units.

Federal republic - a state in which the powers of the central government are restricted and in which the component parts (states, colonies, or provinces) retain a degree of self-government; ultimate sovereign power rests with the voters who chose their governmental representatives.

Islamic republic - a particular form of government adopted by some Muslim states; although such a state is, in theory, a theocracy, it remains a republic, but its laws are required to be compatible with the laws of Islam.

Maoism - the theory and practice of Marxism-Leninism developed in China by Mao Zedong (Mao Tse-tung), which states that a continuous revolution is necessary if the leaders of a communist state are to keep in touch with the people.

Marxism - the political, economic, and social principles espoused by 19th century economist Karl Marx; he viewed the struggle of workers as a progression of historical forces that would proceed from a class struggle of the proletariat (workers) exploited by capitalists (business owners), to a socialist "dictatorship of the proletariat," to, finally, a classless society - Communism.

Marxism-Leninism - an expanded form of communism developed by Lenin from doctrines of Karl Marx; Lenin saw imperialism as the final stage of capitalism and shifted the focus of workers' struggle from developed to underdeveloped countries.

Monarchy - a government in which the supreme power is lodged in the hands of a monarch who reigns over a state or territory, usually for life and by hereditary right; the monarch may be either a sole absolute ruler or a sovereign - such as a king, queen, or prince - with constitutionally limited authority.

Oligarchy - a government in which control is exercised by a small group of individuals whose authority generally is based on wealth or power.

Parliamentary democracy - a political system in which the legislature (parliament) selects the government - a prime minister, premier, or chancellor along with the cabinet ministers - according to party strength as expressed in elections; by this system, the government acquires a dual responsibility: to the people as well as to the parliament.

Parliamentary government (Cabinet-Parliamentary government) - a government in which members of an executive branch (the cabinet and its leader - a prime minister, premier, or chancellor) are nominated to their positions by a legislature or parliament, and are directly responsible to it; this type of government can be dissolved at will by the parliament (legislature) by means of a no confidence vote or the leader of the cabinet may dissolve the parliament if it can no longer function.

Parliamentary monarchy - a state headed by a monarch who is not actively involved in policy formation or implementation (i.e., the exercise of sovereign powers by a monarch in a ceremonial capacity); true governmental leadership is carried out by a cabinet and its head - a prime minister, premier, or chancellor - who are drawn from a legislature (parliament).

Presidential - a system of government where the executive branch exists separately from a legislature (to which it is generally not accountable).

Republic - a representative democracy in which the people's elected deputies (representatives), not the people themselves, vote on legislation.

Socialism - a government in which the means of planning, producing, and distributing goods is controlled by a central government that theoretically seeks a more just and equitable distribution of property and labor; in actuality, most socialist governments have ended up being no more than dictatorships over workers by a ruling elite.

Sultanate - similar to a monarchy, but a government in which the supreme power is in the hands of a sultan (the head of a Muslim state); the sultan may be an absolute ruler or a sovereign with constitutionally limited authority.

Theocracy - a form of government in which a Deity is recognized as the supreme civil ruler, but the Deity's laws are interpreted by ecclesiastical authorities (bishops, mullahs, etc.); a government subject to religious authority.

Totalitarian - a government that seeks to subordinate the individual to the state by controlling not only all political and economic matters, but also the attitudes, values, and beliefs of its population.

**Greenwich Mean Time (GMT):** The mean solar time at the Greenwich Meridian, Greenwich, England, with the hours and days, since 1925, reckoned from midnight. GMT is now a historical term having been replaced by UTC on 1 January 1972. See **Coordinated Universal Time.**

**Gross domestic product:** See **GDP**

**Gross national product:** See **GNP**

**Gross world product:** See **GWP**

**GWP:** This entry gives the gross world product (GWP) or aggregate value of all final goods and services produced worldwide in a given year.

**Heliports:** This entry gives the total number of heliports with hard-surface runways, helipads, or landing areas that support routine sustained helicopter operations exclusively and have support facilities including one or more of the following facilities: lighting, fuel, passenger handling, or maintenance. It includes former airports used exclusively for helicopter operations but excludes heliports limited to day operations and natural clearings that could support helicopter landings and takeoffs.

**HIV/AIDS - adult prevalence rate:** This entry gives an estimate of the percentage of adults (aged 15-49) living with HIV/AIDS. The adult prevalence rate is calculated by dividing the estimated number of adults living with HIV/AIDS at yearend by the total adult population at yearend.

**HIV/AIDS - deaths:** This entry gives an estimate of the number of adults and children who died of AIDS during a given calendar year.

**HIV/AIDS - people living with HIV/AIDS:** This entry gives an estimate of all people (adults and children) alive at yearend with HIV infection, whether or not they have developed symptoms of AIDS.

**Household income or consumption by percentage share:** Data on household income or consumption come from household surveys, the results adjusted for household size. Nations use different standards and procedures in collecting and adjusting the data. Surveys based on income will normally show a more unequal distribution than surveys based on consumption. The quality of surveys is improving with time, yet caution is still necessary in making inter-country comparisons.

**Hydrographic data codes:** See **Data codes**

**Illicit drugs:** This entry gives information on the five categories of illicit drugs - narcotics, stimulants, depressants (sedatives), hallucinogens, and cannabis. These categories include many drugs legally produced and prescribed by doctors as well as those illegally produced and sold outside of medical channels.

Cannabis (*Cannabis sativa*) is the common hemp plant, which provides hallucinogens with some sedative properties, and includes marijuana (pot, Acapulco gold, grass, reefer), tetrahydrocannabinol (THC, Marinol), hashish (hash), and hashish oil (hash oil).
Coca (mostly *Erythroxylum coca*) is a bush with leaves that contain the stimulant used to make cocaine. Coca is not to be confused with cocoa, which comes from cacao seeds and is used in making chocolate, cocoa, and cocoa butter.
Cocaine is a stimulant derived from the leaves of the coca bush.
Depressants (sedatives) are drugs that reduce tension and anxiety and include chloral hydrate, barbiturates (Amytal, Nembutal, Seconal, phenobarbital), benzodiazepines (Librium, Valium), methaqualone (Quaalude), glutethimide (Doriden), and others (Equanil, Placidyl, Valmid).
Drugs are any chemical substances that effect a physical, mental, emotional, or behavioral change in an individual.
Drug abuse is the use of any licit or illicit chemical substance that results in physical, mental, emotional, or behavioral impairment in an individual.

**Hallucinogens** are drugs that affect sensation, thinking, self-awareness, and emotion. Hallucinogens include LSD (acid, microdot), mescaline and peyote (mexc, buttons, cactus), amphetamine variants (PMA, STP, DOB), phencyclidine (PCP, angel dust, hog), phencyclidine analogues (PCE, PCPy, TCP), and others (psilocybin, psilocyn).

**Hashish** is the resinous exudate of the cannabis or hemp plant (*Cannabis sativa*).

**Heroin** is a semisynthetic derivative of morphine.

**Mandrax** is a trade name for methaqualone, a pharmaceutical depressant.

**Marijuana** is the dried leaf of the cannabis or hemp plant (*Cannabis sativa*).

**Methaqualone** is a pharmaceutical depressant, referred to as mandrax in Southwest Asia and Africa.

**Narcotics** are drugs that relieve pain, often induce sleep, and refer to opium, opium derivatives, and synthetic substitutes. Natural narcotics include opium (paregoric, parepectolin), morphine (MS-Contin, Roxanol), codeine (Tylenol with codeine, Empirin with codeine, Robitussin AC), and thebaine. Semisynthetic narcotics include heroin (horse, smack), and hydromorphone (Dilaudid). Synthetic narcotics include meperidine or Pethidine (Demerol, Mepergan), methadone (Dolophine, Methadose), and others (Darvon, Lomotil).

**Opium** is the brown, gummy exudate of the incised, unripe seedpod of the opium poppy.

**Opium poppy** (*Papaver somniferum*) is the source for the natural and semisynthetic narcotics.

**Poppy straw** is the entire cut and dried opium poppy-plant material, other than the seeds. Opium is extracted from poppy straw in commercial operations that produce the drug for medical use.

**Qat** (kat, khat) is a stimulant from the buds or leaves of *Catha edulis* that is chewed or drunk as tea.

**Quaaludes** is the North American slang term for methaqualone, a pharmaceutical depressant.

**Stimulants** are drugs that relieve mild depression, increase energy and activity, and include cocaine (coke, snow, crack), amphetamines (Desoxyn, Dexedrine), ephedrine, ecstasy (clarity, essence, doctor, Adam), phenmetrazine (Preludin), methylphenidate (Ritalin), and others (Cylert, Sanorex, Tenuate).

**Imports:** This entry provides the total US dollar amount of merchandise imports on a c.i.f. (cost, insurance, and freight) or f.o.b. (free on board) basis. These figures are calculated on an exchange rate basis, i.e., not in purchasing power parity (PPP) terms.

**Imports - commodities:** This entry provides a listing of the highest-valued imported products; it sometimes includes the percent of total dollar value.

**Imports - partners:** This entry provides a rank ordering of trading partners starting with the most important; it sometimes includes the percent of total dollar value.

**Independence:** For most countries, this entry gives the date that sovereignty was achieved and from which nation, empire, or trusteeship. For the other countries, the date given may not represent "independence" in the strict sense, but rather some significant nationhood event such as the traditional founding date or the date of unification, federation, confederation, establishment, fundamental change in the form of government, or state succession. Dependent areas include the notation "none" followed by the nature of their dependency status. Also see the **Terminology** note.

## Definitions and Notes *(continued)*

**Industrial production growth rate:** This entry gives the annual percentage increase in industrial production (includes manufacturing, mining, and construction).

**Industries:** This entry provides a rank ordering of industries starting with the largest by value of annual output.

**Infant mortality rate:** This entry gives the number of deaths of infants under one year old in a given year per 1,000 live births in the same year; included is the total death rate, and deaths by sex, *male* and *female*. This rate is often used as an indicator of the level of health in a country.

**Inflation rate (consumer prices):** This entry furnishes the annual percent change in consumer prices compared with the previous year's consumer prices.

**International disputes:** see **Disputes - international**

**International organization participation:** This entry lists in alphabetical order by abbreviation those international organizations in which the subject country is a member or participates in some other way.

**International organizations:** This information is presented in **Appendix B: International Organizations and Groups** which includes the name, abbreviation, date established, aim, and members by category.

**Internet country code:** This entry includes the two-letter codes maintained by the International Organization for Standardization (ISO) in the ISO 3166 Alpha-2 list and used by the Internet Assigned Numbers Authority (IANA) to establish country-coded top-level domains (ccTLDs).

**Internet hosts:** This entry lists the number of Internet hosts available within a country. An Internet host is a computer connected directly to the Internet; normally an Internet Service Provider's (ISP) computer is a host. Internet users may use either a hard-wired terminal, at an institution with a mainframe computer connected directly to the Internet, or may connect remotely by way of a modem via telephone line, cable, or satellite to the Internet Service Provider's host computer. The number of hosts is one indicator of the extent of Internet connectivity.

**Internet users:** This entry gives the number of users within a country that access the Internet. Statistics vary from country to country and may include users who access the Internet at least several times a week to those who access it only once within a period of several months.

**Introduction:** This category includes one entry, **Background**.

**Investment (gross fixed):** This entry records total business spending on fixed assets, such as factories, machinery, equipment, dwellings, and inventories of raw materials, which provide the basis for future production. It is measured gross of the depreciation of the assets, i.e., it includes investment that merely replaces worn-out or scrapped capital.

**Irrigated land:** This entry gives the number of square kilometers of land area that is artificially supplied with water.

**Judicial branch:** This entry contains the name(s) of the highest court(s) and a brief description of the selection process for members.

**Labor force:** This entry contains the total labor force figure.

**Labor force - by occupation:** This entry lists the percentage distribution of the labor force by occupation. The distribution will total less than 100 percent if the data are incomplete.

**Land boundaries:** This entry contains the *total* length of all land boundaries and the individual lengths for each of the contiguous *border countries.* When available, official lengths published by national statistical agencies are used. Because surveying methods may differ, country border lengths reported by contiguous countries may differ.

**Land use:** This entry contains the percentage shares of total land area for three different types of land use: *arable land* - land cultivated for crops like wheat, maize, and rice that are replanted after each harvest; *permanent crops* - land cultivated for crops like citrus, coffee, and rubber that are not replanted after each harvest; includes land under flowering shrubs, fruit trees, nut trees, and vines, but excludes land under trees grown for wood or timber; *other* - any land not arable or under permanent crops; includes permanent meadows and pastures, forests and woodlands, built-on areas, roads, barren land, etc.

**Languages:** This entry provides a rank ordering of languages starting with the largest and sometimes includes the percent of total population speaking that language.

**Legal system:** This entry contains a brief description of the legal system's historical roots, role in government, and acceptance of International Court of Justice (ICJ) jurisdiction.

**Legislative branch:** This entry contains information on the structure (unicameral, bicameral, tricameral), formal name, number of seats, and term of office. *Elections* includes the nature of the election process or accession to power, date of the last election, and date of the next election. *Election results* includes the percent of vote and/or number of seats held by each party in the last election.

**Life expectancy at birth:** This entry contains the average number of years to be lived by a group of people born in the same year, if mortality at each age remains constant in the future. The entry includes *total population* as well as the *male* and *female* components. Life expectancy at birth is also a measure of overall quality of life in a country and summarizes the mortality at all ages. It can also be thought of as indicating the potential return on investment in human capital and is necessary for the calculation of various actuarial measures.

**Literacy:** This entry includes a *definition* of literacy and Census Bureau percentages for the *total population, males,* and *females.* There are no universal definitions and standards of literacy. Unless otherwise specified, all rates are based on the most common definition - the ability to read and write at a specified age. Detailing the standards that individual countries use to assess the ability to read and write is beyond the scope of the *Factbook.* Information on literacy, while not a perfect measure of educational results, is probably the most easily available and valid for international comparisons. Low levels of literacy, and education in general, can impede the economic development of a country in the current rapidly changing, technology-driven world.

## Definitions and Notes *(continued)*

**Location:** This entry identifies the country's regional location, neighboring countries, and adjacent bodies of water.

**Major infectious diseases:** This entry lists major infectious diseases likely to be encountered in countries where the risk of such diseases is assessed to be very high as compared to the United States. These infectious diseases represent risks to US government personnel traveling to the specified country for a period of less than three years. The *degree of risk* is assessed by considering the foreign nature of these infectious diseases, their severity, and the probability of being affected by the diseases present. The diseases listed do not necessarily represent the total disease burden experienced by the local population.

The risk to an individual traveler varies considerably by the specific location, visit duration, type of activities, type of accommodations, time of year, and other factors. Consultation with a travel medicine physician is needed to evaluate individual risk and recommend appropriate preventive measures such as vaccines.

Diseases are organized into the following six exposure categories shown in italics *and listed in typical descending order of risk*. Note: The sequence of exposure categories listed in individual country entries may vary according to local conditions.

*food or waterborne diseases* acquired through eating or drinking on the local economy:

Hepatitis A - viral disease that interferes with the functioning of the liver; spread through consumption of food or water contaminated with fecal matter, principally in areas of poor sanitation; victims exhibit fever, jaundice, and diarrhea; 15% of victims will experience prolonged symptoms over 6-9 months; vaccine available.

Hepatitis E - water-borne viral disease that interferes with the functioning of the liver; most commonly spread through fecal contamination of drinking water; victims exhibit jaundice, fatigue, abdominal pain, and dark colored urine.

Typhoid fever - bacterial disease spread through contact with food or water contaminated by fecal matter or sewage; victims exhibit sustained high fevers; left untreated, mortality rates can reach 20%.

*vectorborne diseases* acquired through the bite of an infected arthropod:

Malaria - caused by single-cell parasitic protozoa *Plasmodium*; transmitted to humans via the bite of the female Anopheles mosquito; parasites multiply in the liver attacking red blood cells resulting in cycles of fever, chills, and sweats accompanied by anemia; death due to damage to vital organs and interruption of blood supply to the brain; endemic in 100, mostly tropical, countries with 90% of cases and the majority of 1.5-2.5 million estimated annual deaths occurring in sub-Saharan Africa.

Dengue fever - mosquito-borne (*Aedes aegypti*) viral disease associated with urban environments; manifests as sudden onset of fever and severe headache; occasionally produces shock and hemorrhage leading to death in 5% of cases.

Yellow fever - mosquito-borne viral disease; severity ranges from influenza-like symptoms to severe hepatitis and hemorrhagic fever; occurs only in tropical South America and sub-Saharan Africa, where most cases are reported; fatality rate is less than 20%.

Japanese Encephalitis - mosquito-borne (*Culex tritaeniorhynchus*) viral disease associated with rural areas in Asia; acute encephalitis can progress to paralysis, coma, and death; fatality rates 30%.

African Trypanosomiasis - caused by the parasitic protozoa *Trypanosoma*; transmitted to humans via the bite of bloodsucking Tsetse flies; infection leads to malaise and irregular fevers and, in advanced cases when the parasites invade the central nervous system, coma and death; endemic in 36 countries of sub-Saharan Africa; cattle and wild animals act as reservoir hosts for the parasites.

Cutaneous Leishmaniasis - caused by the parasitic protozoa *leishmania*; transmitted to humans via the bite of sandflies; results in skin lesions that may become chronic; endemic in 88 countries; 90% of cases occur in Iran, Afghanistan, Syria, Saudi Arabia, Brazil, and Peru; wild and domesticated animals as well as humans can act as reservoirs of infection.

Plague - bacterial disease transmitted by fleas normally associated with rats; person-to-person airborne transmission also possible; recent plague epidemics occurred in areas of Asia, Africa, and South America associated with rural areas or small towns and villages; manifests as fever, headache, and painfully swollen lymph nodes; disease progresses rapidly and without antibiotic treatment leads to pneumonic form with a death rate in excess of 50%.

Crimean-Congo hemorrhagic fever - tick-borne viral disease; infection may also result from exposure to infected animal blood or tissue; geographic distribution includes Africa, Asia, the Middle East, and Eastern Europe; sudden onset of fever, headache, and muscle aches followed by hemorrhaging in the bowels, urine, nose, and gums; mortality rate is approximately 30%.

Rift Valley fever - viral disease affecting domesticated animals and humans; transmission is by mosquito and other biting insects; infection may also occur through handling of infected meat or contact with blood; geographic distribution includes eastern and southern Africa where cattle and sheep are raised; symptoms are generally mild with fever and some liver abnormalities, but the disease may progress to hemorrhagic fever, encephalitis, or ocular disease; fatality rates are low at about 1% of cases.

Chikungunya - mosquito-borne (*Aedes aegypti*) viral disease associated with urban environments, similar to Dengue Fever; characterized by sudden onset of fever, rash, and severe joint pain usually lasting 3-7 days, some cases result in persistent arthritis.

***water contact diseases*** acquired through swimming or wading in freshwater lakes, streams, and rivers:

Leptospirosis - bacterial disease that affects animals and humans; infection occurs through contact with water, food, or soil contaminated by animal urine; symptoms include high fever, severe headache, vomiting, jaundice, and diarrhea; untreated, the disease can result in kidney damage, liver failure, meningitis, or respiratory distress; fatality rates are low but left untreated recovery can take months.

Schistosomiasis - caused by parasitic trematode flatworm *Schistosoma*; fresh water snails act as intermediate host and release larval form of parasite that penetrates the skin of people exposed to contaminated water; worms mature and reproduce in the blood vessels, liver, kidneys, and intestines releasing eggs, which become trapped in tissues triggering an immune response; may manifest as either urinary or intestinal disease resulting in decreased work or learning capacity; mortality, while generally low, may occur in advanced cases usually due to bladder cancer; endemic in 74 developing countries with 80% of infected people living in sub-Saharan Africa; humans act as the reservoir for this parasite.

***aerosolized dust or soil contact disease*** acquired through inhalation of aerosols contaminated with rodent urine:

Lassa fever - viral disease carried by rats of the genus *Mastomys*; endemic in portions of West Africa; infection occurs through direct contact with or consumption of food contaminated by rodent urine or fecal matter containing virus particles; fatality rate can reach 50% in epidemic outbreaks.

*respiratory disease* acquired through close contact with an infectious person: Meningococcal meningitis - bacterial disease causing an inflammation of the lining of the brain and spinal cord; one of the most important bacterial pathogens is *Neisseria meningitidis* because of its potential to cause epidemics; symptoms include stiff neck, high fever, headaches, and vomiting; bacteria are transmitted from person to person by respiratory droplets and facilitated by close and prolonged contact resulting from crowded living conditions, often with a seasonal distribution; death occurs in 5-15% of cases, typically within 24-48 hours of onset of symptoms; highest burden of meningococcal disease occurs in the hyperendemic region of sub-Saharan Africa known as the "Meningitis Belt" which stretches from Senegal east to Ethiopia.

*animal contact disease* acquired through direct contact with local animals: Rabies - viral disease of mammals usually transmitted through the bite of an infected animal, most commonly dogs; virus affects the central nervous system causing brain alteration and death; symptoms initially are non-specific fever and headache progressing to neurological symptoms; death occurs within days of the onset of symptoms.

**Manpower available for military service:** This entry gives the number of males and females falling in the military age range for a country (defined as being ages 16-49) and assumes that every individual is fit to serve.

**Manpower fit for military service:** This entry gives the number of males and females falling in the military age range for a country (defined as being ages 16-49) and who are not otherwise disqualified for health reasons; accounts for the health situation in the country and provides a more realistic estimate of the actual number fit to serve.

**Manpower reaching militarily significant age annually:** This entry gives the number of males and females entering the military manpower pool (i.e., reaching age 16) in any given year and is a measure of the availability of military-age young adults.

**Map references:** This entry includes the name of the *Factbook* reference map on which a country may be found. Note that boundary representations on these maps are not necessarily authoritative. The entry on **Geographic coordinates** may be helpful in finding some smaller countries.

**Maritime claims:** This entry includes the following claims, the definitions of which are excerpted from the United Nations Convention on the Law of the Sea (UNCLOS), which alone contains the full and definitive descriptions:

*territorial sea* - the sovereignty of a coastal state extends beyond its land territory and internal waters to an adjacent belt of sea, described as the territorial sea in the UNCLOS (Part II); this sovereignty extends to the air space over the territorial sea as well as its underlying seabed and subsoil; every state has the right to establish the breadth of its territorial sea up to a limit not exceeding 12 nautical miles; the normal baseline for measuring the breadth of the territorial sea is the mean low-water line along the coast as marked on large-scale charts officially recognized by the coastal state; the UNCLOS describes specific rules for archipelagic states.

**contiguous zone** - according to the UNCLOS (Article 33), this is a zone contiguous to a coastal state's territorial sea, over which it may exercise the control necessary to: prevent infringement of its customs, fiscal, immigration, or sanitary laws and regulations within its territory or territorial sea; punish infringement of the above laws and regulations committed within its territory or territorial sea; the contiguous zone may not extend beyond 24 nautical miles from the baselines from which the breadth of the territorial sea is measured (e.g. the US has claimed a 12-nautical mile contiguous zone in addition to its 12-nautical mile territorial sea).

**exclusive economic zone (EEZ)** - the UNCLOS (Part V) defines the EEZ as a zone beyond and adjacent to the territorial sea in which a coastal state has: sovereign rights for the purpose of exploring and exploiting, conserving and managing the natural resources, whether living or non-living, of the waters superjacent to the seabed and of the seabed and its subsoil, and with regard to other activities for the economic exploitation and exploration of the zone, such as the production of energy from the water, currents, and winds; jurisdiction with regard to the establishment and use of artificial islands, installations, and structures; marine scientific research; the protection and preservation of the marine environment; the outer limit of the exclusive economic zone shall not exceed 200 nautical miles from the baselines from which the breadth of the territorial sea is measured.

**continental shelf** - the UNCLOS (Article 76) defines the continental shelf of a coastal state as comprising the seabed and subsoil of the submarine areas that extend beyond its territorial sea throughout the natural prolongation of its land territory to the outer edge of the continental margin, or to a distance of 200 nautical miles from the baselines from which the breadth of the territorial sea is measured where the outer edge of the continental margin does not extend up to that distance; the continental margin comprises the submerged prolongation of the landmass of the coastal state, and consists of the seabed and subsoil of the shelf, the slope and the rise; wherever the continental margin extends beyond 200 nautical miles from the baseline, coastal states may extend their claim to a distance not to exceed 350 nautical miles from the baseline or 100 nautical miles from the 2500 meter isobath; it does not include the deep ocean floor with its oceanic ridges or the subsoil thereof.

**exclusive fishing zone** - while this term is not used in the UNCLOS, some states (e.g., the United Kingdom) have chosen not to claim an EEZ, but rather to claim jurisdiction over the living resources off their coast; in such cases, the term exclusive fishing zone is often used; the breadth of this zone is normally the same as the EEZ or 200 nautical miles.

**Market value of publicly traded shares:** This entry gives the value of shares issued by publicly traded companies at a price determined in the national stock markets on the final day of the period indicated. It is simply the latest price per share multiplied by the total number of outstanding shares, cumulated over all companies listed on the particular exchange.

**Median age:** This entry is the age that divides a population into two numerically equal groups; that is, half the people are younger than this age and half are older. It is a single index that summarizes the age distribution of a population. Currently, the median age ranges from a low of about 15 in Uganda and Gaza Strip to 40 or more in several European countries and Japan. See the entry for "Age structure" for the importance of a young versus an older age structure and, by implication, a low versus a higher median age.

## Definitions and Notes *(continued)*

**Merchant marine:** Merchant marine may be defined as all ships engaged in the carriage of goods; or all commercial vessels (as opposed to all nonmilitary ships), which excludes tugs, fishing vessels, offshore oil rigs, etc. This entry contains information in four fields - *total*, ships *by type*, *foreign-owned*, and *registered in other countries.*

> *Total* includes the number of ships (1,000 GRT or over), total DWT for those ships, and total GRT for those ships. DWT or dead weight tonnage is the total weight of cargo, plus bunkers, stores, etc., that a ship can carry when immersed to the appropriate load line. GRT or gross register tonnage is a figure obtained by measuring the entire sheltered volume of a ship available for cargo and passengers and converting it to tons on the basis of 100 cubic feet per ton; there is no stable relationship between GRT and DWT.
> Ships *by type* includes a listing of barge carriers, bulk cargo ships, cargo ships, chemical tankers, combination bulk carriers, combination ore/oil carriers, container ships, liquefied gas tankers, livestock carriers, multifunctional large-load carriers, petroleum tankers, passenger ships, passenger/cargo ships, railcar carriers, refrigerated cargo ships, roll-on/roll-off cargo ships, short-sea passenger ships, specialized tankers, and vehicle carriers.
> *Foreign-owned* are ships that fly the flag of one country but belong to owners in another.
> *Registered in other countries* are ships that belong to owners in one country but fly the flag of another.

**Military:** This category includes the entries dealing with a country's military structure, manpower, and expenditures.

**Military - note:** This entry includes miscellaneous military information of significance not included elsewhere.

**Military branches:** This entry lists the service branches subordinate to defense ministries or the equivalent (typically ground, naval, air, and marine forces).

**Military expenditures:** This entry gives spending on defense programs for the most recent year available as a percent of gross domestic product (GDP); the GDP is calculated on an exchange rate basis, i.e., not in terms of purchasing power parity (PPP).

**Military service age and obligation:** This entry gives the required ages for voluntary or conscript military service and the length of service obligation.

**Money figures:** All money figures are expressed in contemporaneous US dollars unless otherwise indicated.

**National holiday:** This entry gives the primary national day of celebration - usually independence day.

**Nationality:** This entry provides the identifying terms for citizens - *noun* and *adjective.*

**Natural gas - consumption:** This entry is the total natural gas consumed in cubic meters (cu m). The discrepancy between the amount of natural gas produced and/or imported and the amount consumed and/or exported is due to the omission of stock changes and other complicating factors.

**Natural gas - exports:** This entry is the total natural gas exported in cubic meters (cu m).

**Natural gas - imports:** This entry is the total natural gas imported in cubic meters (cu m).

**Natural gas - production:** This entry is the total natural gas produced in cubic meters (cu m). The discrepancy between the amount of natural gas produced and/or imported and the amount consumed and/or exported is due to the omission of stock changes and other complicating factors.

**Natural gas - proved reserves:** This entry is the stock of proved reserves of natural gas in cubic meters (cu m). Proved reserves are those quantities of natural gas, which, by analysis of geological and engineering data, can be estimated with a high degree of confidence to be commercially recoverable from a given date forward, from known reservoirs and under current economic conditions.

**Natural hazards:** This entry lists potential natural disasters.

**Natural resources:** This entry lists a country's mineral, petroleum, hydropower, and other resources of commercial importance.

**Net migration rate:** This entry includes the figure for the difference between the number of persons entering and leaving a country during the year per 1,000 persons (based on midyear population). An excess of persons entering the country is referred to as net immigration (e.g., 3.56 migrants/1,000 population); an excess of persons leaving the country as net emigration (e.g., -9.26 migrants/1,000 population). The net migration rate indicates the contribution of migration to the overall level of population change. High levels of migration can cause problems such as increasing unemployment and potential ethnic strife (if people are coming in) or a reduction in the labor force, perhaps in certain key sectors (if people are leaving).

**Oil - consumption:** This entry is the total oil consumed in barrels per day (bbl/day). The discrepancy between the amount of oil produced and/or imported and the amount consumed and/or exported is due to the omission of stock changes, refinery gains, and other complicating factors.

**Oil - exports:** This entry is the total oil exported in barrels per day (bbl/day), including both crude oil and oil products.

**Oil - imports:** This entry is the total oil imported in barrels per day (bbl/day), including both crude oil and oil products.

**Oil - production:** This entry is the total oil produced in barrels per day (bbl/day). The discrepancy between the amount of oil produced and/or imported and the amount consumed and/or exported is due to the omission of stock changes, refinery gains, and other complicating factors.

**Oil - proved reserves:** This entry is the stock of proved reserves of crude oil in barrels (bbl). Proved reserves are those quantities of petroleum which, by analysis of geological and engineering data, can be estimated with a high degree of confidence to be commercially recoverable from a given date forward, from known reservoirs and under current economic conditions.

## Definitions and Notes *(continued)*

**People:** This category includes the entries dealing with the characteristics of the people and their society.

**People - note:** This entry includes miscellaneous demographic information of significance not included elsewhere.

**Personal Names - Capitalization:** The *Factbook* capitalizes the surname or family name of individuals for the convenience of our users who are faced with a world of different cultures and naming conventions. The need for capitalization, bold type, underlining, italics, or some other indicator of the individual's surname is apparent in the following examples: MAO Zedong, Fidel CASTRO Ruz, George W. BUSH, and TUNKU SALAHUDDIN Abdul Aziz Shah ibni Al-Marhum Sultan Hisammuddin Alam Shah. By knowing the surname, a short form without all capital letters can be used with confidence as in President Castro, Chairman Mao, President Bush, or Sultan Tunku Salahuddin. The same system of capitalization is extended to the names of leaders with surnames that are not commonly used such as Queen ELIZABETH II. For Vietnamese names, the given name is capitalized because officials are referred to by their given name rather than by their surname. For example, the president of Vietnam is Tran Duc LUONG. His surname is Tran, but he is referred to by his given name - President LUONG.

**Personal Names - Spelling:** The romanization of personal names in the *Factbook* normally follows the same transliteration system used by the US Board on Geographic Names for spelling place names. At times, however, a foreign leader expressly indicates a preference for, or the media or official documents regularly use, a romanized spelling that differs from the transliteration derived from the US Government standard. In such cases, the *Factbook* uses the alternative spelling.

**Personal Names - Titles:** The *Factbook* capitalizes any valid title (or short form of it) immediately preceding a person's name. A title standing alone is not capitalized. Examples: President PUTIN and President BUSH are chiefs of state. In Russia, the president is chief of state and the premier is the head of the government, while in the US, the president is both chief of state and head of government.

**Petroleum:** See entries under **Oil**.

**Petroleum products:** See entries under **Oil**.

**Pipelines:** This entry gives the lengths and types of pipelines for transporting products like natural gas, crude oil, or petroleum products.

**Piracy:** Piracy is defined by the 1982 United Nations Convention on the Law of the Sea as any illegal act of violence, detention, or depredation directed against a ship, aircraft, persons, or property in a place outside the jurisdiction of any State. Such criminal acts committed in the territorial waters of a littoral state are generally considered to be armed robbery against ships. Information on piracy may be found, where applicable, in the Transportation – note.

**Political parties and leaders:** This entry includes a listing of significant political organizations and their leaders.

**Political pressure groups and leaders:** This entry includes a listing of a country's political, social, labor, or religious organizations that are involved in politics, or that exert political pressure, but whose leaders do not stand for legislative election. International movements or organizations are generally not listed.

**Population:** This entry gives an estimate from the US Bureau of the Census based on statistics from population censuses, vital statistics registration systems, or sample surveys pertaining to the recent past and on assumptions about future trends. The total population presents one overall measure of the potential impact of the country on the world and within its region. Note: Starting with the 1993 *Factbook*, demographic estimates for some countries (mostly African) have explicitly taken into account the effects of the growing impact of the HIV/AIDS epidemic. These countries are currently: The Bahamas, Benin, Botswana, Brazil, Burkina Faso, Burma, Burundi, Cambodia, Cameroon, Central African Republic, Democratic Republic of the Congo, Republic of the Congo, Cote d'Ivoire, Ethiopia, Gabon, Ghana, Guyana, Haiti, Honduras, Kenya, Lesotho, Malawi, Mozambique, Namibia, Nigeria, Rwanda, South Africa, Swaziland, Tanzania, Thailand, Togo, Uganda, Zambia, and Zimbabwe.

**Population growth rate:** The average annual percent change in the population, resulting from a surplus (or deficit) of births over deaths and the balance of migrants entering and leaving a country. The rate may be positive or negative. The growth rate is a factor in determining how great a burden would be imposed on a country by the changing needs of its people for infrastructure (e.g., schools, hospitals, housing, roads), resources (e.g., food, water, electricity), and jobs. Rapid population growth can be seen as threatening by neighboring countries.

**Ports and terminals:** This entry lists major ports and terminals primarily on the basis of the amount of cargo tonnage shipped through the facilities on an annual basis. In some instances, the number of containers handled or ship visits were also considered.

**Public debt:** This entry records the cumulative total of all government borrowings less repayments that are denominated in a country's home currency. Public debt should not be confused with external debt, which reflects the foreign currency liabilities of both the private and public sector and must be financed out of foreign exchange earnings.

**Radio broadcast stations:** This entry includes the total number of AM, FM, and shortwave broadcast stations.

**Railways:** This entry states the *total* route length of the railway network and of its component parts by gauge: *broad*, *standard*, *narrow*, and *dual*. Other gauges are listed under *note*.

**Reference maps:** This section includes world and regional maps.

**Refugees and internally displaced persons:** This entry includes those persons residing in a country as *refugees* or internally displaced persons (*IDPs*). The definition of a refugee according to a United Nations Convention is "a person who is outside his/her country of nationality or habitual residence; has a well-founded fear of persecution because of his/her race, religion, nationality, membership in a particular social group or political opinion; and is unable or unwilling to avail himself/herself of the protection of that country, or to return there, for fear of persecution." The UN established the Office of the UN High Commissioner for

Refugees (UNHCR) in 1950 to handle refugee matters worldwide. The UN Relief and Works Agency for Palestine Refugees in the Near East (UNRWA) has a different operational definition for a Palestinian refugee: "a person whose normal place of residence was Palestine during the period 1 June 1946 to 15 May 1948 and who lost both home and means of livelihood as a result of the 1948 conflict." However, UNHCR also assists some 400,000 Palestinian refugees not covered under the UNRWA definition. The term "internally displaced person" is not specifically covered in the UN Convention; it is used to describe people who have fled their homes for reasons similar to refugees, but who remain within their own national territory and are subject to the laws of that state.

**Religions:** This entry is an ordered listing of religions by adherents starting with the largest group and sometimes includes the percent of total population. The core characteristics and beliefs of the world's major religions are described below.

**Baha'i** - Founded by Mirza Husayn-Ali (known as Baha'u'llah) in Iran in 1852, Baha'i faith emphasizes monotheism and believes in one eternal transcendent God. Its guiding focus is to encourage the unity of all peoples on the earth so that justice and peace may be achieved on earth. Baha'i revelation contends the prophets of major world religions reflect some truth or element of the divine, believes all were manifestations of God given to specific communities in specific times, and that Baha'u'llah is an additional prophet meant to call all humankind. Bahais are an open community, located worldwide, with the greatest concentration of believers in South Asia.

**Buddhism** - Religion or philosophy inspired by the 5th century B.C. teachings of Siddhartha Gautama (also known as Gautama Buddha "the enlightened one"). Buddhism focuses on the goal of spiritual enlightenment centered on an understanding of Gautama Buddha's Four Noble Truths on the nature of suffering, and on the Eightfold Path of spiritual and moral practice, to break the cycle of suffering of which we are a part. Buddhism ascribes to a karmic system of rebirth. Several schools and sects of Buddhism exist, differing often on the nature of the Buddha, the extent to which enlightenment can be achieved - for one or for all, and by whom - religious orders or laity.
*Basic Groupings*
Theravada Buddhism: The oldest Buddhist school, Theravada is practiced mostly in Sri Lanka, Cambodia, Laos, Burma, and Thailand, with minority representation elsewhere in Asia and the West. Theravadans follow the Pali Canon of Buddha's teachings, and believe that one may escape the cycle of rebirth, worldly attachment, and suffering for oneself; this process may take one or several lifetimes.
Mahayana Buddhism, including subsets Zen and Tibetan Buddhism: Forms of Mahayana Buddhism are common in East Asia and Tibet, and parts of the West. Mahayanas have additional scriptures beyond the Pali Canon and believe the Buddha is eternal and still teaching. Unlike Theravada Buddhism, Mahayana schools maintain the Buddha-nature is present in all beings and all will ultimately achieve enlightenment.

**Christianity** - Descending from Judaism, Christianity's central belief maintains Jesus of Nazareth is the promised messiah of the Hebrew Scriptures, and that his life, death, and resurrection are salvific for the world. Christianity is one of the three monotheistic Abrahamic faiths, along with Islam and Judaism, which traces its spiritual lineage to Abraham of the Hebrew Scriptures. Its sacred texts include the Hebrew Bible and the New Testament (or the Christian Gospels).
*Basic Groupings*

Catholicism (or Roman Catholicism): This is the oldest established western Christian church and the world's largest single religious body. It is supranational, and recognizes a hierarchical structure with the Pope, or Bishop of Rome, as its head, located at the Vatican. Catholics believe the Pope is the divinely ordered head of the Church from a direct spiritual legacy of Jesus' apostle Peter. Catholicism is comprised of 23 particular Churches, or Rites - one Western (Latin-Rite) and 22 Eastern. The Latin Rite is by far the largest, making up about 98% of Catholic membership. Eastern-Rite Churches, such as the Maronite Church and the Ukrainian Catholic Church, are in communion with Rome although they preserve their own worship traditions and their immediate hierarchy consists of clergy within their own rite. The Catholic Church has a comprehensive theological and moral doctrine specified for believers in its catechism, which makes it unique among most forms of Christianity.

Mormonism (including the Church of Jesus Christ of Latter-Day Saints): Originating in 1830 in the United States under Joseph Smith, Mormonism is not characterized as a form of Protestant Christianity because it claims additional revealed Christian scriptures after the Hebrew Bible and New Testament. The Book of Mormon maintains there was an appearance of Jesus in the New World following the Christian account of his resurrection, and that the Americas are uniquely blessed continents. Mormonism believes earlier Christian traditions, such as the Roman Catholic, Orthodox, and Protestant reform faiths, are apostasies and that Joseph Smith's revelation of the Book of Mormon is a restoration of true Christianity. Mormons have a hierarchical religious leadership structure, and actively proselytize their faith; they are located primarily in the Americas and in a number of other Western countries.

Orthodox Christianity: The oldest established eastern form of Christianity, the Holy Orthodox Church, has a ceremonial head in the Bishop of Constantinople (Istanbul), also known as a Patriarch, but its various regional forms (e.g., Greek Orthodox, Russian Orthodox, Serbian Orthodox, Ukrainian Orthodox) are autocephalous (independent of Constantinople's authority, and have their own Patriarchs). Orthodox churches are highly nationalist and ethnic. The Orthodox Christian faith shares many theological tenets with the Roman Catholic Church, but diverges on some key premises and does not recognize the governing authority of the Pope.

Protestant Christianity: Protestant Christianity originated in the 16th century as an attempt to reform Roman Catholicism's practices, dogma, and theology. It encompasses several forms or denominations which are extremely varied in structure, beliefs, relationship to state, clergy, and governance. Many protestant theologies emphasize the primary role of scripture in their faith, advocating individual interpretation of Christian texts without the mediation of a final religious authority such as the Roman Pope. The oldest Protestant Christianities include Lutheranism, Calvinism (Presbyterians), and Anglican Christianity (Episcopalians), which have established liturgies, governing structure, and formal clergy. Other variants on Protestant Christianity, including Pentecostal movements and independent churches, may lack one or more of these elements, and their leadership and beliefs are individualized and dynamic.

**Hinduism** - Originating in the Vedic civilization of India (second and first millennium B.C.), Hinduism is an extremely diverse set of beliefs and practices with no single founder or religious authority. Hinduism has many scriptures; the Vedas, the Upanishads, and the Bhagavad-Gita are among some of the most important. Hindus may worship one or many deities, usually with prayer rituals within their own home. The most common figures of devotion are the gods Vishnu, Shiva, and a mother goddess, Devi. Most Hindus believe the soul, or *atman*, is eternal, and goes through a cycle of birth, death, and rebirth (*samsara*) determined by one's positive or negative karma, or the consequences of one's actions. The goal of religious life is to learn to act so as to finally achieve liberation (*moksha*) of one's soul, escaping the rebirth cycle.

**Islam** - The third of the monotheistic Abrahamic faiths, Islam originated with the teachings of Muhammad in the 7th century. Muslims believe Muhammad is the final of all religious prophets (beginning with Abraham) and that the Qu'ran, which is the Islamic scripture, was revealed to him by God. Islam derives from the word submission, and obedience to God is a primary theme in this religion. In order to live an Islamic life, believers must follow the five pillars, or tenets, of Islam, which are the testimony of faith (*shahada*), daily prayer (*salah*), giving alms (*zakah*), fasting during Ramadan (*sawm*), and the pilgrimage to Mecca (*hajj*).

*Basic Groupings*

The two primary branches of Islam are Sunni and Shia, which split from each other over a religio-political leadership dispute about the rightful successor to Muhammad. The Shia believe Muhammad's cousin and son-in-law, Ali, was the only divinely ordained Imam (religious leader), while the Sunni maintain the first three caliphs after Muhammad were also legitimate authorities. In modern Islam, Sunnis and Shia continue to have different views of acceptable schools of Islamic jurisprudence, and who is a proper Islamic religious authority. Islam also has an active mystical branch, Sufism, with various Sunni and Shia subsets.

Sunni Islam accounts for over 75% of the world's Muslim population. It recognizes the Abu Bakr as the first caliph after Muhammad. Sunni has four schools of Islamic doctrine and law - Hanafi, Maliki, Shafi'i, and Hanbali - which uniquely interpret the *Hadith*, or recorded oral traditions of Muhammad. A Sunni Muslim may elect to follow any one of these schools, as all are considered equally valid.

Shia Islam represents 10-20% of Muslims worldwide, and its distinguishing feature is its reverence for Ali as an infallible, divinely inspired leader, and as the first Imam of the Muslim community after Muhammad. A majority of Shia are known as "Twelvers," because they believe that the 11 familial successor imams after Muhammad culminate in a 12th Imam (al-Mahdi) who is hidden in the world and will reappear at its end to redeem the righteous.

*Variants*

Ismaili faith: A sect of Shia Islam, its adherents are also known as "Seveners," because they believe that the rightful seventh Imam in Islamic leadership was Isma'il, the elder son of Imam Jafar al-Sadiq. Ismaili tradition awaits the return of the seventh Imam as the Mahdi, or Islamic messianic figure. Ismailis are located in various parts of the world, particularly South Asia and the Levant.

Alawi faith: Another Shia sect of Islam, the name reflects followers' devotion to the religious authority of Ali. Alawites are a closed, secretive religious group who assert they are Shia Muslims, although outside scholars speculate their beliefs may have a syncretic mix with other faiths originating in the Middle East. Alawis live mostly in Syria, Lebanon, and Turkey.

Druze faith: A highly secretive tradition and a closed community that derives from the Ismaili sect of Islam; its core beliefs are thought to emphasize a combination of Gnostic principles believing that the Fatimid caliph, al-Hakin, is the one who embodies the key aspects of goodness of the universe, which are, the intellect, the word, the soul, the preceder, and the follower. The Druze have a key presence in Syria, Lebanon, and Israel.

**Jainism** - Originating in India, Jain spiritual philosophy believes in an eternal human soul, the eternal universe, and a principle of "the own nature of things." It emphasizes compassion for all living things, seeks liberation of the human soul from reincarnation through enlightenment, and values personal responsibility due to the belief in the immediate consequences of one's behavior. Jain philosophy teaches non-violence and prescribes vegetarianism for monks and laity alike; its adherents are a highly influential religious minority in Indian society.

**Judaism** - One of the first known monotheistic religions, likely dating to between 2000-1500 B.C., Judaism is the native faith of the Jewish people, based upon the belief in a covenant of responsibility between a sole omnipotent creator God and Abraham, the patriarch of Judaism's Hebrew Bible, or *Tanakh*. Divine revelation of principles and prohibitions in the Hebrew Scriptures form the basis of Jewish law, or *halakhah*, which is a key component of the faith. While there are extensive traditions of Jewish halakhic and theological discourse, there is no final dogmatic authority in the tradition. Local communities have their own religious leadership. Modern Judaism has three basic categories of faith: Orthodox, Conservative, and Reform/Liberal. These differ in their views and observance of Jewish law, with the Orthodox representing the most traditional practice, and Reform/Liberal communities the most accommodating of individualized interpretations of Jewish identity and faith.

**Shintoism** - A native animist tradition of Japan, Shinto practice is based upon the premise that every being and object has its own spirit or *kami*. Shinto practitioners worship several particular *kamis*, including the *kamis* of nature, and families often have shrines to their ancestors' *kamis*. Shintoism has no fixed tradition of prayers or prescribed dogma, but is characterized by individual ritual. Respect for the *kamis* in nature is a key Shinto value. Prior to the end of World War II, Shinto was the state religion of Japan, and bolstered the cult of the Japanese emperor.

**Sikhism** - Founded by the Guru Nanak (born 1469), Sikhism believes in a non-anthropomorphic, supreme, eternal, creator God; centering one's devotion to God is seen as a means of escaping the cycle of rebirth. Sikhs follow the teachings of Nanak and nine subsequent gurus. Their scripture, the Guru Granth Sahib - also known as the Adi Granth - is considered the living Guru, or final authority of Sikh faith and theology. Sikhism emphasizes equality of humankind and disavows caste, class, or gender discrimination.

**Taoism** - Chinese philosophy or religion based upon Lao Tzu's Tao Te Ching, which centers on belief in the Tao, or the way, as the flow of the universe and the nature of things. Taoism encourages a principle of non-force, or wu-wei, as the means to live harmoniously with the Tao. Taoists believe the esoteric world is made up of a perfect harmonious balance and nature, while in the manifest world - particularly in the body - balance is distorted. The Three Jewels of the Tao - compassion, simplicity, and humility - serve as the basis for Taoist ethics.

**Zoroastrianism** - Originating from the teachings of Zoroaster in about the 9th or 10th century B.C., Zoroastrianism may be the oldest continuing creedal religion. Its key beliefs center on a transcendent creator God, Ahura Mazda, and the concept of free will. The key ethical tenets of Zoroastrianism expressed in its scripture, the Avesta, are based on a dualistic worldview where one may prevent chaos if one chooses to serve God and exercises good thoughts, good words, and good deeds. Zoroastrianism is generally a closed religion and members are almost always born to Zoroastrian parents. Prior to the spread of Islam, Zoroastrianism dominated greater Iran. Today, though a minority, Zoroastrians remain primarily in Iran, India, and Pakistan.

**Reserves of foreign exchange and gold:** This entry gives the dollar value for the stock of all financial assets that are available to the central monetary authority for use in meeting a country's balance of payments needs as of the end-date of the period specified. This category includes not only foreign currency and gold, but also a country's holdings of Special Drawing Rights in the International Monetary Fund, and its reserve position in the Fund.

**Roadways:** This entry gives the *total* length of the road network and includes the length of the *paved* and *unpaved* portions.

**School life expectancy (primary to tertiary education):** School life expectancy (SLE) is the total number of years of schooling (primary to tertiary) that a child can expect to receive, assuming that the probability of his or her being enrolled in school at any particular future age is equal to the current enrollment ratio at that age. Caution must be maintained when utilizing this indicator in international comparisons. For example, a year or grade completed in one country is not necessarily the same in terms of educational content or quality as a year or grade completed in another country. SLE represents the expected number of years of schooling that will be completed, including years spent repeating one or more grades.

**Sex ratio:** This entry includes the number of males for each female in five age groups - *at birth, under 15 years, 15-64 years, 65 years and over,* and for the *total population.* Sex ratio at birth has recently emerged as an indicator of certain kinds of sex discrimination in some countries. For instance, high sex ratios at birth in some Asian countries are now attributed to sex-selective abortion and infanticide due to a strong preference for sons. This will affect future marriage patterns and fertility patterns. Eventually, it could cause unrest among young adult males who are unable to find partners.

**Stock of direct foreign investment - abroad:** This entry gives the cumulative US dollar value of all investments in foreign countries made directly by residents - primarily companies - of the home country, as of the end of the time period indicated. Direct investment excludes investment through purchase of shares.

**Stock of direct foreign investment - at home:** This entry gives the cumulative US dollar value of all investments in the home country made directly by residents - primarily companies - of other countries as of the end of the time period indicated. Direct investment excludes investment through purchase of shares.

**Stock of domestic credit:** This entry is the total quantity of credit, denominated in the domestic currency, provided by banks to nonbanking institutions. The national currency units have been converted to US dollars at the closing exchange rate on the date of the information.

**Stock of money:** This entry, also known as "M1," comprises the total quantity of currency in circulation (notes and coins) plus demand deposits denominated in the national currency, held by nonbank financial institutions, state and local governments, nonfinancial public enterprises, and the private sector of the economy. The national currency units have been converted to US dollars at the closing exchange rate on the date of the information.

**Stock of quasi money:** This entry comprises the total quantity of time and savings deposits denominated in the national currency, held by nonbank financial institutions, state and local governments, nonfinancial public enterprises, and the private sector of the economy. When added together with "M1" the total money supply is known as "M2." The national currency units have been converted to US dollars at the closing exchange rate on the date of the information.

**Suffrage:** This entry gives the age at enfranchisement and whether the right to vote is universal or restricted.

## Definitions and Notes *(continued)*

**Telephone numbers:** All telephone numbers in *The World Factbook* consist of the country code in brackets, the city or area code (where required) in parentheses, and the local number. The one component that is not presented is the international access code, which varies from country to country. For example, an international direct dial telephone call placed from the US to Madrid, Spain, would be as follows:

011 [34] (1) 577-xxxx, where
011 is the international access code for station-to-station calls;
01 is for calls other than station-to-station calls,
[34] is the country code for Spain,
(1) is the city code for Madrid,
577 is the local exchange, and
xxxx is the local telephone number.

An international direct dial telephone call placed from another country to the US would be as follows:

international access code + [1] (202) 939-xxxx,
where [ 1] is the country code for the US,
(202) is the area code for Washington, DC,
939 is the local exchange,
and xxxx is the local telephone number.

**Telephone system:** This entry includes a brief general assessment of the system with details on the domestic and international components. The following terms and abbreviations are used throughout the entry:

Arabsat - Arab Satellite Communications Organization (Riyadh, Saudi Arabia).

Autodin - Automatic Digital Network (US Department of Defense).

CB - citizen's band mobile radio communications.

Cellular telephone system - the telephones in this system are radio transceivers, with each instrument having its own private radio frequency and sufficient radiated power to reach the booster station in its area (cell), from which the telephone signal is fed to a telephone exchange.

Central American Microwave System - a trunk microwave radio relay system that links the countries of Central America and Mexico with each other.

Coaxial cable - a multichannel communication cable consisting of a central conducting wire, surrounded by and insulated from a cylindrical conducting shell; a large number of telephone channels can be made available within the insulated space by the use of a large number of carrier frequencies.

Comsat - Communications Satellite Corporation (US).

DSN - Defense Switched Network (formerly Automatic Voice Network or Autovon); basic general-purpose, switched voice network of the Defense Communications System (US Department of Defense).

Eutelsat - European Telecommunications Satellite Organization (Paris).

Fiber-optic cable - a multichannel communications cable using a thread of optical glass fibers as a transmission medium in which the signal (voice, video, etc.) is in the form of a coded pulse of light.

GSM - a global system for mobile (cellular) communications devised by the Groupe Special Mobile of the pan-European standardization organization, Conference Europeanne des Posts et Telecommunications (CEPT) in 1982.

HF - high frequency; any radio frequency in the 3,000- to 30,000-kHz range.

Inmarsat - International Maritime Satellite Organization (London); provider of global mobile satellite communications for commercial, distress, and safety applications at sea, in the air, and on land.

## Definitions and Notes *(continued)*

Intelsat - International Telecommunications Satellite Organization (Washington, DC).

Intersputnik - International Organization of Space Communications (Moscow); first established in the former Soviet Union and the East European countries, it is now marketing its services worldwide with earth stations in North America, Africa, and East Asia.

Landline - communication wire or cable of any sort that is installed on poles or buried in the ground.

Marecs - Maritime European Communications Satellite used in the Inmarsat system on lease from the European Space Agency.

Marisat - satellites of the Comsat Corporation that participate in the Inmarsat system.

Medarabtel - the Middle East Telecommunications Project of the International Telecommunications Union (ITU) providing a modern telecommunications network, primarily by microwave radio relay, linking Algeria, Djibouti, Egypt, Jordan, Libya, Morocco, Saudi Arabia, Somalia, Sudan, Syria, Tunisia, and Yemen; it was initially started in Morocco in 1970 by the Arab Telecommunications Union (ATU) and was known at that time as the Middle East Mediterranean Telecommunications Network.

Microwave radio relay - transmission of long distance telephone calls and television programs by highly directional radio microwaves that are received and sent on from one booster station to another on an optical path.

NMT - Nordic Mobile Telephone; an analog cellular telephone system that was developed jointly by the national telecommunications authorities of the Nordic countries (Denmark, Finland, Iceland, Norway, and Sweden).

Orbita - a Russian television service; also the trade name of a packet-switched digital telephone network.

Radiotelephone communications - the two-way transmission and reception of sounds by broadcast radio on authorized frequencies using telephone handsets.

PanAmSat - PanAmSat Corporation (Greenwich, CT).

SAFE - South African Far East Cable

Satellite communication system - a communication system consisting of two or more earth stations and at least one satellite that provide long distance transmission of voice, data, and television; the system usually serves as a trunk connection between telephone exchanges; if the earth stations are in the same country, it is a domestic system.

Satellite earth station - a communications facility with a microwave radio transmitting and receiving antenna and required receiving and transmitting equipment for communicating with satellites.

Satellite link - a radio connection between a satellite and an earth station permitting communication between them, either one-way (down link from satellite to earth station - television receive-only transmission) or two-way (telephone channels).

SHF - super high frequency; any radio frequency in the 3,000- to 30,000-MHz range.

Shortwave - radio frequencies (from 1.605 to 30 MHz) that fall above the commercial broadcast band and are used for communication over long distances.

Solidaridad - geosynchronous satellites in Mexico's system of international telecommunications in the Western Hemisphere.

Statsionar - Russia's geostationary system for satellite telecommunications.

Submarine cable - a cable designed for service under water.

TAT - Trans-Atlantic Telephone; any of a number of high-capacity submarine coaxial telephone cables linking Europe with North America.

Telefax - facsimile service between subscriber stations via the public switched telephone network or the international Datel network.

Telegraph - a telecommunications system designed for unmodulated electric impulse transmission.

Telex - a communication service involving teletypewriters connected by wire through automatic exchanges.

Tropospheric scatter - a form of microwave radio transmission in which the troposphere is used to scatter and reflect a fraction of the incident radio waves back to earth; powerful, highly directional antennas are used to transmit and receive the microwave signals; reliable over-the-horizon communications are realized for distances up to 600 miles in a single hop; additional hops can extend the range of this system for very long distances.

Trunk network - a network of switching centers, connected by multichannel trunk lines.

UHF - ultra high frequency; any radio frequency in the 300- to 3,000-MHz range.

VHF - very high frequency; any radio frequency in the 30- to 300-MHz range.

**Telephones - main lines in use:** This entry gives the total number of main telephone lines in use.

**Telephones - mobile cellular:** This entry gives the total number of mobile cellular telephone subscribers.

**Television broadcast stations:** This entry gives the total number of separate broadcast stations plus any repeater stations.

**Terminology:** Due to the highly structured nature of the *Factbook* database, some collective generic terms have to be used. For example, the word **Country** in the **Country name** entry refers to a wide variety of dependencies, areas of special sovereignty, uninhabited islands, and other entities in addition to the traditional countries or independent states. **Military** is also used as an umbrella term for various civil defense, security, and defense activities in many entries. The **Independence** entry includes the usual colonial independence dates and former ruling states as well as other significant nationhood dates such as the traditional founding date or the date of unification, federation, confederation, establishment, or state succession that are not strictly independence dates. Dependent areas have the nature of their dependency status noted in this same entry.

**Terrain:** This entry contains a brief description of the topography.

**Time difference:** This entry is expressed in *The World Factbook* in two ways. First, it is stated as the difference in hours between the capital of an entity and **Coordinated Universal Time (UTC)** during Standard Time. Additionally, the difference in time between the capital of an entity and that observed in Washington, D.C. is also provided. Note that the time difference assumes both locations are simultaneously observing Standard Time or Daylight Saving Time.

**Time zones:** Ten countries (Australia, Brazil, Canada, Indonesia, Kazakhstan, Mexico, New Zealand, Russia, Spain, and the United States) and the island of Greenland observe more than one official time depending on the number of designated time zones within their boundaries. An illustration of time zones throughout the world and within countries can be seen in the Standard Time Zones of the World map included in the **Reference Maps** section of *The World Factbook*.

**Total fertility rate:** This entry gives a figure for the average number of children that would be born per woman if all women lived to the end of their childbearing years and bore children according to a given fertility rate at each age. The total fertility rate (TFR) is a more direct measure of the level of fertility than the crude birth rate, since it refers to births per woman. This indicator shows the potential for population change in the country. A rate of two children per woman is considered the replacement rate for a population, resulting in relative stability in terms of total numbers. Rates above two children indicate populations growing in size and whose median age is declining. Higher rates may also indicate difficulties for families, in some situations, to feed and educate their children and for women to enter the labor force. Rates below two children indicate populations decreasing in size and growing older. Global fertility rates are in general decline and this trend is most pronounced in industrialized countries, especially Western Europe, where populations are projected to decline dramatically over the next 50 years.

**Total renewable water resources:** This entry provides the long-term average water availability for a country in cubic kilometers of precipitation, recharged ground water, and surface inflows from surrounding countries. The values have been adjusted to account for overlap resulting from surface flow recharge of groundwater sources. Total renewable water resources provides the water total available to a country but does not include water resource totals that have been reserved for upstream or downstream countries through international agreements. Note that these values are averages and do not accurately reflect the total available in any given year. Annual available resources can vary greatly due to short-term and long-term climatic and weather variations.

**Trafficking in persons:** Trafficking in persons is modern-day slavery, involving victims who are forced, defrauded, or coerced into labor or sexual exploitation. The International Labor Organization (ILO), the UN agency charged with addressing labor standards, employment, and social protection issues, estimates that 12.3 million people worldwide are enslaved in forced labor, bonded labor, forced child labor, sexual servitude, and involuntary servitude at any given time. Human trafficking is a multi-dimensional threat, depriving people of their human rights and freedoms, risking global health, promoting social breakdown, inhibiting development by depriving countries of their human capital, and helping fuel the growth of organized crime. In 2000, the US Congress passed the Trafficking Victims Protection Act (TVPA), reauthorized in 2003 and 2005, which provides tools for the US to combat trafficking in persons, both domestically and abroad. One of the law's key components is the creation of the US Department of State's annual *Trafficking in Persons Report*, which assesses the government response (i.e., the *current situation*) in some 150 countries with a significant number of victims trafficked across their borders who are recruited, harbored, transported, provided, or obtained for forced labor or sexual exploitation. Countries in the annual report are rated in three tiers, based on government efforts to combat trafficking. The countries identified in this entry are those listed in the *2008 Trafficking in Persons Report* as *Tier 2 Watch List* or *Tier 3* based on the following *tier rating* definitions:

## Definitions and Notes *(continued)*

*Tier 2 Watch List* countries do not fully comply with the minimum standards for the elimination of trafficking but are making significant efforts to do so, and meet one of the following criteria:

    1. they display high or significantly increasing number of victims,

    2. they have failed to provide evidence of increasing efforts to combat trafficking in persons, or,

    3. they have committed to take action over the next year.

*Tier 3* countries neither satisfy the minimum standards for the elimination of trafficking nor demonstrate a significant effort to do so. Countries in this tier are subject to potential non-humanitarian and non-trade sanctions.

**Transnational issues:** This category includes four entries - **Disputes - international**, **Refugees and internally displaced persons**, **Trafficking in persons**, and **Illicit drugs** - that deal with current issues going beyond national boundaries.

**Transportation:** This category includes the entries dealing with the means for movement of people and goods.

**Transportation - note:** This entry includes miscellaneous transportation information of significance not included elsewhere.

**UTC (Coordinated Universal Time):** See entry for Coordinated Universal Time.

**Unemployment rate:** This entry contains the percent of the labor force that is without jobs. Substantial underemployment might be noted.

**Urbanization:** This entry provides two measures of the degree of urbanization of a population. The first, *urban population*, describes the percentage of the total population living in urban areas, as defined by the country. The second, *rate of urbanization*, describes the projected average rate of change of the size of the urban population over the given period of time. Additionally, the World entry includes a list of the *ten largest urban agglomerations*. An *urban agglomeration* is defined as comprising the city or town proper and also the suburban fringe or thickly settled territory lying outside of, but adjacent to, the boundaries of the city.

**Waterways:** This entry gives the total length of navigable rivers, canals, and other inland bodies of water.

**Weights and Measures:** This information is presented in **Appendix G: Weights and Measures** and includes mathematical notations (mathematical powers and names), metric interrelationships (prefix; symbol; length, weight, or capacity; area; volume), and standard conversion factors.

**Years:** All year references are for the calendar year (CY) unless indicated as fiscal year (FY). The calendar year is an accounting period of 12 months from 1 January to 31 December. The fiscal year is an accounting period of 12 months other than 1 January to 31 December.

---

**Note:** Information for the US and US dependencies was complied from material in the public domain and does not represent Intelligence Community estimates.

# Guide to Country Profiles ( Categories , Fields, and *subfields*)

## Introduction
Background

## Geography
Location
Geographic coordinates
Map references
Area
*total*
*land*
*water*
Area - comparative
Land boundaries
*total*
*border countries*
Coastline
Maritime claims
*territorial sea*
*contiguous zone*
*exclusive economic zone*
*continental shelf*
*exclusive fishing zone*
Climate
Terrain
Elevation extremes
*lowest point*
*highest point*
Natural resources
Land use
*arable land*
*permanent crops*
*other*
Irrigated land
Total renewable water resources
Freshwater withdrawal
*total*
*per capita*
Natural hazards
Environment - current issues
Environment - international agreements
*party to*
*signed, but not ratified*
Geography - note

## People
Population
Age structure
*0-14 years*
*15-64 years*
*65 years and over*
Median age
*total population*
*male*
*female*
Population growth rate
Birth rate
Death rate
Net migration rate
Urbanization
*urban population*
*rate of urbanization*
Sex ratio
*at birth*
*under 15 years*
*15-64 years*
*65 years and over*
*total population*
Infant mortality rate
*total*
*male*
*female*

Life expectancy at birth
*total population*
*male*
*female*
Total fertility rate
HIV/AIDS - adult prevalence rate
HIV/AIDS - people living with HIV/AIDS
HIV/AIDS – deaths
Major infectious diseases
*degree of risk*
*food or waterborne diseases*
*vectorborne diseases*
*water contact diseases*
*aerosolized dust or soil contact disease*
*respiratory disease*
*animal contact disease*
Nationality
*noun*
*adjective*
Ethnic groups
Religions
Languages
Literacy
*definition*
*total population*
*male*
*female*
School life expectancy (primary to tertiary education)
*total*
*male*
*female*
Education expenditures
People - note

## Government
Country name
*conventional long form*
*conventional short form*
*local long form*
*local short form*
*former*
*abbreviation*
Dependency status
Government type
Capital
*name*
*geographic coordinates*
*time difference*
*daylight saving time*
Administrative divisions
Dependent areas
Independence
National holiday
Constitution
Legal system
Suffrage
Executive branch
*chief of state*
*head of government*
*cabinet*
*elections*
*election results*
Legislative branch
*elections*
*election results*
Judicial branch
Political parties and leaders
Political pressure groups and leaders
International organization participation

Diplomatic representation in the US
*chief of mission*
*chancery*
*telephone*
*FAX*
*consulate(s) general*
*consulate(s)*
Diplomatic representation from the US
*chief of mission*
*embassy*
*mailing address*
*telephone*
*FAX*
*consulate(s) general*
*consulate(s)*
*branch office(s)*
Flag description
Government - note

## Economy
Economy - overview
GDP (purchasing power parity)
GDP (official exchange rate)
GDP - real growth rate
GDP - per capita (PPP)
GDP - composition by sector
*agriculture*
*industry*
*services*
Labor force
Labor force - by occupation
*agriculture*
*industry*
*services*
Unemployment rate
Household income or consumption by percentage share
*lowest 10%*
*highest 10%*
Distribution of family income - Gini index
Investment (gross fixed)
Budget
*revenues*
*expenditures*
Public debt
Inflation rate (consumer prices)
Central bank discount rate
Commercial bank prime lending rate
Stock of money
Stock of quasi money
Stock of domestic credit
Market value of publicly traded shares
Agriculture - products
Industries
Industrial production growth rate
Electricity - production
Electricity - consumption
Electricity - exports
Electricity - imports
Oil - production
Oil - consumption
Oil - exports
Oil - imports
Oil - proved reserves
Natural gas – production
Natural gas – consumption
Natural gas – exports
Natural gas - imports
Natural gas - proved reserves
Current account balance

Exports
Exports - commodities
Exports - partners
Imports
Imports - commodities
Imports - partners
Reserves of foreign exchange and gold
Debt - external
Stock of direct foreign investment – at home
Stock of direct foreign investment – abroad
Exchange rates

## Geography
Telephones - main lines in use
Telephones - mobile cellular
Telephone system
*general assessment*
*domestic*
*international*
Radio broadcast stations
Television broadcast stations
Internet country code
Internet hosts
Internet users
Communications - note

## Transportation
Airports
Airports - with paved runways
*total*
*over 3,047 m*
*2,438 to 3047 m*
*1,524 to 2,437 m*
*914 to 1,523 m*
*under 914 m*
Airports - with unpaved runways
*total*
*over 3,047 m*
*2,438 to 3,047 m*
*1,524 to 2,437 m*
*914 to 1,523 m*
*under 914 m*
Heliports
Pipelines
Railways
*total*
*broad gauge*
*standard gauge*
*narrow gauge*
*dual gauge*
Roadways
*total*
*paved*
*unpaved*
Waterways
Merchant marine
*total*
*ships by type*
*foreign owned*
*registered in other countries*
Ports and terminals
Transportation - note

## Guide To Country Profiles *(continued)*

### Military

**Military branches**
**Military service age and obligation**
**Manpower available for militarily service**
    *males age 16-49*
    *females age 16-49*
**Manpower fit for military service**
    *males 16-49*
    *females 16-49*
**Manpower reaching militarily significant age annually**
    *male*
    *female*
**Military expenditures - percent of GDP**
**Military - note**

### Transnational Issues

**Disputes – international**
**Refugees and internally displaced persons**
    *refugees (country of origin)*
    *IDPs*
**Trafficking in persons**
    *current situation*
    *tier rating*
**Illicit drugs**

# World

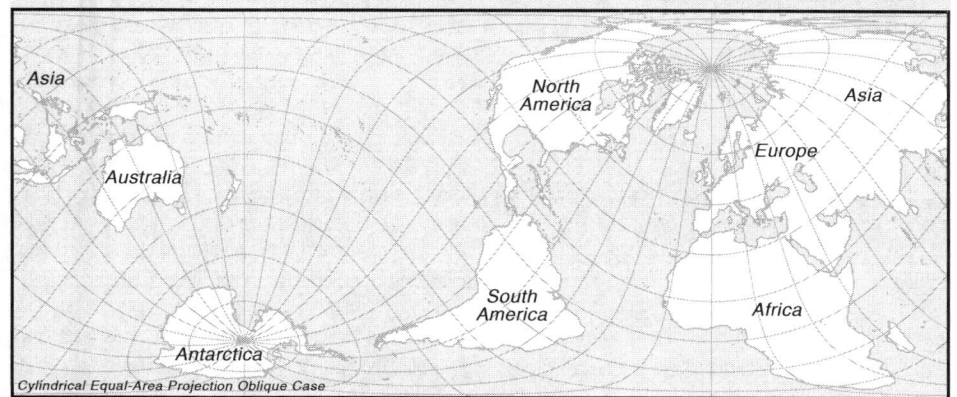

Asia
Australia
Antarctica
North America
South America
Europe
Asia
Africa
*Cylindrical Equal-Area Projection Oblique Case*

## Introduction

**Background:** Globally, the 20th century was marked by: (a) two devastating world wars; (b) the Great Depression of the 1930s; (c) the end of vast colonial empires; (d) rapid advances in science and technology, from the first airplane flight at Kitty Hawk, North Carolina (US) to the landing on the moon; (e) the Cold War between the Western alliance and the Warsaw Pact nations; (f) a sharp rise in living standards in North America, Europe, and Japan; (g) increased concerns about the environment, including loss of forests, shortages of energy and water, the decline in biological diversity, and air pollution; (h) the onset of the AIDS epidemic; and (i) the ultimate emergence of the US as the only world superpower. The planet's population continues to explode: from 1 billion in 1820, to 2 billion in 1930, 3 billion in 1960, 4 billion in 1974, 5 billion in 1988, and 6 billion in 2000. For the 21st century, the continued exponential growth in science and technology raises both hopes (e.g., advances in medicine) and fears (e.g., development of even more lethal weapons of war).

## Geography

**Geographic overview:** The surface of the earth is approximately 70.9% water and 29.1% land. The former portion is divided into large water bodies termed oceans. The World Factbook recognizes and describes five oceans, which are in decreasing order of size: the Pacific Ocean, Atlantic Ocean, Indian Ocean, Southern Ocean, and Arctic Ocean.
The land portion is generally divided into several, large, discrete landmasses termed continents. Depending on the convention used, the number of continents can vary from five to seven. The most common classification recognizes seven, which are (from largest to smallest): Asia, Africa, North America, South America, Antarctica, Europe, and Australia. Asia and Europe are sometimes lumped together into a Eurasian continent resulting in six continents. Alternatively, North and South America are

sometimes grouped as simply the Americas, resulting in a continent total of six (or five, if the Eurasia designation is used).
North America is commonly understood to include the island of Greenland, the isles of the Caribbean, and to extend south all the way to the Isthmus of Panama. The easternmost extent of Europe is generally defined as being the Ural Mountains and the Ural River; on the southeast the Caspian Sea; and on the south the Caucasus Mountains, the Black Sea, and the Mediterranean. Africa's northeast extremity is frequently delimited at the Isthmus of Suez, but for geopolitical purposes, the Egyptian Sinai Peninsula is often included as part of Africa. Asia usually incorporates all the islands of the Philippines, Malaysia, and Indonesia. The islands of the Pacific are often lumped with Australia into a "land mass" termed Oceania or Australasia.
Although the above groupings are the most common, different continental dispositions are recognized or taught in certain parts of the world, with some arrangements more heavily based on cultural spheres rather than physical geographic considerations.

**Map references:** Physical Map of the World, Political Map of the World, Standard Time Zones of the World
**Area:**
*total:* 510.072 million sq km
*land:* 148.94 million sq km
*water:* 361.132 million sq km
*note:* 70.9% of the world's surface is water, 29.1% is land

**Area - comparative:** land area about 16 times the size of the US
**Land boundaries:** the land boundaries in the world total 251,060 km (not counting shared boundaries twice); two nations, China and Russia, each border 14 other countries
*note:* 45 nations and other areas are landlocked, these include: Afghanistan, Andorra, Armenia, Austria, Azerbaijan, Belarus, Bhutan, Bolivia, Botswana, Burkina Faso, Burundi, Central African Republic, Chad, Czech Republic, Ethiopia, Holy See

(Vatican City), Hungary, Kazakhstan, Kosovo, Kyrgyzstan, Laos, Lesotho, Liechtenstein, Luxembourg, Macedonia, Malawi, Mali, Moldova, Mongolia, Nepal, Niger, Paraguay, Rwanda, San Marino, Serbia, Slovakia, Swaziland, Switzerland, Tajikistan, Turkmenistan, Uganda, Uzbekistan, West Bank, Zambia, Zimbabwe; two of these, Liechtenstein and Uzbekistan, are doubly landlocked
**Coastline:** 356,000 km
*note:* 94 nations and other entities are islands that border no other countries, they include: American Samoa, Anguilla, Antigua and Barbuda, Aruba, Ashmore and Cartier Islands, The Bahamas, Bahrain, Baker Island, Barbados, Bermuda, Bouvet Island, British Indian Ocean Territory, British Virgin Islands, Cape Verde, Cayman Islands, Christmas Island, Clipperton Island, Cocos (Keeling) Islands, Comoros, Cook Islands, Coral Sea Islands, Cuba, Cyprus, Dominica, Falkland Islands (Islas Malvinas), Faroe Islands, Fiji, French Polynesia, French Southern and Antarctic Lands, Greenland, Grenada, Guam, Guernsey, Heard Island and McDonald Islands, Howland Island, Iceland, Isle of Man, Jamaica, Jan Mayen, Japan, Jarvis Island, Jersey, Johnston Atoll, Kingman Reef, Kiribati, Madagascar, Maldives, Malta, Marshall Islands, Martinique, Mauritius, Mayotte, Federated States of Micronesia, Midway Islands, Montserrat, Nauru, Navassa Island, New Caledonia, New Zealand, Niue, Norfolk Island, Northern Mariana Islands, Palau, Palmyra Atoll, Paracel Islands, Philippines, Pitcairn Islands, Puerto Rico, Reunion, Saint Barthelemy, Saint Helena, Saint Kitts and Nevis, Saint Lucia, Saint Pierre and Miquelon, Saint Vincent and the Grenadines, Samoa, Sao Tome and Principe, Seychelles, Singapore, Solomon Islands, South Georgia and the South Sandwich Islands, Spratly Islands, Sri Lanka, Svalbard, Tokelau, Tonga, Trinidad and Tobago, Turks and Caicos Islands, Tuvalu, Vanuatu, Virgin Islands, Wake Island, Wallis and Futuna, Taiwan
**Maritime claims:** a variety of situations exist, but in general, most countries make the following claims measured from the mean low-tide baseline as described in the 1982 UN Convention on the Law of the Sea: territorial sea - 12 nm, contiguous zone - 24 nm, and exclusive economic zone - 200 nm; additional zones provide for exploitation of continental shelf resources and an exclusive fishing zone; boundary situations with neighboring states prevent many countries from extending their fishing or economic zones to a full 200 nm
**Climate:** a wide equatorial band of hot and humid tropical climates - bordered north and south by subtropical temperate zones - that separate two large areas of cold and dry polar climates
**Terrain:** the greatest ocean depth is the Mariana Trench at 10,924 m in the Pacific Ocean
**Elevation extremes:**
*lowest point:* Bentley Subglacial Trench -2,555 m
*note:* in the oceanic realm, Challenger Deep in the Mariana Trench is the lowest point, lying -10,924 m below the surface of the Pacific Ocean
*highest point:* Mount Everest 8,850 m

**Natural resources:** the rapid depletion of nonrenewable mineral resources, the depletion of forest areas and wetlands, the extinction of animal and plant species, and the deterioration in air and water quality (especially in some countries of Eastern Europe, the former USSR, and China) pose serious long-term problems that governments and peoples are only beginning to address

**Land use:**
*arable land:* 10.57%
*permanent crops:* 1.04%
*other:* 88.38% (2005)

**Irrigated land:** 2,770,980 sq km (2003)

**Natural hazards:** large areas subject to severe weather (tropical cyclones); natural disasters (earthquakes, landslides, tsunamis, volcanic eruptions)

**Environment - current issues:** large areas subject to overpopulation, industrial disasters, pollution (air, water, acid rain, toxic substances), loss of vegetation (overgrazing, deforestation, desertification), loss of wildlife, soil degradation, soil depletion, erosion; global warming becoming a greater concern

**Geography - note:** the world is now thought to be about 4.55 billion years old, just about one-third of the 13.7-billion-year age estimated for the universe

## People

**Population:** 6,790,062,216 (July 2009 est.)

**Age structure:**
*0-14 years:* 27.2% (male 950,127,898/ female 894,359,186)
*15-64 years:* 65.2% (male 2,235,114,476/ female 2,192,071,874)
*65 years and over:* 7.6% (male 227,748,114/ female 290,640,668) (2009 est.)

**Median age:**
*total:* 28.4 years
*male:* 27.7 years
*female:* 29 years (2009 est.)

**Population growth rate:** 1.167% (2009 est.)

**Birth rate:** 19.95 births/1,000 population (2009 est.)

**Death rate:** 8.2 deaths/1,000 population (2009 est.)

**Urbanization:**
*urban population:* 48.6% of total population (2005)
*rate of urbanization:* 1.98% annual rate of change (2005-10 est.)
*ten largest urban agglomerations:* Tokyo (Japan) - 35,676,000; New York-Newark (US) - 19,040,000; Ciudad de Mexico (Mexico) - 19,028,000; Mumbai (India) - 18,978,000; Sao Paulo (Brazil) - 18,845,000; Delhi (India) - 15,926,000; Shanghai (China) - 14,987,000; Kolkata (India) - 14,787,000; Dhaka (Bangladesh) - 13,458,000; Buenos Aires (Argentina) - 12,795,000 (2007)

**Sex ratio:**
*at birth:* 1.07 male(s)/female
*under 15 years:* 1.06 male(s)/female
*15-64 years:* 1.02 male(s)/female
*65 years and over:* 0.78 male(s)/female
*total population:* 1.01 male(s)/female (2009 est.)

**Infant mortality rate:**
*total:* 40.85 deaths/1,000 live births
*male:* 43.85 deaths/1,000 live births
*female:* 37.67 deaths/1,000 live births (2009 est.)

**Life expectancy at birth:**
*total population:* 66.57 years
*male:* 64.52 years
*female:* 68.76 years (2009 est.)

**Total fertility rate:** 2.58 children born/woman (2009 est.)

**HIV/AIDS - adult prevalence rate:** 0.8% (2007 est.)

**HIV/AIDS - people living with HIV/AIDS:** 33 million (2007 est.)

**HIV/AIDS - deaths:** 2 million (2007 est.)

**Religions:** Christians 33.32% (of which Roman Catholics 16.99%, Protestants 5.78%, Orthodox 3.53%, Anglicans 1.25%), Muslims 21.01%, Hindus 13.26%, Buddhists 5.84%, Sikhs 0.35%, Jews 0.23%, Baha'is 0.12%, other religions 11.78%, non-religious 11.77%, atheists 2.32% (2007 est.)

**Languages:** Mandarin Chinese 13.22%, Spanish 4.88%, English 4.68%, Arabic 3.12%, Hindi 2.74%, Portuguese 2.69%, Bengali 2.59%, Russian 2.2%, Japanese 1.85%, Standard German 1.44%, French 1.2% (2005 est.)
*note:* percents are for "first language" speakers only

**Literacy:**
*definition:* age 15 and over can read and write
*total population:* 82%
*male:* 87%
*female:* 77%
*note:* over two-thirds of the world's 785 million illiterate adults are found in only eight countries (Bangladesh, China, Egypt, Ethiopia, India, Indonesia, Nigeria, and Pakistan); of all the illiterate adults in the world, two-thirds are women; extremely low literacy rates are concentrated in three regions, the Arab states, South and West Asia, and Sub-Saharan Africa, where around one-third of the men and half of all women are illiterate (2005 est.)

## Government

**Administrative divisions:** 265 nations, dependent areas, and other entities

**Legal system:** all members of the UN are parties to the statute that established the International Court of Justice (ICJ) or World Court

## Economy

**Economy - overview:** Global output rose by 3.8% in 2008, down from 5.2% in 2007. Among major economies, growth was led by China (9.8%), Russia (7.4%), and India (7.3%). Worldwide, nations varied widely in their growth results, with Macau (15%), Azerbaijan (13.2%), and Angola (11.6%), registering the highest. Growth rates slowed in all the major industrial countries and most developing countries, because of uncertainties in the financial markets and lowered consumer confidence. Externally, the nation-state, as a bedrock economic-political institution,

is steadily losing control over international flows of people, goods, funds, and technology. Internally, the central government often finds its control over resources slipping as separatist regional movements - typically based on ethnicity - gain momentum, e.g., in many of the successor states of the former Soviet Union, in the former Yugoslavia, in India, in Iraq, in Indonesia, and in Canada. Externally, the central government is losing decisionmaking powers to international bodies, notably the EU. In Western Europe, governments face the difficult political problem of channeling resources away from welfare programs in order to increase investment and strengthen incentives to seek employment. The addition of 80 million people each year to an already overcrowded globe is exacerbating the problems of pollution, desertification, underemployment, epidemics, and famine. Because of their own internal problems and priorities, the industrialized countries devote insufficient resources to deal effectively with the poorer areas of the world, which, at least from an economic point of view, are becoming further marginalized. The introduction of the euro as the common currency of much of Western Europe in January 1999, while paving the way for an integrated economic powerhouse, poses economic risks because of varying levels of income and cultural and political differences among the participating nations. The terrorist attacks on the US on 11 September 2001 accentuated a growing risk to global prosperity, illustrated, for example, by the reallocation of resources away from investment to anti-terrorist programs. The opening of war in March 2003 between a US-led coalition and Iraq added new uncertainties to global economic prospects. The complex political difficulties and the high economic cost of establishing domestic order in Iraq became major global problems that continued through 2008.

**GDP (purchasing power parity):**
$69.49 trillion (2008 est.)
$67.2 trillion (2007)
$65.95 trillion (2006)
*note:* data are in 2008 US dollars

**GDP (official exchange rate):** GWP (gross world product): $62.25 trillion (2008 est.)

**GDP - real growth rate:**
3.8% (2008 est.)
5.2% (2007 est.)
5.3% (2006 est.)

**GDP - per capita (PPP):**
$10,400 (2008 est.)
$10,200 (2007 est.)
$9,800 (2006 est.)
*note:* data are in 2008 US dollars

**GDP - composition by sector:**
*agriculture:* 4%
*industry:* 32%
*services:* 64% (2008 est.)

**Labor force:** 3.167 billion (2008 est.)

**Labor force - by occupation:**
*agriculture:* 40%
*industry:* 20.6%
*services:* 39.4% (2007 est.)

**Unemployment rate:**
30% (2007 est.)
*note:* combined unemployment and underemployment in many non-industrialized countries; developed countries typically 4%-12% unemployment
**Household income or consumption by percentage share:**
*lowest 10%:* 2.5%
*highest 10%:* 29.9% (2002 est.)
**Investment (gross fixed):** 21.9% of GDP (2008 est.)
**Inflation rate (consumer prices):** developed countries 1% to 4% typically; developing countries 5% to 20% typically; national inflation rates vary widely in individual cases, from declining prices in Japan to hyperinflation in one Third World country (Zimbabwe); inflation rates have declined for most countries for the last several years, held in check by increasing international competition from several low wage countries
**Stock of money:** $12.35 trillion (31 December 2007)
**Stock of quasi money:** $27.31 trillion (31 December 2007)
**Stock of domestic credit:** $69.9 trillion (31 December 2007)
**Market value of publicly traded shares:** $66.82 trillion (31 December 2007 est.)
**Industries:** dominated by the onrush of technology, especially in computers, robotics, telecommunications, and medicines and medical equipment; most of these advances take place in OECD nations; only a small portion of non-OECD countries have succeeded in rapidly adjusting to these technological forces; the accelerated development of new industrial (and agricultural) technology is complicating already grim environmental problems
**Industrial production growth rate:** 2.2% (2008 est.)
**Electricity - production:** 19.02 trillion kWh (2007 est.)
**Electricity - consumption:** 17.48 trillion kWh (2007 est.)
**Electricity - exports:** 674 billion kWh (2007 est.)
**Electricity - imports:** 622.6 billion kWh (2007 est.)
**Oil - production:** 85.54 million bbl/day (2007 est.)
**Oil - consumption:** 85.22 million bbl/day (2007 est.)
**Oil - exports:** 66.19 million bbl/day (2005)
**Oil - imports:** 65.41 million bbl/day (2005)
**Oil - proved reserves:** 1.332 trillion bbl (1 January 2008 est.)
**Natural gas - production:** 3.021 trillion cu m (2007 est.)
**Natural gas - consumption:** 3.198 trillion cu m (2007 est.)
**Natural gas - exports:** 929.9 billion cu m (2007 est.)
**Natural gas - imports:** 957.6 billion cu m (2007)
**Natural gas - proved reserves:** 175.4 trillion cu m (1 January 2008 est.)
**Exports:** $16.28 trillion f.o.b. (2008 est.)

**Exports - commodities:** the whole range of industrial and agricultural goods and services
*top ten - share of world trade:* electrical machinery, including computers 14.8%; mineral fuels, including oil, coal, gas, and refined products 14.4%; nuclear reactors, boilers, and parts 14.2%; cars, trucks, and buses 8.9%; scientific and precision instruments 3.5%; plastics 3.4%; iron and steel 2.7%; organic chemicals 2.6%; pharmaceutical products 2.6%; diamonds, pearls, and precious stones 1.9% (2006 est.)
**Exports - partners:** US 13.7%, Germany 7.3%, China 6.2%, France 4.6%, UK 4.5%, Japan 4.1%
*note:* these data show the share of world exports to the specified countries (2007)
**Imports:** $16.21 trillion f.o.b. (2008 est.)
**Imports - commodities:** the whole range of industrial and agricultural goods and services
*top ten - share of world trade:* see listing for exports
**Imports - partners:** China 10.7%, Germany 9.2%, US 8.3%, Japan 5.1%, France 4%
*note:* these data show the share of world imports from the specified countries (2007)
**Debt - external:** $54.62 trillion
*note:* this figure is the sum total of all countries' external debt, both public and private (31 December 2008 est.)
**Stock of direct foreign investment - at home:** World total DFI $16.65 trillion (2008 est.)
**Stock of direct foreign investment - abroad:** World total DFI $16.22 trillion (2008 est.)

## Communications

**Telephones - main lines in use:** 1,263,367,600 (2005)
**Telephones - mobile cellular:** 2,168,433,600 (2005)
**Telephone system:**
*general assessment:* NA
*domestic:* NA
*international:* NA
**Radio broadcast stations:** AM NA, FM NA, shortwave NA
**Television broadcast stations:** NA
**Internet users:** 1,018,057,389 (2005)

## Transportation

**Airports:** total airports - 49,024
*top ten by passengers:* Atlanta (ATL) - 89,379,287; Chicago (ORD) - 76,177,855; London (LHR) - 68,068,304; Tokyo (HND) - 66,823,414; Los Angeles (LAX) - 61,896,075; Paris (CDG) - 59,922,177; Dallas/Fort Worth (DFW) - 59,786,476; Frankfurt (FRA) - 54,161,856; Beijing (PEK) - 53,583,664; Madrid (MAD) - 52,122,702
*top ten by cargo (metric tons):* Memphis (MEM) - 3,840,491; Hong Kong (HKG) - 3,773,964; Anchorage (ANC) - 2,825,511; Shanghai (PVG) - 2,559,310; Inch'on (ICN) - 2,555,580; Paris (CDG) - 2,297,896; Tokyo (NRT) - 2,254,421; Frankfurt (FRA) - 2,127,646; Louisville (SDF) - 2,078,947; Miami (MIA) -1,922,985 (2007)

**Heliports:** 1,359 (2007)
**Railways:**
*total:* 1,370,782 km (2006)
**Roadways:**
*total:* 68,937,575 km (2008)
**Waterways:** 671,886 km (2004)
**Ports and terminals:**
*top ten container ports as measured by Twenty-Foot Equivalent Units (TEUs):* Singapore - 27,935,500; Shanghai - 26,150,000; Hong Kong - 23,999,000; Shenzhen (China) - 21,099,100; Pusan (South Korea) -13,254,703; - Rotterdam - 10,790,604; Dubai (UAE) - 10,650,000; Kaohsiung (Taiwan) - 10,256,829; Hamburg - 9,917,180; Qingdao (China) - 9,462,000 (2007)

## Military

**Military expenditures:** roughly 2% of GDP of gross world product (2005 est.)

## Transnational Issues

**Disputes - international:** stretching over 250,000 km, the world's 322 international land boundaries separate 194 independent states and 71 dependencies, areas of special sovereignty, and other miscellaneous entities; ethnicity, culture, race, religion, and language have divided states into separate political entities as much as history, physical terrain, political fiat, or conquest, resulting in sometimes arbitrary and imposed boundaries; most maritime states have claimed limits that include territorial seas and exclusive economic zones; overlapping limits due to adjacent or opposite coasts create the potential for 430 bilateral maritime boundaries of which 209 have agreements that include contiguous and non-contiguous segments; boundary, borderland/resource, and territorial disputes vary in intensity from managed or dormant to violent or militarized; undemarcated, indefinite, porous, and unmanaged boundaries tend to encourage illegal cross-border activities, uncontrolled migration, and confrontation; territorial disputes may evolve from historical and/or cultural claims, or they may be brought on by resource competition; ethnic and cultural clashes continue to be responsible for much of the territorial fragmentation and internal displacement of the estimated 6.6 million people and cross-border displacements of 8.6 million refugees around the world as of early 2006; just over one million refugees were repatriated in the same period; other sources of contention include access to water and mineral (especially hydrocarbon) resources, fisheries, and arable land; armed conflict prevails not so much between the uniformed armed forces of independent states as between stateless armed entities that detract from the sustenance and welfare of local populations, leaving the community of nations to cope with resultant refugees, hunger, disease, impoverishment, and environmental degradation

**Refugees and internally displaced persons:** the United Nations High Commissioner for Refugees (UNHCR) estimated that in December 2006 there was a global population of 8.8 million registered refugees and as many as 24.5 million IDPs in more than 50 countries; the actual global population of refugees is probably closer to 10 million given the estimated 1.5 million Iraqi refugees displaced throughout the Middle East (2007)

**Trafficking in persons:**

*current situation:* approximately 800,000 people, mostly women and children, are trafficked annually across national borders, not including millions trafficked within their own countries; at least 80% of the victims are female and up to 50% are minors; 75% of all victims are trafficked into commercial sexual exploitation; almost two-thirds of the global victims are trafficked intra-regionally within East Asia and the Pacific (260,000 to 280,000 people) and Europe and Eurasia (170,000 to 210,000 people)

*Tier 2 Watch List:* Albania, Argentina, Armenia, Azerbaijan, Bahrain, Burundi, Cameroon, Central African Republic, Chad, China, Costa Rica, Cote d'Ivoire, Cyprus, Democratic Republic of the Congo, Dominican Republic, Egypt, Equatorial Guinea, Gabon, The Gambia, Guatemala, Guinea, Guinea-Bissau, Guyana, India, Jordan, Libya, Malaysia, Montenegro, Mozambique, Niger, Panama, Republic of the Congo, Russia, South Africa, Sri Lanka, Tajikistan, Uzbekistan, Venezuela, Zambia, Zimbabwe

*Tier 3:* Algeria, Burma, Cuba, Fiji, Iran, Kuwait, Moldova, North Korea, Oman, Papua New Guinea, Qatar, Saudi Arabia, Sudan, Syria (2008)

**Illicit drugs:**

*cocaine:* worldwide coca leaf cultivation in 2007 amounted to 232,500 hectares; Colombia produced slightly more than two-thirds of the worldwide crop, followed by Peru and Bolivia; potential pure cocaine production decreased 7% to 865 metric tons in 2007; Colombia conducts an aggressive coca eradication campaign, but both Peruvian and Bolivian Governments are hesitant to eradicate coca in key growing areas; 551 metric tons of export-quality cocaine (85% pure) is documented to have been seized or destroyed in 2005; US consumption of export quality cocaine is estimated to have been in excess of 380 metric tons

*opiates:* worldwide illicit opium poppy cultivation continued to increase in 2007, with a potential opium production of 8,400 metric tons, reaching the highest levels recorded since estimates began in mid-1980s; Afghanistan is world's primary opium producer, accounting for 95% of the global supply; Southeast Asia - responsible for 9% of global opium - saw marginal increases in production; Latin America produced 1% of global opium, but most was refined into heroin destined for the US market; if all potential opium was processed into pure heroin, the potential global production would be 1,000 metric tons of heroin in 2007

# Afghanistan

## Introduction

**Background:** Ahmad Shah DURRANI unified the Pashtun tribes and founded Afghanistan in 1747. The country served as a buffer between the British and Russian empires until it won independence from notional British control in 1919. A brief experiment in democracy ended in a 1973 coup and a 1978 Communist counter-coup. The Soviet Union invaded in 1979 to support the tottering Afghan Communist regime, touching off a long and destructive war. The USSR withdrew in 1989 under relentless pressure by internationally supported anti-Communist mujahedin rebels. A series of subsequent civil wars saw Kabul finally fall in 1996 to the Taliban, a hardline Pakistani-sponsored movement that emerged in 1994 to end the country's civil war and anarchy. Following the 11 September 2001 terrorist attacks in New York City, a US, Allied, and anti-Taliban Northern Alliance military action toppled the Taliban for sheltering Osama BIN LADIN. The UN-sponsored Bonn Conference in 2001 established a process for political reconstruction that included the adoption of a new constitution, a presidential election in 2004, and National Assembly elections in 2005. In December 2004, Hamid KARZAI became the first democratically elected president of Afghanistan and the National Assembly was inaugurated the following December. Despite gains toward building a stable central government, a resurgent Taliban and continuing provincial instability - particularly in the south and the east -remain serious challenges for the Afghan Government.

## Geography

**Location:** Southern Asia, north and west of Pakistan, east of Iran

**Geographic coordinates:** 33 00 N, 65 00 E

**Map references:** Asia

**Area:**

*total:* 647,500 sq km

*land:* 647,500 sq km

*water:* 0 sq km

**Area - comparative:** slightly smaller than Texas

**Land boundaries:**

*total:* 5,529 km

*border countries:* China 76 km, Iran 936 km, Pakistan 2,430 km, Tajikistan 1,206 km, Turkmenistan 744 km, Uzbekistan 137 km

**Coastline:** 0 km (landlocked)

**Maritime claims:** none (landlocked)

**Climate:** arid to semiarid; cold winters and hot summers

**Terrain:** mostly rugged mountains; plains in north and southwest

**Elevation extremes:**

*lowest point:* Amu Darya 258 m

*highest point:* Nowshak 7,485 m

**Natural resources:** natural gas, petroleum, coal, copper, chromite, talc, barites, sulfur, lead, zinc, iron ore, salt, precious and semiprecious stones

**Land use:**

*arable land:* 12.13%

*permanent crops:* 0.21%

*other:* 87.66% (2005)

**Irrigated land:** 27,200 sq km (2003)

**Total renewable water resources:** 65 cu km (1997)

**Freshwater withdrawal (domestic/industrial/agricultural):**

*total:* 23.26 cu km/yr (2%/0%/98%)

*per capita:* 779 cu m/yr (2000)

**Natural hazards:** damaging earthquakes occur in Hindu Kush mountains; flooding; droughts

**Environment - current issues:** limited natural fresh water resources; inadequate supplies of potable water; soil degradation; overgrazing; deforestation (much of the remaining forests are being cut down for fuel and building materials); desertification; air and water pollution

**Environment - international agreements:**

*party to:* Biodiversity, Climate Change, Desertification, Endangered Species, Environmental Modification, Marine Dumping, Ozone Layer Protection

*signed, but not ratified:* Hazardous Wastes, Law of the Sea, Marine Life Conservation

**Geography - note:** landlocked; the Hindu Kush mountains that run northeast to southwest divide the northern provinces from the rest of the country; the highest peaks are in the northern Vakhan (Wakhan Corridor)

## People

**Population:** 33,609,937 (July 2009 est.)

**Age structure:**

*0-14 years:* 44.5% (male 7,664,670/ female 7,300,446)

*15-64 years:* 53% (male 9,147,846/female 8,679,800)

*65 years and over:* 2.4% (male 394,572/ female 422,603) (2009 est.)

**Median age:**

*total:* 17.6 years

*male:* 17.6 years

*female:* 17.6 years (2009 est.)

# Afghanistan (continued)

**Population growth rate:** 2.629% (2009 est.)
**Birth rate:** 45.46 births/1,000 population (2009 est.)
**Death rate:** 19.56 deaths/1,000 population (2008 est.)
**Net migration rate:** 21 migrant(s)/1,000 population (2009 est.)
**Urbanization:**
*urban population:* 24% of total population (2008)
*rate of urbanization:* 5.4% annual rate of change (2005-10 est.)
**Sex ratio:**
*at birth:* 1.05 male(s)/female
*under 15 years:* 1.05 male(s)/female
*15-64 years:* 1.05 male(s)/female
*65 years and over:* 0.93 male(s)/female
*total population:* 1.05 male(s)/female (2009 est.)
**Infant mortality rate:**
*total:* 151.95 deaths/1,000 live births
*male:* 156.01 deaths/1,000 live births
*female:* 147.7 deaths/1,000 live births (2009 est.)
**Life expectancy at birth:**
*total population:* 44.64 years
*male:* 44.47 years
*female:* 44.81 years (2009 est.)
**Total fertility rate:** 6.53 children born/woman (2009 est.)
**HIV/AIDS - adult prevalence rate:** 0.01% (2001 est.)
**HIV/AIDS - people living with HIV/AIDS:** NA
**HIV/AIDS - deaths:** NA
**Major infectious diseases:**
*degree of risk:* high
*food or waterborne diseases:* bacterial and protozoal diarrhea, hepatitis A, and typhoid fever
*vectorborne disease:* malaria
*animal contact disease:* rabies
*note:* highly pathogenic H5N1 avian influenza has been identified in this country; it poses a negligible risk with extremely rare cases possible among US citizens who have close contact with birds (2009)
**Nationality:**
*noun:* Afghan(s)
*adjective:* Afghan
**Ethnic groups:** Pashtun 42%, Tajik 27%, Hazara 9%, Uzbek 9%, Aimak 4%, Turkmen 3%, Baloch 2%, other 4%
**Religions:** Sunni Muslim 80%, Shia Muslim 19%, other 1%
**Languages:** Afghan Persian or Dari (official) 50%, Pashto (official) 35%, Turkic languages (primarily Uzbek and Turkmen) 11%, 30 minor languages (primarily Balochi and Pashai) 4%, much bilingualism
**Literacy:**
*definition:* age 15 and over can read and write
*total population:* 28.1%
*male:* 43.1%
*female:* 12.6% (2000 est.)
**School life expectancy (primary to tertiary education):**
*total:* 8 years
*male:* 11 years
*female:* 4 years (2004)
**Education expenditures:** NA

## Government

**Country name:**
*conventional long form:* Islamic Republic of Afghanistan
*conventional short form:* Afghanistan
*local long form:* Jomhuri-ye Eslami-ye Afghanestan
*local short form:* Afghanestan
*former:* Republic of Afghanistan
**Government type:** Islamic republic
**Capital:**
*name:* Kabul
*geographic coordinates:* 34 31 N, 69 11 E
*time difference:* UTC+4.5 (9.5 hours ahead of Washington, DC during Standard Time)
**Administrative divisions:** 34 provinces (welayat, singular - welayat); Badakhshan, Badghis, Baghlan, Balkh, Bamyan, Daykundi, Farah, Faryab, Ghazni, Ghor, Helmand, Herat, Jowzjan, Kabul, Kandahar, Kapisa, Khost, Kunar, Kunduz, Laghman, Logar, Nangarhar, Nimroz, Nuristan, Paktika, Paktiya, Panjshir, Parwan, Samangan, Sar-e Pul, Takhar, Uruzgan, Wardak, Zabul
**Independence:** 19 August 1919 (from UK control over Afghan foreign affairs)
**National holiday:** Independence Day, 19 August (1919)
**Constitution:** new constitution drafted 14 December 2003-4 January 2004; signed 16 January 2004; ratified 26 January 2004
**Legal system:** based on mixed civil and Sharia law; has not accepted compulsory ICJ jurisdiction
**Suffrage:** 18 years of age; universal
**Executive branch:**
*chief of state:* President of the Islamic Republic of Afghanistan Hamid KARZAI (since 7 December 2004); First Vice President Ahmad Zia MASOOD; Second Vice President Abdul Karim KHALILI (since 7 December 2004); note - the president is both the chief of state and head of government; former King ZAHIR Shah held the honorific, "Father of the Country," and presided symbolically over certain occasions but lacked any governing authority; the honorific is not hereditary; King ZAHIR Shah died on 23 July 2007
*head of government:* President of the Islamic Republic of Afghanistan Hamid KARZAI (since 7 December 2004); First Vice President Ahmad Zia MASOOD; Second Vice President Abdul Karim KHALILI (since 7 December 2004)
*cabinet:* 25 ministers; note - under the new constitution, ministers are appointed by the president and approved by the National Assembly
*elections:* the president and two vice presidents are elected by direct vote for a five-year term (eligible for a second term); if no candidate receives 50% or more of the vote in the first round of voting, the two candidates with the most votes will participate in a second round; a president can only be elected for two terms; election last held 9 October 2004 (next to be held in August 2009)
*election results:* Hamid KARZAI elected president; percent of vote - Hamid KARZAI 55.4%, Yunus QANUNI 16.3%, Ustad Mohammad MOHAQQEQ 11.6%, Abdul Rashid DOSTAM 10.0%, Abdul Latif PEDRAM 1.4%, Masooda JALAL 1.2%
**Legislative branch:** the bicameral National Assembly consists of the Meshrano Jirga or House of Elders (102 seats, one-third elected from provincial councils for four-year terms, one-third elected from local district councils for three-year terms, and one-third nominated by the president for five-year terms) and the Wolesi Jirga or House of People (no more than 249 seats), directly elected for five-year terms
*note:* on rare occasions the government may convene a Loya Jirga (Grand Council) on issues of independence, national sovereignty, and territorial integrity; it can amend the provisions of the constitution and prosecute the president; it is made up of members of the National Assembly and chairpersons of the provincial and district councils
*elections:* last held 18 September 2005 (next to be held for the Wolesi Jirga by September 2009; next was to be held for the provincial councils to the Meshrano Jirga by September 2008)
*election results:* the single non-transferable vote (SNTV) system used in the election did not make use of political party slates; most candidates ran as independents
**Judicial branch:** the constitution establishes a nine-member Stera Mahkama or Supreme Court (its nine justices are appointed for 10-year terms by the president with approval of the Wolesi Jirga) and subordinate High Courts and Appeals Courts; there is also a minister of justice; a separate Afghan Independent Human Rights Commission established by the Bonn Agreement is charged with investigating human rights abuses and war crimes
**Political parties and leaders:** Afghanistan Peoples' Treaty Party [Sayyed Amir TAHSEEN]; Afghanistan's Islamic Mission Organization [Abdul Rasoul SAYYAF]; Afghanistan's Islamic Nation Party [Toran Noor Aqa Ahmad ZAI]; Afghanistan's National Islamic Party [Rohullah LOUDIN]; Afghanistan's Welfare Party [Meer Asef ZAEEFI]; Afghan Social Democratic Party [Anwarul Haq AHADI]; Afghan Society for the Call to the Koran and Sunna [Mawlawee Samiullah NAJEEBEE]; Comprehensive Movement of Democracy and Development of Afghanistan Party [Sher Mohammad BAZGAR]; Democratic Party of Afghanistan [Tawos ARAB]; Democratic Party of Afghanistan [Abdul Kabir RANJBAR]; Elites People of Afghanistan Party [Abdul Hamid JAWAD]; Freedom and Democracy Movement of Afghanistan [Abdul Raqib Jawid KOHISTANEE]; Freedom Party of Afghanistan [Ilaj Abdul MALEK]; Freedom Party of Afghanistan [Dr. Ghulam Farooq NEJRABEE]; Hizullah-e-Afghanistan [Qari Ahmad ALI]; Human Rights Protection and Development Party of Afghanistan [Baryalai NASRATI]; Islamic Justice Party of Afghanistan [Mohammad Kabir MARZBAN]; Islamic Movement of Afghanistan [Mohammad Ali JAWID]; Islamic Movement of Afghanistan Party [Mohammad Mukhtar MUFLEH]; Islamic Party of Afghanistan

[Mohammad Khalid FAROOQI, Abdul Hadi ARGHANDIWAL]; Islamic Party of the Afghan Land [Mohammad Hassan FEROZKHEL]; Islamic People's Movement of Afghanistan [Ilhaj Said Hussain ANWARY]; Islamic Society of Afghanistan [Ustad RABBANI]; Islamic Unity of the Nation of Afghanistan Party [Qurban Ali URFANI]; Islamic Unity Party of Afghanistan [Mohammad Karim KHALILI]; Islamic Unity Party of the People of Afghanistan [Ustad Mohammad MOHAQQEQ]; Labor and Progress of Afghanistan Party [Zulfiqar OMID]; Muslim People of Afghanistan Party [Besmellah JOYAN]; Muslim Unity Movement Party of Afghanistan [Wazir Mohammad WAHDAT]; National and Islamic Sovereignty Movement Party of Afghanistan [Ahmad Shah AHMADZAI]; National Congress Party of Afghanistan [Abdul Latif PEDRAM]; National Country Party [Ghulam MOHAMMAD]; National Development Party of Afghanistan [Dr. Aref BAKTASH]; National Freedom Seekers Party [Abdul Hadi DABEER]; National Independence Party of Afghanistan [Taj Mohammad WARDAK]; National Islamic Fighters Party of Afghanistan [Amanat NINGARHAREE]; National Islamic Front of Afghanistan [Pir Sayed Ahmad GAILANEE]; National Islamic Moderation Party of Afghanistan [Qara Bik Eized YAAR]; National Islamic Movement of Afghanistan [Sayed NOORULLAH]; National Islamic Unity Party of Afghanistan [Mohammad AKBAREE]; National Movement of Afghanistan [Ahmad Wali MASOOUD]; National Party of Afghanistan [Abdul Rashid ARYAN]; National Patch of Afghanistan Party [Sayed Kamal SADAT]; National Peace Islamic Party of Afghanistan [Shah Mohammood Popal ZAI]; National Peace & Islamic Party of the Tribes of Afghanistan [Abdul Qaher SHARIATEE]; National Peace & Unity Party of Afghanistan [Abdul Qader IMAMI]; National Prosperity and Islamic Party of Afghanistan [Mohammad Osman SALEKZADA]; National Prosperity Party [Mohammad Hassan JAHFAREE]; National Solidarity Movement of Afghanistan [Pir Sayed Eshaq GAILANEE]; National Solidarity Party of Afghanistan [Sayed Mansoor NADREEI]; National Sovereignty Party [Sayed Mustafa KAZEMI]; National Stability Party [Mohammad Same KHAROTI]; National Stance Party [Habibullah JANEBDAR]; National Tribal Unity Islamic Party of Afghanistan [Mohammad Shah KHOGYANI]; National United Front [Burhanuddin RABBANI] (a coalition); National Unity Movement [Sultan Mohammad GHAZI]; National Unity Movement of Afghanistan [Mohammad Nadir AATASH]; National Unity Party of Afghanistan [Abdul Rashid JALILI]; New Afghanistan Party [Mohammad Yunis QANUNI]; Peace and National Welfare Activists Society [Shamsul Haq Noor SHAMS]; Peace Movement [Shahnawaz TANAI]; People's Aspirations Party of Afghanistan [Ilhaj Saraj-u-din ZAFAREE]; People's Freedom Seekers Party of Afghanistan [Feda Mohammad EHSAS]; People's Liberal Freedom Seekers Party of Afghanistan [Ajmal SUHAIL]; People's Message Party of Afghanistan [Noor Aqa WAINEE]; People's Movement of the National Unity of Afghanistan [Abdul Hakim NOORZAI]; People's Party of Afghanistan [Ahmad Shah ASAR]; People's Prosperity Party of Afghanistan [Ustad Mohammad ZAREEF];

People's Sovereignty Movement of Afghanistan [Hayatullah SUBHANEE]; People's Uprising Party of Afghanistan [Sayed Zahir Qayed Omul BELADI]; People's Welfare Party of Afghanistan [Mia Gul WASIQ]; People's Welfare Party of Afghanistan [Mohammad Zubair PAIROZ]; Progressive Democratic Party of Afghanistan [Wali ARYA]; Republican Party [Sebghatullah SANJAR]; Solidarity Party of Afghanistan [Abdul Khaleq NEMAT]; The Afghanistan's Mujahid Nation's Islamic Unity Movement. [Saeedullah SAEED]; The People of Afghanistan's Democratic Movement [Sharif NAZARI]; Tribes Solidarity Party of Afghanistan [Mohammad Zarif NASERI]; Understanding and Democracy Party of Afghanistan [Ahamad SHAHEEN]; United Afghanistan Party [Mohammad Wasil RAHIMEE]; United Islamic Party of Afghanistan [Wahidullah SABAWOON]; Young Afghanistan's Islamic Organization [Sayed Jawad HUSSINEE]; Youth Solidarity Party ofAfghanistan [Mohammad Jamil KARZAI]; note - includes only political parties approved by the Ministry of Justice

**Political pressure groups and leaders:** *other:* religious groups; tribal leaders; ethnically based groups

**International organization participation:** ADB, CP, ECO, FAO, G-77, IAEA, IBRD, ICAO, ICCt, IDA, IDB, IFAD, IFC, IFRCS, ILO, IMF, Interpol, IOC, IOM, ISO (correspondent), ITSO, ITU, MIGA, NAM, OIC, OPCW, OSCE (partner), SAARC, SACEP, SCO (guest), UN, UNCTAD, UNESCO, UNIDO, UNWTO, UPU, WCO, WFTU, WHO, WIPO, WMO, WTO (observer)

**Diplomatic representation in the US:**
*chief of mission:* Ambassador Said Tayeb JAWAD
*chancery:* 2341 Wyoming Avenue NW, Washington, DC 20008
*telephone:* [1] (202) 483-6410
*FAX:* [1] (202) 483-6488
*consulate(s) general:* Los Angeles, New York

**Diplomatic representation from the US:**
*chief of mission:* Ambassador (vacant); Deputy Ambassador Francis J. RICCIARDONE, Jr.
*embassy:* The Great Masood Road, Kabul
*mailing address:* U.S. Embassy Kabul, APO, AE 09806
*telephone:* [93] 0700 108 001
*FAX:* [93] 0700 108 564

**Flag description:** three equal vertical bands of black (hoist side), red, and green, with the national emblem in white centered on the red band and slightly overlapping the other two bands; the center of the emblem features a mosque with pulpit and flags on either side, below the mosque are numerals for the solar year 1298 (1919 in the Gregorian calendar, the year of Afghan independence from the UK); this central image is circled by a border consisting of sheaves of wheat on the left and right, in the upper-center is an Arabic inscription of the Shahada (Muslim creed) below which are rays of the rising sun over the Takbir (Arabic expression meaning "God is great"), and at bottom center is a scroll bearing the name Afghanistan

## Economy

**Economy - overview:** Afghanistan's economy is recovering from decades of conflict. The economy has improved significantly since the fall of the Taliban regime in 2001 largely because of the infusion of international assistance, the recovery of the agricultural sector, and service sector growth. Real GDP growth exceeded 7% in 2008. Despite the progress of the past few years, Afghanistan is extremely poor, landlocked, and highly dependent on foreign aid, agriculture, and trade with neighboring countries. Much of the population continues to suffer from shortages of housing, clean water, electricity, medical care, and jobs. Criminality, insecurity, and the Afghan Government's inability to extend rule of law to all parts of the country pose challenges to future economic growth. It will probably take the remainder of the decade and continuing donor aid and attention to significantly raise Afghanistan's living standards from its current level, among the lowest in the world. International pledges made by more than 60 countries and international financial institutions at the Berlin Donors Conference for Afghan reconstruction in March 2004 reached $8.9 billion for 2004-09. While the international community remains committed to Afghanistan's development, pledging over $57 billion at three donors' conferences since 2002, Kabul will need to overcome a number of challenges. Expanding poppy cultivation and a growing opium trade generate roughly $3 billion in illicit economic activity and looms as one of Kabul's most serious policy concerns. Other long-term challenges include: budget sustainability, job creation, corruption, government capacity, and rebuilding war torn infrastructure.

**GDP (purchasing power parity):**
$23.03 billion (2008 est.)
$21.43 billion (2007)
$19.22 billion (2006)
*note:* data are in 2008 US dollars

**GDP (official exchange rate):** $12.85 billion (2008 est.)

**GDP - real growth rate:**
7.5% (2008 est.)
11.5% (2007 est.)
8.2% (2006 est.)

**GDP - per capita (PPP):**
$800 (2008 est.)
$700 (2007 est.)
$600 (2006 est.)
*note:* data are in 2008 US dollars

**GDP - composition by sector:**
*agriculture:* 31%
*industry:* 26%
*services:* 43%
*note:* data exclude opium production (2008 est.)

**Labor force:** 15 million (2004 est.)

**Labor force - by occupation:**
*agriculture:* 80%
*industry:* 10%
*services:* 10% (2004 est.)

# Afghanistan *(continued)*

**Unemployment rate:**
40% (2008 est.)
40% (2005 est.)
**Population below poverty line:** 53% (2003)
**Household income or consumption by percentage share:**
*lowest 10%:* NA%
*highest 10%:* NA%
**Budget:**
*revenues:* $890 million
*expenditures:* $2.7 billion
*note:* Afghanistan has also received $2.6 billion from the Reconstruction Trust Fund and $63 million from the Law and Order Trust Fund (2007 est.)
**Inflation rate (consumer prices):**
13% (2007 est.)
**Central bank discount rate:** NA
**Commercial bank prime lending rate:** 18.14% (31 December 2007)
**Stock of money:** $1.426 billion (31 December 2007)
**Stock of quasi money:** $958.6 million (31 December 2007)
**Stock of domestic credit:** $20.06 million (31 December 2007)
**Market value of publicly traded shares:** $NA
**Agriculture - products:** opium, wheat, fruits, nuts; wool, mutton, sheepskins, lambskins
**Industries:** small-scale production of textiles, soap, furniture, shoes, fertilizer, cement; handwoven carpets; natural gas, coal, copper
**Industrial production growth rate:** NA%
**Electricity - production:** 839 million kWh (2007 est.)
**Electricity - consumption:** 1.418 billion kWh (2007 est.)
**Electricity - exports:** 0 kWh (2007 est.)
**Electricity - imports:** 608 million kWh (2007 est.)
**Oil - production:** 0 bbl/day (2007 est.)
**Oil - consumption:** 5,036 bbl/day (2006 est.)
**Oil - exports:** 0 bbl/day (2005)
**Oil - imports:** 4,534 bbl/day (2005)
**Oil - proved reserves:** 0 bbl (1 January 2006 est.)
**Natural gas - production:** 20 million cu m (2006 est.)
**Natural gas - consumption:** 20 million cu m (2006 est.)
**Natural gas - exports:** 0 cu m (2007 est.)
**Natural gas - imports:** 0 cu m (2007 est.)
**Natural gas - proved reserves:** 49.55 billion cu m (1 January 2008 est.)
**Current account balance:** -$67 million (2007 est.)
**Exports:** $327 million; note - not including illicit exports or reexports (2007)
**Exports - commodities:** opium, fruits and nuts, handwoven carpets, wool, cotton, hides and pelts, precious and semi-precious gems
**Exports - partners:** India 22.8%, Pakistan 21.8%, US 20.5%, Tajikistan 7.2% (2007)
**Imports:** $4.85 billion (2007)
**Imports - commodities:** capital goods, food, textiles, petroleum products

**Imports - partners:** Pakistan 36.8%, US 11%, India 5%, Germany 4.2% (2007)
**Debt - external:** $8 billion in bilateral debt, mostly to Russia; Afghanistan has $500 million in debt to multilateral development banks (2004)
**Exchange rates:** afghanis (AFA) per US dollar - 50 (2007), 46 (2006), 47.7 (2005), 48 (2004), 49 (2003)

## Communications

**Telephones - main lines in use:** 280,000 (2005)
**Telephones - mobile cellular:** 5.4 million (2008)
**Telephone system:**
*general assessment:* limited landline telephone service; an increasing number of Afghans utilize mobile-cellular phone networks in major cities
*domestic:* aided by the presence of multiple providers, mobile-cellular telephone service is improving rapidly
*international:* country code - 93; five VSAT's installed in Kabul, Herat, Mazar-e-Sharif, Kandahar, and Jalalabad provide international and domestic voice and data connectivity (2007)
**Radio broadcast stations:** AM 21, FM 5, shortwave 1 (broadcasts in Pashto, Dari (Afghan Persian), Urdu, and English) (2006)
**Television broadcast stations:** at least 7 (1 government-run central television station in Kabul and regional stations in 6 of the 34 provinces) (2006)
**Internet country code:** .af
**Internet hosts:** 31 (2008)
**Internet users:** 580,000 (2007)
**Communications - note:** Internet access is growing through Internet cafes as well as public "telekiosks" in Kabul (2005)

## Transportation

**Airports:** 50 (2008)
**Airports - with paved runways:**
*total:* 14
*over 3,047 m:* 4
*2,438 to 3,047 m:* 2
*1,524 to 2,437 m:* 6
*914 to 1,523 m:* 1
*under 914 m:* 1 (2008)
**Airports - with unpaved runways:**
*total:* 36
*over 3,047 m:* 1
*2,438 to 3,047 m:* 5
*1,524 to 2,437 m:* 16
*914 to 1,523 m:* 4
*under 914 m:* 10 (2008)
**Heliports:** 9 (2007)
**Pipelines:** gas 466 km (2008)
**Roadways:**
*total:* 42,150 km
*paved:* 12,350 km
*unpaved:* 29,800 km (2006)
**Waterways:** 1,200 km (chiefly Amu Darya, which handles vessels up to 500 DWT) (2008)
**Ports and terminals:** Kheyrabad, Shir Khan

## Military

**Military branches:** Afghan Armed Forces: Afghan National Army (ANA, includes Afghan National Army Air Corps) (2009)
**Military service age and obligation:** 22 years of age; inductees are contracted into service for a 4-year term (2005)
**Manpower available for military service:**
*males age 16-49:* 7,431,147
*females age 16-49:* 7,004,819 (2008 est.)
**Manpower fit for military service:**
*males age 16-49:* 4,371,193
*females age 16-49:* 4,072,945 (2009 est.)
**Manpower reaching militarily significant age annually:**
*male:* 382,720
*female:* 361,733 (2009 est.)
**Military expenditures:** 1.9% of GDP (2006 est.)

## Transnational Issues

**Disputes - international:** Pakistan has built fences in some portions of its border with Afghanistan which remains open in some areas to foreign terrorists and other illegal activities
**Refugees and internally displaced persons:**
*IDPs:* 132,246 (mostly Pashtuns and Kuchis displaced in south and west due to drought and instability) (2007)
**Illicit drugs:** world's largest producer of opium; poppy cultivation decreased 22% to 157,000 hectares in 2008 but remains at a historically high level; less favorable growing conditions in 2008 reduced potential opium production to 5,500 metric tons, down 31 percent from 2007; if the entire opium crop were processed, 648 metric tons of pure heroin potentially could be produced; the Taliban and other antigovernment groups participate in and profit from the opiate trade, which is a key source of revenue for the Taliban inside Afghanistan; widespread corruption and instability impede counterdrug efforts; most of the heroin consumed in Europe and Eurasia is derived from Afghan opium; vulnerable to drug money laundering through informal financial networks; regional source of hashish (2008)

# Akrotiri
*(UK Sovereign Base Area)*

## Introduction

**Background:** By terms of the 1960 Treaty of Establishment that created the independent Republic of Cyprus, the UK retained full sovereignty and jurisdiction over two areas of almost 254 square kilometers - Akrotiri and Dhekelia. The southernmost and smallest of these is the Akrotiri Sovereign Base Area, which is also referred to as the Western Sovereign Base Area.

## Geography

**Location:** Eastern Mediterranean, peninsula on the southwest coast of Cyprus
**Geographic coordinates:** 34 37 N, 32 58 E
**Map references:** Middle East
**Area:**
*total:* 123 sq km
*note:* includes a salt lake and wetlands
**Area - comparative:** about 0.7 times the size of Washington, DC
**Land boundaries:**
*total:* 47.4 km
*border countries:* Cyprus 47.4 km
**Coastline:** 56.3 km
**Climate:** temperate; Mediterranean with hot, dry summers and cool winters
**Environment - current issues:** hunting around the salt lake; note - breeding place for loggerhead and green turtles; only remaining colony of griffon vultures is on the base
**Geography - note:** British extraterritorial rights also extended to several small off-post sites scattered across Cyprus; of the Sovereign Base Area (SBA) land, 60% is privately owned and farmed, 20% is owned by the Ministry of Defense, and 20% is SBA Crown land

## People

**Population:** approximately 15,700 live on the Sovereign Base Areas of Akrotiri and Dhekelia including 7,700 Cypriots, 3,600 Service and UK-based contract personnel, and 4,400 dependents
**Languages:** English, Greek

## Government

**Country name:**
*conventional long form:* Akrotiri Sovereign Base Area
*conventional short form:* Akrotiri
**Dependency status:** a special form of UK overseas territory; administered by an administrator who is also the Commander, British Forces Cyprus
**Capital:**
*name:* Episkopi Cantonment (base administrative center for Akrotiri and Dhekelia)
*geographic coordinates:* 34 40 N, 32 51 E
*time difference:* UTC+2 (7 hours ahead of Washington, DC during Standard Time)
*daylight saving time:* +1hr, begins last Sunday in March; ends last Sunday in October
**Constitution:** Sovereign Base Areas of Akrotiri and Dhekelia Order in Council 1960, effective 16 August 1960, functions as a basic legal document
**Legal system:** the Sovereign Base Area Administration has its own court system to deal with civil and criminal matters; laws applicable to the Cypriot population are, as far as possible, the same as the laws of the Republic of Cyprus
**Executive branch:**
*chief of state:* Queen ELIZABETH II (since 6 February 1952)
*head of government:* Administrator Major General Jamie GORDON (since October 2008); note - reports to the British Ministry of Defense
*elections:* none; the monarch is hereditary; the administrator is appointed by the monarch
**Diplomatic representation in the US:** none (overseas territory of the UK)
**Diplomatic representation from the US:** none (overseas territory of the UK)
**Flag description:** the flag of the UK is used

## Economy

**Economy - overview:** Economic activity is limited to providing services to the military and their families located in Akrotiri. All food and manufactured goods must be imported.
**Exchange rates:** euros (EUR) per US dollar - 0.6827
*note:* on 1 January 2008 Akrotiri and Dhekelia adopted the euro along with the rest of Cyprus

## Communications

**Radio broadcast stations:** AM NA, FM 1, shortwave NA (British Forces Broadcasting Service (BFBS) provides Radio 1 and Radio 2 service to Akrotiri, Dhekelia, and Nicosia) (2006)

**Television broadcast stations:** 0 (British Forces Broadcasting Service (BFBS) provides multi-channel satellite service to Akrotiri, Dhekelia, and Nicosia) (2006)

## Military

**Military - note:** Akrotiri has a full RAF base, Headquarters for British Forces Cyprus, and Episkopi Support Unit

# Albania

## Introduction

**Background:** Albania declared its independence from the Ottoman Empire in 1912, but was conquered by Italy in 1939. Communist partisans took over the country in 1944. Albania allied itself first with the USSR (until 1960), and then with China (to 1978). In the early 1990s, Albania ended 46 years of xenophobic Communist rule and established a multiparty democracy. The transition has proven challenging as successive governments have tried to deal with high unemployment, widespread corruption, a dilapidated physical infrastructure, powerful organized crime networks, and combative political opponents. Albania has made progress in its democratic development since first holding multiparty elections in 1991, but deficiencies remain. International observers judged elections to be largely free and fair since the restoration of political stability following the collapse of pyramid schemes in 1997; however, there have been claims of electoral fraud in every one of Albania's post-communist elections. In the 2005 general elections, the Democratic Party and its allies won a decisive victory on pledges to reduce crime and corruption, promote economic growth, and decrease the size of government. The election, and particularly the orderly transition of power, was considered an important step forward. Albania joined NATO in April 2009 and is a potential candidate for EU accession. Although Albania's economy continues to grow, the country is still one of the poorest in Europe, hampered by a large informal economy and an inadequate energy and transportation infrastructure.

## Geography

**Location:** Southeastern Europe, bordering the Adriatic Sea and Ionian Sea, between Greece in the south and Montenegro and Kosovo to the north
**Geographic coordinates:** 41 00 N, 20 00 E
**Map references:** Europe

**Area:**
*total:* 28,748 sq km
*land:* 27,398 sq km
*water:* 1,350 sq km
**Area - comparative:** slightly smaller than Maryland
**Land boundaries:**
*total:* 717 km
*border countries:* Greece 282 km, Macedonia 151 km, Montenegro 172 km, Kosovo 112 km
**Coastline:** 362 km
**Maritime claims:**
*territorial sea:* 12 nm
*continental shelf:* 200 m depth or to the depth of exploitation
**Climate:** mild temperate; cool, cloudy, wet winters; hot, clear, dry summers; interior is cooler and wetter
**Terrain:** mostly mountains and hills; small plains along coast
**Elevation extremes:**
*lowest point:* Adriatic Sea 0 m
*highest point:* Maja e Korabit (Golem Korab) 2,764 m
**Natural resources:** petroleum, natural gas, coal, bauxite, chromite, copper, iron ore, nickel, salt, timber, hydropower
**Land use:**
*arable land:* 20.1%
*permanent crops:* 4.21%
*other:* 75.69% (2005)
**Irrigated land:** 3,530 sq km (2003)
**Total renewable water resources:** 41.7 cu km (2001)
**Freshwater withdrawal (domestic/industrial/agricultural):**
*total:* 1.71 cu km/yr (27%/11%/62%)
*per capita:* 546 cu m/yr (2000)
**Natural hazards:** destructive earthquakes; tsunamis occur along southwestern coast; floods; drought
**Environment - current issues:** deforestation; soil erosion; water pollution from industrial and domestic effluents
**Environment - international agreements:**
*party to:* Air Pollution, Biodiversity, Climate Change, Climate Change-Kyoto Protocol, Desertification, Endangered Species, Hazardous Wastes, Law of the Sea, Ozone Layer Protection, Wetlands
*signed, but not ratified:* none of the selected agreements
**Geography - note:** strategic location along Strait of Otranto (links Adriatic Sea to Ionian Sea and Mediterranean Sea)

## People

**Population:** 3,639,453 (July 2009 est.)
**Age structure:**
*0-14 years:* 23.1% (male 440,528/female 400,816)
*15-64 years:* 67.1% (male 1,251,001/female 1,190,841)
*65 years and over:* 9.8% (male 165,557/female 190,710) (2009 est.)

**Median age:**
*total:* 29.9 years
*male:* 29.3 years
*female:* 30.6 years (2009 est.)
**Population growth rate:** 0.546% (2009 est.)
**Birth rate:** 15.29 births/1,000 population (2009 est.)
**Death rate:** 5.44 deaths/1,000 population (2008 est.)
**Net migration rate:** -4.28 migrant(s)/1,000 population (2009 est.)
**Urbanization:**
*urban population:* 47% of total population (2008)
*rate of urbanization:* 1.9% annual rate of change (2005-10 est.)
**Sex ratio:**
*at birth:* 1.1 male(s)/female
*under 15 years:* 1.1 male(s)/female
*15-64 years:* 1.05 male(s)/female
*65 years and over:* 0.87 male(s)/female
*total population:* 1.04 male(s)/female (2009 est.)
**Infant mortality rate:**
*total:* 18.62 deaths/1,000 live births
*male:* 19.05 deaths/1,000 live births
*female:* 18.15 deaths/1,000 live births (2009 est.)
**Life expectancy at birth:**
*total population:* 77.96 years
*male:* 75.28 years
*female:* 80.89 years (2009 est.)
**Total fertility rate:** 2.01 children born/woman (2009 est.)
**HIV/AIDS - adult prevalence rate:** NA
**HIV/AIDS - people living with HIV/AIDS:** NA
**HIV/AIDS - deaths:** NA
**Nationality:**
*noun:* Albanian(s)
*adjective:* Albanian
**Ethnic groups:** Albanian 95%, Greek 3%, other 2% (Vlach, Roma (Gypsy), Serb, Macedonian, Bulgarian) (1989 est.)
*note:* in 1989, other estimates of the Greek population ranged from 1% (official Albanian statistics) to 12% (from a Greek organization)
**Religions:** Muslim 70%, Albanian Orthodox 20%, Roman Catholic 10%
*note:* percentages are estimates; there are no available current statistics on religious affiliation; all mosques and churches were closed in 1967 and religious observances prohibited; in November 1990, Albania began allowing private religious practice
**Languages:** Albanian (official - derived from Tosk dialect), Greek, Vlach, Romani, Slavic dialects
**Literacy:**
*definition:* age 9 and over can read and write
*total population:* 98.7%
*male:* 99.2%
*female:* 98.3% (2001 census)
**School life expectancy (primary to tertiary education):**
*total:* 11 years
*male:* 11 years
*female:* 11 years (2004)
**Education expenditures:** 2.9% of GDP (2002)

# Albania (continued)

## Government

**Country name:**
*conventional long form:* Republic of Albania
*conventional short form:* Albania
*local long form:* Republika e Shqiperise
*local short form:* Shqiperia
*former:* People's Socialist Republic of Albania
**Government type:** emerging democracy
**Capital:**
*name:* Tirana (Tirane)
*geographic coordinates:* 41 19 N, 19 49 E
*time difference:* UTC+1 (6 hours ahead of
Washington, DC during Standard Time)
*daylight saving time:* +1hr, begins last Sunday
in March; ends last Sunday in October
**Administrative divisions:** 12 counties (qarqe,
singular - qark); Berat, Diber, Durres, Elbasan, Fier,
Gjirokaster, Korce, Kukes, Lezhe, Shkoder, Tirane, Vlore
**Independence:** 28 November 1912 (from the
Ottoman Empire)
**National holiday:** Independence Day, 28 November
(1912)
**Constitution:** approved by parliament on 21 October
1998; adopted by popular referendum on
22 November 1998; promulgated 28 November 1998
**Legal system:** has a civil law system; has not
accepted compulsory ICJ jurisdiction; has accepted
jurisdiction of the International Criminal Court for its
citizens
**Suffrage:** 18 years of age; universal
**Executive branch:**
*chief of state:* President of the Republic Bamir TOPI
(since 24 July 2007)
*head of government:* Prime Minister Sali BERISHA
(since 10 September 2005)
*cabinet:* Council of Ministers proposed by the prime
minister, nominated by the president, and approved
by parliament
*elections:* president elected by the Assembly for a
five-year term (eligible for a second term); four
election rounds held between 8 and 20 July 2007
(next election to be held in 2012); prime minister
appointed by the president
*election results:* Bamir TOPI elected president;
Assembly vote, fourth round (three-fifths majority (84
votes) required): Bamir TOPI 85 votes, Neritan CEKA
5 votes
**Legislative branch:** unicameral Assembly or
Kuvendi (140 seats; 100 members elected by direct
popular vote and 40 by proportional vote to serve
four-year terms)
*elections:* last held 3 July 2005 (next to be held in
2009)
*election results:* percent of vote by party - NA; seats
by party - PD 56, PS 42, PR 11, PSD 7, LSI 5, other 19
*note:* Parliament in November 2008 approved an
electoral reform package that will transform the
electoral system from a majority system to a regional
proportional system; the code will also establish an
electoral threshold limiting smaller party
representation

**Judicial branch:** Constitutional Court, Supreme
Court (chairman is elected by the People's Assembly
for a four-year term) and multiple appeals and district
courts
**Political parties and leaders:** Agrarian
Environmentalist Party or PAA [Lufter XHUVELI];
Christian Democratic Party or PDK [Nard NDOKA];
Communist Party of Albania or PKSH [Hysni
MILLOSHI]; Democratic Alliance Party or AD [Neritan
CEKA]; Democratic Party or PD [Sali BERISHA]; G99
Political Movement [Erion VELIAJ]; Liberal Union
Party or BLD [Arjan STAROVA]; National Front Party
(Balli Kombetar) or PBK [Artur ROSHI]; New
Democratic Party or PDR [Genc POLLO]; Republican
Party or PR [Fatmir MEDIU]; Social Democracy Party
of Albania or PDSSh [Paskal MILO]; Social
Democratic Party or PSD [Skender GJINUSHI];
Socialist Movement for Integration or LSI [Ilir META];
Socialist Party or PS [Edi RAMA]; Socialist Party 1991
[Petro KOCI]; Union for Human Rights Party or PBDNj
[Vangjel DULE]
**Political pressure groups and leaders:** Citizens
Advocacy Office [Kreshnik SPAHIU]; Confederation of
Trade Unions of Albania or KSSH [Kastriot MUCO];
Front for Albanian National Unification or FBKSH
[Gafur ADILI]; Mjaft Movement; Omonia [Jani JANI];
Union of Independent Trade Unions of Albania or
BSPSH [Gezim KALAJA]
**International organization participation:** BSEC,
CE, CEI, EAPC, EBRD, FAO, IAEA, IBRD, ICAO,
ICCt, ICRM, IDA, IDB, IFAD, IFC, IFRCS, ILO, IMF,
IMO, Interpol, IOC, IOM, IPU, ISO (correspondent),
ITU, ITUC, MIGA, NATO, OIC, OIF, OPCW, OSCE,
SECI, UN, UNCTAD, UNESCO, UNIDO, UNOMIG,
UNWTO, UPU, WCO, WFTU, WHO, WIPO, WMO,
WTO
**Diplomatic representation in the US:**
*chief of mission:* Ambassador Aleksander
SALLABANDA
*chancery:* 2100 S Street NW, Washington, DC 20008
*telephone:* [1] (202) 223-4942
*FAX:* [1] (202) 628-7342
*consulate(s) general:* New York
**Diplomatic representation from the US:**
*chief of mission:* Ambassador John L. WITHERS, II
*embassy:* Rruga e Elbasanit, Labinoti #103, Tirana
*mailing address:* US Department of State, 9510
Tirana Place, Dulles, VA 20189-9510
*telephone:* [355] (4) 2247285
*FAX:* [355] (4) 2232222
**Flag description:** red with a black two-headed eagle
in the center

## Economy

**Economy - overview:** Lagging behind its Balkan
neighbors, Albania is making the difficult transition to
a more modern open-market economy.
Macroeconomic growth has averaged around 5% over
the last five years and inflation is low and stable. The
government has taken measures to curb violent crime,
and recently adopted a fiscal reform package aimed at
reducing the large gray economy and attracting
foreign investment. The economy is bolstered by
annual remittances from abroad representing about
15% of GDP, mostly from Albanians residing in
Greece and Italy; this helps offset the towering trade
deficit. The agricultural sector, which accounts for
over half of employment but only about one-fifth of
GDP, is limited primarily to small family operations
and subsistence farming because of lack of modern
equipment, unclear property rights, and the
prevalence of small, inefficient plots of land. Energy
shortages because of a reliance on hydropower, and
antiquated and inadequate infrastructure contribute to
Albania's poor business environment and lack of
success in attracting new foreign investment. The
completion of a new thermal power plant near Vlore
has helped diversify generation capacity, and plans to
upgrade transmission lines between Albania and
Montenegro and Kosovo would help relieve the
energy shortages. Also, with help from EU funds, the
government is taking steps to improve the poor
national road and rail network, a long-standing barrier
to sustained economic growth.
**GDP (purchasing power parity):**
$21.82 billion (2008 est.)
$20.57 billion (2007)
$19.4 billion (2006)
*note:* data are in 2008 US dollars
Albania has an informal, and unreported, sector that
may be as large as 50% of official GDP
**GDP (official exchange rate):** $13.52 billion
(2008 est.)
**GDP - real growth rate:**
6.1% (2008 est.)
6% (2007 est.)
5.5% (2006 est.)
**GDP - per capita (PPP):**
$6,000 (2008 est.)
$5,700 (2007 est.)
$5,400 (2006 est.)
*note:* data are in 2008 US dollars
**GDP - composition by sector:**
*agriculture:* 20.6%
*industry:* 19.9%
*services:* 59.5% (2008 est.)
**Labor force:** 1.09 million (not including 352,000
emigrant workers) (September 2006 est.)
**Labor force - by occupation:**
*agriculture:* 58%
*industry:* 15%
*services:* 27% (September 2006 est.)
**Unemployment rate:**
12.5% (2008 est.)
13.2% (2007 est.)
*note:* these are official rates, but actual rates may
exceed 30% due to preponderance of
near-subsistence farming
**Population below poverty line:** 25% (2004 est.)
**Household income or consumption by
percentage share:**
*lowest 10%:* 3.4%
*highest 10%:* 24.4% (2004)

**Distribution of family income - Gini index:** 26.7 (2005)
**Investment (gross fixed):** 22.8% of GDP (2008 est.)
**Budget:**
*revenues:* $3.771 billion
*expenditures:* $4.538 billion (2008 est.)
**Public debt:** 51.2% of GDP (2008 est.)
**Inflation rate (consumer prices):**
4% (2008 est.)
2.9% (2007 est.)
**Central bank discount rate:** 6.25%
(31 December 2007)
**Commercial bank prime lending rate:** 14.1%
(31 December 2007)
**Stock of money:** $2.707 billion (31 December 2007)
**Stock of quasi money:** $6.433 billion
(31 December 2007)
**Stock of domestic credit:** $7.341 billion
(31 December 2007)
**Market value of publicly traded shares:** $NA
**Agriculture - products:** wheat, corn, potatoes, vegetables, fruits, sugar beets, grapes; meat, dairy products
**Industries:** food processing, textiles and clothing; lumber, oil, cement, chemicals, mining, basic metals, hydropower
**Industrial production growth rate:** 3% (2008 est.)
**Electricity - production:** 2.892 billion kWh
(2007 est.)
**Electricity - consumption:** 3.607 billion kWh
(2007 est.)
**Electricity - exports:** 0 kWh (2007 est.)
**Electricity - imports:** 2.8 billion kWh (2007 est.)
**Oil - production:** 6,425 bbl/day (2007 est.)
**Oil - consumption:** 30,900 bbl/day (2006 est.)
**Oil - exports:** 748.9 bbl/day (2005 est.)
**Oil - imports:** 24,860 bbl/day (2005 est.)
**Oil - proved reserves:** 199.1 million bbl
(1 January 2008 est.)
**Natural gas - production:** 30 million cu m
(2006 est.)
**Natural gas - consumption:** 30 million cu m
(2006 est.)
**Natural gas - exports:** 0 cu m (2007 est.)
**Natural gas - imports:** 0 cu m (2007 est.)
**Natural gas - proved reserves:** 849.5 million cu m
(1 January 2008 est.)
**Current account balance:** -$1.639 billion
(2008 est.)
**Exports:** $1.416 billion f.o.b. (2008 est.)
**Exports - commodities:** textiles and footwear; asphalt, metals and metallic ores, crude oil; vegetables, fruits, tobacco
**Exports - partners:** Italy 72%, Greece 8.8%, China 2.7% (2007)
**Imports:** $4.844 billion f.o.b. (2008 est.)
**Imports - commodities:** machinery and equipment, foodstuffs, textiles, chemicals
**Imports - partners:** Italy 27.6%, Greece 14.8%, Turkey 7.4%, China 6.8%, Germany 5.6%, Switzerland 5%, Russia 4.2% (2007)

**Reserves of foreign exchange and gold:** $2.479 billion (31 December 2008 est.)
**Debt - external:** $1.55 billion (2004)
**Exchange rates:** leke (ALL) per US dollar - 79.546 (2008 est.), 92.668 (2007), 98.384 (2006), 102.649 (2005), 102.78 (2004)

## Communications

**Telephones - main lines in use:** 353,600 (2005)
**Telephones - mobile cellular:** 2.3 million (2007)
**Telephone system:**
*general assessment:* despite new investment in fixed lines, the density of main lines remains low with roughly 10 lines per 100 people; cellular telephone use is widespread and generally effective; combined fixed line and mobile telephone density is approximately 75 telephones per 100 persons
*domestic:* offsetting the shortage of fixed line capacity, mobile phone service has been available since 1996; by 2003, two companies were providing mobile services at a greater density than some of Albania's neighbors; Internet broadband services initiated in 2005; Internet cafes are popular in Tirana and have started to spread outside the capital
*international:* country code - 355; submarine cable provides connectivity to Italy, Croatia, and Greece; the Trans-Balkan Line, a combination submarine cable and land fiber-optic system, provides additional connectivity to Bulgaria, Macedonia, and Turkey; international traffic carried by fiber-optic cable and, when necessary, by microwave radio relay from the Tirana exchange to Italy and Greece (2007)
**Radio broadcast stations:** AM 13, FM 46, shortwave 1 (2005)
**Television broadcast stations:** 65 (3 national, 62 local); 2 cable networks (2005)
**Internet country code:** .al
**Internet hosts:** 10,162 (2008)
**Internet users:** 471,200 (2006)

## Transportation

**Airports:** 8 (2008)
**Airports - with paved runways:**
*total:* 3
*2,438 to 3,047 m:* 3 (2008)
**Airports - with unpaved runways:**
*total:* 5
*over 3,047 m:* 1
*1,524 to 2,437 m:* 2
*914 to 1,523 m:* 1
*under 914 m:* 1 (2008)
**Heliports:** 1 (2007)
**Pipelines:** gas 339 km; oil 207 km (2008)
**Railways:**
*total:* 447 km
*standard gauge:* 447 km 1.435-m gauge (2006)
**Roadways:**
*total:* 18,000 km
*paved:* 7,020 km
*unpaved:* 10,980 km (2002)

**Waterways:** 43 km (2008)
**Merchant marine:**
*total:* 24
*by type:* cargo 22, roll on/roll off 2
*foreign-owned:* 1 (Turkey 1)
*registered in other countries:* 2 (Panama 2) (2008)
**Ports and terminals:** Durres, Sarande, Shengjin, Vlore

## Military

**Military branches:** Joint Force Command (includes Land, Naval, and Aviation Brigade Commands), Joint Support Command (includes Logistic Command), Training and Doctrine Command (2009)
**Military service age and obligation:** 19 years of age (2004)
**Manpower available for military service:**
*males age 16-49:* 944,592
*females age 16-49:* 908,527 (2008 est.)
**Manpower fit for military service:**
*males age 16-49:* 800,665
*females age 16-49:* 768,536 (2009 est.)
**Manpower reaching militarily significant age annually:**
*male:* 34,778
*female:* 31,673 (2009 est.)
**Military expenditures:** 1.49% of GDP (2005 est.)

## Transnational Issues

**Disputes - international:** the Albanian Government calls for the protection of the rights of ethnic Albanians in neighboring countries, and the peaceful resolution of interethnic disputes; some ethnic Albanian groups in neighboring countries advocate for a "greater Albania," but the idea has little appeal among Albanian nationals; the mass emigration of unemployed Albanians remains a problem for developed countries, chiefly Greece and Italy
**Trafficking in persons:**
*current situation:* Albania is a source country for women and girls trafficked for the purpose of commercial sexual exploitation and forced labor; it is no longer considered a major country of transit; Albanian victims are trafficked to Greece, Italy, Macedonia, and Kosovo, with many trafficked onward to Western European countries; children were also trafficked to Greece for begging and other forms of child labor; approximately half of all Albanian trafficking victims are under age 18; internal sex trafficking of women and children is on the rise
*tier rating:* Tier 2 Watch List - Albania is on the Tier 2 Watch List for its failure to provide evidence of increasing efforts to combat trafficking in persons in 2007, particularly in the area of victim protection; the government did not appropriately identify trafficking victims during 2007, and has not demonstrated that it is vigorously investigating or prosecuting complicit officials (2008)

## Albania (continued)

**Illicit drugs:** increasingly active transshipment point for Southwest Asian opiates, hashish, and cannabis transiting the Balkan route and - to a lesser extent - cocaine from South America destined for Western Europe; limited opium and expanding cannabis production; ethnic Albanian narcotrafficking organizations active and expanding in Europe; vulnerable to money laundering associated with regional trafficking in narcotics, arms, contraband, and illegal aliens

# Algeria

## Introduction

**Background:** After more than a century of rule by France, Algerians fought through much of the 1950s to achieve independence in 1962. Algeria's primary political party, the National Liberation Front (FLN), has dominated politics ever since. Many Algerians in the subsequent generation were not satisfied, however, and moved to counter the FLN's centrality in Algerian politics. The surprising first round success of the Islamic Salvation Front (FIS) in the December 1991 balloting spurred the Algerian army to intervene and postpone the second round of elections to prevent what the secular elite feared would be an extremist-led government from assuming power. The army began a crackdown on the FIS that spurred FIS supporters to begin attacking government targets. The government later allowed elections featuring pro-government and moderate religious-based parties, but did not appease the activists who progressively widened their attacks. The fighting escalated into an insurgency, which saw intense fighting between 1992-98 and which resulted in over 100,000 deaths - many attributed to indiscriminate massacres of villagers by extremists. The government gained the upper hand by the late-1990s and FIS's armed wing, the Islamic Salvation Army, disbanded in January 2000. However, small numbers of armed militants persist in confronting government forces and conducting ambushes and occasional attacks on villages. The army placed Abdelaziz BOUTEFLIKA in the presidency in 1999 in a fraudulent election but claimed neutrality in his 2004 landslide reelection victory. Longstanding problems continue to face BOUTEFLIKA in his second term, including large-scale unemployment, a shortage of housing, unreliable electrical and water supplies, government inefficiencies and corruption, and the continuing activities of extremist militants. The Salafist Group for Preaching and Combat (GSPC) in 2006 merged with al-Qaida to form al-Qaida in the Lands of the Islamic Maghreb, which since has launched an ongoing series of kidnappings and bombings - including high-profile, mass-casualty suicide attacks targeted against the Algerian government and Western interests. Algeria must also diversify its petroleum-based economy, which has yielded a large cash reserve but which has not been used to redress Algeria's many social and infrastructure problems.

## Geography

**Location:** Northern Africa, bordering the Mediterranean Sea, between Morocco and Tunisia
**Geographic coordinates:** 28 00 N, 3 00 E
**Map references:** Africa
**Area:**
*total:* 2,381,740 sq km
*land:* 2,381,740 sq km
*water:* 0 sq km
**Area - comparative:** slightly less than 3.5 times the size of Texas
**Land boundaries:**
*total:* 6,343 km
*border countries:* Libya 982 km, Mali 1,376 km, Mauritania 463 km, Morocco 1,559 km, Niger 956 km, Tunisia 965 km, Western Sahara 42 km
**Coastline:** 998 km
**Maritime claims:**
*territorial sea:* 12 nm
*exclusive fishing zone:* 32-52 nm
**Climate:** arid to semiarid; mild, wet winters with hot, dry summers along coast; drier with cold winters and hot summers on high plateau; sirocco is a hot, dust/sand-laden wind especially common in summer
**Terrain:** mostly high plateau and desert; some mountains; narrow, discontinuous coastal plain
**Elevation extremes:**
*lowest point:* Chott Melrhir -40 m
*highest point:* Tahat 3,003 m
**Natural resources:** petroleum, natural gas, iron ore, phosphates, uranium, lead, zinc
**Land use:**
*arable land:* 3.17%
*permanent crops:* 0.28%
*other:* 96.55% (2005)
**Irrigated land:** 5,690 sq km (2003)
**Total renewable water resources:** 14.3 cu km (1997)
**Freshwater withdrawal (domestic/industrial/agricultural):**
*total:* 6.07 cu km/yr (22%/13%/65%)
*per capita:* 185 cu m/yr (2000)
**Natural hazards:** mountainous areas subject to severe earthquakes; mudslides and floods in rainy season
**Environment - current issues:** soil erosion from overgrazing and other poor farming practices; desertification; dumping of raw sewage, petroleum refining wastes, and other industrial effluents is leading to the pollution of rivers and coastal waters; Mediterranean Sea, in particular, becoming polluted from oil wastes, soil erosion, and fertilizer runoff; inadequate supplies of potable water

# Algeria *(continued)*

**Environment - international agreements:**

*party to:* Biodiversity, Climate Change, Climate Change-Kyoto Protocol, Desertification, Endangered Species, Environmental Modification, Hazardous Wastes, Law of the Sea, Ozone Layer Protection, Ship Pollution, Wetlands

*signed, but not ratified:* none of the selected agreements

**Geography - note:** second-largest country in Africa (after Sudan)

## People

**Population:** 34,178,188 (July 2009 est.)

**Age structure:**

*0-14 years:* 25.4% (male 4,436,591/female 4,259,729)

*15-64 years:* 69.5% (male 11,976,965/female 11,777,618)

*65 years and over:* 5.1% (male 798,576/female 928,709) (2009 est.)

**Median age:**

*total:* 26.6 years

*male:* 26.3 years

*female:* 26.8 years (2009 est.)

**Population growth rate:** 1.196% (2009 est.)

**Birth rate:** 16.9 births/1,000 population (2009 est.)

**Death rate:** 4.62 deaths/1,000 population (2008 est.)

**Net migration rate:** -0.29 migrant(s)/1,000 population (2009 est.)

**Urbanization:**

*urban population:* 65% of total population (2008)

*rate of urbanization:* 2.5% annual rate of change (2005-10 est.)

**Sex ratio:**

*at birth:* 1.05 male(s)/female

*under 15 years:* 1.04 male(s)/female

*15-64 years:* 1.02 male(s)/female

*65 years and over:* 0.86 male(s)/female

*total population:* 1.01 male(s)/female (2009 est.)

**Infant mortality rate:**

*total:* 27.73 deaths/1,000 live births

*male:* 30.86 deaths/1,000 live births

*female:* 24.45 deaths/1,000 live births (2009 est.)

**Life expectancy at birth:**

*total population:* 74.02 years

*male:* 72.35 years

*female:* 75.77 years (2009 est.)

**Total fertility rate:** 1.79 children born/woman (2009 est.)

**HIV/AIDS - adult prevalence rate:** 0.1%; note - no country specific models provided (2007 est.)

**HIV/AIDS - people living with HIV/AIDS:** 21,000 (2007 est.)

**HIV/AIDS - deaths:** fewer than 1,000 (2007 est.)

**Nationality:**

*noun:* Algerian(s)

*adjective:* Algerian

**Ethnic groups:** Arab-Berber 99%, European less than 1%

*note:* almost all Algerians are Berber in origin, not Arab; the minority who identify themselves as Berber live mostly in the mountainous region of Kabylie east of Algiers; the Berbers are also Muslim but identify with their Berber rather than Arab cultural heritage; Berbers have long agitated, sometimes violently, for autonomy; the government is unlikely to grant autonomy but has offered to begin sponsoring teaching Berber language in schools

**Religions:** Sunni Muslim (state religion) 99%, Christian and Jewish 1%

**Languages:** Arabic (official), French, Berber dialects

**Literacy:**

*definition:* age 15 and over can read and write

*total population:* 69.9%

*male:* 79.6%

*female:* 60.1% (2002 est.)

**School life expectancy (primary to tertiary education):**

*total:* 13 years

*male:* 13 years

*female:* 13 years (2005)

**Education expenditures:** 5.1% of GDP (1999)

## Government

**Country name:**

*conventional long form:* People's Democratic Republic of Algeria

*conventional short form:* Algeria

*local long form:* Al Jumhuriyah al Jaza'iriyah ad Dimuqratiyah ash Sha'biyah

*local short form:* Al Jaza'ir

**Government type:** republic

**Capital:**

*name:* Algiers

*geographic coordinates:* 36 45 N, 3 03 E

*time difference:* UTC+1 (6 hours ahead of Washington, DC during Standard Time)

**Administrative divisions:** 48 provinces (wilayat, singular - wilaya); Adrar, Ain Defla, Ain Temouchent, Alger, Annaba, Batna, Bechar, Bejaia, Biskra, Blida, Bordj Bou Arreridj, Bouira, Boumerdes, Chlef, Constantine, Djelfa, El Bayadh, El Oued, El Tarf, Ghardaia, Guelma, Illizi, Jijel, Khenchela, Laghouat, Mascara, Medea, Mila, Mostaganem, M'Sila, Naama, Oran, Ouargla, Oum el Bouaghi, Relizane, Saida, Setif, Sidi Bel Abbes, Skikda, Souk Ahras, Tamanghasset, Tebessa, Tiaret, Tindouf, Tipaza, Tissemsilt, Tizi Ouzou, Tlemcen

**Independence:** 5 July 1962 (from France)

**National holiday:** Revolution Day, 1 November (1954)

**Constitution:** 8 September 1963; revised 19 November 1976; effective 22 November 1976; revised 3 November 1988, 23 February 1989, 28 November 1996, 10 April 2002, and 12 November 2008

**Legal system:** socialist, based on French and Islamic law; judicial review of legislative acts in ad hoc Constitutional Council composed of various public officials including several Supreme Court justices; has not accepted compulsory ICJ jurisdiction

**Suffrage:** 18 years of age; universal

**Executive branch:**

*chief of state:* President Abdelaziz BOUTEFLIKA (since 28 April 1999)

*head of government:* Prime Minister Ahmed OUYAHIA (since 23 June 2008)

*cabinet:* Cabinet of Ministers appointed by the president

*elections:* president elected by popular vote for a five-year term; note - a November 2008 constitutional amendment abolished presidential term limits; election last held 9 April 2009 (next to be held in April 2014); prime minister appointed by the president

*election results:* Abdelaziz BOUTEFLIKA reelected president for third term; percent of vote - Abdelaziz BOUTEFLIKA 90.2%, Louisa HANOUNE 4.2%, Moussa TOUATI 2.3%, Djahid YOUNSI 1.4%, Ali Fawzi REBIANE less than 1%, Mohamed SAID less than 1%

**Legislative branch:** bicameral Parliament consists of the Council of Nations (Senate) (144 seats; one-third of the members appointed by the president, two-thirds elected by indirect vote to serve six-year terms; the constitution requires half the council to be renewed every three years) and the National People's Assembly or Al-Majlis Al-Shabi Al-Watani (389 seats; members elected by popular vote to serve five-year terms)

*elections:* National People's Assembly - last held 17 May 2007 (next to be held in 2012); Council of Nations (Senate) - last held 28 December 2006 (next to be held in 2009)

*election results:* National People's Assembly - percent of vote by party - NA; seats by party - FLN 136, RND 61, MSP 52, PT 26, RCD 19, FNA 13, other 49, independents 33; Council of Nations - percent of vote by party - NA; seats by party - FLN 29, RND 12, MSP 3, RCD 1, independents 3, presidential appointees (unknown affiliation) 24; note - Council seating reflects the number of replaced council members rather than the whole Council

**Judicial branch:** Supreme Court

**Political parties and leaders:** Ahd 54 [Ali Fauzi REBIANE]; Algerian National Front or FNA [Moussa TOUATI]; National Democratic Rally (Rassemblement National Democratique) or RND [Ahmed OUYAHIA]; National Liberation Front or FLN [Abdelaziz BELKHADEM, secretary general]; National Reform Movement or Islah (formerly MRN) [Ahmed ABDESLAM]; Rally for Culture and Democracy or RCD [Said SADI]; Renaissance Movement or EnNahda Movement [Fatah RABEI]; Socialist Forces Front or FFS [Hocine Ait AHMED]; Society of Peace Movement or MSP [Boudjerra SOLTANI]; Workers Party or PT [Louisa HANOUNE]

*note:* a law banning political parties based on religion was enacted in March 1997

**Political pressure groups and leaders:** The Algerian Human Rights League or LADDH [Hocine ZEHOUANE]; SOS Disparus [Nacera DUTOUR]

**International organization participation:** ABEDA, AfDB, AFESD, AMF, AMU, AU, BIS, FAO, G-15, G-24, G-77, IAEA, IBRD, ICAO, ICC, ICCt (signatory), ICRM, IDA, IDB, IFAD, IFC, IFRCS, IHO, ILO, IMF,

IMO, IMSO, Interpol, IOC, IOM, IPU, ISO, ITSO, ITU, ITUC, LAS, MIGA, MONUC, NAM, OAPEC, OAS (observer), OIC, OPCW, OPEC, OSCE (partner), UN, UNCTAD, UNESCO, UNHCR, UNIDO, UNITAR, UNWTO, UPU, WCO, WFTU, WHO, WIPO, WMO, WTO (observer)

**Diplomatic representation in the US:**
*chief of mission:* Ambassador Abdallah BAALI
*chancery:* 2118 Kalorama Road NW, Washington, DC 20008
*telephone:* [1] (202) 265-2800
*FAX:* [1] (202) 667-2174

**Diplomatic representation from the US:**
*chief of mission:* Ambassador David D. PEARCE
*embassy:* 05 Chemin Cheikh Bachir, El-Ibrahimi, El-Biar 16000 Algiers
*mailing address:* B. P. 408, Alger-Gare, 16030 Algiers
*telephone:* [213] 770-08-2000
*FAX:* [213] 21-60-7355

**Flag description:** two equal vertical bands of green (hoist side) and white; a red, five-pointed star within a red crescent centered over the two-color boundary
*note:* the crescent, star, and color green are traditional symbols of Islam (the state religion)

## Economy

**Economy - overview:** The hydrocarbons sector is the backbone of the economy, accounting for roughly 60% of budget revenues, 30% of GDP, and over 95% of export earnings. Algeria has the eighth-largest reserves of natural gas in the world and is the fourth-largest gas exporter; it ranks 15th in oil reserves. Sustained high oil prices in recent years have helped improve Algeria's financial and macroeconomic indicators. Algeria is running substantial trade surpluses and building up record foreign exchange reserves. Algeria has decreased its external debt to less than 5% of GDP after repaying its Paris Club and London Club debt in 2006. Real GDP has risen due to higher oil output and increased government spending. The government's continued efforts to diversify the economy by attracting foreign and domestic investment outside the energy sector, however, has had little success in reducing high unemployment and improving living standards. Structural reform within the economy, such as development of the banking sector and the construction of infrastructure, moves ahead slowly hampered by corruption and bureaucratic resistance.

**GDP (purchasing power parity):**
$235.5 billion (2008 est.)
$228.6 billion (2007)
$218.6 billion (2006)
*note:* data are in 2008 US dollars
**GDP (official exchange rate):** $171.3 billion (2008 est.)
**GDP - real growth rate:**
3% (2008 est.)
4.6% (2007 est.)
2.2% (2006 est.)

**GDP - per capita (PPP):**
$7,000 (2008 est.)
$6,900 (2007 est.)
$6,600 (2006 est.)
*note:* data are in 2008 US dollars
**GDP - composition by sector:**
*agriculture:* 8.1%
*industry:* 62.5%
*services:* 29.4% (2008 est.)
**Labor force:** 9.44 million (2008 est.)
**Labor force - by occupation:** agriculture 14%, industry 13.4%, construction and public works 10%, trade 14.6%, government 32%, other 16% (2003 est.)
**Unemployment rate:**
12.9% (2008 est.)
11.8% (2007 est.)
**Population below poverty line:** 25% (2005 est.)
**Household income or consumption by percentage share:**
*lowest 10%:* 2.8%
*highest 10%:* 26.8% (1995)
**Distribution of family income - Gini index:** 35.3 (1995)
**Investment (gross fixed):** 24.8% of GDP (2008 est.)
**Budget:**
*revenues:* $73.26 billion
*expenditures:* $51.19 billion (2008 est.)
**Public debt:** 13.8% of GDP (2008 est.)
**Inflation rate (consumer prices):**
3.6% (2008 est.)
3.5% (2007 est.)
**Central bank discount rate:** 4% (31 December 2007)
**Commercial bank prime lending rate:** 8% (31 December 2007)
**Stock of money:** $55.43 billion (31 December 2007)
**Stock of quasi money:** $28.59 billion (31 December 2007)
**Stock of domestic credit:** NA
**Market value of publicly traded shares:** $NA
**Agriculture - products:** wheat, barley, oats, grapes, olives, citrus, fruits; sheep, cattle
**Industries:** petroleum, natural gas, light industries, mining, electrical, petrochemical, food processing
**Industrial production growth rate:** 4.5% (2008 est.)
**Electricity - production:** 33.12 billion kWh (2006 est.)
**Electricity - consumption:** 26.91 billion kWh (2006 est.)
**Electricity - exports:** 300 million kWh (2006 est.)
**Electricity - imports:** 382 million kWh (2006 est.)
**Oil - production:** 2.173 million bbl/day (2007 est.)
**Oil - consumption:** 279,800 bbl/day (2006 est.)
**Oil - exports:** 1.844 million bbl/day (2005 est.)
**Oil - imports:** 13,110 bbl/day (2005 est.)
**Oil - proved reserves:** 12.2 billion bbl (1 January 2008 est.)
**Natural gas - production:** 85.7 billion cu m (2007 est.)
**Natural gas - consumption:** 26.3 billion cu m (2007 est.)

**Natural gas - exports:** 59.4 billion cu m (2007 est.)
**Natural gas - imports:** 0 cu m (2007 est.)
**Natural gas - proved reserves:** 4.502 trillion cu m (1 January 2008 est.)
**Current account balance:** $35.8 billion (2008 est.)
**Exports:** $75.06 billion f.o.b. (2008 est.)
**Exports - commodities:** petroleum, natural gas, and petroleum products 97%
**Exports - partners:** US 29.4%, Italy 13.8%, Spain 9.6%, Canada 8.4%, France 7.4%, Netherlands 5% (2007)
**Imports:** $36.87 billion f.o.b. (2008 est.)
**Imports - commodities:** capital goods, foodstuffs, consumer goods
**Imports - partners:** France 18.7%, China 9%, Italy 8.5%, Spain 6%, US 5.5%, Germany 5.3%, Russia 4.6%, Turkey 4.1% (2007)
**Reserves of foreign exchange and gold:** $150.5 billion (31 December 2008 est.)
**Debt - external:** $2.913 billion (31 December 2008 est.)
**Stock of direct foreign investment - at home:** $14.11 billion (2008 est.)
**Stock of direct foreign investment - abroad:** $1.162 billion (2008 est.)
**Exchange rates:** Algerian dinars (DZD) per US dollar - 63.25 (2008 est.), 69.9 (2007), 72.647 (2006), 73.276 (2005), 72.061 (2004)

## Communications

**Telephones - main lines in use:** 3.068 million (2007)
**Telephones - mobile cellular:** 27.563 million (2007)
**Telephone system:**
*general assessment:* a weak network of fixed-main lines, which remains low at less than 10 telephones per 100 persons, is partially offset by the rapid increase in mobile cellular subscribership; in 2007, combined fixed-line and mobile telephone density surpassed 90 telephones per 100 persons
*domestic:* privatization of Algeria's telecommunications sector began in 2000; three mobile cellular licenses have been issued and, in 2005, a consortium led by Egypt's Orascom Telecom won a 15-year license to build and operate a fixed-line network in Algeria; the license will allow Orascom to develop high-speed data and other specialized services and contribute to meeting the large unfulfilled demand for basic residential telephony; Internet broadband services began in 2003 with approximately 200,000 subscribers in 2006
*international:* country code - 213; landing point for the SEA-ME-WE-4 fiber-optic submarine cable system that provides links to Europe, the Middle East, and Asia; microwave radio relay to Italy, France, Spain, Morocco, and Tunisia; coaxial cable to Morocco and Tunisia; participant in Medarabtel; satellite earth stations - 51 (Intelsat, Intersputnik, and Arabsat) (2007)
**Radio broadcast stations:** AM 25, FM 1, shortwave 8 (1999)

## Algeria (continued)

**Television broadcast stations:** 46 (plus 216 repeaters) (1995)
**Internet country code:** .dz
**Internet hosts:** 477 (2008)
**Internet users:** 3.5 million (2007)

### Transportation

**Airports:** 142 (2008)
**Airports - with paved runways:**
*total:* 57
*over 3,047 m:* 11
*2,438 to 3,047 m:* 28
*1,524 to 2,437 m:* 12
*914 to 1,523 m:* 5
*under 914 m:* 1 (2008)
**Airports - with unpaved runways:**
*total:* 85
*2,438 to 3,047 m:* 3
*1,524 to 2,437 m:* 19
*914 to 1,523 m:* 40
*under 914 m:* 23 (2008)
**Heliports:** 2 (2007)
**Pipelines:** condensate 1,937 km; gas 14,648 km; liquid petroleum gas 2,933 km; oil 7,579 km (2008)
**Railways:**
*total:* 3,973 km
*standard gauge:* 2,888 km 1.435-m gauge (283 km electrified)
*narrow gauge:* 1,085 km 1.055-m gauge (2006)
**Roadways:**
*total:* 108,302 km
*paved:* 76,028 km (includes 645 km of expressways)
*unpaved:* 32,274 km (2004)
**Merchant marine:**
*total:* 33
*by type:* bulk carrier 6, cargo 8, chemical tanker 1, liquefied gas 9, passenger/cargo 3, petroleum tanker 4, roll on/roll off 2
*foreign-owned:* 18 (Jordan 7, UK 11) (2008)
**Ports and terminals:** Algiers, Annaba, Arzew, Bejaia, Djendjene, Jijel, Mostaganem, Oran, Skikda

### Military

**Military branches:** National Popular Army (ANP; includes Land Forces), Algerian National Navy (MRA), Air Force (QJJ), Territorial Air Defense Force (2005)
**Military service age and obligation:** 19-30 years of age for compulsory military service; conscript service obligation - 18 months (6 months basic training, 12 months civil projects) (2006)
**Manpower available for military service:**
*males age 16-49:* 9,736,757
*females age 16-49:* 9,590,978 (2008 est.)
**Manpower fit for military service:**
*males age 16-49:* 8,317,473
*females age 16-49:* 8,367,005 (2009 est.)
**Manpower reaching militarily significant age annually:**
*male:* 375,852
*female:* 362,158 (2009 est.)
**Military expenditures:** 3.3% of GDP (2006)

### Transnational Issues

**Disputes - international:** Algeria, and many other states, rejects Moroccan administration of Western Sahara; the Polisario Front, exiled in Algeria, represents the Sahrawi Arab Democratic Republic; Algeria's border with Morocco remains an irritant to bilateral relations, each nation accusing the other of harboring militants and arms smuggling; Algeria remains concerned about armed bandits operating throughout the Sahel who sometimes destabilize southern Algerian towns; dormant disputes include Libyan claims of about 32,000 sq km still reflected on its maps of southeastern Algeria and the FLN's assertions of a claim to Chirac Pastures in southeastern Morocco
**Refugees and internally displaced persons:**
*refugees (country of origin):* 90,000 (Western Saharan Sahrawi, mostly living in Algerian-sponsored camps in the southwestern Algerian town of Tindouf)
*IDPs:* undetermined (civil war during 1990s) (2007)
**Trafficking in persons:**
*current situation:* Algeria is a transit country for men and women trafficked from sub-Saharan Africa to Europe for the purposes of commercial sexual exploitation and involuntary servitude; Algerian children are trafficked internally for the purpose of domestic servitude or street vending
*tier rating:* Tier 3 - Algeria did not report any serious law enforcement actions to punish traffickers who force women into commercial sexual exploitation or men into involuntary servitude in 2007; the government again reported no investigations of trafficking of children for domestic servitude or improvements in protection services available to victims of trafficking; Algeria still lacks victim protection services, and its failure to distinguish between trafficking and illegal migration may result in the punishment of victims of trafficking (2008)

## American Samoa
*(territory of the US)*

### Introduction

**Background:** Settled as early as 1000 B.C., Samoa was "discovered" by European explorers in the 18th century. International rivalries in the latter half of the 19th century were settled by an 1899 treaty in which Germany and the US divided the Samoan archipelago. The US formally occupied its portion - a smaller group of eastern islands with the excellent harbor of Pago Pago - the following year.

### Geography

**Location:** Oceania, group of islands in the South Pacific Ocean, about half way between Hawaii and New Zealand
**Geographic coordinates:** 14 20 S, 170 00 W
**Map references:** Oceania
**Area:**
*total:* 199 sq km
*land:* 199 sq km
*water:* 0 sq km
*note:* includes Rose Island and Swains Island
**Area - comparative:** slightly larger than Washington, DC
**Land boundaries:** 0 km
**Coastline:** 116 km
**Maritime claims:**
*territorial sea:* 12 nm
*exclusive economic zone:* 200 nm
**Climate:** tropical marine, moderated by southeast trade winds; annual rainfall averages about 3 m; rainy season (November to April), dry season (May to October); little seasonal temperature variation
**Terrain:** five volcanic islands with rugged peaks and limited coastal plains, two coral atolls (Rose Island, Swains Island)
**Elevation extremes:**
*lowest point:* Pacific Ocean 0 m
*highest point:* Lata Mountain 964 m
**Natural resources:** pumice, pumicite

# American Samoa *(continued)*

**Land use:**
*arable land:* 10%
*permanent crops:* 15%
*other:* 75% (2005)
**Irrigated land:** NA
**Natural hazards:** typhoons common from December to March
**Environment - current issues:** limited natural fresh water resources; the water division of the government has spent substantial funds in the past few years to improve water catchments and pipelines
**Geography - note:** Pago Pago has one of the best natural deepwater harbors in the South Pacific Ocean, sheltered by shape from rough seas and protected by peripheral mountains from high winds; strategic location in the South Pacific Ocean

## People

**Population:** 65,628 (July 2009 est.)
**Age structure:**
*0-14 years:* 33.4% (male 11,159/female 10,768)
*15-64 years:* 62.7% (male 20,848/female 20,271)
*65 years and over:* 3.9% (male 1,211/female 1,371) (2009 est.)
**Median age:**
*total:* 23.1 years
*male:* 23 years
*female:* 23.3 years (2009 est.)
**Population growth rate:** 1.222% (2009 est.)
**Birth rate:** 23.31 births/1,000 population (2009 est.)
**Death rate:** 4.13 deaths/1,000 population (2008 est.)
**Net migration rate:** -6.99 migrant(s)/1,000 population (2009 est.)
**Urbanization:**
*urban population:* 92% of total population (2008)
*rate of urbanization:* 2.4% annual rate of change (2005-10 est.)
**Sex ratio:**
*at birth:* 1.06 male(s)/female
*under 15 years:* 1.04 male(s)/female
*15-64 years:* 1.03 male(s)/female
*65 years and over:* 0.88 male(s)/female
*total population:* 1.02 male(s)/female (2009 est.)
**Infant mortality rate:**
*total:* 10.18 deaths/1,000 live births
*male:* 13.3 deaths/1,000 live births
*female:* 6.88 deaths/1,000 live births (2009 est.)
**Life expectancy at birth:**
*total population:* 73.72 years
*male:* 70.8 years
*female:* 76.82 years (2009 est.)
**Total fertility rate:** 3.29 children born/woman (2009 est.)
**HIV/AIDS - adult prevalence rate:** NA
**HIV/AIDS - people living with HIV/AIDS:** NA
**HIV/AIDS - deaths:** NA
**Nationality:**
*noun:* American Samoan(s) (US nationals)
*adjective:* American Samoan
**Ethnic groups:** native Pacific islander 91.6%, Asian 2.8%, white 1.1%, mixed 4.2%, other 0.3% (2000 census)

**Religions:** Christian Congregationalist 50%, Roman Catholic 20%, Protestant and other 30%
**Languages:** Samoan 90.6% (closely related to Hawaiian and other Polynesian languages), English 2.9%, Tongan 2.4%, other Pacific islander 2.1%, other 2%
*note:* most people are bilingual (2000 census)
**Literacy:**
*definition:* age 15 and over can read and write
*total population:* 97%
*male:* 98%
*female:* 97% (1980 est.)
**Education expenditures:** NA

## Government

**Country name:**
*conventional long form:* Territory of American Samoa
*conventional short form:* American Samoa
*abbreviation:* AS
**Dependency status:** unincorporated and unorganized territory of the US; administered by the Office of Insular Affairs, US Department of the Interior
**Government type:** NA
**Capital:**
*name:* Pago Pago
*geographic coordinates:* 14 16 S, 170 42 W
*time difference:* UTC-11 (6 hours behind Washington, DC during Standard Time)
**Administrative divisions:** none (territory of the US); there are no first-order administrative divisions as defined by the US Government, but there are three districts and two islands* at the second order; Eastern, Manu'a, Rose Island*, Swains Island*, Western
**Independence:** none (territory of the US)
**National holiday:** Flag Day, 17 April (1900)
**Constitution:** ratified 2 June 1966; effective 1 July 1967
**Legal system:** NA
**Suffrage:** 18 years of age; universal
**Executive branch:**
*chief of state:* President Barack H. OBAMA (since 20 January 2009); Vice President Joseph R. BIDEN (since 20 January 2009)
*head of government:* Governor Togiola TULAFONO (since 7 April 2003)
*cabinet:* Cabinet made up of 12 department directors
*elections:* under the US Constitution, residents of unincorporated territories, such as American Samoa, do not vote in elections for US president and vice president; however, they may vote in Democratic and Republican presidential primary elections; governor and lieutenant governor elected on the same ticket by popular vote for four-year terms (eligible for a second term); election last held 4 and 18 November 2008 (next to be held in November 2012)
*election results:* Togiola TULAFONO reelected governor; percent of vote - Togiola TULAFONO 56.5%, Afoa Moega LUTU 43.5%
**Legislative branch:** bicameral Fono or Legislative Assembly consists of the Senate (18 seats; members are elected from local chiefs to serve four-year

terms)and the House of Representatives (21 seats; 20 members are elected by popular vote and 1 is an appointed, nonvoting delegate from Swains Island; members serve two-year terms)
*elections:* House of Representatives - last held 4 November 2008 (next to be held in November 2010); Senate - last held 4 November 2008 (next to be held in November 2012)
*election results:* House of Representatives - percent of vote by party - NA; seats by party - NA; Senate - percent of vote by party - NA; seats by party - independents 18
*note:* American Samoa elects one nonvoting representative to the US House of Representatives; election last held on 4 November 2008 (next to be held in November 2010); results - Eni F. H. FALEOMAVAEGA reelected as delegate
**Judicial branch:** High Court (chief justice and associate justices are appointed by the US Secretary of the Interior)
**Political parties and leaders:** Democratic Party [Oreta M. TOGAFAU]; Republican Party [Tautai A. F. FAALEVAO]
**Political pressure groups and leaders:** Population Pressure LAS (addresses the growing population pressures)
**International organization participation:** Interpol (subbureau), IOC, SPC, UPU
**Diplomatic representation in the US:** none (territory of the US)
**Diplomatic representation from the US:** none (territory of the US)
**Flag description:** blue, with a white triangle edged in red that is based on the fly side and extends to the hoist side; a brown and white American bald eagle flying toward the hoist side is carrying two traditional Samoan symbols of authority, a war club known as a "Fa'alaufa'i" (upper; left talon), and a coconut fiber fly whisk known as a "Fue" (lower; right talon); the combination of symbols broadly mimics that seen on the US Great Seal and reflects the relationship between the United States and American Samoa

## Economy

**Economy - overview:** American Samoa has a traditional Polynesian economy in which more than 90% of the land is communally owned. Economic activity is strongly linked to the US with which American Samoa conducts most of its commerce. Tuna fishing and tuna processing plants are the backbone of the private sector, with canned tuna the primary export. Transfers from the US Government add substantially to American Samoa's economic well being. Attempts by the government to develop a larger and broader economy are restrained by Samoa's remote location, its limited transportation, and its devastating hurricanes. Tourism is a promising developing sector.
**GDP (purchasing power parity):**
$575.3 million (2007 est.)
$510.1 million (2003)

**GDP (official exchange rate):** $462.2 million (2005)
**GDP - real growth rate:**
3% (2003)
**GDP - per capita (PPP):**
$8,000 (2007 est.)
$5,800 (2005 est.)
**GDP - composition by sector:**
*agriculture:* NA%
*industry:* NA%
*services:* NA%
**Labor force:** 17,630 (2005)
**Labor force - by occupation:**
*agriculture:* 34%
*industry:* 33%
*services:* 33% (1990)
**Unemployment rate:**
29.8% (2005)
**Population below poverty line:** NA%
**Household income or consumption by percentage share:**
*lowest 10%:* NA%
*highest 10%:* NA%
**Budget:**
*revenues:* $155.4 million (37% in local revenue and 63% in US grants)
*expenditures:* $183.6 million (FY07)
**Inflation rate (consumer prices):**
NA%
**Agriculture - products:** bananas, coconuts, vegetables, taro, breadfruit, yams, copra, pineapples, papayas; dairy products, livestock
**Industries:** tuna canneries (largely supplied by foreign fishing vessels), handicrafts
**Industrial production growth rate:** NA%
**Electricity - production:** 180 million kWh (2006 est.)
**Electricity - consumption:** 167.4 million kWh (2006 est.)
**Electricity - exports:** 0 kWh (2007 est.)
**Electricity - imports:** 0 kWh (2007 est.)
**Oil - production:** 0 bbl/day (2007 est.)
**Oil - consumption:** 4,053 bbl/day (2006 est.)
**Oil - exports:** 0 bbl/day (2005)
**Oil - imports:** 4,066 bbl/day (2005)
**Oil - proved reserves:** 0 bbl (1 January 2006 est.)
**Natural gas - production:** 0 cu m (2007 est.)
**Natural gas - consumption:** 0 cu m (2007 est.)
**Natural gas - exports:** 0 cu m (2007 est.)
**Natural gas - imports:** 0 cu m (2007 est.)
**Natural gas - proved reserves:** 0 cu m (1 January 2006 est.)
**Exports:** $445.6 million (FY04 est.)
**Exports - commodities:** canned tuna 93% (2004 est.)
**Imports:** $308.8 million (FY04 est.)
**Imports - commodities:** materials for canneries 56%, food 8%, petroleum products 7%, machinery and parts 6% (2004 est.)
**Debt - external:** $NA
**Exchange rates:** the US dollar is used

## Communications

**Telephones - main lines in use:** 10,400 (2004)
**Telephones - mobile cellular:** 2,200 (2004)
**Telephone system:**
*general assessment:* NA
*domestic:* good telex, telegraph, facsimile, and cellular telephone services; domestic satellite system with 1 Comsat earth station
*international:* country code - 1-684; satellite earth station - 1 (Intelsat-Pacific Ocean)
**Radio broadcast stations:** AM 2, FM 3, shortwave 0 (2005)
**Television broadcast stations:** 1 (2006)
**Internet country code:** .as
**Internet hosts:** 1,923 (2008)
**Internet users:** NA

## Transportation

**Airports:** 3 (2008)
**Airports - with paved runways:**
*total:* 3
*over 3,047 m:* 1
*914 to 1,523 m:* 1
*under 914 m:* 1 (2008)
**Roadways:**
*total:* 221 km (2007)
**Ports and terminals:** Pago Pago

## Military

**Manpower fit for military service:**
*males age 16-49:* 13,875
*females age 16-49:* 13,517 (2009 est.)
**Manpower reaching militarily significant age annually:**
*male:* 820
*female:* 802 (2009 est.)
**Military - note:** defense is the responsibility of the US

## Transnational Issues

**Disputes - international:** Tokelau periodically asserts claims to American Samoa's Swains Island (Olohega), such as in its 2006 draft independence constitution

# Andorra

## Introduction

**Background:** For 715 years, from 1278 to 1993, Andorrans lived under a unique co-principality, ruled by French and Spanish leaders (from 1607 onward, the French chief of state and the Spanish bishop of Urgel). In 1993, this feudal system was modified with the titular heads of state retained, but the government transformed into a parliamentary democracy. Long isolated and impoverished, mountainous Andorra achieved considerable prosperity since World War II through its tourist industry. Many immigrants (legal and illegal) are attracted to the thriving economy with its lack of income taxes.

## Geography

**Location:** Southwestern Europe, between France and Spain
**Geographic coordinates:** 42 30 N, 1 30 E
**Map references:** Europe
**Area:**
*total:* 468 sq km
*land:* 468 sq km
*water:* 0 sq km
**Area - comparative:** 2.5 times the size of Washington, DC
**Land boundaries:**
*total:* 120.3 km
*border countries:* France 56.6 km, Spain 63.7 km
**Coastline:** 0 km (landlocked)
**Maritime claims:** none (landlocked)
**Climate:** temperate; snowy, cold winters and warm, dry summers
**Terrain:** rugged mountains dissected by narrow valleys
**Elevation extremes:**
*lowest point:* Riu Runer 840 m
*highest point:* Coma Pedrosa 2,946 m
**Natural resources:** hydropower, mineral water, timber, iron ore, lead

# Andorra *(continued)*

**Land use:**
*arable land:* 2.13%
*permanent crops:* 0%
*other:* 97.87% (2005)
**Irrigated land:** NA
**Natural hazards:** avalanches
**Environment - current issues:** deforestation; overgrazing of mountain meadows contributes to soil erosion; air pollution; wastewater treatment and solid waste disposal
**Environment - international agreements:**
*party to:* Biodiversity, Desertification, Hazardous Wastes, Ozone Layer Protection
*signed, but not ratified:* none of the selected agreements
**Geography - note:** landlocked; straddles a number of important crossroads in the Pyrenees

## People

**Population:** 83,888 (July 2009 est.)
**Age structure:**
*0-14 years:* 15.5% (male 6,710/female 6,305)
*15-64 years:* 72.2% (male 31,604/female 28,925)
*65 years and over:* 12.3% (male 5,113/female 5,231) (2009 est.)
**Median age:**
*total:* 39.4 years
*male:* 39.7 years
*female:* 39.1 years (2009 est.)
**Population growth rate:** 1.135% (2009 est.)
**Birth rate:** 10.35 births/1,000 population (2009 est.)
**Death rate:** 5.59 deaths/1,000 population (2008 est.)
**Net migration rate:** 6.89 migrant(s)/1,000 population (2009 est.)
**Urbanization:**
*urban population:* 89% of total population (2008)
*rate of urbanization:* -0.2% annual rate of change (2005-10 est.)
**Sex ratio:**
*at birth:* 1.07 male(s)/female
*under 15 years:* 1.06 male(s)/female
*15-64 years:* 1.09 male(s)/female
*65 years and over:* 0.98 male(s)/female
*total population:* 1.07 male(s)/female (2009 est.)
**Infant mortality rate:**
*total:* 3.76 deaths/1,000 live births
*male:* 3.78 deaths/1,000 live births
*female:* 3.74 deaths/1,000 live births (2009 est.)
**Life expectancy at birth:**
*total population:* 82.51 years
*male:* 80.33 years
*female:* 84.84 years (2009 est.)
**Total fertility rate:** 1.33 children born/woman (2009 est.)
**HIV/AIDS - adult prevalence rate:** NA
**HIV/AIDS - people living with HIV/AIDS:** NA
**HIV/AIDS - deaths:** NA
**Nationality:**
*noun:* Andorran(s)
*adjective:* Andorran

**Ethnic groups:** Spanish 43%, Andorran 33%, Portuguese 11%, French 7%, other 6% (1998)
**Religions:** Roman Catholic (predominant)
**Languages:** Catalan (official), French, Castilian, Portuguese
**Literacy:**
*definition:* NA
*total population:* 100%
*male:* 100%
*female:* 100%
**School life expectancy (primary to tertiary education):**
*total:* 11 years
*male:* 11 years
*female:* 11 years (2006)
**Education expenditures:** 2.3% of GDP (2006)

## Government

**Country name:**
*conventional long form:* Principality of Andorra
*conventional short form:* Andorra
*local long form:* Principat d'Andorra
*local short form:* Andorra
**Government type:** parliamentary democracy (since March 1993) that retains as its chiefs of state a coprincipality; the two princes are the president of France and bishop of Seo de Urgel, Spain, who are represented locally by coprinces' representatives
**Capital:**
*name:* Andorra la Vella
*geographic coordinates:* 42 30 N, 1 31 E
*time difference:* UTC+1 (6 hours ahead of Washington, DC during Standard Time)
*daylight saving time:* +1hr, begins last Sunday in March; ends last Sunday in October
**Administrative divisions:** 7 parishes (parroquies, singular - parroquia); Andorra la Vella, Canillo, Encamp, Escaldes-Engordany, La Massana, Ordino, Sant Julia de Loria
**Independence:** 1278 (formed under the joint suzerainty of the French Count of Foix and the Spanish Bishop of Urgel)
**National holiday:** Our Lady of Meritxell Day, 8 September (1278)
**Constitution:** Andorra's first written constitution was drafted in 1991; approved by referendum 14 March 1993; effective 28 April 1993
**Legal system:** based on French and Spanish civil codes; no judicial review of legislative acts; has not accepted compulsory ICJ jurisdiction
**Suffrage:** 18 years of age; universal
**Executive branch:**
*chief of state:* French Coprince Nicolas SARKOZY (since 16 May 2007); represented by Philippe MASSONI (since 26 July 2002) and Spanish Coprince Bishop Joan-Enric VIVES i SICILIA (since 12 May 2003); represented by Nemesi MARQUES i OSTE (since 30 July 2003)
*head of government:* Executive Council President Jaume BARTUMEU CASSANY (since 5 June 2009)
*cabinet:* Executive Council or Govern designated by the Executive Council president

*elections:* Executive Council president elected by the General Council and formally appointed by the coprinces for a four-year term; election last held 24 April 2005 (next to be held in April-May 2009)
*election results:* Jaume BARTUMEU CASSANY elected executive council president; percent of General Council vote - NA
**Legislative branch:** unicameral General Council of the Valleys or Consell General de las Valls (28 seats; members are elected by direct popular vote, 14 from a single national constituency and 14 to represent each of the seven parishes; to serve four-year terms)
*elections:* last held on 26 April 2009 (next to be held in March-April 2013)
*election results:* percent of vote by party - PS 45.03%, Reformist Coaliton 32.34%, Andorra for Change 18.86%, other 3.77%; seats by party - PS 14, Reformist Coalition 11, Andorra for Change 3
**Judicial branch:** Tribunal of Judges or Tribunal de Batlles; Tribunal of the Courts or Tribunal de Corts; Supreme Court of Justice of Andorra or Tribunal Superior de Justicia d'Andorra; Supreme Council of Justice or Consell Superior de la Justicia; Fiscal Ministry or Ministeri Fiscal; Constitutional Tribunal or Tribunal Constitucional
**Political parties and leaders:** Andorra for Change [Juan Eusebio NOMEN CALVET]; New Center [Vicenc MATEU] (formerly Andorran Democratic Center Party); Liberal Party of Andorra or PLA [Joan Gabriel i ESTANY] (formerly Liberal Union or UL); Reformist Coalition (includes the Liberal Party and New Center) [Joan Gabriel i ESTANY]; Social Democratic Party or PS [Jaume BARTUMEU CASSANY] (formerly part of National Democratic Group or AND)
**Political pressure groups and leaders:** NA
**International organization participation:** CE, FAO, ICAO, ICCt, ICRM, IFRCS, Interpol, IOC, IPU, ITU, OIF, OPCW, OSCE, UN, UNCTAD, UNESCO, Union Latina, UNWTO, WCO, WHO, WIPO, WTO (observer)
**Diplomatic representation in the US:**
*chief of mission:* Ambassador Carles FONT-ROSSELL
*chancery:* 2 United Nations Plaza, 25th Floor, New York, NY 10017
*telephone:* [1] (212) 750-8064
*FAX:* [1] (212) 750-6630
**Diplomatic representation from the US:** the US does not have an embassy in Andorra; the US Ambassador to Spain is accredited to Andorra; US interests in Andorra are represented by the Consulate General's office in Barcelona (Spain); mailing address: Paseo Reina Elisenda de Montcada, 23, 08034 Barcelona, Spain; telephone: [34] (93) 280-2227; FAX: [34] (93) 280-6175
**Flag description:** three equal vertical bands of blue (hoist side), yellow, and red, with the national coat of arms centered in the yellow band; the coat of arms features a quartered shield
*note:* similar to the flags of Chad and Romania, which do not have a national coat of arms in the center, and the flag of Moldova, which does bear a national emblem

# Andorra *(continued)*

## Economy

**Economy - overview:** Tourism, the mainstay of Andorra's tiny, well-to-do economy, accounts for more than 80% of GDP. An estimated 11.6 million tourists visit annually, attracted by Andorra's duty-free status and by its summer and winter resorts. Andorra's comparative advantage has recently eroded as the economies of neighboring France and Spain have been opened up, providing broader availability of goods and lower tariffs. The banking sector, with its partial "tax haven" status, also contributes substantially to the economy. Agricultural production is limited - only 2% of the land is arable - and most food has to be imported. The principal livestock activity is sheep raising. Manufacturing output consists mainly of cigarettes, cigars, and furniture. Andorra is a member of the EU Customs Union and is treated as an EU member for trade in manufactured goods (no tariffs) and as a non-EU member for agricultural products.

**GDP (purchasing power parity):**
$3.66 billion (2007)
$3.588 billion (2006)
$2.77 billion (2005)
**GDP (official exchange rate):** $NA
**GDP - real growth rate:**
2% (2007 est.)
3.5% (2005 est.)
**GDP - per capita (PPP):**
$42,500 (2007)
$38,800 (2005)
**GDP - composition by sector:**
*agriculture:* NA%
*industry:* NA%
*services:* NA%
**Labor force:** 42,230 (2007)
**Labor force - by occupation:**
*agriculture:* 0.3%
*industry:* 20.8%
*services:* 79% (2007)
**Unemployment rate:**
0% (2007)
0% (2006)
**Population below poverty line:** NA%
**Household income or consumption by percentage share:**
*lowest 10%:* NA%
*highest 10%:* NA%
**Budget:**
*revenues:* $496.9 million
*expenditures:* $496.8 million (2007)
**Inflation rate (consumer prices):**
3.9% (2007)
3.2% (2005)
**Agriculture - products:** small quantities of rye, wheat, barley, oats, vegetables; sheep
**Industries:** tourism (particularly skiing), cattle raising, timber, banking, tobacco, furniture
**Industrial production growth rate:** NA%
**Electricity - production:** NA kWh
**Electricity - consumption:** NA kWh

**Electricity - exports:** NA kWh
**Electricity - imports:** NA kWh; note - most electricity supplied by Spain and France; Andorra generates a small amount of hydropower
**Exports:** $117.1 million f.o.b. (2007)
**Exports - commodities:** tobacco products, furniture
**Imports:** $1.789 billion (2007)
**Imports - commodities:** consumer goods, food, electricity
**Debt - external:** $NA
**Exchange rates:** euros (EUR) per US dollar - 0.6827 (2008 est.), 0.7306 (2007), 0.7964 (2006), 0.8041 (2005), 0.8054 (2004)

## Communications

**Telephones - main lines in use:** 37,200 (2007)
**Telephones - mobile cellular:** 68,500 (2007)
**Telephone system:**
*general assessment:* NA
*domestic:* modern system with microwave radio relay connections between exchanges
*international:* country code - 376; landline circuits to France and Spain
**Radio broadcast stations:** AM 0, FM 1, shortwave 0 (easy access to radio and television broadcasts originating in France and Spain) (2007)
**Television broadcast stations:** 1 (2007)
**Internet country code:** .ad
**Internet hosts:** 23,368 (2008)
**Internet users:** 58,900 (2007)

## Transportation

**Roadways:**
*total:* 270 km (1994)

## Military

**Military branches:** no regular military forces, Police Service of Andorra (2008)
**Manpower available for military service:**
*males age 16-49:* 18,685 (2008 est.)
**Manpower fit for military service:**
*males age 16-49:* 18,617
*females age 16-49:* 17,613 (2009 est.)
**Manpower reaching militarily significant age annually:**
*male:* 402
*female:* 373 (2009 est.)
**Military - note:** defense is the responsibility of France and Spain

## Transnational Issues

**Disputes - international:** none

# Angola

## Introduction

**Background:** Angola is rebuilding its country after the end of a 27-year civil war in 2002. Fighting between the Popular Movement for the Liberation of Angola (MPLA), led by Jose Eduardo DOS SANTOS, and the National Union for the Total Independence of Angola (UNITA), led by Jonas SAVIMBI, followed independence from Portugal in 1975. Peace seemed imminent in 1992 when Angola held national elections, but fighting picked up again by 1996. Up to 1.5 million lives may have been lost - and 4 million people displaced - in the quarter century of fighting. SAVIMBI's death in 2002 ended UNITA's insurgency and strengthened the MPLA's hold on power. President DOS SANTOS held legislative elections in September 2008, and announced plans to hold presidential elections in 2009.

## Geography

**Location:** Southern Africa, bordering the South Atlantic Ocean, between Namibia and Democratic Republic of the Congo
**Geographic coordinates:** 12 30 S, 18 30 E
**Map references:** Africa
**Area:**
*total:* 1,246,700 sq km
*land:* 1,246,700 sq km
*water:* 0 sq km
**Area - comparative:** slightly less than twice the size of Texas
**Land boundaries:**
*total:* 5,198 km
*border countries:* Democratic Republic of the Congo 2,511 km (of which 225 km is the boundary of discontiguous Cabinda Province), Republic of the Congo 201 km, Namibia 1,376 km, Zambia 1,110 km
**Coastline:** 1,600 km
**Maritime claims:**
*territorial sea:* 12 nm
*contiguous zone:* 24 nm
*exclusive economic zone:* 200 nm

# Angola (continued)

**Climate:** semiarid in south and along coast to Luanda; north has cool, dry season (May to October) and hot, rainy season (November to April)

**Terrain:** narrow coastal plain rises abruptly to vast interior plateau

**Elevation extremes:**
*lowest point:* Atlantic Ocean 0 m
*highest point:* Morro de Moco 2,620 m

**Natural resources:** petroleum, diamonds, iron ore, phosphates, copper, feldspar, gold, bauxite, uranium

**Land use:**
*arable land:* 2.65%
*permanent crops:* 0.23%
*other:* 97.12% (2005)

**Irrigated land:** 800 sq km (2003)

**Total renewable water resources:** 184 cu km (1987)

**Freshwater withdrawal (domestic/industrial/agricultural):**
*total:* 0.35 cu km/yr (23%/17%/60%)
*per capita:* 22 cu m/yr (2000)

**Natural hazards:** locally heavy rainfall causes periodic flooding on the plateau

**Environment - current issues:** overuse of pastures and subsequent soil erosion attributable to population pressures; desertification; deforestation of tropical rain forest, in response to both international demand for tropical timber and to domestic use as fuel, resulting in loss of biodiversity; soil erosion contributing to water pollution and siltation of rivers and dams; inadequate supplies of potable water

**Environment - international agreements:**
*party to:* Biodiversity, Climate Change, Climate Change-Kyoto Protocol, Desertification, Law of the Sea, Marine Dumping, Ozone Layer Protection, Ship Pollution
*signed, but not ratified:* none of the selected agreements

**Geography - note:** the province of Cabinda is an exclave, separated from the rest of the country by the Democratic Republic of the Congo

## People

**Population:** 12,799,293 (July 2009 est.)

**Age structure:**
*0-14 years:* 43.5% (male 2,812,359/female 2,759,047)
*15-64 years:* 53.7% (male 3,496,726/female 3,382,440)
*65 years and over:* 2.7% (male 153,678/female 195,043) (2009 est.)

**Median age:**
*total:* 18 years
*male:* 18 years
*female:* 18 years (2009 est.)

**Population growth rate:** 2.095% (2009 est.)

**Birth rate:** 43.69 births/1,000 population (2009 est.)

**Death rate:** 24.44 deaths/1,000 population (2008 est.)

**Net migration rate:** 1.34 migrant(s)/1,000 population (2009 est.)

**Urbanization:**
*urban population:* 57% of total population (2008)
*rate of urbanization:* 4.4% annual rate of change (2005-10 est.)

**Sex ratio:**
*at birth:* 1.05 male(s)/female
*under 15 years:* 1.02 male(s)/female
*15-64 years:* 1.03 male(s)/female
*65 years and over:* 0.79 male(s)/female
*total population:* 1.02 male(s)/female (2009 est.)

**Infant mortality rate:**
*total:* 180.21 deaths/1,000 live births
*male:* 192.24 deaths/1,000 live births
*female:* 167.58 deaths/1,000 live births (2009 est.)

**Life expectancy at birth:**
*total population:* 38.2 years
*male:* 37.24 years
*female:* 39.22 years (2009 est.)

**Total fertility rate:** 6.12 children born/woman (2009 est.)

**HIV/AIDS - adult prevalence rate:** 2.1% (2007 est.)

**HIV/AIDS - people living with HIV/AIDS:** 190,000 (2007 est.)

**HIV/AIDS - deaths:** 11,000 (2007 est.)

**Major infectious diseases:**
*degree of risk:* very high
*food or waterborne diseases:* bacterial and protozoal diarrhea, hepatitis A, typhoid fever
*vectorborne diseases:* malaria, African trypanosomiasis (sleeping sickness)
*water contact disease:* schistosomiasis (2009)

**Nationality:**
*noun:* Angolan(s)
*adjective:* Angolan

**Ethnic groups:** Ovimbundu 37%, Kimbundu 25%, Bakongo 13%, mestico (mixed European and native African) 2%, European 1%, other 22%

**Religions:** indigenous beliefs 47%, Roman Catholic 38%, Protestant 15% (1998 est.)

**Languages:** Portuguese (official), Bantu and other African languages

**Literacy:**
*definition:* age 15 and over can read and write
*total population:* 67.4%
*male:* 82.9%
*female:* 54.2% (2001 est.)

**Education expenditures:** 2.4% of GDP (2005)

## Government

**Country name:**
*conventional long form:* Republic of Angola
*conventional short form:* Angola
*local long form:* Republica de Angola
*local short form:* Angola
*former:* People's Republic of Angola

**Government type:** republic; multiparty presidential regime

**Capital:**
*name:* Luanda
*geographic coordinates:* 8 50 S, 13 14 E
*time difference:* UTC+1 (6 hours ahead of Washington, DC during Standard Time)

**Administrative divisions:** 18 provinces (provincias, singular - provincia); Bengo, Benguela, Bie, Cabinda, Cuando Cubango, Cuanza Norte, Cuanza Sul, Cunene, Huambo, Huila, Luanda, Lunda Norte, Lunda Sul, Malanje, Moxico, Namibe, Uige, Zaire

**Independence:** 11 November 1975 (from Portugal)

**National holiday:** Independence Day, 11 November (1975)

**Constitution:** adopted by People's Assembly 25August 1992

**Legal system:** based on Portuguese civil law system and customary law; modified to accommodate political pluralism and increased use of free markets; has not accepted compulsory ICJ jurisdiction

**Suffrage:** 18 years of age; universal

**Executive branch:**
*chief of state:* President Jose Eduardo DOS SANTOS (since 21 September 1979); note - the president is both chief of state and head of government
*head of government:* President Jose Eduardo DOS SANTOS (since 21 September 1979); Antonio Paulo KASSOMA was named prime minister by MPLA on 26 September 2008
*cabinet:* Council of Ministers appointed by the president
*elections:* president elected by universal ballot for a five-year term (eligible for a second consecutive or discontinuous term) under the 1992 constitution; President DOS SANTOS was selected by the party to take over after the death of former President Augustino NETO(1979) under a one-party system and stood for reelection in Angola's first multiparty elections 29-30 September 1992 (next to be held in September 2009)
*election results:* Jose Eduardo DOS SANTOS 49.6%, Jonas SAVIMBI 40.1%, making a run-off election necessary; the run-off was never held leaving DOS SANTOS in his current position as the president

**Legislative branch:** unicameral National Assembly or Assembleia Nacional (220 seats; members elected by proportional vote to serve four-year terms)
*elections:* last held 5-6 September 2008 (next to be held in September 2012)
*election results:* percent of vote by party - MPLA 81.6%, UNITA 10.4%, PRS 3.2%, ND 1.2%, FNLA 1.1%, other 2.5%; seats by party - MPLA 191, UNITA 16, PRS 8, FNLA 3, ND 2

**Judicial branch:** Supreme Court and separate provincial courts (judges are appointed by the president)

**Political parties and leaders:** National Front for the Liberation of Angola or FNLA [Ngola KABANGU]; National Union for the Total Independence of Angola or UNITA (largest opposition party) [Isaias SAMAKUVA]; Popular Movement for the Liberation of Angola or MPLA (ruling party in power since 1975) [Jose Eduardo DOS SANTOS]; Social Renewal Party or PRS [Eduardo KUANGANA]
*note:* nine other parties participated in the legislative election in September but won no seats

**Political pressure groups and leaders:** Front for the Liberation of the Enclave of Cabinda or FLEC [N'zita Henriques TIAGO, Antonio Bento BEMBE] *note:* FLEC's small-scale armed struggle for the independence of Cabinda Province persists despite the signing of a peace accord with the government in August 2006

**International organization participation:** ACP, AfDB, AU, CPLP, FAO, G-77, IAEA, IBRD, ICAO, ICCt (signatory), ICRM, IDA, IFAD, IFC, IFRCS, ILO, IMF, IMO, Interpol, IOC, IOM, IPU, ISO (correspondent), ITSO, ITU, ITUC, MIGA, NAM, OAS (observer), OPEC, SADC, UN, UNCTAD, UNESCO, UNIDO, Union Latina, UNWTO, UPU, WCO, WFTU, WHO, WIPO, WMO, WTO

**Diplomatic representation in the US:**
*chief of mission:* Ambassador Josefina Perpetua Pitra DIAKITE
*chancery:* 2108 16th Street NW, Washington, DC 20009
*telephone:* [1] (202) 785-1156
*FAX:* [1] (202) 785-1258
*consulate(s) general:* Houston, New York

**Diplomatic representation from the US:**
*chief of mission:* Ambassador Dan MOZENA
*embassy:* number 32 Rua Houari Boumedienne (in the Miramar area of Luanda), Luanda
*mailing address:* international mail: Caixa Postal 6468, Luanda; pouch: US Embassy Luanda, US Department of State, 2550 Luanda Place, Washington, DC 20521-2550
*telephone:* [244] (222) 64-1000
*FAX:* [244] (222) 64-1232

**Flag description:** two equal horizontal bands of red (top) and black with a centered yellow emblem consisting of a five-pointed star within half a cogwheel crossed by a machete (in the style of a hammer and sickle)

### Economy

**Economy - overview:** Angola's high growth rate is driven by its oil sector, which has taken advantage of high international oil prices. Oil production and its supporting activities contribute about 85% of GDP. Increased oil production supported growth averaging more than 15% per year from 2004 to 2007. A postwar reconstruction boom and resettlement of displaced persons has led to high rates of growth in construction and agriculture as well. Much of the country's infrastructure is still damaged or undeveloped from the 27-year-long civil war. Remnants of the conflict such as widespread land mines still mar the countryside even though an apparently durable peace was established after the death of rebel leader Jonas SAVIMBI in February 2002. Subsistence agriculture provides the main livelihood for most of the people, but half of the country's food must still be imported. In 2005, the government started using a $2 billion line of credit, since increased to $7 billion, from China to rebuild Angola's public infrastructure, and several large-scale projects were completed in 2006. Angola also has large credit lines from Brazil, Portugal, Germany, Spain, and the EU. The central bank in 2003 implemented an exchange rate stabilization program using foreign exchange reserves to buy kwanzas out of circulation. This policy became more sustainable in 2005 because of strong oil export earnings; it has significantly reduced inflation. Although consumer inflation declined from 325% in 2000 to under 13% in 2008, the stabilization policy has put pressure on international net liquidity. Angola became a member of OPEC in late 2006 and in late 2007 was assigned a production quota of 1.9 million barrels a day, somewhat less than the 2-2.5 million bbl Angola's government had wanted. To fully take advantage of its rich national resources - gold, diamonds, extensive forests, Atlantic fisheries, and large oil deposits - Angola will need to implement government reforms, increase transparency, and reduce corruption. The government has rejected a formal IMF monitored program, although it continues Article IV consultations and ad hoc cooperation. Corruption, especially in the extractive sectors, and the negative effects of large inflows of foreign exchange, are major challenges facing Angola.

**GDP (purchasing power parity):**
$110.3 billion (2008 est.)
$97.43 billion (2007)
$83.49 billion (2006)
*note:* data are in 2008 US dollars

**GDP (official exchange rate):** $95.95 billion (2008 est.)

**GDP - real growth rate:**
13.2% (2008 est.)
16.7% (2007 est.)
19.6% (2006 est.)

**GDP - per capita (PPP):**
$8,800 (2008 est.)
$7,900 (2007 est.)
$7,000 (2006 est.)
*note:* data are in 2008 US dollars

**GDP - composition by sector:**
*agriculture:* 9.2%
*industry:* 65.8%
*services:* 24.6% (2008 est.)

**Labor force:** 7.288 million (2008 est.)

**Labor force - by occupation:**
*agriculture:* 85%
*industry and services:* 15% (2003 est.)

**Unemployment rate:** NA

**Population below poverty line:** 70% (2003 est.)

**Household income or consumption by percentage share:**
*lowest 10%:* NA%
*highest 10%:* NA%

**Investment (gross fixed):** 9% of GDP (2008 est.)

**Budget:**
*revenues:* $27.18 billion
*expenditures:* $20.6 billion (2008 est.)

**Public debt:** 8.7% of GDP (2008 est.)

**Inflation rate (consumer prices):**
12.5% (2008 est.)
12.2% (2007 est.)

**Central bank discount rate:** 19.57% (31 December 2007)

**Commercial bank prime lending rate:** 17.7% (31 December 2007)

**Stock of money:** $4.153 billion (31 December 2007)

**Stock of quasi money:** $7.216 billion (31 December 2007)

**Stock of domestic credit:** $1.385 billion (31 December 2007)

**Agriculture - products:** bananas, sugarcane, coffee, sisal, corn, cotton, manioc (tapioca), tobacco, vegetables, plantains; livestock; forest products; fish

**Industries:** petroleum; diamonds, iron ore, phosphates, feldspar, bauxite, uranium, and gold; cement; basic metal products; fish processing; food processing, brewing, tobacco products, sugar; textiles; ship repair

**Industrial production growth rate:** 12% (2008 est.)

**Electricity - production:** 3.513 billion kWh (2006 est.)

**Electricity - consumption:** 3.084 billion kWh (2006 est.)

**Electricity - exports:** 0 kWh (2007 est.)

**Electricity - imports:** 0 kWh (2007 est.)

**Oil - production:** 1.91 million bbl/day (2008 est.)

**Oil - consumption:** 55,640 bbl/day (2006 est.)

**Oil - exports:** 1.23 million bbl/day (2005)

**Oil - imports:** 19,550 bbl/day (2005)

**Oil - proved reserves:** 9.035 billion bbl (1 January 2008 est.)

**Natural gas - production:** 680 million cu m (2006 est.)

**Natural gas - consumption:** 680 million cu m (2006 est.)

**Natural gas - exports:** 0 cu m (2007 est.)

**Natural gas - imports:** 0 cu m (2007 est.)

**Natural gas - proved reserves:** 269.8 billion cu m (1 January 2008 est.)

**Current account balance:** $21.01 billion (2008 est.)

**Exports:** $72.58 billion f.o.b. (2008 est.)

**Exports - commodities:** crude oil, diamonds, refined petroleum products, coffee, sisal, fish and fish products, timber, cotton

**Exports - partners:** US 32.1%, China 32%, France 5.9%, Taiwan 5.3%, South Africa 4.5% (2007)

**Imports:** $15.25 billion f.o.b. (2008 est.)

**Imports - commodities:** machinery and electrical equipment, vehicles and spare parts; medicines, food, textiles, military goods

**Imports - partners:** Portugal 19.7%, US 10.9%, China 10.5%, Brazil 10.3%, South Africa 6.6%, France 6.3%, UK 4.6%, Germany 4.3% (2007)

**Reserves of foreign exchange and gold:** $24.64 billion (31 December 2008 est.)

**Debt - external:** $7.907 billion (31 December 2008 est.)

**Stock of direct foreign investment - at home:** $19.49 billion (2008 est.)

**Stock of direct foreign investment - abroad:** $227 million (2006 est.)

## Angola (continued)

**Exchange rates:** kwanza (AOA) per US dollar - 75.023 (2008 est.), 76.6 (2007), 80.4 (2006), 88.6 (2005), 83.541 (2004)

### Communications

**Telephones - main lines in use:** 98,200 (2006)
**Telephones - mobile cellular:** 3.307 million (2007)
**Telephone system:**
*general assessment:* system inadequate; fewer than one fixed-line per 100 persons; combined fixed line and mobile telephone density exceeded 25 telephones per 100 persons in 2007
*domestic:* state-owned telecom had monopoly for fixed-lines until 2005; demand outstripped capacity, prices were high, and services poor; Telecom Namibia, through an Angolan company, became the first private licensed operator in Angola's fixed-line telephone network; Angola Telecom established mobile-cellular service in Luanda in 1993 and the network has been extended to larger towns; a privately-owned, mobile-cellular service provider began operations in 2001
*international:* country code - 244; landing point for the SAT-3/WASC fiber-optic submarine cable that provides connectivity to Europe and Asia; satellite earth stations - 29 (2007)
**Radio broadcast stations:** AM 21, FM 6, shortwave 7 (2001)
**Television broadcast stations:** 6 (2000)
**Internet country code:** .ao
**Internet hosts:** 3,562 (2008)
**Internet users:** 100,000 (2007)

### Transportation

**Airports:** 211 (2008)
**Airports - with paved runways:**
*total:* 30
*over 3,047 m:* 5
*2,438 to 3,047 m:* 8
*1,524 to 2,437 m:* 12
*914 to 1,523 m:* 4
*under 914 m:* 1 (2008)
**Airports - with unpaved runways:**
*total:* 181
*over 3,047 m:* 2
*2,438 to 3,047 m:* 5
*1,524 to 2,437 m:* 32
*914 to 1,523 m:* 100
*under 914 m:* 42 (2008)
**Pipelines:** gas 2 km; oil 87 km (2008)
**Railways:**
*total:* 2,761 km
*narrow gauge:* 2,638 km 1.067-m gauge; 123 km 0.600-m gauge (2006)
**Roadways:**
*total:* 51,429 km
*paved:* 5,349 km
*unpaved:* 46,080 km (2001)
**Waterways:** 1,300 km (2008)

**Merchant marine:**
*total:* 6
*by type:* cargo 1, passenger/cargo 2, petroleum tanker 2, roll on/roll off 1
*foreign-owned:* 1 (Spain 1)
*registered in other countries:* 6 (Bahamas 6) (2008)
**Ports and terminals:** Cabinda, Lobito, Luanda, Namibe

### Military

**Military branches:** Angolan Armed Forces (FAA): Army, Navy (Marinha de Guerra Angola, MGA), Angolan National Air Force (Forca Aerea Nacional Angolana, FANA) (2009)
**Military service age and obligation:** 22-24 years of age for compulsory military service; conscript service obligation - 2 years; Angolan citizenship required (2009)
**Manpower available for military service:**
*males age 16-49:* 2,856,492
*females age 16-49:* 2,755,864 (2008 est.)
**Manpower fit for military service:**
*males age 16-49:* 1,467,833
*females age 16-49:* 1,411,468 (2009 est.)
**Manpower reaching militarily significant age annually:**
*male:* 146,738
*female:* 143,478 (2009 est.)
**Military expenditures:** 5.7% of GDP (2006)

### Transnational Issues

**Disputes - international:** Cabindan separatists continue to return to the Angolan exclave from exile in neighboring states and Europe since the 2006 ceasefire and peace agreement
**Refugees and internally displaced persons:**
*refugees (country of origin):* 12,615 (Democratic Republic of Congo)
*IDPs:* 61,700 (27-year civil war ending in 2002; 4 million IDPs already have returned) (2007)
**Illicit drugs:** used as a transshipment point for cocaine destined for Western Europe and other African states, particularly South Africa

## Anguilla
*(overseas territory of the UK)*

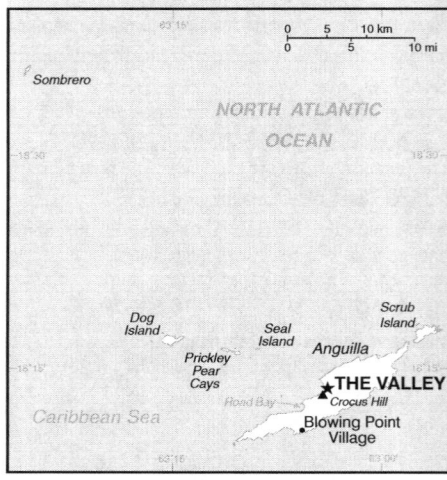

### Introduction

**Background:** Colonized by English settlers from Saint Kitts in 1650, Anguilla was administered by Great Britain until the early 19th century, when the island - against the wishes of the inhabitants - was incorporated into a single British dependency along with Saint Kitts and Nevis. Several attempts at separation failed. In 1971, two years after a revolt, Anguilla was finally allowed to secede; this arrangement was formally recognized in 1980 with Anguilla becoming a separate British dependency.

### Geography

**Location:** Caribbean, islands between the Caribbean Sea and North Atlantic Ocean, east of Puerto Rico
**Geographic coordinates:** 18 15 N, 63 10 W
**Map references:** Central America and the Caribbean
**Area:**
*total:* 102 sq km
*land:* 102 sq km
*water:* 0 sq km
**Area - comparative:** about one-half the size of Washington, DC
**Land boundaries:** 0 km
**Coastline:** 61 km
**Maritime claims:**
*territorial sea:* 3 nm
*exclusive fishing zone:* 200 nm
**Climate:** tropical; moderated by northeast trade winds
**Terrain:** flat and low-lying island of coral and limestone
**Elevation extremes:**
*lowest point:* Caribbean Sea 0 m
*highest point:* Crocus Hill 65 m
**Natural resources:** salt, fish, lobster

# Anguilla (continued)

**Land use:**
*arable land:* 0%
*permanent crops:* 0%
*other:* 100% (mostly rock with sparse scrub oak, few trees, some commercial salt ponds) (2005)
**Irrigated land:** NA
**Natural hazards:** frequent hurricanes and other tropical storms (July to October)
**Environment - current issues:** supplies of potable water sometimes cannot meet increasing demand largely because of poor distribution system
**Geography - note:** the most northerly of the Leeward Islands in the Lesser Antilles

## People

**Population:** 14,436 (July 2009 est.)
**Age structure:**
*0-14 years:* 24.5% (male 1,815/female 1,725)
*15-64 years:* 67.8% (male 4,665/female 5,125)
*65 years and over:* 7.7% (male 534/female 572) (2009 est.)
**Median age:**
*total:* 32.6 years
*male:* 31.5 years
*female:* 33.8 years (2009 est.)
**Population growth rate:** 2.272% (2009 est.)
**Birth rate:** 13.02 births/1,000 population (2009 est.)
**Death rate:** 4.39 deaths/1,000 population (2008 est.)
**Net migration rate:** 14.06 migrant(s)/1,000 population (2009 est.)
**Urbanization:**
*urban population:* 100% of total population (2008)
*rate of urbanization:* 1.4% annual rate of change (2005-10 est.)
**Sex ratio:**
*at birth:* 1.02 male(s)/female
*under 15 years:* 1.05 male(s)/female
*15-64 years:* 0.91 male(s)/female
*65 years and over:* 0.93 male(s)/female
*total population:* 0.94 male(s)/female (2009 est.)
**Infant mortality rate:**
*total:* 3.52 deaths/1,000 live births
*male:* 3.97 deaths/1,000 live births
*female:* 3.05 deaths/1,000 live births (2009 est.)
**Life expectancy at birth:**
*total population:* 80.65 years
*male:* 78.11 years
*female:* 83.26 years (2009 est.)
**Total fertility rate:** 1.75 children born/woman (2009 est.)
**HIV/AIDS - adult prevalence rate:** NA
**HIV/AIDS - people living with HIV/AIDS:** NA
**HIV/AIDS - deaths:** NA
**Nationality:**
*noun:* Anguillan(s)
*adjective:* Anguillan
**Ethnic groups:** black (predominant) 90.1%, mixed, mulatto 4.6%, white 3.7%, other 1.5% (2001 census)
**Religions:** Anglican 29%, Methodist 23.9%, other Protestant 30.2%, Roman Catholic 5.7%, other Christian 1.7%, other 5.2%, none or unspecified 4.3% (2001 census)

**Languages:** English (official)
**Literacy:**
*definition:* age 12 and over can read and write
*total population:* 95%
*male:* 95%
*female:* 95% (1984 est.)
**School life expectancy (primary to tertiary education):**
*total:* 11 years
*male:* 11 years
*female:* 11 years (2006)
**Education expenditures:** 4% of GDP (2005)

## Government

**Country name:**
*conventional long form:* none
*conventional short form:* Anguilla
**Dependency status:** overseas territory of the UK
**Government type:** NA
**Capital:**
*name:* The Valley
*geographic coordinates:* 18 13 N, 63 03 W
*time difference:* UTC-4 (1 hour ahead of Washington, DC during Standard Time)
**Administrative divisions:** none (overseas territory of the UK)
**Independence:** none (overseas territory of the UK)
**National holiday:** Anguilla Day, 30 May (1967)
**Constitution:** Anguilla Constitutional Order 1 April 1982; amended 1990
**Legal system:** based on English common law
**Suffrage:** 18 years of age; universal
**Executive branch:**
*chief of state:* Queen ELIZABETH II (since 6 February 1952); represented by Governor Alistair HARRISON (since 21 April 2009)
*head of government:* Chief Minister Osbourne FLEMING (since 3 March 2000)
*cabinet:* Executive Council appointed by the governor from among the elected members of the House of Assembly
*elections:* the monarch is hereditary; governor appointed by the monarch; following legislative elections, the leader of the majority party or the leader of the majority coalition is usually appointed chief minister by the governor
**Legislative branch:** unicameral House of Assembly (11 seats; 7 members elected by direct popular vote, 2 ex officio members, and 2 appointed; members serve five-year terms)
*elections:* last held 21 February 2005 (next to be held in 2010)
*election results:* percent of vote by party - AUF 38.9%, AUM 19.4%, ANSA 19.2%, APP 9.5%, independents 13%; seats by party - AUF 4, ANSA 2, AUM 1
**Judicial branch:** High Court (judge provided by Eastern Caribbean Supreme Court)
**Political parties and leaders:** Anguilla United Front or AUF [Osbourne FLEMING, Victor BANKS] (a coalition of the Anguilla Democratic Party or ADP and the Anguilla National Alliance or ANA); Anguilla United Movement or AUM [Hubert HUGHES]; Anguilla

Progressive Party or APP [Roy ROGERS]; Anguilla Strategic Alternative or ANSA [Edison BAIRD]
**Political pressure groups and leaders:** NA
**International organization participation:** Caricom (associate), CDB, Interpol (subbureau), OECS, UPU, WFTU
**Diplomatic representation in the US:** none (overseas territory of the UK)
**Diplomatic representation from the US:** none (overseas territory of the UK)
**Flag description:** blue, with the flag of the UK in the upper hoist-side quadrant and the Anguillan coat of arms centered in the outer half of the flag; the coat of arms depicts three orange dolphins in an interlocking circular design on a white background with blue wavy water below

## Economy

**Economy - overview:** Anguilla has few natural resources, and the economy depends heavily on luxury tourism, offshore banking, lobster fishing, and remittances from emigrants. Increased activity in the tourism industry has spurred the growth of the construction sector contributing to economic growth. Anguillan officials have put substantial effort into developing the offshore financial sector, which is small but growing. In the medium term, prospects for the economy will depend largely on the tourism sector and, therefore, on revived income growth in the industrialized nations as well as on favorable weather conditions.
**GDP (purchasing power parity):**
$108.9 million (2004 est.)
**GDP (official exchange rate):** $108.9 million (2004 est.)
**GDP - real growth rate:**
10.2% (2004 est.)
**GDP - per capita (PPP):**
$8,800 (2004 est.)
**GDP - composition by sector:**
*agriculture:* 4%
*industry:* 18%
*services:* 78% (2002 est.)
**Labor force:** 6,049 (2001)
**Labor force - by occupation:** agriculture/fishing/forestry/mining 4%, manufacturing 3%, construction 18%, transportation and utilities 10%, commerce 36%, services 29% (2000 est.)
**Unemployment rate:**
8% (2002)
**Population below poverty line:** 23% (2002)
**Household income or consumption by percentage share:**
*lowest 10%:* NA%
*highest 10%:* NA%
**Budget:**
*revenues:* $22.8 million
*expenditures:* $22.5 million (2000 est.)
**Inflation rate (consumer prices):**
5.3% (2006 est.)
**Central bank discount rate:** 6.5% (31 December 2007)

## Anguilla *(continued)*

**Commercial bank prime lending rate:** 9.76%
(31 December 2007)
**Stock of money:** $23.57 million
(31 December 2007)
**Stock of quasi money:** $470.1 million
(31 December 2007)
**Stock of domestic credit:** $447.7 million
(31 December 2007)
**Agriculture - products:** small quantities of tobacco,
vegetables; cattle raising
**Industries:** tourism, boat building, offshore financial
services
**Industrial production growth rate:** NA
**Electricity - production:** NA kWh
**Current account balance:** -$42.87 million
(2003 est.)
**Exports:** $13 million (2006)
**Exports - commodities:** lobster, fish, livestock, salt,
concrete blocks, rum
**Imports:** $143 million (2006)
**Imports - commodities:** fuels, foodstuffs,
manufactures, chemicals, trucks, textiles
**Debt - external:** $8.8 million (1998)
**Exchange rates:** East Caribbean dollars (XCD)
per US dollar - 2.7 (2007), 2.7 (2006), 2.7 (2005),
2.7 (2004), 2.7 (2003)
*note:* fixed rate since 1976

### Communications

**Telephones - main lines in use:** 6,200 (2002)
**Telephones - mobile cellular:** 1,800 (2002)
**Telephone system:**
*general assessment:* NA
*domestic:* modern internal telephone system
*international:* country code - 1-264; landing point for
the East Caribbean Fiber System (ECFS) submarine
cable with links to 13 other islands in the eastern
Caribbean extending from the British Virgin Islands to
Trinidad; microwave radio relay to island of Saint
Martin (Guadeloupe and Netherlands Antilles) (2007)
**Radio broadcast stations:** AM 2, FM 7,
shortwave 0 (2004)
**Television broadcast stations:** 1 (1997)
**Internet country code:** .ai
**Internet hosts:** 205 (2008)
**Internet users:** 3,000 (2002)

### Transportation

**Airports:** 3 (2008)
**Airports - with paved runways:**
*total:* 1
*1,524 to 2,437 m:* 1 (2008)
**Airports - with unpaved runways:**
*total:* 2
*under 914 m:* 2 (2008)
**Roadways:**
*total:* 175 km
*paved:* 82 km
*unpaved:* 93 km (2004)
**Ports and terminals:** Blowing Point, Road Bay

### Military

**Manpower available for military service:**
*males age 16-49:* 3,538 (2008 est.)
**Manpower fit for military service:**
*males age 16-49:* 2,955
*females age 16-49:* 3,308 (2009 est.)
**Manpower reaching militarily significant age
annually:**
*male:* 107
*female:* 106 (2009 est.)
**Military - note:** defense is the responsibility of the
UK

### Transnational Issues

**Disputes - international:** none
**Illicit drugs:** transshipment point for South American
narcotics destined for the US and Europe

# Antarctica

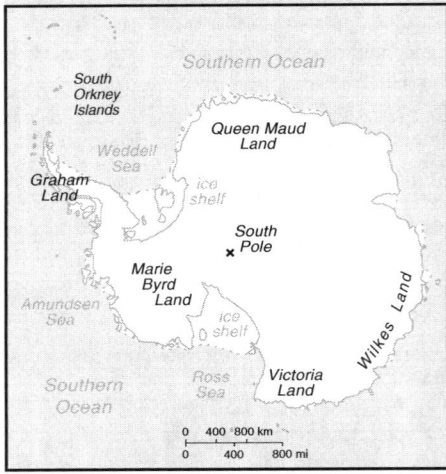

### Introduction

**Background:** Speculation over the existence of a
"southern land" was not confirmed until the early
1820s when British and American commercial
operators and British and Russian national
expeditions began exploring the Antarctic Peninsula
region and other areas south of the Antarctic Circle.
Not until 1840 was it established that Antarctica was
indeed a continent and not just a group of islands.
Several exploration "firsts" were achieved in the early
20th century. Following World War II, there was an
upsurge in scientific research on the continent. A
number of countries have set up a range of year-round
and seasonal stations, camps, and refuges to support
scientific research in Antarctica. Seven have made
territorial claims, but not all countries recognize these
claims. In order to form a legal framework for the
activities of nations on the continent, an Antarctic
Treaty was negotiated that neither denies nor gives
recognition to existing territorial claims; signed in
1959, it entered into force in 1961.

### Geography

**Location:** continent mostly south of the Antarctic
Circle
**Geographic coordinates:** 90 00 S, 0 00 E
**Map references:** Antarctic Region
**Area:**
*total:* 14 million sq km
*land:* 14 million sq km (280,000 sq km ice-free, 13.72
million sq km ice-covered) (est.)
*note:* fifth-largest continent, following Asia, Africa,
North America, and South America, but larger than
Australia and the subcontinent of Europe
**Area - comparative:** slightly less than 1.5 times the
size of the US
**Land boundaries:** 0 km
*note:* see entry on Disputes - international
**Coastline:** 17,968 km

# Antarctica *(continued)*

**Maritime claims:** Australia, Chile, and Argentina claim Exclusive Economic Zone (EEZ) rights or similar over 200 nm extensions seaward from their continental claims, but like the claims themselves, these zones are not accepted by other countries; 21 of 28 Antarctic consultative nations have made no claims to Antarctic territory (although Russia and the US have reserved the right to do so) and do not recognize the claims of the other nations; also see the Disputes - international entry

**Climate:** severe low temperatures vary with latitude, elevation, and distance from the ocean; East Antarctica is colder than West Antarctica because of its higher elevation; Antarctic Peninsula has the most moderate climate; higher temperatures occur in January along the coast and average slightly below freezing

**Terrain:** about 98% thick continental ice sheet and 2% barren rock, with average elevations between 2,000 and 4,000 meters; mountain ranges up to nearly 5,000 meters; ice-free coastal areas include parts of southern Victoria Land, Wilkes Land, the Antarctic Peninsula area, and parts of Ross Island on McMurdo Sound; glaciers form ice shelves along about half of the coastline, and floating ice shelves constitute 11% of the area of the continent

**Elevation extremes:**
*lowest point:* Bentley Subglacial Trench -2,540 m
*highest point:* Vinson Massif 4,897 m
*note:* the lowest known land point in Antarctica is hidden in the Bentley Subglacial Trench; at its surface is the deepest ice yet discovered and the world's lowest elevation not under seawater

**Natural resources:** iron ore, chromium, copper, gold, nickel, platinum and other minerals, and coal and hydrocarbons have been found in small uncommercial quantities; none presently exploited; krill, finfish, and crab have been taken by commercial fisheries

**Land use:**
*arable land:* 0%
*permanent crops:* 0%
*other:* 100% (ice 98%, barren rock 2%) (2005)

**Natural hazards:** katabatic (gravity-driven) winds blow coastward from the high interior; frequent blizzards form near the foot of the plateau; cyclonic storms form over the ocean and move clockwise along the coast; volcanism on Deception Island and isolated areas of West Antarctica; other seismic activity rare and weak; large icebergs may calve from ice shelf

**Environment - current issues:** in 1998, NASA satellite data showed that the Antarctic ozone hole was the largest on record, covering 27 million square kilometers; researchers in 1997 found that increased ultraviolet light passing through the hole damages the DNA of icefish, an Antarctic fish lacking hemoglobin; ozone depletion earlier was shown to harm one-celled Antarctic marine plants; in 2002, significant areas of ice shelves disintegrated in response to regional warming

**Geography - note:** the coldest, windiest, highest (on average), and driest continent; during summer, more solar radiation reaches the surface at the South Pole than is received at the Equator in an equivalent period; mostly uninhabitable

## People

**Population:** no indigenous inhabitants, but there are both permanent and summer-only staffed research stations
*note:* 29 nations, all signatory to the Antarctic Treaty, operate through their National Antarctic Program a number of seasonal-only (summer) and year-round research stations on the continent and its nearby islands south of 60 degrees south latitude (the region covered by the Antarctic Treaty); the population doing and supporting science or engaged in the management and protection of the Antarctic region varies from approximately 4,400 in summer to 1,100 in winter; in addition, approximately 1,000 personnel, including ship's crew and scientists doing onboard research, are present in the waters of the treaty region; peak summer (December-February) population - 4,490 total; Argentina 667, Australia 200, Australia and Romania jointly 13, Belgium 20, Brazil 40, Bulgaria 18, Chile 359, China 90, Czech Republic 20, Ecuador 26, Finland 20, France 125, France and Italy jointly 60, Germany 90, India 65, Italy 102, Japan 125, South Korea 70, NZ 85, Norway 44, Peru 28, Poland 40, Russia 429, South Africa 80, Spain 50, Sweden 20, Ukraine 24, UK 217, US 1,293, Uruguay 70 (2008-2009); winter (June-August) station population - 1,106 total; Argentina 176, Australia 62, Brazil 12, Chile 114, China 29, France 26, France and Italy jointly 13, Germany 9, India 25, Japan 40, South Korea 18, NZ 10, Norway 7, Poland 12, Russia 148, South Africa 10, Ukraine 12, UK 37, US 337, Uruguay 9 (2009); research stations operated within the Antarctic Treaty area (south of 60 degrees south latitude) by National Antarctic Programs: year-round stations - 40 total; Argentina 6, Australia 3, Brazil 1, Chile 6, China 2, France 1, France and Italy jointly 1, Germany 1, India 1, Japan 1, South Korea 1, NZ 1, Norway 1, Poland 1, Russia 5, South Africa 1, Ukraine 1, UK 2, US 3, Uruguay 1 (2009); a range of seasonal-only (summer) stations, camps, and refuges -Argentina, Australia, Belgium, Bulgaria, Brazil, Chile, China, Czech Republic, Ecuador, Finland, France, Germany, India, Italy, Japan, South Korea, New Zealand, Norway, Peru, Poland, Romania (with Australia), Russia, South Africa, Spain, Sweden, Ukraine, UK, US, and Uruguay (2008-2009); in addition, during the austral summer some nations have numerous occupied locations such as tent camps, summer-long temporary facilities, and mobile traverses in support of research (May 2009 est.)

## Government

**Country name:**
*conventional long form:* none
*conventional short form:* Antarctica

**Government type:** Antarctic Treaty Summary - the Antarctic Treaty, signed on 1 December 1959 and entered into force on 23 June 1961, establishes the legal framework for the management of Antarctica; the 32nd Antarctic Treaty Consultative Meeting was held in Baltimore, MD, USA in April 2009; at these periodic meetings, decisions are made by consensus (not by vote) of all consultative member nations; by May 2009, there were 47 treaty member nations: 28 consultative and 19 non-consultative; consultative (decision-making) members include the seven nations that claim portions of Antarctica as national territory (some claims overlap) and 21 non-claimant nations; the US and Russia have reserved the right to make claims; the US does not recognize the claims of others; Antarctica is administered through meetings of the consultative member nations; decisions from these meetings are carried out by these member nations (with respect to their own nationals and operations) in accordance with their own national laws; the years in parentheses indicate when a consultative member-nation acceded to the Treaty and when it was accepted as a consultative member, while no date indicates the country was an original 1959 treaty signatory; claimant nations are - Argentina, Australia, Chile, France, NZ, Norway, and the UK. Nonclaimant consultative nations are - Belgium, Brazil (1975/1983), Bulgaria (1978/1998) China (1983/1985), Ecuador (1987/1990), Finland (1984/1989), Germany (1979/1981), India (1983/1983), Italy (1981/1987), Japan, South Korea (1986/1989), Netherlands (1967/1990), Peru (1981/1989), Poland (1961/1977), Russia, South Africa, Spain (1982/1988), Sweden (1984/1988), Ukraine (1992/2004), Uruguay (1980/1985), and the US; non-consultative members, with year of accession in parentheses, are - Austria (1987), Belarus (2006), Canada (1988), Colombia (1989), Cuba (1984), Czech Republic (1962/1993), Denmark (1965), Estonia (2001), Greece (1987), Guatemala (1991), Hungary (1984), North Korea (1987), Monaco (2008), Papua New Guinea (1981), Romania (1971), Slovakia (1962/1993), Switzerland (1990), Turkey (1996), and Venezuela (1999); note - Czechoslovakia acceded to the Treaty in 1962 and separated into the Czech Republic and Slovakia in 1993; Article 1 - area to be used for peaceful purposes only; military activity, such as weapons testing, is prohibited, but military personnel and equipment may be used for scientific research or any other peaceful purpose; Article 2 - freedom of scientific investigation and cooperation shall continue; Article 3 - free exchange of information and personnel, cooperation with the UN and other international agencies; Article 4 - does not recognize, dispute, or establish territorial claims and no new claims shall be asserted while the treaty is in force; Article 5 - prohibits nuclear explosions or disposal of radioactive wastes; Article 6 - includes under the treaty all land and ice shelves south of 60 degrees 00 minutes south and reserves high seas rights;
Article 7 - treaty-state observers have free access, including aerial observation, to any area and may inspect all stations, installations, and equipment;

advance notice of all expeditions and of the introduction of military personnel must be given; Article 8 - allows for jurisdiction over observers and scientists by their own states; Article 9 - frequent consultative meetings take place among member nations; Article 10 - treaty states will discourage activities by any country in Antarctica that are contrary to the treaty; Article 11 - disputes to be settled peacefully by the parties concerned or, ultimately, by the ICJ; Articles 12, 13, 14 - deal with upholding, interpreting, and amending the treaty among involved nations; other agreements - some 200 recommendations adopted at treaty consultative meetings and ratified by governments include - Agreed Measures for Fauna and Flora (1964) which were later incorporated into the Environmental Protocol; Convention for the Conservation of Antarctic Seals (1972); Convention on the Conservation of Antarctic Marine Living Resources (1980); a mineral resources agreement was signed in 1988 but remains unratified; the Protocol on Environmental Protection to the Antarctic Treaty was signed 4 October 1991 and entered into force 14 January 1998; this agreement provides for the protection of the Antarctic environment through six specific annexes: 1) environmental impact assessment, 2) conservation of Antarctic fauna and flora, 3) waste disposal and waste management, 4) prevention of marine pollution, 5) area protection and management and 6) liability arising from environmental emergencies; it prohibits all activities relating to mineral resources except scientific research; a permanent Antarctic Treaty Secretariat was established in 2004 in Buenos Aires, Argentina

**Legal system:** Antarctica is administered through meetings of the consultative member nations; decisions from these meetings are carried out by these member nations (with respect to their own nationals and operations) in accordance with their own national laws; more generally, access to the Antarctic Treaty area, that is to all areas between 60 and 90 degrees south latitude, is subject to a number of relevant legal instruments and authorization procedures adopted by the states party to the Antarctic Treaty; note - US law, including certain criminal offenses by or against US nationals, such as murder, may apply extraterritorially; some US laws directly apply to Antarctica; for example, the Antarctic Conservation Act, 16 U.S.C. section 2401 et seq., provides civil and criminal penalties for the following activities unless authorized by regulation of statute: the taking of native mammals or birds; the introduction of nonindigenous plants and animals; entry into specially protected areas; the discharge or disposal of pollutants; and the importation into the US of certain items from Antarctica; violation of the Antarctic Conservation Act carries penalties of up to $10,000 in fines and one year in prison; the National Science Foundation and Department of Justice share enforcement responsibilities; Public Law 95-541, the US Antarctic Conservation Act of 1978, as amended in 1996, requires expeditions from the US to Antarctica to notify, in advance, the Office of Oceans, Room 5805, Department of State, Washington, DC 20520, which reports such plans to other nations as required by the Antarctic Treaty; for more information, contact Permit Office, Office of Polar Programs, National Science Foundation, Arlington, Virginia 22230; telephone: (703) 292-8030, or visit its website at www.nsf.gov

## Economy

**Economy - overview:** Fishing off the coast and tourism, both based abroad, account for Antarctica's limited economic activity. Antarctic fisheries in 2006-07 (1 July-30 June) reported landing 126,976 metric tons (estimated fishing from the area covered by the Convention on the Conservation of Antarctic Marine Living Resources (CCAMLR), which extends slightly beyond the Antarctic Treaty area). Unregulated fishing, particularly of Patagonian toothfish (Dissostichus eleginoides - also known as Chilean sea bass), is a serious problem. The CCAMLR determines the recommended catch limits for marine species. A total of 45,652 tourists visited the Antarctic Treaty area in the 2007-08 Antarctic summer, up from the 36,460 visitors in 2006-2007, and the 30,877 visitors in 2005-2006 (estimates provided to the Antarctic Treaty by the International Association of Antarctica Tour Operators (IAATO); this does not include passengers on overflights). Nearly all of them were passengers on commercial (nongovernmental) ships and several yachts that make trips during the summer. Most tourist trips last approximately two weeks.

## Communications

**Telephones - main lines in use:** 0; note - information for US bases only (2001)
**Telephone system:**
*general assessment:* local systems at some research stations
*domestic:* commercial cellular networks operating in a small number of locations
*international:* country code - none allocated; via satellite (including mobile Inmarsat and Iridium systems) to and from all research stations, ships, aircraft, and most field parties (2007)
**Radio broadcast stations:** FM 2, shortwave 1 (information for US bases only); note - many research stations have a local FM radio station (2007)
**Television broadcast stations:** 1 (cable system with 6 channels; American Forces Antarctic Network-McMurdo - information for US bases only) (2002)
**Internet country code:** .aq
**Internet hosts:** 7,748 (2008)

## Transportation

**Airports:** 25 (2008)
**Airports - with unpaved runways:**
*total:* 25
*over 3,047 m:* 4
*2,438 to 3,047 m:* 5
*1,524 to 2,437 m:* 1
*914 to 1,523 m:* 9
*under 914 m:* 6 (2008)

**Heliports:** 53
*note:* all year-round and seasonal stations operated by National Antarctic Programs stations have some kind of helicopter landing facilities, prepared (helipads) or unprepared (2007)
**Ports and terminals:** there are no developed ports and harbors in Antarctica; most coastal stations have sparse and intermittent offshore anchorages; a few stations have basic wharf facilities
**Transportation - note:** US coastal stations include McMurdo (77 51 S, 166 40 E) and Palmer (64 43 S, 64 03 W); government use only except by permit (see Permit Office under "Legal System"); all ships at port are subject to inspection in accordance with Article 7, Antarctic Treaty; relevant legal instruments and authorization procedures adopted by the states parties to the Antarctic Treaty regulating access to the Antarctic Treaty area to all areas between 60 and 90 degrees of latitude south have to be complied with (see "Legal System"); The Hydrographic Commission on Antarctica (HCA), a commission of the International Hydrographic Organization (IHO), is responsible for hydrographic surveying and nautical charting matters in Antarctic Treaty area; it coordinates and facilitates provision of accurate and appropriate charts and other aids to navigation in support of safety of navigation in region; membership of HCA is open to any IHO Member State whose government has acceded to the Antarctic Treaty and which contributes resources or data to IHO Chart coverage of the area

## Military

**Military - note:** the Antarctic Treaty prohibits any measures of a military nature, such as the establishment of military bases and fortifications, the carrying out of military maneuvers, or the testing of any type of weapon; it permits the use of military personnel or equipment for scientific research or for any other peaceful purposes

## Transnational Issues

**Disputes - international:** the Antarctic Treaty freezes, and most states do not recognize, the land and maritime territorial claims made by Argentina, Australia, Chile, France, New Zealand, Norway, and the United Kingdom (some overlapping) for three-fourths of the continent; the US and Russia reserve the right to make claims; no claims have been made in the sector between 90 degrees west and 150 degrees west; the International Whaling Commission created a sanctuary around the entire continent to deter catches by countries claiming to conduct scientific whaling; Australia has established a similar preserve in the waters around its territorial claim

# Antigua and Barbuda

## Introduction

**Background:** The Siboney were the first to inhabit the islands of Antigua and Barbuda in 2400 B.C., but Arawak Indians populated the islands when COLUMBUS landed on his second voyage in 1493. Early settlements by the Spanish and French were succeeded by the English who formed a colony in 1667. Slavery, established to run the sugar plantations on Antigua, was abolished in 1834. The islands became an independent state within the British Commonwealth of Nations in 1981.

## Geography

**Location:** Caribbean, islands between the Caribbean Sea and the North Atlantic Ocean, east-southeast of Puerto Rico
**Geographic coordinates:** 17 03 N, 61 48 W
**Map references:** Central America and the Caribbean
**Area:**
*total:* 442.6 sq km (Antigua 280 sq km; Barbuda 161 sq km)
*land:* 442.6 sq km
*water:* 0 sq km
*note:* includes Redonda, 1.6 sq km
**Area - comparative:** 2.5 times the size of Washington, DC
**Land boundaries:** 0 km
**Coastline:** 153 km
**Maritime claims:**
*territorial sea:* 12 nm
*contiguous zone:* 24 nm
*exclusive economic zone:* 200 nm
*continental shelf:* 200 nm or to the edge of the continental margin
**Climate:** tropical maritime; little seasonal temperature variation
**Terrain:** mostly low-lying limestone and coral islands, with some higher volcanic areas

**Elevation extremes:**
*lowest point:* Caribbean Sea 0 m
*highest point:* Boggy Peak 402 m
**Natural resources:** NEGL; pleasant climate fosters tourism
**Land use:**
*arable land:* 18.18%
*permanent crops:* 4.55%
*other:* 77.27% (2005)
**Irrigated land:** NA
**Total renewable water resources:** 0.1 cu km (2000)
**Freshwater withdrawal (domestic/industrial/agricultural):**
*total:* 0.005 cu km/yr (60%/20%/20%)
*per capita:* 63 cu m/yr (1990)
**Natural hazards:** hurricanes and tropical storms (July to October); periodic droughts
**Environment - current issues:** water management -a major concern because of limited natural fresh water resources - is further hampered by the clearing of trees to increase crop production, causing rainfall to run off quickly
**Environment - international agreements:**
*party to:* Biodiversity, Climate Change, Climate Change-Kyoto Protocol, Desertification, Endangered Species, Environmental Modification, Hazardous Wastes, Law of the Sea, Marine Dumping, Ozone Layer Protection, Ship Pollution, Wetlands, Whaling
*signed, but not ratified:* none of the selected agreements
**Geography - note:** Antigua has a deeply indented shoreline with many natural harbors and beaches; Barbuda has a large western harbor

## People

**Population:** 85,632 (July 2009 est.)
**Age structure:**
*0-14 years:* 26.8% (male 11,660/female 11,303)
*15-64 years:* 66.6% (male 26,597/female 30,414)
*65 years and over:* 6.6% (male 2,456/female 3,202) (2009 est.)
**Median age:**
*total:* 29.7 years
*male:* 28.2 years
*female:* 31.1 years (2009 est.)
**Population growth rate:** 1.303% (2009 est.)
**Birth rate:** 16.59 births/1,000 population (2009 est.)
**Death rate:** 6.14 deaths/1,000 population (2008 est.)
**Net migration rate:** 2.38 migrant(s)/1,000 population (2009 est.)
**Urbanization:**
*urban population:* 30% of total population (2008)
*rate of urbanization:* 0.9% annual rate of change (2005-10 est.)
**Sex ratio:**
*at birth:* 1.05 male(s)/female
*under 15 years:* 1.03 male(s)/female
*15-64 years:* 0.87 male(s)/female
*65 years and over:* 0.77 male(s)/female
*total population:* 0.91 male(s)/female (2009 est.)

**Infant mortality rate:**
*total:* 16.25 deaths/1,000 live births
*male:* 18.76 deaths/1,000 live births
*female:* 13.62 deaths/1,000 live births (2009 est.)
**Life expectancy at birth:**
*total population:* 74.76 years
*male:* 72.81 years
*female:* 76.81 years (2009 est.)
**Total fertility rate:** 2.07 children born/woman (2009 est.)
**HIV/AIDS - adult prevalence rate:** NA
**HIV/AIDS - people living with HIV/AIDS:** NA
**HIV/AIDS - deaths:** NA
**Nationality:**
*noun:* Antiguan(s), Barbudan(s)
*adjective:* Antiguan, Barbudan
**Ethnic groups:** black 91%, mixed 4.4%, white 1.7%, other 2.9% (2001 census)
**Religions:** Anglican 25.7%, Seventh Day Adventist 12.3%, Pentecostal 10.6%, Moravian 10.5%, Roman Catholic 10.4%, Methodist 7.9%, Baptist 4.9%, Church of God 4.5%, other Christian 5.4%, other 2%, none or unspecified 5.8% (2001 census)
**Languages:** English (official), local dialects
**Literacy:**
*definition:* age 15 and over has completed five or more years of schooling
*total population:* 85.8%
*male:* NA
*female:* NA (2003 est.)
**Education expenditures:** 3.9% of GDP (2002)

## Government

**Country name:**
*conventional long form:* none
*conventional short form:* Antigua and Barbuda
**Government type:** constitutional monarchy with a parliamentary system of government and a Commonwealth realm
**Capital:**
*name:* Saint John's
*geographic coordinates:* 17 07 N, 61 51 W
*time difference:* UTC-4 (1 hour ahead of Washington, DC during Standard Time)
**Administrative divisions:** 6 parishes and 2 dependencies*; Barbuda*, Redonda*, Saint George, Saint John, Saint Mary, Saint Paul, Saint Peter, Saint Philip
**Independence:** 1 November 1981 (from the UK)
**National holiday:** Independence Day (National Day), 1 November (1981)
**Constitution:** 1 November 1981
**Legal system:** based on English common law
**Suffrage:** 18 years of age; universal
**Executive branch:**
*chief of state:* Queen ELIZABETH II (since 6 February 1952); represented by Governor General Louisse LAKE-TACK (since 17 July 2007)
*head of government:* Prime Minister Winston Baldwin SPENCER (since 24 March 2004)
*cabinet:* Council of Ministers appointed by the

governor general on the advice of the prime minister
*elections:* the monarch is hereditary; governor general chosen by the monarch on the advice of the prime minister; following legislative elections, the leader of the majority party or the leader of the majority coalition is usually appointed prime minister by the governor general
**Legislative branch:** bicameral Parliament consists of the Senate (17 seats; members appointed by the governor general) and the House of Representatives (17 seats; members are elected by proportional representation to serve five-year terms)
*elections:* House of Representatives - last held 12 March 2009 (next to be held in 2014)
*election results:* percent of vote by party - UPP 50.9%, ALP 47.2%, BPM 1.1%; seats by party - UPP 9, ALP 7, BPM 1
**Judicial branch:** Eastern Caribbean Supreme Court consisting of a High Court of Justice and a Court of Appeal (based in Saint Lucia; two judges of the Supreme Court are residents of the islands and preside over the Court of Summary Jurisdiction); Magistrates' Courts; member of the Caribbean Court of Justice
**Political parties and leaders:** Antigua Labor Party or ALP [Lester Bryant BIRD]; Barbudans for a Better Barbuda [Ordrick SAMUEL]; Barbuda People's Movement or BPM [Thomas H. FRANK]; Barbuda People's Movement for Change [Arthur NIBBS]; United Progressive Party or UPP [Baldwin SPENCER] (a coalition of three parties - Antigua Caribbean Liberation Movement or ACLM, Progressive Labor Movement or PLM, United National Democratic Party or UNDP)
**Political pressure groups and leaders:** Antigua Trades and Labor Union or ATLU [William ROBINSON]; People's Democratic Movement or PDM [Hugh MARSHALL]
**International organization participation:** ACP, C, Caricom, CDB, FAO, G-77, IBRD, ICAO, ICCt, ICRM, IDA, IFAD, IFC, IFRCS, ILO, IMF, IMO, Interpol, IOC, ISO (subscriber), ITU, ITUC, MIGA, NAM, OAS, OECS, OPANAL, OPCW, UN, UNCTAD, UNESCO, UPU, WCL, WFTU, WHO, WIPO, WMO, WTO
**Diplomatic representation in the US:**
*chief of mission:* Ambassador Deborah Mae LOVELL
*chancery:* 3216 New Mexico Avenue NW, Washington, DC 20016
*telephone:* [1] (202) 362-5122
*FAX:* [1] (202) 362-5225
*consulate(s) general:* Miami, New York
**Diplomatic representation from the US:** the US does not have an embassy in Antigua and Barbuda; the US Ambassador to Barbados is accredited to Antigua and Barbuda
**Flag description:** red, with an inverted isosceles triangle based on the top edge of the flag; the triangle contains three horizontal bands of black (top), light blue, and white, with a yellow rising sun in the black band

## Economy

**Economy - overview:** Antigua has a relatively high GDP per capita in comparison to most other Caribbean nations. The economy experienced solid growth from 2003 to 2007, reaching over 12% in 2006 driven by a construction boom in hotels and housing associated with the Cricket World Cup. Growth dropped off in 2008 with the end of the boom. Tourism continues to dominate the economy, accounting for nearly 60% of GDP and 40% of investment. The dual-island nation's agricultural production is focused on the domestic market and constrained by a limited water supply and a labor shortage stemming from the lure of higher wages in tourism and construction. Manufacturing comprises enclave-type assembly for export with major products being bedding, handicrafts, and electronic components. Prospects for economic growth in the medium term will continue to depend on tourist arrivals from the US, Canada, and Europe and potential damages from natural disasters. Since taking office in 2004, the SPENCER government has adopted an ambitious fiscal reform program, and has been successful in reducing its public debt-to-GDP ratio from 120% to about 90%.
**GDP (purchasing power parity):**
$1.61 billion (2008 est.)
$1.577 billion (2007)
$1.486 billion (2006)
*note:* data are in 2008 US dollars
**GDP (official exchange rate):** $1.126 billion (2008 est.)
**GDP - real growth rate:**
2.1% (2008 est.)
6.1% (2007 est.)
12.2% (2006 est.)
**GDP - per capita (PPP):**
$19,000 (2008 est.)
$18,900 (2007 est.)
$18,000 (2006 est.)
*note:* data are in 2008 US dollars
**GDP - composition by sector:**
*agriculture:* 3.8%
*industry:* 22%
*services:* 74.3% (2002 est.)
**Labor force:** 30,000 (1991)
**Labor force - by occupation:**
*agriculture:* 7%
*industry:* 11%
*services:* 82% (1983)
**Unemployment rate:**
11% (2001 est.)
**Population below poverty line:** NA%
**Household income or consumption by percentage share:**
*lowest 10%:* NA%
*highest 10%:* NA%
**Budget:**
*revenues:* $123.7 million
*expenditures:* $145.9 million (2000 est.)
**Inflation rate (consumer prices):**
1.5% (2007 est.)

**Central bank discount rate:** 6.5% (31 December 2007)
**Commercial bank prime lending rate:** 10.44% (31 December 2007)
**Stock of money:** $294.8 million (31 December 2007)
**Stock of quasi money:** $902 million (31 December 2007)
**Stock of domestic credit:** $1.002 billion (31 December 2007)
**Agriculture - products:** cotton, fruits, vegetables, bananas, coconuts, cucumbers, mangoes, sugarcane; livestock
**Industries:** tourism, construction, light manufacturing (clothing, alcohol, household appliances)
**Industrial production growth rate:** NA%
**Electricity - production:** 105 million kWh (2006 est.)
**Electricity - consumption:** 97.65 million kWh (2006 est.)
**Electricity - exports:** 0 kWh (2007 est.)
**Electricity - imports:** 0 kWh (2007 est.)
**Oil - production:** 0 bbl/day (2007 est.)
**Oil - consumption:** 4,109 bbl/day (2006 est.)
**Oil - exports:** 157.7 bbl/day (2005)
**Oil - imports:** 4,556 bbl/day (2005)
**Oil - proved reserves:** 0 bbl (1 January 2006 est.)
**Natural gas - production:** 0 cu m (2007 est.)
**Natural gas - consumption:** 0 cu m (2007 est.)
**Natural gas - exports:** 0 cu m (2007 est.)
**Natural gas - imports:** 0 cu m (2007 est.)
**Natural gas - proved reserves:** 0 cu m (1 January 2006 est.)
**Current account balance:** -$211 million (2007 est.)
**Exports:** $84.3 million (2007 est.)
**Exports - commodities:** petroleum products, bedding, handicrafts, electronic components, transport equipment, food and live animals
**Imports:** $522.8 million (2007 est.)
**Imports - commodities:** food and live animals, machinery and transport equipment, manufactures, chemicals, oil
**Debt - external:** $359.8 million (June 2006)
**Exchange rates:** East Caribbean dollars (XCD) per US dollar - 2.7 (2007), 2.7 (2006), 2.7 (2005), 2.7 (2004), 2.7 (2003)
*note:* fixed rate since 1976

## Communications

**Telephones - main lines in use:** 37,500 (2006)
**Telephones - mobile cellular:** 110,200 (2006)
**Telephone system:**
*general assessment:* NA
*domestic:* good automatic telephone system
*international:* country code - 1-268; landing point for the East Caribbean Fiber System (ECFS) submarine cable with links to 13 other islands in the eastern Caribbean extending from the British Virgin Islands to Trinidad; satellite earth stations - 2; tropospheric scatter to Saba (Netherlands Antilles) and Guadeloupe (2007)

# Antigua and Barbuda *(continued)*

**Radio broadcast stations:** AM 4, FM 2, shortwave 0 (1998)
**Television broadcast stations:** 2 (1997)
**Internet country code:** .ag
**Internet hosts:** 2,215 (2008)
**Internet users:** 60,000 (2007)

## Transportation

**Airports:** 3 (2008)
**Airports - with paved runways:**
*total:* 2
*2,438 to 3,047 m:* 1
*under 914 m:* 1 (2008)
**Airports - with unpaved runways:**
*total:* 1
*under 914 m:* 1 (2008)
**Roadways:**
*total:* 1,165 km
*paved:* 384 km
*unpaved:* 781 km (2002)
**Merchant marine:**
*total:* 1,146
*by type:* barge carrier 2, bulk carrier 50, cargo 651, carrier 4, chemical tanker 5, container 392, liquefied gas 12, petroleum tanker 1, refrigerated cargo 9, roll on/roll off 20
*foreign-owned:* 1,113 (Australia 1, Colombia 2, Cyprus 18, Denmark 19, Estonia 23, France 1, Germany 941, Greece 3, Iceland 12, Italy 1, Latvia 13, Lithuania 5, Netherlands 20, NZ 2, Norway 8, Poland 2, Russia 4, Slovenia 6, Sweden 1, Switzerland 8, Turkey 6, UK 9, US 8) (2008)
**Ports and terminals:** Saint John's

## Military

**Military branches:** Royal Antigua and Barbuda Defense Force (2009)
**Military service age and obligation:** 18 years of age for voluntary military service; no conscription (2008)
**Manpower available for military service:**
*males age 16-49:* 19,560
*females age 16-49:* 18,977 (2008 est.)
**Manpower fit for military service:**
*males age 16-49:* 17,271
*females age 16-49:* 19,586 (2009 est.)
**Manpower reaching militarily significant age annually:**
*male:* 744
*female:* 743 (2009 est.)
**Military expenditures:** NA

## Transnational Issues

**Disputes - international:** none
**Illicit drugs:** considered a minor transshipment point for narcotics bound for the US and Europe; more significant as an offshore financial center

# Arctic Ocean

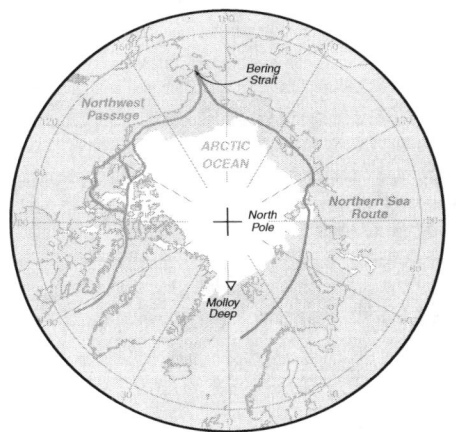

## Introduction

**Background:** The Arctic Ocean is the smallest of the world's five oceans (after the Pacific Ocean, Atlantic Ocean, Indian Ocean, and the recently delimited Southern Ocean). The Northwest Passage (US and Canada) and Northern Sea Route (Norway and Russia) are two important seasonal waterways. A sparse network of air, ocean, river, and land routes circumscribes the Arctic Ocean.

## Geography

**Location:** body of water between Europe, Asia, and North America, mostly north of the Arctic Circle
**Geographic coordinates:** 90 00 N, 0 00 E
**Map references:** Arctic Region
**Area:**
*total:* 14.056 million sq km
*note:* includes Baffin Bay, Barents Sea, Beaufort Sea, Chukchi Sea, East Siberian Sea, Greenland Sea, Hudson Bay, Hudson Strait, Kara Sea, Laptev Sea, Northwest Passage, and other tributary water bodies
**Area - comparative:** slightly less than 1.5 times the size of the US
**Coastline:** 45,389 km
**Climate:** polar climate characterized by persistent cold and relatively narrow annual temperature ranges; winters characterized by continuous darkness, cold and stable weather conditions, and clear skies; summers characterized by continuous daylight, damp and foggy weather, and weak cyclones with rain or snow
**Terrain:** central surface covered by a perennial drifting polar icepack that, on average, is about 3 meters thick, although pressure ridges may be three times that thickness; clockwise drift pattern in the Beaufort Gyral Stream, but nearly straight-line movement from the New Siberian Islands (Russia) to Denmark Strait (between Greenland and Iceland); the icepack is surrounded by open seas during the summer, but more than doubles in size during the winter and extends to the encircling landmasses; the ocean floor is about 50% continental shelf (highest percentage of any ocean) with the remainder a central basin interrupted by three submarine ridges (Alpha Cordillera, Nansen Cordillera, and Lomonosov Ridge)
**Elevation extremes:**
*lowest point:* Fram Basin -4,665 m
*highest point:* sea level 0 m
**Natural resources:** sand and gravel aggregates, placer deposits, polymetallic nodules, oil and gas fields, fish, marine mammals (seals and whales)
**Natural hazards:** ice islands occasionally break away from northern Ellesmere Island; icebergs calved from glaciers in western Greenland and extreme northeastern Canada; permafrost in islands; virtually ice locked from October to June; ships subject to superstructure icing from October to May
**Environment - current issues:** endangered marine species include walruses and whales; fragile ecosystem slow to change and slow to recover from disruptions or damage; thinning polar icepack
**Geography - note:** major chokepoint is the southern Chukchi Sea (northern access to the Pacific Ocean via the Bering Strait); strategic location between North America and Russia; shortest marine link between the extremes of eastern and western Russia; floating research stations operated by the US and Russia; maximum snow cover in March or April about 20 to 50 centimeters over the frozen ocean; snow cover lasts about 10 months

## Economy

**Economy - overview:** Economic activity is limited to the exploitation of natural resources, including petroleum, natural gas, fish, and seals.

## Transportation

**Ports and terminals:** Churchill (Canada), Murmansk (Russia), Prudhoe Bay (US)
**Transportation - note:** sparse network of air, ocean, river, and land routes; the Northwest Passage (North America) and Northern Sea Route (Eurasia) are important seasonal waterways

## Transnational Issues

**Disputes - international:** the littoral states are engaged in various stages of demonstrating the limits of their continental shelves beyond 200 nautical miles from their declared baselines in accordance with Article 76, paragraph 8, of the United Nations Convention on the Law of the Sea; record summer melting of sea ice in the Arctic has restimulated interest in maritime shipping lanes and sea floor exploration

# Argentina

## Introduction

**Background:** In 1816, the United Provinces of the Rio Plata declared their independence from Spain. After Bolivia, Paraguay, and Uruguay went their separate ways, the area that remained became Argentina. The country's population and culture were heavily shaped by immigrants from throughout Europe, but most particularly Italy and Spain, which provided the largest percentage of newcomers from 1860 to 1930. Up until about the mid-20th century, much of Argentina's history was dominated by periods of internal political conflict between Federalists and Unitarians and between civilian and military factions. After World War II, an era of Peronist populism and direct and indirect military interference in subsequent governments was followed by a military junta that took power in 1976. Democracy returned in 1983 after a failed bid to seize the Falkland (Malvinas) Islands by force, and has persisted despite numerous challenges, the most formidable of which was a severe economic crisis in 2001-02 that led to violent public protests and the resignation of several interim presidents.

## Geography

**Location:** Southern South America, bordering the South Atlantic Ocean, between Chile and Uruguay
**Geographic coordinates:** 34 00 S, 64 00 W
**Map references:** South America
**Area:**
*total:* 2,766,890 sq km
*land:* 2,736,690 sq km
*water:* 30,200 sq km
**Area - comparative:** slightly less than three-tenths the size of the US
**Land boundaries:**
*total:* 9,861 km
*border countries:* Bolivia 832 km, Brazil 1,261 km, Chile 5,308 km, Paraguay 1,880 km, Uruguay 580 km
**Coastline:** 4,989 km
**Maritime claims:**
*territorial sea:* 12 nm
*contiguous zone:* 24 nm
*exclusive economic zone:* 200 nm
*continental shelf:* 200 nm or to the edge of the continental margin
**Climate:** mostly temperate; arid in southeast; subantarctic in southwest
**Terrain:** rich plains of the Pampas in northern half, flat to rolling plateau of Patagonia in south, rugged Andes along western border
**Elevation extremes:**
*lowest point:* Laguna del Carbon -105 m (located between Puerto San Julian and Comandante Luis Piedra Buena in the province of Santa Cruz)
*highest point:* Cerro Aconcagua 6,960 m (located in the northwestern corner of the province of Mendoza)
**Natural resources:** fertile plains of the pampas, lead, zinc, tin, copper, iron ore, manganese, petroleum, uranium
**Land use:**
*arable land:* 10.03%
*permanent crops:* 0.36%
*other:* 89.61% (2005)
**Irrigated land:** 15,500 sq km (2003)
**Total renewable water resources:** 814 cu km (2000)
**Freshwater withdrawal (domestic/industrial/agricultural):**
*total:* 29.19 cu km/yr (17%/9%/74%)
*per capita:* 753 cu m/yr (2000)
**Natural hazards:** San Miguel de Tucuman and Mendoza areas in the Andes subject to earthquakes; pamperos are violent windstorms that can strike the pampas and northeast; heavy flooding
**Environment - current issues:** environmental problems (urban and rural) typical of an industrializing economy such as deforestation, soil degradation, desertification, air pollution, and water pollution
*note:* Argentina is a world leader in setting voluntary greenhouse gas targets
**Environment - international agreements:**
*party to:* Antarctic-Environmental Protocol, Antarctic-Marine Living Resources, Antarctic Seals, Antarctic Treaty, Biodiversity, Climate Change, Climate Change-Kyoto Protocol, Desertification, Endangered Species, Environmental Modification, Hazardous Wastes, Law of the Sea, Marine Dumping, Ozone Layer Protection, Ship Pollution, Wetlands, Whaling
*signed, but not ratified:* Marine Life Conservation
**Geography - note:** second-largest country in South America (after Brazil); strategic location relative to sea lanes between the South Atlantic and the South Pacific Oceans (Strait of Magellan, Beagle Channel, Drake Passage); diverse geophysical landscapes range from tropical climates in the north to tundra in the far south; Cerro Aconcagua is the Western Hemisphere's tallest mountain, while Laguna del Carbon is the lowest point in the Western Hemisphere

## People

**Population:** 40,913,584 (July 2009 est.)
**Age structure:**
*0-14 years:* 25.6% (male 5,369,477/ female 5,122,260)
*15-64 years:* 63.5% (male 12,961,725/ female 13,029,265)
*65 years and over:* 10.8% (male 1,819,057/ female 2,611,800) (2009 est.)
**Median age:**
*total:* 30 years
*male:* 29 years
*female:* 31 years (2009 est.)
**Population growth rate:** 1.053% (2009 est.)
**Birth rate:** 17.94 births/1,000 population (2009 est.)
**Death rate:** 7.43 deaths/1,000 population (2008 est.)
**Net migration rate:** 0 migrant(s)/1,000 population (2009 est.)
**Urbanization:**
*urban population:* 92% of total population (2008)
*rate of urbanization:* 1.2% annual rate of change (2005-10 est.)
**Sex ratio:**
*at birth:* 1.05 male(s)/female
*under 15 years:* 1.05 male(s)/female
*15-64 years:* 1 male(s)/female
*65 years and over:* 0.7 male(s)/female
*total population:* 0.97 male(s)/female (2009 est.)
**Infant mortality rate:**
*total:* 11.44 deaths/1,000 live births
*male:* 12.76 deaths/1,000 live births
*female:* 10.06 deaths/1,000 live births (2009 est.)
**Life expectancy at birth:**
*total population:* 76.56 years
*male:* 73.32 years
*female:* 79.97 years (2009 est.)
**Total fertility rate:** 2.35 children born/woman (2009 est.)
**HIV/AIDS - adult prevalence rate:** 0.5% (2007 est.)
**HIV/AIDS - people living with HIV/AIDS:** 120,000 (2007 est.)
**HIV/AIDS - deaths:** 7,000 (2007 est.)
**Major infectious diseases:**
*degree of risk:* intermediate
*food or waterborne diseases:* bacterial diarrhea, hepatitis A
*water contact disease:* leptospirosis (2009)

# Argentina *(continued)*

**Nationality:**
*noun:* Argentine(s)
*adjective:* Argentine
**Ethnic groups:** white (mostly Spanish and Italian) 97%, mestizo (mixed white and Amerindian ancestry), Amerindian, or other non-white groups 3%
**Religions:** nominally Roman Catholic 92% (less than 20% practicing), Protestant 2%, Jewish 2%, other 4%
**Languages:** Spanish (official), Italian, English, German, French
**Literacy:**
*definition:* age 15 and over can read and write
*total population:* 97.2%
*male:* 97.2%
*female:* 97.2% (2001 census)
**School life expectancy (primary to tertiary education):**
*total:* 15 years
*male:* 14 years
*female:* 16 years (2005)
**Education expenditures:** 3.8% of GDP (2004)

## Government

**Country name:**
*conventional long form:* Argentine Republic
*conventional short form:* Argentina
*local long form:* Republica Argentina
*local short form:* Argentina
**Government type:** republic
**Capital:**
*name:* Buenos Aires
*geographic coordinates:* 34 36 S, 58 40 W
*time difference:* UTC-3 (3 hours ahead of Washington, DC during Standard Time)
*daylight saving time:* +1hr, begins first Sunday in October; ends third Saturday in March; note - a new policy of daylight saving time was initiated by the government on 30 December 2007
**Administrative divisions:** 23 provinces (provincias, singular - provincia) and 1 autonomous city* (distrito federal); Buenos Aires, Buenos Aires Capital Federal*, Catamarca, Chaco, Chubut, Cordoba, Corrientes, Entre Rios, Formosa, Jujuy, La Pampa, La Rioja, Mendoza, Misiones, Neuquen, Rio Negro, Salta, San Juan, San Luis, Santa Cruz, Santa Fe, Santiago del Estero, Tierra del Fuego - Antartida e Islas del Atlantico Sur, Tucuman
*note:* the US does not recognize any claims to Antarctica
**Independence:** 9 July 1816 (from Spain)
**National holiday:** Revolution Day, 25 May (1810)
**Constitution:** 1 May 1853; amended many times starting in 1860
**Legal system:** mixture of US and West European legal systems; has not accepted compulsory ICJ jurisdiction
**Suffrage:** 18 years of age; universal and compulsory
**Executive branch:**
*chief of state:* President Cristina FERNANDEZ DE KIRCHNER (since 10 December 2007); Vice President Julio COBOS (since 10 December 2007);

*note* - the president is both the chief of state and head of government
*head of government:* President Cristina FERNANDEZ DE KIRCHNER (since 10 December 2007); Vice President Julio COBOS (since 10 December 2007)
*cabinet:* Cabinet appointed by the president
*elections:* president and vice president elected on the same ticket by popular vote for four-year terms (eligible for a second term); election last held 28 October 2007 (next election to be held in 2011)
*election results:* Cristina FERNANDEZ DE KIRCHNER elected president; percent of vote - Cristina FERNANDEZ DE KIRCHNER 45%, Elisa CARRIO 23%, Roberto LAVAGNA 17%, Alberto Rodriguez SAA 8%
**Legislative branch:** bicameral National Congress or Congreso Nacional consists of the Senate (72 seats; members are elected by direct vote; presently one-third of the members elected every two years to serve six-year terms) and the Chamber of Deputies (257 seats; members are elected by direct vote; one-half of the members elected every two years to serve four-year terms)
*elections:* Senate - last held 28 October 2007 (next to be held in 2009); Chamber of Deputies - last held last held 28 October 2007 (next to be held in 2009)
*election results:* Senate - percent of vote by bloc or party - NA; seats by bloc or party - FpV 12, UCR 4, CC 4, other 4; Chamber of Deputies - percent of vote by bloc or party - NA; seats by bloc or party - FpV 5, UCR 10, PJ 10, PRO 6, CC 16, FJ 2, other 31; note - as of 1 January 2009, the composition of the entire legislature is as follows: Senate - seats by bloc or party - FpV 42, UCR 8, CC 2, other 20; Chamber of Deputies - seats by bloc or party - FpV 119, UCR 24, CC 18, PS 10, PRO 9, other 77
**Judicial branch:** Supreme Court or Corte Suprema (the Supreme Court judges are appointed by the president with approval of the Senate)
*note:* the Supreme Court has seven judges; the Argentine Congress in 2006 passed a bill to gradually reduce the number of Supreme Court judges to five
**Political parties and leaders:** Coalicion Civica (a broad coalition loosely affiliated with Elisa CARRIO); Front for Victory or FpV (a broad coalition, including elements of the UCR and numerous provincial parties) [Nestor KIRCHNER]; Interbloque Federal or IF (a broad coalition of approximately 12 parties including PRO); Justicialist Party or PJ [Nestor KIRCHNER]; Radical Civic Union or UCR [Gerardo MORALES]; Republican Proposal or PRO [Mauricio MACRI] (including Federal Recreate Movement or RECREAR [Esteban BULLRICH]; Socialist Party or PS [Ruben GIUSTINIANI]; Union For All [Patricia BULLRICH]; several provincial parties
**Political pressure groups and leaders:** Argentine Association of Pharmaceutical Labs (CILFA); Argentine Industrial Union (manufacturers' association); Argentine Rural Confederation or CRA (small to medium landowners' association); Argentine Rural Society (large landowners' association); Central of Argentine Workers or CTA (a radical union for

employed and unemployed workers); General Confederation of Labor or CGT (Peronist-leaning umbrella labor organization); White and Blue CGT (dissident CGT labor confederation); Roman Catholic Church
*other:* business organizations; Peronist-dominated labor movement; Piquetero groups (popular protest organizations that can be either pro or anti-government); students
**International organization participation:** AfDB (nonregional members), Australia Group, BCIE, BIS, CAN (associate), FAO, G-15, G-20, G-24, G-77, IADB, IAEA, IBRD, ICAO, ICC, ICCt, ICRM, IDA, IFAD, IFC, IFRCS, IHO, ILO, IMF, IMO, IMSO, Interpol, IOC, IOM, IPU, ISO, ITSO, ITU, ITUC, LAES, LAIA, Mercosur, MIGA, MINURSO, MINUSTAH, NSG, OAS, OPANAL, OPCW, PCA, RG, SICA (observer), UN, UNASUR, UNCTAD, UNESCO, UNFICYP, UNHCR, UNIDO, Union Latina (observer), UNTSO, UNWTO, UPU, WCL, WCO, WFTU, WHO, WIPO, WMO, WTO, ZC
**Diplomatic representation in the US:**
*chief of mission:* Ambassador Hector Marcos TIMERMAN
*chancery:* 1600 New Hampshire Avenue NW, Washington, DC 20009
*telephone:* [1] (202) 238-6400
*FAX:* [1] (202) 332-3171
*consulate(s) general:* Atlanta, Chicago, Houston, Los Angeles, Miami, New York
**Diplomatic representation from the US:**
*chief of mission:* Ambassador Earl Anthony WAYNE
*embassy:* Avenida Colombia 4300, C1425GMN Buenos Aires
*mailing address:* international mail: use embassy street address; APO address: US Embassy Buenos Aires, Unit 4334, APO AA 34034
*telephone:* [54] (11) 5777-4533
*FAX:* [54] (11) 5777-4240
**Flag description:** three equal horizontal bands of light blue (top), white, and light blue; centered in the white band is a radiant yellow sun with a human face known as the Sun of May

## Economy

**Economy - overview:** Argentina benefits from rich natural resources, a highly literate population, an export-oriented agricultural sector, and a diversified industrial base. Although one of the world's wealthiest countries 100 years ago, Argentina suffered during most of the 20th century from recurring economic crises, persistent fiscal and current account deficits, high inflation, mounting external debt, and capital flight. A severe depression, growing public and external indebtedness, and a bank run culminated in 2001 in the most serious economic, social, and political crisis in the country's turbulent history. Interim President Adolfo RODRIGUEZ SAA declared a default - the largest in history - on the government's foreign debt in December of that year, and abruptly resigned only a few days after taking office. His successor, Eduardo DUHALDE, announced an end to the peso's decade-long 1-to-1 peg

# Argentina *(continued)*

to the US dollar in early 2002. The economy bottomed out that year, with real GDP 18% smaller than in 1998 and almost 60% of Argentines under the poverty line. Real GDP rebounded to grow by an average 9% annually over the subsequent five years, taking advantage of previously idled industrial capacity and labor, an audacious debt restructuring and reduced debt burden, excellent international financial conditions, and expansionary monetary and fiscal policies. Inflation also increased, however, during the administration of President Nestor KIRCHNER, which responded with price restraints on businesses, as well as export taxes and restraints, and beginning in early 2007, with understating inflation data. Cristina FERNANDEZ DE KIRCHNER succeeded her husband as President in late 2007, but was stymied in her efforts to hike export taxes still further by protesting farmers. Her government nationalized private pension funds in late 2008, which bolstered government coffers, but failed to assuage investors' concerns about the direction of economic policy.

**GDP (purchasing power parity):**
$575.6 billion (2008 est.)
$537.5 billion (2007)
$494.5 billion (2006)
*note:* data are in 2008 US dollars

**GDP (official exchange rate):** $338.7 billion (2008 est.)

**GDP - real growth rate:**
7.1% (2008 est.)
8.7% (2007 est.)
8.5% (2006 est.)

**GDP - per capita (PPP):**
$14,200 (2008 est.)
$13,400 (2007 est.)
$12,500 (2006 est.)
*note:* data are in 2008 US dollars

**GDP - composition by sector:**
*agriculture:* 9.2%
*industry:* 34.1%
*services:* 56.7% (2008 est.)

**Labor force:** 16.27 million
*note:* urban areas only (2008 est.)

**Labor force - by occupation:**
*agriculture:* 1%
*industry:* 23%
*services:* 76% (2008 est.)

**Unemployment rate:**
7.8% (September 2008)
8.5% (2007 est.)

**Population below poverty line:** 23.4% (January-June 2007)

**Household income or consumption by percentage share:**
*lowest 10%:* 1%
*highest 10%:* 35% (January-March 2007)

**Distribution of family income - Gini index:** 49 (January-March 2007)

**Investment (gross fixed):** 24% of GDP (2008 est.)

**Budget:**
*revenues:* $86.3 billion
*expenditures:* $80.4 billion (2008 est.)

**Public debt:** 51% of GDP (June 2008)

**Inflation rate (consumer prices):**
22% (2008 est.)
8.8% (2007 est.)
*note:* based on non-official estimates; the much lower official rates lack credibility

**Central bank discount rate:** NA

**Commercial bank prime lending rate:** 28% (28 November 2008)

**Stock of money:** $33.93 billion (31 December 2007)

**Stock of quasi money:** $45.92 billion (31 December 2007)

**Stock of domestic credit:** $72.55 billion (31 December 2007)

**Market value of publicly traded shares:** $86.68 billion (31 December 2007)

**Agriculture - products:** sunflower seeds, lemons, soybeans, grapes, corn, tobacco, peanuts, tea, wheat; livestock

**Industries:** food processing, motor vehicles, consumer durables, textiles, chemicals and petrochemicals, printing, metallurgy, steel

**Industrial production growth rate:** 6.5% (2008 est.)

**Electricity - production:** 109.4 billion kWh (2006 est.)

**Electricity - consumption:** 97.72 billion kWh (2006 est.)

**Electricity - exports:** 2.628 billion kWh (2007 est.)

**Electricity - imports:** 10.27 billion kWh (2007 est.)

**Oil - production:** 790,800 bbl/day (2007 est.)

**Oil - consumption:** 440,000 bbl/day (2007 est.)

**Oil - exports:** 339,900 bbl/day (2005)

**Oil - imports:** 23,380 bbl/day (2005)

**Oil - proved reserves:** 2.587 billion bbl (1 January 2008 est.)

**Natural gas - production:** 44.8 billion cu m (2007 est.)

**Natural gas - consumption:** 44.1 billion cu m (2007 est.)

**Natural gas - exports:** 2.6 billion cu m (2007 est.)

**Natural gas - imports:** 1.9 billion cu m (2007 est.)

**Natural gas - proved reserves:** 446 billion cu m (1 January 2008 est.)

**Current account balance:** $6 billion (2008 est.)

**Exports:** $73 billion f.o.b. (2008 est.)

**Exports - commodities:** soybeans and derivatives, petroleum and gas, vehicles, corn, wheat

**Exports - partners:** Brazil 19.1%, China 9.4%, US 7.9%, Chile 7.6% (2007)

**Imports:** $59.9 billion f.o.b. (2008 est.)

**Imports - commodities:** machinery, motor vehicles, petroleum and natural gas, organic chemicals, plastics

**Imports - partners:** Brazil 34.6%, US 12.6%, China 12%, Germany 5% (2007)

**Reserves of foreign exchange and gold:** $45.9 billion (15 December 2008)

**Debt - external:** $135.5 billion (31 December 2008 est.)

**Stock of direct foreign investment - at home:** $69.1 billion (2008 est.)

**Stock of direct foreign investment - abroad:** $26.81 billion (2008 est.)

**Exchange rates:** Argentine pesos (ARS) per US dollar - 3.1636 (2008 est.), 3.1105 (2007), 3.0543 (2006), 2.9037 (2005), 2.9233 (2004)

## Communications

**Telephones - main lines in use:** 9.5 million (2007)

**Telephones - mobile cellular:** 40.402 million (2007)

**Telephone system:**
*general assessment:* by opening the telecommunications market to competition and foreign investment with the "Telecommunications Liberalization Plan of 1998," Argentina encouraged the growth of modern telecommunications technology; fiber-optic cable trunk lines are being installed between all major cities; major networks are entirely digital and the availability of telephone service is improving; fixed-line telephone density is gradually increasing reaching nearly 25 lines per 100 people in 2007; mobile telephone subscribership has been increasing rapidly and has reached a level of 100 telephones per 100 persons
*domestic:* microwave radio relay, fiber-optic cable, and a domestic satellite system with 40 earth stations serve the trunk network; more than 110,000 pay telephones are installed and mobile telephone use is rapidly expanding; broadband services are gaining ground
*international:* country code - 54; landing point for the Atlantis-2, UNISUR, and South America-1 optical submarine cable systems that provide links to Europe, Africa, South and Central America, and US; satellite earth stations - 112; 2 international gateways near Buenos Aires (2007)

**Radio broadcast stations:** AM 260, FM (probably more than 1,000, mostly unlicensed), shortwave 6 (1998)

**Television broadcast stations:** 42 (plus 444 repeaters) (1997)

**Internet country code:** .ar

**Internet hosts:** 3.813 million (2008)

**Internet users:** 9.309 million (2007)

## Transportation

**Airports:** 1,150 (2008)

**Airports - with paved runways:**
*total:* 154
*over 3,047 m:* 4
*2,438 to 3,047 m:* 26
*1,524 to 2,437 m:* 65
*914 to 1,523 m:* 50
*under 914 m:* 9 (2008)

**Airports - with unpaved runways:**
*total:* 996
*over 3,047 m:* 1
*2,438 to 3,047 m:* 1
*1,524 to 2,437 m:* 45
*914 to 1,523 m:* 526
*under 914 m:* 423 (2008)

# Argentina (continued)

**Heliports:** 1 (2007)

**Pipelines:** gas 28,138 km; liquid petroleum gas 41 km; oil 5,939 km; refined products 3,629 km (2008)

**Railways:**

*total:* 31,902 km

*broad gauge:* 20,858 km 1.676-m gauge (141 km electrified)

*standard gauge:* 2,885 km 1.435-m gauge (26 km electrified)

*narrow gauge:* 7,922 km 1.000-m gauge; 237 km 0.750-m gauge (2006)

**Roadways:**

*total:* 231,374 km

*paved:* 69,412 km (includes 734 km of expressways)

*unpaved:* 161,962 km (2004)

**Waterways:** 11,000 km (2007)

**Merchant marine:**

*total:* 46

*by type:* bulk carrier 3, cargo 9, chemical tanker 2, container 1, passenger 1, passenger/cargo 3, petroleum tanker 24, refrigerated cargo 2, roll on/roll off 1

*foreign-owned:* 14 (Brazil 1, Chile 7, Spain 2, UK 4)

*registered in other countries:* 19 (Liberia 3, Panama 8, Paraguay 5, Uruguay 3) (2008)

**Ports and terminals:** Arroyo Seco, Bahia Blanca, Buenos Aires, La Plata, Punta Colorada, Rosario, San Lorenzo-San Martin

## Military

**Military branches:** Argentine Army (Ejercito Argentino), Navy of the Argentine Republic (Armada Republica; includes naval aviation and naval infantry), Argentine Air Force (Fuerza Aerea Argentina, FAA) (2009)

**Military service age and obligation:** 18-24 years of age for voluntary military service (18-21 requires parental permission); no conscription (2001)

**Manpower available for military service:**

*males age 16-49:* 10,029,488

*females age 16-49:* 9,889,002 (2008 est.)

**Manpower fit for military service:**

*males age 16-49:* 8,264,853

*females age 16-49:* 8,268,498 (2009 est.)

**Manpower reaching militarily significant age annually:**

*male:* 341,590

*female:* 326,342 (2009 est.)

**Military expenditures:** 1.3% of GDP (2005 est.)

**Military - note:** the Argentine military is a well-organized force constrained by the country's prolonged economic hardship; the country has recently experienced a strong recovery, and the military is implementing a modernization plan aimed at making the ground forces lighter and more responsive (2008)

## Transnational Issues

**Disputes - international:** Argentina continues to assert its claims to the UK-administered Falkland Islands (Islas Malvinas), South Georgia, and the South Sandwich Islands in its constitution, forcibly occupying the Falklands in 1982, but in 1995 agreed no longer to seek settlement by force; territorial claim in Antarctica partially overlaps UK and Chilean claims; unruly region at convergence of Argentina-Brazil-Paraguay borders is locus of money laundering, smuggling, arms and illegal narcotics trafficking, and fundraising for extremist organizations; uncontested dispute between Brazil and Uruguay over Braziliera/Brasiliera Island in the Quarai/Cuareim River leaves the tripoint with Argentina in question; in 2006, Argentina went to the ICJ to protest, on environmental grounds, the construction of two pulp mills in Uruguay on the Uruguay River, which forms the boundary; both parties presented their pleadings in 2007 with Argentina's reply in January and Uruguay's rejoinder in July 2008; the joint boundary commission, established by Chile and Argentina in 2001 has yet to map and demarcate the delimited boundary in the inhospitable Andean Southern Ice Field (Campo de Hielo Sur)

**Trafficking in persons:**

*current situation:* Argentina is a source, transit, and destination country for men, women, and children trafficked for the purposes of commercial sexual exploitation and forced labor; most victims are trafficked within the country, from rural to urban areas; child sex tourism is a problem; foreign women and children, primarily from Paraguay, Brazil, and the Dominican Republic, are trafficked to Argentina for commercial sexual exploitation; Argentine women and girls are also trafficked to neighboring countries, Mexico, and Western Europe for sexual exploitation; a significant number of Bolivians, Peruvians, and Paraguayans are trafficked into the country for forced labor in sweatshops, agriculture, and as domestic servants

*tier rating:* Tier 2 Watch List - despite some progress, Argentina remains on the Tier 2 Watch List for the third consecutive year for its failure to show evidence of increasing efforts to combat human trafficking, particularly in terms of providing adequate assistance to victims and curbing official complicity with trafficking activity, especially on the provincial and local levels; the Argentine Congress has demonstrated progress by enacting much-needed and first-ever federal anti-trafficking legislation (2008)

**Illicit drugs:** a transshipment country for cocaine headed for Europe, heroin headed for the US, and ephedrine and pseudoephedrine headed for Mexico; some money-laundering activity, especially in the Tri-Border Area; law enforcement corruption; a source for precursor chemicals; increasing domestic consumption of drugs in urban centers, especially cocaine base and synthetic drugs (2008)

# Armenia

## Introduction

**Background:** Armenia prides itself on being the first nation to formally adopt Christianity (early 4th century). Despite periods of autonomy, over the centuries Armenia came under the sway of various empires including the Roman, Byzantine, Arab, Persian, and Ottoman. During World War I in the western portion of Armenia, Ottoman Turkey instituted a policy of forced resettlement coupled with other harsh practices that resulted in an estimated 1 million Armenian deaths. The eastern area of Armenia was ceded by the Ottomans to Russia in 1828; this portion declared its independence in 1918, but was conquered by the Soviet Red Army in 1920. Armenian leaders remain preoccupied with the long conflict with Azerbaijan over Nagorno-Karabakh, a primarily Armenian-populated region, assigned to Soviet Azerbaijan in the 1920s by Moscow. Armenia and Azerbaijan began fighting over the area in 1988; the struggle escalated after both countries attained independence from the Soviet Union in 1991. By May 1994, when a cease-fire took hold, ethnic Armenian forces held not only Nagorno-Karabakh but also a significant portion of Azerbaijan proper. The economies of both sides have been hurt by their inability to make substantial progress toward a peaceful resolution. Turkey closed the common border with Armenia because of the Armenian separatists' control of Nagorno-Karabakh and surrounding areas.

## Geography

**Location:** Southwestern Asia, east of Turkey

**Geographic coordinates:** 40 00 N, 45 00 E

**Map references:** Asia

**Area:**

*total:* 29,743 sq km

*land:* 28,454 sq km

*water:* 1,289 sq km

**Area - comparative:** slightly smaller than Maryland

**Land boundaries:**

*total:* 1,254 km

*border countries:* Azerbaijan-proper 566 km, Azerbaijan-Naxcivan exclave 221 km, Georgia 164 km, Iran 35 km, Turkey 268 km

**Coastline:** 0 km (landlocked)

**Maritime claims:** none (landlocked)

**Climate:** highland continental, hot summers, cold winters

**Terrain:** Armenian Highland with mountains; little forest land; fast flowing rivers; good soil in Aras River valley

**Elevation extremes:**

*lowest point:* Debed River 400 m

*highest point:* Aragats Lerrnagagat' 4,090 m

**Natural resources:** small deposits of gold, copper, molybdenum, zinc, bauxite

**Land use:**

*arable land:* 16.78%

*permanent crops:* 2.01%

*other:* 81.21% (2005)

**Irrigated land:** 2,860 sq km (2003)

**Total renewable water resources:** 10.5 cu km (1997)

**Freshwater withdrawal (domestic/industrial/ agricultural):**

*total:* 2.95 cu km/yr (30%/4%/66%)

*per capita:* 977 cu m/yr (2000)

**Natural hazards:** occasionally severe earthquakes; droughts

**Environment - current issues:** soil pollution from toxic chemicals such as DDT; the energy crisis of the 1990s led to deforestation when citizens scavenged for firewood; pollution of Hrazdan (Razdan) and Aras Rivers; the draining of Sevana Lich (Lake Sevan), a result of its use as a source for hydropower, threatens drinking water supplies; restart of Metsamor nuclear power plant in spite of its location in a seismically active zone

**Environment - international agreements:**

*party to:* Air Pollution, Biodiversity, Climate Change, Climate Change-Kyoto Protocol, Desertification, Environmental Modification, Hazardous Wastes, Law of the Sea, Ozone Layer Protection, Wetlands

*signed, but not ratified:* Air Pollution-Persistent Organic Pollutants

**Geography - note:** landlocked in the Lesser Caucasus Mountains; Sevana Lich (Lake Sevan) is the largest lake in this mountain range

## People

**Population:** 2,967,004 (July 2009 est.)

**Age structure:**

*0-14 years:* 18.2% (male 289,119/female 252,150)

*15-64 years:* 71.1% (male 986,764/female 1,123,708)

*65 years and over:* 10.6% (male 122,996/female 192,267) (2009 est.)

**Median age:**

*total:* 31.5 years

*male:* 28.8 years

*female:* 34.4 years (2009 est.)

**Population growth rate:** -0.03% (2009 est.)

**Birth rate:** 12.65 births/1,000 population (2009 est.)

**Death rate:** 8.34 deaths/1,000 population (2008 est.)

**Net migration rate:** -4.56 migrant(s)/1,000 population (2009 est.)

**Urbanization:**

*urban population:* 64% of total population (2008)

*rate of urbanization:* -0.3% annual rate of change (2005-10 est.)

**Sex ratio:**

*at birth:* 1.14 male(s)/female

*under 15 years:* 1.15 male(s)/female

*15-64 years:* 0.88 male(s)/female

*65 years and over:* 0.64 male(s)/female

*total population:* 0.89 male(s)/female (2009 est.)

**Infant mortality rate:**

*total:* 20.21 deaths/1,000 live births

*male:* 24.97 deaths/1,000 live births

*female:* 14.77 deaths/1,000 live births (2009 est.)

**Life expectancy at birth:**

*total population:* 72.68 years

*male:* 69.06 years

*female:* 76.81 years (2009 est.)

**Total fertility rate:** 1.36 children born/woman (2009 est.)

**HIV/AIDS - adult prevalence rate:** 0.1% (2007 est.)

**HIV/AIDS - people living with HIV/AIDS:** 2,400 (2007 est.)

**HIV/AIDS - deaths:** fewer than 200 (2007 est.)

**Nationality:**

*noun:* Armenian(s)

*adjective:* Armenian

**Ethnic groups:** Armenian 97.9%, Yezidi (Kurd) 1.3%, Russian 0.5%, other 0.3% (2001 census)

**Religions:** Armenian Apostolic 94.7%, other Christian 4%, Yezidi (monotheist with elements of nature worship) 1.3%

**Languages:** Armenian 97.7%, Yezidi 1%, Russian 0.9%, other 0.4% (2001 census)

**Literacy:**

*definition:* age 15 and over can read and write

*total population:* 99.4%

*male:* 99.7%

*female:* 99.2% (2001 census)

**School life expectancy (primary to tertiary education):**

*total:* 11 years

*male:* 11 years

*female:* 12 years (2006)

**Education expenditures:** 3.2% of GDP (2001)

## Government

**Country name:**

*conventional long form:* Republic of Armenia

*conventional short form:* Armenia

*local long form:* Hayastani Hanrapetut'yun

*local short form:* Hayastan

*former:* Armenian Soviet Socialist Republic, Armenian Republic

**Government type:** republic

**Capital:**

*name:* Yerevan

*geographic coordinates:* 40 10 N, 44 30 E

*time difference:* UTC+4 (9 hours ahead of Washington, DC during Standard Time)

*daylight saving time:* +1hr, begins last Sunday in March; ends last Sunday in October

**Administrative divisions:** 11 provinces (marzer, singular - marz); Aragatsotn, Ararat, Armavir, Geghark'unik', Kotayk', Lorri, Shirak, Syunik', Tavush, Vayots' Dzor, Yerevan

**Independence:** 21 September 1991 (from the Soviet Union)

**National holiday:** Independence Day, 21 September (1991)

**Constitution:** adopted by nationwide referendum 5 July 1995; amendments adopted through a nationwide referendum 27 November 2005

**Legal system:** based on civil law system; has not accepted compulsory ICJ jurisdiction

**Suffrage:** 18 years of age; universal

**Executive branch:**

*chief of state:* President Serzh SARGSIAN (since 9 April 2008)

*head of government:* Prime Minister Tigran SARGSIAN (since 9 April 2008)

*cabinet:* Council of Ministers appointed by the prime minister

*elections:* president elected by popular vote for a five-year term (eligible for a second term); election last held 19 February 2008 (next to be held February 2013); prime minister appointed by the president based on majority or plurality support in parliament; the prime minister and Council of Ministers must resign if the National Assembly refuses to accept their program

*election results:* Serzh SARGSIAN elected president; percent of vote - Serzh SARGSIAN 52.9%, Levon TER-PETROSSIAN 21.5%, Artur BAGHDASARIAN 16.7%

**Legislative branch:** unicameral National Assembly (Parliament) or Azgayin Zhoghov (131 seats; members elected by popular vote, 90 members elected by party list and 41 by direct vote; to serve five-year terms)

*elections:* last held 12 May 2007 (next to be held in the spring of 2012)

*election results:* percent of vote by party - HHK 33.9%, Prosperous Armenia 15.1%, ARF (Dashnak) 13.2%, Rule of Law 7.1%, Heritage Party 6%, other 24.7%; seats by party - HHK 64, Prosperous Armenia 18, ARF (Dashnak) 16, Rule of Law 9, Heritage Party 7, independent 17

**Judicial branch:** Constitutional Court; Court of Cassation (Appeals Court)

**Political parties and leaders:** Armenian National Congress or ANC [Levon TER-PETROSSIAN]; Armenian National Movement or ANM [Ararat ZURABIAN]; Armenian People's Party [Tigran KARAPETIAN]; Armenian Ramkavar Azadagan Party Alliance or HRAK (includes former Dashink Party, National Revival Party, and Ramkavar Liberal Party);

# Armenia (continued)

Armenian Revolutionary Federation ("Dashnak" Party) or ARF [Hrant MARKARIAN]; Heritage Party [Raffi HOVHANNISIAN]; National Democratic Party [Shavarsh KOCHARIAN]; National Democratic Union or NDU [Vazgen MANUKIAN]; National Unity Party [Artashes GEGHAMIAN]; People's Party of Armenia [Stepan DEMIRCHIAN]; Prosperous Armenia [Gagik TSAROUKIAN]; Republic Party [Aram SARKISIAN]; Republican Party of Armenia or HHK [Serzh SARGSIAN]; Rule of Law Party (Orinats Yerkir) [Artur BAGHDASARIAN]; Union of Constitutional Rights [Hrant KHACHATURIAN]; United Labor Party [Gurgen ARSENIAN]

**Political pressure groups and leaders:** Aylentrank (Impeachment) [Nikol PASHINIAN]; Yerkrapah Union [Manvel GRIGORIAN]

**International organization participation:** ACCT (observer), ADB, BSEC, CE, CIS, CSTO, EAEC (observer), EAPC, EBRD, FAO, GCTU, IAEA, IBRD, ICAO, ICCt (signatory), ICRM, IDA, IFAD, IFC, IFRCS, ILO, IMF, Interpol, IOC, IOM, IPU, ISO, ITSO, ITU, MIGA, NAM (observer), OAS (observer), OIF (associate member), OPCW, OSCE, PFP, UN, UNCTAD, UNESCO, UNIDO, UNWTO, UPU, WCO, WFTU, WHO, WIPO, WMO, WTO

**Diplomatic representation in the US:**
*chief of mission:* Ambassador Tatoul MARKARIAN
*chancery:* 2225 R Street NW, Washington, DC 20008
*telephone:* [1] (202) 319-1976
*FAX:* [1] (202) 319-2982
*consulate(s) general:* Los Angeles

**Diplomatic representation from the US:**
*chief of mission:* Ambassador Marie L. YOVANOVITCH
*embassy:* 1 American Ave., Yerevan 0082
*mailing address:* American Embassy Yerevan, US Department of State, 7020 Yerevan Place, Washington, DC 20521-7020
*telephone:* [374](10) 464-700
*FAX:* [374](10) 464-742

**Flag description:** three equal horizontal bands of red (top), blue, and orange

## Economy

**Economy - overview:** Since the breakup of the Soviet Union in 1991, Armenia has made progress in implementing many economic reforms including privatization, price reforms, and prudent fiscal policies. The conflict with Azerbaijan over the ethnic Armenian-dominated region of Nagorno-Karabakh contributed to a severe economic decline in the early 1990s. By 1994, however, the Armenian Government launched an ambitious IMF-sponsored economic liberalization program that resulted in positive growth rates. Economic growth has averaged over 10% in recent years. However, with the global economic downturn, Armenia's growth rate dropped to 7.6% in 2008. Armenia has managed to reduce poverty, slash inflation, stabilize its currency, and privatize most small- and medium-sized enterprises. Under the old Soviet central planning system, Armenia developed a modern industrial sector, supplying machine tools, textiles, and other manufactured goods to sister republics, in exchange for raw materials and energy. Armenia has since switched to small-scale agriculture and away from the large agroindustrial complexes of the Soviet era. Nuclear power plants built at Metsamor in the 1970s were closed following the 1988 Spitak Earthquake, though they sustained no damage. One of the two reactors was re-opened in 1995, but the Armenian government is under international pressure to close it due to concerns that the Soviet era design lacks important safeguards. Metsamor provides 40 percent of the country's electricity - hydropower accounts for about one-fourth. Economic ties with Russia remain close, especially in the energy sector. The electricity distribution system was privatized in 2002 and bought by Russia's RAO-UES in 2005. Construction of a pipeline to deliver natural gas from Iran to Armenia was completed in December 2008 and after testing is expected to be operational in Spring 2009, though it is unlikely significant quantities of gas will flow through it until the Yerevan Thermal Power Plant renovation is completed in 2010. Armenia has some mineral deposits (copper, gold, bauxite). Pig iron, unwrought copper, and other nonferrous metals are Armenia's highest valued exports. Armenia's severe trade imbalance has been offset somewhat by international aid, remittances from Armenians working abroad, and foreign direct investment. Armenia joined the WTO in January 2003. The government made some improvements in tax and customs administration in recent years, but anti-corruption measures will be more difficult to implement. Despite strong economic growth, Armenia's unemployment rate remains high. Armenia will need to pursue additional economic reforms in order to improve its economic competitiveness and to build on recent improvements in poverty and unemployment, especially given its economic isolation from two of its nearest neighbors, Turkey and Azerbaijan. The disruption of rail transit into Armenia during the Georgia-Russia conflict in August 2008 highlighted how vulnerable Armenia's supply chains for key goods - such as gasoline - are to instances of regional instability.

**GDP (purchasing power parity):**
$18.92 billion (2008 est.)
$17.58 billion (2007)
$15.45 billion (2006)
*note:* data are in 2008 US dollars

**GDP (official exchange rate):** $12.07 billion (2008 est.)

**GDP - real growth rate:**
7.6% (2008 est.)
13.8% (2007 est.)
13.2% (2006 est.)

**GDP - per capita (PPP):**
$6,400 (2008 est.)
$5,900 (2007 est.)
$5,200 (2006 est.)
*note:* data are in 2008 US dollars

**GDP - composition by sector:**
*agriculture:* 17.2%
*industry:* 36.4%
*services:* 46.4% (2007 est.)

**Labor force:** 1.2 million (2007 est.)

**Labor force - by occupation:**
*agriculture:* 46.2%
*industry:* 15.6%
*services:* 38.2% (2006 est.)

**Unemployment rate:**
7.1% (2007 est.)

**Population below poverty line:** 26.5% (2006 est.)

**Household income or consumption by percentage share:**
*lowest 10%:* 1.6%
*highest 10%:* 41.3% (2004)

**Distribution of family income - Gini index:** 37 (2006)

**Investment (gross fixed):** 34.1% of GDP (2008 est.)

**Budget:**
*revenues:* $2.438 billion
*expenditures:* $2.696 billion; including capital expenditures of $NA (2008 est.)

**Inflation rate (consumer prices):**
10.2% (2008 est.)
4.4% (2007 est.)

**Central bank discount rate:** 7.25%
*note:* this is the Refinancing Rate, the key monetary policy instrument of the Armenian National Bank (2 December 2008)

**Commercial bank prime lending rate:** 17.52% (31 December 2007)

**Stock of money:** $1.507 billion (31 December 2007)

**Stock of quasi money:** $765.2 million (31 December 2007)

**Stock of domestic credit:** $1.256 billion (31 December 2007)

**Market value of publicly traded shares:** $105 million (31 December 2007)

**Agriculture - products:** fruit (especially grapes), vegetables; livestock

**Industries:** diamond-processing, metal-cutting machine tools, forging-pressing machines, electric motors, tires, knitted wear, hosiery, shoes, silk fabric, chemicals, trucks, instruments, microelectronics, jewelry manufacturing, software development, food processing, brandy

**Industrial production growth rate:** 3% (2008 est.)

**Electricity - production:** 5.544 billion kWh (2007 est.)

**Electricity - consumption:** 4.539 billion kWh (2006 est.)

**Electricity - exports:** 322.6 million kWh; note - exports an unknown quantity to Georgia; includes exports to Nagorno-Karabakh region in Azerbaijan (2007 est.)

**Electricity - imports:** 400.6 million kWh; note - imports an unknown quantity from Iran (2007 est.)

**Oil - production:** 0 bbl/day (2007 est.)

**Oil - consumption:** 41,090 bbl/day (2006 est.)

**Oil - exports:** 0 bbl/day (2005)

# Armenia (continued)

**Oil - imports:** 44,670 bbl/day (2005)
**Oil - proved reserves:** 0 bbl (1 January 2006 est.)
**Natural gas - production:** 0 cu m (2007 est.)
**Natural gas - consumption:** 2.05 billion cu m (2007 est.)
**Natural gas - exports:** 0 cu m (2007 est.)
**Natural gas - imports:** 2.05 billion cu m (2007 est.)
**Natural gas - proved reserves:** 0 cu m (1 January 2006)
**Current account balance:** -$877 million (2008 est.)
**Exports:** $1.225 billion f.o.b. (2008 est.)
**Exports - commodities:** pig iron, unwrought copper, nonferrous metals, diamonds, mineral products, foodstuffs, energy
**Exports - partners:** Russia 17.5%, Germany 14.7%, Netherlands 13.5%, Belgium 8.7%, Georgia 7.6%, US 6.6%, Switzerland 4.3%, Bulgaria 4.1%, Ukraine 4% (2007)
**Imports:** $3.546 billion f.o.b. (2008 est.)
**Imports - commodities:** natural gas, petroleum, tobacco products, foodstuffs, diamonds
**Imports - partners:** Russia 15.1%, Ukraine 7.7%, Kazakhstan 7.4%, Germany 6.8%, China 6%, France 4.6%, US 4.5%, Iraq 4.3% (2007)
**Reserves of foreign exchange and gold:** $1.954 billion (31 December 2008 est.)
**Debt - external:** $1.372 billion (31 December 2007 est.)
**Exchange rates:** drams (AMD) per US dollar - 303.93 (2008 est.), 344.06 (2007), 414.69 (2006), 457.69 (2005), 533.45 (2004)

## Communications

**Telephones - main lines in use:** 603,900 (2006)
**Telephones - mobile cellular:** 1,185,400 (2006)
**Telephone system:**
*general assessment:* telecommunications investments have made major inroads in modernizing and upgrading the outdated telecommunications network inherited from the Soviet era; now 100% privately owned and undergoing modernization and expansion; mobile-cellular services monopoly terminated in late 2004 and a second provider began operations in mid-2005
*domestic:* reliable modern landline and mobile-cellular services are available across Yerevan in major cities and towns; significant but ever-shrinking gaps remain in mobile-cellular coverage in rural areas
*international:* country code - 374; Yerevan is connected to the Trans-Asia-Europe fiber-optic cable through Iran; additional international service is available by microwave radio relay and landline connections to the other countries of the Commonwealth of Independent States, through the Moscow international switch, and by satellite to the rest of the world; satellite earth stations - 3 (2007)
**Radio broadcast stations:** AM 9, FM 16, shortwave 1 (2006)
**Television broadcast stations:** 48 (private television stations alongside 2 public networks; major Russian channels widely available) (2006)
**Internet country code:** .am

**Internet hosts:** 26,081 (2008)
**Internet users:** 172,800 (2006)

## Transportation

**Airports:** 11 (2008)
**Airports - with paved runways:**
*total:* 10
*over 3,047 m:* 2
*2,438 to 3,047 m:* 2
*1,524 to 2,437 m:* 4
*914 to 1,523 m:* 2 (2008)
**Airports - with unpaved runways:**
*total:* 1
*914 to 1,523 m:* 1 (2008)
**Pipelines:** gas 2,233 km (2008)
**Railways:**
*total:* 839 km
*broad gauge:* 839 km 1.520-m gauge (828 km electrified)
*note:* some lines are out of service (2006)
**Roadways:**
*total:* 7,700 km
*paved:* 7,700 km (includes 1,561 km of expressways) (2006)

## Military

**Military branches:** Armed Forces: Ground Forces, Air Force and Air Defense, Nagorno-Karabakh Self Defense Force (NKSDF) (2009)
**Military service age and obligation:** 18-27 years of age for voluntary or compulsory military service; 2-year conscript service obligation (2007)
**Manpower available for military service:**
*males age 16-49:* 809,576
*females age 16-49:* 870,864 (2008 est.)
**Manpower fit for military service:**
*males age 16-49:* 642,734
*females age 16-49:* 729,047 (2009 est.)
**Manpower reaching militarily significant age annually:**
*male:* 27,293
*female:* 25,574 (2009 est.)
**Military expenditures:** 6.5% of GDP (FY01)

## Transnational Issues

**Disputes - international:** Armenia supports ethnic Armenian secessionists in Nagorno-Karabakh and since the early 1990s, has militarily occupied 16% of Azerbaijan - Organization for Security and Cooperation in Europe (OSCE) continues to mediate dispute; over 800,000 mostly ethnic Azerbaijanis were driven from the occupied lands and Armenia; about 230,000 ethnic Armenians were driven from their homes in Azerbaijan into Armenia and Nagorno-Karabakh; Azerbaijan seeks transit route through Armenia to connect to Naxcivan exclave; border with Turkey remains closed over Nagorno-Karabakh dispute; ethnic Armenian groups in Javakheti region of Georgia seek greater autonomy; Armenians continue to emigrate, primarily to Russia, seeking employment

**Refugees and internally displaced persons:**
*refugees (country of origin):* 113,295 (Azerbaijan)
*IDPs:* 8,400 (conflict with Azerbaijan over Nagorno-Karabakh, majority have returned home since 1994 ceasefire) (2007)
**Trafficking in persons:**
*current situation:* Armenia is primarily a source country for women and girls trafficked to the UAE and Turkey for the purpose of commercial sexual exploitation; Armenian men and women are trafficked to Turkey and Russia for the purpose of forced labor
*tier rating:* Tier 2 Watch List - Armenia is placed on the Tier 2 Watch List for a fourth consecutive year; its efforts to increase compliance with the minimum standards were assessed based on its commitments to undertake future actions, particularly in the areas of improving victim protection and assistance; while the government elevated anti-trafficking responsibilities to the ministerial level, adopted a new National Action Plan, and drafted a National Referral Mechanism, it has yet to show tangible progress in identifying and protecting victims or in tackling trafficking complicity of government officials; the Armenian Government made some notable improvements in its anti-trafficking law enforcement efforts, but it failed to demonstrate evidence of investigations, prosecutions, convictions, and sentences of officials complicit in trafficking (2008)
**Illicit drugs:** illicit cultivation of small amount of cannabis for domestic consumption; minor transit point for illicit drugs - mostly opium and hashish - moving from Southwest Asia to Russia and to a lesser extent the rest of Europe

# Aruba
*(part of the Kingdom of the Netherlands)*

## Introduction

**Background:** Discovered and claimed for Spain in 1499, Aruba was acquired by the Dutch in 1636. The island's economy has been dominated by three main industries. A 19th century gold rush was followed by prosperity brought on by the opening in 1924 of an oil refinery. The last decades of the 20th century saw a boom in the tourism industry. Aruba seceded from the Netherlands Antilles in 1986 and became a separate, autonomous member of the Kingdom of the Netherlands. Movement toward full independence was halted at Aruba's request in 1990.

## Geography

**Location:** Caribbean, island in the Caribbean Sea, north of Venezuela
**Geographic coordinates:** 12 30 N, 69 58 W
**Map references:** Central America and the Caribbean
**Area:**
*total:* 193 sq km
*land:* 193 sq km
*water:* 0 sq km
**Area - comparative:** slightly larger than Washington, DC
**Land boundaries:** 0 km
**Coastline:** 68.5 km
**Maritime claims:**
*territorial sea:* 12 nm
**Climate:** tropical marine; little seasonal temperature variation
**Terrain:** flat with a few hills; scant vegetation
**Elevation extremes:**
*lowest point:* Caribbean Sea 0 m
*highest point:* Mount Jamanota 188 m
**Natural resources:** NEGL; white sandy beaches
**Land use:**
*arable land:* 10.53%
*permanent crops:* 0%
*other:* 89.47% (2005)

**Irrigated land:** 0.01 sq km (1998 est.)
**Natural hazards:** hurricanes; lies outside the Caribbean hurricane belt and is rarely threatened
**Environment - current issues:** NA
**Geography - note:** a flat, riverless island renowned for its white sand beaches; its tropical climate is moderated by constant trade winds from the Atlantic Ocean; the temperature is almost constant at about 27 degrees Celsius (81 degrees Fahrenheit)

## People

**Population:** 103,065
*note:* estimate based on a revision of the base population, fertility, and mortality numbers, as well as a revision of 1985-99 migration estimates from outmigration to inmigration, which is assumed to continue into the future; the new results are consistent with the 2000 census (July 2009 est.)
**Age structure:**
*0-14 years:* 19.1% (male 9,921/female 9,758)
*15-64 years:* 70.3% (male 34,676/female 37,752)
*65 years and over:* 10.6% (male 4,351/female 6,607) (2009 est.)
**Median age:**
*total:* 37.8 years
*male:* 36 years
*female:* 39.5 years (2009 est.)
**Population growth rate:** 1.478% (2009 est.)
**Birth rate:** 12.79 births/1,000 population (2009 est.)
**Death rate:** 7.65 deaths/1,000 population (2008 est.)
**Net migration rate:** 9.7 migrant(s)/1,000 population (2009 est.)
**Urbanization:**
*urban population:* 47% of total population (2008)
*rate of urbanization:* 0.1% annual rate of change (2005-10 est.)
**Sex ratio:**
*at birth:* 1.02 male(s)/female
*under 15 years:* 1.02 male(s)/female
*15-64 years:* 0.92 male(s)/female
*65 years and over:* 0.66 male(s)/female
*total population:* 0.9 male(s)/female (2009 est.)
**Infant mortality rate:**
*total:* 13.79 deaths/1,000 live births
*male:* 18.28 deaths/1,000 live births
*female:* 9.22 deaths/1,000 live births (2009 est.)
**Life expectancy at birth:**
*total population:* 75.28 years
*male:* 72.25 years
*female:* 78.38 years (2009 est.)
**Total fertility rate:** 1.85 children born/woman (2009 est.)
**HIV/AIDS - adult prevalence rate:** NA
**HIV/AIDS - people living with HIV/AIDS:** NA
**HIV/AIDS - deaths:** NA
**Nationality:**
*noun:* Aruban(s)
*adjective:* Aruban; Dutch
**Ethnic groups:** mixed white/Caribbean Amerindian 80%, other 20%

**Religions:** Roman Catholic 80.8%, Evangelist 4.1%, Protestant 2.5%, Jehovah's Witnesses 1.5%, Methodist 1.2%, Jewish 0.2%, other 5.1%, none or unspecified 4.6%
**Languages:** Papiamento (a Spanish-Portuguese-Dutch-English dialect) 66.3%, Spanish 12.6%, English (widely spoken) 7.7%, Dutch (official) 5.8%, other 2.2%, unspecified or unknown 5.3% (2000 census)
**Literacy:**
*definition:* NA
*total population:* 97.3%
*male:* 97.5%
*female:* 97.1% (2000 census)
**School life expectancy (primary to tertiary education):**
*total:* 14 years
*male:* 13 years
*female:* 14 years (2006)
**Education expenditures:** 4.8% of GDP (2005)

## Government

**Country name:**
*conventional long form:* none
*conventional short form:* Aruba
**Dependency status:** member country of the Kingdom of the Netherlands; full autonomy in internal affairs obtained in 1986 upon separation from the Netherlands Antilles; Dutch Government responsible for defense and foreign affairs
**Government type:** parliamentary democracy
**Capital:**
*name:* Oranjestad
*geographic coordinates:* 12 31 N, 70 02 W
*time difference:* UTC-4 (1 hour ahead of Washington, DC during Standard Time)
**Administrative divisions:** none (part of the Kingdom of the Netherlands)
**Independence:** none (part of the Kingdom of the Netherlands)
**National holiday:** Flag Day, 18 March (1976)
**Constitution:** 1 January 1986
**Legal system:** based on Dutch civil law system, with some English common law influence
**Suffrage:** 18 years of age; universal
**Executive branch:**
*chief of state:* Queen BEATRIX of the Netherlands (since 30 April 1980); represented by Governor General Fredis REFUNJOL (since 11 May 2004)
*head of government:* Prime Minister Nelson O. ODUBER (since 30 October 2001)
*cabinet:* Council of Ministers elected by the Staten
*elections:* the monarch is hereditary; governor general appointed for a six-year term by the monarch; prime minister and deputy prime minister elected by the Staten for four-year terms; election last held in 2005 (next to be held by 2009)
*election results:* Nelson O. ODUBER elected prime minister; percent of legislative vote - NA

**Legislative branch:** unicameral Legislature or Staten (21 seats; members elected by direct popular vote to serve four-year terms)
*elections:* last held 23 September 2005 (next to be held in 2009)
*election results:* percent of vote by party - MEP 43%, AVP 32%, MPA 7%, RED 7%, PDR 6%, OLA 4%, PPA 2%; seats by party - MEP 11, AVP 8, MPA 1, RED 1

**Judicial branch:** Common Court of Justice of Aruba (judges are appointed by the monarch)

**Political parties and leaders:** Aliansa/Aruban Social Movement or MSA [Robert WEVER]; Aruban Liberal Organization or OLA [Glenbert CROES]; Aruban Patriotic Movement or MPA [Monica ARENDS-KOCK]; Aruban Patriotic Party or PPA [Benny NISBET]; Aruban People's Party or AVP [Mike EMAN]; People's Electoral Movement Party or MEP [Nelson O. ODUBER]; Real Democracy or PDR [Andin BIKKER]; RED [Rudy LAMPE]; Workers Political Platform or PTT [Gregorio WOLFF]

**Political pressure groups and leaders:**
*other:* environmental groups

**International organization participation:** Caricom (observer), ILO, IMF, Interpol, IOC, ITUC, UNESCO (associate), UNWTO (associate), UPU, WCL, WFTU, WMO

**Diplomatic representation in the US:** none (represented by the Kingdom of the Netherlands); note - Mr. Henry BAARH, Minister Plenipotentiary for Aruba at the Embassy of the Kingdom of the Netherlands

**Diplomatic representation from the US:** the US does not have an embassy in Aruba; the Consul General to Netherlands Antilles is accredited to Aruba

**Flag description:** blue, with two narrow, horizontal, yellow stripes across the lower portion and a red, four-pointed star outlined in white in the upper hoist-side corner

## Economy

**Economy - overview:** Tourism is the mainstay of the small open Aruban economy with offshore banking and oil refining and storage also important. The rapid growth of the tourism sector over the last decade has resulted in a substantial expansion of other activities. Over 1.5 million tourists per year visit Aruba with 75% of those from the US. Construction continues to boom with hotel capacity five times the 1985 level. In addition, the country's oil refinery reopened in 1993 providing a major source of employment, foreign exchange earnings, and growth. Tourist arrivals have rebounded strongly following a dip after the 11 September 2001 attacks. The island experiences only a brief low season. Hotel occupancy in 2004 averaged 80% compared to 68% throughout the rest of the Caribbean. The government has made cutting the budget and trade deficits a high priority.

**GDP (purchasing power parity):**
$2.258 billion (2005 est.)
$2.205 billion (2004)

**GDP (official exchange rate):** $2.258 billion (2005 est.)

**GDP - real growth rate:**
2.4% (2005 est.)

**GDP - per capita (PPP):**
$21,800 (2004 est.)

**GDP - composition by sector:**
*agriculture:* 0.4%
*industry:* 33.3%
*services:* 66.3% (2002 est.)

**Labor force:** 41,500 (2004 est.)

**Labor force - by occupation:**
*agriculture:* NA%
*industry:* NA%
*services:* NA%
*note:* most employment is in wholesale and retail trade and repair, followed by hotels and restaurants; oil refining

**Unemployment rate:**
6.9% (2005 est.)

**Population below poverty line:** NA%

**Household income or consumption by percentage share:**
*lowest 10%:* NA%
*highest 10%:* NA%

**Budget:**
*revenues:* $507.9 million
*expenditures:* $577.9 million (2005 est.)

**Public debt:** 46.3% of GDP (2005)

**Inflation rate (consumer prices):**
3.4% (2005)

**Central bank discount rate:** 5% (31 December 2007)

**Commercial bank prime lending rate:** 11.01% (31 December 2007)

**Stock of money:** $640.9 million (31 December 2007)

**Stock of quasi money:** $792.9 million (31 December 2007)

**Stock of domestic credit:** $1.348 billion (31 December 2007)

**Agriculture - products:** aloes; livestock; fish

**Industries:** tourism, transshipment facilities, oil refining

**Industrial production growth rate:** NA%

**Electricity - production:** 800 million kWh (2006 est.)

**Electricity - consumption:** 744 million kWh (2006 est.)

**Electricity - exports:** 0 kWh (2007 est.)

**Electricity - imports:** 0 kWh (2007 est.)

**Oil - production:** 2,356 bbl/day (2007 est.)

**Oil - consumption:** 7,102 bbl/day (2006 est.)

**Oil - exports:** 233,300 bbl/day (2005)

**Oil - imports:** 238,200 bbl/day (2005)

**Oil - proved reserves:** NA

**Natural gas - production:** 0 cu m (2007 est.)

**Natural gas - consumption:** 0 cu m (2007 est.)

**Natural gas - exports:** 0 cu m (2007 est.)

**Natural gas - imports:** 0 cu m (2007 est.)

**Natural gas - proved reserves:** 0 cu m (1 January 2006)

**Exports:** $124 million f.o.b.; note - includes oil reexports (2006)

**Exports - commodities:** live animals and animal products, art and collectibles, machinery and electrical equipment, transport equipment

**Exports - partners:** Panama 29.7%, Colombia 17%, Netherlands Antilles 13.2%, US 11.3%, Venezuela 10.9%, Netherlands 9.2% (2007)

**Imports:** $1.054 billion f.o.b. (2006)

**Imports - commodities:** machinery and electrical equipment, crude oil for refining and reexport, chemicals; foodstuffs

**Imports - partners:** US 54.6%, Netherlands 12%, UK 4.7% (2007)

**Debt - external:** $478.6 million (2005 est.)

**Exchange rates:** Aruban guilders/florins (AWG) per US dollar - NA (2007), 1.79 (2006), 1.79 (2005), 1.79 (2004), 1.79 (2003)

## Communications

**Telephones - main lines in use:** 38,700 (2006)

**Telephones - mobile cellular:** 105,700 (2006)

**Telephone system:**
*general assessment:* modern fully automatic telecommunications system
*domestic:* increased competition through privatization; 3 wireless service providers are now licensed
*international:* country code - 297; landing site for the PAN-AM submarine telecommunications cable system that extends from the US Virgin Islands through Aruba to Venezuela, Colombia, Panama, and the west coast of South America; extensive interisland microwave radio relay links (2007)

**Radio broadcast stations:** AM 2, FM 16, shortwave 0 (2004)

**Television broadcast stations:** 1 (1997)

**Internet country code:** .aw

**Internet hosts:** 17,661 (2008)

**Internet users:** 24,000 (2007)

## Transportation

**Airports:** 1 (2008)

**Airports - with paved runways:**
*total:* 1
*2,438 to 3,047 m:* 1 (2008)

**Ports and terminals:** Barcadera, Oranjestad, Sint Nicolaas

## Military

**Military branches:** no regular military forces; the Netherlands maintains a detachment of marines, a frigate, and an amphibious combat detachment in the neighboring Netherlands Antilles (2009)

**Manpower available for military service:**
*males age 16-49:* 24,585
*females age 16-49:* 25,742 (2008 est.)

**Manpower fit for military service:**
*males age 16-49:* 20,287
*females age 16-49:* 21,232 (2009 est.)

# Aruba *(continued)*

**Manpower reaching militarily significant age annually:**
*male:* 722
*female:* 711 (2009 est.)
**Military - note:** defense is the responsibility of the Kingdom of the Netherlands

## Transnational Issues

**Disputes - international:** none
**Illicit drugs:** transit point for US- and Europe-bound narcotics with some accompanying money-laundering activity; relatively high percentage of population consumes cocaine

# Ashmore and Cartier Islands
*(territory of Australia)*

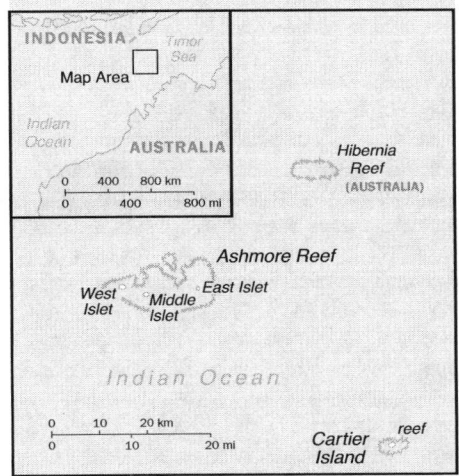

## Introduction

**Background:** These uninhabited islands came under Australian authority in 1931; formal administration began two years later. Ashmore Reef supports a rich and diverse avian and marine habitat; in 1983, it became a National Nature Reserve. Cartier Island, a former bombing range, became a marine reserve in 2000.

## Geography

**Location:** Southeastern Asia, islands in the Indian Ocean, midway between northwestern Australia and Timor island
**Geographic coordinates:** 12 14 S, 123 05 E
**Map references:** Southeast Asia
**Area:**
*total:* 5 sq km
*land:* 5 sq km
*water:* 0 sq km
*note:* includes Ashmore Reef (West, Middle, and East Islets) and Cartier Island
**Area - comparative:** about eight times the size of The Mall in Washington, DC
**Land boundaries:** 0 km
**Coastline:** 74.1 km
**Maritime claims:**
*territorial sea:* 12 nm
*contiguous zone:* 12 nm
*exclusive fishing zone:* 200 nm
*continental shelf:* 200 m depth or to the depth of exploitation
**Climate:** tropical
**Terrain:** low with sand and coral
**Elevation extremes:**
*lowest point:* Indian Ocean 0 m
*highest point:* unnamed location 3 m
**Natural resources:** fish
**Land use:**
*arable land:* 0%
*permanent crops:* 0%
*other:* 100% (all grass and sand) (2005)

**Irrigated land:** 0 sq km
**Natural hazards:** surrounded by shoals and reefs that can pose maritime hazards
**Environment - current issues:** illegal killing of protected wildlife by traditional Indonesian fisherman, as well as fishing by non-traditional Indonesian vessels, are ongoing problems
**Geography - note:** Ashmore Reef National Nature Reserve established in August 1983; Cartier Island Marine Reserve established in 2000

## People

**Population:** no indigenous inhabitants
*note:* Indonesian fishermen are allowed access to the lagoon and fresh water at Ashmore Reef's West Island; access to East and Middle Islands is by permit only

## Government

**Country name:**
*conventional long form:* Territory of Ashmore and Cartier Islands
*conventional short form:* Ashmore and Cartier Islands
**Dependency status:** territory of Australia; administered by the Australian Government Attorney-General's Department
**Legal system:** the laws of the Commonwealth of Australia and the laws of the Northern Territory of Australia, where applicable, apply
**Diplomatic representation in the US:** none (territory of Australia)
**Diplomatic representation from the US:** none (territory of Australia)
**Flag description:** the flag of Australia is used

## Economy

**Economy - overview:** no economic activity

## Transportation

**Ports and terminals:** none; offshore anchorage only

## Military

**Military - note:** defense is the responsibility of Australia; periodic visits by the Royal Australian Navy and Royal Australian Air Force

## Transnational Issues

**Disputes - international:** as the closest Australian territory to Indonesia, these islands became the target of human traffickers for the landing of illegal immigrants; in 2001, the Australian government removed these islands from the Australian Migration Zone making illegal arrivals ineligible for temporary visas and entry into Australia

# Atlantic Ocean

## Introduction

**Background:** The Atlantic Ocean is the second largest of the world's five oceans (after the Pacific Ocean, but larger than the Indian Ocean, Southern Ocean, and Arctic Ocean). The Kiel Canal (Germany), Oresund (Denmark-Sweden), Bosporus (Turkey), Strait of Gibraltar (Morocco-Spain), and the Saint Lawrence Seaway (Canada-US) are important strategic access waterways. The decision by the International Hydrographic Organization in the spring of 2000 to delimit a fifth world ocean, the Southern Ocean, removed the portion of the Atlantic Ocean south of 60 degrees south latitude.

## Geography

**Location:** body of water between Africa, Europe, the Southern Ocean, and the Western Hemisphere
**Geographic coordinates:** 0 00 N, 25 00 W
**Map references:** Political Map of the World
**Area:**
*total:* 76.762 million sq km
*note:* includes Baltic Sea, Black Sea, Caribbean Sea, Davis Strait, Denmark Strait, part of the Drake Passage, Gulf of Mexico, Labrador Sea, Mediterranean Sea, North Sea, Norwegian Sea, almost all of the Scotia Sea, and other tributary water bodies
**Area - comparative:** slightly less than 6.5 times the size of the US
**Coastline:** 111,866 km
**Climate:** tropical cyclones (hurricanes) develop off the coast of Africa near Cape Verde and move westward into the Caribbean Sea; hurricanes can occur from May to December but are most frequent from August to November
**Terrain:** surface usually covered with sea ice in Labrador Sea, Denmark Strait, and coastal portions of the Baltic Sea from October to June; clockwise warm-water gyre (broad, circular system of currents) in the northern Atlantic, counterclockwise warm-water

gyre in the southern Atlantic; the ocean floor is dominated by the Mid-Atlantic Ridge, a rugged north-south centerline for the entire Atlantic basin
**Elevation extremes:**
*lowest point:* Milwaukee Deep in the Puerto Rico Trench -8,605 m
*highest point:* sea level 0 m
**Natural resources:** oil and gas fields, fish, marine mammals (seals and whales), sand and gravel aggregates, placer deposits, polymetallic nodules, precious stones
**Natural hazards:** icebergs common in Davis Strait, Denmark Strait, and the northwestern Atlantic Ocean from February to August and have been spotted as far south as Bermuda and the Madeira Islands; ships subject to superstructure icing in extreme northern Atlantic from October to May; persistent fog can be a maritime hazard from May to September; hurricanes (May to December)
**Environment - current issues:** endangered marine species include the manatee, seals, sea lions, turtles, and whales; drift net fishing is hastening the decline of fish stocks and contributing to international disputes; municipal sludge pollution off eastern US, southern Brazil, and eastern Argentina; oil pollution in Caribbean Sea, Gulf of Mexico, Lake Maracaibo, Mediterranean Sea, and North Sea; industrial waste and municipal sewage pollution in Baltic Sea, North Sea, and Mediterranean Sea
**Geography - note:** major chokepoints include the Dardanelles, Strait of Gibraltar, access to the Panama and Suez Canals; strategic straits include the Strait of Dover, Straits of Florida, Mona Passage, The Sound (Oresund), and Windward Passage; the Equator divides the Atlantic Ocean into the North Atlantic Ocean and South Atlantic Ocean

## Economy

**Economy - overview:** The Atlantic Ocean provides some of the world's most heavily trafficked sea routes, between and within the Eastern and Western Hemispheres. Other economic activity includes the exploitation of natural resources, e.g., fishing, dredging of aragonite sands (The Bahamas), and production of crude oil and natural gas (Caribbean Sea, Gulf of Mexico, and North Sea).

## Transportation

**Ports and terminals:** Alexandria (Egypt), Algiers (Algeria), Antwerp (Belgium), Barcelona (Spain), Buenos Aires (Argentina), Casablanca (Morocco), Colon (Panama), Copenhagen (Denmark), Dakar (Senegal), Gdansk (Poland), Hamburg (Germany), Helsinki (Finland), Las Palmas (Canary Islands, Spain), Le Havre (France), Lisbon (Portugal), London (UK), Marseille (France), Montevideo (Uruguay), Montreal (Canada), Naples (Italy), New Orleans (US), New York (US), Oran (Algeria), Oslo (Norway), Peiraiefs or Piraeus (Greece), Rio de Janeiro (Brazil), Rotterdam (Netherlands), Saint Petersburg (Russia), Stockholm (Sweden)

**Transportation - note:** Kiel Canal and Saint Lawrence Seaway are two important waterways; significant domestic commercial and recreational use of Intracoastal Waterway on central and south Atlantic seaboard and Gulf of Mexico coast of US; the International Maritime Bureau reports the territorial waters of littoral states and offshore Atlantic waters as high risk for piracy and armed robbery against ships, particularly in the Gulf of Guinea off West Africa, the east coast of Brazil, and the Caribbean Sea; numerous commercial vessels have been attacked and hijacked both at anchor and while underway; hijacked vessels are often disguised and cargoes stolen; crews have been robbed and stores or cargoes stolen

## Transnational Issues

**Disputes - international:** some maritime disputes (see littoral states)

# Australia

## Introduction

**Background:** Aboriginal settlers arrived on the continent from Southeast Asia about 40,000 years before the first Europeans began exploration in the 17th century. No formal territorial claims were made until 1770, when Capt. James COOK took possession in the name of Great Britain. Six colonies were created in the late 18th and 19th centuries; they federated and became the Commonwealth of Australia in 1901. The new country took advantage of its natural resources to rapidly develop agricultural and manufacturing industries and to make a major contribution to the British effort in World Wars I and II. In recent decades, Australia has transformed itself into an internationally competitive, advanced market economy. It boasted one of the OECD's fastest growing economies during the 1990s, a performance due in large part to economic reforms adopted in the 1980s. Long-term concerns include climate-change issues such as the depletion of the ozone layer and more frequent droughts, and management and conservation of coastal areas, especially the Great Barrier Reef.

## Geography

**Location:** Oceania, continent between the Indian Ocean and the South Pacific Ocean
**Geographic coordinates:** 27 00 S, 133 00 E
**Map references:** Oceania
**Area:**
*total:* 7,686,850 sq km
*land:* 7,617,930 sq km
*water:* 68,920 sq km
*note:* includes Lord Howe Island and Macquarie Island
**Area - comparative:** slightly smaller than the US contiguous 48 states
**Land boundaries:** 0 km
**Coastline:** 25,760 km

**Maritime claims:**
*territorial sea:* 12 nm
*contiguous zone:* 24 nm
*exclusive economic zone:* 200 nm
*continental shelf:* 200 nm or to the edge of the continental margin
**Climate:** generally arid to semiarid; temperate in south and east; tropical in north
**Terrain:** mostly low plateau with deserts; fertile plain in southeast
**Elevation extremes:**
*lowest point:* Lake Eyre -15 m
*highest point:* Mount Kosciuszko 2,229 m
**Natural resources:** bauxite, coal, iron ore, copper, tin, gold, silver, uranium, nickel, tungsten, mineral sands, lead, zinc, diamonds, natural gas, petroleum
*note:* Australia is the world's largest net exporter of coal accounting for 29% of global coal exports
**Land use:**
*arable land:* 6.15% (includes about 27 million hectares of cultivated grassland)
*permanent crops:* 0.04%
*other:* 93.81% (2005)
**Irrigated land:** 25,450 sq km (2003)
**Total renewable water resources:** 398 cu km (1995)
**Freshwater withdrawal (domestic/industrial/agricultural):**
*total:* 24.06 cu km/yr (15%/10%/75%)
*per capita:* 1,193 cu m/yr (2000)
**Natural hazards:** cyclones along the coast; severe droughts; forest fires
**Environment - current issues:** soil erosion from overgrazing, industrial development, urbanization, and poor farming practices; soil salinity rising due to the use of poor quality water; desertification; clearing for agricultural purposes threatens the natural habitat of many unique animal and plant species; the Great Barrier Reef off the northeast coast, the largest coral reef in the world, is threatened by increased shipping and its popularity as a tourist site; limited natural fresh water resources
**Environment - international agreements:**
*party to:* Antarctic-Environmental Protocol, Antarctic-Marine Living Resources, Antarctic Seals, Antarctic Treaty, Biodiversity, Climate Change, Climate Change-Kyoto Protocol, Desertification, Endangered Species, Environmental Modification, Hazardous Wastes, Law of the Sea, Marine Dumping, Marine Life Conservation, Ozone Layer Protection, Ship Pollution, Tropical Timber 83, Tropical Timber 94, Wetlands, Whaling
*signed, but not ratified:* none of the selected agreements
**Geography - note:** world's smallest continent but sixth-largest country; population concentrated along the eastern and southeastern coasts; the invigorating sea breeze known as the "Fremantle Doctor" affects the city of Perth on the west coast and is one of the most consistent winds in the world

## People

**Population:** 21,262,641 (July 2009 est.)
**Age structure:**
*0-14 years:* 18.6% (male 2,026,975/female 1,923,828)
*15-64 years:* 67.9% (male 7,318,743/female 7,121,613)
*65 years and over:* 13.5% (male 1,306,329/female 1,565,153) (2009 est.)
**Median age:**
*total:* 37.3 years
*male:* 36.6 years
*female:* 38.1 years (2009 est.)
**Population growth rate:** 1.195% (2009 est.)
**Birth rate:** 12.47 births/1,000 population (2009 est.)
**Death rate:** 6.68 deaths/1,000 population (2008 est.)
**Net migration rate:** 6.23 migrant(s)/1,000 population (2009 est.)
**Urbanization:**
*urban population:* 89% of total population (2008)
*rate of urbanization:* 1.2% annual rate of change (2005-10 est.)
**Sex ratio:**
*at birth:* 1.06 male(s)/female
*under 15 years:* 1.05 male(s)/female
*15-64 years:* 1.03 male(s)/female
*65 years and over:* 0.84 male(s)/female
*total population:* 1 male(s)/female (2009 est.)
**Infant mortality rate:**
*total:* 4.75 deaths/1,000 live births
*male:* 5.08 deaths/1,000 live births
*female:* 4.4 deaths/1,000 live births (2009 est.)
**Life expectancy at birth:**
*total population:* 81.63 years
*male:* 79.25 years
*female:* 84.14 years (2009 est.)
**Total fertility rate:** 1.78 children born/woman (2009 est.)
**HIV/AIDS - adult prevalence rate:** 0.2% (2007 est.)
**HIV/AIDS - people living with HIV/AIDS:** 18,000 (2007 est.)
**HIV/AIDS - deaths:** fewer than 100 200 (2007 est.)
**Nationality:**
*noun:* Australian(s)
*adjective:* Australian
**Ethnic groups:** white 92%, Asian 7%, aboriginal and other 1%
**Religions:** Catholic 25.8%, Anglican 18.7%, Uniting Church 5.7%, Presbyterian and Reformed 3%, Eastern Orthodox 2.7%, other Christian 7.9%, Buddhist 2.1%, Muslim 1.7%, other 2.4%, unspecified 11.3%, none 18.7% (2006 Census)
**Languages:** English 78.5%, Chinese 2.5%, Italian 1.6%, Greek 1.3%, Arabic 1.2%, Vietnamese 1%, other 8.2%, unspecified 5.7% (2006 Census)
**Literacy:**
*definition:* age 15 and over can read and write
*total population:* 99%
*male:* 99%
*female:* 99% (2003 est.)

# Australia *(continued)*

**School life expectancy (primary to tertiary education):**
*total:* 20 years
*male:* 20 years
*female:* 21 years (2006)
**Education expenditures:** 4.5% of GDP (2005)

## Government

**Country name:**
*conventional long form:* Commonwealth of Australia
*conventional short form:* Australia
**Government type:** federal parliamentary democracy and a Commonwealth realm
**Capital:**
*name:* Canberra
*geographic coordinates:* 35 17 S, 149 13 E
*time difference:* UTC+10 (15 hours ahead of Washington, DC during Standard Time)
*daylight saving time:* +1hr, begins last Sunday in October; ends last Sunday in March
*note:* Australia is divided into three time zones
**Administrative divisions:** 6 states and 2 territories*; Australian Capital Territory*, New South Wales, Northern Territory*, Queensland, South Australia, Tasmania, Victoria, Western Australia
**Dependent areas:** Ashmore and Cartier Islands, Christmas Island, Cocos (Keeling) Islands, Coral Sea Islands, Heard Island and McDonald Islands, Macquarie Island, Norfolk Island
**Independence:** 1 January 1901 (federation of UK colonies)
**National holiday:** Australia Day, 26 January (1788); ANZAC Day (commemorated as the anniversary of the landing of troops of the Australian and New Zealand Army Corps during World War I at Gallipoli, Turkey), 25 April (1915)
**Constitution:** 9 July 1900; effective 1 January 1901
**Legal system:** based on English common law; accepts compulsory ICJ jurisdiction with reservations
**Suffrage:** 18 years of age; universal and compulsory
**Executive branch:**
*chief of state:* Queen of Australia ELIZABETH II (since 6 February 1952); represented by Governor General Quentin BRYCE (since 5 September 2008)
*head of government:* Prime Minister Kevin RUDD (since 3 December 2007); Deputy Prime Minister Julia GILLARD (since 3 December 2007)
*cabinet:* prime minister nominates, from among members of Parliament, candidates who are subsequently sworn in by the governor general to serve as government ministers
*elections:* the monarch is hereditary; governor general appointed by the monarch on the recommendation of the prime minister; following legislative elections, the leader of the majority party or leader of a majority coalition is sworn in as prime minister by the governor general
**Legislative branch:** bicameral Federal Parliament consists of the Senate (76 seats; 12 members from each of the six states and 2 from each of the two mainland territories; one-half of state members are elected every three years by popular vote to serve

six-year terms while all territory members are elected every three years) and the House of Representatives (150 seats; members elected by popular preferential vote to serve terms of up to three-years; no state can have fewer than 5 representatives)
*elections:* Senate - last held 24 November 2007 (next to be held no later than 2010); House of Representatives - last held 24 November 2007 (next to be called no later than 2010)
*election results:* Senate - percent of vote by party - NA; seats by party - Liberal Party-National Party coalition 37, Australian Labor Party 32, Australian Greens 5, Family First Party 1, independent 1; House of Representatives - percent of vote by party - NA; seats by party - Australian Labor Party 83, Liberal Party 55, National Party 10, independents 2
**Judicial branch:** High Court (the chief justice and six other justices are appointed by the governor general)
**Political parties and leaders:** Australian Democrats [Lyn ALLISON]; Australian Greens [Bob BROWN]; Australian Labor Party [Kevin RUDD]; Country Liberal Party [Terry MILLS]; Family First Party [Steve FIELDING]; Liberal Party [Malcolm TURNBULL]; The Nationals [Warren TRUSS]
**Political pressure groups and leaders:**
*other:* business groups; environmental groups; social groups; trade unions
**International organization participation:** ADB, ANZUS, APEC, ARF, ASEAN (dialogue partner), Australia Group, BIS, C, CP, EAS, EBRD, FAO, G-20, IAEA, IBRD, ICAO, ICC, ICCt, ICRM, IDA, IEA, IFC, IFRCS, IHO, ILO, IMF, IMO, IMSO, Interpol, IOC, IOM, IPU, ISO, ITSO, ITU, ITUC, MIGA, NAM (guest), NEA, NSG, OECD, OPCW, Paris Club, PCA, PIF, SAARC (observer), Sparteca, SPC, UN, UNCTAD, UNESCO, UNHCR, UNMIS, UNMIT, UNRWA, UNTSO, UNWTO, UPU, WCO, WFTU, WHO, WIPO, WMO, WTO, ZC
**Diplomatic representation in the US:**
*chief of mission:* Ambassador Dennis J. RICHARDSON
*chancery:* 1601 Massachusetts Avenue NW, Washington, DC 20036
*telephone:* [1] (202) 797-3000
*FAX:* [1] (202) 797-3168
*consulate(s) general:* Atlanta, Chicago, Honolulu, Los Angeles, New York, San Francisco
**Diplomatic representation from the US:**
*chief of mission:* Ambassador Robert D. McCALLUM, Jr.
*embassy:* Moonah Place, Yarralumla, Canberra, Australian Capital Territory 2600
*mailing address:* APO AP 96549
*telephone:* [61] (02) 6214-5600
*FAX:* [61] (02) 6214-5970
*consulate(s) general:* Melbourne, Perth, Sydney
**Flag description:** blue with the flag of the UK in the upper hoist-side quadrant and a large seven-pointed star in the lower hoist-side quadrant known as the Commonwealth or Federation Star, representing the federation of the colonies of Australia in 1901; the star depicts one point for each of the six original states and

one representing all of Australia's internal and external territories; on the fly half is a representation of the Southern Cross constellation in white with one small five-pointed star and four larger, seven-pointed stars

## Economy

**Economy - overview:** Australia has an enviable, strong economy with a per capita GDP on par with the four dominant West European economies. Emphasis on reforms, low inflation, a housing market boom, and growing ties with China have been key factors over the course of the economy's 17 solid years of expansion. Robust business and consumer confidence and high export prices for raw materials and agricultural products fueled the economy in recent years, particularly in mining states. Drought, robust import demand, and a strong currency pushed the trade deficit up however, while infrastructure bottlenecks and a tight labor market constrained growth in export volumes and stoked inflation through mid-2008. The unwinding of the yen-based carry trade in late 2008 has contributed to a weakening of the Australian dollar. Tight global liquidity has challenged Australia's banking sector, which relies heavily on international wholesale markets for funding. The economy remains relatively healthy despite falling export commodity prices. The government plans to counter slowing growth in 2009 with fiscal stimulus efforts.
**GDP (purchasing power parity):**
$800.5 billion (2008 est.)
$783.2 billion (2007)
$753.1 billion (2006)
*note:* data are in 2008 US dollars
**GDP (official exchange rate):** $1.069 trillion (2008 est.)
**GDP - real growth rate:**
2.2% (2008 est.)
4% (2007 est.)
2.9% (2006 est.)
**GDP - per capita (PPP):**
$38,100 (2008 est.)
$37,700 (2007 est.)
$36,800 (2006 est.)
*note:* data are in 2008 US dollars
**GDP - composition by sector:**
*agriculture:* 2.5%
*industry:* 26.4%
*services:* 71.1% (2008 est.)
**Labor force:** 11.21 million (2008 est.)
**Labor force - by occupation:**
*agriculture:* 3.6%
*industry:* 21.1%
*services:* 75% (2005 est.)
**Unemployment rate:**
4.5% (2008 est.)
4.4% (2007 est.)
**Population below poverty line:** NA%
**Household income or consumption by percentage share:**
*lowest 10%:* 2%
*highest 10%:* 25.4% (1994)

**Distribution of family income - Gini index:** 30.5 (2006)

**Investment (gross fixed):** 27.6% of GDP (2008 est.)

**Budget:**
*revenues:* $343.6 billion
*expenditures:* $340.7 billion (2008 est.)

**Public debt:** 15.4% of GDP

*note:* the Commonwealth government eliminated its net debt in 2006, but continues a gross debt issue to support the market for risk-free securities (2008 est.)

**Inflation rate (consumer prices):**
4.7% (2008 est.)
2.3% (2007 est.)

**Central bank discount rate:** NA

**Commercial bank prime lending rate:** 10.02% (31 December 2007)

**Stock of money:** $298.5 billion (31 December 2007)

**Stock of quasi money:** $667.2 billion (31 December 2007)

**Stock of domestic credit:** $1.312 trillion (31 December 2007)

**Market value of publicly traded shares:** $1.298 trillion (31 December 2007)

**Agriculture - products:** wheat, barley, sugarcane, fruits, cattle, sheep, poultry

**Industries:** mining, industrial and transportation equipment, food processing, chemicals, steel

**Industrial production growth rate:** 3.5% (2008 est.)

**Electricity - production:** 244.2 billion kWh (2007 est.)

**Electricity - consumption:** 220 billion kWh (2006 est.)

**Electricity - exports:** 0 kWh (2007 est.)

**Electricity - imports:** 0 kWh (2007 est.)

**Oil - production:** 600,000 bbl/day (2008 est.)

**Oil - consumption:** 966,200 bbl/day (2007 est.)

**Oil - exports:** 337,400 bbl/day (2005)

**Oil - imports:** 615,000 bbl/day (2005)

**Oil - proved reserves:** 1.5 billion bbl (1 January 2008 est.)

**Natural gas - production:** 43.62 billion cu m (2007 est.)

**Natural gas - consumption:** 29.4 billion cu m (2007 est.)

**Natural gas - exports:** 19.91 billion cu m (2007 est.)

**Natural gas - imports:** 5.689 billion cu m (2007 est.)

**Natural gas - proved reserves:** 849.5 billion cu m (1 January 2008 est.)

**Current account balance:** -$43.84 billion (2008 est.)

**Exports:** $178.9 billion (2008 est.)

**Exports - commodities:** coal, iron ore, gold, meat, wool, alumina, wheat, machinery and transport equipment

**Exports - partners:** Japan 18.9%, China 14.2%, South Korea 8%, US 6%, NZ 5.6%, India 5.5%, UK 4.2% (2007)

**Imports:** $187.2 billion (2008 est.)

**Imports - commodities:** machinery and transport equipment, computers and office machines, telecommunication equipment and parts; crude oil and petroleum products

**Imports - partners:** China 15.5%, US 12.8%, Japan 9.6%, Singapore 5.6%, Germany 5.2%, UK 4.3%, Thailand 4.2% (2007)

**Reserves of foreign exchange and gold:** $25.75 billion (31 December 2008 est.)

**Debt - external:** $1.032 trillion (31 December 2008 est.)

**Stock of direct foreign investment - at home:** $333.1 billion (2008 est.)

**Stock of direct foreign investment - abroad:** $301.1 billion (2008 est.)

**Exchange rates:** Australian dollars (AUD) per US dollar - 1.2059 (2008 est.), 1.2137 (2007), 1.3285 (2006), 1.3095 (2005), 1.3598 (2004)

## Communications

**Telephones - main lines in use:** 9.76 million (2007)

**Telephones - mobile cellular:** 21.26 million (2007)

**Telephone system:**
*general assessment:* excellent domestic and international service
*domestic:* domestic satellite system; significant use of radiotelephone in areas of low population density; rapid growth of mobile cellular telephones
*international:* country code - 61; landing point for the SEA-ME-WE-3 optical telecommunications submarine cable with links to Asia, the Middle East, and Europe; the Southern Cross fiber optic submarine cable provides links to New Zealand and the United States; satellite earth stations - 19 (10 Intelsat - 4 Indian Ocean and 6 Pacific Ocean, 2 Inmarsat - Indian and Pacific Ocean regions, 2 Globalstar, 5 other) (2007)

**Radio broadcast stations:** AM 262, FM 345, shortwave 1 (1998)

**Television broadcast stations:** 104 (1997)

**Internet country code:** .au

**Internet hosts:** 11.134 million (2008)

**Internet users:** 11.24 million (2007)

## Transportation

**Airports:** 462 (2008)

**Airports - with paved runways:**
*total:* 322
*over 3,047 m:* 11
*2,438 to 3,047 m:* 12
*1,524 to 2,437 m:* 144
*914 to 1,523 m:* 141
*under 914 m:* 14 (2008)

**Airports - with unpaved runways:**
*total:* 140
*1,524 to 2,437 m:* 19
*914 to 1,523 m:* 107
*under 914 m:* 14 (2008)

**Heliports:** 1 (2007)

**Pipelines:** gas 27,105 km; liquid petroleum gas 240 km; oil 3,258 km; oil/gas/water 1 km (2008)

**Railways:**
*total:* 38,550 km
*broad gauge:* 3,727 km 1.600-m gauge
*standard gauge:* 20,519 km 1.435-m gauge (1,877 km electrified)
*narrow gauge:* 14,074 km 1.067-m gauge (2,453 km electrified)
*dual gauge:* 230 km dual gauge (2006)

**Roadways:**
*total:* 812,972 km
*paved:* 341,448 km
*unpaved:* 471,524 km (2004)

**Waterways:** 2,000 km (mainly used for recreation on Murray and Murray-Darling river systems) (2006)

**Merchant marine:**
*total:* 50
*by type:* bulk carrier 12, cargo 5, chemical tanker 1, container 1, liquefied gas 4, passenger 7, passenger/cargo 7, petroleum tanker 8, roll on/roll off 5
*foreign-owned:* 24 (Canada 9, France 1, Germany 2, Japan 1, Netherlands 2, Norway 1, Singapore 1, UK 5, US 2)
*registered in other countries:* 28 (Antigua and Barbuda 1, Belize 1, Bermuda 1, Dominica 2, Fiji 1, Marshall Islands 1, NZ 1, Panama 4, Singapore 12, Tonga 1, US 1, Vanuatu 2) (2008)

**Ports and terminals:** Brisbane, Dampier, Fremantle, Gladstone, Hay Point, Melbourne, Newcastle, Port Hedland, Port Kembla, Port Walcott, Sydney

## Military

**Military branches:** Australian Defense Force (ADF): Australian Army, Royal Australian Navy, Royal Australian Air Force, Special Operations Command (2006)

**Military service age and obligation:** 17 years of age for voluntary military service (with parental consent); no conscription; women allowed to serve in Army combat units in non-combat support roles (2008)

**Manpower available for military service:**
*males age 16-49:* 4,999,988
*females age 16-49:* 4,870,043 (2008 est.)

**Manpower fit for military service:**
*males age 16-49:* 4,341,591
*females age 16-49:* 4,179,659 (2009 est.)

**Manpower reaching militarily significant age annually:**
*male:* 144,959
*female:* 137,333 (2009 est.)

**Military expenditures:** 2.4% of GDP (2006)

## Transnational Issues

**Disputes - international:** Timor-Leste and Australia agreed in 2005 to defer the disputed portion of the boundary for 50 years and to split hydrocarbon revenues evenly outside the Joint Petroleum Development Area covered by the 2002 Timor Sea Treaty; dispute with Timor-Leste hampers creation of a revised maritime boundary with Indonesia in the

Timor Sea; regional states continue to express concern over Australia's 2004 declaration of a 1,000-nautical mile-wide maritime identification zone; Australia asserts land and maritime claims to Antarctica; in 2004 Australia submitted its claims to Commission on the Limits of the Continental Shelf (CLCS) to extend its continental margins covering over 3.37 million square kilometers, expanding its seabed roughly 30 percent more than its claimed exclusive economic zone; since 2003, Australia has led the Regional Assistance Mission to the Solomon Islands (RAMSI) to maintain civil and political order and reinforce regional security

**Illicit drugs:**  Tasmania is one of the world's major suppliers of licit opiate products; government maintains strict controls over areas of opium poppy cultivation and output of poppy straw concentrate; major consumer of cocaine and amphetamines

# Austria

## Introduction

**Background:**  Once the center of power for the large Austro-Hungarian Empire, Austria was reduced to a small republic after its defeat in World War I. Following annexation by Nazi Germany in 1938 and subsequent occupation by the victorious Allies in 1945, Austria's status remained unclear for a decade. A State Treaty signed in 1955 ended the occupation, recognized Austria's independence, and forbade unification with Germany. A constitutional law that same year declared the country's "perpetual neutrality" as a condition for Soviet military withdrawal. The Soviet Union's collapse in 1991 and Austria's entry into the European Union in 1995 have altered the meaning of this neutrality. A prosperous, democratic country, Austria entered the EU Economic and Monetary Union in 1999. In January 2009, Austria assumed a nonpermanent seat on the UN Security Council for the 2009-10 term.

## Geography

**Location:**  Central Europe, north of Italy and Slovenia
**Geographic coordinates:**  47 20 N, 13 20 E
**Map references:**  Europe
**Area:**
*total:* 83,870 sq km
*land:* 82,444 sq km
*water:* 1,426 sq km
**Area - comparative:**  slightly smaller than Maine
**Land boundaries:**
*total:* 2,562 km
*border countries:* Czech Republic 362 km, Germany 784 km, Hungary 366 km, Italy 430 km, Liechtenstein 35 km, Slovakia 91 km, Slovenia 330 km, Switzerland 164 km
**Coastline:**  0 km (landlocked)
**Maritime claims:**  none (landlocked)
**Climate:**  temperate; continental, cloudy; cold winters with frequent rain and some snow in lowlands and snow in mountains; moderate summers with occasional showers

**Terrain:**  in the west and south mostly mountains (Alps); along the eastern and northern margins mostly flat or gently sloping
**Elevation extremes:**
*lowest point:* Neusiedler See 115 m
*highest point:* Grossglockner 3,798 m
**Natural resources:**  oil, coal, lignite, timber, iron ore, copper, zinc, antimony, magnesite, tungsten, graphite, salt, hydropower
**Land use:**
*arable land:* 16.59%
*permanent crops:* 0.85%
*other:* 82.56% (2005)
**Irrigated land:**  40 sq km (2003)
**Total renewable water resources:**  84 cu km (2005)
**Freshwater withdrawal (domestic/industrial/agricultural):**
*total:* 3.67 cu km/yr (35%/64%/1%)
*per capita:* 448 cu m/yr (1999)
**Natural hazards:**  landslides; avalanches; earthquakes
**Environment - current issues:**  some forest degradation caused by air and soil pollution; soil pollution results from the use of agricultural chemicals; air pollution results from emissions by coal- and oil-fired power stations and industrial plants and from trucks transiting Austria between northern and southern Europe
**Environment - international agreements:**
*party to:* Air Pollution, Air Pollution-Nitrogen Oxides, Air Pollution-Persistent Organic Pollutants, Air Pollution-Sulfur 85, Air Pollution-Sulphur 94, Air Pollution-Volatile Organic Compounds, Antarctic Treaty, Biodiversity, Climate Change, Climate Change-Kyoto Protocol, Desertification, Endangered Species, Environmental Modification, Hazardous Wastes, Law of the Sea, Ozone Layer Protection, Ship Pollution, Tropical Timber 83, Tropical Timber 94, Wetlands, Whaling
*signed, but not ratified:* none of the selected agreements
**Geography - note:**  landlocked; strategic location at the crossroads of central Europe with many easily traversable Alpine passes and valleys; major river is the Danube; population is concentrated on eastern lowlands because of steep slopes, poor soils, and low temperatures elsewhere

## People

**Population:**  8,210,281 (July 2009 est.)
**Age structure:**
*0-14 years:* 14.5% (male 609,748/female 581,144)
*15-64 years:* 67.5% (male 2,785,091/female 2,756,402)
*65 years and over:* 18% (male 612,613/female 865,283) (2009 est.)
**Median age:**
*total:* 42.2 years
*male:* 41.1 years
*female:* 43.2 years (2009 est.)
**Population growth rate:**  0.052% (2009 est.)

# Austria (continued)

**Birth rate:** 8.65 births/1,000 population (2009 est.)
**Death rate:** 9.91 deaths/1,000 population (2008 est.)
**Net migration rate:** 1.85 migrant(s)/1,000 population (2009 est.)
**Urbanization:**
*urban population:* 67% of total population (2008)
*rate of urbanization:* 0.7% annual rate of change (2005-10 est.)
**Sex ratio:**
*at birth:* 1.05 male(s)/female
*under 15 years:* 1.05 male(s)/female
*15-64 years:* 1.01 male(s)/female
*65 years and over:* 0.71 male(s)/female
*total population:* 0.95 male(s)/female (2009 est.)
**Infant mortality rate:**
*total:* 4.42 deaths/1,000 live births
*male:* 5.39 deaths/1,000 live births
*female:* 3.41 deaths/1,000 live births (2009 est.)
**Life expectancy at birth:**
*total population:* 79.5 years
*male:* 76.6 years
*female:* 82.56 years (2009 est.)
**Total fertility rate:** 1.39 children born/woman (2009 est.)
**HIV/AIDS - adult prevalence rate:** 0.2% (2007 est.)
**HIV/AIDS - people living with HIV/AIDS:** 9,800 (2007 est.)
**HIV/AIDS - deaths:** fewer than 100 (2003 est.)
**Nationality:**
*noun:* Austrian(s)
*adjective:* Austrian
**Ethnic groups:** Austrians 91.1%, former Yugoslavs 4% (includes Croatians, Slovenes, Serbs, and Bosniaks), Turks 1.6%, German 0.9%, other or unspecified 2.4% (2001 census)
**Religions:** Roman Catholic 73.6%, Protestant 4.7%, Muslim 4.2%, other 3.5%, unspecified 2%, none 12% (2001 census)
**Languages:** German (official nationwide) 88.6%, Turkish 2.3%, Serbian 2.2%, Croatian (official in Burgenland) 1.6%, other (includes Slovene, official in Carinthia, and Hungarian, official in Burgenland) 5.3% (2001 census)
**Literacy:**
*definition:* age 15 and over can read and write
*total population:* 98%
*male:* NA
*female:* NA
**School life expectancy (primary to tertiary education):**
*total:* 15 years
*male:* 15 years
*female:* 16 years (2006)
**Education expenditures:** 5.4% of GDP (2005)

## Government

**Country name:**
*conventional long form:* Republic of Austria
*conventional short form:* Austria
*local long form:* Republik Oesterreich
*local short form:* Oesterreich

**Government type:** federal republic
**Capital:**
*name:* Vienna
*geographic coordinates:* 48 12 N, 16 22 E
*time difference:* UTC+1 (6 hours ahead of Washington, DC during Standard Time)
*daylight saving time:* +1hr, begins last Sunday in March; ends last Sunday in October
**Administrative divisions:** 9 states (Bundeslaender, singular - Bundesland); Burgenland, Kaernten (Carinthia), Niederoesterreich (Lower Austria), Oberoesterreich (Upper Austria), Salzburg, Steiermark (Styria), Tirol (Tyrol), Vorarlberg, Wien (Vienna)
**Independence:** 976 (Margravate of Austria established); 17 September 1156 (Duchy of Austria founded); 11 August 1804 (Austrian Empire proclaimed); 12 November 1918 (republic proclaimed)
**National holiday:** National Day, 26 October (1955); note - commemorates the passage of the law on permanent neutrality
**Constitution:** 1920; revised 1929; reinstated 1 May 1945; note - during the period 1 May 1934-1 May 1945 there was a fascist (corporative) constitution in place
**Legal system:** civil law system with Roman law origin; judicial review of legislative acts by the Constitutional Court; separate administrative and civil/penal supreme courts; accepts compulsory ICJ jurisdiction
**Suffrage:** 16 years of age; universal; note - reduced from 18 years of age in 2007
**Executive branch:**
*chief of state:* President Heinz FISCHER (SPOe) (since 8 July 2004)
*head of government:* Chancellor Werner FAYMANN (SPOe) (since 2 December 2008); Vice Chancellor Josef PROELL (OeVP) (since 2 December 2008)
*cabinet:* Council of Ministers chosen by the president on the advice of the chancellor
*elections:* president elected by direct popular vote for a six-year term (eligible for a second term); presidential election last held 25 April 2004 (next to be held in April 2010); chancellor formally chosen by the president but determined by the coalition parties forming a parliamentary majority; vice chancellor chosen by the president on the advice of the chancellor
*election results:* Heinz FISCHER elected president; percent of vote - Heinz FISCHER 52.4%, Benita FERRERO-WALDNER 47.6%
*note:* government coalition - SPOe and OeVP
**Legislative branch:** bicameral Federal Assembly or Bundesversammlung consists of Federal Council or Bundesrat (62 seats; members chosen by state parliaments with each state receiving 3 to 12 members in proportion to its population; members serve five- or six-year terms) and the National Council or Nationalrat (183 seats; members elected by direct popular vote to serve five-year terms)
*elections:* National Council - last held 28 September 2008 (next to be held by September 2013)
*election results:* National Council - percent of vote by

party - SPOe 29.3%, OeVP 26%, FPOe 17.5%, BZOe 10.7%, Greens 10.4%, other 6.1%; seats by party - SPOe 57, OeVP 51, FPOe 34, BZOe 21, Greens 20
**Judicial branch:** Supreme Judicial Court or Oberster Gerichtshof; Administrative Court or Verwaltungsgerichtshof; Constitutional Court or Verfassungsgerichtshof
**Political parties and leaders:** Alliance for the Future of Austria or BZOe [Josef BUCHER]; Austrian People's Party or OeVP [Josef PROELL]; Freedom Party of Austria or FPOe [Heinz Christian STRACHE]; Social Democratic Party of Austria or SPOe [Werner FAYMANN]; The Greens [Eva GLAWISCHNIG]
**Political pressure groups and leaders:** Austrian Trade Union Federation or OeGB (nominally independent but primarily Social Democratic); Federal Economic Chamber; OeVP-oriented Association of Austrian Industrialists or IV; Roman Catholic Church, including its chief lay organization, Catholic Action
*other:* three composite leagues of the Austrian People's Party or OeVP representing business, labor, farmers, and other nongovernment organizations in the areas of environment and human rights
**International organization participation:** ACCT (observer), ADB (nonregional member), AfDB (nonregional member), Australia Group, BIS, BSEC (observer), CE, CEI, CERN, EAPC, EBRD, EIB, EMU, ESA, EU, FAO, G-9, IADB, IAEA, IBRD, ICAO, ICC, ICCt, ICRM, IDA, IEA, IFAD, IFC, IFRCS, ILO, IMF, IMO, Interpol, IOC, IOM, IPU, ISO, ITSO, ITU, ITUC, MIGA, MINURSO, NAM (guest), NEA, NSG, OAS (observer), OECD, OIF (observer), OPCW, OSCE, Paris Club, PCA, PFP, Schengen Convention, SECI (observer), UN, UNCTAD, UNDOF, UNESCO, UNFICYP, UNHCR, UNIDO, UNOMIG, UNTSO, UNWTO, UPU, WCL, WCO, WEU (observer), WFTU, WHO, WIPO, WMO, WTO, ZC
**Diplomatic representation in the US:**
*chief of mission:* Ambassador Christian PROSL
*chancery:* 3524 International Court NW, Washington, DC 20008-3035
*telephone:* [1] (202) 895-6700
*FAX:* [1] (202) 895-6750
*consulate(s) general:* Chicago, Los Angeles, New York
**Diplomatic representation from the US:**
*chief of mission:* Ambassador (vacant); Charge d'Affaires Scott F. KILNER
*embassy:* Boltzmanngasse 16, A-1090, Vienna
*mailing address:* use embassy street address
*telephone:* [43] (1) 31339-0
*FAX:* [43] (1) 3100682
**Flag description:** three equal horizontal bands of red (top), white, and red

## Economy

**Economy - overview:** Austria, with its well-developed market economy and high standard of living, is closely tied to other EU economies, especially Germany's. Its economy features a large service sector, a sound industrial sector, and a small,

# Austria (continued)

but highly developed agricultural sector. Following several years of solid foreign demand for Austrian exports and record employment growth, the global economic downturn in 2008 led to a recession that is likely to persist through 2009. The government's stabilization measures could increase the budget deficit to about 2.8% of GDP in 2009 and above 3% in 2010, from about 0.6% in 2008. The Austrian economy has benefited greatly in the past from strong commercial relations, especially in the banking and insurance sectors, with central, eastern, and southeastern Europe, but these sectors have been vulnerable to recent international financial instabilities, and some of Austria's largest banks have required government support. Even after the global economic outlook improves, Austria will need to continue restructuring, emphasizing knowledge-based sectors of the economy, and encouraging greater labor flexibility and greater labor participation to offset its aging population and exceedingly low fertility rate.

**GDP (purchasing power parity):**
$325 billion (2008 est.)
$319.9 billion (2007)
$314 billion (2006)
note: data are in 2008 US dollars

**GDP (official exchange rate):** $432.4 billion (2008 est.)

**GDP - real growth rate:**
1.6% (2008 est.)
3.1% (2007 est.)
3.4% (2006 est.)

**GDP - per capita (PPP):**
$39,200 (2008 est.)
$39,500 (2007 est.)
$38,300 (2006 est.)
note: data are in 2008 US dollars

**GDP - composition by sector:**
agriculture: 1.9%
industry: 30.6%
services: 67.4% (2008 est.)

**Labor force:** 3.493 million (2008 est.)

**Labor force - by occupation:**
agriculture: 5.5%
industry: 27.5%
services: 67% (2005 est.)

**Unemployment rate:**
3.7% (2008 est.)
4.4% (2007 est.)

**Population below poverty line:** 5.9% (2004)

**Household income or consumption by percentage share:**
lowest 10%: 3.3%
highest 10%: 22.5% (2004)

**Distribution of family income - Gini index:** 26 (2007)

**Investment (gross fixed):** 20.7% of GDP (2008 est.)

**Budget:**
revenues: $198.6 billion
expenditures: $203 billion (2008 est.)

**Public debt:** 58.8% of GDP (2008 est.)

**Inflation rate (consumer prices):**
3.7% (2008 est.)
2.2% (2007 est.)

**Central bank discount rate:** 4%
note: this is the European Central Bank's rate on the marginal lending facility, which offers overnight credit to banks in the euro area

**Commercial bank prime lending rate:** 6.3% (31 December 2007)

**Stock of money:** NA
note: see entry for the European Union for money supply in the euro area; the European Central Bank (ECB) controls monetary policy for the 16 members of the Economic and Monetary Union (EMU); individual members of the EMU do not control the quantity of money and quasi money circulating within their own borders

**Stock of quasi money:** NA

**Stock of domestic credit:** $548.5 billion (31 December 2008)

**Market value of publicly traded shares:** $228.7 billion (31 December 2007)

**Agriculture - products:** grains, potatoes, sugar beets, wine, fruit; dairy products, cattle, pigs, poultry; lumber

**Industries:** construction, machinery, vehicles and parts, food, metals, chemicals, lumber and wood processing, paper and paperboard, communications equipment, tourism

**Industrial production growth rate:** 4.4% (2008 est.)

**Electricity - production:** 59.31 billion kWh (2007 est.)

**Electricity - consumption:** 62.35 billion kWh (2006 est.)

**Electricity - exports:** 18.47 billion kWh (2007 est.)

**Electricity - imports:** 28.5 billion kWh (2007 est.)

**Oil - production:** 24,920 bbl/day (2007 est.)

**Oil - consumption:** 289,400 bbl/day (2007 est.)

**Oil - exports:** 46,300 bbl/day (2005)

**Oil - imports:** 313,500 bbl/day (2005)

**Oil - proved reserves:** 50 million bbl (1 January 2008 est.)

**Natural gas - production:** 1.848 billion cu m (2007 est.)

**Natural gas - consumption:** 8.436 billion cu m (2007 est.)

**Natural gas - exports:** 2.767 billion cu m (2007 est.)

**Natural gas - imports:** 9.658 billion cu m (2007 est.)

**Natural gas - proved reserves:** 16.14 billion cu m (1 January 2008 est.)

**Current account balance:** $10.63 billion (2008 est.)

**Exports:** $163.3 billion f.o.b. (2008 est.)

**Exports - commodities:** machinery and equipment, motor vehicles and parts, paper and paperboard, metal goods, chemicals, iron and steel, textiles, foodstuffs

**Exports - partners:** Germany 29.8%, Italy 8.8%, US 4.9%, Switzerland 4.3% (2007)

**Imports:** $183.4 billion f.o.b. (2008 est.)

**Imports - commodities:** machinery and equipment, motor vehicles, chemicals, metal goods, oil and oil products; foodstuffs

**Imports - partners:** Germany 45.5%, Italy 7.1%, Switzerland 5%, Netherlands 4.3% (2007)

**Reserves of foreign exchange and gold:** $18.22 billion (2008 est.)

**Debt - external:** $752.5 billion (30 June 2007)

**Stock of direct foreign investment - at home:** $276.9 billion (2008 est.)

**Stock of direct foreign investment - abroad:** $275.2 billion (2008 est.)

**Exchange rates:** euros (EUR) per US dollar - 0.6827 (2008 est.), 0.7345 (2007), 0.7964 (2006), 0.8041 (2005), 0.8054 (2004)

## Communications

**Telephones - main lines in use:** 3.374 million (2007)

**Telephones - mobile cellular:** 9.768 million (2007)

**Telephone system:**
general assessment: highly developed and efficient
domestic: fixed-line subscribership has been in decline since the mid-1990s with mobile-cellular subscribership eclipsing it by the late 1990s; the fiber-optic net is very extensive; all telephone applications and Internet services are available
international: country code - 43; satellite earth stations -15; in addition, there are about 600 VSATs (very small aperture terminals) (2007)

**Radio broadcast stations:** AM 2, FM 65 (plus several hundred repeaters), shortwave 1 (2001)

**Television broadcast stations:** 10 (plus more than 1,000 repeaters) (2001)

**Internet country code:** .at

**Internet hosts:** 2.806 million (2008)

**Internet users:** 4.277 million (2007)

## Transportation

**Airports:** 55 (2008)

**Airports - with paved runways:**
total: 25
over 3,047 m: 1
2,438 to 3,047 m: 5
1,524 to 2,437 m: 1
914 to 1,523 m: 3
under 914 m: 15 (2008)

**Airports - with unpaved runways:**
total: 30
1,524 to 2,437 m: 1
914 to 1,523 m: 3
under 914 m: 26 (2008)

**Heliports:** 1 (2007)

**Pipelines:** gas 2,721 km; oil 663 km; refined products 157 km (2008)

**Railways:**
total: 6,383 km
standard gauge: 5,924 km 1.435-m gauge (3,772 km electrified)
narrow gauge: 371 km 1.000-m gauge; 88 km 0.760-m gauge (25 km electrified) (2006)

# Austria *(continued)*

**Roadways:**
*total:* 107,262 km
*paved:* 107,262 km (includes 1,677 km of expressways) (2006)
**Waterways:** 358 km (2007)
**Merchant marine:**
*total:* 4
*by type:* cargo 2, container 2
*foreign-owned:* 2 (Netherlands 2)
*registered in other countries:* 4 (Cyprus 1, Malta 1, Saint Vincent and the Grenadines 2) (2008)
**Ports and terminals:** Enns, Krems, Linz, Vienna

## Military

**Military branches:** Land Forces (KdoLdSK), Air Forces (KdoLuSK)
**Military service age and obligation:** 18-35 years of age for compulsory military service; 16 years of age for male or female voluntary service; service obligation 6 months of training, followed by an 8-year reserve obligation (2008)
**Manpower available for military service:**
*males age 16-49:* 1,986,411
*females age 16-49:* 1,944,834 (2008 est.)
**Manpower fit for military service:**
*males age 16-49:* 1,607,456
*females age 16-49:* 1,576,335 (2009 est.)
**Manpower reaching militarily significant age annually:**
*male:* 50,540
*female:* 48,042 (2009 est.)
**Military expenditures:** 0.9% of GDP (2005 est.)

## Transnational Issues

**Disputes - international:** while threats of international legal action never materialized in 2007, 915,220 Austrians, with the support of the newly elected Freedom Party, signed a petition in January 2008, demanding that Austria block the Czech Republic's accession to the EU unless Prague closed its nuclear power plant in Temelin, bordering Austria
**Illicit drugs:** transshipment point for Southwest Asian heroin and South American cocaine destined for Western Europe; increasing consumption of European-produced synthetic drugs

# Azerbaijan

## Introduction

**Background:** Azerbaijan - a nation with a majority-Turkic and majority-Muslim population - was briefly independent from 1918 to 1920; it regained its independence after the collapse of the Soviet Union in 1991. Despite a 1994 cease-fire, Azerbaijan has yet to resolve its conflict with Armenia over the Azerbaijani Nagorno-Karabakh region (largely Armenian populated). Azerbaijan has lost 16% of its territory and must support some 600,000 internally displaced persons as a result of the conflict. Corruption is ubiquitous, and the government has been accused of authoritarianism. Although the poverty rate has been reduced in recent years, the promise of widespread wealth from development of Azerbaijan's energy sector remains largely unfulfilled.

## Geography

**Location:** Southwestern Asia, bordering the Caspian Sea, between Iran and Russia, with a small European portion north of the Caucasus range
**Geographic coordinates:** 40 30 N, 47 30 E
**Map references:** Asia
**Area:**
*total:* 86,600 sq km
*land:* 86,100 sq km
*water:* 500 sq km
*note:* includes the exclave of Naxcivan Autonomous Republic and the Nagorno-Karabakh region; the region's autonomy was abolished by Azerbaijani Supreme Soviet on 26 November 1991
**Area - comparative:** slightly smaller than Maine
**Land boundaries:**
*total:* 2,013 km
*border countries:* Armenia (with Azerbaijan-proper) 566 km, Armenia (with Azerbaijan-Naxcivan exclave) 221 km, Georgia 322 km, Iran (with Azerbaijan-proper) 432 km, Iran (with Azerbaijan-Naxcivan exclave) 179 km, Russia 284 km, Turkey 9 km

**Coastline:** 0 km (landlocked); note - Azerbaijan borders the Caspian Sea (713 km)
**Maritime claims:** none (landlocked)
**Climate:** dry, semiarid steppe
**Terrain:** large, flat Kur-Araz Ovaligi (Kura-Araks Lowland) (much of it below sea level) with Great Caucasus Mountains to the north, Qarabag Yaylasi (Karabakh Upland) in west; Baku lies on Abseron Yasaqligi (Apsheron Peninsula) that juts into Caspian Sea
**Elevation extremes:**
*lowest point:* Caspian Sea -28 m
*highest point:* Bazarduzu Dagi 4,485 m
**Natural resources:** petroleum, natural gas, iron ore, nonferrous metals, bauxite
**Land use:**
*arable land:* 20.62%
*permanent crops:* 2.61%
*other:* 76.77% (2005)
**Irrigated land:** 14,550 sq km (2003)
**Total renewable water resources:** 30.3 cu km (1997)
**Freshwater withdrawal (domestic/industrial/agricultural):**
*total:* 17.25 cu km/yr (5%/28%/68%)
*per capita:* 2,051 cu m/yr (2000)
**Natural hazards:** droughts
**Environment - current issues:** local scientists consider the Abseron Yasaqligi (Apsheron Peninsula) (including Baku and Sumqayit) and the Caspian Sea to be the ecologically most devastated area in the world because of severe air, soil, and water pollution; soil pollution results from oil spills, from the use of DDT pesticide, and from toxic defoliants used in the production of cotton
**Environment - international agreements:**
*party to:* Air Pollution, Biodiversity, Climate Change, Climate Change-Kyoto Protocol, Desertification, Endangered Species, Hazardous Wastes, Marine Dumping, Ozone Layer Protection, Ship Pollution, Wetlands
*signed, but not ratified:* none of the selected agreements
**Geography - note:** both the main area of the country and the Naxcivan exclave are landlocked

## People

**Population:** 8,238,672 (July 2009 est.)
**Age structure:**
*0-14 years:* 23.9% (male 1,042,132/female 926,495)
*15-64 years:* 69.4% (male 2,807,717/female 2,908,221)
*65 years and over:* 6.7% (male 204,410/female 349,697) (2009 est.)
**Median age:**
*total:* 28.2 years
*male:* 26.6 years
*female:* 30 years (2009 est.)
**Population growth rate:** 0.762% (2009 est.)
**Birth rate:** 17.62 births/1,000 population (2009 est.)
**Death rate:** 8.32 deaths/1,000 population (2008 est.)

# Azerbaijan *(continued)*

**Net migration rate:** -1.69 migrant(s)/1,000 population (2009 est.)

**Urbanization:**

*urban population:* 52% of total population (2008)

*rate of urbanization:* 1% annual rate of change (2005-10 est.)

**Sex ratio:**

*at birth:* 1.13 male(s)/female

*under 15 years:* 1.12 male(s)/female

*15-64 years:* 0.96 male(s)/female

*65 years and over:* 0.58 male(s)/female

*total population:* 0.97 male(s)/female (2009 est.)

**Infant mortality rate:**

*total:* 54.6 deaths/1,000 live births

*male:* 60.2 deaths/1,000 live births

*female:* 48.27 deaths/1,000 live births (2009 est.)

**Life expectancy at birth:**

*total population:* 66.66 years

*male:* 62.53 years

*female:* 71.34 years (2009 est.)

**Total fertility rate:** 2.04 children born/woman (2009 est.)

**HIV/AIDS - adult prevalence rate:** less than 0.2% (2007 est.)

**HIV/AIDS - people living with HIV/AIDS:** 7,800 (2007 est.)

**HIV/AIDS - deaths:** fewer than 100 (2007 est.)

**Nationality:**

*noun:* Azerbaijani(s)

*adjective:* Azerbaijani

**Ethnic groups:** Azeri 90.6%, Dagestani 2.2%, Russian 1.8%, Armenian 1.5%, other 3.9% (1999 census)

*note:* almost all Armenians live in the separatist Nagorno-Karabakh region

**Religions:** Muslim 93.4%, Russian Orthodox 2.5%, Armenian Orthodox 2.3%, other 1.8% (1995 est.)

*note:* religious affiliation is still nominal in Azerbaijan; percentages for actual practicing adherents are much lower

**Languages:** Azerbaijani (Azeri) 90.3%, Lezgi 2.2%, Russian 1.8%, Armenian 1.5%, other 3.3%, unspecified 1% (1999 census)

**Literacy:**

*definition:* age 15 and over can read and write

*total population:* 98.8%

*male:* 99.5%

*female:* 98.2% (1999 census)

**School life expectancy (primary to tertiary education):**

*total:* 11 years

*male:* 11 years

*female:* 11 years (2006)

**Education expenditures:** 2.1% of GDP (2006)

## Government

**Country name:**

*conventional long form:* Republic of Azerbaijan

*conventional short form:* Azerbaijan

*local long form:* Azarbaycan Respublikasi

*local short form:* Azarbaycan

*former:* Azerbaijan Soviet Socialist Republic

**Government type:** republic

**Capital:**

*name:* Baku (Baki, Baky)

*geographic coordinates:* 40 23 N, 49 52 E

*time difference:* UTC+4 (9 hours ahead of Washington, DC during Standard Time)

*daylight saving time:* +1hr, begins last Sunday in March; ends last Sunday in October

**Administrative divisions:** 59 rayons (rayonlar; rayon - singular), 11 cities (saharlar; sahar - singular), 1 autonomous republic (muxtar respublika)

*rayons:* Abseron Rayonu, Agcabadi Rayonu, Agdam Rayonu, Agdas Rayonu, Agstafa Rayonu, Agsu Rayonu, Astara Rayonu, Balakan Rayonu, Barda Rayonu, Beylaqan Rayonu, Bilasuvar Rayonu, Cabrayil Rayonu, Calilabad Rayonu, Daskasan Rayonu, Davaci Rayonu, Fuzuli Rayonu, Gadabay Rayonu, Goranboy Rayonu, Goycay Rayonu, Haciqabul Rayonu, Imisli Rayonu, Ismayilli Rayonu, Kalbacar Rayonu, Kurdamir Rayonu, Lacin Rayonu, Lankaran Rayonu, Lerik Rayonu, Masalli Rayonu, Neftcala Rayonu, Oguz Rayonu, Qabala Rayonu, Qax Rayonu, Qazax Rayonu, Qobustan Rayonu, Quba Rayonu, Qubadli Rayonu, Qusar Rayonu, Saatli Rayonu, Sabirabad Rayonu, Saki Rayonu, Salyan Rayonu, Samaxi Rayonu, Samkir Rayonu, Samux Rayonu, Siyazan Rayonu, Susa Rayonu, Tartar Rayonu, Tovuz Rayonu, Ucar Rayonu, Xacmaz Rayonu, Xanlar Rayonu, Xizi Rayonu, Xocali Rayonu, Xocavand Rayonu, Yardimli Rayonu, Yevlax Rayonu, Zangilan Rayonu, Zaqatala Rayonu, Zardab Rayonu

*cities:* Ali Bayramli Sahari, Baki Sahari, Ganca Sahari, Lankaran Sahari, Mingacevir Sahari, Naftalan Sahari, Saki Sahari, Sumqayit Sahari, Susa Sahari, Xankandi Sahari, Yevlax Sahari

*autonomous republic:* Naxcivan Muxtar Respublikasi

**Independence:** 30 August 1991 (from the Soviet Union)

**National holiday:** Founding of the Democratic Republic of Azerbaijan, 28 May (1918)

**Constitution:** adopted 12 November 1995; modified by referendum 24 August 2002

**Legal system:** based on civil law system; has not accepted compulsory ICJ jurisdiction

**Suffrage:** 18 years of age; universal

**Executive branch:**

*chief of state:* President Ilham ALIYEV (since 31 October 2003)

*head of government:* Prime Minister Artur RASIZADE (since 4 November 2003); First Deputy Prime Minister Yaqub EYYUBOV (since June 2006)

*cabinet:* Council of Ministers appointed by the president and confirmed by the National Assembly

*elections:* president elected by popular vote to a five-year term (eligible for a second term); election last held 15 October 2008 (next to be held in October 2013); prime minister and first deputy prime minister appointed by the president and confirmed by the National Assembly

*election results:* Ilham ALIYEV reelected president; percent of vote - Ilham ALIYEV 89%, Igbal AGHAZADE 2.9%, five other candidates with smaller percentages

*note:* several political parties boycotted the election due to unfair conditions; OSCE observers concluded that the election did not meet international standards

**Legislative branch:** unicameral National Assembly or Milli Mejlis (125 seats; members elected by popular vote to serve five-year terms)

*elections:* last held 6 November 2005 (next to be held in November 2010)

*election results:* percent of vote by party - NA; seats by party - Yeni 58, Azadliq coalition 8, CSP 2, Motherland 2, other parties with single seats 9, independents 42, undetermined 4

**Judicial branch:** Supreme Court

**Political parties and leaders:** Azadliq (Freedom) coalition (Popular Front Party, Liberal Party, Citizens' Development Party); Azerbaijan Democratic Party or ADP [Sardar JALALOGLU]; Azerbaijan Democratic Reforms Party (ADRP) Youth Movement [Ramin HAJILI]; Azerbaijan Popular Front or APF, now split in two [Ali KARIMLI, leader of "Reform" APF party; Mirmahmud MIRALI-OGLU, leader of "Classic" APF party]; Azerbaijan Public Forum [Eldar NAMAZOV]; Citizens' Development Party [Ali ALIYEV]; Civil Solidarity Party or CSP [Sabir RUSTAMKHANLY]; Dalga Youth Movement [Vafa JAFAROVA]; Green Party [Mais GULALIYEV and Tarana MAMMADOVA]; Hope (Umid) Party [Iqbal AGAZADE]; Ireli Youth Movement [Jeyhun OSMANLI, Roya TALIBOVA, Farhad MAMMADOV, Elnara GARIBOVA, Elnur MAMMADOV, Ziya ALIYEV]; Justice Party [Ilyas ISMAILOV]; Liberal Party of Azerbaijan [Lala Shovkat HACIYEVA]; Magam Youth Movement [Emin HUSEYNOV]; Motherland Party [Fazail AGAMALI]; Musavat (Equality) [Isa GAMBAR, chairman]; Musavat Party Youth Movement [Elnur MAMMADLI]; National Democratic Party or Grey Wolves (Nationalist, Pan-Turkic) [Iskender HAMIDOV]; Open Society Party [Rasul GULIYEV, in exile in the US]; Party for National Independence of Azerbaijan or PNIA [Ayaz RUSTAMOV]; Popular Front Party Youth Movement [Seymur KHAZIYEV]; Social Democratic Party of Azerbaijan or SDP [Araz ALIZADE and Ayaz MUTALIBOV (in exile)]; Turkish Nationalist Party [Vugar BAYTURAN]; United Azerbaijan Party [Karrar ABILOV]; United Azerbaijan National Unity Party [Hajibaba AZIMOV]; United Party [Tahir KARIMLI]; Yeni (New) Azerbaijan Party [President Ilham ALIYEV]; Yeni Azerbaijan Party Youth Movement [Ramil HASANOV]; Yox (No) Youth Movement [Ali ISMAYILOV]

*note:* opposition parties regularly factionalize and form new parties;

**Political pressure groups and leaders:** Armenian Nagorno-Karabakh Republic (self-proclaimed); Karabakh Liberation Organization; Sadval, Lezgin movement; Talysh independence movement; Union of Pro-Azerbaijani Forces or UPAF

**International organization participation:** ADB, BSEC, CE, CIS, EAPC, EBRD, ECO, FAO, GCTU, GUAM, IAEA, IBRD, ICAO, ICRM, IDA, IDB, IFAD, IFC, IFRCS, ILO, IMF, IMO, Interpol, IOC, IOM, IPU, ISO, ITSO, ITU, ITUC, MIGA, NAM (observer), OAS

# Azerbaijan (continued)

(observer), OIC, OPCW, OSCE, PFP, SECI (observer), UN, UNCTAD, UNESCO, UNIDO, UNWTO, UPU, WCO, WFTU, WHO, WIPO, WMO, WTO (observer)

**Diplomatic representation in the US:**
*chief of mission:* Ambassador Yashar ALIYEV
*chancery:* 2741 34th Street NW, Washington, DC 20008
*telephone:* [1] (202) 337-3500
*FAX:* [1] (202) 337-5911
*Consulate(s) general:* Los Angeles

**Diplomatic representation from the US:**
*chief of mission:* Ambassador Anne E. DERSE
*embassy:* 83 Azadlig Prospecti, Baku AZ1007
*mailing address:* American Embassy Baku, US Department of State, 7050 Baku Place, Washington, DC 20521-7050
*telephone:* [994] (12) 4980-335 through 337
*FAX:* [994] (12) 4656-671

**Flag description:** three equal horizontal bands of blue (top), red, and green; a crescent and eight-pointed star in white are centered in red band

## Economy

**Economy - overview:** Azerbaijan's high economic growth during 2006-08 is attributable to large and growing oil exports, but the non-energy sector also featured double-digit growth in 2008, spurred by growth in the construction, banking, and real estate sectors. However, the current global economic slowdown presents some challenges for the Azerbaijani economy as oil prices have plummeted since mid-2008 and local banks face a more uncertain international financial environment. Azerbaijan's oil production declined through 1997, but has registered an increase every year since. Negotiation of production-sharing arrangements (PSAs) with foreign firms, which have committed $60 billion to long-term oilfield development, should generate the funds needed to spur future industrial development. Oil production under the first of these PSAs, with the Azerbaijan International Operating Company, began in November 1997. A consortium of Western oil companies built a $4 billion pipeline from Baku to Turkey's Mediterranean port of Ceyhan which will pump 1.2 million barrels a day from a large offshore field when at full capacity. Azerbaijan shares all the formidable problems of the former Soviet republics in making the transition from a command to a market economy, but its considerable energy resources brighten its medium-term prospects. Baku has only recently begun making progress on economic reform, and old economic ties and structures are slowly being replaced. Several other obstacles impede Azerbaijan's economic progress: the need for stepped up foreign investment in the non-energy sector, the continuing conflict with Armenia over the Nagorno-Karabakh region, pervasive corruption, and potential for a sharp downturn in the construction and real estate sectors. Trade with Russia and the other former Soviet republics is declining in importance, while trade is building with Turkey and the nations of Europe. Long-term prospects will depend on world oil prices, the location of new oil and gas pipelines in the region, and Azerbaijan's ability to manage its energy wealth to promote sustainable growth in non-energy sectors of the economy and spur employment.

**GDP (purchasing power parity):**
$73.65 billion (2008 est.)
$66 billion (2007)
$53.48 billion (2006)
*note:* data are in 2008 US dollars

**GDP (official exchange rate):** $53.26 billion (2008 est.)

**GDP - real growth rate:**
11.6% (2008 est.)
23.4% (2007 est.)
30.5% (2006 est.)

**GDP - per capita (PPP):**
$9,000 (2008 est.)
$8,100 (2007 est.)
$6,600 (2006 est.)
*note:* data are in 2008 US dollars

**GDP - composition by sector:**
*agriculture:* 6%
*industry:* 62.6%
*services:* 31.4% (2008 est.)

**Labor force:** 5.782 million (2008 est.)

**Labor force - by occupation:**
*agriculture:* 39.3%
*industry:* 12.1%
*services:* 48.6% (2005)

**Unemployment rate:**
0.8% (2008 est.)
1% (2007 est.)

**Population below poverty line:** 24% (2005 est.)

**Household income or consumption by percentage share:**
*lowest 10%:* 3.1%
*highest 10%:* 29.5% (2001)

**Distribution of family income - Gini index:** 36.5 (2001)

**Investment (gross fixed):** 21% of GDP (2008 est.)

**Budget:**
*revenues:* $14.51 billion
*expenditures:* $15.66 billion (2008 est.)

**Public debt:** 5.2% of GDP (2008 est.)

**Inflation rate (consumer prices):**
21.6% (2008 est.)
16.7% (2007 est.)

**Central bank discount rate:** 8%
*note:* this is the Refinancing Rate, the key policy rate for the National Bank of Azerbaijan (31 December 2008)

**Commercial bank prime lending rate:** 19.13% (31 December 2007)

**Stock of money:** $4.261 billion (31 December 2007)

**Stock of quasi money:** $2.593 billion (31 December 2007)

**Stock of domestic credit:** $5.726 billion (31 December 2007)

**Market value of publicly traded shares:** $NA

**Agriculture - products:** cotton, grain, rice, grapes, fruit, vegetables, tea, tobacco; cattle, pigs, sheep, goats

**Industries:** petroleum and natural gas, petroleum products, oilfield equipment; steel, iron ore; cement; chemicals and petrochemicals; textiles

**Industrial production growth rate:** 12% (2008 est.)

**Electricity - production:** 23.8 billion kWh (2007 est.)

**Electricity - consumption:** 27.5 billion kWh (2007 est.)

**Electricity - exports:** 800 million kWh (2007 est.)

**Electricity - imports:** 500 million kWh (2007 est.)

**Oil - production:** 1.099 million bbl/day (2008 est.)

**Oil - consumption:** 160,000 bbl/day (2007 est.)

**Oil - exports:** 795,600 bbl/day (2007 est.)

**Oil - imports:** 4,267 bbl/day (2005)

**Oil - proved reserves:** 7 billion bbl (1 January 2008 est.)

**Natural gas - production:** 9.77 billion cu m (2007 est.)

**Natural gas - consumption:** 9.77 billion cu m (2007 est.)

**Natural gas - exports:** 0 cu m (2007 est.)

**Natural gas - imports:** 0 cu m (2005)

**Natural gas - proved reserves:** 849.5 billion cu m (1 January 2008 est.)

**Current account balance:** $19.36 billion (2008 est.)

**Exports:** $38.28 billion f.o.b. (2008 est.)

**Exports - commodities:** oil and gas 90%, machinery, cotton, foodstuffs

**Exports - partners:** Turkey 17.4%, Italy 15.5%, Russia 8.7%, Iran 7.2%, Indonesia 6.4%, Israel 6.1%, Georgia 5.7%, US 4.8%, France 4.3% (2007)

**Imports:** $7.496 billion f.o.b. (2008 est.)

**Imports - commodities:** machinery and equipment, oil products, foodstuffs, metals, chemicals

**Imports - partners:** Russia 17.6%, Turkey 10.9%, Germany 8.2%, Ukraine 8.2%, UK 7.2%, Japan 5.2%, China 4.9%, US 4.7% (2007)

**Reserves of foreign exchange and gold:** $8.5 billion (31 December 2008 est.)

**Debt - external:** $2.733 billion (31 December 2008 est.)

**Stock of direct foreign investment - at home:** $7.329 billion (2008 est.)

**Stock of direct foreign investment - abroad:** $5.812 billion (2008 est.)

**Exchange rates:** Azerbaijani manats (AZN) per US dollar - 0.8219 (2008 est.), 0.8581 (2007), 0.8934 (2006), 4,727.1 (2005), 4,913.48 (2004)
*note:* on 1 January 2006 Azerbaijan revalued its currency, with 5,000 old manats equal to 1 new manat

## Communications

**Telephones - main lines in use:** 1.254 million (2007)

**Telephones - mobile cellular:** 4.3 million (2007)

**Telephone system:**
*general assessment:* inadequate; requires considerable expansion and modernization;

# Azerbaijan (continued)

teledensity of 15 main lines per 100 persons is low; mobile-cellular penetration is increasing and is currently about 50 telephones per 100 persons *domestic:* fixed-line telephony and a broad range of other telecom services are controlled by a state-owned telecommunications monopoly and growth has been stagnant; more competition exists in the mobile-cellular market with three providers in 2006; satellite service connects Baku to a modern switch in its exclave of Naxcivan *international:* country code - 994; the Trans-Asia-Europe (TAE) fiber-optic link transits Azerbaijan providing international connectivity to neighboring countries; the old Soviet system of cable and microwave is still serviceable; satellite earth stations - 2 (2007)

**Radio broadcast stations:** AM 10, FM 17, shortwave 1 (1998)
**Television broadcast stations:** 2 (1997)
**Internet country code:** .az
**Internet hosts:** 6,995 (2008)
**Internet users:** 1.036 million (2007)

## Transportation

**Airports:** 35 (2008)
**Airports - with paved runways:**
*total:* 27
*over 3,047 m:* 2
*2,438 to 3,047 m:* 6
*1,524 to 2,437 m:* 13
*914 to 1,523 m:* 4
*under 914 m:* 2 (2008)
**Airports - with unpaved runways:**
*total:* 8
*914 to 1,523 m:* 1
*under 914 m:* 7 (2008)
**Heliports:** 1 (2007)
**Pipelines:** condensate 1 km; gas 3,361 km; oil 1,424 km(2008)
**Railways:**
*total:* 2,122 km
*broad gauge:* 2,122 km 1.520-m gauge (1,278 km electrified) (2006)
**Roadways:**
*total:* 59,141 km
*paved:* 29,210 km
*unpaved:* 29,931 km (2004)
**Merchant marine:**
*total:* 89
*by type:* cargo 26, passenger 2, passenger/cargo 9, petroleum tanker 46, roll on/roll off 3, specialized tanker 3
*registered in other countries:* 3 (Malta 2, Panama 1) (2008)
**Ports and terminals:** Baku (Baki)

## Military

**Military branches:** Army, Navy, Air and Air Defense Forces (2008)
**Military service age and obligation:** men between 18 and 35 are liable for military service; 18 years of age for voluntary military service; length of military service is 18 months and 12 months for university graduates (2006)
**Manpower available for military service:**
*males age 16-49:* 2,278,888
*females age 16-49:* 2,291,770 (2008 est.)
**Manpower fit for military service:**
*males age 16-49:* 1,727,464
*females age 16-49:* 1,944,260 (2009 est.)
**Manpower reaching militarily significant age annually:**
*male:* 90,416
*female:* 85,344 (2009 est.)
**Military expenditures:** 2.6% of GDP (2005 est.)

## Transnational Issues

**Disputes - international:** Armenia supports ethnic Armenian secessionists in Nagorno-Karabakh and since the early 1990s has militarily occupied 16% of Azerbaijan; over 800,000 mostly ethnic Azerbaijanis were driven from the occupied lands and Armenia; about 230,000 ethnic Armenians were driven from their homes in Azerbaijan into Armenia and Nagorno-Karabakh; Azerbaijan seeks transit route through Armenia to connect to Naxcivan exclave; Organization for Security and Cooperation in Europe (OSCE) continues to mediate dispute; Azerbaijan, Kazakhstan, and Russia have ratified Caspian seabed delimitation treaties based on equidistance, while Iran continues to insist on an even one-fifth allocation and challenges Azerbaijan's hydrocarbon exploration in disputed waters; bilateral talks continue with Turkmenistan on dividing the seabed and contested oilfields in the middle of the Caspian; Azerbaijan and Georgia continue to discuss the alignment of their boundary at certain crossing areas
**Refugees and internally displaced persons:**
*refugees (country of origin):* 2,400 (Russia)
*IDPs:* 580,000-690,000 (conflict with Armenia over Nagorno-Karabakh) (2007)
**Trafficking in persons:**
*current situation:* Azerbaijan is primarily a source and transit country for men, women, and children trafficked for the purposes of commercial sexual exploitation and forced labor; women and some children from Azerbaijan are trafficked to Turkey and the UAE for the purpose of sexual exploitation; men and boys are trafficked to Russia for the purpose of forced labor; Azerbaijan serves as a transit country for victims from Uzbekistan, Kyrgyzstan, Kazakhstan, and Moldova trafficked to Turkey and the UAE for sexual exploitation

*tier rating:* Tier 2 Watch List - Azerbaijan is on the Tier 2 Watch List for its failure to provide evidence of increasing efforts to combat trafficking in persons, particularly efforts to investigate, prosecute, and punish traffickers; to address complicity among law enforcement personnel; and to adequately identify and protect victims in Azerbaijan; the government has yet to develop a much-needed mechanism to identify potential trafficking victims and refer them to safety and care; poor treatment of trafficking victims in courtrooms continues to be a problem (2008)
**Illicit drugs:** limited illicit cultivation of cannabis and opium poppy, mostly for CIS consumption; small government eradication program; transit point for Southwest Asian opiates bound for Russia and to a lesser extent the rest of Europe

# Bahamas, The

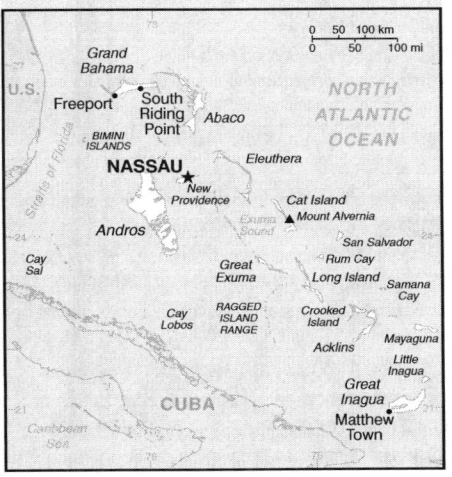

## Introduction

**Background:** Lucayan Indians inhabited the islands when Christopher COLUMBUS first set foot in the New World on San Salvador in 1492. British settlement of the islands began in 1647; the islands became a colony in 1783. Since attaining independence from the UK in 1973, The Bahamas have prospered through tourism and international banking and investment management. Because of its geography, the country is a major transshipment point for illegal drugs, particularly shipments to the US and Europe, and its territory is used for smuggling illegal migrants into the US.

## Geography

**Location:** Caribbean, chain of islands in the North Atlantic Ocean, southeast of Florida, northeast of Cuba

**Geographic coordinates:** 24 15 N, 76 00 W

**Map references:** Central America and the Caribbean

**Area:**
*total:* 13,940 sq km
*land:* 10,070 sq km
*water:* 3,870 sq km

**Area - comparative:** slightly smaller than Connecticut

**Land boundaries:** 0 km

**Coastline:** 3,542 km

**Maritime claims:**
*territorial sea:* 12 nm
*exclusive economic zone:* 200 nm

**Climate:** tropical marine; moderated by warm waters of Gulf Stream

**Terrain:** long, flat coral formations with some low rounded hills

**Elevation extremes:**
*lowest point:* Atlantic Ocean 0 m
*highest point:* Mount Alvernia, on Cat Island 63 m

**Natural resources:** salt, aragonite, timber, arable land

**Land use:**
*arable land:* 0.58%
*permanent crops:* 0.29%
*other:* 99.13% (2005)

**Irrigated land:** 10 sq km (2003)

**Total renewable water resources:** NA

**Natural hazards:** hurricanes and other tropical storms cause extensive flood and wind damage

**Environment - current issues:** coral reef decay; solid waste disposal

**Environment - international agreements:**
*party to:* Biodiversity, Climate Change, Climate Change-Kyoto Protocol, Desertification, Endangered Species, Hazardous Wastes, Law of the Sea, Ozone Layer Protection, Ship Pollution, Wetlands
*signed, but not ratified:* none of the selected agreements

**Geography - note:** strategic location adjacent to US and Cuba; extensive island chain of which 30 are inhabited

## People

**Population:** 309,156
*note:* estimates for this country explicitly take into account the effects of excess mortality due to AIDS; this can result in lower life expectancy, higher infant mortality, higher death rates, lower population growth rates, and changes in the distribution of population by age and sex than would otherwise be expected (July 2009 est.)

**Age structure:**
*0-14 years:* 25.9% (male 40,085/female 39,959)
*15-64 years:* 67.2% (male 102,154/female 105,482)
*65 years and over:* 6.9% (male 8,772/female 12,704) (2009 est.)

**Median age:**
*total:* 28.7 years
*male:* 27.9 years
*female:* 29.5 years (2009 est.)

**Population growth rate:** 0.536% (2009 est.)

**Birth rate:** 16.81 births/1,000 population (2009 est.)

**Death rate:** 9.22 deaths/1,000 population (2008 est.)

**Net migration rate:** -2.13 migrant(s)/1,000 population (2009 est.)

**Urbanization:**
*urban population:* 84% of total population (2008)
*rate of urbanization:* 1.4% annual rate of change (2005-10 est.)

**Sex ratio:**
*at birth:* 1.02 male(s)/female
*under 15 years:* 1 male(s)/female
*15-64 years:* 0.97 male(s)/female
*65 years and over:* 0.69 male(s)/female
*total population:* 0.96 male(s)/female (2009 est.)

**Infant mortality rate:**
*total:* 23.17 deaths/1,000 live births
*male:* 28.21 deaths/1,000 live births
*female:* 18.04 deaths/1,000 live births (2009 est.)

**Life expectancy at birth:**
*total population:* 65.78 years
*male:* 62.63 years
*female:* 68.98 years (2009 est.)

**Total fertility rate:** 2.1 children born/woman (2009 est.)

**HIV/AIDS - adult prevalence rate:** 3% (2007 est.)

**HIV/AIDS - people living with HIV/AIDS:** 6,200 (2007 est.)

**HIV/AIDS - deaths:** fewer than 200 (2007 est.)

**Nationality:**
*noun:* Bahamian(s)
*adjective:* Bahamian

**Ethnic groups:** black 85%, white 12%, Asian and Hispanic 3%

**Religions:** Baptist 35.4%, Anglican 15.1%, Roman Catholic 13.5%, Pentecostal 8.1%, Church of God 4.8%, Methodist 4.2%, other Christian 15.2%, none or unspecified 2.9%, other 0.8% (2000 census)

**Languages:** English (official), Creole (among Haitian immigrants)

**Literacy:**
*definition:* age 15 and over can read and write
*total population:* 95.6%
*male:* 94.7%
*female:* 96.5% (2003 est.)

**Education expenditures:** 3.6% of GDP (2000)

## Government

**Country name:**
*conventional long form:* Commonwealth of The Bahamas
*conventional short form:* The Bahamas

**Government type:** constitutional parliamentary democracy and a Commonwealth realm

**Capital:**
*name:* Nassau
*geographic coordinates:* 25 05 N, 77 21 W
*time difference:* UTC-5 (same time as Washington, DC during Standard Time)
*daylight saving time:* +1hr, begins second Sunday in March; ends first Sunday in November

**Administrative divisions:** 21 districts; Acklins and Crooked Islands, Bimini, Cat Island, Exuma, Freeport, Fresh Creek, Governor's Harbour, Green Turtle Cay, Harbour Island, High Rock, Inagua, Kemps Bay, Long Island, Marsh Harbour, Mayaguana, New Providence, Nichollstown and Berry Islands, Ragged Island, Rock Sound, Sandy Point, San Salvador, and Rum Cay

**Independence:** 10 July 1973 (from the UK)

**National holiday:** Independence Day, 10 July (1973)

**Constitution:** 10 July 1973

**Legal system:** based on English common law

**Suffrage:** 18 years of age; universal

**Executive branch:**
*chief of state:* Queen ELIZABETH II (since 6 February 1952); represented by Governor General Arthur D. HANNA (since 1 February 2006)
*head of government:* Prime Minister Hubert A. INGRAHAM (since 4 May 2007)
*cabinet:* Cabinet appointed by the governor general on the prime minister's recommendation
*elections:* the monarch is hereditary; governor general appointed by the monarch; following legislative

elections, the leader of the majority party or the leader of the majority coalition is usually appointed prime minister by the governor general; the prime minister recommends the deputy prime minister

**Legislative branch:** bicameral Parliament consists of the Senate (16 seats; members appointed by the governor general upon the advice of the prime minister and the opposition leader to serve five-year terms) and the House of Assembly (41 seats; members elected by direct popular vote to serve five-year terms); the government may dissolve the parliament and call elections at any time

*elections:* last held 2 May 2007 (next to be held by May 2012)

*election results:* percent of vote by party - FNM 49.86%, PLP 47.02%; seats by party - FNM 23, PLP 18

**Judicial branch:** Privy Council in London; Courts of Appeal; Supreme (lower) Court; Magistrates' Courts

**Political parties and leaders:** Free National Movement or FNM [Hubert INGRAHAM]; Progressive Liberal Party or PLP [Perry CHRISTIE]

**Political pressure groups and leaders:** Friends of the Environment

*other:* trade unions

**International organization participation:** ACP, C, Caricom, CDB, FAO, G-77, IADB, IBRD, ICAO, ICCt (signatory), ICFTU, ICRM, IDA, IFAD, IFC, IFRCS, ILO, IMF, IMO, IMSO, Interpol, IOC, IOM, ITSO, ITU, LAES, MIGA, NAM, OAS, OPANAL, OPCW (signatory), UN, UNCTAD, UNESCO, UNIDO, UNWTO, UPU, WCO, WFTU, WHO, WIPO, WMO, WTO (observer)

**Diplomatic representation in the US:**

*chief of mission:* Ambassador Cornelius A. SMITH

*chancery:* 2220 Massachusetts Avenue NW, Washington, DC 20008

*telephone:* [1] (202) 319-2660

*FAX:* [1] (202) 319-2668

*consulate(s) general:* Miami, New York

**Diplomatic representation from the US:**

*chief of mission:* Ambassador Ned L. SIEGEL

*embassy:* 42 Queen Street, Nassau, New Providence

*mailing address:* local or express mail address: P. O. Box N-8197, Nassau; US Department of State, 3370 Nassau Place, Washington, DC 20521-3370

*telephone:* [1] (242) 322-1181, 328-2206 (after hours)

*FAX:* [1] (242) 328-2206

**Flag description:** three equal horizontal bands of aquamarine (top), gold, and aquamarine, with a black equilateral triangle based on the hoist side

## Economy

**Economy - overview:** The Bahamas is one of the wealthiest Caribbean countries with an economy heavily dependent on tourism and offshore banking. Tourism together with tourism-driven construction and manufacturing accounts for approximately 60% of GDP and directly or indirectly employs half of the archipelago's labor force. Steady growth in tourism receipts and a boom in construction of new hotels, resorts, and residences had led to solid GDP growth in recent years,

but tourist arrivals have been on the decline since 2006 and will likely drop even further in 2009. Tourism, in turn, depends on growth in the US, the source of more than 80% of the visitors. To help offset the effect of the global economic downturn, particularly on employment, the INGRAHAM administration plans to engage in infrastructure projects. Financial services constitute the second-most important sector of the Bahamian economy and, when combined with business services, account for about 36% of GDP. However, since December 2000, when the government enacted new regulations on the financial sector, many international businesses have left The Bahamas. Manufacturing and agriculture combined contribute approximately a tenth of GDP and show little growth, despite government incentives aimed at those sectors. Overall growth prospects in the short run rest heavily on the fortunes of the tourism sector.

**GDP (purchasing power parity):**
$8.779 billion (2008 est.)
$8.649 billion (2007)
$8.413 billion (2006)
*note:* data are in 2008 US dollars

**GDP (official exchange rate):** $6.935 billion (2008 est.)

**GDP - real growth rate:**
1.5% (2008 est.)
2.8% (2007 est.)
4.6% (2006 est.)

**GDP - per capita (PPP):**
$28,600 (2008 est.)
$28,300 (2007 est.)
$27,700 (2006 est.)
*note:* data are in 2008 US dollars

**GDP - composition by sector:**
*agriculture:* 3%
*industry:* 7%
*services:* 90% (2001 est.)

**Labor force:** 181,900 (2006)

**Labor force - by occupation:** agriculture 5%, industry 5%, tourism 50%, other services 40% (2005 est.)

**Unemployment rate:**
7.6% (2006 est.)

**Population below poverty line:** 9.3% (2004)

**Household income or consumption by percentage share:**
*lowest 10%:* NA%
*highest 10%:* 27% (2000)

**Budget:**
*revenues:* $1.03 billion
*expenditures:* $1.03 billion (FY04/05)

**Inflation rate (consumer prices):**
2.4% (2007 est.)

**Central bank discount rate:** 5.25% (31 December 2007)

**Commercial bank prime lending rate:** 5.5% (31 December 2007)

**Stock of money:** $1.274 billion (31 December 2007)

**Stock of quasi money:** $4.324 billion (31 December 2007)

**Stock of domestic credit:** $7.395 billion (31 December 2007)

**Market value of publicly traded shares:** $NA

**Agriculture - products:** citrus, vegetables; poultry

**Industries:** tourism, banking, cement, oil transshipment, salt, rum, aragonite, pharmaceuticals, spiral-welded steel pipe

**Industrial production growth rate:** NA%

**Electricity - production:** 2.05 billion kWh (2007 est.)

**Electricity - consumption:** 1.793 billion kWh (2006 est.)

**Electricity - exports:** 0 kWh (2007 est.)

**Electricity - imports:** 0 kWh (2007 est.)

**Oil - production:** 0 bbl/day (2007 est.)

**Oil - consumption:** 26,830 bbl/day (2006 est.)

**Oil - exports:** transshipments of 38,740 bbl/day (2005)

**Oil - imports:** 69,780 bbl/day (2005)

**Oil - proved reserves:** 0 bbl (1 January 2006 est.)

**Natural gas - production:** 0 cu m (2007 est.)

**Natural gas - consumption:** 0 cu m (2007 est.)

**Natural gas - exports:** 0 cu m (2007 est.)

**Natural gas - imports:** 0 cu m (2007 est.)

**Natural gas - proved reserves:** 0 cu m (1 January 2006 est.)

**Current account balance:** -$1.442 billion (2007 est.)

**Exports:** $674 million (2006)

**Exports - commodities:** mineral products and salt, animal products, rum, chemicals, fruit and vegetables

**Exports - partners:** US 20.4%, Singapore 15.5%, Spain 14.5%, Poland 14.3%, Germany 6.6%, Guatemala 5.7%, Switzerland 5.2% (2007)

**Imports:** $2.401 billion (2006)

**Imports - commodities:** machinery and transport equipment, manufactures, chemicals, mineral fuels; food and live animals

**Imports - partners:** US 26.7%, South Korea 14.1%, Japan 13.5%, Italy 7.5%, Singapore 5.2%, Venezuela 4.5%, Spain 4.3% (2007)

**Debt - external:** $342.6 million (2004 est.)

**Exchange rates:** Bahamian dollars (BSD) per US dollar - 1 (2008 est.), 1 (2007), 1 (2006), 1 (2005), 1 (2004)

## Communications

**Telephones - main lines in use:** 132,900 (2007)

**Telephones - mobile cellular:** 374,000 (2007)

**Telephone system:**

*general assessment:* modern facilities

*domestic:* totally automatic system; highly developed; the Bahamas Domestic Submarine Network links 14 of the islands and is designed to satisfy increasing demand for voice and broadband internet services

*international:* country code - 1-242; landing point for the Americas Region Caribbean Ring System (ARCOS-1) fiber-optic submarine cable that provides links to South and Central America, parts of the Caribbean, and the US; satellite earth stations - 2 (2007)

**Radio broadcast stations:** AM 3, FM 5, shortwave 0 (2006)

**Television broadcast stations:** 2 (2006)

**Internet country code:** .bs

# Bahamas, The *(continued)*

**Internet hosts:** 41 (2008)
**Internet users:** 120,000 (2007)

## Transportation

**Airports:** 62 (2008)
**Airports - with paved runways:**
*total:* 23
*over 3,047 m:* 2
*2,438 to 3,047 m:* 4
*1,524 to 2,437 m:* 11
*914 to 1,523 m:* 6 (2008)
**Airports - with unpaved runways:**
*total:* 39
*1,524 to 2,437 m:* 5
*914 to 1,523 m:* 12
*under 914 m:* 22 (2008)
**Heliports:** 1 (2007)
**Roadways:**
*total:* 2,717 km
*paved:* 1,560 km
*unpaved:* 1,157 km (2002)
**Merchant marine:**
*total:* 1,223
*by type:* barge carrier 1, bulk carrier 210, cargo 226, carrier 2, chemical tanker 88, combination ore/oil 12, container 65, liquefied gas 77, passenger 109, passenger/cargo 35, petroleum tanker 209, refrigerated cargo 119, roll on/roll off 16, specialized tanker 3, vehicle carrier 51
*foreign-owned:* 1,150 (Angola 6, Belgium 15, Bermuda 12, Brazil 2, Canada 84, China 10, Croatia 1, Cuba 1, Cyprus 25, Denmark 67, Finland 9, France 30, Germany 44, Greece 209, Hong Kong 30, Iceland 1, Indonesia 2, Ireland 2, Isle of Man 1, Italy 4, Japan 87, Jordan 2, Kenya 1, Malaysia 13, Monaco 15, Montenegro 2, Netherlands 9, Nigeria 2, Norway 189, Poland 17, Russia 4, Saudi Arabia 16, Singapore 17, Slovenia 1, South Africa 1, Spain 14, Sweden 4, Switzerland 1, Thailand 5, Trinidad and Tobago 1, Turkey 8, UAE 23, UK 56, US 106, Venezuela 1)
*registered in other countries:* 12 (Bolivia 1, Panama 9, Peru 1, Portugal 1) (2008)
**Ports and terminals:** Freeport, Nassau, South Riding Point

## Military

**Military branches:** Royal Bahamian Defense Force: Land Force, Navy, Air Wing (2009)
**Military service age and obligation:** 18 years of age (est.); no conscription (2008)
**Manpower available for military service:**
*males age 16-49:* 80,200 (2008 est.)
**Manpower fit for military service:**
*males age 16-49:* 50,764
*females age 16-49:* 51,690 (2009 est.)
**Manpower reaching militarily significant age annually:**
*male:* 2,992
*female:* 3,003 (2009 est.)
**Military expenditures:** 0.5% of GDP (2006)

## Transnational Issues

**Disputes - international:** disagrees with the US on the alignment the northern axis of a potential maritime boundary; continues to monitor and interdict drug dealers and Haitian and Cuban refugees in Bahamian waters
**Illicit drugs:** transshipment point for cocaine and marijuana bound for US and Europe; offshore financial center

# Bahrain

## Introduction

**Background:** In 1783, the al-Khalifa family captured Bahrain from the Persians. In order to secure these holdings, it entered into a series of treaties with the UK during the 19th century that made Bahrain a British protectorate. The archipelago attained its independence in 1971. Bahrain's small size and central location among Persian Gulf countries require it to play a delicate balancing act in foreign affairs among its larger neighbors. Facing declining oil reserves, Bahrain has turned to petroleum processing and refining and has transformed itself into an international banking center. King HAMAD bin Isa al-Khalifa, after coming to power in 1999, pushed economic and political reforms to improve relations with the Shia community. Shia political societies participated in 2006 parliamentary and municipal elections. Al Wifaq, the largest Shia political society, won the largest number of seats in the elected chamber of the legislature. However, Shia discontent has resurfaced in recent years with street demonstrations and occasional low-level violence.

## Geography

**Location:** Middle East, archipelago in the Persian Gulf, east of Saudi Arabia
**Geographic coordinates:** 26 00 N, 50 33 E
**Map references:** Middle East
**Area:**
*total:* 665 sq km
*land:* 665 sq km
*water:* 0 sq km
**Area - comparative:** 3.5 times the size of Washington, DC
**Land boundaries:** 0 km
**Coastline:** 161 km
**Maritime claims:**
*territorial sea:* 12 nm
*contiguous zone:* 24 nm
*continental shelf:* extending to boundaries to be determined

## Bahrain (continued)

**Climate:** arid; mild, pleasant winters; very hot, humid summers

**Terrain:** mostly low desert plain rising gently to low central escarpment

**Elevation extremes:**
*lowest point:* Persian Gulf 0 m
*highest point:* Jabal ad Dukhan 122 m

**Natural resources:** oil, associated and nonassociated natural gas, fish, pearls

**Land use:**
*arable land:* 2.82%
*permanent crops:* 5.63%
*other:* 91.55% (2005)

**Irrigated land:** 40 sq km (2003)

**Total renewable water resources:** 0.1 cu km (1997)

**Freshwater withdrawal (domestic/industrial/agricultural):**
*total:* 0.3 cu km/yr (40%/3%/57%)
*per capita:* 411 cu m/yr (2000)

**Natural hazards:** periodic droughts; dust storms

**Environment - current issues:** desertification resulting from the degradation of limited arable land, periods of drought, and dust storms; coastal degradation (damage to coastlines, coral reefs, and sea vegetation) resulting from oil spills and other discharges from large tankers, oil refineries, and distribution stations; lack of freshwater resources (groundwater and seawater are the only sources for all water needs)

**Environment - international agreements:**
*party to:* Biodiversity, Climate Change, Climate Change-Kyoto Protocol, Desertification, Hazardous Wastes, Law of the Sea, Ozone Layer Protection, Wetlands
*signed, but not ratified:* none of the selected agreements

**Geography - note:** close to primary Middle Eastern petroleum sources; strategic location in Persian Gulf, through which much of the Western world's petroleum must transit to reach open ocean

### People

**Population:** 727,785
*note:* includes 235,108 non-nationals (July 2009 est.)

**Age structure:**
*0-14 years:* 25.9% (male 95,224/female 93,241)
*15-64 years:* 70.2% (male 292,941/female 217,729)
*65 years and over:* 3.9% (male 15,106/female 13,544) (2009 est.)

**Median age:**
*total:* 30.1 years
*male:* 33.2 years
*female:* 26.7 years (2009 est.)

**Population growth rate:** 1.285% (2009 est.)

**Birth rate:** 17.02 births/1,000 population (2009 est.)

**Death rate:** 4.29 deaths/1,000 population (2008 est.)

**Net migration rate:** 0.2 migrant(s)/1,000 population (2009 est.)

**Urbanization:**
*urban population:* 89% of total population (2008)
*rate of urbanization:* 1.8% annual rate of change (2005-10 est.)

**Sex ratio:**
*at birth:* 1.03 male(s)/female
*under 15 years:* 1.02 male(s)/female
*15-64 years:* 1.34 male(s)/female
*65 years and over:* 1.12 male(s)/female
*total population:* 1.24 male(s)/female (2009 est.)

**Infant mortality rate:**
*total:* 15.25 deaths/1,000 live births
*male:* 17.81 deaths/1,000 live births
*female:* 12.61 deaths/1,000 live births (2009 est.)

**Life expectancy at birth:**
*total population:* 75.16 years
*male:* 72.64 years
*female:* 77.76 years (2009 est.)

**Total fertility rate:** 2.5 children born/woman (2009 est.)

**HIV/AIDS - adult prevalence rate:** 0.2% (2001 est.)

**HIV/AIDS - people living with HIV/AIDS:** fewer than 600 (2007 est.)

**HIV/AIDS - deaths:** fewer than 200 (2003 est.)

**Nationality:**
*noun:* Bahraini(s)
*adjective:* Bahraini

**Ethnic groups:** Bahraini 62.4%, non-Bahraini 37.6% (2001 census)

**Religions:** Muslim (Shia and Sunni) 81.2%, Christian 9%, other 9.8% (2001 census)

**Languages:** Arabic, English, Farsi, Urdu

**Literacy:**
*definition:* age 15 and over can read and write
*total population:* 86.5%
*male:* 88.6%
*female:* 83.6% (2001 census)

**School life expectancy (primary to tertiary education):**
*total:* 15 years
*male:* 14 years
*female:* 16 years (2006)

**Education expenditures:** 3.9% of GDP (1991)

### Government

**Country name:**
*conventional long form:* Kingdom of Bahrain
*conventional short form:* Bahrain
*local long form:* Mamlakat al Bahrayn
*local short form:* Al Bahrayn
*former:* Dilmun

**Government type:** constitutional monarchy

**Capital:**
*name:* Manama
*geographic coordinates:* 26 14 N, 50 34 E
*time difference:* UTC+3 (8 hours ahead of Washington, DC during Standard Time)

**Administrative divisions:** 5 governorates; Asamah, Janubiyah, Muharraq, Shamaliyah, Wasat
*note:* each governorate administered by an appointed governor

**Independence:** 15 August 1971 (from the UK)

**National holiday:** National Day, 16 December (1971); note - 15 August 1971 was the date of independence from the UK, 16 December 1971 was the date of independence from British protection

**Constitution:** adopted 14 February 2002

**Legal system:** based on Islamic law and English common law; has not accepted compulsory ICJ jurisdiction

**Suffrage:** 20 years of age; universal

**Executive branch:**
*chief of state:* King HAMAD bin Isa Al-Khalifa (since 6 March 1999); Heir Apparent Crown Prince SALMAN bin Hamad (son of the monarch, born 21 October 1969)
*head of government:* Prime Minister KHALIFA bin Salman Al-Khalifa (since 1971); Deputy Prime Ministers ALI bin Khalifa bin Salman Al-Khalifa, MUHAMMAD bin Mubarak Al-Khalifa, Jawad al-ARAIDH
*cabinet:* Cabinet appointed by the monarch
*elections:* the monarchy is hereditary; prime minister appointed by the monarch

**Legislative branch:** bicameral legislature consists of the Consultative Council (40 members appointed by the King) and the Council of Representatives or Chamber of Deputies (40 seats; members directly elected to serve four-year terms)
*elections:* Council of Representatives - last held November-December 2006 (next election to be held in 2010)
*election results:* Council of Representatives - percent of vote by society - NA; seats by society - al Wifaq (Shia) 17, al Asala (Sunni Salafi) 5, al Minbar (Sunni Muslim Brotherhood) 7, independents 11; note - seats by society as of February 2007 - al Wifaq 17, al Asala 8, al Minbar 7, al Mustaqbal (Moderate Sunni pro-government) 4, unassociated independents (all Sunni) 3, independent affiliated with al Wifaq (Sunni oppositionist) 1

**Judicial branch:** High Civil Appeals Court

**Political parties and leaders:** political parties prohibited but political societies were legalized per a July 2005 law

**Political pressure groups and leaders:** Shia activists; Sunni Islamist legislators
*other:* several small leftist and other groups are active

**International organization participation:** ABEDA, AFESD, AMF, FAO, G-77, GCC, IBRD, ICAO, ICC, ICCt (signatory), ICRM, IDA, IDB, IFC, IFRCS, IHO, ILO, IMF, IMO, IMSO, Interpol, IOC, IOM (observer), IPU, ISO, ITSO, ITU, ITUC, LAS, MIGA, NAM, OAPEC, OIC, OPCW, PCA, UN, UNCTAD, UNESCO, UNIDO, UNWTO, UPU, WCO, WFTU, WHO, WIPO, WMO, WTO

**Diplomatic representation in the US:**
*chief of mission:* Ambassador Houda Ibrahim Ezra NUNU
*chancery:* 3502 International Drive NW, Washington, DC 20008
*telephone:* [1] (202) 342-1111
*FAX:* [1] (202) 362-2192
*consulate(s) general:* New York
**Diplomatic representation from the US:**
*chief of mission:* Ambassador J. Adam ERELI
*embassy:* Building #979, Road 3119 (next to Al-Ahli Sports Club), Block 331, Zinj District, Manama
*mailing address:* PSC 451, Box 660, FPO AE 09834-5100; international mail: American Embassy, Box 26431, Manama
*telephone:* [973] 1724-2700
*FAX:* [973] 1727-0547
**Flag description:** red, the traditional color for flags of Persian Gulf states, with a white serrated band (five white points) on the hoist side; the five points represent the five pillars of Islam

### Economy

**Economy - overview:** With its highly developed communication and transport facilities, Bahrain is home to numerous multinational firms with business in the Gulf. Petroleum production and refining account for over 60% of Bahrain's export receipts, over 70% of government revenues, and 11% of GDP (exclusive of allied industries), underpinning Bahrain's strong economic growth in recent years. Aluminum is Bahrain's second major export after oil. Other major segments of Bahrain's economy are the financial and construction sectors. Bahrain is focused on Islamic banking and is competing on an international scale with Malaysia as a worldwide banking center. Bahrain is actively pursuing the diversification and privatization of its economy to reduce the country's dependence on oil. As part of this effort, in August 2006 Bahrain and the US implemented a Free Trade Agreement (FTA), the first FTA between the US and a Gulf state. Continued strong growth hinges on Bahrain's ability to acquire new natural gas supplies as feedstock to support its expanding petrochemical and aluminum industries. Unemployment, especially among the young, and the depletion of oil and underground water resources are long-term economic problems. The global financial crisis is likely to result in slower economic growth for Bahrain during 2009 as tight international credit and a slowing global economy cause funding for many non-oil projects to dry up. Lower oil prices may also cause Bahrain's budget to slip back into deficit.
**GDP (purchasing power parity):**
$26.7 billion (2008 est.)
$25.17 billion (2007)
$23.29 billion (2006)
*note:* data are in 2008 US dollars
**GDP (official exchange rate):** $19.68 billion (2008 est.)

**GDP - real growth rate:**
6.1% (2008 est.)
8.1% (2007 est.)
6.7% (2006 est.)
**GDP - per capita (PPP):**
$37,200 (2008 est.)
$35,500 (2007 est.)
$33,300 (2006 est.)
*note:* data are in 2008 US dollars
**GDP - composition by sector:**
*agriculture:* 0.3%
*industry:* 43.6%
*services:* 56% (2007 est.)
**Labor force:** 463,000
*note:* 44% of the population in the 15-64 age group is non-national (2008 est.)
**Labor force - by occupation:**
*agriculture:* 1%
*industry:* 79%
*services:* 20% (1997 est.)
**Unemployment rate:**
15% (2005 est.)
**Population below poverty line:** NA%
**Household income or consumption by percentage share:**
*lowest 10%:* NA%
*highest 10%:* NA%
**Investment (gross fixed):** 27.3% of GDP (2008 est.)
**Budget:**
*revenues:* $7.226 billion
*expenditures:* $5.806 billion (2008 est.)
**Public debt:** 33.2% of GDP (2008 est.)
**Inflation rate (consumer prices):**
7% (2008 est.)
3.3% (2007 est.)
**Commercial bank prime lending rate:** 8.35% (31 December 2007)
**Stock of money:** $4.169 billion (31 December 2007)
**Stock of quasi money:** $10.63 billion (31 December 2007)
**Stock of domestic credit:** $10.32 billion (31 December 2007)
**Market value of publicly traded shares:** $28.13 billion (31 December 2007)
**Agriculture - products:** fruit, vegetables; poultry, dairy products; shrimp, fish
**Industries:** petroleum processing and refining, aluminum smelting, iron pelletization, fertilizers, Islamic and offshore banking, insurance, ship repairing, tourism
**Industrial production growth rate:** 5.1% (2008 est.)
**Electricity - production:** 9.233 billion kWh (2006 est.)
**Electricity - consumption:** 8.742 billion kWh (2006 est.)
**Electricity - exports:** 0 kWh (2007 est.)
**Electricity - imports:** 0 kWh (2007 est.)
**Oil - production:** 48,610 bbl/day (2007 est.)

**Oil - consumption:** 32,830 bbl/day (2006 est.)
**Oil - exports:** 238,900 bbl/day (2005)
**Oil - imports:** 221,500 bbl/day (2005)
**Oil - proved reserves:** 124.6 million bbl (1 January 2008 est.)
**Natural gas - production:** 11.33 billion cu m (2006 est.)
**Natural gas - consumption:** 11.33 billion cu m (2006 est.)
**Natural gas - exports:** 0 cu m (2007 est.)
**Natural gas - imports:** 0 cu m (2007 est.)
**Natural gas - proved reserves:** 92.03 billion cu m (1 January 2008 est.)
**Current account balance:** $2.269 billion (2008 est.)
**Exports:** $19.17 billion (2008 est.)
**Exports - commodities:** petroleum and petroleum products, aluminum, textiles
**Exports - partners:** Saudi Arabia 3.5%, US 2.5%, UAE 2.5%
*note:* data exclude oil exports (2007)
**Imports:** $15.64 billion (2008 est.)
**Imports - commodities:** crude oil, machinery, chemicals
**Imports - partners:** Saudi Arabia 37.7%, Japan 7.2%, US 6.2%, Germany 4.7%, UK 4.5%, UAE 4.2%, China 4.1% (2007)
**Reserves of foreign exchange and gold:** $4.865 billion (31 December 2008 est.)
**Debt - external:** $10.57 billion (31 December 2008 est.)
**Stock of direct foreign investment - at home:** $15.2 billion (2008 est.)
**Stock of direct foreign investment - abroad:** $9.52 billion (2008 est.)
**Exchange rates:** Bahraini dinars (BHD) per US dollar - 0.376 (2008 est.), 0.376 (2007), 0.376 (2006), 0.376 (2005), 0.376 (2004)

### Communications

**Telephones - main lines in use:** 194,200 (2006)
**Telephones - mobile cellular:** 1.116 million (2007)
**Telephone system:**
*general assessment:* modern system
*domestic:* modern fiber-optic integrated services; digital network with rapidly growing use of mobile-cellular telephones
*international:* country code - 973; landing point for the Fiber-Optic Link Around the Globe (FLAG) submarine cable network that provides links to Asia, Middle East, Europe, and US; tropospheric scatter to Qatar and UAE; microwave radio relay to Saudi Arabia; satellite earth station - 1 (2007)
**Radio broadcast stations:** AM 2, FM 3, shortwave 0 (1998)
**Television broadcast stations:** 4 (1997)
**Internet country code:** .bh
**Internet hosts:** 2,621 (2008)
**Internet users:** 250,000 (2007)

## Bahrain *(continued)*

### Transportation

**Airports:** 3 (2008)
**Airports - with paved runways:**
*total:* 3
*over 3,047 m:* 2
*2,438 to 3,047 m:* 1 (2008)
**Heliports:** 1 (2007)
**Pipelines:** gas 20 km; oil 32 km (2008)
**Roadways:**
*total:* 3,498 km
*paved:* 2,768 km
*unpaved:* 730 km (2003)
**Merchant marine:**
*total:* 9
*by type:* bulk carrier 4, container 4, petroleum tanker 1
*foreign-owned:* 6 (Kuwait 5, UAE 1) (2008)
**Ports and terminals:** Mina' Salman, Sitrah

### Military

**Military branches:** Bahrain Defense Forces (BDF):
Ground Force (includes Air Defense), Naval Force, Air
Force, National Guard
**Military service age and obligation:** 17 years of
age for voluntary military service; 15 years of age for
NCOs, technicians, and cadets; no conscription
(2008)
**Manpower available for military service:**
*males age 16-49:* 210,938
*females age 16-49:* 170,471 (2008 est.)
**Manpower fit for military service:**
*males age 16-49:* 171,004
*females age 16-49:* 144,555 (2009 est.)
**Manpower reaching militarily significant age
annually:**
*male:* 6,612
*female:* 6,499 (2009 est.)
**Military expenditures:** 4.5% of GDP (2006)

### Transnational Issues

**Disputes - international:** none
**Trafficking in persons:**
*current situation:* Bahrain is a destination country for
men and women trafficked for the purposes of
involuntary servitude and commercial sexual
exploitation; men and women from Africa, South Asia,
and Southeast Asia migrate voluntarily to Bahrain to
work as laborers or domestic servants where some
face conditions of involuntary servitude such as
unlawful withholding of passports, restrictions on
movements, non-payment of wages, threats, and
physical or sexual abuse; women from Thailand,
Morocco, Eastern Europe, and Central Asia are
trafficked to Bahrain for the purpose of commercial
sexual exploitation
*tier rating:* Tier 2 Watch List - Bahrain is on the Tier 2
Watch List for failing to show evidence of increased
efforts to combat human trafficking, particularly efforts
that enforce laws against trafficking in persons, and
that prevent the punishment of victims of trafficking;
during 2007, Bahrain passed a comprehensive law

prohibiting all forms of trafficking in persons; the
government also established a specialized
anti-trafficking unit within the Ministry of Interior to
investigate trafficking crimes; however, the
government did not report any prosecutions or
convictions for trafficking offenses during 2007,
despite reports of a substantial problem of involuntary
servitude and sex trafficking (2008)

## Baker Island
*(Territory of the US)*

Description under

United States

Pacific Island

Wildlife Refuges

## Bangladesh

### Introduction

**Background:** Europeans began to set up trading
posts in the area of Bangladesh in the 16th century;
eventually the British came to dominate the region and
it became part of British India. In 1947, West Pakistan
and East Bengal (both primarily Muslim) separated
from India (largely Hindu) and jointly became the new
country of Pakistan. East Bengal became East
Pakistan in 1955, but the awkward arrangement of a
two-part country with its territorial units separated by
1,600 km left the Bengalis marginalized and
dissatisfied. East Pakistan seceded from its union with
West Pakistan in 1971 and was renamed Bangladesh.
A military-backed, emergency caretaker regime
suspended parliamentary elections planned
for January 2007 in an effort to reform the political
system and root out corruption. In contrast to the
strikes and violent street rallies that had marked
Bangladeshi politics in previous years, the
parliamentary elections finally held in late December
2008 were mostly peaceful. Sheikh HASINA Wajed
was reappointed prime minister. About a third of this
extremely poor country floods annually during the
monsoon rainy season, hampering economic
development.

### Geography

**Location:** Southern Asia, bordering the Bay of
Bengal, between Burma and India
**Geographic coordinates:** 24 00 N, 90 00 E
**Map references:** Asia
**Area:**
*total:* 144,000 sq km
*land:* 133,910 sq km
*water:* 10,090 sq km
**Area - comparative:** slightly smaller than Iowa
**Land boundaries:**
*total:* 4,246 km
*border countries:* Burma 193 km, India 4,053 km
**Coastline:** 580 km

# Bangladesh (continued)

**Maritime claims:**
*territorial sea:* 12 nm
*contiguous zone:* 18 nm
*exclusive economic zone:* 200 nm
*continental shelf:* up to the outer limits of the continental margin
**Climate:** tropical; mild winter (October to March); hot, humid summer (March to June); humid, warm rainy monsoon (June to October)
**Terrain:** mostly flat alluvial plain; hilly in southeast
**Elevation extremes:**
*lowest point:* Indian Ocean 0 m
*highest point:* Keokradong 1,230 m
**Natural resources:** natural gas, arable land, timber, coal
**Land use:**
*arable land:* 55.39%
*permanent crops:* 3.08%
*other:* 41.53% (2005)
**Irrigated land:** 47,250 sq km (2003)
**Total renewable water resources:** 1,210.6 cu km (1999)
**Freshwater withdrawal (domestic/industrial/agricultural):**
*total:* 79.4 cu km/yr (3%/1%/96%)
*per capita:* 560 cu m/yr (2000)
**Natural hazards:** droughts; cyclones; much of the country routinely inundated during the summer monsoon season
**Environment - current issues:** many people are landless and forced to live on and cultivate flood-prone land; waterborne diseases prevalent in surface water; water pollution, especially of fishing areas, results from the use of commercial pesticides; ground water contaminated by naturally occurring arsenic; intermittent water shortages because of falling water tables in the northern and central parts of the country; soil degradation and erosion; deforestation; severe overpopulation
**Environment - international agreements:**
*party to:* Biodiversity, Climate Change, Climate Change-Kyoto Protocol, Desertification, Endangered Species, Environmental Modification, Hazardous Wastes, Law of the Sea, Ozone Layer Protection, Ship Pollution, Wetlands
*signed, but not ratified:* none of the selected agreements
**Geography - note:** most of the country is situated on deltas of large rivers flowing from the Himalayas: the Ganges unites with the Jamuna (main channel of the Brahmaputra) and later joins the Meghna to eventually empty into the Bay of Bengal

## People

**Population:** 156,050,883 (July 2009 est.)
**Age structure:**
*0-14 years:* 34.6% (male 27,065,625/female 26,913,961)
*15-64 years:* 61.4% (male 45,222,182/female 50,537,052)
*65 years and over:* 4% (male 3,057,255/female 3,254,808) (2009 est.)

**Median age:**
*total:* 23.3 years
*male:* 22.9 years
*female:* 23.5 years (2009 est.)
**Population growth rate:** 1.292% (2009 est.)
**Birth rate:** 24.68 births/1,000 population (2009 est.)
**Death rate:** 8 deaths/1,000 population (2008 est.)
**Net migration rate:** -2.53 migrant(s)/1,000 population (2009 est.)
**Urbanization:**
*urban population:* 27% of total population (2008)
*rate of urbanization:* 3.5% annual rate of change (2005-10 est.)
**Sex ratio:**
*at birth:* 1.04 male(s)/female
*under 15 years:* 1.01 male(s)/female
*15-64 years:* 0.9 male(s)/female
*65 years and over:* 0.94 male(s)/female
*total population:* 0.93 male(s)/female (2009 est.)
**Infant mortality rate:**
*total:* 59.02 deaths/1,000 live births
*male:* 66.12 deaths/1,000 live births
*female:* 51.64 deaths/1,000 live births (2009 est.)
**Life expectancy at birth:**
*total population:* 60.25 years
*male:* 57.57 years
*female:* 63.03 years (2009 est.)
**Total fertility rate:** 2.74 children born/woman (2009 est.)
**HIV/AIDS - adult prevalence rate:** less than 0.1% (2001 est.)
**HIV/AIDS - people living with HIV/AIDS:** 12,000 (2007 est.)
**HIV/AIDS - deaths:** fewer than 500 (2007 est.)
**Major infectious diseases:**
*degree of risk:* high
*food or waterborne diseases:* bacterial and protozoal diarrhea, hepatitis A and E, and typhoid fever
*vectorborne diseases:* dengue fever and malaria are high risks in some locations
*water contact disease:* leptospirosis
*animal contact disease:* rabies
*note:* highly pathogenic H5N1 avian influenza has been identified in this country; it poses a negligible risk with extremely rare cases possible among US citizens who have close contact with birds (2009)
**Nationality:**
*noun:* Bangladeshi(s)
*adjective:* Bangladeshi
**Ethnic groups:** Bengali 98%, other 2% (includes tribal groups, non-Bengali Muslims) (1998)
**Religions:** Muslim 83%, Hindu 16%, other 1% (1998)
**Languages:** Bangla (official, also known as Bengali), English
**Literacy:**
*definition:* age 15 and over can read and write
*total population:* 47.9%
*male:* 54%
*female:* 41.4% (2001 Census)

**School life expectancy (primary to tertiary education):**
*total:* 8 years
*male:* 8 years
*female:* 8 years (2004)
**Education expenditures:** 2.7% of GDP (2005)

## Government

**Country name:**
*conventional long form:* People's Republic of Bangladesh
*conventional short form:* Bangladesh
*local long form:* Gana Prajatantri Banladesh
*local short form:* Banladesh
*former:* East Bengal, East Pakistan
**Government type:** parliamentary democracy
**Capital:**
*name:* Dhaka
*geographic coordinates:* 23 43 N, 90 24 E
*time difference:* UTC+6 (11 hours ahead of Washington, DC during Standard Time)
**Administrative divisions:** 6 divisions; Barisal, Chittagong, Dhaka, Khulna, Rajshahi, Sylhet
**Independence:** 16 December 1971 (from West Pakistan); note - 26 March 1971 is the date of independence from West Pakistan, 16 December 1971 is known as Victory Day and commemorates the official creation of the state of Bangladesh
**National holiday:** Independence Day, 26 March (1971); note - 26 March 1971 is the date of independence from West Pakistan, 16 December 1971 is Victory Day and commemorates the official creation of the state of Bangladesh
**Constitution:** 4 November 1972; effective 16 December 1972; suspended following coup of 24 March 1982; restored 10 November 1986; amended many times
**Legal system:** based on English common law; has not accepted compulsory ICJ jurisdiction
**Suffrage:** 18 years of age; universal
**Executive branch:**
*chief of state:* President Zillur RAHMAN (since 12 February 2009)
*head of government:* Prime Minister Sheikh HASINA Wajed (since 6 January 2009)
*cabinet:* Cabinet selected by the prime minister and appointed by the president
*elections:* president elected by National Parliament for a five-year term (eligible for a second term); last election held on 11 February 2009 (next scheduled election to be held in 2014)
*election results:* Zillur RAHMAN declared president-elect by the Election Commission on 11 February 2009 (sworn in on 12 February); he ran unopposed as president; percent of National Parliament vote - NA
**Legislative branch:** unicameral National Parliament or Jatiya Sangsad; 300 seats elected by popular vote from single territorial constituencies; members serve five-year terms
*elections:* last held 29 December 2008 (next to be held in 2013)

# Bangladesh (continued)

*election results:* percent of vote by party - AL 49%, BNP 33.2%, JP 7%, JIB 4.6%, other 6.2%; seats by party - AL 230, BNP 30, JP 27, JIB 2, other 11

**Judicial branch:** Supreme Court (the chief justices and other judges are appointed by the president)

**Political parties and leaders:** Awami League or AL [Sheikh HASINA]; Bangladesh Communist Party or BCP [Manjurul A. KHAN]; Bangladesh Nationalist Party or BNP [Khaleda ZIA]; Islami Oikya Jote or IOJ [Mufti Fazlul Haq AMINI]; Jamaat-e-Islami Bangladesh or JIB [Matiur Rahman NIZAMI]; Jatiya Party or JP (Ershad faction) [Hussain Mohammad ERSHAD]; Jatiya Party (Manzur faction) [Naziur Rahman MANZUR]; Liberal Democratic Party or LDP [Badrudozza CHOWDHURY and Oli AHMED]

**Political pressure groups and leaders:** Advocacy to End Gender-based Violence through the MoWCA (Ministry of Women's and Children's Affairs)
*other:* environmentalists; Islamist groups; religious leaders; teachers; union leaders

**International organization participation:** ADB, ARF, BIMSTEC, C, CP, FAO, G-77, IAEA, IBRD, ICAO, ICC, ICCt (signatory), ICRM, IDA, IDB, IFAD, IFC, IFRCS, IHO, ILO, IMF, IMO, IMSO, Interpol, IOC, IOM, ISO, ITSO, ITU, ITUC, MIGA, MINURCAT, MINURSO, MONUC, NAM, OIC, OPCW, SAARC, SACEP, UN, UNAMID, UNCTAD, UNESCO, UNHCR, UNIDO, UNMIL, UNMIS, UNMIT, UNOCI, UNOMIG, UNWTO, UPU, WCL, WCO, WFTU, WHO, WIPO, WMO, WTO

**Diplomatic representation in the US:**
*chief of mission:* Ambassador M. Humayun KABIR
*chancery:* 3510 International Drive NW, Washington, DC 20008
*telephone:* [1] (202) 244-0183
*FAX:* [1] (202) 244-7830/2771
*consulate(s) general:* Los Angeles, New York

**Diplomatic representation from the US:**
*chief of mission:* Ambassador James F. MORIARTY
*embassy:* Madani Avenue, Baridhara, Dhaka 1212
*mailing address:* G. P. O. Box 323, Dhaka 1000
*telephone:* [880] (2) 885-5500
*FAX:* [880] (2) 882-3744

**Flag description:** green field with a large red disk shifted slightly to the hoist side of center; the red disk represents the rising sun and the sacrifice to achieve independence; the green field symbolizes the lush vegetation of Bangladesh

## Economy

**Economy - overview:** The economy has grown 5-6% per year since 1996 despite inefficient state-owned enterprises, delays in exploiting natural gas resources, insufficient power supplies, and slow implementation of economic reforms. Bangladesh remains a poor, overpopulated, and inefficiently-governed nation. Although more than half of GDP is generated through the service sector, nearly two-thirds of Bangladeshis are employed in the agriculture sector, with rice as the single-most-important product. Garment exports and remittances from Bangladeshis working overseas, mainly in the Middle East and East Asia, fuel economic growth. In 2008 Bangladesh pursued a monetary policy aimed at maintaining high employment, but created higher inflation in the process.

**GDP (purchasing power parity):**
$224 billion (2008 est.)
$213.6 billion (2007)
$201.1 billion (2006)
*note:* data are in 2008 US dollars

**GDP (official exchange rate):** $83.04 billion (2008 est.)

**GDP - real growth rate:**
4.9% (2008 est.)
6.2% (2007 est.)
6.4% (2006 est.)

**GDP - per capita (PPP):**
$1,500 (2008 est.)
$1,400 (2007 est.)
$1,300 (2006 est.)
*note:* data are in 2008 US dollars

**GDP - composition by sector:**
*agriculture:* 19.1%
*industry:* 28.6%
*services:* 52.3% (2008 est.)

**Labor force:** 70.86 million
*note:* extensive export of labor to Saudi Arabia, Kuwait, UAE, Oman, Qatar, and Malaysia; workers' remittances estimated at $4.8 billion in 2005-06. (2008 est.)

**Labor force - by occupation:**
*agriculture:* 63%
*industry:* 11%
*services:* 26% (FY95/96)

**Unemployment rate:**
2.5% (2008 est.)
2.5% (2007 est.)

**Population below poverty line:** 45% (2004 est.)

**Household income or consumption by percentage share:**
*lowest 10%:* 3.7%
*highest 10%:* 27.9% (2000)

**Distribution of family income - Gini index:** 33.2 (2005)

**Investment (gross fixed):** 24.3% of GDP (2008 est.)

**Budget:**
*revenues:* $8.831 billion
*expenditures:* $12.54 billion (2008 est.)

**Public debt:** 34.6% of GDP (2008 est.)

**Inflation rate (consumer prices):**
9.4% (2008 est.)
9.1% (2007 est.)

**Central bank discount rate:** 5% (31 December 2007)

**Commercial bank prime lending rate:** 16% (31 December 2007)

**Stock of money:** $8.444 billion (31 December 2007)

**Stock of quasi money:** $32.4 billion (31 December 2007)

**Stock of domestic credit:** $40.15 billion (31 December 2007)

**Market value of publicly traded shares:** $6.793 billion (31 December 2007)

**Agriculture - products:** rice, jute, tea, wheat, sugarcane, potatoes, tobacco, pulses, oilseeds, spices, fruit; beef, milk, poultry

**Industries:** cotton textiles, jute, garments, tea processing, paper newsprint, cement, chemical fertilizer, light engineering, sugar

**Industrial production growth rate:** 6.9% (2008 est.)

**Electricity - production:** 22.78 billion kWh (2007 est.)

**Electricity - consumption:** 21.37 billion kWh (2006 est.)

**Electricity - exports:** 0 kWh (2007 est.)

**Electricity - imports:** 0 kWh (2007 est.)

**Oil - production:** 6,746 bbl/day (2007 est.)

**Oil - consumption:** 89,940 bbl/day (2006 est.)

**Oil - exports:** 1,351 bbl/day (2005)

**Oil - imports:** 83,220 bbl/day (2005)

**Oil - proved reserves:** 28 million bbl (1 January 2008 est.)

**Natural gas - production:** 15.7 billion cu m (2007 est.)

**Natural gas - consumption:** 15.7 billion cu m (2007 est.)

**Natural gas - exports:** 0 cu m (2007 est.)

**Natural gas - imports:** 0 cu m (2007 est.)

**Natural gas - proved reserves:** 141.6 billion cu m (1 January 2008 est.)

**Current account balance:** -$55 million (2008 est.)

**Exports:** $13.97 billion (2008 est.)

**Exports - commodities:** garments, jute and jute goods, leather, frozen fish and seafood

**Exports - partners:** US 23%, Germany 13%, UK 9.1%, France 5.5%, Belgium 4% (2007)

**Imports:** $20.17 billion (2008 est.)

**Imports - commodities:** machinery and equipment, chemicals, iron and steel, textiles, foodstuffs, petroleum products, cement

**Imports - partners:** China 15%, India 14.3%, Kuwait 8.3%, Singapore 6.2%, Hong Kong 4.2% (2007)

**Reserves of foreign exchange and gold:** $5.934 billion (31 December 2008 est.)

**Debt - external:** $21.72 billion (31 December 2008 est.)

**Stock of direct foreign investment - at home:** $5.618 billion (2008 est.)

**Stock of direct foreign investment - abroad:** $104 million (2008 est.)

**Exchange rates:** taka (BDT) per US dollar - 68.554 (2008 est.), 69.893 (2007), 69.031 (2006), 64.328 (2005), 59.513 (2004)

## Communications

**Telephones - main lines in use:** 1.187 million (2007)

**Telephones - mobile cellular:** 34.37 million (2007)

# Bangladesh (continued)

**Telephone system:**

*general assessment:* inadequate for a modern country; fixed-line telephone density remains less than 1 per 100 persons; mobile-cellular telephone subscribership has been increasing rapidly and is approaching 25 per 100 persons

*domestic:* modernizing; introducing digital systems; trunk systems include VHF and UHF microwave radio relay links, and some fiber-optic cable in cities

*international:* country code - 880; landing point for the SEA-ME-WE-4 fiber-optic submarine cable system that provides links to Europe, the Middle East, and Asia; satellite earth stations - 6; international radiotelephone communications and landline service to neighboring countries (2007)

**Radio broadcast stations:** AM 15, FM 13, shortwave 2 (2006)

**Television broadcast stations:** 15 (1999)

**Internet country code:** .bd

**Internet hosts:** 1,440 (2008)

**Internet users:** 500,000 (2007)

## Transportation

**Airports:** 17 (2008)

**Airports - with paved runways:**

*total:* 16

*over 3,047 m:* 1

*2,438 to 3,047 m:* 3

*1,524 to 2,437 m:* 5

*914 to 1,523 m:* 1

*under 914 m:* 6 (2008)

**Airports - with unpaved runways:**

*total:* 1

*1,524 to 2,437 m:* 1 (2008)

**Pipelines:** gas 2,597 km (2008)

**Railways:**

*total:* 2,768 km

*broad gauge:* 946 km 1.676-m gauge

*narrow gauge:* 1,822 km 1.000-m gauge (2006)

**Roadways:**

*total:* 239,226 km

*paved:* 22,726 km

*unpaved:* 216,500 km (2003)

**Waterways:** 8,370 km

*note:* includes up to 3,060 km main cargo routes; network reduced to 5,200 km in dry season (2007)

**Merchant marine:**

*total:* 40

*by type:* bulk carrier 3, cargo 27, container 5, passenger/cargo 1, petroleum tanker 4

*foreign-owned:* 1 (China 1)

*registered in other countries:* 10 (Comoros 2, Honduras 1, Malta 2, Panama 2, Singapore 2, Togo 1) (2008)

**Ports and terminals:** Chittagong, Mongla Port

**Transportation - note:** the International Maritime Bureau reports the territorial waters of Bangladesh as high risk for armed robbery against ships; numerous commercial vessels have been attacked both at anchor and while underway; crews have been robbed and stores or cargoes stolen

## Military

**Military branches:** Bangladesh Defense Force: Bangladesh Army (Sena Bahini), Bangladesh Navy (Noh Bahini, BN), Bangladesh Air Force (Biman Bahini, BAF) (2009)

**Military service age and obligation:** 16 years of age for voluntary military service; 17 years of age for officers (both with parental consent); conscription legally possible in emergency, but has never been implemented (2008)

**Manpower available for military service:**

*males age 16-49:* 41,199,340 (2008 est.)

**Manpower fit for military service:**

*males age 16-49:* 24,946,041

*females age 16-49:* 31,409,069 (2009 est.)

**Manpower reaching militarily significant age annually:**

*male:* 1,538,865

*female:* 1,666,670 (2009 est.)

**Military expenditures:** 1.5% of GDP (2006)

## Transnational Issues

**Disputes - international:** discussions with India remain stalled to delimit a small section of river boundary, exchange territory for 51 small Bangladeshi exclaves in India and 111 small Indian exclaves in Bangladesh, allocate divided villages, and stop illegal cross-border trade, migration, violence, and transit of terrorists through the porous border; Bangladesh protests India's fencing and walling off high-traffic sections of the porous boundary; a joint Bangladesh-India boundary commission resurveyed and reconstructed 92 missing pillars in 2007; dispute with India over New Moore/South Talpatty/Purbasha Island in the Bay of Bengal deters maritime boundary delimitation; after 21 years, Bangladesh resumes talks with Burma on delimiting a maritime boundary

**Refugees and internally displaced persons:**

*refugees (country of origin):* 26,268 (Burma)

*IDPs:* 65,000 (land conflicts, religious persecution) (2007)

**Illicit drugs:** transit country for illegal drugs produced in neighboring countries

# Barbados

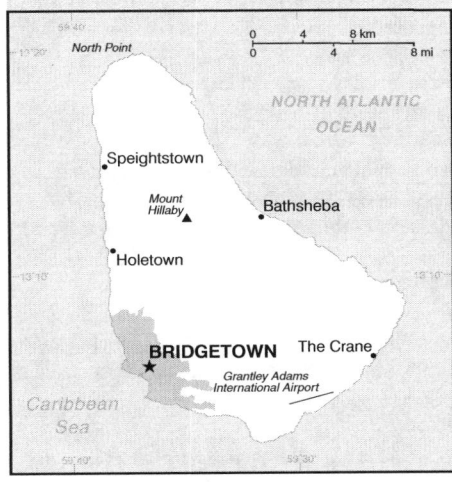

## Introduction

**Background:** The island was uninhabited when first settled by the British in 1627. Slaves worked the sugar plantations established on the island until 1834 when slavery was abolished. The economy remained heavily dependent on sugar, rum, and molasses production through most of the 20th century. The gradual introduction of social and political reforms in the 1940s and 1950s led to complete independence from the UK in 1966. In the 1990s, tourism and manufacturing surpassed the sugar industry in economic importance.

## Geography

**Location:** Caribbean, island in the North Atlantic Ocean, northeast of Venezuela

**Geographic coordinates:** 13 10 N, 59 32 W

**Map references:** Central America and the Caribbean

**Area:**

*total:* 431 sq km

*land:* 431 sq km

*water:* 0 sq km

**Area - comparative:** 2.5 times the size of Washington, DC

**Land boundaries:** 0 km

**Coastline:** 97 km

**Maritime claims:**

*territorial sea:* 12 nm

*exclusive economic zone:* 200 nm

**Climate:** tropical; rainy season (June to October)

**Terrain:** relatively flat; rises gently to central highland region

**Elevation extremes:**

*lowest point:* Atlantic Ocean 0 m

*highest point:* Mount Hillaby 336 m

**Natural resources:** petroleum, fish, natural gas

**Land use:**

*arable land:* 37.21%

*permanent crops:* 2.33%

*other:* 60.46% (2005)

**Irrigated land:** 50 sq km (2003)
**Total renewable water resources:** 0.1 cu km (2003)
**Freshwater withdrawal (domestic/industrial/agricultural):**
*total:* 0.09 cu km/yr (33%/44%/22%)
*per capita:* 333 cu m/yr (2000)
**Natural hazards:** infrequent hurricanes; periodic landslides
**Environment - current issues:** pollution of coastal waters from waste disposal by ships; soil erosion; illegal solid waste disposal threatens contamination of aquifers
**Environment - international agreements:**
*party to:* Biodiversity, Climate Change, Climate Change-Kyoto Protocol, Desertification, Endangered Species, Hazardous Wastes, Law of the Sea, Marine Dumping, Ozone Layer Protection, Ship Pollution, Wetlands
*signed, but not ratified:* none of the selected agreements
**Geography - note:** easternmost Caribbean island

## People

**Population:** 284,589 (July 2009 est.)
**Age structure:**
*0-14 years:* 19.2% (male 27,383/female 27,352)
*15-64 years:* 71.3% (male 99,829/female 103,049)
*65 years and over:* 9.5% (male 10,464/female 16,512) (2009 est.)
**Median age:**
*total:* 35.8 years
*male:* 34.7 years
*female:* 36.9 years (2009 est.)
**Population growth rate:** 0.383% (2009 est.)
**Birth rate:** 12.55 births/1,000 population (2009 est.)
**Death rate:** 8.58 deaths/1,000 population (2008 est.)
**Net migration rate:** -0.31 migrant(s)/1,000 population (2009 est.)
**Urbanization:**
*urban population:* 40% of total population (2008)
*rate of urbanization:* 1.5% annual rate of change (2005-10 est.)
**Sex ratio:**
*at birth:* 1.01 male(s)/female
*under 15 years:* 1 male(s)/female
*15-64 years:* 0.97 male(s)/female
*65 years and over:* 0.63 male(s)/female
*total population:* 0.94 male(s)/female (2009 est.)
**Infant mortality rate:**
*total:* 12.29 deaths/1,000 live births
*male:* 13.89 deaths/1,000 live births
*female:* 10.67 deaths/1,000 live births (2009 est.)
**Life expectancy at birth:**
*total population:* 73.94 years
*male:* 71.65 years
*female:* 76.26 years (2009 est.)
**Total fertility rate:** 1.68 children born/woman (2009 est.)
**HIV/AIDS - adult prevalence rate:** 1.2% (2007 est.)
**HIV/AIDS - people living with HIV/AIDS:** 2,200 (2007 est.)

**HIV/AIDS - deaths:** fewer than 100 (2007 est.)
**Nationality:**
*noun:* Barbadian(s) or Bajan (colloquial)
*adjective:* Barbadian or Bajan (colloquial)
**Ethnic groups:** black 90%, white 4%, Asian and mixed 6%
**Religions:** Protestant 63.4% (Anglican 28.3%, Pentecostal 18.7%, Methodist 5.1%, other 11.3%), Roman Catholic 4.2%, other Christian 7%, other 4.8%, none or unspecified 20.6% (2008 est.)
**Languages:** English
**Literacy:**
*definition:* age 15 and over has ever attended school
*total population:* 99.7%
*male:* 99.7%
*female:* 99.7% (2002 est.)
**School life expectancy (primary to tertiary education):**
*total:* 13 years
*male:* 13 years
*female:* 14 years (2001)
**Education expenditures:** 6.9% of GDP (2005)

## Government

**Country name:**
*conventional long form:* none
*conventional short form:* Barbados
**Government type:** parliamentary democracy and a Commonwealth realm
**Capital:**
*name:* Bridgetown
*geographic coordinates:* 13 06 N, 59 37 W
*time difference:* UTC-4 (1 hour ahead of Washington, DC during Standard Time)
**Administrative divisions:** 11 parishes and 1 city*; Bridgetown*, Christ Church, Saint Andrew, Saint George, Saint James, Saint John, Saint Joseph, Saint Lucy, Saint Michael, Saint Peter, Saint Philip, Saint Thomas
**Independence:** 30 November 1966 (from the UK)
**National holiday:** Independence Day, 30 November (1966)
**Constitution:** 30 November 1966
**Legal system:** English common law; no judicial review of legislative acts; accepts compulsory ICJ jurisdiction with reservations
**Suffrage:** 18 years of age; universal
**Executive branch:**
*chief of state:* Queen ELIZABETH II (since 6 February 1952); represented by Governor General Sir Clifford Straughn HUSBANDS (since 1 June 1996)
*head of government:* Prime Minister David THOMPSON (since 16 January 2008)
*cabinet:* Cabinet appointed by the governor general on the advice of the prime minister
*elections:* the monarch is hereditary; governor general appointed by the monarch; following legislative elections, the leader of the majority party or the leader of the majority coalition is usually appointed prime minister by the governor general; the prime minister recommends the deputy prime minister

**Legislative branch:** bicameral Parliament consists of the Senate (21 seats; members appointed by the governor general - 12 on the advice of the Prime Minister, 2 on the advice of the opposition leader, and 7 at his discretion) and the House of Assembly (30 seats; members are elected by direct popular vote to serve five-year terms)
*elections:* House of Assembly - last held 15 January 2008 (next to be called in 2013)
*election results:* House of Assembly - percent of vote by party - DLP 52.5%, BLP 47.3%; seats by party - DLP 20, BLP 10
**Judicial branch:** Supreme Court of Judicature consists of a High Court and a Court of Appeal (judges are appointed by the Service Commissions for the Judicial and Legal Services); Caribbean Court of Justice or CCJ is the highest court of appeal; based in Port of Spain, Trinidad and Tobago
**Political parties and leaders:** Barbados Labor Party or BLP [Mia MOTTLEY]; Democratic Labor Party or DLP [David THOMPSON]; People's Empowerment Party or PEP [David COMISSIONG]
**Political pressure groups and leaders:** Barbados Secondary Teachers' Union or BSTU [Patrick FROST]; Barbados Union of Teachers or BUT [Herbert GITTENS]; Congress of Trade Unions and Staff Associations of Barbados or CTUSAB, (includes the BWU, NUPW, BUT, and BSTU) [Leroy TROTMAN]; Barbados Workers Union or BWU [Leroy TROTMAN]; Clement Payne Labor Union [David COMISSIONG]; National Union of Public Workers [Joseph GODDARD]
**International organization participation:** ACP, C, Caricom, CDB, FAO, G-77, IADB, IBRD, ICAO, ICCt, ICRM, IDA, IFAD, IFC, IFRCS, ILO, IMF, IMO, Interpol, IOC, ISO, ITSO, ITU, ITUC, LAES, MIGA, NAM, OAS, OPANAL, OPCW, UN, UNCTAD, UNESCO, UNIDO, UPU, WCO, WFTU, WHO, WIPO, WMO, WTO
**Diplomatic representation in the US:**
*chief of mission:* Ambassador John BEALE
*chancery:* 2144 Wyoming Avenue NW, Washington, DC 20008
*telephone:* [1] (202) 939-9200
*FAX:* [1] (202) 332-7467
*consulate(s) general:* Miami, New York
*consulate(s):* Los Angeles
**Diplomatic representation from the US:**
*chief of mission:* Ambassador Mary M. OURISMAN
*embassy:* U.S. Embassy, Wildey Business Park, Wildey, St. Michael BB 14006
*mailing address:* P. O. Box 302, Bridgetown BB 11000; CMR 1014, APO AA 34055
*telephone:* [1] (246) 227-4399
*FAX:* [1] (246) 431-0179
**Flag description:** three equal vertical bands of blue (hoist side), gold, and blue with the head of a black trident centered on the gold band; the trident head represents independence and a break with the past (the colonial coat of arms contained a complete trident)

# Barbados *(continued)*

## Economy

**Economy - overview:** Historically, the Barbadian economy was dependent on sugarcane cultivation and related activities. However, in recent years the economy has diversified into light industry and tourism with about three-quarters of GDP and 80% of exports being attributed to services. Growth has rebounded since 2003, bolstered by increases in construction projects and tourism revenues, reflecting its success in the higher-end segment, but the sector will likely face declining revenues with the global economic downturn. The country enjoys one of the highest per capita incomes in the region. Offshore finance and information services are important foreign exchange earners and thrive from having the same time zone as eastern US financial centers and a relatively highly educated workforce. The government continues its efforts to reduce unemployment, to encourage direct foreign investment, and to privatize remaining state-owned enterprises. The public debt-to-GDP ratio of about 80% will likely widen as the THOMPSON administration engages in a more expansionary fiscal policy.

**GDP (purchasing power parity):**
$5.466 billion (2008 est.)
$5.386 billion (2007)
$5.214 billion (2006)
*note:* data are in 2008 US dollars

**GDP (official exchange rate):** $3.777 billion (2008 est.)

**GDP - real growth rate:**
1.5% (2008 est.)
3.3% (2007 est.)
3.9% (2006 est.)

**GDP - per capita (PPP):**
$19,300 (2008 est.)
$19,100 (2007 est.)
$18,500 (2006 est.)
*note:* data are in 2008 US dollars

**GDP - composition by sector:**
*agriculture:* 6%
*industry:* 16%
*services:* 78% (2000 est.)

**Labor force:** 128,500 (2001 est.)

**Labor force - by occupation:**
*agriculture:* 10%
*industry:* 15%
*services:* 75% (1996 est.)

**Unemployment rate:**
10.7% (2003 est.)

**Population below poverty line:** NA%

**Household income or consumption by percentage share:**
*lowest 10%:* NA%
*highest 10%:* NA%

**Budget:**
*revenues:* $847 million (including grants)
*expenditures:* $886 million (2000 est.)

**Inflation rate (consumer prices):**
5.5% (2007 est.)

**Central bank discount rate:** 12% (31 December 2007)

**Commercial bank prime lending rate:** 10.8% (31 December 2007)

**Stock of money:** $1.478 billion (31 December 2007)

**Stock of quasi money:** $2.717 billion (31 December 2007)

**Stock of domestic credit:** $3.533 billion (31 December 2007)

**Market value of publicly traded shares:** $5.599 billion (31 December 2007)

**Agriculture - products:** sugarcane, vegetables, cotton

**Industries:** tourism, sugar, light manufacturing, component assembly for export

**Industrial production growth rate:** -3.2% (2000 est.)

**Electricity - production:** 1.003 billion kWh (2007 est.)

**Electricity - consumption:** 939.9 million kWh (2007 est.)

**Electricity - exports:** 0 kWh (2007 est.)

**Electricity - imports:** 0 kWh (2007 est.)

**Oil - production:** 1,111 bbl/day (2007 est.)

**Oil - consumption:** 8,674 bbl/day (2006 est.)

**Oil - exports:** 1,750 bbl/day (2005)

**Oil - imports:** 10,710 bbl/day (2005)

**Oil - proved reserves:** 2.2 million bbl (1 January 2008 est.)

**Natural gas - production:** 29.17 million cu m (2006 est.)

**Natural gas - consumption:** 29.17 million cu m (2006 est.)

**Natural gas - exports:** 0 cu m (2007 est.)

**Natural gas - imports:** 0 cu m (2007 est.)

**Natural gas - proved reserves:** 141.6 million cu m (1 January 2008 est.)

**Current account balance:** -$254 million (2007 est.)

**Exports:** $385 million (2006)

**Exports - commodities:** manufactures, sugar and molasses, rum, other foods and beverages, chemicals, electrical components

**Exports - partners:** Trinidad and Tobago 15.5%, Jamaica 13.5%, UK 9.4%, US 9.3%, Brazil 8.3%, Saint Lucia 7.2%, Saint Vincent and the Grenadines 4.5% (2007)

**Imports:** $1.586 billion (2006)

**Imports - commodities:** consumer goods, machinery, foodstuffs, construction materials, chemicals, fuel, electrical components

**Imports - partners:** US 30.5%, Trinidad and Tobago 27.6%, UK 6.5% (2007)

**Reserves of foreign exchange and gold:** $620 million (2007)

**Debt - external:** $668 million (2003)

**Exchange rates:** Barbadian dollars (BBD) per US dollar - NA (2007), 2 (2006), 2 (2005), 2 (2004), 2 (2003)

## Communications

**Telephones - main lines in use:** 134,900 (2005)

**Telephones - mobile cellular:** 237,100 (2006)

**Telephone system:**
*general assessment:* fixed-line teledensity of roughly 50 per 100 persons; mobile-cellular telephone density of about 85 per 100 persons
*domestic:* island-wide automatic telephone system
*international:* country code - 1-246; landing point for the East Caribbean Fiber System (ECFS) submarine cable with links to 13 other islands in the eastern Caribbean extending from the British Virgin Islands to Trinidad; satellite earth stations - 1 (Intelsat -Atlantic Ocean); tropospheric scatter to Trinidad and Saint Lucia (2007)

**Radio broadcast stations:** AM 2, FM 6, shortwave 0 (2004)

**Television broadcast stations:** 1 (plus 2 cable channels) (2004)

**Internet country code:** .bb

**Internet hosts:** 104 (2008)

**Internet users:** 160,000 (2005)

## Transportation

**Airports:** 1 (2008)

**Airports - with paved runways:**
*total:* 1
*over 3,047 m:* 1 (2008)

**Roadways:**
*total:* 1,600 km
*paved:* 1,600 km (2004)

**Merchant marine:**
*total:* 85
*by type:* bulk carrier 15, cargo 50, chemical tanker 7, passenger 1, passenger/cargo 1, petroleum tanker 3, refrigerated cargo 6, roll on/roll off 2
*foreign-owned:* 80 (Canada 9, Greece 12, India 1, Iran 2, Lebanon 1, Norway 38, Sweden 7, Syria 1, UK 9)
*registered in other countries:* 1 (Saint Vincent and the Grenadines 1) (2008)

**Ports and terminals:** Bridgetown

## Military

**Military branches:** Royal Barbados Defense Force: Troops Command, Barbados Coast Guard (2007)

**Military service age and obligation:** 18 years of age for voluntary military service (younger requires parental consent); no conscription (2008)

**Manpower available for military service:**
*males age 16-49:* 75,265
*females age 16-49:* 75,389 (2008 est.)

**Manpower fit for military service:**
*males age 16-49:* 58,596
*females age 16-49:* 58,866 (2009 est.)

**Manpower reaching militarily significant age annually:**
*male:* 2,015
*female:* 2,007 (2009 est.)

**Military expenditures:** 0.5% of GDP (2006 est.)

## Barbados (continued)

**Military - note:** the Royal Barbados Defense Force includes a land-based Troop Command and a small Coast Guard; the primary role of the land element is to defend the island against external aggression; the Command consists of a single, part-time battalion with a small regular cadre that is deployed throughout the island; it increasingly supports the police in patrolling the coastline to prevent smuggling and other illicit activities (2007)

### Transnational Issues

**Disputes - international:** Barbados and Trinidad and Tobago abide by the April 2006 Permanent Court of Arbitration decision delimiting a maritime boundary and limiting catches of flying fish in Trinidad and Tobago's exclusive economic zone; joins other Caribbean states to counter Venezuela's claim that Aves Island sustains human habitation, a criterion under the UN Convention on the Law of the Sea (UNCLOS), which permits Venezuela to extend its EEZ/continental shelf over a large portion of the eastern Caribbean Sea

**Illicit drugs:** one of many Caribbean transshipment points for narcotics bound for Europe and the US; offshore financial center

# Belarus

### Introduction

**Background:** After seven decades as a constituent republic of the USSR, Belarus attained its independence in 1991. It has retained closer political and economic ties to Russia than any of the other former Soviet republics. Belarus and Russia signed a treaty on a two-state union on 8 December 1999 envisioning greater political and economic integration. Although Belarus agreed to a framework to carry out the accord, serious implementation has yet to take place. Since his election in July 1994 as the country's first president, Aleksandr LUKASHENKO has steadily consolidated his power through authoritarian means. Government restrictions on freedom of speech and the press, peaceful assembly, and religion remain in place.

### Geography

**Location:** Eastern Europe, east of Poland
**Geographic coordinates:** 53 00 N, 28 00 E
**Map references:** Europe
**Area:**
*total:* 207,600 sq km
*land:* 207,600 sq km
*water:* 0 sq km
**Area - comparative:** slightly smaller than Kansas
**Land boundaries:**
*total:* 3,306 km
*border countries:* Latvia 171 km, Lithuania 680 km, Poland 605 km, Russia 959 km, Ukraine 891 km
**Coastline:** 0 km (landlocked)
**Maritime claims:** none (landlocked)
**Climate:** cold winters, cool and moist summers; transitional between continental and maritime
**Terrain:** generally flat and contains much marshland
**Elevation extremes:**
*lowest point:* Nyoman River 90 m
*highest point:* Dzyarzhynskaya Hara 346 m

**Natural resources:** forests, peat deposits, small quantities of oil and natural gas, granite, dolomitic limestone, marl, chalk, sand, gravel, clay
**Land use:**
*arable land:* 26.77%
*permanent crops:* 0.6%
*other:* 72.63% (2005)
**Irrigated land:** 1,310 sq km (2003)
**Total renewable water resources:** 58 cu km (1997)
**Freshwater withdrawal (domestic/industrial/agricultural):**
*total:* 2.79 cu km/yr (23%/47%/30%)
*per capita:* 286 cu m/yr (2000)
**Natural hazards:** NA
**Environment - current issues:** soil pollution from pesticide use; southern part of the country contaminated with fallout from 1986 nuclear reactor accident at Chornobyl' in northern Ukraine
**Environment - international agreements:**
*party to:* Air Pollution, Air Pollution-Nitrogen Oxides, Air Pollution-Sulfur 85, Biodiversity, Climate Change, Climate Change-Kyoto Protocol, Desertification, Endangered Species, Environmental Modification, Hazardous Wastes, Law of the Sea, Marine Dumping, Ozone Layer Protection, Ship Pollution, Wetlands
*signed, but not ratified:* none of the selected agreements
**Geography - note:** landlocked; glacial scouring accounts for the flatness of Belarusian terrain and for its 11,000 lakes

### People

**Population:** 9,648,533 (July 2009 est.)
**Age structure:**
*0-14 years:* 14.3% (male 707,550/female 667,560)
*15-64 years:* 71.3% (male 3,337,253/female 3,540,916)
*65 years and over:* 14.5% (male 446,746/female 948,508) (2009 est.)
**Median age:**
*total:* 38.6 years
*male:* 35.6 years
*female:* 41.6 years (2009 est.)
**Population growth rate:** -0.378% (2009 est.)
**Birth rate:** 9.71 births/1,000 population (2009 est.)
**Death rate:** 13.92 deaths/1,000 population (2008 est.)
**Net migration rate:** 0.38 migrant(s)/1,000 population (2009 est.)
**Urbanization:**
*urban population:* 73% of total population (2008)
*rate of urbanization:* 0% annual rate of change (2005-10 est.)
**Sex ratio:**
*at birth:* 1.06 male(s)/female
*under 15 years:* 1.06 male(s)/female
*15-64 years:* 0.94 male(s)/female
*65 years and over:* 0.47 male(s)/female
*total population:* 0.87 male(s)/female (2009 est.)

# Belarus (continued)

**Infant mortality rate:**

*total:* 6.43 deaths/1,000 live births

*male:* 7.45 deaths/1,000 live births

*female:* 5.36 deaths/1,000 live births (2009 est.)

**Life expectancy at birth:**

*total population:* 70.63 years

*male:* 64.95 years

*female:* 76.67 years (2009 est.)

**Total fertility rate:** 1.24 children born/woman (2009 est.)

**HIV/AIDS - adult prevalence rate:** 0.2% (2007 est.)

**HIV/AIDS - people living with HIV/AIDS:** 13,000 (2007 est.)

**HIV/AIDS - deaths:** 1,100 (2007 est.)

**Nationality:**

*noun:* Belarusian(s)

*adjective:* Belarusian

**Ethnic groups:** Belarusian 81.2%, Russian 11.4%, Polish 3.9%, Ukrainian 2.4%, other 1.1% (1999 census)

**Religions:** Eastern Orthodox 80%, other (including Roman Catholic, Protestant, Jewish, and Muslim) 20% (1997 est.)

**Languages:** Belarusian, Russian, other

**Literacy:**

*definition:* age 15 and over can read and write

*total population:* 99.6%

*male:* 99.8%

*female:* 99.4% (1999 census)

**School life expectancy (primary to tertiary education):**

*total:* 15 years

*male:* 14 years

*female:* 15 years (2006)

**Education expenditures:** 6.1% of GDP (2006)

## Government

**Country name:**

*conventional long form:* Republic of Belarus

*conventional short form:* Belarus

*local long form:* Respublika Byelarus'

*local short form:* Byelarus'

*former:* Belorussian (Byelorussian) Soviet Socialist Republic

**Government type:** republic in name, although in fact a dictatorship

**Capital:**

*name:* Minsk

*geographic coordinates:* 53 54 N, 27 34 E

*time difference:* UTC+2 (7 hours ahead of Washington, DC during Standard Time)

*daylight saving time:* +1hr, begins last Sunday in March; ends last Sunday in October

**Administrative divisions:** 6 provinces (voblastsi, singular - voblasts') and 1 municipality* (horad); Brest, Homyel', Horad Minsk*, Hrodna, Mahilyow, Minsk, Vitsyebsk

*note:* administrative divisions have the same names as their administrative centers

**Independence:** 25 August 1991 (from the Soviet Union)

**National holiday:** Independence Day, 3 July (1944); note - 3 July 1944 was the date Minsk was liberated from German troops, 25 August 1991 was the date of independence from the Soviet Union

**Constitution:** 15 March 1994; revised by national referendum of 24 November 1996 giving the presidency greatly expanded powers and became effective 27 November 1996; revised again 17 October 2004 removing presidential term limits

**Legal system:** based on civil law system; has not accepted compulsory ICJ jurisdiction

**Suffrage:** 18 years of age; universal

**Executive branch:**

*chief of state:* President Aleksandr LUKASHENKO (since 20 July 1994)

*head of government:* Prime Minister Sergey SIDORSKIY (since 19 December 2003); First Deputy Prime Minister Vladimir SEMASHKO (since December 2003)

*cabinet:* Council of Ministers

*elections:* president elected by popular vote for a five-year term; first election took place 23 June and 10July 1994; according to the 1994 constitution, the next election should have been held in 1999, however, Aleksandr LUKASHENKO extended his term to 2001 via a November 1996 referendum; subsequent election held 9 September 2001; an October 2004 referendum ended presidential term limits and allowed the president to run in a third election, which was held on 19 March 2006; prime minister and deputy prime ministers appointed by the president

*election results:* Aleksandr LUKASHENKO reelected president; percent of vote - Aleksandr LUKASHENKO 82.6%, Aleksandr MILINKEVICH 6%, Aleksandr KOZULIN 2.3%; note - election marred by electoral fraud

**Legislative branch:** bicameral National Assembly or Natsionalnoye Sobranie consists of the Council of the Republic or Soviet Respubliki (64 seats; 56 members elected by regional councils and eight members appointed by the president, to serve four-year terms) and the Chamber of Representatives or Palata Predstaviteley (110 seats; members elected by popular vote to serve four-year terms)

*elections:* Palata Predstaviteley - last held 28 September and 3 October 2008 (next to be held fall of 2012); international observers determined that despite minor improvements the election ultimately fell short of democratic standards; pro-LUKASHENKO candidates won every seat

*election results:* Soviet Respubliki - percent of vote by party - NA; seats by party - NA; Palata Predstaviteley -percent of vote by party - NA; seats by party - NA

**Judicial branch:** Supreme Court (judges are appointed by the president); Constitutional Court (half of the judges appointed by the president and half appointed by the Chamber of Representatives)

**Political parties and leaders:**

*pro-government parties:* Agrarian Party or AP [Mikhail SHIMANSKY]; Communist Party of Belarus or KPB; Belarusian Patriotic Movement (Belarusian Patriotic Party) or BPR [Nikolay ULAKHOVICH, chairman]; Liberal Democratic Party [Sergey GAYDUKEVICH]; Republican Party of Labor and Justice [Viktor SOKOLOV]; Social-Sports Party [Vladimir ALEXANDROVICH]

*opposition parties:* Belarusian Christian Democracy Party (unregistered) [Pavel SEVERINETS]; Belarusian Party of Communists or PKB [Sergey KALYAKIN]; Belarusian Party of Labor (unregistered) [Aleksandr BUKHVOSTOV, Leonid LEMESHONAK]; Belarusian Popular Front or BPF [Levon BARSHCHEVSKIY]; Belarusian Social-Democratic Gramada [Stanislav SHUSHKEVICH]; Belarusian Social Democratic Party Hramada (People's Assembly) or BSDPH [Anatoliy LEVKOVICH]; European Coalition [Nikolay STATKEVICH]; Green Party [Oleg GROMYKO]; Party of Freedom and Progress (unregistered) [Vladimir NOVOSYAD]; United Civic Party or UCP [Anatoliy LEBEDKO]; Women's Party Hope (Nadezhda) [Valentina MATUSEVICH, chairperson]

*other opposition includes:* Christian Conservative BPF [Zyanon PAZNIAK]; Ecological Party of Greens [Mikhail KARTASH]; Party of Popular Accord [Sergey YERMAKK]; Republican Party [Vladimir BELAZOR]

**Political pressure groups and leaders:** Assembly of Pro-Democratic NGOs [Sergey MATSKEVICH]; Belarusian Congress of Democratic Trade Unions [Aleksandr YAROSHUK]; Belarusian Helsinki Committee [Tatiana PROTKO]; Belarusian Organization of Working Women [Irina ZHIKHAR]; BPF-Youth [Franak VYACHORKA]; Charter 97 [Andrey SANNIKOV]; For Freedom [Aleksandr MILINKEVICH]; Lenin Communist Union of Youth (youth wing of the Belarusian Party of Communists or PKB); National Strike Committee of Entrepreneurs [Aleksandr VASILYEV, Valery LEVONEVSKY]; Partnership NGO [Nikolay ASTREYKA]; Perspektiva kiosk watchdog NGO [Anatol SHUMCHENKO]; Vyasna [Ales BYALATSKY]; Women's Independent Democratic Movement [Ludmila PETINA]; Young Belarus (Malady Belarus) [Artur FINKEVICH]; Youth Front (Malady Front) [Dmitriy DASHKEVICH]; Zubr youth group [Vladimir KOBETS]

**International organization participation:** BSEC (observer), CEI, CIS, CSTO, EAEC, EAPC, EBRD, FAO, GCTU, IAEA, IBRD, ICAO, ICRM, IDA, IFC, IFRCS, ILO, IMF, IMSO, Interpol, IOC, IOM, IPU, ISO, ITU, ITUC, MIGA, NAM, NSG, OPCW, OSCE, PCA, PFP, UN, UNCTAD, UNESCO, UNIDO, UNWTO, UPU, WCO, WFTU, WHO, WIPO, WMO, WTO (observer)

**Diplomatic representation in the US:**

*chief of mission:* Ambassador (vacant); Charge D'Affaires Oleg KRAVCHENKO

*chancery:* 1619 New Hampshire Avenue NW, Washington, DC 20009

*telephone:* [1] (202) 986-1604

*FAX:* [1] (202) 986-1805

*consulate(s) general:* New York

**Diplomatic representation from the US:**

*chief of mission:* Ambassador (vacant); Charge

# Belarus (continued)

d'Affaires Jonathan MOORE
*embassy:* 46 Starovilenskaya Street, Minsk 220002
*mailing address:* PSC 78, Box B Minsk, APO 09723
*telephone:* [375] (17) 210-12-83, 217-7347 through 7348
*FAX:* [375] (17) 234-7853
**Flag description:** red horizontal band (top) and green horizontal band one-half the width of the red band; a white vertical stripe on the hoist side bears Belarusian national ornamentation in red

## Economy

**Economy - overview:** Belarus has seen little structural reform since 1995, when President LUKASHENKO launched the country on the path of "market socialism." In keeping with this policy, LUKASHENKO reimposed administrative controls over prices and currency exchange rates and expanded the state's right to intervene in the management of private enterprises. Since 2005, the government has re-nationalized a number of private companies. In addition, businesses have been subject to pressure by central and local governments, e.g., arbitrary changes in regulations, numerous rigorous inspections, retroactive application of new business regulations, and arrests of "disruptive" businessmen and factory owners. A wide range of redistributive policies has helped those at the bottom of the ladder; the Gini coefficient is among the lowest in the world. Because of these restrictive economic policies, Belarus has had trouble attracting foreign investment. Nevertheless, government statistics indicate GDP growth has been strong in recent years, reaching more than 9% in 2008, despite the roadblocks of a tough, centrally directed economy with a high rate of inflation. Belarus receives discounted oil and natural gas from Russia and much of Belarus' growth can be attributed to the re-export of Russian oil at market prices. Trade with Russia - by far its largest single trade partner - decreased in 2007-08, largely as a result of a change in the way the Value Added Tax (VAT) on trade was collected. Russia has introduced an export duty on oil shipped to Belarus, which will increase gradually through 2009, and a requirement that Belarusian duties on re-exported Russian oil be shared with Russia - 80% was slated to go to Russia in 2008, and 85% in 2009. Russia also increased Belarusian natural gas prices from $47 per thousand cubic meters (tcm) in 2006 to $100 per tcm in 2007, and to $128 per tcm in 2008, and plans to increase prices gradually to world levels by 2011. Russia's recent policy of bringing energy prices for Belarus to world market levels may result in a slowdown in economic growth in Belarus over the next few years. Some policy measures, including improving energy efficiency and diversifying exports, have been introduced, but external borrowing has been the main mechanism used to manage the growing pressures on the economy. Belarus felt the effects of the global financial crisis in late 2008 and reached agreement with Russia in November for a $2 billion stabilization loan and with the IMF for a $2.5 billion stand-by agreement in January 2009. In line with IMF conditionality, Belarus devalued the ruble approximately 20% in January 2009 and has tightened some fiscal and monetary policies. Belarus's economic growth is likely to slow in 2009 as it faces decreasing demand for its exports, and will find it difficult to increase external borrowing if the credit markets continue to tighten.

**GDP (purchasing power parity):**
$114.1 billion (2008 est.)
$104.5 billion (2007)
$96.59 billion (2006)
*note:* data are in 2008 US dollars

**GDP (official exchange rate):** $57.68 billion (2008 est.)

**GDP - real growth rate:**
9.2% (2008 est.)
8.2% (2007 est.)
9.9% (2006 est.)

**GDP - per capita (PPP):**
$11,800 (2008 est.)
$10,700 (2007 est.)
$9,900 (2006 est.)
*note:* data are in 2008 US dollars

**GDP - composition by sector:**
*agriculture:* 8.4%
*industry:* 41.5%
*services:* 50.1% (2008 est.)

**Labor force:** 4.3 million (31 December 2005)

**Labor force - by occupation:**
*agriculture:* 14%
*industry:* 34.7%
*services:* 51.3% (2003 est.)

**Unemployment rate:**
1.6% (2005)
*note:* officially registered unemployed; large number of underemployed workers

**Population below poverty line:** 27.1% (2003 est.)

**Household income or consumption by percentage share:**
*lowest 10%:* 3.4%
*highest 10%:* 23.5% (2002)

**Distribution of family income - Gini index:** 27.9 (2005)

**Investment (gross fixed):** 31.5% of GDP (2008 est.)

**Budget:**
*revenues:* $25.23 billion
*expenditures:* $26.05 billion (2008 est.)

**Inflation rate (consumer prices):**
15.5% (2008 est.)
8.4% (2007 est.)

**Central bank discount rate:** 10% (31 December 2007)

**Commercial bank prime lending rate:** 8.58% (31 December 2007)

**Stock of money:** $4.065 billion (31 December 2007)

**Stock of quasi money:** $6.823 billion (31 December 2007)

**Stock of domestic credit:** $12.16 billion (31 December 2007)

**Market value of publicly traded shares:** $NA

**Agriculture - products:** grain, potatoes, vegetables, sugar beets, flax; beef, milk

**Industries:** metal-cutting machine tools, tractors, trucks, earthmovers, motorcycles, televisions, synthetic fibers, fertilizer, textiles, radios, refrigerators

**Industrial production growth rate:** 11.5% (2008 est.)

**Electricity - production:** 29.91 billion kWh (2006 est.)

**Electricity - consumption:** 30.43 billion kWh (2006 est.)

**Electricity - exports:** 5.789 billion kWh (2006 est.)

**Electricity - imports:** 10.15 billion kWh (2006 est.)

**Oil - production:** 33,700 bbl/day (2007 est.)

**Oil - consumption:** 179,700 bbl/day (2006 est.)

**Oil - exports:** 256,400 bbl/day (2005 est.)

**Oil - imports:** 394,100 bbl/day (2005 est.)

**Oil - proved reserves:** 198 million bbl (1 January 2008 est.)

**Natural gas - production:** 164 million cu m (2007 est.)

**Natural gas - consumption:** 21.76 billion cu m (2007 est.)

**Natural gas - exports:** 0 cu m (2007 est.)

**Natural gas - imports:** 21.6 billion cu m (2007 est.)

**Natural gas - proved reserves:** 2.832 billion cu m (1 January 2008 est.)

**Current account balance:** -$3.832 billion (2008 est.)

**Exports:** $31.81 billion f.o.b. (2008 est.)

**Exports - commodities:** machinery and equipment, mineral products, chemicals, metals, textiles, foodstuffs

**Exports - partners:** Russia 36.5%, Netherlands 17.8%, UK 6.3%, Ukraine 6.1%, Poland 5%, Latvia 4.1% (2007)

**Imports:** $36.64 billion f.o.b. (2008 est.)

**Imports - commodities:** mineral products, machinery and equipment, chemicals, foodstuffs, metals

**Imports - partners:** Russia 59.9%, Germany 7.6%, Ukraine 5.4% (2007)

**Reserves of foreign exchange and gold:** $3.775 billion (November 2008 est.)

**Debt - external:** $9.127 billion (31 December 2008 est.)

**Exchange rates:** Belarusian rubles (BYB/BYR) per US dollar - 2,130 (2008 est.), 2,145 (2007), 2,144.6 (2006), 2,150 (2005), 2,160.26 (2004)

## Communications

**Telephones - main lines in use:** 3.672 million (2007)

**Telephones - mobile cellular:** 6.96 million (2007)

**Telephone system:**
*general assessment:* Belarus lags behind its neighbors in upgrading telecommunications infrastructure; state-owned Beltelcom is the sole provider of fixed-line local and long distance service; fixed-line teledensity of roughly 35 per 100 persons;

# Belarus (continued)

mobile-cellular telephone density of about 70 per 100 persons; modernization of the network progressing with roughly two-thirds of switching equipment now digital
*domestic:* fixed-line penetration is improving although rural areas continue to be underserved; 3 GSM wireless networks are experiencing rapid growth; strict government controls on telecommunications technologies
*international:* country code - 375; Belarus is a member of the Trans-European Line (TEL), Trans-Asia-Europe (TAE) fiber-optic line, and has access to the Trans-Siberia Line (TSL); 3 fiber-optic segments provide connectivity to Latvia, Poland, Russia, and Ukraine; worldwide service is available to Belarus through this infrastructure; additional analog lines to Russia; Intelsat, Eutelsat, and Intersputnik earth stations (2007)
**Radio broadcast stations:** AM 28, FM 37, shortwave 11 (1998)
**Television broadcast stations:** 47 (plus 27 repeaters) (1995)
**Internet country code:** .by
**Internet hosts:** 68,118 (2008)
**Internet users:** 6 million (2007)

## Transportation

**Airports:** 65 (2008)
**Airports - with paved runways:**
*total:* 35
*over 3,047 m:* 2
*2,438 to 3,047 m:* 22
*1,524 to 2,437 m:* 4
*914 to 1,523 m:* 1
*under 914 m:* 6 (2008)
**Airports - with unpaved runways:**
*total:* 30
*2,438 to 3,047 m:* 1
*1,524 to 2,437 m:* 1
*914 to 1,523 m:* 2
*under 914 m:* 26 (2008)
**Heliports:** 1 (2007)
**Pipelines:** gas 5,250 km; oil 1,528 km; refined products 1,730 km (2008)
**Railways:**
*total:* 5,512 km
*broad gauge:* 5,497 km 1.520-m gauge (874 km electrified)
*standard gauge:* 15 km 1.435 m (2006)
**Roadways:**
*total:* 94,797 km
*paved:* 84,028 km
*unpaved:* 10,769 km (2005)
**Waterways:** 2,500 km (use limited by location on perimeter of country and by shallowness) (2003)
**Ports and terminals:** Mazyr

## Military

**Military branches:** Belarus Armed Forces: Land Force, Air and Air Defense Force (2009)
**Military service age and obligation:** 18-27 years of age for compulsory military service; conscript service obligation - 18 months (2005)
**Manpower available for military service:**
*males age 16-49:* 2,491,643
*females age 16-49:* 2,528,779 (2008 est.)
**Manpower fit for military service:**
*males age 16-49:* 1,720,049
*females age 16-49:* 2,069,898 (2009 est.)
**Manpower reaching militarily significant age annually:**
*male:* 60,009
*female:* 56,834 (2009 est.)
**Military expenditures:** 1.4% of GDP (2005 est.)

## Transnational Issues

**Disputes - international:** Boundary demarcated with Latvia and Lithuania in 2006; 1997 boundary delimitation treaty with Ukraine remains unratified over unresolved financial claims, preventing demarcation and diminishing border security
**Illicit drugs:** limited cultivation of opium poppy and cannabis, mostly for the domestic market; transshipment point for illicit drugs to and via Russia, and to the Baltics and Western Europe; a small and lightly regulated financial center; anti-money-laundering legislation does not meet international standards and was weakened further when know-your-customer requirements were curtailed in 2008; few investigations or prosecutions of money-laundering activities (2008)

# Belgium

## Introduction

**Background:** Belgium became independent from the Netherlands in 1830; it was occupied by Germany during World Wars I and II. The country prospered in the past half century as a modern, technologically advanced European state and member of NATO and the EU. Tensions between the Dutch-speaking Flemings of the north and the French-speaking Walloons of the south have led in recent years to constitutional amendments granting these regions formal recognition and autonomy.

## Geography

**Location:** Western Europe, bordering the North Sea, between France and the Netherlands
**Geographic coordinates:** 50 50 N, 4 00 E
**Map references:** Europe
**Area:**
*total:* 30,528 sq km
*land:* 30,278 sq km
*water:* 250 sq km
**Area - comparative:** about the size of Maryland
**Land boundaries:**
*total:* 1,385 km
*border countries:* France 620 km, Germany 167 km, Luxembourg 148 km, Netherlands 450 km
**Coastline:** 66.5 km
**Maritime claims:**
*territorial sea:* 12 nm
*contiguous zone:* 24 nm
*exclusive economic zone:* geographic coordinates define outer limit
*continental shelf:* median line with neighbors
**Climate:** temperate; mild winters, cool summers; rainy, humid, cloudy
**Terrain:** flat coastal plains in northwest, central rolling hills, rugged mountains of Ardennes Forest in southeast

# Belgium (continued)

**Elevation extremes:**
*lowest point:* North Sea 0 m
*highest point:* Signal de Botrange 694 m
**Natural resources:** construction materials, silica sand, carbonates
**Land use:**
*arable land:* 27.42%
*permanent crops:* 0.69%
*other:* 71.89%
*note:* includes Luxembourg (2005)
**Irrigated land:** 400 sq km (2003)
**Total renewable water resources:** 20.8 cu km (2005)
**Freshwater withdrawal (domestic/industrial/agricultural):**
*total:* 7.44 cu km/yr (13%/85%/1%)
*per capita:* 714 cu m/yr (1998)
**Natural hazards:** flooding is a threat along rivers and in areas of reclaimed coastal land, protected from the sea by concrete dikes
**Environment - current issues:** the environment is exposed to intense pressures from human activities: urbanization, dense transportation network, industry, extensive animal breeding and crop cultivation; air and water pollution also have repercussions for neighboring countries; uncertainties regarding federal and regional responsibilities (now resolved) had slowed progress in tackling environmental challenges
**Environment - international agreements:**
*party to:* Air Pollution, Air Pollution-Nitrogen Oxides, Air Pollution-Persistent Organic Pollutants, Air Pollution-Sulfur 85, Air Pollution-Sulfur 94, Air Pollution-Volatile Organic Compounds, Antarctic-Environmental Protocol, Antarctic-Marine Living Resources, Antarctic Seals, Antarctic Treaty, Biodiversity, Climate Change, Climate Change-Kyoto Protocol, Desertification, Endangered Species, Environmental Modification, Hazardous Wastes, Law of the Sea, Marine Dumping, Marine Life Conservation, Ozone Layer Protection, Ship Pollution, Tropical Timber 83, Tropical Timber 94, Wetlands, Whaling
*signed, but not ratified:* none of the selected agreements
**Geography - note:** crossroads of Western Europe; most West European capitals within 1,000 km of Brussels, the seat of both the European Union and NATO

## People

**Population:** 10,414,336 (July 2009 est.)
**Age structure:**
*0-14 years:* 16.1% (male 857,373/female 822,303)
*15-64 years:* 66.3% (male 3,480,072/female 3,419,721)
*65 years and over:* 17.6% (male 760,390/female 1,074,477) (2009 est.)
**Median age:**
*total:* 41.7 years
*male:* 40.4 years
*female:* 43 years (2009 est.)

**Population growth rate:** 0.094% (2009 est.)
**Birth rate:** 10.15 births/1,000 population (2009 est.)
**Death rate:** 10.38 deaths/1,000 population (2008 est.)
**Net migration rate:** 1.22 migrant(s)/1,000 population (2009 est.)
**Urbanization:**
*urban population:* 97% of total population (2008)
*rate of urbanization:* 0.3% annual rate of change (2005-10 est.)
**Sex ratio:**
*at birth:* 1.04 male(s)/female
*under 15 years:* 1.04 male(s)/female
*15-64 years:* 1.02 male(s)/female
*65 years and over:* 0.71 male(s)/female
*total population:* 0.96 male(s)/female (2009 est.)
**Infant mortality rate:**
*total:* 4.44 deaths/1,000 live births
*male:* 4.99 deaths/1,000 live births
*female:* 3.87 deaths/1,000 live births (2009 est.)
**Life expectancy at birth:**
*total population:* 79.22 years
*male:* 76.06 years
*female:* 82.53 years (2009 est.)
**Total fertility rate:** 1.65 children born/woman (2009 est.)
**HIV/AIDS - adult prevalence rate:** 0.2% (2007 est.)
**HIV/AIDS - people living with HIV/AIDS:** 15,000 (2007 est.)
**HIV/AIDS - deaths:** fewer than 100 (2007 est.)
**Nationality:**
*noun:* Belgian(s)
*adjective:* Belgian
**Ethnic groups:** Fleming 58%, Walloon 31%, mixed or other 11%
**Religions:** Roman Catholic 75%, other (includes Protestant) 25%
**Languages:** Dutch (official) 60%, French (official) 40%, German (official) less than 1%, legally bilingual (Dutch and French)
**Literacy:**
*definition:* age 15 and over can read and write
*total population:* 99%
*male:* 99%
*female:* 99% (2003 est.)
**School life expectancy (primary to tertiary education):**
*total:* 16 years
*male:* 16 years
*female:* 16 years (2006)
**Education expenditures:** 6% of GDP (2004)

## Government

**Country name:**
*conventional long form:* Kingdom of Belgium
*conventional short form:* Belgium
*local long form:* Royaume de Belgique/Koninkrijk Belgie
*local short form:* Belgique/Belgie
**Government type:** federal parliamentary democracy under a constitutional monarchy

**Capital:**
*name:* Brussels
*geographic coordinates:* 50 50 N, 4 20 E
*time difference:* UTC+1 (6 hours ahead of Washington, DC during Standard Time)
*daylight saving time:* +1hr, begins last Sunday in March; ends last Sunday in October
**Administrative divisions:** 10 provinces (French: provinces, singular - province; Dutch: provincies, singular - provincie) and 3 regions* (French: regions; Dutch: gewesten); Brussels* (Bruxelles) capital region; Flanders* region (five provinces): Antwerpen (Antwerp), Limburg, Oost-Vlaanderen (East Flanders), Vlaams-Brabant (Flemish Brabant), West-Vlaanderen (West Flanders); Wallonia* region (five provinces): Brabant Wallon (Walloon Brabant), Hainaut, Liege, Luxembourg, Namur
*note:* as a result of the 1993 constitutional revision that furthered devolution into a federal state, there are now three levels of government (federal, regional, and linguistic community) with a complex division of responsibilities
**Independence:** 4 October 1830 (a provisional government declared independence from the Netherlands); 21 July 1831 (King LEOPOLD I ascended to the throne)
**National holiday:** 21 July (1831) ascension to the Throne of King LEOPOLD I
**Constitution:** 7 February 1831; amended many times; revised 14 July 1993 to create a federal state
**Legal system:** based on civil law system influenced by English constitutional theory; judicial review of legislative acts; accepts compulsory ICJ jurisdiction with reservations
**Suffrage:** 18 years of age; universal and compulsory
**Executive branch:**
*chief of state:* King ALBERT II (since 9 August 1993); Heir Apparent Prince PHILIPPE, son of the monarch
*head of government:* Prime Minister Herman VAN ROMPUY (30 December 2008)
*cabinet:* Council of Ministers are formally appointed by the monarch
*elections:* the monarchy is hereditary and constitutional; following legislative elections, the leader of the majority party or the leader of the majority coalition is usually appointed prime minister by the monarch and then approved by parliament
**Legislative branch:** bicameral Parliament consists of a Senate or Senaat in Dutch, Senat in French (71 seats; 40 members are directly elected by popular vote, 31 are indirectly elected; members serve four-year terms) and a Chamber of Deputies or Kamer van Volksvertegenwoordigers in Dutch, Chambre des Representants in French (150 seats; members are directly elected by popular vote on the basis of proportional representation to serve four-year terms)
*elections:* Senate and Chamber of Deputies - last held 10 June 2007 (next to be held no later than June 2011)
*election results:* Senate - percent of vote by party - CDV/N-VA 19.4%, Open VLD 12.4%, MR 12.3%, VB 11.9%, PS 10.2%, SP.A-Spirit 10%, CDH 5.9%, Ecolo 5.8%, Groen! 3.6%, Dedecker List 3.4%, FN 2.3%,

# Belgium (continued)

other 2.8%; seats by party - CDV 12, MR 11, Open VLD 9, VB 8, PS 7, SP.A 6, CDH 5, Ecolo 5, Groen! 2, LDD 1, FN 1, independents 4; Chamber of Deputies - percent of vote by party - CDV/N-VA 18.5%, MR 12.5%, VB 12%, Open VLD 11.8%, PS 10.9%, SP.A-Spirit 10.3%, CDH 6.1%, Ecolo 5.1%, Dedecker List 4%, Groen! 4%, FN 2%, other 2.8%; seats by party - CDV 23, N-VA 7, MR 23, VB 17, Open VLD 18, PS 20, SP.A 14, CDH 10, Ecolo 8, Dedecker List 5, Groen! 4, FN 1

*note:* as a result of the 1993 constitutional revision that furthered devolution into a federal state, there are now three levels of government (federal, regional, and linguistic community) with a complex division of responsibilities; this reality leaves six governments, each with its own legislative assembly

**Judicial branch:** Supreme Court of Justice or Hof van Cassatie (in Dutch) or Cour de Cassation (in French) (judges are appointed for life by the government; candidacies have to be submitted by the High Justice Council)

**Political parties and leaders:**
*Flemish parties:* Christian Democratic and Flemish or CDV [Marianne THYSSEN]; Dedecker List [Jean-Marie DEDECKER]; Flemish Liberals and Democrats or Open VLD [Bart SOMERS]; Groen! [Mieke VOGELS] (formerly AGALEV, Flemish Greens); New Flemish Alliance or N-VA [Bart DE WEVER]; Social Liberal Party or SLP [Geert LAMBERT]; note - prior to 19 April 2008, known as Spirit; Social Progressive Alternative or SP.A [Caroline GENNEZ]; Vlaams Belang (Flemish Interest) or VB [Bruno VALKENIERS]
*Francophone parties:* Ecolo (Francophone Greens) [Jean-Michel JAVAUX, Isabelle DURANT]; Humanist and Democratic Center or CDH [Joelle MILQUET]; National Front or FN [Daniel HUYGENS]; Reform Movement or MR [Didier REYNDERS]; Socialist Party or PS [Elio DI RUPO]; other minor parties

**Political pressure groups and leaders:** Christian, Socialist, and Liberal Trade Unions; Federation of Belgian Industries
*other:* numerous other associations representing bankers, manufacturers, middle-class artisans, and the legal and medical professions; various organizations represent the cultural interests of Flanders and Wallonia; various peace groups such as Pax Christi and groups representing immigrants

**International organization participation:** ACCT, ADB (nonregional members), AfDB (nonregional members), Australia Group, Benelux, BIS, CE, CERN, EAPC, EBRD, EIB, EMU, ESA, EU, FAO, G-9, G-10, IADB, IAEA, IBRD, ICAO, ICC, ICCt, ICRM, IDA, IEA, IFAD, IFC, IFRCS, IHO, ILO, IMF, IMO, IMSO, Interpol, IOC, IOM, IPU, ISO, ITSO, ITU, ITUC, MIGA, MONUC, NATO, NEA, NSG, OAS (observer), OECD, OIF, OPCW, OSCE, Paris Club, PCA, Schengen Convention, SECI (observer), UN, UNCTAD, UNESCO, UNHCR, UNIDO, UNIFIL, UNMIS, UNRWA, UNTSO, UPU, WADB (nonregional), WCL, WCO, WEU, WFTU, WHO, WIPO, WMO, WTO, ZC

**Diplomatic representation in the US:**
*chief of mission:* Ambassador Jan MATTHYSEN
*chancery:* 3330 Garfield Street NW, Washington, DC 20008
*telephone:* [1] (202) 333-6900
*FAX:* [1] (202) 333-3079
*consulate(s) general:* Atlanta, Los Angeles, New York

**Diplomatic representation from the US:**
*chief of mission:* Ambassador (vacant); Charge d'Affaires Wayne BUSH
*embassy:* 27 Boulevard du Regent [Regentlaan], B-1000 Brussels
*mailing address:* PSC 82, Box 002, APO AE 09710
*telephone:* [32] (2) 508-2111
*FAX:* [32] (2) 511-2725

**Flag description:** three equal vertical bands of black (hoist side), yellow, and red
*note:* the design was based on the flag of France

## Economy

**Economy - overview:** This modern, private-enterprise economy has capitalized on its central geographic location, highly developed transport network, and diversified industrial and commercial base. Industry is concentrated mainly in the populous Flemish area in the north. With few natural resources, Belgium must import substantial quantities of raw materials and export a large volume of manufactures, making its economy unusually dependent on the state of world markets. Roughly three-quarters of its trade is with other EU countries. Public debt is more than 80% of GDP. On the positive side, the government succeeded in balancing its budget during the 2000-2008 period, and income distribution is relatively equal. Belgium began circulating the euro currency in January 2002. Economic growth and foreign direct investment dropped in 2008. In 2009 Belgium is likely to have negative growth, growing unemployment, and a 3% budget deficit, stemming from the worldwide banking crisis.

**GDP (purchasing power parity):**
$390.5 billion (2008 est.)
$385.5 billion (2007)
$375.7 billion (2006)
*note:* data are in 2008 US dollars

**GDP (official exchange rate):** $495.4 billion (2008)

**GDP - real growth rate:**
1.3% (2008)
2.6% (2007 est.)
3% (2006 est.)

**GDP - per capita (PPP):**
$37,500 (2008 est.)
$37,100 (2007 est.)
$36,200 (2006 est.)
*note:* data are in 2008 US dollars

**GDP - composition by sector:**
*agriculture:* 1%
*industry:* 24.2%
*services:* 74.9% (2008 est.)

**Labor force:** 4.99 million (2008)

**Labor force - by occupation:**
*agriculture:* 2%
*industry:* 25%
*services:* 73% (2007 est.)

**Unemployment rate:**
6.5% (2008)
7.5% (2007 est.)

**Population below poverty line:** 15.2% (2007 est.)

**Household income or consumption by percentage share:**
*lowest 10%:* 3.4%
*highest 10%:* 28.4% (2000)

**Distribution of family income - Gini index:** 28 (2005)

**Investment (gross fixed):** 21.3% of GDP (2008 est.)

**Budget:**
*revenues:* $251.3 billion
*expenditures:* $254.2 billion (2008 est.)

**Public debt:** 80.8% of GDP (2008)

**Inflation rate (consumer prices):**
4.5% (2008)
1.8% (2007 est.)

**Central bank discount rate:** 4%
*note:* this is the European Central Bank's rate on the marginal lending facility, which offers overnight credit to banks in the euro area

**Commercial bank prime lending rate:** 2.1% (30 January 2009)

**Stock of money:** $953.6 million
*note:* see entry for the European Union for money supply in the euro area; the European Central Bank (ECB) controls monetary policy for the 16 members of the Economic and Monetary Union (EMU); individual members of the EMU do not control the quantity of money and quasi money circulating within their own borders (31 December 2007)

**Stock of quasi money:** NA

**Stock of domestic credit:** $767.7 billion (31 December 2007)

**Market value of publicly traded shares:** $386.4 billion (31 December 2007)

**Agriculture - products:** sugar beets, fresh vegetables, fruits, grain, tobacco; beef, veal, pork, milk

**Industries:** engineering and metal products, motor vehicle assembly, transportation equipment, scientific instruments, processed food and beverages, chemicals, basic metals, textiles, glass, petroleum

**Industrial production growth rate:** 2% (2008 est.)

**Electricity - production:** 82.94 billion kWh (2007 est.)

**Electricity - consumption:** 85.54 billion kWh (2006 est.)

**Electricity - exports:** 9.035 billion kWh (2007 est.)

**Electricity - imports:** 15.78 billion kWh (2007 est.)

**Oil - production:** 8,671 bbl/day (2007 est.)

**Oil - consumption:** 628,500 bbl/day (2007 est.)

**Oil - exports:** 528,700 bbl/day (2005)

**Oil - imports:** 1.119 million bbl/day (2005)

**Oil - proved reserves:** 0 bbl (1 January 2006 est.)

## Belgium *(continued)*

**Natural gas - production:** 0 cu m (2007 est.)
**Natural gas - consumption:** 17.39 billion cu m (2007 est.)
**Natural gas - exports:** 0 cu m (2007 est.)
**Natural gas - imports:** 17.34 billion cu m (2007 est.)
**Natural gas - proved reserves:** 0 cu m (1 January 2006)
**Current account balance:** $3.972 billion (2008 est.)
**Exports:** $372.9 billion f.o.b. (2008 est.)
**Exports - commodities:** machinery and equipment, chemicals, finished diamonds, metals and metal products, foodstuffs
**Exports - partners:** Germany 19.5%, France 16.7%, Netherlands 11.9%, UK 7.6%, US 5.7%, Italy 5.2% (2007)
**Imports:** $375.2 billion f.o.b. (2008 est.)
**Imports - commodities:** raw materials, machinery and equipment, chemicals, raw diamonds, pharmaceuticals, foodstuffs, transportation equipment, oil products
**Imports - partners:** Germany 17.7%, Netherlands 17.6%, France 11.2%, UK 6.2%, US 5.4%, Ireland 4.9%, China 4.1% (2007)
**Reserves of foreign exchange and gold:** $16.51 billion (2007 est.)
**Debt - external:** $1.313 trillion (30 June 2007)
**Stock of direct foreign investment - at home:** $733.9 billion (2008 est.)
**Stock of direct foreign investment - abroad:** $581.9 billion (2008 est.)
**Exchange rates:** euros (EUR) per US dollar - 0.6827 (2008), 0.7345 (2007), 0.7964 (2006), 0.8041 (2005), 0.8054 (2004)

### Communications

**Telephones - main lines in use:** 4.668 million (2007)
**Telephones - mobile cellular:** 10.23 million (2007)
**Telephone system:**
*general assessment:* highly developed, technologically advanced, and completely automated domestic and international telephone and telegraph facilities
*domestic:* nationwide cellular telephone system; extensive cable network; limited microwave radio relay network
*international:* country code - 32; landing point for a number of submarine cables that provide links to Europe, the Middle East, and Asia; satellite earth stations - 7 (Intelsat - 3) (2007)
**Radio broadcast stations:** AM 7, FM 79, shortwave 1 (1998)
**Television broadcast stations:** 25 (plus 10 repeaters) (1997)
**Internet country code:** .be
**Internet hosts:** 3.841 million (2008)
**Internet users:** 5.22 million (2007)

### Transportation

**Airports:** 42 (2008)
**Airports - with paved runways:**
*total:* 27
*over 3,047 m:* 6
*2,438 to 3,047 m:* 8
*1,524 to 2,437 m:* 3
*914 to 1,523 m:* 1
*under 914 m:* 9 (2008)
**Airports - with unpaved runways:**
*total:* 15
*914 to 1,523 m:* 1
*under 914 m:* 14 (2008)
**Heliports:** 1 (2007)
**Pipelines:** gas 1,330 km; oil 158 km; refined products 535 km (2008)
**Railways:**
*total:* 3,536 km
*standard gauge:* 3,536 km 1.435-m gauge (2,950 km electrified) (2006)
**Roadways:**
*total:* 152,256 km
*paved:* 119,079 km (includes 1,763 km of expressways)
*unpaved:* 33,177 km (2006)
**Waterways:** 2,043 km (1,528 km in regular commercial use) (2008)
**Merchant marine:**
*total:* 79
*by type:* bulk carrier 20, cargo 9, chemical tanker 1, container 6, liquefied gas 20, passenger 2, petroleum tanker 11, roll on/roll off 10
*foreign-owned:* 6 (Denmark 4, France 2)
*registered in other countries:* 111 (Bahamas 15, Cyprus 2, France 6, Gibraltar 2, Greece 16, Hong Kong 3, Liberia 4, Luxembourg 7, Malta 15, Mozambique 2, Netherlands 2, Netherlands Antilles 1, Panama 2, Portugal 8, Russia 4, Saint Kitts and Nevis 1, Saint Vincent and the Grenadines 8, Sierra Leone 1, Singapore 8, Vanuatu 4) (2008)
**Ports and terminals:** Antwerp, Gent, Liege, Zeebrugge

### Military

**Military branches:** Belgian Armed Forces: Land Operations Command, Naval Operations Command, Air Operations Command (2009)
**Military service age and obligation:** 18 years of age for voluntary military service; conscription suspended (2008)
**Manpower available for military service:**
*males age 16-49:* 2,407,128
*females age 16-49:* 2,340,039 (2008 est.)
**Manpower fit for military service:**
*males age 16-49:* 1,962,409
*females age 16-49:* 1,905,178 (2009 est.)
**Manpower reaching militarily significant age annually:**
*male:* 62,722
*female:* 59,969 (2009 est.)
**Military expenditures:** 1.3% of GDP (2005 est.)

### Transnational Issues

**Disputes - international:** none
**Illicit drugs:** growing producer of synthetic drugs and cannabis; transit point for US-bound ecstasy; source of precursor chemicals for South American cocaine processors; transshipment point for cocaine, heroin, hashish, and marijuana entering Western Europe; despite a strengthening of legislation, the country remains vulnerable to money laundering related to narcotics, automobiles, alcohol, and tobacco; significant domestic consumption of ecstasy

# Belize

## Introduction

**Background:** Belize was the site of several Mayan city states until their decline at the end of the first millennium A.D. The British and Spanish disputed the region in the 17th and 18th centuries; it formally became the colony of British Honduras in 1854. Territorial disputes between the UK and Guatemala delayed the independence of Belize until 1981. Guatemala refused to recognize the new nation until 1992 and the two countries are involved in an ongoing border dispute. Guatemala and Belize are gearing up for a simultaneous referendum to determine if this dispute will go before the International Court of Justice at The Hague. Tourism has become the mainstay of the economy. Current concerns include an unsustainable foreign debt, high unemployment, growing involvement in the South American drug trade, growing urban crime, and increasing incidences of HIV/AIDS.

## Geography

**Location:** Central America, bordering the Caribbean Sea, between Guatemala and Mexico
**Geographic coordinates:** 17 15 N, 88 45 W
**Map references:** Central America and the Caribbean
**Area:**
*total:* 22,966 sq km
*land:* 22,806 sq km
*water:* 160 sq km
**Area - comparative:** slightly smaller than Massachusetts
**Land boundaries:**
*total:* 516 km
*border countries:* Guatemala 266 km, Mexico 250 km
**Coastline:** 386 km
**Maritime claims:**
*territorial sea:* 12 nm in the north, 3 nm in the south; note - from the mouth of the Sarstoon River to Ranguana Cay, Belize's territorial sea is 3 nm;

according to Belize's Maritime Areas Act, 1992, the purpose of this limitation is to provide a framework for negotiating a definitive agreement on territorial differences with Guatemala
*exclusive economic zone:* 200 nm
**Climate:** tropical; very hot and humid; rainy season (May to November); dry season (February to May)
**Terrain:** flat, swampy coastal plain; low mountains in south
**Elevation extremes:**
*lowest point:* Caribbean Sea 0 m
*highest point:* Doyle's Delight 1,160 m
**Natural resources:** arable land potential, timber, fish, hydropower
**Land use:**
*arable land:* 3.05%
*permanent crops:* 1.39%
*other:* 95.56% (2005)
**Irrigated land:** 30 sq km (2003)
**Total renewable water resources:** 18.6 cu km (2000)
**Freshwater withdrawal (domestic/industrial/agricultural):**
*total:* 0.15 cu km/yr (7%/73%/20%)
*per capita:* 556 cu m/yr (2000)
**Natural hazards:** frequent, devastating hurricanes (June to November) and coastal flooding (especially in south)
**Environment - current issues:** deforestation; water pollution from sewage, industrial effluents, agricultural runoff; solid and sewage waste disposal
**Environment - international agreements:**
*party to:* Biodiversity, Climate Change, Climate Change-Kyoto Protocol, Desertification, Endangered Species, Hazardous Wastes, Law of the Sea, Ozone Layer Protection, Ship Pollution, Wetlands, Whaling
*signed, but not ratified:* none of the selected agreements
**Geography - note:** only country in Central America without a coastline on the North Pacific Ocean

## People

**Population:** 307,899 (July 2009 est.)
**Age structure:**
*0-14 years:* 37.9% (male 59,462/female 57,117)
*15-64 years:* 58.6% (male 91,298/female 89,170)
*65 years and over:* 3.5% (male 5,185/female 5,667) (2009 est.)
**Median age:**
*total:* 20.4 years
*male:* 20.3 years
*female:* 20.6 years (2009 est.)
**Population growth rate:** 2.154% (2009 est.)
**Birth rate:** 27.33 births/1,000 population (2009 est.)
**Death rate:** 5.77 deaths/1,000 population (2008 est.)
**Net migration rate:** NA
**Urbanization:**
*urban population:* 52% of total population (2008)
*rate of urbanization:* 3.1% annual rate of change (2005-10 est.)

**Sex ratio:**
*at birth:* 1.05 male(s)/female
*under 15 years:* 1.04 male(s)/female
*15-64 years:* 1.02 male(s)/female
*65 years and over:* 0.92 male(s)/female
*total population:* 1.03 male(s)/female (2009 est.)
**Infant mortality rate:**
*total:* 23.07 deaths/1,000 live births
*male:* 26 deaths/1,000 live births
*female:* 19.99 deaths/1,000 live births (2009 est.)
**Life expectancy at birth:**
*total population:* 68.2 years
*male:* 66.44 years
*female:* 70.05 years (2009 est.)
**Total fertility rate:** 3.36 children born/woman (2009 est.)
**HIV/AIDS - adult prevalence rate:** 2.1% (2007 est.)
**HIV/AIDS - people living with HIV/AIDS:** 3,600 (2007 est.)
**HIV/AIDS - deaths:** fewer than 200 (2007 est.)
**Major infectious diseases:**
*degree of risk:* high
*food or waterborne diseases:* bacterial diarrhea, hepatitis A, and typhoid fever
*vectorborne diseases:* dengue fever and malaria
*water contact disease:* leptospirosis (2009)
**Nationality:**
*noun:* Belizean(s)
*adjective:* Belizean
**Ethnic groups:** mestizo 48.7%, Creole 24.9%, Maya 10.6%, Garifuna 6.1%, other 9.7% (2000 census)
**Religions:** Roman Catholic 49.6%, Protestant 27% (Pentecostal 7.4%, Anglican 5.3%, Seventh-Day Adventist 5.2%, Mennonite 4.1%, Methodist 3.5%, Jehovah's Witnesses 1.5%), other 14%, none 9.4% (2000)
**Languages:** Spanish 46%, Creole 32.9%, Mayan dialects 8.9%, English 3.9% (official), Garifuna 3.4% (Carib), German 3.3%, other 1.4%, unknown 0.2% (2000 census)
**Literacy:**
*definition:* age 15 and over can read and write
*total population:* 76.9%
*male:* 76.7%
*female:* 77.1% (2000 census)
**School life expectancy (primary to tertiary education):**
*total:* 13 years
*male:* 13 years
*female:* 13 years (2004)
**Education expenditures:** 5.3% of GDP (2004)

## Government

**Country name:**
*conventional long form:* none
*conventional short form:* Belize
*former:* British Honduras
**Government type:** parliamentary democracy and a Commonwealth realm

# Belize (continued)

**Capital:**
*name:* Belmopan
*geographic coordinates:* 17 15 N, 88 46 W
*time difference:* UTC-6 (1 hour behind Washington, DC during Standard Time)
**Administrative divisions:** 6 districts; Belize, Cayo, Corozal, Orange Walk, Stann Creek, Toledo
**Independence:** 21 September 1981 (from the UK)
**National holiday:** Independence Day, 21 September (1981)
**Constitution:** 21 September 1981
**Legal system:** English law; has not accepted compulsory ICJ jurisdiction
**Suffrage:** 18 years of age; universal
**Executive branch:**
*chief of state:* Queen ELIZABETH II (since 6 February 1952); represented by Governor General Sir Colville YOUNG, Sr. (since 17 November 1993)
*head of government:* Prime Minister Dean BARROW (since 8 February 2008); Deputy Prime Minister Gaspar VEGA (since 12 February 2008)
*cabinet:* Cabinet appointed by the governor general on the advice of the prime minister
*elections:* the monarch is hereditary; governor general appointed by the monarch; following legislative elections, the leader of the majority party or the leader of the majority coalition is usually appointed prime minister by the governor general; prime minister recommends the deputy prime minister
**Legislative branch:** bicameral National Assembly consists of the Senate (12 seats; members appointed by the governor general - 6 on the advice of the prime minister, 3 on the advice of the leader of the opposition, and 1 each on the advice of the Belize Council of Churches and Evangelical Association of Churches, the Belize Chamber of Commerce and Industry and the Belize Better Business Bureau, and the National Trade Union Congress and the Civil Society Steering Committee; to serve five-year terms) and the House of Representatives (31 seats; members are elected by direct popular vote to serve five-year terms)
*elections:* House of Representatives - last held 6 February 2008 (next to be held in 2013)
*election results:* percent of vote by party - UDP 56.3%, PUP 40.9%; seats by party - UDP 25, PUP 6
**Judicial branch:** Summary Jurisdiction Courts (criminal) and District Courts (civil jurisdiction); Supreme Court (the chief justice is appointed by the governor general on the advice of the prime minister); Court of Appeal; Privy Council in the UK; member of the Caribbean Court of Justice (CCJ)
**Political parties and leaders:** National Alliance for Belizean Rights or NABR; National Reform Party or NRP [Cornelius DUECK]; People's National Party or PNP [Wil MAHEIA]; People's United Party or PUP [John BRICENO]; United Democratic Party or UDP [Dean BARROW]; Vision Inspired by the People or VIP [Paul MORGAN]; We the People Reform Movement or WTP [Hipolito BAUTISTA]

**Political pressure groups and leaders:** Society for the Promotion of Education and Research or SPEAR [Gustavo PERERA]; Association of Concerned Belizeans or ACB [David VASQUEZ]; National Trade Union Congress of Belize or NTUC/B [Rene GOMEZ]
**International organization participation:** ACP, C, Caricom, CDB, FAO, G-77, IADB, IAEA, IBRD, ICAO, ICCt, ICRM, IDA, IFAD, IFC, IFRCS, ILO, IMF, IMO, Interpol, IOC, IOM, ITU, ITUC, LAES, MIGA, NAM, OAS, OPANAL, OPCW, PCA, RG, SICA, UN, UNCTAD, UNESCO, UNIDO, UPU, WCL, WCO, WFTU, WHO, WIPO, WMO, WTO
**Diplomatic representation in the US:**
*chief of mission:* Ambassador Nestor MENDEZ
*chancery:* 2535 Massachusetts Avenue NW, Washington, DC 20008
*telephone:* [1] (202) 332-9636
*FAX:* [1] (202) 332-6888
*consulate(s) general:* Los Angeles
**Diplomatic representation from the US:**
*chief of mission:* Ambassador (vacant); Charge d'Affaires J.A. DIFFILY
*embassy:* Floral Park Road, Belmopan City, Cayo District
*mailing address:* P.O. Box 497, Belmopan City, Cayo District, Belize
*telephone:* [501] 822-4011
*FAX:* [501] 822-4012
**Flag description:** blue with a narrow red stripe along the top and the bottom edges; centered is a large white disk bearing the coat of arms; the coat of arms features a shield flanked by two workers in front of a mahogany tree with the related motto SUB UMBRA FLOREO (I Flourish in the Shade) on a scroll at the bottom, all encircled by a green garland

## Economy

**Economy - overview:** In this small, essentially private-enterprise economy, tourism is the number one foreign exchange earner followed by exports of marine products, citrus, cane sugar, bananas, and garments. The government's expansionary monetary and fiscal policies, initiated in September 1998, led to sturdy GDP growth averaging nearly 4% in 1999-2007, though growth slipped to 3.8% in 2008 as a result of the global slowdown, natural disasters, and the drop in the price of oil. Oil discoveries in 2006 bolstered the economic growth. Exploration efforts continue and a small increase in production is expected in 2009. Major concerns continue to be the sizable trade deficit and unsustainable foreign debt equivalent to nearly 70% of GDP. In February 2007, the government restructured nearly all of its public external commercial debt, which helped reduce interest payments and relieve some of the country's liquidity concerns. A key short-term objective remains the reduction of poverty with the help of international donors.
**GDP (purchasing power parity):**
$2.82 billion (2008 est.)
$2.459 billion (2007)
$2.421 billion (2006)
*note:* data are in 2008 US dollars

**GDP (official exchange rate):** $1.383 billion (2008 est.)
**GDP - real growth rate:**
3.8% (2008 est.)
1.6% (2007 est.)
5.3% (2006 est.)
**GDP - per capita (PPP):**
$8,600 (2008 est.)
$8,300 (2007 est.)
$8,400 (2006 est.)
*note:* data are in 2008 US dollars
**GDP - composition by sector:**
*agriculture:* 29%
*industry:* 16.9%
*services:* 54.1% (2008 est.)
**Labor force:** 113,000
*note:* shortage of skilled labor and all types of technical personnel (2006 est.)
**Labor force - by occupation:**
*agriculture:* 19.5%
*industry:* 17.9%
*services:* 61.9% (2005)
**Unemployment rate:**
8.5% (2007)
9.4% (2006)
**Population below poverty line:** 33.5% (2002 est.)
**Household income or consumption by percentage share:**
*lowest 10%:* NA%
*highest 10%:* NA%
**Investment (gross fixed):** 24.5% of GDP (2008 est.)
**Budget:**
*revenues:* $335.5 million
*expenditures:* $361.5 million (2008 est.)
**Inflation rate (consumer prices):**
4.5% (2008 est.)
2.3% (2007 est.)
**Central bank discount rate:** 12% (31 December 2007)
**Commercial bank prime lending rate:** 14.33% (31 December 2007)
**Stock of money:** $323.9 million (31 December 2007)
**Stock of quasi money:** $549 million (31 December 2007)
**Stock of domestic credit:** $877.6 million (31 December 2007)
**Market value of publicly traded shares:** $NA
**Agriculture - products:** bananas, cacao, citrus, sugar; fish, cultured shrimp; lumber; garments
**Industries:** garment production, food processing, tourism, construction, oil
**Industrial production growth rate:** 1.8% (2008 est.)
**Electricity - production:** 213.5 million kWh (2007 est.)
**Electricity - consumption:** 193.3 million kWh (2006 est.)
**Electricity - exports:** 0 kWh (2007 est.)
**Electricity - imports:** 0 kWh (2007 est.)

# Belize (continued)

**Oil - production:** 3,000 bbl/day (2007 est.)
**Oil - consumption:** 7,000 bbl/day (2006 est.)
**Oil - exports:** 1,960 bbl/day (2006)
**Oil - imports:** 7,122 bbl/day (2005)
**Oil - proved reserves:** 6.7 million bbl (1 January 2008 est.)
**Natural gas - production:** 0 cu m (2007 est.)
**Natural gas - consumption:** 0 cu m (2007 est.)
**Natural gas - exports:** 0 cu m (2007 est.)
**Natural gas - imports:** 0 cu m (2007 est.)
**Natural gas - proved reserves:** 0 cu m (1 January 2006 est.)
**Current account balance:** -$32 million (2008 est.)
**Exports:** $496 million f.o.b. (2008 est.)
**Exports - commodities:** sugar, bananas, citrus, clothing, fish products, molasses, wood, crude oil
**Exports - partners:** US 28.7%, UK 16.3%, Thailand 5.8%, Cote d'Ivoire 5.4%, Finland 4.2%, Spain 4% (2007)
**Imports:** $718 million f.o.b. (2008 est.)
**Imports - commodities:** machinery and transport equipment, manufactured goods; fuels, chemicals, pharmaceuticals; food, beverages, tobacco
**Imports - partners:** US 31.2%, Mexico 13.6%, Cuba 8.5%, Guatemala 8%, Russia 4.6% (2007)
**Reserves of foreign exchange and gold:** $117 million (31 December 2008 est.)
**Debt - external:** $1.2 billion (June 2005 est.)
**Exchange rates:** Belizean dollars (BZD) per US dollar - 2 (2008), 2 (2007), 2 (2006), 2 (2005), 2 (2004)

## Communications

**Telephones - main lines in use:** 33,900 (2007)
**Telephones - mobile cellular:** 118,300 (2007)
**Telephone system:**
*general assessment:* above-average system; fixed-line teledensity of 12 per 100 persons; mobile-cellular telephone density of about 40 per 100 persons
*domestic:* trunk network depends primarily on microwave radio relay
*international:* country code - 501; landing point for the Americas Region Caribbean Ring System (ARCOS-1) fiber-optic telecommunications submarine cable that provides links to South and Central America, parts of the Caribbean, and the US; satellite earth station - 8 (Intelsat - 2, unknown - 6) (2007)
**Radio broadcast stations:** AM 1, FM 16, shortwave 0 (2006)
**Television broadcast stations:** 7 (2008)
**Internet country code:** .bz
**Internet hosts:** 2,751 (2008)
**Internet users:** 32,000 (2007)

## Transportation

**Airports:** 44 (2008)
**Airports - with paved runways:**
*total:* 4
*2,438 to 3,047 m:* 1
*914 to 1,523 m:* 1
*under 914 m:* 2 (2008)
**Airports - with unpaved runways:**
*total:* 40
*2,438 to 3,047 m:* 1
*914 to 1,523 m:* 12
*under 914 m:* 27 (2008)
**Roadways:**
*total:* 3,007 km
*paved:* 575 km
*unpaved:* 2,432 km (2006)
**Waterways:** 825 km (navigable only by small craft) (2008)
**Merchant marine:**
*total:* 216
*by type:* barge carrier 1, bulk carrier 32, cargo 152, chemical tanker 2, container 1, passenger 1, petroleum tanker 9, refrigerated cargo 12, roll on/roll off 5, specialized tanker 1
*foreign-owned:* 178 (Australia 1, China 71, Croatia 2, Cyprus 1, Estonia 6, Greece 1, Iceland 2, Italy 3, Japan 8, South Korea 1, Latvia 12, Norway 3, Peru 1, Russia 31, Singapore 2, Spain 1, Turkey 15, Ukraine 7, UAE 5, UK 5) (2008)
**Ports and terminals:** Belize City, Big Creek

## Military

**Military branches:** Belize Defense Force (BDF): Army, BDF Air Wing, BDF Volunteer Guard (2009)
**Military service age and obligation:** 18 years of age for voluntary military service; laws allow for conscription only if volunteers are insufficient; conscription has never been implemented; volunteers typically outnumber available positions by 3:1 (2008)
**Manpower available for military service:**
*males age 16-49:* 74,605
*females age 16-49:* 72,926 (2008 est.)
**Manpower fit for military service:**
*males age 16-49:* 56,135
*females age 16-49:* 54,732 (2009 est.)
**Manpower reaching militarily significant age annually:**
*male:* 3,632
*female:* 3,500 (2009 est.)
**Military expenditures:** 1.4% of GDP (2006)

## Transnational Issues

**Disputes - international:** OAS-initiated Agreement on the Framework for Negotiations and Confidence Building Measures saw cooperation in repatriation of Guatemalan squatters and other areas, but Guatemalan land and maritime claims in Belize and the Caribbean Sea remain unresolved; the Line of Adjacency created under the 2002 Differendum serves in lieu of the contiguous international boundary to control squatting in the sparsely inhabited rain forests of Belize's border region; Honduras claims Belizean-administered Sapodilla Cays in its constitution but agreed to a joint ecological park under the Differendum
**Illicit drugs:** transshipment point for cocaine; small-scale illicit producer of cannabis, primarily for local consumption; offshore sector money-laundering activity related to narcotics trafficking and other crimes (2008)

# Benin

## Introduction

**Background:** Present day Benin was the site of Dahomey, a prominent West African kingdom that rose in the 15th century. The territory became a French Colony in 1872 and achieved independence on 1 August 1960, as the Republic of Benin. A succession of military governments ended in 1972 with the rise to power of Mathieu KEREKOU and the establishment of a government based on Marxist-Leninist principles. A move to representative government began in 1989. Two years later, free elections ushered in former Prime Minister Nicephore SOGLO as president, marking the first successful transfer of power in Africa from a dictatorship to a democracy. KEREKOU was returned to power by elections held in 1996 and 2001, though some irregularities were alleged. KEREKOU stepped down at the end of his second term in 2006 and was succeeded by Thomas YAYI Boni, a political outsider and independent. YAYI has begun a high profile fight against corruption and has strongly promoted accelerating Benin's economic growth.

## Geography

**Location:** Western Africa, bordering the Bight of Benin, between Nigeria and Togo

**Geographic coordinates:** 9 30 N, 2 15 E

**Map references:** Africa

**Area:**
*total:* 112,620 sq km
*land:* 110,620 sq km
*water:* 2,000 sq km

**Area - comparative:** slightly smaller than Pennsylvania

**Land boundaries:**
*total:* 1,989 km
*border countries:* Burkina Faso 306 km, Niger 266 km, Nigeria 773 km, Togo 644 km

**Coastline:** 121 km

**Maritime claims:**
*territorial sea:* 200 nm

**Climate:** tropical; hot, humid in south; semiarid in north

**Terrain:** mostly flat to undulating plain; some hills and low mountains

**Elevation extremes:**
*lowest point:* Atlantic Ocean 0 m
*highest point:* Mont Sokbaro 658 m

**Natural resources:** small offshore oil deposits, limestone, marble, timber

**Land use:**
*arable land:* 23.53%
*permanent crops:* 2.37%
*other:* 74.1% (2005)

**Irrigated land:** 120 sq km (2003)

**Total renewable water resources:** 25.8 cu km (2001)

**Freshwater withdrawal (domestic/industrial/agricultural):**
*total:* 0.13 cu km/yr (32%/23%/45%)
*per capita:* 15 cu m/yr (2001)

**Natural hazards:** hot, dry, dusty harmattan wind may affect north from December to March

**Environment - current issues:** inadequate supplies of potable water; poaching threatens wildlife populations; deforestation; desertification

**Environment - international agreements:**
*party to:* Biodiversity, Climate Change, Climate Change-Kyoto Protocol, Desertification, Endangered Species, Environmental Modification, Hazardous Wastes, Law of the Sea, Ozone Layer Protection, Ship Pollution, Wetlands, Whaling
*signed, but not ratified:* none of the selected agreements

**Geography - note:** sandbanks create difficult access to a coast with no natural harbors, river mouths, or islands

## People

**Population:** 8,791,832
*note:* estimates for this country explicitly take into account the effects of excess mortality due to AIDS; this can result in lower life expectancy, higher infant mortality, higher death rates, lower population growth rates, and changes in the distribution of population by age and sex than would otherwise be expected (July 2009 est.)

**Age structure:**
*0-14 years:* 45.2% (male 2,028,493/female 1,948,353)
*15-64 years:* 52.1% (male 2,275,662/female 2,308,945)
*65 years and over:* 2.6% (male 94,569/female 135,810) (2009 est.)

**Median age:**
*total:* 17.2 years
*male:* 16.8 years
*female:* 17.7 years (2009 est.)

**Population growth rate:** 2.977% (2009 est.)

**Birth rate:** 39.22 births/1,000 population (2009 est.)

**Death rate:** 9.69 deaths/1,000 population (2008 est.)

**Net migration rate:** 0 migrant(s)/1,000 population (2009 est.)

**Urbanization:**
*urban population:* 41% of total population (2008)
*rate of urbanization:* 4% annual rate of change (2005-10 est.)

**Sex ratio:**
*at birth:* 1.05 male(s)/female
*under 15 years:* 1.04 male(s)/female
*15-64 years:* 0.99 male(s)/female
*65 years and over:* 0.7 male(s)/female
*total population:* 1 male(s)/female (2009 est.)

**Infant mortality rate:**
*total:* 64.64 deaths/1,000 live births
*male:* 68.07 deaths/1,000 live births
*female:* 61.04 deaths/1,000 live births (2009 est.)

**Life expectancy at birth:**
*total population:* 59 years
*male:* 57.83 years
*female:* 60.23 years (2009 est.)

**Total fertility rate:** 5.49 children born/woman (2009 est.)

**HIV/AIDS - adult prevalence rate:** 1.2% (2007 est.)

**HIV/AIDS - people living with HIV/AIDS:** 64,000 (2007 est.)

**HIV/AIDS - deaths:** 3,300 (2007 est.)

**Major infectious diseases:**
*degree of risk:* very high
*food or waterborne diseases:* bacterial and protozoal diarrhea, hepatitis A, and typhoid fever
*vectorborne diseases:* malaria and yellow fever
*respiratory disease:* meningococcal meningitis
*animal contact disease:* rabies (2009)

**Nationality:**
*noun:* Beninese (singular and plural)
*adjective:* Beninese

**Ethnic groups:** Fon and related 39.2%, Adja and related 15.2%, Yoruba and related 12.3%, Bariba and related 9.2%, Peulh and related 7%, Ottamari and related 6.1%, Yoa-Lokpa and related 4%, Dendi and related 2.5%, other 1.6% (includes Europeans), unspecified 2.9% (2002 census)

**Religions:** Christian 42.8% (Catholic 27.1%, Celestial 5%, Methodist 3.2%, other Protestant 2.2%, other 5.3%), Muslim 24.4%, Vodoun 17.3%, other 15.5% (2002 census)

**Languages:** French (official), Fon and Yoruba (most common vernaculars in south), tribal languages (at least six major ones in north)

**Literacy:**
*definition:* age 15 and over can read and write
*total population:* 34.7%
*male:* 47.9%
*female:* 23.3% (2002 census)

**School life expectancy (primary to tertiary education):**
*total:* 7 years
*male:* 9 years
*female:* 6 years (2001)

**Education expenditures:** 4.4% of GDP (2004)

# Benin (continued)

## Government

**Country name:**
*conventional long form:* Republic of Benin
*conventional short form:* Benin
*local long form:* Republique du Benin
*local short form:* Benin
*former:* Dahomey
**Government type:** republic
**Capital:**
*name:* Porto-Novo (official capital)
*geographic coordinates:* 6 29 N, 2 37 E
*time difference:* UTC+1 (6 hours ahead of Washington, DC during Standard Time)
*note:* Cotonou (seat of government)
**Administrative divisions:** 12 departments; Alibori, Atakora, Atlantique, Borgou, Collines, Kouffo, Donga, Littoral, Mono, Oueme, Plateau, Zou
**Independence:** 1 August 1960 (from France)
**National holiday:** National Day, 1 August (1960)
**Constitution:** adopted by referendum 2 December 1990
**Legal system:** based on French civil law and customary law; has not accepted compulsory ICJ jurisdiction
**Suffrage:** 18 years of age; universal
**Executive branch:**
*chief of state:* President Thomas YAYI Boni (since 6 April 2006); note - the president is both the chief of state and head of government
*head of government:* President Thomas YAYI Boni (since 6 April 2006)
*cabinet:* Council of Ministers appointed by the president
*elections:* president elected by popular vote for a five-year term (eligible for a second term); runoff election held 19 March 2006 (next to be held in March 2011)
*election results:* Thomas YAYI Boni elected president; percent of vote - Thomas YAYI Boni 74.5%, Adrien HOUNGBEDJI 25.5%
**Legislative branch:** unicameral National Assembly or Assemblee Nationale (83 seats; members are elected by direct popular vote to serve four-year terms)
*elections:* last held 31 March 2007 (next to be held by March 2011)
*election results:* percent of vote by party - NA; seats by party - FCBE 35, ADD 20, PRD 10, other and independents 18
**Judicial branch:** Constitutional Court or Cour Constitutionnelle; Supreme Court or Cour Supreme; High Court of Justice
**Political parties and leaders:** Alliance for Dynamic Democracy or ADD; Alliance of Progress Forces or AFP; African Movement for Democracy and Progress or MADEP [Sefou FAGBOHOUN]; Benin Renaissance or RB [Rosine SOGLO]; Democratic Renewal Party or PRD [Adrien HOUNGBEDJI]; Force Cowrie for an Emerging Benin or FCBE; Impulse for Progress and Democracy or IPD [Theophile NATA]; Key Force or FC [Lazare S»HOU...TO]; Movement for

the People's Alternative or MAP [Olivier CAPO-CHICHI]; Rally for Democracy and Progress or RDP [Dominique HOUNGNINOU]; Social Democrat Party or PSD [Bruno AMOUSSOU]; Union for the Relief or UPR [Issa SALIFOU]; Union for Democracy and National Solidarity or UDS [Sacca LAFIA]
*note:* approximately 20 additional minor parties
**Political pressure groups and leaders:**
*other:* economic groups; environmentalists; political groups; teachers' unions and other educational groups
**International organization participation:** ACCT, ACP, AfDB, AU, ECOWAS, Entente, FAO, FZ, G-77, IAEA, IBRD, ICAO, ICCt, ICRM, IDA, IDB, IFAD, IFC, IFRCS, ILO, IMF, IMO, Interpol, IOC, IOM, IPU, ISO (correspondent), ITSO, ITU, ITUC, MIGA, MONUC, NAM, OAS (observer), OIC, OIF, OPCW, PCA, UN, UNCTAD, UNESCO, UNHCR, UNIDO, UNMIL, UNMIS, UNOCI, UNWTO, UPU, WADB (regional), WAEMU, WCL, WCO, WFTU, WHO, WIPO, WMO, WTO
**Diplomatic representation in the US:**
*chief of mission:* Ambassador Cyrille Segbe OGUIN
*chancery:* 2124 Kalorama Road NW, Washington, DC 20008
*telephone:* [1] (202) 232-6656
*FAX:* [1] (202) 265-1996
**Diplomatic representation from the US:**
*chief of mission:* Ambassador Gayleatha B. BROWN
*embassy:* Rue Caporal Bernard Anani, Cotonou
*mailing address:* 01 B. P. 2012, Cotonou
*telephone:* [229] 21-30-06-50
*FAX:* [229] 21-30-03-84
**Flag description:** two equal horizontal bands of yellow (top) and red (bottom) with a vertical green band on the hoist side

## Economy

**Economy - overview:** The economy of Benin remains underdeveloped and dependent on subsistence agriculture, cotton production, and regional trade. Growth in real output has averaged around 5% in the past seven years, but rapid population growth has offset much of this increase. Inflation has subsided over the past several years. In order to raise growth still further, Benin plans to attract more foreign investment, place more emphasis on tourism, facilitate the development of new food processing systems and agricultural products, and encourage new information and communication technology. Specific projects to improve the business climate by reforms to the land tenure system, the commercial justice system, and the financial sector were included in Benin's $307 million Millennium Challenge Account grant signed in February 2006. The 2001 privatization policy continues in telecommunications, water, electricity, and agriculture though the government annulled the privatization of Benin's state cotton company in November 2007 after the discovery of irregularities in the bidding process. The Paris Club and bilateral creditors have eased the

external debt situation, with Benin benefiting from a G8 debt reduction announced in July 2005, while pressing for more rapid structural reforms. An insufficient electrical supply continues to adversely affect Benin's economic growth though the government recently has taken steps to increase domestic power production.
**GDP (purchasing power parity):**
$12.84 billion (2008 est.)
$12.25 billion (2007)
$11.72 billion (2006)
*note:* data are in 2008 US dollars
**GDP (official exchange rate):** $6.94 billion (2008 est.)
**GDP - real growth rate:**
4.8% (2008 est.)
4.5% (2007 est.)
3.8% (2006 est.)
**GDP - per capita (PPP):**
$1,500 (2008 est.)
$1,500 (2007 est.)
$1,500 (2006 est.)
*note:* data are in 2008 US dollars
**GDP - composition by sector:**
*agriculture:* 33.2%
*industry:* 14.5%
*services:* 52.3% (2007 est.)
**Labor force:** 5.38 million (2007 est.)
**Unemployment rate:**
NA%
**Population below poverty line:** 37.4% (2007 est.)
**Household income or consumption by percentage share:**
*lowest 10%:* 3.1%
*highest 10%:* 29% (2003)
**Distribution of family income - Gini index:** 36.5 (2003)
**Investment (gross fixed):** 19.5% of GDP (2008 est.)
**Budget:**
*revenues:* $1.436 billion
*expenditures:* $1.729 billion (2008 est.)
**Inflation rate (consumer prices):**
5.2% (2008 est.)
1.3% (2007 est.)
**Central bank discount rate:** 4.25% (31 December 2007)
**Commercial bank prime lending rate:** NA
**Stock of money:** $1.324 billion (31 December 2007)
**Stock of quasi money:** $627.2 million (31 December 2007)
**Stock of domestic credit:** $520.6 million (31 December 2007)
**Market value of publicly traded shares:** $NA
**Agriculture - products:** cotton, corn, cassava (tapioca), yams, beans, palm oil, peanuts, cashews; livestock
**Industries:** textiles, food processing, construction materials, cement
**Industrial production growth rate:** 5.5% (2008 est.)

**Electricity - production:** 120 million kWh (2006 est.)
**Electricity - consumption:** 595 million kWh (2006 est.)
**Electricity - exports:** 0 kWh (2007 est.)
**Electricity - imports:** 590 million kWh (2006 est.)
**Oil - production:** 0 bbl/day (2007 est.)
**Oil - consumption:** 9,232 bbl/day (2007 est.)
**Oil - exports:** 6,484 bbl/day (2005)
**Oil - imports:** 16,830 bbl/day (2007 est.)
**Oil - proved reserves:** 8 million bbl (1 January 2008 est.)
**Natural gas - production:** 0 cu m (2007 est.)
**Natural gas - consumption:** 0 cu m (2007 est.)
**Natural gas - exports:** 0 cu m (2007 est.)
**Natural gas - imports:** 0 cu m (2007 est.)
**Natural gas - proved reserves:** 1.133 billion cu m (1 January 2008 est.)
**Current account balance:** -$485 million (2008 est.)
**Exports:** $776 million f.o.b. (2008 est.)
**Exports - commodities:** cotton, cashews, shea butter, textiles, palm products, seafood
**Exports - partners:** China 24.7%, India 8.2%, Niger 6.6%, Togo 5.4%, Nigeria 5.3%, Belgium 4.6% (2007)
**Imports:** $1.355 billion f.o.b. (2008 est.)
**Imports - commodities:** foodstuffs, capital goods, petroleum products
**Imports - partners:** China 44.5%, France 8.2%, US 6.5%, Thailand 6.3%, Malaysia 4.8% (2007)
**Reserves of foreign exchange and gold:** $1.292 billion (31 December 2008 est.)
**Debt - external:** $1.2 billion (2007)
**Exchange rates:** Communaute Financiere Africaine francs (XOF) per US dollar - 447.81 (2008 est.), 493.51 (2007), 522.59 (2006), 527.47 (2005), 528.29 (2004)
*note:* since 1 January 1999, the West African CFA franc (XOF) has been pegged to the euro at a rate of 655.957 CFA francs per euro; West African CFA franc (XOF) coins and banknotes are not accepted in countries using Central African CFA francs (XAF), and vice versa, even though the two currencies trade at par

## Communications

**Telephones - main lines in use:** 110,300 (2007)
**Telephones - mobile cellular:** 1.895 million (2007)
**Telephone system:**
*general assessment:* inadequate; fixed-line network characterized by aging, deteriorating equipment with fixed-line teledensity stuck at 1 per 100 persons; mobile-cellular telephone subscribership is increasing
*domestic:* system of open-wire, microwave radio relay, and cellular connections; multiple mobile-cellular providers
*international:* country code - 229; landing point for the SAT-3/WASC fiber-optic submarine cable that provides connectivity to Europe and Asia; satellite earth stations - 7 (Intelsat-Atlantic Ocean) (2007)

**Radio broadcast stations:** AM 1, FM 34, shortwave 1 (2007)
**Television broadcast stations:** 6 (2007)
**Internet country code:** .bj
**Internet hosts:** 848 (2008)
**Internet users:** 150,000 (2007)

## Transportation

**Airports:** 5 (2008)
**Airports - with paved runways:**
*total:* 1
*1,524 to 2,437 m:* 1 (2008)
**Airports - with unpaved runways:**
*total:* 4
*2,438 to 3,047 m:* 1
*1,524 to 2,437 m:* 1
*914 to 1,523 m:* 2 (2008)
**Railways:**
*total:* 758 km
*narrow gauge:* 758 km 1.000-m gauge (2006)
**Roadways:**
*total:* 16,000 km
*paved:* 1,400 km
*unpaved:* 14,600 km (2006)
**Waterways:** 150 km (on River Niger along northern border) (2007)
**Ports and terminals:** Cotonou

## Military

**Military branches:** Benin Armed Forces (FAB): Army (l'Arme de Terre), Benin Navy (Forces Navales Beninois, FNB), Benin People's Air Force (Force Aerienne Populaire de Benin, FAPB) (2008)
**Military service age and obligation:** 21 years of age for compulsory and voluntary military service; in practice, volunteers may be taken at the age of 18; both sexes are eligible for military service; conscript tour of duty - 18 months (2006)
**Manpower available for military service:**
*males age 16-49:* 1,908,457
*females age 16-49:* 1,882,421 (2008 est.)
**Manpower fit for military service:**
*males age 16-49:* 1,279,053
*females age 16-49:* 1,292,438 (2009 est.)
**Manpower reaching militarily significant age annually:**
*male:* 101,549
*female:* 97,856 (2009 est.)
**Military expenditures:** 1.7% of GDP (2006)

## Transnational Issues

**Disputes - international:** in September 2007, Economic Community of West African States (ECOWAS) intervened to attempt to resolve the dispute over two villages along the Benin-Burkina Faso border that remain from 2005 ICJ decision; much of Benin-Niger boundary, including tripoint with Nigeria, remains undemarcated; in 2005, Nigeria ceded thirteen villages to Benin, but border relations remain strained by rival cross-border gang clashes;

talks continue between Benin and Togo on funding the Adjrala hydroelectric dam on the Mona River
**Refugees and internally displaced persons:**
*refugees (country of origin):* 9,444 (Togo) (2007)
**Illicit drugs:** transshipment point used by traffickers for cocaine destined for Western Europe; vulnerable to money laundering due to poorly enforced financial regulations (2008)

# Bermuda
*(overseas territory of the UK)*

## Introduction

**Background:** Bermuda was first settled in 1609 by shipwrecked English colonists headed for Virginia. Tourism to the island to escape North American winters first developed in Victorian times. Tourism continues to be important to the island's economy, although international business has overtaken it in recent years. Bermuda has developed into a highly successful offshore financial center. Although a referendum on independence from the UK was soundly defeated in 1995, the present government has reopened debate on the issue.

## Geography

**Location:** North America, group of islands in the North Atlantic Ocean, east of South Carolina (US)
**Geographic coordinates:** 32 20 N, 64 45 W
**Map references:** North America
**Area:**
*total:* 53.3 sq km
*land:* 53.3 sq km
*water:* 0 sq km
**Area - comparative:** about one-third the size of Washington, DC
**Land boundaries:** 0 km
**Coastline:** 103 km
**Maritime claims:**
*territorial sea:* 12 nm
*exclusive fishing zone:* 200 nm
**Climate:** subtropical; mild, humid; gales, strong winds common in winter
**Terrain:** low hills separated by fertile depressions
**Elevation extremes:**
*lowest point:* Atlantic Ocean 0 m
*highest point:* Town Hill 76 m
**Natural resources:** limestone, pleasant climate fostering tourism

**Land use:**
*arable land:* 20%
*permanent crops:* 0%
*other:* 80% (55% developed, 45% rural/open space) (2005)
**Irrigated land:** NA
**Natural hazards:** hurricanes (June to November)
**Environment - current issues:** sustainable development
**Geography - note:** consists of about 138 coral islands and islets with ample rainfall, but no rivers or freshwater lakes; some land was leased by US Government from 1941 to 1995

## People

**Population:** 67,837 (July 2009 est.)
**Age structure:**
*0-14 years:* 18.3% (male 6,271/female 6,163)
*15-64 years:* 67.5% (male 22,555/female 23,215)
*65 years and over:* 14.2% (male 3,979/female 5,654) (2009 est.)
**Median age:**
*total:* 41.3 years
*male:* 39.9 years
*female:* 42.7 years (2009 est.)
**Population growth rate:** 0.647% (2009 est.)
**Birth rate:** 11.57 births/1,000 population (2009 est.)
**Death rate:** 7.98 deaths/1,000 population (2008 est.)
**Net migration rate:** 2.2 migrant(s)/1,000 population (2009 est.)
**Urbanization:**
*urban population:* 100% of total population (2008)
*rate of urbanization:* 0.3% annual rate of change (2005-10 est.)
**Sex ratio:**
*at birth:* 1.02 male(s)/female
*under 15 years:* 1.02 male(s)/female
*15-64 years:* 0.97 male(s)/female
*65 years and over:* 0.7 male(s)/female
*total population:* 0.94 male(s)/female (2009 est.)
**Infant mortality rate:**
*total:* 2.46 deaths/1,000 live births
*male:* 2.57 deaths/1,000 live births
*female:* 2.35 deaths/1,000 live births (2009 est.)
**Life expectancy at birth:**
*total population:* 80.43 years
*male:* 77.2 years
*female:* 83.72 years (2009 est.)
**Total fertility rate:** 1.99 children born/woman (2009 est.)
**HIV/AIDS - adult prevalence rate:** 0.297% (2005)
**HIV/AIDS - people living with HIV/AIDS:** 163 (2005)
**HIV/AIDS - deaths:** 392 (2005)
**Nationality:**
*noun:* Bermudian(s)
*adjective:* Bermudian
**Ethnic groups:** black 54.8%, white 34.1%, mixed 6.4%, other races 4.3%, unspecified 0.4% (2000 census)
**Religions:** Anglican 23%, Roman Catholic 15%, African Methodist Episcopal 11%, other Protestant 18%, other 12%, unaffiliated 6%, unspecified 1%, none 14% (2000 census)

**Languages:** English (official), Portuguese
**Literacy:**
*definition:* age 15 and over can read and write
*total population:* 98%
*male:* 98%
*female:* 99% (2005 est.)
**School life expectancy (primary to tertiary education):**
*total:* 13 years
*male:* 13 years
*female:* 14 years (2005)
**Education expenditures:** 1.2% of GDP (2006)

## Government

**Country name:**
*conventional long form:* none
*conventional short form:* Bermuda
*former:* Somers Islands
**Dependency status:** overseas territory of the UK
**Government type:** parliamentary; self-governing territory
**Capital:**
*name:* Hamilton
*geographic coordinates:* 32 17 N, 64 47 W
*time difference:* UTC-4 (1 hour ahead of Washington, DC during Standard Time)
*daylight saving time:* +1hr, begins second Sunday in March; ends first Sunday in November
**Administrative divisions:** 9 parishes and 2 municipalities*; Devonshire, Hamilton, Hamilton*, Paget, Pembroke, Saint George*, Saint George's, Sandys, Smith's, Southampton, Warwick
**Independence:** none (overseas territory of the UK)
**National holiday:** Bermuda Day, 24 May
**Constitution:** 8 June 1968; amended 1989 and 2003
**Legal system:** English law
**Suffrage:** 18 years of age; universal
**Executive branch:**
*chief of state:* Queen ELIZABETH II (since 6 February 1952); represented by Governor Sir Richard GOZNEY (since 12 December 2007)
*head of government:* Premier Ewart BROWN (since 30 October 2006); Deputy Premier Paula COX
*cabinet:* Cabinet nominated by the premier, appointed by the governor
*elections:* the monarch is hereditary; governor appointed by the monarch; following legislative elections, the leader of the majority party or the leader of the majority coalition is usually appointed premier by the governor
**Legislative branch:** bicameral Parliament consists of the Senate (11 seats; members appointed by the governor, the premier, and the opposition) and the House of Assembly (36 seats; members are elected by popular vote to serve up to five-year terms)
*elections:* last general election held 18 December 2007 (next to be held not later than 2012)
*election results:* percent of vote by party - PLP 52.5%, UBP 47.3%; seats by party - PLP 22, UBP 14
**Judicial branch:** Supreme Court; Court of Appeal; Magistrate Courts

# Bermuda (continued)

**Political parties and leaders:** Progressive Labor Party or PLP [Ewart BROWN]; United Bermuda Party or UBP [Kim SWAN]

**Political pressure groups and leaders:** Bermuda Employer's Union [Eddie SAINTS]; Bermuda Industrial Union or BIU [Derrick BURGESS]; Bermuda Public Services Union or BPSU [Ed BALL]; Bermuda Union of Teachers [Michael CHARLES]

**International organization participation:** Caricom (associate), Interpol (subbureau), IOC, ITUC, UPU, WCO, WFTU

**Diplomatic representation in the US:** none (overseas territory of the UK)

**Diplomatic representation from the US:**
*chief of mission:* Consul General Gregory W. SLAYTON
*consulate(s) general:* Crown Hill, 16 Middle Road, Devonshire DVO3
*mailing address:* P. O. Box HM325, Hamilton HMBX; American Consulate General Hamilton, US Department of State, 5300 Hamilton Place, Washington, DC 20520-5300
*telephone:* [1] (441) 295-1342
*FAX:* [1] (441) 295-1592, 296-9233

**Flag description:** red, with the flag of the UK in the upper hoist-side quadrant and the Bermudian coat of arms (white and green shield with a red lion holding a scrolled shield showing the sinking of the ship Sea Venture off Bermuda in 1609) centered on the outer half of the flag

## Economy

**Economy - overview:** Bermuda enjoys the third highest per capita income in the world more than 50% higher than that of the US. Its economy is primarily based on providing financial services for international business and luxury facilities for tourists. A number of reinsurance companies relocated to the island following the 11 September 2001 attacks and again after Hurricane Katrina in August 2005 contributing to the expansion of an already robust international business sector. Bermuda's tourism industry - which derives over 80% of its visitors from the US - continues to struggle but remains the island's number two industry. Most capital equipment and food must be imported. Bermuda's industrial sector is small, although construction continues to be important; the average cost of a house in June 2003 had risen to $976,000. Agriculture is limited with only 20% of the land being arable.

**GDP (purchasing power parity):**
$4.5 billion (2004 est.)

**GDP (official exchange rate):** $NA

**GDP - real growth rate:**
4.6% (2004 est.)

**GDP - per capita (PPP):**
$69,900 (2004 est.)

**GDP - composition by sector:**
*agriculture:* 1%
*industry:* 10%
*services:* 89% (2002 est.)

**Labor force:** 38,360 (2004)

**Labor force - by occupation:** agriculture and fishing 3%, laborers 17%, clerical 19%, professional and technical 21%, administrative and managerial 15%, sales 7%, services 19% (2004 est.)

**Unemployment rate:**
2.1% (2004 est.)

**Population below poverty line:** 19% (2000)

**Household income or consumption by percentage share:**
*lowest 10%:* NA%
*highest 10%:* NA%

**Budget:**
*revenues:* $738 million
*expenditures:* $665 million (FY04/05)

**Inflation rate (consumer prices):**
2.8% (November 2005)

**Market value of publicly traded shares:** $2.731 billion (31 December 2007)

**Agriculture - products:** bananas, vegetables, citrus, flowers; dairy products, honey

**Industries:** international business, tourism, light manufacturing

**Industrial production growth rate:** NA%

**Electricity - production:** 675.6 million kWh (2007 est.)

**Electricity - consumption:** 619.8 million kWh (2006 est.)

**Electricity - exports:** 0 kWh (2007 est.)

**Electricity - imports:** 0 kWh (2007 est.)

**Oil - production:** 0 bbl/day (2007 est.)

**Oil - consumption:** 4,566 bbl/day (2006 est.)

**Oil - exports:** 0 bbl/day (2005)

**Oil - imports:** 4,378 bbl/day (2005)

**Oil - proved reserves:** 0 bbl (1 January 2006 est.)

**Natural gas - production:** 0 cu m (2007 est.)

**Natural gas - consumption:** 0 cu m (2007 est.)

**Natural gas - exports:** 0 cu m (2007 est.)

**Natural gas - imports:** 0 cu m (2007 est.)

**Natural gas - proved reserves:** 0 cu m (1 January 2006 est.)

**Exports:** $763 million (2006)

**Exports - commodities:** reexports of pharmaceuticals

**Exports - partners:** Spain 13.8%, Germany 11.7%, Switzerland 8.8%, Denmark 6.6%, UK 6% (2007)

**Imports:** $1.162 billion (2006)

**Imports - commodities:** clothing, fuels, machinery and transport equipment, construction materials, chemicals, food and live animals

**Imports - partners:** South Korea 36.4%, US 15.7%, Germany 13.2%, Italy 11.8% (2007)

**Debt - external:** $160 million (FY99/00)

**Stock of direct foreign investment - at home:** $NA

**Stock of direct foreign investment - abroad:** $NA

**Exchange rates:** Bermudian dollars (BMD) per US dollar - 1.0000 (fixed rate pegged to the US dollar)

## Communications

**Telephones - main lines in use:** 57,700 (2006)
**Telephones - mobile cellular:** 60,100 (2006)

**Telephone system:**
*general assessment:* good
*domestic:* fully automatic digital telephone system; fiber optic trunk lines
*international:* country code - 1-441; landing point for the Atlantica-1 telecommunications submarine cable that extends from the US to Brazil; satellite earth stations - 3 (2007)

**Radio broadcast stations:** AM 5, FM 3, shortwave 0 (2005)

**Television broadcast stations:** 3 (2005)

**Internet country code:** .bm

**Internet hosts:** 1,628 (2008)

**Internet users:** 48,000 (2007)

## Transportation

**Airports:** 1 (2008)

**Airports - with paved runways:**
*total:* 1
*2,438 to 3,047 m:* 1 (2008)

**Roadways:**
*total:* 447 km
*paved:* 447 km
*note:* public roads - 225 km; private roads - 222 km (2007)

**Merchant marine:**
*total:* 137
*by type:* bulk carrier 23, chemical tanker 3, container 22, liquefied gas 33, passenger 24, passenger/cargo 5, petroleum tanker 18, refrigerated cargo 9
*foreign-owned:* 115 (Australia 1, China 10, France 1, Germany 22, Greece 9, Hong Kong 4, Ireland 1, Israel 3, Japan 2, Nigeria 11, Norway 5, Sweden 20, UK 3, US 23)
*registered in other countries:* 50 (Bahamas 12, Marshall Islands 4, Philippines 34) (2008)

**Ports and terminals:** Hamilton, Saint George

## Military

**Military branches:** Bermuda Regiment (2008)

**Military service age and obligation:** 18-23 years of age; eligible men required to register for conscription as needed into the Bermuda Regiment, which is largely voluntary; term of service 39 months (2007)

**Manpower available for military service:**
*males age 16-49:* 15,623 (2008 est.)

**Manpower fit for military service:**
*males age 16-49:* 12,496
*females age 16-49:* 12,486 (2009 est.)

**Manpower reaching militarily significant age annually:**
*male:* 426
*female:* 413 (2009 est.)

**Military expenditures:** 0.11% of GDP (2005 est.)

**Military - note:** defense is the responsibility of the UK

## Transnational Issues

**Disputes - international:** none

# Bhutan

## Introduction

**Background:** In 1865, Britain and Bhutan signed the Treaty of Sinchulu, under which Bhutan would receive an annual subsidy in exchange for ceding some border land to British India. Under British influence, a monarchy was set up in 1907; three years later, a treaty was signed whereby the British agreed not to interfere in Bhutanese internal affairs and Bhutan allowed Britain to direct its foreign affairs. This role was assumed by independent India after 1947. Two years later, a formal Indo-Bhutanese accord returned the areas of Bhutan annexed by the British, formalized the annual subsidies the country received, and defined India's responsibilities in defense and foreign relations. A refugee issue of over 100,000 Bhutanese in Nepal remains unresolved; 90% of the refugees are housed in seven United Nations Office of the High Commissioner for Refugees (UNHCR) camps. In March 2005, King Jigme Singye WANGCHUCK unveiled the government's draft constitution - which would introduce major democratic reforms - and pledged to hold a national referendum for its approval. In December 2006, the King abdicated the throne to his son, Jigme Khesar Namgyel WANGCHUCK, in order to give him experience as head of state before the democratic transition. In early 2007, India and Bhutan renegotiated their treaty to allow Bhutan greater autonomy in conducting its foreign policy, although Thimphu continues to coordinate policy decisions in this area with New Delhi. In July 2007, seven ministers of Bhutan's ten-member cabinet resigned to join the political process, and the cabinet acted as a caretaker regime until democratic elections for seats to the country's first parliament were completed in March 2008. The king ratified the country's first constitution in July 2008.

## Geography

**Location:** Southern Asia, between China and India
**Geographic coordinates:** 27 30 N, 90 30 E
**Map references:** Asia
**Area:**
*total:* 47,000 sq km
*land:* 47,000 sq km
*water:* 0 sq km
**Area - comparative:** about one-half the size of Indiana
**Land boundaries:**
*total:* 1,075 km
*border countries:* China 470 km, India 605 km
**Coastline:** 0 km (landlocked)
**Maritime claims:** none (landlocked)
**Climate:** varies; tropical in southern plains; cool winters and hot summers in central valleys; severe winters and cool summers in Himalayas
**Terrain:** mostly mountainous with some fertile valleys and savanna
**Elevation extremes:**
*lowest point:* Drangme Chhu 97 m
*highest point:* Kula Kangri 7,553 m
**Natural resources:** timber, hydropower, gypsum, calcium carbonate
**Land use:**
*arable land:* 2.3%
*permanent crops:* 0.43%
*other:* 97.27% (2005)
**Irrigated land:** 400 sq km (2003)
**Total renewable water resources:** 95 cu km (1987)
**Freshwater withdrawal (domestic/industrial/agricultural):**
*total:* 0.43 cu km/yr (5%/1%/94%)
*per capita:* 199 cu m/yr (2000)
**Natural hazards:** violent storms from the Himalayas are the source of the country's name, which translates as Land of the Thunder Dragon; frequent landslides during the rainy season
**Environment - current issues:** soil erosion; limited access to potable water
**Environment - international agreements:**
*party to:* Biodiversity, Climate Change, Climate Change-Kyoto Protocol, Desertification, Endangered Species, Hazardous Wastes, Ozone Layer Protection
*signed, but not ratified:* Law of the Sea
**Geography - note:** landlocked; strategic location between China and India; controls several key Himalayan mountain passes

## People

**Population:** 691,141
*note:* the Factbook population estimate is consistent with the first modern census of Bhutan, conducted in 2005; previous Factbook population estimates for this country, which were on the order of three times the total population reported here, were based on Bhutanese government publications that did not include the census (July 2009 est.)

**Age structure:**
*0-14 years:* 30.2% (male 106,410/female 102,164)
*15-64 years:* 64.3% (male 235,988/female 208,484)
*65 years and over:* 5.5% (male 20,169/female 17,926) (2009 est.)
**Median age:**
*total:* 23.9 years
*male:* 24.5 years
*female:* 23.3 years (2009 est.)
**Population growth rate:** 1.267% (2009 est.)
**Birth rate:** 20.07 births/1,000 population (2009 est.)
**Death rate:** 7.54 deaths/1,000 population (2008 est.)
**Net migration rate:** NA
**Urbanization:**
*urban population:* 35% of total population (2008)
*rate of urbanization:* 4.9% annual rate of change (2005-10 est.)
**Sex ratio:**
*at birth:* 1.05 male(s)/female
*under 15 years:* 1.04 male(s)/female
*15-64 years:* 1.13 male(s)/female
*65 years and over:* 1.12 male(s)/female
*total population:* 1.1 male(s)/female (2009 est.)
**Infant mortality rate:**
*total:* 49.36 deaths/1,000 live births
*male:* 50.38 deaths/1,000 live births
*female:* 48.29 deaths/1,000 live births (2009 est.)
**Life expectancy at birth:**
*total population:* 66.13 years
*male:* 65.33 years
*female:* 66.97 years (2009 est.)
**Total fertility rate:** 2.38 children born/woman (2009 est.)
**HIV/AIDS - adult prevalence rate:** less than 0.1% (2007 est.)
**HIV/AIDS - people living with HIV/AIDS:** fewer than 100 (2007 est.)
**HIV/AIDS - deaths:** NA
**Major infectious diseases:**
*degree of risk:* intermediate
*food or waterborne diseases:* bacterial and protozoal diarrhea, hepatitis A, and typhoid fever
*vectorborne diseases:* dengue fever and malaria
*water contact disease:* leptospirosis (2009)
**Nationality:**
*noun:* Bhutanese (singular and plural)
*adjective:* Bhutanese
**Ethnic groups:** Bhote 50%, ethnic Nepalese 35% (includes Lhotsampas - one of several Nepalese ethnic groups), indigenous or migrant tribes 15%
**Religions:** Lamaistic Buddhist 75%, Indian- and Nepalese-influenced Hinduism 25%
**Languages:** Dzongkha (official), Bhotes speak various Tibetan dialects, Nepalese speak various Nepalese dialects
**Literacy:**
*definition:* age 15 and over can read and write
*total population:* 47%
*male:* 60%
*female:* 34% (2003 est.)

# Bhutan *(continued)*

**School life expectancy (primary to tertiary education):**
*total:* 10 years
*male:* 11 years
*female:* 10 years (2006)
**Education expenditures:** 7% of GDP (2005)

## Government

**Country name:**
*conventional long form:* Kingdom of Bhutan
*conventional short form:* Bhutan
*local long form:* Druk Gyalkhap
*local short form:* Druk Yul
**Government type:** constitutional monarchy
**Capital:**
*name:* Thimphu
*geographic coordinates:* 27 29 N, 89 36 E
*time difference:* UTC+6 (11 hours ahead of Washington, DC during Standard Time)
**Administrative divisions:** 20 districts (dzongkhag, singular and plural); Bumthang, Chhukha, Chirang, Daga, Gasa, Geylegphug, Ha, Lhuntshi, Mongar, Paro, Pemagatsel, Punakha, Samchi, Samdrup Jongkhar, Shemgang, Tashigang, Tashi Yangtse, Thimphu, Tongsa, Wangdi Phodrang
**Independence:** 1907 (became a unified kingdom under its first hereditary king)
**National holiday:** National Day (Ugyen WANGCHUCK became first hereditary king), 17 December (1907)
**Constitution:** ratified 18 July 2008
**Legal system:** based on Indian law and English common law; has not accepted compulsory ICJ jurisdiction
**Suffrage:** 18 years of age; universal
**Executive branch:**
*chief of state:* King Jigme Khesar Namgyel WANGCHUCK (since 14 December 2006); note - King Jigme Singye WANGCHUCK abdicated the throne on 14 December 2006 and his son immediately succeeded him; the nearly two-year delay between the former King's abdication and his son's coronation on 6 November 2008 was to ensure an astrologically auspicious coronation date and to give the new King-who had limited experience-deeper administrative expertise under the guidance of this father
*head of government:* Prime Minister Jigme THINLEY (since 9 April 2008)
*cabinet:* Council of Ministers (Lhengye Shungtsog) nominated by the monarch, approved by the National Assembly; members serve fixed, five-year terms; note -there is also a Royal Advisory Council (Lodoi Tsokde), members nominated by the monarch
*elections:* the monarch is hereditary, but democratic reforms in July 1998 grant the National Assembly authority to remove the monarch with two-thirds vote; election of a new National Assembly occurred in March 2008; the leader of the majority party is nominated as the prime minister

**Legislative branch:** bicameral Parliament consists of the non-partisan National Council (25 seats; 20 members elected by each of the 20 electoral districts (dzongkhags) for four-year terms and 5 members nominated by the King); and the National Assembly (47 seats; members elected by direct, popular vote for five-year terms)
*elections:* National Council elections last held on 31 December 2007 and 29 January 2008 (next to be held by December 2012); National Assembly elections last held on 24 March 2008 (next to be held by March 2013)
*election results:* National Council - NA; National Assembly - percent of vote by party - DPT 67%, PDP 33%; seats by party - DPT 45, PDP 2
**Judicial branch:** Supreme Court of Appeal (the monarch); High Court (judges appointed by the monarch); note - the draft constitution establishes a Supreme Court that will serve as chief court of appeal
**Political parties and leaders:** Bhutan Peace and Prosperity Party (Druk Phuensum Tshogpa) or DPT [Jigme THINLEY]; People's Democratic Party or PDP [Tshering TOBGAY]
**Political pressure groups and leaders:** United Front for Democracy (exiled); Druk National Congress (exiled)
*other:* Buddhist clergy; ethnic Nepalese organizations leading militant antigovernment campaign; Indian merchant community
**International organization participation:** ADB, BIMSTEC, CP, FAO, G-77, IBRD, ICAO, IDA, IFAD, IFC, IMF, Interpol, IOC, IOM (observer), ISO (correspondent), ITSO, ITU, NAM, OPCW, SAARC, SACEP, UN, UNCTAD, UNESCO, UNIDO, UNWTO, UPU, WCO, WFTU, WHO, WIPO, WMO, WTO (observer)
**Diplomatic representation in the US:** none; note - the Permanent Mission to the UN for Bhutan has consular jurisdiction in the US; address: 763 First Avenue, New York, NY 10017; telephone [1] (212) 682-2268; FAX [1] (212) 661-0551
*consulate(s) general:* New York
**Diplomatic representation from the US:** the US and Bhutan have no formal diplomatic relations, although informal contact is maintained between the Bhutanese and US Embassy in New Delhi (India)
**Flag description:** divided diagonally from the lower hoist-side corner; the upper triangle is yellow and the lower triangle is orange; centered along the dividing line is a large black and white dragon facing away from the hoist side

## Economy

**Economy - overview:** The economy, one of the world's smallest and least developed, is based on agriculture and forestry, which provide the main livelihood for more than 60% of the population. Agriculture consists largely of subsistence farming and animal husbandry. Rugged mountains dominate the terrain and make the building of roads and other infrastructure difficult and expensive. The economy is closely aligned with India's through strong trade and monetary links and dependence on India's financial assistance. The industrial sector is technologically backward, with most production of the cottage industry type. Most development projects, such as road construction, rely on Indian migrant labor. Model education, social, and environment programs are underway with support from multilateral development organizations. Each economic program takes into account the government's desire to protect the country's environment and cultural traditions. For example, the government, in its cautious expansion of the tourist sector, encourages visits by upscale, environmentally conscientious tourists. Detailed controls and uncertain policies in areas such as industrial licensing, trade, labor, and finance continue to hamper foreign investment. Hydropower exports to India have boosted Bhutan's overall growth, even though GDP fell in 2008 as a result of a slowdown in India, its predominant export market. New hydropower projects will be the driving force behind Bhutan's ability to create employment and sustain growth in the coming years.
**GDP (purchasing power parity):**
$3.789 billion (2008 est.)
$3.238 billion (2007)
$2.768 billion (2006)
*note:* data are in 2008 US dollars
**GDP (official exchange rate):** $1.368 billion (2008 est.)
**GDP - real growth rate:**
6.6% (2008 est.)
17% (2007 est.)
7.8% (2006 est.)
**GDP - per capita (PPP):**
$5,600 (2008 est.)
$4,800 (2007 est.)
$4,200 (2006 est.)
*note:* data are in 2008 US dollars
**GDP - composition by sector:**
*agriculture:* 22.3%
*industry:* 37.9%
*services:* 39.8% (2006)
**Labor force:** NA
*note:* major shortage of skilled labor
**Labor force - by occupation:**
*agriculture:* 63%
*industry:* 6%
*services:* 31% (2004 est.)
**Unemployment rate:**
2.5% (2004)
**Population below poverty line:** 31.7% (2003)
**Household income or consumption by percentage share:**
*lowest 10%:* NA%
*highest 10%:* NA%
**Budget:**
*revenues:* $272 million
*expenditures:* $350 million
*note:* the government of India finances nearly three-fifths of Bhutan's budget expenditures (2005)
**Public debt:** 81.4% of GDP (2004)

# Bhutan *(continued)*

**Inflation rate (consumer prices):**
4.9% (2007 est.)
**Commercial bank prime lending rate:** 14%
(31 December 2007)
**Stock of money:** $381.1 million
(31 December 2007)
**Stock of quasi money:** $220.3 million
(31 December 2007)
**Stock of domestic credit:** $169.9 million
(31 December 2007)
**Market value of publicly traded shares:** $NA
**Agriculture - products:** rice, corn, root crops, citrus,
foodgrains; dairy products, eggs
**Industries:** cement, wood products, processed
fruits, alcoholic beverages, calcium carbide, tourism
**Industrial production growth rate:** NA
**Electricity - production:** 4.475 billion kWh
(2007 est.)
**Electricity - consumption:** 528.8 million kWh
(2007 est.)
**Electricity - exports:** 3.644 billion kWh (2007 est.)
**Electricity - imports:** 11 million kWh (2007 est.)
**Oil - production:** 0 bbl/day (2007 est.)
**Oil - consumption:** 1,250 bbl/day (2006 est.)
**Oil - exports:** 0 bbl/day (2005)
**Oil - imports:** 1,152 bbl/day (2005)
**Oil - proved reserves:** 0 bbl (1 January 2006 est.)
**Natural gas - production:** 0 cu m (2007 est.)
**Natural gas - consumption:** 0 cu m (2007 est.)
**Natural gas - exports:** 0 cu m (2007 est.)
**Natural gas - imports:** 0 cu m (2007 est.)
**Natural gas - proved reserves:** 0 cu m
(1 January 2006 est.)
**Current account balance:** $116 million (2007 est.)
**Exports:** $350 million f.o.b. (2006)
**Exports - commodities:** electricity (to India),
cardamom, gypsum, timber, handicrafts, cement, fruit,
precious stones, spices
**Exports - partners:** India 58.6%, Hong Kong 30.1%,
Bangladesh 7.3% (2007)
**Imports:** $320 million c.i.f. (2006)
**Imports - commodities:** fuel and lubricants, grain,
aircraft, machinery and parts, vehicles, fabrics, rice
**Imports - partners:** India 74.5%, Japan 7.4%,
Sweden 3.2% (2007)
**Debt - external:** $713.3 million (2006)
**Exchange rates:** ngultrum (BTN) per US dollar -
41.487 (2007), 45.279 (2006), 44.101 (2005), 45.317
(2004), 46.583 (2003)
*note:* the ngultrum is pegged to the Indian rupee

## Communications

**Telephones - main lines in use:** 29,900 (2007)
**Telephones - mobile cellular:** 149,400 (2007)
**Telephone system:**
*general assessment:* urban towns and district
headquarters have telecommunications services
*domestic:* very low teledensity; domestic service is
very poor especially in rural areas; wireless service
available since 2003
*international:* country code - 975; international telephone

and telegraph service via landline and microwave relay
through India; satellite earth station - 1 Intelsat (2007)
**Radio broadcast stations:** AM 0, FM 9,
shortwave 1 (2007)
**Television broadcast stations:** 1 (2007)
**Internet country code:** .bt
**Internet hosts:** 9,046 (2008)
**Internet users:** 40,000 (2007)

## Transportation

**Airports:** 2 (2008)
**Airports - with paved runways:**
*total:* 1
*1,524 to 2,437 m:* 1 (2008)
**Airports - with unpaved runways:**
*total:* 1
*914 to 1,523 m:* 1 (2008)
**Roadways:**
*total:* 8,050 km
*paved:* 4,991 km
*unpaved:* 3,059 km (2003)

## Military

**Military branches:** Royal Bhutan Army (includes
Royal Bodyguard and Royal Bhutan Police) (2009)
**Military service age and obligation:** 18 years of
age for voluntary military service; no conscription
(2008)
**Manpower available for military service:**
*males age 16-49:* 190,104
*females age 16-49:* 167,289 (2008 est.)
**Manpower fit for military service:**
*males age 16-49:* 150,210
*females age 16-49:* 135,991 (2009 est.)
**Manpower reaching militarily significant age
annually:**
*male:* 7,668
*female:* 7,379 (2009 est.)
**Military expenditures:** 1% of GDP (2005 est.)

## Transnational Issues

**Disputes - international:** Bhutan cooperates with
India to expel Indian Nagaland separatists; lacking
any treaty describing the boundary, Bhutan and China
continue negotiations to establish a common
boundary alignment to resolve territorial disputes
arising from substantial cartographic discrepancies,
the largest of which lie in Bhutan's northwest and
along the Chumbi salient

# Bolivia

## Introduction

**Background:** Bolivia, named after independence
fighter Simon BOLIVAR, broke away from Spanish rule in
1825; much of its subsequent history has consisted of a
series of nearly 200 coups and countercoups.
Democratic civilian rule was established in 1982, but
leaders have faced difficult problems of deep-seated
poverty, social unrest, and illegal drug production. In
December 2005, Bolivians elected Movement Toward
Socialism leader Evo MORALES president - by the
widest margin of any leader since the restoration of
civilian rule in 1982 - after he ran on a promise to change
the country's traditional political class and empower the
nation's poor, indigenous majority. However, since taking
office, his controversial strategies have exacerbated
racial and economic tensions between the Amerindian
populations of the Andean west and the non-indigenous
communities of the eastern lowlands.

## Geography

**Location:** Central South America, southwest of Brazil
**Geographic coordinates:** 17 00 S, 65 00 W
**Map references:** South America
**Area:**
*total:* 1,098,580 sq km
*land:* 1,084,390 sq km
*water:* 14,190 sq km
**Area - comparative:** slightly less than three times
the size of Montana
**Land boundaries:**
*total:* 6,940 km
*border countries:* Argentina 832 km, Brazil 3,423 km,
Chile 860 km, Paraguay 750 km, Peru 1,075 km
**Coastline:** 0 km (landlocked)
**Maritime claims:** none (landlocked)
**Climate:** varies with altitude; humid and tropical to
cold and semiarid
**Terrain:** rugged Andes Mountains with a highland
plateau (Altiplano), hills, lowland plains of the
Amazon Basin

# Bolivia *(continued)*

**Elevation extremes:**
*lowest point:* Rio Paraguay 90 m
*highest point:* Nevado Sajama 6,542 m
**Natural resources:** tin, natural gas, petroleum, zinc, tungsten, antimony, silver, iron, lead, gold, timber, hydropower
**Land use:**
*arable land:* 2.78%
*permanent crops:* 0.19%
*other:* 97.03% (2005)
**Irrigated land:** 1,320 sq km (2003)
**Total renewable water resources:** 622.5 cu km (2000)
**Freshwater withdrawal (domestic/industrial/agricultural):**
*total:* 1.44 cu km/yr (13%/7%/81%)
*per capita:* 157 cu m/yr (2000)
**Natural hazards:** flooding in the northeast (March-April)
**Environment - current issues:** the clearing of land for agricultural purposes and the international demand for tropical timber are contributing to deforestation; soil erosion from overgrazing and poor cultivation methods (including slash-and-burn agriculture); desertification; loss of biodiversity; industrial pollution of water supplies used for drinking and irrigation
**Environment - international agreements:**
*party to:* Biodiversity, Climate Change, Climate Change-Kyoto Protocol, Desertification, Endangered Species, Hazardous Wastes, Law of the Sea, Marine Dumping, Ozone Layer Protection, Ship Pollution, Tropical Timber 83, Tropical Timber 94, Wetlands
*signed, but not ratified:* Environmental Modification, Marine Life Conservation
**Geography - note:** landlocked; shares control of Lago Titicaca, world's highest navigable lake (elevation 3,805 m), with Peru

## People

**Population:** 9,775,246 (July 2009 est.)
**Age structure:**
*0-14 years:* 35.5% (male 1,767,310/female 1,701,744)
*15-64 years:* 60% (male 2,877,605/female 2,992,043)
*65 years and over:* 4.5% (male 193,196/female 243,348) (2009 est.)
**Median age:**
*total:* 21.9 years
*male:* 21.3 years
*female:* 22.6 years (2009 est.)
**Population growth rate:** 1.772% (2009 est.)
**Birth rate:** 25.82 births/1,000 population (2009 est.)
**Death rate:** 7.35 deaths/1,000 population (2008 est.)
**Net migration rate:** -1.05 migrant(s)/1,000 population (2009 est.)
**Urbanization:**
*urban population:* 66% of total population (2008)
*rate of urbanization:* 2.5% annual rate of change (2005-10 est.)

**Sex ratio:**
*at birth:* 1.05 male(s)/female
*under 15 years:* 1.04 male(s)/female
*15-64 years:* 0.96 male(s)/female
*65 years and over:* 0.79 male(s)/female
*total population:* 0.98 male(s)/female (2009 est.)
**Infant mortality rate:**
*total:* 44.66 deaths/1,000 live births
*male:* 48.56 deaths/1,000 live births
*female:* 40.57 deaths/1,000 live births (2009 est.)
**Life expectancy at birth:**
*total population:* 66.89 years
*male:* 64.2 years
*female:* 69.72 years (2009 est.)
**Total fertility rate:** 3.17 children born/woman (2009 est.)
**HIV/AIDS - adult prevalence rate:** 0.2% (2007 est.)
**HIV/AIDS - people living with HIV/AIDS:** 8,100 (2007 est.)
**HIV/AIDS - deaths:** fewer than 500 (2007 est.)
**Major infectious diseases:**
*degree of risk:* high
*food or waterborne diseases:* bacterial diarrhea, hepatitis A, and typhoid fever
*vectorborne diseases:* dengue fever, malaria, and yellow fever
*water contact disease:* leptospirosis (2009)
**Nationality:**
*noun:* Bolivian(s)
*adjective:* Bolivian
**Ethnic groups:** Quechua 30%, mestizo (mixed white and Amerindian ancestry) 30%, Aymara 25%, white 15%
**Religions:** Roman Catholic 95%, Protestant (Evangelical Methodist) 5%
**Languages:** Spanish 60.7% (official), Quechua 21.2% (official), Aymara 14.6% (official), foreign languages 2.4%, other 1.2% (2001 census)
**Literacy:**
*definition:* age 15 and over can read and write
*total population:* 86.7%
*male:* 93.1%
*female:* 80.7% (2001 census)
**Education expenditures:** 6.4% of GDP (2003)

## Government

**Country name:**
*conventional long form:* Plurinational State of Bolivia
*conventional short form:* Bolivia
*local long form:* Estado Plurinacional de Bolivia
*local short form:* Bolivia
**Government type:** republic; note - the new constitution defines Bolivia as a "Social Unitarian State"
**Capital:**
*name:* La Paz (administrative capital)
*geographic coordinates:* 16 30 S, 68 09 W
*time difference:* UTC-4 (1 hour ahead of Washington, DC during Standard Time)
*note:* Sucre (constitutional capital)

**Administrative divisions:** 9 departments (departamentos, singular - departamento); Beni, Chuquisaca, Cochabamba, La Paz, Oruro, Pando, Potosi, Santa Cruz, Tarija
**Independence:** 6 August 1825 (from Spain)
**National holiday:** Independence Day, 6 August (1825)
**Constitution:** 2 February 1967; revised in August 1994; voters approved a new constitution on 25 January 2009
**Legal system:** based on Spanish law and Napoleonic Code; has not accepted compulsory ICJ jurisdiction; the 2009 Constitution incorporates indigenous community justice into Bolivia's judicial system
**Suffrage:** 18 years of age, universal and compulsory (married); 21 years of age, universal and compulsory (single)
**Executive branch:**
*chief of state:* President Juan Evo MORALES Ayma (since 22 January 2006); Vice President Alvaro GARCIA Linera (since 22 January 2006); note - the president is both chief of state and head of government
*head of government:* President Juan Evo MORALES Ayma (since 22 January 2006); Vice President Alvaro GARCIA Linera (since 22 January 2006)
*cabinet:* Cabinet appointed by the president
*elections:* president and vice president elected on the same ticket by popular vote for a single five-year term; election last held 18 December 2005 (next to be held in December 2009)
*election results:* Juan Evo MORALES Ayma elected president; percent of vote - Juan Evo MORALES Ayma 53.7%; Jorge Fernando QUIROGA Ramirez 28.6%; Samuel DORIA MEDINA Arana 7.8%; Michiaki NAGATANI Morishit 6.5%; Felipe QUISPE Huanca 2.2%; Guildo ANGULA Cabrera 0.7%
**Legislative branch:** bicameral National Congress or Congreso Nacional consists of Chamber of Senators or Camara de Senadores (27 seats; members are elected by proportional representation from party lists to serve five-year terms) and Chamber of Deputies or Camara de Diputados (130 seats; 70 members are directly elected from their districts and 60 are elected by proportional representation from party lists to serve five-year terms); note - under representational rules established by the 2009 Constitution, the National Congress will become the Plurinational Legislative Assembly or Asamblea Legislativa Plurinacional; the number of Deputies will remain at 130, but the number of Senators will rise to 36
*elections:* Chamber of Senators and Chamber of Deputies - last held 18 December 2005 (next to be held in December 2009)
*election results:* Chamber of Senators - percent of vote by party - NA; seats by party - PODEMOS 13, MAS 12, UN 1, MNR 1; Chamber of Deputies - percent of vote by party - NA; seats by party - MAS 73, PODEMOS 43, UN 8, MNR 6
**Judicial branch:** Supreme Court or Corte Suprema (judges appointed for 10-year terms by National Congress); District Courts (one in each department);

# Bolivia (continued)

provincial and local courts (to try minor cases); Constitutional Tribunal (five primary or titulares and five alternate or suplente magistrates appointed by Congress; to rule on constitutional issues); National Electoral Court (six members elected by Congress, Supreme Court, the president, and the political party with the highest vote in the last election for four-year terms); note - under the 2009 Constitution, all Constitutional and Supreme Court judges will be elected by popular vote

**Political parties and leaders:** Free Bolivia Movement or MBL [Franz BARRIOS]; Movement Toward Socialism or MAS [Juan Evo MORALES Ayma]; Movement Without Fear or MSM [Juan DEL GRANADO]; National Revolutionary Movement or MNR [Mirta QUEVEDO]; National Unity [Samuel DORIA MEDINA Arana]; Poder Democratico Nacional or PODEMOS [Jorge Fernando QUIROGA Ramirez]; Social Alliance [Rene JOAQUINO]

**Political pressure groups and leaders:** Sole Confederation of Campesino Workers of Bolivia or CSUTCB

*other:* Cocalero groups; indigenous organizations; labor unions

**International organization participation:** CAN, FAO, G-77, IADB, IAEA, IBRD, ICAO, ICCt, ICRM, IDA, IFAD, IFC, IFRCS, ILO, IMF, IMO, Interpol, IOC, IOM, IPU, ISO (correspondent), ITSO, ITU, LAES, LAIA, Mercosur (associate), MIGA, MINURCAT, MINUSTAH, MONUC, NAM, OAS, OPANAL, OPCW, PCA, RG, UN, UNASUR, UNCTAD, UNESCO, UNFICYP, UNIDO, Union Latina, UNMIL, UNMIS, UNOCI, UNWTO, UPU, WCL, WCO, WFTU, WHO, WIPO, WMO, WTO

**Diplomatic representation in the US:**
*chief of mission:* Ambassador (vacant); Charge d'Affaires Erika DUENAS
*chancery:* 3014 Massachusetts Avenue NW, Washington, DC 20008
*telephone:* [1] (202) 483-4410
*FAX:* [1] (202) 328-3712
*consulate(s) general:* Los Angeles, Miami, New York, San Francisco
*note:* as of September 2008, the US has expelled the Bolivian ambassador to the US

**Diplomatic representation from the US:**
*chief of mission:* Ambassador (vacant); Charge d'Affaires Krishna URS
*embassy:* Avenida Arce 2780, Casilla 425, La Paz
*mailing address:* P. O. Box 425, La Paz; APO AA 34032
*telephone:* [591] (2) 216-8000
*FAX:* [591] (2) 216-8111
*note:* as of September 2008, the Bolivian Government has expelled the US Ambassador to Bolivia

**Flag description:** three equal horizontal bands of red (top), yellow, and green with the coat of arms centered on the yellow band
*note:* similar to the flag of Ghana, which has a large black five-pointed star centered in the yellow band

## Economy

**Economy - overview:** Bolivia is one of the poorest and least developed countries in Latin America. Following a disastrous economic crisis during the early 1980s, reforms spurred private investment, stimulated economic growth, and cut poverty rates in the 1990s. The period 2003-05 was characterized by political instability, racial tensions, and violent protests against plans - subsequently abandoned - to export Bolivia's newly discovered natural gas reserves to large northern hemisphere markets. In 2005, the government passed a controversial hydrocarbons law that imposed significantly higher royalties and required foreign firms then operating under risk-sharing contracts to surrender all production to the state energy company. In early 2008, higher earnings for mining and hydrocarbons exports pushed the current account surplus to 9.4% of GDP and the government's higher tax take produced a fiscal surplus after years of large deficits. Private investment as a share of GDP, however, remains among the lowest in Latin America, and inflation remained at double-digit levels in 2008. The decline in commodity prices in late 2008, the lack of foreign investment in the mining and hydrocarbon sectors, and the suspension of trade benefits with the United States will pose challenges for the Bolivian economy in 2009.

**GDP (purchasing power parity):**
$43.08 billion (2008 est.)
$40.8 billion (2007)
$39 billion (2006)
*note:* data are in 2008 US dollars

**GDP (official exchange rate):** $18.94 billion (2008 est.)

**GDP - real growth rate:**
5.6% (2008 est.)
4.6% (2007 est.)
4.8% (2006 est.)

**GDP - per capita (PPP):**
$4,500 (2008 est.)
$4,300 (2007 est.)
$4,200 (2006 est.)
*note:* data are in 2008 US dollars

**GDP - composition by sector:**
*agriculture:* 11.3%
*industry:* 36.9%
*services:* 51.8% (2008 est.)

**Labor force:** 4.457 million (2008 est.)

**Labor force - by occupation:**
*agriculture:* 40%
*industry:* 17%
*services:* 43% (2006 est.)

**Unemployment rate:**
7.5% (2008 est.)
7.5% (2007 est.)
*note:* data are for urban areas; widespread underemployment

**Population below poverty line:** 60% (2006 est.)

**Household income or consumption by percentage share:**
*lowest 10%:* 0.3%
*highest 10%:* 47.2% (2002)

**Distribution of family income - Gini index:** 59.2 (2006)

**Investment (gross fixed):** 16.7% of GDP (2008 est.)

**Budget:**
*revenues:* $8.044 billion
*expenditures:* $7.341 billion (2008 est.)

**Public debt:** 52.7% of GDP (2008 est.)

**Inflation rate (consumer prices):**
11.5% (2008 est.)
8.7% (2007 est.)

**Central bank discount rate:** 6.5% (31 December 2007)

**Commercial bank prime lending rate:** 12.86% (31 December 2007)

**Stock of money:** $3.032 billion (31 December 2007)

**Stock of quasi money:** $4.729 billion (31 December 2007)

**Stock of domestic credit:** $4.759 billion (31 December 2007)

**Market value of publicly traded shares:** $2.263 billion (31 December 2007)

**Agriculture - products:** soybeans, coffee, coca, cotton, corn, sugarcane, rice, potatoes; timber

**Industries:** mining, smelting, petroleum, food and beverages, tobacco, handicrafts, clothing

**Industrial production growth rate:** 7.4% (2008 est.)

**Electricity - production:** 5.668 billion kWh (2007 est.)

**Electricity - consumption:** 5.092 billion kWh (2007 est.)

**Electricity - exports:** 0 kWh (2007 est.)

**Electricity - imports:** 0 kWh (2007 est.)

**Oil - production:** 61,790 bbl/day (2007 est.)

**Oil - consumption:** 31,500 bbl/day (2007 est.)

**Oil - exports:** 18,500 bbl/day (2007 est.)

**Oil - imports:** 8,600 bbl/day (2007 est.)

**Oil - proved reserves:** 465 million bbl (1 January 2008 est.)

**Natural gas - production:** 14.7 billion cu m (2007 est.)

**Natural gas - consumption:** 3 billion cu m (2007 est.)

**Natural gas - exports:** 11.7 billion cu m (2007 est.)

**Natural gas - imports:** 0 cu m (2007 est.)

**Natural gas - proved reserves:** 750.4 billion cu m (1 January 2008 est.)

**Current account balance:** $1.789 billion (2008 est.)

**Exports:** $6.384 billion f.o.b. (2008 est.)

**Exports - commodities:** natural gas, soybeans and soy products, crude petroleum, zinc ore, tin

**Exports - partners:** Brazil 46%, US 9.8%, Japan 7.6%, Argentina 5.8%, South Korea 4.8%, Peru 4.1% (2007)

**Imports:** $4.782 billion f.o.b. (2008 est.)

**Imports - commodities:** petroleum products, plastics, paper, aircraft and aircraft parts, prepared foods, automobiles, insecticides, soybeans

**Imports - partners:** Brazil 29.9%, Argentina 16.2%, Chile 10.5%, US 9.8%, Peru 8.1% (2007)

**Reserves of foreign exchange and gold:** $7.864 billion (31 December 2008 est.)
**Debt - external:** $4.603 billion (31 December 2008 est.)
**Stock of direct foreign investment - at home:** $6.88 billion (31 December 2004)
**Stock of direct foreign investment - abroad:** $NA
**Exchange rates:** bolivianos (BOB) per US dollar - 7.253 (2008 est.), 7.8616 (2007), 8.0159 (2006), 8.0661 (2005), 7.9363 (2004)

## Communications

**Telephones - main lines in use:** 678,200 (2007)
**Telephones - mobile cellular:** 3.254 million (2007)
**Telephone system:**
*general assessment:* privatization begun in 1995; reliability has steadily improved; new subscribers face bureaucratic difficulties; most telephones are concentrated in La Paz and other cities; mobile-cellular telephone use expanding rapidly; fixed-line teledensity of 7 per 100 persons; mobile-cellular telephone density of 35 per 100 persons
*domestic:* primary trunk system, which is being expanded, employs digital microwave radio relay; some areas are served by fiber-optic cable; mobile cellular systems are being expanded
*international:* country code - 591; satellite earth station -1 Intelsat (Atlantic Ocean) (2007)
**Radio broadcast stations:** AM 171, FM 73, shortwave 77 (1999)
**Television broadcast stations:** 48 (1997)
**Internet country code:** .bo
**Internet hosts:** 68,428 (2008)
**Internet users:** 1 million (2007)

## Transportation

**Airports:** 1,009 (2008)
**Airports - with paved runways:**
*total:* 16
*over 3,047 m:* 4
*2,438 to 3,047 m:* 4
*1,524 to 2,437 m:* 5
*914 to 1,523 m:* 3 (2008)
**Airports - with unpaved runways:**
*total:* 993
*over 3,047 m:* 1
*2,438 to 3,047 m:* 4
*1,524 to 2,437 m:* 58
*914 to 1,523 m:* 186
*under 914 m:* 744 (2008)
**Pipelines:** gas 4,883 km; liquid petroleum gas 47 km; oil 2,475 km; refined products 1,589 km (2008)
**Railways:**
*total:* 3,504 km
*narrow gauge:* 3,504 km 1.000-m gauge (2006)
**Roadways:**
*total:* 62,479 km
*paved:* 3,749 km
*unpaved:* 58,730 km (2004)
**Waterways:** 10,000 km (commercially navigable) (2007)

**Merchant marine:**
*total:* 23
*by type:* bulk carrier 1, cargo 11, carrier 1, passenger/cargo 1, petroleum tanker 7, refrigerated cargo 1, specialized tanker 1
*foreign-owned:* 7 (Bahamas 1, China 1, Iran 1, Singapore 1, Syria 2, Taiwan 1) (2008)
**Ports and terminals:** Puerto Aguirre (inland port on the Paraguay/Parana waterway at the Bolivia/Brazil border); Bolivia has free port privileges in maritime ports in Argentina, Brazil, Chile, and Paraguay

## Military

**Military branches:** Bolivian Armed Forces: Bolivian Army (Ejercito Boliviano, EB), Bolivian Navy (Fuerza Naval Boliviana, FNB; includes marines), Bolivian Air Force (Fuerza Aerea Boliviana, FAB) (2009)
**Military service age and obligation:** 18-49 years of age for 12-month compulsory military service; when annual number of volunteers falls short of goal, compulsory recruitment is effected, including conscription of boys as young as 14; 15-19 years of age for voluntary premilitary service, provides exemption from further military service (2009)
**Manpower available for military service:**
*males age 16-49:* 2,295,746
*females age 16-49:* 2,366,828 (2008 est.)
**Manpower fit for military service:**
*males age 16-49:* 1,666,697
*females age 16-49:* 1,906,396 (2009 est.)
**Manpower reaching militarily significant age annually:**
*male:* 108,304
*female:* 104,882 (2009 est.)
**Military expenditures:** 1.9% of GDP (2006)

## Transnational Issues

**Disputes - international:** Chile and Peru rebuff Bolivia's reactivated claim to restore the Atacama corridor, ceded to Chile in 1884, but Chile offers instead unrestricted but not sovereign maritime access through Chile for Bolivian natural gas and other commodities; an accord placed the long-disputed Isla Suarez/Ilha de Guajara-Mirim, a fluvial island on the Rio Mamore, under Bolivian administration in 1958, but sovereignty remains in dispute
**Illicit drugs:** world's third-largest cultivator of coca (after Colombia and Peru) with an estimated 29,500 hectares under cultivation in 2007, increased slightly when compared to 2006; third largest producer of cocaine, estimated at 120 metric tons potential pure cocaine in 2007; transit country for Peruvian and Colombian cocaine destined for Brazil, Argentina, Chile, Paraguay, and Europe; cultivation generally increasing since 2000, despite eradication and alternative crop programs; weak border controls; some money-laundering activity related to narcotics trade; major cocaine consumption (2008)

# Bosnia and Herzegovina

## Introduction

**Background:** Bosnia and Herzegovina's declaration of sovereignty in October 1991 was followed by a declaration of independence from the former Yugoslavia on 3 March 1992 after a referendum boycotted by ethnic Serbs. The Bosnian Serbs - supported by neighboring Serbia and Montenegro - responded with armed resistance aimed at partitioning the republic along ethnic lines and joining Serb-held areas to form a "Greater Serbia." In March 1994, Bosniaks and Croats reduced the number of warring factions from three to two by signing an agreement creating a joint Bosniak/Croat Federation of Bosnia and Herzegovina. On 21 November 1995, in Dayton, Ohio, the warring parties initialed a peace agreement that brought to a halt three years of interethnic civil strife (the final agreement was signed in Paris on 14 December 1995). The Dayton Peace Accords retained Bosnia and Herzegovina's international boundaries and created a joint multi-ethnic and democratic government charged with conducting foreign, diplomatic, and fiscal policy. Also recognized was a second tier of government comprised of two entities roughly equal in size: the Bosniak/Croat Federation of Bosnia and Herzegovina and the Bosnian Serb-led Republika Srpska (RS). The Federation and RS governments were charged with overseeing most government functions. The Office of the High Representative (OHR) was established to oversee the implementation of the civilian aspects of the agreement. In 1995-96, a NATO-led international peacekeeping force (IFOR) of 60,000 troops served in Bosnia to implement and monitor the military aspects of the agreement. IFOR was succeeded by a smaller, NATO-led Stabilization Force (SFOR) whose mission was to deter renewed hostilities. European Union peacekeeping troops (EUFOR) replaced SFOR in December 2004; their mission is to maintain peace and stability throughout the country. EUFOR's mission changed from peacekeeping to civil policing in October 2007, with its presence reduced from nearly 7,000 to less than 2,500 troops.

# Bosnia and Herzegovina *(continued)*

## Geography

**Location:** Southeastern Europe, bordering the Adriatic Sea and Croatia

**Geographic coordinates:** 44 00 N, 18 00 E

**Map references:** Europe

**Area:**
*total:* 51,209.2 sq km
*land:* 51,197 sq km
*water:* 12.2 sq km

**Area - comparative:** slightly smaller than West Virginia

**Land boundaries:**
*total:* 1,538 km
*border countries:* Croatia 932 km, Montenegro 249 km, Serbia 357 km

**Coastline:** 20 km

**Maritime claims:** no data available

**Climate:** hot summers and cold winters; areas of high elevation have short, cool summers and long, severe winters; mild, rainy winters along coast

**Terrain:** mountains and valleys

**Elevation extremes:**
*lowest point:* Adriatic Sea 0 m
*highest point:* Maglic 2,386 m

**Natural resources:** coal, iron ore, bauxite, copper, lead, zinc, chromite, cobalt, manganese, nickel, clay, gypsum, salt, sand, forests, hydropower

**Land use:**
*arable land:* 19.61%
*permanent crops:* 1.89%
*other:* 78.5% (2005)

**Irrigated land:** 30 sq km (2003)

**Total renewable water resources:** 37.5 cu km (2003)

**Natural hazards:** destructive earthquakes

**Environment - current issues:** air pollution from metallurgical plants; sites for disposing of urban waste are limited; water shortages and destruction of infrastructure because of the 1992-95 civil strife; deforestation

**Environment - international agreements:**
*party to:* Air Pollution, Biodiversity, Climate Change, Climate Change-Kyoto Protocol, Desertification, Hazardous Wastes, Law of the Sea, Marine Life Conservation, Ozone Layer Protection, Wetlands
*signed, but not ratified:* none of the selected agreements

**Geography - note:** within Bosnia and Herzegovina's recognized borders, the country is divided into a joint Bosniak/Croat Federation (about 51% of the territory) and the Bosnian Serb-led Republika Srpska or RS (about 49% of the territory); the region called Herzegovina is contiguous to Croatia and Montenegro, and traditionally has been settled by an ethnic Croat majority in the west and an ethnic Serb majority in the east

## People

**Population:** 4,613,414 (July 2009 est.)

**Age structure:**
*0-14 years:* 14.5% (male 344,760/female 323,303)
*15-64 years:* 70.7% (male 1,645,274/female 1,617,136)
*65 years and over:* 14.8% (male 279,781/female 403,160) (2009 est.)

**Median age:**
*total:* 39.8 years
*male:* 38.7 years
*female:* 41 years (2009 est.)

**Population growth rate:** 0.339% (2009 est.)

**Birth rate:** 8.85 births/1,000 population (2009 est.)

**Death rate:** 8.54 deaths/1,000 population (2008 est.)

**Net migration rate:** 3.17 migrant(s)/1,000 population (2009 est.)

**Urbanization:**
*urban population:* 47% of total population (2008)
*rate of urbanization:* 1.4% annual rate of change (2005-10 est.)

**Sex ratio:**
*at birth:* 1.07 male(s)/female
*under 15 years:* 1.07 male(s)/female
*15-64 years:* 1.02 male(s)/female
*65 years and over:* 0.69 male(s)/female
*total population:* 0.97 male(s)/female (2009 est.)

**Infant mortality rate:**
*total:* 9.1 deaths/1,000 live births
*male:* 10.44 deaths/1,000 live births
*female:* 7.67 deaths/1,000 live births (2009 est.)

**Life expectancy at birth:**
*total population:* 78.5 years
*male:* 74.92 years
*female:* 82.34 years (2009 est.)

**Total fertility rate:** 1.25 children born/woman (2009 est.)

**HIV/AIDS - adult prevalence rate:** less than 0.1% (2007 est.)

**HIV/AIDS - people living with HIV/AIDS:** 900 (2007 est.)

**HIV/AIDS - deaths:** 100 (2001 est.)

**Nationality:**
*noun:* Bosnian(s), Herzegovinian(s)
*adjective:* Bosnian, Herzegovinian

**Ethnic groups:** Bosniak 48%, Serb 37.1%, Croat 14.3%, other 0.6% (2000)
*note:* Bosniak has replaced Muslim as an ethnic term in part to avoid confusion with the religious term Muslim - an adherent of Islam

**Religions:** Muslim 40%, Orthodox 31%, Roman Catholic 15%, other 14%

**Languages:** Bosnian, Croatian, Serbian

**Literacy:**
*definition:* age 15 and over can read and write
*total population:* 96.7%
*male:* 99%
*female:* 94.4% (2000 est.)

**Education expenditures:** NA

## Government

**Country name:**
*conventional long form:* none
*conventional short form:* Bosnia and Herzegovina
*local long form:* none
*local short form:* Bosna i Hercegovina
*former:* People's Republic of Bosnia and Herzegovina, Socialist Republic of Bosnia and Herzegovina

**Government type:** emerging federal democratic republic

**Capital:**
*name:* Sarajevo
*geographic coordinates:* 43 52 N, 18 25 E
*time difference:* UTC+1 (6 hours ahead of Washington, DC during Standard Time)
*daylight saving time:* +1hr, begins last Sunday in March; ends last Sunday in October

**Administrative divisions:** 2 first-order administrative divisions and 1 internationally supervised district* - Brcko district (Brcko Distrikt)*, the Bosniak/Croat Federation of Bosnia and Herzegovina (Federacija Bosna i Hercegovina) and the Bosnian Serb-led Republika Srpska; note - Brcko district is in northeastern Bosnia and is an administrative unit under the sovereignty of Bosnia and Herzegovina; the district remains under international supervision

**Independence:** 1 March 1992 (from Yugoslavia; referendum for independence completed 1 March 1992; independence declared 3 March 1992)

**National holiday:** National Day, 25 November (1943)

**Constitution:** the Dayton Peace Accords, signed 14 December 1995 in Paris, included a new constitution now in force; note - each of the entities also has its own constitution

**Legal system:** based on civil law system; has not accepted compulsory ICJ jurisdiction

**Suffrage:** 18 years of age, 16 if employed; universal

**Executive branch:**
*chief of state:* Chairman of the Presidency Nebojsa RADMANOVIC (chairman since 6 November 2008; presidency member since 1 October 2006 - Serb); other members of the three-member presidency rotating (every eight months): Haris SILAJDZIC (presidency member since 1 October 2006 - Bosniak); and Zeljko KOMSIC (presidency member since 1 October 2006 - Croat)
*head of government:* Chairman of the Council of Ministers Nikola SPIRIC (since 11 January 2007)
*cabinet:* Council of Ministers nominated by the council chairman; approved by the National House of Representatives
*elections:* the three members of the presidency (one Bosniak, one Croat, one Serb) are elected by popular vote for a four-year term (eligible for a second term, but then ineligible for four years); the chairmanship rotates every eight months and resumes where it left off following each national election; election last held 1 October 2006 (next to be held in 2010); the chairman of the Council of Ministers is appointed by the presidency and confirmed by the National House of Representatives

## Bosnia and Herzegovina (continued)

*election results:* percent of vote - Nebojsa RADMANOVIC with 53.3% of the votes for the Serb seat; Zeljko KOMSIC with 39.6% of the votes for the Croat seat; Haris SILAJDZIC with 62.8% of the votes for the Bosniak seat
*note:* President of the Federation of Bosnia and Herzegovina: Borjana KRISTO (since 21 February 2007); Vice Presidents Spomenka MICIC (since NA 2007) and Mirsad KEBO (since NA 2007); President of the Republika Srpska: Rajko KUSMANOVIC (since 28 December 2007)

**Legislative branch:** bicameral Parliamentary Assembly or Skupstina consists of the House of Peoples or Dom Naroda (15 seats, 5 Bosniak, 5 Croat, 5 Serb; members elected by the Bosniak/Croat Federation's House of Representatives and the Republika Srpska's National Assembly to serve four-year terms); and the national House of Representatives or Predstavnicki Dom (42 seats, 28 seats allocated for the Federation of Bosnia and Herzegovina and 14 seats for the Republika Srpska; members elected by popular vote on the basis of proportional representation, to serve four-year terms); note - Bosnia's election law specifies four-year terms for the state and first-order administrative division entity legislatures
*elections:* House of Peoples - last constituted in January 2003 (next to be constituted in 2007); national House of Representatives - elections last held 1 October 2006 (next to be held in 2010)
*election results:* House of Peoples - percent of vote by party/coalition - NA; seats by party/coalition - NA; national House of Representatives - percent of vote by party/coalition - NA; seats by party/coalition - SDA 9, SBiH 8, SNSD 7, SDP 5, SDS 3, HDZ-BH 3, HDZ1990 2, other 5
*note:* the Bosniak/Croat Federation has a bicameral legislature that consists of a House of Peoples (58 seats - 17 Bosniak, 17 Croat, 17 Serb, 7 other); last constituted December 2002; and a House of Representatives (98 seats; members elected by popular vote to serve four-year terms); elections last held 1 October 2006 (next to be held in October 2010); percent of vote by party - NA; seats by party/coalition -SDA 28, SBiH 24, SDP 17, HDZ-BH 8, HDZ1990 7, other 14; the Republika Srpska has a National Assembly (83 seats; members elected by popular vote to serve four-year terms); elections last held 1 October 2006 (next to be held in the fall of 2010); percent of vote by party - NA; seats by party/coalition - SNSD 41, SDS 17, PDP 8, DNS 4, SBiH 4, SPRS 3, SDA 3, other 3; as a result of the 2002 constitutional reform process, a 28-member Republika Srpska Council of Peoples (COP) was established in the Republika Srpska National Assembly including eight Croats, eight Bosniaks, eight Serbs, and four members of the smaller communities
**Judicial branch:** BH Constitutional Court (consists of nine members: four members are selected by the Bosniak/Croat Federation's House of Representatives, two members by the Republika Srpska's National Assembly, and three non-Bosnian

members by the president of the European Court of Human Rights); BH State Court (consists of nine judges and three divisions - Administrative, Appellate and Criminal - having jurisdiction over cases related to state-level law and appellate jurisdiction over cases initiated in the entities); a War Crimes Chamber opened in March 2005
*note:* the entities each have a Supreme Court; each entity also has a number of lower courts; there are 10 cantonal courts in the Federation, plus a number of municipal courts; the Republika Srpska has five municipal courts

**Political parties and leaders:** Alliance of Independent Social Democrats or SNSD [Milorad DODIK]; Bosnian Party or BOSS [Mirnes AJANOVIC]; Bosnian Patriotic Party of BPS [Sefer HALILOVIC]; Civic Democratic Party or GDS [Ibrahim SPAHIC]; Croat Christian Democratic Union of Bosnia and Herzegovina or HKDU [Marin TOPIC]; Croat Party of Rights or HSP [Zvonko JURISIC]; Croat Peasants Party or HSS [Marko TADIC]; Croatian Democratic Union of Bosnia and Herzegovina or HDZ-BH [Dragan COVIC]; Croatian Democratic Union 1990 or HDZ1990 [Bozo LJUBIC]; Croatian Peoples Union [Milenko BRKIC]; Democratic National Union or DNZ [Rifet DOLIC]; Democratic Party of DP [Dragan CAVIC]; Democratic Peoples Alliance or DNS [Marko PAVIC]; Liberal Democratic Party or LDS [Rasim KADIC]; Nasa Stranka or NS [Bojan BAJIC]; New Croat Initiative or NHI [Kresimir ZUBAK]; Party for Bosnia and Herzegovina or SBiH [Haris SILAJDZIC]; Party for Democratic Action or SDA [Sulejman TIHIC]; Party for Work and Progress or RzB [Mladen IVANKOVIC-LIJANOVIC]; Party of Democratic Progress or PDP [Mladen IVANIC]; Serb Democratic Party or SDS [Mladen BOSIC]; Serb Radical Party of the Republika Srpska or SRS-RS [Milanko MIHAJLICA]; Serb Radical Party-Dr. Vojislav Seselj or SRS-VS [Radislav KANJERIC]; Social Democratic Party of BIH or SDP [Zlatko LAGUMDZIJA]; Social Democratic Union or SDU [Sejfudin TOKIC]; Socialist Party of Republika Srpska or SPRS [Petar DJOKIC]
**Political pressure groups and leaders:**
*other:* displaced persons associations; student councils; war veterans
**International organization participation:** BIS, CE, CEI, EAPC, EBRD, FAO, G-77, IAEA, IBRD, ICAO, ICCt, ICRM, IDA, IFAD, IFC, IFRCS, ILO, IMF, IMO, IMSO, Interpol, IOC, IOM, IPU, ISO, ITSO, ITU, ITUC, MIGA, MONUC, NAM (observer), OAS (observer), OIC (observer), OPCW, OSCE, PFP, SECI, UN, UNCTAD, UNESCO, UNIDO, UNWTO, UPU, WCO, WFTU, WHO, WIPO, WMO, WTO (observer)
**Diplomatic representation in the US:**
*chief of mission:* Ambassador Mitar KUJUNDZIC
*chancery:* 2109 E Street NW, Washington, DC 20037
*telephone:* [1] (202) 337-1500
*FAX:* [1] (202) 337-1502
*consulate(s) general:* Chicago, New York
**Diplomatic representation from the US:**
*chief of mission:* Ambassador Charles L. ENGLISH
*embassy:* Alipasina 43, 71000 Sarajevo

*mailing address:* use embassy street address
*telephone:* [387] (33) 445-700
*FAX:* [387] (33) 659-722
*branch office(s):* Banja Luka, Mostar
**Flag description:** a wide medium blue vertical band on the fly side with a yellow isosceles triangle abutting the band and the top of the flag; the remainder of the flag is medium blue with seven full five-pointed white stars and two half stars top and bottom along the hypotenuse of the triangle

### Economy

**Economy - overview:** The interethnic warfare in Bosnia and Herzegovina caused production to plummet by 80% from 1992 to 1995 and unemployment to soar. With an uneasy peace in place, output recovered in 1996-99 at high percentage rates from a low base; but output growth slowed in 2000-02. Part of the lag in output was made up in 2003-08 when GDP growth exceeded 5% per year. Banking reform accelerated in 2001 as all the Communist-era payments bureaus were shut down; foreign banks, primarily from Western Europe, now control most of the banking sector. The konvertibilna marka (convertible mark or BAM)- the national currency introduced in 1998 - is pegged to the euro, and confidence in the currency and the banking sector has increased. Bosnia's private sector is growing and foreign investment is slowly increasing, but government spending, at nearly 40% of adjusted GDP, remains high because of redundant government offices at the state, entity and municipal level. Implementing privatization, however, has been slow, particularly in the Federation where political division between ethnically-based political parties makes agreement on economic policy more difficult. A sizeable current account deficit and high unemployment rate remain the two most serious macroeconomic problems. Successful implementation of a value-added tax in 2006 provided a predictable source of revenue for the government and helped rein in gray market activity. National-level statistics have also improved over time but a large share of economic activity remains unofficial and unrecorded. Bosnia and Herzegovina became a full member of the Central European Free Trade Agreement in September 2007. Bosnia's economy has been largely sheltered from the global financial downtown although key economic indicators have worsened. Key exporters in the metal, automobile and wood processing industries have reported a worsening performance and have announced layoffs and output reductions.
**GDP (purchasing power parity):**
$29.9 billion (2008 est.)
$28.32 billion (2007)
$26.51 billion (2006)
*note:* data are in 2008 US dollars
Bosnia has a large informal sector that may be as much as 50% of official GDP

# Bosnia and Herzegovina *(continued)*

**GDP (official exchange rate):** $19.36 billion (2008 est.)

**GDP - real growth rate:**
5.6% (2008 est.)
6.8% (2007 est.)
6.7% (2006 est.)

**GDP - per capita (PPP):**
$6,500 (2008 est.)
$6,200 (2007 est.)
$5,900 (2006 est.)
*note:* data are in 2008 US dollars

**GDP - composition by sector:**
*agriculture:* 10.2%
*industry:* 23.9%
*services:* 66% (2006 est.)

**Labor force:** 1.196 million (2007)

**Labor force - by occupation:**
*agriculture:* 19.8%
*industry:* 32.6%
*services:* 47.6% (2007)

**Unemployment rate:**
29% (2007 est.)
45.5% (31 December 2004 est.)
*note:* official rate; gray economy may reduce actual unemployment to 25-30%

**Population below poverty line:** 25% (2004 est.)

**Household income or consumption by percentage share:**
*lowest 10%:* 3.9%
*highest 10%:* 21.4% (2001)

**Distribution of family income - Gini index:** 56.2 (2007)

**Budget:**
*revenues:* $8.607 billion
*expenditures:* $8.962 billion (2008 est.)

**Public debt:** 40% of GDP (2008 est.)

**Inflation rate (consumer prices):**
8% (2008 est.)
1.6% (2007 est.)

**Commercial bank prime lending rate:** 7.17% (31 December 2007)

**Stock of money:** $5.13 billion (31 December 2007)

**Stock of quasi money:** $5.597 billion (31 December 2007)

**Stock of domestic credit:** $8.895 billion (31 December 2007)

**Market value of publicly traded shares:** $NA

**Agriculture - products:** wheat, corn, fruits, vegetables; livestock

**Industries:** steel, coal, iron ore, lead, zinc, manganese, bauxite, vehicle assembly, textiles, tobacco products, wooden furniture, tank and aircraft assembly, domestic appliances, oil refining

**Industrial production growth rate:** 6.3% (2008 est.)

**Electricity - production:** 12.84 billion kWh (2006 est.)

**Electricity - consumption:** 8.501 billion kWh (2006 est.)

**Electricity - exports:** 5.123 billion kWh (2006 est.)

**Electricity - imports:** 3.015 billion kWh (2006 est.)

**Oil - production:** 0 bbl/day (2007 est.)

**Oil - consumption:** 27,590 bbl/day (2006 est.)

**Oil - exports:** 0 bbl/day (2005)

**Oil - imports:** 27,370 bbl/day (2005)

**Oil - proved reserves:** 0 bbl (1 January 2006 est.)

**Natural gas - production:** 0 cu m (2007 est.)

**Natural gas - consumption:** 400 million cu m (2006 est.)

**Natural gas - exports:** 0 cu m (2007 est.)

**Natural gas - imports:** NA cu m

**Natural gas - proved reserves:** 0 cu m (1 January 2006)

**Current account balance:** -$2.85 billion (2008 est.)

**Exports:** $5.092 billion f.o.b. (2008 est.)

**Exports - commodities:** metals, clothing, wood products

**Exports - partners:** Croatia 21%, Slovenia 16.5%, Italy 16.1%, Germany 13.3%, Austria 9.6%, Hungary 5.7% (2007)

**Imports:** $11.94 billion f.o.b. (2008 est.)

**Imports - commodities:** machinery and equipment, chemicals, fuels, foodstuffs

**Imports - partners:** Croatia 24.7%, Slovenia 13.3%, Germany 13.1%, Italy 10.4%, Austria 7%, Turkey 6.5%, Hungary 5.4% (2007)

**Reserves of foreign exchange and gold:** $5.2 billion (31 December 2008 est.)

**Debt - external:** $8.353 billion (31 December 2008 est.)

**Exchange rates:** konvertibilna markas (BAM) per US dollar - 1.3083 (2008 est.), 1.4419 (2007), 1.5576 (2006), 1.5727 (2005), 1.5752 (2004)
*note:* the convertible mark is pegged to the euro

## Communications

**Telephones - main lines in use:** 1.065 million (2007)

**Telephones - mobile cellular:** 2.45 million (2007)

**Telephone system:**
*general assessment:* post-war reconstruction of the telecommunications network, aided by a internationally sponsored program under ERBD, resulted in sharp increases in the number of main telephone lines available; mobile cellular subscribership has been increasing rapidly
*domestic:* fixed-line teledensity roughly 25 per 100 persons; mobile-cellular telephone density exceeds 50 per 100 persons
*international:* country code - 387; no satellite earth stations (2007)

**Radio broadcast stations:** AM 8, FM 16, shortwave 1 (1998)

**Television broadcast stations:** 33 (plus 277 repeaters) (September 1995)

**Internet country code:** .ba

**Internet hosts:** 56,032 (2008)

**Internet users:** 1.055 million (2007)

## Transportation

**Airports:** 25 (2008)

**Airports - with paved runways:**
*total:* 7
*2,438 to 3,047 m:* 4
*1,524 to 2,437 m:* 1
*under 914 m:* 2 (2008)

**Airports - with unpaved runways:**
*total:* 18
*1,524 to 2,437 m:* 1
*914 to 1,523 m:* 7
*under 914 m:* 10 (2008)

**Heliports:** 5 (2007)

**Railways:**
*total:* 608 km
*standard gauge:* 608 km 1.435-m gauge (2006)

**Roadways:**
*total:* 21,846 km
*paved:* 11,425 km (4,714 km of interurban roads)
*unpaved:* 10,421 km (2006)

**Waterways:** Sava River (northern border) open to shipping but use limited (2008)

**Ports and terminals:** Bosanska Gradiska, Bosanski Brod, Bosanski Samac, and Brcko (all inland waterway ports on the Sava River), Orasje

## Military

**Military branches:** Bosnia and Herzegovina Armed Forces (OSBiH): Army of Bosnia and Herzegovina, Air and Air Defense Forces of Bosnia and Herzegovina (Zrakoplovstvo i Protuzracna Obrana, ZPO) (2009)

**Military service age and obligation:** 18 years of age for voluntary military service; conscription abolished January 2006; 4-month service obligation (2009)

**Manpower available for military service:**
*males age 16-49:* 1,212,007
*females age 16-49:* 1,170,645 (2008 est.)

**Manpower fit for military service:**
*males age 16-49:* 991,953
*females age 16-49:* 959,226 (2009 est.)

**Manpower reaching militarily significant age annually:**
*male:* 27,368
*female:* 25,644 (2009 est.)

**Military expenditures:** 4.5% of GDP (2005 est.)

## Transnational Issues

**Disputes - international:** sections along the Drina River remain in dispute between Bosnia and Herzegovina and Serbia; discussions continue with Croatia on several small disputed sections of the boundary related to maritime access that hinder final ratification of the 1999 border agreement

**Refugees and internally displaced persons:**
*refugees (country of origin):* 7,269 (Croatia)
*IDPs:* 131,600 (Bosnian Croats, Serbs, and Bosniaks displaced in 1992-95 war) (2007)

**Illicit drugs:** increasingly a transit point for heroin being trafficked to Western Europe; minor transit point for marijuana; remains highly vulnerable to money-laundering activity given a primarily cash-based and unregulated economy, weak law enforcement, and instances of corruption

# Botswana

## Introduction

**Background:** Formerly the British protectorate of Bechuanaland, Botswana adopted its new name upon independence in 1966. Four decades of uninterrupted civilian leadership, progressive social policies, and significant capital investment have created one of the most dynamic economies in Africa. Mineral extraction, principally diamond mining, dominates economic activity, though tourism is a growing sector due to the country's conservation practices and extensive nature preserves. Botswana has one of the world's highest known rates of HIV/AIDS infection, but also one of Africa's most progressive and comprehensive programs for dealing with the disease.

## Geography

**Location:** Southern Africa, north of South Africa
**Geographic coordinates:** 22 00 S, 24 00 E
**Map references:** Africa
**Area:**
*total:* 600,370 sq km
*land:* 585,370 sq km
*water:* 15,000 sq km
**Area - comparative:** slightly smaller than Texas
**Land boundaries:**
*total:* 4,013 km
*border countries:* Namibia 1,360 km, South Africa 1,840 km, Zimbabwe 813 km
**Coastline:** 0 km (landlocked)
**Maritime claims:** none (landlocked)
**Climate:** semiarid; warm winters and hot summers
**Terrain:** predominantly flat to gently rolling tableland; Kalahari Desert in southwest
**Elevation extremes:**
*lowest point:* junction of the Limpopo and Shashe Rivers 513 m
*highest point:* Tsodilo Hills 1,489 m
**Natural resources:** diamonds, copper, nickel, salt, soda ash, potash, coal, iron ore, silver

**Land use:**
*arable land:* 0.65%
*permanent crops:* 0.01%
*other:* 99.34% (2005)
**Irrigated land:** 10 sq km (2003)
**Total renewable water resources:** 14.7 cu km (2001)
**Freshwater withdrawal (domestic/industrial/agricultural):**
*total:* 0.19 cu km/yr (41%/18%/41%)
*per capita:* 107 cu m/yr (2000)
**Natural hazards:** periodic droughts; seasonal August winds blow from the west, carrying sand and dust across the country, which can obscure visibility
**Environment - current issues:** overgrazing; desertification; limited fresh water resources
**Environment - international agreements:**
*party to:* Biodiversity, Climate Change, Climate Change-Kyoto Protocol, Desertification, Endangered Species, Hazardous Wastes, Law of the Sea, Ozone Layer Protection, Wetlands
*signed, but not ratified:* none of the selected agreements
**Geography - note:** landlocked; population concentrated in eastern part of the country

## People

**Population:** 1,990,876
*note:* estimates for this country explicitly take into account the effects of excess mortality due to AIDS; this can result in lower life expectancy, higher infant mortality, higher death rates, lower population growth rates, and changes in the distribution of population by age and sex than would otherwise be expected (July 2009 est.)
**Age structure:**
*0-14 years:* 34.8% (male 352,399/female 340,058)
*15-64 years:* 61.4% (male 613,714/female 608,003)
*65 years and over:* 3.9% (male 31,155/female 45,547) (2009 est.)
**Median age:**
*total:* 21.7 years
*male:* 21.5 years
*female:* 21.9 years (2009 est.)
**Population growth rate:** 1.937% (2009 est.)
**Birth rate:** 22.89 births/1,000 population (2009 est.)
**Death rate:** 14.02 deaths/1,000 population (2008 est.)
**Net migration rate:** 5 migrant(s)/1,000 population
*note:* there is an increasing flow of Zimbabweans into South Africa and Botswana in search of better economic opportunities (2009 est.)
**Urbanization:**
*urban population:* 60% of total population (2008)
*rate of urbanization:* 2.5% annual rate of change (2005-10 est.)
**Sex ratio:**
*at birth:* 1.03 male(s)/female
*under 15 years:* 1.04 male(s)/female
*15-64 years:* 1.01 male(s)/female
*65 years and over:* 0.68 male(s)/female
*total population:* 1 male(s)/female (2009 est.)

**Infant mortality rate:**
*total:* 12.59 deaths/1,000 live births
*male:* 13.43 deaths/1,000 live births
*female:* 11.73 deaths/1,000 live births (2009 est.)
**Life expectancy at birth:**
*total population:* 61.85 years
*male:* 61.72 years
*female:* 61.99 years (2009 est.)
**Total fertility rate:** 2.6 children born/woman (2009 est.)
**HIV/AIDS - adult prevalence rate:** 23.9% (2007 est.)
**HIV/AIDS - people living with HIV/AIDS:** 300,000 (2007 est.)
**HIV/AIDS - deaths:** 11,000 (2007 est.)
**Major infectious diseases:**
*degree of risk:* high
*food or waterborne diseases:* bacterial diarrhea, hepatitis A, and typhoid fever
*vectorborne disease:* malaria (2009)
**Nationality:**
*noun:* Motswana (singular), Batswana (plural)
*adjective:* Motswana (singular), Batswana (plural)
**Ethnic groups:** Tswana (or Setswana) 79%, Kalanga 11%, Basarwa 3%, other, including Kgalagadi and white 7%
**Religions:** Christian 71.6%, Badimo 6%, other 1.4%, unspecified 0.4%, none 20.6% (2001 census)
**Languages:** Setswana 78.2%, Kalanga 7.9%, Sekgalagadi 2.8%, English 2.1% (official), other 8.6%, unspecified 0.4% (2001 census)
**Literacy:**
*definition:* age 15 and over can read and write
*total population:* 81.2%
*male:* 80.4%
*female:* 81.8% (2003 est.)
**School life expectancy (primary to tertiary education):**
*total:* 12 years
*male:* 12 years
*female:* 12 years (2005)
**Education expenditures:** 8.7% of GDP (2007)

## Government

**Country name:**
*conventional long form:* Republic of Botswana
*conventional short form:* Botswana
*local long form:* Republic of Botswana
*local short form:* Botswana
*former:* Bechuanaland
**Government type:** parliamentary republic
**Capital:**
*name:* Gaborone
*geographic coordinates:* 24 45 S, 25 55 E
*time difference:* UTC+2 (7 hours ahead of Washington, DC during Standard Time)
**Administrative divisions:** 9 districts and 5 town councils*; Central, Francistown*, Gaborone*, Ghanzi, Jwaneng*, Kgalagadi, Kgatleng, Kweneng, Lobatse*, Northeast, Northwest, Selebi-Pikwe*, Southeast, Southern

# Botswana (continued)

**Independence:** 30 September 1966 (from the UK)
**National holiday:** Independence Day (Botswana Day), 30 September (1966)
**Constitution:** March 1965; effective 30 September 1966
**Legal system:** based on Roman-Dutch law and local customary law; judicial review limited to matters of interpretation; accepts compulsory ICJ jurisdiction with reservations
**Suffrage:** 18 years of age; universal
**Executive branch:**
*chief of state:* President Seretse Khama Ian KHAMA (since 1 April 2008); Vice President Mompati MERAFHE (since 1 April 2008); note - the president is both the chief of state and head of government
*head of government:* President Seretse Khama Ian KHAMA (since 1 April 2008); Vice President Mompati MERAFHE (since 1 April 2008)
*cabinet:* Cabinet appointed by the president
*elections:* president indirectly elected for a five-year term (eligible for a second term); election last held 20 October 2004 (next to be held in October 2009); vice president appointed by the president
*election results:* Festus G. MOGAE elected president; percent of National Assembly vote - 52%: note - MOGAE stepped down on 1 April 2008 and designated KHAMA to serve out the remainder of his term
**Legislative branch:** bicameral Parliament consists of the House of Chiefs (a largely advisory 15-member body with 8 ex-officio members consisting of the chiefs of the principal tribes, and 7 non-permanent members serving 5-year terms, consisting of 4 elected subchiefs and 3 members selected by the other 12 members) and the National Assembly (63 seats, 57 members are directly elected by popular vote, 4 are appointed by the majority party, and 2, the President and Attorney-General, serve as ex-officio members; members serve five-year terms)
*elections:* National Assembly elections last held 30 October 2004 (next to be held in October 2009)
*election results:* percent of vote by party - BDP 51.7%, BNF 26.1%, BCP 16.6%, other 5%; seats by party - BDP 44, BNF 12, BCP 1
**Judicial branch:** High Court; Court of Appeal; Magistrates' Courts (one in each district)
**Political parties and leaders:** Botswana Alliance Movement or BAM [Ephraim Lepetu SETSHWAELO]; Botswana Congress Party or BCP [Gilson SALESHANDO]; Botswana Democratic Party or BDP [Ian KHAMA]; Botswana National Front or BNF [Otswoletse MOUPO]; Botswana Peoples Party or BPP [Bernard BALIKANI]; MELS Movement of Botswana or MELS [Themba JOINA]; New Democratic Front or NDF [Dick BAYFORD]
*note:* a number of minor parties joined forces in 1999 to form the BAM but did not capture any parliamentary seats - includes the United Action Party [Ephraim Lepetu SETSHWAELO]; the Independence Freedom Party or IFP [Motsamai MPHO]; the Botswana Progressive Union [D. K. KWELE]

**Political pressure groups and leaders:** First People of the Kalahari (Bushman organization); Pitso Ya Ba Tswana; Society for the Promotion of Ikalanga Language (Kalanga elites)
*other:* diamond mining companies
**International organization participation:** ACP, AfDB, AU, C, FAO, G-77, IAEA, IBRD, ICAO, ICCt, ICRM, IDA, IFAD, IFC, IFRCS, ILO, IMF, Interpol, IOC, IPU, ISO, ITSO, ITU, ITUC, MIGA, NAM, OPCW, SACU, SADC, UN, UNCTAD, UNESCO, UNIDO, UNMIS, UNWTO, UPU, WCO, WFTU, WHO, WIPO, WMO, WTO
**Diplomatic representation in the US:**
*chief of mission:* Ambassador Lapologang Caesar LEKOA
*chancery:* 1531-1533 New Hampshire Avenue NW, Washington, DC 20036
*telephone:* [1] (202) 244-4990
*FAX:* [1] (202) 244-4164
**Diplomatic representation from the US:**
*chief of mission:* Ambassador Stephen J. NOLAN
*embassy:* Embassy Enclave (off Khama Crescent), Gaborone
*mailing address:* Embassy Enclave, P. O. Box 90, Gaborone
*telephone:* [267] 395-3982
*FAX:* [267] 395-6947
**Flag description:** light blue with a horizontal white-edged black stripe in the center

## Economy

**Economy - overview:** Botswana has maintained one of the world's highest economic growth rates since independence in 1966, though growth fell below 5% in 2007-08. Through fiscal discipline and sound management, Botswana has transformed itself from one of the poorest countries in the world to a middle-income country with a per capita GDP of $13,300 in 2008. Two major investment services rank Botswana as the best credit risk in Africa. Diamond mining has fueled much of the expansion and currently accounts for more than one-third of GDP and for 70-80% of export earnings. Tourism, financial services, subsistence farming, and cattle raising are other key sectors. On the downside, the government must deal with high rates of unemployment and poverty. Unemployment officially was 23.8% in 2004, but unofficial estimates place it closer to 40%. HIV/AIDS infection rates are the second highest in the world and threaten Botswana's impressive economic gains. An expected leveling off in diamond mining production overshadows long-term prospects.
**GDP (purchasing power parity):**
$26.04 billion (2008 est.)
$25.24 billion (2007)
$24.43 billion (2006)
*note:* data are in 2008 US dollars
**GDP (official exchange rate):** $13.81 billion (2008 est.)
**GDP - real growth rate:**
3.2% (2008 est.)
3.3% (2007 est.)
5.3% (2006 est.)

**GDP - per capita (PPP):**
$13,300 (2008 est.)
$13,200 (2007 est.)
$13,000 (2006 est.)
*note:* data are in 2008 US dollars
**GDP - composition by sector:**
*agriculture:* 1.6%
*industry:* 52.6% (including 36% mining)
*services:* 45.8% (2008 est.)
**Labor force:** 288,400 formal sector employees (2004)
**Labor force - by occupation:**
*agriculture:* NA%
*industry:* NA%
*services:* NA%
**Unemployment rate:**
7.5% (2007 est.)
**Population below poverty line:** 30.3% (2003)
**Household income or consumption by percentage share:**
*lowest 10%:* NA%
*highest 10%:* NA%
**Distribution of family income - Gini index:** 63 (1993)
**Investment (gross fixed):** 23.9% of GDP (2008 est.)
**Budget:**
*revenues:* $4.556 billion
*expenditures:* $4.127 billion (2008 est.)
**Public debt:** 5.1% of GDP (2008 est.)
**Inflation rate (consumer prices):**
12.5% (2008 est.)
7.1% (2007 est.)
**Central bank discount rate:** 14.5% (31 December 2007)
**Commercial bank prime lending rate:** 16.22% (31 December 2007)
**Stock of money:** $1.026 billion (31 December 2007)
**Stock of quasi money:** $4.336 billion (31 December 2007)
**Stock of domestic credit:** NA
**Market value of publicly traded shares:** $5.887 billion (31 December 2007)
**Agriculture - products:** livestock, sorghum, maize, millet, beans, sunflowers, groundnuts
**Industries:** diamonds, copper, nickel, salt, soda ash, potash; livestock processing; textiles
**Industrial production growth rate:** 2.4% (2008 est.)
**Electricity - production:** 979 million kWh (2006 est.)
**Electricity - consumption:** 2.574 billion kWh (2006 est.)
**Electricity - exports:** 0 kWh (2007 est.)
**Electricity - imports:** 1.959 billion kWh (2007 est.)
**Oil - production:** 0 bbl/day (2007 est.)
**Oil - consumption:** 11,640 bbl/day (2006 est.)
**Oil - exports:** 0 bbl/day (2005)
**Oil - imports:** 14,500 bbl/day (2005)
**Oil - proved reserves:** 0 bbl (1 January 2006 est.)
**Natural gas - production:** 0 cu m (2007 est.)

## Botswana *(continued)*

**Natural gas - consumption:** 0 cu m (2007 est.)
**Natural gas - exports:** 0 cu m (2007 est.)
**Natural gas - imports:** 0 cu m (2007 est.)
**Natural gas - proved reserves:** 0 cu m (1 January 2006 est.)
**Current account balance:** $1.611 billion (2008 est.)
**Exports:** $5.127 billion f.o.b. (2008 est.)
**Exports - commodities:** diamonds, copper, nickel, soda ash, meat, textiles
**Imports:** $3.931 billion f.o.b. (2008 est.)
**Imports - commodities:** foodstuffs, machinery, electrical goods, transport equipment, textiles, fuel and petroleum products, wood and paper products, metal and metal products
**Reserves of foreign exchange and gold:** $10.28 billion (31 December 2008 est.)
**Debt - external:** $395 million (31 December 2008 est.)
**Exchange rates:** pulas (BWP) per US dollar - 6.7907 (2008 est.), 6.2035 (2007), 5.8447 (2006), 5.1104 (2005), 4.6929 (2004)

### Communications

**Telephones - main lines in use:** 136,900 (2006)
**Telephones - mobile cellular:** 1.427 million (2007)
**Telephone system:**
*general assessment:* the system is expanding with the growth of mobile-cellular service and participation in regional development; system is fully digital with fiber-optic cables linking the major population centers in the east; fixed-line connections declined in recent years and now stand at roughly 8 per 100 persons; mobile-cellular telephone density currently is about 80 per 100 persons
*domestic:* small system of open-wire lines, microwave radio relay links, and a few radiotelephone communication stations; mobile-cellular service is growing fast
*international:* country code - 267; international calls are made via satellite, using international direct dialing; 2 international exchanges; digital microwave radio relay links to Namibia, Zambia, Zimbabwe, and South Africa; satellite earth station - 1 Intelsat (Indian Ocean) (2007)
**Radio broadcast stations:** AM 8, FM 13, shortwave 4 (2001)
**Television broadcast stations:** 2 (1 state-owned, 1 private)
**Internet country code:** .bw
**Internet hosts:** 6,374 (2008)
**Internet users:** 80,000 (2007)

### Transportation

**Airports:** 77 (2008)
**Airports - with paved runways:**
*total:* 10
*2,438 to 3,047 m:* 2
*1,524 to 2,437 m:* 7
*914 to 1,523 m:* 1 (2008)

**Airports - with unpaved runways:**
*total:* 67
*1,524 to 2,437 m:* 3
*914 to 1,523 m:* 54
*under 914 m:* 10 (2008)
**Railways:**
*total:* 888 km
*narrow gauge:* 888 km 1.067-m gauge (2006)
**Roadways:**
*total:* 25,798 km
*paved:* 8,410 km
*unpaved:* 17,388 km (2005)

### Military

**Military branches:** Botswana Defense Force: Ground Forces (includes Air Arm) (2009)
**Military service age and obligation:** 18 is the apparent age of voluntary military service; the official qualifications for determining minimum age are unknown (2001)
**Manpower available for military service:**
*males age 16-49:* 487,853
*females age 16-49:* 464,278 (2008 est.)
**Manpower fit for military service:**
*males age 16-49:* 341,190
*females age 16-49:* 315,588 (2009 est.)
**Manpower reaching militarily significant age annually:**
*male:* 23,420
*female:* 22,904 (2009 est.)
**Military expenditures:** 3.3% of GDP (2006)

### Transnational Issues

**Disputes - international:** Botswana still struggles to seal its border from thousands of Zimbabweans who flee economic collapse and political persecution; Namibia has long supported, and in 2004 Zimbabwe dropped objections to, plans between Botswana and Zambia to build a bridge over the Zambezi River at Kazungula crossing, thereby de facto recognizing the short, but not clearly delimited, Botswana-Zambia boundary

# Bouvet Island
*(territory of Norway)*

### Introduction

**Background:** This uninhabited volcanic island is almost entirely covered by glaciers and is difficult to approach. It was discovered in 1739 by a French naval officer after whom the island was named. No claim was made until 1825, when the British flag was raised. In 1928, the UK waived its claim in favor of Norway, which had occupied the island the previous year. In 1971, Norway designated Bouvet Island and the adjacent territorial waters a nature reserve. Since 1977, it has run an automated meteorological station on the island.

### Geography

**Location:** island in the South Atlantic Ocean, southwest of the Cape of Good Hope (South Africa)
**Geographic coordinates:** 54 26 S, 3 24 E
**Map references:** Antarctic Region
**Area:**
*total:* 49 sq km
*land:* 49 sq km
*water:* 0 sq km
**Area - comparative:** about 0.3 times the size of Washington, DC
**Land boundaries:** 0 km
**Coastline:** 29.6 km
**Maritime claims:**
*territorial sea:* 4 nm
**Climate:** antarctic
**Terrain:** volcanic; coast is mostly inaccessible
**Elevation extremes:**
*lowest point:* South Atlantic Ocean 0 m
*highest point:* Olav Peak 935 m
**Natural resources:** none
**Land use:**
*arable land:* 0%
*permanent crops:* 0%
*other:* 100% (93% ice) (2005)
**Irrigated land:** 0 sq km
**Natural hazards:** NA

# Bouvet Island (continued)

**Environment - current issues:** NA
**Geography - note:** covered by glacial ice; declared a nature reserve by Norway

## People

**Population:** uninhabited

## Government

**Country name:**
*conventional long form:* none
*conventional short form:* Bouvet Island
**Dependency status:** territory of Norway; administered by the Polar Department of the Ministry of Justice and Oslo Police
**Legal system:** the laws of Norway, where applicable, apply
**Flag description:** the flag of Norway is used

## Economy

**Economy - overview:** no economic activity; declared a nature reserve

## Communications

**Internet country code:** .bv
**Internet hosts:** 6 (2008)
**Communications - note:** automatic meteorological station

## Transportation

**Ports and terminals:** none; offshore anchorage only

## Military

**Military - note:** defense is the responsibility of Norway

## Transnational Issues

**Disputes - international:** none

# Brazil

## Introduction

**Background:** Following more than three centuries under Portuguese rule, Brazil peacefully gained its independence in 1822, maintaining a monarchical system of government until the abolition of slavery in 1888 and the subsequent proclamation of a republic by the military in 1889. Brazilian coffee exporters politically dominated the country until populist leader Getulio VARGAS rose to power in 1930. By far the largest and most populous country in South America, Brazil underwent more than half a century of populist and military government until 1985, when the military regime peacefully ceded power to civilian rulers. Brazil continues to pursue industrial and agricultural growth and development of its interior. Exploiting vast natural resources and a large labor pool, it is today South America's leading economic power and a regional leader. Highly unequal income distribution and crime remain pressing problems.

## Geography

**Location:** Eastern South America, bordering the Atlantic Ocean
**Geographic coordinates:** 10 00 S, 55 00 W
**Map references:** South America
**Area:**
*total:* 8,511,965 sq km
*land:* 8,456,510 sq km
*water:* 55,455 sq km
*note:* includes Arquipelago de Fernando de Noronha, Atol das Rocas, Ilha da Trindade, Ilhas Martin Vaz, and Penedos de Sao Pedro e Sao Paulo
**Area - comparative:** slightly smaller than the US
**Land boundaries:**
*total:* 16,885 km
*border countries:* Argentina 1,261 km, Bolivia 3,423 km, Colombia 1,644 km, French Guiana 730 km, Guyana 1,606 km, Paraguay 1,365 km, Peru 2,995 km, Suriname 593 km, Uruguay 1,068 km, Venezuela 2,200 km

**Coastline:** 7,491 km
**Maritime claims:**
*territorial sea:* 12 nm
*contiguous zone:* 24 nm
*exclusive economic zone:* 200 nm
*continental shelf:* 200 nm or to edge of the continental margin
**Climate:** mostly tropical, but temperate in south
**Terrain:** mostly flat to rolling lowlands in north; some plains, hills, mountains, and narrow coastal belt
**Elevation extremes:**
*lowest point:* Atlantic Ocean 0 m
*highest point:* Pico da Neblina 3,014 m
**Natural resources:** bauxite, gold, iron ore, manganese, nickel, phosphates, platinum, tin, uranium, petroleum, hydropower, timber
**Land use:**
*arable land:* 6.93%
*permanent crops:* 0.89%
*other:* 92.18% (2005)
**Irrigated land:** 29,200 sq km (2003)
**Total renewable water resources:** 8,233 cu km (2000)
**Freshwater withdrawal (domestic/industrial/agricultural):**
*total:* 59.3 cu km/yr (20%/18%/62%)
*per capita:* 318 cu m/yr (2000)
**Natural hazards:** recurring droughts in northeast; floods and occasional frost in south
**Environment - current issues:** deforestation in Amazon Basin destroys the habitat and endangers a multitude of plant and animal species indigenous to the area; there is a lucrative illegal wildlife trade; air and water pollution in Rio de Janeiro, Sao Paulo, and several other large cities; land degradation and water pollution caused by improper mining activities; wetland degradation; severe oil spills
**Environment - international agreements:**
*party to:* Antarctic-Environmental Protocol, Antarctic-Marine Living Resources, Antarctic Seals, Antarctic Treaty, Biodiversity, Climate Change, Climate Change-Kyoto Protocol, Desertification, Endangered Species, Environmental Modification, Hazardous Wastes, Law of the Sea, Marine Dumping, Ozone Layer Protection, Ship Pollution, Tropical Timber 83, Tropical Timber 94, Wetlands, Whaling
*signed, but not ratified:* none of the selected agreements
**Geography - note:** largest country in South America; shares common boundaries with every South American country except Chile and Ecuador

## People

**Population:** 198,739,269
*note:* Brazil conducted a census in August 2000, which reported a population of 169,872,855; that figure was about 3.8% lower than projections by the US Census Bureau, and is close to the implied underenumeration of 4.6% for the 1991 census (July 2009 est.)

# Brazil (continued)

**Age structure:**
*0-14 years:* 26.7% (male 27,092,880/female 26,062,244)
*15-64 years:* 66.8% (male 65,804,108/female 67,047,725)
*65 years and over:* 6.4% (male 5,374,230/female 7,358,082) (2009 est.)

**Median age:**
*total:* 28.6 years
*male:* 27.8 years
*female:* 29.3 years (2009 est.)

**Population growth rate:** 1.199% (2009 est.)
**Birth rate:** 18.43 births/1,000 population (2009 est.)
**Death rate:** 6.35 deaths/1,000 population (2008 est.)
**Net migration rate:** -0.09 migrant(s)/1,000 population (2009 est.)

**Urbanization:**
*urban population:* 86% of total population (2008)
*rate of urbanization:* 1.8% annual rate of change (2005-10 est.)

**Sex ratio:**
*at birth:* 1.05 male(s)/female
*under 15 years:* 1.04 male(s)/female
*15-64 years:* 0.98 male(s)/female
*65 years and over:* 0.73 male(s)/female
*total population:* 0.98 male(s)/female (2009 est.)

**Infant mortality rate:**
*total:* 22.58 deaths/1,000 live births
*male:* 26.16 deaths/1,000 live births
*female:* 18.83 deaths/1,000 live births (2009 est.)

**Life expectancy at birth:**
*total population:* 71.99 years
*male:* 68.43 years
*female:* 75.73 years (2009 est.)

**Total fertility rate:** 2.21 children born/woman (2009 est.)

**HIV/AIDS - adult prevalence rate:** 0.6% (2007 est.)
**HIV/AIDS - people living with HIV/AIDS:** 730,000 (2007 est.)
**HIV/AIDS - deaths:** 15,000 (2007 est.)

**Nationality:**
*noun:* Brazilian(s)
*adjective:* Brazilian

**Ethnic groups:** white 53.7%, mulatto (mixed white and black) 38.5%, black 6.2%, other (includes Japanese, Arab, Amerindian) 0.9%, unspecified 0.7% (2000 census)

**Religions:** Roman Catholic (nominal) 73.6%, Protestant 15.4%, Spiritualist 1.3%, Bantu/voodoo 0.3%, other 1.8%, unspecified 0.2%, none 7.4% (2000 census)

**Languages:** Portuguese (official and most widely spoken language); note - less common languages include Spanish (border areas and schools), German, Italian, Japanese, English, and a large number of minor Amerindian languages

**Literacy:**
*definition:* age 15 and over can read and write
*total population:* 88.6%
*male:* 88.4%
*female:* 88.8% (2004 est.)

**School life expectancy (primary to tertiary education):**
*total:* 14 years
*male:* 14 years
*female:* 15 years (2005)

**Education expenditures:** 4% of GDP (2004)

## Government

**Country name:**
*conventional long form:* Federative Republic of Brazil
*conventional short form:* Brazil
*local long form:* Republica Federativa do Brasil
*local short form:* Brasil

**Government type:** federal republic

**Capital:**
*name:* Brasilia
*geographic coordinates:* 15 47 S, 47 55 W
*time difference:* UTC-3 (2 hours ahead of Washington, DC during Standard Time)
*daylight saving time:* +1hr, begins third Sunday in October; ends third Sunday in February
*note:* Brazil is divided into four time zones, including one for the Fernando de Noronha Islands

**Administrative divisions:** 26 states (estados, singular - estado) and 1 federal district* (distrito federal); Acre, Alagoas, Amapa, Amazonas, Bahia, Ceara, Distrito Federal*, Espirito Santo, Goias, Maranhao, Mato Grosso, Mato Grosso do Sul, Minas Gerais, Para, Paraiba, Parana, Pernambuco, Piaui, Rio de Janeiro, Rio Grande do Norte, Rio Grande do Sul, Rondonia, Roraima, Santa Catarina, Sao Paulo, Sergipe, Tocantins

**Independence:** 7 September 1822 (from Portugal)
**National holiday:** Independence Day, 7 September (1822)
**Constitution:** 5 October 1988
**Legal system:** based on Roman codes; has not accepted compulsory ICJ jurisdiction
**Suffrage:** voluntary between 16 and 18 years of age and over 70; compulsory over 18 and under 70 years of age; note - military conscripts do not vote

**Executive branch:**
*chief of state:* President Luiz Inacio LULA DA SILVA (since 1 January 2003); Vice President Jose ALENCAR (since 1 January 2003); note - the president is both the chief of state and head of government
*head of government:* President Luiz Inacio LULA DA SILVA (since 1 January 2003); Vice President Jose ALENCAR (since 1 January 2003)
*cabinet:* Cabinet appointed by the president
*elections:* president and vice president elected on the same ticket by popular vote for a single four-year term; election last held 1 October 2006 with runoff 29 October 2006 (next to be held 3 October 2010 and, if necessary, 31 October 2010)
*election results:* Luiz Inacio LULA DA SILVA (PT) reelected president - 60.83%, Geraldo ALCKMIN (PSDB) 39.17%

**Legislative branch:** bicameral National Congress or Congresso Nacional consists of the Federal Senate or Senado Federal (81 seats; 3 members from each state and federal district elected according to the principle of majority to serve eight-year terms; one-third and two-thirds elected every four years, alternately) and the Chamber of Deputies or Camara dos Deputados (513 seats; members are elected by proportional representation to serve four-year terms)
*elections:* Federal Senate - last held 1 October 2006 for one-third of the Senate (next to be held in October 2010 for two-thirds of the Senate); Chamber of Deputies - last held 1 October 2006 (next to be held in October 2010)
*election results:* Federal Senate - percent of vote by party - NA; seats by party - PFL 6, PSDB 5, PMDB 4, PTB 3, PT 2, PDT 1, PSB 1, PL 1, PPS 1, PRTB 1, PP 1, PCdoB 1; Chamber of Deputies - percent of vote by party - NA; seats by party - PMDB 89, PT 83, PFL 65, PSDB 65, PP 42, PSB 27, PDT 24, PL 23, PTB 22, PPS 21, PCdoB 13, PV 13, PSC 9, other 17; note - as of 1 January 2009, the composition of the entire legislature is as follows: Federal Senate - seats by party - PMDB 21, DEM (formerly PFL) 12, PSDB 13, PT 12, PTB 7, PDT 5, PR 4, PSB 2, PCdoB 1, PRB 1, PP 1, PSC 1, PSOL 1; Chamber of Deputies - seats by party - PMDB 95, PT 79, PSDB 59, DEM (formerly PFL) 53, PR 44, PP 40, PSB 29, PDT 25, PTB 19, PPS 14, PV 14, PCdoB 13, PSC 11, PMN 5, PRB 4, PHS 3, PSOL 3, PTC 1, PTdoB 1

**Judicial branch:** Supreme Federal Tribunal or STF (11 ministers are appointed for life by the president and confirmed by the Senate); Higher Tribunal of Justice; Regional Federal Tribunals (judges are appointed for life); note - though appointed "for life," judges, like all federal employees, have a mandatory retirement age of 70

**Political parties and leaders:** Brazilian Democratic Movement Party or PMDB [Federal Deputy Michel TEMER]; Brazilian Labor Party or PTB [Roberto JEFFERSON]; Brazilian Renewal Labor Party or PRTB [Jose Levy FIDELIX da Cruz]; Brazilian Republican Party or PRB [Vitor Paulo Araujo DOS SANTOS]; Brazilian Social Democracy Party or PSDB [Senator Sergio GUERRA]; Brazilian Socialist Party or PSB [Governor Eduardo Henrique Accioly CAMPOS]; Christian Labor Party or PTC [Daniel TOURINHO]; Communist Party of Brazil or PCdoB [Jose Renato RABELO]; Democratic Labor Party or PDT [Carlos Roberto LUPI]; the Democrats or DEM (formerly Liberal Front Party or PFL) [Federal Deputy Rodrigo MAIA]; Freedom and Socialism Party or PSOL [Heloisa HELENA]; Green Party or PV [Jose Luiz de Franca PENNA]; Humanist Party of Solidarity or PHS [Paulo Roberto MATOS]; Labor Party of Brazil or PTdoB [Luis Henrique de Oliveira RESENDE]; Liberal Front Party or PFL (now known as the Democrats or DEM); National Mobilization Party or PMN [Oscar Noronha FILHO]; Party of the Republic or PR [Sergio TAMER]; Popular Socialist Party or PPS [Federal Deputy Fernando CORUJA]; Progressive Party or PP [Francisco DORNELLES]; Social Christian Party or PSC [Vitor Jorge Abdala NOSSEIS]; Workers' Party or PT [Ricardo Jose Ribeiro BERZOINI]

# Brazil (continued)

**Political pressure groups and leaders:** Landless Workers' Movement or MST
*other:* labor unions and federations; large farmers' associations; religious groups including evangelical Christian churches and the Catholic Church
**International organization participation:** AfDB (nonregional member), BIS, CAN (associate), CPLP, FAO, G-15, G-20, G-24, G-77, IADB, IAEA, IBRD, ICAO, ICC, ICCt, ICRM, IDA, IFAD, IFC, IFRCS, IHO, ILO, IMF, IMO, IMSO, Interpol, IOC, IOM, IPU, ISO, ITSO, ITU, ITUC, LAES, LAIA, Mercosur, MIGA, MINURCAT, MINURSO, MINUSTAH, NAM (observer), NSG, OAS, OPANAL, OPCW, PCA, RG, SICA (observer), UN, UNASUR, UNCTAD, UNESCO, UNFICYP, UNHCR, UNIDO, Union Latina, UNITAR, UNMIL, UNMIS, UNMIT, UNOCI, UNWTO, UPU, WCL, WCO, WFTU, WHO, WIPO, WMO, WTO
**Diplomatic representation in the US:**
*chief of mission:* Ambassador Antonio de Aguiar PATRIOTA
*chancery:* 3006 Massachusetts Avenue NW, Washington, DC 20008
*telephone:* [1] (202) 238-2700
*FAX:* [1] (202) 238-2827
*consulate(s) general:* Boston, Chicago, Houston, Los Angeles, Miami, New York, San Francisco
**Diplomatic representation from the US:**
*chief of mission:* Ambassador Clifford M. SOBEL
*embassy:* Avenida das Nacoes, Quadra 801, Lote 3, Distrito Federal Cep 70403-900, Brasilia
*mailing address:* Unit 3500, APO AA 34030
*telephone:* [55] (61) 3312-7000
*FAX:* [55] (61) 3225-9136
*consulate(s) general:* Rio de Janeiro, Sao Paulo
*consulate(s):* Recife
**Flag description:** green with a large yellow diamond in the center bearing a blue celestial globe with 27 white five-pointed stars (one for each state and the Federal District) arranged in the same pattern as the night sky over Brazil; the globe has a white equatorial band with the motto ORDEM E PROGRESSO (Order and Progress)

## Economy

**Economy - overview:** Characterized by large and well-developed agricultural, mining, manufacturing, and service sectors, Brazil's economy outweighs that of all other South American countries and Brazil is expanding its presence in world markets. From 2003 to 2007, Brazil ran record trade surpluses and recorded its first current account surpluses since 1992. Productivity gains coupled with high commodity prices contributed to the surge in exports. Brazil improved its debt profile in 2006 by shifting its debt burden toward real denominated and domestically held instruments. LULA DA SILVA restated his commitment to fiscal responsibility by maintaining the country's primary surplus during the 2006 election. Following his second inauguration in October of that year, LULA DA SILVA announced a package of further economic reforms to reduce taxes and increase investment in infrastructure. Brazil's debt achieved investment grade status early in 2008, but the government's attempt to achieve strong growth while reducing the debt burden created inflationary pressures. For most of 2008, the Central Bank embarked on a restrictive monetary policy to stem these pressures. Since the onset of the global financial crisis in September, Brazil's currency and its stock market - Bovespa - have significantly lost value, -41% for Bovespa for the year ending 30 December 2008. Brazil incurred another current account deficit in 2008, as world demand and prices for commodities dropped in the second-half of the year.
**GDP (purchasing power parity):**
$1.99 trillion (2008 est.)
$1.892 trillion (2007)
$1.795 trillion (2006)
*note:* data are in 2008 US dollars
**GDP (official exchange rate):** $1.665 trillion (2008 est.)
**GDP - real growth rate:**
5.2% (2008 est.)
5.4% (2007 est.)
4% (2006 est.)
**GDP - per capita (PPP):**
$10,100 (2008 est.)
$9,800 (2007 est.)
$9,400 (2006 est.)
*note:* data are in 2008 US dollars
**GDP - composition by sector:**
*agriculture:* 5.5%
*industry:* 28.5%
*services:* 66% (2008 est.)
**Labor force:** 100.9 million (2008 est.)
**Labor force - by occupation:**
*agriculture:* 20%
*industry:* 14%
*services:* 66% (2003 est.)
**Unemployment rate:**
8% (2008 est.)
9.3% (2007 est.)
**Population below poverty line:** 31% (2005)
**Household income or consumption by percentage share:**
*lowest 10%:* 0.9%
*highest 10%:* 44.8% (2004)
**Distribution of family income - Gini index:** 56.7 (2005)
**Investment (gross fixed):** 18.6% of GDP (2008 est.)
**Budget:**
*revenues:* NA
*expenditures:* NA
**Public debt:** 40.7% of GDP (2008 est.)
**Inflation rate (consumer prices):**
5.8% (2008 est.)
3.6% (2007 est.)
**Central bank discount rate:** 17.85% (31 December 2007)
**Commercial bank prime lending rate:** 43.72% (31 December 2007)

**Stock of money:** $131.1 billion (31 December 2007)
**Stock of quasi money:** $792.8 billion (31 December 2007)
**Stock of domestic credit:** $1.377 trillion (31 December 2007)
**Market value of publicly traded shares:** $1.37 trillion (31 December 2007)
**Agriculture - products:** coffee, soybeans, wheat, rice, corn, sugarcane, cocoa, citrus; beef
**Industries:** textiles, shoes, chemicals, cement, lumber, iron ore, tin, steel, aircraft, motor vehicles and parts, other machinery and equipment
**Industrial production growth rate:** 4.4% (2008 est.)
**Electricity - production:** 437.3 billion kWh (2007 est.)
**Electricity - consumption:** 402.2 billion kWh (2007 est.)
**Electricity - exports:** 2.034 billion kWh (2007 est.)
**Electricity - imports:** 40.47 billion kWh; note - supplied by Paraguay (2007 est.)
**Oil - production:** 2.277 million bbl/day (2007 est.)
**Oil - consumption:** 2.372 million bbl/day (2007 est.)
**Oil - exports:** 481,100 bbl/day (2005)
**Oil - imports:** 648,800 bbl/day (2005)
**Oil - proved reserves:** 12.18 billion bbl (1 January 2008 est.)
**Natural gas - production:** 9.8 billion cu m (2007 est.)
**Natural gas - consumption:** 19.8 billion cu m (2007 est.)
**Natural gas - exports:** 0 cu m (2007 est.)
**Natural gas - imports:** 10 billion cu m (2007 est.)
**Natural gas - proved reserves:** 347.7 billion cu m (1 January 2008 est.)
**Current account balance:** -$27.33 billion (2008 est.)
**Exports:** $200 billion f.o.b. (2008 est.)
**Exports - commodities:** transport equipment, iron ore, soybeans, footwear, coffee, autos
**Exports - partners:** US 16.1%, Argentina 9.2%, China 6.8%, Netherlands 5.6%, Germany 4.6% (2007)
**Imports:** $176 billion f.o.b. (2008 est.)
**Imports - commodities:** machinery, electrical and transport equipment, chemical products, oil, automotive parts, electronics
**Imports - partners:** US 15.7%, China 10.5%, Argentina 8.6%, Germany 7.2%, Nigeria 4.4% (2007)
**Reserves of foreign exchange and gold:** $197.4 billion (31 December 2008 est.)
**Debt - external:** $236.6 billion (31 December 2008 est.)
**Stock of direct foreign investment - at home:** $280.9 billion (2008 est.)
**Stock of direct foreign investment - abroad:** $119.1 billion (2008 est.)
**Exchange rates:** reals (BRL) per US dollar - 1.8644 (2008 est.), 1.85 (2007 est.), 2.1761 (2006), 2.4344 (2005), 2.9251 (2004)

# Brazil (continued)

## Communications

**Telephones - main lines in use:** 39.4 million (2007)
**Telephones - mobile cellular:** 120.98 million (2007)
**Telephone system:**

*general assessment:* good working system; fixed-line connections have remained relatively stable in recent years and stand at about 20 per 100 persons; less expensive mobile cellular technology is a major driver in expanding telephone service to the low-income segment of the population with mobile-cellular telephone density reaching nearly 65 per 100 persons
*domestic:* extensive microwave radio relay system and a domestic satellite system with 64 earth stations; mobile-cellular usage has more than tripled in the past 5 years
*international:* country code - 55; landing point for a number of submarine cables, including Atlantis 2, that provide direct links to South and Central America, the Caribbean, the US, Africa, and Europe; satellite earth stations - 3 Intelsat (Atlantic Ocean), 1 Inmarsat (Atlantic Ocean region east), connected by microwave relay system to Mercosur Brazilsat B3 satellite earth station (2007)

**Radio broadcast stations:** AM 1,365, FM 296, shortwave 161 (of which 91 are collocated with AM stations) (1999)
**Television broadcast stations:** 138 (1997)
**Internet country code:** .br
**Internet hosts:** 9.573 million (2008)
**Internet users:** 50 million (2007)

## Transportation

**Airports:** 4,176 (2008)
**Airports - with paved runways:**
*total:* 734
*over 3,047 m:* 7
*2,438 to 3,047 m:* 26
*1,524 to 2,437 m:* 169
*914 to 1,523 m:* 476
*under 914 m:* 56 (2008)
**Airports - with unpaved runways:**
*total:* 3,442
*1,524 to 2,437 m:* 85
*914 to 1,523 m:* 1,541
*under 914 m:* 1,816 (2008)
**Heliports:** 16 (2007)
**Pipelines:** condensate/gas 62 km; gas 9,892 km; liquid petroleum gas 353 km; oil 4,517 km; refined products 4,465 km (2008)
**Railways:**
*total:* 29,295 km
*broad gauge:* 4,932 km 1.600-m gauge (939 km electrified)
*standard gauge:* 194 km 1.440-m gauge
*narrow gauge:* 23,773 km 1.000-m gauge (581 km electrified)
*dual gauge:* 396 km 1.000 m and 1.600-m gauges (three rails) (78 km electrified) (2006)

**Roadways:**
*total:* 1,751,868 km
*paved:* 96,353 km
*unpaved:* 1,655,515 km (2004)
**Waterways:** 50,000 km (most in areas remote from industry and population) (2008)
**Merchant marine:**
*total:* 136
*by type:* bulk carrier 19, cargo 22, carrier 1, chemical tanker 7, container 11, liquefied gas 12, passenger/cargo 12, petroleum tanker 45, roll on/roll off 7
*foreign-owned:* 25 (Chile 1, Denmark 2, Germany 6, Greece 1, Mexico 1, Norway 5, Spain 9)
*registered in other countries:* 8 (Argentina 1, Bahamas 2, Ghana 1, Liberia 3, Marshall Islands 1) (2008)
**Ports and terminals:** Guaiba, Ilha Grande, Paranagua, Rio Grande, Santos, Sao Sebastiao, Tubarao
**Transportation - note:** the International Maritime Bureau reports the territorial and offshore waters in the Atlantic Ocean as a significant risk for piracy and armed robbery against ships; numerous commercial vessels have been attacked and hijacked both at anchor and while underway; crews have been robbed and stores or cargoes stolen

## Military

**Military branches:** Brazilian Army (Exercito Brasileiro, EB), Brazilian Navy (Marinha do Brasil (MB), includes Naval Air and Marine Corps (Corpo de Fuzileiros Navais)), Brazilian Air Force (Forca Aerea Brasileira, FAB) (2009)
**Military service age and obligation:** 21-45 years of age for compulsory military service; conscript service obligation - 9 to 12 months; 17-45 years of age for voluntary service; an increasing percentage of the ranks are "long-service" volunteer professionals; women were allowed to serve in the armed forces beginning in early 1980s when the Brazilian Army became the first army in South America to accept women into career ranks; women serve in Navy and Air Force only in Women's Reserve Corps (2001)
**Manpower available for military service:**
*males age 16-49:* 52,449,957
*females age 16-49:* 52,375,921 (2008 est.)
**Manpower fit for military service:**
*males age 16-49:* 38,043,555
*females age 16-49:* 44,267,520 (2009 est.)
**Manpower reaching militarily significant age annually:**
*male:* 1,690,031
*female:* 1,630,851 (2009 est.)
**Military expenditures:** 2.6% of GDP (2006 est.)

## Transnational Issues

**Disputes - international:** unruly region at convergence of Argentina-Brazil-Paraguay borders is locus of money laundering, smuggling, arms and illegal narcotics trafficking, and fundraising for extremist organizations; uncontested boundary dispute with Uruguay over Isla Brasilera at the confluence of the Quarai/Cuareim and Invernada rivers, that form a tripoint with Argentina; the Itaipu Dam reservoir covers over a once contested section of Brazil-Paraguay boundary west of Guaira Falls on the Rio Parana; an accord placed the long-disputed Isla Suarez/Ilha de Guajara-Mirim, a fluvial island on the Rio Mamore, under Bolivian administration in 1958, but sovereignty remains in dispute
**Illicit drugs:** second-largest consumer of cocaine in the world; illicit producer of cannabis; trace amounts of coca cultivation in the Amazon region, used for domestic consumption; government has a large-scale eradication program to control cannabis; important transshipment country for Bolivian, Colombian, and Peruvian cocaine headed for Europe; also used by traffickers as a way station for narcotics air transshipments between Peru and Colombia; upsurge in drug-related violence and weapons smuggling; important market for Colombian, Bolivian, and Peruvian cocaine; illicit narcotics proceeds are often laundered through the financial system; significant illicit financial activity in the Tri-Border Area (2008)

# British Indian Ocean Territory
*(overseas territory of the UK)*

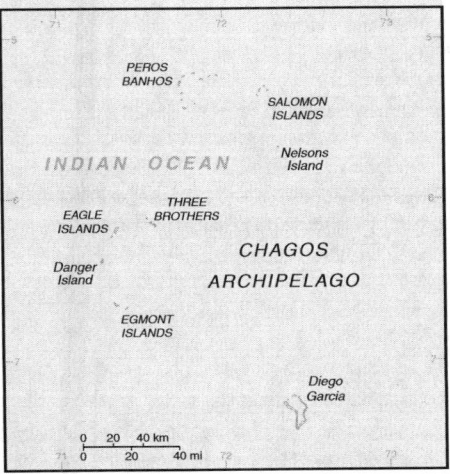

## Introduction

**Background:** Formerly administered as part of the British Crown Colony of Mauritius, the British Indian Ocean Territory (BIOT) was established as an overseas territory of the UK in 1965. A number of the islands of the territory were later transferred to the Seychelles when it attained independence in 1976. Subsequently, BIOT has consisted only of the six main island groups comprising the Chagos Archipelago. The largest and most southerly of the islands, Diego Garcia, contains a joint UK-US naval support facility. All of the remaining islands are uninhabited. Between 1967 and 1973, former agricultural workers, earlier residents in the islands, were relocated primarily to Mauritius, but also to the Seychelles. Negotiations between 1971 and 1982 resulted in the establishment of a trust fund by the British Government as compensation for the displaced islanders, known as Chagossians. Beginning in 1998, the islanders pursued a series of lawsuits against the British Government seeking further compensation and the right to return to the territory. In 2006 and 2007, British court rulings invalidated the immigration policies contained in the 2004 BIOT Constitution Order that had excluded the islanders from the archipelago, but upheld the special military status of Diego Garcia. In 2008, the House of Lords, as the final court of appeal in the UK, ruled in favor of the British Government by overturning the lower court rulings and finding no right of return on the part of the Chagossians.

## Geography

**Location:** archipelago in the Indian Ocean, south of India, about halfway between Africa and Indonesia
**Geographic coordinates:** 6 00 S, 71 30 E; note - Diego Garcia 7 20 S, 72 25 E
**Map references:** Political Map of the World

**Area:**
*total:* 54,400 sq km
*land:* 60 sq km; Diego Garcia 44 sq km
*water:* 54,340 sq km
*note:* includes the entire Chagos Archipelago of 55 islands
**Area - comparative:** land area is about 0.3 times the size of Washington, DC
**Land boundaries:** 0 km
**Coastline:** 698 km
**Maritime claims:**
*territorial sea:* 3 nm
*exclusive fishing zone:* 200 nm
**Climate:** tropical marine; hot, humid, moderated by trade winds
**Terrain:** flat and low (most areas do not exceed two meters in elevation)
**Elevation extremes:**
*lowest point:* Indian Ocean 0 m
*highest point:* unnamed location on Diego Garcia 15 m
**Natural resources:** coconuts, fish, sugarcane
**Land use:**
*arable land:* 0%
*permanent crops:* 0%
*other:* 100% (2005)
**Irrigated land:** 0 sq km
**Natural hazards:** NA
**Environment - current issues:** NA
**Geography - note:** archipelago of 55 islands; Diego Garcia, largest and southernmost island, occupies strategic location in central Indian Ocean; island is site of joint US-UK military facility

## People

**Population:** no indigenous inhabitants
*note:* approximately 1,200 former agricultural workers resident in the Chagos Archipelago, often referred to as Chagossians or Ilois, were relocated to Mauritius and the Seychelles in the 1960s and 1970s; in November 2004, approximately 4,000 UK and US military personnel and civilian contractors were living on the island of Diego Garcia

## Government

**Country name:**
*conventional long form:* British Indian Ocean Territory
*conventional short form:* none
*abbreviation:* BIOT
**Dependency status:** overseas territory of the UK; administered by a commissioner, resident in the Foreign and Commonwealth Office in London
**Legal system:** the laws of the UK, where applicable, apply
**Executive branch:**
*chief of state:* Queen ELIZABETH II (since 6 February 1952)
*head of government:* Commissioner Colin ROBERTS (since July 2008); Administrator Joanne YEADON (since December 2007); note - both reside in the UK and are represented by the officer commanding British Forces on Diego Garcia
*cabinet:* NA

*elections:* none; the monarch is hereditary; commissioner and administrator appointed by the monarch
**Diplomatic representation in the US:** none (overseas territory of the UK)
**Diplomatic representation from the US:** none (overseas territory of the UK)
**Flag description:** white with six blue wavy horizontal stripes; the flag of the UK is in the upper hoist-side quadrant; the striped section bears a palm tree and yellow crown centered on the outer half of the flag

## Economy

**Economy - overview:** All economic activity is concentrated on the largest island of Diego Garcia, where a joint UK-US military facility is located. Construction projects and various services needed to support the military installation are performed by military and contract employees from the UK, Mauritius, the Philippines, and the US. There are no industrial or agricultural activities on the islands. The territory earns foreign exchange by selling fishing licenses and postage stamps.
**Electricity - production:** NA kWh; note - electricity supplied by the US military
**Electricity - consumption:** NA kWh
**Exchange rates:** the US dollar is used

## Communications

**Telephones - main lines in use:** NA
**Telephone system:**
*general assessment:* separate facilities for military and public needs are available
*domestic:* all commercial telephone services are available, including connection to the Internet
*international:* country code (Diego Garcia) - 246; international telephone service is carried by satellite (2000)
**Radio broadcast stations:** AM 1, FM 2, shortwave 0 (1998)
**Television broadcast stations:** 1 (1997)
**Internet country code:** .io
**Internet hosts:** 89 (2008)

## Transportation

**Airports:** 1 (2008)
**Airports - with paved runways:**
*total:* 1
*over 3,047 m:* 1 (2008)
**Roadways:**
*note:* short section of paved road between port and airfield on Diego Garcia
**Ports and terminals:** Diego Garcia

## Military

**Military - note:** defense is the responsibility of the UK; the US lease on Diego Garcia expires in 2016

**Disputes - international:** Mauritius claims the Chagos Archipelago including Diego Garcia; in 2001, the former inhabitants of the Chagos Archipelago, evicted in 1967 and 1973 and now residing chiefly in Mauritius, were granted UK citizenship and the right to repatriation; in May 2007, the UK Court of Appeals upheld the May 2006 High Court of London judgment reversing the UK government's 2004 Orders of Council that banned habitation on the islands; a small group of Chagossians visited Diego Garcia in April 2006; repatriation is complicated by the exclusive US military lease of Diego Garcia that restricts access to the largest viable island in the chain

# British Virgin Islands
*(overseas territory of the UK)*

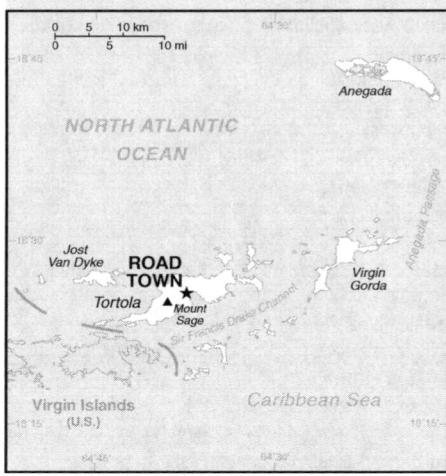

## Introduction

**Background:** First inhabited by Arawak and later by Carib Indians, the Virgin Islands were settled by the Dutch in 1648 and then annexed by the English in 1672. The islands were part of the British colony of the Leeward Islands from 1872-1960; they were granted autonomy in 1967. The economy is closely tied to the larger and more populous US Virgin Islands to the west; the US dollar is the legal currency.

## Geography

**Location:** Caribbean, between the Caribbean Sea and the North Atlantic Ocean, east of Puerto Rico
**Geographic coordinates:** 18 30 N, 64 30 W
**Map references:** Central America and the Caribbean
**Area:**
*total:* 153 sq km
*land:* 153 sq km
*water:* 0 sq km
*note:* comprised of 16 inhabited and more than 20 uninhabited islands; includes the islands of Tortola, Anegada, Virgin Gorda, Jost van Dyke
**Area - comparative:** about 0.9 times the size of Washington, DC
**Land boundaries:** 0 km
**Coastline:** 80 km
**Maritime claims:**
*territorial sea:* 3 nm
*exclusive fishing zone:* 200 nm
**Climate:** subtropical; humid; temperatures moderated by trade winds
**Terrain:** coral islands relatively flat; volcanic islands steep, hilly
**Elevation extremes:**
*lowest point:* Caribbean Sea 0 m
*highest point:* Mount Sage 521 m
**Natural resources:** NEGL

**Land use:**
*arable land:* 20%
*permanent crops:* 6.67%
*other:* 73.33% (2005)
**Irrigated land:** NA
**Natural hazards:** hurricanes and tropical storms (July to October)
**Environment - current issues:** limited natural fresh water resources (except for a few seasonal streams and springs on Tortola, most of the islands' water supply comes from wells and rainwater catchments)
**Geography - note:** strong ties to nearby US Virgin Islands and Puerto Rico

## People

**Population:** 24,491 (July 2009 est.)
**Age structure:**
*0-14 years:* 19.8% (male 2,454/female 2,387)
*15-64 years:* 74.4% (male 9,346/female 8,881)
*65 years and over:* 5.8% (male 734/female 689) (2009 est.)
**Median age:**
*total:* 32.3 years
*male:* 32.4 years
*female:* 32.2 years (2009 est.)
**Population growth rate:** 1.837% (2009 est.)
**Birth rate:** 14.62 births/1,000 population (2009 est.)
**Death rate:** 4.37 deaths/1,000 population (2008 est.)
**Net migration rate:** 8.13 migrant(s)/1,000 population (2009 est.)
**Urbanization:**
*urban population:* 40% of total population (2008)
*rate of urbanization:* 1.7% annual rate of change (2005-10 est.)
**Sex ratio:**
*at birth:* 1.05 male(s)/female
*under 15 years:* 1.03 male(s)/female
*15-64 years:* 1.05 male(s)/female
*65 years and over:* 1.06 male(s)/female
*total population:* 1.05 male(s)/female (2009 est.)
**Infant mortality rate:**
*total:* 14.65 deaths/1,000 live births
*male:* 16.61 deaths/1,000 live births
*female:* 12.58 deaths/1,000 live births (2009 est.)
**Life expectancy at birth:**
*total population:* 77.26 years
*male:* 76.03 years
*female:* 78.55 years (2009 est.)
**Total fertility rate:** 1.71 children born/woman (2009 est.)
**HIV/AIDS - adult prevalence rate:** NA
**HIV/AIDS - people living with HIV/AIDS:** NA
**HIV/AIDS - deaths:** NA
**Nationality:**
*noun:* British Virgin Islander(s)
*adjective:* British Virgin Islander
**Ethnic groups:** black 83.4%, white 7%, other 9.6% (includes Indian and mixed) (2004 Census)

# British Virgin Islands (continued)

**Religions:** Protestant 86% (Methodist 33%, Anglican 17%, Church of God 9%, Seventh-Day Adventist 6%, Baptist 4%, Jehovah's Witnesses 2%, other 15%), Roman Catholic 10%, other 2%, none 2% (1991)
**Languages:** English (official)
**Literacy:**
*definition:* age 15 and over can read and write
*total population:* 97.8% (1991 est.)
*male:* NA
*female:* NA
**School life expectancy (primary to tertiary education):**
*total:* 17 years
*male:* 15 years
*female:* 19 years (2005)
**Education expenditures:** 3.7% of GDP (2006)

## Government

**Country name:**
*conventional long form:* none
*conventional short form:* British Virgin Islands
*abbreviation:* BVI
**Dependency status:** overseas territory of the UK; internal self-governing
**Government type:** NA
**Capital:**
*name:* Road Town
*geographic coordinates:* 18 27 N, 64 37 W
*time difference:* UTC-4 (1 hour ahead of Washington, DC during Standard Time)
**Administrative divisions:** none (overseas territory of the UK)
**Independence:** none (overseas territory of the UK)
**National holiday:** Territory Day, 1 July (1956)
**Constitution:** 13 June 2007
**Legal system:** English law
**Suffrage:** 18 years of age; universal
**Executive branch:**
*chief of state:* Queen ELIZABETH II (since 6 February 1952); represented by Governor David PEAREY (since 18 April 2006)
*head of government:* Premier Ralph T. O'NEAL (since 23 August 2007)
*cabinet:* Executive Council appointed by the governor from members of the House of Assembly
*elections:* the monarch is hereditary; governor appointed by the monarch; following legislative elections, the leader of the majority party or the leader of the majority coalition is usually appointed premier by the governor
**Legislative branch:** unicameral House of Assembly (13 elected seats and 1 non-voting ex officio member in the attorney general; members are elected by direct popular vote, 1 member from each of nine electoral districts, 4 at-large members; members serve four-year terms)
*elections:* last held 20 August 2007 (next to be held in 2011)
*election results:* percent of vote by party - VIP 45.2%, NDP 39.6%, independent 15.2%; seats by party - VIP 10, NDP 2, independent 1

**Judicial branch:** Eastern Caribbean Supreme Court, consisting of the High Court of Justice and the Court of Appeal (one judge of the Supreme Court is a resident of the islands and presides over the High Court); Magistrate's Court; Juvenile Court; Court of Summary Jurisdiction
**Political parties and leaders:** Concerned Citizens Movement or CCM [Ethlyn SMITH]; National Democratic Party or NDP [Orlando SMITH]; United Party or UP [Gregory MADURO]; Virgin Islands Party or VIP [Ralph T. O'NEAL]
**Political pressure groups and leaders:** The Family Support Network; The Women's Desk
*other:* environmentalists
**International organization participation:** Caricom (associate), CDB, Interpol (subbureau), IOC, OECS, UNESCO (associate), UPU, WFTU
**Diplomatic representation in the US:** none (overseas territory of the UK)
**Diplomatic representation from the US:** none (overseas territory of the UK)
**Flag description:** blue, with the flag of the UK in the upper hoist-side quadrant and the Virgin Islander coat of arms centered in the outer half of the flag; the coat of arms depicts a woman flanked on either side by a vertical column of six oil lamps above a scroll bearing the Latin word VIGILATE (Be Watchful)

## Economy

**Economy - overview:** The economy, one of the most stable and prosperous in the Caribbean, is highly dependent on tourism generating an estimated 45% of the national income. An estimated 820,000 tourists, mainly from the US, visited the islands in 2005. In the mid-1980s, the government began offering offshore registration to companies wishing to incorporate in the islands, and incorporation fees now generate substantial revenues. Roughly 400,000 companies were on the offshore registry by yearend 2000. The adoption of a comprehensive insurance law in late 1994, which provides a blanket of confidentiality with regulated statutory gateways for investigation of criminal offenses, made the British Virgin Islands even more attractive to international business. Livestock raising is the most important agricultural activity; poor soils limit the islands' ability to meet domestic food requirements. Because of traditionally close links with the US Virgin Islands, the British Virgin Islands has used the US dollar as its currency since 1959.
**GDP (purchasing power parity):**
$853.4 million (2004 est.)
**GDP (official exchange rate):** $839.7 million (2003)
**GDP - real growth rate:**
1% (2002 est.)
**GDP - per capita (PPP):**
$38,500 (2004 est.)
**GDP - composition by sector:**
*agriculture:* 1.8%
*industry:* 6.2%
*services:* 92% (1996 est.)
**Labor force:** 12,770 (2004)

**Labor force - by occupation:**
*agriculture:* 0.6%
*industry:* 40%
*services:* 59.4% (2005)
**Unemployment rate:**
3.6% (1997)
**Population below poverty line:** NA%
**Household income or consumption by percentage share:**
*lowest 10%:* NA%
*highest 10%:* NA%
**Budget:**
*revenues:* $204.7 million
*expenditures:* $180.4 million (2004)
**Inflation rate (consumer prices):**
2% (2005)
**Agriculture - products:** fruits, vegetables; livestock, poultry; fish
**Industries:** tourism, light industry, construction, rum, concrete block, offshore financial center
**Industrial production growth rate:** NA%
**Electricity - production:** 45 million kWh (2006 est.)
**Electricity - consumption:** 41.85 million kWh (2006 est.)
**Electricity - exports:** 0 kWh (2007 est.)
**Electricity - imports:** 0 kWh (2007 est.)
**Oil - production:** 0 bbl/day (2007 est.)
**Oil - consumption:** 650 bbl/day (2006 est.)
**Oil - exports:** 0 bbl/day (2005)
**Oil - imports:** 649.8 bbl/day (2005)
**Oil - proved reserves:** 0 bbl (1 January 2006 est.)
**Natural gas - production:** 0 cu m (2007 est.)
**Natural gas - consumption:** 0 cu m (2007 est.)
**Natural gas - exports:** 0 cu m (2007 est.)
**Natural gas - imports:** 0 cu m (2007 est.)
**Natural gas - proved reserves:** 0 cu m (1 January 2006 est.)
**Current account balance:** $134.3 million (1999)
**Exports:** $25.3 million (2002)
**Exports - commodities:** rum, fresh fish, fruits, animals; gravel, sand
**Imports:** $187 million f.o.b. (2002 est.)
**Imports - commodities:** building materials, automobiles, foodstuffs, machinery
**Debt - external:** $36.1 million (1997)
**Exchange rates:** the US dollar is used

## Communications

**Telephones - main lines in use:** 11,700 (2002)
**Telephones - mobile cellular:** 8,000 (2002)
**Telephone system:**
*general assessment:* worldwide telephone service
*domestic:* NA
*international:* country code - 1-284; connected via submarine cable to Bermuda; the East Caribbean Fiber System (ECFS) submarine cable provides connectivity to 13 other islands in the eastern Caribbean (2007)
**Radio broadcast stations:** AM 1, FM 5, shortwave 0 (2004)

**Television broadcast stations:** 1 (plus 1 cable company) (1997)
**Internet country code:** .vg
**Internet hosts:** 465 (2008)
**Internet users:** 4,000 (2002)

## Transportation

**Airports:** 4 (2008)
**Airports - with paved runways:**
*total:* 2
*914 to 1,523 m:* 1
*under 914 m:* 1 (2008)
**Airports - with unpaved runways:**
*total:* 2
*914 to 1,523 m:* 2 (2008)
**Roadways:**
*total:* 200 km
*paved:* 200 km (2007)
**Merchant marine:**
*registered in other countries:* 1 (Panama 1) (2008)
**Ports and terminals:** Road Town

## Military

**Manpower available for military service:**
*males age 16-49:* 7,101 (2008 est.)
**Manpower fit for military service:**
*males age 16-49:* 5,979
*females age 16-49:* 5,738 (2009 est.)
**Manpower reaching militarily significant age annually:**
*male:* 178
*female:* 173 (2009 est.)
**Military - note:** defense is the responsibility of the UK

## Transnational Issues

**Disputes - international:** none
**Illicit drugs:** transshipment point for South American narcotics destined for the US and Europe; large offshore financial center makes it vulnerable to money laundering

# Brunei

## Introduction

**Background:** The Sultanate of Brunei's influence peaked between the 15th and 17th centuries when its control extended over coastal areas of northwest Borneo and the southern Philippines. Brunei subsequently entered a period of decline brought on by internal strife over royal succession, colonial expansion of European powers, and piracy. In 1888, Brunei became a British protectorate; independence was achieved in 1984. The same family has ruled Brunei for over six centuries. Brunei benefits from extensive petroleum and natural gas fields, the source of one of the highest per capita GDPs in Asia.

## Geography

**Location:** Southeastern Asia, bordering the South China Sea and Malaysia
**Geographic coordinates:** 4 30 N, 114 40 E
**Map references:** Southeast Asia
**Area:**
*total:* 5,770 sq km
*land:* 5,270 sq km
*water:* 500 sq km
**Area - comparative:** slightly smaller than Delaware
**Land boundaries:**
*total:* 381 km
*border countries:* Malaysia 381 km
**Coastline:** 161 km
**Maritime claims:**
*territorial sea:* 12 nm
*exclusive economic zone:* 200 nm or to median line
**Climate:** tropical; hot, humid, rainy
**Terrain:** flat coastal plain rises to mountains in east; hilly lowland in west
**Elevation extremes:**
*lowest point:* South China Sea 0 m
*highest point:* Bukit Pagon 1,850 m
**Natural resources:** petroleum, natural gas, timber

**Land use:**
*arable land:* 2.08%
*permanent crops:* 0.87%
*other:* 97.05% (2005)
**Irrigated land:** 10 sq km (2003)
**Total renewable water resources:** 8.5 cu km (1999)
**Freshwater withdrawal (domestic/industrial/agricultural):**
*total:* 0.09
*per capita:* 243 cu m/yr (1994)
**Natural hazards:** typhoons, earthquakes, and severe flooding are rare
**Environment - current issues:** seasonal smoke/haze resulting from forest fires in Indonesia
**Environment - international agreements:**
*party to:* Biodiversity, Climate Change, Desertification, Endangered Species, Hazardous Wastes, Law of the Sea, Ozone Layer Protection, Ship Pollution
*signed, but not ratified:* none of the selected agreements
**Geography - note:** close to vital sea lanes through South China Sea linking Indian and Pacific Oceans; two parts physically separated by Malaysia; almost an enclave within Malaysia

## People

**Population:** 388,190 (July 2009 est.)
**Age structure:**
*0-14 years:* 26.6% (male 53,282/female 50,141)
*15-64 years:* 70.1% (male 135,640/female 136,292)
*65 years and over:* 3.3% (male 6,199/female 6,636) (2009 est.)
**Median age:**
*total:* 27.8 years
*male:* 27.7 years
*female:* 27.8 years (2009 est.)
**Population growth rate:** 1.759% (2009 est.)
**Birth rate:** 18.2 births/1,000 population (2009 est.)
**Death rate:** 3.28 deaths/1,000 population (2008 est.)
**Net migration rate:** 2.69 migrant(s)/1,000 population (2009 est.)
**Urbanization:**
*urban population:* 75% of total population (2008)
*rate of urbanization:* 2.6% annual rate of change (2005-10 est.)
**Sex ratio:**
*at birth:* 1.05 male(s)/female
*under 15 years:* 1.06 male(s)/female
*15-64 years:* 1 male(s)/female
*65 years and over:* 0.93 male(s)/female
*total population:* 1.01 male(s)/female (2009 est.)
**Infant mortality rate:**
*total:* 12.27 deaths/1,000 live births
*male:* 14.68 deaths/1,000 live births
*female:* 9.75 deaths/1,000 live births (2009 est.)
**Life expectancy at birth:**
*total population:* 75.74 years
*male:* 73.52 years
*female:* 78.07 years (2009 est.)

# Brunei (continued)

**Total fertility rate:** 1.91 children born/woman (2009 est.)

**HIV/AIDS - adult prevalence rate:** less than 0.1% (2003 est.)

**HIV/AIDS - people living with HIV/AIDS:** fewer than 200 (2003 est.)

**HIV/AIDS - deaths:** fewer than 200 (2003 est.)

**Nationality:**
*noun:* Bruneian(s)
*adjective:* Bruneian

**Ethnic groups:** Malay 66.3%, Chinese 11.2%, indigenous 3.4%, other 19.1% (2004 est.)

**Religions:** Muslim (official) 67%, Buddhist 13%, Christian 10%, other (includes indigenous beliefs) 10%

**Languages:** Malay (official), English, Chinese

**Literacy:**
*definition:* age 15 and over can read and write
*total population:* 92.7%
*male:* 95.2%
*female:* 90.2% (2001 census)

**School life expectancy (primary to tertiary education):**
*total:* 14 years
*male:* 14 years
*female:* 14 years (2006)

**Education expenditures:** 5.2% of GDP (2000)

## Government

**Country name:**
*conventional long form:* Brunei Darussalam
*conventional short form:* Brunei
*local long form:* Negara Brunei Darussalam
*local short form:* Brunei

**Government type:** constitutional sultanate

**Capital:**
*name:* Bandar Seri Begawan
*geographic coordinates:* 4 53 N, 114 56 E
*time difference:* UTC+8 (13 hours ahead of Washington, DC during Standard Time)

**Administrative divisions:** 4 districts (daerah-daerah, singular - daerah); Belait, Brunei-Muara, Temburong, Tutong

**Independence:** 1 January 1984 (from the UK)

**National holiday:** National Day, 23 February (1984); note - 1 January 1984 was the date of independence from the UK, 23 February 1984 was the date of independence from British protection

**Constitution:** 29 September 1959 (some provisions suspended under a State of Emergency since December 1962, others since independence on 1 January 1984)

**Legal system:** based on English common law; for Muslims, Islamic Sharia law supersedes civil law in a number of areas; has not accepted compulsory ICJ jurisdiction

**Suffrage:** 18 years of age for village elections; universal

**Executive branch:**
*chief of state:* Sultan and Prime Minister Sir HASSANAL Bolkiah (since 5 October 1967); note - the monarch is both the chief of state and head of government

*head of government:* Sultan and Prime Minister Sir HASSANAL Bolkiah (since 5 October 1967)
*cabinet:* Council of Cabinet Ministers appointed and presided over by the monarch; deals with executive matters; note - there is also a Religious Council (members appointed by the monarch) that advises on religious matters, a Privy Council (members appointed by the monarch) that deals with constitutional matters, and the Council of Succession (members appointed by the monarch) that determines the succession to the throne if the need arises
*elections:* none; the monarch is hereditary

**Legislative branch:** The Sultan appointed a council with 29 members as of 2 September 2005; the council has met in March of each year since then
*elections:* last held in March 1962 (date of next election NA)
*note:* The Legislative Council met on 25 September 2004 for first time in 20 years with 21 members appointed by the Sultan; it passed constitutional amendments calling for a 45-seat council with 15 elected members

**Judicial branch:** Supreme Court - chief justice and judges are sworn in by monarch for three-year terms; Judicial Committee of Privy Council in London is final court of appeal for civil cases; Sharia courts deal with Islamic laws (2006)

**Political parties and leaders:** National Development Party or NDP [YASSIN Affendi]
*note:* Brunei National Solidarity Party or PPKB [Abdul LATIF bin Chuchu] and People's Awareness Party or PAKAR [Awang Haji MAIDIN bin Haji Ahmad] were deregistered; parties are small and have limited activity

**Political pressure groups and leaders:** NA

**International organization participation:** ADB, APEC, APT, ARF, ASEAN, C, EAS, G-77, IBRD, ICAO, ICRM, IDB, IFRCS, ILO, IMF, IMO, IMSO, Interpol, IOC, ISO (correspondent), ITSO, ITU, NAM, OIC, OPCW, UN, UNCTAD, UNESCO, UNWTO, UPU, WCO, WFTU, WHO, WIPO, WMO, WTO

**Diplomatic representation in the US:**
*chief of mission:* Ambassador (vacant); Charge d'Affaires Angela SHIM
*chancery:* 3520 International Court NW, Washington, DC 20008
*telephone:* [1] (202) 237-1838
*FAX:* [1] (202) 885-0560

**Diplomatic representation from the US:**
*chief of mission:* Ambassador William E. TODD
*embassy:* Third Floor, Teck Guan Plaza, Jalan Sultan, Bandar Seri Begawan, BS8811
*mailing address:* PSC 470 (BSB), FPO AP 96507; P.O. Box 2991, Bandar Seri Begawan BS8675, Negara Brunei Darussalam
*telephone:* [673] 222-0384
*FAX:* [673] 222-5293

**Flag description:** yellow with two diagonal bands of white (top, almost double width) and black starting from the upper hoist side; the national emblem in red is superimposed at the center; the emblem includes a swallow-tailed flag on top of a winged column within an upturned crescent above a scroll and flanked by two upraised hands

## Economy

**Economy - overview:** Brunei has a small well-to-do economy that encompasses a mixture of foreign and domestic entrepreneurship, government regulation, welfare measures, and village tradition. Crude oil and natural gas production account for just over half of GDP and more than 90% of exports. Per capita GDP is among the highest in Asia, and substantial income from overseas investment supplements income from domestic production. The government provides for all medical services and free education through the university level and subsidizes rice and housing. Brunei's leaders are concerned that steadily increased integration into the world economy will undermine internal social cohesion. Plans for the future include upgrading the labor force, reducing unemployment, strengthening the banking and tourist sectors, increasing agricultural production, and, in general, further widening the economic base beyond oil and gas.

**GDP (purchasing power parity):**
$20.25 billion (2008 est.)
$20.13 billion (2007)
$20.01 billion (2006)
*note:* data are in 2008 US dollars

**GDP (official exchange rate):** $17.18 billion (2008 est.)

**GDP - real growth rate:**
0.4% (2008 est.)
0.6% (2007 est.)
5.1% (2006 est.)

**GDP - per capita (PPP):**
$53,100 (2008 est.)
$53,700 (2007 est.)
$54,400 (2006 est.)
*note:* data are in 2008 US dollars

**GDP - composition by sector:**
*agriculture:* 0.7%
*industry:* 75%
*services:* 25% (2005 est.)

**Labor force:** 188,800 (2008 est.)

**Labor force - by occupation:**
*agriculture:* 4.5%
*industry:* 63.1%
*services:* 32.4% (2003 est.)

**Unemployment rate:**
3.7% (2008)
4% (2006)

**Population below poverty line:** NA%

**Household income or consumption by percentage share:**
*lowest 10%:* NA%
*highest 10%:* NA%

**Budget:**
*revenues:* $6.889 billion
*expenditures:* $4 billion (2008 est.)

**Inflation rate (consumer prices):**
0.3% (2007 est.)

**Commercial bank prime lending rate:** 5.5% (February 2009)

**Stock of money:** $2.674 billion (31 December 2007)

**Stock of quasi money:** $4.258 billion (31 December 2007)

**Stock of domestic credit:** $2.38 billion (31 December 2007)

**Market value of publicly traded shares:** $NA

**Agriculture - products:** rice, vegetables, fruits; chickens, water buffalo, cattle, goats, eggs

**Industries:** petroleum, petroleum refining, liquefied natural gas, construction

**Industrial production growth rate:** 1.8% (2006 est.)

**Electricity - production:** 3.145 billion kWh (2007 est.)

**Electricity - consumption:** 2.758 billion kWh (2007 est.)

**Electricity - exports:** 0 kWh (2007 est.)

**Electricity - imports:** 0 kWh (2007 est.)

**Oil - production:** 192,600 bbl/day (1st quarter 2008 est.)

**Oil - consumption:** 13,200 bbl/day (2006 est.)

**Oil - exports:** 200,000 bbl/day (2005)

**Oil - imports:** 304 bbl/day (2005)

**Oil - proved reserves:** 1.1 billion bbl (1 January 2008 est.)

**Natural gas - production:** 13.8 billion cu m (2006 est.)

**Natural gas - consumption:** 3.99 billion cu m (2006 est.)

**Natural gas - exports:** 9.4 billion cu m (2007 est.)

**Natural gas - imports:** 0 cu m (2007 est.)

**Natural gas - proved reserves:** 390.8 billion cu m (1 January 2008 est.)

**Current account balance:** $7.101 billion (2007 est.)

**Exports:** $8.25 billion f.o.b. (2007)

**Exports - commodities:** crude oil, natural gas, garments

**Exports - partners:** Japan 32.8%, Indonesia 24.4%, Australia 13.4%, South Korea 12.2%, US 5.5% (2007)

**Imports:** $2.055 billion c.i.f. (2007 est.)

**Imports - commodities:** machinery and transport equipment, manufactured goods, food, chemicals

**Imports - partners:** UK 46.4%, Singapore 19.5%, Malaysia 11.3% (2007)

**Debt - external:** $0 (2005)

**Exchange rates:** Bruneian dollars (BND) per US dollar - NA (2007), 1.5886 (2006), 1.6644 (2005), 1.6902 (2004), 1.7422 (2003)

## Communications

**Telephones - main lines in use:** 79,200 (2007)

**Telephones - mobile cellular:** 339,800 (2007)

**Telephone system:**

*general assessment:* service throughout the country is excellent; international service is good to Southeast Asia, Middle East, Western Europe, and the US

*domestic:* every service available

*international:* country code - 673; landing point for the SEA-ME-WE-3 optical telecommunications submarine cable that provides links to Asia, the Middle East, and Europe; the Asia-America Gateway submarine cable network, scheduled for completion by late 2008, will provide new links to Asia and the US; satellite earth stations - 2 Intelsat (1 Indian Ocean and 1 Pacific Ocean) (2007)

**Radio broadcast stations:** AM 1, FM 2 (transmitting on 18 different frequencies), shortwave 0 (British Forces Broadcasting Service (BFBS) station transmits two FM signals with English and Nepali service) (2006)

**Television broadcast stations:** 4 (includes 2 UHF stations broadcasting a subscription service) (2006)

**Internet country code:** .bn

**Internet hosts:** 14,950 (2008)

**Internet users:** 199,532 (2007)

## Transportation

**Airports:** 2 (2008)

**Airports - with paved runways:**

*total:* 1

*over 3,047 m:* 1 (2008)

**Airports - with unpaved runways:**

*total:* 1

*914 to 1,523 m:* 1 (2008)

**Heliports:** 3 (2007)

**Pipelines:** gas 37 km; oil 18 km (2008)

**Roadways:**

*total:* 3,650 km

*paved:* 2,819 km

*unpaved:* 831 km (2005)

**Waterways:** 209 km (navigable by craft drawing less than 1.2 m) (2008)

**Merchant marine:**

*total:* 8

*by type:* liquefied gas 8

*foreign-owned:* 1 (UK 1) (2008)

**Ports and terminals:** Lumut, Muara, Seria

## Military

**Military branches:** Royal Brunei Armed Forces (RBAF): Royal Brunei Land Forces, Royal Brunei Navy, Royal Brunei Air Force (Tentera Udara Diraja Brunei) (2009)

**Military service age and obligation:** 18 years of age (est.) for voluntary military service; non-Malays are ineligible to serve (2007)

**Manpower available for military service:**

*males age 16-49:* 108,356

*females age 16-49:* 110,153 (2008 est.)

**Manpower fit for military service:**

*males age 16-49:* 92,543

*females age 16-49:* 95,301 (2009 est.)

**Manpower reaching militarily significant age annually:**

*male:* 3,460

*female:* 3,399 (2009 est.)

**Military expenditures:** 4.5% of GDP (2006)

## Transnational Issues

**Disputes - international:** Brunei and Malaysia agreed in September 2008 to resolve their offshore and deepwater seabed dispute, resume hydrocarbon exploration, and renounce any territorial claims on land; Brunei established an exclusive economic fishing zone encompassing Louisa Reef in the southern Spratly Islands in 1984, but makes no public territorial claim to the offshore reefs; the 2002 "Declaration on the Conduct of Parties in the South China Sea" has eased tensions in the Spratly Islands but falls short of a legally binding "code of conduct" desired by several of the disputants

**Illicit drugs:** drug trafficking and illegally importing controlled substances are serious offenses in Brunei and carry a mandatory death penalty

# Bulgaria

## Introduction

**Background:** The Bulgars, a Central Asian Turkic tribe, merged with the local Slavic inhabitants in the late 7th century to form the first Bulgarian state. In succeeding centuries, Bulgaria struggled with the Byzantine Empire to assert its place in the Balkans, but by the end of the 14th century the country was overrun by the Ottoman Turks. Northern Bulgaria attained autonomy in 1878 and all of Bulgaria became independent from the Ottoman Empire in 1908. Having fought on the losing side in both World Wars, Bulgaria fell within the Soviet sphere of influence and became a People's Republic in 1946. Communist domination ended in 1990, when Bulgaria held its first multiparty election since World War II and began the contentious process of moving toward political democracy and a market economy while combating inflation, unemployment, corruption, and crime. The country joined NATO in 2004 and the EU in 2007.

## Geography

**Location:** Southeastern Europe, bordering the Black Sea, between Romania and Turkey
**Geographic coordinates:** 43 00 N, 25 00 E
**Map references:** Europe
**Area:**
*total:* 110,910 sq km
*land:* 110,550 sq km
*water:* 360 sq km
**Area - comparative:** slightly larger than Tennessee
**Land boundaries:**
*total:* 1,808 km
*border countries:* Greece 494 km, Macedonia 148 km, Romania 608 km, Serbia 318 km, Turkey 240 km
**Coastline:** 354 km
**Maritime claims:**
*territorial sea:* 12 nm
*contiguous zone:* 24 nm
*exclusive economic zone:* 200 nm

**Climate:** temperate; cold, damp winters; hot, dry summers
**Terrain:** mostly mountains with lowlands in north and southeast
**Elevation extremes:**
*lowest point:* Black Sea 0 m
*highest point:* Musala 2,925 m
**Natural resources:** bauxite, copper, lead, zinc, coal, timber, arable land
**Land use:**
*arable land:* 29.94%
*permanent crops:* 1.9%
*other:* 68.16% (2005)
**Irrigated land:** 5,880 sq km (2003)
**Total renewable water resources:** 19.4 cu km (2005)
**Freshwater withdrawal (domestic/industrial/agricultural):**
*total:* 6.92 cu km/yr (3%/78%/19%)
*per capita:* 895 cu m/yr (2003)
**Natural hazards:** earthquakes; landslides
**Environment - current issues:** air pollution from industrial emissions; rivers polluted from raw sewage, heavy metals, detergents; deforestation; forest damage from air pollution and resulting acid rain; soil contamination from heavy metals from metallurgical plants and industrial wastes
**Environment - international agreements:**
*party to:* Air Pollution, Air Pollution-Nitrogen Oxides, Air Pollution-Persistent Organic Pollutants, Air Pollution-Sulfur 85, Air Pollution-Sulfur 94, Air Pollution-Volatile Organic Compounds, Antarctic-Environmental Protocol, Antarctic-Marine Living Resources, Antarctic Treaty, Biodiversity, Climate Change, Climate Change-Kyoto Protocol, Desertification, Endangered Species, Environmental Modification, Hazardous Wastes, Law of the Sea, Marine Dumping, Ozone Layer Protection, Ship Pollution, Wetlands
*signed, but not ratified:* none of the selected agreements
**Geography - note:** strategic location near Turkish Straits; controls key land routes from Europe to Middle East and Asia

## People

**Population:** 7,204,687 (July 2009 est.)
**Age structure:**
*0-14 years:* 13.8% (male 509,544/female 484,816)
*15-64 years:* 68.5% (male 2,426,060/female 2,508,772)
*65 years and over:* 17.7% (male 518,711/female 756,784) (2009 est.)
**Median age:**
*total:* 41.4 years
*male:* 39.2 years
*female:* 43.6 years (2009 est.)
**Population growth rate:** -0.79% (2009 est.)
**Birth rate:** 9.51 births/1,000 population (2009 est.)
**Death rate:** 14.3 deaths/1,000 population (2008 est.)

**Net migration rate:** -3.11 migrant(s)/1,000 population (2009 est.)
**Urbanization:**
*urban population:* 71% of total population (2008)
*rate of urbanization:* -0.3% annual rate of change (2005-10 est.)
**Sex ratio:**
*at birth:* 1.06 male(s)/female
*under 15 years:* 1.05 male(s)/female
*15-64 years:* 0.97 male(s)/female
*65 years and over:* 0.68 male(s)/female
*total population:* 0.92 male(s)/female (2009 est.)
**Infant mortality rate:**
*total:* 17.87 deaths/1,000 live births
*male:* 21.28 deaths/1,000 live births
*female:* 14.25 deaths/1,000 live births (2009 est.)
**Life expectancy at birth:**
*total population:* 73.09 years
*male:* 69.48 years
*female:* 76.91 years (2009 est.)
**Total fertility rate:** 1.41 children born/woman (2009 est.)
**HIV/AIDS - adult prevalence rate:** less than 0.1% (2001 est.)
**HIV/AIDS - people living with HIV/AIDS:** 346 (2001 est.)
**HIV/AIDS - deaths:** 100 (2001 est.)
**Nationality:**
*noun:* Bulgarian(s)
*adjective:* Bulgarian
**Ethnic groups:** Bulgarian 83.9%, Turk 9.4%, Roma 4.7%, other 2% (including Macedonian, Armenian, Tatar, Circassian) (2001 census)
**Religions:** Bulgarian Orthodox 82.6%, Muslim 12.2%, other Christian 1.2%, other 4% (2001 census)
**Languages:** Bulgarian 84.5%, Turkish 9.6%, Roma 4.1%, other and unspecified 1.8% (2001 census)
**Literacy:**
*definition:* age 15 and over can read and write
*total population:* 98.2%
*male:* 98.7%
*female:* 97.7% (2001 census)
**School life expectancy (primary to tertiary education):**
*total:* 14 years
*male:* 13 years
*female:* 14 years (2006)
**Education expenditures:** 4.5% of GDP (2005)

## Government

**Country name:**
*conventional long form:* Republic of Bulgaria
*conventional short form:* Bulgaria
*local long form:* Republika Balgariya
*local short form:* Balgariya
**Government type:** parliamentary democracy
**Capital:**
*name:* Sofia
*geographic coordinates:* 42 41 N, 23 19 E
*time difference:* UTC+2 (7 hours ahead of Washington, DC during Standard Time)

# Bulgaria (continued)

*daylight saving time:* +1hr, begins last Sunday in March; ends last Sunday in October

**Administrative divisions:** 28 provinces (oblasti, singular - oblast); Blagoevgrad, Burgas, Dobrich, Gabrovo, Khaskovo, Kurdzhali, Kyustendil, Lovech, Montana, Pazardzhik, Pernik, Pleven, Plovdiv, Razgrad, Ruse, Shumen, Silistra, Sliven, Smolyan, Sofiya, Sofiya-Grad, Stara Zagora, Turgovishte, Varna, Veliko Turnovo, Vidin, Vratsa, Yambol

**Independence:** 3 March 1878 (as an autonomous principality within the Ottoman Empire); 22 September 1908 (complete independence from the Ottoman Empire)

**National holiday:** Liberation Day, 3 March (1878)

**Constitution:** adopted 12 July 1991

**Legal system:** civil and criminal law based on Roman law; accepts compulsory ICJ jurisdiction with reservations

**Suffrage:** 18 years of age; universal

**Executive branch:**
*chief of state:* President Georgi PARVANOV (since 22 January 2002); Vice President Angel MARIN (since 22 January 2002)
*head of government:* Prime Minister Sergei STANISHEV (since 16 August 2005); Deputy Prime Ministers Ivaylo KALFIN, Daniel VULCHEV, and Emel ETEM (since 16 August 2005) and Meglena PLUGCHIEVA (since 25 April 2008)
*cabinet:* Council of Ministers nominated by the prime minister and elected by the National Assembly
*elections:* president and vice president elected on the same ticket by popular vote for a five-year term (eligible for a second term); election last held 22 and 29 October 2006 (next to be held in 2011); chairman of the Council of Ministers (prime minister) elected by the National Assembly; deputy prime ministers nominated by the prime minister and elected by the National Assembly
*election results:* Georgi PARVANOV reelected president; percent of vote - Georgi PARVANOV 77.3%, Volen SIDEROV 22.7%; Sergei STANISHEV elected prime minister, result of legislative vote - 168 to 67

**Legislative branch:** unicameral National Assembly or Narodno Sabranie (240 seats; members elected by popular vote to serve four-year terms)
*elections:* last held 25 June 2005 (next to be held mid-2009)
*election results:* percent of vote by party - CfB 31.1%, NDSV 19.9%, MRF 12.7%, ATAKA 8.2%, UDF 7.7%, DSB 6.5%, BPU 5.2%, other 8.7%; seats by party - CfB 83, NDSV 53, MRF 33, UDF 20, ATAKA 17, DSB 17, BPU 13, independents 4; note - seats by party as of February 2009 - CfB 81, NDSV 35, MRF 34, UDF 18, Bulgarian New Democracy 16, DSB 13, Movement Forward 11, ATAKA 11, independents 21

**Judicial branch:** independent judiciary comprised of judges, prosecutors and investigating magistrates who are appointed, promoted, demoted, and dismissed by a 25-member Supreme Judicial Council (consists of the chairmen of the two Supreme Courts, the Chief Prosecutor, and 22 members, half of whom are elected by the National Assembly and the other half by the bodies of the judiciary for a 5-year term in office); three levels of case review; 182 courts of which two Supreme Courts act as the last instance on civil and criminal cases (the Supreme Court of Cassation) and appeals of government decisions (the Supreme Administrative Court)

**Political parties and leaders:** ATAKA (Attack Coalition) (coalition of parties headed by the Attack National Union); Attack National Union [Volen SIDEROV]; Agrarian National Union or ANU [Stefan LICHEV]; Bulgarian New Democracy [Borislav RALCHEV]; Bulgarian Socialist Party or BSP [Sergei STANISHEV]; Citizens for the European Development of Bulgaria or GERB [Tsvetan TSVETANOV]; Coalition for Bulgaria or CfB (coalition of parties dominated by BSP) [Sergei STANISHEV]; Democrats for a Strong Bulgaria or DSB [Ivan KOSTOV]; Gergyovden [Petar STOYANOVICH]; Internal Macedonian Revolutionary Organization or IMRO [Krasimir KARAKACHANOV]; Liberal Initiative for Democratic European Development or LIDER [Khristo KOVACHKI]; Movement for Rights and Freedoms or MRF [Ahmed DOGAN]; Movement Forward (LIDER, IMRO, ANU, Gergyovden); National Movement for Stability and Progress or NDSV [Simeon SAXE-COBURG-GOTHA] (formerly National Movement Simeon II or NMS2); New Time [Emil KOSHLUKOV]; Union of Democratic Forces or UDF [Martin DIMITROV]; Union of Free Democrats or UFD [Stefan SOFIYANSKI]; United Agrarians [Anastasia MOZER]; United Democratic Forces or UtDF (a coalition of center-right parties dominated by UDF)

**Political pressure groups and leaders:** Confederation of Independent Trade Unions of Bulgaria or CITUB; Podkrepa Labor Confederation
*other:* numerous regional, ethnic, and national interest groups with various agendas

**International organization participation:** ACCT, Australia Group, BIS, BSEC, CE, CEI, CERN, EAPC, EBRD, EIB, EU, FAO, G- 9, IAEA, IBRD, ICAO, ICC, ICCt, ICRM, IFC, IFRCS, ILO, IMF, IMO, IMSO, Interpol, IOC, IOM, IPU, ISO, ITSO, ITU, ITUC, MIGA, NAM (guest), NATO, NSG, OAS (observer), OIF, OPCW, OSCE, PCA, SECI, UN, UNCTAD, UNESCO, UNIDO, UNMIL, UNMIS, UNWTO, UPU, WCL, WCO, WEU (associate affiliate), WFTU, WHO, WIPO, WMO, WTO, ZC

**Diplomatic representation in the US:**
*chief of mission:* Ambassador Latchezar PETKOV
*chancery:* 1621 22nd Street NW, Washington, DC 20008
*telephone:* [1] (202) 387-0174
*FAX:* [1] (202) 234-7973
*consulate(s) general:* Chicago, Los Angeles, New York

**Diplomatic representation from the US:**
*chief of mission:* Ambassador Nancy McELDOWNEY
*embassy:* 16 Kozyak Street, Sofia 1407
*mailing address:* American Embassy Sofia, US Department of State, 5740 Sofia Place, Washington, DC 20521-5740
*telephone:* [359] (2) 937-5100
*FAX:* [359] (2) 937-5320

**Flag description:** three equal horizontal bands of white (top), green, and red
*note:* the national emblem, formerly on the hoist side of the white stripe, has been removed

## Economy

**Economy - overview:** Bulgaria, a former Communist country that entered the EU on 1 January 2007, has experienced strong growth since a major economic downturn in 1996. Successive governments have demonstrated a commitment to economic reforms and responsible fiscal planning, but have failed so far to rein in rising inflation and large current account deficits. Bulgaria has averaged more than 6% growth since 2004, attracting significant amounts of foreign direct investment, but corruption in the public administration, a weak judiciary, and the presence of organized crime remain significant challenges.

**GDP (purchasing power parity):**
$93.78 billion (2008 est.)
$88.48 billion (2007)
$83.31 billion (2006)
*note:* data are in 2008 US dollars

**GDP (official exchange rate):** $49.43 billion (2008)

**GDP - real growth rate:**
6% (2008)
6.2% (2007 est.)
6.3% (2006 est.)

**GDP - per capita (PPP):**
$12,900 (2008 est.)
$12,100 (2007 est.)
$11,300 (2006 est.)
*note:* data are in 2008 US dollars

**GDP - composition by sector:**
*agriculture:* 4.6%
*industry:* 28.7%
*services:* 66.7% (2008 est.)

**Labor force:** 2.44 million (2008)

**Labor force - by occupation:**
*agriculture:* 7.5%
*industry:* 35.5%
*services:* 57% (2007 est.)

**Unemployment rate:**
6.3% (2008)
7.7% (2007 est.)

**Population below poverty line:** 14.1% (2003 est.)

**Household income or consumption by percentage share:**
*lowest 10%:* 3%
*highest 10%:* 25.5% (2007)

**Distribution of family income - Gini index:** 30.7 (2007)

# Bulgaria (continued)

**Investment (gross fixed):** 38.3% of GDP (2008)
**Budget:**
*revenues:* $20.43 billion
*expenditures:* $18.93 billion (2008)
**Public debt:** 16.7% of GDP (2008)
**Inflation rate (consumer prices):**
7.8% (2008)
9.8% (2007 est.)
**Central bank discount rate:** 5.77%
(31 December 2008)
**Commercial bank prime lending rate:** 10%
(31 December 2007)
**Stock of money:** $14.86 billion (31 December 2008)
**Stock of quasi money:** $34.17 billion (31 December 2008)
**Stock of domestic credit:** $33.3 billion
(31 December 2008)
**Market value of publicly traded shares:** $21.79 billion (31 December 2007)
**Agriculture - products:** vegetables, fruits, tobacco, wine, wheat, barley, sunflowers, sugar beets; livestock
**Industries:** electricity, gas, water; food, beverages, tobacco; machinery and equipment, base metals, chemical products, coke, refined petroleum, nuclear fuel
**Industrial production growth rate:** 3.9% (2008)
**Electricity - production:** 42.43 billion kWh (2007)
**Electricity - consumption:** 28.8 billion kWh
(2007 est.)
**Electricity - exports:** 7.992 billion kWh (2007 est.)
**Electricity - imports:** 3.243 billion kWh (2007 est.)
**Oil - production:** 3,520 bbl/day (2007)
**Oil - consumption:** 142,400 bbl/day (2007)
**Oil - exports:** 2,480 bbl/day (2007)
**Oil - imports:** 145,200 bbl/day (2007)
**Oil - proved reserves:** 15 million bbl
(1 January 2008 est.)
**Natural gas - production:** 0 cu m (2007 est.)
**Natural gas - consumption:** 3.5 billion cu m
(2007 est.)
**Natural gas - exports:** 0 cu m (2007)
**Natural gas - imports:** 3.229 billion cu m (2007)
**Natural gas - proved reserves:** 5.663 billion cu m
(1 January 2008 est.)
**Current account balance:** -$12.11 billion (2008)
**Exports:** $22.3 billion f.o.b. (2008)
**Exports - commodities:** clothing, footwear, iron and steel, machinery and equipment, fuels
**Exports - partners:** Turkey 11.5%, Germany 10.3%, Italy 10.2%, Greece 9.1%, Belgium 6.2%, Romania 4.9% (2007)
**Imports:** $35.3 billion f.o.b. (2008)
**Imports - commodities:** machinery and equipment; metals and ores; chemicals and plastics; fuels, minerals, and raw materials
**Imports - partners:** Russia 12.3%, Germany 12.3%, Italy 8.7%, Ukraine 7.2%, Turkey 6.9%, Greece 6.2%, Romania 4.5%, Austria 4.3% (2007)
**Reserves of foreign exchange and gold:** $18.59 billion (31 December 2008)
**Debt - external:** $54.01 billion (30 November 2008)

**Stock of direct foreign investment - at home:**
$45.13 billion (2008)
**Stock of direct foreign investment - abroad:**
$1.402 billion (2008)
**Exchange rates:** leva (BGN) per US dollar - 1.3171 (2008 est.), 1.4366 (2007), 1.5576 (2006), 1.5741 (2005), 1.5751 (2004)

## Communications

**Telephones - main lines in use:** 2.3 million (2007)
**Telephones - mobile cellular:** 9.897 million (2007)
**Telephone system:**
*general assessment:* an extensive but antiquated telecommunications network inherited from the Soviet era; quality has improved; the Bulgaria Telecommunications Company's fixed-line monopoly terminated in 2005 when alternative fixed-line operators were given access to its network; a drop in fixed-line connections in recent years has been more than offset by a sharp increase in mobile-cellular telephone use fostered by multiple service providers; the number of cellular telephone subscriptions now exceeds the population
*domestic:* a fairly modern digital cable trunk line now connects switching centers in most of the regions; the others are connected by digital microwave radio relay
*international:* country code - 359; submarine cable provides connectivity to Ukraine and Russia; a combination submarine cable and land fiber-optic system provides connectivity to Italy, Albania, and Macedonia; satellite earth stations - 3 (1 Intersputnik in the Atlantic Ocean region, 2 Intelsat in the Atlantic and Indian Ocean regions) (2007)
**Radio broadcast stations:** AM 31, FM 63, shortwave 2 (2001)
**Television broadcast stations:** 39 (plus 1,242 repeaters) (2001)
**Internet country code:** .bg
**Internet hosts:** 513,470 (2008)
**Internet users:** 1.899 million (2007)

## Transportation

**Airports:** 204 (2008)
**Airports - with paved runways:**
*total:* 127
*over 3,047 m:* 2
*2,438 to 3,047 m:* 18
*1,524 to 2,437 m:* 15
*under 914 m:* 92 (2008)
**Airports - with unpaved runways:**
*total:* 77
*1,524 to 2,437 m:* 1
*914 to 1,523 m:* 7
*under 914 m:* 69 (2008)
**Heliports:** 4 (2007)
**Pipelines:** gas 2,926 km; oil 339 km; refined products 156 km (2008)
**Railways:**
*total:* 4,294 km
*standard gauge:* 4,049 km 1.435-m gauge (2,710 km electrified)
*narrow gauge:* 245 km 0.760-m gauge (2006)

**Roadways:**
*total:* 40,231 km
*paved:* 39,587 km (includes 331 km of expressways)
*unpaved:* 644 km (2005)
**Waterways:** 470 km (2008)
**Merchant marine:**
*total:* 74
*by type:* bulk carrier 37, cargo 14, chemical tanker 5, container 6, liquefied gas 2, passenger/cargo 2, petroleum tanker 3, roll on/roll off 4, specialized tanker 1
*foreign-owned:* 65 (Germany 63, Ireland 1, Russia 1)
*registered in other countries:* 31 (Comoros 2, Malta 5, Panama 3, Saint Vincent and the Grenadines 15, Slovakia 6) (2008)
**Ports and terminals:** Burgas, Varna

## Military

**Military branches:** Bulgarian Armed Forces: Ground Forces, Naval Forces, Bulgarian Air Forces (Bulgarski Voennovazdyshni Sily, BVVS) (2009)
**Military service age and obligation:** 18-27 years of age for voluntary military service; as of May 2006, 67% of the Bulgarian Army comprised of professional soldiers; conscription ended January 2008; Air Forces and Naval Forces became fully professional at the end of 2006 (2008)
**Manpower available for military service:**
*males age 16-49:* 1,701,979
*females age 16-49:* 1,691,092 (2008 est.)
**Manpower fit for military service:**
*males age 16-49:* 1,351,312
*females age 16-49:* 1,381,017 (2009 est.)
**Manpower reaching militarily significant age annually:**
*male:* 38,263
*female:* 36,374 (2009 est.)
**Military expenditures:** 2.6% of GDP (2005 est.)

## Transnational Issues

**Disputes - international:** none
**Illicit drugs:** major European transshipment point for Southwest Asian heroin and, to a lesser degree, South American cocaine for the European market; limited producer of precursor chemicals; vulnerable to money laundering because of corruption, organized crime; some money laundering of drug-related proceeds through financial institutions (2008)

# Burkina Faso

## Introduction

**Background:** Burkina Faso (formerly Upper Volta) achieved independence from France in 1960. Repeated military coups during the 1970s and 1980s were followed by multiparty elections in the early 1990s. Current President Blaise COMPAORE came to power in a 1987 military coup and has won every election since then. Burkina Faso's high population density and limited natural resources result in poor economic prospects for the majority of its citizens. Recent unrest in Cote d'Ivoire and northern Ghana has hindered the ability of several hundred thousand seasonal Burkinabe farm workers to find employment in neighboring countries. In January 2008, Burkina Faso assumed a nonpermanent seat on the UN Security Council for the 2008-09 term.

## Geography

**Location:** Western Africa, north of Ghana
**Geographic coordinates:** 13 00 N, 2 00 W
**Map references:** Africa
**Area:**
*total:* 274,200 sq km
*land:* 273,800 sq km
*water:* 400 sq km
**Area - comparative:** slightly larger than Colorado
**Land boundaries:**
*total:* 3,193 km
*border countries:* Benin 306 km, Cote d'Ivoire 584 km, Ghana 549 km, Mali 1,000 km, Niger 628 km, Togo 126 km
**Coastline:** 0 km (landlocked)
**Maritime claims:** none (landlocked)
**Climate:** tropical; warm, dry winters; hot, wet summers
**Terrain:** mostly flat to dissected, undulating plains; hills in west and southeast

**Elevation extremes:**
*lowest point:* Mouhoun (Black Volta) River 200 m
*highest point:* Tena Kourou 749 m
**Natural resources:** manganese, limestone, marble; small deposits of gold, phosphates, pumice, salt
**Land use:**
*arable land:* 17.66%
*permanent crops:* 0.22%
*other:* 82.12% (2005)
**Irrigated land:** 250 sq km (2003)
**Total renewable water resources:** 17.5 cu km (2001)
**Freshwater withdrawal (domestic/industrial/agricultural):**
*total:* 0.8 cu km/yr (13%/1%/86%)
*per capita:* 60 cu m/yr (2000)
**Natural hazards:** recurring droughts
**Environment - current issues:** recent droughts and desertification severely affecting agricultural activities, population distribution, and the economy; overgrazing; soil degradation; deforestation
**Environment - international agreements:**
*party to:* Biodiversity, Climate Change, Climate Change-Kyoto Protocol, Desertification, Endangered Species, Hazardous Wastes, Law of the Sea, Marine Life Conservation, Ozone Layer Protection, Wetlands
*signed, but not ratified:* none of the selected agreements
**Geography - note:** landlocked savanna cut by the three principal rivers of the Black, Red, and White Voltas

## People

**Population:** 15,746,232
*note:* estimates for this country explicitly take into account the effects of excess mortality due to AIDS; this can result in lower life expectancy, higher infant mortality, higher death rates, lower population growth rates, and changes in the distribution of population by age and sex than would otherwise be expected (July 2009 est.)
**Age structure:**
*0-14 years:* 46.2% (male 3,646,661/female 3,621,648)
*15-64 years:* 51.3% (male 4,025,917/female 4,054,865)
*65 years and over:* 2.5% (male 156,895/female 240,246) (2009 est.)
**Median age:**
*total:* 16.8 years
*male:* 16.6 years
*female:* 17 years (2009 est.)
**Population growth rate:** 3.103% (2009 est.)
**Birth rate:** 44.33 births/1,000 population (2009 est.)
**Death rate:** 13.59 deaths/1,000 population (2008 est.)
**Net migration rate:** NA
**Urbanization:**
*urban population:* 20% of total population (2008)
*rate of urbanization:* 5% annual rate of change (2005-10 est.)

**Sex ratio:**
*at birth:* 1.03 male(s)/female
*under 15 years:* 1.01 male(s)/female
*15-64 years:* 0.99 male(s)/female
*65 years and over:* 0.65 male(s)/female
*total population:* 0.99 male(s)/female (2009 est.)
**Infant mortality rate:**
*total:* 84.49 deaths/1,000 live births
*male:* 92.09 deaths/1,000 live births
*female:* 76.66 deaths/1,000 live births (2009 est.)
**Life expectancy at birth:**
*total population:* 52.95 years
*male:* 51.04 years
*female:* 54.91 years (2009 est.)
**Total fertility rate:** 6.28 children born/woman (2009 est.)
**HIV/AIDS - adult prevalence rate:** 1.6% (2007 est.)
**HIV/AIDS - people living with HIV/AIDS:** 130,000 (2007 est.)
**HIV/AIDS - deaths:** 9,200 (2007 est.)
**Major infectious diseases:**
*degree of risk:* very high
*food or waterborne diseases:* bacterial and protozoal diarrhea, hepatitis A, and typhoid fever
*vectorborne disease:* malaria and yellow fever
*water contact disease:* schistosomiasis
*respiratory disease:* meningococcal meningitis
*animal contact disease:* rabies
*note:* highly pathogenic H5N1 avian influenza has been identified in this country; it poses a negligible risk with extremely rare cases possible among US citizens who have close contact with birds (2009)
**Nationality:**
*noun:* Burkinabe (singular and plural)
*adjective:* Burkinabe
**Ethnic groups:** Mossi over 40%, other approximately 60% (includes Gurunsi, Senufo, Lobi, Bobo, Mande, and Fulani)
**Religions:** Muslim 50%, indigenous beliefs 40%, Christian (mainly Roman Catholic) 10%
**Languages:** French (official), native African languages belonging to Sudanic family spoken by 90% of the population
**Literacy:**
*definition:* age 15 and over can read and write
*total population:* 21.8%
*male:* 29.4%
*female:* 15.2% (2003 est.)
**School life expectancy (primary to tertiary education):**
*total:* 5 years
*male:* 5 years
*female:* 4 years (2006)
**Education expenditures:** 4.2% of GDP (2006)

## Government

**Country name:**
*conventional long form:* none
*conventional short form:* Burkina Faso
*local long form:* none
*local short form:* Burkina Faso
*former:* Upper Volta, Republic of Upper Volta

# Burkina Faso *(continued)*

**Government type:** parliamentary republic
**Capital:**
*name:* Ouagadougou
*geographic coordinates:* 12 22 N, 1 31 W
*time difference:* UTC 0 (5 hours ahead of Washington, DC during Standard Time)
**Administrative divisions:** 45 provinces; Bale, Bam, Banwa, Bazega, Bougouriba, Boulgou, Boulkiemde, Comoe, Ganzourgou, Gnagna, Gourma, Houet, Ioba, Kadiogo, Kenedougou, Komondjari, Kompienga, Kossi, Koulpelogo, Kouritenga, Kourweogo, Leraba, Loroum, Mouhoun, Nahouri, Namentenga, Nayala, Noumbiel, Oubritenga, Oudalan, Passore, Poni, Sanguie, Sanmatenga, Seno, Sissili, Soum, Sourou, Tapoa, Tuy, Yagha, Yatenga, Ziro, Zondoma, Zoundweogo
**Independence:** 5 August 1960 (from France)
**National holiday:** Republic Day, 11 December (1958)
**Constitution:** approved by referendum 2 June 1991; formally adopted 11 June 1991; last amended January 2002
**Legal system:** based on French civil law system and customary law; has not accepted compulsory ICJ jurisdiction
**Suffrage:** 18 years of age; universal
**Executive branch:**
*chief of state:* President Blaise COMPAORE (since 15 October 1987)
*head of government:* Prime Minister Tertius ZONGO (since 4 June 2007)
*cabinet:* Council of Ministers appointed by the president on the recommendation of the prime minister
*elections:* president elected by popular vote for a five-year term (eligible for a second term); election last held 13 November 2005 (next to be held in 2010); in April 2000, the constitution was amended reducing the presidential term from seven to five years, enforceable as of 2005; prime minister appointed by the president with the consent of the legislature
*election results:* Blaise COMPAORE reelected president; percent of popular vote - Blaise COMPAORE 80.3%, Benewende Stanislas SANKARA 4.9%
**Legislative branch:** unicameral National Assembly or Assemblee Nationale (111 seats; members are elected by popular vote to serve five-year terms)
*elections:* National Assembly election last held 6 May 2007 (next to be held in May 2012)
*election results:* percent of vote by party - NA; seats by party - CDP 73, ADF-RDA 14, UPR 5, UNIR-MS 4, CFD-B 3, UPS 2, PDP-PS 2, RDB 2, PDS 2, PAREN 1, PAI 1, RPC 1, UDPS 1
**Judicial branch:** Supreme Court; Appeals Court
**Political parties and leaders:** African Democratic Rally-Alliance for Democracy and Federation or ADF-RDA [Gilbert OUEDRAOGO]; Citizen's Popular Rally or RPC [Antoine QUARE]; Coalition of Democratic Forces of Burkina or CFD-B [Amadou Diemdioda DICKO]; Congress for Democracy and Progress or CDP [Roch Marc-Christian KABORE];

Democratic and Popular Rally or RDP [Nana THIBAUT]; Movement for Tolerance and Progress or MTP [Nayabtigungou Congo KABORE]; Party for African Independence or PAI [Soumane TOURE]; Party for Democracy and Progress-Socialist Party or PDP-PS [Ali LANKOANDE]; Party for Democracy and Socialism or PDS [Felix SOUBEIGA]; Party for National Rebirth or PAREN [Jeanne TRAORE]; Rally for the Development of Burkina or RDB [Antoine KARGOUGOU]; Rally of Ecologists of Burkina Faso or RDEB [Ram OUEDRAGO]; Republican Party for Integration and Solidarity or PARIS; Union for Democracy and Social Progress or UDPS [Fidele HIEN]; Union for Rebirth - Sankarist Movement or UNIR-MS [Benewende STANISLAS]; Union for the Republic or UPR [Toussaint Abel COULIBALY]; Union of Sankarist Parties or UPS [Ernest Nongma OUEDRAOGO]
**Political pressure groups and leaders:** Burkinabe General Confederation of Labor or CGTB [Tole SAGNON]; Burkinabe Movement for Human Rights or MBDHP [Chrysigone ZOUGMORE]; Group of 14 February [Benewende STANISLAS]; National Confederation of Burkinabe Workers or CNTB [Laurent OUEDRAOGO]; National Organization of Free Unions or ONSL [Paul KABORE]
*other:* watchdog/political action groups throughout the country in both organizations and communities
**International organization participation:** ACCT, ACP, AfDB, AU, ECOWAS, Entente, FAO, FZ, G-77, IAEA, IBRD, ICAO, ICC, ICCt, ICRM, IDA, IDB, IFAD, IFC, IFRCS, ILO, IMF, Interpol, IOC, IOM, IPU, ISO (correspondent), ITSO, ITU, ITUC, MIGA, MONUC, NAM, OIC, OIF, OPCW, PCA, UN, UNAMID, UNCTAD, UNESCO, UNIDO, UNITAR, UNMIS, UNOCI, UNWTO, UPU, WADB (regional), WAEMU, WCL, WCO, WFTU, WHO, WIPO, WMO, WTO
**Diplomatic representation in the US:**
*chief of mission:* Ambassador Paramanga Ernest YONLI
*chancery:* 2340 Massachusetts Avenue NW, Washington, DC 20008
*telephone:* [1] (202) 332-5577
*FAX:* [1] (202) 667-1882
**Diplomatic representation from the US:**
*chief of mission:* Ambassador Jeanine E. JACKSON
*embassy:* 602 Avenue Raoul Follereau, Koulouba, Secteur 4
*mailing address:* 01 B. P. 35, Ouagadougou 01; pouch mail - US Department of State, 2440 Ouagadougou Place, Washington, DC 20521-2440
*telephone:* [226] 50-30-67-23
*FAX:* [226] 50-30-38-90
**Flag description:** two equal horizontal bands of red (top) and green with a yellow five-pointed star in the center
*note:* uses the popular pan-African colors of Ethiopia

## Economy

**Economy - overview:** One of the poorest countries in the world, landlocked Burkina Faso has few natural resources and a weak industrial base. About 90% of the population is engaged in subsistence agriculture, which is vulnerable to periodic drought. Cotton is the main cash crop and the government has joined with three other cotton producing countries in the region - Mali, Niger, and Chad - to lobby in the World Trade Organization for fewer subsidies to producers in other competing countries. Since 1998, Burkina Faso has embarked upon a gradual but successful privatization of state-owned enterprises. Having revised its investment code in 2004, Burkina Faso hopes to attract foreign investors. Thanks to this new code and other legislation favoring the mining sector, the country has seen an upswing in gold exploration and production. While the bitter internal crisis in neighboring Cote d'Ivoire is beginning to be resolved, it is still having a negative effect on Burkina Faso's trade and employment. Burkina Faso received a Millennium Challenge Corporation (MCC) threshold grant to improve girls' education at the primary school level, and signed an MCC compact that focuses on the areas of infrastructure, agriculture, and land reform in July 2008.
**GDP (purchasing power parity):**
$17.82 billion (2008 est.)
$17.05 billion (2007)
$16.46 billion (2006)
*note:* data are in 2008 US dollars
**GDP (official exchange rate):** $8.242 billion (2008 est.)
**GDP - real growth rate:**
4.5% (2008 est.)
3.6% (2007 est.)
5.5% (2006 est.)
**GDP - per capita (PPP):**
$1,200 (2008 est.)
$1,200 (2007 est.)
$1,100 (2006 est.)
*note:* data are in 2008 US dollars
**GDP - composition by sector:**
*agriculture:* 29.1%
*industry:* 19.9%
*services:* 51% (2008 est.)
**Labor force:** 5 million
*note:* a large part of the male labor force migrates annually to neighboring countries for seasonal employment (2003)
**Labor force - by occupation:**
*agriculture:* 90%
*industry and services:* 10% (2000 est.)
**Unemployment rate:**
77% (2004)
**Population below poverty line:** 46.4% (2004)
**Household income or consumption by percentage share:**
*lowest 10%:* 2.8%
*highest 10%:* 32.2% (2004)

# Burkina Faso *(continued)*

**Distribution of family income - Gini index:** 39.5 (2007)
**Investment (gross fixed):** 24.5% of GDP (2008 est.)
**Budget:**
*revenues:* $1.799 billion
*expenditures:* $2.337 billion (2008 est.)
**Inflation rate (consumer prices):**
7.3% (2008 est.)
-0.2% (2007 est.)
**Central bank discount rate:** 4.25% (31 December 2007)
**Commercial bank prime lending rate:** NA
**Stock of money:** $1.051 billion (31 December 2007)
**Stock of quasi money:** $663 million (31 December 2007)
**Stock of domestic credit:** $905.1 million (31 December 2007)
**Market value of publicly traded shares:** $NA
**Agriculture - products:** cotton, peanuts, shea nuts, sesame, sorghum, millet, corn, rice; livestock
**Industries:** cotton lint, beverages, agricultural processing, soap, cigarettes, textiles, gold
**Industrial production growth rate:** 4.5% (2008 est.)
**Electricity - production:** 611.6 million kWh (2007 est.)
**Electricity - consumption:** 509.3 million kWh (2006 est.)
**Electricity - exports:** 0 kWh (2007 est.)
**Electricity - imports:** 0 kWh (2007 est.)
**Oil - production:** 0 bbl/day (2007 est.)
**Oil - consumption:** 8,470 bbl/day (2006 est.)
**Oil - exports:** 0 bbl/day (2005)
**Oil - imports:** 8,446 bbl/day (2005)
**Oil - proved reserves:** 0 bbl (1 January 2006 est.)
**Natural gas - production:** 0 cu m (2007 est.)
**Natural gas - consumption:** 0 cu m (2007 est.)
**Natural gas - exports:** 0 cu m (2007 est.)
**Natural gas - imports:** 0 cu m (2007 est.)
**Natural gas - proved reserves:** 0 cu m (1 January 2006 est.)
**Current account balance:** -$908 million (2008 est.)
**Exports:** $809 million f.o.b. (2008 est.)
**Exports - commodities:** cotton, livestock, gold
**Exports - partners:** China 29.6%, Singapore 15.7%, Thailand 7.2%, Ghana 6.4%, Niger 4.8% (2007)
**Imports:** $1.665 billion f.o.b. (2008 est.)
**Imports - commodities:** capital goods, foodstuffs, petroleum
**Imports - partners:** Cote d'Ivoire 25.8%, France 20.6%, Togo 7.1% (2007)
**Reserves of foreign exchange and gold:** $1.264 billion (31 December 2008 est.)
**Debt - external:** $1.33 billion (2007)
**Exchange rates:** Communaute Financiere Africaine francs (XOF) per US dollar - 447.81 (2008 est.), 493.51 (2007), 522.59 (2006), 527.47 (2005), 528.29 (2004)

*note:* since 1 January 1999, the West African CFA franc (XOF) has been pegged to the euro at a rate of 655.957 CFA francs per euro; West African CFA franc (XOF) coins and banknotes are not accepted in countries using Central African CFA francs (XAF), and vice versa, even though the two currencies trade at par

## Communications

**Telephones - main lines in use:** 94,800 (2006)
**Telephones - mobile cellular:** 1.611 million (2007)
**Telephone system:**
*general assessment:* services only fair; in 2006 the government sold a 51 percent stake in the national telephone company and ultimately plans to retain only a 23 percent stake in the company; fixed-line connections stand at less than 1 per 100 persons; mobile-cellular usage, fostered by multiple providers, is increasing rapidly from a low base
*domestic:* microwave radio relay, open-wire, and radiotelephone communication stations
*international:* country code - 226; satellite earth station -1 Intelsat (Atlantic Ocean) (2007)
**Radio broadcast stations:** AM 2, FM 26, shortwave 3 (2007)
**Television broadcast stations:** 3 (1 national, 2 private)
**Internet country code:** .bf
**Internet hosts:** 116 (2008)
**Internet users:** 80,000 (2006)

## Transportation

**Airports:** 26 (2008)
**Airports - with paved runways:**
*total:* 2
*over 3,047 m:* 1
*2,438 to 3,047 m:* 1 (2008)
**Airports - with unpaved runways:**
*total:* 24
*1,524 to 2,437 m:* 4
*914 to 1,523 m:* 12
*under 914 m:* 8 (2008)
**Railways:**
*total:* 622 km
*narrow gauge:* 622 km 1.000-m gauge
*note:* another 660 km of this railway extends into Cote d'Ivoire (2006)
**Roadways:**
*total:* 92,495 km
*paved:* 3,857 km
*unpaved:* 88,638 km (2004)

## Military

**Military branches:** Army, Air Force of Burkina Faso (Force Aerienne de Burkina Faso, FABF), National Gendarmerie (2009)
**Military service age and obligation:** 18 years of age for voluntary military service; women may serve in supporting roles (2009)

**Manpower available for military service:**
*males age 16-49:* 3,364,288 (2008 est.)
**Manpower fit for military service:**
*males age 16-49:* 2,197,557
*females age 16-49:* 2,191,978 (2009 est.)
**Manpower reaching militarily significant age annually:**
*male:* 182,540
*female:* 180,051 (2009 est.)
**Military expenditures:** 1.2% of GDP (2006)

## Transnational Issues

**Disputes - international:** in September 2007, Economic Community of West African States (ECOWAS) intervened to attempt to resolve the dispute over two villages along the Benin-Burkina Faso border that remain from a 2005 ICJ decision; in recent years citizens and rogue security forces rob and harass local populations on both sides of the poorly defined Burkina Faso-Niger border; despite the presence of more than 9,000 UN forces (UNOCI) in Cote d'Ivoire since 2004, ethnic conflict continues to spread into neighboring states who can no longer send their migrant workers to work in Ivorian cocoa plantations

# Burma

## Introduction

**Background:** Britain conquered Burma over a period of 62 years (1824-1886) and incorporated it into its Indian Empire. Burma was administered as a province of India until 1937 when it became a separate, self-governing colony; independence from the Commonwealth was attained in 1948. Gen. NE WIN dominated the government from 1962 to 1988, first as military ruler, then as self-appointed president, and later as political kingpin. In September 1988, the military deposed NE WIN and established a new ruling junta. Despite multiparty legislative elections in 1990 that resulted in the main opposition party - the National League for Democracy (NLD) - winning a landslide victory, the junta refused to hand over power. NLD leader and Nobel Peace Prize recipient AUNG SAN SUU KYI, who was under house arrest from 1989 to 1995 and 2000 to 2002, was imprisoned in May 2003 and subsequently transferred to house arrest. After the ruling junta in August 2007 unexpectedly increased fuel prices, tens of thousands of Burmese marched in protest, led by prodemocracy activists and Buddhist monks. In late September 2007, the government brutally suppressed the protests, killing at least 13 people and arresting thousands for participating in the demonstrations. Since then, the regime has continued to raid homes and monasteries and arrest persons suspected of participating in the pro-democracy protests. The junta appointed Labor Minister AUNG KYI in October 2007 as liaison to AUNG SAN SUU KYI, who remains under house arrest and virtually incommunicado with her party and supporters. Burma in early May 2008 was struck by Cyclone Nargis which official estimates claimed left over 80,000 dead and 50,000 injured. Despite this tragedy, the junta proceeded with its May constitutional referendum, the first vote in Burma since 1990, setting the stage for the 2010 parliamentary elections.

## Geography

**Location:** Southeastern Asia, bordering the Andaman Sea and the Bay of Bengal, between Bangladesh and Thailand

**Geographic coordinates:** 22 00 N, 98 00 E

**Map references:** Southeast Asia

**Area:**
*total:* 678,500 sq km
*land:* 657,740 sq km
*water:* 20,760 sq km

**Area - comparative:** slightly smaller than Texas

**Land boundaries:**
*total:* 5,876 km
*border countries:* Bangladesh 193 km, China 2,185 km, India 1,463 km, Laos 235 km, Thailand 1,800 km

**Coastline:** 1,930 km

**Maritime claims:**
*territorial sea:* 12 nm
*contiguous zone:* 24 nm
*exclusive economic zone:* 200 nm
*continental shelf:* 200 nm or to the edge of the continental margin

**Climate:** tropical monsoon; cloudy, rainy, hot, humid summers (southwest monsoon, June to September); less cloudy, scant rainfall, mild temperatures, lower humidity during winter (northeast monsoon, December to April)

**Terrain:** central lowlands ringed by steep, rugged highlands

**Elevation extremes:**
*lowest point:* Andaman Sea 0 m
*highest point:* Hkakabo Razi 5,881 m

**Natural resources:** petroleum, timber, tin, antimony, zinc, copper, tungsten, lead, coal, marble, limestone, precious stones, natural gas, hydropower

**Land use:**
*arable land:* 14.92%
*permanent crops:* 1.31%
*other:* 83.77% (2005)

**Irrigated land:** 18,700 sq km (2003)

**Total renewable water resources:** 1,045.6 cu km (1999)

**Freshwater withdrawal (domestic/industrial/agricultural):**
*total:* 33.23 cu km/yr (1%/1%/98%)
*per capita:* 658 cu m/yr (2000)

**Natural hazards:** destructive earthquakes and cyclones; flooding and landslides common during rainy season (June to September); periodic droughts

**Environment - current issues:** deforestation; industrial pollution of air, soil, and water; inadequate sanitation and water treatment contribute to disease

**Environment - international agreements:**
*party to:* Biodiversity, Climate Change, Climate Change-Kyoto Protocol, Desertification, Endangered Species, Law of the Sea, Ozone Layer Protection, Ship Pollution, Tropical Timber 83, Tropical Timber 94
*signed, but not ratified:* none of the selected agreements

**Geography - note:** strategic location near major Indian Ocean shipping lanes

## People

**Population:** 48,137,741
*note:* estimates for this country take into account the effects of excess mortality due to AIDS; this can result in lower life expectancy, higher infant mortality, higher death rates, lower population growth rates, and changes in the distribution of population by age and sex than would otherwise be expected (July 2009 est.)

**Age structure:**
*0-14 years:* 25.3% (male 6,193,263/female 5,990,658)
*15-64 years:* 69.3% (male 16,510,648/female 16,828,462)
*65 years and over:* 5.4% (male 1,121,412/female 1,493,298) (2009 est.)

**Median age:**
*total:* 28.2 years
*male:* 27.7 years
*female:* 28.8 years (2009 est.)

**Population growth rate:** 0.783% (2009 est.)
**Birth rate:** 16.97 births/1,000 population (2009 est.)
**Death rate:** 9.23 deaths/1,000 population (2008 est.)
**Net migration rate:** NA

**Urbanization:**
*urban population:* 33% of total population (2008)
*rate of urbanization:* 2.9% annual rate of change (2005-10 est.)

**Sex ratio:**
*at birth:* 1.06 male(s)/female
*under 15 years:* 1.03 male(s)/female
*15-64 years:* 0.98 male(s)/female
*65 years and over:* 0.75 male(s)/female
*total population:* 0.98 male(s)/female (2009 est.)

**Infant mortality rate:**
*total:* 47.61 deaths/1,000 live births
*male:* 53.78 deaths/1,000 live births
*female:* 41.07 deaths/1,000 live births (2009 est.)

**Life expectancy at birth:**
*total population:* 63.39 years
*male:* 61.17 years
*female:* 65.74 years (2009 est.)

**Total fertility rate:** 1.89 children born/woman (2009 est.)

# Burma (continued)

**HIV/AIDS - adult prevalence rate:** 0.7% (2007 est.)
**HIV/AIDS - people living with HIV/AIDS:** 240,000 (2007 est.)
**HIV/AIDS - deaths:** 25,000 (2007 est.)
**Major infectious diseases:**
*degree of risk:* very high
*food or waterborne diseases:* bacterial and protozoal diarrhea, hepatitis A, and typhoid fever
*vectorborne diseases:* dengue fever and malaria
*water contact disease:* leptospirosis
*animal contact disease:* rabies
*note:* highly pathogenic H5N1 avian influenza has been identified in this country; it poses a negligible risk with extremely rare cases possible among US citizens who have close contact with birds (2009)
**Nationality:**
*noun:* Burmese (singular and plural)
*adjective:* Burmese
**Ethnic groups:** Burman 68%, Shan 9%, Karen 7%, Rakhine 4%, Chinese 3%, Indian 2%, Mon 2%, other 5%
**Religions:** Buddhist 89%, Christian 4% (Baptist 3%, Roman Catholic 1%), Muslim 4%, animist 1%, other 2%
**Languages:** Burmese, minority ethnic groups have their own languages
**Literacy:**
*definition:* age 15 and over can read and write
*total population:* 89.9%
*male:* 93.9%
*female:* 86.4% (2006 est.)
**School life expectancy (primary to tertiary education):**
*total:* 8 years
*male:* 8 years
*female:* 8 years (2001)
**Education expenditures:** 1.2% of GDP (2001)

## Government

**Country name:**
*conventional long form:* Union of Burma
*conventional short form:* Burma
*local long form:* Pyidaungzu Myanma Naingngandaw (translated by the US Government as Union of Myanmar and by the Burmese as Union of Myanmar)
*local short form:* Myanma Naingngandaw
*former:* Socialist Republic of the Union of Burma
*note:* since 1989 the military authorities in Burma have promoted the name Myanmar as a conventional name for their state; this decision was not approved by any sitting legislature in Burma, and the US Government did not adopt the name, which is a derivative of the Burmese short-form name Myanma Naingngandaw
**Government type:** military junta
**Capital:**
*name:* Rangoon (Yangon)
*geographic coordinates:* 16 48 N, 96 09 E
*time difference:* UTC+6.5 (11.5 hours ahead of Washington, DC during Standard Time)
*note:* Nay Pyi Taw is administrative capital

**Administrative divisions:** 7 divisions (taing-myar, singular - taing) and 7 states* (pyi ne-myar, singular - pyi ne)
*divisions:* Ayeyarwady, Bago, Magway, Mandalay, Sagaing, Tanintharyi, Yangon
*states:* Chin, Kachin, Kayah, Kayin, Mon, Rakhine, Shan
**Independence:** 4 January 1948 (from the UK)
**National holiday:** Independence Day, 4 January (1948); Union Day, 12 February (1947)
**Constitution:** 3 January 1974; suspended since 18 September 1988; a new constitution was approved on 10 May 2008; note - new constitution will take effect when a new parliament is convened following elections scheduled for 2010
**Legal system:** based on English common law; has not accepted compulsory ICJ jurisdiction
**Suffrage:** 18 years of age; universal
**Executive branch:**
*chief of state:* Chairman of the State Peace and Development Council (SPDC) Sr. Gen. THAN SHWE (since 23 April 1992)
*head of government:* Prime Minister, Lt. Gen THEIN SEIN (since 24 October 2007)
*cabinet:* Cabinet is overseen by SPDC; military junta assumed power 18 September 1988 under name State Law and Order Restoration Council (SLORC)
*elections:* none
**Legislative branch:** a unicameral People's Assembly or Pyithu Hluttaw consisting of 485 seats with members elected by popular vote was elected in 1990 but was never seated; according to the terms of the constitution approved on 10 May 2008, a bicameral Pyidaungsu Hluttaw consisting of an upper house with a maximum of 224 seats and a lower house with a maximum of 440 seats will be selected in elections in 2010
*elections:* last held 27 May 1990, but Assembly never allowed by junta to convene (junta has announced plans to hold elections in 2010)
*election results:* percent of vote by party - NA; seats by party - NLD 392 (opposition), SNLD 23 (opposition), NUP 10 (pro-government), other 60
**Judicial branch:** remnants of the British-era legal system are in place, but there is no guarantee of a fair public trial; the judiciary is not independent of the executive
**Political parties and leaders:** National League for Democracy or NLD [AUNG SHWE, AUNG SAN SUU KYI]; National Unity Party or NUP (pro-regime) [TUN YE]; Shan Nationalities League for Democracy or SNLD [HKUN HTUN OO]; and numerous other smaller parties
**Political pressure groups and leaders:** Ethnic Nationalities Council or ENC (based in Thailand); Federation of Trade Unions-Burma or FTUB (exile trade union and labor advocates); National Coalition Government of the Union of Burma or NCGUB (self-proclaimed government in exile) ["Prime Minister" Dr. SEIN WIN] consists of individuals, some legitimately elected to the People's Assembly in 1990 (the group fled to a border area and joined insurgents

in December 1990 to form parallel government in exile); Kachin Independence Organization or KIO; Karen National Union or KNU; Karenni National People's Party or KNPP; National Council-Union of Burma or NCUB (exile coalition of opposition groups); United Wa State Army or UWSA; Union Solidarity and Development Association or USDA (pro-regime, a social and political mass-member organization) [HTAY OO, general secretary]; 88 Generation Students (pro-democracy movement) [TOE KYAW HLAING]
*other:* several Shan factions
**International organization participation:** ADB, APT, ARF, ASEAN, BIMSTEC, CP, EAS, FAO, G-77, IAEA, IBRD, ICAO, ICRM, IDA, IFAD, IFC, IFRCS, IHO, ILO, IMF, IMO, Interpol, IOC, ISO (correspondent), ITU, NAM, OPCW (signatory), SAARC (observer), UN, UNCTAD, UNESCO, UNIDO, UPU, WCO, WFTU, WHO, WIPO, WMO, WTO
**Diplomatic representation in the US:**
*chief of mission:* Ambassador (vacant); Charge d'Affaires MYINT LWIN
*chancery:* 2300 S Street NW, Washington, DC 20008
*telephone:* [1] (202) 332-3344
*FAX:* [1] (202) 332-4351
*consulate(s) general:* New York
**Diplomatic representation from the US:**
*chief of mission:* Charge d'Affaires Larry M. DINGER - note: The United States does not maintain an ambassador in Burma
*embassy:* 110 University Avenue, Kamayut Township, Rangoon
*mailing address:* Box B, APO AP 96546
*telephone:* [95] (1) 536-509, 535-756, 538-038
*FAX:* [95] (1) 650-306
**Flag description:** red with a blue rectangle in the upper hoist-side corner bearing 14, white, five-pointed stars encircling a cogwheel containing a stalk of rice; the 14 stars represent the seven administrative divisions and seven states

## Economy

**Economy - overview:** Burma, a resource-rich country, suffers from pervasive government controls, inefficient economic policies, and rural poverty. Despite Burma's increasing oil and gas revenue, socio-economic conditions have deteriorated because of the regime's mismanagement of the economy. The economy suffers from serious macroeconomic imbalances - including rising inflation, fiscal deficits, multiple official exchange rates that overvalue the Burmese kyat, a distorted interest rate regime, unreliable statistics, and an inability to reconcile national accounts to determine a realistic GDP figure. Most overseas development assistance ceased after the junta began to suppress the democracy movement in 1988 and subsequently refused to honor the results of the 1990 legislative elections. In response to the government of Burma's attack in May 2003 on AUNG SAN SUU KYI and her convoy, the US imposed new economic sanctions in August 2003 including a ban on imports of Burmese products and a ban on provision of financial services by US persons. Further, a poor investment climate hampers the inflow of foreign investment. Foreign investors have shied away from nearly every sector except for natural gas and power generation. The business climate is widely perceived as opaque, corrupt, and highly inefficient. The most productive sectors will continue to be in extractive industries - especially oil and gas, mining, and timber - with the latter causing significant environmental degradation. Other areas, such as manufacturing and services, are struggling with inadequate infrastructure, unpredictable import/export policies, deteriorating health and education systems, and endemic corruption. A major banking crisis in 2003 shuttered 20 private banks and disrupted the economy. As of 2008, the largest private banks operated under tight restrictions, limiting the private sector's access to formal credit. The September 2007 crackdown on prodemocracy demonstrators, including thousands of monks, strained the economy as the tourism industry, which directly employs about 500,000 people, suffered dramatic declines in foreign visitor levels. In November 2007, the European Union announced new sanctions banning investment and trade in Burmese gems, timber, and precious stones, while the United States expanded its sanctions list to include more Burmese government and military officials and their family members, as well as prominent regime business cronies, their family members, and associated companies. Official statistics are inaccurate. In July 2008 the President signed into law the Tom Lantos JADE (Junta's Anti-Democratic Efforts) Act of 2008, imposing new targeted sanctions on the regime. Published statistics on foreign trade are greatly understated because of the size of the black market and unofficial border trade -often estimated to be as large as the official economy. Though the Burmese government has good economic relations with its neighbors, better investment and business climates and an improved political situation are needed to promote serious foreign investment, exports, and tourism.

**GDP (purchasing power parity):**
$55.04 billion (2008 est.)
$54.55 billion (2007)
$52.76 billion (2006)
*note:* data are in 2008 US dollars
**GDP (official exchange rate):** $13.7 billion (2008 est.)
**GDP - real growth rate:**
0.9% (2008 est.)
3.4% (2007 est.)
3.4% (2006 est.)
**GDP - per capita (PPP):**
$1,200 (2008 est.)
$1,200 (2007 est.)
$1,100 (2006 est.)
*note:* data are in 2008 US dollars

**GDP - composition by sector:**
*agriculture:* 40.9%
*industry:* 19.7%
*services:* 39.3% (2008 est.)
**Labor force:** 30.04 million (2008 est.)
**Labor force - by occupation:**
*agriculture:* 70%
*industry:* 7%
*services:* 23% (2001)
**Unemployment rate:**
9.4% (2008 est.)
5.2% (2007 est.)
**Population below poverty line:** 32.7% (2007 est.)
**Household income or consumption by percentage share:**
*lowest 10%:* 2.8%
*highest 10%:* 32.4% (1998)
**Investment (gross fixed):** 14.1% of GDP (2008 est.)
**Budget:**
*revenues:* $983.6 million
*expenditures:* $1.775 billion (2008 est.)
**Inflation rate (consumer prices):**
27.3% (2008 est.)
35% (2007 est.)
**Central bank discount rate:** 12% (31 December 2007)
**Commercial bank prime lending rate:** 17% (31 December 2007)
**Stock of money:** $598 billion
*note:* this number reflects the vastly overvalued official exchange rate of 5.38 kyat per dollar; at the unofficial black market rate of 1305 kyat per dollar, the stock of kyats would equal only US$2.465 billion and Burma's velocity of money (the number of times money turns over in the course of a year) would be six, in line with the velocity of money for other countries in the region (31 December 2007)
**Stock of quasi money:** $216.9 billion (31 December 2007)
**Stock of domestic credit:** $887.7 billion (31 December 2007)
**Market value of publicly traded shares:** $NA
**Agriculture - products:** rice, pulses, beans, sesame, groundnuts, sugarcane; hardwood; fish and fish products
**Industries:** agricultural processing; wood and wood products; copper, tin, tungsten, iron; cement, construction materials; pharmaceuticals; fertilizer; oil and natural gas; garments, jade and gems
**Industrial production growth rate:** 7.1% (2008 est.)
**Electricity - production:** 5.961 billion kWh (2006 est.)
**Electricity - consumption:** 4.289 billion kWh (2006 est.)
**Electricity - exports:** 0 kWh (2007 est.)
**Electricity - imports:** 0 kWh (2007 est.)
**Oil - production:** 21,900 bbl/day (2007 est.)
**Oil - consumption:** 43,140 bbl/day (2006 est.)
**Oil - exports:** 5,000 bbl/day (2006 est.)

**Oil - imports:** 22,180 bbl/day (2005 est.)
**Oil - proved reserves:** 50 million bbl (1 January 2008 est.)
**Natural gas - production:** 12.6 billion cu m (2006 est.)
**Natural gas - consumption:** 3.62 billion cu m (2006 est.)
**Natural gas - exports:** 9.9 billion cu m (2007 est.)
**Natural gas - imports:** 0 cu m (2007 est.)
**Natural gas - proved reserves:** 283.2 billion cu m (1 January 2008 est.)
**Current account balance:** $762 million (2008 est.)
**Exports:** $6.149 billion f.o.b.
*note:* official export figures are grossly underestimated due to the value of timber, gems, narcotics, rice, and other products smuggled to Thailand, China, and Bangladesh (2008 est.)
**Exports - commodities:** natural gas, wood products, pulses, beans, fish, rice, clothing, jade and gems
**Exports - partners:** Thailand 44.3%, India 14.5%, China 7.1%, Japan 5.7% (2007)
**Imports:** $3.589 billion f.o.b.
*note:* import figures are grossly underestimated due to the value of consumer goods, diesel fuel, and other products smuggled in from Thailand, China, Malaysia, and India (2008 est.)
**Imports - commodities:** fabric, petroleum products, fertilizer, plastics, machinery, transport equipment; cement, construction materials, crude oil; food products, edible oil
**Imports - partners:** China 33.7%, Thailand 19.1%, Singapore 15.5%, South Korea 5.8%, Indonesia 5.2%, Malaysia 4.2% (2007)
**Reserves of foreign exchange and gold:** $2.262 billion (31 December 2008 est.)
**Debt - external:** $7.17 billion (31 December 2008 est.)
**Exchange rates:** kyats (MMK) per US dollar - 1,205 (2008 est.), 1,296 (2007), 1,280 (2006), 5.761 (2005), 5.7459 (2004)
*note:* unofficial exchange rates ranged in 2004 from 815 kyat/US dollar to nearly 970 kyat/US dollar, and by yearend 2005, the unofficial exchange rate was 1,075 kyat/US dollar; data shown for 2003-05 are official exchange rates

## Communications

**Telephones - main lines in use:** 503,900 (2005)
**Telephones - mobile cellular:** 214,200 (2006)
**Telephone system:**
*general assessment:* meets minimum requirements for local and intercity service for business and government
*domestic:* system barely capable of providing basic service; cellular phone system is grossly underdeveloped with a subscribership base of less than 1 per 100 persons
*international:* country code - 95; landing point for the SEA-ME-WE-3 optical telecommunications submarine cable that provides links to Asia, the Middle East, and Europe; satellite earth stations - 2, Intelsat (Indian Ocean) and ShinSat (2007)

# Burma (continued)

**Radio broadcast stations:** AM 1, FM 2, shortwave 3 (2007)
**Television broadcast stations:** 4 (2008)
**Internet country code:** .mm
**Internet hosts:** 108 (2008)
**Internet users:** 40,000 (2007)

## Transportation

**Airports:** 84 (2008)
**Airports - with paved runways:**
*total:* 31
*over 3,047 m:* 10
*2,438 to 3,047 m:* 10
*1,524 to 2,437 m:* 9
*under 914 m:* 2 (2008)
**Airports - with unpaved runways:**
*total:* 53
*over 3,047 m:* 1
*1,524 to 2,437 m:* 9
*914 to 1,523 m:* 13
*under 914 m:* 30 (2008)
**Heliports:** 4 (2007)
**Pipelines:** gas 2,228 km; oil 558 km (2008)
**Railways:**
*total:* 3,955 km
*narrow gauge:* 3,955 km 1.000-m gauge (2006)
**Roadways:**
*total:* 27,000 km
*paved:* 3,200 km
*unpaved:* 23,800 km (2006)
**Waterways:** 12,800 km (2008)
**Merchant marine:**
*total:* 24
*by type:* bulk carrier 1, cargo 17, passenger 2, passenger/cargo 3, specialized tanker 1
*foreign-owned:* 3 (Cyprus 1, Germany 1, Japan 1)
*registered in other countries:* 1 (Panama 1) (2008)
**Ports and terminals:** Moulmein, Rangoon, Sittwe

## Military

**Military branches:** Myanmar Armed Forces (Tatmadaw): Army, Navy, Air Force (Tatmadaw Lay) (2008)
**Military service age and obligation:** 18 years of age for voluntary military service for both sexes; forced conscription of children, although officially prohibited, reportedly continues (2007)
**Manpower available for military service:**
*males age 16-49:* 13,402,788
*females age 16-49:* 13,437,042 (2008 est.)
**Manpower fit for military service:**
*males age 16-49:* 9,146,312
*females age 16-49:* 9,520,852 (2009 est.)
**Manpower reaching militarily significant age annually:**
*male:* 426,110
*female:* 417,674 (2009 est.)
**Military expenditures:** 2.1% of GDP (2005 est.)

## Transnational Issues

**Disputes - international:** over half of Burma's population consists of diverse ethnic groups who have substantial numbers of kin in neighboring countries; Thailand must deal with Karen and other ethnic refugees, asylum seekers, and rebels, as well as illegal cross-border activities from Burma; Thailand is studying the feasibility of jointly constructing the Hatgyi Dam on the Salween River near the border with Burma; citing environmental, cultural, and social concerns, China is reconsidering construction of 13 dams on the Salween River but energy-starved Burma with backing from Thailand remains intent on building five hydro-electric dams downstream, despite identical regional and international protests; India seeks cooperation from Burma to keep Indian Nagaland separatists, such as the United Liberation Front of Assam, from hiding in remote Burmese Uplands; after 21 years, Bangladesh resumes talks with Burma on delimiting a maritime boundary in January 2008
**Refugees and internally displaced persons:**
*IDPs:* 503,000 (government offensives against ethnic insurgent groups near the eastern borders; most IDPs are ethnic Karen, Karenni, Shan, Tavoyan, and Mon) (2007)
**Trafficking in persons:**
*current situation:* Burma is a source country for women, children, and men trafficked for the purpose of forced labor and commercial sexual exploitation; Burmese women and children are trafficked to East and Southeast Asia for commercial sexual exploitation, domestic servitude, and forced labor; Burmese children are subjected to conditions of forced labor in Thailand as hawkers, beggars, and for work in shops, agriculture, fish processing, and small-scale industries; women are trafficked for commercial sexual exploitation to Malaysia and China; some trafficking victims transit Burma from Bangladesh to Malaysia and from China to Thailand; internal trafficking occurs primarily from villages to urban centers and economic hubs for labor in industrial zones, agricultural estates, and commercial sexual exploitation; military and civilian officials continue to use a significant amount of forced labor; ethnic insurgent groups also used compulsory labor of adults and unlawful recruitment of children; the military junta's gross economic mismanagement, human rights abuses, and its policy of using forced labor are the top causal factors for Burma's significant trafficking problem
*tier rating:* Tier 3 - Burma does not fully comply with the minimum standards for the elimination of trafficking and is not making significant efforts to do so; military and civilian officials remain directly involved in significant acts of forced labor and unlawful conscription of child soldiers (2008)

**Illicit drugs:** remains world's second largest producer of illicit opium with an estimated production in 2008 of 340 metric tons, an increase of 26%, and poppy cultivation in 2008 totaled 22,500 hectares, a 4% increase from 2007; production in the United Wa State Army's areas of greatest control remains low; Shan state is the source of 94% of Burma's poppy cultivation; lack of government will to take on major narcotrafficking groups and lack of serious commitment against money laundering continues to hinder the overall antidrug effort; major source of methamphetamine and heroin for regional consumption (2008)

# Burundi

## Introduction

**Background:** Burundi's first democratically elected president was assassinated in October 1993 after only 100 days in office, triggering widespread ethnic violence between Hutu and Tutsi factions. More than 200,000 Burundians perished during the conflict that spanned almost a dozen years. Hundreds of thousands of Burundians were internally displaced or became refugees in neighboring countries. An internationally brokered power-sharing agreement between the Tutsi-dominated government and the Hutu rebels in 2003 paved the way for a transition process that led to an integrated defense force, established a new constitution in 2005, and elected a majority Hutu government in 2005. The new government, led by President Pierre NKURUNZIZA, signed a South African brokered ceasefire with the country's last rebel group in September of 2006 but still faces many challenges.

## Geography

**Location:** Central Africa, east of Democratic Republic of the Congo
**Geographic coordinates:** 3 30 S, 30 00 E
**Map references:** Africa
**Area:**
*total:* 27,830 sq km
*land:* 25,650 sq km
*water:* 2,180 sq km
**Area - comparative:** slightly smaller than Maryland
**Land boundaries:**
*total:* 974 km
*border countries:* Democratic Republic of the Congo 233 km, Rwanda 290 km, Tanzania 451 km
**Coastline:** 0 km (landlocked)
**Maritime claims:** none (landlocked)
**Climate:** equatorial; high plateau with considerable altitude variation (772 m to 2,670 m above sea level); average annual temperature varies with altitude from 23 to 17 degrees centigrade but is generally moderate as

the average altitude is about 1,700 m; average annual rainfall is about 150 cm; two wet seasons (February to May and September to November), and two dry seasons (June to August and December to January)
**Terrain:** hilly and mountainous, dropping to a plateau in east, some plains
**Elevation extremes:**
*lowest point:* Lake Tanganyika 772 m
*highest point:* Heha 2,670 m
**Natural resources:** nickel, uranium, rare earth oxides, peat, cobalt, copper, platinum, vanadium, arable land, hydropower, niobium, tantalum, gold, tin, tungsten, kaolin, limestone
**Land use:**
*arable land:* 35.57%
*permanent crops:* 13.12%
*other:* 51.31% (2005)
**Irrigated land:** 210 sq km (2003)
**Total renewable water resources:** 3.6 cu km (1987)
**Freshwater withdrawal (domestic/industrial/agricultural):**
*total:* 0.29 cu km/yr (17%/6%/77%)
*per capita:* 38 cu m/yr (2000)
**Natural hazards:** flooding; landslides; drought
**Environment - current issues:** soil erosion as a result of overgrazing and the expansion of agriculture into marginal lands; deforestation (little forested land remains because of uncontrolled cutting of trees for fuel); habitat loss threatens wildlife populations
**Environment - international agreements:**
*party to:* Biodiversity, Climate Change, Climate Change-Kyoto Protocol, Desertification, Endangered Species, Hazardous Wastes, Ozone Layer Protection, Wetlands
*signed, but not ratified:* Law of the Sea
**Geography - note:** landlocked; straddles crest of the Nile-Congo watershed; the Kagera, which drains into Lake Victoria, is the most remote headstream of the White Nile

## People

**Population:** 8,988,091
*note:* estimates for this country explicitly take into account the effects of excess mortality due to AIDS; this can result in lower life expectancy, higher infant mortality, higher death rates, lower population growth rates, and changes in the distribution of population by age and sex than would otherwise be expected (July 2009 est.)
**Age structure:**
*0-14 years:* 46.2% (male 2,087,315/female 2,063,518)
*15-64 years:* 51.3% (male 2,291,123/female 2,320,839)
*65 years and over:* 2.5% (male 89,444/female 135,852) (2009 est.)
**Median age:**
*total:* 16.7 years
*male:* 16.5 years
*female:* 17 years (2009 est.)

**Population growth rate:** 3.279% (2009 est.)
**Birth rate:** 41.42 births/1,000 population (2009 est.)
**Death rate:** 12.91 deaths/1,000 population (2008 est.)
**Net migration rate:** 4.04 migrant(s)/1,000 population (2009 est.)
**Urbanization:**
*urban population:* 10% of total population (2008)
*rate of urbanization:* 6.8% annual rate of change (2005-10 est.)
**Sex ratio:**
*at birth:* 1.03 male(s)/female
*under 15 years:* 1.01 male(s)/female
*15-64 years:* 0.99 male(s)/female
*65 years and over:* 0.66 male(s)/female
*total population:* 0.99 male(s)/female (2009 est.)
**Infant mortality rate:**
*total:* 59.64 deaths/1,000 live births
*male:* 66.32 deaths/1,000 live births
*female:* 52.76 deaths/1,000 live births (2009 est.)
**Life expectancy at birth:**
*total population:* 52.09 years
*male:* 51.2 years
*female:* 53.01 years (2009 est.)
**Total fertility rate:** 6.33 children born/woman (2009 est.)
**HIV/AIDS - adult prevalence rate:** 2% (2007 est.)
**HIV/AIDS - people living with HIV/AIDS:** 110,000 (2007 est.)
**HIV/AIDS - deaths:** 11,000 (2007 est.)
**Major infectious diseases:**
*degree of risk:* very high
*food or waterborne diseases:* bacterial and protozoal diarrhea, hepatitis A, and typhoid fever
*vectorborne disease:* malaria
*water contact disease:* schistosomiasis
*animal contact disease:* rabies (2009)
**Nationality:**
*noun:* Burundian(s)
*adjective:* Burundian
**Ethnic groups:** Hutu (Bantu) 85%, Tutsi (Hamitic) 14%, Twa (Pygmy) 1%, Europeans 3,000, South Asians 2,000
**Religions:** Christian 67% (Roman Catholic 62%, Protestant 5%), indigenous beliefs 23%, Muslim 10%
**Languages:** Kirundi (official), French (official), Swahili (along Lake Tanganyika and in the Bujumbura area)
**Literacy:**
*definition:* age 15 and over can read and write
*total population:* 59.3%
*male:* 67.3%
*female:* 52.2% (2000 est.)
**School life expectancy (primary to tertiary education):**
*total:* 7 years
*male:* 8 years
*female:* 7 years (2006)
**Education expenditures:** 5.1% of GDP (2005)

# Burundi (continued)

**Country name:**

*conventional long form:* Republic of Burundi

*conventional short form:* Burundi

*local long form:* Republique du Burundi/Republika y'u Burundi

*local short form:* Burundi

*former:* Urundi

**Government type:** republic

**Capital:**

*name:* Bujumbura

*geographic coordinates:* 3 22 S, 29 21 E

*time difference:* UTC+2 (7 hours ahead of Washington, DC during Standard Time)

**Administrative divisions:** 17 provinces; Bubanza, Bujumbura Mairie, Bujumbura Rurale, Bururi, Cankuzo, Cibitoke, Gitega, Karuzi, Kayanza, Kirundo, Makamba, Muramvya, Muyinga, Mwaro, Ngozi, Rutana, Ruyigi

**Independence:** 1 July 1962 (from UN trusteeship under Belgian administration)

**National holiday:** Independence Day, 1 July (1962)

**Constitution:** ratified by popular referendum 28 February 2005

**Legal system:** based on German and Belgian civil codes and customary law; has not accepted compulsory ICJ jurisdiction

**Suffrage:** 18 years of age; universal (adult)

**Executive branch:**

*chief of state:* President Pierre NKURUNZIZA (since 26 August 2005); First Vice President Yves SAVINGUVU - Tutsi (since 9 November 2007); Second Vice President Gabriel NTISEZERANA - Hutu (since 9 February 2007); note - the president is both the chief of state and head of government

*head of government:* President Pierre NKURUNZIZA (since 26 August 2005); First Vice President Yves SAVINGUVU - Tutsi (since 9 November 2007); Second Vice President Gabriel NTISEZERANA - Hutu (since 9 February 2007)

*cabinet:* Council of Ministers appointed by president

*elections:* the president is elected by popular vote to a five-year term (eligible for a second term); note - the constitution adopted in February 2005 permits the post-transition president to be elected by a two-thirds majority of the parliament; vice presidents nominated by the president, endorsed by parliament

*election results:* Pierre NKURUNZIZA was elected president by the parliament by a vote of 151 to 9; note -the constitution adopted in February 2005 permits the post-transition president to be elected by a two-thirds majority of the legislature

**Legislative branch:** bicameral Parliament or Parlement, consists of a Senate (54 seats; 34 members elected by indirect vote to serve five-year terms, with remaining seats assigned to ethnic groups and former chiefs of state) and a National Assembly or Assemblee Nationale (minimum 100 seats, 60% Hutu and 40% Tutsi with at least 30% being women; additional seats appointed by a National Independent Electoral Commission to ensure ethnic

representation; members are elected by popular vote to serve five-year terms)

*elections:* Senate - last held 29 July 2005 (next to be held in 2010); National Assembly - last held 4 July 2005 (next to be held in 2010)

*election results:* Senate - percent of vote by party - NA%; seats by party - CNDD-FDD 30, FRODEBU 3, CNDD 1; National Assembly - percent of vote by party -CNDD-FDD 58.6%, FRODEBU 21.7%, UPRONA 7.2%, CNDD 4.1%, MRC-Rurenzangemero 2.1%, others 6.2%; seats by party - CNDD-FDD 59, FRODEBU 25, UPRONA 10, CNDD 4, MRC-Rurenzangemero 2

**Judicial branch:** Supreme Court or Cour Supreme; Constitutional Court; High Court of Justice (composed of the Supreme Court and the Constitutional Court)

**Political parties and leaders:**

*governing parties:* Burundi Democratic Front or FRODEBU [Leonce NGENDAKUMANA]; National Council for the Defense of Democracy - Front for the Defense of Democracy or CNDD-FDD [Jeremie NGENDAKUMANA]; Unity for National Progress or UPRONA [Aloys RUBUKA]

*note:* a multiparty system was introduced after 1998, included are: National Council for the Defense of Democracy or CNDD [Leonard NYANGOMA]; National Resistance Movement for the Rehabilitation of the Citizen or MRC-Rurenzangemero [Epitace BANYAGANAKANDI]; Party for National Redress or PARENA [Jean-Baptiste BAGAZA]

**Political pressure groups and leaders:**

Observatoire de lutte contre la corruption et les malversations economiques or OLUCOME [Gabriel RUFYIRI] (anti-corruption pressure group)

*other:* Hutu and Tutsi militias (loosely organized)

**International organization participation:** ACCT, ACP, AfDB, AU, CEPGL, COMESA, EAC, FAO, G-77, IBRD, ICAO, ICCt, ICRM, IDA, IFAD, IFC, IFRCS, ILO, IMF, Interpol, IOC, IOM, IPU, ISO (subscriber), ITU, ITUC, MIGA, NAM, OIF, OPCW, UN, UNAMID, UNCTAD, UNESCO, UNIDO, UNWTO, UPU, WCO, WFTU, WHO, WIPO, WMO, WTO

**Diplomatic representation in the US:**

*chief of mission:* Ambassador Celestin NIYONGABO

*chancery:* Suite 212, 2233 Wisconsin Avenue NW, Washington, DC 20007

*telephone:* [1] (202) 342-2574

*FAX:* [1] (202) 342-2578

**Diplomatic representation from the US:**

*chief of mission:* Ambassador Patricia Newton MOLLER

*embassy:* Avenue des Etats-Unis, Bujumbura

*mailing address:* B. P. 1720, Bujumbura

*telephone:* [257] 223454

*FAX:* [257] 222926

**Flag description:** divided by a white diagonal cross into red panels (top and bottom) and green panels (hoist side and fly side) with a white disk superimposed at the center bearing three red six-pointed stars outlined in green arranged in a triangular design (one star above, two stars below)

**Economy - overview:** Burundi is a landlocked, resource-poor country with an underdeveloped manufacturing sector. The economy is predominantly agricultural with more than 90% of the population dependent on subsistence agriculture. Economic growth depends on coffee and tea exports, which account for 90% of foreign exchange earnings. The ability to pay for imports rests primarily on weather conditions and international coffee and tea prices. The Tutsi minority, 14% of the population, dominates the coffee trade. An ethnic-based war that lasted for over a decade resulted in more than 200,000 deaths, forced more than 48,000 refugees into Tanzania, and displaced 140,000 others internally. Only one in two children go to school, and approximately one in 15 adults has HIV/AIDS. Food, medicine, and electricity remain in short supply. Burundi's GDP grew around 4% annually in 2006-08. Political stability and the end of the civil war have improved aid flows and economic activity has increased, but underlying weaknesses - a high poverty rate, poor education rates, a weak legal system, and low administrative capacity - risk undermining planned economic reforms. Burundi will continue to remain heavily dependent on aid from bilateral and multilateral donors; the delay of funds after a corruption scandal cut off bilateral aid in 2007 reduced government's revenues and its ability to pay salaries.

**GDP (purchasing power parity):**

$3.103 billion (2008 est.)

$2.969 billion (2007)

$2.866 billion (2006)

*note:* data are in 2008 US dollars

**GDP (official exchange rate):** $903 million (2008 est.)

**GDP - real growth rate:**

4.5% (2008 est.)

3.6% (2007 est.)

5.1% (2006 est.)

**GDP - per capita (PPP):**

$400 (2008 est.)

$400 (2007 est.)

$400 (2006 est.)

*note:* data are in 2008 US dollars

**GDP - composition by sector:**

*agriculture:* 32.9%

*industry:* 21.3%

*services:* 45.8% (2008 est.)

**Labor force:** 2.99 million (2002)

**Labor force - by occupation:**

*agriculture:* 93.6%

*industry:* 2.3%

*services:* 4.1% (2002 est.)

**Unemployment rate:**

NA%

**Population below poverty line:** 68% (2002 est.)

**Household income or consumption by percentage share:**

*lowest 10%:* 1.7%

*highest 10%:* 32.8% (1998)

# Burundi (continued)

**Distribution of family income - Gini index:** 42.4 (1998)

**Investment (gross fixed):** 28.4% of GDP (2008 est.)

**Budget:**
*revenues:* $292.2 million
*expenditures:* $351.3 million; including capital expenditures of $NA (2008 est.)

**Inflation rate (consumer prices):**
12% (2008 est.)
8.3% (2007 est.)

**Central bank discount rate:** 10.12% (31 December 2007)

**Commercial bank prime lending rate:** 16.84% (31 December 2007)

**Stock of money:** $208.7 million (31 December 2007)

**Stock of quasi money:** $141 million (31 December 2007)

**Stock of domestic credit:** $342 million (31 December 2007)

**Market value of publicly traded shares:** $NA

**Agriculture - products:** coffee, cotton, tea, corn, sorghum, sweet potatoes, bananas, manioc (tapioca); beef, milk, hides

**Industries:** light consumer goods such as blankets, shoes, soap; assembly of imported components; public works construction; food processing

**Industrial production growth rate:** 8% (2008 est.)

**Electricity - production:** 87 million kWh (2006 est.)

**Electricity - consumption:** 120.9 million kWh (2006 est.)

**Electricity - exports:** 0 kWh (2007 est.)

**Electricity - imports:** 40 million kWh; note - supplied by the Democratic Republic of the Congo (2007 est.)

**Oil - production:** 0 bbl/day (2007 est.)

**Oil - consumption:** 2,956 bbl/day (2006 est.)

**Oil - exports:** 0 bbl/day (2005)

**Oil - imports:** 2,635 bbl/day (2005)

**Oil - proved reserves:** 0 bbl (1 January 2006 est.)

**Natural gas - production:** 0 cu m (2007 est.)

**Natural gas - consumption:** 0 cu m (2007 est.)

**Natural gas - exports:** 0 cu m (2007 est.)

**Natural gas - imports:** 0 cu m (2007 est.)

**Natural gas - proved reserves:** 0 cu m (1 January 2006 est.)

**Current account balance:** -$120 million (2008 est.)

**Exports:** $47 million f.o.b. (2008 est.)

**Exports - commodities:** coffee, tea, sugar, cotton, hides

**Exports - partners:** Germany 31.3%, Pakistan 6.8%, Belgium 5.8%, Sweden 4.3%, Rwanda 4.3%, France 4.2%, Sudan 4% (2007)

**Imports:** $307 million f.o.b. (2008 est.)

**Imports - commodities:** capital goods, petroleum products, foodstuffs

**Imports - partners:** Saudi Arabia 17%, Kenya 11.4%, Belgium 8.7%, France 6.1%, Uganda 5.4%, Germany 5.4%, India 4.8%, Pakistan 4.2% (2007)

**Reserves of foreign exchange and gold:** $134 million (31 December 2008 est.)

**Debt - external:** $1.2 billion (2003)

**Exchange rates:** Burundi francs (BIF) per US dollar -1,198 (2008 est.), 1,065 (2007), 1,030 (2006), 1,138 (2005), 1,100.91 (2004)

## Communications

**Telephones - main lines in use:** 35,000 (2006)

**Telephones - mobile cellular:** 250,000 (2007)

**Telephone system:**
*general assessment:* primitive system; telephone density one of the lowest in the world; fixed-line connections stand at well less than 1 per 100 persons; mobile-cellular usage is increasing but remains at a meager 3 per 100 persons
*domestic:* sparse system of open-wire, radiotelephone communications, and low-capacity microwave radio relay
*international:* country code - 257; satellite earth station -1 Intelsat (Indian Ocean) (2007)

**Radio broadcast stations:** AM 0, FM 4, shortwave 1 (2001)

**Television broadcast stations:** 1 (2001)

**Internet country code:** .bi

**Internet hosts:** 162 (2008)

**Internet users:** 60,000 (2006)

## Transportation

**Airports:** 8 (2008)

**Airports - with paved runways:**
*total:* 1
*over 3,047 m:* 1 (2008)

**Airports - with unpaved runways:**
*total:* 7
*914 to 1,523 m:* 4
*under 914 m:* 3 (2008)

**Heliports:** 1 (2007)

**Roadways:**
*total:* 12,322 km
*paved:* 1,286 km
*unpaved:* 11,036 km (2004)

**Waterways:** mainly on Lake Tanganyika (2008)

**Ports and terminals:** Bujumbura

## Military

**Military branches:** National Defense Force (Forces de Defense Nationales, FDN): Army (includes Naval Detachment and Air Wing), Gendarmerie (2008)

**Military service age and obligation:** 16 years of age for compulsory and voluntary military service; children as young as 10 years of age have been conscripted into the armed forces; the enrollment of children is still not prohibited (2007)

**Manpower available for military service:**
*males age 16-49:* 1,878,544
*females age 16-49:* 1,851,676 (2008 est.)

**Manpower fit for military service:**
*males age 16-49:* 1,124,072
*females age 16-49:* 1,102,729 (2009 est.)

**Manpower reaching militarily significant age annually:**
*male:* 101,402
*female:* 101,897 (2009 est.)

**Military expenditures:** 5.9% of GDP (2006 est.)

## Transnational Issues

**Disputes - international:** Burundi and Rwanda dispute sections of border on the Akanyaru/Kanyaru and the Kagera/Nyabarongo rivers, which have changed course since the 1960s, when the boundary was delimited; cross-border conflicts among Tutsi, Hutu, other ethnic groups, associated political rebels, armed gangs, and various government forces persist in the Great Lakes region

**Refugees and internally displaced persons:**
*refugees (country of origin):* 9,849 (Democratic Republic of the Congo)
*IDPs:* 100,000 (armed conflict between government and rebels; most IDPs in northern and western Burundi) (2007)

**Trafficking in persons:**
*current situation:* Burundi is a source country for children trafficked for the purposes of child soldiering, domestic servitude, and commercial sexual exploitation; a small number of Burundian children may be trafficked internally for domestic servitude or commercial sexual exploitation; in early 2008, Burundian children were allegedly trafficked to Uganda, via Rwanda, for agricultural labor and commercial sexual exploitation
*tier rating:* Tier 2 Watch List - Burundi is on the Tier 2 Watch List for the second consecutive year for its failure to provide sufficient evidence of increasing efforts to combat trafficking in persons in 2007; the government's inability to provide adequate protective services to children accused of association with armed groups and to conduct anti-trafficking law enforcement activities continue to be causes for concern; Burundi has not ratified the 2000 UN TIP Protocol (2008)

# Cambodia

## Introduction

**Background:** Most Cambodians consider themselves to be Khmers, descendants of the Angkor Empire that extended over much of Southeast Asia and reached its zenith between the 10th and 13th centuries. Attacks by the Thai and Cham (from present-day Vietnam) weakened the empire, ushering in a long period of decline. The king placed the country under French protection in 1863 and it became part of French Indochina in 1887. Following Japanese occupation in World War II, Cambodia gained full independence from France in 1953. In April 1975, after a five-year struggle, Communist Khmer Rouge forces captured Phnom Penh and evacuated all cities and towns. At least 1.5 million Cambodians died from execution, forced hardships, or starvation during the Khmer Rouge regime under POL POT. A December 1978 Vietnamese invasion drove the Khmer Rouge into the countryside, began a 10-year Vietnamese occupation, and touched off almost 13 years of civil war. The 1991 Paris Peace Accords mandated democratic elections and a ceasefire, which was not fully respected by the Khmer Rouge. UN-sponsored elections in 1993 helped restore some semblance of normalcy under a coalition government. Factional fighting in 1997 ended the first coalition government, but a second round of national elections in 1998 led to the formation of another coalition government and renewed political stability. The remaining elements of the Khmer Rouge surrendered in early 1999. Some of the surviving Khmer Rouge leaders are awaiting trial by a UN-sponsored tribunal for crimes against humanity. Elections in July 2003 were relatively peaceful, but it took one year of negotiations between contending political parties before a coalition government was formed. In October 2004, King Norodom SIHANOUK abdicated the throne and his son, Prince Norodom SIHAMONI, was selected to succeed him. Local elections were held in Cambodia in April 2007, and there was little in the way of pre-election violence that preceded prior elections. National elections in July 2008 were relatively peaceful.

## Geography

**Location:** Southeastern Asia, bordering the Gulf of Thailand, between Thailand, Vietnam, and Laos
**Geographic coordinates:** 13 00 N, 105 00 E
**Map references:** Southeast Asia
**Area:**
*total:* 181,040 sq km
*land:* 176,520 sq km
*water:* 4,520 sq km
**Area - comparative:** slightly smaller than Oklahoma
**Land boundaries:**
*total:* 2,572 km
*border countries:* Laos 541 km, Thailand 803 km, Vietnam 1,228 km
**Coastline:** 443 km
**Maritime claims:**
*territorial sea:* 12 nm
*contiguous zone:* 24 nm
*exclusive economic zone:* 200 nm
*continental shelf:* 200 nm
**Climate:** tropical; rainy, monsoon season (May to November); dry season (December to April); little seasonal temperature variation
**Terrain:** mostly low, flat plains; mountains in southwest and north
**Elevation extremes:**
*lowest point:* Gulf of Thailand 0 m
*highest point:* Phnum Aoral 1,810 m
**Natural resources:** oil and gas, timber, gemstones, iron ore, manganese, phosphates, hydropower potential
**Land use:**
*arable land:* 20.44%
*permanent crops:* 0.59%
*other:* 78.97% (2005)
**Irrigated land:** 2,700 sq km (2003)
**Total renewable water resources:** 476.1 cu km (1999)
**Freshwater withdrawal (domestic/industrial/agricultural):**
*total:* 4.08 cu km/yr (1%/0%/98%)
*per capita:* 290 cu m/yr (2000)
**Natural hazards:** monsoonal rains (June to November); flooding; occasional droughts
**Environment - current issues:** illegal logging activities throughout the country and strip mining for gems in the western region along the border with Thailand have resulted in habitat loss and declining biodiversity (in particular, destruction of mangrove swamps threatens natural fisheries); soil erosion; in rural areas, most of the population does not have access to potable water; declining fish stocks because of illegal fishing and overfishing
**Environment - international agreements:**
*party to:* Biodiversity, Climate Change, Climate Change-Kyoto Protocol, Desertification, Endangered Species, Hazardous Wastes, Marine Life Conservation, Ozone Layer Protection, Ship Pollution, Tropical Timber 94, Wetlands, Whaling
*signed, but not ratified:* Law of the Sea
**Geography - note:** a land of paddies and forests dominated by the Mekong River and Tonle Sap

## People

**Population:** 14,494,293
*note:* estimates for this country take into account the effects of excess mortality due to AIDS; this can result in lower life expectancy, higher infant mortality, higher death rates, lower population growth rates, and changes in the distribution of population by age and sex than would otherwise be expected (July 2009 est.)
**Age structure:**
*0-14 years:* 32.6% (male 2,388,922/female 2,336,439)
*15-64 years:* 63.8% (male 4,498,568/female 4,743,677)
*65 years and over:* 3.6% (male 197,649/female 329,038) (2009 est.)
**Median age:**
*total:* 22.1 years
*male:* 21.4 years
*female:* 22.8 years (2009 est.)
**Population growth rate:** 1.765% (2009 est.)
**Birth rate:** 25.73 births/1,000 population (2009 est.)
**Death rate:** 8.16 deaths/1,000 population (2008 est.)
**Net migration rate:** NA
**Urbanization:**
*urban population:* 22% of total population (2008)
*rate of urbanization:* 4.6% annual rate of change (2005-10 est.)
**Sex ratio:**
*at birth:* 1.04 male(s)/female
*under 15 years:* 1.02 male(s)/female
*15-64 years:* 0.95 male(s)/female
*65 years and over:* 0.6 male(s)/female
*total population:* 0.96 male(s)/female (2009 est.)
**Infant mortality rate:**
*total:* 54.79 deaths/1,000 live births
*male:* 61.84 deaths/1,000 live births
*female:* 47.42 deaths/1,000 live births (2009 est.)
**Life expectancy at birth:**
*total population:* 62.1 years
*male:* 60.03 years
*female:* 64.27 years (2009 est.)
**Total fertility rate:** 3.04 children born/woman (2009 est.)
**HIV/AIDS - adult prevalence rate:** 0.8% (2007 est.)
**HIV/AIDS - people living with HIV/AIDS:** 75,000 (2007 est.)
**HIV/AIDS - deaths:** 6,900 (2007 est.)
**Major infectious diseases:**
*degree of risk:* very high
*food or waterborne diseases:* bacterial and protozoal diarrhea, hepatitis A, and typhoid fever
*vectorborne diseases:* dengue fever, Japanese encephalitis, and malaria
*note:* highly pathogenic H5N1 avian influenza has been identified in this country; it poses a negligible risk with extremely rare cases possible among US citizens who have close contact with birds (2009)
**Nationality:**
*noun:* Cambodian(s)
*adjective:* Cambodian

# Cambodia (continued)

**Ethnic groups:** Khmer 90%, Vietnamese 5%, Chinese 1%, other 4%

**Religions:** Buddhist 96.4%, Muslim 2.1%, other 1.3%, unspecified 0.2% (1998 census)

**Languages:** Khmer (official) 95%, French, English

**Literacy:**
*definition:* age 15 and over can read and write
*total population:* 73.6%
*male:* 84.7%
*female:* 64.1% (2004 est.)

**School life expectancy (primary to tertiary education):**
*total:* 10 years
*male:* 10 years
*female:* 9 years (2006)

**Education expenditures:** 1.7% of GDP (2004)

## Government

**Country name:**
*conventional long form:* Kingdom of Cambodia
*conventional short form:* Cambodia
*local long form:* Preahreacheanachakr Kampuchea (phonetic pronunciation)
*local short form:* Kampuchea
*former:* Khmer Republic, Democratic Kampuchea, People's Republic of Kampuchea, State of Cambodia

**Government type:** multiparty democracy under a constitutional monarchy

**Capital:**
*name:* Phnom Penh
*geographic coordinates:* 11 33 N, 104 55 E
*time difference:* UTC+7 (12 hours ahead of Washington, DC during Standard Time)

**Administrative divisions:** 23 provinces (khaitt, singular and plural) and 1 municipality (krong, singular and plural)
*provinces:* Banteay Mean Cheay, Batdambang, Kampong Cham, Kampong Chhnang, Kampong Spoe, Kampong Thum, Kampot, Kandal, Kaoh Kong, Keb, Krachen, Mondol Kiri, Otdar Mean Cheay, Pailin, Pouthisat, Preah Seihanu (Sihanoukville), Preah Vihear, Prey Veng, Rotanah Kiri, Siem Reab, Stoeng Treng, Svay Rieng, Takev
*municipalities:* Phnum Penh (Phnom Penh)

**Independence:** 9 November 1953 (from France)

**National holiday:** Independence Day, 9 November (1953)

**Constitution:** promulgated 21 September 1993

**Legal system:** primarily a civil law mixture of French-influenced codes from the United Nations Transitional Authority in Cambodia (UNTAC) period, royal decrees, and acts of the legislature, with influences of customary law and remnants of communist legal theory; increasing influence of common law; accepts compulsory ICJ jurisdiction with reservations

**Suffrage:** 18 years of age; universal

**Executive branch:**
*chief of state:* King Norodom SIHAMONI (since 29 October 2004)
*head of government:* Prime Minister HUN SEN (since 14 January 1985) [co-prime minister from 1993 to 1997];

Permanent Deputy Prime Minister MEN SAM AN (since 25 September 2008); Deputy Prime Ministers SAR KHENG (since 3 February 1992); SOK AN, TEA BANH, HOR NAMHONG, NHEK BUNCHHAY (since 16 July 2004); BIN CHHIN (since 5 September 2007); KEAT CHHON, YIM CHHAI LY (since 24 September 2008); KE KIMYAN (since 12 March 2009)
*cabinet:* Council of Ministers named by the prime minister and appointed by the monarch
*elections:* the king is chosen by a Royal Throne Council from among all eligible males of royal descent; following legislative elections, a member of the majority party or majority coalition is named prime minister by the Chairman of the National Assembly and appointed by the king

**Legislative branch:** bicameral, consists of the Senate (61 seats; 2 members appointed by the monarch, 2 elected by the National Assembly, and 57 elected by parliamentarians and commune councils; members serve five-year terms) and the National Assembly (123 seats; members elected by popular vote to serve five-year terms)
*elections:* Senate - last held 22 January 2006 (next to be held in January 2011); National Assembly - last held 27 July 2008 (next to be held in July 2013)
*election results:* Senate - percent of vote by party - CPP 69%, FUNCINPEC 21%, SRP 10%; seats by party - CPP 45, FUNCINPEC 10, SRP 2; National Assembly - percent of vote by party - CPP 58%, SRP 22%, HRP 7%; NRP 6%; FUNCINPEC 5%; others 2%; seats by party - CPP 90, SRP 26, HRP 3, FUNCINPEC 2, NRP 2

**Judicial branch:** Supreme Council of the Magistracy (provided for in the constitution and formed in December 1997); Supreme Court (and lower courts) exercises judicial authority

**Political parties and leaders:** Cambodian People's Party or CPP [CHEA SIM]; Human Rights Party or HRP [KHEM SOKHA, also spelled KEM SOKHA]; National United Front for an Independent, Neutral, Peaceful, and Cooperative Cambodia or FUNCINPEC [KEV PUT REAKSMEI]; Norodom Ranariddh Party or NRP [CHHIM SEAK LENG]; Sam Rangsi Party or SRP [SAM RANGSI, also spelled SAM RAINSY]

**Political pressure groups and leaders:**
Cambodian Freedom Fighters or CFF; Partnership for Transparency Fund or PTF (anti-corruption organization); Students Movement for Democracy; The Committee for Free and Fair Elections or Comfrel
*other:* human rights organizations; vendors

**International organization participation:** ACCT, ADB, APT, ARF, ASEAN, EAS, FAO, G-77, IBRD, ICAO, ICCt, ICRM, IDA, IFAD, IFC, IFRCS, ILO, IMF, IMO, Interpol, IOC, IOM, IPU, ISO (subscriber), ITU, MIGA, NAM, OIF, OPCW, PCA, UN, UNCTAD, UNESCO, UNIDO, UNMIS, UNWTO, UPU, WCO, WFTU, WHO, WIPO, WMO, WTO

**Diplomatic representation in the US:**
*chief of mission:* Ambassador HENG HEM
*chancery:* 4530 16th Street NW, Washington, DC 20011
*telephone:* [1] (202) 726-7742
*FAX:* [1] (202) 726-8381

**Diplomatic representation from the US:**
*chief of mission:* Ambassador Carol A. RODLEY
*embassy:* #1, Street 96, Sangkat Wat Phnom, Khan Daun Penh, Phnom Penh
*mailing address:* Box P, APO AP 96546
*telephone:* [855] (23) 728-000
*FAX:* [855] (23) 728-600

**Flag description:** three horizontal bands of blue (top), red (double width), and blue with a white three-towered temple representing Angkor Wat outlined in black in the center of the red band
*note:* only national flag to incorporate an actual building in its design

## Economy

**Economy - overview:** From 2004 to 2007, the economy grew about 10% per year, driven largely by an expansion in the garment sector, construction, agriculture, and tourism. Growth dropped below 7% in 2008 as a result of the global economic slowdown. With the January 2005 expiration of a WTO Agreement on Textiles and Clothing, Cambodian textile producers were forced to compete directly with lower-priced countries such as China, India, Vietnam, and Bangladesh. The garment industry currently employs more than 320,000 people and contributes more than 85% of Cambodia's exports. In 2005, exploitable oil deposits were found beneath Cambodia's territorial waters, representing a new revenue stream for the government if commercial extraction begins. Mining also is attracting significant investor interest, particularly in the northern parts of the country, and the government has said opportunities exist for mining bauxite, gold, iron and gems. In 2006, a US-Cambodia bilateral Trade and Investment Framework Agreement (TIFA) was signed and several rounds of discussions have been held since 2007. The tourism industry has continued to grow rapidly, with foreign arrivals exceeding 2 million per year in 2007-08, however, economic troubles abroad will dampen growth in 2009. Rubber exports declined more than 15% in 2008 due to falling world market prices. The global financial crisis is weakening demand for Cambodian exports, and construction is declining due to a shortage of credit. The long-term development of the economy remains a daunting challenge. The Cambodian government is working with bilateral and multilateral donors, including the World Bank and IMF, to address the country's many pressing needs. The major economic challenge for Cambodia over the next decade will be fashioning an economic environment in which the private sector can create enough jobs to handle Cambodia's demographic imbalance. More than 50% of the population is less than 21 years old. The population lacks education and productive skills, particularly in the poverty-ridden countryside, which suffers from an almost total lack of basic infrastructure.

**GDP (purchasing power parity):**
$27.95 billion (2008 est.)
$26.62 billion (2007)
$24.15 billion (2006)
*note:* data are in 2008 US dollars

**GDP (official exchange rate):** $10.3 billion (2008 est.)

**GDP - real growth rate:**
6.8% (2008 est.)
10.2% (2007 est.)
10.8% (2006 est.)

**GDP - per capita (PPP):**
$2,000 (2008 est.)
$1,900 (2007 est.)
$1,800 (2006 est.)
*note:* data are in 2008 US dollars

**GDP - composition by sector:**
*agriculture:* 29%
*industry:* 30%
*services:* 41% (2007 est.)

**Labor force:** 8.6 million (2008 est.)

**Labor force - by occupation:**
*agriculture:* 75%
*industry:* NA%
*services:* NA% (2004 est.)

**Unemployment rate:**
3.5% (2007 est.)
2.5% (2000 est.)

**Population below poverty line:** 35% (2004)

**Household income or consumption by percentage share:**
*lowest 10%:* 2.9%
*highest 10%:* 34.8% (2004)

**Distribution of family income - Gini index:** 43 (2007 est.)

**Investment (gross fixed):** 21.3% of GDP (2008 est.)

**Budget:**
*revenues:* $1.264 billion
*expenditures:* $1.478 billion (2008 est.)

**Inflation rate (consumer prices):**
20.2% (2008 est.)
5.9% (2007 est.)

**Central bank discount rate:** 5.25% (31 December 2007)

**Stock of money:** $513.6 million (31 December 2007)

**Stock of quasi money:** $2.309 billion (31 December 2007)

**Stock of domestic credit:** $1.131 billion (31 December 2007)

**Market value of publicly traded shares:** $NA

**Agriculture - products:** rice, rubber, corn, vegetables, cashews, tapioca, silk

**Industries:** tourism, garments, construction, rice milling, fishing, wood and wood products, rubber, cement, gem mining, textiles

**Industrial production growth rate:** 8.4% (2008 est.)

**Electricity - production:** 1.163 billion kWh (2006 est.)

**Electricity - consumption:** 1.178 billion kWh (2006 est.)

**Electricity - exports:** 0 kWh (2007 est.)

**Electricity - imports:** 110 million kWh (2006 est.)

**Oil - production:** 0 bbl/day (2007 est.)

**Oil - consumption:** 3,736 bbl/day (2006 est.)

**Oil - exports:** 0 bbl/day (2005)

**Oil - imports:** 3,618 bbl/day (2005)

**Oil - proved reserves:** 0 bbl (1 January 2006 est.)

**Natural gas - production:** 0 cu m (2007 est.)

**Natural gas - consumption:** 0 cu m (2007 est.)

**Natural gas - exports:** 0 cu m (2007 est.)

**Natural gas - imports:** 0 cu m (2007 est.)

**Natural gas - proved reserves:** 0 cu m (1 January 2006 est.)

**Current account balance:** -$1.27 billion (2008 est.)

**Exports:** $4.616 billion f.o.b. (2008 est.)

**Exports - commodities:** clothing, timber, rubber, rice, fish, tobacco, footwear

**Exports - partners:** US 58.1%, Germany 7.3%, UK 5.2%, Canada 4.6%, Vietnam 4.5% (2007)

**Imports:** $6.424 billion f.o.b. (2008 est.)

**Imports - commodities:** petroleum products, cigarettes, gold, construction materials, machinery, motor vehicles, pharmaceutical products

**Imports - partners:** Thailand 23.1%, Vietnam 16.9%, China 15%, Hong Kong 10.4%, Singapore 7.5%, Taiwan 7.2%, South Korea 4.8% (2007)

**Reserves of foreign exchange and gold:** $2.375 billion (31 December 2008 est.)

**Debt - external:** $4.317 billion (31 December 2008 est.)

**Exchange rates:** riels (KHR) per US dollar - 4,070.94 (2008 est.), 4,006 (2007), 4,103 (2006), 4,092.5 (2005), 4,016.25 (2004)

## Communications

**Telephones - main lines in use:** 37,500 (2007)

**Telephones - mobile cellular:** 2.583 million (2007)

**Telephone system:**
*general assessment:* mobile-phone systems are widely used in urban areas to bypass deficiencies in the fixed-line network; fixed-line connections stand at well less than 1 per 100 persons; mobile-cellular usage, aided by increasing competition among service providers, is increasing and stands at nearly 20 per 100 persons
*domestic:* adequate landline and/or cellular service in Phnom Penh and other provincial cities; mobile-phone coverage is rapidly expanding in rural areas
*international:* country code - 855; adequate but expensive landline and cellular service available to all countries from Phnom Penh and major provincial cities; satellite earth station - 1 Intersputnik (Indian Ocean region) (2007)

**Radio broadcast stations:** AM 1, FM 50, shortwave NA (2008)

**Television broadcast stations:** 8 (including 2 TV relay stations with French and Vietnamese broadcasts); excludes 18 regional relay stations (2008)

**Internet country code:** .kh

**Internet hosts:** 1,230 (2008)

**Internet users:** 70,000 (2007)

## Transportation

**Airports:** 17 (2008)

**Airports - with paved runways:**
*total:* 6
*2,438 to 3,047 m:* 2
*1,524 to 2,437 m:* 2
*914 to 1,523 m:* 2 (2008)

**Airports - with unpaved runways:**
*total:* 11
*1,524 to 2,437 m:* 1
*914 to 1,523 m:* 9
*under 914 m:* 1 (2008)

**Heliports:** 1 (2007)

**Railways:**
*total:* 602 km
*narrow gauge:* 602 km 1.000-m gauge (2006)

**Roadways:**
*total:* 38,257 km
*paved:* 2,406 km
*unpaved:* 35,851 km (2004)

**Waterways:** 2,400 km (mainly on Mekong River) (2008)

**Merchant marine:**
*total:* 626
*by type:* bulk carrier 41, cargo 530, carrier 3, chemical tanker 10, container 8, passenger/cargo 6, petroleum tanker 11, refrigerated cargo 15, roll on/roll off 1, vehicle carrier 1
*foreign-owned:* 467 (Canada 2, China 193, Cyprus 7, Egypt 13, Gabon 1, Greece 3, Hong Kong 8, Indonesia 2, Japan 1, South Korea 22, Latvia 1, Lebanon 8, Netherlands 1, Romania 1, Russia 83, Singapore 4, Syria 48, Taiwan 1, Turkey 26, Ukraine 34, UAE 2, US 6) (2008)

**Ports and terminals:** Phnom Penh, Kampong Saom (Sihanoukville)

## Military

**Military branches:** Royal Cambodian Armed Forces: Royal Cambodian Army, Royal Khmer Navy, Royal Cambodian Air Force (2009)

**Military service age and obligation:** conscription law of October 2006 requires all males between 18-30 to register for military service; 18-month service obligation (2006)

**Manpower available for military service:**
*males age 16-49:* 3,759,034
*females age 16-49:* 3,784,333 (2008 est.)

**Manpower fit for military service:**
*males age 16-49:* 2,673,383
*females age 16-49:* 2,763,256 (2009 est.)

**Manpower reaching militarily significant age annually:**
*male:* 177,881
*female:* 175,332 (2009 est.)

**Military expenditures:** 3% of GDP (2005 est.)

# Cambodia (continued)

**Disputes - international:** Cambodia and Thailand dispute sections of boundary with missing boundary markers and claims of Thai encroachments into Cambodian territory; maritime boundary with Vietnam is hampered by unresolved dispute over sovereignty of offshore islands; Thailand accuses Cambodia of obstructing inclusion of Thai areas near Preah Vihear temple ruins, awarded to Cambodia by ICJ decision in 1962, as part of a planned UN World Heritage site
**Illicit drugs:** narcotics-related corruption reportedly involving some in the government, military, and police; limited methamphetamine production; vulnerable to money laundering due to its cash-based economy and porous borders

# Cameroon

## Introduction

**Background:** The former French Cameroon and part of British Cameroon merged in 1961 to form the present country. Cameroon has generally enjoyed stability, which has permitted the development of agriculture, roads, and railways, as well as a petroleum industry. Despite a slow movement toward democratic reform, political power remains firmly in the hands of President Paul BIYA.

## Geography

**Location:** Western Africa, bordering the Bight of Biafra, between Equatorial Guinea and Nigeria
**Geographic coordinates:** 6 00 N, 12 00 E
**Map references:** Africa
**Area:**
*total:* 475,440 sq km
*land:* 469,440 sq km
*water:* 6,000 sq km
**Area - comparative:** slightly larger than California
**Land boundaries:**
*total:* 4,591 km
*border countries:* Central African Republic 797 km, Chad 1,094 km, Republic of the Congo 523 km, Equatorial Guinea 189 km, Gabon 298 km, Nigeria 1,690 km
**Coastline:** 402 km
**Maritime claims:**
*territorial sea:* 12 nm
*contiguous zone:* 24 nm
**Climate:** varies with terrain, from tropical along coast to semiarid and hot in north
**Terrain:** diverse, with coastal plain in southwest, dissected plateau in center, mountains in west, plains in north
**Elevation extremes:**
*lowest point:* Atlantic Ocean 0 m
*highest point:* Fako 4,095 m (on Mt. Cameroon)
**Natural resources:** petroleum, bauxite, iron ore, timber, hydropower

**Land use:**
*arable land:* 12.54%
*permanent crops:* 2.52%
*other:* 84.94% (2005)
**Irrigated land:** 260 sq km (2003)
**Total renewable water resources:** 285.5 cu km (2003)
**Freshwater withdrawal (domestic/industrial/ agricultural):**
*total:* 0.99 cu km/yr (18%/8%/74%)
*per capita:* 61 cu m/yr (2000)
**Natural hazards:** volcanic activity with periodic releases of poisonous gases from Lake Nyos and Lake Monoun volcanoes
**Environment - current issues:** waterborne diseases are prevalent; deforestation; overgrazing; desertification; poaching; overfishing
**Environment - international agreements:**
*party to:* Biodiversity, Climate Change, Climate Change-Kyoto Protocol, Desertification, Endangered Species, Hazardous Wastes, Law of the Sea, Ozone Layer Protection, Tropical Timber 83, Tropical Timber 94, Wetlands, Whaling
*signed, but not ratified:* none of the selected agreements
**Geography - note:** sometimes referred to as the hinge of Africa; throughout the country there are areas of thermal springs and indications of current or prior volcanic activity; Mount Cameroon, the highest mountain in Sub-Saharan west Africa, is an active volcano

## People

**Population:** 18,879,301
*note:* estimates for this country explicitly take into account the effects of excess mortality due to AIDS; this can result in lower life expectancy, higher infant mortality, higher death rates, lower population growth rates, and changes in the distribution of population by age and sex than would otherwise be expected (July 2009 est.)
**Age structure:**
*0-14 years:* 40.9% (male 3,891,762/female 3,822,870)
*15-64 years:* 55.9% (male 5,298,143/female 5,250,493)
*65 years and over:* 3.3% (male 283,289/female 332,744) (2009 est.)
**Median age:**
*total:* 19.2 years
*male:* 19 years
*female:* 19.3 years (2009 est.)
**Population growth rate:** 2.19% (2009 est.)
**Birth rate:** 34.1 births/1,000 population (2009 est.)
**Death rate:** 12.41 deaths/1,000 population (2008 est.)
**Net migration rate:** NA
**Urbanization:**
*urban population:* 57% of total population (2008)
*rate of urbanization:* 3.5% annual rate of change (2005-10 est.)

# Cameroon (continued)

**Sex ratio:**

*at birth:* 1.03 male(s)/female

*under 15 years:* 1.02 male(s)/female

*15-64 years:* 1.01 male(s)/female

*65 years and over:* 0.85 male(s)/female

*total population:* 1.01 male(s)/female (2009 est.)

**Infant mortality rate:**

*total:* 63.34 deaths/1,000 live births

*male:* 68.08 deaths/1,000 live births

*female:* 58.47 deaths/1,000 live births (2009 est.)

**Life expectancy at birth:**

*total population:* 53.69 years

*male:* 52.89 years

*female:* 54.52 years (2009 est.)

**Total fertility rate:** 4.33 children born/woman (2009 est.)

**HIV/AIDS - adult prevalence rate:** 5.1% (2007 est.)

**HIV/AIDS - people living with HIV/AIDS:** 540,000 (2007 est.)

**HIV/AIDS - deaths:** 39,000 (2007 est.)

**Major infectious diseases:**

*degree of risk:* very high

*food or waterborne diseases:* bacterial and protozoal diarrhea, hepatitis A and E, and typhoid fever

*vectorborne diseases:* malaria and yellow fever

*water contact disease:* schistosomiasis

*respiratory disease:* meningococcal meningitis

*animal contact disease:* rabies (2009)

**Nationality:**

*noun:* Cameroonian(s)

*adjective:* Cameroonian

**Ethnic groups:** Cameroon Highlanders 31%, Equatorial Bantu 19%, Kirdi 11%, Fulani 10%, Northwestern Bantu 8%, Eastern Nigritic 7%, other African 13%, non-African less than 1%

**Religions:** indigenous beliefs 40%, Christian 40%, Muslim 20%

**Languages:** 24 major African language groups, English (official), French (official)

**Literacy:**

*definition:* age 15 and over can read and write

*total population:* 67.9%

*male:* 77%

*female:* 59.8% (2001 est.)

**School life expectancy (primary to tertiary education):**

*total:* 9 years

*male:* 10 years

*female:* 8 years (2006)

**Education expenditures:** 3.3% of GDP (2006)

## Government

**Country name:**

*conventional long form:* Republic of Cameroon

*conventional short form:* Cameroon

*local long form:* Republique du Cameroun/ Republic of Cameroon

*local short form:* Cameroun/Cameroon

*former:* French Cameroon, British Cameroon, Federal Republic of Cameroon, United Republic of Cameroon

**Government type:** republic; multiparty presidential regime

**Capital:**

*name:* Yaounde

*geographic coordinates:* 3 52 N, 11 31 E

*time difference:* UTC+1 (6 hours ahead of Washington, DC during Standard Time)

**Administrative divisions:** 10 provinces; Adamaoua, Centre, Est, Extreme-Nord, Littoral, Nord, Nord-Ouest, Ouest, Sud, Sud-Ouest

**Independence:** 1 January 1960 (from French-administered UN trusteeship)

**National holiday:** Republic Day (National Day), 20 May (1972)

**Constitution:** approved by referendum 20 May 1972; adopted 2 June 1972; revised January 1996

**Legal system:** based on French civil law system, with common law influence; accepts compulsory ICJ jurisdiction

**Suffrage:** 20 years of age; universal

**Executive branch:**

*chief of state:* President Paul BIYA (since 6 November 1982)

*head of government:* Prime Minister Philemon YANG (since 30 June 2009)

*cabinet:* Cabinet appointed by the president from proposals submitted by the prime minister

*elections:* president elected by popular vote for a seven-year term (eligible for a second term); election last held 11 October 2004 (next to be held by October 2011); prime minister appointed by the president

*election results:* President Paul BIYA reelected; percent of vote - Paul BIYA 70.9%, John FRU NDI 17.4%, Adamou Ndam NJOYA 4.5%, Garga Haman ADJI 3.7%

**Legislative branch:** unicameral National Assembly or Assemblee Nationale (180 seats; members are elected by direct popular vote to serve five-year terms); note - the president can either lengthen or shorten the term of the legislature

*elections:* last held 22 July 2007 (next to be held in 2012)

*election results:* percent of vote by party - NA; seats by party - CPDM 140, SDF 14, UDC 4, UNDP 4, MP 1, vacant 17

*note:* the constitution calls for an upper chamber for the legislature, to be called a Senate, but it has yet to be established

**Judicial branch:** Supreme Court (judges are appointed by the president); High Court of Justice (consists of nine judges and six substitute judges; elected by the National Assembly)

**Political parties and leaders:** Cameroonian Democratic Union or UDC [Adamou Ndam NJOYA]; Cameroon People's Democratic Movement or CPDM [Paul BIYA]; Movement for the Defense of the Republic or MDR [Dakole DAISSALA]; Movement for the Liberation and Development of Cameroon or MLDC [Marcel YONDO]; National Union for Democracy and Progress or UNDP [Maigari BELLO BOUBA]; Progressive Movement or MP; Social Democratic Front or SDF [John FRU NDI]; Union of Peoples of Cameroon or UPC [Augustin Frederic KODOCK]

**Political pressure groups and leaders:** Human Rights Defense Group [Albert MUKONG, president]; Southern Cameroon National Council [Ayamba Ette OTUN]

**International organization participation:** ACCT, ACP, AfDB, AU, BDEAC, C, CEMAC, FAO, FZ, G-77, IAEA, IBRD, ICAO, ICC, ICCt (signatory), ICRM, IDA, IDB, IFAD, IFC, IFRCS, ILO, IMF, IMO, IMSO, Interpol, IOC, IOM, IPU, ISO (correspondent), ITSO, ITU, ITUC, MIGA, NAM, OIC, OIF, OPCW, PCA, UN, UNCTAD, UNESCO, UNIDO, UNWTO, UPU, WCL, WCO, WFTU, WHO, WIPO, WMO, WTO

**Diplomatic representation in the US:**

*chief of mission:* Ambassador Joseph FOE-ATANGANA

*chancery:* 2349 Massachusetts Avenue NW, Washington, DC 20008

*telephone:* [1] (202) 265-8790

*FAX:* [1] (202) 387-3826

**Diplomatic representation from the US:**

*chief of mission:* Ambassador Janet E. GARVEY

*embassy:* Avenue Rosa Parks, Yaounde

*mailing address:* P. O. Box 817, Yaounde; pouch: American Embassy, US Department of State, Washington, DC 20521-2520

*telephone:* [237] 2220 15 00; Consular: [237] 2220 16 03

*FAX:* [237] 2220 16 00 Ext. 4531; Consular FAX: [237] 2220 17 52

*branch office(s):* Douala

**Flag description:** three equal vertical bands of green (hoist side), red, and yellow, with a yellow five-pointed star centered in the red band

*note:* uses the popular pan-African colors of Ethiopia

## Economy

**Economy - overview:** Because of its modest oil resources and favorable agricultural conditions, Cameroon has one of the best-endowed primary commodity economies in sub-Saharan Africa. Still, it faces many of the serious problems facing other underdeveloped countries, such as stagnating per capita income, a relatively inequitable distribution of income, a top-heavy civil service, and a generally unfavorable climate for business enterprise. International oil and cocoa prices have a significant impact on the economy. Since 1990, the government has embarked on various IMF and World Bank programs designed to spur business investment, increase efficiency in agriculture, improve trade, and recapitalize the nation's banks. The IMF is pressing for more reforms, including increased budget transparency, privatization, and poverty reduction programs.

**GDP (purchasing power parity):**

$42.76 billion (2008 est.)

$41.16 billion (2007)

$39.84 billion (2006)

*note:* data are in 2008 US dollars

**GDP (official exchange rate):** $25 billion (2008 est.)

# Cameroon (continued)

**GDP - real growth rate:**
3.9% (2008 est.)
3.3% (2007 est.)
3.2% (2006 est.)
**GDP - per capita (PPP):**
$2,300 (2008 est.)
$2,300 (2007 est.)
$2,300 (2006 est.)
*note:* data are in 2008 US dollars
**GDP - composition by sector:**
*agriculture:* 43.5%
*industry:* 16%
*services:* 40.5% (2008 est.)
**Labor force:** 6.716 million (2008 est.)
**Labor force - by occupation:**
*agriculture:* 70%
*industry:* 13%
*services:* 17% (2001 est.)
**Unemployment rate:**
30% (2001 est.)
**Population below poverty line:** 48% (2000 est.)
**Household income or consumption by percentage share:**
*lowest 10%:* 2.3%
*highest 10%:* 35.4% (2001)
**Distribution of family income - Gini index:** 44.6 (2001)
**Investment (gross fixed):** 17.6% of GDP (2008 est.)
**Budget:**
*revenues:* $5.371 billion
*expenditures:* $4.319 billion (2008 est.)
**Public debt:** 11.9% of GDP (2008 est.)
**Inflation rate (consumer prices):**
4.4% (2008 est.)
1.1% (2007 est.)
**Commercial bank prime lending rate:** 15% (31 December 2007)
**Stock of money:** $2.616 billion (31 December 2007)
**Stock of quasi money:** $1.698 billion (31 December 2007)
**Stock of domestic credit:** $1.3 billion (31 December 2007)
**Market value of publicly traded shares:** $NA
**Agriculture - products:** coffee, cocoa, cotton, rubber, bananas, oilseed, grains, root starches; livestock; timber
**Industries:** petroleum production and refining, aluminum production, food processing, light consumer goods, textiles, lumber, ship repair
**Industrial production growth rate:** 4.7% (2008 est.)
**Electricity - production:** 3.903 billion kWh (2006 est.)
**Electricity - consumption:** 3.323 billion kWh (2006 est.)
**Electricity - exports:** 0 kWh (2007 est.)
**Electricity - imports:** 0 kWh (2007 est.)
**Oil - production:** 87,400 bbl/day (2008 est.)
**Oil - consumption:** 24,500 bbl/day (2006 est.)
**Oil - exports:** 108,800 bbl/day (2005)

**Oil - imports:** 50,750 bbl/day (2005)
**Oil - proved reserves:** 200 million bbl (1 January 2008 est.)
**Natural gas - production:** 20 million cu m (2006 est.)
**Natural gas - consumption:** 20 million cu m (2006 est.)
**Natural gas - exports:** 0 cu m (2007 est.)
**Natural gas - imports:** 0 cu m (2007 est.)
**Natural gas - proved reserves:** 135.1 billion cu m (1 January 2008 est.)
**Current account balance:** $377 million (2008 est.)
**Exports:** $5.246 billion f.o.b. (2008 est.)
**Exports - commodities:** crude oil and petroleum products, lumber, cocoa beans, aluminum, coffee, cotton
**Exports - partners:** Spain 19.8%, Italy 15.7%, France 11.7%, South Korea 9.4%, Netherlands 6.1%, US 5.7% (2007)
**Imports:** $4.362 billion f.o.b. (2008 est.)
**Imports - commodities:** machinery, electrical equipment, transport equipment, fuel, food
**Imports - partners:** France 23.4%, Nigeria 12.8%, China 9%, Belgium 5.8%, US 4% (2007)
**Reserves of foreign exchange and gold:** $3.788 billion (31 December 2008 est.)
**Debt - external:** $2.36 billion (31 December 2008 est.)
**Exchange rates:** Cooperation Financiere en Afrique Centrale francs (XAF) per US dollar - 447.81 (2008 est.), 493.51 (2007), 522.59 (2006), 527.47 (2005), 528.29 (2004)
*note:* since 1 January 1999, the Central African CFA franc (XAF) has been pegged to the euro at a rate of 655.957 CFA francs per euro; Central African CFA franc (XAF) coins and banknotes are not accepted in countries using West African CFA francs (XOF), and vice versa, even though the two currencies trade at par

## Communications

**Telephones - main lines in use:** 130,700 (2006)
**Telephones - mobile cellular:** 4.536 million (2007)
**Telephone system:**
*general assessment:* fixed-line connections stand at less than 1 per 100 persons; equipment is old and outdated, and connections with many parts of the country are unreliable; mobile-cellular usage, in part a reflection of the poor condition and general inadequacy of the fixed-line network, increased more than 6-fold between 2002 and 2007 reaching a subscribership base of 25 per 100 persons
*domestic:* cable, microwave radio relay, and tropospheric scatter
*international:* country code - 237; landing point for the SAT-3/WASC fiber-optic submarine cable that provides connectivity to Europe and Asia; satellite earth stations - 2 Intelsat (Atlantic Ocean) (2007)
**Radio broadcast stations:** AM 2, FM 9, shortwave 3 (2001)

**Television broadcast stations:** 1 (2001)
**Internet country code:** .cm
**Internet hosts:** 69 (2008)
**Internet users:** 370,000 (2006)

## Transportation

**Airports:** 34 (2008)
**Airports - with paved runways:**
*total:* 10
*over 3,047 m:* 2
*2,438 to 3,047 m:* 4
*1,524 to 2,437 m:* 3
*914 to 1,523 m:* 1 (2008)
**Airports - with unpaved runways:**
*total:* 24
*1,524 to 2,437 m:* 4
*914 to 1,523 m:* 14
*under 914 m:* 6 (2008)
**Pipelines:** oil 889 km (2008)
**Railways:**
*total:* 987 km
*narrow gauge:* 987 km 1.000-m gauge (2006)
**Roadways:**
*total:* 50,000 km
*paved:* 5,000 km
*unpaved:* 45,000 km (2004)
**Waterways:** navigation mainly on Benue River; limited during rainy season (2008)
**Ports and terminals:** Douala, Limboh Terminal

## Military

**Military branches:** Cameroon Armed Forces: Army, Navy (includes naval infantry), Air Force (Armee de l'Air du Cameroun, AAC) (2009)
**Military service age and obligation:** 18 years of age for voluntary military service; no conscription; the government makes periodic calls for volunteers (2006)
**Manpower available for military service:**
*males age 16-49:* 4,321,175
*females age 16-49:* 4,228,625 (2008 est.)
**Manpower fit for military service:**
*males age 16-49:* 2,645,601
*females age 16-49:* 2,574,948 (2009 est.)
**Manpower reaching militarily significant age annually:**
*male:* 213,027
*female:* 208,642 (2009 est.)
**Military expenditures:** 1.3% of GDP (2006)

## Transnational Issues

**Disputes - international:** Joint Border Commission with Nigeria reviewed 2002 ICJ ruling on the entire boundary and bilaterally resolved differences, including June 2006 Greentree Agreement that immediately ceded sovereignty of the Bakassi Peninsula to Cameroon with a full phase-out of Nigerian control and patriation of residents in 2008; Cameroon and Nigeria agree on maritime delimitation in March 2008; sovereignty dispute between

Equatorial Guinea and Cameroon over an island at the mouth of the Ntem River; only Nigeria and Cameroon have heeded the Lake Chad Commission's admonition to ratify the delimitation treaty, which also includes the Chad-Niger and Niger-Nigeria boundaries

**Refugees and internally displaced persons:**
*refugees (country of origin):* 20,000-30,000 (Chad); 3,000 (Nigeria); 24,000 (Central African Republic) (2007)

**Trafficking in persons:**
*current situation:* Cameroon is a source, transit, and destination country for women and children trafficked for the purposes of forced labor and commercial sexual exploitation; most victims are children trafficked within country, with girls primarily trafficked for domestic servitude and sexual exploitation; both boys and girls are also trafficked within Cameroon for forced labor in sweatshops, bars, restaurants, and on tea and cocoa plantations; children are trafficked into Cameroon from neighboring states for forced labor in agriculture, fishing, street vending, and spare-parts shops; Cameroon is a transit country for children trafficked between Gabon and Nigeria, and from Nigeria to Saudi Arabia; it is a source country for women transported by sex-trafficking rings to Europe
*tier rating:* Tier 2 Watch List - Cameroon is on the Tier 2 Watch List for its failure to provide evidence of increasing efforts to combat human trafficking in 2007, particularly in terms of efforts to prosecute and convict trafficking offenders; while Cameroon reported some arrests of traffickers, none of them were prosecuted or punished; the government does not identify trafficking victims among vulnerable populations nor does it monitor the number of victims it intercepts (2008)

# Canada

## Introduction

**Background:** A land of vast distances and rich natural resources, Canada became a self-governing dominion in 1867 while retaining ties to the British crown. Economically and technologically the nation has developed in parallel with the US, its neighbor to the south across an unfortified border. Canada faces the political challenges of meeting public demands for quality improvements in health care and education services, as well as responding to separatist concerns in predominantly francophone Quebec. Canada also aims to develop its diverse energy resources while maintaining its commitment to the environment.

## Geography

**Location:** Northern North America, bordering the North Atlantic Ocean on the east, North Pacific Ocean on the west, and the Arctic Ocean on the north, north of the conterminous US
**Geographic coordinates:** 60 00 N, 95 00 W
**Map references:** North America
**Area:**
*total:* 9,984,670 sq km
*land:* 9,093,507 sq km
*water:* 891,163 sq km
**Area - comparative:** somewhat larger than the US
**Land boundaries:**
*total:* 8,893 km
*border countries:* US 8,893 km (includes 2,477 km with Alaska)
**Coastline:** 202,080 km
**Maritime claims:**
*territorial sea:* 12 nm
*contiguous zone:* 24 nm
*exclusive economic zone:* 200 nm
*continental shelf:* 200 nm or to the edge of the continental margin

**Climate:** varies from temperate in south to subarctic and arctic in north
**Terrain:** mostly plains with mountains in west and lowlands in southeast
**Elevation extremes:**
*lowest point:* Atlantic Ocean 0 m
*highest point:* Mount Logan 5,959 m
**Natural resources:** iron ore, nickel, zinc, copper, gold, lead, molybdenum, potash, diamonds, silver, fish, timber, wildlife, coal, petroleum, natural gas, hydropower
**Land use:**
*arable land:* 4.57%
*permanent crops:* 0.65%
*other:* 94.78% (2005)
**Irrigated land:** 7,850 sq km (2003)
**Total renewable water resources:** 3,300 cu km (1985)
**Freshwater withdrawal (domestic/industrial/agricultural):**
*total:* 44.72 cu km/yr (20%/69%/12%)
*per capita:* 1,386 cu m/yr (1996)
**Natural hazards:** continuous permafrost in north is a serious obstacle to development; cyclonic storms form east of the Rocky Mountains, a result of the mixing of air masses from the Arctic, Pacific, and North American interior, and produce most of the country's rain and snow east of the mountains
**Environment - current issues:** air pollution and resulting acid rain severely affecting lakes and damaging forests; metal smelting, coal-burning utilities, and vehicle emissions impacting on agricultural and forest productivity; ocean waters becoming contaminated due to agricultural, industrial, mining, and forestry activities
**Environment - international agreements:**
*party to:* Air Pollution, Air Pollution-Nitrogen Oxides, Air Pollution-Persistent Organic Pollutants, Air Pollution-Sulfur 85, Air Pollution-Sulfur 94,

# Canada (continued)

Antarctic-Environmental Protocol, Antarctic-Marine Living Resources, Antarctic Seals, Antarctic Treaty, Biodiversity, Climate Change, Climate Change-Kyoto Protocol, Desertification, Endangered Species, Environmental Modification, Hazardous Wastes, Law of the Sea, Marine Dumping, Ozone Layer Protection, Ship Pollution, Tropical Timber 83, Tropical Timber 94, Wetlands

*signed, but not ratified:* Air Pollution-Volatile Organic Compounds, Marine Life Conservation

**Geography - note:** second-largest country in world (after Russia); strategic location between Russia and US via north polar route; approximately 90% of the population is concentrated within 160 km of the US border

## People

**Population:** 33,487,208 (July 2009 est.)

**Age structure:**

*0-14 years:* 16.1% (male 2,761,711/ female 2,626,836)

*15-64 years:* 68.7% (male 11,633,950/ female 11,381,735)

*65 years and over:* 15.2% (male 2,220,189/ female 2,862,787) (2009 est.)

**Median age:**

*total:* 40.4 years

*male:* 39.3 years

*female:* 41.5 years (2009 est.)

**Population growth rate:** 0.817% (2009 est.)

**Birth rate:** 10.28 births/1,000 population (2009 est.)

**Death rate:** 7.61 deaths/1,000 population (2008 est.)

**Net migration rate:** 5.63 migrant(s)/1,000 population (2009 est.)

**Urbanization:**

*urban population:* 80% of total population (2008)

*rate of urbanization:* 1% annual rate of change (2005-10 est.)

**Sex ratio:**

*at birth:* 1.06 male(s)/female

*under 15 years:* 1.05 male(s)/female

*15-64 years:* 1.02 male(s)/female

*65 years and over:* 0.78 male(s)/female

*total population:* 0.98 male(s)/female (2009 est.)

**Infant mortality rate:**

*total:* 5.04 deaths/1,000 live births

*male:* 5.37 deaths/1,000 live births

*female:* 4.69 deaths/1,000 live births (2009 est.)

**Life expectancy at birth:**

*total population:* 81.23 years

*male:* 78.69 years

*female:* 83.91 years (2009 est.)

**Total fertility rate:** 1.58 children born/woman (2009 est.)

**HIV/AIDS - adult prevalence rate:** 0.4% (2007 est.)

**HIV/AIDS - people living with HIV/AIDS:** 73,000 (2007 est.)

**HIV/AIDS - deaths:** fewer than 500 (2007 est.)

**Nationality:**

*noun:* Canadian(s)

*adjective:* Canadian

**Ethnic groups:** British Isles origin 28%, French origin 23%, other European 15%, Amerindian 2%, other, mostly Asian, African, Arab 6%, mixed background 26%

**Religions:** Roman Catholic 42.6%, Protestant 23.3% (including United Church 9.5%, Anglican 6.8%, Baptist 2.4%, Lutheran 2%), other Christian 4.4%, Muslim 1.9%, other and unspecified 11.8%, none 16% (2001 census)

**Languages:** English (official) 59.3%, French (official) 23.2%, other 17.5%

**Literacy:**

*definition:* age 15 and over can read and write

*total population:* 99%

*male:* 99%

*female:* 99% (2003 est.)

**School life expectancy (primary to tertiary education):**

*total:* 17 years

*male:* 17 years

*female:* 17 years (2004)

**Education expenditures:** 5.2% of GDP (2002)

## Government

**Country name:**

*conventional long form:* none

*conventional short form:* Canada

**Government type:** a parliamentary democracy, a federation, and a Commonwealth realm

**Capital:**

*name:* Ottawa

*geographic coordinates:* 45 25 N, 75 42 W

*time difference:* UTC-5 (same time as Washington, DC during Standard Time)

*daylight saving time:* +1hr, begins second Sunday in March; ends first Sunday in November

*note:* Canada is divided into six time zones

**Administrative divisions:** 10 provinces and 3 territories*; Alberta, British Columbia, Manitoba, New Brunswick, Newfoundland and Labrador, Northwest Territories*, Nova Scotia, Nunavut*, Ontario, Prince Edward Island, Quebec, Saskatchewan, Yukon Territory*

**Independence:** 1 July 1867 (union of British North American colonies); 11 December 1931 (recognized by UK)

**National holiday:** Canada Day, 1 July (1867)

**Constitution:** made up of unwritten and written acts, customs, judicial decisions, and traditions; the written part of the constitution consists of the Constitution Act of 29 March 1867, which created a federation of four provinces, and the Constitution Act of 17 April 1982, which transferred formal control over the constitution from Britain to Canada, and added a Canadian Charter of Rights and Freedoms as well as procedures for constitutional amendments

**Legal system:** based on English common law, except in Quebec, where civil law system based on French law prevails; accepts compulsory ICJ jurisdiction with reservations

**Suffrage:** 18 years of age; universal

**Executive branch:**

*head of state:* Queen ELIZABETH II (since 6 February 1952); represented by Governor General Michaelle JEAN (since 27 September 2005)

*head of government:* Prime Minister Stephen HARPER (since 6 February 2006)

*cabinet:* Federal Ministry chosen by the prime minister usually from among the members of his own party sitting in Parliament

*elections:* the monarchy is hereditary; governor general appointed by the monarch on the advice of the prime minister for a five-year term; following legislative elections, the leader of the majority party or the leader of the majority coalition in the House of Commons is automatically designated prime minister by the governor general

**Legislative branch:** bicameral Parliament or Parlement consists of the Senate or Senat (105 seats; members appointed by the governor general with the advice of the prime minister and serve until reaching 75 years of age) and the House of Commons or Chambre des Communes (308 seats; members elected by direct, popular vote to serve a maximum of five-year terms starting in 2009 elections)

*elections:* House of Commons - last held 14 October 2008 (next to be held no later than 19 October 2012)

*election results:* House of Commons - percent of vote by party - Conservative Party 37.6%, Liberal Party 26.2%, New Democratic Party 18.2%, Bloc Quebecois 10%, Greens 6.8%, other 1%; seats by party - Conservative Party 143, Liberal Party 77, New Democratic Party 37, Bloc Quebecois 49, other 2

**Judicial branch:** Supreme Court of Canada (judges are appointed by the prime minister through the governor general); Federal Court of Canada; Federal Court of Appeal; Provincial Courts (these are named variously Court of Appeal, Court of Queens Bench, Superior Court, Supreme Court, and Court of Justice)

**Political parties and leaders:** Bloc Quebecois [Gilles DUCEPPE]; Conservative Party of Canada [Stephen HARPER] (a merger of the Canadian Alliance and the Progressive Conservative Party); Green Party [Elizabeth MAY]; Liberal Party [Michael IGNATIEFF]; New Democratic Party [Jack LAYTON]

**Political pressure groups and leaders:**

*other:* agricultural sector; automobile industry; business groups; chemical industry; commercial banks; communications sector; energy industry; environmentalists; public administration groups; steel industry; trade unions

**International organization participation:** ACCT, ADB (nonregional member), AfDB (nonregional member), APEC, Arctic Council, ARF, ASEAN (dialogue partner), Australia Group, BIS, C, CDB, CE (observer), EAPC, EBRD, ESA (cooperating state), FAO, G-20, G-7, G-8, G-10, IADB, IAEA, IBRD, ICAO, ICC, ICCt, ICRM, IDA, IEA, IFAD, IFC, IFRCS, IHO, ILO, IMF, IMO, IMSO, Interpol, IOC, IOM, IPU, ISO, ITSO, ITU, ITUC, MIGA, MINUSTAH, MONUC, NAFTA, NAM (guest), NATO, NEA, NSG, OAS, OECD, OIF, OPCW, OSCE, Paris Club, PCA, PIF (partner), SECI (observer), UN, UNAMID, UNCTAD,

# Canada (continued)

UNDOF, UNESCO, UNFICYP, UNHCR, UNMIS, UNRWA, UNTSO, UNWTO, UPU, WCL, WCO, WFTU, WHO, WIPO, WMO, WTO, ZC

**Diplomatic representation in the US:**
*chief of mission:* Ambassador Michael WILSON
*chancery:* 501 Pennsylvania Avenue NW, Washington, DC 20001
*telephone:* [1] (202) 682-1740
*FAX:* [1] (202) 682-7701
*consulate(s) general:* Atlanta, Boston, Buffalo, Chicago, Dallas, Denver, Detroit, Los Angeles, Miami, Minneapolis, New York, Phoenix, San Diego, San Francisco, Seattle, Tucson
*consulate(s):* Anchorage, Houston, Philadelphia, Princeton (New Jersey), Raleigh, San Jose (California), Tucson

**Diplomatic representation from the US:**
*chief of mission:* Ambassador David H. WILKINS
*embassy:* 490 Sussex Drive, Ottawa, Ontario K1N 1G8
*mailing address:* P. O. Box 5000, Ogdensburg, NY 13669-0430; P.O. Box 866, Station B, Ottawa, Ontario K1P 5T1
*telephone:* [1] (613) 688-5335
*FAX:* [1] (613) 688-3082
*consulate(s) general:* Calgary, Halifax, Montreal, Quebec, Toronto, Vancouver, Winnipeg

**Flag description:** two vertical bands of red (hoist and fly side, half width) with white square between them; an 11-pointed red maple leaf is centered in the white square; the official colors of Canada are red and white

## Economy

**Economy - overview:** As an affluent, high-tech industrial society in the trillion-dollar class, Canada resembles the US in its market-oriented economic system, pattern of production, and affluent living standards. Since World War II, the impressive growth of the manufacturing, mining, and service sectors has transformed the nation from a largely rural economy into one primarily industrial and urban. The 1989 US-Canada Free Trade Agreement (FTA) and the 1994 North American Free Trade Agreement (NAFTA) (which includes Mexico) touched off a dramatic increase in trade and economic integration with the US, its principle trading partner. Canada enjoys a substantial trade surplus with the US, which absorbs nearly 80% of Canadian exports each year. Canada is the US's largest foreign supplier of energy, including oil, gas, uranium, and electric power. Given its great natural resources, skilled labor force, and modern capital plant, Canada has enjoyed solid economic growth, and prudent fiscal management has produced consecutive balanced budgets from 1997 to 2007. In 2008, growth slowed sharply as a result of the global economic downturn, US housing slump, plunging auto sector demand, and a drop in world commodity prices. Public finances, too, are set to deteriorate for the first time in a decade. Tight global credit conditions have further restrained business and housing investment, despite the conservative lending practices and strong capitalization that made Canada's major banks among the most stable in the world.

**GDP (purchasing power parity):**
$1.307 trillion (2008 est.)
$1.299 trillion (2007)
$1.265 trillion (2006)
*note:* data are in 2008 US dollars

**GDP (official exchange rate):** $1.564 trillion (2008 est.)

**GDP - real growth rate:**
0.6% (2008 est.)
2.7% (2007 est.)
3.1% (2006 est.)

**GDP - per capita (PPP):**
$39,300 (2008 est.)
$39,400 (2007 est.)
$38,700 (2006 est.)
*note:* data are in 2008 US dollars

**GDP - composition by sector:**
*agriculture:* 2%
*industry:* 28.4%
*services:* 69.6% (2008 est.)

**Labor force:** 18.18 million (2008 est.)

**Labor force - by occupation:** agriculture 2%, manufacturing 13%, construction 6%, services 76%, other 3% (2006)

**Unemployment rate:**
6.1% (2008 est.)
6% (2007 est.)

**Population below poverty line:** 10.8%; note - this figure is the Low Income Cut-Off (LICO), a calculation that results in higher figures than found in many comparable economies; Canada does not have an official poverty line (2005)

**Household income or consumption by percentage share:**
*lowest 10%:* 2.6%
*highest 10%:* 24.8% (2000)

**Distribution of family income - Gini index:** 32.1 (2005)

**Investment (gross fixed):** 22.6% of GDP (2008 est.)

**Budget:**
*revenues:* $608.3 billion
*expenditures:* $606 billion (2008 est.)

**Public debt:** 62.3% of GDP (2008 est.)

**Inflation rate (consumer prices):**
1% (January 2009 est.)
2.1% (2007 est.)

**Central bank discount rate:** 3.5% (January 2009)

**Commercial bank prime lending rate:** 6.1% (31 December 2007)

**Stock of money:** $391.6 billion (31 December 2007)

**Stock of quasi money:** $1.381 trillion (31 December 2007)

**Stock of domestic credit:** $2.382 trillion (31 December 2007)

**Market value of publicly traded shares:** $2.187 trillion (31 December 2007)

**Agriculture - products:** wheat, barley, oilseed, tobacco, fruits, vegetables; dairy products; forest products; fish

**Industries:** transportation equipment, chemicals, processed and unprocessed minerals, food products, wood and paper products, fish products, petroleum and natural gas

**Industrial production growth rate:** -1% (2008 est.)

**Electricity - production:** 612.6 billion kWh (2007 est.)

**Electricity - consumption:** 530 billion kWh (2006 est.)

**Electricity - exports:** 50.12 billion kWh (2007 est.)

**Electricity - imports:** 19.66 billion kWh (2007 est.)

**Oil - production:** 3.425 million bbl/day (2007 est.)

**Oil - consumption:** 2.371 million bbl/day (2007 est.)

**Oil - exports:** 2.225 million bbl/day (2005)

**Oil - imports:** 1.229 million bbl/day (2005)

**Oil - proved reserves:** 178.6 billion bbl
*note:* includes oil sands (1 January 2008 est.)

**Natural gas - production:** 187 billion cu m (2007 est.)

**Natural gas - consumption:** 92.9 billion cu m (2007 est.)

**Natural gas - exports:** 107.3 billion cu m (2007 est.)

**Natural gas - imports:** 13.2 billion cu m (2007 est.)

**Natural gas - proved reserves:** 1.648 trillion cu m (1 January 2008 est.)

**Current account balance:** $12.82 billion (2008 est.)

**Exports:** $461.8 billion f.o.b. (2008 est.)

**Exports - commodities:** motor vehicles and parts, industrial machinery, aircraft, telecommunications equipment; chemicals, plastics, fertilizers; wood pulp, timber, crude petroleum, natural gas, electricity, aluminum

**Exports - partners:** US 78.9%, UK 2.8%, China 2.1% (2007)

**Imports:** $436.7 billion f.o.b. (2008 est.)

**Imports - commodities:** machinery and equipment, motor vehicles and parts, crude oil, chemicals, electricity, durable consumer goods

**Imports - partners:** US 54.1%, China 9.4%, Mexico 4.2% (2007)

**Reserves of foreign exchange and gold:** $41.08 billion (2007 est.)

**Debt - external:** $758.6 billion (30 June 2007)

**Stock of direct foreign investment - at home:** $586.6 billion (2008 est.)

**Stock of direct foreign investment - abroad:** $547.2 billion (2008 est.)

**Exchange rates:** Canadian dollars (CAD) per US dollar - 1.0364 (2008 est.), 1.0724 (2007), 1.1334 (2006), 1.2118 (2005), 1.301 (2004)

# Canada (continued)

## Communications

**Telephones - main lines in use:** 21 million (2006)
**Telephones - mobile cellular:** 18.749 million (2006)
**Telephone system:**
*general assessment:* excellent service provided by modern technology
*domestic:* domestic satellite system with about 300 earth stations
*international:* country code - 1; submarine cables provide links to the US and Europe; satellite earth stations - 7 (5 Intelsat - 4 Atlantic Ocean and 1 Pacific Ocean, and 2 Intersputnik - Atlantic Ocean region) (2007)
**Radio broadcast stations:** AM 245, FM 582, shortwave 6 (2004)
**Television broadcast stations:** 148 (2007)
**Internet country code:** .ca
**Internet hosts:** 5.119 million (2008)
**Internet users:** 28 million (2007)

## Transportation

**Airports:** 1,369 (2008)
**Airports - with paved runways:**
*total:* 514
*over 3,047 m:* 18
*2,438 to 3,047 m:* 16
*1,524 to 2,437 m:* 152
*914 to 1,523 m:* 251
*under 914 m:* 77 (2008)
**Airports - with unpaved runways:**
*total:* 855
*1,524 to 2,437 m:* 70
*914 to 1,523 m:* 367
*under 914 m:* 418 (2008)
**Heliports:** 11 (2007)
**Pipelines:** crude and refined oil 23,564 km; liquid petroleum gas 74,980 km (2006)
**Railways:**
*total:* 48,068 km
*standard gauge:* 48,068 km 1.435-m gauge (2006)
**Roadways:**
*total:* 1,042,300 km
*paved:* 415,600 km (includes 17,000 km of expressways)
*unpaved:* 626,700 km (2006)
**Waterways:** 636 km
*note:* Saint Lawrence Seaway of 3,769 km, including the Saint Lawrence River of 3,058 km, shared with United States (2008)
**Merchant marine:**
*total:* 175
*by type:* bulk carrier 60, cargo 13, carrier 1, chemical tanker 10, combination ore/oil 1, container 2, passenger 6, passenger/cargo 64, petroleum tanker 12, roll on/roll off 6
*foreign-owned:* 17 (Germany 3, Netherlands 1, Norway 3, US 10)
*registered in other countries:* 206 (Australia 9, Bahamas 84, Barbados 9, Cambodia 2, Cyprus 2, Denmark 1, Honduras 1, Hong Kong 44, Liberia 7,

Malta 1, Marshall Islands 6, Norway 10, Panama 18, Saint Vincent and the Grenadines 1, Spain 4, Taiwan 2, Vanuatu 5) (2008)
**Ports and terminals:** Fraser River Port, Halifax, Hamilton, Montreal, Port-Cartier, Quebec City, Saint John (New Brunswick), Sept-Isles, Vancouver

## Military

**Military branches:** Canadian Forces: Land Forces Command (LFC), Maritime Command (MARCOM), Air Command (AIRCOM), Canada Command (homeland security) (2009)
**Military service age and obligation:** 17 years of age for male and female voluntary military service (with parental consent); 16 years of age for reserve and military college applicants; Canadian citizenship or permanent residence status required; maximum 34 years of age; service obligation 3-9 years (2008)
**Manpower available for military service:**
*males age 16-49:* 8,072,010
*females age 16-49:* 7,813,462 (2008 est.)
**Manpower fit for military service:**
*males age 16-49:* 6,647,513
*females age 16-49:* 6,413,748 (2009 est.)
**Manpower reaching militarily significant age annually:**
*male:* 223,238
*female:* 210,797 (2009 est.)
**Military expenditures:** 1.1% of GDP (2005 est.)

## Transnational Issues

**Disputes - international:** managed maritime boundary disputes with the US at Dixon Entrance, Beaufort Sea, Strait of Juan de Fuca, and the Gulf of Maine including the disputed Machias Seal Island and North Rock; Canada, the US, and other countries dispute the status of the Northwest Passage; US works closely with Canada to intensify security measures for monitoring and controlling legal and illegal movement of people, transport, and commodities across the international border; sovereignty dispute with Denmark over Hans Island in the Kennedy Channel between Ellesmere Island and Greenland; commencing the collection of technical evidence for submission to the Commission on the Limits of the Continental Shelf in support of claims for continental shelf beyond 200 nautical miles from its declared baselines in the Arctic, as stipulated in Article 76, paragraph 8, of the United Nations Convention on the Law of the Sea
**Illicit drugs:** illicit producer of cannabis for the domestic drug market and export to US; use of hydroponics technology permits growers to plant large quantities of high-quality marijuana indoors; increasing ecstasy production, some of which is destined for the US; vulnerable to narcotics money laundering because of its mature financial services sector

# Cape Verde

## Introduction

**Background:** The uninhabited islands were discovered and colonized by the Portuguese in the 15th century; Cape Verde subsequently became a trading center for African slaves and later an important coaling and resupply stop for whaling and transatlantic shipping. Following independence in 1975, and a tentative interest in unification with Guinea-Bissau, a one-party system was established and maintained until multi-party elections were held in 1990. Cape Verde continues to exhibit one of Africa's most stable democratic governments. Repeated droughts during the second half of the 20th century caused significant hardship and prompted heavy emigration. As a result, Cape Verde's expatriate population is greater than its domestic one. Most Cape Verdeans have both African and Portuguese antecedents.

## Geography

**Location:** Western Africa, group of islands in the North Atlantic Ocean, west of Senegal
**Geographic coordinates:** 16 00 N, 24 00 W
**Map references:** Political Map of the World
**Area:**
*total:* 4,033 sq km
*land:* 4,033 sq km
*water:* 0 sq km
**Area - comparative:** slightly larger than Rhode Island
**Land boundaries:** 0 km
**Coastline:** 965 km
**Maritime claims:** measured from claimed archipelagic baselines
*territorial sea:* 12 nm
*contiguous zone:* 24 nm
*exclusive economic zone:* 200 nm
**Climate:** temperate; warm, dry summer; precipitation meager and very erratic
**Terrain:** steep, rugged, rocky, volcanic

# Cape Verde *(continued)*

**Elevation extremes:**
*lowest point:* Atlantic Ocean 0 m
*highest point:* Mt. Fogo 2,829 m (a volcano on Fogo Island)
**Natural resources:** salt, basalt rock, limestone, kaolin, fish, clay, gypsum
**Land use:**
*arable land:* 11.41%
*permanent crops:* 0.74%
*other:* 87.85% (2005)
**Irrigated land:** 30 sq km (2003)
**Total renewable water resources:** 0.3 cu km (1990)
**Freshwater withdrawal (domestic/industrial/agricultural):**
*total:* 0.02 cu km/yr (7%/2%/91%)
*per capita:* 39 cu m/yr (2000)
**Natural hazards:** prolonged droughts; seasonal harmattan wind produces obscuring dust; volcanically and seismically active
**Environment - current issues:** soil erosion; deforestation due to demand for wood used as fuel; water shortages; desertification; environmental damage has threatened several species of birds and reptiles; illegal beach sand extraction; overfishing
**Environment - international agreements:**
*party to:* Biodiversity, Climate Change, Climate Change-Kyoto Protocol, Desertification, Endangered Species, Environmental Modification, Hazardous Wastes, Law of the Sea, Marine Dumping, Ozone Layer Protection, Ship Pollution, Wetlands
*signed, but not ratified:* none of the selected agreements
**Geography - note:** strategic location 500 km from west coast of Africa near major north-south sea routes; important communications station; important sea and air refueling site

## People

**Population:** 429,474 (July 2009 est.)
**Age structure:**
*0-14 years:* 35.2% (male 76,012/female 74,993)
*15-64 years:* 58.5% (male 123,376/female 127,653)
*65 years and over:* 6.4% (male 10,040/female 17,400) (2009 est.)
**Median age:**
*total:* 21.1 years
*male:* 20.4 years
*female:* 21.9 years (2009 est.)
**Population growth rate:** 0.561% (2009 est.)
**Birth rate:** 23.5 births/1,000 population (2009 est.)
**Death rate:** 6.26 deaths/1,000 population (2008 est.)
**Net migration rate:** -11.67 migrant(s)/1,000 population (2009 est.)
**Urbanization:**
*urban population:* 60% of total population (2008)
*rate of urbanization:* 3.5% annual rate of change (2005-10 est.)

**Sex ratio:**
*at birth:* 1.03 male(s)/female
*under 15 years:* 1.01 male(s)/female
*15-64 years:* 0.97 male(s)/female
*65 years and over:* 0.58 male(s)/female
*total population:* 0.95 male(s)/female (2009 est.)
**Infant mortality rate:**
*total:* 41.35 deaths/1,000 live births
*male:* 47.39 deaths/1,000 live births
*female:* 35.12 deaths/1,000 live births (2009 est.)
**Life expectancy at birth:**
*total population:* 71.61 years
*male:* 68.27 years
*female:* 75.05 years (2009 est.)
**Total fertility rate:** 3.07 children born/woman (2009 est.)
**HIV/AIDS - adult prevalence rate:** 0.035% (2001 est.)
**HIV/AIDS - people living with HIV/AIDS:** 775 (2001)
**HIV/AIDS - deaths:** 225 (as of 2001)
**Nationality:**
*noun:* Cape Verdean(s)
*adjective:* Cape Verdean
**Ethnic groups:** Creole (mulatto) 71%, African 28%, European 1%
**Religions:** Roman Catholic (infused with indigenous beliefs), Protestant (mostly Church of the Nazarene)
**Languages:** Portuguese, Crioulo (a blend of Portuguese and West African words)
**Literacy:**
*definition:* age 15 and over can read and write
*total population:* 76.6%
*male:* 85.8%
*female:* 69.2% (2003 est.)
**School life expectancy (primary to tertiary education):**
*total:* 12 years
*male:* 11 years
*female:* 12 years (2006)
**Education expenditures:** 6.3% of GDP (2006)

## Government

**Country name:**
*conventional long form:* Republic of Cape Verde
*conventional short form:* Cape Verde
*local long form:* Republica de Cabo Verde
*local short form:* Cabo Verde
**Government type:** republic
**Capital:**
*name:* Praia
*geographic coordinates:* 14 55 N, 23 31 W
*time difference:* UTC-1 (4 hours ahead of Washington, DC during Standard Time)
**Administrative divisions:** 17 municipalities (concelhos, singular - concelho); Boa Vista, Brava, Maio, Mosteiros, Paul, Praia, Porto Novo, Ribeira Grande, Sal, Santa Catarina, Santa Cruz, Sao Domingos, Sao Filipe, Sao Miguel, Sao Nicolau, Sao Vicente, Tarrafal
**Independence:** 5 July 1975 (from Portugal)

**National holiday:** Independence Day, 5 July (1975)
**Constitution:** 25 September 1992; a major revision on 23 November 1995 substantially increased the powers of the president; a 1999 revision created the position of national ombudsman (Provedor de Justica)
**Legal system:** based on the legal system of Portugal; has not accepted compulsory ICJ jurisdiction
**Suffrage:** 18 years of age; universal
**Executive branch:**
*chief of state:* President Pedro Verona PIRES (since 22 March 2001)
*head of government:* Prime Minister Jose Maria Pereira NEVES (since 1 February 2001)
*cabinet:* Council of Ministers appointed by the president on the recommendation of the prime minister
*elections:* president elected by popular vote for a five-year term (eligible for a second term); election last held 12 February 2006 (next to be held in February 2011); prime minister nominated by the National Assembly and appointed by the president
*election results:* Pedro PIRES reelected president; percent of vote - Pedro PIRES (PAICV) 51.2%, Carlos VIEGA (MPD) 48.8%
**Legislative branch:** unicameral National Assembly or Assembleia Nacional (72 seats; members are elected by popular vote to serve five-year terms)
*elections:* last held 22 January 2006 (next to be held in January 2011)
*election results:* percent of vote by party - PAICV 52.3%, MPD 44%, UCID 2.7%; seats by party - PAICV 41, MPD 29, UCID 2
**Judicial branch:** Supreme Tribunal of Justice or Supremo Tribunal de Justia
**Political parties and leaders:** African Party for Independence of Cape Verde or PAICV [Jose Maria Pereira NEVES, chairman]; Democratic Christian Party or PDC [Manuel RODRIGUES]; Democratic Renovation Party or PRD [Victor FIDALGO]; Democratic and Independent Cape Verdean Union or UCID [Antonio MONTEIRO]; Movement for Democracy or MPD [Jorge SANTOS]; Party for Democratic Convergence or PCD [Dr. Eurico MONTEIRO]; Party of Work and Solidarity or PTS [Isaias RODRIGUES]; Social Democratic Party or PSD [Joao ALEM]
**Political pressure groups and leaders:**
*other:* environmentalists; political pressure groups
**International organization participation:** ACCT, ACP, AfDB, AU, CPLP, ECOWAS, FAO, G-77, IBRD, ICAO, ICCt (signatory), ICRM, IDA, IFAD, IFC, IFRCS, ILO, IMF, IMO, Interpol, IOC, IOM, IPU, ITSO, ITU, ITUC, MIGA, NAM, OIF, OPCW, UN, UNCTAD, UNESCO, UNIDO, Union Latina, UNWTO, UPU, WCO, WFTU, WHO, WIPO, WMO, WTO
**Diplomatic representation in the US:**
*chief of mission:* Ambassador Fatima Lima VEIGA
*chancery:* 3415 Massachusetts Avenue NW, Washington, DC 20007
*telephone:* [1] (202) 965-6820
*FAX:* [1] (202) 965-1207
*consulate(s) general:* Boston

# Cape Verde (continued)

**Diplomatic representation from the US:**
*chief of mission:* Ambassador Marianne M. MYLES
*embassy:* Rua Abilio Macedo n6, Praia
*mailing address:* C. P. 201, Praia
*telephone:* [238] 2-60-89-00
*FAX:* [238] 2-61-13-55

**Flag description:** five unequal horizontal bands; the top-most band of blue - equal to one half the width of the flag - is followed by three bands of white, red, and white, each equal to 1/12 of the width, and a bottom stripe of blue equal to one quarter of the flag width; a circle of 10, yellow, five-pointed stars, each representing one of the islands, is centered on the red stripe and positioned 3/8 of the length of the flag from the hoist side

## Economy

**Economy - overview:** This island economy suffers from a poor natural resource base, including serious water shortages exacerbated by cycles of long-term drought. The economy is service-oriented, with commerce, transport, tourism, and public services accounting for about three-fourths of GDP. Although nearly 70% of the population lives in rural areas, the share of food production in GDP is low. About 82% of food must be imported. The fishing potential, mostly lobster and tuna, is not fully exploited. Cape Verde annually runs a high trade deficit, financed by foreign aid and remittances from emigrants; remittances supplement GDP by more than 20%. Economic reforms are aimed at developing the private sector and attracting foreign investment to diversify the economy. Future prospects depend heavily on the maintenance of aid flows, the encouragement of tourism, remittances, and the momentum of the government's development program. Cape Verde became a member of the WTO in July 2008.

**GDP (purchasing power parity):**
$1.635 billion (2008 est.)
$1.542 billion (2007)
$1.443 billion (2006)
*note:* data are in 2008 US dollars

**GDP (official exchange rate):** $1.845 billion (2008 est.)

**GDP - real growth rate:**
6% (2008 est.)
6.9% (2007 est.)
10.8% (2006 est.)

**GDP - per capita (PPP):**
$3,800 (2008 est.)
$3,600 (2007 est.)
$3,400 (2006 est.)
*note:* data are in 2008 US dollars

**GDP - composition by sector:**
*agriculture:* 9%
*industry:* 16.9%
*services:* 74.1% (2008 est.)

**Labor force:** 120,600 (1990)

**Unemployment rate:**
21% (2000 est.)

**Population below poverty line:** 30% (2000)

**Household income or consumption by percentage share:**
*lowest 10%:* NA%
*highest 10%:* NA%

**Investment (gross fixed):** 41.3% of GDP (2008 est.)

**Budget:**
*revenues:* $525.4 million
*expenditures:* $585.3 million (2008 est.)

**Inflation rate (consumer prices):**
5% (2008 est.)
4.4% (2007 est.)

**Central bank discount rate:** 8.5% (31 December 2007)

**Commercial bank prime lending rate:** 10.55% (31 December 2007)

**Stock of money:** $574 million (31 December 2007)

**Stock of quasi money:** $689 million (31 December 2007)

**Stock of domestic credit:** $1.049 billion (31 December 2007)

**Agriculture - products:** bananas, corn, beans, sweet potatoes, sugarcane, coffee, peanuts; fish

**Industries:** food and beverages, fish processing, shoes and garments, salt mining, ship repair

**Industrial production growth rate:** 8% (2008 est.)

**Electricity - production:** 47 million kWh (2006 est.)

**Electricity - consumption:** 43.71 million kWh (2006 est.)

**Electricity - exports:** 0 kWh (2007 est.)

**Electricity - imports:** 0 kWh (2007 est.)

**Oil - production:** 0 bbl/day (2007 est.)

**Oil - consumption:** 2,117 bbl/day (2006 est.)

**Oil - exports:** 0 bbl/day (2005)

**Oil - imports:** 1,785 bbl/day (2005)

**Oil - proved reserves:** 0 bbl (1 January 2006 est.)

**Natural gas - production:** 0 cu m (2007 est.)

**Natural gas - consumption:** 0 cu m (2007 est.)

**Natural gas - exports:** 0 cu m (2007 est.)

**Natural gas - imports:** 0 cu m (2007 est.)

**Natural gas - proved reserves:** 0 cu m (1 January 2006 est.)

**Current account balance:** -$167 million (2008 est.)

**Exports:** $102 million f.o.b. (2008 est.)

**Exports - commodities:** fuel, shoes, garments, fish, hides

**Exports - partners:** Spain 37.2%, Portugal 29.9%, Morocco 7%, US 6.6% (2007)

**Imports:** $887 million f.o.b. (2008 est.)

**Imports - commodities:** foodstuffs, industrial products, transport equipment, fuels

**Imports - partners:** Portugal 40.7%, Netherlands 10.9%, France 6.5%, Spain 5.6%, Cote d'Ivoire 4.9%, Brazil 4.7%, Italy 4.7% (2007)

**Reserves of foreign exchange and gold:** $459 million (31 December 2008 est.)

**Debt - external:** $325 million (2002)

**Exchange rates:** Cape Verdean escudos (CVE) per US dollar - 73.84 (2008 est.), 81.235 (2007), 87.946 (2006), 88.67 (2005), 88.808 (2004)

## Communications

**Telephones - main lines in use:** 71,600 (2006)

**Telephones - mobile cellular:** 148,000 (2007)

**Telephone system:**
*general assessment:* effective system, extensive modernization from 1996-2000 following partial privatization in 1995
*domestic:* major service provider is Cabo Verde Telecom (CVT); fiber-optic ring, completed in 2001, links all islands providing Internet access and ISDN services; cellular service introduced in 1998; broadband services launched in 2004
*international:* country code - 238; landing point for the Atlantis-2 fiber-optic transatlantic telephone cable that provides links to South America, Senegal, and Europe; HF radiotelephone to Senegal and Guinea-Bissau; satellite earth station - 1 Intelsat (Atlantic Ocean) (2007)

**Radio broadcast stations:** AM 0, FM 22 (plus 12 repeaters), shortwave 0 (2001)

**Television broadcast stations:** 1 (plus 7 repeaters) (2001)

**Internet country code:** .cv

**Internet hosts:** 20 (2008)

**Internet users:** 37,000 (2007)

## Transportation

**Airports:** 10 (2008)

**Airports - with paved runways:**
*total:* 9
*over 3,047 m:* 1
*1,524 to 2,437 m:* 3
*914 to 1,523 m:* 3
*under 914 m:* 2 (2008)

**Roadways:**
*total:* 1,350 km
*paved:* 932 km
*unpaved:* 418 km (2000)

**Merchant marine:**
*total:* 8
*by type:* cargo 2, chemical tanker 1, passenger/cargo 5
*foreign-owned:* 2 (Spain 1, UK 1) (2008)

**Ports and terminals:** Porto Grande

## Military

**Military branches:** People's Revolutionary Armed Forces (FARP): Army, Coast Guard (includes maritime air wing) (2007)

**Military service age and obligation:** 18 years of age (est.) for selective compulsory military service; 14-month conscript service obligation (2006)

**Manpower available for military service:**
*males age 16-49:* 103,650
*females age 16-49:* 103,553 (2008 est.)

**Manpower fit for military service:**
*males age 16-49:* 84,967
*females age 16-49:* 90,154 (2009 est.)

# Cape Verde *(continued)*

**Manpower reaching militarily significant age annually:**
*male:* 5,471
*female:* 5,349 (2009 est.)
**Military expenditures:** 0.7% of GDP (2005)

## Transnational Issues

**Disputes - international:** none
**Illicit drugs:** used as a transshipment point for Latin American cocaine destined for Western Europe, particularly because of Lusophone links to Brazil, Portugal, and Guinea-Bissau; has taken steps to deter drug money laundering, including a 2002 anti-money laundering reform that criminalizes laundering the proceeds of narcotics trafficking and other crimes and the establishment in 2008 of a Financial Intelligence Unit (2008)

# Cayman Islands
*(overseas territory of the UK)*

## Introduction

**Background:** The Cayman Islands were colonized from Jamaica by the British during the 18th and 19th centuries and were administered by Jamaica after 1863. In 1959, the islands became a territory within the Federation of the West Indies. When the Federation dissolved in 1962, the Cayman Islands chose to remain a British dependency.

## Geography

**Location:** Caribbean, three-island group (Grand Cayman, Cayman Brac, Little Cayman) in Caribbean Sea, 240 km south of Cuba and 268 km northwest of Jamaica
**Geographic coordinates:** 19 30 N, 80 30 W
**Map references:** Central America and the Caribbean
**Area:**
*total:* 262 sq km
*land:* 262 sq km
*water:* 0 sq km
**Area - comparative:** 1.5 times the size of Washington, DC
**Land boundaries:** 0 km
**Coastline:** 160 km
**Maritime claims:**
*territorial sea:* 12 nm
*exclusive fishing zone:* 200 nm
**Climate:** tropical marine; warm, rainy summers (May to October) and cool, relatively dry winters (November to April)
**Terrain:** low-lying limestone base surrounded by coral reefs
**Elevation extremes:**
*lowest point:* Caribbean Sea 0 m
*highest point:* The Bluff (Cayman Brac) 43 m
**Natural resources:** fish, climate and beaches that foster tourism

**Land use:**
*arable land:* 3.85%
*permanent crops:* 0%
*other:* 96.15% (2005)
**Irrigated land:** NA
**Natural hazards:** hurricanes (July to November)
**Environment - current issues:** no natural fresh water resources; drinking water supplies must be met by rainwater catchments
**Geography - note:** important location between Cuba and Central America

## People

**Population:** 49,035
*note:* most of the population lives on Grand Cayman (July 2009 est.)
**Age structure:**
*0-14 years:* 19.6% (male 4,824/female 4,783)
*15-64 years:* 71.1% (male 16,994/female 17,884)
*65 years and over:* 9.3% (male 2,139/female 2,411) (2009 est.)
**Median age:**
*total:* 38.1 years
*male:* 37.7 years
*female:* 38.6 years (2009 est.)
**Population growth rate:** 2.394% (2009 est.)
**Birth rate:** 12.36 births/1,000 population (2009 est.)
**Death rate:** 4.83 deaths/1,000 population (2008 est.)
**Net migration rate:** 16.48 migrant(s)/1,000 population
*note:* major destination for Cubans trying to migrate to the US (2009 est.)
**Urbanization:**
*urban population:* 100% of total population (2008)
*rate of urbanization:* 1.5% annual rate of change (2005-10 est.)
**Sex ratio:**
*at birth:* 1.02 male(s)/female
*under 15 years:* 1.01 male(s)/female
*15-64 years:* 0.95 male(s)/female
*65 years and over:* 0.89 male(s)/female
*total population:* 0.96 male(s)/female (2009 est.)
**Infant mortality rate:**
*total:* 6.94 deaths/1,000 live births
*male:* 7.96 deaths/1,000 live births
*female:* 5.9 deaths/1,000 live births (2009 est.)
**Life expectancy at birth:**
*total population:* 80.44 years
*male:* 77.8 years
*female:* 83.14 years (2009 est.)
**Total fertility rate:** 1.88 children born/woman (2009 est.)
**HIV/AIDS - adult prevalence rate:** NA
**HIV/AIDS - people living with HIV/AIDS:** NA
**HIV/AIDS - deaths:** NA
**Nationality:**
*noun:* Caymanian(s)
*adjective:* Caymanian
**Ethnic groups:** mixed 40%, white 20%, black 20%, expatriates of various ethnic groups 20%

# Cayman Islands *(continued)*

**Religions:** Church of God 26%, United Church 11.8% (Presbyterian and Congregational), Roman Catholic 11%, Baptist 8.7%, Seventh Day Adventist 8.2%, Anglican 5.7%, Pentecostal 5.3%, other Christian 2.7%, non-denominational 5.8%, other 3.8%, none 9.8%, unspecified 1.1% (1999 census)

**Languages:** English 95%, Spanish 3.2%, other 1.8% (1999 census)

**Literacy:**
*definition:* age 15 and over has ever attended school
*total population:* 98%
*male:* 98%
*female:* 98% (1970 est.)

**School life expectancy (primary to tertiary education):**
*total:* 13 years
*male:* 12 years
*female:* 13 years (2001)

**Education expenditures:** 2.8% of GDP (2005)

## Government

**Country name:**
*conventional long form:* none
*conventional short form:* Cayman Islands
**Dependency status:** overseas territory of the UK
**Government type:** British crown colony
**Capital:**
*name:* George Town (on Grand Cayman)
*geographic coordinates:* 19 18 N, 81 23 W
*time difference:* UTC-5 (same time as Washington, DC during Standard Time)
**Administrative divisions:** 8 districts; Creek, Eastern, Midland, South Town, Spot Bay, Stake Bay, West End, Western
**Independence:** none (overseas territory of the UK)
**National holiday:** Constitution Day, first Monday in July
**Constitution:** 1959; revised 1962, 1972, and 1994
**Legal system:** British common law and local statutes
**Suffrage:** 18 years of age; universal
**Executive branch:**
*chief of state:* Queen ELIZABETH II (since 6 February 1952); represented by Governor Stuart JACK (since 23 November 2005)
*head of government:* Leader of Government Business McKeeva BUSH (since 27 May 2009)
*cabinet:* The Cabinet (three members appointed by the governor, five members elected by the Legislative Assembly)
*elections:* the monarch is hereditary; the governor is appointed by the monarch; following legislative elections, the leader of the majority party or coalition is appointed by the governor Leader of Government Business
**Legislative branch:** unicameral Legislative Assembly (18 seats; 3 appointed members from The Cabinet and 15 elected by popular vote; to serve four-year terms)
*elections:* last held 20 May 2009 (next to be held not later than May 2013)
*election results:* percent of vote by party - NA; seats by party - UDP 9, PPM 5, independent 1

**Judicial branch:** Summary Court; Grand Court; Cayman Islands Court of Appeal
**Political parties and leaders:** United Democratic Party or UDP [McKeeva BUSH]; People's Progressive Movement or PPM [Kurt TIBBETTS]
**Political pressure groups and leaders:** National Trust
*other:* environmentalists
**International organization participation:** Caricom (associate), CDB, Interpol (subbureau), IOC, UNESCO (associate), UPU, WFTU
**Diplomatic representation in the US:** none (overseas territory of the UK)
**Diplomatic representation from the US:** none (overseas territory of the UK)
**Flag description:** blue, with the flag of the UK in the upper hoist-side quadrant and the Caymanian coat of arms centered on the outer half of the flag; the coat of arms includes a pineapple and turtle above a shield with three stars (representing the three islands) and a scroll at the bottom bearing the motto HE HATH FOUNDED IT UPON THE SEAS

## Economy

**Economy - overview:** With no direct taxation, the islands are a thriving offshore financial center. More than 68,000 companies were registered in the Cayman Islands as of 2003, including almost 500 banks, 800 insurers, and 5,000 mutual funds. A stock exchange was opened in 1997. Tourism is also a mainstay, accounting for about 70% of GDP and 75% of foreign currency earnings. The tourist industry is aimed at the luxury market and caters mainly to visitors from North America. Total tourist arrivals exceeded 2.1 million in 2003, with about half from the US. About 90% of the islands' food and consumer goods must be imported. The Caymanians enjoy one of the highest outputs per capita and one of the highest standards of living in the world.
**GDP (purchasing power parity):**
$1.939 billion (2004 est.)
$1.922 billion (2003)
**GDP (official exchange rate):** $NA
**GDP - real growth rate:**
0.9% (2004 est.)
**GDP - per capita (PPP):**
$43,800 (2004 est.)
**GDP - composition by sector:**
*agriculture:* 1.4%
*industry:* 3.2%
*services:* 95.4% (1994 est.)
**Labor force:** 23,450 (2004)
**Labor force - by occupation:**
*agriculture:* 1.4%
*industry:* 12.6%
*services:* 86% (1995)
**Unemployment rate:**
4.4% (2004)
**Population below poverty line:** NA%

**Household income or consumption by percentage share:**
*lowest 10%:* NA%
*highest 10%:* NA%
**Budget:**
*revenues:* $423.8 million
*expenditures:* $392.6 million (2004)
**Inflation rate (consumer prices):**
4.4% (2004)
**Market value of publicly traded shares:** $183.5 million (31 December 2007)
**Agriculture - products:** vegetables, fruit; livestock; turtle farming
**Industries:** tourism, banking, insurance and finance, construction, construction materials, furniture
**Industrial production growth rate:** NA%
**Electricity - production:** 546.1 million kWh (2007 est.)
**Electricity - consumption:** 546.1 million kWh (2007 est.)
**Electricity - exports:** 0 kWh (2007 est.)
**Electricity - imports:** 0 kWh (2007 est.)
**Oil - production:** 0 bbl/day (2007 est.)
**Oil - consumption:** 2,767 bbl/day (2006 est.)
**Oil - exports:** 0 bbl/day (2005)
**Oil - imports:** 2,818 bbl/day (2005)
**Oil - proved reserves:** 0 bbl (1 January 2006 est.)
**Natural gas - production:** 0 cu m (2007 est.)
**Natural gas - consumption:** 0 cu m (2007 est.)
**Natural gas - exports:** 0 cu m (2007 est.)
**Natural gas - imports:** 0 cu m (2007 est.)
**Natural gas - proved reserves:** 0 cu m (1 January 2006 est.)
**Exports:** $2.52 million (2004)
**Exports - commodities:** turtle products, manufactured consumer goods
**Imports:** $866.9 million f.o.b. (2004)
**Imports - commodities:** foodstuffs, manufactured goods
**Debt - external:** $70 million (1996)
**Stock of direct foreign investment - at home:** $NA
**Stock of direct foreign investment - abroad:** $NA
**Exchange rates:** Caymanian dollars (KYD) per US dollar - NA (2007), 0.8496 (2006)

## Communications

**Telephones - main lines in use:** 38,000 (2002)
**Telephones - mobile cellular:** 33,800 (2004)
**Telephone system:**
*general assessment:* reasonably good system
*domestic:* liberalization of telecom market in 2003; introduction of competition in the mobile-cellular market in 2004
*international:* country code - 1-345; landing point for the MAYA-1 submarine telephone cable network that provides links to the US and parts of Central and South America; submarine cable provides connectivity to Jamaica; satellite earth station - 1 Intelsat (Atlantic Ocean) (2007)

## Cayman Islands *(continued)*

**Radio broadcast stations:** AM 1, FM 4, shortwave 0 (2004)
**Television broadcast stations:** 4 with cable system (2004)
**Internet country code:** .ky
**Internet hosts:** 4,648 (2008)
**Internet users:** 22,000 (2007)

### Transportation

**Airports:** 3 (2008)
**Airports - with paved runways:**
*total:* 2
*1,524 to 2,437 m:* 2 (2008)
**Airports - with unpaved runways:**
*total:* 1
*914 to 1,523 m:* 1 (2008)
**Roadways:**
*total:* 785 km
*paved:* 785 km (2007)
**Merchant marine:**
*total:* 109
*by type:* bulk carrier 30, cargo 2, chemical tanker 42, petroleum tanker 15, refrigerated cargo 10, roll on/roll off 3, vehicle carrier 7
*foreign-owned:* 107 (Denmark 3, Germany 15, Greece 16, Italy 4, Japan 13, Norway 1, Singapore 10, UK 3, US 42) (2008)
**Ports and terminals:** Cayman Brac, George Town

### Military

**Military branches:** no regular military forces; Royal Cayman Islands Police Force (2007)
**Manpower available for military service:**
*males age 16-49:* 11,790 (2008 est.)
**Manpower fit for military service:**
*males age 16-49:* 9,735
*females age 16-49:* 10,145 (2009 est.)
**Manpower reaching militarily significant age annually:**
*male:* 334
*female:* 345 (2009 est.)
**Military - note:** defense is the responsibility of the UK

### Transnational Issues

**Disputes - international:** none
**Illicit drugs:** major offshore financial center; vulnerable to drug transshipment to the US and Europe (2008)

# Central African Republic

### Introduction

**Background:** The former French colony of Ubangi-Shari became the Central African Republic upon independence in 1960. After three tumultuous decades of misrule - mostly by military governments - civilian rule was established in 1993 and lasted for one decade. President Ange-Felix PATASSE's civilian government was plagued by unrest, and in March 2003 he was deposed in a military coup led by General Francois BOZIZE, who established a transitional government. Though the government has the tacit support of civil society groups and the main parties, a wide field of candidates contested the municipal, legislative, and presidential elections held in March and May of 2005 in which General BOZIZE was affirmed as president. The government still does not fully control the countryside, where pockets of lawlessness persist. Unrest in neighboring nations, Chad, Sudan, and the DRC, continues to affect stability in the Central African Republic as well.

### Geography

**Location:** Central Africa, north of Democratic Republic of the Congo
**Geographic coordinates:** 7 00 N, 21 00 E
**Map references:** Africa
**Area:**
*total:* 622,984 sq km
*land:* 622,984 sq km
*water:* 0 sq km
**Area - comparative:** slightly smaller than Texas
**Land boundaries:**
*total:* 5,203 km
*border countries:* Cameroon 797 km, Chad 1,197 km, Democratic Republic of the Congo 1,577 km, Republic of the Congo 467 km, Sudan 1,165 km
**Coastline:** 0 km (landlocked)
**Maritime claims:** none (landlocked)
**Climate:** tropical; hot, dry winters; mild to hot, wet summers

**Terrain:** vast, flat to rolling, monotonous plateau; scattered hills in northeast and southwest
**Elevation extremes:**
*lowest point:* Oubangui River 335 m
*highest point:* Mont Ngaoui 1,420 m
**Natural resources:** diamonds, uranium, timber, gold, oil, hydropower
**Land use:**
*arable land:* 3.1%
*permanent crops:* 0.15%
*other:* 96.75% (2005)
**Irrigated land:** 20 sq km (2003)
**Total renewable water resources:** 144.4 cu km (2003)
**Freshwater withdrawal (domestic/industrial/agricultural):**
*total:* 0.03 cu km/yr (80%/16%/4%)
*per capita:* 7 cu m/yr (2000)
**Natural hazards:** hot, dry, dusty harmattan winds affect northern areas; floods are common
**Environment - current issues:** tap water is not potable; poaching has diminished the country's reputation as one of the last great wildlife refuges; desertification; deforestation
**Environment - international agreements:**
*party to:* Biodiversity, Climate Change, Climate Change-Kyoto Protocol, Desertification, Endangered Species, Hazardous Wastes, Ozone Layer Protection, Tropical Timber 94, Wetlands
*signed, but not ratified:* Law of the Sea
**Geography - note:** landlocked; almost the precise center of Africa

### People

**Population:** 4,511,488
*note:* estimates for this country explicitly take into account the effects of excess mortality due to AIDS; this can result in lower life expectancy, higher infant mortality, higher death rates, lower population growth rates, and changes in the distribution of population by age and sex than would otherwise be expected (July 2009 est.)
**Age structure:**
*0-14 years:* 40.9% (male 928,277/female 917,739)
*15-64 years:* 55% (male 1,235,940/female 1,244,958)
*65 years and over:* 4.1% (male 71,439/female 113,135) (2009 est.)
**Median age:**
*total:* 18.8 years
*male:* 18.5 years
*female:* 19.1 years (2009 est.)
**Population growth rate:** 1.491% (2009 est.)
**Birth rate:** 32.75 births/1,000 population (2009 est.)
**Death rate:** 18.04 deaths/1,000 population (2008 est.)
**Net migration rate:** NA
**Urbanization:**
*urban population:* 39% of total population (2008)
*rate of urbanization:* 2.3% annual rate of change (2005-10 est.)

# Central African Republic (continued)

**Sex ratio:**
*at birth:* 1.03 male(s)/female
*under 15 years:* 1.01 male(s)/female
*15-64 years:* 0.99 male(s)/female
*65 years and over:* 0.63 male(s)/female
*total population:* 0.98 male(s)/female (2009 est.)

**Infant mortality rate:**
*total:* 80.62 deaths/1,000 live births
*male:* 87.22 deaths/1,000 live births
*female:* 73.82 deaths/1,000 live births (2009 est.)

**Life expectancy at birth:**
*total population:* 44.47 years
*male:* 44.4 years
*female:* 44.54 years (2009 est.)

**Total fertility rate:** 4.14 children born/woman (2009 est.)

**HIV/AIDS - adult prevalence rate:** 6.3% (2007 est.)

**HIV/AIDS - people living with HIV/AIDS:** 160,000 (2007 est.)

**HIV/AIDS - deaths:** 11,000 (2007 est.)

**Major infectious diseases:**
*degree of risk:* very high
*food or waterborne diseases:* bacterial and protozoal diarrhea, hepatitis A, and typhoid fever
*vectorborne disease:* malaria
*respiratory disease:* meningococcal meningitis
*water contact disease:* schistosomiasis
*animal contact disease:* rabies (2009)

**Nationality:**
*noun:* Central African(s)
*adjective:* Central African

**Ethnic groups:** Baya 33%, Banda 27%, Mandjia 13%, Sara 10%, Mboum 7%, M'Baka 4%, Yakoma 4%, other 2%

**Religions:** indigenous beliefs 35%, Protestant 25%, Roman Catholic 25%, Muslim 15%
*note:* animistic beliefs and practices strongly influence the Christian majority

**Languages:** French (official), Sangho (lingua franca and national language), tribal languages

**Literacy:**
*definition:* age 15 and over can read and write
*total population:* 48.6%
*male:* 64.8%
*female:* 33.5% (2000 est.)

**Education expenditures:** 1.4% of GDP (2006)

## Government

**Country name:**
*conventional long form:* Central African Republic
*conventional short form:* none
*local long form:* Republique Centrafricaine
*local short form:* none
*former:* Ubangi-Shari, Central African Empire
*abbreviation:* CAR

**Government type:** republic

**Capital:**
*name:* Bangui
*geographic coordinates:* 4 22 N, 18 35 E
*time difference:* UTC+1 (6 hours ahead of Washington, DC during Standard Time)

**Administrative divisions:** 14 prefectures (prefectures, singular - prefecture), 2 economic prefectures* (prefectures economiques, singular - prefecture economique), and 1 commune**; Bamingui-Bangoran, Bangui**, Basse-Kotto, Haute-Kotto, Haut-Mbomou, Kemo, Lobaye, Mambere-Kadei, Mbomou, Nana-Grebizi*, Nana-Mambere, Ombella-Mpoko, Ouaka, Ouham, Ouham-Pende, Sangha-Mbaere*, Vakaga

**Independence:** 13 August 1960 (from France)

**National holiday:** Republic Day, 1 December (1958)

**Constitution:** ratified by popular referendum 5 December 2004; effective 27 December 2004

**Legal system:** based on French law; has not accepted compulsory ICJ jurisdiction

**Suffrage:** 21 years of age; universal

**Executive branch:**
*chief of state:* President Francois BOZIZE (since 15 March 2003 coup)
*head of government:* Prime Minister Faustin-Archange TOUADERA (since 22 January 2008)
*cabinet:* Council of Ministers
*elections:* under the new constitution, the president elected to a five-year term (eligible for a second term); elections last held 13 March and 8 May 2005 (next to be held in 2010); prime minister appointed by the political party with a parliamentary majority
*election results:* Francois BOZIZE elected president; percent of second round balloting - Francois BOZIZE (KNK) 64.6%, Martin ZIGUELE (MLPC) 35.4%

**Legislative branch:** unicameral National Assembly or Assemblee Nationale (105 seats; members are elected by popular vote to serve five-year terms)
*elections:* last held 13 March 2005 and 8 May 2005 (next to be held in 2010)
*election results:* percent of vote by party - NA; seats by party - KNK 42, MLPC 11, RDC 8, PSD 4, FPP 2, ADP 2, LONDO 1, independents 34, other 1

**Judicial branch:** Supreme Court or Cour Supreme; Constitutional Court (three judges appointed by the president, three by the president of the National Assembly, and three by fellow judges); Court of Appeal; Criminal Courts; Inferior Courts

**Political parties and leaders:** Alliance for Democracy and Progress or ADP [Jacques MBOLIEDAS]; Central African Democratic Rally or RDC [Andre KOLINGBA]; Civic Forum or FC [Gen. Timothee MALENDOMA]; Democratic Forum for Modernity or FODEM [Charles MASSI]; Liberal Democratic Party or PLD [Nestor KOMBO-NAGUEMON]; Londo Association or LONDO; Movement for Democracy and Development or MDD [David DACKO]; Movement for the Liberation of the Central African People or MLPC [Ange-Felix PATASSE] (the party of deposed president); National Convergence or KNK; Patriotic Front for Progress or FPP [Abel GOUMBA]; People's Union for the Republic or UPR [Pierre Sammy MAKFOY]; National Unity Party or PUN [Jean-Paul NGOUPANDE]; Social Democratic Party or PSD [Enoch LAKOUE]

**Political pressure groups and leaders:** Monam (combating gender-base violence)

**International organization participation:** ACCT, ACP, AfDB, AU, BDEAC, CEMAC, FAO, FZ, G-77, IAEA, IBRD, ICAO, ICCt, ICRM, IDA, IFAD, IFC, IFRCS, ILO, IMF, Interpol, IOC, ITSO, ITU, ITUC, MIGA, NAM, OIC (observer), OIF, OPCW, UN, UNCTAD, UNESCO, UNIDO, UNWTO, UPU, WCL, WCO, WFTU, WHO, WIPO, WMO, WTO

**Diplomatic representation in the US:**
*chief of mission:* Ambassador Emmanuel TOUABOY
*chancery:* 1618 22nd Street NW, Washington, DC 20008
*telephone:* [1] (202) 483-7800
*FAX:* [1] (202) 332-9893

**Diplomatic representation from the US:**
*chief of mission:* Ambassador Frederick B. COOK
*embassy:* Avenue David Dacko, Bangui
*mailing address:* B. P. 924, Bangui
*telephone:* [236] 61 02 00
*FAX:* [236] 61 44 94
*note:* the embassy is currently operating with a minimal staff

**Flag description:** four equal horizontal bands of blue (top), white, green, and yellow with a vertical red band in center; a yellow five-pointed star to the hoist side of the blue band

## Economy

**Economy - overview:** Subsistence agriculture, together with forestry, remains the backbone of the economy of the Central African Republic (CAR), with more than 70% of the population living in outlying areas. The agricultural sector generates more than half of GDP. Timber has accounted for about 16% of export earnings and the diamond industry, for 40%. Important constraints to economic development include the CAR's landlocked position, a poor transportation system, a largely unskilled work force, and a legacy of misdirected macroeconomic policies. Factional fighting between the government and its opponents remains a drag on economic revitalization. Distribution of income is extraordinarily unequal. Grants from France and the international community can only partially meet humanitarian needs.

**GDP (purchasing power parity):**
$3.239 billion (2008 est.)
$3.13 billion (2007)
$3.004 billion (2006)
*note:* data are in 2008 US dollars

**GDP (official exchange rate):** $2.087 billion (2008 est.)

**GDP - real growth rate:**
3.5% (2008 est.)
4.2% (2007 est.)
4% (2006 est.)

**GDP - per capita (PPP):**
$700 (2008 est.)
$700 (2007 est.)
$700 (2006 est.)
*note:* data are in 2008 US dollars

**GDP - composition by sector:**
*agriculture:* 55%
*industry:* 20%
*services:* 25% (2001 est.)
**Labor force:** 1.857 million (2006)
**Unemployment rate:**
8% (2001 est.)
*note:* 23% unemployment for Bangui
**Population below poverty line:** NA%
**Household income or consumption by percentage share:**
*lowest 10%:* 0.7%
*highest 10%:* 47.7% (1993)
**Distribution of family income - Gini index:** 61.3 (1993)
**Budget:**
*revenues:* $250 million
*expenditures:* $273 million (2007 est.)
**Inflation rate (consumer prices):**
0.9% (2007 est.)
**Central bank discount rate:** 5.25% (31 December 2007)
**Commercial bank prime lending rate:** 15% (31 December 2007)
**Stock of money:** $218.3 million (31 December 2007)
**Stock of quasi money:** $47.58 million (31 December 2007)
**Stock of domestic credit:** $320.2 million (31 December 2007)
**Market value of publicly traded shares:** $NA
**Agriculture - products:** timber, cotton, coffee, tobacco, manioc (tapioca), yams, millet, corn, bananas; timber
**Industries:** gold and diamond mining, logging, brewing, textiles, footwear, assembly of bicycles and motorcycles
**Industrial production growth rate:** 3% (2002)
**Electricity - production:** 110 million kWh (2006 est.)
**Electricity - consumption:** 102.3 million kWh (2006 est.)
**Electricity - exports:** 0 kWh (2007 est.)
**Electricity - imports:** 0 kWh (2007 est.)
**Oil - production:** 0 bbl/day (2007 est.)
**Oil - consumption:** 2,322 bbl/day (2006 est.)
**Oil - exports:** 0 bbl/day (2005)
**Oil - imports:** 2,057 bbl/day (2005)
**Oil - proved reserves:** 0 bbl (1 January 2006 est.)
**Natural gas - production:** 0 cu m (2007 est.)
**Natural gas - consumption:** 0 cu m (2007 est.)
**Natural gas - exports:** 0 cu m (2007 est.)
**Natural gas - imports:** 0 cu m (2007 est.)
**Natural gas - proved reserves:** 0 cu m (1 January 2006)
**Current account balance:** -$77 million (2007 est.)
**Exports:** $146.7 million f.o.b. (2007 est.)
**Exports - commodities:** diamonds, timber, cotton, coffee, tobacco
**Exports - partners:** Belgium 22.7%, Indonesia 19.3%, Italy 7.7%, France 7.1%, Spain 6.9%,

Democratic Republic of the Congo 6.8%, China 4.9%, Turkey 4.7% (2007)
**Imports:** $237.3 million f.o.b. (2007 est.)
**Imports - commodities:** food, textiles, petroleum products, machinery, electrical equipment, motor vehicles, chemicals, pharmaceuticals
**Imports - partners:** France 16.6%, Netherlands 13%, Cameroon 9.7%, US 6.3% (2007)
**Debt - external:** $1.153 billion (2007 est.)
**Exchange rates:** Cooperation Financiere en Afrique Centrale francs (XAF) per US dollar - 447.81 (2008 est.), 481.8 (2007), 522.59 (2006), 527.47 (2005), 528.29 (2004)
*note:* since 1 January 1999, the Central African CFA franc (XAF) has been pegged to the euro at a rate of 655.957 CFA francs per euro; Central African CFA franc (XAF) coins and banknotes are not accepted in countries using West African CFA francs (XOF), and vice versa, even though the two currencies trade at par

## Communications

**Telephones - main lines in use:** 12,000 (2006)
**Telephones - mobile cellular:** 130,000 (2007)
**Telephone system:**
*general assessment:* limited telephone service; fixed-line connections for well less than 1 per 100 persons coupled with mobile-cellular usage of only about 3 per 100 persons; most fixed-line and cellular telephone services are concentrated in Bangui
*domestic:* network consists principally of microwave radio relay and low-capacity, low-powered radiotelephone communication
*international:* country code - 236; satellite earth station -1 Intelsat (Atlantic Ocean) (2007)
**Radio broadcast stations:** AM 1, FM 5, shortwave 1 (2001)
**Television broadcast stations:** 1 (2001)
**Internet country code:** .cf
**Internet hosts:** 21 (2008)
**Internet users:** 13,000 (2006)

## Transportation

**Airports:** 44 (2008)
**Airports - with paved runways:**
*total:* 2
*2,438 to 3,047 m:* 1
*1,524 to 2,437 m:* 1 (2008)
**Airports - with unpaved runways:**
*total:* 42
*2,438 to 3,047 m:* 1
*1,524 to 2,437 m:* 11
*914 to 1,523 m:* 19
*under 914 m:* 11 (2008)
**Roadways:**
*total:* 24,307 km (2000)
**Waterways:** 2,800 km (primarily on the Oubangui and Sangha rivers) (2007)
**Ports and terminals:** Bangui, Nola, Salo, Nzinga

## Military

**Military branches:** Central African Armed Forces (Forces Armees Centrafricaines, FACA): Ground Forces, General Directorate of Gendarmerie Inspection (DGIG), Military Air Service, National Police (2008)
**Military service age and obligation:** 18 years of age for selective military service; 2-year conscript service obligation (2008)
**Manpower available for military service:**
*males age 16-49:* 1,032,828
*females age 16-49:* 999,330 (2008 est.)
**Manpower fit for military service:**
*males age 16-49:* 552,907
*females age 16-49:* 512,611 (2009 est.)
**Manpower reaching militarily significant age annually:**
*male:* 55,484
*female:* 55,168 (2009 est.)
**Military expenditures:** 1.1% of GDP (2006 est.)

## Transnational Issues

**Disputes - international:** periodic skirmishes over water and grazing rights among related pastoral populations along the border with southern Sudan persist
**Refugees and internally displaced persons:**
*refugees (country of origin):* 7,900 (Sudan); 3,700 (Democratic Republic of the Congo); note - UNHCR resumed repatriation of Southern Sudanese refugees in 2006
*IDPs:* 197,000 (ongoing unrest following coup in 2003) (2007)
**Trafficking in persons:**
*current situation:* Central African Republic is a source, transit, and destination country for men, women, and children trafficked for the purposes of forced labor and sexual exploitation; the majority of victims are children trafficked within the country for sexual exploitation, domestic servitude, street vending, and forced agricultural, mine, market and restaurant labor; to a lesser extent, children are trafficked from the Central African Republic to Cameroon, Nigeria, and the Democratic Republic of Congo; rebels conscript children into armed forces within the country
*tier rating:* Tier 2 Watch List - Central African Republic is on the Tier 2 Watch List for the third consecutive year for its failure to show evidence of increasing efforts to combat trafficking in 2007; efforts to address trafficking through vigorous law enforcement measures and victim protection efforts were minimal, though awareness about trafficking appeared to be increasing in the country; the government does not actively investigate cases, work to identify trafficking victims among vulnerable populations, or rescue and provide care to victims; the government has not taken measures to reduce demand for commercial sex acts (2008)

# Chad

## Introduction

**Background:** Chad, part of France's African holdings until 1960, endured three decades of civil warfare as well as invasions by Libya before a semblance of peace was finally restored in 1990. The government eventually drafted a democratic constitution, and held flawed presidential elections in 1996 and 2001. In 1998, a rebellion broke out in northern Chad, which has sporadically flared up despite several peace agreements between the government and the rebels. In 2005, new rebel groups emerged in western Sudan and made probing attacks into eastern Chad, despite signing peace agreements in December 2006 and October 2007. Power remains in the hands of an ethnic minority. In June 2005, President Idriss DEBY held a referendum successfully removing constitutional term limits and won another controversial election in 2006. Sporadic rebel campaigns continued throughout 2006 and 2007, and the capital experienced a significant rebel threat in early 2008.

## Geography

**Location:** Central Africa, south of Libya
**Geographic coordinates:** 15 00 N, 19 00 E
**Map references:** Africa
**Area:**
*total:* 1.284 million sq km
*land:* 1,259,200 sq km
*water:* 24,800 sq km
**Area - comparative:** slightly more than three times the size of California
**Land boundaries:**
*total:* 5,968 km
*border countries:* Cameroon 1,094 km, Central African Republic 1,197 km, Libya 1,055 km, Niger 1,175 km, Nigeria 87 km, Sudan 1,360 km
**Coastline:** 0 km (landlocked)
**Maritime claims:** none (landlocked)
**Climate:** tropical in south, desert in north
**Terrain:** broad, arid plains in center, desert in north, mountains in northwest, lowlands in south
**Elevation extremes:**
*lowest point:* Djourab Depression 160 m
*highest point:* Emi Koussi 3,415 m
**Natural resources:** petroleum, uranium, natron, kaolin, fish (Lake Chad), gold, limestone, sand and gravel, salt
**Land use:**
*arable land:* 2.8%
*permanent crops:* 0.02%
*other:* 97.18% (2005)
**Irrigated land:** 300 sq km (2003)
**Total renewable water resources:** 43 cu km (1987)
**Freshwater withdrawal (domestic/industrial/agricultural):**
*total:* 0.23 cu km/yr (17%/0%/83%)
*per capita:* 24 cu m/yr (2000)
**Natural hazards:** hot, dry, dusty harmattan winds occur in north; periodic droughts; locust plagues
**Environment - current issues:** inadequate supplies of potable water; improper waste disposal in rural areas contributes to soil and water pollution; desertification
**Environment - international agreements:**
*party to:* Biodiversity, Climate Change, Desertification, Endangered Species, Hazardous Wastes, Ozone Layer Protection, Wetlands
*signed, but not ratified:* Law of the Sea, Marine Dumping
**Geography - note:** landlocked; Lake Chad is the most significant water body in the Sahel

## People

**Population:** 10,329,208 (July 2009 est.)
**Age structure:**
*0-14 years:* 46.7% (male 2,445,841/ female 2,381,319)
*15-64 years:* 50.4% (male 2,386,428/ female 2,816,050)
*65 years and over:* 2.9% (male 126,351/ female 173,219) (2009 est.)

**Median age:**
*total:* 16.5 years
*male:* 15.3 years
*female:* 17.7 years (2009 est.)
**Population growth rate:** 2.069% (2009 est.)
**Birth rate:** 40.86 births/1,000 population (2009 est.)
**Death rate:** 16.39 deaths/1,000 population (2008 est.)
**Net migration rate:** -4.08 migrant(s)/1,000 population (2009 est.)
**Urbanization:**
*urban population:* 27% of total population (2008)
*rate of urbanization:* 4.7% annual rate of change (2005-10 est.)
**Sex ratio:**
*at birth:* 1.04 male(s)/female
*under 15 years:* 1.03 male(s)/female
*15-64 years:* 0.85 male(s)/female
*65 years and over:* 0.73 male(s)/female
*total population:* 0.92 male(s)/female (2009 est.)
**Infant mortality rate:**
*total:* 98.69 deaths/1,000 live births
*male:* 104.72 deaths/1,000 live births
*female:* 92.42 deaths/1,000 live births (2009 est.)
**Life expectancy at birth:**
*total population:* 47.7 years
*male:* 46.67 years
*female:* 48.77 years (2009 est.)
**Total fertility rate:** 5.31 children born/woman (2009 est.)
**HIV/AIDS - adult prevalence rate:** 3.5% (2007 est.)
**HIV/AIDS - people living with HIV/AIDS:** 200,000 (2007 est.)
**HIV/AIDS - deaths:** 14,000 (2007 est.)
**Major infectious diseases:**
*degree of risk:* very high
*food or waterborne diseases:* bacterial and protozoal diarrhea, hepatitis A, and typhoid fever
*vectorborne disease:* malaria
*water contact disease:* schistosomiasis
*respiratory disease:* meningococcal meningitis
*animal contact disease:* rabies (2009)
**Nationality:**
*noun:* Chadian(s)
*adjective:* Chadian
**Ethnic groups:** Sara 27.7%, Arab 12.3%, Mayo-Kebbi 11.5%, Kanem-Bornou 9%, Ouaddai 8.7%, Hadjarai 6.7%, Tandjile 6.5%, Gorane 6.3%, Fitri-Batha 4.7%, other 6.4%, unknown 0.3% (1993 census)
**Religions:** Muslim 53.1%, Catholic 20.1%, Protestant 14.2%, animist 7.3%, other 0.5%, unknown 1.7%, atheist 3.1% (1993 census)
**Languages:** French (official), Arabic (official), Sara (in south), more than 120 different languages and dialects
**Literacy:**
*definition:* age 15 and over can read and write French or Arabic
*total population:* 25.7%
*male:* 40.8%
*female:* 12.8% (2000 est.)

# Chad *(continued)*

**School life expectancy (primary to tertiary education):**
*total:* 6 years
*male:* 7 years
*female:* 4 years (2005)
**Education expenditures:** 1.9% of GDP (2005)

## Government

**Country name:**
*conventional long form:* Republic of Chad
*conventional short form:* Chad
*local long form:* Republique du Tchad/Jumhuriyat Tshad
*local short form:* Tchad/Tshad
**Government type:** republic
**Capital:**
*name:* N'Djamena
*geographic coordinates:* 12 06 N, 15 02 E
*time difference:* UTC+1 (6 hours ahead of Washington, DC during Standard Time)
**Administrative divisions:** 18 regions (regions, singular - region); Batha, Borkou-Ennedi-Tibesti, Chari-Baguirmi, Guera, Hadjer-Lamis, Kanem, Lac, Logone Occidental, Logone Oriental, Mandoul, Mayo-Kebbi Est, Mayo-Kebbi Ouest, Moyen-Chari, Ouaddai, Salamat, Tandjile, Ville de N'Djamena, Wadi Fira
**Independence:** 11 August 1960 (from France)
**National holiday:** Independence Day, 11 August (1960)
**Constitution:** passed by referendum 31 March 1996; a June 2005 referendum removed constitutional term limits
**Legal system:** based on French civil law system and Chadian customary law; has not accepted compulsory ICJ jurisdiction
**Suffrage:** 18 years of age; universal
**Executive branch:**
*chief of state:* President Lt. Gen. Idriss DEBY Itno (since 4 December 1990)
*head of government:* Prime Minister Youssof Saleh ABBAS (since 16 April 2008)
*cabinet:* Council of State, members appointed by the president on the recommendation of the prime minister
*elections:* president elected by popular vote to serve five-year term; if no candidate receives at least 50% of the total vote, the two candidates receiving the most votes must stand for a second round of voting; last held 3 May 2006 (next to be held by May 2011); prime minister appointed by the president
*election results:* Lt. Gen. Idriss DEBY Itno reelected president; percent of vote - Lt. Gen. Idriss DEBY 64.7%, Delwa Kassire KOUMAKOYE 15.1%, Albert Pahimi PADACKE 7.8%, Mahamat ABDOULAYE 7.1%, Brahim KOULAMALLAH 5.3%; note - a June 2005 national referendum altered the constitution removing presidential term limits and permitting Lt. Gen. Idriss DEBY Itno to run for reelection

**Legislative branch:** unicameral National Assembly (155 seats; members elected by popular vote to serve four-year terms); note - the 1996 constitution called for a Senate that has never been formed
*elections:* National Assembly - last held 21 April 2002 (next to be held by 2009); note - legislative elections, originally scheduled for 2006, were first delayed by National Assembly action and subsequently by an accord, signed in August 2007, between government and opposition parties
*election results:* percent of vote by party - NA; seats by party - MPS 110, RDP 12, FAR 9, RNDP 5, UNDR 5, URD 3, other 11
**Judicial branch:** Supreme Court; Court of Appeal; Criminal Courts; Magistrate Courts
**Political parties and leaders:** Federation Action for the Republic or FAR [Ngarledjy YORONGAR]; National Rally for Development and Progress or RNDP [Delwa Kassire KOUMAKOYE]; National Union for Democracy and Renewal or UNDR [Saleh KEBZABO]; Party for Liberty and Development or PLD [Ibni Oumar Mahamat SALEH]; Patriotic Salvation Movement or MPS [Mahamat Saleh AHMAT, chairman]; Rally for Democracy and Progress or RDP [Lol Mahamat CHOUA]; Union for Renewal and Democracy or URD [Gen. Wadal Abdelkader KAMOUGUE]
**Political pressure groups and leaders:**
rebel groups
**International organization participation:** ACCT, ACP, AfDB, AU, BDEAC, CEMAC, FAO, FZ, G-77, IAEA, IBRD, ICAO, ICCt, ICRM, IDA, IDB, IFAD, IFC, IFRCS, ILO, IMF, Interpol, IOC, ITSO, ITU, ITUC, MIGA, NAM, OIC, OIF, OPCW, UN, UNCTAD, UNESCO, UNIDO, UNOCI, UNWTO, UPU, WCL, WCO, WFTU, WHO, WIPO, WMO, WTO
**Diplomatic representation in the US:**
*chief of mission:* Ambassador Mahamat Adam BECHIR
*chancery:* 2002 R Street NW, Washington, DC 20009
*telephone:* [1] (202) 462-4009
*FAX:* [1] (202) 265-1937
**Diplomatic representation from the US:**
*chief of mission:* Ambassador Louis NIGRO
*embassy:* Avenue Felix Eboue, N'Djamena
*mailing address:* B. P. 413, N'Djamena
*telephone:* [235] 251-62-11, 251-70-09, 251-77-59
*FAX:* [235] 251-56-54
**Flag description:** three equal vertical bands of blue (hoist side), yellow, and red
*note:* similar to the flag of Romania; also similar to the flags of Andorra and Moldova, both of which have a national coat of arms centered in the yellow band; design was based on the flag of France

## Economy

**Economy - overview:** Chad's primarily agricultural economy will continue to be boosted by major foreign direct investment projects in the oil sector that began in 2000. At least 80% of Chad's population relies on subsistence farming and livestock raising for its

livelihood. Chad's economy has long been handicapped by its landlocked position, high energy costs, and a history of instability. Chad relies on foreign assistance and foreign capital for most public and private sector investment projects. A consortium led by two US companies has been investing $3.7 billion to develop oil reserves - estimated at 1 billion barrels - in southern Chad. Chinese companies are also expanding exploration efforts and plan to build a refinery. The nation's total oil reserves are estimated at 1.5 billion barrels. Oil production came on stream in late 2003. Chad began to export oil in 2004. Cotton, cattle, and gum arabic provide the bulk of Chad's non-oil export earnings.
**GDP (purchasing power parity):**
$16.26 billion (2008 est.)
$15.99 billion (2007)
$15.79 billion (2006)
*note:* data are in 2008 US dollars
**GDP (official exchange rate):** $9.106 billion (2008 est.)
**GDP - real growth rate:**
1.7% (2008 est.)
1.3% (2007 est.)
0.2% (2006 est.)
**GDP - per capita (PPP):**
$1,600 (2008 est.)
$1,600 (2007 est.)
$1,600 (2006 est.)
*note:* data are in 2008 US dollars
**GDP - composition by sector:**
*agriculture:* 20.5%
*industry:* 48%
*services:* 31.5% (2008 est.)
**Labor force:** 3.747 million (2006)
**Labor force - by occupation:**
*agriculture:* 80% (subsistence farming, herding, and fishing)
*industry and services:* 20% (2006 est.)
**Unemployment rate:**
NA%
**Population below poverty line:** 80% (2001 est.)
**Household income or consumption by percentage share:**
*lowest 10%:* NA%
*highest 10%:* NA%
**Investment (gross fixed):** 8.5% of GDP (2008 est.)
**Budget:**
*revenues:* $2.142 billion
*expenditures:* $2.125 billion (2008 est.)
**Inflation rate (consumer prices):**
10% (2008 est.)
4% (2007 est.)
**Central bank discount rate:** 5.25% (31 December 2007)
**Commercial bank prime lending rate:** 15% (31 December 2007)
**Stock of money:** $874.5 million (31 December 2007)
**Stock of quasi money:** $55.23 million (31 December 2007)
**Stock of domestic credit:** $82.81 million (31 December 2007)

# Chad (continued)

**Market value of publicly traded shares:** $NA

**Agriculture - products:** cotton, sorghum, millet, peanuts, rice, potatoes, manioc (tapioca); cattle, sheep, goats, camels

**Industries:** oil, cotton textiles, meatpacking, brewing, natron (sodium carbonate), soap, cigarettes, construction materials

**Industrial production growth rate:** 2% (2008 est.)

**Electricity - production:** 95 million kWh (2006 est.)

**Electricity - consumption:** 88.35 million kWh (2006 est.)

**Electricity - exports:** 0 kWh (2007 est.)

**Electricity - imports:** 0 kWh (2007 est.)

**Oil - production:** 156,000 bbl/day (2008 est.)

**Oil - consumption:** 1,352 bbl/day (2006 est.)

**Oil - exports:** 176,700 bbl/day (2005)

**Oil - imports:** 1,492 bbl/day (2005)

**Oil - proved reserves:** 1.5 billion bbl (1 January 2008 est.)

**Natural gas - production:** 0 cu m (2007 est.)

**Natural gas - consumption:** 0 cu m (2007 est.)

**Natural gas - exports:** 0 cu m (2007 est.)

**Natural gas - imports:** 0 cu m (2007 est.)

**Natural gas - proved reserves:** 0 cu m (1 January 2006 est.)

**Current account balance:** $527 million (2008 est.)

**Exports:** $5.501 billion f.o.b. (2008 est.)

**Exports - commodities:** oil, cattle, cotton, gum arabic

**Exports - partners:** US 89.5%, Japan 3.7%, China 3.4% (2007)

**Imports:** $1.47 billion f.o.b. (2008 est.)

**Imports - commodities:** machinery and transportation equipment, industrial goods, foodstuffs, textiles

**Imports - partners:** France 20.4%, Cameroon 16.1%, US 10.9%, China 10%, Germany 7.5%, Saudi Arabia 4.4% (2007)

**Reserves of foreign exchange and gold:** $1.12 billion (31 December 2008 est.)

**Debt - external:** $1.6 billion (2005 est.)

**Stock of direct foreign investment - at home:** $4.5 billion (2006 est.)

**Stock of direct foreign investment - abroad:** $NA

**Exchange rates:** Cooperation Financiere en Afrique Centrale francs (XAF) per US dollar - 447.81 (2008 est.), 480.1 (2007), 522.59 (2006), 527.47 (2005), 528.29 (2004)

*note:* since 1 January 1999, the Central African CFA franc (XAF) has been pegged to the euro at a rate of 655.957 CFA francs per euro; Central African CFA franc (XAF) coins and banknotes are not accepted in countries using West African CFA francs (XOF), and vice versa, even though the two currencies trade at par

## Communications

**Telephones - main lines in use:** 13,000 (2006)

**Telephones - mobile cellular:** 918,400 (2007)

**Telephone system:**

*general assessment:* primitive system with high costs and low telephone density; fixed-line connections for only about 1 per 1000 persons coupled with mobile-cellular usage of only about 9 per 100 persons

*domestic:* fair system of radiotelephone communication stations

*international:* country code - 235; satellite earth station -1 Intelsat (Atlantic Ocean) (2007)

**Radio broadcast stations:** AM 2, FM 4, shortwave 5 (2001)

**Television broadcast stations:** 1 (2001)

**Internet country code:** .td

**Internet hosts:** 5 (2008)

**Internet users:** 60,000 (2006)

## Transportation

**Airports:** 53 (2008)

**Airports - with paved runways:**

*total:* 8

*over 3,047 m:* 2

*2,438 to 3,047 m:* 3

*1,524 to 2,437 m:* 2

*under 914 m:* 1 (2008)

**Airports - with unpaved runways:**

*total:* 45

*2,438 to 3,047 m:* 1

*1,524 to 2,437 m:* 13

*914 to 1,523 m:* 21

*under 914 m:* 10 (2008)

**Pipelines:** oil 250 km (2008)

**Roadways:**

*total:* 33,400 km

*paved:* 267 km

*unpaved:* 33,133 km (2002)

**Waterways:** Chari and Legone rivers are navigable only in wet season (2008)

## Military

**Military branches:** Armed Forces: Chadian National Army (Armee Nationale du Tchad, ANT), Chadian Air Force (Force Aerienne Tchadienne, FAT), Gendarmerie (2008)

**Military service age and obligation:** 20 years of age for conscripts, with 3-year service obligation; 18 years of age for volunteers; no minimum age restriction for volunteers with consent from a guardian; women are subject to 1 year of compulsory military or civic service at age of 21 (2004)

**Manpower available for military service:**

*males age 16-49:* 1,906,545

*females age 16-49:* 2,258,758 (2008 est.)

**Manpower fit for military service:**

*males age 16-49:* 1,103,006

*females age 16-49:* 1,315,620 (2009 est.)

**Manpower reaching militarily significant age annually:**

*male:* 121,080

*female:* 121,585 (2009 est.)

**Military expenditures:** 4.2% of GDP (2006)

## Transnational Issues

**Disputes - international:** since 2003, Janjawid armed militia and the Sudanese military have driven hundreds of thousands of Darfur residents into Chad; Chad remains an important mediator in the Sudanese civil conflict, reducing tensions with Sudan arising from cross-border banditry; Chadian Aozou rebels reside in southern Libya; only Nigeria and Cameroon have heeded the Lake Chad Commission's admonition to ratify the delimitation treaty, which also includes the Chad-Niger and Niger-Nigeria boundaries

**Refugees and internally displaced persons:**

*refugees (country of origin):* 234,000 (Sudan); 54,200 (Central African Republic)

*IDPs:* 178,918 (2007)

**Trafficking in persons:**

*current situation:* Chad is a source, transit, and destination country for children trafficked for the purposes of forced labor and commercial sexual exploitation; the majority of children are trafficked within Chad for involuntary domestic servitude, forced cattle herding, forced begging, forced labor in petty commerce or the fishing industry, or for commercial sexual exploitation; to a lesser extent, Chadian children are also trafficked to Cameroon, the Central African Republic, and Nigeria for cattle herding; children may also be trafficked from Cameroon and the Central African Republic to Chad's oil producing regions for sexual exploitation

*tier rating:* Tier 2 Watch List - Chad is on the Tier 2 Watch List for its failure to provide evidence of increasing efforts to combat human trafficking in 2007; Chad was destabilized during 2007 by civil conflict leading to a declared state of emergency in February 2008, and a steady influx of refugees fleeing Sudan and the Central African Republic; the government demonstrated insufficient overall efforts to combat trafficking; Chad has not ratified the 2000 UN TIP Protocol (2008)

# Chile

## Introduction

**Background:** Prior to the coming of the Spanish in the 16th century, northern Chile was under Inca rule while the indigenous Mapuche inhabited central and southern Chile. Although Chile declared its independence in 1810, decisive victory over the Spanish was not achieved until 1818. In the War of the Pacific (1879-83), Chile defeated Peru and Bolivia and won its present northern regions. It was not until the 1880s that the Mapuche Indians were completely subjugated. After a series of elected governments, a three-year-old Marxist government of Salvador ALLENDE was overthrown in 1973 by a military coup led by Augusto PINOCHET, who ruled until a freely elected president was installed in 1990. Sound economic policies, maintained consistently since the 1980s, have contributed to steady growth, reduced poverty rates by over half, and have helped secure the country's commitment to democratic and representative government. Chile has increasingly assumed regional and international leadership roles befitting its status as a stable, democratic nation.

## Geography

**Location:** Southern South America, bordering the South Pacific Ocean, between Argentina and Peru

**Geographic coordinates:** 30 00 S, 71 00 W

**Map references:** South America

**Area:**
*total:* 756,950 sq km
*land:* 748,800 sq km
*water:* 8,150 sq km
*note:* includes Easter Island (Isla de Pascua) and Isla Sala y Gomez

**Area - comparative:** slightly smaller than twice the size of Montana

**Land boundaries:**
*total:* 6,339 km
*border countries:* Argentina 5,308 km, Bolivia 860 km, Peru 171 km

**Coastline:** 6,435 km

**Maritime claims:**
*territorial sea:* 12 nm
*contiguous zone:* 24 nm
*exclusive economic zone:* 200 nm
*continental shelf:* 200/350 nm

**Climate:** temperate; desert in north; Mediterranean in central region; cool and damp in south

**Terrain:** low coastal mountains; fertile central valley; rugged Andes in east

**Elevation extremes:**
*lowest point:* Pacific Ocean 0 m
*highest point:* Nevado Ojos del Salado 6,880 m

**Natural resources:** copper, timber, iron ore, nitrates, precious metals, molybdenum, hydropower

**Land use:**
*arable land:* 2.62%
*permanent crops:* 0.43%
*other:* 96.95% (2005)

**Irrigated land:** 19,000 sq km (2003)

**Total renewable water resources:** 922 cu km (2000)

**Freshwater withdrawal (domestic/industrial/agricultural):**
*total:* 12.55 cu km/yr (11%/25%/64%)
*per capita:* 770 cu m/yr (2000)

**Natural hazards:** severe earthquakes; active volcanism; tsunamis

**Environment - current issues:** widespread deforestation and mining threaten natural resources; air pollution from industrial and vehicle emissions; water pollution from raw sewage

**Environment - international agreements:**
*party to:* Antarctic-Environmental Protocol, Antarctic-Marine Living Resources, Antarctic Seals, Antarctic Treaty, Biodiversity, Climate Change, Climate Change-Kyoto Protocol, Desertification, Endangered Species, Environmental Modification, Hazardous Wastes, Law of the Sea, Marine Dumping, Ozone Layer Protection, Ship Pollution, Wetlands, Whaling
*signed, but not ratified:* none of the selected agreements

**Geography - note:** strategic location relative to sea lanes between Atlantic and Pacific Oceans (Strait of Magellan, Beagle Channel, Drake Passage); Atacama Desert is one of world's driest regions

## People

**Population:** 16,601,707 (July 2009 est.)

**Age structure:**
*0-14 years:* 23.2% (male 1,966,017/ female 1,877,963)
*15-64 years:* 67.8% (male 5,625,963/ female 5,628,146)
*65 years and over:* 9.1% (male 627,746/ female 875,872) (2009 est.)

**Median age:**
*total:* 31.4 years
*male:* 30.4 years
*female:* 32.4 years (2009 est.)

**Population growth rate:** 0.881% (2009 est.)

**Birth rate:** 14.64 births/1,000 population (2009 est.)

**Death rate:** 5.77 deaths/1,000 population (2008 est.)

**Net migration rate:** NA

**Urbanization:**
*urban population:* 88% of total population (2008)
*rate of urbanization:* 1.3% annual rate of change (2005-10 est.)

**Sex ratio:**
*at birth:* 1.05 male(s)/female
*under 15 years:* 1.05 male(s)/female
*15-64 years:* 1 male(s)/female
*65 years and over:* 0.72 male(s)/female
*total population:* 0.98 male(s)/female (2009 est.)

**Infant mortality rate:**
*total:* 7.71 deaths/1,000 live births
*male:* 8.49 deaths/1,000 live births
*female:* 6.88 deaths/1,000 live births (2009 est.)

**Life expectancy at birth:**
*total population:* 77.34 years
*male:* 74.07 years
*female:* 80.77 years (2009 est.)

**Total fertility rate:** 1.92 children born/woman (2009 est.)

**HIV/AIDS - adult prevalence rate:** 0.3% (2007 est.)

**HIV/AIDS - people living with HIV/AIDS:** 31,000 (2007 est.)

**HIV/AIDS - deaths:** 1,100 (2007 est.)

**Nationality:**
*noun:* Chilean(s)
*adjective:* Chilean

**Ethnic groups:** white and white-Amerindian 95.4%, Mapuche 4%, other indigenous groups 0.6% (2002 census)

**Religions:** Roman Catholic 70%, Evangelical 15.1%, Jehovah's Witness 1.1%, other Christian 1%, other 4.6%, none 8.3% (2002 census)

**Languages:** Spanish (official), Mapudungun, German, English

**Literacy:**
*definition:* age 15 and over can read and write
*total population:* 95.7%
*male:* 95.8%
*female:* 95.6% (2002 census)

# Chile (continued)

**School life expectancy (primary to tertiary education):**
*total:* 14 years
*male:* 14 years
*female:* 14 years (2006)
**Education expenditures:** 3.2% of GDP (2006)

## Government

**Country name:**
*conventional long form:* Republic of Chile
*conventional short form:* Chile
*local long form:* Republica de Chile
*local short form:* Chile
**Government type:** republic
**Capital:**
*name:* Santiago
*geographic coordinates:* 33 27 S, 70 40 W
*time difference:* UTC-4 (1 hour ahead of Washington, DC during Standard Time)
*daylight saving time:* +1hr, begins second Sunday in October; ends second Sunday in March
**Administrative divisions:** 15 regions (regiones, singular - region); Aisen del General Carlos Ibanez del Campo, Antofagasta, Araucania, Arica y Parinacota, Atacama, Biobio, Coquimbo, Libertador General Bernardo O'Higgins, Los Lagos, Los Rios, Magallanes y de la Antartica Chilena, Maule, Region Metropolitana (Santiago), Tarapaca, Valparaiso
*note:* the US does not recognize claims to Antarctica
**Independence:** 18 September 1810 (from Spain)
**National holiday:** Independence Day, 18 September (1810)
**Constitution:** 11 September 1980, effective 11 March 1981; amended 1989, 1991, 1997, 1999, 2000, 2003, and 2005
**Legal system:** based on Code of 1857 derived from Spanish law and subsequent codes influenced by French and Austrian law; judicial review of legislative acts in the Supreme Court; has not accepted compulsory ICJ jurisdiction; note - in June 2005, Chile completed overhaul of its criminal justice system to a new, US-style adversarial system
**Suffrage:** 18 years of age; universal and compulsory
**Executive branch:**
*chief of state:* President Michelle BACHELET Jeria (since 11 March 2006); note - the president is both the chief of state and head of government
*head of government:* President Michelle BACHELET Jeria (since 11 March 2006)
*cabinet:* Cabinet appointed by the president
*elections:* president elected by popular vote for a single four-year term; election last held 11 December 2005, with runoff election held 15 January 2006 (next to be held in December 2009)
*election results:* Michelle BACHELET Jeria elected president; percent of vote - Michelle BACHELET Jeria 53.5%; Sebastian PINERA Echenique 46.5%
**Legislative branch:** bicameral National Congress or Congreso Nacional consists of the Senate or Senado (38 seats; members elected by popular vote to serve eight-year terms; one-half elected every four years) and the Chamber of Deputies or Camara de

Diputados (120 seats; members are elected by popular vote to serve four-year terms)
*elections:* Senate - last held 11 December 2005 (next to be held in December 2009); Chamber of Deputies - last held 11 December 2005 (next to be held in December 2009)
*election results:* Senate - percent of vote by party - NA; seats by party - CPD 20 (PDC 6, PS 8, PPD 3, PRSD 3), APC 17 (UDI 9, RN 8), independent 1; Chamber of Deputies - percent of vote by party - NA; seats by party - CPD 65 (PDC 21, PPD 22, PS 15, PRSD 7), APC 54 (UDI 34, RN 20), independent 1; note - as of 8 January 2008: Senate - seats by party - CPD 18, (PDC 5, PS 8, PPD 2, PRSD 3), APC 16 (UDI 9, RN 7), independent 4; Chamber of Deputies - seats by party - CPD 57 (PDC 16, PPD 19, PS 15, PRSD 7), APC 53 (UDI 33, RN 20), independent 10.
**Judicial branch:** Supreme Court or Corte Suprema (judges are appointed by the president and ratified by the Senate from lists of candidates provided by the court itself; the president of the Supreme Court is elected every three years by the 20-member court); Constitutional Tribunal (eight-members - two each from the Senate, Chamber of Deputies, Supreme Court, and National Secuirty Council - review the constitutionality of laws approved by Congress)
**Political parties and leaders:** Alliance for Chile (Alianza) or APC (including National Renewal or RN [Carlos LARRAIN Pena] and Independent Democratic Union or UDI [Juan Antonio COLOMA Correa]); Coalition of Parties for Democracy (Concertacion) or CPD (including Christian Democratic Party or PDC [Juan Carlos LATORRE Carmona], Socialist Party or PS [Camilo ESCALONA Medina], Party for Democracy or PPD [Pepe AUTH Stewart], and Radical Social Democratic Party or PRSD [Jose Antonio GOMEZ Urrutia]); Communist Party or PC [Guillermo TEILLIER del Valle]; Humanist Party [Marilen CABRERA Olmos]
**Political pressure groups and leaders:** Roman Catholic Church, particularly conservative groups such as Opus Dei; United Labor Central or CUT includes trade unionists from the country's five largest labor confederations
*other:* revitalized university student federations at all major universities
**International organization participation:** APEC, BIS, CAN (associate), FAO, G-15, G-77, IADB, IAEA, IBRD, ICAO, ICC, ICCt (signatory), ICRM, IDA, IFAD, IFC, IFRCS, IHO, ILO, IMF, IMO, IMSO, Interpol, IOC, IOM, IPU, ISO, ITSO, ITU, ITUC, LAES, LAIA, Mercosur (associate), MIGA, MINUSTAH, NAM, OAS, OECD (accession state), OPANAL, OPCW, PCA, RG, SICA (observer), UN, UNASUR, UNCTAD, UNESCO, UNHCR, UNIDO, Union Latina, UNMOGIP, UNTSO, UNWTO, UPU, WCL, WCO, WFTU, WHO, WIPO, WMO, WTO
**Diplomatic representation in the US:**
*chief of mission:* Ambassador Jose Maria GONI Carrasco
*chancery:* 1732 Massachusetts Avenue NW, Washington, DC 20036
*telephone:* [1] (202) 785-1746
*FAX:* [1] (202) 887-5579

*consulate(s) general:* Chicago, Houston, Los Angeles, Miami, New York, Philadelphia, San Francisco, San Juan (Puerto Rico)
**Diplomatic representation from the US:**
*chief of mission:* Ambassador Paul E. SIMONS
*embassy:* Avenida Andres Bello 2800, Las Condes, Santiago
*mailing address:* APO AA 34033
*telephone:* [56] (2) 330-3000
*FAX:* [56] (2) 330-3710, 330-3160
**Flag description:** two equal horizontal bands of white (top) and red; a blue square the same height as the white band at the hoist-side end of the white band; the square bears a white five-pointed star in the center representing a guide to progress and honor; blue symbolizes the sky, white is for the snow-covered Andes, and red represents the blood spilled to achieve independence
*note:* design was influenced by the US flag

## Economy

**Economy - overview:** Chile has a market-oriented economy characterized by a high level of foreign trade and a reputation for strong financial institutions and sound policy that have given it the strongest sovereign bond rating in South America. Exports account for 40% of GDP, with commodities making up some three-quarters of total exports. Copper alone provides one-third of government revenue. During the early 1990s, Chile's reputation as a role model for economic reform was strengthened when the democratic government of Patricio AYLWIN - which took over from the military in 1990 - deepened the economic reform initiated by the military government. Growth in real GDP averaged 8% during 1991-97, but fell to half that level in 1998 because of tight monetary policies implemented to keep the current account deficit in check and because of lower export earnings - the latter a product of the global financial crisis. A severe drought exacerbated the situation in 1999, reducing crop yields and causing hydroelectric shortfalls and electricity rationing, and Chile experienced negative economic growth for the first time in more than 15 years. In the years since then, growth has averaged 4% per year. Chile deepened its longstanding commitment to trade liberalization with the signing of a free trade agreement with the US, which took effect on 1 January 2004. Chile claims to have more bilateral or regional trade agreements than any other country. It has 57 such agreements (not all of them full free trade agreements), including with the European Union, Mercosur, China, India, South Korea, and Mexico. Over the past five years, foreign direct investment inflows have quadrupled to some $17 billion in 2008. The Chilean government conducts a rule-based countercyclical fiscal policy, accumulating surpluses in sovereign wealth funds during periods of high copper prices and economic growth, and allowing deficit spending only during periods of low copper prices and growth. As of September 2008, those sovereign wealth funds - kept mostly outside the country and separate from Central Bank reserves - amounted to more than $20 billion.

**GDP (purchasing power parity):**
$245.3 billion (2008 est.)
$237.2 billion (2007)
$225.7 billion (2006)
*note:* data are in 2008 US dollars
**GDP (official exchange rate):** $181.5 billion
(2008 est.)
**GDP - real growth rate:**
4% (2008 est.)
5.1% (2007 est.)
4.3% (2006 est.)
**GDP - per capita (PPP):**
$14,900 (2008 est.)
$14,500 (2007 est.)
$14,000 (2006 est.)
*note:* data are in 2008 US dollars
**GDP - composition by sector:**
*agriculture:* 4.8%
*industry:* 50.5%
*services:* 44.7% (2008 est.)
**Labor force:** 7.32 million (2008 est.)
**Labor force - by occupation:**
*agriculture:* 13.2%
*industry:* 23%
*services:* 63.9% (2005)
**Unemployment rate:**
7.5% (August-October 2008)
7% (2007 est.)
**Population below poverty line:** 18.2% (2005)
**Household income or consumption by
percentage share:**
*lowest 10%:* 1.4%
*highest 10%:* 45% (2003)
**Distribution of family income - Gini index:** 54.9
(2003)
**Investment (gross fixed):** 23.7% of GDP
(2008 est.)
**Budget:**
*revenues:* $46.5 billion
*expenditures:* $37.7 billion (2008 est.)
**Public debt:** 3.8% of GDP (2008 est.)
**Inflation rate (consumer prices):**
8.8% (2008 est.)
4.4% (2007 est.)
**Central bank discount rate:** 6% (31 December
2007)
**Commercial bank prime lending rate:** 8.67%
(31 December 2007)
**Stock of money:** $16.6 billion (31 December 2007)
**Stock of quasi money:** $80.42 billion
(31 December 2007)
**Stock of domestic credit:** $127.1 billion
(31 December 2007)
**Market value of publicly traded shares:** $212.9
billion (31 December 2007)
**Agriculture - products:** grapes, apples, pears,
onions, wheat, corn, oats, peaches, garlic, asparagus,
beans; beef, poultry, wool; fish; timber
**Industries:** copper, other minerals, foodstuffs, fish
processing, iron and steel, wood and wood products,
transport equipment, cement, textiles

**Industrial production growth rate:** 1.7%
(2008 est.)
**Electricity - production:** 50.37 billion kWh
(2006 est.)
**Electricity - consumption:** 45.52 billion kWh
(2006 est.)
**Electricity - exports:** 0 kWh (2007 est.)
**Electricity - imports:** 1.628 billion kWh (2007 est.)
**Oil - production:** 11,610 bbl/day (2007 est.)
**Oil - consumption:** 253,000 bbl/day (2006 est.)
**Oil - exports:** 32,500 bbl/day (2005)
**Oil - imports:** 222,900 bbl/day (2006 est.)
**Oil - proved reserves:** 150 million bbl
(1 January 2008 est.)
**Natural gas - production:** 1.8 billion cu m
(2007 est.)
**Natural gas - consumption:** 4.2 billion cu m
(2007 est.)
**Natural gas - exports:** 0 cu m (2007 est.)
**Natural gas - imports:** 2.4 billion cu m (2007 est.)
**Natural gas - proved reserves:** 97.97 billion cu m
(1 January 2008 est.)
**Current account balance:** -$1.574 billion
(2008 est.)
**Exports:** $69.1 billion f.o.b. (2008 est.)
**Exports - commodities:** copper, fruit, fish products,
paper and pulp, chemicals, wine
**Exports - partners:** China 14.8%, US 12.5%, Japan
10.5%, Netherlands 5.8%, South Korea 5.7%, Italy
5.1%, Brazil 5% (2007)
**Imports:** $59.17 billion f.o.b. (2008 est.)
**Imports - commodities:** petroleum and petroleum
products, chemicals, electrical and
telecommunications equipment, industrial machinery,
vehicles, natural gas
**Imports - partners:** US 16.7%, China 11.2%, Brazil
10.3%, Argentina 9.9% (2007)
**Reserves of foreign exchange and gold:** $21.99
billion (31 December 2008 est.)
**Debt - external:** $64.57 billion
(31 December 2008 est.)
**Stock of direct foreign investment - at home:**
$108.9 billion (2008 est.)
**Stock of direct foreign investment - abroad:**
$29.98 billion (2008 est.)
**Exchange rates:** Chilean pesos (CLP) per US
dollar -509.02 (2008 est.), 526.25 (2007), 530.29
(2006), 560.09 (2005), 609.37 (2004)

## Communications

**Telephones - main lines in use:** 3.379 million
(2007)
**Telephones - mobile cellular:** 13.955 million (2007)
**Telephone system:**
*general assessment:* privatization begun in 1988;
most advanced telecommunications infrastructure in
South America; modern system based on extensive
microwave radio relay facilities; fixed-line connections
have dropped in recent years as mobile-cellular usage
continues to increase, reaching a level of 85
telephones per 100 persons

*domestic:* extensive microwave radio relay links;
domestic satellite system with 3 earth stations
*international:* country code - 56; submarine cables
provide links to the US and to Central and South
America; satellite earth stations - 2 Intelsat (Atlantic
Ocean) (2007)
**Radio broadcast stations:** AM 180, FM 64,
shortwave 17 (1998)
**Television broadcast stations:** 63 (plus 121
repeaters) (1997)
**Internet country code:** .cl
**Internet hosts:** 847,215 (2008)
**Internet users:** 5.57 million (2007)

## Transportation

**Airports:** 357 (2008)
**Airports - with paved runways:**
*total:* 80
*over 3,047 m:* 5
*2,438 to 3,047 m:* 8
*1,524 to 2,437 m:* 22
*914 to 1,523 m:* 24
*under 914 m:* 21 (2008)
**Airports - with unpaved runways:**
*total:* 277
*2,438 to 3,047 m:* 2
*1,524 to 2,437 m:* 12
*914 to 1,523 m:* 52
*under 914 m:* 211 (2008)
**Pipelines:** gas 2,676 km; liquid petroleum gas 519
km; oil 892 km; refined products 769 km (2008)
**Railways:**
*total:* 6,585 km
*broad gauge:* 2,831 km 1.676-m gauge (1,317 km
electrified)
*narrow gauge:* 3,754 km 1.000-m gauge (2006)
**Roadways:**
*total:* 80,505 km
*paved:* 16,745 km (includes 2,414 km of
expressways)
*unpaved:* 63,760 km (2004)
**Merchant marine:**
*total:* 44
*by type:* bulk carrier 9, cargo 7, chemical tanker 8,
container 1, liquefied gas 2, passenger 4, passenger/
cargo 2, petroleum tanker 7, roll on/roll off 1, vehicle
carrier 3
*registered in other countries:* 40 (Argentina 7, Brazil
1, Cyprus 1, Isle of Man 6, Marshall Islands 4, Norway
2, Panama 12, Singapore 6, Venezuela 1) (2008)
**Ports and terminals:** Coronel, Huasco, Lirquen,
Puerto Ventanas, San Antonio, San Vicente,
Valparaiso

## Military

**Military branches:** Army of the Nation, Chilean Navy
(Armada de Chile, includes naval air, marine corps,
and Maritime Territory and Merchant Marine
Directorate (Directemar)), Chilean Air Force (Fuerza
Aerea de Chile, FACh), Carabineros Corps (Cuerpo
de Carabineros) (2008)

**Military service age and obligation:** 18-45 years of age for voluntary male and female military service, although the right to compulsory recruitment is retained; service obligation - 12 months for Army, 22 months for Navy and Air Force (2008)

**Manpower available for military service:**
*males age 16-49:* 4,242,912
*females age 16-49:* 4,182,509 (2008 est.)

**Manpower fit for military service:**
*males age 16-49:* 3,573,165
*females age 16-49:* 3,523,649 (2009 est.)

**Manpower reaching militarily significant age annually:**
*male:* 145,766
*female:* 139,648 (2009 est.)

**Military expenditures:** 2.7% of GDP (2006)

## Transnational Issues

**Disputes - international:** Chile and Peru rebuff Bolivia's reinvigorated claim to restore the Atacama corridor, ceded to Chile in 1884, but Chile has offered instead unrestricted but not sovereign maritime access through Chile to Bolivian gas and other commodities; Chile rejects Peru's unilateral legislation to change its latitudinal maritime boundary with Chile to an equidistance line with a southwestern axis favoring Peru, in October 2007, Peru took its maritime complaint with Chile to the ICJ; territorial claim in Antarctica (Chilean Antarctic Territory) partially overlaps Argentine and British claims; the joint boundary commission, established by Chile and Argentina in 2001, has yet to map and demarcate the delimited boundary in the inhospitable Andean Southern Ice Field (Campo de Hielo Sur)

**Illicit drugs:** transshipment country for cocaine destined for Europe and the region; some money laundering activity, especially through the Iquique Free Trade Zone; imported precursors passed on to Bolivia; domestic cocaine consumption is rising, making Chile a significant consumer of cocaine (2008)

# China
*(also see separate Hong Kong, Macau, and Taiwan entries)*

## Introduction

**Background**
For centuries China stood as a leading civilization, outpacing the rest of the world in the arts and sciences, but in the 19th and early 20th centuries, the country was beset by civil unrest, major famines, military defeats, and foreign occupation. After World War II, the Communists under MAO Zedong established an autocratic socialist system that, while ensuring China's sovereignty, imposed strict controls over everyday life and cost the lives of tens of millions of people. After 1978, MAO's successor DENG Xiaoping and other leaders focused on market-oriented economic development and by 2000 output had quadrupled. For much of the population, living standards have improved dramatically and the room for personal choice has expanded, yet political controls remain tight.

## Geography

**Location:** Eastern Asia, bordering the East China Sea, Korea Bay, Yellow Sea, and South China Sea, between North Korea and Vietnam
**Geographic coordinates:** 35 00 N, 105 00 E
**Map references:** Asia
**Area:**
*total:* 9,596,960 sq km
*land:* 9,326,410 sq km
*water:* 270,550 sq km
**Area - comparative:** slightly smaller than the US
**Land boundaries:**
*total:* 22,117 km
*border countries:* Afghanistan 76 km, Bhutan 470 km, Burma 2,185 km, India 3,380 km, Kazakhstan 1,533 km, North Korea 1,416 km, Kyrgyzstan 858 km, Laos 423 km, Mongolia 4,677 km, Nepal 1,236 km, Pakistan 523 km, Russia (northeast) 3,605 km, Russia (northwest) 40 km, Tajikistan 414 km, Vietnam 1,281 km
*regional borders:* Hong Kong 30 km, Macau 0.34 km

**Coastline:** 14,500 km
**Maritime claims:**
*territorial sea:* 12 nm
*contiguous zone:* 24 nm
*exclusive economic zone:* 200 nm
*continental shelf:* 200 nm or to the edge of the continental margin
**Climate:** extremely diverse; tropical in south to subarctic in north
**Terrain:** mostly mountains, high plateaus, deserts in west; plains, deltas, and hills in east
**Elevation extremes:**
*lowest point:* Turpan Pendi -154 m
*highest point:* Mount Everest 8,850 m
**Natural resources:** coal, iron ore, petroleum, natural gas, mercury, tin, tungsten, antimony, manganese, molybdenum, vanadium, magnetite, aluminum, lead, zinc, uranium, hydropower potential (world's largest)
**Land use:**
*arable land:* 14.86%
*permanent crops:* 1.27%
*other:* 83.87% (2005)
**Irrigated land:** 545,960 sq km (2003)
**Total renewable water resources:** 2,829.6 cu km (1999)
**Freshwater withdrawal (domestic/industrial/agricultural):**
*total:* 549.76 cu km/yr (7%/26%/68%)
*per capita:* 415 cu m/yr (2000)
**Natural hazards:** frequent typhoons (about five per year along southern and eastern coasts); damaging floods; tsunamis; earthquakes; droughts; land subsidence
**Environment - current issues:** air pollution (greenhouse gases, sulfur dioxide particulates) from reliance on coal produces acid rain; water shortages, particularly in the north; water pollution from untreated wastes; deforestation; estimated loss of one-fifth of agricultural land since 1949 to soil erosion and economic development; desertification; trade in endangered species

# China (continued)

**Environment - international agreements:**
*party to:* Antarctic-Environmental Protocol, Antarctic Treaty, Biodiversity, Climate Change, Climate Change-Kyoto Protocol, Desertification, Endangered Species, Environmental Modification, Hazardous Wastes, Law of the Sea, Marine Dumping, Ozone Layer Protection, Ship Pollution, Tropical Timber 83, Tropical Timber 94, Wetlands, Whaling
*signed, but not ratified:* none of the selected agreements
**Geography - note:** world's fourth largest country (after Russia, Canada, and US); Mount Everest on the border with Nepal is the world's tallest peak

## People

**Population:** 1,338,612,968 (July 2009 est.)
**Age structure:**
*0-14 years:* 19.8% (male 140,877,745/ female 124,290,090)
*15-64 years:* 72.1% (male 495,724,889/ female 469,182,087)
*65 years and over:* 8.1% (male 51,774,115/ female 56,764,042) (2009 est.)
**Median age:**
*total:* 34.1 years
*male:* 33.5 years
*female:* 34.7 years (2009 est.)
**Population growth rate:** 0.655% (2009 est.)
**Birth rate:** 14 births/1,000 population (2009 est.)
**Death rate:** 7.03 deaths/1,000 population (2008 est.)
**Net migration rate:** -0.39 migrant(s)/1,000 population (2009 est.)
**Urbanization:**
*urban population:* 43% of total population (2008)
*rate of urbanization:* 2.7% annual rate of change (2005-10 est.)
**Sex ratio:**
*at birth:* 1.1 male(s)/female
*under 15 years:* 1.13 male(s)/female
*15-64 years:* 1.06 male(s)/female
*65 years and over:* 0.91 male(s)/female
*total population:* 1.06 male(s)/female (2009 est.)
**Infant mortality rate:**
*total:* 20.25 deaths/1,000 live births
*male:* 18.87 deaths/1,000 live births
*female:* 21.77 deaths/1,000 live births (2009 est.)
**Life expectancy at birth:**
*total population:* 73.47 years
*male:* 71.61 years
*female:* 75.52 years (2009 est.)
**Total fertility rate:** 1.79 children born/woman (2009 est.)
**HIV/AIDS - adult prevalence rate:** 0.1% (2007 est.)
**HIV/AIDS - people living with HIV/AIDS:** 700,000 (2007 est.)
**HIV/AIDS - deaths:** 39,000 (2007 est.)
**Major infectious diseases:**
*degree of risk:* intermediate
*food or waterborne diseases:* bacterial diarrhea, hepatitis A, and typhoid fever
*vectorborne diseases:* Japanese encephalitis and dengue fever
*soil contact disease:* hantaviral hemorrhagic fever with renal syndrome (HFRS)
*animal contact disease:* rabies
*note:* highly pathogenic H5N1 avian influenza has been identified in this country; it poses a negligible risk with extremely rare cases possible among US citizens who have close contact with birds (2009)
**Nationality:**
*noun:* Chinese (singular and plural)
*adjective:* Chinese
**Ethnic groups:** Han Chinese 91.5%, Zhuang, Manchu, Hui, Miao, Uyghur, Tujia, Yi, Mongol, Tibetan, Buyi, Dong, Yao, Korean, and other nationalities 8.5% (2000 census)
**Religions:** Daoist (Taoist), Buddhist, Christian 3%-4%, Muslim 1%-2%
*note:* officially atheist (2002 est.)
**Languages:** Standard Chinese or Mandarin (Putonghua, based on the Beijing dialect), Yue (Cantonese), Wu (Shanghainese), Minbei (Fuzhou), Minnan (Hokkien-Taiwanese), Xiang, Gan, Hakka dialects, minority languages (see Ethnic groups entry)
**Literacy:**
*definition:* age 15 and over can read and write
*total population:* 90.9%
*male:* 95.1%
*female:* 86.5% (2000 census)
**School life expectancy (primary to tertiary education):**
*total:* 11 years
*male:* 11 years
*female:* 11 years (2006)
**Education expenditures:** 1.9% of GDP (1999)

## Government

**Country name:**
*conventional long form:* People's Republic of China
*conventional short form:* China
*local long form:* Zhonghua Renmin Gongheguo
*local short form:* Zhongguo
*abbreviation:* PRC
**Government type:** Communist state
**Capital:**
*name:* Beijing
*geographic coordinates:* 39 55 N, 116 23 E
*time difference:* UTC+8 (13 hours ahead of Washington, DC during Standard Time)
*note:* despite its size, all of China falls within one time zone; many people in Xinjiang Province observe an unofficial "Xinjiang timezone" of UTC+6, two hours behind Beijing
**Administrative divisions:** 23 provinces (sheng, singular and plural), 5 autonomous regions (zizhiqu, singular and plural), and 4 municipalities (shi, singular and plural)
*provinces:* Anhui, Fujian, Gansu, Guangdong, Guizhou, Hainan, Hebei, Heilongjiang, Henan, Hubei, Hunan, Jiangsu, Jiangxi, Jilin, Liaoning, Qinghai, Shaanxi, Shandong, Shanxi, Sichuan, Yunnan, Zhejiang; (see note on Taiwan)
*autonomous regions:* Guangxi, Nei Mongol, Ningxia, Xinjiang Uygur, Xizang (Tibet)
*municipalities:* Beijing, Chongqing, Shanghai, Tianjin
*note:* China considers Taiwan its 23rd province; see separate entries for the special administrative regions of Hong Kong and Macau
**Independence:** 221 BC (unification under the Qin or Ch'in Dynasty); 1 January 1912 (Qing or Ch'ing Dynasty replaced by the Republic of China); 1 October 1949 (People's Republic of China established)
**National holiday:** Anniversary of the Founding of the People's Republic of China, 1 October (1949)
**Constitution:** most recent promulgation 4 December 1982 with amendments in 1988 and 1993
**Legal system:** based on civil law system; derived from Soviet and continental civil code legal principles; legislature retains power to interpret statutes; constitution ambiguous on judicial review of legislation; has not accepted compulsory ICJ jurisdiction
**Suffrage:** 18 years of age; universal
**Executive branch:**
*chief of state:* President HU Jintao (since 15 March 2003); Vice President XI Jinping (since 15 March 2008)
*head of government:* Premier WEN Jiabao (since 16 March 2003); Executive Vice Premier LI Keqiang (17 March 2008), Vice Premier HUI Liangyu (since 17 March 2003), Vice Premier ZHANG Deijiang (since 17 March 2008), and Vice Premier WANG Qishan (since 17 March 2008)
*cabinet:* State Council appointed by National People's Congress
*elections:* president and vice president elected by National People's Congress for a five-year term (eligible for a second term); elections last held 15-17 March 2008 (next to be held in mid-March 2013); premier nominated by president, confirmed by National People's Congress
*election results:* HU Jintao elected president by National People's Congress with a total of 2,963 votes; XI Jinping elected vice president with a total of 2,919 votes
**Legislative branch:** unicameral National People's Congress or Quanguo Renmin Daibiao Dahui (2,987 seats; members elected by municipal, regional, and provincial people's congresses, and People's Liberation Army to serve five-year terms)
*elections:* last held December 2007-February 2008; date of next election - late 2012 to early 2013
*election results:* percent of vote - NA; seats - 2,987
*note:* only members of the CCP, its eight allied parties, and sympathetic independent candidates are elected
**Judicial branch:** Supreme People's Court (judges appointed by the National People's Congress); Local People's Courts (comprise higher, intermediate, and basic courts); Special People's Courts (primarily military, maritime, railway transportation, and forestry courts)
**Political parties and leaders:** Chinese Communist Party or CCP [HU Jintao]; eight registered small parties controlled by CCP

# China (continued)

**Political pressure groups and leaders:** the China Democracy Party; the Falungong spiritual movement
*note:* no substantial political opposition groups exist, although the government has identified the organizations listed above as subversive groups
**International organization participation:** ADB, AfDB (nonregional member), APEC, APT, Arctic Council (observer), ARF, ASEAN (dialogue partner), BIS, CDB, EAS, FAO, G-20, G-24 (observer), G-77, IAEA, IBRD, ICAO, ICC, ICRM, IDA, IFAD, IFC, IFRCS, IHO, ILO, IMF, IMO, IMSO, Interpol, IOC, IOM (observer), IPU, ISO, ITSO, ITU, LAIA (observer), MIGA, MINURSO, MONUC, NAM (observer), NSG, OAS (observer), OPCW, PCA, PIF (partner), SAARC (observer), SCO, SICA (observer), UN, UN Security Council, UNAMID, UNCTAD, UNESCO, UNHCR, UNIDO, UNIFIL, UNITAR, UNMIL, UNMIS, UNMIT, UNOCI, UNTSO, UNWTO, UPU, WCO, WFTU, WHO, WIPO, WMO, WTO, ZC
**Diplomatic representation in the US:**
*chief of mission:* Ambassador ZHOU Wenzhong
*chancery:* 12 International Place NW, Washington, DC 20008
*telephone:* [1] (202) 328-2500
*FAX:* [1] (202) 328-2582
*consulate(s) general:* Chicago, Houston, Los Angeles, New York, San Francisco
**Diplomatic representation from the US:**
*chief of mission:* Ambassador (vacant); Charge d'Affaires Daniel PICCUTA
*embassy:* 55 An Jia Lou Lu, 100600 Beijing
*mailing address:* PSC 461, Box 50, FPO AP 96521-0002
*telephone:* [86] (10) 8531-3000
*FAX:* [86] (10) 8531-3300
*consulate(s) general:* Chengdu, Guangzhou, Shanghai, Shenyang, Wuhan
**Flag description:** red with a large yellow five-pointed star and four smaller yellow five-pointed stars (arranged in a vertical arc toward the middle of the flag) in the upper hoist-side corner

## Economy

**Economy - overview:** China's economy during the past 30 years has changed from a centrally planned system that was largely closed to international trade to a more market-oriented economy that has a rapidly growing private sector and is a major player in the global economy. Reforms started in the late 1970s with the phasing out of collectivized agriculture, and expanded to include the gradual liberalization of prices, fiscal decentralization, increased autonomy for state enterprises, the foundation of a diversified banking system, the development of stock markets, the rapid growth of the non-state sector, and the opening to foreign trade and investment. Annual inflows of foreign direct investment rose to nearly $84 billion in 2007. China has generally implemented reforms in a gradualist or piecemeal fashion. In recent years, China has re-invigorated its support for leading state-owned enterprises in sectors it considers

important to "economic security," explicitly looking to foster globally competitive national champions. After keeping its currency tightly linked to the US dollar for years, China in July 2005 revalued its currency by 2.1% against the US dollar and moved to an exchange rate system that references a basket of currencies. Cumulative appreciation of the renminbi against the US dollar since the end of the dollar peg was more than 20% by late 2008, but the exchange rate has changed little since the onset of the global financial crisis. The restructuring of the economy and resulting efficiency gains have contributed to a more than tenfold increase in GDP since 1978. Measured on a purchasing power parity (PPP) basis that adjusts for price differences, China in 2008 stood as the second-largest economy in the world after the US, although in per capita terms the country is still lower middle-income. The Chinese government faces numerous economic development challenges, including: (a) strengthening its social safety net, including pension and health system reform, to counteract a high domestic savings rate and correspondingly low domestic demand; (b) sustaining adequate job growth for tens of millions of migrants, new entrants to the work force, and workers laid off from state-owned enterprises deemed not worth saving; (c) reducing corruption and other economic crimes; and (d) containing environmental damage and social strife related to the economy's rapid transformation. Economic development has been more rapid in coastal provinces than in the interior, and approximately 200 million rural laborers and their dependents have relocated to urban areas to find work. One demographic consequence of the "one child" policy is that China is now one of the most rapidly aging countries in the world. Deterioration in the environment - notably air pollution, soil erosion, and the steady fall of the water table, especially in the north - is another long-term problem. China continues to lose arable land because of erosion and economic development. In 2007 China intensified government efforts to improve environmental conditions, tying the evaluation of local officials to environmental targets, publishing a national climate change policy, and establishing a high level leading group on climate change, headed by Premier WEN Jiabao. The Chinese government seeks to add energy production capacity from sources other than coal and oil. In late 2008, as China commemorated the 30th anniversary of its historic economic reforms, the global economic downturn began to slow foreign demand for Chinese exports for the first time in many years. The government vowed to continue reforming the economy and emphasized the need to increase domestic consumption in order to make China less dependent on foreign exports for GDP growth in the future.
**GDP (purchasing power parity):**
$7.8 trillion (2008 est.)
$7.104 trillion (2007)
$6.475 trillion (2006)
*note:* data are in 2008 US dollars

**GDP (official exchange rate):** $4.222 trillion (2008 est.)
**GDP - real growth rate:**
9.8% (2008 est.)
13% (2007 est.)
11.6% (2006 est.)
**GDP - per capita (PPP):**
$6,000 (2008 est.)
$5,500 (2007 est.)
$4,900 (2006 est.)
*note:* data are in 2008 US dollars
**GDP - composition by sector:**
*agriculture:* 10.6%
*industry:* 49.2%
*services:* 40.2% (2008 est.)
**Labor force:** 807.7 million (2008 est.)
**Labor force - by occupation:**
*agriculture:* 43%
*industry:* 25%
*services:* 32% (2006 est.)
**Unemployment rate:**
4% (2008 est.)
4% (2007 est.)
*note:* official data for urban areas only; including migrants may boost total unemployment to 9%; substantial unemployment and underemployment in rural areas
**Population below poverty line:** 8%
*note:* 21.5 million rural population live below the official "absolute poverty" line (approximately $90 per year); and an additional 35.5 million rural population above that but below the official "low income" line (approximately $125 per year) (2006 est.)
**Household income or consumption by percentage share:**
*lowest 10%:* 1.6%
*highest 10%:* 34.9% (2004)
**Distribution of family income - Gini index:** 47 (2007)
**Investment (gross fixed):** 40.2% of GDP (2008 est.)
**Budget:**
*revenues:* $868.6 billion
*expenditures:* $850.5 billion (2008 est.)
**Public debt:** 15.7% of GDP (2008 est.)
**Inflation rate (consumer prices):**
6% (2008 est.)
4.8% (2007 est.)
**Central bank discount rate:** 3.06% (17 December 2007)
**Commercial bank prime lending rate:** 5.58% (17 December 2007)
**Stock of money:** $2.3 trillion (31 October 2008)
**Stock of quasi money:** $4.331 trillion (31 October 2008)
**Stock of domestic credit:** $5.316 trillion (31 October 2008)
**Market value of publicly traded shares:** $6.226 trillion (31 December 2007 est.)
**Agriculture - products:** rice, wheat, potatoes, corn, peanuts, tea, millet, barley, apples, cotton, oilseed; pork; fish

# China (continued)

**Industries:** mining and ore processing, iron, steel, aluminum, and other metals, coal; machine building; armaments; textiles and apparel; petroleum; cement; chemicals; fertilizers; consumer products, including footwear, toys, and electronics; food processing; transportation equipment, including automobiles, rail cars and locomotives, ships, and aircraft; telecommunications equipment, commercial space launch vehicles, satellites

**Industrial production growth rate:** 10.7% (2008 est.)

**Electricity - production:** 3.256 trillion kWh (2007)

**Electricity - consumption:** 3.271 trillion kWh (2007)

**Electricity - exports:** 14.56 billion kWh (2007 est.)

**Electricity - imports:** 4.251 billion kWh (2007 est.)

**Oil - production:** 3.725 million bbl/day (2008 est.)

**Oil - consumption:** 7.88 million bbl/day (2007 est.)

**Oil - exports:** 399,000 bbl/day (2007)

**Oil - imports:** 4.21 million bbl/day (2007)

**Oil - proved reserves:** 16 billion bbl (1 January 2008 est.)

**Natural gas - production:** 69.27 billion cu m (2007 est.)

**Natural gas - consumption:** 70.51 billion cu m (2007 est.)

**Natural gas - exports:** 5.36 billion cu m (2007 est.)

**Natural gas - imports:** 3.871 billion cu m (2007 est.)

**Natural gas - proved reserves:** 2.265 trillion cu m (1 January 2008 est.)

**Current account balance:** $368.2 billion (2008 est.)

**Exports:** $1.465 trillion f.o.b. (2008 est.)

**Exports - commodities:** electrical and other machinery, including data processing equipment, apparel, textiles, iron and steel, optical and medical equipment

**Exports - partners:** US 19.1%, Hong Kong 15.1%, Japan 8.4%, South Korea 4.6%, Germany 4% (2007)

**Imports:** $1.156 trillion f.o.b. (2008 est.)

**Imports - commodities:** electrical and other machinery, oil and mineral fuels, optical and medical equipment, metal ores, plastics, organic chemicals

**Imports - partners:** Japan 14%, South Korea 10.9%, Taiwan 10.5%, US 7.3%, Germany 4.7% (2007)

**Reserves of foreign exchange and gold:** $2.033 trillion (31 December 2008 est.)

**Debt - external:** $420.8 billion (31 December 2008 est.)

**Stock of direct foreign investment - at home:** $758.9 billion (2007 est.)

**Stock of direct foreign investment - abroad:** $139.3 billion (2008 est.)

**Exchange rates:** Renminbi yuan (RMB) per US dollar - 6.9385 (2008 est.), 7.61 (2007), 7.97 (2006), 8.1943 (2005), 8.2768 (2004)

## Communications

**Telephones - main lines in use:** 365.4 million (2007)

**Telephones - mobile cellular:** 547.286 million (2007)

**Telephone system:**

*general assessment:* domestic and international services are increasingly available for private use; unevenly distributed domestic system serves principal cities, industrial centers, and many towns; China continues to develop its telecommunications infrastructure, and is partnering with foreign providers to expand its global reach; China in the summer of 2008 began a major restructuring of its telecommunications industry, resulting in the consolidation of its six telecom service operators to three, China Telecom, China Mobile and China Unicom, each providing both fixed-line and mobile services

*domestic:* interprovincial fiber-optic trunk lines and cellular telephone systems have been installed; mobile-cellular subscribership is increasing rapidly; the number of Internet users exceeded 250 million by summer 2008; a domestic satellite system with 55 earth stations is in place

*international:* country code - 86; a number of submarine cables provide connectivity to Asia, the Middle East, Europe, and the US; satellite earth stations - 7 (5 Intelsat - 4 Pacific Ocean and 1 Indian Ocean; 1 Intersputnik - Indian Ocean region; and 1 Inmarsat - Pacific and Indian Ocean regions) (2007)

**Radio broadcast stations:** AM 369, FM 259, shortwave 45 (1998)

**Television broadcast stations:** 3,240 (of which 209 are operated by China Central Television, 31 are provincial TV stations, and nearly 3,000 are local city stations) (1997)

**Internet country code:** .cn

**Internet hosts:** 14.306 million (2008)

**Internet users:** 253 million (2008)

## Transportation

**Airports:** 477 (2008)

**Airports - with paved runways:**
*total:* 413
*over 3,047 m:* 59
*2,438 to 3,047 m:* 132
*1,524 to 2,437 m:* 129
*914 to 1,523 m:* 21
*under 914 m:* 72 (2008)

**Airports - with unpaved runways:**
*total:* 64
*over 3,047 m:* 3
*2,438 to 3,047 m:* 5
*1,524 to 2,437 m:* 12
*914 to 1,523 m:* 17
*under 914 m:* 27 (2008)

**Heliports:** 35 (2007)

**Pipelines:** gas 28,132 km; oil 20,204 km; refined products 9,746 km (2008)

**Railways:**
*total:* 75,438 km
*standard gauge:* 75,438 km 1.435-m gauge (20,151 km electrified) (2005)

**Roadways:**
*total:* 1,930,544 km
*paved:* 1,575,571 km (includes 41,005 km of expressways)
*unpaved:* 354,973 km (2005)

**Waterways:** 110,000 km navigable (2008)

**Merchant marine:**
*total:* 1,826
*by type:* barge carrier 4, bulk carrier 451, cargo 689, carrier 2, chemical tanker 69, combination ore/oil 1, container 162, liquefied gas 44, passenger 8, passenger/cargo 83, petroleum tanker 244, refrigerated cargo 33, roll on/roll off 10, specialized tanker 9, vehicle carrier 17
*foreign-owned:* 20 (Ecuador 1, Greece 2, Hong Kong 12, Indonesia 1, Japan 2, South Korea 1, Norway 1)
*registered in other countries:* 1,441 (Bahamas 10, Bangladesh 1, Belize 71, Bermuda 10, Bolivia 1, Cambodia 193, Cyprus 10, France 5, Georgia 10, Germany 2, Honduras 3, Hong Kong 324, India 1, Indonesia 2, Kiribati 15, South Korea 1, Liberia 11, Malta 12, Marshall Islands 7, Mongolia 1, Norway 36, Panama 532, Philippines 4, Saint Vincent and the Grenadines 94, Sierra Leone 15, Singapore 14, Thailand 1, Tuvalu 16, unknown 39) (2008)

**Ports and terminals:** Dalian, Guangzhou, Ningbo, Qingdao, Qinhuangdao, Shanghai, Shenzhen, Tianjin

## Military

**Military branches:** People's Liberation Army (PLA): Ground Forces, Navy (includes marines and naval aviation), Air Force (includes airborne forces), and Second Artillery Corps (strategic missile force); People's Armed Police (PAP); PLA Reserve Force (2009)

**Military service age and obligation:** 18-22 years of age for selective compulsory military service, with 24-month service obligation; no minimum age for voluntary service (all officers are volunteers); 18-19 years of age for women high school graduates who meet requirements for specific military jobs (2007)

**Manpower available for military service:**
*males age 16-49:* 375,009,345
*females age 16-49:* 354,314,328 (2008 est.)

**Manpower fit for military service:**
*males age 16-49:* 314,459,083
*females age 16-49:* 296,763,134 (2009 est.)

**Manpower reaching militarily significant age annually:**
*male:* 10,621,373
*female:* 9,533,880 (2009 est.)

**Military expenditures:** 4.3% of GDP (2006)

# China (continued)

## Transnational Issues

**Disputes - international:** continuing talks and confidence-building measures work toward reducing tensions over Kashmir that nonetheless remains militarized with portions under the de facto administration of China (Aksai Chin), India (Jammu and Kashmir), and Pakistan (Azad Kashmir and Northern Areas); India does not recognize Pakistan's ceding historic Kashmir lands to China in 1964; China and India continue their security and foreign policy dialogue started in 2005 related to the dispute over most of their rugged, militarized boundary, regional nuclear proliferation, and other matters; China claims most of India's Arunachal Pradesh to the base of the Himalayas; lacking any treaty describing the boundary, Bhutan and China continue negotiations to establish a common boundary alignment to resolve territorial disputes due to cartographic discrepancies; Chinese maps show an international boundary symbol off the coasts of the littoral states of the South China Seas, where China has interrupted Vietnamese hydrocarbon exploration; China asserts sovereignty over the Spratly Islands together with Malaysia, Philippines, Taiwan, Vietnam, and possibly Brunei; the 2002 "Declaration on the Conduct of Parties in the South China Sea" eased tensions in the Spratly's but is not the legally binding "code of conduct" sought by some parties; Vietnam and China continue to expand construction of facilities in the Spratly's and in March 2005, the national oil companies of China, the Philippines, and Vietnam signed a joint accord on marine seismic activities in the Spratly Islands; China occupies some of the Paracel Islands also claimed by Vietnam and Taiwan; China and Taiwan continue to reject both Japan's claims to the uninhabited islands of Senkaku-shoto (Diaoyu Tai) and Japan's unilaterally declared equidistance line in the East China Sea, the site of intensive hydrocarbon exploration and exploitation; certain islands in the Yalu and Tumen rivers are in dispute with North Korea; North Korea and China seek to stem illegal migration to China by North Koreans, fleeing privations and oppression, by building a fence along portions of the border and imprisoning North Koreans deported by China; China and Russia have demarcated the once disputed islands at the Amur and Ussuri confluence and in the Argun River in accordance with their 2004 Agreement; China and Tajikistan have begun demarcating the revised boundary agreed to in the delimitation of 2002; the decade-long demarcation of the China-Vietnam land boundary is expected to be completed by the end of 2008, while the maritime boundary delimitation and fisheries agreements in the Gulf of Tonkin, ratified in June 2004, have been implemented; citing environmental, cultural, and social concerns, China has reconsidered construction of 13 dams on the Salween River, but energy-starved Burma, with backing from Thailand, remains intent on building five hydro-electric dams downstream despite regional and international protests; Chinese and Hong Kong authorities met in March 2008 to resolve ownership and use of lands recovered in Shenzhen River channelization, including 96-hectare Lok Ma Chau Loop; Hong Kong developing plans to reduce 2,000 out of 2,800 hectares of its restricted Closed Area by 2010

**Refugees and internally displaced persons:**
*refugees (country of origin):* 300,897 (Vietnam); estimated 30,000-50,000 (North Korea)
*IDPs:* 90,000 (2007)

**Trafficking in persons:**
*current situation:* China is a source, transit, and destination country for men, women, and children trafficked for the purposes of sexual exploitation and forced labor; the majority of trafficking in China occurs within the country's borders, but there is also considerable international trafficking of Chinese citizens to Africa, Asia, Europe, Latin America, the Middle East, and North America; Chinese women are lured abroad through false promises of legitimate employment, only to be forced into commercial sexual exploitation, largely in Taiwan, Thailand, Malaysia, and Japan; women and children are trafficked to China from Mongolia, Burma, North Korea, Russia, and Vietnam for forced labor, marriage, and prostitution; some North Korean women and children seeking to leave their country voluntarily cross the border into China and are then sold into prostitution, marriage, or forced labor
*tier rating:* Tier 2 Watch List - China is on the Tier 2 Watch List for the fourth consecutive year for its failure to provide evidence of increasing efforts to combat human trafficking, particularly in terms of punishment of trafficking crimes and the protection of Chinese and foreign victims of trafficking; victims are sometimes punished for unlawful acts that were committed as a direct result of their being trafficked, such as violations of prostitution or immigration/emigration controls; the Chinese Government continued to treat North Korean victims of trafficking solely as economic migrants, routinely deporting them back to horrendous conditions in North Korea; additional challenges facing the Chinese Government include the enormous size of its trafficking problem and the significant level of corruption and complicity in trafficking by some local government officials (2008)

**Illicit drugs:** major transshipment point for heroin produced in the Golden Triangle region of Southeast Asia; growing domestic consumption of synthetic drugs, and heroin from Southeast and Southwest Asia; source country for methamphetamine and heroin chemical precursors, despite new regulations on its large chemical industry (2008)

# Christmas Island
*(territory of Australia)*

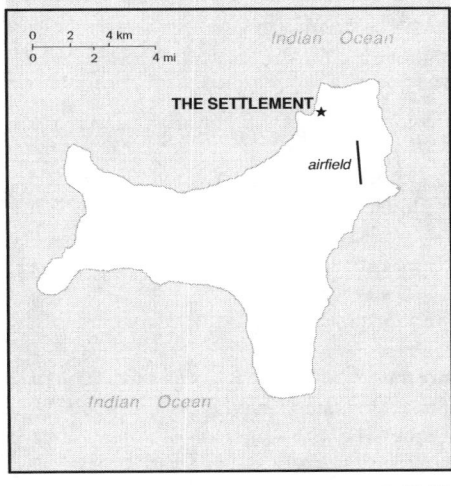

## Introduction

**Background:** Named in 1643 for the day of its discovery, the island was annexed and settlement began by the UK in 1888. Phosphate mining began in the 1890s. The UK transferred sovereignty to Australia in 1958. Almost two-thirds of the island has been declared a national park.

## Geography

**Location:** Southeastern Asia, island in the Indian Ocean, south of Indonesia
**Geographic coordinates:** 10 30 S, 105 40 E
**Map references:** Southeast Asia
**Area:**
*total:* 135 sq km
*land:* 135 sq km
*water:* 0 sq km
**Area - comparative:** about three-quarters the size of Washington, DC
**Land boundaries:** 0 km
**Coastline:** 138.9 km
**Maritime claims:**
*territorial sea:* 12 nm
*contiguous zone:* 12 nm
*exclusive fishing zone:* 200 nm
**Climate:** tropical with a wet season (December to April) and dry season; heat and humidity moderated by trade winds
**Terrain:** steep cliffs along coast rise abruptly to central plateau
**Elevation extremes:**
*lowest point:* Indian Ocean 0 m
*highest point:* Murray Hill 361 m
**Natural resources:** phosphate, beaches
**Land use:**
*arable land:* 0%
*permanent crops:* 0%
*other:* 100% (mainly tropical rainforest; 63% of the island is a national park) (2005)

# Christmas Island (continued)

**Irrigated land:** NA
**Natural hazards:** the narrow fringing reef surrounding the island can be a maritime hazard
**Environment - current issues:** loss of rainforest; impact of phosphate mining
**Geography - note:** located along major sea lanes of Indian Ocean

## People

**Population:** 1,402 (July 2009 est.)
**Age structure:**
*0-14 years:* NA
*15-64 years:* NA
*65 years and over:* NA
**Population growth rate:** 0% (2009 est.)
**Birth rate:** NA
**Death rate:** NA
**Net migration rate:** NA
**Sex ratio:** NA
**Infant mortality rate:**
*total:* NA
*male:* NA
*female:* NA
**Life expectancy at birth:**
*total population:* NA
*male:* NA
*female:* NA
**Total fertility rate:** NA
**HIV/AIDS - adult prevalence rate:** NA
**HIV/AIDS - people living with HIV/AIDS:** NA
**HIV/AIDS - deaths:** NA
**Nationality:**
*noun:* Christmas Islander(s)
*adjective:* Christmas Island
**Ethnic groups:** Chinese 70%, European 20%, Malay 10%
*note:* no indigenous population (2001)
**Religions:** Buddhist 36%, Muslim 25%, Christian 18%, other 21% (1997)
**Languages:** English (official), Chinese, Malay
**Literacy:** NA

## Government

**Country name:**
*conventional long form:* Territory of Christmas Island
*conventional short form:* Christmas Island
**Dependency status:** non-self governing territory of Australia; administered from Canberra by the Australian Government Attorney-General's Department
**Government type:** NA
**Capital:**
*name:* The Settlement
*geographic coordinates:* 10 25 S, 105 43 E
*time difference:* UTC+7 (12 hours ahead of Washington, DC during Standard Time)
**Administrative divisions:** none (territory of Australia)
**Independence:** none (territory of Australia)
**National holiday:** Australia Day, 26 January (1788)

**Constitution:** Christmas Island Act of 1958-59 (1 October 1958) as amended by the Territories Law Reform Act of 1992
**Legal system:** under the authority of the governor general of Australia and Australian law
**Suffrage:** 18 years of age
**Executive branch:**
*chief of state:* Queen ELIZABETH II (since 6 February 1952) represented by the Australian governor general
*head of government:* Administrator Neil LUCAS (since 30 January 2006)
*elections:* the monarch is hereditary; administrator appointed by the governor general of Australia and represents the monarch and Australia
**Legislative branch:** unicameral Christmas Island Shire Council (9 seats; members elected by popular vote to serve four-year terms)
*elections:* held every two years with half the members standing for election; last held 20 October 2007 (next to be held in 2009)
*election results:* percent of vote - NA; seats - independents 9
**Judicial branch:** Supreme Court; District Court; Magistrate's Court
**Political parties and leaders:** none
**Political pressure groups and leaders:** none
**International organization participation:** none
**Diplomatic representation in the US:** none (territory of Australia)
**Diplomatic representation from the US:** none (territory of Australia)
**Flag description:** territorial flag; divided diagonally from upper hoist to lower fly; the upper triangle is green with a yellow image of the Golden Bosun Bird superimposed, the lower triangle is blue with the Southern Cross constellation, representing Australia, superimposed; a centered yellow disk displays a green map of the island
*note:* the flag of Australia is used for official purposes

## Economy

**Economy - overview:** Phosphate mining had been the only significant economic activity, but in December 1987 the Australian government closed the mine. In 1991, the mine was reopened. With the support of the government, a $34 million casino opened in 1993, but closed in 1998. The Australian government in 2001 agreed to support the creation of a commercial space-launching site on the island expected to begin operations in the near future.
**GDP (purchasing power parity):** $NA
**Labor force:** NA
**Budget:**
*revenues:* $NA
*expenditures:* $NA
**Agriculture - products:** NA
**Industries:** tourism, phosphate extraction (near depletion)
**Exports:** $NA
**Exports - commodities:** phosphate
**Imports:** $NA

**Imports - commodities:** consumer goods
**Exchange rates:** Australian dollars (AUD) per US dollar - 1.2059 (2008 est.), 1.2137 (2007), 1.3285 (2006), 1.3095 (2005), 1.3598 (2004)

## Communications

**Telephones - main lines in use:** NA
**Telephone system:**
*general assessment:* service provided by the Australian network
*domestic:* GSM mobile telephone service replaced older analog system in February 2005
*international:* country code - 61-8; satellite earth station - 1 (Intelsat provides telephone and telex service) (2005)
**Radio broadcast stations:** AM 1, FM 2, shortwave 0 (2006)
**Television broadcast stations:** 0 (TV broadcasts received via satellite from mainland Australia) (2006)
**Internet country code:** .cx
**Internet hosts:** 1,821 (2008)
**Internet users:** 464 (2001)

## Transportation

**Airports:** 1 (2008)
**Airports - with paved runways:**
*total:* 1
*1,524 to 2,437 m:* 1 (2008)
**Roadways:**
*total:* 140 km
*paved:* 30 km
*unpaved:* 110 km (2007)
**Ports and terminals:** Flying Fish Cove

## Military

**Military - note:** defense is the responsibility of Australia

## Transnational Issues

**Disputes - international:** none

# Clipperton Island
*(possession of France)*

## Introduction

**Background:** This isolated island was named for John CLIPPERTON, a pirate who made it his hideout early in the 18th century. Annexed by France in 1855, it was seized by Mexico in 1897. Arbitration eventually awarded the island to France, which took possession in 1935.

## Geography

**Location:** Middle America, atoll in the North Pacific Ocean, 1,120 km southwest of Mexico
**Geographic coordinates:** 10 17 N, 109 13 W
**Map references:** Political Map of the World
**Area:**
*total:* 6 sq km
*land:* 6 sq km
*water:* 0 sq km
**Area - comparative:** about 12 times the size of The Mall in Washington, DC
**Land boundaries:** 0 km
**Coastline:** 11.1 km
**Maritime claims:**
*territorial sea:* 12 nm
*exclusive economic zone:* 200 nm
**Climate:** tropical; humid, average temperature 20-32 degrees C, wet season (May to October)
**Terrain:** coral atoll
**Elevation extremes:**
*lowest point:* Pacific Ocean 0 m
*highest point:* Rocher Clipperton 29 m
**Natural resources:** fish
**Land use:**
*arable land:* 0%
*permanent crops:* 0%
*other:* 100% (all coral) (2005)
**Irrigated land:** 0 sq km
**Natural hazards:** NA
**Environment - current issues:** NA
**Geography - note:** reef 12 km in circumference

## People

**Population:** uninhabited

## Government

**Country name:**
*conventional long form:* none
*conventional short form:* Clipperton Island
*local long form:* none
*local short form:* Ile Clipperton
*former:* sometimes called Ile de la Passion
**Dependency status:** possession of France; administered directly by the Minister of Overseas France
**Legal system:** the laws of France, where applicable, apply
**Flag description:** the flag of France is used

## Economy

**Economy - overview:** Although 115 species of fish have been identified in the territorial waters of Clipperton Island, the only economic activity is tuna fishing.

## Transportation

**Ports and terminals:** none; offshore anchorage only

## Military

**Military - note:** defense is the responsibility of France

## Transnational Issues

**Disputes - international:** none

# Cocos (Keeling) Islands
*(territory of Australia)*

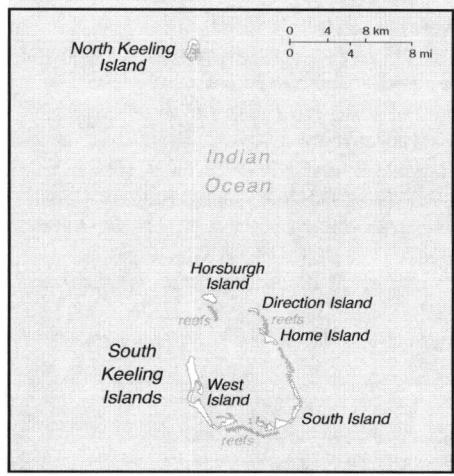

## Introduction

**Background:** There are 27 coral islands in the group. Captain William KEELING discovered the islands in 1609, but they remained uninhabited until the 19th century. From the 1820s to 1978, members of the CLUNIE-ROSS family controlled the islands and the copra produced from local coconuts. Annexed by the UK in 1857, the Cocos Islands were transferred to the Australian Government in 1955. The population on the two inhabited islands generally is split between the ethnic Europeans on West Island and the ethnic Malays on Home Island.

## Geography

**Location:** Southeastern Asia, group of islands in the Indian Ocean, southwest of Indonesia, about halfway from Australia to Sri Lanka
**Geographic coordinates:** 12 30 S, 96 50 E
**Map references:** Southeast Asia
**Area:**
*total:* 14 sq km
*land:* 14 sq km
*water:* 0 sq km
*note:* includes the two main islands of West Island and Home Island
**Area - comparative:** about 24 times the size of The Mall in Washington, DC
**Land boundaries:** 0 km
**Coastline:** 26 km
**Maritime claims:**
*territorial sea:* 12 nm
*exclusive fishing zone:* 200 nm
**Climate:** tropical with high humidity, moderated by the southeast trade winds for about nine months of the year
**Terrain:** flat, low-lying coral atolls
**Elevation extremes:**
*lowest point:* Indian Ocean 0 m
*highest point:* unnamed location 5 m
**Natural resources:** fish

# Cocos (Keeling) Islands *(continued)*

**Land use:**
*arable land:* 0%
*permanent crops:* 0%
*other:* 100% (2005)
**Irrigated land:** NA
**Natural hazards:** cyclone season is October to April
**Environment - current issues:** fresh water resources are limited to rainwater accumulations in natural underground reservoirs
**Geography - note:** islands are thickly covered with coconut palms and other vegetation; site of a World War I naval battle in November 1914 between the Australian light cruiser HMAS Sydney and the German raider SMS Emden; after being heavily damaged in the engagement, the Emden was beached by her captain on North Keeling Island

## People

**Population:** 596 (July 2009 est.)
**Age structure:**
*0-14 years:* NA
*15-64 years:* NA
*65 years and over:* NA
**Population growth rate:** 0% (2009 est.)
**Birth rate:** NA
**Death rate:** NA
**Net migration rate:** NA
**Infant mortality rate:**
*total:* NA
*male:* NA
*female:* NA
**Life expectancy at birth:**
*total population:* NA
*male:* NA
*female:* NA
**Total fertility rate:** NA
**HIV/AIDS - adult prevalence rate:** NA
**HIV/AIDS - people living with HIV/AIDS:** NA
**HIV/AIDS - deaths:** NA
**Nationality:**
*noun:* Cocos Islander(s)
*adjective:* Cocos Islander
**Ethnic groups:** Europeans, Cocos Malays
**Religions:** Sunni Muslim 80%, other 20% (2002 est.)
**Languages:** Malay (Cocos dialect), English
**Literacy:** NA

## Government

**Country name:**
*conventional long form:* Territory of Cocos (Keeling) Islands
*conventional short form:* Cocos (Keeling) Islands
**Dependency status:** non-self governing territory of Australia; administered from Canberra by the Australian Government Attorney-General's Department
**Government type:** NA
**Capital:**
*name:* West Island
*geographic coordinates:* 12 10 S, 96 50 E
*time difference:* UTC+6.5 (11.5 hours ahead of Washington, DC during Standard Time)

**Administrative divisions:** none (territory of Australia)
**Independence:** none (territory of Australia)
**National holiday:** Australia Day, 26 January (1788)
**Constitution:** Cocos (Keeling) Islands Act of 1955 (23 November 1955) as amended by the Territories Law Reform Act of 1992
**Legal system:** based upon the laws of Australia and local laws
**Suffrage:** 18 years of age
**Executive branch:**
*chief of state:* Queen ELIZABETH II (since 6 February 1952); represented by the Australian governor general
*head of government:* Administrator (nonresident) Neil LUCAS (since 30 January 2006)
*cabinet:* NA
*elections:* the monarch is hereditary; administrator appointed by the governor general of Australia and represents the monarch and Australia
**Legislative branch:** unicameral Cocos (Keeling) Islands Shire Council (7 seats)
*elections:* held every two years with half the members standing for election; last held in May 2007 (next to be held in May 2009)
**Judicial branch:** Supreme Court; Magistrate's Court
**Political parties and leaders:** none
**Political pressure groups and leaders:** The Cocos Islands Youth Support Centre
**International organization participation:** none
**Diplomatic representation in the US:** none (territory of Australia)
**Diplomatic representation from the US:** none (territory of Australia)
**Flag description:** the flag of Australia is used

## Economy

**Economy - overview:** Grown throughout the islands, coconuts are the sole cash crop. Small local gardens and fishing contribute to the food supply, but additional food and most other necessities must be imported from Australia. There is a small tourist industry.
**GDP (purchasing power parity):** $NA
**Labor force:** NA
**Labor force - by occupation:**
*note:* the Cocos Islands Cooperative Society Ltd. employs construction workers, stevedores, and lighterage workers; tourism employs others
**Unemployment rate:**
60% (2000 est.)
**Budget:**
*revenues:* $NA
*expenditures:* $NA
**Agriculture - products:** vegetables, bananas, pawpaws, coconuts
**Industries:** copra products and tourism
**Exports:** $NA
**Exports - commodities:** copra
**Imports:** $NA
**Imports - commodities:** foodstuffs
**Exchange rates:** Australian dollars (AUD) per US dollar - 1.2059 (2008 est.), 1.2137 (2007), 1.3285 (2006), 1.3095 (2005), 1.3598 (2004)

## Communications

**Telephones - main lines in use:** 287 (1992)
**Telephone system:**
*general assessment:* connected within Australia's telecommunication system; a local mobile-cellular network is in operation
*domestic:* NA
*international:* country code - 61; telephone, telex, and facsimile communications with Australia and elsewhere via satellite; satellite earth station - 1 (Intelsat) (2001)
**Radio broadcast stations:** AM 1, FM 2, shortwave 0 (2004)
**Television broadcast stations:** 4 (2007)
**Internet country code:** .cc
**Internet users:** NA

## Transportation

**Airports:** 1 (2008)
**Airports - with paved runways:**
*total:* 1
*1,524 to 2,437 m:* 1 (2008)
**Roadways:**
*total:* 22 km
*paved:* 10 km
*unpaved:* 12 km (2006)
**Ports and terminals:** Port Refuge

## Military

**Military - note:** defense is the responsibility of Australia; the territory has a five-person police force

## Transnational Issues

**Disputes - international:** none

# Colombia

**Background:** Colombia was one of the three countries that emerged from the collapse of Gran Colombia in 1830 (the others are Ecuador and Venezuela). A four-decade long conflict between government forces and anti-government insurgent groups, principally the Revolutionary Armed Forces of Colombia (FARC) heavily funded by the drug trade, escalated during the 1990s. The insurgents lack the military or popular support necessary to overthrow the government and violence has been decreasing since about 2002, but insurgents continue attacks against civilians and large areas of the countryside are under guerrilla influence or are contested by security forces. More than 31,000 former paramilitaries had demobilized by the end of 2006 and the United Self Defense Forces of Colombia (AUC) as a formal organization had ceased to function. In the wake of the paramilitary demobilization, emerging criminal groups arose, whose members include some former paramilitaries. The Colombian Government has stepped up efforts to reassert government control throughout the country, and now has a presence in every one of its administrative departments. However, neighboring countries worry about the violence spilling over their borders.

## Geography

**Location:** Northern South America, bordering the Caribbean Sea, between Panama and Venezuela, and bordering the North Pacific Ocean, between Ecuador and Panama
**Geographic coordinates:** 4 00 N, 72 00 W
**Map references:** South America
**Area:**
*total:* 1,138,910 sq km
*land:* 1,038,700 sq km
*water:* 100,210 sq km
*note:* includes Isla de Malpelo, Roncador Cay, and Serrana Bank

**Area - comparative:** slightly less than twice the size of Texas
**Land boundaries:**
*total:* 6,309 km
*border countries:* Brazil 1,644 km, Ecuador 590 km, Panama 225 km, Peru 1,800 km, Venezuela 2,050 km
**Coastline:** 3,208 km (Caribbean Sea 1,760 km, North Pacific Ocean 1,448 km)
**Maritime claims:**
*territorial sea:* 12 nm
*exclusive economic zone:* 200 nm
*continental shelf:* 200 m depth or to the depth of exploitation
**Climate:** tropical along coast and eastern plains; cooler in highlands
**Terrain:** flat coastal lowlands, central highlands, high Andes Mountains, eastern lowland plains
**Elevation extremes:**
*lowest point:* Pacific Ocean 0 m
*highest point:* Pico Cristobal Colon 5,775 m
*note:* nearby Pico Simon Bolivar also has the same elevation
**Natural resources:** petroleum, natural gas, coal, iron ore, nickel, gold, copper, emeralds, hydropower
**Land use:**
*arable land:* 2.01%
*permanent crops:* 1.37%
*other:* 96.62% (2005)
**Irrigated land:** 9,000 sq km (2003)
**Total renewable water resources:** 2,132 cu km (2000)
**Freshwater withdrawal (domestic/industrial/agricultural):**
*total:* 10.71 cu km/yr (50%/4%/46%)
*per capita:* 235 cu m/yr (2000)
**Natural hazards:** highlands subject to volcanic eruptions; occasional earthquakes; periodic droughts
**Environment - current issues:** deforestation; soil and water quality damage from overuse of pesticides; air pollution, especially in Bogota, from vehicle emissions
**Environment - international agreements:**
*party to:* Antarctic Treaty, Biodiversity, Climate Change, Climate Change-Kyoto Protocol, Desertification, Endangered Species, Hazardous Wastes, Marine Life Conservation, Ozone Layer Protection, Ship Pollution, Tropical Timber 83, Tropical Timber 94, Wetlands
*signed, but not ratified:* Law of the Sea
**Geography - note:** only South American country with coastlines on both the North Pacific Ocean and Caribbean Sea

## People

**Population:** 45,644,023 (July 2009 est.)
**Age structure:**
*0-14 years:* 28.9% (male 6,679,701/female 6,522,976)
*15-64 years:* 65.4% (male 14,571,536/female 15,297,179)
*65 years and over:* 5.6% (male 1,103,391/female 1,469,240) (2009 est.)

**Median age:**
*total:* 27.1 years
*male:* 26.1 years
*female:* 28 years (2009 est.)
**Population growth rate:** 1.377% (2009 est.)
**Birth rate:** 19.57 births/1,000 population (2009 est.)
**Death rate:** 5.54 deaths/1,000 population (2008 est.)
**Net migration rate:** -0.26 migrant(s)/1,000 population (2009 est.)
**Urbanization:**
*urban population:* 74% of total population (2008)
*rate of urbanization:* 1.7% annual rate of change (2005-10 est.)
**Sex ratio:**
*at birth:* 1.03 male(s)/female
*under 15 years:* 1.02 male(s)/female
*15-64 years:* 0.95 male(s)/female
*65 years and over:* 0.75 male(s)/female
*total population:* 0.96 male(s)/female (2009 est.)
**Infant mortality rate:**
*total:* 18.9 deaths/1,000 live births
*male:* 22.53 deaths/1,000 live births
*female:* 15.14 deaths/1,000 live births (2009 est.)
**Life expectancy at birth:**
*total population:* 72.81 years
*male:* 68.98 years
*female:* 76.76 years (2009 est.)
**Total fertility rate:** 2.46 children born/woman (2009 est.)
**HIV/AIDS - adult prevalence rate:** 0.6% (2007 est.)
**HIV/AIDS - people living with HIV/AIDS:** 170,000 (2007 est.)
**HIV/AIDS - deaths:** 9,800 (2007 est.)
**Major infectious diseases:**
*degree of risk:* high
*food or waterborne diseases:* bacterial diarrhea
*vectorborne diseases:* dengue fever, malaria, and yellow fever
*water contact disease:* leptospirosis (2009)
**Nationality:**
*noun:* Colombian(s)
*adjective:* Colombian
**Ethnic groups:** mestizo 58%, white 20%, mulatto 14%, black 4%, mixed black-Amerindian 3%, Amerindian 1%
**Religions:** Roman Catholic 90%, other 10%
**Languages:** Spanish
**Literacy:**
*definition:* age 15 and over can read and write
*total population:* 90.4%
*male:* 90.1%
*female:* 90.7% (2005 census)
**School life expectancy (primary to tertiary education):**
*total:* 12 years
*male:* 12 years
*female:* 13 years (2006)
**Education expenditures:** 4.7% of GDP (2006)

# Colombia (continued)

## Government

**Country name:**
*conventional long form:* Republic of Colombia
*conventional short form:* Colombia
*local long form:* Republica de Colombia
*local short form:* Colombia
**Government type:** republic; executive branch dominates government structure
**Capital:**
*name:* Bogota
*geographic coordinates:* 4 36 N, 74 05 W
*time difference:* UTC-5 (same time as Washington, DC during Standard Time)
**Administrative divisions:** 32 departments (departamentos, singular - departamento) and 1 capital district* (distrito capital); Amazonas, Antioquia, Arauca, Atlantico, Bogota*, Bolivar, Boyaca, Caldas, Caqueta, Casanare, Cauca, Cesar, Choco, Cordoba, Cundinamarca, Guainia, Guaviare, Huila, La Guajira, Magdalena, Meta, Narino, Norte de Santander, Putumayo, Quindio, Risaralda, San Andres y Providencia, Santander, Sucre, Tolima, Valle del Cauca, Vaupes, Vichada
**Independence:** 20 July 1810 (from Spain)
**National holiday:** Independence Day, 20 July (1810)
**Constitution:** 5 July 1991; amended many times
**Legal system:** based on Spanish law; a new criminal code modeled after US procedures was enacted into law in 2004 and reached full implemention in January 2008; judicial review of executive and legislative acts; has not accepted compulsory ICJ jurisdiction
**Suffrage:** 18 years of age; universal
**Executive branch:**
*chief of state:* President Alvaro URIBE Velez (since 7 August 2002); Vice President Francisco SANTOS (since 7 August 2002); note - the president is both the chief of state and head of government
*head of government:* President Alvaro URIBE Velez (since 7 August 2002); Vice President Francisco SANTOS (since 7 August 2002)
*cabinet:* Cabinet consists of a coalition of the three largest parties that supported President URIBE's reelection - the PSUN, PC, and CR - and independents
*elections:* president and vice president elected by popular vote for a four-year term (eligible for a second term); election last held 28 May 2006 (next to be held in May 2010)
*election results:* President Alvaro URIBE Velez reelected president; percent of vote - Alvaro URIBE Velez 62%, Carlos GAVIRIA Diaz 22%, Horacio SERPA Uribe 12%, other 4%
**Legislative branch:** bicameral Congress or Congreso consists of the Senate or Senado (102 seats; members are elected by popular vote to serve four-year terms) and the House of Representatives or Camara de Representantes (166 seats; members are elected by popular vote to serve four-year terms)
*elections:* Senate - last held 12 March 2006 (next to be held in March 2010); House of Representatives - last held 12 March 2006 (next to be held in March 2010)

*election results:* Senate - percent of vote by party - NA; seats by party - PSUN 20, PC 18, PL 18, CR 15, PDI 10, other parties 21; House of Representatives - percent of vote by party - NA; seats by party - PL 35, PSUN 33, PC 29, CR 20, PDA 8, other parties 41
**Judicial branch:** four roughly coequal, supreme judicial organs; Supreme Court of Justice or Corte Suprema de Justicia (highest court of criminal law; judges are selected by their peers from the nominees of the Superior Judicial Council for eight-year terms); Council of State (highest court of administrative law; judges are selected from the nominees of the Superior Judicial Council for eight-year terms); Constitutional Court (guards integrity and supremacy of the constitution; rules on constitutionality of laws, amendments to the constitution, and international treaties); Superior Judicial Council (administers and disciplines the civilian judiciary; resolves jurisdictional conflicts arising between other courts; members are elected by three sister courts and Congress for eight-year terms)
**Political parties and leaders:** Colombian Conservative Party or PC [Efrain Jose CEPEDA Sarabia]; Alternative Democratic Pole or PDA [Carlos GAVIRIA Diaz]; Liberal Party or PL [Cesar GAVIRIA Trujillo]; Radical Change or CR [German VARGAS Lleras]; Social National Unity Party or U Party [Carlos FERRO Solanilla]
*note:* Colombia has 15 formally recognized political parties, and numerous unofficial parties that did not meet the vote threshold in the March 2006 legislative elections required for recognition
**Political pressure groups and leaders:** National Liberation Army or ELN; Revolutionary Armed Forces of Colombia or FARC
*note:* two largest insurgent groups active in Colombia
**International organization participation:** BCIE, CAN, Caricom (observer), CDB, FAO, G-3, G-24, G-77, IADB, IAEA, IBRD, ICAO, ICC, ICCt, ICRM, IDA, IFAD, IFC, IFRCS, IHO, ILO, IMF, IMO, IMSO, Interpol, IOC, IOM, IPU, ISO, ITSO, ITU, ITUC, LAES, LAIA, Mercosur (associate), MIGA, NAM, OAS, OPANAL, OPCW, PCA, RG, UN, UNASUR, UNCTAD, UNESCO, UNHCR, UNIDO, Union Latina, UNWTO, UPU, WCL, WCO, WFTU, WHO, WIPO, WMO, WTO
**Diplomatic representation in the US:**
*chief of mission:* Ambassador Carolina BARCO Isakson
*chancery:* 2118 Leroy Place NW, Washington, DC 20008
*telephone:* [1] (202) 387-8338
*FAX:* [1] (202) 232-8643
*consulate(s) general:* Atlanta, Boston, Chicago, Houston, Los Angeles, Miami, New York, San Francisco, San Juan (Puerto Rico), Washington, DC
**Diplomatic representation from the US:**
*chief of mission:* Ambassador William R. BROWNFIELD
*embassy:* Calle 24 Bis No. 48-50, Bogota, D.C.
*mailing address:* Carrera 45 No. 24B-27, Bogota, D.C.
*telephone:* [57] (1) 315-0811
*FAX:* [57] (1) 315-2197

**Flag description:** three horizontal bands of yellow (top, double-width), blue, and red
*note:* similar to the flag of Ecuador, which is longer and bears the Ecuadorian coat of arms superimposed in the center

## Economy

**Economy - overview:** Colombia has experienced accelerating growth between 2002 and 2007, with expansion above 7% in 2007, chiefly due to advancements in domestic security, to rising commodity prices, and to President URIBE's promarket economic policies. Colombia's sustained growth helped reduce poverty by 20% and cut unemployment by 25% since 2002. Additionally, investor friendly reforms to Colombia's hydrocarbon sector and the US-Colombia Trade Promotion Agreement (CTPA) negotiations have attracted record levels of foreign investment. Inequality, underemployment,and narcotrafficking remain significant challenges, and Colombia's infrastructure requires significant updating in order to sustain expansion. Economic growth slipped in 2008 as a result of the global financial crisis and weakening demand for Colombia's exports. In response, URIBE's administration has cut capital controls, arranged for emergency credit lines from multilateral institutions, and promoted investment incentives such as Colombia's modernized free trade zone mechanism, legal stability contracts, and new bilateral investment treaties and trade agreements. The government has also encouraged exporters to diversify their customer base away from the United States and Venezuela, Colombia's largest trading partners. Nevertheless, the business sector continues to be concerned about the impact of a global recession on Colombia's exports, as well as the approval of the CTPA, which is stalled in the US Congress.
**GDP (purchasing power parity):**
$399.4 billion (2008 est.)
$385.9 billion (2007)
$359 billion (2006)
*note:* data are in 2008 US dollars
**GDP (official exchange rate):** $249.8 billion (2008 est.)
**GDP - real growth rate:**
3.5% (2008 est.)
7.5% (2007 est.)
6.9% (2006 est.)
**GDP - per capita (PPP):**
$8,900 (2008 est.)
$8,700 (2007 est.)
$8,200 (2006 est.)
*note:* data are in 2008 US dollars
**GDP - composition by sector:**
*agriculture:* 9.4%
*industry:* 36.6%
*services:* 54% (2008 est.)
**Labor force:** 21.3 million (2008 est.)
**Labor force - by occupation:**
*agriculture:* 22.4%
*industry:* 18.8%
*services:* 58.8% (2005 est.)

# Colombia (continued)

**Unemployment rate:**
11.8% (2008 est.)
11.2% (2007 est.)
**Population below poverty line:** 49.2% (2005)
**Household income or consumption by percentage share:**
*lowest 10%:* 7.9%
*highest 10%:* 34.3% (2004)
**Distribution of family income - Gini index:** 53.8 (2005)
**Investment (gross fixed):** 23.1% of GDP (2008 est.)
**Budget:**
*revenues:* $76.42 billion
*expenditures:* $78.49 billion; including capital expenditures of $NA (2008 est.)
**Public debt:** 48% of GDP (2008 est.)
**Inflation rate (consumer prices):**
7.7% (2008 est.)
5.5% (2007 est.)
**Central bank discount rate:** 9.5% (31 December 2008)
**Commercial bank prime lending rate:** 15.6% (31 December 2008)
**Stock of money:** $21.81 billion (31 December 2007)
**Stock of quasi money:** $27.25 billion (31 December 2007)
**Stock of domestic credit:** $57.2 billion (31 December 2008)
**Market value of publicly traded shares:** $87 billion (31 December 2008)
**Agriculture - products:** coffee, cut flowers, bananas, rice, tobacco, corn, sugarcane, cocoa beans, oilseed, vegetables; forest products; shrimp
**Industries:** textiles, food processing, oil, clothing and footwear, beverages, chemicals, cement; gold, coal, emeralds
**Industrial production growth rate:** 2.5% (2008 est.)
**Electricity - production:** 53.6 billion kWh (2007)
**Electricity - consumption:** 52.8 billion kWh (2007)
**Electricity - exports:** 876.7 million kWh (2007)
**Electricity - imports:** 38.4 million kWh (2007)
**Oil - production:** 588,000 bbl/day (2008 est.)
**Oil - consumption:** 267,000 bbl/day (2007 est.)
**Oil - exports:** 294,000 bbl/day (2008 est.)
**Oil - imports:** 12,480 bbl/day (2005)
**Oil - proved reserves:** 1.506 billion bbl (1 January 2008 est.)
**Natural gas - production:** 7.22 billion cu m (2006 est.)
**Natural gas - consumption:** 7.22 billion cu m (2006 est.)
**Natural gas - exports:** 0 cu m (2007 est.)
**Natural gas - imports:** 0 cu m (2007 est.)
**Natural gas - proved reserves:** 122.9 billion cu m (1 January 2008 est.)
**Current account balance:** -$5.592 billion (2008 est.)
**Exports:** $41.08 billion f.o.b. (2008 est.)

**Exports - commodities:** petroleum, coffee, coal, nickel, emeralds, apparel, bananas, cut flowers
**Exports - partners:** US 35.4%, Venezuela 17.4%, Ecuador 4.3% (2007)
**Imports:** $38.88 billion f.o.b. (2008 est.)
**Imports - commodities:** industrial equipment, transportation equipment, consumer goods, chemicals, paper products, fuels, electricity
**Imports - partners:** US 26.2%, China 10.1%, Mexico 9.3%, Brazil 7.3%, Venezuela 4.2% (2007)
**Reserves of foreign exchange and gold:** $23.66 billion (31 December 2008 est.)
**Debt - external:** $41.68 billion (31 December 2008 est.)
**Stock of direct foreign investment - at home:** $65.69 billion (2008 est.)
**Stock of direct foreign investment - abroad:** $10.88 billion (2008 est.)
**Exchange rates:** Colombian pesos (COP) per US dollar - 2,243.6 (2008), 2,013.8 (2007), 2,358.6 (2006), 2,320.75 (2005), 2,628.61 (2004)

## Communications

**Telephones - main lines in use:** 7.936 million (2007)
**Telephones - mobile cellular:** 33.941 million (2007)
**Telephone system:**
*general assessment:* modern system in many respects; telecommunications sector liberalized during the 1990s; multiple providers of both fixed-line and mobile-cellular services; fixed-line connections stand at about 18 per 100 persons; mobile cellular usage is about 75 per 100 persons; competition among cellular service providers is resulting in falling local and international calling rates and contributing to the steep decline in the market share of fixed line services
*domestic:* nationwide microwave radio relay system; domestic satellite system with 41 earth stations; fiber-optic network linking 50 cities
*international:* country code - 57; submarine cables provide links to the US, parts of the Caribbean, and Central and South America; satellite earth stations - 10 (6 Intelsat, 1 Inmarsat, 3 fully digitalized international switching centers) (2007)
**Radio broadcast stations:** AM 454, FM 34, shortwave 27 (1999)
**Television broadcast stations:** 60 (1997)
**Internet country code:** .co
**Internet hosts:** 1.554 million (2008)
**Internet users:** 12.1 million (2007)

## Transportation

**Airports:** 991 (2008)
**Airports - with paved runways:**
*total:* 107
*over 3,047 m:* 2
*2,438 to 3,047 m:* 8
*1,524 to 2,437 m:* 39
*914 to 1,523 m:* 46
*under 914 m:* 12 (2008)

**Airports - with unpaved runways:**
*total:* 884
*over 3,047 m:* 1
*1,524 to 2,437 m:* 35
*914 to 1,523 m:* 227
*under 914 m:* 621 (2008)
**Heliports:** 2 (2007)
**Pipelines:** gas 4,560 km; oil 6,094 km; refined products 3,383 km (2008)
**Railways:**
*total:* 3,304 km
*standard gauge:* 150 km 1.435-m gauge
*narrow gauge:* 3,154 km 0.914-m gauge (2006)
**Roadways:**
*total:* 164,257 km (2005)
**Waterways:** 18,000 km (2008)
**Merchant marine:**
*total:* 17
*by type:* cargo 13, petroleum tanker 3, specialized tanker 1
*registered in other countries:* 6 (Antigua and Barbuda 2, Panama 4) (2008)
**Ports and terminals:** Barranquilla, Buenaventura, Cartagena, Santa Marta, Turbo

## Military

**Military branches:** National Army (Ejercito Nacional), National Navy (Armada Nacional, includes Naval Aviation, Naval Infantry (Infanteria de Marina, Colmar), and Coast Guard), Colombian Air Force (Fuerza Aerea de Colombia, FAC) (2008)
**Military service age and obligation:** 18-24 years of age for compulsory and voluntary military service; service obligation - 18 months (2004)
**Manpower available for military service:**
*males age 16-49:* 11,478,109
*females age 16-49:* 11,809,279 (2008 est.)
**Manpower fit for military service:**
*males age 16-49:* 8,212,944
*females age 16-49:* 10,045,435 (2009 est.)
**Manpower reaching militarily significant age annually:**
*male:* 446,432
*female:* 437,164 (2009 est.)
**Military expenditures:** 3.4% of GDP (2005 est.)

## Transnational Issues

**Disputes - international:** in December 2007, ICJ allocates San Andres, Providencia, and Santa Catalina islands to Colombia under 1928 Treaty but does not rule on 82 degrees W meridian as maritime boundary with Nicaragua; managed dispute with Venezuela over maritime boundary and Venezuelan-administered Los Monjes Islands near the Gulf of Venezuela; Colombian-organized illegal narcotics, guerrilla, and paramilitary activities penetrate all neighboring borders and have caused Colombian citizens to flee mostly into neighboring countries; Colombia, Honduras, Nicaragua, Jamaica, and the US assert various claims to Bajo Nuevo and Serranilla Bank

## Colombia (continued)

**Refugees and internally displaced persons:**
*IDPs:* 1.8-3.5 million (conflict between government and illegal armed groups and drug traffickers) (2007)
**Illicit drugs:** illicit producer of coca, opium poppy, and cannabis; world's leading coca cultivator with 167,000 hectares in coca cultivation in 2007, a 6% increase over 2006, producing a potential of 535 mt of pure cocaine; the world's largest producer of coca derivatives; supplies cocaine to nearly all of the US market and the great majority of other international drug markets; in 2005, aerial eradication dispensed herbicide to treat over 130,000 hectares but aggressive replanting on the part of coca growers means Colombia remains a key producer; a significant portion of narcotics proceeds are either laundered or invested in Colombia through the black market peso exchange; important supplier of heroin to the US market; opium poppy cultivation is estimated to have fallen 25% between 2006 and 2007; most Colombian heroin is destined for the US market (2008)

# Comoros

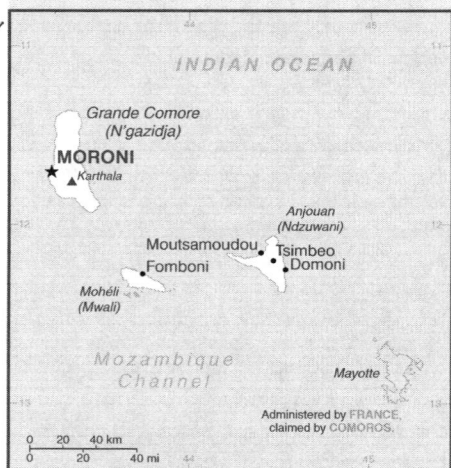

## Introduction

**Background:** Comoros has endured more than 20 coups or attempted coups since gaining independence from France in 1975. In 1997, the islands of Anjouan and Moheli declared independence from Comoros. In 1999, military chief Col. AZALI seized power in a bloodless coup, and helped negotiate the 2000 Fomboni Accords power-sharing agreement in which the federal presidency rotates among the three islands, and each island maintains its own local government. AZALI won the 2002 Presidential election, and each island in the archipelago elected its own president. AZALI stepped down in 2006 and President SAMBI was elected to office. In 2007, BACAR effected Anjouan's de-facto secession from the Union, refusing to step down in favor of fresh Anjouanais elections when Comoros' other islands held legitimate elections in July. The African Union (AU) initially attempted to resolve the political crisis by applying sanctions and a naval blockade on Anjouan, but in March 2008, AU and Comoran soldiers seized the island. The move was generally welcomed by the island's inhabitants.

## Geography

**Location:** Southern Africa, group of islands at the northern mouth of the Mozambique Channel, about two-thirds of the way between northern Madagascar and northern Mozambique
**Geographic coordinates:** 12 10 S, 44 15 E
**Map references:** Africa
**Area:**
*total:* 2,170 sq km
*land:* 2,170 sq km
*water:* 0 sq km
**Area - comparative:** slightly more than 12 times the size of Washington, DC
**Land boundaries:** 0 km

**Coastline:** 340 km
**Maritime claims:**
*territorial sea:* 12 nm
*exclusive economic zone:* 200 nm
**Climate:** tropical marine; rainy season (November to May)
**Terrain:** volcanic islands, interiors vary from steep mountains to low hills
**Elevation extremes:**
*lowest point:* Indian Ocean 0 m
*highest point:* Le Karthala 2,360 m
**Natural resources:** NEGL
**Land use:**
*arable land:* 35.87%
*permanent crops:* 23.32%
*other:* 40.81% (2005)
**Irrigated land:** NA
**Total renewable water resources:** 1.2 cu km (2003)
**Freshwater withdrawal (domestic/industrial/ agricultural):**
*total:* 0.01 cu km/yr (48%/5%/47%)
*per capita:* 13 cu m/yr (1999)
**Natural hazards:** cyclones possible during rainy season (December to April); Le Karthala on Grand Comore is an active volcano
**Environment - current issues:** soil degradation and erosion results from crop cultivation on slopes without proper terracing; deforestation
**Environment - international agreements:**
*party to:* Biodiversity, Climate Change, Climate Change-Kyoto Protocol, Desertification, Endangered Species, Hazardous Wastes, Law of the Sea, Ozone Layer Protection, Ship Pollution, Wetlands
*signed, but not ratified:* none of the selected agreements
**Geography - note:** important location at northern end of Mozambique Channel

## People

**Population:** 752,438 (July 2009 est.)
**Age structure:**
*0-14 years:* 42.2% (male 159,282/female 158,073)
*15-64 years:* 54.8% (male 203,533/female 208,591)
*65 years and over:* 3.1% (male 10,474/female 12,485) (2009 est.)
**Median age:**
*total:* 18.8 years
*male:* 18.5 years
*female:* 19.1 years (2009 est.)
**Population growth rate:** 2.766% (2009 est.)
**Birth rate:** 35.23 births/1,000 population (2009 est.)
**Death rate:** 7.76 deaths/1,000 population (2008 est.)
**Net migration rate:** NA
**Urbanization:**
*urban population:* 28% of total population (2008)
*rate of urbanization:* 2.7% annual rate of change (2005-10 est.)

# Comoros (continued)

**Sex ratio:**
*at birth:* 1.03 male(s)/female
*under 15 years:* 1.01 male(s)/female
*15-64 years:* 0.98 male(s)/female
*65 years and over:* 0.84 male(s)/female
*total population:* 0.98 male(s)/female (2009 est.)
**Infant mortality rate:**
*total:* 66.57 deaths/1,000 live births
*male:* 74.5 deaths/1,000 live births
*female:* 58.4 deaths/1,000 live births (2009 est.)
**Life expectancy at birth:**
*total population:* 63.47 years
*male:* 61.07 years
*female:* 65.94 years (2009 est.)
**Total fertility rate:** 4.84 children born/woman
(2009 est.)
**HIV/AIDS - adult prevalence rate:** less than 0.1%
(2007 est.)
**HIV/AIDS - people living with HIV/AIDS:** NA
(2007 est.)
**HIV/AIDS - deaths:** NA
**Nationality:**
*noun:* Comoran(s)
*adjective:* Comoran
**Ethnic groups:** Antalote, Cafre, Makoa, Oimatsaha,
Sakalava
**Religions:** Sunni Muslim 98%, Roman Catholic 2%
**Languages:** Arabic (official), French (official),
Shikomoro (a blend of Swahili and Arabic)
**Literacy:**
*definition:* age 15 and over can read and write
*total population:* 56.5%
*male:* 63.6%
*female:* 49.3% (2003 est.)
**School life expectancy (primary to tertiary
education):**
*total:* 8 years
*male:* 9 years
*female:* 7 years (2004)
**Education expenditures:** 3.8% of GDP (2002)

## Government

**Country name:**
*conventional long form:* Union of the Comoros
*conventional short form:* Comoros
*local long form:* Udzima wa Komori (Comorian);
Union des Comores (French); Jumhuriyat al Qamar al
Muttahidah (Arabic)
*local short form:* Komori (Comorian); Comores
(French); Juzur al Qamar (Arabic)
**Government type:** republic
**Capital:**
*name:* Moroni
*geographic coordinates:* 11 42 S, 43 14 E
*time difference:* UTC+3 (8 hours ahead of
Washington, DC during Standard Time)
**Administrative divisions:** 3 islands and 4
municipalities*; Grande Comore (N'gazidja), Anjouan
(Ndzuwani), Domoni*, Fomboni*, Moheli (Mwali),
Moroni*, Mutsamudu*
**Independence:** 6 July 1975 (from France)

**National holiday:** Independence Day, 6 July (1975)
**Constitution:** 23 December 2001
**Legal system:** French and Islamic law in a new
consolidated code; has not accepted compulsory ICJ
jurisdiction
**Suffrage:** 18 years of age; universal
**Executive branch:**
*chief of state:* President Ahmed Abdallah SAMBI
(since 26 May 2006)
*head of government:* President Ahmed Abdallah
SAMBI (since 26 May 2006)
*cabinet:* Council of Ministers appointed by the
president
*elections:* as defined by the 2001 constitution, the
presidency rotates every four years among the
elected presidents from the three main islands in the
Union; election last held 14 May 2006 (next to be held
by May 2010)
*election results:* Ahmed Abdallah SAMBI elected
president; percent of vote - Ahmed Abdallah SAMBI
58.0%, Ibrahim HALIDI 28.3%, Mohamed
DJAANFAMI 13.7%
**Legislative branch:** unicameral Assembly of the
Union (33 seats; 15 deputies are selected by the
individual islands' local assemblies and 18 by
universal suffrage; to serve for five years);
*elections:* last held 18 and 25 April 2004 (next to be
held in 2009)
*election results:* percent of vote by party - NA; seats
by party - CdIA 12, CRC 6; note - 15 additional seats
are filled by deputies from local island assemblies
**Judicial branch:** Supreme Court or Cour Supremes
(two members appointed by the president, two
members elected by the Federal Assembly, one
elected by the Council of each island, and others are
former presidents of the republic)
**Political parties and leaders:** Convention for the
Renewal of the Comoros or CRC [AZALI Assowmani];
Camp of the Autonomous Islands or CdIA (a coalition
of parties organized by the islands' presidents in
opposition to the Union President); Front National
pour la Justice or FNJ [Ahmed RACHID] (Islamic party
in opposition); Mouvement pour la Democratie et le
Progress or MDP-NGDC [Abbas DJOUSSOUF]; Parti
Comorien pour la Democratie et le Progress or PCDP
[Ali MROUDJAE]; Rassemblement National pour le
Development or RND [Omar TAMOU, Abdoulhamid
AFFRAITANE]
**Political pressure groups and leaders:**
*other:* environmentalists
**International organization participation:** ACCT,
ACP, AfDB, AMF, AU, COMESA, FAO, FZ, G-77,
IBRD, ICAO, ICCt, ICRM, IDA, IDB, IFAD, IFC,
IFRCS, ILO, IMF, IMO, IMSO, InOC, Interpol, IOC,
IPU, ITSO, ITU, ITUC, LAS, NAM, OIC, OIF, OPCW,
UN, UNCTAD, UNESCO, UNIDO, UPU, WCO,
WFTU, WHO, WIPO, WMO, WTO (observer)
**Diplomatic representation in the US:**
*chief of mission:* Representative to the UN and
Ambassador to the US Mohamed TOIHIRI
*chancery:* Mission to the US, 866 United Nations
Plaza, Suite 418, New York, NY 10017
*telephone:* [1] (212) 750-1637

**Diplomatic representation from the US:** the US
does not have an embassy in Comoros; the
ambassador to Madagascar is accredited to Comoros
**Flag description:** four equal horizontal bands of
yellow (top), white, red, and blue, with a green
isosceles triangle based on the hoist; centered within
the triangle is a white crescent with the convex side
facing the hoist and four white, five-pointed stars
placed vertically in a line between the points of the
crescent; the horizontal bands and the four stars
represent the four main islands of the archipelago -
Mwali, N'gazidja, Nzwani, and Mahore (Mayotte -
territorial collectivity of France, but claimed by
Comoros)
*note:* the crescent, stars, and color green are
traditional symbols of Islam

## Economy

**Economy - overview:** One of the world's poorest
countries, Comoros is made up of three islands that
have inadequate transportation links, a young and
rapidly increasing population, and few natural
resources. The low educational level of the labor force
contributes to a subsistence level of economic activity,
high unemployment, and a heavy dependence on
foreign grants and technical assistance. Agriculture,
including fishing, hunting, and forestry, contributes
40% to GDP, employs 80% of the labor force, and
provides most of the exports. The country is not
self-sufficient in food production; rice, the main staple,
accounts for the bulk of imports. The government -
which is hampered by internal political disputes - is
struggling to upgrade education and technical training,
privatize commercial and industrial enterprises,
improve health services, diversify exports, promote
tourism, and reduce the high population growth rate.
The political problems have inhibited growth, which
has averaged only about 1% in 2006-08. Remittances
from 150,000 Comorans abroad help supplement
GDP.
**GDP (purchasing power parity):**
$741.4 million (2008 est.)
$737.7 million (2007)
$730.4 million (2006)
*note:* data are in 2008 US dollars
**GDP (official exchange rate):** $557 million
(2008 est.)
**GDP - real growth rate:**
0.5% (2008 est.)
1% (2007 est.)
1.3% (2006 est.)
**GDP - per capita (PPP):**
$1,000 (2008 est.)
$1,000 (2007 est.)
$1,100 (2006 est.)
*note:* data are in 2008 US dollars
**GDP - composition by sector:**
*agriculture:* 40%
*industry:* 4%
*services:* 56% (2001 est.)
**Labor force:** 144,500 (1996 est.)

# Comoros *(continued)*

**Labor force - by occupation:**
*agriculture:* 80%
*industry and services:* 20% (1996 est.)
**Unemployment rate:**
20% (1996 est.)
**Population below poverty line:** 60% (2002 est.)
**Household income or consumption by percentage share:**
*lowest 10%:* NA%
*highest 10%:* NA%
**Budget:**
*revenues:* $27.6 million
*expenditures:* $NA (2001 est.)
**Inflation rate (consumer prices):**
3% (2007 est.)
**Central bank discount rate:** 5.36% (31 December 2007)
**Commercial bank prime lending rate:** 10.5% (31 December 2007)
**Stock of money:** $76.68 million (31 December 2007)
**Stock of quasi money:** $23.39 million (31 December 2007)
**Stock of domestic credit:** $45.09 million (31 December 2007)
**Agriculture - products:** vanilla, cloves, ylang-ylang, perfume essences, copra, coconuts, bananas, cassava (tapioca)
**Industries:** fishing, tourism, perfume distillation
**Industrial production growth rate:** -2% (1999 est.)
**Electricity - production:** 20 million kWh (2006 est.)
**Electricity - consumption:** 18.6 million kWh (2006 est.)
**Electricity - exports:** 0 kWh (2007 est.)
**Electricity - imports:** 0 kWh (2007 est.)
**Oil - production:** 0 bbl/day (2007 est.)
**Oil - consumption:** 712.3 bbl/day (2006 est.)
**Oil - exports:** 0 bbl/day (2005)
**Oil - imports:** 755.4 bbl/day (2005)
**Oil - proved reserves:** 0 bbl (1 January 2006 est.)
**Natural gas - production:** 0 cu m (2007 est.)
**Natural gas - consumption:** 0 cu m (2007 est.)
**Natural gas - exports:** 0 cu m (2007 est.)
**Natural gas - imports:** 0 cu m (2007 est.)
**Natural gas - proved reserves:** 0 cu m (1 January 2006 est.)
**Current account balance:** $8 million (2007 est.)
**Exports:** $32 million f.o.b. (2006)
**Exports - commodities:** vanilla, ylang-ylang (perfume essence), cloves, copra
**Exports - partners:** Turkey 38%, France 27.5%, Singapore 9.2%, Saudi Arabia 4.1% (2007)
**Imports:** $143 million f.o.b. (2006)
**Imports - commodities:** rice and other foodstuffs, consumer goods, petroleum products, cement, transport equipment
**Imports - partners:** France 18.2%, UAE 10.8%, South Africa 8.5%, Pakistan 7.2%, Kenya 5.7%, China 5.4%, India 5% (2007)

**Debt - external:** $232 million (2000 est.)
**Exchange rates:** Comoran francs (KMF) per US dollar - 361.4 (2007), 391.8 (2006), 395.6 (2005), 396.21 (2004), 435.9 (2003)
*note:* the Comoran franc is pegged to the euro at a rate of 491.9677 Comoran francs per euro

## Communications

**Telephones - main lines in use:** 19,100 (2006)
**Telephones - mobile cellular:** 40,000 (2007)
**Telephone system:**
*general assessment:* sparse system of microwave radio relay and HF radiotelephone communication stations; fixed-line connections only about 3 per 100 persons; mobile cellular usage about 5 per 100 persons
*domestic:* HF radiotelephone communications and microwave radio relay
*international:* country code - 269; HF radiotelephone communications to Madagascar and Reunion
**Radio broadcast stations:** AM 1, FM 4, shortwave 1 (2001)
**Television broadcast stations:** NA
**Internet country code:** .km
**Internet hosts:** 8 (2008)
**Internet users:** 21,000 (2006)

## Transportation

**Airports:** 4 (2008)
**Airports - with paved runways:**
*total:* 4
*2,438 to 3,047 m:* 1
*914 to 1,523 m:* 3 (2008)
**Roadways:**
*total:* 880 km
*paved:* 673 km
*unpaved:* 207 km (2002)
**Merchant marine:**
*total:* 136
*by type:* bulk carrier 15, cargo 87, carrier 2, chemical tanker 5, container 2, passenger 1, passenger/cargo 1, petroleum tanker 9, refrigerated cargo 5, roll on/roll off 8, specialized tanker 1
*foreign-owned:* 68 (Bangladesh 2, Bulgaria 2, Cyprus 1, Greece 6, India 2, Kenya 1, Kuwait 1, Lebanon 4, Norway 1, Pakistan 4, Philippines 1, Russia 12, Saudi Arabia 1, Singapore 1, Syria 4, Turkey 8, Ukraine 8, UAE 7, US 2) (2008)
**Ports and terminals:** Mayotte, Mutsamudu

## Military

**Military branches:** National Development Army (AND): Comoran Security Force; Comoran Federal Police (2008)
**Manpower available for military service:**
*males age 16-49:* 167,850
*females age 16-49:* 167,362 (2008 est.)
**Manpower fit for military service:**
*males age 16-49:* 125,747
*females age 16-49:* 135,707 (2009 est.)

**Manpower reaching militarily significant age annually:**
*male:* 8,203
*female:* 8,188 (2009 est.)
**Military expenditures:** 2.8% of GDP (2006)

## Transnational Issues

**Disputes - international:** claims French-administered Mayotte and challenges France's and Madagascar's claims to Banc du Geyser, a drying reef in the Mozambique Channel; in May 2008, African Union forces are called in to assist the Comoros military recapture Anjouan Island from rebels who seized it in 2001

# Congo, Democratic Republic of the

## Introduction

**Background:** Established as a Belgian colony in 1908, the Republic of the Congo gained its independence in 1960, but its early years were marred by political and social instability. Col. Joseph MOBUTU seized power and declared himself president in a November 1965 coup. He subsequently changed his name - to MOBUTU Sese Seko - as well as that of the country - to Zaire. MOBUTU retained his position for 32 years through several sham elections, as well as through the use of brutal force. Ethnic strife and civil war, touched off by a massive inflow of refugees in 1994 from fighting in Rwanda and Burundi, led in May 1997 to the toppling of the MOBUTU regime by a rebellion backed by Rwanda and Uganda and fronted by Laurent KABILA. He renamed the country the Democratic Republic of the Congo (DRC), but in August 1998 his regime was itself challenged by a second insurrection again backed by Rwanda and Uganda. Troops from Angola, Chad, Namibia, Sudan, and Zimbabwe intervened to support KABILA's regime. A cease-fire was signed in July 1999 by the DRC, Congolese armed rebel groups, Angola, Namibia, Rwanda, Uganda, and Zimbabwe but sporadic fighting continued. Laurent KABILA was assassinated in January 2001 and his son, Joseph KABILA, was named head of state. In October 2002, the new president was successful in negotiating the withdrawal of Rwandan forces occupying eastern Congo; two months later, the Pretoria Accord was signed by all remaining warring parties to end the fighting and establish a government of national unity. A transitional government was set up in July 2003. Joseph KABILA as president and four vice presidents represented the former government, former rebel groups, the political opposition, and civil society. The transitional government held a successful constitutional referendum in December 2005 and elections for the presidency, National Assembly, and provincial legislatures in 2006. KABILA was inaugurated president in December 2006. The National Assembly was installed in September 2006. Its president, Vital KAMERHE, was chosen in December. Provincial assemblies were constituted in early 2007, and elected governors and national senators in January 2007.

## Geography

**Location:** Central Africa, northeast of Angola
**Geographic coordinates:** 0 00 N, 25 00 E
**Map references:** Africa
**Area:**
*total:* 2,345,410 sq km
*land:* 2,267,600 sq km
*water:* 77,810 sq km
**Area - comparative:** slightly less than one-fourth the size of the US
**Land boundaries:**
*total:* 10,730 km
*border countries:* Angola 2,511 km (of which 225 km is the boundary of Angola's discontiguous Cabinda Province), Burundi 233 km, Central African Republic 1,577 km, Republic of the Congo 2,410 km, Rwanda 217 km, Sudan 628 km, Tanzania 459 km, Uganda 765 km, Zambia 1,930 km
**Coastline:** 37 km
**Maritime claims:**
*territorial sea:* 12 nm
*exclusive economic zone:* boundaries with neighbors
**Climate:** tropical; hot and humid in equatorial river basin; cooler and drier in southern highlands; cooler and wetter in eastern highlands; north of Equator - wet season (April to October), dry season (December to February); south of Equator - wet season (November to March), dry season (April to October)
**Terrain:** vast central basin is a low-lying plateau; mountains in east
**Elevation extremes:**
*lowest point:* Atlantic Ocean 0 m
*highest point:* Pic Marguerite on Mont Ngaliema (Mount Stanley) 5,110 m
**Natural resources:** cobalt, copper, niobium, tantalum, petroleum, industrial and gem diamonds, gold, silver, zinc, manganese, tin, uranium, coal, hydropower, timber
**Land use:**
*arable land:* 2.86%
*permanent crops:* 0.47%
*other:* 96.67% (2005)
**Irrigated land:** 110 sq km (2003)
**Total renewable water resources:** 1,283 cu km (2001)
**Freshwater withdrawal (domestic/industrial/agricultural):**
*total:* 0.36 cu km/yr (53%/17%/31%)
*per capita:* 6 cu m/yr (2000)
**Natural hazards:** periodic droughts in south; Congo River floods (seasonal); in the east, in the Great Rift Valley, there are active volcanoes

**Environment - current issues:** poaching threatens wildlife populations; water pollution; deforestation; refugees responsible for significant deforestation, soil erosion, and wildlife poaching; mining of minerals (coltan - a mineral used in creating capacitors, diamonds, and gold) causing environmental damage
**Environment - international agreements:**
*party to:* Biodiversity, Climate Change, Climate Change-Kyoto Protocol, Desertification, Endangered Species, Hazardous Wastes, Law of the Sea, Marine Dumping, Ozone Layer Protection, Tropical Timber 83, Tropical Timber 94, Wetlands
*signed, but not ratified:* Environmental Modification
**Geography - note:** straddles equator; has narrow strip of land that controls the lower Congo River and is only outlet to South Atlantic Ocean; dense tropical rain forest in central river basin and eastern highlands

## People

**Population:** 68,692,542
*note:* estimates for this country explicitly take into account the effects of excess mortality due to AIDS; this can result in lower life expectancy, higher infant mortality, higher death rates, lower population growth rates, and changes in the distribution of population by age and sex than would otherwise be expected (July 2009 est.)
**Age structure:**
*0-14 years:* 46.9% (male 16,161,301/female 16,038,024)
*15-64 years:* 50.6% (male 17,289,453/female 17,483,027)
*65 years and over:* 2.5% (male 699,667/female 1,021,070) (2009 est.)
**Median age:**
*total:* 16.4 years
*male:* 16.2 years
*female:* 16.6 years (2009 est.)
**Population growth rate:** 3.208% (2009 est.)
**Birth rate:** 42.63 births/1,000 population (2009 est.)
**Death rate:** 11.88 deaths/1,000 population (2008 est.)
**Net migration rate:** 1.07 migrant(s)/1,000 population (2009 est.)
**Urbanization:**
*urban population:* 34% of total population (2008)
*rate of urbanization:* 5.1% annual rate of change (2005-10 est.)
**Sex ratio:**
*at birth:* 1.03 male(s)/female
*under 15 years:* 1.01 male(s)/female
*15-64 years:* 0.99 male(s)/female
*65 years and over:* 0.68 male(s)/female
*total population:* 0.99 male(s)/female (2009 est.)
**Infant mortality rate:**
*total:* 81.21 deaths/1,000 live births
*male:* 89.11 deaths/1,000 live births
*female:* 73.07 deaths/1,000 live births (2009 est.)
**Life expectancy at birth:**
*total population:* 54.36 years
*male:* 52.58 years
*female:* 56.2 years (2009 est.)

**Total fertility rate:** 6.2 children born/woman (2009 est.)

**HIV/AIDS - adult prevalence rate:** 4.2% (2003 est.)

**HIV/AIDS - people living with HIV/AIDS:** 1.1 million (2003 est.)

**HIV/AIDS - deaths:** 100,000 (2003 est.)

**Major infectious diseases:**

*degree of risk:* very high

*food or waterborne diseases:* bacterial and protozoal diarrhea, hepatitis A, and typhoid fever

*vectorborne diseases:* malaria, plague, and African trypanosomiasis (sleeping sickness)

*water contact disease:* schistosomiasis

*animal contact disease:* rabies (2009)

**Nationality:**

*noun:* Congolese (singular and plural)

*adjective:* Congolese or Congo

**Ethnic groups:** over 200 African ethnic groups of which the majority are Bantu; the four largest tribes - Mongo, Luba, Kongo (all Bantu), and the Mangbetu-Azande (Hamitic) make up about 45% of the population

**Religions:** Roman Catholic 50%, Protestant 20%, Kimbanguist 10%, Muslim 10%, other (includes syncretic sects and indigenous beliefs) 10%

**Languages:** French (official), Lingala (a lingua franca trade language), Kingwana (a dialect of Kiswahili or Swahili), Kikongo, Tshiluba

**Literacy:**

*definition:* age 15 and over can read and write French, Lingala, Kingwana, or Tshiluba

*total population:* 67.2%

*male:* 80.9%

*female:* 54.1% (2001 est.)

**School life expectancy (primary to tertiary education):**

*total:* 9 years

*male:* 10 years

*female:* 8 years (2003)

**Education expenditures:** NA

## Government

**Country name:**

*conventional long form:* Democratic Republic of the Congo

*conventional short form:* DRC

*local long form:* Republique Democratique du Congo

*local short form:* RDC

*former:* Congo Free State, Belgian Congo, Congo/ Leopoldville, Congo/Kinshasa, Zaire

*abbreviation:* DRC

**Government type:** republic

**Capital:**

*name:* Kinshasa

*geographic coordinates:* 4 19 S, 15 18 E

*time difference:* UTC+1 (six hours ahead of Washington, DC during Standard Time)

**Administrative divisions:** 10 provinces (provinces, singular - province) and 1 city* (ville); Bandundu, Bas-Congo, Equateur, Kasai-Occidental, Kasai-Oriental, Katanga, Kinshasa*, Maniema, Nord-Kivu, Orientale, Sud-Kivu

*note:* according to the Constitution adopted in December 2005, the current administrative divisions will be subdivided into 26 new provinces by 2009

**Independence:** 30 June 1960 (from Belgium)

**National holiday:** Independence Day, 30 June (1960)

**Constitution:** 18 February 2006

**Legal system:** a new constitution was adopted by referendum 18 December 2005; accepts compulsory ICJ jurisdiction with reservations

**Suffrage:** 18 years of age; universal and compulsory

**Executive branch:**

*chief of state:* President Joseph KABILA (since 17 January 2001); note - following the assassination of his father, Joseph KABILA succeeded to the presidency which he retained through the 2003-06 transition; he was subsequently elected president in October 2006

*head of government:* Prime Minister Adolphe MUZITO (since 10 October 2008)

*cabinet:* Ministers of State appointed by the president

*elections:* under the new constitution the president is elected by popular vote for a five-year term (eligible for a second term); elections last held 30 July 2006 and 29 October 2006 (next to be held in 2011); prime minister appointed by the president

*election results:* Joseph KABILA elected president; percent of vote (second round) - Joseph KABILA 58%, Jean-Pierre BEMBA Gombo 42%

*note:* Joseph KABILA succeeded his father, Laurent Desire KABILA, following the latter's assassination in January 2001; negotiations with rebel leaders led to the establishment of a transitional government in July 2003 with free elections held on 30 July 2006 and a run-off on 29 October 2006 confirming Joseph KABILA as president

**Legislative branch:** bicameral legislature consists of a Senate (108 seats; members elected by provincial assemblies to serve five-year terms) and a National Assembly (500 seats; 61 members elected by majority vote in single-member constituencies, 439 members elected by open list proportional-representation in multi-member constituencies; to serve five-year terms)

*elections:* Senate - last held 19 January 2007 (next to be held by 2012); National Assembly - last held 30 July 2006 (next to be held in 2011)

*election results:* Senate - percent of vote by party - NA; seats by party - PPRD 22, MLC 14, FR 7, RCD 7, PDC 6, CDC 3, MSR 3, PALU 2, independents 26, others 18 (political parties that won a single seat); National Assembly - percent of vote by party - NA; seats by party - PPRD 111, MLC 64, PALU 34, MSR 27, FR 26, RCD 15, independents 63, others 160 (includes 63 political parties that won 10 or fewer seats)

**Judicial branch:** Constitutional Court; Appeals Court or Cour de Cassation; Council of State; High Military Court; plus civil and military courts and tribunals

**Political parties and leaders:** Christian Democrat Party or PDC [Jose ENDUNDO]; Congolese Rally for Democracy or RCD [Azarias RUBERWA]; Convention of Christian Democrats or CDC; Forces of Renewal or FR [Mbusa NYAMWISI]; Movement for the Liberation of the Congo or MLC [Jean-Pierre BEMBA]; People's Party for Reconstruction and Democracy or PPRD [Joseph KABILA]; Social Movement for Renewal or MSR [Pierre LUMBI]; Unified Lumumbist Party or PALU [Antoine GIZENGA]; Union for Democracy and Social Progress or UDPS [Etienne TSHISEKEDI]; Union of Mobutuist Democrats or UDEMO [MOBUTU Nzanga]

**Political pressure groups and leaders:** MONUC - UN organization working with the government; FARDC (Forces ArmÈes de la RÈpublique DÈmocratique du Congo) - Army of the Democratic Republic of the Congo which commits atrocities on citizens; FDLA (Forces Democratiques de Liberation du Rwanda) - Rwandan militia group

**International organization participation:** ACCT, ACP, AfDB, AU, CEPGL, COMESA, FAO, G-24, G-77, IAEA, IBRD, ICAO, ICCt, ICRM, IDA, IFAD, IFC, IFRCS, IHO (suspended), ILO, IMF, IMO, Interpol, IOC, IOM, IPU, ISO, ITSO, ITU, ITUC, MIGA, NAM, OIF, OPCW, PCA, SADC, UN, UNCTAD, UNESCO, UNHCR, UNIDO, UNWTO, UPU, WCL, WCO, WFTU, WHO, WIPO, WMO, WTO

**Diplomatic representation in the US:**

*chief of mission:* Ambassador Faida MITIFU

*chancery:* 1800 New Hampshire Avenue NW, Washington, DC 20009: note - Consular Office at 1726 M Street, NW, Washington, DC, 20036

*telephone:* [1] (202) 234-7690 through 7691

*FAX:* [1] (202) 234-2609

**Diplomatic representation from the US:**

*chief of mission:* Ambassador William GARVELINK

*embassy:* 310 Avenue des Aviateurs, Kinshasa

*mailing address:* Unit 31550, APO AE 09828

*telephone:* [243] (81) 225-5872

*FAX:* [243] (81) 301-0561

**Flag description:** sky blue field divided diagonally from the lower hoist corner to upper fly corner by a red stripe bordered by two narrow yellow stripes; a yellow, five-pointed star appears in the upper hoist corner

## Economy

**Economy - overview:** The economy of the Democratic Republic of the Congo - a nation endowed with vast potential wealth - is slowly recovering from two decades of decline. Conflict that began in August 1998 has dramatically reduced national output and government revenue, increased external debt, and resulted in the deaths of more than 5 million people from violence, famine, and disease. Foreign businesses curtailed operations due to uncertainty about the outcome of the conflict, lack of infrastructure, and the difficult operating environment. Conditions began to improve in late 2002 with the withdrawal of a large portion of the invading foreign troops. The transitional government reopened relations with international financial institutions and international donors, and President KABILA began implementing reforms, although progress has been slow and the International Monetary Fund curtailed their program for the DRC at the end of March 2006 because of fiscal overruns. Much economic activity still occurs in the informal sector, and is not reflected in GDP data. Renewed activity in the mining sector, the source of most export income, boosted Kinshasa's fiscal position and GDP growth from 2006-2008, however, renewed strife in the second half of 2008, combined with a fall in world market prices for the DRC's key mineral exports inflicted major damage on the economy and halted growth. Government reforms may lead to increased government revenues, outside budget assistance, and foreign direct investment, although an uncertain legal framework, corruption, a lack of transparency in government policy are long-term problems. The DRC government has applied to the IMF for an Exogenous Shock Facility in the amount of $200 million to help it deal with its deteriorating financial situation, and the World Bank will consider a separate $100 million in emergency funding. The global recession probably will cut economic growth in 2009 to half its 2008 level.

**GDP (purchasing power parity):**
$21.05 billion (2008 est.)
$19.49 billion (2007)
$18.22 billion (2006)
*note:* data are in 2008 US dollars

**GDP (official exchange rate):** $12.96 billion (2008 est.)

**GDP - real growth rate:**
8% (2008 est.)
7% (2007 est.)
6.4% (2006 est.)

**GDP - per capita (PPP):**
$300 (2008 est.)
$300 (2007 est.)
$300 (2006 est.)
*note:* data are in 2008 US dollars

**GDP - composition by sector:**
*agriculture:* 55%
*industry:* 11%
*services:* 34% (2000 est.)

**Labor force:** 15 million (2006 est.)

**Labor force - by occupation:**
*agriculture:* NA%
*industry:* NA%
*services:* NA%

**Unemployment rate:**
NA%

**Population below poverty line:** NA%

**Household income or consumption by percentage share:**
*lowest 10%:* NA%
*highest 10%:* NA%

**Budget:**
*revenues:* $700 million
*expenditures:* $2 billion (2006 est.)

**Inflation rate (consumer prices):**
16.7% (2007 est.)

**Central bank discount rate:** 5.25% (31 December 2007)

**Commercial bank prime lending rate:** NA

**Stock of money:** $597 million (31 December 2007)

**Stock of quasi money:** $677.9 million (31 December 2007)

**Stock of domestic credit:** $559.5 million (31 December 2007)

**Market value of publicly traded shares:** $NA

**Agriculture - products:** coffee, sugar, palm oil, rubber, tea, quinine, cassava (tapioca), palm oil, bananas, root crops, corn, fruits; wood products

**Industries:** mining (diamonds, gold, copper, cobalt, coltan, zinc), mineral processing, consumer products (including textiles, footwear, cigarettes, processed foods and beverages), cement, commercial ship repair

**Industrial production growth rate:** NA%

**Electricity - production:** 7.243 billion kWh (2006 est.)

**Electricity - consumption:** 5.158 billion kWh (2006 est.)

**Electricity - exports:** 1.799 billion kWh (2006 est.)

**Electricity - imports:** 6 million kWh (2006 est.)

**Oil - production:** 22,160 bbl/day (2007 est.)

**Oil - consumption:** 10,460 bbl/day (2006 est.)

**Oil - exports:** 19,820 bbl/day (2005)

**Oil - imports:** 8,220 bbl/day (2006 est.)

**Oil - proved reserves:** 180 million bbl (1 January 2008 est.)

**Natural gas - production:** 0 cu m (2007 est.)

**Natural gas - consumption:** 0 cu m (2007 est.)

**Natural gas - exports:** 0 cu m (2007 est.)

**Natural gas - imports:** 0 cu m (2007 est.)

**Natural gas - proved reserves:** 991.1 million cu m (1 January 2008 est.)

**Current account balance:** -$402 million (2007 est.)

**Exports:** $6.1 billion f.o.b. (2007)

**Exports - commodities:** diamonds, gold, copper, cobalt, wood products, crude oil, coffee

**Exports - partners:** Belgium 23.6%, China 21.7%, US 9.8%, Finland 9.1%, Brazil 9.1%, France 6.8%, Zambia 6% (2007)

**Imports:** $5.2 billion f.o.b. (2007)

**Imports - commodities:** foodstuffs, mining and other machinery, transport equipment, fuels

**Imports - partners:** South Africa 22.5%, Belgium 10.3%, Zambia 8.9%, Zimbabwe 7.5%, France 6.8%, Kenya 6.3%, US 4.1%, Cote d'Ivoire 4.1% (2007)

**Debt - external:** $10 billion (2007 est.)

**Exchange rates:** Congolese francs (CDF) per US dollar - NA (2007), 464.69 (2006), 437.86 (2005), 401.04 (2004), 405.34 (2003)

## Communications

**Telephones - main lines in use:** 9,700 (2006)

**Telephones - mobile cellular:** 6.592 million (2007)

**Telephone system:**
*general assessment:* inadequate; state-owned fixed-line operator has been unable to expand fixed-line connections and there are now fewer than 10,000 connections - less than 1 per 1000 persons; given the backdrop of a wholly inadequate fixed-line infrastructure, the use of cellular services has surged and subscribership in 2007 reached 6.6 million - 10 per 100 persons
*domestic:* barely adequate wire and microwave radio relay service in and between urban areas; domestic satellite system with 14 earth stations
*international:* country code - 243; satellite earth station -1 Intelsat (Atlantic Ocean) (2007)

**Radio broadcast stations:** AM 3, FM 11, shortwave 2 (2001)

**Television broadcast stations:** 4 (2001)

**Internet country code:** .cd

**Internet hosts:** 3,211 (2008)

**Internet users:** 230,400 (2007)

## Transportation

**Airports:** 200 (2008)

**Airports - with paved runways:**
*total:* 26
*over 3,047 m:* 4
*2,438 to 3,047 m:* 2
*1,524 to 2,437 m:* 17
*914 to 1,523 m:* 2
*under 914 m:* 1 (2008)

**Airports - with unpaved runways:**
*total:* 174
*2,438 to 3,047 m:* 1
*1,524 to 2,437 m:* 17
*914 to 1,523 m:* 89
*under 914 m:* 67 (2008)

**Pipelines:** gas 37 km; oil 39 km; refined products 756 km (2008)

**Railways:**
*total:* 5,138 km
*narrow gauge:* 3,987 km 1.067-m gauge (858 km electrified); 125 km 1.000-m gauge; 1,026 km 0.600-m gauge (2006)

**Roadways:**
*total:* 153,497 km
*paved:* 2,794 km
*unpaved:* 150,703 km (2004)

**Waterways:** 15,000 km (2008)

**Merchant marine:**
*total:* 1
*by type:* petroleum tanker 1
*foreign-owned:* 1 (Congo, Republic of the 1) (2008)

**Ports and terminals:** Banana, Boma, Bukavu, Bumba, Goma, Kalemie, Kindu, Kinshasa, Kisangani, Matadi, Mbandaka

## Military

**Military branches:** Armed Forces of the Democratic Republic of the Congo (Forces d'Armees de la Republique Democratique du Congo, FARDC): Army, National Navy (La Marine Nationale), Congolese Air Force (Force Aerienne Congolaise, FAC) (2008)

**Military service age and obligation:** 18-45 years of age for military service

**Manpower available for military service:**
*males age 16-49:* 14,101,263 (2008 est.)

# Congo, Democratic Republic of the (continued)

**Manpower fit for military service:**
*males age 16-49:* 8,925,355
*females age 16-49:* 9,047,356 (2009 est.)
**Manpower reaching militarily significant age annually:**
*male:* 814,199
*female:* 811,238 (2009 est.)
**Military expenditures:** 2.5% of GDP (2006)

## Transnational Issues

**Disputes - international:** heads of the Great Lakes states and UN pledged in 2004 to abate tribal, rebel, and militia fighting in the region, including northeast Congo, where the UN Organization Mission in the Democratic Republic of the Congo (MONUC), organized in 1999, maintains over 16,500 uniformed peacekeepers; members of Uganda's Lords Resistance Army forces continue to seek refuge in Congo's Garamba National Park as peace talks with the Uganda government evolve; the location of the boundary in the broad Congo River with the Republic of the Congo is indefinite except in the Pool Malebo/Stanley Pool area; Uganda and DROC dispute Rukwanzi island in Lake Albert and other areas on the Semliki River with hydrocarbon potential; boundary commission continues discussions over Congolese-administered triangle of land on the right bank of the Lunkinda river claimed by Zambia near the DROC village of Pweto

**Refugees and internally displaced persons:**
*refugees (country of origin):* 132,295 (Angola); 37,313 (Rwanda); 17,777 (Burundi); 13,904 (Uganda); 6,181 (Sudan); 5,243 (Republic of Congo)
*IDPs:* 1.4 million (fighting between government forces and rebels since mid-1990s; most IDPs are in eastern provinces) (2007)

**Trafficking in persons:**
*current situation:* Democratic Republic of the Congo is a source and destination country for men, women, and children trafficked for the purposes of forced labor and sexual exploitation; much of this trafficking occurs within the country's unstable eastern provinces and is perpetrated by armed groups outside government control
*tier rating:* Tier 2 Watch List - Democratic Republic of the Congo is on the Tier 2 Watch List for its failure to provide evidence of increasing efforts to combat trafficking in persons in 2007; while some significant initial advances were noted, the government's capacity to apprehend, convict, or imprison traffickers remained weak; the government lacks sufficient financial, technical, and human resources to effectively address not only trafficking crimes, but also to provide basic levels of security in some parts of the country (2008)

**Illicit drugs:** one of Africa's biggest producers of cannabis, but mostly for domestic consumption; traffickers exploit lax shipping controls to transit pseudoephedrine through the capital; while rampant corruption and inadequate supervision leaves the banking system vulnerable to money laundering, the lack of a well-developed financial system limits the country's utility as a money-laundering center (2008)

# Congo, Republic of the

## Introduction

**Background:** Upon independence in 1960, the former French region of Middle Congo became the Republic of the Congo. A quarter century of experimentation with Marxism was abandoned in 1990 and a democratically elected government took office in 1992. A brief civil war in 1997 restored former Marxist President Denis SASSOU-NGUESSO, and ushered in a period of ethnic and political unrest. Southern-based rebel groups agreed to a final peace accord in March 2003, but the calm is tenuous and refugees continue to present a humanitarian crisis. The Republic of Congo was once one of Africa's largest petroleum producers, but with declining production it will need new offshore oil finds to sustain its oil earnings over the long term.

## Geography

**Location:** Western Africa, bordering the South Atlantic Ocean, between Angola and Gabon
**Geographic coordinates:** 1 00 S, 15 00 E
**Map references:** Africa
**Area:**
*total:* 342,000 sq km
*land:* 341,500 sq km
*water:* 500 sq km
**Area - comparative:** slightly smaller than Montana
**Land boundaries:**
*total:* 5,504 km
*border countries:* Angola 201 km, Cameroon 523 km, Central African Republic 467 km, Democratic Republic of the Congo 2,410 km, Gabon 1,903 km
**Coastline:** 169 km
**Maritime claims:**
*territorial sea:* 200 nm
**Climate:** tropical; rainy season (March to June); dry season (June to October); persistent high temperatures and humidity; particularly enervating climate astride the Equator

**Terrain:** coastal plain, southern basin, central plateau, northern basin
**Elevation extremes:**
*lowest point:* Atlantic Ocean 0 m
*highest point:* Mount Berongou 903 m
**Natural resources:** petroleum, timber, potash, lead, zinc, uranium, copper, phosphates, gold, magnesium, natural gas, hydropower
**Land use:**
*arable land:* 1.45%
*permanent crops:* 0.15%
*other:* 98.4% (2005)
**Irrigated land:** 20 sq km (2003)
**Total renewable water resources:** 832 cu km (1987)
**Freshwater withdrawal (domestic/industrial/agricultural):**
*total:* 0.03 cu km/yr (59%/29%/12%)
*per capita:* 8 cu m/yr (2000)
**Natural hazards:** seasonal flooding
**Environment - current issues:** air pollution from vehicle emissions; water pollution from the dumping of raw sewage; tap water is not potable; deforestation
**Environment - international agreements:**
*party to:* Biodiversity, Climate Change, Climate Change-Kyoto Protocol, Desertification, Endangered Species, Hazardous Wastes, Law of the Sea, Ozone Layer Protection, Ship Pollution, Tropical Timber 83, Tropical Timber 94, Wetlands
*signed, but not ratified:* none of the selected agreements
**Geography - note:** about 70% of the population lives in Brazzaville, Pointe-Noire, or along the railroad between them

## People

**Population:** 4,012,809
*note:* estimates for this country explicitly take into account the effects of excess mortality due to AIDS; this can result in lower life expectancy, higher infant mortality, higher death rates, lower population growth rates, and changes in the distribution of population by age and sex than would otherwise be expected (July 2009 est.)

**Age structure:**
*0-14 years:* 45.9% (male 927,599/female 915,540)
*15-64 years:* 51.2% (male 1,021,975/female 1,034,119)
*65 years and over:* 2.8% (male 46,687/female 66,889) (2009 est.)
**Median age:**
*total:* 16.8 years
*male:* 16.6 years
*female:* 17.1 years (2009 est.)
**Population growth rate:** 2.754% (2009 est.)
**Birth rate:** 41.37 births/1,000 population (2009 est.)
**Death rate:** 12.28 deaths/1,000 population (2008 est.)
**Net migration rate:** -1.82 migrant(s)/1,000 population (2009 est.)

# Congo, Republic of the (continued)

**Urbanization:**

*urban population:* 61% of total population (2008)

*rate of urbanization:* 2.7% annual rate of change (2005-10 est.)

**Sex ratio:**

*at birth:* 1.03 male(s)/female

*under 15 years:* 1.01 male(s)/female

*15-64 years:* 0.99 male(s)/female

*65 years and over:* 0.7 male(s)/female

*total population:* 0.99 male(s)/female (2009 est.)

**Infant mortality rate:**

*total:* 79.78 deaths/1,000 live births

*male:* 85.29 deaths/1,000 live births

*female:* 74.1 deaths/1,000 live births (2009 est.)

**Life expectancy at birth:**

*total population:* 54.15 years

*male:* 52.9 years

*female:* 55.43 years (2009 est.)

**Total fertility rate:** 5.84 children born/woman (2009 est.)

**HIV/AIDS - adult prevalence rate:** 3.5% (2007 est.)

**HIV/AIDS - people living with HIV/AIDS:** 79,000 (2007 est.)

**HIV/AIDS - deaths:** 6,400 (2007 est.)

**Major infectious diseases:**

*degree of risk:* very high

*food or waterborne diseases:* bacterial and protozoal diarrhea, hepatitis A, and typhoid fever

*vectorborne disease:* malaria and African trypanosomiasis (sleeping sickness)

*animal contact disease:* rabies

*water contact disease:* schistosomiasis (2009)

**Nationality:**

*noun:* Congolese (singular and plural)

*adjective:* Congolese or Congo

**Ethnic groups:** Kongo 48%, Sangha 20%, M'Bochi 12%, Teke 17%, Europeans and other 3%

**Religions:** Christian 50%, animist 48%, Muslim 2%

**Languages:** French (official), Lingala and Monokutuba (lingua franca trade languages), many local languages and dialects (of which Kikongo is the most widespread)

**Literacy:**

*definition:* age 15 and over can read and write

*total population:* 83.8%

*male:* 89.6%

*female:* 78.4% (2003 est.)

**School life expectancy (primary to tertiary education):**

*total:* 9 years

*male:* 10 years

*female:* 8 years (2003)

**Education expenditures:** 1.9% of GDP (2005)

## Government

**Country name:**

*conventional long form:* Republic of the Congo

*conventional short form:* Congo (Brazzaville)

*local long form:* Republique du Congo

*local short form:* none

*former:* Middle Congo, Congo/Brazzaville, Congo

**Government type:** republic

**Capital:**

*name:* Brazzaville

*geographic coordinates:* 4 15 S, 15 17 E

*time difference:* UTC+1 (six hours ahead of Washington, DC during Standard Time)

**Administrative divisions:** 10 regions (regions, singular - region) and 1 commune*; Bouenza, Brazzaville*, Cuvette, Cuvette-Ouest, Kouilou, Lekoumou, Likouala, Niari, Plateaux, Pool, Sangha

**Independence:** 15 August 1960 (from France)

**National holiday:** Independence Day, 15 August (1960)

**Constitution:** approved by referendum 20 January 2002

**Legal system:** based on French civil law system and customary law; has not accepted compulsory ICJ jurisdiction

**Suffrage:** 18 years of age; universal

**Executive branch:**

*chief of state:* President Denis SASSOU-NGUESSO (since 25 October 1997, following the civil war in which he toppled elected president Pascal LISSOUBA);

*head of government:* Prime Minister Isidore MVOUBA (since 7 January 2005)

*cabinet:* Council of Ministers appointed by the president

*elections:* president elected by popular vote for a seven-year term (eligible for a second term); election last held 10 March 2002 (next to be held in July 2009)

*election results:* Denis SASSOU-NGUESSO reelected president; percent of vote - Denis SASSOU-NGUESSO 89.4%, Joseph Kignoumbi Kia MBOUNGOU 2.7%

**Legislative branch:** bicameral Parliament consists of the Senate (72 seats; members are elected by indirect vote to serve five-year terms) and the National Assembly (137 seats; members are elected by popular vote to serve five-year terms)

*elections:* Senate - last held 5 August 2008 (next to be held in 2013); National Assembly - last held 24 June and 5 August 2007 (next to be held in 2012)

*election results:* Senate - percent of vote by party - NA; seats by party - RMP 33, FDU 23, UPADS 2, independents 7, other 7; National Assembly - percent of vote by party - NA; seats by party - PCT 46, MCDDI 11, UPADS 11, MAR 5, MSD 5, independents 37, other 22

**Judicial branch:** Supreme Court or Cour Supreme

**Political parties and leaders:** Action Movement for Renewal or MAR; Congolese Movement for Democracy and Integral Development or MCDDI [Michel MAMPOUYA]; Congolese Labour Party or PCT; Movement for Solidarity and Development or MSD; Pan-African Union for Social Development or UPADS [Martin MBERI]; Rally of the Presidential Majority or RMP; Rally for Democracy and Social Progress or RDPS [Jean-Pierre Thystere TCHICAYA, president]; Rally for Democracy and the Republic or RDR [Raymond Damasge NGOLLO]; Union for Democracy and Republic or UDR; United Democratic Forces or FDU [Sebastian EBAO]; many less important parties

**Political pressure groups and leaders:** Congolese Trade Union Congress or CSC; General Union of Congolese Pupils and Students or UGEEC; Revolutionary Union of Congolese Women or URFC; Union of Congolese Socialist Youth or UJSC

**International organization participation:** ACCT, ACP, AfDB, AU, BDEAC, CEMAC, FAO, FZ, G-77, IBRD, ICAO, ICCt, ICRM, IDA, IFAD, IFC, IFRCS, ILO, IMF, IMO, Interpol, IOC, IOM, IPU, ITSO, ITU, ITUC, MIGA, NAM, OIF, OPCW, UN, UNCTAD, UNESCO, UNIDO, UNITAR, UNWTO, UPU, WCL, WCO, WFTU, WHO, WIPO, WMO, WTO

**Diplomatic representation in the US:**

*chief of mission:* Ambassador Serge MOMBOULI

*chancery:* 4891 Colorado Avenue NW, Washington, DC 20011

*telephone:* [1] (202) 726-5500

*FAX:* [1] (202) 726-1860

**Diplomatic representation from the US:**

*chief of mission:* Ambassador Allan EASTHAM

*embassy:* Boulevard de la Revolution, BDEAC Building, 4th Floor, Brazzaville; note - a new embassy is expected to open in 2009

*mailing address:* B.P. 1015, Brazzaville

*telephone:* [242] 281-1481, 281-3368; note - until the new embassy in Brazzaville becomes operational, some duties will still be handled in the US embassy in Kinshasha, Democratic Republic of the Congo

**Flag description:** divided diagonally from the lower hoist side by a yellow band; the upper triangle (hoist side) is green and the lower triangle is red

*note:* uses the popular pan-African colors of Ethiopia

## Economy

**Economy - overview:** The economy is a mixture of subsistence agriculture, an industrial sector based largely on oil, and support services, and a government characterized by budget problems and overstaffing. Oil has supplanted forestry as the mainstay of the economy, providing a major share of government revenues and exports. In the early 1980s, rapidly rising oil revenues enabled the government to finance large-scale development projects with GDP growth averaging 5% annually, one of the highest rates in Africa. The government has mortgaged a substantial portion of its oil earnings through oil-backed loans that have contributed to a growing debt burden and chronic revenue shortfalls. Economic reform efforts have been undertaken with the support of international organizations, notably the World Bank and the IMF. However, the reform program came to a halt in June 1997 when civil war erupted. Denis SASSOU-NGUESSO, who returned to power when the war ended in October 1997, publicly expressed interest in moving forward on economic reforms and privatization and in renewing cooperation with international financial institutions. Economic progress was badly hurt by slumping oil prices and the resumption of armed conflict in December 1998, which worsened the republic's budget deficit. The current administration presides over an uneasy internal peace and faces difficult economic challenges of stimulating recovery and reducing poverty. Recovery of oil prices has boosted the economy's GDP and near-term prospects. In March 2006, the World Bank and the International Monetary Fund (IMF) approved Heavily Indebted Poor Countries (HIPC) treatment for Congo.

**GDP (purchasing power parity):**
$15.6 billion (2008 est.)
$14.43 billion (2007)
$14.67 billion (2006)
*note:* data are in 2008 US dollars

**GDP (official exchange rate):** $13.35 billion (2008 est.)

**GDP - real growth rate:**
8.1% (2008 est.)
-1.6% (2007 est.)
6.2% (2006 est.)

**GDP - per capita (PPP):**
$4,000 (2008 est.)
$3,800 (2007 est.)
$4,000 (2006 est.)
*note:* data are in 2008 US dollars

**GDP - composition by sector:**
*agriculture:* 5.6%
*industry:* 57.1%
*services:* 37.3% (2006 est.)

**Labor force:** NA

**Unemployment rate:**
NA%

**Population below poverty line:** NA%

**Household income or consumption by percentage share:**
*lowest 10%:* NA%
*highest 10%:* NA%

**Investment (gross fixed):** 19.3% of GDP (2008 est.)

**Budget:**
*revenues:* $5.363 billion
*expenditures:* $2.758 billion (2008 est.)

**Inflation rate (consumer prices):**
5% (2008 est.)
2.7% (2007 est.)

**Commercial bank prime lending rate:** 15% (31 December 2007)

**Stock of money:** $1.4 billion (31 December 2007)

**Stock of quasi money:** $204.3 million (31 December 2007)

**Stock of domestic credit:** NA

**Market value of publicly traded shares:** $NA

**Agriculture - products:** cassava (tapioca), sugar, rice, corn, peanuts, vegetables, coffee, cocoa; forest products

**Industries:** petroleum extraction, cement, lumber, brewing, sugar, palm oil, soap, flour, cigarettes

**Industrial production growth rate:** 15% (2008 est.)

**Electricity - production:** 444 million kWh (2006 est.)

**Electricity - consumption:** 564 million kWh (2006 est.)

**Electricity - exports:** 0 kWh (2007 est.)

**Electricity - imports:** 411 million kWh (2006 est.)

**Oil - production:** 261,000 bbl/day (2008 est.)

**Oil - consumption:** 7,677 bbl/day (2006 est.)

**Oil - exports:** 230,200 bbl/day (2005 est.)

**Oil - imports:** 1,702 bbl/day (2005)

**Oil - proved reserves:** 1.6 billion bbl (1 January 2008 est.)

**Natural gas - production:** 180 million cu m (2006 est.)

**Natural gas - consumption:** 180 million cu m (2006 est.)

**Natural gas - exports:** 0 cu m (2007 est.)

**Natural gas - imports:** 0 cu m (2007 est.)

**Natural gas - proved reserves:** 90.61 billion cu m (1 January 2008 est.)

**Current account balance:** $406 million (2008 est.)

**Exports:** $9.009 billion f.o.b. (2008 est.)

**Exports - commodities:** petroleum, lumber, plywood, sugar, cocoa, coffee, diamonds

**Exports - partners:** US 41%, China 36.5%, Taiwan 3.6% (2007)

**Imports:** $2.722 billion f.o.b. (2008 est.)

**Imports - commodities:** capital equipment, construction materials, foodstuffs

**Imports - partners:** France 18.1%, South Korea 14.7%, China 12.6%, Italy 10.3%, India 4.7%, US 4.2% (2007)

**Reserves of foreign exchange and gold:** $3.845 billion (31 December 2008 est.)

**Debt - external:** $5 billion (2000 est.)

**Exchange rates:** Cooperation Financiere en Afrique Centrale francs (XAF) per US dollar - 447.81 (2008 est.), 483.6 (2007), 522.59 (2006), 527.47 (2005), 528.29 (2004)
*note:* since 1 January 1999, the Central African CFA franc (XAF) has been pegged to the euro at a rate of 655.957 CFA francs per euro; Central African CFA franc (XAF) coins and banknotes are not accepted in countries using West African CFA francs (XOF), and vice versa, even though the two currencies trade at par

## Communications

**Telephones - main lines in use:** 15,900 (2005)

**Telephones - mobile cellular:** 1.334 million (2007)

**Telephone system:**
*general assessment:* services barely adequate for government use; key exchanges are in Brazzaville, Pointe-Noire, and Loubomo; intercity lines frequently out of order; fixed-line infrastructure inadequate providing less than 1 connection per 100 persons; in the absence of an adequate fixed line infrastructure, mobile-cellular subscribership has surged reaching 35 per 100 persons
*domestic:* primary network consists of microwave radio relay and coaxial cable
*international:* country code - 242; satellite earth station -1 Intelsat (Atlantic Ocean)

**Radio broadcast stations:** AM 1, FM 5, shortwave 3 (2001)

**Television broadcast stations:** 1 (2001)

**Internet country code:** .cg

**Internet hosts:** 5 (2008)

**Internet users:** 70,000 (2006)

## Transportation

**Airports:** 24 (2008)

**Airports - with paved runways:**
*total:* 6
*over 3,047 m:* 2
*2,438 to 3,047 m:* 1
*1,524 to 2,437 m:* 3 (2008)

**Airports - with unpaved runways:**
*total:* 18
*1,524 to 2,437 m:* 7
*914 to 1,523 m:* 10
*under 914 m:* 1 (2008)

**Pipelines:** gas 7 km; oil 207 km (2008)

**Railways:**
*total:* 894 km
*narrow gauge:* 894 km 1.067-m gauge (2006)

**Roadways:**
*total:* 17,289 km
*paved:* 864 km
*unpaved:* 16,425 km (2004)

**Waterways:** 1,120 km (commercially navigable on Congo and Oubanqui rivers) (2008)

**Merchant marine:**
*registered in other countries:* 1 (Congo, Democratic Republic of the 1) (2008)

**Ports and terminals:** Brazzaville, Djeno, Impfondo, Ouesso, Oyo, Pointe-Noire

## Military

**Military branches:** Congolese Armed Forces (Forces Armees Congolaises, FAC): Army, Navy, Congolese Air Force (Armee de l'Air Congolaise), Gendarmerie, Special Presidential Security Guard (GSSP) (2008)

**Military service age and obligation:** 18 years of age for voluntary military service; women allowed to serve (2007)

**Manpower available for military service:**
*males age 16-49:* 842,771
*females age 16-49:* 833,624 (2008 est.)

**Manpower fit for military service:**
*males age 16-49:* 538,202
*females age 16-49:* 527,649 (2009 est.)

**Manpower reaching militarily significant age annually:**
*male:* 46,976
*female:* 46,490 (2009 est.)

**Military expenditures:** 3.1% of GDP (2006)

## Transnational Issues

**Disputes - international:** the location of the boundary in the broad Congo River with the Democratic Republic of the Congo is indefinite except in the Pool Malebo/Stanley Pool area

## Congo, Republic of the *(continued)*

**Refugees and internally displaced persons:**
*refugees (country of origin):* 46,341 (Democratic Republic of Congo); 6,564 (Rwanda)
*IDPs:* 48,000 (multiple civil wars since 1992; most IDPs are ethnic Lari) (2007)
**Trafficking in persons:**
*current situation:* Republic of the Congo is a source and destination country for children trafficked for the purposes of forced labor and commercial sexual exploitation; girls are trafficked from rural areas within the country for commercial sexual exploitation, forced street vending, and domestic servitude; children are trafficked from other African countries for domestic servitude, forced market vending, and forced labor in the fishing industry
*tier rating:* Tier 2 Watch List - Republic of the Congo is on the Tier 2 Watch List for its failure to show evidence of increasing efforts to combat trafficking in persons in 2007; struggling to recover from six years of civil conflict that ended in 2003, the Republic of the Congo's capacity to address trafficking is handicapped; the government neither monitors its borders for trafficking activity nor provides specialized anti-trafficking training for law enforcement officials; the government does not encourage victims to assist in trafficking investigations or prosecutions, and has not taken measures to reduce demand for commercial sex acts in the Republic of the Congo (2008)

# Cook Islands
*(self-governing in free association with New Zealand)*

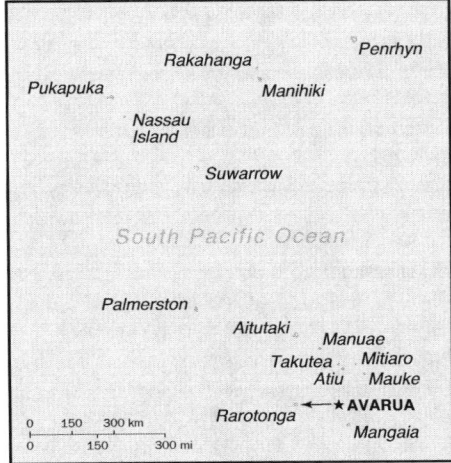

## Introduction

**Background:** Named after Captain COOK, who sighted them in 1770, the islands became a British protectorate in 1888. By 1900, administrative control was transferred to New Zealand; in 1965, residents chose self-government in free association with New Zealand. The emigration of skilled workers to New Zealand and government deficits are continuing problems.

## Geography

**Location:** Oceania, group of islands in the South Pacific Ocean, about half way between Hawaii and New Zealand
**Geographic coordinates:** 21 14 S, 159 46 W
**Map references:** Oceania
**Area:**
*total:* 236.7 sq km
*land:* 236.7 sq km
*water:* 0 sq km
**Area - comparative:** 1.3 times the size of Washington, DC
**Land boundaries:** 0 km
**Coastline:** 120 km
**Maritime claims:**
*territorial sea:* 12 nm
*exclusive economic zone:* 200 nm
*continental shelf:* 200 nm or to the edge of the continental margin
**Climate:** tropical oceanic; moderated by trade winds; a dry season from April to November and a more humid season from December to March
**Terrain:** low coral atolls in north; volcanic, hilly islands in south
**Elevation extremes:**
*lowest point:* Pacific Ocean 0 m
*highest point:* Te Manga 652 m
**Natural resources:** NEGL
**Land use:**
*arable land:* 16.67%
*permanent crops:* 8.33%
*other:* 75% (2005)

**Irrigated land:** NA
**Natural hazards:** typhoons (November to March)
**Environment - current issues:** NA
**Environment - international agreements:**
*party to:* Biodiversity, Climate Change, Climate Change-Kyoto Protocol, Desertification, Hazardous Wastes, Law of the Sea, Ozone Layer Protection
**Geography - note:** the northern Cook Islands are seven low-lying, sparsely populated, coral atolls; the southern Cook Islands, where most of the population lives, consist of eight elevated, fertile, volcanic isles, including the largest, Rarotonga, at 67 sq km

### People

**Population:** 11,870 (July 2009 est.)
**Age structure:**
*0-14 years:* 27.1% (male 1,704/female 1,508)
*15-64 years:* 63.7% (male 3,898/female 3,664)
*65 years and over:* 9.2% (male 540/female 556) (2009 est.)
**Median age:**
*total:* 30.5 years
*male:* 29.8 years
*female:* 31.1 years (2009 est.)
**Population growth rate:** -3.302% (2009 est.)
**Birth rate:** 16.18 births/1,000 population (2009 est.)
**Death rate:** NA
**Urbanization:**
*urban population:* 74% of total population (2008)
*rate of urbanization:* -0.7% annual rate of change (2005-10 est.)
**Sex ratio:**
*at birth:* 1.05 male(s)/female
*under 15 years:* 1.13 male(s)/female
*15-64 years:* 1.06 male(s)/female
*65 years and over:* 0.97 male(s)/female
*total population:* 1.07 male(s)/female (2009 est.)
**Infant mortality rate:**
*total:* 16.9 deaths/1,000 live births
*male:* 20.57 deaths/1,000 live births
*female:* 13.04 deaths/1,000 live births (2009 est.)
**Life expectancy at birth:**
*total population:* 74.22 years
*male:* 71.46 years
*female:* 77.13 years (2009 est.)
**Total fertility rate:** 2.49 children born/woman (2009 est.)
**HIV/AIDS - adult prevalence rate:** NA
**HIV/AIDS - people living with HIV/AIDS:** NA
**HIV/AIDS - deaths:** NA
**Nationality:**
*noun:* Cook Islander(s)
*adjective:* Cook Islander
**Ethnic groups:** Cook Island Maori (Polynesian) 87.7%, part Cook Island Maori 5.8%, other 6.5% (2001 census)
**Religions:** Cook Islands Christian Church 55.9%, Roman Catholic 16.8%, Seventh-Day Adventists 7.9%, Church of Latter Day Saints 3.8%, other Protestant 5.8%, other 4.2%, unspecified 2.6%, none 3% (2001 census)

**Languages:** English (official), Maori
**Literacy:**
*definition:* NA
*total population:* 95%
*male:* NA
*female:* NA
**School life expectancy (primary to tertiary education):**
*total:* 10 years
*male:* 10 years
*female:* 10 years (2005)
**Education expenditures:** 0.2% of GDP (2001)
**People - note:** 2001 census counted a resident population of 15,017

## Government

**Country name:**
*conventional long form:* none
*conventional short form:* Cook Islands
*former:* Harvey Islands
**Dependency status:** self-governing in free association with New Zealand; Cook Islands is fully responsible for internal affairs; New Zealand retains responsibility for external affairs and defense, in consultation with the Cook Islands
**Government type:** self-governing parliamentary democracy
**Capital:**
*name:* Avarua
*geographic coordinates:* 21 12 S, 159 46 W
*time difference:* UTC-10 (5 hours behind Washington, DC during Standard Time)
**Administrative divisions:** none
**Independence:** none (became self-governing in free association with New Zealand on 4 August 1965 and has the right at any time to move to full independence by unilateral action)
**National holiday:** Constitution Day, first Monday in August (1965)
**Constitution:** 4 August 1965
**Legal system:** based on New Zealand law and English common law
**Suffrage:** 18 years of age; universal (adult)
**Executive branch:**
*chief of state:* Queen ELIZABETH II (since 6 February 1952) represented by Sir Frederick GOODWIN (since 9 February 2001); New Zealand High Commissioner Tia BARRETT (since December 2008), representative of New Zealand
*head of government:* Prime Minister Jim MARURAI (since 14 December 2004); Deputy Prime Minister Terepai MAOATE (since 9 August 2005)
*cabinet:* Cabinet chosen by the prime minister; collectively responsible to Parliament
*elections:* the monarch is hereditary; the UK representative is appointed by the monarch; the New Zealand high commissioner is appointed by the New Zealand Government; following legislative elections, the leader of the majority party or the leader of the majority coalition usually becomes prime minister

**Legislative branch:** bicameral Parliament consisting of a House of Ariki (or upper house) made up of traditional leaders and a Legislative Assembly (or lower house) (24 seats; members elected by popular vote to serve four-year terms)
*note:* the House of Ariki advises on traditional matters and maintains considerable influence but has no legislative powers
*elections:* last held 26 September 2006 (next to be held by 2011)
*election results:* percent of vote by party - Demo 51.9%, CIP 45.5%, independent 2.7%; seats by party -Demo 15, CIP 8, independent 1
**Judicial branch:** High Court
**Political parties and leaders:** Cook Islands Party or CIP [Henry PUNA]; Democratic Party or Demo [Dr. Terepai MAOATE]
**Political pressure groups and leaders:** Reform Conference (lobby for political system changes)
*other:* various groups lobbying for political change
**International organization participation:** ACP, ADB, FAO, ICAO, ICCt, ICRM, IFAD, IFRCS, IMSO, IOC, ITUC, OPCW, PIF, Sparteca, SPC, UNESCO, UPU, WHO, WMO
**Diplomatic representation in the US:** none (self-governing in free association with New Zealand)
**Diplomatic representation from the US:** none (self-governing in free association with New Zealand)
**Flag description:** blue, with the flag of the UK in the upper hoist-side quadrant and a large circle of 15 white five-pointed stars (one for every island) centered in the outer half of the flag

## Economy

**Economy - overview:** Like many other South Pacific island nations, the Cook Islands' economic development is hindered by the isolation of the country from foreign markets, the limited size of domestic markets, lack of natural resources, periodic devastation from natural disasters, and inadequate infrastructure. Agriculture, employing more than one-quarter of the working population, provides the economic base with major exports made up of copra and citrus fruit. Black pearls are the Cook Islands' leading export. Manufacturing activities are limited to fruit processing, clothing, and handicrafts. Trade deficits are offset by remittances from emigrants and by foreign aid overwhelmingly from New Zealand. In the 1980s and 1990s, the country lived beyond its means, maintaining a bloated public service and accumulating a large foreign debt. Subsequent reforms, including the sale of state assets, the strengthening of economic management, the encouragement of tourism, and a debt restructuring agreement, have rekindled investment and growth.
**GDP (purchasing power parity):**
$183.2 million (2005 est.)
**GDP (official exchange rate):** $183.2 million (2005 est.)
**GDP - real growth rate:**
0.1% (2005 est.)

**GDP - per capita (PPP):**
$9,100 (2005 est.)
**GDP - composition by sector:**
*agriculture:* 15.1%
*industry:* 9.6%
*services:* 75.3% (2004)
**Labor force:** 6,820 (2001)
**Labor force - by occupation:**
*agriculture:* 29%
*industry:* 15%
*services:* 56% (1995)
**Unemployment rate:**
13.1% (2005)
**Population below poverty line:** NA%
**Household income or consumption by percentage share:**
*lowest 10%:* NA%
*highest 10%:* NA%
**Budget:**
*revenues:* $70.95 million
*expenditures:* $69.05 million (FY05/06)
**Inflation rate (consumer prices):**
2.1% (2005 est.)
**Agriculture - products:** copra, citrus, pineapples, tomatoes, beans, pawpaws, bananas, yams, taro, coffee; pigs, poultry
**Industries:** fruit processing, tourism, fishing, clothing, handicrafts
**Industrial production growth rate:** 1% (2002)
**Electricity - production:** 30 million kWh (2006 est.)
**Electricity - consumption:** 27.9 million kWh (2006 est.)
**Electricity - exports:** 0 kWh (2007 est.)
**Electricity - imports:** 0 kWh (2007 est.)
**Oil - production:** 0 bbl/day (2007 est.)
**Oil - consumption:** 463.7 bbl/day (2006 est.)
**Oil - exports:** 0 bbl/day (2005)
**Oil - imports:** 475.5 bbl/day (2005)
**Oil - proved reserves:** 0 bbl (1 January 2006 est.)
**Natural gas - production:** 0 cu m (2007 est.)
**Natural gas - consumption:** 0 cu m (2007 est.)
**Natural gas - exports:** 0 cu m (2007 est.)
**Natural gas - imports:** 0 cu m (2007 est.)
**Natural gas - proved reserves:** 0 cu m (1 January 2006 est.)
**Current account balance:** $26.67 million (2005)
**Exports:** $5.222 million (2005)
**Exports - commodities:** copra, papayas, fresh and canned citrus fruit, coffee; fish; pearls and pearl shells; clothing
**Imports:** $81.04 million f.o.b. (2005)
**Imports - commodities:** foodstuffs, textiles, fuels, timber, capital goods
**Debt - external:** $141 million (1996 est.)
**Exchange rates:** NZ dollars (NZD) per US dollar - 1.4151 (2008 est.), 1.3811 (2007), 1.5408 (2006), 1.4203 (2005), 1.5087 (2004)

## Communications

**Telephones - main lines in use:** 6,200 (2002)
**Telephones - mobile cellular:** 1,500 (2002)

**Telephone system:**

*general assessment:* Telecom Cook Islands offers international direct dialing, Internet, email, fax, and Telex

*domestic:* individual islands are connected by a combination of satellite earth stations, microwave systems, and VHF and HF radiotelephone; within the islands, service is provided by small exchanges connected to subscribers by open-wire, cable, and fiber-optic cable

*international:* country code - 682; satellite earth station -1 Intelsat (Pacific Ocean)

**Radio broadcast stations:** AM 1, FM 1, shortwave 0 (2004)

**Television broadcast stations:** 1 (outer islands receive satellite broadcasts) (2004)

**Internet country code:** .ck

**Internet hosts:** 2,234 (2008)

**Internet users:** 3,600 (2002)

## Transportation

**Airports:** 9 (2008)

**Airports - with paved runways:**

*total:* 1

*1,524 to 2,437 m:* 1 (2008)

**Airports - with unpaved runways:**

*total:* 8

*1,524 to 2,437 m:* 3

*914 to 1,523 m:* 4

*under 914 m:* 1 (2008)

**Roadways:**

*total:* 320 km

*paved:* 33 km

*unpaved:* 287 km (2003)

**Merchant marine:**

*total:* 26

*by type:* cargo 14, chemical tanker 1, petroleum tanker 1, refrigerated cargo 8, roll on/roll off 2

*foreign-owned:* 17 (Latvia 1, Lithuania 1, NZ 1, Nigeria 1, Norway 5, Sweden 8) (2008)

**Ports and terminals:** Avatiu

## Military

**Military branches:** no regular military forces; National Police Department (2007)

**Manpower fit for military service:**

*males age 16-49:* 2,334

*females age 16-49:* 2,286 (2009 est.)

**Manpower reaching militarily significant age annually:**

*male:* 148

*female:* 125 (2009 est.)

**Military - note:** defense is the responsibility of New Zealand in consultation with the Cook Islands and at its request

## Transnational Issues

**Disputes - international:** none

# Coral Sea Islands
*(territory of Australia)*

## Introduction

**Background:** Scattered over more than three-quarters of a million square kilometers of ocean, the Coral Sea Islands were declared a territory of Australia in 1969. They are uninhabited except for a small meteorological staff on the Willis Islets. Automated weather stations, beacons, and a lighthouse occupy many other islands and reefs.

## Geography

**Location:** Oceania, islands in the Coral Sea, northeast of Australia

**Geographic coordinates:** 18 00 S, 152 00 E

**Map references:** Oceania

**Area:**

*total:* less than 3 sq km

*land:* less than 3 sq km

*water:* 0 sq km

*note:* includes numerous small islands and reefs scattered over a sea area of about 780,000 sq km with the Willis Islets the most important

**Area - comparative:** NA

**Land boundaries:** 0 km

**Coastline:** 3,095 km

**Maritime claims:**

*territorial sea:* 3 nm

*exclusive fishing zone:* 200 nm

**Climate:** tropical

**Terrain:** sand and coral reefs and islands (or cays)

**Elevation extremes:**

*lowest point:* Pacific Ocean 0 m

*highest point:* unnamed location on Cato Island 6 m

**Natural resources:** NEGL

**Land use:**

*arable land:* 0%

*permanent crops:* 0%

*other:* 100% (mostly grass or scrub cover) (2005)

**Irrigated land:** 0 sq km

**Natural hazards:** occasional tropical cyclones

**Environment - current issues:** no permanent fresh water resources

**Geography - note:** important nesting area for birds and turtles

## People

**Population:** no indigenous inhabitants

*note:* there is a staff of three to four at the meteorological station on Willis Island (July 2007 est.)

## Government

**Country name:**

*conventional long form:* Coral Sea Islands Territory

*conventional short form:* Coral Sea Islands

**Dependency status:** territory of Australia; administered from Canberra by the Australian Government Attorney-General's Department

**Legal system:** the laws of Australia, where applicable, apply

**Executive branch:** administered from Canberra by the Australian Attorney-General's Department

**Diplomatic representation in the US:** none (territory of Australia)

**Diplomatic representation from the US:** none (territory of Australia)

**Flag description:** the flag of Australia is used

## Economy

**Economy - overview:** no economic activity

## Communications

**Communications - note:** there are automatic weather stations on many of the isles and reefs relaying data to the mainland

## Transportation

**Ports and terminals:** none; offshore anchorage only

## Military

**Military - note:** defense is the responsibility of Australia

## Transnational Issues

**Disputes - international:** none

# Costa Rica

## Introduction

**Background:** Although explored by the Spanish early in the 16th century, initial attempts at colonizing Costa Rica proved unsuccessful due to a combination of factors, including: disease from mosquito-infested swamps, brutal heat, resistance by natives, and pirate raids. It was not until 1563 that a permanent settlement of Cartago was established in the cooler, fertile central highlands. The area remained a colony for some two and a half centuries. In 1821, Costa Rica became one of several Central American provinces that jointly declared their independence from Spain. Two years later it joined the United Provinces of Central America, but this federation disintegrated in 1838, at which time Costa Rica proclaimed its sovereignty and independence. Since the late 19th century, only two brief periods of violence have marred the country's democratic development. Although it still maintains a large agricultural sector, Costa Rica has expanded its economy to include strong technology and tourism industries. The standard of living is relatively high. Land ownership is widespread. In January 2008, Costa Rica assumed a nonpermanent seat on the UN Security Council for the 2008-09 term.

## Geography

**Location:** Central America, bordering both the Caribbean Sea and the North Pacific Ocean, between Nicaragua and Panama
**Geographic coordinates:** 10 00 N, 84 00 W
**Map references:** Central America and the Caribbean
**Area:**
*total:* 51,100 sq km
*land:* 50,660 sq km
*water:* 440 sq km
*note:* includes Isla del Coco

**Area - comparative:** slightly smaller than West Virginia
**Land boundaries:**
*total:* 639 km
*border countries:* Nicaragua 309 km, Panama 330 km
**Coastline:** 1,290 km
**Maritime claims:**
*territorial sea:* 12 nm
*exclusive economic zone:* 200 nm
*continental shelf:* 200 nm
**Climate:** tropical and subtropical; dry season (December to April); rainy season (May to November); cooler in highlands
**Terrain:** coastal plains separated by rugged mountains including over 100 volcanic cones, of which several are major volcanoes
**Elevation extremes:**
*lowest point:* Pacific Ocean 0 m
*highest point:* Cerro Chirripo 3,810 m
**Natural resources:** hydropower
**Land use:**
*arable land:* 4.4%
*permanent crops:* 5.87%
*other:* 89.73% (2005)
**Irrigated land:** 1,080 sq km (2003)
**Total renewable water resources:** 112.4 cu km (2000)
**Freshwater withdrawal (domestic/industrial/ agricultural):**
*total:* 2.68 cu km/yr (29%/17%/53%)
*per capita:* 619 cu m/yr (2000)
**Natural hazards:** occasional earthquakes, hurricanes along Atlantic coast; frequent flooding of lowlands at onset of rainy season and landslides; active volcanoes
**Environment - current issues:** deforestation and land use change, largely a result of the clearing of land for cattle ranching and agriculture; soil erosion; coastal marine pollution; fisheries protection; solid waste management; air pollution
**Environment - international agreements:**
*party to:* Biodiversity, Climate Change, Climate Change-Kyoto Protocol, Desertification, Endangered Species, Environmental Modification, Hazardous Wastes, Law of the Sea, Marine Dumping, Ozone Layer Protection, Wetlands, Whaling
*signed, but not ratified:* Marine Life Conservation
**Geography - note:** four volcanoes, two of them active, rise near the capital of San Jose in the center of the country; one of the volcanoes, Irazu, erupted destructively in 1963-65

## People

**Population:** 4,253,877 (July 2009 est.)
**Age structure:**
*0-14 years:* 26.7% (male 581,916/female 555,216)
*15-64 years:* 67.1% (male 1,443,606/ female 1,411,168)
*65 years and over:* 6.2% (male 120,969/ female 141,002) (2009 est.)

**Median age:**
*total:* 27.5 years
*male:* 27.1 years
*female:* 28 years (2009 est.)
**Population growth rate:** 1.356% (2009 est.)
**Birth rate:** 17.43 births/1,000 population (2009 est.)
**Death rate:** 4.31 deaths/1,000 population (2008 est.)
**Net migration rate:** 0.47 migrant(s)/1,000 population (2009 est.)
**Urbanization:**
*urban population:* 63% of total population (2008)
*rate of urbanization:* 2.3% annual rate of change (2005-10 est.)
**Sex ratio:**
*at birth:* 1.05 male(s)/female
*under 15 years:* 1.05 male(s)/female
*15-64 years:* 1.02 male(s)/female
*65 years and over:* 0.86 male(s)/female
*total population:* 1.02 male(s)/female (2009 est.)
**Infant mortality rate:**
*total:* 8.77 deaths/1,000 live births
*male:* 9.66 deaths/1,000 live births
*female:* 7.83 deaths/1,000 live births (2009 est.)
**Life expectancy at birth:**
*total population:* 77.58 years
*male:* 74.96 years
*female:* 80.34 years (2009 est.)
**Total fertility rate:** 2.14 children born/woman (2009 est.)
**HIV/AIDS - adult prevalence rate:** 0.4% (2007 est.)
**HIV/AIDS - people living with HIV/AIDS:** 9,700 (2007 est.)
**HIV/AIDS - deaths:** fewer than 200 (2007 est.)
**Major infectious diseases:**
*degree of risk:* intermediate
*food or waterborne diseases:* bacterial diarrhea
*vectorborne diseases:* dengue fever (2009)
**Nationality:**
*noun:* Costa Rican(s)
*adjective:* Costa Rican
**Ethnic groups:** white (including mestizo) 94%, black 3%, Amerindian 1%, Chinese 1%, other 1%
**Religions:** Roman Catholic 76.3%, Evangelical 13.7%, Jehovah's Witnesses 1.3%, other Protestant 0.7%, other 4.8%, none 3.2%
**Languages:** Spanish (official), English
**Literacy:**
*definition:* age 15 and over can read and write
*total population:* 94.9%
*male:* 94.7%
*female:* 95.1% (2000 census)
**School life expectancy (primary to tertiary education):**
*total:* 12 years
*male:* 12 years
*female:* 12 years (2005)
**Education expenditures:** 4.9% of GDP (2004)

# Costa Rica *(continued)*

## Government

**Country name:**
*conventional long form:* Republic of Costa Rica
*conventional short form:* Costa Rica
*local long form:* Republica de Costa Rica
*local short form:* Costa Rica
**Government type:** democratic republic
**Capital:**
*name:* San Jose
*geographic coordinates:* 9 56 N, 84 05 W
*time difference:* UTC-6 (1 hour behind Washington, DC during Standard Time)
**Administrative divisions:** 7 provinces (provincias, singular - provincia); Alajuela, Cartago, Guanacaste, Heredia, Limon, Puntarenas, San Jose
**Independence:** 15 September 1821 (from Spain)
**National holiday:** Independence Day, 15 September (1821)
**Constitution:** 7 November 1949
**Legal system:** based on Spanish civil law system; judicial review of legislative acts in the Supreme Court; has accepted compulsory ICJ jurisdiction
**Suffrage:** 18 years of age; universal and compulsory
**Executive branch:**
*chief of state:* President Oscar ARIAS Sanchez (since 8 May 2006); First Vice President (vacant); Second Vice President (vacant); note - the president is both the chief of state and head of government
*head of government:* President Oscar ARIAS Sanchez (since 8 May 2006); First Vice President (vacant); Second Vice President (vacant)
*cabinet:* Cabinet selected by the president
*elections:* president and vice presidents elected on the same ticket by popular vote for a single four-year term; election last held 5 February 2006 (next to be held in February 2010)
*election results:* Oscar ARIAS Sanchez elected president; percent of vote - Oscar ARIAS Sanchez (PLN) 40.9%; Otton SOLIS (PAC) 39.8%, Otto GUEVARA Guth (PML) 8%, Ricardo TOLEDO (PUSC) 3%
**Legislative branch:** unicameral Legislative Assembly or Asamblea Legislativa (57 seats; members are elected by direct, popular vote to serve four-year terms)
*elections:* last held 5 February 2006 (next to be held in February 2010)
*election results:* percent of vote by party - NA; seats by party - PLN 25, PAC 17, PML 6, PUSC 5, PASE 1, PFA 1, PRN 1, PUN 1; note - as of 1 January 2009: seats by party - PLN 25, PAC 16, PML 5, PUSC 5, PASE 1, PFA 1, PRN 1, independent 3
**Judicial branch:** Supreme Court or Corte Suprema (22 justices are elected for renewable eight-year terms by the Legislative Assembly)
**Political parties and leaders:** Authentic Member from Heredia [Jose SALAS]; Citizen Action Party or PAC [Epsy CAMPBELL Barr]; Costa Rican Renovation Party or PRC [Gerardo Justo OROZCO Alvarez]; Democratic Force Party or PFD [Marco NUNEZ Gonzalez]; General Union Party or PUGEN

[Carlos Alberto FERNANDEZ Vega]; Homeland First or PP [Juan Jose VARGAS Fallas]; Independent Worker Party or PIO [Jose Alberto CUBERO Carmona]; Libertarian Movement Party or PML [Otto GUEVARA Guth]; National Christian Alliance Party or ANC [Juan Carlos CHAVEZ Mora]; National Integration Party or PIN [Walter MUNOZ Cespedes]; National Liberation Party or PLN [Francisco Antonio PACHECO Fernandez]; National Patriotic Party or PPN [Daniel Enrique REYNOLDS Vargas]; National Restoration Party or PRN [Fabio Enrique DELGADO Hernandez]; National Union Party or PUN [Arturo ACOSTA Mora]; Nationalist Democratic Alliance or ADN [Jose Miguel VILLALOBOS Umana]; Patriotic Union or UP [Jose Miguel CORRALES Bolanos]; Social Christian Unity Party or PUSC [Luis FISHMAN Zonzinski]; Union for Change Party or UPC [Antonio ALVAREZ Desanti]; United Leftist Coalition or IU [Humberto VARGAS Carbonel]
**Political pressure groups and leaders:** Authentic Confederation of Democratic Workers or CATD (Communist Party affiliate); Chamber of Coffee Growers; Confederated Union of Workers or CUT (Communist Party affiliate); Costa Rican Confederation of Democratic Workers or CCTD (Liberation Party affiliate); Costa Rican Exporter's Chamber or CADEXCO; Costa Rican Solidarity Movement; Costa Rican Union of Private Sector Enterprises or UCCAEP [Rafael CARRILLO]; Federation of Public Service Workers or FTSP; National Association for Economic Development or ANFE; National Association of Educators or ANDE; National Association of Public and Private Employees or ANEP [Albino VARGAS]; Rerum Novarum or CTRN (PLN affiliate) [Gilbert BROWN]
**International organization participation:** BCIE, CACM, FAO, G-77, IADB, IAEA, IBRD, ICAO, ICC, ICCt, ICRM, IDA, IFAD, IFC, IFRCS, ILO, IMF, IMO, IMSO, Interpol, IOC, IOM, IPU, ISO, ITSO, ITU, ITUC, LAES, LAIA (observer), MIGA, NAM (observer), OAS, OPANAL, OPCW, PCA, RG, SICA, UN, UNCTAD, UNESCO, UNHCR, UNIDO, Union Latina, UNWTO, UPU, WCL, WCO, WFTU, WHO, WIPO, WMO, WTO
**Diplomatic representation in the US:**
*chief of mission:* Ambassador (vacant); Charge d'Affaires Laura DACHNER
*chancery:* 2114 S Street NW, Washington, DC 20008
*telephone:* [1] (202) 234-2945
*FAX:* [1] (202) 265-4795
*consulate(s) general:* Atlanta, Chicago, Houston, Los Angeles, Miami, New Orleans, New York, San Francisco, San Juan (Puerto Rico)
**Diplomatic representation from the US:**
*chief of mission:* Ambassador Peter CIANCHETTE
*embassy:* Calle 120 Avenida O, Pavas, San Jose
*mailing address:* APO AA 34020
*telephone:* [506] 519-2000
*FAX:* [506] 519-2305
**Flag description:** five horizontal bands of blue (top), white, red (double width), white, and blue, with the coat of arms in a white elliptical disk on the hoist side of the red band; above the coat of arms a light blue

ribbon contains the words, AMERICA CENTRAL, and just below it near the top of the coat of arms is a white ribbon with the words, REPUBLICA COSTA RICA

## Economy

**Economy - overview:** Costa Rica's basically stable economy depends on tourism, agriculture, and electronics exports. Exports have become more diversified in the past 10 years due to the growth of the high-tech manufacturing sector, which is dominated by the microprocessor industry and the production of medical devices. Tourism continues to bring in foreign exchange, as Costa Rica's impressive biodiversity makes it a key destination for ecotourism. Foreign investors remain attracted by the country's political stability and relatively high education levels, as well as the fiscal incentives offered in the free-trade zones. Costa Rica has attracted one of the highest levels of foreign direct investment per capita in Latin America. Poverty has remained around 20% for nearly 20 years, and the strong social safety net that had been put into place by the government has eroded due to increased financial constraints on government expenditures. Immigration from Nicaragua has increasingly become a concern for the government. The estimated 300,000-500,000 Nicaraguans in Costa Rica legally and illegally are an important source of - mostly unskilled - labor, but also place heavy demands on the social welfare system. Under the ARIAS administration, the government has made strides in reducing internal and external debt - in 2007, Costa Rica had its first budget surplus in 50 years. Reducing inflation remains a difficult problem because of rising commodity import prices and labor market rigidities, though lower oil prices will decrease upward pressures. The Central Bank is moving towards a more flexible exchange rate system to focus on inflation targeting by 2010. The US-Central American Free Trade Agreement (CAFTA) entered into force on 1 January 2009, after significant delays within the Costa Rican legislature. Nevertheless, economic growth has slowed in 2009 as the global downturn reduced export demand and invesment inflows.
**GDP (purchasing power parity):**
$48.48 billion (2008 est.)
$47.07 billion (2007)
$44.07 billion (2006)
*note:* data are in 2008 US dollars
**GDP (official exchange rate):** $30.38 billion (2008 est.)
**GDP - real growth rate:**
3% (2008 est.)
6.8% (2007 est.)
8.8% (2006 est.)
**GDP - per capita (PPP):**
$11,600 (2008 est.)
$11,400 (2007 est.)
$10,800 (2006 est.)
*note:* data are in 2008 US dollars

# Costa Rica *(continued)*

**GDP - composition by sector:**
*agriculture:* 7.6%
*industry:* 29.1%
*services:* 63.3% (2008 est.)
**Labor force:** 1.957 million
*note:* this official estimate excludes Nicaraguans living in Costa Rica (2008 est.)
**Labor force - by occupation:**
*agriculture:* 14%
*industry:* 22%
*services:* 64% (2006 est.)
**Unemployment rate:**
5.6% (2008 est.)
4.6% (2007 est.)
**Population below poverty line:** 16% (2006 est.)
**Household income or consumption by percentage share:**
*lowest 10%:* 1%
*highest 10%:* 37.4% (2003)
**Distribution of family income - Gini index:** 48 (2008)
**Investment (gross fixed):** 23% of GDP (2008 est.)
**Budget:**
*revenues:* $4.604 billion
*expenditures:* $4.552 billion (2008 est.)
**Public debt:** 38.4% of GDP (2008)
**Inflation rate (consumer prices):**
13.9% (2008 est.)
9.4% (2007 est.)
**Central bank discount rate:** 17% (31 December 2007)
**Commercial bank prime lending rate:** 12.8% (31 December 2007)
**Stock of money:** $4.504 billion (31 December 2007)
**Stock of quasi money:** $2.87 billion (31 December 2007)
**Stock of domestic credit:** $12.91 billion (31 December 2007)
**Market value of publicly traded shares:** $2.035 billion (31 December 2007)
**Agriculture - products:** bananas, pineapples, coffee, melons, ornamental plants, sugar, corn, rice, beans, potatoes; beef, poultry, dairy; timber
**Industries:** microprocessors, food processing, medical equipment, textiles and clothing, construction materials, fertilizer, plastic products
**Industrial production growth rate:** -0.8% (2008 est.)
**Electricity - production:** 8.918 billion kWh (2007)
**Electricity - consumption:** 7.779 billion kWh (2006 est.)
**Electricity - exports:** 77.16 million kWh (2008 est.)
**Electricity - imports:** 203.2 million kWh (2007 est.)
**Oil - production:** 0 bbl/day (2004)
**Oil - consumption:** 44,000 bbl/day (January 2009)
**Oil - exports:** 2,115 bbl/day (2005)
**Oil - imports:** 43,110 bbl/day (2005)
**Oil - proved reserves:** NA bbl
**Natural gas - production:** 0 cu m (2007 est.)
**Natural gas - consumption:** 0 cu m (2007 est.)
**Natural gas - exports:** 0 cu m (2007 est.)

**Natural gas - imports:** 0 cu m (2007 est.)
**Natural gas - proved reserves:** 0 cu m (1 January 2006 est.)
**Current account balance:** -$5.698 billion (2008 est.)
**Exports:** $9.675 billion (2008 est.)
**Exports - commodities:** bananas, pineapples, coffee, melons, ornamental plants, sugar; seafood; electronic components, medical equipment
**Exports - partners:** US 25.7%, China 14.1%, Netherlands 10.9%, UK 6.3%, Mexico 5% (2007)
**Imports:** $15.37 billion (2008 est.)
**Imports - commodities:** raw materials, consumer goods, capital equipment, petroleum, construction materials
**Imports - partners:** US 41%, Mexico 6.1%, Venezuela 5.7%, Japan 5.4%, China 5.1%, Brazil 4.3% (2007)
**Reserves of foreign exchange and gold:** $3.573 billion (31 December 2008 est.)
**Debt - external:** $7.401 billion (31 December 2008 est.)
**Stock of direct foreign investment - at home:** $18.96 billion (31 December 2008)
**Stock of direct foreign investment - abroad:** $574 million (2008 est.)
**Exchange rates:** Costa Rican colones (CRC) per US dollar - 530.41 (2008 est.), 519.53 (2007), 511.3 (2006), 477.79 (2005), 437.91 (2004)

## Communications

**Telephones - main lines in use:** 1.437 million (2007)
**Telephones - mobile cellular:** 1.503 million (2007)
**Telephone system:**
*general assessment:* good domestic telephone service in terms of breadth of coverage; restricted cellular telephone service; state-run monopoly provider is struggling with the demand for new lines, resulting in long waiting times
*domestic:* point-to-point and point-to-multi-point microwave, fiber-optic, and coaxial cable link rural areas; Internet service is available
*international:* country code - 506; landing point for the Americas Region Caribbean Ring System (ARCOS-1) fiber-optic telecommunications submarine cable and the MAYA-1 submarine cable that provide links to South and Central America, parts of the Caribbean, and the US; connected to Central American Microwave System; satellite earth stations - 2 Intelsat (Atlantic Ocean) (2007)
**Radio broadcast stations:** AM 65, FM 51, shortwave 19 (2002)
**Television broadcast stations:** 20 (plus 43 repeaters) (2002)
**Internet country code:** .cr
**Internet hosts:** 16,440 (2008)
**Internet users:** 1.5 million (2007)

## Transportation

**Airports:** 149 (2008)
**Airports - with paved runways:**
*total:* 37
*2,438 to 3,047 m:* 2
*1,524 to 2,437 m:* 2
*914 to 1,523 m:* 22
*under 914 m:* 11 (2008)
**Airports - with unpaved runways:**
*total:* 112
*914 to 1,523 m:* 18
*under 914 m:* 94 (2008)
**Pipelines:** refined products 796 km (2008)
**Railways:**
*total:* 278 km
*narrow gauge:* 278 km 1.067-m gauge
*note:* none of the railway network is in use (2007)
**Roadways:**
*total:* 35,330 km
*paved:* 8,621 km
*unpaved:* 26,709 km (2004)
**Waterways:** 730 km (seasonally navigable by small craft) (2008)
**Merchant marine:**
*total:* 1
*by type:* passenger/cargo 1 (2008)
**Ports and terminals:** Caldera, Puerto Limon

## Military

**Military branches:** no regular military forces; Ministry of Public Security, Government, and Police (2009)
**Manpower available for military service:**
*males age 16-49:* 1,134,205
*females age 16-49:* 1,095,763 (2008 est.)
**Manpower fit for military service:**
*males age 16-49:* 971,224
*females age 16-49:* 936,978 (2009 est.)
**Manpower reaching militarily significant age annually:**
*male:* 40,698
*female:* 38,808 (2009 est.)
**Military expenditures:** 0.4% of GDP (2006)

## Transnational Issues

**Disputes - international:** the ICJ has given Costa Rica until January 2008 to reply and Nicaragua until July 2008 to rejoin before rendering its decision on the navigation, security, and commercial rights of Costa Rican vessels on the Rìo San Juan over which Nicaragua retains sovereignty
**Refugees and internally displaced persons:**
*refugees (country of origin):* 9,699-11,500 (Colombia) (2007)
**Trafficking in persons:**
*current situation:* Costa Rica is a source, transit, and destination country for men, women, and children trafficked for the purposes of commercial sexual exploitation and forced labor; women and girls from neighboring states, Russia, Uzbekistan, and the

Philippines are trafficked into the country for sexual exploitation; Costa Rica also serves as a transit point for victims trafficked to North America and Europe; the government identifies child sex tourism as a serious problem; men, women, and children are also trafficked within the country for forced labor in fishing and construction, and as domestic servants
*tier rating:* Tier 2 Watch List - Costa Rica is on the Tier 2 Watch List for its failure to provide evidence of increasing efforts to combat human trafficking, particularly in terms of its failure to improve its inadequate assistance to victims; while Costa Rican officials recognize human trafficking as a serious problem, the lack of a stronger response by the government is of concern (2008)

**Illicit drugs:** transshipment country for cocaine and heroin from South America; illicit production of cannabis in remote areas; domestic cocaine consumption, particularly crack cocaine, is rising; significant consumption of amphetamines; seizures of smuggled cash in Costa Rica and at the main border crossing to enter Costa Rica from Nicaragua have risen in recent years (2008)

# Cote d'Ivoire

## Introduction

**Background:** Close ties to France since independence in 1960, the development of cocoa production for export, and foreign investment made Cote d'Ivoire one of the most prosperous of the West African states, but did not protect it from political turmoil. In December 1999, a military coup - the first ever in Cote d'Ivoire's history - overthrew the government. Junta leader Robert GUEI blatantly rigged elections held in late 2000 and declared himself the winner. Popular protest forced him to step aside and brought Laurent GBAGBO into power. Ivorian dissidents and disaffected members of the military launched a failed coup attempt in September 2002. Rebel forces claimed the northern half of the country, and in January 2003 were granted ministerial positions in a unity government under the auspices of the Linas-Marcoussis Peace Accord. President GBAGBO and rebel forces resumed implementation of the peace accord in December 2003 after a three-month stalemate, but issues that sparked the civil war, such as land reform and grounds for citizenship, remained unresolved. In March 2007 President GBAGBO and former New Force rebel leader Guillaume SORO signed the Ouagadougou Political Agreement. As a result of the agreement, SORO joined GBAGBO's government as Prime Minister and the two agreed to reunite the country by dismantling the zone of confidence separating North from South, integrate rebel forces into the national armed forces, and hold elections. Several thousand French and UN troops remain in Cote d'Ivoire to help the parties implement their commitments and to support the peace process.

## Geography

**Location:** Western Africa, bordering the North Atlantic Ocean, between Ghana and Liberia
**Geographic coordinates:** 8 00 N, 5 00 W
**Map references:** Africa
**Area:**
*total:* 322,460 sq km
*land:* 318,000 sq km
*water:* 4,460 sq km
**Area - comparative:** slightly larger than New Mexico
**Land boundaries:**
*total:* 3,110 km
*border countries:* Burkina Faso 584 km, Ghana 668 km, Guinea 610 km, Liberia 716 km, Mali 532 km
**Coastline:** 515 km
**Maritime claims:**
*territorial sea:* 12 nm
*exclusive economic zone:* 200 nm
*continental shelf:* 200 nm
**Climate:** tropical along coast, semiarid in far north; three seasons - warm and dry (November to March), hot and dry (March to May), hot and wet (June to October)
**Terrain:** mostly flat to undulating plains; mountains in northwest
**Elevation extremes:**
*lowest point:* Gulf of Guinea 0 m
*highest point:* Mont Nimba 1,752 m
**Natural resources:** petroleum, natural gas, diamonds, manganese, iron ore, cobalt, bauxite, copper, gold, nickel, tantalum, silica sand, clay, cocoa beans, coffee, palm oil, hydropower
**Land use:**
*arable land:* 10.23%
*permanent crops:* 11.16%
*other:* 78.61% (2005)
**Irrigated land:** 730 sq km (2003)
**Total renewable water resources:** 81 cu km (2001)
**Freshwater withdrawal (domestic/industrial/agricultural):**
*total:* 0.93 cu km/yr (24%/12%/65%)
*per capita:* 51 cu m/yr (2000)
**Natural hazards:** coast has heavy surf and no natural harbors; during the rainy season torrential flooding is possible
**Environment - current issues:** deforestation (most of the country's forests - once the largest in West Africa - have been heavily logged); water pollution from sewage and industrial and agricultural effluents
**Environment - international agreements:**
*party to:* Biodiversity, Climate Change, Climate Change-Kyoto Protocol, Desertification, Endangered Species, Hazardous Wastes, Law of the Sea, Marine Dumping, Ozone Layer Protection, Ship Pollution, Tropical Timber 83, Tropical Timber 94, Wetlands, Whaling
*signed, but not ratified:* none of the selected agreements
**Geography - note:** most of the inhabitants live along the sandy coastal region; apart from the capital area, the forested interior is sparsely populated

# Cote d'Ivoire *(continued)*

## People

**Population:** 20,617,068

*note:* estimates for this country explicitly take into account the effects of excess mortality due to AIDS; this can result in lower life expectancy, higher infant mortality, higher death rates, lower population growth rates, and changes in the distribution of population by age and sex than would otherwise be expected (July 2009 est.)

**Age structure:**

*0-14 years:* 40.6% (male 4,215,912/female 4,146,077)

*15-64 years:* 56.6% (male 5,942,642/female 5,720,108)

*65 years and over:* 2.9% (male 296,074/female 296,255) (2009 est.)

**Median age:**

*total:* 19.2 years

*male:* 19.4 years

*female:* 19.1 years (2009 est.)

**Population growth rate:** 2.133% (2009 est.)

**Birth rate:** 32.11 births/1,000 population (2009 est.)

**Death rate:** 11.17 deaths/1,000 population (2008 est.)

**Net migration rate:** NA

**Urbanization:**

*urban population:* 49% of total population (2008)

*rate of urbanization:* 3.2% annual rate of change (2005-10 est.)

**Sex ratio:**

*at birth:* 1.03 male(s)/female

*under 15 years:* 1.02 male(s)/female

*15-64 years:* 1.04 male(s)/female

*65 years and over:* 1 male(s)/female

*total population:* 1.03 male(s)/female (2009 est.)

**Infant mortality rate:**

*total:* 68.06 deaths/1,000 live births

*male:* 75.17 deaths/1,000 live births

*female:* 60.73 deaths/1,000 live births (2009 est.)

**Life expectancy at birth:**

*total population:* 55.45 years

*male:* 54.64 years

*female:* 56.28 years (2009 est.)

**Total fertility rate:** 4.12 children born/woman (2009 est.)

**HIV/AIDS - adult prevalence rate:** 3.9% (2007 est.)

**HIV/AIDS - people living with HIV/AIDS:** 480,000 (2007 est.)

**HIV/AIDS - deaths:** 38,000 (2007 est.)

**Major infectious diseases:**

*degree of risk:* very high

*food or waterborne diseases:* bacterial diarrhea, hepatitis A, and typhoid fever

*vectorborne diseases:* malaria and yellow fever

*water contact:* schistosomiasis

*animal contact disease:* rabies

*note:* highly pathogenic H5N1 avian influenza has been identified in this country; it poses a negligible risk with extremely rare cases possible among US citizens who have close contact with birds (2009)

**Nationality:**

*noun:* Ivoirian(s)

*adjective:* Ivoirian

**Ethnic groups:** Akan 42.1%, Voltaiques or Gur 17.6%, Northern Mandes 16.5%, Krous 11%, Southern Mandes 10%, other 2.8% (includes 130,000 Lebanese and 14,000 French) (1998)

**Religions:** Muslim 38.6%, Christian 32.8%, indigenous 11.9%, none 16.7% (2008 est.)

*note:* the majority of foreigners (migratory workers) are Muslim (70%) and Christian (20%)

**Languages:** French (official), 60 native dialects with Dioula the most widely spoken

**Literacy:**

*definition:* age 15 and over can read and write

*total population:* 48.7%

*male:* 60.8%

*female:* 38.6% (2000 est.)

**Education expenditures:** 4.6% of GDP (2001)

## Government

**Country name:**

*conventional long form:* Republic of Cote d'Ivoire

*conventional short form:* Cote d'Ivoire

*local long form:* Republique de Cote d'Ivoire

*local short form:* Cote d'Ivoire

*note:* pronounced coat-div-whar

*former:* Ivory Coast

**Government type:** republic; multiparty presidential regime established 1960

*note:* the government is currently operating under a power-sharing agreement mandated by international mediators

**Capital:**

*name:* Yamoussoukro

*geographic coordinates:* 6 49 N, 5 17 W

*time difference:* UTC 0 (5 hours ahead of Washington, DC during Standard Time)

*note:* although Yamoussoukro has been the official capital since 1983, Abidjan remains the commercial and administrative center; the US, like other countries, maintains its Embassy in Abidjan

**Administrative divisions:** 19 regions; Agneby, Bafing, Bas-Sassandra, Denguele, Dix-Huit Montagnes, Fromager, Haut-Sassandra, Lacs, Lagunes, Marahoue, Moyen-Cavally, Moyen-Comoe, N'zi-Comoe, Savanes, Sud-Bandama, Sud-Comoe, Vallee du Bandama, Worodougou, Zanzan

**Independence:** 7 August 1960 (from France)

**National holiday:** Independence Day, 7 August (1960)

**Constitution:** approved by referendum 23 July 2000

**Legal system:** based on French civil law system and customary law; judicial review in the Constitutional Chamber of the Supreme Court; accepts compulsory ICJ jurisdiction with reservations

**Suffrage:** 18 years of age; universal

**Executive branch:**

*chief of state:* President Laurent GBAGBO (since 26 October 2000)

*head of government:* Prime Minister Guillaume SORO (since 4 April 2007)

*cabinet:* Council of Ministers appointed by the president; note - under the current power-sharing agreement the prime minister and the president share the authority to appoint ministers

*elections:* president elected by popular vote for a five-year term (no term limits); election last held 26 October 2000 (elections were to be held in 2008 but have been repeatedly postponed by the government; the UN Security Council has extended the government's mandate); prime minister appointed by the president

*election results:* Laurent GBAGBO elected president; percent of vote - Laurent GBAGBO 59.4%, Robert GUEI 32.7%, Francis WODIE 5.7%, other 2.2%

**Legislative branch:** unicameral National Assembly or Assemblee Nationale (225 seats; members are elected in single- and multi-district elections by direct popular vote to serve five-year terms)

*elections:* elections last held 10 December 2000 with by-elections on 14 January 2001 (elections originally scheduled for 2005 have been repeatedly postponed by the government)

*election results:* percent of vote by party - NA; seats by party - FPI 96, PDCI-RDA 94, RDR 5, PIT 4, other 2, independents 22, vacant 2

*note:* a Senate was scheduled to be created in October 2006 elections that never took place

**Judicial branch:** Supreme Court or Cour Supreme consists of four chambers: Judicial Chamber for criminal cases, Audit Chamber for financial cases, Constitutional Chamber for judicial review cases, and Administrative Chamber for civil cases; there is no legal limit to the number of members

**Political parties and leaders:** Citizen's Democratic Union or UDCY [Theodore MEL EG]; Democratic Party of Cote d'Ivoire or PDCI [Henri Konan BEDIE]; Ivorian Popular Front or FPI [Pascale Affi N'GUESSAN]; Ivorian Worker's Party or PIT [Francis WODIE]; Opposition Movement of the Future or MFA [Innocent Augustin ANAKY]; Rally of the Republicans or RDR [Alassane OUATTARA]; Union for Democracy and Peace in Cote d'Ivoire or UDPCI [Toikeuse MABRI]; over 144 smaller registered parties

**Political pressure groups and leaders:** Federation of University and High School Students of Cote d'Ivoire or FESCI [Serges KOFFI]; Rally of Houphouetists for Democracy and Peace or RHDP [Alphonse DJEDJE MADY]; Young Patriots [Charles BLE GOUDE]

**International organization participation:** ACCT, ACP, AfDB, AU, ECOWAS, Entente, FAO, FZ, G-24, G-77, IAEA, IBRD, ICAO, ICCt (signatory), ICRM, IDA, IDB, IFAD, IFC, IFRCS, ILO, IMF, IMO, Interpol, IOC, IOM, IPU, ITSO, ITU, ITUC, MIGA, NAM, OIC, OIF, OPCW, UN, UNCTAD, UNESCO, UNHCR, UNIDO, Union Latina, UNWTO, UPU, WADB (regional), WAEMU, WCL, WCO, WFTU, WHO, WIPO, WMO, WTO

**Diplomatic representation in the US:**

*chief of mission:* Ambassador Yao Charles KOFFI

*chancery:* 3421 Massachusetts Avenue NW, Washington, DC 20007

*telephone:* [1] (202) 797-0300

*FAX:* [1] (202) 244-3088

# Cote d'Ivoire *(continued)*

**Diplomatic representation from the US:**
*chief of mission:* Ambassador Wanda L. NESBITT
*embassy:* Cocody Riviera Golf 01, Abidjan
*mailing address:* B. P. 1712, Abidjan 01
*telephone:* [225] 22 49 40 00
*FAX:* [225] 22 49 43 32
**Flag description:** three equal vertical bands of orange (hoist side), white, and green
*note:* similar to the flag of Ireland, which is longer and has the colors reversed - green (hoist side), white, and orange; also similar to the flag of Italy, which is green (hoist side), white, and red; design was based on the flag of France

## Economy

**Economy - overview:** Cote d'Ivoire is the world's largest producer and exporter of cocoa beans and a significant producer and exporter of coffee and palm oil. Consequently, the economy is highly sensitive to fluctuations in international prices for these products, and, to a lesser extent, in climatic conditions. Despite government attempts to diversify the economy, it is still heavily dependent on agriculture and related activities, engaging roughly 68% of the population. Since 2006, oil and gas production have become more important engines of economic activity than cocoa. According to IMF statistics, earnings from oil and refined products were $1.3 billion in 2006, while cocoa-related revenues were $1 billion during the same period. Cote d'Ivoire's offshore oil and gas production has resulted in substantial crude oil exports and provides sufficient natural gas to fuel electricity exports to Ghana, Togo, Benin, Mali and Burkina Faso. Oil exploration by a number of consortiums of private companies continues offshore, and President GBAGBO has expressed hope that daily crude output could reach 200,000 barrels per day (b/d) by the end of the decade. Since the end of the civil war in 2003, political turmoil has continued to damage the economy, resulting in the loss of foreign investment and slow economic growth. GDP grew by nearly 2% in 2007 and 3% in 2008. Per capita income has declined by 15% since 1999.
**GDP (purchasing power parity):**
$34 billion (2008 est.)
$33.1 billion (2007)
$32.58 billion (2006)
*note:* data are in 2008 US dollars
**GDP (official exchange rate):** $23.78 billion (2008 est.)
**GDP - real growth rate:**
2.7% (2008 est.)
1.6% (2007 est.)
-0.3% (2006 est.)
**GDP - per capita (PPP):**
$1,700 (2008 est.)
$1,700 (2007 est.)
$1,700 (2006 est.)
*note:* data are in 2008 US dollars

**GDP - composition by sector:**
*agriculture:* 27.9%
*industry:* 21.9%
*services:* 50.1% (2008 est.)
**Labor force:** 7.035 million (68% agricultural) (2008 est.)
**Labor force - by occupation:**
*agriculture:* 68%
*industry and services:* NA (2007 est.)
**Unemployment rate:**
*note:* unemployment may have climbed to 40-50% as a result of the civil war
**Population below poverty line:** 42% (2006 est.)
**Household income or consumption by percentage share:**
*lowest 10%:* 2%
*highest 10%:* 34% (2002)
**Distribution of family income - Gini index:** 44.6 (2002)
**Investment (gross fixed):** 9.5% of GDP (2008 est.)
**Budget:**
*revenues:* $4.725 billion
*expenditures:* $5.082 billion (2008 est.)
**Public debt:** 58.3% of GDP (2008 est.)
**Inflation rate (consumer prices):**
6.1% (2008 est.)
1.9% (2007 est.)
**Central bank discount rate:** 4.25% (31 December 2007)
**Commercial bank prime lending rate:** NA
**Stock of money:** $4.451 billion (31 December 2007)
**Stock of quasi money:** $1.915 billion (31 December 2007)
**Stock of domestic credit:** $4.404 billion (31 December 2007)
**Market value of publicly traded shares:** $8.353 billion (31 December 2007)
**Agriculture - products:** coffee, cocoa beans, bananas, palm kernels, corn, rice, manioc (tapioca), sweet potatoes, sugar, cotton, rubber; timber
**Industries:** foodstuffs, beverages; wood products, oil refining, truck and bus assembly, textiles, fertilizer, building materials, electricity, ship construction and repair
**Industrial production growth rate:** 5% (2008 est.)
**Electricity - production:** 5.274 billion kWh (2006 est.)
**Electricity - consumption:** 3.177 billion kWh (2006 est.)
**Electricity - exports:** 1.066 billion kWh (2006 est.)
**Electricity - imports:** 0 kWh (2007 est.)
**Oil - production:** 54,400 bbl/day (2008 est.)
**Oil - consumption:** 25,950 bbl/day (2006 est.)
**Oil - exports:** 84,940 bbl/day (2005)
**Oil - imports:** 71,850 bbl/day (2005)
**Oil - proved reserves:** 100 million bbl (1 January 2008 est.)
**Natural gas - production:** 1.3 billion cu m (2006 est.)
**Natural gas - consumption:** 1.3 billion cu m (2006 est.)

**Natural gas - exports:** 0 cu m (2007 est.)
**Natural gas - imports:** 0 cu m (2007 est.)
**Natural gas - proved reserves:** 28.32 billion cu m (1 January 2008 est.)
**Current account balance:** $407 million (2008 est.)
**Exports:** $11.96 billion f.o.b. (2008 est.)
**Exports - commodities:** cocoa, coffee, timber, petroleum, cotton, bananas, pineapples, palm oil, fish
**Exports - partners:** Germany 9.7%, Nigeria 9.2%, Netherlands 8.4%, France 7.3%, US 7%, Burkina Faso 4.4% (2007)
**Imports:** $7.948 billion f.o.b. (2008 est.)
**Imports - commodities:** fuel, capital equipment, foodstuffs
**Imports - partners:** Nigeria 31.1%, France 16.7%, China 7.3% (2007)
**Reserves of foreign exchange and gold:** $3.3 billion (31 December 2008 est.)
**Debt - external:** $14.46 billion (31 December 2008 est.)
**Stock of direct foreign investment - at home:** $NA
**Stock of direct foreign investment - abroad:** $NA
**Exchange rates:** Communaute Financiere Africaine francs (XOF) per US dollar - 447.81 (2008 est.), 481.83 (2007), 522.89 (2006), 527.47 (2005), 528.29 (2004)
*note:* since 1 January 1999, the West African CFA franc (XOF) has been pegged to the euro at a rate of 655.957 CFA francs per euro; West African CFA franc (XOF) coins and banknotes are not accepted in countries using Central African CFA francs (XAF), and vice versa, even though the two currencies trade at par

## Communications

**Telephones - main lines in use:** 730,000 (2007)
**Telephones - mobile cellular:** 7.05 million (2007)
**Telephone system:**
*general assessment:* well developed by African standards; telecommunications sector privatized in late 1990s and operational fixed-lines have more than quadrupled since that time; with multiple cellular service providers competing in the market, cellular usage has increased sharply to roughly 40 per 100 persons
*domestic:* open-wire lines and microwave radio relay; 90% digitalized
*international:* country code - 225; landing point for the SAT-3/WASC fiber-optic submarine cable that provides connectivity to Europe and Asia; satellite earth stations - 2 Intelsat (1 Atlantic Ocean and 1 Indian Ocean) (2007)
**Radio broadcast stations:** AM 2, FM 9, shortwave 3 (1998)
**Television broadcast stations:** 14 (1998)
**Internet country code:** .ci
**Internet hosts:** 5,569 (2008)
**Internet users:** 300,000 (2006)

# Cote d'Ivoire (continued)

## Transportation

**Airports:** 31 (2008)
**Airports - with paved runways:**
*total:* 7
*over 3,047 m:* 1
*2,438 to 3,047 m:* 2
*1,524 to 2,437 m:* 4 (2008)
**Airports - with unpaved runways:**
*total:* 24
*1,524 to 2,437 m:* 6
*914 to 1,523 m:* 13
*under 914 m:* 5 (2008)
**Pipelines:** condensate 86 km; gas 180 km; oil 92 km (2008)
**Railways:**
*total:* 660 km
*narrow gauge:* 660 km 1.000 meter gauge
*note:* an additional 622 km of this railroad extends into Burkina Faso (2006)
**Roadways:**
*total:* 80,000 km
*paved:* 6,500 km
*unpaved:* 73,500 km
*note:* includes intercity and urban roads; another 20,000 km of dirt roads are in poor condition and 150,000 km of dirt roads are impassable (2006)
**Waterways:** 980 km (navigable rivers, canals, and numerous coastal lagoons) (2008)
**Ports and terminals:** Abidjan, Espoir, San-Pedro

## Military

**Military branches:** Cote d'Ivoire Defense and Security Forces (FDSCI): Army, Navy, Air Force (2006)
**Military service age and obligation:** 18 years of age for compulsory and voluntary male and female military service (2008)
**Manpower available for military service:**
*males age 16-49:* 4,369,735
*females age 16-49:* 4,287,042 (2008 est.)
**Manpower fit for military service:**
*males age 16-49:* 3,122,106
*females age 16-49:* 2,936,391 (2009 est.)
**Manpower reaching militarily significant age annually:**
*male:* 236,159
*female:* 232,617 (2009 est.)
**Military expenditures:** 1.6% of GDP (2005 est.)

## Transnational Issues

**Disputes - international:** despite the presence of over 9,000 UN forces (UNOCI) in Cote d'Ivoire since 2004, ethnic conflict still leaves displaced hundreds of thousands of Ivorians in and out of the country as well as driven out migrants from neighboring states who worked in Ivorian cocoa plantations; the March 2007 peace deal between Ivorian rebels and the government brought significant numbers of rebels out of hiding in neighboring states

**Refugees and internally displaced persons:**
*refugees (country of origin):* 25,615 (Liberia)
*IDPs:* 709,000 (2002 coup; most IDPs are in western regions) (2007)
**Trafficking in persons:**
Cote d'Ivoire is a source, transit, and destination country for women and children trafficked for forced labor and commercial sexual exploitation; trafficking within the country is more prevalent than international trafficking and the majority of victims are children; women and girls are trafficked from northern areas to southern cities for domestic servitude, restaurant labor, and sexual exploitation; boys are trafficked internally for agricultural and service labor and transnationally for forced labor in agriculture, mining, construction, and in the fishing industry; women and girls are trafficked to and from other West and Central African countries for domestic servitude and forced street vending
*tier rating:* Tier 2 Watch List - Cote d'Ivoire is on the Tier 2 Watch List for its failure to provide evidence of increasing efforts to eliminate trafficking in 2007, particularly with regard to its law enforcement efforts and protection of sex trafficking victims; in addition, Ivoirian law does not prohibit all forms of trafficking, and Cote d'Ivoire has not ratified the 2000 UN TIP Protocol (2008)
**Illicit drugs:** illicit producer of cannabis, mostly for local consumption; utility as a narcotic transshipment point to Europe reduced by ongoing political instability; while rampant corruption and inadequate supervision leave the banking system vulnerable to money laundering, the lack of a developed financial system limits the country's utility as a major money-laundering center (2008)

# Croatia

## Introduction

**Background:** The lands that today comprise Croatia were part of the Austro-Hungarian Empire until the close of World War I. In 1918, the Croats, Serbs, and Slovenes formed a kingdom known after 1929 as Yugoslavia. Following World War II, Yugoslavia became a federal independent Communist state under the strong hand of Marshal TITO. Although Croatia declared its independence from Yugoslavia in 1991, it took four years of sporadic, but often bitter, fighting before occupying Serb armies were mostly cleared from Croatian lands. Under UN supervision, the last Serb-held enclave in eastern Slavonia was returned to Croatia in 1998. In January 2008, Croatia assumed a nonpermanent seat on the UN Security Council for the 2008-09 term, and in April 2008 it joined NATO. Croatia is a candidate for eventual EU accession.

## Geography

**Location:** Southeastern Europe, bordering the Adriatic Sea, between Bosnia and Herzegovina and Slovenia
**Geographic coordinates:** 45 10 N, 15 30 E
**Map references:** Europe
**Area:**
*total:* 56,542 sq km
*land:* 56,414 sq km
*water:* 128 sq km
**Area - comparative:** slightly smaller than West Virginia
**Land boundaries:**
*total:* 1,982 km
*border countries:* Bosnia and Herzegovina 932 km, Hungary 329 km, Serbia 241 km, Montenegro 25 km, Slovenia 455 km
**Coastline:** 5,835 km (mainland 1,777 km, islands 4,058 km)
**Maritime claims:**
*territorial sea:* 12 nm
*continental shelf:* 200 m depth or to the depth of exploitation

# Croatia *(continued)*

**Climate:** Mediterranean and continental; continental climate predominant with hot summers and cold winters; mild winters, dry summers along coast

**Terrain:** geographically diverse; flat plains along Hungarian border, low mountains and highlands near Adriatic coastline and islands

**Elevation extremes:**
*lowest point:* Adriatic Sea 0 m
*highest point:* Dinara 1,830 m

**Natural resources:** oil, some coal, bauxite, low-grade iron ore, calcium, gypsum, natural asphalt, silica, mica, clays, salt, hydropower

**Land use:**
*arable land:* 25.82%
*permanent crops:* 2.19%
*other:* 71.99% (2005)

**Irrigated land:** 110 sq km (2003)

**Total renewable water resources:** 105.5 cu km (1998)

**Natural hazards:** destructive earthquakes

**Environment - current issues:** air pollution (from metallurgical plants) and resulting acid rain is damaging the forests; coastal pollution from industrial and domestic waste; landmine removal and reconstruction of infrastructure consequent to 1992-95 civil strife

**Environment - international agreements:**
*party to:* Air Pollution, Air Pollution-Nitrogen Oxides, Air Pollution-Persistent Organic Pollutants, Air Pollution-Sulfur 94, Air Pollution-Volatile Organic Compounds, Biodiversity, Climate Change, Climate Change-Kyoto Protocol, Desertification, Endangered Species, Hazardous Wastes, Law of the Sea, Marine Dumping, Ozone Layer Protection, Ship Pollution, Wetlands, Whaling
*signed, but not ratified:* none of the selected agreements

**Geography - note:** controls most land routes from Western Europe to Aegean Sea and Turkish Straits; most Adriatic Sea islands lie off the coast of Croatia - some 1,200 islands, islets, ridges, and rocks

## People

**Population:** 4,489,409 (July 2009 est.)

**Age structure:**
*0-14 years:* 15.6% (male 358,360/female 340,098)
*15-64 years:* 67.5% (male 1,506,364/female 1,522,789)
*65 years and over:* 17% (male 295,960/female 465,838) (2009 est.)

**Median age:**
*total:* 41 years
*male:* 39.1 years
*female:* 42.8 years (2009 est.)

**Population growth rate:** -0.052% (2009 est.)

**Birth rate:** 9.64 births/1,000 population (2009 est.)

**Death rate:** 11.66 deaths/1,000 population (2008 est.)

**Net migration rate:** 1.59 migrant(s)/1,000 population (2009 est.)

**Urbanization:**
*urban population:* 57% of total population (2008)
*rate of urbanization:* 0.4% annual rate of change (2005-10 est.)

**Sex ratio:**
*at birth:* 1.06 male(s)/female
*under 15 years:* 1.05 male(s)/female
*15-64 years:* 0.99 male(s)/female
*65 years and over:* 0.64 male(s)/female
*total population:* 0.93 male(s)/female (2009 est.)

**Infant mortality rate:**
*total:* 6.37 deaths/1,000 live births
*male:* 6.42 deaths/1,000 live births
*female:* 6.33 deaths/1,000 live births (2009 est.)

**Life expectancy at birth:**
*total population:* 75.35 years
*male:* 71.72 years
*female:* 79.18 years (2009 est.)

**Total fertility rate:** 1.42 children born/woman (2009 est.)

**HIV/AIDS - adult prevalence rate:** less than 0.1% (2007 est.)

**HIV/AIDS - people living with HIV/AIDS:** 200 (2007 est.)

**HIV/AIDS - deaths:** fewer than 10 (2001 est.)

**Major infectious diseases:**
*degree of risk:* intermediate
*food or waterborne diseases:* bacterial diarrhea
*vectorborne diseases:* tickborne encephalitis
*note:* highly pathogenic H5N1 avian influenza has been identified in this country; it poses a negligible risk with extremely rare cases possible among US citizens who have close contact with birds (2009)

**Nationality:**
*noun:* Croat(s), Croatian(s)
*adjective:* Croatian

**Ethnic groups:** Croat 89.6%, Serb 4.5%, other 5.9% (including Bosniak, Hungarian, Slovene, Czech, and Roma) (2001 census)

**Religions:** Roman Catholic 87.8%, Orthodox 4.4%, other Christian 0.4%, Muslim 1.3%, other and unspecified 0.9%, none 5.2% (2001 census)

**Languages:** Croatian 96.1%, Serbian 1%, other and undesignated 2.9% (including Italian, Hungarian, Czech, Slovak, and German) (2001 census)

**Literacy:**
*definition:* age 15 and over can read and write
*total population:* 98.1%
*male:* 99.3%
*female:* 97.1% (2001 census)

**School life expectancy (primary to tertiary education):**
*total:* 14 years
*male:* 13 years
*female:* 14 years (2006)

**Education expenditures:** 4.5% of GDP (2004)

## Government

**Country name:**
*conventional long form:* Republic of Croatia
*conventional short form:* Croatia
*local long form:* Republika Hrvatska
*local short form:* Hrvatska
*former:* People's Republic of Croatia, Socialist Republic of Croatia

**Government type:** presidential/parliamentary democracy

**Capital:**
*name:* Zagreb
*geographic coordinates:* 45 48 N, 16 00 E
*time difference:* UTC+1 (6 hours ahead of Washington, DC during Standard Time)
*daylight saving time:* +1hr, begins last Sunday in March; ends last Sunday in October

**Administrative divisions:** 20 counties (zupanije, zupanija - singular) and 1 city* (grad - singular); Bjelovarsko-Bilogorska, Brodsko-Posavska, Dubrovacko-Neretvanska (Dubrovnik-Neretva), Istarska (Istria), Karlovacka, Koprivnicko-Krizevacka, Krapinsko-Zagorska, Licko-Senjska (Lika-Senj), Medimurska, Osjecko-Baranjska, Pozesko-Slavonska (Pozega-Slavonia), Primorsko-Goranska, Sibensko-Kninska, Sisacko-Moslavacka, Splitsko-Dalmatinska (Split-Dalmatia), Varazdinska, Viroviticko-Podravska, Vukovarsko-Srijemska, Zadarska, Zagreb*, Zagrebacka

**Independence:** 25 June 1991 (from Yugoslavia)

**National holiday:** Independence Day, 8 October (1991); note - 25 June 1991 was the day the Croatian parliament voted for independence; following a three-month moratorium to allow the European Community to solve the Yugoslav crisis peacefully, Parliament adopted a decision on 8 October 1991 to sever constitutional relations with Yugoslavia

**Constitution:** adopted on 22 December 1990; revised 2000, 2001

**Legal system:** based on Austro-Hungarian law system with Communist law influences; has not accepted compulsory ICJ jurisdiction

**Suffrage:** 18 years of age; universal (16 years of age, if employed)

**Executive branch:**
*chief of state:* President Stjepan (Stipe) MESIC (since 18 February 2000)
*head of government:* Prime Minister Ivo SANADER (since 9 December 2003); Deputy Prime Ministers Jadranka KOSOR (since 23 December 2003), Damir POLANCEC (since 15 February 2005), Djurdja ADLESIC (since 12 January 2008), Slobodan UZELAC (since 12 January 2008)
*cabinet:* Council of Ministers named by the prime minister and approved by the parliamentary Assembly
*elections:* president elected by popular vote for a five-year term (eligible for a second term); election last held 16 January 2005 (next to be held in January 2010); the leader of the majority party or the leader of the majority coalition is usually appointed prime minister by the president and then approved by the Assembly

# Croatia (continued)

*election results:* Stjepan MESIC reelected president; percent of vote in the second round - Stjepan MESIC 66%, Jadranka KOSOR 34%

**Legislative branch:** unicameral Assembly or Sabor (153 seats; members elected from party lists by popular vote to serve four-year terms)

*elections:* last held 25 November 2007 (next to be held in November 2011)

*election results:* percent of vote by party - NA; number of seats by party - HDZ 66, SDP 57, HNS 6, HSS 6, HDSSB 3, IDS 3, SDSS 3, other 9

**Judicial branch:** Supreme Court; Constitutional Court; judges for both courts are appointed for eight-year terms by the Judicial Council of the Republic, which is elected by the Assembly

**Political parties and leaders:** Croatian Democratic Congress of Slavonia and Baranja or HDSSB [Vladimir SISLJAGIC]; Croatian Democratic Union or HDZ [Ivo SANADER]; Croatian Party of the Right or HSP [Anto DJAPIC]; Croatian Peasant Party or HSS [Josip FRISCIC]; Croatian Pensioner Party or HSU [Silvano HRELJA]; Croatian People's Party or HNS [Radimir CACIC]; Croatian Social Liberal Party or HSLS [Djurdja ADLESIC]; Independent Democratic Serb Party or SDSS [Vojislav STANIMIROVIC]; Istrian Democratic Assembly or IDS [Ivan JAKOVCIC]; Social Democratic Party of Croatia or SDP [Zoran MILANOVIC]

**Political pressure groups and leaders:**
*other:* human rights groups

**International organization participation:** ACCT (observer), Australia Group, BIS, BSEC (observer), CE, CEI, EAPC, EBRD, FAO, IADB, IAEA, IBRD, ICAO, ICC, ICCt, ICRM, IDA, IFAD, IFC, IFRCS, IHO, ILO, IMF, IMO, IMSO, Interpol, IOC, IOM, IPU, ISO, ITSO, ITU, ITUC, MIGA, MINURSO, MINUSTAH, NAM (observer), NATO, NSG, OAS (observer), OIF (observer), OPCW, OSCE, PCA, SECI, UN, UNCTAD, UNDOF, UNESCO, UNFICYP, UNIDO, UNIFIL, UNMIL, UNMIS, UNMOGIP, UNOCI, UNOMIG, UNWTO, UPU, WCO, WFTU, WHO, WIPO, WMO, WTO, ZC

**Diplomatic representation in the US:**
*chief of mission:* Ambassador Kolinda GRABAR-KITAROVIC
*chancery:* 2343 Massachusetts Avenue NW, Washington, DC 20008
*telephone:* [1] (202) 588-5899
*FAX:* [1] (202) 588-8936
*consulate(s) general:* Chicago, Los Angeles, New York

**Diplomatic representation from the US:**
*chief of mission:* Ambassador Robert A. BRADTKE
*embassy:* 2 Thomas Jefferson Street, 10010 Zagreb
*mailing address:* use street address
*telephone:* [385] (1) 661-2200
*FAX:* [385] (1) 661-2373

**Flag description:** three equal horizontal bands of red (top), white, and blue, superimposed by the Croatian coat of arms (red and white checkered)

## Economy

**Economy - overview:** Once one of the wealthiest of the Yugoslav republics, Croatia's economy suffered badly during the 1991-95 war as output collapsed and the country missed the early waves of investment in Central and Eastern Europe that followed the fall of the Berlin Wall. Since 2000, however, Croatia's economic fortunes have begun to improve slowly, with moderate but steady GDP growth between 4% and 6% led by a rebound in tourism and credit-driven consumer spending. Inflation over the same period has remained tame and the currency, the kuna, stable. Nevertheless, difficult problems still remain, including a stubbornly high unemployment rate, a growing trade deficit and uneven regional development. The state retains a large role in the economy, as privatization efforts often meet stiff public and political resistance. While macroeconomic stabilization has largely been achieved, structural reforms lag because of deep resistance on the part of the public and lack of strong support from politicians. The EU accession process should accelerate fiscal and structural reform. While long term growth prospects for the economy remain strong, Croatia will face significant pressure as a result of the global financial crisis. Croatia's high foreign debt, anemic export sector, strained state budget, and over-reliance on tourism revenue will result in higher risk to economic stability over the medium term.

**GDP (purchasing power parity):**
$73.36 billion (2008 est.)
$70 billion (2007)
$66.92 billion (2006)
*note:* data are in 2008 US dollars

**GDP (official exchange rate):** $63.95 billion (2008 est.)

**GDP - real growth rate:**
4.8% (2008 est.)
5.6% (2007 est.)
4.8% (2006 est.)

**GDP - per capita (PPP):**
$16,100 (2008 est.)
$15,700 (2007 est.)
$14,900 (2006 est.)
*note:* data are in 2008 US dollars

**GDP - composition by sector:**
*agriculture:* 7%
*industry:* 31.6%
*services:* 61.4% (2008 est.)

**Labor force:** 1.781 million (2008)

**Labor force - by occupation:**
*agriculture:* 5%
*industry:* 31.3%
*services:* 63.6% (2008)

**Unemployment rate:**
14.8% (2008 est.)
11.8% (2007 est.)

**Population below poverty line:** 11% (2003)

**Household income or consumption by percentage share:**
*lowest 10%:* 3.4%
*highest 10%:* 24.5% (2003 est.)

**Distribution of family income - Gini index:** 29 (2008)

**Investment (gross fixed):** 31.5% of GDP (2008 est.)

**Budget:**
*revenues:* $23.71 billion
*expenditures:* $23.46 billion (2008 est.)

**Public debt:** 48.9% of GDP (2008 est.)

**Inflation rate (consumer prices):**
6.3% (2008 est.)
4.5% (2007 est.)

**Central bank discount rate:** 9% (31 December 2008)

**Commercial bank prime lending rate:** 9.33% (31 December 2008)

**Stock of money:** $10.43 billion (31 December 2008)

**Stock of quasi money:** $31.77 billion (31 December 2008)

**Stock of domestic credit:** $47.83 billion (31 December 2008)

**Market value of publicly traded shares:** $53.02 billion (31 December 2008)

**Agriculture - products:** wheat, corn, sugar beets, sunflower seed, barley, alfalfa, clover, olives, citrus, grapes, soybeans, potatoes; livestock, dairy products

**Industries:** chemicals and plastics, machine tools, fabricated metal, electronics, pig iron and rolled steel products, aluminum, paper, wood products, construction materials, textiles, shipbuilding, petroleum and petroleum refining, food and beverages, tourism

**Industrial production growth rate:** 2.9% (2008 est.)

**Electricity - production:** 12.25 billion kWh (2007)

**Electricity - consumption:** 18.61 billion kWh (2007)

**Electricity - exports:** 1.451 billion kWh (2007)

**Electricity - imports:** 7.511 billion kWh (2007)

**Oil - production:** 17,580 bbl/day (2007 est.)

**Oil - consumption:** 101,200 bbl/day (2007 est.)

**Oil - exports:** 0 bbl/day (2007)

**Oil - imports:** 83,800 bbl/day (2007)

**Oil - proved reserves:** 79.15 million bbl (1 January 2008 est.)

**Natural gas - production:** 2.892 billion cu m (2007)

**Natural gas - consumption:** 3.3 billion cu m (2007)

**Natural gas - exports:** 751.7 million cu m (2007)

**Natural gas - imports:** 1.055 billion cu m (2007)

**Natural gas - proved reserves:** 40.9 billion cu m (1 January 2008 est.)

**Current account balance:** -$6.156 billion (2008 est.)

**Exports:** $12.36 billion f.o.b. (2008)

**Exports - commodities:** transport equipment, machinery, textiles, chemicals, foodstuffs, fuels

**Exports - partners:** Italy 19.3%, Bosnia and Herzegovina 13.9%, Germany 10.2%, Slovenia 8.4%, Austria 6.2% (2007)

**Imports:** $25.84 billion f.o.b. (2008)

# Croatia *(continued)*

**Imports - commodities:** machinery, transport and electrical equipment; chemicals, fuels and lubricants; foodstuffs

**Imports - partners:** Italy 16.1%, Germany 14.4%, Russia 10.1%, China 6.2%, Slovenia 6%, Austria 5.3% (2007)

**Reserves of foreign exchange and gold:** $14.14 billion (31 December 2008 est.)

**Debt - external:** $53.3 billion (31 December 2008 est.)

**Stock of direct foreign investment - at home:** $19.5 billion (2008)

**Stock of direct foreign investment - abroad:** $2.1 billion (2008)

**Exchange rates:** kuna (HRK) per US dollar - 4.98 (2008 est.), 5.3735 (2007), 5.8625 (2006), 5.9473 (2005), 6.0358 (2004)

## Communications

**Telephones - main lines in use:** 1.825 million (2007)

**Telephones - mobile cellular:** 5.035 million (2007)

**Telephone system:**
*general assessment:* the telecommunications network has improved steadily since the mid-1990s; the number of fixed telephone lines holding steady at about 40 per 100 persons; the number of cellular telephone subscriptions exceeds the population
*domestic:* more than 90 percent of local lines are digital
*international:* country code - 385; digital international service is provided through the main switch in Zagreb; Croatia participates in the Trans-Asia-Europe (TEL) fiber-optic project, which consists of 2 fiber-optic trunk connections with Slovenia and a fiber-optic trunk line from Rijeka to Split and Dubrovnik; the ADRIA-1 submarine cable provides connectivity to Albania and Greece (2007)

**Radio broadcast stations:** AM 16, FM 98, shortwave 5 (1999)

**Television broadcast stations:** 36 (plus 321 repeaters) (1995)

**Internet country code:** .hr

**Internet hosts:** 1.111 million (2008)

**Internet users:** 1.995 million (2007)

## Transportation

**Airports:** 68 (2008)
**Airports - with paved runways:**
*total:* 23
*over 3,047 m:* 2
*2,438 to 3,047 m:* 6
*1,524 to 2,437 m:* 2
*914 to 1,523 m:* 4
*under 914 m:* 9 (2008)
**Airports - with unpaved runways:**
*total:* 45
*1,524 to 2,437 m:* 1
*914 to 1,523 m:* 7
*under 914 m:* 37 (2008)
**Heliports:** 2 (2007)
**Pipelines:** gas 1,327 km; oil 583 km (2008)

**Railways:**
*total:* 2,726 km
*standard gauge:* 2,726 km 1.435-m gauge (1,199 km electrified) (2006)
**Roadways:**
*total:* 28,788 km (includes 877 km of expressways) (2006)
**Waterways:** 785 km (2008)
**Merchant marine:**
*total:* 80
*by type:* bulk carrier 25, cargo 11, chemical tanker 3, passenger/cargo 30, petroleum tanker 8, refrigerated cargo 1, roll on/roll off 2
*registered in other countries:* 30 (Bahamas 1, Belize 2, Liberia 2, Malta 9, Marshall Islands 6, Panama 3, Saint Vincent and the Grenadines 7) (2008)
**Ports and terminals:** Omisalj, Ploce, Rijeka, Sibenik, Vukovar (on Danube River)

## Military

**Military branches:** Armed Forces of the Republic of Croatia (Oruzane Snage Republike Hrvatske, OSRH), consists of five major commands directly subordinate to a General Staff: Ground Forces (Hrvatska Kopnena Vojska, HKoV), Naval Forces (Hrvatska Ratna Mornarica, HRM; includes coast guard), Air Force and Air Defense Command, Joint Education and Training Command, Logistics Command; Military Police Force supports each of the three Croatian military forces (2009)

**Military service age and obligation:** 18-27 years of age for compulsory military service; 16 years of age with consent for voluntary service; 6-month conscript service obligation; full conversion to voluntary military service by 2010 (2006)

**Manpower available for military service:**
*males age 16-49:* 1,035,712
*females age 16-49:* 1,037,896 (2008 est.)
**Manpower fit for military service:**
*males age 16-49:* 770,798
*females age 16-49:* 849,957 (2009 est.)
**Manpower reaching militarily significant age annually:**
*male:* 27,620
*female:* 26,154 (2009 est.)
**Military expenditures:** 2.39% of GDP (2005 est.)

## Transnational Issues

**Disputes - international:** dispute remains with Bosnia and Herzegovina over several small sections of the boundary related to maritime access that hinders ratification of the 1999 border agreement; the Croatia-Slovenia land and maritime boundary agreement, which would have ceded most of Pirin Bay and maritime access to Slovenia and several villages to Croatia, remains unratified and in dispute; Slovenia also protests Croatia's 2003 claim to an exclusive economic zone in the Adriatic; as a European Union peripheral state, Slovenia imposed a hard border Schengen regime with non-member Croatia in December 2007

**Refugees and internally displaced persons:**
*IDPs:* 2,900-7,000 (Croats and Serbs displaced in 1992-95 war) (2007)
**Illicit drugs:** transit point along the Balkan route for Southwest Asian heroin to Western Europe; has been used as a transit point for maritime shipments of South American cocaine bound for Western Europe (2008)

# Cuba

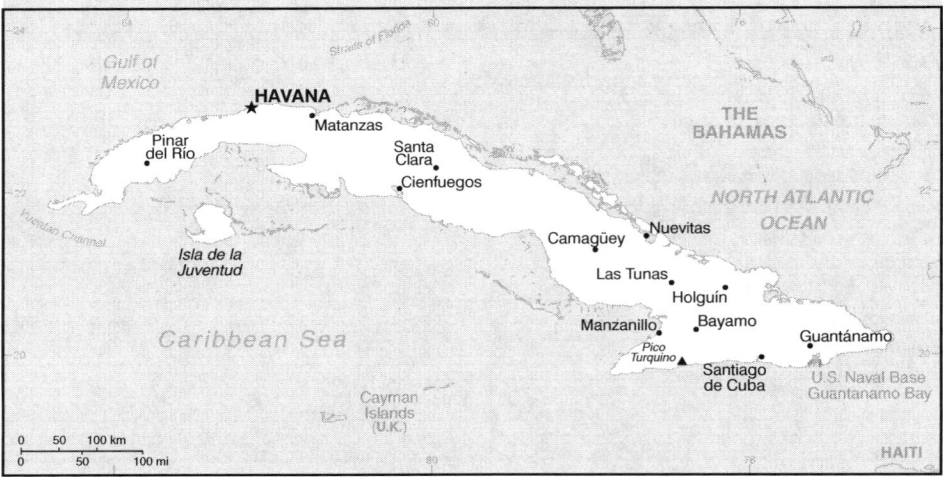

## Introduction

**Background:** The native Amerindian population of Cuba began to decline after the European discovery of the island by Christopher COLUMBUS in 1492 and following its development as a Spanish colony during the next several centuries. Large numbers of African slaves were imported to work the coffee and sugar plantations, and Havana became the launching point for the annual treasure fleets bound for Spain from Mexico and Peru. Spanish rule eventually provoked an independence movement and occasional rebellions that were harshly suppressed. US intervention during the Spanish-American War in 1898 assisted the Cubans in overthrowing Spanish rule. The Treaty of Paris established Cuban independence from the US in 1902 after which the island experienced a string of governments mostly dominated by the military and corrupt politicians. Fidel CASTRO led a rebel army to victory in 1959; his iron rule held the subsequent regime together for nearly five decades. He stepped down as president in February 2008 in favor of his younger brother Raul CASTRO. Cuba's Communist revolution, with Soviet support, was exported throughout Latin America and Africa during the 1960s, 1970s, and 1980s. The country faced a severe economic downturn in 1990 following the withdrawal of former Soviet subsidies worth $4 billion to $6 billion annually. Cuba portrays its difficulties as the result of the US embargo in place since 1961. Illicit migration to the US - using homemade rafts, alien smugglers, air flights, or via the southwest border - is a continuing problem. The US Coast Guard intercepted 2,656 individuals attempting to cross the Straits of Florida in fiscal year 2007.

## Geography

**Location:** Caribbean, island between the Caribbean Sea and the North Atlantic Ocean, 150 km south of Key West, Florida

**Geographic coordinates:** 21 30 N, 80 00 W

**Map references:** Central America and the Caribbean

**Area:**
*total:* 110,860 sq km
*land:* 110,860 sq km
*water:* 0 sq km

**Area - comparative:** slightly smaller than Pennsylvania

**Land boundaries:**
*total:* 29 km
*border countries:* US Naval Base at Guantanamo Bay 29 km
*note:* Guantanamo Naval Base is leased by the US and remains part of Cuba

**Coastline:** 3,735 km

**Maritime claims:**
*territorial sea:* 12 nm
*contiguous zone:* 24 nm
*exclusive economic zone:* 200 nm

**Climate:** tropical; moderated by trade winds; dry season (November to April); rainy season (May to October)

**Terrain:** mostly flat to rolling plains, with rugged hills and mountains in the southeast

**Elevation extremes:**
*lowest point:* Caribbean Sea 0 m
*highest point:* Pico Turquino 2,005 m

**Natural resources:** cobalt, nickel, iron ore, chromium, copper, salt, timber, silica, petroleum, arable land

**Land use:**
*arable land:* 27.63%
*permanent crops:* 6.54%
*other:* 65.83% (2005)

**Irrigated land:** 8,700 sq km (2003)

**Total renewable water resources:** 38.1 cu km (2000)

**Freshwater withdrawal (domestic/industrial/agricultural):**
*total:* 8.2 cu km/yr (19%/12%/69%)
*per capita:* 728 cu m/yr (2000)

**Natural hazards:** the east coast is subject to hurricanes from August to November (in general, the country averages about one hurricane every other year); droughts are common

**Environment - current issues:** air and water pollution; biodiversity loss; deforestation

**Environment - international agreements:**
*party to:* Antarctic Treaty, Biodiversity, Climate Change, Climate Change-Kyoto Protocol, Desertification, Endangered Species, Environmental Modification, Hazardous Wastes, Law of the Sea, Marine Dumping, Ozone Layer Protection, Ship Pollution, Wetlands
*signed, but not ratified:* Marine Life Conservation

**Geography - note:** largest country in Caribbean and westernmost island of the Greater Antilles

## People

**Population:** 11,451,652 (July 2009 est.)

**Age structure:**
*0-14 years:* 18.3% (male 1,077,745/female 1,020,393)
*15-64 years:* 70.4% (male 4,035,691/female 4,030,103)
*65 years and over:* 11.2% (male 584,478/female 703,242) (2009 est.)

**Median age:**
*total:* 37.3 years
*male:* 36.6 years
*female:* 38 years (2009 est.)

**Population growth rate:** 0.233% (2009 est.)

**Birth rate:** 11.13 births/1,000 population (2009 est.)

**Death rate:** 7.19 deaths/1,000 population (2008 est.)

**Net migration rate:** -1.56 migrant(s)/1,000 population (2009 est.)

**Urbanization:**
*urban population:* 76% of total population (2008)
*rate of urbanization:* 0% annual rate of change (2005-10 est.)

**Sex ratio:**
*at birth:* 1.06 male(s)/female
*under 15 years:* 1.06 male(s)/female
*15-64 years:* 1 male(s)/female
*65 years and over:* 0.83 male(s)/female
*total population:* 0.99 male(s)/female (2009 est.)

**Infant mortality rate:**
*total:* 5.82 deaths/1,000 live births
*male:* 6.51 deaths/1,000 live births
*female:* 5.09 deaths/1,000 live births (2009 est.)

**Life expectancy at birth:**
*total population:* 77.45 years
*male:* 75.19 years
*female:* 79.85 years (2009 est.)

# Cuba *(continued)*

**Total fertility rate:** 1.61 children born/woman (2009 est.)

**HIV/AIDS - adult prevalence rate:** less than 0.1% (2007 est.)

**HIV/AIDS - people living with HIV/AIDS:** 6,200 (2007 est.)

**HIV/AIDS - deaths:** fewer than 100 (2007 est.)

**Major infectious diseases:**

*degree of risk:* intermediate

*food or waterborne diseases:* bacterial diarrhea and hepatitis A

*vectorborne diseases:* dengue fever (2009)

**Nationality:**

*noun:* Cuban(s)

*adjective:* Cuban

**Ethnic groups:** white 65.1%, mulatto and mestizo 24.8%, black 10.1% (2002 census)

**Religions:** nominally 85% Roman Catholic prior to CASTRO assuming power; Protestants, Jehovah's Witnesses, Jews, and Santeria are also represented

**Languages:** Spanish

**Literacy:**

*definition:* age 15 and over can read and write

*total population:* 99.8%

*male:* 99.8%

*female:* 99.8% (2002 census)

**School life expectancy (primary to tertiary education):**

*total:* 16 years

*male:* 15 years

*female:* 17 years (2006)

**Education expenditures:** 9.1% of GDP (2006)

**People - note:** illicit emigration is a continuing problem; Cubans attempt to depart the island and enter the US using homemade rafts, alien smugglers, direct flights, or falsified visas; Cubans also use non-maritime routes to enter the US including direct flights to Miami and over-land via the southwest border

## Government

**Country name:**

*conventional long form:* Republic of Cuba

*conventional short form:* Cuba

*local long form:* Republica de Cuba

*local short form:* Cuba

**Government type:** Communist state

**Capital:**

*name:* Havana

*geographic coordinates:* 23 07 N, 82 21 W

*time difference:* UTC-5 (same time as Washington, DC during Standard Time)

*daylight saving time:* +1hr, begins last Sunday in March; ends last Sunday in October

**Administrative divisions:** 14 provinces (provincias, singular - provincia) and 1 special municipality* (municipio especial); Camaguey, Ciego de Avila, Cienfuegos, Ciudad de La Habana, Granma, Guantanamo, Holguin, Isla de la Juventud*, La Habana, Las Tunas, Matanzas, Pinar del Rio, Sancti Spiritus, Santiago de Cuba, Villa Clara

**Independence:** 20 May 1902 (from Spain 10 December 1898; administered by the US from 1898 to 1902); not acknowledged by the Cuban Government as a day of independence

**National holiday:** Triumph of the Revolution, 1 January (1959)

**Constitution:** 24 February 1976; amended July 1992 and June 2002

**Legal system:** based on Spanish civil law and influenced by American legal concepts with large elements of Communist legal theory; has not accepted compulsory ICJ jurisdiction

**Suffrage:** 16 years of age; universal

**Executive branch:**

*chief of state:* President of the Council of State and President of the Council of Ministers Gen. Raul CASTRO Ruz (president since 24 February 2008); First Vice President of the Council of State and First Vice President of the Council of Ministers Gen. Jose Ramon MACHADO Ventura (since 24 February 2008); note - the president is both the chief of state and head of government

*head of government:* President of the Council of State and President of the Council of Ministers Gen. Raul CASTRO Ruz (president since 24 February 2008); First Vice President of the Council of State and First Vice President of the Council of Ministers Gen. Jose Ramon MACHADO Ventura (since 24 February 2008)

*cabinet:* Council of Ministers proposed by the president of the Council of State and appointed by the National Assembly or the 31-member Council of State, elected by the assembly to act on its behalf when it is not in session

*elections:* president and vice presidents elected by the National Assembly for a term of five years; election last held 24 February 2008 (next to be held in 2013)

*election results:* Gen. Raul CASTRO Ruz elected president; percent of legislative vote - 100%; Gen. Jose Ramon MACHADO Ventura elected vice president; percent of legislative vote - 100%

**Legislative branch:** unicameral National Assembly of People's Power or Asemblea Nacional del Poder Popular (number of seats in the National Assembly is based on population; 614 seats; members elected directly from slates approved by special candidacy commissions to serve five-year terms)

*elections:* last held 20 January 2008 (next to be held in January 2013)

*election results:* Cuba's Communist Party is the only legal party, and officially sanctioned candidates run unopposed

**Judicial branch:** People's Supreme Court or Tribunal Supremo Popular (president, vice president, and other judges are elected by the National Assembly)

**Political parties and leaders:** Cuban Communist Party or PCC [Fidel CASTRO Ruz, first secretary]

**Political pressure groups and leaders:** Human Rights Watch; National Association of Small Farmers

**International organization participation:** ACP, FAO, G-77, IAEA, ICAO, ICC, ICRM, IFAD, IFRCS, IHO, ILO, IMO, IMSO, Interpol, IOC, IOM (observer), IPU, ISO, ITSO, ITU, LAES, LAIA, NAM, OAS (excluded from formal participation since 1962), OPANAL, OPCW, PCA, UN, UNCTAD, UNESCO, UNIDO, Union Latina, UNITAR, UNWTO, UPU, WCL, WCO, WFTU, WHO, WIPO, WMO, WTO

**Diplomatic representation in the US:** none; note - Cuba has an Interests Section in the Swiss Embassy, headed by Principal Officer Jorge BOLANOS Suarez; address: Cuban Interests Section, Swiss Embassy, 2630 16th Street NW, Washington, DC 20009; telephone: [1] (202) 797-8518; FAX: [1] (202) 797-8521

**Diplomatic representation from the US:** none; note - the US has an Interests Section in the Swiss Embassy, headed by Chief of Mission Jonathan D. FARRAR; address: USINT, Swiss Embassy, Calzada between L and M Streets, Vedado, Havana; telephone: [53] (7) 833-3551 through 3559 (operator assistance required); FAX: [53] (7) 833-1653; protecting power in Cuba is Switzerland

**Flag description:** five equal horizontal bands of blue (top, center, and bottom) alternating with white; a red equilateral triangle based on the hoist side bears a white, five-pointed star in the center

## Economy

**Economy - overview:** The government continues to balance the need for economic loosening against a desire for firm political control. It has rolled back limited reforms undertaken in the 1990s to increase enterprise efficiency and alleviate serious shortages of food, consumer goods, and services. The average Cuban's standard of living remains at a lower level than before the downturn of the 1990s, which was caused by the loss of Soviet aid and domestic inefficiencies. Since late 2000, Venezuela has been providing oil on preferential terms, and it currently supplies about 100,000 barrels per day of petroleum products. Cuba has been paying for the oil, in part, with the services of Cuban personnel in Venezuela including some 30,000 medical professionals.

**GDP (purchasing power parity):**

$108.2 billion (2008 est.)

$103.7 billion (2007)

$96.7 billion (2006)

*note:* data are in 2008 US dollars

**GDP (official exchange rate):** $55.18 billion (2008 est.)

**GDP - real growth rate:**

4.3% (2008 est.)

7.3% (2007 est.)

12.1% (2006 est.)

**GDP - per capita (PPP):**

$9,500 (2008 est.)

$9,100 (2007 est.)

$8,500 (2006 est.)

*note:* data are in 2008 US dollars

**GDP - composition by sector:**
*agriculture:* 4.4%
*industry:* 22.8%
*services:* 72.8% (2008 est.)
**Labor force:** 4.962 million
*note:* state sector 78%, non-state sector 22%
(2008 est.)
**Labor force - by occupation:**
*agriculture:* 20%
*industry:* 19.4%
*services:* 60.6% (2005)
**Unemployment rate:**
1.8% (2008 est.)
1.8% (2007 est.)
**Population below poverty line:** NA%
**Household income or consumption by percentage share:**
*lowest 10%:* NA%
*highest 10%:* NA%
**Investment (gross fixed):** 11.6% of GDP
(2008 est.)
**Budget:**
*revenues:* $41.06 billion
*expenditures:* $43.33 billion (2008 est.)
**Public debt:** 32.8% of GDP (2008 est.)
**Inflation rate (consumer prices):**
4.2% (2008 est.)
3.1% (2007 est.)
**Central bank discount rate:** %NA
**Commercial bank prime lending rate:** %NA
**Stock of money:** $NA
**Stock of quasi money:** $NA
**Stock of domestic credit:** $NA
**Agriculture - products:** sugar, tobacco, citrus, coffee, rice, potatoes, beans; livestock
**Industries:** sugar, petroleum, tobacco, construction, nickel, steel, cement, agricultural machinery, pharmaceuticals
**Industrial production growth rate:** 6% (2008 est.)
**Electricity - production:** 17.62 billion kWh
(2007 est.)
**Electricity - consumption:** 14.67 billion kWh
(2007 est.)
**Electricity - exports:** 0 kWh (2007 est.)
**Electricity - imports:** 0 kWh (2007 est.)
**Oil - production:** 61,300 bbl/day (2008 est.)
**Oil - consumption:** 203,500 bbl/day (2006 est.)
**Oil - exports:** 0 bbl/day (2006)
**Oil - imports:** 123,200 bbl/day (2005)
**Oil - proved reserves:** 124 million bbl (1 January 2008 est.)
**Natural gas - production:** 1.218 billion cu m (2007)
**Natural gas - consumption:** 1.218 billion cu m (2007)
**Natural gas - exports:** 0 cu m (2007 est.)
**Natural gas - imports:** 0 cu m (2007 est.)
**Natural gas - proved reserves:** 70.79 billion cu m (1 January 2008 est.)
**Current account balance:** -$330 million (2008 est.)
**Exports:** $3.497 billion f.o.b. (2008 est.)

**Exports - commodities:** sugar, nickel, tobacco, fish, medical products, citrus, coffee
**Exports - partners:** China 27.5%, Canada 26.9%, Netherlands 11.1%, Spain 4.7% (2007)
**Imports:** $11.74 billion f.o.b. (2008 est.)
**Imports - commodities:** petroleum, food, machinery and equipment, chemicals
**Imports - partners:** Venezuela 29.6%, China 13.4%, Spain 10.4%, Canada 6%, US 5.1% (2007)
**Reserves of foreign exchange and gold:** $4.347 billion (31 December 2008 est.)
**Debt - external:** $18.25 billion (convertible currency); another $15-20 billion owed to Russia (31 December 2008 est.)
**Stock of direct foreign investment - at home:** $11.24 billion (2006 est.)
**Stock of direct foreign investment - abroad:** $4.138 billion (2006 est.)
**Exchange rates:** Cuban pesos (CUP) per US dollar -0.9259 (2008 est.), 0.9259 (2007), 0.9231 (2006)
*note:* Cuba has two currencies in circulation: the Cuban peso (CUP) and the convertible peso (CUC); in April 2005 the official exchange rate changed from $1 per CUC to $1.08 per CUC (0.93 CUC per $1) both for individuals and enterprises; individuals can buy 24 Cuban pesos (CUP) for each CUC sold or sell 25 Cuban pesos for each CUC bought; enterprises, however, must exchange CUP and CUC at a 1:1 ratio.

### Communications

**Telephones - main lines in use:** 1.043 million (2007)
**Telephones - mobile cellular:** 198,300 (2007)
**Telephone system:**
*general assessment:* greater investment beginning in 1994 and the establishment of a new Ministry of Information Technology and Communications in 2000 has resulted in improvements in the system; wireless service is expensive and must be paid in convertible pesos, which effectively limits mobile cellular subscribership
*domestic:* national fiber-optic system under development; 95% of switches digitized by end of 2006; fixed telephone line density remains low at less than 10 per 100 inhabitants; domestic cellular service expanding but remains at only about 2 per 100 persons
*international:* country code - 53; fiber-optic cable laid to but not linked to US network; satellite earth station -1 Intersputnik (Atlantic Ocean region) (2007)
**Radio broadcast stations:** AM 169, FM 55, shortwave 1 (1998)
**Television broadcast stations:** 58 (1997)
**Internet country code:** .cu
**Internet hosts:** 3,664 (2008)
**Internet users:** 1.31 million
*note:* private citizens are prohibited from buying computers or accessing the Internet without special authorization; foreigners may access the Internet in large hotels but are subject to firewalls; some Cubans

buy illegal passwords on the black market or take advantage of public outlets to access limited email and the government-controlled "intranet" (2007)

### Transportation

**Airports:** 147 (2008)
**Airports - with paved runways:**
*total:* 70
*over 3,047 m:* 7
*2,438 to 3,047 m:* 9
*1,524 to 2,437 m:* 18
*914 to 1,523 m:* 5
*under 914 m:* 31 (2008)
**Airports - with unpaved runways:**
*total:* 77
*1,524 to 2,437 m:* 1
*914 to 1,523 m:* 20
*under 914 m:* 56 (2008)
**Pipelines:** gas 41 km; oil 230 km (2008)
**Railways:**
*total:* 4,226 km
*standard gauge:* 4,226 km 1.435-m gauge (140 km electrified)
*note:* an additional 7,742 km of track is used by sugar plantations; about 65% of this track is standard gauge; the rest is narrow gauge (2006)
**Roadways:**
*total:* 60,858 km
*paved:* 29,820 km (includes 638 km of expressway)
*unpaved:* 31,038 km (2000)
**Waterways:** 240 km (2008)
**Merchant marine:**
*total:* 11
*by type:* bulk carrier 2, cargo 3, passenger 1, petroleum tanker 3, refrigerated cargo 2
*foreign-owned:* 1 (Spain 1)
*registered in other countries:* 13 (Bahamas 1, Cyprus 1, Netherlands Antilles 1, Panama 10) (2008)
**Ports and terminals:** Cienfuegos, Havana, Matanzas

### Military

**Military branches:** Revolutionary Armed Forces (Fuerzas Armadas Revolucionarias, FAR): Revolutionary Army (ER; includes Territorial Militia Troops (Milicia de Tropas de Territoriales, MTT)), Revolutionary Navy (Marina de Guerra Revolucionaria, MGR; includes Marine Corps), Revolutionary Air and Air Defense Force (DAAFAR), Youth Labor Army (Ejercito Juvenil del Trabajo, EJT) (2009)
**Military service age and obligation:** 17-28 years of age for compulsory military service; 2-year service obligation; both sexes subject to military service (2006)
**Manpower available for military service:**
*males age 16-49:* 3,094,388
*females age 16-49:* 3,024,876 (2008 est.)
**Manpower fit for military service:**
*males age 16-49:* 2,532,495
*females age 16-49:* 2,468,631 (2009 est.)

## Cuba *(continued)*

**Manpower reaching militarily significant age annually:**

*male:* 75,969

*female:* 72,253 (2009 est.)

**Military expenditures:** 3.8% of GDP (2006 est.)

**Military - note:** the collapse of the Soviet Union deprived the Cuban Army of its major economic and logistic support and had a significant impact on equipment numbers and serviceability; the army remains well trained and professional in nature; while the lack of replacement parts for its existing equipment and the current severe shortage of fuel have increasingly affected operational capabilities, Cuba remains able to offer considerable resistance to any regional power (2008)

### Transnational Issues

**Disputes - international:** US Naval Base at Guantanamo Bay is leased to US and only mutual agreement or US abandonment of the facility can terminate the lease

**Trafficking in persons:**

*current situation:* Cuba is principally a source country for women and children trafficked within the country for the purpose of commercial sexual exploitation and possibly for forced labor; the country is a destination for sex tourism including child sex tourism, which is a problem in many areas of the country; some Cuban nationals willingly migrate to the United States but are subsequently exploited for forced labor by their smugglers; Cuba is also a transit point for the smuggling of migrants from China, Sri Lanka, Bangladesh, Lebanon, and other nations to the United States and Canada

*tier rating:* Tier 3 - Cuba does not fully comply with the minimum standards for the elimination of trafficking and is not making significant efforts to do so; exact information about trafficking in Cuba is difficult to obtain because the government does not acknowledge or condemn human trafficking as a problem in Cuba; tangible efforts to prosecute offenders, protect victims, or prevent human trafficking activity do not appear to have been made during 2007; Cuba has not ratified the 2000 UN TIP Protocol (2008)

**Illicit drugs:** territorial waters and air space serve as transshipment zone for US- and European-bound drugs; established the death penalty for certain drug-related crimes in 1999 (2008)

# Cyprus

## Introduction

**Background:** A former British colony, Cyprus became independent in 1960 following years of resistance to British rule. Tensions between the Greek Cypriot majority and Turkish Cypriot minority came to a head in December 1963, when violence broke out in the capital of Nicosia. Despite the deployment of UN peacekeepers in 1964, sporadic intercommunal violence continued forcing most Turkish Cypriots into enclaves throughout the island. In 1974, a Greek Government-sponsored attempt to seize control of Cyprus was met by military intervention from Turkey, which soon controlled more than a third of the island. In 1983, the Turkish-held area declared itself the "Turkish Republic of Northern Cyprus" ("TRNC"), but it is recognized only by Turkey. The election of a new Cypriot president in 2008 served as the impetus for the UN to encourage both the Turkish and Cypriot Governments to reopen unification negotiations. In September 2008, the leaders of the Greek Cypriot and Turkish Cypriot communities started negotiations under UN auspices aimed at reuniting the divided island. The entire island entered the EU on 1 May 2004, although the EU acquis - the body of common rights and obligations - applies only to the areas under direct government control, and is suspended in the areas administered by Turkish Cypriots. However, individual Turkish Cypriots able to document their eligibility for Republic of Cyprus citizenship legally enjoy the same rights accorded to other citizens of European Union states.

## Geography

**Location:** Middle East, island in the Mediterranean Sea, south of Turkey

**Geographic coordinates:** 35 00 N, 33 00 E

**Map references:** Middle East

**Area:**

*total:* 9,250 sq km (of which 3,355 sq km are in north Cyprus)

*land:* 9,240 sq km

*water:* 10 sq km

**Area - comparative:** about 0.6 times the size of Connecticut

**Land boundaries:**

*total:* 150.4 km (approximately)

*border sovereign base areas:* Akrotiri 47.4 km, Dhekelia 103 km (approximately)

**Coastline:** 648 km

**Maritime claims:**

*territorial sea:* 12 nm

*contiguous zone:* 24 nm

*continental shelf:* 200 m depth or to the depth of exploitation

**Climate:** temperate; Mediterranean with hot, dry summers and cool winters

**Terrain:** central plain with mountains to north and south; scattered but significant plains along southern coast

**Elevation extremes:**

*lowest point:* Mediterranean Sea 0 m

*highest point:* Mount Olympus 1,951 m

**Natural resources:** copper, pyrites, asbestos, gypsum, timber, salt, marble, clay earth pigment

**Land use:**

*arable land:* 10.81%

*permanent crops:* 4.32%

*other:* 84.87% (2005)

**Irrigated land:** 400 sq km (2003)

**Total renewable water resources:** 0.4 cu km (2005)

**Freshwater withdrawal (domestic/industrial/agricultural):**

*total:* 0.21 cu km/yr (27%/1%/71%)

*per capita:* 250 cu m/yr (2000)

# Cyprus (continued)

**Natural hazards:** moderate earthquake activity; droughts

**Environment - current issues:** water resource problems (no natural reservoir catchments, seasonal disparity in rainfall, sea water intrusion to island's largest aquifer, increased salination in the north); water pollution from sewage and industrial wastes; coastal degradation; loss of wildlife habitats from urbanization

**Environment - international agreements:**
*party to:* Air Pollution, Air Pollution-Nitrogen Oxides, Air Pollution-Persistent Organic Pollutants, Air Pollution-Sulfur 94, Biodiversity, Climate Change, Climate Change-Kyoto Protocol, Desertification, Endangered Species, Environmental Modification, Hazardous Wastes, Law of the Sea, Marine Dumping, Ozone Layer Protection, Ship Pollution, Wetlands
*signed, but not ratified:* none of the selected agreements

**Geography - note:** the third largest island in the Mediterranean Sea (after Sicily and Sardinia)

## People

**Population:** 796,740 (July 2009 est.)
**Age structure:**
*0-14 years:* 19.1% (male 77,959/female 74,591)
*15-64 years:* 68.5% (male 276,890/female 269,267)
*65 years and over:* 12.3% (male 42,961/female 55,072) (2009 est.)
**Median age:**
*total:* 35.5 years
*male:* 34.5 years
*female:* 36.6 years (2009 est.)
**Population growth rate:** 0.519% (2009 est.)
**Birth rate:** 12.57 births/1,000 population (2009 est.)
**Death rate:** 7.76 deaths/1,000 population (2008 est.)
**Net migration rate:** 0.42 migrant(s)/1,000 population (2009 est.)
**Urbanization:**
*urban population:* 70% of total population (2008)
*rate of urbanization:* 1.3% annual rate of change (2005-10 est.)
**Sex ratio:**
*at birth:* 1.05 male(s)/female
*under 15 years:* 1.04 male(s)/female
*15-64 years:* 1.03 male(s)/female
*65 years and over:* 0.78 male(s)/female
*total population:* 1 male(s)/female (2009 est.)
**Infant mortality rate:**
*total:* 6.6 deaths/1,000 live births
*male:* 8.14 deaths/1,000 live births
*female:* 4.98 deaths/1,000 live births (2009 est.)
**Life expectancy at birth:**
*total population:* 78.33 years
*male:* 75.91 years
*female:* 80.86 years (2009 est.)
**Total fertility rate:** 1.77 children born/woman (2009 est.)
**HIV/AIDS - adult prevalence rate:** 0.1% (2003 est.)
**HIV/AIDS - people living with HIV/AIDS:** fewer than 1,000 (2007 est.)

**HIV/AIDS - deaths:** NA
**Nationality:**
*noun:* Cypriot(s)
*adjective:* Cypriot
**Ethnic groups:** Greek 77%, Turkish 18%, other 5% (2001)
**Religions:** Greek Orthodox 78%, Muslim 18%, other (includes Maronite and Armenian Apostolic) 4%
**Languages:** Greek, Turkish, English
**Literacy:**
*definition:* age 15 and over can read and write
*total population:* 97.6%
*male:* 98.9%
*female:* 96.3% (2001 census)
**School life expectancy (primary to tertiary education):**
*total:* 14 years
*male:* 13 years
*female:* 14 years (2006)
**Education expenditures:** 6.3% of GDP (2004)

## Government

**Country name:**
*conventional long form:* Republic of Cyprus
*conventional short form:* Cyprus
*local long form:* Kypriaki Dimokratia/Kibris Cumhuriyeti
*local short form:* Kypros/Kibris
*note:* the Turkish Cypriot community, which administers the northern part of the island, refers to itself as the "Turkish Republic of Northern Cyprus" ("TRNC")
**Government type:** republic
*note:* a separation of the two ethnic communities inhabiting the island began following the outbreak of communal strife in 1963; this separation was further solidified after the Turkish intervention in July 1974 that followed a Greek junta-supported coup attempt gave the Turkish Cypriots de facto control in the north; Greek Cypriots control the only internationally recognized government; on 15 November 1983 Turkish Cypriot "President" Rauf DENKTASH declared independence and the formation of a "Turkish Republic of Northern Cyprus" ("TRNC"), which is recognized only by Turkey
**Capital:**
*name:* Nicosia (Lefkosia)
*geographic coordinates:* 35 10 N, 33 22 E
*time difference:* UTC+2 (7 hours ahead of Washington, DC during Standard Time)
*daylight saving time:* +1hr, begins last Sunday in March; ends last Sunday in October
**Administrative divisions:** 6 districts; Famagusta, Kyrenia, Larnaca, Limassol, Nicosia, Paphos; note - Turkish Cypriot area's administrative divisions include Kyrenia, all but a small part of Famagusta, and small parts of Nicosia (Lefkosia)
**Independence:** 16 August 1960 (from the UK); note -Turkish Cypriots proclaimed self-rule on 13 February 1975 and independence in 1983, but these proclamations are only recognized by Turkey

**National holiday:** Independence Day, 1 October (1960); note - Turkish Cypriots celebrate 15 November (1983) as Independence Day
**Constitution:** 16 August 1960
*note:* from December 1963, the Turkish Cypriots no longer participated in the government; negotiations to create the basis for a new or revised constitution to govern the island and for better relations between Greek and Turkish Cypriots have been held intermittently since the mid-1960s; in 1975, following the 1974 Turkish intervention, Turkish Cypriots created their own constitution and governing bodies within the "Turkish Federated State of Cyprus," which became the "Turkish Republic of Northern Cyprus (TRNC)" when the Turkish Cypriots declared their independence in 1983; a new constitution for the "TRNC" passed by referendum on 5 May 1985, although the "TRNC" remains unrecognized by any country other than Turkey
**Legal system:** based on English common law, with civil law modifications; accepts compulsory ICJ jurisdiction with reservations
**Suffrage:** 18 years of age; universal
**Executive branch:**
*chief of state:* President Demetris CHRISTOFIAS (since 28 February 2008); note - the president is both the chief of state and head of government; post of vice president is currently vacant; under the 1960 constitution, the post is reserved for a Turkish Cypriot
*head of government:* President Demetris CHRISTOFIAS (since 28 February 2008)
*cabinet:* Council of Ministers appointed jointly by the president and vice president
*elections:* president elected by popular vote for a five-year term; election last held 17 and 24 February 2008 (next to be held in February 2013)
*election results:* Demetris CHRISTOFIAS elected president; percent of vote (first round) - Ioannis KASOULIDES 33.5%, Demetris CHRISTOFIAS 33.3%, Tassos PAPADOPOULOS 31.8%; (second round) Demetris CHRISTOFIAS 53.4%, Ioannis KASOULIDES 46.6%
*note:* Mehmet Ali TALAT became "president" of the "TRNC", 24 April 2005, after "presidential" elections on 17 April 2005; results - Mehmet Ali TALAT 55.6%, Dervis EROGLU 22.7%; Ferdi Sabit SOYER is "TRNC prime minister" and heads the Council of Ministers (cabinet) in coalition with "Foreign Minister and Deputy Prime Minister" Turgay AVCI
**Legislative branch:** unicameral - area under government control: House of Representatives or Vouli Antiprosopon (80 seats; 56 assigned to the Greek Cypriots, 24 to Turkish Cypriots; note - only those assigned to Greek Cypriots are filled; members are elected by popular vote to serve five-year terms); area administered by Turkish Cypriots: Assembly of the Republic or Cumhuriyet Meclisi (50 seats; members are elected by popular vote to serve five-year terms)

# Cyprus (continued)

*elections:* area under government control: last held 21 May 2006 (next to be held in 2010); area administered by Turkish Cypriots: last held 19 April 2009 (next to be held in 2014)

*election results:* area under government control: House of Representatives - percent of vote by party - AKEL 31.1%, DISY 30.3%, DIKO 17.9%, EDEK 8.9%, EURO.KO 5.8%, Greens 2.0%; seats by party - AKEL 18, DISY 18, DIKO 11, EDEK 4, EURO.KO 4, Greens 1; area administered by Turkish Cypriots: Assembly of the Republic - percent of vote by party - UBP 44.1%, CTP 29.3%, DP 10.6%, other 16%; seats by party - UBP 26, CTP 15, DP 5, other 4

**Judicial branch:** Supreme Court (judges are appointed jointly by the president and vice president) *note:* there is also a Supreme Court in the area administered by Turkish Cypriots

**Political parties and leaders:**

*area under government control:* Democratic Party or DIKO [Marios KAROYIAN]; Democratic Rally or DISY [Nikos ANASTASIADES]; European Party or EURO.KO [Demetris SYLLOURIS]; Fighting Democratic Movement or ADIK [Dinos MIKHAILIDES]; Green Party of Cyprus [George PERDIKIS]; Movement for Social Democrats or EDEK [Yiannakis OMIROU]; Progressive Party of the Working People or AKEL (Communist Party) [Andros KYPRIANOU]; United Democrats or EDI [Michalis PAPAPETROU]

*area administered by Turkish Cypriots:* Centrist Party or HP [Rasit PERTEV]; Communal Democracy Party or TDP [Mehmet CAKICIL]; Cyprus Socialist Party or KSP [Yusuf ALKIM]; Democratic Party or DP [Serder DENKTASH]; Freedom and Reform Party or ORP [Turgay AVCI]; National Unity Party or UBP [Dervis EROGLU]; Nationalist Justice Party or MAP [Ata TEPE]; New Cyprus Party or YKP [Murat KANATLI]; Politics for the People Party or HIS [Ahmet YONLUER]; Republican Turkish Party or CTP [Ferdi Sabit SOYER]; United Cyprus Party or BKP [Izzet IZCAN]

**Political pressure groups and leaders:** Confederation of Cypriot Workers or SEK (pro-West); Confederation of Revolutionary Labor Unions or Dev-Is; Federation of Turkish Cypriot Labor Unions or Turk-Sen; Pan-Cyprian Labor Federation or PEO (Communist controlled)

**International organization participation:** Australia Group, C, CE, EBRD, EIB, EMU, EU, FAO, IAEA, IBRD, ICAO, ICC, ICCt, IFAD, IFC, IHO, ILO, IMF, IMO, IMSO, Interpol, IOC, IOM, IPU, ISO, ITSO, ITU, ITUC, MIGA, NAM (guest), NSG, OAS (observer), OIF (associate member), OPCW, OSCE, PCA, UN, UNCTAD, UNESCO, UNHCR, UNIDO, UNIFIL, UNWTO, UPU, WCL, WCO, WFTU, WHO, WIPO, WMO, WTO

**Diplomatic representation in the US:**

*chief of mission:* Ambassador Andreas KAKOURIS
*chancery:* 2211 R Street NW, Washington, DC 20008
*telephone:* [1] (202) 462-5772, 462-0873
*FAX:* [1] (202) 483-6710
*consulate(s) general:* New York

*note:* representative of the Turkish Cypriot community in the US is Hilmi AKIL; office at 1667 K Street NW, Washington, DC; telephone [1] (202) 887-6198

**Diplomatic representation from the US:**

*chief of mission:* Ambassador Frank C. URBANCIC, Jr.
*embassy:* corner of Metochiou and Ploutarchou Streets, 2407 Engomi, Nicosia
*mailing address:* P. O. Box 24536, 1385 Nicosia
*telephone:* [357] (22) 393939
*FAX:* [357] (22) 780944

**Flag description:** white with a copper-colored silhouette of the island (the name Cyprus is derived from the Greek word for copper) above two green crossed olive branches in the center of the flag; the branches symbolize the hope for peace and reconciliation between the Greek and Turkish communities
*note:* the "Turkish Republic of Northern Cyprus" flag has a white field with narrow horizontal red stripes positioned a small distance from the top and bottom edges between which is centered a red crescent and a red five-pointed star

## Economy

**Economy - overview:** The area of the Republic of Cyprus under government control has a market economy dominated by the service sector, which accounts for 78% of GDP. Tourism, financial services, and real estate are the most important sectors. Erratic growth rates over the past decade reflect the economy's reliance on tourism, which often fluctuates with political instability in the region and economic conditions in Western Europe. Nevertheless, the economy in the area under government control has grown at a rate well above the EU average since 2000. Cyprus joined the European Exchange Rate Mechanism (ERM2) in May 2005 and adopted the euro as its national currency on 1 January 2008. An aggressive austerity program in the preceding years, aimed at paving the way for the euro, helped turn a soaring fiscal deficit (6.3% in 2003) into a surplus of 1.2% in 2008, and reduced inflation to 5.1%. This prosperity will come under pressure in 2009, as construction and tourism slow in the face of reduced foreign demand triggered by the ongoing global financial crisis. Growth is expected to slow to less than 2%, which would be its lowest level since 2003. As in the area administered by Turkish Cypriots, water shortages are a perennial problem; a few desalination plants have been added to existing plants over the last year and are now on line. After 10 years of drought, the country received substantial rainfall from 2001-04. Since then, rainfall has been well below average, making water rationing a necessity.

**GDP (purchasing power parity):**
$22.69 billion (2008 est.)
$21.9 billion (2007)
$20.98 billion (2006)
*note:* data are in 2008 US dollars

**GDP (official exchange rate):** $25.59 billion (2008 est.)

**GDP - real growth rate:**
3.6% (2008 est.)
4.4% (2007 est.)
4.1% (2006 est.)

**GDP - per capita (PPP):**
$28,600 (2008 est.)
$27,800 (2007 est.)
$26,700 (2006 est.)
*note:* data are in 2008 US dollars

**GDP - composition by sector:**
*agriculture:* 2.6%
*industry:* 19.1%
*services:* 78.3% (2008 est.)

**Labor force:** 403,000 (2008 est.)

**Labor force - by occupation:**
*agriculture:* 8.5%
*industry:* 20.5%
*services:* 71% (2006 est.)

**Unemployment rate:**
3.8% (2008 est.)
3.9% (2007 est.)

**Population below poverty line:** NA%

**Household income or consumption by percentage share:**
*lowest 10%:* NA%
*highest 10%:* NA%

**Distribution of family income - Gini index:** 29 (2005)

**Investment (gross fixed):** 21.4% of GDP (2008 est.)

**Budget:**
*revenues:* $11.33 billion
*expenditures:* $11.2 billion (2008 est.)

**Public debt:** 49% of GDP (2008 est.)

**Inflation rate (consumer prices):**
5.1% (2008 est.)
2.4% (2007 est.)

**Central bank discount rate:** 4%
*note:* this is the European Central Bank's rate on the marginal lending facility, which offers overnight credit to banks in the euro area (31 December 2008)

**Commercial bank prime lending rate:** 6.74% (31 December 2007)

**Stock of money:** $4.094 billion
*note:* this figure represents the US dollar value of Cypriot pounds in circulation prior to Cyprus joining the Economic and Monetary Union (EMU); see entry for the European Union for money supply in the euro area; the European Central Bank (ECB) controls monetary policy for the 16 members of the EMU; individual members of the EMU do not control the quantity of money and quasi money circulating within their own borders (31 December 2007)

**Stock of quasi money:** $43.93 billion (31 December 2007)

**Stock of domestic credit:** $52.09 billion (31 December 2007)

**Market value of publicly traded shares:** $29.48 billion (31 December 2007)

# Cyprus (continued)

**Agriculture - products:** citrus, vegetables, barley, grapes, olives, vegetables; poultry, pork, lamb; dairy, cheese

**Industries:** tourism, food and beverage processing, cement and gypsum production, ship repair and refurbishment, textiles, light chemicals, metal products, wood, paper, stone, and clay products

**Industrial production growth rate:** 2.8% (2008 est.)

**Electricity - production:** 4.52 billion kWh (2007 est.)

**Electricity - consumption:** 4.151 billion kWh (2006 est.)

**Electricity - exports:** 0 kWh (2007 est.)
**Electricity - imports:** 0 kWh (2007 est.)
**Oil - production:** 0 bbl/day (2008 est.)
**Oil - consumption:** 57,830 bbl/day (2006 est.)
**Oil - exports:** 0 bbl/day (2005)
**Oil - imports:** 55,970 bbl/day (2005)
**Oil - proved reserves:** NA bbl
**Natural gas - production:** 0 cu m (2007 est.)
**Natural gas - consumption:** 0 cu m (2007 est.)
**Natural gas - exports:** 0 cu m (2007 est.)
**Natural gas - imports:** 0 cu m (2007 est.)
**Natural gas - proved reserves:** 0 cu m (1 January 2006)

**Current account balance:** -$2.609 billion (2008 est.)

**Exports:** $1.53 billion f.o.b. (2008 est.)

**Exports - commodities:** citrus, potatoes, pharmaceuticals, cement, and clothing

**Exports - partners:** Greece 21.1%, UK 14.3%, Germany 6.6% (2007)

**Imports:** $8.689 billion f.o.b. (2008 est.)

**Imports - commodities:** consumer goods, petroleum and lubricants, intermediate goods, machinery, transport equipment

**Imports - partners:** Greece 17.7%, Italy 10.2%, UK 9.6%, Germany 9.4%, Israel 6.5%, France 5.4%, China 5.3%, Netherlands 4.1% (2007)

**Reserves of foreign exchange and gold:** $1.476 billion (31 December 2008 est.)

**Debt - external:** $28.84 billion (31 December 2008 est.)

**Stock of direct foreign investment - at home:** $15.04 billion (2008 est.)

**Stock of direct foreign investment - abroad:** $6.403 billion (2008 est.)

**Exchange rates:** euros (EUR) per US dollar - 0.6827 (2008 est.), Cypriot pounds (CYP) per US dollar - 0.4286 (2007), 0.4586 (2006), 0.4641 (2005), 0.4686 (2004)

**Economy of the area administered by Turkish Cypriots:**
*Economy - overview:* The Turkish Cypriot economy has roughly 40% of the per capita GDP of the south, and economic growth tends to be volatile, given the north's relative isolation, bloated public sector, reliance on the Turkish lira, and small market size. Agriculture and services, together, employ more than half of the work force. The Turkish Cypriot economy grew around 10.6% in 2006, fueled by growth in the construction and education sectors, as well as increased employment of Turkish Cypriots in the area under government control. GDP declined about 2.0% in 2007. The Turkish Cypriots are heavily dependent on transfers from the Turkish Government. Ankara directly finances about one-third of the "TRNC's" budget. Aid from Turkey has exceeded $400 million annually in recent years. The Turkish Cypriot economy probably will experience a sharp slowdown in 2008-2009 due to the global financial crisis, because the Turkish Cypriot financial sector is dominated by mainland Turkish banks, and because of its reliance on British and Turkish tourism, which has declined due to the recession.
*GDP (purchasing power parity):* $1.829 billion (2007 est.)
*GDP - real growth rate:* -2% (2007 est.)
*GDP - per capita:* $11,700 (2007 est.)
*GDP - composition by sector:* agriculture: 8.6%, industry: 22.5%, services: 69.1% (2006 est.)
*Labor force:* 95,030 (2007 est.)
*Labor force - by occupation:* agriculture: 14.5%, industry: 29%, services: 56.5% (2004)
*Unemployment rate:* 9.4% (2005 est.)
*Population below poverty line:* %NA
*Inflation rate:* 11.4% (2006)
*Budget:* revenues: $2.5 billion, expenditures: $2.5 billion (2006)
*Agriculture - products:* citrus fruit, dairy, potatoes, grapes, olives, poultry, lamb
*Industries:* foodstuffs, textiles, clothing, ship repair, clay, gypsum, copper, furniture
*Industrial production growth rate:* -0.3% (2007 est.)
*Electricity production:* 998.9 million kWh (2005)
*Electricity consumption:* 797.9 million kWh (2005)
*Exports:* $68.1 million, f.o.b. (2007 est.)
*Export - commodities:* citrus, dairy, potatoes, textiles
*Export - partners:* Turkey 40%; direct trade between the area administered by Turkish Cypriots and the area under government control remains limited
*Imports:* $1.2 billion, f.o.b. (2007 est.)
*Import - commodities:* vehicles, fuel, cigarettes, food, minerals, chemicals, machinery
*Import - partners:* Turkey 60%; direct trade between the area administered by Turkish Cypriots and the area under government control remains limited
*Reserves of foreign exchange and gold:* $NA
*Debt - external:* $NA
*Currency (code):* Turkish new lira (YTL)
*Exchange rates:* Turkish new lira per US dollar: 1.319 (2007) 1.4286 (2006) 1.3436 (2005) 1.4255 (2004) 1.5009 (2003)

## Communications

**Telephones - main lines in use:** area under government control: 376,000 (2007); area administered by Turkish Cypriots: 86,228 (2002)
**Telephones - mobile cellular:** area under government control: 962,200 (2007); area administered by Turkish Cypriots: 147,522 (2002)

**Telephone system:**
*general assessment:* excellent in both area under government control and area administered by Turkish Cypriots
*domestic:* open-wire, fiber-optic cable, and microwave radio relay
*international:* country code - 357 (area administered by Turkish Cypriots uses the country code of Turkey - 90); a number of submarine cables, including the SEA-ME-WE-3, combine to provide connectivity to Western Europe, the Middle East, and Asia; tropospheric scatter; satellite earth stations - 8 (3 Intelsat - 1 Atlantic Ocean and 2 Indian Ocean, 2 Eutelsat, 2 Intersputnik, and 1 Arabsat)

**Radio broadcast stations:**
*area under government control:* AM 5, FM 76, shortwave 0
*area administered by Turkish Cypriots:* AM 1, FM 20, shortwave 1 (2004)

**Television broadcast stations:**
*area under government control:* 8
*area administered by Turkish Cypriots:* 2 (plus 4 relay) (2004)

**Internet country code:** .cy
**Internet hosts:** 143,099 (2008)
**Internet users:** 380,000 (2007)

## Transportation

**Airports:** 16 (2008)
**Airports - with paved runways:**
*total:* 13
*2,438 to 3,047 m:* 6
*1,524 to 2,437 m:* 3
*914 to 1,523 m:* 3
*under 914 m:* 1 (2008)
**Airports - with unpaved runways:**
*total:* 3
*1,524 to 2,437 m:* 1
*under 914 m:* 2 (2008)
**Heliports:** 10 (2007)
**Roadways:**
*total:* 14,630 km (area under government control: 12,280 km; area administered by Turkish Cypriots: 2,350 km)
*paved:* area under government control: 7,979 km (includes 257 km of expressways); area administered by Turkish Cypriots: 1,370 km
*unpaved:* area under government control: 4,301 km; area administered by Turkish Cypriots: 980 km (2006)
**Merchant marine:**
*total:* 858
*by type:* bulk carrier 295, cargo 182, chemical tanker 63, container 193, liquefied gas 10, passenger 5, passenger/cargo 24, petroleum tanker 58, refrigerated cargo 10, roll on/roll off 12, specialized tanker 1, vehicle carrier 5
*foreign-owned:* 690 (Austria 1, Belgium 2, Canada 2, Chile 1, China 10, Cuba 1, Denmark 4, Estonia 5, Germany 189, Greece 259, Hong Kong 2, India 2, Iran 10, Ireland 3, Israel 4, Italy 7, Japan 21, South Korea 1, Latvia 1, Lebanon 1, Netherlands 22, Norway 18,

# Cyprus (continued)

Philippines 1, Poland 18, Portugal 1, Russia 50, Singapore 3, Slovenia 4, Spain 6, Sweden 2, Syria 2, Ukraine 4, UAE 9, UK 19, US 5)
*registered in other countries:* 256 (Antigua and Barbuda 18, Bahamas 25, Belize 1, Burma 1, Cambodia 7, Comoros 1, Georgia 1, Germany 2, Gibraltar 1, Greece 7, Liberia 63, Malta 31, Marshall Islands 37, Netherlands 8, Netherlands Antilles 21, Panama 19, Poland 1, Russia 2, Saint Kitts and Nevis 1, Saint Vincent and the Grenadines 1, Samoa 1, Singapore 1, Tonga 1, Turkey 2, UK 2, unknown 1) (2008)
**Ports and terminals:** area under government control: Larnaca, Limassol, Vasilikos; area administered by Turkish Cypriots: Famagusta, Kyrenia

## Military

**Military branches:** Republic of Cyprus: Greek Cypriot National Guard (Ethniki Forea, EF; includes naval and air elements); northern Cyprus: Turkish Cypriot Security Force (GKK) (2009)
**Military service age and obligation:** Greek Cypriot National Guard (GCNG): 18-50 years of age for compulsory military service for all Greek Cypriot males; 17 years of age for voluntary service; women may volunteer for a 3-year term; length of normal service is 25 months (2009)
**Manpower available for military service:**
*Greek Cypriot National Guard (GCNG): males age 16-49:* 199,767
*females age 16-49:* 190,665 (2008 est.)
**Manpower fit for military service:**
*Greek Cypriot National Guard (GCNG): males age 16-49:* 165,615
*females age 16-49:* 159,362 (2009 est.)
**Manpower reaching militarily significant age annually:**
*male:* 6,241
*female:* 5,979 (2009 est.)
**Military expenditures:** 3.8% of GDP (2005 est.)

## Transnational Issues

**Disputes - international:** hostilities in 1974 divided the island into two de facto autonomous entities, the internationally recognized Cypriot Government and a Turkish-Cypriot community (north Cyprus); the 1,000-strong UN Peacekeeping Force in Cyprus (UNFICYP) has served in Cyprus since 1964 and maintains the buffer zone between north and south; on 1 May 2004, Cyprus entered the European Union still divided, with the EU's body of legislation and standards (acquis communitaire) suspended in the north; Turkey protests Cypriot Government creating hydrocarbon blocks and maritime boundary with Lebanon in March 2007
**Refugees and internally displaced persons:**
*IDPs:* 210,000 (both Turkish and Greek Cypriots; many displaced for over 30 years) (2007)

**Trafficking in persons:**
*current situation:* Cyprus is primarily a destination country for a large number of women trafficked from Eastern and Central Europe, the Philippines, and the Dominican Republic for the purpose of sexual exploitation; traffickers continued to fraudulently recruit victims for work as dancers in cabarets and nightclubs on short-term "artiste" visas, for work in pubs and bars on employment visas, or for illegal work on tourist or student visas
*tier rating:* Tier 2 Watch List - Cyprus is on the Tier 2 Watch List for a third consecutive year for failure to show evidence of increasing efforts to combat human trafficking during 2007; although Cyprus passed a new trafficking law and opened a government trafficking shelter, these efforts are outweighed by its failure to show tangible and critically needed progress in the areas of law enforcement, victim protection, and the prevention of trafficking (2008)
**Illicit drugs:** minor transit point for heroin and hashish via air routes and container traffic to Europe, especially from Lebanon and Turkey; some cocaine transits as well; despite a strengthening of anti-money-laundering legislation, remains vulnerable to money laundering; reporting of suspicious transactions in offshore sector remains weak (2008)

# Czech Republic

## Introduction

**Background:** Following the First World War, the closely related Czechs and Slovaks of the former Austro-Hungarian Empire merged to form Czechoslovakia. During the interwar years, the new country's leaders were frequently preoccupied with meeting the demands of other ethnic minorities within the republic, most notably the Sudeten Germans and the Ruthenians (Ukrainians). After World War II, a truncated Czechoslovakia fell within the Soviet sphere of influence. In 1968, an invasion by Warsaw Pact troops ended the efforts of the country's leaders to liberalize Communist party rule and create "socialism with a human face." Anti-Soviet demonstrations the following year ushered in a period of harsh repression. With the collapse of Soviet authority in 1989, Czechoslovakia regained its freedom through a peaceful "Velvet Revolution." On 1 January 1993, the country underwent a "velvet divorce" into its two national components, the Czech Republic and Slovakia. The Czech Republic joined NATO in 1999 and the European Union in 2004.

## Geography

**Location:** Central Europe, between Germany, Poland, Slovikia, and Austria
**Geographic coordinates:** 49 45 N, 15 30 E
**Map references:** Europe
**Area:**
*total:* 78,866 sq km
*land:* 77,276 sq km
*water:* 1,590 sq km
**Area - comparative:** slightly smaller than South Carolina
**Land boundaries:**
*total:* 1,989 km
*border countries:* Austria 362 km, Germany 815 km, Poland 615 km, Slovakia 197 km
**Coastline:** 0 km (landlocked)
**Maritime claims:** none (landlocked)

# Czech Republic (continued)

**Climate:** temperate; cool summers; cold, cloudy, humid winters

**Terrain:** Bohemia in the west consists of rolling plains, hills, and plateaus surrounded by low mountains; Moravia in the east consists of very hilly country

**Elevation extremes:**
*lowest point:* Elbe River 115 m
*highest point:* Snezka 1,602 m

**Natural resources:** hard coal, soft coal, kaolin, clay, graphite, timber

**Land use:**
*arable land:* 38.82%
*permanent crops:* 3%
*other:* 58.18% (2005)

**Irrigated land:** 240 sq km (2003)

**Total renewable water resources:** 16 cu km (2005)

**Freshwater withdrawal (domestic/industrial/agricultural):**
*total:* 1.91 cu km/yr (41%/57%/2%)
*per capita:* 187 cu m/yr (2002)

**Natural hazards:** flooding

**Environment - current issues:** air and water pollution in areas of northwest Bohemia and in northern Moravia around Ostrava present health risks; acid rain damaging forests; efforts to bring industry up to EU code should improve domestic pollution

**Environment - international agreements:**
*party to:* Air Pollution, Air Pollution-Nitrogen Oxides, Air Pollution-Persistent Organic Pollutants, Air Pollution-Sulfur 85, Air Pollution-Sulfur 94, Air Pollution-Volatile Organic Compounds, Antarctic-Environmental Protocol, Antarctic Treaty, Biodiversity, Climate Change, Climate Change-Kyoto Protocol, Desertification, Endangered Species, Environmental Modification, Hazardous Wastes, Law of the Sea, Ozone Layer Protection, Ship Pollution, Wetlands, Whaling
*signed, but not ratified:* none of the selected agreements

**Geography - note:** landlocked; strategically located astride some of oldest and most significant land routes in Europe; Moravian Gate is a traditional military corridor between the North European Plain and the Danube in central Europe

## People

**Population:** 10,211,904 (July 2009 est.)

**Age structure:**
*0-14 years:* 13.6% (male 712,045/female 673,657)
*15-64 years:* 71% (male 3,641,887/female 3,604,044)
*65 years and over:* 15.5% (male 623,882/female 956,389) (2009 est.)

**Median age:**
*total:* 40.1 years
*male:* 38.6 years
*female:* 41.9 years (2009 est.)

**Population growth rate:** -0.094% (2009 est.)

**Birth rate:** 8.83 births/1,000 population (2009 est.)

**Death rate:** 10.69 deaths/1,000 population (2008 est.)

**Net migration rate:** 0.97 migrant(s)/1,000 population (2009 est.)

**Urbanization:**
*urban population:* 73% of total population (2008)
*rate of urbanization:* 0% annual rate of change (2005-10 est.)

**Sex ratio:**
*at birth:* 1.06 male(s)/female
*under 15 years:* 1.06 male(s)/female
*15-64 years:* 1.01 male(s)/female
*65 years and over:* 0.65 male(s)/female
*total population:* 0.95 male(s)/female (2009 est.)

**Infant mortality rate:**
*total:* 3.79 deaths/1,000 live births
*male:* 4.13 deaths/1,000 live births
*female:* 3.43 deaths/1,000 live births (2009 est.)

**Life expectancy at birth:**
*total population:* 76.81 years
*male:* 73.54 years
*female:* 80.28 years (2009 est.)

**Total fertility rate:** 1.24 children born/woman (2009 est.)

**HIV/AIDS - adult prevalence rate:** less than 0.1% (2001 est.)

**HIV/AIDS - people living with HIV/AIDS:** 1,500 (2007 est.)

**HIV/AIDS - deaths:** fewer than 10 (2001 est.)

**Nationality:**
*noun:* Czech(s)
*adjective:* Czech

**Ethnic groups:** Czech 90.4%, Moravian 3.7%, Slovak 1.9%, other 4% (2001 census)

**Religions:** Roman Catholic 26.8%, Protestant 2.1%, other 3.3%, unspecified 8.8%, unaffiliated 59% (2001 census)

**Languages:** Czech 94.9%, Slovak 2%, other 2.3%, unidentified 0.8% (2001 census)

**Literacy:**
*definition:* NA
*total population:* 99%
*male:* 99%
*female:* 99% (2003 est.)

**School life expectancy (primary to tertiary education):**
*total:* 15 years
*male:* 15 years
*female:* 15 years (2006)

**Education expenditures:** 4.4% of GDP (2004)

## Government

**Country name:**
*conventional long form:* Czech Republic
*conventional short form:* Czech Republic
*local long form:* Ceska Republika
*local short form:* Cesko

**Government type:** parliamentary democracy

**Capital:**
*name:* Prague
*geographic coordinates:* 50 05 N, 14 28 E
*time difference:* UTC+1 (6 hours ahead of Washington, DC during Standard Time)
*daylight saving time:* +1hr, begins last Sunday in March; ends last Sunday in October

**Administrative divisions:** 13 regions (kraje, singular - kraj) and 1 capital city* (hlavni mesto); Jihocesky (South Bohemia), Jihomoravsky (South Moravia), Karlovarsky, Kralovehradecky, Liberecky, Moravskoslezsky (Moravia-Silesia), Olomoucky, Pardubicky, Plzensky (Pilsen), Praha (Prague)*, Stredocesky (Central Bohemia), Ustecky, Vysocina, Zlinsky

**Independence:** 1 January 1993 (Czechoslovakia split into the Czech Republic and Slovakia)

**National holiday:** Czech Founding Day, 28 October (1918)

**Constitution:** ratified 16 December 1992, effective 1 January 1993; amended 1997, 2000, 2001 (twice), 2002

**Legal system:** civil law system based on Austro-Hungarian codes; legal code modified to bring it in line with Organization on Security and Cooperation in Europe (OSCE) obligations and to expunge Marxist-Leninist legal theory

**Suffrage:** 18 years of age; universal

**Executive branch:**
*chief of state:* President Vaclav KLAUS (since 7 March 2003)
*head of government:* Prime Minister Jan FISCHER (since 9 April 2009); Deputy Prime Ministers Petr NECAS (since 9 January 2007), Martin BURSIK (since 9 January 2007), and Vlasta PARKANOVA (since 23 January 2008)
*cabinet:* Cabinet appointed by the president on the recommendation of the prime minister
*elections:* president elected by Parliament for a five-year term (eligible for a second term); last successful election held 15 February 2008 (after earlier elections held 8 and 9 February 2008 were inconclusive; next election to be held in 2013); prime minister appointed by the president
*election results:* Vaclav KLAUS reelected president on 15 February 2008; Vaclav KLAUS 141 votes, Jan SVEJNAR 111 votes (third round; combined votes of both chambers of parliament)

**Legislative branch:** bicameral Parliament or Parlament consists of the Senate or Senat (81 seats; members are elected by popular vote to serve six-year terms; one-third elected every two years) and the Chamber of Deputies or Poslanecka Snemovna (200 seats; members are elected by popular vote to serve four-year terms)
*elections:* Senate - last held in two rounds 17-18 and 24-25 October 2008 (next to be held by October 2010); Chamber of Deputies - last held 2-3 June 2006 (next to be held by June 2010)
*election results:* Senate - percent of vote by party - NA; seats by party - ODS 36, CSSD 29, KDU-CSL 7, Open Democracy Club 6, others 3; Chamber of Deputies - percent of vote by party - ODS 35.4%, CSSD 32.3%, KSCM 12.8%, KDU-CSL 7.2%, Greens 6.3%, other 6%; seats by party - ODS 81, CSSD 74, KSCM 26, KDU-CSL 13, Greens 6; note - seats by party as of December 2008 - ODS 79, CSSD 71, KSCM 26, KDU-CSL 13, Greens 4, unaffiliated 7 (former CSSD, ODS, and Green Party members)

# Czech Republic (continued)

**Judicial branch:** Supreme Court; Constitutional Court; chairman and deputy chairmen are appointed by the president for a 10-year term

**Political parties and leaders:** Association of Independent Candidates-European Democrats or SNK-ED [Helmut DOHNALEK]; Christian Democratic Union-Czechoslovak People's Party or KDU-CSL [Jiri CUNEK]; Civic Democratic Party or ODS [Mirek TOPOLANEK]; Communist Party of Bohemia and Moravia or KSCM [Vojtech FILIP]; Czech Social Democratic Party or CSSD [Jiri PAROUBEK]; Free Citizens' Party or SSO [Petr MACH]; Green Party [Martin BURSIK]; Independent Democrats (NEZDEM) [Vladimir ZELEZNY]; Party of Open Society (SOS) [Pavel NOVACEK]; Path of Change [Jiri LOBKOWITZ]; Union of Freedom-Democratic Union or US-DEU [Jan CERNY]

**Political pressure groups and leaders:** Czech-Moravian Confederation of Trade Unions or CMKOS [Milan STECH]

**International organization participation:** ACCT (observer), Australia Group, BIS, BSEC (observer), CE, CEI, CERN, EAPC, EBRD, EIB, ESA (cooperating state), EU, FAO, IAEA, IBRD, ICAO, ICC, ICCt (signatory), ICRM, IDA, IEA, IFC, IFRCS, ILO, IMF, IMO, IMSO, Interpol, IOC, IOM, IPU, ISO, ITSO, ITU, ITUC, MIGA, MONUC, NAM (guest), NATO, NEA, NSG, OAS (observer), OECD, OIF (observer), OPCW, OSCE, PCA, Schengen Convention, UN, UNCTAD, UNESCO, UNIDO, UNMIL, UNOMIG, UNWTO, UPU, WCL, WCO, WEU (associate), WFTU, WHO, WIPO, WMO, WTO, ZC

**Diplomatic representation in the US:**
*chief of mission:* Ambassador Petr KOLAR
*chancery:* 3900 Spring of Freedom Street NW, Washington, DC 20008
*telephone:* [1] (202) 274-9100
*FAX:* [1] (202) 966-8540
*consulate(s) general:* Chicago, Los Angeles, New York

**Diplomatic representation from the US:**
*chief of mission:* Ambassador Richard W. GRABER
*embassy:* Trziste 15, 118 01 Prague 1
*mailing address:* use embassy street address
*telephone:* [420] 257 022 000
*FAX:* [420] 257 022 809

**Flag description:** two equal horizontal bands of white (top) and red with a blue isosceles triangle based on the hoist side
*note:* identical to the flag of the former Czechoslovakia

## Economy

**Economy - overview:** The Czech Republic is one of the most stable and prosperous of the post-Communist states of Central and Eastern Europe. Maintaining an open investment climate has been a key element of the Czech Republic's transition from a communist, centrally planned economy to a functioning market economy. As a member of the European Union, with an advantageous location in the center of Europe, a relatively low cost structure, and a well-qualified labor force, the Czech Republic is an attractive destination for foreign investment. Prior to its EU accession in 2004, the Czech government harmonized its laws and regulations with those of the European Union. The government plans to meet the criteria for joining the euro area around 2012. The small, open, export-driven Czech economy grew by over 6% annually from 2005-2007 and the strong growth continued throughout the first three quarters of 2008. Despite the global financial crisis, the conservative Czech financial system has remained relatively healthy. The rate of Czech economic growth, however, began to fall in the fourth quarter of 2008, mainly due to a significant drop in demand for Czech exports in Western Europe. This trend is expected to continue, with many analysts predicting the Czech economy to contract slightly in 2009.

**GDP (purchasing power parity):**
$266.3 billion (2008 est.)
$257.3 billion (2007)
$242.7 billion (2006)
*note:* data are in 2008 US dollars

**GDP (official exchange rate):** $217.2 billion (2008 est.)

**GDP - real growth rate:**
3.9% (2008 est.)
6% (2007 est.)
6.8% (2006 est.)

**GDP - per capita (PPP):**
$26,100 (2008 est.)
$25,200 (2007 est.)
$23,700 (2006 est.)
*note:* data are in 2008 US dollars

**GDP - composition by sector:**
*agriculture:* 2.6%
*industry:* 38.7%
*services:* 58.7% (2008 est.)

**Labor force:** 5.37 million (2008 est.)

**Labor force - by occupation:**
*agriculture:* 3.6%
*industry:* 40.2%
*services:* 56.2% (2007)

**Unemployment rate:**
6% (2008)
6.6% (2007 est.)

**Population below poverty line:** NA%

**Household income or consumption by percentage share:**
*lowest 10%:* 4.3%
*highest 10%:* 22.4% (1996)

**Distribution of family income - Gini index:** 26 (2005)

**Investment (gross fixed):** 27.8% of GDP (2008 est.)

**Budget:**
*revenues:* $94.96 billion
*expenditures:* $99.46 billion (2008 est.)

**Public debt:** 29.4% of GDP (2008 est.)

**Inflation rate (consumer prices):**
3.6% (2008)
2.9% (2007 est.)

**Central bank discount rate:** 1.25% (31 December 2008)

**Commercial bank prime lending rate:** 5.79% (31 December 2007)

**Stock of money:** $84.43 billion (31 December 2007)

**Stock of quasi money:** $58.77 billion (31 December 2007)

**Stock of domestic credit:** $103.9 billion (31 December 2007)

**Market value of publicly traded shares:** $73.42 billion (31 December 2007)

**Agriculture - products:** wheat, potatoes, sugar beets, hops, fruit; pigs, poultry

**Industries:** motor vehicles, metallurgy, machinery and equipment, glass, armaments

**Industrial production growth rate:** 7% (2008 est.)

**Electricity - production:** 82.88 billion kWh (2007 est.)

**Electricity - consumption:** 61.52 billion kWh (2006 est.)

**Electricity - exports:** 26.36 billion kWh (2007 est.)

**Electricity - imports:** 10.2 billion kWh (2007 est.)

**Oil - production:** 13,530 bbl/day (2007 est.)

**Oil - consumption:** 207,400 bbl/day (2007 est.)

**Oil - exports:** 27,360 bbl/day (2005)

**Oil - imports:** 224,600 bbl/day (2005)

**Oil - proved reserves:** 15 million bbl (1 January 2008 est.)

**Natural gas - production:** 172 million cu m (2007 est.)

**Natural gas - consumption:** 8.622 billion cu m (2007 est.)

**Natural gas - exports:** 402 million cu m (2007 est.)

**Natural gas - imports:** 8.628 billion cu m (2007 est.)

**Natural gas - proved reserves:** 3.964 billion cu m (1 January 2008 est.)

**Current account balance:** -$6.46 billion (2008 est.)

**Exports:** $145.8 billion f.o.b. (2008 est.)

**Exports - commodities:** machinery and transport equipment 52%, raw materials and fuel 9%, chemicals 5% (2003)

**Exports - partners:** Germany 30.7%, Slovakia 8.7%, Poland 5.9%, France 5.4%, UK 5.1%, Italy 4.9%, Austria 4.6% (2007)

**Imports:** $141.4 billion f.o.b. (2008 est.)

**Imports - commodities:** machinery and transport equipment 46%, raw materials and fuels 15%, chemicals 10% (2003)

**Imports - partners:** Germany 31.8%, Netherlands 6.7%, Slovakia 6.4%, Poland 6.3%, Austria 5.1%, China 5.1%, Russia 4.5%, Italy 4.4%, France 4.1% (2007)

**Reserves of foreign exchange and gold:** $37 billion (31 December 2008)

**Debt - external:** $88.74 billion (31 December 2008 est.)

**Stock of direct foreign investment - at home:** $107.6 billion (2008 est.)

**Stock of direct foreign investment - abroad:** $7.721 billion (2008 est.)

# Czech Republic *(continued)*

**Exchange rates:** koruny (CZK) per US dollar - 17.064 (2008), 20.53 (2007), 22.596 (2006), 23.957 (2005), 25.7 (2004)

## Communications

**Telephones - main lines in use:** 2.888 million (2006)

**Telephones - mobile cellular:** 13.075 million (2007)

**Telephone system:**

*general assessment:* privatization and modernization of the Czech telecommunication system got a late start but is advancing steadily; access to the fixed-line telephone network expanded throughout the 1990s but the number of fixed line connections has been dropping since then; mobile telephone usage increased sharply beginning in the mid-1990s and the number of cellular telephone subscriptions now greatly exceeds the population

*domestic:* virtually all exchanges now digital; existing copper subscriber systems enhanced with Asymmetric Digital Subscriber Line (ADSL) equipment to accommodate Internet and other digital signals; trunk systems include fiber-optic cable and microwave radio relay

*international:* country code - 420; satellite earth stations - 6 (2 Intersputnik - Atlantic and Indian Ocean regions, 1 Intelsat, 1 Eutelsat, 1 Inmarsat, 1 Globalstar) (2007)

**Radio broadcast stations:** AM 31, FM 304, shortwave 17 (2000)

**Television broadcast stations:** 71 (2008)

**Internet country code:** .cz

**Internet hosts:** 2.434 million (2008)

**Internet users:** 4.4 million (2007)

## Transportation

**Airports:** 122 (2008)

**Airports - with paved runways:**
*total:* 45
*over 3,047 m:* 2
*2,438 to 3,047 m:* 10
*1,524 to 2,437 m:* 13
*914 to 1,523 m:* 2
*under 914 m:* 18 (2008)

**Airports - with unpaved runways:**
*total:* 77
*1,524 to 2,437 m:* 1
*914 to 1,523 m:* 26
*under 914 m:* 50 (2008)

**Heliports:** 1 (2007)

**Pipelines:** gas 7,010 km; oil 547 km; refined products 94 km (2008)

**Railways:**
*total:* 9,597 km
*standard gauge:* 9,597 km 1.435-m gauge (3,041 km electrified) (2006)

**Roadways:**
*total:* 128,512 km
*paved:* 128,512 km (includes 657 km of expressways) (2007)

**Waterways:** 664 km (principally on Elbe, Vltava, Oder, and other navigable rivers, lakes, and canals) (2008)

**Merchant marine:**
*registered in other countries:* 1 (Saint Vincent and the Grenadines 1) (2008)
**Ports and terminals:** Decin, Prague, Usti nad Labem

## Military

**Military branches:** Army of the Czech Republic (ACR): Joint Forces Command (includes Land Forces and Air Forces), Support and Training Forces Command (2009)

**Military service age and obligation:** 18-28 years of age for voluntary and 19-28 for compulsory military service (2008)

**Manpower available for military service:**
*males age 16-49:* 2,522,383
*females age 16-49:* 2,425,095 (2008 est.)

**Manpower fit for military service:**
*males age 16-49:* 2,095,038
*females age 16-49:* 2,011,531 (2009 est.)

**Manpower reaching militarily significant age annually:**
*male:* 60,150
*female:* 57,157 (2009 est.)

**Military expenditures:** 1.46% of GDP (2007 est.)

## Transnational Issues

**Disputes - international:** while threats of international legal action never materialized in 2007, 915,220 Austrians, with the support of the popular Freedom Party, signed a petition in January 2008, demanding that Austria block the Czech Republic's accession to the EU unless Prague closes its controversial Soviet-style nuclear plant in Temelin, bordering Austria

**Illicit drugs:** transshipment point for Southwest Asian heroin and minor transit point for Latin American cocaine to Western Europe; producer of synthetic drugs for local and regional markets; susceptible to money laundering related to drug trafficking, organized crime; significant consumer of ecstasy (2008)

# Denmark

## Introduction

**Background:** Once the seat of Viking raiders and later a major north European power, Denmark has evolved into a modern, prosperous nation that is participating in the general political and economic integration of Europe. It joined NATO in 1949 and the EEC (now the EU) in 1973. However, the country has opted out of certain elements of the European Union's Maastricht Treaty, including the European Economic and Monetary Union (EMU), European defense cooperation, and issues concerning certain justice and home affairs.

## Geography

**Location:** Northern Europe, bordering the Baltic Sea and the North Sea, on a peninsula north of Germany (Jutland); also includes two major islands (Sjaelland and Fyn)

**Geographic coordinates:** 56 00 N, 10 00 E

**Map references:** Europe

**Area:**
*total:* 43,094 sq km
*land:* 42,394 sq km
*water:* 700 sq km
*note:* includes the island of Bornholm in the Baltic Sea and the rest of metropolitan Denmark (the Jutland Peninsula, and the major islands of Sjaelland and Fyn), but excludes the Faroe Islands and Greenland

**Area - comparative:** slightly less than twice the size of Massachusetts

**Land boundaries:**
*total:* 68 km
*border countries:* Germany 68 km

**Coastline:** 7,314 km

**Maritime claims:**
*territorial sea:* 12 nm
*contiguous zone:* 24 nm
*exclusive economic zone:* 200 nm
*continental shelf:* 200 m depth or to the depth of exploitation

# Denmark (continued)

**Climate:** temperate; humid and overcast; mild, windy winters and cool summers

**Terrain:** low and flat to gently rolling plains

**Elevation extremes:**
*lowest point:* Lammefjord -7 m
*highest point:* Yding Skovhoej 173 m

**Natural resources:** petroleum, natural gas, fish, salt, limestone, chalk, stone, gravel and sand

**Land use:**
*arable land:* 52.59%
*permanent crops:* 0.19%
*other:* 47.22% (2005)

**Irrigated land:** 4,490 sq km (2003)

**Total renewable water resources:** 6.1 cu km (2003)

**Freshwater withdrawal (domestic/industrial/agricultural):**
*total:* 0.67 cu km/yr (32%/26%/42%)
*per capita:* 123 cu m/yr (2002)

**Natural hazards:** flooding is a threat in some areas of the country (e.g., parts of Jutland, along the southern coast of the island of Lolland) that are protected from the sea by a system of dikes

**Environment - current issues:** air pollution, principally from vehicle and power plant emissions; nitrogen and phosphorus pollution of the North Sea; drinking and surface water becoming polluted from animal wastes and pesticides

**Environment - international agreements:**
*party to:* Air Pollution, Air Pollution-Nitrogen Oxides, Air Pollution-Persistent Organic Pollutants, Air Pollution-Sulfur 85, Air Pollution-Sulfur 94, Air Pollution-Volatile Organic Compounds, Antarctic Treaty, Biodiversity, Climate Change, Climate Change-Kyoto Protocol, Desertification, Endangered Species, Environmental Modification, Hazardous Wastes, Law of the Sea, Marine Dumping, Marine Life Conservation, Ozone Layer Protection, Ship Pollution, Tropical Timber 83, Tropical Timber 94, Wetlands, Whaling
*signed, but not ratified:* none of the selected agreements

**Geography - note:** controls Danish Straits (Skagerrak and Kattegat) linking Baltic and North Seas; about one-quarter of the population lives in greater Copenhagen

## People

**Population:** 5,500,510 (July 2009 est.)

**Age structure:**
*0-14 years:* 18.1% (male 511,882/female 485,782)
*15-64 years:* 65.8% (male 1,817,800/female 1,798,964)
*65 years and over:* 16.1% (male 387,142/female 498,940) (2009 est.)

**Median age:**
*total:* 40.5 years
*male:* 39.6 years
*female:* 41.3 years (2009 est.)

**Population growth rate:** 0.28% (2009 est.)

**Birth rate:** 10.54 births/1,000 population (2009 est.)

**Death rate:** 10.25 deaths/1,000 population (2008 est.)

**Net migration rate:** 2.48 migrant(s)/1,000 population (2009 est.)

**Urbanization:**
*urban population:* 87% of total population (2008)
*rate of urbanization:* 0.5% annual rate of change (2005-10 est.)

**Sex ratio:**
*at birth:* 1.06 male(s)/female
*under 15 years:* 1.05 male(s)/female
*15-64 years:* 1.01 male(s)/female
*65 years and over:* 0.78 male(s)/female
*total population:* 0.98 male(s)/female (2009 est.)

**Infant mortality rate:**
*total:* 4.34 deaths/1,000 live births
*male:* 4.39 deaths/1,000 live births
*female:* 4.29 deaths/1,000 live births (2009 est.)

**Life expectancy at birth:**
*total population:* 78.3 years
*male:* 75.96 years
*female:* 80.78 years (2009 est.)

**Total fertility rate:** 1.74 children born/woman (2009 est.)

**HIV/AIDS - adult prevalence rate:** 0.2% (2007 est.)

**HIV/AIDS - people living with HIV/AIDS:** 4,800 (2007 est.)

**HIV/AIDS - deaths:** fewer than 100 (2003 est.)

**Nationality:**
*noun:* Dane(s)
*adjective:* Danish

**Ethnic groups:** Scandinavian, Inuit, Faroese, German, Turkish, Iranian, Somali

**Religions:** Evangelical Lutheran 95%, other Christian (includes Protestant and Roman Catholic) 3%, Muslim 2%

**Languages:** Danish, Faroese, Greenlandic (an Inuit dialect), German (small minority)
*note:* English is the predominant second language

**Literacy:**
*definition:* age 15 and over can read and write
*total population:* 99%
*male:* 99%
*female:* 99% (2003 est.)

**School life expectancy (primary to tertiary education):**
*total:* 17 years
*male:* 16 years
*female:* 17 years (2006)

**Education expenditures:** 8.3% of GDP (2005)

## Government

**Country name:**
*conventional long form:* Kingdom of Denmark
*conventional short form:* Denmark
*local long form:* Kongeriget Danmark
*local short form:* Danmark

**Government type:** constitutional monarchy

**Capital:**
*name:* Copenhagen
*geographic coordinates:* 55 40 N, 12 35 E
*time difference:* UTC+1 (6 hours ahead of Washington, DC during Standard Time)
*daylight saving time:* +1hr, begins last Sunday in March; ends last Sunday in October
*note:* applies to continental Denmark only, not to its North Atlantic components

**Administrative divisions:** metropolitan Denmark - 5 regions (regioner, singular - region); Hovedstaden, Midtjylland, Nordjylland, Sjaelland, Syddanmark
*note:* an extensive local government reform merged 271 municipalities into 98 and 13 counties into five regions, effective 1 January 2007

**Independence:** first organized as a unified state in 10th century; in 1849 became a constitutional monarchy

**National holiday:** none designated; Constitution Day, 5 June (1849) is generally viewed as the National Day

**Constitution:** 5 June 1953; note - constitution allowed for a unicameral legislature and a female chief of state

**Legal system:** civil law system; judicial review of legislative acts; accepts compulsory ICJ jurisdiction with reservations

**Suffrage:** 18 years of age; universal

**Executive branch:**
*chief of state:* Queen MARGRETHE II (since 14 January 1972); Heir Apparent Crown Prince FREDERIK, elder son of the monarch (born 26 May 1968)
*head of government:* Prime Minister Lars Lokke RASMUSSEN (since 5 April 2009)
*cabinet:* Council of State appointed by the monarch
*elections:* the monarch is hereditary; following legislative elections, the leader of the majority party or the leader of the majority coalition is usually appointed prime minister by the monarch

**Legislative branch:** unicameral People's Assembly or Folketing (179 seats, including 2 from Greenland and 2 from the Faroe Islands; members are elected by popular vote on the basis of proportional representation to serve four-year terms unless the Folketing is dissolved earlier)
*elections:* last held 13 November 2007 (next to be held in 2011)
*election results:* percent of vote by party - Liberal Party 26.2%, Social Democrats 25.5%, Danish People's Party 13.9%, Socialist People's Party 13.0%, Conservative People's Party 10.4%, Social Liberal Party 5.1%, New Alliance 2.8%, Red-Green Unity List 2.2%, other 0.9%; seats by party - Liberal Party 46, Social Democrats 45, Danish People's Party 25, Socialist People's Party 23, Conservative People's Party 18, Social Liberal Party 9, New Alliance 5, Red-Green Alliance 4; note - does not include the two seats from Greenland and the two seats from the Faroe Islands

# Denmark (continued)

**Judicial branch:** Supreme Court (judges are appointed for life by the monarch)

**Political parties and leaders:** Christian Democrats [Bjarne Hartung KIRKEGAARD] (was Christian People's Party); Conservative Party [Lene ESPERSEN] (sometimes known as Conservative People's Party); Danish People's Party [Pia KJAERSGAARD]; Liberal Party [Anders Fogh RASMUSSEN]; Liberal Alliance [Naser KHADER](formerly known as New Alliance); Red-Green Unity List (Alliance) [collective leadership] (bloc includes Left Socialist Party, Communist Party of Denmark, Socialist Workers' Party); Social Democratic Party [Helle THORNING-SCHMIDT]; Social Liberal Party [Margrethe VESTAGER]; Socialist People's Party [Villy SOEVNDAL]

**Political pressure groups and leaders:** Danish Free Press Society (freedom of speech); Danish National Socialist Movement or DNSB [Jonni HANSEN] (neo-Nazi organization)
*other:* human rights groups

**International organization participation:** ADB (nonregional member), AfDB (nonregional member), Arctic Council, Australia Group, BIS, CBSS, CE, CERN, EAPC, EBRD, EIB, ESA, EU, FAO, G-9, IADB, IAEA, IBRD, ICAO, ICC, ICCt, ICRM, IDA, IEA, IFAD, IFC, IFRCS, IHO, ILO, IMF, IMO, IMSO, Interpol, IOC, IOM, IPU, ISO, ITSO, ITU, ITUC, MIGA, MONUC, NATO, NC, NEA, NIB, NSG, OAS (observer), OECD, OPCW, OSCE, Paris Club, PCA, Schengen Convention, UN, UNCTAD, UNESCO, UNHCR, UNIDO, UNMIL, UNMIS, UNMOGIP, UNOMIG, UNRWA, UNTSO, UPU, WCO, WEU (observer), WFTU, WHO, WIPO, WMO, WTO, ZC

**Diplomatic representation in the US:**
*chief of mission:* Ambassador Friis Arne PETERSEN
*chancery:* 3200 Whitehaven Street NW, Washington, DC 20008
*telephone:* [1] (202) 234-4300
*FAX:* [1] (202) 328-1470
*consulate(s) general:* Chicago, New York

**Diplomatic representation from the US:**
*chief of mission:* Ambassador James P. CAIN
*embassy:* Dag Hammarskjolds Alle 24, 2100 Copenhagen
*mailing address:* PSC 73, APO AE 09716
*telephone:* [45] 33 41 71 00
*FAX:* [45] 35 43 02 23

**Flag description:** red with a white cross that extends to the edges of the flag; the vertical part of the cross is shifted to the hoist side; the banner is referred to as the Dannebrog (Danish flag)
*note:* the shifted design element was subsequently adopted by the other Nordic countries of Finland, Iceland, Norway, and Sweden

## Economy

**Economy - overview:** This thoroughly modern market economy features high-tech agriculture, up-to-date small-scale and corporate industry, extensive government welfare measures, an equitable distribution of income, comfortable living standards, a stable currency, a stable political system, and high dependence on foreign trade. Unemployment is low and capacity constraints limit growth potential. Denmark is a net exporter of food and energy and enjoys a comfortable balance of payments surplus. The government has been successful in meeting, and even exceeding, the economic convergence criteria for participating in the third phase (a common European currency) of the European Economic and Monetary Union (EMU), but so far Denmark has decided not to join 16 other EU members in the euro. Nonetheless, the Danish krone remains pegged to the euro. Denmark's fiscal position is among the strongest in the EU. Economic growth gained momentum in 2004 and the upturn continued through 2006. After a long consumption-driven upswing, Denmark's economy began slowing in early 2007 with the end of a housing boom. This cyclical slowdown has been exacerbated by the global financial crisis through increased borrowing costs and lower export demand, consumer confidence, and investment. The slowing global economy cut GDP by 0.6% in 2008. A major long-term issue will be the sharp decline in the ratio of workers to retirees.

**GDP (purchasing power parity):**
$204.9 billion (2008 est.)
$206.2 billion (2007)
$202.9 billion (2006)
*note:* data are in 2008 US dollars

**GDP (official exchange rate):** $369.6 billion (2008 est.)

**GDP - real growth rate:**
-0.6% (2008 est.)
1.6% (2007 est.)
3.3% (2006 est.)

**GDP - per capita (PPP):**
$37,400 (2008 est.)
$37,700 (2007 est.)
$37,200 (2006 est.)
*note:* data are in 2008 US dollars

**GDP - composition by sector:**
*agriculture:* 1.4%
*industry:* 25.9%
*services:* 72.7% (2008 est.)

**Labor force:** 2.86 million (2008 est.)

**Labor force - by occupation:**
*agriculture:* 2.9%
*industry:* 23.8%
*services:* 72.7% (2005 est.)

**Unemployment rate:**
2% (2008 est.)
2.8% (2007 est.)

**Population below poverty line:** NA%

**Household income or consumption by percentage share:**
*lowest 10%:* 2%
*highest 10%:* 24% (2000 est.)

**Distribution of family income - Gini index:** 24 (2005)

**Investment (gross fixed):** 22.4% of GDP (2008 est.)

**Budget:**
*revenues:* $192 billion
*expenditures:* $177.6 billion (2008 est.)

**Public debt:** 21.8% of GDP (2008 est.)

**Inflation rate (consumer prices):**
3.5% (2008 est.)
1.7% (2007 est.)

**Central bank discount rate:** 4% (31 December 2007)

**Commercial bank prime lending rate:** NA

**Stock of money:** $148.7 billion (31 December 2007)

**Stock of quasi money:** $81.64 billion (31 December 2007)

**Stock of domestic credit:** $684.7 billion (31 December 2007)

**Market value of publicly traded shares:** $277.7 billion (31 December 2007)

**Agriculture - products:** barley, wheat, potatoes, sugar beets; pork, dairy products; fish

**Industries:** iron, steel, nonferrous metals, chemicals, food processing, machinery and transportation equipment, textiles and clothing, electronics, construction, furniture and other wood products, shipbuilding and refurbishment, windmills, pharmaceuticals, medical equipment

**Industrial production growth rate:** 0.4% (2008 est.)

**Electricity - production:** 36.99 billion kWh (2007 est.)

**Electricity - consumption:** 34.68 billion kWh (2006 est.)

**Electricity - exports:** 11.38 billion kWh (2007 est.)

**Electricity - imports:** 10.43 billion kWh (2007 est.)

**Oil - production:** 313,800 bbl/day (2007 est.)

**Oil - consumption:** 190,600 bbl/day (2007 est.)

**Oil - exports:** 320,000 bbl/day (2006)

**Oil - imports:** 164,000 bbl/day (2006 est.)

**Oil - proved reserves:** 1.188 billion bbl (1 January 2008 est.)

**Natural gas - production:** 9.223 billion cu m (2007 est.)

**Natural gas - consumption:** 4.555 billion cu m (2007 est.)

**Natural gas - exports:** 4.517 billion cu m (2007 est.)

**Natural gas - imports:** 0 cu m (2007 est.)

**Natural gas - proved reserves:** 70.51 billion cu m (1 January 2008 est.)

**Current account balance:** $4.333 billion (2008 est.)

**Exports:** $119.5 billion f.o.b. (2008 est.)

**Exports - commodities:** machinery and instruments, meat and meat products, dairy products, fish, pharmaceuticals, furniture, windmills

**Exports - partners:** Germany 17.4%, Sweden 14.5%, UK 8%, US 6.1%, Norway 5.7%, France 4.8%, Netherlands 4.8% (2007)

**Imports:** $120.7 billion f.o.b. (2008 est.)

**Imports - commodities:** machinery and equipment, raw materials and semimanufactures for industry, chemicals, grain and foodstuffs, consumer goods

**Imports - partners:** Germany 21.6%, Sweden 14.4%, Netherlands 7.1%, Norway 6%, China 5.4%, UK 5.3%, Italy 4.1%, France 4% (2007)

# Denmark *(continued)*

**Reserves of foreign exchange and gold:** $34.32 billion (2006 est.)
**Debt - external:** $492.6 billion (30 June 2007)
**Stock of direct foreign investment - at home:** $133.6 billion (2008 est.)
**Stock of direct foreign investment - abroad:** $163.2 billion (2008 est.)
**Exchange rates:** Danish kroner (DKK) per US dollar -5.0236 (2008 est.), 5.4797 (2007), 5.9468 (2006), 5.9969 (2005), 5.9911 (2004)

## Communications

**Telephones - main lines in use:** 2.824 million (2007)
**Telephones - mobile cellular:** 6.243 million (2007)
**Telephone system:**
*general assessment:* excellent telephone and telegraph services
*domestic:* buried and submarine cables and microwave radio relay form trunk network, 4 cellular mobile communications systems
*international:* country code - 45; a series of fiber-optic submarine cables link Denmark with Canada, Faroe Islands, Germany, Iceland, Netherlands, Norway, Poland, Russia, Sweden, and UK; satellite earth stations - 18 (6 Intelsat, 10 Eutelsat, 1 Orion, 1 Inmarsat (Blaavand-Atlantic-East)); note - the Nordic countries (Denmark, Finland, Iceland, Norway, and Sweden) share the Danish earth station and the Eik, Norway, station for worldwide Inmarsat access
**Radio broadcast stations:** AM 1, FM 355, shortwave 0 (1998)
**Television broadcast stations:** 172 (2008)
**Internet country code:** .dk
**Internet hosts:** 3.642 million (2008)
**Internet users:** 3.5 million (2007)

## Transportation

**Airports:** 92 (2008)
**Airports - with paved runways:**
*total:* 28
*over 3,047 m:* 2
*2,438 to 3,047 m:* 7
*1,524 to 2,437 m:* 4
*914 to 1,523 m:* 12
*under 914 m:* 3 (2008)
**Airports - with unpaved runways:**
*total:* 64
*914 to 1,523 m:* 3
*under 914 m:* 61 (2008)
**Pipelines:** gas 2,858 km; oil 107 km (2008)
**Railways:**
*total:* 2,644 km
*standard gauge:* 2,644 km 1.435-m gauge (636 km electrified) (2007)
**Roadways:**
*total:* 72,362 km
*paved:* 72,362 km (includes 1,032 km of expressways) (2006)
**Waterways:** 400 km (2008)

**Merchant marine:**
*total:* 327
*by type:* bulk carrier 8, cargo 63, carrier 2, chemical tanker 78, container 84, liquefied gas 2, passenger/cargo 42, petroleum tanker 29, refrigerated cargo 7, roll on/roll off 8, specialized tanker 4
*foreign-owned:* 26 (Canada 1, Germany 1, Germany 9, Greece 4, Iceland 2, Norway 3, Sweden 6)
*registered in other countries:* 534 (Antigua and Barbuda 19, Bahamas 67, Belgium 4, Brazil 2, Cayman Islands 3, Cyprus 4, Egypt 1, Estonia 1, France 2, Germany 1, Gibraltar 7, Hong Kong 24, Isle of Man 29, Italy 3, Jamaica 2, Liberia 12, Lithuania 5, Luxembourg 1, Malta 30, Marshall Islands 10, Mexico 2, Netherlands 29, Netherlands Antilles 2, Norway 25, Panama 40, Portugal 3, Saint Vincent and the Grenadines 16, Singapore 87, South Africa 1, Spain 2, Sweden 4, Togo 1, UAE 1, UK 62, US 31, Venezuela 1) (2008)
**Ports and terminals:** Aalborg, Aarhus, Copenhagen, Ensted, Esbjerg, Fredericia, Kalundborg

## Military

**Military branches:** Defense Command: Army Operational Command, Admiral Danish Fleet, Island Command Greenland, Tactical Air Command, Home Guard (2008)
**Military service age and obligation:** 18 years of age for compulsory and voluntary military service; conscripts serve an initial training period that varies from 4 to 12 months according to specialization; reservists are assigned to mobilization units following completion of their conscript service; women eligible to volunteer for military service (2004)
**Manpower available for military service:**
*males age 16-49:* 1,235,067
*females age 16-49:* 1,215,418 (2008 est.)
**Manpower fit for military service:**
*males age 16-49:* 1,013,223
*females age 16-49:* 998,837 (2009 est.)
**Manpower reaching militarily significant age annually:**
*male:* 37,231
*female:* 35,306 (2009 est.)
**Military expenditures:** 1.3% of GDP (2007 est.)

## Transnational Issues

**Disputes - international:** Iceland, the UK, and Ireland dispute Denmark's claim that the Faroe Islands' continental shelf extends beyond 200 nm; Faroese continue to study proposals for full independence; sovereignty dispute with Canada over Hans Island in the Kennedy Channel between Ellesmere Island and Greenland

# Dhekelia
*(UK sovereign base area)*

## Introduction

**Background:** By terms of the 1960 Treaty of Establishment that created the independent Republic of Cyprus, the UK retained full sovereignty and jurisdiction over two areas of almost 254 square kilometers - Akrotiri and Dhekelia. The larger of these is the Dhekelia Sovereign Base Area, which is also referred to as the Eastern Sovereign Base Area.

## Geography

**Location:** Eastern Mediterranean, on the southeast coast of Cyprus near Famagusta
**Geographic coordinates:** 34 59 N, 33 45 E
**Map references:** Middle East
**Area:**
*total:* 130.8 sq km
*note:* area surrounds three Cypriot enclaves
**Area - comparative:** about three-quarters the size of Washington, DC
**Land boundaries:**
*total:* 103 km (approximately)
*border countries:* Cyprus 103 km (approximately)
**Coastline:** 27.5 km
**Climate:** temperate; Mediterranean with hot, dry summers and cool winters
**Environment - current issues:** netting and trapping of small migrant songbirds in the spring and autumn
**Geography - note:** British extraterritorial rights also extended to several small off-post sites scattered across Cyprus; of the Sovereign Base Area land 60% is privately owned and farmed, 20% is owned by the Ministry of Defense, and 20% is SBA Crown land

## People

**Population:** approximately 15,700 live on the Sovereign Base Areas of Akrotiri and Dhekelia including 7,700 Cypriots, 3,600 Service and UK Based Contract personnel, and 4,400 dependents
**Languages:** English, Greek

# Dhekelia (continued)

## Government

**Country name:**
*conventional long form:* Dhekelia Sovereign Base Area
*conventional short form:* Dhekelia
**Dependency status:** a special form of UK overseas territory; administered by an administrator who is also the Commander, British Forces Cyprus
**Capital:**
*name:* Episkopi Cantonment (base administrative center for Akrotiri and Dhekelia); located in Akrotiri
*geographic coordinates:* 34 40 N, 32 51 E
*time difference:* UTC+2 (7 hours ahead of Washington, DC during Standard Time)
*daylight saving time:* +1hr, begins last Sunday in March; ends last Sunday in October
**Constitution:** Sovereign Base Areas of Akrotiri and Dhekelia Order in Council 1960, effective 16 August 1960, functions as a basic legal document
**Legal system:** the Sovereign Base Area Administration has its own court system to deal with civil and criminal matters; laws applicable to the Cypriot population are, as far as possible, the same as the laws of the Republic of Cyprus
**Executive branch:**
*chief of state:* Queen ELIZABETH II (since 6 February 1952)
*head of government:* Administrator Major General Jamie GORDON (since October 2008); note - reports to the British Ministry of Defense
*elections:* none; the monarch is hereditary; the administrator is appointed by the monarch
**Diplomatic representation in the US:** none (overseas territory of the UK)
**Diplomatic representation from the US:** none (overseas territory of the UK)
**Flag description:** the flag of the UK is used

## Economy

**Economy - overview:** Economic activity is limited to providing services to the military and their families located in Dhekelia. All food and manufactured goods must be imported.
**Industries:** none
**Exchange rates:** euros (EUR) per US dollar - 0.6827 (2008)
*note:* on 1 January 2008, Dhekelia and Akrotiri adopted the euro along with the rest of Cyprus

## Communications

**Radio broadcast stations:** AM NA, FM 1 (located in Akrotiri), shortwave NA (British Forces Broadcasting Service (BFBS) provides Radio 1 and Radio 2 service to Akrotiri, Dhekelia, and Nicosia) (2006)
**Television broadcast stations:** 0 (British Forces Broadcasting Service (BFBS) provides multi-channel satellite service to Akrotiri, Dhekelia, and Nicosia) (2006)

## Military

**Military - note:** includes Dhekelia Garrison and Ayios Nikolaos Station connected by a roadway

# Djibouti

## Introduction

**Background:** The French Territory of the Afars and the Issas became Djibouti in 1977. Hassan Gouled APTIDON installed an authoritarian one-party state and proceeded to serve as president until 1999. Unrest among the Afars minority during the 1990s led to a civil war that ended in 2001 following the conclusion of a peace accord between Afar rebels and the Issa-dominated government. In 1999, Djibouti's first multi-party presidential elections resulted in the election of Ismail Omar GUELLEH; he was re-elected to a second and final term in 2005. Djibouti occupies a strategic geographic location at the mouth of the Red Sea and serves as an important transshipment location for goods entering and leaving the east African highlands. The present leadership favors close ties to France, which maintains a significant military presence in the country, but also has strong ties with the US. Djibouti hosts the only US military base in sub-Saharan Africa and is a front-line state in the global war on terrorism.

## Geography

**Location:** Eastern Africa, bordering the Gulf of Aden and the Red Sea, between Eritrea and Somalia
**Geographic coordinates:** 11 30 N, 43 00 E
**Map references:** Africa
**Area:**
*total:* 23,000 sq km
*land:* 22,980 sq km
*water:* 20 sq km
**Area - comparative:** slightly smaller than Massachusetts
**Land boundaries:**
*total:* 516 km
*border countries:* Eritrea 109 km, Ethiopia 349 km, Somalia 58 km
**Coastline:** 314 km

**Maritime claims:**
*territorial sea:* 12 nm
*contiguous zone:* 24 nm
*exclusive economic zone:* 200 nm
**Climate:** desert; torrid, dry
**Terrain:** coastal plain and plateau separated by central mountains
**Elevation extremes:**
*lowest point:* Lac Assal -155 m
*highest point:* Moussa Ali 2,028 m
**Natural resources:** geothermal areas, gold, clay, granite, limestone, marble, salt, diatomite, gypsum, pumice, petroleum
**Land use:**
*arable land:* 0.04%
*permanent crops:* 0%
*other:* 99.96% (2005)
**Irrigated land:** 10 sq km (2003)
**Total renewable water resources:** 0.3 cu km (1997)
**Freshwater withdrawal (domestic/industrial/agricultural):**
*total:* 0.02 cu km/yr (84%/0%/16%)
*per capita:* 25 cu m/yr (2000)
**Natural hazards:** earthquakes; droughts; occasional cyclonic disturbances from the Indian Ocean bring heavy rains and flash floods
**Environment - current issues:** inadequate supplies of potable water; limited arable land; desertification; endangered species
**Environment - international agreements:**
*party to:* Biodiversity, Climate Change, Climate Change-Kyoto Protocol, Desertification, Endangered Species, Hazardous Wastes, Law of the Sea, Ozone Layer Protection, Ship Pollution, Wetlands
*signed, but not ratified:* none of the selected agreements
**Geography - note:** strategic location near world's busiest shipping lanes and close to Arabian oilfields; terminus of rail traffic into Ethiopia; mostly wasteland; Lac Assal (Lake Assal) is the lowest point in Africa

## People

**Population:** 516,055 (July 2009 est.)
**Age structure:**
*0-14 years:* 43.3% (male 112,135/female 111,343)
*15-64 years:* 53% (male 141,298/female 132,360)
*65 years and over:* 3.7% (male 9,502/female 9,417) (2009 est.)
**Median age:**
*total:* 18.1 years
*male:* 18.5 years
*female:* 17.8 years (2009 est.)
**Population growth rate:** 1.903% (2009 est.)
**Birth rate:** 38.13 births/1,000 population (2009 est.)
**Death rate:** 19.16 deaths/1,000 population (2008 est.)
**Net migration rate:** NA
**Urbanization:**
*urban population:* 87% of total population (2008)
*rate of urbanization:* 2.2% annual rate of change (2005-10 est.)

# Djibouti (continued)

**Sex ratio:**
*at birth:* 1.03 male(s)/female
*under 15 years:* 1.01 male(s)/female
*15-64 years:* 1.07 male(s)/female
*65 years and over:* 1.01 male(s)/female
*total population:* 1.04 male(s)/female (2009 est.)

**Infant mortality rate:**
*total:* 97.51 deaths/1,000 live births
*male:* 104.98 deaths/1,000 live births
*female:* 89.82 deaths/1,000 live births (2009 est.)

**Life expectancy at birth:**
*total population:* 43.37 years
*male:* 41.89 years
*female:* 44.89 years (2009 est.)

**Total fertility rate:** 5.06 children born/woman (2009 est.)

**HIV/AIDS - adult prevalence rate:** 3.1% (2007 est.)

**HIV/AIDS - people living with HIV/AIDS:** 16,000 (2007 est.)

**HIV/AIDS - deaths:** 1,100 (2007 est.)

**Major infectious diseases:**
*degree of risk:* high
*food or waterborne diseases:* bacterial and protozoal diarrhea, hepatitis A and E, and typhoid fever
*vectorborne disease:* malaria
*note:* highly pathogenic H5N1 avian influenza has been identified in this country; it poses a negligible risk with extremely rare cases possible among US citizens who have close contact with birds (2009)

**Nationality:**
*noun:* Djiboutian(s)
*adjective:* Djiboutian

**Ethnic groups:** Somali 60%, Afar 35%, other 5% (includes French, Arab, Ethiopian, and Italian)

**Religions:** Muslim 94%, Christian 6%

**Languages:** French (official), Arabic (official), Somali, Afar

**Literacy:**
*definition:* age 15 and over can read and write
*total population:* 67.9%
*male:* 78%
*female:* 58.4% (2003 est.)

**School life expectancy (primary to tertiary education):**
*total:* 4 years
*male:* 5 years
*female:* 4 years (2006)

**Education expenditures:** 8.4% of GDP (2006)

## Government

**Country name:**
*conventional long form:* Republic of Djibouti
*conventional short form:* Djibouti
*local long form:* Republique de Djibouti/Jumhuriyat Jibuti
*local short form:* Djibouti/Jibuti
*former:* French Territory of the Afars and Issas, French Somaliland

**Government type:** republic

**Capital:**
*name:* Djibouti
*geographic coordinates:* 11 35 N, 43 09 E
*time difference:* UTC+3 (8 hours ahead of Washington, DC during Standard Time)

**Administrative divisions:** 6 districts (cercles, singular - cercle); Ali Sabieh, Arta, Dikhil, Djibouti, Obock, Tadjourah

**Independence:** 27 June 1977 (from France)

**National holiday:** Independence Day, 27 June (1977)

**Constitution:** approved by referendum 4 September 1992; note - constitution allows for multiparties

**Legal system:** based on French civil law system, traditional practices, and Islamic law; accepts ICJ jurisdiction with reservations

**Suffrage:** 18 years of age; universal

**Executive branch:**
*chief of state:* President Ismail Omar GUELLEH (since 8 May 1999)
*head of government:* Prime Minister Mohamed Dileita DILEITA (since 4 March 2001)
*cabinet:* Council of Ministers responsible to the president
*elections:* president elected by popular vote for a six-year term (eligible for a second term); election last held 8 April 2005 (next to be held by April 2011); prime minister appointed by the president
*election results:* Ismail Omar GUELLEH reelected president; percent of vote - Ismail Omar GUELLEH 100%

**Legislative branch:** unicameral Chamber of Deputies or Chambre des Deputes (65 seats; members elected by popular vote for five-year terms)
*elections:* last held 8 February 2008 (next to be held 2013)
*election results:* percent of vote by party - NA; seats - UMP (coalition of parties associated with President Ismail Omar GUELLAH) 65

**Judicial branch:** Supreme Court or Cour Supreme

**Political parties and leaders:** Democratic National Party or PND [ADEN Robleh Awaleh]; Democratic Renewal Party or PRD [Abdillahi HAMARITEH]; Djibouti Development Party or PDD [Mohamed Daoud CHEHEM]; Front pour la Restauration de l'Unite Democratique or FRUD [Ali Mohamed DAOUD]; People's Progress Assembly or RPP [Ismail Omar GUELLEH] (governing party); Peoples Social Democratic Party or PPSD [Moumin Bahdon FARAH]; Republican Alliance for Democracy or ARD [Ahmed YOUSSOUF]; Union for a Presidential Majority or UMP (a coalition of parties including RPP, FRUD, PND, and PPSD) [Mohamed Dileita DILEITA]; Union for Democracy and Justice or UDJ

**Political pressure groups and leaders:** Union for Presidential Majority UMP (coalition includes RPP, FRUD, PPSD and PND); Union for Democratic Changeover or UAD (opposition coalition includes ARD, MRDD, and UDJ)

**International organization participation:** ACCT, ACP, AfDB, AFESD, AMF, AU, COMESA, FAO, G-77, IBRD, ICAO, ICCt, ICRM, IDA, IDB, IFAD, IFC, IFRCS, IGAD, ILO, IMF, IMO, Interpol, IOC, ITU, ITUC, LAS, MIGA, MINURSO, NAM, OIC, OIF, OPCW, UN, UNCTAD, UNESCO, UNIDO, UNWTO, UPU, WCO, WFTU, WHO, WIPO, WMO, WTO

**Diplomatic representation in the US:**
*chief of mission:* Ambassador Roble OLHAYE Oudine
*chancery:* Suite 515, 1156 15th Street NW, Washington, DC 20005
*telephone:* [1] (202) 331-0270
*FAX:* [1] (202) 331-0302

**Diplomatic representation from the US:**
*chief of mission:* Ambassador James C. SWAN
*embassy:* Plateau du Serpent, Boulevard Marechal Joffre, Djibouti
*mailing address:* B. P. 185, Djibouti
*telephone:* [253] 35 39 95
*FAX:* [253] 35 39 40

**Flag description:** two equal horizontal bands of light blue (top) and light green with a white isosceles triangle based on the hoist side bearing a red five-pointed star in the center

## Economy

**Economy - overview:** The economy is based on service activities connected with the country's strategic location and status as a free trade zone in the Horn of Africa. Two-thirds of Djibouti's inhabitants live in the capital city; the remainder are mostly nomadic herders. Scanty rainfall limits crop production to fruits and vegetables, and most food must be imported. Djibouti provides services as both a transit port for the region and an international transshipment and refueling center. Imports and exports from landlocked neighbor Ethiopia represent 85% of port activity at Djibouti's container terminal. Djibouti has few natural resources and little industry. The nation is, therefore, heavily dependent on foreign assistance to help support its balance of payments and to finance development projects. An unemployment rate of nearly 60% in urban areas continues to be a major problem. While inflation is not a concern, due to the fixed tie of the Djiboutian franc to the US dollar, the artificially high value of the Djiboutian franc adversely affects Djibouti's balance of payments. Per capita consumption dropped an estimated 35% between 1999 and 2006 because of recession, civil war, and a high population growth rate (including immigrants and refugees). Faced with a multitude of economic difficulties, the government has fallen in arrears on long-term external debt and has been struggling to meet the stipulations of foreign aid donors.

**GDP (purchasing power parity):**
$1.889 billion (2008 est.)
$1.782 billion (2007)
$1.693 billion (2006)
*note:* data are in 2008 US dollars

**GDP (official exchange rate):** $973 million (2008 est.)

# Djibouti (continued)

**GDP - real growth rate:**
6% (2008 est.)
5.3% (2007 est.)
4.8% (2006 est.)
**GDP - per capita (PPP):**
$3,700 (2008 est.)
$3,600 (2007 est.)
$3,500 (2006 est.)
*note:* data are in 2008 US dollars
**GDP - composition by sector:**
*agriculture:* 3.2%
*industry:* 14.9%
*services:* 81.9% (2006 est.)
**Labor force:** 282,000 (2000)
**Labor force - by occupation:**
*agriculture:* NA%
*industry:* NA%
*services:* NA%
**Unemployment rate:**
59% (2007 est.)
*note:* data are for urban areas, 83% in rural areas
**Population below poverty line:** 42% (2007 est.)
**Household income or consumption by percentage share:**
*lowest 10%:* NA%
*highest 10%:* NA%
**Budget:**
*revenues:* $135 million
*expenditures:* $182 million (1999 est.)
**Inflation rate (consumer prices):**
5% (2007 est.)
**Commercial bank prime lending rate:** NA
**Stock of money:** $380 million (31 December 2007)
**Stock of quasi money:** $284.1 million
(31 December 2007)
**Stock of domestic credit:** $224.7 million
(31 December 2007)
**Agriculture - products:** fruits, vegetables; goats, sheep, camels, animal hides
**Industries:** construction, agricultural processing
**Electricity - production:** 250 million kWh
(2006 est.)
**Electricity - consumption:** 232.5 million kWh
(2006 est.)
**Electricity - exports:** 0 kWh (2007 est.)
**Electricity - imports:** 0 kWh (2007 est.)
**Oil - production:** 0 bbl/day (2007 est.)
**Oil - consumption:** 12,170 bbl/day (2006 est.)
**Oil - exports:** 19.18 bbl/day (2005)
**Oil - imports:** 11,810 bbl/day (2005)
**Oil - proved reserves:** 0 bbl (1 January 2006 est.)
**Natural gas - production:** 0 cu m (2007 est.)
**Natural gas - consumption:** 0 cu m (2007 est.)
**Natural gas - exports:** 0 cu m (2007 est.)
**Natural gas - imports:** 0 cu m (2007 est.)
**Natural gas - proved reserves:** 0 cu m (1 January 2006 est.)
**Current account balance:** -$212 million (2007 est.)
**Exports:** $340 million f.o.b. (2006)
**Exports - commodities:** reexports, hides and skins, coffee (in transit)

**Exports - partners:** Somalia 66.4%, Ethiopia
21.5%, Yemen 3.4% (2007)
**Imports:** $1.555 billion f.o.b. (2006)
**Imports - commodities:** foods, beverages, transport equipment, chemicals, petroleum products
**Imports - partners:** Saudi Arabia 21%, India 18.1%, China 9.4%, Ethiopia 4.7%, Malaysia 4.6%, Japan 4.2% (2007)
**Debt - external:** $428 million (2006)
**Exchange rates:** Djiboutian francs (DJF) per US dollar - 177.71 (2007), 174.75 (2006), 177.72 (2005), 177.72 (2004), 177.72 (2003)

## Communications

**Telephones - main lines in use:** 10,800 (2005)
**Telephones - mobile cellular:** 45,000 (2007)
**Telephone system:**
*general assessment:* telephone facilities in the city of Djibouti are adequate, as are the microwave radio relay connections to outlying areas of the country
*domestic:* microwave radio relay network; mobile cellular coverage is primarily limited to the area in and around Djibouti city
*international:* country code - 253; landing point for the SEA-ME-WE-3 optical telecommunications submarine cable with links to Asia, the Middle East, and Europe; satellite earth stations - 2 (1 Intelsat - Indian Ocean and 1 Arabsat); Medarabtel regional microwave radio relay telephone network (2007)
**Radio broadcast stations:** AM 1, FM 2, shortwave 0 (2001)
**Television broadcast stations:** 1 (2001)
**Internet country code:** .dj
**Internet hosts:** 161 (2008)
**Internet users:** 11,000 (2006)

## Transportation

**Airports:** 13 (2008)
**Airports - with paved runways:**
*total:* 3
*over 3,047 m:* 1
*2,438 to 3,047 m:* 1
*1,524 to 2,437 m:* 1 (2008)
**Airports - with unpaved runways:**
*total:* 10
*1,524 to 2,437 m:* 2
*914 to 1,523 m:* 5
*under 914 m:* 3 (2008)
**Railways:**
*total:* 100 km (Djibouti segment of the Addis Ababa-Djibouti railway)
*narrow gauge:* 100 km 1.000-m gauge
*note:* railway is under joint control of Djibouti and Ethiopia but is largely inoperable (2006)
**Roadways:**
*total:* 3,065 km
*paved:* 1,226 km
*unpaved:* 1,839 km (2000)
**Ports and terminals:** Djibouti

**Transportation - note:** the International Maritime Bureau reports offshore waters in the Gulf of Aden are high risk for piracy; numerous vessels, including commercial shipping and pleasure craft, have been attacked and hijacked both at anchor and while underway; crew, passengers, and cargo are held for ransom

## Military

**Military branches:** Djibouti National Army (includes Navy and Air Force)
**Military service age and obligation:** 18 years of age for voluntary military service; 16-25 years of age for voluntary military training; no conscription (2008)
**Manpower available for military service:**
*males age 16-49:* 111,274
*females age 16-49:* 105,168 (2008 est.)
**Manpower fit for military service:**
*males age 16-49:* 55,173
*females age 16-49:* 52,825 (2009 est.)
**Manpower reaching militarily significant age annually:**
*male:* 5,778
*female:* 5,771 (2009 est.)
**Military expenditures:** 3.8% of GDP (2006)

## Transnational Issues

**Disputes - international:** Djibouti maintains economic ties and border accords with "Somaliland" leadership while maintaining some political ties to various factions in Somalia; Kuwait is chief investor in the 2008 restoration and upgrade of the Ethiopian-Djibouti rail link
**Refugees and internally displaced persons:**
*refugees (country of origin):* 8,642 (Somalia) (2007)

# Dominica

## Introduction

**Background:** Dominica was the last of the Caribbean islands to be colonized by Europeans due chiefly to the fierce resistance of the native Caribs. France ceded possession to Great Britain in 1763, which made the island a colony in 1805. In 1980, two years after independence, Dominica's fortunes improved when a corrupt and tyrannical administration was replaced by that of Mary Eugenia CHARLES, the first female prime minister in the Caribbean, who remained in office for 15 years. Some 3,000 Carib Indians still living on Dominica are the only pre-Columbian population remaining in the eastern Caribbean.

## Geography

**Location:** Caribbean, island between the Caribbean Sea and the North Atlantic Ocean, about half way between Puerto Rico and Trinidad and Tobago
**Geographic coordinates:** 15 25 N, 61 20 W
**Map references:** Central America and the Caribbean
**Area:**
*total:* 754 sq km
*land:* 754 sq km
*water:* 0 sq km
**Area - comparative:** slightly more than four times the size of Washington, DC
**Land boundaries:** 0 km
**Coastline:** 148 km
**Maritime claims:**
*territorial sea:* 12 nm
*contiguous zone:* 24 nm
*exclusive economic zone:* 200 nm
**Climate:** tropical; moderated by northeast trade winds; heavy rainfall
**Terrain:** rugged mountains of volcanic origin
**Elevation extremes:**
*lowest point:* Caribbean Sea 0 m
*highest point:* Morne Diablatins 1,447 m

**Natural resources:** timber, hydropower, arable land
**Land use:**
*arable land:* 6.67%
*permanent crops:* 21.33%
*other:* 72% (2005)
**Irrigated land:** NA
**Total renewable water resources:** NA
**Freshwater withdrawal (domestic/industrial/agricultural):**
*total:* 0.02 cu km/yr
*per capita:* 213 cu m/yr (1996)
**Natural hazards:** flash floods are a constant threat; destructive hurricanes can be expected during the late summer months
**Environment - current issues:** NA
**Environment - international agreements:**
*party to:* Biodiversity, Climate Change, Climate Change-Kyoto Protocol, Desertification, Endangered Species, Environmental Modification, Hazardous Wastes, Law of the Sea, Ozone Layer Protection, Ship Pollution, Whaling
*signed, but not ratified:* none of the selected agreements
**Geography - note:** known as "The Nature Island of the Caribbean" due to its spectacular, lush, and varied flora and fauna, which are protected by an extensive natural park system; the most mountainous of the Lesser Antilles, its volcanic peaks are cones of lava craters and include Boiling Lake, the second-largest, thermally active lake in the world

## People

**Population:** 72,660 (July 2009 est.)
**Age structure:**
*0-14 years:* 24% (male 8,910/female 8,518)
*15-64 years:* 65.8% (male 24,532/female 23,301)
*65 years and over:* 10.2% (male 3,187/female 4,212) (2009 est.)
**Median age:**
*total:* 29.8 years
*male:* 29.4 years
*female:* 30.2 years (2009 est.)
**Population growth rate:** 0.208% (2009 est.)
**Birth rate:** 15.73 births/1,000 population (2009 est.)
**Death rate:** 8.32 deaths/1,000 population (2008 est.)
**Net migration rate:** -5.45 migrant(s)/1,000 population (2009 est.)
**Urbanization:**
*urban population:* 74% of total population (2008)
*rate of urbanization:* 0.2% annual rate of change (2005-10 est.)
**Sex ratio:**
*at birth:* 1.05 male(s)/female
*under 15 years:* 1.05 male(s)/female
*15-64 years:* 1.05 male(s)/female
*65 years and over:* 0.76 male(s)/female
*total population:* 1.02 male(s)/female (2009 est.)
**Infant mortality rate:**
*total:* 13.65 deaths/1,000 live births
*male:* 18.34 deaths/1,000 live births
*female:* 8.73 deaths/1,000 live births (2009 est.)

**Life expectancy at birth:**
*total population:* 75.55 years
*male:* 72.61 years
*female:* 78.64 years (2009 est.)
**Total fertility rate:** 2.09 children born/woman (2009 est.)
**HIV/AIDS - adult prevalence rate:** NA
**HIV/AIDS - people living with HIV/AIDS:** NA
**HIV/AIDS - deaths:** NA
**Nationality:**
*noun:* Dominican(s)
*adjective:* Dominican
**Ethnic groups:** black 86.8%, mixed 8.9%, Carib Amerindian 2.9%, white 0.8%, other 0.7% (2001 census)
**Religions:** Roman Catholic 61.4%, Seventh Day Adventist 6%, Pentecostal 5.6%, Baptist 4.1%, Methodist 3.7%, Church of God 1.2%, Jehovah's Witnesses 1.2%, other Christian 7.7%, Rastafarian 1.3%, other or unspecified 1.6%, none 6.1% (2001 census)
**Languages:** English (official), French patois
**Literacy:**
*definition:* age 15 and over has ever attended school
*total population:* 94%
*male:* 94%
*female:* 94% (2003 est.)
**School life expectancy (primary to tertiary education):**
*total:* 13 years
*male:* 13 years
*female:* 14 years (2005)
**Education expenditures:** 5% of GDP (1999)

## Government

**Country name:**
*conventional long form:* Commonwealth of Dominica
*conventional short form:* Dominica
**Government type:** parliamentary democracy
**Capital:**
*name:* Roseau
*geographic coordinates:* 15 18 N, 61 24 W
*time difference:* UTC-4 (1 hour ahead of Washington, DC during Standard Time)
**Administrative divisions:** 10 parishes; Saint Andrew, Saint David, Saint George, Saint John, Saint Joseph, Saint Luke, Saint Mark, Saint Patrick, Saint Paul, Saint Peter
**Independence:** 3 November 1978 (from the UK)
**National holiday:** Independence Day, 3 November (1978)
**Constitution:** 3 November 1978
**Legal system:** based on English common law; accepts ICJ jurisdiction
**Suffrage:** 18 years of age; universal
**Executive branch:**
*chief of state:* President Nicholas J. O. LIVERPOOL (since October 2003)
*head of government:* Prime Minister Roosevelt SKERRIT (since 8 January 2004)

# Dominica (continued)

cabinet: Cabinet appointed by the president on the advice of the prime minister

elections: president elected by the House of Assembly for a five-year term; election last held 1 October 2003 (next to be held in 2013); prime minister appointed by the president

election results: Nicholas LIVERPOOL consented to a second term in 2008 at the request of the prime minister and leader of the opposition

**Legislative branch:** unicameral House of Assembly (30 seats; 9 members appointed, 21 elected by popular vote; to serve five-year terms)

elections: last held 5 May 2005 (next to be held by 5August 2010); note - tradition dictates that the election will be held within five years of the last election, but technically it is five years from the first seating of parliament (12 May 2005) plus a 90-day grace period

election results: percent of vote by party - DLP 52.1%, UWP 43.6%, DFP 3.2%, other 1.1%; seats by party - DLP 12, UWP 8, independent 1

**Judicial branch:** Eastern Caribbean Supreme Court, consisting of the Court of Appeal and the High Court (located in Saint Lucia; one of the six judges must reside in Dominica and preside over the Court of Summary Jurisdiction)

**Political parties and leaders:** Dominica Freedom Party or DFP [Charles SAVARIN]; Dominica Labor Party or DLP [Roosevelt SKERRIT]; Dominica United Workers Party or UWP [Earl WILLIAMS]

**Political pressure groups and leaders:** Dominica Liberation Movement or DLM (a small leftist party)

**International organization participation:** ACCT, ACP, C, Caricom, CDB, FAO, G-77, IBRD, ICCt, ICRM, IDA, IFAD, IFC, IFRCS, ILO, IMF, IMO, Interpol, IOC, ISO (subscriber), ITU, ITUC, MIGA, NAM, OAS, OECS, OIF, OPANAL, OPCW, UN, UNCTAD, UNESCO, UNIDO, UPU, WCL, WFTU, WHO, WIPO, WMO, WTO

**Diplomatic representation in the US:**

chief of mission: Ambassador (vacant); Charge d'Affaires Judith Ann ROLLE

chancery: 3216 New Mexico Avenue NW, Washington, DC 20016

telephone: [1] (202) 364-6781

FAX: [1] (202) 364-6791

consulate(s) general: New York

**Diplomatic representation from the US:** the US does not have an embassy in Dominica; the US Ambassador to Barbados is accredited to Dominica

**Flag description:** green, with a centered cross of three equal bands - the vertical part is yellow (hoist side), black, and white and the horizontal part is yellow (top), black, and white; superimposed in the center of the cross is a red disk bearing a sisserou parrot encircled by 10 green, five-pointed stars edged in yellow; the 10 stars represent the 10 administrative divisions (parishes)

## Economy

**Economy - overview:** The Dominican economy depends on agriculture, primarily bananas, and remains highly vulnerable to climatic conditions and international economic developments. Tourism has increased as the government seeks to promote Dominica as an "ecotourism" destination and has developed a new tourism development plan with assistance from the EU. Hurricane Dean struck the island in August 2007 causing damages equivalent to 20% of GDP. In 2003, the government began a comprehensive restructuring of the economy - including elimination of price controls, privatization of the state banana company, and tax increases - to address Dominica's economic and financial crisis of 2001-02 and to meet IMF targets. This restructuring paved the way for the current economic recovery - real growth for 2006 reached a two-decade high - and will help to reduce the debt burden, which remains at about 100% of GDP. In order to diversify the island's production base, the government is attempting to develop an offshore financial sector and has signed an agreement with the EU to develop geothermal energy resources.

**GDP (purchasing power parity):**
$719.8 million (2008 est.)
$701.5 million (2007)
$691.2 million (2006)
note: data are in 2008 US dollars

**GDP (official exchange rate):** $365 million (2008 est.)

**GDP - real growth rate:**
2.6% (2008 est.)
1.5% (2007 est.)
4% (2006 est.)

**GDP - per capita (PPP):**
$9,900 (2008 est.)
$9,700 (2007 est.)
$9,600 (2006 est.)
note: data are in 2008 US dollars

**GDP - composition by sector:**
agriculture: 17.7%
industry: 32.8%
services: 49.5% (2004 est.)

**Labor force:** 25,000 (2000 est.)

**Labor force - by occupation:**
agriculture: 40%
industry: 32%
services: 28% (2000 est.)

**Unemployment rate:**
23% (2000 est.)

**Population below poverty line:** 30% (2002 est.)

**Household income or consumption by percentage share:**
lowest 10%: NA%
highest 10%: NA%

**Budget:**
revenues: $73.9 million
expenditures: $84.4 million (2001)

**Inflation rate (consumer prices):**
2.7% (2007 est.)

**Central bank discount rate:** 6.5% (31 December 2007)

**Commercial bank prime lending rate:** 9.17% (31 December 2007)

**Stock of money:** $73.71 million (31 December 2007)

**Stock of quasi money:** $269.1 million (31 December 2007)

**Stock of domestic credit:** $193.1 million (31 December 2007)

**Agriculture - products:** bananas, citrus, mangoes, root crops, coconuts, cocoa; forest and fishery potential not exploited

**Industries:** soap, coconut oil, tourism, copra, furniture, cement blocks, shoes

**Industrial production growth rate:** NA

**Electricity - production:** 90 million kWh (2006 est.)

**Electricity - consumption:** 83.7 million kWh (2006 est.)

**Electricity - exports:** 0 kWh (2007 est.)

**Electricity - imports:** 0 kWh (2007 est.)

**Oil - production:** 0 bbl/day (2007 est.)

**Oil - consumption:** 850.5 bbl/day (2006 est.)

**Oil - exports:** 0 bbl/day (2005)

**Oil - imports:** 669.6 bbl/day (2005)

**Oil - proved reserves:** 0 bbl (1 January 2006 est.)

**Natural gas - production:** 0 cu m (2007 est.)

**Natural gas - consumption:** 0 cu m (2007 est.)

**Natural gas - exports:** 0 cu m (2007 est.)

**Natural gas - imports:** 0 cu m (2007 est.)

**Natural gas - proved reserves:** 0 cu m (1 January 2006 est.)

**Current account balance:** -$72 million (2007 est.)

**Exports:** $94 million f.o.b. (2006)

**Exports - commodities:** bananas, soap, bay oil, vegetables, grapefruit, oranges

**Exports - partners:** China 24.4%, Jamaica 10.3%, Antigua and Barbuda 10.1%, Guyana 8.5%, UK 8.2%, Trinidad and Tobago 5.5%, Saint Lucia 4.6%, Saint Kitts & Nevis 4% (2007)

**Imports:** $296 million f.o.b. (2006)

**Imports - commodities:** manufactured goods, machinery and equipment, food, chemicals

**Imports - partners:** US 24.1%, China 21.2%, Trinidad and Tobago 13.2%, Japan 11.1% (2007)

**Debt - external:** $213 million (2004)

**Exchange rates:** East Caribbean dollars (XCD) per US dollar - 2.7 (2007), 2.7 (2006), 2.7 (2005), 2.7 (2004), 2.7 (2003)

## Communications

**Telephones - main lines in use:** 21,000 (2004)

**Telephones - mobile cellular:** 41,800 (2004)

**Telephone system:**

general assessment: NA

domestic: fully automatic network

international: country code - 1-767; landing point for the East Caribbean Fiber Optic System (ECFS) submarine cable with links to 13 other islands in the eastern Caribbean extending from the British Virgin Islands to Trinidad; microwave radio relay and SHF radiotelephone links to Martinique and Guadeloupe; VHF and UHF radiotelephone links to Saint Lucia

**Radio broadcast stations:** AM 2, FM 4, shortwave 0 (2003)

# Dominica *(continued)*

**Television broadcast stations:** 1 (2004)
**Internet country code:** .dm
**Internet hosts:** 29 (2008)
**Internet users:** 26,500 (2006)

## Transportation

**Airports:** 2 (2008)
**Airports - with paved runways:**
*total:* 2
*914 to 1,523 m:* 2 (2008)
**Roadways:**
*total:* 780 km
*paved:* 393 km
*unpaved:* 387 km (2000)
**Merchant marine:**
*total:* 53
*by type:* bulk carrier 14, cargo 27, chemical tanker 3, petroleum tanker 5, refrigerated cargo 2, roll on/roll off 1, vehicle carrier 1
*foreign-owned:* 47 (Australia 2, Estonia 7, Greece 10, India 2, Latvia 1, Norway 1, Russia 3, Saudi Arabia 2, Singapore 7, Syria 2, Turkey 5, Ukraine 4, UAE 1) (2008)
**Ports and terminals:** Portsmouth, Roseau

## Military

**Military branches:** no regular military forces; Commonwealth of Dominica Police Force (includes Coast Guard) (2008)
**Manpower available for military service:**
*males age 16-49:* 18,584 (2008 est.)
**Manpower fit for military service:**
*males age 16-49:* 15,821
*females age 16-49:* 15,291 (2009 est.)
**Manpower reaching militarily significant age annually:**
*male:* 776
*female:* 731 (2009 est.)
**Military expenditures:** NA (2006)

## Transnational Issues

**Disputes - international:** Dominica is the only Caribbean state to challenge Venezuela's sovereignty claim over Aves Island and joins the other island nations in challenging whether the feature sustains human habitation, a criterion under the UN Convention on the Law of the Sea (UNCLOS), which permits Venezuela to extend its Exclusive Economic Zone (EEZ) and continental shelf claims over a large portion of the eastern Caribbean Sea
**Illicit drugs:** transshipment point for narcotics bound for the US and Europe; minor cannabis producer (2008)

# Dominican Republic

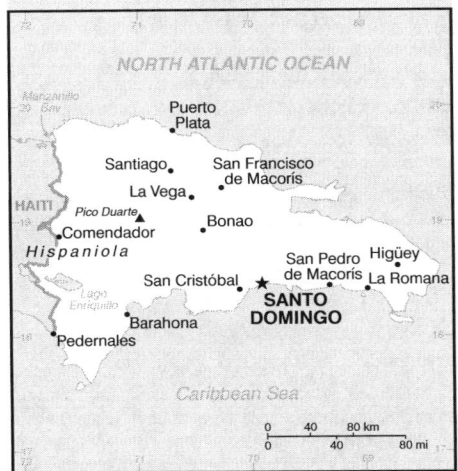

## Introduction

**Background:** Explored and claimed by Christopher COLUMBUS on his first voyage in 1492, the island of Hispaniola became a springboard for Spanish conquest of the Caribbean and the American mainland. In 1697, Spain recognized French dominion over the western third of the island, which in 1804 became Haiti. The remainder of the island, by then known as Santo Domingo, sought to gain its own independence in 1821 but was conquered and ruled by the Haitians for 22 years; it finally attained independence as the Dominican Republic in 1844. In 1861, the Dominicans voluntarily returned to the Spanish Empire, but two years later they launched a war that restored independence in 1865. A legacy of unsettled, mostly non-representative rule followed, capped by the dictatorship of Rafael Leonidas TRUJILLO from 1930-61. Juan BOSCH was elected president in 1962 but was deposed in a military coup in 1963. In 1965, the United States led an intervention in the midst of a civil war sparked by an uprising to restore BOSCH. In 1966, Joaquin BALAGUER defeated BOSCH in an election to become president. BALAGUER maintained a tight grip on power for most of the next 30 years when international reaction to flawed elections forced him to curtail his term in 1996. Since then, regular competitive elections have been held in which opposition candidates have won the presidency. Former President (1996-2000) Leonel FERNANDEZ Reyna won election to a second term in 2004 following a constitutional amendment allowing presidents to serve more than one term.

## Geography

**Location:** Caribbean, eastern two-thirds of the island of Hispaniola, between the Caribbean Sea and the North Atlantic Ocean, east of Haiti
**Geographic coordinates:** 19 00 N, 70 40 W
**Map references:** Central America and the Caribbean

**Area:**
*total:* 48,730 sq km
*land:* 48,380 sq km
*water:* 350 sq km
**Area - comparative:** slightly more than twice the size of New Hampshire
**Land boundaries:**
*total:* 360 km
*border countries:* Haiti 360 km
**Coastline:** 1,288 km
**Maritime claims:** measured from claimed archipelagic straight baselines
*territorial sea:* 6 nm
*contiguous zone:* 24 nm
*exclusive economic zone:* 200 nm
*continental shelf:* 200 nm or to the edge of the continental margin
**Climate:** tropical maritime; little seasonal temperature variation; seasonal variation in rainfall
**Terrain:** rugged highlands and mountains with fertile valleys interspersed
**Elevation extremes:**
*lowest point:* Lago Enriquillo -46 m
*highest point:* Pico Duarte 3,175 m
**Natural resources:** nickel, bauxite, gold, silver
**Land use:**
*arable land:* 22.49%
*permanent crops:* 10.26%
*other:* 67.25% (2005)
**Irrigated land:** 2,750 sq km (2003)
**Total renewable water resources:** 21 cu km (2000)
**Freshwater withdrawal (domestic/industrial/agricultural):**
*total:* 3.39 cu km/yr (32%/2%/66%)
*per capita:* 381 cu m/yr (2000)
**Natural hazards:** lies in the middle of the hurricane belt and subject to severe storms from June to October; occasional flooding; periodic droughts
**Environment - current issues:** water shortages; soil eroding into the sea damages coral reefs; deforestation
**Environment - international agreements:**
*party to:* Biodiversity, Climate Change, Climate Change-Kyoto Protocol, Desertification, Endangered Species, Hazardous Wastes, Marine Dumping, Marine Life Conservation, Ozone Layer Protection, Ship Pollution, Wetlands
*signed, but not ratified:* Law of the Sea
**Geography - note:** shares island of Hispaniola with Haiti

## People

**Population:** 9,650,054 (July 2009 est.)
**Age structure:**
*0-14 years:* 31.4% (male 1,543,141/female 1,488,016)
*15-64 years:* 62.7% (male 3,087,351/female 2,960,319)
*65 years and over:* 5.9% (male 264,476/female 306,751) (2009 est.)

# Dominican Republic (continued)

**Median age:**
*total:* 24.9 years
*male:* 24.8 years
*female:* 25.1 years (2009 est.)
**Population growth rate:** 1.489% (2009 est.)
**Birth rate:** 22.39 births/1,000 population (2009 est.)
**Death rate:** 5.3 deaths/1,000 population (2008 est.)
**Net migration rate:** -2.22 migrant(s)/1,000 population (2009 est.)
**Urbanization:**
*urban population:* 69% of total population (2008)
*rate of urbanization:* 2.6% annual rate of change (2005-10 est.)
**Sex ratio:**
*at birth:* 1.04 male(s)/female
*under 15 years:* 1.04 male(s)/female
*15-64 years:* 1.04 male(s)/female
*65 years and over:* 0.86 male(s)/female
*total population:* 1.03 male(s)/female (2009 est.)
**Infant mortality rate:**
*total:* 25.96 deaths/1,000 live births
*male:* 28 deaths/1,000 live births
*female:* 23.84 deaths/1,000 live births (2009 est.)
**Life expectancy at birth:**
*total population:* 73.7 years
*male:* 71.88 years
*female:* 75.6 years (2009 est.)
**Total fertility rate:** 2.76 children born/woman (2009 est.)
**HIV/AIDS - adult prevalence rate:** 1.1% (2007 est.)
**HIV/AIDS - people living with HIV/AIDS:** 62,000 (2007 est.)
**HIV/AIDS - deaths:** 4,100 (2007 est.)
**Major infectious diseases:**
*degree of risk:* high
*food or waterborne diseases:* bacterial diarrhea, hepatitis A, and typhoid fever
*vectorborne diseases:* dengue fever and malaria
*water contact disease:* leptospirosis (2009)
**Nationality:**
*noun:* Dominican(s)
*adjective:* Dominican
**Ethnic groups:** mixed 73%, white 16%, black 11%
**Religions:** Roman Catholic 95%, other 5%
**Languages:** Spanish
**Literacy:**
*definition:* age 15 and over can read and write
*total population:* 87%
*male:* 86.8%
*female:* 87.2% (2002 census)
**School life expectancy (primary to tertiary education):**
*total:* 12 years
*male:* 12 years
*female:* 13 years (2004)
**Education expenditures:** 3.6% of GDP (2006)

**Country name:**
*conventional long form:* Dominican Republic
*conventional short form:* The Dominican
*local long form:* Republica Dominicana
*local short form:* La Dominicana
**Government type:** democratic republic
**Capital:**
*name:* Santo Domingo
*geographic coordinates:* 18 28 N, 69 54 W
*time difference:* UTC-4 (1 hour ahead of Washington, DC during Standard Time)
**Administrative divisions:** 31 provinces (provincias, singular - provincia) and 1 district* (distrito); Azua, Bahoruco, Barahona, Dajabon, Distrito Nacional*, Duarte, El Seibo, Elias Pina, Espaillat, Hato Mayor, Independencia, La Altagracia, La Romana, La Vega, Maria Trinidad Sanchez, Monsenor Nouel, Monte Cristi, Monte Plata, Pedernales, Peravia, Puerto Plata, Salcedo, Samana, San Cristobal, San Jose de Ocoa, San Juan, San Pedro de Macoris, Sanchez Ramirez, Santiago, Santiago Rodriguez, Santo Domingo, Valverde
**Independence:** 27 February 1844 (from Haiti)
**National holiday:** Independence Day, 27 February (1844)
**Constitution:** 28 November 1966; amended 25 July 2002
**Legal system:** based on French civil codes; Criminal Procedures Code modified in 2004 to include important elements of an accusatory system; accepts compulsory ICJ jurisdiction
**Suffrage:** 18 years of age, universal and compulsory; married persons regardless of age; note -members of the armed forces and national police cannot vote
**Executive branch:**
*chief of state:* President Leonel FERNANDEZ Reyna (since 16 August 2004); Vice President Rafael ALBURQUERQUE de Castro (since 16 August 2004); note - the president is both the chief of state and head of government
*head of government:* President Leonel FERNANDEZ Reyna (since 16 August 2004); Vice President Rafael ALBURQUERQUE de Castro (since 16 August 2004)
*cabinet:* Cabinet nominated by the president
*elections:* president and vice president elected on the same ticket by popular vote for four-year terms (eligible for a second consecutive term); election last held 16 May 2008 (next to be held in May 2012)
*election results:* Leonel FERNANDEZ reelected president; percent of vote - Leonel FERNANDEZ 53.6%, Miguel VARGAS 41%, Amable ARISTY less than 5%
**Legislative branch:** bicameral National Congress or Congreso Nacional consists of the Senate or Senado (32 seats; members are elected by popular vote to serve four-year terms) and the House of Representatives or Camara de Diputados (178 seats; members are elected by popular vote to serve four-year terms)

*elections:* Senate - last held 16 May 2006 (next to be held in May 2010); House of Representatives - last held 16 May 2006 (next to be held in May 2010)
*election results:* Senate - percent of vote by party - NA; seats by party - PLD 22, PRD 6, PRSC 4; House of Representatives - percent of vote by party - NA; seats by party - PLD 96, PRD 60, PRSC 22
**Judicial branch:** Supreme Court or Corte Suprema (judges are appointed by the National Judicial Council comprised of the president, the leaders of both chambers of congress, the president of the Supreme Court, and an additional non-governing party congressional representative)
**Political parties and leaders:** Dominican Liberation Party or PLD [Leonel FERNANDEZ Reyna]; Dominican Revolutionary Party or PRD [Ramon ALBURQUERQUE]; National Progressive Front [Vincent CASTILLO, Pelegrin CASTILLO]; Social Christian Reformist Party or PRSC [Enrique ANTUN]
**Political pressure groups and leaders:** Citizen Participation Group (Participacion Ciudadania); Collective of Popular Organizations or COP; Foundation for Institution-Building and Justice (FINJUS)
**International organization participation:** ACP, BCIE, Caricom (observer), FAO, G-77, IADB, IAEA, IBRD, ICAO, ICC, ICCt, ICRM, IDA, IFAD, IFC, IFRCS, IHO (suspended), ILO, IMF, IMO, Interpol, IOC, IOM, IPU, ISO (correspondent), ITSO, ITU, ITUC, LAES, LAIA (observer), MIGA, NAM, OAS, OPANAL, OPCW (signatory), PCA, RG, SICA (associated member), UN, UNCTAD, UNESCO, UNIDO, Union Latina, UNWTO, UPU, WCL, WCO, WFTU, WHO, WIPO, WMO, WTO
**Diplomatic representation in the US:**
*chief of mission:* Ambassador (vacant); Charge d'Affaires Wellington BENCOSME
*chancery:* 1715 22nd Street NW, Washington, DC 20008
*telephone:* [1] (202) 332-6280
*FAX:* [1] (202) 265-8057
*consulate(s) general:* Anchorage, Boston, Chicago, Mayaguez (Puerto Rico), Miami, New Orleans, New York, San Juan (Puerto Rico), Sun Valley (California)
**Diplomatic representation from the US:**
*chief of mission:* Ambassador P. Robert FANNIN
*embassy:* corner of Calle Cesar Nicolas Penson and Calle Leopoldo Navarro, Santo Domingo
*mailing address:* Unit 5500, APO AA 34041-5500
*telephone:* [1] (809) 221-2171
*FAX:* [1] (809) 686-7437
**Flag description:** a centered white cross that extends to the edges divides the flag into four rectangles - the top ones are blue (hoist side) and red, and the bottom ones are red (hoist side) and blue; a small coat of arms featuring a shield supported by an olive branch (left) and a palm branch (right) is at the center of the cross; above the shield a blue ribbon displays the motto, DIOS, PATRIA, LIBERTAD (God, Fatherland, Liberty), and below the shield, REPUBLICA DOMINICANA appears on a red ribbon

# Dominican Republic *(continued)*

## Economy

**Economy - overview:** The Dominican Republic has enjoyed strong GDP growth since 2005 and continued to post sound gains through mid-2008. The global recession, however, had a significant impact on GDP growth in the latter half of the year as tourism and remittances, two of the Dominican Republic's most important economic contributors, showed signs of slowing. The economy is highly dependent upon the US, the destination for about two-thirds of exports. Remittances from the US amount to about a tenth of GDP, equivalent to almost half of exports and three-quarters of tourism receipts. The country has long been viewed primarily as an exporter of sugar, coffee, and tobacco but in recent years the service sector has overtaken agriculture as the economy's largest employer due to growth in tourism and free trade zones. Although 2007 saw inflation around 6%, the rate grew to over 12% in 2008. High food prices, driven by the effects of consecutive tropical storms on agricultural products, and education prices were significant contributors to the jump. The effects of the global financial crisis and the US recession are projected to negatively affect GDP growth in 2009 with a rebound expected in 2010. Although the economy is growing at a respectable rate, high unemployment and underemployment remains an important challenge. The country suffers from marked income inequality; the poorest half of the population receives less than one-fifth of GNP, while the richest 10% enjoys nearly 40% of national income. The Central America-Dominican Republic Free Trade Agreement (CAFTA-DR) came into force in March 2007, which should boost investment and exports and reduce losses to the Asian garment industry.

**GDP (purchasing power parity):**
$77.43 billion (2008 est.)
$74.1 billion (2007)
$68.29 billion (2006)
*note:* data are in 2008 US dollars

**GDP (official exchange rate):** $45.69 billion (2008 est.)

**GDP - real growth rate:**
4.5% (2008 est.)
8.5% (2007 est.)
10.7% (2006 est.)

**GDP - per capita (PPP):**
$8,100 (2008 est.)
$7,900 (2007 est.)
$7,400 (2006 est.)
*note:* data are in 2008 US dollars

**GDP - composition by sector:**
*agriculture:* 11.3%
*industry:* 23.5%
*services:* 65.2% (2008 est.)

**Labor force:** 4.119 million (2008 est.)

**Labor force - by occupation:**
*agriculture:* 14.6%
*industry:* 22.3%
*services:* 63.1% (2005)

**Unemployment rate:**
15.4% (2008 est.)
15.6% (2007 est.)

**Population below poverty line:** 42.2% (2004)

**Household income or consumption by percentage share:**
*lowest 10%:* 1.4%
*highest 10%:* 41.1% (2004)

**Distribution of family income - Gini index:** 49.9 (2005)

**Investment (gross fixed):** 19.6% of GDP (2008 est.)

**Budget:**
*revenues:* $7.947 billion
*expenditures:* $9.069 billion (2008 est.)

**Public debt:** 39.1% of GDP (2008 est.)

**Inflation rate (consumer prices):**
12.2% (2008 est.)
6.1% (2007 est.)

**Commercial bank prime lending rate:** 15.83% (31 December 2007)

**Stock of money:** $4.074 billion (31 December 2007)

**Stock of quasi money:** $5.631 billion (31 December 2007)

**Stock of domestic credit:** $15.92 billion (31 December 2007)

**Market value of publicly traded shares:** $NA

**Agriculture - products:** sugarcane, coffee, cotton, cocoa, tobacco, rice, beans, potatoes, corn, bananas; cattle, pigs, dairy products, beef, eggs

**Industries:** tourism, sugar processing, ferronickel and gold mining, textiles, cement, tobacco

**Industrial production growth rate:** 3.2% (2008 est.)

**Electricity - production:** 13.37 billion kWh (2006 est.)

**Electricity - consumption:** 11.81 billion kWh (2006 est.)

**Electricity - exports:** 0 kWh (2007 est.)

**Electricity - imports:** 0 kWh (2007 est.)

**Oil - production:** 12 bbl/day (2004)

**Oil - consumption:** 117,300 bbl/day (2006 est.)

**Oil - exports:** 0 bbl/day (2005)

**Oil - imports:** 116,600 bbl/day (2005)

**Oil - proved reserves:** NA bbl

**Natural gas - production:** 0 cu m (2007 est.)

**Natural gas - consumption:** 250 million cu m (2006 est.)

**Natural gas - exports:** 0 cu m (2007 est.)

**Natural gas - imports:** 239.8 million cu m (2005)

**Natural gas - proved reserves:** 0 cu m (1 January 2006 est.)

**Current account balance:** -$4.23 billion (2008 est.)

**Exports:** $7.17 billion f.o.b. (2008 est.)

**Exports - commodities:** ferronickel, sugar, gold, silver, coffee, cocoa, tobacco, meats, consumer goods

**Exports - partners:** US 66.4%, Belgium 3.7%, Finland 3.2% (2007)

**Imports:** $16.02 billion f.o.b. (2008 est.)

**Imports - commodities:** foodstuffs, petroleum, cotton and fabrics, chemicals and pharmaceuticals

**Imports - partners:** US 46%, Venezuela 8.1%, Mexico 5.9%, Colombia 4.7% (2007)

**Reserves of foreign exchange and gold:** $2.162 billion (31 December 2008 est.)

**Debt - external:** $11.7 billion (31 December 2008 est.)

**Stock of direct foreign investment - at home:** $14.75 billion (2008 est.)

**Stock of direct foreign investment - abroad:** $59 million (2008 est.)

**Exchange rates:** Dominican pesos (DOP) per US dollar - 34.775 (2008 est.), 33.113 (2007), 33.406 (2006), 30.409 (2005), 42.12 (2004)

## Communications

**Telephones - main lines in use:** 907,000 (2007)

**Telephones - mobile cellular:** 5.513 million (2007)

**Telephone system:**
*general assessment:* relatively efficient system based on island-wide microwave radio relay network
*domestic:* fixed telephone line density is about 10 per 100 persons; multiple providers of mobile cellular service with a subscribership of roughly 60 per 100 persons
*international:* country code - 1-809; landing point for the Americas Region Caribbean Ring System (ARCOS-1) fiber-optic telecommunications submarine cable that provides links to South and Central America, parts of the Caribbean, and US; satellite earth station - 1 Intelsat (Atlantic Ocean) (2007)

**Radio broadcast stations:** AM 120, FM 56, shortwave 4 (1998)

**Television broadcast stations:** 25 (2003)

**Internet country code:** .do

**Internet hosts:** 105,546 (2008)

**Internet users:** 1.677 million (2007)

## Transportation

**Airports:** 36 (2008)

**Airports - with paved runways:**
*total:* 18
*over 3,047 m:* 3
*2,438 to 3,047 m:* 4
*1,524 to 2,437 m:* 5
*914 to 1,523 m:* 5
*under 914 m:* 1 (2008)

**Airports - with unpaved runways:**
*total:* 18
*1,524 to 2,437 m:* 2
*914 to 1,523 m:* 3
*under 914 m:* 13 (2008)

**Railways:**
*total:* 517 km
*standard gauge:* 375 km 1.435-m gauge
*narrow gauge:* 142 km 0.762-m gauge
*note:* additional 1,226 km operated by sugar companies in 1.076 m, 0.889 m, and 0.762-m gauges (2006)

**Roadways:**
*total:* 19,705 km
*paved:* 9,872 km
*unpaved:* 9,833 km (2002)

**Merchant marine:**
*total:* 1
*by type:* cargo 1
*registered in other countries:* 1 (Panama 1) (2008)
**Ports and terminals:** Boca Chica, Caucedo, Puerto Plata, Rio Haina, Santo Domingo

## Military

**Military branches:** Army, Navy, Air Force (Fuerza Aerea Dominicana, FAD) (2007)
**Military service age and obligation:** 18 years of age for voluntary military service (2007)
**Manpower available for military service:**
*males age 16-49:* 2,440,203
*females age 16-49:* 2,326,694 (2008 est.)
**Manpower fit for military service:**
*males age 16-49:* 2,056,774
*females age 16-49:* 1,921,836 (2009 est.)
**Manpower reaching militarily significant age annually:**
*male:* 97,766
*female:* 93,922 (2009 est.)
**Military expenditures:** 0.8% of GDP (2006)

## Transnational Issues

**Disputes - international:** Haitian migrants cross the porous border into the Dominican Republic to find work; illegal migrants from the Dominican Republic cross the Mona Passage each year to Puerto Rico to find better work
**Trafficking in persons:**
*current situation:* the Dominican Republic is a source, transit, and destination country for men, women, and children trafficked for the purposes of commercial sexual exploitation and forced labor; a large number of Dominican women are trafficked into prostitution and sexual exploitation in Western Europe, Australia, Central and South America, and Caribbean destinations; a significant number of women, boys, and girls are trafficked within the country for sexual exploitation and domestic servitude
*tier rating:* Tier 2 Watch List - for a second consecutive year, the Dominican Republic is on the Tier 2 Watch List for its failure to show evidence of increasing efforts to combat human trafficking, particularly in terms of not adequately investigating and prosecuting public officials who may be complicit with trafficking activity, and inadequate government efforts to protect trafficking victims; the government has taken measures to reduce demand for commercial sex acts with children through criminal prosecutions (2008)
**Illicit drugs:** transshipment point for South American drugs destined for the US and Europe; has become a transshipment point for ecstasy from the Netherlands and Belgium destined for US and Canada; substantial money laundering activity in particular by Colombian narcotics traffickers; significant amphetamine consumption (2008)

# Ecuador

## Introduction

**Background:** What is now Ecuador formed part of the northern Inca Empire until the Spanish conquest in 1533. Quito became a seat of Spanish colonial government in 1563 and part of the Viceroyalty of New Granada in 1717. The territories of the Viceroyalty - New Granada (Colombia), Venezuela, and Quito - gained their independence between 1819 and 1822 and formed a federation known as Gran Colombia. When Quito withdrew in 1830, the traditional name was changed in favor of the "Republic of the Equator." Between 1904 and 1942, Ecuador lost territories in a series of conflicts with its neighbors. A border war with Peru that flared in 1995 was resolved in 1999. Although Ecuador marked 25 years of civilian governance in 2004, the period has been marred by political instability. Protests in Quito have contributed to the mid-term ouster of Ecuador's last three democratically elected Presidents. In September 2008, voters approved a new constitution; Ecuador's twentieth since gaining independence. General elections, under the new constitutional framework, are expected in April 2009.

## Geography

**Location:** Western South America, bordering the Pacific Ocean at the Equator, between Colombia and Peru
**Geographic coordinates:** 2 00 S, 77 30 W
**Map references:** South America
**Area:**
*total:* 283,560 sq km
*land:* 276,840 sq km
*water:* 6,720 sq km
*note:* includes Galapagos Islands
**Area - comparative:** slightly smaller than Nevada
**Land boundaries:**
*total:* 2,010 km
*border countries:* Colombia 590 km, Peru 1,420 km
**Coastline:** 2,237 km

**Maritime claims:**
*territorial sea:* 200 nm
*continental shelf:* 100 nm from 2,500-m isobath
**Climate:** tropical along coast, becoming cooler inland at higher elevations; tropical in Amazonian jungle lowlands
**Terrain:** coastal plain (costa), inter-Andean central highlands (sierra), and flat to rolling eastern jungle (oriente)
**Elevation extremes:**
*lowest point:* Pacific Ocean 0 m
*highest point:* Chimborazo 6,267 m
*note:* due to the fact that the earth is not a perfect sphere and has an equatorial bulge, the highest point on the planet furthest from its center is Mount Chimborazo not Mount Everest, which is merely the highest point above sea-level
**Natural resources:** petroleum, fish, timber, hydropower
**Land use:**
*arable land:* 5.71%
*permanent crops:* 4.81%
*other:* 89.48% (2005)
**Irrigated land:** 8,650 sq km (2003)
**Total renewable water resources:** 432 cu km (2000)
**Freshwater withdrawal (domestic/industrial/agricultural):**
*total:* 16.98 cu km/yr (12%/5%/82%)
*per capita:* 1,283 cu m/yr (2000)
**Natural hazards:** frequent earthquakes; landslides; volcanic activity; floods; periodic droughts
**Environment - current issues:** deforestation; soil erosion; desertification; water pollution; pollution from oil production wastes in ecologically sensitive areas of the Amazon Basin and Galapagos Islands
**Environment - international agreements:**
*party to:* Antarctic-Environmental Protocol, Antarctic Treaty, Biodiversity, Climate Change, Climate Change-Kyoto Protocol, Desertification, Endangered Species, Hazardous Wastes, Ozone Layer Protection, Ship Pollution, Tropical Timber 83, Tropical Timber 94, Wetlands
*signed, but not ratified:* none of the selected agreements
**Geography - note:** Cotopaxi in Andes is highest active volcano in world

## People

**Population:** 14,573,101 (July 2009 est.)
**Age structure:**
*0-14 years:* 31.1% (male 2,312,610/female 2,220,378)
*15-64 years:* 62.7% (male 4,506,908/female 4,636,703)
*65 years and over:* 6.2% (male 432,144/female 464,358) (2009 est.)
**Median age:**
*total:* 25 years
*male:* 24.4 years
*female:* 25.6 years (2009 est.)

**Population growth rate:** 1.497% (2009 est.)
**Birth rate:** 20.77 births/1,000 population (2009 est.)
**Death rate:** 4.21 deaths/1,000 population (2008 est.)
**Net migration rate:** -0.81 migrant(s)/1,000 population (2009 est.)
**Urbanization:**
*urban population:* 66% of total population (2008)
*rate of urbanization:* 2.1% annual rate of change (2005-10 est.)
**Sex ratio:**
*at birth:* 1.05 male(s)/female
*under 15 years:* 1.04 male(s)/female
*15-64 years:* 0.97 male(s)/female
*65 years and over:* 0.93 male(s)/female
*total population:* 0.99 male(s)/female (2009 est.)
**Infant mortality rate:**
*total:* 20.9 deaths/1,000 live births
*male:* 24.4 deaths/1,000 live births
*female:* 17.24 deaths/1,000 live births (2009 est.)
**Life expectancy at birth:**
*total population:* 75.3 years
*male:* 72.37 years
*female:* 78.37 years (2009 est.)
**Total fertility rate:** 2.51 children born/woman (2009 est.)
**HIV/AIDS - adult prevalence rate:** 0.3% (2007 est.)
**HIV/AIDS - people living with HIV/AIDS:** 26,000 (2007 est.)
**HIV/AIDS - deaths:** 1,400 (2007 est.)
**Major infectious diseases:**
*degree of risk:* high
*food or waterborne diseases:* bacterial diarrhea, hepatitis A, and typhoid fever
*vectorborne diseases:* dengue fever and malaria
*water contact disease:* leptospirosis (2009)
**Nationality:**
*noun:* Ecuadorian(s)
*adjective:* Ecuadorian
**Ethnic groups:** mestizo (mixed Amerindian and white) 65%, Amerindian 25%, Spanish and others 7%, black 3%
**Religions:** Roman Catholic 95%, other 5%
**Languages:** Spanish (official), Amerindian languages (especially Quechua)
**Literacy:**
*definition:* age 15 and over can read and write
*total population:* 91%
*male:* 92.3%
*female:* 89.7% (2001 census)
**Education expenditures:** 1% of GDP (2001)

## Government

**Country name:**
*conventional long form:* Republic of Ecuador
*conventional short form:* Ecuador
*local long form:* Republica del Ecuador
*local short form:* Ecuador
**Government type:** republic
**Capital:**
*name:* Quito
*geographic coordinates:* 0 13 S, 78 30 W
*time difference:* UTC-5 (same time as Washington, DC during Standard Time)

**Administrative divisions:** 24 provinces (provincias, singular - provincia); Azuay, Bolivar, Canar, Carchi, Chimborazo, Cotopaxi, El Oro, Esmeraldas, Galapagos, Guayas, Imbabura, Loja, Los Rios, Manabi, Morona-Santiago, Napo, Orellana, Pastaza, Pichincha, Santa Elena, Santo Domingo de los Tsachilas, Sucumbios, Tungurahua, Zamora-Chinchipe
**Independence:** 24 May 1822 (from Spain)
**National holiday:** Independence Day (independence of Quito), 10 August (1809)
**Constitution:** 20 October 2008
**Legal system:** based on civil law system; has not accepted compulsory ICJ jurisdiction
**Suffrage:** 18 years of age; universal, compulsory for literate persons ages 18-65, optional for other eligible voters
**Executive branch:**
*chief of state:* President Rafael CORREA Delgado (since 15 January 2007); Vice President Lenin MORENO Garces (since 15 January 2007); note - the president is both the chief of state and head of government
*head of government:* President Rafael CORREA Delgado (since 15 January 2007); Vice President Lenin MORENO Garces (since 15 January 2007)
*cabinet:* Cabinet appointed by the president
*elections:* the president and vice president are elected on the same ticket by popular vote for a four-year term and can be re-elected for another consecutive term; election last held 26 April 2009 (next to be held 2013)
*election results:* President Rafael CORREA Delgado reelected president; percent of vote - Rafael CORREA Delgado 51.7%; Lucio GUTIERREZ 28%; Alvaro NOBOA 11.6%; other 8.7%; note - official results pending
**Legislative branch:** unicameral National Congress or Congreso Nacional (100 seats; members are elected through a party-list proportional representation system to serve four-year terms)
*elections:* last held 15 October 2006 (next to be held 26 April 2009)
*election results:* percent of vote by party - NA; seats by party - PRIAN 28; PSP 24; PSC 13; ID 7; PRE 6; MUPP-NP 6; RED 5; UDC 5; other 6; note - defections by members of National Congress are commonplace, resulting in frequent changes in the numbers of seats held by the various parties
*note:* when a Constituent Assembly was convened to draft a new constitution, the National Congress was placed on indefinite recess and replaced by a legislative committee; the legislative committee will continue to function until a new National Assembly is elected in April 2009
**Judicial branch:** Supreme Court or Corte Suprema (according to the Constitution, new justices are elected by the full Supreme Court; in December 2004, however, Congress successfully replaced the entire court by a simple majority resolution)

**Political parties and leaders:** Alianza PAIS Movement [Rafael Vicente CORREA Delgado]; Christian Democratic Union or UDC [Diego ORDONEZ Guerrero]; Democratic Left or ID [Andres PAEZ Benalcazar]; Ethical and Democratic Network or RED [Leon ROLDOS]; Institutional Renewal and National Action Party or PRIAN [Alvaro NOBOA]; Pachakutik Plurinational Unity Movement - New Country or MUPP-NP [Jorge GUAMAN]; Patriotic Society Party or PSP [Lucio GUTIERREZ Borbua]; Popular Democratic Movement or MPD [Ciro GUZMAN Aldaz]; Roldosist Party or PRE [Abdala BUCARAM Ortiz, director]; Social Christian Party or PSC [Pascual DEL CIOPPO]; Socialist Party - Broad Front or PS-FA [Gustavo AYALA Cruz]
**Political pressure groups and leaders:** Confederation of Indigenous Nationalities of Ecuador or CONAIE [Marlon SANTI, president]; Coordinator of Social Movements or CMS [F. Napoleon SANTOS]; Federation of Indigenous Evangelists of Ecuador or FEINE [Marco MURILLO, president]; National Federation of Indigenous Afro-Ecuatorianos and Peasants or FENOCIN [Pedro DE LA CRUZ, president]
**International organization participation:** CAN, FAO, G-77, IADB, IAEA, IBRD, ICAO, ICC, ICCt, ICRM, IDA, IFAD, IFC, IFRCS, IHO, ILO, IMF, IMO, Interpol, IOC, IOM, IPU, ISO, ITSO, ITU, ITUC, LAES, LAIA, Mercosur (associate), MIGA, MINURCAT, MINUSTAH, NAM, OAS, OPANAL, OPCW, OPEC, PCA, RG, UN, UNASUR, UNCTAD, UNESCO, UNHCR, UNIDO, Union Latina, UNMIL, UNMIS, UNOCI, UNWTO, UPU, WCL, WCO, WFTU, WHO, WIPO, WMO, WTO
**Diplomatic representation in the US:**
*chief of mission:* Ambassador Luis Benigno GALLEGOS Chiriboga
*chancery:* 2535 15th Street NW, Washington, DC 20009
*telephone:* [1] (202) 234-7200
*FAX:* [1] (202) 667-3482
*consulate(s) general:* Chicago, Houston, Los Angeles, Miami, New Orleans, New York, Newark (New Jersey), San Francisco
**Diplomatic representation from the US:**
*chief of mission:* Ambassador Heather HODGES
*embassy:* Avenida Avigiras E12-170 y Avenida Eloy Alfaro, Quito
*mailing address:* Avenida Guayacanes N52-205 y Avenida Avigiras
*telephone:* [593] (2) 398-5000
*FAX:* [593] (2) 398-5100
*consulate(s) general:* Guayaquil
**Flag description:** three horizontal bands of yellow (top, double width), blue, and red with the coat of arms superimposed at the center of the flag; similar to the flag of Colombia, which is shorter and does not bear a coat of arms

# Ecuador (continued)

## Economy

**Economy - overview:** Ecuador is substantially dependent on its petroleum resources, which have accounted for more than half of the country's export earnings and one-fourth of public sector revenues in recent years. In 1999/2000, Ecuador suffered a severe economic crisis, with GDP contracting by more than 6%. Poverty increased significantly, the banking system collapsed, and Ecuador defaulted on its external debt later that year. In March 2000, Congress approved a series of structural reforms that also provided for the adoption of the US dollar as legal tender. Dollarization stabilized the economy, and positive growth returned in the years that followed, helped by high oil prices, remittances, and increased non-traditional exports. From 2002-06 the economy grew 5.5%, the highest five-year average in 25 years. The poverty rate declined but remained high at 38% in 2006. In 2006 the government imposed a windfall revenue tax on foreign oil companies, leading to the suspension of free trade negotiations with the US. These measures led to a drop in petroleum production in 2007. President Rafael CORREA raised the specter of debt default and followed through on those threats in December 2008 by defaulting on some commercial bond obligations. He also decreed a higher windfall revenue tax on private oil companies, then renegotiated their contracts to overcome the debilitating effect of the tax. This generated economic uncertainty; private investment has dropped and economic growth has slowed.

**GDP (purchasing power parity):**
$107.1 billion (2008 est.)
$101.1 billion (2007)
$98.73 billion (2006)
*note:* data are in 2008 US dollars

**GDP (official exchange rate):** $54.67 billion (2008 est.)

**GDP - real growth rate:**
5.9% (2008 est.)
2.4% (2007 est.)
3.9% (2006 est.)

**GDP - per capita (PPP):**
$7,500 (2008 est.)
$7,200 (2007 est.)
$7,100 (2006 est.)
*note:* data are in 2008 US dollars

**GDP - composition by sector:**
*agriculture:* 6.6%
*industry:* 33.9%
*services:* 59.5% (2008 est.)

**Labor force:** 4.64 million (urban) (2008 est.)

**Labor force - by occupation:**
*agriculture:* 8.3%
*industry:* 21.2%
*services:* 70.4% (2005)

**Unemployment rate:**
8.7% (2008 est.)
8.8% (2007 est.)

**Population below poverty line:** 38.3% (2006)

**Household income or consumption by percentage share:**
*lowest 10%:* 2%
*highest 10%:* 35%
*note:* data for urban households only (October 2006)

**Distribution of family income - Gini index:** 46
*note:* data are for urban households (2006)

**Investment (gross fixed):** 23.3% of GDP (2008 est.)

**Budget:**
*revenues:* $19.44 billion
*expenditures:* planned $17.79 billion (2008 est.)

**Public debt:** 29.2% of GDP (2008 est.)

**Inflation rate (consumer prices):**
8.6% (2008 est.)
2.3% (2007 est.)

**Central bank discount rate:** 10.72% (31 December 2007)

**Commercial bank prime lending rate:** 12.5% (15 October 2008)

**Stock of money:** $4.395 billion (31 December 2007)

**Stock of quasi money:** $7.974 billion (31 December 2007)

**Stock of domestic credit:** $8.926 billion (31 December 2007)

**Market value of publicly traded shares:** $4.266 billion (31 December 2007)

**Agriculture - products:** bananas, coffee, cocoa, rice, potatoes, manioc (tapioca), plantains, sugarcane; cattle, sheep, pigs, beef, pork, dairy products; balsa wood; fish, shrimp

**Industries:** petroleum, food processing, textiles, wood products, chemicals

**Industrial production growth rate:** 2% (2008 est.)

**Electricity - production:** 14.84 billion kWh (2006 est.)

**Electricity - consumption:** 12.9 billion kWh (2006 est.)

**Electricity - exports:** 38.53 million kWh (2006 est.)

**Electricity - imports:** 861 million kWh (2006 est.)

**Oil - production:** 511,600 bbl/day (2007 est.)

**Oil - consumption:** 160,500 bbl/day (2006 est.)

**Oil - exports:** 421,700 bbl/day (2005 est.)

**Oil - imports:** 47,060 bbl/day (2005)

**Oil - proved reserves:** 4.517 billion bbl (1 January 2008 est.)

**Natural gas - production:** 280 million cu m (2006 est.)

**Natural gas - consumption:** 280 million cu m (2006 est.)

**Natural gas - exports:** 0 cu m (2007 est.)

**Natural gas - imports:** 0 cu m (2007 est.)

**Natural gas - proved reserves:** 9.369 billion cu m (1 January 2006 est.)

**Current account balance:** $2.008 billion (2008 est.)

**Exports:** $19.4 billion (2008 est.)

**Exports - commodities:** petroleum, bananas, cut flowers, shrimp, cacao, coffee, hemp, wood, fish

**Exports - partners:** US 41.9%, Peru 8.5%, Chile 4.9%, Russia 4.8%, Colombia 4.7% (2007)

**Imports:** $16.6 billion f.o.b. (2008 est.)

**Imports - commodities:** industrial materials, fuels and lubricants, nondurable consumer goods

**Imports - partners:** US 23.7%, Colombia 10.3%, China 7.6%, Brazil 5.3%, Japan 4.3% (2007)

**Reserves of foreign exchange and gold:** $6.492 billion (31 December 2008 est.)

**Debt - external:** $16.96 billion (31 December 2008 est.)

**Stock of direct foreign investment - at home:** $16.81 billion (2008 est.)

**Stock of direct foreign investment - abroad:** $598 million (2008 est.)

**Exchange rates:** the US dollar is used; the sucre was eliminated in 2000

## Communications

**Telephones - main lines in use:** 1.805 million (2007)

**Telephones - mobile cellular:** 10.086 million (2007)

**Telephone system:**
*general assessment:* generally elementary but being expanded
*domestic:* fixed-line services provided by three state-owned enterprises; plans to transfer the state-owned operators to private ownership have repeatedly failed; fixed-line density stands at about 13 per 100 persons; mobile cellular use has surged and has a subscribership of nearly 75 per 100 persons
*international:* country code - 593; landing point for the PAN-AM submarine telecommunications cable that provides links to the west coast of South America, Panama, Colombia, Venezuela, and extending onward to Aruba and the US Virgin Islands in the Caribbean; satellite earth station - 1 Intelsat (Atlantic Ocean) (2007)

**Radio broadcast stations:** AM 392, FM 35, shortwave 29 (2001)

**Television broadcast stations:** 7 (plus 14 repeaters) (2000)

**Internet country code:** .ec

**Internet hosts:** 45,404 (2008)

**Internet users:** 1.549 million (2006)

## Transportation

**Airports:** 418 (2008)

**Airports - with paved runways:**
*total:* 102
*over 3,047 m:* 3
*2,438 to 3,047 m:* 4
*1,524 to 2,437 m:* 16
*914 to 1,523 m:* 27
*under 914 m:* 52 (2008)

**Airports - with unpaved runways:**
*total:* 316
*914 to 1,523 m:* 35
*under 914 m:* 281 (2008)

**Heliports:** 1 (2007)

**Pipelines:** extra heavy crude 435 km; gas 5 km; oil 1,374 km; refined products 1,301 km (2008)

**Railways:**
*total:* 966 km
*narrow gauge:* 966 km 1.067-m gauge (2006)
**Roadways:**
*total:* 43,670 km
*paved:* 6,472 km
*unpaved:* 37,198 km (2006)
**Waterways:** 1,500 km (most inaccessible) (2008)
**Merchant marine:**
*total:* 37
*by type:* cargo 1, chemical tanker 1, liquefied gas 1, passenger 8, petroleum tanker 24, refrigerated cargo 1, specialized tanker 1
*foreign-owned:* 1 (US 1)
*registered in other countries:* 5 (China 1, Panama 4) (2008)
**Ports and terminals:** Esmeraldas, Guayaquil, Manta, Puerto Bolivar

## Military

**Military branches:** Army, Navy (includes Naval Infantry, Naval Aviation, Coast Guard), Air Force (Fuerza Aerea Ecuatoriana, FAE) (2007)
**Military service age and obligation:** 20 years of age for selective conscript military service; 12-month service obligation (2008)
**Manpower available for military service:**
*males age 16-49:* 3,536,602
*females age 16-49:* 3,559,188 (2008 est.)
**Manpower fit for military service:**
*males age 16-49:* 2,708,470
*females age 16-49:* 3,165,489 (2009 est.)
**Manpower reaching militarily significant age annually:**
*male:* 148,010
*female:* 143,291 (2009 est.)
**Military expenditures:** 2.8% of GDP (2006)

## Transnational Issues

**Disputes - international:** organized illegal narcotics operations in Colombia penetrate across Ecuador's shared border, which thousands of Colombians also cross to escape the violence in their home country
**Refugees and internally displaced persons:**
*refugees (country of origin):* 11,526 (Colombia); note -UNHCR estimates as many as 250,000 Columbians are seeking asylum in Ecuador, many of whom do not register as refugees for fear of deportation (2007)
**Illicit drugs:** significant transit country for cocaine originating in Colombia and Peru, with much of the US-bound cocaine passing through Ecuadorian Pacific waters; importer of precursor chemicals used in production of illicit narcotics; attractive location for cash-placement by drug traffickers laundering money because of dollarization and weak anti-money-laundering regime; increased activity on the northern frontier by trafficking groups and Colombian insurgents (2008)

# Egypt

## Introduction

**Background:** The regularity and richness of the annual Nile River flood, coupled with semi-isolation provided by deserts to the east and west, allowed for the development of one of the world's great civilizations. A unified kingdom arose circa 3200 B.C., and a series of dynasties ruled in Egypt for the next three millennia. The last native dynasty fell to the Persians in 341 B.C., who in turn were replaced by the Greeks, Romans, and Byzantines. It was the Arabs who introduced Islam and the Arabic language in the 7th century and who ruled for the next six centuries. A local military caste, the Mamluks took control about 1250 and continued to govern after the conquest of Egypt by the Ottoman Turks in 1517. Following the completion of the Suez Canal in 1869, Egypt became an important world transportation hub, but also fell heavily into debt. Ostensibly to protect its investments, Britain seized control of Egypt's government in 1882, but nominal allegiance to the Ottoman Empire continued until 1914. Partially independent from the UK in 1922, Egypt acquired full sovereignty with the overthrow of the British-backed monarchy in 1952. The completion of the Aswan High Dam in 1971 and the resultant Lake Nasser have altered the time-honored place of the Nile River in the agriculture and ecology of Egypt. A rapidly growing population (the largest in the Arab world), limited arable land, and dependence on the Nile all continue to overtax resources and stress society. The government has struggled to meet the demands of Egypt's growing population through economic reform and massive investment in communications and physical infrastructure.

## Geography

**Location:** Northern Africa, bordering the Mediterranean Sea, between Libya and the Gaza Strip, and the Red Sea north of Sudan, and includes the Asian Sinai Peninsula
**Geographic coordinates:** 27 00 N, 30 00 E

**Map references:** Africa
**Area:**
*total:* 1,001,450 sq km
*land:* 995,450 sq km
*water:* 6,000 sq km
**Area - comparative:** slightly more than three times the size of New Mexico
**Land boundaries:**
*total:* 2,665 km
*border countries:* Gaza Strip 11 km, Israel 266 km, Libya 1,115 km, Sudan 1,273 km
**Coastline:** 2,450 km
**Maritime claims:**
*territorial sea:* 12 nm
*contiguous zone:* 24 nm
*exclusive economic zone:* 200 nm
*continental shelf:* 200 m depth or to the depth of exploitation
**Climate:** desert; hot, dry summers with moderate winters
**Terrain:** vast desert plateau interrupted by Nile valley and delta
**Elevation extremes:**
*lowest point:* Qattara Depression -133 m
*highest point:* Mount Catherine 2,629 m
**Natural resources:** petroleum, natural gas, iron ore, phosphates, manganese, limestone, gypsum, talc, asbestos, lead, zinc
**Land use:**
*arable land:* 2.92%
*permanent crops:* 0.5%
*other:* 96.58% (2005)
**Irrigated land:** 34,220 sq km (2003)
**Total renewable water resources:** 86.8 cu km (1997)
**Freshwater withdrawal (domestic/industrial/agricultural):**
*total:* 68.3 cu km/yr (8%/6%/86%)
*per capita:* 923 cu m/yr (2000)
**Natural hazards:** periodic droughts; frequent earthquakes; flash floods; landslides; hot, driving windstorm called khamsin occurs in spring; dust storms; sandstorms
**Environment - current issues:** agricultural land being lost to urbanization and windblown sands; increasing soil salination below Aswan High Dam; desertification; oil pollution threatening coral reefs, beaches, and marine habitats; other water pollution from agricultural pesticides, raw sewage, and industrial effluents; limited natural fresh water resources away from the Nile, which is the only perennial water source; rapid growth in population overstraining the Nile and natural resources
**Environment - international agreements:**
*party to:* Biodiversity, Climate Change, Climate Change-Kyoto Protocol, Desertification, Endangered Species, Environmental Modification, Hazardous Wastes, Law of the Sea, Marine Dumping, Ozone Layer Protection, Ship Pollution, Tropical Timber 83, Tropical Timber 94, Wetlands
*signed, but not ratified:* none of the selected agreements

# Egypt (continued)

**Geography - note:** controls Sinai Peninsula, only land bridge between Africa and remainder of Eastern Hemisphere; controls Suez Canal, a sea link between Indian Ocean and Mediterranean Sea; size, and juxtaposition to Israel, establish its major role in Middle Eastern geopolitics; dependence on upstream neighbors; dominance of Nile basin issues; prone to influxes of refugees

## People

**Population:** 83,082,869 (July 2009 est.)
**Age structure:**
*0-14 years:* 31.4% (male 13,345,500/ female 12,743,878)
*15-64 years:* 63.8% (male 26,823,127/ female 26,169,421)
*65 years and over:* 4.8% (male 1,701,068/female 2,299,875) (2009 est.)
**Median age:**
*total:* 24.8 years
*male:* 24.4 years
*female:* 25.2 years (2009 est.)
**Population growth rate:** 1.642% (2009 est.)
**Birth rate:** 21.7 births/1,000 population (2009 est.)
**Death rate:** 5.09 deaths/1,000 population (2008 est.)
**Net migration rate:** -0.2 migrant(s)/1,000 population (2009 est.)
**Urbanization:**
*urban population:* 43% of total population (2008)
*rate of urbanization:* 1.8% annual rate of change (2005-10 est.)
**Sex ratio:**
*at birth:* 1.05 male(s)/female
*under 15 years:* 1.05 male(s)/female
*15-64 years:* 1.02 male(s)/female
*65 years and over:* 0.74 male(s)/female
*total population:* 1.02 male(s)/female (2009 est.)
**Infant mortality rate:**
*total:* 27.26 deaths/1,000 live births
*male:* 28.93 deaths/1,000 live births
*female:* 25.51 deaths/1,000 live births (2009 est.)
**Life expectancy at birth:**
*total population:* 72.12 years
*male:* 69.56 years
*female:* 74.81 years (2009 est.)
**Total fertility rate:** 2.66 children born/woman (2009 est.)
**HIV/AIDS - adult prevalence rate:** less than 0.1% (2001 est.)
**HIV/AIDS - people living with HIV/AIDS:** 9,200 (2007 est.)
**HIV/AIDS - deaths:** fewer than 500 (2007 est.)
**Major infectious diseases:**
*degree of risk:* intermediate
*food or waterborne diseases:* bacterial diarrhea, hepatitis A, and typhoid fever
*vectorborne disease:* Rift Valley fever
*water contact disease:* schistosomiasis
*note:* highly pathogenic H5N1 avian influenza has been identified in this country; it poses a negligible risk with extremely rare cases possible among US citizens who have close contact with birds (2009)

**Nationality:**
*noun:* Egyptian(s)
*adjective:* Egyptian
**Ethnic groups:** Egyptian 99.6%, other 0.4% (2006 census)
**Religions:** Muslim (mostly Sunni) 90%, Coptic 9%, other Christian 1%
**Languages:** Arabic (official), English and French widely understood by educated classes
**Literacy:**
*definition:* age 15 and over can read and write
*total population:* 71.4%
*male:* 83%
*female:* 59.4% (2005 est.)
**Education expenditures:** 4.2% of GDP (2006)

## Government

**Country name:**
*conventional long form:* Arab Republic of Egypt
*conventional short form:* Egypt
*local long form:* Jumhuriyat Misr al-Arabiyah
*local short form:* Misr
*former:* United Arab Republic (with Syria)
**Government type:** republic
**Capital:**
*name:* Cairo
*geographic coordinates:* 30 03 N, 31 15 E
*time difference:* UTC+2 (7 hours ahead of Washington, DC during Standard Time)
*daylight saving time:* +1hr, begins last Friday in April; ends last Thursday in September
**Administrative divisions:** 26 governorates (muhafazat, singular - muhafazah); Ad Daqahliyah, Al Bahr al Ahmar (Red Sea), Al Buhayrah (El Beheira), Al Fayyum (El Faiyum), Al Gharbiyah, Al Iskandariyah (Alexandria), Al Isma'iliyah (Ismailia), Al Jizah (Giza), Al Minufiyah (El Monofia), Al Minya, Al Qahirah (Cairo), Al Qalyubiyah, Al Wadi al Jadid (New Valley), As Suways (Suez), Ash Sharqiyah, Aswan, Asyut, Bani Suwayf (Beni Suef), Bur Sa'id (Port Said), Dumyat (Damietta), Janub Sina' (South Sinai), Kafr ash Shaykh, Matruh (Western Desert), Qina (Qena), Shamal Sina' (North Sinai), Suhaj (Sohag)
**Independence:** 28 February 1922 (from the UK)
**National holiday:** Revolution Day, 23 July (1952)
**Constitution:** 11 September 1971; amended 22 May 1980, 25 May 2005, and 26 March 2007
**Legal system:** based on Islamic and civil law (particularly Napoleonic codes); judicial review by Supreme Court and Council of State (oversees validity of administrative decisions); accepts compulsory ICJ jurisdiction with reservations
**Suffrage:** 18 years of age; universal and compulsory
**Executive branch:**
*chief of state:* President Mohamed Hosni MUBARAK (since 14 October 1981)
*head of government:* Prime Minister Ahmed Mohamed NAZIF (since 9 July 2004)
*cabinet:* Cabinet appointed by the president

*elections:* president elected by popular vote for six-year term (no term limits); note - a national referendum in May 2005 approved a constitutional amendment that changed the presidential election to a multicandidate popular vote; previously the president was nominated by the People's Assembly and the nomination was validated by a national, popular referendum; last referendum held 26 September 1999; first election under terms of constitutional amendment held 7 September 2005; next election scheduled for 2011
*election results:* Hosni MUBARAK reelected president; percent of vote - Hosni MUBARAK 88.6%, Ayman NOUR 7.6%, Noman GOMAA 2.9%
**Legislative branch:** bicameral system consists of the Advisory Council or Majlis al-Shura (Shura Council) that traditionally functions only in a consultative role but 2007 constitutional amendments could grant the Council new powers (264 seats; 176 elected by popular vote, 88 appointed by the president; members serve six-year terms; mid-term elections for half of the elected members) and the People's Assembly or Majlis al-Sha'b (454 seats; 444 elected by popular vote, 10 appointed by the president; members serve five-year terms)
*elections:* Advisory Council - last held June 2007 (next to be held May-June 2010); People's Assembly - three-phase voting - last held 7 and 20 November, 1 December 2005; (next to be held November-December 2010)
*election results:* Advisory Council - percent of vote by party - NA; seats by party - NDP 84, Tagammu 1, independents 3; People's Assembly - percent of vote by party - NA; seats by party - NDP 311, NWP 6, Tagammu 2, Tomorrow Party 1, independents 112 (12 seats to be determined by rerun elections, 10 seats appointed by President)
**Judicial branch:** Supreme Constitutional Court
**Political parties and leaders:** National Democratic Party or NDP (governing party) [Mohamed Hosni MUBARAK]; National Progressive Unionist Grouping or Tagammu [Rifaat EL-SAID]; New Wafd Party or NWP [Mahmoud ABAZA]; Tomorrow Party [Moussa Mustafa MOUSSA]
*note:* formation of political parties must be approved by the government; only parties with representation in elected bodies are listed
**Political pressure groups and leaders:** Muslim Brotherhood (technically illegal)
*note:* despite a constitutional ban against religious-based parties and political activity, the technically illegal Muslim Brotherhood constitutes Hosni MUBARAK's potentially most significant political opposition; MUBARAK has alternated between tolerating limited political activity by the Brotherhood (its members, who ran as independents, hold 88 seats in the People's Assembly) and blocking its influence; civic society groups are sanctioned, but constrained in practical terms; only trade unions and professional associations affiliated with the government are officially sanctioned; Internet social networking groups and bloggers

# Egypt (continued)

**International organization participation:** ABEDA, ACCT, AfDB, AFESD, AMF, AU, BSEC (observer), CAEU, COMESA, EBRD, FAO, G-15, G-24, G-77, IAEA, IBRD, ICAO, ICC, ICCt (signatory), ICRM, IDA, IDB, IFAD, IFC, IFRCS, IHO, ILO, IMF, IMO, IMSO, Interpol, IOC, IOM, IPU, ISO, ITSO, ITU, LAS, MIGA, MINURCAT, MINURSO, MONUC, NAM, OAPEC, OAS (observer), OIC, OIF, OSCE (partner), PCA, UN, UNAMID, UNCTAD, UNESCO, UNHCR, UNIDO, UNMIL, UNMIS, UNOMIG, UNRWA, UNWTO, UPU, WCO, WFTU, WHO, WIPO, WMO, WTO

**Diplomatic representation in the US:**
*chief of mission:* Ambassador Sameh Hassan SHOUKRY
*chancery:* 3521 International Court NW, Washington, DC 20008
*telephone:* [1] (202) 895-5400
*FAX:* [1] (202) 244-4319
*consulate(s) general:* Chicago, Houston, New York, San Francisco

**Diplomatic representation from the US:**
*chief of mission:* Ambassador Margaret SCOBEY
*embassy:* 8 Kamal El Din Salah St., Garden City, Cairo
*mailing address:* Unit 64900, Box 15, APO AE 09839-4900; 5 Tawfik Diab Street, Garden City, Cairo
*telephone:* [20] (2) 2797-3300
*FAX:* [20] (2) 2797-3200

**Flag description:** three equal horizontal bands of red (top), white, and black; the national emblem (a gold Eagle of Saladin facing the hoist side with a shield superimposed on its chest above a scroll bearing the name of the country in Arabic) centered in the white band; design is based on the Arab Liberation flag and similar to the flag of Syria, which has two green stars in the white band, Iraq, which has an Arabic inscription centered in the white band, and Yemen, which has a plain white band

## Economy

**Economy - overview:** Occupying the northeast corner of the African continent, Egypt is bisected by the highly fertile Nile valley, where most economic activity takes place. Egypt's economy was highly centralized during the rule of former President Gamal Abdel NASSER but has opened up considerably under former President Anwar EL-SADAT and current President Mohamed Hosni MUBARAK. Cairo has aggressively pursued economic reforms to encourage inflows of foreign investment and facilitate GDP growth. In 2005, Prime Minister Ahmed NAZIF's government reduced personal and corporate tax rates, reduced energy subsidies, and privatized several enterprises. The stock market boomed, and GDP grew about 7% each year since 2006. Despite these achievements, the government has failed to raise living standards for the average Egyptian, and has had to continue providing subsidies for basic necessities. The subsidies have contributed to a sizeable budget deficit - roughly 7% of GDP in 2007-08 - and represent a significant drain on the economy. Foreign direct investment has increased significantly in the past two years, but the NAZIF government will need to continue its aggressive pursuit of reforms in order to sustain the spike in investment and growth and begin to improve economic conditions for the broader population. Egypt's export sectors - particularly natural gas - have bright prospects.

**GDP (purchasing power parity):**
$442.6 billion (2008 est.)
$414.1 billion (2007)
$386.6 billion (2006)
*note:* data are in 2008 US dollars

**GDP (official exchange rate):** $158.3 billion (2008 est.)

**GDP - real growth rate:**
6.9% (2008 est.)
7.1% (2007 est.)
6.8% (2006 est.)

**GDP - per capita (PPP):**
$5,400 (2008 est.)
$5,200 (2007 est.)
$4,900 (2006 est.)
*note:* data are in 2008 US dollars

**GDP - composition by sector:**
*agriculture:* 13.4%
*industry:* 37.6%
*services:* 48.9% (2008 est.)

**Labor force:** 24.72 million (2008 est.)

**Labor force - by occupation:**
*agriculture:* 32%
*industry:* 17%
*services:* 51% (2001 est.)

**Unemployment rate:**
8.7% (2008 est.)
9.1% (2007 est.)

**Population below poverty line:** 20% (2005 est.)

**Household income or consumption by percentage share:**
*lowest 10%:* 3.7%
*highest 10%:* 29.5% (2000)

**Distribution of family income - Gini index:** 34.4 (2001)

**Investment (gross fixed):** 17% of GDP (2008 est.)

**Budget:**
*revenues:* $40.46 billion
*expenditures:* $51.38 billion (2008 est.)

**Public debt:** 84.7% of GDP (2008 est.)

**Inflation rate (consumer prices):**
18% (2008 est.)
9.5% (2007 est.)

**Central bank discount rate:** 9% (31 December 2007)

**Commercial bank prime lending rate:** 12.51% (31 December 2007)

**Stock of money:** $27.6 billion (31 December 2007)

**Stock of quasi money:** $102.6 billion (31 December 2007)

**Stock of domestic credit:** $113.9 billion (31 December 2007)

**Market value of publicly traded shares:** $139.3 billion (31 December 2007)

**Agriculture - products:** cotton, rice, corn, wheat, beans, fruits, vegetables; cattle, water buffalo, sheep, goats

**Industries:** textiles, food processing, tourism, chemicals, pharmaceuticals, hydrocarbons, construction, cement, metals, light manufactures

**Industrial production growth rate:** 7.7% (2008 est.)

**Electricity - production:** 109.1 billion kWh (2006 est.)

**Electricity - consumption:** 96.2 billion kWh (2006 est.)

**Electricity - exports:** 557 million kWh (2006 est.)

**Electricity - imports:** 208 million kWh (2006 est.)

**Oil - production:** 664,000 bbl/day (2007 est.)

**Oil - consumption:** 652,700 bbl/day (2006 est.)

**Oil - exports:** 204,700 bbl/day (2005 est.)

**Oil - imports:** 140,000 bbl/day (2005)

**Oil - proved reserves:** 3.7 billion bbl (1 January 2008 est.)

**Natural gas - production:** 47.5 billion cu m (2007 est.)

**Natural gas - consumption:** 31.8 billion cu m (2007 est.)

**Natural gas - exports:** 15.7 billion cu m (2007 est.)

**Natural gas - imports:** 0 cu m (2007 est.)

**Natural gas - proved reserves:** 1.656 trillion cu m (1 January 2008 est.)

**Current account balance:** $1.483 billion (2008 est.)

**Exports:** $33.36 billion f.o.b. (2008 est.)

**Exports - commodities:** crude oil and petroleum products, cotton, textiles, metal products, chemicals

**Exports - partners:** US 9.7%, Italy 9.5%, Spain 7.6%, Syria 5.5%, Saudi Arabia 4.9%, UK 4.2% (2007)

**Imports:** $56.43 billion f.o.b. (2008 est.)

**Imports - commodities:** machinery and equipment, foodstuffs, chemicals, wood products, fuels

**Imports - partners:** US 11.7%, China 9.7%, Italy 6.4%, Germany 6.3%, Saudi Arabia 4.7%, Russia 4.3% (2007)

**Reserves of foreign exchange and gold:** $36.91 billion (31 December 2008 est.)

**Debt - external:** $28.84 billion (31 December 2008 est.)

**Stock of direct foreign investment - at home:** $59.03 billion (2008 est.)

**Stock of direct foreign investment - abroad:** $2.28 billion (2008 est.)

**Exchange rates:** Egyptian pounds (EGP) per US dollar - 5.4 (2008 est.), 5.67 (2007), 5.725 (2006), 5.78 (2005), 6.1962 (2004)

## Communications

**Telephones - main lines in use:** 11.229 million (2007)

**Telephones - mobile cellular:** 30.065 million (2007)

**Telephone system:**

*general assessment:* large system; underwent extensive upgrading during 1990s and is reasonably modern; Telecom Egypt, the landline monopoly, has been increasing service availability and in 2007 fixed-line density stood at 14 per 100 persons; as of 2007 there were three mobile-cellular networks and service is expanding rapidly

*domestic:* principal centers at Alexandria, Cairo, Al Mansurah, Ismailia, Suez, and Tanta are connected by coaxial cable and microwave radio relay

*international:* country code - 20; landing point for both the SEA-ME-WE-3 and SEA-ME-WE-4 submarine cable networks; linked to the international submarine cable FLAG (Fiber-Optic Link Around the Globe); satellite earth stations - 4 (2 Intelsat - Atlantic Ocean and Indian Ocean, 1 Arabsat, and 1 Inmarsat); tropospheric scatter to Sudan; microwave radio relay to Israel; a participant in Medarabtel (2007)

**Radio broadcast stations:** AM 42 (plus 15 repeaters), FM 11, shortwave 3 (1999)

**Television broadcast stations:** 98 (September 1995)

**Internet country code:** .eg

**Internet hosts:** 175,342 (2008)

**Internet users:** 8.62 million (2007)

## Transportation

**Airports:** 85 (2008)

**Airports - with paved runways:**

*total:* 71

*over 3,047 m:* 15

*2,438 to 3,047 m:* 35

*1,524 to 2,437 m:* 15

*914 to 1,523 m:* 2

*under 914 m:* 4 (2008)

**Airports - with unpaved runways:**

*total:* 14

*2,438 to 3,047 m:* 1

*1,524 to 2,437 m:* 3

*914 to 1,523 m:* 5

*under 914 m:* 5 (2008)

**Heliports:** 3 (2007)

**Pipelines:** condensate 320 km; condensate/gas 13 km; gas 5,586 km; liquid petroleum gas 956 km; oil 4,314 km; oil/gas/water 3 km; refined products 895 km; unknown 59 km; water 9 km (2008)

**Railways:**

*total:* 5,063 km

*standard gauge:* 5,063 km 1.435-m gauge (62 km electrified) (2006)

**Roadways:**

*total:* 92,370 km

*paved:* 74,820 km

*unpaved:* 17,550 km (2004)

**Waterways:** 3,500 km

*note:* includes Nile River, Lake Nasser, Alexandria-Cairo Waterway, and numerous smaller canals in delta; Suez Canal (193.5 km including approaches) navigable by oceangoing vessels drawing up to 17.68 m (2007)

**Merchant marine:**

*total:* 67

*by type:* bulk carrier 11, cargo 28, container 2, passenger/cargo 4, petroleum tanker 13, roll on/roll off 9

*foreign-owned:* 10 (Denmark 1, Greece 8, Lebanon 1)

*registered in other countries:* 58 (Cambodia 13, Georgia 12, Honduras 3, North Korea 1, Malta 1, Moldova 1, Panama 17, Saint Kitts and Nevis 2, Saint Vincent and the Grenadines 3, Saudi Arabia 1, Sierra Leone 3, Togo 1) (2008)

**Ports and terminals:** Ayn Sukhnah, Alexandria, Damietta, El Dekheila, Sidi Kurayr, Suez

## Military

**Military branches:** Army, Navy, Air Force, Air Defense Command

**Military service age and obligation:** 18-30 years of age for male conscript military service; service obligation 12-36 months, followed by a 9-year reserve obligation (2008)

**Manpower available for military service:**

*males age 16-49:* 21,247,777

*females age 16-49:* 20,406,408 (2008 est.)

**Manpower fit for military service:**

*males age 16-49:* 18,490,522

*females age 16-49:* 17,719,905 (2009 est.)

**Manpower reaching militarily significant age annually:**

*male:* 831,157

*female:* 792,330 (2009 est.)

**Military expenditures:** 3.4% of GDP (2005 est.)

## Transnational Issues

**Disputes - international:** while Sudan retains claim to the Hala'ib Triangle north of the 1899 Treaty boundary along the 22nd Parallel, both states withdrew their military presence in the 1990s and Egypt has invested in and effectively administers the area; Egypt no longer shows its administration of the Bir Tawil trapezoid in Sudan on its maps; Gazan breaches in the security wall with Egypt in January 2008 highlight difficulties in monitoring the Sinai border

**Refugees and internally displaced persons:**

*refugees (country of origin):* 60,000 - 80,000 (Iraq); 70,198 (Palestinian Territories); 12,157 (Sudan) (2007)

**Trafficking in persons:**

*current situation:* Egypt is a transit country for women trafficked from Eastern European countries to Israel for sexual exploitation, and is a source for children trafficked within the country for commercial sexual exploitation and domestic servitude, although the extent to which children are trafficked internally is unknown; children were also recruited for domestic and agricultural work; some of these children face conditions of involuntary servitude, such as restrictions on movement, non-payment of wages, threats, and physical or sexual abuse

*tier rating:* Tier 2 Watch List - Egypt is on the Tier 2 Watch List for the third year in a row because it did not provide evidence of increasing efforts to investigate and prosecute traffickers; however, in July 2007, the government established the "National Coordinating Committee to Combat and Prevent Trafficking in Persons," which improved inter-governmental coordination on anti-trafficking initiatives; Egypt made no discernible efforts to punish trafficking crimes in 2007 and the Egyptian penal code does not prohibit all forms of trafficking; Egypt did not increase its services to trafficking victims during the reporting period (2008)

**Illicit drugs:** transit point for cannabis, heroin, and opium moving to Europe, Israel, and North Africa; transit stop for Nigerian drug couriers; concern as money laundering site due to lax enforcement of financial regulations

# El Salvador

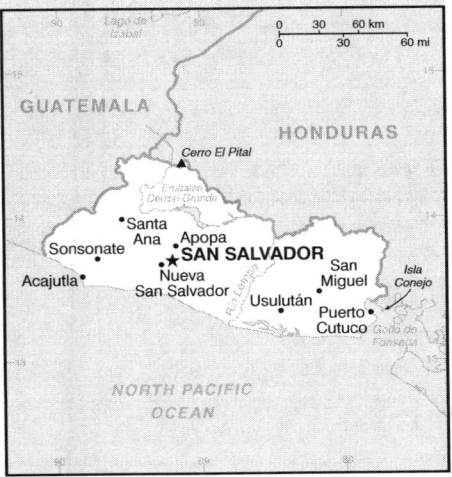

## Introduction

**Background:** El Salvador achieved independence from Spain in 1821 and from the Central American Federation in 1839. A 12-year civil war, which cost about 75,000 lives, was brought to a close in 1992 when the government and leftist rebels signed a treaty that provided for military and political reforms.

## Geography

**Location:** Central America, bordering the North Pacific Ocean, between Guatemala and Honduras
**Geographic coordinates:** 13 50 N, 88 55 W
**Map references:** Central America and the Caribbean
**Area:**
*total:* 21,040 sq km
*land:* 20,720 sq km
*water:* 320 sq km
**Area - comparative:** slightly smaller than Massachusetts
**Land boundaries:**
*total:* 545 km
*border countries:* Guatemala 203 km, Honduras 342 km
**Coastline:** 307 km
**Maritime claims:**
*territorial sea:* 12 nm
*contiguous zone:* 24 nm
*exclusive economic zone:* 200 nm
**Climate:** tropical; rainy season (May to October); dry season (November to April); tropical on coast; temperate in uplands
**Terrain:** mostly mountains with narrow coastal belt and central plateau
**Elevation extremes:**
*lowest point:* Pacific Ocean 0 m
*highest point:* Cerro El Pital 2,730 m
**Natural resources:** hydropower, geothermal power, petroleum, arable land

**Land use:**
*arable land:* 31.37%
*permanent crops:* 11.88%
*other:* 56.75% (2005)
**Irrigated land:** 450 sq km (2003)
**Total renewable water resources:** 25.2 cu km (2001)
**Freshwater withdrawal (domestic/industrial/agricultural):**
*total:* 1.28 cu km/yr (25%/16%/59%)
*per capita:* 186 cu m/yr (2000)
**Natural hazards:** known as the Land of Volcanoes; frequent and sometimes destructive earthquakes and volcanic activity; extremely susceptible to hurricanes
**Environment - current issues:** deforestation; soil erosion; water pollution; contamination of soils from disposal of toxic wastes
**Environment - international agreements:**
*party to:* Biodiversity, Climate Change, Climate Change-Kyoto Protocol, Desertification, Endangered Species, Hazardous Wastes, Ozone Layer Protection, Wetlands
*signed, but not ratified:* Law of the Sea
**Geography - note:** smallest Central American country and only one without a coastline on Caribbean Sea

## People

**Population:** 7,185,218 (July 2009 est.)
**Age structure:**
*0-14 years:* 35.4% (male 1,299,608/female 1,245,617)
*15-64 years:* 59.3% (male 2,033,423/female 2,225,810)
*65 years and over:* 5.3% (male 166,224/female 214,536) (2009 est.)
**Median age:**
*total:* 22.5 years
*male:* 21.3 years
*female:* 23.6 years (2009 est.)
**Population growth rate:** 1.656% (2009 est.)
**Birth rate:** 25.31 births/1,000 population (2009 est.)
**Death rate:** 5.53 deaths/1,000 population (2008 est.)
**Net migration rate:** -3.27 migrant(s)/1,000 population (2009 est.)
**Urbanization:**
*urban population:* 61% of total population (2008)
*rate of urbanization:* 1.9% annual rate of change (2005-10 est.)
**Sex ratio:**
*at birth:* 1.05 male(s)/female
*under 15 years:* 1.04 male(s)/female
*15-64 years:* 0.91 male(s)/female
*65 years and over:* 0.78 male(s)/female
*total population:* 0.95 male(s)/female (2009 est.)
**Infant mortality rate:**
*total:* 21.52 deaths/1,000 live births
*male:* 24.38 deaths/1,000 live births
*female:* 18.52 deaths/1,000 live births (2009 est.)

**Life expectancy at birth:**
*total population:* 72.33 years
*male:* 68.72 years
*female:* 76.11 years (2009 est.)
**Total fertility rate:** 3 children born/woman (2009 est.)
**HIV/AIDS - adult prevalence rate:** 0.8% (2007 est.)
**HIV/AIDS - people living with HIV/AIDS:** 35,000 (2007 est.)
**HIV/AIDS - deaths:** 1,700 (2007 est.)
**Major infectious diseases:**
*degree of risk:* high
*food or waterborne diseases:* bacterial diarrhea, hepatitis A, and typhoid fever
*vectorborne diseases:* dengue fever
*water contact disease:* leptospirosis (2009)
**Nationality:**
*noun:* Salvadoran(s)
*adjective:* Salvadoran
**Ethnic groups:** mestizo 90%, white 9%, Amerindian 1%
**Religions:** Roman Catholic 57.1%, Protestant 21.2%, Jehovah's Witnesses 1.9%, Mormon 0.7%, other religions 2.3%, none 16.8% (2003 est.)
**Languages:** Spanish, Nahua (among some Amerindians)
**Literacy:**
*definition:* age 10 and over can read and write
*total population:* 80.2%
*male:* 82.8%
*female:* 77.7% (2003 est.)
**School life expectancy (primary to tertiary education):**
*total:* 12 years
*male:* 12 years
*female:* 12 years (2006)
**Education expenditures:** 3.1% of GDP (2006)

## Government

**Country name:**
*conventional long form:* Republic of El Salvador
*conventional short form:* El Salvador
*local long form:* Republica de El Salvador
*local short form:* El Salvador
**Government type:** republic
**Capital:**
*name:* San Salvador
*geographic coordinates:* 13 42 N, 89 12 W
*time difference:* UTC-6 (1 hour behind Washington, DC during Standard Time)
**Administrative divisions:** 14 departments (departamentos, singular - departamento); Ahuachapan, Cabanas, Chalatenango, Cuscatlan, La Libertad, La Paz, La Union, Morazan, San Miguel, San Salvador, San Vicente, Santa Ana, Sonsonate, Usulutan
**Independence:** 15 September 1821 (from Spain)
**National holiday:** Independence Day, 15 September (1821)
**Constitution:** 20 December 1983

# El Salvador *(continued)*

**Legal system:** based on civil and Roman law with traces of common law; judicial review of legislative acts in the Supreme Court; has not accepted compulsory ICJ jurisdiction

**Suffrage:** 18 years of age; universal

**Executive branch:**

*chief of state:* President Mauricio FUNES Cartagena (since 1 June 2009); Vice President Salvador SANCHEZ CEREN (since 1 June 2009); note - the president is both the chief of state and head of government

*head of government:* President Mauricio FUNES Cartagena (since 1 June 2009); Vice President Salvador SANCHEZ CEREN (since 1 June 2009)

*cabinet:* Council of Ministers selected by the president

*elections:* president and vice president elected on the same ticket by popular vote for a single five-year term; election last held 15 March 2009 (next to be held in March 2014)

*election results:* Mauricio FUNES Cartagena elected president; percent of vote - Mauricio FUNES Cartagena 51.3%, Rodrigo AVILA 48.7%

**Legislative branch:** unicameral Legislative Assembly or Asamblea Legislativa (84 seats; members are elected by direct, popular vote to serve three-year terms)

*elections:* last held 18 January 2009 (next to be held in March 2012)

*election results:* percent of vote by party - NA; seats by party - FMLN 35, ARENA 32, PCN 11, PDC 5, CD 1

**Judicial branch:** Supreme Court or Corte Suprema (15 judges are selected by the Legislative Assembly; the 15 judges are assigned to four Supreme Court chambers - constitutional, civil, penal, and administrative conflict)

**Political parties and leaders:** Christian Democratic Party or PDC [Rodolfo PARKER]; Democratic Convergence or CD [Hector DADA HIREZI] (formerly United Democratic Center or CDU); Farabundo Marti National Liberation Front or FMLN [Medardo GONZALEZ]; National Conciliation Party or PCN [Ciro CRUZ ZEPEDA]; Nationalist Republican Alliance or ARENA [Rodrigo AVILA]; Popular Social Christian Party or PPSC [Rene AGUILUZ]; Revolutionary Democratic Front or FDR [Julio Cesar HERNANDEZ Carcamo]

**Political pressure groups and leaders:** labor organizations - Electrical Industry Union of El Salvador or SIES; Federation of the Construction Industry, Similar Transport and other activities, or FESINCONTRANS; National Confederation of Salvadoran Workers or CNTS; National Union of Salvadoran Workers or UNTS; Port Industry Union of El Salvador or SIPES; Salvadoran Union of Ex-Petrolleros and Peasant Workers or USEPOC; Salvadoran Workers Central or CTS; Workers Union of Electrical Corporation or STCEL; business organizations - National Association of Small Enterprise or ANEP; Salvadoran Assembly Industry Association or ASIC; Salvadoran Industrial Association or ASI

**International organization participation:** BCIE, CACM, FAO, G-77, IADB, IAEA, IBRD, ICAO, ICC, ICRM, IDA, IFAD, IFC, IFRCS, ILO, IMF, IMO, Interpol, IOC, IOM, IPU, ISO (correspondent), ITSO, ITU, ITUC, MIGA, MINURSO, NAM (observer), OAS, OPANAL, OPCW, PCA, RG, SICA, UN, UNCTAD, UNESCO, UNIDO, UNIFIL, Union Latina, UNMIL, UNMIS, UNOCI, UNWTO, UPU, WCL, WCO, WFTU, WHO, WIPO, WMO, WTO

**Diplomatic representation in the US:**

*chief of mission:* Ambassador Rene Antonio LEON Rodriguez

*chancery:* 1400 16th Street, Washington, DC 20036

*telephone:* [1] (202) 265-9671

*FAX:* [1] (202) 234-3763

*consulate(s) general:* Chicago, Dallas, Duluth (Georgia), Houston, Las Vegas, Los Angeles, Miami, New York (2), Nogales (Arizona), Santa Ana (California), San Francisco, Washington (DC), Woodbridge (Virginia)

*consulate(s):* Boston, Elizabeth (New Jersey)

**Diplomatic representation from the US:**

*chief of mission:* Ambassador (vacant); Charge d'Affaires Robert BLAU

*embassy:* Final Boulevard Santa Elena Sur, Antiguo Cuscatlan, La Libertad, San Salvador

*mailing address:* Unit 3450, APO AA 34023; 3450 San Salvador Place, Washington, DC 20521-3450

*telephone:* [503] 2501-2999

*FAX:* [503] 2501-2150

**Flag description:** three equal horizontal bands of blue (top), white, and blue with the national coat of arms centered in the white band; the coat of arms features a round emblem encircled by the words REPUBLICA DE EL SALVADOR EN LA AMERICA CENTRAL; similar to the flag of Nicaragua, which has a different coat of arms centered in the white band - it features a triangle encircled by the words REPUBLICA DE NICARAGUA on top and AMERICA CENTRAL on the bottom; also similar to the flag of Honduras, which has five blue stars arranged in an X pattern centered in the white band

## Economy

**Economy - overview:** The smallest country in Central America, El Salvador has the third largest economy, but growth has been modest in recent years. Economic growth will decelerate in 2009 due to the global slowdown and to El Salvador's dependence on exports to the US and remittances from the US. El Salvador leads the region in remittances per capita with inflows equivalent to nearly all export income. In 2006 El Salvador was the first country to ratify the Central America-Dominican Republic Free Trade Agreement (CAFTA). CAFTA has bolstered the export of processed foods, sugar, and ethanol, and supported investment in the maquila sector. The SACA administration has sought to diversify the economy, focusing on regional transportation and tourism. El Salvador has promoted an open trade and investment environment, and has embarked on a wave of privatizations extending to telecom, electricity distribution, banking, and pension funds. In late 2006, the government and the Millennium Challenge Corporation signed a five-year, $461 million compact to stimulate economic growth and reduce poverty in the country's northern region through investments in education, public services, enterprise development, and transportation infrastructure. With the adoption of the US dollar as its currency in 2001, El Salvador lost control over monetary policy and must concentrate on maintaining a disciplined fiscal policy.

**GDP (purchasing power parity):**

$43.94 billion (2008 est.)

$42.57 billion (2007)

$40.66 billion (2006)

*note:* data are in 2008 US dollars

**GDP (official exchange rate):** $22.28 billion (2008 est.)

**GDP - real growth rate:**

3.2% (2008 est.)

4.7% (2007 est.)

4.2% (2006 est.)

**GDP - per capita (PPP):**

$6,200 (2008 est.)

$6,100 (2007 est.)

$6,000 (2006 est.)

*note:* data are in 2008 US dollars

**GDP - composition by sector:**

*agriculture:* 11.2%

*industry:* 24.7%

*services:* 64.1% (2008 est.)

**Labor force:** 2.958 million (2008 est.)

**Labor force - by occupation:**

*agriculture:* 19%

*industry:* 23%

*services:* 58% (2006 est.)

**Unemployment rate:**

6.3% (2008 est.)

6.2% (2007 est.)

*note:* data are official rates; but the economy has much underemployment

**Population below poverty line:** 30.7% (2006 est.)

**Household income or consumption by percentage share:**

*lowest 10%:* 0.7%

*highest 10%:* 38.8% (2002)

**Distribution of family income - Gini index:** 52.4 (2002)

**Investment (gross fixed):** 16% of GDP (2008 est.)

**Budget:**

*revenues:* $3.928 billion

*expenditures:* $4.226 billion (2008 est.)

**Public debt:** 26.7% of GDP (2008 est.)

**Inflation rate (consumer prices):**

4.7% (2008 est.)

4.6% (2007 est.)

**Commercial bank prime lending rate:** NA

**Stock of money:** $1.802 billion (31 December 2007)

**Stock of quasi money:** $764.1 million (31 December 2007)

**Stock of domestic credit:** $9.221 billion (31 December 2008)

# El Salvador (continued)

**Market value of publicly traded shares:** $6.743 billion (31 December 2007)
**Agriculture - products:** coffee, sugar, corn, rice, beans, oilseed, cotton, sorghum; beef, dairy products
**Industries:** food processing, beverages, petroleum, chemicals, fertilizer, textiles, furniture, light metals
**Industrial production growth rate:** 3.8% (2008 est.)
**Electricity - production:** 5.338 billion kWh (2007 est.)
**Electricity - consumption:** 4.426 billion kWh (2007 est.)
**Electricity - exports:** 8.64 million kWh (2007 est.)
**Electricity - imports:** 11.08 million kWh (2007 est.)
**Oil - production:** 0 bbl/day (2005)
**Oil - consumption:** 44,330 bbl/day (2006 est.)
**Oil - exports:** 4,963 bbl/day (2006)
**Oil - imports:** 45,210 bbl/day (2006)
**Oil - proved reserves:** 0 bbl (1 January 2006 est.)
**Natural gas - production:** 0 cu m (2007 est.)
**Natural gas - consumption:** 0 cu m (2007 est.)
**Natural gas - exports:** 0 cu m (2007 est.)
**Natural gas - imports:** 0 cu m (2007 est.)
**Natural gas - proved reserves:** 0 cu m (1 January 2006 est.)
**Current account balance:** -$1.119 billion (2008 est.)
**Exports:** $4.55 billion (2008 est.)
**Exports - commodities:** offshore assembly exports, coffee, sugar, textiles and apparel, gold, ethanol, chemicals, electricity, iron and steel manufactures
**Exports - partners:** US 51%, Guatemala 13.6%, Honduras 11.2%, Nicaragua 5.5% (2007)
**Imports:** $9.75 billion (2008 est.)
**Imports - commodities:** raw materials, consumer goods, capital goods, fuels, foodstuffs, petroleum, electricity
**Imports - partners:** US 35.7%, Mexico 9.8%, Guatemala 8.5%, China 4.7% (2007)
**Reserves of foreign exchange and gold:** $2.541 billion (31 December 2008 est.)
**Debt - external:** $9.422 billion (31 November 2008 est.)
**Stock of direct foreign investment - at home:** $6.693 billion (2008 est.)
**Stock of direct foreign investment - abroad:** $366 million (2008 est.)
**Exchange rates:** the US dollar became El Salvador's currency in 2001

## Communications

**Telephones - main lines in use:** 1.08 million (2007)
**Telephones - mobile cellular:** 6.137 million (2007)
**Telephone system:**
*general assessment:* multiple mobile-cellular service providers are expanding services rapidly and in 2007 mobile-cellular density stood at nearly 90 per 100 persons; growth in fixed-line services has slowed in the face of mobile-cellular competition
*domestic:* nationwide microwave radio relay system
*international:* country code - 503; satellite earth station -1 Intelsat (Atlantic Ocean); connected to Central American Microwave System (2007)
**Radio broadcast stations:** AM 52, FM 144, shortwave 0 (2005)
**Television broadcast stations:** 5 (1997)
**Internet country code:** .sv
**Internet hosts:** 11,434 (2008)
**Internet users:** 700,000 (2006)

## Transportation

**Airports:** 65 (2008)
**Airports - with paved runways:**
*total:* 4
*over 3,047 m:* 1
*1,524 to 2,437 m:* 1
*914 to 1,523 m:* 2 (2008)
**Airports - with unpaved runways:**
*total:* 61
*1,524 to 2,437 m:* 1
*914 to 1,523 m:* 13
*under 914 m:* 47 (2008)
**Heliports:** 1 (2007)
**Railways:**
*total:* 562 km
*narrow gauge:* 562 km 0.914-m gauge
*note:* railways have been inoperable since 2005 because of disuse and high costs that led to a lack of maintenance (2007)
**Roadways:**
*total:* 10,886 km
*paved:* 2,827 km (includes 327 km of expressways)
*unpaved:* 8,059 km (2000)
**Waterways:** Rio Lempa partially navigable for small craft (2008)
**Ports and terminals:** Acajutla, Puerto Cutuco

## Military

**Military branches:** Salvadoran Army (ES), Salvadoran Navy (FNES), Salvadoran Air Force (Fuerza Aerea Salvadorena, FAS) (2008)
**Military service age and obligation:** 18 years of age for selective compulsory military service; 16 years of age for voluntary service; service obligation - 8 months, but 11 months for officers and NCOs (2008)
**Manpower available for military service:**
*males age 16-49:* 1,634,816
*females age 16-49:* 1,775,474 (2008 est.)
**Manpower fit for military service:**
*males age 16-49:* 1,201,290
*females age 16-49:* 1,547,278 (2009 est.)
**Manpower reaching militarily significant age annually:**
*male:* 77,473
*female:* 74,655 (2009 est.)
**Military expenditures:** 5% of GDP (2006)

## Transnational Issues

**Disputes - international:** International Court of Justice (ICJ) ruled on the delimitation of "bolsones" (disputed areas) along the El Salvador-Honduras boundary, in 1992, with final agreement by the parties in 2006 after an Organization of American States (OAS) survey and a further ICJ ruling in 2003; the 1992 ICJ ruling advised a tripartite resolution to a maritime boundary in the Gulf of Fonseca advocating Honduran access to the Pacific; El Salvador continues to claim tiny Conejo Island, not identified in the ICJ decision, off Honduras in the Gulf of Fonseca
**Illicit drugs:** transshipment point for cocaine; small amounts of marijuana produced for local consumption; significant use of cocaine

# Equatorial Guinea

## Introduction

**Background:** Equatorial Guinea gained independence in 1968 after 190 years of Spanish rule. This tiny country, composed of a mainland portion plus five inhabited islands, is one of the smallest on the African continent. President Teodoro OBIANG NGUEMA MBASOGO has ruled the country since 1979 when he seized power in a coup. Although nominally a constitutional democracy since 1991, the 1996 and 2002 presidential elections - as well as the 1999 and 2004 legislative elections - were widely seen as flawed. The president exerts almost total control over the political system and has discouraged political opposition. Equatorial Guinea has experienced rapid economic growth due to the discovery of large offshore oil reserves, and in the last decade has become Sub-Saharan Africa's third largest oil exporter. Despite the country's economic windfall from oil production resulting in a massive increase in government revenue in recent years, there have been few improvements in the population's living standards.

## Geography

**Location:** Western Africa, bordering the Bight of Biafra, between Cameroon and Gabon
**Geographic coordinates:** 2 00 N, 10 00 E
**Map references:** Africa
**Area:**
*total:* 28,051 sq km
*land:* 28,051 sq km
*water:* 0 sq km
**Area - comparative:** slightly smaller than Maryland
**Land boundaries:**
*total:* 539 km
*border countries:* Cameroon 189 km, Gabon 350 km
**Coastline:** 296 km
**Maritime claims:**
*territorial sea:* 12 nm
*exclusive economic zone:* 200 nm

**Climate:** tropical; always hot, humid
**Terrain:** coastal plains rise to interior hills; islands are volcanic
**Elevation extremes:**
*lowest point:* Atlantic Ocean 0 m
*highest point:* Pico Basile 3,008 m
**Natural resources:** petroleum, natural gas, timber, gold, bauxite, diamonds, tantalum, sand and gravel, clay
**Land use:**
*arable land:* 4.63%
*permanent crops:* 3.57%
*other:* 91.8% (2005)
**Irrigated land:** NA
**Total renewable water resources:** 26 cu km (2001)
**Freshwater withdrawal (domestic/industrial/agricultural):**
*total:* 0.11 cu km/yr (83%/16%/1%)
*per capita:* 220 cu m/yr (2000)
**Natural hazards:** violent windstorms; flash floods
**Environment - current issues:** tap water is not potable; deforestation
**Environment - international agreements:**
*party to:* Biodiversity, Climate Change, Climate Change-Kyoto Protocol, Desertification, Endangered Species, Hazardous Wastes, Law of the Sea, Marine Dumping, Ozone Layer Protection, Ship Pollution, Wetlands
*signed, but not ratified:* none of the selected agreements
**Geography - note:** insular and continental regions widely separated

## People

**Population:** 633,441 (July 2009 est.)
**Age structure:**
*0-14 years:* 41.9% (male 134,823/female 130,308)
*15-64 years:* 54% (male 167,820/female 174,238)
*65 years and over:* 4.1% (male 11,574/female 14,678) (2009 est.)
**Median age:**
*total:* 18.9 years
*male:* 18.3 years
*female:* 19.6 years (2009 est.)
**Population growth rate:** 2.703% (2009 est.)
**Birth rate:** 36.52 births/1,000 population (2009 est.)
**Death rate:** 9.72 deaths/1,000 population (2008 est.)
**Net migration rate:** NA
**Urbanization:**
*urban population:* 39% of total population (2008)
*rate of urbanization:* 2.8% annual rate of change (2005-10 est.)
**Sex ratio:**
*at birth:* 1.03 male(s)/female
*under 15 years:* 1.03 male(s)/female
*15-64 years:* 0.96 male(s)/female
*65 years and over:* 0.79 male(s)/female
*total population:* 0.98 male(s)/female (2009 est.)
**Infant mortality rate:**
*total:* 81.58 deaths/1,000 live births
*male:* 82.68 deaths/1,000 live births
*female:* 80.46 deaths/1,000 live births (2009 est.)

**Life expectancy at birth:**
*total population:* 61.61 years
*male:* 60.71 years
*female:* 62.54 years (2009 est.)
**Total fertility rate:** 5.08 children born/woman (2009 est.)
**HIV/AIDS - adult prevalence rate:** 3.4% (2007 est.)
**HIV/AIDS - people living with HIV/AIDS:** 11,000 (2007 est.)
**HIV/AIDS - deaths:** 370 (2001 est.)
**Major infectious diseases:**
*degree of risk:* very high
*food or waterborne diseases:* bacterial and protozoal diarrhea, hepatitis A, and typhoid fever
*vectorborne disease:* malaria and yellow fever
*animal contact disease:* rabies (2009)
**Nationality:**
*noun:* Equatorial Guinean(s) or Equatoguinean(s)
*adjective:* Equatorial Guinean or Equatoguinean
**Ethnic groups:** Fang 85.7%, Bubi 6.5%, Mdowe 3.6%, Annobon 1.6%, Bujeba 1.1%, other 1.4% (1994 census)
**Religions:** nominally Christian and predominantly Roman Catholic, pagan practices
**Languages:** Spanish 67.6% (official), other 32.4% (includes French (official), Fang, Bubi) (1994 census)
**Literacy:**
*definition:* age 15 and over can read and write
*total population:* 87%
*male:* 93.4%
*female:* 80.5% (2000 est.)
**School life expectancy (primary to tertiary education):**
*total:* 10 years
*male:* 10 years
*female:* 9 years (2000)
**Education expenditures:** 0.6% of GDP (2003)

## Government

**Country name:**
*conventional long form:* Republic of Equatorial Guinea
*conventional short form:* Equatorial Guinea
*local long form:* Republica de Guinea Ecuatorial/Republique de Guinee equatoriale
*local short form:* Guinea Ecuatorial/Guinee equatoriale
*former:* Spanish Guinea
**Government type:** republic
**Capital:**
*name:* Malabo
*geographic coordinates:* 3 45 N, 8 47 E
*time difference:* UTC+1 (6 hours ahead of Washington, DC during Standard Time)
**Administrative divisions:** 7 provinces (provincias, singular - provincia); Annobon, Bioko Norte, Bioko Sur, Centro Sur, Kie-Ntem, Litoral, Wele-Nzas
**Independence:** 12 October 1968 (from Spain)
**National holiday:** Independence Day, 12 October (1968)

**Constitution:** approved by national referendum 17 November 1991; amended January 1995

**Legal system:** partly based on Spanish civil law and tribal custom; has not accepted compulsory ICJ jurisdiction

**Suffrage:** 18 years of age; universal

**Executive branch:**

*chief of state:* President Brig. Gen. (Ret.) Teodoro OBIANG NGUEMA MBASOGO (since 3 August 1979 when he seized power in a military coup)

*head of government:* Prime Minister Ignacio Milan TANG (since 8 July 2008);

*cabinet:* Council of Ministers appointed by the president

*elections:* president elected by popular vote for a seven-year term (no term limits); election last held 15 December 2002 (next to be held December 2009); prime minister and deputy prime ministers appointed by the president

*election results:* Teodoro OBIANG NGUEMA MBASOGO reelected president; percent of vote - Teodoro OBIANG NGUEMA MBASOGO 97.1%, Celestino Bonifacio BACALE 2.2%; elections marred by widespread fraud

**Legislative branch:** unicameral House of People's Representatives or Camara de Representantes del Pueblo (100 seats; members directly elected by popular vote to serve five-year terms)

*elections:* last held 4 May 2008 (next to be held in 2012)

*election results:* percent of vote by party - NA; seats by party - PDGE 89, EC 10, CPDS 1

*note:* Parliament has little power since the constitution vests all executive authority in the president

**Judicial branch:** Supreme Tribunal

**Political parties and leaders:** Convergence Party for Social Democracy or CPDS [Placido MICO Abogo]; Democratic Party for Equatorial Guinea or PDGE (ruling party) [Teodoro OBIANG NGUEMA MBASOGO]; Electoral Coalition or EC; Party for Progress of Equatorial Guinea or PPGE [Severo MOTO]; Popular Action of Equatorial Guinea or APGE [Avelino MOCACHE]; Popular Union or UP

**Political pressure groups and leaders:** ASODEGUE (Madrid-based pressure group for democratic reform); Global Witness (anti-corruption)

**International organization participation:** ACP, AfDB, AU, BDEAC, CEMAC, CPLP (associate), FAO, FZ, G-77, IBRD, ICAO, ICRM, IDA, IFAD, IFC, IFRCS, ILO, IMF, IMO, Interpol, IOC, ITSO, ITU, MIGA, NAM, OAS (observer), OIF, OPCW, UN, UNCTAD, UNESCO, UNIDO, UNWTO, UPU, WFTU, WHO, WIPO, WTO (observer)

**Diplomatic representation in the US:**

*chief of mission:* Ambassador Purificacion ANGUE ONDO

*chancery:* 2020 16th Street NW, Washington, DC 20009

*telephone:* [1] (202) 518-5700

*FAX:* [1] (202) 518-5252

**Diplomatic representation from the US:**

*chief of mission:* Ambassador (vacant)

*embassy:* K-3, Carreterade Aeropuerto, al lado de Restaurante El Paraiso, Malabo; note - relocated embassy is opened for limited functions; inquiries should continue to be directed to the US Embassy in Yaounde, Cameroon

*mailing address:* B.P. 817, Yaounde, Cameroon; US Embassy Yaounde, US Department of State, Washington, DC 20521-2520

*telephone:* [237] 2220-1500

*FAX:* [237] 2220-1572

**Flag description:** three equal horizontal bands of green (top), white, and red, with a blue isosceles triangle based on the hoist side and the coat of arms centered in the white band; the coat of arms has six yellow six-pointed stars (representing the mainland and five offshore islands) above a gray shield bearing a silk-cotton tree and below which is a scroll with the motto UNIDAD, PAZ, JUSTICIA (Unity, Peace, Justice)

## Economy

**Economy - overview:** The discovery and exploitation of large oil reserves have contributed to dramatic economic growth in recent years. Forestry, farming, and fishing are also major components of GDP. Subsistence farming predominates. Although pre-independence Equatorial Guinea counted on cocoa production for hard currency earnings, the neglect of the rural economy under successive regimes has diminished potential for agriculture-led growth (the government has stated its intention to reinvest some oil revenue into agriculture). A number of aid programs sponsored by the World Bank and the IMF have been cut off since 1993, because of corruption and mismanagement. No longer eligible for concessional financing because of large oil revenues, the government has been trying to agree on a "shadow" fiscal management program with the World Bank and IMF. Government officials and their family members own most businesses. Undeveloped natural resources include titanium, iron ore, manganese, uranium, and alluvial gold. Growth remained strong in 2008, led by oil.

**GDP (purchasing power parity):**
$19.37 billion (2008 est.)
$17.42 billion (2007)
$15.91 billion (2006)
*note:* data are in 2008 US dollars

**GDP (official exchange rate):** $20.16 billion (2008 est.)

**GDP - real growth rate:**
11.2% (2008 est.)
9.5% (2007 est.)
-1.9% (2006 est.)

**GDP - per capita (PPP):**
$31,400 (2008 est.)
$29,000 (2007 est.)
$27,300 (2006 est.)
*note:* data are in 2008 US dollars

**GDP - composition by sector:**

*agriculture:* 2.7%

*industry:* 92.6%

*services:* 4.6% (2008 est.)

**Labor force:** NA

**Unemployment rate:** 30% (1998 est.)

**Population below poverty line:** NA%

**Household income or consumption by percentage share:**

*lowest 10%:* NA%

*highest 10%:* NA%

**Investment (gross fixed):** 30% of GDP (2008 est.)

**Budget:**

*revenues:* $7.056 billion

*expenditures:* $3.779 billion (2008 est.)

**Public debt:** 9.3% of GDP (2008 est.)

**Inflation rate (consumer prices):**
7.5% (2008 est.)
6% (2007 est.)

**Central bank discount rate:** 5.25% (31 December 2007)

**Commercial bank prime lending rate:** 15% (31 December 2007)

**Stock of money:** $835.2 million (31 December 2007)

**Stock of quasi money:** $174.5 million (31 December 2007)

**Stock of domestic credit:** NA

**Agriculture - products:** coffee, cocoa, rice, yams, cassava (tapioca), bananas, palm oil nuts; livestock; timber

**Industries:** petroleum, fishing, sawmilling, natural gas

**Industrial production growth rate:** 12.5% (2008 est.)

**Electricity - production:** 27 million kWh (2006 est.)

**Electricity - consumption:** 25.11 million kWh (2006 est.)

**Electricity - exports:** 0 kWh (2007 est.)

**Electricity - imports:** 0 kWh (2007 est.)

**Oil - production:** 368,500 bbl/day (2007 est.)

**Oil - consumption:** 918.3 bbl/day (2006 est.)

**Oil - exports:** 375,400 bbl/day (2005)

**Oil - imports:** 1,070 bbl/day (2005)

**Oil - proved reserves:** 1.1 billion bbl (1 January 2008 est.)

**Natural gas - production:** 1.3 billion cu m (2006 est.)

**Natural gas - consumption:** 1.3 billion cu m (2006 est.)

**Natural gas - exports:** 0 cu m (2007 est.)

**Natural gas - imports:** 0 cu m (2007 est.)

**Natural gas - proved reserves:** 36.81 billion cu m (1 January 2008 est.)

**Current account balance:** $1.837 billion (2008 est.)

**Exports:** $15.82 billion f.o.b. (2008 est.)

**Exports - commodities:** petroleum, methanol, timber, cocoa

**Exports - partners:** US 20.6%, China 18.8%, Spain 13.9%, Taiwan 13.4%, France 7.5%, Japan 6.5%, Portugal 6.4% (2007)
**Imports:** $3.211 billion f.o.b. (2008 est.)
**Imports - commodities:** petroleum sector equipment, other equipment
**Imports - partners:** US 19.6%, Spain 13.7%, Cote d'Ivoire 11.9%, France 9.6%, China 7.7%, Italy 6.6%, UK 6.4%, Netherlands 4.1% (2007)
**Reserves of foreign exchange and gold:** $5.517 billion (31 December 2008 est.)
**Debt - external:** $1.652 billion (31 December 2008 est.)
**Exchange rates:** Cooperation Financiere en Afrique Centrale francs (XAF) per US dollar - 447.81 (2008 est.), 481.83 (2007), 522.4 (2006), 527.47 (2005), 528.29 (2004)
*note:* since 1 January 1999, the Central African CFA franc (XAF) has been pegged to the euro at a rate of 655.957 CFA francs per euro; Central African CFA franc (XAF) coins and banknotes are not accepted in countries using West African CFA francs (XOF), and vice versa, even though the two currencies trade at par

## Communications

**Telephones - main lines in use:** 10,000 (2005)
**Telephones - mobile cellular:** 220,000 (2007)
**Telephone system:**
*general assessment:* digital fixed-line network in most major urban areas and good mobile coverage
*domestic:* fixed-line density is about 2 per 100 persons; mobile-cellular subscribership has been increasing and in 2007 stood at about 40 percent of the population
*international:* country code - 240; international communications from Bata and Malabo to African and European countries; satellite earth station - 1 Intelsat (Indian Ocean) (2007)
**Radio broadcast stations:** AM 0, FM 3, shortwave 5 (2001)
**Television broadcast stations:** 1 (2001)
**Internet country code:** .gq
**Internet hosts:** 9 (2008)
**Internet users:** 8,000 (2006)

## Transportation

**Airports:** 6 (2008)
**Airports - with paved runways:**
*total:* 5
*2,438 to 3,047 m:* 1
*1,524 to 2,437 m:* 1
*914 to 1,523 m:* 1
*under 914 m:* 2 (2008)
**Pipelines:** gas 38 km (2008)
**Roadways:**
*total:* 2,880 km (2000)
**Merchant marine:**
*total:* 1
*by type:* cargo 1 (2008)
**Ports and terminals:** Bata, Malabo

## Military

**Military branches:** National Guard (Guardia Nacional (Army), with Coast Guard (Navy) and Air Wing) (2008)
**Military service age and obligation:** 18 years of age (est.) for compulsory military service (2008)
**Manpower available for military service:**
*males age 16-49:* 136,725
*females age 16-49:* 138,018 (2008 est.)
**Manpower fit for military service:**
*males age 16-49:* 105,468
*females age 16-49:* 107,919 (2009 est.)
**Manpower reaching militarily significant age annually:**
*male:* 6,983
*female:* 6,726 (2009 est.)
**Military expenditures:** 0.1% of GDP (2006 est.)

## Transnational Issues

**Disputes - international:** in 2002, ICJ ruled on an equidistance settlement of Cameroon-Equatorial Guinea-Nigeria maritime boundary in the Gulf of Guinea, but a dispute between Equatorial Guinea and Cameroon over an island at the mouth of the Ntem River and imprecisely defined maritime coordinates in the ICJ decision delay final delimitation; UN urges Equatorial Guinea and Gabon to resolve the sovereignty dispute over Gabon-occupied Mbane and lesser islands and to create a maritime boundary in the hydrocarbon-rich Corisco Bay
**Trafficking in persons:**
*current situation:* Equatorial Guinea is primarily a destination country for children trafficked for the purpose of forced labor and possibly for the purpose of sexual exploitation; children have been trafficked from nearby countries for domestic servitude, market labor, ambulant vending, and possibly sexual exploitation; women may also be trafficked to Equatorial Guinea from Cameroon, Benin, other neighboring countries, and China for sexual exploitation
*tier rating:* Tier 2 Watch List - Equatorial Guinea is on the Tier 2 Watch List for its failure to provide evidence of increasing efforts to eliminate trafficking, particularly in the areas of prosecuting and convicting trafficking offenders and failing to formalize mechanisms to provide assistance to victims; although the government made some effort to enforce laws against child labor exploitation, it failed to report any trafficking prosecutions or convictions in 2007; the government continued to lack shelters or formal procedures for providing care to victims (2008)

# Eritrea

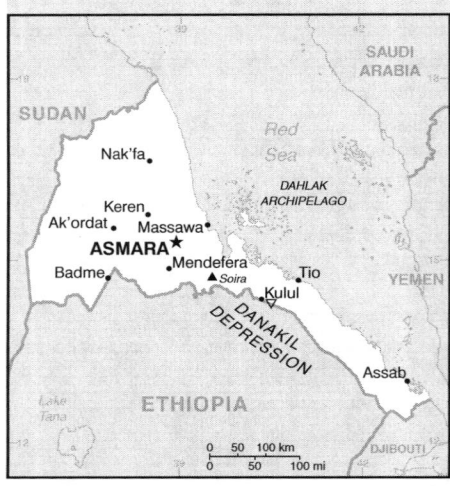

## Introduction

**Background:** Eritrea was awarded to Ethiopia in 1952 as part of a federation. Ethiopia's annexation of Eritrea as a province 10 years later sparked a 30-year struggle for independence that ended in 1991 with Eritrean rebels defeating governmental forces; independence was overwhelmingly approved in a 1993 referendum. A two-and-a-half-year border war with Ethiopia that erupted in 1998 ended under UN auspices in December 2000. Eritrea hosted a UN peacekeeping operation that monitored a 25 km-wide Temporary Security Zone (TSZ) on the border with Ethiopia. Eritrea's denial of fuel to the mission caused the UN to withdraw the mission and terminate its mandate 31 July 2008. An international commission, organized to resolve the border dispute, posted its findings in 2002. However, both parties have been unable to reach agreement on implementing the decision. On 30 November 2007, the Eritrea-Ethiopia Boundary Commission remotely demarcated the border by coordinates and dissolved itself, leaving Ethiopia still occupying several tracts of disputed territory, including the town of Badme. Eritrea accepted the EEBC's "virtual demarcation" decision and called on Ethiopia to remove its troops from the TSZ which it states is Eritrean territory. Ethiopia has not accepted the virtual demarcation decision.

## Geography

**Location:** Eastern Africa, bordering the Red Sea, between Djibouti and Sudan
**Geographic coordinates:** 15 00 N, 39 00 E
**Map references:** Africa
**Area:**
*total:* 121,320 sq km
*land:* 121,320 sq km
*water:* 0 sq km
**Area - comparative:** slightly larger than Pennsylvania

# Eritrea (continued)

**Land boundaries:**
*total:* 1,626 km
*border countries:* Djibouti 109 km, Ethiopia 912 km, Sudan 605 km
**Coastline:** 2,234 km (mainland on Red Sea 1,151 km, islands in Red Sea 1,083 km)
**Maritime claims:**
*territorial sea:* 12 nm
**Climate:** hot, dry desert strip along Red Sea coast; cooler and wetter in the central highlands (up to 61 cm of rainfall annually, heaviest June to September); semiarid in western hills and lowlands
**Terrain:** dominated by extension of Ethiopian north-south trending highlands, descending on the east to a coastal desert plain, on the northwest to hilly terrain and on the southwest to flat-to-rolling plains
**Elevation extremes:**
*lowest point:* near Kulul within the Danakil Depression -75 m
*highest point:* Soira 3,018 m
**Natural resources:** gold, potash, zinc, copper, salt, possibly oil and natural gas, fish
**Land use:**
*arable land:* 4.78%
*permanent crops:* 0.03%
*other:* 95.19% (2005)
**Irrigated land:** 210 sq km (2003)
**Total renewable water resources:** 6.3 cu km (2001)
**Freshwater withdrawal (domestic/industrial/ agricultural):**
*total:* 0.3 cu km/yr (3%/0%/97%)
*per capita:* 68 cu m/yr (2000)
**Natural hazards:** frequent droughts; locust swarms
**Environment - current issues:** deforestation; desertification; soil erosion; overgrazing; loss of infrastructure from civil warfare
**Environment - international agreements:**
*party to:* Biodiversity, Climate Change, Climate Change-Kyoto Protocol, Desertification, Endangered Species, Hazardous Wastes, Ozone Layer Protection
*signed, but not ratified:* none of the selected agreements
**Geography - note:** strategic geopolitical position along world's busiest shipping lanes; Eritrea retained the entire coastline of Ethiopia along the Red Sea upon de jure independence from Ethiopia on 24 May 1993

## People

**Population:** 5,647,168 (July 2009 est.)
**Age structure:**
*0-14 years:* 42.8% (male 1,212,848/female 1,202,240)
*15-64 years:* 53.7% (male 1,483,169/female 1,547,078)
*65 years and over:* 3.6% (male 92,009/female 109,824) (2009 est.)
**Median age:**
*total:* 18.4 years
*male:* 18 years
*female:* 18.8 years (2009 est.)

**Population growth rate:** 2.577% (2009 est.)
**Birth rate:** 34.2 births/1,000 population (2009 est.)
**Death rate:** 8.63 deaths/1,000 population (2008 est.)
**Net migration rate:** NA
**Urbanization:**
*urban population:* 21% of total population (2008)
*rate of urbanization:* 5.4% annual rate of change (2005-10 est.)
**Sex ratio:**
*at birth:* 1.03 male(s)/female
*under 15 years:* 1.01 male(s)/female
*15-64 years:* 0.96 male(s)/female
*65 years and over:* 0.84 male(s)/female
*total population:* 0.98 male(s)/female (2009 est.)
**Infant mortality rate:**
*total:* 43.33 deaths/1,000 live births
*male:* 48.97 deaths/1,000 live births
*female:* 37.51 deaths/1,000 live births (2009 est.)
**Life expectancy at birth:**
*total population:* 61.78 years
*male:* 59.71 years
*female:* 63.9 years (2009 est.)
**Total fertility rate:** 4.72 children born/woman (2009 est.)
**HIV/AIDS - adult prevalence rate:** 1.3% (2007 est.)
**HIV/AIDS - people living with HIV/AIDS:** 38,000 (2007 est.)
**HIV/AIDS - deaths:** 2,600 (2007 est.)
**Major infectious diseases:**
*degree of risk:* high
*food or waterborne diseases:* bacterial diarrhea, hepatitis A, and typhoid fever
*vectorborne disease:* malaria (2009)
**Nationality:**
*noun:* Eritrean(s)
*adjective:* Eritrean
**Ethnic groups:** Tigrinya 50%, Tigre and Kunama 40%, Afar 4%, Saho (Red Sea coast dwellers) 3%, other 3%
**Religions:** Muslim, Coptic Christian, Roman Catholic, Protestant
**Languages:** Afar, Arabic, Tigre and Kunama, Tigrinya, other Cushitic languages
**Literacy:**
*definition:* age 15 and over can read and write
*total population:* 58.6%
*male:* 69.9%
*female:* 47.6% (2003 est.)
**School life expectancy (primary to tertiary education):**
*total:* 5 years
*male:* 6 years
*female:* 4 years (2004)
**Education expenditures:** 2.4% of GDP (2006)

## Government

**Country name:**
*conventional long form:* State of Eritrea
*conventional short form:* Eritrea
*local long form:* Hagere Ertra
*local short form:* Ertra
*former:* Eritrea Autonomous Region in Ethiopia

**Government type:** transitional government
*note:* following a successful referendum on independence for the Autonomous Region of Eritrea on 23-25 April 1993, a National Assembly, composed entirely of the People's Front for Democracy and Justice or PFDJ, was established as a transitional legislature; a Constitutional Commission was also established to draft a constitution; ISAIAS Afworki was elected president by the transitional legislature; the constitution, ratified in May 1997, did not enter into effect, pending parliamentary and presidential elections; parliamentary elections were scheduled in December 2001, but were postponed indefinitely; currently the sole legal party is the People's Front for Democracy and Justice (PFDJ)
**Capital:**
*name:* Asmara (Asmera)
*geographic coordinates:* 15 20 N, 38 56 E
*time difference:* UTC+3 (8 hours ahead of Washington, DC during Standard Time)
**Administrative divisions:** 6 regions (zobatat, singular - zoba); Anseba, Debub (Southern), Debubawi K'eyih Bahri (Southern Red Sea), Gash Barka, Ma'akel (Central), Semenawi Keyih Bahri (Northern Red Sea)
**Independence:** 24 May 1993 (from Ethiopia)
**National holiday:** Independence Day, 24 May (1993)
**Constitution:** adopted on 23 May 1997, but has not yet been fully implemented
**Legal system:** primary basis is the Ethiopian legal code of 1957 with revisions; new civil, commercial, and penal codes have not yet been promulgated; government also issues unilateral proclamations setting laws and policies; also relies on customary and post-independence-enacted laws and, for civil cases involving Muslims, Islamic law; does not accept compulsory ICJ jurisdiction
**Suffrage:** 18 years of age; universal
**Executive branch:**
*chief of state:* President ISAIAS Afworki (since 8 June 1993); note - the president is both the chief of state and head of government and is head of the State Council and National Assembly
*head of government:* President ISAIAS Afworki (since 8 June 1993)
*cabinet:* State Council is the collective executive authority; members appointed by the president
*elections:* president elected by the National Assembly for a five-year term (eligible for a second term); the most recent and only election held 8 June 1993 (next election date uncertain as the National Assembly did not hold a presidential election in December 2001 as anticipated)
*election results:* ISAIAS Afworki elected president; percent of National Assembly vote - ISAIAS Afworki 95%, other 5%
**Legislative branch:** unicameral National Assembly (150 seats; members elected by direct popular vote to serve five-year terms)
*elections:* in May 1997, following the adoption of the new constitution, 75 members of the PFDJ Central

# Eritrea *(continued)*

Committee (the old Central Committee of the EPLF), 60 members of the 527-member Constituent Assembly, which had been established in 1997 to discuss and ratify the new constitution, and 15 representatives of Eritreans living abroad were formed into a Transitional National Assembly to serve as the country's legislative body until countrywide elections to a National Assembly were held; although only 75 of 150 members of the Transitional National Assembly were elected, the constitution stipulates that once past the transition stage, all members of the National Assembly will be elected by secret ballot of all eligible voters; National Assembly elections scheduled for December 2001 were postponed indefinitely

**Judicial branch:** High Court - regional, subregional, and village courts; also have military and special courts

**Political parties and leaders:** People's Front for Democracy and Justice or PFDJ [ISAIAS Afworki] (the only party recognized by the government); note - a National Assembly committee drafted a law on political parties in January 2001, but the full National Assembly has yet to debate or vote on it

**Political pressure groups and leaders:** Eritrean Democratic Party (EDP) [HAGOS, Mesfin]; Eritrean Islamic Jihad or EIJ (includes Eritrean Islamic Jihad Movement or EIJM also known as the Abu Sihel Movement); Eritrean Islamic Salvation or EIS (also known as the Arafa Movement); Eritrean Liberation Front or ELF [ABDULLAH Muhammed]; Eritrean National Alliance or ENA (a coalition including EIJ, EIS, ELF, and a number of ELF factions) [HERUY Tedla Biru]; Eritrean Public Forum or EPF [ARADOM Iyob]

**International organization participation:** ACP, AfDB, AU, COMESA, FAO, G-77, IAEA, IBRD, ICAO, ICCt (signatory), IDA, IFAD, IFC, IFRCS (observer), ILO, IMF, IMO, Interpol, IOC, ISO (correspondent), ITU, ITUC, LAS (observer), MIGA, NAM, OPCW, PCA, UN, UNCTAD, UNESCO, UNIDO, UNWTO, UPU, WCO, WFTU, WHO, WIPO, WMO

**Diplomatic representation in the US:**
*chief of mission:* Ambassador GHIRMAI Ghebremariam
*chancery:* 1708 New Hampshire Avenue NW, Washington, DC 20009
*telephone:* [1] (202) 319-1991
*FAX:* [1] (202) 319-1304
*consulate(s) general:* Oakland (California)

**Diplomatic representation from the US:**
*chief of mission:* Ambassador Ronald MCMULLEN
*embassy:* 179 Ala Street, Asmara
*mailing address:* P. O. Box 211, Asmara
*telephone:* [291] (1) 120004
*FAX:* [291] (1) 127584

**Flag description:** red isosceles triangle (based on the hoist side) dividing the flag into two right triangles; the upper triangle is green, the lower one is blue; a gold wreath encircling a gold olive branch is centered on the hoist side of the red triangle

## Economy

**Economy - overview:** Since independence from Ethiopia in 1993, Eritrea has faced the economic problems of a small, desperately poor country, accentuated by the recent implementation of restrictive economic policies. Eritrea has a command economy under the control of the sole political party, the People's Front for Democracy and Justice (PFDJ). Like the economies of many African nations, the economy is largely based on subsistence agriculture, with 80% of the population involved in farming and herding. The Ethiopian-Eritrea war in 1998-2000 severely hurt Eritrea's economy. GDP growth fell to zero in 1999 and to -12.1% in 2000. The May 2000 Ethiopian offensive into northern Eritrea caused some $600 million in property damage and loss, including losses of $225 million in livestock and 55,000 homes. The attack prevented planting of crops in Eritrea's most productive region, causing food production to drop by 62%. Despite the fighting, Eritrea developed its transportation infrastructure, asphalting new roads, improving its ports, and repairing war-damaged roads and bridges. Since the war's conclusion, the government has maintained a firm grip on the economy, expanding the use of the military and party-owned businesses to complete Eritrea's development agenda. The government strictly controls the use of foreign currency by limiting access and availability. Few private enterprises remain in Eritrea. Eritrea's economy depends heavily on taxes paid by members of the diaspora. Erratic rainfall and the delayed demobilization of agriculturalists from the military continue to interfere with agricultural production, and Eritrea's recent harvests have been unable to meet the food needs of the country. The Government continues to place its hope for additional revenue on the development of several international mining projects. Despite difficulties for international companies in working with the Eritrean Government, a Canadian mining company signed a contract with the Government in 2007 and plans to begin mineral extraction in 2010. Eritrea also opened a free trade zone at the port of Massawa in 2008. Eritrea's economic future depends upon its ability to master social problems such as illiteracy, unemployment, and low skills, and more importantly, on the government's willingness to support a true market economy.

**GDP (purchasing power parity):**
$3.946 billion (2008 est.)
$3.868 billion (2007)
$3.83 billion (2006)
*note:* data are in 2008 US dollars

**GDP (official exchange rate):** $1.479 billion (2008 est.)

**GDP - real growth rate:**
2% (2008 est.)
1% (2007 est.)
-1% (2006 est.)

**GDP - per capita (PPP):**
$700 (2008 est.)
$700 (2007 est.)
$700 (2006 est.)
*note:* data are in 2008 US dollars

**GDP - composition by sector:**
*agriculture:* 17.4%
*industry:* 23.2%
*services:* 59.4% (2008 est.)

**Labor force:** NA

**Labor force - by occupation:**
*agriculture:* 80%
*industry and services:* 20% (2004 est.)

**Unemployment rate:**
NA%

**Population below poverty line:** 50% (2004 est.)

**Household income or consumption by percentage share:**
*lowest 10%:* NA%
*highest 10%:* NA%

**Investment (gross fixed):** 21.2% of GDP (2008 est.)

**Budget:**
*revenues:* $234.5 million
*expenditures:* $523.1 million (2008 est.)

**Inflation rate (consumer prices):**
18% (2008 est.)
17% (2007 est.)

**Stock of money:** $749.1 million (31 December 2007)

**Stock of quasi money:** $932.9 million (31 December 2007)

**Stock of domestic credit:** $1.711 billion (31 December 2007)

**Agriculture - products:** sorghum, lentils, vegetables, corn, cotton, tobacco, sisal; livestock, goats; fish

**Industries:** food processing, beverages, clothing and textiles, light manufacturing, salt, cement

**Industrial production growth rate:** 2% (2008 est.)

**Electricity - production:** 253 million kWh (2006 est.)

**Electricity - consumption:** 216 million kWh (2006 est.)

**Electricity - exports:** 0 kWh (2007 est.)

**Electricity - imports:** 0 kWh (2007 est.)

**Oil - production:** 0 bbl/day (2007 est.)

**Oil - consumption:** 5,186 bbl/day (2006 est.)

**Oil - exports:** 54.74 bbl/day (2005)

**Oil - imports:** 4,924 bbl/day (2005)

**Oil - proved reserves:** 0 bbl (1 January 2006 est.)

**Natural gas - production:** 0 cu m (2007 est.)

**Natural gas - consumption:** 0 cu m (2007 est.)

**Natural gas - exports:** 0 cu m (2007 est.)

**Natural gas - imports:** 0 cu m (2007 est.)

**Natural gas - proved reserves:** 0 cu m (1 January 2006 est.)

**Current account balance:** -$247 million (2008 est.)

**Exports:** $14 million f.o.b. (2008 est.)

**Exports - commodities:** livestock, sorghum, textiles, food, small manufactures

**Exports - partners:** Italy 34.4%, China 16.2%, Sudan 15.2%, France 9.4%, Saudi Arabia 5.2%, Australia 4.4% (2007)

**Imports:** $601 million f.o.b. (2008 est.)

## Eritrea *(continued)*

**Imports - commodities:** machinery, petroleum products, food, manufactured goods
**Imports - partners:** Saudi Arabia 19.1%, Italy 15.1%, China 11.1%, Turkey 8.3%, Germany 7.2%, Ukraine 5.1% (2007)
**Reserves of foreign exchange and gold:** $27 million (31 December 2008 est.)
**Debt - external:** $311 million (2000 est.)
**Exchange rates:** nakfa (ERN) per US dollar - 15.38 (2008 est.), 15.5 (2007), 15.4 (2006), 14.5 (2005), 13.788 (2004)
*note:* the official exchange rate is 15 nakfa to the dollar

### Communications

**Telephones - main lines in use:** 37,500 (2006)
**Telephones - mobile cellular:** 70,000 (2007)
**Telephone system:**
*general assessment:* inadequate; combined fixed-line and mobile cellular subscribership is only about 2 per 100 persons
*domestic:* inadequate; most telephones are in Asmara; government is seeking international tenders to improve the system (2002)
*international:* country code - 291; note - international connections exist
**Radio broadcast stations:** AM 2, FM NA, shortwave 2 (2000)
**Television broadcast stations:** 2 (2006)
**Internet country code:** .er
**Internet hosts:** 1,074 (2008)
**Internet users:** 120,000 (2007)

### Transportation

**Airports:** 14 (2008)
**Airports - with paved runways:**
*total:* 4
*over 3,047 m:* 2
*2,438 to 3,047 m:* 2 (2008)
**Airports - with unpaved runways:**
*total:* 10
*over 3,047 m:* 1
*2,438 to 3,047 m:* 1
*1,524 to 2,437 m:* 3
*914 to 1,523 m:* 3
*under 914 m:* 2 (2008)
**Heliports:** 1 (2007)
**Railways:**
*total:* 306 km
*narrow gauge:* 306 km 0.950-m gauge (2006)
**Roadways:**
*total:* 4,010 km
*paved:* 874 km
*unpaved:* 3,136 km (2000)
**Merchant marine:**
*total:* 5
*by type:* cargo 2, liquefied gas 1, petroleum tanker 1, roll on/roll off 1 (2008)
**Ports and terminals:** Assab, Massawa

### Military

**Military branches:** Eritrean Armed Forces: Ground Forces, Navy, Air Force (2008)
**Military service age and obligation:** 18-40 years of age for male and female voluntary and compulsory military service; 16-month conscript service obligation (2006)
**Manpower available for military service:**
*males age 16-49:* 1,108,836
*females age 16-49:* 1,096,120 (2008 est.)
**Manpower fit for military service:**
*males age 16-49:* 834,018
*females age 16-49:* 887,495 (2009 est.)
**Manpower reaching militarily significant age annually:**
*male:* 62,265
*female:* 62,328 (2009 est.)
**Military expenditures:** 6.3% of GDP (2006 est.)

### Transnational Issues

**Disputes - international:** Eritrea and Ethiopia agreed to abide by 2002 Ethiopia-Eritrea Boundary Commission's (EEBC) delimitation decision but, neither party responded to the revised line detailed in the November 2006 EEBC Demarcation Statement; UN Peacekeeping Mission to Ethiopia and Eritrea (UNMEE), which has monitored the 25-km-wide Temporary Security Zone in Eritrea since 2000, is extended for six months in 2007 despite Eritrean restrictions on its operations and reduced force of 17,000; Sudan accuses Eritrea of supporting eastern Sudanese rebel groups
**Refugees and internally displaced persons:**
*IDPs:* 32,000 (border war with Ethiopia from 1998-2000; most IDPs are near the central border region) (2007)

# Estonia

### Introduction

**Background:** After centuries of Danish, Swedish, German, and Russian rule, Estonia attained independence in 1918. Forcibly incorporated into the USSR in 1940 - an action never recognized by the US -it regained its freedom in 1991, with the collapse of the Soviet Union. Since the last Russian troops left in 1994, Estonia has been free to promote economic and political ties with Western Europe. It joined both NATO and the EU in the spring of 2004.

### Geography

**Location:** Eastern Europe, bordering the Baltic Sea and Gulf of Finland, between Latvia and Russia
**Geographic coordinates:** 59 00 N, 26 00 E
**Map references:** Europe
**Area:**
*total:* 45,226 sq km
*land:* 43,211 sq km
*water:* 2,015 sq km
*note:* includes 1,520 islands in the Baltic Sea
**Area - comparative:** slightly smaller than New Hampshire and Vermont combined
**Land boundaries:**
*total:* 633 km
*border countries:* Latvia 343 km, Russia 290 km
**Coastline:** 3,794 km
**Maritime claims:**
*territorial sea:* 12 nm
*exclusive economic zone:* limits fixed in coordination with neighboring states
**Climate:** maritime; wet, moderate winters, cool summers
**Terrain:** marshy, lowlands; flat in the north, hilly in the south
**Elevation extremes:**
*lowest point:* Baltic Sea 0 m
*highest point:* Suur Munamagi 318 m
**Natural resources:** oil shale, peat, phosphorite, clay, limestone, sand, dolomite, arable land, sea mud

# Estonia (continued)

**Land use:**
*arable land:* 12.05%
*permanent crops:* 0.35%
*other:* 87.6% (2005)
**Irrigated land:** 40 sq km (2003)'
**Total renewable water resources:** 21.1 cu km (2005)
**Freshwater withdrawal (domestic/industrial/ agricultural):**
*total:* 1.41 cu km/yr (56%/39%/5%)
*per capita:* 1,060 cu m/yr (2002)
**Natural hazards:** sometimes flooding occurs in the spring
**Environment - current issues:** air polluted with sulfur dioxide from oil-shale burning power plants in northeast; however, the amount of pollutants emitted to the air have fallen steadily, the emissions of 2000 were 80% less than in 1980; the amount of unpurified wastewater discharged to water bodies in 2000 was one-20th the level of 1980; in connection with the start-up of new water purification plants, the pollution load of wastewater decreased; Estonia has more than 1,400 natural and manmade lakes, the smaller of which in agricultural areas need to be monitored; coastal seawater is polluted in certain locations
**Environment - international agreements:**
*party to:* Air Pollution, Air Pollution-Nitrogen Oxides, Air Pollution-Persistent Organic Pollutants, Air Pollution-Sulfur 85, Air Pollution-Volatile Organic Compounds, Antarctic Treaty, Biodiversity, Climate Change, Climate Change-Kyoto Protocol, Endangered Species, Hazardous Wastes, Law of the Sea, Ozone Layer Protection, Ship Pollution, Wetlands
*signed, but not ratified:* none of the selected agreements
**Geography - note:** the mainland terrain is flat, boggy, and partly wooded; offshore lie more than 1,500 islands

## People

**Population:** 1,299,371 (July 2009 est.)
**Age structure:**
*0-14 years:* 14.9% (male 99,748/female 94,051)
*15-64 years:* 67.5% (male 417,816/female 459,246)
*65 years and over:* 17.6% (male 75,486/female 153,024) (2009 est.)
**Median age:**
*total:* 39.9 years
*male:* 36.5 years
*female:* 43.5 years (2009 est.)
**Population growth rate:** -0.632% (2009 est.)
**Birth rate:** 10.37 births/1,000 population (2009 est.)
**Death rate:** 13.35 deaths/1,000 population (2008 est.)
**Net migration rate:** -3.26 migrant(s)/1,000 population (2009 est.)
**Urbanization:**
*urban population:* 69% of total population (2008)
*rate of urbanization:* -0.3% annual rate of change (2005-10 est.)

**Sex ratio:**
*at birth:* 1.06 male(s)/female
*under 15 years:* 1.06 male(s)/female
*15-64 years:* 0.91 male(s)/female
*65 years and over:* 0.49 male(s)/female
*total population:* 0.84 male(s)/female (2009 est.)
**Infant mortality rate:**
*total:* 7.32 deaths/1,000 live births
*male:* 8.48 deaths/1,000 live births
*female:* 6.08 deaths/1,000 live births (2009 est.)
**Life expectancy at birth:**
*total population:* 72.82 years
*male:* 67.45 years
*female:* 78.53 years (2009 est.)
**Total fertility rate:** 1.42 children born/woman (2009 est.)
**HIV/AIDS - adult prevalence rate:** 1.3% (2007 est.)
**HIV/AIDS - people living with HIV/AIDS:** 9,900 (2007 est.)
**HIV/AIDS - deaths:** fewer than 500 (2007 est.)
**Major infectious diseases:**
*degree of risk:* intermediate
*food or waterborne diseases:* bacterial diarrhea
*vectorborne disease:* tickborne encephalitis (2009)
**Nationality:**
*noun:* Estonian(s)
*adjective:* Estonian
**Ethnic groups:** Estonian 67.9%, Russian 25.6%, Ukrainian 2.1%, Belarusian 1.3%, Finn 0.9%, other 2.2% (2000 census)
**Religions:** Evangelical Lutheran 13.6%, Orthodox 12.8%, other Christian (including Methodist, Seventh-Day Adventist, Roman Catholic, Pentecostal) 1.4%, unaffiliated 34.1%, other and unspecified 32%, none 6.1% (2000 census)
**Languages:** Estonian (official) 67.3%, Russian 29.7%, other 2.3%, unknown 0.7% (2000 census)
**Literacy:**
*definition:* age 15 and over can read and write
*total population:* 99.8%
*male:* 99.8%
*female:* 99.8% (2000 census)
**School life expectancy (primary to tertiary education):**
*total:* 16 years
*male:* 15 years
*female:* 17 years (2006)
**Education expenditures:** 5.1% of GDP (2004)

## Government

**Country name:**
*conventional long form:* Republic of Estonia
*conventional short form:* Estonia
*local long form:* Eesti Vabariik
*local short form:* Eesti
*former:* Estonian Soviet Socialist Republic
**Government type:** parliamentary republic
**Capital:**
*name:* Tallinn
*geographic coordinates:* 59 26 N, 24 43 E

*time difference:* UTC+2 (7 hours ahead of Washington, DC during Standard Time)
*daylight saving time:* +1hr, begins last Sunday in March; ends last Sunday in October
**Administrative divisions:** 15 counties (maakonnad, singular - maakond); Harjumaa (Tallinn), Hiiumaa (Kardla), Ida-Virumaa (Johvi), Jarvamaa (Paide), Jogevamaa (Jogeva), Laanemaa (Haapsalu), Laane-Virumaa (Rakvere), Parnumaa (Parnu), Polvamaa (Polva), Raplamaa (Rapla), Saaremaa (Kuressaare), Tartumaa (Tartu), Valgamaa (Valga), Viljandimaa (Viljandi), Vorumaa (Voru)
*note:* counties have the administrative center name following in parentheses
**Independence:** 20 August 1991 (from the Soviet Union)
**National holiday:** Independence Day, 24 February (1918); note - 24 February 1918 was the date Estonia declared its independence from Soviet Russia; 20 August 1991 was the date it declared its independence from the Soviet Union
**Constitution:** adopted 28 June 1992
**Legal system:** based on civil law system; accepts compulsory ICJ jurisdiction with reservations
**Suffrage:** 18 years of age; universal for all Estonian citizens
**Executive branch:**
*chief of state:* President Toomas Hendrik ILVES (since 9 October 2006)
*head of government:* Prime Minister Andrus ANSIP (since 12 April 2005)
*cabinet:* Ministers appointed by the prime minister, approved by Parliament
*elections:* president elected by Parliament for a five-year term (eligible for a second term); if a candidate does not secure two-thirds of the votes after three rounds of balloting in the Parliament, then an electoral assembly (made up of Parliament plus members of local councils) elects the president, choosing between the two candidates with the largest number of votes; election last held 23 September 2006 (next to be held in the fall of 2011); prime minister nominated by the president and approved by Parliament
*election results:* Toomas Hendrik ILVES elected president on 23 September 2006 by a 345-member electoral assembly; ILVES received 174 votes to incumbent Arnold RUUTEL's 162; remaining 9 ballots left blank or invalid
**Legislative branch:** unicameral Parliament or Riigikogu (101 seats; members are elected by popular vote to serve four-year terms)
*elections:* last held 4 March 2007 (next to be held in March 2011)
*election results:* percent of vote by party - Estonian Reform Party 27.8%, Center Party of Estonia 26.1%, Union of Pro Patria and Res Publica 17.9%, Social Democratic Party 10.6%, Estonian Greens 7.1%, Estonian People's Union 7.1%, other 5%; seats by party - Estonian Reform Party 31, Center Party 29, Union of Pro Patria and Res Publica 19, Social Democratic Party 10, Estonian Greens 6, Estonian People's Union 6

# Estonia (continued)

**Judicial branch:** Supreme Court (chairman appointed for life by Parliament)

**Political parties and leaders:** Center Party of Estonia (Keskerakond) [Edgar SAVISAAR]; Estonian Greens (Rohelised) [Marek STRANDBERG]; Estonian People's Union (Rahvaliit) [Villu REILJAN]; Estonian Reform Party (Reformierakond) [Andrus ANSIP]; Social Democratic Party (formerly People's Party Moodukad or Moderates) [Ivari PADAR]; Union of Pro Patria and Res Publica (Isamaa je Res Publica Liit) [Mart LAAR]

**Political pressure groups and leaders:** Nochnoy Dozor/Night Watch anti-fascist movement (leader Alexander KOROBOV)

**International organization participation:** Australia Group, BA, BIS, CBSS, CE, EAPC, EBRD, EIB, EU, FAO, IAEA, IBRD, ICAO, ICCt, ICRM, IDA, IFC, IFRCS, IHO, ILO, IMF, IMO, Interpol, IOC, IOM, IPU, ISO (correspondent), ITU, ITUC, MIGA, NATO, NIB, NSG, OAS (observer), OECD (accession state), OPCW, OSCE, PCA, Schengen Convention, UN, UNCTAD, UNESCO, UNHCR, UNITAR, UNTSO, UPU, WCO, WEU (associate partner), WFTU, WHO, WIPO, WMO, WTO

**Diplomatic representation in the US:**
*chief of mission:* Ambassador Vaino REINART
*chancery:* 2131 Massachusetts Avenue NW, Washington, DC 20008
*telephone:* [1] (202) 588-0101
*FAX:* [1] (202) 588-0108
*consulate(s) general:* New York

**Diplomatic representation from the US:**
*chief of mission:* Ambassador (vacant); Charge d'Affaires Karen DECKER
*embassy:* Kentmanni 20, 15099 Tallinn
*mailing address:* use embassy street address
*telephone:* [372] 668-8100
*FAX:* [372] 668-8265

**Flag description:** pre-1940 flag restored by Supreme Soviet in May 1990 - three equal horizontal bands of blue (top), black, and white

## Economy

**Economy - overview:** Estonia, a 2004 European Union entrant, has a modern market-based economy and one of the highest per capita income levels in Central Europe. Estonia's successive governments have pursued a free market, pro-business economic agenda and have wavered little in their commitment to pro-market reforms. Tallinn's priority has been to sustain high growth rates - on average 8% per year from 2003 to 2007. The economy benefits from strong electronics and telecommunications sectors and strong trade ties with Finland, Sweden, and Germany. The current government has pursued relatively sound fiscal policies, resulting in balanced budgets and low public debt. Rapid growth, however, has made it difficult to keep inflation and large current-account deficits from soaring, putting downward pressure on the country's currency. The government has not given up on adopting the euro, but has repeatedly postponed its target date. Estonia's

economy slowed down markedly and even fell into recession in mid-2008, primarily as a result of an investment and consumption slump following the bursting of the real estate market bubble.

**GDP (purchasing power parity):**
$27.72 billion (2008 est.)
$28.73 billion (2007)
$27.02 billion (2006)
*note:* data are in 2008 US dollars

**GDP (official exchange rate):** $23.46 billion (2008 est.)

**GDP - real growth rate:**
-3% (2008 est.)
6.3% (2007 est.)
10.4% (2006 est.)

**GDP - per capita (PPP):**
$21,200 (2008 est.)
$21,800 (2007 est.)
$20,400 (2006 est.)
*note:* data are in 2008 US dollars

**GDP - composition by sector:**
*agriculture:* 2.9%
*industry:* 32.3%
*services:* 64.8% (2008 est.)

**Labor force:** 686,000 (2008 est.)

**Labor force - by occupation:**
*agriculture:* 4.7%
*industry:* 33.7%
*services:* 61.6% (2007)

**Unemployment rate:**
6.2% (30 September 2008 est.)
4.7% (2007 est.)

**Population below poverty line:** 5% (2003)

**Household income or consumption by percentage share:**
*lowest 10%:* 2.5%
*highest 10%:* 27.6% (2003)

**Distribution of family income - Gini index:** 34 (2008)

**Investment (gross fixed):** 29.4% of GDP (2008 est.)

**Budget:**
*revenues:* $8.92 billion
*expenditures:* $9.091 billion (2008 est.)

**Public debt:** 3.8% of GDP (2008 est.)

**Inflation rate (consumer prices):**
10.4% (2008 est.)
6.6% (2007 est.)

**Commercial bank prime lending rate:** 6.46% (31 December 2007)

**Stock of money:** $7.158 billion (31 December 2007)

**Stock of quasi money:** $4.253 billion (31 December 2007)

**Stock of domestic credit:** $21.35 billion (31 December 2007)

**Market value of publicly traded shares:** $6.037 billion (31 December 2007)

**Agriculture - products:** potatoes, vegetables; livestock and dairy products; fish

**Industries:** engineering, electronics, wood and wood products, textiles; information technology, telecommunications

**Industrial production growth rate:** 2.5% (2008 est.)

**Electricity - production:** 12.19 billion kWh (2007)

**Electricity - consumption:** 7.18 billion kWh (2007)

**Electricity - exports:** 2.765 billion kWh (2007)

**Electricity - imports:** 345 million kWh (2007)

**Oil - production:** 7,430 bbl/day (2007 est.)

**Oil - consumption:** 30,440 bbl/day (2006 est.)

**Oil - exports:** 7,000 bbl/day (2005)

**Oil - imports:** 28,170 bbl/day (2005)

**Oil - proved reserves:** 0 bbl (1 January 2006 est.)

**Natural gas - production:** 0 cu m (2007)

**Natural gas - consumption:** 1.003 billion cu m (2007)

**Natural gas - exports:** 0 cu m (2007)

**Natural gas - imports:** 1.003 billion cu m (2007 est.)

**Natural gas - proved reserves:** 0 cu m (1 January 2006 est.)

**Current account balance:** -$3.037 billion (2008 est.)

**Exports:** $13.16 billion f.o.b. (2008 est.)

**Exports - commodities:** machinery and equipment 29%, wood and paper 13%, metals 10%, food products 8%, textiles 5%, chemical products (2007)

**Exports - partners:** Finland 17.9%, Sweden 13.2%, Latvia 11.4%, Russia 8.9%, Lithuania 5.8%, Germany 5.2%, US 4.1% (2007)

**Imports:** $16.23 billion f.o.b. (2008 est.)

**Imports - commodities:** machinery and equipment 35%, textiles 19%, mineral fuels 19%, chemical products 9%, foodstuffs 6% (2001)

**Imports - partners:** Finland 15.9%, Germany 12.8%, Sweden 10.1%, Russia 10%, Latvia 7.6%, Lithuania 6.9%, Poland 4.5% (2007)

**Reserves of foreign exchange and gold:** $3.657 billion (31 December 2008 est.)

**Debt - external:** $29.5 billion (31 December 2008 est.)

**Stock of direct foreign investment - at home:** $18.94 billion (2008 est.)

**Stock of direct foreign investment - abroad:** $6.723 billion (2008 est.)

**Exchange rates:** krooni (EEK) per US dollar - 10.7 (2008), 11.535 (2007), 12.473 (2006), 12.584 (2005), 12.596 (2004)
*note:* the krooni is pegged to the euro

## Communications

**Telephones - main lines in use:** 495,500 (2007)

**Telephones - mobile cellular:** 1.982 million (2007)

**Telephone system:**
*general assessment:* foreign investment in the form of joint business ventures greatly improved telephone service; substantial fiber-optic cable systems carry telephone, TV, and radio traffic in the digital mode; Internet services are widely available; schools and libraries are connected to the Internet, a large percentage of the population files income-tax returns online, and online voting was used for the first time in the 2005 local elections
*domestic:* a wide range of high quality voice, data, and Internet services is available throughout the country

# Estonia (continued)

*international:* country code - 372; fiber-optic cables to Finland, Sweden, Latvia, and Russia provide worldwide packet-switched service; 2 international switches are located in Tallinn (2001)
**Radio broadcast stations:** AM 0, FM 32, shortwave 0 (2007)
**Television broadcast stations:** 4 (2007)
**Internet country code:** .ee
**Internet hosts:** 645,495 (2008)
**Internet users:** 780,000 (2007)

## Transportation

**Airports:** 19 (2008)
**Airports - with paved runways:**
*total:* 13
*over 3,047 m:* 1
*2,438 to 3,047 m:* 8
*1,524 to 2,437 m:* 1
*914 to 1,523 m:* 3 (2008)
**Airports - with unpaved runways:**
*total:* 6
*over 3,047 m:* 1
*1,524 to 2,437 m:* 2
*under 914 m:* 3 (2008)
**Heliports:** 1 (2007)
**Pipelines:** gas 859 km (2008)
**Railways:**
*total:* 816 km
*broad gauge:* 816 km 1.520 m/1.524-m gauge (131 km electrified) (2007)
**Roadways:**
*total:* 57,016 km
*paved:* 12,926 km (includes 99 km of expressways)
*unpaved:* 44,090 km (2005)
**Waterways:** 320 km (2008)
**Merchant marine:**
*total:* 29
*by type:* cargo 5, passenger/cargo 21, petroleum tanker 2, chemical tanker 1
*foreign-owned:* 4 (Denmark 1, Germany 1, Norway 2)
*registered in other countries:* 85 (Antigua and Barbuda 23, Belize 6, Cyprus 5, Dominica 7, Finland 2, Latvia 2, Liberia 1, Malta 11, Norway 1, Panama 5, Saint Kitts and Nevis 3, Saint Vincent and the Grenadines 16, Sweden 2, Vanuatu 1) (2008)
**Ports and terminals:** Kuivastu, Kunda, Muuga, Tallinn, Virtsu

## Military

**Military branches:** Estonian Defense Forces: Land Force, Navy, Air Force (Eesti Ohuvagi), Volunteer Defense League (Kaitseliit, KL) (2009)
**Military service age and obligation:** obligation for compulsory service ages 16-60, with conscription "likely" ages 18-27; service requirement 8-11 months (2009)
**Manpower available for military service:**
*males age 16-49:* 306,273
*females age 16-49:* 317,852 (2008 est.)
**Manpower fit for military service:**
*males age 16-49:* 216,483
*females age 16-49:* 260,408 (2009 est.)

**Manpower reaching militarily significant age annually:**
*male:* 7,583
*female:* 7,111 (2009 est.)
**Military expenditures:** 2% of GDP (2005 est.)

## Transnational Issues

**Disputes - international:** Russia recalled its signature to the 1996 technical border agreement with Estonia in 2005, rather than concede to Estonia's appending prepared a unilateral declaration referencing Soviet occupation and territorial losses; Russia demands better accommodation of Russian-speaking population in Estonia; Estonian citizen groups continue to press for realignment of the boundary based on the 1920 Tartu Peace Treaty that would bring the now divided ethnic Setu people and parts of the Narva region within Estonia; as a member state that forms part of the EU's external border, Estonia must implement the strict Schengen border rules with Russia
**Illicit drugs:** growing producer of synthetic drugs; increasingly important transshipment zone for cannabis, cocaine, opiates, and synthetic drugs since joining the European Union and the Schengen Accord; potential money laundering related to organized crime and drug trafficking is a concern, as is possible use of the gambling sector to launder funds; major use of opiates and ecstasy

# Ethiopia

## Introduction

**Background:** Unique among African countries, the ancient Ethiopian monarchy maintained its freedom from colonial rule with the exception of a short-lived Italian occupation from 1936-41. In 1974, a military junta, the Derg, deposed Emperor Haile SELASSIE (who had ruled since 1930) and established a socialist state. Torn by bloody coups, uprisings, wide-scale drought, and massive refugee problems, the regime was finally toppled in 1991 by a coalition of rebel forces, the Ethiopian People's Revolutionary Democratic Front (EPRDF). A constitution was adopted in 1994, and Ethiopia's first multiparty elections were held in 1995. A border war with Eritrea late in the 1990s ended with a peace treaty in December 2000. The Eritrea-Ethiopia Border Commission in November 2007 remotely demarcated the border by geographical coordinates, but final demarcation of the boundary on the ground is currently on hold because of Ethiopian objections to an international commission's finding requiring it to surrender territory considered sensitive to Ethiopia.

## Geography

**Location:** Eastern Africa, west of Somalia
**Geographic coordinates:** 8 00 N, 38 00 E
**Map references:** Africa
**Area:**
*total:* 1,127,127 sq km
*land:* 1,119,683 sq km
*water:* 7,444 sq km
**Area - comparative:** slightly less than twice the size of Texas
**Land boundaries:**
*total:* 5,328 km
*border countries:* Djibouti 349 km, Eritrea 912 km, Kenya 861 km, Somalia 1,600 km, Sudan 1,606 km
**Coastline:** 0 km (landlocked)
**Maritime claims:** none (landlocked)
**Climate:** tropical monsoon with wide topographic-induced variation

# Ethiopia *(continued)*

**Terrain:** high plateau with central mountain range divided by Great Rift Valley

**Elevation extremes:**
*lowest point:* Danakil Depression -125 m
*highest point:* Ras Dejen 4,533 m

**Natural resources:** small reserves of gold, platinum, copper, potash, natural gas, hydropower

**Land use:**
*arable land:* 10.01%
*permanent crops:* 0.65%
*other:* 89.34% (2005)

**Irrigated land:** 2,900 sq km (2003)

**Total renewable water resources:** 110 cu km (1987)

**Freshwater withdrawal (domestic/industrial/ agricultural):**
*total:* 5.56 cu km/yr (6%/0%/94%)
*per capita:* 72 cu m/yr (2002)

**Natural hazards:** geologically active Great Rift Valley susceptible to earthquakes, volcanic eruptions; frequent droughts

**Environment - current issues:** deforestation; overgrazing; soil erosion; desertification; water shortages in some areas from water-intensive farming and poor management

**Environment - international agreements:**
*party to:* Biodiversity, Climate Change, Climate Change-Kyoto Protocol, Desertification, Endangered Species, Hazardous Wastes, Ozone Layer Protection
*signed, but not ratified:* Environmental Modification, Law of the Sea

**Geography - note:** landlocked - entire coastline along the Red Sea was lost with the de jure independence of Eritrea on 24 May 1993; the Blue Nile, the chief headstream of the Nile by water volume, rises in T'ana Hayk (Lake Tana) in northwest Ethiopia; three major crops are believed to have originated in Ethiopia: coffee, grain sorghum, and castor bean

## People

**Population:** 85,237,338
*note:* estimates for this country explicitly take into account the effects of excess mortality due to AIDS; this can result in lower life expectancy, higher infant mortality, higher death rates, lower population growth rates, and changes in the distribution of population by age and sex than would otherwise be expected (July 2009 est.)

**Age structure:**
*0-14 years:* 46.1% (male 19,596,784/female 19,688,887)
*15-64 years:* 51.2% (male 21,376,495/female 22,304,812)
*65 years and over:* 2.7% (male 975,923/female 1,294,437) (2009 est.)

**Median age:**
*total:* 16.9 years
*male:* 16.6 years
*female:* 17.2 years (2009 est.)

**Population growth rate:** 3.208% (2009 est.)

**Birth rate:** 43.66 births/1,000 population (2009 est.)

**Death rate:** 11.83 deaths/1,000 population (2008 est.)

**Net migration rate:** -0.02 migrant(s)/1,000 population
*note:* repatriation of Ethiopian refugees residing in Sudan is expected to continue for several years; some Sudanese, Somali, and Eritrean refugees, who fled to Ethiopia from the fighting or famine in their own countries, continue to return to their homes (2009 est.)

**Urbanization:**
*urban population:* 17% of total population (2008)
*rate of urbanization:* 4.3% annual rate of change (2005-10 est.)

**Sex ratio:**
*at birth:* 1.03 male(s)/female
*under 15 years:* 1 male(s)/female
*15-64 years:* 0.96 male(s)/female
*65 years and over:* 0.75 male(s)/female
*total population:* 0.97 male(s)/female (2009 est.)

**Infant mortality rate:**
*total:* 80.8 deaths/1,000 live births
*male:* 92.06 deaths/1,000 live births
*female:* 69.2 deaths/1,000 live births (2009 est.)

**Life expectancy at birth:**
*total population:* 55.41 years
*male:* 52.92 years
*female:* 57.97 years (2009 est.)

**Total fertility rate:** 6.12 children born/woman (2009 est.)

**HIV/AIDS - adult prevalence rate:** 2.1% (2007 est.)

**HIV/AIDS - people living with HIV/AIDS:** 980,000 (2007 est.)

**HIV/AIDS - deaths:** 67,000 (2007 est.)

**Major infectious diseases:**
*degree of risk:* high
*food or waterborne diseases:* bacterial and protozoal diarrhea, hepatitis A and E, and typhoid fever
*vectorborne diseases:* malaria
*respiratory disease:* meningococcal meningitis
*animal contact disease:* rabies
*water contact disease:* schistosomiasis (2009)

**Nationality:**
*noun:* Ethiopian(s)
*adjective:* Ethiopian

**Ethnic groups:** Oromo 32.1%, Amara 30.1%, Tigraway 6.2%, Somalie 5.9%, Guragie 4.3%, Sidama 3.5%, Welaita 2.4%, other 15.4% (1994 census)

**Religions:** Christian 60.8% (Orthodox 50.6%, Protestant 10.2%), Muslim 32.8%, traditional 4.6%, other 1.8% (1994 census)

**Languages:** Amarigna 32.7%, Oromigna 31.6%, Tigrigna 6.1%, Somaligna 6%, Guaragigna 3.5%, Sidamigna 3.5%, Hadiyigna 1.7%, other 14.8%, English (major foreign language taught in schools) (1994 census)

**Literacy:**
*definition:* age 15 and over can read and write
*total population:* 42.7%
*male:* 50.3%
*female:* 35.1% (2003 est.)

**School life expectancy (primary to tertiary education):**
*total:* 8 years
*male:* 8 years
*female:* 7 years (2007)

**Education expenditures:** 6% of GDP (2006)

## Government

**Country name:**
*conventional long form:* Federal Democratic Republic of Ethiopia
*conventional short form:* Ethiopia
*local long form:* Ityop'iya Federalawi Demokrasiyawi Ripeblik
*local short form:* Ityop'iya
*former:* Abyssinia, Italian East Africa
*abbreviation:* FDRE

**Government type:** federal republic

**Capital:**
*name:* Addis Ababa
*geographic coordinates:* 9 02 N, 38 42 E
*time difference:* UTC+3 (8 hours ahead of Washington, DC during Standard Time)

**Administrative divisions:** 9 ethnically based states (kililoch, singular - kilil) and 2 self-governing administrations* (astedaderoch, singular - astedader); Adis Abeba* (Addis Ababa), Afar, Amara (Amhara), Binshangul Gumuz, Dire Dawa*, Gambela Hizboch (Gambela Peoples), Hareri Hizb (Harari People), Oromiya (Oromia), Sumale (Somali), Tigray, Ye Debub Biheroch Bihereseboch na Hizboch (Southern Nations, Nationalities and Peoples)

**Independence:** oldest independent country in Africa and one of the oldest in the world - at least 2,000 years

**National holiday:** National Day (defeat of MENGISTU regime), 28 May (1991)

**Constitution:** ratified 8 December 1994, effective 22 August 1995

**Legal system:** based on civil law; currently transitional mix of national and regional courts; has not accepted compulsory ICJ jurisdiction

**Suffrage:** 18 years of age; universal

**Executive branch:**
*chief of state:* President GIRMA Woldegiorgis (since 8 October 2001)
*head of government:* Prime Minister MELES Zenawi (since August 1995)
*cabinet:* Council of Ministers as provided for in the December 1994 constitution; ministers are selected by the prime minister and approved by the House of People's Representatives
*elections:* president elected by the House of People's Representatives for a six-year term (eligible for a second term); election last held 9 October 2007 (next to be held in October 2013); prime minister designated by the party in power following legislative elections
*election results:* GIRMA Woldegiorgis elected president; percent of vote by the House of People's Representatives - 79%

# Ethiopia (continued)

**Legislative branch:** bicameral Parliament consists of the House of Federation (or upper chamber responsible for interpreting the constitution and federal-regional issues) (108 seats; members are chosen by state assemblies to serve five-year terms) and the House of People's Representatives (or lower chamber responsible for passing legislation) (547 seats; members are directly elected by popular vote from single-member districts to serve five-year terms)
*elections:* last held 15 May 2005 (next to be held in 2010)
*election results:* percent of vote - NA; seats by party - EPRDF 327, CUD 109, UEDF 52, SPDP 23, OFDM 11, BGPDUF 8, ANDP 8, independent 1, others 6, undeclared 2
*note:* some seats still remain vacant as detained opposition MPs did not take their seats
**Judicial branch:** Federal Supreme Court (the president and vice president of the Federal Supreme Court are recommended by the prime minister and appointed by the House of People's Representatives; for other federal judges, the prime minister submits to the House of People's Representatives for appointment candidates selected by the Federal Judicial Administrative Council)
**Political parties and leaders:** Afar National Democratic Party or ANDP [Mohammed Kedir]; Benishangul Gumuz People's Democratic Unity Front or BGPDUF [Mulualem BESSE]; Coalition for Unity and Democratic Party or CUDP; Gurage Nationalities' Democratic Movement or GNDM; Oromo Federalist Democratic Movement or OFDM [BULCHA Demeksa]; Omoro People's Congress or OPC [IMERERA Gudina]; Somali People's Democratic Party or SPDP; United Ethiopian Democratic Forces or UEDF [BEYENE Petros]
**Political pressure groups and leaders:** Ethiopian People's Patriotic Front or EPPF; Ogaden National Liberation Front or ONLF; Oromo Liberation Front or OLF [DAOUD Ibsa]
**International organization participation:** ACP, AfDB, AU, COMESA, FAO, G-24, G-77, IAEA, IBRD, ICAO, ICRM, IDA, IFAD, IFC, IFRCS, IGAD, ILO, IMF, IMO, Interpol, IOC, IOM (observer), IPU, ISO, ITSO, ITU, ITUC, MIGA, NAM, OPCW, PCA, UN, UNAMID, UNCTAD, UNESCO, UNHCR, UNIDO, UNMIL, UNOCI, UNWTO, UPU, WCO, WFTU, WHO, WIPO, WMO, WTO (observer)
**Diplomatic representation in the US:**
*chief of mission:* Ambassador Samuel ASSEFA
*chancery:* 3506 International Drive NW, Washington, DC 20008
*telephone:* [1] (202) 364-1200
*FAX:* [1] (202) 587-0195
*consulate(s) general:* Los Angeles
*consulate(s):* New York
**Diplomatic representation from the US:**
*chief of mission:* Ambassador Donald Y. YAMAMOTO
*embassy:* Entoto Street, Addis Ababa
*mailing address:* P. O. Box 1014, Addis Ababa
*telephone:* [251] 11-517-40-00
*FAX:* [251] 11-517-40-01

**Flag description:** three equal horizontal bands of green (top), yellow, and red, with a yellow pentagram and single yellow rays emanating from the angles between the points on a light blue disk centered on the three bands; Ethiopia is the oldest independent country in Africa, and the three main colors of her flag were so often adopted by other African countries upon independence that they became known as the pan-African colors

## Economy

**Economy - overview:** Ethiopia's poverty-stricken economy is based on agriculture, accounting for almost half of GDP, 60% of exports, and 80% of total employment. The agricultural sector suffers from frequent drought and poor cultivation practices. Coffee is critical to the Ethiopian economy with exports of some $350 million in 2006, but historically low prices have seen many farmers switching to qat to supplement income. The war with Eritrea in 1998-2000 and recurrent drought have buffeted the economy, in particular coffee production. In November 2001, Ethiopia qualified for debt relief from the Highly Indebted Poor Countries (HIPC) initiative, and in December 2005 the IMF forgave Ethiopia's debt. Under Ethiopia's constitution, the state owns all land and provides long-term leases to the tenants; the system continues to hamper growth in the industrial sector as entrepreneurs are unable to use land as collateral for loans. Drought struck again late in 2002, leading to a 3.3% decline in GDP in 2003. Normal weather patterns helped agricultural and GDP growth recover during 2004-08.
**GDP (purchasing power parity):**
$66.29 billion (2008 est.)
$61.09 billion (2007)
$54.99 billion (2006)
*note:* data are in 2008 US dollars
**GDP (official exchange rate):** $25.08 billion (2008 est.)
**GDP - real growth rate:**
8.5% (2008 est.)
11.1% (2007 est.)
10.9% (2006 est.)
**GDP - per capita (PPP):**
$800 (2008 est.)
$800 (2007 est.)
$700 (2006 est.)
*note:* data are in 2008 US dollars
**GDP - composition by sector:**
*agriculture:* 45.9%
*industry:* 12.9%
*services:* 41.2% (2008 est.)
**Labor force:** 27.27 million (1999)
**Labor force - by occupation:**
*agriculture:* 80.2%
*industry:* 6.6%
*services:* 13.2% (2005)
**Unemployment rate:**
NA%
**Population below poverty line:** 38.7% (FY05/06 est.)

**Household income or consumption by percentage share:**
*lowest 10%:* 3.9%
*highest 10%:* 25.5% (2000)
**Distribution of family income - Gini index:** 30 (2000)
**Investment (gross fixed):** 25.4% of GDP (2008 est.)
**Budget:**
*revenues:* $4.586 billion
*expenditures:* $5.729 billion (2008 est.)
**Public debt:** 34.4% of GDP (2008 est.)
**Inflation rate (consumer prices):**
41% (2008 est.)
17.2% (2007 est.)
**Commercial bank prime lending rate:** 7% (31 December 2006)
**Stock of money:** $3.651 billion (31 December 2006)
**Stock of quasi money:** $3.258 billion (31 December 2007)
**Stock of domestic credit:** $6.694 billion (31 December 2006)
**Market value of publicly traded shares:** $NA
**Agriculture - products:** cereals, pulses, coffee, oilseed, cotton, sugarcane, potatoes, qat, cut flowers; hides, cattle, sheep, goats; fish
**Industries:** food processing, beverages, textiles, leather, chemicals, metals processing, cement
**Industrial production growth rate:** 6% (2008 est.)
**Electricity - production:** 3.268 billion kWh (2006 est.)
**Electricity - consumption:** 2.941 billion kWh (2006 est.)
**Electricity - exports:** 0 kWh (2007 est.)
**Electricity - imports:** 0 kWh (2007 est.)
**Oil - production:** 7.334 bbl/day (2007 est.)
**Oil - consumption:** 30,450 bbl/day (2006 est.)
**Oil - exports:** 0 bbl/day (2005)
**Oil - imports:** 29,820 bbl/day (2005)
**Oil - proved reserves:** 428,000 bbl (1 January 2008 est.)
**Natural gas - production:** 0 cu m (2007 est.)
**Natural gas - consumption:** 0 cu m (2007 est.)
**Natural gas - exports:** 0 cu m (2007 est.)
**Natural gas - imports:** 0 cu m (2007 est.)
**Natural gas - proved reserves:** 24.92 billion cu m (1 January 2008 est.)
**Current account balance:** -$1.609 billion (2008 est.)
**Exports:** $1.439 billion f.o.b. (2008 est.)
**Exports - commodities:** coffee, qat, gold, leather products, live animals, oilseeds
**Exports - partners:** Germany 8.2%, Saudi Arabia 7%, US 6.9%, Djibouti 6.6%, China 6.5%, Italy 6.5%, Japan 5.9%, Netherlands 4.8% (2007)
**Imports:** $6.218 billion f.o.b. (2008 est.)
**Imports - commodities:** food and live animals, petroleum and petroleum products, chemicals, machinery, motor vehicles, cereals, textiles
**Imports - partners:** Saudi Arabia 17%, China 15.9%, India 7.8%, Italy 5.1% (2007)

# Ethiopia *(continued)*

**Reserves of foreign exchange and gold:** $1.008 billion (31 December 2008 est.)

**Debt - external:** $3.158 billion (31 December 2008 est.)

**Exchange rates:** birr (ETB) per US dollar - 9.57 (2008 est.), 8.96 (2007), 8.69 (2006), 8.68 (2005), 8.6356 (2004)

*note:* since 24 October 2001, exchange rates are determined on a daily basis via interbank transactions regulated by the Central Bank

## Communications

**Telephones - main lines in use:** 880,100 (2007)

**Telephones - mobile cellular:** 1.208 million (2007)

**Telephone system:**

*general assessment:* inadequate telephone system; the number of fixed lines and mobile telephones is increasing from a very small base; combined fixed and mobile-cellular teledensity is only about 2 per 100 persons

*domestic:* open-wire; microwave radio relay; radio communication in the HF, VHF, and UHF frequencies; 2 domestic satellites provide the national trunk service

*international:* country code - 251; open-wire to Sudan and Djibouti; microwave radio relay to Kenya and Djibouti; satellite earth stations - 3 Intelsat (1 Atlantic Ocean and 2 Pacific Ocean)

**Radio broadcast stations:** AM 8, FM 0, shortwave 1 (2001)

**Television broadcast stations:** 1 (plus 24 repeaters) (2001)

**Internet country code:** .et

**Internet hosts:** 128 (2008)

**Internet users:** 291,000 (2007)

## Transportation

**Airports:** 63 (2008)

**Airports - with paved runways:**

*total:* 16

*over 3,047 m:* 3

*2,438 to 3,047 m:* 6

*1,524 to 2,437 m:* 5

*914 to 1,523 m:* 1

*under 914 m:* 1 (2008)

**Airports - with unpaved runways:**

*total:* 47

*over 3,047 m:* 1

*2,438 to 3,047 m:* 4

*1,524 to 2,437 m:* 10

*914 to 1,523 m:* 23

*under 914 m:* 9 (2008)

**Railways:**

*total:* 699 km (Ethiopian segment of the Addis Ababa-Djibouti railroad)

*narrow gauge:* 699 km 1.000-m gauge

*note:* railway is under joint control of Djibouti and Ethiopia but is largely inoperable (2006)

**Roadways:**

*total:* 36,469 km

*paved:* 6,980 km

*unpaved:* 29,489 km (2004)

**Merchant marine:**

*total:* 9

*by type:* cargo 8, roll on/roll off 1 (2008)

**Ports and terminals:** Ethiopia is landlocked and uses ports of Djibouti in Djibouti and Berbera in Somalia

## Military

**Military branches:** Ethiopian National Defense Force (ENDF): Ground Forces, Ethiopian Air Force (ETAF) (2008)

*note:* Ethiopia is landlocked and has no navy; following the secession of Eritrea, Ethiopian naval facilities remained in Eritrean possession

**Military service age and obligation:** 18 years of age for compulsory and voluntary military service; theoretically, no compulsory military service, but the military can conduct call-ups when necessary and compliance is compulsory (2008)

**Manpower available for military service:**

*males age 16-49:* 17,666,967

*females age 16-49:* 17,530,211 (2008 est.)

**Manpower fit for military service:**

*males age 16-49:* 11,078,847

*females age 16-49:* 12,017,073 (2009 est.)

**Manpower reaching militarily significant age annually:**

*male:* 908,384

*female:* 916,354 (2009 est.)

**Military expenditures:** 3% of GDP (2006)

## Transnational Issues

**Disputes - international:** Eritrea and Ethiopia agreed to abide by the 2002 Eritrea-Ethiopia Boundary Commission's (EEBC) delimitation decision, but neither party responded to the revised line detailed in the November 2006 EEBC Demarcation Statement; UN Peacekeeping Mission to Ethiopia and Eritrea (UNMEE), which has monitored the 25-km-wide Temporary Security Zone in Eritrea since 2000, is extended for six months in 2007 despite Eritrean restrictions on its operations and reduced force of 17,000; the undemarcated former British administrative line has little meaning as a political separation to rival clans within Ethiopia's Ogaden and southern Somalia's Oromo region; Ethiopian forces invaded southern Somalia and routed Islamist Courts from Mogadishu in January 2007; "Somaliland" secessionists provide port facilities in Berbera and trade ties to landlocked Ethiopia; civil unrest in eastern Sudan has hampered efforts to demarcate the porous boundary with Ethiopia

**Refugees and internally displaced persons:**

*refugees (country of origin):* 66,980 (Sudan); 16,576 (Somalia); 13,078 (Eritrea)

*IDPs:* 200,000 (border war with Eritrea from 1998-2000, ethnic clashes in Gambela, and ongoing Ethiopian military counterinsurgency in Somali region; most IDPs are in Tigray and Gambela Provinces) (2007)

**Illicit drugs:** transit hub for heroin originating in Southwest and Southeast Asia and destined for Europe, as well as cocaine destined for markets in southern Africa; cultivates qat (khat) for local use and regional export, principally to Djibouti and Somalia (legal in all three countries); the lack of a well-developed financial system limits the country's utility as a money laundering center

# European Union

Entry

follows

country listing

# Falkland Islands (Islas Malvinas)

*(overseas territory of the UK; also claimed by Argentina)*

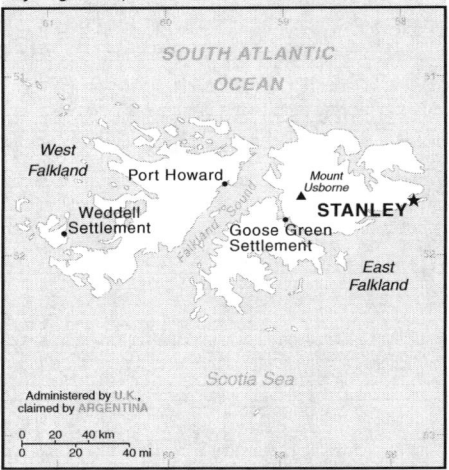

## Introduction

**Background:** Although first sighted by an English navigator in 1592, the first landing (English) did not occur until almost a century later in 1690, and the first settlement (French) was not established until 1764. The colony was turned over to Spain two years later and the islands have since been the subject of a territorial dispute, first between Britain and Spain, then between Britain and Argentina. The UK asserted its claim to the islands by establishing a naval garrison there in 1833. Argentina invaded the islands on 2 April 1982. The British responded with an expeditionary force that landed seven weeks later and after fierce fighting forced an Argentine surrender on 14 June 1982.

## Geography

**Location:** Southern South America, islands in the South Atlantic Ocean, east of southern Argentina
**Geographic coordinates:** 51 45 S, 59 00 W
**Map references:** South America
**Area:**
*total:* 12,173 sq km
*land:* 12,173 sq km
*water:* 0 sq km
*note:* includes the two main islands of East and West Falkland and about 200 small islands
**Area - comparative:** slightly smaller than Connecticut
**Land boundaries:** 0 km
**Coastline:** 1,288 km
**Maritime claims:**
*territorial sea:* 12 nm
*continental shelf:* 200 nm
*exclusive fishing zone:* 200 nm
**Climate:** cold marine; strong westerly winds, cloudy, humid; rain occurs on more than half of days in year; average annual rainfall is 24 inches in Stanley; occasional snow all year, except in January and February, but does not accumulate

**Terrain:** rocky, hilly, mountainous with some boggy, undulating plains
**Elevation extremes:**
*lowest point:* Atlantic Ocean 0 m
*highest point:* Mount Usborne 705 m
**Natural resources:** fish, squid, wildlife, calcified seaweed, sphagnum moss
**Land use:**
*arable land:* 0%
*permanent crops:* 0%
*other:* 100% (99% permanent pastures, 1% other) (2005)
**Irrigated land:** NA
**Natural hazards:** strong winds persist throughout the year
**Environment - current issues:** overfishing by unlicensed vessels is a problem; reindeer were introduced to the islands in 2001 for commercial reasons; this is the only commercial reindeer herd in the world unaffected by the 1986 Chornobyl disaster
**Geography - note:** deeply indented coast provides good natural harbors; short growing season

## People

**Population:** 3,140 (July 2008 est.)
**Age structure:**
*0-14 years:* NA
*15-64 years:* NA
*65 years and over:* NA
**Population growth rate:** 0.011% (2009 est.)
**Birth rate:** NA
**Death rate:** NA
**Net migration rate:** NA
**Urbanization:**
*urban population:* 92% of total population (2008)
*rate of urbanization:* 1.2% annual rate of change (2005-10 est.)
**Infant mortality rate:**
*total:* NA
*male:* NA
*female:* NA (2008 est.)
**Life expectancy at birth:**
*total population:* NA
*male:* NA
*female:* NA
**Total fertility rate:** NA
**HIV/AIDS - adult prevalence rate:** NA
**HIV/AIDS - people living with HIV/AIDS:** NA
**HIV/AIDS - deaths:** NA
**Nationality:**
*noun:* Falkland Islander(s)
*adjective:* Falkland Island
**Ethnic groups:** British
**Religions:** Christian 67.2%, none 31.5%, other 1.3% (2006 census)
**Languages:** English
**Literacy:** NA

## Government

**Country name:**
*conventional long form:* none
*conventional short form:* Falkland Islands (Islas Malvinas)
**Dependency status:** overseas territory of the UK; also claimed by Argentina
**Government type:** NA
**Capital:**
*name:* Stanley
*geographic coordinates:* 51 42 S, 57 51 W
*time difference:* UTC-4 (1 hour ahead of Washington, DC during Standard Time)
*daylight saving time:* +1hr, begins first Sunday in September; ends third Sunday in April
**Administrative divisions:** none (overseas territory of the UK; also claimed by Argentina)
**Independence:** none (overseas territory of the UK; also claimed by Argentina)
**National holiday:** Liberation Day, 14 June (1982)
**Constitution:** 3 October 1985; amended 1997 and 1998
**Legal system:** English common law
**Suffrage:** 18 years of age; universal
**Executive branch:**
*chief of state:* Queen ELIZABETH II (since 6 February 1952)
*head of government:* Governor Alan HUCKLE (since 25 August 2006); Chief Executive Dr. Tim THOROGOOD (since 3 January 2008)
*cabinet:* Executive Council; three members elected by the Legislative Council, two ex officio members (chief executive and the financial secretary), and the governor
*elections:* the monarchy is hereditary; governor appointed by the monarch
**Legislative branch:** unicameral Legislative Council (10 seats; 2 members are ex officio and 8 are elected by popular vote; to serve four-year terms); presided over by the governor
*elections:* last held 17 November 2005 (next to be held in November 2009)
*election results:* percent of vote - NA; seats - independents 8
**Judicial branch:** Supreme Court (chief justice is a nonresident); Magistrates Court (senior magistrate presides over civil and criminal divisions); Court of Summary Jurisdiction
**Political parties and leaders:** none; all independents
**Political pressure groups and leaders:** Falkland Islands Association (supports freedom of the people from external causes)
**International organization participation:** UPU
**Diplomatic representation in the US:** none (overseas territory of the UK; also claimed by Argentina)
**Diplomatic representation from the US:** none (overseas territory of the UK; also claimed by Argentina)

# Falkland Islands (Islas Malvinas) *(continued)*

**Flag description:** blue with the flag of the UK in the upper hoist-side quadrant and the Falkland Island coat of arms centered on the outer half of the flag; the coat of arms contains a white ram (sheep raising was once the major economic activity) above the sailing ship Desire (whose crew discovered the islands) with a scroll at the bottom bearing the motto DESIRE THE RIGHT

## Economy

**Economy - overview:** The economy was formerly based on agriculture, mainly sheep farming, but today fishing contributes the bulk of economic activity. In 1987, the government began selling fishing licenses to foreign trawlers operating within the Falkland Islands' exclusive fishing zone. These license fees total more than $40 million per year, which help support the island's health, education, and welfare system. Squid accounts for 75% of the fish taken. Dairy farming supports domestic consumption; crops furnish winter fodder. Exports feature shipments of high-grade wool to the UK and the sale of postage stamps and coins. The islands are now self-financing except for defense. The British Geological Survey announced a 200-mile oil exploration zone around the islands in 1993, and early seismic surveys suggest substantial reserves capable of producing 500,000 barrels per day; to date, no exploitable site has been identified. An agreement between Argentina and the UK in 1995 seeks to defuse licensing and sovereignty conflicts that would dampen foreign interest in exploiting potential oil reserves. Tourism, especially eco-tourism, is increasing rapidly, with about 30,000 visitors in 2001. Another large source of income is interest paid on money the government has in the bank. The British military presence also provides a sizeable economic boost.

**GDP (purchasing power parity):** $105.1 million (2002 est.)

**GDP (official exchange rate):** $105.1 million (2002 est.)

**GDP - real growth rate:** NA%

**GDP - per capita (PPP):** $35,400 (2002 est.)

**GDP - composition by sector:**
*agriculture:* 95%
*industry:* NA%
*services:* NA% (1996)

**Labor force:** 1,724 (est.) (1996)

**Labor force - by occupation:**
*agriculture:* 95% (mostly sheepherding and fishing)
*industry and services:* 5% (1996)

**Unemployment rate:**

**Population below poverty line:** NA%

**Household income or consumption by percentage share:**
*lowest 10%:* NA%
*highest 10%:* NA%

**Budget:**
*revenues:* $66.2 million
*expenditures:* $67.9 million (FY98/99 est.)

**Inflation rate (consumer prices):** 3.6% (1998)

**Agriculture - products:** fodder and vegetable crops; sheep, dairy products; fish, squid

**Industries:** fish and wool processing; tourism

**Industrial production growth rate:** NA%

**Electricity - production:** 16 million kWh (2006 est.)

**Electricity - consumption:** 14.88 million kWh (2006 est.)

**Electricity - exports:** 0 kWh (2007 est.)

**Electricity - imports:** 0 kWh (2007 est.)

**Oil - production:** 0 bbl/day (2007 est.)

**Oil - consumption:** 252.3 bbl/day (2006 est.)

**Oil - exports:** 0 bbl/day (2005)

**Oil - imports:** 248.9 bbl/day (2005)

**Oil - proved reserves:** 0 bbl (1 January 2006 est.)

**Natural gas - production:** 0 cu m (2007 est.)

**Natural gas - consumption:** 0 cu m (2007 est.)

**Natural gas - exports:** 0 cu m (2007 est.)

**Natural gas - imports:** 0 cu m (2007 est.)

**Natural gas - proved reserves:** 0 cu m (1 January 2006 est.)

**Exports:** $125 million (2004 est.)

**Exports - commodities:** wool, hides, meat, fish, squid

**Imports:** $90 million (2004 est.)

**Imports - commodities:** fuel, food and drink, building materials, clothing

**Debt - external:** $NA

**Exchange rates:** Falkland pounds (FKP) per US dollar - 0.5302 (2008), 0.4993 (2007), 0.5418 (2006), 0.5493 (2005), 0.5462 (2004)
*note:* the Falkland pound is at par with the British pound

## Communications

**Telephones - main lines in use:** 2,400 (2002)

**Telephones - mobile cellular:** 0 (2001)

**Telephone system:**
*general assessment:* NA
*domestic:* government-operated radiotelephone and private VHF/CB radiotelephone networks provide effective service to almost all points on both islands
*international:* country code - 500; satellite earth station -1 Intelsat (Atlantic Ocean) with links through London to other countries

**Radio broadcast stations:** AM 1, FM 7, shortwave 0 (British Forces Broadcasting Service (BFBS) provides Radio 1 and Radio 2 service) (2006)

**Television broadcast stations:** 2 (British Forces Broadcasting Service (BFBS) provides multi-channel satellite service to members of UK Forces as well as islanders); cable television is available in Stanley (2006)

**Internet country code:** .fk

**Internet hosts:** 91 (2008)

**Internet users:** 1,900 (2002)

## Transportation

**Airports:** 6 (2008)

**Airports - with paved runways:**
*total:* 2
*2,438 to 3,047 m:* 1
*914 to 1,523 m:* 1 (2008)

**Airports - with unpaved runways:**
*total:* 4
*under 914 m:* 4 (2008)

**Roadways:**
*total:* 440 km
*paved:* 50 km
*unpaved:* 390 km (2008)

**Ports and terminals:** Stanley

## Military

**Military branches:** no regular military forces

**Military expenditures:** NA

**Military - note:** defense is the responsibility of the UK

## Transnational Issues

**Disputes - international:** Argentina, which claims the islands in its constitution and briefly occupied them by force in 1982, agreed in 1995 to no longer seek settlement by force; UK continues to reject Argentine requests for sovereignty talks

# Faroe Islands
*(part of the Kingdom of Denmark)*

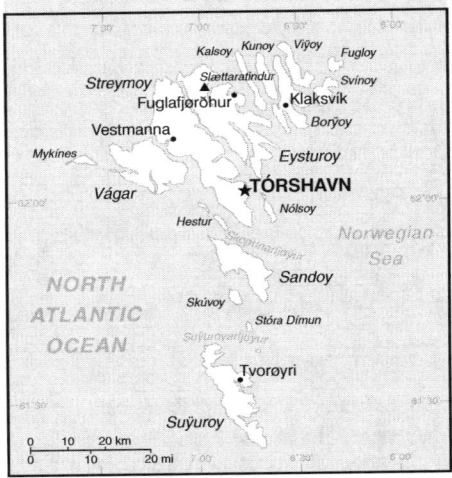

## Introduction

**Background:** The population of the Faroe Islands is largely descended from Viking settlers who arrived in the 9th century. The islands have been connected politically to Denmark since the 14th century. A high degree of self government was attained in 1948.

## Geography

**Location:** Northern Europe, island group between the Norwegian Sea and the North Atlantic Ocean, about half way between Iceland and Norway
**Geographic coordinates:** 62 00 N, 7 00 W
**Map references:** Europe
**Area:**
*total:* 1,399 sq km
*land:* 1,399 sq km
*water:* 0 sq km (some lakes and streams)
**Area - comparative:** eight times the size of Washington, DC
**Land boundaries:** 0 km
**Coastline:** 1,117 km
**Maritime claims:**
*territorial sea:* 3 nm
*continental shelf:* 200 nm or agreed boundaries or median line
*exclusive fishing zone:* 200 nm or agreed boundaries or median line
**Climate:** mild winters, cool summers; usually overcast; foggy, windy
**Terrain:** rugged, rocky, some low peaks; cliffs along most of coast
**Elevation extremes:**
*lowest point:* Atlantic Ocean 0 m
*highest point:* Slaettaratindur 882 m
**Natural resources:** fish, whales, hydropower, possible oil and gas
**Land use:**
*arable land:* 2.14%
*permanent crops:* 0%
*other:* 97.86% (2005)

**Irrigated land:** 0 sq km
**Natural hazards:** NA
**Environment - current issues:** NA
**Environment - international agreements:**
*party to:* Marine Dumping - associate member to the London Convention and Ship Pollution
**Geography - note:** archipelago of 17 inhabited islands and one uninhabited island, and a few uninhabited islets; strategically located along important sea lanes in northeastern Atlantic; precipitous terrain limits habitation to small coastal lowlands

## People

**Population:** 48,856 (July 2009 est.)
**Age structure:**
*0-14 years:* 21.6% (male 5,451/female 5,108)
*15-64 years:* 64% (male 16,708/female 14,544)
*65 years and over:* 14.4% (male 3,324/female 3,721) (2009 est.)
**Median age:**
*total:* 36.9 years
*male:* 36.3 years
*female:* 37.7 years (2009 est.)
**Population growth rate:** 0.397% (2009 est.)
**Birth rate:** 13.04 births/1,000 population (2009 est.)
**Death rate:** 8.67 deaths/1,000 population (2008 est.)
**Net migration rate:** -0.41 migrant(s)/1,000 population (2009 est.)
**Urbanization:**
*urban population:* 41% of total population (2008)
*rate of urbanization:* 2% annual rate of change (2005-10 est.)
**Sex ratio:**
*at birth:* 1.07 male(s)/female
*under 15 years:* 1.07 male(s)/female
*15-64 years:* 1.15 male(s)/female
*65 years and over:* 0.89 male(s)/female
*total population:* 1.09 male(s)/female (2009 est.)
**Infant mortality rate:**
*total:* 6.32 deaths/1,000 live births
*male:* 6.56 deaths/1,000 live births
*female:* 6.06 deaths/1,000 live births (2009 est.)
**Life expectancy at birth:**
*total population:* 79.44 years
*male:* 77 years
*female:* 82.05 years (2009 est.)
**Total fertility rate:** 2.44 children born/woman (2009 est.)
**HIV/AIDS - adult prevalence rate:** NA
**HIV/AIDS - people living with HIV/AIDS:** NA
**HIV/AIDS - deaths:** NA
**Nationality:**
*noun:* Faroese (singular and plural)
*adjective:* Faroese
**Ethnic groups:** Scandinavian
**Religions:** Evangelical Lutheran 83.8%, other and unspecified 16.2% (2006 administrative data)
**Languages:** Faroese (derived from Old Norse), Danish
**Literacy:** NA; note - probably 99%, the same as Denmark proper

## Government

**Country name:**
*conventional long form:* none
*conventional short form:* Faroe Islands
*local long form:* none
*local short form:* Foroyar
**Dependency status:** part of the Kingdom of Denmark; self-governing overseas administrative division of Denmark since 1948
**Government type:** NA
**Capital:**
*name:* Torshavn
*geographic coordinates:* 62 01 N, 6 46 W
*time difference:* UTC 0 (5 hours ahead of Washington, DC during Standard Time)
*daylight saving time:* +1hr, begins last Sunday in March; ends last Sunday in October
**Administrative divisions:** none (part of the Kingdom of Denmark; self-governing overseas administrative division of Denmark); there are no first-order administrative divisions as defined by the US Government, but there are 34 municipalities
**Independence:** none (part of the Kingdom of Denmark; self-governing overseas administrative division of Denmark)
**National holiday:** Olaifest (Olavasoka), 29 July
**Constitution:** 5 June 1953 (Danish constitution)
**Legal system:** the laws of Denmark, where applicable, apply
**Suffrage:** 18 years of age; universal
**Executive branch:**
*chief of state:* Queen MARGRETHE II of Denmark (since 14 January 1972), represented by High Commissioner Birgit KLEIS, chief administrative officer (since 1 November 2001)
*head of government:* Prime Minister Kaj Leo JOHANNESSEN (since 26 September 2008)
*cabinet:* Landsstyri appointed by the prime minister
*elections:* the monarch is hereditary; high commissioner appointed by the monarch; following legislative elections, the leader of the majority party or the leader of the majority coalition is usually elected prime minister by the Faroese Parliament; election last held 19 January 2008 (next to be held no later than January 2012)
*election results:* Joannes EIDESGAARD elected prime minister; governing coalition collapses in September 2008, Kaj Leo JOHANNESSEN becomes Prime Minister
**Legislative branch:** unicameral Faroese Parliament or Logting (33 seats; members are elected by popular vote on a proportional basis from the seven constituencies to serve four-year terms)
*elections:* last held 19 January 2008 (next to be held no later than January 2012)
*election results:* percent of vote by party - Union Party 21%, Social Democratic Party 19.4%, Republican Party 23.3%, People's Party 20.1%, Center Party 8.4%, Self-Government Party 7.2%, other 0.6%; seats by party - Republican Party 8, Union Party 7, Social Democratic Party 6, People's Party 7, Center Party 3, Independence Party 2

# Faroe Islands (continued)

note: election of two seats to the Danish Parliament was last held on 13 November 2007 (next to be held no later than November 2011); results - percent of vote by party - NA; seats by party - Republican Party 1, Union Party 1

**Judicial branch:** none

**Political parties and leaders:** Center Party [Jenis A. RANA]; Independence Party [Kari P. HOJGAARD]; People's Party [Jorgen NICLASEN]; Republican Party [Hogni HOYDAL]; Social Democratic Party [Joannes EIDESGAARD]; Self-Government Party [Kari P. HOJGAARD]; Union Party [Kaj Leo JOHANNESEN]

**Political pressure groups and leaders:** Sea Shepard [Paul WATSON] (preservation of small whales)

other: conservationists

**International organization participation:** Arctic Council, FAO, IMO (associate), NC, NIB, UPU

**Diplomatic representation in the US:** none (self-governing overseas administrative division of Denmark)

**Diplomatic representation from the US:** none (self-governing overseas administrative division of Denmark)

**Flag description:** white with a red cross outlined in blue extending to the edges of the flag; the vertical part of the cross is shifted toward the hoist side in the style of the Dannebrog (Danish flag)

## Economy

**Economy - overview:** The Faroese economy is dependent on fishing, which makes the economy vulnerable to price swings. The sector accounts for 95% of exports and nearly half of GDP. Since 2003 the Faroese economy has picked up as a result of higher prices for fish and for housing. Unemployment is minimal and government finances are relatively sound. Oil finds close to the Islands give hope for economically recoverable deposits, which could eventually lay the basis for a more diversified economy and lessen dependence on Danish economic assistance. Aided by a substantial annual subsidy (about 15% of GDP) from Denmark, the Faroese have a standard of living not far below the Danes and other Scandinavians.

**GDP (purchasing power parity):** $1 billion (2001 est.)

**GDP (official exchange rate):** $1.7 billion (2005 est.)

**GDP - real growth rate:** 2.4% (2005 est.)

**GDP - per capita (PPP):** $31,000 (2001 est.)

**GDP - composition by sector:**
agriculture: 27%
industry: 11%
services: 62% (1999)

**Labor force:** 24,250 (October 2000)

**Labor force - by occupation:**
agriculture: 11.2%
industry: 21.9%
services: 66.9% (2007)

**Unemployment rate:**
1.4% (2007)
2.1% (2006)

**Population below poverty line:** NA%

**Household income or consumption by percentage share:**
lowest 10%: NA%
highest 10%: NA%

**Budget:**
revenues: $588 million
expenditures: $623 million (2005)

**Inflation rate (consumer prices):**
1.8% (2005)

**Agriculture - products:** milk, potatoes, vegetables; sheep; salmon, other fish

**Industries:** fishing, fish processing, small ship repair and refurbishment, handicrafts

**Industrial production growth rate:** 8% (1999 est.)

**Electricity - production:** 295 million kWh (2006 est.)

**Electricity - consumption:** 274.4 million kWh (2006 est.)

**Electricity - exports:** 0 kWh (2007 est.)

**Electricity - imports:** 0 kWh (2007 est.)

**Oil - production:** 0 bbl/day (2007 est.)

**Oil - consumption:** 4,628 bbl/day (2006 est.)

**Oil - exports:** 0 bbl/day (2005)

**Oil - imports:** 4,636 bbl/day (2005)

**Oil - proved reserves:** 0 bbl (1 January 2006 est.)

**Natural gas - production:** 0 cu m (2007 est.)

**Natural gas - consumption:** 0 cu m (2007 est.)

**Natural gas - exports:** 0 cu m (2007 est.)

**Natural gas - imports:** 0 cu m (2007 est.)

**Natural gas - proved reserves:** 0 cu m (1 January 2006 est.)

**Exports:** $634 million f.o.b. (2006)

**Exports - commodities:** fish and fish products 94%, stamps, ships (1999)

**Exports - partners:** Denmark 29.6%, UK 24.5%, Norway 13.3%, Nigeria 10.5%, Netherlands 6.8% (2007)

**Imports:** $751 million c.i.f. (2006)

**Imports - commodities:** consumer goods 36%, raw materials and semi-manufactures 32%, machinery and transport equipment 29%, fuels, fish, salt (1999)

**Imports - partners:** Denmark 51.9%, Norway 21.6%, Sweden 5%, UK 4.6% (2007)

**Debt - external:** $64 million (1999)

**Exchange rates:** Danish kroner (DKK) per US dollar -5.0236 (2008 est.), 5.4797 (2007), 5.9468 (2006), 5.9969 (2005), 5.9911 (2004)

## Communications

**Telephones - main lines in use:** 23,000 (2006)

**Telephones - mobile cellular:** 50,000 (2006)

**Telephone system:**
general assessment: good international communications; good domestic facilities
domestic: digitalization was completed in 1998; both NMT (analog) and GSM (digital) mobile telephone systems are installed

international: country code - 298; satellite earth stations - 1 Orion; 1 fiber-optic submarine cable to the Shetland Islands, linking the Faroe Islands with Denmark and Iceland; fiber-optic submarine cable connection to Canada-Europe cable

**Radio broadcast stations:** AM 1, FM 13, shortwave 0 (1998)

**Television broadcast stations:** 3 (plus 43 repeaters) (September 1995)

**Internet country code:** .fo

**Internet hosts:** 8,516 (2008)

**Internet users:** 34,000 (2006)

## Transportation

**Airports:** 1 (2008)

**Airports - with paved runways:**
total: 1
914 to 1,523 m: 1 (2008)

**Roadways:**
total: 463 km (2006)

**Merchant marine:**
total: 12
by type: cargo 9, passenger/cargo 3
foreign-owned: 5 (Iceland 1, Norway 4) (2008)

**Ports and terminals:** Torshavn, Vagur

## Military

**Military branches:** no regular military forces

**Manpower available for military service:**
males age 16-49: 11,725 (2008 est.)

**Manpower fit for military service:**
males age 16-49: 9,759
females age 16-49: 8,311 (2009 est.)

**Manpower reaching militarily significant age annually:**
male: 386
female: 375 (2009 est.)

**Military expenditures:** NA

**Military - note:** defense is the responsibility of Denmark

## Transnational Issues

**Disputes - international:** because anticipated offshore hydrocarbon resources have not been realized, earlier Faroese proposals for full independence have been deferred; Iceland, the UK, and Ireland dispute Denmark's claim that the Faroe Islands' continental shelf extends beyond 200 nm

# Fiji

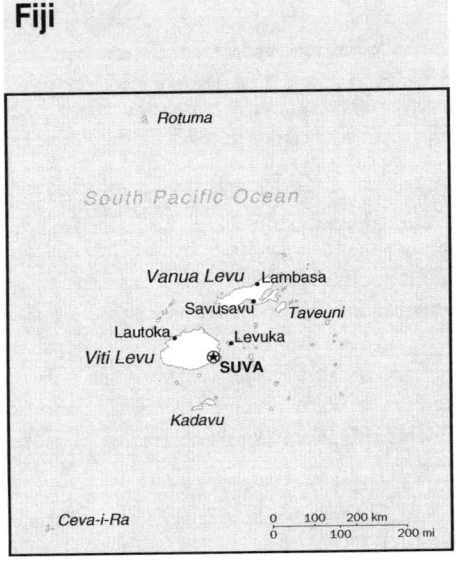

## Introduction

**Background:** Fiji became independent in 1970 after nearly a century as a British colony. Democratic rule was interrupted by two military coups in 1987 caused by concern over a government perceived as dominated by the Indian community (descendants of contract laborers brought to the islands by the British in the 19th century). The coups and a 1990 constitution that cemented native Melanesian control of Fiji led to heavy Indian emigration; the population loss resulted in economic difficulties, but ensured that Melanesians became the majority. A new constitution enacted in 1997 was more equitable. Free and peaceful elections in 1999 resulted in a government led by an Indo-Fijian, but a civilian-led coup in May 2000 ushered in a prolonged period of political turmoil. Parliamentary elections held in August 2001 provided Fiji with a democratically elected government led by Prime Minister Laisenia QARASE. Re-elected in May 2006, QARASE was ousted in a December 2006 military coup led by Commodore Voreqe BAINIMARAMA, who initially appointed himself acting president but in January 2007 became interim prime minister. Since taking power BAINIMARAMA has neutralized his opponents, crippled Fiji's democratic institutions, and refused to hold elections.

## Geography

**Location:** Oceania, island group in the South Pacific Ocean, about two-thirds of the way from Hawaii to New Zealand
**Geographic coordinates:** 18 00 S, 175 00 E
**Map references:** Oceania
**Area:**
*total:* 18,270 sq km
*land:* 18,270 sq km
*water:* 0 sq km
**Area - comparative:** slightly smaller than New Jersey

**Land boundaries:** 0 km
**Coastline:** 1,129 km
**Maritime claims:** measured from claimed archipelagic straight baselines
*territorial sea:* 12 nm
*exclusive economic zone:* 200 nm
*continental shelf:* 200 m depth or to the depth of exploitation; rectilinear shelf claim added
**Climate:** tropical marine; only slight seasonal temperature variation
**Terrain:** mostly mountains of volcanic origin
**Elevation extremes:**
*lowest point:* Pacific Ocean 0 m
*highest point:* Tomanivi 1,324 m
**Natural resources:** timber, fish, gold, copper, offshore oil potential, hydropower
**Land use:**
*arable land:* 10.95%
*permanent crops:* 4.65%
*other:* 84.4% (2005)
**Irrigated land:** 30 sq km (2003)
**Total renewable water resources:** 28.6 cu km (1987)
**Freshwater withdrawal (domestic/industrial/agricultural):**
*total:* 0.07 cu km/yr (14%/14%/71%)
*per capita:* 82 cu m/yr (2000)
**Natural hazards:** cyclonic storms can occur from November to January
**Environment - current issues:** deforestation; soil erosion
**Environment - international agreements:**
*party to:* Biodiversity, Climate Change, Climate Change-Kyoto Protocol, Desertification, Endangered Species, Law of the Sea, Marine Life Conservation, Ozone Layer Protection, Tropical Timber 83, Tropical Timber 94, Wetlands
*signed, but not ratified:* none of the selected agreements
**Geography - note:** includes 332 islands; approximately 110 are inhabited

## People

**Population:** 944,720 (July 2009 est.)
**Age structure:**
*0-14 years:* 30.3% (male 146,327/female 140,327)
*15-64 years:* 64.9% (male 307,077/female 305,886)
*65 years and over:* 4.8% (male 20,300/female 24,803) (2009 est.)
**Median age:**
*total:* 25.5 years
*male:* 25 years
*female:* 26 years (2009 est.)
**Population growth rate:** 1.379% (2009 est.)
**Birth rate:** 21.92 births/1,000 population (2009 est.)
**Death rate:** 5.66 deaths/1,000 population (2008 est.)
**Net migration rate:** -2.47 migrant(s)/1,000 population (2009 est.)

**Urbanization:**
*urban population:* 52% of total population (2008)
*rate of urbanization:* 1.6% annual rate of change (2005-10 est.)
**Sex ratio:**
*at birth:* 1.05 male(s)/female
*under 15 years:* 1.04 male(s)/female
*15-64 years:* 1 male(s)/female
*65 years and over:* 0.82 male(s)/female
*total population:* 1.01 male(s)/female (2009 est.)
**Infant mortality rate:**
*total:* 11.58 deaths/1,000 live births
*male:* 12.74 deaths/1,000 live births
*female:* 10.35 deaths/1,000 live births (2009 est.)
**Life expectancy at birth:**
*total population:* 70.73 years
*male:* 68.18 years
*female:* 73.41 years (2009 est.)
**Total fertility rate:** 2.65 children born/woman (2009 est.)
**HIV/AIDS - adult prevalence rate:** 0.1% (2007 est.)
**HIV/AIDS - people living with HIV/AIDS:** 600 (2003 est.)
**HIV/AIDS - deaths:** fewer than 200 (2003 est.)
**Nationality:**
*noun:* Fijian(s)
*adjective:* Fijian
**Ethnic groups:** Fijian 57.3% (predominantly Melanesian with a Polynesian admixture), Indian 37.6%, Rotuman 1.2%, other 3.9% (European, other Pacific Islanders, Chinese) (2007 census)
**Religions:** Christian 64.5% (Methodist 34.6%, Roman Catholic 9.1%, Assembly of God 5.7%, Seventh Day Adventist 3.9%, Anglican 0.8%, other 10.4%), Hindu 27.9%, Muslim 6.3%, Sikh 0.3%, other or unspecified 0.3%, none 0.7% (2007 census)
**Languages:** English (official), Fijian (official), Hindustani
**Literacy:**
*definition:* age 15 and over can read and write
*total population:* 93.7%
*male:* 95.5%
*female:* 91.9% (2003 est.)
**School life expectancy (primary to tertiary education):**
*total:* 13 years
*male:* 13 years
*female:* 13 years (2005)
**Education expenditures:** 6.5% of GDP (2004)

## Government

**Country name:**
*conventional long form:* Republic of the Fiji Islands
*conventional short form:* Fiji
*local long form:* Republic of the Fiji Islands/Matanitu ko Viti
*local short form:* Fiji/Viti

# Fiji (continued)

**Government type:** republic
**Capital:**
*name:* Suva (on Viti Levu)
*geographic coordinates:* 18 08 S, 178 25 E
*time difference:* UTC+12 (17 hours ahead of Washington, DC during Standard Time)
**Administrative divisions:** 4 divisions and 1 dependency*; Central, Eastern, Northern, Rotuma*, Western
**Independence:** 10 October 1970 (from the UK)
**National holiday:** Independence Day, second Monday of October (1970)
**Constitution:** enacted 25 July 1997; effective 28 July 1998; note - it encourages multiculturalism and makes multiparty government mandatory
**Legal system:** based on British system; has not accepted compulsory ICJ jurisdiction
**Suffrage:** 21 years of age; universal
**Executive branch:**
*chief of state:* President Ratu Josefa ILOILOVATU Uluivuda (since 18 July 2000); note - ILOILOVATU was reaffirmed as president by the Great Council of Chiefs in a statement issued on 22 December and reappointed by the coup leader Commodore Voreqe BAINIMARAMA in January 2007
*head of government:* Prime Minister Laisenia QARASE (since 10 September 2000); note - although QARASE is still the legal prime minister, he has been confined to his home island; the president appointed Commodore Voreqe BAINIMARAMA interim prime minister under the military regime
*cabinet:* Cabinet appointed by the prime minister from among the members of Parliament and is responsible to Parliament; note - coup leader Commodore Voreqe BAINIMARAMA has appointed an interim cabinet
*elections:* president elected by the Great Council of Chiefs for a five-year term (eligible for a second term); prime minister appointed by the president; election last held 8 March 2006
*election results:* Ratu Josefa ILOILOVATU Uluivuda elected president by the Great Council of Chiefs; percent of vote - NA
**Legislative branch:** bicameral Parliament consists of the Senate (32 seats; 14 appointed by the president on the advice of the Great Council of Chiefs, 9 appointed by the president on the advice of the Prime Minister, 8 on the advice of the opposition leader, and 1 appointed on the advice of the council of Rotuma) and the House of Representatives (71 seats; 23 reserved for ethnic Fijians, 19 reserved for ethnic Indians, 3 reserved for other ethnic groups, 1 reserved for the council of Rotuma constituency encompassing the whole of Fiji, and 25 open seats; members serve five-year terms)
*elections:* House of Representatives - last held 6-13 May 2006 (next to be held in 2011)
*election results:* House of Representatives - percent of vote by party - SDL 44.6%, FLP 39.2%, UPP 0.8%, independents 4.9%, other 10.5%; seats by party - SDL 36, FLP 31, UPP 2, independents 2

**Judicial branch:** Supreme Court (judges are appointed by the president); Court of Appeal; High Court; Magistrates' Courts
**Political parties and leaders:** Dodonu Ni Taukei Party or DNT [Fereti S. DEWA]; Fiji Democratic Party or FDP [Filipe BOLE] (a merger of the Christian Democrat Alliance or VLV [Poesci Waqalevu BUNE], Fijian Association Party or FAP, Fijian Political Party or SVT (primarily Fijian) [Sitiveni RABUKA], and New Labor Unity Party or NLUP [Ofa SWANN]); Fiji Labor Party or FLP [Mahendra CHAUDHRY]; General Voters Party or GVP (became part of United General Party); Girmit Heritage Party or GHP; Justice and Freedom Party or AIM; Lio 'On Famor Rotuma Party or LFR; National Federation Party or NFP (primarily Indian) [Pramond RAE]; Nationalist Vanua Takolavo Party or NVTLP [Saula TELAWA]; Party of National Unity or PANU [Ponipate LESAVUA]; Party of the Truth or POTT; United Fiji Party/Sogosogo Duavata ni Lewenivanua or SDL [Laisenia QARASE]; United Peoples Party or UPP [Millis Mick BEDDOES]
**Political pressure groups and leaders:** Group Against Racial Discrimination or GARD [Dr. Anirudk SINGH] (for restoration of a democratic government); Viti Landowners Association
**International organization participation:** ACP, ADB, C (suspended), CP, FAO, G-77, IBRD, ICAO, ICCt, ICRM, IDA, IFAD, IFC, IFRCS, IHO, ILO, IMF, IMO, Interpol, IOC, ISO, ITSO, ITU, ITUC, MIGA, OPCW, PCA, PIF, Sparteca, SPC, UN, UNCTAD, UNESCO, UNIDO, UNMIS, UNMIT, UNWTO, UPU, WCO, WFTU, WHO, WIPO, WMO, WTO
**Diplomatic representation in the US:**
*chief of mission:* Ambassador Winston THOMPSON
*chancery:* 2000 M Street, NW, Suite 710, Washington, DC 20036
*telephone:* [1] (202) 466-8320
*FAX:* [1] (202) 466-8325
**Diplomatic representation from the US:**
*chief of mission:* Ambassador C. Steven McGANN
*embassy:* 31 Loftus Street, Suva
*mailing address:* P. O. Box 218, Suva
*telephone:* [679] 331-4466
*FAX:* [679] 330-0081
**Flag description:** light blue with the flag of the UK in the upper hoist-side quadrant and the Fijian shield centered on the outer half of the flag; the shield depicts a yellow lion above a white field quartered by the cross of Saint George featuring stalks of sugarcane, a palm tree, bananas, and a white dove

## Economy

**Economy - overview:** Fiji, endowed with forest, mineral, and fish resources, is one of the most developed of the Pacific island economies though still with a large subsistence sector. Sugar exports, remittances from Fijians working abroad, and a growing tourist industry - with 400,000 to 500,000 tourists annually - are the major sources of foreign exchange. Fiji's sugar has special access to European Union markets but will be harmed by the EU's decision to cut sugar subsidies. Sugar processing makes up one-third of industrial activity but is not efficient. Fiji's tourism industry was damaged by the December 2006 coup and is facing an uncertain recovery time. In 2007 tourist arrivals were down almost 6%, with substantial job losses in the service sector, and GDP dipped nearly 7%. The coup has created a difficult business climate. The EU has suspended all aid until the interim government takes steps toward new elections. Long-term problems include low investment, uncertain land ownership rights, and the government's inability to manage its budget. Overseas remittances from Fijians working in Kuwait and Iraq have decreased significantly. Fiji's current account deficit reached 23% of GDP in 2006.
**GDP (purchasing power parity):**
$3.616 billion (2008 est.)
$3.573 billion (2007)
$3.825 billion (2006)
*note:* data are in 2008 US dollars
**GDP (official exchange rate):** $3.783 billion (2008 est.)
**GDP - real growth rate:**
1.2% (2008 est.)
-6.6% (2007 est.)
3.4% (2006 est.)
**GDP - per capita (PPP):**
$3,900 (2008 est.)
$3,900 (2007 est.)
$4,200 (2006 est.)
*note:* data are in 2008 US dollars
**GDP - composition by sector:**
*agriculture:* 8.9%
*industry:* 13.5%
*services:* 77.6% (2004 est.)
**Labor force:** 117,500 (2006 est.)
**Labor force - by occupation:**
*agriculture:* 70%
*industry and services:* 30% (2001 est.)
**Unemployment rate:**
7.6% (1999)
**Population below poverty line:** 25.5% (FY90/91)
**Household income or consumption by percentage share:**
*lowest 10%:* NA%
*highest 10%:* NA%
**Budget:**
*revenues:* $1.363 billion
*expenditures:* $1.376 billion (2006)
**Inflation rate (consumer prices):**
4.8% (2007)
**Central bank discount rate:** 9.25% (31 December 2007)
**Commercial bank prime lending rate:** 9.01% (31 December 2007)
**Stock of money:** $1.042 billion (31 December 2007)
**Stock of quasi money:** $1.088 billion (31 December 2007)
**Stock of domestic credit:** $1.948 billion (31 December 2007)

**Market value of publicly traded shares:** $522.2 million (31 December 2007)

**Agriculture - products:** sugarcane, coconuts, cassava (tapioca), rice, sweet potatoes, bananas; cattle, pigs, horses, goats; fish

**Industries:** tourism, sugar, clothing, copra, gold, silver, lumber, small cottage industries

**Industrial production growth rate:** NA%

**Electricity - production:** 928 million kWh (2007 est.)

**Electricity - consumption:** 1.016 billion kWh (2006 est.)

**Electricity - exports:** 0 kWh (2007 est.)

**Electricity - imports:** 0 kWh (2007 est.)

**Oil - production:** 0 bbl/day (2007 est.)

**Oil - consumption:** 9,971 bbl/day (2006 est.)

**Oil - exports:** 2,848 bbl/day (2005)

**Oil - imports:** 10,900 bbl/day (2005)

**Oil - proved reserves:** 0 bbl (1 January 2006 est.)

**Natural gas - production:** 0 cu m (2007 est.)

**Natural gas - consumption:** 0 cu m (2007 est.)

**Natural gas - exports:** 0 cu m (2007 est.)

**Natural gas - imports:** 0 cu m (2007 est.)

**Natural gas - proved reserves:** 0 cu m (1 January 2006 est.)

**Current account balance:** -$507 million (2007 est.)

**Exports:** $1.202 billion f.o.b. (2006)

**Exports - commodities:** sugar, garments, gold, timber, fish, molasses, coconut oil

**Exports - partners:** US 17.3%, UK 11.3%, Australia 10%, Samoa 5.4%, Tonga 4.7%, NZ 4.5%, Japan 4.1% (2007)

**Imports:** $3.12 billion c.i.f. (2006)

**Imports - commodities:** manufactured goods, machinery and transport equipment, petroleum products, food, chemicals

**Imports - partners:** Singapore 30.4%, Australia 21.6%, NZ 17.7%, China 4.5% (2007)

**Debt - external:** $127 million (2004 est.)

**Stock of direct foreign investment - at home:** $NA

**Stock of direct foreign investment - abroad:** $NA

**Exchange rates:** Fijian dollars (FJD) per US dollar - NA (2007), 1.7313 (2006), 1.691 (2005), 1.7331 (2004), 1.8958 (2003)

## Communications

**Telephones - main lines in use:** 108,400 (2007)

**Telephones - mobile cellular:** 437,000 (2007)

**Telephone system:**

*general assessment:* modern local, interisland, and international (wire/radio integrated) public and special-purpose telephone, telegraph, and teleprinter facilities; regional radio communications center

*domestic:* telephone or radio telephone links to almost all inhabited islands; most towns and large villages have automatic telephone exchanges and direct dialing; combined fixed and mobile-cellular density is about 60 per 100 persons

*international:* country code - 679; access to important cable links between US and Canada as well as between NZ and Australia; satellite earth stations - 2 Inmarsat (Pacific Ocean) (2007)

**Radio broadcast stations:** AM 13, FM 40, shortwave 0 (1998)

**Television broadcast stations:** NA

**Internet country code:** .fj

**Internet hosts:** 12,592 (2008)

**Internet users:** 80,000 (2006)

## Transportation

**Airports:** 28 (2008)

**Airports - with paved runways:**

*total:* 3

*over 3,047 m:* 1

*1,524 to 2,437 m:* 1

*914 to 1,523 m:* 1 (2008)

**Airports - with unpaved runways:**

*total:* 25

*914 to 1,523 m:* 7

*under 914 m:* 18 (2008)

**Railways:**

*total:* 597 km

*narrow gauge:* 597 km 0.600-m gauge

*note:* belongs to the government-owned Fiji Sugar Corporation; used to haul sugarcane during the harvest season, which runs from May to December (2006)

**Roadways:**

*total:* 3,440 km

*paved:* 1,692 km

*unpaved:* 1,748 km (2000)

**Waterways:** 203 km

*note:* 122 km navigable by motorized craft and 200-metric-ton barges (2008)

**Merchant marine:**

*total:* 9

*by type:* passenger 3, passenger/cargo 4, roll on/roll off 2

*foreign-owned:* 1 (Australia 1) (2008)

**Ports and terminals:** Lautoka, Suva

## Military

**Military branches:** Republic of Fiji Military Forces (RFMF): Land Forces, Naval Forces (2009)

**Military service age and obligation:** 18 years of age for voluntary military service; reserve obligation to age 45 (2006)

**Manpower available for military service:**

*males age 16-49:* 242,567

*females age 16-49:* 238,556 (2008 est.)

**Manpower fit for military service:**

*males age 16-49:* 192,363

*females age 16-49:* 204,410 (2009 est.)

**Manpower reaching militarily significant age annually:**

*male:* 9,107

*female:* 8,755 (2009 est.)

**Military expenditures:** 2.2% of GDP (2005 est.)

## Transnational Issues

**Disputes - international:** none

**Trafficking in persons:**

*current situation:* Fiji is a source country for children trafficked for the purpose of commercial sexual exploitation and a destination country for a small number of women from China and India trafficked for the purposes of forced labor and commercial sexual exploitation

*tier rating:* Tier 3 - Fiji does not fully comply with the minimum standards for the elimination of trafficking and is not making significant efforts to do so; the government has demonstrated no action to investigate or prosecute traffickers, assist victims, take steps to reduce the demand for commercial sex acts, or support any anti-trafficking information or education campaigns; Fiji has not ratified the 2000 UN TIP Protocol (2008)

# Finland

## Introduction

**Background:** Finland was a province and then a grand duchy under Sweden from the 12th to the 19th centuries, and an autonomous grand duchy of Russia after 1809. It won its complete independence in 1917. During World War II, it was able to successfully defend its freedom and resist invasions by the Soviet Union - albeit with some loss of territory. In the subsequent half century, the Finns made a remarkable transformation from a farm/forest economy to a diversified modern industrial economy; per capita income is now among the highest in Western Europe. A member of the European Union since 1995, Finland was the only Nordic state to join the euro system at its initiation in January 1999.

## Geography

**Location:** Northern Europe, bordering the Baltic Sea, Gulf of Bothnia, and Gulf of Finland, between Sweden and Russia

**Geographic coordinates:** 64 00 N, 26 00 E
**Map references:** Europe
**Area:**
*total:* 338,145 sq km
*land:* 304,473 sq km
*water:* 33,672 sq km
**Area - comparative:** slightly smaller than Montana
**Land boundaries:**
*total:* 2,654 km
*border countries:* Norway 727 km, Sweden 614 km, Russia 1,313 km
**Coastline:** 1,250 km
**Maritime claims:**
*territorial sea:* 12 nm (in the Gulf of Finland - 3 nm)
*contiguous zone:* 24 nm
*exclusive fishing zone:* 12 nm; extends to continental shelf boundary with Sweden
*continental shelf:* 200 m depth or to the depth of exploitation
**Climate:** cold temperate; potentially subarctic but comparatively mild because of moderating influence of the North Atlantic Current, Baltic Sea, and more than 60,000 lakes
**Terrain:** mostly low, flat to rolling plains interspersed with lakes and low hills
**Elevation extremes:**
*lowest point:* Baltic Sea 0 m
*highest point:* Haltiatunturi 1,328 m
**Natural resources:** timber, iron ore, copper, lead, zinc, chromite, nickel, gold, silver, limestone
**Land use:**
*arable land:* 6.54%
*permanent crops:* 0.02%
*other:* 93.44% (2005)
**Irrigated land:** 640 sq km (2003)
**Total renewable water resources:** 110 cu km (2005)
**Freshwater withdrawal (domestic/industrial/agricultural):**
*total:* 2.33 cu km/yr (14%/84%/3%)
*per capita:* 444 cu m/yr (1999)
**Natural hazards:** NA
**Environment - current issues:** air pollution from manufacturing and power plants contributing to acid rain; water pollution from industrial wastes, agricultural chemicals; habitat loss threatens wildlife populations
**Environment - international agreements:**
*party to:* Air Pollution, Air Pollution-Nitrogen Oxides, Air Pollution-Persistent Organic Pollutants, Air Pollution-Sulfur 85, Air Pollution-Sulfur 94, Air Pollution-Volatile Organic Compounds, Antarctic-Environmental Protocol, Antarctic-Marine Living Resources, Antarctic Treaty, Biodiversity, Climate Change, Climate Change-Kyoto Protocol, Desertification, Endangered Species, Environmental Modification, Hazardous Wastes, Law of the Sea, Marine Dumping, Marine Life Conservation, Ozone Layer Protection, Ship Pollution, Tropical Timber 83, Tropical Timber 94, Wetlands, Whaling
*signed, but not ratified:* none of the selected agreements

**Geography - note:** long boundary with Russia; Helsinki is northernmost national capital on European continent; population concentrated on small southwestern coastal plain

## People

**Population:** 5,250,275 (July 2009 est.)
**Age structure:**
*0-14 years:* 16.4% (male 438,425/female 422,777)
*15-64 years:* 66.8% (male 1,773,495/female 1,732,792)
*65 years and over:* 16.8% (male 357,811/female 524,975) (2009 est.)
**Median age:**
*total:* 42.1 years
*male:* 40.5 years
*female:* 43.7 years (2009 est.)
**Population growth rate:** 0.098% (2009 est.)
**Birth rate:** 10.38 births/1,000 population (2009 est.)
**Death rate:** 10 deaths/1,000 population (2008 est.)
**Net migration rate:** 0.68 migrant(s)/1,000 population (2009 est.)
**Urbanization:**
*urban population:* 63% of total population (2008)
*rate of urbanization:* 0.8% annual rate of change (2005-10 est.)
**Sex ratio:**
*at birth:* 1.04 male(s)/female
*under 15 years:* 1.04 male(s)/female
*15-64 years:* 1.02 male(s)/female
*65 years and over:* 0.68 male(s)/female
*total population:* 0.96 male(s)/female (2009 est.)
**Infant mortality rate:**
*total:* 3.47 deaths/1,000 live births
*male:* 3.78 deaths/1,000 live births
*female:* 3.15 deaths/1,000 live births (2009 est.)
**Life expectancy at birth:**
*total population:* 78.97 years
*male:* 75.48 years
*female:* 82.61 years (2009 est.)
**Total fertility rate:** 1.73 children born/woman (2009 est.)
**HIV/AIDS - adult prevalence rate:** less than 0.1% (2007 est.)
**HIV/AIDS - people living with HIV/AIDS:** 2,400 (2007 est.)
**HIV/AIDS - deaths:** fewer than 100 (2003 est.)
**Nationality:**
*noun:* Finn(s)
*adjective:* Finnish
**Ethnic groups:** Finn 93.4%, Swede 5.6%, Russian 0.5%, Estonian 0.3%, Roma (Gypsy) 0.1%, Sami 0.1% (2006)
**Religions:** Lutheran Church of Finland 82.5%, Orthodox Church 1.1%, other Christian 1.1%, other 0.1%, none 15.1% (2006)
**Languages:** Finnish 91.2% (official), Swedish 5.5% (official), other 3.3% (small Sami- and Russian-speaking minorities) (2007)

## Finland (continued)

**Literacy:**
*definition:* age 15 and over can read and write
*total population:* 100%
*male:* 100%
*female:* 100% (2000 est.)
**School life expectancy (primary to tertiary education):**
*total:* 17 years
*male:* 17 years
*female:* 18 years (2006)
**Education expenditures:** 6.4% of GDP (2005)

### Government

**Country name:**
*conventional long form:* Republic of Finland
*conventional short form:* Finland
*local long form:* Suomen tasavalta/Republiken Finland
*local short form:* Suomi/Finland
**Government type:** republic
**Capital:**
*name:* Helsinki
*geographic coordinates:* 60 10 N, 24 56 E
*time difference:* UTC+2 (7 hours ahead of Washington, DC during Standard Time)
*daylight saving time:* +1hr, begins last Sunday in March; ends last Sunday in October
**Administrative divisions:** 6 provinces (laanit, singular - laani); Ahvenanmaan Laani (Aland), Etela-Suomen Laani (Southern Finland), Ita-Suomen Laani (Eastern Finland), Lansi-Suomen Laani (Western Finland), Lapin Laani (Lapland), Oulun Laani
**Independence:** 6 December 1917 (from Russia)
**National holiday:** Independence Day, 6 December (1917)
**Constitution:** 1 March 2000
**Legal system:** civil law system based on Swedish law; the president may request the Supreme Court to review laws; accepts compulsory ICJ jurisdiction with reservations
**Suffrage:** 18 years of age; universal
**Executive branch:**
*chief of state:* President Tarja HALONEN (since 1 March 2000)
*head of government:* Prime Minister Matti VANHANEN (since 24 June 2003); Deputy Prime Minister Jyrki KATAINEN (since 19 April 2007)
*cabinet:* Council of State or Valtioneuvosto appointed by the president, responsible to parliament
*elections:* president elected by popular vote for a six-year term (eligible for a second term); election last held 15 January 2006 (next to be held in January 2012); the president appoints the prime minister and deputy prime minister from the majority party or the majority coalition after parliamentary elections and the parliament must approve the appointment; Prime Minister VANHANEN reelected 17 April 2007
*election results:* percent of vote - Tarja HALONEN (SDP) 46.3%, Sauli NIINISTO (Kok) 24.1%, Matti VANHANEN (Kesk) 18.6%, Heidi HAUTALA

(VIHR) 3.5%; a runoff election between HALONEN and NIINISTO was held 29 January 2006 - HALONEN 51.8%, NIINISTO 48.2%; Matti VANHANEN reelected prime minister; election results 121-71
*note:* government coalition - Kesk, KOK, VIHR, and SFP
**Legislative branch:** unicameral Parliament or Eduskunta (200 seats; members are elected by popular vote on a proportional basis to serve four-year terms)
*elections:* last held 18 March 2007 (next to be held March 2011)
*election results:* percent of vote by party - Kesk 23.1%, Kok 22.3%, SDP 21.4%, VAS 8.8%, VIHR 8.5%, KD 4.9%, SFP 4.5%, True Finns 4.1%, other 3.4%; seats by party - Kesk 51, Kok 50, SDP 45, VAS 17, VIHR 15, SFP 9, KD 7, True Finns 5, other 1
**Judicial branch:** Supreme Court or Korkein Oikeus (judges appointed by the president)
**Political parties and leaders:** Center Party or Kesk [Matti VANHANEN]; Christian Democrats or KD [Paivi RASANEN]; Green Party or VIHR [Tarja CRONBERG]; Left Alliance or VAS [Martti KORHONEN] (composed of People's Democratic League and Democratic Alternative); National Coalition Party (conservative) or Kok [Jyrki KATAINEN]; Social Democratic Party or SDP [Jutta URPILAINEN]; Swedish People's Party or SFP [Stefan WALLIN]; True Finns [Timo SOINI]
**International organization participation:** ADB (nonregional member), AfDB (nonregional member), Arctic Council, Australia Group, BIS, CBSS, CE, CERN, EAPC, EBRD, EIB, EMU, ESA, EU, FAO, G-9, IADB, IAEA, IBRD, ICAO, ICC, ICCt, ICRM, IDA, IEA, IFAD, IFC, IFRCS, IHO, ILO, IMF, IMO, IMSO, Interpol, IOC, IOM, IPU, ISO, ITSO, ITU, ITUC, MIGA, NAM (guest), NC, NEA, NIB, NSG, OAS (observer), OECD, OPCW, OSCE, Paris Club, PCA, PFP, Schengen Convention, UN, UNCTAD, UNESCO, UNHCR, UNIDO, UNMIL, UNMIS, UNMOGIP, UNTSO, UPU, WCO, WEU (observer), WFTU, WHO, WIPO, WMO, WTO, ZC
**Diplomatic representation in the US:**
*chief of mission:* Ambassador Pekka LINTU
*chancery:* 3301 Massachusetts Avenue NW, Washington, DC 20008
*telephone:* [1] (202) 298-5800
*FAX:* [1] (202) 298-6030
*consulate(s) general:* Los Angeles, New York
**Diplomatic representation from the US:**
*chief of mission:* Ambassador Barbara BARRETT
*embassy:* Itainen Puistotie 14B, 00140 Helsinki
*mailing address:* APO AE 09723
*telephone:* [358] (9) 616250
*FAX:* [358] (9) 6162 5800
**Flag description:** white with a blue cross extending to the edges of the flag; the vertical part of the cross is shifted to the hoist side in the style of the Dannebrog (Danish flag)

### Economy

**Economy - overview:** Finland has a highly industrialized, largely free-market economy with per capita output roughly that of the UK, France, Germany, and Italy. Its key economic sector is manufacturing - principally the wood, metals, engineering, telecommunications, and electronics industries. Trade is important; Finland's ratio of exports to GDP has risen from a quarter to 37% over the past 15 years. Finland excels in high-tech exports such as mobile phones. Except for timber and several minerals, Finland depends on imports of raw materials, energy, and some components for manufactured goods. Because of the climate, agricultural development is limited to maintaining self-sufficiency in basic products. Forestry, an important export earner, provides a secondary occupation for the rural population. Although Finland has been one of the best performing economies within the EU in recent years and its banks and financial markets have avoided the worst of global financial crisis, the world slowdown has hit export growth and domestic demand and will serve as a brake on economic growth in 2009 and 2010. The slowdown of construction, other investment, and exports will cause unemployment to rise. During 2009, unemployment will climb to over 8% of the labor force. Long-term challenges include the need to address a rapidly aging population and decreasing productivity that threaten competitiveness, fiscal sustainability, and economic growth.
**GDP (purchasing power parity):**
$195.2 billion (2008 est.)
$192.1 billion (2007)
$184.3 billion (2006)
*note:* data are in 2008 US dollars
**GDP (official exchange rate):** $281.2 billion (2008 est.)
**GDP - real growth rate:**
1.5% (2008 est.)
4.2% (2007 est.)
4.9% (2006 est.)
**GDP - per capita (PPP):**
$37,200 (2008 est.)
$36,700 (2007 est.)
$35,200 (2006 est.)
*note:* data are in 2008 US dollars
**GDP - composition by sector:**
*agriculture:* 2.8%
*industry:* 33.2%
*services:* 64% (2008 est.)
**Labor force:** 2.53 million (2008)
**Labor force - by occupation:** agriculture and forestry 4.5%, industry 18.3%, construction 7.3%, commerce 16%, finance, insurance, and business services 14.5%, transport and communications 7%, public services 32.4% (2008)
**Unemployment rate:**
6.4% (2008 est.)
6.9% (2007 est.)

# Finland (continued)

**Population below poverty line:** NA%
**Household income or consumption by percentage share:**
*lowest 10%:* 3.6%
*highest 10%:* 24.7% (2007)
**Distribution of family income - Gini index:** 29.5 (2007)
**Investment (gross fixed):** 20.5% of GDP (2008 est.)
**Budget:**
*revenues:* $66.48 billion
*expenditures:* $65.3 billion (2008)
**Public debt:** 33% of GDP (2008 est.)
**Inflation rate (consumer prices):**
4.1% (2008 est.)
2.5% (2007 est.)
**Central bank discount rate:** 4%
*note:* this is the European Central Bank's rate on the marginal lending facility, which offers overnight credit to banks in the euro area
**Commercial bank prime lending rate:** 5.04% (December 2008)
**Stock of money:** NA
*note:* see entry for the European Union for money supply in the euro area; the European Central Bank (ECB) controls monetary policy for the 16 members of the Economic and Monetary Union (EMU); individual members of the EMU do not control the quantity of money and quasi money circulating within their own borders
**Stock of quasi money:** NA
**Stock of domestic credit:** $240.7 billion (31 December 2007)
**Market value of publicly traded shares:** $369.2 billion (31 December 2007)
**Agriculture - products:** barley, wheat, sugar beets, potatoes; dairy cattle; fish
**Industries:** metals and metal products, electronics, machinery and scientific instruments, shipbuilding, pulp and paper, foodstuffs, chemicals, textiles, clothing
**Industrial production growth rate:** 4% (2008 est.)
**Electricity - production:** 74.1 billion kWh (2008)
**Electricity - consumption:** 86.9 billion kWh (2008)
**Electricity - exports:** 3.2 billion kWh (2008)
**Electricity - imports:** 16 billion kWh (2008)
**Oil - production:** 8,951 bbl/day (2007 est.)
**Oil - consumption:** 217,500 bbl/day (2008)
**Oil - exports:** 124,300 bbl/day (2007)
**Oil - imports:** 331,200 bbl/day (2007)
**Oil - proved reserves:** NA bbl
**Natural gas - production:** 0 cu m (2007 est.)
**Natural gas - consumption:** 2.268 billion cu m (2007 est.)
**Natural gas - exports:** 0 cu m (2007 est.)
**Natural gas - imports:** 4.576 billion cu m (2007 est.)
**Natural gas - proved reserves:** 0 cu m (1 January 2006)
**Current account balance:** $10.29 billion (2008)
**Exports:** $104.3 billion f.o.b. (2008 est.)

**Exports - commodities:** electrical and optical equipment, machinery, transport equipment, paper and pulp, chemicals, basic metals; timber
**Exports - partners:** Germany 10.9%, Sweden 10.7%, Russia 10.3%, US 6.4%, UK 5.8%, Netherlands 5.6% (2007)
**Imports:** $93.28 billion f.o.b. (2008 est.)
**Imports - commodities:** foodstuffs, petroleum and petroleum products, chemicals, transport equipment, iron and steel, machinery, textile yarn and fabrics, grains
**Imports - partners:** Germany 15.8%, Russia 14%, Sweden 13.7%, Netherlands 6.8%, China 5.5%, UK 4.9% (2007)
**Reserves of foreign exchange and gold:** $9.3 billion (31 December 2008 est.)
**Debt - external:** $271.2 billion (30 June 2007)
**Stock of direct foreign investment - at home:** $94.57 billion (2008 est.)
**Stock of direct foreign investment - abroad:** $121.9 billion (2008 est.)
**Exchange rates:** euros (EUR) per US dollar - 0.6827 (2008 est.), 0.7345 (2007), 0.7964 (2006), 0.8041 (2005), 0.8054 (2004)

## Communications

**Telephones - main lines in use:** 1.74 million (2007)
**Telephones - mobile cellular:** 6.08 million (2007)
**Telephone system:**
*general assessment:* modern system with excellent service
*domestic:* digital fiber-optic fixed-line network and an extensive cellular network provide domestic needs
*international:* country code - 358; submarine cables provide links to Estonia and Sweden; satellite earth stations - access to Intelsat transmission service via a Swedish satellite earth station, 1 Inmarsat (Atlantic and Indian Ocean regions); note - Finland shares the Inmarsat earth station with the other Nordic countries (Denmark, Iceland, Norway, and Sweden)
**Radio broadcast stations:** AM 2, FM 59, shortwave 2 (2008)
**Television broadcast stations:** 120 (plus 431 repeaters) (1999); note - on 1 September 2007, Finland began broadcasting all television signals digitally; analog broadcasts via cable networks were discontinued 29 February 2008
**Internet country code:** .fi; note - Aland Islands assigned .ax
**Internet hosts:** 3.877 million (2008)
**Internet users:** 3.6 million (2007)

## Transportation

**Airports:** 148 (2008)
**Airports - with paved runways:**
*total:* 75
*over 3,047 m:* 3
*2,438 to 3,047 m:* 26
*1,524 to 2,437 m:* 10
*914 to 1,523 m:* 22
*under 914 m:* 14 (2008)

**Airports - with unpaved runways:**
*total:* 73
*914 to 1,523 m:* 3
*under 914 m:* 70 (2008)
**Pipelines:** gas 694 km (2008)
**Railways:**
*total:* 5,741 km
*broad gauge:* 5,741 km 1.524-m gauge (2,619 km electrified) (2006)
**Roadways:**
*total:* 78,821 km
*paved:* 50,854 km (includes 700 km of expressways)
*unpaved:* 27,967 km (2008)
**Waterways:** 7,842 km
*note:* includes Saimaa Canal system of 3,577 km; southern part leased from Russia (2008)
**Merchant marine:**
*total:* 98
*by type:* bulk carrier 3, cargo 28, carrier 1, chemical tanker 6, container 3, passenger 5, passenger/cargo 18, petroleum tanker 5, roll on/roll off 27, vehicle carrier 2
*foreign-owned:* 8 (Estonia 2, Germany 1, Norway 3, Sweden 2)
*registered in other countries:* 47 (Bahamas 9, Germany 4, Gibraltar 3, Netherlands 14, Norway 1, Panama 2, Saint Kitts and Nevis 1, Sweden 12, UK 1) (2008)
**Ports and terminals:** Hamina, Helsinki, Kokkola, Kotka, Naantali, Pori, Raahe, Rauma, Turku

## Military

**Military branches:** Finnish Defense Forces (FDF): Army, Navy (includes Coastal Defense Forces), Air Force (Suomen Ilmavoimat) (2007)
**Military service age and obligation:** 18 years of age for male voluntary and compulsory - and female voluntary - national military and nonmilitary service; service obligation 6-12 months; mandatory retirement at age 60 (2008)
**Manpower available for military service:**
*males age 16-49:* 1,169,910
*females age 16-49:* 1,121,187 (2008 est.)
**Manpower fit for military service:**
*males age 16-49:* 962,479
*females age 16-49:* 920,297 (2009 est.)
**Manpower reaching militarily significant age annually:**
*male:* 33,784
*female:* 32,621 (2009 est.)
**Military expenditures:** 2% of GDP (2005 est.)

## Transnational Issues

**Disputes - international:** various groups in Finland advocate restoration of Karelia and other areas ceded to the Soviet Union, but the Finnish Government asserts no territorial demands

# France

## Introduction

**Background:** Although ultimately a victor in World Wars I and II, France suffered extensive losses in its empire, wealth, manpower, and rank as a dominant nation-state. Nevertheless, France today is one of the most modern countries in the world and is a leader among European nations. Since 1958, it has constructed a hybrid presidential-parliamentary governing system resistant to the instabilities experienced in earlier more purely parliamentary administrations. In recent years, its reconciliation and cooperation with Germany have proved central to the economic integration of Europe, including the introduction of a common exchange currency, the euro, in January 1999. At present, France is at the forefront of efforts to develop the EU's military capabilities to supplement progress toward an EU foreign policy.

## Geography

**Location:**
*metropolitan France:* Western Europe, bordering the Bay of Biscay and English Channel, between Belgium and Spain, southeast of the UK; bordering the Mediterranean Sea, between Italy and Spain
*French Guiana:* Northern South America, bordering the North Atlantic Ocean, between Brazil and Suriname
*Guadeloupe:* Caribbean, islands between the Caribbean Sea and the North Atlantic Ocean, southeast of Puerto Rico
*Martinique:* Caribbean, island between the Caribbean Sea and North Atlantic Ocean, north of Trinidad and Tobago
*Reunion:* Southern Africa, island in the Indian Ocean, east of Madagascar

**Geographic coordinates:**
*metropolitan France:* 46 00 N, 2 00 E
*French Guiana:* 4 00 N, 53 00 W
*Guadeloupe:* 16 15 N, 61 35 W
*Martinique:* 14 40 N, 61 00 W
*Reunion:* 21 06 S, 55 36 E

**Map references:**
*metropolitan France:* Europe
*French Guiana:* South America
*Guadeloupe:* Central America and the Caribbean
*Martinique:* Central America and the Caribbean
*Reunion:* World

**Area:**
*total:* 643,427 sq km; 547,030 sq km (metropolitan France)
*land:* 640,053 sq km; 545,630 sq km (metropolitan France)
*water:* 3,374 sq km; 1,400 sq km (metropolitan France)
*note:* the first numbers include the overseas regions of French Guiana, Guadeloupe, Martinique, and Reunion

**Area - comparative:** slightly less than the size of Texas

**Land boundaries:**
*metropolitan France - total:* 2,889 km
*border countries:* Andorra 56.6 km, Belgium 620 km, Germany 451 km, Italy 488 km, Luxembourg 73 km, Monaco 4.4 km, Spain 623 km, Switzerland 573 km
*French Guiana - total:* 1,183 km
*border countries:* Brazil 673 km, Suriname 510 km

**Coastline:**
*total:* 4,668 km
*metropolitan France:* 3,427 km

**Maritime claims:**
*territorial sea:* 12 nm
*contiguous zone:* 24 nm
*exclusive economic zone:* 200 nm (does not apply to the Mediterranean)
*continental shelf:* 200 m depth or to the depth of exploitation

**Climate:**
*metropolitan France:* generally cool winters and mild summers, but mild winters and hot summers along the Mediterranean; occasional strong, cold, dry, north-to-northwesterly wind known as mistral
*French Guiana:* tropical; hot, humid; little seasonal temperature variation
*Guadeloupe and Martinique:* subtropical tempered by trade winds; moderately high humidity; rainy season (June to October); vulnerable to devastating cyclones (hurricanes) every eight years on average
*Reunion:* tropical, but temperature moderates with elevation; cool and dry (May to November), hot and rainy (November to April)

**Terrain:**
*metropolitan France:* mostly flat plains or gently rolling hills in north and west; remainder is mountainous, especially Pyrenees in south, Alps in east
*French Guiana:* low-lying coastal plains rising to hills and small mountains
*Guadeloupe:* Basse-Terre is volcanic in origin with interior mountains; Grande-Terre is low limestone formation; most of the seven other islands are volcanic in origin
*Martinique:* mountainous with indented coastline; dormant volcano
*Reunion:* mostly rugged and mountainous; fertile lowlands along coast

**Elevation extremes:**
*lowest point:* Rhone River delta -2 m
*highest point:* Mont Blanc 4,807 m

**Natural resources:**
*metropolitan France:* coal, iron ore, bauxite, zinc, uranium, antimony, arsenic, potash, feldspar, fluorspar, gypsum, timber, fish
*French Guiana:* gold deposits, petroleum, kaolin, niobium, tantalum, clay

**Land use:**
*arable land:* 33.46%
*permanent crops:* 2.03%
*other:* 64.51%
*note:* French Guiana - arable land 0.13%, permanent crops 0.04%, other 99.83% (90% forest, 10% other); Guadeloupe - arable land 11.70%, permanent crops 2.92%, other 85.38%; Martinique - arable land 9.09%, permanent crops 10.0%, other 80.91%; Reunion - arable land 13.94%, permanent crops 1.59%, other 84.47% (2005)

**Irrigated land:**
*total:* 26,190 sq km;
*metropolitan France:* 26,000 sq km (2003)

**Total renewable water resources:** 189 cu km (2005)

**Freshwater withdrawal (domestic/industrial/agricultural):**
*total:* 33.16 cu km/yr (16%/74%/10%)
*per capita:* 548 cu m/yr (2000)

**Natural hazards:**
*metropolitan France:* flooding; avalanches; midwinter windstorms; drought; forest fires in south near the Mediterranean
*overseas departments:* hurricanes (cyclones); flooding; volcanic activity (Guadeloupe, Martinique, Reunion)

**Environment - current issues:** some forest damage from acid rain; air pollution from industrial and vehicle emissions; water pollution from urban wastes, agricultural runoff

**Environment - international agreements:**
*party to:* Air Pollution, Air Pollution-Nitrogen Oxides, Air Pollution-Persistent Organic Pollutants, Air Pollution-Sulfur 85, Air Pollution-Sulfur 94, Air Pollution-Volatile Organic Compounds, Antarctic-Environmental Protocol, Antarctic-Marine Living Resources, Antarctic Seals, Antarctic Treaty, Biodiversity, Climate Change, Climate Change-Kyoto Protocol, Desertification, Endangered Species, Hazardous Wastes, Law of the Sea, Marine Dumping, Marine Life Conservation, Ozone Layer Protection, Ship Pollution, Tropical Timber 83, Tropical Timber 94, Wetlands, Whaling
*signed, but not ratified:* none of the selected agreements

**Geography - note:** largest West European nation

# France (continued)

## People

**Population:**
*total:* 64,057,792
*note:* 62,150,775 in metropolitan France (July 2009 est.)

**Age structure:**
*0-14 years:* 18.6% (male 6,129,729/female 5,838,925)
*15-64 years:* 65% (male 20,963,124/female 20,929,280)
*65 years and over:* 16.4% (male 4,403,248/female 6,155,767) (2009 est.)

**Median age:**
*total:* 39.4 years
*male:* 38 years
*female:* 40.9 years (2009 est.)

**Population growth rate:** 0.549% (2009 est.)
**Birth rate:** 12.57 births/1,000 population (2009 est.)
**Death rate:** 8.48 deaths/1,000 population (2008 est.)
**Net migration rate:** 1.48 migrant(s)/1,000 population (2009 est.)

**Urbanization:**
*urban population:* 77% of total population (2008)
*rate of urbanization:* 0.8% annual rate of change (2005-10 est.)

**Sex ratio:**
*at birth:* 1.05 male(s)/female
*under 15 years:* 1.05 male(s)/female
*15-64 years:* 1 male(s)/female
*65 years and over:* 0.72 male(s)/female
*total population:* 0.96 male(s)/female (2009 est.)

**Infant mortality rate:**
*total:* 3.33 deaths/1,000 live births
*male:* 3.66 deaths/1,000 live births
*female:* 2.99 deaths/1,000 live births (2009 est.)

**Life expectancy at birth:**
*total population:* 80.98 years
*male:* 77.79 years
*female:* 84.33 years (2009 est.)

**Total fertility rate:** 1.98 children born/woman (2009 est.)

**HIV/AIDS - adult prevalence rate:** 0.4% (2007 est.)
**HIV/AIDS - people living with HIV/AIDS:** 140,000 (2007 est.)
**HIV/AIDS - deaths:** 1,600 (2007 est.)

**Nationality:**
*noun:* Frenchman(men), Frenchwoman(women)
*adjective:* French

**Ethnic groups:** Celtic and Latin with Teutonic, Slavic, North African, Indochinese, Basque minorities
*overseas departments:* black, white, mulatto, East Indian, Chinese, Amerindian

**Religions:** Roman Catholic 83%-88%, Protestant 2%, Jewish 1%, Muslim 5%-10%, unaffiliated 4%
*overseas departments:* Roman Catholic, Protestant, Hindu, Muslim, Buddhist, pagan

**Languages:** French 100%, rapidly declining regional dialects and languages (Provencal, Breton, Alsatian, Corsican, Catalan, Basque, Flemish)
*overseas departments:* French, Creole patois

**Literacy:**
*definition:* age 15 and over can read and write
*total population:* 99%
*male:* 99%
*female:* 99% (2003 est.)

**School life expectancy (primary to tertiary education):**
*total:* 16 years
*male:* 16 years
*female:* 17 years (2006)

**Education expenditures:** 5.7% of GDP (2005)

## Government

**Country name:**
*conventional long form:* French Republic
*conventional short form:* France
*local long form:* Republique francaise
*local short form:* France

**Government type:** republic

**Capital:**
*name:* Paris
*geographic coordinates:* 48 52 N, 2 20 E
*time difference:* UTC+1 (6 hours ahead of Washington, DC during Standard Time)
*daylight saving time:* +1hr, begins last Sunday in March; ends last Sunday in October
*note:* applies to metropolitan France only, not to its overseas departments, collectivities, or territories

**Administrative divisions:** 26 regions (regions, singular - region); Alsace, Aquitaine, Auvergne, Basse-Normandie (Lower Normandy), Bourgogne (Burgundy), Bretagne (Brittany), Centre, Champagne-Ardenne, Corse (Corsica), Franche-Comte, Guadeloupe, Guyane (French Guiana), Haute-Normandie (Upper Normandy), Ile-de-France, Languedoc-Roussillon, Limousin, Lorraine, Martinique, Midi-Pyrenees, Nord-Pas-de-Calais, Pays de la Loire, Picardie, Poitou-Charentes, Provence-Alpes-Cote d'Azur, Reunion, Rhone-Alpes
*note:* France is divided into 22 metropolitan regions (including the "territorial collectivity" of Corse or Corsica) and 4 overseas regions (including French Guiana, Guadeloupe, Martinique, and Reunion) and is subdivided into 96 metropolitan departments and 4 overseas departments (which are the same as the overseas regions)

**Dependent areas:** Clipperton Island, French Polynesia, French Southern and Antarctic Lands, Mayotte, New Caledonia, Saint Barthelemy, Saint Martin, Wallis and Futuna
*note:* the US does not recognize claims to Antarctica; New Caledonia has been considered a "sui generis" collectivity of France since 1998, a unique status falling between that of an independent country and a French overseas department

**Independence:** 486 (Frankish tribes unified); 843 (Western Francia established from the division of the Carolingian Empire)

**National holiday:** Fete de la Federation, 14 July (1790); note - although often incorrectly referred to as Bastille Day, the celebration actually commemorates the holiday held on the first anniversary of the storming of the Bastille (on 14 July 1789) and the establishment of a constitutional monarchy; other names for the holiday are Fete Nationale (National Holiday) and quatorze juillet (14th of July)

**Constitution:** adopted by referendum 28 September 1958; effective 4 October 1958; amended many times
*note:* amended concerning election of president in 1962; amended to comply with provisions of 1992 EC Maastricht Treaty, 1997 Amsterdam Treaty, 2003 Treaty of Nice; amended to tighten immigration laws in 1993; amended in 2000 to change the seven-year presidential term to a five-year term; amended in 2005 to make the EU constitutional treaty compatible with the Constitution of France and to ensure that the decision to ratify EU accession treaties would be made by referendum

**Legal system:** civil law system with indigenous concepts; review of administrative but not legislative acts; has not accepted compulsory ICJ jurisdiction

**Suffrage:** 18 years of age; universal

**Executive branch:**
*chief of state:* President Nicolas SARKOZY (since 16 May 2007)
*head of government:* Prime Minister Francois FILLON (since 17 May 2007)
*cabinet:* Council of Ministers appointed by the president at the suggestion of the prime minister
*elections:* president elected by popular vote for a five-year term (changed from seven-year term in October 2000); election last held 22 April and 6 May 2007 (next to be held spring 2012); prime minister nominated by the National Assembly majority and appointed by the president
*election results:* Nicolas SARKOZY wins the election; first round: percent of vote - Nicolas SARKOZY 31.18%, Segolene ROYAL 25.87%, Francois BAYROU 18.57%, Jean-Marie LE PEN 10.44%, others 13.94%; second round: SARKOZY 53.1% and ROYAL 46.9%

**Legislative branch:** bicameral Parliament or Parlement consists of the Senate or Senat (343 seats, 321 for metropolitan France and overseas departments, 2 for New Caledonia, 2 for Mayotte, 1 for Saint-Pierre and Miquelon, 1 for Saint-Barthelemy, 1 for Saint-Martin, 3 for overseas territories, and 12 for French nationals abroad; members are indirectly elected by an electoral college to serve six-year terms; one third elected every three years); note - between 2006 and 2011, 15 new seats will be added to the Senate for a total of 348 seats - 326 for metropolitan France and overseas departments, 2 for New Caledonia, 2 for Mayotte, 1 for Saint-Pierre and Miquelon, 1 for Saint-Barthelemy, 1 for Saint-Martin, 3 for overseas territories, and 12 for French nationals abroad; starting in 2008, members will be indirectly elected by an electoral college to serve six-year terms with one-half elected every three years; and the National Assembly or Assemblee Nationale (577 seats, 555 for metropolitan France, 15 for overseas departments, 7 for dependencies; members are elected by popular vote under a single-member majority system to serve five-year terms)

*elections:* Senate - last held 21 September 2008 (next to be held in September 2014); National Assembly - last held 10 and 17 June 2007 (next to be held in June 2012)

*election results:* Senate - percent of vote by party - NA; seats by party - UMP 151, PS 116, UC-UDF 29, CRC 23, RDSE 17, other 7; National Assembly - percent of vote by party - UMP 46.37%, PS 42.25%, miscellaneous left wing parties 2.47%, PCF 2.28%, NC 2.12%, PRG 1.65%, miscellaneous right wing parties 1.17%, the Greens 0.45%, other 1.24%; seats by party - UMP 313, PS 186, NC 22, miscellaneous left wing parties 15, PCF 15, miscellaneous right wing parties 9, PRG 7, the Greens 4, other 6

**Judicial branch:** Supreme Court of Appeals or Cour de Cassation (judges are appointed by the president from nominations of the High Council of the Judiciary); Constitutional Council or Conseil Constitutionnel (three members appointed by the president, three appointed by the president of the National Assembly, and three appointed by the president of the Senate); Council of State or Conseil d'Etat

**Political parties and leaders:** Communist, Republican and Citizen or CRC; Democratic Movement or MoDem [Francois BAYROU] (previously Union for French Democracy or UDF); Democratic and Social European Rally or RDSE [Yvon COLLIN] (mainly Radical Republican and Socialist Parties, and PRG); French Communist Party or PCF [Marie-George BUFFET]; Greens [Cecile DUFLOT]; Left Radical Party or PRG [Jean-Michel BAYLET] (previously Radical Socialist Party or PRS and the Left Radical Movement or MRG); Movement for France or MPF [Philippe DE VILLIERS]; National Front or FN [Jean-Marie LE PEN]; New Center or NC [Herve MORIN]; Radical Party [Jean-Louis BORLOO]; Rally for France or RPF [Charles PASQUA]; Republican and Citizen Movement or MRC [Jean Pierre CHEVENEMENT and Georges SARRE]; Socialist Party or PS [Martine AUBRY]; Union Centrist-UDF or UC-UDF [Michel MERCIER]; Union for a Popular Movement or UMP [Xavier BERTRAND]

**Political pressure groups and leaders:** Confederation Francaise Democratique du Travail or CFDT, left-leaning labor union with approximately 803,000 members; Confederation Generale des Cadres or CGC, independent white-collar union with 196,000 members; Confederation Generale du Travail or CGT, historically communist labor union with approximately 700,000 members; Confederation Generale du Travail - Force Ouvriere or FO, independent labor union with an estimated 300,000 members; Mouvement des Entreprises de France or MEDEF, employers' union with 750,000 companies as members (claimed)

*French Guiana:* conservationists; gold mining pressure groups; hunting pressure groups

*Guadeloupe:* Christian Movement for the Liberation of Guadeloupe or KLPG; General Federation of Guadeloupe Workers or CGT-G; General Union of Guadeloupe Workers or UGTG; Movement for an Independent Guadeloupe or MPGI; The Socialist Renewal Movement

*Martinique:* Caribbean Revolutionary Alliance or ARC; Central Union for Martinique Workers or CSTM; Frantz Fanon Circle; League of Workers and Peasants; Proletarian Action Group or GAP

*Reunion:* NA

**International organization participation:** ADB (nonregional member), AfDB (nonregional member), Arctic Council (observer), Australia Group, BDEAC, BIS, BSEC (observer), CBSS (observer), CE, CERN, EAPC, EBRD, EIB, EMU, ESA, EU, FAO, FZ, G-20, G-5, G-7, G-8, G-10, IADB, IAEA, IBRD, ICAO, ICC, ICCt, ICRM, IDA, IEA, IFAD, IFC, IFRCS, IHO, ILO, IMF, IMO, IMSO, InOC, Interpol, IOC, IOM, IPU, ISO, ITSO, ITU, ITUC, MIGA, MINURCAT, MINURSO, MINUSTAH, MONUC, NATO, NEA, NSG, OAS (observer), OECD, OIF, OPCW, OSCE, Paris Club, PCA, PIF (partner), Schengen Convention, SECI (observer), SPC, UN, UN Security Council, UNAMID, UNCTAD, UNESCO, UNHCR, UNIDO, UNIFIL, Union Latina, UNITAR, UNMIL, UNOCI, UNOMIG, UNRWA, UNTSO, UNWTO, UPU, WADB (nonregional), WCL, WCO, WEU, WFTU, WHO, WIPO, WMO, WTO, ZC

**Diplomatic representation in the US:**

*chief of mission:* Ambassador Pierre VIMONT

*chancery:* 4101 Reservoir Road NW, Washington, DC 20007

*telephone:* [1] (202) 944-6000

*FAX:* [1] (202) 944-6166

*consulate(s) general:* Atlanta, Boston, Chicago, Houston, Los Angeles, Miami, New Orleans, New York, San Francisco

**Diplomatic representation from the US:**

*chief of mission:* Ambassador (vacant); Charge d'Affaires Mark A. PEKALA

*embassy:* 2 Avenue Gabriel, 75382 Paris Cedex 08

*mailing address:* PSC 116, APO AE 09777

*telephone:* [33] (1) 43-12-22-22

*FAX:* [33] (1) 42 66 97 83

*consulate(s) general:* Marseille, Strasbourg

**Flag description:** three equal vertical bands of blue (hoist side), white, and red; known as the "Le drapeau tricolore" (French Tricolor), the origin of the flag dates to 1790 and the French Revolution; the design and/or colors are similar to a number of other flags, including those of Belgium, Chad, Ireland, Cote d'Ivoire, Luxembourg, and Netherlands; the official flag for all French dependent areas

## Economy

**Economy - overview:** France is in the midst of transition from a well-to-do modern economy that has featured extensive government ownership and intervention to one that relies more on market mechanisms. The government has partially or fully privatized many large companies, banks, and insurers, and has ceded stakes in such leading firms as Air France, France Telecom, Renault, and Thales. It maintains a strong presence in some sectors, particularly power, public transport, and defense industries. The telecommunications sector is gradually being opened to competition. France's leaders remain committed to a capitalism in which they maintain social equity by means of laws, tax policies, and social spending that reduce income disparity and the impact of free markets on public health and welfare. Widespread opposition to labor reform has in recent years hampered the government's ability to revitalize the economy. During 2007-08, the government implemented several important labor reforms, including a de facto extension of the 35-hour workweek by allowing employees to work longer overtime hours. During 2009, the government is expected to delay or even renounce other reform efforts due to the on-going financial crisis. GDP growth dropped to 0.7% in 2008; the French government plans to increase public investment and continue injecting capital into the banking sector to alleviate the negative effects of the crisis during 2009. As a result of lower fiscal revenues and increased expenditures the general government deficit is expected to exceed the euro-zone ceiling 3% of GDP. France's tax burden remains one of the highest in Europe - at nearly 50% of GDP in 2005. With at least 75 million foreign tourists per year, France is the most visited country in the world and maintains the third largest income in the world from tourism.

**GDP (purchasing power parity):**

$2.097 trillion (2008 est.)

$2.083 trillion (2007)

$2.074 trillion (2006)

*note:* data are in 2008 US dollars

**GDP (official exchange rate):** $2.978 trillion (2008 est.)

**GDP - real growth rate:**

0.7% (2008 est.)

2.1% (2007 est.)

2.4% (2006 est.)

**GDP - per capita (PPP):**

$32,700 (2008 est.)

$33,300 (2007 est.)

$32,800 (2006 est.)

*note:* data are in 2008 US dollars

**GDP - composition by sector:**

*agriculture:* 2.2%

*industry:* 20.3%

*services:* 77.4% (2008 est.)

**Labor force:** 28.5 million (2008 est.)

**Labor force - by occupation:**

*agriculture:* 3.8%

*industry:* 24.3%

*services:* 71.8% (2005)

**Unemployment rate:**

7.4% (2008 est.)

7.9% (2007 est.)

**Population below poverty line:** 6.2% (2004)

**Household income or consumption by percentage share:**

*lowest 10%:* 3%

*highest 10%:* 24.8% (2004)

# France *(continued)*

**Distribution of family income - Gini index:** 32.7 (2008)
**Investment (gross fixed):** 21% of GDP (2008 est.)
**Budget:**
*revenues:* $1.439 trillion
*expenditures:* $1.525 trillion (2008 est.)
**Public debt:** 67% of GDP (2008 est.)
**Inflation rate (consumer prices):**
1% (2008 est.)
1.5% (2007 est.)
**Central bank discount rate:** NA
**Commercial bank prime lending rate:** 6.6% (2008)
**Stock of money:** NA
*note:* see entry for the European Union for money supply in the euro area; the European Central Bank (ECB) controls monetary policy for the 16 members of the Economic and Monetary Union (EMU); individual members of the EMU do not control the quantity of money and quasi money circulating within their own borders
**Stock of quasi money:** NA
**Stock of domestic credit:** $5.739 trillion (April 2008)
**Market value of publicly traded shares:** $2.771 trillion (31 December 2007)
**Agriculture - products:** wheat, cereals, sugar beets, potatoes, wine grapes; beef, dairy products; fish
**Industries:** machinery, chemicals, automobiles, metallurgy, aircraft, electronics; textiles, food processing; tourism
**Industrial production growth rate:** -8% (2008 est.)
**Electricity - production:** 570 billion kWh (2007 est.)
**Electricity - consumption:** 480 billion kWh (2007 est.)
**Electricity - exports:** 67.6 billion kWh (2007)
**Electricity - imports:** 10.8 billion kWh (2007)
**Oil - production:** 71,400 bbl/day (2007)
**Oil - consumption:** 1.95 million bbl/day (2007)
**Oil - exports:** 584,700 bbl/day (2005)
**Oil - imports:** 2.465 million bbl/day (2005)
**Oil - proved reserves:** 122 million bbl (1 January 2008 est.)
**Natural gas - production:** 953 million cu m (2007 est.)
**Natural gas - consumption:** 42.69 billion cu m (2007 est.)
**Natural gas - exports:** 966 million cu m (2007 est.)
**Natural gas - imports:** 42.9 billion cu m (2007 est.)
**Natural gas - proved reserves:** 7.277 billion cu m (1 January 2008 est.)
**Current account balance:** -$58 billion (2008 est.)
**Exports:** $761 billion f.o.b. (2008 est.)
**Exports - commodities:** machinery and transportation equipment, aircraft, plastics, chemicals, pharmaceutical products, iron and steel, beverages
**Exports - partners:** Germany 14.9%, Spain 9.3%, Italy 8.9%, UK 8.1%, Belgium 7.3%, US 6.1%, Netherlands 4.1% (2007)
**Imports:** $833 billion f.o.b. (2008 est.)
**Imports - commodities:** machinery and equipment, vehicles, crude oil, aircraft, plastics, chemicals

**Imports - partners:** Germany 18.9%, Belgium 11.4%, Italy 8.4%, Spain 7.1%, Netherlands 7%, UK 5.6%, US 4.4%, China 4% (2007)
**Reserves of foreign exchange and gold:** $204.4 billion (2008)
**Debt - external:** $5.37 trillion (30 September 2008)
**Stock of direct foreign investment - at home:** $1.234 trillion (2008 est.)
**Stock of direct foreign investment - abroad:** $1.889 trillion (2008 est.)
**Exchange rates:** euros (EUR) per US dollar - 0.6827 (2008 est.), 0.7345 (2007), 0.7964 (2006), 0.8041 (2005), 0.8054 (2004)

## Communications

**Telephones - main lines in use:** 35.533 million; 34.8 million (metropolitan France) (2007)
**Telephones - mobile cellular:** 56.719 million; 55.358 million (metropolitan France) (2007)
**Telephone system:**
*general assessment:* highly developed
*domestic:* extensive cable and microwave radio relay; extensive use of fiber-optic cable; domestic satellite system
*international:* country code - 33; numerous submarine cables provide links throughout Europe, Asia, Australia, the Middle East, and US; satellite earth stations - more than 3 (2 Intelsat (with total of 5 antennas - 2 for Indian Ocean and 3 for Atlantic Ocean), NA Eutelsat, 1 Inmarsat - Atlantic Ocean region); HF radiotelephone communications with more than 20 countries
*overseas departments:* country codes: French Guiana - 594; Guadeloupe - 590; Martinique - 596; Reunion - 262
**Radio broadcast stations:** AM 41, FM about 3,500 (this figure is an approximation and includes many repeaters), shortwave 2 (1998)
**Television broadcast stations:** 584 (plus 9,676 repeaters) (1995)
**Internet country code:** metropolitan France - .fr; French Guiana - .gf; Guadeloupe - .gp; Martinique - .mq; Reunion - .re
**Internet hosts:** 14.256 million; 14,256,000 (metropolitan France) (2008)
**Internet users:** 31.295 million; 30.838 million (metropolitan France) (2007)

## Transportation

**Airports:** 475 (2008)
**Airports - with paved runways:**
*total:* 295
*over 3,047 m:* 14
*2,438 to 3,047 m:* 26
*1,524 to 2,437 m:* 98
*914 to 1,523 m:* 82
*under 914 m:* 75 (2008)
**Airports - with unpaved runways:**
*total:* 180
*1,524 to 2,437 m:* 3
*914 to 1,523 m:* 71
*under 914 m:* 106 (2008)

**Heliports:** 3 (2007)
**Pipelines:** gas 14,688 km; oil 3,036 km; refined products 5,080 km (2008)
**Railways:**
*total:* 29,370 km
*standard gauge:* 29,203 km 1.435-m gauge (14,778 kmelectrified)
*narrow gauge:* 167 km 1.000-m gauge (2006)
**Roadways:**
*total:* 951,500 km
*paved:* 951,500 km (metropolitan France; includes 10,950 km of expressways)
*note:* there are another 5,100 km of roadways in overseas departments (2006)
**Waterways:**
*metropolitan France:* 8,501 km (1,621 km accessible to craft of 3,000 metric tons)
*French Guiana:* 3,760 km (460 km navigable by small oceangoing vessels and coastal and river steamers, 3,300 km by native craft) (2008)
**Merchant marine:**
*total:* 138
*by type:* bulk carrier 2, cargo 1, chemical tanker 32, container 25, liquefied gas 12, passenger 3, passenger/cargo 33, petroleum tanker 23, roll on/roll off 7
*foreign-owned:* 38 (Belgium 6, China 5, Denmark 2, Germany 1, Italy 2, Japan 1, NZ 1, Norway 5, Saudi Arabia 1, Singapore 2, Sweden 9, Switzerland 3)
*registered in other countries:* 127 (Antigua and Barbuda 1, Australia 1, Bahamas 30, Belgium 2, Bermuda 1, Hong Kong 1, Indonesia 1, Isle of Man 1, Italy 2, Liberia 5, Luxembourg 17, Malta 5, Morocco 14, Netherlands 1, Norway 3, Panama 5, Saint Vincent and the Grenadines 6, Singapore 1, Taiwan 1, UK 23, Wallis and Futuna 6) (2008)
**Ports and terminals:** Bordeaux, Calais, Dunkerque, Le Havre, Marseille, Nantes, Paris, Rouen, Strasbourg

## Military

**Military branches:** Army (Armee de Terre; includes Marines, Foreign Legion, Army Light Aviation), Navy (Marine Nationale, includes Naval Air, Maritime Gendarmerie (Coast Guard)), Air Force (Armee de l'Air, includes Air Defense), National Gendarmerie (2009)
**Military service age and obligation:** 17-40 years of age for male or female voluntary military service; no conscription; 12-month service obligation; women serve in noncombat military posts (2008)
**Manpower available for military service:**
*males age 16-49:* 14,646,427
*females age 16-49:* 14,379,630 (2008 est.)
**Manpower fit for military service:**
*males age 16-49:* 12,087,606
*females age 16-49:* 11,811,260 (2009 est.)
**Manpower reaching militarily significant age annually:**
*male:* 391,480
*female:* 373,334 (2009 est.)

# France (continued)

**Military expenditures:** 2.6% of GDP (2005 est.)

**T r a n s n a t i o n a l   I s s u e s**

**Disputes - international:** Madagascar claims the French territories of Bassas da India, Europa Island, Glorioso Islands, and Juan de Nova Island; Comoros claims Mayotte; Mauritius claims Tromelin Island; territorial dispute between Suriname and the French overseas department of French Guiana; France asserts a territorial claim in Antarctica (Adelie Land); France and Vanuatu claim Matthew and Hunter Islands, east of New Caledonia

**Illicit drugs:**

*metropolitan France:* transshipment point for South American cocaine, Southwest Asian heroin, and European synthetics

*French Guiana:* small amount of marijuana grown for local consumption; minor transshipment point to Europe

*Martinique:* transshipment point for cocaine and marijuana bound for the US and Europe

# French Polynesia
*(overseas lands of France)*

## Introduction

**Background:** The French annexed various Polynesian island groups during the 19th century. In September 1995, France stirred up widespread protests by resuming nuclear testing on the Mururoa atoll after a three-year moratorium. The tests were suspended in January 1996. In recent years, French Polynesia's autonomy has been considerably expanded.

## Geography

**Location:** Oceania, archipelagoes in the South Pacific Ocean about half way between South America and Australia

**Geographic coordinates:** 15 00 S, 140 00 W

**Map references:** Oceania

**Area:**
*total:* 4,167 sq km (118 islands and atolls)
*land:* 3,660 sq km
*water:* 507 sq km

**Area - comparative:** slightly less than one-third the size of Connecticut

**Land boundaries:** 0 km

**Coastline:** 2,525 km

**Maritime claims:**
*territorial sea:* 12 nm
*exclusive economic zone:* 200 nm

**Climate:** tropical, but moderate

**Terrain:** mixture of rugged high islands and low islands with reefs

**Elevation extremes:**
*lowest point:* Pacific Ocean 0 m
*highest point:* Mont Orohena 2,241 m

**Natural resources:** timber, fish, cobalt, hydropower

**Land use:**
*arable land:* 0.75%
*permanent crops:* 5.5%
*other:* 93.75% (2005)

**Irrigated land:** 10 sq km (2003)

**Natural hazards:** occasional cyclonic storms in January

**Environment - current issues:** NA

**Geography - note:** includes five archipelagoes (four volcanic, one coral); Makatea in French Polynesia is one of the three great phosphate rock islands in the Pacific Ocean - the others are Banaba (Ocean Island) in Kiribati and Nauru

## People

**Population:** 287,032 (July 2009 est.)

**Age structure:**
*0-14 years:* 24.3% (male 35,631/female 34,097)
*15-64 years:* 68.9% (male 102,537/female 95,317)
*65 years and over:* 6.8% (male 9,821/female 9,629) (2009 est.)

**Median age:**
*total:* 29.1 years
*male:* 29.4 years
*female:* 28.8 years (2009 est.)

**Population growth rate:** 1.391% (2009 est.)

**Birth rate:** 15.91 births/1,000 population (2009 est.)

**Death rate:** 4.67 deaths/1,000 population (2008 est.)

**Net migration rate:** 2.73 migrant(s)/1,000 population (2009 est.)

**Urbanization:**
*urban population:* 52% of total population (2008)
*rate of urbanization:* 1.3% annual rate of change (2005-10 est.)

**Sex ratio:**
*at birth:* 1.05 male(s)/female
*under 15 years:* 1.04 male(s)/female
*15-64 years:* 1.08 male(s)/female
*65 years and over:* 1.02 male(s)/female
*total population:* 1.06 male(s)/female (2009 est.)

**Infant mortality rate:**
*total:* 7.55 deaths/1,000 live births
*male:* 8.67 deaths/1,000 live births
*female:* 6.38 deaths/1,000 live births (2009 est.)

**Life expectancy at birth:**
*total population:* 76.71 years
*male:* 74.26 years
*female:* 79.29 years (2009 est.)

**Total fertility rate:** 1.92 children born/woman (2009 est.)

**HIV/AIDS - adult prevalence rate:** NA

**HIV/AIDS - people living with HIV/AIDS:** NA

**HIV/AIDS - deaths:** NA

**Nationality:**
*noun:* French Polynesian(s)
*adjective:* French Polynesian

**Ethnic groups:** Polynesian 78%, Chinese 12%, local French 6%, metropolitan French 4%

**Religions:** Protestant 54%, Roman Catholic 30%, other 10%, no religion 6%

**Languages:** French 61.1% (official), Polynesian 31.4% (official), Asian languages 1.2%, other 0.3%, unspecified 6% (2002 census)

**Literacy:**
*definition:* age 14 and over can read and write
*total population:* 98%
*male:* 98%
*female:* 98% (1977 est.)

**Education expenditures:** NA

# French Polynesia (continued)

## Government

**Country name:**
*conventional long form:* Overseas Lands of French Polynesia
*conventional short form:* French Polynesia
*local long form:* Pays d'outre-mer de la Polynesie Francaise
*local short form:* Polynesie Francaise
*former:* French Colony of Oceania
**Dependency status:** overseas lands of France; overseas territory of France from 1946-2004
**Government type:** NA
**Capital:**
*name:* Papeete
*geographic coordinates:* 17 32 S, 149 34 W
*time difference:* UTC-10 (5 hours behind Washington, DC during Standard Time)
**Administrative divisions:** none (overseas lands of France); there are no first-order administrative divisions as defined by the US Government, but there are five archipelagic divisions named Archipel des Marquises, Archipel des Tuamotu, Archipel des Tubuai, Iles du Vent, Iles Sous-le-Vent
**Independence:** none (overseas lands of France)
**National holiday:** Bastille Day, 14 July (1789)
**Constitution:** 4 October 1958 (French Constitution)
**Legal system:** the laws of France, where applicable, apply
**Suffrage:** 18 years of age; universal
**Executive branch:**
*chief of state:* President Nicolas SARKOZY (since 16 May 2007), represented by High Commissioner of the Republic Adolphe COLRAT (since 7 July 2008)
*head of government:* President of French Polynesia Oscar TEMARU (since 7 February 2009); President of the Territorial Assembly Eduoard FRITCH (since 12 February 2009)
*cabinet:* Council of Ministers; president submits a list of members of the Territorial Assembly for approval by them to serve as ministers
*elections:* French president elected by popular vote for a five-year term; high commissioner appointed by the French president on the advice of the French Ministry of Interior; president of the territorial government and the president of the Territorial Assembly are elected by the members of the assembly for five-year terms (no term limits)
**Legislative branch:** unicameral Territorial Assembly or Assemblee Territoriale (57 seats; members are elected by popular vote to serve five-year terms)
*elections:* last held 27 January 2008 (first round) and 10 February 2008 (second round) (next to be held in 2013)
*election results:* percent of vote by party - Our Home alliance 45.2%, Union for Democracy alliance 37.2%, Popular Rally (Tahoeraa Huiraatira) 17.2% other 0.5%; seats by party - Our Home alliance 27, Union for Democracy alliance 20, Popular Rally 10
*note:* one seat was elected to the French Senate on 21 September 2008 (next to be held in September 2014); results - percent of vote by party - NA; seats by party - PS 1, independent 1; two seats were elected to the French National Assembly on 10-17 June 2007 (next to be held in 2012); results - percent of vote by party - NA; seats by party - UMP 2
**Judicial branch:** Court of Appeal or Cour d'Appel; Court of the First Instance or Tribunal de Premiere Instance; Court of Administrative Law or Tribunal Administratif
**Political parties and leaders:** Alliance for a New Democracy or ADN [Nicole BOUTEAU and Philip SCHYLE](includes the parties The New Star and This Country is Yours); Independent Front for the Liberation of Polynesia (Tavini Huiraatira) [Oscar TEMARU]; New Fatherland Party (Ai'a Api) [Emile VERNAUDON]; Our Home alliance; Popular Rally (Tahoeraa Huiraatira) [Gaston FLOSSE]; Union for Democracy alliance or UPD [Oscar TEMARU]
**Political pressure groups and leaders:** NA
**International organization participation:** FZ, ITUC, PIF (associate member), SPC, UPU, WMO
**Diplomatic representation in the US:** none (overseas lands of France)
**Diplomatic representation from the US:** none (overseas lands of France)
**Flag description:** two narrow red horizontal bands encase a wide white band; centered on the white band is a disk with a blue and white wave pattern on the lower half and a gold and white ray pattern on the upper half; a stylized red, blue, and white ship rides on the wave pattern; the French flag is used for official occasions
**Government - note:** under certain acts of France, French Polynesia has acquired autonomy in all areas except those relating to police and justice, monetary policy, tertiary education, immigration, and defense and foreign affairs; the duties of its president are fashioned after those of the French prime minister

## Economy

**Economy - overview:** Since 1962, when France stationed military personnel in the region, French Polynesia has changed from a subsistence agricultural economy to one in which a high proportion of the work force is either employed by the military or supports the tourist industry. With the halt of French nuclear testing in 1996, the military contribution to the economy fell sharply. Tourism accounts for about one-fourth of GDP and is a primary source of hard currency earnings. Other sources of income are pearl farming and deep-sea commercial fishing. The small manufacturing sector primarily processes agricultural products. The territory benefits substantially from development agreements with France aimed principally at creating new businesses and strengthening social services.
**GDP (purchasing power parity):**
$4.718 billion (2004 est.)
$4.58 billion (2003)
**GDP (official exchange rate):** $6.1 billion (2004)
**GDP - real growth rate:**
2.7% (2005)
5.1% (2002)
**GDP - per capita (PPP):**
$18,000 (2004 est.)
$17,500 (2003 est.)
**GDP - composition by sector:**
*agriculture:* 3.5%
*industry:* 20.4%
*services:* 76.1% (2005)
**Labor force:** 113,400 (2006)
**Labor force - by occupation:**
*agriculture:* 13%
*industry:* 19%
*services:* 68% (2002)
**Unemployment rate:**
11.7% (2005)
**Population below poverty line:** NA%
**Household income or consumption by percentage share:**
*lowest 10%:* NA%
*highest 10%:* NA%
**Budget:**
*revenues:* $865 million
*expenditures:* $644.1 million (1999)
**Inflation rate (consumer prices):**
1.1% (2007)
1.1% (2006 est.)
**Market value of publicly traded shares:** $NA
**Agriculture - products:** fish; coconuts, vanilla, vegetables, fruits, coffee; poultry, beef, dairy products
**Industries:** tourism, pearls, agricultural processing, handicrafts, phosphates
**Industrial production growth rate:** NA%
**Electricity - production:** 475 million kWh (2006 est.)
**Electricity - consumption:** 441.8 million kWh (2006 est.)
**Electricity - exports:** 0 kWh (2007 est.)
**Electricity - imports:** 0 kWh (2007 est.)
**Oil - production:** 0 bbl/day (2007 est.)
**Oil - consumption:** 6,082 bbl/day (2006 est.)
**Oil - exports:** 0 bbl/day (2005)
**Oil - imports:** 6,271 bbl/day (2005)
**Oil - proved reserves:** 0 bbl (1 January 2006 est.)
**Natural gas - production:** 0 cu m (2007 est.)
**Natural gas - consumption:** 0 cu m (2007 est.)
**Natural gas - exports:** 0 cu m (2007 est.)
**Natural gas - imports:** 0 cu m (2007 est.)
**Natural gas - proved reserves:** 0 cu m (1 January 2006 est.)
**Exports:** $211 million f.o.b. (2005 est.)
**Exports - commodities:** cultured pearls, coconut products, mother-of-pearl, vanilla, shark meat
**Imports:** $1.706 billion f.o.b. (2005 est.)
**Imports - commodities:** fuels, foodstuffs, machinery and equipment
**Debt - external:** $NA
**Exchange rates:** Comptoirs Francais du Pacifique francs (XPF) per US dollar - 87.59 (2007), 94.97 (2006), 95.89 (2005), 96.04 (2004), 105.66 (2003)
*note:* pegged at the rate of 119.25 XPF to the euro

# French Polynesia (continued)

## Communications

**Telephones - main lines in use:** 53,600 (2006)
**Telephones - mobile cellular:** 174,800 (2007)
**Telephone system:**
*general assessment:* NA
*domestic:* NA
*international:* country code - 689; satellite earth station -1 Intelsat (Pacific Ocean)
**Radio broadcast stations:** AM 2, FM 14, shortwave 2 (1998)
**Television broadcast stations:** 7 (plus 17 repeaters) (1997)
**Internet country code:** .pf
**Internet hosts:** 14,070 (2008)
**Internet users:** 75,000 (2007)

## Transportation

**Airports:** 55 (2008)
**Airports - with paved runways:**
*total:* 48
*over 3,047 m:* 2
*1,524 to 2,437 m:* 5
*914 to 1,523 m:* 34
*under 914 m:* 7 (2008)
**Airports - with unpaved runways:**
*total:* 7
*914 to 1,523 m:* 3
*under 914 m:* 4 (2008)
**Heliports:** 1 (2007)
**Roadways:**
*total:* 2,590 km
*paved:* 1,735 km
*unpaved:* 855 km (1999)
**Merchant marine:**
*total:* 15
*by type:* cargo 6, passenger 2, passenger/cargo 5, refrigerated cargo 1, roll on/roll off 1
*registered in other countries:* 2 (Wallis and Futuna 2) (2008)
**Ports and terminals:** Papeete

## Military

**Military branches:** no regular military forces (2009)
**Manpower available for military service:**
*males age 16-49:* 79,540 (2008 est.)
**Manpower fit for military service:**
*males age 16-49:* 65,408
*females age 16-49:* 64,421 (2009 est.)
**Manpower reaching militarily significant age annually:**
*male:* 2,665
*female:* 2,552 (2009 est.)
**Military - note:** defense is the responsibility of France

## Transnational Issues

**Disputes - international:** none

# French Southern and Antarctic Lands
*(overseas territory of France)*

## Introduction

**Background:** In February 2007, the Iles Eparses became an integral part of the French Southern and Antarctic Lands (TAAF). The Southern Lands are now divided into five administrative districts, two of which are archipelagos, Iles Crozet and Iles Kerguelen; the third is a district composed of two volcanic islands, Ile Saint-Paul and Ile Amsterdam; the fourth, Iles Eparses, consists of five scattered tropical islands around Madagascar. They contain no permanent inhabitants and are visited only by researchers studying the native fauna, scientists at the various scientific stations, fishermen, and military personnel. The fifth district is the Antarctic portion, which consists of "Adelie Land," a thin slice of the Antarctic continent discovered and claimed by the French in 1840.
*Ile Amsterdam:* Discovered but not named in 1522 by the Spanish, the island subsequently received the appellation of Nieuw Amsterdam from a Dutchman; it was claimed by France in 1843. A short-lived attempt at cattle farming began in 1871. A French meteorological station established on the island in 1949 is still in use.
*Ile Saint Paul:* Claimed by France since 1893, the island was a fishing industry center from 1843 to 1914. In 1928, a spiny lobster cannery was established, but when the company went bankrupt in 1931, seven workers were abandoned. Only two survived until 1934 when rescue finally arrived.
*Iles Crozet:* A large archipelago formed from the Crozet Plateau, Iles Crozet is divided into two main groups: L'Occidental (the West), which includes Ile aux Cochons, Ilots des Apotres, Ile des Pingouins, and the reefs Brisants de l'Heroine; and L'Oriental (the east), which includes Ile d'Est and Ile de la Possession (the largest island of the Crozets). Discovered and claimed by France in 1772, the islands were used for seal hunting and as a base for whaling. Originally administered as a dependency of Madagascar, they became part of the TAAF in 1955.
*Iles Kerguelen:* This island group, discovered in 1772, is made up of one large island (Ile Kerguelen) and about 300 smaller islands. A permanent group of 50 to 100 scientists resides at the main base at Port-aux-Francais.
*Adelie Land:* The only non-insular district of the TAAF is the Antarctic claim known as "Adelie Land." The US Government does not recognize it as a French dependency.
*Bassas da India:* A French possession since 1897, this atoll is a volcanic rock surrounded by reefs and is awash at high tide.
*Europa Island:* This heavily wooded island has been a French possession since 1897; it is the site of a small military garrison that staffs a weather station.
*Glorioso Islands:* A French possession since 1892, the Glorioso Islands are composed of two lushly vegetated coral islands (Ile Glorieuse and Ile du Lys) and three rock islets. A military garrison operates a weather and radio station on Ile Glorieuse.
*Juan de Nova Island:* Named after a famous 15th century Spanish navigator and explorer, the island has been a French possession since 1897. It has been exploited for its guano and phosphate. Presently a small military garrison oversees a meteorological station.
*Tromelin Island:* First explored by the French in 1776, the island came under the jurisdiction of Reunion in 1814. At present, it serves as a sea turtle sanctuary and is the site of an important meteorological station.

## Geography

**Location:** southeast and east of Africa, islands in the southern Indian Ocean, some near Madagascar and others about equidistant between Africa, Antarctica, and Australia; note - French Southern and Antarctic Lands include Ile Amsterdam, Ile Saint-Paul, Iles Crozet, Iles Kerguelen, Bassas da India, Europa Island, Glorioso Islands, Juan de Nova Island, and Tromelin Island in the southern Indian Ocean, along with the French-claimed sector of Antarctica, "Adelie Land"; the US does not recognize the French claim to "Adelie Land"
**Geographic coordinates:**
*Ile Amsterdam (Ile Amsterdam et Ile Saint-Paul):* 37 50 S, 77 32 E
*Ile Saint-Paul (Ile Amsterdam et Ile Saint-Paul):* 38 72 S, 77 53 E
*Iles Crozet:* 46 25 S, 51 00 E
*Iles Kerguelen:* 49 15 S, 69 35 E
*Bassas da India (Iles Eparses):* 21 30 S, 39 50 E
*Europa Island (Iles Eparses):* 22 20 S, 40 22 E
*Glorioso Islands (Iles Eparses):* 11 30 S, 47 20 E
*Juan de Nova Island (Iles Eparses):* 17 03 S, 42 45 E
*Tromelin Island (Iles Eparses):* 15 52 S, 54 25 E
**Map references:** Antarctic Region, Africa
**Area:**
*Ile Amsterdam (Ile Amsterdam et Ile Saint-Paul):* total - 55 sq km; land - 55 sq km; water - 0 sq km
*Ile Saint-Paul (Ile Amsterdam et Ile Saint-Paul):* total -7 sq km; land - 7 sq km; water - 0 sq km
*Iles Crozet:* total - 352 sq km; land - 352 sq km; water -0 sq km
*Iles Kerguelen:* total - 7,215 sq km; land - 7,215 sq km; water - 0 sq km
*Bassas da India (Iles Eparses):* total - 80 sq km; land -0.2 sq km; water - 79.8 sq km (lagoon)
*Europa Island (Iles Eparses):* total - 28 sq km; land - 28 sq km; water - 0 sq km
*Glorioso Islands (Iles Eparses):* total - 5 sq km; land - 5 sq km; water - 0 sq km
*Juan de Nova Island (Iles Eparses):* total - 4.4 sq km; land - 4.4 sq km; water - 0 sq km
*Tromelin Island (Iles Eparses):* total - 1 sq km; land - 1 sq km; water - 0 sq km
*note:* excludes "Adelie Land" claim of about 500,000 sq km in Antarctica that is not recognized by the US

# French Southern and Antarctic Lands (continued)

**Juan de Nova Island**

0  1  2 km
0  1  2 mi

*Mozambique Channel*

weather station ■ airstrip

**Europa Island**

*reefs*

weather station ■
airstrip

*reefs*

*Mozambique Channel*

0  1  2 km
0  1  2 mi

**Glorioso Islands**

0  2  4 km
0  2  4 mi

*INDIAN OCEAN*

*Wreck Rock*

*Île du Lys*

weather ■ station

airstrip

*Verte Rocks*

*Île Glorieuse*

*South Rock*

**Tromelin Island**

*reef*

*INDIAN OCEAN*

weather ■ station

airstrip

0  0.2  0.4 km
0  0.2  0.4 mi

40                          60

TANZ.

SEYCHELLES

COMOROS

Glorioso Islands
(Fr. S. and Ant. Lands)

Mayotte
(administered by FRANCE;
claimed by COMOROS)

Tromelin Island
(Fr. S. and Ant. Lands)

MOZ.

Juan de
Nova Island
(Fr. S. and Ant. Lands)

MADAGASCAR

MAURITIUS

*Mozambique Channel*

20

Bassas
da India
(Fr. S. and Ant.
Lands)

Europa
Island
(Fr. S. and Ant.
Lands)

Reunion
(FRANCE)

*Tropic of Capricorn*

INDIAN

OCEAN

Île Amsterdam
(Fr. S. and Ant. Lands)

Île Saint-Paul
(Fr. S. and Ant. Lands)

40

**Îles Crozet**

*INDIAN OCEAN*

*ÎLOTS DES APÔTRES*

*Île aux Cochons*

*Île de la Possession*

*Île de l'Est*

*ÎLES DES PINGOUINS*

Base
Alfred
Faure

0  20  40 km
0  20  40 mi

PRINCE EDWARD
ISLANDS
(SOUTH AFRICA)

ÎLES
CROZET
(Fr. S. and Ant.
Lands)

ÎLES KERGUELEN
(Fr. S. and Ant. Lands)

0        300        600 kilometers
0        300        600 miles

**Îles Amsterdam and Saint-Paul**

Martin-de-Viviès

*Île Amsterdam*

*INDIAN OCEAN*

*Île Saint-Paul*

0  10  20 km
0  10  20 mi

**Îles Kerguelen**

*ÎLES NUAGEUSES*

*ÎLES LEYGUES*

*Île Foch*

*Golfe des Baleiniers*

*Cabotte St. Barbara Croix*

*Île Kerguelen*

Port-aux-
Français

*Île de l'Ouest*

*Mont. Ross* ▲

*Baie d'Audierne*

0  20  40 km
0  20  40 mi

*Map scales vary*

# French Southern and Antarctic Lands (continued)

**Area - comparative:**
*Ile Amsterdam (Ile Amsterdam et Ile Saint-Paul):* less than one-half the size of Washington, DC
*Ile Saint-Paul (Ile Amsterdam et Ile Saint-Paul):* more than 10 times the size of The Mall in Washington, DC
*Iles Crozet:* about twice the size of Washington, DC
*Iles Kerguelen:* slightly larger than Delaware
*Bassas da India (Iles Eparses):* land area about one-third the size of The Mall in Washington, DC
*Europa Island (Iles Eparses):* about one-sixth the size of Washington, DC
*Glorioso Islands (Iles Eparses):* about eight times the size of The Mall in Washington, DC
*Juan de Nova Island (Iles Eparses):* about seven times the size of The Mall in Washington, DC
*Tromelin Island (Iles Eparses):* about 1.7 times the size of The Mall in Washington, DC

**Land boundaries:** 0 km

**Coastline:**
*Ile Amsterdam (Ile Amsterdam et Ile Saint-Paul):* 28 km
*Ile Saint-Paul (Ile Amsterdam et Ile Saint-Paul): Iles Kerguelen:* 2,800 km
*Bassas da India (Iles Eparses):* 35.2 km
*Europa Island (Iles Eparses):* 22.2 km
*Glorioso Islands (Iles Eparses):* 35.2 km
*Juan de Nova Island (Iles Eparses):* 24.1 km
*Tromelin Island (Iles Eparses):* 3.7 km

**Maritime claims:**
*territorial sea:* 12 nm
*exclusive economic zone:* 200 nm from Iles Kerguelen and Iles Eparses (does not include the rest of French Southern and Antarctic Lands); Juan de Nova Island and Tromelin Island claim a continental shelf of 200-m depth or to the depth of exploitation

**Climate:**
*Ile Amsterdam et Ile Saint-Paul:* oceanic with persistent westerly winds and high humidity
*Iles Crozet:* windy, cold, wet, and cloudy
*Iles Kerguelen:* oceanic, cold, overcast, windy
*Iles Eparses:* tropical

**Terrain:**
*Ile Amsterdam (Ile Amsterdam et Ile Saint-Paul):* a volcanic island with steep coastal cliffs; the center floor of the volcano is a large plateau
*Ile Saint-Paul (Ile Amsterdam et Ile Saint-Paul):* triangular in shape, the island is the top of a volcano, rocky with steep cliffs on the eastern side; has active thermal springs
*Iles Crozet:* a large archipelago formed from the Crozet Plateau is divided into two groups of islands
*Iles Kerguelen:* the interior of the large island of Ile Kerguelen is composed of rugged terrain of high mountains, hills, valleys, and plains with a number of peninsulas stretching off its coasts
*Bassas da India (Iles Eparses):* atoll, awash at high tide; shallow (15 m) lagoon
*Europa Island, Glorioso Islands, Juan de Nova Island:* low, flat, and sandy
*Tromelin Island (Iles Eparses):* low, flat, sandy; likely volcanic seamount

**Elevation extremes:**
*lowest point:* Indian Ocean 0 m
*highest point:* Mont de la Dives on Ile Amsterdam (Ile Amsterdam et Ile Saint-Paul) 867 m; unnamed location on Ile Saint-Paul (Ile Amsterdam et Ile Saint-Paul) 272 m; Pic Marion-Dufresne in Iles Crozet 1,090 m; Mont Ross in Iles Kerguelen 1,850 m; unnamed location on Bassas de India (Iles Eparses) 2.4 m; unnamed location on Europa Island (Iles Eparses) 24 m; unnamed location on Glorioso Islands (Iles Eparses) 12 m; unnamed location on Juan de Nova Island (Iles Eparses) 10 m; unnamed location on Tromelin Island (Iles Eparses) 7 m

**Natural resources:** fish, crayfish
*note:* Glorioso Islands and Tromelin Island (Iles Eparses) have guano, phosphates, and coconuts

**Land use:** Ile Amsterdam (Ile Amsterdam et Ile Saint-Paul) - 100% trees, grasses, ferns, and moss; Ile Saint-Paul (Ile Amsterdam et Ile Saint-Paul) - 100% grass, ferns, and moss; Iles Crozet - 100% tossock grass, heath, and fern; Iles Kerguelen - 100% tossock grass and Kerguelen cabbage; Bassas da India (Iles Eparses) - 100% rock, coral reef, and sand; Europa Island (Iles Eparses) - 100% mangrove swamp and dry woodlands; Glorioso Islands (Iles Eparses) - 100% lush vegetation and coconut palms; Juan de Nova Island (Iles Eparses) - 90% forest, 10% other; Tromelin Island (Iles Eparses) - 100% grasses and scattered brush (2005)

**Irrigated land:** 0 sq km

**Natural hazards:** Ile Amsterdam and Ile Saint-Paul are inactive volcanoes; Iles Eparses subject to periodic cyclones; Bassas da India is a maritime hazard since it is under water for a period of three hours prior to and following the high tide and surrounded by reefs

**Environment - current issues:** introduction of foreign species on Iles Crozet has caused severe damage to the original ecosystem; overfishing of Patagonian toothfish around Iles Crozet and Iles Kerguelen

**Geography - note:** islands component is widely scattered across remote locations in the southern Indian Ocean
*Bassas da India (Iles Eparses):* the atoll is a circular reef that sits atop a long-extinct, submerged volcano
*Europa Island and Juan de Nova Island (Iles Eparses):* wildlife sanctuary for seabirds and sea turtles
*Glorioso Island (Iles Eparses):* the islands and rocks are surrounded by an extensive reef system
*Tromelin Island (Iles Eparses):* climatologically important location for forecasting cyclones in the western Indian Ocean; wildlife sanctuary (seabirds, tortoises)

**Population:** no indigenous inhabitants
*Ile Amsterdam (Ile Amsterdam et Ile Saint-Paul):* has no permanent residents but has a meteorological station
*Ile Saint-Paul (Ile Amsterdam et Ile Saint-Paul):* is uninhabited but is frequently visited by fishermen and has a scientific research cabin for short stays
*Iles Crozet:* are uninhabited except for 18 to 30 people staffing the Alfred Faure research station on Ile del la Possession
*Iles Kerguelen:* 50 to 100 scientists are located at the main base at Port-aux-Francais on Ile Kerguelen
*Bassas da India (Iles Eparses):* uninhabitable
*Europa Island, Glorioso Islands, Juan de Nova Island (Iles Eparses):* a small French military garrison and a few meteorologists on each possession; visited by scientists
*Tromelin Island (Iles Eparses):* uninhabited, except for visits by scientists

**Country name:**
*conventional long form:* Territory of the French Southern and Antarctic Lands
*conventional short form:* French Southern and Antarctic Lands
*local long form:* Territoire des Terres Australes et Antarctiques Francaises
*local short form:* Terres Australes et Antarctiques Francaises
*abbreviation:* TAAF

**Dependency status:** overseas territory of France since 1955; administered from Paris by Administrateur Superieur Eric PILLOTON (since 10 April 2007)

**Administrative divisions:** none (overseas territory of France); there are no first-order administrative divisions as defined by the US Government, but there are five administrative districts named Iles Crozet, Iles Eparses, Iles Kerguelen, Ile Saint-Paul et Ile Amsterdam; the fifth district is the "Adelie Land" claim in Antarctica that is not recognized by the US

**Legal system:** the laws of France, where applicable, apply

**Executive branch:**
*chief of state:* President Nicolas SARKOZY (since 16 May 2007), represented by Senior Administrator Rollon MOUCHEL-BLAISOT (16 October 2008)

**International organization participation:** UPU

**Diplomatic representation in the US:** none (overseas territory of France)

**Diplomatic representation from the US:** none (overseas territory of France)

**Flag description:** the flag of France is used

## Economy

**Economy - overview:** Economic activity is limited to servicing meteorological and geophysical research stations, military bases, and French and other fishing fleets. The fish catches landed on Iles Kerguelen by foreign ships are exported to France and Reunion.

## Communications

**Internet country code:** .tf
**Internet hosts:** 38 (2008)
**Communications - note:** one or more meteorological stations on each possession; note - meteorological station on Tromelin Island (Iles Eparses) is important for forecasting cyclones

## Transportation

**Airports:** 4 (note - one each on Europa Island, Glorioso Islands, Juan de Nova Island, and Tromelin Island in the Iles Eparses district) (2006)
**Ports and terminals:** none; offshore anchorage only
**Transportation - note:**
*aids to navigation - lighthouses:* Europa Island 18m; Juan de Nova Island (W side) 37m; Tromelin Island (NW point) 11m (all in the Iles Eparses district)

## Military

**Military - note:** defense is the responsibility of France

## Transnational Issues

**Disputes - international:** French claim to "Adelie Land" in Antarctica is not recognized by the US
*Bassas da India, Europa Island, Glorioso Islands, Juan de Nova Island (Iles Eparses):* claimed by Madagascar
*Tromelin Island (Iles Eparses):* claimed by Mauritius

# Gabon

## Introduction

**Background:** Until recently, only two autocratic presidents had ruled Gabon since its independence from France in 1960. The recent president of Gabon, El Hadj Omar BONGO Ondimba -one of the longest-serving heads of state in the world - had dominated the country's political scene for four decades. President BONGO introduced a nominal multiparty system and a new constitution in the early 1990s. However, allegations of electoral fraud during local elections in 2002-03 and the presidential elections in 2005 exposed the weaknesses of formal political structures in Gabon. President BONGO died in June 2009 and was replaced in accordance with the constitution by Rose Francine ROGOMBE, the president of the Senate. New elections are planned for the summer of 2009. This will be the first Gabonese elections in which BONGO is not participating. Despite political conditions, a small population, abundant natural resources, and considerable foreign support have helped make Gabon one of the more prosperous and stable African countries.

## Geography

**Location:** Western Africa, bordering the Atlantic Ocean at the Equator, between Republic of the Congo and Equatorial Guinea
**Geographic coordinates:** 1 00 S, 11 45 E
**Map references:** Africa
**Area:**
*total:* 267,667 sq km
*land:* 257,667 sq km
*water:* 10,000 sq km
**Area - comparative:** slightly smaller than Colorado
**Land boundaries:**
*total:* 2,551 km
*border countries:* Cameroon 298 km, Republic of the Congo 1,903 km, Equatorial Guinea 350 km
**Coastline:** 885 km

**Maritime claims:**
*territorial sea:* 12 nm
*contiguous zone:* 24 nm
*exclusive economic zone:* 200 nm
**Climate:** tropical; always hot, humid
**Terrain:** narrow coastal plain; hilly interior; savanna in east and south
**Elevation extremes:**
*lowest point:* Atlantic Ocean 0 m
*highest point:* Mont Iboundji 1,575 m
**Natural resources:** petroleum, natural gas, diamond, niobium, manganese, uranium, gold, timber, iron ore, hydropower
**Land use:**
*arable land:* 1.21%
*permanent crops:* 0.64%
*other:* 98.15% (2005)
**Irrigated land:** 70 sq km (2003)
**Total renewable water resources:** 164 cu km (1987)
**Freshwater withdrawal (domestic/industrial/agricultural):**
*total:* 0.12 cu km/yr (50%/8%/42%)
*per capita:* 87 cu m/yr (2000)
**Natural hazards:** NA
**Environment - current issues:** deforestation; poaching
**Environment - international agreements:**
*party to:* Biodiversity, Climate Change, Climate Change-Kyoto Protocol, Desertification, Endangered Species, Hazardous Wastes, Law of the Sea, Marine Dumping, Ozone Layer Protection, Ship Pollution, Tropical Timber 83, Tropical Timber 94, Wetlands, Whaling
*signed, but not ratified:* none of the selected agreements
**Geography - note:** a small population and oil and mineral reserves have helped Gabon become one of Africa's wealthier countries; in general, these circumstances have allowed the country to maintain and conserve its pristine rain forest and rich biodiversity

## People

**Population:** 1,514,993
*note:* estimates for this country explicitly take into account the effects of excess mortality due to AIDS; this can result in lower life expectancy, higher infant mortality, higher death rates, lower population growth rates, and changes in the distribution of population by age and sex than would otherwise be expected (July 2009 est.)
**Age structure:**
*0-14 years:* 42.1% (male 320,414/female 318,027)
*15-64 years:* 53.9% (male 407,461/female 409,633)
*65 years and over:* 3.9% (male 24,799/female 34,659) (2009 est.)
**Median age:**
*total:* 18.6 years
*male:* 18.4 years
*female:* 18.9 years (2009 est.)

**Population growth rate:** 1.934% (2009 est.)
**Birth rate:** 35.57 births/1,000 population (2009 est.)
**Death rate:** 12.59 deaths/1,000 population (2008 est.)
**Net migration rate:** -3.48 migrant(s)/1,000 population (2009 est.)
**Urbanization:**
*urban population:* 85% of total population (2008)
*rate of urbanization:* 2.1% annual rate of change (2005-10 est.)
**Sex ratio:**
*at birth:* 1.03 male(s)/female
*under 15 years:* 1.01 male(s)/female
*15-64 years:* 1 male(s)/female
*65 years and over:* 0.72 male(s)/female
*total population:* 0.99 male(s)/female (2009 est.)
**Infant mortality rate:**
*total:* 51.78 deaths/1,000 live births
*male:* 60.17 deaths/1,000 live births
*female:* 43.15 deaths/1,000 live births (2009 est.)
**Life expectancy at birth:**
*total population:* 53.11 years
*male:* 52.19 years
*female:* 54.05 years (2009 est.)
**Total fertility rate:** 4.65 children born/woman (2009 est.)
**HIV/AIDS - adult prevalence rate:** 5.9% (2007 est.)
**HIV/AIDS - people living with HIV/AIDS:** 49,000 (2007 est.)
**HIV/AIDS - deaths:** 2,300 (2007 est.)
**Major infectious diseases:**
*degree of risk:* very high
*food or waterborne diseases:* bacterial diarrhea, hepatitis A, and typhoid fever
*vectorborne disease:* malaria and chikungunya
*water contact disease:* schistosomiasis
*animal contact disease:* rabies (2009)
**Nationality:**
*noun:* Gabonese (singular and plural)
*adjective:* Gabonese
**Ethnic groups:** Bantu tribes, including four major tribal groupings (Fang, Bapounou, Nzebi, Obamba); other Africans and Europeans, 154,000, including 10,700 French and 11,000 persons of dual nationality
**Religions:** Christian 55%-75%, animist, Muslim less than 1%
**Languages:** French (official), Fang, Myene, Nzebi, Bapounou/Eschira, Bandjabi
**Literacy:**
*definition:* age 15 and over can read and write
*total population:* 63.2%
*male:* 73.7%
*female:* 53.3% (1995 est.)
**Education expenditures:** 3.8% of GDP (2000)

## Government

**Country name:**
*conventional long form:* Gabonese Republic
*conventional short form:* Gabon
*local long form:* Republique Gabonaise
*local short form:* Gabon
**Government type:** republic; multiparty presidential regime
**Capital:**
*name:* Libreville
*geographic coordinates:* 0 23 N, 9 27 E
*time difference:* UTC+1 (6 hours ahead of Washington, DC during Standard Time)
**Administrative divisions:** 9 provinces; Estuaire, Haut-Ogooue, Moyen-Ogooue, Ngounie, Nyanga, Ogooue-Ivindo, Ogooue-Lolo, Ogooue-Maritime, Woleu-Ntem
**Independence:** 17 August 1960 (from France)
**National holiday:** Independence Day, 17 August (1960)
**Constitution:** adopted 14 March 1991
**Legal system:** based on French civil law system and customary law; judicial review of legislative acts in Constitutional Chamber of the Supreme Court; has not accepted compulsory ICJ jurisdiction
**Suffrage:** 21 years of age; universal
**Executive branch:**
*chief of state:* President (interim) Rose Francine ROGOMBE (since 10 June 2009)
*head of government:* Prime Minister Jean Eyeghe NDONG (since 20 January 2006)
*cabinet:* Council of Ministers appointed by the prime minister in consultation with the president
*elections:* president elected by popular vote for a seven-year term (no term limits); election last held 27 November 2005 (next to be held in summer 2012); prime minister appointed by the president
*election results:* President El Hadj Omar BONGO OndimbaPresident El Hadj Omar BONGO Ondimba reelected; percent of vote - El Hadj Omar BONGO Ondimba 79.2%, Pierre MAMBOUNDOU 13.6%, Zacharie MYBOTO 6.6%
*note:* President BONGO died on 8 June 2009 after serving as president for 32 years, in accordance with the constitution he was replaced on an interim basis by the president of the Senate, Rose Francine ROGOMBE on 10 June 2009, new elections should be held within 45 days
**Legislative branch:** bicameral legislature consists of the Senate (91 seats; members elected by members of municipal councils and departmental assemblies to serve six-year terms) and the National Assembly or Assemblee Nationale (120 seats; members are elected by direct, popular vote to serve five-year terms)
*elections:* Senate - last held 26 January and 9 February 2003 (next to be held by January 2009); National Assembly - last held 17 and 24 December 2006 (next to be held in December 2011)

*election results:* Senate - percent of vote by party - NA; seats by party - PDG 53, RNB 20, PGP 4, ADERE 3, RDP 1, CLR 1, independents 9; National Assembly -percent of vote by party - NA; seats by party - PDG 82, RPG 8, UPG 8, UGDD 4, ADERE 3, CLR 2, PGP-Ndaot 2, PSD 2, independents 4, others 5
**Judicial branch:** Supreme Court or Cour Supreme consisting of three chambers - Judicial, Administrative, and Accounts; Constitutional Court; Courts of Appeal; Court of State Security; County Courts
**Political parties and leaders:** Circle of Liberal Reformers or CLR [General Jean Boniface ASSELE]; Congress for Democracy and Justice or CDJ [Jules Aristide Bourdes OGOULIGUENDE]; Democratic and Republican Alliance or ADERE [Divungui-di-Ndinge DIDJOB]; Gabonese Democratic Party or PDG (former sole party) [Simplice Nguedet MANZELA]; Gabonese Party for Progress or PGP [Benoit Mouity NZAMBA]; Gabonese Union for Democracy and Development or UGDD [Zacherie MYBOTO]; National Rally of Woodcutters or RNB; National Rally of Woodcutters-Rally for Gabon or RNB-RPG (Bucherons) [Fr. Paul M'BA-ABESSOLE]; Party of Development and Social Solidarity or PDS [Seraphin Ndoat REMBOGO]; People's Unity Party or PUP [Louis Gaston MAYILA]; Social Democratic Party or PSD [Pierre Claver MAGANGA-MOUSSAVOU]; Union for Democracy and Social Integration or UDIS; Union of Gabonese Patriots or UPG [Pierre MAMBOUNDOU]
**Political pressure groups and leaders:** NA
**International organization participation:** ACCT, ACP, AfDB, AU, BDEAC, CEMAC, FAO, FZ, G-24, G-77, IAEA, IBRD, ICAO, ICCt, ICRM, IDA, IDB, IFAD, IFC, IFRCS, ILO, IMF, IMO, IMSO, Interpol, IOC, IOM, IPU, ISO (correspondent), ITSO, ITU, ITUC, MIGA, MINURCAT, NAM, OIC, OIF, OPCW, UN, UNAMID, UNCTAD, UNESCO, UNIDO, UNMIS, UNWTO, UPU, WCL, WCO, WFTU, WHO, WIPO, WMO, WTO
**Diplomatic representation in the US:**
*chief of mission:* Ambassador Carlos BOUNGOU
*chancery:* Suite 200, 2034 20th Street NW, Washington, DC 20009
*telephone:* [1] (202) 797-1000
*FAX:* [1] (202) 332-0668
*consulate(s):* New York
**Diplomatic representation from the US:**
*chief of mission:* Ambassador Eunice S. REDDICK
*embassy:* Boulevard du Bord de Mer, Libreville
*mailing address:* Centre Ville, B. P. 4000, Libreville; pouch:2270 Libreville Place, Washington, DC 20521-2270
*telephone:* [241] 76 20 03 through 76 20 04, after hours - 07380171
*FAX:* [241] 74 55 07
**Flag description:** three equal horizontal bands of green (top), yellow, and blue

# Gabon *(continued)*

## Economy

**Economy - overview:** Gabon enjoys a per capita income four times that of most sub-Saharan African nations, but because of high income inequality, a large proportion of the population remains poor. Gabon depended on timber and manganese until oil was discovered offshore in the early 1970s. The oil sector now accounts for more than 50% of GDP. Gabon continues to face fluctuating prices for its oil, timber, and manganese exports. Despite the abundance of natural wealth, poor fiscal management hobbles the economy. In 1997, an IMF mission to Gabon criticized the government for overspending on off-budget items, overborrowing from the central bank, and slipping on its schedule for privatization and administrative reform. The rebound of oil prices since 1999 have helped growth, but drops in production have hampered Gabon from fully realizing potential gains, and will continue to temper the gains for most of this decade. In December 2000, Gabon signed a new agreement with the Paris Club to reschedule its official debt. A follow-up bilateral repayment agreement with the US was signed in December 2001. Gabon signed a 14-month Stand-By Arrangement with the IMF in May 2007, and received Paris Club debt rescheduling later that year.

**GDP (purchasing power parity):**
$21.44 billion (2008 est.)
$20.7 billion (2007)
$19.6 billion (2006)
*note:* data are in 2008 US dollars

**GDP (official exchange rate):** $15.91 billion (2008 est.)

**GDP - real growth rate:**
3.6% (2008 est.)
5.6% (2007 est.)
1.2% (2006 est.)

**GDP - per capita (PPP):**
$14,400 (2008 est.)
$14,200 (2007 est.)
$13,700 (2006 est.)
*note:* data are in 2008 US dollars

**GDP - composition by sector:**
*agriculture:* 5.7%
*industry:* 57.2%
*services:* 37% (2008 est.)

**Labor force:** 592,000 (2008 est.)

**Labor force - by occupation:**
*agriculture:* 60%
*industry:* 15%
*services:* 25% (2000 est.)

**Unemployment rate:**
21% (2006 est.)

**Population below poverty line:** NA%

**Household income or consumption by percentage share:**
*lowest 10%:* NA%
*highest 10%:* NA%

**Investment (gross fixed):** 32% of GDP (2008 est.)

**Budget:**
*revenues:* $4.463 billion
*expenditures:* $2.746 billion (2008 est.)

**Public debt:** 26.3% of GDP (2008 est.)

**Inflation rate (consumer prices):**
5% (2008 est.)
5% (2007 est.)

**Central bank discount rate:** 5.25% (31 December 2007)

**Commercial bank prime lending rate:** 15% (31 December 2007)

**Stock of money:** $1.547 billion (31 December 2007)

**Stock of quasi money:** $799.3 million (31 December 2007)

**Stock of domestic credit:** $359.8 million (31 December 2007)

**Market value of publicly traded shares:** $NA

**Agriculture - products:** cocoa, coffee, sugar, palm oil, rubber; cattle; okoume (a tropical softwood); fish

**Industries:** petroleum extraction and refining; manganese, gold; chemicals, ship repair, food and beverages, textiles, lumbering and plywood, cement

**Industrial production growth rate:** 1.5% (2008 est.)

**Electricity - production:** 1.671 billion kWh (2006 est.)

**Electricity - consumption:** 1.365 billion kWh (2006 est.)

**Electricity - exports:** 0 kWh (2007 est.)

**Electricity - imports:** 0 kWh (2007 est.)

**Oil - production:** 243,900 bbl/day (2007 est.)

**Oil - consumption:** 13,170 bbl/day (2006 est.)

**Oil - exports:** 255,500 bbl/day (2005)

**Oil - imports:** 2,485 bbl/day (2005)

**Oil - proved reserves:** 2 billion bbl (1 January 2008 est.)

**Natural gas - production:** 100 million cu m (2006 est.)

**Natural gas - consumption:** 100 million cu m (2006 est.)

**Natural gas - exports:** 0 cu m (2007 est.)

**Natural gas - imports:** 0 cu m (2007 est.)

**Natural gas - proved reserves:** 28.32 billion cu m (1 January 2008 est.)

**Current account balance:** $2.026 billion (2008 est.)

**Exports:** $9.743 billion f.o.b. (2008 est.)

**Exports - commodities:** crude oil 70%, timber, manganese, uranium (2001)

**Exports - partners:** US 32.5%, China 15.8%, France 9.4%, Malaysia 6%, Trinidad and Tobago 5% (2007)

**Imports:** $2.83 billion f.o.b. (2008 est.)

**Imports - commodities:** machinery and equipment, foodstuffs, chemicals, construction materials

**Imports - partners:** France 27.7%, US 19.1%, Belgium 5.4%, Netherlands 4.7%, China 4.1% (2007)

**Reserves of foreign exchange and gold:** $1.859 billion (31 December 2008 est.)

**Debt - external:** $3.173 billion (31 December 2008 est.)

**Exchange rates:** Cooperation Financiere en Afrique Centrale francs (XAF) per US dollar - 447.81 (2008 est.), 481.83 (2007), 522.89 (2006), 527.47 (2005), 528.29 (2004)
*note:* since 1 January 1999, the Central African CFA franc (XAF) has been pegged to the euro at a rate of 655.957 CFA francs per euro; Central African CFA franc (XAF) coins and banknotes are not accepted in countries using West African CFA francs (XOF), and vice versa, even though the two currencies trade at par

## Communications

**Telephones - main lines in use:** 26,500 (2007)
**Telephones - mobile cellular:** 1.169 million (2007)
**Telephone system:**
*general assessment:* adequate service by African standards and improving with the help of a growing mobile cell network system with multiple providers; mobile-cellular subscribership reached 80 per 100 persons in 2007
*domestic:* adequate system of cable, microwave radio relay, tropospheric scatter, radiotelephone communication stations, and a domestic satellite system with 12 earth stations
*international:* country code - 241; landing point for the SAT-3/WASC fiber-optic submarine cable that provides connectivity to Europe and Asia; satellite earth stations - 3 Intelsat (Atlantic Ocean) (2007)

**Radio broadcast stations:** AM 6, FM 7 (plus 11 repeaters), shortwave 4 (2001)

**Television broadcast stations:** 4 (plus 4 repeaters) (2001)

**Internet country code:** .ga

**Internet hosts:** 88 (2008)

**Internet users:** 145,000 (2007)

## Transportation

**Airports:** 39 (2008)
**Airports - with paved runways:**
*total:* 12
*over 3,047 m:* 1
*2,438 to 3,047 m:* 1
*1,524 to 2,437 m:* 9
*914 to 1,523 m:* 1 (2008)

**Airports - with unpaved runways:**
*total:* 27
*1,524 to 2,437 m:* 5
*914 to 1,523 m:* 10
*under 914 m:* 12 (2008)

**Pipelines:** gas 240 km; oil 723 km (2008)

**Railways:**
*total:* 814 km
*standard gauge:* 814 km 1.435-m gauge (2006)

**Roadways:**
*total:* 9,170 km
*paved:* 937 km
*unpaved:* 8,233 km (2004)

**Waterways:** 1,600 km (310 km on Ogooue River) (2008)

**Merchant marine:**
*registered in other countries:* 2 (Cambodia 1, Panama 1) (2008)
**Ports and terminals:** Gamba, Libreville, Lucinda, Port-Gentil

## Military

**Military branches:** Army, Navy, Air Force, National Gendarmerie, National Police
**Military service age and obligation:** 20 years of age for compulsory and voluntary military service (2007)
**Manpower available for military service:**
*males age 16-49:* 331,181
*females age 16-49:* 332,498 (2008 est.)
**Manpower fit for military service:**
*males age 16-49:* 195,519
*females age 16-49:* 190,519 (2009 est.)
**Manpower reaching militarily significant age annually:**
*male:* 16,933
*female:* 16,942 (2009 est.)
**Military expenditures:** 3.4% of GDP (2005 est.)

## Transnational Issues

**Disputes - international:** UN urges Equatorial Guinea and Gabon to resolve the sovereignty dispute over Gabon-occupied Mbane Island and lesser islands and to establish a maritime boundary in hydrocarbon-rich Corisco Bay
**Refugees and internally displaced persons:**
*refugees (country of origin):* 7,178 (Republic of Congo) (2007)
**Trafficking in persons:**
*current situation:* Gabon is predominantly a destination country for children trafficked from other African countries for the purpose of forced labor; girls are primarily trafficked for domestic servitude, forced market vending, forced restaurant labor, and sexual exploitation, while boys are trafficked for forced street hawking and forced labor in small workshops
*tier rating:* Tier 2 Watch List - Gabon is on the Tier 2 Watch List for its failure to provide evidence of increasing efforts to combat human trafficking in 2007, particularly in terms of efforts to convict and punish trafficking offenders; the government has not reported the convictions or sentences of any trafficking offenders; the government did not take steps to reduce demand for commercial sex acts (2008)

# Gambia, The

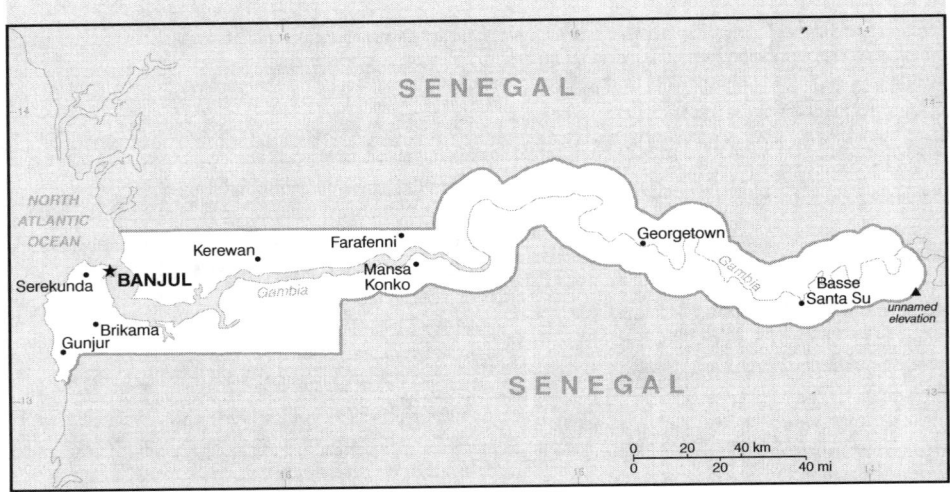

## Introduction

**Background:** The Gambia gained its independence from the UK in 1965. Geographically surrounded by Senegal, it formed a short-lived federation of Senegambia between 1982 and 1989. In 1991 the two nations signed a friendship and cooperation treaty, but tensions have flared up intermittently since then. Yahya A. J. J. JAMMEH led a military coup in 1994 that overthrew the president and banned political activity. A new constitution and presidential elections in 1996, followed by parliamentary balloting in 1997, completed a nominal return to civilian rule. JAMMEH has been elected president in all subsequent elections, including most recently in late 2006.

## Geography

**Location:** Western Africa, bordering the North Atlantic Ocean and Senegal
**Geographic coordinates:** 13 28 N, 16 34 W
**Map references:** Africa
**Area:**
*total:* 11,300 sq km
*land:* 10,000 sq km
*water:* 1,300 sq km
**Area - comparative:** slightly less than twice the size of Delaware
**Land boundaries:**
*total:* 740 km
*border countries:* Senegal 740 km
**Coastline:** 80 km
**Maritime claims:**
*territorial sea:* 12 nm
*contiguous zone:* 18 nm
*exclusive fishing zone:* 200 nm
*continental shelf:* extent not specified
**Climate:** tropical; hot, rainy season (June to November); cooler, dry season (November to May)

**Terrain:** flood plain of the Gambia River flanked by some low hills
**Elevation extremes:**
*lowest point:* Atlantic Ocean 0 m
*highest point:* unnamed location 53 m
**Natural resources:** fish, titanium (rutile and ilmenite), tin, zircon, silica sand, clay, petroleum
**Land use:**
*arable land:* 27.88%
*permanent crops:* 0.44%
*other:* 71.68% (2005)
**Irrigated land:** 20 sq km (2003)
**Total renewable water resources:** 8 cu km (1982)
**Freshwater withdrawal (domestic/industrial/agricultural):**
*total:* 0.03 cu km/yr (23%/12%/65%)
*per capita:* 20 cu m/yr (2000)
**Natural hazards:** drought (rainfall has dropped by 30% in the last 30 years)
**Environment - current issues:** deforestation; desertification; water-borne diseases prevalent
**Environment - international agreements:**
*party to:* Biodiversity, Climate Change, Climate Change-Kyoto Protocol, Desertification, Endangered Species, Hazardous Wastes, Law of the Sea, Ozone Layer Protection, Ship Pollution, Wetlands, Whaling
*signed, but not ratified:* none of the selected agreements
**Geography - note:** almost an enclave of Senegal; smallest country on the continent of Africa

## People

**Population:** 1,782,893 (July 2009 est.)
**Age structure:**
*0-14 years:* 43.6% (male 390,806/female 387,172)
*15-64 years:* 53.6% (male 473,478/female 481,315)
*65 years and over:* 2.8% (male 25,071/female 25,051) (2009 est.)

**Median age:**
*total:* 17.9 years
*male:* 17.8 years
*female:* 18.1 years (2009 est.)
**Population growth rate:** 2.668% (2009 est.)
**Birth rate:** 37.87 births/1,000 population (2009 est.)
**Death rate:** 11.74 deaths/1,000 population (2008 est.)
**Net migration rate:** 0.3 migrant(s)/1,000 population (2009 est.)
**Urbanization:**
*urban population:* 57% of total population (2008)
*rate of urbanization:* 4.2% annual rate of change (2005-10 est.)
**Sex ratio:**
*at birth:* 1.03 male(s)/female
*under 15 years:* 1.01 male(s)/female
*15-64 years:* 0.98 male(s)/female
*65 years and over:* 1 male(s)/female
*total population:* 1 male(s)/female (2009 est.)
**Infant mortality rate:**
*total:* 67.33 deaths/1,000 live births
*male:* 73.56 deaths/1,000 live births
*female:* 60.91 deaths/1,000 live births (2009 est.)
**Life expectancy at birth:**
*total population:* 55.35 years
*male:* 53.43 years
*female:* 57.34 years (2009 est.)
**Total fertility rate:** 5.04 children born/woman (2009 est.)
**HIV/AIDS - adult prevalence rate:** 0.9% (2007 est.)
**HIV/AIDS - people living with HIV/AIDS:** 8,200 (2007 est.)
**HIV/AIDS - deaths:** 600 (2003 est.)
**Major infectious diseases:**
*degree of risk:* very high
*food or waterborne diseases:* bacterial and protozoal diarrhea, hepatitis A, and typhoid fever
*vectorborne diseases:* malaria
*water contact disease:* schistosomiasis
*respiratory disease:* meningococcal meningitis
*animal contact disease:* rabies (2009)
**Nationality:**
*noun:* Gambian(s)
*adjective:* Gambian
**Ethnic groups:** African 99% (Mandinka 42%, Fula 18%, Wolof 16%, Jola 10%, Serahuli 9%, other 4%), non-African 1% (2003 census)
**Religions:** Muslim 90%, Christian 8%, indigenous beliefs 2%
**Languages:** English (official), Mandinka, Wolof, Fula, other indigenous vernaculars
**Literacy:**
*definition:* age 15 and over can read and write
*total population:* 40.1%
*male:* 47.8%
*female:* 32.8% (2003 est.)
**School life expectancy (primary to tertiary education):**
*total:* 7 years
*male:* 7 years
*female:* 7 years (2004)
**Education expenditures:** 2% of GDP (2004)

## Government

**Country name:**
*conventional long form:* Republic of The Gambia
*conventional short form:* The Gambia
**Government type:** republic
**Capital:**
*name:* Banjul
*geographic coordinates:* 13 27 N, 16 34 W
*time difference:* UTC 0 (5 hours ahead of Washington, DC during Standard Time)
**Administrative divisions:** 5 divisions and 1 city*; Banjul*, Central River, Lower River, North Bank, Upper River, Western
**Independence:** 18 February 1965 (from the UK)
**National holiday:** Independence Day, 18 February (1965)
**Constitution:** approved by national referendum 8 August 1996; effective 16 January 1997
**Legal system:** based on a composite of English common law, Islamic law, and customary law; accepts compulsory ICJ jurisdiction with reservations
**Suffrage:** 18 years of age; universal
**Executive branch:**
*chief of state:* President Yahya A. J. J. JAMMEH (since 18 October 1996); note - from 1994 to 1996 he was chairman of the Junta; Vice President Isatou NJIE-SAIDY (since 20 March 1997); note - the president is both the chief of state and head of government
*head of government:* President Yahya A. J. J. JAMMEH (since 18 October 1996); Vice President Isatou NJIE-SAIDY (since 20 March 1997)
*cabinet:* Cabinet appointed by the president
*elections:* president elected by popular vote for a five-year term (no term limits); election last held 22 September 2006 (next to be held in 2011)
*election results:* Yahya A. J. J. JAMMEH reelected president; percent of vote - Yahya A. J. J. JAMMEH 67.3%, Ousainou DARBOE 26.6%, Halifa SALLAH 6.0%
**Legislative branch:** unicameral National Assembly (53 seats; 48 members elected by popular vote, 5 appointed by the president; to serve five-year terms)
*elections:* last held 25 January 2007 (next to be held in 2012)
*election results:* percent of vote by party - NA; seats by party - APRC 47, UDP 4, NADD 1, independent 1
**Judicial branch:** Supreme Court
**Political parties and leaders:** Alliance for Patriotic Reorientation and Construction or APRC (the ruling party) [Yahya A. J. J. JAMMEH]; Gambia People's Democratic Party or GPDP [Henry GOMEZ]; National Alliance for Democracy and Development or NADD [Halifa SALLAH]; National Convention Party or NCP [Sheriff DIBBA]; National Reconciliation Party or NRP [Hamat N. K. BAH]; People's Democratic Organization for Independence and Socialism or PDOIS [Halifa SALLAH]; United Democratic Party or UDP [Ousainou DARBOE]

**Political pressure groups and leaders:** National Environment Agency or NEA; West African Peace Building Network-Gambian Chapter or WANEB-GAMBIA; Youth Employment Network Gambia or YENGambia
*other:* special needs group advocates; teachers and principals
**International organization participation:** ABEDA, ACP, AfDB, AU, C, ECOWAS, FAO, G-77, IBRD, ICAO, ICCt, ICRM, IDA, IDB, IFAD, IFC, IFRCS, ILO, IMF, IMO, Interpol, IOC, IOM, IPU, ITSO, ITU, ITUC, MIGA, MINURCAT, NAM, OIC, OPCW, UN, UNAMID, UNCTAD, UNESCO, UNIDO, UNMIL, UNOCI, UNWTO, UPU, WCL, WCO, WFTU, WHO, WIPO, WMO, WTO
**Diplomatic representation in the US:**
*chief of mission:* Ambassador (vacant); Charge d'Affaires Abdul Rahman COLE
*chancery:* Suite 600, 1424 K Street NW, Washington, DC 20005
*telephone:* [1] (202) 785-1379, 1399, 1425
*FAX:* [1] (202) 785-1430
**Diplomatic representation from the US:**
*chief of mission:* Ambassador Barry L. WELLS
*embassy:* Kairaba Avenue, Fajara, Banjul
*mailing address:* P. M. B. No. 19, Banjul
*telephone:* [220] 439-2856, 437-6169, 437-6170
*FAX:* [220] 439-2475
**Flag description:** three equal horizontal bands of red (top), blue with white edges, and green

## Economy

**Economy - overview:** The Gambia has no confirmed mineral or natural resource deposits and has a limited agricultural base. About 75% of the population depends on crops and livestock for its livelihood. Small-scale manufacturing activity features the processing of peanuts, fish, and hides. Reexport trade normally constitutes a major segment of economic activity, but a 1999 government-imposed preshipment inspection plan, and instability of the Gambian dalasi (currency) have drawn some of the reexport trade away from The Gambia. The Gambia's natural beauty and proximity to Europe has made it one of the larger markets for tourism in West Africa. The government's 1998 seizure of the private peanut firm Alimenta eliminated the largest purchaser of Gambian groundnuts. Despite an announced program to begin privatizing key parastatals, no plans have been made public that would indicate that the government intends to follow through on its promises. Unemployment and underemployment rates remain extremely high; short-run economic progress depends on sustained bilateral and multilateral aid, on responsible government economic management, on continued technical assistance from the IMF and bilateral donors, and on expected growth in the construction sector.
**GDP (purchasing power parity):**
$2.264 billion (2008 est.)
$2.146 billion (2007)
$2.019 billion (2006)
*note:* data are in 2008 US dollars

**GDP (official exchange rate):** $779 million (2008 est.)

**GDP - real growth rate:**
5.5% (2008 est.)
6.3% (2007 est.)
6.5% (2006 est.)

**GDP - per capita (PPP):**
$1,300 (2008 est.)
$1,300 (2007 est.)
$1,200 (2006 est.)
*note:* data are in 2008 US dollars

**GDP - composition by sector:**
*agriculture:* 33%
*industry:* 8.7%
*services:* 58.3% (2008 est.)

**Labor force:** 400,000 (1996)

**Labor force - by occupation:**
*agriculture:* 75%
*industry:* 19%
*services:* 6% (1996)

**Unemployment rate:**
NA%

**Population below poverty line:** NA%

**Household income or consumption by percentage share:**
*lowest 10%:* 1.8%
*highest 10%:* 37% (1998)

**Distribution of family income - Gini index:** 50.2 (1998)

**Investment (gross fixed):** 24.7% of GDP (2008 est.)

**Budget:**
*revenues:* $194.3 million
*expenditures:* $228.8 million (2008 est.)

**Inflation rate (consumer prices):**
6% (2008 est.)
5.1% (2007 est.)

**Central bank discount rate:** 10% (31 December 2007)

**Commercial bank prime lending rate:** 27.92% (31 December 2007)

**Stock of money:** $186.7 million (31 December 2007)

**Stock of quasi money:** $180.4 million (31 December 2007)

**Stock of domestic credit:** $169.9 million (31 December 2007)

**Market value of publicly traded shares:** $NA

**Agriculture - products:** rice, millet, sorghum, peanuts, corn, sesame, cassava (tapioca), palm kernels; cattle, sheep, goats

**Industries:** processing peanuts, fish, and hides; tourism, beverages, agricultural machinery assembly, woodworking, metalworking, clothing

**Industrial production growth rate:** 5.9% (2008 est.)

**Electricity - production:** 200.2 million kWh (2007 est.)

**Electricity - consumption:** 143.6 million kWh (2006 est.)

**Electricity - exports:** 0 kWh (2007 est.)

**Electricity - imports:** 0 kWh (2007 est.)

**Oil - production:** 0 bbl/day (2007 est.)
**Oil - consumption:** 2,082 bbl/day (2006 est.)
**Oil - exports:** 41.62 bbl/day (2005)
**Oil - imports:** 2,123 bbl/day (2005)
**Oil - proved reserves:** 0 bbl (1 January 2006 est.)

**Natural gas - production:** 0 cu m (2007 est.)
**Natural gas - consumption:** 0 cu m (2007 est.)
**Natural gas - exports:** 0 cu m (2007 est.)
**Natural gas - imports:** 0 cu m (2007 est.)
**Natural gas - proved reserves:** 0 cu m (1 January 2006 est.)

**Current account balance:** -$116 million (2008 est.)

**Exports:** $111 million f.o.b. (2008 est.)

**Exports - commodities:** peanut products, fish, cotton lint, palm kernels, re-exports

**Exports - partners:** India 37.7%, China 17.5%, UK 8.7%, France 5.1%, Belgium 4.2% (2007)

**Imports:** $301 million f.o.b. (2008 est.)

**Imports - commodities:** foodstuffs, manufactures, fuel, machinery and transport equipment

**Imports - partners:** China 23.7%, Senegal 11.5%, Cote d'Ivoire 8.3%, Brazil 8%, Netherlands 5.2% (2007)

**Reserves of foreign exchange and gold:** $144 million (31 December 2008 est.)

**Debt - external:** $628.8 million (2003 est.)

**Exchange rates:** dalasis (GMD) per US dollar - 22.75 (2008 est.), 27.79 (2007), 28.066 (2006), 28.575 (2005), 30.03 (2004)

## Communications

**Telephones - main lines in use:** 76,400 (2007)

**Telephones - mobile cellular:** 795,900 (2007)

**Telephone system:**
*general assessment:* adequate; a packet switched data network is available; two mobile-cellular service providers
*domestic:* adequate network of microwave radio relay and open-wire; combined fixed-line and mobile-cellular teledensity reached 50 telephones per 100 persons in 2007
*international:* country code - 220; microwave radio relay links to Senegal and Guinea-Bissau; satellite earth station - 1 Intelsat (Atlantic Ocean) (2007)

**Radio broadcast stations:** AM 3, FM 2, shortwave 0 (2001)

**Television broadcast stations:** 1 (government-owned) (1997)

**Internet country code:** .gm

**Internet hosts:** 320 (2008)

**Internet users:** 100,200 (2007)

## Transportation

**Airports:** 1 (2008)

**Airports - with paved runways:**
*total:* 1
*over 3,047 m:* 1 (2008)

**Roadways:**
*total:* 3,742 km
*paved:* 723 km
*unpaved:* 3,019 km (2004)

**Waterways:** 390 km (on River Gambia; small ocean-going vessels can reach 190 km) (2008)

**Merchant marine:**
*total:* 5
*by type:* passenger/cargo 4, petroleum tanker 1 (2008)

**Ports and terminals:** Banjul

## Military

**Military branches:** Office of the Chief of Defense: Gambian National Army (National Guard, GNA), Gambian Navy (GN) (2009)

**Military service age and obligation:** 18 years of age for voluntary military service; no conscription (2008)

**Manpower available for military service:**
*males age 16-49:* 379,668
*females age 16-49:* 384,438 (2008 est.)

**Manpower fit for military service:**
*males age 16-49:* 238,454
*females age 16-49:* 253,680 (2009 est.)

**Manpower reaching militarily significant age annually:**
*male:* 20,238
*female:* 20,167 (2009 est.)

**Military expenditures:** 0.5% of GDP (2006)

## Transnational Issues

**Disputes - international:** attempts to stem refugees, cross-border raids, arms smuggling, and other illegal activities by separatists from southern Senegal's Casamance region, as well as from conflicts in other west African states

**Refugees and internally displaced persons:**
*refugees (country of origin):* 5,955 (Sierra Leone) (2007)

**Trafficking in persons:**
*current situation:* The Gambia is a source, transit, and destination country for children and women trafficked for the purposes of forced labor and commercial sexual exploitation; women and girls, and to a lesser extent boys, are trafficked for sexual exploitation - in particular to meet the demand for European sex tourism - and for domestic servitude; boys are trafficked within the country for forced begging and street vending; Gambian women and children may be trafficked to Europe through trafficking schemes disguised as migrant smuggling
*tier rating:* Tier 2 Watch List - for a second consecutive year, The Gambia is on the Tier 2 Watch List for its failure to provide evidence of increasing efforts to eliminate trafficking; The Gambia failed to report any trafficking arrests, prosecutions, or convictions in 2007, and the government demonstrated weak victim protection efforts during the reporting period (2008)

# Gaza Strip

## Introduction

**Background:** The September 1993 Israel-PLO Declaration of Principles on Interim Self-Government Arrangements provided for a transitional period of Palestinian self-rule in the West Bank and Gaza Strip. Under a series of agreements signed between May 1994 and September 1999, Israel transferred to the Palestinian Authority (PA) security and civilian responsibility for Palestinian-populated areas of the West Bank and Gaza. Negotiations to determine the permanent status of the West Bank and Gaza stalled following the outbreak of an intifada in September 2000, as Israeli forces reoccupied most Palestinian-controlled areas. In April 2003, the Quartet (US, EU, UN, and Russia) presented a roadmap to a final settlement of the conflict by 2005 based on reciprocal steps by the two parties leading to two states, Israel and a democratic Palestine. The proposed date for a permanent status agreement was postponed indefinitely due to violence and accusations that both sides had not followed through on their commitments. Following Palestinian leader Yasir ARAFAT's death in late 2004, Mahmud ABBAS was elected PA president in January 2005. A month later, Israel and the PA agreed to the Sharm el-Sheikh Commitments in an effort to move the peace process forward. In September 2005, Israel unilaterally withdrew all its settlers and soldiers and dismantled its military facilities in the Gaza Strip and withdrew settlers and redeployed soldiers from four small northern West Bank settlements. Nonetheless, Israel controls maritime, airspace, and most access to the Gaza Strip. A November 2005 PA-Israeli agreement authorized the reopening of the Rafah border crossing between the Gaza Strip and Egypt under joint PA and Egyptian control. In January 2006, the Islamic Resistance Movement, HAMAS, won control of the Palestinian Legislative Council (PLC). The international community refused to accept the HAMAS-led government because it did not recognize Israel, would not renounce violence, and refused to honor previous peace agreements

between Israel and the PA. HAMAS took control of the PA government in March 2006, but President ABBAS had little success negotiating with HAMAS to present a political platform acceptable to the international community so as to lift economic sanctions on Palestinians. The PLC was unable to convene throughout most of 2006 as a result of Israel's detention of many HAMAS PLC members and Israeli-imposed travel restrictions on other PLC members. Violent clashes took place between Fatah and HAMAS supporters in the Gaza Strip in 2006 and early 2007, resulting in numerous Palestinian deaths and injuries. ABBAS and HAMAS Political Bureau Chief MISHAL in February 2007 signed the Mecca Agreement in Saudi Arabia that resulted in the formation of a Palestinian National Unity Government (NUG) headed by HAMAS member Ismail HANIYA. However, fighting continued in the Gaza Strip, and in June, HAMAS militants succeeded in a violent takeover of all military and governmental institutions in the Gaza Strip. ABBAS dismissed the NUG and through a series of Presidential decrees formed a PA government in the West Bank led by independent Salam FAYYAD. HAMAS rejected the NUG's dismissal and has called for resuming talks with Fatah, but ABBAS has ruled out negotiations until HAMAS agrees to a return of PA control over the Gaza Strip and recognizes the FAYYAD-led government. FAYYAD and his PA government initiated a series of security and economic reforms to improve conditions in the West Bank. ABBAS participated in talks with Israel's Prime Minister OLMERT and secured the release of some Palestinian prisoners and previously withheld customs revenue. During a November 2007 international meeting in Annapolis Maryland, ABBAS and OLMERT agreed to resume peace negotiations with the goal of reaching a final peace settlement. Late November 2007 through June 2008 witnessed a substantial increase in Israeli-Palestinian violence. An Egyptian-brokered truce in June 2008 between Israel and HAMAS brought about a five-month pause in hostilities, but spiraling end-of-year violence culminated with massive Israeli air assaults on HAMAS installations in late December followed by Israeli ground attacks in early January 2009. Israel in mid January unilaterally stopped the attacks and HAMAS responded by suspending rocket and mortarfire. The fighting resulted in the deaths of an estimated 1,100 to 1,400 Palestinians and left tens of thousands of people homeless. International donors pledged $4.5 billion in aid to rebuild the Gaza Strip, but by mid-May 2009 only a small fraction of the aid had been delivered.

## Geography

**Location:** Middle East, bordering the Mediterranean Sea, between Egypt and Israel
**Geographic coordinates:** 31 25 N, 34 20 E
**Map references:** Middle East
**Area:**
*total:* 360 sq km
*land:* 360 sq km
*water:* 0 sq km

**Area - comparative:** slightly more than twice the size of Washington, DC
**Land boundaries:**
*total:* 62 km
*border countries:* Egypt 11 km, Israel 51 km
**Coastline:** 40 km
**Maritime claims:** Israeli-occupied with current status subject to the Israeli-Palestinian Interim Agreement - permanent status to be determined through further negotiation
**Climate:** temperate, mild winters, dry and warm to hot summers
**Terrain:** flat to rolling, sand- and dune-covered coastal plain
**Elevation extremes:**
*lowest point:* Mediterranean Sea 0 m
*highest point:* Abu 'Awdah (Joz Abu 'Auda) 105 m
**Natural resources:** arable land, natural gas
**Land use:**
*arable land:* 29%
*permanent crops:* 21%
*other:* 50% (2002)
**Irrigated land:** 155 sq km; (note - includes West Bank) (2003)
**Natural hazards:** droughts
**Environment - current issues:** desertification; salination of fresh water; sewage treatment; water-borne disease; soil degradation; depletion and contamination of underground water resources
**Geography - note:** strategic strip of land along Mideast-North African trade routes has experienced an incredibly turbulent history; the town of Gaza itself has been besieged countless times in its history

## People

**Population:** 1,551,859 (July 2009 est.)
**Age structure:**
*0-14 years:* 44.4% (male 353,489/female 334,770)
*15-64 years:* 53% (male 420,618/female 402,297)
*65 years and over:* 2.6% (male 16,483/female 24,202) (2009 est.)
**Median age:**
*total:* 17.4 years
*male:* 17.2 years
*female:* 17.5 years (2009 est.)
**Population growth rate:** 3.349% (2009 est.)
**Birth rate:** 36.93 births/1,000 population (2009 est.)
**Death rate:** 3.53 deaths/1,000 population (2008 est.)
**Net migration rate:** 0 migrant(s)/1,000 population (2009 est.)
**Urbanization:**
*urban population:* 72% of total population (2008)
*rate of urbanization:* 3.3% annual rate of change (2005-10 est.)
**Sex ratio:**
*at birth:* 1.06 male(s)/female
*under 15 years:* 1.06 male(s)/female
*15-64 years:* 1.05 male(s)/female
*65 years and over:* 0.68 male(s)/female
*total population:* 1.04 male(s)/female (2009 est.)

# Gaza Strip *(continued)*

**Infant mortality rate:**
*total:* 18.35 deaths/1,000 live births
*male:* 19.53 deaths/1,000 live births
*female:* 17.09 deaths/1,000 live births (2009 est.)
**Life expectancy at birth:**
*total population:* 73.42 years
*male:* 71.82 years
*female:* 75.12 years (2009 est.)
**Total fertility rate:** 5.03 children born/woman
(2009 est.)
**HIV/AIDS - adult prevalence rate:** NA
**HIV/AIDS - people living with HIV/AIDS:** NA
**HIV/AIDS - deaths:** NA
**Nationality:**
*noun:* NA
*adjective:* NA
**Ethnic groups:** Palestinian Arab
**Religions:** Muslim (predominantly Sunni) 99.3%,
Christian 0.7%
**Languages:** Arabic, Hebrew (spoken by many
Palestinians), English (widely understood)
**Literacy:**
*definition:* age 15 and over can read and write
*total population:* 92.4%
*male:* 96.7%
*female:* 88% (2004 est.)
**School life expectancy (primary to tertiary
education):**
*total:* 14 years
*male:* 13 years
*female:* 14 years (2006)
**Education expenditures:** NA

## Government

**Country name:**
*conventional long form:* none
*conventional short form:* Gaza Strip
*local long form:* none
*local short form:* Qita Ghazzah

## Economy

**Economy - overview:** High population density,
limited land access, and strict internal and external
security controls have kept economic conditions in the
Gaza Strip - the smaller of the two areas under the
Palestinian Authority (PA) - even more degraded than in
the West Bank. The beginning of the second intifada in
September 2000 sparked an economic downturn,
largely the result of Israeli closure policies; these
policies, which were imposed to address security
concerns in Israel, disrupted labor and trade access to
and from the Gaza Strip. In 2001, and even more
severely in 2003, Israeli military measures in PA areas
resulted in the destruction of capital, the disruption of
administrative structures, and widespread business
closures. The Israeli withdrawal from the Gaza Strip in
September 2005 offered some medium-term
opportunities for economic growth, but Israeli-imposed
crossings closures, which became more restrictive after
HAMAS violently took over the territory in June 2007,
have resulted in widespread private sector layoffs and

shortages of most goods. The status of the crossings,
which are closed to all but the most basic goods, has
not changed following Israel's military offensive into the
Gaza Strip in early 2009.
**GDP (purchasing power parity):**
$11.95 billion (2008 est.)
$5.034 billion (2006)
$5.327 billion (2005)
*note:* data are in 2008 US dollars
**GDP (official exchange rate):** $6.641 billion
(includes West Bank) (2008 est.)
**GDP - real growth rate:**
0.8% (2008 est.)
-8% (2006 est.)
4.9% (2005 est.)
**GDP - per capita (PPP):**
$2,900 (2008 est.)
$1,100 (2006 est.)
*note:* data are in 2008 US dollars
**GDP - composition by sector:**
*agriculture:* 8%
*industry:* 13%
*services:* 79% (includes West Bank) (2007 est.)
**Labor force:** 267,000 (2006)
**Labor force - by occupation:**
*agriculture:* 12%
*industry:* 5%
*services:* 83% (June 2008)
**Unemployment rate:**
41.3% (June 2008)
34.8% (2006)
**Population below poverty line:** 80% (2007 est.)
**Household income or consumption by
percentage share:**
*lowest 10%:* NA%
*highest 10%:* NA%
**Budget:**
*revenues:* $1.149 billion
*expenditures:* $2.31 billion
*note:* includes West Bank (2006)
**Inflation rate (consumer prices):**
11.5% (2008)
3.6% (2006)
*note:* includes West Bank
**Commercial bank prime lending rate:** 7.73%
(31 December 2006)
**Stock of money:** $1.574 billion (31 December 2007)
**Stock of quasi money:** $3.048 billion (31 December
2007)
**Stock of domestic credit:** $1.455 billion
(31 December 2007)
**Agriculture - products:** olives, citrus fruit,
vegetables, flowers, beef, dairy products
**Industries:** textiles, food processing
**Industrial production growth rate:** 2.4% (includes
West Bank) (2005)
**Electricity - production:** 140,000 kWh (2005)
**Electricity - consumption:** 230,000 kWh (2005)
**Electricity - exports:** 0 kWh (2008)
**Electricity - imports:** 90,000 kWh; note - from Israeli
Electric Company (2005)

**Exports:** $339 million f.o.b.; (includes West Bank)
(2006)
**Exports - commodities:** citrus, flowers, textiles
**Imports:** $2.84 billion c.i.f.; (includes West Bank)
(2006)
**Imports - commodities:** food, consumer goods,
construction materials
**Debt - external:** $1.3 billion (2007 est.)
**Exchange rates:** new Israeli shekels (ILS) per US
dollar - 3.56 (2008 est.), 4.14 (2007), 4.4565 (2006),
4.4877 (2005), 4.482 (2004)

## Communications

**Telephones - main lines in use:** 350,400 (includes
West Bank) (2007)
**Telephones - mobile cellular:** 1.026 million
(includes West Bank) (2007)
**Telephone system:**
*general assessment:* NA
*domestic:* Israeli company BEZEK and the Palestinian
company PALTEL are responsible for fixed line
services; the Palestinian JAWAL company provides
cellular services
*international:* country code - 970 (2004)
**Radio broadcast stations:** AM 0, FM 10,
shortwave 0 (2008)
**Television broadcast stations:** 1 (2008)
**Internet country code:** .ps; note - same as West
Bank
**Internet users:** 355,500 (includes West Bank) (2007)

## Transportation

**Airports:** 1 (2008)
**Airports - with paved runways:**
*total:* 1
*over 3,047 m:* 1 (2008)
**Airports - with unpaved runways:**
*total:* 1
*under 914 m:* 1 (2008)
**Heliports:** 1 (2007)
**Roadways:**
*note:* see entry for West Bank
**Ports and terminals:** Gaza

## Military

**Military branches:** Palestinian Authority security
forces have operated only in the West Bank, not in the
Gaza Strip, since Hamas seized power in June 2007;
law and order and other security functions are
performed by Hamas security organizations (2008)
**Manpower available for military service:**
*males age 16-49:* 337,670 (2008 est.)
**Manpower fit for military service:**
*males age 16-49:* 312,003
*females age 16-49:* 297,380 (2009 est.)
**Manpower reaching militarily significant age
annually:**
*male:* 19,147
*female:* 18,200 (2009 est.)
**Military expenditures:** NA

# Gaza Strip *(continued)*

**Disputes - international:** West Bank and Gaza Strip are Israeli-occupied with current status subject to the Israeli-Palestinian Interim Agreement - permanent status to be determined through further negotiation; Israel removed settlers and military personnel from the Gaza Strip in August 2005

**Refugees and internally displaced persons:**
*refugees (country of origin):* 1.017 million (Palestinian Refugees (UNRWA)) (2007)

# Georgia

## Introduction

**Background:** The region of present-day Georgia contained the ancient kingdoms of Colchis and Kartli-Iberia. The area came under Roman influence in the first centuries A.D. and Christianity became the state religion in the 330s. Domination by Persians, Arabs, and Turks was followed by a Georgian golden age (11th-13th centuries) that was cut short by the Mongol invasion of 1236. Subsequently, the Ottoman and Persian empires competed for influence in the region. Georgia was absorbed into the Russian Empire in the 19th century. Independent for three years (1918-1921) following the Russian revolution, it was forcibly incorporated into the USSR until the Soviet Union dissolved in 1991. An attempt by the incumbent Georgian government to manipulate national legislative elections in November 2003 touched off widespread protests that led to the resignation of Eduard SHEVARDNADZE, president since 1995. New elections in early 2004 swept Mikheil SAAKASHVILI into power along with his National Movement party. Progress on market reforms and democratization has been made in the years since independence, but this progress has been complicated by Russian assistance and support to the breakaway regions of Abkhazia and South Ossetia. After a series of Russian and separatist provocations in summer 2008, Georgian military action in South Ossetia in early August led to a Russian military response that not only occupied the breakaway areas, but large portions of Georgia proper as well. Russian troops pulled back from most occupied Georgian territory, but in late August 2008 Russia unilaterally recognized the independence of Abkhazia and South Ossetia. This action was strongly condemned by most of the world's nations and international organizations.

## Geography

**Location:** Southwestern Asia, bordering the Black Sea, between Turkey and Russia

**Geographic coordinates:** 42 00 N, 43 30 E

**Map references:** Asia

**Area:**
*total:* 69,700 sq km
*land:* 69,700 sq km
*water:* 0 sq km

**Area - comparative:** slightly smaller than South Carolina

**Land boundaries:**
*total:* 1,461 km
*border countries:* Armenia 164 km, Azerbaijan 322 km, Russia 723 km, Turkey 252 km

**Coastline:** 310 km

**Maritime claims:**
*territorial sea:* 12 nm
*exclusive economic zone:* 200 nm

**Climate:** warm and pleasant; Mediterranean-like on Black Sea coast

**Terrain:** largely mountainous with Great Caucasus Mountains in the north and Lesser Caucasus Mountains in the south; Kolkhet'is Dablobi (Kolkhida Lowland) opens to the Black Sea in the west; Mtkvari River Basin in the east; good soils in river valley flood plains, foothills of Kolkhida Lowland

**Elevation extremes:**
*lowest point:* Black Sea 0 m
*highest point:* Mt'a Shkhara 5,201 m

**Natural resources:** forests, hydropower, manganese deposits, iron ore, copper, minor coal and oil deposits; coastal climate and soils allow for important tea and citrus growth

**Land use:**
*arable land:* 11.51%
*permanent crops:* 3.79%
*other:* 84.7% (2005)

**Irrigated land:** 4,690 sq km (2003)
**Total renewable water resources:** 63.3 cu km (1997)
**Freshwater withdrawal (domestic/industrial/agricultural):**
*total:* 3.61 cu km/yr (20%/21%/59%)
*per capita:* 808 cu m/yr (2000)
**Natural hazards:** earthquakes
**Environment - current issues:** air pollution, particularly in Rust'avi; heavy pollution of Mtkvari River and the Black Sea; inadequate supplies of potable water; soil pollution from toxic chemicals
**Environment - international agreements:**
*party to:* Air Pollution, Biodiversity, Climate Change, Climate Change-Kyoto Protocol, Desertification, Endangered Species, Hazardous Wastes, Law of the Sea, Ozone Layer Protection, Ship Pollution, Wetlands
*signed, but not ratified:* none of the selected agreements
**Geography - note:** strategically located east of the Black Sea; Georgia controls much of the Caucasus Mountains and the routes through them

## People

**Population:** 4,615,807 (July 2009 est.)
**Age structure:**
*0-14 years:* 16.1% (male 395,929/female 345,071)
*15-64 years:* 67.6% (male 1,503,360/female 1,616,234)
*65 years and over:* 16.4% (male 302,103/female 453,110) (2009 est.)
**Median age:**
*total:* 38.6 years
*male:* 36.1 years
*female:* 41 years (2009 est.)
**Population growth rate:** -0.325% (2009 est.)
**Birth rate:** 10.66 births/1,000 population (2009 est.)
**Death rate:** 9.51 deaths/1,000 population (2008 est.)
**Net migration rate:** -4.26 migrant(s)/1,000 population (2009 est.)
**Urbanization:**
*urban population:* 53% of total population (2008)
*rate of urbanization:* -0.6% annual rate of change (2005-10 est.)
**Sex ratio:**
*at birth:* 1.13 male(s)/female
*under 15 years:* 1.15 male(s)/female
*15-64 years:* 0.93 male(s)/female
*65 years and over:* 0.67 male(s)/female
*total population:* 0.91 male(s)/female (2009 est.)
**Infant mortality rate:**
*total:* 16.22 deaths/1,000 live births
*male:* 18.21 deaths/1,000 live births
*female:* 13.97 deaths/1,000 live births (2009 est.)
**Life expectancy at birth:**
*total population:* 76.72 years
*male:* 73.41 years
*female:* 80.45 years (2009 est.)
**Total fertility rate:** 1.44 children born/woman (2009 est.)

**HIV/AIDS - adult prevalence rate:** less than 0.1% (2007 est.)
**HIV/AIDS - people living with HIV/AIDS:** 2,700 (2007 est.)
**HIV/AIDS - deaths:** fewer than 200 (2003 est.)
**Nationality:**
*noun:* Georgian(s)
*adjective:* Georgian
**Ethnic groups:** Georgian 83.8%, Azeri 6.5%, Armenian 5.7%, Russian 1.5%, other 2.5% (2002 census)
**Religions:** Orthodox Christian 83.9%, Muslim 9.9%, Armenian-Gregorian 3.9%, Catholic 0.8%, other 0.8%, none 0.7% (2002 census)
**Languages:** Georgian 71% (official), Russian 9%, Armenian 7%, Azeri 6%, other 7%
*note:* Abkhaz is the official language in Abkhazia
**Literacy:**
*definition:* age 15 and over can read and write
*total population:* 100%
*male:* 100%
*female:* 100% (2004 est.)
**School life expectancy (primary to tertiary education):**
*total:* 12 years
*male:* 12 years
*female:* 13 years (2006)
**Education expenditures:** 3.1% of GDP (2006)

## Government

**Country name:**
*conventional long form:* none
*conventional short form:* Georgia
*local long form:* none
*local short form:* Sak'art'velo
*former:* Georgian Soviet Socialist Republic
**Government type:** republic
**Capital:**
*name:* T'bilisi
*geographic coordinates:* 41 43 N, 44 47 E
*time difference:* UTC+4 (9 hours ahead of Washington, DC during Standard Time)
**Administrative divisions:** 9 regions (mkharebi, singular - mkhare), 1 city (k'alak'i), and 2 autonomous republics (avtomnoy respubliki, singular - avtom respublika)
*regions:* Guria, Imereti, Kakheti, Kvemo Kartli, Mtskheta-Mtianeti, Racha-Lechkhumi and Kvemo Svaneti, Samegrelo and Zemo Svaneti, Samtskhe-Javakheti, Shida Kartli
*city:* Tbilisi
*autonomous republics:* Abkhazia or Ap'khazet'is Avtonomiuri Respublika (Sokhumi), Ajaria or Acharis Avtonomiuri Respublika (Bat'umi)
*note:* the administrative centers of the two autonomous republics are shown in parentheses
**Independence:** 9 April 1991 (from the Soviet Union)
**National holiday:** Independence Day, 26 May (1918); note - 26 May 1918 was the date of independence from Soviet Russia, 9 April 1991 was the date of independence from the Soviet Union

**Constitution:** adopted 24 August 1995
**Legal system:** based on civil law system; accepts compulsory ICJ jurisdiction
**Suffrage:** 18 years of age; universal
**Executive branch:**
*chief of state:* President Mikheil SAAKASHVILI (since 25 January 2004); the president is both the chief of state and head of government for the power ministries: state security (includes interior) and defense
*head of government:* President Mikheil SAAKASHVILI (since 25 January 2004); Prime Minister Nikoloz GILAURI (since 6 February 2009); the president is both the chief of state and head of government for the power ministries: state security (includes interior) and defense; the prime minister is head of the remaining ministries of government
*cabinet:* Cabinet of Ministers
*elections:* president elected by popular vote for a five-year term (eligible for a second term); election last held 5 January 2008 (next to be held January 2013)
*election results:* Mikheil SAAKASHVILI reelected president; percent of vote - Mikheil SAAKASHVILI 53.5%, Levan GACHECHILADZE 25.7%, Badri PATARKATSISHVILI 7.1%
**Legislative branch:** unicameral Parliament or Parlamenti (also known as Supreme Council or Umaghlesi Sabcho) (150 seats; 75 members elected by proportional representation, 75 from single-seat constituencies; to serve five-year terms)
*elections:* last held 21 May 2008 (next to be held in spring 2012)
*election results:* percent of vote by party - United National Movement 59.2%, National Council-New Rights 17.7%, Christian Democratic Movement 8.8%, Labor Party 7.4%, Republican Party 3.8%; seats by party - United National Movement 120, National Council-New Rights 16, Christian Democratic Movement 6, Labor Party 6, Republican Party 2
**Judicial branch:** Supreme Court (judges elected by the Supreme Council on the president's or chairman of the Supreme Court's recommendation); Constitutional Court; first and second instance courts
**Political parties and leaders:** Christian Democratic Movement [Giorgi TARGAMADZE]; Democratic Movement United Georgia [Nino BURJANADZE]; Georgian People's Front [Nodar NATADZE]; Georgian United Communist Party or UCPG [Panteleimon GIORGADZE]; Georgia's Way Party [Salome ZOURABICHVILI]; Greens [Giorgi GACHECHILADZE]; Industry Will Save Georgia (Industrialists) or IWSG [Georgi TOPADZE]; Labor Party [Shalva NATELASHVILI]; National Council-New Rights (bloc forming joint opposition) [Levan GACHECHILADZE]; National Democratic Party or NDP [Bachuki KARDAVA]; United National Movement [Mikheil SAAKASHVILI]; New Rights [David GAMKRELIDZE]; Republican Party [David USUPASHVILI]; Socialist Party or SPG [Irakli MINDELI]; Traditionalists [Akaki ASATIANI]; Union of National Forces-Conservatives [Koba DAVITASHVILI and Zviad DZIDZIGURI]

## Georgia (continued)

**Political pressure groups and leaders:** separatists in the breakaway regions of Abkhazia and South Ossetia

**International organization participation:** ACCT (observer), ADB, BSEC, CE, CIS, EAPC, EBRD, FAO, GCTU, GUAM, IAEA, IBRD, ICAO, ICC, ICCt, ICRM, IDA, IFAD, IFC, IFRCS, ILO, IMF, IMO, Interpol, IOC, IOM, IPU, ISO (correspondent), ITSO, ITU, ITUC, MIGA, OAS (observer), OIF (observer), OPCW, OSCE, PFP, SECI (observer), UN, UNCTAD, UNESCO, UNIDO, UNWTO, UPU, WCO, WFTU, WHO, WIPO, WMO, WTO

**Diplomatic representation in the US:**
*chief of mission:* Ambassador Batu KUTELIA
*chancery:* 2209 Massachusetts Avenue NW, Washington, DC 20008
*telephone:* [1] (202) 387-2390
*FAX:* [1] (202) 393-4537
*consulate(s) general:* New York

**Diplomatic representation from the US:**
*chief of mission:* Ambassador John F. TEFFT
*embassy:* 11 George Balanchine Street, T'bilisi 0131
*mailing address:* 7060 T'bilisi Place, Washington, DC 20521-7060
*telephone:* [995] (32) 27-70-00
*FAX:* [995] (32) 53-23-10

**Flag description:** white rectangle, in its central portion a red cross connecting all four sides of the flag; in each of the four corners is a small red bolnur-katskhuri cross; the five-cross flag appears to date back to the 14th century

### Economy

**Economy - overview:** Georgia's economy sustained GDP growth of close to 10% in 2006 and 12% in 2007, based on strong inflows of foreign investment and robust government spending. However, growth slowed to less than 3% in 2008 and is expected to slow further in 2009. Georgia's main economic activities include the cultivation of agricultural products such as grapes, citrus fruits, and hazelnuts; mining of manganese and copper; and output of a small industrial sector producing alcoholic and nonalcoholic beverages, metals, machinery, aircraft and chemicals. Areas of recent improvement include growth in the construction, banking services, and mining sectors, but reduced availability of external investment and the slowing regional economy are emerging risks. The country imports nearly all its needed supplies of natural gas and oil products. It has sizeable hydropower capacity, a growing component of its energy supplies. Georgia has overcome the chronic energy shortages of the past by renovating hydropower plants and by bringing in newly available supplies from Azerbaijan. It also has an increased ability to pay for more expensive gas imports from Russia. The construction on the Baku-T'bilisi-Ceyhan oil pipeline, the Baku-T'bilisi-Erzerum gas pipeline, and the Kars-Akhalkalaki Railroad are part of a strategy to capitalize on Georgia's strategic location between Europe and Asia and develop its role as a transit point for gas, oil and other goods. Georgia has historically suffered from a chronic failure to collect tax revenues; however, the government has made great progress and has reformed the tax code, improved tax administration, increased tax enforcement, and cracked down on corruption since coming to power in 2004. Government revenues have increased nearly four fold since 2003. Due to improvements in customs and tax enforcement, smuggling is a declining problem. The country is pinning its hopes for long-term growth on a determined effort to reduce regulation, taxes, and corruption in order to attract foreign investment, but the economy faces a more difficult investment climate both domestically and internationally.

**GDP (purchasing power parity):**
$21.6 billion (2008 est.)
$21.09 billion (2007)
$18.77 billion (2006)
*note:* data are in 2008 US dollars

**GDP (official exchange rate):** $13.28 billion (2008 est.)

**GDP - real growth rate:**
2.4% (2008 est.)
12.4% (2007 est.)
9.4% (2006 est.)

**GDP - per capita (PPP):**
$4,700 (2008 est.)
$4,500 (2007 est.)
$4,000 (2006 est.)
*note:* data are in 2008 US dollars

**GDP - composition by sector:**
*agriculture:* 12.8%
*industry:* 28.4%
*services:* 58.8% (2008 est.)

**Labor force:** 2.02 million (2007 est.)

**Labor force - by occupation:**
*agriculture:* 55.6%
*industry:* 8.9%
*services:* 35.5% (2006 est.)

**Unemployment rate:**
13.6% (2006 est.)

**Population below poverty line:** 31% (2006)

**Household income or consumption by percentage share:**
*lowest 10%:* 2.4%
*highest 10%:* 27% (2005)

**Distribution of family income - Gini index:** 40.8 (2005)

**Investment (gross fixed):** 29.5% of GDP (2008 est.)

**Budget:**
*revenues:* $3.778 billion
*expenditures:* $4.182 billion (2008 est.)

**Inflation rate (consumer prices):**
11.3% (2008 est.)
9.3% (2007 est.)

**Central bank discount rate:** 8%
*note:* this is the Refinancing Rate, the key monetary policy rate of the Georgian National Bank (25 December 2008)

**Commercial bank prime lending rate:** 20.41% (31 December 2007)

**Stock of money:** $1.154 billion (31 December 2007)

**Stock of quasi money:** $1.379 billion (31 December 2007)

**Stock of domestic credit:** $3.374 billion (31 December 2007)

**Market value of publicly traded shares:** $1.389 billion (31 December 2007)

**Agriculture - products:** citrus, grapes, tea, hazelnuts, vegetables; livestock

**Industries:** steel, aircraft, machine tools, electrical appliances, mining (manganese and copper), chemicals, wood products, wine

**Industrial production growth rate:** 6% (2008 est.)

**Electricity - production:** 7.116 billion kWh (2006 est.)

**Electricity - consumption:** 6.694 billion kWh (2006 est.)

**Electricity - exports:** 635 million kWh (2007 est.)

**Electricity - imports:** 532 million kWh (2007 est.)

**Oil - production:** 979.1 bbl/day (2007 est.)

**Oil - consumption:** 12,980 bbl/day (2006 est.)

**Oil - exports:** 2,492 bbl/day (2005)

**Oil - imports:** 15,820 bbl/day (2005)

**Oil - proved reserves:** 35 million bbl (1 January 2008 est.)

**Natural gas - production:** 10 million cu m (2007 est.)

**Natural gas - consumption:** 1.49 billion cu m (2007 est.)

**Natural gas - exports:** 0 cu m (2007 est.)

**Natural gas - imports:** 1.48 billion cu m (2007 est.)

**Natural gas - proved reserves:** 8.495 billion cu m (1 January 2008 est.)

**Current account balance:** -$3.334 billion (2008 est.)

**Exports:** $2.761 billion (2008 est.)

**Exports - commodities:** scrap metal, wine, mineral water, ores, vehicles, fruits and nuts

**Exports - partners:** Turkey 13%, US 11.2%, Azerbaijan 6.3%, UK 5.4%, Bulgaria 5.1%, Ukraine 5%, Armenia 4.8%, Turkmenistan 4.5%, Canada 4.2% (2007)

**Imports:** $7.304 billion f.o.b. (2008 est.)

**Imports - commodities:** fuels, vehicles, machinery and parts, grain and other foods, pharmaceuticals

**Imports - partners:** Turkey 14%, Russia 12.3%, Ukraine 8.5%, Azerbaijan 7.3%, Germany 6.8%, US 5%, Bulgaria 4.6% (2007)

**Reserves of foreign exchange and gold:** $1.522 billion (31 December 2008 est.)

**Debt - external:** $4.5 billion (2007)

**Exchange rates:** laris (GEL) per US dollar - 1.47 (2008 est.), 1.7 (2007), 1.78 (2006), 1.8127 (2005), 1.9167 (2004)

### Communications

**Telephones - main lines in use:** 556,100 (2007)
**Telephones - mobile cellular:** 2.6 million (2007)
**Telephone system:**
*general assessment:* fixed-line telecommunications network has only limited coverage outside Tbilisi; long

list of people waiting for fixed line connections; multiple mobile-cellular providers provide services to an increasing subscribership throughout the country *domestic:* cellular telephone networks now cover the entire country; mobile-cellular teledensity approaching 60 per 100 people; urban fixed-line telephone density is about 20 per 100 people; rural telephone density is about 4 per 100 people; intercity facilities include a fiber-optic line between T'bilisi and K'ut'aisi; nationwide pager service is available *international:* country code - 995; the Georgia-Russia fiber optic submarine cable provides connectivity to Russia; international service is available by microwave, landline, and satellite through the Moscow switch; international electronic mail and telex service are available

**Radio broadcast stations:** AM 7, FM 12, shortwave 4 (1998)

**Television broadcast stations:** 12 (plus repeaters) (1998)

**Internet country code:** .ge
**Internet hosts:** 27,905 (2008)
**Internet users:** 360,000 (2007)

### Transportation

**Airports:** 23 (2008)
**Airports - with paved runways:**
*total:* 19
*over 3,047 m:* 1
*2,438 to 3,047 m:* 7
*1,524 to 2,437 m:* 5
*914 to 1,523 m:* 4
*under 914 m:* 2 (2008)
**Airports - with unpaved runways:**
*total:* 4
*1,524 to 2,437 m:* 1
*914 to 1,523 m:* 2
*under 914 m:* 1 (2008)
**Heliports:** 3 (2007)
**Pipelines:** gas 1,591 km; oil 1,253 km (2008)
**Railways:**
*total:* 1,612 km
*broad gauge:* 1,575 km 1.520-m gauge (1,575 electrified)
*narrow gauge:* 37 km 0.912-m gauge (37 electrified) (2006)
**Roadways:**
*total:* 20,329 km
*paved:* 7,854 km (includes 13 km of expressways)
*unpaved:* 12,475 km (2006)
**Merchant marine:**
*total:* 191
*by type:* bulk carrier 18, cargo 148, carrier 2, chemical tanker 1, container 4, liquefied gas 1, passenger/cargo 2, petroleum tanker 4, refrigerated cargo 5, roll on/roll off 4, vehicle carrier 2
*foreign-owned:* 153 (China 10, Cyprus 1, Egypt 12, Germany 2, Greece 5, Hong Kong 2, Israel 2, Lebanon 4, Monaco 4, Nigeria 1, Romania 16, Russia 12, Syria 49, Turkey 14, Ukraine 18, UAE 1) (2008)

**Ports and terminals:** Bat'umi, P'ot'i
**Transportation - note:** large parts of transportation network are in poor condition because of lack of maintenance and repair

### Military

**Military branches:** Georgian Armed Forces: Land Forces, Air and Air Defense Forces
*note:* naval forces have been incorporated into the coast guard (2009)
**Military service age and obligation:** 18 to 34 years of age for compulsory and voluntary active duty military service; conscript service obligation - 18 months (2005)
**Manpower available for military service:**
*males age 16-49:* 1,113,251
*females age 16-49:* 1,168,021 (2008 est.)
**Manpower fit for military service:**
*males age 16-49:* 908,282
*females age 16-49:* 959,290 (2009 est.)
**Manpower reaching militarily significant age annually:**
*male:* 32,355
*female:* 30,809 (2009 est.)
**Military expenditures:** 0.59% of GDP (2005 est.)
**Military - note:** a CIS peacekeeping force of Russian troops is deployed in the Abkhazia region of Georgia together with a UN military observer group; a Russian peacekeeping battalion is deployed in South Ossetia

### Transnational Issues

**Disputes - international:** Russia and Georgia agree on delimiting 80% of their common border, leaving certain small, strategic segments and the maritime boundary unresolved; OSCE observers monitor volatile areas such as the Pankisi Gorge in the Akhmeti region and the Argun Gorge in Abkhazia; UN Observer Mission in Georgia has maintained a peacekeeping force in Georgia since 1993; Meshkheti Turks scattered throughout the former Soviet Union seek to return to Georgia; boundary with Armenia remains undemarcated; ethnic Armenian groups in Javakheti region of Georgia seek greater autonomy from the Georgian government; Azerbaijan and Georgia continue to discuss the alignment of their boundary at certain crossing areas
**Refugees and internally displaced persons:**
*refugees (country of origin):* 1,100 (Russia)
*IDPs:* 220,000-240,000 (displaced from Abkhazia and South Ossetia) (2007)
**Illicit drugs:** limited cultivation of cannabis and opium poppy, mostly for domestic consumption; used as transshipment point for opiates via Central Asia to Western Europe and Russia

# Germany

### Introduction

**Background:** As Europe's largest economy and second most populous nation (after Russia), Germany is a key member of the continent's economic, political, and defense organizations. European power struggles immersed Germany in two devastating World Wars in the first half of the 20th century and left the country occupied by the victorious Allied powers of the US, UK, France, and the Soviet Union in 1945. With the advent of the Cold War, two German states were formed in 1949: the western Federal Republic of Germany (FRG) and the eastern German Democratic Republic (GDR). The democratic FRG embedded itself in key Western economic and security organizations, the EC, which became the EU, and NATO, while the Communist GDR was on the front line of the Soviet-led Warsaw Pact. The decline of the USSR and the end of the Cold War allowed for German unification in 1990. Since then, Germany has expended considerable funds to bring Eastern productivity and wages up to Western standards. In January 1999, Germany and 10 other EU countries introduced a common European exchange currency, the euro.

### Geography

**Location:** Central Europe, bordering the Baltic Sea and the North Sea, between the Netherlands and Poland, south of Denmark
**Geographic coordinates:** 51 00 N, 9 00 E
**Map references:** Europe
**Area:**
*total:* 357,021 sq km
*land:* 349,223 sq km
*water:* 7,798 sq km
**Area - comparative:** slightly smaller than Montana
**Land boundaries:**
*total:* 3,621 km
*border countries:* Austria 784 km, Belgium 167 km, Czech Republic 646 km, Denmark 68 km, France 451 km, Luxembourg 138 km, Netherlands 577 km, Poland 456 km, Switzerland 334 km

# Germany (continued)

**Coastline:** 2,389 km
**Maritime claims:**
*territorial sea:* 12 nm
*exclusive economic zone:* 200 nm
*continental shelf:* 200 m depth or to the depth of exploitation
**Climate:** temperate and marine; cool, cloudy, wet winters and summers; occasional warm mountain (foehn) wind
**Terrain:** lowlands in north, uplands in center, Bavarian Alps in south
**Elevation extremes:**
*lowest point:* Neuendorf bei Wilster -3.54 m
*highest point:* Zugspitze 2,963 m
**Natural resources:** coal, lignite, natural gas, iron ore, copper, nickel, uranium, potash, salt, construction materials, timber, arable land
**Land use:**
*arable land:* 33.13%
*permanent crops:* 0.6%
*other:* 66.27% (2005)
**Irrigated land:** 4,850 sq km (2003)
**Total renewable water resources:** 188 cu km (2005)
**Freshwater withdrawal (domestic/industrial/ agricultural):**
*total:* 38.01 cu km/yr (12%/68%/20%)
*per capita:* 460 cu m/yr (2001)
**Natural hazards:** flooding
**Environment - current issues:** emissions from coal-burning utilities and industries contribute to air pollution; acid rain, resulting from sulfur dioxide emissions, is damaging forests; pollution in the Baltic Sea from raw sewage and industrial effluents from rivers in eastern Germany; hazardous waste disposal; government established a mechanism for ending the use of nuclear power over the next 15 years; government working to meet EU commitment to identify nature preservation areas in line with the EU's Flora, Fauna, and Habitat directive
**Environment - international agreements:**
*party to:* Air Pollution, Air Pollution-Nitrogen Oxides, Air Pollution-Persistent Organic Pollutants, Air Pollution-Sulfur 85, Air Pollution-Sulfur 94, Air Pollution-Volatile Organic Compounds, Antarctic-Environmental Protocol, Antarctic-Marine Living Resources, Antarctic Seals, Antarctic Treaty, Biodiversity, Climate Change, Climate Change-Kyoto Protocol, Desertification, Endangered Species, Environmental Modification, Hazardous Wastes, Law of the Sea, Marine Dumping, Ozone Layer Protection, Ship Pollution, Tropical Timber 83, Tropical Timber 94, Wetlands, Whaling
*signed, but not ratified:* none of the selected agreements
**Geography - note:** strategic location on North European Plain and along the entrance to the Baltic Sea

## People

**Population:** 82,329,758 (July 2009 est.)
**Age structure:**
*0-14 years:* 13.7% (male 5,768,366/female 5,470,516)
*15-64 years:* 66.1% (male 27,707,761/female 26,676,759)
*65 years and over:* 20.3% (male 7,004,805/female 9,701,551) (2009 est.)
**Median age:**
*total:* 43.8 years
*male:* 42.6 years
*female:* 45.2 years (2009 est.)
**Population growth rate:** -0.053% (2009 est.)
**Birth rate:** 8.18 births/1,000 population (2009 est.)
**Death rate:** 10.8 deaths/1,000 population (2008 est.)
**Net migration rate:** 2.19 migrant(s)/1,000 population (2009 est.)
**Urbanization:**
*urban population:* 74% of total population (2008)
*rate of urbanization:* 0.1% annual rate of change (2005-10 est.)
**Sex ratio:**
*at birth:* 1.06 male(s)/female
*under 15 years:* 1.05 male(s)/female
*15-64 years:* 1.04 male(s)/female
*65 years and over:* 0.72 male(s)/female
*total population:* 0.97 male(s)/female (2009 est.)
**Infant mortality rate:**
*total:* 3.99 deaths/1,000 live births
*male:* 4.41 deaths/1,000 live births
*female:* 3.55 deaths/1,000 live births (2009 est.)
**Life expectancy at birth:**
*total population:* 79.26 years
*male:* 76.26 years
*female:* 82.42 years (2009 est.)
**Total fertility rate:** 1.41 children born/woman (2009 est.)
**HIV/AIDS - adult prevalence rate:** 0.1% (2007 est.)
**HIV/AIDS - people living with HIV/AIDS:** 53,000 (2007 est.)
**HIV/AIDS - deaths:** fewer than 500 (2007 est.)
**Nationality:**
*noun:* German(s)
*adjective:* German
**Ethnic groups:** German 91.5%, Turkish 2.4%, other 6.1% (made up largely of Greek, Italian, Polish, Russian, Serbo-Croatian, Spanish)
**Religions:** Protestant 34%, Roman Catholic 34%, Muslim 3.7%, unaffiliated or other 28.3%
**Languages:** German
**Literacy:**
*definition:* age 15 and over can read and write
*total population:* 99%
*male:* 99%
*female:* 99% (2003 est.)
**School life expectancy (primary to tertiary education):**
*total:* 16 years
*male:* 16 years
*female:* 16 years (2006)

**Education expenditures:** 4.6% of GDP (2004)
**People - note:** second most populous country in Europe after Russia

## Government

**Country name:**
*conventional long form:* Federal Republic of Germany
*conventional short form:* Germany
*local long form:* Bundesrepublik Deutschland
*local short form:* Deutschland
*former:* German Empire, German Republic, German Reich
**Government type:** federal republic
**Capital:**
*name:* Berlin
*geographic coordinates:* 52 31 N, 13 24 E
*time difference:* UTC+1 (6 hours ahead of Washington, DC during Standard Time)
*daylight saving time:* +1hr, begins last Sunday in March; ends last Sunday in October
**Administrative divisions:** 16 states (Laender, singular - Land); Baden-Wuerttemberg, Bayern (Bavaria), Berlin, Brandenburg, Bremen, Hamburg, Hessen, Mecklenburg-Vorpommern (Mecklenburg-Western Pomerania), Niedersachsen (Lower Saxony), Nordrhein-Westfalen (North Rhine-Westphalia), Rheinland-Pfalz (Rhineland-Palatinate), Saarland, Sachsen (Saxony), Sachsen-Anhalt (Saxony-Anhalt), Schleswig-Holstein, Thueringen (Thuringia); note - Bayern, Sachsen, and Thueringen refer to themselves as free states (Freistaaten, singular - Freistaat)
**Independence:** 18 January 1871 (German Empire unification); divided into four zones of occupation (UK, US, USSR, and later, France) in 1945 following World War II; Federal Republic of Germany (FRG or West Germany) proclaimed 23 May 1949 and included the former UK, US, and French zones; German Democratic Republic (GDR or East Germany) proclaimed 7 October 1949 and included the former USSR zone; West Germany and East Germany unified 3 October 1990; all four powers formally relinquished rights 15 March 1991
**National holiday:** Unity Day, 3 October (1990)
**Constitution:** 23 May 1949, known as Basic Law; became constitution of the united Germany 3 October 1990
**Legal system:** civil law system with indigenous concepts; judicial review of legislative acts in the Federal Constitutional Court; has not accepted compulsory ICJ jurisdiction
**Suffrage:** 18 years of age; universal
**Executive branch:**
*chief of state:* President Horst KOEHLER (since 1 July 2004)
*head of government:* Chancellor Angela MERKEL (since 22 November 2005)
*cabinet:* Cabinet or Bundesminister (Federal Ministers) appointed by the president on the recommendation of the chancellor
*elections:* president elected for a five-year term

# Germany (continued)

(eligible for a second term) by a Federal Convention, including all members of the Federal Assembly and an equal number of delegates elected by the state parliaments; election last held 23 May 2004 (next scheduled for 23 May 2009); chancellor elected by an absolute majority of the Federal Assembly for a four-year term; Bundestag vote for Chancellor last held 22 November 2005 (next will follow the national elections to be held by 27 September 2009)
*election results:* Horst KOEHLER elected president; received 604 votes of the Federal Convention against 589 for Gesine SCHWAN; Angela MERKEL elected chancellor; vote by Federal Assembly 397 to 202 with 12 abstentions
**Legislative branch:** bicameral legislature consists of the Federal Council or Bundesrat (69 votes; state governments sit in the Council; each has three to six votes in proportion to population and are required to vote as a block)and the Federal Assembly or Bundestag (614 seats; members elected by popular vote for a four-year term under a system of personalized proportional representation; a party must win 5% of the national vote or three direct mandates to gain proportional representation and caucus recognition)
*elections:* Bundestag - last held on 18 September 2005 (next to be held no later than autumn 2009); note -there are no elections for the Bundesrat; composition is determined by the composition of the state-level governments; the composition of the Bundesrat has the potential to change any time one of the 16 states holds an election
*election results:* Bundestag - percent of vote by party -CDU/CSU 35.2%, SPD 34.3%, FDP 9.8%, Left 8.7%, Greens 8.1%, other 3.9%; seats by party - CDU/CSU 225, SPD 222, FDP 61, Left 53, Greens 51, independents 2
**Judicial branch:** Federal Constitutional Court or Bundesverfassungsgericht (half the judges are elected by the Bundestag and half by the Bundesrat)
**Political parties and leaders:** Alliance '90/Greens [Claudia ROTH and Cem OEZDEMIR]; Christian Democratic Union or CDU [Angela MERKEL]; Christian Social Union or CSU [Horst SEEHOFER]; Free Democratic Party or FDP [Guido WESTERWELLE]; Left Party or Die Linke [Lothar BISKY and Oskar LAFONTAINE]; Social Democratic Party or SPD [Franz MUENTEFERING]
**Political pressure groups and leaders:**
*other:* business associations and employers' organizations; religious, trade unions, immigrant, expellee, and veterans groups
**International organization participation:** ADB (nonregional member), AfDB (nonregional member), Arctic Council (observer), Australia Group, BIS, BSEC (observer), CBSS, CDB, CE, CERN, EAPC, EBRD, EIB, EMU, ESA, EU, FAO, G-20, G-5, G-7, G-8, G-10, IADB, IAEA, IBRD, ICAO, ICC, ICCt, ICRM, IDA, IEA, IFAD, IFC, IFRCS, IHO, ILO, IMF, IMO, IMSO, Interpol, IOC, IOM, IPU, ISO, ITSO, ITU, ITUC, MIGA, NAM (guest), NATO, NEA, NSG, OAS (observer), OECD, OPCW, OSCE, Paris Club, PCA, Schengen Convention, SECI (observer), SICA (observer), UN, UNCTAD, UNESCO, UNHCR, UNIDO, UNIFIL, UNMIL, UNMIS, UNOMIG, UNRWA, UNWTO, UPU, WADB (nonregional), WCO, WEU, WFTU, WHO, WIPO, WMO, WTO, ZC
**Diplomatic representation in the US:**
*chief of mission:* Ambassador Klaus SCHARIOTH
*chancery:* 4645 Reservoir Road NW, Washington, DC 20007
*telephone:* [1] (202) 298-4000
*FAX:* [1] (202) 298-4249
*consulate(s) general:* Atlanta, Boston, Chicago, Houston, Los Angeles, Miami, New York, San Francisco
**Diplomatic representation from the US:**
*chief of mission:* Ambassador (vacant); Charge d'Affaires John KOENIG
*embassy:* Pariser Platz 2, 10117 Berlin; note - new embassy opened 4 July 2008
*mailing address:* PSC 120, Box 1000, APO AE 09265, Clayallee 170, 14195 Berlin
*telephone:* [49] (030) 2385174
*FAX:* [49] (030) 8305-1215
*consulate(s) general:* Duesseldorf, Frankfurt am Main, Hamburg, Leipzig, Munich
**Flag description:** three equal horizontal bands of black (top), red, and gold

## Economy

**Economy - overview:** The German economy - the fifth largest economy in the world in PPP terms and Europe's largest - began to contract in the second quarter of 2008 as the strong euro, high oil prices, tighter credit markets, and slowing growth abroad took their toll on Germany's export-dependent economy. At 1.3% in 2008, GDP growth is expected to be negative in 2009. Recent stimulus and lender relief efforts will make demands on Germany's federal budget and undercut plans to balance its budget by 2011. The reforms launched by the former government of Chancellor Gerhard SCHOEDER, deemed necessary due to chronically high unemployment and low average growth, led to strong growth in 2007, while unemployment in 2008 fell below 8%, a new post-reunification low. Germany's aging population, combined with high chronic unemployment, has pushed social security outlays to a level exceeding contributions, but higher government revenues from the cyclical upturn in 2006-07 and a 3% rise in the value-added tax cut Germany's budget deficit to within the EU's 3% debt limit in 2007. The current government of Chancellor Angela MERKEL has initiated other reform measures, such as a gradual increase in the mandatory retirement age from 65 to 67 and measures to increase female participation in the labor market. The modernization and integration of the eastern German economy - where unemployment still exceeds 30% in some municipalities - continues to be a costly long-term process, with annual transfers from west to east amounting to roughly $80 billion. While corporate restructuring and growing capital markets have set strong foundations to help Germany meet the longer-term challenges of European economic integration and globalization, Germany's export-oriented economy has proved a disadvantage in the context of weak global demand.
**GDP (purchasing power parity):**
$2.863 trillion (2008 est.)
$2.816 trillion (2007)
$2.806 trillion (2006)
*note:* data are in 2008 US dollars
**GDP (official exchange rate):** $3.818 trillion (2008 est.)
**GDP - real growth rate:**
1.3% (2008 est.)
2.5% (2007 est.)
3% (2006 est.)
**GDP - per capita (PPP):**
$34,800 (2008 est.)
$34,900 (2007 est.)
$34,000 (2006 est.)
*note:* data are in 2008 US dollars
**GDP - composition by sector:**
*agriculture:* 0.9%
*industry:* 30.1%
*services:* 69% (2008 est.)
**Labor force:** 43.62 million (2008 est.)
**Labor force - by occupation:**
*agriculture:* 2.4%
*industry:* 29.7%
*services:* 67.8% (2005)
**Unemployment rate:**
7.9% (2008 est.)
9% (2007 est.)
*note:* this is the International Labor Organization's estimated rate for international comparisons; Germany's Federal Employment Office estimated a seasonally adjusted rate of 10.8%
**Population below poverty line:** 11% (2001 est.)
**Household income or consumption by percentage share:**
*lowest 10%:* 3.2%
*highest 10%:* 22.1% (2000)
**Distribution of family income - Gini index:** 27 (2006)
**Investment (gross fixed):** 18.9% of GDP (2008 est.)
**Budget:**
*revenues:* $1.614 trillion
*expenditures:* $1.579 trillion (2008 est.)
**Public debt:** 62.6% of GDP (2008 est.)
**Inflation rate (consumer prices):**
2.8% (2008 est.)
2.3% (2007 est.)
**Central bank discount rate:** 4%
*note:* this is the European Central Bank's rate on the marginal lending facility, which offers overnight credit to banks in the euro area
**Commercial bank prime lending rate:** 5.96% (31 December 2007)

# Germany (continued)

**Stock of money:** NA

*note:* see entry for the European Union for money supply in the euro area; the European Central Bank (ECB) controls monetary policy for the 16 members of the Economic and Monetary Union (EMU); individual members of the EMU do not control the quantity of money and quasi money circulating within their own borders

**Stock of quasi money:** NA

**Stock of domestic credit:** $5.081 trillion (31 December 2007)

**Market value of publicly traded shares:** $2.106 trillion (31 December 2007)

**Agriculture - products:** potatoes, wheat, barley, sugar beets, fruit, cabbages; cattle, pigs, poultry

**Industries:** among the world's largest and most technologically advanced producers of iron, steel, coal, cement, chemicals, machinery, vehicles, machine tools, electronics, food and beverages, shipbuilding, textiles

**Industrial production growth rate:** 2.2% (2008 est.)

**Electricity - production:** 594.7 billion kWh (2007 est.)

**Electricity - consumption:** 549.1 billion kWh (2006 est.)

**Electricity - exports:** 62.31 billion kWh (2007 est.)

**Electricity - imports:** 42.87 billion kWh (2007 est.)

**Oil - production:** 148,100 bbl/day (2007 est.)

**Oil - consumption:** 2.456 million bbl/day (2007 est.)

**Oil - exports:** 563,400 bbl/day (2005)

**Oil - imports:** 3.026 million bbl/day (2005)

**Oil - proved reserves:** 367 million bbl (1 January 2008 est.)

**Natural gas - production:** 17.96 billion cu m (2007 est.)

**Natural gas - consumption:** 97.44 billion cu m (2007 est.)

**Natural gas - exports:** 12.22 billion cu m (2007 est.)

**Natural gas - imports:** 88.35 billion cu m (2007 est.)

**Natural gas - proved reserves:** 254.8 billion cu m (1 January 2008 est.)

**Current account balance:** $267.1 billion (2008 est.)

**Exports:** $1.53 trillion f.o.b. (2008 est.)

**Exports - commodities:** machinery, vehicles, chemicals, metals and manufactures, foodstuffs, textiles

**Exports - partners:** France 9.7%, US 7.5%, UK 7.3%, Italy 6.7%, Netherlands 6.4%, Austria 5.4%, Belgium 5.3%, Spain 5% (2007)

**Imports:** $1.202 trillion f.o.b. (2008 est.)

**Imports - commodities:** machinery, vehicles, chemicals, foodstuffs, textiles, metals

**Imports - partners:** Netherlands 12%, France 8.6%, Belgium 7.8%, China 6.2%, Italy 5.8%, UK 5.6%, US 4.5%, Austria 4.4% (2007)

**Reserves of foreign exchange and gold:** $136.2 billion (31 December 2007 est.)

**Debt - external:** $4.489 trillion (30 June 2007)

**Stock of direct foreign investment - at home:** $924.7 billion (2008 est.)

**Stock of direct foreign investment - abroad:** $1.36 trillion (2008 est.)

**Exchange rates:** euros (EUR) per US dollar - 0.6827 (2008 est.), 0.7345 (2007), 0.7964 (2006), 0.8041 (2005), 0.8054 (2004)

## Communications

**Telephones - main lines in use:** 53.75 million (2007)

**Telephones - mobile cellular:** 97.151 million (2007)

**Telephone system:**

*general assessment:* Germany has one of the world's most technologically advanced telecommunications systems; as a result of intensive capital expenditures since reunification, the formerly backward system of the eastern part of the country, dating back to World War II, has been modernized and integrated with that of the western part

*domestic:* Germany is served by an extensive system of automatic telephone exchanges connected by modern networks of fiber-optic cable, coaxial cable, microwave radio relay, and a domestic satellite system; cellular telephone service is widely available, expanding rapidly, and includes roaming service to many foreign countries

*international:* country code - 49; Germany's international service is excellent worldwide, consisting of extensive land and undersea cable facilities as well as earth stations in the Inmarsat, Intelsat, Eutelsat, and Intersputnik satellite systems (2001)

**Radio broadcast stations:** AM 51, FM 787, shortwave 4 (1998)

**Television broadcast stations:** 373 (plus 8,042 repeaters) (1995)

**Internet country code:** .de

**Internet hosts:** 22.606 million (2008)

**Internet users:** 42.5 million (2007)

## Transportation

**Airports:** 549 (2008)

**Airports - with paved runways:**

*total:* 331

*over 3,047 m:* 13

*2,438 to 3,047 m:* 52

*1,524 to 2,437 m:* 59

*914 to 1,523 m:* 73

*under 914 m:* 134 (2008)

**Airports - with unpaved runways:**

*total:* 218

*1,524 to 2,437 m:* 3

*914 to 1,523 m:* 34

*under 914 m:* 181 (2008)

**Heliports:** 28 (2007)

**Pipelines:** gas 24,364 km; oil 3,379 km; refined products 3,843 km (2008)

**Railways:**

*total:* 48,215 km

*standard gauge:* 47,962 km 1.435-m gauge (20,278 km electrified)

*narrow gauge:* 229 km 1.000-m gauge (16 km electrified); 24 km 0.750-m gauge (2006)

**Roadways:**

*total:* 644,480 km

*paved:* 644,480 km (includes 12,400 km of expressways)

*note:* includes local roads (2006)

**Waterways:** 7,467 km

*note:* Rhine River carries most goods; Main-Danube Canal links North Sea and Black Sea (2008)

**Merchant marine:**

*total:* 393

*by type:* bulk carrier 2, cargo 43, chemical tanker 13, container 284, liquefied gas 5, passenger 5, passenger/cargo 27, petroleum tanker 11, roll on/roll off 3

*foreign-owned:* 11 (China 2, Cyprus 2, Denmark 1, Finland 4, Netherlands 1, Sweden 1)

*registered in other countries:* 2,998 (Antigua and Barbuda 941, Australia 2, Bahamas 44, Bermuda 22, Brazil 6, Bulgaria 63, Burma 1, Canada 3, Cayman Islands 15, Cyprus 189, Denmark 9, Denmark 1, Estonia 1, Finland 1, France 1, Georgia 2, Gibraltar 129, Hong Kong 6, India 2, Indonesia 1, Isle of Man 56, Jamaica 4, Liberia 849, Luxembourg 5, Malaysia 1, Malta 91, Marshall Islands 235, Mongolia 4, Morocco 2, Netherlands 75, Netherlands Antilles 43, Norway 1, NZ 1, Panama 44, Portugal 20, Russia 1, Saint Vincent and the Grenadines 3, Singapore 24, Slovakia 3, Spain 5, Sri Lanka 5, Sweden 5, Turkey 1, UK 76, US 5) (2008)

**Ports and terminals:** Bremen, Bremerhaven, Duisburg, Hamburg, Karlsruhe, Lubeck, Rostock, Wilhemshaven

## Military

**Military branches:** Federal Armed Forces (Bundeswehr): Army (Heer), Navy (Deutsche Marine, includes naval air arm), Air Force (Luftwaffe), Joint Support Services (Streitkraeftbasis), Central Medical Service (Zentraler Sanitaetsdienst) (2009)

**Military service age and obligation:** 18 years of age (conscripts serve a 9-month tour of compulsory military service) (2004)

**Manpower available for military service:**

*males age 16-49:* 19,594,118

*females age 16-49:* 18,543,955 (2008 est.)

**Manpower fit for military service:**

*males age 16-49:* 15,747,493

*females age 16-49:* 14,899,416 (2009 est.)

**Manpower reaching militarily significant age annually:**

*male:* 431,508

*female:* 409,111 (2009 est.)

**Military expenditures:** 1.5% of GDP (2005 est.)

## Transnational Issues

**Disputes - international:** none

**Illicit drugs:** source of precursor chemicals for South American cocaine processors; transshipment point for and consumer of Southwest Asian heroin, Latin American cocaine, and European-produced synthetic drugs; major financial center

# Ghana

## Introduction

**Background:** Formed from the merger of the British colony of the Gold Coast and the Togoland trust territory, Ghana in 1957 became the first sub-Saharan country in colonial Africa to gain its independence. Ghana endured a long series of coups before Lt. Jerry RAWLINGS took power in 1981 and banned political parties. After approving a new constitution and restoring multiparty politics in 1992, RAWLINGS won presidential elections in 1992 and 1996, but was constitutionally prevented from running for a third term in 2000. John KUFUOR succeeded him and was reelected in 2004. Kufuor is constitutionally barred from running for a third term in upcoming Presidential elections, which are scheduled for December 2008.

## Geography

**Location:** Western Africa, bordering the Gulf of Guinea, between Cote d'Ivoire and Togo
**Geographic coordinates:** 8 00 N, 2 00 W
**Map references:** Africa
**Area:**
*total:* 239,460 sq km
*land:* 230,940 sq km
*water:* 8,520 sq km
**Area - comparative:** slightly smaller than Oregon
**Land boundaries:**
*total:* 2,094 km
*border countries:* Burkina Faso 549 km, Cote d'Ivoire 668 km, Togo 877 km
**Coastline:** 539 km
**Maritime claims:**
*territorial sea:* 12 nm
*contiguous zone:* 24 nm
*exclusive economic zone:* 200 nm
*continental shelf:* 200 nm
**Climate:** tropical; warm and comparatively dry along southeast coast; hot and humid in southwest; hot and dry in north

**Terrain:** mostly low plains with dissected plateau in south-central area
**Elevation extremes:**
*lowest point:* Atlantic Ocean 0 m
*highest point:* Mount Afadjato 880 m
**Natural resources:** gold, timber, industrial diamonds, bauxite, manganese, fish, rubber, hydropower, petroleum, silver, salt, limestone
**Land use:**
*arable land:* 17.54%
*permanent crops:* 9.22%
*other:* 73.24% (2005)
**Irrigated land:** 310 sq km (2003)
**Total renewable water resources:** 53.2 cu km (2001)
**Freshwater withdrawal (domestic/industrial/ agricultural):**
*total:* 0.98 cu km/yr (24%/10%/66%)
*per capita:* 44 cu m/yr (2000)
**Natural hazards:** dry, dusty, northeastern harmattan winds occur from January to March; droughts
**Environment - current issues:** recurrent drought in north severely affects agricultural activities; deforestation; overgrazing; soil erosion; poaching and habitat destruction threatens wildlife populations; water pollution; inadequate supplies of potable water
**Environment - international agreements:**
*party to:* Biodiversity, Climate Change, Climate Change-Kyoto Protocol, Desertification, Endangered Species, Environmental Modification, Hazardous Wastes, Law of the Sea, Ozone Layer Protection, Ship Pollution, Tropical Timber 83, Tropical Timber 94, Wetlands
*signed, but not ratified:* Marine Life Conservation
**Geography - note:** Lake Volta is the world's largest artificial lake

## People

**Population:** 23,832,495
*note:* estimates for this country explicitly take into account the effects of excess mortality due to AIDS; this can result in lower life expectancy, higher infant mortality, higher death rates, lower population growth rates, and changes in the distribution of population by age and sex than would otherwise be expected (July 2009 est.)
**Age structure:**
*0-14 years:* 37.3% (male 4,503,331/ female 4,393,104)
*15-64 years:* 59.1% (male 7,039,696/ female 7,042,208)
*65 years and over:* 3.6% (male 393,364/ female 460,792) (2009 est.)
**Median age:**
*total:* 20.7 years
*male:* 20.5 years
*female:* 21 years (2009 est.)
**Population growth rate:** 1.882% (2009 est.)
**Birth rate:** 28.58 births/1,000 population (2009 est.)
**Death rate:** 9.39 deaths/1,000 population (2008 est.)

**Net migration rate:** -0.53 migrant(s)/1,000 population (2009 est.)
**Urbanization:**
*urban population:* 50% of total population (2008)
*rate of urbanization:* 3.5% annual rate of change (2005-10 est.)
**Sex ratio:**
*at birth:* 1.03 male(s)/female
*under 15 years:* 1.02 male(s)/female
*15-64 years:* 1 male(s)/female
*65 years and over:* 0.85 male(s)/female
*total population:* 1 male(s)/female (2009 est.)
**Infant mortality rate:**
*total:* 51.09 deaths/1,000 live births
*male:* 55.32 deaths/1,000 live births
*female:* 46.74 deaths/1,000 live births (2009 est.)
**Life expectancy at birth:**
*total population:* 59.85 years
*male:* 58.98 years
*female:* 60.75 years (2009 est.)
**Total fertility rate:** 3.68 children born/woman (2009 est.)
**HIV/AIDS - adult prevalence rate:** 1.9% (2007 est.)
**HIV/AIDS - people living with HIV/AIDS:** 260,000 (2007 est.)
**HIV/AIDS - deaths:** 21,000 (2007 est.)
**Major infectious diseases:**
*degree of risk:* very high
*food or waterborne diseases:* bacterial and protozoal diarrhea, hepatitis A, and typhoid fever
*vectorborne diseases:* malaria
*water contact disease:* schistosomiasis
*respiratory disease:* meningococcal meningitis
*animal contact disease:* rabies
*note:* highly pathogenic H5N1 avian influenza has been identified in this country; it poses a negligible risk with extremely rare cases possible among US citizens who have close contact with birds (2009)
**Nationality:**
*noun:* Ghanaian(s)
*adjective:* Ghanaian
**Ethnic groups:** Akan 45.3%, Mole-Dagbon 15.2%, Ewe 11.7%, Ga-Dangme 7.3%, Guan 4%, Gurma 3.6%, Grusi 2.6%, Mande-Busanga 1%, other tribes 1.4%, other 7.8% (2000 census)
**Religions:** Christian 68.8% (Pentecostal/ Charismatic 24.1%, Protestant 18.6%, Catholic 15.1%, other 11%), Muslim 15.9%, traditional 8.5%, other 0.7%, none 6.1% (2000 census)
**Languages:** Asante 14.8%, Ewe 12.7%, Fante 9.9%, Boron (Brong) 4.6%, Dagomba 4.3%, Dangme 4.3%, Dagarte (Dagaba) 3.7%, Akyem 3.4%, Ga 3.4%, Akuapem 2.9%, other 36.1% (includes English (official)) (2000 census)
**Literacy:**
*definition:* age 15 and over can read and write
*total population:* 57.9%
*male:* 66.4%
*female:* 49.8% (2000 census)

# Ghana (continued)

**School life expectancy (primary to tertiary education):**
*total:* 9 years
*male:* 10 years
*female:* 9 years (2007)
**Education expenditures:** 5.4% of GDP (2005)

## Government

**Country name:**
*conventional long form:* Republic of Ghana
*conventional short form:* Ghana
*former:* Gold Coast
**Government type:** constitutional democracy
**Capital:**
*name:* Accra
*geographic coordinates:* 5 33 N, 0 13 W
*time difference:* UTC 0 (5 hours ahead of Washington, DC during Standard Time)
**Administrative divisions:** 10 regions; Ashanti, Brong-Ahafo, Central, Eastern, Greater Accra, Northern, Upper East, Upper West, Volta, Western
**Independence:** 6 March 1957 (from the UK)
**National holiday:** Independence Day, 6 March (1957)
**Constitution:** approved 28 April 1992
**Legal system:** based on English common law and customary law; has not accepted compulsory ICJ jurisdiction
**Suffrage:** 18 years of age; universal
**Executive branch:**
*chief of state:* President John Evans Atta MILLS (since 7 January 2009); Vice President John Dramani MAHAMA (since 7 January 2009); note - the president is both the chief of state and head of government
*head of government:* President John Evans Atta MILLS (since 7 January 2009); Vice President John Dramani MAHAMA (since 7 January 2009)
*cabinet:* Council of Ministers; president nominates members subject to approval by Parliament
*elections:* president and vice president elected on the same ticket by popular vote for four-year terms (eligible for a second term); election last held 7 December 2008 with a second round held 28 December 2008 (next to be held 7 December 2012)
*election results:* John Evans Atta MILLS elected president in run-off election; percent of vote - John Evans Atta MILLS 50.23%, Nana Addo Dankwa AKUFO-ADDO 49.77%
**Legislative branch:** unicameral Parliament (230 seats; members are elected by direct, popular vote to serve four-year terms)
*elections:* last held 7 December 2008 (next to be held 7 December 2012)
*election results:* percent of vote by party - NA; seats by party - NDC 114, NPP 107, PNC 2, CPP 1, independent 4, other 2
**Judicial branch:** Supreme Court
**Political parties and leaders:** Convention People's Party or CPP [Ladi NYLANDER]; Democratic Freedom Party or DFP [Alhaji Abudu Rahman

ISSAKAH]; Every Ghanaian Living Everywhere or EGLE; Great Consolidated Popular Party or GCPP [Dan LARTEY]; National Democratic Congress or NDC [Dr. Kwabena ADJEI]; New Patriotic Party or NPP [Peter MAC-MANU]; People's National Convention or PNC [Alhaji Amed RAMADAN]; Reform Party [Kyeretwie OPUKU]; United Renaissance Party or URP [Charles WAYO]
**Political pressure groups and leaders:** Christian Aid (water rights); Committee for Joint Action or CJA (education reform); National Coalition Against the Privatization of Water or CAP (water rights); Oxfam (water rights); Public Citizen (water rights); Students Coalition Against EPA [Kwabena Ososukene OKAI] (education reform); Third World Network (education reform)
**International organization participation:** ACP, AfDB, AU, C, ECOWAS, FAO, G-24, G-77, IAEA, IBRD, ICAO, ICC, ICCt, ICRM, IDA, IFAD, IFC, IFRCS, ILO, IMF, IMO, IMSO, Interpol, IOC, IOM, IPU, ISO, ITSO, ITU, ITUC, MIGA, MINURCAT, MINURSO, MONUC, NAM, OAS (observer), OIF (associate member), OPCW, UN, UNAMID, UNCTAD, UNESCO, UNHCR, UNIDO, UNIFIL, UNITAR, UNMIL, UNOCI, UNOMIG, UNWTO, UPU, WCL, WCO, WFTU, WHO, WIPO, WMO, WTO
**Diplomatic representation in the US:**
*chief of mission:* Ambassador (vacant); Deputy Chief of Mission Adolphus K. ARTHUR
*chancery:* 3512 International Drive NW, Washington, DC 20008
*telephone:* [1] (202) 686-4520
*FAX:* [1] (202) 686-4527
*consulate(s) general:* New York
**Diplomatic representation from the US:**
*chief of mission:* Ambassador Donald G. TEITELBAUM
*embassy:* 24 4th Circular Rd. Cantonments, Accra
*mailing address:* P. O. Box 194, Accra
*telephone:* [233] (21) 741-000
*FAX:* [233] (21) 741-389
**Flag description:** three equal horizontal bands of red (top), yellow, and green, with a large black five-pointed star centered in the yellow band; uses the popular pan-African colors of Ethiopia; similar to the flag of Bolivia, which has a coat of arms centered in the yellow band

## Economy

**Economy - overview:** Well endowed with natural resources, Ghana has roughly twice the per capita output of the poorest countries in West Africa. Even so, Ghana remains heavily dependent on international financial and technical assistance. Gold and cocoa production, and individual remittances, are major sources of foreign exchange. The domestic economy continues to revolve around agriculture, which accounts for about 35% of GDP and employs about 55% of the work force, mainly small landholders. Ghana signed a Millennium Challenge Corporation (MCC) Compact in 2006, which aims to assist in

transforming Ghana's agricultural sector. Ghana opted for debt relief under the Heavily Indebted Poor Country (HIPC) program in 2002, and is also benefiting from the Multilateral Debt Relief Initiative that took effect in 2006. Thematic priorities under its current Growth and Poverty Reduction Strategy, which also provides the framework for development partner assistance, are: macroeconomic stability; private sector competitiveness; human resource development; and good governance and civic responsibility. Sound macro-economic management along with high prices for gold and cocoa helped sustain GDP growth in 2008.
**GDP (purchasing power parity):**
$34.04 billion (2008 est.)
$32.02 billion (2007)
$30.18 billion (2006)
*note:* data are in 2008 US dollars
**GDP (official exchange rate):** $17.72 billion (2008 est.)
**GDP - real growth rate:**
6.3% (2008 est.)
6.1% (2007 est.)
6.4% (2006 est.)
**GDP - per capita (PPP):**
$1,500 (2008 est.)
$1,400 (2007 est.)
$1,300 (2006 est.)
*note:* data are in 2008 US dollars
**GDP - composition by sector:**
*agriculture:* 37.3%
*industry:* 25.3%
*services:* 37.5% (2006 est.)
**Labor force:** 11.52 million (2008 est.)
**Labor force - by occupation:**
*agriculture:* 56%
*industry:* 15%
*services:* 29% (2005 est.)
**Unemployment rate:**
11% (2000 est.)
**Population below poverty line:** 28.5% (2007 est.)
**Household income or consumption by percentage share:**
*lowest 10%:* 2.2%
*highest 10%:* 30.1% (1999)
**Distribution of family income - Gini index:** 39.4 (2005-06)
**Investment (gross fixed):** 31.9% of GDP (2008 est.)
**Budget:**
*revenues:* $4.021 billion
*expenditures:* $5.521 billion (2008 est.)
**Public debt:** 66.5% of GDP (2008 est.)
**Inflation rate (consumer prices):**
16.4% (2008 est.)
10.7% (2007 est.)
**Central bank discount rate:** 13.5% (31 December 2007)
**Commercial bank prime lending rate:** NA
**Stock of money:** $2.179 billion (31 December 2006)
**Stock of quasi money:** $2.174 billion (31 December 2006)

# Ghana (continued)

**Stock of domestic credit:** $4.173 billion
(31 December 2006)
**Market value of publicly traded shares:** $2.38
billion (31 December 2007)
**Agriculture - products:** cocoa, rice, cassava
(tapioca), peanuts, corn, shea nuts, bananas; timber
**Industries:** mining, lumbering, light manufacturing,
aluminum smelting, food processing, cement, small
commercial ship building
**Industrial production growth rate:** 6.5%
(2008 est.)
**Electricity - production:** 8.204 billion kWh
(2006 est.)
**Electricity - consumption:** 6.76 billion kWh
(2006 est.)
**Electricity - exports:** 755 million kWh (2006 est.)
**Electricity - imports:** 629 million kWh (2006 est.)
**Oil - production:** 7,571 bbl/day (2007 est.)
**Oil - consumption:** 49,300 bbl/day (2006 est.)
**Oil - exports:** 5,709 bbl/day (2005)
**Oil - imports:** 45,520 bbl/day (2005)
**Oil - proved reserves:** 15 million bbl (1 January
2008 est.)
**Natural gas - production:** 0 cu m (2007 est.)
**Natural gas - consumption:** 0 cu m (2007 est.)
**Natural gas - exports:** 0 cu m (2007 est.)
**Natural gas - imports:** 0 cu m (2007 est.)
**Natural gas - proved reserves:** 22.65 billion cu m
(1 January 2008 est.)
**Current account balance:** -$1.807 billion
(2008 est.)
**Exports:** $5.439 billion f.o.b. (2008 est.)
**Exports - commodities:** gold, cocoa, timber, tuna,
bauxite, aluminum, manganese ore, diamonds,
horticulture
**Exports - partners:** Netherlands 11%, UK 9%,
France 6.2%, US 5.9%, Germany 4.6%, Belgium
4.4% (2007)
**Imports:** $9.816 billion f.o.b. (2008 est.)
**Imports - commodities:** capital equipment,
petroleum, foodstuffs
**Imports - partners:** Nigeria 15.1%, China 14.9%,
UK 5.2%, US 5.1% (2007)
**Reserves of foreign exchange and gold:** $2.301
billion (31 December 2008 est.)
**Debt - external:** $5.697 billion (31 December
2008 est.)
**Stock of direct foreign investment - at home:**
$NA
**Stock of direct foreign investment - abroad:** $NA
**Exchange rates:** cedis (GHC) per US dollar - 1.1
(2008 est.), 0.95 (2007), 9,174.8 (2006), 9,072.5
(2005), 9,004.6 (2004)
*note:* in 2007 Ghana revalued its currency with 10,000
old cedis equal to 1 new cedis

## Communications

**Telephones - main lines in use:** 376,500 (2007)
**Telephones - mobile cellular:** 7.604 million (2007)
**Telephone system:**
*general assessment:* outdated and unreliable
fixed-line infrastructure heavily concentrated in Accra;
competition among multiple mobile-cellular providers
has spurred growth with subscribership about 35 per
100 persons and rising
*domestic:* primarily microwave radio relay; wireless
local loop has been installed
*international:* country code - 233; landing point for the
SAT-3/WASC fiber-optic submarine cable that
provides connectivity to Europe and Asia; satellite
earth stations - 4 Intelsat (Atlantic Ocean); microwave
radio relay link to Panaftel system connects Ghana to
its neighbors (2007)
**Radio broadcast stations:** AM 0, FM 86, shortwave
3 (2007)
**Television broadcast stations:** 7 (2007)
**Internet country code:** .gh
**Internet hosts:** 24,018 (2008)
**Internet users:** 650,000 (2007)

## Transportation

**Airports:** 11 (2008)
**Airports - with paved runways:**
*total:* 7
*over 3,047 m:* 1
*2,438 to 3,047 m:* 1
*1,524 to 2,437 m:* 3
*914 to 1,523 m:* 2 (2008)
**Airports - with unpaved runways:**
*total:* 4
*914 to 1,523 m:* 3
*under 914 m:* 1 (2008)
**Pipelines:** oil 5 km; refined products 309 km (2008)
**Railways:**
*total:* 953 km
*narrow gauge:* 953 km 1.067-m gauge (2006)
**Roadways:**
*total:* 62,221 km
*paved:* 9,955 km
*unpaved:* 52,266 km (2006)
**Waterways:** 1,293 km
*note:* 168 km for launches and lighters on Volta,
Ankobra, and Tano rivers; 1,125 km of arterial and
feeder waterways on Lake Volta (2008)
**Merchant marine:**
*total:* 4
*by type:* petroleum tanker 1, refrigerated cargo 3
*foreign-owned:* 1 (Brazil 1) (2008)
**Ports and terminals:** Tema

## Military

**Military branches:** Ghanaian Army, Ghanaian
Navy, Ghanaian Air Force (2008)
**Military service age and obligation:** 18 years of
age for voluntary military service; no conscription
(2008)
**Manpower available for military service:**
*males age 16-49:* 5,802,096
*females age 16-49:* 5,729,939 (2008 est.)
**Manpower fit for military service:**
*males age 16-49:* 3,849,113
*females age 16-49:* 3,840,083 (2009 est.)
**Manpower reaching militarily significant age
annually:**
*male:* 272,954
*female:* 266,186 (2009 est.)
**Military expenditures:** 0.8% of GDP (2006 est.)

## Transnational Issues

**Disputes - international:** Ghana struggles to
accommodate returning nationals who worked in the
cocoa plantations and escaped fighting in Cote
d'Ivoire
**Refugees and internally displaced persons:**
*refugees (country of origin):* 35,653 (Liberia); 8,517
(Togo) (2007)
**Illicit drugs:** illicit producer of cannabis for the
international drug trade; major transit hub for
Southwest and Southeast Asian heroin and, to a
lesser extent, South American cocaine destined for
Europe and the US; widespread crime and money
laundering problem, but the lack of a well developed
financial infrastructure limits the country's utility as a
money laundering center; significant domestic
cocaine and cannabis use

# Gibraltar
*(overseas territory of the UK)*

## Introduction

**Background:** Strategically important, Gibraltar was reluctantly ceded to Great Britain by Spain in the 1713 Treaty of Utrecht; the British garrison was formally declared a colony in 1830. In a referendum held in 1967, Gibraltarians voted overwhelmingly to remain a British dependency. The subsequent granting of autonomy in 1969 by the UK led to Spain closing the border and severing all communication links. A series of talks were held by the UK and Spain between 1997 and 2002 on establishing temporary joint sovereignty over Gibraltar. In response to these talks, the Gibraltar Government called a referendum in late 2002 in which the majority of citizens voted overwhelmingly against any sharing of sovereignty with Spain. Since the referendum, tripartite talks on other issues have been held with Spain, the UK, and Gibraltar, and in September 2006 a three-way agreement was signed. Spain agreed to remove restrictions on air movements, to speed up customs procedures, to implement international telephone dialing, and to allow mobile roaming agreements. Britain agreed to pay increased pensions to Spaniards who had been employed in Gibraltar before the border closed. Spain will be allowed to open a cultural institute from which the Spanish flag will fly. A new noncolonial constitution came into effect in 2007, but the UK retains responsibility for defense, foreign relations, internal security, and financial stability.

## Geography

**Location:** Southwestern Europe, bordering the Strait of Gibraltar, which links the Mediterranean Sea and the North Atlantic Ocean, on the southern coast of Spain
**Geographic coordinates:** 36 08 N, 5 21 W
**Map references:** Europe
**Area:**
*total:* 6.5 sq km
*land:* 6.5 sq km
*water:* 0 sq km

**Area - comparative:** slightly less than one-half the size of Rhode Island
**Land boundaries:**
*total:* 1.2 km
*border countries:* Spain 1.2 km
**Coastline:** 12 km
**Maritime claims:**
*territorial sea:* 3 nm
**Climate:** Mediterranean with mild winters and warm summers
**Terrain:** a narrow coastal lowland borders the Rock of Gibraltar
**Elevation extremes:**
*lowest point:* Mediterranean Sea 0 m
*highest point:* Rock of Gibraltar 426 m
**Natural resources:** none
**Land use:**
*arable land:* 0%
*permanent crops:* 0%
*other:* 100% (2005)
**Irrigated land:** NA
**Natural hazards:** NA
**Environment - current issues:** limited natural freshwater resources: large concrete or natural rock water catchments collect rainwater (no longer used for drinking water) and adequate desalination plant
**Geography - note:** strategic location on Strait of Gibraltar that links the North Atlantic Ocean and Mediterranean Sea

## People

**Population:** 28,034 (July 2009 est.)
**Age structure:**
*0-14 years:* 16.7% (male 2,393/female 2,276)
*15-64 years:* 66.9% (male 9,532/female 9,219)
*65 years and over:* 16.5% (male 2,125/female 2,489) (2009 est.)
**Median age:**
*total:* 40.5 years
*male:* 39.9 years
*female:* 41 years (2009 est.)
**Population growth rate:** 0.111% (2009 est.)
**Birth rate:** 10.67 births/1,000 population (2009 est.)
**Death rate:** 9.46 deaths/1,000 population (2008 est.)
**Net migration rate:** 0 migrant(s)/1,000 population (2009 est.)
**Urbanization:**
*urban population:* 100% of total population (2008)
*rate of urbanization:* 0.1% annual rate of change (2005-10 est.)
**Sex ratio:**
*at birth:* 1.05 male(s)/female
*under 15 years:* 1.05 male(s)/female
*15-64 years:* 1.03 male(s)/female
*65 years and over:* 0.85 male(s)/female
*total population:* 1 male(s)/female (2009 est.)
**Infant mortality rate:**
*total:* 4.83 deaths/1,000 live births
*male:* 5.37 deaths/1,000 live births
*female:* 4.27 deaths/1,000 live births (2009 est.)

**Life expectancy at birth:**
*total population:* 80.19 years
*male:* 77.3 years
*female:* 83.22 years (2009 est.)
**Total fertility rate:** 1.65 children born/woman (2009 est.)
**HIV/AIDS - adult prevalence rate:** NA
**HIV/AIDS - people living with HIV/AIDS:** NA
**HIV/AIDS - deaths:** NA
**Nationality:**
*noun:* Gibraltarian(s)
*adjective:* Gibraltar
**Ethnic groups:** Spanish, Italian, English, Maltese, Portuguese, German, North Africans
**Religions:** Roman Catholic 78.1%, Church of England 7%, other Christian 3.2%, Muslim 4%, Jewish 2.1%, Hindu 1.8%, other or unspecified 0.9%, none 2.9% (2001 census)
**Languages:** English (used in schools and for official purposes), Spanish, Italian, Portuguese
**Literacy:**
*definition:* NA
*total population:* above 80%
*male:* NA
*female:* NA
**Education expenditures:** NA

## Government

**Country name:**
*conventional long form:* none
*conventional short form:* Gibraltar
**Dependency status:** overseas territory of the UK
**Government type:** NA
**Capital:**
*name:* Gibraltar
*geographic coordinates:* 36 08 N, 5 21 W
*time difference:* UTC+1 (6 hours ahead of Washington, DC during Standard Time)
*daylight saving time:* +1hr, begins last Sunday in March; ends last Sunday in October
**Administrative divisions:** none (overseas territory of the UK)
**Independence:** none (overseas territory of the UK)
**National holiday:** National Day, 10 September (1967); note - day of the national referendum to decide whether to remain with the UK or go with Spain
**Constitution:** 5 June 2006; came into force 2 January 2007
**Legal system:** the laws of the UK, where applicable, apply
**Suffrage:** 18 years of age; universal; and British citizens who have been residents six months or more
**Executive branch:**
*chief of state:* Queen ELIZABETH II (since 6 February 1952); represented by Governor Sir Robert FULTON (since 27 October 2006)
*head of government:* Chief Minister Peter CARUANA (since 17 May 1996)
*cabinet:* Council of Ministers appointed from among the 17 elected members of the Parliament by the governor in consultation with the chief minister

*elections:* the monarch is hereditary; governor appointed by the monarch; following legislative elections, the leader of the majority party or the leader of the majority coalition is usually appointed chief minister by the governor

**Legislative branch:** unicameral Parliament (18 seats: 17 members elected by popular vote, 1 for the Speaker appointed by Parliament; members serve four-year terms)

*elections:* last held 11 October 2007 (next to be held not later than October 2011)

*election results:* percent of vote by party - GSD 49.3%, GSLP 31.8%, Gibraltar Liberal Party 13.6%; seats by party - GSD 10, GSLP 4, Gibraltar Liberal Party 3

**Judicial branch:** Supreme Court; Court of Appeal

**Political parties and leaders:** Gibraltar Liberal Party [Joseph GARCIA]; Gibraltar Social Democrats or GSD [Peter CARUANA]; Gibraltar Socialist Labor Party or GSLP [Joseph John BOSSANO]

**Political pressure groups and leaders:** Chamber of Commerce; Gibraltar Representatives Organization; Women's Association

**International organization participation:** Interpol (subbureau), UPU

**Diplomatic representation in the US:** none (overseas territory of the UK)

**Diplomatic representation from the US:** none (overseas territory of the UK)

**Flag description:** two horizontal bands of white (top, double width) and red with a three-towered red castle in the center of the white band; hanging from the castle gate is a gold key centered in the red band

## Economy

**Economy - overview:** Self-sufficient Gibraltar benefits from an extensive shipping trade, offshore banking, and its position as an international conference center. The British military presence has been sharply reduced and now contributes about 7% to the local economy, compared with 60% in 1984. The financial sector, tourism (almost 5 million visitors in 1998), shipping services fees, and duties on consumer goods also generate revenue. The financial sector, the shipping sector, and tourism each contribute 25%-30% of GDP. Telecommunications accounts for another 10%. In recent years, Gibraltar has seen major structural change from a public to a private sector economy, but changes in government spending still have a major impact on the level of employment.

**GDP (purchasing power parity):**
$1.066 billion (2005 est.)
$769 million (2000)

**GDP (official exchange rate):** $1.066 billion (2005 est.)

**GDP - real growth rate:**
7% (2005 est.)

**GDP - per capita (PPP):**
$38,200 (2005 est.)
$27,900 (2000 est.)

**GDP - composition by sector:**
*agriculture:* NA%
*industry:* NA%
*services:* NA%

**Labor force:** 12,690 (including non-Gibraltar laborers) (2001)

**Labor force - by occupation:**
*agriculture:* negligible
*industry:* 40%
*services:* 60% (2001)

**Unemployment rate:**
3% (2005 est.)

**Population below poverty line:** NA%

**Household income or consumption by percentage share:**
*lowest 10%:* NA%
*highest 10%:* NA%

**Budget:**
*revenues:* $455.1 million
*expenditures:* $423.6 million (2005 est.)

**Public debt:** 15.7% of GDP (2005 est.)

**Inflation rate (consumer prices):**
2.9% (2005)

**Agriculture - products:** none

**Industries:** tourism, banking and finance, ship repairing, tobacco

**Industrial production growth rate:** NA%

**Electricity - production:** 142 million kWh (2006 est.)

**Electricity - consumption:** 142 million kWh (2006 est.)

**Electricity - exports:** 0 kWh (2007 est.)

**Electricity - imports:** 0 kWh (2007 est.)

**Oil - production:** 0 bbl/day (2007 est.)

**Oil - consumption:** 22,620 bbl/day (2006 est.)

**Oil - exports:** 0 bbl/day (2005)

**Oil - imports:** 25,080 bbl/day (2005)

**Oil - proved reserves:** 0 bbl (1 January 2006 est.)

**Natural gas - production:** 0 cu m (2007 est.)

**Natural gas - consumption:** 0 cu m (2007 est.)

**Natural gas - exports:** 0 cu m (2007 est.)

**Natural gas - imports:** 0 cu m (2007 est.)

**Natural gas - proved reserves:** 0 cu m (1 January 2006 est.)

**Exports:** $271 million f.o.b. (2004 est.)

**Exports - commodities:** (principally reexports) petroleum 51%, manufactured goods 41%, other 8%

**Imports:** $2.967 billion c.i.f. (2004 est.)

**Imports - commodities:** fuels, manufactured goods, and foodstuffs

**Debt - external:** $NA

**Exchange rates:** Gibraltar pounds (GIP) per US dollar - 0.4993 (2007), 0.5434 (2006), 0.5504 (2005), 0.5462 (2004), 0.6125 (2003)
*note:* the Gibraltar pound is at par with the British pound

## Communications

**Telephones - main lines in use:** 24,512 (2002)
**Telephones - mobile cellular:** 9,797 (2002)
**Telephone system:**
*general assessment:* adequate, automatic domestic system and adequate international facilities
*domestic:* automatic exchange facilities
*international:* country code - 350; radiotelephone; microwave radio relay; satellite earth station - 1 Intelsat (Atlantic Ocean)
**Radio broadcast stations:** AM 1, FM 5, shortwave 0 (1998)
**Television broadcast stations:** 1 (plus 3 repeaters) (1997)
**Internet country code:** .gi
**Internet hosts:** 1,904 (2008)
**Internet users:** 6,200 (2002)

## Transportation

**Airports:** 1 (2008)
**Airports - with paved runways:**
*total:* 1
*1,524 to 2,437 m:* 1 (2008)
**Roadways:**
*total:* 29 km
*paved:* 29 km (2007)
**Merchant marine:**
*total:* 240
*by type:* bulk carrier 5, cargo 125, chemical tanker 51, container 43, passenger 1, petroleum tanker 10, roll on/roll off 5
*foreign-owned:* 225 (Belgium 2, Cyprus 1, Denmark 7, Finland 3, Germany 129, Greece 6, Iceland 1, Morocco 4, Netherlands 21, Norway 33, Sweden 13, UAE 3, UK 2)
*registered in other countries:* 7 (Liberia 5, Panama 1, Saint Vincent and the Grenadines 1) (2008)
**Ports and terminals:** Gibraltar

## Military

**Military branches:** Royal Gibraltar Regiment (2007)
**Manpower available for military service:**
*males age 16-49:* 6,308 (2008 est.)
**Manpower fit for military service:**
*males age 16-49:* 5,234
*females age 16-49:* 5,242 (2009 est.)
**Manpower reaching militarily significant age annually:**
*male:* 186
*female:* 179 (2009 est.)
**Military - note:** defense is the responsibility of the UK; the Royal Gibraltar Regiment replaced the last British regular infantry forces in 1992

## Transnational Issues

**Disputes - international:** in 2002, Gibraltar residents voted overwhelmingly by referendum to reject any "shared sovereignty" arrangement; the government of Gibraltar insists on equal participation in talks between the UK and Spain; Spain disapproves of UK plans to grant Gibraltar even greater autonomy

# Greece

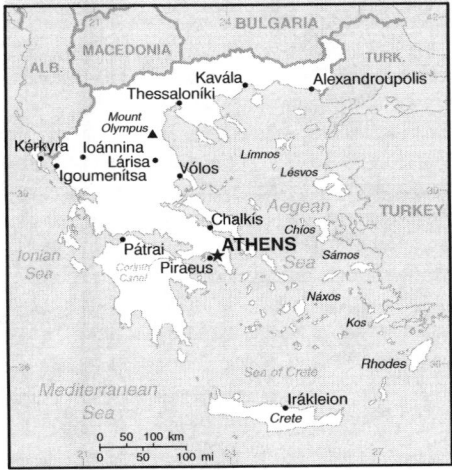

## Introduction

**Background:** Greece achieved independence from the Ottoman Empire in 1829. During the second half of the 19th century and the first half of the 20th century, it gradually added neighboring islands and territories, most with Greek-speaking populations. In World War II, Greece was first invaded by Italy (1940) and subsequently occupied by Germany (1941-44); fighting endured in a protracted civil war between supporters of the king and Communist rebels. Following the latter's defeat in 1949, Greece joined NATO in 1952. A military dictatorship, which in 1967 suspended many political liberties and forced the king to flee the country, lasted seven years. The 1974 democratic elections and a referendum created a parliamentary republic and abolished the monarchy. In 1981, Greece joined the EC (now the EU); it became the 12th member of the European Economic and Monetary Union in 2001.

## Geography

**Location:** Southern Europe, bordering the Aegean Sea, Ionian Sea, and the Mediterranean Sea, between Albania and Turkey
**Geographic coordinates:** 39 00 N, 22 00 E
**Map references:** Europe
**Area:**
*total:* 131,940 sq km
*land:* 130,800 sq km
*water:* 1,140 sq km
**Area - comparative:** slightly smaller than Alabama
**Land boundaries:**
*total:* 1,228 km
*border countries:* Albania 282 km, Bulgaria 494 km, Turkey 206 km, Macedonia 246 km
**Coastline:** 13,676 km
**Maritime claims:**
*territorial sea:* 12 nm
*continental shelf:* 200 m depth or to the depth of exploitation

**Climate:** temperate; mild, wet winters; hot, dry summers
**Terrain:** mostly mountains with ranges extending into the sea as peninsulas or chains of islands
**Elevation extremes:**
*lowest point:* Mediterranean Sea 0 m
*highest point:* Mount Olympus 2,917 m
**Natural resources:** lignite, petroleum, iron ore, bauxite, lead, zinc, nickel, magnesite, marble, salt, hydropower potential
**Land use:**
*arable land:* 20.45%
*permanent crops:* 8.59%
*other:* 70.96% (2005)
**Irrigated land:** 14,530 sq km (2003)
**Total renewable water resources:** 72 cu km (2005)
**Freshwater withdrawal (domestic/industrial/agricultural):**
*total:* 8.7 cu km/yr (16%/3%/81%)
*per capita:* 782 cu m/yr (1997)
**Natural hazards:** severe earthquakes
**Environment - current issues:** air pollution; water pollution
**Environment - international agreements:**
*party to:* Air Pollution, Air Pollution-Nitrogen Oxides, Air Pollution-Sulfur 94, Antarctic-Environmental Protocol, Antarctic-Marine Living Resources, Antarctic Treaty, Biodiversity, Climate Change, Climate Change-Kyoto Protocol, Desertification, Endangered Species, Environmental Modification, Hazardous Wastes, Law of the Sea, Marine Dumping, Ozone Layer Protection, Ship Pollution, Tropical Timber 83, Tropical Timber 94, Wetlands
*signed, but not ratified:* Air Pollution-Persistent Organic Pollutants, Air Pollution-Volatile Organic Compounds
**Geography - note:** strategic location dominating the Aegean Sea and southern approach to Turkish Straits; a peninsular country, possessing an archipelago of about 2,000 islands

## People

**Population:** 10,737,428 (July 2009 est.)
**Age structure:**
*0-14 years:* 14.3% (male 788,722/female 742,270)
*15-64 years:* 66.6% (male 3,568,660/female 3,578,344)
*65 years and over:* 19.2% (male 902,617/female 1,156,815) (2009 est.)
**Median age:**
*total:* 41.8 years
*male:* 40.7 years
*female:* 42.9 years (2009 est.)
**Population growth rate:** 0.127% (2009 est.)
**Birth rate:** 9.45 births/1,000 population (2009 est.)
**Death rate:** 10.42 deaths/1,000 population (2008 est.)
**Net migration rate:** 2.33 migrant(s)/1,000 population (2009 est.)
**Urbanization:**
*urban population:* 61% of total population (2008)
*rate of urbanization:* 0.6% annual rate of change (2005-10 est.)

**Sex ratio:**
*at birth:* 1.06 male(s)/female
*under 15 years:* 1.06 male(s)/female
*15-64 years:* 1 male(s)/female
*65 years and over:* 0.78 male(s)/female
*total population:* 0.96 male(s)/female (2009 est.)
**Infant mortality rate:**
*total:* 5.16 deaths/1,000 live births
*male:* 5.68 deaths/1,000 live births
*female:* 4.62 deaths/1,000 live births (2009 est.)
**Life expectancy at birth:**
*total population:* 79.66 years
*male:* 77.11 years
*female:* 82.37 years (2009 est.)
**Total fertility rate:** 1.37 children born/woman (2009 est.)
**HIV/AIDS - adult prevalence rate:** 0.2% (2007 est.)
**HIV/AIDS - people living with HIV/AIDS:** 11,000 (2007 est.)
**HIV/AIDS - deaths:** fewer than 100 (2007 est.)
**Nationality:**
*noun:* Greek(s)
*adjective:* Greek
**Ethnic groups:** population: Greek 93%, other (foreign citizens) 7% (2001 census)
*note:* percents represent citizenship, since Greece does not collect data on ethnicity
**Religions:** Greek Orthodox 98%, Muslim 1.3%, other 0.7%
**Languages:** Greek 99% (official), other 1% (includes English and French)
**Literacy:**
*definition:* age 15 and over can read and write
*total population:* 96%
*male:* 97.8%
*female:* 94.2% (2001 census)
**School life expectancy (primary to tertiary education):**
*total:* 17 years
*male:* 17 years
*female:* 17 years (2006)
**Education expenditures:** 4.4% of GDP (2005)

## Government

**Country name:**
*conventional long form:* Hellenic Republic
*conventional short form:* Greece
*local long form:* Elliniki Dhimokratia
*local short form:* Ellas or Ellada
*former:* Kingdom of Greece
**Government type:** parliamentary republic
**Capital:**
*name:* Athens
*geographic coordinates:* 37 59 N, 23 44 E
*time difference:* UTC+2 (7 hours ahead of Washington, DC during Standard Time)
*daylight saving time:* +1hr, begins last Sunday in March; ends last Sunday in October
**Administrative divisions:** 51 prefectures (nomoi, singular - nomos) and 1 autonomous region*; Achaia, Agion Oros* (Mt. Athos), Aitolia kai Akarnania, Argolis,

Arkadia, Arta, Attiki, Chalkidiki, Chanion, Chios, Dodekanisos, Drama, Evros, Evrytania, Evvoia, Florina, Fokidos, Fthiotis, Grevena, Ileia, Imathia, Ioannina, Irakleion, Karditsa, Kastoria, Kavala, Kefallinia, Kerkyra, Kilkis, Korinthia, Kozani, Kyklades, Lakonia, Larisa, Lasithi, Lefkas, Lesvos, Magnisia, Messinia, Pella, Pieria, Preveza, Rethynnis, Rodopi, Samos, Serrai, Thesprotia, Thessaloniki, Trikala, Voiotia, Xanthi, Zakynthos

**Independence:** 1829 (from the Ottoman Empire)

**National holiday:** Independence Day, 25 March (1821)

**Constitution:** 11 June 1975; amended March 1986 and April 2001

**Legal system:** based on codified Roman law; judiciary divided into civil, criminal, and administrative courts; accepts compulsory ICJ jurisdiction with reservations

**Suffrage:** 18 years of age; universal and compulsory

**Executive branch:**

*chief of state:* President Karolos PAPOULIAS (since 12 March 2005)

*head of government:* Prime Minister Konstandinos (Kostas) KARAMANLIS (since 7 March 2004)

*cabinet:* Cabinet appointed by the president on the recommendation of the prime minister

*elections:* president elected by parliament for a five-year term (eligible for a second term); election last held 8 February 2005 (next to be held by February 2010); president appoints leader of the party securing plurality of vote in election to become prime minister and form a government

*election results:* Karolos PAPOULIAS elected president; number of parliamentary votes, 279 out of 300

**Legislative branch:** unicameral Parliament or Vouli ton Ellinon (300 seats; members are elected by direct popular vote to serve four-year terms)

*elections:* last held 16 September 2007 (next to be held by 2011)

*election results:* percent of vote by party - ND 41.8%, PASOK 38.1%, KKE 8.2%, Synaspismos 5%, LAOS 3.8%, other 3.1%; seats by party - ND 152, PASOK 102, KKE 22, Synaspismos 14, LAOS 10

**Judicial branch:** Supreme Judicial Court; Special Supreme Tribunal; all judges are appointed for life by the president after consultation with a judicial council

**Political parties and leaders:** Coalition of the Radical Left or SYRIZA [Alekos ALAVANOS]; Communist Party (Marxist-Leninist) [Gr. KONSTANTOPOULOS]; Communist Party of Greece or KKE [Aleka PAPARIGA]; Democratic Revival [Stelios PAPATHEMELIS]; Democratic Universal Hellas [Stergio KRIKELISI]; Ecologist Greens [Ioanna KONTOULI]; Fighting Socialist Party [Nikos KARGOPOULOS]; Greek Ecologists [Dimosthenis VERGIS]; Liberal Alliance [Foris PERIKOS]; Liberal Party [Manolis KALIGIANNIS]; Light-Truth-Justice [Konstantinos MELISSOURGOS]; New Democracy or ND [Konstandinos KARAMANLIS]; Organization for the Reconstruction of the Communist Party of Greece [Ilias ZAFIROPOULOS]; Panhellenic Socialist

Movement or PASOK [Yiorgos PAPANDREOU]; Popular Orthodox Rally or LAOS [Yeoryios KARATZAFERIS]; Radical Left Front [D. DESILLAS]; Regional Urban Development [Nikolaos KOLITIS]; Salvation Party Christian Democracy [Alkiviadis STOILIS]; Union of Centrists [Vassilis LEVENTIS]; United Anti-Capitalist Left [Konstantinos PAPDAKIS]

**Political pressure groups and leaders:** Civil Servants Confederation or ADEDY [Spyros PAPASPYROS]; Federation of Greek Industries or SEV [Dimitris DASKALOPOULOS]; General Confederation of Greek Workers or GSEE [Ioannis PANAGOPOULOS]

**International organization participation:** Australia Group, BIS, BSEC, CE, CERN, EAPC, EBRD, EIB, EMU, ESA, EU, FAO, IAEA, IBRD, ICAO, ICC, ICCt, ICRM, IDA, IEA, IFAD, IFC, IFRCS, IHO, ILO, IMF, IMO, IMSO, Interpol, IOC, IOM, IPU, ISO, ITSO, ITU, ITUC, MIGA, MINURSO, NAM (guest), NATO, NEA, NSG, OAS (observer), OECD, OIF, OPCW, OSCE, PCA, Schengen Convention, SECI, UN, UNCTAD, UNESCO, UNHCR, UNIDO, UNIFIL, UNMIS, UNOMIG, UNWTO, UPU, WCO, WEU, WFTU, WHO, WIPO, WMO, WTO, ZC

**Diplomatic representation in the US:**

*chief of mission:* Ambassador Alexandros P. MALLIAS

*chancery:* 2217 Massachusetts Avenue NW, Washington, DC 20008

*telephone:* [1] (202) 939-1300

*FAX:* [1] (202) 939-1324

*consulate(s) general:* Boston, Chicago, Los Angeles, New York, San Francisco, Tampa

*consulate(s):* Atlanta, Houston, New Orleans

**Diplomatic representation from the US:**

*chief of mission:* Ambassador Daniel V. SPECKHARD

*embassy:* 91 Vasilisis Sophias Avenue, 10160 Athens

*mailing address:* PSC 108, APO AE 09842-0108

*telephone:* [30] (210) 721-2951

*FAX:* [30] (210) 645-6282

*consulate(s) general:* Thessaloniki

**Flag description:** nine equal horizontal stripes of blue alternating with white; there is a blue square in the upper hoist-side corner bearing a white cross; the cross symbolizes Greek Orthodoxy, the established religion of the country

## Economy

**Economy - overview:** Greece has a capitalist economy with the public sector accounting for about 40% of GDP and with per capita GDP about two-thirds that of the leading euro-zone economies. Tourism provides 15% of GDP. Immigrants make up nearly one-fifth of the work force, mainly in agricultural and unskilled jobs. Greece is a major beneficiary of EU aid, equal to about 3.3% of annual GDP. The Greek economy grew by nearly 4.0% per year between 2003 and 2007, due partly to infrastructural spending related to the 2004 Athens Olympic Games, and in part to an increased availability of credit, which has

sustained record levels of consumer spending. But growth dropped to 2.8% in 2008, as a result of the world financial crisis and tightening credit conditions. Greece violated the EU's Growth and Stability Pact budget deficit criteria of no more than 3% of GDP from 2001 to 2006, but finally met that criteria in 2007-08. Public debt, inflation, and unemployment are above the euro-zone average, but are falling. The Greek Government continues to grapple with cutting government spending, reducing the size of the public sector, and reforming the labor and pension systems, in the face of often vocal opposition from the country's powerful labor unions and the general public. The economy remains an important domestic political issue in Greece and, while the ruling New Democracy government has had some success in improving economic growth and reducing the budget deficit, Athens faces long-term challenges in its effort to continue its economic reforms, especially social security reform and privatization.

**GDP (purchasing power parity):**

$343.6 billion (2008 est.)

$334.2 billion (2007)

$321.4 billion (2006)

*note:* data are in 2008 US dollars

**GDP (official exchange rate):** $373.5 billion (2008 est.)

**GDP - real growth rate:**

2.8% (2008 est.)

4% (2007 est.)

4.2% (2006 est.)

**GDP - per capita (PPP):**

$32,000 (2008 est.)

$31,200 (2007 est.)

$30,100 (2006 est.)

*note:* data are in 2008 US dollars

**GDP - composition by sector:**

*agriculture:* 3.5%

*industry:* 23.4%

*services:* 73.1% (2008 est.)

**Labor force:** 4.96 million (2008 est.)

**Labor force - by occupation:**

*agriculture:* 12.4%

*industry:* 22.4%

*services:* 65.1% (2005 est.)

**Unemployment rate:**

8% (2008 est.)

8.3% (2007 est.)

**Population below poverty line:** NA%

**Household income or consumption by percentage share:**

*lowest 10%:* 2.5%

*highest 10%:* 26% (2000 est.)

**Distribution of family income - Gini index:** 33 (2005)

**Investment (gross fixed):** 24.9% of GDP (2008 est.)

**Budget:**

*revenues:* $132.4 billion

*expenditures:* $143.8 billion (2008 est.)

**Public debt:** 90.1% of GDP (2008 est.)

# Greece (continued)

**Inflation rate (consumer prices):**
4.4% (2008 est.)
2.9% (2007 est.)
**Central bank discount rate:** 4%
*note:* this is the European Central Bank's rate on the marginal lending facility, which offers overnight credit to banks in the euro area
**Commercial bank prime lending rate:** 7.71% (31 December 2007)
**Stock of money:** NA
*note:* see entry for the European Union for money supply in the euro area; the European Central Bank (ECB) controls monetary policy for the 16 members of the Economic and Monetary Union (EMU); individual members of the EMU do not control the quantity of money and quasi money circulating within their own borders
**Stock of quasi money:** NA
**Stock of domestic credit:** $392.4 billion (31 December 2007)
**Market value of publicly traded shares:** $264.9 billion (31 December 2007)
**Agriculture - products:** wheat, corn, barley, sugar beets, olives, tomatoes, wine, tobacco, potatoes; beef, dairy products
**Industries:** tourism, food and tobacco processing, textiles, chemicals, metal products; mining, petroleum
**Industrial production growth rate:** 3.2% (2008 est.)
**Electricity - production:** 59.33 billion kWh (2007 est.)
**Electricity - consumption:** 55.98 billion kWh (2006 est.)
**Electricity - exports:** 269 million kWh (2007 est.)
**Electricity - imports:** 5.894 billion kWh (2007 est.)
**Oil - production:** 4,265 bbl/day (2007 est.)
**Oil - consumption:** 441,400 bbl/day (2007 est.)
**Oil - exports:** 125,100 bbl/day (2005)
**Oil - imports:** 527,200 bbl/day (2005)
**Oil - proved reserves:** 10 million bbl (1 January 2008 est.)
**Natural gas - production:** 24 million cu m (2007 est.)
**Natural gas - consumption:** 4.069 billion cu m (2007 est.)
**Natural gas - exports:** 0 cu m (2007 est.)
**Natural gas - imports:** 4.1 billion cu m (2007 est.)
**Natural gas - proved reserves:** 1.982 billion cu m (1 January 2008 est.)
**Current account balance:** -$36.26 billion (2008 est.)
**Exports:** $27.4 billion f.o.b. (2008 est.)
**Exports - commodities:** food and beverages, manufactured goods, petroleum products, chemicals, textiles
**Exports - partners:** Germany 11.6%, Italy 10.8%, Cyprus 6.6%, Bulgaria 6.5%, UK 5.5%, Romania 4.5%, France 4.2%, US 4.2% (2007)
**Imports:** $82.28 billion f.o.b. (2008 est.)
**Imports - commodities:** machinery, transport equipment, fuels, chemicals

**Imports - partners:** Germany 12.9%, Italy 11.7%, Russia 5.6%, France 5.6%, China 5%, Netherlands 5% (2007)
**Reserves of foreign exchange and gold:** $2.425 billion (31 December 2008 est.)
**Debt - external:** $92.19 billion (31 December 2008 est.)
**Stock of direct foreign investment - at home:** $55.19 billion (2008 est.)
**Stock of direct foreign investment - abroad:** $25.33 billion (2008 est.)
**Exchange rates:** euros (EUR) per US dollar - 0.6827 (2008 est.), 0.7345 (2007), 0.7964 (2006), 0.8041 (2005), 0.8054 (2004)

## Communications

**Telephones - main lines in use:** 6.227 million (2007)
**Telephones - mobile cellular:** 11.997 million (2007)
**Telephone system:**
*general assessment:* adequate, modern networks reach all areas; good mobile telephone and international service
*domestic:* microwave radio relay trunk system; extensive open-wire connections; submarine cable to offshore islands
*international:* country code - 30; landing point for the SEA-ME-WE-3 optical telecommunications submarine cable that provides links to Europe, Middle East, and Asia; a number of smaller submarine cables provide connectivity to various parts of Europe, the Middle East, and Cyprus; tropospheric scatter; satellite earth stations - 4 (2 Intelsat - 1 Atlantic Ocean and 1 Indian Ocean, 1 Eutelsat, and 1 Inmarsat - Indian Ocean region)
**Radio broadcast stations:** AM 26, FM 88, shortwave 4 (1998)
**Television broadcast stations:** 36 (plus 1,341 repeaters); also 2 stations in the American Armed Forces Radio and Television Service (1995)
**Internet country code:** .gr
**Internet hosts:** 1.626 million (2008)
**Internet users:** 2.54 million (2007)

## Transportation

**Airports:** 81 (2008)
**Airports - with paved runways:**
*total:* 66
*over 3,047 m:* 5
*2,438 to 3,047 m:* 15
*1,524 to 2,437 m:* 20
*914 to 1,523 m:* 17
*under 914 m:* 9 (2008)
**Airports - with unpaved runways:**
*total:* 15
*914 to 1,523 m:* 3
*under 914 m:* 12 (2008)
**Heliports:** 9 (2007)
**Pipelines:** gas 1,197 km; oil 75 km (2008)

**Railways:**
*total:* 2,571 km
*standard gauge:* 1,565 km 1.435-m gauge (764 km electrified)
*narrow gauge:* 961 km 1.000-m gauge; 22 km 0.750-m gauge
*dual gauge:* 23 km combined 1.435 m and 1.000-m gauges (three rail system) (2006)
**Roadways:**
*total:* 117,533 km
*paved:* 107,895 km (includes 880 km of expressways)
*unpaved:* 9,638 km (2005)
**Waterways:** 6 km
*note:* Corinth Canal (6 km) crosses the Isthmus of Corinth; shortens sea voyage by 325 km (2008)
**Merchant marine:**
*total:* 869
*by type:* bulk carrier 260, cargo 66, carrier 1, chemical tanker 66, combination ore/oil 2, container 45, liquefied gas 10, passenger 13, passenger/cargo 115, petroleum tanker 274, roll on/roll off 15, specialized tanker 2
*foreign-owned:* 64 (Belgium 16, Cyprus 7, Turkey 1, UK 32, US 8)
*registered in other countries:* 2,357 (Antigua and Barbuda 3, Bahamas 209, Barbados 12, Belize 1, Bermuda 9, Brazil 1, Cambodia 3, Cayman Islands 16, China 2, Comoros 6, Cyprus 259, Denmark 4, Dominica 10, Egypt 8, Georgia 5, Gibraltar 6, Honduras 4, Hong Kong 22, Isle of Man 50, Italy 6, Jamaica 6, North Korea 1, Lebanon 2, Liberia 358, Maldives 1, Malta 452, Marshall Islands 269, Norway 3, Panama 510, Philippines 4, Portugal 4, Russia 1, Saint Kitts and Nevis 3, Saint Vincent and the Grenadines 71, Sao Tome and Principe 1, Saudi Arabia 3, Sierra Leone 1, Singapore 15, Slovakia 2, Turkey 1, UAE 3, Uruguay 1, Vanuatu 1, Venezuela 3, unknown 5) (2008)
**Ports and terminals:** Agioitheodoroi, Aspropyrgos, Pachi, Piraeus, Thessaloniki

## Military

**Military branches:** Hellenic Army (Ellinikos Stratos, ES), Hellenic Navy (Ellinikos Polemiko Navtiko, EPN), Hellenic Air Force (Elliniki Polimiki Aeroporia, EPA) (2009)
**Military service age and obligation:** 19-45 years of age for compulsory military service; during wartime the law allows for recruitment beginning January of the year of inductee's 18th birthday, thus including 17 year olds; 17 years of age for volunteers; conscript service obligation - 1 year for all services; women are eligible for voluntary military service (2008)
**Manpower available for military service:**
*males age 16-49:* 2,535,174
*females age 16-49:* 2,517,273 (2008 est.)
**Manpower fit for military service:**
*males age 16-49:* 2,067,878
*females age 16-49:* 2,050,289 (2009 est.)

# Greece *(continued)*

**Manpower reaching militarily significant age annually:**
*male:* 53,401
*female:* 50,084 (2009 est.)
**Military expenditures:** 4.3% of GDP (2005 est.)

## Transnational Issues

**Disputes - international:** Greece and Turkey continue discussions to resolve their complex maritime, air, territorial, and boundary disputes in the Aegean Sea; Cyprus question with Turkey; Greece rejects the use of the name Macedonia or Republic of Macedonia; the mass migration of unemployed Albanians still remains a problem for developed countries, chiefly Greece and Italy

**Illicit drugs:** a gateway to Europe for traffickers smuggling cannabis and heroin from the Middle East and Southwest Asia to the West and precursor chemicals to the East; some South American cocaine transits or is consumed in Greece; money laundering related to drug trafficking and organized crime

# Greenland
*(part of the Kingdom of Denmark)*

## Introduction

**Background:** Greenland, the world's largest island, is about 81% ice-capped. Vikings reached the island in the 10th century from Iceland; Danish colonization began in the 18th century, and Greenland was made an integral part of Denmark in 1953. It joined the European Community (now the EU) with Denmark in 1973, but withdrew in 1985 over a dispute centered on stringent fishing quotas. Greenland was granted self-government in 1979 by the Danish parliament; the law went into effect the following year. Greenland voted in favor of increased self-rule in November 2008 and acquired complete responsibilty for internal affairs in June 2009. Denmark, however, continues to exercise control of Greenland's foreign affairs in consultation with Greenland's Home Rule Government.

## Geography

**Location:** Northern North America, island between the Arctic Ocean and the North Atlantic Ocean, northeast of Canada
**Geographic coordinates:** 72 00 N, 40 00 W
**Map references:** Arctic Region
**Area:**
*total:* 2,166,086 sq km
*land:* 2,166,086 sq km (410,449 sq km ice-free, 1,755,637 sq km ice-covered) (2000 est.)
**Area - comparative:** slightly more than three times the size of Texas
**Land boundaries:** 0 km
**Coastline:** 44,087 km
**Maritime claims:**
*territorial sea:* 3 nm
*exclusive fishing zone:* 200 nm or agreed boundaries or median line
*continental shelf:* 200 nm or agreed boundaries or median line
**Climate:** arctic to subarctic; cool summers, cold winters
**Terrain:** flat to gradually sloping icecap covers all but a narrow, mountainous, barren, rocky coast
**Elevation extremes:**
*lowest point:* Atlantic Ocean 0 m
*highest point:* Gunnbjorn 3,700 m
**Natural resources:** coal, iron ore, lead, zinc, molybdenum, diamonds, gold, platinum, niobium, tantalite, uranium, fish, seals, whales, hydropower, possible oil and gas
**Land use:**
*arable land:* 0%
*permanent crops:* 0%
*other:* 100% (2005)
**Irrigated land:** NA
**Natural hazards:** continuous permafrost over northern two-thirds of the island
**Environment - current issues:** protection of the arctic environment; preservation of the Inuit traditional way of life, including whaling and seal hunting
**Geography - note:** dominates North Atlantic Ocean between North America and Europe; sparse population confined to small settlements along coast; close to one-quarter of the population lives in the capital, Nuuk; world's second largest ice cap

## People

**Population:** 57,600 (July 2009 est.)
**Age structure:**
*0-14 years:* 23% (male 6,727/female 6,533)
*15-64 years:* 70.1% (male 21,696/female 18,669)
*65 years and over:* 6.9% (male 2,000/female 1,975) (2009 est.)
**Median age:**
*total:* 33.5 years
*male:* 34.9 years
*female:* 31.9 years (2009 est.)
**Population growth rate:** 0.062% (2009 est.)
**Birth rate:** 14.76 births/1,000 population (2009 est.)

# Greenland (continued)

**Death rate:** 8.23 deaths/1,000 population (2008 est.)
**Net migration rate:** -5.99 migrant(s)/1,000 population (2009 est.)
**Urbanization:**
*urban population:* 84% of total population (2008)
*rate of urbanization:* 0.9% annual rate of change (2005-10 est.)
**Sex ratio:**
*at birth:* 1.05 male(s)/female
*under 15 years:* 1.03 male(s)/female
*15-64 years:* 1.16 male(s)/female
*65 years and over:* 1.01 male(s)/female
*total population:* 1.12 male(s)/female (2009 est.)
**Infant mortality rate:**
*total:* 10.72 deaths/1,000 live births
*male:* 12.26 deaths/1,000 live births
*female:* 9.1 deaths/1,000 live births (2009 est.)
**Life expectancy at birth:**
*total population:* 70.07 years
*male:* 67.44 years
*female:* 72.85 years (2009 est.)
**Total fertility rate:** 2.19 children born/woman (2009 est.)
**HIV/AIDS - adult prevalence rate:** NA
**HIV/AIDS - people living with HIV/AIDS:** 100 (1999)
**HIV/AIDS - deaths:** NA
**Nationality:**
*noun:* Greenlander(s)
*adjective:* Greenlandic
**Ethnic groups:** Greenlander 88% (Inuit and Greenland-born whites), Danish and others 12% (2000)
**Religions:** Evangelical Lutheran
**Languages:** Greenlandic (East Inuit), Danish, English
**Literacy:**
*definition:* age 15 and over can read and write
*total population:* 100%
*male:* 100%
*female:* 100% (2001 est.)
**Education expenditures:** NA

## Government

**Country name:**
*conventional long form:* none
*conventional short form:* Greenland
*local long form:* none
*local short form:* Kalaallit Nunaat
**Dependency status:** part of the Kingdom of Denmark; self-governing overseas administrative division of Denmark since 1979
**Government type:** parliamentary democracy within a constitutional monarchy
**Capital:**
*name:* Nuuk (Godthab)
*geographic coordinates:* 64 11 N, 51 45 W
*time difference:* UTC-3 (2 hours ahead of Washington, DC during Standard Time)
*daylight saving time:* +1hr, begins last Sunday in March; ends last Sunday in October
*note:* Greenland is divided into four time zones

**Administrative divisions:** 3 districts (landsdele); Avannaa (Nordgronland), Tunu (Ostgronland), Kitaa (Vestgronland)
*note:* there are 18 municipalities in Greenland
**Independence:** none (extensive self-rule as part of the Kingdom of Denmark; foreign affairs is the responsibility of Denmark, but Greenland actively participates in international agreements relating to Greenland)
**National holiday:** June 21 (longest day)
**Constitution:** 5 June 1953 (Danish constitution)
**Legal system:** the laws of Denmark, where applicable, apply
**Suffrage:** 18 years of age; universal
**Executive branch:**
*chief of state:* Queen MARGRETHE II of Denmark (since 14 January 1972), represented by High Commissioner Soren MOLLER (since April 2005)
*head of government:* Prime Minister Hans ENOKSEN (since 14 December 2002)
*cabinet:* Home Rule Government is elected by the Parliament (Landsting) on the basis of the strength of parties
*elections:* the monarchy is hereditary; high commissioner appointed by the monarch; prime minister is elected by parliament (usually the leader of the majority party);
*election results:* Hans ENOKSEN reelected prime minister
*note:* government coalition - Siumut and Inuit Ataqatigiit
**Legislative branch:** unicameral Parliament or Landsting (31 seats; members are elected by popular vote on the basis of proportional representation to serve four-year terms)
*elections:* last held on 15 November 2005 (next to be held by December 2009)
*election results:* percent of vote by party - Inuit Ataqatigiit 43.7%, Siumut 26.5%, Demokratiit 12.7%, Atassut 10.9%; Kattusseqatigiit 3.8%, other 2.4%; seats by party - IA 14, Siumut 9, Demokraatiit 4, Atassut 3, Kattusseqatigiit 1
*note:* two representatives were elected to the Danish Parliament or Folketing on 13 November 2007 (next to be held in November 2011); percent of vote by party - NA; seats by party - Siumut 1, Inuit Ataqatigiit 1
**Judicial branch:** High Court or Landsret (appeals can be made to the Ostre Landsret or Eastern Division of the High Court or Supreme Court in Copenhagen)
**Political parties and leaders:** Atassut Party (Solidarity) [Finn KARLSEN] (a conservative party favoring continuing close relations with Denmark); Demokratiit [Per BERTHELSEN]; Inuit Ataqatigiit or IA (Eskimo Brotherhood) [Josef MOTZFELDT] (a leftist party favoring complete independence from Denmark rather than home rule); Kattusseqatigiit (Candidate List) (an independent right-of-center party with no official platform); Siumut (Forward Party) [Hans ENOKSEN] (a social democratic party advocating more distinct Greenlandic identity and greater autonomy from Denmark)

**Political pressure groups and leaders:**
*other:* conservationists; environmentalists
**International organization participation:** Arctic Council, NC, NIB, UPU
**Diplomatic representation in the US:** none (self-governing overseas administrative division of Denmark)
**Diplomatic representation from the US:** none (self-governing overseas administrative division of Denmark)
**Flag description:** two equal horizontal bands of white (top) and red with a large disk slightly to the hoist side of center - the top half of the disk is red, the bottom half is white

## Economy

**Economy - overview:** The economy remains critically dependent on exports of fish and a substantial subsidy from the Danish Government, which supplies about half of government revenues. The public sector, including publicly-owned enterprises and the municipalities, plays the dominant role in the economy. Several interesting hydrocarbon and mineral exploration activities are ongoing and in 2007 a US firm signed an agreement with the Greenland Home Rule government to study the feasibility of building a multi-billion dollar aluminum smelter and hydropower plant.
**GDP (purchasing power parity):**
$1.1 billion (2001 est.)
**GDP (official exchange rate):** $1.7 billion (2005)
**GDP - real growth rate:**
2% (2005 est.)
**GDP - per capita (PPP):**
$20,000 (2001 est.)
**GDP - composition by sector:**
*agriculture:* NA%
*industry:* NA%
*services:* NA%
**Labor force:** 32,120 (2004)
**Unemployment rate:**
9.3% (2005 est.)
**Population below poverty line:** NA%
**Household income or consumption by percentage share:**
*lowest 10%:* NA%
*highest 10%:* NA%
**Budget:**
*revenues:* $1.36 billion
*expenditures:* $1.27 billion (2005)
**Inflation rate (consumer prices):**
1% (2005 est.)
**Agriculture - products:** forage crops, garden and greenhouse vegetables; sheep, reindeer; fish
**Industries:** fish processing (mainly shrimp and Greenland halibut); gold, niobium, tantalite, uranium, iron and diamond mining; handicrafts, hides and skins, small shipyards
**Industrial production growth rate:** NA%
**Electricity - production:** 305 million kWh (2006 est.)

# Greenland *(continued)*

**Electricity - consumption:** 283.7 million kWh (2006 est.)

**Electricity - exports:** 0 kWh (2007 est.)

**Electricity - imports:** 0 kWh (2007 est.)

**Oil - production:** 0 bbl/day (2007 est.)

**Oil - consumption:** 3,927 bbl/day (2006 est.)

**Oil - exports:** 149.5 bbl/day (2005)

**Oil - imports:** 4,089 bbl/day (2005)

**Oil - proved reserves:** 0 bbl (1 January 2006 est.)

**Natural gas - production:** 0 cu m (2007 est.)

**Natural gas - consumption:** 0 cu m (2007 est.)

**Natural gas - exports:** 0 cu m (2007 est.)

**Natural gas - imports:** 0 cu m (2007 est.)

**Natural gas - proved reserves:** 0 cu m (1 January 2006 est.)

**Exports:** $480 million f.o.b. (2006)

**Exports - commodities:** fish and fish products 94% (prawns 63%) (2001 est.)

**Exports - partners:** Denmark 61.8%, Japan 9.9%, Canada 7.3%, China 5.8% (2007)

**Imports:** $712 million c.i.f. (2006)

**Imports - commodities:** machinery and transport equipment, manufactured goods, food, petroleum products

**Imports - partners:** Denmark 68.1%, Sweden 19.3%, Canada 2.5% (2007)

**Debt - external:** $25 million (1999)

**Exchange rates:** Danish kroner (DKK) per US dollar -5.0236 (2008 est.), 5.4797 (2007), 5.9468 (2006), 5.9969 (2005), 5.9911 (2004)

## Communications

**Telephones - main lines in use:** 36,000 (2006)

**Telephones - mobile cellular:** 66,400 (2007)

**Telephone system:**
*general assessment:* adequate domestic and international service provided by satellite, cables and microwave radio relay; totally digitalized in 1995
*domestic:* microwave radio relay and satellite
*international:* country code - 299; satellite earth stations - 15 (12 Intelsat, 1 Eutelsat, 2 Americom GE-2 (all Atlantic Ocean)) (2000)

**Radio broadcast stations:** AM 5, FM 14, shortwave 0 (2008)

**Television broadcast stations:** 1 (plus some local low-power stations, and 3 American Forces Radio and Television Service (AFRTS) stations (1997)

**Internet country code:** .gl

**Internet hosts:** 14,132 (2008)

**Internet users:** 52,000 (2007)

## Transportation

**Airports:** 15 (2008)

**Airports - with paved runways:**
*total:* 10
*2,438 to 3,047 m:* 2
*1,524 to 2,437 m:* 1
*914 to 1,523 m:* 1
*under 914 m:* 6 (2008)

**Airports - with unpaved runways:**
*total:* 5
*1,524 to 2,437 m:* 1
*914 to 1,523 m:* 2
*under 914 m:* 2 (2008)

**Roadways:**
*note:* although there are short roads in towns, there are no roads between towns; inter-urban transport takes place either by sea or air (2005)

**Merchant marine:**
*total:* 2
*by type:* cargo 1, passenger 1 (2008)

**Ports and terminals:** Sisimiut

## Military

**Military branches:** no regular military forces

**Manpower available for military service:**
*males age 16-49:* 15,221 (2008 est.)

**Manpower fit for military service:**
*males age 16-49:* 10,809
*females age 16-49:* 11,437 (2009 est.)

**Manpower reaching militarily significant age annually:**
*male:* 532
*female:* 491 (2009 est.)

**Military - note:** defense is the responsibility of Denmark

## Transnational Issues

**Disputes - international:** managed dispute between Canada and Denmark over Hans Island in the Kennedy Channel between Canada's Ellesmere Island and Greenland

# Grenada

## Introduction

**Background:** Carib Indians inhabited Grenada when COLUMBUS discovered the island in 1498, but it remained uncolonized for more than a century. The French settled Grenada in the 17th century, established sugar estates, and imported large numbers of African slaves. Britain took the island in 1762 and vigorously expanded sugar production. In the 19th century, cacao eventually surpassed sugar as the main export crop; in the 20th century, nutmeg became the leading export. In 1967, Britain gave Grenada autonomy over its internal affairs. Full independence was attained in 1974 making Grenada one of the smallest independent countries in the Western Hemisphere. Grenada was seized by a Marxist military council on 19 October 1983. Six days later the island was invaded by US forces and those of six other Caribbean nations, which quickly captured the ringleaders and their hundreds of Cuban advisers. Free elections were reinstituted the following year and have continued since that time. Hurricane Ivan struck Grenada in September of 2004 causing severe damage.

## Geography

**Location:** Caribbean, island between the Caribbean Sea and Atlantic Ocean, north of Trinidad and Tobago

**Geographic coordinates:** 12 07 N, 61 40 W

**Map references:** Central America and the Caribbean

**Area:**
*total:* 344 sq km
*land:* 344 sq km
*water:* 0 sq km

**Area - comparative:** twice the size of Washington, DC

**Land boundaries:** 0 km

**Coastline:** 121 km

**Maritime claims:**
*territorial sea:* 12 nm
*exclusive economic zone:* 200 nm

# Grenada (continued)

**Climate:** tropical; tempered by northeast trade winds

**Terrain:** volcanic in origin with central mountains

**Elevation extremes:**

*lowest point:* Caribbean Sea 0 m

*highest point:* Mount Saint Catherine 840 m

**Natural resources:** timber, tropical fruit, deepwater harbors

**Land use:**

*arable land:* 5.88%

*permanent crops:* 29.41%

*other:* 64.71% (2005)

**Irrigated land:** NA

**Total renewable water resources:** NA

**Natural hazards:** lies on edge of hurricane belt; hurricane season lasts from June to November

**Environment - current issues:** NA

**Environment - international agreements:**

*party to:* Biodiversity, Climate Change, Climate Change-Kyoto Protocol, Desertification, Endangered Species, Law of the Sea, Ozone Layer Protection, Whaling

*signed, but not ratified:* none of the selected agreements

**Geography - note:** the administration of the islands of the Grenadines group is divided between Saint Vincent and the Grenadines and Grenada

## People

**Population:** 90,739 (July 2009 est.)

**Age structure:**

*0-14 years:* 32% (male 14,608/female 14,410)

*15-64 years:* 65.2% (male 31,278/female 27,873)

*65 years and over:* 2.8% (male 1,268/female 1,302) (2009 est.)

**Median age:**

*total:* 22.8 years

*male:* 23.3 years

*female:* 22.3 years (2009 est.)

**Population growth rate:** 0.468% (2009 est.)

**Birth rate:** 21.32 births/1,000 population (2009 est.)

**Death rate:** 6.31 deaths/1,000 population (2008 est.)

**Net migration rate:** -10.55 migrant(s)/1,000 population (2009 est.)

**Urbanization:**

*urban population:* 31% of total population (2008)

*rate of urbanization:* 0.3% annual rate of change (2005-10 est.)

**Sex ratio:**

*at birth:* 1 male(s)/female

*under 15 years:* 1.01 male(s)/female

*15-64 years:* 1.12 male(s)/female

*65 years and over:* 0.97 male(s)/female

*total population:* 1.08 male(s)/female (2009 est.)

**Infant mortality rate:**

*total:* 13.23 deaths/1,000 live births

*male:* 12.95 deaths/1,000 live births

*female:* 13.52 deaths/1,000 live births (2009 est.)

**Life expectancy at birth:**

*total population:* 65.95 years

*male:* 64.06 years

*female:* 67.85 years (2009 est.)

**Total fertility rate:** 2.23 children born/woman (2009 est.)

**HIV/AIDS - adult prevalence rate:** NA

**HIV/AIDS - people living with HIV/AIDS:** NA

**HIV/AIDS - deaths:** NA

**Nationality:**

*noun:* Grenadian(s)

*adjective:* Grenadian

**Ethnic groups:** black 82%, mixed black and European 13%, European and East Indian 5%, and trace of Arawak/Carib Amerindian

**Religions:** Roman Catholic 53%, Anglican 13.8%, other Protestant 33.2%

**Languages:** English (official), French patois

**Literacy:**

*definition:* age 15 and over can read and write

*total population:* 96%

*male:* NA

*female:* NA (2003 est.)

**School life expectancy (primary to tertiary education):**

*total:* 12 years

*male:* 12 years

*female:* 12 years (2005)

**Education expenditures:** 5.2% of GDP (2003)

## Government

**Country name:**

*conventional long form:* none

*conventional short form:* Grenada

**Government type:** parliamentary democracy and a Commonwealth realm

**Capital:**

*name:* Saint George's

*geographic coordinates:* 12 03 N, 61 45 W

*time difference:* UTC-4 (1 hour ahead of Washington, DC during Standard Time)

**Administrative divisions:** 6 parishes and 1 dependency*; Carriacou and Petite Martinique*, Saint Andrew, Saint David, Saint George, Saint John, Saint Mark, Saint Patrick

**Independence:** 7 February 1974 (from the UK)

**National holiday:** Independence Day, 7 February (1974)

**Constitution:** 19 December 1973

**Legal system:** based on English common law; has not accepted compulsory ICJ jurisdiction

**Suffrage:** 18 years of age; universal

**Executive branch:**

*chief of state:* Queen ELIZABETH II (since 6 February 1952); represented by Governor General Carlyle Arnold GLEAN (since 27 November 2008)

*head of government:* Prime Minister Tillman THOMAS (since 9 July 2008)

*cabinet:* Cabinet appointed by the governor general on the advice of the prime minister

*elections:* the monarch is hereditary; governor general appointed by the monarch; following legislative elections, the leader of the majority party or the leader of the majority coalition is usually appointed prime minister by the governor general

**Legislative branch:** bicameral Parliament consists of the Senate (13 seats, 10 appointed by the government and 3 by the leader of the opposition) and the House of Representatives (15 seats; members are elected by popular vote to serve five-year terms)

*elections:* last held on 8 July 2008 (next to be held in 2013)

*election results:* House of Representatives - percent of vote by party - NA; seats by party - NDC 11, NNP 4

**Judicial branch:** Eastern Caribbean Supreme Court, consisting of a court of Appeal and a High Court of Justice (two High Court judges are assigned to and reside in Grenada); Itinerant Court of Appeal three judges; member of the Caribbean Court of Justice (CCJ)

**Political parties and leaders:** Grenada United Labor Party or GULP [Gloria Payne BANFIELD]; National Democratic Congress or NDC [Tillman THOMAS]; New National Party or NNP [Keith MITCHELL]

**Political pressure groups and leaders:** Committee for Human Rights in Grenada or CHRG; New Jewel Movement Support Group; The British Grenada Friendship Society; The New Jewel 19 Committee

**International organization participation:** ACP, C, Caricom, CDB, FAO, G-77, IBRD, ICAO, ICRM, IDA, IFAD, IFC, IFRCS, ILO, IMF, IMO, Interpol, IOC, ITU, ITUC, MIGA, NAM, OAS, OECS, OPANAL, OPCW, UN, UNCTAD, UNESCO, UNIDO, UPU, WFTU, WHO, WIPO, WTO

**Diplomatic representation in the US:**

*chief of mission:* Ambassador Denis G. ANTOINE

*chancery:* 1701 New Hampshire Avenue NW, Washington, DC 20009

*telephone:* [1] (202) 265-2561

*FAX:* [1] (202) 265-2468

*consulate(s) general:* New York

**Diplomatic representation from the US:**

*chief of mission:* the US Ambassador to Barbados is accredited to Grenada

*embassy:* Lance-aux-Epines Stretch, Saint George's

*mailing address:* P. O. Box 54, Saint George's

*telephone:* [1] (473) 444-1173 through 1177

*FAX:* [1] (473) 444-4820

**Flag description:** a rectangle divided diagonally into yellow triangles (top and bottom) and green triangles (hoist side and outer side), with a red border around the flag; there are seven yellow, five-pointed stars with three centered in the top red border, three centered in the bottom red border, and one on a red disk superimposed at the center of the flag; there is also a symbolic nutmeg pod on the hoist-side triangle (Grenada is the world's second-largest producer of nutmeg, after Indonesia); the seven stars represent the seven administrative divisions

## Economy

**Economy - overview:** Grenada relies on tourism as its main source of foreign exchange especially since the construction of an international airport in 1985.

# Grenada (continued)

Hurricanes Ivan (2004) and Emily (2005) severely damaged the agricultural sector - particularly nutmeg and cocoa cultivation - which had been a key driver of economic growth. Grenada has rebounded from the devastating effects of the hurricanes but is now saddled with the debt burden from the rebuilding process. Public debt-to-GDP is nearly 110%, leaving the THOMAS administration limited room to engage in public investments and social spending. Strong performances in construction and manufacturing, together with the development of tourism and an offshore financial industry, have also contributed to growth in national output; however, economic growth will likely slow in 2009 because of the global economic slowdown's effects on tourism and remittances.

**GDP (purchasing power parity):**
$1.211 billion (2008 est.)
$1.168 billion (2007)
$1.12 billion (2006)
*note:* data are in 2008 US dollars

**GDP (official exchange rate):** $657 million (2008 est.)

**GDP - real growth rate:**
3.7% (2008 est.)
4.3% (2007 est.)
-1.1% (2006 est.)

**GDP - per capita (PPP):**
$13,400 (2008 est.)
$13,000 (2007 est.)
$12,500 (2006 est.)
*note:* data are in 2008 US dollars

**GDP - composition by sector:**
*agriculture:* 5.4%
*industry:* 18%
*services:* 76.6% (2003)

**Labor force:** 42,300 (1996)

**Labor force - by occupation:**
*agriculture:* 24%
*industry:* 14%
*services:* 62% (1999 est.)

**Unemployment rate:**
12.5% (2000)

**Population below poverty line:** 32% (2000)

**Household income or consumption by percentage share:**
*lowest 10%:* NA%
*highest 10%:* NA%

**Budget:**
*revenues:* $85.8 million
*expenditures:* $102.1 million (1997)

**Inflation rate (consumer prices):**
3.7% (2007 est.)

**Central bank discount rate:** 6.5% (31 December 2007)

**Commercial bank prime lending rate:** 9.76% (31 December 2007)

**Stock of money:** $151.2 million (31 December 2007)

**Stock of quasi money:** $533.4 million (31 December 2007)

**Stock of domestic credit:** $575.8 million (31 December 2007)

**Market value of publicly traded shares:** $NA

**Agriculture - products:** bananas, cocoa, nutmeg, mace, citrus, avocados, root crops, sugarcane, corn, vegetables

**Industries:** food and beverages, textiles, light assembly operations, tourism, construction

**Electricity - production:** 167.2 million kWh (2006 est.)

**Electricity - consumption:** 144.2 million kWh (2006 est.)

**Electricity - exports:** 0 kWh (2007 est.)

**Electricity - imports:** 0 kWh (2007 est.)

**Oil - production:** 0 bbl/day (2007 est.)

**Oil - consumption:** 2,043 bbl/day (2006 est.)

**Oil - exports:** 0 bbl/day (2005)

**Oil - imports:** 1,844 bbl/day (2005)

**Oil - proved reserves:** 0 bbl (1 January 2006 est.)

**Natural gas - production:** 0 cu m (2007 est.)

**Natural gas - consumption:** 0 cu m (2007 est.)

**Natural gas - exports:** 0 cu m (2007 est.)

**Natural gas - imports:** 0 cu m (2007 est.)

**Natural gas - proved reserves:** 0 cu m (1 January 2006 est.)

**Current account balance:** -$138 million (2007 est.)

**Exports:** $38 million (2006)

**Exports - commodities:** bananas, cocoa, nutmeg, fruit and vegetables, clothing, mace

**Exports - partners:** Jamaica 92.8%, Saint Lucia 1.3%, US 1.2% (2007)

**Imports:** $343 million f.o.b. (2006)

**Imports - commodities:** food, manufactured goods, machinery, chemicals, fuel

**Imports - partners:** Trinidad and Tobago 36.5%, US 23.3%, Italy 4.1% (2007)

**Debt - external:** $347 million (2004)

**Exchange rates:** East Caribbean dollars (XCD) per US dollar - 2.7 (2007), 2.7 (2006), 2.7 (2005), 2.7 (2004), 2.7 (2003)

## Communications

**Telephones - main lines in use:** 27,700 (2006)

**Telephones - mobile cellular:** 46,200 (2006)

**Telephone system:**
*general assessment:* automatic, islandwide telephone system
*domestic:* interisland VHF and UHF radiotelephone links
*international:* country code - 1-473; landing point for the East Caribbean Fiber Optic System (ECFS) submarine cable with links to 13 other islands in the eastern Caribbean extending from the British Virgin Islands to Trinidad; SHF radiotelephone links to Trinidad and Tobago and Saint Vincent; VHF and UHF radio links to Trinidad

**Radio broadcast stations:** AM 2, FM 13, shortwave 0 (1998)

**Television broadcast stations:** 2 (1997)

**Internet country code:** .gd

**Internet hosts:** 9 (2008)

**Internet users:** 23,000 (2007)

## Transportation

**Airports:** 3 (2008)

**Airports - with paved runways:**
*total:* 3
*2,438 to 3,047 m:* 1
*1,524 to 2,437 m:* 1
*under 914 m:* 1 (2008)

**Roadways:**
*total:* 1,127 km
*paved:* 687 km
*unpaved:* 440 km (2000)

**Ports and terminals:** Saint George's

## Military

**Military branches:** no regular military forces; Royal Grenada Police Force (includes Coast Guard) (2007)

**Manpower available for military service:**
*males age 16-49:* 27,309 (2008 est.)

**Manpower fit for military service:**
*males age 16-49:* 20,483
*females age 16-49:* 20,923 (2009 est.)

**Manpower reaching militarily significant age annually:**
*male:* 982
*female:* 937 (2009 est.)

**Military expenditures:** NA

## Transnational Issues

**Disputes - international:** none

**Illicit drugs:** small-scale cannabis cultivation; lesser transshipment point for marijuana and cocaine to US

# Guam
*(territory of the US)*

## Introduction

**Background:** Guam was ceded to the US by Spain in 1898. Captured by the Japanese in 1941, it was retaken by the US three years later. The military installation on the island is one of the most strategically important US bases in the Pacific.

## Geography

**Location:** Oceania, island in the North Pacific Ocean, about three-quarters of the way from Hawaii to the Philippines
**Geographic coordinates:** 13 28 N, 144 47 E
**Map references:** Oceania
**Area:**
*total:* 541.3 sq km
*land:* 541.3 sq km
*water:* 0 sq km
**Area - comparative:** three times the size of Washington, DC
**Land boundaries:** 0 km
**Coastline:** 125.5 km
**Maritime claims:**
*territorial sea:* 12 nm
*exclusive economic zone:* 200 nm
**Climate:** tropical marine; generally warm and humid, moderated by northeast trade winds; dry season (January to June), rainy season (July to December); little seasonal temperature variation
**Terrain:** volcanic origin, surrounded by coral reefs; relatively flat coralline limestone plateau (source of most fresh water), with steep coastal cliffs and narrow coastal plains in north, low hills in center, mountains in south
**Elevation extremes:**
*lowest point:* Pacific Ocean 0 m
*highest point:* Mount Lamlam 406 m
**Natural resources:** aquatic wildlife (supporting tourism), fishing (largely undeveloped)

**Land use:**
*arable land:* 3.64%
*permanent crops:* 18.18%
*other:* 78.18% (2005)
**Irrigated land:** NA
**Natural hazards:** frequent squalls during rainy season; relatively rare but potentially destructive typhoons (June - December)
**Environment - current issues:** extirpation of native bird population by the rapid proliferation of the brown tree snake, an exotic, invasive species
**Geography - note:** largest and southernmost island in the Mariana Islands archipelago; strategic location in western North Pacific Ocean

## People

**Population:** 178,430 (July 2009 est.)
**Age structure:**
*0-14 years:* 27.8% (male 25,651/female 23,904)
*15-64 years:* 65.2% (male 59,304/female 56,995)
*65 years and over:* 7% (male 5,786/female 6,790) (2009 est.)
**Median age:**
*total:* 29.1 years
*male:* 28.8 years
*female:* 29.4 years (2009 est.)
**Population growth rate:** 1.365% (2009 est.)
**Birth rate:** 18.22 births/1,000 population (2009 est.)
**Death rate:** 4.65 deaths/1,000 population (2008 est.)
**Net migration rate:** NA
**Urbanization:**
*urban population:* 93% of total population (2008)
*rate of urbanization:* 1.3% annual rate of change (2005-10 est.)
**Sex ratio:**
*at birth:* 1.06 male(s)/female
*under 15 years:* 1.07 male(s)/female
*15-64 years:* 1.04 male(s)/female
*65 years and over:* 0.85 male(s)/female
*total population:* 1.03 male(s)/female
**Infant mortality rate:**
*total:* 6.05 deaths/1,000 live births
*male:* 6.47 deaths/1,000 live births
*female:* 5.6 deaths/1,000 live births (2009 est.)
**Life expectancy at birth:**
*total population:* 78.01 years
*male:* 74.97 years
*female:* 81.23 years (2009 est.)
**Total fertility rate:** 2.54 children born/woman (2009 est.)
**HIV/AIDS - adult prevalence rate:** NA
**HIV/AIDS - people living with HIV/AIDS:** NA
**HIV/AIDS - deaths:** NA
**Nationality:**
*noun:* Guamanian(s) (US citizens)
*adjective:* Guamanian
**Ethnic groups:** Chamorro 37.1%, Filipino 26.3%, other Pacific islander 11.3%, white 6.9%, other Asian 6.3%, other ethnic origin or race 2.3%, mixed 9.8% (2000 census)

**Religions:** Roman Catholic 85%, other 15% (1999 est.)
**Languages:** English 38.3%, Chamorro 22.2%, Philippine languages 22.2%, other Pacific island languages 6.8%, Asian languages 7%, other languages 3.5% (2000 census)
**Literacy:**
*definition:* age 15 and over can read and write
*total population:* 99%
*male:* 99%
*female:* 99% (1990 est.)
**Education expenditures:** NA

## Government

**Country name:**
*conventional long form:* Territory of Guam
*conventional short form:* Guam
*local long form:* Guahan
*local short form:* Guahan
**Dependency status:** organized, unincorporated territory of the US with policy relations between Guam and the US under the jurisdiction of the Office of Insular Affairs, US Department of the Interior
**Government type:** NA
**Capital:**
*name:* Hagatna (Agana)
*geographic coordinates:* 13 28 N, 144 44 E
*time difference:* UTC+10 (15 hours ahead of Washington, DC during Standard Time)
**Administrative divisions:** none (territory of the US)
**Independence:** none (territory of the US)
**National holiday:** Discovery Day, first Monday in March (1521)
**Constitution:** Organic Act of Guam, 1 August 1950
**Legal system:** modeled on US; US federal laws apply
**Suffrage:** 18 years of age; universal; US citizens but do not vote in US presidential elections
**Executive branch:**
*chief of state:* President Barack H. OBAMA (since 20 January 2009); Vice President Joseph R. BIDEN (since 20 January 2009)
*head of government:* Governor Felix P. CAMACHO (since 6 January 2003); Lieutenant Governor Dr. Michael W. CRUZ (since 1 January 2007)
*cabinet:* heads of executive departments; appointed by the governor with the consent of the Guam legislature
*elections:* under the US Constitution, residents of unincorporated territories, such as Guam, do not vote in elections for US president and vice president; however, they may vote in Democratic and Republican presidential primary elections; governor and lieutenant governor elected on the same ticket by popular vote for four-year term (can serve two consecutive terms, then must wait a full term before running again); election last held 7 November 2006 (next to be held in November 2010)
*election results:* Felix P. CAMACHO reelected governor; Dr. Michael W. CRUZ elected lieutenant governor; percent of vote - NA

**Legislative branch:** unicameral Legislature (15 seats; members are elected by popular vote to serve two-year terms)
*elections:* last held 4 November 2008 (next to be held in November 2010)
*election results:* percent of vote by party - NA; seats by party - Democratic Party 10, Republican Party 5
*note:* Guam elects one nonvoting delegate to the US House of Representatives; election last held 4 November 2008 (next to be held in November 2010); results - percent of vote by party - NA; seats by party - Democratic Party 1
**Judicial branch:** Federal District Court (judge is appointed by the president); Territorial Superior Court (judges appointed for eight-year terms by the governor)
**Political parties and leaders:** Democratic Party [leader Michael PHILLIPS]; Republican Party [Philip J. FLORES] (controls the legislature)
**Political pressure groups and leaders:** Guam Federation of Teachers' Union; Guam Waterworks Authority Workers
*other:* activists; indigenous groups
**International organization participation:** IOC, SPC, UPU
**Diplomatic representation in the US:** none (territory of the US)
**Diplomatic representation from the US:** none (territory of the US)
**Flag description:** territorial flag is dark blue with a narrow red border on all four sides; centered is a red-bordered, pointed, vertical ellipse containing a beach scene, outrigger canoe with sail, and a palm tree with the word GUAM superimposed in bold red letters; US flag is the national flag

## E c o n o m y

**Economy - overview:** The economy depends largely on US military spending and tourism. Total US grants, wage payments, and procurement outlays amounted to $1.3 billion in 2004. Over the past 30 years, the tourist industry has grown to become the largest income source following national defense. The Guam economy continues to experience expansion in both its tourism and military sectors.
**GDP (purchasing power parity):**
$2.5 billion (2005 est.)
**GDP (official exchange rate):** $2.773 billion (2001)
**GDP - real growth rate:** NA%
**GDP - per capita (PPP):**
$15,000 (2005 est.)
**GDP - composition by sector:**
*agriculture:* NA%
*industry:* NA%
*services:* NA%
**Labor force:** 62,050 (2002 est.)
**Labor force - by occupation:**
*agriculture:* 26%
*industry:* 10%
*services:* 64% (2004 est.)
**Unemployment rate:**
11.4% (2002 est.)

**Population below poverty line:** 23% (2001 est.)
**Household income or consumption by percentage share:**
*lowest 10%:* NA%
*highest 10%:* NA%
**Budget:**
*revenues:* $319.6 million
*expenditures:* $427.8 million (2002 est.)
**Inflation rate (consumer prices):**
2.5% (2005 est.)
**Agriculture - products:** fruits, copra, vegetables; eggs, pork, poultry, beef
**Industries:** US military, tourism, construction, transshipment services, concrete products, printing and publishing, food processing, textiles
**Industrial production growth rate:** NA%
**Electricity - production:** 1.789 billion kWh (2006 est.)
**Electricity - consumption:** 1.664 billion kWh (2006 est.)
**Electricity - exports:** 0 kWh (2007 est.)
**Electricity - imports:** 0 kWh (2007 est.)
**Oil - production:** 0 bbl/day (2007 est.)
**Oil - consumption:** 12,780 bbl/day (2007 est.)
**Oil - exports:** 0 bbl/day (2005)
**Oil - imports:** 13,530 bbl/day (2005)
**Oil - proved reserves:** 0 bbl (1 January 2006 est.)
**Natural gas - production:** 0 cu m (2007 est.)
**Natural gas - consumption:** 0 cu m (2007 est.)
**Natural gas - exports:** 0 cu m (2007 est.)
**Natural gas - imports:** 0 cu m (2007 est.)
**Natural gas - proved reserves:** 0 cu m (1 January 2006 est.)
**Exports:** $45 million f.o.b. (2004 est.)
**Exports - commodities:** transshipments of refined petroleum products, construction materials, fish, food and beverage products
**Imports:** $701 million f.o.b. (2004 est.)
**Imports - commodities:** petroleum and petroleum products, food, manufactured goods
**Debt - external:** $NA
**Exchange rates:** the US dollar is used

## C o m m u n i c a t i o n s

**Telephones - main lines in use:** 65,500 (2003)
**Telephones - mobile cellular:** 98,000 (2004)
**Telephone system:**
*general assessment:* modern system, integrated with US facilities for direct dialing, including free use of 800 numbers
*domestic:* modern digital system, including cellular mobile service and local access to the Internet
*international:* country code - 1-671; major landing point for submarine cables between Asia and the US (Guam is a trans-Pacific communications hub for major carriers linking the US and Asia); satellite earth stations - 2 Intelsat (Pacific Ocean)
**Radio broadcast stations:** AM 3, FM 11, shortwave 2 (2005)
**Television broadcast stations:** 3 (2006)
**Internet country code:** .gu

**Internet hosts:** 36 (2008)
**Internet users:** 65,000 (2005)

## T r a n s p o r t a t i o n

**Airports:** 5; note - 2 serviceable (2008)
**Airports - with paved runways:**
*total:* 4
*over 3,047 m:* 2
*2,438 to 3,047 m:* 1 - closed
*914 to 1,523 m:* 1 - closed (2008)
**Airports - with unpaved runways:**
*total:* 1
*under 914 m:* 1 (2008)
**Roadways:**
*total:* 1,045 km (2007)
**Ports and terminals:** Apra Harbor

## M i l i t a r y

**Manpower fit for military service:**
*males age 16-49:* 37,563
*females age 16-49:* 36,083 (2009 est.)
**Manpower reaching militarily significant age annually:**
*male:* 1,677
*female:* 1,581 (2009 est.)
**Military - note:** defense is the responsibility of the US

## T r a n s n a t i o n a l   I s s u e s

**Disputes - international:** none

# Guatemala

## Introduction

**Background:** The Mayan civilization flourished in Guatemala and surrounding regions during the first millennium A.D. After almost three centuries as a Spanish colony, Guatemala won its independence in 1821. During the second half of the 20th century, it experienced a variety of military and civilian governments, as well as a 36-year guerrilla war. In 1996, the government signed a peace agreement formally ending the conflict, which had left more than 100,000 people dead and had created, by some estimates, some 1 million refugees.

## Geography

**Location:** Central America, bordering the North Pacific Ocean, between El Salvador and Mexico, and bordering the Gulf of Honduras (Caribbean Sea) between Honduras and Belize
**Geographic coordinates:** 15 30 N, 90 15 W
**Map references:** Central America and the Caribbean
**Area:**
*total:* 108,890 sq km
*land:* 108,430 sq km
*water:* 460 sq km
**Area - comparative:** slightly smaller than Tennessee
**Land boundaries:**
*total:* 1,687 km
*border countries:* Belize 266 km, El Salvador 203 km, Honduras 256 km, Mexico 962 km
**Coastline:** 400 km
**Maritime claims:**
*territorial sea:* 12 nm
*exclusive economic zone:* 200 nm
*continental shelf:* 200 m depth or to the depth of exploitation

**Climate:** tropical; hot, humid in lowlands; cooler in highlands
**Terrain:** mostly mountains with narrow coastal plains and rolling limestone plateau
**Elevation extremes:**
*lowest point:* Pacific Ocean 0 m
*highest point:* Volcan Tajumulco 4,211 m
**Natural resources:** petroleum, nickel, rare woods, fish, chicle, hydropower
**Land use:**
*arable land:* 13.22%
*permanent crops:* 5.6%
*other:* 81.18% (2005)
**Irrigated land:** 1,300 sq km (2003)
**Total renewable water resources:** 111.3 cu km (2000)
**Freshwater withdrawal (domestic/industrial/agricultural):**
*total:* 2.01 cu km/yr (6%/13%/80%)
*per capita:* 160 cu m/yr (2000)
**Natural hazards:** numerous volcanoes in mountains, with occasional violent earthquakes; Caribbean coast extremely susceptible to hurricanes and other tropical storms
**Environment - current issues:** deforestation in the Peten rainforest; soil erosion; water pollution
**Environment - international agreements:**
*party to:* Antarctic Treaty, Biodiversity, Climate Change, Climate Change-Kyoto Protocol, Desertification, Endangered Species, Environmental Modification, Hazardous Wastes, Law of the Sea, Marine Dumping, Ozone Layer Protection, Ship Pollution, Wetlands, Whaling
*signed, but not ratified:* none of the selected agreements
**Geography - note:** no natural harbors on west coast

## People

**Population:** 13,276,517 (July 2009 est.)
**Age structure:**
*0-14 years:* 39.4% (male 2,664,058/ female 2,573,006)
*15-64 years:* 56.8% (male 3,655,184/ female 3,884,331)
*65 years and over:* 3.8% (male 231,652/ female 268,286) (2009 est.)
**Median age:**
*total:* 19.4 years
*male:* 18.9 years
*female:* 20 years (2009 est.)
**Population growth rate:** 2.066% (2009 est.)
**Birth rate:** 27.98 births/1,000 population (2009 est.)
**Death rate:** 5.19 deaths/1,000 population (2008 est.)
**Net migration rate:** -2.21 migrant(s)/1,000 population (2009 est.)
**Urbanization:**
*urban population:* 49% of total population (2008)
*rate of urbanization:* 3.4% annual rate of change (2005-10 est.)

**Sex ratio:**
*at birth:* 1.05 male(s)/female
*under 15 years:* 1.03 male(s)/female
*15-64 years:* 0.94 male(s)/female
*65 years and over:* 0.86 male(s)/female
*total population:* 0.97 male(s)/female (2009 est.)
**Infant mortality rate:**
*total:* 27.84 deaths/1,000 live births
*male:* 30.2 deaths/1,000 live births
*female:* 25.35 deaths/1,000 live births (2009 est.)
**Life expectancy at birth:**
*total population:* 70.29 years
*male:* 68.49 years
*female:* 72.19 years (2009 est.)
**Total fertility rate:** 3.47 children born/woman (2009 est.)
**HIV/AIDS - adult prevalence rate:** 0.8% (2007 est.)
**HIV/AIDS - people living with HIV/AIDS:** 59,000 (2007 est.)
**HIV/AIDS - deaths:** 3,900 (2007 est.)
**Major infectious diseases:**
*degree of risk:* high
*food or waterborne diseases:* bacterial diarrhea, hepatitis A, and typhoid fever
*vectorborne disease:* dengue fever and malaria
*water contact disease:* leptospirosis (2009)
**Nationality:**
*noun:* Guatemalan(s)
*adjective:* Guatemalan
**Ethnic groups:** Mestizo (mixed Amerindian-Spanish -in local Spanish called Ladino) and European 59.4%, K'iche 9.1%, Kaqchikel 8.4%, Mam 7.9%, Q'eqchi 6.3%, other Mayan 8.6%, indigenous non-Mayan 0.2%, other 0.1% (2001 census)
**Religions:** Roman Catholic, Protestant, indigenous Mayan beliefs
**Languages:** Spanish 60%, Amerindian languages 40% (23 officially recognized Amerindian languages, including Quiche, Cakchiquel, Kekchi, Mam, Garifuna, and Xinca)
**Literacy:**
*definition:* age 15 and over can read and write
*total population:* 69.1%
*male:* 75.4%
*female:* 63.3% (2002 census)
**School life expectancy (primary to tertiary education):**
*total:* 10 years
*male:* 11 years
*female:* 10 years (2006)
**Education expenditures:** 2.6% of GDP (2006)

## Government

**Country name:**
*conventional long form:* Republic of Guatemala
*conventional short form:* Guatemala
*local long form:* Republica de Guatemala
*local short form:* Guatemala
**Government type:** constitutional democratic republic

# Guatemala (continued)

**Capital:**

*name:* Guatemala

*geographic coordinates:* 14 37 N, 90 31 W

*time difference:* UTC-6 (1 hour behind Washington, DC during Standard Time)

*daylight saving time:* +1hr, begins last Sunday in April; ends last Friday in September; note - there is no DST planned for 2007-2009

**Administrative divisions:** 22 departments (departamentos, singular - departamento); Alta Verapaz, Baja Verapaz, Chimaltenango, Chiquimula, El Progreso, Escuintla, Guatemala, Huehuetenango, Izabal, Jalapa, Jutiapa, Peten, Quetzaltenango, Quiche, Retalhuleu, Sacatepequez, San Marcos, Santa Rosa, Solola, Suchitepequez, Totonicapan, Zacapa

**Independence:** 15 September 1821 (from Spain)

**National holiday:** Independence Day, 15 September (1821)

**Constitution:** 31 May 1985, effective 14 January 1986; suspended 25 May 1993; reinstated 5 June 1993; amended November 1993

**Legal system:** civil law system; judicial review of legislative acts; has not accepted compulsory ICJ jurisdiction

**Suffrage:** 18 years of age; universal; note - active duty members of the armed forces may not vote and are restricted to their barracks on election day

**Executive branch:**

*chief of state:* President Alvaro COLOM Caballeros (since 14 January 2008); Vice President Jose Rafael ESPADA (since 14 January 2008); note - the president is both the chief of state and head of government

*head of government:* President Alvaro COLOM Caballeros (since 14 January 2008); Vice President Jose Rafael ESPADA (since 14 January 2008)

*cabinet:* Council of Ministers appointed by the president

*elections:* president elected by popular vote for a four-year term (may not serve consecutive terms); election last held 9 September 2007; runoff held 4 November 2007 (next to be held September 2011)

*election results:* Alvaro COLOM Caballeros elected president; percent of vote - Alvaro COLOM Caballeros 52.8%, Otto PEREZ Molina 47.2%

**Legislative branch:** unicameral Congress of the Republic or Congreso de la Republica (158 seats; members are elected by popular vote to serve four-year terms)

*elections:* last held 9 September 2007 (next to be held in September 2011)

*election results:* percent of vote by party - UNE 30.4%, GANA 23.4%, PP 18.9%, FRG 9.5%, PU 5.1%, other 12.7%; seats by party - UNE 48, GANA 37, PP 30, FRG 15, PU 8, CASA 5, EG 4, PAN 4, UCN 4, URNG 2, UD 1

**Judicial branch:** Constitutional Court or Corte de Constitucionalidad is Guatemala's highest court (five judges are elected for concurrent five-year terms); Supreme Court of Justice or Corte Suprema de Justicia (13 members serve concurrent five-year terms and elect a president of the Court each year from among their number; the president of the Supreme Court of Justice also supervises trial judges around the country, who are named to five-year terms)

**Political parties and leaders:** Center of Social Action or CASA [Eduardo SUGER]; Democracy Front or FRENTE [Alfonso CABRERA]; Democratic Union or UD [Manuel CONDE Orellana]; Encounter for Guatemala or EG [Nineth MONTENGRO]; Grand National Alliance or GANA [Alfredo VILLA]; Guatemalan National Revolutionary Unity or URNG [Hector NUILA]; Guatemalan Republican Front or FRG [Efrain RIOS Montt]; National Advancement Party or PAN [Juan Guillermo GUTIERREZ]; National Unity for Hope or UNE [Juan Jose ALFARO Lemus]; Nationalist Change Union or UCN [Mario ESTRADA]; Patriot Party or PP [Ret. Gen. Otto PEREZ Molina]; Unionista Party or PU [Fritz GARCIA-GALLONT]

**Political pressure groups and leaders:** Agrarian Owners Group or UNAGRO; Alliance Against Impunity or AAI; Committee for Campesino Unity or CUC; Coordinating Committee of Agricultural, Commercial, Industrial, and Financial Associations or CACIF; Mutual Support Group or GAM

**International organization participation:** BCIE, CACM, FAO, G-24, G-77, IADB, IAEA, IBRD, ICAO, ICC, ICRM, IDA, IFAD, IFC, IFRCS, IHO, ILO, IMF, IMO, Interpol, IOC, IOM, IPU, ISO (correspondent), ITSO, ITU, ITUC, LAES, LAIA (observer), MIGA, MINUSTAH, MONUC, NAM, OAS, OPANAL, OPCW, PCA, RG, SICA, UN, UNCTAD, UNESCO, UNIDO, UNIFIL, Union Latina, UNMIS, UNOCI, UNWTO, UPU, WCL, WCO, WFTU, WHO, WIPO, WMO, WTO

**Diplomatic representation in the US:**

*chief of mission:* Ambassador Francisco VILLAGRAN de Leon

*chancery:* 2220 R Street NW, Washington, DC 20008

*telephone:* [1] (202) 745-4952

*FAX:* [1] (202) 745-1908

*consulate(s) general:* Atlanta, Chicago, Denver, Houston, Los Angeles, Miami, New York, Phoenix, Providence, San Francisco

**Diplomatic representation from the US:**

*chief of mission:* Ambassador Stephen G. MCFARLAND

*embassy:* 7-01 Avenida Reforma, Zone 10, Guatemala City

*mailing address:* APO AA 34024

*telephone:* [502] 2326-4000

*FAX:* [502] 2326-4654

**Flag description:** three equal vertical bands of light blue (hoist side), white, and light blue, with the coat of arms centered in the white band; the coat of arms includes a green and red quetzal (the national bird) and a scroll bearing the inscription LIBERTAD 15 DE SEPTIEMBRE DE 1821 (the original date of independence from Spain) all superimposed on a pair of crossed rifles and a pair of crossed swords and framed by a wreath

## Economy

**Economy - overview:** Guatemala is the most populous of the Central American countries with a GDP per capita roughly one-half that of Argentina, Brazil, and Chile. The agricultural sector accounts for about one-tenth of GDP, two-fifths of exports, and half of the labor force. Coffee, sugar, and bananas are the main products, with sugar exports benefiting from increased global demand for ethanol. The 1996 signing of peace accords, which ended 36 years of civil war, removed a major obstacle to foreign investment, and Guatemala since then has pursued important reforms and macroeconomic stabilization. The Central American Free Trade Agreement (CAFTA) entered into force in July 2006 and has since spurred increased investment in the export sector, but concerns over security, the lack of skilled workers and poor infrastructure continued to hamper foreign participation. The distribution of income remains highly unequal with more than half of the population below the national poverty line. Other ongoing challenges include increasing government revenues, negotiating further assistance from international donors, curtailing drug trafficking and rampant crime, and narrowing the trade deficit. Given Guatemala's large expatriate community in the United States, it is the top remittance recipient in Central America, with inflows serving as a primary source of foreign income equivalent to nearly two-thirds of exports. Economic growth will slow in 2009 as export demand from US and other Central American markets drop and foreign investment slows amid the global slowdown.

**GDP (purchasing power parity):**

$68.02 billion (2008 est.)

$65.53 billion (2007)

$62 billion (2006)

*note:* data are in 2008 US dollars

**GDP (official exchange rate):** $36.28 billion (2008 est.)

**GDP - real growth rate:**

3.8% (2008 est.)

5.7% (2007 est.)

5.3% (2006 est.)

**GDP - per capita (PPP):**

$5,200 (2008 est.)

$5,100 (2007 est.)

$5,000 (2006 est.)

*note:* data are in 2008 US dollars

**GDP - composition by sector:**

*agriculture:* 13.2%

*industry:* 25.8%

*services:* 61% (2008 est.)

**Labor force:** 4.054 million (2008 est.)

**Labor force - by occupation:**

*agriculture:* 50%

*industry:* 15%

*services:* 35% (1999 est.)

**Unemployment rate:**

3.2% (2005 est.)

**Population below poverty line:** 56.2% (2004 est.)

# Guatemala (continued)

**Household income or consumption by percentage share:**
*lowest 10%:* 0.9%
*highest 10%:* 43.4% (2002)
**Distribution of family income - Gini index:** 55.1 (2007)
**Investment (gross fixed):** 20.3% of GDP (2008 est.)
**Budget:**
*revenues:* $4.944 billion
*expenditures:* $5.647 billion (2008 est.)
**Public debt:** 23.7% of GDP (2008 est.)
**Inflation rate (consumer prices):**
12.2% (2008 est.)
6.8% (2007 est.)
**Central bank discount rate:** NA
**Commercial bank prime lending rate:** 12.84% (31 December 2007)
**Stock of money:** $6.227 billion (31 December 2007)
**Stock of quasi money:** $8.928 billion (31 December 2007)
**Stock of domestic credit:** $13.96 billion (31 December 2007)
**Market value of publicly traded shares:** $NA
**Agriculture - products:** sugarcane, corn, bananas, coffee, beans, cardamom; cattle, sheep, pigs, chickens
**Industries:** sugar, textiles and clothing, furniture, chemicals, petroleum, metals, rubber, tourism
**Industrial production growth rate:** 3.5% (2008 est.)
**Electricity - production:** 7.643 billion kWh (2006 est.)
**Electricity - consumption:** 6.617 billion kWh (2006 est.)
**Electricity - exports:** 131.9 million kWh (2007 est.)
**Electricity - imports:** 8.11 million kWh (2007 est.)
**Oil - production:** 15,820 bbl/day (2007 est.)
**Oil - consumption:** 74,230 bbl/day (2006 est.)
**Oil - exports:** 15,560 bbl/day (2006 est.)
**Oil - imports:** 72,960 bbl/day (2006 est.)
**Oil - proved reserves:** 83.07 million bbl (1 January 2008 est.)
**Natural gas - production:** 0 cu m (2007 est.)
**Natural gas - consumption:** 0 cu m (2007 est.)
**Natural gas - exports:** 0 cu m (2007 est.)
**Natural gas - imports:** 0 cu m (2007 est.)
**Natural gas - proved reserves:** 2.96 billion cu m (1 January 2006 est.)
**Current account balance:** -$3.316 billion (2008 est.)
**Exports:** $8.028 billion f.o.b. (2008 est.)
**Exports - commodities:** coffee, sugar, petroleum, apparel, bananas, fruits and vegetables, cardamom
**Exports - partners:** US 42.2%, El Salvador 9.6%, Honduras 8.6%, Mexico 6.5%, Costa Rica 4.5% (2007)
**Imports:** $15.42 billion f.o.b. (2008 est.)
**Imports - commodities:** fuels, machinery and transport equipment, construction materials, grain, fertilizers, electricity

**Imports - partners:** US 34.9%, Mexico 9.9%, China 6.8%, El Salvador 4.6%, Costa Rica 4.1% (2007)
**Reserves of foreign exchange and gold:** $4.229 billion (31 December 2008 est.)
**Debt - external:** $6.337 billion (31 December 2008 est.)
**Exchange rates:** quetzales (GTQ) per US dollar - 7.5895 (2008 est.), 7.6833 (2007), 7.6026 (2006), 7.6339 (2005), 7.9465 (2004)

## Communications

**Telephones - main lines in use:** 1.355 million (2006)
**Telephones - mobile cellular:** 10.15 million (2007)
**Telephone system:**
*general assessment:* fairly modern network centered in the city of Guatemala
*domestic:* state-owned telecommunications company privatized in the late 1990s opening the way for competition; fixed-line teledensity 11 per 100 persons; fixed-line investments are being concentrated on improving rural connectivity; mobile-cellular teledensity 80 per 100 persons
*international:* country code - 502; landing point for both the Americas Region Caribbean Ring System (ARCOS-1) and the SAM-1 fiber optic submarine cable system that together provide connectivity to South and Central America, parts of the Caribbean, and the US; connected to Central American Microwave System; satellite earth station - 1 Intelsat (Atlantic Ocean)
**Radio broadcast stations:** AM 130, FM 487, shortwave 15 (2000)
**Television broadcast stations:** 26 (plus 27 repeaters) (1997)
**Internet country code:** .gt
**Internet hosts:** 124,095 (2008)
**Internet users:** 1.32 million (2006)

## Transportation

**Airports:** 374 (2008)
**Airports - with paved runways:**
*total:* 12
*2,438 to 3,047 m:* 3
*1,524 to 2,437 m:* 2
*914 to 1,523 m:* 4
*under 914 m:* 3 (2008)
**Airports - with unpaved runways:**
*total:* 362
*2,438 to 3,047 m:* 1
*1,524 to 2,437 m:* 5
*914 to 1,523 m:* 86
*under 914 m:* 270 (2008)
**Pipelines:** oil 480 km (2008)
**Railways:**
*total:* 886 km
*narrow gauge:* 886 km 0.914-m gauge (2006)
**Roadways:**
*total:* 14,095 km
*paved:* 4,863 km (includes 75 km of expressways)
*unpaved:* 9,232 km (2000)

**Waterways:** 990 km
*note:* 260 km navigable year round; additional 730 km navigable during high-water season (2007)
**Ports and terminals:** Puerto Quetzal, Santo Tomas de Castilla

## Military

**Military branches:** Army, Navy (includes Marines), Air Force
**Military service age and obligation:** all male citizens between the ages of 18 and 50 are liable for military service; conscript service obligation varies from 12 to 24 months; women can serve as officers (2008)
**Manpower available for military service:**
*males age 16-49:* 2,861,696
*females age 16-49:* 3,062,967 (2008 est.)
**Manpower fit for military service:**
*males age 16-49:* 2,401,297
*females age 16-49:* 2,725,572 (2009 est.)
**Manpower reaching militarily significant age annually:**
*male:* 165,910
*female:* 163,760 (2009 est.)
**Military expenditures:** 0.4% of GDP (2006)

## Transnational Issues

**Disputes - international:** annual ministerial meetings under the OAS-initiated Agreement on the Framework for Negotiations and Confidence Building Measures continue to address Guatemalan land and maritime claims in Belize and the Caribbean Sea; the Line of Adjacency created under the 2002 Differendum serves in lieu of the contiguous international boundary to control squatting in the sparsely inhabited rain forests of Belize's border region; Mexico must deal with thousands of impoverished Guatemalans and other Central Americans who cross the porous border looking for work in Mexico and the United States
**Refugees and internally displaced persons:**
*IDPs:* undetermined (the UN does not estimate there are any IDPs, although some NGOs estimate over 200,000 IDPs as a result of over three decades of internal conflict that ended in 1996) (2007)
**Trafficking in persons:**
*current situation:* Guatemala is a source, transit, and destination country for Guatemalans and Central Americans trafficked for the purposes of commercial sexual exploitation and forced labor; human trafficking is a significant and growing problem in the country; Guatemalan women and children are trafficked within the country for commercial sexual exploitation, primarily to Mexico and the United States; Guatemalan men, women, and children are also trafficked within the country, and to Mexico and the United States, for forced labor
*tier rating:* Tier 2 Watch List - for a second consecutive year, Guatemala is on the Tier 2 Watch List for its failure to provide evidence of increasing efforts to combat trafficking in persons, particularly

# Guatemala (continued)

with respect to ensuring that trafficking offenders are appropriately prosecuted for their crimes; while prosecutors initiated trafficking prosecutions, they continued to face problems in court with application of Guatemala's comprehensive anti-trafficking law; the government made modest improvements to its protection efforts, but assistance remained inadequate overall in 2007 (2008)

**Illicit drugs:** major transit country for cocaine and heroin; in 2005, cultivated 100 hectares of opium poppy after reemerging as a potential source of opium in 2004; potential production of less than 1 metric ton of pure heroin; marijuana cultivation for mostly domestic consumption; proximity to Mexico makes Guatemala a major staging area for drugs (particularly for cocaine); money laundering is a serious problem; corruption is a major problem

# Guernsey
*(British crown dependency)*

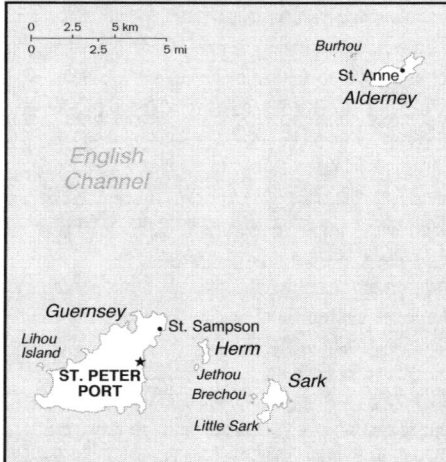

## Introduction

**Background:** Guernsey and the other Channel Islands represent the last remnants of the medieval Dukedom of Normandy, which held sway in both France and England. The islands were the only British soil occupied by German troops in World War II. Guernsey is a British crown dependency, but is not part of the UK. However, the UK Government is constitutionally responsible for its defense and international representation.

## Geography

**Location:** Western Europe, islands in the English Channel, northwest of France
**Geographic coordinates:** 49 28 N, 2 35 W
**Map references:** Europe
**Area:**
*total:* 78 sq km
*land:* 78 sq km
*water:* 0 sq km
*note:* includes Alderney, Guernsey, Herm, Sark, and some other smaller islands
**Area - comparative:** about one-half the size of Washington, DC
**Land boundaries:** 0 km
**Coastline:** 50 km
**Maritime claims:**
*territorial sea:* 3 nm
*exclusive fishing zone:* 12 nm
**Climate:** temperate with mild winters and cool summers; about 50% of days are overcast
**Terrain:** mostly level with low hills in southwest
**Elevation extremes:**
*lowest point:* Atlantic Ocean 0 m
*highest point:* unnamed location on Sark 114 m
**Natural resources:** cropland
**Land use:**
*arable land:* NA
*permanent crops:* NA
*other:* NA

**Irrigated land:** NA
**Natural hazards:** NA
**Environment - current issues:** NA
**Geography - note:** large, deepwater harbor at Saint Peter Port

## People

**Population:** 65,870 (July 2009 est.)
**Age structure:**
*0-14 years:* 14.4% (male 4,793/female 4,668)
*15-64 years:* 67.5% (male 22,058/female 22,433)
*65 years and over:* 18.1% (male 5,078/female 6,840) (2009 est.)
**Median age:**
*total:* 42.5 years
*male:* 41.4 years
*female:* 43.4 years (2009 est.)
**Population growth rate:** 0.21% (2009 est.)
**Birth rate:** 8.46 births/1,000 population (2009 est.)
**Death rate:** 10.09 deaths/1,000 population (2008 est.)
**Net migration rate:** 3.8 migrant(s)/1,000 population (2009 est.)
**Urbanization:**
*urban population:* 31% of total population (2008)
*rate of urbanization:* 0.6% annual rate of change (2005-10 est.)
**Sex ratio:**
*at birth:* 1.03 male(s)/female
*under 15 years:* 1.03 male(s)/female
*15-64 years:* 0.98 male(s)/female
*65 years and over:* 0.74 male(s)/female
*total population:* 0.94 male(s)/female (2009 est.)
**Infant mortality rate:**
*total:* 4.47 deaths/1,000 live births
*male:* 4.98 deaths/1,000 live births
*female:* 3.93 deaths/1,000 live births (2009 est.)
**Life expectancy at birth:**
*total population:* 80.77 years
*male:* 77.76 years
*female:* 83.88 years (2009 est.)
**Total fertility rate:** 1.41 children born/woman (2009 est.)
**HIV/AIDS - adult prevalence rate:** NA
**HIV/AIDS - people living with HIV/AIDS:** NA
**HIV/AIDS - deaths:** NA
**Nationality:**
*noun:* Channel Islander(s)
*adjective:* Channel Islander
**Ethnic groups:** UK and Norman-French descent with small percentages from other European countries
**Religions:** Anglican, Roman Catholic, Presbyterian, Baptist, Congregational, Methodist
**Languages:** English, French, Norman-French dialect spoken in country districts
**Literacy:** NA
**Education expenditures:** NA

# Guernsey *(continued)*

## Government

**Country name:**
*conventional long form:* Bailiwick of Guernsey
*conventional short form:* Guernsey
**Dependency status:** British crown dependency
**Government type:** parliamentary democracy
**Capital:**
*name:* Saint Peter Port
*geographic coordinates:* 49 27 N, 2 32 W
*time difference:* UTC 0 (5 hours ahead of Washington, DC during Standard Time)
*daylight saving time:* +1hr, begins last Sunday in March; ends last Sunday in October
**Administrative divisions:** none (British crown dependency); there are no first-order administrative divisions as defined by the US Government, but there are 10 parishes including Castel, Forest, Saint Andrew, Saint Martin, Saint Peter Port, Saint Pierre du Bois, Saint Sampson, Saint Saviour, Torteval, Vale
**Independence:** none (British crown dependency)
**National holiday:** Liberation Day, 9 May (1945)
**Constitution:** unwritten; partly statutes, partly common law and practice
**Legal system:** the laws of the UK, where applicable, apply; justice is administered by the Royal Court
**Suffrage:** 16 years of age; universal
**Executive branch:**
*chief of state:* Queen ELIZABETH II (since 6 February 1952), represented by Lieutenant Governor Sir Fabian MALBON (since 28 October 2005)
*head of government:* Chief Minister Lyndon TROTT (since 1 May 2008)
*cabinet:* Policy Council elected by the States of Deliberation
*elections:* the monarch is hereditary; lieutenant governor appointed by the monarch; chief minister is elected by States of Deliberation
*election results:* Lyndon TROTT elected chief minister, percent of vote of the States of Deliberation NA
**Legislative branch:** unicameral States of Deliberation (45 seats; members are elected by popular vote for four years); note - Alderney and Sark have parliaments
*elections:* last held 23 April 2008 (next to be held in 2012)
*election results:* percent of vote - NA; seats - all independents
**Judicial branch:** Royal Court (judges elected by an electoral college and the bailiff)
**Political parties and leaders:** none; all independents
**Political pressure groups and leaders:** Stop Traffic Endangering Pedestrian Safety or STEPS; No More Masts [Colin FALLAIZE]
**International organization participation:** UPU
**Diplomatic representation in the US:** none (British crown dependency)
**Diplomatic representation from the US:** none (British crown dependency)

**Flag description:** white with the red cross of Saint George (patron saint of England) extending to the edges of the flag and a yellow equal-armed cross of William the Conqueror superimposed on the Saint George cross

## Economy

**Economy - overview:** Financial services - banking, fund management, insurance - account for about 23% of employment and about 55% of total income in this tiny, prosperous Channel Island economy. Tourism, manufacturing, and horticulture, mainly tomatoes and cut flowers, have been declining. Financial services, construction, retail, and the public sector have been growing. Light tax and death duties make Guernsey a popular tax haven. The evolving economic integration of the EU nations is changing the environment under which Guernsey operates.
**GDP (purchasing power parity):**
$2.742 billion (2005)
**GDP (official exchange rate):** $2.742 billion (2005)
**GDP - real growth rate:**
3% (2005 est.)
**GDP - per capita (PPP):**
$44,600 (2005)
**GDP - composition by sector:**
*agriculture:* 3%
*industry:* 10%
*services:* 87% (2000)
**Labor force:** 31,470 (March 2006)
**Unemployment rate:**
0.9% (March 2006 est.)
**Population below poverty line:** NA%
**Household income or consumption by percentage share:**
*lowest 10%:* NA%
*highest 10%:* NA%
**Budget:**
*revenues:* $563.6 million
*expenditures:* $530.9 million (2005)
**Inflation rate (consumer prices):**
3.4% (June 2006)
**Agriculture - products:** tomatoes, greenhouse flowers, sweet peppers, eggplant, fruit; Guernsey cattle
**Industries:** tourism, banking
**Industrial production growth rate:** NA%
**Electricity - production:** NA kWh
**Electricity - consumption:** NA kWh
**Electricity - exports:** 0 kWh (2002)
**Electricity - imports:** 0 kWh (2002)
**Exports:** $NA
**Exports - commodities:** tomatoes, flowers and ferns, sweet peppers, eggplant, other vegetables
**Imports:** $NA
**Imports - commodities:** coal, gasoline, oil, machinery and equipment
**Debt - external:** $NA

**Exchange rates:** Guernsey pound 0.5302 (2008 est.), 0.4993 (2007), 0.5418 (2006), 0.5493 (2005), 0.5462 (2004)
*note:* the Guernsey pound is at par with the British pound

## Communications

**Telephones - main lines in use:** 45,100 (2005)
**Telephones - mobile cellular:** 43,800 (2004)
**Telephone system:**
*general assessment:* NA
*domestic:* NA
*international:* 1 submarine cable
**Radio broadcast stations:** AM 1, FM 1, shortwave 0 (1998)
**Television broadcast stations:** 1 (1997)
**Internet country code:** .gg
**Internet hosts:** 156 (2008)
**Internet users:** 36,000 (2005)

## Transportation

**Airports:** 2 (2008)
**Airports - with paved runways:**
*total:* 2
*914 to 1,523 m:* 1
*under 914 m:* 1 (2008)
**Ports and terminals:** Saint Peter Port, Saint Sampson

## Military

**Manpower fit for military service:**
*males age 16-49:* 12,447
*females age 16-49:* 12,566 (2009 est.)
**Manpower reaching militarily significant age annually:**
*male:* 362
*female:* 351 (2009 est.)
**Military - note:** defense is the responsibility of the UK

## Transnational Issues

**Disputes - international:** none

# Guinea

## Introduction

**Background:** Guinea has had a history of authoritarian rule since gaining its independence from France in 1958. Lansana CONTE came to power in 1984 when the military seized the government after the death of the first president, Sekou TOURE. Guinea did not hold democratic elections until 1993 when Gen. CONTE (head of the military government) was elected president of the civilian government. He was reelected in 1998 and again in 2003, though all the polls were marred by irregularities. History repeated itself in December 2008 when following President CONTE's death, Capt. Moussa Dadis CAMARA led a military coup, seizing power and suspending the constitution as well as political and union activity. Guinea has maintained some semblance of internal stability despite spillover effects from conflict in Sierra Leone and Liberia. As those countries have rebuilt, however, Guinea's own vulnerability to political and economic crisis has increased. Declining economic conditions and popular dissatisfaction with corruption and bad governance prompted two massive strikes in 2006, and a third nationwide strike in early 2007.

## Geography

**Location:** Western Africa, bordering the North Atlantic Ocean, between Guinea-Bissau and Sierra Leone
**Geographic coordinates:** 11 00 N, 10 00 W
**Map references:** Africa
**Area:**
*total:* 245,857 sq km
*land:* 245,857 sq km
*water:* 0 sq km
**Area - comparative:** slightly smaller than Oregon
**Land boundaries:**
*total:* 3,399 km
*border countries:* Cote d'Ivoire 610 km, Guinea-Bissau 386 km, Liberia 563 km, Mali 858 km, Senegal 330 km, Sierra Leone 652 km

**Coastline:** 320 km
**Maritime claims:**
*territorial sea:* 12 nm
*exclusive economic zone:* 200 nm
**Climate:** generally hot and humid; monsoonal-type rainy season (June to November) with southwesterly winds; dry season (December to May) with northeasterly harmattan winds
**Terrain:** generally flat coastal plain, hilly to mountainous interior
**Elevation extremes:**
*lowest point:* Atlantic Ocean 0 m
*highest point:* Mont Nimba 1,752 m
**Natural resources:** bauxite, iron ore, diamonds, gold, uranium, hydropower, fish, salt
**Land use:**
*arable land:* 4.47%
*permanent crops:* 2.64%
*other:* 92.89% (2005)
**Irrigated land:** 950 sq km (2003)
**Total renewable water resources:** 226 cu km (1987)
**Freshwater withdrawal (domestic/industrial/agricultural):**
*total:* 1.51 cu km/yr (8%/2%/90%)
*per capita:* 161 cu m/yr (2000)
**Natural hazards:** hot, dry, dusty harmattan haze may reduce visibility during dry season
**Environment - current issues:** deforestation; inadequate supplies of potable water; desertification; soil contamination and erosion; overfishing, overpopulation in forest region; poor mining practices have led to environmental damage
**Environment - international agreements:**
*party to:* Biodiversity, Climate Change, Climate Change-Kyoto Protocol, Desertification, Endangered Species, Hazardous Wastes, Law of the Sea, Ozone Layer Protection, Ship Pollution, Wetlands, Whaling
*signed, but not ratified:* none of the selected agreements
**Geography - note:** the Niger and its important tributary the Milo have their sources in the Guinean highlands

## People

**Population:** 10,057,975 (July 2009 est.)
**Age structure:**
*0-14 years:* 42.8% (male 2,175,852/female 2,128,518)
*15-64 years:* 53.7% (male 2,701,184/female 2,704,161)
*65 years and over:* 3.5% (male 153,053/female 195,207) (2009 est.)
**Median age:**
*total:* 18.5 years
*male:* 18.2 years
*female:* 18.7 years (2009 est.)
**Population growth rate:** 2.572% (2009 est.)
**Birth rate:** 37.52 births/1,000 population (2009 est.)

**Death rate:** 11.29 deaths/1,000 population (2008 est.)
**Net migration rate:** -0.8 migrant(s)/1,000 population (2009 est.)
**Urbanization:**
*urban population:* 34% of total population (2008)
*rate of urbanization:* 3.5% annual rate of change (2005-10 est.)
**Sex ratio:**
*at birth:* 1.03 male(s)/female
*under 15 years:* 1.02 male(s)/female
*15-64 years:* 1 male(s)/female
*65 years and over:* 0.78 male(s)/female
*total population:* 1 male(s)/female (2009 est.)
**Infant mortality rate:**
*total:* 65.22 deaths/1,000 live births
*male:* 68.7 deaths/1,000 live births
*female:* 61.63 deaths/1,000 live births (2009 est.)
**Life expectancy at birth:**
*total population:* 57.09 years
*male:* 55.63 years
*female:* 58.6 years (2009 est.)
**Total fertility rate:** 5.2 children born/woman (2009 est.)
**HIV/AIDS - adult prevalence rate:** 1.6% (2007 est.)
**HIV/AIDS - people living with HIV/AIDS:** 87,000 (2007 est.)
**HIV/AIDS - deaths:** 4,500 (2007 est.)
**Major infectious diseases:**
*degree of risk:* very high
*food or waterborne diseases:* bacterial and protozoal diarrhea, hepatitis A, and typhoid fever
*vectorborne diseases:* malaria and yellow fever
*water contact disease:* schistosomiasis
*animal contact disease:* rabies
*aerosolized dust or soil contact disease:* Lassa fever (2009)
**Nationality:**
*noun:* Guinean(s)
*adjective:* Guinean
**Ethnic groups:** Peuhl 40%, Malinke 30%, Soussou 20%, smaller ethnic groups 10%
**Religions:** Muslim 85%, Christian 8%, indigenous beliefs 7%
**Languages:** French (official); note - each ethnic group has its own language
**Literacy:**
*definition:* age 15 and over can read and write
*total population:* 29.5%
*male:* 42.6%
*female:* 18.1% (2003 est.)
**School life expectancy (primary to tertiary education):**
*total:* 8 years
*male:* 10 years
*female:* 7 years (2006)
**Education expenditures:** 1.6% of GDP (2005)

# Guinea (continued)

## Government

**Country name:**
*conventional long form:* Republic of Guinea
*conventional short form:* Guinea
*local long form:* Republique de Guinee
*local short form:* Guinee
*former:* French Guinea
**Government type:** republic
**Capital:**
*name:* Conakry
*geographic coordinates:* 9 33 N, 13 42 W
*time difference:* UTC 0 (5 hours ahead of Washington, DC during Standard Time)
**Administrative divisions:** 33 prefectures and 1 special zone (zone special)*; Beyla, Boffa, Boke, Conakry*, Coyah, Dabola, Dalaba, Dinguiraye, Dubreka, Faranah, Forecariah, Fria, Gaoual, Gueckedou, Kankan, Kerouane, Kindia, Kissidougou, Koubia, Koundara, Kouroussa, Labe, Lelouma, Lola, Macenta, Mali, Mamou, Mandiana, Nzerekore, Pita, Siguiri, Telimele, Tougue, Yomou
**Independence:** 2 October 1958 (from France)
**National holiday:** Independence Day, 2 October (1958)
**Constitution:** 23 December 1990 (Loi Fundamentale)
**Legal system:** based on French civil law system, customary law, and decree; accepts compulsory ICJ jurisdiction with reservations
**Suffrage:** 18 years of age; universal
**Executive branch:**
*chief of state:* Capt. Moussa Dadis CAMARA, President of the National Council for Democracy and Development, who led a military coup following the death of President Lansana CONTE on 22 December 2008
*head of government:* Prime Minister Kabine KOMARA (since 30 December 2008)
*cabinet:* Council of Ministers appointed by the president
*elections:* president elected by popular vote for a seven-year term (no term limits); candidate must receive a majority of the votes cast to be elected president; election last held 21 December 2003 (ad hoc election scheduled for 13 December 2009); the prime minister is appointed by the president
*election results:* Lansana CONTE reelected president; percent of vote - Lansana CONTE 95.3%, Mamadou Bhoye BARRY 4.6%
**Legislative branch:** unicameral People's National Assembly or Assemblee Nationale Populaire (114 seats; members are elected by a mixed system of direct popular vote and proportional party lists)
*elections:* last held 30 June 2002 (legislative elections due in 2007 were first rescheduled for 2008 and subsequently rescheduled for 11 October 2009)
*election results:* percent of vote by party - PUP 61.6%, UPR 26.6%, other 11.8%; seats by party - PUP 85, UPR 20, other 9

**Judicial branch:** Court of First Instance or Tribunal de Premiere Instance; Court of Appeal or Cour d'Appel; Supreme Court or Cour Supreme
**Political parties and leaders:** National Union for Progress or UPN [Mamadou Bhoye BARRY]; Party for Unity and Progress or PUP (the governing party) [Sekou KONATE]; People's Party of Guinea or PPG [Charles Pascal TOLNO]; Rally for the Guinean People or RPG [Alpha CONDE]; Union of Democratic Forces of Guinea or UFDG [Cellou Dalein DIALLO]; Union of Republican Forces or UFR [Sidya TOURE]; Union for Progress of Guinea or UPG [Jean-Marie DORE, secretary-general]; Union for Progress and Renewal or UPR [Ousmane BAH]
**Political pressure groups and leaders:** National Confederation of Guinean Workers-Labor Union of Guinean Workers or CNTG-USTG Alliance (includes National Confederation of Guinean Workers or CNTG [Rabiatou Sarah DIALLO] and Labor Union of Guinean Workers or USTG [Dr. Ibrahima FOFANA]); National Council of Civil Society Organizations of Guinea or CNOSCG [Ben Sekou SYLLA]; Syndicate of Guinean Teachers and Researchers or SLECG [Dr. Louis M'Bemba SOUMAH]
**International organization participation:** ACP, AfDB, AU, ECOWAS, FAO, G-77, IBRD, ICAO, ICCt, ICRM, IDA, IDB, IFAD, IFC, IFRCS, ILO, IMF, IMO, Interpol, IOC, IOM, IPU, ISO (correspondent), ITSO, ITU, ITUC, MIGA, MINURSO, NAM, OIC, OIF, OPCW, UN, UNCTAD, UNESCO, UNHCR, UNIDO, UNMIS, UNOCI, UNWTO, UPU, WCL, WCO, WFTU, WHO, WIPO, WMO, WTO
**Diplomatic representation in the US:**
*chief of mission:* Ambassador Mory Karamoko KABA
*chancery:* 2112 Leroy Place NW, Washington, DC 20008
*telephone:* [1] (202) 483-9420
*FAX:* [1] (202) 483-8688
**Diplomatic representation from the US:**
*chief of mission:* Ambassador (vacant); Charge d'Affaires Elizabeth RASPOLIC
*embassy:* Koloma, Conakry, east of Hamdallaye Circle
*mailing address:* B. P. 603, Transversale No. 2, Centre Administratif de Koloma, Commune de Ratoma, Conakry
*telephone:* [224] 65-10-40-00
*FAX:* [224] 65-10-42-97
**Flag description:** three equal vertical bands of red (hoist side), yellow, and green; uses the popular pan-African colors of Ethiopia

## Economy

**Economy - overview:** Guinea possesses major mineral, hydropower, and agricultural resources, yet remains an underdeveloped nation. The country has almost half of the world's bauxite reserves. The mining sector accounts for more than 70% of exports. Long-run improvements in government fiscal arrangements, literacy, and the legal framework are needed if the country is to move out of poverty.

Investor confidence has been sapped by rampant corruption, a lack of electricity and other infrastructure, a lack of skilled workers, and the political uncertainty because of the death of President Lansana CONTE in December 2008. Guinea is trying to reengage with the IMF and World Bank, which cut off most assistance in 2003, and is working closely with technical advisors from the U.S. Treasury Department, the World Bank and IMF, seeking to return to a fully funded program. Growth rose slightly in 2006-08, primarily due to increases in global demand and commodity prices on world markets, but the standard of living fell. The Guinea franc depreciated sharply as the prices for basic necessities like food and fuel rose beyond the reach of most Guineans. Dissatisfaction with economic conditions prompted nationwide strikes in February and June 2006.
**GDP (purchasing power parity):**
$10.44 billion (2008 est.)
$10.15 billion (2007)
$9.997 billion (2006)
*note:* data are in 2008 US dollars
**GDP (official exchange rate):** $4.454 billion (2008 est.)
**GDP - real growth rate:**
2.9% (2008 est.)
1.5% (2007 est.)
2.2% (2006 est.)
**GDP - per capita (PPP):**
$1,100 (2008 est.)
$1,100 (2007 est.)
$1,100 (2006 est.)
*note:* data are in 2008 US dollars
**GDP - composition by sector:**
*agriculture:* 22.4%
*industry:* 40.9%
*services:* 36.6% (2008 est.)
**Labor force:** 3.7 million (2006 est.)
**Labor force - by occupation:**
*agriculture:* 76%
*industry and services:* 24% (2006 est.)
**Unemployment rate:**
NA%
**Population below poverty line:** 47% (2006 est.)
**Household income or consumption by percentage share:**
*lowest 10%:* 1.9%
*highest 10%:* 41% (2006)
**Distribution of family income - Gini index:** 38.1 (2006)
**Investment (gross fixed):** 11.7% of GDP (2008 est.)
**Budget:**
*revenues:* $315 million
*expenditures:* $796.5 million (2008 est.)
**Inflation rate (consumer prices):**
30% (2008 est.)
23.4% (2007 est.)
**Central bank discount rate:** 22.25% (31 December 2005)
**Commercial bank prime lending rate:** NA

**Stock of money:** $309.8 million (31 December 2005)

**Stock of quasi money:** NA

**Stock of domestic credit:** $422.1 million (31 December 2005)

**Market value of publicly traded shares:** $NA

**Agriculture - products:** rice, coffee, pineapples, palm kernels, cassava (tapioca), bananas, sweet potatoes; cattle, sheep, goats; timber

**Industries:** bauxite, gold, diamonds, iron; alumina refining; light manufacturing, and agricultural processing

**Industrial production growth rate:** 8% (2008 est.)

**Electricity - production:** 800 million kWh

*note:* excludes electricity generated at interior mining sites (2006 est.)

**Electricity - consumption:** 744 million kWh (2006 est.)

**Electricity - exports:** 0 kWh (2007 est.)

**Electricity - imports:** 0 kWh (2007 est.)

**Oil - production:** 0 bbl/day (2007 est.)

**Oil - consumption:** 8,559 bbl/day (2006 est.)

**Oil - exports:** 0 bbl/day (2005)

**Oil - imports:** 8,811 bbl/day (2005)

**Oil - proved reserves:** 0 bbl (1 January 2006 est.)

**Natural gas - production:** 0 cu m (2007 est.)

**Natural gas - consumption:** 0 cu m (2007 est.)

**Natural gas - exports:** 0 cu m (2007 est.)

**Natural gas - imports:** 0 cu m (2007 est.)

**Natural gas - proved reserves:** 0 cu m (1 January 2006 est.)

**Current account balance:** -$535 million (2008 est.)

**Exports:** $1.202 billion f.o.b. (2008 est.)

**Exports - commodities:** bauxite, alumina, gold, diamonds, coffee, fish, agricultural products

**Exports - partners:** Russia 10.8%, Ukraine 9.6%, Spain 8.8%, US 7.5%, Germany 7.4%, South Korea 7.2%, France 7%, Ireland 5.5%, China 5% (2007)

**Imports:** $1.392 billion f.o.b. (2008 est.)

**Imports - commodities:** petroleum products, metals, machinery, transport equipment, textiles, grain and other foodstuffs

**Imports - partners:** China 10%, France 7%, Netherlands 6.3% (2007)

**Reserves of foreign exchange and gold:** $92 million (31 December 2008 est.)

**Debt - external:** $3.529 billion (31 December 2008 est.)

**Exchange rates:** Guinean francs (GNF) per US dollar - 5,500 (2008 est.), 4,122.8 (2007), 5,350 (2006), 3,644.3 (2005), 2,225 (2004)

## Communications

**Telephones - main lines in use:** 26,300 (2005)

**Telephones - mobile cellular:** 189,000 (2005)

**Telephone system:**

*general assessment:* inadequate system of open-wire lines, small radiotelephone communication stations, and new microwave radio relay system

*domestic:* Conakry reasonably well served; coverage elsewhere remains inadequate and large companies tend to rely on their own systems for nationwide links; combined fixed and mobile-cellular teledensity is about 2 per 100 persons

*international:* country code - 224; satellite earth station -1 Intelsat (Atlantic Ocean)

**Radio broadcast stations:** AM 0, FM 5, shortwave 3 (2006)

**Television broadcast stations:** 6 (2001)

**Internet country code:** .gn

**Internet hosts:** 16 (2008)

**Internet users:** 50,000 (2006)

## Transportation

**Airports:** 17 (2008)

**Airports - with paved runways:**

*total:* 5

*over 3,047 m:* 1

*2,438 to 3,047 m:* 1

*1,524 to 2,437 m:* 3 (2008)

**Airports - with unpaved runways:**

*total:* 12

*1,524 to 2,437 m:* 6

*914 to 1,523 m:* 4

*under 914 m:* 2 (2008)

**Railways:**

*total:* 837 km

*standard gauge:* 175 km 1.435-m gauge

*narrow gauge:* 662 km 1.000-m gauge (2006)

**Roadways:**

*total:* 44,348 km

*paved:* 4,342 km

*unpaved:* 40,006 km (2003)

**Waterways:** 1,300 km (navigable by shallow-draft native craft) (2008)

**Ports and terminals:** Conakry, Kamsar

## Military

**Military branches:** National Armed Forces: Army, Navy (Armee de Mer or Marine Guineenne, includes Marines), Air Force (2009)

**Military service age and obligation:** 18-25 years of age for compulsory or voluntary military service; 18-month conscript service obligation (2009)

**Manpower available for military service:**

*males age 16-49:* 2,230,049

*females age 16-49:* 2,193,236 (2008 est.)

**Manpower fit for military service:**

*males age 16-49:* 1,396,278

*females age 16-49:* 1,435,387 (2009 est.)

**Manpower reaching militarily significant age annually:**

*male:* 110,281

*female:* 107,879 (2009 est.)

**Military expenditures:** 1.7% of GDP (2006)

## Transnational Issues

**Disputes - international:** conflicts among rebel groups, warlords, and youth gangs in neighboring states have spilled over into Guinea, resulting in domestic instability; Sierra Leone considers Guinea's definition of the flood plain limits to define the left bank boundary of the Makona and Moa rivers excessive and protests Guinea's continued occupation of these lands, including the hamlet of Yenga, occupied since 1998

**Refugees and internally displaced persons:**

*refugees (country of origin):* 21,856 (Liberia); 5,259 (Sierra Leone); 3,900 (Cote d'Ivoire)

*IDPs:* 19,000 (cross-border incursions from Cote d'Ivoire, Liberia, Sierra Leone) (2007)

**Trafficking in persons:**

*current situation:* Guinea is a source, transit, and destination country for men, women, and children trafficked for the purposes of forced labor and sexual exploitation; the majority of victims are children, and internal trafficking is more prevalent than transnational trafficking; within the country, girls are trafficked primarily for domestic servitude and sexual exploitation, while boys are trafficked for forced agricultural labor, and as forced beggars, street vendors, shoe shiners, and laborers in gold and diamond mines; some Guinean men are also trafficked for agricultural labor within Guinea; transnationally, girls are trafficked into Guinea for domestic servitude and likely also for sexual exploitation

*tier rating:* Tier 2 Watch List - Guinea is on the Tier 2 Watch List for its failure to provide evidence of increasing efforts to eliminate trafficking over 2006; Guinea demonstrated minimal law enforcement efforts for a second year in a row, while protection efforts diminished over efforts in 2006; the government did not report any trafficking convictions in 2007; due to a lack of resources, the government does not provide shelter services for trafficking victims; the government took no measures to reduce the demand for commercial sexual exploitation (2008)

# Guinea-Bissau

## Introduction

**Background:** Since independence from Portugal in 1974, Guinea-Bissau has experienced considerable political and military upheaval. In 1980, a military coup established authoritarian dictator Joao Bernardo 'Nino' VIEIRA as president. Despite setting a path to a market economy and multiparty system, VIEIRA's regime was characterized by the suppression of political opposition and the purging of political rivals. Several coup attempts through the 1980s and early 1990s failed to unseat him. In 1994 VIEIRA was elected president in the country's first free elections. A military mutiny and resulting civil war in 1998 eventually led to VIEIRA's ouster in May 1999. In February 2000, a transitional government turned over power to opposition leader Kumba YALA, after he was elected president in transparent polling. In September 2003, after only three years in office, YALA was ousted by the military in a bloodless coup, and businessman Henrique ROSA was sworn in as interim president. In 2005, former President VIEIRA was re-elected president pledging to pursue economic development and national reconciliation. He was assassinated in March 2009; new elections are to take place in June 2009.

## Geography

**Location:** Western Africa, bordering the North Atlantic Ocean, between Guinea and Senegal
**Geographic coordinates:** 12 00 N, 15 00 W
**Map references:** Africa
**Area:**
*total:* 36,120 sq km
*land:* 28,000 sq km
*water:* 8,120 sq km
**Area - comparative:** slightly less than three times the size of Connecticut
**Land boundaries:**
*total:* 724 km
*border countries:* Guinea 386 km, Senegal 338 km

**Coastline:** 350 km
**Maritime claims:**
*territorial sea:* 12 nm
*exclusive economic zone:* 200 nm
**Climate:** tropical; generally hot and humid; monsoonal-type rainy season (June to November) with southwesterly winds; dry season (December to May) with northeasterly harmattan winds
**Terrain:** mostly low coastal plain rising to savanna in east
**Elevation extremes:**
*lowest point:* Atlantic Ocean 0 m
*highest point:* unnamed location in the northeast corner of the country 300 m
**Natural resources:** fish, timber, phosphates, bauxite, clay, granite, limestone, unexploited deposits of petroleum
**Land use:**
*arable land:* 8.31%
*permanent crops:* 6.92%
*other:* 84.77% (2005)
**Irrigated land:** 250 sq km (2003)
**Total renewable water resources:** 31 cu km (2003)
**Freshwater withdrawal (domestic/industrial/agricultural):**
*total:* 0.18 cu km/yr (13%/5%/82%)
*per capita:* 113 cu m/yr (2000)
**Natural hazards:** hot, dry, dusty harmattan haze may reduce visibility during dry season; brush fires
**Environment - current issues:** deforestation; soil erosion; overgrazing; overfishing
**Environment - international agreements:**
*party to:* Biodiversity, Climate Change, Climate Change-Kyoto Protocol, Desertification, Endangered Species, Hazardous Wastes, Law of the Sea, Ozone Layer Protection, Wetlands
*signed, but not ratified:* none of the selected agreements
**Geography - note:** this small country is swampy along its western coast and low-lying inland

## People

**Population:** 1,533,964 (July 2009 est.)
**Age structure:**
*0-14 years:* 40.8% (male 312,253/female 313,609)
*15-64 years:* 56.1% (male 414,924/female 445,639)
*65 years and over:* 3.1% (male 19,191/female 28,348) (2009 est.)
**Median age:**
*total:* 19.3 years
*male:* 18.7 years
*female:* 19.8 years (2009 est.)
**Population growth rate:** 2.019% (2009 est.)
**Birth rate:** 35.97 births/1,000 population (2009 est.)
**Death rate:** 16.05 deaths/1,000 population (2008 est.)
**Net migration rate:** 0 migrant(s)/1,000 population (2009 est.)
**Urbanization:**
*urban population:* 30% of total population (2008)
*rate of urbanization:* 3.2% annual rate of change (2005-10 est.)

**Sex ratio:**
*at birth:* 1.03 male(s)/female
*under 15 years:* 1 male(s)/female
*15-64 years:* 0.93 male(s)/female
*65 years and over:* 0.68 male(s)/female
*total population:* 0.95 male(s)/female (2009 est.)
**Infant mortality rate:**
*total:* 99.82 deaths/1,000 live births
*male:* 109.89 deaths/1,000 live births
*female:* 89.45 deaths/1,000 live births (2009 est.)
**Life expectancy at birth:**
*total population:* 47.9 years
*male:* 46.07 years
*female:* 49.79 years (2009 est.)
**Total fertility rate:** 4.65 children born/woman (2009 est.)
**HIV/AIDS - adult prevalence rate:** 1.8% (2007 est.)
**HIV/AIDS - people living with HIV/AIDS:** 16,000 (2007 est.)
**HIV/AIDS - deaths:** 1,100 (2007 est.)
**Major infectious diseases:**
*degree of risk:* very high
*food or waterborne diseases:* bacterial and protozoal diarrhea, hepatitis A, and typhoid fever
*vectorborne diseases:* malaria and yellow fever
*water contact disease:* schistosomiasis
*animal contact disease:* rabies (2009)
**Nationality:**
*noun:* Guinean(s)
*adjective:* Guinean
**Ethnic groups:** African 99% (includes Balanta 30%, Fula 20%, Manjaca 14%, Mandinga 13%, Papel 7%), European and mulatto less than 1%
**Religions:** Muslim 50%, indigenous beliefs 40%, Christian 10%
**Languages:** Portuguese (official), Crioulo, African languages
**Literacy:**
*definition:* age 15 and over can read and write
*total population:* 42.4%
*male:* 58.1%
*female:* 27.4% (2003 est.)
**School life expectancy (primary to tertiary education):**
*total:* 5 years
*male:* 7 years
*female:* 4 years (2001)
**Education expenditures:** 5.2% of GDP (1999)

## Government

**Country name:**
*conventional long form:* Republic of Guinea-Bissau
*conventional short form:* Guinea-Bissau
*local long form:* Republica da Guine-Bissau
*local short form:* Guine-Bissau
*former:* Portuguese Guinea
**Government type:** republic
**Capital:**
*name:* Bissau
*geographic coordinates:* 11 51 N, 15 35 W
*time difference:* UTC 0 (5 hours ahead of Washington, DC during Standard Time)

**Administrative divisions:** 9 regions (regioes, singular - regiao); Bafata, Biombo, Bissau, Bolama, Cacheu, Gabu, Oio, Quinara, Tombali; note - Bolama may have been renamed Bolama/Bijagos

**Independence:** 24 September 1973 (declared); 10 September 1974 (from Portugal)

**National holiday:** Independence Day, 24 September (1973)

**Constitution:** 16 May 1984; amended 4 May 1991, 4 December 1991, 26 February 1993, 9 June 1993, and in 1996

**Legal system:** based on French civil law; accepts compulsory ICJ jurisdiction

**Suffrage:** 18 years of age; universal

**Executive branch:**

*chief of state:* President Raimundo PEREIRA, who as Parliamentary Speaker succeeded President VIERA following VIERA's assassination on 2 March 2009; a presidential election is scheduled for 28 June 2009

*head of government:* Prime Minister Carlos GOMES Junior (since 25 December 2008)

*cabinet:* NA

*elections:* president elected by popular vote for a five-year term (no term limits); election last held 24July 2005 (next to be held 28 June 2009 following the assassination of President VIERA); prime minister appointed by the president after consultation with party leaders in the legislature

*election results:* Joao Bernardo VIEIRA elected president; percent of vote, second ballot - Joao Bernardo VIEIRA 52.4%, Malam Bacai SANHA 47.6%

**Legislative branch:** unicameral National People's Assembly or Assembleia Nacional Popular (100 seats; members are elected by popular vote to serve four-year terms)

*elections:* last held 16 November 2008 (next to be held 2012)

*election results:* percent of vote by party - PAIGC 49.8%, PRS 25.3%, PRID 7.5%, PND 2.4%, AD 1.4%, other parties 13.6%; seats by party - PAIGC 67, PRS 28, PRID 3, PND 1, AD 1

**Judicial branch:** Supreme Court or Supremo Tribunal da Justica (consists of nine justices appointed by the president and serve at his pleasure; final court of appeals in criminal and civil cases); Regional Courts (one in each of nine regions; first court of appeals for Sectoral Court decisions; hear all felony cases and civil cases valued at more than $1,000); 24 Sectoral Courts (judges are not necessarily trained lawyers; they hear civil cases valued at less than $1,000 and misdemeanor criminal cases)

**Political parties and leaders:** African Party for the Independence of Guinea-Bissau and Cape Verde or PAIGC [Carlos GOMES Junior]; Party for Social Renewal or PRS [Kumba YALA]; Democratic Alliance or AD [Victor MANDINGA]; Democratic Social Front or FDS [Rafael BARBOSA]; Electoral Union or UE [Joaquim BALDE]; Guinea-Bissau Civic Forum/Social Democracy or FCGSD [Antonieta Rosa GOMES]; Guinea-Bissau Democratic Party or PDG; Guinea-Bissau Socialist Democratic Party or PDSG

[Serifo BALDE]; Labor and Solidarity Party or PST [Iancuba INDJAI]; New Democracy Party or PND; Party for Democratic Convergence or PCD [Victor MANDINGA]; Party for Renewal and Progress or PRP; Progress Party or PP; Republican Party for Independence and Development or PRID [Aristides GOMES]; Union for Change or UM [Amine SAAD]; Union of Guinean Patriots or UPG [Francisca VAZ]; United Platform or UP (coalition formed by PCD, FDS, FLING, and RGB-MB); United Popular Alliance or APU; United Social Democratic Party or PUSD [Frnacisco FADUL]

**Political pressure groups and leaders:** NA

**International organization participation:** ACP, AfDB, AU, CPLP, ECOWAS, FAO, FZ, G-77, IBRD, ICAO, ICCt (signatory), ICRM, IDA, IDB, IFAD, IFC, IFRCS, ILO, IMF, IMO, Interpol, IOC, IOM, ITSO, ITU, ITUC, MIGA, NAM, OIC, OIF, OPCW, UN, UNCTAD, UNESCO, UNIDO, Union Latina, UNWTO, UPU, WADB (regional), WAEMU, WFTU, WHO, WIPO, WMO, WTO

**Diplomatic representation in the US:**

*chief of mission:* none; note - Guinea-Bissau does not have official representation in Washington, DC

**Diplomatic representation from the US:** the US Embassy suspended operations on 14 June 1998 in the midst of violent conflict between forces loyal to then President VIEIRA and military-led junta; the US Ambassador to Senegal is accredited to Guinea-Bissau

**Flag description:** two equal horizontal bands of yellow (top) and green with a vertical red band on the hoist side; there is a black five-pointed star centered in the red band; uses the popular pan-African colors of Ethiopia

## Economy

**Economy - overview:** One of the five poorest countries in the world, Guinea-Bissau depends mainly on farming and fishing. Cashew crops have increased remarkably in recent years, and the country now ranks fifth in cashew production. Guinea-Bissau exports fish and seafood along with small amounts of peanuts, palm kernels, and timber. Rice is the major crop and staple food. However, intermittent fighting between Senegalese-backed government troops and a military junta destroyed much of the country's infrastructure and caused widespread damage to the economy in 1998; the civil war led to a 28% drop in GDP that year, with partial recovery in 1999-2002. Before the war, trade reform and price liberalization were the most successful part of the country's structural adjustment program under IMF sponsorship. The tightening of monetary policy and the development of the private sector had also begun to reinvigorate the economy. Because of high costs, the development of petroleum, phosphate, and other mineral resources is not a near-term prospect. Offshore oil prospecting is underway in several sectors but has not yet led to commercially viable crude deposits. The inequality of income distribution is one of the most extreme in the

world. The government and international donors continue to work out plans to forward economic development from a lamentably low base. In December 2003, the World Bank, IMF, and UNDP were forced to step in to provide emergency budgetary support in the amount of $107 million for 2004, representing over 80% of the total national budget. Government drift and indecision, however, resulted in continued low growth in 2002-06. Higher raw material prices boosted growth in 2007 and 2008.

**GDP (purchasing power parity):**

$857 million (2008 est.)

$830.4 million (2007)

$808.6 million (2006)

*note:* data are in 2008 US dollars

**GDP (official exchange rate):** $442 million (2008 est.)

**GDP - real growth rate:**

3.2% (2008 est.)

2.7% (2007 est.)

1.8% (2006 est.)

**GDP - per capita (PPP):**

$600 (2008 est.)

$600 (2007 est.)

$600 (2006 est.)

*note:* data are in 2008 US dollars

**GDP - composition by sector:**

*agriculture:* 62%

*industry:* 12%

*services:* 26% (1999 est.)

**Labor force:** 480,000 (1999)

**Labor force - by occupation:**

*agriculture:* 82%

*industry and services:* 18% (2000 est.)

**Unemployment rate:**

NA%

**Population below poverty line:** NA%

**Household income or consumption by percentage share:**

*lowest 10%:* 0.5%

*highest 10%:* 42.4% (1991)

**Budget:**

*revenues:* $NA

*expenditures:* $NA

**Inflation rate (consumer prices):**

3.8% (2007 est.)

**Central bank discount rate:** 4.25% (31 December 2007)

**Stock of money:** $142.5 million (31 December 2007)

**Stock of quasi money:** $12.04 million (31 December 2007)

**Stock of domestic credit:** $46.44 million (31 December 2007)

**Market value of publicly traded shares:** $NA

**Agriculture - products:** rice, corn, beans, cassava (tapioca), cashew nuts, peanuts, palm kernels, cotton; timber; fish

**Industries:** agricultural products processing, beer, soft drinks

**Industrial production growth rate:** 4.7% (2003 est.)

# Guinea-Bissau *(continued)*

**Electricity - production:** 60 million kWh (2006 est.)
**Electricity - consumption:** 55.8 million kWh (2006 est.)
**Electricity - exports:** 0 kWh (2007 est.)
**Electricity - imports:** 0 kWh (2007 est.)
**Oil - production:** 0 bbl/day (2007 est.)
**Oil - consumption:** 2,520 bbl/day (2006 est.)
**Oil - exports:** 0 bbl/day (2005)
**Oil - imports:** 2,560 bbl/day (2005)
**Oil - proved reserves:** 0 bbl (1 January 2006 est.)
**Natural gas - production:** 0 cu m (2007 est.)
**Natural gas - consumption:** 0 cu m (2007 est.)
**Natural gas - exports:** 0 cu m (2007 est.)
**Natural gas - imports:** 0 cu m (2007 est.)
**Natural gas - proved reserves:** 0 cu m (1 January 2006 est.)
**Current account balance:** -$6 million (2007 est.)
**Exports:** $133 million f.o.b. (2006)
**Exports - commodities:** cashew nuts, shrimp, peanuts, palm kernels, sawn lumber
**Exports - partners:** Brazil 56.2%, India 33.6%, Nigeria 8.3% (2007)
**Imports:** $200 million f.o.b. (2006)
**Imports - commodities:** foodstuffs, machinery and transport equipment, petroleum products
**Imports - partners:** Portugal 21.7%, Senegal 16.8%, France 6%, Pakistan 4.7% (2007)
**Debt - external:** $941.5 million (2000 est.)
**Exchange rates:** Communaute Financiere Africaine francs (XOF) per US dollar - 447.81 (2008 est.), 493.51 (2007), 522.59 (2006), 527.47 (2005), 528.29 (2004)
*note:* since 1 January 1999, the West African CFA franc (XOF) has been pegged to the euro at a rate of 655.957 CFA francs per euro; West African CFA franc (XOF) coins and banknotes are not accepted in countries using Central African CFA francs (XAF), and vice versa, even though the two currencies trade at par

## Communications

**Telephones - main lines in use:** 4,600 (2007)
**Telephones - mobile cellular:** 296,200 (2007)
**Telephone system:**
*general assessment:* small system
*domestic:* combination of microwave radio relay, open-wire lines, radiotelephone, and cellular communications; fixed-line teledensity less than 1 per 100 persons; mobile-cellular teledensity reached 20 per 100 in 2007
*international:* country code - 245
**Radio broadcast stations:** AM 1 (transmitter out of service), FM 4, shortwave 0 (2001)
**Television broadcast stations:** 1 (2007)
**Internet country code:** .gw
**Internet hosts:** 82 (2008)
**Internet users:** 37,000 (2006)

## Transportation

**Airports:** 9 (2008)
**Airports - with paved runways:**
*total:* 2
*over 3,047 m:* 1
*1,524 to 2,437 m:* 1 (2008)
**Airports - with unpaved runways:**
*total:* 7
*1,524 to 2,437 m:* 1
*914 to 1,523 m:* 3
*under 914 m:* 3 (2008)
**Roadways:**
*total:* 3,455 km
*paved:* 965 km
*unpaved:* 2,490 km (2002)
**Waterways:** rivers are navigable for some distance; many inlets and creeks give shallow-water access to much of interior (2008)
**Ports and terminals:** Bissau, Buba, Cacheu, Farim

## Military

**Military branches:** People's Revolutionary Armed Force (FARP): Army, Navy, Air Force; paramilitary force
**Military service age and obligation:** 18-25 years of age for selective compulsory military service; 16 years of age or younger with parental consent, for voluntary service (2009)
**Manpower available for military service:**
*males age 16-49:* 344,087
*females age 16-49:* 347,886 (2008 est.)
**Manpower fit for military service:**
*males age 16-49:* 194,110
*females age 16-49:* 200,660 (2009 est.)
**Manpower reaching militarily significant age annually:**
*male:* 16,957
*female:* 17,172 (2009 est.)
**Military expenditures:** 3.1% of GDP (2005 est.)

## Transnational Issues

**Disputes - international:** in 2006, political instability within Senegal's Casamance region resulted in thousands of Senegalese refugees, cross-border raids, and arms smuggling into Guinea-Bissau
**Refugees and internally displaced persons:**
*refugees (country of origin):* 7,454 (Senegal) (2007)
**Trafficking in persons:**
*current situation:* Guinea-Bissau is a source country for children trafficked primarily for forced begging and forced agricultural labor to other West African countries
*tier rating:* Tier 2 Watch List - for the second year in a row, Guinea-Bissau is on the Tier 2 Watch List for its failure to combat severe forms of trafficking in persons, as evidenced by the continued failure to pass an anti-trafficking law and inadequate efforts to investigate or prosecute trafficking crimes or convict and punish trafficking offenders (2008)

**Illicit drugs:** increasingly important transit country for South American cocaine enroute to Europe; enabling environment for trafficker operations thanks to pervasive corruption; archipelago-like geography around the capital facilitates drug smuggling

# Guyana

## Introduction

**Background:** Originally a Dutch colony in the 17th century, by 1815 Guyana had become a British possession. The abolition of slavery led to black settlement of urban areas and the importation of indentured servants from India to work the sugar plantations. This ethnocultural divide has persisted and has led to turbulent politics. Guyana achieved independence from the UK in 1966, and since then it has been ruled mostly by socialist-oriented governments. In 1992, Cheddi JAGAN was elected president in what is considered the country's first free and fair election since independence. After his death five years later, his wife, Janet JAGAN, became president but resigned in 1999 due to poor health. Her successor, Bharrat JAGDEO, was reelected in 2001 and again in 2006.

## Geography

**Location:** Northern South America, bordering the North Atlantic Ocean, between Suriname and Venezuela
**Geographic coordinates:** 5 00 N, 59 00 W
**Map references:** South America
**Area:**
*total:* 214,970 sq km
*land:* 196,850 sq km
*water:* 18,120 sq km
**Area - comparative:** slightly smaller than Idaho
**Land boundaries:**
*total:* 2,949 km
*border countries:* Brazil 1,606 km, Suriname 600 km, Venezuela 743 km
**Coastline:** 459 km
**Maritime claims:**
*territorial sea:* 12 nm
*exclusive economic zone:* 200 nm
*continental shelf:* 200 nm or to the outer edge of the continental margin

**Climate:** tropical; hot, humid, moderated by northeast trade winds; two rainy seasons (May to August, November to January)
**Terrain:** mostly rolling highlands; low coastal plain; savanna in south
**Elevation extremes:**
*lowest point:* Atlantic Ocean 0 m
*highest point:* Mount Roraima 2,835 m
**Natural resources:** bauxite, gold, diamonds, hardwood timber, shrimp, fish
**Land use:**
*arable land:* 2.23%
*permanent crops:* 0.14%
*other:* 97.63% (2005)
**Irrigated land:** 1,500 sq km (2003)
**Total renewable water resources:** 241 cu km (2000)
**Freshwater withdrawal (domestic/industrial/agricultural):**
*total:* 1.64 cu km/yr (2%/1%/98%)
*per capita:* 2,187 cu m/yr (2000)
**Natural hazards:** flash floods are a constant threat during rainy seasons
**Environment - current issues:** water pollution from sewage and agricultural and industrial chemicals; deforestation
**Environment - international agreements:**
*party to:* Biodiversity, Climate Change, Climate Change-Kyoto Protocol, Desertification, Endangered Species, Hazardous Wastes, Law of the Sea, Ozone Layer Protection, Ship Pollution, Tropical Timber 83, Tropical Timber 94
*signed, but not ratified:* none of the selected agreements
**Geography - note:** the third-smallest country in South America after Suriname and Uruguay; substantial portions of its western and eastern territories are claimed by Venezuela and Suriname respectively

## People

**Population:** 772,298
*note:* estimates for this country explicitly take into account the effects of excess mortality due to AIDS; this can result in lower life expectancy, higher infant mortality, higher death rates, lower population growth rates, and changes in the distribution of population by age and sex than would otherwise be expected (July 2009 est.)
**Age structure:**
*0-14 years:* 25.7% (male 101,319/female 97,505)
*15-64 years:* 68.7% (male 268,058/female 262,595)
*65 years and over:* 5.5% (male 17,938/female 24,883) (2009 est.)
**Median age:**
*total:* 28.7 years
*male:* 28.2 years
*female:* 29.2 years (2009 est.)
**Population growth rate:** 0.181% (2009 est.)
**Birth rate:** 17.56 births/1,000 population (2009 est.)
**Death rate:** 8.29 deaths/1,000 population (2008 est.)

**Net migration rate:** -7.44 migrant(s)/1,000 population (2009 est.)
**Urbanization:**
*urban population:* 28% of total population (2008)
*rate of urbanization:* 0% annual rate of change (2005-10 est.)
**Sex ratio:**
*at birth:* 1.05 male(s)/female
*under 15 years:* 1.04 male(s)/female
*15-64 years:* 1.02 male(s)/female
*65 years and over:* 0.72 male(s)/female
*total population:* 1.01 male(s)/female (2009 est.)
**Infant mortality rate:**
*total:* 29.65 deaths/1,000 live births
*male:* 33.02 deaths/1,000 live births
*female:* 26.11 deaths/1,000 live births (2009 est.)
**Life expectancy at birth:**
*total population:* 66.68 years
*male:* 64.09 years
*female:* 69.4 years (2009 est.)
**Total fertility rate:** 2.03 children born/woman (2009 est.)
**HIV/AIDS - adult prevalence rate:** 2.5% (2007 est.)
**HIV/AIDS - people living with HIV/AIDS:** 13,000 (2007 est.)
**HIV/AIDS - deaths:** fewer than 1,000 (2007 est.)
**Major infectious diseases:**
*degree of risk:* high
*food or waterborne diseases:* bacterial and protozoal diarrhea, hepatitis A, and typhoid fever
*vectorborne diseases:* dengue fever and malaria
*water contact disease:* leptospirosis (2009)
**Nationality:**
*noun:* Guyanese (singular and plural)
*adjective:* Guyanese
**Ethnic groups:** East Indian 43.5%, black (African) 30.2%, mixed 16.7%, Amerindian 9.1%, other 0.5% (2002 census)
**Religions:** Hindu 28.4%, Pentecostal 16.9%, Roman Catholic 8.1%, Anglican 6.9%, Seventh Day Adventist 5%, Methodist 1.7%, Jehovah Witness 1.1%, other Christian 17.7%, Muslim 7.2%, other 4.3%, none 4.3% (2002 census)
**Languages:** English, Amerindian dialects, Creole, Caribbean Hindustani (a dialect of Hindi), Urdu
**Literacy:**
*definition:* age 15 and over has ever attended school
*total population:* 98.8%
*male:* 99.1%
*female:* 98.5% (2003 est.)
**School life expectancy (primary to tertiary education):**
*total:* 13 years
*male:* 13 years
*female:* 14 years (2005)
**Education expenditures:** 8.3% of GDP (2006)

# Guyana (continued)

## Government

**Country name:**
*conventional long form:* Cooperative Republic of Guyana
*conventional short form:* Guyana
*former:* British Guiana
**Government type:** republic
**Capital:**
*name:* Georgetown
*geographic coordinates:* 6 48 N, 58 10 W
*time difference:* UTC-4 (1 hour ahead of Washington, DC during Standard Time)
**Administrative divisions:** 10 regions; Barima-Waini, Cuyuni-Mazaruni, Demerara-Mahaica, East Berbice-Corentyne, Essequibo Islands-West Demerara, Mahaica-Berbice, Pomeroon-Supenaam, Potaro-Siparuni, Upper Demerara-Berbice, Upper Takutu-Upper Essequibo
**Independence:** 26 May 1966 (from the UK)
**National holiday:** Republic Day, 23 February (1970)
**Constitution:** 6 October 1980
**Legal system:** based on English common law with certain admixtures of Roman-Dutch law; has not accepted compulsory ICJ jurisdiction
**Suffrage:** 18 years of age; universal
**Executive branch:**
*chief of state:* President Bharrat JAGDEO (since 11 August 1999); note - assumed presidency after resignation of President Janet JAGAN and was reelected in 2001, and again in 2006
*head of government:* Prime Minister Samuel HINDS (since October 1992, except for a period as chief of state after the death of President Cheddi JAGAN on 6 March 1997)
*cabinet:* Cabinet of Ministers appointed by the president, responsible to the legislature
*elections:* president elected by popular vote as leader of a party list in parliamentary elections, which must be held at least every five years (no term limits); elections last held 28 August 2006 (next to be held by August 2011); prime minister appointed by the president
*election results:* President Bharrat JAGDEO reelected; percent of vote 54.6%
**Legislative branch:** unicameral National Assembly (65 seats; members elected by popular vote, also not more than 4 non-elected non-voting ministers and 2 non-elected non-voting parliamentary secretaries appointed by the president; to serve five-year terms)
*elections:* last held 28 August 2006 (next to be held by August 2011)
*election results:* percent of vote by party - PPP/C 54.6%, PNC/R 34%, AFC 8.1%, other 3.3%; seats by party - PPP/C 36, PNC/R 22, AFC 5, other 2
**Judicial branch:** Supreme Court of Judicature, consisting of the High Court and the Court of Appeal, with right of final appeal to the Caribbean Court of Justice (CCJ)
**Political parties and leaders:** Alliance for Change or AFC [Raphael TROTMAN and Khemraj RAMJATTAN]; Guyana Action Party or GAP [Paul HARDY]; Justice for All Party [C.N. SHARMA];

People's National Congress/Reform or PNC/R [Robert Herman Orlando CORBIN]; People's Progressive Party/Civic or PPP/C [Bharrat JAGDEO]; Rise, Organize, and Rebuild or ROAR [Ravi DEV]; The United Force or TUF [Manzoor NADIR]; The Unity Party [Joey JAGAN]; Vision Guyana [Peter RAMSAROOP]; Working People's Alliance or WPA [Rupert ROOPNARAINE]
**Political pressure groups and leaders:** Amerindian People's Association; Guyana Bar Association; Guyana Citizens Initiative; Guyana Human Rights Association; Guyana Public Service Union or GPSU; Private Sector Commission; Trades Union Congress
**International organization participation:** ACP, C, Caricom, CDB, FAO, G-77, IADB, IBRD, ICAO, ICCt, ICRM, IDA, IFAD, IFC, IFRCS, ILO, IMF, IMO, Interpol, IOC, IOM (observer), ISO (subscriber), ITU, ITUC, LAES, MIGA, NAM, OAS, OIC, OPANAL, OPCW, PCA, RG, UN, UNASUR, UNCTAD, UNESCO, UNIDO, UPU, WCL, WCO, WFTU, WHO, WIPO, WMO, WTO
**Diplomatic representation in the US:**
*chief of mission:* Ambassador Bayney KARRAN
*chancery:* 2490 Tracy Place NW, Washington, DC 20008
*telephone:* [1] (202) 265-6900
*FAX:* [1] (202) 232-1297
*consulate(s) general:* New York
**Diplomatic representation from the US:**
*chief of mission:* Ambassador John Melvin JONES
*embassy:* US Embassy, 100 Young and Duke Streets, Kingston, Georgetown
*mailing address:* P. O. Box 10507, Georgetown; US Embassy, 3170 Georgetown Place, Washington DC 20521-3170
*telephone:* [592] 225-4900 through 4909
*FAX:* [592] 225-8497
**Flag description:** green, with a red isosceles triangle (based on the hoist side) superimposed on a long, yellow arrowhead; there is a narrow, black border between the red and yellow, and a narrow, white border between the yellow and the green

## Economy

**Economy - overview:** The Guyanese economy exhibited moderate economic growth in recent years and is based largely on agriculture and extractive industries. The economy is heavily dependent upon the export of six commodities - sugar, gold, bauxite, shrimp, timber, and rice - which represent nearly 60% of the country's GDP and are highly susceptible to adverse weather conditions and fluctuations in commodity prices. Economic recovery since the 2005 flood-related contraction has been buoyed by increases in remittances and foreign direct investment in the sugar and rice industries as well as the mining sector. The bauxite mining sector should benefit in the near term from restructuring and partial privatization, and the state-owned sugar industry will conduct efficiency increasing modernizations. Export earnings from agriculture and mining have remained flat as rising commodity prices have offset declining production, while

the import bill has risen, driven by higher energy costs. Chronic problems include a shortage of skilled labor and a deficient infrastructure. The government is juggling a sizable external debt against the urgent need for expanded public investment. In March 2007, the Inter-American Development Bank, Guyana's principal donor, canceled Guyana's nearly $470 million debt, equivalent to nearly 48% of GDP, which along with other Highly Indebted Poor Country (HIPC) debt forgiveness brought the debt-to-GDP ratio down from 183% in 2006 to 120% in 2007. Guyana became heavily indebted as a result of the inward-looking, state-led development model pursued in the 1970s and 1980s. Guyana's entrance into the Caricom Single Market and Economy (CSME) in January 2006 has broadened the country's export market, primarily in the raw materials sector.
**GDP (purchasing power parity):**
$3.01 billion (2008 est.)
$2.878 billion (2007)
$2.733 billion (2006)
*note:* data are in 2008 US dollars
**GDP (official exchange rate):** $1.134 billion (2008 est.)
**GDP - real growth rate:**
3.2% (2008 est.)
5.3% (2007 est.)
5.1% (2006 est.)
**GDP - per capita (PPP):**
$3,900 (2008 est.)
$3,700 (2007 est.)
$3,600 (2006 est.)
*note:* data are in 2008 US dollars
**GDP - composition by sector:**
*agriculture:* 31.9%
*industry:* 21%
*services:* 47.2% (2008 est.)
**Labor force:** 418,000 (2001 est.)
**Labor force - by occupation:**
*agriculture:* NA%
*industry:* NA%
*services:* NA%
**Unemployment rate:**
11% (2007)
**Population below poverty line:** NA%
**Household income or consumption by percentage share:**
*lowest 10%:* 1.3%
*highest 10%:* 33.8% (1999)
**Distribution of family income - Gini index:** 43.2 (1999)
**Investment (gross fixed):** 40.5% of GDP (2008 est.)
**Budget:**
*revenues:* $463.7 million
*expenditures:* $536 million (2008 est.)
**Inflation rate (consumer prices):**
7.8% (2008 est.)
12.3% (2007 est.)
**Central bank discount rate:** 6.5% (31 December 2007)
**Commercial bank prime lending rate:** 14.61% (31 December 2007)

**Stock of money:** $315.2 million
(31 December 2007)
**Stock of quasi money:** $728.8 million
(31 December 2007)
**Stock of domestic credit:** $739.3 million
(31 December 2007)
**Market value of publicly traded shares:** $262.4
million (31 December 2007)
**Agriculture - products:** sugarcane, rice, shrimp,
fish, edible oils; beef, pork, poultry
**Industries:** bauxite, sugar, rice milling, timber,
textiles, gold mining
**Industrial production growth rate:** 1% (2008 est.)
**Electricity - production:** 600 million kWh (2007)
**Electricity - consumption:** 600 million kWh (2007)
**Electricity - exports:** 0 kWh (2007 est.)
**Electricity - imports:** 0 kWh (2007 est.)
**Oil - production:** 0 bbl/day (2007 est.)
**Oil - consumption:** 10,440 bbl/day (2006 est.)
**Oil - exports:** 0 bbl/day (2005)
**Oil - imports:** 10,960 bbl/day (2005)
**Oil - proved reserves:** 0 bbl (1 January 2006 est.)
**Natural gas - production:** 0 cu m (2007 est.)
**Natural gas - consumption:** 0 cu m (2007 est.)
**Natural gas - exports:** 0 cu m (2007 est.)
**Natural gas - imports:** 0 cu m (2007 est.)
**Natural gas - proved reserves:** 0 cu m
(1 January 2006 est.)
**Current account balance:** -$246 million (2008 est.)
**Exports:** $736.9 million f.o.b. (2008 est.)
**Exports - commodities:** sugar, gold, bauxite,
alumina, rice, shrimp, molasses, rum, timber
**Exports - partners:** Canada 18.7%, US 16.5%, UK
9.1%, Portugal 7.6%, Trinidad and Tobago 5.2%,
France 4.7%, Netherlands 4.6%, Jamaica 4% (2007)
**Imports:** $1.162 billion f.o.b. (2008 est.)
**Imports - commodities:** manufactures, machinery,
petroleum, food
**Imports - partners:** Trinidad and Tobago 26.2%, US
20.5%, Cuba 7.2%, China 7.1%, UK 5.4% (2007)
**Reserves of foreign exchange and gold:** $309.7
million (30 September 2008)
**Debt - external:** $804.3 million (30 September 2008)
**Exchange rates:** Guyanese dollars (GYD) per US
dollar - 203.86 (2008 est.), 201.89 (2007), 200.28
(2006), 200.79 (2005), 198.31 (2004)

## Communications

**Telephones - main lines in use:** 110,100 (2005)
**Telephones - mobile cellular:** 281,400 (2005)
**Telephone system:**
*general assessment:* fair system for long-distance
service
*domestic:* microwave radio relay network for trunk
lines; fixed-line teledensity is about 15 per 100
persons; many areas still lack fixed-line telephone
services; mobile-cellular teledensity reached 37 per
100 persons in 2005
*international:* country code - 592; tropospheric scatter
to Trinidad; satellite earth station - 1 Intelsat (Atlantic
Ocean)

**Radio broadcast stations:** AM 3, FM 3, shortwave
1 (1998)
**Television broadcast stations:** 3 (1 public station;
2 private stations which relay US satellite services)
(1997)
**Internet country code:** .gy
**Internet hosts:** 6,218 (2008)
**Internet users:** 190,000 (2007)

## Transportation

**Airports:** 96 (2008)
**Airports - with paved runways:**
*total:* 10
*1,524 to 2,437 m:* 3
*under 914 m:* 7 (2008)
**Airports - with unpaved runways:**
*total:* 86
*1,524 to 2,437 m:* 1
*914 to 1,523 m:* 14
*under 914 m:* 71 (2008)
**Roadways:**
*total:* 7,970 km
*paved:* 590 km
*unpaved:* 7,380 km (2000)
**Waterways:** 330 km
*note:* Berbice, Demerara, and Essequibo rivers are
navigable by oceangoing vessels for 150 km, 100 km,
and 80 km respectively (2008)
**Merchant marine:**
*total:* 8
*by type:* cargo 6, petroleum tanker 1, refrigerated
cargo 1
*registered in other countries:* 3 (Saint Vincent and the
Grenadines 2, unknown 1) (2008)
**Ports and terminals:** Georgetown

## Military

**Military branches:** Guyana Defense Force: Army
(includes Coast Guard, Air Corps) (2008)
**Military service age and obligation:** 18-25 years of
age for voluntary military service; no conscription
(2008)
**Manpower available for military service:**
*males age 16-49:* 220,797 (2008 est.)
**Manpower fit for military service:**
*males age 16-49:* 150,307
*females age 16-49:* 144,622 (2009 est.)
**Manpower reaching militarily significant age
annually:**
*male:* 6,625
*female:* 6,365 (2009 est.)
**Military expenditures:** 1.8% of GDP (2006)

## Transnational Issues

**Disputes - international:** all of the area west of the
Essequibo River is claimed by Venezuela preventing
any discussion of a maritime boundary; Guyana has
expressed its intention to join Barbados in asserting
claims before UNCLOS that Trinidad and Tobago's
maritime boundary with Venezuela extends into their
waters; Suriname claims a triangle of land between
the New and Kutari/Koetari rivers in a historic dispute
over the headwaters of the Courantyne; Guyana
seeks arbitration under provisions of the UN
Convention on the Law of the Sea (UNCLOS) to
resolve the long-standing dispute with Suriname over
the axis of the territorial sea boundary in potentially
oil-rich waters
**Trafficking in persons:**
*current situation:* Guyana is a source, transit, and
destination country for men, women, and children
trafficked for the purposes of commercial sexual
exploitation and forced labor; most trafficking appears
to take place in remote mining camps in the country's
interior; some women and girls are trafficked from
northern Brazil; reporting from other nations suggests
Guyanese women and girls are trafficked for sexual
exploitation to neighboring countries and Guyanese
men and boys are subject to labor exploitation in
construction and agriculture; trafficking victims from
Suriname, Brazil, and Venezuela transit Guyana en
route to Caribbean destinations
*tier rating:* Tier 2 Watch List - for a second
consecutive year, Guyana is on the Tier 2 Watch List
for failing to provide evidence of increasing efforts to
combat trafficking, particularly in the area of law
enforcement actions against trafficking offenders; the
government has yet to produce an anti-trafficking
conviction under the comprehensive Combating of
Trafficking in Persons Act, which became law in 2005;
the government operates no shelters for trafficking
victims, but did include limited funding for
anti-trafficking NGOs in its 2008 budget; the
government did not make any effort to reduce demand
for commercial sex acts during 2007 (2008)
**Illicit drugs:** transshipment point for narcotics from
South America - primarily Venezuela - to Europe and
the US; producer of cannabis; rising money
laundering related to drug trafficking and human
smuggling

# Haiti

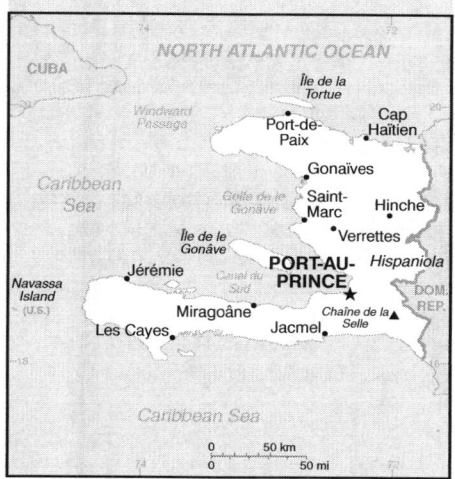

## Introduction

**Background:** The native Taino Amerindians - who inhabited the island of Hispaniola when it was discovered by COLUMBUS in 1492 - were virtually annihilated by Spanish settlers within 25 years. In the early 17th century, the French established a presence on Hispaniola. In 1697, Spain ceded to the French the western third of the island, which later became Haiti. The French colony, based on forestry and sugar-related industries, became one of the wealthiest in the Caribbean but only through the heavy importation of African slaves and considerable environmental degradation. In the late 18th century, Haiti's nearly half million slaves revolted under Toussaint L'OUVERTURE. After a prolonged struggle, Haiti became the first black republic to declare independence in 1804. The poorest country in the Western Hemisphere, Haiti has been plagued by political violence for most of its history. After an armed rebellion led to the forced resignation and exile of President Jean-Bertrand ARISTIDE in February 2004, an interim government took office to organize new elections under the auspices of the United Nations Stabilization Mission in Haiti (MINUSTAH). Continued violence and technical delays prompted repeated postponements, but Haiti finally did inaugurate a democratically elected president and parliament in May of 2006.

## Geography

**Location:** Caribbean, western one-third of the island of Hispaniola, between the Caribbean Sea and the North Atlantic Ocean, west of the Dominican Republic

**Geographic coordinates:** 19 00 N, 72 25 W

**Map references:** Central America and the Caribbean

**Area:**
*total:* 27,750 sq km
*land:* 27,560 sq km
*water:* 190 sq km

**Area - comparative:** slightly smaller than Maryland

**Land boundaries:**
*total:* 360 km
*border countries:* Dominican Republic 360 km

**Coastline:** 1,771 km

**Maritime claims:**
*territorial sea:* 12 nm
*contiguous zone:* 24 nm
*exclusive economic zone:* 200 nm
*continental shelf:* to depth of exploitation

**Climate:** tropical; semiarid where mountains in east cut off trade winds

**Terrain:** mostly rough and mountainous

**Elevation extremes:**
*lowest point:* Caribbean Sea 0 m
*highest point:* Chaine de la Selle 2,680 m

**Natural resources:** bauxite, copper, calcium carbonate, gold, marble, hydropower

**Land use:**
*arable land:* 28.11%
*permanent crops:* 11.53%
*other:* 60.36% (2005)

**Irrigated land:** 920 sq km (2003)

**Total renewable water resources:** 14 cu km (2000)

**Freshwater withdrawal (domestic/industrial/agricultural):**
*total:* 0.99 cu km/yr (5%/1%/94%)
*per capita:* 116 cu m/yr (2000)

**Natural hazards:** lies in the middle of the hurricane belt and subject to severe storms from June to October; occasional flooding and earthquakes; periodic droughts

**Environment - current issues:** extensive deforestation (much of the remaining forested land is being cleared for agriculture and used as fuel); soil erosion; inadequate supplies of potable water

**Environment - international agreements:**
*party to:* Biodiversity, Climate Change, Climate Change-Kyoto Protocol, Desertification, Law of the Sea, Marine Dumping, Marine Life Conservation, Ozone Layer Protection
*signed, but not ratified:* Hazardous Wastes

**Geography - note:** shares island of Hispaniola with Dominican Republic (western one-third is Haiti, eastern two-thirds is the Dominican Republic)

## People

**Population:** 9,035,536
*note:* estimates for this country explicitly take into account the effects of excess mortality due to AIDS; this can result in lower life expectancy, higher infant mortality, higher death rates, lower population growth rates, and changes in the distribution of population by age and sex than would otherwise be expected (July 2009 est.)

**Age structure:**
*0-14 years:* 38.1% (male 1,735,917/female 1,704,383)
*15-64 years:* 58.5% (male 2,621,059/female 2,665,447)
*65 years and over:* 3.4% (male 120,040/female 188,690) (2009 est.)

**Median age:**
*total:* 20.2 years
*male:* 19.8 years
*female:* 20.7 years (2009 est.)

**Population growth rate:** 1.838% (2009 est.)

**Birth rate:** 29.1 births/1,000 population (2009 est.)

**Death rate:** 10.15 deaths/1,000 population (2008 est.)

**Net migration rate:** -2.07 migrant(s)/1,000 population (2009 est.)

**Urbanization:**
*urban population:* 47% of total population (2008)
*rate of urbanization:* 4.5% annual rate of change (2005-10 est.)

**Sex ratio:**
*at birth:* 1.03 male(s)/female
*under 15 years:* 1.02 male(s)/female
*15-64 years:* 0.98 male(s)/female
*65 years and over:* 0.64 male(s)/female
*total population:* 0.98 male(s)/female (2009 est.)

**Infant mortality rate:**
*total:* 59.69 deaths/1,000 live births
*male:* 66.18 deaths/1,000 live births
*female:* 53.01 deaths/1,000 live births (2009 est.)

**Life expectancy at birth:**
*total population:* 60.78 years
*male:* 59.13 years
*female:* 62.48 years (2009 est.)

**Total fertility rate:** 3.81 children born/woman (2009 est.)

**HIV/AIDS - adult prevalence rate:** 2.2% (2007 est.)

**HIV/AIDS - people living with HIV/AIDS:** 120,000 (2007 est.)

**HIV/AIDS - deaths:** 7,200 (2007 est.)

**Major infectious diseases:**
*degree of risk:* high
*food or waterborne diseases:* bacterial and protozoal diarrhea, hepatitis A and E, and typhoid fever
*vectorborne diseases:* dengue fever and malaria
*water contact disease:* leptospirosis (2009)

**Nationality:**
*noun:* Haitian(s)
*adjective:* Haitian

**Ethnic groups:** black 95%, mulatto and white 5%

**Religions:** Roman Catholic 80%, Protestant 16% (Baptist 10%, Pentecostal 4%, Adventist 1%, other 1%), none 1%, other 3%
*note:* roughly half of the population practices voodoo

**Languages:** French (official), Creole (official)

**Literacy:**
*definition:* age 15 and over can read and write
*total population:* 52.9%
*male:* 54.8%
*female:* 51.2% (2003 est.)

**Education expenditures:** 1.4% of GDP (1991)

# Haiti *(continued)*

## Government

**Country name:**
*conventional long form:* Republic of Haiti
*conventional short form:* Haiti
*local long form:* Republique d'Haiti/Repiblik d' Ayiti
*local short form:* Haiti/Ayiti
**Government type:** republic
**Capital:**
*name:* Port-au-Prince
*geographic coordinates:* 18 32 N, 72 20 W
*time difference:* UTC-5 (same time as Washington, DC during Standard Time)
*daylight saving time:* +1hr, begins first Sunday in April; ends last Sunday in October
**Administrative divisions:** 10 departments (departements, singular - departement); Artibonite, Centre, Grand 'Anse, Nippes, Nord, Nord-Est, Nord-Ouest, Ouest, Sud, Sud-Est
**Independence:** 1 January 1804 (from France)
**National holiday:** Independence Day, 1 January (1804)
**Constitution:** approved March 1987
*note:* suspended June 1988 with most articles reinstated March 1989; constitutional government ousted in a military coup in September 1991, although in October 1991 military government claimed to be observing the constitution; returned to constitutional rule in October 1994; constitution, while technically in force between 2004-2006, was not enforced; returned to constitutional rule in May 2006
**Legal system:** based on Roman civil law system; accepts compulsory ICJ jurisdiction
**Suffrage:** 18 years of age; universal
**Executive branch:**
*chief of state:* President Rene PREVAL (since 14 May 2006)
*head of government:* Prime Minister Michele PIERRE-LOUIS (since 5 September 2008)
*cabinet:* Cabinet chosen by the prime minister in consultation with the president
*elections:* president elected by popular vote for a five-year term (may not serve consecutive terms); election last held 7 February 2006 (next to be held in 2011); prime minister appointed by the president, ratified by the National Assembly
*election results:* Rene PREVAL elected president; percent of vote - Rene PREVAL 51%
**Legislative branch:** bicameral National Assembly or Assemblee Nationale consists of the Senate (30 seats; members elected by popular vote to serve six-year terms; one-third elected every two years) and the Chamber of Deputies (99 seats; members are elected by popular vote to serve four-year terms); note -in reestablishing the Senate, the candidate in each department receiving the most votes in the last election serves six years, the candidate with the second most votes serves four years, and the candidate with the third most votes serves two years
*elections:* Senate - last held 21 April 2006 with run-off elections on 3 December 2006 (next regular election, for one third of seats, to be held in 2008); Chamber of

Deputies - last held 21 April 2006 with run-off elections on 3 December 2006 and 29 April 2007 (next regular election to be held in 2010)
*election results:* Senate - percent of vote by party - NA; seats by party - L'ESPWA 11, FUSION 5, OPL 4, FL 3, LAAA 2, UNCRH 2, PONT 2, ALYANS 1; Chamber of Deputies - percent of vote by party - NA; seats by party - L'ESPWA 23, FUSION 17, FRN 12, OPL 10, ALYANS 10, LAAA 5, MPH 3, MOCHRENA 3, other 10; results for six other seats contested on 3 December 2006 remain unknown
**Judicial branch:** Supreme Court or Cour de Cassation
**Political parties and leaders:** Artibonite in Action or LAAA [Youri LATORTUE]; Assembly of Progressive National Democrats or RDNP [Leslie MANIGAT]; Convention for Democratic Unity or KID [Evans PAUL]; Cooperative Action to Build Haiti or KONBA [Evans LESCOUFALIR]; Democratic Alliance or ALYANS [Evans PAUL] (coalition composed of KID and PPRH); Effort and Solidarity to Create an Alternative for the People or ESKAMP [Joseph JASME]; For Us All or PONT [Jean-Marie CHERESTAL]; Front for Hope or L'ESPWA [Rene PREVAL] (alliance of ESKAMP, PLB, and grass-roots organizations Grand-Anse Resistance Committee, the Central Plateau Peasants' Group, and Kombit Sudest); Haitian Christian Democratic Party or PDCH [Osner FEVRY and Marie-Denise CLAUDE]; Haitian Democratic and Reform Movement or MODEREH [Dany TOUSSAINT and Pierre Soncon PRINCE]; Heads Together or Tet-Ansanm [Dr. Gerard BLOT]; Independent Movement for National Reconciliation or MIRN [Luc FLEURINORD]; Justice for Peace and National Development or JPDN [Rigaud DUPLAN]; Fanmi Lavalas or FL [Rudy HERIVEAUX]; Liberal Party of Haiti or PLH [Gehy MICHEL]; Merging of Haitian Social Democratic Parties or FUSION or FPSDH [Serge GILLES] (coalition of Ayiti Capable, Haitian National Revolutionary Party, and National Congress of Democratic Movements); Mobilization for Haiti's Development or MPH [Samir MOURRA]; Mobilization for National Development or MDN [Hubert de RONCERAY]; Movement for National Reconstruction or MRN [Jean Henold BUTEAU]; Movement for the Installation of Democracy in Haiti or MIDH [Marc BAZIN]; National Christian Union for the Reconstruction of Haiti or UNCRH [Marie Claude GERMAIN]; National Front for the Reconstruction of Haiti or FRN [Guy PHILIPPE]; New Christian Movement for a New Haiti or MOCHRENA [Luc MESADIEU]; Open the Gate Party or PLB [Anes LUBIN]; Popular Party for the Renewal of Haiti or PPRH [Claude ROMAIN]; Struggling People's Organization or OPL [Edgard LEBLANC]; Union of Nationalist and Progressive Haitians or UNITE [Edouard FRANCISQUE]
**Political pressure groups and leaders:** Autonomous Organizations of Haitian Workers or CATH [Fignole ST-CYR]; Confederation of Haitian Workers or CTH; Federation of Workers Trade Unions or FOS; General Organization of Independent Haitian

Workers [Patrick NUMAS]; Grand-Anse Resistance Committee, or KOREGA; National Popular Assembly or APN; Papaye Peasants Movement or MPP [Chavannes JEAN-BAPTISTE]; Popular Organizations Gathering Power or PROP; Protestant Federation of Haiti; Roman Catholic Church
**International organization participation:** ACP, Caricom, CDB, FAO, G-77, IADB, IAEA, IBRD, ICAO, ICCt (signatory), ICRM, IDA, IFAD, IFC, IFRCS, ILO, IMF, IMO, Interpol, IOC, IOM, ITSO, ITU, ITUC, LAES, MIGA, NAM, OAS, OIF, OPANAL, OPCW, PCA, UN, UNCTAD, UNESCO, UNIDO, Union Latina, UNWTO, UPU, WCL, WCO, WFTU, WHO, WIPO, WMO, WTO
**Diplomatic representation in the US:**
*chief of mission:* Ambassador Raymond JOSEPH
*chancery:* 2311 Massachusetts Avenue NW, Washington, DC 20008
*telephone:* [1] (202) 332-4090
*FAX:* [1] (202) 745-7215
*consulate(s) general:* Boston, Chicago, Miami, New York, San Juan (Puerto Rico)
*consulate(s):* Orlando (Florida)
**Diplomatic representation from the US:**
*chief of mission:* Ambassador Janet A. SANDERSON
*embassy:* Tabarre 41, Route de Tabarre, Port-au-Prince
*mailing address:* use mailing address
*telephone:* [509] 229-8000
*FAX:* [509] 229-8028
**Flag description:** two equal horizontal bands of blue (top) and red with a centered white rectangle bearing the coat of arms, which contains a palm tree flanked by flags and two cannons above a scroll bearing the motto L'UNION FAIT LA FORCE (Union Makes Strength)

## Economy

**Economy - overview:** Haiti is the poorest country in the Western Hemisphere with 80% of the population living under the poverty line and 54% in abject poverty. Two-thirds of all Haitians depend on the agricultural sector, mainly small-scale subsistence farming, and remain vulnerable to damage from frequent natural disasters, exacerbated by the country's widespread deforestation. While the economy has recovered in recent years, registering positive growth since 2005, four tropical storms in 2008 severely damaged the transportation infrastructure and agricultural sector. US economic engagement under the Haitian Hemispheric Opportunity through Partnership Encouragement (HOPE) Act, passed in December 2006, has boosted apparel exports and investment by providing tariff-free access to the US. HOPE II, passed in October 2008, has further improved the export environment for the apparel sector by extending preferences to 2018; the apparel sector accounts for two-thirds of Haitian exports and nearly one-tenth of GDP. Remittances are the primary source of foreign exchange, equaling nearly a quarter of GDP and more than twice the earnings from exports. Haiti suffers from high inflation, a lack of investment because of insecurity and limited infrastructure, and a severe trade deficit. In 2005, Haiti paid its arrears to the World Bank, paving the way for reengagement with the Bank. Haiti is expected to receive debt forgiveness for about $525 million of its debt through the Highly-Indebted Poor Country (HIPC) initiative by mid-2009. The government relies on formal international economic assistance for fiscal sustainability.

**GDP (purchasing power parity):**
$11.59 billion (2008 est.)
$11.33 billion (2007)
$10.98 billion (2006)
*note:* data are in 2008 US dollars

**GDP (official exchange rate):** $6.966 billion (2008 est.)

**GDP - real growth rate:**
2.3% (2008 est.)
3.2% (2007 est.)
2.3% (2006 est.)

**GDP - per capita (PPP):**
$1,300 (2008 est.)
$1,300 (2007 est.)
$1,300 (2006 est.)
*note:* data are in 2008 US dollars

**GDP - composition by sector:**
*agriculture:* 28%
*industry:* 20%
*services:* 52% (2004 est.)

**Labor force:** 3.6 million
*note:* shortage of skilled labor, unskilled labor abundant (1995)

**Labor force - by occupation:**
*agriculture:* 66%
*industry:* 9%
*services:* 25% (1995)

**Unemployment rate:**
NA%
*note:* widespread unemployment and underemployment; more than two-thirds of the labor force do not have formal jobs

**Population below poverty line:** 80% (2003 est.)

**Household income or consumption by percentage share:**
*lowest 10%:* 0.7%
*highest 10%:* 47.7% (2001)

**Distribution of family income - Gini index:** 59.2 (2001)

**Investment (gross fixed):** 28.9% of GDP (2008 est.)

**Budget:**
*revenues:* $820.6 million
*expenditures:* $965.2 million (2008 est.)

**Inflation rate (consumer prices):**
15.8% (2008 est.)
8.5% (2007 est.)

**Commercial bank prime lending rate:** 46.99% (31 December 2007)

**Stock of money:** $704.7 million (31 December 2007)

**Stock of quasi money:** $1.561 billion (31 December 2007)

**Stock of domestic credit:** $1.537 billion (31 December 2007)

**Market value of publicly traded shares:** $NA

**Agriculture - products:** coffee, mangoes, sugarcane, rice, corn, sorghum; wood

**Industries:** sugar refining, flour milling, textiles, cement, light assembly based on imported parts

**Industrial production growth rate:** 1.2% (2008 est.)

**Electricity - production:** 549 million kWh (2006 est.)

**Electricity - consumption:** 330 million kWh (2006 est.)

**Electricity - exports:** 0 kWh (2007 est.)

**Electricity - imports:** 0 kWh (2007 est.)

**Oil - production:** 0 bbl/day (2007 est.)

**Oil - consumption:** 12,370 bbl/day (2006 est.)

**Oil - exports:** 0 bbl/day (2005)

**Oil - imports:** 11,980 bbl/day (2005)

**Oil - proved reserves:** 0 bbl (1 January 2006 est.)

**Natural gas - production:** 0 cu m (2007 est.)

**Natural gas - consumption:** 0 cu m (2007 est.)

**Natural gas - exports:** 0 cu m (2007 est.)

**Natural gas - imports:** 0 cu m (2007 est.)

**Natural gas - proved reserves:** 0 cu m (1 January 2006 est.)

**Current account balance:** -$664 million (2008 est.)

**Exports:** $491 million f.o.b. (2008 est.)

**Exports - commodities:** apparel, manufactures, oils, cocoa, mangoes, coffee

**Exports - partners:** US 72.9%, Dominican Republic 8.8%, Canada 3.3% (2007)

**Imports:** $2.095 billion f.o.b. (2008 est.)

**Imports - commodities:** food, manufactured goods, machinery and transport equipment, fuels, raw materials

**Imports - partners:** US 41.2%, Netherlands Antilles 14.9%, China 4.7%, Brazil 4.4% (2007)

**Reserves of foreign exchange and gold:** $482 million (31 December 2008 est.)

**Debt - external:** $1.463 billion (31 December 2008 est.)

**Exchange rates:** gourdes (HTG) per US dollar - 39.216 (2008 est.), 37.138 (2007), 40.232 (2006), 40.449 (2005), 38.352 (2004)

## Communications

**Telephones - main lines in use:** 108,300 (2007)

**Telephones - mobile cellular:** 2.5 million (2007)

**Telephone system:**
*general assessment:* telecommunications infrastructure is among the least developed in Latin America and the Caribbean; domestic facilities barely adequate; international facilities slightly better; mobile-cellular telephone services are expanding rapidly due, in part, to the introduction of low-cost GSM phones in 2006
*domestic:* coaxial cable and microwave radio relay trunk service
*international:* country code - 509; satellite earth station -1 Intelsat (Atlantic Ocean)

**Radio broadcast stations:** AM 41, FM 26, shortwave 0 (1999)

**Television broadcast stations:** 2 (plus a cable TV service) (1997)

**Internet country code:** .ht

**Internet hosts:** 7 (2008)

**Internet users:** 1 million (2007)

## Transportation

**Airports:** 14 (2008)

**Airports - with paved runways:**
*total:* 4
*2,438 to 3,047 m:* 1
*914 to 1,523 m:* 3 (2008)

**Airports - with unpaved runways:**
*total:* 10
*914 to 1,523 m:* 1
*under 914 m:* 9 (2008)

**Roadways:**
*total:* 4,160 km
*paved:* 1,011 km
*unpaved:* 3,149 km (2000)

**Ports and terminals:** Cap-Haitien

## Military

**Military branches:** no regular military forces - small Coast Guard; the regular Haitian Armed Forces (FAdH) - Army, Navy, and Air Force - have been demobilized but still exist on paper until or unless they are constitutionally abolished (2009)

**Manpower available for military service:**
*males age 16-49:* 2,047,083
*females age 16-49:* 2,047,953 (2008 est.)

**Manpower fit for military service:**
*males age 16-49:* 1,518,840
*females age 16-49:* 1,530,043 (2009 est.)

**Manpower reaching militarily significant age annually:**
*male:* 108,444
*female:* 106,243 (2009 est.)

**Military expenditures:** 0.4% of GDP (2006)

## Transnational Issues

**Disputes - international:** since 2004, about 8,000 peacekeepers from the UN Stabilization Mission in Haiti (MINUSTAH) maintain civil order in Haiti; despite efforts to control illegal migration, Haitians cross into the Dominican Republic and sail to neighboring countries; Haiti claims US-administered Navassa Island

**Illicit drugs:** Caribbean transshipment point for cocaine en route to the US and Europe; substantial bulk cash smuggling activity; Colombian narcotics traffickers favor Haiti for illicit financial transactions; pervasive corruption; significant consumer of cannabis

# Heard Island and McDonald Islands
*(territory of Australia)*

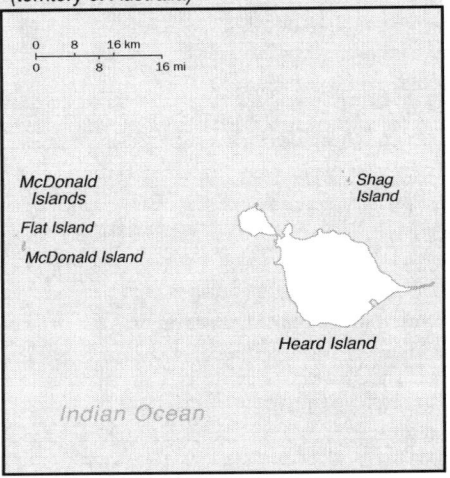

## Introduction

**Background:** These uninhabited, barren, sub-Antarctic islands were transferred from the UK to Australia in 1947. Populated by large numbers of seal and bird species, the islands have been designated a nature preserve.

## Geography

**Location:** islands in the Indian Ocean, about two-thirds of the way from Madagascar to Antarctica
**Geographic coordinates:** 53 06 S, 72 31 E
**Map references:** Antarctic Region
**Area:**
*total:* 412 sq km
*land:* 412 sq km
*water:* 0 sq km
**Area - comparative:** slightly more than two times the size of Washington, DC
**Land boundaries:** 0 km
**Coastline:** 101.9 km
**Maritime claims:**
*territorial sea:* 12 nm
*exclusive fishing zone:* 200 nm
**Climate:** antarctic
**Terrain:** Heard Island - 80% ice-covered, bleak and mountainous, dominated by a large massif (Big Ben) and an active volcano (Mawson Peak); McDonald Islands - small and rocky
**Elevation extremes:**
*lowest point:* Indian Ocean 0 m
*highest point:* Mawson Peak, on Big Ben 2,745 m
**Natural resources:** fish
**Land use:**
*arable land:* 0%
*permanent crops:* 0%
*other:* 100% (2005)
**Irrigated land:** 0 sq km
**Natural hazards:** Mawson Peak, an active volcano, is on Heard Island
**Environment - current issues:** NA

**Geography - note:** Mawson Peak on Heard Island is the highest Australian mountain (at 2,745 meters, it is taller than Mt. Kosciuszko in Australia proper), and one of only two active volcanoes located in Australian territory, the other being McDonald Island; in 1992, McDonald Island broke its dormancy and began erupting; it has erupted several times since, the most recent being in 2005

## People

**Population:** uninhabited

## Government

**Country name:**
*conventional long form:* Territory of Heard Island and McDonald Islands
*conventional short form:* Heard Island and McDonald Islands
*abbreviation:* HIMI
**Dependency status:** territory of Australia; administered from Canberra by the Australian Antarctic Division of the Department of the Environment, Water, Heritage and the Arts
**Legal system:** the laws of Australia, where applicable, apply
**Diplomatic representation in the US:** none (territory of Australia)
**Diplomatic representation from the US:** none (territory of Australia)
**Flag description:** the flag of Australia is used

## Economy

**Economy - overview:** The islands have no indigenous economic activity, but the Australian Government allows limited fishing in the surrounding waters.

## Communications

**Internet country code:** .hm

## Transportation

**Ports and terminals:** none; offshore anchorage only

## Military

**Military - note:** defense is the responsibility of Australia; Australia conducts fisheries patrols

## Transnational Issues

**Disputes - international:** none

# Holy See (Vatican City)

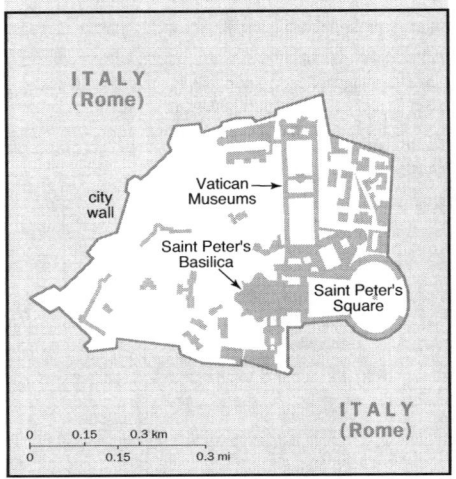

## Introduction

**Background:** Popes in their secular role ruled portions of the Italian peninsula for more than a thousand years until the mid 19th century, when many of the Papal States were seized by the newly united Kingdom of Italy. In 1870, the pope's holdings were further circumscribed when Rome itself was annexed. Disputes between a series of "prisoner" popes and Italy were resolved in 1929 by three Lateran Treaties, which established the independent state of Vatican City and granted Roman Catholicism special status in Italy. In 1984, a concordat between the Holy See and Italy modified certain of the earlier treaty provisions, including the primacy of Roman Catholicism as the Italian state religion. Present concerns of the Holy See include religious freedom, international development, the environment, the Middle East, China, the decline of religion in Europe, terrorism, interreligious dialogue and reconciliation, and the application of church doctrine in an era of rapid change and globalization. About one billion people worldwide profess the Catholic faith.

## Geography

**Location:** Southern Europe, an enclave of Rome (Italy)
**Geographic coordinates:** 41 54 N, 12 27 E
**Map references:** Europe
**Area:**
*total:* 0.44 sq km
*land:* 0.44 sq km
*water:* 0 sq km
**Area - comparative:** about 0.7 times the size of The Mall in Washington, DC
**Land boundaries:**
*total:* 3.2 km
*border countries:* Italy 3.2 km
**Coastline:** 0 km (landlocked)
**Maritime claims:** none (landlocked)

# Holy See (Vatican City) *(continued)*

**Climate:** temperate; mild, rainy winters (September to May) with hot, dry summers (May to September)
**Terrain:** urban; low hill
**Elevation extremes:**
*lowest point:* unnamed location 19 m
*highest point:* unnamed location 75 m
**Natural resources:** none
**Land use:**
*arable land:* 0%
*permanent crops:* 0%
*other:* 100% (urban area) (2005)
**Irrigated land:** 0 sq km
**Natural hazards:** NA
**Environment - current issues:** NA
**Environment - international agreements:**
*party to:* Ozone Layer Protection
*signed, but not ratified:* Air Pollution, Environmental Modification
**Geography - note:** landlocked; enclave in Rome, Italy; world's smallest state; beyond the territorial boundary of Vatican City, the Lateran Treaty of 1929 grants the Holy See extraterritorial authority over 23 sites in Rome and five outside of Rome, including the Pontifical Palace at Castel Gandolfo (the Pope's summer residence)

## People

**Population:** 826 (July 2009 est.)
**Population growth rate:** 0.003% (2009 est.)
**Urbanization:**
*urban population:* 100% of total population (2008)
*rate of urbanization:* 0.1% annual rate of change (2005-10 est.)
**HIV/AIDS - adult prevalence rate:** NA
**HIV/AIDS - people living with HIV/AIDS:** NA
**HIV/AIDS - deaths:** NA
**Nationality:**
*noun:* none
*adjective:* none
**Ethnic groups:** Italians, Swiss, other
**Religions:** Roman Catholic
**Languages:** Italian, Latin, French, various other languages
**Literacy:**
*definition:* NA
*total population:* 100%
*male:* 100%
*female:* 100%

## Government

**Country name:**
*conventional long form:* The Holy See (State of the Vatican City)
*conventional short form:* Holy See (Vatican City)
*local long form:* Santa Sede (Stato della Citta del Vaticano)
*local short form:* Santa Sede (Citta del Vaticano)
**Government type:** ecclesiastical

**Capital:**
*name:* Vatican City
*geographic coordinates:* 41 54 N, 12 27 E
*time difference:* UTC+1 (6 hours ahead of Washington, DC during Standard Time)
*daylight saving time:* +1hr, begins last Sunday in March; ends last Sunday in October
**Administrative divisions:** none
**Independence:** 11 February 1929 (from Italy); note - the three treaties signed with Italy on 11 February 1929 acknowledged, among other things, the full sovereignty of the Vatican and established its territorial extent; however, the origin of the Papal States, which over the years have varied considerably in extent, may be traced back to the 8th century
**National holiday:** Election Day of Pope BENEDICT XVI, 19 April (2005)
**Constitution:** Fundamental Law promulgated by Pope JOHN PAUL II on 26 November 2000, effective 22 February 2001 (replaced the first Fundamental Law of 1929)
**Legal system:** based on Code of Canon Law and revisions to it
**Suffrage:** limited to cardinals less than 80 years old
**Executive branch:**
*chief of state:* Pope BENEDICT XVI (since 19 April 2005)
*head of government:* Secretary of State Cardinal Tarcisio BERTONE (since 15 September 2006)
*cabinet:* Pontifical Commission for the State of Vatican City appointed by the pope
*elections:* pope elected for life by the College of Cardinals; election last held 19 April 2005 (next to be held after the death of the current pope); secretary of state appointed by the pope
*election results:* Joseph RATZINGER elected Pope BENEDICT XVI
**Legislative branch:** unicameral Pontifical Commission for Vatican City State
**Judicial branch:** there are three tribunals responsible for civil and criminal matters within Vatican City; three other tribunals rule on issues pertaining to the Holy See
*note:* judicial duties were established by the Motu Proprio of Pope PIUS XII on 1 May 1946
**Political parties and leaders:** none
**Political pressure groups and leaders:** none (exclusive of influence exercised by church officers)
**International organization participation:** CE (observer), IAEA, Interpol, IOM (observer), ITSO, ITU, ITUC, NAM (guest), OAS (observer), OPCW, OSCE, UN (observer), UNCTAD, UNHCR, Union Latina (observer), UNWTO (observer), UPU, WFTU, WIPO, WTO (observer)
**Diplomatic representation in the US:**
*chief of mission:* Apostolic Nuncio Archbishop Pietro SAMBI
*chancery:* 3339 Massachusetts Avenue NW, Washington, DC 20008
*telephone:* [1] (202) 333-7121
*FAX:* [1] (202) 337-4036

**Diplomatic representation from the US:**
*chief of mission:* Ambassador (vacant); Charge d'Affaires Julieta NOYES
*embassy:* Villa Domiziana, Via delle Terme Deciane 26, 00153 Rome
*mailing address:* PSC 833, Box 66, APO AE 09624
*telephone:* [39] (06) 4674-3428
*FAX:* [39] (06) 575-3411
**Flag description:** two vertical bands of yellow (hoist side) and white with the arms of the Holy See, consisting of the crossed keys of Saint Peter surmounted by the three-tiered papal tiara, centered in the white band

## Economy

**Economy - overview:** The Holy See is supported financially by a variety of sources, including investments, real estate income, and donations from Catholic individuals, dioceses, and institutions; these help fund the Roman Curia (Vatican bureaucracy), diplomatic missions, and media outlets. The separate Vatican City State budget includes the Vatican museums and post office and is supported financially by the sale of stamps, coins, medals, and tourist mementos; by fees for admission to museums; and by publications sales. Moreover, an annual collection taken up in dioceses and direct donations go to a non-budgetary fund known as Peter's Pence, which is used directly by the Pope for charity, disaster relief, and aid to churches in developing nations. The incomes and living standards of lay workers are comparable to those of counterparts who work in the city of Rome.
**GDP (purchasing power parity):** $NA
**Labor force:** NA
**Labor force - by occupation:**
*note:* essentially services with a small amount of industry; nearly all dignitaries, priests, nuns, guards, and the approximately 3,000 lay workers live outside the Vatican
**Population below poverty line:** NA%
**Budget:**
*revenues:* $374 million
*expenditures:* $388 million (2007)
**Industries:** printing; production of coins, medals, postage stamps; mosaics and staff uniforms; worldwide banking and financial activities
**Electricity - production:** NA kWh
**Electricity - consumption:** NA kWh
**Electricity - imports:** NA kWh; note - electricity supplied by Italy; a small portion of electricity is self-produced from solar panels
**Exchange rates:** euros (EUR) per US dollar - 0.6827 (2008 est.), 0.7345 (2007), 0.7964 (2006), 0.8041 (2005), 0.8054 (2004)

**Holy See (Vatican City)** *(continued)*

**Telephones - main lines in use:** 5,120 (2005)
**Telephone system:**
*general assessment:* automatic digital exchange
*domestic:* connected via fiber optic cable to Telecom Italia network
*international:* country code - 39; uses Italian system
**Radio broadcast stations:** AM 5, FM 3, shortwave 5 (2008)
**Television broadcast stations:** 1 (2008)
**Internet country code:** .va
**Internet hosts:** 55 (2008)
**Internet users:** 93 (2000)

## Military

**Military branches:** Pontifical Swiss Guard (Corpo della Guardia Svizzera Pontificia) (2009)
**Military - note:** defense is the responsibility of Italy; ceremonial and limited security duties performed by Pontifical Swiss Guard

## Transnational Issues

**Disputes - international:** none

# Honduras

## Introduction

**Background:** Once part of Spain's vast empire in the New World, Honduras became an independent nation in 1821. After two and a half decades of mostly military rule, a freely elected civilian government came to power in 1982. During the 1980s, Honduras proved a haven for anti-Sandinista contras fighting the Marxist Nicaraguan Government and an ally to Salvadoran Government forces fighting leftist guerrillas. The country was devastated by Hurricane Mitch in 1998, which killed about 5,600 people and caused approximately $2 billion in damage.

## Geography

**Location:** Central America, bordering the Caribbean Sea, between Guatemala and Nicaragua and bordering the Gulf of Fonseca (North Pacific Ocean), between El Salvador and Nicaragua
**Geographic coordinates:** 15 00 N, 86 30 W
**Map references:** Central America and the Caribbean
**Area:**
*total:* 112,090 sq km
*land:* 111,890 sq km
*water:* 200 sq km
**Area - comparative:** slightly larger than Tennessee
**Land boundaries:**
*total:* 1,520 km
*border countries:* Guatemala 256 km, El Salvador 342 km, Nicaragua 922 km
**Coastline:** 820 km
**Maritime claims:**
*territorial sea:* 12 nm
*contiguous zone:* 24 nm
*exclusive economic zone:* 200 nm
*continental shelf:* natural extension of territory or to 200 nm
**Climate:** subtropical in lowlands, temperate in mountains
**Terrain:** mostly mountains in interior, narrow coastal plains

**Elevation extremes:**
*lowest point:* Caribbean Sea 0 m
*highest point:* Cerro Las Minas 2,870 m
**Natural resources:** timber, gold, silver, copper, lead, zinc, iron ore, antimony, coal, fish, hydropower
**Land use:**
*arable land:* 9.53%
*permanent crops:* 3.21%
*other:* 87.26% (2005)
**Irrigated land:** 800 sq km (2003)
**Total renewable water resources:** 95.9 cu km (2000)
**Freshwater withdrawal (domestic/industrial/agricultural):**
*total:* 0.86 cu km/yr (8%/12%/80%)
*per capita:* 119 cu m/yr (2000)
**Natural hazards:** frequent, but generally mild, earthquakes; extremely susceptible to damaging hurricanes and floods along the Caribbean coast
**Environment - current issues:** urban population expanding; deforestation results from logging and the clearing of land for agricultural purposes; further land degradation and soil erosion hastened by uncontrolled development and improper land use practices such as farming of marginal lands; mining activities polluting Lago de Yojoa (the country's largest source of fresh water), as well as several rivers and streams, with heavy metals
**Environment - international agreements:**
*party to:* Biodiversity, Climate Change, Climate Change-Kyoto Protocol, Desertification, Endangered Species, Hazardous Wastes, Law of the Sea, Marine Dumping, Ozone Layer Protection, Ship Pollution, Tropical Timber 83, Tropical Timber 94, Wetlands
*signed, but not ratified:* none of the selected agreements
**Geography - note:** has only a short Pacific coast but a long Caribbean shoreline, including the virtually uninhabited eastern Mosquito Coast

## People

**Population:** 7,792,854
*note:* estimates for this country explicitly take into account the effects of excess mortality due to AIDS; this can result in lower life expectancy, higher infant mortality, higher death rates, lower population growth rates, and changes in the distribution of population by age and sex than would otherwise be expected (July 2009 est.)
**Age structure:**
*0-14 years:* 38.1% (male 1,514,544/female 1,451,862)
*15-64 years:* 58.3% (male 2,278,508/female 2,267,527)
*65 years and over:* 3.6% (male 125,991/female 154,422) (2009 est.)
**Median age:**
*total:* 20.3 years
*male:* 20 years
*female:* 20.7 years (2009 est.)
**Population growth rate:** 1.956% (2009 est.)

# Honduras (continued)

**Birth rate:** 26.27 births/1,000 population (2009 est.)
**Death rate:** 5.36 deaths/1,000 population (2008 est.)
**Net migration rate:** -1.3 migrant(s)/1,000 population (2009 est.)
**Urbanization:**
*urban population:* 48% of total population (2008)
*rate of urbanization:* 2.9% annual rate of change (2005-10 est.)
**Sex ratio:**
*at birth:* 1.05 male(s)/female
*under 15 years:* 1.04 male(s)/female
*15-64 years:* 1 male(s)/female
*65 years and over:* 0.82 male(s)/female
*total population:* 1.01 male(s)/female (2009 est.)
**Infant mortality rate:**
*total:* 24.03 deaths/1,000 live births
*male:* 26.97 deaths/1,000 live births
*female:* 20.94 deaths/1,000 live births (2009 est.)
**Life expectancy at birth:**
*total population:* 69.4 years
*male:* 67.86 years
*female:* 71.02 years (2009 est.)
**Total fertility rate:** 3.27 children born/woman (2009 est.)
**HIV/AIDS - adult prevalence rate:** 0.7% (2007 est.)
**HIV/AIDS - people living with HIV/AIDS:** 28,000 (2007 est.)
**HIV/AIDS - deaths:** 1,900 (2007 est.)
**Major infectious diseases:**
*degree of risk:* high
*food or waterborne diseases:* bacterial diarrhea, hepatitis A, and typhoid fever
*vectorborne diseases:* dengue fever and malaria
*water contact disease:* leptospirosis (2009)
**Nationality:**
*noun:* Honduran(s)
*adjective:* Honduran
**Ethnic groups:** mestizo (mixed Amerindian and European) 90%, Amerindian 7%, black 2%, white 1%
**Religions:** Roman Catholic 97%, Protestant 3%
**Languages:** Spanish, Amerindian dialects
**Literacy:**
*definition:* age 15 and over can read and write
*total population:* 80%
*male:* 79.8%
*female:* 80.2% (2001 census)
**School life expectancy (primary to tertiary education):**
*total:* 11 years
*male:* 11 years
*female:* 12 years (2004)
**Education expenditures:** 3.8% of GDP (1991)

## Government

**Country name:**
*conventional long form:* Republic of Honduras
*conventional short form:* Honduras
*local long form:* Republica de Honduras
*local short form:* Honduras
**Government type:** democratic constitutional republic

**Capital:**
*name:* Tegucigalpa
*geographic coordinates:* 14 06 N, 87 13 W
*time difference:* UTC-6 (1 hour behind Washington, DC during Standard Time)
*daylight saving time:* +1hr, begins second Sunday in March; ends first Sunday in November
**Administrative divisions:** 18 departments (departamentos, singular - departamento); Atlantida, Choluteca, Colon, Comayagua, Copan, Cortes, El Paraiso, Francisco Morazan, Gracias a Dios, Intibuca, Islas de la Bahia, La Paz, Lempira, Ocotepeque, Olancho, Santa Barbara, Valle, Yoro
**Independence:** 15 September 1821 (from Spain)
**National holiday:** Independence Day, 15 September (1821)
**Constitution:** 11 January 1982, effective 20 January 1982; amended many times
**Legal system:** rooted in Roman and Spanish civil law with increasing influence of English common law; recent judicial reforms include abandoning Napoleonic legal codes in favor of the oral adversarial system; accepts ICJ jurisdiction with reservations
**Suffrage:** 18 years of age; universal and compulsory
**Executive branch:**
*chief of state:* President Jose Manuel ZELAYA Rosales (since 27 January 2006); Vice President Commissioner Aristides MEJIA Carranza (since 1 February 2009); note - the president is both the chief of state and head of government; because the president and vice president are elected on the same ticket, the position of "vice president commissioner" was created after Vice President Elvin SANTOS resigned in late 2008 to run for president in the November 2009 election
*head of government:* President Jose Manuel ZELAYA Rosales (since 27 January 2006); Vice President Commissioner Aristides MEJIA Carranza (since 1 February 2009)
*cabinet:* Cabinet appointed by president
*elections:* president elected by popular vote for a four-year term; election last held 27 November 2005 (next to be held in November 2009)
*election results:* Jose Manuel ZELAYA Rosales elected president - 49.8%, Porfirio "Pepe" LOBO Sosa 46.1%, other 4.1%
**Legislative branch:** unicameral National Congress or Congreso Nacional (128 seats; members are elected proportionally by department to serve four-year terms)
*elections:* last held 27 November 2005 (next to be held in November 2009)
*election results:* percent of vote by party - NA; seats by party - PL 62, PN 55, PUD 5, PDC 4, PINU 2
**Judicial branch:** Supreme Court of Justice or Corte Suprema de Justicia (15 judges are elected for seven-year terms by the National Congress)
**Political parties and leaders:** Christian Democratic Party or PDC [Felicito AVILA]; Democratic Unification Party or PUD [Cesar HAM]; Liberal Party or PL [Patricia RODAS]; National Innovation and Unity Party or PINU [Jorge AQUILAR Paredes]; National Party of Honduras or PN [Porfirio LOBO]

**Political pressure groups and leaders:** Committee for the Defense of Human Rights in Honduras or CODEH; Confederation of Honduran Workers or CTH; Coordinating Committee of Popular Organizations or CCOP; General Workers Confederation or CGT; Honduran Council of Private Enterprise or COHEP; National Association of Honduran Campesinos or ANACH; National Union of Campesinos or UNC; Popular Bloc or BP; United Confederation of Honduran Workers or CUTH
**International organization participation:** BCIE, CACM, FAO, G-77, IADB, IAEA, IBRD, ICAO, ICCt, ICRM, IDA, IFAD, IFC, IFRCS, ILO, IMF, IMO, Interpol, IOC, IOM, ISO (subscriber), ITSO, ITU, ITUC, LAES, LAIA (observer), MIGA, MINURSO, NAM, OAS, OPANAL, OPCW, PCA, RG, SICA, UN, UNCTAD, UNESCO, UNIDO, Union Latina, UNWTO, UPU, WCL, WCO, WFTU, WHO, WIPO, WMO, WTO
**Diplomatic representation in the US:**
*chief of mission:* Ambassador Roberto FLORES BERMUDEZ
*chancery:* Suite 4-M, 3007 Tilden Street NW, Washington, DC 20008
*telephone:* [1] (202) 966-7702
*FAX:* [1] (202) 966-9751
*consulate(s) general:* Atlanta, Chicago, Houston, Los Angeles, Miami, New Orleans, New York, Phoenix, San Francisco
*honorary consulate(s):* Jacksonville
**Diplomatic representation from the US:**
*chief of mission:* Ambassador Hugo LLORENS
*embassy:* Avenida La Paz, Apartado Postal No. 3453, Tegucigalpa
*mailing address:* American Embassy, APO AA 34022, Tegucigalpa
*telephone:* [504] 236-9320, 238-5114
*FAX:* [504] 238-4357
**Flag description:** three equal horizontal bands of blue (top), white, and blue, with five blue, five-pointed stars arranged in an X pattern centered in the white band; the stars represent the members of the former Federal Republic of Central America - Costa Rica, El Salvador, Guatemala, Honduras, and Nicaragua; similar to the flag of El Salvador, which features a round emblem encircled by the words REPUBLICA DE EL SALVADOR EN LA AMERICA CENTRAL centered in the white band; also similar to the flag of Nicaragua, which features a triangle encircled by the word REPUBLICA DE NICARAGUA on top and AMERICA CENTRAL on the bottom, centered in the white band

## Economy

**Economy - overview:** Honduras, the second poorest country in Central America, has an extraordinarily unequal distribution of income and high unemployment. The economy relies heavily on a narrow range of exports, notably bananas and coffee, making it vulnerable to natural disasters and shifts in commodity prices; however, investments in the maquila and non-traditional export sectors are slowly

# Honduras (continued)

diversifying the economy. Economic growth remains dependent on the US economy its largest trading partner, and will decline in 2009 as a result of reduction in export demand and tightening global credit markets. Remittances represent over a quarter of GDP or nearly three-quarters of exports. The US-Central America Free Trade Agreement (CAFTA) came into force in 2006 and has helped foster investment. Despite improvements in tax collections, the government's fiscal deficit is growing due to increases in current expenditures and financial losses from the state energy and telephone companies.

**GDP (purchasing power parity):**
$33.63 billion (2008 est.)
$32.34 billion (2007)
$30.42 billion (2006)
*note:* data are in 2008 US dollars

**GDP (official exchange rate):** $13.78 billion (2008 est.)

**GDP - real growth rate:**
4% (2008 est.)
6.3% (2007 est.)
6.3% (2006 est.)

**GDP - per capita (PPP):**
$4,400 (2008 est.)
$4,300 (2007 est.)
$4,200 (2006 est.)
*note:* data are in 2008 US dollars

**GDP - composition by sector:**
*agriculture:* 13.4%
*industry:* 28.2%
*services:* 58.5% (2008 est.)

**Labor force:** 2.892 million (2008 est.)

**Labor force - by occupation:**
*agriculture:* 39.2%
*industry:* 20.9%
*services:* 39.8% (2005 est.)

**Unemployment rate:**
27.8% (2007 est.)

**Population below poverty line:** 50.7% (2004)

**Household income or consumption by percentage share:**
*lowest 10%:* 1.2%
*highest 10%:* 42.2% (2003)

**Distribution of family income - Gini index:** 53.8 (2003)

**Investment (gross fixed):** 31.5% of GDP (2008 est.)

**Budget:**
*revenues:* $2.628 billion
*expenditures:* $3.183 billion; including capital expenditures of $106 million (2008 est.)

**Public debt:** 21% of GDP (2008 est.)

**Inflation rate (consumer prices):**
11.9% (2008 est.)
6.9% (2007 est.)

**Central bank discount rate:** NA

**Commercial bank prime lending rate:** 16.61% (31 December 2007)

**Stock of money:** $1.573 billion (31 December 2007)

**Stock of quasi money:** $5.266 billion (31 December 2007)

**Stock of domestic credit:** $6.298 billion (31 December 2007)

**Market value of publicly traded shares:** $NA

**Agriculture - products:** bananas, coffee, citrus; beef; timber; shrimp, tilapia, lobster; corn, African palm

**Industries:** sugar, coffee, textiles, clothing, wood products

**Industrial production growth rate:** 4% (2008 est.)

**Electricity - production:** 5.753 billion kWh (2006 est.)

**Electricity - consumption:** 4.233 billion kWh (2006 est.)

**Electricity - exports:** 0 kWh (2007 est.)

**Electricity - imports:** 11.8 million kWh (2007 est.)

**Oil - production:** 0 bbl/day (2007 est.)

**Oil - consumption:** 46,830 bbl/day (2006 est.)

**Oil - exports:** 417.9 bbl/day (2005)

**Oil - imports:** 44,040 bbl/day (2005)

**Oil - proved reserves:** 0 bbl (1 January 2006 est.)

**Natural gas - production:** 0 cu m (2007 est.)

**Natural gas - consumption:** 0 cu m (2007 est.)

**Natural gas - exports:** 0 cu m (2007 est.)

**Natural gas - imports:** 0 cu m (2007 est.)

**Natural gas - proved reserves:** 0 cu m (1 January 2006 est.)

**Current account balance:** -$2.047 billion (2008 est.)

**Exports:** $6.236 billion f.o.b. (2008 est.)

**Exports - commodities:** coffee, shrimp, bananas, gold, palm oil, fruit, lobster, lumber

**Exports - partners:** US 67.2%, El Salvador 4.9%, Guatemala 3.9% (2007)

**Imports:** $10.2 billion f.o.b. (2008 est.)

**Imports - commodities:** machinery and transport equipment, industrial raw materials, chemical products, fuels, foodstuffs

**Imports - partners:** US 52.4%, Guatemala 7.1%, El Salvador 5.2%, Mexico 4.5%, Costa Rica 4.2% (2007)

**Reserves of foreign exchange and gold:** $2.096 billion (31 December 2008 est.)

**Debt - external:** $3.602 billion (31 December 2008 est.)

**Exchange rates:** lempiras (HNL) per US dollar - 18.983 (2008 est.), 18.9 (2007), 18.895 (2006), 18.92 (2005), 18.206 (2004)

## Communications

**Telephones - main lines in use:** 821,200 (2007)

**Telephones - mobile cellular:** 4.185 million (2007)

**Telephone system:**
*general assessment:* telecommunications infrastructure is among the least developed in Latin America; fixed-line connections are limited; multiple providers of mobile-cellular services
*domestic:* beginning in 2003, private sub-operators allowed to provide fixed-lines in order to expand telephone coverage; fixed-line teledensity has increased to about 10 per 100 persons; mobile-cellular telephone service has been increasing rapidly and subscribership in 2007 approached 60 per 100 persons

*international:* country code - 504; landing point for both the Americas Region Caribbean Ring System (ARCOS-1) and the MAYA-1 fiber optic submarine cable system that together provide connectivity to South and Central America, parts of the Caribbean, and the US; satellite earth stations - 2 Intelsat (Atlantic Ocean); connected to Central American Microwave System

**Radio broadcast stations:** AM 241, FM 53, shortwave 12 (1998)

**Television broadcast stations:** 11 (plus 17 repeaters) (1997)

**Internet country code:** .hn

**Internet hosts:** 13,370 (2008)

**Internet users:** 424,200 (2007)

## Transportation

**Airports:** 108 (2008)

**Airports - with paved runways:**
*total:* 12
*2,438 to 3,047 m:* 3
*1,524 to 2,437 m:* 2
*914 to 1,523 m:* 4
*under 914 m:* 3 (2008)

**Airports - with unpaved runways:**
*total:* 96
*1,524 to 2,437 m:* 2
*914 to 1,523 m:* 17
*under 914 m:* 77 (2008)

**Railways:**
*total:* 699 km
*narrow gauge:* 279 km 1.067-m gauge; 420 km 0.914-m gauge (2006)

**Roadways:**
*total:* 13,600 km
*paved:* 2,775 km
*unpaved:* 10,825 km (2000)

**Waterways:** 465 km (most navigable only by small craft) (2008)

**Merchant marine:**
*total:* 123
*by type:* bulk carrier 10, cargo 57, chemical tanker 6, container 1, liquefied gas 1, passenger 4, passenger/cargo 7, petroleum tanker 25, refrigerated cargo 7, roll on/roll off 4, specialized tanker 1
*foreign-owned:* 42 (Bangladesh 1, Canada 1, China 3, Egypt 3, Greece 4, Hong Kong 1, Israel 1, Japan 4, South Korea 6, Lebanon 1, Mexico 1, Singapore 12, Taiwan 2, Tanzania 1, Vietnam 1) (2008)

**Ports and terminals:** La Ceiba, Puerto Cortes, San Lorenzo, Tela

## Military

**Military branches:** Army, Navy (includes Naval Infantry), Honduran Air Force (Fuerza Aerea Hondurena, FAH) (2008)

**Military service age and obligation:** 18 years of age for voluntary 2 to 3-year military service (2004)

**Manpower available for military service:**
*males age 16-49:* 1,868,940
*females age 16-49:* 1,825,770 (2008 est.)

## Honduras (continued)

**Manpower fit for military service:**
*males age 16-49:* 1,397,938
*females age 16-49:* 1,402,398 (2009 est.)
**Manpower reaching militarily significant age annually:**
*male:* 92,638
*female:* 88,993 (2009 est.)
**Military expenditures:** 0.6% of GDP (2006 est.)

### Transnational Issues

**Disputes - international:** International Court of Justice (ICJ) ruled on the delimitation of "bolsones" (disputed areas) along the El Salvador-Honduras border in 1992 with final settlement by the parties in 2006 after an Organization of American States (OAS) survey and a further ICJ ruling in 2003; the 1992 ICJ ruling advised a tripartite resolution to a maritime boundary in the Gulf of Fonseca with consideration of Honduran access to the Pacific; El Salvador continues to claim tiny Conejo Island, not mentioned in the ICJ ruling, off Honduras in the Gulf of Fonseca; Honduras claims the Belizean-administered Sapodilla Cays off the coast of Belize in its constitution, but agreed to a joint ecological park around the cays should Guatemala consent to a maritime corridor in the Caribbean under the OAS-sponsored 2002 Belize-Guatemala Differendum; memorials and countermemorials were filed by the parties in Nicaragua's 1999 and 2001 proceedings against Honduras and Colombia at the ICJ over the maritime boundary and territorial claims in the western Caribbean Sea - final public hearings are scheduled for 2007

**Illicit drugs:** transshipment point for drugs and narcotics; illicit producer of cannabis, cultivated on small plots and used principally for local consumption; corruption is a major problem; some money-laundering activity

# Hong Kong
*(special administrative region of China)*

### Introduction

**Background:** Occupied by the UK in 1841, Hong Kong was formally ceded by China the following year; various adjacent lands were added later in the 19th century. Pursuant to an agreement signed by China and the UK on 19 December 1984, Hong Kong became the Hong Kong Special Administrative Region (SAR) of the People's Republic of China on 1 July 1997. In this agreement, China promised that, under its "one country, two systems" formula, China's socialist economic system would not be imposed on Hong Kong and that Hong Kong would enjoy a high degree of autonomy in all matters except foreign and defense affairs for the next 50 years.

### Geography

**Location:** Eastern Asia, bordering the South China Sea and China
**Geographic coordinates:** 22 15 N, 114 10 E
**Map references:** Southeast Asia
**Area:**
*total:* 1,092 sq km
*land:* 1,042 sq km
*water:* 50 sq km
**Area - comparative:** six times the size of Washington, DC
**Land boundaries:**
*total:* 30 km
*regional border:* China 30 km
**Coastline:** 733 km
**Maritime claims:**
*territorial sea:* 3 nm
**Climate:** subtropical monsoon; cool and humid in winter, hot and rainy from spring through summer, warm and sunny in fall
**Terrain:** hilly to mountainous with steep slopes; lowlands in north
**Elevation extremes:**
*lowest point:* South China Sea 0 m
*highest point:* Tai Mo Shan 958 m

**Natural resources:** outstanding deepwater harbor, feldspar
**Land use:**
*arable land:* 5.05%
*permanent crops:* 1.01%
*other:* 93.94% (2001)
**Irrigated land:** 20 sq km (1998 est.)
**Natural hazards:** occasional typhoons
**Environment - current issues:** air and water pollution from rapid urbanization
**Environment - international agreements:**
*party to:* Marine Dumping (associate member), Ship Pollution (associate member)
**Geography - note:** more than 200 islands

### People

**Population:** 7,055,071 (July 2009 est.)
**Age structure:**
*0-14 years:* 12.2% (male 450,833/female 411,997)
*15-64 years:* 74.6% (male 2,551,256/female 2,713,532)
*65 years and over:* 13.1% (male 434,090/female 493,363) (2009 est.)
**Median age:**
*total:* 42.3 years
*male:* 41.9 years
*female:* 42.6 years (2009 est.)
**Population growth rate:** 0.504% (2009 est.)
**Birth rate:** 7.42 births/1,000 population (2009 est.)
**Death rate:** 6.6 deaths/1,000 population (2008 est.)
**Net migration rate:** 4.38 migrant(s)/1,000 population (2009 est.)
**Urbanization:**
*urban population:* 100% of total population (2008)
*rate of urbanization:* 1% annual rate of change (2005-10 est.)
**Sex ratio:**
*at birth:* 1.08 male(s)/female
*under 15 years:* 1.09 male(s)/female
*15-64 years:* 0.94 male(s)/female
*65 years and over:* 0.88 male(s)/female
*total population:* 0.95 male(s)/female (2009 est.)
**Infant mortality rate:**
*total:* 2.92 deaths/1,000 live births
*male:* 3.1 deaths/1,000 live births
*female:* 2.73 deaths/1,000 live births (2009 est.)
**Life expectancy at birth:**
*total population:* 81.86 years
*male:* 79.16 years
*female:* 84.79 years (2009 est.)
**Total fertility rate:** 1.02 children born/woman (2009 est.)
**HIV/AIDS - adult prevalence rate:** 0.1% (2003 est.)
**HIV/AIDS - people living with HIV/AIDS:** 2,600 (2003 est.)
**HIV/AIDS - deaths:** fewer than 200 (2003 est.)
**Nationality:**
*noun:* Chinese/Hong Konger
*adjective:* Chinese/Hong Kong
**Ethnic groups:** Chinese 95%, Filipino 1.6%, Indonesian 1.3%, other 2.1% (2006 census)

# Hong Kong *(continued)*

**Religions:** eclectic mixture of local religions 90%, Christian 10%

**Languages:** Chinese (Cantonese) 89.2% (official), other Chinese dialects 6.4%, English 3.2% (official), other 1.2% (2001 census)

**Literacy:**
*definition:* age 15 and over has ever attended school
*total population:* 93.5%
*male:* 96.9%
*female:* 89.6% (2002)

**School life expectancy (primary to tertiary education):**
*total:* 14 years
*male:* 14 years
*female:* 13 years (2006)

**Education expenditures:** 3.9% of GDP (2006)

## Government

**Country name:**
*conventional long form:* Hong Kong Special Administrative Region
*conventional short form:* Hong Kong
*local long form:* Xianggang Tebie Xingzhengqu
*local short form:* Xianggang
*abbreviation:* HK

**Dependency status:** special administrative region of China

**Government type:** limited democracy

**Administrative divisions:** none (special administrative region of China)

**Independence:** none (special administrative region of China)

**National holiday:** National Day (Anniversary of the Founding of the People's Republic of China), 1 October (1949); note - 1 July 1997 is celebrated as Hong Kong Special Administrative Region Establishment Day

**Constitution:** Basic Law, approved in March 1990 by China's National People's Congress, is Hong Kong's "mini-constitution"

**Legal system:** based on English common law

**Suffrage:** direct election - 18 years of age for half the legislature and a majority of seats in 18 district councils; universal for permanent residents living in the territory of Hong Kong for the past seven years; indirect election - limited to about 220,000 members of functional constituencies and an 800-member election committee drawn from broad regional groupings, central government bodies, and municipal organizations

**Executive branch:**
*chief of state:* President of China HU Jintao (since 15 March 2003)
*head of government:* Chief Executive Donald TSANG Yam-kuen (since 24 June 2005)
*cabinet:* Executive Council or ExCo consists of 15 official members and 14 non-official members
*elections:* chief executive elected for five-year term by 800-member electoral committee; last held on 25 March 2007 (next to be held in 2012)
*election results:* Donald TSANG elected chief executive receiving 84.1% of the vote of the election committee; Alan LEONG Kah-kit received 15.9%

**Legislative branch:** unicameral Legislative Council or LegCo (60 seats; 30 seats indirectly elected by functional constituencies, 30 elected by popular vote; members serve four-year terms)
*elections:* last held 7 September 2008 (next to be held in September 2012)
*election results:* percent of vote by party - pro-democracy 57%; pro-Beijing 40%, independent 3%; seats by parties - (pro-Beijing 35) DAB 13, Liberal Party 7, FTU 1, others 14; (pro-democracy 23) Democratic Party 8, Civic Party 5, CTU 3, League of Social Democrats 3, ADPL 2, The Frontier 1, NWSC 1; others 11; independents and non-voting LegCo president 2

**Judicial branch:** Court of Final Appeal in the Hong Kong Special Administrative Region

**Political parties and leaders:** Association for Democracy and People's Livelihood or ADPL [Frederick FUNG Kin-kee]; Civic Party [KUAN Hsin-chi]; Democratic Alliance for the Betterment and Progress of Hong Kong or DAB [TAM Yiu Cheng]; Democratic Party [Albert HO Chun-yan]; League of Social Democrats [Raymond WONG Yuk-man]; Liberal Party [Miriam LAU Kin-yee]
*note:* political blocs include: pro-democracy - ADPL, Civic Party; Democratic Party, League of Social Democrats; pro-Beijing - DAB, Liberal Party, The Professional Forum (an informal group of three generally pro-government and pro-business LegCo members from functional constituencies and one independent elected from a geographic constituency); there is no political party ordinance, so there are no registered political parties; politically active groups register as societies or companies

**Political pressure groups and leaders:** Chinese General Chamber of Commerce (pro-China); Chinese Manufacturers' Association of Hong Kong; Confederation of Trade Unions or CTU (pro-democracy) [LAU Chin-shek, president; LEE Cheuk-yan, general secretary]; Federation of Hong Kong Industries; Federation of Trade Unions or FTU (pro-China) [CHENG Yiu-tong, executive councilor]; Hong Kong Alliance in Support of the Patriotic Democratic Movement in China [Szeto WAH, chairman]; Hong Kong and Kowloon Trade Union Council (pro-Taiwan); Hong Kong General Chamber of Commerce; Hong Kong Professional Teachers' Union [CHEUNG Man-kwong, president]; Neighborhood and Workers' Service Center or NWSC [LEUNG Yiu-chung, LegCo member] (pro-democracy); Civic Act-up [Cyd HO Sau-lan, LegCo member] (pro-democracy)

**International organization participation:** ADB, APEC, BIS, ICC, IHO, IMF, IMO (associate), IOC, ISO (correspondent), ITUC, UNWTO (associate), UPU, WCL, WCO, WFTU, WMO, WTO

**Diplomatic representation in the US:** none (special administrative region of China); Hong Kong Economic and Trade Office in Washington, New York, and San Francisco carries out normal liaison and communication with the US Government and other US entities

**Diplomatic representation from the US:**
*chief of mission:* Consul General Joseph R. DONOVAN, Jr.
*consulate(s) general:* 26 Garden Road, Hong Kong
*mailing address:* PSC 461, Box 1, FPO AP 96521-0006
*telephone:* [852] 2523-9011
*FAX:* [852] 2845-1598

**Flag description:** red with a stylized, white, five-petal bauhinia flower in the center

## Economy

**Economy - overview:** Hong Kong has a free market economy highly dependent on international trade and finance, which has left it heavily exposed to the global economic slowdown that began in 2008. The total value of goods and services trade, including the sizable share of reexports, was equivalent to 404% of GDP in 2007. The territory has become increasingly integrated with mainland China over the past few years through trade, tourism, and financial links. The mainland has long been Hong Kong's largest trading partner, accounting for nearly 49% of Hong Kong's exports trade by value in 2008. As a result of China's easing of travel restrictions, the number of mainland tourists to the territory has surged from 4.5 million in 2001 to 16.9 million in 2008, when they outnumbered visitors from all other countries combined. Hong Kong has also established itself as the premier stock market for Chinese firms seeking to list abroad. More than one-third of the firms listed on the Hong Kong Stock Exchange are now mainland Chinese companies, and they account for 60% of the Exchange's market capitalization. During the past decade, as Hong Kong's manufacturing industry moved to the mainland, its service industry has grown rapidly and now accounts for more than 90% of the territory's GDP. Hong Kong's natural resources are limited, and food and raw materials must be imported. GDP growth averaged a strong 5% from 1989 to 2007, but the global financial crisis caused a sharp slowdown in the second half of 2008, pushing the territory into recession. Hong Kong continues to link its currency closely to the US dollar, maintaining an arrangement established in 1983.

**GDP (purchasing power parity):**
$307.6 billion (2008 est.)
$299.5 billion (2007)
$281.5 billion (2006)
*note:* data are in 2008 US dollars

**GDP (official exchange rate):** $223.8 billion (2008 est.)

**GDP - real growth rate:**
2.8% (2008 est.)
6.4% (2007 est.)
7% (2006 est.)

**GDP - per capita (PPP):**
$43,800 (2008 est.)
$42,900 (2007 est.)
$40,600 (2006 est.)
*note:* data are in 2008 US dollars

**GDP - composition by sector:**
*agriculture:* 0%
*industry:* 7.9%
*services:* 92% (2008 est.)

## Hong Kong *(continued)*

**Labor force:** 3.67 million (2008 est.)
**Labor force - by occupation:** manufacturing 6.1%, construction 1.9%, wholesale and retail trade, restaurants, and hotels 42.9%, financing, insurance, and real estate 21.4%, transport and communications 7.9%, community and social services 19.7%
*note:* above data exclude public sector (2008 est.)
**Unemployment rate:**
4.1% (December 2008 est.)
4% (2007 est.)
**Population below poverty line:** NA%
**Household income or consumption by percentage share:**
*lowest 10%:* NA%
*highest 10%:* NA%
**Distribution of family income - Gini index:** 53.3 (2007)
**Investment (gross fixed):** 20.6% of GDP (2008 est.)
**Budget:**
*revenues:* $36.62 billion
*expenditures:* $38.89 billion (2008 est.)
**Public debt:** 14.5% of GDP (2008 est.)
**Inflation rate (consumer prices):**
2.1% (2008 est.)
2% (2007 est.)
**Central bank discount rate:** 0.5% (31 December 2008)
**Commercial bank prime lending rate:** 5% (31 December 2008)
**Stock of money:** $63.03 billion (31 December 2008)
**Stock of quasi money:** $352.4 billion (31 December 2008)
**Stock of domestic credit:** $272.4 billion (31 December 2008)
**Market value of publicly traded shares:** $1.32 trillion (31 December 2008)
**Agriculture - products:** fresh vegetables; poultry, pork; fish
**Industries:** textiles, clothing, tourism, banking, shipping, electronics, plastics, toys, watches, clocks
**Industrial production growth rate:** 0% (2008 est.)
**Electricity - production:** 38.4 billion kWh (2008 est.)
**Electricity - consumption:** 44.6 billion kWh (2008 est.)
**Electricity - exports:** 3.7 billion kWh (2008 est.)
**Electricity - imports:** 11 billion kWh (2008 est.)
**Oil - production:** 0 bbl/day (2008)
**Oil - consumption:** 315,400 bbl/day (2008 est.)
**Oil - exports:** 19,480 bbl/day (2008)
**Oil - imports:** 334,900 bbl/day (2008)
**Oil - proved reserves:** 0 bbl (1 January 2008)
**Natural gas - production:** 0 cu m (2008)
**Natural gas - consumption:** 3.08 billion cu m (2008 est.)
**Natural gas - exports:** 0 cu m (2008)
**Natural gas - imports:** 3.08 billion cu m (2008 est.)
**Natural gas - proved reserves:** 0 cu m (1 January 2006 est.)
**Current account balance:** $22.44 billion (2008 est.)
**Exports:** $362.1 billion f.o.b., including reexports (2008)

**Exports - commodities:** electrical machinery and appliances, textiles, apparel, footwear, watches and clocks, toys, plastics, precious stones, printed material
**Exports - partners:** China 48.7%, US 13.7%, Japan 4.5% (2007)
**Imports:** $387.9 billion (2008 est.)
**Imports - commodities:** raw materials and semi-manufactures, consumer goods, capital goods, foodstuffs, fuel (most is re-exported)
**Imports - partners:** China 46.3%, Japan 10%, Taiwan 7.1%, Singapore 6.8%, US 4.9%, South Korea 4.2% (2007)
**Reserves of foreign exchange and gold:** $165.9 billion (31 December 2008)
**Debt - external:** $78.84 billion (31 December 2008 est.)
**Stock of direct foreign investment - at home:** $1.235 trillion (2008 est.)
**Stock of direct foreign investment - abroad:** $1.079 trillion (2008 est.)
**Exchange rates:** Hong Kong dollars (HKD) per US dollar - 7.751 (2008), 7.802 (2007), 7.7678 (2006), 7.7773 (2005), 7.788 (2004)

### Communications

**Telephones - main lines in use:** 3.875 million (2007)
**Telephones - mobile cellular:** 10.55 million (2007)
**Telephone system:**
*general assessment:* modern facilities provide excellent domestic and international services
*domestic:* microwave radio relay links and extensive fiber-optic network
*international:* country code - 852; multiple international submarine cables provide connections to Asia, US, Australia, the Middle East, and Western Europe; satellite earth stations - 3 Intelsat (1 Pacific Ocean and 2 Indian Ocean); coaxial cable to Guangzhou, China
**Radio broadcast stations:** AM 6, FM 10, shortwave 0 (2008)
**Television broadcast stations:** 2 (2 TV networks, each broadcasting on 2 channels) (2008)
**Internet country code:** .hk
**Internet hosts:** 817,766 (2008)
**Internet users:** 3.961 million (2007)

### Transportation

**Airports:** 2 (2008)
**Airports - with paved runways:**
*total:* 2
*over 3,047 m:* 1
*1,524 to 2,437 m:* 1 (2008)
**Heliports:** 5 (2007)
**Roadways:**
*total:* 2,009 km
*paved:* 2,009 km (2007)
**Merchant marine:**
*total:* 1,114
*by type:* barge carrier 2, bulk carrier 525, cargo 142, carrier 3, chemical tanker 68, combination ore/oil 2, container 205, liquefied gas 22, passenger 6,

passenger/cargo 5, petroleum tanker 114, roll on/roll off 4, specialized tanker 9, vehicle carrier 7
*foreign-owned:* 703 (Belgium 3, Canada 44, China 324, Denmark 24, France 1, Germany 6, Greece 22, Indonesia 7, Iran 15, Japan 111, South Korea 3, Norway 40, Philippines 1, Portugal 1, Russia 2, Singapore 18, Syria 1, Taiwan 11, UAE 1, UK 39, US 29)
*registered in other countries:* 357 (Bahamas 30, Bermuda 4, Cambodia 8, China 12, Cyprus 2, Georgia 2, Honduras 1, India 1, Jamaica 1, Kiribati 4, Liberia 44, Malaysia 14, Malta 1, Marshall Islands 4, Mexico 1, Netherlands Antilles 2, Norway 20, Panama 130, Philippines 1, Portugal 2, Saint Vincent and the Grenadines 6, Seychelles 1, Sierra Leone 1, Singapore 47, Tuvalu 7, UK 2, Vietnam 1, unknown 8) (2008)
**Ports and terminals:** Hong Kong

### Military

**Military branches:** no regular indigenous military forces; Hong Kong garrison of China's People's Liberation Army (PLA) includes elements of the PLA Ground Forces, PLA Navy, and PLA Air Force; these forces are under the direct leadership of the Central Military Commission in Beijing and under administrative control of the adjacent Guangzhou Military Region (2009)
**Manpower available for military service:**
*males age 16-49:* 1,772,820
*females age 16-49:* 1,941,448 (2008 est.)
**Manpower fit for military service:**
*males age 16-49:* 1,421,406
*females age 16-49:* 1,543,443 (2009 est.)
**Manpower reaching militarily significant age annually:**
*male:* 42,330
*female:* 38,797 (2009 est.)
**Military expenditures:** NA
**Military - note:** defense is the responsibility of China

### Transnational Issues

**Disputes - international:** none
**Illicit drugs:** despite strenuous law enforcement efforts, faces difficult challenges in controlling transit of heroin and methamphetamine to regional and world markets; modern banking system provides conduit for money laundering; rising indigenous use of synthetic drugs, especially among young people

## Howland Island
*(territory of the US)*

Description under

United States

Pacific Island

Wildlife Refuges

# Hungary

## Introduction

**Background:** Hungary became a Christian kingdom in A.D. 1000 and for many centuries served as a bulwark against Ottoman Turkish expansion in Europe. The kingdom eventually became part of the polyglot Austro-Hungarian Empire, which collapsed during World War I. The country fell under Communist rule following World War II. In 1956, a revolt and an announced withdrawal from the Warsaw Pact were met with a massive military intervention by Moscow. Under the leadership of Janos KADAR in 1968, Hungary began liberalizing its economy, introducing so-called "Goulash Communism." Hungary held its first multiparty elections in 1990 and initiated a free market economy. It joined NATO in 1999 and the EU in 2004.

## Geography

**Location:** Central Europe, northwest of Romania
**Geographic coordinates:** 47 00 N, 20 00 E
**Map references:** Europe
**Area:**
*total:* 93,030 sq km
*land:* 92,340 sq km
*water:* 690 sq km
**Area - comparative:** slightly smaller than Indiana
**Land boundaries:**
*total:* 2,185 km
*border countries:* Austria 366 km, Croatia 329 km, Romania 443 km, Serbia 166 km, Slovakia 676 km, Slovenia 102 km, Ukraine 103 km
**Coastline:** 0 km (landlocked)
**Maritime claims:** none (landlocked)
**Climate:** temperate; cold, cloudy, humid winters; warm summers
**Terrain:** mostly flat to rolling plains; hills and low mountains on the Slovakian border

**Elevation extremes:**
*lowest point:* Tisza River 78 m
*highest point:* Kekes 1,014 m
**Natural resources:** bauxite, coal, natural gas, fertile soils, arable land
**Land use:**
*arable land:* 49.58%
*permanent crops:* 2.06%
*other:* 48.36% (2005)
**Irrigated land:** 2,300 sq km (2003)
**Total renewable water resources:** 120 cu km (2005)
**Freshwater withdrawal (domestic/industrial/agricultural):**
*total:* 21.03 cu km/yr (9%/59%/32%)
*per capita:* 2,082 cu m/yr (2001)
**Environment - current issues:** the upgrading of Hungary's standards in waste management, energy efficiency, and air, soil, and water pollution to meet EU requirements will require large investments
**Environment - international agreements:**
*party to:* Air Pollution, Air Pollution-Nitrogen Oxides, Air Pollution-Persistent Organic Pollutants, Air Pollution-Sulfur 85, Air Pollution-Sulfur 94, Air Pollution-Volatile Organic Compounds, Antarctic Treaty, Biodiversity, Climate Change, Climate Change-Kyoto Protocol, Desertification, Endangered Species, Environmental Modification, Hazardous Wastes, Law of the Sea, Marine Dumping, Ozone Layer Protection, Ship Pollution, Wetlands, Whaling
*signed, but not ratified:* none of the selected agreements
**Geography - note:** landlocked; strategic location astride main land routes between Western Europe and Balkan Peninsula as well as between Ukraine and Mediterranean basin; the north-south flowing Duna (Danube) and Tisza Rivers divide the country into three large regions

## People

**Population:** 9,905,596 (July 2009 est.)
**Age structure:**
*0-14 years:* 15% (male 763,553/female 720,112)
*15-64 years:* 69.3% (male 3,384,961/female 3,475,135)
*65 years and over:* 15.8% (male 566,067/female 995,768) (2009 est.)
**Median age:**
*total:* 39.4 years
*male:* 37.1 years
*female:* 42 years (2009 est.)
**Population growth rate:** -0.257% (2009 est.)
**Birth rate:** 9.51 births/1,000 population (2009 est.)
**Death rate:** 12.99 deaths/1,000 population (2008 est.)
**Net migration rate:** 0.87 migrant(s)/1,000 population (2009 est.)
**Urbanization:**
*urban population:* 68% of total population (2008)
*rate of urbanization:* 0.3% annual rate of change (2005-10 est.)
**Sex ratio:**
*at birth:* 1.06 male(s)/female
*under 15 years:* 1.06 male(s)/female
*15-64 years:* 0.97 male(s)/female
*65 years and over:* 0.57 male(s)/female
*total population:* 0.91 male(s)/female (2009 est.)
**Infant mortality rate:**
*total:* 7.86 deaths/1,000 live births
*male:* 8.57 deaths/1,000 live births
*female:* 7.12 deaths/1,000 live births (2009 est.)
**Life expectancy at birth:**
*total population:* 73.44 years
*male:* 69.27 years
*female:* 77.87 years (2009 est.)
**Total fertility rate:** 1.35 children born/woman (2009 est.)
**HIV/AIDS - adult prevalence rate:** 0.1% (2007 est.)
**HIV/AIDS - people living with HIV/AIDS:** 3,300 (2007 est.)
**HIV/AIDS - deaths:** fewer than 100 (2001 est.)
**Major infectious diseases:**
*degree of risk:* intermediate
*food or waterborne diseases:* bacterial diarrhea and hepatitis A
*vectorborne diseases:* tickborne encephalitis (2009)
**Nationality:**
*noun:* Hungarian(s)
*adjective:* Hungarian
**Ethnic groups:** Hungarian 92.3%, Roma 1.9%, other or unknown 5.8% (2001 census)
**Religions:** Roman Catholic 51.9%, Calvinist 15.9%, Lutheran 3%, Greek Catholic 2.6%, other Christian 1%, other or unspecified 11.1%, unaffiliated 14.5% (2001 census)
**Languages:** Hungarian 93.6%, other or unspecified 6.4% (2001 census)
**Literacy:**
*definition:* age 15 and over can read and write
*total population:* 99.4%
*male:* 99.5%
*female:* 99.3% (2003 est.)

**School life expectancy (primary to tertiary education):**
*total:* 15 years
*male:* 15 years
*female:* 16 years (2006)
**Education expenditures:** 5.5% of GDP (2005)

## Government

**Country name:**
*conventional long form:* Republic of Hungary
*conventional short form:* Hungary
*local long form:* Magyar Koztarsasag
*local short form:* Magyarorszag
**Government type:** parliamentary democracy
**Capital:**
*name:* Budapest
*geographic coordinates:* 47 30 N, 19 05 E
*time difference:* UTC+1 (6 hours ahead of Washington, DC during Standard Time)
*daylight saving time:* +1hr, begins last Sunday in March; ends last Sunday in October
**Administrative divisions:** 19 counties (megyek, singular - megye), 23 urban counties (singular - megyei varos), and 1 capital city (fovaros)
*counties:* Bacs-Kiskun, Baranya, Bekes, Borsod-Abauj-Zemplen, Csongrad, Fejer, Gyor-Moson-Sopron, Hajdu-Bihar, Heves, Jasz-Nagykun-Szolnok, Komarom-Esztergom, Nograd, Pest, Somogy, Szabolcs-Szatmar-Bereg, Tolna, Vas, Veszprem, Zala
*urban counties:* Bekescsaba, Debrecen, Dunaujvaros, Eger, Erd, Gyor, Hodmezovasarhely, Kaposvar, Kecskemet, Miskolc, Nagykanizsa, Nyiregyhaza, Pecs, Salgotarjan, Sopron, Szeged, Szekesfehervar, Szekszard, Szolnok, Szombathely, Tatabanya, Veszprem, Zalaegerszeg
*capital city:* Budapest
**Independence:** 25 December 1000 (crowning of King STEPHEN I, traditional founding date)
**National holiday:** Saint Stephen's Day, 20 August
**Constitution:** 18 August 1949, effective 20 August 1949; revised 19 April 1972; 18 October 1989; and 1997
*note:* 18 October 1989 revision ensured legal rights for individuals and constitutional checks on the authority of the prime minister and also established the principle of parliamentary oversight; 1997 amendment streamlined the judicial system
**Legal system:** based on the German-Austrian legal system; accepts compulsory ICJ jurisdiction with reservations
**Suffrage:** 18 years of age; universal
**Executive branch:**
*chief of state:* President Laszlo SOLYOM (since 5 August 2005)
*head of government:* Prime Minister Gordon BAJNAI (since 14 April 2009)
*cabinet:* Council of Ministers prime minister elected by the National Assembly on the recommendation of the president; other ministers proposed by the prime minister and appointed and relieved of their duties by the president

*elections:* president elected by the National Assembly for a five-year term (eligible for a second term); election last held 6-7 June 2005 (next to be held by June 2010); prime minister elected by the National Assembly on the recommendation of the president; election last held 14 April 2009
*election results:* Laszlo SOLYOM elected president by a simple majority in the third round of voting, 185 to 182; Gordon BAJNAI elected prime minister; result of legislative vote - 204 to 0
*note:* to be elected, the president must win two-thirds of legislative vote in the first two rounds or a simple majority in the third round
**Legislative branch:** unicameral National Assembly or Orszaggyules (386 seats; members are elected by popular vote under a system of proportional and direct representation to serve four-year terms)
*elections:* last held 9 and 23 April 2006 (next to be held in April 2010)
*election results:* percent of vote by party (5% or more of the vote required for parliamentary representation in the first round) - MSzP 43.2%, Fidesz-KDNP 42%, SzDSz 6.5%, MDF 5%, other 3.3%; seats by party - MSzP 190, Fidesz-KDNP 164, SzDSz 20, MDF 11, independent 1; seats by party as of January 2009 - MSzP 190, Fidesz-KDNP 161, SzDSz 19, MDF 10, independent 5, vacant 1
**Judicial branch:** Constitutional Court (judges are elected by the National Assembly for nine-year terms)
**Political parties and leaders:** Alliance of Free Democrats or SzDSz [Gabor FODOR]; Christian Democratic People's Party or KDNP [Zsolt SEMJEN]; Hungarian Civic Alliance or Fidesz [Viktor ORBAN, chairman]; Hungarian Democratic Forum or MDF [Ibolya DAVID]; Hungarian Socialist Party or MSzP [Ildiko LENDVAI]
**Political pressure groups and leaders:** Air Work Group (works to reduce air pollution in towns and cities); Company For Freedom Rights (Tarsasag a Szabadsagjogokert) or TASZ (personal data protection); Danube Circle (protests the building of the Gabchikovo-Nagymaros dam); Green Future (protests the impact of lead contamination of local factory on health of the people); environmentalists: Hungarian Ornithological and Nature Conservation Society (Magyar Madartani Egyesulet) or MME; Green Alternative (Zold Alternativa)
**International organization participation:** Australia Group, BIS, CE, CEI, CERN, EAPC, EBRD, EIB, ESA (cooperating state), EU, FAO, G-9, IAEA, IBRD, ICAO, ICC, ICCt, ICRM, IDA, IEA, IFC, IFRCS, ILO, IMF, IMO, IMSO, Interpol, IOC, IOM, IPU, ISO, ITSO, ITU, ITUC, MIGA, MINURSO, NAM (guest), NATO, NEA, NSG, OAS (observer), OECD, OIF (observer), OPCW, OSCE, PCA, Schengen Convention, SECI, UN, UNCTAD, UNESCO, UNFICYP, UNHCR, UNIDO, UNIFIL, UNOMIG, UNWTO, UPU, WCL, WCO, WEU (associate), WFTU, WHO, WIPO, WMO, WTO, ZC
**Diplomatic representation in the US:**
*chief of mission:* Ambassador Ferenc SOMOGYI
*chancery:* 3910 Shoemaker Street NW, Washington, DC 20008

*telephone:* [1] (202) 362-6730
*FAX:* [1] (202) 966-8135
*consulate(s) general:* Chicago, Los Angeles, New York
**Diplomatic representation from the US:**
*chief of mission:* Ambassador April H. FOLEY
*embassy:* Szabadsag ter 12, H-1054 Budapest
*mailing address:* pouch: American Embassy Budapest, 5270 Budapest Place, US Department of State, Washington, DC 20521-5270
*telephone:* [36] (1) 475-4400
*FAX:* [36] (1) 475-4764
**Flag description:** three equal horizontal bands of red (top), white, and green

## Economy

**Economy - overview:** Hungary has made the transition from a centrally planned to a market economy, with a per capita income nearly two-thirds that of the EU-25 average. The private sector accounts for more than 80% of GDP. Foreign ownership of and investment in Hungarian firms is widespread, with cumulative foreign direct investment totaling more than $60 billion since 1989. The government's IMF-mandated austerity measures, imposed since late 2006, have reduced the budget deficit from over 9% of GDP in 2006 to 3.3% in 2008. Hungary's impending inability to service its short-term debt - brought on by the global credit crunch in late 2008 - led Budapest to seek and receive an IMF-arranged financial assistance package worth over $25 billion. The global financial crisis, declining exports, and low domestic consumption and fixed asset accumulation, dampened by government austerity measures, will result in a negative growth rate of about -1.5% to -2.5% in 2009.
**GDP (purchasing power parity):**
$205.7 billion (2008 est.)
$208.9 billion (2007)
$193.2 billion (2006)
*note:* data are in 2008 US dollars
**GDP (official exchange rate):** $131.4 billion (2008 est.)
**GDP - real growth rate:**
-1.5% (2008 est.)
1.3% (2007 est.)
3.9% (2006 est.)
**GDP - per capita (PPP):**
$19,800 (2008 est.)
$19,700 (2007 est.)
$19,400 (2006 est.)
*note:* data are in 2008 US dollars
**GDP - composition by sector:**
*agriculture:* 3.2%
*industry:* 31.9%
*services:* 65% (2008 est.)
**Labor force:** 4.2 million (2008 est.)
**Labor force - by occupation:**
*agriculture:* 5%
*industry:* 32.4%
*services:* 62.6% (2005)

**Unemployment rate:**
8% (2008 est.)
7.3% (2007 est.)
**Population below poverty line:** 8.6% (1993 est.)
**Household income or consumption by percentage share:**
*lowest 10%:* 4%
*highest 10%:* 22.2% (2002)
**Distribution of family income - Gini index:** 28 (2005)
**Investment (gross fixed):** 15.2% of GDP
(January - September 2008)
**Budget:**
*revenues:* $76.2 billion
*expenditures:* $81.5 billion (2008 est.)
**Public debt:** 73.8% of GDP (2008 est.)
**Inflation rate (consumer prices):**
6.1% (2008 est.)
8% (2007 est.)
**Central bank discount rate:** 9.5% (1 January 2009)
**Commercial bank prime lending rate:** 9.48%
(26 January 2009)
**Stock of money:** $36.78 billion (31 December 2007)
**Stock of quasi money:** $43.07 billion
(31 December 2007)
**Stock of domestic credit:** $109.5 billion
(31 December 2007)
**Market value of publicly traded shares:** $21.9
billion (31 December 2008)
**Agriculture - products:** wheat, corn, sunflower seed, potatoes, sugar beets; pigs, cattle, poultry, dairy products
**Industries:** mining, metallurgy, construction materials, processed foods, textiles, chemicals (especially pharmaceuticals), motor vehicles
**Industrial production growth rate:** 0.4%
(2008 est.)
**Electricity - production:** 37.66 billion kWh
(2007 est.)
**Electricity - consumption:** 37.11 billion kWh
(2006 est.)
**Electricity - exports:** 10.69 billion kWh (2007 est.)
**Electricity - imports:** 14.68 billion kWh (2007 est.)
**Oil - production:** 32,580 bbl/day (2007 est.)
**Oil - consumption:** 162,800 bbl/day (2007 est.)
**Oil - exports:** 66,660 bbl/day (2005)
**Oil - imports:** 178,400 bbl/day (2005)
**Oil - proved reserves:** 20.18 million bbl
(1 January 2008 est.)
**Natural gas - production:** 2.545 billion cu m
(2007 est.)
**Natural gas - consumption:** 13.36 billion cu m
(2007 est.)
**Natural gas - exports:** 138 million cu m (2007 est.)
**Natural gas - imports:** 10.45 billion cu m (2007 est.)
**Natural gas - proved reserves:** 8.098 billion cu m
(1 January 2008 est.)
**Current account balance:** -$6.89 billion (2008 est.)
**Exports:** $109.3 billion f.o.b. (2008 est.)
**Exports - commodities:** machinery and equipment 61.1%, other manufactures 28.7%, food products 6.5%, raw materials 2%, fuels and electricity 1.6% (2003)

**Exports - partners:** Germany 28.1%, Italy 5.6%, France 4.7%, Austria 4.6%, Romania 4.5%, UK 4.5%, Slovakia 4.2%, Poland 4.2% (2007)
**Imports:** $107.5 billion f.o.b. (2008 est.)
**Imports - commodities:** machinery and equipment 51.6%, other manufactures 35.7%, fuels and electricity 7.7%, food products 3.1%, raw materials 2.0% (2003)
**Imports - partners:** Germany 26.6%, China 7.8%, Russia 6.9%, Austria 6.1%, Italy 4.5%, France 4.3%, Netherlands 4.3% (2007)
**Reserves of foreign exchange and gold:** $30.95 billion (31 December 2008)
**Debt - external:** $144.2 billion (31 December 2008 est.)
**Stock of direct foreign investment - at home:** $152.4 billion (2008 est.)
**Stock of direct foreign investment - abroad:** $79.56 billion (2008 est.)
**Exchange rates:** forints (HUF) per US dollar - 171.8 (2008), 183.83 (2007), 210.39 (2006), 199.58 (2005), 202.75 (2004)

## Communications

**Telephones - main lines in use:** 3.251 million (2007)
**Telephones - mobile cellular:** 11.03 million (2007)
**Telephone system:**
*general assessment:* the telephone system has been modernized and is capable of satisfying all requests for telecommunication service
*domestic:* the system is digitalized and highly automated; trunk services are carried by fiber-optic cable and digital microwave radio relay; a program for fiber-optic subscriber connections was initiated in 1996; competition among mobile-cellular service providers has led to a sharp increase in the use of mobile cellular phones since 2000 and a decrease in the number of fixed-line connections
*international:* country code - 36; Hungary has fiber-optic cable connections with all neighboring countries; the international switch is in Budapest; satellite earth stations - 2 Intelsat (Atlantic Ocean and Indian Ocean regions), 1 Inmarsat, 1 very small aperture terminal (VSAT) system of ground terminals
**Radio broadcast stations:** AM 5, FM 90, shortwave 1 (2008)
**Television broadcast stations:** 95 (2008)
**Internet country code:** .hu
**Internet hosts:** 1.879 million (2008)
**Internet users:** 4.2 million (2007)

## Transportation

**Airports:** 46 (2008)
**Airports - with paved runways:**
*total:* 20
*over 3,047 m:* 2
*2,438 to 3,047 m:* 8
*1,524 to 2,437 m:* 4
*914 to 1,523 m:* 4
*under 914 m:* 2 (2008)

**Airports - with unpaved runways:**
*total:* 26
*2,438 to 3,047 m:* 2
*1,524 to 2,437 m:* 3
*914 to 1,523 m:* 11
*under 914 m:* 10 (2008)
**Heliports:** 5 (2007)
**Pipelines:** gas 4,407 km; oil 987 km; refined products 335 km (2008)
**Railways:**
*total:* 8,057 km
*broad gauge:* 36 km 1.524-m gauge
*standard gauge:* 7,802 km 1.435-m gauge (2,628 km electrified)
*narrow gauge:* 219 km 0.760-m gauge (2006)
**Roadways:**
*total:* 159,568 km
*paved:* 70,050 km (30,874 km of interurban roads including 626 km of expressways)
*unpaved:* 89,518 km (2005)
**Waterways:** 1,622 km (most on Danube River) (2008)
**Ports and terminals:** Budapest, Dunaujvaros, Gyor-Gonyu, Csepel, Baja, Mohacs

## Military

**Military branches:** Ground Forces, Hungarian Air Force (Magyar Legiero, ML) (2009)
**Military service age and obligation:** 18-50 years of age for voluntary military service; no conscription; 6-month service obligation (2008)
**Manpower available for military service:**
*males age 16-49:* 2,391,400
*females age 16-49:* 2,337,240 (2008 est.)
**Manpower fit for military service:**
*males age 16-49:* 1,887,755
*females age 16-49:* 1,934,019 (2009 est.)
**Manpower reaching militarily significant age annually:**
*male:* 60,248
*female:* 57,280 (2009 est.)
**Military expenditures:** 1.75% of GDP (2005 est.)

## Transnational Issues

**Disputes - international:** bilateral government, legal, technical and economic working group negotiations continue in 2006 with Slovakia over Hungary's failure to complete its portion of the Gabcikovo-Nagymaros hydroelectric dam project along the Danube; as a member state that forms part of the EU's external border, Hungary has implemented the strict Schengen border rules
**Illicit drugs:** transshipment point for Southwest Asian heroin and cannabis and for South American cocaine destined for Western Europe; limited producer of precursor chemicals, particularly for amphetamine and methamphetamine; efforts to counter money laundering, related to organized crime and drug trafficking, are improving, but remain vulnerable; significant consumer of ecstasy

# Iceland

## Introduction

**Background:** Settled by Norwegian and Celtic (Scottish and Irish) immigrants during the late 9th and 10th centuries A.D., Iceland boasts the world's oldest functioning legislative assembly, the Althing, established in 930. Independent for over 300 years, Iceland was subsequently ruled by Norway and Denmark. Fallout from the Askja volcano of 1875 devastated the Icelandic economy and caused widespread famine. Over the next quarter century, 20% of the island's population emigrated, mostly to Canada and the US. Limited home rule from Denmark was granted in 1874 and complete independence attained in 1944. Literacy, longevity, and social cohesion are first-rate by world standards.

## Geography

**Location:** Northern Europe, island between the Greenland Sea and the North Atlantic Ocean, northwest of the United Kingdom
**Geographic coordinates:** 65 00 N, 18 00 W
**Map references:** Arctic Region
**Area:**
*total:* 103,000 sq km
*land:* 100,250 sq km
*water:* 2,750 sq km
**Area - comparative:** slightly smaller than Kentucky
**Land boundaries:** 0 km
**Coastline:** 4,970 km
**Maritime claims:**
*territorial sea:* 12 nm
*exclusive economic zone:* 200 nm
*continental shelf:* 200 nm or to the edge of the continental margin
**Climate:** temperate; moderated by North Atlantic Current; mild, windy winters; damp, cool summers
**Terrain:** mostly plateau interspersed with mountain peaks, icefields; coast deeply indented by bays and fiords

**Elevation extremes:**
*lowest point:* Atlantic Ocean 0 m
*highest point:* Hvannadalshnukur 2,110 m (at Vatnajokull glacier)
**Natural resources:** fish, hydropower, geothermal power, diatomite
**Land use:**
*arable land:* 0.07%
*permanent crops:* 0%
*other:* 99.93% (2005)
**Irrigated land:** NA
**Total renewable water resources:** 170 cu km (2005)
**Freshwater withdrawal (domestic/industrial/agricultural):**
*total:* 0.17 cu km/yr (34%/66%/0%)
*per capita:* 567 cu m/yr (2003)
**Natural hazards:** earthquakes and volcanic activity
**Environment - current issues:** water pollution from fertilizer runoff; inadequate wastewater treatment
**Environment - international agreements:**
*party to:* Air Pollution, Air Pollution-Persistent Organic Pollutants, Biodiversity, Climate Change, Climate Change-Kyoto Protocol, Desertification, Endangered Species, Hazardous Wastes, Kyoto Protocol, Law of the Sea, Marine Dumping, Ozone Layer Protection, Ship Pollution, Transboundary Air Pollution, Wetlands, Whaling
*signed, but not ratified:* Environmental Modification, Marine Life Conservation
**Geography - note:** strategic location between Greenland and Europe; westernmost European country; Reykjavik is the northernmost national capital in the world; more land covered by glaciers than in all of continental Europe

## People

**Population:** 306,694 (July 2009 est.)
**Age structure:**
*0-14 years:* 20.7% (male 32,268/female 31,308)
*15-64 years:* 67.1% (male 104,158/female 101,584)
*65 years and over:* 12.2% (male 16,952/female 20,424) (2009 est.)
**Median age:**
*total:* 35.1 years
*male:* 34.6 years
*female:* 35.6 years (2009 est.)
**Population growth rate:** 0.741% (2009 est.)
**Birth rate:** 13.43 births/1,000 population (2009 est.)
**Death rate:** 6.81 deaths/1,000 population (2008 est.)
**Net migration rate:** 0.83 migrant(s)/1,000 population (2009 est.)
**Urbanization:**
*urban population:* 92% of total population (2008)
*rate of urbanization:* 0.8% annual rate of change (2005-10 est.)
**Sex ratio:**
*at birth:* 1.04 male(s)/female
*under 15 years:* 1.03 male(s)/female
*15-64 years:* 1.02 male(s)/female
*65 years and over:* 0.83 male(s)/female
*total population:* 1 male(s)/female (2009 est.)

**Infant mortality rate:**
*total:* 3.23 deaths/1,000 live births
*male:* 3.38 deaths/1,000 live births
*female:* 3.08 deaths/1,000 live births (2009 est.)
**Life expectancy at birth:**
*total population:* 80.67 years
*male:* 78.53 years
*female:* 82.9 years (2009 est.)
**Total fertility rate:** 1.9 children born/woman (2009 est.)
**HIV/AIDS - adult prevalence rate:** 0.2% (2007 est.)
**HIV/AIDS - people living with HIV/AIDS:** 220 (2007 est.)
**HIV/AIDS - deaths:** fewer than 100 (2003 est.)
**Nationality:**
*noun:* Icelander(s)
*adjective:* Icelandic
**Ethnic groups:** homogeneous mixture of descendants of Norse and Celts 94%, population of foreign origin 6%
**Religions:** Lutheran Church of Iceland 80.7%, Roman Catholic Church 2.5%, Reykjavik Free Church 2.4%, Hafnarfjorour Free Church 1.6%, other religions 3.6%, unaffiliated 3%, other or unspecified 6.2% (2006 est.)
**Languages:** Icelandic, English, Nordic languages, German widely spoken
**Literacy:**
*definition:* age 15 and over can read and write
*total population:* 99%
*male:* 99%
*female:* 99% (2003 est.)
**School life expectancy (primary to tertiary education):**
*total:* 18 years
*male:* 17 years
*female:* 19 years (2006)
**Education expenditures:** 7.6% of GDP (2004)

## Government

**Country name:**
*conventional long form:* Republic of Iceland
*conventional short form:* Iceland
*local long form:* Lydveldid Island
*local short form:* Island
**Government type:** constitutional republic
**Capital:**
*name:* Reykjavik
*geographic coordinates:* 64 09 N, 21 57 W
*time difference:* UTC 0 (5 hours ahead of Washington, DC during Standard Time)
**Administrative divisions:** 8 regions; Austurland, Hofudhborgarsvaedhi, Nordhurland Eystra, Nordhurland Vestra, Sudhurland, Sudhurnes, Vestfirdhir, Vesturland
**Independence:** 1 December 1918 (became a sovereign state under the Danish Crown); 17 June 1944 (from Denmark)
**National holiday:** Independence Day, 17 June (1944)

**Constitution:** 16 June 1944, effective 17 June 1944; amended many times

**Legal system:** civil law system based on Danish law; has not accepted compulsory ICJ jurisdiction

**Suffrage:** 18 years of age; universal

**Executive branch:**

*chief of state:* President Olafur Ragnar GRIMSSON (since 1 August 1996)

*head of government:* Prime Minister Johanna SIGURDARDOTTIR (since 2 February 2009);

*cabinet:* Cabinet appointed by the prime minister

*2004 election results:* Olafur Ragnar GRIMSSON 85.6%, Baldur AGUSTSSON 12.5%, Astthor MAGNUSSON 1.9%

*elections:* president, a largely ceremonial post, is elected by popular vote for a four-year term (no term limits); election last held 28 June 2004 (next to be held in June 2012); following legislative elections, the leader of the majority party or the leader of the majority coalition is usually the prime minister

*note:* the election for president planned for 28 June 2008 was never held because Olafur Ragnar GRIMSSON had no challengers; he was sworn in on 1 August 2008; a coalition government of the Social Democratic Alliance and the Left-Green Movement, headed by Johanna SIGURDARDOTTIR, assumed office 1 February 2009

**Legislative branch:** unicameral Parliament or Althing (63 seats; members are elected by popular vote to serve four-year terms)

*elections:* last held 25 April 2009 (next to be held in 2013)

*election results:* percent of vote by party - Social Democratic Alliance 29.8%, Independence Party 23.7%, Left-Green Movement 21.7%, Progressive Party 14.8%, Citizens' Movement 7.2%, other 2.8%; seats by party - Social Democratic Alliance 20, Independence Party 16, Left-Green Alliance 14, Progressive Party 9, Citizens' Movement 4

**Judicial branch:** Supreme Court or Haestirettur (justices are appointed for life by the Minister of Justice); eight district courts (justices are appointed for life by the Minister of Justice)

**Political parties and leaders:** Citizens' Movement; Independence Party or IP [Bjarni BENEDIKTSSON, Jr.]; Left-Green Movement or LGM [Steingrimur SIGFUSSON]; Liberal Party or LP [Gudjon KRISTJANSSON]; Progressive Party or PP [Sigmundur David GUNNLAUGSSON; Social Democratic Alliance or SDA [Johanna SIGUROARDOTTIR] (includes People's Alliance or PA, Social Democratic Party or SDP, Women's List)

**Political pressure groups and leaders:** People's Voices [Hordur TORFARSON]; New Times; Civic Action Association [Gunnar SIGURDSSON]; The Association of Military Opponents [Stefan PALSSON]

**International organization participation:** Arctic Council, Australia Group, BIS, CBSS, CE, EAPC, EBRD, EFTA, FAO, IAEA, IBRD, ICAO, ICC, ICCt, ICRM, IDA, IFAD, IFC, IFRCS, IHO, ILO, IMF, IMO, IMSO, Interpol, IOC, IPU, ISO, ITSO, ITU, ITUC, MIGA, NATO, NC, NEA, NIB, OAS (observer), OECD, OPCW, OSCE, PCA, Schengen Convention, UN, UNCTAD, UNESCO, UPU, WCO, WEU (associate), WFTU, WHO, WIPO, WMO, WTO

**Diplomatic representation in the US:**

*chief of mission:* Ambassador Hjalmar HANNESSON

*chancery:* Suite 1200, 1156 15th Street NW, Washington, DC 20005-1704

*telephone:* [1] (202) 265-6653

*FAX:* [1] (202) 265-6656

*consulate(s) general:* New York

**Diplomatic representation from the US:**

*chief of mission:* Ambassador Hjalmar HANNESSON

*embassy:* Laufasvegur 21, 101 Reykjavik

*mailing address:* US Department of State, 5640 Reykjavik Place, Washington, D.C. 20521-5640

*telephone:* [354] 562-9100

*FAX:* [354] 562-9118

**Flag description:** blue with a red cross outlined in white extending to the edges of the flag; the vertical part of the cross is shifted to the hoist side in the style of the Dannebrog (Danish flag)

## Economy

**Economy - overview:** Iceland's Scandinavian-type social-market economy combines a capitalist structure and free-market principles with an extensive welfare system, including generous housing subsidies. Prior to the 2008 crisis, Iceland had achieved high growth, low unemployment, and a remarkably even distribution of income. Government economic priorities have included stabilizing the krona, reducing the current account deficit, containing inflation, restructuring the financial sector, and diversifying the economy. The economy depends heavily on the fishing industry, which provides 40% of export earnings and employs 5% of the work force. It remains sensitive to declining fish stocks as well as to fluctuations in world prices for its main exports: fish and fish products, aluminum, and ferrosilicon. Iceland's economy has been diversifying into manufacturing and service industries in the last decade, with new developments in software production, biotechnology, and tourism. Abundant geothermal sources have attracted substantial foreign investment in the aluminum and hydropower sectors and boosted economic growth, although the financial crisis has put several investment projects on hold. Much of Iceland's economic growth in recent years came as the result of a boom in domestic demand following the rapid expansion of the country's financial sector. Domestic banks expanded aggressively in foreign markets, and consumers and businesses borrowed heavily in foreign-currency loans, following the privatization of the sector in the early 2000s. Worsening global financial conditions throughout 2008 resulted in a sharp depreciation of the krona vis-a-vis other major currencies. The foreign exposure of Icelandic banks, whose loans and other assets totaled more than 10 times the country's GDP, became unsustainable. Iceland's three largest banks collapsed in late 2008. The country negotiated over $10 billion in loans from the IMF and other countries to stabilize its currency and financial sector, and to guarantee foreign deposits in Icelandic banks. A protracted recession is expected in 2009 and 2010 with GDP likely to contract and unemployment likely to surpass 10%. The collapse of the financial system has led to a major shift in opinion in favor of joining the EU and adopting the euro. Previous opposition to this move stemmed from Icelanders' concern about losing control of their fishing resources. Iceland's coalition government collapsed in January 2009 following protests over growing joblessness and losses to personal savings.

**GDP (purchasing power parity):**

$12.15 billion (2008 est.)

$12.59 billion (2007)

$12.01 billion (2006)

*note:* data are in 2008 US dollars

**GDP (official exchange rate):** $19.02 billion (2008 est.)

**GDP - real growth rate:**

-3.5% (2008 est.)

4.9% (2007 est.)

4.4% (2006 est.)

**GDP - per capita (PPP):**

$39,900 (2008 est.)

$41,700 (2007 est.)

$40,100 (2006 est.)

*note:* data are in 2008 US dollars

**GDP - composition by sector:**

*agriculture:* 5%

*industry:* 26.5%

*services:* 68.5% (2008 est.)

**Labor force:** 166,000 (2008 est.)

**Labor force - by occupation:**

*agriculture:* 3%

*industry:* 19%

*services:* 78% (2007)

**Unemployment rate:**

1.6% (2008 est.)

1% (2007 est.)

*note:* this figure climbed to 9.4% as of February 2009

**Population below poverty line:** NA%

**Household income or consumption by percentage share:**

*lowest 10%:* NA%

*highest 10%:* NA%

**Distribution of family income - Gini index:** 25 (2005)

**Investment (gross fixed):** 21.9% of GDP (2008 est.)

**Budget:**

*revenues:* $7.582 billion

*expenditures:* $7.159 billion (2008 est.)

**Public debt:** 23% of GDP (2008 est.)

**Inflation rate (consumer prices):**

13.4% (2008 est.)

5.1% (2007 est.)

**Central bank discount rate:** 15.25% (31 December 2007)

**Commercial bank prime lending rate:** 19.29% (31 December 2007)

# Iceland (continued)

**Stock of money:** $6.64 billion (31 December 2007)
**Stock of quasi money:** $15.05 billion (31 December 2006)
**Stock of domestic credit:** $49.67 billion (31 December 2006)
**Market value of publicly traded shares:** $40.56 billion (31 December 2007)
**Agriculture - products:** potatoes, green vegetables; mutton, dairy products; fish
**Industries:** fish processing; aluminum smelting, ferrosilicon production; geothermal power, tourism
**Industrial production growth rate:** 5.5% (2008 est.)
**Electricity - production:** 11.71 billion kWh (2007 est.)
**Electricity - consumption:** 9.312 billion kWh (2006 est.)
**Electricity - exports:** 0 kWh (2007 est.)
**Electricity - imports:** 0 kWh (2007 est.)
**Oil - production:** 0 bbl/day (2007 est.)
**Oil - consumption:** 21,120 bbl/day (2007 est.)
**Oil - exports:** 860.8 bbl/day (2005)
**Oil - imports:** 17,450 bbl/day (2005)
**Oil - proved reserves:** 0 bbl (1 January 2006 est.)
**Natural gas - production:** 0 cu m (2007 est.)
**Natural gas - consumption:** 0 cu m (2007 est.)
**Natural gas - exports:** 0 cu m (2007 est.)
**Natural gas - imports:** 0 cu m (2007 est.)
**Natural gas - proved reserves:** 0 cu m (1 January 2006 est.)
**Current account balance:** -$3.257 billion (2008 est.)
**Exports:** $6.846 billion f.o.b. (2008 est.)
**Exports - commodities:** fish and fish products 70%, aluminum, animal products, ferrosilicon, diatomite
**Exports - partners:** Netherlands 21.3%, Germany 13.3%, UK 13.2%, Ireland 7.7%, US 7.3%, Spain 4.6%, Japan 4.3% (2007)
**Imports:** $6.543 billion f.o.b. (2008 est.)
**Imports - commodities:** machinery and equipment, petroleum products, foodstuffs, textiles
**Imports - partners:** US 13.7%, Germany 12.2%, Sweden 10.2%, Denmark 7.5%, Netherlands 5.7%, UK 5.4%, China 5.1%, Norway 4.6% (2007)
**Reserves of foreign exchange and gold:** $2.5 billion (31 December 2008 est.)
**Debt - external:** $3.073 billion (2002)
**Stock of direct foreign investment - at home:** $NA
**Stock of direct foreign investment - abroad:** $NA
**Exchange rates:** Icelandic kronur (ISK) per US dollar - 85.619 (2008 est.), 63.391 (2007), 70.195 (2006), 62.982 (2005), 70.192 (2004)

## Communications

**Telephones - main lines in use:** 186,700 (2007)
**Telephones - mobile cellular:** 347,500 (2007)
**Telephone system:**
*general assessment:* telecommunications infrastructure is modern and fully digitized, with satellite-earth stations, fiber-optic cables, and an extensive broadband network
*domestic:* liberalization of the telecommunications sector beginning in the late 1990s has led to increased competition especially in the mobile services segment of the market
*international:* country code - 354; the CANTAT-3 and FARICE-1 submarine cable systems provide connectivity to Canada, the Faroe Islands, UK, Denmark, and Germany; a planned new section of the Hibernia-Atlantic submarine cable will provide additional connectivity to Canada, US, and Ireland; satellite earth stations - 2 Intelsat (Atlantic Ocean), 1 Inmarsat (Atlantic and Indian Ocean regions); note - Iceland shares the Inmarsat earth station with the other Nordic countries (Denmark, Finland, Norway, and Sweden)
**Radio broadcast stations:** AM 3, FM about 70, shortwave 1 (2008)
**Television broadcast stations:** 14 (plus 156 repeaters) (1997)
**Internet country code:** .is
**Internet hosts:** 263,980 (2008)
**Internet users:** 202,300 (2007)

## Transportation

**Airports:** 99 (2008)
**Airports - with paved runways:**
*total:* 6
*over 3,047 m:* 1
*1,524 to 2,437 m:* 3
*914 to 1,523 m:* 2 (2008)
**Airports - with unpaved runways:**
*total:* 93
*1,524 to 2,437 m:* 3
*914 to 1,523 m:* 27
*under 914 m:* 63 (2008)
**Roadways:**
*total:* 13,058 km
*paved/oiled gravel:* 4,397 km (does not include urban roads)
*unpaved:* 8,661 km (2007)
**Merchant marine:**
*total:* 2
*by type:* passenger/cargo 2
*registered in other countries:* 37 (Antigua and Barbuda 12, Bahamas 1, Belize 2, Denmark 2, Faroe Islands 1, Gibraltar 1, Malta 5, Marshall Islands 3, Norway 3, Saint Vincent and the Grenadines 7) (2008)
**Ports and terminals:** Grundartangi, Hafnarfjordur, Reykjavik

## Military

**Military branches:** no regular military forces; Icelandic National Police (2008)
**Manpower available for military service:**
*males age 16-49:* 74,896 (2008 est.)
**Manpower fit for military service:**
*males age 16-49:* 62,576
*females age 16-49:* 61,159 (2009 est.)
**Manpower reaching militarily significant age annually:**
*male:* 2,369
*female:* 2,349 (2009 est.)
**Military expenditures:** 0% of GDP (2005 est.)
**Military - note:** Iceland has no standing military force; under a 1951 bilateral agreement - still valid - its defense was provided by the US-manned Icelandic Defense Force (IDF) headquartered at Keflavik; however, all US military forces in Iceland were withdrawn as of October 2006; although wartime defense of Iceland remains a NATO commitment, in April 2007, Iceland and Norway signed a bilateral agreement providing for Norwegian aerial surveillance and defense of Icelandic airspace (2008)

## Transnational Issues

**Disputes - international:** Iceland, the UK, and Ireland dispute Denmark's claim that the Faroe Islands' continental shelf extends beyond 200 nm

# India

**Background:** Aryan tribes from the northwest infiltrated onto the Indian subcontinent about 1500 B.C.; their merger with the earlier Dravidian inhabitants created the classical Indian culture. The Maurya Empire of the 4th and 3rd centuries B.C. - which reached its zenith under ASHOKA - united much of South Asia. The Golden Age ushered in by the Gupta dynasty (4th to 6th centuries A.D.) saw a flowering of Indian science, art, and culture. Arab incursions starting in the 8th century and Turkic in the 12th were followed by those of European traders, beginning in the late 15th century. By the 19th century, Britain had assumed political control of virtually all Indian lands. Indian armed forces in the British army played a vital role in both World Wars. Nonviolent resistance to British colonialism led by Mohandas GANDHI and Jawaharlal NEHRU brought independence in 1947. The subcontinent was divided into the secular state of India and the smaller Muslim state of Pakistan. A third war between the two countries in 1971 resulted in East Pakistan becoming the separate nation of Bangladesh. India's nuclear weapons testing in 1998 caused Pakistan to conduct its own tests that same year. Despite impressive gains in economic investment and output, India faces pressing problems such as significant overpopulation, environmental degradation, extensive poverty, and widespread corruption.

## Geography

**Location:** Southern Asia, bordering the Arabian Sea and the Bay of Bengal, between Burma and Pakistan
**Geographic coordinates:** 20 00 N, 77 00 E
**Map references:** Asia
**Area:**
*total:* 3,287,590 sq km
*land:* 2,973,190 sq km
*water:* 314,400 sq km

**Area - comparative:** slightly more than one-third the size of the US
**Land boundaries:**
*total:* 14,103 km
*border countries:* Bangladesh 4,053 km, Bhutan 605 km, Burma 1,463 km, China 3,380 km, Nepal 1,690 km, Pakistan 2,912 km
**Coastline:** 7,000 km
**Maritime claims:**
*territorial sea:* 12 nm
*contiguous zone:* 24 nm
*exclusive economic zone:* 200 nm
*continental shelf:* 200 nm or to the edge of the continental margin
**Climate:** varies from tropical monsoon in south to temperate in north
**Terrain:** upland plain (Deccan Plateau) in south, flat to rolling plain along the Ganges, deserts in west, Himalayas in north
**Elevation extremes:**
*lowest point:* Indian Ocean 0 m
*highest point:* Kanchenjunga 8,598 m
**Natural resources:** coal (fourth-largest reserves in the world), iron ore, manganese, mica, bauxite, titanium ore, chromite, natural gas, diamonds, petroleum, limestone, arable land
**Land use:**
*arable land:* 48.83%
*permanent crops:* 2.8%
*other:* 48.37% (2005)
**Irrigated land:** 558,080 sq km (2003)
**Total renewable water resources:** 1,907.8 cu km (1999)
**Freshwater withdrawal (domestic/industrial/agricultural):**
*total:* 645.84 cu km/yr (8%/5%/86%)
*per capita:* 585 cu m/yr (2000)
**Natural hazards:** droughts; flash floods, as well as widespread and destructive flooding from monsoonal rains; severe thunderstorms; earthquakes
**Environment - current issues:** deforestation; soil erosion; overgrazing; desertification; air pollution from industrial effluents and vehicle emissions; water pollution from raw sewage and runoff of agricultural pesticides; tap water is not potable throughout the country; huge and growing population is overstraining natural resources
**Environment - international agreements:**
*party to:* Antarctic-Environmental Protocol, Antarctic-Marine Living Resources, Antarctic Treaty, Biodiversity, Climate Change, Climate Change-Kyoto Protocol, Desertification, Endangered Species, Environmental Modification, Hazardous Wastes, Law of the Sea, Ozone Layer Protection, Ship Pollution, Tropical Timber 83, Tropical Timber 94, Wetlands, Whaling
*signed, but not ratified:* none of the selected agreements
**Geography - note:** dominates South Asian subcontinent; near important Indian Ocean trade routes; Kanchenjunga, third tallest mountain in the world, lies on the border with Nepal

## People

**Population:** 1,166,079,217 (July 2009 est.)
**Age structure:**
*0-14 years:* 31.1% (male 190,075,426/ female 172,799,553)
*15-64 years:* 63.6% (male 381,446,079/ female 359,802,209)
*65 years and over:* 5.3% (male 29,364,920/ female 32,591,030) (2009 est.)
**Median age:**
*total:* 25.3 years
*male:* 24.9 years
*female:* 25.8 years (2009 est.)
**Population growth rate:** 1.548% (2009 est.)
**Birth rate:** 21.76 births/1,000 population (2009 est.)
**Death rate:** 6.4 deaths/1,000 population (2008 est.)
**Net migration rate:** -0.05 migrant(s)/1,000 population (2009 est.)
**Urbanization:**
*urban population:* 29% of total population (2008)
*rate of urbanization:* 2.4% annual rate of change (2005-10 est.)
**Sex ratio:**
*at birth:* 1.12 male(s)/female
*under 15 years:* 1.1 male(s)/female
*15-64 years:* 1.06 male(s)/female
*65 years and over:* 0.9 male(s)/female
*total population:* 1.06 male(s)/female (2009 est.)
**Infant mortality rate:**
*total:* 30.15 deaths/1,000 live births
*male:* 34.61 deaths/1,000 live births
*female:* 25.17 deaths/1,000 live births (2009 est.)
**Life expectancy at birth:**
*total population:* 69.89 years
*male:* 67.46 years
*female:* 72.61 years (2009 est.)
**Total fertility rate:** 2.72 children born/woman (2009 est.)
**HIV/AIDS - adult prevalence rate:** 0.3% (2007 est.)
**HIV/AIDS - people living with HIV/AIDS:** 2.4 million (2007 est.)
**HIV/AIDS - deaths:** 310,000 (2001 est.)
**Major infectious diseases:**
*degree of risk:* high
*food or waterborne diseases:* bacterial diarrhea, hepatitis A and E, and typhoid fever
*vectorborne diseases:* chikungunya, dengue fever, Japanese encephalitis, and malaria
*animal contact disease:* rabies
*water contact disease:* leptospirosis
*note:* highly pathogenic H5N1 avian influenza has been identified in this country; it poses a negligible risk with extremely rare cases possible among US citizens who have close contact with birds (2009)
**Nationality:**
*noun:* Indian(s)
*adjective:* Indian
**Ethnic groups:** Indo-Aryan 72%, Dravidian 25%, Mongoloid and other 3% (2000)

# India (continued)

**Religions:** Hindu 80.5%, Muslim 13.4%, Christian 2.3%, Sikh 1.9%, other 1.8%, unspecified 0.1% (2001 census)

**Languages:** Hindi 41%, Bengali 8.1%, Telugu 7.2%, Marathi 7%, Tamil 5.9%, Urdu 5%, Gujarati 4.5%, Kannada 3.7%, Malayalam 3.2%, Oriya 3.2%, Punjabi 2.8%, Assamese 1.3%, Maithili 1.2%, other 5.9%

*note:* English enjoys associate status but is the most important language for national, political, and commercial communication; Hindi is the most widely spoken language and primary tongue of 41% of the people; there are 14 other official languages: Bengali, Telugu, Marathi, Tamil, Urdu, Gujarati, Malayalam, Kannada, Oriya, Punjabi, Assamese, Kashmiri, Sindhi, and Sanskrit; Hindustani is a popular variant of Hindi/Urdu spoken widely throughout northern India but is not an official language (2001 census)

**Literacy:**
*definition:* age 15 and over can read and write
*total population:* 61%
*male:* 73.4%
*female:* 47.8% (2001 census)

**School life expectancy (primary to tertiary education):**
*total:* 10 years
*male:* 11 years
*female:* 9 years (2005)

**Education expenditures:** 3.2% of GDP (2005)

## Government

**Country name:**
*conventional long form:* Republic of India
*conventional short form:* India
*local long form:* Republic of India/Bharatiya Ganarajya
*local short form:* India/Bharat

**Government type:** federal republic

**Capital:**
*name:* New Delhi
*geographic coordinates:* 28 36 N, 77 12 E
*time difference:* UTC+5.5 (10.5 hours ahead of Washington, DC during Standard Time)

**Administrative divisions:** 28 states and 7 union territories*; Andaman and Nicobar Islands*, Andhra Pradesh, Arunachal Pradesh, Assam, Bihar, Chandigarh*, Chhattisgarh, Dadra and Nagar Haveli*, Daman and Diu*, Delhi*, Goa, Gujarat, Haryana, Himachal Pradesh, Jammu and Kashmir, Jharkhand, Karnataka, Kerala, Lakshadweep*, Madhya Pradesh, Maharashtra, Manipur, Meghalaya, Mizoram, Nagaland, Orissa, Puducherry*, Punjab, Rajasthan, Sikkim, Tamil Nadu, Tripura, Uttar Pradesh, Uttarakhand, West Bengal

**Independence:** 15 August 1947 (from the UK)

**National holiday:** Republic Day, 26 January (1950)

**Constitution:** 26 January 1950; amended many times

**Legal system:** based on English common law; judicial review of legislative acts; accepts compulsory ICJ jurisdiction with reservations; separate personal law codes apply to Muslims, Christians, and Hindus

**Suffrage:** 18 years of age; universal

**Executive branch:**
*chief of state:* President Pratibha PATIL (since 25 July 2007); Vice President Hamid ANSARI (since 11 August 2007)
*head of government:* Prime Minister Manmohan SINGH (since 22 May 2004)
*cabinet:* Cabinet appointed by the president on the recommendation of the prime minister
*elections:* president elected by an electoral college consisting of elected members of both houses of Parliament and the legislatures of the states for a five-year term (no term limits); election last held in July 2007 (next to be held in July 2012); vice president elected by both houses of Parliament for a five-year term; election last held in August 2007 (next to be held August 2012); prime minister chosen by parliamentary members of the majority party following legislative elections; election last held April - May 2004 (next to be held no later than May 2009)
*election results:* Pratibha PATIL elected president; percent of vote - 65.8%; Bhairon Singh SHEKHAWAT -34.2%

**Legislative branch:** bicameral Parliament or Sansad consists of the Council of States or Rajya Sabha (a body consisting of not more than 250 members up to 12 of whom are appointed by the president, the remainder are chosen by the elected members of the state and territorial assemblies; members serve six-year terms) and the People's Assembly or Lok Sabha (545 seats; 543 elected by popular vote, 2 appointed by the president; members serve five-year terms)
*elections:* People's Assembly - last held in five phases 16, 22-23, 30 April and 7, 13 May 2009 (next must be held by May 2014)
*election results:* People's Assembly - percent of vote by party - NA; seats by party - INC 206, BJP 116, SP 23, BSP 21, JD (U) 20, AITC 19, DMK 18, CPI-M 16, BJD 14, SS 11, AIADMK 9, NCP 9, other 61, vacant 2

**Judicial branch:** Supreme Court (one chief justice and 25 associate justices are appointed by the president and remain in office until they reach the age of 65 or are removed for "proved misbehavior")

**Political parties and leaders:** All India Anna Dravida Munnetra Kazhagam or AIADMK [J. JAYALALITHAA]; All India Trinamool Congress or AITC [Mamata BANERJEE]; Bahujan Samaj Party or BSP [Kumari MAYAWATI]; Bharatiya Janata Party or BJP [Rajnath SINGH]; Biju Janata Dal or BJD [Naveen PATNAIK]; Communist Party of India or CPI [Ardhendu Bhushan BARDHAN]; Communist Party of India-Marxist or CPI-M [Prakash KARAT]; Dravida Munnetra Kazaghan or DMK [M. KARUNANIDHI]; Indian National Congress or INC [Sonia GANDHI]; Janata Dal (United) or JD(U) [Sharad YADAV]; Jharkhand Mukti Morcha or JMM [Shibu SOREN]; Left Front (an alliance of Indian leftist parties); Lok Jan Shakti Party or LJSP [Ram Vilas PASWAN]; Nationalist Congress Party or NCP [Sharad PAWAR]; Pattali Makkal Katchi or PMK [S. RAMADOSS]; Rashtriya Janata Dal or RJD [Laloo Prasad YADAV];

Samajwadi Party or SP [Mulayam Singh YADAV]; Shiromani Akali Dal or SAD [Parkash Singh BADAL]; Shiv Sena or SS [Bal THACKERAY]; note - India has dozens of national and regional political parties; only parties or coalitions with four or more seats in the People's Assembly are listed

**Political pressure groups and leaders:** All Parties Hurriyat Conference in the Kashmir Valley (separatist group); Bajrang Dal (religious organization); National Socialist Council of Nagaland in the northeast (separatist group); Rashtriya Swayamsevak Sangh (religious organization); Vishwa Hindu Parishad (religious organization

*other:* numerous religious or militant/chauvinistic organizations; various separatist groups seeking greater communal and/or regional autonomy

**International organization participation:** ADB, AfDB (nonregional member), ARF, ASEAN (dialogue partner), BIMSTEC, BIS, C, CERN (observer), CP, EAS, FAO, G-15, G-20, G-24, G-77, IAEA, IBRD, ICAO, ICC, ICRM, IDA, IFAD, IFC, IFRCS, IHO, ILO, IMF, IMO, IMSO, Interpol, IOC, IOM, IPU, ISO, ITSO, ITU, ITUC, LAS (observer), MIGA, MONUC, NAM, OAS (observer), OPCW, PCA, PIF (partner), SAARC, SACEP, SCO (observer), UN, UNCTAD, UNDOF, UNESCO, UNHCR, UNIDO, UNIFIL, UNITAR, UNMIS, UNMIT, UNOCI, UNWTO, UPU, WCL, WCO, WFTU, WHO, WIPO, WMO, WTO

**Diplomatic representation in the US:**
*chief of mission:* Ambassador Meera SHANKAR
*chancery:* 2107 Massachusetts Avenue NW, Washington, DC 20008; note - Consular Wing located at 2536 Massachusetts Avenue NW, Washington, DC 20008
*telephone:* [1] (202) 939-7000
*FAX:* [1] (202) 265-4351
*consulate(s) general:* Chicago, Houston, New York, San Francisco

**Diplomatic representation from the US:**
*chief of mission:* Ambassador (vacant); Charge d'Affaires A. Peter BURLEIGH
*embassy:* Shantipath, Chanakyapuri, New Delhi 110021
*mailing address:* use embassy street address
*telephone:* [91] (011) 2419-8000
*FAX:* [91] (11) 2419-0017
*consulate(s) general:* Chennai (Madras), Kolkata (Calcutta), Mumbai (Bombay)

**Flag description:** three equal horizontal bands of saffron (subdued orange) (top), white, and green, with a blue chakra (24-spoked wheel) centered in the white band; similar to the flag of Niger, which has a small orange disk centered in the white band

## Economy

**Economy - overview:** India's diverse economy encompasses traditional village farming, modern agriculture, handicrafts, a wide range of modern industries, and a multitude of services. Services are the major source of economic growth, accounting for more than half of India's output with less than one third of its labor force. Slightly more than half of the work force is in agriculture, leading the United Progressive Alliance (UPA) government to articulate a rural economic development program that includes creating basic infrastructure to improve the lives of the rural poor and boost economic performance. The government has reduced controls on foreign trade and investment. Higher limits on foreign direct investment were permitted in a few key sectors, such as telecommunications. However, tariff spikes in sensitive categories, including agriculture, and incremental progress on economic reforms still hinder foreign access to India's vast and growing market. Privatization of government-owned industries remains stalled and continues to generate political debate; populist pressure from within the UPA government had restrained needed initiatives. The economy has posted an average growth rate of more than 7% in the decade since 1997, reducing poverty by about 10 percentage points. India achieved 9.6% GDP growth in 2006, 9.0% in 2007, and 6.6% in 2008, significantly expanding manufactures through late 2008. India also is capitalizing on its large numbers of well-educated people skilled in the English language to become a major exporter of software services and software workers. Strong growth combined with easy consumer credit, a real estate boom, and fast-rising commodity prices fueled inflation concerns from mid-2006 to August 2008. Rising tax revenues from better tax administration and economic expansion helped New Delhi make progress in reducing its fiscal deficit for three straight years before skyrocketing global commodity prices more than doubled the cost of government energy and fertilizer subsidies. The ballooning subsidies, amidst slowing growth, brought the return of a large fiscal deficit in 2008. In the long run, the huge and growing population is the fundamental social, economic, and environmental problem.

**GDP (purchasing power parity):**
$3.267 trillion (2008 est.)
$3.065 trillion (2007)
$2.812 trillion (2006)
*note:* data are in 2008 US dollars

**GDP (official exchange rate):** $1.237 trillion (2008 est.)

**GDP - real growth rate:**
6.6% (2008 est.)
9% (2007 est.)
9.6% (2006 est.)

**GDP - per capita (PPP):**
$2,800 (2008 est.)
$2,700 (2007 est.)
$2,500 (2006 est.)
*note:* data are in 2008 US dollars

**GDP - composition by sector:**
*agriculture:* 17.2%
*industry:* 29.1%
*services:* 53.7% (2008 est.)

**Labor force:** 523.5 million (2008 est.)

**Labor force - by occupation:**
*agriculture:* 60%
*industry:* 12%
*services:* 28% (2003)

**Unemployment rate:**
6.8% (2008 est.)
7.2% (2007 est.)

**Population below poverty line:** 25% (2007 est.)

**Household income or consumption by percentage share:**
*lowest 10%:* 3.6%
*highest 10%:* 31.1% (2004)

**Distribution of family income - Gini index:** 36.8 (2004)

**Investment (gross fixed):** 39% of GDP (2008 est.)

**Budget:**
*revenues:* $153.5 billion
*expenditures:* $205.3 billion (2008 est.)

**Public debt:** 78% of GDP (federal and state debt combined) (2008 est.)

**Inflation rate (consumer prices):**
7.8% (2008 est.)
6.4% (2007 est.)

**Central bank discount rate:** 5.5% (31 January 2009)

**Commercial bank prime lending rate:** 8.5% (31 January 2009)

**Stock of money:** $250.9 billion (31 December 2007)

**Stock of quasi money:** $647.3 billion (31 December 2007)

**Stock of domestic credit:** $769.3 billion (31 December 2007)

**Market value of publicly traded shares:** $650 billion (31 December 2008)

**Agriculture - products:** rice, wheat, oilseed, cotton, jute, tea, sugarcane, potatoes; onions, dairy products, sheep, goats, poultry; fish

**Industries:** textiles, chemicals, food processing, steel, transportation equipment, cement, mining, petroleum, machinery, software

**Industrial production growth rate:** 4.8% (2008 est.)

**Electricity - production:** 665.3 billion kWh (2007 est.)

**Electricity - consumption:** 517.2 billion kWh (2006 est.)

**Electricity - exports:** 378 million kWh (2006 est.)

**Electricity - imports:** 3.189 billion kWh (2006 est.)

**Oil - production:** 880,500 bbl/day (2007 est.)

**Oil - consumption:** 2.722 million bbl/day (2007 est.)

**Oil - exports:** 450,700 bbl/day (2005 est.)

**Oil - imports:** 2.159 million bbl/day (2005 est.)

**Oil - proved reserves:** 5.625 billion bbl (1 January 2008 est.)

**Natural gas - production:** 31.7 billion cu m (2007 est.)

**Natural gas - consumption:** 41.7 billion cu m (2007 est.)

**Natural gas - exports:** 0 cu m (2007 est.)

**Natural gas - imports:** 10 billion cu m (2007 est.)

**Natural gas - proved reserves:** 1.075 trillion cu m (1 January 2008 est.)

**Current account balance:** -$38.39 billion (2008 est.)

**Exports:** $175.7 billion f.o.b. (2008 est.)

**Exports - commodities:** petroleum products, textile goods, gems and jewelry, engineering goods, chemicals, leather manufactures

**Exports - partners:** US 15%, China 8.7%, UAE 8.7%, UK 4.4% (2007)

**Imports:** $287.5 billion f.o.b. (2008 est.)

**Imports - commodities:** crude oil, machinery, gems, fertilizer, chemicals

**Imports - partners:** China 10.6%, US 7.8%, Germany 4.4%, Singapore 4.4% (2007)

**Reserves of foreign exchange and gold:** $250 billion (31 December 2008 est.)

**Debt - external:** $163.8 billion (31 December 2008 est.)

**Stock of direct foreign investment - at home:** $142.9 billion (2008 est.)

**Stock of direct foreign investment - abroad:** $54.21 billion (2008 est.)

**Exchange rates:** Indian rupees (INR) per US dollar - 43.319 (2008 est.), 41.487 (2007), 45.3 (2006), 44.101 (2005), 45.317 (2004)

## Communications

**Telephones - main lines in use:** 37.75 million (2009)

**Telephones - mobile cellular:** 362.3 million (2009)

**Telephone system:**
*general assessment:* recent deregulation and liberalization of telecommunications laws and policies have prompted rapid growth; local and long distance service provided throughout all regions of the country, with services primarily concentrated in the urban areas; steady improvement is taking place with the recent admission of private and private-public investors, but combined fixed and mobile telephone density remains low at about 35 for each 100 persons nationwide and much lower for persons in rural areas; extremely rapid growth in cellular service with modest declines in fixed lines
*domestic:* mobile cellular service introduced in 1994 and organized nationwide into four metropolitan areas and 19 telecom circles each with multiple private service providers and one or more state-owned service providers; in recent years significant trunk capacity added in the form of fiber-optic cable and one of the world's largest domestic satellite systems, the Indian National Satellite system (INSAT), with 6 satellites supporting 33,000 very small aperture terminals (VSAT)
*international:* country code - 91; a number of major international submarine cable systems, including Sea-Me-We-3 with landing sites at Cochin and Mumbai (Bombay), Sea-Me-We-4 with a landing site at Chennai, Fiber-Optic Link Around the Globe (FLAG) with a landing site at Mumbai (Bombay), South Africa - Far East (SAFE) with a landing site at Cochin, the i2i cable network linking to Singapore with landing sites at Mumbai (Bombay) and Chennai (Madras), and Tata Indicom linking Singapore and Chennai (Madras), provide a significant increase in the bandwidth available for both voice and data traffic;

satellite earth stations - 8 Intelsat (Indian Ocean) and 1 Inmarsat (Indian Ocean region); 9 gateway exchanges operating from Mumbai (Bombay), New Delhi, Kolkata (Calcutta), Chennai (Madras), Jalandhar, Kanpur, Gandhinagar, Hyderabad, and Ernakulam (2008)

**Radio broadcast stations:** AM 153, FM 91, shortwave 68 (1998)

**Television broadcast stations:** 562 (1997)

**Internet country code:** .in

**Internet hosts:** 2.707 million (2008)

**Internet users:** 80 million (2007)

## Transportation

**Airports:** 345 (2008)

**Airports - with paved runways:**

*total:* 251

*over 3,047 m:* 19

*2,438 to 3,047 m:* 55

*1,524 to 2,437 m:* 77

*914 to 1,523 m:* 84

*under 914 m:* 16 (2008)

**Airports - with unpaved runways:**

*total:* 94

*2,438 to 3,047 m:* 1

*1,524 to 2,437 m:* 7

*914 to 1,523 m:* 39

*under 914 m:* 47 (2008)

**Heliports:** 30 (2007)

**Pipelines:** condensate/gas 2 km; gas 6,061 km; liquid petroleum gas 2,156 km; oil 7,678 km; refined products 6,876 km (2008)

**Railways:**

*total:* 63,221 km

*broad gauge:* 46,807 km 1.676-m gauge (17,343 km electrified)

*narrow gauge:* 13,290 km 1.000-m gauge (165 km electrified); 3,124 km 0.762-m gauge and 0.610-m gauge (2006)

**Roadways:**

*total:* 3,316,452 km (includes 200 km of expressways) (2006)

**Waterways:** 14,500 km

*note:* 5,200 km on major rivers and 485 km on canals suitable for mechanized vessels (2008)

**Merchant marine:**

*total:* 501

*by type:* bulk carrier 102, cargo 241, carrier 1, chemical tanker 19, container 13, liquefied gas 18, passenger 3, passenger/cargo 11, petroleum tanker 92, roll on/roll off 1

*foreign-owned:* 12 (China 1, Germany 2, Hong Kong 1, UAE 6, UK 2)

*registered in other countries:* 61 (Barbados 1, Comoros 2, Cyprus 2, Dominica 2, Liberia 2, Malta 2, Marshall Islands 1, Panama 27, Saint Kitts and Nevis 1, Saint Vincent and the Grenadines 7, Singapore 13, unknown 1) (2008)

**Ports and terminals:** Chennai, Haldia, Jawaharal Nehru, Kandla, Kolkata (Calcutta), Mormugao, Mumbai (Bombay), New Mangalore, Vishakhapatnam

## Military

**Military branches:** Army, Navy (includes naval air arm), Air Force (Bharatiya Vayu Sena), Coast Guard (2009)

**Military service age and obligation:** 16 years of age for voluntary military service; no conscription; women officers allowed in noncombat roles only (2008)

**Manpower available for military service:**

*males age 16-49:* 301,094,084

*females age 16-49:* 283,047,141 (2008 est.)

**Manpower fit for military service:**

*males age 16-49:* 237,042,868

*females age 16-49:* 243,276,310 (2009 est.)

**Manpower reaching militarily significant age annually:**

*male:* 11.795 million

*female:* 10,820,590 (2009 est.)

**Military expenditures:** 2.5% of GDP (2006)

## Transnational Issues

**Disputes - international:** since China and India launched a security and foreign policy dialogue in 2005, consolidated discussions related to the dispute over most of their rugged, militarized boundary, regional nuclear proliferation, Indian claims that China transferred missiles to Pakistan, and other matters continue; various talks and confidence-building measures have cautiously begun to defuse tensions over Kashmir, particularly since the October 2005 earthquake in the region; Kashmir nevertheless remains the site of the world's largest and most militarized territorial dispute with portions under the de facto administration of China (Aksai Chin), India (Jammu and Kashmir), and Pakistan (Azad Kashmir and Northern Areas); India and Pakistan have maintained the 2004 cease fire in Kashmir and initiated discussions on defusing the armed stand-off in the Siachen glacier region; Pakistan protests India's fencing the highly militarized Line of Control and construction of the Baglihar Dam on the Chenab River in Jammu and Kashmir, which is part of the larger dispute on water sharing of the Indus River and its tributaries; UN Military Observer Group in India and Pakistan (UNMOGIP) has maintained a small group of peacekeepers since 1949; India does not recognize Pakistan's ceding historic Kashmir lands to China in 1964; to defuse tensions and prepare for discussions on a maritime boundary, India and Pakistan seek technical resolution of the disputed boundary in Sir Creek estuary at the mouth of the Rann of Kutch in the Arabian Sea; Pakistani maps continue to show its Junagadh claim in Indian Gujarat State; discussions with Bangladesh remain stalled to delimit a small section of river boundary, to exchange territory for 51 Bangladeshi exclaves in India and 111 Indian exclaves in Bangladesh, to allocate divided villages, and to stop illegal cross-border trade, migration, violence, and transit of terrorists through the porous border; Bangladesh protests India's attempts to fence off high-traffic sections of the border; dispute with Bangladesh over New Moore/South Talpatty/Purbasha Island in the Bay of Bengal deters maritime boundary delimitation; India seeks cooperation from Bhutan and Burma to keep Indian Nagaland and Assam separatists from hiding in remote areas along the borders; Joint Border Committee with Nepal continues to examine contested boundary sections, including the 400 square kilometer dispute over the source of the Kalapani River; India maintains a strict border regime to keep out Maoist insurgents and control illegal cross-border activities from Nepal

**Refugees and internally displaced persons:**

*refugees (country of origin):* 77,200 (Tibet/China); 69,609 (Sri Lanka); 9,472 (Afghanistan)

*IDPs:* at least 600,000 (about half are Kashmiri Pandits from Jammu and Kashmir) (2007)

**Trafficking in persons:**

*current situation:* India is a source, destination, and transit country for men, women, and children trafficked for the purposes of forced labor and commercial sexual exploitation; internal forced labor may constitute India's largest trafficking problem; men, women, and children are held in debt bondage and face forced labor working in brick kilns, rice mills, agriculture, and embroidery factories; women and girls are trafficked within the country for the purposes of commercial sexual exploitation and forced marriage; children are subjected to forced labor as factory workers, domestic servants, beggars, and agriculture workers, and have been used as armed combatants by some terrorist and insurgent groups; India is also a destination for women and girls from Nepal and Bangladesh trafficked for the purpose of commercial sexual exploitation; Indian women are trafficked to the Middle East for commercial sexual exploitation; men and women from Bangladesh and Nepal are trafficked through India for forced labor and commercial sexual exploitation in the Middle East

*tier rating:* Tier 2 Watch List - India is on the Tier 2 Watch List for a fifth consecutive year for its failure to provide evidence of increasing efforts to combat human trafficking in 2007; despite the reported extent of the trafficking crisis in India, government authorities made uneven efforts to prosecute traffickers and protect trafficking victims; government authorities continued to rescue victims of commercial sexual exploitation and forced child labor and child armed combatants, and began to show progress in law enforcement against these forms of trafficking; a critical challenge overall is the lack of punishment for traffickers, effectively resulting in impunity for acts of human trafficking; India has not ratified the 2000 UN TIP Protocol (2008)

**Illicit drugs:** world's largest producer of licit opium for the pharmaceutical trade, but an undetermined quantity of opium is diverted to illicit international drug markets; transit point for illicit narcotics produced in neighboring countries and throughout Southwest Asia; illicit producer of methaqualone; vulnerable to narcotics money laundering through the hawala system; licit ketamine and precursor production

# Indian Ocean

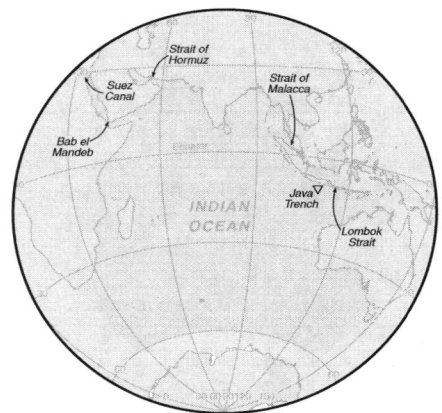

## Introduction

**Background:** The Indian Ocean is the third largest of the world's five oceans (after the Pacific Ocean and Atlantic Ocean, but larger than the Southern Ocean and Arctic Ocean). Four critically important access waterways are the Suez Canal (Egypt), Bab el Mandeb (Djibouti-Yemen), Strait of Hormuz (Iran-Oman), and Strait of Malacca (Indonesia-Malaysia). The decision by the International Hydrographic Organization in the spring of 2000 to delimit a fifth ocean, the Southern Ocean, removed the portion of the Indian Ocean south of 60 degrees south latitude.

## Geography

**Location:** body of water between Africa, the Southern Ocean, Asia, and Australia
**Geographic coordinates:** 20 00 S, 80 00 E
**Map references:** Political Map of the World
**Area:**
*total:* 68.556 million sq km
*note:* includes Andaman Sea, Arabian Sea, Bay of Bengal, Flores Sea, Great Australian Bight, Gulf of Aden, Gulf of Oman, Java Sea, Mozambique Channel, Persian Gulf, Red Sea, Savu Sea, Strait of Malacca, Timor Sea, and other tributary water bodies
**Area - comparative:** about 5.5 times the size of the US
**Coastline:** 66,526 km
**Climate:** northeast monsoon (December to April), southwest monsoon (June to October); tropical cyclones occur during May/June and October/November in the northern Indian Ocean and January/February in the southern Indian Ocean

**Terrain:** surface dominated by counterclockwise gyre (broad, circular system of currents) in the southern Indian Ocean; unique reversal of surface currents in the northern Indian Ocean; low atmospheric pressure over southwest Asia from hot, rising, summer air results in the southwest monsoon and southwest-to-northeast winds and currents, while high pressure over northern Asia from cold, falling, winter air results in the northeast monsoon and northeast-to-southwest winds and currents; ocean floor is dominated by the Mid-Indian Ocean Ridge and subdivided by the Southeast Indian Ocean Ridge, Southwest Indian Ocean Ridge, and Ninetyeast Ridge
**Elevation extremes:**
*lowest point:* Java Trench -7,258 m
*highest point:* sea level 0 m
**Natural resources:** oil and gas fields, fish, shrimp, sand and gravel aggregates, placer deposits, polymetallic nodules
**Natural hazards:** occasional icebergs pose navigational hazard in southern reaches
**Environment - current issues:** endangered marine species include the dugong, seals, turtles, and whales; oil pollution in the Arabian Sea, Persian Gulf, and Red Sea
**Geography - note:** major chokepoints include Bab el Mandeb, Strait of Hormuz, Strait of Malacca, southern access to the Suez Canal, and the Lombok Strait

## Economy

**Economy - overview:** The Indian Ocean provides major sea routes connecting the Middle East, Africa, and East Asia with Europe and the Americas. It carries a particularly heavy traffic of petroleum and petroleum products from the oilfields of the Persian Gulf and Indonesia. Its fish are of great and growing importance to the bordering countries for domestic consumption and export. Fishing fleets from Russia, Japan, South Korea, and Taiwan also exploit the Indian Ocean, mainly for shrimp and tuna. Large reserves of hydrocarbons are being tapped in the offshore areas of Saudi Arabia, Iran, India, and western Australia. An estimated 40% of the world's offshore oil production comes from the Indian Ocean. Beach sands rich in heavy minerals and offshore placer deposits are actively exploited by bordering countries, particularly India, South Africa, Indonesia, Sri Lanka, and Thailand.

## Transportation

**Ports and terminals:** Chennai (Madras; India), Colombo (Sri Lanka), Durban (South Africa), Jakarta (Indonesia), Kolkata (Calcutta; India) Melbourne (Australia), Mumbai (Bombay; India), Richards Bay (South Africa)

**Transportation - note:** the International Maritime Bureau reports the territorial waters of littoral states and offshore waters as high risk for piracy and armed robbery against ships, particularly in the Gulf of Aden, along the east coast of Africa, the Bay of Bengal, and the Strait of Malacca; numerous vessels, including commercial shipping and pleasure craft, have been attacked and hijacked both at anchor and while underway; hijacked vessels are often disguised and cargoes stolen; crew and passengers are often held for ransom, murdered, or cast adrift

## Transnational Issues

**Disputes - international:** some maritime disputes (see littoral states)

---

# Indonesia

## Introduction

**Background:** The Dutch began to colonize Indonesia in the early 17th century; Japan occupied the islands from 1942 to 1945. Indonesia declared its independence after Japan's surrender, but it required four years of intermittent negotiations, recurring hostilities, and UN mediation before the Netherlands agreed to transfer sovereignty in 1949. Indonesia's first free parliamentary election after decades of repressive rule took place in 1999. Indonesia is now the world's third-largest democracy, the world's largest archipelagic state, and home to the world's largest Muslim population. Current issues include: alleviating poverty, improving education, preventing terrorism, consolidating democracy after four decades of authoritarianism, implementing economic and financial reforms, stemming corruption, holding the military and police accountable for past human rights violations, addressing climate change, and controlling avian influenza. In 2005, Indonesia reached a historic peace agreement with armed separatists in Aceh, which led to democratic elections in December 2006. Indonesia continues to face a low intensity separatist movement in Papua.

## Geography

**Location:** Southeastern Asia, archipelago between the Indian Ocean and the Pacific Ocean
**Geographic coordinates:** 5 00 S, 120 00 E
**Map references:** Southeast Asia
**Area:**
*total:* 1,919,440 sq km
*land:* 1,826,440 sq km
*water:* 93,000 sq km
**Area - comparative:** slightly less than three times the size of Texas

**Land boundaries:**
*total:* 2,830 km
*border countries:* Timor-Leste 228 km, Malaysia 1,782 km, Papua New Guinea 820 km
**Coastline:** 54,716 km
**Maritime claims:** measured from claimed archipelagic straight baselines
*territorial sea:* 12 nm
*exclusive economic zone:* 200 nm
**Climate:** tropical; hot, humid; more moderate in highlands
**Terrain:** mostly coastal lowlands; larger islands have interior mountains
**Elevation extremes:**
*lowest point:* Indian Ocean 0 m
*highest point:* Puncak Jaya 5,030 m
**Natural resources:** petroleum, tin, natural gas, nickel, timber, bauxite, copper, fertile soils, coal, gold, silver
**Land use:**
*arable land:* 11.03%
*permanent crops:* 7.04%
*other:* 81.93% (2005)
**Irrigated land:** 45,000 sq km (2003)
**Total renewable water resources:** 2,838 cu km (1999)
**Freshwater withdrawal (domestic/industrial/agricultural):**
*total:* 82.78 cu km/yr (8%/1%/91%)
*per capita:* 372 cu m/yr (2000)
**Natural hazards:** occasional floods; severe droughts; tsunamis; earthquakes; volcanoes; forest fires
**Environment - current issues:** deforestation; water pollution from industrial wastes, sewage; air pollution in urban areas; smoke and haze from forest fires
**Environment - international agreements:**
*party to:* Biodiversity, Climate Change, Climate Change-Kyoto Protocol, Desertification, Endangered Species, Hazardous Wastes, Law of the Sea, Ozone Layer Protection, Ship Pollution, Tropical Timber 83, Tropical Timber 94, Wetlands
*signed, but not ratified:* Marine Life Conservation
**Geography - note:** archipelago of 17,508 islands (6,000 inhabited); straddles equator; strategic location astride or along major sea lanes from Indian Ocean to Pacific Ocean

## People

**Population:** 240,271,522 (July 2009 est.)
**Age structure:**
*0-14 years:* 28.1% (male 34,337,341/female 33,162,207)
*15-64 years:* 66% (male 79,549,569/female 78,918,321)
*65 years and over:* 6% (male 6,335,208/female 7,968,876) (2009 est.)
**Median age:**
*total:* 27.6 years
*male:* 27.1 years
*female:* 28.1 years (2009 est.)
**Population growth rate:** 1.136% (2009 est.)
**Birth rate:** 18.84 births/1,000 population (2009 est.)
**Death rate:** 6.24 deaths/1,000 population (2008 est.)
**Net migration rate:** -1.24 migrant(s)/1,000 population (2009 est.)
**Urbanization:**
*urban population:* 52% of total population (2008)
*rate of urbanization:* 3.3% annual rate of change (2005-10 est.)
**Sex ratio:**
*at birth:* 1.05 male(s)/female
*under 15 years:* 1.03 male(s)/female
*15-64 years:* 1.01 male(s)/female
*65 years and over:* 0.8 male(s)/female
*total population:* 1 male(s)/female (2009 est.)
**Infant mortality rate:**
*total:* 29.97 deaths/1,000 live births
*male:* 34.93 deaths/1,000 live births
*female:* 24.77 deaths/1,000 live births (2009 est.)
**Life expectancy at birth:**
*total population:* 70.76 years
*male:* 68.26 years
*female:* 73.38 years (2009 est.)
**Total fertility rate:** 2.31 children born/woman (2009 est.)
**HIV/AIDS - adult prevalence rate:** 0.2% (2007 est.)
**HIV/AIDS - people living with HIV/AIDS:** 270,000 (2007 est.)
**HIV/AIDS - deaths:** 8,700 (2007 est.)
**Major infectious diseases:**
*degree of risk:* high
*food or waterborne diseases:* bacterial diarrhea, hepatitis A and E, and typhoid fever
*vectorborne diseases:* chikungunya, dengue fever, and malaria
*note:* highly pathogenic H5N1 avian influenza has been identified in this country; it poses a negligible risk with extremely rare cases possible among US citizens who have close contact with birds (2009)

**Nationality:**
*noun:* Indonesian(s)
*adjective:* Indonesian
**Ethnic groups:** Javanese 40.6%, Sundanese 15%, Madurese 3.3%, Minangkabau 2.7%, Betawi 2.4%, Bugis 2.4%, Banten 2%, Banjar 1.7%, other or unspecified 29.9% (2000 census)
**Religions:** Muslim 86.1%, Protestant 5.7%, Roman Catholic 3%, Hindu 1.8%, other or unspecified 3.4% (2000 census)
**Languages:** Bahasa Indonesia (official, modified form of Malay), English, Dutch, local dialects (the most widely spoken of which is Javanese)
**Literacy:**
*definition:* age 15 and over can read and write
*total population:* 90.4%
*male:* 94%
*female:* 86.8% (2004 est.)
**School life expectancy (primary to tertiary education):**
*total:* 11 years
*male:* 12 years
*female:* 11 years (2005)
**Education expenditures:** 3.6% of GDP (2006)

## Government

**Country name:**
*conventional long form:* Republic of Indonesia
*conventional short form:* Indonesia
*local long form:* Republik Indonesia
*local short form:* Indonesia
*former:* Netherlands East Indies, Dutch East Indies
**Government type:** republic
**Capital:**
*name:* Jakarta
*geographic coordinates:* 6 10 S, 106 49 E
*time difference:* UTC+7 (12 hours ahead of Washington, DC during Standard Time)
*note:* Indonesia is divided into three time zones
**Administrative divisions:** 30 provinces (provinsi-provinsi, singular - provinsi), 2 special regions* (daerah-daerah istimewa, singular - daerah istimewa), and 1 special capital city district** (daerah khusus ibukota); Aceh*, Bali, Banten, Bengkulu, Gorontalo, Jakarta Raya**, Jambi, Jawa Barat, Jawa Tengah, Jawa Timur, Kalimantan Barat, Kalimantan Selatan, Kalimantan Tengah, Kalimantan Timur, Kepulauan Bangka Belitung, Kepulauan Riau, Lampung, Maluku, Maluku Utara, Nusa Tenggara Barat, Nusa Tenggara Timur, Papua, Papua Barat, Riau, Sulawesi Barat, Sulawesi Selatan, Sulawesi Tengah, Sulawesi Tenggara, Sulawesi Utara, Sumatera Barat, Sumatera Selatan, Sumatera Utara, Yogyakarta*
*note:* following the implementation of decentralization beginning on 1 January 2001, the 465 regencies and municipalities have become the key administrative units responsible for providing most government services

**Independence:** 17 August 1945 (declared); 27 December 1949 (by the Netherlands)
*note:* in August 2005, the Netherlands announced it recognized de facto Indonesian independence on 17 August 1945
**National holiday:** Independence Day, 17 August (1945)
**Constitution:** August 1945; abrogated by Federal Constitution of 1949 and Provisional Constitution of 1950, restored 5 July 1959; series of amendments concluded in 2002
**Legal system:** based on Roman-Dutch law, substantially modified by indigenous concepts and by new criminal procedures and election codes; has not accepted compulsory ICJ jurisdiction
**Suffrage:** 17 years of age; universal and married persons regardless of age
**Executive branch:**
*chief of state:* President Susilo Bambang YUDHOYONO (since 20 October 2004); Vice President Muhammad Yusuf KALLA (since 20 October 2004); note - the president is both the chief of state and head of government
*head of government:* President Susilo Bambang YUDHOYONO (since 20 October 2004); Vice President Muhammad Yusuf KALLA (since 20 October 2004)
*cabinet:* Cabinet appointed by the president
*elections:* president and vice president were elected for five-year terms (eligible for a second term) by direct vote of the citizenry; last held 20 September 2004 (next to be held on 8 July 2009)
*election results:* Susilo Bambang YUDHOYONO elected president receiving 60.6% of vote; MEGAWATI Sukarnoputri received 39.4%
**Legislative branch:** People's Consultative Assembly (Majelis Permusyawaratan Rakyat or MPR) is the upper house, consists of members of DPR and DPD, has role in inaugurating and impeaching the president and in amending the constitution, does not formulate national policy; House of Representatives or Dewan Perwakilan Rakyat (DPR) (550 seats, members elected to serve five-year terms), formulates and passes legislation at the national level; House of Regional Representatives (Dewan Perwakilan Daerah or DPD), constitutionally mandated role includes providing legislative input to DPR on issues affecting regions
*elections:* last held 9 April 2009 (next to be held in 2014)
*election results:* percent of vote by party - PD 20.9%, GOLKAR 14.5%, PDI-P 14.0%, PKS 7.9%, PAN 6.0%, PPP 5.3%, PKB 4.9%, GERINDRA 4.5%, HANURA 3.8%, others 18.2%; seats by party - PD 148, GOLKAR 108, PDI-P 93, PKS 59, PAN 42, PPP 39, PKB 26, GERINDRA 30, HANURA 15
*note:* 29 other parties received less than 2.5% of the vote so did not obtain any seats; because of election rules, the number of seats won does not always follow the percentage of votes received by parties

**Judicial branch:** Supreme Court or Mahkamah Agung is the final court of appeal but does not have the power of judicial review (justices are appointed by the president from a list of candidates selected by the legislature); in March 2004 the Supreme Court assumed administrative and financial responsibility for the lower court system from the Ministry of Justice and Human Rights; Constitutional Court or Mahkamah Konstitusi (invested by the president on 16 August 2003) has the power of judicial review, jurisdiction over the results of a general election, and reviews actions to dismiss a president from office; Labor Court under supervision of Supreme Court began functioning in January 2006; the Anti-Corruption Court has jurisdiction over corruption cases brought by the independent Corruption Eradication Commission; in 2006, the Constitutional Court declared the mechanism by which the Anti-Corruption Court was established unconstitutional and gave the parliament until the end of 2009 to pass Anti-Corruption Court legislation
**Political parties and leaders:** Democrat Party or PD [Hadi UTOMO]; Functional Groups Party or GOLKAR [Yusuf KALLA]; Great Indonesia Movement Party or GERINDRA [WIRANTO]; Indonesia Democratic Party-Struggle or PDI-P [MEGAWATI Sukarnoputri]; National Awakening Party or PKB [Muhaiman ISKANDAR]; National Mandate Party or PAN [Sutrisno BACHIR]; People's Conscience Party or HANURA [SUHARDI]; Prosperous Justice Party or PKS [Tifatul SEMBIRING]; United Development Party or PPP [Suryadharma ALI]
**Political pressure groups and leaders:** Indonesian Women's Coalition (Koalisi Perempuan - human rights group); Islamic Defenders Front or FPI; National Alliance for Freedom of Religion and Faith; Oil Palm Watch (environmental)
**International organization participation:** ADB, APEC, APT, ARF, ASEAN, BIS, CP, EAS, FAO, G-15, G-20, G-77, IAEA, IBRD, ICAO, ICC, ICRM, IDA, IDB, IFAD, IFC, IFRCS, IHO, ILO, IMF, IMO, IMSO, Interpol, IOC, IOM (observer), IPU, ISO, ITSO, ITU, ITUC, MIGA, MONUC, NAM, OIC, OPCW, OPEC, PIF (partner), UN, UNAMID, UNCTAD, UNESCO, UNIDO, UNIFIL, UNMIL, UNMIS, UNOMIG, UNWTO, UPU, WCL, WCO, WFTU, WHO, WIPO, WMO, WTO
**Diplomatic representation in the US:**
*chief of mission:* Ambassador SUDJADNAN Parnohadiningrat
*chancery:* 2020 Massachusetts Avenue NW, Washington, DC 20036
*telephone:* [1] (202) 775-5200
*FAX:* [1] (202) 775-5365
*consulate(s) general:* Chicago, Houston, Los Angeles, New York, San Francisco
**Diplomatic representation from the US:**
*chief of mission:* Ambassador Cameron R. HUME
*embassy:* Jalan 1 Medan Merdeka Selatan 4-5, Jakarta 10110
*mailing address:* Unit 8129, Box 1, FPO AP 96520
*telephone:* [62] (21) 3435-9000
*FAX:* [62] (21) 3435-9922
*consulate(s) general:* Surabaya

# Indonesia *(continued)*

**Flag description:** two equal horizontal bands of red (top) and white; similar to the flag of Monaco, which is shorter; also similar to the flag of Poland, which is white (top) and red

## Economy

**Economy - overview:** Indonesia, a vast polyglot nation, has made significant economic advances under the administration of President YUDHOYONO, but faces challenges stemming from the global financial crisis and world economic downturn. Indonesia's debt-to-GDP ratio in recent years has declined steadily because of increasingly robust GDP growth and sound fiscal stewardship. The government has introduced significant reforms in the financial sector, including in the areas of tax and customs, the use of Treasury bills, and capital market supervision. Indonesia's investment law, passed in March 2007, seeks to address some of the concerns of foreign and domestic investors. Indonesia still struggles with poverty and unemployment, inadequate infrastructure, corruption, a complex regulatory environment, and unequal resource distribution among regions. The non-bank financial sector, including pension funds and insurance, remains weak, and despite efforts to broaden and deepen capital markets, they remain underdeveloped. Economic difficulties in early 2008 centered on high global food and oil prices and their impact on Indonesia's poor and on the budget. The onset of the global financial crisis dampened inflationary pressures, but increased risk aversion for emerging market assets resulted in large losses in the stock market, significant depreciation of the rupiah, and a difficult environment for bond issuance. As global demand has slowed and prices for Indonesia's commodity exports have fallen, Indonesia faces the prospect of growth significantly below the 6-plus percent recorded in 2007 and 2008.

**GDP (purchasing power parity):**
$915.9 billion (2008 est.)
$863.1 billion (2007)
$811.1 billion (2006)
*note:* data are in 2008 US dollars

**GDP (official exchange rate):** $510.8 billion (2008 est.)

**GDP - real growth rate:**
6.1% (2008 est.)
6.4% (2007 est.)
5.5% (2006 est.)

**GDP - per capita (PPP):**
$3,900 (2008 est.)
$3,700 (2007 est.)
$3,500 (2006 est.)
*note:* data are in 2008 US dollars

**GDP - composition by sector:**
*agriculture:* 13.5%
*industry:* 45.6%
*services:* 40.8% (2008 est.)

**Labor force:** 112 million (2008 est.)

**Labor force - by occupation:**
*agriculture:* 42.1%
*industry:* 18.6%
*services:* 39.3% (2005 est.)

**Unemployment rate:**
8.4% (2008 est.)
9.1% (2007 est.)

**Population below poverty line:** 17.8% (2006)

**Household income or consumption by percentage share:**
*lowest 10%:* 3.6%
*highest 10%:* 28.5% (2002)

**Distribution of family income - Gini index:** 39.4 (2005)

**Investment (gross fixed):** 23.6% of GDP (2008)

**Budget:**
*revenues:* $101.1 billion
*expenditures:* $101.6 billion (2008 est.)

**Public debt:** 30.1% of GDP (2008 est.)

**Inflation rate (consumer prices):**
11.1% (2008 est.)
6.3% (2007 est.)

**Central bank discount rate:** 9.25% (31 December 2008)

**Commercial bank prime lending rate:** 15.13% (31 December 2008)

**Stock of money:** $41.8 billion (31 December 2008)

**Stock of quasi money:** $120 billion (31 December 2008)

**Stock of domestic credit:** $134.8 billion (31 December 2008)

**Market value of publicly traded shares:** $111.5 billion (31 December 2008)

**Agriculture - products:** rice, cassava (tapioca), peanuts, rubber, cocoa, coffee, palm oil, copra; poultry, beef, pork, eggs

**Industries:** petroleum and natural gas, textiles, apparel, footwear, mining, cement, chemical fertilizers, plywood, rubber, food, tourism

**Industrial production growth rate:** 2.8% (2008 est.)

**Electricity - production:** 142.4 billion kWh (2007 est.)

**Electricity - consumption:** 121.2 billion kWh (2007 est.)

**Electricity - exports:** 0 kWh (2007 est.)

**Electricity - imports:** 0 kWh (2007 est.)

**Oil - production:** 977,000 bbl/day (2008 est.)

**Oil - consumption:** 1.564 million bbl/day (2008 est.)

**Oil - exports:** 85,000 bbl/day (2008 est.)

**Oil - imports:** 672,000 bbl/day (2008 est.)

**Oil - proved reserves:** 3.99 billion bbl (1 January 2007 est.)

**Natural gas - production:** 56 billion cu m (2007 est.)

**Natural gas - consumption:** 23.4 billion cu m (2007 est.)

**Natural gas - exports:** 32.6 billion cu m (2007 est.)

**Natural gas - imports:** 0 cu m (2007 est.)

**Natural gas - proved reserves:** 2.659 trillion cu m (1 January 2008 est.)

**Current account balance:** $1 billion (2008 est.)

**Exports:** $136.8 billion f.o.b. (2008 est.)

**Exports - commodities:** oil and gas, electrical appliances, plywood, textiles, rubber

**Exports - partners:** Japan 20.7%, US 10.2%, Singapore 9.2%, China 8.5%, South Korea 6.6%, Malaysia 4.5%, India 4.3% (2007)

**Imports:** $128.8 billion f.o.b. (2008 est.)

**Imports - commodities:** machinery and equipment, chemicals, fuels, foodstuffs

**Imports - partners:** Singapore 13.2%, China 11.5%, Japan 8.8%, Malaysia 8.6%, US 6.4%, Thailand 5.8%, Saudi Arabia 4.5%, South Korea 4.3%, Australia 4% (2007)

**Reserves of foreign exchange and gold:** $51.54 billion (31 December 2008)

**Debt - external:** $151.7 billion (30 September 2008)

**Stock of direct foreign investment - at home:** $63.46 billion (2008 est.)

**Stock of direct foreign investment - abroad:** $4.277 billion (2008 est.)

**Exchange rates:** Indonesian rupiah (IDR) per US dollar - 9,698.9 (2008), 9,143 (2007), 9,159.3 (2006), 9,704.7 (2005), 8,938.9 (2004)

## Communications

**Telephones - main lines in use:** 17.828 million (2007)

**Telephones - mobile cellular:** 81.835 million (2007)

**Telephone system:**
*general assessment:* domestic service fair, international service good
*domestic:* interisland microwave system and HF radio police net; domestic satellite communications system; coverage provided by existing network has been expanded by use of over 200,000 telephone kiosks many located in remote areas; mobile cellular subscribership growing rapidly
*international:* country code - 62; landing point for both the SEA-ME-WE-3 and SEA-ME-WE-4 submarine cable networks that provide links throughout Asia, the Middle East, and Europe; satellite earth stations - 2 Intelsat (1 Indian Ocean and 1 Pacific Ocean)

**Radio broadcast stations:** AM 678, FM 43, shortwave 82 (1998)

**Television broadcast stations:** 54 local TV stations (11 national TV networks; each with its group of local transmitters) (2006)

**Internet country code:** .id

**Internet hosts:** 753,200 (2008)

**Internet users:** 13 million (2007)

## Transportation

**Airports:** 669 (2008)

**Airports - with paved runways:**
*total:* 163
*over 3,047 m:* 4
*2,438 to 3,047 m:* 17
*1,524 to 2,437 m:* 52
*914 to 1,523 m:* 54
*under 914 m:* 36 (2008)

## Indonesia (continued)

**Airports - with unpaved runways:**
*total:* 506
*1,524 to 2,437 m:* 5
*914 to 1,523 m:* 26
*under 914 m:* 475 (2008)
**Heliports:** 17 (2007)
**Pipelines:** condensate 735 km; condensate/gas 73 km; gas 5,797 km; oil 5,721 km; oil/gas/water 12 km; refined products 1,370 km; water 44 km (2008)
**Railways:**
*total:* 6,458 km
*narrow gauge:* 5,961 km 1.067-m gauge (125 km electrified); 497 km 0.750-m gauge (2006)
**Roadways:**
*total:* 391,009 km
*paved:* 216,714 km
*unpaved:* 174,295 km (2005)
**Waterways:** 21,579 km (2008)
**Merchant marine:**
*total:* 971
*by type:* bulk carrier 54, cargo 514, chemical tanker 35, container 80, liquefied gas 7, passenger 44, passenger/cargo 68, petroleum tanker 143, refrigerated cargo 2, roll on/roll off 10, specialized tanker 10, vehicle carrier 4
*foreign-owned:* 43 (China 2, France 1, Germany 1, Japan 6, Norway 1, Philippines 1, Singapore 27, Taiwan 2, UAE 2)
*registered in other countries:* 114 (Bahamas 2, Cambodia 2, China 1, Hong Kong 7, Liberia 2, Mongolia 1, Panama 31, Singapore 66, unknown 2) (2008)
**Ports and terminals:** Banjarmasin, Belawan, Ciwandan, Kotabaru, Krueg Geukueh, Palembang, Panjang, Sungai Pakning, Tanjung Perak, Tanjung Priok
**Transportation - note:** the International Maritime Bureau reports the territorial and offshore waters in the Strait of Malacca and South China Sea as high risk for piracy and armed robbery against ships; numerous commercial vessels have been attacked and hijacked both at anchor and while underway; hijacked vessels are often disguised and cargo diverted to ports in East Asia; crews have been murdered or cast adrift

### Military

**Military branches:** Indonesian Armed Forces (Tentara Nasional Indonesia, TNI): Army (TNI-Angkatan Darat (TNI-AD)), Navy (TNI-Angkatan Laut (TNI-AL); includes marines, naval air arm), Air Force (TNI-Angkatan Udara (TNI-AU)), National Air Defense Command (Kommando Pertahanan Udara Nasional (Kohanudnas)) (2009)
**Military service age and obligation:** 18 years of age for selective compulsory and voluntary military service; 2-year conscript service obligation, with reserve obligation to age 45 (officers); Indonesian citizens only (2008)
**Manpower available for military service:**
*males age 16-49:* 63,800,825
*females age 16-49:* 61,729,717 (2008 est.)

**Manpower fit for military service:**
*males age 16-49:* 52,997,922
*females age 16-49:* 52,503,046 (2009 est.)
**Manpower reaching militarily significant age annually:**
*male:* 2,197,323
*female:* 2,126,412 (2009 est.)
**Military expenditures:** 3% of GDP (2005 est.)

### Transnational Issues

**Disputes - international:** Indonesia has a stated foreign policy objective of establishing stable fixed land and maritime boundaries with all of its neighbors; Timor-Leste-Indonesia Boundary Committee has resolved all but a small portion of the land boundary, but discussions on maritime boundaries are stalemated over sovereignty of the uninhabited coral island of Pulau Batek/Fatu Sinai in the north and alignment with Australian claims in the south; many refugees from Timor-Leste who left in 2003 still reside in Indonesia and refuse repatriation; a 1997 treaty between Indonesia and Australia settled some parts of their maritime boundary but outstanding issues remain; ICJ's award of Sipadan and Ligitan islands to Malaysia in 2002 left the sovereignty of Unarang rock and the maritime boundary in the Ambalat oil block in the Celebes Sea in dispute; the ICJ decision has prompted Indonesia to assert claims to and to establish a presence on its smaller outer islands; Indonesia and Singapore continue to work on finalization of their 1973 maritime boundary agreement by defining unresolved areas north of Indonesia's Batam Island; Indonesian secessionists, squatters, and illegal migrants create repatriation problems for Papua New Guinea; piracy remains a problem in the Malacca Strait; maritime delimitation talks continue with Palau; Indonesian groups challenge Australia's claim to Ashmore Reef; Australia has closed parts of the Ashmore and Cartier Reserve to Indonesian traditional fishing and placed restrictions on certain catches
**Refugees and internally displaced persons:**
*IDPs:* 200,000-350,000 (government offensives against rebels in Aceh; most IDPs in Aceh, Central Kalimantan, Central Sulawesi Provinces, and Maluku) (2007)
**Illicit drugs:** illicit producer of cannabis largely for domestic use; producer of methamphetamine and ecstasy

# Iran

### Introduction

**Background:** Known as Persia until 1935, Iran became an Islamic republic in 1979 after the ruling monarchy was overthrown and Shah Mohammad Reza PAHLAVI was forced into exile. Conservative clerical forces established a theocratic system of government with ultimate political authority vested in a learned religious scholar referred to commonly as the Supreme Leader who, according to the constitution, is accountable only to the Assembly of Experts. US-Iranian relations have been strained since a group of Iranian students seized the US Embassy in Tehran on 4 November 1979 and held it until 20 January 1981. During 1980-88, Iran fought a bloody, indecisive war with Iraq that eventually expanded into the Persian Gulf and led to clashes between US Navy and Iranian military forces between 1987 and 1988. Iran has been designated a state sponsor of terrorism for its activities in Lebanon and elsewhere in the world and remains subject to US, UN, and EU economic sanctions and export controls because of its continued involvement in terrorism and its nuclear weapons ambitions. Following the election of reformer Hojjat ol-Eslam Mohammad KHATAMI as president in 1997 and similarly a reformer Majles (parliament) in 2000, a campaign to foster political reform in response to popular dissatisfaction was initiated. The movement floundered as conservative politicians, through the control of unelected institutions, prevented reform measures from being enacted and increased repressive measures. Starting with nationwide municipal elections in 2003 and continuing through Majles elections in 2004, conservatives reestablished control over Iran's elected government institutions, which culminated with the August 2005 inauguration of hardliner Mahmud AHMADI-NEJAD as president. The UN Security Council has passed a number of resolutions (1696 in July 2006, 1737 in December 2006, 1747 in March 2007, 1803 in March 2008, and 1835 in September 2008) calling for Iran to suspend

# Iran *(continued)*

its uranium enrichment and reprocessing activities and comply with its IAEA obligations and responsibilities. Resolutions 1737, 1477, and 1803 subject a number of Iranian individuals and entities involved in Iran's nuclear and ballistic missile programs to sanctions. Additionally, several Iranian entities are subject to US sanctions under Executive Order 13382 designations for proliferation activities and EO 13224 designations for support of terrorism.

## Geography

**Location:** Middle East, bordering the Gulf of Oman, the Persian Gulf, and the Caspian Sea, between Iraq and Pakistan

**Geographic coordinates:** 32 00 N, 53 00 E

**Map references:** Middle East

**Area:**
*total:* 1.648 million sq km
*land:* 1.636 million sq km
*water:* 12,000 sq km

**Area - comparative:** slightly larger than Alaska

**Land boundaries:**
*total:* 5,440 km
*border countries:* Afghanistan 936 km, Armenia 35 km, Azerbaijan-proper 432 km, Azerbaijan-Naxcivan exclave 179 km, Iraq 1,458 km, Pakistan 909 km, Turkey 499 km, Turkmenistan 992 km

**Coastline:** 2,440 km; note - Iran also borders the Caspian Sea (740 km)

**Maritime claims:**
*territorial sea:* 12 nm
*contiguous zone:* 24 nm
*exclusive economic zone:* bilateral agreements or median lines in the Persian Gulf
*continental shelf:* natural prolongation

**Climate:** mostly arid or semiarid, subtropical along Caspian coast

**Terrain:** rugged, mountainous rim; high, central basin with deserts, mountains; small, discontinuous plains along both coasts

**Elevation extremes:**
*lowest point:* Caspian Sea -28 m
*highest point:* Kuh-e Damavand 5,671 m

**Natural resources:** petroleum, natural gas, coal, chromium, copper, iron ore, lead, manganese, zinc, sulfur

**Land use:**
*arable land:* 9.78%
*permanent crops:* 1.29%
*other:* 88.93% (2005)

**Irrigated land:** 76,500 sq km (2003)

**Total renewable water resources:** 137.5 cu km (1997)

**Freshwater withdrawal (domestic/industrial/agricultural):**
*total:* 72.88 cu km/yr (7%/2%/91%)
*per capita:* 1,048 cu m/yr (2000)

**Natural hazards:** periodic droughts, floods; dust storms, sandstorms; earthquakes

**Environment - current issues:** air pollution, especially in urban areas, from vehicle emissions, refinery operations, and industrial effluents; deforestation; overgrazing; desertification; oil pollution in the Persian Gulf; wetland losses from drought; soil degradation (salination); inadequate supplies of potable water; water pollution from raw sewage and industrial waste; urbanization

**Environment - international agreements:**
*party to:* Biodiversity, Climate Change, Climate Change-Kyoto Protocol, Desertification, Endangered Species, Hazardous Wastes, Marine Dumping, Ozone Layer Protection, Ship Pollution, Wetlands
*signed, but not ratified:* Environmental Modification, Law of the Sea, Marine Life Conservation

**Geography - note:** strategic location on the Persian Gulf and Strait of Hormuz, which are vital maritime pathways for crude oil transport

## People

**Population:** 66,429,284 (July 2009 est.)

**Age structure:**
*0-14 years:* 21.7% (male 7,394,841/female 7,022,076)
*15-64 years:* 72.9% (male 24,501,544/female 23,914,172)
*65 years and over:* 5.4% (male 1,725,828/female 1,870,823) (2009 est.)

**Median age:**
*total:* 27 years
*male:* 26.8 years
*female:* 27.2 years (2009 est.)

**Population growth rate:** 0.883% (2009 est.)

**Birth rate:** 17.17 births/1,000 population (2009 est.)

**Death rate:** 5.69 deaths/1,000 population (2008 est.)

**Net migration rate:** -2.62 migrant(s)/1,000 population (2009 est.)

**Urbanization:**
*urban population:* 68% of total population (2008)
*rate of urbanization:* 2.1% annual rate of change (2005-10 est.)

**Sex ratio:**
*at birth:* 1.05 male(s)/female
*under 15 years:* 1.05 male(s)/female
*15-64 years:* 1.02 male(s)/female
*65 years and over:* 0.92 male(s)/female
*total population:* 1.02 male(s)/female (2009 est.)

**Infant mortality rate:**
*total:* 35.78 deaths/1,000 live births
*male:* 35.98 deaths/1,000 live births
*female:* 35.56 deaths/1,000 live births (2009 est.)

**Life expectancy at birth:**
*total population:* 71.14 years
*male:* 69.65 years
*female:* 72.72 years (2009 est.)

**Total fertility rate:** 1.71 children born/woman (2009 est.)

**HIV/AIDS - adult prevalence rate:** 0.2% (2007 est.)

**HIV/AIDS - people living with HIV/AIDS:** 86,000 (2007 est.)

**HIV/AIDS - deaths:** 4,300 (2007 est.)

**Major infectious diseases:**
*degree of risk:* intermediate
*food or waterborne diseases:* bacterial diarrhea
*vectorborne diseases:* Crimean Congo hemorrhagic fever and malaria
*note:* highly pathogenic H5N1 avian influenza has been identified in this country; it poses a negligible risk with extremely rare cases possible among US citizens who have close contact with birds (2009)

**Nationality:**
*noun:* Iranian(s)
*adjective:* Iranian

**Ethnic groups:** Persian 51%, Azeri 24%, Gilaki and Mazandarani 8%, Kurd 7%, Arab 3%, Lur 2%, Baloch 2%, Turkmen 2%, other 1%

**Religions:** Muslim 98% (Shia 89%, Sunni 9%), other (includes Zoroastrian, Jewish, Christian, and Baha'i) 2%

**Languages:** Persian and Persian dialects 58%, Turkic and Turkic dialects 26%, Kurdish 9%, Luri 2%, Balochi 1%, Arabic 1%, Turkish 1%, other 2%

**Literacy:**
*definition:* age 15 and over can read and write
*total population:* 77%
*male:* 83.5%
*female:* 70.4% (2002 est.)

**School life expectancy (primary to tertiary education):**
*total:* 13 years
*male:* 13 years
*female:* 13 years (2005)

**Education expenditures:** 5.1% of GDP (2006)

## Government

**Country name:**
*conventional long form:* Islamic Republic of Iran
*conventional short form:* Iran
*local long form:* Jomhuri-ye Eslami-ye Iran
*local short form:* Iran
*former:* Persia

**Government type:** theocratic republic

**Capital:**
*name:* Tehran
*geographic coordinates:* 35 40 N, 51 25 E
*time difference:* UTC+3.5 (8.5 hours ahead of Washington, DC during Standard Time)

**Administrative divisions:** 30 provinces (ostanha, singular - ostan); Ardabil, Azarbayjan-e Gharbi, Azarbayjan-e Sharqi, Bushehr, Chahar Mahall va Bakhtiari, Esfahan, Fars, Gilan, Golestan, Hamadan, Hormozgan, Ilam, Kerman, Kermanshah, Khorasan-e Jonubi, Khorasan-e Razavi, Khorasan-e Shomali, Khuzestan, Kohgiluyeh va Buyer Ahmad, Kordestan, Lorestan, Markazi, Mazandaran, Qazvin, Qom, Semnan, Sistan va Baluchestan, Tehran, Yazd, Zanjan

**Independence:** 1 April 1979 (Islamic Republic of Iran proclaimed)

**National holiday:** Republic Day, 1 April (1979)

**Constitution:** 2-3 December 1979; revised in 1989
*note:* the revision in 1989 expanded powers of the presidency and eliminated the prime ministership

# Iran (continued)

**Legal system:** based on Sharia law system; has not accepted compulsory ICJ jurisdiction

**Suffrage:** 18 years of age; universal

**Executive branch:**

*chief of state:* Supreme Leader Ali Hoseini-KHAMENEI (since 4 June 1989)

*head of government:* President Mahmud AHMADI-NEJAD (since 3 August 2005); First Vice President Parviz DAVUDI (since 11 September 2005)

*cabinet:* Council of Ministers selected by the president with legislative approval; the Supreme Leader has some control over appointments to the more sensitive ministries

*note:* also considered part of the Executive branch of government are three oversight bodies: 1) Assembly of Experts (Majles-Khebregan), a popularly elected body charged with determining the succession of the Supreme Leader, reviewing his performance, and deposing him if deemed necessary; 2) Expediency Council or the Council for the Discernment of Expediency (Majma-e-Tashkise-Maslahat-e-Nezam) exerts supervisory authority over the executive, judicial, and legislative branches and resolves legislative issues on which the Majles and the Council of Guardians disagree and since 1989 has been used to advise national religious leaders on matters of national policy; in 2005 the Council's powers were expanded to act as a supervisory body for the government; 3) Council of Guardians of the Constitution or Council of Guardians or Guardians Council (Shora-ye Negaban-e Qanun-e Assassi) determines whether proposed legislation is both constitutional and faithful to Islamic law, vets candidates for suitability, and supervises national elections

*elections:* Supreme Leader is appointed for life by the Assembly of Experts; president is elected by popular vote for a four-year term (eligible for a second term and third nonconsecutive term); last held 17 June 2005 with a two-candidate runoff on 24 June 2005 (next presidential election slated for 12 June 2009)

*election results:* Mahmud AHMADI-NEJAD elected president; percent of vote - Mahmud AHMADI-NEJAD 62%, Ali Akbar Hashemi-RAFSANJANI 36%

**Legislative branch:** unicameral Islamic Consultative Assembly or Majles-e-Shura-ye-Eslami or Majles (290 seats; members elected by popular vote to serve four-year terms)

*elections:* last held 14 March 2008 with a runoff held 25 April 2008 (next to be held in 2012)

*election results:* percent of vote - NA; seats by party - conservatives/Islamists 167, reformers 39, independents 74, religious minorities 5, other 5

**Judicial branch:** The Supreme Court (Qeveh Qazaieh) and the four-member High Council of the Judiciary have a single head and overlapping responsibilities; together they supervise the enforcement of all laws and establish judicial and legal policies; lower courts include a special clerical court, a revolutionary court, and a special administrative court

**Political parties and leaders:** formal political parties are a relatively new phenomenon in Iran and most conservatives still prefer to work through political pressure groups rather than parties; often political parties or coalitions are formed prior to elections and disbanded soon thereafter; a loose pro-reform coalition called the 2nd Khordad Front, which includes political parties as well as less formal groups and organizations, achieved considerable success in elections for the sixth Majles in early 2000; groups in the coalition included the Islamic Iran Participation Front (IIPF), Executives of Construction Party (Kargozaran), Solidarity Party, Islamic Labor Party, Mardom Salari, Mojahedin of the Islamic Revolution Organization (MIRO), and Militant Clerics Society (Ruhaniyun); the coalition participated in the seventh Majles elections in early 2004; following his defeat in the 2005 presidential elections, former MCS Secretary General and sixth Majles Speaker Mehdi KARUBI formed the National Trust Party; a new conservative group, Islamic Iran Developers Coalition (Abadgaran), took a leading position in the new Majles after winning a majority of the seats in February 2004; following the 2004 Majles elections, traditional and hardline conservatives have attempted to close ranks under the United Front of Principlists and the Broad Popular Coalition of Principlists; several reformist groups, such as the Islamic Revolution, came together as a reformist coalition in advance of the 2008 Majles elections; the IIPF has repeatedly complained that the overwhelming majority of its candidates have been unfairly disqualified from the 2008 elections

**Political pressure groups and leaders:** groups that generally support the Islamic Republic: Ansar-e Hizballah-Islamic Coalition Party (Motalefeh); Followers of the Line of the Imam and the Leader; Islamic Engineers Society; Tehran Militant Clergy Association (Ruhaniyat); active pro-reform student group: Office of Strengthening Unity (OSU); opposition groups: Baluchistan People's Party (BPP); Freedom Movement of Iran; Marz-e Por Gohar; National Front; and various ethnic and Monarchist organizations; armed political groups that have been repressed by the government: Democratic Party of Iranian Kurdistan (KDPI); Jundallah; Komala; Mujahedin-e Khalq Organization (MEK or MKO); People's Fedayeen; People's Free Life Party of Kurdistan (PJAK)

**International organization participation:** CP, ECO, FAO, G-15, G-24, G-77, IAEA, IBRD, ICAO, ICC, ICCt (signatory), ICRM, IDA, IDB, IFAD, IFC, IFRCS, IHO, ILO, IMF, IMO, IMSO, Interpol, IOC, IOM, IPU, ISO, ITSO, ITU, MIGA, NAM, OIC, OPCW, OPEC, PCA, SAARC (observer), SCO (observer), UN, UNCTAD, UNESCO, UNHCR, UNIDO, UNITAR, UNWTO, UPU, WCL, WCO, WFTU, WHO, WIPO, WMO, WTO (observer)

**Diplomatic representation in the US:** none; note - Iran has an Interests Section in the Pakistani Embassy; address: Iranian Interests Section, Pakistani Embassy, 2209 Wisconsin Avenue NW, Washington, DC 20007; telephone: [1] (202) 965-4990; FAX [1] (202) 965-1073

**Diplomatic representation from the US:** none; note - the US Interests Section is located in the Embassy of Switzerland No. 39 Shahid Mousavi (Golestan 5th), Pasdaran Ave., Tehran, Iran; telephone [98] 21 2254 2178/2256 5273; FAX [98] 21 2258 0432

**Flag description:** three equal horizontal bands of green (top), white, and red; the national emblem (a stylized representation of the word Allah in the shape of a tulip, a symbol of martyrdom) in red is centered in the white band; ALLAH AKBAR (God is Great) in white Arabic script is repeated 11 times along the bottom edge of the green band and 11 times along the top edge of the red band

## Economy

**Economy - overview:** Iran's economy is marked by an inefficient state sector, reliance on the oil sector, which provides the majority of government revenues, and statist policies, which create major distortions throughout the system. Most economic activity is controlled by the state. Private sector activity is typically limited to small-scale workshops, farming, and services. Price controls, subsidies, and other rigidities weigh down the economy, undermining the potential for private-sector-led growth. Significant informal market activity flourishes. Corruption and shortages of goods are widespread. President Mahmud AHMADI-NEJAD has proposed reforms to Iran's system of price controls and subsidies, particularly on food and energy. However, previous government-led efforts at reform - such as fuel rationing in July 2007 and the imposition of the Value-Added Tax (VAT) in October 2008 - were met with stiff resistance and violent protests. High oil prices in recent years allowed Iran to greatly increase its export earnings and amass nearly $100 billion in foreign exchange reserves. But with oil prices currently below $40 per barrel, the Iranian government is facing difficulties. Tehran has formulated a 2009 budget that anticipates lower oil prices. The government has drawn down the country's Oil Stabilization Fund, and may be dipping into foreign exchange reserves. Iran continues to suffer from double-digit unemployment and inflation - inflation climbed to a 28% annual rate in 2008. Underemployment among Iran's educated youth has convinced many to seek jobs overseas, resulting in a significant "brain drain."

**GDP (purchasing power parity):**
$842 billion (2008 est.)
$790.6 billion (2007)
$733.2 billion (2006)
note: data are in 2008 US dollars

**GDP (official exchange rate):** $382.3 billion (2008 est.)

**GDP - real growth rate:**
6.5% (2008 est.)
7.8% (2007 est.)
5.8% (2006 est.)

# Iran (continued)

**GDP - per capita (PPP):**
$12,800 (2008 est.)
$12,100 (2007 est.)
$11,300 (2006 est.)
*note:* data are in 2008 US dollars
**GDP - composition by sector:**
*agriculture:* 10.8%
*industry:* 44.3%
*services:* 44.9% (2008 est.)
**Labor force:** 24.35 million
*note:* shortage of skilled labor (2008 est.)
**Labor force - by occupation:**
*agriculture:* 25%
*industry:* 31%
*services:* 45% (June 2007)
**Unemployment rate:**
12.5% (2008 est.)
12% (2007 est.)
*note:* data are according to the Iranian Government
**Population below poverty line:** 18% (2007 est.)
**Household income or consumption by percentage share:**
*lowest 10%:* 2%
*highest 10%:* 33.7% (1998)
**Distribution of family income - Gini index:** 44.5 (2006)
**Investment (gross fixed):** 27.7% of GDP (2008 est.)
**Budget:**
*revenues:* $51 billion
*expenditures:* $103 billion (FY09/10 est.)
**Public debt:** 25% of GDP (2008 est.)
**Inflation rate (consumer prices):**
28% (2008 est.)
17.1% (2007 est.)
*note:* official Iranian estimate
**Commercial bank prime lending rate:** 12% (31 December 2007)
**Stock of money:** $46.13 billion (31 December 2007)
**Stock of quasi money:** $68.71 billion (31 December 2007)
**Stock of domestic credit:** $109.7 billion (31 December 2007)
**Market value of publicly traded shares:** $45.57 billion (31 December 2007)
**Agriculture - products:** wheat, rice, other grains, sugar beets, sugar cane, fruits, nuts, cotton; dairy products, wool; caviar
**Industries:** petroleum, petrochemicals, fertilizers, caustic soda, textiles, cement and other construction materials, food processing (particularly sugar refining and vegetable oil production), ferrous and non-ferrous metal fabrication, armaments
**Industrial production growth rate:** 4.5% excluding oil (2008 est.)
**Electricity - production:** 193 billion kWh (2006 est.)
**Electricity - consumption:** 145 billion kWh (2006 est.)
**Electricity - exports:** 2.775 billion kWh (2006 est.)
**Electricity - imports:** 2.54 billion kWh (2006 est.)
**Oil - production:** 4.7 million bbl/day (2007 est.)

**Oil - consumption:** 1.6 million bbl/day (2007 est.)
**Oil - exports:** 2.8 million bbl/day (2007 est.)
**Oil - imports:** 210,000 bbl/day (2007)
**Oil - proved reserves:** 138.4 billion bbl based on Iranian claims (1 January 2008 est.)
**Natural gas - production:** 111.9 billion cu m (2007 est.)
**Natural gas - consumption:** 111.8 billion cu m (2007 est.)
**Natural gas - exports:** 6.2 billion cu m (2007 est.)
**Natural gas - imports:** 6.1 billion cu m (2007 est.)
**Natural gas - proved reserves:** 26.85 trillion cu m (1 January 2008 est.)
**Current account balance:** $27.47 billion (2008 est.)
**Exports:** $106.4 billion f.o.b. (2008 est.)
**Exports - commodities:** petroleum 80%, chemical and petrochemical products, fruits and nuts, carpets
**Exports - partners:** China 15%, Japan 14.3%, Turkey 7.4%, South Korea 7.3%, Italy 6.4% (2007)
**Imports:** $67.79 billion f.o.b. (2008 est.)
**Imports - commodities:** industrial raw materials and intermediate goods, capital goods, foodstuffs and other consumer goods, technical services
**Imports - partners:** China 14.2%, Germany 9.6%, UAE 9.1%, South Korea 6.3%, Russia 5.7%, Italy 5% (2007)
**Reserves of foreign exchange and gold:** $96.56 billion (31 December 2008 est.)
**Debt - external:** $21.77 billion (31 December 2008 est.)
**Stock of direct foreign investment - at home:** $6.954 billion (2008 est.)
**Stock of direct foreign investment - abroad:** $993 million (2008 est.)
**Exchange rates:** Iranian rials (IRR) per US dollar - 9,142.8 (2008 est.), 9,407.5 (2007), 9,227.1 (2006), 8,964 (2005), 8,614 (2004)
*note:* Iran has been using a managed floating exchange rate regime since unifying multiple exchange rates in March 2002

## Communications

**Telephones - main lines in use:** 23.835 million (2007)
**Telephones - mobile cellular:** 29.77 million (2007)
**Telephone system:**
*general assessment:* currently being modernized and expanded with the goal of not only improving the efficiency and increasing the volume of the urban service but also bringing telephone service to several thousand villages, not presently connected
*domestic:* the addition of new fiber cables and modern switching and exchange systems installed by Iran's state-owned telecom company have improved and expanded the main line network greatly; main line availability has more than doubled to nearly 24 million lines since 2000; additionally, mobile service has increased dramatically serving nearly 30 million subscribers in 2007
*international:* country code - 98; submarine fiber-optic cable to UAE with access to Fiber-Optic Link Around

the Globe (FLAG); Trans-Asia-Europe (TAE) fiber-optic line runs from Azerbaijan through the northern portion of Iran to Turkmenistan with expansion to Georgia and Azerbaijan; HF radio and microwave radio relay to Turkey, Azerbaijan, Pakistan, Afghanistan, Turkmenistan, Syria, Kuwait, Tajikistan, and Uzbekistan; satellite earth stations - 13 (9 Intelsat and 4 Inmarsat) (2007)
**Radio broadcast stations:** AM 72, FM 6, shortwave 5 (1998)
**Television broadcast stations:** 29 (plus 450 repeaters) (1997)
**Internet country code:** .ir
**Internet hosts:** 2,860 (2008)
**Internet users:** 23 million (2007)

## Transportation

**Airports:** 317 (2008)
**Airports - with paved runways:**
*total:* 130
*over 3,047 m:* 40
*2,438 to 3,047 m:* 29
*1,524 to 2,437 m:* 23
*914 to 1,523 m:* 32
*under 914 m:* 6 (2008)
**Airports - with unpaved runways:**
*total:* 187
*over 3,047 m:* 1
*2,438 to 3,047 m:* 1
*1,524 to 2,437 m:* 10
*914 to 1,523 m:* 144
*under 914 m:* 31 (2008)
**Heliports:** 14 (2007)
**Pipelines:** condensate 7 km; condensate/gas 12 km; gas 19,246 km; liquid petroleum gas 570 km; oil 7,018 km; refined products 7,936 km (2008)
**Railways:**
*total:* 8,367 km
*broad gauge:* 94 km 1.676-m gauge
*standard gauge:* 8,273 km 1.435-m gauge (146 km electrified) (2006)
**Roadways:**
*total:* 172,927 km
*paved:* 125,908 km (includes 1,429 km of expressways)
*unpaved:* 47,019 km (2006)
**Waterways:** 850 km (on Karun River; additional service on Lake Urmia) (2008)
**Merchant marine:**
*total:* 74
*by type:* bulk carrier 18, cargo 34, chemical tanker 4, container 6, liquefied gas 1, passenger/cargo 4, petroleum tanker 2, refrigerated cargo 2, roll on/roll off 3
*foreign-owned:* 1 (UAE 1)
*registered in other countries:* 115 (Barbados 2, Bolivia 1, Cyprus 10, Hong Kong 15, Malta 79, Panama 7, Saint Vincent and the Grenadines 1) (2008)
**Ports and terminals:** Assaluyeh, Bandar Abbas, Bandar-e-Eman Khomeyni

## Military

**Military branches:** Islamic Republic of Iran Regular Forces (Artesh): Ground Forces, Navy, Air Force of the Military of the Islamic Republic of Iran (Niru-ye Hava'i-ye Artesh-e Jomhuri-ye Eslami-ye Iran, IRIAF; Air Defense Command being formed); Islamic Revolutionary Guard Corps (Sepah-e Pasdaran-e Enqelab-e Eslami, IRGC): Ground Forces, Navy, Air Force, Qods Force (special operations), and Basij Force (Popular Mobilization Army); Law Enforcement Forces (2008)

**Military service age and obligation:** 19 years of age for compulsory military service; 16 years of age for volunteers; 17 years of age for Law Enforcement Forces; 15 years of age for Basij Forces (Popular Mobilization Army); conscript military service obligation - 18 months; women exempt from military service (2008)

**Manpower available for military service:**
*males age 16-49:* 20,212,275
*females age 16-49:* 19,638,751 (2008 est.)

**Manpower fit for military service:**
*males age 16-49:* 17,658,573
*females age 16-49:* 17,148,290 (2009 est.)

**Manpower reaching militarily significant age annually:**
*male:* 700,213
*female:* 664,846 (2009 est.)

**Military expenditures:** 2.5% of GDP (2006)

## Transnational Issues

**Disputes - international:** Iran protests Afghanistan's limiting flow of dammed tributaries to the Helmand River in periods of drought; Iraq's lack of a maritime boundary with Iran prompts jurisdiction disputes beyond the mouth of the Shatt al Arab in the Persian Gulf; Iran and UAE dispute Tunb Islands and Abu Musa Island, which are occupied by Iran; Iran stands alone among littoral states in insisting upon a division of the Caspian Sea into five equal sectors

**Refugees and internally displaced persons:**
*refugees (country of origin):* 914,268 (Afghanistan); 54,024 (Iraq) (2007)

**Trafficking in persons:**
*current situation:* Iran is a source, transit, and destination country for women trafficked for the purposes of sexual exploitation and involuntary servitude; Iranian women are trafficked internally for the purpose of forced prostitution and for forced marriages to settle debts; Iranian children are trafficked internally and Afghan children are trafficked into Iran for the purpose of forced marriages, commercial sexual exploitation, and involuntary servitude as beggars or laborers
*tier rating:* Tier 3 - Iran did not provide evidence of law enforcement activities against trafficking, and credible reports indicate that Iranian authorities punish victims of trafficking with beatings, imprisonment, and execution; Iran has not ratified the 2000 UN TIP Protocol (2008)

**Illicit drugs:** despite substantial interdiction efforts and considerable control measures along the border with Afghanistan, Iran remains one of the primary transshipment routes for Southwest Asian heroin to Europe; suffers one of the highest opiate addiction rates in the world, and has an increasing problem with synthetic drugs; lacks anti-money laundering laws; has reached out to neighboring countries to share counter-drug intelligence

# Iraq

## Introduction

**Background:** Formerly part of the Ottoman Empire, Iraq was occupied by Britain during the course of World War I; in 1920, it was declared a League of Nations mandate under UK administration. In stages over the next dozen years, Iraq attained its independence as a kingdom in 1932. A "republic" was proclaimed in 1958, but in actuality a series of strongmen ruled the country until 2003. The last was SADDAM Husayn. Territorial disputes with Iran led to an inconclusive and costly eight-year war (1980-88). In August 1990, Iraq seized Kuwait but was expelled by US-led, UN coalition forces during the Gulf War of January-February 1991. Following Kuwait's liberation, the UN Security Council (UNSC) required Iraq to scrap all weapons of mass destruction and long-range missiles and to allow UN verification inspections. Continued Iraqi noncompliance with UNSC resolutions over a period of 12 years led to the US-led invasion of Iraq in March 2003 and the ouster of the SADDAM Husayn regime. US forces remained in Iraq under a UNSC mandate until 31 December 2008 and under a bilateral Security Agreement thereafter, helping to provide security and to support the freely elected government. In October 2005, Iraqis approved a constitution in a national referendum and, pursuant to this document, elected a 275-member Council of Representatives (CoR) in December 2005. After the election, Ibrahim al-JAAFARI was selected as prime minister; he was replaced by Nuri al-MALIKI in May 2006. The CoR approved most cabinet ministers in May 2006, marking the transition to Iraq's first constitutional government in nearly a half century. On 31 January 2009, Iraq held elections for provincial councils in all provinces except for the three provinces comprising the Kurdistan Regional Government and at-Ta'mim (Kirkuk) province.

# Iraq (continued)

## Geography

**Location:** Middle East, bordering the Persian Gulf, between Iran and Kuwait

**Geographic coordinates:** 33 00 N, 44 00 E

**Map references:** Middle East

**Area:**
*total:* 437,072 sq km
*land:* 432,162 sq km
*water:* 4,910 sq km

**Area - comparative:** slightly more than twice the size of Idaho

**Land boundaries:**
*total:* 3,650 km
*border countries:* Iran 1,458 km, Jordan 181 km, Kuwait 240 km, Saudi Arabia 814 km, Syria 605 km, Turkey 352 km

**Coastline:** 58 km

**Maritime claims:**
*territorial sea:* 12 nm
*continental shelf:* not specified

**Climate:** mostly desert; mild to cool winters with dry, hot, cloudless summers; northern mountainous regions along Iranian and Turkish borders experience cold winters with occasionally heavy snows that melt in early spring, sometimes causing extensive flooding in central and southern Iraq

**Terrain:** mostly broad plains; reedy marshes along Iranian border in south with large flooded areas; mountains along borders with Iran and Turkey

**Elevation extremes:**
*lowest point:* Persian Gulf 0 m
*highest point:* unnamed peak; 3,611 m; note - this peak is neither Gundah Zhur 3,607 m nor Kuh-e Hajji-Ebrahim 3,595 m

**Natural resources:** petroleum, natural gas, phosphates, sulfur

**Land use:**
*arable land:* 13.12%
*permanent crops:* 0.61%
*other:* 86.27% (2005)

**Irrigated land:** 35,250 sq km (2003)

**Total renewable water resources:** 96.4 cu km (1997)

**Freshwater withdrawal (domestic/industrial/agricultural):**
*total:* 42.7 cu km/yr (3%/5%/92%)
*per capita:* 1,482 cu m/yr (2000)

**Natural hazards:** dust storms; sandstorms; floods

**Environment - current issues:** government water control projects have drained most of the inhabited marsh areas east of An Nasiriyah by drying up or diverting the feeder streams and rivers; a once sizable population of Marsh Arabs, who inhabited these areas for thousands of years, has been displaced; furthermore, the destruction of the natural habitat poses serious threats to the area's wildlife populations; inadequate supplies of potable water; development of the Tigris and Euphrates rivers system contingent upon agreements with upstream riparian Turkey; air and water pollution; soil degradation (salination) and erosion; desertification

**Environment - international agreements:**
*party to:* Biodiversity, Law of the Sea, Ozone Layer Protection
*signed, but not ratified:* Environmental Modification

**Geography - note:** strategic location on Shatt al Arab waterway and at the head of the Persian Gulf

## People

**Population:** 28,945,657 (July 2009 est.)

**Age structure:**
*0-14 years:* 38.8% (male 5,709,688/ female 5,531,359)
*15-64 years:* 58.2% (male 8,529,956/ female 8,310,164)
*65 years and over:* 3% (male 408,266/ female 456,224) (2009 est.)

**Median age:**
*total:* 20.4 years
*male:* 20.3 years
*female:* 20.5 years (2009 est.)

**Population growth rate:** 2.507% (2009 est.)

**Birth rate:** 30.1 births/1,000 population (2009 est.)

**Death rate:** 5.14 deaths/1,000 population (2008 est.)

**Net migration rate:** NA

**Urbanization:**
*urban population:* 67% of total population (2008)
*rate of urbanization:* 1.7% annual rate of change (2005-10 est.)

**Sex ratio:**
*at birth:* 1.05 male(s)/female
*under 15 years:* 1.03 male(s)/female
*15-64 years:* 1.03 male(s)/female
*65 years and over:* 0.9 male(s)/female
*total population:* 1.02 male(s)/female (2009 est.)

**Infant mortality rate:**
*total:* 43.82 deaths/1,000 live births
*male:* 49.38 deaths/1,000 live births
*female:* 37.98 deaths/1,000 live births (2009 est.)

**Life expectancy at birth:**
*total population:* 69.94 years
*male:* 68.6 years
*female:* 71.34 years (2009 est.)

**Total fertility rate:** 3.86 children born/woman (2009 est.)

**HIV/AIDS - adult prevalence rate:** less than 0.1% (2001 est.)

**HIV/AIDS - people living with HIV/AIDS:** fewer than 500 (2003 est.)

**HIV/AIDS - deaths:** NA

**Major infectious diseases:**
*degree of risk:* intermediate
*food or waterborne diseases:* bacterial diarrhea, hepatitis A, and typhoid fever
*note:* highly pathogenic H5N1 avian influenza has been identified in this country; it poses a negligible risk with extremely rare cases possible among US citizens who have close contact with birds (2009)

**Nationality:**
*noun:* Iraqi(s)
*adjective:* Iraqi

**Ethnic groups:** Arab 75%-80%, Kurdish 15%-20%, Turkoman, Assyrian, or other 5%

**Religions:** Muslim 97% (Shia 60%-65%, Sunni 32%-37%), Christian or other 3%

**Languages:** Arabic, Kurdish (official in Kurdish regions), Turkoman (a Turkish dialect), Assyrian (Neo-Aramaic), Armenian

**Literacy:**
*definition:* age 15 and over can read and write
*total population:* 74.1%
*male:* 84.1%
*female:* 64.2% (2000 est.)

**School life expectancy (primary to tertiary education):**
*total:* 10 years
*male:* 11 years
*female:* 8 years (2005)

**Education expenditures:** NA

## Government

**Country name:**
*conventional long form:* Republic of Iraq
*conventional short form:* Iraq
*local long form:* Al Jumhuriyah al-Iraqiyah
*local short form:* Al Iraq

**Government type:** parliamentary democracy

**Capital:**
*name:* Baghdad
*geographic coordinates:* 33 20 N, 44 23 E
*time difference:* UTC+3 (8 hours ahead of Washington, DC during Standard Time)

**Administrative divisions:** 18 governorates (muhafazat, singular - muhafazah) and 1 region*; Al Anbar, Al Basrah, Al Muthanna, Al Qadisiyah, An Najaf, Arbil, As Sulaymaniyah, At Ta'mim, Babil, Baghdad, Dahuk, Dhi Qar, Diyala, Karbala', Kurdistan Regional Government*, Maysan, Ninawa, Salah ad Din, Wasit

**Independence:** 3 October 1932 (from League of Nations mandate under British administration); note - on 28 June 2004 the Coalition Provisional Authority transferred sovereignty to the Iraqi-controlled Government

**National holiday:** Republic Day, July 14 (1958); note - the Government of Iraq has yet to declare an official national holiday but still observes Republic Day

**Constitution:** ratified on 15 October 2005 (subject to review by the Constitutional Review Committee and a possible public referendum )

**Legal system:** based on European civil and Islamic law under the framework outlined in the Iraqi Constitution; has not accepted compulsory ICJ jurisdiction

**Suffrage:** 18 years of age; universal

**Executive branch:**
*chief of state:* President Jalal TALABANI (since 6 April 2005); Vice Presidents Adil ABD AL-MAHDI and Tariq al-HASHIMI (since 22 April 2006); note - the president and vice presidents comprise the Presidency Council)
*head of government:* Prime Minister Nuri al-MALIKI (since 20 May 2006); Deputy Prime Ministers Barham

SALIH (since 20 May 2006)and Rafi al-ISSAWI
(since 19 July 2008)

*cabinet:* 36 ministers appointed by the Presidency
Council, plus Prime Minister Nuri al-MALIKI and
Deputy Prime Ministers Barham SALIH and Rafi
al-ISSAWI

*elections:* held 15 December 2005 to elect a
275-member Council of Representatives

**Legislative branch:** unicameral Council of
Representatives (consisting of 275 members elected
by a closed-list, proportional representation system)

*elections:* last held 15 December 2005 to elect a
275-member Council of Representatives (next to be
held December 2009); the Council of Representatives
elected the Presidency Council and approved the
prime minister and two deputy prime ministers

*election results:* Council of Representatives - percent
of vote by party - Unified Iraqi Alliance 41%, Kurdistan
Alliance 22%, Tawafuq Coalition 15%, Iraqi National
List 8%, Iraqi Front for National Dialogue 4%, other
10%; number of seats by party (as of November
2007) -Unified Iraqi Alliance (including the Sadrist bloc
with 30 and Fadilah with 15) 130, Kurdistan Alliance
53, Tawafuq Front 44, Iraqi National List 25, Fadilah
15, Iraqi Front for National Dialogue 11, other 12

**Judicial branch:** the Iraq Constitution calls for the
federal judicial power to be comprised of the Higher
Judicial Council, Federal Supreme Court, Federal
Court of Cassation, Public Prosecution Department,
Judiciary Oversight Commission and other federal
courts that are regulated in accordance with the law

**Political parties and leaders:** Assyrian Democratic
Movement [Yunadim KANNA]; Badr Organization [Hadi
al-AMIRI]; Constitutional Monarchy Movement or CMM
[Sharif Ali Bin al-HUSAYN]; Da'wa al-Islamiya Party [Nuri
al-MALIKI]; General Conference of Iraqi People [Adnan
al-DULAYMI]; Independent Iraqi Alliance or IIA [Falah
al-NAQIB]; Iraqi Communist Party [Hamid MAJID]; Iraqi
Front for National Dialogue [Salih al-MUTLAQ]; Iraqi
Hizballah [Karim Mahmud al-MUHAMMADAWI]; Iraqi
Independent Democrats or IID [Adnan PACHACHI,
Mahdi al-HAFIZ]; Iraqi Islamic Party or IIP [Tariq
al-HASHIMI]; Iraqi National Accord or INA [Ayad
ALLAWI]; Iraqi National Congress or INC [Ahmad
CHALABI]; Iraqi National Council for Dialogue or INCD
[Khalaf Ulayan al-Khalifawi al-DULAYMI]; Iraqi National
Unity Movement or INUM [Ahmad al-KUBAYSI]; Islamic
Action Organization or IAO [Ayatollah Muhammad
al-MUDARRISI]; Islamic Supreme Council of Iraq or ISCI
[Abd al-Aziz al-HAKIM]; Jama'at al Fadilah or JAF
[Muhammad Ali al-YAQUBI]; Kurdistan Democratic Party
or KDP [Masud BARZANI]; Kurdistan Islamic Union
[Salah ad-Din Muhammad BAHA al-DIN]; Patriotic Union
of Kurdistan or PUK [Jalal TALABANI]; Sadrist Trend
[Muqtada al-SADR] (not an organized political party, but
it fields independent candidates affiliated with Muqtada
al-SADR); Sahawa al-Iraq [Ahmad al-RISHAWI]

*note:* the Kurdistan Alliance, Iraqi National List,
Tawafuq Front, Iraqi Front for National Dialogue, and
Unified Iraqi Alliance were only electoral slates
consisting of the representatives from the various Iraqi
political parties

**Political pressure groups and leaders:** Sunni
militias; Shia militias, some associated with political
parties

**International organization participation:** ABEDA,
AFESD (suspended), AMF, CAEU, FAO, G-77, IAEA,
IBRD, ICAO, ICRM, IDA, IDB, IFAD, IFC, IFRCS, ILO,
IMF, IMO, IMSO, Interpol, IOC, ISO, ITSO, ITU, LAS,
MIGA, NAM, OAPEC, OIC, OPEC, PCA, UN,
UNCTAD, UNESCO, UNIDO, UNWTO, UPU, WCO,
WFTU, WHO, WIPO, WMO, WTO (observer)

**Diplomatic representation in the US:**

*chief of mission:* Ambassador Samir Shakir
al-SUMAYDI

*chancery:* 3421 Massachusetts Ave, NW,
Washington, DC 20007

*telephone:* [1] (202) 742-1600

*FAX:* [1] (202) 333-1129

**Diplomatic representation from the US:**

*chief of mission:* Ambassador Christopher R. HILL

*embassy:* Baghdad

*mailing address:* APO AE 09316

*telephone:* 1-240-553-0589 ext. 5340 or 5635; note -
Consular Section

*FAX:* NA

**Flag description:** three equal horizontal bands of
red (top), white, and black; the Takbir (Arabic
expression meaning "God is great") in green Arabic
script is centered in the white band; similar to the flag
of Syria, which has two stars but no script, Yemen,
which has a plain white band, and that of Egypt, which
has a gold Eagle of Saladin centered in the white
band; design is based upon the Arab Liberation
colors; Council of Representatives approved this flag
as a compromise temporary replacement for Ba'athist
Saddam-era flag

## Economy

**Economy - overview:** Decreasing insurgent attacks
and an improving security environment in many parts of
the country are helping to spur economic activity. Iraq's
economy is dominated by the oil sector, which has
traditionally provided over 90% of foreign exchange
earnings. Oil exports are around levels seen before
Operation Iraqi Freedom. Total government revenues
have benefited from high oil prices in recent years;
however, revenues have declined significantly since the
oil price drop in fall 2008. Iraq is making some progress
in building the institutions needed to implement economic
policy. In March 2009 Iraq concluded a Stand-By
Arrangement (SBA) with the IMF that details economic
reforms. The SBA allows an 80% reduction of the debt
owed to Paris Club creditor nations. The International
Compact with Iraq was established in May 2007 to
integrate Iraq into the regional and global economy, and
the Iraqi government is seeking to pass laws to
strengthen its economy. This legislation includes a
hydrocarbon law to establish a modern legal framework
to allow Iraq to develop its resources and a revenue
sharing law to equitably divide oil revenues within the
nation, although both are still under contentious political
negotiation. Some foreign entities have expressed

interest in reinvigorating Iraq's industrial sector. The
government of Iraq is pursuing a strategy to gain foreign
participation in joint ventures with State-owned
enterprises. Provincial Councils are also using their own
budgets to promote and facilitate investment at the local
level. The Central Bank has been successful in
controlling inflation through appreciation of the dinar
against the US dollar. However, Iraq's challenge will be to
use macroeconomic gains to improve the lives of
ordinary Iraqis. Reducing corruption and implementing
structural reforms, such as bank restructuring and
developing the private sector, will be key to Iraq's
economic success.

**GDP (purchasing power parity):**
$112.8 billion (2008 est.)
$104.6 billion (2007)
$103.1 billion (2006)
*note:* data are in 2008 US dollars

**GDP (official exchange rate):** $93.8 billion
(2008 est.)

**GDP - real growth rate:**
9.8% (2008 est.)
1.5% (2007 est.)
6.2% (2006 est.)

**GDP - per capita (PPP):**
$4,000 (2008 est.)
$3,800 (2007 est.)
$3,800 (2006 est.)
*note:* data are in 2008 US dollars

**GDP - composition by sector:**
*agriculture:* 5%
*industry:* 68%
*services:* 27% (2006 est.)

**Labor force:** 7.74 million (2008 est.)

**Labor force - by occupation:**
*agriculture:* NA%
*industry:* NA%
*services:* NA%

**Unemployment rate:**
18.2% (2008 est.)
18% (2006 est.)
*note:* official data; unofficial estimates as high as 30%

**Population below poverty line:** NA%

**Household income or consumption by
percentage share:**
*lowest 10%:* NA%
*highest 10%:* NA%

**Budget:**
*revenues:* $42.4 billion
*expenditures:* $49.9 billion (FY08 est.)

**Inflation rate (consumer prices):**
6.8% (2008 est.)
4.7% (2007 est.)

**Central bank discount rate:** 15%
(31 December 2008)

**Commercial bank prime lending rate:** 19.74%
(31 December 2007)

**Stock of money:** $18.81 billion (31 December 2007)

**Stock of quasi money:** $3.67 billion
(31 December 2007)

**Stock of domestic credit:** NA

# Iraq *(continued)*

**Market value of publicly traded shares:** $1.878 billion (31 March 2008)

**Agriculture - products:** wheat, barley, rice, vegetables, dates, cotton; cattle, sheep, poultry

**Industries:** petroleum, chemicals, textiles, leather, construction materials, food processing, fertilizer, metal fabrication/processing

**Industrial production growth rate:** 10.5% (2008 est.)

**Electricity - production:** 36.92 billion kWh (2008 est.)

**Electricity - consumption:** 39.88 billion kWh (2008 est.)

**Electricity - exports:** 0 kWh (2008)

**Electricity - imports:** 2.95 billion kWh (2008 est.)

**Oil - production:** 2.42 million bbl/day (2008 est.)

**Oil - consumption:** 295,000 bbl/day (2007 est.)

**Oil - exports:** 1.83 million bbl/day (2008 est.)

**Oil - imports:** 104,300 bbl/day (2005)

**Oil - proved reserves:** 115 billion bbl (1 January 2008 est.)

**Natural gas - production:** 15.66 billion cu m (2008 est.)

**Natural gas - consumption:** 9.454 billion cu m

*note:* 1.48 billion cu m were flared (2008 est.)

**Natural gas - exports:** 0 cu m (2007 est.)

**Natural gas - imports:** 0 cu m (2007 est.)

**Natural gas - proved reserves:** 3.17 trillion cu m (1 January 2008 est.)

**Current account balance:** $22.6 billion (2008 est.)

**Exports:** $66.1 billion f.o.b. (2008 est.)

**Exports - commodities:** crude oil 84%, crude materials excluding fuels 8%, food and live animals 5%

**Exports - partners:** US 36.8%, Italy 12.6%, South Korea 9.5%, Taiwan 6.3%, Spain 5.2%, Canada 4.7%, France 4.4%, Netherlands 4.2% (2007)

**Imports:** $43.5 billion f.o.b. (2008 est.)

**Imports - commodities:** food, medicine, manufactures

**Imports - partners:** Syria 30.5%, Turkey 19.8%, US 11.1%, Jordan 5%, China 4.8% (2007)

**Reserves of foreign exchange and gold:** $46.8 billion (31 December 2008 est.)

**Debt - external:** $40.4 billion (31 December 2008 est.)

**Exchange rates:** New Iraqi dinars (NID) per US dollar - 1,176 (2008), 1,255 (2007), 1,466 (2006), 1,475 (2005), 1,890 (second half, 2003)

## Communications

**Telephones - main lines in use:** 1.547 million (2005)

**Telephones - mobile cellular:** 14.021 million (2007)

**Telephone system:**

*general assessment:* the 2003 liberation of Iraq severely disrupted telecommunications throughout Iraq including international connections; widespread government efforts to rebuild domestic and international communications through fiber optic links are in progress; the mobile cellular market has expanded rapidly with an estimated 14 million current users in 2007

*domestic:* repairs to switches and lines destroyed during 2003 continue; additional switching capacity is improving access; cellular service is available and centered on 3 GSM networks which are being expanded beyond their regional roots, improving country-wide connectivity; wireless local loop licenses have been issued with the hope of overcoming the lack of fixed-line infrastructure

*international:* country code - 964; satellite earth stations - 4 (2 Intelsat - 1 Atlantic Ocean and 1 Indian Ocean, 1 Intersputnik - Atlantic Ocean region, and 1 Arabsat (inoperative)); local microwave radio relay connects border regions to Jordan, Kuwait, Syria, and Turkey; planned international fiber-optic connections to Iran (terrestrial) with a link to the Fiber-Optic Link Around the Globe (FLAG) submarine fiber-optic cable (2007)

**Radio broadcast stations:** 52 (station frequency types NA) (2008)

**Television broadcast stations:** 47 (2008)

**Internet country code:** .iq

**Internet hosts:** 3 (2008)

**Internet users:** 54,000 (2007)

## Transportation

**Airports:** 105 (2008)

**Airports - with paved runways:**

*total:* 75

*over 3,047 m:* 19

*2,438 to 3,047 m:* 37

*1,524 to 2,437 m:* 5

*914 to 1,523 m:* 6

*under 914 m:* 8 (2008)

**Airports - with unpaved runways:**

*total:* 30

*over 3,047 m:* 3

*2,438 to 3,047 m:* 4

*1,524 to 2,437 m:* 4

*914 to 1,523 m:* 13

*under 914 m:* 6 (2008)

**Heliports:** 17 (2007)

**Pipelines:** gas 2,501 km; liquid petroleum gas 918 km; oil 5,418 km; refined products 1,637 km (2008)

**Railways:**

*total:* 2,272 km

*standard gauge:* 2,272 km 1.435-m gauge (2006)

**Roadways:**

*total:* 44,900 km

*paved:* 37,851 km

*unpaved:* 7,049 km (2002)

**Waterways:** 5,279 km

*note:* Euphrates River (2,815 km), Tigris River (1,899 km), and Third River (565 km) are principal waterways (2008)

**Merchant marine:**

*total:* 14

*by type:* cargo 10, petroleum tanker 4 (2008)

**Ports and terminals:** Al Basrah, Khawr az Zubayr, Umm Qasr

## Military

**Military branches:** Iraqi Armed Forces: Iraqi Army (includes Iraqi Special Operations Force, Iraqi Intervention Force), Iraqi Navy (former Iraqi Coastal Defense Force), Iraqi Air Force (former Iraqi Army Air Corps) (2005)

**Military service age and obligation:** 18-49 years of age for voluntary military service (2008)

**Manpower available for military service:**

*males age 16-49:* 7,086,200

*females age 16-49:* 6,808,954 (2008 est.)

**Manpower fit for military service:**

*males age 16-49:* 6,203,425

*females age 16-49:* 6,065,009 (2009 est.)

**Manpower reaching militarily significant age annually:**

*male:* 313,500

*female:* 304,923 (2009 est.)

**Military expenditures:** 8.6% of GDP (2006)

## Transnational Issues

**Disputes - international:** coalition forces assist Iraqis in monitoring internal and cross-border security; approximately two million Iraqis have fled the conflict in Iraq, with the majority taking refuge in Syria and Jordan, and lesser numbers to Egypt, Lebanon, Iran, and Turkey; Iraq's lack of a maritime boundary with Iran prompts jurisdiction disputes beyond the mouth of the Shatt al Arab in the Persian Gulf; Turkey has expressed concern over the autonomous status of Kurds in Iraq

**Refugees and internally displaced persons:**

*refugees (country of origin):* 10,000-15,000 (Palestinian Territories); 11,773 (Iran); 16,832 (Turkey)

*IDPs:* 2.4 million (ongoing US-led war and ethno-sectarian violence) (2007)

# Ireland

## Introduction

**Background:** Celtic tribes arrived on the island between 600-150 B.C. Invasions by Norsemen that began in the late 8th century were finally ended when King Brian BORU defeated the Danes in 1014. English invasions began in the 12th century and set off more than seven centuries of Anglo-Irish struggle marked by fierce rebellions and harsh repressions. A failed 1916 Easter Monday Rebellion touched off several years of guerrilla warfare that in 1921 resulted in independence from the UK for 26 southern counties; six northern (Ulster) counties remained part of the UK. In 1949, Ireland withdrew from the British Commonwealth; it joined the European Community in 1973. Irish governments have sought the peaceful unification of Ireland and have cooperated with Britain against terrorist groups. A peace settlement for Northern Ireland is gradually being implemented despite some difficulties. In 2006, the Irish and British governments developed and began to implement the St. Andrews Agreement, building on the Good Friday Agreement approved in 1998.

## Geography

**Location:** Western Europe, occupying five-sixths of the island of Ireland in the North Atlantic Ocean, west of Great Britain
**Geographic coordinates:** 53 00 N, 8 00 W
**Map references:** Europe
**Area:**
*total:* 70,280 sq km
*land:* 68,890 sq km
*water:* 1,390 sq km
**Area - comparative:** slightly larger than West Virginia
**Land boundaries:**
*total:* 360 km
*border countries:* UK 360 km
**Coastline:** 1,448 km
**Maritime claims:**
*territorial sea:* 12 nm
*exclusive fishing zone:* 200 nm

**Climate:** temperate maritime; modified by North Atlantic Current; mild winters, cool summers; consistently humid; overcast about half the time
**Terrain:** mostly level to rolling interior plain surrounded by rugged hills and low mountains; sea cliffs on west coast
**Elevation extremes:**
*lowest point:* Atlantic Ocean 0 m
*highest point:* Carrauntoohil 1,041 m
**Natural resources:** natural gas, peat, copper, lead, zinc, silver, barite, gypsum, limestone, dolomite
**Land use:**
*arable land:* 16.82%
*permanent crops:* 0.03%
*other:* 83.15% (2005)
**Irrigated land:** NA
**Total renewable water resources:** 46.8 cu km (2003)
**Freshwater withdrawal (domestic/industrial/agricultural):**
*total:* 1.18 cu km/yr (23%/77%/0%)
*per capita:* 284 cu m/yr (1994)
**Natural hazards:** NA
**Environment - current issues:** water pollution, especially of lakes, from agricultural runoff
**Environment - international agreements:**
*party to:* Air Pollution, Air Pollution-Nitrogen Oxides, Air Pollution-Sulfur 94, Biodiversity, Climate Change, Climate Change-Kyoto Protocol, Desertification, Endangered Species, Environmental Modification, Hazardous Wastes, Law of the Sea, Marine Dumping, Ozone Layer Protection, Ship Pollution, Tropical Timber 83, Tropical Timber 94, Wetlands, Whaling
*signed, but not ratified:* Air Pollution-Persistent Organic Pollutants, Marine Life Conservation
**Geography - note:** strategic location on major air and sea routes between North America and northern Europe; over 40% of the population resides within 100 kmof Dublin

## People

**Population:** 4,203,200 (July 2009 est.)
**Age structure:**
*0-14 years:* 20.9% (male 454,571/female 424,022)
*15-64 years:* 67.1% (male 1,411,336/female 1,409,760)
*65 years and over:* 12% (male 224,850/female 278,661) (2009 est.)
**Median age:**
*total:* 35 years
*male:* 34.2 years
*female:* 35.7 years (2009 est.)
**Population growth rate:** 1.12% (2009 est.)
**Birth rate:** 14.23 births/1,000 population (2009 est.)
**Death rate:** 7.77 deaths/1,000 population (2008 est.)
**Net migration rate:** 4.71 migrant(s)/1,000 population (2009 est.)
**Urbanization:**
*urban population:* 61% of total population (2008)
*rate of urbanization:* 2.2% annual rate of change (2005-10 est.)

**Sex ratio:**
*at birth:* 1.07 male(s)/female
*under 15 years:* 1.07 male(s)/female
*15-64 years:* 1 male(s)/female
*65 years and over:* 0.81 male(s)/female
*total population:* 0.99 male(s)/female (2009 est.)
**Infant mortality rate:**
*total:* 5.05 deaths/1,000 live births
*male:* 5.53 deaths/1,000 live births
*female:* 4.54 deaths/1,000 live births (2009 est.)
**Life expectancy at birth:**
*total population:* 78.24 years
*male:* 75.6 years
*female:* 81.06 years (2009 est.)
**Total fertility rate:** 1.85 children born/woman (2009 est.)
**HIV/AIDS - adult prevalence rate:** 0.2% (2007 est.)
**HIV/AIDS - people living with HIV/AIDS:** 5,500 (2007 est.)
**HIV/AIDS - deaths:** fewer than 100 (2007 est.)
**Nationality:**
*noun:* Irishman(men), Irishwoman(women), Irish (collective plural)
*adjective:* Irish
**Ethnic groups:** Irish 87.4%, other white 7.5%, Asian 1.3%, black 1.1%, mixed 1.1%, unspecified 1.6% (2006 census)
**Religions:** Roman Catholic 87.4%, Church of Ireland 2.9%, other Christian 1.9%, other 2.1%, unspecified 1.5%, none 4.2% (2006 census)
**Languages:** English (official) is the language generally used, Irish (Gaelic or Gaeilge) (official) spoken mainly in areas along the western coast
**Literacy:**
*definition:* age 15 and over can read and write
*total population:* 99%
*male:* 99%
*female:* 99% (2003 est.)
**School life expectancy (primary to tertiary education):**
*total:* 18 years
*male:* 17 years
*female:* 18 years (2006)
**Education expenditures:** 4.7% of GDP (2005)

## Government

**Country name:**
*conventional long form:* none
*conventional short form:* Ireland
*local long form:* none
*local short form:* Eire
**Government type:** republic, parliamentary democracy
**Capital:**
*name:* Dublin
*geographic coordinates:* 53 19 N, 6 14 W
*time difference:* UTC 0 (5 hours ahead of Washington, DC during Standard Time)
*daylight saving time:* +1hr, begins last Sunday in March; ends last Sunday in October

# Ireland (continued)

**Administrative divisions:** 26 counties; Carlow, Cavan, Clare, Cork, Donegal, Dublin, Galway, Kerry, Kildare, Kilkenny, Laois, Leitrim, Limerick, Longford, Louth, Mayo, Meath, Monaghan, Offaly, Roscommon, Sligo, Tipperary, Waterford, Westmeath, Wexford, Wicklow

**Independence:** 6 December 1921 (from the UK by treaty)

**National holiday:** Saint Patrick's Day, 17 March

**Constitution:** adopted 1 July 1937 by plebiscite; effective 29 December 1937

**Legal system:** based on English common law substantially modified by indigenous concepts; judicial review of legislative acts in Supreme Court; has not accepted compulsory ICJ jurisdiction

**Suffrage:** 18 years of age; universal

**Executive branch:**
*chief of state:* President Mary MCALEESE (since 11 November 1997)
*head of government:* Prime Minister Brian COWEN (since 7 May 2008)
*cabinet:* Cabinet appointed by the president with previous nomination by the prime minister and approval of the House of Representatives
*elections:* president elected by popular vote for a seven-year term (eligible for a second term); election last held 31 October 1997 (next scheduled for October 2011); note - Mary MCALEESE appointed to a second term when no other candidate qualified for the 2004 presidential election; prime minister (taoiseach) nominated by the House of Representatives and appointed by the president
*election results:* Mary MCALEESE elected president; percent of vote - Mary MCALEESE 44.8%, Mary BANOTTI 29.6%
*note:* government coalition - Fianna Fail, the Green Party, the Progressive Democrats (disbanding), and independent members of Parliament

**Legislative branch:** bicameral Parliament or Oireachtas consists of the Senate or Seanad Eireann (60 seats; 49 members elected by the universities and from candidates put forward by five vocational panels, 11 are nominated by the prime minister; members serve five-year terms) and the House of Representatives or Dail Eireann (166 seats; members are elected by popular vote on the basis of proportional representation to serve five-year terms)
*elections:* Senate - last held in July 2007 (next to be held by July 2012); House of Representatives - last held 24 May 2007 (next to be held by May 2012)
*election results:* Senate - percent of vote by party - NA; seats by party - Fianna Fail 28, Fine Gael 14, Labor Party 6, Progressive Democrats 2, Green Party 2, Sein Fein 1, independents 7; House of Representatives - percent of vote by party - Fianna Fail 41.6%, Fine Gael 27.3%, Labor Party 10.1%, Sinn Fein 6.9%, Green Party 4.7%, Progressive Democrats 2.7%, other 6.7%; seats by party - Fianna Fail 78, Fine Gael 51, Labor Party 20, Sinn Fein 4, Green Party 6, Progressive Democrats 2, independents 4, Speaker of the Dail 1
*note:* on 8 November 2008, delegates voted to disband the party, but as of January 2009, the party was still operating

**Judicial branch:** Supreme Court (judges appointed by the president on the advice of the prime minister and cabinet)

**Political parties and leaders:** Fianna Fail [Brian COWEN]; Fine Gael [Enda KENNY]; Green Party [John GORMLEY]; Labor Party [Eamon GILMORE]; Progressive Democrats [Ciaran CANNON] (disbanding); Sinn Fein [Gerry ADAMS]; Socialist Party [Joe HIGGINS]; The Workers' Party [Mick FINNEGAN]

**Political pressure groups and leaders:** Families Acting for Innocent Relatives or FAIR [Brian McCONNELL] (seek compensation for victims of violence); Families Against Intimidation and Terror or FAIT (oppose terrorism); Gaeltacht Civil Rights Campaign (Coiste Cearta Sibhialta na Gaeilge) or CCSG (encourages the use of the Irish language and campaigns for greater civil rights in Irish speaking areas); Irish Republican Army or IRA (terrorist group); Keep Ireland Open (environmental group); Midland Railway Action Group or MRAG [Willie ALLEN] (transportation promoters); Rail Users Ireland (formerly the Platform 11 - transportation promoters); 32 Country Sovereignty Movement or 32CSM (supports a fully sovereign Ireland); Ulster Defence Association or UDA (terrorist group)

**International organization participation:** ADB (nonregional member), Australia Group, BIS, CE, EAPC, EBRD, EIB, EMU, ESA, EU, FAO, IAEA, IBRD, ICAO, ICC, ICCt, ICRM, IDA, IEA, IFAD, IFC, IFRCS, IHO, ILO, IMF, IMO, Interpol, IOC, IOM, IPU, ISO, ITSO, ITU, ITUC, MIGA, MINURSO, MONUC, NEA, NSG, OAS (observer), OECD, OPCW, OSCE, Paris Club, PCA, PFP, UN, UNCTAD, UNESCO, UNHCR, UNIDO, UNIFIL, UNMIL, UNOCI, UNTSO, UPU, WCO, WEU (observer), WFTU, WHO, WIPO, WMO, WTO, ZC

**Diplomatic representation in the US:**
*chief of mission:* Ambassador Michael COLLINS
*chancery:* 2234 Massachusetts Avenue NW, Washington, DC 20008
*telephone:* [1] (202) 462-3939
*FAX:* [1] (202) 232-5993
*consulate(s) general:* Boston, Chicago, New York, San Francisco

**Diplomatic representation from the US:**
*chief of mission:* Ambassador (vacant); Charge d'Affaires Robert J. FAUCHER
*embassy:* 42 Elgin Road, Ballsbridge, Dublin 4
*mailing address:* use embassy street address
*telephone:* [353] (1) 668-8777
*FAX:* [353] (1) 668-9946

**Flag description:** three equal vertical bands of green (hoist side), white, and orange; similar to the flag of Cote d'Ivoire, which is shorter and has the colors reversed - orange (hoist side), white, and green; also similar to the flag of Italy, which is shorter and has colors of green (hoist side), white, and red

## Economy

**Economy - overview:** Ireland is a small, modern, trade-dependent economy. GDP growth averaged 6% in 1995-2007, but economic activity dropped sharply in 2008 and Ireland entered into a recession for the first time in more than a decade with the onset of the world financial crisis and subsequent severe slowdown in the property and construction markets. Agriculture, once the most important sector, is now dwarfed by industry and services. Although the export sector, dominated by foreign multinationals, remains a key component of Ireland's economy, construction most recently fueled economic growth along with strong consumer spending and business investment. Property prices rose more rapidly in Ireland in the decade up to 2006 than in any other developed world economy. Per capita GDP also surged during Ireland's high-growth years, and in 2007 surpassed that of the United States. The Irish Government has implemented a series of national economic programs designed to curb price and wage inflation, invest in infrastructure, increase labor force skills, and promote foreign investment. In 2008 the COWEN government moved to guarantee all bank deposits, recapitalize the banking system, and establish partly-public venture capital funds in response to the country's economic downturn. Ireland joined in circulating the euro on 1 January 2002 along with 11 other EU nations.

**GDP (purchasing power parity):**
$191.9 billion (2008 est.)
$195.3 billion (2007)
$184.2 billion (2006)
*note:* data are in 2008 US dollars

**GDP (official exchange rate):** $285 billion (2008 est.)

**GDP - real growth rate:**
-1.7% (2008 est.)
6% (2007 est.)
5.7% (2006 est.)

**GDP - per capita (PPP):**
$46,200 (2008 est.)
$47,500 (2007 est.)
$45,300 (2006 est.)
*note:* data are in 2008 US dollars

**GDP - composition by sector:**
*agriculture:* 5%
*industry:* 46%
*services:* 49% (2002 est.)

**Labor force:** 2.27 million (2008 est.)

**Labor force - by occupation:**
*agriculture:* 6%
*industry:* 27%
*services:* 67% (2006 est.)

**Unemployment rate:**
6.2% (2008 est.)
4.6% (2007 est.)

**Population below poverty line:** 7% (2005 est.)

**Household income or consumption by percentage share:**
*lowest 10%:* 2.9%
*highest 10%:* 27.2% (2000)

**Distribution of family income - Gini index:** 32 (2005)

**Investment (gross fixed):** 19.8% of GDP (2008 est.)

**Budget:**
*revenues:* $93.84 billion
*expenditures:* $110.8 billion (2008 est.)

**Public debt:** 31.5% of GDP (2008 est.)

**Inflation rate (consumer prices):**
4% (2008 est.)
4.9% (2007 est.)

**Central bank discount rate:** 4%
*note:* this is the European Central Bank's rate on the marginal lending facility, which offers overnight credit to banks in the euro area

**Commercial bank prime lending rate:** 6.52% (31 December 2007)

**Stock of money:** NA
*note:* see entry for the European Union for money supply in the euro area; the European Central Bank (ECB) controls monetary policy for the 16 members of the Economic and Monetary Union (EMU); individual members of the EMU do not control the quantity of money and quasi money circulating within their own borders

**Stock of quasi money:** NA

**Stock of domestic credit:** $768.9 billion (31 December 2007)

**Market value of publicly traded shares:** $144 billion (31 December 2007)

**Agriculture - products:** turnips, barley, potatoes, sugar beets, wheat; beef, dairy products

**Industries:** steel, lead, zinc, silver, aluminum, barite, and gypsum mining processing; food products, brewing, textiles, clothing; chemicals, pharmaceuticals; machinery, rail transportation equipment; glass and crystal; software, tourism

**Industrial production growth rate:** 5% (2007 est.)

**Electricity - production:** 25.77 billion kWh (2007 est.)

**Electricity - consumption:** 25.67 billion kWh (2006 est.)

**Electricity - exports:** 82 million kWh (2007 est.)

**Electricity - imports:** 1.412 billion kWh (2007 est.)

**Oil - production:** 0 bbl/day (2005 est.)

**Oil - consumption:** 200,900 bbl/day (2007 est.)

**Oil - exports:** 29,780 bbl/day (2005)

**Oil - imports:** 194,000 bbl/day (2005)

**Oil - proved reserves:** 0 bbl (1 January 2006 est.)

**Natural gas - production:** 457 million cu m (2007 est.)

**Natural gas - consumption:** 4.984 billion cu m (2007 est.)

**Natural gas - exports:** 0 cu m (2007 est.)

**Natural gas - imports:** 4.552 billion cu m (2007 est.)

**Natural gas - proved reserves:** 9.911 billion cu m (1 January 2008 est.)

**Current account balance:** -$8.621 billion (2008 est.)

**Exports:** $128 billion f.o.b. (2008 est.)

**Exports - commodities:** machinery and equipment, computers, chemicals, pharmaceuticals; live animals, animal products

**Exports - partners:** UK 18.7%, US 17.9%, Belgium 14.5%, Germany 7.4%, France 5.8% (2007)

**Imports:** $91.27 billion f.o.b. (2008 est.)

**Imports - commodities:** data processing equipment, other machinery and equipment, chemicals, petroleum and petroleum products, textiles, clothing

**Imports - partners:** UK 38.3%, US 11.3%, Germany 9.7%, Netherlands 5%, France 4.2% (2007)

**Reserves of foreign exchange and gold:** $926.2 million (2006 est.)

**Debt - external:** $1.841 trillion (30 June 2007)

**Stock of direct foreign investment - at home:** $216 billion (2008 est.)

**Stock of direct foreign investment - abroad:** $149.1 billion (2008 est.)

**Exchange rates:** euros (EUR) per US dollar - 0.6827 (2008 est.), 0.7345 (2007), 0.7964 (2006), 0.8041 (2005), 0.8054 (2004)

## Communications

**Telephones - main lines in use:** 2.112 million (2007)

**Telephones - mobile cellular:** 4.94 million (2007)

**Telephone system:**
*general assessment:* modern digital system using cable and microwave radio relay
*domestic:* system privatized but dominated by former state monopoly operator; increasing levels of broadband access
*international:* country code - 353; landing point for the Hibernia-Atlantic submarine cable with links to the US, Canada, and UK; satellite earth station - 1 Intelsat (Atlantic Ocean)

**Radio broadcast stations:** AM 9, FM 106, shortwave 0 (1998)

**Television broadcast stations:** 4 (many repeaters); (projected digital broadcasting scheduled to be launched in 2009) (2008)

**Internet country code:** .ie

**Internet hosts:** 1.242 million (2008)

**Internet users:** 1.708 million (2007)

## Transportation

**Airports:** 37 (2008)

**Airports - with paved runways:**
*total:* 17
*over 3,047 m:* 1
*2,438 to 3,047 m:* 1
*1,524 to 2,437 m:* 4
*914 to 1,523 m:* 5
*under 914 m:* 6 (2008)

**Airports - with unpaved runways:**
*total:* 20
*914 to 1,523 m:* 2
*under 914 m:* 18 (2008)

**Pipelines:** gas 1,550 km (2008)

**Railways:**
*total:* 3,237 km
*broad gauge:* 1,872 km 1.600-m gauge (37 km electrified)
*narrow gauge:* 1,365 km 0.914-m gauge (operated by the Irish Peat Board to transport peat to power stations and briquetting plants) (2006)

**Roadways:**
*total:* 96,602 km
*paved:* 96,602 km (includes 200 km of expressways) (2003)

**Waterways:** 956 km (pleasure craft only) (2008)

**Merchant marine:**
*total:* 29
*by type:* cargo 25, chemical tanker 2, container 1, roll on/roll off 1
*foreign-owned:* 2 (US 2)
*registered in other countries:* 21 (Bahamas 2, Bermuda 1, Bulgaria 1, Cyprus 3, Isle of Man 1, Marshall Islands 1, Netherlands 10, Slovakia 1, UK 1) (2008)

**Ports and terminals:** Cork, Dublin, Shannon Foynes

## Military

**Military branches:** Irish Defense Forces (Oglaigh na h-Eireann): Army (includes Naval Service and Air Corps (Aer-Chor na h-Eireann)) (2009)

**Military service age and obligation:** 17-25 years of age for male or female voluntary military service (17-27 years of age for the Naval Service); enlistees 16 years of age can be recruited for apprentice specialist positions; maximum obligation 12 years; 17-35 years of age for the Reserve Defense Forces; EU citizenship or 5-year residence in Ireland required (2008)

**Manpower available for military service:**
*males age 16-49:* 1,024,635
*females age 16-49:* 1,024,276 (2008 est.)

**Manpower fit for military service:**
*males age 16-49:* 857,162
*females age 16-49:* 854,416 (2009 est.)

**Manpower reaching militarily significant age annually:**
*male:* 28,072
*female:* 26,400 (2009 est.)

**Military expenditures:** 0.9% of GDP (2005 est.)

## Transnational Issues

**Disputes - international:** Ireland, Iceland, and the UK dispute Denmark's claim that the Faroe Islands' continental shelf extends beyond 200 nm

**Illicit drugs:** transshipment point for and consumer of hashish from North Africa to the UK and Netherlands and of European-produced synthetic drugs; increasing consumption of South American cocaine; minor transshipment point for heroin and cocaine destined for Western Europe; despite recent legislation, narcotics-related money laundering - using bureaux de change, trusts, and shell companies involving the offshore financial community - remains a concern

# Isle of Man
*(British crown dependency)*

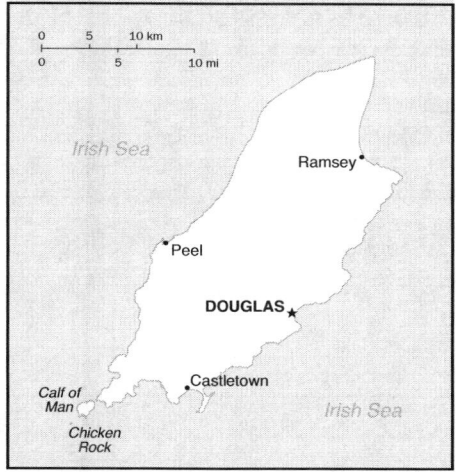

## Introduction

**Background:** Part of the Norwegian Kingdom of the Hebrides until the 13th century when it was ceded to Scotland, the isle came under the British crown in 1765. Current concerns include reviving the almost extinct Manx Gaelic language. Isle of Man is a British crown dependency but is not part of the UK. However, the UK Government remains constitutionally responsible for its defense and international representation.

## Geography

**Location:** Western Europe, island in the Irish Sea, between Great Britain and Ireland
**Geographic coordinates:** 54 15 N, 4 30 W
**Map references:** Europe
**Area:**
*total:* 572 sq km
*land:* 572 sq km
*water:* 0 sq km
**Area - comparative:** slightly more than three times the size of Washington, DC
**Land boundaries:** 0 km
**Coastline:** 160 km
**Maritime claims:**
*territorial sea:* 12 nm
*exclusive fishing zone:* 12 nm
**Climate:** temperate; cool summers and mild winters; overcast about a third of the time
**Terrain:** hills in north and south bisected by central valley
**Elevation extremes:**
*lowest point:* Irish Sea 0 m
*highest point:* Snaefell 621 m
**Natural resources:** none
**Land use:**
*arable land:* 9%
*permanent crops:* 0%
*other:* 91% (permanent pastures, forests, mountain, and heathland) (2002)

**Irrigated land:** 0 sq km
**Natural hazards:** NA
**Environment - current issues:** waste disposal (both household and industrial); transboundary air pollution
**Geography - note:** one small islet, the Calf of Man, lies to the southwest and is a bird sanctuary

## People

**Population:** 76,512 (July 2009 est.)
**Age structure:**
*0-14 years:* 16.9% (male 6,612/female 6,300)
*15-64 years:* 66% (male 25,433/female 25,083)
*65 years and over:* 17.1% (male 5,408/female 7,676) (2009 est.)
**Median age:**
*total:* 40.2 years
*male:* 39 years
*female:* 41.4 years (2009 est.)
**Population growth rate:** 0.524% (2009 est.)
**Birth rate:** 10.77 births/1,000 population (2009 est.)
**Death rate:** 11.02 deaths/1,000 population (2008 est.)
**Net migration rate:** 5.23 migrant(s)/1,000 population (2009 est.)
**Urbanization:**
*urban population:* 51% of total population (2008)
*rate of urbanization:* -0.2% annual rate of change (2005-10 est.)
**Sex ratio:**
*at birth:* 1.05 male(s)/female
*under 15 years:* 1.05 male(s)/female
*15-64 years:* 1.01 male(s)/female
*65 years and over:* 0.7 male(s)/female
*total population:* 0.96 male(s)/female (2009 est.)
**Infant mortality rate:**
*total:* 5.37 deaths/1,000 live births
*male:* 6.11 deaths/1,000 live births
*female:* 4.58 deaths/1,000 live births (2009 est.)
**Life expectancy at birth:**
*total population:* 78.82 years
*male:* 75.86 years
*female:* 81.93 years (2009 est.)
**Total fertility rate:** 1.65 children born/woman (2009 est.)
**HIV/AIDS - adult prevalence rate:** NA
**HIV/AIDS - people living with HIV/AIDS:** NA
**HIV/AIDS - deaths:** NA
**Nationality:**
*noun:* Manxman (men), Manxwoman (women)
*adjective:* Manx
**Ethnic groups:** Manx (Norse-Celtic descent), Britons
**Religions:** Anglican, Roman Catholic, Methodist, Baptist, Presbyterian, Society of Friends
**Languages:** English, Manx Gaelic
**Literacy:** NA
**Education expenditures:** NA

## Government

**Country name:**
*conventional long form:* none
*conventional short form:* Isle of Man
*abbreviation:* I.O.M.
**Dependency status:** British crown dependency
**Government type:** parliamentary democracy
**Capital:**
*name:* Douglas
*geographic coordinates:* 54 09 N, 4 29 W
*time difference:* UTC 0 (five hours ahead of Washington, DC during Standard Time)
*daylight saving time:* +1hr, begins last Sunday in March; ends last Sunday in October
**Administrative divisions:** none; there are no first-order administrative divisions as defined by the US Government, but there are 24 local authorities each with its own elections
**Independence:** none (British crown dependency)
**National holiday:** Tynwald Day, 5 July
**Constitution:** unwritten; note - The Isle of Man Constitution Act of 1961 does not embody the unwritten Manx Constitution
**Legal system:** the laws of the UK, where applicable, apply and Manx statutes
**Suffrage:** 16 years of age; universal
**Executive branch:**
*chief of state:* Lord of Mann Queen ELIZABETH II (since 6 February 1952); represented by Lieutenant Governor Sir Paul K. HADDACKS (since 17 October 2005)
*head of government:* Chief Minister Tony BROWN (since 14 December 2006)
*cabinet:* Council of Ministers
*elections:* the monarch is hereditary; lieutenant governor appointed by the monarch; the chief minister is elected by the Tynwald for a five-year term; election last held 14 December 2006 (next to be held in December 2011)
*election results:* House of Keys speaker Tony BROWN elected chief minister by the Tynwald
**Legislative branch:** bicameral Tynwald consists of the Legislative Council (11 seats; members composed of the President of Tynwald, the Lord Bishop of Sodor and Man, a nonvoting attorney general, and 8 others named by the House of Keys) and the House of Keys (24 seats; members are elected by popular vote to serve five-year terms)
*elections:* House of Keys - last held 23 November 2006 (next to be held in November 2011)
*election results:* House of Keys - percent of vote by party - NA; seats by party - Liberal Vannin Party 2, Man Labor Party 1, independents 21
**Judicial branch:** High Court of Justice (justices are appointed by the Lord Chancellor of England on the nomination of the lieutenant governor)
**Political parties and leaders:** Alliance for Progressive Government; Liberal Vannin Party [Peter KARRAN]; Man Labor Party; Man Nationalist Party (Mec Vannin) [Bernard MOFFATT]
*note:* most members sit as independents

# Isle of Man (continued)

**Political pressure groups and leaders:** Alliance for Progressive Government or APG (a government watchdog); Mec Vannin (political party advocating a sovereign state and environment policies); note - has only had one member elected to the Tynwald
**International organization participation:** UPU
**Diplomatic representation in the US:** none (British crown dependency)
**Diplomatic representation from the US:** none (British crown dependency)
**Flag description:** red with the Three Legs of Man emblem (Trinacria), in the center; the three legs are joined at the thigh and bent at the knee; in order to have the toes pointing clockwise on both sides of the flag, a two-sided emblem is used

## Economy

**Economy - overview:** Offshore banking, manufacturing, and tourism are key sectors of the economy. The government offers incentives to high-technology companies and financial institutions to locate on the island; this has paid off in expanding employment opportunities in high-income industries. As a result, agriculture and fishing, once the mainstays of the economy, have declined in their contributions to GDP. The Isle of Man also attracts online gambling sites and the film industry. Trade is mostly with the UK. The Isle of Man enjoys free access to EU markets.
**GDP (purchasing power parity):**
$2.719 billion (2005 est.)
**GDP (official exchange rate):** $2.719 billion (2005 est.)
**GDP - real growth rate:**
5.2% (2005)
**GDP - per capita (PPP):**
$35,000 (2005 est.)
**GDP - composition by sector:**
*agriculture:* 1%
*industry:* 13%
*services:* 86% (2000 est.)
**Labor force:** 39,690 (2001)
**Labor force - by occupation:** agriculture, forestry, and fishing 3%, manufacturing 11%, construction 10%, transport and communication 8%, wholesale and retail distribution 11%, professional and scientific services 18%, public administration 6%, banking and finance 18%, tourism 2%, entertainment and catering 3%, miscellaneous services 10% (2001)
**Unemployment rate:**
1.5% (December 2006 est.)
**Population below poverty line:** NA%
**Household income or consumption by percentage share:**
*lowest 10%:* NA%
*highest 10%:* NA%
**Budget:**
*revenues:* $965 million
*expenditures:* $943 million (FY05/06 est.)
**Inflation rate (consumer prices):**
3.1% (December 2006 est.)

**Market value of publicly traded shares:** $NA
**Agriculture - products:** cereals, vegetables; cattle, sheep, pigs, poultry
**Industries:** financial services, light manufacturing, tourism
**Exports:** $NA
**Exports - commodities:** tweeds, herring, processed shellfish, beef, lamb
**Imports:** $NA
**Imports - commodities:** timber, fertilizers, fish
**Debt - external:** $NA
**Exchange rates:** Manx pounds (IMP) per US dollar - 0.5302 (2008 est.), 0.4993 (2007), 0.5418 (2006), 0.5493 (2005), 0.5462 (2004)
*note:* the Manx pound is at par with the British pound

## Communications

**Telephones - main lines in use:** 51,000 (1999)
**Telephone system:**
*general assessment:* NA
*domestic:* landline, telefax, mobile cellular telephone system
*international:* fiber-optic cable, microwave radio relay, satellite earth station, submarine cable
**Radio broadcast stations:** AM 1, FM 1, shortwave 0 (1998)
**Television broadcast stations:** 0 (receives broadcasts from the UK and satellite) (1999)
**Internet country code:** .im
**Internet hosts:** 426 (2008)
**Internet users:** NA

## Transportation

**Airports:** 1 (2008)
**Airports - with paved runways:**
*total:* 1
*1,524 to 2,437 m:* 1 (2008)
**Railways:**
*total:* 65 km
*standard gauge:* 7 km 1.067-m gauge (7 km electrified)
*narrow gauge:* 58 km 0.914-m gauge (29 km electrified)
*note:* primarily summer tourist attractions (2006)
**Roadways:**
*total:* 500 km (2008)
**Merchant marine:**
*total:* 273
*by type:* bulk carrier 31, cargo 50, chemical tanker 48, container 12, liquefied gas 41, passenger/cargo 1, petroleum tanker 73, refrigerated cargo 4, roll on/roll off 8, vehicle carrier 5
*foreign-owned:* 181 (Chile 6, Denmark 29, France 1, Germany 56, Greece 50, Ireland 1, Japan 6, Monaco 3, Netherlands 1, Norway 20, Singapore 1, Sweden 1, Turkey 2, US 4)
*registered in other countries:* 7 (Bahamas 1, Liberia 5, Marshall Islands 1) (2008)
**Ports and terminals:** Douglas, Ramsey

## Military

**Manpower fit for military service:**
*males age 16-49:* 14,691
*females age 16-49:* 14,338 (2009 est.)
**Manpower reaching militarily significant age annually:**
*male:* 466
*female:* 446 (2009 est.)
**Military - note:** defense is the responsibility of the UK

## Transnational Issues

**Disputes - international:** none

# Israel

*(also see separate Gaza Strip and West Bank entries)*

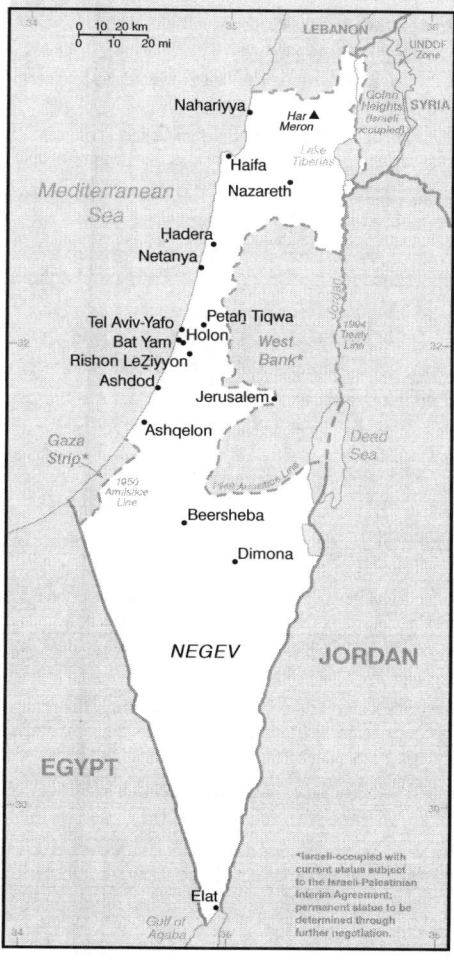

## Introduction

**Background:** Following World War II, the British withdrew from their mandate of Palestine, and the UN partitioned the area into Arab and Jewish states, an arrangement rejected by the Arabs. Subsequently, the Israelis defeated the Arabs in a series of wars without ending the deep tensions between the two sides. The territories Israel occupied since the 1967 war are not included in the Israel country profile, unless otherwise noted. On 25 April 1982, Israel withdrew from the Sinai pursuant to the 1979 Israel-Egypt Peace Treaty. In keeping with the framework established at the Madrid Conference in October 1991, bilateral negotiations were conducted between Israel and Palestinian representatives and Syria to achieve a permanent settlement. Israel and Palestinian officials signed on 13 September 1993 a Declaration of Principles (also known as the "Oslo Accords") guiding an interim period of Palestinian self-rule. Outstanding territorial and other disputes with Jordan were resolved in the 26 October 1994 Israel-Jordan Treaty of Peace. In addition, on 25 May 2000, Israel withdrew unilaterally

from southern Lebanon, which it had occupied since 1982. In April 2003, US President BUSH, working in conjunction with the EU, UN, and Russia - the "Quartet" - took the lead in laying out a roadmap to a final settlement of the conflict by 2005, based on reciprocal steps by the two parties leading to two states, Israel and a democratic Palestine. However, progress toward a permanent status agreement was undermined by Israeli-Palestinian violence between September 2003 and February 2005. An Israeli-Palestinian agreement reached at Sharm al-Sheikh in February 2005, along with an internally-brokered Palestinian cease-fire, significantly reduced the violence. In the summer of 2005, Israel unilaterally disengaged from the Gaza Strip, evacuating settlers and its military while retaining control over most points of entry into the Gaza Strip. The election of HAMAS in January 2006 to head the Palestinian Legislative Council froze relations between Israel and the Palestinian Authority (PA). Ehud OLMERT became prime minister in March 2006; he shelved plans to unilaterally evacuate from most of the West Bank following an Israeli military operation in Gaza in June-July 2006 and a 34-day conflict with Hizballah in Lebanon in June-August 2006. OLMERT in June 2007 resumed talks with the PA after HAMAS seized control of the Gaza Strip and PA President Mahmoud ABBAS formed a new government without HAMAS. OLMERT in September 2008 resigned in the wake of several corruption allegations, but remained prime minister until the new coalition government under former Prime Minister Binyamin NETANYAHU was completed in late March 2009, following the February general election.

## Geography

**Location:** Middle East, bordering the Mediterranean Sea, between Egypt and Lebanon
**Geographic coordinates:** 31 30 N, 34 45 E
**Map references:** Middle East
**Area:**
*total:* 20,770 sq km
*land:* 20,330 sq km
*water:* 440 sq km
**Area - comparative:** slightly smaller than New Jersey
**Land boundaries:**
*total:* 1,017 km
*border countries:* Egypt 266 km, Gaza Strip 51 km, Jordan 238 km, Lebanon 79 km, Syria 76 km, West Bank 307 km
**Coastline:** 273 km
**Maritime claims:**
*territorial sea:* 12 nm
*continental shelf:* to depth of exploitation
**Climate:** temperate; hot and dry in southern and eastern desert areas
**Terrain:** Negev desert in the south; low coastal plain; central mountains; Jordan Rift Valley

**Elevation extremes:**
*lowest point:* Dead Sea -408 m
*highest point:* Har Meron 1,208 m
**Natural resources:** timber, potash, copper ore, natural gas, phosphate rock, magnesium bromide, clays, sand
**Land use:**
*arable land:* 15.45%
*permanent crops:* 3.88%
*other:* 80.67% (2005)
**Irrigated land:** 1,940 sq km (2003)
**Total renewable water resources:** 1.7 cu km (2001)
**Freshwater withdrawal (domestic/industrial/agricultural):**
*total:* 2.05 cu km/yr (31%/7%/62%)
*per capita:* 305 cu m/yr (2000)
**Natural hazards:** sandstorms may occur during spring and summer; droughts; periodic earthquakes
**Environment - current issues:** limited arable land and natural fresh water resources pose serious constraints; desertification; air pollution from industrial and vehicle emissions; groundwater pollution from industrial and domestic waste, chemical fertilizers, and pesticides
**Environment - international agreements:**
*party to:* Biodiversity, Climate Change, Climate Change-Kyoto Protocol, Desertification, Endangered Species, Hazardous Wastes, Ozone Layer Protection, Ship Pollution, Wetlands, Whaling
*signed, but not ratified:* Marine Life Conservation
**Geography - note:** there are about 340 Israeli civilian sites - including 100 small outpost communities in the West Bank - as well as 42 sites in the Golan Heights, 0 in the Gaza Strip, and 29 in East Jerusalem (July 2008 est.); Lake Tiberias (Sea of Galilee) is an important freshwater source

## People

**Population:** 7,233,701
*note:* includes about 187,000 Israeli settlers in the West Bank, about 20,000 in the Israeli-occupied Golan Heights, and fewer than 177,000 in East Jerusalem (July 2009 est.)
**Age structure:**
*0-14 years:* 27.9% (male 1,031,629/female 984,230)
*15-64 years:* 62.3% (male 2,283,034/female 2,221,301)
*65 years and over:* 9.9% (male 311,218/female 402,289) (2009 est.)
**Median age:**
*total:* 29.1 years
*male:* 28.4 years
*female:* 29.8 years (2009 est.)
**Population growth rate:** 1.671% (2009 est.)
**Birth rate:** 19.77 births/1,000 population (2009 est.)
**Death rate:** 5.41 deaths/1,000 population (2008 est.)
**Net migration rate:** 2.37 migrant(s)/1,000 population (2009 est.)

## Israel (continued)

**Urbanization:**
*urban population:* 92% of total population (2008)
*rate of urbanization:* 1.7% annual rate of change
(2005-10 est.)
**Sex ratio:**
*at birth:* 1.05 male(s)/female
*under 15 years:* 1.05 male(s)/female
*15-64 years:* 1.03 male(s)/female
*65 years and over:* 0.77 male(s)/female
*total population:* 1 male(s)/female (2009 est.)
**Infant mortality rate:**
*total:* 4.22 deaths/1,000 live births
*male:* 4.39 deaths/1,000 live births
*female:* 4.05 deaths/1,000 live births (2009 est.)
**Life expectancy at birth:**
*total population:* 80.73 years
*male:* 78.62 years
*female:* 82.95 years (2009 est.)
**Total fertility rate:** 2.75 children born/woman
(2009 est.)
**HIV/AIDS - adult prevalence rate:** 0.1% (2007 est.)
**HIV/AIDS - people living with HIV/AIDS:** 5,100
(2007 est.)
**HIV/AIDS - deaths:** fewer than 200 (2007 est.)
**Nationality:**
*noun:* Israeli(s)
*adjective:* Israeli
**Ethnic groups:** Jewish 76.4% (of which Israel-born
67.1%, Europe/America-born 22.6%, Africa-born
5.9%, Asia-born 4.2%), non-Jewish 23.6% (mostly
Arab) (2004)
**Religions:** Jewish 76.4%, Muslim 16%, Arab
Christians 1.7%, other Christian 0.4%, Druze 1.6%,
unspecified 3.9% (2004)
**Languages:** Hebrew (official), Arabic used officially
for Arab minority, English most commonly used
foreign language
**Literacy:**
*definition:* age 15 and over can read and write
*total population:* 97.1%
*male:* 98.5%
*female:* 95.9% (2004 est.)
**School life expectancy (primary to tertiary
education):**
*total:* 15 years
*male:* 15 years
*female:* 16 years (2006)
**Education expenditures:** 6.9% of GDP (2004)

### Government

**Country name:**
*conventional long form:* State of Israel
*conventional short form:* Israel
*local long form:* Medinat Yisra'el
*local short form:* Yisra'el
**Government type:** parliamentary democracy
**Capital:**
*name:* Jerusalem
*geographic coordinates:* 31 46 N, 35 14 E
*time difference:* UTC+2 (7 hours ahead of
Washington, DC during Standard Time)

*daylight saving time:* +1hr, begins last Friday
in March; ends the Sunday between the holidays of
Rosh Hashana and Yom Kippur
*note:* Israel proclaimed Jerusalem as its capital in
1950, but the US, like nearly all other countries,
maintains its Embassy in Tel Aviv
**Administrative divisions:** 6 districts (mehozot,
singular - mehoz); Central, Haifa, Jerusalem,
Northern, Southern, Tel Aviv
**Independence:** 14 May 1948 (from League of
Nations mandate under British administration)
**National holiday:** Independence Day, 14 May
(1948); note - Israel declared independence on
14 May 1948, but the Jewish calendar is lunar and the
holiday may occur in April or May
**Constitution:** no formal constitution; some of the
functions of a constitution are filled by the Declaration
of Establishment (1948), the Basic Laws of the
parliament (Knesset), and the Israeli citizenship law;
note - since May 2003 the Constitution, Law, and
Justice Committee of the Knesset has been working
on a draft constitution
**Legal system:** mixture of English common law,
British Mandate regulations, and, in personal matters,
Jewish, Christian, and Muslim legal systems; has not
accepted compulsory ICJ jurisdiction
**Suffrage:** 18 years of age; universal
**Executive branch:**
*chief of state:* President Shimon PERES (since
15July 2007)
*head of government:* Prime Minister Binjamin
NETANYAHU (since 31 March 2009); Vice Prime
Minister Silvan SHALOM (since 31 March 2009); Vice
Prime Minister Moshe YAALON (since 31 March 2009)
*cabinet:* Cabinet selected by prime minister and
approved by the Knesset
*elections:* president is largely a ceremonial role and is
elected by the Knesset for a seven-year term
(one-term limit); election last held 13 June 2007 (next
to be held in 2014 but can be called earlier); following
legislative elections, the president assigns a Knesset
member - traditionally the leader of the largest party -
the task of forming a governing coalition
*election results:* Shimon PERES elected president;
number of votes in first round - Shimon PERES 58,
Reuven RIVLIN 37, Colette AVITAL 21; PERES elected
president in second round with 86 votes (unopposed)
**Legislative branch:** unicameral Knesset (120 seats;
members elected by popular vote to serve four-year
terms)
*elections:* last held 10 February 2009 (next scheduled
election to be held in 2013)
*election results:* percent of vote by party - Kadima
23.2%, Likud-Ahi 22.3%, Yisrael Beiteinu 12.1%,
Labor 10.2%, SHAS 8.8%, United Torah Judaism
4.5%, United Arab List 3.5%, NU 3.4%, Hadash 3.4%,
The Jewish Home 3%, The New Movement-Meretz
3%, Balad 2.6%; seats by party - Kadima 28,
Likud-Ahi 27, Yisrael Beiteinu 15, Labor 13, SHAS 11,
United Torah Judaism 5, United Arab List 4, NU 4,
HADASH 4, The Jewish Home 3, The New
Movement-Meretz 3, Balad 3

**Judicial branch:** Supreme Court (justices appointed
by Judicial Selection Committee - made up of all three
branches of the government; mandatory retirement
age is 70)
**Political parties and leaders:** Balad [Azmi
BISHARA]; Democratic Front for Peace and Equality
(HADASH) [Muhammad BARAKEH]; Kadima [Tzipora
"Tzipi" LIVNI]; Labor Party [Ehud BARAK]; Likud
[Binyamin NETANYAHU]; National Union [Yaakov
KATZ]; The Jewish Home (HaBayit HaYehudi) [Daniel
HERSCHKOWITZ]; SHAS [Eliyahu YISHAI]; The New
Movement-Meretz [Haim ORON]; United Arab
List-Ta'al [Ibrahim SARSUR]; United Torah Judaism
or UTJ [Yaakov LITZMAN]; Yisrael Beiteinu [Avigdor
LIEBERMAN]
**Political pressure groups and leaders:** B'Tselem
[Jessica MONTELL, Executive Director] monitors
human rights abuses; Peace Now [Yariv
OPPENHEIMER, Secretary General] supports
territorial concessions in the West Bank and Gaza
Strip; YESHA Council of Settlements [Danny DAYAN,
Chairman] promotes settler interests and opposes
territorial compromise
**International organization participation:** BIS,
BSEC (observer), CERN (observer), EBRD, FAO,
IADB, IAEA, IBRD, ICAO, ICC, ICCt (signatory),
ICRM, IDA, IFAD, IFC, IFRCS, ILO, IMF, IMO, IMSO,
Interpol, IOC, IOM, IPU, ISO, ITSO, ITU, ITUC, MIGA,
OAS (observer), OECD (accession state), OPCW
(signatory), OSCE (partner), PCA, SECI (observer),
UN, UNCTAD, UNESCO, UNHCR, UNIDO, UNWTO,
UPU, WCO, WFTU, WHO, WIPO, WMO, WTO
**Diplomatic representation in the US:**
*chief of mission:* Ambassador Salai MERIDOR
*chancery:* 3514 International Drive NW,
Washington, DC 20008
*telephone:* [1] (202) 364-5500
*FAX:* [1] (202) 364-5607
*consulate(s) general:* Atlanta, Boston, Chicago,
Houston, Los Angeles, Miami, New York,
Philadelphia, San Francisco
**Diplomatic representation from the US:**
*chief of mission:* Ambassador James B.
CUNNINGHAM
*embassy:* 71 Hayarkon Street, Tel Aviv 63903
*mailing address:* PSC 98, Box 29, APO AE 09830
*telephone:* [972] (3) 519-7575
*FAX:* [972] (3) 516-4390
*consulate(s) general:* Jerusalem; note - an
independent US mission, established in 1928, whose
members are not accredited to a foreign government
**Flag description:** white with a blue hexagram
(six-pointed linear star) known as the Magen David
(Shield of David) centered between two equal
horizontal blue bands near the top and bottom edges
of the flag

# Israel (continued)

## Economy

**Economy - overview:** Israel has a technologically advanced market economy with substantial, though diminishing, government participation. It depends on imports of crude oil, grains, raw materials, and military equipment. Despite limited natural resources, Israel has intensively developed its agricultural and industrial sectors over the past 20 years. Israel imports substantial quantities of grain but is largely self-sufficient in other agricultural products. Cut diamonds, high-technology equipment, and agricultural products (fruits and vegetables) are the leading exports. Israel usually posts sizable trade deficits, which are covered by large transfer payments from abroad and by foreign loans. Roughly half of the government's external debt is owed to the US, its major source of economic and military aid. Israel's GDP, after contracting slightly in 2001 and 2002 due to the Palestinian conflict and troubles in the high-technology sector, has grown by about 5% per year since 2003. The economy grew an estimated 3.9% in 2008, slowed by the global financial crisis. The government's prudent fiscal policy and structural reforms over the past few years have helped to induce strong foreign investment, tax revenues, and private consumption, setting the economy on a solid growth path.

**GDP (purchasing power parity):**
$200.7 billion (2008 est.)
$193.2 billion (2007)
$183.3 billion (2006)
*note:* data are in 2008 US dollars
**GDP (official exchange rate):** $188.7 billion (2008 est.)
**GDP - real growth rate:**
3.9% (2008 est.)
5.4% (2007 est.)
5.1% (2006 est.)
**GDP - per capita (PPP):**
$28,200 (2008 est.)
$27,600 (2007 est.)
$26,700 (2006 est.)
*note:* data are in 2008 US dollars
**GDP - composition by sector:**
*agriculture:* 2.7%
*industry:* 31.7%
*services:* 65.6% (2008 est.)
**Labor force:** 2.95 million (2008 est.)
**Labor force - by occupation:**
*agriculture:* 2%
*industry:* 16%
*services:* 82% (30 September 2008)
**Unemployment rate:**
6.1% (2008 est.)
7.3% (2007 est.)
**Population below poverty line:** 21.6%
*note:* Israel's poverty line is $7.30 per person per day (2005)
**Household income or consumption by percentage share:**
*lowest 10%:* 2.6%
*highest 10%:* 24.2% (2007)

**Distribution of family income - Gini index:** 38.6 (2005)
**Investment (gross fixed):** 18% of GDP (2008 est.)
**Budget:**
*revenues:* $68.44 billion
*expenditures:* $70.06 billion (2008 est.)
**Public debt:** 75.7% of GDP (2008 est.)
**Inflation rate (consumer prices):**
4.7% (2008 est.)
0.5% (2007 est.)
**Central bank discount rate:** 4% (31 December 2007)
**Commercial bank prime lending rate:** 6.27% (31 December 2007)
**Stock of money:** $15.36 billion (31 December 2006)
**Stock of quasi money:** $154.3 billion (31 December 2007)
**Stock of domestic credit:** $113.4 billion (31 December 2006)
**Market value of publicly traded shares:** $236.4 billion (31 December 2007)
**Agriculture - products:** citrus, vegetables, cotton; beef, poultry, dairy products
**Industries:** high-technology projects (including aviation, communications, computer-aided design and manufactures, medical electronics, fiber optics), wood and paper products, potash and phosphates, food, beverages, and tobacco, caustic soda, cement, construction, metals products, chemical products, plastics, diamond cutting, textiles, footwear
**Industrial production growth rate:** 4.1% (2008 est.)
**Electricity - production:** 48.7 billion kWh (2006 est.)
**Electricity - consumption:** 44.74 billion kWh (2006 est.)
**Electricity - exports:** 1.844 billion kWh (2006 est.)
**Electricity - imports:** 0 kWh (2007 est.)
**Oil - production:** 5,966 bbl/day (2007 est.)
**Oil - consumption:** 232,300 bbl/day (2006 est.)
**Oil - exports:** 82,910 bbl/day (2005)
**Oil - imports:** 334,300 bbl/day (2005)
**Oil - proved reserves:** 1.94 million bbl (1 January 2008 est.)
**Natural gas - production:** 2.35 billion cu m (2006 est.)
**Natural gas - consumption:** 2.27 billion cu m (2006 est.)
**Natural gas - exports:** 0 cu m (2007 est.)
**Natural gas - imports:** 0 cu m (2007 est.)
**Natural gas - proved reserves:** 30.44 billion cu m (1 January 2008 est.)
**Current account balance:** $1.893 billion (2008 est.)
**Exports:** $54.16 billion f.o.b. (2008 est.)
**Exports - commodities:** machinery and equipment, software, cut diamonds, agricultural products, chemicals, textiles and apparel
**Exports - partners:** US 35%, Belgium 7.5%, Hong Kong 5.8% (2007)
**Imports:** $62.52 billion f.o.b. (2008 est.)

**Imports - commodities:** raw materials, military equipment, investment goods, rough diamonds, fuels, grain, consumer goods
**Imports - partners:** US 13.9%, Belgium 7.9%, Germany 6.2%, China 6.1%, Switzerland 5.1%, UK 4.7%, Italy 4.1% (2007)
**Reserves of foreign exchange and gold:** $38.66 billion (31 December 2008 est.)
**Debt - external:** $91.25 billion (31 December 2008 est.)
**Stock of direct foreign investment - at home:** $68.06 billion (2008 est.)
**Stock of direct foreign investment - abroad:** $51.94 billion (2008 est.)
**Exchange rates:** new Israeli shekels (ILS) per US dollar - 3.56 (2008 est.), 4.14 (2007), 4.4565 (2006), 4.4877 (2005), 4.482 (2004)

## Communications

**Telephones - main lines in use:** 3.005 million (2006)
**Telephones - mobile cellular:** 8.902 million (2007)
**Telephone system:**
*general assessment:* most highly developed system in the Middle East although not the largest
*domestic:* good system of coaxial cable and microwave radio relay; all systems are digital; four privately-owned mobile-cellular service providers with countrywide coverage; mobile-cellular teledensity is 140 per 100 persons
*international:* country code - 972; submarine cables provide links to Europe, Cyprus, and parts of the Middle East; satellite earth stations - 3 Intelsat (2 Atlantic Ocean and 1 Indian Ocean) (2007)
**Radio broadcast stations:** AM 23, FM 15, shortwave 2 (1998)
**Television broadcast stations:** 17 (plus 36 repeaters) (1995)
**Internet country code:** .il
**Internet hosts:** 1.415 million (2008)
**Internet users:** 2 million (2007)

## Transportation

**Airports:** 47 (2008)
**Airports - with paved runways:**
*total:* 30
*over 3,047 m:* 2
*2,438 to 3,047 m:* 5
*1,524 to 2,437 m:* 7
*914 to 1,523 m:* 10
*under 914 m:* 6 (2008)
**Airports - with unpaved runways:**
*total:* 17
*1,524 to 2,437 m:* 1
*914 to 1,523 m:* 2
*under 914 m:* 14 (2008)
**Heliports:** 3 (2007)
**Pipelines:** gas 176 km; oil 442 km; refined products 261 km (2008)
**Railways:**
*total:* 853 km
*standard gauge:* 853 km 1.435-m gauge (2006)

# Israel (continued)

**Roadways:**
*total:* 17,870 km
*paved:* 17,870 km (includes 146 km of expressways) (2007)

**Merchant marine:**
*total:* 11
*by type:* cargo 2, container 9
*registered in other countries:* 60 (Bermuda 3, Cyprus 4, Georgia 2, Honduras 1, Liberia 23, Malta 18, Panama 3, Saint Vincent and the Grenadines 2, Slovakia 4) (2008)

**Ports and terminals:** Ashdod, Elat (Eilat), Hadera, Haifa

## Military

**Military branches:** Israel Defense Forces (IDF), Israel Naval Forces (INF), Israel Air Force (IAF) (2007)

**Military service age and obligation:** 18 years of age for compulsory (Jews, Druzes) and voluntary (Christians, Muslims, Circassians) military service; both sexes are obligated to military service; conscript service obligation - 36 months for enlisted men, 21 months for enlisted women, 48 months for officers; reserve obligation to age 41-51 (men), 24 (women) (2008)

**Manpower available for military service:**
*males age 16-49:* 1,717,362
*females age 16-49:* 1,636,574 (2008 est.)

**Manpower fit for military service:**
*males age 16-49:* 1,474,966
*females age 16-49:* 1,404,712 (2009 est.)

**Manpower reaching militarily significant age annually:**
*male:* 61,223
*female:* 58,219 (2009 est.)

**Military expenditures:** 7.3% of GDP (2006)

## Transnational Issues

**Disputes - international:** West Bank and Gaza Strip are Israeli-occupied with current status subject to the Israeli-Palestinian Interim Agreement - permanent status to be determined through further negotiation; Israel continues construction of a "seam line" separation barrier along parts of the Green Line and within the West Bank; Israel withdrew its settlers and military from the Gaza Strip and from four settlements in the West Bank in August 2005; Golan Heights is Israeli-occupied (Lebanon claims the Shab'a Farms area of Golan Heights); since 1948, about 350 peacekeepers from the UN Truce Supervision Organization (UNTSO) headquartered in Jerusalem monitor ceasefires, supervise armistice agreements, prevent isolated incidents from escalating, and assist other UN personnel in the region

**Refugees and internally displaced persons:**
*IDPs:* 150,000-420,000 (Arab villagers displaced from homes in northern Israel) (2007)

**Illicit drugs:** increasingly concerned about ecstasy, cocaine, and heroin abuse; drugs arrive in country from Lebanon and, increasingly, from Jordan; money-laundering center

# Italy

## Introduction

**Background:** Italy became a nation-state in 1861 when the regional states of the peninsula, along with Sardinia and Sicily, were united under King Victor EMMANUEL II. An era of parliamentary government came to a close in the early 1920s when Benito MUSSOLINI established a Fascist dictatorship. His alliance with Nazi Germany led to Italy's defeat in World War II. A democratic republic replaced the monarchy in 1946 and economic revival followed. Italy was a charter member of NATO and the European Economic Community (EEC). It has been at the forefront of European economic and political unification, joining the Economic and Monetary Union in 1999. Persistent problems include illegal immigration, organized crime, corruption, high unemployment, sluggish economic growth, and the low incomes and technical standards of southern Italy compared with the prosperous north.

## Geography

**Location:** Southern Europe, a peninsula extending into the central Mediterranean Sea, northeast of Tunisia
**Geographic coordinates:** 42 50 N, 12 50 E
**Map references:** Europe
**Area:**
*total:* 301,230 sq km
*land:* 294,020 sq km
*water:* 7,210 sq km
*note:* includes Sardinia and Sicily
**Area - comparative:** slightly larger than Arizona
**Land boundaries:**
*total:* 1,899.2 km
*border countries:* Austria 430 km, France 488 km, Holy See (Vatican City) 3.2 km, San Marino 39 km, Slovenia 199 km, Switzerland 740 km
**Coastline:** 7,600 km
**Maritime claims:**
*territorial sea:* 12 nm
*continental shelf:* 200-m depth or to the depth of exploitation

**Climate:** predominantly Mediterranean; Alpine in far north; hot, dry in south
**Terrain:** mostly rugged and mountainous; some plains, coastal lowlands
**Elevation extremes:**
*lowest point:* Mediterranean Sea 0 m
*highest point:* Mont Blanc (Monte Bianco) de Courmayeur 4,748 m (a secondary peak of Mont Blanc)
**Natural resources:** coal, mercury, zinc, potash, marble, barite, asbestos, pumice, fluorspar, feldspar, pyrite (sulfur), natural gas and crude oil reserves, fish, arable land
**Land use:**
*arable land:* 26.41%
*permanent crops:* 9.09%
*other:* 64.5% (2005)
**Irrigated land:** 27,500 sq km (2003)
**Total renewable water resources:** 175 cu km (2005)
**Freshwater withdrawal (domestic/industrial/agricultural):**
*total:* 41.98 cu km/yr (18%/37%/45%)
*per capita:* 723 cu m/yr (1998)
**Natural hazards:** regional risks include landslides, mudflows, avalanches, earthquakes, volcanic eruptions, flooding; land subsidence in Venice
**Environment - current issues:** air pollution from industrial emissions such as sulfur dioxide; coastal and inland rivers polluted from industrial and agricultural effluents; acid rain damaging lakes; inadequate industrial waste treatment and disposal facilities
**Environment - international agreements:**
*party to:* Air Pollution, Air Pollution-Nitrogen Oxides, Air Pollution-Persistent Organic Pollutants, Air Pollution-Sulfur 85, Air Pollution-Sulfur 94, Air Pollution-Volatile Organic Compounds, Antarctic-Environmental Protocol, Antarctic-Marine Living Resources, Antarctic Seals, Antarctic Treaty, Biodiversity, Climate Change, Climate Change-Kyoto Protocol, Desertification, Endangered Species, Environmental Modification, Hazardous Wastes, Law of the Sea, Marine Dumping, Ozone Layer Protection, Ship Pollution, Tropical Timber 83, Tropical Timber 94, Wetlands, Whaling
*signed, but not ratified:* none of the selected agreements
**Geography - note:** strategic location dominating central Mediterranean as well as southern sea and air approaches to Western Europe

## People

**Population:** 58,126,212 (July 2009 est.)
**Age structure:**
*0-14 years:* 13.5% (male 4,056,156/female 3,814,070)
*15-64 years:* 66.3% (male 19,530,696/female 18,981,084)
*65 years and over:* 20.2% (male 4,903,762/female 6,840,444) (2009 est.)

# Italy (continued)

**Median age:**

*total:* 43.3 years

*male:* 41.8 years

*female:* 44.8 years (2009 est.)

**Population growth rate:** -0.047% (2009 est.)

**Birth rate:** 8.18 births/1,000 population (2009 est.)

**Death rate:** 10.61 deaths/1,000 population (2008 est.)

**Net migration rate:** 2.06 migrant(s)/1,000 population (2009 est.)

**Urbanization:**

*urban population:* 68% of total population (2008)

*rate of urbanization:* 0.4% annual rate of change (2005-10 est.)

**Sex ratio:**

*at birth:* 1.07 male(s)/female

*under 15 years:* 1.06 male(s)/female

*15-64 years:* 1.03 male(s)/female

*65 years and over:* 0.72 male(s)/female

*total population:* 0.96 male(s)/female (2009 est.)

**Infant mortality rate:**

*total:* 5.51 deaths/1,000 live births

*male:* 6.07 deaths/1,000 live births

*female:* 4.91 deaths/1,000 live births (2009 est.)

**Life expectancy at birth:**

*total population:* 80.2 years

*male:* 77.26 years

*female:* 83.33 years (2009 est.)

**Total fertility rate:** 1.31 children born/woman (2009 est.)

**HIV/AIDS - adult prevalence rate:** 0.4% (2007 est.)

**HIV/AIDS - people living with HIV/AIDS:** 150,000 (2007 est.)

**HIV/AIDS - deaths:** 1,900 (2007 est.)

**Nationality:**

*noun:* Italian(s)

*adjective:* Italian

**Ethnic groups:** Italian (includes small clusters of German-, French-, and Slovene-Italians in the north and Albanian-Italians and Greek-Italians in the south)

**Religions:** Roman Catholic 90% (approximately; about one-third practicing), other 10% (includes mature Protestant and Jewish communities and a growing Muslim immigrant community)

**Languages:** Italian (official), German (parts of Trentino-Alto Adige region are predominantly German speaking), French (small French-speaking minority in Valle d'Aosta region), Slovene (Slovene-speaking minority in the Trieste-Gorizia area)

**Literacy:**

*definition:* age 15 and over can read and write

*total population:* 98.4%

*male:* 98.8%

*female:* 98% (2001 census)

**School life expectancy (primary to tertiary education):**

*total:* 16 years

*male:* 16 years

*female:* 17 years (2006)

**Education expenditures:** 4.5% of GDP (2005)

## Government

**Country name:**

*conventional long form:* Italian Republic

*conventional short form:* Italy

*local long form:* Repubblica Italiana

*local short form:* Italia

*former:* Kingdom of Italy

**Government type:** republic

**Capital:**

*name:* Rome

*geographic coordinates:* 41 54 N, 12 29 E

*time difference:* UTC+1 (6 hours ahead of Washington, DC during Standard Time)

*daylight saving time:* +1hr, begins last Sunday in March; ends last Sunday in October

**Administrative divisions:** 15 regions (regioni, singular - regione) and 5 autonomous regions* (regioni autonome, singular - regione autonoma); Abruzzo, Basilicata, Calabria, Campania, Emilia-Romagna, Friuli-Venezia Giulia*, Lazio (Latium), Liguria, Lombardia, Marche, Molise, Piemonte (Piedmont), Puglia (Apulia), Sardegna* (Sardinia), Sicilia*, Toscana (Tuscany), Trentino-Alto Adige* (Trentino-South Tyrol), Umbria, Valle d'Aosta* (Aosta Valley), Veneto (Venetia)

**Independence:** 17 March 1861 (Kingdom of Italy proclaimed; Italy was not finally unified until 1870)

**National holiday:** Republic Day, 2 June (1946)

**Constitution:** passed 11 December 1947, effective 1 January 1948; amended many times

**Legal system:** based on civil law system; appeals treated as new trials; judicial review under certain conditions in Constitutional Court; has not accepted compulsory ICJ jurisdiction

**Suffrage:** 18 years of age; universal (except in senatorial elections, where minimum age is 25)

**Executive branch:**

*chief of state:* President Giorgio NAPOLITANO (since 15 May 2006)

*head of government:* Prime Minister Silvio BERLUSCONI (since 8 May 2008) note - in Italy the prime minister is referred to as the president of the Council of Ministers

*cabinet:* Council of Ministers nominated by the prime minister and approved by the president

*elections:* president elected by an electoral college consisting of both houses of parliament and 58 regional representatives for a seven-year term (no term limits); election last held 10 May 2006 (next to be held in May 2013); prime minister appointed by the president and confirmed by parliament

*election results:* Giorgio NAPOLITANO elected president on the fourth round of voting; electoral college vote - 543

**Legislative branch:** bicameral Parliament or Parlamento consists of the Senate or Senato della Repubblica (315 seats; members elected by proportional vote with the winning coalition in each region receiving 55% of seats from that region; to serve five-year terms) and the Chamber of Deputies or Camera dei Deputati (630 seats; members elected by popular vote with the winning national coalition receiving 54% of chamber seats; to serve five-year terms)

*elections:* Senate - last held 13-14 April 2008 (next to be held April 2013); Chamber of Deputies - last held 13-14 April 2008 (next to be held April 2013)

*election results:* Senate - percent of vote by party - NA; seats by party - S. BERLUSCONI coalition 174 (PdL 147, LN 25, MpA 2), W. VELTRONI coalition 132 (PD 118, IdV 3), UdC 3, other 6; Chamber of Deputies -percent of vote by party - NA; seats by party -S. BERLUSCONI coalition 344 (PdL 276, LN 60, MpA 8), W. VELTRONI coalition 246 (PD 217, IdV 29), UdC 36, other 4

**Judicial branch:** Constitutional Court or Corte Costituzionale (composed of 15 judges: one-third appointed by the president, one-third elected by parliament, one-third elected by the ordinary and administrative Supreme Courts)

**Political parties and leaders:**

*Silvio BERLUSCONI coalition:* People of Freedom or PdL [Silvio BERLUSCONI]; Lega Nord or LN [Umberto BOSSI]; Movement for Autonomy or MpA [Raffaele LOMBARDO]

*Walter VELTRONI coalition:* Democratic Party or PD [Walter VELTRONI]; Italy of Values or IdV [Antonio DI PIETRO]

*other non-allied parties:* Union of the Center or UdC [Savino PEZZOTTA]

**Political pressure groups and leaders:** manufacturers and merchants associations - Confcommercio; Confindustria; organized farm groups - Confcoltivatori; Confagricoltura; Roman Catholic Church; three major trade union confederations - Confederazione Generale Italiana del Lavoro or CGIL [Guglielmo EPIFANI] which is left wing; Confederazione Italiana dei Sindacati Lavoratori or CISL [Raffaele BONANNO], which is Roman Catholic centrist; Unione Italiana del Lavoro or UIL [Luigi ANGELETTI] which is lay centrist)

**International organization participation:** ADB (nonregional member), AfDB (nonregional member), Arctic Council (observer), Australia Group, BIS, BSEC (observer), CBSS (observer), CDB, CE, CEI, CERN, EAPC, EBRD, EIB, EMU, ESA, EU, FAO, G-20, G-7, G-8, G-10, IADB, IAEA, IBRD, ICAO, ICC, ICCt, ICRM, IDA, IEA, IFAD, IFC, IFRCS, IHO, ILO, IMF, IMO, IMSO, Interpol, IOC, IOM, IPU, ISO, ITSO, ITU, ITUC, LAIA (observer), MIGA, MINURSO, NAM (guest), NATO, NEA, NSG, OAS (observer), OECD, OPCW, OSCE, Paris Club, PCA, Schengen Convention, SECI (observer), SICA (observer), UN, UNCTAD, UNESCO, UNHCR, UNIDO, UNIFIL, Union Latina, UNMOGIP, UNRWA, UNTSO, UNWTO, UPU, WCL, WCO, WEU, WFTU, WHO, WIPO, WMO, WTO, ZC

# Italy (continued)

**Diplomatic representation in the US:**
*chief of mission:* Ambassador Giovanni CASTELLANETA
*chancery:* 3000 Whitehaven Street NW, Washington, DC 20008
*telephone:* [1] (202) 612-4400
*FAX:* [1] (202) 518-2151
*consulate(s) general:* Boston, Chicago, Houston, Miami, New York, Los Angeles, Philadelphia, San Francisco
*consulate(s):* Detroit

**Diplomatic representation from the US:**
*chief of mission:* Ambassador (vacant); Charge d'Affaires Elizabeth DIBBLE
*embassy:* Via Vittorio Veneto 121, 00187-Rome
*mailing address:* PSC 59, Box 100, APO AE 09624
*telephone:* [39] (06) 46741
*FAX:* [39] (06) 488-2672, 4674-2356
*consulate(s) general:* Florence, Milan, Naples

**Flag description:** three equal vertical bands of green (hoist side), white, and red; similar to the flag of Ireland, which is longer and is green (hoist side), white, and orange; also similar to the flag of the Cote d'Ivoire, which has the colors reversed - orange (hoist side), white, and green; inspired by the French flag brought to Italy by Napoleon in 1797

## Economy

**Economy - overview:** Italy has a diversified industrial economy, which is divided into a developed industrial north, dominated by private companies, and a less-developed, welfare-dependent, agricultural south, with high unemployment. The Italian economy is driven in large part by the manufacture of high-quality consumer goods produced by small and medium-sized enterprises. Italy also has a sizable underground economy, which by some estimates accounts for as much as 15% of GDP. These activities are most common within the agriculture, construction, and service sectors. Italy has moved slowly on implementing needed structural reforms, such as lightening the high tax burden and overhauling Italy's rigid labor market and over-generous pension system and these conditions will be exacerbated by the recent global financial crisis. The Italian government is seeking to rein in government spending, but the leadership faces a severe economic constraint: Italy's official debt remains above 100% of GDP, and the fiscal deficit - 1.5% of GDP in 2007 - could approach 3% in 2009 as political pressure to stimulate the economy and the costs of servicing Italy's debt rise. The economy will continue to contract through 2009 as the global demand for exports drop.

**GDP (purchasing power parity):**
$1.821 trillion (2008 est.)
$1.834 trillion (2007)
$1.809 trillion (2006)
*note:* data are in 2008 US dollars
**GDP (official exchange rate):** $2.399 trillion (2008 est.)

**GDP - real growth rate:**
-0.7% (2008 est.)
1.4% (2007 est.)
1.9% (2006 est.)
**GDP - per capita (PPP):**
$31,000 (2008 est.)
$31,500 (2007 est.)
$31,100 (2006 est.)
*note:* data are in 2008 US dollars
**GDP - composition by sector:**
*agriculture:* 2%
*industry:* 26.7%
*services:* 71.3% (2008 est.)
**Labor force:** 25.09 million (2008 est.)
**Labor force - by occupation:**
*agriculture:* 4.2%
*industry:* 30.7%
*services:* 65.1% (2005)
**Unemployment rate:**
6.8% (2008 est.)
6.2% (2007 est.)
**Population below poverty line:** NA%
**Household income or consumption by percentage share:**
*lowest 10%:* 2.3%
*highest 10%:* 26.8% (2000)
**Distribution of family income - Gini index:** 32 (2006)
**Investment (gross fixed):** 20.5% of GDP (2008 est.)
**Budget:**
*revenues:* $1.139 trillion
*expenditures:* $1.203 trillion (2008 est.)
**Public debt:** 103.7% of GDP (2008 est.)
**Inflation rate (consumer prices):**
3.6% (2008 est.)
1.8% (2007 est.)
**Central bank discount rate:** 4%
*note:* this is the European Central Bank's rate on the marginal lending facility, which offers overnight credit to banks in the euro area
**Commercial bank prime lending rate:** 10.93% (31 December 2007)
**Stock of money:** NA
*note:* see entry for the European Union for money supply in the euro area; the European Central Bank (ECB) controls monetary policy for the 16 members of the Economic and Monetary Union (EMU); individual members of the EMU do not control the quantity of money and quasi money circulating within their own borders
**Stock of quasi money:** NA
**Stock of domestic credit:** $3.084 trillion (31 December 2007)
**Market value of publicly traded shares:** $1.073 trillion (31 December 2007)
**Agriculture - products:** fruits, vegetables, grapes, potatoes, sugar beets, soybeans, grain, olives; beef, dairy products; fish
**Industries:** tourism, machinery, iron and steel, chemicals, food processing, textiles, motor vehicles, clothing, footwear, ceramics

**Industrial production growth rate:** -0.2% (2008 est.)
**Electricity - production:** 292.1 billion kWh (2007 est.)
**Electricity - consumption:** 316.3 billion kWh (2006 est.)
**Electricity - exports:** 1.916 billion kWh (2007 est.)
**Electricity - imports:** 34.56 billion kWh (2007 est.)
**Oil - production:** 166,600 bbl/day (2007 est.)
**Oil - consumption:** 1.702 million bbl/day (2007 est.)
**Oil - exports:** 616,700 bbl/day (2005)
**Oil - imports:** 2.223 million bbl/day (2005)
**Oil - proved reserves:** 406.5 million bbl (1 January 2008 est.)
**Natural gas - production:** 9.706 billion cu m (2007 est.)
**Natural gas - consumption:** 84.89 billion cu m (2007 est.)
**Natural gas - exports:** 68 million cu m (2007 est.)
**Natural gas - imports:** 73.95 billion cu m (2007 est.)
**Natural gas - proved reserves:** 94.15 billion cu m (1 January 2008 est.)
**Current account balance:** -$68.82 billion (2008 est.)
**Exports:** $566.1 billion f.o.b. (2008 est.)
**Exports - commodities:** engineering products, textiles and clothing, production machinery, motor vehicles, transport equipment, chemicals; food, beverages and tobacco; minerals, and nonferrous metals
**Exports - partners:** Germany 12.9%, France 11.4%, Spain 7.4%, US 6.8%, UK 5.8% (2007)
**Imports:** $566.8 billion f.o.b. (2008 est.)
**Imports - commodities:** engineering products, chemicals, transport equipment, energy products, minerals and nonferrous metals, textiles and clothing; food, beverages, and tobacco
**Imports - partners:** Germany 16.9%, France 9%, China 5.9%, Netherlands 5.5%, Belgium 4.3%, Spain 4.2% (2007)
**Reserves of foreign exchange and gold:** $104 billion (31 December 2008 est.)
**Debt - external:** $1.06 trillion (31 December 2008 est.)
**Stock of direct foreign investment - at home:** $374.8 billion (2008 est.)
**Stock of direct foreign investment - abroad:** $547.7 billion (2008 est.)
**Exchange rates:** euros (EUR) per US dollar - 0.6827 (2008 est.), 0.7345 (2007), 0.7964 (2006), 0.8041 (2005), 0.8054 (2004)

## Communications

**Telephones - main lines in use:** 26.89 million (2006)
**Telephones - mobile cellular:** 78.571 million (2006)
**Telephone system:**
*general assessment:* modern, well developed, fast; fully automated telephone, telex, and data services
*domestic:* high-capacity cable and microwave radio relay trunks

# Italy (continued)

*international:* country code - 39; a series of submarine cables provide links to Asia, Middle East, Europe, North Africa, and US; satellite earth stations - 3 Intelsat (with a total of 5 antennas - 3 for Atlantic Ocean and 2 for Indian Ocean), 1 Inmarsat (Atlantic Ocean region), and NA Eutelsat

**Radio broadcast stations:** AM about 100, FM about 4,600, shortwave 9 (1998)

**Television broadcast stations:** 358 (plus 4,728 repeaters) (1995)

**Internet country code:** .it

**Internet hosts:** 17.702 million (2008)

**Internet users:** 32 million (2007)

## Transportation

**Airports:** 132 (2008)

**Airports - with paved runways:**

*total:* 101

*over 3,047 m:* 8

*2,438 to 3,047 m:* 30

*1,524 to 2,437 m:* 16

*914 to 1,523 m:* 34

*under 914 m:* 13 (2008)

**Airports - with unpaved runways:**

*total:* 31

*1,524 to 2,437 m:* 1

*914 to 1,523 m:* 11

*under 914 m:* 19 (2008)

**Heliports:** 5 (2007)

**Pipelines:** gas 17,544 km; oil 1,241 km (2008)

**Railways:**

*total:* 19,460 km

*standard gauge:* 18,038 km 1.435-m gauge (11,354 kmelectrified)

*narrow gauge:* 123 km 1.000-m gauge (123 km electrified); 1,299 km 0.950-m gauge (161 km electrified) (2006)

**Roadways:**

*total:* 487,700 km

*paved:* 487,700 km (includes 6,700 km of expressways) (2005)

**Waterways:** 2,400 km

*note:* used for commercial traffic; of limited overall value compared to road and rail (2008)

**Merchant marine:**

*total:* 609

*by type:* bulk carrier 60, cargo 47, carrier 2, chemical tanker 159, combination ore/oil 1, container 25, liquefied gas 27, passenger 22, passenger/cargo 154, petroleum tanker 35, refrigerated cargo 4, roll on/roll off 33, specialized tanker 13, vehicle carrier 27

*foreign-owned:* 64 (Denmark 3, France 2, Greece 6, Japan 1, Lebanon 1, Nigeria 1, Norway 2, Portugal 1, Sweden 1, Switzerland 8, Taiwan 13, Turkey 1, UK 7, US 17)

*registered in other countries:* 208 (Antigua and Barbuda 1, Bahamas 4, Belize 3, Cayman Islands 4, Cyprus 7, France 2, Liberia 41, Malta 50, Marshall Islands 3, Netherlands 1, Norway 4, Panama 28, Portugal 12, Russia 4, Saint Kitts and Nevis 1, Saint Vincent and the Grenadines 17, Singapore 5, Slovakia 2, Spain 2, Sweden 9, Turkey 3, UK 5) (2008)

**Ports and terminals:** Augusta, Genoa, Livorno, Ravenna, Sarroch, Taranto, Trieste, Venice

## Military

**Military branches:** Italian Army (Esercito Italiano, EI), Italian Navy (Marina Militare Italiana, MMI), Italian Air Force (Aeronautica Militare Italiana, AMI), Carabinieri Corps (Arma dei Carabinieri, CC) (2009)

**Military service age and obligation:** 18-27 year of age for voluntary military service; conscription abolished January 2005; women may serve in any military branch; 10-month service obligation, with a reserve obligation to age 45 (Army and Air Force) or 39 (Navy) (2006)

**Manpower available for military service:**

*males age 16-49:* 13,884,079

*females age 16-49:* 13,158,378 (2008 est.)

**Manpower fit for military service:**

*males age 16-49:* 11,197,487

*females age 16-49:* 10,574,250 (2009 est.)

**Manpower reaching militarily significant age annually:**

*male:* 287,845

*female:* 270,384 (2009 est.)

**Military expenditures:** 1.8% of GDP (2005 est.)

## Transnational Issues

**Disputes - international:** Italy's long coastline and developed economy entices tens of thousands of illegal immigrants from southeastern Europe and northern Africa

**Illicit drugs:** important gateway for and consumer of Latin American cocaine and Southwest Asian heroin entering the European market; money laundering by organized crime and from smuggling

# Jamaica

## Introduction

**Background:** The island - discovered by Christopher COLUMBUS in 1494 - was settled by the Spanish early in the 16th century. The native Taino Indians, who had inhabited Jamaica for centuries, were gradually exterminated and replaced by African slaves. England seized the island in 1655 and established a plantation economy based on sugar, cocoa, and coffee. The abolition of slavery in 1834 freed a quarter million slaves, many of whom became small farmers. Jamaica gradually obtained increasing independence from Britain. In 1958 it joined other British Caribbean colonies in forming the Federation of the West Indies. Jamaica gained full independence when it withdrew from the Federation in 1962. Deteriorating economic conditions during the 1970s led to recurrent violence as rival gangs affiliated with the major political parties evolved into powerful organized crime networks involved in international drug smuggling and money laundering. Violent crime, drug trafficking, and poverty pose significant challenges to the government today. Nonetheless, many rural and resort areas remain relatively safe and contribute substantially to the economy.

## Geography

**Location:** Caribbean, island in the Caribbean Sea, south of Cuba
**Geographic coordinates:** 18 15 N, 77 30 W
**Map references:** Central America and the Caribbean
**Area:**
*total:* 10,991 sq km
*land:* 10,831 sq km
*water:* 160 sq km
**Area - comparative:** slightly smaller than Connecticut
**Land boundaries:** 0 km
**Coastline:** 1,022 km

**Maritime claims:** measured from claimed archipelagic straight baselines
*territorial sea:* 12 nm
*contiguous zone:* 24 nm
*exclusive economic zone:* 200 nm
*continental shelf:* 200 nm or to edge of the continental margin
**Climate:** tropical; hot, humid; temperate interior
**Terrain:** mostly mountains, with narrow, discontinuous coastal plain
**Elevation extremes:**
*lowest point:* Caribbean Sea 0 m
*highest point:* Blue Mountain Peak 2,256 m
**Natural resources:** bauxite, gypsum, limestone
**Land use:**
*arable land:* 15.83%
*permanent crops:* 10.01%
*other:* 74.16% (2005)
**Irrigated land:** 250 sq km (2002)
**Total renewable water resources:** 9.4 cu km (2000)
**Freshwater withdrawal (domestic/industrial/ agricultural):**
*total:* 0.41 cu km/yr (34%/17%/49%)
*per capita:* 155 cu m/yr (2000)
**Natural hazards:** hurricanes (especially July to November)
**Environment - current issues:** heavy rates of deforestation; coastal waters polluted by industrial waste, sewage, and oil spills; damage to coral reefs; air pollution in Kingston results from vehicle emissions
**Environment - international agreements:**
*party to:* Biodiversity, Climate Change, Climate Change-Kyoto Protocol, Desertification, Endangered Species, Hazardous Wastes, Law of the Sea, Marine Dumping, Marine Life Conservation, Ozone Layer Protection, Ship Pollution, Wetlands
*signed, but not ratified:* none of the selected agreements

## People

**Population:** 2,825,928 (July 2009 est.)
**Age structure:**
*0-14 years:* 31.4% (male 451,310/female 436,466)
*15-64 years:* 61.1% (male 851,372/female 875,132)
*65 years and over:* 7.5% (male 94,833/female 116,815) (2009 est.)
**Median age:**
*total:* 23.7 years
*male:* 23.1 years
*female:* 24.2 years (2009 est.)
**Population growth rate:** 0.755% (2009 est.)
**Birth rate:** 19.68 births/1,000 population (2009 est.)
**Death rate:** 6.37 deaths/1,000 population (2008 est.)
**Net migration rate:** -5.7 migrant(s)/1,000 population (2009 est.)
**Urbanization:**
*urban population:* 53% of total population (2008)
*rate of urbanization:* 0.9% annual rate of change (2005-10 est.)
**Sex ratio:**
*at birth:* 1.05 male(s)/female
*under 15 years:* 1.03 male(s)/female
*15-64 years:* 0.97 male(s)/female
*65 years and over:* 0.81 male(s)/female
*total population:* 0.98 male(s)/female (2009 est.)
**Infant mortality rate:**
*total:* 15.22 deaths/1,000 live births
*male:* 15.81 deaths/1,000 live births
*female:* 14.61 deaths/1,000 live births (2009 est.)
**Life expectancy at birth:**
*total population:* 73.53 years
*male:* 71.83 years
*female:* 75.3 years (2009 est.)
**Total fertility rate:** 2.25 children born/woman (2009 est.)
**HIV/AIDS - adult prevalence rate:** 1.6% (2007 est.)
**HIV/AIDS - people living with HIV/AIDS:** 27,000 (2007 est.)
**HIV/AIDS - deaths:** 1,500 (2007 est.)
**Nationality:**
*noun:* Jamaican(s)
*adjective:* Jamaican
**Ethnic groups:** black 91.2%, mixed 6.2%, other or unknown 2.6% (2001 census)
**Religions:** Protestant 62.5% (Seventh-Day Adventist 10.8%, Pentecostal 9.5%, Other Church of God 8.3%, Baptist 7.2%, New Testament Church of God 6.3%, Church of God in Jamaica 4.8%, Church of God of Prophecy 4.3%, Anglican 3.6%, other Christian 7.7%), Roman Catholic 2.6%, other or unspecified 14.2%, none 20.9%, (2001 census)
**Languages:** English, English patois
**Literacy:**
*definition:* age 15 and over has ever attended school
*total population:* 87.9%
*male:* 84.1%
*female:* 91.6% (2003 est.)

# Jamaica (continued)

**School life expectancy (primary to tertiary education):**
*total:* 12 years
*male:* 11 years
*female:* 12 years (2003)
**Education expenditures:** 5.3% of GDP (2005)

## Government

**Country name:**
*conventional long form:* none
*conventional short form:* Jamaica
**Government type:** constitutional parliamentary democracy and a Commonwealth realm
**Capital:**
*name:* Kingston
*geographic coordinates:* 18 00 N, 76 48 W
*time difference:* UTC-5 (same time as Washington, DC during Standard Time)
**Administrative divisions:** 14 parishes; Clarendon, Hanover, Kingston, Manchester, Portland, Saint Andrew, Saint Ann, Saint Catherine, Saint Elizabeth, Saint James, Saint Mary, Saint Thomas, Trelawny, Westmoreland
*note:* for local government purposes, Kingston and Saint Andrew were amalgamated in 1923 into the present single corporate body known as the Kingston and Saint Andrew Corporation
**Independence:** 6 August 1962 (from the UK)
**National holiday:** Independence Day, 6 August (1962)
**Constitution:** 6 August 1962
**Legal system:** based on English common law; has not accepted compulsory ICJ jurisdiction
**Suffrage:** 18 years of age; universal
**Executive branch:**
*chief of state:* Queen ELIZABETH II (since 6 February 1952); represented by Governor General Dr. Patrick L. ALLEN (since 26 February 2009)
*head of government:* Prime Minister Bruce GOLDING (since 11 September 2007)
*cabinet:* Cabinet appointed by the governor general on the advice of the prime minister
*elections:* the monarch is hereditary; governor general appointed by the monarch on the recommendation of the prime minister; following legislative elections, the leader of the majority party or the leader of the majority coalition in the House of Representatives is appointed prime minister by the governor general; the deputy prime minister is recommended by the prime minister
**Legislative branch:** bicameral Parliament consists of the Senate (a 21-member body appointed by the governor general on the recommendations of the prime minister and the leader of the opposition; ruling party is allocated 13 seats, and the opposition is allocated 8 seats) and the House of Representatives (60 seats; members are elected by popular vote to serve five-year terms)
*elections:* last held 3 September 2007 (next to be held no later than October 2012)
*election results:* percent of vote by party - JLP 50.1%, PNP 49.8%; seats by party - JLP 33, PNP 27

**Judicial branch:** Supreme Court (judges appointed by the governor general on the advice of the prime minister); Court of Appeal; Privy Council in UK; member of the Caribbean Court of Justice (CCJ)
**Political parties and leaders:** Jamaica Labor Party or JLP [Bruce GOLDING]; People's National Party or PNP [Portia SIMPSON-MILLER]; National Democratic Movement or NDM [Michael WILLIAMS]
**Political pressure groups and leaders:** New Beginnings Movement or NBM; Rastafarians (black religious/racial cultists, pan-Africanists)
**International organization participation:** ACP, C, Caricom, CDB, FAO, G-15, G-77, IADB, IAEA, IBRD, ICAO, ICCt (signatory), ICRM, IFAD, IFC, IFRCS, IHO, ILO, IMF, IMO, Interpol, IOC, IOM, ISO, ITSO, ITU, LAES, MIGA, NAM, OAS, OPANAL, OPCW, UN, UNCTAD, UNESCO, UNIDO, UNWTO, UPU, WCO, WFTU, WHO, WIPO, WMO, WTO
**Diplomatic representation in the US:**
*chief of mission:* Ambassador Anthony JOHNSON
*chancery:* 1520 New Hampshire Avenue NW, Washington, DC 20036
*telephone:* [1] (202) 452-0660
*FAX:* [1] (202) 452-0081
*consulate(s) general:* Miami, New York
**Diplomatic representation from the US:**
*chief of mission:* Ambassador Brenda LaGrange JOHNSON
*embassy:* 142 Old Hope Road, Kingston 6
*mailing address:* P.O. Box 541, Kingston 5
*telephone:* [1] (876) 702-6000
*FAX:* [1] (876) 702-6001
**Flag description:** diagonal yellow cross divides the flag into four triangles - green (top and bottom) and black (hoist side and outer side)

## Economy

**Economy - overview:** The Jamaican economy is heavily dependent on services, which now account for more than 60% of GDP. The country continues to derive most of its foreign exchange from tourism, remittances, and bauxite/alumina. Remittances account for nearly 20% of GDP and are equivalent to tourism revenues. Jamaica's economy, already saddled with the lowest economic growth in Latin America, will face increasing difficulties as the global economy slows. The economy faces serious long-term problems: a sizable merchandise trade deficit, large-scale unemployment and underemployment, and a debt-to-GDP ratio of almost 130%. Jamaica's onerous debt burden - the fourth highest per capita - is the result of government bailouts to ailing sectors of the economy, most notably the financial sector in the mid-to-late 1990s. It hinders government spending on infrastructure and social programs as debt servicing accounts for nearly half of government expenditures. Inflation rose sharply in 2008 as a result of high prices for imported food and oil and should fall in 2009 with the decline in international oil prices. High unemployment exacerbates the serious crime problem, including

gang violence that is fueled by the drug trade. The GOLDING administration faces the difficult prospect of having to achieve fiscal discipline in order to maintain debt payments while simultaneously attacking a serious and growing crime problem that is hampering economic growth.
**GDP (purchasing power parity):**
$20.88 billion (2008 est.)
$21 billion (2007)
$20.69 billion (2006)
*note:* data are in 2008 US dollars
**GDP (official exchange rate):** $13.47 billion (2008 est.)
**GDP - real growth rate:**
-0.6% (2008 est.)
1.5% (2007 est.)
2.4% (2006 est.)
**GDP - per capita (PPP):**
$7,400 (2008 est.)
$7,500 (2007 est.)
$7,500 (2006 est.)
*note:* data are in 2008 US dollars
**GDP - composition by sector:**
*agriculture:* 5.2%
*industry:* 32.9%
*services:* 61.8% (2008 est.)
**Labor force:** 1.261 million (2008 est.)
**Labor force - by occupation:**
*agriculture:* 17%
*industry:* 19%
*services:* 64% (2006)
**Unemployment rate:**
10.1% (2008 est.)
9.9% (2007 est.)
**Population below poverty line:** 14.8% (2003 est.)
**Household income or consumption by percentage share:**
*lowest 10%:* 2.1%
*highest 10%:* 35.8% (2004)
**Distribution of family income - Gini index:** 45.5 (2004)
**Investment (gross fixed):** 34.9% of GDP (2008 est.)
**Budget:**
*revenues:* $4.166 billion
*expenditures:* $4.838 billion (2008 est.)
**Public debt:** 124.1% of GDP (2008 est.)
**Inflation rate (consumer prices):**
22.5% (2008 est.)
9.5% (2007 est.)
**Central bank discount rate:** %NA
**Commercial bank prime lending rate:** 17.2% (31 December 2007)
**Stock of money:** $1.369 billion (31 December 2007)
**Stock of quasi money:** $4.54 billion (31 December 2007)
**Stock of domestic credit:** $6.609 billion (31 December 2007)
**Market value of publicly traded shares:** $12.33 billion (31 December 2007)

## Jamaica (continued)

**Agriculture - products:** sugarcane, bananas, coffee, citrus, yams, ackees, vegetables; poultry, goats, milk; crustaceans, mollusks
**Industries:** tourism, bauxite/alumina, agro processing, light manufactures, rum, cement, metal, paper, chemical products, telecommunications
**Industrial production growth rate:** 1.5% (2008 est.)
**Electricity - production:** 7.04 billion kWh (2006 est.)
**Electricity - consumption:** 6.1 billion kWh (2006 est.)
**Electricity - exports:** 0 kWh (2007 est.)
**Electricity - imports:** 0 kWh (2007 est.)
**Oil - production:** 0 bbl/day (2005 est.)
**Oil - consumption:** 73,370 bbl/day (2006 est.)
**Oil - exports:** 1,535 bbl/day (2005)
**Oil - imports:** 71,280 bbl/day (2005)
**Oil - proved reserves:** 0 bbl (1 January 2006 est.)
**Natural gas - production:** 0 cu m (2007 est.)
**Natural gas - consumption:** 0 cu m (2007 est.)
**Natural gas - exports:** 0 cu m (2007 est.)
**Natural gas - imports:** 0 cu m (2007 est.)
**Natural gas - proved reserves:** 0 cu m (1 January 2006 est.)
**Current account balance:** -$2.448 billion (2008 est.)
**Exports:** $2.569 billion f.o.b. (2008 est.)
**Exports - commodities:** alumina, bauxite, sugar, rum, coffee, yams, beverages, chemicals, wearing apparel, mineral fuels
**Exports - partners:** US 37.2%, Canada 15%, UK 9.7%, Netherlands 9.1% (2007)
**Imports:** $7.191 billion f.o.b. (2008 est.)
**Imports - commodities:** food and other consumer goods, industrial supplies, fuel, parts and accessories of capital goods, machinery and transport equipment, construction materials
**Imports - partners:** US 37.2%, Trinidad and Tobago 14.5%, Grenada 9.7%, Venezuela 8.3%, Brazil 4.2% (2007)
**Reserves of foreign exchange and gold:** $2.05 billion (31 December 2008 est.)
**Debt - external:** $10.38 billion (31 December 2008 est.)
**Exchange rates:** Jamaican dollars (JMD) per US dollar - 72.236 (2008 est.), 69.034 (2007), 65.768 (2006), 62.51 (2005), 61.197 (2004)

### Communications

**Telephones - main lines in use:** 342,000 (2006)
**Telephones - mobile cellular:** 2.495 million (2006)
**Telephone system:**
*general assessment:* fully automatic domestic telephone network
*domestic:* the 1999 agreement to open the market for telecommunications services resulted in rapid growth in mobile-cellular telephone usage while the number of fixed-lines in use has declined; combined mobile-cellular teledensity now exceeds 100 per 100 persons
*international:* country code - 1-876; the Fibralink

submarine cable network provides enhanced delivery of business and broadband traffic and is linked to the Americas Region Caribbean Ring System (ARCOS-1) submarine cable in the Dominican Republic; the link to ARCOS-1 provides seamless connectivity to US, parts of the Caribbean, Central America, and South America; satellite earth stations - 2 Intelsat (Atlantic Ocean) (2006)
**Radio broadcast stations:** AM 10, FM 13, shortwave 0 (1998)
**Television broadcast stations:** 7 (1997)
**Internet country code:** .jm
**Internet hosts:** 1,292 (2008)
**Internet users:** 1.5 million (2007)

### Transportation

**Airports:** 27 (2008)
**Airports - with paved runways:**
*total:* 12
*2,438 to 3,047 m:* 2
*914 to 1,523 m:* 3
*under 914 m:* 7 (2008)
**Airports - with unpaved runways:**
*total:* 15
*under 914 m:* 15 (2008)
**Roadways:**
*total:* 21,552 km
*paved:* 15,937 km (includes 33 km of expressways)
*unpaved:* 5,615 km (2005)
**Merchant marine:**
*total:* 20
*by type:* bulk carrier 6, cargo 6, carrier 1, container 4, roll on/roll off 3
*foreign-owned:* 17 (Denmark 2, Germany 4, Greece 6, Hong Kong 1, Latvia 1, Russia 3) (2008)
**Ports and terminals:** Kingston, Port Esquivel, Port Kaiser, Port Rhoades, Rocky Point

### Military

**Military branches:** Jamaica Defense Force: Ground Forces, Coast Guard, Air Wing (2007)
**Military service age and obligation:** 18 years of age for voluntary military service; younger recruits may be conscripted with parental consent (2001)
**Manpower available for military service:**
*males age 16-49:* 688,480
*females age 16-49:* 709,548 (2008 est.)
**Manpower fit for military service:**
*males age 16-49:* 573,520
*females age 16-49:* 586,426 (2009 est.)
**Manpower reaching militarily significant age annually:**
*male:* 31,833
*female:* 31,257 (2009 est.)
**Military expenditures:** 0.6% of GDP (2006 est.)

### Transnational Issues

**Disputes - international:** none
**Illicit drugs:** transshipment point for cocaine from South America to North America and Europe; illicit cultivation and consumption of cannabis; government has an active manual cannabis eradication program; corruption is a major concern; substantial money-laundering activity; Colombian narcotics traffickers favor Jamaica for illicit financial transactions

# Jan Mayen
*(territory of Norway)*

## Introduction

**Background:** This desolate, arctic, mountainous island was named after a Dutch whaling captain who indisputably discovered it in 1614 (earlier claims are inconclusive). Visited only occasionally by seal hunters and trappers over the following centuries, the island came under Norwegian sovereignty in 1929. The long dormant Haakon VII Toppen/Beerenberg volcano resumed activity in 1970; the most recent eruption occurred in 1985. It is the northernmost active volcano on earth.

## Geography

**Location:** Northern Europe, island between the Greenland Sea and the Norwegian Sea, northeast of Iceland
**Geographic coordinates:** 71 00 N, 8 00 W
**Map references:** Arctic Region
**Area:**
*total:* 377 sq km
*land:* 377 sq km
*water:* 0 sq km
**Area - comparative:** slightly more than twice the size of Washington, DC
**Land boundaries:** 0 km
**Coastline:** 124.1 km
**Maritime claims:**
*territorial sea:* 4 nm
*contiguous zone:* 10 nm
*exclusive economic zone:* 200 nm
*continental shelf:* 200 m depth or to the depth of exploitation
**Climate:** arctic maritime with frequent storms and persistent fog
**Terrain:** volcanic island, partly covered by glaciers
**Elevation extremes:**
*lowest point:* Norwegian Sea 0 m
*highest point:* Haakon VII Toppen/Beerenberg 2,277 m
**Natural resources:** none

**Land use:**
*arable land:* 0%
*permanent crops:* 0%
*other:* 100% (2005)
**Irrigated land:** 0 sq km
**Natural hazards:** dominated by the volcano Haakon VII Toppen/Beerenberg; volcanic activity resumed in 1970; the most recent eruption occurred in 1985
**Environment - current issues:** NA
**Geography - note:** barren volcanic island with some moss and grass

### People

**Population:** no indigenous inhabitants
*note:* personnel operate the Long Range Navigation (Loran-C) base and the weather and coastal services radio station

### Government

**Country name:**
*conventional long form:* none
*conventional short form:* Jan Mayen
**Dependency status:** territory of Norway; since August 1994, administered from Oslo through the county governor (fylkesmann) of Nordland; however, authority has been delegated to a station commander of the Norwegian Defense Communication Service
**Legal system:** the laws of Norway, where applicable, apply
**Flag description:** the flag of Norway is used

### Economy

**Economy - overview:** Jan Mayen is a volcanic island with no exploitable natural resources. Economic activity is limited to providing services for employees of Norway's radio and meteorological stations on the island.

### Communications

**Radio broadcast stations:** NA; note - there is one radio and meteorological station (1998)

### Transportation

**Airports:** 1 (2008)
**Airports - with unpaved runways:**
*total:* 1
*1,524 to 2,437 m:* 1 (2008)
**Ports and terminals:** none; offshore anchorage only

### Military

**Military - note:** defense is the responsibility of Norway

### Transnational Issues

**Disputes - international:** none

# Japan

## Introduction

**Background:** In 1603, a Tokugawa shogunate (military dictatorship) ushered in a long period of isolation from foreign influence in order to secure its power. For more than two centuries this policy enabled Japan to enjoy stability and a flowering of its indigenous culture. Following the Treaty of Kanagawa with the US in 1854, Japan opened its ports and began to intensively modernize and industrialize. During the late 19th and early 20th centuries, Japan became a regional power that was able to defeat the forces of both China and Russia. It occupied Korea, Formosa (Taiwan), and southern Sakhalin Island. In 1931-32 Japan occupied Manchuria, and in 1937 it launched a full-scale invasion of China. Japan attacked US forces in 1941 - triggering America's entry into World War II - and soon occupied much of East and Southeast Asia. After its defeat in World War II, Japan recovered to become an economic power and a staunch ally of the US. While the emperor retains his throne as a symbol of national unity, elected politicians - with heavy input from bureaucrats and business executives - wield actual decisionmaking power. The economy experienced a major slowdown starting in the 1990s following three decades of unprecedented growth, but Japan still remains a major economic power, both in Asia and globally. In January 2009, Japan assumed a nonpermanent seat on the UN Security Council for the 2009-10 term.

## Geography

**Location:** Eastern Asia, island chain between the North Pacific Ocean and the Sea of Japan, east of the Korean Peninsula
**Geographic coordinates:** 36 00 N, 138 00 E
**Map references:** Asia
**Area:**
*total:* 377,835 sq km
*land:* 374,744 sq km
*water:* 3,091 sq km

# Japan (continued)

*note:* includes Bonin Islands (Ogasawara-gunto), Daito-shoto, Minami-jima, Okino-tori-shima, Ryukyu Islands (Nansei-shoto), and Volcano Islands (Kazan-retto)

**Area - comparative:** slightly smaller than California

**Land boundaries:** 0 km

**Coastline:** 29,751 km

**Maritime claims:**

*territorial sea:* 12 nm; between 3 nm and 12 nm in the international straits - La Perouse or Soya, Tsugaru, Osumi, and Eastern and Western Channels of the Korea or Tsushima Strait

*contiguous zone:* 24 nm

*exclusive economic zone:* 200 nm

**Climate:** varies from tropical in south to cool temperate in north

**Terrain:** mostly rugged and mountainous

**Elevation extremes:**

*lowest point:* Hachiro-gata -4 m

*highest point:* Mount Fuji 3,776 m

**Natural resources:** negligible mineral resources, fish

*note:* with virtually no energy natural resources, Japan is the world's largest importer of coal and liquefied natural gas as well as the second largest importer of oil

**Land use:**

*arable land:* 11.64%

*permanent crops:* 0.9%

*other:* 87.46% (2005)

**Irrigated land:** 25,920 sq km (2003)

**Total renewable water resources:** 430 cu km (1999)

**Freshwater withdrawal (domestic/industrial/ agricultural):**

*total:* 88.43 cu km/yr (20%/18%/62%)

*per capita:* 690 cu m/yr (2000)

**Natural hazards:** many dormant and some active volcanoes; about 1,500 seismic occurrences (mostly tremors) every year; tsunamis; typhoons

**Environment - current issues:** air pollution from power plant emissions results in acid rain; acidification of lakes and reservoirs degrading water quality and threatening aquatic life; Japan is one of the largest consumers of fish and tropical timber, contributing to the depletion of these resources in Asia and elsewhere

**Environment - international agreements:**

*party to:* Antarctic-Environmental Protocol, Antarctic-Marine Living Resources, Antarctic Seals, Antarctic Treaty, Biodiversity, Climate Change, Climate Change-Kyoto Protocol, Desertification, Endangered Species, Environmental Modification, Hazardous Wastes, Law of the Sea, Marine Dumping, Ozone Layer Protection, Ship Pollution, Tropical Timber 83, Tropical Timber 94, Wetlands, Whaling

*signed, but not ratified:* none of the selected agreements

**Geography - note:** strategic location in northeast Asia

## People

**Population:** 127,078,679 (July 2009 est.)

**Age structure:**

*0-14 years:* 13.5% (male 8,804,465/female 8,344,800)

*15-64 years:* 64.3% (male 41,187,425/female 40,533,876)

*65 years and over:* 22.2% (male 11,964,694/female 16,243,419) (2009 est.)

**Median age:**

*total:* 44.2 years

*male:* 42.4 years

*female:* 46.1 years (2009 est.)

**Population growth rate:** -0.191% (2009 est.)

**Birth rate:** 7.64 births/1,000 population (2009 est.)

**Death rate:** 9.26 deaths/1,000 population (2008 est.)

**Net migration rate:** NA

**Urbanization:**

*urban population:* 66% of total population (2008)

*rate of urbanization:* 0.2% annual rate of change (2005-10 est.)

**Sex ratio:**

*at birth:* 1.06 male(s)/female

*under 15 years:* 1.06 male(s)/female

*15-64 years:* 1.02 male(s)/female

*65 years and over:* 0.74 male(s)/female

*total population:* 0.95 male(s)/female (2009 est.)

**Infant mortality rate:**

*total:* 2.79 deaths/1,000 live births

*male:* 2.99 deaths/1,000 live births

*female:* 2.58 deaths/1,000 live births (2009 est.)

**Life expectancy at birth:**

*total population:* 82.12 years

*male:* 78.8 years

*female:* 85.62 years (2009 est.)

**Total fertility rate:** 1.21 children born/woman (2009 est.)

**HIV/AIDS - adult prevalence rate:** less than 0.1% (2003 est.)

**HIV/AIDS - people living with HIV/AIDS:** 9,600 (2007 est.)

**HIV/AIDS - deaths:** fewer than 100 (2007 est.)

**Nationality:**

*noun:* Japanese (singular and plural)

*adjective:* Japanese

**Ethnic groups:** Japanese 98.5%, Koreans 0.5%, Chinese 0.4%, other 0.6%

*note:* up to 230,000 Brazilians of Japanese origin migrated to Japan in the 1990s to work in industries; some have returned to Brazil (2004)

**Religions:** Shintoism 83.9%, Buddhism 71.4%, Christianity 2%, other 7.8%

*note:* total adherents exceeds 100% because many people belong to both Shintoism and Buddhism (2005)

**Languages:** Japanese

**Literacy:**

*definition:* age 15 and over can read and write

*total population:* 99%

*male:* 99%

*female:* 99% (2002)

**School life expectancy (primary to tertiary education):**

*total:* 15 years

*male:* 15 years

*female:* 15 years (2006)

**Education expenditures:** 3.5% of GDP (2005)

## Government

**Country name:**

*conventional long form:* none

*conventional short form:* Japan

*local long form:* Nihon-koku/Nippon-koku

*local short form:* Nihon/Nippon

**Government type:** a parliamentary government with a constitutional monarchy

**Capital:**

*name:* Tokyo

*geographic coordinates:* 35 41 N, 139 45 E

*time difference:* UTC+9 (14 hours ahead of Washington, DC during Standard Time)

**Administrative divisions:** 47 prefectures; Aichi, Akita, Aomori, Chiba, Ehime, Fukui, Fukuoka, Fukushima, Gifu, Gunma, Hiroshima, Hokkaido, Hyogo, Ibaraki, Ishikawa, Iwate, Kagawa, Kagoshima, Kanagawa, Kochi, Kumamoto, Kyoto, Mie, Miyagi, Miyazaki, Nagano, Nagasaki, Nara, Niigata, Oita, Okayama, Okinawa, Osaka, Saga, Saitama, Shiga, Shimane, Shizuoka, Tochigi, Tokushima, Tokyo, Tottori, Toyama, Wakayama, Yamagata, Yamaguchi, Yamanashi

**Independence:** 660 B.C. (traditional date of the founding of the nation by Emperor JIMMU; first recognized by Emperor Meiji in 1873)

**National holiday:** Birthday of Emperor AKIHITO, 23 December (1933)

**Constitution:** 3 May 1947

**Legal system:** modeled after German civil law system with English-American influence; judicial review of legislative acts in the Supreme Court; accepts compulsory ICJ jurisdiction with reservations

**Suffrage:** 20 years of age; universal

**Executive branch:**

*chief of state:* Emperor AKIHITO (since 7 January 1989)

*head of government:* Prime Minister Taro ASO (since 24 September 2008)

*cabinet:* Cabinet appointed by the prime minister

*elections:* Diet designates prime minister; constitution requires that prime minister commands parliamentary majority; following legislative elections, leader of majority party or leader of majority coalition in House of Representatives usually becomes prime minister; monarch is hereditary

**Legislative branch:** bicameral Diet or Kokkai consists of the House of Councillors or Sangi-in (242 seats - members elected for fixed six-year terms; half reelected every three years; 146 members in multi-seat constituencies and 96 by proportional representation) and the House of Representatives or Shugi-in (480 seats - members elected for maximum four-year terms; 300 in single-seat constituencies; 180

# Japan (continued)

members by proportional representation in 11 regional blocs); the prime minister has the right to dissolve the House of Representatives at any time with the concurrence of the cabinet.

*elections:* House of Councillors - last held 29 July 2007 (next to be held in July 2010); House of Representatives - last held 11 September 2005 (next election by October 2009)

*election results:* House of Councillors - percent of vote by party - NA; seats by party - DPJ 109, LDP 83, Komeito 20, JCP 7, SDP 5, others 18
House of Representatives - percent of vote by party (in single-seat constituencies) - LDP 47.8%, DPJ 36.4%, others 15.8%; seats by party - LDP 296, DPJ 113, Komeito 31, JCP 9, SDP 7, others 24 (2007)

**Judicial branch:** Supreme Court (chief justice is appointed by the monarch after designation by the cabinet; all other justices are appointed by the cabinet)

**Political parties and leaders:** Democratic Party of Japan or DPJ [Yukio HATOYAMA]; Japan Communist Party or JCP [Kazuo SHII]; Komeito [Akihiro OTA]; Liberal Democratic Party or LDP [Taro ASO]; Social Democratic Party or SDP [Mizuho FUKUSHIMA]

**Political pressure groups and leaders:**
*other:* business groups; trade unions

**International organization participation:** ADB, AfDB (nonregional member), APEC, APT, ARF, ASEAN (dialogue partner), Australia Group, BIS, CE (observer), CERN (observer), CP, EAS, EBRD, FAO, G-20, G-5, G-7, G-8, G-10, IADB, IAEA, IBRD, ICAO, ICC, ICCt, ICRM, IDA, IEA, IFAD, IFC, IFRCS, IHO, ILO, IMF, IMO, IMSO, Interpol, IOC, IOM, IPU, ISO, ITSO, ITU, ITUC, LAIA, MIGA, NEA, NSG, OAS (observer), OECD, OPCW, OSCE (partner), Paris Club, PCA, PIF (partner), SAARC (observer), SECI (observer), UN, UNCTAD, UNDOF, UNESCO, UNHCR, UNIDO, UNITAR, UNRWA, UNWTO, UPU, WCL, WCO, WFTU, WHO, WIPO, WMO, WTO, ZC

**Diplomatic representation in the US:**
*chief of mission:* Ambassador Ichiro FUJISAKI
*chancery:* 2520 Massachusetts Avenue NW, Washington, DC 20008
*telephone:* [1] (202) 238-6700
*FAX:* [1] (202) 328-2187
*consulate(s) general:* Atlanta, Boston, Chicago, Denver, Detroit, Agana (Guam), Honolulu, Houston, Los Angeles, Miami, New York, Portland (Oregon), San Francisco, Seattle
*consulate(s):* Anchorage, Nashville

**Diplomatic representation from the US:**
*chief of mission:* Ambassador (vacant); Charge d'Affaires James P. ZUMWALT
*embassy:* 1-10-5 Akasaka, Minato-ku, Tokyo 107-8420
*mailing address:* Unit 9800, Box 300, APO AP 96303-0300
*telephone:* [81] (03) 3224-5000
*FAX:* [81] (03) 3505-1862
*consulate(s) general:* Naha (Okinawa), Osaka-Kobe, Sapporo
*consulate(s):* Fukuoka, Nagoya

**Flag description:** white with a large red disk (representing the sun without rays) in the center

## Economy

**Economy - overview:** In the years following World War II, government-industry cooperation, a strong work ethic, mastery of high technology, and a comparatively small defense allocation (1% of GDP) helped Japan advance with extraordinary speed to the rank of second most technologically powerful economy in the world after the US. Today, measured on a purchasing power parity (PPP) basis, Japan is the third-largest economy in the world after the US and China. Two notable characteristic of the post-war economy were the close interlocking structures of manufacturers, suppliers, and distributors, known as keiretsu, and the guarantee of lifetime employment for a substantial portion of the urban labor force. Both features are now eroding under the dual pressures of global competition and domestic demographic change. Japan's industrial sector is heavily dependent on imported raw materials and fuels. A tiny agricultural sector is highly subsidized and protected, with crop yields among the highest in the world. Usually self sufficient in rice, Japan imports about 60% of its food on a caloric basis. Japan maintains one of the world's largest fishing fleets and accounts for nearly 15% of the global catch. For three decades, overall real economic growth had been spectacular - a 10% average in the 1960s, a 5% average in the 1970s, and a 4% average in the 1980s. Growth slowed markedly in the 1990s, averaging just 1.7%, largely because of the after effects of inefficient investment and an asset price bubble in the late 1980s that required a protracted period of time for firms to reduce excess debt, capital, and labor. In October 2007 Japan's longest post-war period of economic expansion ended after 69 months and Japan entered into recession in 2008, with 2009 marking a return to near 0% interest rates. The 10-year privatization of Japan Post, which has functioned not only as the national postal delivery system but also, through its banking and insurance facilities as Japan's largest financial institution, was completed in October 2007, marking a major milestone in the process of structural reform. The Japanese financial sector was not heavily exposed to sub-prime mortgages or their derivative instruments and weathered the initial effect of the global credit crunch, but a sharp downturn in business investment and global demand for Japan's exports in late 2008 pushed Japan further into a recession. Japan's huge government debt, which totals 170% of GDP, and the aging of the population are two major long-run problems. Debate continues on the role of and effects of reform in restructuring the economy.

**GDP (purchasing power parity):**
$4.348 trillion (2008 est.)
$4.365 trillion (2007)
$4.263 trillion (2006)
*note:* data are in 2008 US dollars

**GDP (official exchange rate):** $4.844 trillion (2008 est.)

**GDP - real growth rate:**
-0.4% (2008 est.)
2.4% (2007 est.)
2% (2006 est.)

**GDP - per capita (PPP):**
$34,200 (2008 est.)
$34,300 (2007 est.)
$33,400 (2006 est.)
*note:* data are in 2008 US dollars

**GDP - composition by sector:**
*agriculture:* 1.4%
*industry:* 26.4%
*services:* 72.1% (2008 est.)

**Labor force:** 66.15 million (2008 est.)

**Labor force - by occupation:**
*agriculture:* 4.4%
*industry:* 27.9%
*services:* 66.4% (2005)

**Unemployment rate:**
4.2% (2008 est.)
3.8% (2007 est.)

**Population below poverty line:** NA%

**Household income or consumption by percentage share:**
*lowest 10%:* 4.8%
*highest 10%:* 21.7% (1993)

**Distribution of family income - Gini index:** 38.1 (2002)

**Investment (gross fixed):** 22.5% of GDP (2008 est.)

**Budget:**
*revenues:* $1.672 trillion
*expenditures:* $1.823 trillion (2008 est.)

**Public debt:** 170.4% of GDP (2008 est.)

**Inflation rate (consumer prices):**
1.8% (2008 est.)
0.1% (2007 est.)

**Central bank discount rate:** 0.1% (19 December 2008)

**Commercial bank prime lending rate:** 1.68% (November 2008)

**Stock of money:** $4.37 trillion (31 December 2007)

**Stock of quasi money:** $4.783 trillion (31 December 2007)

**Stock of domestic credit:** $9.653 trillion (31 December 2007)

**Market value of publicly traded shares:** $4.453 trillion (31 December 2007)

**Agriculture - products:** rice, sugar beets, vegetables, fruit; pork, poultry, dairy products, eggs; fish

**Industries:** among world's largest and technologically advanced producers of motor vehicles, electronic equipment, machine tools, steel and nonferrous metals, ships, chemicals, textiles, processed foods

**Industrial production growth rate:** 0.5% (2008 est.)

**Electricity - production:** 1.195 trillion kWh (2007 est.)

**Electricity - consumption:** 1.08 trillion kWh (2006 est.)
**Electricity - exports:** 0 kWh (2007 est.)
**Electricity - imports:** 0 kWh (2007 est.)
**Oil - production:** 132,400 bbl/day (2007)
**Oil - consumption:** 5.007 million bbl/day (2007)
**Oil - exports:** 240,000 bbl/day (2007)
**Oil - imports:** 5.032 million bbl/day (2007)
**Oil - proved reserves:** 44.12 million bbl (1 January 2008 est.)
**Natural gas - production:** 3.729 billion cu m (2007 est.)
**Natural gas - consumption:** 100.3 billion cu m (2007 est.)
**Natural gas - exports:** 0 cu m (2007 est.)
**Natural gas - imports:** 95.62 billion cu m (2007 est.)
**Natural gas - proved reserves:** 20.9 billion cu m (1 January 2008 est.)
**Current account balance:** $187.8 billion (2008 est.)
**Exports:** $776.8 billion f.o.b. (2008 est.)
**Exports - commodities:** transport equipment, motor vehicles, semiconductors, electrical machinery, chemicals
**Exports - partners:** US 20.4%, China 15.3%, South Korea 7.6%, Taiwan 6.3%, Hong Kong 5.4% (2007)
**Imports:** $696.2 billion f.o.b. (2008 est.)
**Imports - commodities:** machinery and equipment, fuels, foodstuffs, chemicals, textiles, raw materials
**Imports - partners:** China 20.5%, US 11.6%, Saudi Arabia 5.7%, UAE 5.2%, Australia 5%, South Korea 4.4%, Indonesia 4.2% (2007)
**Reserves of foreign exchange and gold:** $954.1 billion (31 December 2007 est.)
**Debt - external:** $1.492 trillion (30 June 2007)
**Stock of direct foreign investment - at home:** $139.7 billion (2008 est.)
**Stock of direct foreign investment - abroad:** $597 billion (2008 est.)
**Exchange rates:** yen (JPY) per US dollar - 103.58 (2008 est.), 117.99 (2007), 116.18 (2006), 110.22 (2005), 108.19 (2004)

## Communications

**Telephones - main lines in use:** 51.232 million (2007)
**Telephones - mobile cellular:** 107.339 million (2007)
**Telephone system:**
*general assessment:* excellent domestic and international service
*domestic:* high level of modern technology and excellent service of every kind
*international:* country code - 81; numerous submarine cables provide links throughout Asia, Australia, the Middle East, Europe, and US; satellite earth stations - 5 Intelsat (4 Pacific Ocean and 1 Indian Ocean), 1 Intersputnik (Indian Ocean region), and 1 Inmarsat (Pacific and Indian Ocean regions
**Radio broadcast stations:** AM 215 (plus 370 repeaters), FM 89 (plus 485 repeaters), shortwave 21 (2001)

**Television broadcast stations:** 211 (plus 7,341 repeaters); in addition, US Forces are served by 3 TV stations and 2 TV cable services (1999)
**Internet country code:** .jp
**Internet hosts:** 39.909 million (2008)
**Internet users:** 88.11 million (2007)

## Transportation

**Airports:** 175 (2008)
**Airports - with paved runways:**
*total:* 144
*over 3,047 m:* 7
*2,438 to 3,047 m:* 41
*1,524 to 2,437 m:* 40
*914 to 1,523 m:* 28
*under 914 m:* 28 (2008)
**Airports - with unpaved runways:**
*total:* 31
*914 to 1,523 m:* 4
*under 914 m:* 27 (2008)
**Heliports:** 14 (2007)
**Pipelines:** gas 3,862 km; oil 167 km; oil/gas/water 53 km (2008)
**Railways:**
*total:* 23,474 km
*standard gauge:* 3,204 km 1.435-m gauge (3,204 km electrified)
*narrow gauge:* 77 km 1.372-m gauge (77 km electrified); 20,182 km 1.067-m gauge (13,334 km electrified); 11 km 0.762-m gauge (11 km electrified) (2006)
**Roadways:**
*total:* 1,196,999 km
*paved:* 949,101 km (includes 7,383 km of expressways)
*unpaved:* 247,898 km (2006)
**Waterways:** 1,770 km (seagoing vessels use inland seas) (2007)
**Merchant marine:**
*total:* 683
*by type:* bulk carrier 136, cargo 30, carrier 3, chemical tanker 27, container 11, liquefied gas 59, passenger 12, passenger/cargo 135, petroleum tanker 156, refrigerated cargo 2, roll on/roll off 51, vehicle carrier 61
*registered in other countries:* 3,074 (Australia 1, Bahamas 87, Belize 8, Bermuda 2, Burma 1, Cambodia 1, Cayman Islands 13, China 2, Cyprus 21, France 1, Honduras 4, Hong Kong 111, Indonesia 6, Isle of Man 6, Italy 1, South Korea 20, Liberia 116, Malaysia 4, Malta 8, Marshall Islands 17, Nigeria 1, Norway 29, Panama 2335, Philippines 81, Portugal 15, Saint Kitts and Nevis 3, Saint Vincent and the Grenadines 3, Singapore 131, Thailand 4, UK 4, US 7, Vanuatu 29, Vietnam 1, unknown 1) (2008)
**Ports and terminals:** Chiba, Kawasaki, Kobe, Mizushima, Moji, Nagoya, Osaka, Tokyo, Tomakomai, Yohohama

## Military

**Military branches:** Japanese Ministry of Defense (MOD): Ground Self-Defense Force (Rikujou Jietai, GSDF), Maritime Self-Defense Force (Kaijou Jietai, MSDF), Air Self-Defense Force (Koku Jieitai, ASDF) (2009)
**Military service age and obligation:** 18 years of age for voluntary military service (2001)
**Manpower available for military service:**
*males age 16-49:* 27,819,804
*females age 16-49:* 26,863,794 (2008 est.)
**Manpower fit for military service:**
*males age 16-49:* 22,757,136
*females age 16-49:* 21,920,703 (2009 est.)
**Manpower reaching militarily significant age annually:**
*male:* 621,254
*female:* 589,270 (2009 est.)
**Military expenditures:** 0.8% of GDP (2006)

## Transnational Issues

**Disputes - international:** the sovereignty dispute over the islands of Etorofu, Kunashiri, and Shikotan, and the Habomai group, known in Japan as the "Northern Territories" and in Russia as the "Southern Kuril Islands," occupied by the Soviet Union in 1945, now administered by Russia and claimed by Japan, remains the primary sticking point to signing a peace treaty formally ending World War II hostilities; Japan and South Korea claim Liancourt Rocks (Take-shima/ Dokdo) occupied by South Korea since 1954; China and Taiwan dispute both Japan's claims to the uninhabited islands of the Senkaku-shoto (Diaoyu Tai) and Japan's unilaterally declared exclusive economic zone in the East China Sea, the site of intensive hydrocarbon prospecting

# Jarvis Island
*(territory of the US)*

Description under

United States

Pacific Island

Wildlife Refuges

# Jersey
*(British crown dependency)*

## Introduction

**Background:** Jersey and the other Channel Islands represent the last remnants of the medieval Dukedom of Normandy that held sway in both France and England. These islands were the only British soil occupied by German troops in World War II. Jersey is a British crown dependency but is not part of the UK. However, the UK Government is constitutionally responsible for its defense and international representation.

## Geography

**Location:** Western Europe, island in the English Channel, northwest of France
**Geographic coordinates:** 49 15 N, 2 10 W
**Map references:** Europe
**Area:**
*total:* 116 sq km
*land:* 116 sq km
*water:* 0 sq km
**Area - comparative:** about two-thirds the size of Washington, DC
**Land boundaries:** 0 km
**Coastline:** 70 km
**Maritime claims:**
*territorial sea:* 3 nm
*exclusive fishing zone:* 12 nm
**Climate:** temperate; mild winters and cool summers
**Terrain:** gently rolling plain with low, rugged hills along north coast
**Elevation extremes:**
*lowest point:* Atlantic Ocean 0 m
*highest point:* unnamed location 143 m
**Natural resources:** arable land
**Land use:**
*arable land:* 0%
*permanent crops:* 0%
*other:* 100% (2005)
**Irrigated land:** NA
**Natural hazards:** NA
**Environment - current issues:** NA

**Geography - note:** largest and southernmost of Channel Islands; about 30% of population concentrated in Saint Helier

## People

**Population:** 91,626 (July 2009 est.)
**Age structure:**
*0-14 years:* 16.1% (male 7,623/female 7,087)
*15-64 years:* 67.7% (male 30,914/female 31,081)
*65 years and over:* 16.3% (male 6,614/female 8,307) (2009 est.)
**Median age:**
*total:* 42.9 years
*male:* 42.1 years
*female:* 43.6 years (2009 est.)
**Population growth rate:** 0.211% (2009 est.)
**Birth rate:** 8.63 births/1,000 population (2009 est.)
**Death rate:** 9.36 deaths/1,000 population (2008 est.)
**Net migration rate:** 2.73 migrant(s)/1,000 population (2009 est.)
**Urbanization:**
*urban population:* 31% of total population (2008)
*rate of urbanization:* 0.6% annual rate of change (2005-10 est.)
**Sex ratio:**
*at birth:* 1.08 male(s)/female
*under 15 years:* 1.08 male(s)/female
*15-64 years:* 1 male(s)/female
*65 years and over:* 0.8 male(s)/female
*total population:* 0.97 male(s)/female (2009 est.)
**Infant mortality rate:**
*total:* 4.73 deaths/1,000 live births
*male:* 5.09 deaths/1,000 live births
*female:* 4.34 deaths/1,000 live births (2009 est.)
**Life expectancy at birth:**
*total population:* 79.75 years
*male:* 77.23 years
*female:* 82.46 years (2009 est.)
**Total fertility rate:** 1.57 children born/woman (2009 est.)
**HIV/AIDS - adult prevalence rate:** NA
**HIV/AIDS - people living with HIV/AIDS:** NA
**HIV/AIDS - deaths:** NA
**Nationality:**
*noun:* Channel Islander(s)
*adjective:* Channel Islander
**Ethnic groups:** Jersey 51.1%, Britons 34.8%, Irish, French, and other white 6.6%, Portuguese/Madeiran 6.4%, other 1.1% (2001 census)
**Religions:** Anglican, Roman Catholic, Baptist, Congregational New Church, Methodist, Presbyterian
**Languages:** English 94.5% (official), Portuguese 4.6%, other 0.9% (2001 census)
**Literacy:** NA
**Education expenditures:** NA

## Government

**Country name:**
*conventional long form:* Bailiwick of Jersey
*conventional short form:* Jersey
**Dependency status:** British crown dependency
**Government type:** parliamentary democracy

**Capital:**
*name:* Saint Helier
*geographic coordinates:* 49 11 N, 2 06 W
*time difference:* UTC 0 (5 hours ahead of Washington, DC during Standard Time)
*daylight saving time:* +1hr, begins last Sunday in March; ends last Sunday in October
**Administrative divisions:** none (British crown dependency); there are no first-order administrative divisions as defined by the US Government, but there are 12 parishes including Grouville, Saint Brelade, Saint Clement, Saint Helier, Saint John, Saint Lawrence, Saint Martin, Saint Mary, Saint Ouen, Saint Peter, Saint Saviour, and Trinity
**Independence:** none (British crown dependency)
**National holiday:** Liberation Day, 9 May (1945)
**Constitution:** unwritten; partly statutes, partly common law and practice
**Legal system:** the laws of the UK, where applicable, apply and local statutes; justice is administered by the Royal Court
**Suffrage:** 16 years of age; universal
**Executive branch:**
*chief of state:* Queen ELIZABETH II (since 6 February 1952); represented by Lieutenant Governor Andrew RIDGEWAY (since 14 June 2006)
*head of government:* Chief Minister Terry LE SUEUR (12 December 2008); Bailiff Philip Martin BAILHACHE (since February 1995)
*cabinet:* Cabinet (since December 2005)
*elections:* ministers of the Cabinet including the chief minister are elected by the Assembly of States; the monarch is hereditary; lieutenant governor and bailiff appointed by the monarch
**Legislative branch:** unicameral Assembly of the States of Jersey (58 seats; 55 are voting members, of which 12 are senators elected for six-year terms, 12 are constables or heads of parishes elected for three-year terms, 29 are deputies elected for three-year terms, the bailiff and the deputy bailiff, and 3 non-voting members includes the Dean of Jersey, the Attorney General, and the Solicitor General appointed by the monarch)
*elections:* last held 15 October 2008 for senators and 26 November 2008 for deputies (next to be held in 2011)
*election results:* percent of vote - NA; seats - independents 55
**Judicial branch:** Royal Court (judges elected by an electoral college and the bailiff)
**Political parties and leaders:** two declared parties: Centre Party; Jersey Democratic Alliance
*note:* all senators and deputies elected in 2008 were independents
**Political pressure groups and leaders:** Institute of Directors, Jersey branch (provides business support); Jersey Hospitality Association [Robert JONES] (trade association); Jersey Rights Association [David ROTHERHAM] (human rights); La Societe Jersiaise (education and conservation group); Progress Jersey [Darius J. PEARCE, Daren O'TOOLE, Gino RISOLI] (human rights); Royal Jersey Agriculture and Horticultural Society or RJA&HS (development and management of the Jersey breed of cattle); Save Jersey's Heritage (protects heritage through building preservation)

## Jersey *(continued)*

**Diplomatic representation in the US:** none (British crown dependency)
**Diplomatic representation from the US:** none (British crown dependency)
**Flag description:** white with a diagonal red cross extending to the corners of the flag; in the upper quadrant, surmounted by a yellow crown, a red shield with the three lions of England in yellow

### Economy

**Economy - overview:** Jersey's economy is based on international financial services, agriculture, and tourism. In 2005 the finance sector accounted for about 50% of the island's output. Potatoes, cauliflower, tomatoes, and especially flowers are important export crops, shipped mostly to the UK. The Jersey breed of dairy cattle is known worldwide and represents an important export income earner. Milk products go to the UK and other EU countries. Tourism accounts for one-quarter of GDP. In recent years, the government has encouraged light industry to locate in Jersey, with the result that an electronics industry has developed, displacing more traditional industries. All raw material and energy requirements are imported, as well as a large share of Jersey's food needs. Light taxes and death duties make the island a popular tax haven. Living standards come close to those of the UK.
**GDP (purchasing power parity):**
$5.1 billion (2005 est.)
**GDP (official exchange rate):** $5.1 billion (2005 est.)
**GDP - real growth rate:** NA%
**GDP - per capita (PPP):**
$57,000 (2005 est.)
**GDP - composition by sector:**
*agriculture:* 1%
*industry:* 2%
*services:* 97% (2005)
**Labor force:** 53,560 (June 2006)
**Unemployment rate:**
2.2% (2006 est.)
**Population below poverty line:** NA%
**Household income or consumption by percentage share:**
*lowest 10%:* NA%
*highest 10%:* NA%
**Budget:**
*revenues:* $829 million
*expenditures:* $851 million (2005)
**Inflation rate (consumer prices):**
3.7% (December 2006)
**Market value of publicly traded shares:** $NA
**Agriculture - products:** potatoes, cauliflower, tomatoes; beef, dairy products
**Industries:** tourism, banking and finance, dairy, electronics
**Industrial production growth rate:** NA%
**Electricity - consumption:** 630.1 million kWh (2004 est.)
**Electricity - imports:** NA kWh; note - electricity supplied by France
**Exports:** $NA
**Exports - commodities:** light industrial and electrical goods, dairy cattle, foodstuffs, textiles

**Imports:** $NA
**Imports - commodities:** machinery and transport equipment, manufactured goods, foodstuffs, mineral fuels, chemicals
**Debt - external:** $NA
**Exchange rates:** Jersey pounds per US dollar 0.5302 (2008 est.), 0.4993 (2007), 0.5418 (2006), 0.5493 (2005), 0.5462 (2004)
*note:* the Jersey pound is at par with the British pound

### Communications

**Telephones - main lines in use:** 73,900 (2001)
**Telephones - mobile cellular:** 83,900 (2004)
**Telephone system:**
*general assessment:* state owned, partially-competitive market; increasingly modern, with some broadband access
*domestic:* digital telephone system launch announced in 2006 and currently being implemented
*international:* submarine cable connectivity to Guernsey, the UK, and France (2008)
**Radio broadcast stations:** AM NA, FM 1, shortwave 0 (UK radio broadcasts carried via local relays) (2008)
**Television broadcast stations:** 2 (UK television carried by local relays with a switch to digital broadcasts scheduled for 2010) (2008)
**Internet country code:** .je
**Internet hosts:** 190 (2008)
**Internet users:** 27,000 (2005)

### Transportation

**Airports:** 1 (2008)
**Airports - with paved runways:**
*total:* 1
*1,524 to 2,437 m:* 1 (2008)
**Roadways:**
*total:* 358 km (2002)
**Ports and terminals:** Gorey, Saint Aubin, Saint Helier

### Military

**Manpower fit for military service:**
*males age 16-49:* 16,920
*females age 16-49:* 16,826 (2009 est.)
**Manpower reaching militarily significant age annually:**
*male:* 586
*female:* 541 (2009 est.)
**Military - note:** defense is the responsibility of the UK

### Transnational Issues

**Disputes - international:** none

## Johnston Atoll
*(territory of the US)*

Description under

United States

Pacific Island

Wildlife Refuges

## Jordan

Golan Heights (Israeli occupied)

*Israeli occupied with current status subject to the Israeli-Palestinian Interim Agreement; permanent status to be determined through further negotiation.

### Introduction

**Background:** Following World War I and the dissolution of the Ottoman Empire, the UK received a mandate to govern much of the Middle East. Britain separated out a semi-autonomous region of Transjordan from Palestine in the early 1920s, and the area gained its independence in 1946; it adopted the name of Jordan in 1950. The country's long-time ruler was King HUSSEIN (1953-99). A pragmatic leader, he successfully navigated competing pressures from the major powers (US, USSR, and UK), various Arab states, Israel, and a large internal Palestinian population. Jordan lost the West Bank to Israel in the 1967 war and barely managed to defeat Palestinian rebels who threatened to overthrow the monarchy in 1970. King HUSSEIN in 1988 permanently relinquished Jordanian claims to the West Bank. In 1989, he reinstituted parliamentary elections and initiated a gradual political liberalization; political parties were legalized in 1992. In 1994, he signed a peace treaty with Israel. King ABDALLAH II, the son of King HUSSEIN, assumed the throne following his father's death in February 1999. Since then, he has consolidated his power and undertaken an aggressive economic reform program. Jordan acceded to the World Trade Organization in 2000, and began to participate in the European Free Trade Association in 2001. In 2003, Jordan staunchly supported the Coalition ouster of Saddam in Iraq and following the outbreak of insurgent violence in Iraq, absorbed thousands of displaced Iraqis. Municipal elections were held in July 2007 under a system in which 20% of seats in all municipal councils were reserved by quota for women. Parliamentary elections were held in November 2007 and saw independent pro-government candidates win the vast majority of seats. In November 2007, King ABDALLAH instructed his new prime minister to focus on socioeconomic reform, developing a healthcare and housing network for civilians and military personnel, and improving the educational system.

# Jordan *(continued)*

## Geography

**Location:** Middle East, northwest of Saudi Arabia
**Geographic coordinates:** 31 00 N, 36 00 E
**Map references:** Middle East
**Area:**
*total:* 92,300 sq km
*land:* 91,971 sq km
*water:* 329 sq km
**Area - comparative:** slightly smaller than Indiana
**Land boundaries:**
*total:* 1,635 km
*border countries:* Iraq 181 km, Israel 238 km, Saudi Arabia 744 km, Syria 375 km, West Bank 97 km
**Coastline:** 26 km
**Maritime claims:**
*territorial sea:* 3 nm
**Climate:** mostly arid desert; rainy season in west (November to April)
**Terrain:** mostly desert plateau in east, highland area in west; Great Rift Valley separates East and West Banks of the Jordan River
**Elevation extremes:**
*lowest point:* Dead Sea -408 m
*highest point:* Jabal Ram 1,734 m
**Natural resources:** phosphates, potash, shale oil
**Land use:**
*arable land:* 3.32%
*permanent crops:* 1.18%
*other:* 95.5% (2005)
**Irrigated land:** 750 sq km (2003)
**Total renewable water resources:** 0.9 cu km (1997)
**Freshwater withdrawal (domestic/industrial/agricultural):**
*total:* 1.01 cu km/yr (21%/4%/75%)
*per capita:* 177 cu m/yr (2000)
**Natural hazards:** droughts; periodic earthquakes
**Environment - current issues:** limited natural fresh water resources; deforestation; overgrazing; soil erosion; desertification
**Environment - international agreements:**
*party to:* Biodiversity, Climate Change, Climate Change-Kyoto Protocol, Desertification, Endangered Species, Hazardous Wastes, Law of the Sea, Marine Dumping, Ozone Layer Protection, Wetlands
*signed, but not ratified:* none of the selected agreements
**Geography - note:** strategic location at the head of the Gulf of Aqaba and as the Arab country that shares the longest border with Israel and the occupied West Bank

## People

**Population:** 6,342,948 (July 2009 est.)
**Age structure:**
*0-14 years:* 31.3% (male 1,014,183/female 973,538)
*15-64 years:* 64.5% (male 2,183,638/female 1,904,420)
*65 years and over:* 4.2% (male 128,759/female 138,410) (2009 est.)
**Median age:**
*total:* 24.3 years
*male:* 25 years
*female:* 23.6 years (2009 est.)
**Population growth rate:** 2.264% (2009 est.)
**Birth rate:** 19.55 births/1,000 population (2009 est.)
**Death rate:** 2.72 deaths/1,000 population (2008 est.)
**Net migration rate:** 5.83 migrant(s)/1,000 population (2009 est.)
**Urbanization:**
*urban population:* 78% of total population (2008)
*rate of urbanization:* 3.1% annual rate of change (2005-10 est.)
**Sex ratio:**
*at birth:* 1.06 male(s)/female
*under 15 years:* 1.04 male(s)/female
*15-64 years:* 1.15 male(s)/female
*65 years and over:* 0.93 male(s)/female
*total population:* 1.1 male(s)/female (2009 est.)
**Infant mortality rate:**
*total:* 14.97 deaths/1,000 live births
*male:* 17.91 deaths/1,000 live births
*female:* 11.86 deaths/1,000 live births (2009 est.)
**Life expectancy at birth:**
*total population:* 78.87 years
*male:* 76.34 years
*female:* 81.56 years (2009 est.)
**Total fertility rate:** 2.39 children born/woman (2009 est.)
**HIV/AIDS - adult prevalence rate:** less than 0.1% (2001 est.)
**HIV/AIDS - people living with HIV/AIDS:** 600 (2007 est.)
**HIV/AIDS - deaths:** fewer than 500 (2003 est.)
**Nationality:**
*noun:* Jordanian(s)
*adjective:* Jordanian
**Ethnic groups:** Arab 98%, Circassian 1%, Armenian 1%
**Religions:** Sunni Muslim 92%, Christian 6% (majority Greek Orthodox, but some Greek and Roman Catholics, Syrian Orthodox, Coptic Orthodox, Armenian Orthodox, and Protestant denominations), other 2% (several small Shia Muslim and Druze populations) (2001 est.)
**Languages:** Arabic (official), English widely understood among upper and middle classes
**Literacy:**
*definition:* age 15 and over can read and write
*total population:* 89.9%
*male:* 95.1%
*female:* 84.7% (2003 est.)
**School life expectancy (primary to tertiary education):**
*total:* 13 years
*male:* 13 years
*female:* 13 years (2006)
**Education expenditures:** 4.9% of GDP (1999)

## Government

**Country name:**
*conventional long form:* Hashemite Kingdom of Jordan
*conventional short form:* Jordan
*local long form:* Al Mamlakah al Urduniyah al Hashimiyah
*local short form:* Al Urdun
*former:* Transjordan
**Government type:** constitutional monarchy
**Capital:**
*name:* Amman
*geographic coordinates:* 31 57 N, 35 56 E
*time difference:* UTC+2 (7 hours ahead of Washington, DC during Standard Time)
*daylight saving time:* +1hr, begins last Thursday in March; ends last Friday in September
**Administrative divisions:** 12 governorates (muhafazat, singular - muhafazah); Ajlun, Al 'Aqabah, Al Balqa', Al Karak, Al Mafraq, 'Amman, At Tafilah, Az Zarqa', Irbid, Jarash, Ma'an, Madaba
**Independence:** 25 May 1946 (from League of Nations mandate under British administration)
**National holiday:** Independence Day, 25 May (1946)
**Constitution:** 1 January 1952; amended many times
**Legal system:** based on Islamic law and French codes; judicial review of legislative acts in a specially provided High Tribunal; has not accepted compulsory ICJ jurisdiction
**Suffrage:** 18 years of age; universal
**Executive branch:**
*chief of state:* King ABDALLAH II (since 7 February 1999); Prince HUSSEIN (born 1994), eldest son of King ABDALLAH II, is considered to be first in line to inherit the throne
*head of government:* Prime Minister Nader al-DAHABI (since 25 November 2007)
*cabinet:* Cabinet appointed by the prime minister in consultation with the monarch
*elections:* the monarch is hereditary; prime minister appointed by the monarch
**Legislative branch:** bicameral National Assembly or Majlis al-'Umma consists of the Senate, also called the House of Notables or Majlis al-Ayan (55 seats; members appointed by the monarch to serve four-year terms) and the Chamber of Deputies, also called the House of Representatives or Majlis al-Nuwaab (110 seats; members elected using a single, non-transferable vote system in multi-member districts to serve four-year terms); note - six seats are reserved for women, nine seats are reserved for Christian candidates, nine seats are reserved for Bedouin candidates, and three seats are reserved for Jordanians of Chechen or Circassian descent
*elections:* Chamber of Deputies - last held 20 November 2007 (next scheduled to be held in 2011)
*election results:* Chamber of Deputies - percent of vote by party - NA; seats by party - IAF 6, independents and other 104; note - seven women serve in the Assembly, six of whom filled women's quota seats and one was directly elected

# Jordan (continued)

**Judicial branch:** Court of Cassation (Supreme Court)

**Political parties and leaders:** Arab Ba'ath Socialist Party [Fuad DABBOUR]; Ba'ath Arab Progressive Party [Tayseer al-HAMSI]; Call Party [Mohammed Abu BAKR]; Democratic People's Party [Ahmad Yusuf 'ALIYA]; Democratic Popular Unity Party [Sa'ed DIAB]; Islamic Action Front [Zaki Beni-IRSHAID]; Islamic Center Party [Marwan al-FA'OURI; Jordanian Communist Party [Munir HAMARNEH]; Jordanian National Party [Mona Abu BAKR]; Jordanian United Front [Amjad al-MAJALI]; Life Party [Thaher 'AMROU]; Message Party [Hazem QASHOU]; National Constitution Party [Ahmed al-SHUNAQ]; National Movement for Direct Democracy [Mohammed al-QAQ];

**Political pressure groups and leaders:** Anti-Normalization Committee [Ali Abu SUKKAR, president vice chairman]; Jordan Bar Association [Saleh al-ARMUTI, chairman]; Jordanian Press Association [Sayf al-SHARIF, president]; Jordanian Muslim Brotherhood [Dr. Hamam SAID, controller general]

**International organization participation:** ABEDA, AFESD, AMF, CAEU, FAO, G-77, IAEA, IBRD, ICAO, ICC, ICCt, ICRM, IDA, IDB, IFAD, IFC, IFRCS, ILO, IMF, IMO, Interpol, IOC, IOM, IPU, ISO, ITSO, ITU, ITUC, LAS, MIGA, MINURCAT, MINUSTAH, MONUC, NAM, OIC, OPCW, OSCE (partner), PCA, UN, UNAMID, UNCTAD, UNESCO, UNHCR, UNIDO, UNMIL, UNMIS, UNOCI, UNOMIG, UNRWA, UNWTO, UPU, WCO, WFTU, WHO, WIPO, WMO, WTO

**Diplomatic representation in the US:**
*chief of mission:* Ambassador ZEID Ra'ad Zeid al-Hussein, Prince
*chancery:* 3504 International Drive NW, Washington, DC 20008
*telephone:* [1] (202) 966-2664
*FAX:* [1] (202) 966-3110

**Diplomatic representation from the US:**
*chief of mission:* Ambassador Robert S. BEECROFT
*embassy:* Abdoun, Amman
*mailing address:* P. O. Box 354, Amman 11118 Jordan; Unit 70200, Box 5, DPO AE 09892-0200
*telephone:* [962] (6) 590-6000
*FAX:* [962] (6) 592-0121

**Flag description:** three equal horizontal bands of black (top), representing the Abbassid Caliphate, white, representing the Ummayyad Caliphate, and green, representing the Fatimid Caliphate; a red isosceles triangle on the hoist side, representing the Great Arab Revolt of 1916, and bearing a small white seven-pointed star symbolizing the seven verses of the opening Sura (Al-Fatiha) of the Holy Koran; the seven points on the star represent faith in One God, humanity, national spirit, humility, social justice, virtue, and aspirations; design is based on the Arab Revolt flag of World War I

## Economy

**Economy - overview:** Jordan is a small Arab country with insufficient supplies of water, oil, and other natural resources. Poverty, unemployment, and inflation are fundamental problems, but King ABDALLAH II, since assuming the throne in 1999, has undertaken some broad economic reforms in a long-term effort to improve living standards. Since Jordan's graduation from its most recent IMF program in 2002, Amman has continued to follow IMF guidelines, practicing careful monetary policy, making substantial headway with privatization, and opening the trade regime. Jordan's exports have significantly increased under the free trade accord with the US and Jordanian Qualifying Industrial Zones (QIZ), which allow Jordan to export goods with some Israeli content duty free to the US. In 2006 and 2008, Jordan used privatization proceeds to significantly reduce its debt-to-GDP ratio. These measures have helped improve productivity and have made Jordan more attractive for foreign investment. The government ended subsidies for petroleum and other consumer goods in 2008 in an effort to control the budget. The main challenges facing Jordan are reducing dependence on foreign grants, reducing the growing budget deficit, attracting investments, and creating jobs. Jordan is currently exploring nuclear power generation to forestall energy shortfalls. Jordan's conservative banking sector has been largely protected from the worldwide financial crisis, but many businesses, particularly in the tourism and real estate sector, are predicting a slow-down in 2009.

**GDP (purchasing power parity):**
$30.76 billion (2008 est.)
$29.07 billion (2007)
$27.42 billion (2006)
*note:* data are in 2008 US dollars

**GDP (official exchange rate):** $19.12 billion (2008 est.)

**GDP - real growth rate:**
5.8% (2008 est.)
6% (2007 est.)
6.3% (2006 est.)

**GDP - per capita (PPP):**
$5,000 (2008 est.)
$4,800 (2007 est.)
$4,600 (2006 est.)
*note:* data are in 2008 US dollars

**GDP - composition by sector:**
*agriculture:* 3.6%
*industry:* 10.1%
*services:* 86.3% (2008 est.)

**Labor force:** 1.615 million (2008 est.)

**Labor force - by occupation:**
*agriculture:* 2.7%
*industry:* 20%
*services:* 77.4% (2001 est.)

**Unemployment rate:**
12.9% (2008 est.)
13.5% (2007 est.)
*note:* official rate; unofficial rate is approximately 30%

**Population below poverty line:** 14.2% (2002)

**Household income or consumption by percentage share:**
*lowest 10%:* 2.7%
*highest 10%:* 30.6% (2003)

**Distribution of family income - Gini index:** 39.7 (2007)

**Investment (gross fixed):** 34.1% of GDP (2008 est.)

**Budget:**
*revenues:* $5.999 billion
*expenditures:* $7.87 billion (2008 est.)

**Public debt:** 58.3% of GDP (2008 est.)

**Inflation rate (consumer prices):**
14.9% (2008 est.)
5.4% (2007 est.)

**Central bank discount rate:** 6.25% (31 December 2008)

**Commercial bank prime lending rate:** 8.45% (31 December 2008)

**Stock of money:** $7.87 billion (31 December 2008)

**Stock of quasi money:** $17.98 billion (31 December 2008)

**Stock of domestic credit:** $25.05 billion (31 December 2008)

**Market value of publicly traded shares:** $35.8 billion (31 December 2008)

**Agriculture - products:** citrus, tomatoes, cucumbers, olives; sheep, poultry, stone fruits, strawberries, dairy

**Industries:** clothing, fertilizers, potash, phosphate mining, pharmaceuticals, petroleum refining, cement, inorganic chemicals, light manufacturing, tourism

**Industrial production growth rate:** 1.8% (2008 est.)

**Electricity - production:** 10.08 billion kWh (2007 est.)

**Electricity - consumption:** 9.852 billion kWh (2006 est.)

**Electricity - exports:** 13 million kWh (2006 est.)

**Electricity - imports:** 472 million kWh (2006 est.)

**Oil - production:** 0 bbl/day (2005 est.)

**Oil - consumption:** 110,700 bbl/day (2006 est.)

**Oil - exports:** 0 bbl/day (2005 est.)

**Oil - imports:** 112,300 bbl/day (2005 est.)

**Oil - proved reserves:** 1 million bbl (1 January 2008 est.)

**Natural gas - production:** 320 million cu m (2006 est.)

**Natural gas - consumption:** 2.25 billion cu m (2006 est.)

**Natural gas - exports:** 0 cu m (2007 est.)

**Natural gas - imports:** 2.4 billion cu m (2007 est.)

**Natural gas - proved reserves:** 6.031 billion cu m (1 January 2008 est.)

**Current account balance:** -$4.87 billion (2008 est.)

**Exports:** $6.521 billion f.o.b. (2008 est.)

**Exports - commodities:** clothing, fertilizers, potash, phosphates, vegetables, pharmaceuticals

# Jordan (continued)

**Exports - partners:** US 22.4%, Iraq 12.9%, India 8.3%, UAE 7.8%, Saudi Arabia 7.5%, Syria 4.9% (2007)
**Imports:** $15.65 billion f.o.b. (2008 est.)
**Imports - commodities:** crude oil, machinery, transport equipment, iron, cereals
**Imports - partners:** Saudi Arabia 21%, China 9.7%, Germany 7.5%, US 4.7%, Egypt 4.4% (2007)
**Reserves of foreign exchange and gold:** $7.884 billion (31 December 2008 est.)
**Debt - external:** $6.597 billion (31 December 2008 est.)
**Stock of direct foreign investment - at home:** $20.38 billion (2008 est.)
**Exchange rates:** Jordanian dinars (JOD) per US dollar - 0.709 (2008 est.), 0.709 (2007), 0.709 (2006), 0.709 (2005), 0.709 (2004)

## Communications

**Telephones - main lines in use:** 585,500 (2007)
**Telephones - mobile cellular:** 4.771 million (2007)
**Telephone system:**
*general assessment:* service has improved recently with increased use of digital switching equipment; microwave radio relay transmission and coaxial and fiber-optic cable are employed on trunk lines; growing mobile-cellular usage in both urban and rural areas is reducing use of fixed-line services; Internet penetration remains modest and slow-growing
*domestic:* 1995 telecommunications law opened all non-fixed-line services to private competition; in 2005, monopoly over fixed-line services terminated and the entire telecommunications sector was opened to competition; mobile-cellular usage is increasing rapidly and teledensity reached 80 per 100 persons in 2007
*international:* country code - 962; landing point for the Fiber-Optic Link Around the Globe (FLAG) submarine cable network that provides links to Asia, Middle East, Europe; satellite earth stations - 33 (3 Intelsat, 1 Arabsat, and 29 land and maritime Inmarsat terminals); fiber-optic cable to Saudi Arabia and microwave radio relay link with Egypt and Syria; participant in Medarabtel (2007)
**Radio broadcast stations:** FM 31 (2007)
**Television broadcast stations:** 22 (2007)
**Internet country code:** .jo
**Internet hosts:** 21,150 (2008)
**Internet users:** 1.127 million (2007)

## Transportation

**Airports:** 17 (2008)
**Airports - with paved runways:**
*total:* 15
*over 3,047 m:* 7
*2,438 to 3,047 m:* 6
*914 to 1,523 m:* 1
*under 914 m:* 1 (2008)

**Airports - with unpaved runways:**
*total:* 2
*under 914 m:* 2 (2008)
**Heliports:** 1 (2007)
**Pipelines:** gas 439 km; oil 49 km (2008)
**Railways:**
*total:* 505 km
*narrow gauge:* 505 km 1.050-m gauge (2006)
**Roadways:**
*total:* 7,694 km
*paved:* 7,694 km (2006)
**Merchant marine:**
*total:* 21
*by type:* cargo 8, container 1, passenger/cargo 7, petroleum tanker 2, roll on/roll off 3
*foreign-owned:* 13 (UAE 13)
*registered in other countries:* 24 (Algeria 7, Bahamas 2, Panama 13, Syria 2) (2008)
**Ports and terminals:** Al 'Aqabah

## Military

**Military branches:** Jordanian Armed Forces (JAF): Royal Jordanian Land Force, Royal Jordanian Navy, Royal Jordanian Air Force (Al-Quwwat al-Jawwiya al-Malakiya al-Urduniya, RJAF), Special Operations Command (Socom); Public Security Directorate (normally falls under Ministry of Interior, but comes under JAF in wartime or crisis) (2008)
**Military service age and obligation:** 17 years of age for voluntary military service; conscription at age 18 was suspended in 1999, although all males under age 37 are required to register; women not subject to conscription, but can volunteer to serve in non-combat military positions (2004)
**Manpower available for military service:**
*males age 16-49:* 1,812,551
*females age 16-49:* 1,559,155 (2008 est.)
**Manpower fit for military service:**
*males age 16-49:* 1,593,919
*females age 16-49:* 1,382,097 (2009 est.)
**Manpower reaching militarily significant age annually:**
*male:* 69,830
*female:* 67,292 (2009 est.)
**Military expenditures:** 8.6% of GDP (2006)

## Transnational Issues

**Disputes - international:** approximately two million Iraqis have fled the conflict in Iraq, with the majority taking refuge in Syria and Jordan; 2004 Agreement settles border dispute with Syria pending demarcation
**Refugees and internally displaced persons:**
*refugees (country of origin):* 1,835,704 (Palestinian Refugees (UNRWA)); 500,000 (Iraq)
*IDPs:* 160,000 (1967 Arab-Israeli War) (2007)

**Trafficking in persons:**
*current situation:* Jordan is a destination and transit country for women and men from South and Southeast Asia trafficked for the purpose of forced labor; Jordan is also a destination for women from Eastern Europe and Morocco for prostitution; women from Bangladesh, Sri Lanka, Indonesia, and the Philippines migrate willingly to work as domestic servants, but some are subjected to conditions of forced labor, including unlawful withholding of passports, restrictions on movement, non-payment of wages, threats, and physical or sexual abuse
*tier rating:* Tier 2 Watch List - Jordan is on the Tier 2 Watch List for its failure to provide evidence of increasing efforts to combat trafficking in persons in 2007, particularly in the area of law enforcement against trafficking for forced labor; the government made minimal efforts to investigate or prosecute numerous allegations related to exploitation of foreign domestic workers; Jordan failed for a second year to criminally prosecute and punish those who committed acts of forced labor; Jordan also continues to lack victim protection services; Jordan has not ratified the 2000 UN TIP Protocol (2008)

# Kazakhstan

RUSSIA
Petropavlovsk
Qostanay (Kostanay)
Oral (Ural'sk)
Pavlodar
ASTANA
Semey (Semipalatinsk)
Öskemen (Ust-Kamenogorsk)
Aqtöbe (Aktobe)
Qaraghandy (Karaganda)
MONG.
Atyraū (Atyrau)
Lake Balkhash
Baykonur Cosmodrome
Bayqongyr (Baykonyr)
Aral Sea
Qyzylorda (Kyzylorda)
Aqtaū (Aktau)
Sır Darya
CHINA
Khan Tängiri Shyngy
Almaty
Caspian Sea
AZER.
Taraz
Shymkent
KYRGYZSTAN
Naryn
UZBEKISTAN
TURKMENISTAN
0 100 200 km
0 100 200 mi
RUSSIA

## Introduction

**Background:** Native Kazakhs, a mix of Turkic and Mongol nomadic tribes who migrated into the region in the 13th century, were rarely united as a single nation. The area was conquered by Russia in the 18th century, and Kazakhstan became a Soviet Republic in 1936. During the 1950s and 1960s agricultural "Virgin Lands" program, Soviet citizens were encouraged to help cultivate Kazakhstan's northern pastures. This influx of immigrants (mostly Russians, but also some other deported nationalities) skewed the ethnic mixture and enabled non-Kazakhs to outnumber natives. Independence in 1991 caused many of these newcomers to emigrate. Kazakhstan's economy is larger than those of all the other Central Asian states combined, largely due to the country's vast natural resources and a recent history of political stability. Current issues include: developing a cohesive national identity; expanding the development of the country's vast energy resources and exporting them to world markets; achieving a sustainable economic growth; diversifying the economy outside the oil, gas, and mining sectors; enhancing Kazakhstan's competitiveness; and strengthening relations with neighboring states and other foreign powers.

## Geography

**Location:** Central Asia, northwest of China; a small portion west of the Ural (Zhayyq) River in eastern-most Europe
**Geographic coordinates:** 48 00 N, 68 00 E
**Map references:** Asia
**Area:**
*total:* 2,717,300 sq km
*land:* 2,669,800 sq km
*water:* 47,500 sq km
**Area - comparative:** slightly less than four times the size of Texas

**Land boundaries:**
*total:* 12,185 km
*border countries:* China 1,533 km, Kyrgyzstan 1,224 km, Russia 6,846 km, Turkmenistan 379 km, Uzbekistan 2,203 km
**Coastline:** 0 km (landlocked); note - Kazakhstan borders the Aral Sea, now split into two bodies of water (1,070 km), and the Caspian Sea (1,894 km)
**Maritime claims:** none (landlocked)
**Climate:** continental, cold winters and hot summers, arid and semiarid
**Terrain:** vast flat steppe extending from the Volga in the west to the Altai Mountains in the east and from the plains of western Siberia in the north to oases and deserts of Central Asia in the south
**Elevation extremes:**
*lowest point:* Vpadina Kaundy -132 m
*highest point:* Khan Tangiri Shyngy (Pik Khan-Tengri) 6,995 m
**Natural resources:** major deposits of petroleum, natural gas, coal, iron ore, manganese, chrome ore, nickel, cobalt, copper, molybdenum, lead, zinc, bauxite, gold, uranium
**Land use:**
*arable land:* 8.28%
*permanent crops:* 0.05%
*other:* 91.67% (2005)
**Irrigated land:** 35,560 sq km (2003)
**Total renewable water resources:** 109.6 cu km (1997)
**Freshwater withdrawal (domestic/industrial/agricultural):**
*total:* 35 cu km/yr (2%/17%/82%)
*per capita:* 2,360 cu m/yr (2000)
**Natural hazards:** earthquakes in the south; mudslides around Almaty
**Environment - current issues:** radioactive or toxic chemical sites associated with former defense industries and test ranges scattered throughout the

country pose health risks for humans and animals; industrial pollution is severe in some cities; because the two main rivers that flowed into the Aral Sea have been diverted for irrigation, it is drying up and leaving behind a harmful layer of chemical pesticides and natural salts; these substances are then picked up by the wind and blown into noxious dust storms; pollution in the Caspian Sea; soil pollution from overuse of agricultural chemicals and salination from poor infrastructure and wasteful irrigation practices
**Environment - international agreements:**
*party to:* Air Pollution, Biodiversity, Climate Change, Desertification, Endangered Species, Environmental Modification, Hazardous Wastes, Ozone Layer Protection, Ship Pollution, Wetlands
*signed, but not ratified:* Climate Change-Kyoto Protocol
**Geography - note:** landlocked; Russia leases approximately 6,000 sq km of territory enclosing the Baykonur Cosmodrome; in January 2004, Kazakhstan and Russia extended the lease to 2050

## People

**Population:** 15,399,437 (July 2009 est.)
**Age structure:**
*0-14 years:* 21.8% (male 1,717,469/female 1,643,920)
*15-64 years:* 70.2% (male 5,279,292/female 5,534,607)
*65 years and over:* 7.9% (male 426,494/female 797,655) (2009 est.)
**Median age:**
*total:* 29.6 years
*male:* 28.1 years
*female:* 31.3 years (2009 est.)
**Population growth rate:** 0.392% (2009 est.)
**Birth rate:** 16.6 births/1,000 population (2009 est.)
**Death rate:** 9.39 deaths/1,000 population (2008 est.)
**Net migration rate:** -3.3 migrant(s)/1,000 population (2009 est.)
**Urbanization:**
*urban population:* 58% of total population (2008)
*rate of urbanization:* 1.2% annual rate of change (2005-10 est.)
**Sex ratio:**
*at birth:* 1.06 male(s)/female
*under 15 years:* 1.04 male(s)/female
*15-64 years:* 0.95 male(s)/female
*65 years and over:* 0.54 male(s)/female
*total population:* 0.93 male(s)/female (2009 est.)
**Infant mortality rate:**
*total:* 25.73 deaths/1,000 live births
*male:* 30.15 deaths/1,000 live births
*female:* 21.06 deaths/1,000 live births (2009 est.)
**Life expectancy at birth:**
*total population:* 67.87 years
*male:* 62.58 years
*female:* 73.47 years (2009 est.)
**Total fertility rate:** 1.88 children born/woman (2009 est.)

# Kazakhstan (continued)

**HIV/AIDS - adult prevalence rate:** 0.1% (2007 est.)
**HIV/AIDS - people living with HIV/AIDS:** 12,000 (2007 est.)
**HIV/AIDS - deaths:** fewer than 500 (2007 est.)
**Nationality:**
*noun:* Kazakhstani(s)
*adjective:* Kazakhstani
**Ethnic groups:** Kazakh (Qazaq) 53.4%, Russian 30%, Ukrainian 3.7%, Uzbek 2.5%, German 2.4%, Tatar 1.7%, Uygur 1.4%, other 4.9% (1999 census)
**Religions:** Muslim 47%, Russian Orthodox 44%, Protestant 2%, other 7%
**Languages:** Kazakh (Qazaq, state language) 64.4%, Russian (official, used in everyday business, designated the "language of interethnic communication") 95% (2001 est.)
**Literacy:**
*definition:* age 15 and over can read and write
*total population:* 99.5%
*male:* 99.8%
*female:* 99.3% (1999 est.)
**School life expectancy (primary to tertiary education):**
*total:* 15 years
*male:* 15 years
*female:* 16 years (2007)
**Education expenditures:** 2.3% of GDP (2005)

## Government

**Country name:**
*conventional long form:* Republic of Kazakhstan
*conventional short form:* Kazakhstan
*local long form:* Qazaqstan Respublikasy
*local short form:* Qazaqstan
*former:* Kazakh Soviet Socialist Republic
**Government type:** republic; authoritarian presidential rule, with little power outside the executive branch
**Capital:**
*name:* Astana
*geographic coordinates:* 51 10 N, 71 25 E
*time difference:* UTC+6 (11 hours ahead of Washington, DC during Standard Time)
*note:* Kazakhstan is divided into two time zones
**Administrative divisions:** 14 provinces (oblystar, singular - oblys) and 3 cities* (qalalar, singular - qala); Almaty Oblysy, Almaty Qalasy*, Aqmola Oblysy (Astana), Aqtobe Oblysy, Astana Qalasy*, Atyrau Oblysy, Batys Qazaqstan Oblysy (Oral), Bayqongyr Qalasy*, Mangghystau Oblysy (Aqtau), Ongtustik Qazaqstan Oblysy (Shymkent), Pavlodar Oblysy, Qaraghandy Oblysy, Qostanay Oblysy, Qyzylorda Oblysy, Shyghys Qazaqstan Oblysy (Oskemen), Soltustik Qazaqstan Oblysy (Petropavlovsk), Zhambyl Oblysy (Taraz)
*note:* administrative divisions have the same names as their administrative centers (exceptions have the administrative center name following in parentheses); in 1995, the Governments of Kazakhstan and Russia entered into an agreement whereby Russia would lease for a period of 20 years an area of 6,000 sq km enclosing the Baykonur space launch facilities and the city of Bayqongyr (Baykonur, formerly Leninsk); in 2004, a new agreement extended the lease to 2050
**Independence:** 16 December 1991 (from the Soviet Union)
**National holiday:** Independence Day, 16 December (1991)
**Constitution:** first post-independence constitution adopted 28 January 1993; new constitution adopted by national referendum 30 August 1995
**Legal system:** based on Islamic law and Roman law; has not accepted compulsory ICJ jurisdiction
**Suffrage:** 18 years of age; universal
**Executive branch:**
*chief of state:* President Nursultan A. NAZARBAYEV (chairman of the Supreme Soviet from 22 February 1990, elected president 1 December 1991)
*head of government:* Prime Minister Karim MASIMOV (since 10 January 2007); First Deputy Prime Minister Umirzak SHUKEYEV (since 3 March 2009) and Deputy Prime Ministers Yerbol ORYNBAYEV (since 29 October 2007) and Serik AKHMETOV (since 3 March 2009)
*cabinet:* Council of Ministers appointed by the president
*elections:* president elected by popular vote for a five-year term; election last held 4 December 2005 (next to be held in 2012); prime minister and first deputy prime minister appointed by the president, with Mazhilis approval; note - constitutional amendments of May 2007 shortened the presidential term from seven years to five years and established a two-consecutive-term limit; changes will take effect after NAZARBAYEV's term ends; he, and only he, is allowed to run for president indefinitely
*election results:* Nursultan A. NAZARBAYEV reelected president; percent of vote - Nursultan A. NAZARBAYEV 91.1%, Zharmakhan A. TUYAKBAI 6.6%, Alikhan M. BAIMENOV 1.6%
**Legislative branch:** bicameral Parliament consists of the Senate (47 seats; 15 members are appointed by the president; other members are elected by local assemblies; members serve six-year terms, but elections are staggered with half of the members up for re-election every three years) and the Mazhilis (107 seats; 9 out of the 107 Mazhilis members are elected by the Assembly of the People of Kazakhstan, a presidentially appointed advisory body designed to represent the country's ethnic minorities; non-appointed members are popularly elected to serve five-year terms)
*elections:* Senate - (indirect) last held October 2008; next to be held in 2011; Mazhilis - last held 18 August 2007 (next to be held in 2012)
*election results:* Senate - percent of vote by party - NA; seats by party - Nur Otan 16; Mazhilis - percent of vote by party - Nur-Otan 88.1%, NSDP 4.6%, Ak Zhol 3.3%, Auyl 1.6%, Communist People's Party 1.3%, Patriots Party .8% Ruhaniyat .4%; seats by party - Nur-Otan 98; note - parties must achieve a threshold of 7% of the electorate to qualify for seats in the Mazhilis

**Judicial branch:** Supreme Court (44 members); Constitutional Council (seven members)
**Political parties and leaders:** Adilet (Justice) [Maksut NARIKBAYEV, Zeynulla ALSHIMBAYEV, Serik ABDRAHMANOV, Bakhytbek AKHMETZHAN, Yerkin ONGARBAYEV, Tolegan SYDYKOV] (formerly Democratic Party of Kazakhstan); Agrarian and Industrial Union of Workers Block or AIST (Agrarian Party and Civic Party); Ak Zhol Party (Bright Path) [Alikhan BAIMENOV]; Alga [Vladimir KOZLOV] (unregistered); Auyl (Village) [Gani KALIYEV]; Azat Party (formerly True Ak Zhol Party) [Bolat ABILOV]; Communist Party of Kazakhstan or KPK [Serikbolsyn ABDILDIN]; Communist People's Party of Kazakhstan [Vladislav KOSAREV]; National Social Democratic Party (NSDP)[Zharmakhan TUYAKBAY]; Nur-Otan [Bakhytzhan ZHUMAGULOV] (the Agrarian, Asar, and Civic parties merged with Otan); Patriots' Party [Gani KASYMOV]; Rukhaniyat (Spirituality) [Altynshash ZHAGANOVA]
**Political pressure groups and leaders:** Adil-Soz [Tamara KALEYEVA]; Almaty Helsinki Group [Ninel FOKINA]; Confederation of Free Trade Unions [Sergei BELKIN]; For Fair Elections [Yevgeniy ZHOVTIS, Sabit ZHUSUPOV, Sergey DUVANOV, Ibrash NUSUPBAYEV]; Kazakhstan International Bureau on Human Rights [Yevgeniy ZHOVTIS, executive director]; Pan-National Social Democratic Party of Kazakhstan [Zharmakhan TUYAKBAI]; Pensioners Movement or Pokoleniye [Irina SAVOSTINA, chairwoman]; Republican Network of International Monitors [Dos KUSHIM]; Transparency International [Sergei ZLOTNIKOV]
**International organization participation:** ADB, CIS, CSTO, EAEC, EAPC, EBRD, ECO, FAO, GCTU, IAEA, IBRD, ICAO, ICRM, IDA, IDB, IFAD, IFC, IFRCS, ILO, IMF, IMO, Interpol, IOC, IOM, IPU, ISO, ITSO, ITU, MIGA, NAM (observer), NSG, OAS (observer), OIC, OPCW, OSCE, PFP, SCO, UN, UNCTAD, UNESCO, UNIDO, UNWTO, UPU, WCL, WCO, WFTU, WHO, WIPO, WMO, WTO (observer)
**Diplomatic representation in the US:**
*chief of mission:* Ambassador Yerlan IDRISOV
*chancery:* 1401 16th Street NW, Washington, DC 20036
*telephone:* [1] (202) 232-5488
*FAX:* [1] (202) 232-5845
*consulate(s) general:* Los Angeles
*consulate(s):* New York
**Diplomatic representation from the US:**
*chief of mission:* Ambassador Richard E. HOAGLAND
*embassy:* Ak Bulak 4, Str. 23-22, Building #3, Astana 010010
*mailing address:* use embassy street address
*telephone:* [7] (7172) 70-21-00
*FAX:* [7] (7172) 34-08-90
**Flag description:** sky blue background representing the endless sky and a gold sun with 32 rays above a soaring golden steppe eagle in the center; on the hoist side is a "national ornamentation" in gold

# Kazakhstan (continued)

## Economy

**Economy - overview:** Kazakhstan, the largest of the former Soviet republics in territory, excluding Russia, possesses enormous fossil fuel reserves and plentiful supplies of other minerals and metals. It also has a large agricultural sector featuring livestock and grain. Kazakhstan's industrial sector rests on the extraction and processing of these natural resources. Kazakhstan enjoyed double-digit growth in 2000-01 and 8% or more per year in 2002-07 - thanks largely to its booming energy sector, but also to economic reform, good harvests, and increased foreign investment; growth slowed to 3% in 2008, however, as a result of declining oil prices and a softening world economy. Inflation reached 10% in 2007 and 18% in 2008. In the energy sector, the opening of the Caspian Pipeline Consortium in 2001, from western Kazakhstan's Tengiz oilfield to the Black Sea, substantially raised export capacity. In 2006, Kazakhstan completed the Atasu-Alashankou portion of an oil pipeline to China that is planned in future construction to extend from the country's Caspian coast eastward to the Chinese border. The country has embarked upon an industrial policy designed to diversify the economy away from overdependence on the oil sector by developing its manufacturing potential. The policy changed the corporate tax code to favor domestic industry as a means to reduce the influence of foreign investment and foreign personnel. The government has engaged in several disputes with foreign oil companies over the terms of production agreements, most recently, with regard to the Kashagan project in 2007-08. Since 2007, Astana has provided financial support to the banking sector which has been struggling with poor asset quality and large foreign loans.

**GDP (purchasing power parity):**
$176.9 billion (2008 est.)
$171.7 billion (2007)
$158.3 billion (2006)
note: data are in 2008 US dollars

**GDP (official exchange rate):** $141.2 billion (2008 est.)

**GDP - real growth rate:**
3% (2008 est.)
8.5% (2007 est.)
10.6% (2006 est.)

**GDP - per capita (PPP):**
$11,500 (2008 est.)
$11,200 (2007 est.)
$10,400 (2006 est.)
note: data are in 2008 US dollars

**GDP - composition by sector:**
agriculture: 5.8%
industry: 39.4%
services: 54.7% (2008 est.)

**Labor force:** 8.358 million (2008 est.)

**Labor force - by occupation:**
agriculture: 31.5%
industry: 18.4%
services: 50% (2005 est.)

**Unemployment rate:**
6.9% (2008 est.)
7.3% (2007 est.)

**Population below poverty line:** 13.8% (2007)

**Household income or consumption by percentage share:**
lowest 10%: 3.3%
highest 10%: 26.5% (2004 est.)

**Distribution of family income - Gini index:** 30.4 (2005)

**Investment (gross fixed):** 27.8% of GDP (2008 est.)

**Budget:**
revenues: $29.64 billion
expenditures: $32.6 billion (2008 est.)

**Public debt:** 9.1% of GDP (2008 est.)

**Inflation rate (consumer prices):**
18.6% (2008 est.)
10.8% (2007 est.)

**Central bank discount rate:** 11% (31 December 2007)

**Stock of money:** $12.74 billion (31 December 2007)

**Stock of quasi money:** $25.75 billion (31 December 2007)

**Stock of domestic credit:** $43.75 billion (31 December 2007)

**Market value of publicly traded shares:** $41.38 billion (31 December 2007)

**Agriculture - products:** grain (mostly spring wheat), cotton; livestock

**Industries:** oil, coal, iron ore, manganese, chromite, lead, zinc, copper, titanium, bauxite, gold, silver, phosphates, sulfur, iron and steel; tractors and other agricultural machinery, electric motors, construction materials

**Industrial production growth rate:** 0.7% (2008 est.)

**Electricity - production:** 74.93 billion kWh (2007 est.)

**Electricity - consumption:** 61.81 billion kWh (2006 est.)

**Electricity - exports:** 3.528 billion kWh (2007 est.)

**Electricity - imports:** 3.665 billion kWh (2007 est.)

**Oil - production:** 1.445 million bbl/day (2007 est.)

**Oil - consumption:** 243,100 bbl/day (2006 est.)

**Oil - exports:** 1.236 million bbl/day (2005 est.)

**Oil - imports:** 127,600 bbl/day (2005)

**Oil - proved reserves:** 30 billion bbl (1 January 2008 est.)

**Natural gas - production:** 27.88 billion cu m (2007 est.)

**Natural gas - consumption:** 30.58 billion cu m (2007 est.)

**Natural gas - exports:** 8.1 billion cu m (2007 est.)

**Natural gas - imports:** 10.8 billion cu m (2007 est.)

**Natural gas - proved reserves:** 2.832 trillion cu m (1 January 2008 est.)

**Current account balance:** $326 million (2008 est.)

**Exports:** $66.57 billion f.o.b. (2008 est.)

**Exports - commodities:** oil and oil products 59%, ferrous metals 19%, chemicals 5%, machinery 3%, grain, wool, meat, coal (2001)

**Exports - partners:** China 15.5%, Germany 11.5%, Russia 11.2%, Italy 7.2%, France 6.7% (2007)

**Imports:** $37.53 billion f.o.b. (2008 est.)

**Imports - commodities:** machinery and equipment, metal products, foodstuffs

**Imports - partners:** Russia 35.4%, China 22.1%, Germany 8% (2007)

**Reserves of foreign exchange and gold:** $22.36 billion (31 December 2008 est.)

**Debt - external:** $103.6 billion (31 December 2008 est.)

**Stock of direct foreign investment - at home:** $47.66 billion (2008 est.)

**Stock of direct foreign investment - abroad:** $2.188 billion (2008 est.)

**Exchange rates:** tenge (KZT) per US dollar - 120.25 (2008 est.), 122.55 (2007), 126.09 (2006), 132.88 (2005), 136.04 (2004)

## Communications

**Telephones - main lines in use:** 3.237 million (2007)

**Telephones - mobile cellular:** 12.588 million (2007)

**Telephone system:**
general assessment: inherited an outdated telecommunications network from the Soviet era requiring modernization
domestic: intercity by landline and microwave radio relay; number of fixed-line connections is gradually increasing and fixed-line teledensity is about 20 per 100 persons; mobile-cellular usage is increasing rapidly and subscriptions now exceed 80 per 100 persons
international: country code - 7; international traffic with other former Soviet republics and China carried by landline and microwave radio relay and with other countries by satellite and by the Trans-Asia-Europe (TAE) fiber-optic cable; satellite earth stations - 2 Intelsat (2007)

**Radio broadcast stations:** AM 60, FM 18, shortwave 9 (2008)

**Television broadcast stations:** 12 (plus 9 repeaters) (1998)

**Internet country code:** .kz

**Internet hosts:** 36,417 (2008)

**Internet users:** 1.901 million (2006)

## Transportation

**Airports:** 95 (2008)

**Airports - with paved runways:**
total: 64
over 3,047 m: 10
2,438 to 3,047 m: 26
1,524 to 2,437 m: 16
914 to 1,523 m: 4
under 914 m: 8 (2008)

## Kazakhstan (continued)

**Airports - with unpaved runways:**
*total:* 31
*over 3,047 m:* 5
*2,438 to 3,047 m:* 6
*1,524 to 2,437 m:* 4
*914 to 1,523 m:* 3
*under 914 m:* 13 (2008)
**Heliports:** 5 (2007)
**Pipelines:** condensate 658 km; gas 11,146 km; oil 10,376 km; refined products 1,095 km; water 1,465 km(2008)
**Railways:**
*total:* 13,700 km
*broad gauge:* 13,700 km 1.520-m gauge (3,700 km electrified) (2006)
**Roadways:**
*total:* 91,563 km
*paved:* 83,717 km
*unpaved:* 7,846 km (2006)
**Waterways:** 4,000 km (on the Ertis ((Irtysh)) River (80%) and Syr Darya ((Syrdariya)) River) (2008)
**Merchant marine:**
*total:* 5
*by type:* petroleum tanker 4, refrigerated cargo 1 (2008)
**Ports and terminals:** Aqtau (Shevchenko), Atyrau (Gur'yev), Oskemen (Ust-Kamenogorsk), Pavlodar, Semey (Semipalatinsk)

### Military

**Military branches:** Kazakh Armed Forces: Ground Forces, Navy, Air Mobile Forces, Air Defense Forces (2009)
**Military service age and obligation:** 18 years of age for compulsory military service; conscript service obligation - 2 years; minimum age for volunteers NA (2004)
**Manpower available for military service:**
*males age 16-49:* 4,176,731
*females age 16-49:* 4,219,636 (2008 est.)
**Manpower fit for military service:**
*males age 16-49:* 2,888,931
*females age 16-49:* 3,550,014 (2009 est.)
**Manpower reaching militarily significant age annually:**
*male:* 139,262
*female:* 133,047 (2009 est.)
**Military expenditures:** 0.9% of GDP (Ministry of Defense expenditures) (FY02)

### Transnational Issues

**Disputes - international:** Kyrgyzstan has yet to ratify the 2001 boundary delimitation with Kazakhstan; field demarcation of the boundaries with Turkmenistan commenced in 2005, and with Uzbekistan in 2004; demarcation is scheduled to get underway with Russia in 2007; demarcation with China was completed in 2002; creation of a seabed boundary with Turkmenistan in the Caspian Sea remains under discussion; equidistant seabed treaties have been ratified with Azerbaijan and Russia in the Caspian

Sea, but no resolution has been made on dividing the water column among any of the littoral states
**Refugees and internally displaced persons:**
*refugees (country of origin):* 3,700 (Russia); 508 (Afghanistan) (2007)
**Illicit drugs:** significant illicit cultivation of cannabis for CIS markets, as well as limited cultivation of opium poppy and ephedra (for the drug ephedrine); limited government eradication of illicit crops; transit point for Southwest Asian narcotics bound for Russia and the rest of Europe; significant consumer of opiates

# Kenya

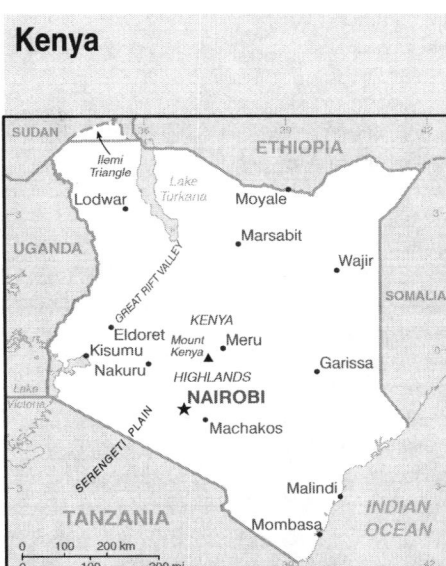

### Introduction

**Background:** Founding president and liberation struggle icon Jomo KENYATTA led Kenya from independence in 1963 until his death in 1978, when President Daniel Toroitich arap MOI took power in a constitutional succession. The country was a de facto one-party state from 1969 until 1982 when the ruling Kenya African National Union (KANU) made itself the sole legal party in Kenya. MOI acceded to internal and external pressure for political liberalization in late 1991. The ethnically fractured opposition failed to dislodge KANU from power in elections in 1992 and 1997, which were marred by violence and fraud, but were viewed as having generally reflected the will of the Kenyan people. President MOI stepped down in December 2002 following fair and peaceful elections. Mwai KIBAKI, running as the candidate of the multiethnic, united opposition group, the National Rainbow Coalition (NARC), defeated KANU candidate Uhuru KENYATTA and assumed the presidency following a campaign centered on an anticorruption platform. KIBAKI's NARC coalition splintered in 2005 over the constitutional review process. Government defectors joined with KANU to form a new opposition coalition, the Orange Democratic Movement, which defeated the government's draft constitution in a popular referendum in November 2005. KIBAKI's reelection in December 2007 brought charges of vote rigging from ODM candidate Raila ODINGA and unleashed two months of violence in which as many as 1,500 people died. UN-sponsored talks in late February produced a powersharing accord bringing ODINGA into the government in the restored position of prime minister.

### Geography

**Location:** Eastern Africa, bordering the Indian Ocean, between Somalia and Tanzania
**Geographic coordinates:** 1 00 N, 38 00 E

# Kenya (continued)

**Map references:** Africa

**Area:**
*total:* 582,650 sq km
*land:* 569,250 sq km
*water:* 13,400 sq km

**Area - comparative:** slightly more than twice the size of Nevada

**Land boundaries:**
*total:* 3,477 km
*border countries:* Ethiopia 861 km, Somalia 682 km, Sudan 232 km, Tanzania 769 km, Uganda 933 km

**Coastline:** 536 km

**Maritime claims:**
*territorial sea:* 12 nm
*exclusive economic zone:* 200 nm
*continental shelf:* 200 m depth or to the depth of exploitation

**Climate:** varies from tropical along coast to arid in interior

**Terrain:** low plains rise to central highlands bisected by Great Rift Valley; fertile plateau in west

**Elevation extremes:**
*lowest point:* Indian Ocean 0 m
*highest point:* Mount Kenya 5,199 m

**Natural resources:** limestone, soda ash, salt, gemstones, fluorspar, zinc, diatomite, gypsum, wildlife, hydropower

**Land use:**
*arable land:* 8.01%
*permanent crops:* 0.97%
*other:* 91.02% (2005)

**Irrigated land:** 1,030 sq km (2003)

**Total renewable water resources:** 30.2 cu km (1990)

**Freshwater withdrawal (domestic/industrial/agricultural):**
*total:* 1.58 cu km/yr (30%/6%/64%)
*per capita:* 46 cu m/yr (2000)

**Natural hazards:** recurring drought; flooding during rainy seasons

**Environment - current issues:** water pollution from urban and industrial wastes; degradation of water quality from increased use of pesticides and fertilizers; water hyacinth infestation in Lake Victoria; deforestation; soil erosion; desertification; poaching

**Environment - international agreements:**
*party to:* Biodiversity, Climate Change, Climate Change-Kyoto Protocol, Desertification, Endangered Species, Hazardous Wastes, Law of the Sea, Marine Dumping, Marine Life Conservation, Ozone Layer Protection, Ship Pollution, Wetlands, Whaling
*signed, but not ratified:* none of the selected agreements

**Geography - note:** the Kenyan Highlands comprise one of the most successful agricultural production regions in Africa; glaciers are found on Mount Kenya, Africa's second highest peak; unique physiography supports abundant and varied wildlife of scientific and economic value

## People

**Population:** 39,002,772
*note:* estimates for this country explicitly take into account the effects of excess mortality due to AIDS; this can result in lower life expectancy, higher infant mortality, higher death rates, lower population growth rates, and changes in the distribution of population by age and sex than would otherwise be expected (July 2009 est.)

**Age structure:**
*0-14 years:* 42.3% (male 8,300,393/female 8,181,898)
*15-64 years:* 55.1% (male 10,784,119/female 10,702,999)
*65 years and over:* 2.6% (male 470,218/female 563,145) (2009 est.)

**Median age:**
*total:* 18.7 years
*male:* 18.6 years
*female:* 18.8 years (2009 est.)

**Population growth rate:** 2.691% (2009 est.)

**Birth rate:** 36.64 births/1,000 population (2009 est.)

**Death rate:** 10.3 deaths/1,000 population (2008 est.)

**Net migration rate:** 0 migrant(s)/1,000 population (2009 est.)

**Urbanization:**
*urban population:* 22% of total population (2008)
*rate of urbanization:* 4% annual rate of change (2005-10 est.)

**Sex ratio:**
*at birth:* 1.02 male(s)/female
*under 15 years:* 1.01 male(s)/female
*15-64 years:* 1.01 male(s)/female
*65 years and over:* 0.84 male(s)/female
*total population:* 1 male(s)/female (2009 est.)

**Infant mortality rate:**
*total:* 54.7 deaths/1,000 live births
*male:* 57.56 deaths/1,000 live births
*female:* 51.78 deaths/1,000 live births (2009 est.)

**Life expectancy at birth:**
*total population:* 57.86 years
*male:* 57.49 years
*female:* 58.24 years (2009 est.)

**Total fertility rate:** 4.56 children born/woman (2009 est.)

**HIV/AIDS - adult prevalence rate:** 6.7% (2003 est.)

**HIV/AIDS - people living with HIV/AIDS:** 1.2 million (2003 est.)

**HIV/AIDS - deaths:** 150,000 (2003 est.)

**Major infectious diseases:**
*degree of risk:* high
*food or waterborne diseases:* bacterial and protozoal diarrhea, hepatitis A, and typhoid fever
*vectorborne disease:* malaria and Rift Valley fever
*water contact disease:* schistosomiasis
*animal contact disease:* rabies (2009)

**Nationality:**
*noun:* Kenyan(s)
*adjective:* Kenyan

**Ethnic groups:** Kikuyu 22%, Luhya 14%, Luo 13%, Kalenjin 12%, Kamba 11%, Kisii 6%, Meru 6%, other African 15%, non-African (Asian, European, and Arab) 1%

**Religions:** Protestant 45%, Roman Catholic 33%, Muslim 10%, indigenous beliefs 10%, other 2%
*note:* a large majority of Kenyans are Christian, but estimates for the percentage of the population that adheres to Islam or indigenous beliefs vary widely

**Languages:** English (official), Kiswahili (official), numerous indigenous languages

**Literacy:**
*definition:* age 15 and over can read and write
*total population:* 85.1%
*male:* 90.6%
*female:* 79.7% (2003 est.)

**School life expectancy (primary to tertiary education):**
*total:* 10 years
*male:* 10 years
*female:* 9 years (2004)

**Education expenditures:** 6.9% of GDP (2006)

## Government

**Country name:**
*conventional long form:* Republic of Kenya
*conventional short form:* Kenya
*local long form:* Republic of Kenya/Jamhuri ya Kenya
*local short form:* Kenya
*former:* British East Africa

**Government type:** republic

**Capital:**
*name:* Nairobi
*geographic coordinates:* 1 17 S, 36 49 E
*time difference:* UTC+3 (8 hours ahead of Washington, DC during Standard Time)

**Administrative divisions:** 7 provinces and 1 area*; Central, Coast, Eastern, Nairobi Area*, North Eastern, Nyanza, Rift Valley, Western

**Independence:** 12 December 1963 (from the UK)

**National holiday:** Independence Day, 12 December (1963)

**Constitution:** 12 December 1963; amended as a republic 1964; reissued with amendments 1979, 1982, 1986, 1988, 1991, 1992, 1997, 2001; note - a new draft constitution was defeated by popular referendum in 2005

**Legal system:** based on Kenyan statutory law, Kenyan and English common law, tribal law, and Islamic law; judicial review in High Court; accepts compulsory ICJ jurisdiction with reservations; constitutional amendment of 1982 making Kenya a de jure one-party state repealed in 1991

**Suffrage:** 18 years of age; universal

**Executive branch:**
*chief of state:* President Mwai KIBAKI (since 30 December 2002); Vice President Stephene Kalonzo MUSYOKA (since 10 January 2008);
*head of government:* President Mwai KIBAKI (since 30 December 2002); Vice President Stephene Kalonzo MUSYOKA (since 10 January 2008); note -

# Kenya *(continued)*

the roles of the president and prime minister are not well defined at this juncture; constitutionally, the president remains chief of state and head of government, but the prime minister is charged with coordinating government business

*cabinet:* Cabinet appointed by the president and headed by the prime minister, who is the leader of the largest party in parliament

*elections:* president elected by popular vote for a five-year term (eligible for a second term); in addition to receiving the largest number of votes in absolute terms, the presidential candidate must also win 25% or more of the vote in at least five of Kenya's seven provinces and one area to avoid a runoff; election last held 27 December 2007 (next to be held in December 2012); vice president appointed by the president

*election results:* President Mwai KIBAKI reelected; percent of vote - Mwai KIBAKI 46%, Raila ODINGA 44%, Kalonzo MUSYOKA 9%

**Legislative branch:** unicameral National Assembly or Bunge usually referred to as Parliament (224 seats; 210 members elected by popular vote to serve five-year terms, 12 nominated members who are appointed by the president but selected by the parties in proportion to their parliamentary vote totals, 2 ex-officio members)

*elections:* last held 27 December 2007 (next to be held in December 2012)

*election results:* percent of vote by party - NA; seats by party - ODM 99, PNU 46, ODM-K 16, KANU 14 other 35; ex-officio 2; seats appointed by the president -ODM 6, PNU 3, ODM-K 2, KANU 1

**Judicial branch:** Court of Appeal (chief justice is appointed by the president); High Court

**Political parties and leaders:** Forum for the Restoration of Democracy-Kenya or FORD-Kenya [Musikari KOMBO]; Forum for the Restoration of Democracy-People or FORD-People [Reuben OYONDI]; Kenya African National Union or KANU [Uhuru KENYATTA]; National Rainbow Coalition-Kenya or NARC-Kenya [Martha KARUA]; Orange Democratic Movement or ODM [Raila ODINGA]; Orange Democratic Movement-Kenya or ODM-K [Kalonzo MUSYOKA]; Party of National Unity or PNU [Mwai KIBAKI]; Shirikisho Party of Kenya or SPK [Chirau Ali MWAKWERE]

**Political pressure groups and leaders:** Council of Islamic Preachers of Kenya or CIPK [Sheikh Idris MOHAMMED]; Kenya Human Rights Commission [L. Muthoni WANYEKI]; Muslim Human Rights Forum [Ali-Amin KIMATHI]; National Convention Executive Council or NCEC, a proreform coalition of political parties and nongovernment organizations [Ndung'u WAINANA]; National Muslim Leaders Forum or NAMLEF [Abdullahi ABDI]; Protestant National Council of Churches of Kenya or NCCK [Canon Peter Karanja MWANGI]; Roman Catholic and other Christian churches; Supreme Council of Kenya Muslims or SUPKEM [Shaykh Abdul Gafur al-BUSAIDY]

*other:* labor unions

**International organization participation:** ACP, AfDB, AU, C, COMESA, EAC, EADB, FAO, G-15, G-77, IAEA, IBRD, ICAO, ICCt, ICRM, IDA, IFAD, IFC, IFRCS, IGAD, ILO, IMF, IMO, IMSO, Interpol, IOC, IOM, IPU, ISO, ITSO, ITU, ITUC, MIGA, MINURSO, MONUC, NAM, OPCW, PCA, UN, UNAMID, UNCTAD, UNESCO, UNHCR, UNIDO, UNMIL, UNMIS, UNOCI, UNWTO, UPU, WCO, WFTU, WHO, WIPO, WMO, WTO

**Diplomatic representation in the US:**

*chief of mission:* Ambassador Peter Rateng Oginga OGEGO

*chancery:* 2249 R Street NW, Washington, DC 20008

*telephone:* [1] (202) 387-6101

*FAX:* [1] (202) 462-3829

*consulate(s) general:* Los Angeles

*consulate(s):* New York

**Diplomatic representation from the US:**

*chief of mission:* Ambassador Michael RANNEBERGER

*embassy:* US Embassy, United Nations Avenue, Nairobi; P. O. Box 606 Village Market, Nairobi 00621

*mailing address:* Box 21A, Unit 64100, APO AE 09831

*telephone:* [254] (20) 363-6000

*FAX:* [254] (20) 363-410

**Flag description:** three equal horizontal bands of black (top), red, and green; the red band is edged in white; a large warrior's shield covering crossed spears is superimposed at the center

## Economy

**Economy - overview:** The regional hub for trade and finance in East Africa, Kenya has been hampered by corruption and by reliance upon several primary goods whose prices have remained low. In 1997, the IMF suspended Kenya's Enhanced Structural Adjustment Program due to the government's failure to maintain reforms and curb corruption. A severe drought from 1999 to 2000 compounded Kenya's problems, causing water and energy rationing and reducing agricultural output. As a result, GDP contracted by 0.2% in 2000. The IMF, which had resumed loans in 2000 to help Kenya through the drought, again halted lending in 2001 when the government failed to institute several anticorruption measures. Despite the return of strong rains in 2001, weak commodity prices, endemic corruption, and low investment limited Kenya's economic growth to 1.2%. Growth lagged at 1.1% in 2002 because of erratic rains, low investor confidence, meager donor support, and political infighting up to the elections. In the key December 2002 elections, Daniel Arap MOI's 24-year-old reign ended, and a new opposition government took on the formidable economic problems facing the nation. After some early progress in rooting out corruption and encouraging donor support, the KIBAKI government was rocked by high-level graft scandals in 2005 and 2006. In 2006, the World Bank and IMF delayed loans pending action by the government on corruption. The international

financial institutions and donors have since resumed lending, despite little action on the government's part to deal with corruption. Post-election violence in early 2008, coupled with the effects of the global financial crisis on remittance and exports, reduced GDP growth to 2.2% in 2008, down from 7% the previous year.

**GDP (purchasing power parity):**
$61.83 billion (2008 est.)
$60.5 billion (2007)
$56.56 billion (2006)
*note:* data are in 2008 US dollars

**GDP (official exchange rate):** $31.42 billion (2008 est.)

**GDP - real growth rate:**
2.2% (2008 est.)
7% (2007 est.)
6.4% (2006 est.)

**GDP - per capita (PPP):**
$1,600 (2008 est.)
$1,600 (2007 est.)
$1,600 (2006 est.)
*note:* data are in 2008 US dollars

**GDP - composition by sector:**
*agriculture:* 23.8%
*industry:* 16.7%
*services:* 59.5% (2007 est.)

**Labor force:** 9.45 million (2007 est.)

**Labor force - by occupation:**
*agriculture:* 75%
*industry and services:* 25% (2003 est.)

**Unemployment rate:**
40% (2008 est.)
40% (2001 est.)

**Population below poverty line:** 50% (2000 est.)

**Household income or consumption by percentage share:**
*lowest 10%:* 2%
*highest 10%:* 37.2% (2000)

**Distribution of family income - Gini index:** 42.5 (2008 est.)

**Investment (gross fixed):** 21.6% of GDP (2008 est.)

**Budget:**
*revenues:* $6.617 billion
*expenditures:* $8.196 billion (2008 est.)

**Public debt:** 40.6% of GDP (2008 est.)

**Inflation rate (consumer prices):**
25.5% (2008 est.)
9.7% (2007 est.)

**Commercial bank prime lending rate:** 14.8% (31 December 2008)

**Stock of money:** $5.932 billion (31 December 2007)

**Stock of quasi money:** $6.273 billion (31 December 2007)

**Stock of domestic credit:** $10.43 billion (31 December 2007)

**Market value of publicly traded shares:** $13.39 billion (31 December 2007)

**Agriculture - products:** tea, coffee, corn, wheat, sugarcane, fruit, vegetables; dairy products, beef, pork, poultry, eggs

# Kenya (continued)

**Industries:** small-scale consumer goods (plastic, furniture, batteries, textiles, clothing, soap, cigarettes, flour), agricultural products, horticulture, oil refining; aluminum, steel, lead; cement, commercial ship repair, tourism

**Industrial production growth rate:** 3.6% (2008 est.)

**Electricity - production:** 5.223 billion kWh (2008 est.)

**Electricity - consumption:** 4.863 billion kWh (2008 est.)

**Electricity - exports:** 58.3 million kWh (2007 est.)

**Electricity - imports:** 22.5 million kWh (2007 est.)

**Oil - production:** 0 bbl/day (2008 est.)

**Oil - consumption:** 65,530 bbl/day (2006 est.)

**Oil - exports:** 5,137 bbl/day (2005)

**Oil - imports:** 72,780 bbl/day (2005)

**Oil - proved reserves:** 0 bbl (1 January 2006 est.)

**Natural gas - production:** 0 cu m (2007 est.)

**Natural gas - consumption:** 0 cu m (2007 est.)

**Natural gas - exports:** 0 cu m (2007 est.)

**Natural gas - imports:** 0 cu m (2007 est.)

**Natural gas - proved reserves:** 0 cu m (1 January 2006 est.)

**Current account balance:** -$1.859 billion (2008 est.)

**Exports:** $4.882 billion f.o.b. (2008 est.)

**Exports - commodities:** tea, horticultural products, coffee, petroleum products, fish, cement

**Exports - partners:** Uganda 16.9%, UK 9.3%, Tanzania 8.2%, Netherlands 8.2%, US 6.4%, Pakistan 5.2% (2007)

**Imports:** $10.77 billion f.o.b. (2008 est.)

**Imports - commodities:** machinery and transportation equipment, petroleum products, motor vehicles, iron and steel, resins and plastics

**Imports - partners:** UAE 11.4%, China 9.9%, India 8.7%, Saudi Arabia 8%, South Africa 6.9%, US 6.2%, Japan 5.9%, UK 4.6% (2007)

**Reserves of foreign exchange and gold:** $2.875 billion (31 December 2008 est.)

**Debt - external:** $6.749 billion (31 December 2008 est.)

**Stock of direct foreign investment - at home:** $2.541 billion (2008 est.)

**Stock of direct foreign investment - abroad:** $47 million (2008 est.)

**Exchange rates:** Kenyan shillings (KES) per US dollar - 68.358 (2008 est.), 68.309 (2007), 72.101 (2006), 75.554 (2005), 79.174 (2004)

## Communications

**Telephones - main lines in use:** 264,800 (2007)

**Telephones - mobile cellular:** 11.44 million (2007)

**Telephone system:**
*general assessment:* inadequate; fixed-line telephone system is small and inefficient; trunks are primarily microwave radio relay; business data commonly transferred by a very small aperture terminal (VSAT) system
*domestic:* no recent growth in fixed-line infrastructure

and the sole provider, Telkom Kenya, is slated for privatization; multiple providers in the mobile-cellular segment of the market fostering a boom in mobile-cellular telephone usage
*international:* country code - 254; satellite earth stations - 4 Intelsat

**Radio broadcast stations:** AM 24, FM 82, shortwave 6 (2008)

**Television broadcast stations:** 8 (2008)

**Internet country code:** .ke

**Internet hosts:** 27,376 (2008)

**Internet users:** 3 million (2007)

## Transportation

**Airports:** 180 (2008)

**Airports - with paved runways:**
*total:* 16
*over 3,047 m:* 4
*2,438 to 3,047 m:* 1
*1,524 to 2,437 m:* 4
*914 to 1,523 m:* 6
*under 914 m:* 1 (2008)

**Airports - with unpaved runways:**
*total:* 164
*1,524 to 2,437 m:* 10
*914 to 1,523 m:* 105
*under 914 m:* 49 (2008)

**Pipelines:** oil 4 km; refined products 928 km (2008)

**Railways:**
*total:* 2,778 km
*narrow gauge:* 2,778 km 1.000-m gauge (2006)

**Roadways:**
*total:* 63,265 km (interurban roads)
*paved:* 8,933 km
*unpaved:* 54,332 km
*note:* there also are 100,000 km of rural roads and 14,500 km of urban roads for a national total of 177,765 km (2004)

**Waterways:** part of Lake Victoria system is within boundaries of Kenya (2007)

**Merchant marine:**
*total:* 1
*by type:* petroleum tanker 1
*registered in other countries:* 6 (Bahamas 1, Comoros 1, Saint Vincent and the Grenadines 2, Tuvalu 1, unknown 1) (2008)

**Ports and terminals:** Mombasa

## Military

**Military branches:** Kenyan Armed Forces: Kenyan Army, Kenyan Navy, Kenyan Air Force (2008)

**Military service age and obligation:** 18 years of age (est.) for voluntary service, with a 9-year obligation (2007)

**Manpower available for military service:**
*males age 16-49:* 9,044,685
*females age 16-49:* 8,805,736 (2008 est.)

**Manpower fit for military service:**
*males age 16-49:* 5,935,480
*females age 16-49:* 5,662,755 (2009 est.)

**Manpower reaching militarily significant age annually:**
*male:* 412,656
*female:* 408,657 (2009 est.)

**Military expenditures:** 2.8% of GDP (2006)

## Transnational Issues

**Disputes - international:** Kenya served as an important mediator in brokering Sudan's north-south separation in February 2005; Kenya provides shelter to almost a quarter of a million refugees, including Ugandans who flee across the border periodically to seek protection from Lord's Resistance Army (LRA) rebels; Kenya works hard to prevent the clan and militia fighting in Somalia from spreading across the border, which has long been open to nomadic pastoralists; the boundary that separates Kenya's and Sudan's sovereignty is unclear in the "Ilemi Triangle," which Kenya has administered since colonial times

**Refugees and internally displaced persons:**
*refugees (country of origin):* 173,702 (Somalia); 73,004 (Sudan); 16,428 (Ethiopia)
*IDPs:* 250,000-400,000 (2007 post-election violence; KANU attacks on opposition tribal groups in 1990s) (2007)

**Illicit drugs:** widespread harvesting of small plots of marijuana; transit country for South Asian heroin destined for Europe and North America; Indian methaqualone also transits on way to South Africa; significant potential for money-laundering activity given the country's status as a regional financial center; massive corruption, and relatively high levels of narcotics-associated activities

## Kingman Reef
*(territory of the US)*

Description under

United States

Pacific Island

Wildlife Refuges

# Kiribati

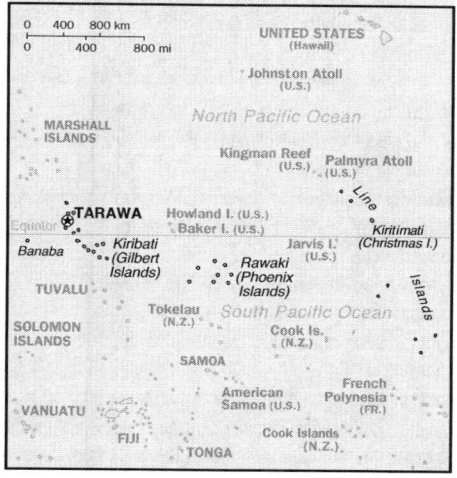

## Introduction

**Background:** The Gilbert Islands became a British protectorate in 1892 and a colony in 1915; they were captured by the Japanese in the Pacific War in 1941. The islands of Makin and Tarawa were the sites of major US amphibious victories over entrenched Japanese garrisons in 1943. The Gilbert Islands were granted self-rule by the UK in 1971 and complete independence in 1979 under the new name of Kiribati. The US relinquished all claims to the sparsely inhabited Phoenix and Line Island groups in a 1979 treaty of friendship with Kiribati.

## Geography

**Location:** Oceania, group of 33 coral atolls in the Pacific Ocean, straddling the Equator; the capital Tarawa is about half way between Hawaii and Australia; note - on 1 January 1995, Kiribati proclaimed that all of its territory was in the same time zone as its Gilbert Islands group (UTC +12) even though the Phoenix Islands and the Line Islands under its jurisdiction were on the other side of the International Date Line
**Geographic coordinates:** 1 25 N, 173 00 E
**Map references:** Oceania
**Area:**
*total:* 811 sq km
*land:* 811 sq km
*water:* 0 sq km
*note:* includes three island groups - Gilbert Islands, Line Islands, Phoenix Islands
**Area - comparative:** four times the size of Washington, DC
**Land boundaries:** 0 km
**Coastline:** 1,143 km
**Maritime claims:**
*territorial sea:* 12 nm
*exclusive economic zone:* 200 nm
**Climate:** tropical; marine, hot and humid, moderated by trade winds

**Terrain:** mostly low-lying coral atolls surrounded by extensive reefs
**Elevation extremes:**
*lowest point:* Pacific Ocean 0 m
*highest point:* unnamed location on Banaba 81 m
**Natural resources:** phosphate (production discontinued in 1979)
**Land use:**
*arable land:* 2.74%
*permanent crops:* 47.95%
*other:* 49.31% (2005)
**Irrigated land:** NA
**Natural hazards:** typhoons can occur any time, but usually November to March; occasional tornadoes; low level of some of the islands make them sensitive to changes in sea level
**Environment - current issues:** heavy pollution in lagoon of south Tarawa atoll due to heavy migration mixed with traditional practices such as lagoon latrines and open-pit dumping; ground water at risk
**Environment - international agreements:**
*party to:* Biodiversity, Climate Change, Climate Change-Kyoto Protocol, Desertification, Hazardous Wastes, Law of the Sea, Marine Dumping, Ozone Layer Protection, Whaling
*signed, but not ratified:* none of the selected agreements
**Geography - note:** 21 of the 33 islands are inhabited; Banaba (Ocean Island) in Kiribati is one of the three great phosphate rock islands in the Pacific Ocean - the others are Makatea in French Polynesia, and Nauru

## People

**Population:** 112,850 (July 2009 est.)
**Age structure:**
*0-14 years:* 37.6% (male 21,488/female 20,899)
*15-64 years:* 59% (male 32,871/female 33,690)
*65 years and over:* 3.5% (male 1,656/female 2,246) (2009 est.)
**Median age:**
*total:* 20.8 years
*male:* 20.3 years
*female:* 21.3 years (2009 est.)
**Population growth rate:** 2.235% (2009 est.)
**Birth rate:** 30.2 births/1,000 population (2009 est.)
**Death rate:** 7.97 deaths/1,000 population (2008 est.)
**Net migration rate:** NA
**Urbanization:**
*urban population:* 44% of total population (2008)
*rate of urbanization:* 1.8% annual rate of change (2005-10 est.)
**Sex ratio:**
*at birth:* 1.05 male(s)/female
*under 15 years:* 1.03 male(s)/female
*15-64 years:* 0.98 male(s)/female
*65 years and over:* 0.74 male(s)/female
*total population:* 0.99 male(s)/female (2009 est.)
**Infant mortality rate:**
*total:* 43.48 deaths/1,000 live births
*male:* 48.35 deaths/1,000 live births
*female:* 38.36 deaths/1,000 live births (2009 est.)

**Life expectancy at birth:**
*total population:* 63.22 years
*male:* 60.14 years
*female:* 66.45 years (2009 est.)
**Total fertility rate:** 4.04 children born/woman (2009 est.)
**HIV/AIDS - adult prevalence rate:** NA
**HIV/AIDS - people living with HIV/AIDS:** NA
**HIV/AIDS - deaths:** NA
**Nationality:**
*noun:* I-Kiribati (singular and plural)
*adjective:* I-Kiribati
**Ethnic groups:** Micronesian 98.8%, other 1.2% (2000 census)
**Religions:** Roman Catholic 52%, Protestant (Congregational) 40%, other (includes Seventh-Day Adventist, Muslim, Baha'i, Latter-day Saints, Church of God) 8% (1999)
**Languages:** I-Kiribati, English (official)
**Literacy:** NA
**School life expectancy (primary to tertiary education):**
*total:* 12 years
*male:* 12 years
*female:* 13 years (2005)
**Education expenditures:** 17.8% of GDP (2002)

## Government

**Country name:**
*conventional long form:* Republic of Kiribati
*conventional short form:* Kiribati
*local long form:* Republic of Kiribati
*local short form:* Kiribati
*note:* pronounced keer-ree-bahss
*former:* Gilbert Islands
**Government type:** republic
**Capital:**
*name:* Tarawa
*geographic coordinates:* 1 19 N, 172 58 E
*time difference:* UTC+12 (17 hours ahead of Washington, DC during Standard Time)
**Administrative divisions:** 3 units; Gilbert Islands, Line Islands, Phoenix Islands; note - in addition, there are 6 districts (Banaba, Central Gilberts, Line Islands, Northern Gilberts, Southern Gilberts, Tarawa) and 21 island councils - one for each of the inhabited islands (Abaiang, Abemama, Aranuka, Arorae, Banaba, Beru, Butaritari, Kanton, Kiritimati, Kuria, Maiana, Makin, Marakei, Nikunau, Nonouti, Onotoa, Tabiteuea, Tabuaeran, Tamana, Tarawa, Teraina)
**Independence:** 12 July 1979 (from the UK)
**National holiday:** Independence Day, 12 July (1979)
**Constitution:** 12 July 1979
**Legal system:** English common law supplemented by local, customary law
**Suffrage:** 18 years of age; universal
**Executive branch:**
*chief of state:* President Anote TONG (since 10 July 2003); Vice President Teima ONORIO; note - the president is both the chief of state and head of government

# Kiribati (continued)

*head of government:* President Anote TONG (since 10 July 2003); Vice President Teima ONORIO

*cabinet:* 12-member cabinet appointed by the president from among the members of the House of Parliament

*elections:* the House of Parliament chooses the presidential candidates from among its members and then those candidates compete in a general election; president is elected by popular vote for a four-year term (eligible for two more terms); election last held 17 October 2007 (next to be held in 2011); vice president appointed by the president

*election results:* Anote TONG 63.7%, Nabuti MWEMWENIKARAWA 32.9%

**Legislative branch:** unicameral House of Parliament or Maneaba Ni Maungatabu (46 seats; 44 members elected by popular vote, 1 ex officio member - the attorney general, 1 nominated by the Rabi Council of Leaders (representing Banaba Island); serve four-year terms)

*elections:* legislative elections were held in two rounds - the first round on 22 August 2007 and the second round on 30 August 2007 (next to be held in 2011)

*election results:* percent of vote by party - NA; seats by party - NA, other 2 (includes attorney general)

**Judicial branch:** Court of Appeal; High Court; 26 Magistrates' courts; judges at all levels are appointed by the president

**Political parties and leaders:** Boutokaan Te Koaua Party or BTK [Taberannang TIMEON]; Maneaban Te Mauri Party or MTM [Teburoro TITO]; Maurin Kiribati Pati or MKP; National Progressive Party or NPP [Dr. Harry TONG]

*note:* there is no tradition of formally organized political parties in Kiribati; they more closely resemble factions or interest groups because they have no party headquarters, formal platforms, or party structures

**Political pressure groups and leaders:** NA

**International organization participation:** ACP, ADB, C, FAO, IBRD, ICAO, ICRM, IDA, IFAD, IFC, IFRCS, ILO, IMF, IMO, IOC, ITU, ITUC, OPCW, PIF, Sparteca, SPC, UN, UNCTAD, UNESCO, UPU, WHO, WMO

**Diplomatic representation in the US:** Kiribati does not have an embassy in the US; there is an honorary consulate in Honolulu

**Diplomatic representation from the US:** the US does not have an embassy in Kiribati; the ambassador to Fiji is accredited to Kiribati

**Flag description:** the upper half is red with a yellow frigate bird flying over a yellow rising sun, and the lower half is blue with three horizontal wavy white stripes to represent the ocean

## Economy

**Economy - overview:** A remote country of 33 scattered coral atolls, Kiribati has few natural resources and is one of the least developed Pacific Islands. Commercially viable phosphate deposits were exhausted at the time of independence from the UK in 1979. Copra and fish now represent the bulk of production and exports. The economy has fluctuated widely in recent years. Economic development is constrained by a shortage of skilled workers, weak infrastructure, and remoteness from international markets. Tourism provides more than one-fifth of GDP. Private sector initiatives and a financial sector are in the early stages of development. Foreign financial aid from the EU, UK, US, Japan, Australia, New Zealand, Canada, UN agencies, and Taiwan accounts for 20-25% of GDP. Remittances from seamen on merchant ships abroad account for more than $5 million each year. Kiribati receives around $15 million annually for the government budget from an Australian trust fund.

**GDP (purchasing power parity):**
$357.4 million (2008 est.)
$344.6 million (2007)
$337.9 million (2006)
*note:* data are in 2008 US dollars

**GDP (official exchange rate):** $71 million (2008 est.)

**GDP - real growth rate:**
3.7% (2008 est.)
2% (2007 est.)
2.4% (2006 est.)

**GDP - per capita (PPP):**
$3,200 (2008 est.)
$3,200 (2007 est.)
$3,200 (2006 est.)
*note:* data are in 2008 US dollars

**GDP - composition by sector:**
*agriculture:* 8.9%
*industry:* 24.2%
*services:* 66.8% (2004)

**Labor force:** 7,870 economically active, not including subsistence farmers (2001 est.)

**Labor force - by occupation:**
*agriculture:* 2.7%
*industry:* 32%
*services:* 65.3% (2000)

**Unemployment rate:**
2% (1992 est.)

**Population below poverty line:** NA%

**Household income or consumption by percentage share:**
*lowest 10%:* NA%
*highest 10%:* NA%

**Budget:**
*revenues:* $55.52 million
*expenditures:* $59.71 million (FY05)

**Inflation rate (consumer prices):**
0.2% (2007 est.)

**Market value of publicly traded shares:** $NA

**Agriculture - products:** copra, taro, breadfruit, sweet potatoes, vegetables; fish

**Industries:** fishing, handicrafts

**Industrial production growth rate:** NA

**Electricity - production:** 10 million kWh (2006 est.)

**Electricity - consumption:** 9.3 million kWh (2006 est.)

**Electricity - exports:** 0 kWh (2007 est.)

**Electricity - imports:** 0 kWh (2007 est.)

**Oil - production:** 0 bbl/day (2007 est.)

**Oil - consumption:** 232.4 bbl/day (2006 est.)

**Oil - exports:** 0 bbl/day (2005)

**Oil - imports:** 259.1 bbl/day (2005)

**Oil - proved reserves:** 0 bbl (1 January 2006 est.)

**Natural gas - production:** 0 cu m (2007 est.)

**Natural gas - consumption:** 0 cu m (2007 est.)

**Natural gas - exports:** 0 cu m (2007 est.)

**Natural gas - imports:** 0 cu m (2007 est.)

**Natural gas - proved reserves:** 0 cu m (1 January 2006 est.)

**Current account balance:** -$21 million (2007 est.)

**Exports:** $17 million f.o.b. (2004 est.)

**Exports - commodities:** copra 62%, coconuts, seaweed, fish

**Imports:** $62 million c.i.f. (2004 est.)

**Imports - commodities:** foodstuffs, machinery and equipment, miscellaneous manufactured goods, fuel

**Debt - external:** $10 million (1999 est.)

**Exchange rates:** Australian dollars (AUD) per US dollar - 1.2059 (2008 est.), 1.2137 (2007), 1.3285 (2006), 1.3095 (2005), 1.3598 (2004)

## Communications

**Telephones - main lines in use:** 4,500 (2002)

**Telephones - mobile cellular:** 700 (2005)

**Telephone system:**
*general assessment:* generally good quality national and international service
*domestic:* wire line service available on Tarawa and Kiritimati (Christmas Island); connections to outer islands by HF/VHF radiotelephone; wireless service available in Tarawa since 1999
*international:* country code - 686; Kiribati is being linked to the Pacific Ocean Cooperative Telecommunications Network, which should improve telephone service; satellite earth station - 1 Intelsat (Pacific Ocean)

**Radio broadcast stations:** AM 1, FM 2, shortwave 1 (may be inactive) (2002)

**Television broadcast stations:** 1 (possibly inactive) (2002)

**Internet country code:** .ki

**Internet hosts:** 9 (2008)

**Internet users:** 2,000 (2007)

## Transportation

**Airports:** 19 (2008)

**Airports - with paved runways:**
*total:* 4
*1,524 to 2,437 m:* 4 (2008)

**Airports - with unpaved runways:**
*total:* 15
*914 to 1,523 m:* 11
*under 914 m:* 4 (2008)

**Roadways:**
*total:* 670 km (2000)

**Waterways:** 5 km (small network of canals in Line Islands) (2007)

**Merchant marine:**

*total:* 43

*by type:* bulk carrier 2, cargo 18, chemical tanker 3, petroleum tanker 6, refrigerated cargo 14

*foreign-owned:* 31 (China 15, Hong Kong 4, South Korea 2, Singapore 4, Taiwan 5, Turkey 1) (2008)

**Ports and terminals:** Betio

## Military

**Military branches:** no regular military forces (constitutionally prohibited); Police Force (2009)

**Manpower available for military service:**

*males age 16-49:* 26,377 (2008 est.)

**Manpower fit for military service:**

*males age 16-49:* 18,129

*females age 16-49:* 20,643 (2009 est.)

**Manpower reaching militarily significant age annually:**

*male:* 1,264

*female:* 1,242 (2009 est.)

**Military expenditures:** NA

**Military - note:** Kiribati does not have military forces; defense assistance is provided by Australia and NZ

## Transnational Issues

**Disputes - international:** none

# Korea, North

## Introduction

**Background:** An independent kingdom for much of its long history, Korea was occupied by Japan beginning in 1905 following the Russo-Japanese War. Five years later, Japan formally annexed the entire peninsula. Following World War II, Korea was split with the northern half coming under Soviet-sponsored Communist control. After failing in the Korean War (1950-53) to conquer the US-backed Republic of Korea (ROK) in the southern portion by force, North Korea (DPRK), under its founder President KIM Il Sung, adopted a policy of ostensible diplomatic and economic "self-reliance" as a check against outside influence. The DPRK demonized the US as the ultimate threat to its social system through state-funded propaganda, and molded political, economic, and military policies around the core ideological objective of eventual unification of Korea under Pyongyang's control. KIM's son, the current ruler KIM Jong Il, was officially designated as his father's successor in 1980, assuming a growing political and managerial role until the elder KIM's death in 1994. After decades of economic mismanagement and resource misallocation, the DPRK since the mid-1990s has relied heavily on international aid to feed its population. North Korea's history of regional military provocations, proliferation of military-related items, long-range missile development, WMD programs including nuclear weapons test in 2006 and 2009, and massive conventional armed forces are of major concern to the international community.

## Geography

**Location:** Eastern Asia, northern half of the Korean Peninsula bordering the Korea Bay and the Sea of Japan, between China and South Korea

**Geographic coordinates:** 40 00 N, 127 00 E

**Map references:** Asia

**Area:**

*total:* 120,540 sq km

*land:* 120,410 sq km

*water:* 130 sq km

**Area - comparative:** slightly smaller than Mississippi

**Land boundaries:**

*total:* 1,673 km

*border countries:* China 1,416 km, South Korea 238 km, Russia 19 km

**Coastline:** 2,495 km

**Maritime claims:**

*territorial sea:* 12 nm

*exclusive economic zone:* 200 nm

*note:* military boundary line 50 nm in the Sea of Japan and the exclusive economic zone limit in the Yellow Sea where all foreign vessels and aircraft without permission are banned

**Climate:** temperate with rainfall concentrated in summer

**Terrain:** mostly hills and mountains separated by deep, narrow valleys; coastal plains wide in west, discontinuous in east

**Elevation extremes:**

*lowest point:* Sea of Japan 0 m

*highest point:* Paektu-san 2,744 m

**Natural resources:** coal, lead, tungsten, zinc, graphite, magnesite, iron ore, copper, gold, pyrites, salt, fluorspar, hydropower

**Land use:**

*arable land:* 22.4%

*permanent crops:* 1.66%

*other:* 75.94% (2005)

**Irrigated land:** 14,600 sq km (2003)

**Total renewable water resources:** 77.1 cu km (1999)

**Freshwater withdrawal (domestic/industrial/ agricultural):**

*total:* 9.02 cu km/yr (20%/25%/55%)

*per capita:* 401 cu m/yr (2000)

**Natural hazards:** late spring droughts often followed by severe flooding; occasional typhoons during the early fall

**Environment - current issues:** water pollution; inadequate supplies of potable water; waterborne disease; deforestation; soil erosion and degradation

**Environment - international agreements:**

*party to:* Antarctic Treaty, Biodiversity, Climate Change, Climate Change-Kyoto Protocol, Desertification, Environmental Modification, Hazardous Wastes, Ozone Layer Protection, Ship Pollution

*signed, but not ratified:* Law of the Sea

**Geography - note:** strategic location bordering China, South Korea, and Russia; mountainous interior is isolated and sparsely populated

# Korea, North *(continued)*

## People

**Population:** 22,665,345 (July 2009 est.)
**Age structure:**
*0-14 years:* 21.3% (male 2,440,439/female 2,376,557)
*15-64 years:* 69.4% (male 7,776,889/female 7,945,399)
*65 years and over:* 9.4% (male 820,504/female 1,305,557) (2009 est.)
**Median age:**
*total:* 33.5 years
*male:* 32.1 years
*female:* 34.9 years (2009 est.)
**Population growth rate:** 0.42% (2009 est.)
**Birth rate:** 14.82 births/1,000 population (2009 est.)
**Death rate:** 7.29 deaths/1,000 population (2008 est.)
**Net migration rate:** -0.09 migrant(s)/1,000 population (2009 est.)
**Urbanization:**
*urban population:* 63% of total population (2008)
*rate of urbanization:* 0.9% annual rate of change (2005-10 est.)
**Sex ratio:**
*at birth:* 1.06 male(s)/female
*under 15 years:* 1.03 male(s)/female
*15-64 years:* 0.98 male(s)/female
*65 years and over:* 0.63 male(s)/female
*total population:* 0.95 male(s)/female (2009 est.)
**Infant mortality rate:**
*total:* 51.34 deaths/1,000 live births
*male:* 58.64 deaths/1,000 live births
*female:* 43.6 deaths/1,000 live births (2009 est.)
**Life expectancy at birth:**
*total population:* 63.81 years
*male:* 61.23 years
*female:* 66.53 years (2009 est.)
**Total fertility rate:** 1.96 children born/woman (2009 est.)
**HIV/AIDS - adult prevalence rate:** NA
**HIV/AIDS - people living with HIV/AIDS:** NA
**HIV/AIDS - deaths:** NA
**Nationality:**
*noun:* Korean(s)
*adjective:* Korean
**Ethnic groups:** racially homogeneous; there is a small Chinese community and a few ethnic Japanese
**Religions:** traditionally Buddhist and Confucianist, some Christian and syncretic Chondogyo (Religion of the Heavenly Way)
*note:* autonomous religious activities now almost nonexistent; government-sponsored religious groups exist to provide illusion of religious freedom
**Languages:** Korean
**Literacy:**
*definition:* age 15 and over can read and write
*total population:* 99%
*male:* 99%
*female:* 99%
**Education expenditures:** NA

## Government

**Country name:**
*conventional long form:* Democratic People's Republic of Korea
*conventional short form:* North Korea
*local long form:* Choson-minjujuui-inmin-konghwaguk
*local short form:* Choson
*abbreviation:* DPRK
**Government type:** Communist state one-man dictatorship
**Capital:**
*name:* Pyongyang
*geographic coordinates:* 39 01 N, 125 45 E
*time difference:* UTC+9 (14 hours ahead of Washington, DC during Standard Time)
**Administrative divisions:** 9 provinces (do, singular and plural) and 4 municipalities* (si, singular and plural); Chagang-do (Chagang), Hamgyong-bukto (North Hamgyong), Hamgyong-namdo (South Hamgyong), Hwanghae-bukto (North Hwanghae), Hwanghae-namdo (South Hwanghae), Kaesong-si (Kaesong)*, Kangwon-do (Kangwon), Najin Sonbong-si (Najin-Sonbong)*, Namp'o-si (Namp'o)*, P'yongan-bukto (North P'yongan), P'yongan-namdo (South P'yongan), P'yongyang-si (Pyongyang)*, Yanggang-do (Yanggang)
**Independence:** 15 August 1945 (from Japan)
**National holiday:** Founding of the Democratic People's Republic of Korea (DPRK), 9 September (1948)
**Constitution:** adopted 1948; completely revised 27 December 1972, revised again in April 1992, and September 1998
**Legal system:** based on Prussian civil law system with Japanese influences and Communist legal theory; no judicial review of legislative acts; has not accepted compulsory ICJ jurisdiction
**Suffrage:** 17 years of age; universal
**Executive branch:**
*chief of state:* KIM Jong Il (since July 1994); note - on 9 April 2009, rubberstamp Supreme People's Assembly (SPA) reelected KIM Jong Il chairman of the National Defense Commission, a position accorded nation's "highest administrative authority"; SPA reelected KIM Yong Nam in 2003 president of its Presidium also with responsibility of representing state and receiving diplomatic credentials
*head of government:* Premier KIM Yong Il (since 11 April 2007); Vice Premier KWAK Pom Gi (since 5 September 1998), Vice Premier O Su Yong (since 13 April 2009), Vice Premier RO Tu Chol (since 3 September 2003), Vice Premier THAE Jong Su (since 16 October 2007)
*cabinet:* Naegak (cabinet) members, except for Minister of People's Armed Forces, are appointed by SPA
*elections:* last held in September 2003; date of next election NA
*election results:* KIM Jong Il and KIM Yong Nam were only nominees for positions and ran unopposed

**Legislative branch:** unicameral Supreme People's Assembly or Ch'oego Inmin Hoeui (687 seats; members elected by popular vote to serve five-year terms)
*elections:* last held 8 March 2009 (next due to be held in March 2014)
*election results:* percent of vote by party - NA; seats by party - NA; ruling party approves a list of candidates who are elected without opposition; a token number of seats are reserved for minor parties
**Judicial branch:** Central Court (judges are elected by the Supreme People's Assembly)
**Political parties and leaders:** major party - Korean Workers' Party or KWP [KIM Jong Il]; minor parties - Chondoist Chongu Party [RYU Mi Yong] (under KWP control), Social Democratic Party [KIM Yong Dae] (under KWP control)
**Political pressure groups and leaders:** none
**International organization participation:** ARF, FAO, G-77, ICAO, ICRM, IFAD, IFRCS, IHO, IMO, IOC, IPU, ISO, ITSO, ITU, NAM, UN, UNCTAD, UNESCO, UNIDO, UNWTO, UPU, WFTU, WHO, WIPO, WMO
**Diplomatic representation in the US:** none; North Korea has a Permanent Mission to the UN in New York
**Diplomatic representation from the US:** none; note - Swedish Embassy in Pyongyang represents the US as consular protecting power
**Flag description:** three horizontal bands of blue (top), red (triple width), and blue; the red band is edged in white; on the hoist side of the red band is a white disk with a red five-pointed star

## Economy

**Economy - overview:** North Korea, one of the world's most centrally directed and least open economies, faces chronic economic problems. Industrial capital stock is nearly beyond repair as a result of years of underinvestment and shortages of spare parts. Large-scale military spending draws off resources needed for investment and civilian consumption. Industrial and power output have declined in parallel from pre-1990 levels. Severe flooding in the summer of 2007 aggravated chronic food shortages caused by on-going systemic problems including a lack of arable land, collective farming practices, and persistent shortages of tractors and fuel. Large-scale international food aid deliveries have allowed the people of North Korea to escape widespread starvation since famine threatened in 1995, but the population continues to suffer from prolonged malnutrition and poor living conditions. Since 2002, the government has allowed private "farmers' markets" to begin selling a wider range of goods. It also permitted some private farming - on an experimental basis - in an effort to boost agricultural output. In October 2005, the government tried to reverse some of these policies by forbidding private sales of grains and reinstituting a centralized food rationing system. By December 2005, the government terminated most international humanitarian assistance operations in North Korea (calling instead for developmental assistance only) and restricted the activities of remaining international and non-governmental aid organizations such as the World Food Program. External food aid now comes primarily from China and South Korea in the form of grants and long-term concessional loans. In May 2008, the US agreed to give 500,000 metric tons of food to North Korea via the World Food Program and US nongovernmental organizations; Pyongyang began receiving these shipments in mid-2008. During the October 2007 summit, South Korea also agreed to develop some of North Korea's infrastructure, natural resources, and light industry, but inter-Korean economic cooperation slowed in 2008 as Pyongyang restricted tourism and manufacturing joint ventures in the North, and food aid from South Korea was suspended. Firm political control remains the Communist government's overriding concern, which will likely inhibit the loosening of economic regulations.

**GDP (purchasing power parity):**
$40 billion (2008 est.)
*note:* North Korea does not publish any reliable National Income Accounts data; the datum shown here is derived from purchasing power parity (PPP) GDP estimates for North Korea that were made by Angus MADDISON in a study conducted for the OECD; his figure for 1999 was extrapolated to 2008 using estimated real growth rates for North Korea's GDP and an inflation factor based on the US GDP deflator; the result was rounded to the nearest $10 billion.
*note:* data are in 2008 US dollars
**GDP (official exchange rate):** $26.2 billion (2008 est.)
**GDP - real growth rate:**
-2.3% (2008 est.)
**GDP - per capita (PPP):**
$1,700 (2008 est.)
*note:* data are in 2008 US dollars
**GDP - composition by sector:**
*agriculture:* 23.3%
*industry:* 43.1%
*services:* 33.6% (2002 est.)
**Labor force:** 20 million
*note:* estimates vary widely (2004 est.)
**Labor force - by occupation:**
*agriculture:* 37%
*industry and services:* 63% (2004 est.)
**Unemployment rate:**
NA%
**Population below poverty line:** NA%
**Household income or consumption by percentage share:**
*lowest 10%:* NA%
*highest 10%:* NA%
**Budget:**
*revenues:* $2.88 billion
*expenditures:* $2.98 billion (2005)

**Inflation rate (consumer prices):**
NA%
**Agriculture - products:** rice, corn, potatoes, soybeans, pulses; cattle, pigs, pork, eggs
**Industries:** military products; machine building, electric power, chemicals; mining (coal, iron ore, limestone, magnesite, graphite, copper, zinc, lead, and precious metals), metallurgy; textiles, food processing; tourism
**Industrial production growth rate:** NA%
**Electricity - production:** 21.72 billion kWh (2007 est.)
**Electricity - consumption:** 18.18 billion kWh (2006 est.)
**Electricity - exports:** 0 kWh (2007 est.)
**Electricity - imports:** 0 kWh (2007 est.)
**Oil - production:** 141 bbl/day (2007 est.)
**Oil - consumption:** 24,000 bbl/day (2006 est.)
**Oil - exports:** 0 bbl/day (2006)
**Oil - imports:** 10,520 bbl/day (2007 est.)
**Oil - proved reserves:** NA bbl
**Natural gas - production:** 0 cu m (2007 est.)
**Natural gas - consumption:** 0 cu m (2007 est.)
**Natural gas - exports:** 0 cu m (2007 est.)
**Natural gas - imports:** 0 cu m (2007 est.)
**Natural gas - proved reserves:** 0 cu m (1 January 2007)
**Exports:** $1.684 billion f.o.b. (2007)
**Exports - commodities:** minerals, metallurgical products, manufactures (including armaments), textiles, agricultural and fishery products
**Exports - partners:** South Korea 45%, China 35%, Thailand 5% (2007)
**Imports:** $3.055 billion c.i.f. (2007)
**Imports - commodities:** petroleum, coking coal, machinery and equipment, textiles, grain
**Imports - partners:** China 27%, South Korea 16%, Thailand 9%, Russia 7% (2006)
**Debt - external:** $12.5 billion (2001 est.)
**Exchange rates:** North Korean won (KPW) per US dollar - 140 (2007), 141 (2006), 170 (December 2004), market rate: North Korean won per US dollar - 3,400 (October 2008)

## Communications

**Telephones - main lines in use:** 1.18 million (2007)
**Telephone system:**
*general assessment:* inadequate system; currently mobile cellular telephone services are available in Pyongyang only
*domestic:* fiber-optic links installed between cities; telephone directories unavailable; mobile cellular service, initiated in 2002, suspended in 2004; Orascom Telecom, an Egyptian company, launched mobile service on December 15, 2008 for the Pyongyang area only
*international:* country code - 850; satellite earth stations - 2 (1 Intelsat - Indian Ocean, 1 Russian - Indian Ocean region); other international connections through Moscow and Beijing (2008)

**Radio broadcast stations:** AM 17 (including 11 stations of Korean Central Broadcasting Station; North Korea has a "national intercom" cable radio station wired throughout the country that is a significant source of information for the average North Korean citizen; it is wired into most residences and workplaces and carries news and commentary), FM 14, shortwave 14 (2006)
**Television broadcast stations:** 4 (includes Korean Central Television, Mansudae Television, Korean Educational and Cultural Network, and Kaesong Television targeting South Korea) (2003)
**Internet country code:** .kp
**Internet users:** NA

## Transportation

**Airports:** 78 (2008)
**Airports - with paved runways:**
*total:* 36
*over 3,047 m:* 2
*2,438 to 3,047 m:* 22
*1,524 to 2,437 m:* 8
*914 to 1,523 m:* 1
*under 914 m:* 3 (2008)
**Airports - with unpaved runways:**
*total:* 42
*2,438 to 3,047 m:* 3
*1,524 to 2,437 m:* 17
*914 to 1,523 m:* 14
*under 914 m:* 8 (2008)
**Heliports:** 23 (2007)
**Pipelines:** oil 154 km (2008)
**Railways:**
*total:* 5,235 km
*standard gauge:* 5,235 km 1.435-m gauge (3,500 km electrified) (2006)
**Roadways:**
*total:* 25,554 km
*paved:* 724 km
*unpaved:* 24,830 km (2006)
**Waterways:** 2,250 km (most navigable only by small craft) (2008)
**Merchant marine:**
*total:* 167
*by type:* bulk carrier 11, cargo 121, carrier 1, chemical tanker 4, container 3, passenger/cargo 3, petroleum tanker 19, refrigerated cargo 4, roll on/roll off 1
*foreign-owned:* 19 (Egypt 1, Greece 1, Lebanon 1, Lithuania 1, Romania 4, Syria 1, UAE 8, Yemen 2)
*registered in other countries:* 2 (Mongolia 1, Panama 1) (2008)
**Ports and terminals:** Ch'ongjin, Haeju, Hungnam (Hamhung), Kimch'aek, Kosong, Najin, Namp'o, Sinuiju, Songnim, Sonbong (formerly Unggi), Ungsang, Wonsan

## Military

**Military branches:** North Korean People's Army: Ground Forces, Navy, Air Force; civil security forces (2005)

**Military service age and obligation:** 17 years of age (2004)

**Manpower available for military service:**
*males age 16-49:* 6,225,747
*females age 16-49:* 6,188,270 (2008 est.)

**Manpower fit for military service:**
*males age 16-49:* 4,104,964
*females age 16-49:* 4,492,374 (2009 est.)

**Manpower reaching militarily significant age annually:**
*male:* 191,759
*female:* 184,641 (2009 est.)

**Military expenditures:** NA

## Transnational Issues

**Disputes - international:** risking arrest, imprisonment, and deportation, tens of thousands of North Koreans cross into China to escape famine, economic privation, and political oppression; North Korea and China dispute the sovereignty of certain islands in Yalu and Tumen rivers; Military Demarcation Line within the 4-km wide Demilitarized Zone has separated North from South Korea since 1953; periodic incidents in the Yellow Sea with South Korea which claims the Northern Limiting Line as a maritime boundary; North Korea supports South Korea in rejecting Japan's claim to Liancourt Rocks (Tok-do/Take-shima)

**Refugees and internally displaced persons:**
*IDPs:* undetermined (flooding in mid-2007 and famine during mid-1990s) (2007)

**Trafficking in persons:**
*current situation:* North Korea is a source country for men, women, and children trafficked for the purposes of forced labor and commercial sexual exploitation; the most common form of trafficking involves North Korean women and girls who cross the border into China voluntarily; additionally, North Korean women and girls are lured out of North Korea to escape poor social and economic conditions by the promise of food, jobs, and freedom, only to be forced into prostitution, marriage, or exploitative labor arrangements once in China
*tier rating:* Tier 3 - North Korea does not fully comply with minimum standards for the elimination of trafficking and is not making significant efforts to do so; the government does not acknowledge the existence of human rights abuses in the country or recognize trafficking, either within the country or transnationally; North Korea has not ratified the 2000 UN TIP Protocol (2008)

**Illicit drugs:** for years, from the 1970s into the 2000s, citizens of the Democratic People's Republic of (North) Korea (DPRK), many of them diplomatic employees of the government, were apprehended abroad while trafficking in narcotics, including two in Turkey in December 2004; police investigations in Taiwan and Japan in recent years have linked North Korea to large illicit shipments of heroin and methamphetamine, including an attempt by the North Korean merchant ship Pong Su to deliver 150 kg of heroin to Australia in April 2003

# Korea, South

## Introduction

**Background:** An independent Korean state or collection of states has existed almost continuously for several millennia. Between its initial unification in the 7th century - from three predecessor Korean states - until the 20th century, Korea existed as a single independent country. In 1905, following the Russo-Japanese War, Korea became a protectorate of imperial Japan, and in 1910 it was annexed as a colony. Korea regained its independence following Japan's surrender to the United States in 1945. After World War II, a Republic of Korea (ROK) was set up in the southern half of the Korean Peninsula while a Communist-style government was installed in the north (the DPRK). During the Korean War (1950-53), US troops and UN forces fought alongside soldiers from the ROK to defend South Korea from DPRK attacks supported by China and the Soviet Union. An armistice was signed in 1953, splitting the peninsula along a demilitarized zone at about the 38th parallel. Thereafter, South Korea achieved rapid economic growth with per capita income rising to roughly 14 times the level of North Korea. In 1993, KIM Young-sam became South Korea's first civilian president following 32 years of military rule. South Korea today is a fully functioning modern democracy. In June 2000, a historic first North-South summit took place between the South's President KIM Dae-jung and the North's leader KIM Jong Il. In October 2007, a second North-South summit took place between the South's President ROH Moo-hyun and the North Korean leader. Harsh rhetoric and unwillingness by North Korea to engage with President LEE Myung-bak following his February 2008 inauguration has strained inter-Korean relations.

## Geography

**Location:** Eastern Asia, southern half of the Korean Peninsula bordering the Sea of Japan and the Yellow Sea

**Geographic coordinates:** 37 00 N, 127 30 E

**Map references:** Asia

**Area:**
*total:* 98,480 sq km
*land:* 98,190 sq km
*water:* 290 sq km

**Area - comparative:** slightly larger than Indiana

**Land boundaries:**
*total:* 238 km
*border countries:* North Korea 238 km

**Coastline:** 2,413 km

**Maritime claims:**
*territorial sea:* 12 nm; between 3 nm and 12 nm in the Korea Strait
*contiguous zone:* 24 nm
*exclusive economic zone:* 200 nm
*continental shelf:* not specified

**Climate:** temperate, with rainfall heavier in summer than winter

**Terrain:** mostly hills and mountains; wide coastal plains in west and south

**Elevation extremes:**
*lowest point:* Sea of Japan 0 m
*highest point:* Halla-san 1,950 m

**Natural resources:** coal, tungsten, graphite, molybdenum, lead, hydropower potential

**Land use:**
*arable land:* 16.58%
*permanent crops:* 2.01%
*other:* 81.41% (2005)

**Irrigated land:** 8,780 sq km (2003)

**Total renewable water resources:** 69.7 cu km (1999)

**Freshwater withdrawal (domestic/industrial/agricultural):**
*total:* 18.59 cu km/yr (36%/16%/48%)
*per capita:* 389 cu m/yr (2000)

**Natural hazards:** occasional typhoons bring high winds and floods; low-level seismic activity common in southwest

**Environment - current issues:** air pollution in large cities; acid rain; water pollution from the discharge of sewage and industrial effluents; drift net fishing

**Environment - international agreements:**
*party to:* Antarctic-Environmental Protocol, Antarctic-Marine Living Resources, Antarctic Treaty, Biodiversity, Climate Change, Climate Change-Kyoto Protocol, Desertification, Endangered Species, Environmental Modification, Hazardous Wastes, Law of the Sea, Marine Dumping, Ozone Layer Protection, Ship Pollution, Tropical Timber 83, Tropical Timber 94, Wetlands, Whaling
*signed, but not ratified:* none of the selected agreements

**Geography - note:** strategic location on Korea Strait

# Korea, South *(continued)*

## People

**Population:** 48,508,972 (July 2009 est.)
**Age structure:**
*0-14 years:* 16.8% (male 4,278,581/female 3,887,516)
*15-64 years:* 72.3% (male 17,897,053/female 17,196,840)
*65 years and over:* 10.8% (male 2,104,589/female 3,144,393) (2009 est.)
**Median age:**
*total:* 37.3 years
*male:* 36 years
*female:* 38.5 years (2009 est.)
**Population growth rate:** 0.266% (2009 est.)
**Birth rate:** 8.93 births/1,000 population (2009 est.)
**Death rate:** 5.73 deaths/1,000 population (2008 est.)
**Net migration rate:** -0.33 migrant(s)/1,000 population (2009 est.)
**Urbanization:**
*urban population:* 81% of total population (2008)
*rate of urbanization:* 0.6% annual rate of change (2005-10 est.)
**Sex ratio:**
*at birth:* 1.07 male(s)/female
*under 15 years:* 1.1 male(s)/female
*15-64 years:* 1.04 male(s)/female
*65 years and over:* 0.67 male(s)/female
*total population:* 1 male(s)/female (2009 est.)
**Infant mortality rate:**
*total:* 4.26 deaths/1,000 live births
*male:* 4.49 deaths/1,000 live births
*female:* 4.02 deaths/1,000 live births (2009 est.)
**Life expectancy at birth:**
*total population:* 78.72 years
*male:* 75.45 years
*female:* 82.22 years (2009 est.)
**Total fertility rate:** 1.21 children born/woman (2009 est.)
**HIV/AIDS - adult prevalence rate:** less than 0.1% (2007 est.)
**HIV/AIDS - people living with HIV/AIDS:** 13,000 (2007 est.)
**HIV/AIDS - deaths:** fewer than 500 (2007 est.)
**Nationality:**
*noun:* Korean(s)
*adjective:* Korean
**Ethnic groups:** homogeneous (except for about 20,000 Chinese)
**Religions:** Christian 26.3% (Protestant 19.7%, Roman Catholic 6.6%), Buddhist 23.2%, other or unknown 1.3%, none 49.3% (1995 census)
**Languages:** Korean, English widely taught in junior high and high school
**Literacy:**
*definition:* age 15 and over can read and write
*total population:* 97.9%
*male:* 99.2%
*female:* 96.6% (2002)

**School life expectancy (primary to tertiary education):**
*total:* 17 years
*male:* 18 years
*female:* 15 years (2007)
**Education expenditures:** 4.6% of GDP (2004)

## Government

**Country name:**
*conventional long form:* Republic of Korea
*conventional short form:* South Korea
*local long form:* Taehan-min'guk
*local short form:* Han'guk
*abbreviation:* ROK
**Government type:** republic
**Capital:**
*name:* Seoul
*geographic coordinates:* 37 33 N, 126 59 E
*time difference:* UTC+9 (14 hours ahead of Washington, DC during Standard Time)
**Administrative divisions:** 9 provinces (do, singular and plural) and 7 metropolitan cities* (gwangyoksi, singular and plural); Cheju-do, Cholla-bukto (North Cholla), Cholla-namdo (South Cholla), Ch'ungch'ong-bukto (North Ch'ungch'ong), Ch'ungch'ong-namdo (South Ch'ungch'ong), Inch'on-gwangyoksi (Inch'on)*, Kangwon-do, Kwangju-gwangyoksi (Kwangju)*, Kyonggi-do, Kyongsang-bukto (North Kyongsang), Kyongsang-namdo (South Kyongsang), Pusan-gwangyoksi (Pusan)*, Soul-t'ukpyolsi (Seoul)*, Taegu-gwangyoksi (Taegu)*, Taejon-gwangyoksi (Taejon)*, Ulsan-gwangyoksi (Ulsan)*
**Independence:** 15 August 1945 (from Japan)
**National holiday:** Liberation Day, 15 August (1945)
**Constitution:** 17 July 1948; note - amended or rewritten nine times; current constitution approved on 29 October 1987
**Legal system:** combines elements of continental European civil law systems, Anglo-American law, and Chinese classical thought; has not accepted compulsory ICJ jurisdiction
**Suffrage:** 19 years of age; universal
**Executive branch:**
*chief of state:* President LEE Myung-bak (since 25 February 2008)
*head of government:* Prime Minister HAN Seung-soo (since 29 February 2008)
*cabinet:* State Council appointed by the president on the prime minister's recommendation
*elections:* president elected by popular vote for a single five-year term; election last held 19 December 2007 (next to be held in December 2012); prime minister appointed by president with consent of National Assembly
*election results:* LEE Myung-bak elected president on 19 December 2007; percent of vote - LEE Myung-bak (GNP) 48.7%; CHUNG Dong-young (UNDP) 26.1%); LEE Hoi-chang (independent) 15.1; others 10.1%

**Legislative branch:** unicameral National Assembly or Kukhoe (299 seats; 243 members elected in single-seat constituencies, 56 elected by proportional representation; to serve four-year terms)
*elections:* last held 9 April 2008 (next to be held in April 2012)
*election results:* percent of vote by party - NA; seats by party - GNP 172, UDP 83, LFP 20, Pro-Park Alliance 8, DLP 5, CKP 1, independents 9
**Judicial branch:** Supreme Court (justices appointed by the president with consent of National Assembly); Constitutional Court (justices appointed by the president based partly on nominations by National Assembly and Chief Justice of the court)
**Political parties and leaders:** Democratic Party or DP [CHUNG Sye-kyun] (formerly the United Democratic Party or UDP); Democratic Labor Party or DLP [KANG Ki-kabi]; Grand National Party or GNP [KANG Jae-sup]; Liberty Forward Party or LFP [LEE Hoi-chang]; Pro-Park Alliance or PPA [SUH Choung-won]; Renewal Korea Party or RKP [MOON Kook-hyun]
**Political pressure groups and leaders:** Federation of Korean Industries; Federation of Korean Trade Unions; Korean Confederation of Trade Unions; Korean National Council of Churches; Korean Traders Association; Korean Veterans' Association; National Council of Labor Unions; National Democratic Alliance of Korea; National Federation of Farmers' Associations; National Federation of Student Associations
**International organization participation:** ADB, AfDB (nonregional member), APEC, APT, ARF, ASEAN (dialogue partner), Australia Group, BIS, CP, EAS, EBRD, FAO, G-20, IADB, IAEA, IBRD, ICAO, ICC, ICCt, ICRM, IDA, IEA, IFAD, IFC, IFRCS, IHO, ILO, IMF, IMO, IMSO, Interpol, IOC, IOM, IPU, ISO, ITSO, ITU, ITUC, LAIA, MIGA, NEA, NSG, OAS (observer), OECD, OPCW, OSCE (partner), PCA, PIF (partner), SAARC (observer), UN, UNCTAD, UNESCO, UNHCR, UNIDO, UNIFIL, UNMIL, UNMIS, UNMOGIP, UNOMIG, UNWTO, UPU, WCL, WCO, WFTU, WHO, WIPO, WMO, WTO, ZC
**Diplomatic representation in the US:**
*chief of mission:* Ambassador HAN Duck-soo
*chancery:* 2450 Massachusetts Avenue NW, Washington, DC 20008
*telephone:* [1] (202) 939-5600
*FAX:* [1] (202) 387-0205
*consulate(s) general:* Agana (Guam), Atlanta, Boston, Chicago, Honolulu, Houston, Los Angeles, New York, San Francisco, Seattle
**Diplomatic representation from the US:**
*chief of mission:* Ambassador Kathleen STEPHENS
*embassy:* 32 Sejongno, Jongno-gu, Seoul 110-710
*mailing address:* US Embassy Seoul, APO AP 96205-5550
*telephone:* [82] (2) 397-4114
*FAX:* [82] (2) 738-8845
**Flag description:** white with a red (top) and blue yin-yang symbol in the center; there is a different black trigram from the ancient I Ching (Book of Changes) in each corner of the white field

## Economy

**Economy - overview:** Since the 1960s, South Korea has achieved an incredible record of growth and integration into the high-tech modern world economy. Four decades ago, GDP per capita was comparable with levels in the poorer countries of Africa and Asia. In 2004, South Korea joined the trillion dollar club of world economies. In 2008, its GDP per capita was roughly the same as that of the Czech Republic and New Zealand. Initially, this success was achieved by a system of close government/business ties including directed credit, import restrictions, sponsorship of specific industries, and a strong labor effort. The government promoted the import of raw materials and technology at the expense of consumer goods and encouraged savings and investment over consumption. The Asian financial crisis of 1997-98 exposed longstanding weaknesses in South Korea's development model including high debt/equity ratios, massive foreign borrowing, and an undisciplined financial sector. GDP plunged by 6.9% in 1998, then recovered by 9% in 1999-2000. Korea adopted numerous economic reforms following the crisis, including greater openness to foreign investment and imports. Growth fell back to 3.3% in 2001 because of the slowing global economy, falling exports, and the perception that much-needed corporate and financial reforms had stalled. Led by consumer spending and exports, growth in 2002 was an impressive 7% despite anemic global growth. Between 2003 and 2007, growth moderated to about 4-5% annually. A downturn in consumer spending was offset by rapid export growth. In 2008, inflation increased in the face of rising oil and food prices before easing in the fourth quarter. Korea was hit hard by the global financial turmoil that began in September 2008. Stock prices fell by more than 40% for the year and the value of the won fell by approximately 26%. Korean GDP shrank in the fourth quarter and GDP growth for the year was just 2.5%. The Korean government adopted several measures to combat the credit crunch and stimulate the economy.

**GDP (purchasing power parity):**
$1.278 trillion (2008 est.)
$1.247 trillion (2007)
$1.173 trillion (2006)
*note:* data are in 2008 US dollars

**GDP (official exchange rate):** $857.5 billion (2008 est.)

**GDP - real growth rate:**
2.5% (2008 est.)
5% (2007 est.)
5.1% (2006 est.)

**GDP - per capita (PPP):**
$26,000 (2008 est.)
$25,500 (2007 est.)
$24,400 (2006 est.)
*note:* data are in 2008 US dollars

**GDP - composition by sector:**
*agriculture:* 3%
*industry:* 39.5%
*services:* 57.6% (2008 est.)

**Labor force:** 24.35 million (2008 est.)

**Labor force - by occupation:**
*agriculture:* 7.2%
*industry:* 25.1%
*services:* 67.7% (2007)

**Unemployment rate:**
3.2% (2008 est.)
3.3% (2007 est.)

**Population below poverty line:** 15% (2003 est.)

**Household income or consumption by percentage share:**
*lowest 10%:* 2.7%
*highest 10%:* 24.2% (2007)

**Distribution of family income - Gini index:** 31.3 (2007)

**Investment (gross fixed):** 27.1% of GDP (2008 est.)

**Budget:**
*revenues:* $232.2 billion
*expenditures:* $222.9 billion (2008 est.)

**Public debt:** 32.7% of GDP (2008 est.)

**Inflation rate (consumer prices):**
4.7% (2008 est.)
2.5% (2007 est.)

**Central bank discount rate:** 3% (31 December 2008)

**Commercial bank prime lending rate:** 7% (31 December 2008)

**Stock of money:** $80.66 billion (31 December 2008)

**Stock of quasi money:** $478 billion (31 December 2008)

**Stock of domestic credit:** $937 billion (31 December 2008)

**Market value of publicly traded shares:** $623 billion (31 December 2008)

**Agriculture - products:** rice, root crops, barley, vegetables, fruit; cattle, pigs, chickens, milk, eggs; fish

**Industries:** electronics, telecommunications, automobile production, chemicals, shipbuilding, steel

**Industrial production growth rate:** 4.5% (2008 est.)

**Electricity - production:** 440 billion kWh (2008 est.)

**Electricity - consumption:** 385.1 billion kWh (2008 est.)

**Electricity - exports:** 0 kWh (2008 est.)

**Electricity - imports:** 0 kWh (2008 est.)

**Oil - production:** 20,970 bbl/day (2007 est.)

**Oil - consumption:** 2.08 million bbl/day (2008 est.)

**Oil - exports:** 910,000 bbl/day
*note:* exports consist of oil derivatives (gasoline, light oil, and diesel), not crude oil (2008 est.)

**Oil - imports:** 2.37 million bbl/day (2008)

**Oil - proved reserves:** NA bbl

**Natural gas - production:** 640 million cu m (2007 est.)

**Natural gas - consumption:** 37 billion cu m (2007 est.)

**Natural gas - exports:** 0 cu m (2007 est.)

**Natural gas - imports:** 34.4 billion cu m (2007 est.)

**Natural gas - proved reserves:** 50 billion cu m (1 January 2008 est.)

**Current account balance:** -$6.41 billion (2008)

**Exports:** $419 billion f.o.b. (2008)

**Exports - commodities:** semiconductors, wireless telecommunications equipment, motor vehicles, computers, steel, ships, petrochemicals

**Exports - partners:** China 22.1%, US 12.4%, Japan 7.1%, Hong Kong 5% (2007)

**Imports:** $435 billion f.o.b. (2008 est.)

**Imports - commodities:** machinery, electronics and electronic equipment, oil, steel, transport equipment, organic chemicals, plastics

**Imports - partners:** China 17.7%, Japan 15.8%, US 10.5%, Saudi Arabia 5.9% (2007)

**Reserves of foreign exchange and gold:** $201.2 billion (31 December 2008)

**Debt - external:** $380.5 billion (31 December 2008)

**Stock of direct foreign investment - at home:** $103.7 billion (30 June 2008)

**Stock of direct foreign investment - abroad:** $74.6 billion (30 June 2008)

**Exchange rates:** South Korean won (KRW) per US dollar - 1,101.7 (2008 est.), 929.2 (2007), 954.8 (2006), 1,024.1 (2005), 1,145.3 (2004)

## Communications

**Telephones - main lines in use:** 23.905 million (2007)

**Telephones - mobile cellular:** 43.5 million (2007)

**Telephone system:**
*general assessment:* excellent domestic and international services featuring rapid incorporation of new technologies
*domestic:* combined fixed-line and mobile-cellular telephone subscribership roughly 140 per 100 persons; rapid assimilation of a full range of telecommunications technologies leading to a boom in e-commerce
*international:* country code - 82; numerous submarine cables provide links throughout Asia, Australia, the Middle East, Europe, and US; satellite earth stations - 66

**Radio broadcast stations:** AM 96, FM 322, shortwave 1 (2008)

**Television broadcast stations:** 57 (plus 103 cable operators and 119 relay cable operators) (2008)

**Internet country code:** .kr

**Internet hosts:** 333,823 (2008)

**Internet users:** 35.59 million (2007)

## Transportation

**Airports:** 113 (2008)

**Airports - with paved runways:**
*total:* 71
*over 3,047 m:* 3
*2,438 to 3,047 m:* 22
*1,524 to 2,437 m:* 12
*914 to 1,523 m:* 12
*under 914 m:* 22 (2008)

# Korea, South *(continued)*

**Airports - with unpaved runways:**
*total:* 42
*914 to 1,523 m:* 2
*under 914 m:* 40 (2008)
**Heliports:** 536 (2007)
**Pipelines:** gas 1,423 km; refined products 827 km (2008)
**Railways:**
*total:* 3,381 km
*standard gauge:* 3,381 km 1.435-m gauge (1,843 km electrified) (2008)
**Roadways:**
*total:* 103,029 km
*paved:* 80,642 km (includes 3,367 km of expressways)
*unpaved:* 22,387 km (2008)
**Waterways:** 1,608 km (most navigable only by small craft) (2008)
**Merchant marine:**
*total:* 812
*by type:* bulk carrier 212, cargo 226, carrier 2, chemical tanker 133, container 80, liquefied gas 33, passenger 5, passenger/cargo 26, petroleum tanker 61, refrigerated cargo 16, roll on/roll off 9, specialized tanker 4, vehicle carrier 5
*foreign-owned:* 31 (China 1, Japan 20, Norway 2, UK 1, US 7)
*registered in other countries:* 363 (Belize 1, Cambodia 22, China 1, Cyprus 1, Honduras 6, Hong Kong 3, Kiribati 2, Liberia 3, Malta 2, Marshall Islands 10, Mongolia 1, Netherlands 1, Panama 303, Russia 1, Singapore 3, Tuvalu 1, unknown 2) (2008)
**Ports and terminals:** Inch'on, P'ohang, Pusan, Ulsan

## Military

**Military branches:** Republic of Korea Army, Navy (includes Marine Corps), Air Force (2009)
**Military service age and obligation:** 20-30 years of age for compulsory military service, with middle school education required; conscript service obligation - 24-28 months, depending on the military branch involved (to be reduced to 18 months beginning 2016); 18-26 years of age for voluntary military service; women, in service since 1950, admitted to 7 service branches, including infantry, but excluded from artillery, armor, anti-air, and chaplaincy corps; some 4,000 women serve as commissioned and noncommissioned officers, approx. 2.3% of all officers (2008)
**Manpower available for military service:**
*males age 16-49:* 13,691,809
*females age 16-49:* 13,029,859 (2008 est.)
**Manpower fit for military service:**
*males age 16-49:* 10,991,263
*females age 16-49:* 10,356,604 (2009 est.)
**Manpower reaching militarily significant age annually:**
*male:* 371,728
*female:* 322,605 (2009 est.)
**Military expenditures:** 2.7% of GDP (2006)

## Transnational Issues

**Disputes - international:** Military Demarcation Line within the 4-km wide Demilitarized Zone has separated North from South Korea since 1953; periodic incidents with North Korea in the Yellow Sea over the Northern Limiting Line, which South Korea claims as a maritime boundary; South Korea and Japan claim Liancourt Rocks (Tok-do/Take-shima), occupied by South Korea since 1954

# Kosovo

## Introduction

**Background:** Ethnic Serbs migrated to the territories of modern Kosovo in the 7th century but did not fully incorporate them into the Serbian realm until the early 13th century. The defeat of the Serbian empire at the Battle of Kosovo in 1389 led to five centuries of Ottoman rule during which large numbers of Turks and Albanians moved to Kosovo. By the end of the 19th century, Albanians replaced the Serbs as the dominant ethnic group in Kosovo. Serbia reacquired control over Kosovo from the Ottoman Empire during the First Balkan War of 1912. Kosovo became an autonomous province of Serbia with status almost equivalent to that of a republic under the 1974 Constitution of the Socialist Federal Republic of Yugoslavia. Despite legislative concessions, Albanian nationalism increased in the 1980s, which led to riots and calls for Kosovo's independence. At the same time, Serb nationalist leaders, such as Slobodan MILOSEVIC, exploited Kosovo Serb claims of maltreatment to secure votes from supporters, many of whom viewed Kosovo as their cultural heartland. Under MILOSEVIC's leadership, Serbia instituted a new constitution in 1989 that revoked Kosovo's status as an autonomous province of Serbia. Kosovo Albanian leaders responded in 1991 by organizing a referendum that declared Kosovo independent. Under MILOSEVIC, Serbia carried out repressive measures against the Albanians in the early 1990s as the unofficial Kosovo government, led by Ibrahim RUGOVA, used passive resistance in an attempt to try to gain international assistance and recognition of an independent Kosovo. Albanians dissatisfied with RUGOVA's passive strategy in the 1990s created the Kosovo Liberation Army and launched an insurgency. Starting in 1998, Serbian military, police, and paramilitary forces conducted a counterinsurgency campaign that resulted in massacres and massive expulsions of ethnic Albanians. International attempts to mediate the conflict failed, and MILOSEVIC's rejection of a proposed settlement led to a three-month NATO bombing campaign against Serbia beginning in March 1999 that forced Serbia to agree to withdraw its military and police forces from Kosovo. UN Security Council Resolution 1244 (1999) placed Kosovo under a transitional administration, the UN Interim Administration Mission in Kosovo (UNMIK), pending a determination of Kosovo's future status. A UN-led process began in late 2005 to determine Kosovo's final status. The negotiations ran in stages between 2006 and 2007, but ended without agreement between Belgrade and Pristina. On 17 February 2008, the Kosovo Assembly declared Kosovo independent. Since then, over fifty countries have recognized Kosovo. Serbia continues to reject Kosovo's independence and subsequently has sought an advisory opinion with the backing of the General Assembly from the International Court of Justice on the legality under international law of Kosovo's independence declaration.

## Geography

**Location:** Southeast Europe, between Serbia and Macedonia
**Geographic coordinates:** 42 35 N, 21 00 E
**Map references:** Europe
**Area:**
*total:* 10,887 sq km
*land:* 10,887 sq km
*water:* 0 sq km
**Area - comparative:** slightly larger than Delaware
**Land boundaries:**
*total:* 702 km
*border countries:* Albania 112 km, Macedonia 159 km, Montenegro 79 km, Serbia 352 km
**Coastline:** 0 km (landlocked)
**Maritime claims:** none (landlocked)
**Climate:** influenced by continental air masses resulting in relatively cold winters with heavy snowfall and hot, dry summers and autumns; Mediterranean and alpine influences create regional variation; maximum rainfall between October and December
**Terrain:** flat fluvial basin with an elevation of 400-700 mabove sea level surrounded by several high mountain ranges with elevations of 2,000 to 2,500 m
**Elevation extremes:**
*lowest point:* Drini i Bardhe/Beli Drim 297 m (located on the border with Albania)
*highest point:* Gjeravica/Deravica 2,656 m
**Natural resources:** nickel, lead, zinc, magnesium, lignite, kaolin, chrome, bauxite

## People

**Population:** 1,804,838 (July 2009 est.)
**Age structure:**
*0-14 years:* 27.7% (male 260,678/female 239,779)
*15-64 years:* 65.7% (male 617,890/female 567,939)
*65 years and over:* 6.6% (male 50,463/female 68,089) (2009 est.)

**Median age:**
*total:* 25.9 years
*male:* 25.4 years
*female:* 26.4 years (2009 est.)
**Sex ratio:**
*at birth:* 1.09 male(s)/female
*under 15 years:* 1.09 male(s)/female
*15-64 years:* 1.09 male(s)/female
*65 years and over:* 0.74 male(s)/female
*total population:* 1.06 male(s)/female (2009 est.)
**Nationality:**
*noun:* Kosovar (Albanian), Kosovac (Serbian)
*adjective:* Kosovar (Albanian), Kosovski (Serbian)
*note:* Kosovan, a neutral term, is sometimes also used as a noun or adjective
**Ethnic groups:** Albanians 88%, Serbs 7%, other 5% (Bosniak, Gorani, Roma, Turk, Ashkali, Egyptian)
**Religions:** Muslim, Serbian Orthodox, Roman Catholic
**Languages:** Albanian (official), Serbian (official), Bosnian, Turkish, Roma
**Literacy:**
*definition:* age 15 and over can read and write
*total population:* 91.9%
*male:* 96.6%
*female:* 87.5% (2007 Census)

## Government

**Country name:**
*conventional long form:* Republic of Kosovo
*conventional short form:* Kosovo
*local long form:* Republika e Kosoves (Republika Kosovo)
*local short form:* Kosova (Kosovo)
**Government type:** republic
**Capital:**
*name:* Pristina (Prishtine, Prishtina)
*geographic coordinates:* 42 40 N, 21 10 E
*time difference:* UTC+1 (6 hours ahead of Washington, DC during Standard Time)
*daylight saving time:* +1hr, begins last Sunday in March; ends last Sunday in October
**Administrative divisions:** 30 municipalities (komunat, singular - komuna in Albanian; opstine, singular - opstina in Serbian); Decan (Decani), Dragash (Dragas), Ferizaj (Urosevac), Fushe Kosove (Kosovo Polje), Gjakove (Dakovica), Gjilan (Gnjilane), Gllogovc/Drenas (Glogovac), Istog (Istok), Kacanik, Kamenice/Dardana (Kamenica), Kline (Klina), Leposaviq (Leposavic), Lipjan (Lipljan), Malisheve (Malisevo), Mitrovice (Mitrovica), Novoberde (Novo Brdo), Obiliq (Obilic), Peje (Pec), Podujeve (Podujevo), Prishtine (Pristina), Prizren, Rahovec (Orahovac), Shterpce (Strpce), Shtime (Stimlje), Skenderaj (Srbica), Suhareke (Suva Reka), Viti (Vitina), Vushtrri (Vucitrn), Zubin Potok, Zvecan
**Independence:** 17 February 2008 (from Serbia)
**National holiday:** Independence Day, 17 February (2008)
**Constitution:** adopted by the Kosovo Assembly on 9 April 2008; effective 15 June 2008

**Legal system:** evolving legal system based on terms of UN Special Envoy Martti AHTISAARI's Plan for Kosovo's supervised independence
**Suffrage:** 18 years of age; universal
**Executive branch:**
*chief of state:* President Fatmir SEJDIU (since 10 February 2006)
*head of government:* Prime Minister Hashim THACI (since 9 January 2008)
*cabinet:* ministers; elected by the Kosovo Assembly
*elections:* the president is elected for a five-year term by the Kosovo Assembly; election last held 9 January 2008 (next to be held by in 2013); the prime minister is elected by the Kosovo Assembly
*election results:* Fatmir SEJDIU reelected president after three rounds; first round: Fatmir SEJDIU 62, Naim MALOKU 37; second round: Fatmir SEJDIU 61, Naim MALOKU 37; third round: Fatmir SEJDIU 68; and Hashim THACI elected to be prime minister by the Assembly
**Legislative branch:** unicameral national Assembly (120 seats; 100 seats directly elected, 10 seats guaranteed for ethnic Serbs, 10 seats guaranteed for other ethnic minorities; to serve four-year terms)
*elections:* last held 17 November 2007 (next to be held in 2011)
*election results:* percent of vote by party - PDK 34.3%, LDK 22.6%, AKR 12.3%, LDD 10.0%, AAK 9.6%, other 11.2%; seats by party - PDK 37, LDK 25, AKR 13, LDD 11, AAK 10, other 4
**Judicial branch:** Supreme Court; district courts; municipal courts
*note:* the Kosovo Constitution dictates that the Supreme Court of Kosovo is the highest judicial authority, and provides for a Kosovo Judicial Council (KJC) that proposes to the president candidates for appointment or reappointment as judges and prosecutors; the KJC is also responsible for decisions on the promotion and transfer of judges and disciplinary proceedings against judges; at least 15 percent of Supreme Court and district court judges shall be from non-majority communities
**Political parties and leaders:** Albanian Christian Democratic Party of Kosovo or PShDK [Tome MARKU]; Alliance for the Future of Kosovo or AAK [Ramush HARADINAJ]; Alliance for a New Kosovo or AKR [Behgjet PACOLLI]; Alliance of Independent Social Democrats of Kosovo and Metohija or SDSKIM [Slavisa PETKOVIC]; Autonomous Liberal Party of SLS [Slobodan PETROVIC]; Bosniak Vakat Coalition [Dzezair MURATI]; Citizens' Initiative of Gora or GIG [Mursel] HALJILJI]; Council of Independent Social Democrats of Kosovo or SNSDKIM [Ljubisa ZIVIC]; Democratic Action Party or SDA [Numan BALIC]; Democratic Ashkali Party of Kosovo or PDAK; Democratic League of Dardania or LDD [Nexhat DACI]; Democratic League of Kosovo or LDK [Fatmir SEJDIU]; Democratic Party of Ashkali of Kosovo or PDAK [Sabit RAHMANI]; Democratic Party of Kosovo or PDK [Hashim THACI]; Democratic Party Vatan [Sadik IDRIZI]; Democratic Union of Ashkalis or BDA [Sabit RRAHMANI]; Justice Party or PD [Sylejman

# Kosovo (continued)

QERKEZI]; Kosovo Democratic Turkish Party of KDTP [Mahir YAGCILAR]; Liberal Party of Kosovo or PLK [Gjergi DEDAJ]; New Democratic Initiative of Kosovo or IRDK [Xhevdet NEZIRAJ]; New Democratic Party or ND [Branislav GRBIC]; New Kosovo Alliance or AKR [Behxhet PACOLLI]; Popular Movement of Kosovo or LPK [Emrush XHEMAJLI]; Reform Party Ora [Teuta SAHATCIA]; Serb National Party or SNS [Mihailo SCEPANOVIC]; Serbian Kosovo and Metohija Party or SKMS [Dragisa MIRIC]; Serbian List for Kosovo and Metohija [Oliver IVANOVIC]; Social Democratic Party of Kosovo or PSDK [Agim CEKU]; United Roma Party of Kosovo or PREBK [Haxhi Zylfi MERXHA]

**Political pressure groups and leaders:** Council for the Defense of Human Rights and Freedom (human rights); Humanitarian Law Centre (human rights); Movement for Self-Determination; Serb National Council (SNV)

**International organization participation:** ITUC, WFTU

**Diplomatic representation in the US:**
*chief of mission:* Ambassador (vacant); Charge d'Affaires Avni SPAHIU
*chancery:* 900 19th Street, NW, Suite 400, Washington, DC 2006
*telephone:* 202-436-3581

**Diplomatic representation from the US:**
*chief of mission:* Ambassador Tina KAIDANOW
*embassy:* Arberia/Dragodan, Nazim Hikmet 30, Pristina, Kosovo
*mailing address:* use embassy street address
*telephone:* [381] 38 59 59 3000
*FAX:* [381] 38 549 890

**Flag description:** centered on a dark blue field is the geographical shape of Kosovo in a gold color surmounted by six white, five-pointed stars - each representing one of the major ethnic groups of Kosovo - arrayed in a slight arc

## Economy

**Economy - overview:** Over the past few years Kosovo's economy has shown significant progress in transitioning to a market-based system and maintaining macroeconomic stability, but it is still highly dependent on the international community and the diaspora for financial and technical assistance. Remittances from the diaspora - located mainly in Germany and Switzerland - are estimated to account for about 15% of GDP, and donor-financed activities and aid for another 15%. Kosovo's citizens are the poorest in Europe with an average annual per capita income of only $2,300. Unemployment, around 40% of the population, is a significant problem that encourages outward migration and black market activity. Most of Kosovo's population lives in rural towns outside of the capital, Pristina. Inefficient, near-subsistence farming is common - the result of small plots, limited mechanization, and lack of technical expertise. With international assistance, Kosovo has been able to privatize 50% of its

state-owned enterprises (SOEs) by number, and over 90% of SOEs by value. Minerals and metals - including lignite, lead, zinc, nickel, chrome, aluminum, magnesium, and a wide variety of construction materials - once formed the backbone of industry, but output has declined because of ageing equipment and insufficient investment. A limited and unreliable electricity supply due to technical and financial problems is a major impediment to economic development. Kosovo's Ministry of Energy and Mining has solicited expressions of interest from private investors to develop a new power plant in order to address Kosovo and the region's unmet and growing demands for power. The official currency of Kosovo is the euro, but the Serbian dinar is also used in Serb enclaves. Kosovo's tie to the euro has helped keep core inflation low. Kosovo has one of the most open economies in the region, and continues to work with the international community on measures to improve the business environment and attract foreign investment.

**GDP (purchasing power parity):**
$5 billion (2007 est.)

**GDP (official exchange rate):** $3.237 billion (2007 est.)

**GDP - real growth rate:**
5.1% (2007 est.)

**GDP - per capita (PPP):**
$2,300 (2007 est.)

**GDP - composition by sector:**
*agriculture:* 20%
*industry:* 20%
*services:* 60% (2007 est.)

**Labor force:** 550,000 (2007 est.)

**Labor force - by occupation:**
*agriculture:* 16.5%
*industry:* NA
*services:* NA (2007 est.)

**Unemployment rate:**
40% (2007 est.)

**Population below poverty line:** 37% (2007 est.)

**Distribution of family income - Gini index:** 30 (FY05/06)

**Investment (gross fixed):** 30% of GDP (2007 est.)

**Budget:**
*revenues:* $1.19 billion
*expenditures:* $1.22 billion (2007 est.)

**Public debt:** NA

**Inflation rate (consumer prices):**
5.3% (2007 est.)

**Agriculture - products:** wheat, corn, berries, potatoes, peppers

**Industries:** mineral mining, construction materials, base metals, leather, machinery, appliances

**Electricity - production:** 832 million kWh (2006)

**Electricity - consumption:** 4.281 billion kWh (2006)

**Oil - production:** 0 bbl/day (2007)

**Oil - consumption:** NA bbl/day

**Oil - proved reserves:** NA bbl

**Natural gas - production:** 0 cu m (2007)

**Natural gas - consumption:** 0 cu m (2007)

**Natural gas - proved reserves:** NA cu m

**Current account balance:** -$964 million (2007)

**Exports:** $527 million (2007)

**Exports - commodities:** mining and processed metal products, scrap metals, leather products, machinery, appliances

**Imports:** $2.6 billion f.o.b. (2007)

**Imports - commodities:** foodstuffs, wood, petroleum, chemicals, machinery and electrical equipment

**Reserves of foreign exchange and gold:** $NA

**Debt - external:** $NA

**Exchange rates:** euros (EUR) per US dollar - 0.6827 (2008), 0.7345 (2007)

## Communications

**Telephones - main lines in use:** 106,300 (2006)

**Telephones - mobile cellular:** 562,000 (2006)

## Transportation

**Airports:** 10 (2008)

**Airports - with paved runways:**
*total:* 6
*2,438 to 3,047 m:* 1
*1,524 to 2,437 m:* 1
*under 914 m:* 4 (2008)

**Airports - with unpaved runways:**
*total:* 4
*under 914 m:* 4 (2008)

**Heliports:** 2 (2008)

**Railways:**
*total:* 430 km
*standard gauge:* 430 km 1.435-m gauge (2005)

**Roadways:**
*total:* 1,924 km
*paved:* 1,666 km
*unpaved:* 258 km (2006)

## Military

**Manpower fit for military service:**
*males age 16-49:* 428,685
*females age 16-49:* 388,848 (2009 est.)

## Transnational Issues

**Disputes - international:** Serbia with several other states protest the US and other states' recognition of Kosovo's declaring itself as a sovereign and independent state in February 2008; ethnic Serbian municipalities along Kosovo's northern border challenge final status of Kosovo-Serbia boundary; several thousand NATO-led KFOR peacekeepers under UNMIK authority continue to keep the peace within Kosovo between the ethnic Albanian majority and the Serb minority in Kosovo; Kosovo and Macedonia completed demarcation of their boundary in September 2008

**Refugees and internally displaced persons:**
*IDP's:* 21,000 (2007)

# Kuwait

## Introduction

**Background:** Britain oversaw foreign relations and defense for the ruling Kuwaiti AL-SABAH dynasty from 1899 until independence in 1961. Kuwait was attacked and overrun by Iraq on 2 August 1990. Following several weeks of aerial bombardment, a US-led, UN coalition began a ground assault on 23 February 1991 that liberated Kuwait in four days. Kuwait spent more than $5 billion to repair oil infrastructure damaged during 1990-91. The AL-SABAH family has ruled since returning to power in 1991 and reestablished an elected legislature that in recent years has become increasingly assertive. The country witnessed the historic election in May 2009 of four women to its National Assembly.

## Geography

**Location:** Middle East, bordering the Persian Gulf, between Iraq and Saudi Arabia
**Geographic coordinates:** 29 30 N, 45 45 E
**Map references:** Middle East
**Area:**
*total:* 17,820 sq km
*land:* 17,820 sq km
*water:* 0 sq km
**Area - comparative:** slightly smaller than New Jersey
**Land boundaries:**
*total:* 462 km
*border countries:* Iraq 240 km, Saudi Arabia 222 km
**Coastline:** 499 km
**Maritime claims:**
*territorial sea:* 12 nm
**Climate:** dry desert; intensely hot summers; short, cool winters
**Terrain:** flat to slightly undulating desert plain
**Elevation extremes:**
*lowest point:* Persian Gulf 0 m
*highest point:* unnamed location 306 m

**Natural resources:** petroleum, fish, shrimp, natural gas
**Land use:**
*arable land:* 0.84%
*permanent crops:* 0.17%
*other:* 98.99% (2005)
**Irrigated land:** 130 sq km (2003)
**Total renewable water resources:** 0.02 cu km (1997)
**Freshwater withdrawal (domestic/industrial/agricultural):**
*total:* 0.44 cu km/yr (45%/2%/52%)
*per capita:* 164 cu m/yr (2000)
**Natural hazards:** sudden cloudbursts are common from October to April and bring heavy rain, which can damage roads and houses; sandstorms and dust storms occur throughout the year but are most common between March and August
**Environment - current issues:** limited natural fresh water resources; some of world's largest and most sophisticated desalination facilities provide much of the water; air and water pollution; desertification
**Environment - international agreements:**
*party to:* Biodiversity, Climate Change, Climate Change-Kyoto Protocol, Desertification, Endangered Species, Environmental Modification, Hazardous Wastes, Law of the Sea, Ozone Layer Protection
*signed, but not ratified:* Marine Dumping
**Geography - note:** strategic location at head of Persian Gulf

## People

**Population:** 2,691,158
*note:* includes 1,291,354 non-nationals (July 2009 est.)
**Age structure:**
*0-14 years:* 26.4% (male 361,150/female 348,518)
*15-64 years:* 70.7% (male 1,219,075/female 683,587)
*65 years and over:* 2.9% (male 49,163/female 29,665) (2009 est.)
**Median age:**
*total:* 26.2 years
*male:* 28.1 years
*female:* 22.7 years (2009 est.)
**Population growth rate:** 3.547%
*note:* this rate reflects a return to pre-Gulf crisis immigration of expatriates (2009 est.)
**Birth rate:** 21.81 births/1,000 population (2009 est.)
**Death rate:** 2.37 deaths/1,000 population (2008 est.)
**Net migration rate:** 16.02 migrant(s)/1,000 population (2009 est.)
**Urbanization:**
*urban population:* 98% of total population (2008)
*rate of urbanization:* 2.5% annual rate of change (2005-10 est.)
**Sex ratio:**
*at birth:* 1.04 male(s)/female
*under 15 years:* 1.04 male(s)/female
*15-64 years:* 1.78 male(s)/female
*65 years and over:* 1.66 male(s)/female
*total population:* 1.54 male(s)/female (2009 est.)

**Infant mortality rate:**
*total:* 8.96 deaths/1,000 live births
*male:* 9.94 deaths/1,000 live births
*female:* 7.95 deaths/1,000 live births (2009 est.)
**Life expectancy at birth:**
*total population:* 77.71 years
*male:* 76.51 years
*female:* 78.95 years (2009 est.)
**Total fertility rate:** 2.76 children born/woman (2009 est.)
**HIV/AIDS - adult prevalence rate:** 0.12% (2001 est.)
**HIV/AIDS - people living with HIV/AIDS:** NA (2007 est.)
**HIV/AIDS - deaths:** NA
**Nationality:**
*noun:* Kuwaiti(s)
*adjective:* Kuwaiti
**Ethnic groups:** Kuwaiti 45%, other Arab 35%, South Asian 9%, Iranian 4%, other 7%
**Religions:** Muslim 85% (Sunni 70%, Shia 30%), other (includes Christian, Hindu, Parsi) 15%
**Languages:** Arabic (official), English widely spoken
**Literacy:**
*definition:* age 15 and over can read and write
*total population:* 93.3%
*male:* 94.4%
*female:* 91% (2005 census)
**School life expectancy (primary to tertiary education):**
*total:* 13 years
*male:* 12 years
*female:* 13 years (2006)
**Education expenditures:** 3.8% of GDP (2006)

## Government

**Country name:**
*conventional long form:* State of Kuwait
*conventional short form:* Kuwait
*local long form:* Dawlat al Kuwayt
*local short form:* Al Kuwayt
**Government type:** constitutional emirate
**Capital:**
*name:* Kuwait
*geographic coordinates:* 29 22 N, 47 58 E
*time difference:* UTC+3 (8 hours ahead of Washington, DC during Standard Time)
**Administrative divisions:** 6 governorates (muhafazat, singular - muhafazah); Al Ahmadi, Al 'Asimah, Al Farwaniyah, Al Jahra', Hawalli, Mubarak al Kabir
**Independence:** 19 June 1961 (from the UK)
**National holiday:** National Day, 25 February (1950)
**Constitution:** approved and promulgated 11 November 1962
**Legal system:** civil law system with Islamic law significant in personal matters; has not accepted compulsory ICJ jurisdiction
**Suffrage:** 21 years of age; universal (adult); note - males in the military or police are not allowed to vote; adult females were allowed to vote as of 16 May 2005; all voters must have been citizens for 20 years

# Kuwait (continued)

**Executive branch:**

*chief of state:* Amir SABAH al-Ahmad al-Jabir al-Sabah (since 29 January 2006); Crown Prince NAWAF al-Ahmad al-Jabir al-Sabah

*head of government:* Prime Minister NASIR al-MUHAMMAD al-Ahmad al-Sabah (since 3 April 2007); First Deputy Prime Minister JABIR MUBAREK al-Hamad al-Sabah (since 9 February 2006); Deputy Prime Ministers MUHAMMAD al-Sabah al-Salim al-Sabah (since 9 February 2006) and Faysal al-HAJJI (since 5 April 2007)

*cabinet:* Council of Ministers appointed by the prime minister and approved by the amir

*elections:* none; the amir is hereditary; the amir appoints the prime minister and deputy prime ministers

**Legislative branch:** unicameral National Assembly or Majlis al-Umma (50 seats; members elected by popular vote to serve four-year terms; all cabinet ministers are also ex officio voting members of the National Assembly)

*elections:* last held 16 May 2009 (next election to be held in 2013)

*election results:* percent of vote by bloc - NA; seats by bloc - Sunni Muslim groups 11, liberals 7, Shiite Muslim groups 6, Popular Action Bloc 3, unaffiliated tribal groups 23

**Judicial branch:** High Court of Appeal

**Political parties and leaders:** none; formation of political parties is in practice illegal but is not forbidden by law

**Political pressure groups and leaders:**

*other:* Islamists; merchants; political groups; secular liberals and pro-governmental deputies; Shia activists; tribal groups

**International organization participation:** ABEDA, AfDB (nonregional member), AFESD, AMF, BDEAC, CAEU, FAO, G-77, GCC, IAEA, IBRD, ICAO, ICC, ICCt (signatory), ICRM, IDA, IDB, IFAD, IFC, IFRCS, IHO, ILO, IMF, IMO, IMSO, Interpol, IOC, IPU, ISO, ITSO, ITU, ITUC, LAS, MIGA, NAM, OAPEC, OIC, OPCW, OPEC, PCA, UN, UNCTAD, UNESCO, UNIDO, UNITAR, UNWTO, UPU, WCO, WFTU, WHO, WIPO, WMO, WTO

**Diplomatic representation in the US:**

*chief of mission:* Ambassador SALIM al-Abdallah al-Jabir al-Sabah

*chancery:* 2940 Tilden Street NW, Washington, DC 20008

*telephone:* [1] (202) 966-0702

*FAX:* [1] (202) 364-2868

*consulate(s) general:* Los Angeles

**Diplomatic representation from the US:**

*chief of mission:* Ambassador Deborah K. JONES

*embassy:* Bayan 36302, Block 13, Al-Masjed Al-Aqsa Street (near the Bayan palace), Kuwait City

*mailing address:* P. O. Box 77 Safat 13001 Kuwait; or PSC 1280 APO AE 09880-9000

*telephone:* [965] 259-1001

*FAX:* [965] 538-0282

**Flag description:** three equal horizontal bands of green (top), white, and red with a black trapezoid based on the hoist side; design, which dates to 1961, based on the Arab revolt flag of World War I

## Economy

**Economy - overview:** Kuwait is a small, rich, relatively open economy with self-reported crude oil reserves of about 104 billion barrels - 8% of world reserves. Petroleum accounts for nearly half of GDP, 95% of export revenues, and 80% of government income. Kuwait experienced rapid economic growth over the last several years on the back of high oil prices and in 2008 posted its tenth consecutive budget surplus. As a result of this positive fiscal situation, the need for economic reforms was less urgent and the government did not push through new initiatives. The drop in oil prices in late 2008 will reduce Kuwait's fiscal surplus in 2009. The global financial crisis may slow the pace of investment and development projects, but Kuwait has vowed to use its considerable financial resources to stabilize the economy if necessary.

**GDP (purchasing power parity):**
$149.1 billion (2008 est.)
$137.4 billion (2007)
$131.2 billion (2006)
*note:* data are in 2008 US dollars

**GDP (official exchange rate):** $159.7 billion (2008 est.)

**GDP - real growth rate:**
8.5% (2008 est.)
4.7% (2007 est.)
6.3% (2006 est.)

**GDP - per capita (PPP):**
$57,400 (2008 est.)
$54,800 (2007 est.)
$54,300 (2006 est.)
*note:* data are in 2008 US dollars

**GDP - composition by sector:**
*agriculture:* 0.3%
*industry:* 52.2%
*services:* 47.5% (2008 est.)

**Labor force:** 2.225 million
*note:* non-Kuwaitis represent about 80% of the labor force (2008 est.)

**Labor force - by occupation:**
*agriculture:* NA%
*industry:* NA%
*services:* NA%

**Unemployment rate:**
2.2% (2004 est.)

**Population below poverty line:** NA%

**Household income or consumption by percentage share:**
*lowest 10%:* NA%
*highest 10%:* NA%

**Investment (gross fixed):** 18.4% of GDP (2008 est.)

**Budget:**
*revenues:* $113.3 billion
*expenditures:* $63.55 billion (2008 est.)

**Public debt:** 7.2% of GDP (2008 est.)

**Inflation rate (consumer prices):**
11.7% (2008 est.)
5.5% (2007 est.)

**Central bank discount rate:** 6.25% (31 December 2007)

**Commercial bank prime lending rate:** 8.54% (31 December 2007)

**Stock of money:** $15.12 billion (31 December 2007)

**Stock of quasi money:** $55.2 billion (31 December 2007)

**Stock of domestic credit:** $78.25 billion (31 December 2007)

**Market value of publicly traded shares:** $188 billion (31 December 2007)

**Agriculture - products:** practically no crops; fish

**Industries:** petroleum, petrochemicals, cement, shipbuilding and repair, water desalination, food processing, construction materials

**Industrial production growth rate:** 8% (2008 est.)

**Electricity - production:** 44.75 billion kWh (2006 est.)

**Electricity - consumption:** 39.54 billion kWh (2006 est.)

**Electricity - exports:** 0 kWh (2007 est.)

**Electricity - imports:** 0 kWh (2007 est.)

**Oil - production:** 2.613 million bbl/day (2007 est.)

**Oil - consumption:** 334,700 bbl/day (2006 est.)

**Oil - exports:** 2.356 million bbl/day (2005)

**Oil - imports:** 8,022 bbl/day (2005)

**Oil - proved reserves:** 104 billion bbl (1 January 2008 est.)

**Natural gas - production:** 12.5 billion cu m (2006 est.)

**Natural gas - consumption:** 12.5 billion cu m (2006 est.)

**Natural gas - exports:** 0 cu m (2007 est.)

**Natural gas - imports:** 0 cu m (2007 est.)

**Natural gas - proved reserves:** 1.586 trillion cu m (1 January 2008 est.)

**Current account balance:** $65.21 billion (2008 est.)

**Exports:** $95.46 billion f.o.b. (2008 est.)

**Exports - commodities:** oil and refined products, fertilizers

**Exports - partners:** Japan 19.9%, South Korea 17%, Taiwan 11.2%, Singapore 9.9%, US 8.4%, Netherlands 4.8%, China 4.4% (2007)

**Imports:** $26.54 billion f.o.b. (2008 est.)

**Imports - commodities:** food, construction materials, vehicles and parts, clothing

**Imports - partners:** US 12.7%, Japan 8.5%, Germany 7.3%, China 6.8%, South Korea 6.6%, Saudi Arabia 6.2%, Italy 5.8%, UK 4.6% (2007)

**Reserves of foreign exchange and gold:** $10.64 billion (31 December 2008 est.)

**Debt - external:** $38.82 billion (31 December 2008 est.)

**Stock of direct foreign investment - at home:** $1.22 billion (2008 est.)

**Stock of direct foreign investment - abroad:** $28.29 billion (2008 est.)

# Kuwait (continued)

**Exchange rates:** Kuwaiti dinars (KD) per US dollar - 0.2679 (2008 est.), 0.2844 (2007), 0.29 (2006), 0.292 (2005), 0.2947 (2004)

## Communications

**Telephones - main lines in use:** 517,000 (2006)
**Telephones - mobile cellular:** 2.774 million (2007)
**Telephone system:**
*general assessment:* the quality of service is excellent
*domestic:* new telephone exchanges provide a large capacity for new subscribers; trunk traffic is carried by microwave radio relay, coaxial cable, and open-wire and fiber-optic cable; a cellular telephone system operates throughout Kuwait, and the country is well supplied with pay telephones
*international:* country code - 965; linked to international submarine cable Fiber-Optic Link Around the Globe (FLAG); linked to Bahrain, Qatar, UAE via the Fiber-Optic Gulf (FOG) cable; coaxial cable and microwave radio relay to Saudi Arabia; satellite earth stations - 6 (3 Intelsat - 1 Atlantic Ocean and 2 Indian Ocean, 1 Inmarsat - Atlantic Ocean, and 2 Arabsat)
**Radio broadcast stations:** AM 6, FM 11, shortwave 1 (1998)
**Television broadcast stations:** 13 (plus several satellite channels) (1997)
**Internet country code:** .kw
**Internet hosts:** 3,289 (2008)
**Internet users:** 900,000 (2007)

## Transportation

**Airports:** 7 (2008)
**Airports - with paved runways:**
*total:* 4
*over 3,047 m:* 1
*2,438 to 3,047 m:* 2
*1,524 to 2,437 m:* 1 (2008)
**Airports - with unpaved runways:**
*total:* 3
*1,524 to 2,437 m:* 1
*under 914 m:* 2 (2008)
**Heliports:** 4 (2007)
**Pipelines:** gas 269 km; oil 540 km; refined products 57 km (2008)
**Roadways:**
*total:* 5,749 km
*paved:* 4,887 km
*unpaved:* 862 km (2004)
**Merchant marine:**
*total:* 38
*by type:* bulk carrier 2, cargo 1, carrier 3, container 6, liquefied gas 4, petroleum tanker 22
*registered in other countries:* 34 (Bahrain 5, Comoros 1, Libya 1, Panama 2, Qatar 7, Saint Kitts and Nevis 1, Saudi Arabia 7, UAE 10) (2008)
**Ports and terminals:** Ash Shu'aybah, Ash Shuwaykh, Az Zawr (Mina' Sa'ud), Mina' 'Abd Allah, Mina' al Ahmadi

## Military

**Military branches:** Kuwaiti Land Forces (KLF), Kuwaiti Navy, Kuwaiti Air Force (Al-Quwwat al-Jawwiya al-Kuwaitiya), Kuwaiti National Guard (KNG) (2008)
**Military service age and obligation:** 18-30 years of age for compulsory and 18-25 years of age for voluntary military service; women age 18-30 may be subject to compulsory military service; conscription suspended in 2001 (2009)
**Manpower available for military service:**
*males age 16-49:* 1,032,408
*females age 16-49:* 568,657 (2008 est.)
**Manpower fit for military service:**
*males age 16-49:* 935,525
*females age 16-49:* 519,854 (2009 est.)
**Manpower reaching militarily significant age annually:**
*male:* 18,122
*female:* 18,865 (2009 est.)
**Military expenditures:** 5.3% of GDP (2006)

## Transnational Issues

**Disputes - international:** Kuwait and Saudi Arabia continue negotiating a joint maritime boundary with Iran; no maritime boundary exists with Iraq in the Persian Gulf
**Trafficking in persons:**
*current situation:* Kuwait is a destination country for men and women who migrate legally from South and Southeast Asia for domestic or low-skilled labor, but are subjected to conditions of involuntary servitude by employers in Kuwait including conditions of physical and sexual abuse, non-payment of wages, confinement to the home, and withholding of passports to restrict their freedom of movement; Kuwait is reportedly a transit point for South and East Asian workers recruited for low-skilled work in Iraq; some of these workers are deceived as to the true location and nature of this work, and others are subjected to conditions of involuntary servitude in Iraq
*tier rating:* Tier 3 - insufficient efforts in 2007 to prosecute and punish abusive employers and those who traffic women for sexual exploitation; the government failed for the fourth year in a row to live up to promises to provide shelter and protective services for victims of involuntary domestic servitude and other forms of trafficking (2008)

# Kyrgyzstan

## Freshwater withdrawal (domestic/industrial/agricultural):
*total:* 10.08 cu km/yr (3%/3%/94%)
*per capita:* 1,916 cu m/yr (2000)
**Natural hazards:** NA
**Environment - current issues:** water pollution; many people get their water directly from contaminated streams and wells; as a result, water-borne diseases are prevalent; increasing soil salinity from faulty irrigation practices
**Environment - international agreements:**
*party to:* Air Pollution, Biodiversity, Climate Change, Climate Change-Kyoto Protocol, Desertification, Hazardous Wastes, Ozone Layer Protection, Wetlands
*signed, but not ratified:* none of the selected agreements
**Geography - note:** landlocked; entirely mountainous, dominated by the Tien Shan range; 94% of the country is 1,000 m above sea level, with an average elevation of 2,750 m; many tall peaks, glaciers, and high-altitude lakes

## Introduction

**Background:** A Central Asian country of incredible natural beauty and proud nomadic traditions, most of Kyrgyzstan was formally annexed to Russia in 1876. The Kyrgyz staged a major revolt against the Tsarist Empire in 1916 in which almost one-sixth of the Kyrgyz population was killed. Kyrgyzstan became a Soviet republic in 1936 and achieved independence in 1991 when the USSR dissolved. Nationwide demonstrations in the spring of 2005 resulted in the ouster of President Askar AKAEV, who had run the country since 1990. Subsequent presidential elections in July 2005 were won overwhelmingly by former prime minister Kurmanbek BAKIEV. The political opposition organized demonstrations in Bishkek in April, May, and November 2006 resulting in the adoption of a new constitution that transferred some of the president's powers to parliament and the government. In December 2006, the Kyrgyzstani parliament voted to adopt new amendments, restoring some of the presidential powers lost in the November 2006 constitutional change. By late-September 2007, both previous versions of the constitution were declared illegal, and the country reverted to the AKAEV-era 2003 constitution, which was subsequently modified in a flawed referendum initiated by BAKIEV. The president then dissolved parliament, called for early elections, and gained control of the new parliament through his newly-created political party, Ak Jol, in December 2007 elections. Current concerns include: privatization of state-owned enterprises, negative trends in democracy and political freedoms, endemic corruption, improving interethnic relations, electricity generation, rising food prices, and combating terrorism.

## Geography

**Location:** Central Asia, west of China
**Geographic coordinates:** 41 00 N, 75 00 E
**Map references:** Asia
**Area:**
*total:* 198,500 sq km
*land:* 191,300 sq km
*water:* 7,200 sq km
**Area - comparative:** slightly smaller than South Dakota
**Land boundaries:**
*total:* 3,051 km
*border countries:* China 858 km, Kazakhstan 1,224 km, Tajikistan 870 km, Uzbekistan 1,099 km
**Coastline:** 0 km (landlocked)
**Maritime claims:** none (landlocked)
**Climate:** dry continental to polar in high Tien Shan Mountains; subtropical in southwest (Fergana Valley); temperate in northern foothill zone
**Terrain:** peaks of Tien Shan and associated valleys and basins encompass entire nation
**Elevation extremes:**
*lowest point:* Kara-Daryya (Karadar'ya) 132 m
*highest point:* Jengish Chokusu (Pik Pobedy) 7,439 m
**Natural resources:** abundant hydropower; significant deposits of gold and rare earth metals; locally exploitable coal, oil, and natural gas; other deposits of nepheline, mercury, bismuth, lead, and zinc
**Land use:**
*arable land:* 6.55%
*permanent crops:* 0.28%
*other:* 93.17%
*note:* Kyrgyzstan has the world's largest natural-growth walnut forest (2005)
**Irrigated land:** 10,720 sq km (2003)
**Total renewable water resources:** 46.5 cu km (1997)

## People

**Population:** 5,431,747 (July 2009 est.)
**Age structure:**
*0-14 years:* 29.7% (male 822,128/female 789,425)
*15-64 years:* 64.5% (male 1,717,497/female 1,787,551)
*65 years and over:* 5.8% (male 123,045/female 192,101) (2009 est.)
**Median age:**
*total:* 24.4 years
*male:* 23.6 years
*female:* 25.3 years (2009 est.)
**Population growth rate:** 1.396% (2009 est.)
**Birth rate:** 23.44 births/1,000 population (2009 est.)
**Death rate:** 6.97 deaths/1,000 population (2008 est.)
**Net migration rate:** -2.57 migrant(s)/1,000 population (2009 est.)
**Urbanization:**
*urban population:* 36% of total population (2008)
*rate of urbanization:* 1.6% annual rate of change (2005-10 est.)
**Sex ratio:**
*at birth:* 1.05 male(s)/female
*under 15 years:* 1.04 male(s)/female
*15-64 years:* 0.96 male(s)/female
*65 years and over:* 0.64 male(s)/female
*total population:* 0.96 male(s)/female (2009 est.)
**Infant mortality rate:**
*total:* 31.26 deaths/1,000 live births
*male:* 36.19 deaths/1,000 live births
*female:* 26.06 deaths/1,000 live births (2009 est.)
**Life expectancy at birth:**
*total population:* 69.43 years
*male:* 65.43 years
*female:* 73.64 years (2009 est.)
**Total fertility rate:** 2.65 children born/woman (2009 est.)

# Kyrgyzstan *(continued)*

**HIV/AIDS - adult prevalence rate:** less than 0.1% (2007 est.)

**HIV/AIDS - people living with HIV/AIDS:** 4,200 (2007 est.)

**HIV/AIDS - deaths:** fewer than 200 (2007 est.)

**Nationality:**

*noun:* Kyrgyzstani(s)

*adjective:* Kyrgyzstani

**Ethnic groups:** Kyrgyz 64.9%, Uzbek 13.8%, Russian 12.5%, Dungan 1.1%, Ukrainian 1%, Uygur 1%, other 5.7% (1999 census)

**Religions:** Muslim 75%, Russian Orthodox 20%, other 5%

**Languages:** Kyrgyz 64.7% (official), Uzbek 13.6%, Russian 12.5% (official), Dungun 1%, other 8.2% (1999 census)

**Literacy:**

*definition:* age 15 and over can read and write

*total population:* 98.7%

*male:* 99.3%

*female:* 98.1% (1999 census)

**School life expectancy (primary to tertiary education):**

*total:* 12 years

*male:* 12 years

*female:* 13 years (2006)

**Education expenditures:** 4.9% of GDP (2005)

## Government

**Country name:**

*conventional long form:* Kyrgyz Republic

*conventional short form:* Kyrgyzstan

*local long form:* Kyrgyz Respublikasy

*local short form:* Kyrgyzstan

*former:* Kirghiz Soviet Socialist Republic

**Government type:** republic

**Capital:**

*name:* Bishkek

*geographic coordinates:* 42 52 N, 74 36 E

*time difference:* UTC+6 (11 hours ahead of Washington, DC during Standard Time)

**Administrative divisions:** 7 provinces (oblastlar, singular - oblasty) and 1 city* (shaar); Batken Oblasty, Bishkek Shaary*, Chuy Oblasty (Bishkek), Jalal-Abad Oblasty, Naryn Oblasty, Osh Oblasty, Talas Oblasty, Ysyk-Kol Oblasty (Karakol)

*note:* administrative divisions have the same names as their administrative centers (exceptions have the administrative center name following in parentheses)

**Independence:** 31 August 1991 (from the Soviet Union)

**National holiday:** Independence Day, 31 August (1991)

**Constitution:** approved by referendum in November 2006

*note:* under the old constitution adopted on 5 May 1993, an amendment proposed by President Askar AKAEV and passed in a national referendum on 2 February 2003 significantly expanded the powers of the president at the expense of the legislature; during large-scale demonstrations in November 2006,

President BAKIEV and the opposition negotiated a new constitution granting greater powers to the parliament and the government; amendments added on 30 December 2006 redistributed some power back to the president, but both November and December 2006 versions were annulled in September 2007, and a new version was approved by referendum on 21 October 2007; the BAKIEV-initiated referendum was criticized by Western observers for voting irregularities, particularly ballot stuffing

**Legal system:** based on French and Russian laws; has not accepted compulsory ICJ jurisdiction

**Suffrage:** 18 years of age; universal

**Executive branch:**

*chief of state:* President Kurmanbek BAKIEV (since 14 August 2005)

*head of government:* Prime Minister Igor CHUDINOV (since 24 December 2007); First Deputy Prime Minister Omurbek BABANOV (since 26 January 2009)

*cabinet:* Cabinet of Ministers proposed by the prime minister, appointed by the president; ministers in charge of defense and security, appointed solely by the president

*elections:* Kurmanbek BAKIEV elected by popular vote for a five-year term (eligible for a second term); election last held 10 July 2005 (next scheduled for 2010); prime minister nominated by the parliamentary party holding more than 50% of the seats; if no such party exists, the president selects the party that will nominate a prime minister

*election results:* Kurmanbek BAKIEV elected president; percent of vote - Kurmanbek BAKIEV 88.6%, Tursunbai BAKIR-UULU 3.9%, other candidates 7.5%

**Legislative branch:** unicameral Supreme Council or Jorgorku Kengesh (90 seats; members are elected by popular vote to serve five-year terms)

*elections:* last held 16 December 2007 (next to be held in 2012)

*election results:* Supreme Council - percent of vote by party - NA; seats by party - Ak Jol 71, Social Democratic Party 11, KCP 8

**Judicial branch:** Supreme Court; Constitutional Court (judges of both the Supreme and Constitutional Courts are appointed for 10-year terms by the Jorgorku Kengesh on the recommendation of the president; their mandatory retirement age is 70 years); Higher Court of Arbitration; Local Courts (judges appointed by the president on the recommendation of the National Council on Legal Affairs for a probationary period of five years, then 10 years)

**Political parties and leaders:** Ak Jol (Good Luck) [Avtandil ARABAEV, Elmira IBRAIMOVA, Vladimir NIFADYEV, co-chairs]; Ak Shumkar (Gerfalcon) [Temir SARIYEV]; Ar-Namys (Dignity) Party [Emil ALIEV]; Asaba (Banner National Revival Party) [Sovetbek JAMALDINOV]]; Ata-Meken (Fatherland) [Omurbek TEKEBAEV]; Democratic Movement of Kyrgyzstan or DDK [Viktor TCHETRNOMORETS]; Erkindik (Freedom) Party [Topchubek TURGUNALIEV]; For Justice Movement [Alikbek JEKSHENKULOV]; Green Party [Erkin BULEKBAEV];

Moya Strana (My Country Party of Action) [Medet SADYRKULOV]; Party of Communists of Kyrgyzstan or KCP [Iskhak MASALIEV]; Party of Justice and Progress [Muratbek IMANALIEV]; Party of Peasants [Esengul ISAKOV]; Republican Party of Labor and Unity [Tabaldy OROZALIEV]; Revolutionary Committee [Azimbek BEKNAZAROV]; Sanjira (Tree of Life) [Ednan KARABAEV]; Social Democratic Party of Kyrgyzstan [Almaz ATAMBAEV]; Svoboda Vybora (Free Choice) Party [Vyacheslav LISOVSKIY]; Turan Party [Kanybek IMANALIYEV]; Uluu Birimdik (Solidarity) Party [Emilbek KAPTAGAEV]; Union of Democratic Forces [Osmon ARTYKBAEV]; United Kyrgyzstan [Amangeldi MURALIEV]

**Political pressure groups and leaders:** Adilet Legal Clinic [Cholpon JAKUPOVA]; Coalition for Democracy and Civil Society [Dinara OSHURAKHUNOVA]; Interbilim [Asiya SASYKBAEVA]

**International organization participation:** ADB, CIS, CSTO, EAEC, EAPC, EBRD, ECO, FAO, GCTU, IAEA, IBRD, ICAO, ICCt (signatory), ICRM, IDA, IDB, IFAD, IFC, IFRCS, ILO, IMF, Interpol, IOC, IOM, IPU, ISO (correspondent), ITSO, ITU, MIGA, MINURCAT, NAM (observer), OIC, OPCW, OSCE, PCA, PFP, SCO, UN, UNCTAD, UNESCO, UNIDO, UNMIL, UNMIS, UNWTO, UPU, WCO, WFTU, WHO, WIPO, WMO, WTO

**Diplomatic representation in the US:**

*chief of mission:* Ambassador Zamira SYDYKOVA

*chancery:* 2360 Massachusetts Ave. NW, Washington, DC 20008

*telephone:* [1] (202) 449-9822

*FAX:* [1] (202) 386-7550

*consulate(s):* New York

**Diplomatic representation from the US:**

*chief of mission:* Ambassador Tatiana C. GFOELLER

*embassy:* 171 Prospect Mira, Bishkek 720016

*mailing address:* use embassy street address

*telephone:* [996] (312) 551-241, (517) 777-217

*FAX:* [996] (312) 551-264

**Flag description:** red field with a yellow sun in the center having 40 rays representing the 40 Kyrgyz tribes; on the obverse side the rays run counterclockwise, on the reverse, clockwise; in the center of the sun is a red ring crossed by two sets of three lines, a stylized representation of the roof of the traditional Kyrgyz yurt

## Economy

**Economy - overview:** Kyrgyzstan is a poor, mountainous country with a predominantly agricultural economy. Cotton, tobacco, wool, and meat are the main agricultural products, although only tobacco and cotton are exported in any quantity. Industrial exports include gold, mercury, uranium, natural gas, and electricity. Following independence, Kyrgyzstan was progressive in carrying out market reforms such as an improved regulatory system and land reform. Kyrgyzstan was the first Commonwealth of Independent States (CIS) country to be accepted into the World Trade Organization. Much of the government's stock in enterprises has been sold. Drops in production had been severe after the breakup of the Soviet Union in December 1991, but by mid-1995, production began to recover and exports began to increase. The economy is heavily weighted toward gold export and a drop in output at the main Kumtor gold mine sparked a 0.5% decline in GDP in 2002 and a 0.6% decline in 2005. The government made steady strides in controlling its substantial fiscal deficit, nearly closing the gap between revenues and expenditures in 2006, before boosting expenditures more than 20% in 2007-08. The government and international financial institutions have been engaged in a comprehensive medium-term poverty reduction and economic growth strategy. In 2005, Bishkek agreed to pursue much-needed tax reform and, in 2006, became eligible for the heavily indebted poor countries (HIPC) initiative. Progress fighting corruption, further restructuring of domestic industry, and success in attracting foreign investment are keys to future growth. GDP grew more than 6% annually in 2007-08, partly due to higher gold prices internationally, but growth is likely to decline from that level in 2009, due to declining demand and lower commodity prices in the wake of the international financial crisis.

**GDP (purchasing power parity):**
$11.41 billion (2008 est.)
$10.77 billion (2007)
$9.951 billion (2006)
*note:* data are in 2008 US dollars
**GDP (official exchange rate):** $5.05 billion (2008 est.)
**GDP - real growth rate:**
6% (2008 est.)
8.2% (2007 est.)
3.1% (2006 est.)
**GDP - per capita (PPP):**
$2,100 (2008 est.)
$2,000 (2007 est.)
$1,900 (2006 est.)
*note:* data are in 2008 US dollars
**GDP - composition by sector:**
*agriculture:* 32.4%
*industry:* 18.6%
*services:* 49% (2008 est.)
**Labor force:** 2.7 million (2000)
**Labor force - by occupation:**
*agriculture:* 48%
*industry:* 12.5%
*services:* 39.5% (2005 est.)
**Unemployment rate:**
18% (2004 est.)
**Population below poverty line:** 40% (2004 est.)
**Household income or consumption by percentage share:**
*lowest 10%:* 3.8%
*highest 10%:* 24.3% (2003)
**Distribution of family income - Gini index:** 30.3 (2003)

**Investment (gross fixed):** 25.8% of GDP (2008 est.)
**Budget:**
*revenues:* $1.17 billion
*expenditures:* $1.192 billion (2008 est.)
**Inflation rate (consumer prices):**
22.5% (2008 est.)
10.2% (2007 est.)
**Commercial bank prime lending rate:** 25.32% (31 December 2007)
**Stock of money:** $911.1 million (31 December 2007)
**Stock of quasi money:** $303.7 million (31 December 2007)
**Stock of domestic credit:** $558.3 million (31 December 2007)
**Market value of publicly traded shares:** $121 million (31 December 2007)
**Agriculture - products:** tobacco, cotton, potatoes, vegetables, grapes, fruits and berries; sheep, goats, cattle, wool
**Industries:** small machinery, textiles, food processing, cement, shoes, sawn logs, refrigerators, furniture, electric motors, gold, rare earth metals
**Industrial production growth rate:** 4.3% (2008 est.)
**Electricity - production:** 15.62 billion kWh (2006 est.)
**Electricity - consumption:** 8.997 billion kWh (2006 est.)
**Electricity - exports:** 2.387 billion kWh (2007 est.)
**Electricity - imports:** 0 kWh (2007 est.)
**Oil - production:** 964.7 bbl/day (2007 est.)
**Oil - consumption:** 12,330 bbl/day (2006 est.)
**Oil - exports:** 2,534 bbl/day (2005)
**Oil - imports:** 14,240 bbl/day (2005)
**Oil - proved reserves:** 40 million bbl (1 January 2008 est.)
**Natural gas - production:** 18 million cu m (2007 est.)
**Natural gas - consumption:** 768 million cu m (2007 est.)
**Natural gas - exports:** 0 cu m (2007 est.)
**Natural gas - imports:** 750 million cu m (2007 est.)
**Natural gas - proved reserves:** 5.663 billion cu m (1 January 2008 est.)
**Current account balance:** -$574 million (2008 est.)
**Exports:** $1.676 billion f.o.b. (2008 est.)
**Exports - commodities:** cotton, wool, meat, tobacco; gold, mercury, uranium, natural gas, hydropower; machinery; shoes
**Exports - partners:** Russia 20.7%, Switzerland 19.9%, Kazakhstan 18%, Afghanistan 10.4%, Uzbekistan 7.6%, China 5.5% (2007)
**Imports:** $3.476 billion f.o.b. (2008 est.)
**Imports - commodities:** oil and gas, machinery and equipment, chemicals, foodstuffs
**Imports - partners:** Russia 40.5%, China 14.7%, Kazakhstan 12.9%, Uzbekistan 5% (2007)
**Reserves of foreign exchange and gold:** $1.426 billion (31 December 2008 est.)

**Debt - external:** $2.966 billion (30 June 2007)
**Stock of direct foreign investment - at home:** $NA
**Stock of direct foreign investment - abroad:** $NA
**Exchange rates:** soms (KGS) per US dollar - 36.108 (2008 est.), 37.746 (2007), 40.149 (2006), 41.012 (2005), 42.65 (2004)

## Communications

**Telephones - main lines in use:** 482,100 (2007)
**Telephones - mobile cellular:** 2.152 million (2007)
**Telephone system:**
*general assessment:* telecommunications infrastructure is being upgraded; loans from the European Bank for Reconstruction and Development (EBRD) are being used to install a digital network, digital radio-relay stations, and fiber-optic links
*domestic:* fixed line penetration remains low and concentrated in urban areas; multiple mobile cellular service providers with growing coverage; mobile cellular subscribership reached 40 per 100 persons in 2007
*international:* country code - 996; connections with other CIS countries by landline or microwave radio relay and with other countries by leased connections with Moscow international gateway switch and by satellite; satellite earth stations - 2 (1 Intersputnik, 1 Intelsat); connected internationally by the Trans-Asia-Europe (TAE) fiber-optic line (2007)
**Radio broadcast stations:** AM 3 (plus 10 repeater stations), FM 23, shortwave NA (2007)
**Television broadcast stations:** 8 (2 countrywide and 6 regional stations; state-owned); note - there are about 20 private TV stations, most of which rebroadcast other channels (2007)
**Internet country code:** .kg
**Internet hosts:** 56,905 (2008)
**Internet users:** 750,000 (2007)

## Transportation

**Airports:** 30 (2008)
**Airports - with paved runways:**
*total:* 18
*over 3,047 m:* 1
*2,438 to 3,047 m:* 3
*1,524 to 2,437 m:* 11
*under 914 m:* 3 (2008)
**Airports - with unpaved runways:**
*total:* 12
*1,524 to 2,437 m:* 1
*914 to 1,523 m:* 1
*under 914 m:* 10 (2008)
**Pipelines:** gas 254 km; oil 16 km (2008)
**Railways:**
*total:* 470 km
*broad gauge:* 470 km 1.520-m gauge (2006)
**Roadways:**
*total:* 18,500 km
*paved:* 16,909 km (includes 140 km of expressways)
*unpaved:* 1,591 km (2003)

**Waterways:** 600 km (2008)
**Ports and terminals:** Balykchy (Ysyk-Kol or Rybach'ye)

## Military

**Military branches:** Ground Forces, Air Force (includes Air Defense Forces), National Guard (2009)
**Military service age and obligation:** 18 years of age for compulsory military service (2001)
**Manpower available for military service:**
*males age 16-49:* 1,398,878
*females age 16-49:* 1,419,374 (2008 est.)
**Manpower fit for military service:**
*males age 16-49:* 1,083,777
*females age 16-49:* 1,229,406 (2009 est.)
**Manpower reaching militarily significant age annually:**
*male:* 57,659
*female:* 55,557 (2009 est.)
**Military expenditures:** 1.4% of GDP (2005 est.)

## Transnational Issues

**Disputes - international:** Kyrgyzstan has yet to ratify the 2001 boundary delimitation with Kazakhstan; disputes in Isfara Valley delay completion of delimitation with Tajikistan; delimitation of 130 km of border with Uzbekistan is hampered by serious disputes around enclaves and other areas
**Illicit drugs:** limited illicit cultivation of cannabis and opium poppy for CIS markets; limited government eradication of illicit crops; transit point for Southwest Asian narcotics bound for Russia and the rest of Europe; major consumer of opiates

# Laos

## Introduction

**Background:** Modern-day Laos has its roots in the ancient Lao kingdom of Lan Xang, established in the 14th Century under King FA NGUM. For 300 years Lan Xang had influence reaching into present-day Cambodia and Thailand, as well as over all of what is now Laos. After centuries of gradual decline, Laos came under the domination of Siam (Thailand) from the late 18th century until the late 19th century when it became part of French Indochina. The Franco-Siamese Treaty of 1907 defined the current Lao border with Thailand. In 1975, the Communist Pathet Lao took control of the government ending a six-century-old monarchy and instituting a strict socialist regime closely aligned to Vietnam. A gradual return to private enterprise and the liberalization of foreign investment laws began in 1986. Laos became a member of ASEAN in 1997.

## Geography

**Location:** Southeastern Asia, northeast of Thailand, west of Vietnam
**Geographic coordinates:** 18 00 N, 105 00 E
**Map references:** Southeast Asia
**Area:**
*total:* 236,800 sq km
*land:* 230,800 sq km
*water:* 6,000 sq km
**Area - comparative:** slightly larger than Utah
**Land boundaries:**
*total:* 5,083 km
*border countries:* Burma 235 km, Cambodia 541 km, China 423 km, Thailand 1,754 km, Vietnam 2,130 km
**Coastline:** 0 km (landlocked)
**Maritime claims:** none (landlocked)
**Climate:** tropical monsoon; rainy season (May to November); dry season (December to April)
**Terrain:** mostly rugged mountains; some plains and plateaus

**Elevation extremes:**
*lowest point:* Mekong River 70 m
*highest point:* Phou Bia 2,817 m
**Natural resources:** timber, hydropower, gypsum, tin, gold, gemstones
**Land use:**
*arable land:* 4.01%
*permanent crops:* 0.34%
*other:* 95.65% (2005)
**Irrigated land:** 1,750 sq km (2003)
**Total renewable water resources:** 333.6 cu km (2003)
**Freshwater withdrawal (domestic/industrial/ agricultural):**
*total:* 3 cu km/yr (4%/6%/90%)
*per capita:* 507 cu m/yr (2000)
**Natural hazards:** floods, droughts
**Environment - current issues:** unexploded ordnance; deforestation; soil erosion; most of the population does not have access to potable water
**Environment - international agreements:**
*party to:* Biodiversity, Climate Change, Climate Change-Kyoto Protocol, Desertification, Endangered Species, Environmental Modification, Law of the Sea, Ozone Layer Protection
*signed, but not ratified:* none of the selected agreements
**Geography - note:** landlocked; most of the country is mountainous and thickly forested; the Mekong River forms a large part of the western boundary with Thailand

## People

**Population:** 6,834,942 (July 2009 est.)
**Age structure:**
*0-14 years:* 40.8% (male 1,400,126/female 1,386,480)
*15-64 years:* 56.1% (male 1,898,995/female 1,936,892)
*65 years and over:* 3.1% (male 92,070/female 120,379) (2009 est.)
**Median age:**
*total:* 19.3 years
*male:* 19 years
*female:* 19.6 years (2009 est.)
**Population growth rate:** 2.316% (2009 est.)
**Birth rate:** 33.94 births/1,000 population (2009 est.)
**Death rate:** 11.02 deaths/1,000 population (2008 est.)
**Net migration rate:** NA
**Urbanization:**
*urban population:* 31% of total population (2008)
*rate of urbanization:* 5.6% annual rate of change (2005-10 est.)
**Sex ratio:**
*at birth:* 1.05 male(s)/female
*under 15 years:* 1.01 male(s)/female
*15-64 years:* 0.98 male(s)/female
*65 years and over:* 0.76 male(s)/female
*total population:* 0.98 male(s)/female (2009 est.)

# Laos (continued)

**Infant mortality rate:**

*total:* 77.82 deaths/1,000 live births

*male:* 86.94 deaths/1,000 live births

*female:* 68.25 deaths/1,000 live births (2009 est.)

**Life expectancy at birth:**

*total population:* 56.68 years

*male:* 54.56 years

*female:* 58.9 years (2009 est.)

**Total fertility rate:** 4.41 children born/woman (2009 est.)

**HIV/AIDS - adult prevalence rate:** 0.2% (2007 est.)

**HIV/AIDS - people living with HIV/AIDS:** 5,500 (2007 est.)

**HIV/AIDS - deaths:** fewer than 100 (2007 est.)

**Major infectious diseases:**

*degree of risk:* very high

*food or waterborne diseases:* bacterial and protozoal diarrhea, hepatitis A, and typhoid fever

*vectorborne diseases:* dengue fever and malaria

*note:* highly pathogenic H5N1 avian influenza has been identified in this country; it poses a negligible risk with extremely rare cases possible among US citizens who have close contact with birds (2008) (2009)

**Nationality:**

*noun:* Lao(s) or Laotian(s)

*adjective:* Lao or Laotian

**Ethnic groups:** Lao 55%, Khmou 11%, Hmong 8%, other (over 100 minor ethnic groups) 26% (2005 census)

**Religions:** Buddhist 67%, Christian 1.5%, other and unspecified 31.5% (2005 census)

**Languages:** Lao (official), French, English, and various ethnic languages

**Literacy:**

*definition:* age 15 and over can read and write

*total population:* 68.7%

*male:* 77%

*female:* 60.9% (2001 est.)

**School life expectancy (primary to tertiary education):**

*total:* 9 years

*male:* 10 years

*female:* 8 years (2006)

**Education expenditures:** 3% of GDP (2006)

## Government

**Country name:**

*conventional long form:* Lao People's Democratic Republic

*conventional short form:* Laos

*local long form:* Sathalanalat Paxathipatai Paxaxon Lao

*local short form:* Pathet Lao (unofficial)

**Government type:** Communist state

**Capital:**

*name:* Vientiane (Viangchan)

*geographic coordinates:* 17 58 N, 102 36 E

*time difference:* UTC+7 (12 hours ahead of Washington, DC during Standard Time)

**Administrative divisions:** 16 provinces (khoueng, singular and plural) and 1 capital city* (nakhon luang, singular and plural); Attapu, Bokeo, Bolikhamxai, Champasak, Houaphan, Khammouan, Louangnamtha, Louangphrabang, Oudomxai, Phongsali, Salavan, Savannakhet, Viangchan (Vientiane)*, Viangchan, Xaignabouli, Xekong, Xiangkhoang

**Independence:** 19 July 1949 (from France)

**National holiday:** Republic Day, 2 December (1975)

**Constitution:** promulgated 14 August 1991

**Legal system:** based on traditional customs, French legal norms and procedures, and socialist practice; has not accepted compulsory ICJ jurisdiction

**Suffrage:** 18 years of age; universal

**Executive branch:**

*chief of state:* President Lt. Gen. CHOUMMALI Saignason (since 8 June 2006); Vice President BOUN-GNANG Volachit (since 8 June 2006)

*head of government:* Prime Minister BOUASONE Bouphavanh (since 8 June 2006); Deputy Prime Ministers Maj. Gen. ASANG Laoli (since May 2002), Maj. Gen. DOUANGCHAI Phichit (since 8 June 2006), SOMSAVAT Lengsavat (since 26 February 1998), and THONGLOUN Sisoulit (since 27 March 2001)

*cabinet:* Ministers appointed by president, approved by National Assembly

*elections:* president and vice president elected by National Assembly for five-year terms; election last held 8 June 2006 (next to be held in 2011); prime minister nominated by president and elected by National Assembly for five-year term

*election results:* CHOUMMALI Saignason elected president; BOUN-GNANG Volachit elected vice president; percent of National Assembly vote - 100%; BOUASONE Bouphavanh elected prime minister; percent of National Assembly vote - 97%

**Legislative branch:** unicameral National Assembly (115 seats; members elected by popular vote from a list of candidates selected by the Lao People's Revolutionary Party to serve five-year terms)

*elections:* last held 30 April 2006 (next to be held in 2011)

*election results:* percent of vote by party - NA; seats by party - LPRP 113, independents 2

**Judicial branch:** People's Supreme Court (the president of the People's Supreme Court is elected by the National Assembly on the recommendation of the National Assembly Standing Committee; the vice president of the People's Supreme Court and the judges are appointed by the National Assembly Standing Committee)

**Political parties and leaders:** Lao People's Revolutionary Party or LPRP [CHOUMMALI Saignason]; other parties proscribed

**Political pressure groups and leaders:** NA

**International organization participation:** ADB, APT, ARF, ASEAN, CP, EAS, FAO, G-77, IBRD, ICAO, ICRM, IDA, IFAD, IFC, IFRCS, ILO, IMF, Interpol, IOC, IPU, ISO (subscriber), ITU, MIGA, NAM, OIF, OPCW, PCA, UN, UNCTAD, UNESCO, UNIDO, UNWTO, UPU, WCO, WFTU, WHO, WIPO, WMO, WTO (observer)

**Diplomatic representation in the US:**

*chief of mission:* Ambassador PHIANE Philakone

*chancery:* 2222 S Street NW, Washington, DC 20008

*telephone:* [1] (202) 332-6416

*FAX:* [1] (202) 332-4923

**Diplomatic representation from the US:**

*chief of mission:* Ambassador Ravic R. HUSO

*embassy:* 19 Rue Bartholonie, That Dam, Vientiane

*mailing address:* American Embassy Vientiane, APO AP 96546

*telephone:* [856] 21-26-7000

*FAX:* [856] 21-26-7190

**Flag description:** three horizontal bands of red (top), blue (double width), and red with a large white disk centered in the blue band

## Economy

**Economy - overview:** The government of Laos, one of the few remaining one-party Communist states, began decentralizing control and encouraging private enterprise in 1986. The results, starting from an extremely low base, were striking - growth averaged 6% per year from 1988-2008 except during the short-lived drop caused by the Asian financial crisis that began in 1997. Despite this high growth rate, Laos remains a country with an underdeveloped infrastructure, particularly in rural areas. It has no railroads, a rudimentary road system, and limited external and internal telecommunications, though the government is sponsoring major improvements in the road system with support from Japan and China. Electricity is available in urban areas and in many rural districts. Subsistence agriculture, dominated by rice, accounts for about 40% of GDP and provides 80% of total employment. The government depends upon aid from international donors for over 80% of its capital investment. The economy has until recently benefited from high foreign investment in hydropower, mining, and construction. The fiscal crisis of late 2008, and the rapid drop in commodity prices - especially copper - has slowed these investments. Several policy changes since 2004 may help spur growth. Laos, which gained Normal Trade Relations status with the US in 2004, is taking steps to join the World Trade Organization. Related trade policy reforms will improve the business environment. On the fiscal side, a value-added tax (VAT) regime, which began with a few large businesses in early 2009, should slowly help streamline the government's inefficient tax system. Economic prospects will improve gradually as the administration continues to simplify investment procedures and as a more competitive banking sector extends credit to small farmers and small entrepreneurs. The government appears committed to raising the country's profile among investors. Foreign donors have praised the Lao government for its efforts to improve the investment regime. The World Bank has declared that Laos' goal of graduating from the UN Development Program's list of least-developed countries by 2020 could be achievable.

# Laos (continued)

**GDP (purchasing power parity):**
$13.99 billion (2008 est.)
$13.01 billion (2007)
$12.1 billion (2006)
*note:* data are in 2008 US dollars
**GDP (official exchange rate):** $5.187 billion
(2008 est.)
**GDP - real growth rate:**
7.5% (2008 est.)
7.5% (2007 est.)
8.3% (2006 est.)
**GDP - per capita (PPP):**
$2,100 (2008 est.)
$2,000 (2007 est.)
$1,900 (2006 est.)
*note:* data are in 2008 US dollars
**GDP - composition by sector:**
*agriculture:* 39.2%
*industry:* 34.3%
*services:* 26.6% (2008 est.)
**Labor force:** 2.1 million (2006 est.)
**Labor force - by occupation:**
*agriculture:* 80%
*industry and services:* 20% (2005 est.)
**Unemployment rate:**
2.4% (2005 est.)
**Population below poverty line:** 30.7% (2005 est.)
**Household income or consumption by
percentage share:**
*lowest 10%:* 3.4%
*highest 10%:* 28.5% (2002)
**Distribution of family income - Gini index:** 34.6
(2002)
**Budget:**
*revenues:* $809.6 million
*expenditures:* $954 million (2008 est.)
**Inflation rate (consumer prices):**
8.5% (2008 est.)
4.5% (2007 est.)
**Central bank discount rate:** 12.67% (31 December
2007)
**Commercial bank prime lending rate:** 28.5%
(31 December 2007)
**Stock of money:** $327.9 million (31 December 2007)
**Stock of quasi money:** $717.9 million
(31 December 2007)
**Stock of domestic credit:** $285.8 million
(31 December 2007)
**Agriculture - products:** sweet potatoes,
vegetables, corn, coffee, sugarcane, tobacco, cotton,
tea, peanuts, rice; water buffalo, pigs, cattle, poultry
**Industries:** copper, tin, gold, and gypsum mining;
timber, electric power, agricultural processing,
construction, garments, cement, tourism
**Industrial production growth rate:** 11% (2008 est.)
**Electricity - production:** 1.639 billion kWh
(2006 est.)
**Electricity - consumption:** 1.344 billion kWh
(2006 est.)
**Electricity - exports:** 547 million kWh (2006 est.)
**Electricity - imports:** 367 million kWh (2006 est.)

**Oil - production:** 0 bbl/day (2007 est.)
**Oil - consumption:** 2,996 bbl/day (2006 est.)
**Oil - exports:** 0 bbl/day (2005)
**Oil - imports:** 3,036 bbl/day (2005)
**Oil - proved reserves:** 0 bbl (1 January 2006 est.)
**Natural gas - production:** 0 cu m (2007 est.)
**Natural gas - consumption:** 0 cu m (2007 est.)
**Natural gas - exports:** 0 cu m (2007 est.)
**Natural gas - imports:** 0 cu m (2007 est.)
**Natural gas - proved reserves:** 0 cu m
(1 January 2006 est.)
**Current account balance:** -$37 million (2008 est.)
**Exports:** $1.033 billion (2008 est.)
**Exports - commodities:** wood products, coffee,
electricity, tin, copper, gold
**Exports - partners:** Thailand 32.7%, Vietnam
14.3%, China 5.9%, South Korea 4.8% (2007)
**Imports:** $1.278 billion f.o.b. (2008 est.)
**Imports - commodities:** machinery and equipment,
vehicles, fuel, consumer goods
**Imports - partners:** Thailand 68.5%, China 9.3%,
Vietnam 5.5% (2007)
**Reserves of foreign exchange and gold:** $765
million (31 December 2008 est.)
**Debt - external:** $3.179 billion (2006)
**Exchange rates:** kips (LAK) per US dollar - 8,760.69
(2008 est.), 9,658 (2007), 10,235 (2006), 10,820
(2005), 10,585.5 (2004)

## Communications

**Telephones - main lines in use:** 94,800 (2007)
**Telephones - mobile cellular:** 1.478 million (2007)
**Telephone system:**
*general assessment:* service to general public is poor
but improving; the government relies on a radiotelephone
network to communicate with remote areas
*domestic:* multiple service providers; mobile cellular
usage growing rapidly; combined fixed-line and
mobile-cellular subscribership about 25 per 100 persons
*international:* country code - 856; satellite earth
station -1 Intersputnik (Indian Ocean region) (2007)
**Radio broadcast stations:** AM 7, FM 14, shortwave
2 (2006)
**Television broadcast stations:** 7 (includes 1 station
relaying Vietnam Television from Hanoi) (2006)
**Internet country code:** .la
**Internet hosts:** 1,015 (2008)
**Internet users:** 100,000 (2007)

## Transportation

**Airports:** 42 (2008)
**Airports - with paved runways:**
*total:* 10
*2,438 to 3,047 m:* 2
*1,524 to 2,437 m:* 5
*914 to 1,523 m:* 3 (2008)
**Airports - with unpaved runways:**
*total:* 32
*1,524 to 2,437 m:* 1
*914 to 1,523 m:* 9
*under 914 m:* 22 (2008)

**Pipelines:** refined products 540 km (2008)
**Roadways:**
*total:* 29,811 km
*paved:* 4,010 km
*unpaved:* 25,801 km (2006)
**Waterways:** 4,600 km
*note:* primarily Mekong and tributaries; 2,900
additional km are intermittently navigable by craft
drawing less than 0.5 m (2008)
**Merchant marine:**
*total:* 1 ship (1000 GRT or over) 2,370 GRT/3,
110 DWT
*by type:* cargo 1 (2008)

## Military

**Military branches:** Lao People's Armed Forces
(LPAF): Lao People's Army (LPA; includes Riverine
Force), Air Force (2009)
**Military service age and obligation:** 15 years of
age for compulsory military service; minimum
18-month conscript service obligation (2006)
**Manpower available for military service:**
*males age 16-49:* 1,549,774
*females age 16-49:* 1,570,702 (2008 est.)
**Manpower fit for military service:**
*males age 16-49:* 1,023,205
*females age 16-49:* 1,085,197 (2009 est.)
**Manpower reaching militarily significant age
annually:**
*male:* 75,310
*female:* 74,498 (2009 est.)
**Military expenditures:** 0.5% of GDP (2006)
**Military - note:** serving one of the world's least
developed countries, the Lao People's Armed Forces
(LPAF) is small, poorly funded, and ineffectively
resourced; its mission focus is border and internal
security, primarily in countering ethnic Hmong insurgent
groups; together with the Lao People's Revolutionary
Party and the government, the Lao People's Army (LPA)
is the third pillar of state machinery, and as such is
expected to suppress political and civil unrest and similar
national emergencies, but the LPA also has upgraded
skills to respond to avian influenza outbreaks; there is no
perceived external threat to the state and the LPA
maintains strong ties with the neighboring Vietnamese
military (2008)

## Transnational Issues

**Disputes - international:** Southeast Asian states
have enhanced border surveillance to check the
spread of avian flu; talks continue on completion of
demarcation with Thailand but disputes remain over
islands in the Mekong River; concern among Mekong
Commission members that China's construction of
dams on the Mekong River will affect water levels
**Illicit drugs:** estimated opium poppy cultivation in
2008 was 1,900 hectares, about a 73% increase from
2007; estimated potential opium production in 2008
more than tripled to 17 metric tons; unsubstantiated
reports of domestic methamphetamine production;
growing domestic methamphetamine problem (2007)

# Latvia

## Introduction

**Background:** The name "Latvia" originates from the ancient Latgalians, one of four eastern Baltic tribes that formed the ethnic core of the Latvian people (ca. 8th-12th centuries A.D.). The region subsequently came under the control of Germans, Poles, Swedes, and finally, Russians. A Latvian republic emerged following World War I, but it was annexed by the USSR in 1940 - an action never recognized by the US and many other countries. Latvia reestablished its independence in 1991 following the breakup of the Soviet Union. Although the last Russian troops left in 1994, the status of the Russian minority (some 30% of the population) remains of concern to Moscow. Latvia joined both NATO and the EU in the spring of 2004.

## Geography

**Location:** Eastern Europe, bordering the Baltic Sea, between Estonia and Lithuania
**Geographic coordinates:** 57 00 N, 25 00 E
**Map references:** Europe
**Area:**
*total:* 64,589 sq km
*land:* 63,589 sq km
*water:* 1,000 sq km
**Area - comparative:** slightly larger than West Virginia
**Land boundaries:**
*total:* 1,382 km
*border countries:* Belarus 171 km, Estonia 343 km, Lithuania 576 km, Russia 292 km
**Coastline:** 498 km
**Maritime claims:**
*territorial sea:* 12 nm
*exclusive economic zone:* 200 nm
*continental shelf:* 200 m depth or to the depth of exploitation
**Climate:** maritime; wet, moderate winters
**Terrain:** low plain

**Elevation extremes:**
*lowest point:* Baltic Sea 0 m
*highest point:* Galzina Kalns 312 m
**Natural resources:** peat, limestone, dolomite, amber, hydropower, wood, arable land
**Land use:**
*arable land:* 28.19%
*permanent crops:* 0.45%
*other:* 71.36% (2005)
**Irrigated land:** 200 sq km
*note:* land in Latvia is often too wet and in need of drainage not irrigation; approximately 16,000 sq km or 85% of agricultural land has been improved by drainage (2003)
**Total renewable water resources:** 49.9 cu km (2005)
**Freshwater withdrawal (domestic/industrial/ agricultural):**
*total:* 0.25 cu km/yr (55%/33%/12%)
*per capita:* 108 cu m/yr (2003)
**Natural hazards:** NA
**Environment - current issues:** Latvia's environment has benefited from a shift to service industries after the country regained independence; the main environmental priorities are improvement of drinking water quality and sewage system, household, and hazardous waste management, as well as reduction of air pollution; in 2001, Latvia closed the EU accession negotiation chapter on environment committing to full enforcement of EU environmental directives by 2010
**Environment - international agreements:**
*party to:* Air Pollution, Air Pollution-Persistent Organic Pollutants, Biodiversity, Climate Change, Climate Change-Kyoto Protocol, Desertification, Endangered Species, Hazardous Wastes, Law of the Sea, Ozone Layer Protection, Ship Pollution, Wetlands
*signed, but not ratified:* none of the selected agreements
**Geography - note:** most of the country is composed of fertile, low-lying plains, with some hills in the east

## People

**Population:** 2,231,503 (July 2009 est.)
**Age structure:**
*0-14 years:* 13.3% (male 152,472/female 145,161)
*15-64 years:* 69.6% (male 756,469/female 797,505)
*65 years and over:* 17% (male 124,432/female 255,464) (2009 est.)
**Median age:**
*total:* 40.1 years
*male:* 37.1 years
*female:* 43.3 years (2009 est.)
**Population growth rate:** -0.614% (2009 est.)
**Birth rate:** 9.78 births/1,000 population (2009 est.)
**Death rate:** 13.63 deaths/1,000 population (2008 est.)
**Net migration rate:** -2.3 migrant(s)/1,000 population (2009 est.)

**Urbanization:**
*urban population:* 68% of total population (2008)
*rate of urbanization:* -0.5% annual rate of change (2005-10 est.)
**Sex ratio:**
*at birth:* 1.05 male(s)/female
*under 15 years:* 1.05 male(s)/female
*15-64 years:* 0.95 male(s)/female
*65 years and over:* 0.49 male(s)/female
*total population:* 0.86 male(s)/female (2009 est.)
**Infant mortality rate:**
*total:* 8.77 deaths/1,000 live births
*male:* 10.63 deaths/1,000 live births
*female:* 6.82 deaths/1,000 live births (2009 est.)
**Life expectancy at birth:**
*total population:* 72.15 years
*male:* 66.98 years
*female:* 77.59 years (2009 est.)
**Total fertility rate:** 1.3 children born/woman (2009 est.)
**HIV/AIDS - adult prevalence rate:** 0.8% (2007 est.)
**HIV/AIDS - people living with HIV/AIDS:** 10,000 (2007 est.)
**HIV/AIDS - deaths:** fewer than 500 (2007 est.)
**Major infectious diseases:**
*degree of risk:* intermediate
*food or waterborne diseases:* bacterial diarrhea
*vectorborne diseases:* tickborne encephalitis (2009)
**Nationality:**
*noun:* Latvian(s)
*adjective:* Latvian
**Ethnic groups:** Latvian 57.7%, Russian 29.6%, Belarusian 4.1%, Ukrainian 2.7%, Polish 2.5%, Lithuanian 1.4%, other 2% (2002)
**Religions:** Lutheran 19.6%, Orthodox 15.3%, other Christian 1%, other 0.4%, unspecified 63.7% (2006)
**Languages:** Latvian (official) 58.2%, Russian 37.5%, Lithuanian and other 4.3% (2000 census)
**Literacy:**
*definition:* age 15 and over can read and write
*total population:* 99.7%
*male:* 99.8%
*female:* 99.7% (2000 census)
**School life expectancy (primary to tertiary education):**
*total:* 16 years
*male:* 14 years
*female:* 17 years (2006)
**Education expenditures:** 5.1% of GDP (2004)

## Government

**Country name:**
*conventional long form:* Republic of Latvia
*conventional short form:* Latvia
*local long form:* Latvijas Republika
*local short form:* Latvija
*former:* Latvian Soviet Socialist Republic
**Government type:** parliamentary democracy

**Capital:**
*name:* Riga
*geographic coordinates:* 56 57 N, 24 06 E
*time difference:* UTC+2 (7 hours ahead of Washington, DC during Standard Time)
*daylight saving time:* +1hr, begins last Sunday in March; ends last Sunday in October
**Administrative divisions:** 26 counties (singular - rajons) and 7 municipalities*: Aizkraukles Rajons, Aluksnes Rajons, Balvu Rajons, Bauskas Rajons, Cesu Rajons, Daugavpils*, Daugavpils Rajons, Dobeles Rajons, Gulbenes Rajons, Jekabpils Rajons, Jelgava*, Jelgavas Rajons, Jurmala*, Kraslavas Rajons, Kuldigas Rajons, Liepaja*, Liepajas Rajons, Limbazu Rajons, Ludzas Rajons, Madonas Rajons, Ogres Rajons, Preilu Rajons, Rezekne*, Rezeknes Rajons, Riga*, Rigas Rajons, Saldus Rajons, Talsu Rajons, Tukuma Rajons, Valkas Rajons, Valmieras Rajons, Ventspils*, Ventspils Rajons
**Independence:** 18 November 1918 (from the Soviet Russia)
**National holiday:** Independence Day, 18 November (1918); note - 18 November 1918 was the date Latvia declared itself independent from Soviet Russia; 4 May 1990 is when it declared the renewal of independence; 21 August 1991 was the date of de facto independence from the Soviet Union
**Constitution:** 15 February 1922; restored to force by the Constitutional Law of the Republic of Latvia adopted by the Supreme Council on 21 August 1991; multiple amendments since
**Legal system:** based on civil law system with traces of Socialist legal traditions and practices; has not accepted compulsory ICJ jurisdiction
**Suffrage:** 18 years of age; universal for Latvian citizens
**Executive branch:**
*chief of state:* President Valdis ZATLERS (since 8 July 2007)
*head of government:* Prime Minister Valdis DOMBROVSKIS (since 12 March 2009)
*cabinet:* Council of Ministers nominated by the prime minister and appointed by Parliament
*elections:* president elected by Parliament for a four-year term (eligible for a second term); election last held 31 May 2007 (next to be held in 2011); prime minister appointed by the president, confirmed by Parliament
*election results:* Valdis ZATLERS elected president; parliamentary vote - Valdis ZATLERS 58, Aivars ENDZINS 39
**Legislative branch:** unicameral Parliament or Saeima (100 seats; members are elected by proportional representation from party lists by popular vote to serve four-year terms)
*elections:* last held 7 October 2006 (next to be held in October 2010)
*election results:* percent of vote by party - TP 19.5%, ZZS 16.7%, JL 16.4%, SC 14.4%; LPP/LC 8.6%; TB/LNNK 6.9%; PCTVL 6%; seats by party - TP 23, ZZS 18, JL 18, SC 17, LPP/LC 10, TB/LNNK 8, PCTVL 6; note - seats by party as of January 2009 - TP 21, SC 18, ZZS 17, JL 14, LPP/LC 10, Civic Union 7, TB/LNNK 5, PCTVL 5, independents 3
**Judicial branch:** Supreme Court (judges' appointments are confirmed by parliament); Constitutional Court (judges' appointments are confirmed by parliament)
**Political parties and leaders:** Civic Union [Sandra KALNIETE, Girts Valdis KRISTOVSKIS]; First Party of Latvia/Latvia's Way or LPP/LC [Ainars SLESERS, Ivars GODMANIS]; For Human Rights in a United Latvia or PCTVL [Jakovs PLINERS, Tatjana ZDANOKA]; For the Fatherland and Freedom/Latvian National Independence Movement or TB/LNNK [Roberts ZILE, Maris GRINBLATS]; Harmony Center or SC [Nils USAKOVS, Janis URBANOVICS]; New Era Party or JL [Solvita ABOLTINA, Dzintars ZAKIS]; People's Party or TP [Mareks SEGLINS]; Society for Different Politics or SCP [Aigars STOKENBERGS; Artis PABRIKS]; The Union of Latvian Greens and Farmers Party or ZZS [Augusts BRIGMANIS]
**Political pressure groups and leaders:** Free Trade Union Confederation of Latvia [Peteris KRIGERS], Employers' Confederation of Latvia [Elina EGLE], Farmers' Parliament [Juris LAZDINS]
**International organization participation:** Australia Group, BA, BIS, CBSS, CE, EAPC, EBRD, EIB, EU, FAO, IAEA, IBRD, ICAO, ICCt, ICRM, IDA, IFC, IFRCS, IHO, ILO, IMF, IMO, IMSO, Interpol, IOC, IOM, IPU, ISO (correspondent), ITU, ITUC, MIGA, NATO, NIB, NSG, OAS (observer), OIF (observer), OPCW, OSCE, PCA, Schengen Convention, UN, UNCTAD, UNESCO, UNWTO, UPU, WCO, WEU (associate partner), WFTU, WHO, WIPO, WMO, WTO
**Diplomatic representation in the US:**
*chief of mission:* Ambassador Andrejs PILDEGOVICS
*chancery:* 2306 Massachusetts Ave. NW, Washington, DC 20008
*telephone:* [1] (202) 328-2840
*FAX:* [1] (202) 328-2860
**Diplomatic representation from the US:**
*chief of mission:* Ambassador (vacant); Charge d'Affaires Bruce ROGERS
*embassy:* 7 Raina Boulevard, Riga LV-1510
*mailing address:* American Embassy Riga, PSC 78, Box Riga, APO AE 09723
*telephone:* [371] 670-36200
*FAX:* [371] 678-20047
**Flag description:** three horizontal bands of maroon (top), white (half-width), and maroon

## Economy

**Economy - overview:** Latvia's economy experienced GDP growth of more than 10% per year during 2006-07; but entered a recession in 2008 as a result of an unsustainable current account deficit and large debt exposure amid the softening world economy. The IMF, EU, and other donors provided assistance to Latvia as part of an agreement to defend the currency's peg to the euro and reduce the fiscal deficit to about 5% of GDP. The majority of companies, banks, and real estate have been privatized, although the state still holds sizable stakes in a few large enterprises. Latvia officially joined the World Trade Organization in February 1999. EU membership, a top foreign policy goal, came in May 2004. The current account deficit and inflation remain major concerns.
**GDP (purchasing power parity):**
$38.98 billion (2008 est.)
$40.86 billion (2007)
$37.04 billion (2006)
*note:* data are in 2008 US dollars
**GDP (official exchange rate):** $33.9 billion (2008 est.)
**GDP - real growth rate:**
-5% (2008 est.)
10.3% (2007 est.)
12.2% (2006 est.)
**GDP - per capita (PPP):**
$17,800 (2008 est.)
$18,100 (2007 est.)
$16,300 (2006 est.)
*note:* data are in 2008 US dollars
**GDP - composition by sector:**
*agriculture:* 3.3%
*industry:* 22.3%
*services:* 74.4% (2008 est.)
**Labor force:** 1.169 million (2008 est.)
**Labor force - by occupation:**
*agriculture:* 12.1%
*industry:* 25.8%
*services:* 61.8% (2005 est.)
**Unemployment rate:**
5.5% (2008 est.)
5.7% (2007 est.)
**Population below poverty line:** NA%
**Household income or consumption by percentage share:**
*lowest 10%:* 2.5%
*highest 10%:* 29.1% (2003)
**Distribution of family income - Gini index:** 36 (2005)
**Investment (gross fixed):** 30.2% of GDP (2008 est.)
**Budget:**
*revenues:* $12.33 billion
*expenditures:* $12.84 billion (2008 est.)
**Public debt:** 17% of GDP (year-end 2008)
**Inflation rate (consumer prices):**
10.5% (2008 est.)
10.1% (2007 est.)

# Latvia (continued)

**Central bank discount rate:** 6% (31 December 2007)

**Commercial bank prime lending rate:** 16.8% (31 December 2008)

**Stock of money:** $6.148 billion (31 December 2008)

**Stock of quasi money:** $4.815 billion (31 December 2008)

**Stock of domestic credit:** $30.49 billion (31 December 2008)

**Market value of publicly traded shares:** $2.144 billion (31 December 2008)

**Agriculture - products:** grain, sugar beets, potatoes, vegetables; beef, pork, milk, eggs; fish

**Industries:** buses, vans, street and railroad cars; synthetic fibers, agricultural machinery, fertilizers, washing machines, radios, electronics, pharmaceuticals, processed foods, textiles; note - dependent on imports for energy and raw materials

**Industrial production growth rate:** -3.2% (2008 est.)

**Electricity - production:** 4.734 billion kWh (2006 est.)

**Electricity - consumption:** 6.424 billion kWh (2006 est.)

**Electricity - exports:** 1.676 billion kWh (2007 est.)

**Electricity - imports:** 4.671 billion kWh (2007 est.)

**Oil - production:** 0 bbl/day (2007 est.)

**Oil - consumption:** 35,180 bbl/day (2006 est.)

**Oil - exports:** 10,070 bbl/day (2005)

**Oil - imports:** 45,340 bbl/day (2005)

**Oil - proved reserves:** 0 bbl (1 January 2006 est.)

**Natural gas - production:** 0 cu m (2007 est.)

**Natural gas - consumption:** 2.04 billion cu m (2007 est.)

**Natural gas - exports:** 0 cu m (2007 est.)

**Natural gas - imports:** 2.04 billion cu m (2007 est.)

**Current account balance:** -$2.1 billion (2008 est.)

**Exports:** $8.364 billion f.o.b. (2008 est.)

**Exports - commodities:** wood and wood products, machinery and equipment, metals, textiles, foodstuffs

**Exports - partners:** Lithuania 15.1%, Estonia 13.8%, Russia 13%, Germany 8.3%, Sweden 7.4%, UK 6.5% (2007)

**Imports:** $14.19 billion f.o.b. (2008 est.)

**Imports - commodities:** machinery and equipment, chemicals, fuels, vehicles

**Imports - partners:** Germany 15.1%, Lithuania 13.8%, Russia 8.7%, Estonia 8%, Poland 6.9%, Finland 5.1%, Sweden 4.9% (2007)

**Reserves of foreign exchange and gold:** $5.09 billion (31 December 2008 est.)

**Debt - external:** $43.9 billion (31 December 2008 est.)

**Stock of direct foreign investment - at home:** $11.21 billion (2008 est.)

**Stock of direct foreign investment - abroad:** $879 million (2008 est.)

**Exchange rates:** lati (LVL) per US dollar - 0.4701 (2008 est.), 0.5162 (2007), 0.5597 (2006), 0.5647 (2005), 0.5402 (2004)

## Communications

**Telephones - main lines in use:** 644,000 (2007)

**Telephones - mobile cellular:** 2.217 million (2007)

**Telephone system:**

*general assessment:* recent efforts focused on bringing competition to the telecommunications sector; the number of fixed lines is decreasing as wireless telephone service expands

*domestic:* number of telecommunications operators has grown rapidly since the fixed-line market opened to competition in 2003; combined fixed-line and mobile-cellular subscribership is roughly 125 per 100 persons

*international:* country code - 371; the Latvian network is now connected via fiber optic cable to Estonia, Finland, and Sweden (2007)

**Radio broadcast stations:** AM 8, FM 62, shortwave 1 (2008)

**Television broadcast stations:** 37 (plus 31 repeaters) (2008)

**Internet country code:** .lv

**Internet hosts:** 220,082 (2008)

**Internet users:** 1.177 million (2007)

## Transportation

**Airports:** 43 (2008)

**Airports - with paved runways:**
*total:* 20
*2,438 to 3,047 m:* 6
*1,524 to 2,437 m:* 3
*914 to 1,523 m:* 3
*under 914 m:* 8 (2008)

**Airports - with unpaved runways:**
*total:* 23
*914 to 1,523 m:* 1
*under 914 m:* 22 (2008)

**Pipelines:** gas 948 km; refined products 415 km (2008)

**Railways:**
*total:* 2,303 km
*broad gauge:* 2,270 km 1.520-m gauge (257 km electrified)
*narrow gauge:* 33 km 0.750-m gauge (2006)

**Roadways:**
*total:* 69,675 km
*paved:* 69,675 km (2006)

**Waterways:** 300 km (2007)

**Merchant marine:**
*total:* 22
*by type:* cargo 8, chemical tanker 3, liquefied gas 2, passenger/cargo 5, petroleum tanker 2, roll on/roll off 2
*foreign-owned:* 2 (Estonia 2)
*registered in other countries:* 118 (Antigua and Barbuda 13, Belize 12, Cambodia 1, Cook Islands 1, Cyprus 1, Dominica 1, Jamaica 1, Liberia 21, Malta 19, Marshall Islands 16, Panama 8, Russia 2, Saint Kitts and Nevis 5, Saint Vincent and the Grenadines 17) (2008)

**Ports and terminals:** Riga, Ventspils

## Military

**Military branches:** National Armed Forces (Nacionalo Brunoto Speku): Ground Forces, Navy (Latvijas Juras Speki; includes Coast Guard (Latvijas Kara Flotes)), Latvian Air Force (Latvijas Gaisa Speki), Border Guard, Latvian Home Guard (Latvijas Zemessardze) (2009)

**Military service age and obligation:** 18 years of age for voluntary male and female military service; conscription abolished January 2007; under current law, every citizen is entitled to serve in the armed forces for life (2009)

**Manpower available for military service:**
*males age 16-49:* 568,683
*females age 16-49:* 565,826 (2008 est.)

**Manpower fit for military service:**
*males age 16-49:* 410,374
*females age 16-49:* 463,144 (2009 est.)

**Manpower reaching militarily significant age annually:**
*male:* 12,901
*female:* 12,497 (2009 est.)

**Military expenditures:** 1.2% of GDP (2005 est.)

## Transnational Issues

**Disputes - international:** Russia demands better Latvian treatment of ethnic Russians in Latvia; as of January 2007, ground demarcation of the boundary with Belarus was complete and mapped with final ratification documentation in preparation; the Latvian parliament has not ratified its 1998 maritime boundary treaty with Lithuania, primarily due to concerns over oil exploration rights; as a member state that forms part of the EU's external border, Latvia has implemented the strict Schengen border rules with Russia

**Illicit drugs:** transshipment and destination point for cocaine, synthetic drugs, opiates, and cannabis from Southwest Asia, Western Europe, Latin America, and neighboring Balkan countries; despite improved legislation, vulnerable to money laundering due to nascent enforcement capabilities and comparatively weak regulation of offshore companies and the gaming industry; CIS organized crime (including counterfeiting, corruption, extortion, stolen cars, and prostitution) accounts for most laundered proceeds

# Lebanon

## Introduction

**Background:** Following the capture of Syria from the Ottoman Empire by Anglo-French forces in 1918, France received a mandate over this territory and separated out the region of Lebanon in 1920. France granted this area independence in 1943. A lengthy civil war (1975-1990) devastated the country, but Lebanon has since made progress toward rebuilding its political institutions. Under the Ta'if Accord - the blueprint for national reconciliation - the Lebanese established a more equitable political system, particularly by giving Muslims a greater voice in the political process while institutionalizing sectarian divisions in the government. Since the end of the war, Lebanon has conducted several successful elections. Most militias have been disbanded, with the exception of Hizballah, designated by the US State Department as a Foreign Terrorist Organization, and Palestinian militant groups. During Lebanon's civil war, the Arab League legitimized in the Ta'if Accord Syria's troop deployment, numbering about 16,000 based mainly east of Beirut and in the Bekaa Valley. Israel's withdrawal from southern Lebanon in May 2000 and the passage in September 2004 of UNSCR 1559 - a resolution calling for Syria to withdraw from Lebanon and end its interference in Lebanese affairs - encouraged some Lebanese groups to demand that Syria withdraw its forces as well. The assassination of former Prime Minister Rafiq HARIRI and 22 others in February 2005 led to massive demonstrations in Beirut against the Syrian presence ("the Cedar Revolution"), and Syria withdrew the remainder of its military forces in April 2005. In May-June 2005, Lebanon held its first legislative elections since the end of the civil war free of foreign interference, handing a majority to the bloc led by Saad HARIRI, the slain prime minister's son. In July 2006, Hizballah kidnapped two Israeli soldiers leading to a 34-day conflict with Israel in which approximately 1,200 Lebanese civilians were killed. UNSCR 1701 ended

the war in August 2006, and Lebanese Armed Forces (LAF) deployed throughout the country for the first time in decades, charged with securing Lebanon's borders against weapons smuggling and maintaining a weapons-free zone in south Lebanon with the help of the UN Interim Force in Lebanon (UNIFIL). The LAF in May-September 2007 battled Sunni extremist group Fatah al-Islam in the Nahr al-Barid Palestinian refugee camp, winning a decisive victory, but destroying the camp and displacing 30,000 Palestinian residents. Lebanese politicians in November 2007 were unable to agree on a successor to Emile LAHUD when he stepped down as president, creating a political vacuum until the election of Army Commander Michel SULAYMAN in May 2008 and the formation of a new unity government in July 2008.

## Geography

**Location:** Middle East, bordering the Mediterranean Sea, between Israel and Syria
**Geographic coordinates:** 33 50 N, 35 50 E
**Map references:** Middle East
**Area:**
*total:* 10,400 sq km
*land:* 10,230 sq km
*water:* 170 sq km
**Area - comparative:** about 0.7 times the size of Connecticut
**Land boundaries:**
*total:* 454 km
*border countries:* Israel 79 km, Syria 375 km
**Coastline:** 225 km
**Maritime claims:**
*territorial sea:* 12 nm
**Climate:** Mediterranean; mild to cool, wet winters with hot, dry summers; Lebanon mountains experience heavy winter snows
**Terrain:** narrow coastal plain; El Beqaa (Bekaa Valley) separates Lebanon and Anti-Lebanon Mountains
**Elevation extremes:**
*lowest point:* Mediterranean Sea 0 m
*highest point:* Qurnat as Sawda' 3,088 m
**Natural resources:** limestone, iron ore, salt, water-surplus state in a water-deficit region, arable land
**Land use:**
*arable land:* 16.35%
*permanent crops:* 13.75%
*other:* 69.9% (2005)
**Irrigated land:** 1,040 sq km (2003)
**Total renewable water resources:** 4.8 cu km (1997)
**Freshwater withdrawal (domestic/industrial/agricultural):**
*total:* 1.38 cu km/yr (33%/1%/67%)
*per capita:* 385 cu m/yr (2000)
**Natural hazards:** dust storms, sandstorms

**Environment - current issues:** deforestation; soil erosion; desertification; air pollution in Beirut from vehicular traffic and the burning of industrial wastes; pollution of coastal waters from raw sewage and oil spills
**Environment - international agreements:**
*party to:* Biodiversity, Climate Change, Climate Change-Kyoto Protocol, Desertification, Hazardous Wastes, Law of the Sea, Ozone Layer Protection, Ship Pollution, Wetlands
*signed, but not ratified:* Environmental Modification, Marine Life Conservation
**Geography - note:** Nahr el Litani is the only major river in Near East not crossing an international boundary; rugged terrain historically helped isolate, protect, and develop numerous factional groups based on religion, clan, and ethnicity

## People

**Population:** 4,017,095 (July 2009 est.)
**Age structure:**
*0-14 years:* 25.8% (male 528,047/female 506,838)
*15-64 years:* 67.1% (male 1,294,485/female 1,399,047)
*65 years and over:* 7.2% (male 130,148/female 158,530) (2009 est.)
**Median age:**
*total:* 29.3 years
*male:* 28 years
*female:* 30.5 years (2009 est.)
**Population growth rate:** 1.107% (2009 est.)
**Birth rate:** 17.1 births/1,000 population (2009 est.)
**Death rate:** 6.06 deaths/1,000 population (2008 est.)
**Net migration rate:** NA
**Urbanization:**
*urban population:* 87% of total population (2008)
*rate of urbanization:* 1.2% annual rate of change (2005-10 est.)
**Sex ratio:**
*at birth:* 1.05 male(s)/female
*under 15 years:* 1.04 male(s)/female
*15-64 years:* 0.92 male(s)/female
*65 years and over:* 0.82 male(s)/female
*total population:* 0.95 male(s)/female (2009 est.)
**Infant mortality rate:**
*total:* 21.82 deaths/1,000 live births
*male:* 24.26 deaths/1,000 live births
*female:* 19.26 deaths/1,000 live births (2009 est.)
**Life expectancy at birth:**
*total population:* 73.66 years
*male:* 71.15 years
*female:* 76.31 years (2009 est.)
**Total fertility rate:** 1.85 children born/woman (2009 est.)
**HIV/AIDS - adult prevalence rate:** 0.1% (2007 est.)
**HIV/AIDS - people living with HIV/AIDS:** 3,000 (2007 est.)
**HIV/AIDS - deaths:** fewer than 200 (2007 est.)
**Nationality:**
*noun:* Lebanese (singular and plural)
*adjective:* Lebanese

# Lebanon (continued)

**Ethnic groups:** Arab 95%, Armenian 4%, other 1%
*note:* many Christian Lebanese do not identify themselves as Arab but rather as descendents of the ancient Canaanites and prefer to be called Phoenicians
**Religions:** Muslim 59.7% (Shia, Sunni, Druze, Isma'ilite, Alawite or Nusayri), Christian 39% (Maronite Catholic, Greek Orthodox, Melkite Catholic, Armenian Orthodox, Syrian Catholic, Armenian Catholic, Syrian Orthodox, Roman Catholic, Chaldean, Assyrian, Copt, Protestant), other 1.3%
*note:* 17 religious sects recognized
**Languages:** Arabic (official), French, English, Armenian
**Literacy:**
*definition:* age 15 and over can read and write
*total population:* 87.4%
*male:* 93.1%
*female:* 82.2% (2003 est.)
**School life expectancy (primary to tertiary education):**
*total:* 13 years
*male:* 13 years
*female:* 13 years (2006)
**Education expenditures:** 2.7% of GDP (2006)

## Government

**Country name:**
*conventional long form:* Lebanese Republic
*conventional short form:* Lebanon
*local long form:* Al Jumhuriyah al Lubnaniyah
*local short form:* Lubnan
*former:* Greater Lebanon
**Government type:** republic
**Capital:**
*name:* Beirut
*geographic coordinates:* 33 52 N, 35 30 E
*time difference:* UTC+2 (7 hours ahead of Washington, DC during Standard Time)
*daylight saving time:* +1hr, begins last Sunday in March; ends last Sunday in October
**Administrative divisions:** 6 governorates (mohafazat, singular - mohafazah); Beqaa, Beyrouth, Liban-Nord, Liban-Sud, Mont-Liban, Nabatiye
*Note:* two new governorates - Aakar and Baalbek-Hermel - have been legislated but not yet implemented
**Independence:** 22 November 1943 (from League of Nations mandate under French administration)
**National holiday:** Independence Day, 22 November (1943)
**Constitution:** 23 May 1926; amended a number of times, most recently Charter of Lebanese National Reconciliation (Ta'if Accord) of October 1989
**Legal system:** mixture of Ottoman law, canon law, Napoleonic code, and civil law; no judicial review of legislative acts; has not accepted compulsory ICJ jurisdiction
**Suffrage:** 21 years of age; compulsory for all males; authorized for women at age 21 with elementary education; excludes military personnel

**Executive branch:**
*chief of state:* President Michel SULAYMAN (since 25 May 2008)
*head of government:* Prime Minister Saad HARIRI (since 27 June 2009)
*cabinet:* Cabinet chosen by the prime minister in consultation with the president and members of the National Assembly
*elections:* president elected by the National Assembly for a six-year term (may not serve consecutive terms); election last held 25 May 2008 (next to be held in 2014); the prime minister and deputy prime minister appointed by the president in consultation with the National Assembly
*election results:* Michel SULAYMAN elected president; National Assembly vote - 118 for, 6 abstentions, 3 invalidated
**Legislative branch:** unicameral National Assembly or Majlis Alnuwab (Arabic) or Assemblee Nationale (French) (128 seats; members elected by popular vote on the basis of sectarian proportional representation to serve four-year terms)
*elections:* last held on 7 June 2009 (next to be held in 2013)
*election results:* percent of vote by group - March 8 Coalition 54.7%, March 14 Coalition 45.3%; seats by group - March 8 Coalition 57; March 14 Coalition 71
**Judicial branch:** four Courts of Cassation (three courts for civil and commercial cases and one court for criminal cases); Constitutional Council (called for in Ta'if Accord - rules on constitutionality of laws); Supreme Council (hears charges against the president and prime minister as needed)
**Political parties and leaders:**
*14 March Coalition:* Democratic Gathering Bloc [Walid JUNBLATT, leader of Progressive Socialist Party]; Democratic Left [Ilyas ATALLAH]; Democratic Renewal Movement [Nassib LAHUD]; Future Movement Bloc [Sa'ad HARIRI]; Kataeb Party [Amine GEMAYEL]; Lebanese Forces [Samir JA'JA]; Tripoli Independent Bloc
*8 March Coalition:* Development and Resistance Bloc [Nabih BERRI, leader of Amal Movement]; Free Patriotic Movement [Michel AWN]; Loyalty to the Resistance Bloc [Mohammad RA'AD] (includes Hizballah Party [Hassan NASRALLAH]); Nasserite Popular Movement [Ussama SAAD]; Popular Bloc [Elias SKAFF]; Syrian Ba'th Party [Sayez SHUKR]; Syrian Social Nationalist Party [Ali QANSO]
*Independent:* Metn Bloc [Michel MURR]; Tashnaq
**Political pressure groups and leaders:** Hizballah military wing
*other:* Palestinian militias; Maronite Christians; Sunnis and their militias; Shi'as and their militias
**International organization participation:** ABEDA, ACCT, AFESD, AMF, FAO, G-24, G-77, IAEA, IBRD, ICAO, ICC, ICRM, IDA, IDB, IFAD, IFC, IFRCS, ILO, IMF, IMO, IMSO, Interpol, IOC, IPU, ISO, ITSO, ITU, LAS, MIGA, NAM, OAS (observer), OIC, OIF, PCA, UN, UNCTAD, UNESCO, UNHCR, UNIDO, UNRWA, UNWTO, UPU, WCO, WFTU, WHO, WIPO, WMO, WTO (observer)

**Diplomatic representation in the US:**
*chief of mission:* Ambassador Antoine CHEDID
*chancery:* 2560 28th Street NW, Washington, DC 20008
*telephone:* [1] (202) 939-6300
*FAX:* [1] (202) 939-6324
*consulate(s) general:* Detroit, New York, Los Angeles
**Diplomatic representation from the US:**
*chief of mission:* Ambassador Michele J. SISON
*embassy:* Awkar, Lebanon; (Awkar facing the Municipality)
*mailing address:* P. O. Box 70-840, Antelias, Lebanon; from US: US Embassy Beirut, 6070 Beirut Place, Washington, DC 20521-6070
*telephone:* [961] (4) 542600, 543600
*FAX:* [961] (4) 544136
**Flag description:** three horizontal bands consisting of red (top), white (middle, double width), and red (bottom) with a green cedar tree centered in the white band

## Economy

**Economy - overview:** Lebanon has a free-market economy and a strong laissez-faire commercial tradition. The government does not restrict foreign investment; however, the investment climate suffers from red tape, corruption, arbitrary licensing decisions, high taxes, tariffs, and fees, archaic legislation, and weak intellectual property rights. The Lebanese economy is service-oriented; main growth sectors include banking and tourism. The 1975-90 civil war seriously damaged Lebanon's economic infrastructure, cut national output by half, and all but ended Lebanon's position as a Middle Eastern entrepot and banking hub. In the years since, Lebanon has rebuilt much of its war-torn physical and financial infrastructure by borrowing heavily - mostly from domestic banks. In an attempt to reduce the ballooning national debt, the Rafiq HARIRI government in 2000 began an austerity program, reining in government expenditures, increasing revenue collection, and passing legislation to privatize state enterprises, but economic and financial reform initiatives stalled and public debt continued to grow despite receipt of more than $2 billion in bilateral assistance at the 2002 Paris II Donors Conference. The Israeli-Hizballah conflict in July-August 2006 caused an estimated $3.6 billion in infrastructure damage, and prompted international donors to pledge nearly $1 billion in recovery and reconstruction assistance. Donors met again in January 2007 at the Paris III Donor Conference and pledged more than $7.5 billion to Lebanon for development projects and budget support, conditioned on progress on Beirut's fiscal reform and privatization program. An 18-month political stalemate and sporadic sectarian and political violence hampered economic activity, particularly tourism, retail sales, and investment, until the new government was formed in July 2008. Political stability since the Doha Accord of May 2008 has helped to boost investment and tourism, but economic growth is likely to slow in 2009 as a result of the global economic recession.

# Lebanon *(continued)*

**GDP (purchasing power parity):**
$44.07 billion (2008 est.)
$41.46 billion (2007)
$39.86 billion (2006)
*note:* data are in 2008 US dollars
**GDP (official exchange rate):** $28.02 billion
(2008 est.)
**GDP - real growth rate:**
7% (2008 est.)
4% (2007 est.)
-4.3% (2006 est.)
**GDP - per capita (PPP):**
$11,100 (2008 est.)
$10,600 (2007 est.)
$10,300 (2006 est.)
*note:* data are in 2008 US dollars
**GDP - composition by sector:**
*agriculture:* 5.1%
*industry:* 19.1%
*services:* 75.8% (2008 est.)
**Labor force:** 1.1 million
*note:* in addition, there are as many as 1 million
foreign workers (2007 est.)
**Labor force - by occupation:**
*agriculture:* NA%
*industry:* NA%
*services:* NA%
**Unemployment rate:**
9.2% (2007 est.)
**Population below poverty line:** 28% (1999 est.)
**Household income or consumption by
percentage share:**
*lowest 10%:* NA%
*highest 10%:* NA%
**Investment (gross fixed):** 24.1% of GDP
(2008 est.)
**Budget:**
*revenues:* $7 billion
*expenditures:* $10 billion (2008 est.)
**Public debt:** 163.5% of GDP (2008 est.)
**Inflation rate (consumer prices):**
10% (2008 est.)
4.2% (2007 est.)
**Central bank discount rate:** 12% (31 December
2007)
**Commercial bank prime lending rate:** 10.26%
(31 December 2007)
**Stock of money:** $2.7 billion (31 December 2008)
**Stock of quasi money:** $657 billion (31 December
2008)
**Stock of domestic credit:** $45.51 billion
(31 December 2007)
**Market value of publicly traded shares:** $9.3
billion (31 December 2008)
**Agriculture - products:** citrus, grapes, tomatoes,
apples, vegetables, potatoes, olives, tobacco; sheep,
goats
**Industries:** banking, tourism, food processing, wine,
jewelry, cement, textiles, mineral and chemical
products, wood and furniture products, oil refining,
metal fabricating

**Industrial production growth rate:** NA%
**Electricity - production:** 8.764 billion kWh
(2006 est.)
**Electricity - consumption:** 8.161 billion kWh
(2006 est.)
**Electricity - exports:** 0 kWh (2007 est.)
**Electricity - imports:** 929 million kWh (2006 est.)
**Oil - production:** 0 bbl/day (2007 est.)
**Oil - consumption:** 106,000 bbl/day (2006 est.)
**Oil - exports:** 0 bbl/day (2005)
**Oil - imports:** 97,590 bbl/day (2005)
**Oil - proved reserves:** 0 bbl (1 January 2006 est.)
**Natural gas - production:** 0 cu m (2007 est.)
**Natural gas - consumption:** 0 cu m (2007 est.)
**Natural gas - exports:** 0 cu m (2007 est.)
**Natural gas - imports:** 0 cu m (2007 est.)
**Natural gas - proved reserves:** 0 cu m (1 January
2006 est.)
**Current account balance:** -$4.344 billion
(2008 est.)
**Exports:** $3.5 billion f.o.b. (2008 est.)
**Exports - commodities:** jewelry, base metals,
chemicals, miscellaneous consumer goods, fruit and
vegetables, tobacco, construction minerals, electric
power machinery and switchgear, textile fibers, paper
**Exports - partners:** Syria 25.2%, UAE 11.8%,
Switzerland 8.2%, Saudi Arabia 5.6% (2007)
**Imports:** $16.1 billion f.o.b. (2008 est.)
**Imports - commodities:** petroleum products, cars,
medicinal products, clothing, meat and live animals,
consumer goods, paper, textile fabrics, tobacco,
electrical machinery and equipment, chemicals
**Imports - partners:** Syria 12.1%, Italy 8.5%, France
8.3%, US 7%, China 5.9%, Germany 5.3%, Saudi
Arabia 4.8% (2007)
**Reserves of foreign exchange and gold:** $25.1
billion (31 December 2008)
**Debt - external:** $21.2 billion (31 December 2008)
**Stock of direct foreign investment - at home:**
$NA
**Stock of direct foreign investment - abroad:** $NA
**Exchange rates:** Lebanese pounds (LBP) per US
dollar - 1,507.5 (2008 est.), 1,507.5 (2007), 1,507.5
(2006), 1,507.5 (2005), 1,507.5 (2004)

## Communications

**Telephones - main lines in use:** 681,400 (2006)
**Telephones - mobile cellular:** 1.26 million (2007)
**Telephone system:**
*general assessment:* repair of the
telecommunications system, severely damaged
during the civil war, now complete
*domestic:* two wireless networks provide good
service; combined fixed-line and mobile-cellular
subscribership 50 per 100 persons
*international:* country code - 961; submarine cable
links to Cyprus, Egypt, and Syria; satellite earth
stations - 2 Intelsat (1 Indian Ocean and 1 Atlantic
Ocean); coaxial cable to Syria (2007)

**Radio broadcast stations:** AM 20, FM 32 (plus
about a dozen unlicensed stations operating),
shortwave 4 (2007)
**Television broadcast stations:** 15 (plus 5
repeaters) (1995)
**Internet country code:** .lb
**Internet hosts:** 36,681 (2008)
**Internet users:** 950,000 (2006)

## Transportation

**Airports:** 7 (2008)
**Airports - with paved runways:**
*total:* 5
*over 3,047 m:* 1
*2,438 to 3,047 m:* 2
*914 to 1,523 m:* 1
*under 914 m:* 1 (2008)
**Airports - with unpaved runways:**
*total:* 2
*914 to 1,523 m:* 2 (2008)
**Pipelines:** gas 43 km (2008)
**Railways:**
*total:* 401 km
*standard gauge:* 319 km 1.435 m
*narrow gauge:* 82 km 1.050 m
*note:* rail system unusable because of the damage
done during fighting in the 1980s and in 2006 (2006)
**Roadways:**
*total:* 6,970 km (includes 170 km of expressways)
(2005)
**Merchant marine:**
*total:* 33
*by type:* bulk carrier 3, cargo 13, carrier 11,
passenger/cargo 1, refrigerated cargo 1, roll on/roll off
2, vehicle carrier 2
*foreign-owned:* 4 (Greece 2, Syria 2)
*registered in other countries:* 55 (Barbados 1,
Cambodia 8, Comoros 4, Cyprus 1, Egypt 1,
Georgia 4, Honduras 1, Italy 1, North Korea 1,
Liberia 2, Malta 11, Mongolia 2, Panama 5, Saint
Vincent and the Grenadines 6, Sierra Leone 1,
Syria 3, Togo 1, unknown 2) (2008)
**Ports and terminals:** Beirut, Tripoli

## Military

**Military branches:** Lebanese Armed Forces (LAF):
Army (includes Navy), Air Force (Al Quwwat al
Jawwiya al Lubnaniya) (2009)
**Military service age and obligation:** 18-30 years of
age for voluntary military service; no conscription (2007)
**Manpower available for military service:**
*males age 16-49:* 1,106,879
*females age 16-49:* 1,122,595 (2008 est.)
**Manpower fit for military service:**
*males age 16-49:* 948,765
*females age 16-49:* 954,663 (2009 est.)
**Manpower reaching militarily significant age
annually:**
*male:* 33,018
*female:* 31,800 (2009 est.)
**Military expenditures:** 3.1% of GDP (2005 est.)

# Lebanon (continued)

Lebanon (continued)

## Transnational Issues

**Disputes - international:** lacking a treaty or other documentation describing the boundary, portions of the Lebanon-Syria boundary are unclear with several sections in dispute; since 2000, Lebanon has claimed Shab'a Farms area in the Israeli-occupied Golan Heights; the roughly 2,000-strong UN Interim Force in Lebanon (UNIFIL) has been in place since 1978

**Refugees and internally displaced persons:**
*refugees (country of origin):* 405,425 (Palestinian refugees (UNRWA)); 50,000-60,000 (Iraq)
*IDPs:* 17,000 (1975-90 civil war, Israeli invasions); 200,000 (July-August 2006 war) (2007)

**Illicit drugs:** cannabis cultivation dramatically reduced to 2,500 hectares in 2002 despite continued significant cannabis consumption; opium poppy cultivation minimal; small amounts of Latin American cocaine and Southwest Asian heroin transit country on way to European markets and for Middle Eastern consumption; money laundering of drug proceeds fuels concern that extremists are benefiting from drug trafficking

# Lesotho

## Introduction

**Background:** Basutoland was renamed the Kingdom of Lesotho upon independence from the UK in 1966. The Basuto National Party ruled for the first two decades. King MOSHOESHOE was exiled in 1990, but returned to Lesotho in 1992 and was reinstated in 1995. Constitutional government was restored in 1993 after seven years of military rule. In 1998, violent protests and a military mutiny following a contentious election prompted a brief but bloody intervention by South African and Botswanan military forces under the aegis of the Southern African Development Community. Subsequent constitutional reforms restored relative political stability. Peaceful parliamentary elections were held in 2002, but the National Assembly elections of February 2007 were hotly contested and aggrieved parties continue to periodically demonstrate their distrust of the results.

## Geography

**Location:** Southern Africa, an enclave of South Africa
**Geographic coordinates:** 29 30 S, 28 30 E
**Map references:** Africa
**Area:**
*total:* 30,355 sq km
*land:* 30,355 sq km
*water:* 0 sq km
**Area - comparative:** slightly smaller than Maryland
**Land boundaries:**
*total:* 909 km
*border countries:* South Africa 909 km
**Coastline:** 0 km (landlocked)
**Maritime claims:** none (landlocked)
**Climate:** temperate; cool to cold, dry winters; hot, wet summers
**Terrain:** mostly highland with plateaus, hills, and mountains

**Elevation extremes:**
*lowest point:* junction of the Orange and Makhaleng Rivers 1,400 m
*highest point:* Thabana Ntlenyana 3,482 m
**Natural resources:** water, agricultural and grazing land, diamonds, sand, clay, building stone
**Land use:**
*arable land:* 10.87%
*permanent crops:* 0.13%
*other:* 89% (2005)
**Irrigated land:** 30 sq km (2003)
**Total renewable water resources:** 5.2 cu km (1987)
**Freshwater withdrawal (domestic/industrial/agricultural):**
*total:* 0.05 cu km/yr (40%/40%/20%)
*per capita:* 28 cu m/yr (2000)
**Natural hazards:** periodic droughts
**Environment - current issues:** population pressure forcing settlement in marginal areas results in overgrazing, severe soil erosion, and soil exhaustion; desertification; Highlands Water Project controls, stores, and redirects water to South Africa
**Environment - international agreements:**
*party to:* Biodiversity, Climate Change, Climate Change-Kyoto Protocol, Desertification, Endangered Species, Hazardous Wastes, Law of the Sea, Marine Life Conservation, Ozone Layer Protection, Wetlands
*signed, but not ratified:* none of the selected agreements
**Geography - note:** landlocked, completely surrounded by South Africa; mountainous, more than 80% of the country is 1,800 m above sea level

## People

**Population:** 2,130,819
*note:* estimates for this country explicitly take into account the effects of excess mortality due to AIDS; this can result in lower life expectancy, higher infant mortality, higher death rates, lower population growth rates, and changes in the distribution of population by age and sex than would otherwise be expected (July 2009 est.)
**Age structure:**
*0-14 years:* 34.8% (male 373,159/female 368,271)
*15-64 years:* 60.2% (male 629,346/female 654,054)
*65 years and over:* 5% (male 42,074/female 63,915) (2009 est.)
**Median age:**
*total:* 21.4 years
*male:* 20.9 years
*female:* 22 years (2009 est.)
**Population growth rate:** 0.116% (2009 est.)
**Birth rate:** 24.14 births/1,000 population (2009 est.)
**Death rate:** 22.33 deaths/1,000 population (2008 est.)
**Net migration rate:** -0.78 migrant(s)/1,000 population (2009 est.)
**Urbanization:**
*urban population:* 25% of total population (2008)
*rate of urbanization:* 3.5% annual rate of change (2005-10 est.)

# Lesotho *(continued)*

**Sex ratio:**

*at birth:* 1.03 male(s)/female

*under 15 years:* 1.01 male(s)/female

*15-64 years:* 0.96 male(s)/female

*65 years and over:* 0.66 male(s)/female

*total population:* 0.96 male(s)/female (2009 est.)

**Infant mortality rate:**

*total:* 77.4 deaths/1,000 live births

*male:* 81.75 deaths/1,000 live births

*female:* 72.92 deaths/1,000 live births (2009 est.)

**Life expectancy at birth:**

*total population:* 40.38 years

*male:* 41.18 years

*female:* 39.54 years (2009 est.)

**Total fertility rate:** 3.06 children born/woman
(2009 est.)

**HIV/AIDS - adult prevalence rate:** 23.2%
(2007 est.)

**HIV/AIDS - people living with HIV/AIDS:** 270,000
(2007 est.)

**HIV/AIDS - deaths:** 18,000 (2007 est.)

**Nationality:**

*noun:* Mosotho (singular), Basotho (plural)

*adjective:* Basotho

**Ethnic groups:** Sotho 99.7%, Europeans, Asians,
and other 0.3%,

**Religions:** Christian 80%, indigenous beliefs 20%

**Languages:** Sesotho (southern Sotho), English
(official), Zulu, Xhosa

**Literacy:**

*definition:* age 15 and over can read and write

*total population:* 84.8%

*male:* 74.5%

*female:* 94.5% (2003 est.)

**School life expectancy (primary to tertiary
education):**

*total:* 10 years

*male:* 10 years

*female:* 10 years (2006)

**Education expenditures:** 13% of GDP (2006)

## Government

**Country name:**

*conventional long form:* Kingdom of Lesotho

*conventional short form:* Lesotho

*local long form:* Kingdom of Lesotho

*local short form:* Lesotho

*former:* Basutoland

**Government type:** parliamentary constitutional
monarchy

**Capital:**

*name:* Maseru

*geographic coordinates:* 29 19 S, 27 29 E

*time difference:* UTC+2 (7 hours ahead of
Washington, DC during Standard Time)

**Administrative divisions:** 10 districts; Berea,
Butha-Buthe, Leribe, Mafeteng, Maseru, Mohale's Hoek,
Mokhotlong, Qacha's Nek, Quthing, Thaba-Tseka

**Independence:** 4 October 1966 (from the UK)

**National holiday:** Independence Day,
4 October (1966)

**Constitution:** 2 April 1993

**Legal system:** based on English common law and
Roman-Dutch law; judicial review of legislative acts in
High Court and Court of Appeal; accepts compulsory
ICJ jurisdiction with reservations

**Suffrage:** 18 years of age; universal

**Executive branch:**

*chief of state:* King LETSIE III (since 7 February
1996); note - King LETSIE III formerly occupied the
throne from November 1990 to February 1995 while
his father was in exile

*head of government:* Prime Minister Pakalitha
MOSISILI (since 23 May 1998)

*cabinet:* Cabinet

*elections:* according to the constitution, the leader of
the majority party in the Assembly automatically
becomes prime minister; the monarch is hereditary,
but, under the terms of the constitution that came into
effect after the March 1993 election, the monarch is a
"living symbol of national unity" with no executive or
legislative powers; under traditional law the college of
chiefs has the power to depose the monarch,
determine who is next in the line of succession, or who
shall serve as regent in the event that the successor is
not of mature age

**Legislative branch:** bicameral Parliament consists
of the Senate (33 members - 22 principal chiefs and
11 other members appointed by the ruling party) and
the Assembly (120 seats, 80 by popular vote and 40
by proportional vote; members elected by popular
vote for five-year terms)

*elections:* last held 17 February 2007 (next to be held
in 2012)

*election results:* percent of vote by party - NA; seats
by party - LCD 61, NIP 21, ABC 17, LWP 10, ACP 4,
BNP 3, other 4

**Judicial branch:** High Court (chief justice appointed
by the monarch acting on the advice of the prime
minister); Court of Appeal; Magistrate Courts;
customary or traditional court

**Political parties and leaders:** Alliance of Congress
Parties or ACP including the Lesotho People's
Congress or LCP [Kelebone MAOPE], the
Basotholand African Congress or BAC [Khauhelo
RALITAPOLE], and a faction of the Basotho Congress
Party or BCP [Ntsukunyane MPHANYA]; All Basotho
Convention or ABC [Thomas THABANE]; Basotho
Batho Democratic Party or BBDP; Basotho Congress
Party or BCP; Basotho Democratic National Party or
BDNP [Thabang NYEOE]; Basotho National Party or
BNP [Maj. Gen. Justin Metsing LEKHANYA];
Basotholand African National Congress or BANC;
Christian Democratic Party or CDP [Enerst
RAMOKOENA]; Lesotho Congress for Democracy or
LCD (the governing party) [Pakalitha MOSISILI];
Lesotho Workers Party or LWP [Macaefa BILLY];
National Independent Party or NIP [Anthony
MANYELI]

**Political pressure groups and leaders:** Media
Institute of Southern Africa, Lesotho chapter [Thabang
MATJAMA] (pushes for media freedom)

**International organization participation:** ACP,
AfDB, AU, C, FAO, G-77, IBRD, ICAO, ICCt, ICRM, IDA,
IFAD, IFC, IFRCS, ILO, IMF, Interpol, IOC, IPU, ISO
(subscriber), ITU, MIGA, NAM, OPCW, SACU, SADC,
UN, UNCTAD, UNESCO, UNHCR, UNIDO, UNWTO,
UPU, WCO, WFTU, WHO, WIPO, WMO, WTO

**Diplomatic representation in the US:**

*chief of mission:* Ambassador (vacant); Charge
d'Affaires Mabasia MOHOBANE

*chancery:* 2511 Massachusetts Avenue NW,
Washington, DC 20008

*telephone:* [1] (202) 797-5533 through 5536

*FAX:* [1] (202) 234-6815

**Diplomatic representation from the US:**

*chief of mission:* Ambassador Robert NOLAN

*embassy:* 254 Kingsway, Maseru West (Consular
Section)

*mailing address:* P. O. Box 333, Maseru 100, Lesotho

*telephone:* [266] 22 312666

*FAX:* [266] 22 310116

**Flag description:** three horizontal stripes of blue
(top), white, and green in the proportions of 3:4:3; the
colors represent rain, peace, and prosperity
respectively; centered in the white stripe is a black
Basotho hat representing the indigenous people; the
flag was unfurled in October 2006 to celebrate 40
years of independence

## Economy

**Economy - overview:** Small, landlocked, and
mountainous, Lesotho relies on remittances from
miners employed in South Africa and customs duties
from the Southern Africa Customs Union for the
majority of government revenue. However, the
government has recently strengthened its tax system
to reduce dependency on customs duties. Completion
of a major hydropower facility in January 1998
permitted the sale of water to South Africa and
generated royalties for Lesotho. Lesotho produces
about 90% of its own electrical power needs. As the
number of mineworkers has declined steadily over the
past several years, a small manufacturing base has
developed based on farm products that support the
milling, canning, leather, and jute industries, as well as
a rapidly expanding apparel-assembly sector. The
latter has grown significantly mainly due to Lesotho
qualifying for the trade benefits contained in the Africa
Growth and Opportunity Act. The economy is still
primarily based on subsistence agriculture, especially
livestock, although drought has decreased agricultural
activity. The extreme inequality in the distribution of
income remains a major drawback. Lesotho has
signed an Interim Poverty Reduction and Growth
Facility with the IMF. In July 2007, Lesotho signed a
Millennium Challenge Account Compact with the US
worth $362.5 million.

**GDP (purchasing power parity):**

$3.37 billion (2008 est.)

$3.155 billion (2007)

$3.011 billion (2006)

*note:* data are in 2008 US dollars

# Lesotho *(continued)*

**GDP (official exchange rate):** $1.652 billion (2008 est.)

**GDP - real growth rate:**
6.8% (2008 est.)
4.8% (2007 est.)
6.2% (2006 est.)

**GDP - per capita (PPP):**
$1,600 (2008 est.)
$1,500 (2007 est.)
$1,400 (2006 est.)
*note:* data are in 2008 US dollars

**GDP - composition by sector:**
*agriculture:* 15.1%
*industry:* 46.7%
*services:* 38.2% (2008 est.)

**Labor force:** 838,000 (2000 est.)

**Labor force - by occupation:**
*agriculture:* 86% of resident population engaged in subsistence agriculture; roughly 35% of the active male wage earners work in South Africa
*industry and services:* 14% (2002 est.)

**Unemployment rate:**
45% (2002)

**Population below poverty line:** 49% (1999)

**Household income or consumption by percentage share:**
*lowest 10%:* 0.9%
*highest 10%:* 43.4% (2002 est.)

**Distribution of family income - Gini index:** 63.2 (1995)

**Investment (gross fixed):** 39.2% of GDP (2008 est.)

**Budget:**
*revenues:* $523 million
*expenditures:* $479.5 million (2008 est.)

**Inflation rate (consumer prices):**
10% (2008 est.)
8% (2007 est.)

**Central bank discount rate:** 12.82% (31 December 2007)

**Commercial bank prime lending rate:** 14.13% (31 December 2007)

**Stock of money:** $439.2 million (31 December 2007)

**Stock of quasi money:** $160.2 million (31 December 2007)

**Stock of domestic credit:** NA

**Agriculture - products:** corn, wheat, pulses, sorghum, barley; livestock

**Industries:** food, beverages, textiles, apparel assembly, handicrafts, construction, tourism

**Industrial production growth rate:** 12% (2008 est.)

**Electricity - production:** 200 million kWh
*note:* electricity supplied by South Africa (2006 est.)

**Electricity - consumption:** 226 million kWh (2006 est.)

**Electricity - exports:** 0 kWh (2007 est.)

**Electricity - imports:** 50 million kWh; note - electricity supplied by South Africa (2007 est.)

**Oil - production:** 0 bbl/day (2007 est.)

**Oil - consumption:** 1,400 bbl/day (2006 est.)

**Oil - exports:** 0 bbl/day (2005)

**Oil - imports:** 1,500 bbl/day (2005)

**Oil - proved reserves:** 0 bbl (1 January 2006 est.)

**Natural gas - production:** 0 cu m (2007 est.)

**Natural gas - consumption:** 0 cu m (2007 est.)

**Natural gas - exports:** 0 cu m (2007 est.)

**Natural gas - imports:** 0 cu m (2007 est.)

**Natural gas - proved reserves:** 0 cu m (1 January 2006 est.)

**Current account balance:** $666 million (2008 est.)

**Exports:** $1.06 billion f.o.b. (2008 est.)

**Exports - commodities:** manufactures 75% (clothing, footwear, road vehicles), wool and mohair, food and live animals (2000)

**Exports - partners:** US 71.5%, Belgium 25.6%, Canada 1.2% (2007)

**Imports:** $1.339 billion f.o.b. (2008 est.)

**Imports - commodities:** food; building materials, vehicles, machinery, medicines, petroleum products

**Imports - partners:** China 30%, Hong Kong 29.6%, India 10%, South Korea 6.6%, Germany 6.4%, Pakistan 4.6% (2007)

**Reserves of foreign exchange and gold:** $799 million (31 December 2008 est.)

**Debt - external:** $628 million (31 December 2008 est.)

**Exchange rates:** maloti (LSL) per US dollar - 7.75 (2008 est.), 7.25 (2007), 6.85 (2006), 6.3593 (2005), 6.4597 (2004)

## Communications

**Telephones - main lines in use:** 53,100 (2006)

**Telephones - mobile cellular:** 456,000 (2007)

**Telephone system:**
*general assessment:* rudimentary system consisting of a modest but growing number of landlines, a small microwave radio relay system, and a small radiotelephone communication system; mobile-cellular telephone system is expanding
*domestic:* privatized in 2001, Telecom Lesotho tasked with providing an additional 50,000 fixed-line connections within five years, a target not met; mobile-cellular service is expanding with a subscribership approaching 25 per 100 persons; rural services are scant
*international:* country code - 266; satellite earth station -1 Intelsat (Atlantic Ocean) (2007)

**Radio broadcast stations:** AM 1, FM 3, shortwave 1 (2007)

**Television broadcast stations:** 1 (2007)

**Internet country code:** .ls

**Internet hosts:** 83 (2008)

**Internet users:** 70,000 (2007)

## Transportation

**Airports:** 28 (2008)

**Airports - with paved runways:**
*total:* 3
*over 3,047 m:* 1
*914 to 1,523 m:* 1
*under 914 m:* 1 (2008)

**Airports - with unpaved runways:**
*total:* 25
*914 to 1,523 m:* 4
*under 914 m:* 21 (2008)

**Roadways:**
*total:* 7,091 km
*paved:* 1,404 km
*unpaved:* 5,687 km (2003)

## Military

**Military branches:** Lesotho Defense Force (LDF): Army (includes Air Wing) (2008)

**Military service age and obligation:** 18-24 years of age for voluntary military service; no conscription (2008)

**Manpower available for military service:**
*males age 16-49:* 525,203
*females age 16-49:* 522,485 (2008 est.)

**Manpower fit for military service:**
*males age 16-49:* 267,083
*females age 16-49:* 240,868 (2009 est.)

**Manpower reaching militarily significant age annually:**
*male:* 26,039
*female:* 25,964 (2009 est.)

**Military expenditures:** 2.6% of GDP (2006)

**Military - note:** Lesotho's declared policy is maintenance of its independent sovereignty and preservation of internal security; in practice, external security is guaranteed by South Africa; restructuring of the Lesotho Defense Force (LDF) and Ministry of Defense and Public Service over the past five years has focused on subordinating the defense apparatus to civilian control and restoring the LDF's cohesion; the restructuring has considerably improved capabilities and professionalism, but the LDF is disproportionately large for a small, poor country; the government has outlined a reduction to a planned 1,500-man strength, but these plans have met with vociferous resistance from the political opposition and from inside the LDF (2008)

## Transnational Issues

**Disputes - international:** none

# Liberia

## Introduction

**Background:** Settlement of freed slaves from the US in what is today Liberia began in 1822; by 1847, the Americo-Liberians were able to establish a republic. William TUBMAN, president from 1944-71, did much to promote foreign investment and to bridge the economic, social, and political gaps between the descendents of the original settlers and the inhabitants of the interior. In 1980, a military coup led by Samuel DOE ushered in a decade of authoritarian rule. In December 1989, Charles TAYLOR launched a rebellion against DOE's regime that led to a prolonged civil war in which DOE himself was killed. A period of relative peace in 1997 allowed for elections that brought TAYLOR to power, but major fighting resumed in 2000. An August 2003 peace agreement ended the war and prompted the resignation of former president Charles TAYLOR, who faces war crimes charges in The Hague related to his involvement in Sierra Leone's civil war. After two years of rule by a transitional government, democratic elections in late 2005 brought President Ellen JOHNSON SIRLEAF to power. The UN Mission in Liberia (UNMIL) maintains a strong presence throughout the country, but the security situation is still fragile and the process of rebuilding the social and economic structure of this war-torn country will take many years.

## Geography

**Location:** Western Africa, bordering the North Atlantic Ocean, between Cote d'Ivoire and Sierra Leone
**Geographic coordinates:** 6 30 N, 9 30 W
**Map references:** Africa
**Area:**
*total:* 111,370 sq km
*land:* 96,320 sq km
*water:* 15,050 sq km
**Area - comparative:** slightly larger than Tennessee

**Land boundaries:**
*total:* 1,585 km
*border countries:* Guinea 563 km, Cote d'Ivoire 716 km, Sierra Leone 306 km
**Coastline:** 579 km
**Maritime claims:**
*territorial sea:* 200 nm
**Climate:** tropical; hot, humid; dry winters with hot days and cool to cold nights; wet, cloudy summers with frequent heavy showers
**Terrain:** mostly flat to rolling coastal plains rising to rolling plateau and low mountains in northeast
**Elevation extremes:**
*lowest point:* Atlantic Ocean 0 m
*highest point:* Mount Wuteve 1,380 m
**Natural resources:** iron ore, timber, diamonds, gold, hydropower
**Land use:**
*arable land:* 3.43%
*permanent crops:* 1.98%
*other:* 94.59% (2005)
**Irrigated land:** 30 sq km (2003)
**Total renewable water resources:** 232 cu km (1987)
**Freshwater withdrawal (domestic/industrial/agricultural):**
*total:* 0.11 cu km/yr (27%/18%/55%)
*per capita:* 34 cu m/yr (2000)
**Natural hazards:** dust-laden harmattan winds blow from the Sahara (December to March)
**Environment - current issues:** tropical rain forest deforestation; soil erosion; loss of biodiversity; pollution of coastal waters from oil residue and raw sewage
**Environment - international agreements:**
*party to:* Biodiversity, Climate Change, Climate Change-Kyoto Protocol, Desertification, Endangered Species, Hazardous Wastes, Law of the Sea, Ozone Layer Protection, Ship Pollution, Tropical Timber 83, Tropical Timber 94, Wetlands
*signed, but not ratified:* Environmental Modification, Marine Life Conservation
**Geography - note:** facing the Atlantic Ocean, the coastline is characterized by lagoons, mangrove swamps, and river-deposited sandbars; the inland grassy plateau supports limited agriculture

## People

**Population:** 3,441,790 (July 2009 est.)
**Age structure:**
*0-14 years:* 44.1% (male 760,989/female 758,554)
*15-64 years:* 53% (male 904,770/female 920,704)
*65 years and over:* 2.8% (male 47,013/female 49,760) (2009 est.)
**Median age:**
*total:* 18 years
*male:* 17.9 years
*female:* 18.2 years (2009 est.)
**Population growth rate:** 2.665% (2009 est.)
**Birth rate:** 42.25 births/1,000 population (2009 est.)

**Death rate:** 21.45 deaths/1,000 population (2008 est.)
**Net migration rate:** 5.13 migrant(s)/1,000 population (2009 est.)
**Urbanization:**
*urban population:* 60% of total population (2008)
*rate of urbanization:* 5.6% annual rate of change (2005-10 est.)
**Sex ratio:**
*at birth:* 1.03 male(s)/female
*under 15 years:* 1 male(s)/female
*15-64 years:* 0.98 male(s)/female
*65 years and over:* 0.94 male(s)/female
*total population:* 0.99 male(s)/female (2009 est.)
**Infant mortality rate:**
*total:* 138.24 deaths/1,000 live births
*male:* 153.55 deaths/1,000 live births
*female:* 122.46 deaths/1,000 live births (2009 est.)
**Life expectancy at birth:**
*total population:* 41.84 years
*male:* 40.71 years
*female:* 43 years (2009 est.)
**Total fertility rate:** 5.79 children born/woman (2009 est.)
**HIV/AIDS - adult prevalence rate:** 1.7% (2007 est.)
**HIV/AIDS - people living with HIV/AIDS:** 35,000 (2007 est.)
**HIV/AIDS - deaths:** 2,300 (2007 est.)
**Major infectious diseases:**
*degree of risk:* very high
*food or waterborne diseases:* bacterial and protozoal diarrhea, hepatitis A, and typhoid fever
*vectorborne diseases:* malaria and yellow fever
*water contact disease:* schistosomiasis
*aerosolized dust or soil contact disease:* Lassa fever
*animal contact disease:* rabies (2009)
**Nationality:**
*noun:* Liberian(s)
*adjective:* Liberian
**Ethnic groups:** indigenous African 95% (including Kpelle, Bassa, Gio, Kru, Grebo, Mano, Krahn, Gola, Gbandi, Loma, Kissi, Vai, Dei, Bella, Mandingo, and Mende), Americo-Liberians 2.5% (descendants of immigrants from the US who had been slaves), Congo People 2.5% (descendants of immigrants from the Caribbean who had been slaves)
**Religions:** Christian 40%, Muslim 20%, indigenous beliefs 40%
**Languages:** English 20% (official), some 20 ethnic group languages few of which can be written or used in correspondence
**Literacy:**
*definition:* age 15 and over can read and write
*total population:* 57.5%
*male:* 73.3%
*female:* 41.6% (2003 est.)
**School life expectancy (primary to tertiary education):**
*total:* 10 years
*male:* 11 years
*female:* 8 years (2000)
**Education expenditures:** NA

# Liberia (continued)

## Government

**Country name:**
*conventional long form:* Republic of Liberia
*conventional short form:* Liberia
**Government type:** republic
**Capital:**
*name:* Monrovia
*geographic coordinates:* 6 18 N, 10 48 W
*time difference:* UTC 0 (5 hours ahead of Washington, DC during Standard Time)
**Administrative divisions:** 15 counties; Bomi, Bong, Gbarpolu, Grand Bassa, Grand Cape Mount, Grand Gedeh, Grand Kru, Lofa, Margibi, Maryland, Montserrado, Nimba, River Cess, River Gee, Sinoe
**Independence:** 26 July 1847
**National holiday:** Independence Day, 26 July (1847)
**Constitution:** 6 January 1986
**Legal system:** dual system of statutory law based on Anglo-American common law for the modern sector and customary law based on unwritten tribal practices for indigenous sector; accepts compulsory ICJ jurisdiction with reservations
**Suffrage:** 18 years of age; universal
**Executive branch:**
*chief of state:* President Ellen JOHNSON SIRLEAF (since 16 January 2006); note - the President is both the chief of state and head of government
*head of government:* President Ellen JOHNSON SIRLEAF (since 16 January 2006)
*cabinet:* Cabinet appointed by the president and confirmed by the Senate
*elections:* president elected by popular vote for a six-year term (eligible for a second term); election last held 8 November 2005 (next to be held in 2011)
*election results:* Ellen JOHNSON SIRLEAF elected president; percent of vote, second round - Ellen JOHNSON SIRLEAF 59.6%, George WEAH 40.4%
**Legislative branch:** bicameral National Assembly consists of the Senate (30 seats; note - number of seats changed in 11 October 2005 elections; members elected by popular vote to serve nine-year terms) and the House of Representatives (64 seats; members elected by popular vote to serve six-year terms)
*elections:* Senate - last held 11 October 2005 (next to be held in 2011); House of Representatives - last held 11 October 2005 (next to be held in 2011)
*election results:* Senate - percent of vote by party - NA; seats by party - COTOL 7, NPP 4, CDC 3, LP 3, UP 3, APD 3, other 7; House of Representatives - percent of vote by party - NA; seats by party - CDC 15, LP 9, COTOL 8, UP 8, APD 5, NPP 4, other 15
*note:* junior senators - those who received the second most votes in each county in the 11 October 2005 election - will only serve a six-year first term because the Liberian constitution mandates staggered Senate elections to ensure continuity of government; all senators will be eligible for nine-year terms thereafter
**Judicial branch:** Supreme Court

**Political parties and leaders:** Alliance for Peace and Democracy or APD [Togba-na TIPOTEH]; Coalition for the Transformation of Liberia or COTOL [H. Varney SHERMAN]; Congress for Democratic Change or CDC [George WEAH]; Liberty Party or LP [Charles BRUMSKINE]; National Patriotic Party or NPP [Roland MASSAQUOI]; Unity Party or UP [Ellen JOHNSON SIRLEAF]
**Political pressure groups and leaders:**
*other:* demobilized former military officers
**International organization participation:** ACP, AfDB, AU, ECOWAS, FAO, G-77, IAEA, IBRD, ICAO, ICCt, ICRM, IDA, IFAD, IFC, IFRCS, ILO, IMF, IMO, IMSO, Interpol, IOC, IOM, IPU, ITU, ITUC, MIGA, NAM, OPCW, UN, UNCTAD, UNESCO, UNIDO, UPU, WCL, WCO, WFTU, WHO, WIPO, WMO, WTO (observer)
**Diplomatic representation in the US:**
*chief of mission:* Ambassador Milton Nathaniel BARNES
*chancery:* 5201 16th Street NW, Washington, DC 20011
*telephone:* [1] (202) 723-0437
*FAX:* [1] (202) 723-0436
*consulate(s) general:* New York
**Diplomatic representation from the US:**
*chief of mission:* Ambassador Linda THOMAS-GREENFIELD
*embassy:* 111 United Nations Drive, P. O. Box 98, Mamba Point, 1000 Monrovia, 10
*mailing address:* use embassy street address
*telephone:* [231] 7-705-4826
*FAX:* [231] 7-701-0370
**Flag description:** 11 equal horizontal stripes of red (top and bottom) alternating with white; there is a white five-pointed star on a blue square in the upper hoist-side corner; the design was based on the US flag

## Economy

**Economy - overview:** Civil war and government mismanagement destroyed much of Liberia's economy, especially the infrastructure in and around the capital, Monrovia. Many businesses fled the country, taking capital and expertise with them, but with the conclusion of fighting and the installation of a democratically-elected government in 2006, some have returned. Richly endowed with water, mineral resources, forests, and a climate favorable to agriculture, Liberia had been a producer and exporter of basic products - primarily raw timber and rubber. Local manufacturing, mainly foreign owned, had been small in scope. President JOHNSON SIRLEAF, a Harvard-trained banker and administrator, has taken steps to reduce corruption, build support from international donors, and encourage private investment. Embargos on timber and diamond exports have been lifted, opening new sources of revenue for the government. The reconstruction of infrastructure and the raising of incomes in this ravaged economy will largely depend on generous financial and technical assistance from donor countries and foreign investment in key sectors, such as infrastructure and power generation.

**GDP (purchasing power parity):**
$1.532 billion (2008 est.)
$1.425 billion (2007)
$1.303 billion (2006)
*note:* data are in 2008 US dollars
**GDP (official exchange rate):** $926 million (2008 est.)
**GDP - real growth rate:**
7.5% (2008 est.)
9.4% (2007 est.)
7.8% (2006 est.)
**GDP - per capita (PPP):**
$500 (2008 est.)
$400 (2007 est.)
$400 (2006 est.)
*note:* data are in 2008 US dollars
**GDP - composition by sector:**
*agriculture:* 76.9%
*industry:* 5.4%
*services:* 17.7% (2002 est.)
**Labor force - by occupation:**
*agriculture:* 70%
*industry:* 8%
*services:* 22% (2000 est.)
**Unemployment rate:**
85% (2003 est.)
**Population below poverty line:** 80% (2000 est.)
**Household income or consumption by percentage share:**
*lowest 10%:* NA%
*highest 10%:* NA%
**Budget:**
*revenues:* NA
*expenditures:* NA
**Inflation rate (consumer prices):**
11.2% (2007 est.)
**Commercial bank prime lending rate:** 15.05% (31 December 2007)
**Stock of money:** $145.6 million (31 December 2007)
**Stock of quasi money:** $49.89 million (31 December 2007)
**Stock of domestic credit:** $1.157 billion (31 December 2007)
**Market value of publicly traded shares:** $NA
**Agriculture - products:** rubber, coffee, cocoa, rice, cassava (tapioca), palm oil, sugarcane, bananas; sheep, goats; timber
**Industries:** rubber processing, palm oil processing, timber, diamonds
**Industrial production growth rate:** NA%
**Electricity - production:** 320 million kWh (2006 est.)
**Electricity - consumption:** 297.6 million kWh (2006 est.)
**Electricity - exports:** 0 kWh (2007 est.)
**Electricity - imports:** 0 kWh (2007 est.)
**Oil - production:** 0 bbl/day (2007 est.)
**Oil - consumption:** 3,687 bbl/day (2006 est.)
**Oil - exports:** 23.37 bbl/day (2005)
**Oil - imports:** 3,593 bbl/day (2005)

# Liberia *(continued)*

**Oil - proved reserves:** 0 bbl (1 January 2006 est.)
**Natural gas - production:** 0 cu m (2007 est.)
**Natural gas - consumption:** 0 cu m (2007 est.)
**Natural gas - exports:** 0 cu m (2007 est.)
**Natural gas - imports:** 0 cu m (2007 est.)
**Natural gas - proved reserves:** 0 cu m (1 January 2006 est.)
**Current account balance:** -$224 million (2007)
**Exports:** $1.197 billion f.o.b. (2006)
**Exports - commodities:** rubber, timber, iron, diamonds, cocoa, coffee
**Exports - partners:** Malaysia 27.5%, Poland 18.5%, Germany 11.5%, US 10.5%, Spain 8.2%, Norway 5.5% (2007)
**Imports:** $7.143 billion f.o.b. (2006)
**Imports - commodities:** fuels, chemicals, machinery, transportation equipment, manufactured goods; foodstuffs
**Imports - partners:** South Korea 31.4%, Singapore 22.1%, Japan 14.9%, China 10.1% (2007)
**Debt - external:** $3.2 billion (2005 est.)
**Stock of direct foreign investment - at home:** $NA
**Stock of direct foreign investment - abroad:** $NA
**Exchange rates:** Liberian dollars (LRD) per US dollar - NA (2007), 59.43 (2006), 53.098 (2005), 54.906 (2004), 59.379 (2003)

## Communications

**Telephones - main lines in use:** 6,900 (2002)
**Telephones - mobile cellular:** 563,000 (2007)
**Telephone system:**
*general assessment:* the limited services available are found almost exclusively in the capital Monrovia; coverage extended to a number of other towns and rural areas by four mobile-cellular network operators
*domestic:* fixed line service stagnant and extremely limited; mobile-cellular subscription base growing and teledensity approaching 20 per 100 persons
*international:* country code - 231; satellite earth station -1 Intelsat (Atlantic Ocean) (2007)
**Radio broadcast stations:** AM 0, FM 10, shortwave 2 (2007)
**Television broadcast stations:** 4 (plus 4 repeaters) (2007)
**Internet country code:** .lr
**Internet hosts:** 7 (2008)
**Internet users:** 1,000 (2002)

## Transportation

**Airports:** 52 (2008)
**Airports - with paved runways:**
*total:* 2
*over 3,047 m:* 1
*1,524 to 2,437 m:* 1 (2008)
**Airports - with unpaved runways:**
*total:* 50
*1,524 to 2,437 m:* 5
*914 to 1,523 m:* 9
*under 914 m:* 36 (2008)

**Railways:**
*total:* 490 km
*standard gauge:* 345 km 1.435-m gauge
*narrow gauge:* 145 km 1.067-m gauge
*note:* sections of railway are inoperable because of damage suffered during civil wars from 1980 to 2003 (2008)
**Roadways:**
*total:* 10,600 km
*paved:* 657 km
*unpaved:* 9,943 km (2000)
**Merchant marine:**
*total:* 2,204
*by type:* barge carrier 3, bulk carrier 390, cargo 107, chemical tanker 241, combination ore/oil 7, container 750, liquefied gas 84, passenger 1, passenger/cargo 3, petroleum tanker 460, refrigerated cargo 103, roll on/roll off 7, specialized tanker 12, vehicle carrier 36
*foreign-owned:* 2,109 (Argentina 3, Belgium 4, Brazil 3, Canada 7, China 11, Croatia 2, Cyprus 63, Denmark 12, Estonia 1, France 5, Germany 849, Gibraltar 5, Greece 358, Hong Kong 44, India 2, Indonesia 2, Isle of Man 5, Israel 23, Italy 41, Japan 116, South Korea 3, Latvia 21, Lebanon 2, Mexico 2, Monaco 8, Netherlands 6, Nigeria 2, Norway 40, Poland 13, Qatar 4, Romania 2, Russia 94, Saudi Arabia 27, Singapore 32, Slovenia 3, Sweden 10, Switzerland 13, Taiwan 91, Turkey 7, Ukraine 25, UAE 23, UK 20, US 98, Uruguay 3, Vietnam 4) (2008)
**Ports and terminals:** Buchanan, Monrovia

## Military

**Military branches:** Armed Forces of Liberia (AFL): Army, Navy, Air Force
**Military service age and obligation:** 16 years of age for voluntary military service; no conscription (2008)
**Manpower available for military service:**
*males age 16-49:* 729,813
*females age 16-49:* 741,223 (2008 est.)
**Manpower fit for military service:**
*males age 16-49:* 387,417
*females age 16-49:* 382,334 (2009 est.)
**Manpower reaching militarily significant age annually:**
*male:* 34,059
*female:* 33,281 (2009 est.)
**Military expenditures:** 1.3% of GDP (2006 est.)

## Transnational Issues

**Disputes - international:** although civil unrest continues to abate with the assistance of 18,000 UN Mission in Liberia (UNMIL) peacekeepers, as of January 2007, Liberian refugees still remain in Guinea, Cote d'Ivoire, Sierra Leone, and Ghana; Liberia, in turn, shelters refugees fleeing turmoil in Cote d'Ivoire; despite the presence of over 9,000 UN forces (UNOCI) in Cote d'Ivoire since 2004, ethnic conflict continues to spread into neighboring states who can no longer send their migrant workers to Ivorian cocoa plantations; UN sanctions ban Liberia from exporting diamonds and timber

**Refugees and internally displaced persons:**
*refugees (country of origin):* 12,600 (Cote d'Ivoire)
*IDPs:* 13,000 (civil war from 1990-2004; IDP resettlement began in November 2004) (2007)
**Illicit drugs:** transshipment point for Southeast and Southwest Asian heroin and South American cocaine for the European and US markets; corruption, criminal activity, arms-dealing, and diamond trade provide significant potential for money laundering, but the lack of well-developed financial system limits the country's utility as a major money-laundering center

# Libya

## Introduction

**Background:** The Italians supplanted the Ottoman Turks in the area around Tripoli in 1911 and did not relinquish their hold until 1943 when defeated in World War II. Libya then passed to UN administration and achieved independence in 1951. Following a 1969 military coup, Col. Muammar Abu Minyar al-QADHAFI began to espouse his own political system, the Third Universal Theory. The system is a combination of socialism and Islam derived in part from tribal practices and is supposed to be implemented by the Libyan people themselves in a unique form of "direct democracy." QADHAFI has always seen himself as a revolutionary and visionary leader. He used oil funds during the 1970s and 1980s to promote his ideology outside Libya, supporting subversives and terrorists abroad to hasten the end of Marxism and capitalism. In addition, beginning in 1973, he engaged in military operations in northern Chad's Aozou Strip - to gain access to minerals and to use as a base of influence in Chadian politics - but was forced to retreat in 1987. UN sanctions in 1992 isolated QADHAFI politically following the downing of Pan AM Flight 103 over Lockerbie, Scotland. During the 1990s, QADHAFI began to rebuild his relationships with Europe. UN sanctions were suspended in April 1999 and finally lifted in September 2003 after Libya accepted responsibility for the Lockerbie bombing. In December 2003, Libya announced that it had agreed to reveal and end its programs to develop weapons of mass destruction and to renounce terrorism. QADHAFI has made significant strides in normalizing relations with Western nations since then. He has received various Western European leaders as well as many working-level and commercial delegations, and made his first trip to Western Europe in 15 years when he traveled to Brussels in April 2004. The US rescinded Libya's designation as a state sponsor of terrorism in June 2006. In January 2008, Libya assumed a nonpermanent seat on the UN Security Council for the 2008-09 term. In August 2008, the US and Libya signed a bilateral comprehensive claims settlement agreement to compensate claimants in both countries who allege injury or death at the hands of the other country, including the Lockerbie bombing, the LaBelle disco bombing, and the UTA 772 bombing. In October 2008, the US Government received $1.5 billion pursuant to the agreement to distribute to US national claimants, and as a result effectively normalized its bilateral relationship with Libya. The two countries then exchanged ambassadors for the first time since 1973 in January 2009.

## Geography

**Location:** Northern Africa, bordering the Mediterranean Sea, between Egypt and Tunisia
**Geographic coordinates:** 25 00 N, 17 00 E
**Map references:** Africa
**Area:**
*total:* 1,759,540 sq km
*land:* 1,759,540 sq km
*water:* 0 sq km
**Area - comparative:** slightly larger than Alaska
**Land boundaries:**
*total:* 4,348 km
*border countries:* Algeria 982 km, Chad 1,055 km, Egypt 1,115 km, Niger 354 km, Sudan 383 km, Tunisia 459 km
**Coastline:** 1,770 km
**Maritime claims:**
*territorial sea:* 12 nm
*note:* Gulf of Sidra closing line - 32 degrees, 30 minutes north
*exclusive fishing zone:* 62 nm
**Climate:** Mediterranean along coast; dry, extreme desert interior
**Terrain:** mostly barren, flat to undulating plains, plateaus, depressions
**Elevation extremes:**
*lowest point:* Sabkhat Ghuzayyil -47 m
*highest point:* Bikku Bitti 2,267 m
**Natural resources:** petroleum, natural gas, gypsum
**Land use:**
*arable land:* 1.03%
*permanent crops:* 0.19%
*other:* 98.78% (2005)
**Irrigated land:** 4,700 sq km (2003)
**Total renewable water resources:** 0.6 cu km (1997)
**Freshwater withdrawal (domestic/industrial/agricultural):**
*total:* 4.27 cu km/yr (14%/3%/83%)
*per capita:* 730 cu m/yr (2000)
**Natural hazards:** hot, dry, dust-laden ghibli is a southern wind lasting one to four days in spring and fall; dust storms, sandstorms
**Environment - current issues:** desertification; limited natural fresh water resources; the Great Manmade River Project, the largest water development scheme in the world, is being built to bring water from large aquifers under the Sahara to coastal cities

**Environment - international agreements:**
*party to:* Biodiversity, Climate Change, Climate Change-Kyoto Protocol, Desertification, Endangered Species, Hazardous Wastes, Marine Dumping, Ozone Layer Protection, Ship Pollution, Wetlands
*signed, but not ratified:* Law of the Sea
**Geography - note:** more than 90% of the country is desert or semidesert

## People

**Population:** 6,310,434
*note:* includes 166,510 non-nationals (July 2009 est.)
**Age structure:**
*0-14 years:* 33% (male 1,064,866/female 1,019,790)
*15-64 years:* 62.7% (male 2,033,478/female 1,920,755)
*65 years and over:* 4.3% (male 133,092/female 138,453) (2009 est.)
**Median age:**
*total:* 23.9 years
*male:* 24 years
*female:* 23.8 years (2009 est.)
**Population growth rate:** 2.17% (2009 est.)
**Birth rate:** 25.15 births/1,000 population (2009 est.)
**Death rate:** 3.46 deaths/1,000 population (2008 est.)
**Net migration rate:** NA
**Urbanization:**
*urban population:* 78% of total population (2008)
*rate of urbanization:* 2.2% annual rate of change (2005-10 est.)
**Sex ratio:**
*at birth:* 1.05 male(s)/female
*under 15 years:* 1.04 male(s)/female
*15-64 years:* 1.06 male(s)/female
*65 years and over:* 0.96 male(s)/female
*total population:* 1.05 male(s)/female (2009 est.)
**Infant mortality rate:**
*total:* 21.05 deaths/1,000 live births
*male:* 23.21 deaths/1,000 live births
*female:* 18.78 deaths/1,000 live births (2009 est.)
**Life expectancy at birth:**
*total population:* 77.26 years
*male:* 74.98 years
*female:* 79.65 years (2009 est.)
**Total fertility rate:** 3.08 children born/woman (2009 est.)
**HIV/AIDS - adult prevalence rate:** 0.3% (2001 est.)
**HIV/AIDS - people living with HIV/AIDS:** 10,000 (2001 est.)
**HIV/AIDS - deaths:** NA
**Nationality:**
*noun:* Libyan(s)
*adjective:* Libyan
**Ethnic groups:** Berber and Arab 97%, other 3% (includes Greeks, Maltese, Italians, Egyptians, Pakistanis, Turks, Indians, and Tunisians)
**Religions:** Sunni Muslim 97%, other 3%
**Languages:** Arabic, Italian, English, all are widely understood in the major cities

# Libya *(continued)*

**Literacy:**
*definition:* age 15 and over can read and write
*total population:* 82.6%
*male:* 92.4%
*female:* 72% (2003 est.)
**School life expectancy (primary to tertiary education):**
*total:* 17 years
*male:* 16 years
*female:* 17 years (2003)
**Education expenditures:** 2.7% of GDP (1999)

## Government

**Country name:**
*conventional long form:* Great Socialist People's Libyan Arab Jamahiriya
*conventional short form:* Libya
*local long form:* Al Jamahiriyah al Arabiyah al Libiyah ash Shabiyah al Ishtirakiyah al Uthma
*local short form:* none
**Government type:** Jamahiriya (a state of the masses) in theory, governed by the populace through local councils; in practice, an authoritarian state
**Capital:**
*name:* Tripoli (Tarabulus)
*geographic coordinates:* 32 53 N, 13 10 E
*time difference:* UTC+2 (7 hours ahead of Washington, DC during Standard Time)
**Administrative divisions:** 25 municipalities (baladiyat, singular - baladiyah); Ajdabiya, Al 'Aziziyah, Al Fatih, Al Jabal al Akhdar, Al Jufrah, Al Khums, Al Kufrah, An Nuqat al Khams, Ash Shati', Awbari, Az Zawiyah, Banghazi, Darnah, Ghadamis, Gharyan, Misratah, Murzuq, Sabha, Sawfajjin, Surt, Tarabulus, Tarhunah, Tubruq, Yafran, Zlitan; note - the 25 municipalities may have been replaced by 13 regions
**Independence:** 24 December 1951 (from UN trusteeship)
**National holiday:** Revolution Day, 1 September (1969)
**Constitution:** none; note - following the September 1969 military overthrow of the Libyan government, the Revolutionary Command Council replaced the existing constitution with the Constitutional Proclamation in December 1969; in March 1977, Libya adopted the Declaration of the Establishment of the People's Authority
**Legal system:** based on Italian and French civil law systems and Islamic law; separate religious courts; no constitutional provision for judicial review of legislative acts; has not accepted compulsory ICJ jurisdiction
**Suffrage:** 18 years of age; universal and technically compulsory
**Executive branch:**
*chief of state:* Revolutionary Leader Col. Muammar Abu Minyar al-QADHAFI (since 1 September 1969); note - holds no official title, but is de facto chief of state
*head of government:* Secretary of the General People's Committee (Prime Minister) al-Baghdadi Ali al-MAHMUDI (since 5 March 2006)

*cabinet:* General People's Committee established by the General People's Congress
*elections:* national elections are indirect through a hierarchy of people's committees; head of government elected by the General People's Congress; election last held March 2006 (next to be held March 2009)
*election results:* NA
**Legislative branch:** unicameral General People's Congress (760 seats; members elected indirectly through a hierarchy of people's committees)
**Judicial branch:** Supreme Court
**Political parties and leaders:** none
**Political pressure groups and leaders:**
*other:* Arab nationalist movements; anti-QADHAFI Libyan exile Movement; Islamic elements
**International organization participation:** ABEDA, AfDB, AFESD, AMF, AMU, AU, CAEU, COMESA, FAO, G-77, IAEA, IBRD, ICAO, ICRM, IDA, IDB, IFAD, IFC, IFRCS, ILO, IMF, IMO, IMSO, Interpol, IOC, IOM, IPU, ISO, ITSO, ITU, LAS, MIGA, NAM, OAPEC, OIC, OPCW, OPEC, PCA, UN, UNAMID, UNCTAD, UNESCO, UNIDO, UNWTO, UPU, WCL, WCO, WFTU, WHO, WIPO, WMO, WTO (observer)
**Diplomatic representation in the US:**
*chief of mission:* Ambassador Ali Suleiman AUJALI
*chancery:* 2600 Virginia Avenue NW, Suite 705, Washington, DC 20037
*telephone:* [1] (202) 944-9601
*FAX:* [1] (202) 944-9060
**Diplomatic representation from the US:**
*chief of mission:* Ambassador Gene A. CRETZ
*embassy:* off Jaraba Street, behind the Libyan-Swiss clinic, Ben Ashour
*mailing address:* US Embassy, 8850 Tripoli Place, Washington, DC 20521-8850
*telephone:* [218] 91-220-3239
**Flag description:** plain green; green is the traditional color of Islam (the state religion)

## Economy

**Economy - overview:** The Libyan economy depends primarily upon revenues from the oil sector, which contribute about 95% of export earnings, about one-quarter of GDP, and 60% of public sector wages. The expected weakness in world hydrocarbon prices throughout 2009 will reduce Libyan government tax income and constrain Libyan economic growth in 2009. Substantial revenues from the energy sector coupled with a small population give Libya one of the highest per capita GDPs in Africa, but little of this income flows down to the lower orders of society. Libyan officials in the past five years have made progress on economic reforms as part of a broader campaign to reintegrate the country into the international fold. This effort picked up steam after UN sanctions were lifted in September 2003 and as Libya announced in December 2003 that it would abandon programs to build weapons of mass destruction. UN Sanctions against Libya were lifted in September 2003. The process of lifting US unilateral sanctions

began in the spring of 2004; all sanctions were removed by June 2006, helping Libya attract greater foreign direct investment, especially in the energy sector. Libyan oil and gas licensing rounds continue to draw high international interest; the National Oil Company set a goal of nearly doubling oil production to 3 million bbl/day by 2012. Libya faces a long road ahead in liberalizing the socialist-oriented economy, but initial steps - including applying for WTO membership, reducing some subsidies, and announcing plans for privatization - are laying the groundwork for a transition to a more market-based economy. The non-oil manufacturing and construction sectors, which account for more than 20% of GDP, have expanded from processing mostly agricultural products to include the production of petrochemicals, iron, steel, and aluminum. Climatic conditions and poor soils severely limit agricultural output, and Libya imports about 75% of its food. Libya's primary agricultural water source remains the Great Manmade River Project, but significant resources are being invested in desalinization research to meet growing water demands.
**GDP (purchasing power parity):**
$88.86 billion (2008 est.)
$83.59 billion (2007)
$78.27 billion (2006)
*note:* data are in 2008 US dollars
**GDP (official exchange rate):** $108.5 billion (2008 est.)
**GDP - real growth rate:**
6.3% (2008 est.)
6.8% (2007 est.)
5.9% (2006 est.)
**GDP - per capita (PPP):**
$14,400 (2008 est.)
$13,800 (2007 est.)
$13,300 (2006 est.)
*note:* data are in 2008 US dollars
**GDP - composition by sector:**
*agriculture:* 1.5%
*industry:* 61.7%
*services:* 36.8% (2008 est.)
**Labor force:** 1.916 million (2008 est.)
**Labor force - by occupation:**
*agriculture:* 17%
*industry:* 23%
*services:* 59% (2004 est.)
**Unemployment rate:**
30% (2004 est.)
**Population below poverty line:** 7.4% (2005 est.)
**Household income or consumption by percentage share:**
*lowest 10%:* NA%
*highest 10%:* NA%
**Investment (gross fixed):** 8.1% of GDP (2008 est.)
**Budget:**
*revenues:* $56.35 billion
*expenditures:* $29.12 billion (2008 est.)
**Public debt:** 3.6% of GDP (2008 est.)

# Libya (continued)

**Inflation rate (consumer prices):**
10.5% (2008 est.)
6.3% (2007 est.)
**Central bank discount rate:** 4% (31 December 2007)
**Commercial bank prime lending rate:** 6% (31 December 2007)
**Stock of money:** $18.04 billion (31 December 2007)
**Stock of quasi money:** $3.192 billion (31 December 2007)
**Stock of domestic credit:** NA
**Market value of publicly traded shares:** $NA
**Agriculture - products:** wheat, barley, olives, dates, citrus, vegetables, peanuts, soybeans; cattle
**Industries:** petroleum, iron and steel, food processing, textiles, handicrafts, cement
**Industrial production growth rate:** 5.8% (2008 est.)
**Electricity - production:** 23.98 billion kWh (2007 est.)
**Electricity - consumption:** 20.71 billion kWh (2006 est.)
**Electricity - exports:** 0 kWh (2007 est.)
**Electricity - imports:** 0 kWh (2007 est.)
**Oil - production:** 1.845 million bbl/day (2007 est.)
**Oil - consumption:** 278,700 bbl/day (2006 est.)
**Oil - exports:** 1.455 million bbl/day (2005)
**Oil - imports:** 575.3 bbl/day (2005)
**Oil - proved reserves:** 41.46 billion bbl (1 January 2008 est.)
**Natural gas - production:** 14.8 billion cu m (2006 est.)
**Natural gas - consumption:** 6.39 billion cu m (2006 est.)
**Natural gas - exports:** 9.9 billion cu m (2007 est.)
**Natural gas - imports:** 0 cu m (2007 est.)
**Natural gas - proved reserves:** 1.419 trillion cu m (1 January 2008 est.)
**Current account balance:** $43.33 billion (2008 est.)
**Exports:** $66.13 billion f.o.b. (2008 est.)
**Exports - commodities:** crude oil, refined petroleum products, natural gas, chemicals
**Exports - partners:** Italy 40.5%, Germany 12.2%, US 7.4%, Spain 7.4%, France 6.3% (2007)
**Imports:** $20.64 billion f.o.b. (2008 est.)
**Imports - commodities:** machinery, semi-finished goods, food, transport equipment, consumer products
**Imports - partners:** Italy 18.9%, Germany 7.7%, China 7.3%, Tunisia 6.8%, France 5.7%, Turkey 5.4%, US 4.3% (2007)
**Reserves of foreign exchange and gold:** $99.45 billion (31 December 2008 est.)
**Debt - external:** $5.521 billion (31 December 2008 est.)
**Stock of direct foreign investment - at home:** $8.736 billion (2008 est.)
**Stock of direct foreign investment - abroad:** $4.783 billion (2008 est.)
**Exchange rates:** Libyan dinars (LYD) per US dollar - 1.2112 (2008 est.), 1.2604 (2007), 1.3108 (2006), 1.3084 (2005), 1.305 (2004)

## Communications

**Telephones - main lines in use:** 852,300 (2005)
**Telephones - mobile cellular:** 4.5 million (2007)
**Telephone system:**
*general assessment:* telecommunications system is state-owned and service is poor, but investment is being made to upgrade; state retains monopoly in fixed-line services; mobile cellular telephone system became operational in 1996; multiple providers for a mobile telephone system that is growing rapidly; combined fixed line and mobile telephone density approached 90 telephones per 100 persons in 2007
*domestic:* microwave radio relay, coaxial cable, cellular, tropospheric scatter, and a domestic satellite system with 14 earth stations
*international:* country code - 218; satellite earth stations - 4 Intelsat, NA Arabsat, and NA Intersputnik; submarine cables to France and Italy; microwave radio relay to Tunisia and Egypt; tropospheric scatter to Greece; participant in Medarabtel (2007)
**Radio broadcast stations:** AM 16, FM 3, shortwave 3 (2001)
**Television broadcast stations:** 12 (plus 1 repeater) (1999)
**Internet country code:** .ly
**Internet hosts:** 31 (2008)
**Internet users:** 260,000 (2006)

## Transportation

**Airports:** 140 (2008)
**Airports - with paved runways:**
*total:* 58
*over 3,047 m:* 23
*2,438 to 3,047 m:* 6
*1,524 to 2,437 m:* 22
*914 to 1,523 m:* 6
*under 914 m:* 1 (2008)
**Airports - with unpaved runways:**
*total:* 82
*over 3,047 m:* 5
*2,438 to 3,047 m:* 1
*1,524 to 2,437 m:* 16
*914 to 1,523 m:* 41
*under 914 m:* 19 (2008)
**Heliports:** 2 (2007)
**Pipelines:** condensate 776 km; gas 2,860 km; oil 6,987 km (2008)
**Railways:** 0 km
*note:* Libya plans to build seven lines totaling 2,757 km of 1.435-m gauge track (2006)
**Roadways:**
*total:* 100,024 km
*paved:* 57,214 km
*unpaved:* 42,810 km (2003)
**Merchant marine:**
*total:* 17
*by type:* cargo 9, liquefied gas 3, petroleum tanker 4, roll on/roll off 1
*foreign-owned:* 4 (Kuwait 1, Norway 1, Syria 2)
*registered in other countries:* 3 (Malta 3) (2008)

**Ports and terminals:** As Sidrah, Az Zuwaytinah, Marsa al Burayqah, Ra's Lanuf, Tripoli, Zawiyah

## Military

**Military branches:** Armed Peoples on Duty (APOD, Army), Libyan Arab Navy, Libyan Arab Air Force (Al-Quwwat al-Jawwiya al-Jamahiriya al-Arabia al-Libyya, LAAF), Libyan Coast Guard (2008)
**Military service age and obligation:** 17 years of age (2004)
**Manpower available for military service:**
*males age 16-49:* 1,682,183
*females age 16-49:* 1,611,001 (2008 est.)
**Manpower fit for military service:**
*males age 16-49:* 1,466,578
*females age 16-49:* 1,409,684 (2009 est.)
**Manpower reaching militarily significant age annually:**
*male:* 60,710
*female:* 58,219 (2009 est.)
**Military expenditures:** 3.9% of GDP (2005 est.)

## Transnational Issues

**Disputes - international:** Libya has claimed more than 32,000 sq km in southeastern Algeria and about 25,000 sq km in the Tommo region of Niger in a currently dormant dispute; various Chadian rebels from the Aozou region reside in southern Libya
**Refugees and internally displaced persons:**
*refugees (country of origin):* 8,000 (Palestinian Territories) (2007)
**Trafficking in persons:**
*current situation:* Libya is a transit and destination country for men and women from sub-Saharan Africa and Asia trafficked for the purposes of forced labor and commercial sexual exploitation
*tier rating:* Tier 2 Watch List - Libya is on the Tier 2 Watch List for its failure to provide evidence of increasing efforts to address trafficking in persons in 2007 when compared to 2006, particularly in the area of investigating and prosecuting trafficking offenses; Libya did not publicly release any data on investigations or punishment of any trafficking offenses (2008)

# Liechtenstein

## Introduction

**Background:** The Principality of Liechtenstein was established within the Holy Roman Empire in 1719. Occupied by both French and Russian troops during the Napoleanic wars, it became a sovereign state in 1806 and joined the Germanic Confederation in 1815. Liechtenstein became fully independent in 1866 when the Confederation dissolved. Until the end of World War I, it was closely tied to Austria, but the economic devastation caused by that conflict forced Liechtenstein to enter into a customs and monetary union with Switzerland. Since World War II (in which Liechtenstein remained neutral), the country's low taxes have spurred outstanding economic growth. In 2000, shortcomings in banking regulatory oversight resulted in concerns about the use of financial institutions for money laundering. However, Liechtenstein implemented anti-money-laundering legislation and a Mutual Legal Assistance Treaty with the US that went into effect in 2003.

## Geography

**Location:** Central Europe, between Austria and Switzerland
**Geographic coordinates:** 47 16 N, 9 32 E
**Map references:** Europe
**Area:**
*total:* 160 sq km
*land:* 160 sq km
*water:* 0 sq km
**Area - comparative:** about 0.9 times the size of Washington, DC
**Land boundaries:**
*total:* 76 km
*border countries:* Austria 34.9 km, Switzerland 41.1 km
**Coastline:** 0 km (doubly landlocked)
**Maritime claims:** none (landlocked)
**Climate:** continental; cold, cloudy winters with frequent snow or rain; cool to moderately warm, cloudy, humid summers

**Terrain:** mostly mountainous (Alps) with Rhine Valley in western third
**Elevation extremes:**
*lowest point:* Ruggeller Riet 430 m
*highest point:* Vorder-Grauspitz 2,599 m
**Natural resources:** hydroelectric potential, arable land
**Land use:**
*arable land:* 25%
*permanent crops:* 0%
*other:* 75% (2005)
**Irrigated land:** NA
**Natural hazards:** NA
**Environment - current issues:** NA
**Environment - international agreements:**
*party to:* Air Pollution, Air Pollution-Nitrogen Oxides, Air Pollution-Persistent Organic Pollutants, Air Pollution-Sulfur 85, Air Pollution-Sulfur 94, Air Pollution-Volatile Organic Compounds, Biodiversity, Climate Change, Climate Change-Kyoto Protocol, Desertification, Endangered Species, Hazardous Wastes, Ozone Layer Protection, Wetlands
*signed, but not ratified:* Law of the Sea
**Geography - note:** along with Uzbekistan, one of only two doubly landlocked countries in the world; variety of microclimatic variations based on elevation

## People

**Population:** 34,761 (July 2009 est.)
**Age structure:**
*0-14 years:* 16.6% (male 2,877/female 2,901)
*15-64 years:* 69.4% (male 11,917/female 12,220)
*65 years and over:* 13.9% (male 2,085/female 2,761) (2009 est.)
**Median age:**
*total:* 41 years
*male:* 40.4 years
*female:* 41.5 years (2009 est.)
**Population growth rate:** 0.702% (2009 est.)
**Birth rate:** 9.75 births/1,000 population (2009 est.)
**Death rate:** 7.42 deaths/1,000 population (2008 est.)
**Net migration rate:** 4.66 migrant(s)/1,000 population (2009 est.)
**Urbanization:**
*urban population:* 14% of total population (2008)
*rate of urbanization:* 0.5% annual rate of change (2005-10 est.)
**Sex ratio:**
*at birth:* 1.01 male(s)/female
*under 15 years:* 0.99 male(s)/female
*15-64 years:* 0.98 male(s)/female
*65 years and over:* 0.76 male(s)/female
*total population:* 0.94 male(s)/female (2009 est.)
**Infant mortality rate:**
*total:* 4.25 deaths/1,000 live births
*male:* 5.54 deaths/1,000 live births
*female:* 2.95 deaths/1,000 live births (2009 est.)
**Life expectancy at birth:**
*total population:* 80.06 years
*male:* 76.59 years
*female:* 83.53 years (2009 est.)

**Total fertility rate:** 1.52 children born/woman (2009 est.)
**HIV/AIDS - adult prevalence rate:** NA
**HIV/AIDS - people living with HIV/AIDS:** NA
**HIV/AIDS - deaths:** NA
**Nationality:**
*noun:* Liechtensteiner(s)
*adjective:* Liechtenstein
**Ethnic groups:** Liechtensteiner 65.6%, other 34.4% (2000 census)
**Religions:** Roman Catholic 76.2%, Protestant 7%, unknown 10.6%, other 6.2% (June 2002)
**Languages:** German (official), Alemannic dialect
**Literacy:**
*definition:* age 10 and over can read and write
*total population:* 100%
*male:* 100%
*female:* 100%
**School life expectancy (primary to tertiary education):**
*total:* 15 years
*male:* 16 years
*female:* 13 years (2004)
**Education expenditures:** NA

## Government

**Country name:**
*conventional long form:* Principality of Liechtenstein
*conventional short form:* Liechtenstein
*local long form:* Fuerstentum Liechtenstein
*local short form:* Liechtenstein
**Government type:** constitutional monarchy
**Capital:**
*name:* Vaduz
*geographic coordinates:* 47 08 N, 9 31 E
*time difference:* UTC+1 (6 hours ahead of Washington, DC during Standard Time)
*daylight saving time:* +1hr, begins last Sunday in March; ends last Sunday in October
**Administrative divisions:** 11 communes (Gemeinden, singular - Gemeinde); Balzers, Eschen, Gamprin, Mauren, Planken, Ruggell, Schaan, Schellenberg, Triesen, Triesenberg, Vaduz
**Independence:** 23 January 1719 (Principality of Liechtenstein established); 12 July 1806 (independence from the Holy Roman Empire)
**National holiday:** Assumption Day, 15 August
**Constitution:** 5 October 1921; amended 15 September 2003
**Legal system:** local civil and penal codes based on civil law system; accepts compulsory ICJ jurisdiction with reservations
**Suffrage:** 18 years of age; universal
**Executive branch:**
*chief of state:* Prince HANS ADAM II (since 13 November 1989, assumed executive powers 26 August 1984); Heir Apparent Prince ALOIS, son of the monarch (born 11 June 1968); note - on 15 August 2004, HANS ADAM transferred the official duties of the ruling prince to ALOIS, but HANS ADAM retains status of chief of state

# Liechtenstein (continued)

*head of government:* Head of Government Klaus TSCHUTSCHER (since 25 March 2009)
*cabinet:* Cabinet elected by the Parliament, confirmed by the monarch
*elections:* the monarch is hereditary; following legislative elections, the leader of the majority party in the Landtag is usually appointed the head of government by the monarch and the leader of the largest minority party in the Landtag is usually appointed the deputy head of government by the monarch if there is a coalition government
**Legislative branch:** unicameral Parliament or Landtag (25 seats; members are elected by popular vote under proportional representation to serve four-year terms)
*elections:* last held 8 February 2009 (next to be held February 2013)
*election results:* percent of vote by party - VU 47.6%, FBP 43.5%, FL 8.9%; seats by party - VU 13, FBP 11, FL 1
**Judicial branch:** Supreme Court or Oberster Gerichtshof; Court of Appeal or Obergericht
**Political parties and leaders:** Die Freie Liste (The Free List) or FL [Claudia HEEB-FLECK and Egon MATT]; Fortschrittliche Buergerpartei (Progressive Citizens' Party) or FBP [Marcus VOGT]; Vaterlaendische Union (Fatherland Union) or VU [Adolf HEEB]
**Political pressure groups and leaders:** NA
**International organization participation:** CE, EBRD, EFTA, IAEA, ICCt, ICRM, IFRCS, Interpol, IOC, IPU, ITSO, ITU, OPCW, OSCE, PCA, UN, UNCTAD, UPU, WCL, WIPO, WTO
**Diplomatic representation in the US:**
*chief of mission:* Ambassador Claudia FRITSCHE
*chancery:* 2900 K Street, NW, Suite 602B, Washington, DC 20007
*telephone:* [1] (202) 331-0590
*FAX:* [1] (202) 331-3221
**Diplomatic representation from the US:** the US does not have an embassy in Liechtenstein; the US Ambassador to Switzerland is accredited to Liechtenstein
**Flag description:** two equal horizontal bands of blue (top) and red with a gold crown on the hoist side of the blue band

## Economy

**Economy - overview:** Despite its small size and limited natural resources, Liechtenstein has developed into a prosperous, highly industrialized, free-enterprise economy with a vital financial service sector and the highest per capita income in the world. The Liechtenstein economy is widely diversified with a large number of small businesses. Low business taxes - the maximum tax rate is 20% - and easy incorporation rules have induced many holding companies to establish nominal offices in Liechtenstein, providing 30% of state revenues. The country participates in a customs union with Switzerland and uses the Swiss franc as its national currency. It imports more than 90% of its energy requirements.

Liechtenstein has been a member of the European Economic Area (an organization serving as a bridge between the European Free Trade Association (EFTA) and the EU) since May 1995. The government is working to harmonize its economic policies with those of an integrated Europe. In 2008 Liechtenstein came under renewed international pressure - particularly from Germany - to improve transparency in its banking and tax systems.
**GDP (purchasing power parity):**
$4.16 billion (2007)
$4.035 billion (2006)
**GDP (official exchange rate):** $4.993 billion (2007)
**GDP - real growth rate:**
3.1% (2007 est.)
**GDP - per capita (PPP):**
$118,000 (2007 est.)
**GDP - composition by sector:**
*agriculture:* 8%
*industry:* 39%
*services:* 54% (2007)
**Labor force:** 31,000 of whom 13,900 commute from Austria, Switzerland, and Germany to work each day (31 December 2006)
**Labor force - by occupation:**
*agriculture:* 1.7%
*industry:* 43.5%
*services:* 55.4% (31 December 2006)
**Unemployment rate:**
1.5% (31 December 2007)
1.3% (September 2002)
**Population below poverty line:** NA%
**Household income or consumption by percentage share:**
*lowest 10%:* NA%
*highest 10%:* NA%
**Budget:**
*revenues:* $424.2 million
*expenditures:* $414.1 million (1998 est.)
**Inflation rate (consumer prices):**
1% (2001
**Market value of publicly traded shares:** $NA
**Agriculture - products:** wheat, barley, corn, potatoes; livestock, dairy products
**Industries:** electronics, metal manufacturing, dental products, ceramics, pharmaceuticals, food products, precision instruments, tourism, optical instruments
**Industrial production growth rate:** NA%
**Exports:** $2.47 billion (1996)
**Exports - commodities:** small specialty machinery, connectors for audio and video, parts for motor vehicles, dental products, hardware, prepared foodstuffs, electronic equipment, optical products
**Imports:** $917.3 million (1996)
**Imports - commodities:** agricultural products, raw materials, energy products, machinery, metal goods, textiles, foodstuffs, motor vehicles
**Debt - external:** $0 (2001)
**Exchange rates:** Swiss francs (CHF) per US dollar - 1.0774 (2008 est.), 1.1973 (2007), 1.2539 (2006), 1.2452 (2005), 1.2435 (2004)

## Communications

**Telephones - main lines in use:** 20,000 (2005)
**Telephones - mobile cellular:** 27,500 (2005)
**Telephone system:**
*general assessment:* automatic telephone system
*domestic:* NA
*international:* country code - 423; linked to Swiss networks by cable and microwave radio relay
**Radio broadcast stations:** AM 0, FM 4, shortwave 0 (1998)
**Television broadcast stations:** NA (linked to Swiss networks) (1997)
**Internet country code:** .li
**Internet hosts:** 7,639 (2008)
**Internet users:** 22,000 (2006)

## Transportation

**Pipelines:** gas 20 km (2008)
**Railways:** 9 km 1.435-m gauge (electrified)
*note:* belongs to the Austrian Railway System connecting Austria and Switzerland (2006)
**Roadways:**
*total:* 380 km
*paved:* 380 km (2007)
**Waterways:** 28 km (2008)

## Military

**Military branches:** no regular military forces (constitutionally prohibited); Principality of Liechtenstein National Police (Landespolizei, LP) (2008)
**Manpower available for military service:**
*males age 16-49:* 8,102 (2008 est.)
**Manpower fit for military service:**
*males age 16-49:* 6,584
*females age 16-49:* 6,801 (2009 est.)
**Manpower reaching militarily significant age annually:**
*male:* 199
*female:* 222 (2009 est.)
**Military - note:** Liechtenstein has no military forces, but is interested in European security policy and is an active member of the Organization for Security and Cooperation in Europe (OSCE)

## Transnational Issues

**Disputes - international:** none
**Illicit drugs:** has strengthened money laundering controls, but money laundering remains a concern due to Liechtenstein's sophisticated offshore financial services sector

# Lithuania

## Introduction

**Background:** Lithuanian lands were united under MINDAUGAS in 1236; over the next century, through alliances and conquest, Lithuania extended its territory to include most of present-day Belarus and Ukraine. By the end of the 14th century Lithuania was the largest state in Europe. An alliance with Poland in 1386 led the two countries into a union through the person of a common ruler. In 1569, Lithuania and Poland formally united into a single dual state, the Polish-Lithuanian Commonwealth. This entity survived until 1795, when its remnants were partitioned by surrounding countries. Lithuania regained its independence following World War I but was annexed by the USSR in 1940 - an action never recognized by the US and many other countries. On 11 March 1990, Lithuania became the first of the Soviet republics to declare its independence, but Moscow did not recognize this proclamation until September of 1991 (following the abortive coup in Moscow). The last Russian troops withdrew in 1993. Lithuania subsequently restructured its economy for integration into Western European institutions; it joined both NATO and the EU in the spring of 2004.

## Geography

**Location:** Eastern Europe, bordering the Baltic Sea, between Latvia and Russia
**Geographic coordinates:** 56 00 N, 24 00 E
**Map references:** Europe
**Area:**
*total:* 65,300 sq km
*land:* NA sq km
*water:* NA sq km
**Area - comparative:** slightly larger than West Virginia
**Land boundaries:**
*total:* 1,574 km
*border countries:* Belarus 680 km, Latvia 576 km, Poland 91 km, Russia (Kaliningrad) 227 km

**Coastline:** 90 km
**Maritime claims:**
*territorial sea:* 12 nm
**Climate:** transitional, between maritime and continental; wet, moderate winters and summers
**Terrain:** lowland, many scattered small lakes, fertile soil
**Elevation extremes:**
*lowest point:* Baltic Sea 0 m
*highest point:* Juozapines Kalnas 294 m
**Natural resources:** peat, arable land, amber
**Land use:**
*arable land:* 44.81%
*permanent crops:* 0.9%
*other:* 54.29% (2005)
**Irrigated land:** 70 sq km (2003)
**Total renewable water resources:** 24.5 cu km (2005)
**Freshwater withdrawal (domestic/industrial/agricultural):**
*total:* 3.33 cu km/yr (78%/15%/7%)
*per capita:* 971 cu m/yr (2003)
**Natural hazards:** NA
**Environment - current issues:** contamination of soil and groundwater with petroleum products and chemicals at military bases
**Environment - international agreements:**
*party to:* Air Pollution, Air Pollution-Nitrogen Oxides, Air Pollution-Persistent Organic Pollutants, Air Pollution-Sulphur 85, Air Pollution-Sulphur 94, Air Pollution-Volatile Organic Compounds, Biodiversity, Climate Change, Climate Change-Kyoto Protocol, Desertification, Endangered Species, Environmental Modification, Hazardous Wastes, Law of the Sea, Ozone Layer Protection, Ship Pollution, Wetlands
*signed, but not ratified:* none of the selected agreements
**Geography - note:** fertile central plains are separated by hilly uplands that are ancient glacial deposits

## People

**Population:** 3,555,179 (July 2009 est.)
**Age structure:**
*0-14 years:* 14.2% (male 258,423/female 245,115)
*15-64 years:* 69.6% (male 1,214,743/female 1,261,413)
*65 years and over:* 16.2% (male 198,714/female 376,771) (2009 est.)
**Median age:**
*total:* 39.3 years
*male:* 36.8 years
*female:* 41.9 years (2009 est.)
**Population growth rate:** -0.279% (2009 est.)
**Birth rate:** 9.11 births/1,000 population (2009 est.)
**Death rate:** 11.12 deaths/1,000 population (2008 est.)
**Net migration rate:** -0.72 migrant(s)/1,000 population (2009 est.)

**Urbanization:**
*urban population:* 67% of total population (2008)
*rate of urbanization:* -0.4% annual rate of change (2005-10 est.)
**Sex ratio:**
*at birth:* 1.06 male(s)/female
*under 15 years:* 1.05 male(s)/female
*15-64 years:* 0.96 male(s)/female
*65 years and over:* 0.53 male(s)/female
*total population:* 0.89 male(s)/female (2009 est.)
**Infant mortality rate:**
*total:* 6.47 deaths/1,000 live births
*male:* 7.73 deaths/1,000 live births
*female:* 5.13 deaths/1,000 live births (2009 est.)
**Life expectancy at birth:**
*total population:* 74.9 years
*male:* 69.98 years
*female:* 80.1 years (2009 est.)
**Total fertility rate:** 1.23 children born/woman (2009 est.)
**HIV/AIDS - adult prevalence rate:** 0.1% (2007 est.)
**HIV/AIDS - people living with HIV/AIDS:** 2,200 (2007 est.)
**HIV/AIDS - deaths:** fewer than 200 (2007 est.)
**Major infectious diseases:**
*degree of risk:* intermediate
*food or waterborne diseases:* bacterial diarrhea
*vectorborne diseases:* tickborne encephalitis (2009)
**Nationality:**
*noun:* Lithuanian(s)
*adjective:* Lithuanian
**Ethnic groups:** Lithuanian 83.4%, Polish 6.7%, Russian 6.3%, other or unspecified 3.6% (2001 census)
**Religions:** Roman Catholic 79%, Russian Orthodox 4.1%, Protestant (including Lutheran and Evangelical Christian Baptist) 1.9%, other or unspecified 5.5%, none 9.5% (2001 census)
**Languages:** Lithuanian (official) 82%, Russian 8%, Polish 5.6%, other and unspecified 4.4% (2001 census)
**Literacy:**
*definition:* age 15 and over can read and write
*total population:* 99.6%
*male:* 99.6%
*female:* 99.6% (2001 census)
**School life expectancy (primary to tertiary education):**
*total:* 16 years
*male:* 15 years
*female:* 17 years (2006)
**Education expenditures:** 5% of GDP (2005)

## Government

**Country name:**
*conventional long form:* Republic of Lithuania
*conventional short form:* Lithuania
*local long form:* Lietuvos Respublika
*local short form:* Lietuva
*former:* Lithuanian Soviet Socialist Republic
**Government type:** parliamentary democracy

# Lithuania (continued)

**Capital:**
*name:* Vilnius
*geographic coordinates:* 54 41 N, 25 19 E
*time difference:* UTC+2 (7 hours ahead of Washington, DC during Standard Time)
*daylight saving time:* +1hr, begins last Sunday in March; ends last Sunday in October
**Administrative divisions:** 10 counties (apskritys, singular - apskritis); Alytaus, Kauno, Klaipedos, Marijampoles, Panevezio, Siauliu, Taurages, Telsiu, Utenos, Vilniaus
**Independence:** 11 March 1990 (declared); 6 September 1991 (recognized by the Soviet Union)
**National holiday:** Independence Day, 16 February (1918); note - 16 February 1918 was the date Lithuania declared its independence from Soviet Russia and established its statehood; 11 March 1990 was the date it declared its independence from the Soviet Union
**Constitution:** adopted 25 October 1992; last amended 13 July 2004
**Legal system:** based on civil law system; legislative acts can be appealed to the constitutional court; has not accepted compulsory ICJ jurisdiction
**Suffrage:** 18 years of age; universal
**Executive branch:**
*chief of state:* President Valdas ADAMKUS (since 12 July 2004)
*head of government:* Prime Minister Andrius KUBILIUS (since 27 November 2008)
*cabinet:* Council of Ministers appointed by the president on the nomination of the prime minister
*elections:* president elected by popular vote for a five-year term (eligible for a second term); election last held 17 May 2009 (next to be held in May 2014); prime minister appointed by the president on the approval of the Parliament
*election results:* Dalia GRYBAUSKAITE elected president; percent of vote - Dalia GRYBAUSKAITE 69.1%, Algirdas BUTKEVICIUS 11.8%, Valentinas MAZURONIS 6.2%, others 12.9%; Andrius KUBILIUS' government approved by Parliament 83-40 with 5 abstentions
*note:* Dalia GRYBAUSKAITE is to assume office on 12 July 2009
**Legislative branch:** unicameral Parliament or Seimas (141 seats; 71 members are elected by popular vote, 70 are elected by proportional representation; serve four-year terms)
*elections:* last held 12 and 26 October 2008 (next to be held October 2012)
*election results:* percent of vote by party - TS-LKD 19.7%, TPP 15.1%, TT 12.7%, LSDP 11.7%, KDP+J 9%, LRLS 5.7%, LCS 5.3%, LLRA 4.8%, LVLS 3.7%, NS 3.6%, other 8.7%; seats by faction - TS-LKD 44, LSDP 26, TPP 16, TT 15, LRLS 11, KDP+J 10, LCS 8, LLRA 3, LVLS 3, NS 1, independent 4
**Judicial branch:** Constitutional Court; Supreme Court; Court of Appeal; judges for all courts appointed by the president

**Political parties and leaders:** Civil Democracy Party or PDP [Viktor MUNTIANAS]; Coalition of Labor Party and Youth or KDP+J [Viktor USPASKICH]; Electoral Action of Lithuanian Poles or LLRA [Valdemar TOMASZEVSKI]; Homeland Union - Lithuanian Christian Democrats or TS-LKD [Andrius KUBILIUS]; Lithuanian Peasant Popular Union or LVLS [Kazimiera PRUNSKIENE]; Liberal and Center Union or LCS [Arturas ZUOKAS]; Liberal Movement or LRLS [Eligijus MASIULIS]; National Revival or TPP [Arunas VALINSKAS]; New Union (Social Liberal) or NS [Arturas PAULAUSKAS]; Order and Justice Party or TT [Rolandas PAKSAS]; Social Democratic Party or LSDP [Gediminas KIRKILAS]; Young Lithuania and New Nationalists [Stanislovas BUSKEVICIUS]
**Political pressure groups and leaders:** Europe House (promotes the EU); European Movement (promotes the EU); Lithuanian Future Forum (promotes the EU)
**International organization participation:** Australia Group, BA, BIS, CBSS, CE, EAPC, EBRD, EIB, EU, FAO, IAEA, IBRD, ICAO, ICC, ICCt, ICRM, IDA, IFC, IFRCS, ILO, IMF, IMO, Interpol, IOC, IOM, IPU, ISO, ITU, ITUC, MIGA, NATO, NIB, NSG, OIF (observer), OPCW, OSCE, PCA, Schengen Convention, UN, UNCTAD, UNESCO, UNIDO, UNOMIG, UNWTO, UPU, WCL, WCO, WEU (associate partner), WFTU, WHO, WIPO, WMO, WTO
**Diplomatic representation in the US:**
*chief of mission:* Ambassador Audrius BRUZGA
*chancery:* 2622 16th Street NW, Washington, DC 20009
*telephone:* [1] (202) 234-5860
*FAX:* [1] (202) 328-0466
*consulate(s) general:* Chicago, New York
**Diplomatic representation from the US:**
*chief of mission:* Ambassador John A. CLOUD
*embassy:* Akmenu gatve 6, Vilnius, LT-03106
*mailing address:* American Embassy, Akmenu Gatve 6, Vilnius LT-03106
*telephone:* [370] (5) 266 5500
*FAX:* [370] (5) 266 5510
**Flag description:** three equal horizontal bands of yellow (top), green, and red

## Economy

**Economy - overview:** Lithuania's economy grew on average 8% per year for the four years prior to 2008, driven by exports and domestic consumer demand. Unemployment stood at 4.8% in 2008, while wages grew at double digit rates. The current account deficit rose to roughly 15% of GDP in 2007-08. Lithuania has gained membership in the World Trade Organization and joined the EU in May 2004. Despite Lithuania's EU accession, Lithuania's trade with its Central and Eastern European neighbors, and Russia in particular, accounts for a growing percentage of total trade. Privatization of the large, state-owned utilities is nearly complete. Foreign government and business support have helped in the transition from the old command economy to a market economy.

**GDP (purchasing power parity):**
$63.25 billion (2008 est.)
$61.29 billion (2007)
$56.28 billion (2006)
*note:* data are in 2008 US dollars
**GDP (official exchange rate):** $48.75 billion (2008 est.)
**GDP - real growth rate:**
3.2% (2008 est.)
8.9% (2007 est.)
7.8% (2006 est.)
**GDP - per capita (PPP):**
$17,700 (2008 est.)
$17,100 (2007 est.)
$15,700 (2006 est.)
*note:* data are in 2008 US dollars
**GDP - composition by sector:**
*agriculture:* 4.3%
*industry:* 32.8%
*services:* 62.8% (2008 est.)
**Labor force:** 1.601 million (2008 est.)
**Labor force - by occupation:**
*agriculture:* 14%
*industry:* 29.1%
*services:* 56.9% (2005)
**Unemployment rate:**
4.8% (2008 est.)
3.5% (2007 est.)
*note:* based on survey data, official registered unemployment of 5.7%
**Population below poverty line:** 4% (2003)
**Household income or consumption by percentage share:**
*lowest 10%:* 2.7%
*highest 10%:* 27.7% (2003)
**Distribution of family income - Gini index:** 36 (2005)
**Investment (gross fixed):** 27.8% of GDP (2008 est.)
**Budget:**
*revenues:* $15.4 billion
*expenditures:* $15.86 billion (2008 est.)
**Public debt:** 11.9% of GDP (2008 est.)
**Inflation rate (consumer prices):**
11% (2008 est.)
5.7% (2007 est.)
**Central bank discount rate:** 4.85% (31 December 2007)
**Commercial bank prime lending rate:** 6.86% (31 December 2007)
**Stock of money:** $11.84 billion (31 December 2007)
**Stock of quasi money:** $6.917 billion (31 December 2007)
**Stock of domestic credit:** $25.05 billion (31 December 2007)
**Market value of publicly traded shares:** $10.13 billion (31 December 2007)
**Agriculture - products:** grain, potatoes, sugar beets, flax, vegetables; beef, milk, eggs; fish

# Lithuania (continued)

**Industries:** metal-cutting machine tools, electric motors, television sets, refrigerators and freezers, petroleum refining, shipbuilding (small ships), furniture making, textiles, food processing, fertilizers, agricultural machinery, optical equipment, electronic components, computers, amber jewelry
**Industrial production growth rate:** 4.6% (2008 est.)
**Electricity - production:** 11.91 billion kWh (2006 est.)
**Electricity - consumption:** 10.4 billion kWh (2006 est.)
**Electricity - exports:** 7.217 billion kWh (2007 est.)
**Electricity - imports:** 5.846 billion kWh (2007 est.)
**Oil - production:** 8,250 bbl/day (2007 est.)
**Oil - consumption:** 57,170 bbl/day (2006 est.)
**Oil - exports:** 148,400 bbl/day (2005)
**Oil - imports:** 206,700 bbl/day (2005)
**Oil - proved reserves:** 12 million bbl (1 January 2008 est.)
**Natural gas - production:** 0 cu m (2007 est.)
**Natural gas - consumption:** 3.44 billion cu m (2007 est.)
**Natural gas - exports:** 0 cu m (2007 est.)
**Natural gas - imports:** 3.44 billion cu m (2007 est.)
**Natural gas - proved reserves:** 0 cu m (1 January 2006 est.)
**Current account balance:** -$6.775 billion (2008 est.)
**Exports:** $23.48 billion f.o.b. (2008 est.)
**Exports - commodities:** mineral products 23%, textiles and clothing 16%, machinery and equipment 11%, chemicals 6%, wood and wood products 5%, foodstuffs 5% (2001)
**Exports - partners:** Russia 15%, Latvia 12.9%, Germany 10.5%, Poland 6.3%, Estonia 5.8%, UK 4.6%, Denmark 4.1%, Belarus 4% (2007)
**Imports:** $30.26 billion f.o.b. (2008 est.)
**Imports - commodities:** mineral products, machinery and equipment, transport equipment, chemicals, textiles and clothing, metals
**Imports - partners:** Russia 18%, Germany 15%, Poland 10.6%, Latvia 5.5%, Netherlands 4.3% (2007)
**Reserves of foreign exchange and gold:** $8.397 billion (31 December 2008 est.)
**Debt - external:** $35.46 billion (31 December 2008 est.)
**Stock of direct foreign investment - at home:** $16.43 billion (2008 est.)
**Stock of direct foreign investment - abroad:** $2.142 billion (2008 est.)
**Exchange rates:** litai (LTL) per US dollar - 2.3251 (2008 est.), 2.5362 (2007), 2.7498 (2006), 2.774 (2005), 2.7806 (2004)

## Communications

**Telephones - main lines in use:** 799,400 (2007)
**Telephones - mobile cellular:** 4.912 million (2007)
**Telephone system:**
*general assessment:* adequate; being modernized to provide improved international capability and better residential access
*domestic:* rapid expansion of mobile-cellular services has resulted in a steady decline in the number of main line subscriptions; mobile-cellular teledensity has increased to about 135 per 100 persons while fixed-line teledensity has dropped to 22 per 100 persons
*international:* country code - 370; major international connections to Denmark, Sweden, and Norway by submarine cable for further transmission by satellite; landline connections to Latvia and Poland (2007)
**Radio broadcast stations:** AM 29, FM 142, shortwave 1 (2001)
**Television broadcast stations:** 44 (may have as many as 100 transmitters, including repeater stations) (2008)
**Internet country code:** .lt
**Internet hosts:** 812,083 (2008)
**Internet users:** 1.333 million (2007)

## Transportation

**Airports:** 87 (2008)
**Airports - with paved runways:**
*total:* 31
*over 3,047 m:* 3
*2,438 to 3,047 m:* 1
*1,524 to 2,437 m:* 7
*914 to 1,523 m:* 2
*under 914 m:* 18 (2008)
**Airports - with unpaved runways:**
*total:* 56
*over 3,047 m:* 1
*914 to 1,523 m:* 3
*under 914 m:* 52 (2008)
**Pipelines:** gas 1,695 km; refined products 114 km (2008)
**Railways:**
*total:* 1,771 km
*broad gauge:* 1,749 km 1.524-m gauge (122 km electrified)
*standard gauge:* 22 km 1.435-m gauge (2006)
**Roadways:**
*total:* 80,715 km
*paved:* 71,301 km (includes 309 km of expressways)
*unpaved:* 9,414 km (2007)
**Waterways:** 441 km (2007)
**Merchant marine:**
*total:* 45
*by type:* cargo 23, container 2, passenger/cargo 6, petroleum tanker 1, refrigerated cargo 13
*foreign-owned:* 6 (Denmark 5, Ukraine 1)
*registered in other countries:* 28 (Antigua and Barbuda 5, Cook Islands 1, North Korea 1, Malta 1, Norway 1, Panama 7, Saint Vincent and the Grenadines 9, unknown 3) (2008)
**Ports and terminals:** Klaipeda

## Military

**Military branches:** Ground Forces, Naval Forces, Air Forces (Karines Oro Pajegos), National Defense Volunteer Forces (2009)
**Military service age and obligation:** 19-26 years of age for compulsory military service; 18 years of age for volunteers; 12-month conscript service obligation; male registration required at age 16 (2009)
**Manpower available for military service:**
*males age 16-49:* 915,187
*females age 16-49:* 906,097 (2008 est.)
**Manpower fit for military service:**
*males age 16-49:* 677,689
*females age 16-49:* 743,468 (2009 est.)
**Manpower reaching militarily significant age annually:**
*male:* 23,556
*female:* 22,404 (2009 est.)
**Military expenditures:** 1.2% of GDP (2007 est.)

## Transnational Issues

**Disputes - international:** Lithuania and Russia committed to demarcating their boundary in 2006 in accordance with the land and maritime treaty ratified by Russia in May 2003 and by Lithuania in 1999; Lithuania operates a simplified transit regime for Russian nationals traveling from the Kaliningrad coastal exclave into Russia, while still conforming, as a EU member state having an external border with a non-EU member, to strict Schengen border rules; the Latvian parliament has not ratified its 1998 maritime boundary treaty with Lithuania, primarily due to concerns over potential hydrocarbons; as of January 2007, ground demarcation of the boundary with Belarus was complete and mapped with final ratification documents in preparation
**Illicit drugs:** transshipment and destination point for cannabis, cocaine, ecstasy, and opiates from Southwest Asia, Latin America, Western Europe, and neighboring Baltic countries; growing production of high-quality amphetamines, but limited production of cannabis, methamphetamines; susceptible to money laundering despite changes to banking legislation

# Luxembourg

## Introduction

**Background:** Founded in 963, Luxembourg became a grand duchy in 1815 and an independent state under the Netherlands. It lost more than half of its territory to Belgium in 1839, but gained a larger measure of autonomy. Full independence was attained in 1867. Overrun by Germany in both World Wars, it ended its neutrality in 1948 when it entered into the Benelux Customs Union and when it joined NATO the following year. In 1957, Luxembourg became one of the six founding countries of the European Economic Community (later the European Union), and in 1999 it joined the euro currency area.

## Geography

**Location:** Western Europe, between France and Germany
**Geographic coordinates:** 49 45 N, 6 10 E
**Map references:** Europe
**Area:**
*total:* 2,586 sq km
*land:* 2,586 sq km
*water:* 0 sq km
**Area - comparative:** slightly smaller than Rhode Island
**Land boundaries:**
*total:* 359 km
*border countries:* Belgium 148 km, France 73 km, Germany 138 km
**Coastline:** 0 km (landlocked)
**Maritime claims:** none (landlocked)
**Climate:** modified continental with mild winters, cool summers
**Terrain:** mostly gently rolling uplands with broad, shallow valleys; uplands to slightly mountainous in the north; steep slope down to Moselle flood plain in the southeast
**Elevation extremes:**
*lowest point:* Moselle River 133 m
*highest point:* Buurgplaatz 559 m

**Natural resources:** iron ore (no longer exploited), arable land
**Land use:**
*arable land:* 27.42%
*permanent crops:* 0.69%
*other:* 71.89% (includes Belgium) (2005)
**Irrigated land:** NA
**Total renewable water resources:** 1.6 cu km (2005)
**Freshwater withdrawal (domestic/industrial/agricultural):**
*total:* 0.06 cu km/yr (42%/45%/13%)
*per capita:* 121 cu m/yr (1999)
**Natural hazards:** NA
**Environment - current issues:** air and water pollution in urban areas, soil pollution of farmland
**Environment - international agreements:**
*party to:* Air Pollution, Air Pollution-Nitrogen Oxides, Air Pollution-Persistent Organic Pollutants, Air Pollution-Sulfur 85, Air Pollution-Sulfur 94, Air Pollution-Volatile Organic Compounds, Biodiversity, Climate Change, Climate Change-Kyoto Protocol, Desertification, Endangered Species, Hazardous Wastes, Law of the Sea, Marine Dumping, Ozone Layer Protection, Ship Pollution, Tropical Timber 83, Tropical Timber 94, Wetlands
*signed, but not ratified:* Environmental Modification
**Geography - note:** landlocked; the only Grand Duchy in the world

## People

**Population:** 491,775 (July 2009 est.)
**Age structure:**
*0-14 years:* 18.5% (male 46,918/female 44,052)
*15-64 years:* 66.7% (male 165,342/female 162,681)
*65 years and over:* 14.8% (male 29,839/female 42,943) (2009 est.)
**Median age:**
*total:* 39.2 years
*male:* 38.2 years
*female:* 40.2 years (2009 est.)
**Population growth rate:** 1.172% (2009 est.)
**Birth rate:** 11.73 births/1,000 population (2009 est.)
**Death rate:** 8.43 deaths/1,000 population (2008 est.)
**Net migration rate:** 8.44 migrant(s)/1,000 population (2009 est.)
**Urbanization:**
*urban population:* 82% of total population (2008)
*rate of urbanization:* 1% annual rate of change (2005-10 est.)
**Sex ratio:**
*at birth:* 1.07 male(s)/female
*under 15 years:* 1.06 male(s)/female
*15-64 years:* 1.02 male(s)/female
*65 years and over:* 0.7 male(s)/female
*total population:* 0.97 male(s)/female (2009 est.)
**Infant mortality rate:**
*total:* 4.56 deaths/1,000 live births
*male:* 4.56 deaths/1,000 live births
*female:* 4.55 deaths/1,000 live births (2009 est.)

**Life expectancy at birth:**
*total population:* 79.33 years
*male:* 76.07 years
*female:* 82.81 years (2009 est.)
**Total fertility rate:** 1.78 children born/woman (2009 est.)
**HIV/AIDS - adult prevalence rate:** 0.2% (2007 est.)
**HIV/AIDS - people living with HIV/AIDS:** fewer than 500 (2003 est.)
**HIV/AIDS - deaths:** fewer than 100 (2003 est.)
**Nationality:**
*noun:* Luxembourger(s)
*adjective:* Luxembourg
**Ethnic groups:** Luxembourger 63.1%, Portuguese 13.3%, French 4.5%, Italian 4.3%, German 2.3%, other EU 7.3%, other 5.2% (2000 census)
**Religions:** Roman Catholic 87%, other (includes Protestant, Jewish, and Muslim) 13% (2000)
**Languages:** Luxembourgish (national language), German (administrative language), French (administrative language)
**Literacy:**
*definition:* age 15 and over can read and write
*total population:* 100%
*male:* 100%
*female:* 100% (2000 est.)
**School life expectancy (primary to tertiary education):**
*total:* 14 years
*male:* 13 years
*female:* 14 years (2006)
**Education expenditures:** 3.4% of GDP (1999)

## Government

**Country name:**
*conventional long form:* Grand Duchy of Luxembourg
*conventional short form:* Luxembourg
*local long form:* Grand Duche de Luxembourg
*local short form:* Luxembourg
**Government type:** constitutional monarchy
**Capital:**
*name:* Luxembourg
*geographic coordinates:* 49 36 N, 6 07 E
*time difference:* UTC+1 (6 hours ahead of Washington, DC during Standard Time)
*daylight saving time:* +1hr, begins last Sunday in March; ends last Sunday in October
**Administrative divisions:** 3 districts; Diekirch, Grevenmacher, Luxembourg
**Independence:** 1839 (from the Netherlands)
**National holiday:** National Day (Birthday of Grand Duchess Charlotte) 23 June; note - the actual date of birth was 23 January 1896, but the festivities were shifted by five months to allow observance during a more favorable time of year
**Constitution:** 17 October 1868; occasional revisions
**Legal system:** based on civil law system; accepts compulsory ICJ jurisdiction
**Suffrage:** 18 years of age; universal and compulsory

**Executive branch:**

*chief of state:* Grand Duke HENRI (since 7 October 2000); Heir Apparent Prince GUILLAUME (son of the monarch, born 11 November 1981)

*head of government:* Prime Minister Jean-Claude JUNCKER (since 20 January 1995); Deputy Prime Minister Jean ASSELBORN (since 31 July 2004)

*cabinet:* Council of Ministers recommended by the prime minister and appointed by the monarch

*elections:* the monarch is hereditary; following popular elections to the Chamber of Deputies, the leader of the majority party or the leader of the majority coalition is usually appointed prime minister by the monarch; the deputy prime minister is appointed by the monarch; they are responsible to the Chamber of Deputies

*note:* government coalition - CSV and LSAP

**Legislative branch:** unicameral Chamber of Deputies or Chambre des Deputes (60 seats; members are elected by popular vote to serve five-year terms)

*elections:* last held 13 June 2004 (next to be held by June 2009)

*election results:* percent of vote by party - CSV 36.1%, LSAP 23.4%, DP 16.1%, Green Party 11.6%, ADR 10%, other 2.8%; seats by party - CSV 24, LSAP 14, DP 10, Green Party 7, ADR 5

*note:* there is also a Council of State that serves as an advisory body to the Chamber of Deputies; the Council of State has 21 members appointed by the Grand Duke on the advice of the prime minister

**Judicial branch:** judicial courts and tribunals (three Justices of the Peace, two district courts, and one Supreme Court of Appeals); administrative courts and tribunals (State Prosecutor's Office, administrative courts and tribunals, and the Constitutional Court); judges for all courts are appointed for life by the monarch

**Political parties and leaders:** Alternative Democratic Reform Party or ADR [Robert MEHLEN]; Christian Social People's Party or CSV [Francois BILTGEN]; Democratic Party or DP [Claude MEISCH]; Green Party [Francois BAUSCH]; dei Lenk/la Gauche (the Left); Luxembourg Socialist Workers' Party or LSAP [Alex BODRY]; other minor parties

**Political pressure groups and leaders:** ABBL (bankers' association); ALEBA (financial sector trade union); Centrale Paysanne (federation of agricultural producers); CEP (professional sector chamber); CGFP (trade union representing civil service); Chambre de Commerce (Chamber of Commerce); Chambre des Metiers (Chamber of Artisans); FEDIL (federation of industrialists); Greenpeace (environment protection); LCGP (center-right trade union); Mouvement Ecologique (protection of ecology); OGBL (center-left trade union)

**International organization participation:** ADB (nonregional member), Australia Group, Benelux, CE, EAPC, EBRD, EIB, EMU, ESA, EU, FAO, IAEA, IBRD, ICAO, ICC, ICCt, ICRM, IDA, IEA, IFAD, IFC, IFRCS, ILO, IMF, IMO, Interpol, IOC, IOM, IPU, ISO, ITSO, ITU, ITUC, MIGA, NATO, NEA, NSG, OAS (observer), OECD, OIF, OPCW, OSCE, PCA, Schengen Convention, UN, UNCTAD, UNESCO, UNHCR, UNIDO, UNIFIL, UNRWA, UPU, WCL, WCO, WEU, WFTU, WHO, WIPO, WMO, WTO, ZC

**Diplomatic representation in the US:**

*chief of mission:* Ambassador Jean-Paul SENNINGER

*chancery:* 2200 Massachusetts Avenue NW, Washington, DC 20008

*telephone:* [1] (202) 265-4171 through 72

*FAX:* [1] (202) 328-8270

*consulate(s) general:* New York, San Francisco

**Diplomatic representation from the US:**

*chief of mission:* Ambassador Ann WAGNER

*embassy:* 22 Boulevard Emmanuel Servais, L-2535 Luxembourg City

*mailing address:* American Embassy Luxembourg, Unit 1410, APO AE 09126-1410 (official mail); American Embassy Luxembourg, PSC 9, Box 9500, APO AE 09123 (personal mail)

*telephone:* [352] 46 01 23

*FAX:* [352] 46 14 01

**Flag description:** three equal horizontal bands of red (top), white, and light blue; similar to the flag of the Netherlands, which uses a darker blue and is shorter; design was based on the flag of France

## Economy

**Economy - overview:** This stable, high-income economy - benefiting from its proximity to France, Belgium, and Germany - has historically featured solid growth, low inflation, and low unemployment. The industrial sector, initially dominated by steel, has become increasingly diversified to include chemicals, rubber, and other products. Growth in the financial sector, which now accounts for about 28% of GDP, has more than compensated for the decline in steel. Most banks are foreign owned and have extensive foreign dealings. Agriculture is based on small family-owned farms. The economy depends on foreign and cross-border workers for about 60% of its labor force. Although Luxembourg, like all EU members, suffered from the global economic slump in the early part of this decade, the country continues to enjoy an extraordinarily high standard of living - GDP per capita ranks third in the world, after Liechtenstein and Qatar. After two years of strong economic growth in 2006-07, turmoil in the world financial markets slowed Luxembourg's economy in 2008, but growth remained above the European average and is likely to remain so in 2009.

**GDP (purchasing power parity):**

$39.42 billion (2008 est.)

$39.18 billion (2007)

$37.51 billion (2006)

*note:* data are in 2008 US dollars

**GDP (official exchange rate):** $57.61 billion (2008 est.)

**GDP - real growth rate:**

3.6% (2008 est.)

4.5% (2007 est.)

6.1% (2006 est.)

**GDP - per capita (PPP):**

$81,100 (2008 est.)

$81,600 (2007 est.)

$79,100 (2006 est.)

*note:* data are in 2008 US dollars

**GDP - composition by sector:**

*agriculture:* 0.4%

*industry:* 13.6%

*services:* 86% (2007 est.)

**Labor force:** 207,100 of whom 125,400 are foreign cross-border workers commuting primarily from France, Belgium, and Germany (2008 est.)

**Labor force - by occupation:**

*agriculture:* 2.2%

*industry:* 17.2%

*services:* 80.6% (2007 est.)

**Unemployment rate:**

4.7% (2008 est.)

4.4% (2007 est.)

**Population below poverty line:** NA%

**Household income or consumption by percentage share:**

*lowest 10%:* 3.5%

*highest 10%:* 23.8% (2000)

**Distribution of family income - Gini index:** 26 (2005)

**Investment (gross fixed):** 19.3% of GDP (2008 est.)

**Budget:**

*revenues:* $22.25 billion

*expenditures:* $22.08 billion (2008 est.)

**Public debt:** 7.2% of GDP (2008 est.)

**Inflation rate (consumer prices):**

4% (2008 est.)

2.3% (2007 est.)

**Central bank discount rate:** 4%

*note:* this is the European Central Bank's rate on the marginal lending facility, which offers overnight credit to banks in the euro area

**Stock of money:** NA

*note:* see entry for the European Union for money supply in the euro area; the European Central Bank (ECB) controls monetary policy for the 16 members of the Economic and Monetary Union (EMU); individual members of the EMU do not control the quantity of money and quasi money circulating within their own borders

**Stock of quasi money:** NA

**Stock of domestic credit:** $357.9 billion (31 December 2007)

**Market value of publicly traded shares:** $166.1 billion (31 December 2007)

**Agriculture - products:** wine, grapes, barley, oats, potatoes, wheat, fruits; dairy products, livestock products

**Industries:** banking and financial services, iron and steel, information technology, telecommunications, cargo transportation, food processing, chemicals, metal products, engineering, tires, glass, aluminum, tourism

**Industrial production growth rate:** 1.7% (2007 est.)

# Luxembourg (continued)

**Electricity - production:** 3.01 billion kWh (2007 est.)
**Electricity - consumption:** 6.748 billion kWh (2006 est.)
**Electricity - exports:** 2.887 billion kWh (2007 est.)
**Electricity - imports:** 6.847 billion kWh (2007 est.)
**Oil - production:** 0 bbl/day (2007 est.)
**Oil - consumption:** 60,640 bbl/day (2007 est.)
**Oil - exports:** 281.5 bbl/day (2005)
**Oil - imports:** 63,760 bbl/day (2005)
**Oil - proved reserves:** 0 bbl (1 January 2006 est.)
**Natural gas - production:** 0 cu m (2007 est.)
**Natural gas - consumption:** 1.329 billion cu m (2007 est.)
**Natural gas - exports:** 0 cu m (2007 est.)
**Natural gas - imports:** 1.329 billion cu m (2007 est.)
**Natural gas - proved reserves:** 0 cu m (1 January 2006 est.)
**Current account balance:** $3.186 billion (2008 est.)
**Exports:** $20.78 billion f.o.b. (2008 est.)
**Exports - commodities:** machinery and equipment, steel products, chemicals, rubber products, glass
**Exports - partners:** Germany 21.1%, France 16.3%, Belgium 10.1%, Italy 7.4%, UK 7.1%, Netherlands 5.4%, Spain 5% (2007)
**Imports:** $28.12 billion c.i.f. (2008 est.)
**Imports - commodities:** minerals, metals, foodstuffs, quality consumer goods
**Imports - partners:** Belgium 27.4%, Germany 23.8%, China 17.1%, France 9.2%, Netherlands 5% (2007)
**Reserves of foreign exchange and gold:** $205.5 million (2006 est.)
**Debt - external:** $NA
**Stock of direct foreign investment - at home:** $NA
**Stock of direct foreign investment - abroad:** $NA
**Exchange rates:** euros (EUR) per US dollar - 0.6827 (2008 est.), 0.7345 (2007), 0.7964 (2006), 0.8041 (2005), 0.8054 (2004)

## Communications

**Telephones - main lines in use:** 248,200 (2007)
**Telephones - mobile cellular:** 604,200 (2007)
**Telephone system:**
*general assessment:* highly developed, completely automated and efficient system, mainly buried cables
*domestic:* fixed line teledensity over 50 per 100 persons; nationwide cellular telephone system with market for mobile-cellular phones virtually saturated
*international:* country code - 352 (2007)
**Radio broadcast stations:** AM 2, FM 9, shortwave 2 (1999)
**Television broadcast stations:** 5 (1999)
**Internet country code:** .lu
**Internet hosts:** 180,756 (2008)
**Internet users:** 345,000 (2007)

## Transportation

**Airports:** 2 (2008)
**Airports - with paved runways:**
*total:* 1
*over 3,047 m:* 1 (2008)
**Airports - with unpaved runways:**
*total:* 1
*under 914 m:* 1 (2008)
**Heliports:** 1 (2007)
**Pipelines:** gas 155 km (2008)
**Railways:**
*total:* 275 km
*standard gauge:* 275 km 1.435-m gauge (243 km electrified) (2006)
**Roadways:**
*total:* 5,227 km
*paved:* 5,227 km (includes 147 km of expressways) (2004)
**Waterways:** 37 km (on Moselle River) (2008)
**Merchant marine:**
*total:* 45
*by type:* bulk carrier 6, cargo 3, chemical tanker 15, container 4, liquefied gas 1, passenger 3, passenger/cargo 1, petroleum tanker 3, roll on/roll off 9
*foreign-owned:* 44 (Belgium 7, Denmark 1, France 17, Germany 5, Netherlands 2, UK 8, US 4)
*registered in other countries:* 1 (Ukraine 1) (2008)
**Ports and terminals:** Mertert

## Military

**Military branches:** Army (2009)
**Military service age and obligation:** 17-25 years of age for male and female voluntary military service; soldiers under 18 are not deployed into combat or with peacekeeping missions; no conscription; Luxembourg citizen or EU citizen with 3-year residence in Luxembourg (2008)
**Manpower available for military service:**
*males age 16-49:* 116,305
*females age 16-49:* 114,566 (2008 est.)
**Manpower fit for military service:**
*males age 16-49:* 95,840
*females age 16-49:* 94,641 (2009 est.)
**Manpower reaching militarily significant age annually:**
*male:* 3,170
*female:* 2,995 (2009 est.)
**Military expenditures:** 0.9% of GDP (2005 est.)

## Transnational Issues

**Disputes - international:** none

# Macau
*(special administrative region of China)*

## Introduction

**Background:** Colonized by the Portuguese in the 16th century, Macau was the first European settlement in the Far East. Pursuant to an agreement signed by China and Portugal on 13 April 1987, Macau became the Macau Special Administrative Region (SAR) of the People's Republic of China on 20 December 1999. In this agreement, China promised that, under its "one country, two systems" formula, China's socialist economic system would not be practiced in Macau, and that Macau would enjoy a high degree of autonomy in all matters except foreign and defense affairs for the next 50 years.

## Geography

**Location:** Eastern Asia, bordering the South China Sea and China
**Geographic coordinates:** 22 10 N, 113 33 E
**Map references:** Southeast Asia
**Area:**
*total:* 28.2 sq km
*land:* 28.2 sq km
*water:* 0 sq km
**Area - comparative:** less than one-sixth the size of Washington, DC
**Land boundaries:**
*total:* 0.34 km
*regional border:* China 0.34 km
**Coastline:** 41 km
**Maritime claims:** not specified
**Climate:** subtropical; marine with cool winters, warm summers
**Terrain:** generally flat
**Elevation extremes:**
*lowest point:* South China Sea 0 m
*highest point:* Coloane Alto 172 m
**Natural resources:** NEGL
**Land use:**
*arable land:* 0%
*permanent crops:* 0%
*other:* 100% (2005)

# Macau (continued)

**Irrigated land:** NA
**Natural hazards:** typhoons
**Environment - current issues:** NA
**Environment - international agreements:**
*party to:* Marine Dumping (associate member), Ship Pollution (associate member)
**Geography - note:** essentially urban; an area of land reclaimed from the sea measuring 5.2 sq km and known as Cotai now connects the islands of Coloane and Taipa; the island area is connected to the mainland peninsula by three bridges

## People

**Population:** 559,846 (July 2009 est.)
**Age structure:**
*0-14 years:* 16.1% (male 47,853/female 42,019)
*15-64 years:* 76.2% (male 199,593/female 227,010)
*65 years and over:* 7.7% (male 20,245/female 23,126) (2009 est.)
**Median age:**
*total:* 35.2 years
*male:* 35.9 years
*female:* 34.6 years (2009 est.)
**Population growth rate:** 1.995% (2009 est.)
**Birth rate:** 8.88 births/1,000 population (2009 est.)
**Death rate:** 3.43 deaths/1,000 population (2008 est.)
**Net migration rate:** 14.56 migrant(s)/1,000 population (2009 est.)
**Urbanization:**
*urban population:* 100% of total population (2008)
*rate of urbanization:* 0.7% annual rate of change (2005-10 est.)
**Sex ratio:**
*at birth:* 1.05 male(s)/female
*under 15 years:* 1.14 male(s)/female
*15-64 years:* 0.88 male(s)/female
*65 years and over:* 0.88 male(s)/female
*total population:* 0.92 male(s)/female (2009 est.)
**Infant mortality rate:**
*total:* 3.22 deaths/1,000 live births
*male:* 3.37 deaths/1,000 live births
*female:* 3.05 deaths/1,000 live births (2009 est.)
**Life expectancy at birth:**
*total population:* 84.36 years
*male:* 81.39 years
*female:* 87.47 years (2009 est.)
**Total fertility rate:** 0.91 children born/woman (2009 est.)
**HIV/AIDS - adult prevalence rate:** NA
**HIV/AIDS - people living with HIV/AIDS:** NA
**HIV/AIDS - deaths:** NA
**Nationality:**
*noun:* Chinese
*adjective:* Chinese
**Ethnic groups:** Chinese 94.3%, other 5.7% (includes Macanese - mixed Portuguese and Asian ancestry) (2006 census)
**Religions:** Buddhist 50%, Roman Catholic 15%, none or other 35% (1997 est.)

**Languages:** Cantonese 85.7%, Hokkien 4%, Mandarin 3.2%, other Chinese dialects 2.7%, English 1.5%, Tagalog 1.3%, other 1.6% (2001 census)
**Literacy:**
*definition:* age 15 and over can read and write
*total population:* 91.3%
*male:* 95.3%
*female:* 87.8% (2001 census)
**School life expectancy (primary to tertiary education):**
*total:* 15 years
*male:* 16 years
*female:* 14 years (2006)
**Education expenditures:** 2.4% of GDP (2005)

## Government

**Country name:**
*conventional long form:* Macau Special Administrative Region
*conventional short form:* Macau
*local long form:* Aomen Tebie Xingzhengqu (Chinese); Regiao Administrativa Especial de Macau (Portuguese)
*local short form:* Aomen (Chinese); Macau (Portuguese)
**Dependency status:** special administrative region of China
**Government type:** limited democracy
**Administrative divisions:** none (special administrative region of the People's Republic of China)
**Independence:** none (special administrative region of China)
**National holiday:** National Day (Anniversary of the Founding of the People's Republic of China), 1 October (1949); note - 20 December 1999 is celebrated as Macau Special Administrative Region Establishment Day
**Constitution:** Basic Law, approved on 31 March 1993 by China's National People's Congress, is Macau's "mini-constitution"
**Legal system:** based on Portuguese civil law system
**Suffrage:** direct election 18 years of age for some non-executive positions, universal for permanent residents living in Macau for the past seven years; indirect election limited to organizations registered as "corporate voters" (257 are currently registered) and a 300-member Election Committee drawn from broad regional groupings, municipal organizations, and central government bodies
**Executive branch:**
*chief of state:* President of China HU Jintao (since 15 March 2003)
*head of government:* Chief Executive Edmund HO Hau-wah (since 20 December 1999)
*cabinet:* Executive Council consists of one government secretary, three legislators, four businessmen, one pro-Beijing unionist, and one pro-Beijing educator
*elections:* chief executive chosen by a 300-member

Election Committee for a five-year term (eligible for a second term); election last held 29 August 2004 (next to be held on 26 July 2009)
*election results:* Edmund HO Hau-wah reelected received 296 votes; three members submitted blank ballots; one member was absent
**Legislative branch:** unicameral Legislative Assembly (29 seats; 12 members elected by popular vote, 10 by indirect vote, and 7 appointed by the chief executive; serve four-year terms)
*elections:* last held 25 September 2005 (next to be held in the fall of 2009)
*election results:* percent of vote - New Democratic Macau Association 18.8%, Macau United Citizens' Association 16.6%, Union for Development 13.3%, Union for Promoting Progress 9.6%, Macau Development Alliance 9.3%, others 32.4%; seats by political group - New Democratic Macau Association 2, Macau United Citizens' Association 2, Union for Development 2, Union for Promoting Progress 2, Macau Development Alliance 1, New Hope 1, Convergence for Development 1, General Union for the Good of Macau 1; 10 seats filled by professional and business groups; seven members appointed by chief executive
**Judicial branch:** Court of Final Appeal in Macau Special Administrative Region
**Political parties and leaders:** New Hope [Jose Maria Pereira COUTINHO]; Development Union [KWAN Tsui-hang]; Macau Development Alliance [Angela LEONG On-kei]; Macau United Citizens' Association [CHAN Meng-kam]; New Democratic Macau Association [Antonio NG Kuok-cheong]; Union for Promoting Progress [LEONG Heng-teng]
*note:* there is no political party ordinance, so there are no registered political parties; politically active groups register as societies or companies
**Political pressure groups and leaders:** Civic Power [Agnes LAM Lok-fong]; Macau Society of Tourism and Entertainment or STDM [Stanley HO]; Macau Worker's Union [HO Heng-kuok]; Roman Catholic Church; Union for Democracy Development [Antonio NG Kuok-cheong]
**International organization participation:** IHO, IMF, IMO (associate), ISO (correspondent), UNESCO (associate), UNWTO (associate), UPU, WCO, WFTU, WMO, WTO
**Diplomatic representation in the US:** none (special administrative region of China)
**Diplomatic representation from the US:** the US has no offices in Macau; US Consulate General in Hong Kong is accredited to Macau
**Flag description:** light green with a lotus flower above a stylized bridge and water in white, beneath an arc of five gold, five-pointed stars: one large in center of arc and four smaller

## Economy

**Economy - overview:** Macau's economy has enjoyed strong growth in recent years on the back of its expanding tourism and gaming sectors. After

# Macau *(continued)*

opening up its locally-controlled casino industry to foreign competition in 2001, the territory attracted tens of billions of dollars in foreign investment, transforming Macao into the world's largest gaming center. By 2006, Macau's gaming revenue surpassed that of the Las Vegas strip, and gaming-related taxes accounted for 75% of total government revenue. In 2008, government revenue from gaming was set to double 2006 collections. The expanding casino sector, and China's decision beginning in 2002 to relax travel restrictions, reenergized Macau's tourism industry. This city of just over 500,000 hosted more than 30 million visitors in 2008. Almost 60% of these came from mainland China, despite increasing restrictions on travel to the SAR. Macau's traditional manufacturing industry has been in a slow decline since the termination of the Multi-Fiber Agreement in 2005. In 2008, exports of textiles and garments generated only $1.1 billion, compared to $13.7 billion in gross gaming receipts. The Closer Economic Partnership Agreement (CEPA) between Macau and mainland China that came into effect on 1 January 2004 offers many Macau-made products tariff-free access to the mainland. Macau's currency, the Pataca, is closely tied to the Hong Kong dollar, which is also freely accepted in the territory.

**GDP (purchasing power parity):**
$18.14 billion (2008 est.)
$12.5 billion (2006)
*note:* data are in 2008 US dollars

**GDP (official exchange rate):** $22.04 billion (2008 est.)

**GDP - real growth rate:**
15% (2008)
16.6% (2006)

**GDP - per capita (PPP):**
$30,000 (2007)
$28,400 (2006)

**GDP - composition by sector:**
*agriculture:* 0.1%
*industry:* 2.8%
*services:* 97.1% (2007 est.)

**Labor force:** 337,400 (2008 est.)

**Labor force - by occupation:** manufacturing 7.4%, construction 12.6%, transport and communications 5%, wholesale and retail trade 12.5%, restaurants and hotels 12.7%, gambling 14%, public sector 6%, financial services 2.1%, other services and agriculture 27.7% (2008)

**Unemployment rate:**
3% (2008)
3.1% (2006)

**Population below poverty line:** NA%

**Household income or consumption by percentage share:**
*lowest 10%:* NA%
*highest 10%:* NA%

**Budget:**
*revenues:* $6.2 billion
*expenditures:* $2.9 billion (2008)

**Inflation rate (consumer prices):**
6.2% (December 2008)
7.2% (2006)

**Commercial bank prime lending rate:** 5.25% (31 December 2008)

**Stock of money:** $2.66 billion (31 December 2008)

**Stock of quasi money:** $20.5 billion (31 December 2008)

**Stock of domestic credit:** $11.5 billion (31 December 2008)

**Market value of publicly traded shares:** $2.3 billion (31 December 2008 est.)

**Agriculture - products:** only 2% of land area is cultivated, mainly by vegetable growers; fishing, mostly for crustaceans, is important; some of the catch is exported to Hong Kong

**Industries:** tourism, gambling, clothing, textiles, electronics, footwear, toys

**Industrial production growth rate:** NA

**Electricity - production:** 1.106 billion kWh (2008 est.)

**Electricity - consumption:** 3.311 billion kWh (2008 est.)

**Electricity - exports:** 0 kWh (2008 est.)

**Electricity - imports:** 2.215 billion kWh (2008 est.)

**Oil - production:** 0 bbl/day (2008 est.)

**Oil - consumption:** 7,942 bbl/day (2008 est.)

**Oil - exports:** 0 bbl/day (2008)

**Oil - imports:** 5,027 bbl/day (2008 est.)

**Oil - proved reserves:** 0 bbl (1 January 2008 est.)

**Natural gas - production:** 0 cu m (2008 est.)

**Natural gas - consumption:** 81.6 million cu m (2008 est.)

**Natural gas - exports:** 0 cu m (2008 est.)

**Natural gas - imports:** 81.9 million cu m (2008 est.)

**Natural gas - proved reserves:** 300,000 cu m (1 January 2008 est.)

**Exports:** $2 billion f.o.b.; note - includes reexports (2008 est.)

**Exports - commodities:** clothing, textiles, footwear, toys, electronics, machinery and parts

**Exports - partners:** US 40.6%, China 14.8%, Hong Kong 13.1%, Germany 6.4%, UK 4% (2007)

**Imports:** $5.4 billion c.i.f. (2008 est.)

**Imports - commodities:** raw materials and semi-manufactured goods, consumer goods (foodstuffs, beverages, tobacco), capital goods, mineral fuels and oils

**Imports - partners:** China 42.6%, Hong Kong 10.1%, Japan 9%, US 5.6%, Germany 4.4%, France 4.2% (2007)

**Debt - external:** $0 (2006)

**Stock of direct foreign investment - at home:** $7.9 billion (2007)

**Stock of direct foreign investment - abroad:** $1.9 billion (2007)

**Exchange rates:** patacas (MOP) per US dollar - 8.011 (2007), 8.0015 (2006), 8.011 (2005), 8.022 (2004), 8.021 (2003)

## Communications

**Telephones - main lines in use:** 177,851 (2008)
**Telephones - mobile cellular:** 856,200 (2008)
**Telephone system:**
*general assessment:* fairly modern communication facilities maintained for domestic and international services
*domestic:* termination of monopoly over mobile-cellular telephone services in 2001 spurred sharp increase in subscriptions with mobile-cellular teledensity approaching 190 per 100 persons in 2008; fixed-line subscribership appears to have peaked and is now in decline
*international:* country code - 853; landing point for the SEA-ME-WE-3 submarine cable network that provides links to Asia, the Middle East, and Europe; HF radiotelephone communication facility; satellite earth station - 1 Intelsat (Indian Ocean) (2008)

**Radio broadcast stations:** AM 1, FM 2, shortwave 0 (2008)

**Television broadcast stations:** 1 (2008)

**Internet country code:** .mo

**Internet hosts:** 263 (2008)

**Internet users:** 300,000 (2007)

## Transportation

**Airports:** 1 (2008)

**Airports - with paved runways:**
*total:* 1
*over 3,047 m:* 1 (2008)

**Heliports:** 1 (2007)

**Roadways:**
*total:* 384 km
*paved:* 384 km (2006)

**Ports and terminals:** Macau

## Military

**Military branches:** no regular military forces; defense is the responsibility of China (2009)

**Manpower available for military service:**
*males age 16-49:* 121,825 (2008 est.)

**Manpower fit for military service:**
*males age 16-49:* 122,962
*females age 16-49:* 148,809 (2009 est.)

**Manpower reaching militarily significant age annually:**
*male:* 4,578
*female:* 4,052 (2009 est.)

**Military - note:** defense is the responsibility of China

## Transnational Issues

**Disputes - international:** none

**Illicit drugs:** transshipment point for drugs going into mainland China; consumer of opiates and amphetamines

# Macedonia

## Introduction

**Background:** Macedonia gained its independence peacefully from Yugoslavia in 1991, but Greece's objection to the new state's use of what it considered a Hellenic name and symbols delayed international recognition, which occurred under the provisional designation of "the Former Yugoslav Republic of Macedonia." In 1995, Greece lifted a 20-month trade embargo and the two countries agreed to normalize relations. The United States began referring to Macedonia by its constitutional name, Republic of Macedonia, in 2004 and negotiations continue between Greece and Macedonia to resolve the name issue. Some ethnic Albanians, angered by perceived political and economic inequities, launched an insurgency in 2001 that eventually won the support of the majority of Macedonia's Albanian population and led to the internationally-brokered Framework Agreement, which ended the fighting by establishing a set of new laws enhancing the rights of minorities. Fully implementing the Framework Agreement and stimulating economic growth and development continue to be challenges for Macedonia, although progress has been made on both fronts over the past several years.

## Geography

**Location:** Southeastern Europe, north of Greece
**Geographic coordinates:** 41 50 N, 22 00 E
**Map references:** Europe
**Area:**
*total:* 25,333 sq km
*land:* 24,856 sq km
*water:* 477 sq km
**Area - comparative:** slightly larger than Vermont
**Land boundaries:**
*total:* 766 km
*border countries:* Albania 151 km, Bulgaria 148 km, Greece 246 km, Kosovo 159 km, Serbia 62 km
**Coastline:** 0 km (landlocked)
**Maritime claims:** none (landlocked)

**Climate:** warm, dry summers and autumns; relatively cold winters with heavy snowfall
**Terrain:** mountainous territory covered with deep basins and valleys; three large lakes, each divided by a frontier line; country bisected by the Vardar River
**Elevation extremes:**
*lowest point:* Vardar River 50 m
*highest point:* Golem Korab (Maja e Korabit) 2,764 m
**Natural resources:** low-grade iron ore, copper, lead, zinc, chromite, manganese, nickel, tungsten, gold, silver, asbestos, gypsum, timber, arable land
**Land use:**
*arable land:* 22.01%
*permanent crops:* 1.79%
*other:* 76.2% (2005)
**Irrigated land:** 550 sq km (2003)
**Total renewable water resources:** 6.4 cu km (2001)
**Freshwater withdrawal (domestic/industrial/agricultural):**
*total:* 2.27
*per capita:* 1,118 cu m/yr (2000)
**Natural hazards:** high seismic risks
**Environment - current issues:** air pollution from metallurgical plants
**Environment - international agreements:**
*party to:* Air Pollution, Biodiversity, Climate Change, Climate Change-Kyoto Protocol, Desertification, Endangered Species, Hazardous Wastes, Law of the Sea, Ozone Layer Protection, Wetlands
*signed, but not ratified:* none of the selected agreements
**Geography - note:** landlocked; major transportation corridor from Western and Central Europe to Aegean Sea and Southern Europe to Western Europe

## People

**Population:** 2,066,718 (July 2009 est.)
**Age structure:**
*0-14 years:* 19.2% (male 206,054/female 191,354)
*15-64 years:* 69.4% (male 722,823/female 710,830)
*65 years and over:* 11.4% (male 102,231/female 133,426) (2009 est.)
**Median age:**
*total:* 35.1 years
*male:* 34.1 years
*female:* 36.2 years (2009 est.)
**Population growth rate:** 0.262% (2009 est.)
**Birth rate:** 11.97 births/1,000 population (2009 est.)
**Death rate:** 8.81 deaths/1,000 population (2008 est.)
**Net migration rate:** -0.52 migrant(s)/1,000 population (2009 est.)
**Urbanization:**
*urban population:* 67% of total population (2008)
*rate of urbanization:* 0.8% annual rate of change (2005-10 est.)
**Sex ratio:**
*at birth:* 1.08 male(s)/female
*under 15 years:* 1.08 male(s)/female
*15-64 years:* 1.02 male(s)/female
*65 years and over:* 0.77 male(s)/female
*total population:* 1 male(s)/female (2009 est.)

**Infant mortality rate:**
*total:* 9.01 deaths/1,000 live births
*male:* 9.21 deaths/1,000 live births
*female:* 8.8 deaths/1,000 live births (2009 est.)
**Life expectancy at birth:**
*total population:* 74.68 years
*male:* 72.18 years
*female:* 77.38 years (2009 est.)
**Total fertility rate:** 1.58 children born/woman (2009 est.)
**HIV/AIDS - adult prevalence rate:** less than 0.1% (2007 est.)
**HIV/AIDS - people living with HIV/AIDS:** fewer than 200 (2007 est.)
**HIV/AIDS - deaths:** fewer than 100 (2003 est.)
**Nationality:**
*noun:* Macedonian(s)
*adjective:* Macedonian
**Ethnic groups:** Macedonian 64.2%, Albanian 25.2%, Turkish 3.9%, Roma (Gypsy) 2.7%, Serb 1.8%, other 2.2% (2002 census)
**Religions:** Macedonian Orthodox 64.7%, Muslim 33.3%, other Christian 0.37%, other and unspecified 1.63% (2002 census)
**Languages:** Macedonian 66.5%, Albanian 25.1%, Turkish 3.5%, Roma 1.9%, Serbian 1.2%, other 1.8% (2002 census)
**Literacy:**
*definition:* age 15 and over can read and write
*total population:* 96.1%
*male:* 98.2%
*female:* 94.1% (2002 census)
**School life expectancy (primary to tertiary education):**
*total:* 12 years
*male:* 12 years
*female:* 12 years (2005)
**Education expenditures:** 3.5% of GDP (2002)

## Government

**Country name:**
*conventional long form:* Republic of Macedonia
*conventional short form:* Macedonia
*local long form:* Republika Makedonija
*local short form:* Makedonija
*note:* the provisional designation used by the UN, EU, and NATO is the "former Yugoslav Republic of Macedonia" (FYROM)
*former:* People's Republic of Macedonia, Socialist Republic of Macedonia
**Government type:** parliamentary democracy
**Capital:**
*name:* Skopje
*geographic coordinates:* 42 00 N, 21 26 E
*time difference:* UTC+1 (6 hours ahead of Washington, DC during Standard Time)
*daylight saving time:* +1hr, begins last Sunday in March; ends last Sunday in October
**Administrative divisions:** 84 municipalities (opstini, singular - opstina); Aerodrom (Skopje), Aracinovo, Berovo, Bitola, Bogdanci, Bogovinje, Bosilovo, Brvenica, Butel (Skopje), Cair (Skopje), Caska,

# Macedonia (continued)

Centar (Skopje), Centar Zupa, Cesinovo, Cucer Sandevo, Debar, Debarca, Delcevo, Demir Hisar, Demir Kapija, Dojran, Dolneni, Dorce Petrov (Gjorce Petrov) (Skopje), Drugovo, Gazi Baba (Skopje), Gevgelija, Gostivar, Gradsko, Ilinden, Jegunovce, Karbinci, Karpos (Skopje), Kavadarci, Kicevo, Kisela Voda (Skopje), Kocani, Konce, Kratovo, Kriva Palanka, Krivogastani, Krusevo, Kumanovo, Lipkovo, Lozovo, Makedonska Kamenica, Makedonski Brod, Mavrovo i Rostusa, Mogila, Negotino, Novaci, Novo Selo, Ohrid, Oslomej, Pehcevo, Petrovec, Plasnica, Prilep, Probistip, Radovis, Rankovce, Resen, Rosoman, Saraj (Skopje), Sopiste, Staro Nagoricane, Stip, Struga, Strumica, Studenicani, Suto Orizari (Skopje), Sveti Nikole, Tearce, Tetovo, Valandovo, Vasilevo, Veles, Vevcani, Vinica, Vranestica, Vrapciste, Zajas, Zelenikovo, Zelino, Zrnovci
*note:* the 10 municipalities followed by Skopje in parentheses collectively constitute the larger Skopje Municipality

**Independence:** 8 September 1991 (referendum by registered voters endorsed independence from Yugoslavia)

**National holiday:** Ilinden Uprising Day, 2 August (1903); note - also known as Saint Elijah's Day

**Constitution:** adopted 17 November 1991, effective 20 November 1991; amended November 2001 and in 2005
*note:* amended November 2001 by a series of new constitutional amendments strengthening minority rights and in 2005 with amendments related to the judiciary

**Legal system:** based on civil law system; judicial review of legislative acts; has not accepted compulsory ICJ jurisdiction

**Suffrage:** 18 years of age; universal

**Executive branch:**
*chief of state:* President Georgi IVANOV (since 12 May 2009)
*head of government:* Prime Minister Nikola GRUEVSKI (since 26 August 2006)
*cabinet:* Council of Ministers elected by the majority vote of all the deputies in the Assembly; note - current cabinet formed by the government coalition parties VMRO/DPMNE, BDI/DUI, and several small parties
*elections:* president elected by popular vote for a five-year term (eligible for a second term); two-round election: first round held 22 March 2009, second round held 5 April 2009 (next to be held in March 2014); prime minister elected by the Assembly following legislative elections
*election results:* Gjorge IVANOV elected president on second-round ballot; percent of vote - Gjorge IVANOV 63.14%, Ljubomir FRCKOSKI 36.86%

**Legislative branch:** unicameral Assembly or Sobranie (120 seats; members elected by popular vote from party lists based on the percentage of the overall vote the parties gain in each of six electoral districts; members serve four-year terms)
*elections:* last held 1 June and 15 June 2008 (next to be held by July 2012)
*election results:* percent of vote by party -

VMRO-DPMNE-led block 49%, SDSM-led block 24%, BDI/DUI 13%, PDSh/DPA 8%, other 6%; seats by party - VMRO-DPMNE-led block 63, SDSM-led block 27, BDI/DUI 18, PDSh/DPA 11, PEI 1

**Judicial branch:** Supreme Court; Constitutional Court; Republican Judicial Council
*note:* the Assembly appoints the judges

**Political parties and leaders:** Democratic Alliance [Pavle TRAJANOV]; Democratic League of Bosniaks [Rafet MUMINOVIC]; Democratic Party of Albanians or PDSh/DPA [Menduh THACI]; Democratic Party of Serbs [Ivan STOILJKOVIC]; Democratic Party of Turks [Kenan HASIPI]; Democratic Renewal of Macedonia [Liljana POPOVSKA]; Democratic Union of Albanians or BDSh [Bardyl MAHMUTI]; Democratic Union of Vlachs for Macedonia [Mitko KOSTOV]; Democratic Union for Integration or BDI/DUI [Ali AHMETI]; For a Better Macedonia coalition [Nikola GRUEVSKI] (includes VMRO-DPMNE, SP, Democratic Union, Democratic Renewal of Macedonia, Democratic Party of Turks, Democratic Party of Serbs, SR, and smaller parties); Internal Macedonian Revolutionary Organization-Democratic Party for Macedonian National Unity or VMRO-DPMNE [Nikola GRUEVSKI]; League for Democracy [Gjorgi MARJANOVIC]; Liberal Democratic Party or LDP [Jovan MANSIEVSKI]; Liberal Party [Stojan ANDOV]; National Alternative [Harun ALIU]; National Democratic Union or BDK [Hysni SHAQIR]; New Democracy of DR/ND [Imer SELMANI]; New Social Democratic Party or NSDP [Tito PETKOVSKI]; Party for Democratic Prosperity or PPD/PDP [Sefedin HARUNI]; Party for European Future or PEI [Fijat CANOSKI]; Party of Free Democrats or PSD [Ljubco JORDANOVSKI]; Social Democratic Alliance of Macedonia or SDSM [Zoran ZAEV]; Socialist Party of Macedonia or SP [Ljubisav IVANOV-ZINGO]; Sun-Coalition for Europe [Radmila SKERINSKA] (includes SDSM, NSDP, LDP, Liberal Party and smaller parties); Union of Romas or SR [Shaban SALIU]; United Party for Emancipation or OPE [Nezdet MUSTAFA]

**Political pressure groups and leaders:** Federation of Free Trade Unions [Svetlana PETROVIC]; Federation of Trade Unions [Vanco MURATOVSKI]; Trade Union of Education, Science and Culture [Dojcin CVETANOSKI]; World Macedonian Congress [Todor PETROV]

**International organization participation:** BIS, CE, CEI, EAPC, EBRD, FAO, IAEA, IBRD, ICAO, ICCt, ICRM, IDA, IFAD, IFC, IFRCS, ILO, IMF, IMO, Interpol, IOC, IOM (observer), IPU, ISO, ITU, ITUC, MIGA, OIF, OPCW, OSCE, PCA, PFP, SECI, UN, UNCTAD, UNESCO, UNHCR, UNIDO, UNIFIL, UNWTO, UPU, WCL, WCO, WFTU, WHO, WIPO, WMO, WTO

**Diplomatic representation in the US:**
*chief of mission:* Ambassador Zoran JOLEVSKI
*chancery:* 2129 Wyoming Avenue NW, Washington, DC 20008
*telephone:* [1] (202) 667-0501
*FAX:* [1] (202) 667-2131
*consulate(s) general:* Southfield (Michigan)

**Diplomatic representation from the US:**
*chief of mission:* Ambassador Philip T. REEKER
*embassy:* Bul. Ilindenska bb, 1000 Skopje
*mailing address:* American Embassy Skopje, US Department of State, 7120 Skopje Place, Washington, DC 20521-7120 (pouch)
*telephone:* [389] 2 311-6180
*FAX:* [389] 2 311-7103

**Flag description:** a yellow sun with eight broadening rays extending to the edges of the red field

## Economy

**Economy - overview:** Having a small, open economy makes Macedonia vulnerable to economic developments in Europe and dependent on regional integration and progress toward EU membership for continued economic growth. At independence in September 1991, Macedonia was the least developed of the Yugoslav republics, producing a mere 5% of the total federal output of goods and services. The collapse of Yugoslavia ended transfer payments from the central government and eliminated advantages from inclusion in a de facto free trade area. An absence of infrastructure, UN sanctions on the downsized Yugoslavia, and a Greek economic embargo over a dispute about the country's constitutional name and flag hindered economic growth until 1996. GDP subsequently rose each year through 2000. In 2001, during a civil conflict, the economy shrank 4.5% because of decreased trade, intermittent border closures, increased deficit spending on security needs, and investor uncertainty. Growth averaged 4% per year during 2003-06 and 5% per year during 2007-08. Macedonia has maintained macroeconomic stability with low inflation, but it has so far lagged the region in attracting foreign investment and creating jobs, despite making extensive fiscal and business sector reforms. Official unemployment remains high at nearly 35%, but may be overstated based on the existence of an extensive gray market, estimated to be more than 20% of GDP, that is not captured by official statistics. In the wake of the global economic downturn, Macedonia has experienced decreased foreign direct investment, lowered credit, and a slowdown of export growth. The Government of Macedonia now predicts growth in 2009 to be no more than 3%.

**GDP (purchasing power parity):**
$18.52 billion (2008 est.)
$17.71 billion (2007)
$16.85 billion (2006)
*note:* data are in 2008 US dollars
Macedonia has a large informal sector

**GDP (official exchange rate):** $9.624 billion (2008 est.)

**GDP - real growth rate:**
4.6% (2008 est.)
5.1% (2007 est.)
3.7% (2006 est.)

**GDP - per capita (PPP):**
$9,000 (2008 est.)
$8,600 (2007 est.)
$8,200 (2006 est.)
*note:* data are in 2008 US dollars

# Macedonia *(continued)*

**GDP - composition by sector:**
*agriculture:* 11.4%
*industry:* 27.2%
*services:* 61.4% (2008 est.)
**Labor force:** 900,000 (2008 est.)
**Labor force - by occupation:**
*agriculture:* 19.6%
*industry:* 30.4%
*services:* 50% (September 2007)
**Unemployment rate:**
34.5% (2008 est.)
34.9% (2007 est.)
**Population below poverty line:** 29.8% (2006)
**Household income or consumption by percentage share:**
*lowest 10%:* 2.4%
*highest 10%:* 29.6% (2003)
**Distribution of family income - Gini index:** 39 (2003)
**Investment (gross fixed):** 18% of GDP (2008 est.)
**Budget:**
*revenues:* $2.889 billion
*expenditures:* $2.985 billion (2008 est.)
**Public debt:** 35.9% of GDP (2008 est.)
**Inflation rate (consumer prices):**
8.4% (2008 est.)
2.3% (2007 est.)
**Central bank discount rate:** 6.5% (31 December 2007)
**Commercial bank prime lending rate:** 10.23% (31 December 2007)
**Stock of money:** $1.173 billion (31 December 2007)
**Stock of quasi money:** $3.127 billion (31 December 2007)
**Stock of domestic credit:** $2.924 billion (31 December 2007)
**Market value of publicly traded shares:** $2.715 billion (31 December 2007)
**Agriculture - products:** grapes, wine, tobacco, vegetables, fruits; milk, eggs
**Industries:** food processing, beverages, textiles, chemicals, iron, steel, cement, energy, pharmaceuticals
**Industrial production growth rate:** 1.8% (2008 est.)
**Electricity - production:** 6.051 billion kWh (2007)
**Electricity - consumption:** 8.651 billion kWh (2007)
**Electricity - exports:** 0 kWh (2007 est.)
**Electricity - imports:** 2.6 billion kWh (2007)
**Oil - production:** 0 bbl/day (2007)
**Oil - consumption:** 19,590 bbl/day (2006 est.)
**Oil - exports:** 6,768 bbl/day (2005)
**Oil - imports:** 26,470 bbl/day (2005)
**Oil - proved reserves:** 0 bbl (1 January 2008 est.)
**Natural gas - production:** 0 cu m (2007 est.)
**Natural gas - consumption:** 100 million cu m (2006 est.)
**Natural gas - exports:** 0 cu m (2007 est.)
**Natural gas - imports:** 102.8 million cu m (2007)
**Natural gas - proved reserves:** 0 cu m (1 January 2008 est.)

**Current account balance:** -$740 million (2008 est.)
**Exports:** $4.397 billion f.o.b. (2008 est.)
**Exports - commodities:** food, beverages, tobacco; textiles, miscellaneous manufactures, iron and steel
**Exports - partners:** Serbia and Montenegro 19.2%, Germany 14.5%, Greece 10.4%, Italy 10.1%, Bulgaria 9.8%, Croatia 5.6%, Belgium 5%, Spain 5% (2007)
**Imports:** $6.663 billion f.o.b. (2008 est.)
**Imports - commodities:** machinery and equipment, automobiles, chemicals, fuels, food products
**Imports - partners:** Germany 13.2%, Greece 12.9%, Bulgaria 9.6%, Serbia and Montenegro 7.7%, Turkey 6.6%, Italy 6.3%, Slovenia 5% (2007)
**Reserves of foreign exchange and gold:** $2.43 billion (31 December 2008 est.)
**Debt - external:** $4.624 billion (31 December 2008 est.)
**Stock of direct foreign investment - at home:** $2.405 billion (2007 est.)
**Stock of direct foreign investment - abroad:** $NA
**Exchange rates:** Macedonian denars (MKD) per US dollar - 41.414 (2008 est.), 44.732 (2007), 48.978 (2006), 48.92 (2005), 49.41 (2004)

## Communications

**Telephones - main lines in use:** 463,600 (2007)
**Telephones - mobile cellular:** 1.518 million (2007)
**Telephone system:**
*general assessment:* competition from the mobile-cellular segment of the telecommunications market has led to a drop in fixed-line telephone subscriptions
*domestic:* combined fixed line and mobile telephone density approaching 100 per 100 persons
*international:* country code - 389 (2007)
**Radio broadcast stations:** AM 29, FM 32, shortwave 0 (2008)
**Television broadcast stations:** 52 (2007)
**Internet country code:** .mk
**Internet hosts:** 36,905 (2008)
**Internet users:** 685,000 (2007)

## Transportation

**Airports:** 17 (2008)
**Airports - with paved runways:**
*total:* 10
*2,438 to 3,047 m:* 2
*under 914 m:* 8 (2008)
**Airports - with unpaved runways:**
*total:* 7
*914 to 1,523 m:* 3
*under 914 m:* 4 (2008)
**Pipelines:** gas 268 km; oil 120 km (2008)
**Railways:**
*total:* 699 km
*standard gauge:* 699 km 1.435-m gauge (223 km electrified) (2006)
**Roadways:**
*total:* 13,182 km (includes 208 km of expressways) (2002)

## Military

**Military branches:** Army of the Republic of Macedonia (ARM): Joint Operational Command, with subordinate Air Wing (Makedonsko Voeno Vozduhoplovstvo, MVV), Special Operations Regiment (2009)
**Military service age and obligation:** 18 years of age for voluntary military service; no conscription (2007)
**Manpower available for military service:**
*males age 16-49:* 532,856
*females age 16-49:* 513,684 (2008 est.)
**Manpower fit for military service:**
*males age 16-49:* 444,247
*females age 16-49:* 427,556 (2009 est.)
**Manpower reaching militarily significant age annually:**
*male:* 14,596
*female:* 13,881 (2009 est.)
**Military expenditures:** 6% of GDP (2005 est.)

## Transnational Issues

**Disputes - international:** Kosovo and Macedonia completed demarcation of their boundary in September 2008; Greece continues to reject the use of the name Macedonia or Republic of Macedonia
**Refugees and internally displaced persons:**
*IDPs:* fewer than 1,000 (ethnic conflict in 2001) (2007)
**Illicit drugs:** major transshipment point for Southwest Asian heroin and hashish; minor transit point for South American cocaine destined for Europe; although not a financial center and most criminal activity is thought to be domestic, money laundering is a problem due to a mostly cash-based economy and weak enforcement

# Madagascar

## Introduction

**Background:** Formerly an independent kingdom, Madagascar became a French colony in 1896 but regained independence in 1960. During 1992-93, free presidential and National Assembly elections were held ending 17 years of single-party rule. In 1997, in the second presidential race, Didier RATSIRAKA, the leader during the 1970s and 1980s, was returned to the presidency. The 2001 presidential election was contested between the followers of Didier RATSIRAKA and Marc RAVALOMANANA, nearly causing secession of half of the country. In April 2002, the High Constitutional Court announced RAVALOMANANA the winner. RAVALOMANANA achieved a second term following a landslide victory in the generally free and fair presidential elections of 2006. In early 2009, protests due to increasing restrictions on opposition press and activities resulted in RAVALOMANANA stepping down and the presidency was conferred to the mayor of Antananarivo, Andry RAJOELINA. Early elections are likely.

## Geography

**Location:** Southern Africa, island in the Indian Ocean, east of Mozambique
**Geographic coordinates:** 20 00 S, 47 00 E
**Map references:** Africa
**Area:**
*total:* 587,040 sq km
*land:* 581,540 sq km
*water:* 5,500 sq km
**Area - comparative:** slightly less than twice the size of Arizona
**Land boundaries:** 0 km
**Coastline:** 4,828 km
**Maritime claims:**
*territorial sea:* 12 nm
*contiguous zone:* 24 nm
*exclusive economic zone:* 200 nm
*continental shelf:* 200 nm or 100 nm from the 2,500-m isobath
**Climate:** tropical along coast, temperate inland, arid in south
**Terrain:** narrow coastal plain, high plateau and mountains in center
**Elevation extremes:**
*lowest point:* Indian Ocean 0 m
*highest point:* Maromokotro 2,876 m
**Natural resources:** graphite, chromite, coal, bauxite, salt, quartz, tar sands, semiprecious stones, mica, fish, hydropower
**Land use:**
*arable land:* 5.03%
*permanent crops:* 1.02%
*other:* 93.95% (2005)
**Irrigated land:** 10,860 sq km (2003)
**Total renewable water resources:** 337 cu km (1984)
**Freshwater withdrawal (domestic/industrial/agricultural):**
*total:* 14.96 cu km/yr (3%/2%/96%)
*per capita:* 804 cu m/yr (2000)
**Natural hazards:** periodic cyclones; drought; and locust infestation
**Environment - current issues:** soil erosion results from deforestation and overgrazing; desertification; surface water contaminated with raw sewage and other organic wastes; several endangered species of flora and fauna unique to the island
**Environment - international agreements:**
*party to:* Biodiversity, Climate Change, Climate Change-Kyoto Protocol, Desertification, Endangered Species, Hazardous Wastes, Law of the Sea, Marine Life Conservation, Ozone Layer Protection, Ship Pollution, Wetlands
*signed, but not ratified:* none of the selected agreements
**Geography - note:** world's fourth-largest island; strategic location along Mozambique Channel

## People

**Population:** 20,653,556 (July 2009 est.)
**Age structure:**
*0-14 years:* 43.5% (male 4,523,033/female 4,460,473)
*15-64 years:* 53.5% (male 5,483,684/female 5,557,098)
*65 years and over:* 3% (male 280,677/female 348,591) (2009 est.)
**Median age:**
*total:* 18 years
*male:* 17.8 years
*female:* 18.2 years (2009 est.)
**Population growth rate:** 3% (2009 est.)
**Birth rate:** 38.14 births/1,000 population (2009 est.)
**Death rate:** 8.32 deaths/1,000 population (2008 est.)
**Net migration rate:** NA
**Urbanization:**
*urban population:* 29% of total population (2008)
*rate of urbanization:* 3.8% annual rate of change (2005-10 est.)
**Sex ratio:**
*at birth:* 1.03 male(s)/female
*under 15 years:* 1.01 male(s)/female
*15-64 years:* 0.99 male(s)/female
*65 years and over:* 0.8 male(s)/female
*total population:* 0.99 male(s)/female (2009 est.)
**Infant mortality rate:**
*total:* 54.2 deaths/1,000 live births
*male:* 59.12 deaths/1,000 live births
*female:* 49.13 deaths/1,000 live births (2009 est.)
**Life expectancy at birth:**
*total population:* 62.89 years
*male:* 60.93 years
*female:* 64.91 years (2009 est.)
**Total fertility rate:** 5.14 children born/woman (2009 est.)
**HIV/AIDS - adult prevalence rate:** 0.1% (2007 est.)
**HIV/AIDS - people living with HIV/AIDS:** 14,000 (2007 est.)
**HIV/AIDS - deaths:** fewer than 1,000 (2007 est.)
**Major infectious diseases:**
*degree of risk:* very high
*food or waterborne diseases:* bacterial and protozoal diarrhea, hepatitis A, and typhoid fever
*vectorborne diseases:* chikungunya, malaria, and plague
*water contact disease:* schistosomiasis (2009)
**Nationality:**
*noun:* Malagasy (singular and plural)
*adjective:* Malagasy
**Ethnic groups:** Malayo-Indonesian (Merina and related Betsileo), Cotiers (mixed African, Malayo-Indonesian, and Arab ancestry - Betsimisaraka, Tsimihety, Antaisaka, Sakalava), French, Indian, Creole, Comoran
**Religions:** indigenous beliefs 52%, Christian 41%, Muslim 7%
**Languages:** English (official), French (official), Malagasy (official)

**Literacy:**
*definition:* age 15 and over can read and write
*total population:* 68.9%
*male:* 75.5%
*female:* 62.5% (2003 est.)
**School life expectancy (primary to tertiary education):**
*total:* 9 years
*male:* 10 years
*female:* 9 years (2006)
**Education expenditures:** 3.1% of GDP (2006)

## Government

**Country name:**
*conventional long form:* Republic of Madagascar
*conventional short form:* Madagascar
*local long form:* Republique de Madagascar/ Repoblikan'i Madagasikara
*local short form:* Madagascar/Madagasikara
*former:* Malagasy Republic
**Government type:** republic
**Capital:**
*name:* Antananarivo
*geographic coordinates:* 18 55 S, 47 31 E
*time difference:* UTC+3 (8 hours ahead of Washington, DC during Standard Time)
**Administrative divisions:** 6 provinces (faritany); Antananarivo, Antsiranana, Fianarantsoa, Mahajanga, Toamasina, Toliara
**Independence:** 26 June 1960 (from France)
**National holiday:** Independence Day, 26 June (1960)
**Constitution:** passed by referendum 19 August 1992
**Legal system:** based on French civil law system and traditional Malagasy law; accepts compulsory ICJ jurisdiction with reservations
**Suffrage:** 18 years of age; universal
**Executive branch:**
*chief of state:* President Andry RAJOELINA (since 18 March 2009)
*head of government:* Prime Minister Roindefo ZAFITSIMIVALO (since 18 March 2009)
*cabinet:* Council of Ministers appointed by the prime minister
*elections:* president elected by popular vote for a five-year term (eligible for a second term); election last held 3 December 2006 (next to be held in December 2011); prime minister appointed by the president
*election results:* percent of vote - Marc RAVALOMANANA 54.8%, Jean LAHINIRIKO 11.7%, Roland RATSIRAKA 10.1%, Herizo RAZAFIMAHALEO 9.1%, Norbert RATSIRAHONANA 4.2%, Ny Hasina ANDRIAMANJATO 4.2%, Elia RAVELOMANANTSOA 2.6%, Pety RAKOTONIAINA 1.7%, other 1.6%; note - RAVALOMANANA stepped down on 17 March 2009
*note:* on 17 March 2009, democratically elected President Marc RAVALOMANANA stepped down handing the government over to the military, which in turn conferred the presidency on opposition leader and Antananarivo mayor Andry RAJOELINA, who will head the High Transition Authority

**Legislative branch:** bicameral legislature consists of a Senate or Senat (100 seats; two-thirds of the seats filled by regional assemblies; the remaining one-third of seats appointed by the president; to serve four-year terms) and a National Assembly or Assemblee Nationale (127 seats - reduced from 160 seats by an April 2007 national referendum; members are elected by popular vote to serve four-year terms)
*elections:* National Assembly - last held 23 September 2007 (next to be held in 2011)
*election results:* National Assembly - percent of vote by party - NA; seats by party - TIM 106, LEADER/ Fanilo 1, independents 20
**Judicial branch:** Supreme Court or Cour Supreme; High Constitutional Court or Haute Cour Constitutionnelle
**Political parties and leaders:** Association for the Rebirth of Madagascar or AREMA [Pierrot RAJAONARIVELO]; Democratic Party for Union in Madagascar or PSDUM [Jean LAHINIRIKO]; Economic Liberalism and Democratic Action for National Recovery or LEADER/Fanilo [Herizo RAZAFIMAHALEO]; Fihaonana Party or FP [Guy-Willy RAZANAMASY]; I Love Madagascar or TIM [Marc RAVALOMANANA]; Renewal of the Social Democratic Party or RPSD [Evariste MARSON]
**Political pressure groups and leaders:** Committee for the Defense of Truth and Justice or KMMR; Committee for National Reconciliation or CRN [Albert Zafy]; National Council of Christian Churches or FFKM
**International organization participation:** ACP, AfDB, AU, COMESA, FAO, G-77, IAEA, IBRD, ICAO, ICC, ICCt, ICRM, IDA, IFAD, IFC, IFRCS, ILO, IMF, IMO, InOC, Interpol, IOC, IOM, IPU, ISO (correspondent), ITSO, ITU, ITUC, MIGA, NAM, OIF, OPCW, SADC, UN, UNCTAD, UNESCO, UNHCR, UNIDO, UNWTO, UPU, WCL, WCO, WFTU, WHO, WIPO, WMO, WTO
**Diplomatic representation in the US:**
*chief of mission:* Ambassador Jocelyn Bertin RADIFERA
*chancery:* 2374 Massachusetts Avenue NW, Washington, DC 20008
*telephone:* [1] (202) 265-5525 through 5526
*FAX:* [1] (202) 265-3034
*consulate(s) general:* Los Angeles, New York
**Diplomatic representation from the US:**
*chief of mission:* Ambassador R. Niels MARQUARDT
*embassy:* 14-16 Rue Rainitovo, Antsahavola, Antananarivo 101
*mailing address:* B. P. 620, Antsahavola, Antananarivo
*telephone:* [261] (20) 22-212-57, 22-212-73, 22-209-56
*FAX:* [261] (20) 22-345-39
**Flag description:** two equal horizontal bands of red (top) and green with a vertical white band of the same width on hoist side

## Economy

**Economy - overview:** Having discarded past socialist economic policies, Madagascar has since the mid 1990s followed a World Bank- and IMF-led policy of privatization and liberalization. This strategy placed the country on a slow and steady growth path from an extremely low level. Agriculture, including fishing and forestry, is a mainstay of the economy, accounting for more than one-fourth of GDP and employing 80% of the population. Exports of apparel have boomed in recent years primarily due to duty-free access to the US. Deforestation and erosion, aggravated by the use of firewood as the primary source of fuel, are serious concerns. President RAVALOMANANA has worked aggressively to revive the economy following the 2002 political crisis, which triggered a 12% drop in GDP that year. Poverty reduction and combating corruption will be the centerpieces of economic policy for the next few years.
**GDP (purchasing power parity):**
$20.76 billion (2008 est.)
$19.4 billion (2007)
$18.27 billion (2006)
*note:* data are in 2008 US dollars
**GDP (official exchange rate):** $9.729 billion (2008 est.)
**GDP - real growth rate:**
7% (2008 est.)
6.2% (2007 est.)
5% (2006 est.)
**GDP - per capita (PPP):**
$1,000 (2008 est.)
$1,000 (2007 est.)
$1,000 (2006 est.)
*note:* data are in 2008 US dollars
**GDP - composition by sector:**
*agriculture:* 26%
*industry:* 15.9%
*services:* 58.1% (2008 est.)
**Labor force:** 7.3 million (2000)
**Population below poverty line:** 50% (2004 est.)
**Household income or consumption by percentage share:**
*lowest 10%:* 1.9%
*highest 10%:* 36.6% (2001)
**Distribution of family income - Gini index:** 47.5 (2001)
**Investment (gross fixed):** 27.2% of GDP (2008 est.)
**Budget:**
*revenues:* $1.688 billion
*expenditures:* $2.066 billion (2008 est.)
**Inflation rate (consumer prices):**
9.2% (2008 est.)
10.3% (2007 est.)
**Commercial bank prime lending rate:** 45% (31 December 2007)
**Stock of money:** $1.161 billion (31 December 2007)
**Stock of quasi money:** $577.4 million (31 December 2007)

**Stock of domestic credit:** $767.5 million (31 December 2007)

**Market value of publicly traded shares:** $NA

**Agriculture - products:** coffee, vanilla, sugarcane, cloves, cocoa, rice, cassava (tapioca), beans, bananas, peanuts; livestock products

**Industries:** meat processing, seafood, soap, breweries, tanneries, sugar, textiles, glassware, cement, automobile assembly plant, paper, petroleum, tourism

**Industrial production growth rate:** 8% (2008 est.)

**Electricity - production:** 1.045 billion kWh (2007 est.)

**Electricity - consumption:** 907 million kWh (2006 est.)

**Electricity - exports:** 0 kWh (2007 est.)

**Electricity - imports:** 0 kWh (2007 est.)

**Oil - production:** 92.18 bbl/day (2007 est.)

**Oil - consumption:** 18,190 bbl/day (2006 est.)

**Oil - exports:** 480.3 bbl/day (2005)

**Oil - imports:** 17,100 bbl/day (2005)

**Oil - proved reserves:** 0 bbl (1 January 2006 est.)

**Natural gas - production:** 0 cu m (2007 est.)

**Natural gas - consumption:** 0 cu m (2007 est.)

**Natural gas - exports:** 0 cu m (2007 est.)

**Natural gas - imports:** 0 cu m (2007 est.)

**Natural gas - proved reserves:** 0 cu m (1 January 2006 est.)

**Current account balance:** -$1.088 billion (2008 est.)

**Exports:** $1.316 billion f.o.b. (2008 est.)

**Exports - commodities:** coffee, vanilla, shellfish, sugar, cotton cloth, chromite, petroleum products

**Exports - partners:** France 31.8%, US 26.6%, Germany 6.1%, UK 4.9%, Italy 4.4% (2007)

**Imports:** $2.541 billion f.o.b. (2008 est.)

**Imports - commodities:** capital goods, petroleum, consumer goods, food

**Imports - partners:** France 13.6%, China 13%, Iran 8.1%, South Africa 6.4%, Hong Kong 4.9%, Mauritius 4.8% (2007)

**Reserves of foreign exchange and gold:** $996 million (31 December 2008 est.)

**Debt - external:** $4.6 billion (2002)

**Stock of direct foreign investment - at home:** $NA

**Stock of direct foreign investment - abroad:** $NA

**Exchange rates:** Malagasy ariary (MGA) per US dollar - 1,654.78 (2008 est.), 1,880 (2007), 2,161.4 (2006), 2,003 (2005), 1,868.9 (2004)

## Communications

**Telephones - main lines in use:** 133,900 (2007)

**Telephones - mobile cellular:** 2.218 million (2007)

**Telephone system:**
*general assessment:* system is above average for the region; Antananarivo's main telephone exchange modernized in the late 1990s, but the rest of the analogue-based telephone system is poorly developed; have added more than 50,000 new fixed lines since 2005

*domestic:* combined fixed-line and mobile telephone density only about 12 per 100 persons

*international:* country code - 261; submarine cable to Bahrain; satellite earth stations - 2 (1 Intelsat - Indian Ocean, 1 Intersputnik - Atlantic Ocean region) (2007)

**Radio broadcast stations:** AM 2, FM 9, shortwave 6 (2001)

**Television broadcast stations:** 1 (plus 36 repeaters) (2001)

**Internet country code:** .mg

**Internet hosts:** 11,016 (2008)

**Internet users:** 110,000 (2006)

## Transportation

**Airports:** 90 (2008)

**Airports - with paved runways:**
*total:* 27
*over 3,047 m:* 1
*2,438 to 3,047 m:* 2
*1,524 to 2,437 m:* 6
*914 to 1,523 m:* 17
*under 914 m:* 1 (2008)

**Airports - with unpaved runways:**
*total:* 63
*1,524 to 2,437 m:* 2
*914 to 1,523 m:* 39
*under 914 m:* 22 (2008)

**Railways:**
*total:* 854 km
*narrow gauge:* 854 km 1.000-m gauge (2006)

**Roadways:**
*total:* 65,663 km
*paved:* 7,617 km
*unpaved:* 58,046 km (2003)

**Waterways:** 600 km
*note:* 432 km navigable (2008)

**Merchant marine:**
*total:* 8
*by type:* cargo 4, passenger/cargo 2, petroleum tanker 2 (2008)

**Ports and terminals:** Antsiranana, Mahajanga, Toamasina, Toliara

## Military

**Military branches:** People's Armed Forces: Intervention Force, Development Force, and Aeronaval Force (navy and air); National Gendarmerie

**Military service age and obligation:** 18-25 years of age for male-only compulsory military service; 18-month conscript service obligation (either military or equivalent civil service); 20-30 years of age for National Gendarmerie recruits (35 years of age for those with military experience) (2008)

**Manpower available for military service:**
*males age 16-49:* 4,443,341
*females age 16-49:* 4,441,124 (2008 est.)

**Manpower fit for military service:**
*males age 16-49:* 3,150,043
*females age 16-49:* 3,404,988 (2009 est.)

**Manpower reaching militarily significant age annually:**
*male:* 236,500
*female:* 235,994 (2009 est.)

**Military expenditures:** 1% of GDP (2006)

## Transnational Issues

**Disputes - international:** claims Bassas da India, Europa Island, Glorioso Islands, and Juan de Nova Island (all administered by France)

**Illicit drugs:** illicit producer of cannabis (cultivated and wild varieties) used mostly for domestic consumption; transshipment point for heroin

# Malawi

## Introduction

**Background:** Established in 1891, the British protectorate of Nyasaland became the independent nation of Malawi in 1964. After three decades of one-party rule under President Hastings Kamuzu BANDA the country held multiparty elections in 1994, under a provisional constitution that came into full effect the following year. Current President Bingu wa MUTHARIKA, elected in May 2004 after a failed attempt by the previous president to amend the constitution to permit another term, struggled to assert his authority against his predecessor and subsequently started his own party, the Democratic Progressive Party (DPP) in 2005. As president, MUTHARIKA has overseen substantial economic improvement but because of political deadlock in the legislature, his minority party has been unable to pass significant legislation, and anti-corruption measures have stalled. Population growth, increasing pressure on agricultural lands, corruption, and the spread of HIV/AIDS pose major problems for Malawi.

## Geography

**Location:** Southern Africa, east of Zambia
**Geographic coordinates:** 13 30 S, 34 00 E
**Map references:** Africa
**Area:**
*total:* 118,480 sq km
*land:* 94,080 sq km
*water:* 24,400 sq km
**Area - comparative:** slightly smaller than Pennsylvania
**Land boundaries:**
*total:* 2,881 km
*border countries:* Mozambique 1,569 km, Tanzania 475 km, Zambia 837 km
**Coastline:** 0 km (landlocked)
**Maritime claims:** none (landlocked)
**Climate:** sub-tropical; rainy season (November to May); dry season (May to November)
**Terrain:** narrow elongated plateau with rolling plains, rounded hills, some mountains
**Elevation extremes:**
*lowest point:* junction of the Shire River and international boundary with Mozambique 37 m
*highest point:* Sapitwa (Mount Mlanje) 3,002 m
**Natural resources:** limestone, arable land, hydropower, unexploited deposits of uranium, coal, and bauxite
**Land use:**
*arable land:* 20.68%
*permanent crops:* 1.18%
*other:* 78.14% (2005)
**Irrigated land:** 560 sq km (2003)
**Total renewable water resources:** 17.3 cu km (2001)
**Freshwater withdrawal (domestic/industrial/ agricultural):**
*total:* 1.01 cu km/yr (15%/5%/80%)
*per capita:* 78 cu m/yr (2000)
**Natural hazards:** NA
**Environment - current issues:** deforestation; land degradation; water pollution from agricultural runoff, sewage, industrial wastes; siltation of spawning grounds endangers fish populations
**Environment - international agreements:**
*party to:* Biodiversity, Climate Change, Climate Change-Kyoto Protocol, Desertification, Endangered Species, Environmental Modification, Hazardous Wastes, Marine Life Conservation, Ozone Layer Protection, Ship Pollution, Wetlands
*signed, but not ratified:* Law of the Sea
**Geography - note:** landlocked; Lake Nyasa, some 580 km long, is the country's most prominent physical feature

## People

**Population:** 14,268,711
*note:* estimates for this country explicitly take into account the effects of excess mortality due to AIDS; this can result in lower life expectancy, higher infant mortality, higher death rates, lower population growth rates, and changes in the distribution of population by age and sex than would otherwise be expected (July 2009 est.)
**Age structure:**
*0-14 years:* 45.8% (male 3,272,790/ female 3,258,893)
*15-64 years:* 51.5% (male 3,696,857/ female 3,656,918)
*65 years and over:* 2.7% (male 162,863/ female 220,390) (2009 est.)
**Median age:**
*total:* 16.8 years
*male:* 16.8 years
*female:* 16.9 years (2009 est.)
**Population growth rate:** 2.388% (2009 est.)
**Birth rate:** 41.48 births/1,000 population (2009 est.)
**Death rate:** 17.89 deaths/1,000 population (2008 est.)
**Net migration rate:** NA
**Urbanization:**
*urban population:* 19% of total population (2008)
*rate of urbanization:* 5.2% annual rate of change (2005-10 est.)
**Sex ratio:**
*at birth:* 1.02 male(s)/female
*under 15 years:* 1 male(s)/female
*15-64 years:* 1.01 male(s)/female
*65 years and over:* 0.74 male(s)/female
*total population:* 1 male(s)/female (2009 est.)
**Infant mortality rate:**
*total:* 89.05 deaths/1,000 live births
*male:* 93.15 deaths/1,000 live births
*female:* 84.88 deaths/1,000 live births (2009 est.)
**Life expectancy at birth:**
*total population:* 43.82 years
*male:* 44.07 years
*female:* 43.57 years (2009 est.)
**Total fertility rate:** 5.59 children born/woman (2009 est.)
**HIV/AIDS - adult prevalence rate:** 11.9% (2007 est.)
**HIV/AIDS - people living with HIV/AIDS:** 930,000 (2007 est.)
**HIV/AIDS - deaths:** 68,000 (2007 est.)
**Major infectious diseases:**
*degree of risk:* very high
*food or waterborne diseases:* bacterial and protozoal diarrhea, hepatitis A, and typhoid fever
*vectorborne diseases:* malaria and plague
*water contact disease:* schistosomiasis
*animal contact disease:* rabies (2009)
**Nationality:**
*noun:* Malawian(s)
*adjective:* Malawian
**Ethnic groups:** Chewa, Nyanja, Tumbuka, Yao, Lomwe, Sena, Tonga, Ngoni, Ngonde, Asian, European
**Religions:** Christian 79.9%, Muslim 12.8%, other 3%, none 4.3% (1998 census)
**Languages:** Chichewa 57.2% (official), Chinyanja 12.8%, Chiyao 10.1%, Chitumbuka 9.5%, Chisena 2.7%, Chilomwe 2.4%, Chitonga 1.7%, other 3.6% (1998 census)

# Malawi (continued)

**Literacy:**

*definition:* age 15 and over can read and write

*total population:* 62.7%

*male:* 76.1%

*female:* 49.8% (2003 est.)

**School life expectancy (primary to tertiary education):**

*total:* 9 years

*male:* 10 years

*female:* 9 years (2004)

**Education expenditures:** 5.8% of GDP (2003)

## Government

**Country name:**

*conventional long form:* Republic of Malawi

*conventional short form:* Malawi

*local long form:* Dziko la Malawi

*local short form:* Malawi

*former:* British Central African Protectorate, Nyasaland Protectorate, Nyasaland

**Government type:** multiparty democracy

**Capital:**

*name:* Lilongwe

*geographic coordinates:* 13 59 S, 33 47 E

*time difference:* UTC+2 (7 hours ahead of Washington, DC during Standard Time)

**Administrative divisions:** 28 districts; Balaka, Blantyre, Chikwawa, Chiradzulu, Chitipa, Dedza, Dowa, Karonga, Kasungu, Likoma, Lilongwe, Machinga (Kasupe), Mangochi, Mchinji, Mulanje, Mwanza, Mzimba, Neno, Ntcheu, Nkhata Bay, Nkhotakota, Nsanje, Ntchisi, Phalombe, Rumphi, Salima, Thyolo, Zomba

**Independence:** 6 July 1964 (from the UK)

**National holiday:** Independence Day (Republic Day), 6 July (1964)

**Constitution:** 18 May 1994

**Legal system:** based on English common law and customary law; judicial review of legislative acts in the Supreme Court of Appeal; accepts compulsory ICJ jurisdiction with reservations

**Suffrage:** 18 years of age; universal

**Executive branch:**

*chief of state:* President Bingu wa MUTHARIKA (since 24 May 2004); note - the president is both the chief of state and head of government

*head of government:* President Bingu wa MUTHARIKA (since 24 May 2004)

*cabinet:* 46-member Cabinet named by the president

*elections:* president elected by popular vote for a five-year term (eligible for a second term); election last held 19 May 2009 (next to be held in May 2014)

*election results:* Bingu wa MUTHARIKA elected president; percent of vote - Bingu wa MUTHARIKA 66%, John TEMBO 30.7%, other 3.3%

**Legislative branch:** unicameral National Assembly (193 seats; members elected by popular vote to serve five-year terms)

*elections:* last held 19 May 2009 (next to be held in May 2014)

*election results:* percent of vote by party - NA; seats by party - DPP 114, MCP 26, UDF 17, independents 32, other 4

**Judicial branch:** Supreme Court of Appeal; High Court (chief justice appointed by the president, puisne judges appointed on the advice of the Judicial Service Commission); magistrate's courts

**Political parties and leaders:** Alliance for Democracy or AFORD [Dindi NYASULU]; Congress of Democrats or CODE [Ralph KASAMBARA]; Democratic Progressive Party or DPP [Bingu wa MUTHARIKA]; Malawi Congress Party or MCP [John TEMBO]; Malawi Democratic Party or MDP [Kampelo KALUA]; Malawi Forum for Unity and Development or MAFUNDE [George MNESA]; Maravi People's Party [Uladi MUSSA]; National Unity Party or NUP [Harry CHIUME]; New Rainbow Coalition Party [Beatrice MWALE]; New Republican Party [Gwanda CHAKUWAMBA]; People's Progressive Movement or PPM [Aleke BANDA]; People's Transformation Movement or PETRA [Kamuzu CHIBAMBO]; Republican Party or RP [Stanley MASAULI]; United Democratic Front or UDF [Bakili MULUZI]; United Democratic Party [Kenedy KALAMBO]

**Political pressure groups and leaders:** Agri-Ecology Media (agriculture and environmental group); Council for NGOs in Malawi or CONGOMA (human rights, democracy, and development); Human Rights Consultative Committee or HRCC (human rights); Malawi Law Society (human rights and law reform); Malawi Movement for the Restoration of Democracy or MMRD (acts to restore and maintain democracy); Public Affairs Committee or PAC (promotes democracy, development, peace and unity)

**International organization participation:** ACP, AfDB, AU, C, COMESA, FAO, G-77, IAEA, IBRD, ICAO, ICCt, ICRM, IDA, IFAD, IFC, IFRCS, ILO, IMF, IMO, Interpol, IOC, ISO (correspondent), ITSO, ITU, ITUC, MIGA, MONUC, NAM, OPCW, SADC, UN, UNAMID, UNCTAD, UNESCO, UNIDO, UNMIL, UNMIS, UNWTO, UPU, WCL, WCO, WFTU, WHO, WIPO, WMO, WTO

**Diplomatic representation in the US:**

*chief of mission:* Ambassador Hawa NDILOWE

*chancery:* 1029 Vermont Avenue, Suite 1000, Washington, DC 20005

*telephone:* [1] (202) 721-0270

*FAX:* [1] (202) 721-0288

**Diplomatic representation from the US:**

*chief of mission:* Ambassador Peter W. BODDE

*embassy:* 16 Jomo Kenyatta Road, Lilongwe 3

*mailing address:* P. O. Box 30016, Lilongwe 3, Malawi

*telephone:* [265] (1) 773 166

*FAX:* [265] (1) 770 471

**Flag description:** three equal horizontal bands of black (top), red, and green with a radiant, rising, red sun centered in the black band

**Government - note:** no party has a majority in the fractured legislature

## Economy

**Economy - overview:** Landlocked Malawi ranks among the world's most densely populated and least developed countries. The economy is predominately agricultural with about 85% of the population living in rural areas. Agriculture accounts for more than one-third of GDP and 90% of export revenues. The performance of the tobacco sector is key to short-term growth as tobacco accounts for more than half of exports. The economy depends on substantial inflows of economic assistance from the IMF, the World Bank, and individual donor nations. In December 2007, the US granted Malawi eligibility status to receive financial support within the Millennium Challenge Corporation (MCC) initiative. Malawi will now begin a consultative process to develop a five-year program before funding can begin. In 2006, Malawi was approved for relief under the Heavily Indebted Poor Countries (HIPC) program. The government faces many challenges including developing a market economy, improving educational facilities, facing up to environmental problems, dealing with the rapidly growing problem of HIV/AIDS, and satisfying foreign donors that fiscal discipline is being tightened. In 2005, President MUTHARIKA championed an anticorruption campaign. Since 2005 President MUTHARIKA'S government has exhibited improved financial discipline under the guidance of Finance Minister Goodall GONDWE and signed a three year Poverty Reduction and Growth Facility worth $56 million with the IMF. Improved relations with the IMF lead other international donors to resume aid as well.

**GDP (purchasing power parity):**

$11.56 billion (2008 est.)

$10.85 billion (2007)

$10.05 billion (2006)

*note:* data are in 2008 US dollars

**GDP (official exchange rate):** $4.082 billion (2008 est.)

**GDP - real growth rate:**

6.5% (2008 est.)

8% (2007 est.)

7.9% (2006 est.)

**GDP - per capita (PPP):**

$800 (2008 est.)

$800 (2007 est.)

$800 (2006 est.)

*note:* data are in 2008 US dollars

**GDP - composition by sector:**

*agriculture:* 38.1%

*industry:* 17.7%

*services:* 44.2% (2008 est.)

**Labor force:** 4.5 million (2001 est.)

**Labor force - by occupation:**

*agriculture:* 90%

*industry and services:* 10% (2003 est.)

**Unemployment rate:**

NA%

**Population below poverty line:** 53% (2004)

**Household income or consumption by percentage share:**
*lowest 10%:* 2.9%
*highest 10%:* 31.8% (2004)
**Distribution of family income - Gini index:** 39 (2004)
**Investment (gross fixed):** 8.6% of GDP (2008 est.)
**Budget:**
*revenues:* $1.227 billion
*expenditures:* $1.337 billion (2008 est.)
**Public debt:** 49.1% of GDP (2008 est.)
**Inflation rate (consumer prices):**
9% (2008 est.)
7.9% (2007 est.)
**Central bank discount rate:** 15% (31 December 2007)
**Commercial bank prime lending rate:** 27.72% (31 December 2007)
**Stock of money:** $361.5 million (31 December 2007)
**Stock of quasi money:** $250.4 million (31 December 2007)
**Stock of domestic credit:** $406.2 million (31 December 2007)
**Market value of publicly traded shares:** $NA
**Agriculture - products:** tobacco, sugarcane, cotton, tea, corn, potatoes, cassava (tapioca), sorghum, pulses, groundnuts, Macadamia nuts; cattle, goats
**Industries:** tobacco, tea, sugar, sawmill products, cement, consumer goods
**Industrial production growth rate:** 6% (2008 est.)
**Electricity - production:** 1.13 billion kWh (2006 est.)
**Electricity - consumption:** 1.051 billion kWh (2006 est.)
**Electricity - exports:** 0 kWh (2007 est.)
**Electricity - imports:** 0 kWh (2007 est.)
**Oil - production:** 0 bbl/day (2007 est.)
**Oil - consumption:** 6,160 bbl/day (2006 est.)
**Oil - exports:** 0 bbl/day (2005)
**Oil - imports:** 6,788 bbl/day (2005)
**Oil - proved reserves:** 0 bbl (1 January 2006 est.)
**Natural gas - production:** 0 cu m (2007 est.)
**Natural gas - consumption:** 0 cu m (2007 est.)
**Natural gas - exports:** 0 cu m (2007 est.)
**Natural gas - imports:** 0 cu m (2007 est.)
**Natural gas - proved reserves:** 0 cu m (1 January 2006 est.)
**Current account balance:** -$420 million (2008 est.)
**Exports:** $679 million f.o.b. (2008 est.)
**Exports - commodities:** tobacco 53%, tea, sugar, cotton, coffee, peanuts, wood products, apparel
**Exports - partners:** Germany 11.7%, South Africa 10%, Egypt 9.2%, Zimbabwe 8.2%, US 7.3%, Russia 5.8%, Netherlands 4.5% (2007)
**Imports:** $1.023 billion f.o.b. (2008 est.)
**Imports - commodities:** food, petroleum products, semimanufactures, consumer goods, transportation equipment

**Imports - partners:** South Africa 36.1%, India 8.5%, Tanzania 6.1%, US 6.1%, China 4.9% (2007)
**Reserves of foreign exchange and gold:** $221 million (31 December 2008 est.)
**Debt - external:** $974 million (31 December 2008 est.)
**Stock of direct foreign investment - at home:** $NA
**Stock of direct foreign investment - abroad:** $NA
**Exchange rates:** Malawian kwachas (MWK) per US dollar - 142.41 (2008 est.), 141.12 (2007), 135.96 (2006), 108.894 (2005), 108.898 (2004)

## Communications

**Telephones - main lines in use:** 175,200 (2007)
**Telephones - mobile cellular:** 1.051 million (2007)
**Telephone system:**
*general assessment:* rudimentary
*domestic:* fixed-line subscribership about 1 per 100 persons; privatization of Malawi Telecommunications (MTL), a necessary step in bringing improvement to telecommunications services, completed in 2006; mobile-cellular services are expanding but cellular network coverage is limited and is based around the main urban areas; mobile cellular subscribership roughly 8 per 100 persons
*international:* country code - 265; satellite earth stations - 2 Intelsat (1 Indian Ocean, 1 Atlantic Ocean)
**Radio broadcast stations:** AM 9, FM 5 (plus 15 repeater stations), shortwave 2 (plus one shortwave station on standby) (2001)
**Television broadcast stations:** 1 (2001)
**Internet country code:** .mw
**Internet hosts:** 107 (2008)
**Internet users:** 139,500 (2007)

## Transportation

**Airports:** 34 (2008)
**Airports - with paved runways:**
*total:* 6
*over 3,047 m:* 1
*1,524 to 2,437 m:* 1
*914 to 1,523 m:* 4 (2008)
**Airports - with unpaved runways:**
*total:* 28
*1,524 to 2,437 m:* 1
*914 to 1,523 m:* 14
*under 914 m:* 13 (2008)
**Railways:**
*total:* 797 km
*narrow gauge:* 797 km 1.067-m gauge (2006)
**Roadways:**
*total:* 15,451 km
*paved:* 6,956 km
*unpaved:* 8,495 km (2003)
**Waterways:** 700 km (on Lake Nyasa (Lake Malawi) and Shire River) (2008)
**Ports and terminals:** Chipoka, Monkey Bay, Nkhata Bay, Nkhotakota, Chilumba

## Military

**Military branches:** Malawi Armed Forces: Army (includes Air Wing and Naval Detachment) (2009)
**Military service age and obligation:** 18 years of age for voluntary military service; standard obligation is 2 years of active duty and 5 years of reserve service (2007)
**Manpower available for military service:**
*males age 16-49:* 3,050,444 (2008 est.)
**Manpower fit for military service:**
*males age 16-49:* 1,732,621
*females age 16-49:* 1,562,107 (2009 est.)
**Manpower reaching militarily significant age annually:**
*male:* 174,044
*female:* 173,828 (2009 est.)
**Military expenditures:** 1.3% of GDP (2006)

## Transnational Issues

**Disputes - international:** disputes with Tanzania over the boundary in Lake Nyasa (Lake Malawi) and the meandering Songwe River remain dormant

# Malaysia

## Introduction

**Background:** During the late 18th and 19th centuries, Great Britain established colonies and protectorates in the area of current Malaysia; these were occupied by Japan from 1942 to 1945. In 1948, the British-ruled territories on the Malay Peninsula formed the Federation of Malaya, which became independent in 1957. Malaysia was formed in 1963 when the former British colonies of Singapore and the East Malaysian states of Sabah and Sarawak on the northern coast of Borneo joined the Federation. The first several years of the country's history were marred by a Communist insurgency, Indonesian confrontation with Malaysia, Philippine claims to Sabah, and Singapore's secession from the Federation in 1965. During the 22-year term of Prime Minister MAHATHIR bin Mohamad (1981-2003), Malaysia was successful in diversifying its economy from dependence on exports of raw materials to expansion in manufacturing, services, and tourism.

## Geography

**Location:** Southeastern Asia, peninsula bordering Thailand and northern one-third of the island of Borneo, bordering Indonesia, Brunei, and the South China Sea, south of Vietnam
**Geographic coordinates:** 2 30 N, 112 30 E
**Map references:** Southeast Asia
**Area:**
*total:* 329,750 sq km
*land:* 328,550 sq km
*water:* 1,200 sq km
**Area - comparative:** slightly larger than New Mexico
**Land boundaries:**
*total:* 2,669 km
*border countries:* Brunei 381 km, Indonesia 1,782 km, Thailand 506 km

**Coastline:** 4,675 km (Peninsular Malaysia 2,068 km, East Malaysia 2,607 km)
**Maritime claims:**
*territorial sea:* 12 nm
*exclusive economic zone:* 200 nm
*continental shelf:* 200 m depth or to the depth of exploitation; specified boundary in the South China Sea
**Climate:** tropical; annual southwest (April to October) and northeast (October to February) monsoons
**Terrain:** coastal plains rising to hills and mountains
**Elevation extremes:**
*lowest point:* Indian Ocean 0 m
*highest point:* Gunung Kinabalu 4,100 m
**Natural resources:** tin, petroleum, timber, copper, iron ore, natural gas, bauxite
**Land use:**
*arable land:* 5.46%
*permanent crops:* 17.54%
*other:* 77% (2005)
**Irrigated land:** 3,650 sq km (2003)
**Total renewable water resources:** 580 cu km (1999)
**Freshwater withdrawal (domestic/industrial/agricultural):**
*total:* 9.02 cu km/yr (17%/21%/62%)
*per capita:* 356 cu m/yr (2000)
**Natural hazards:** flooding; landslides; forest fires
**Environment - current issues:** air pollution from industrial and vehicular emissions; water pollution from raw sewage; deforestation; smoke/haze from Indonesian forest fires
**Environment - international agreements:**
*party to:* Biodiversity, Climate Change, Climate Change-Kyoto Protocol, Desertification, Endangered Species, Hazardous Wastes, Law of the Sea, Marine Life Conservation, Ozone Layer Protection, Ship Pollution, Tropical Timber 83, Tropical Timber 94, Wetlands
*signed, but not ratified:* none of the selected agreements

**Geography - note:** strategic location along Strait of Malacca and southern South China Sea

## People

**Population:** 25,715,819 (July 2009 est.)
**Age structure:**
*0-14 years:* 31.4% (male 4,153,621/female 3,914,962)
*15-64 years:* 63.6% (male 8,210,373/female 8,143,043)
*65 years and over:* 5% (male 569,245/female 724,575) (2009 est.)
**Median age:**
*total:* 24.9 years
*male:* 24.3 years
*female:* 25.6 years (2009 est.)
**Population growth rate:** 1.723% (2009 est.)
**Birth rate:** 22.24 births/1,000 population (2009 est.)
**Death rate:** 5.02 deaths/1,000 population (2008 est.)
**Net migration rate:** NA
*note:* does not reflect net flow of an unknown number of illegal immigrants from other countries in the region (2009 est.)
**Urbanization:**
*urban population:* 70% of total population (2008)
*rate of urbanization:* 3% annual rate of change (2005-10 est.)
**Sex ratio:**
*at birth:* 1.07 male(s)/female
*under 15 years:* 1.06 male(s)/female
*15-64 years:* 1.01 male(s)/female
*65 years and over:* 0.79 male(s)/female
*total population:* 1.01 male(s)/female (2009 est.)
**Infant mortality rate:**
*total:* 15.87 deaths/1,000 live births
*male:* 18.32 deaths/1,000 live births
*female:* 13.24 deaths/1,000 live births (2009 est.)
**Life expectancy at birth:**
*total population:* 73.29 years
*male:* 70.56 years
*female:* 76.21 years (2009 est.)
**Total fertility rate:** 2.95 children born/woman (2009 est.)
**HIV/AIDS - adult prevalence rate:** 0.5% (2007 est.)
**HIV/AIDS - people living with HIV/AIDS:** 80,000 (2007 est.)
**HIV/AIDS - deaths:** 3,900 (2007 est.)
**Major infectious diseases:**
*degree of risk:* high
*food or waterborne diseases:* bacterial diarrhea
*vectorborne diseases:* dengue fever and malaria
*note:* highly pathogenic H5N1 avian influenza has been identified in this country; it poses a negligible risk with extremely rare cases possible among US citizens who have close contact with birds (2009)
**Nationality:**
*noun:* Malaysian(s)
*adjective:* Malaysian
**Ethnic groups:** Malay 50.4%, Chinese 23.7%, indigenous 11%, Indian 7.1%, others 7.8% (2004 est.)

**Religions:** Muslim 60.4%, Buddhist 19.2%, Christian 9.1%, Hindu 6.3%, Confucianism, Taoism, other traditional Chinese religions 2.6%, other or unknown 1.5%, none 0.8% (2000 census)

**Languages:** Bahasa Malaysia (official), English, Chinese (Cantonese, Mandarin, Hokkien, Hakka, Hainan, Foochow), Tamil, Telugu, Malayalam, Panjabi, Thai

*note:* in East Malaysia there are several indigenous languages; most widely spoken are Iban and Kadazan

**Literacy:**
*definition:* age 15 and over can read and write
*total population:* 88.7%
*male:* 92%
*female:* 85.4% (2000 census)

**School life expectancy (primary to tertiary education):**
*total:* 13 years
*male:* 12 years
*female:* 13 years (2005)

**Education expenditures:** 6.2% of GDP (2004)

## Government

**Country name:**
*conventional long form:* none
*conventional short form:* Malaysia
*local long form:* none
*local short form:* Malaysia
*former:* Federation of Malaya

**Government type:** constitutional monarchy
*note:* nominally headed by paramount ruler (commonly referred to as the King) and a bicameral Parliament consisting of a nonelected upper house and an elected lower house; all Peninsular Malaysian states have hereditary rulers (commonly referred to as sultans) except Melaka and Pulau Pinang (Penang); those two states along with Sabah and Sarawak in East Malaysia have governors appointed by government; powers of state governments are limited by federal constitution; under terms of federation, Sabah and Sarawak retain certain constitutional prerogatives (e.g., right to maintain their own immigration controls)

**Capital:**
*name:* Kuala Lumpur
*geographic coordinates:* 3 10 N, 101 42 E
*time difference:* UTC+8 (13 hours ahead of Washington, DC during Standard Time)
*note:* Putrajaya is referred to as administrative center not capital; Parliament meets in Kuala Lumpur

**Administrative divisions:** 13 states (negeri-negeri, singular - negeri) Johor, Kedah, Kelantan, Melaka, Negeri Sembilan, Pahang, Perak, Perlis, Pulau Pinang, Sabah, Sarawak, Selangor, and Terengganu; and one federal territory (wilayah persekutuan) with three components, city of Kuala Lumpur, Labuan, and Putrajaya

**Independence:** 31 August 1957 (from the UK)

**National holiday:** Independence Day/Malaysia Day, 31 August (1957)

**Constitution:** 31 August 1957; amended many times, the latest in 2007

**Legal system:** based on English common law; judicial review of legislative acts in the Supreme Court at request of supreme head of the federation; Islamic law is applied to Muslims in matters of family law and religion; has not accepted compulsory ICJ jurisdiction

**Suffrage:** 21 years of age; universal

**Executive branch:**
*chief of state:* King - Sultan MIZAN Zainal Abidin (since 13 December 2006); (the position of the king is primarily ceremonial)
*head of government:* Prime Minister Mohamed NAJIB bin Abdul Razak (since 3 April 2009); Deputy Prime Minister MUHYIDDIN bin Mohamed Yassin (since 9 April 2009)
*cabinet:* Cabinet appointed by the prime minister from among the members of Parliament with consent of the king
*elections:* kings are elected by and from the hereditary rulers of nine of the states for five-year terms; election last held on 3 November 2006 (next to be held in 2011); prime minister designated from among the members of the House of Representatives; following legislative elections, the leader who commands the support of the majority of members in the House becomes prime minister (since independence this has been the leader of the UMNO party)
*election results:* Sultan MIZAN Zainal Abidin elected king; in practice, selection is based on principle of rotation among rulers of states

**Legislative branch:** bicameral Parliament or Parlimen consists of Senate or Dewan Negara (70 seats; 44 appointed by the king, 26 elected by 13 state legislatures; serve three-year terms with limit of two terms) and House of Representatives or Dewan Rakyat (222 seats; members elected by popular vote; serve up to five-year terms)
*elections:* House of Representatives - last held on 8 March 2008 (next to be held by June 2013)
*election results:* House of Representatives - percent of vote - BN coalition 50.3%, opposition parties 46.8%, others 2.9%; seats - BN coalition 140, opposition parties 82

**Judicial branch:** Civil Courts include Federal Court, Court of Appeal, High Court of Malaya on peninsula Malaysia, and High Court of Sabah and Sarawak in states of Borneo (judges are appointed by the king on the advice of the prime minister); Sharia Courts include Sharia Appeal Court, Sharia High Court, and Sharia Subordinate Courts at state-level and deal with religious and family matters such as custody, divorce, and inheritance only for Muslims; decisions of Sharia courts cannot be appealed to civil courts

**Political parties and leaders:**
*National Front (Barisan Nasional) or BN (ruling coalition) consists of the following parties:* Gerakan Rakyat Malaysia Party or PGRM [KOH Tsu Koon]; Liberal Democratic Party (Parti Liberal Demokratik - Sabah) or LDP [LIEW Vui Keong]; Malaysian Chinese Association (Persatuan China Malaysia) or MCA [ONG Tee Keat]; Malaysian Indian Congress (Kongres India Malaysia) or MIC [S. Samy VELLU]; Parti Bersatu Rakyat Sabah or PBRS [Joseph KURUP]; Parti Bersatu Sabah or PBS [Joseph PAIRIN Kitingan]; Parti Pesaka Bumiputera Bersatu or PBB [Abdul TAIB Mahmud]; Parti Rakyat Sarawak or PRS [James MASING]; Sarawak United People's Party (Parti Bersatu Rakyat Sarawak) or SUPP [George CHAN Hong Nam]; United Malays National Organization or UMNO [NAJIB bin Abdul Razak]; United Pasokmomogun Kadazandusun Murut Organization (Pertubuhan Pasko Momogun Kadazan Dusun Bersatu) or UPKO [Bernard DOMPOK]; People's Progressive Party (Parti Progresif Penduduk Malaysia) or PPP [M.Kayveas]; Sarawak Progressive Democratic Party or SPDP [William MAWAN])
*People's Alliance (Pakatan Rakyat) or PR (opposition coalition) consists of the following parties:* Democratic Action Party (Parti Tindakan Demokratik) or DAP [KARPAL Singh]; Islamic Party of Malaysia (Parti Islam se Malaysia) or PAS [Abdul HADI Awang]; People's Justice Party (Parti Keadilan Rakyat) or PKR [WAN AZIZAH Wan Ismail]; Sarawak National Party or SNAP [Edwin DUNDANG]
*independent party:* Sabah Progressive Party (Parti Progresif Saban) or SAPP [YONG Teck Lee]

**Political pressure groups and leaders:** Bar Council BERSIH (electoral reform coalition); PEMBELA (Muslim NGO coalition)
*other:* religious groups; women's groups; youth groups

**International organization participation:** ADB, APEC, APT, ARF, ASEAN, BIS, C, CP, EAS, FAO, G-15, G-77, IAEA, IBRD, ICAO, ICC, ICRM, IDA, IDB, IFAD, IFC, IFRCS, IHO, ILO, IMF, IMO, IMSO, Interpol, IOC, IPU, ISO, ITSO, ITU, ITUC, MIGA, MINURSO, MONUC, NAM, OIC, OPCW, PCA, PIF (partner), UN, UNCTAD, UNESCO, UNIDO, UNIFIL, UNMIL, UNMIS, UNMIT, UNWTO, UPU, WCL, WCO, WFTU, WHO, WIPO, WMO, WTO

**Diplomatic representation in the US:**
*chief of mission:* Ambassador (vacant); Charge d'Affaires Ilango KARUPPANNAN
*chancery:* 3516 International Court NW, Washington, DC 20008
*telephone:* [1] (202) 572-9700
*FAX:* [1] (202) 572-9882
*consulate(s) general:* Los Angeles, New York

**Diplomatic representation from the US:**
*chief of mission:* Ambassador James R. KEITH
*embassy:* 376 Jalan Tun Razak, 50400 Kuala Lumpur
*mailing address:* US Embassy Kuala Lumpur, APO AP 96535-8152
*telephone:* [60] (3) 2168-5000
*FAX:* [60] (3) 2142-2207

**Flag description:** 14 equal horizontal stripes of red (top) alternating with white (bottom); there is a blue rectangle in the upper hoist-side corner bearing a yellow crescent and a yellow 14-pointed star; the crescent and the star are traditional symbols of Islam; the design was based on the flag of the US

# Malaysia (continued)

## Economy

**Economy - overview:** Malaysia, a middle-income country, has transformed itself since the 1970s from a producer of raw materials into an emerging multi-sector economy. After coming to office in 2003, former Prime Minister ABDULLAH tried to move the economy farther up the value-added production chain by attracting investments in high technology industries, medical technology, and pharmaceuticals. The Government of Malaysia is continuing efforts to boost domestic demand to wean the economy off of its dependence on exports. Nevertheless, exports - particularly of electronics - remain a significant driver of the economy. As an oil and gas exporter, Malaysia has profited from higher world energy prices, although the rising cost of domestic gasoline and diesel fuel forced Kuala Lumpur to reduce government subsidies. Malaysia "unpegged" the ringgit from the US dollar in 2005 and the currency appreciated 6% per year against the dollar in 2006-08. Although this has helped to hold down the price of imports, inflationary pressures began to build in 2007 - in 2008 inflation stood at nearly 6%, year-over-year. The government presented its five-year national development agenda in April 2006 through the Ninth Malaysia Plan, a comprehensive blueprint for the allocation of the national budget from 2006-10. ABDULLAH unveiled a series of ambitious development schemes for several regions that have had trouble attracting business investment. Real GDP growth averaged about 6% per year under ABDULLAH, but regions outside of Kuala Lumpur and the manufacturing hub Penang did not fare as well. The central bank maintains healthy foreign exchange reserves and the regulatory regime has limited Malaysia's exposure to riskier financial instruments and the global financial crisis. Decreasing worldwide demand for consumer goods is expected to hurt economic growth in 2009 and beyond, however.

**GDP (purchasing power parity):**
$386.6 billion (2008 est.)
$367.8 billion (2007)
$346 billion (2006)
*note:* data are in 2008 US dollars

**GDP (official exchange rate):** $214.7 billion (2008 est.)

**GDP - real growth rate:**
5.1% (2008 est.)
6.3% (2007 est.)
5.8% (2006 est.)

**GDP - per capita (PPP):**
$15,300 (2008 est.)
$14,800 (2007 est.)
$14,200 (2006 est.)
*note:* data are in 2008 US dollars

**GDP - composition by sector:**
*agriculture:* 9.7%
*industry:* 44.6%
*services:* 45.7% (2008 est.)

**Labor force:** 11.2 million (2008 est.)

**Labor force - by occupation:**
*agriculture:* 13%
*industry:* 36%
*services:* 51% (2005 est.)

**Unemployment rate:**
3.7% (2008 est.)
3.2% (2007 est.)

**Population below poverty line:** 5.1% (2002 est.)

**Household income or consumption by percentage share:**
*lowest 10%:* 1.4%
*highest 10%:* 39.2% (2003 est.)

**Distribution of family income - Gini index:** 46.1 (2002)

**Investment (gross fixed):** 20.7% of GDP (2008 est.)

**Budget:**
*revenues:* $44.32 billion
*expenditures:* $55.01 billion (2008 est.)

**Public debt:** 42.7% of GDP (2008 est.)

**Inflation rate (consumer prices):**
5.8% (2008 est.)
2% (2007 est.)
*note:* approximately 30% of goods are price-controlled

**Commercial bank prime lending rate:** 6.41% (31 December 2007)

**Stock of money:** $49.41 billion (31 December 2007)

**Stock of quasi money:** $187.6 billion (31 December 2007)

**Stock of domestic credit:** $220 billion (31 December 2007)

**Market value of publicly traded shares:** $325.7 billion (31 December 2007)

**Agriculture - products:** Peninsular Malaysia - rubber, palm oil, cocoa, rice; Sabah - subsistence crops, rubber, timber, coconuts, rice; Sarawak - rubber, pepper, timber

**Industries:** Peninsular Malaysia - rubber and oil palm processing and manufacturing, light manufacturing, electronics, tin mining and smelting, logging, timber processing; Sabah - logging, petroleum production; Sarawak - agriculture processing, petroleum production and refining, logging

**Industrial production growth rate:** 4% (2008 est.)

**Electricity - production:** 102.9 billion kWh (2007 est.)

**Electricity - consumption:** 95.98 billion kWh (2006 est.)

**Electricity - exports:** 2.524 billion kWh (2006 est.)

**Electricity - imports:** 0 kWh (2007 est.)

**Oil - production:** 753,700 bbl/day (2008 est.)

**Oil - consumption:** 501,100 bbl/day (2006 est.)

**Oil - exports:** 546,300 bbl/day (2005)

**Oil - imports:** 308,500 bbl/day (2005)

**Oil - proved reserves:** 4 billion bbl (1 January 2008 est.)

**Natural gas - production:** 64.5 billion cu m (2007 est.)

**Natural gas - consumption:** 32.9 billion cu m (2007 est.)

**Natural gas - exports:** 31.6 billion cu m (2007 est.)

**Natural gas - imports:** 0 cu m (2007 est.)

**Natural gas - proved reserves:** 2.35 trillion cu m (1 January 2008 est.)

**Current account balance:** $27.44 billion (2008 est.)

**Exports:** $195.7 billion f.o.b. (2008 est.)

**Exports - commodities:** electronic equipment, petroleum and liquefied natural gas, wood and wood products, palm oil, rubber, textiles, chemicals

**Exports - partners:** US 15.6%, Singapore 14.6%, Japan 9.1%, China 8.8%, Thailand 5%, Hong Kong 4.6% (2007)

**Imports:** $156.2 billion f.o.b. (2008 est.)

**Imports - commodities:** electronics, machinery, petroleum products, plastics, vehicles, iron and steel products, chemicals

**Imports - partners:** Japan 13%, China 12.9%, Singapore 11.5%, US 10.8%, Taiwan 5.7%, Thailand 5.3%, South Korea 4.9%, Germany 4.6%, Indonesia 4.2% (2007)

**Reserves of foreign exchange and gold:** $104.4 billion (31 December 2008 est.)

**Debt - external:** $54.11 billion (31 December 2008 est.)

**Stock of direct foreign investment - at home:** $92.76 billion (2008 est.)

**Stock of direct foreign investment - abroad:** $50.08 billion (2008 est.)

**Exchange rates:** ringgits (MYR) per US dollar - 3.33 (2008 est.), 3.46 (2007), 3.6683 (2006), 3.8 (2005), 3.8 (2004)

## Communications

**Telephones - main lines in use:** 4.35 million (2007)

**Telephones - mobile cellular:** 23.347 million (2007)

**Telephone system:**
*general assessment:* modern system; international service excellent
*domestic:* good intercity service provided on Peninsular Malaysia mainly by microwave radio relay; adequate intercity microwave radio relay network between Sabah and Sarawak via Brunei; domestic satellite system with 2 earth stations; combined fixed-line and mobile cellular teledensity exceeds 110 per 100 persons
*international:* country code - 60; landing point for several major international submarine cable networks that provide connectivity to Asia, Middle East, and Europe; satellite earth stations - 2 Intelsat (1 Indian Ocean, 1 Pacific Ocean) (2007)

**Radio broadcast stations:** AM 35, FM 391, shortwave 15 (2001)

**Television broadcast stations:** 88 (mainland Malaysia 51, Sabah 16, and Sarawak 21) (2006)

**Internet country code:** .my

**Internet hosts:** 377,716 (2008)

**Internet users:** 15.868 million (2007)

# Malaysia (continued)

## Transportation

**Airports:** 116 (2008)
**Airports - with paved runways:**
*total:* 36 ,
*over 3,047 m:* 5
*2,438 to 3,047 m:* 10
*1,524 to 2,437 m:* 7
*914 to 1,523 m:* 8
*under 914 m:* 6 (2008)
**Airports - with unpaved runways:**
*total:* 80
*914 to 1,523 m:* 8
*under 914 m:* 72 (2008)
**Heliports:** 2 (2007)
**Pipelines:** condensate 3 km; gas 1,965 km; oil 31 km; refined products 114 km (2008)
**Railways:**
*total:* 1,890 km
*standard gauge:* 57 km 1.435-m gauge (57 km electrified)
*narrow gauge:* 1,833 km 1.000-m gauge (150 km electrified) (2006)
**Roadways:**
*total:* 98,721 km
*paved:* 80,280 km (includes 1,821 km of expressways)
*unpaved:* 18,441 km (2004)
**Waterways:** 7,200 km
*note:* Peninsular Malaysia 3,200 km; Sabah 1,500 km; Sarawak 2,500 km (2008)
**Merchant marine:**
*total:* 306
*by type:* bulk carrier 12, cargo 97, carrier 1, chemical tanker 34, container 46, liquefied gas 33, passenger/cargo 5, petroleum tanker 71, roll on/roll off 3, vehicle carrier 4
*foreign-owned:* 40 (Germany 1, Hong Kong 14, Japan 4, Russia 2, Singapore 16, Sweden 3)
*registered in other countries:* 68 (Bahamas 13, Marshall Islands 3, Norway 1, Panama 12, Philippines 1, Saint Kitts and Nevis 1, Singapore 27, Thailand 3, Tuvalu 1, US 2, unknown 4) (2008)
**Ports and terminals:** Bintulu, Johor Bahru, Kuantan, Labuan, George Town (Penang), Port Kelang, Tanjung Pelepas
**Transportation - note:** the International Maritime Bureau reports the territorial and offshore waters in the Strait of Malacca and South China Sea as high risk for piracy and armed robbery against ships; numerous commercial vessels have been attacked and hijacked both at anchor and while underway; hijacked vessels are often disguised and cargo diverted to ports in East Asia; crews have been murdered or cast adrift

## Military

**Military branches:** Malaysian Armed Forces (Angkatan Tentera Malaysia, ATM): Malaysian Army (Tentera Darat Malaysia), Royal Malaysian Navy (Tentera Laut Diraja Malaysia, TLDM), Royal Malaysian Air Force (Tentera Udara Diraja Malaysia, TUDM) (2009)

**Military service age and obligation:** 18 years of age for voluntary military service (2005)
**Manpower available for military service:**
*males age 16-49:* 6,440,338
*females age 16-49:* 6,280,826 (2008 est.)
**Manpower fit for military service:**
*males age 16-49:* 5,493,946
*females age 16-49:* 5,409,524 (2009 est.)
**Manpower reaching militarily significant age annually:**
*male:* 266,267
*female:* 252,543 (2009 est.)
**Military expenditures:** 2.03% of GDP (2005 est.)

## Transnational Issues

**Disputes - international:** Malaysia has asserted sovereignty over the Spratly Islands together with China, Philippines, Taiwan, Vietnam, and possibly Brunei; while the 2002 "Declaration on the Conduct of Parties in the South China Sea" has eased tensions over the Spratly Islands, it is not the legally binding "code of conduct" sought by some parties; Malaysia was not party to the March 2005 joint accord among the national oil companies of China, the Philippines, and Vietnam on conducting marine seismic activities in the Spratly Islands; disputes continue over deliveries of fresh water to Singapore, Singapore's land reclamation, bridge construction, and maritime boundaries in the Johor and Singapore Straits; in November 2007, the ICJ will hold public hearings in response to the memorials and countermemorials filed by the parties in 2003 and 2005 over sovereignty of Pedra Branca Island/Pulau Batu Puteh, Middle Rocks and South Ledge; ICJ awarded Ligitan and Sipadan islands, also claimed by Indonesia and Philippines, to Malaysia but left maritime boundary and sovereignty of Unarang rock in the hydrocarbon-rich Celebes Sea in dispute; separatist violence in Thailand's predominantly Muslim southern provinces prompts measures to close and monitor border with Malaysia to stem terrorist activities; Philippines retains a dormant claim to Malaysia's Sabah State in northern Borneo; Brunei and Malaysia agreed in September 2008 to resolve their offshore and deepwater seabed dispute, resume hydrocarbon exploration and renounce any territorial claims on land; piracy remains a problem in the Malacca Strait
**Refugees and internally displaced persons:**
*refugees (country of origin):* 15,174 (Indonesia); 21,544 (Burma) (2007)
**Trafficking in persons:**
*current situation:* Malaysia is a destination and, to a lesser extent, a source and transit country for women and children trafficked for the purpose of commercial sexual exploitation, and men, women, and children for forced labor; Malaysia is mainly a destination country for men, women, and children who migrate willingly from South and Southeast Asia to work, some of whom are subjected to conditions of involuntary servitude by Malaysian employers in the domestic, agricultural, construction, plantation, and industrial sectors; to a lesser extent, some Malaysian women, primarily of Chinese ethnicity, are trafficked abroad for commercial sexual exploitation
*tier rating:* Tier 2 Watch List - Malaysia improved from Tier 3 to the Tier 2 Watch List for 2008 when it enacted comprehensive anti-trafficking legislation in July 2007; however, it did not take action against exploitative employers or labor traffickers in 2007; the government has not ratified the 2000 UN TIP Protocol (2008)
**Illicit drugs:** drug trafficking prosecuted vigorously and carries severe penalties; heroin still primary drug of abuse, but synthetic drug demand remains strong; continued ecstasy and methamphetamine producer for domestic users and, to a lesser extent, the regional drug market

# Maldives

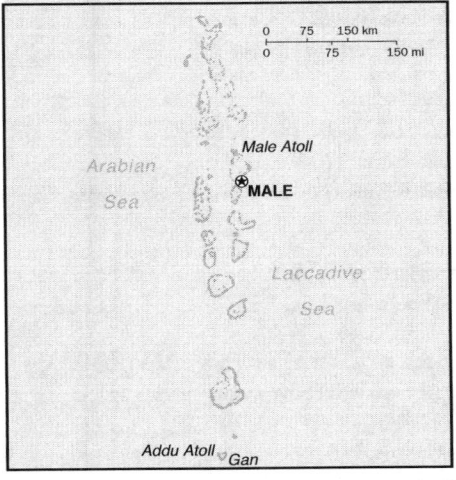

## Introduction

**Background:** The Maldives was long a sultanate, first under Dutch and then under British protection. It became a republic in 1968, three years after independence. President Maumoon Abdul GAYOOM dominated the islands' political scene for 30 years, elected to six successive terms by single-party referendums. Following riots in the capital Male in August 2004, the president and his government pledged to embark upon democratic reforms including a more representative political system and expanded political freedoms. Progress was sluggish, however, and many promised reforms were slow to be realized. Nonetheless, political parties were legalized in 2005. In June 2008, a constituent assembly - termed the "Special Majlis" - finalized a new constitution, which was ratified by the president in August. The first-ever presidential elections under a multi-candidate, multi-party system were held in October 2008. GAYOOM was defeated in a runoff poll by Mohamed NASHEED, a political activist who had been jailed several years earlier by the former regime. Challenges facing the new president include strengthening democracy and combating poverty and drug abuse.

## Geography

**Location:** Southern Asia, group of atolls in the Indian Ocean, south-southwest of India
**Geographic coordinates:** 3 15 N, 73 00 E
**Map references:** Asia
**Area:**
*total:* 300 sq km
*land:* 300 sq km
*water:* 0 sq km
**Area - comparative:** about 1.7 times the size of Washington, DC
**Land boundaries:** 0 km
**Coastline:** 644 km

**Maritime claims:** measured from claimed archipelagic straight baselines
*territorial sea:* 12 nm
*contiguous zone:* 24 nm
*exclusive economic zone:* 200 nm
**Climate:** tropical; hot, humid; dry, northeast monsoon (November to March); rainy, southwest monsoon (June to August)
**Terrain:** flat, with white sandy beaches
**Elevation extremes:**
*lowest point:* Indian Ocean 0 m
*highest point:* unnamed location on Wilingili island in the Addu Atoll 2.4 m
**Natural resources:** fish
**Land use:**
*arable land:* 13.33%
*permanent crops:* 30%
*other:* 56.67% (2005)
**Irrigated land:** NA
**Total renewable water resources:** 0.03 cu km (1999)
**Freshwater withdrawal (domestic/industrial/agricultural):**
*total:* 0.003 cu km/yr (98%/2%/0%)
*per capita:* 9 cu m/yr (1987)
**Natural hazards:** low level of islands makes them sensitive to sea level rise
**Environment - current issues:** depletion of freshwater aquifers threatens water supplies; global warming and sea level rise; coral reef bleaching
**Environment - international agreements:**
*party to:* Biodiversity, Climate Change, Climate Change-Kyoto Protocol, Desertification, Hazardous Wastes, Law of the Sea, Ozone Layer Protection, Ship Pollution
*signed, but not ratified:* none of the selected agreements
**Geography - note:** 1,190 coral islands grouped into 26 atolls (200 inhabited islands, plus 80 islands with tourist resorts); archipelago with strategic location astride and along major sea lanes in Indian Ocean

## People

**Population:** 396,334 (July 2009 est.)
**Age structure:**
*0-14 years:* 22.3% (male 45,038/female 43,291)
*15-64 years:* 73.8% (male 180,874/female 111,703)
*65 years and over:* 3.9% (male 7,711/female 7,717) (2009 est.)
**Median age:**
*total:* 25.7 years
*male:* 26.5 years
*female:* 24.3 years (2009 est.)
**Population growth rate:** -0.168% (2009 est.)
**Birth rate:** 14.55 births/1,000 population (2009 est.)
**Death rate:** 3.66 deaths/1,000 population (2008 est.)
**Net migration rate:** -12.58 migrant(s)/1,000 population (2009 est.)
**Urbanization:**
*urban population:* 38% of total population (2008)
*rate of urbanization:* 5.3% annual rate of change (2005-10 est.)

**Sex ratio:**
*at birth:* 1.05 male(s)/female
*under 15 years:* 1.04 male(s)/female
*15-64 years:* 1.62 male(s)/female
*65 years and over:* 1 male(s)/female
*total population:* 1.44 male(s)/female (2009 est.)
**Infant mortality rate:**
*total:* 29.53 deaths/1,000 live births
*male:* 32.04 deaths/1,000 live births
*female:* 26.89 deaths/1,000 live births (2009 est.)
**Life expectancy at birth:**
*total population:* 73.97 years
*male:* 71.78 years
*female:* 76.28 years (2009 est.)
**Total fertility rate:** 1.9 children born/woman (2009 est.)
**HIV/AIDS - adult prevalence rate:** 0.1% (2001 est.)
**HIV/AIDS - people living with HIV/AIDS:** fewer than 100 (2001 est.)
**HIV/AIDS - deaths:** NA
**Nationality:**
*noun:* Maldivian(s)
*adjective:* Maldivian
**Ethnic groups:** South Indians, Sinhalese, Arabs
**Religions:** Sunni Muslim
**Languages:** Maldivian Dhivehi (dialect of Sinhala, script derived from Arabic), English spoken by most government officials
**Literacy:**
*definition:* age 15 and over can read and write
*total population:* 96.3%
*male:* 96.2%
*female:* 96.4% (2000 census)
**School life expectancy (primary to tertiary education):**
*total:* 12 years
*male:* 12 years
*female:* 12 years (2006)
**Education expenditures:** 8% of GDP (2006)

## Government

**Country name:**
*conventional long form:* Republic of Maldives
*conventional short form:* Maldives
*local long form:* Dhivehi Raajjeyge Jumhooriyyaa
*local short form:* Dhivehi Raajje
**Government type:** republic
**Capital:**
*name:* Male
*geographic coordinates:* 4 10 N, 73 30 E
*time difference:* UTC+5 (10 hours ahead of Washington, DC during Standard Time)
**Administrative divisions:** 19 atolls (atholhu, singular and plural) and the capital city*; Alifu, Baa, Dhaalu, Faafu, Gaafu Alifu, Gaafu Dhaalu, Gnaviyani, Haa Alifu, Haa Dhaalu, Kaafu, Laamu, Lhaviyani, Maale* (Male), Meemu, Noonu, Raa, Seenu, Shaviyani, Thaa, Vaavu
**Independence:** 26 July 1965 (from the UK)
**National holiday:** Independence Day, 26 July (1965)

# Maldives (continued)

**Constitution:** new constitution ratified 7 August 2008

**Legal system:** based on Islamic law with admixtures of English common law primarily in commercial matters; has not accepted compulsory ICJ jurisdiction

**Suffrage:** 21 years of age; universal

**Executive branch:**

*chief of state:* President Mohamed "Anni" NASHEED (since 11 November 2008); Vice President Mohamed WAHEED Hassan Maniku (since 11 November 2008); note - the president is both the chief of state and head of government

*head of government:* President Mohamed "Anni" NASHEED (since 11 November 2008); Vice President Mohamed WAHEED Hassan Maniku (since 11 November 2008)

*cabinet:* Cabinet of Ministers appointed by the president

*elections:* under the new constitution, the president is elected by direct vote; president elected for a five-year term (eligible for a second term); election last held 8 and 28 October 2008 (next to be held in 2013)

*election results:* Mohamed NASHEED elected president; percent of vote - NASHEED 54.25%, Maumoon Abdul GAYOOM 45.75%

**Legislative branch:** unicameral People's Council or Majlis (50 seats; 42 members elected by popular vote, 8 appointed by the president; serve five-year terms)

*elections:* last held 22 January 2005 (next to be held on 9 May 2009)

*election results:* percent of vote - NA; seats - independents 50

**Judicial branch:** Supreme Court; Supreme Court judges are appointed by the president with approval of voting members of the People's Council; High Court; Trial Courts; all lower court judges are appointed by the Judicial Service Commission

**Political parties and leaders:** Adhaalath (Justice) Party or AP [Abdul Majeed Abdul BARI]; Dhivehi Quamee Party or DQP [Hassan SAEED]; Dhivehi Rayyithunge Party (Maldivian People's Party) or DRP [Maumoon Abdul GAYOOM]; Islamic Democratic Party or IDP [Omar NASEER]; Maldivian Democratic Party or MDP [Mohamed NASHEED]; Republican (Jumhoore) Party [Gasim IBRAHIM]; Social Liberal Party or SLP [Ibrahim ISMAIL]

**Political pressure groups and leaders:**

*other:* various unregistered political parties

**International organization participation:** ADB, C, CP, FAO, G-77, IBRD, ICAO, IDA, IDB, IFAD, IFC, IMF, IMO, Interpol, IOC, IPU, ITU, MIGA, NAM, OIC, OPCW, SAARC, SACEP, UN, UNCTAD, UNESCO, UNIDO, UNWTO, UPU, WCO, WFTU, WHO, WIPO, WMO, WTO

**Diplomatic representation in the US:**

*chief of mission:* Ambassador (vacant)

*chancery:* 800 2nd Avenue, Suite 400E, New York, NY 10017

*telephone:* [1] (212) 599-6194

*FAX:* [1] (212) 599-6195

**Diplomatic representation from the US:** the US does not have an embassy in Maldives; the US Ambassador to Sri Lanka, Ambassador Robert O. BLAKE, Jr., is accredited to Maldives and makes periodic visits

**Flag description:** red with a large green rectangle in the center bearing a vertical white crescent; the closed side of the crescent is on the hoist side of the flag

## Economy

**Economy - overview:** Tourism, Maldives' largest industry, accounts for 28% of GDP and more than 60% of foreign exchange receipts. Over 90% of government tax revenue comes from import duties and tourism-related taxes. Fishing is the second leading sector. Agriculture and manufacturing continue to play a lesser role in the economy, constrained by the limited availability of cultivable land and the shortage of domestic labor. Most staple foods must be imported. Industry, which consists mainly of garment production, boat building, and handicrafts, accounts for about 7% of GDP. The Maldivian Government began an economic reform program in 1989 initially by lifting import quotas and opening some exports to the private sector. Subsequently, it has liberalized regulations to allow more foreign investment. Real GDP growth averaged over 7.5% per year for more than a decade. In late December 2004, a major tsunami left more than 100 dead, 12,000 displaced, and property damage exceeding $300 million. As a result of the tsunami, the GDP contracted by about 4.6% in 2005. A rebound in tourism, post-tsunami reconstruction, and development of new resorts helped the economy recover quickly, with GDP growth registering 18% in 2006. Growth slowed in 2007-08, but remained above 5% per year. The trade deficit expanded sharply as a result of high oil prices and imports of construction material. Government spending on social needs, subsidies, and civil servant salaries have created a large budget deficit and inflation has picked up sharply, reaching nearly 13% in October 2008 due to high oil and food prices. Diversifying beyond tourism and fishing, reforming public finance, and increasing employment are the major challenges facing the government. Over the longer term Maldivian authorities worry about the impact of erosion and possible global warming on their low-lying country; 80% of the area is 1 meter or less above sea level.

**GDP (purchasing power parity):**

$1.738 billion (2008 est.)

$1.636 billion (2007)

$1.516 billion (2006)

*note:* data are in 2008 US dollars

**GDP (official exchange rate):** $1.259 billion (2008 est.)

**GDP - real growth rate:**

5.7% (2008 est.)

7.6% (2007 est.)

18% (2006 est.)

**GDP - per capita (PPP):**

$5,000 (2008 est.)

$4,500 (2007 est.)

$4,400 (2006 est.)

*note:* data are in 2008 US dollars

**GDP - composition by sector:**

*agriculture:* 7%

*industry:* 17%

*services:* 76% (2006 est.)

**Labor force:** 128,800 (2006)

**Labor force - by occupation:**

*agriculture:* 22%

*industry:* 18%

*services:* 60% (1995)

**Unemployment rate:**

14.4% (2006 est.)

**Population below poverty line:** 21% (2004)

**Household income or consumption by percentage share:**

*lowest 10%:* NA%

*highest 10%:* NA%

**Budget:**

*revenues:* $762 million (including foreign grants)

*expenditures:* $884 million (2008 est.)

**Inflation rate (consumer prices):**

12.8% (October 2008 est.)

5% (2007 est.)

**Central bank discount rate:** 13% (31 December 2008)

**Commercial bank prime lending rate:** 8% (31 December 2008)

**Stock of money:** $475 million (31 December 2008)

**Stock of quasi money:** $487 million (31 December 2008)

**Stock of domestic credit:** $1.548 billion (31 December 2008)

**Market value of publicly traded shares:** $NA

**Agriculture - products:** coconuts, corn, sweet potatoes; fish

**Industries:** tourism, fish processing, shipping, boat building, coconut processing, garments, woven mats, rope, handicrafts, coral and sand mining

**Industrial production growth rate:** -0.9% (2004 est.)

**Electricity - production:** 270 million kWh (2007 est.)

**Electricity - consumption:** 203.7 million kWh (2006 est.)

**Electricity - exports:** 0 kWh (2008 est.)

**Electricity - imports:** 0 kWh (2008 est.)

**Oil - production:** 0 bbl/day (2008 est.)

**Oil - consumption:** 5,490 bbl/day (2006 est.)

**Oil - exports:** 1,499 bbl/day (2005)

**Oil - imports:** 5,362 bbl/day (2005)

**Oil - proved reserves:** 0 bbl (1 January 2008 est.)

**Natural gas - production:** 0 cu m (2008 est.)

**Natural gas - consumption:** 0 cu m (2008 est.)

**Natural gas - exports:** 0 cu m (2008 est.)

**Natural gas - imports:** 0 cu m (2008 est.)

**Natural gas - proved reserves:** 0 cu m (1 January 2008 est.)

**Current account balance:** -$638 million (2008 est.)

## Maldives *(continued)*

**Exports:** $113 million f.o.b. (2008 est.)
**Exports - commodities:** fish
**Exports - partners:** Thailand 28.3%, UK 17.6%, France 8.8%, Sri Lanka 8.6%, Algeria 8.2%, Japan 6.4%, Italy 4.1% (2007)
**Imports:** $1.276 billion f.o.b. (2008 est.)
**Imports - commodities:** petroleum products, ships, foodstuffs, clothing, intermediate and capital goods
**Imports - partners:** Canada 35.2%, Singapore 15%, UAE 10.2%, India 7.4%, Malaysia 7.1% (2007)
**Debt - external:** $477 million (2008 est.)
**Exchange rates:** rufiyaa (MVR) per US dollar - 12.8 (2008), 12.8 (2007), 12.8 (2006), 12.8 (2005), 12.8 (2004)

### Communications

**Telephones - main lines in use:** 33,200 (2007)
**Telephones - mobile cellular:** 317,800 (2007)
**Telephone system:**
*general assessment:* telephone services have improved; each island now has at least 1 public telephone, and there are mobile cellular networks with a rapidly expanding subscribership approaching 90 per 100 persons
*domestic:* interatoll communication through microwave links; all inhabited islands and resorts are connected with telephone and fax service
*international:* country code - 960; linked to international submarine cable Fiber-Optic Link Around the Globe (FLAG); satellite earth station - 3 Intelsat (Indian Ocean) (2007)
**Radio broadcast stations:** AM 1, FM 1, shortwave 1 (1998)
**Television broadcast stations:** 1 (2006)
**Internet country code:** .mv
**Internet hosts:** 1,600 (2008)
**Internet users:** 33,000 (2007)

### Transportation

**Airports:** 5 (2008)
**Airports - with paved runways:**
*total:* 3
*over 3,047 m:* 1
*2,438 to 3,047 m:* 1
*914 to 1,523 m:* 1 (2008)
**Airports - with unpaved runways:**
*total:* 2
*914 to 1,523 m:* 2 (2008)
**Roadways:**
*total:* 88 km
*paved roads:* 88 km - 60 km in Male; 14 km on Addu Atolis; 14 km on Laamu
*note:* village roads are mainly compacted coral (2006)
**Merchant marine:**
*total:* 29
*by type:* bulk carrier 1, cargo 23, petroleum tanker 3, refrigerated cargo 2
*foreign-owned:* 1 (Greece 1)
*registered in other countries:* 2 (Panama 1, Tuvalu 1) (2008)
**Ports and terminals:** Male

### Military

**Military branches:** Maldives National Defense Force (MNDF): Rapid Reaction Force, Security Protection Group, Coast Guard (2009)
**Military service age and obligation:** 18 years of age for voluntary military service; no conscription (2008)
**Manpower available for military service:**
*males age 16-49:* 89,505
*females age 16-49:* 85,745 (2008 est.)
**Manpower fit for military service:**
*males age 16-49:* 138,746
*females age 16-49:* 82,247 (2009 est.)
**Manpower reaching militarily significant age annually:**
*male:* 4,576
*female:* 3,942 (2009 est.)
**Military expenditures:** 5.5% of GDP (2005 est.)
**Military - note:** the Maldives National Defense Force (MNDF), with its small size and with little serviceable equipment, is inadequate to prevent external aggression and is primarily tasked to reinforce the Maldives Police Service (MPS) and ensure security in the exclusive economic zone (2008)

### Transnational Issues

**Disputes - international:** none
**Refugees and internally displaced persons:**
*IDPs:* 1,000-10,000 (December 2004 tsunami victims) (2007)

# Mali

### Introduction

**Background:** The Sudanese Republic and Senegal became independent of France in 1960 as the Mali Federation. When Senegal withdrew after only a few months, what formerly made up the Sudanese Republic was renamed Mali. Rule by dictatorship was brought to a close in 1991 by a military coup - led by the current president Amadou TOURE - enabling Mali's emergence as one of the strongest democracies on the continent. President Alpha KONARE won Mali's first democratic presidential election in 1992 and was reelected in 1997. In keeping with Mali's two-term constitutional limit, KONARE stepped down in 2002 and was succeeded by Amadou TOURE, who was subsequently elected to a second term in 2007. The elections were widely judged to be free and fair.

### Geography

**Location:** Western Africa, southwest of Algeria
**Geographic coordinates:** 17 00 N, 4 00 W
**Map references:** Africa
**Area:**
*total:* 1.24 million sq km
*land:* 1.22 million sq km
*water:* 20,000 sq km
**Area - comparative:** slightly less than twice the size of Texas
**Land boundaries:**
*total:* 7,243 km
*border countries:* Algeria 1,376 km, Burkina Faso 1,000 km, Guinea 858 km, Cote d'Ivoire 532 km, Mauritania 2,237 km, Niger 821 km, Senegal 419 km
**Coastline:** 0 km (landlocked)
**Maritime claims:** none (landlocked)
**Climate:** subtropical to arid; hot and dry (February to June); rainy, humid, and mild (June to November); cool and dry (November to February)
**Terrain:** mostly flat to rolling northern plains covered by sand; savanna in south, rugged hills in northeast

# Mali *(continued)*

**Elevation extremes:**
*lowest point:* Senegal River 23 m
*highest point:* Hombori Tondo 1,155 m
**Natural resources:** gold, phosphates, kaolin, salt, limestone, uranium, gypsum, granite, hydropower
*note:* bauxite, iron ore, manganese, tin, and copper deposits are known but not exploited
**Land use:**
*arable land:* 3.76%
*permanent crops:* 0.03%
*other:* 96.21% (2005)
**Irrigated land:** 2,360 sq km (2003)
**Total renewable water resources:** 100 cu km (2001)
**Freshwater withdrawal (domestic/industrial/agricultural):**
*total:* 6.55 cu km/yr (9%/1%/90%)
*per capita:* 484 cu m/yr (2000)
**Natural hazards:** hot, dust-laden harmattan haze common during dry seasons; recurring droughts; occasional Niger River flooding
**Environment - current issues:** deforestation; soil erosion; desertification; inadequate supplies of potable water; poaching
**Environment - international agreements:**
*party to:* Biodiversity, Climate Change, Climate Change-Kyoto Protocol, Desertification, Endangered Species, Hazardous Wastes, Law of the Sea, Ozone Layer Protection, Wetlands, Whaling
*signed, but not ratified:* none of the selected agreements
**Geography - note:** landlocked; divided into three natural zones: the southern, cultivated Sudanese; the central, semiarid Sahelian; and the northern, arid Saharan

## People

**Population:** 12,666,987 (July 2009 est.)
**Age structure:**
*0-14 years:* 48.3% (male 3,089,406/female 3,023,341)
*15-64 years:* 48.7% (male 3,065,167/female 3,101,914)
*65 years and over:* 3.1% (male 151,718/female 235,441) (2009 est.)
**Median age:**
*total:* 15.8 years
*male:* 15.5 years
*female:* 16.2 years (2009 est.)
**Population growth rate:** 2.765% (2009 est.)
**Birth rate:** 49.15 births/1,000 population (2009 est.)
**Death rate:** 16.16 deaths/1,000 population (2008 est.)
**Net migration rate:** -5.67 migrant(s)/1,000 population (2009 est.)
**Urbanization:**
*urban population:* 32% of total population (2008)
*rate of urbanization:* 4.8% annual rate of change (2005-10 est.)

**Sex ratio:**
*at birth:* 1.03 male(s)/female
*under 15 years:* 1.02 male(s)/female
*15-64 years:* 0.99 male(s)/female
*65 years and over:* 0.64 male(s)/female
*total population:* 0.99 male(s)/female (2009 est.)
**Infant mortality rate:**
*total:* 102.05 deaths/1,000 live births
*male:* 111.56 deaths/1,000 live births
*female:* 92.26 deaths/1,000 live births (2009 est.)
**Life expectancy at birth:**
*total population:* 50.35 years
*male:* 48.38 years
*female:* 52.38 years (2009 est.)
**Total fertility rate:** 7.29 children born/woman (2009 est.)
**HIV/AIDS - adult prevalence rate:** 1.5% (2007 est.)
**HIV/AIDS - people living with HIV/AIDS:** 100,000 (2007 est.)
**HIV/AIDS - deaths:** 5,800 (2007 est.)
**Major infectious diseases:**
*degree of risk:* very high
*food or waterborne diseases:* bacterial and protozoal diarrhea, hepatitis A, and typhoid fever
*vectorborne disease:* malaria
*water contact disease:* schistosomiasis
*respiratory disease:* meningococcal meningitis (2009)
**Nationality:**
*noun:* Malian(s)
*adjective:* Malian
**Ethnic groups:** Mande 50% (Bambara, Malinke, Soninke), Peul 17%, Voltaic 12%, Songhai 6%, Tuareg and Moor 10%, other 5%
**Religions:** Muslim 90%, Christian 1%, indigenous beliefs 9%
**Languages:** French (official), Bambara 80%, numerous African languages
**Literacy:**
*definition:* age 15 and over can read and write
*total population:* 46.4%
*male:* 53.5%
*female:* 39.6% (2003 est.)
**School life expectancy (primary to tertiary education):**
*total:* 7 years
*male:* 8 years
*female:* 5 years (2005)
**Education expenditures:** 4.5% of GDP (2006)

## Government

**Country name:**
*conventional long form:* Republic of Mali
*conventional short form:* Mali
*local long form:* Republique de Mali
*local short form:* Mali
*former:* French Sudan and Sudanese Republic
**Government type:** republic
**Capital:**
*name:* Bamako
*geographic coordinates:* 12 39 N, 8 00 W
*time difference:* UTC 0 (5 hours ahead of Washington, DC during Standard Time)

**Administrative divisions:** 8 regions (regions, singular - region); Gao, Kayes, Kidal, Koulikoro, Mopti, Segou, Sikasso, Tombouctou
**Independence:** 22 September 1960 (from France)
**National holiday:** Independence Day, 22 September (1960)
**Constitution:** adopted 12 January 1992
**Legal system:** based on French civil law system and customary law; judicial review of legislative acts in Constitutional Court; has not accepted compulsory ICJ jurisdiction
**Suffrage:** 18 years of age; universal
**Executive branch:**
*chief of state:* President Amadou Toumani TOURE (since 8 June 2002)
*head of government:* Prime Minister Modibo SIDIBE (since 28 September 2007)
*cabinet:* Council of Ministers appointed by the prime minister
*elections:* president elected by popular vote for a five-year term (eligible for a second term); election last held on 29 April 2007 (next to be held in April 2012); prime minister appointed by the president
*election results:* Amadou Toumani TOURE reelected president; percent of vote - Amadou Toumani TOURE 71.2%, Ibrahim Boubacar KEITA 19.2%, other 9.6%
**Legislative branch:** unicameral National Assembly or Assemblee Nationale (147 seats; members elected by popular vote to serve five-year terms)
*elections:* last held on 1 and 22 July 2007 (next to be held in July 2012)
*election results:* percent of vote by party - NA; seats by party - ADP coalition 113 (including ADEMA 51, URD 34, MPR 8, CNID 7, UDD 3, and other 10), FDR coalition 15 (including RPM 11, PARENA 4), SADI 4, independent 15
**Judicial branch:** Supreme Court or Cour Supreme
**Political parties and leaders:** Alliance for Democratic Change (political group comprised mainly of Tuareg from Mali's northern region); African Solidarity for Democracy and Independence or SADI [Oumar MARIKO, secretary general]; Alliance for Democracy and Progress or ADP (a coalition of political parties including ADEMA and URD formed in December 2006 to support the presidential candidacy of Amadou TOURE); Alliance for Democracy or ADEMA [Diounconda TRAORE]; Convergence 2007 [Soumeylou Boubeye MAIGA]; Front for Democracy and the Republic or FDR (a coalition of political parties including RPM and PARENA formed to oppose the presidential candidacy of Amadou TOURE); National Congress for Democratic Initiative or CNID [Mountaga TALL]; Party for Democracy and Progress or PDP [Mady KONATE]; Party for National Renewal or PARENA [Tiebile DRAME]; Patriotic Movement for Renewal or MPR [Choguel MAIGA]; Rally for Democracy and Labor or RDT [Amadou Ali NIANGADOU]; Rally for Mali or RPM [Ibrahim Boubacar KEITA]; Sudanese Union/African Democratic Rally or US/RDA [Mamadou Basir GOLOGO]; Union for Democracy and Development or UDD [Moussa Balla COULIBALY]; Union for Republic and Democracy or URD [Soumaila CISSE]

# Mali *(continued)*

**Political pressure groups and leaders:**
*other:* the army; Islamic authorities; rebels in the northern region; state-run cotton company CMDT; tuaregs

**International organization participation:** ACP, AfDB, AU, ECOWAS, FAO, FZ, G-77, IAEA, IBRD, ICAO, ICCt, ICRM, IDA, IDB, IFAD, IFC, IFRCS, ILO, IMF, Interpol, IOC, IOM, IPU, ITSO, ITU, ITUC, MIGA, MINURCAT, MONUC, NAM, OIC, OIF, OPCW, UN, UNAMID, UNCTAD, UNESCO, UNIDO, UNMIL, UNMIS, UNWTO, UPU, WADB (regional), WAEMU, WCO, WFTU, WHO, WIPO, WMO, WTO

**Diplomatic representation in the US:**
*chief of mission:* Ambassador Abdoulaye DIOP
*chancery:* 2130 R Street NW, Washington, DC 20008
*telephone:* [1] (202) 332-2249, 939-8950
*FAX:* [1] (202) 332-6603

**Diplomatic representation from the US:**
*chief of mission:* Ambassador Gillian A. MILOVANOVIC
*embassy:* located just off the Roi Bin Fahad Aziz Bridge just west of the Bamako central district
*mailing address:* ACI 2000, Rue 243, Porte 297, Bamako
*telephone:* [223] 270-2300
*FAX:* [223] 270-2479

**Flag description:** three equal vertical bands of green (hoist side), yellow, and red; uses the popular pan-African colors of Ethiopia

## Economy

**Economy - overview:** Mali is among the 25 poorest countries in the world, with 65% of its land area desert or semidesert and with a highly unequal distribution of income. Economic activity is largely confined to the riverine area irrigated by the Niger. About 10% of the population is nomadic and some 80% of the labor force is engaged in farming and fishing. Industrial activity is concentrated on processing farm commodities. Mali is heavily dependent on foreign aid and vulnerable to fluctuations in world prices for gold and cotton, its main exports. The government has continued its successful implementation of an IMF-recommended structural adjustment program that is helping the economy grow, diversify, and attract foreign investment. Mali has invested in tourism and a tractor assembly factory. Mali's adherence to economic reform and the 50% devaluation of the CFA franc in January 1994 have pushed up economic growth to a 5% average in 1996-2008. Worker remittances and external trade routes for the landlocked country have been jeopardized by continued unrest in neighboring Cote d'Ivoire, however, Mali is building a road network that will connect it to all adjacent countries and it has a railway line to Senegal.

**GDP (purchasing power parity):**
$14.48 billion (2008 est.)
$13.89 billion (2007)
$13.52 billion (2006)
*note:* data are in 2008 US dollars

**GDP (official exchange rate):** $8.776 billion (2008 est.)

**GDP - real growth rate:**
4.2% (2008 est.)
2.8% (2007 est.)
5.3% (2006 est.)

**GDP - per capita (PPP):**
$1,200 (2008 est.)
$1,200 (2007 est.)
$1,200 (2006 est.)
*note:* data are in 2008 US dollars

**GDP - composition by sector:**
*agriculture:* 45%
*industry:* 17%
*services:* 38% (2001 est.)

**Labor force:** 5.4 million (2007 est.)

**Labor force - by occupation:**
*agriculture:* 80%
*industry and services:* 20% (2005 est.)

**Unemployment rate:**
30% (2004 est.)

**Population below poverty line:** 36.1% (2005 est.)

**Household income or consumption by percentage share:**
*lowest 10%:* 2.4%
*highest 10%:* 30.2% (2001)

**Distribution of family income - Gini index:** 40.1 (2001)

**Budget:**
*revenues:* $1.5 billion
*expenditures:* $1.8 billion (2006 est.)

**Inflation rate (consumer prices):**
2.5% (2007 est.)

**Central bank discount rate:** 4.25% (31 December 2007)

**Commercial bank prime lending rate:** NA

**Stock of money:** $1.58 billion (31 December 2007)

**Stock of quasi money:** $697.1 million (31 December 2007)

**Stock of domestic credit:** $1.099 billion (31 December 2007)

**Market value of publicly traded shares:** $NA

**Agriculture - products:** cotton, millet, rice, corn, vegetables, peanuts; cattle, sheep, goats

**Industries:** food processing; construction; phosphate and gold mining

**Industrial production growth rate:** NA%

**Electricity - production:** 505 million kWh (2006 est.)

**Electricity - consumption:** 469.7 million kWh (2006 est.)

**Electricity - exports:** 0 kWh; note - recent hydropower developments may be providing electricity to Senegal and Mauritania (2007 est.)

**Electricity - imports:** 0 kWh (2007 est.)

**Oil - production:** 0 bbl/day (2007 est.)

**Oil - consumption:** 4,640 bbl/day (2006 est.)

**Oil - exports:** 0 bbl/day (2006)

**Oil - imports:** 4,860 bbl/day (2005 est.)

**Oil - proved reserves:** 0 bbl (1 January 2006 est.)

**Natural gas - production:** 0 cu m (2007 est.)

**Natural gas - consumption:** 0 cu m (2007 est.)

**Natural gas - exports:** 0 cu m (2007 est.)

**Natural gas - imports:** 0 cu m (2007 est.)

**Natural gas - proved reserves:** 0 cu m (1 January 2006 est.)

**Current account balance:** -$446 million (2007 est.)

**Exports:** $294 million f.o.b. (2006)

**Exports - commodities:** cotton, gold, livestock

**Exports - partners:** China 19.6%, Thailand 10.5%, Brazil 4.6%, France 4.5%, Indonesia 4.5% (2007)

**Imports:** $2.358 billion f.o.b. (2006)

**Imports - commodities:** petroleum, machinery and equipment, construction materials, foodstuffs, textiles

**Imports - partners:** France 12.9%, Senegal 12.7%, Cote d'Ivoire 10.9%, China 4.9% (2007)

**Debt - external:** $2.8 billion (2002)

**Exchange rates:** Communaute Financiere Africaine francs (XOF) per US dollar - 447.81 (2008 est.), 493.51 (2007), 522.59 (2006), 527.47 (2005), 528.29 (2004)
*note:* since 1 January 1999, the West African CFA franc (XOF) has been pegged to the euro at a rate of 655.957 CFA francs per euro; West African CFA franc (XOF) coins and banknotes are not accepted in countries using Central African CFA francs (XAF), and vice versa, even though the two currencies trade at par

## Communications

**Telephones - main lines in use:** 85,000 (2007)

**Telephones - mobile cellular:** 2.483 million (2007)

**Telephone system:**
*general assessment:* domestic system unreliable but improving; provides only minimal service
*domestic:* fixed-line availability is gradually increasing, but subscribership remains less than 1 per 100 persons; increasing use of local radio loops to extend network coverage to remote areas; mobile-cellular subscribership has increased sharply to 20 per 100 persons
*international:* country code - 223; satellite earth stations - 2 Intelsat (1 Atlantic Ocean, 1 Indian Ocean) (2007)

**Radio broadcast stations:** AM 1, FM 230 (27 regional and government stations, and 203 private stations), shortwave 1 (2001)

**Television broadcast stations:** 2 (plus repeaters) (2007)

**Internet country code:** .ml

**Internet hosts:** 387 (2008)

**Internet users:** 100,000 (2007)

## Transportation

**Airports:** 26 (2008)

**Airports - with paved runways:**
*total:* 8
*2,438 to 3,047 m:* 4
*1,524 to 2,437 m:* 3
*914 to 1,523 m:* 1 (2008)

## Mali (continued)

**Airports - with unpaved runways:**
*total:* 18
*2,438 to 3,047 m:* 1
*1,524 to 2,437 m:* 4
*914 to 1,523 m:* 6
*under 914 m:* 7 (2008)
**Railways:**
*total:* 729 km
*narrow gauge:* 729 km 1.000-m gauge (2006)
**Roadways:**
*total:* 18,709 km
*paved:* 3,368 km
*unpaved:* 15,341 km (2004)
**Waterways:** 1,800 km (2008)
**Ports and terminals:** Koulikoro

### Military

**Military branches:** Malian Armed Forces: Army, Republic of Mali Air Force (Force Aerienne de la Republique du Mali, FARM), National Guard (2008)
**Military service age and obligation:** 18 years of age for compulsory and voluntary military service; conscript service obligation - 2 years (2008)
**Manpower available for military service:**
*males age 16-49:* 2,603,700
*females age 16-49:* 2,441,776 (2008 est.)
**Manpower fit for military service:**
*males age 16-49:* 1,649,772
*females age 16-49:* 1,579,601 (2009 est.)
**Manpower reaching militarily significant age annually:**
*male:* 147,846
*female:* 140,543 (2009 est.)
**Military expenditures:** 1.9% of GDP (2006)

### Transnational Issues

**Disputes - international:** none
**Refugees and internally displaced persons:**
*refugees (country of origin):* 6,300 (Mauritania) (2007)

# Malta

### Introduction

**Background:** Great Britain formally acquired possession of Malta in 1814. The island staunchly supported the UK through both World Wars and remained in the Commonwealth when it became independent in 1964. A decade later Malta became a republic. Since about the mid-1980s, the island has transformed itself into a freight transshipment point, a financial center, and a tourist destination. Malta became an EU member in May 2004 and began using the euro as currency in 2008.

### Geography

**Location:** Southern Europe, islands in the Mediterranean Sea, south of Sicily (Italy)
**Geographic coordinates:** 35 50 N, 14 35 E
**Map references:** Europe
**Area:**
*total:* 316 sq km
*land:* 316 sq km
*water:* 0 sq km
**Area - comparative:** slightly less than twice the size of Washington, DC
**Land boundaries:** 0 km
**Coastline:** 196.8 km (excludes 56.01 km for the island of Gozo)
**Maritime claims:**
*territorial sea:* 12 nm
*contiguous zone:* 24 nm
*continental shelf:* 200 m depth or to the depth of exploitation
*exclusive fishing zone:* 25 nm
**Climate:** Mediterranean; mild, rainy winters; hot, dry summers
**Terrain:** mostly low, rocky, flat to dissected plains; many coastal cliffs
**Elevation extremes:**
*lowest point:* Mediterranean Sea 0 m
*highest point:* Ta'Dmejrek 253 m (near Dingli)

**Natural resources:** limestone, salt, arable land
**Land use:**
*arable land:* 31.25%
*permanent crops:* 3.13%
*other:* 65.62% (2005)
**Irrigated land:** 20 sq km (2003)
**Total renewable water resources:** 0.07 cu km (2005)
**Freshwater withdrawal (domestic/industrial/agricultural):**
*total:* 0.02 cu km/yr (74%/1%/25%)
*per capita:* 50 cu m/yr (2000)
**Natural hazards:** NA
**Environment - current issues:** limited natural fresh water resources; increasing reliance on desalination
**Environment - international agreements:**
*party to:* Air Pollution, Biodiversity, Climate Change, Climate Change-Kyoto Protocol, Desertification, Endangered Species, Hazardous Wastes, Law of the Sea, Marine Dumping, Ozone Layer Protection, Ship Pollution, Wetlands
*signed, but not ratified:* none of the selected agreements
**Geography - note:** the country comprises an archipelago, with only the three largest islands (Malta, Ghawdex or Gozo, and Kemmuna or Comino) being inhabited; numerous bays provide good harbors; Malta and Tunisia are discussing the commercial exploitation of the continental shelf between their countries, particularly for oil exploration

### People

**Population:** 405,165 (July 2009 est.)
**Age structure:**
*0-14 years:* 16.1% (male 33,526/female 31,780)
*15-64 years:* 69.4% (male 142,491/female 138,769)
*65 years and over:* 14.5% (male 25,406/female 33,193) (2009 est.)
**Median age:**
*total:* 39.5 years
*male:* 38.1 years
*female:* 40.9 years (2009 est.)
**Population growth rate:** 0.4% (2009 est.)
**Birth rate:** 10.36 births/1,000 population (2009 est.)
**Death rate:** 8.29 deaths/1,000 population (2008 est.)
**Net migration rate:** 2.02 migrant(s)/1,000 population (2009 est.)
**Urbanization:**
*urban population:* 94% of total population (2008)
*rate of urbanization:* 0.6% annual rate of change (2005-10 est.)
**Sex ratio:**
*at birth:* 1.06 male(s)/female
*under 15 years:* 1.06 male(s)/female
*15-64 years:* 1.03 male(s)/female
*65 years and over:* 0.76 male(s)/female
*total population:* 0.99 male(s)/female (2009 est.)
**Infant mortality rate:**
*total:* 3.75 deaths/1,000 live births
*male:* 4.2 deaths/1,000 live births
*female:* 3.27 deaths/1,000 live births (2009 est.)

# Malta (continued)

## Life expectancy at birth:
*total population:* 79.44 years
*male:* 77.21 years
*female:* 81.8 years (2009 est.)
**Total fertility rate:** 1.51 children born/woman (2009 est.)
**HIV/AIDS - adult prevalence rate:** 0.1% (2007 est.)
**HIV/AIDS - people living with HIV/AIDS:** fewer than 500 (2007 est.)
**HIV/AIDS - deaths:** fewer than 100 (2003 est.)
**Nationality:**
*noun:* Maltese (singular and plural)
*adjective:* Maltese
**Ethnic groups:** Maltese (descendants of ancient Carthaginians and Phoenicians with strong elements of Italian and other Mediterranean stock)
**Religions:** Roman Catholic 98%
**Languages:** Maltese (official) 90.2%, English (official) 6%, multilingual 3%, other 0.8% (2005 census)
**Literacy:**
*definition:* age 10 and over can read and write
*total population:* 92.8%
*male:* 92%
*female:* 93.6% (2003 est.)
**School life expectancy (primary to tertiary education):**
*total:* 15 years
*male:* 15 years
*female:* 15 years (2005)
**Education expenditures:** 5.1% of GDP (2004)

## Government

**Country name:**
*conventional long form:* Republic of Malta
*conventional short form:* Malta
*local long form:* Repubblika ta' Malta
*local short form:* Malta
**Government type:** republic
**Capital:**
*name:* Valletta
*geographic coordinates:* 35 53 N, 14 30 E
*time difference:* UTC+1 (6 hours ahead of Washington, DC during Standard Time)
*daylight saving time:* +1hr, begins last Sunday in March; ends last Sunday in October
**Administrative divisions:** none (administered directly from Valletta); note - local councils carry out administrative orders
**Independence:** 21 September 1964 (from the UK)
**National holiday:** Independence Day, 21 September (1964)
**Constitution:** 1964; amended many times
**Legal system:** based on English common law and Roman civil law; accepts compulsory ICJ jurisdiction with reservations
**Suffrage:** 18 years of age; universal

## Executive branch:
*chief of state:* President George ABELA (since 4 April 2009)
*head of government:* Prime Minister Lawrence GONZI (since 23 March 2004)
*cabinet:* Cabinet appointed by the president on the advice of the prime minister
*elections:* president elected by the House of Representatives for a five-year term (eligible for a second term); election last held on 12 January 2009 (next to be held by April 2014); following legislative elections, the leader of the majority party or leader of a majority coalition is usually appointed prime minister by the president for a five-year term; the deputy prime minister is appointed by the president on the advice of the prime minister
*election results:* George ABELA elected president by the House of Representatives
**Legislative branch:** unicameral House of Representatives (normally 65 seats; members are elected by popular vote on the basis of proportional representation to serve five-year terms; note - the current Parliament is composed of 69 seats; when the political party winning the plurality of votes does not win a majority of seats, the constitution provides that a sufficient number of seats will be added to Parliament to ensure that the party that won the elections has a majority in Parliament)
*elections:* last held on 8 March 2008 (next to be held by March 2013)
*election results:* percent of vote by party - PN 49.3%, MLP 48.9%, other 1.8%; seats by party - PN 35, MLP 34
**Judicial branch:** Constitutional Court; Court of Appeal; judges for both courts are appointed by the president on the advice of the prime minister
**Political parties and leaders:** Alternativa Demokratika/Alliance for Social Justice or AD [Arnold CASSOLA]; Azzjoni Nazzjonaili or AN [Josi MUSCAT]; Malta Labor Party or MLP [Joseph MUSCAT]; Nationalist Party or PN [Lawrence GONZI]
**Political pressure groups and leaders:** Alleanza Liberal-Demokratika Maltra or ALDM (for divorce, abortion, gay marriage, the rights existent in other EU member states); Alleanza Nazzionali Repubblikana or ANR (for traditional values, anti-immigration); Alternattiva Demokratika (pro-environment); Azzjoni Nazzjonali or AN (freedom to participate in democratic government); Flimkien Ghal-Ambjent Ahjar (pro-environment); Ghazdatal-Konsumaturi (consumer rights)
*other:* environmentalists
**International organization participation:** Australia Group, C, CE, EAPC, EBRD, EIB, EMU, EU, FAO, IAEA, IBRD, ICAO, ICCt, ICRM, IFAD, IFC, IFRCS, ILO, IMF, IMO, IMSO, Interpol, IOC, IOM, IPU, ISO, ITSO, ITU, ITUC, MIGA, NSG, OPCW, OSCE, PCA, PFP, Schengen Convention, UN, UNCTAD, UNESCO, UNIDO, UNWTO, UPU, WCL, WCO, WFTU, WHO, WIPO, WMO, WTO

## Diplomatic representation in the US:
*chief of mission:* Ambassador Mark MICELI-FARRUGIA
*chancery:* 2017 Connecticut Avenue NW, Washington, DC 20008
*telephone:* [1] (202) 462-3611 through 3612
*FAX:* [1] (202) 387-5470
*consulate(s):* New York
**Diplomatic representation from the US:**
*chief of mission:* Ambassador (vacant); Charge d'Affaires Jason DAVIS
*embassy:* 3rd Floor, Development House, Saint Anne Street, Floriana, VLT 01
*mailing address:* P. O. Box 535, Valletta, CMR01
*telephone:* [356] 2561 4000
*FAX:* [356] 21 243229
**Flag description:** two equal vertical bands of white (hoist side) and red; in the upper hoist-side corner is a representation of the George Cross, edged in red

## Economy

**Economy - overview:** Malta produces only about 20% of its food needs, has limited fresh water supplies, and has few domestic energy sources. Malta's geographic position between the EU and Africa makes it a recipient of illegal immigration, which has strained Malta's political and economic resources. The financial services industry has grown in recent years, but is not fully modernized. Malta's economy is dependent on foreign trade, manufacturing - especially electronics and pharmaceuticals - and tourism all of which have been negatively affected by the global economic downturn. Malta adopted the euro on 1 January 2008. The Maltese government in 2009 will be challenged to contain the budget deficit, which ballooned in 2008 to about 4.1% of GDP, placing it above the euro zone's 3% maximum.
**GDP (purchasing power parity):**
$9.801 billion (2008 est.)
$9.695 billion (2007)
$9.329 billion (2006)
*note:* data are in 2008 US dollars
**GDP (official exchange rate):** $8.584 billion (2008 est.)
**GDP - real growth rate:**
2.5% (2008 est.)
3.9% (2007 est.)
3.2% (2006 est.)
**GDP - per capita (PPP):**
$24,200 (2008 est.)
$24,100 (2007 est.)
$23,300 (2006 est.)
*note:* data are in 2008 US dollars
**GDP - composition by sector:**
*agriculture:* 1.4%
*industry:* 18%
*services:* 80.6% (2007 est.)
**Labor force:** 173,000 (2008)

# Malta (continued)

**Labor force - by occupation:**
*agriculture:* 2.3%
*industry:* 29.6%
*services:* 68% (2005 est.)
**Unemployment rate:**
6.4% (2007)
**Population below poverty line:** NA%
**Household income or consumption by percentage share:**
*lowest 10%:* NA%
*highest 10%:* NA%
**Distribution of family income - Gini index:** 26 (2007)
**Investment (gross fixed):** 20% of GDP (2008 est.)
**Budget:**
*revenues:* $3.457 billion
*expenditures:* $3.653 billion (2008 est.)
**Inflation rate (consumer prices):**
4.4% (2008 est.)
1.3% (2007 est.)
**Central bank discount rate:** NA
**Commercial bank prime lending rate:** 6.24% (31 December 2007)
**Stock of money:** $4.639 billion
*note:* this figure represents the US dollar value of Maltese liri in circulation prior to Malta joining the Economic and Monetary Union (EMU); see entry for the European Union for money supply in the euro area; the European Central Bank (ECB) controls monetary policy for the 16 members of the EMU; individual members of the EMU do not control the quantity of money and quasi money circulating within their own borders (31 December 2008)
**Stock of quasi money:** $8.771 billion (31 December 2008 est.)
**Stock of domestic credit:** $10 billion (31 December 2008 est.)
**Market value of publicly traded shares:** $5.633 billion (31 December 2007)
**Agriculture - products:** potatoes, cauliflower, grapes, wheat, barley, tomatoes, citrus, cut flowers, green peppers; pork, milk, poultry, eggs
**Industries:** tourism, electronics, ship building and repair, construction, food and beverages, pharmaceuticals, footwear, clothing, tobacco
**Industrial production growth rate:** NA%
**Electricity - production:** 2.146 billion kWh (2007 est.)
**Electricity - consumption:** 1.85 billion kWh (2006 est.)
**Electricity - exports:** 0 kWh (2007 est.)
**Electricity - imports:** 0 kWh (2007 est.)
**Oil - production:** 0 bbl/day (2007 est.)
**Oil - consumption:** 18,680 bbl/day (2006 est.)
**Oil - exports:** 0 bbl/day (2005)
**Oil - imports:** 18,910 bbl/day (2005)
**Oil - proved reserves:** 0 bbl (1 January 2006 est.)
**Natural gas - production:** 0 cu m (2007 est.)
**Natural gas - consumption:** 0 cu m (2007 est.)
**Natural gas - exports:** 0 cu m (2007 est.)
**Natural gas - imports:** 0 cu m (2007 est.)

**Natural gas - proved reserves:** 0 cu m (1 January 2006 est.)
**Current account balance:** -$538 million (2008 est.)
**Exports:** $3.491 billion f.o.b. (2008 est.)
**Exports - commodities:** machinery and transport equipment, manufactures
**Exports - partners:** Singapore 14.4%, Germany 13.7%, France 12.6%, US 11.3%, UK 10%, Hong Kong 6.1%, Japan 4.9%, Italy 4% (2007)
**Imports:** $4.963 billion f.o.b. (2008 est.)
**Imports - commodities:** machinery and transport equipment, manufactured and semi-manufactured goods; food, drink, tobacco
**Imports - partners:** Italy 26%, UK 15%, France 9.5%, Germany 8.8%, Singapore 5.2% (2007)
**Reserves of foreign exchange and gold:** $4.15 billion (31 December 2008 est.)
**Debt - external:** $188.8 million (2005)
**Stock of direct foreign investment - at home:** $NA
**Stock of direct foreign investment - abroad:** $NA
**Exchange rates:** euros (EUR) per US dollar - 0.6827 (2008 est.), Maltese liri per US dollar - 0.3106 (2007), 0.37 (2006), 0.34578 (2005), 0.34466 (2004), 0.37723 (2003)

## Communications

**Telephones - main lines in use:** 198,100 (2007)
**Telephones - mobile cellular:** 371,500 (2007)
**Telephone system:**
*general assessment:* automatic system is adequate; fixed-line teledensity 50 per 100 persons; mobile-cellular teledensity about 90 per 100 persons
*domestic:* submarine cable and microwave radio relay between islands
*international:* country code - 356; submarine cable connects to Italy; satellite earth station - 1 Intelsat (Atlantic Ocean) (2007)
**Radio broadcast stations:** AM 1, FM 18, shortwave 6 (1999)
**Television broadcast stations:** 5 (2006)
**Internet country code:** .mt
**Internet hosts:** 26,494 (2008)
**Internet users:** 158,000 (2007)

## Transportation

**Airports:** 1 (2008)
**Airports - with paved runways:**
*total:* 1
*over 3,047 m:* 1 (2008)
**Roadways:**
*total:* 2,227 km
*paved:* 2,014 km
*unpaved:* 213 km (2005)
**Merchant marine:**
*total:* 1,438
*by type:* bulk carrier 459, cargo 411, carrier 2, chemical tanker 171, container 80, liquefied gas 25, passenger 29, passenger/cargo 15, petroleum tanker 159, refrigerated cargo 32, roll on/roll off 37, specialized tanker 1, vehicle carrier 17

*foreign-owned:* 1,343 (Austria 1, Azerbaijan 2, Bangladesh 2, Belgium 15, Bulgaria 5, Canada 1, China 12, Croatia 9, Cyprus 31, Denmark 30, Egypt 1, Estonia 11, France 5, Germany 91, Greece 452, Hong Kong 1, Iceland 5, India 2, Iran 79, Israel 18, Italy 50, Japan 8, South Korea 2, Latvia 19, Lebanon 11, Libya 3, Lithuania 1, Norway 93, Pakistan 2, Poland 24, Portugal 3, Romania 8, Russia 58, Slovenia 4, Spain 3, Sweden 2, Switzerland 20, Syria 6, Turkey 176, Ukraine 30, UAE 5, UK 19, US 23)
*registered in other countries:* 3 (Panama 3) (2008)
**Ports and terminals:** Marsaxlokk (Malta Freeport), Valletta

## Military

**Military branches:** Armed Forces of Malta (AFM; includes air and maritime elements) (2007)
**Military service age and obligation:** 17 years 6 months of age for voluntary military service; no conscription (2008)
**Manpower available for military service:**
*males age 16-49:* 96,309
*females age 16-49:* 92,242 (2008 est.)
**Manpower fit for military service:**
*males age 16-49:* 80,186
*females age 16-49:* 76,426 (2009 est.)
**Manpower reaching militarily significant age annually:**
*male:* 2,695
*female:* 2,533 (2009 est.)
**Military expenditures:** 0.7% of GDP (2006 est.)

## Transnational Issues

**Disputes - international:** none
**Illicit drugs:** minor transshipment point for hashish from North Africa to Western Europe

# Marshall Islands

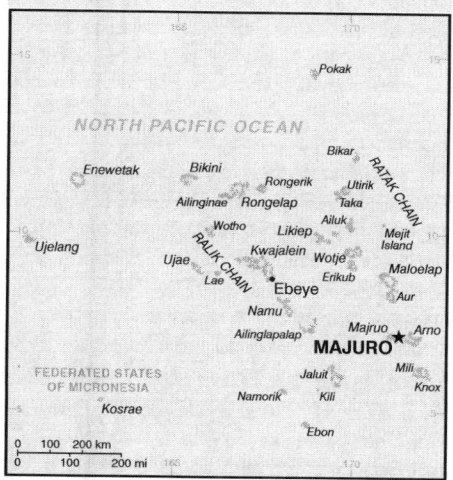

## Introduction

**Background:** After almost four decades under US administration as the easternmost part of the UN Trust Territory of the Pacific Islands, the Marshall Islands attained independence in 1986 under a Compact of Free Association. Compensation claims continue as a result of US nuclear testing on some of the atolls between 1947 and 1962. The Marshall Islands hosts the US Army Kwajalein Atoll (USAKA) Reagan Missile Test Site, a key installation in the US missile defense network.

## Geography

**Location:** Oceania, two archipelagic island chains of 29 atolls, each made up of many small islets, and five single islands in the North Pacific Ocean, about half way between Hawaii and Australia
**Geographic coordinates:** 9 00 N, 168 00 E
**Map references:** Oceania
**Area:**
*total:* 181.3 sq km
*land:* 181.3 sq km
*water:* 0 sq km
*note:* the archipelago includes 11,673 sq km of lagoon waters and includes the atolls of Bikini, Enewetak, Kwajalein, Majuro, Rongelap, and Utirik
**Area - comparative:** about the size of Washington, DC
**Land boundaries:** 0 km
**Coastline:** 370.4 km
**Maritime claims:**
*territorial sea:* 12 nm
*contiguous zone:* 24 nm
*exclusive economic zone:* 200 nm
**Climate:** tropical; hot and humid; wet season May to November; islands border typhoon belt
**Terrain:** low coral limestone and sand islands
**Elevation extremes:**
*lowest point:* Pacific Ocean 0 m
*highest point:* unnamed location on Likiep 10 m

**Natural resources:** coconut products, marine products, deep seabed minerals
**Land use:**
*arable land:* 11.11%
*permanent crops:* 44.44%
*other:* 44.45% (2005)
**Irrigated land:** 0 sq km
**Natural hazards:** infrequent typhoons
**Environment - current issues:** inadequate supplies of potable water; pollution of Majuro lagoon from household waste and discharges from fishing vessels
**Environment - international agreements:**
*party to:* Biodiversity, Climate Change, Climate Change-Kyoto Protocol, Desertification, Hazardous Wastes, Law of the Sea, Ozone Layer Protection, Ship Pollution, Wetlands, Whaling
*signed, but not ratified:* none of the selected agreements
**Geography - note:** the islands of Bikini and Enewetak are former US nuclear test sites; Kwajalein atoll, famous as a World War II battleground, surrounds the world's largest lagoon and is used as a US missile test range; the island city of Ebeye is the second largest settlement in the Marshall Islands, after the capital of Majuro, and one of the most densely populated locations in the Pacific

## People

**Population:** 64,522 (July 2009 est.)
**Age structure:**
*0-14 years:* 38.6% (male 12,683/female 12,217)
*15-64 years:* 58.5% (male 19,302/female 18,459)
*65 years and over:* 2.9% (male 902/female 959) (2009 est.)
**Median age:**
*total:* 21.2 years
*male:* 21.3 years
*female:* 21.2 years (2009 est.)
**Population growth rate:** 2.08% (2009 est.)
**Birth rate:** 30.7 births/1,000 population (2009 est.)
**Death rate:** 4.57 deaths/1,000 population (2008 est.)
**Net migration rate:** -5.41 migrant(s)/1,000 population (2009 est.)
**Urbanization:**
*urban population:* 71% of total population (2008)
*rate of urbanization:* 2.7% annual rate of change (2005-10 est.)
**Sex ratio:**
*at birth:* 1.05 male(s)/female
*under 15 years:* 1.04 male(s)/female
*15-64 years:* 1.05 male(s)/female
*65 years and over:* 0.94 male(s)/female
*total population:* 1.04 male(s)/female (2009 est.)
**Infant mortality rate:**
*total:* 25.45 deaths/1,000 live births
*male:* 28.58 deaths/1,000 live births
*female:* 22.17 deaths/1,000 live births (2009 est.)
**Life expectancy at birth:**
*total population:* 71.19 years
*male:* 69.15 years
*female:* 73.34 years (2009 est.)

**Total fertility rate:** 3.59 children born/woman (2009 est.)
**HIV/AIDS - adult prevalence rate:** NA
**HIV/AIDS - people living with HIV/AIDS:** NA
**HIV/AIDS - deaths:** NA
**Nationality:**
*noun:* Marshallese (singular and plural)
*adjective:* Marshallese
**Ethnic groups:** Marshallese 92.1%, mixed Marshallese 5.9%, other 2% (2006)
**Religions:** Protestant 54.8%, Assembly of God 25.8%, Roman Catholic 8.4%, Bukot nan Jesus 2.8%, Mormon 2.1%, other Christian 3.6%, other 1%, none 1.5% (1999 census)
**Languages:** Marshallese (official) 98.2%, other languages 1.8% (1999 census)
*note:* English (official), widely spoken as a second language
**Literacy:**
*definition:* age 15 and over can read and write
*total population:* 93.7%
*male:* 93.6%
*female:* 93.7% (1999)
**School life expectancy (primary to tertiary education):**
*total:* 13 years
*male:* 13 years
*female:* 13 years (2003)
**Education expenditures:** 11.8% of GDP (2004)

## Government

**Country name:**
*conventional long form:* Republic of the Marshall Islands
*conventional short form:* Marshall Islands
*local long form:* Republic of the Marshall Islands
*local short form:* Marshall Islands
*abbreviation:* RMI
*former:* Trust Territory of the Pacific Islands, Marshall Islands District
**Government type:** constitutional government in free association with the US; the Compact of Free Association entered into force 21 October 1986 and the Amended Compact entered into force in May 2004
**Capital:**
*name:* Majuro
*geographic coordinates:* 7 06 N, 171 23 E
*time difference:* UTC+12 (17 hours ahead of Washington, DC during Standard Time)
**Administrative divisions:** 33 municipalities; Ailinginae, Ailinglaplap, Ailuk, Arno, Aur, Bikar, Bikini, Bokak, Ebon, Enewetak, Erikub, Jabat, Jaluit, Jemo, Kili, Kwajalein, Lae, Lib, Likiep, Majuro, Maloelap, Mejit, Mili, Namorik, Namu, Rongelap, Rongrik, Toke, Ujae, Ujelang, Utirik, Wotho, Wotje
**Independence:** 21 October 1986 (from the US-administered UN trusteeship)
**National holiday:** Constitution Day, 1 May (1979)
**Constitution:** 1 May 1979

**Legal system:** based on adapted Trust Territory laws, acts of the legislature, municipal, common, and customary laws; has not accepted compulsory ICJ jurisdiction

**Suffrage:** 18 years of age; universal

**Executive branch:**

*chief of state:* President Litokwa TOMEING (since 7 January 2008); note - the president is both the chief of state and head of government

*head of government:* President Litokwa TOMEING (since 7 January 2008)

*cabinet:* Cabinet selected by the president from among the members of the legislature

*elections:* president elected by Parliament from among its members for a four-year term; election last held 7 January 2008 (next to be held in 2012)

*election results:* Litokwa TOMEING elected president; TOMEING received 18 votes to 15 for incumbent Kessai Hesa NOTE

**Legislative branch:** unicameral legislature or Nitijela (33 seats; members elected by popular vote to serve four-year terms)

*elections:* last held 19 November 2007 (next to be held by November 2011)

*election results:* percent of vote by party - NA; seats by party - independents 4

*note:* the Council of Chiefs or Ironij is a 12-member body comprised of tribal chiefs that advises on matters affecting customary law and practice

**Judicial branch:** Supreme Court; High Court; Traditional Rights Court

**Political parties and leaders:** traditionally there have been no formally organized political parties; what has existed more closely resembles factions or interest groups because they do not have party headquarters, formal platforms, or party structures; the following two "groupings" have competed in legislative balloting in recent years - Aelon Kein Ad Party [Michael KABUA] and United Democratic Party or UDP [Litokwa TOMEING]

**Political pressure groups and leaders:** NA

**International organization participation:** ACP, ADB, FAO, G-77, IAEA, IBRD, ICAO, ICCt, IDA, IFC, ILO, IMF, IMO, IMSO, Interpol, IOC, ITU, OPCW, PIF, Sparteca, SPC, UN, UNCTAD, UNESCO, WHO

**Diplomatic representation in the US:**

*chief of mission:* Ambassador (vacant); Charge d'Affaires Charles A. PAUL

*chancery:* 2433 Massachusetts Avenue NW, Washington, DC 20008

*telephone:* [1] (202) 234-5414

*FAX:* [1] (202) 232-3236

*consulate(s) general:* Honolulu

**Diplomatic representation from the US:**

*chief of mission:* Ambassador Clyde BISHOP

*embassy:* Oceanside, Mejen Weto, Long Island, Majuro

*mailing address:* P. O. Box 1379, Majuro, Republic of the Marshall Islands 96960-1379

*telephone:* [692] 247-4011

*FAX:* [692] 247-4012

**Flag description:** blue with two stripes radiating from the lower hoist-side corner - orange (top) and white; there is a white star with four large rays and 20 small rays on the hoist side above the two stripes

## Economy

**Economy - overview:** US Government assistance is the mainstay of this tiny island economy. The Marshall Islands received more than $1 billion in aid from the US from 1986-2002. Agricultural production, primarily subsistence, is concentrated on small farms; the most important commercial crops are coconuts and breadfruit. Small-scale industry is limited to handicrafts, tuna processing, and copra. The tourist industry, now a small source of foreign exchange employing less than 10% of the labor force, remains the best hope for future added income. The islands have few natural resources, and imports far exceed exports. Under the terms of the Amended Compact of Free Association, the US will provide millions of dollars per year to the Marshall Islands (RMI) through 2023, at which time a Trust Fund made up of US and RMI contributions will begin perpetual annual payouts. Government downsizing, drought, a drop in construction, the decline in tourism, and less income from the renewal of fishing vessel licenses have held GDP growth to an average of 1% over the past decade.

**GDP (purchasing power parity):**
$133.5 million (2008 est.)
$115 million (2001)
*note:* data are in 2008 US dollars

**GDP (official exchange rate):** $161.7 million (2008 est.)

**GDP - real growth rate:**
-0.3% (2008 est.)
3.5% (2005 est.)

**GDP - per capita (PPP):**
$2,500 (2008 est.)
$2,900 (2005 est.)
*note:* data are in 2008 US dollars

**GDP - composition by sector:**
*agriculture:* 31.7%
*industry:* 14.9%
*services:* 53.4% (2004 est.)

**Labor force:** 14,680 (2000)

**Labor force - by occupation:**
*agriculture:* 21.4%
*industry:* 20.9%
*services:* 57.7% (2000)

**Unemployment rate:**
36% (2006 est.)
30.9% (2000 est.)

**Population below poverty line:** NA%

**Household income or consumption by percentage share:**
*lowest 10%:* NA%
*highest 10%:* NA%

**Budget:**
*revenues:* $123.3 million
*expenditures:* $1.213 billion (2008)

**Inflation rate (consumer prices):**
12.9% (2008 est.)
3% (2005 est.)

**Agriculture - products:** coconuts, tomatoes, melons, taro, breadfruit, fruits; pigs, chickens

**Industries:** copra, tuna processing, tourism, craft items (from seashells, wood, and pearls)

**Industrial production growth rate:** NA%

**Exports:** $19.4 million f.o.b. (2008 est.)

**Exports - commodities:** copra cake, coconut oil, handicrafts, fish

**Imports:** $79.4 million f.o.b. (2008 est.)

**Imports - commodities:** foodstuffs, machinery and equipment, fuels, beverages and tobacco

**Debt - external:** $87 million (2008 est.)

**Exchange rates:** the US dollar is used

## Communications

**Telephones - main lines in use:** 4,500 (2004)

**Telephones - mobile cellular:** 700 (2005)

**Telephone system:**

*general assessment:* digital switching equipment; modern services include telex, cellular, Internet, international calling, caller ID, and leased data circuits

*domestic:* Majuro Atoll and Ebeye and Kwajalein islands have regular, seven-digit, direct-dial telephones; other islands interconnected by high frequency radiotelephone (used mostly for government purposes) and mini-satellite telephones

*international:* country code - 692; satellite earth stations - 2 Intelsat (Pacific Ocean); US Government satellite communications system on Kwajalein (2005)

**Radio broadcast stations:** AM 1, FM 3, shortwave 0 (additionally, the American Armed Forces Radio and Television Service (Central Pacific Network) operates one FM and one AM station on Kwajalein Island) (2005)

**Television broadcast stations:** 2 (both are US military stations; Marshalls Broadcasting Service, a cable company, operates on Majuro) (2005)

**Internet country code:** .mh

**Internet hosts:** 3 (2008)

**Internet users:** 2,200 (2006)

## Transportation

**Airports:** 15 (2008)

**Airports - with paved runways:**
*total:* 4
*1,524 to 2,437 m:* 3
*914 to 1,523 m:* 1 (2008)

**Airports - with unpaved runways:**
*total:* 11
*914 to 1,523 m:* 10
*under 914 m:* 1 (2008)

**Roadways:**
*total:* 2,028 km (includes 75 km of expressways) (2007)

**Merchant marine:**

*total:* 1,049

*by type:* barge carrier 1, bulk carrier 284, cargo 71, carrier 1, chemical tanker 191, combination ore/oil 4, container 188, liquefied gas 47, passenger 5, passenger/cargo 1, petroleum tanker 221, refrigerated cargo 13, roll on/roll off 14, specialized tanker 2, vehicle carrier 6

*foreign-owned:* 990 (Australia 1, Bermuda 4, Brazil 1, Canada 6, Chile 4, China 7, Croatia 6, Cyprus 37, Denmark 10, Germany 235, Greece 269, Hong Kong 4, Iceland 3, India 1, Ireland 1, Isle of Man 1, Italy 3, Japan 17, South Korea 10, Latvia 16, Malaysia 3, Mexico 4, Monaco 13, Netherlands 8, Norway 66, Pakistan 1, Panama 1, Romania 1, Russia 9, Saudi Arabia 5, Singapore 18, Slovenia 4, Spain 1, Sweden 1, Switzerland 12, Taiwan 1, Turkey 50, UAE 15, UK 10, US 123) (2008)

**Ports and terminals:** Majuro

### Military

**Military branches:** no regular military forces; under the 1983 Compact of Free Association, the US has full authority and responsibility for security and defense of the Marshall Islands; Marshall Islands Police (2009)

**Manpower available for military service:**

*males age 16-49:* 15,708 (2008 est.)

**Manpower fit for military service:**

*males age 16-49:* 13,041

*females age 16-49:* 13,199 (2009 est.)

**Manpower reaching militarily significant age annually:**

*male:* 540

*female:* 521 (2009 est.)

**Military expenditures:** NA

**Military - note:** defense is the responsibility of the US

### Transnational Issues

**Disputes - international:** claims US territory of Wake Island

# Mauritania

### Introduction

**Background:** Independent from France in 1960, Mauritania annexed the southern third of the former Spanish Sahara (now Western Sahara) in 1976, but relinquished it after three years of raids by the Polisario guerrilla front seeking independence for the territory. Maaouya Ould Sid Ahmed TAYA seized power in a coup in 1984 and ruled Mauritania with a heavy hand for more than two decades. A series of presidential elections that he held were widely seen as flawed. A bloodless coup in August 2005 deposed President TAYA and ushered in a military council that oversaw a transition to democratic rule. Independent candidate Sidi Ould Cheikh ABDALLAHI was inaugurated in April 2007 as Mauritania's first freely and fairly elected president. His term ended prematurely in August 2008 when a military junta deposed him and ushered in a military council government. Meanwhile, the country continues to experience ethnic tensions among its black population (Afro-Mauritanians) and White and Black Moor (Arab-Berber) communities.

### Geography

**Location:** Northern Africa, bordering the North Atlantic Ocean, between Senegal and Western Sahara

**Geographic coordinates:** 20 00 N, 12 00 W

**Map references:** Africa

**Area:**

*total:* 1,030,700 sq km

*land:* 1,030,400 sq km

*water:* 300 sq km

**Area - comparative:** slightly larger than three times the size of New Mexico

**Land boundaries:**

*total:* 5,074 km

*border countries:* Algeria 463 km, Mali 2,237 km, Senegal 813 km, Western Sahara 1,561 km

**Coastline:** 754 km

**Maritime claims:**

*territorial sea:* 12 nm

*contiguous zone:* 24 nm

*exclusive economic zone:* 200 nm

*continental shelf:* 200 nm or to the edge of the continental margin

**Climate:** desert; constantly hot, dry, dusty

**Terrain:** mostly barren, flat plains of the Sahara; some central hills

**Elevation extremes:**

*lowest point:* Sebkhet Te-n-Dghamcha -5 m

*highest point:* Kediet Ijill 915 m

**Natural resources:** iron ore, gypsum, copper, phosphate, diamonds, gold, oil, fish

**Land use:**

*arable land:* 0.2%

*permanent crops:* 0.01%

*other:* 99.79% (2005)

**Irrigated land:** 490 sq km (2002)

**Total renewable water resources:** 11.4 cu km (1997)

**Freshwater withdrawal (domestic/industrial/agricultural):**

*total:* 1.7 cu km/yr (9%/3%/88%)

*per capita:* 554 cu m/yr (2000)

**Natural hazards:** hot, dry, dust/sand-laden sirocco wind blows primarily in March and April; periodic droughts

**Environment - current issues:** overgrazing, deforestation, and soil erosion aggravated by drought are contributing to desertification; limited natural fresh water resources away from the Senegal, which is the only perennial river; locust infestation

**Environment - international agreements:**

*party to:* Biodiversity, Climate Change, Climate Change-Kyoto Protocol, Desertification, Endangered Species, Hazardous Wastes, Law of the Sea, Ozone Layer Protection, Ship Pollution, Wetlands, Whaling

*signed, but not ratified:* none of the selected agreements

**Geography - note:** most of the population concentrated in the cities of Nouakchott and Nouadhibou and along the Senegal River in the southern part of the country

### People

**Population:** 3,129,486 (July 2009 est.)

**Age structure:**

*0-14 years:* 41% (male 643,436/female 638,793)

*15-64 years:* 55.7% (male 818,778/female 923,046)

*65 years and over:* 3.4% (male 44,836/female 60,597) (2009 est.)

**Median age:**

*total:* 19.2 years

*male:* 18.3 years

*female:* 20 years (2009 est.)

**Population growth rate:** 2.399% (2009 est.)

**Birth rate:** 34.11 births/1,000 population (2009 est.)

**Death rate:** 11.61 deaths/1,000 population (2008 est.)

**Net migration rate:** -0.96 migrant(s)/1,000 population (2009 est.)

# Mauritania *(continued)*

**Urbanization:**

*urban population:* 41% of total population (2008)
*rate of urbanization:* 3% annual rate of change
(2005-10 est.)

**Sex ratio:**

*at birth:* 1.03 male(s)/female
*under 15 years:* 1.01 male(s)/female
*15-64 years:* 0.89 male(s)/female
*65 years and over:* 0.74 male(s)/female
*total population:* 0.93 male(s)/female (2009 est.)

**Infant mortality rate:**

*total:* 63.42 deaths/1,000 live births
*male:* 68.65 deaths/1,000 live births
*female:* 58.03 deaths/1,000 live births (2009 est.)

**Life expectancy at birth:**

*total population:* 60.37 years
*male:* 58.22 years
*female:* 62.59 years (2009 est.)

**Total fertility rate:** 4.45 children born/woman
(2009 est.)

**HIV/AIDS - adult prevalence rate:** 0.8% (2007 est.)

**HIV/AIDS - people living with HIV/AIDS:** 14,000
(2007 est.)

**HIV/AIDS - deaths:** fewer than 1,000 (2007 est.)

**Major infectious diseases:**

*degree of risk:* high
*food or waterborne diseases:* bacterial and protozoal
diarrhea, hepatitis A, and typhoid fever
*vectorborne diseases:* malaria and Rift Valley fever
*respiratory disease:* meningococcal meningitis
*animal contact disease:* rabies (2009)

**Nationality:**

*noun:* Mauritanian(s)
*adjective:* Mauritanian

**Ethnic groups:** mixed Moor/black 40%, Moor 30%,
black 30%

**Religions:** Muslim 100%

**Languages:** Arabic (official and national), Pulaar,
Soninke, Wolof (all national languages), French,
Hassaniya

**Literacy:**

*definition:* age 15 and over can read and write
*total population:* 51.2%
*male:* 59.5%
*female:* 43.4% (2000 census)

**School life expectancy (primary to tertiary
education):**

*total:* 8 years
*male:* 8 years
*female:* 8 years (2006)

**Education expenditures:** 2.9% of GDP (2006)

## Government

**Country name:**

*conventional long form:* Islamic Republic of
Mauritania
*conventional short form:* Mauritania
*local long form:* Al Jumhuriyah al Islamiyah al
Muritaniyah
*local short form:* Muritaniyah

**Government type:** military junta

**Capital:**

*name:* Nouakchott
*geographic coordinates:* 18 07 N, 16 02 W
*time difference:* UTC 0 (5 hours ahead of Washington,
DC during Standard Time)

**Administrative divisions:** 12 regions (regions,
singular - region) and 1 capital district*; Adrar,
Assaba, Brakna, Dakhlet Nouadhibou, Gorgol,
Guidimaka, Hodh Ech Chargui, Hodh El Gharbi,
Inchiri, Nouakchott*, Tagant, Tiris Zemmour, Trarza

**Independence:** 28 November 1960 (from France)

**National holiday:** Independence Day, 28 November
(1960)

**Constitution:** 12 July 1991

**Legal system:** a combination of Islamic law and
French civil law; has not accepted compulsory ICJ
jurisdiction

**Suffrage:** 18 years of age; universal

**Executive branch:**

*chief of state:* Ba Mamadou MBARE, as President of
the Senate is Acting President following the resignation
of Gen. Mohamed Ould Abdul AZIZ; note -AZIZ, who
deposed democratically elected President Sidi Ould
Cheikh ABDELLAHI in a coup and installed himself as
President of Military High Council of State on 6 August
2008, resigned from all political military positions as
required under the constitution to become a candidate
in the 18 July 2009 presidential election
*head of government:* Prime Minister Moulaye Ould
Mohamed LAGHDAF (since 14 August 2008)
*cabinet:* Council of Ministers
*elections:* following the August 2008 coup, the Military
High Council of State pledged to hold a new
presidential election now scheduled for 18 July 2009;
under Mauritania's constitution, the president is
elected by popular vote for a five-year term; election
last held 11 March 2007 with a runoff between the two
leading candidates held on 25 March 2007; prime
minister appointed by the president
*election results:* percent of vote - (second round) Sidi
Ould Cheikh ABDELLAHI 52.8%, Ahmed Ould
DADDAH 47.2%

**Legislative branch:** bicameral legislature consists
of the Senate or Majlis al-Shuyukh (56 seats; 53
members elected by municipal leaders and 3
members elected by Mauritanians abroad to serve
six-year terms; a portion of seats up for election every
two years) and the National Assembly or Majlis
al-Watani (95 seats; members elected by popular vote
to serve five-year terms)
*elections:* Senate - last held 21 January and
4 February 2007 (next to be held in 2009); National
Assembly - last held 19 November and 3 December
2006 (next to be held in 2011); note - it is unclear when
the Senate elections originally scheduled for 2009 will
be held
*election results:* Senate - percent of vote by party -
NA; seats by party - Mithaq (coalition of independents
and parties associated with the former regime) 37,
CFCD (coalition of political parties) 15,
representatives of the diaspora 3, undecided 1;

National Assembly - percent of vote by party - NA;
seats by party - Mithaq 51 (independents 37, PRDR 7,
UDP 3, RDU 3, Alternative (El-Badil) 1), CFCD 41
(RFD 16, UFP 9, APP 6, Centrist Reformists 4,
HATEM-PMUC 3, RD 2, PUDS 1), RNDLE 1, UCD 1,
FP 1

**Judicial branch:** Supreme Court or Cour Supreme;
Court of Appeals; lower courts

**Political parties and leaders:** Alternative or El-Badil
[Mohamed Yahdhi Ould MOCTAR HACEN]; Centrist
Reformists (independent moderate Islamists)
[Mohamed Jamil MANSOUR]; Coalition for Forces for
Democratic Change or CFCD (coalition of political
parties including APP, Centrist Reformists
(independent moderate Islamists), HATEM-PMUC,
PUDS, RD, RFD, UFP); Democratic Renewal or RD
[Moustapha Ould ABDEIDARRAHMANE]; Mauritanian
Party for Unity and Change or HATEM-PMUC [Saleh
Ould HANENA]; Mithaq (coalition of independents and
parties associated with the former regime including
Alternative or El-Badil, PRDR, UDP, RDU); National
Pact for Democracy and Development or PNDD-ADIL
(independents supporting President Abdellahi) [Yahya
Ould Ahmed Ould WAGHEF]; National Rally for
Freedom, Democracy and Equality or RNDLE; National
Rally for Reform and Development or Tawassoul
(moderate Islamists) [Mohamed Jemil Ould
MANSOUR]; Popular Front or FP [Ch'bih Ould CHEIKH
MALAININE]; Popular Progressive Alliance or APP
[Messoud Ould BOULKHEIR]; Rally of Democratic
Forces or RFD [Ahmed Ould DADDAH]; Rally for
Democracy and Unity or RDU [Ahmed Ould SIDI
BABA]; Republican Party for Democracy and Renewal
or PRDR [Boullah Ould MOGUEYA]; Socialist and
Democratic Unity Party or PUDS; Union for Democracy
and Progress or UDP [Naha Mint MOUKNASS]; Union
of Democratic Center or UCD [Cheikh Sid'Ahmed Ould
BABA]; Union of the Forces for Progress or UFP
[Mohamed Ould MAOULOUD];

**Political pressure groups and leaders:** General
Confederation of Mauritanian Workers or CGTM
[Abdallahi Ould MOHAMED, secretary general];
Independent Confederation of Mauritanian Workers or
CLTM [Samory Ould BEYE]; Mauritanian Workers
Union or UTM [Mohamed Ely Ould BRAHIM,
secretary general]
*other:* Arab nationalists; Ba'thists; Islamists

**International organization participation:** ABEDA,
ACP, AfDB, AFESD, AMF, AMU, AU, CAEU, FAO,
G-77, IAEA, IBRD, ICAO, ICRM, IDA, IDB, IFAD, IFC,
IFRCS, ILO, IMF, IMO, Interpol, IOC, IOM, IPU, ITSO,
ITU, ITUC, LAS, MIGA, NAM, OIC, OIF, OPCW, UN,
UNCTAD, UNESCO, UNIDO, UNWTO, UPU, WCL,
WCO, WFTU, WHO, WIPO, WMO, WTO

**Diplomatic representation in the US:**

*chief of mission:* Ambassador Ibrahima DIA
*chancery:* 2129 Leroy Place NW, Washington, DC
20008
*telephone:* [1] (202) 232-5700 through 5701
*FAX:* [1] (202) 319-2623

# Mauritania (continued)

## Diplomatic representation from the US:
*chief of mission:* Ambassador Mark M. BOULWARE
*embassy:* 288 Rue Abdallaye, Rue 42-100 (between Presidency building and Spanish Embassy), Nouakchott
*mailing address:* BP 222, Nouakchott
*telephone:* [222] 525-2660 through 2663
*FAX:* [222] 525-1592
**Flag description:** green with a yellow five-pointed star above a yellow, horizontal crescent; the closed side of the crescent is down; the crescent, star, and color green are traditional symbols of Islam

## Economy

**Economy - overview:** Half the population still depends on agriculture and livestock for a livelihood, even though many of the nomads and subsistence farmers were forced into the cities by recurrent droughts in the 1970s and 1980s. Mauritania has extensive deposits of iron ore, which account for nearly 40% of total exports. The nation's coastal waters are among the richest fishing areas in the world, but overexploitation by foreigners threatens this key source of revenue. The country's first deepwater port opened near Nouakchott in 1986. Before 2000, drought and economic mismanagement resulted in a buildup of foreign debt. In February 2000, Mauritania qualified for debt relief under the Heavily Indebted Poor Countries (HIPC) initiative and nearly all of its foreign debt has since been forgiven. In December 2007 donors pledged $2.1 billion at a triennial Consultative Group review. A new investment code approved in December 2001 improved the opportunities for direct foreign investment. Mauritania and the IMF agreed to a three-year Poverty Reduction and Growth Facility (PRGF) arrangement in 2006 and Mauritania made satisfactory progress, but IMF and World Bank have suspended their programs in Mauritania since the August 2008 coup. Oil prospects, while initially promising, have largely failed to materialize. The Government continues to emphasize reduction of poverty, improvement of health and education, and privatization of the economy.
**GDP (purchasing power parity):**
$6.31 billion (2008 est.)
$6.096 billion (2007)
$6.036 billion (2006)
*note:* data are in 2008 US dollars
**GDP (official exchange rate):** $3.625 billion (2008 est.)
**GDP - real growth rate:**
3.5% (2008 est.)
1% (2007 est.)
11.4% (2006 est.)
**GDP - per capita (PPP):**
$2,100 (2008 est.)
$2,000 (2007 est.)
$2,100 (2006 est.)
*note:* data are in 2008 US dollars

**GDP - composition by sector:**
*agriculture:* 12.5%
*industry:* 46.7%
*services:* 40.7% (2008 est.)
**Labor force:** 786,000 (2001)
**Labor force - by occupation:**
*agriculture:* 50%
*industry:* 10%
*services:* 40% (2001 est.)
**Unemployment rate:**
30% (2008 est.)
20% (2004 est.)
**Population below poverty line:** 40% (2004 est.)
**Household income or consumption by percentage share:**
*lowest 10%:* 2.5%
*highest 10%:* 29.5% (2000)
**Distribution of family income - Gini index:** 39 (2000)
**Budget:**
*revenues:* $770 million
*expenditures:* $770 million (2007 est.)
**Inflation rate (consumer prices):**
7.3% (2007 est.)
**Central bank discount rate:** NA
**Stock of money:** NA
**Stock of quasi money:** NA
**Stock of domestic credit:** NA
**Market value of publicly traded shares:** $NA
**Agriculture - products:** dates, millet, sorghum, rice, corn; cattle, sheep
**Industries:** fish processing, oil production, mining of iron ore, gold, and copper; gypsum deposits have never been exploited
**Industrial production growth rate:** 2% (2000 est.)
**Electricity - production:** 412.3 million kWh (2006 est.)
**Electricity - consumption:** 383.4 million kWh (2006 est.)
**Electricity - exports:** 0 kWh (2007 est.)
**Electricity - imports:** 0 kWh (2007 est.)
**Oil - production:** 14,990 bbl/day (2007 est.)
**Oil - consumption:** 19,320 bbl/day (2006 est.)
**Oil - exports:** 14,990 bbl/day (2007 est.)
**Oil - imports:** 23,630 bbl/day (2005)
**Oil - proved reserves:** 100 million bbl (1 January 2008 est.)
**Natural gas - production:** 0 cu m (2007 est.)
**Natural gas - consumption:** 0 cu m (2007 est.)
**Natural gas - exports:** 0 cu m (2007 est.)
**Natural gas - imports:** 0 cu m (2007 est.)
**Natural gas - proved reserves:** 28.32 billion cu m (1 January 2008 est.)
**Current account balance:** -$184 million (2007 est.)
**Exports:** $1.395 billion f.o.b. (2006)
**Exports - commodities:** iron ore, fish and fish products, gold, copper, petroleum
**Exports - partners:** China 30.5%, France 9.5%, Italy 8.5%, Spain 8.5%, Japan 5.5%, Netherlands 5.3%, Belgium 5%, Cote d'Ivoire 4.7% (2007)

**Imports:** $1.475 billion f.o.b. (2006)
**Imports - commodities:** machinery and equipment, petroleum products, capital goods, foodstuffs, consumer goods
**Imports - partners:** France 16.5%, China 8.1%, Spain 6.7%, US 6.1%, Belgium 5.8%, Brazil 5.7% (2007)
**Debt - external:** $NA
**Exchange rates:** ouguiyas (MRO) per US dollar - NA (2007), 271.3 (2006), 267.04 (2005), 265.8 (2004), 263.03 (2003)

## Communications

**Telephones - main lines in use:** 34,900 (2006)
**Telephones - mobile cellular:** 1.3 million (2007)
**Telephone system:**
*general assessment:* limited system of cable and open-wire lines, minor microwave radio relay links, and radiotelephone communications stations; mobile-cellular services expanding rapidly
*domestic:* Mauritel, the national telecommunications company, was privatized in 2001 but remains the monopoly provider of fixed-line services; fixed-line teledensity 1 per 100 persons; mobile-cellular network coverage extends mainly to urban areas with a teledensity approaching 40 per 100 persons; mostly cable and open-wire lines; a domestic satellite telecommunications system links Nouakchott with regional capitals
*international:* country code - 222; satellite earth stations - 3 (1 Intelsat - Atlantic Ocean, 2 Arabsat)
**Radio broadcast stations:** AM 1, FM 14, shortwave 1 (2001)
**Television broadcast stations:** 1 (2002)
**Internet country code:** .mr
**Internet hosts:** 34 (2008)
**Internet users:** 30,000 (2006)

## Transportation

**Airports:** 24 (2008)
**Airports - with paved runways:**
*total:* 8
*2,438 to 3,047 m:* 4
*1,524 to 2,437 m:* 4 (2008)
**Airports - with unpaved runways:**
*total:* 16
*1,524 to 2,437 m:* 8
*914 to 1,523 m:* 7
*under 914 m:* 1 (2008)
**Railways:** 717 km
*standard gauge:* 717 km 1.435-m gauge (2006)
**Roadways:**
*total:* 11,066 km
*paved:* 2,966 km
*unpaved:* 8,100 km (2006)
**Waterways:** some navigation possible on Senegal River
**Ports and terminals:** Nouadhibou, Nouakchott

**Military branches:** Mauritanian Armed Forces: Army, Mauritanian Navy (Marine Mauritanienne; includes naval infantry), Islamic Air Force of Mauritania (Force Aerienne Islamique de Mauritanie, FAIM) (2008)

**Military service age and obligation:** 18 years of age (est.); conscript service obligation - 2 years; majority of servicemen believed to be volunteers; service in Air Force and Navy is voluntary (2006)

**Manpower available for military service:**
*males age 16-49:* 740,675
*females age 16-49:* 744,709 (2008 est.)

**Manpower fit for military service:**
*males age 16-49:* 450,289
*females age 16-49:* 544,598 (2009 est.)

**Manpower reaching militarily significant age annually:**
*male:* 34,546
*female:* 35,272 (2009 est.)

**Military expenditures:** 5.5% of GDP (2006)

## Transnational Issues

**Disputes - international:** Mauritanian claims to Western Sahara remain dormant

# Mauritius

Agalega Islands, Cargados Carajos Shoals, and Rodrigues are not shown.

## Introduction

**Background:** Although known to Arab and Malay sailors as early as the 10th century, Mauritius was first explored by the Portuguese in the 16th century and subsequently settled by the Dutch - who named it in honor of Prince Maurits van NASSAU - in the 17th century. The French assumed control in 1715, developing the island into an important naval base overseeing Indian Ocean trade, and establishing a plantation economy of sugar cane. The British captured the island in 1810, during the Napoleonic Wars. Mauritius remained a strategically important British naval base, and later an air station, playing an important role during World War II for anti-submarine and convoy operations, as well as the collection of signals intelligence. Independence from the UK was attained in 1968. A stable democracy with regular free elections and a positive human rights record, the country has attracted considerable foreign investment and has earned one of Africa's highest per capita incomes. Recent poor weather, declining sugar prices, and declining textile and apparel production, have slowed economic growth, leading to some protests over standards of living in the Creole community.

## Geography

**Location:** Southern Africa, island in the Indian Ocean, east of Madagascar

**Geographic coordinates:** 20 17 S, 57 33 E

**Map references:** Political Map of the World

**Area:**
*total:* 2,040 sq km
*land:* 2,030 sq km
*water:* 10 sq km
*note:* includes Agalega Islands, Cargados Carajos Shoals (Saint Brandon), and Rodrigues

**Area - comparative:** almost 11 times the size of Washington, DC

**Land boundaries:** 0 km

**Coastline:** 177 km

**Maritime claims:** measured from claimed archipelagic straight baselines
*territorial sea:* 12 nm
*exclusive economic zone:* 200 nm
*continental shelf:* 200 nm or to the edge of the continental margin

**Climate:** tropical, modified by southeast trade winds; warm, dry winter (May to November); hot, wet, humid summer (November to May)

**Terrain:** small coastal plain rising to discontinuous mountains encircling central plateau

**Elevation extremes:**
*lowest point:* Indian Ocean 0 m
*highest point:* Mont Piton 828 m

**Natural resources:** arable land, fish

**Land use:**
*arable land:* 49.02%
*permanent crops:* 2.94%
*other:* 48.04% (2005)

**Irrigated land:** 220 sq km (2003)

**Total renewable water resources:** 2.2 cu km (2001)

**Freshwater withdrawal (domestic/industrial/agricultural):**
*total:* 0.61 cu km/yr (25%/14%/60%)
*per capita:* 488 cu m/yr (2000)

**Natural hazards:** cyclones (November to April); almost completely surrounded by reefs that may pose maritime hazards

**Environment - current issues:** water pollution, degradation of coral reefs

**Environment - international agreements:**
*party to:* Antarctic-Marine Living Resources, Biodiversity, Climate Change, Climate Change-Kyoto Protocol, Desertification, Endangered Species, Environmental Modification, Hazardous Wastes, Law of the Sea, Marine Life Conservation, Ozone Layer Protection, Ship Pollution, Wetlands
*signed, but not ratified:* none of the selected agreements

**Geography - note:** the main island, from which the country derives its name, is of volcanic origin and is almost entirely surrounded by coral reefs; home of the dodo, a large flightless bird related to pigeons, driven to extinction by the end of the 17th century through a combination of hunting and the introduction of predatory species

## People

**Population:** 1,284,264 (July 2009 est.)

**Age structure:**
*0-14 years:* 22.5% (male 147,136/female 142,121)
*15-64 years:* 70.4% (male 449,176/female 455,057)
*65 years and over:* 7.1% (male 36,309/female 54,465) (2009 est.)

**Median age:**
*total:* 31.9 years
*male:* 31 years
*female:* 32.7 years (2009 est.)

# Mauritius (continued)

**Population growth rate:** 0.776% (2009 est.)
**Birth rate:** 14.41 births/1,000 population (2009 est.)
**Death rate:** 6.55 deaths/1,000 population (2008 est.)
**Net migration rate:** -0.06 migrant(s)/1,000 population (2009 est.)
**Urbanization:**
*urban population:* 42% of total population (2008)
*rate of urbanization:* 0.9% annual rate of change (2005-10 est.)
**Sex ratio:**
*at birth:* 1.05 male(s)/female
*under 15 years:* 1.03 male(s)/female
*15-64 years:* 0.99 male(s)/female
*65 years and over:* 0.67 male(s)/female
*total population:* 0.97 male(s)/female (2009 est.)
**Infant mortality rate:**
*total:* 12.2 deaths/1,000 live births
*male:* 14.51 deaths/1,000 live births
*female:* 9.77 deaths/1,000 live births (2009 est.)
**Life expectancy at birth:**
*total population:* 74 years
*male:* 70.53 years
*female:* 77.65 years (2009 est.)
**Total fertility rate:** 1.81 children born/woman (2009 est.)
**HIV/AIDS - adult prevalence rate:** 1.7% (2007 est.)
**HIV/AIDS - people living with HIV/AIDS:** 13,000 (2007 est.)
**HIV/AIDS - deaths:** fewer than 100 (2001 est.)
**Nationality:**
*noun:* Mauritian(s)
*adjective:* Mauritian
**Ethnic groups:** Indo-Mauritian 68%, Creole 27%, Sino-Mauritian 3%, Franco-Mauritian 2%
**Religions:** Hindu 48%, Roman Catholic 23.6%, Muslim 16.6%, other Christian 8.6%, other 2.5%, unspecified 0.3%, none 0.4% (2000 census)
**Languages:** Creole 80.5%, Bhojpuri 12.1%, French 3.4%, English (official; spoken by less than 1% of the population), other 3.7%, unspecified 0.3% (2000 census)
**Literacy:**
*definition:* age 15 and over can read and write
*total population:* 84.4%
*male:* 88.4%
*female:* 80.5% (2000 census)
**School life expectancy (primary to tertiary education):**
*total:* 14 years
*male:* 14 years
*female:* 13 years (2005)
**Education expenditures:** 3.9% of GDP (2006)

## Government

**Country name:**
*conventional long form:* Republic of Mauritius
*conventional short form:* Mauritius
*local long form:* Republic of Mauritius
*local short form:* Mauritius
**Government type:** parliamentary democracy

**Capital:**
*name:* Port Louis
*geographic coordinates:* 20 09 S, 57 29 E
*time difference:* UTC+4 (9 hours ahead of Washington, DC during Standard Time)
**Administrative divisions:** 9 districts and 3 dependencies*; Agalega Islands*, Black River, Cargados Carajos Shoals*, Flacq, Grand Port, Moka, Pamplemousses, Plaines Wilhems, Port Louis, Riviere du Rempart, Rodrigues*, Savanne
**Independence:** 12 March 1968 (from the UK)
**National holiday:** Independence Day, 12 March (1968)
**Constitution:** 12 March 1968; amended 12 March 1992
**Legal system:** based on French civil law system with elements of English common law in certain areas; accepts compulsory ICJ jurisdiction with reservations
**Suffrage:** 18 years of age; universal
**Executive branch:**
*chief of state:* President Sir Anerood JUGNAUTH (since 7 October 2003); Vice President Abdool Raouf BUNDHUN (since 25 February 2002)
*head of government:* Prime Minister Navinchandra RAMGOOLAM (since 5 July 2005)
*cabinet:* Council of Ministers appointed by the president on the recommendation of the prime minister
*elections:* president and vice president elected by the National Assembly for five-year terms (eligible for a second term); election last held 19 September 2008 (next to be held in 2013); prime minister and deputy prime minister appointed by the president, responsible to the National Assembly
*election results:* Sir Anerood JUGNAUTH reelected president by unanimous vote; percent of vote by the National Assembly - NA%
**Legislative branch:** unicameral National Assembly (70 seats; 62 members elected by popular vote, 8 appointed by the election commission to give representation to various ethnic minorities; to serve five-year terms)
*elections:* last held on 3 July 2005 (next to be held in 2010)
*election results:* percent of vote by party - NA; seats by party - AS 38, MSM/MMM 22, OPR 2; appointed seats - AS 4, MSM/MMM 2, OPR 2
**Judicial branch:** Supreme Court
**Political parties and leaders:** Alliance Sociale or AS [Navinchandra RAMGOOLAM] (governing coalition - includes MLD, MMSM, MR, MSD, PMXD); Mauritian Labor Party or MLP [Navinchandra RAMGOOLAM]; Mauritian Militant Movement or MMM [Paul BERENGER]; Mauritian Socialist Militant Movement or MMSM [Madan DULLOO]; Militant Socialist Movement or MSM [Pravind JUGNAUTH]; Mouvement Republicain or MR [Jayarama VALAYDEN]; Parti Mauricien Xavier Duval or PMXD [Xavier Luc DUVAL]; Rodrigues Movement or MR [Joseph (Nicholas) Von MALLY]; Rodrigues Peoples Organization or OPR [Serge CLAIR]

**Political pressure groups and leaders:**
*other:* various labor unions
**International organization participation:** ACP, AfDB, AU, C, COMESA, CPLP (associate), FAO, G-77, IAEA, IBRD, ICAO, ICCt, ICRM, IDA, IFAD, IFC, IFRCS, IHO, ILO, IMF, IMO, IMSO, InOC, Interpol, IOC, IOM, IPU, ISO, ITSO, ITU, ITUC, MIGA, NAM, OIF, OPCW, PCA, SAARC (observer), SADC, UN, UNCTAD, UNESCO, UNIDO, UNWTO, UPU, WCL, WCO, WFTU, WHO, WIPO, WMO, WTO
**Diplomatic representation in the US:**
*chief of mission:* Ambassador Keerteecoomar RUHEE
*chancery:* 4301 Connecticut Avenue NW, Suite 441, Washington, DC 20008
*telephone:* [1] (202) 244-1491 through 1492
*FAX:* [1] (202) 966-0983
**Diplomatic representation from the US:**
*chief of mission:* Ambassador Cesar CABRERA
*embassy:* 4th Floor, Rogers House, John Kennedy Street, Port Louis
*mailing address:* international mail: P. O. Box 544, Port Louis; US mail: American Embassy, Port Louis, US Department of State, Washington, DC 20521-2450
*telephone:* [230] 202-4400
*FAX:* [230] 208-9534
**Flag description:** four equal horizontal bands of red (top), blue, yellow, and green

## Economy

**Economy - overview:** Since independence in 1968, Mauritius has developed from a low-income, agriculturally based economy to a middle-income diversified economy with growing industrial, financial, and tourist sectors. For most of the period, annual growth has been in the order of 5% to 6%. This remarkable achievement has been reflected in more equitable income distribution, increased life expectancy, lowered infant mortality, and a much-improved infrastructure. The economy rests on sugar, tourism, textiles and apparel, and financial services, and is expanding into fish processing, information and communications technology, and hospitality and property development. Sugarcane is grown on about 90% of the cultivated land area and accounts for 15% of export earnings. The government's development strategy centers on creating vertical and horizontal clusters of development in these sectors. Mauritius has attracted more than 32,000 offshore entities, many aimed at commerce in India, South Africa, and China. Investment in the banking sector alone has reached over $1 billion. Mauritius, with its strong textile sector, has been well poised to take advantage of the Africa Growth and Opportunity Act (AGOA).
**GDP (purchasing power parity):**
$15.36 billion (2008 est.)
$14.6 billion (2007)
$13.86 billion (2006)
*note:* data are in 2008 US dollars

# Mauritius *(continued)*

**GDP (official exchange rate):** $8.128 billion (2008 est.)

**GDP - real growth rate:**
5.2% (2008 est.)
5.4% (2007 est.)
5.1% (2006 est.)

**GDP - per capita (PPP):**
$12,100 (2008 est.)
$11,600 (2007 est.)
$11,100 (2006 est.)
*note:* data are in 2008 US dollars

**GDP - composition by sector:**
*agriculture:* 4.5%
*industry:* 24.9%
*services:* 70.6% (2008 est.)

**Labor force:** 584,000 (2008 est.)

**Labor force - by occupation:** agriculture and fishing 9%, construction and industry 30%, transportation and communication 7%, trade, restaurants, hotels 22%, finance 6%, other services 25% (2007)

**Unemployment rate:**
7.6% (2008 est.)
8.8% (2007 est.)

**Population below poverty line:** 8% (2006 est.)

**Household income or consumption by percentage share:**
*lowest 10%:* NA%
*highest 10%:* NA%

**Distribution of family income - Gini index:** 39 (2006 est.)

**Investment (gross fixed):** 27.1% of GDP (2008 est.)

**Budget:**
*revenues:* $1.866 billion
*expenditures:* $2.243 billion; including capital expenditures of $NA (2008 est.)

**Public debt:** 57.2% of GDP (2008 est.)

**Inflation rate (consumer prices):**
10.1% (2008 est.)
8.8% (2007 est.)

**Commercial bank prime lending rate:** 21.87% (31 December 2007)

**Stock of money:** $1.673 billion (31 December 2007)

**Stock of quasi money:** $6.759 billion (31 December 2007)

**Stock of domestic credit:** $8.582 billion (31 December 2007)

**Market value of publicly traded shares:** $5.666 billion (31 December 2007)

**Agriculture - products:** sugarcane, tea, corn, potatoes, bananas, pulses; cattle, goats; fish

**Industries:** food processing (largely sugar milling), textiles, clothing, mining, chemicals, metal products, transport equipment, nonelectrical machinery, tourism

**Industrial production growth rate:** 4.5% (2008 est.)

**Electricity - production:** 2.321 billion kWh (2007 est.)

**Electricity - consumption:** 2.058 billion kWh (2006 est.)

**Electricity - exports:** 0 kWh (2007 est.)

**Electricity - imports:** 0 kWh (2007 est.)

**Oil - production:** 0 bbl/day (2007 est.)

**Oil - consumption:** 22,450 bbl/day (2006 est.)

**Oil - exports:** 0 bbl/day (2006)

**Oil - imports:** 23,650 bbl/day (2006)

**Oil - proved reserves:** 0 bbl (1 January 2006 est.)

**Natural gas - production:** 0 cu m (2007 est.)

**Natural gas - consumption:** 0 cu m (2007 est.)

**Natural gas - exports:** 0 cu m (2007 est.)

**Natural gas - imports:** 0 cu m (2007 est.)

**Natural gas - proved reserves:** 0 cu m (1 January 2006 est.)

**Current account balance:** -$982 million (2008 est.)

**Exports:** $2.36 billion f.o.b. (2008 est.)

**Exports - commodities:** clothing and textiles, sugar, cut flowers, molasses, fish

**Exports - partners:** UK 35.1%, France 14.4%, US 7.7%, Madagascar 6.3%, Italy 5.8% (2007)

**Imports:** $4.503 billion f.o.b. (2008 est.)

**Imports - commodities:** manufactured goods, capital equipment, foodstuffs, petroleum products, chemicals

**Imports - partners:** India 21.2%, China 11.4%, France 10.7%, South Africa 7.4% (2007)

**Reserves of foreign exchange and gold:** $1.909 billion (31 December 2008 est.)

**Debt - external:** $2.55 billion (31 December 2008 est.)

**Stock of direct foreign investment - at home:** $NA

**Stock of direct foreign investment - abroad:** $NA

**Exchange rates:** Mauritian rupees (MUR) per US dollar - 27.973 (2008 est.), 31.798 (2007), 31.656 (2006), 29.496 (2005), 27.499 (2004)

## Communications

**Telephones - main lines in use:** 357,300 (2006)

**Telephones - mobile cellular:** 936,000 (2007)

**Telephone system:**
*general assessment:* small system with good service
*domestic:* monopoly over fixed-line services terminated in 2005; fixed-line teledensity roughly 30 per 100 persons; mobile-cellular services launched in 1989 with teledensity in 2007 reaching 75 per 100 persons
*international:* country code - 230; landing point for the SAFE submarine cable that provides links to Asia and South Africa where it connects to the SAT-3/WASC submarine cable that provides further links to parts of East Africa, and Europe; satellite earth station - 1 Intelsat (Indian Ocean); new microwave link to Reunion; HF radiotelephone links to several countries

**Radio broadcast stations:** AM 4, FM 9, shortwave 0 (2001)

**Television broadcast stations:** 2 (plus several repeaters) (1997)

**Internet country code:** .mu

**Internet hosts:** 9,609 (2008)

**Internet users:** 340,000 (2007)

## Transportation

**Airports:** 5 (2008)

**Airports - with paved runways:**
*total:* 2
*over 3,047 m:* 1
*914 to 1,523 m:* 1 (2008)

**Airports - with unpaved runways:**
*total:* 3
*914 to 1,523 m:* 2
*under 914 m:* 1 (2008)

**Roadways:**
*total:* 2,028 km
*paved:* 2,028 km (includes 75 km of expressways) (2007)

**Merchant marine:**
*total:* 3
*by type:* passenger/cargo 2, refrigerated cargo 1 (2008)

**Ports and terminals:** Port Louis

## Military

**Military branches:** no regular military forces; National Police Force, Special Mobile Force, National Coast Guard (2008)

**Manpower available for military service:**
*males age 16-49:* 341,018 (2008 est.)

**Manpower fit for military service:**
*males age 16-49:* 277,690
*females age 16-49:* 282,211 (2009 est.)

**Manpower reaching militarily significant age annually:**
*male:* 10,901
*female:* 10,796 (2009 est.)

**Military expenditures:** 0.3% of GDP (2006 est.)

## Transnational Issues

**Disputes - international:** Mauritius claims the Chagos Archipelago (UK-administered British Indian Ocean Territory), and its former inhabitants, who reside chiefly in Mauritius; claims French-administered Tromelin Island

**Illicit drugs:** consumer and transshipment point for heroin from South Asia; small amounts of cannabis produced and consumed locally; significant offshore financial industry creates potential for money laundering, but corruption levels are relatively low and the government appears generally to be committed to regulating its banking industry

# Mayotte
*(overseas collectivity of France)*

Administered by FRANCE, claimed by COMOROS.

## Introduction

**Background:** Mayotte was ceded to France along with the other islands of the Comoros group in 1843. It was the only island in the archipelago that voted in 1974 to retain its link with France and forego independence.

## Geography

**Location:** Southern Indian Ocean, island in the Mozambique Channel, about half way between northern Madagascar and northern Mozambique

**Geographic coordinates:** 12 50 S, 45 10 E

**Map references:** Africa

**Area:**
*total:* 374 sq km
*land:* 374 sq km
*water:* 0 sq km

**Area - comparative:** slightly more than twice the size of Washington, DC

**Land boundaries:** 0 km

**Coastline:** 185.2 km

**Maritime claims:**
*territorial sea:* 12 nm
*exclusive economic zone:* 200 nm

**Climate:** tropical; marine; hot, humid, rainy season during northeastern monsoon (November to May); dry season is cooler (May to November)

**Terrain:** generally undulating, with deep ravines and ancient volcanic peaks

**Elevation extremes:**
*lowest point:* Indian Ocean 0 m
*highest point:* Benara 660 m

**Natural resources:** NEGL

**Land use:**
*arable land:* NA%
*permanent crops:* NA%
*other:* NA%

**Irrigated land:** NA

**Natural hazards:** cyclones during rainy season

**Environment - current issues:** NA

**Geography - note:** part of Comoro Archipelago (18 islands)

## People

**Population:** 223,765 (July 2009 est.)

**Age structure:**
*0-14 years:* 45.3% (male 50,985/female 50,413)
*15-64 years:* 52.9% (male 63,395/female 54,882)
*65 years and over:* 1.8% (male 2,085/female 2,005) (2009 est.)

**Median age:**
*total:* 17.2 years
*male:* 18.1 years
*female:* 16.4 years (2009 est.)

**Population growth rate:** 3.317% (2009 est.)

**Birth rate:** 39.26 births/1,000 population (2009 est.)

**Death rate:** 7.36 deaths/1,000 population (2008 est.)

**Net migration rate:** 1.11 migrant(s)/1,000 population (2009 est.)

**Sex ratio:**
*at birth:* 1.03 male(s)/female
*under 15 years:* 1.01 male(s)/female
*15-64 years:* 1.16 male(s)/female
*65 years and over:* 1.04 male(s)/female
*total population:* 1.08 male(s)/female (2009 est.)

**Infant mortality rate:**
*total:* 56.29 deaths/1,000 live births
*male:* 61.89 deaths/1,000 live births
*female:* 50.53 deaths/1,000 live births (2009 est.)

**Life expectancy at birth:**
*total population:* 62.91 years
*male:* 60.65 years
*female:* 65.24 years (2009 est.)

**Total fertility rate:** 5.5 children born/woman (2009 est.)

**HIV/AIDS - adult prevalence rate:** NA

**HIV/AIDS - people living with HIV/AIDS:** NA

**HIV/AIDS - deaths:** NA

**Nationality:**
*noun:* Mahorais (singular and plural)
*adjective:* Mahoran

**Ethnic groups:** NA

**Religions:** Muslim 97%, Christian (mostly Roman Catholic) 3%

**Languages:** Mahorian (a Swahili dialect), French (official language) spoken by 35% of the population

**Literacy:** NA

**Education expenditures:** NA

## Government

**Country name:**
*conventional long form:* Territorial Collectivity of Mayotte
*conventional short form:* Mayotte

**Dependency status:** departmental collectivity of France

**Government type:** NA

**Capital:**
*name:* Mamoudzou
*geographic coordinates:* 12 46 S, 45 13 E
*time difference:* UTC+3 (8 hours ahead of Washington, DC during Standard Time)

**Administrative divisions:** none (territorial overseas collectivity of France)

**Independence:** none (territorial overseas collectivity of France)

**National holiday:** Bastille Day, 14 July (1789)

**Constitution:** 4 October 1958 (French Constitution)

**Legal system:** the laws of France, where applicable, apply

**Suffrage:** 18 years of age; universal

**Executive branch:**
*chief of state:* President Nicolas SARKOZY (since 16 May 2007); represented by Prefect Denis ROBIN (since 28 July 2008)
*head of government:* President of the General Council Ahmed Attoumani DOUCHINA (since March 2008)
*cabinet:* NA
*elections:* French president elected by popular vote for a five-year term; prefect appointed by the French president on the advice of the French Ministry of the Interior; president of the General Council elected by the members of the General Council for a six-year term; next election to be held in 2010

**Legislative branch:** unicameral General Council or Conseil General (19 seats; members are elected by popular vote to serve three-year terms)
*elections:* last held 9 and 16 March 2008 (next to be held in 2011)
*election results:* percent of vote by party - NA; seats by party - UMP 8, Diverse Right 4, independents 4, Citizens and Republic Movement 1, Democratic Movement 1, Diverse Left 1; note - political parties are the same as parties in France
*note:* Mayotte elects two members of the French Senate; elections last held 21 September 2008 (next to be held in September 2014); results - percent of vote by party - NA; seats by party - UC-UDF 1, UMP 1; Mayotte also elects one member to the French National Assembly; elections last held 10-17 June 2007 (next to be held in 2012); results - percent of vote by party - NA; seats by party - independent 1

**Judicial branch:** Supreme Court or Tribunal Superieur d'Appel

**Political parties and leaders:** Democratic Front or FD [Youssouf MOUSSA]; Mahoran Popular Movement or MPM [Ahmed MADI]; Federation of Mahorans or UMP-RPR [Mansour KAMARDINE]; Force of the Rally and the Alliance for Democracy or FRAP; Movement for Department Status Mayotte or MDM [Mouhoutar SALIM]; Renewed Communist Party of Mayotte or MRC [Omar SIMBA]; Socialist Party or PS [Ibrahim ABUBACAR] (local branch of French Parti Socialiste); Union for French Democracy or UDF [Henri JEAN-BAPTISTE]

**Political pressure groups and leaders:** NA

# Mayotte *(continued)*

**International organization participation:** InOC, UPU, WFTU

**Diplomatic representation in the US:** none (territorial overseas collectivity of France)

**Diplomatic representation from the US:** none (territorial overseas collectivity of France)

**Flag description:** unofficial, local flag with the coat of arms of Mayotte centered on a white field, above which the name of the island appears in red capital letters; the main elements of the coat of arms, flanked on either side by a seahorse, appear above a scroll with the motto RA HACHIRI (We are Vigilant); the only official flag is the national flag of France

## Economy

**Economy - overview:** Economic activity is based primarily on the agricultural sector, including fishing and livestock raising. Mayotte is not self-sufficient and must import a large portion of its food requirements, mainly from France. The economy and future development of the island are heavily dependent on French financial assistance, an important supplement to GDP. Mayotte's remote location is an obstacle to the development of tourism.

**GDP (purchasing power parity):**
$953.6 million (2005 est.)

**GDP (official exchange rate):** $NA

**GDP - real growth rate:** NA%

**GDP - per capita (PPP):**
$4,900 (2005 est.)

**GDP - composition by sector:**
*agriculture:* NA%
*industry:* NA%
*services:* NA%

**Labor force:** 44,560 (2002)

**Unemployment rate:**
25.4% (2005)

**Population below poverty line:** NA%

**Household income or consumption by percentage share:**
*lowest 10%:* NA%
*highest 10%:* NA%

**Budget:**
*revenues:* $420 million
*expenditures:* $394 million (2005)

**Inflation rate (consumer prices):**
1.7% (2005)

**Market value of publicly traded shares:** $NA

**Agriculture - products:** vanilla, ylang-ylang (perfume essence), coffee, copra, fish, livestock

**Industries:** newly created lobster and shrimp industry, construction

**Industrial production growth rate:** NA%

**Electricity - production:** NA kWh

**Electricity - consumption:** 139.2 million kWh (2005)

**Exports:** $6.5 million f.o.b. (2005)

**Exports - commodities:** ylang-ylang (perfume essence), vanilla, copra, coconuts, coffee, cinnamon

**Imports:** $341 million f.o.b.; note - excludes petroleum imports (2005)

**Imports - commodities:** food, machinery and equipment, transportation equipment, metals, chemicals

**Debt - external:** $NA

**Exchange rates:** euros (EUR) per US dollar - 0.6734 (2008 est.), 0.7345 (2007), 0.7964 (2006), 0.8041 (2005), 0.8054 (2004)

## Communications

**Telephones - main lines in use:** 10,000 (2002)

**Telephones - mobile cellular:** 48,100 (2005)

**Telephone system:**
*general assessment:* small system administered by French Department of Posts and Telecommunications
*domestic:* NA
*international:* country code - 262; microwave radio relay and HF radiotelephone communications to Comoros

**Radio broadcast stations:** AM 1, FM 5, shortwave 0 (2001)

**Television broadcast stations:** 3 (2001)

**Internet country code:** .yt

**Internet hosts:** 1 (2008)

**Internet users:** NA

## Transportation

**Airports:** 1 (2008)

**Airports - with paved runways:**
*total:* 1
*1,524 to 2,437 m:* 1 (2008)

**Ports and terminals:** Dzaoudzi

## Military

**Manpower fit for military service:**
*males age 16-49:* 35,849
*females age 16-49:* 34,456 (2009 est.)

**Manpower reaching militarily significant age annually:**
*male:* 2,517
*female:* 2,511 (2009 est.)

**Military - note:** defense is the responsibility of France; a small contingent of French forces is stationed on the island

## Transnational Issues

**Disputes - international:** claimed by Comoros

# Mexico

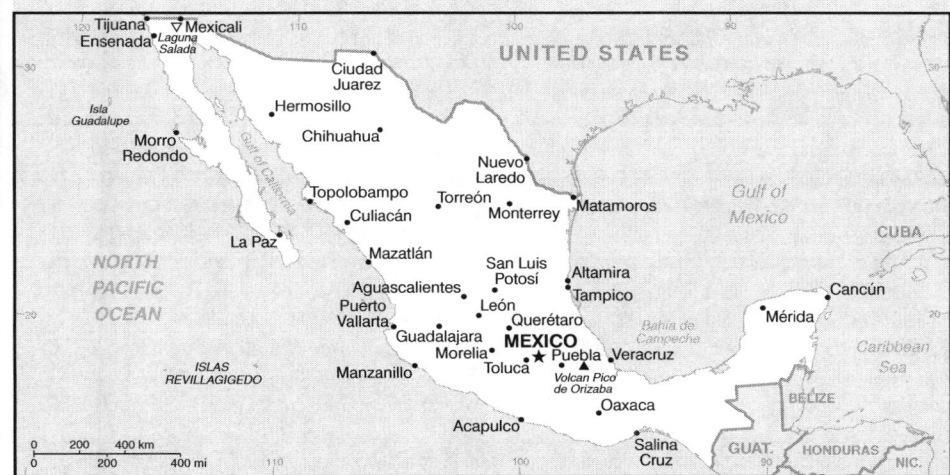

**Background:** The site of advanced Amerindian civilizations, Mexico came under Spanish rule for three centuries before achieving independence early in the 19th century. A devaluation of the peso in late 1994 threw Mexico into economic turmoil, triggering the worst recession in over half a century. The nation had been making an impressive recovery until the global financial crisis hit in late 2008. Ongoing economic and social concerns include low real wages, underemployment for a large segment of the population, inequitable income distribution, and few advancement opportunities for the largely Amerindian population in the impoverished southern states. The elections held in 2000 marked the first time since the 1910 Mexican Revolution that an opposition candidate -Vicente FOX of the National Action Party (PAN) - defeated the party in government, the Institutional Revolutionary Party (PRI). He was succeeded in 2006 by another PAN candidate Felipe CALDERON. In January 2009, Mexico assumed a nonpermanent seat on the UN Security Council for the 2009-10 term.

## Geography

**Location:** Middle America, bordering the Caribbean Sea and the Gulf of Mexico, between Belize and the United States and bordering the North Pacific Ocean, between Guatemala and the United States
**Geographic coordinates:** 23 00 N, 102 00 W
**Map references:** North America
**Area:**
*total:* 1,972,550 sq km
*land:* 1,923,040 sq km
*water:* 49,510 sq km
**Area - comparative:** slightly less than three times the size of Texas

**Land boundaries:**
*total:* 4,353 km
*border countries:* Belize 250 km, Guatemala 962 km, US 3,141 km
**Coastline:** 9,330 km
**Maritime claims:**
*territorial sea:* 12 nm
*contiguous zone:* 24 nm
*exclusive economic zone:* 200 nm
*continental shelf:* 200 nm or to the edge of the continental margin
**Climate:** varies from tropical to desert
**Terrain:** high, rugged mountains; low coastal plains; high plateaus; desert
**Elevation extremes:**
*lowest point:* Laguna Salada -10 m
*highest point:* Volcan Pico de Orizaba 5,700 m
**Natural resources:** petroleum, silver, copper, gold, lead, zinc, natural gas, timber
**Land use:**
*arable land:* 12.66%
*permanent crops:* 1.28%
*other:* 86.06% (2005)
**Irrigated land:** 63,200 sq km (2003)
**Total renewable water resources:** 457.2 cu km (2000)
**Freshwater withdrawal (domestic/industrial/agricultural):**
*total:* 78.22 cu km/yr (17%/5%/77%)
*per capita:* 731 cu m/yr (2000)
**Natural hazards:** tsunamis along the Pacific coast, volcanoes and destructive earthquakes in the center and south, and hurricanes on the Pacific, Gulf of Mexico, and Caribbean coasts
**Environment - current issues:** scarcity of hazardous waste disposal facilities; rural to urban migration; natural fresh water resources scarce and polluted in north, inaccessible and poor quality in center and extreme southeast; raw sewage and

industrial effluents polluting rivers in urban areas; deforestation; widespread erosion; desertification; deteriorating agricultural lands; serious air and water pollution in the national capital and urban centers along US-Mexico border; land subsidence in Valley of Mexico caused by groundwater depletion
*note:* the government considers the lack of clean water and deforestation national security issues
**Environment - international agreements:**
*party to:* Biodiversity, Climate Change, Climate Change-Kyoto Protocol, Desertification, Endangered Species, Hazardous Wastes, Law of the Sea, Marine Dumping, Marine Life Conservation, Ozone Layer Protection, Ship Pollution, Wetlands, Whaling
*signed, but not ratified:* none of the selected agreements
**Geography - note:** strategic location on southern border of US; corn (maize), one of the world's major grain crops, is thought to have originated in Mexico

## People

**Population:** 111,211,789 (July 2009 est.)
**Age structure:**
*0-14 years:* 29.1% (male 16,544,223/female 15,861,141)
*15-64 years:* 64.6% (male 34,734,571/female 37,129,793)
*65 years and over:* 6.2% (male 3,130,518/female 3,811,543) (2009 est.)
**Median age:**
*total:* 26.3 years
*male:* 25.3 years
*female:* 27.3 years (2009 est.)
**Population growth rate:** 1.13% (2009 est.)
**Birth rate:** 19.71 births/1,000 population (2009 est.)
**Death rate:** 4.78 deaths/1,000 population (2008 est.)
**Net migration rate:** -3.61 migrant(s)/1,000 population (2009 est.)
**Urbanization:**
*urban population:* 77% of total population (2008)
*rate of urbanization:* 1.5% annual rate of change (2005-10 est.)
**Sex ratio:**
*at birth:* 1.05 male(s)/female
*under 15 years:* 1.04 male(s)/female
*15-64 years:* 0.94 male(s)/female
*65 years and over:* 0.82 male(s)/female
*total population:* 0.96 male(s)/female (2009 est.)
**Infant mortality rate:**
*total:* 18.42 deaths/1,000 live births
*male:* 20.3 deaths/1,000 live births
*female:* 16.44 deaths/1,000 live births (2009 est.)
**Life expectancy at birth:**
*total population:* 76.06 years
*male:* 73.25 years
*female:* 79 years (2009 est.)
**Total fertility rate:** 2.34 children born/woman (2009 est.)
**HIV/AIDS - adult prevalence rate:** 0.3% (2007 est.)
**HIV/AIDS - people living with HIV/AIDS:** 200,000 (2007 est.)

# Mexico (continued)

**HIV/AIDS - deaths:** 11,000 (2007 est.)

**Major infectious diseases:**

*degree of risk:* intermediate

*food or waterborne diseases:* bacterial diarrhea, hepatitis A, and typhoid fever

*vectorborne disease:* dengue fever

*water contact disease:* leptospirosis (2009)

**Nationality:**

*noun:* Mexican(s)

*adjective:* Mexican

**Ethnic groups:** mestizo (Amerindian-Spanish) 60%, Amerindian or predominantly Amerindian 30%, white 9%, other 1%

**Religions:** Roman Catholic 76.5%, Protestant 6.3% (Pentecostal 1.4%, Jehovah's Witnesses 1.1%, other 3.8%), other 0.3%, unspecified 13.8%, none 3.1% (2000 census)

**Languages:** Spanish only 92.7%, Spanish and indigenous languages 5.7%, indigenous only 0.8%, unspecified 0.8%; note - indigenous languages include various Mayan, Nahuatl, and other regional languages (2005)

**Literacy:**

*definition:* age 15 and over can read and write

*total population:* 91%

*male:* 92.4%

*female:* 89.6% (2004 est.)

**School life expectancy (primary to tertiary education):**

*total:* 13 years

*male:* 14 years

*female:* 13 years (2006)

**Education expenditures:** 5.5% of GDP (2005)

## Government

**Country name:**

*conventional long form:* United Mexican States

*conventional short form:* Mexico

*local long form:* Estados Unidos Mexicanos

*local short form:* Mexico

**Government type:** federal republic

**Capital:**

*name:* Mexico (Distrito Federal)

*geographic coordinates:* 19 26 N, 99 08 W

*time difference:* UTC-6 (1 hour behind Washington, DC during Standard Time)

*daylight saving time:* +1hr, begins first Sunday in April; ends last Sunday in October

*note:* Mexico is divided into three time zones

**Administrative divisions:** 31 states (estados, singular - estado) and 1 federal district* (distrito federal); Aguascalientes, Baja California, Baja California Sur, Campeche, Chiapas, Chihuahua, Coahuila de Zaragoza, Colima, Distrito Federal*, Durango, Guanajuato, Guerrero, Hidalgo, Jalisco, Mexico, Michoacan de Ocampo, Morelos, Nayarit, Nuevo Leon, Oaxaca, Puebla, Queretaro de Arteaga, Quintana Roo, San Luis Potosi, Sinaloa, Sonora, Tabasco, Tamaulipas, Tlaxcala, Veracruz-Llave, Yucatan, Zacatecas

**Independence:** 16 September 1810 (declared); 27 September 1821 (recognized by Spain)

**National holiday:** Independence Day, 16 September (1810)

**Constitution:** 5 February 1917

**Legal system:** mixture of US constitutional theory and civil law system; judicial review of legislative acts; accepts compulsory ICJ jurisdiction with reservations

**Suffrage:** 18 years of age; universal and compulsory (but not enforced)

**Executive branch:**

*chief of state:* President Felipe de Jesus CALDERON Hinojosa (since 1 December 2006); note - the president is both the chief of state and head of government

*head of government:* President Felipe de Jesus CALDERON Hinojosa (since 1 December 2006)

*cabinet:* Cabinet appointed by the president; note - appointment of attorney general requires consent of the Senate

*elections:* president elected by popular vote for a single six-year term; election last held on 2 July 2006 (next to be held 1 July 2012)

*election results:* Felipe CALDERON elected president; percent of vote - Felipe CALDERON 35.89%, Andres Manuel LOPEZ OBRADOR 35.31%, Roberto MADRAZO 22.26%, other 6.54%

**Legislative branch:** bicameral National Congress or Congreso de la Union consists of the Senate or Camara de Senadores (128 seats; 96 members are elected by popular vote to serve six-year terms, and 32 seats are allocated on the basis of each party's popular vote) and the Chamber of Deputies or Camara de Diputados (500 seats; 300 members are elected by popular vote; remaining 200 members are allocated on the basis of each party's popular vote; to serve three-year terms)

*elections:* Senate - last held 2 July 2006 for all of the seats (next to be held 1 July 2012); Chamber of Deputies - last held 2 July 2006 (next to be held 5 July 2009)

*election results:* Senate - percent of vote by party - NA; seats by party - PAN 52, PRI 33, PRD 26, PVEM 6, CD 5, PT 5, independent 1; Chamber of Deputies - percent of vote by party - NA; seats by party - PAN 207, PRD 127, PRI 106, PVEM 17, CD 17, PT 11, other 15

**Judicial branch:** Supreme Court of Justice or Suprema Corte de Justicia de la Nacion (justices or ministros are appointed by the president with consent of the Senate)

**Political parties and leaders:** Convergence for Democracy or CD [Luis MALDONADO Venegas]; Institutional Revolutionary Party or PRI [Beatriz PAREDES]; Labor Party or PT [Alberto ANAYA Gutierrez]; Mexican Green Ecological Party or PVEM [Jorge Emilio GONZALEZ Martinez]; National Action Party (Partido Accion Nacional) or PAN [German MARTINEZ Cazares]; New Alliance Party (Partido Nueva Alianza) or PNA [Jorge Antonio KAHWAGI Macari]; Party of the Democratic Revolution (Partido de la Revolucion Democratica) or PRD [Leonel COTA Montano]; Social Democratic and Peasant Alternative Party (Partido Alternativa Socialdemocrata y Campesina) or Alternativa [Alberto BEGNE Guerra]

**Political pressure groups and leaders:** Broad Progressive Front or FAP; Businessmen's Coordinating Council or CCE; Confederation of Employers of the Mexican Republic or COPARMEX; Confederation of Industrial Chambers or CONCAMIN; Confederation of Mexican Workers or CTM; Confederation of National Chambers of Commerce or CONCANACO; Coordinator for Foreign Trade Business Organizations or COECE; Federation of Unions Providing Goods and Services or FESEBES; National Chamber of Transformation Industries or CANACINTRA; National Peasant Confederation or CNC; National Small Business Chamber or CANACOPE; National Syndicate of Education Workers or SNTE; National Union of Workers or UNT; Popular Assembly of the People of Oaxaca or APPO; Roman Catholic Church

**International organization participation:** APEC, BCIE, BIS, CAN (observer), Caricom (observer), CDB, CE (observer), CSN (observer), EBRD, FAO, G-20, G-3, G-15, G-24, IADB, IAEA, IBRD, ICAO, ICC, ICCt, ICRM, IDA, IFAD, IFC, IFRCS, IHO, ILO, IMF, IMO, IMSO, Interpol, IOC, IOM, IPU, ISO, ITSO, ITU, ITUC, LAES, LAIA, MIGA, NAFTA, NAM (observer), NEA, OAS, OECD, OPANAL, OPCW, PCA, RG, SICA (observer), UN, UNASUR (observer), UNCTAD, UNESCO, UNHCR, UNIDO, Union Latina, UNWTO, UPU, WCL, WCO, WFTU, WHO, WIPO, WMO, WTO

**Diplomatic representation in the US:**

*chief of mission:* Ambassador Arturo SARUKHAN Casamitjana

*chancery:* 1911 Pennsylvania Avenue NW, Washington, DC 20006

*telephone:* [1] (202) 728-1600

*FAX:* [1] (202) 728-1698

*consulate(s) general:* Atlanta, Austin, Boston, Chicago, Dallas, Denver, El Paso, Houston, Laredo (Texas), Los Angeles, Miami, New York, Nogales (Arizona), Phoenix, Sacramento, Saint Paul (Minnesota), San Antonio, San Diego, San Francisco, San Jose, San Juan (Puerto Rico)

*consulate(s):* Albuquerque, Brownsville (Texas), Calexico (California), Del Rio (Texas), Detroit, Douglas (Arizona), Eagle Pass (Texas), Fresno (California), Indianapolis (Indiana), Kansas City (Missouri), Laredo (Texas), Las Vegas, Little Rock (Arkansas), McAllen (Texas), New Orleans, Omaha, Orlando, Oxnard (California), Philadelphia, Portland (Oregon), Presidio (Texas), Raleigh, Salt Lake City, San Bernardino, Santa Ana (California), Seattle, Tucson, Yuma (Arizona)

**Diplomatic representation from the US:**

*chief of mission:* Ambassador Antonio O. GARZA, Jr.

*embassy:* Paseo de la Reforma 305, Colonia Cuauhtemoc, 06500 Mexico, Distrito Federal

*mailing address:* P. O. Box 9000, Brownsville, TX 78520-9000

*telephone:* [52] (55) 5080-2000

*FAX:* [52] (55) 5511-9980

*consulate(s) general:* Ciudad Juarez, Guadalajara, Monterrey, Tijuana

*consulate(s):* Hermosillo, Matamoros, Merida, Nogales, Nuevo Laredo

# Mexico (continued)

**Flag description:** three equal vertical bands of green (hoist side), white, and red; the coat of arms (an eagle with a snake in its beak perched on a cactus) is centered in the white band

## Economy

**Economy - overview:** Mexico has a free market economy in the trillion dollar class. It contains a mixture of modern and outmoded industry and agriculture, increasingly dominated by the private sector. Recent administrations have expanded competition in seaports, railroads, telecommunications, electricity generation, natural gas distribution, and airports. Per capita income is one-fourth that of the US; income distribution remains highly unequal. Trade with the US and Canada has nearly tripled since the implementation of NAFTA in 1994. Mexico has 12 free trade agreements with over 40 countries including, Guatemala, Honduras, El Salvador, the European Free Trade Area, and Japan, putting more than 90% of trade under free trade agreements. In 2007, during its first year in office, the Felipe CALDERON administration was able to garner support from the opposition to successfully pass a pension and a fiscal reform. The administration continues to face many economic challenges including the need to upgrade infrastructure, modernize labor laws, and allow private investment in the energy sector. CALDERON has stated that his top economic priorities remain reducing poverty and creating jobs.

**GDP (purchasing power parity):**
$1.559 trillion (2008 est.)
$1.538 trillion (2007)
$1.49 trillion (2006)
*note:* data are in 2008 US dollars

**GDP (official exchange rate):** $1.143 trillion (2008 est.)

**GDP - real growth rate:**
1.4% (2008 est.)
3.2% (2007 est.)
4.9% (2006 est.)

**GDP - per capita (PPP):**
$14,200 (2008 est.)
$14,100 (2007 est.)
$13,900 (2006 est.)
*note:* data are in 2008 US dollars

**GDP - composition by sector:**
*agriculture:* 3.7%
*industry:* 34.1%
*services:* 62.2% (2008 est.)

**Labor force:** 45.5 million (2008 est.)

**Labor force - by occupation:**
*agriculture:* 15.1%
*industry:* 25.7%
*services:* 59% (2005)

**Unemployment rate:**
4.1% (October 2008)
3.7% (2007 est.)
*note:* underemployment is perhaps 25%

**Population below poverty line:** 13.8% using food-based definition of poverty; asset based poverty amounted to more than 40% (2006)

**Household income or consumption by percentage share:**
*lowest 10%:* 1.2%
*highest 10%:* 37% (2006)

**Distribution of family income - Gini index:** 47.9 (2006)

**Investment (gross fixed):** 22.9% of GDP (2008 est.)

**Budget:**
*revenues:* $256.7 billion
*expenditures:* $256.8 billion (2008 est.)

**Public debt:** 20.3% of GDP (2008 est.)

**Inflation rate (consumer prices):**
6.2% (2008 est.)
4% (2007 est.)

**Central bank discount rate:** NA

**Commercial bank prime lending rate:** 7.56% (31 December 2007)

**Stock of money:** $103.5 billion (31 December 2007)

**Stock of quasi money:** $168.4 billion (31 December 2007)

**Stock of domestic credit:** $349.1 billion (31 December 2007)

**Market value of publicly traded shares:** $397.7 billion (31 December 2007)

**Agriculture - products:** corn, wheat, soybeans, rice, beans, cotton, coffee, fruit, tomatoes; beef, poultry, dairy products; wood products

**Industries:** food and beverages, tobacco, chemicals, iron and steel, petroleum, mining, textiles, clothing, motor vehicles, consumer durables, tourism

**Industrial production growth rate:** 0% (2008 est.)

**Electricity - production:** 243.3 billion kWh (2007 est.)

**Electricity - consumption:** 202 billion kWh (2007 est.)

**Electricity - exports:** 1.278 billion kWh (2007 est.)

**Electricity - imports:** 484.2 million kWh (2007 est.)

**Oil - production:** 3.501 million bbl/day (2007 est.)

**Oil - consumption:** 2.119 million bbl/day (2007 est.)

**Oil - exports:** 2.204 million bbl/day (2005)

**Oil - imports:** 385,400 bbl/day (2005)

**Oil - proved reserves:** 11.65 billion bbl (1 January 2008 est.)

**Natural gas - production:** 55.98 billion cu m (2007 est.)

**Natural gas - consumption:** 68.29 billion cu m (2007 est.)

**Natural gas - exports:** 2.973 billion cu m (2007 est.)

**Natural gas - imports:** 11.69 billion cu m (2007 est.)

**Natural gas - proved reserves:** 392.2 billion cu m (1 January 2008 est.)

**Current account balance:** -$13.45 billion (2008 est.)

**Exports:** $294 billion f.o.b. (2008 est.)

**Exports - commodities:** manufactured goods, oil and oil products, silver, fruits, vegetables, coffee, cotton

**Exports - partners:** US 82.2%, Canada 2.4%, Germany 1.5% (2007)

**Imports:** $305.9 billion f.o.b. (2008 est.)

**Imports - commodities:** metalworking machines, steel mill products, agricultural machinery, electrical equipment, car parts for assembly, repair parts for motor vehicles, aircraft, and aircraft parts

**Imports - partners:** US 49.6%, China 10.5%, Japan 5.8%, South Korea 4.5% (2007)

**Reserves of foreign exchange and gold:** $91.99 billion (31 December 2008 est.)

**Debt - external:** $181.2 billion (31 December 2008 est.)

**Stock of direct foreign investment - at home:** $278.9 billion (2008 est.)

**Stock of direct foreign investment - abroad:** $43.01 billion (2008 est.)

**Exchange rates:** Mexican pesos (MXN) per US dollar - 11.016 (2008 est.), 10.8 (2007), 10.899 (2006), 10.898 (2005), 11.286 (2004)

## Communications

**Telephones - main lines in use:** 19.754 million (2007)

**Telephones - mobile cellular:** 68.254 million (2007)

**Telephone system:**
*general assessment:* adequate telephone service for business and government, but the population is poorly served; mobile subscribers far outnumber fixed-line subscribers; domestic satellite system with 120 earth stations; extensive microwave radio relay network; considerable use of fiber-optic cable and coaxial cable
*domestic:* low telephone density with about 18 fixed lines per 100 persons; privatized in December 1990; despite the opening to competition in January 1997, Telmex remains dominant; legal challenges to Telmex's alleged anti-competitive behavior in the mobile and fixed-line markets culminated in a World Trade Organization ruling in 2004 against Mexico prompting some strengthening of the powers granted Mexico's telecom regulator; mobile cellular teledensity approaching 65 per 100 persons
*international:* country code - 52; Columbus-2 fiber-optic submarine cable with access to the US, Virgin Islands, Canary Islands, Spain, and Italy; the Americas Region Caribbean Ring System (ARCOS-1) and the MAYA-1 submarine cable system together provide access to Central America, parts of South America and the Caribbean, and the US; satellite earth stations - 120 (32 Intelsat, 2 Solidaridad (giving Mexico improved access to South America, Central America, and much of the US as well as enhancing domestic communications), 1 Panamsat, numerous Inmarsat mobile earth stations); linked to Central American Microwave System of trunk connections (2007)

**Radio broadcast stations:** AM 850, FM 545, shortwave 15 (2003)

**Television broadcast stations:** 236 (plus repeaters) (1997)

**Internet country code:** .mx

**Internet hosts:** 10.653 million (2008)

**Internet users:** 22.812 million (2007)

## Transportation

**Airports:** 1,848 (2008)
**Airports - with paved runways:**
total: 243
over 3,047 m: 12
2,438 to 3,047 m: 29
1,524 to 2,437 m: 85
914 to 1,523 m: 81
under 914 m: 36 (2008)
**Airports - with unpaved runways:**
total: 1,605
over 3,047 m: 1
2,438 to 3,047 m: 1
1,524 to 2,437 m: 64
914 to 1,523 m: 426
under 914 m: 1,113 (2008)
**Heliports:** 1 (2007)
**Pipelines:** gas 22,705 km; liquid petroleum gas 1,875 km; oil 8,688 km; oil/gas/water 228 km; refined products 6,520 km (2006)
**Railways:**
total: 17,665 km
standard gauge: 17,665 km 1.435-m gauge (2006)
**Roadways:**
total: 356,945 km
paved: 178,473 km (includes 6,279 km of expressways)
unpaved: 178,472 km (2006)
**Waterways:** 2,900 km (navigable rivers and coastal canals) (2008)
**Merchant marine:**
total: 55
by type: bulk carrier 2, cargo 7, chemical tanker 5, liquefied gas 4, passenger/cargo 11, petroleum tanker 23, roll on/roll off 3
foreign-owned: 4 (Denmark 2, Hong Kong 1, UAE 1)
registered in other countries: 20 (Brazil 1, Honduras 1, Liberia 2, Marshall Islands 4, Panama 2, Portugal 1, Spain 3, Venezuela 5, unknown 1) (2008)
**Ports and terminals:** Altamira, Coatzacoalcos, Manzanillo, Morro Redondo, Salina Cruz, Tampico, Veracruz

## Military

**Military branches:** Secretariat of National Defense (Secretaria de Defensa Nacional, Sedena): Army (Ejercito, includes Mexican Air Force (Fuerza Aerea Mexicana, FAM)); Secretariat of the Navy (Secretaria de Marina, Semar): Mexican Navy (Armada de Mexico, ARM, includes Naval Air Force (FAN) and naval infantry) (2009)
**Military service age and obligation:** 18 years of age for compulsory military service, conscript service obligation - 12 months; 16 years of age with consent for voluntary enlistment; conscripts serve only in the Army; Navy and Air Force service is all voluntary; women are eligible for voluntary military service (2007)
**Manpower available for military service:**
males age 16-49: 27,774,688

females age 16-49: 29,376,791 (2008 est.)
**Manpower fit for military service:**
males age 16-49: 22,541,654
females age 16-49: 25,149,027 (2009 est.)
**Manpower reaching militarily significant age annually:**
male: 1,109,981
female: 1,072,094 (2009 est.)
**Military expenditures:** 0.5% of GDP (2006 est.)

## Transnational Issues

**Disputes - international:** abundant rainfall in recent years along much of the Mexico-US border region has ameliorated periodically strained water-sharing arrangements; the US has intensified security measures to monitor and control legal and illegal personnel, transport, and commodities across its border with Mexico; Mexico must deal with thousands of impoverished Guatemalans and other Central Americans who cross the porous border looking for work in Mexico and the United States
**Refugees and internally displaced persons:**
IDPs: 5,500-10,000 (government's quashing of Zapatista uprising in 1994 in eastern Chiapas Region) (2007)
**Illicit drugs:** major drug-producing nation; cultivation of opium poppy in 2007 rose to 6,900 hectares yielding a potential production of 18 metric tons of pure heroin, or 50 metric tons of "black tar" heroin, the dominant form of Mexican heroin in the western United States; marijuana cultivation increased to 8,900 hectares in 2007 and yielded a potential production of 15,800 metric tons; government conducts the largest independent illicit-crop eradication program in the world; continues as the primary transshipment country for US-bound cocaine from South America, with an estimated 90% of annual cocaine movements toward the US stopping in Mexico; major drug syndicates control the majority of drug trafficking throughout the country; producer and distributor of ecstasy; significant money-laundering center; major supplier of heroin and largest foreign supplier of marijuana and methamphetamine to the US market (2007)

# Micronesia, Federated States of

## Introduction

**Background:** In 1979 the Federated States of Micronesia, a UN Trust Territory under US administration, adopted a constitution. In 1986 independence was attained under a Compact of Free Association with the US, which was amended and renewed in 2004. Present concerns include large-scale unemployment, overfishing, and overdependence on US aid.

## Geography

**Location:** Oceania, island group in the North Pacific Ocean, about three-quarters of the way from Hawaii to Indonesia
**Geographic coordinates:** 6 55 N, 158 15 E
**Map references:** Oceania
**Area:**
total: 702 sq km
land: 702 sq km
water: 0 sq km (fresh water only)
note: includes Pohnpei (Ponape), Chuuk (Truk) Islands, Yap Islands, and Kosrae (Kosaie)
**Area - comparative:** four times the size of Washington, DC (land area only)
**Land boundaries:** 0 km
**Coastline:** 6,112 km
**Maritime claims:**
territorial sea: 12 nm
exclusive economic zone: 200 nm
**Climate:** tropical; heavy year-round rainfall, especially in the eastern islands; located on southern edge of the typhoon belt with occasionally severe damage
**Terrain:** islands vary geologically from high mountainous islands to low, coral atolls; volcanic outcroppings on Pohnpei, Kosrae, and Chuuk
**Elevation extremes:**
lowest point: Pacific Ocean 0 m
highest point: Dolohmwar (Totolom) 791 m

# Micronesia, Federated States of (continued)

**Natural resources:** forests, marine products, deep-seabed minerals, phosphate

**Land use:**
*arable land:* 5.71%
*permanent crops:* 45.71%
*other:* 48.58% (2005)

**Irrigated land:** NA

**Natural hazards:** typhoons (June to December)

**Environment - current issues:** overfishing, climate change, pollution

**Environment - international agreements:**
*party to:* Biodiversity, Climate Change, Climate Change-Kyoto Protocol, Desertification, Hazardous Wastes, Law of the Sea, Ozone Layer Protection
*signed, but not ratified:* none of the selected agreements

**Geography - note:** four major island groups totaling 607 islands

## People

**Population:** 107,434 (July 2009 est.)

**Age structure:**
*0-14 years:* 34.8% (male 19,010/female 18,411)
*15-64 years:* 62.3% (male 33,286/female 33,629)
*65 years and over:* 2.9% (male 1,317/female 1,781) (2009 est.)

**Median age:**
*total:* 22 years
*male:* 21.5 years
*female:* 22.5 years (2009 est.)

**Population growth rate:** -0.238% (2009 est.)

**Birth rate:** 23.1 births/1,000 population (2009 est.)

**Death rate:** 4.53 deaths/1,000 population (2008 est.)

**Net migration rate:** -21.03 migrant(s)/1,000 population (2009 est.)

**Urbanization:**
*urban population:* 22% of total population (2008)
*rate of urbanization:* 0.8% annual rate of change (2005-10 est.)

**Sex ratio:**
*at birth:* 1.05 male(s)/female
*under 15 years:* 1.03 male(s)/female
*15-64 years:* 0.99 male(s)/female
*65 years and over:* 0.74 male(s)/female
*total population:* 1 male(s)/female (2009 est.)

**Infant mortality rate:**
*total:* 26.1 deaths/1,000 live births
*male:* 28.79 deaths/1,000 live births
*female:* 23.27 deaths/1,000 live births (2009 est.)

**Life expectancy at birth:**
*total population:* 70.94 years
*male:* 69.06 years
*female:* 72.93 years (2009 est.)

**Total fertility rate:** 2.89 children born/woman (2009 est.)

**HIV/AIDS - adult prevalence rate:** NA

**HIV/AIDS - people living with HIV/AIDS:** NA

**HIV/AIDS - deaths:** NA

**Nationality:**
*noun:* Micronesian(s)
*adjective:* Micronesian; Chuukese, Kosraen(s), Pohnpeian(s), Yapese

**Ethnic groups:** Chuukese 48.8%, Pohnpeian 24.2%, Kosraean 6.2%, Yapese 5.2%, Yap outer islands 4.5%, Asian 1.8%, Polynesian 1.5%, other 6.4%, unknown 1.4% (2000 census)

**Religions:** Roman Catholic 50%, Protestant 47%, other 3%

**Languages:** English (official and common language), Chuukese, Kosrean, Pohnpeian, Yapese, Ulithian, Woleaian, Nukuoro, Kapingamarangi

**Literacy:**
*definition:* age 15 and over can read and write
*total population:* 89%
*male:* 91%
*female:* 88% (1980 est.)

**Education expenditures:** 7.3% of GDP (2000)

## Government

**Country name:**
*conventional long form:* Federated States of Micronesia
*conventional short form:* none
*local long form:* Federated States of Micronesia
*local short form:* none
*former:* Trust Territory of the Pacific Islands, Ponape, Truk, and Yap Districts
*abbreviation:* FSM

**Government type:** constitutional government in free association with the US; the Compact of Free Association entered into force 3 November 1986 and the Amended Compact entered into force May 2004

**Capital:**
*name:* Palikir
*geographic coordinates:* 6 55 N, 158 09 E
*time difference:* UTC+11 (16 hours ahead of Washington, DC during Standard Time)

**Administrative divisions:** 4 states; Chuuk (Truk), Kosrae (Kosaie), Pohnpei (Ponape), Yap

**Independence:** 3 November 1986 (from the US-administered UN trusteeship)

**National holiday:** Constitution Day, 10 May (1979)

**Constitution:** 10 May 1979

**Legal system:** based on adapted Trust Territory laws, acts of the legislature, municipal, common, and customary laws; has not accepted compulsory ICJ jurisdiction

**Suffrage:** 18 years of age; universal

**Executive branch:**
*chief of state:* President Emanuel MORI (since 11 May 2007); Vice President Alik L. ALIK (since 11 May 2007); note - the president is both the chief of state and head of government
*head of government:* President Emanuel MORI (since 11 May 2007); Vice President Alik L. ALIK (since 11 May 2007)
*cabinet:* Cabinet includes the vice president and the heads of the eight executive departments
*elections:* president and vice president elected by

Congress from among the four senators at large for a four-year term (eligible for a second term); election last held 11 May 2007 (next to be held May 2011); note - a proposed constitutional amendment to establish popular elections for president and vice president failed
*election results:* Emanuel MORI elected president; percent of Congress vote - NA; Alik L. ALIK elected vice president; percent of Congress vote - NA

**Legislative branch:** unicameral Congress (14 seats; 4 - one elected from each state to serve four-year terms and 10 - elected from single-member districts delineated by population to serve two-year terms; members elected by popular vote)
*elections:* last held 3 March 2009 (next to be held in March 2011)
*election results:* percent of vote - NA%; seats - independents 14

**Judicial branch:** Supreme Court

**Political parties and leaders:** no formal parties

**Political pressure groups and leaders:** NA

**International organization participation:** ACP, ADB, FAO, G-77, IBRD, ICAO, ICRM, IDA, IFC, IFRCS, IMF, IOC, ITSO, ITU, MIGA, OPCW, PIF, Sparteca, SPC, UN, UNCTAD, UNESCO, WHO, WMO

**Diplomatic representation in the US:**
*chief of mission:* Ambassador Yosiwo GEORGE
*chancery:* 1725 N Street NW, Washington, DC 20036
*telephone:* [1] (202) 223-4383
*FAX:* [1] (202) 223-4391
*consulate(s) general:* Honolulu, Tamuning (Guam)

**Diplomatic representation from the US:**
*chief of mission:* Ambassador Miriam K. HUGHES
*embassy:* 101 Upper Pics Road, Kolonia
*mailing address:* P. O. Box 1286, Kolonia, Pohnpei, 96941
*telephone:* [691] 320-2187
*FAX:* [691] 320-2186

**Flag description:** light blue with four white five-pointed stars centered; the stars are arranged in a diamond pattern

## Economy

**Economy - overview:** Economic activity consists primarily of subsistence farming and fishing. The islands have few mineral deposits worth exploiting, except for high-grade phosphate. The potential for a tourist industry exists, but the remote location, a lack of adequate facilities, and limited air connections hinder development. Under the original terms of the Compact of Free Association, the US provided $1.3 billion in grant aid during the period 1986-2001; the level of aid has been subsequently reduced. The Amended Compact of Free Association with the US guarantees the Federated States of Micronesia (FSM) millions of dollars in annual aid through 2023, and establishes a Trust Fund into which the US and the FSM make annual contributions in order to provide annual payouts to the FSM in perpetuity after 2023. The country's medium-term economic outlook appears fragile due not only to the reduction in US assistance but also to the current slow growth of the private sector.

**GDP (purchasing power parity):**
$238.1 million (2008 est.)
$277 million (2002)
*note:* data are in 2008 US dollars
GDP supplemented by grant aid, averaging perhaps $100 million annually

**GDP (official exchange rate):** $238.1 million (2008)

**GDP - real growth rate:**
NA
0.3% (2005 est.)

**GDP - per capita (PPP):**
$2,200 (2008 est.)
$2,300 (2005 est.)
*note:* data are in 2008 US dollars

**GDP - composition by sector:**
*agriculture:* 28.9%
*industry:* 15.2%
*services:* 55.9% (2004 est.)

**Labor force:** 16,360 (2008)

**Labor force - by occupation:**
*agriculture:* 0.9%
*industry:* 34.4%
*services:* 64.7%
*note:* two-thirds are government employees (FY05 est.)

**Unemployment rate:**
22% (2000 est.)

**Population below poverty line:** 26.7% (2000)

**Household income or consumption by percentage share:**
*lowest 10%:* NA%
*highest 10%:* NA%

**Budget:**
*revenues:* $166 million ($69 million less grants)
*expenditures:* $152.7 million (FY07 est.)

**Inflation rate (consumer prices):**
2.2% (2005)

**Commercial bank prime lending rate:** 14.03% (31 December 2007)

**Stock of money:** $22.45 million (31 December 2007)

**Stock of quasi money:** $72.49 million (31 December 2007)

**Stock of domestic credit:** $NA

**Market value of publicly traded shares:** $NA

**Agriculture - products:** black pepper, tropical fruits and vegetables, coconuts, bananas, cassava (tapioca), sakau (kava), betel nuts, sweet potatoes; pigs, chickens; fish; Kosraen citrus

**Industries:** tourism, construction; fish processing, specialized aquaculture; craft items (from shell, wood, and pearls)

**Industrial production growth rate:** NA%

**Electricity - production:** 192 million kWh (2002)

**Electricity - consumption:** 178.6 million kWh (2002)

**Electricity - exports:** 0 kWh (2002)

**Electricity - imports:** 0 kWh (2002)

**Current account balance:** -$34.3 million (FY05 est.)

**Exports:** $14 million (f.o.b.) (2004 est.)

**Exports - commodities:** fish, garments, bananas, black pepper, sakau (kava), betel nut

**Imports:** $132.7 million f.o.b. (2004)

**Imports - commodities:** food, manufactured goods, machinery and equipment, beverages

**Debt - external:** $60.8 million (FY05 est.)

**Exchange rates:** the US dollar is used

## Communications

**Telephones - main lines in use:** 8,700 (2007)

**Telephones - mobile cellular:** 27,400 (2007)

**Telephone system:**
*general assessment:* adequate system
*domestic:* islands interconnected by shortwave radiotelephone (used mostly for government purposes), satellite (Intelsat) ground stations, and some coaxial and fiber-optic cable; cellular service available on Kosrae, Pohnpei, and Yap
*international:* country code - 691; satellite earth stations - 5 Intelsat (Pacific Ocean) (2002)

**Radio broadcast stations:** AM 5, FM 1, shortwave 0 (2004)

**Television broadcast stations:** 3 (cable TV also available) (2004)

**Internet country code:** .fm

**Internet hosts:** 866 (2008)

**Internet users:** 15,000 (2007)

## Transportation

**Airports:** 6 (2008)

**Airports - with paved runways:**
*total:* 6
*1,524 to 2,437 m:* 4
*914 to 1,523 m:* 2 (2008)

**Roadways:**
*total:* 240 km
*paved:* 42 km
*unpaved:* 198 km (2000)

**Merchant marine:**
*total:* 3
*by type:* cargo 1, passenger/cargo 2 (2008)

**Ports and terminals:** Tomil Harbor

## Military

**Military branches:** no regular military forces; defense is the responsibility of the US (2009)

**Manpower available for military service:**
*males age 16-49:* 26,686 (2008 est.)

**Manpower fit for military service:**
*males age 16-49:* 21,845
*females age 16-49:* 23,401 (2009 est.)

**Manpower reaching militarily significant age annually:**
*male:* 1,273
*female:* 1,212 (2009 est.)

**Military - note:** defense is the responsibility of the US

## Transnational Issues

**Disputes - international:** none

**Illicit drugs:** major consumer of cannabis

# Midway Islands
*(territory of the US)*

Description under

United States

Pacific Island

Wildlife Refuges

# Moldova

## Introduction

**Background:** Part of Romania during the interwar period, Moldova was incorporated into the Soviet Union at the close of World War II. Although independent from the USSR since 1991, Russian forces have remained on Moldovan territory east of the Dniester River supporting the Slavic majority population, mostly Ukrainians and Russians, who have proclaimed a "Transnistria" republic. One of the poorest nations in Europe, Moldova became the first former Soviet state to elect a Communist as its president in 2001.

## Geography

**Location:** Eastern Europe, northeast of Romania
**Geographic coordinates:** 47 00 N, 29 00 E
**Map references:** Europe
**Area:**
*total:* 33,843 sq km
*land:* 33,371 sq km
*water:* 472 sq km
**Area - comparative:** slightly larger than Maryland

**Land boundaries:**
*total:* 1,390 km
*border countries:* Romania 450 km, Ukraine 940 km
**Coastline:** 0 km (landlocked)
**Maritime claims:** none (landlocked)
**Climate:** moderate winters, warm summers
**Terrain:** rolling steppe, gradual slope south to Black Sea
**Elevation extremes:**
*lowest point:* Dniester River 2 m
*highest point:* Dealul Balanesti 430 m
**Natural resources:** lignite, phosphorites, gypsum, arable land, limestone
**Land use:**
*arable land:* 54.52%
*permanent crops:* 8.81%
*other:* 36.67% (2005)
**Irrigated land:** 3,000 sq km (2003)
**Total renewable water resources:** 11.7 cu km (1997)
**Freshwater withdrawal (domestic/industrial/agricultural):**
*total:* 2.31 cu km/yr (10%/58%/33%)
*per capita:* 549 cu m/yr (2000)
**Natural hazards:** landslides
**Environment - current issues:** heavy use of agricultural chemicals, including banned pesticides such as DDT, has contaminated soil and groundwater; extensive soil erosion from poor farming methods
**Environment - international agreements:**
*party to:* Air Pollution, Air Pollution-Persistent Organic Pollutants, Biodiversity, Climate Change, Climate Change-Kyoto Protocol, Desertification, Endangered Species, Hazardous Wastes, Ozone Layer Protection, Ship Pollution, Wetlands
*signed, but not ratified:* none of the selected agreements
**Geography - note:** landlocked; well endowed with various sedimentary rocks and minerals including sand, gravel, gypsum, and limestone

## People

**Population:** 4,320,748 (July 2009 est.)
**Age structure:**
*0-14 years:* 15.9% (male 353,495/female 334,592)
*15-64 years:* 73.3% (male 1,536,263/female 1,629,882)
*65 years and over:* 10.8% (male 172,070/female 294,446) (2009 est.)
**Median age:**
*total:* 34.6 years
*male:* 32.7 years
*female:* 36.7 years (2009 est.)
**Population growth rate:** -0.079% (2009 est.)
**Birth rate:** 11.12 births/1,000 population (2009 est.)
**Death rate:** 10.8 deaths/1,000 population (2008 est.)
**Net migration rate:** -1.13 migrant(s)/1,000 population (2009 est.)
**Urbanization:**
*urban population:* 42% of total population (2008)
*rate of urbanization:* -1.5% annual rate of change (2005-10 est.)

**Sex ratio:**
*at birth:* 1.06 male(s)/female
*under 15 years:* 1.06 male(s)/female
*15-64 years:* 0.94 male(s)/female
*65 years and over:* 0.58 male(s)/female
*total population:* 0.91 male(s)/female (2009 est.)
**Infant mortality rate:**
*total:* 13.13 deaths/1,000 live births
*male:* 14.57 deaths/1,000 live births
*female:* 11.6 deaths/1,000 live births (2009 est.)
**Life expectancy at birth:**
*total population:* 70.8 years
*male:* 67.1 years
*female:* 74.71 years (2009 est.)
**Total fertility rate:** 1.27 children born/woman (2009 est.)
**HIV/AIDS - adult prevalence rate:** 0.4% (2007 est.)
**HIV/AIDS - people living with HIV/AIDS:** 8,900 (2007 est.)
**HIV/AIDS - deaths:** fewer than 100 (2007 est.)
**Nationality:**
*noun:* Moldovan(s)
*adjective:* Moldovan
**Ethnic groups:** Moldovan/Romanian 78.2%, Ukrainian 8.4%, Russian 5.8%, Gagauz 4.4%, Bulgarian 1.9%, other 1.3% (2004 census)
*note:* internal disputes with ethnic Slavs in the Transnistrian region
**Religions:** Eastern Orthodox 98%, Jewish 1.5%, Baptist and other 0.5% (2000)
**Languages:** Moldovan (official, virtually the same as the Romanian language), Russian, Gagauz (a Turkish dialect)
**Literacy:**
*definition:* age 15 and over can read and write
*total population:* 99.1%
*male:* 99.7%
*female:* 98.6% (2005 est.)
**School life expectancy (primary to tertiary education):**
*total:* 12 years
*male:* 12 years
*female:* 13 years (2006)
**Education expenditures:** 7.6% of GDP (2006)

## Government

**Country name:**
*conventional long form:* Republic of Moldova
*conventional short form:* Moldova
*local long form:* Republica Moldova
*local short form:* Moldova
*former:* Moldavian Soviet Socialist Republic, Moldovan Soviet Socialist Republic
**Government type:** republic
**Capital:**
*name:* Chisinau (Kishinev)
*note:* pronounced kee-shee-now
*geographic coordinates:* 47 00 N, 28 51 E
*time difference:* UTC+2 (7 hours ahead of Washington, DC during Standard Time)
*daylight saving time:* +1hr, begins last Sunday in March; ends last Sunday in October

# Moldova (continued)

**Administrative divisions:** 32 raions (raioane, singular - raionul), 3 municipalities (municipiul), 1 autonomous territorial unit (unitatea teritoriala autonoma), and 1 territorial unit (unitatea teritoriala)
*raions:* Anenii Noi, Basarabeasca, Briceni, Cahul, Cantemir, Calarasi, Causeni, Cimislia, Criuleni, Donduseni, Drochia, Dubasari, Edinet, Falesti, Floresti, Glodeni, Hincesti, Ialoveni, Leova, Nisporeni, Ocnita, Orhei, Rezina, Riscani, Singerei, Soldanesti, Soroca, Stefan-Voda, Straseni, Taraclia, Telenesti, Ungheni
*municipalities:* Balti, Bender, Chisinau
*autonomous territorial unit:* Gagauzia
*territorial unit:* Stinga Nistrului (Transnistria)
**Independence:** 27 August 1991 (from the Soviet Union)
**National holiday:** Independence Day, 27 August (1991)
**Constitution:** adopted 29 July 1994; effective 27August 1994; note - replaced 1979 Soviet constitution
**Legal system:** based on civil law system; Constitutional Court reviews legality of legislative acts and governmental decisions of resolution; accepts many UN and Organization for Security and Cooperation in Europe (OSCE) documents; has not accepted compulsory ICJ jurisdiction
**Suffrage:** 18 years of age; universal
**Executive branch:**
*chief of state:* President Vladimir VORONIN (since 4 April 2001)
*head of government:* Prime Minister Zinaida GRECEANII (since 31 March 2008); First Deputy Prime Minister Igor DODON (since 31 March 2008)
*cabinet:* Cabinet selected by president, subject to approval of Parliament
*elections:* president elected by Parliament for a four-year term (eligible for a second term); election last held 4 April 2005 (next to be held 5 April 2009); note - prime minister designated by the president upon consultation with Parliament; within 15 days from designation, the prime minister-designate must request a vote of confidence from the Parliament regarding his/her work program and entire cabinet; prime minister designated 21 March 2008; cabinet received a vote of confidence 31 March 2008
*election results:* Vladimir VORONIN reelected president; parliamentary votes - Vladimir VORONIN 75, Gheorghe DUCA 1; Zinaida GRECEANII designated prime minister; parliamentary votes of confidence - 56 of 101
**Legislative branch:** unicameral Parliament or Parlamentul (101 seats; members elected by popular vote to serve four-year terms)
*elections:* last held 5 April 2009 (next to be held in 2013)
*election results:* percent of vote by party - PCRM 49.5%, PL 13.1%, PLDM 12.4%, AMN 9.8%; seats by party - PCRM 60, PL 15, PLDM 15, AMN 11
**Judicial branch:** Supreme Court; Constitutional Court (the sole authority for constitutional judicature)

**Political parties and leaders:** Centrist Union or UCM [Vasile TARLEV]; Christian Democratic People's Party or PPCD [Iurie ROSCA]; Communist Party of the Republic of Moldova or PCRM [Vladimir VORONIN]; Democratic Party or PD [Dumitru DIACOV]; Liberal Democratic Party or PLDM [Vladmir FILAT]; Liberal Party or PL [Mihai GHIMPU]; National Liberal Party or PNL [Vitalia PAVLICENKO]; Our Moldova Alliance or AMN [Serafim URECHEAN]; Party for Social Democracy or PDSM [Dumitru BRAGHIS]
**Political pressure groups and leaders:** NA
**International organization participation:** BSEC, CE, CEI, CIS, EAEC (observer), EAPC, EBRD, FAO, GCTU, GUAM, IAEA, IBRD, ICAO, ICCt (signatory), IDA, IFAD, IFC, IFRCS, ILO, IMF, IMO, Interpol, IOC, IOM, IPU, ISO (correspondent), ITU, MIGA, OIF, OPCW, OSCE, PFP, SECI, UN, UNCTAD, UNESCO, UNIDO, Union Latina, UNMIL, UNMIS, UNOCI, UNOMIG, UNWTO, UPU, WCO, WFTU, WHO, WIPO, WMO, WTO
**Diplomatic representation in the US:**
*chief of mission:* Ambassador Nicolae CHIRTOACA
*chancery:* 2101 S Street NW, Washington, DC 20008
*telephone:* [1] (202) 667-1130
*FAX:* [1] (202) 667-1204
**Diplomatic representation from the US:**
*chief of mission:* Ambassador Asif CHAUDHRY
*embassy:* 103 Mateevici Street, Chisinau MD-2009
*mailing address:* use embassy street address
*telephone:* [373] (22) 40-8300
*FAX:* [373] (22) 23-3044
**Flag description:** three equal vertical bands of blue (hoist side), yellow, and red; emblem in center of flag is of a Roman eagle of gold outlined in black with a red beak and talons carrying a yellow cross in its beak and a green olive branch in its right talons and a yellow scepter in its left talons; on its breast is a shield divided horizontally red over blue with a stylized ox head, star, rose, and crescent all in black-outlined yellow; same color scheme as Romania

## Economy

**Economy - overview:** Moldova remains one of the poorest countries in Europe despite recent progress from its small economic base. It enjoys a favorable climate and good farmland but has no major mineral deposits. As a result, the economy depends heavily on agriculture, featuring fruits, vegetables, wine, and tobacco. Moldova must import almost all of its energy supplies. Moldova's dependence on Russian energy was underscored at the end of 2005, when a Russian-owned electrical station in Moldova's separatist Transnistria region cut off power to Moldova and Russia's Gazprom cut off natural gas in disputes over pricing, and again in January 2009, during a similar dispute. Russia's decision to ban Moldovan wine and agricultural products, coupled with its decision to double the price Moldova paid for Russian natural gas, slowed GDP growth in 2006. However, in 2007-08 growth returned to the 6% level Moldova had achieved in 2000-05, boosted by Russia's partial

removal of the bans, solid fixed capital investment, and strong domestic demand driven by remittances from abroad. Economic reforms have been slow because of corruption and strong political forces backing government controls. Nevertheless, the government's primary goal of EU integration has resulted in some market-oriented progress. The granting of EU trade preferences and increased exports to Russia will encourage higher growth rates, but the agreements are unlikely to serve as a panacea, given the extent to which export success depends on higher quality standards and other factors. The economy remains vulnerable to higher fuel prices, poor agricultural weather, and the skepticism of foreign investors. Also, the presence of an illegal separatist regime in Moldova's Transnistria region continues to be a drag on the Moldovan economy. The deteriorating global economic crisis did not seriously effect the Moldovan economy in 2008 due to its low exposure to the international financial system, but a global economic slowdown, particularly in the EU and Russia, could hurt the economy in 2009 as Moldova relies heavily on remittances from Moldovans abroad.
**GDP (purchasing power parity):**
$10.63 billion (2008 est.)
$9.954 billion (2007)
$9.664 billion (2006)
*note:* data are in 2008 US dollars
**GDP (official exchange rate):** $6.197 billion (2008 est.)
**GDP - real growth rate:**
7.3% (2008)
3% (2007 est.)
4.8% (2006 est.)
**GDP - per capita (PPP):**
$2,500 (2008 est.)
$2,300 (2007 est.)
$2,200 (2006 est.)
*note:* data are in 2008 US dollars
**GDP - composition by sector:**
*agriculture:* 17.3%
*industry:* 21.5%
*services:* 61.2% (2008 est.)
**Labor force:** 1.327 million (2008 est.)
**Labor force - by occupation:**
*agriculture:* 40.6%
*industry:* 16%
*services:* 43.3% (2005)
**Unemployment rate:**
2.1% (2007 est.)
**Population below poverty line:** 29.5% (2005)
**Household income or consumption by percentage share:**
*lowest 10%:* 3.2%
*highest 10%:* 26.4% (2003)
**Distribution of family income - Gini index:** 33.2 (2003)
**Investment (gross fixed):** 36.1% of GDP (2008 est.)

# Moldova (continued)

**Budget:**
*revenues:* $1.95 billion
*expenditures:* $2.01 billion (2008)
**Public debt:** 21.3% of GDP (2008 est.)
**Inflation rate (consumer prices):**
7.5% (2008)
12.3% (2007 est.)
**Commercial bank prime lending rate:** 18.83%
(31 December 2007)
**Stock of money:** $965 million (31 December 2007)
**Stock of quasi money:** $1.449 billion (31 December 2007)
**Stock of domestic credit:** $1.896 billion
(31 December 2007)
**Market value of publicly traded shares:** $573.9
million (2004)
**Agriculture - products:** vegetables, fruits, wine,
grain, sugar beets, sunflower seed, tobacco; beef,
milk
**Industries:** sugar, vegetable oil, food processing,
agricultural machinery; foundry equipment,
refrigerators and freezers, washing machines;
hosiery, shoes, textiles
**Industrial production growth rate:** 6% (2008 est.)
**Electricity - production:** 3.824 billion kWh
(2006 est.)
**Electricity - consumption:** 5.806 billion kWh
(2006 est.)
**Electricity - exports:** 229 million kWh (2006 est.)
**Electricity - imports:** 3.741 billion kWh (2006 est.)
**Oil - production:** 0 bbl/day (2007 est.)
**Oil - consumption:** 15,770 bbl/day (2006 est.)
**Oil - exports:** 50.03 bbl/day (2005)
**Oil - imports:** 14,450 bbl/day (2005)
**Oil - proved reserves:** 0 bbl (1 January 2006 est.)
**Natural gas - production:** 50 million cu m
(2006 est.)
**Natural gas - consumption:** 2.44 billion cu m
(2007 est.)
**Natural gas - exports:** 0 cu m (2007 est.)
**Natural gas - imports:** 2.44 billion cu m (2007 est.)
**Natural gas - proved reserves:** 0 cu m (1 January
2006 est.)
**Current account balance:** -$903 million (2008 est.)
**Exports:** $1.79 billion f.o.b. (2008 est.)
**Exports - commodities:** foodstuffs, textiles,
machinery
**Exports - partners:** Russia 25.3%, Romania 13%,
Italy 10%, Ukraine 8.7%, Germany 8.5%, Poland
6.2%, Belarus 4.2% (2007)
**Imports:** $5 billion f.o.b. (2008 est.)
**Imports - commodities:** mineral products and fuel,
machinery and equipment, chemicals, textiles
**Imports - partners:** Russia 20.5%, Ukraine 15.8%,
Romania 15%, Germany 8.7%, Italy 5.7%,
Poland 4.1% (2007)
**Reserves of foreign exchange and gold:** $1.65
billion (31 December 2008 est.)
**Debt - external:** $4.092 billion (31 December
2008 est.)

**Stock of direct foreign investment - at home:**
$1.813 billion (2008)
**Stock of direct foreign investment - abroad:** $NA
**Exchange rates:** Moldovan lei (MDL) per US dollar -
10.326 (2008 est.), 12.177 (2007), 13.131 (2006),
12.6 (2005), 12.33 (2004)

## Communications

**Telephones - main lines in use:** 1.08 million (2007)
**Telephones - mobile cellular:** 1.883 million (2007)
**Telephone system:**
*general assessment:* inadequate, outmoded, poor
service outside Chisinau; some modernization is
under way
*domestic:* depending on location, new subscribers
may face long wait for service; multiple private
operators of GSM mobile-cellular telephone service
are operating; GPRS system is being introduced; a
CDMA mobile telephone network began operations in
2007; combined fixed-line and mobile-cellular
teledensity 70 per 100 persons
*international:* country code - 373; service through
Romania and Russia via landline; satellite earth
stations - at least 3 (Intelsat, Eutelsat, and
Intersputnik) (2007)
**Radio broadcast stations:** AM 2, FM 29,
shortwave NA (2006)
**Television broadcast stations:** 40 (2006)
**Internet country code:** .md
**Internet hosts:** 223,869 (2008)
**Internet users:** 700,000 (2007)

## Transportation

**Airports:** 11 (2008)
**Airports - with paved runways:**
*total:* 5
*over 3,047 m:* 1
*2,438 to 3,047 m:* 2
*1,524 to 2,437 m:* 2 (2008)
**Airports - with unpaved runways:**
*total:* 6
*1,524 to 2,437 m:* 3
*914 to 1,523 m:* 1
*under 914 m:* 2 (2008)
**Pipelines:** gas 1,906 km (2008)
**Railways:**
*total:* 1,138 km
*broad gauge:* 1,124 km 1.520-m gauge
*standard gauge:* 14 km 1.435-m gauge (2006)
**Roadways:**
*total:* 12,666 km
*paved:* 12,117 km
*unpaved:* 549 km (2007)
**Waterways:** 424 km (on Dniester and Prut rivers)
(2008)
**Merchant marine:**
*total:* 39
*by type:* bulk carrier 2, cargo 32, chemical tanker 2,
combination ore/oil 2, petroleum tanker 1
*foreign-owned:* 17 (Egypt 1, Romania 3, Russia 3,
Syria 1, Turkey 3, Ukraine 5, Yemen 1) (2008)

## Military

**Military branches:** National Army: Land Forces,
Rapid Reaction Forces, Air and Air Defense Forces
(2009)
**Military service age and obligation:** 18 years of
age for compulsory military service; 17 years of age
for voluntary service; male registration required at age
16; 12-month service obligation (2009)
**Manpower available for military service:**
*males age 16-49:* 1,161,924
*females age 16-49:* 1,187,771 (2008 est.)
**Manpower fit for military service:**
*males age 16-49:* 877,665
*females age 16-49:* 987,356 (2009 est.)
**Manpower reaching militarily significant age
annually:**
*male:* 31,633
*female:* 30,214 (2009 est.)
**Military expenditures:** 0.4% of GDP (2005 est.)

## Transnational Issues

**Disputes - international:** Moldova and Ukraine
operate joint customs posts to monitor the transit of
people and commodities through Moldova's
break-away Transnistria region, which remains under
OSCE supervision
**Trafficking in persons:**
*current situation:* Moldova is a major source and, to a
lesser extent, a transit country for women and girls
trafficked for the purpose of commercial sexual
exploitation; Moldovan women are trafficked to the
Middle East, Eastern Europe, and Western Europe;
girls and young women are trafficked within the
country from rural areas to Chisinau; children are also
trafficked to neighboring countries for forced labor and
begging; labor trafficking of men to work in the
construction, agriculture, and service sectors of
Russia is increasingly a problem
*tier rating:* Tier 3 - Moldova does not fully comply with
the minimum standards for the elimination of
trafficking and is not making significant efforts to do
so; the government failed to follow-up on allegations
of officials complicit in trafficking cited in the 2007
Report, and it did not demonstrate proactive efforts to
identify trafficking victims (2008)
**Illicit drugs:** limited cultivation of opium poppy and
cannabis, mostly for CIS consumption; transshipment
point for illicit drugs from Southwest Asia via Central
Asia to Russia, Western Europe, and possibly the US;
widespread crime and underground economic activity

# Monaco

## Introduction

**Background:** The Genoese built a fortress on the site of present-day Monaco in 1215. The current ruling Grimaldi family secured control in the late 13th century, and a principality was established in 1338. Economic development was spurred in the late 19th century with a railroad linkup to France and the opening of a casino. Since then, the principality's mild climate, splendid scenery, and gambling facilities have made Monaco world famous as a tourist and recreation center.

## Geography

**Location:** Western Europe, bordering the Mediterranean Sea on the southern coast of France, near the border with Italy
**Geographic coordinates:** 43 44 N, 7 24 E
**Map references:** Europe
**Area:**
*total:* 1.95 sq km
*land:* 1.95 sq km
*water:* 0 sq km
**Area - comparative:** about three times the size of The Mall in Washington, DC
**Land boundaries:**
*total:* 4.4 km
*border countries:* France 4.4 km
**Coastline:** 4.1 km
**Maritime claims:**
*territorial sea:* 12 nm
*exclusive economic zone:* 12 nm
**Climate:** Mediterranean with mild, wet winters and hot, dry summers
**Terrain:** hilly, rugged, rocky
**Elevation extremes:**
*lowest point:* Mediterranean Sea 0 m
*highest point:* Mont Agel 140 m
**Natural resources:** none

**Land use:**
*arable land:* 0%
*permanent crops:* 0%
*other:* 100% (urban area) (2005)
**Irrigated land:** NA
**Natural hazards:** NA
**Environment - current issues:** NA
**Environment - international agreements:**
*party to:* Air Pollution, Air Pollution-Sulfur 94, Air Pollution-Volatile Organic Compounds, Biodiversity, Climate Change, Climate Change-Kyoto Protocol, Desertification, Endangered Species, Hazardous Wastes, Law of the Sea, Marine Dumping, Ozone Layer Protection, Ship Pollution, Wetlands, Whaling
*signed, but not ratified:* none of the selected agreements
**Geography - note:** second-smallest independent state in the world (after Holy See); almost entirely urban

## People

**Population:** 32,965 (July 2009 est.)
**Age structure:**
*0-14 years:* 14.6% (male 2,466/female 2,349)
*15-64 years:* 62.4% (male 10,184/female 10,395)
*65 years and over:* 23% (male 3,068/female 4,503) (2009 est.)
**Median age:**
*total:* 45.7 years
*male:* 43.6 years
*female:* 47.7 years (2009 est.)
**Population growth rate:** 0.394% (2009 est.)
**Birth rate:** 9.1 births/1,000 population (2009 est.)
**Death rate:** 12.96 deaths/1,000 population (2008 est.)
**Net migration rate:** 7.58 migrant(s)/1,000 population (2009 est.)
**Urbanization:**
*urban population:* 100% of total population (2008)
*rate of urbanization:* 0.3% annual rate of change (2005-10 est.)
**Sex ratio:**
*at birth:* 1.06 male(s)/female
*under 15 years:* 1.05 male(s)/female
*15-64 years:* 0.98 male(s)/female
*65 years and over:* 0.68 male(s)/female
*total population:* 0.91 male(s)/female (2009 est.)
**Infant mortality rate:**
*total:* 5 deaths/1,000 live births
*male:* 5.77 deaths/1,000 live births
*female:* 4.19 deaths/1,000 live births (2009 est.)
**Life expectancy at birth:**
*total population:* 80.09 years
*male:* 76.3 years
*female:* 84.09 years (2009 est.)
**Total fertility rate:** 1.75 children born/woman (2009 est.)
**HIV/AIDS - adult prevalence rate:** NA
**HIV/AIDS - people living with HIV/AIDS:** NA
**HIV/AIDS - deaths:** NA
**Nationality:**
*noun:* Monegasque(s) or Monacan(s)
*adjective:* Monegasque or Monacan

**Ethnic groups:** French 47%, Monegasque 16%, Italian 16%, other 21%
**Religions:** Roman Catholic 90%, other 10%
**Languages:** French (official), English, Italian, Monegasque
**Literacy:**
*definition:* age 15 and over can read and write
*total population:* 99%
*male:* 99%
*female:* 99% (2003 est.)
**Education expenditures:** 4.4% of GDP (2004)

## Government

**Country name:**
*conventional long form:* Principality of Monaco
*conventional short form:* Monaco
*local long form:* Principaute de Monaco
*local short form:* Monaco
**Government type:** constitutional monarchy
**Capital:**
*name:* Monaco
*geographic coordinates:* 43 44 N, 7 25 E
*time difference:* UTC+1 (6 hours ahead of Washington, DC during Standard Time)
*daylight saving time:* +1hr, begins last Sunday in March; ends last Sunday in October
**Administrative divisions:** none; there are no first-order administrative divisions as defined by the US Government, but there are four quarters (quartiers, singular - quartier); Fontvieille, La Condamine, Monaco-Ville, Monte-Carlo
**Independence:** 1419 (beginning of rule by the House of Grimaldi)
**National holiday:** National Day (Saint Rainier's Day), 19 November (1857)
**Constitution:** 17 December 1962; modified 2 April 2002
**Legal system:** based on French law; has not accepted compulsory ICJ jurisdiction
**Suffrage:** 18 years of age; universal
**Executive branch:**
*chief of state:* Prince ALBERT II (since 6 April 2005)
*head of government:* Minister of State Jean-Paul PROUST (since 1 June 2005)
*cabinet:* Council of Government is under the authority of the monarch
*elections:* the monarchy is hereditary; minister of state appointed by the monarch from a list of three French national candidates presented by the French Government
**Legislative branch:** unicameral National Council or Conseil National (24 seats; 16 members elected by list majority system, 8 by proportional representation; to serve five-year terms)
*elections:* last held 3 February 2008 (next to be held in February 2013)
*election results:* percent of vote by party - UPM 52.2%, REM 40.5%, Monaco Together 7.3%; seats by party - UPM 21, REM 3
**Judicial branch:** Supreme Court or Tribunal Supreme (judges appointed by the monarch on the basis of nominations by the National Council)

# Monaco (continued)

**Political parties and leaders:** Union for Monaco or UPM (including National Union for the Future of Monaco or UNAM); Rally and Issues for Monaco or REM; Monaco Together

**Political pressure groups and leaders:** NA

**International organization participation:** CE, FAO, IAEA, ICAO, ICC, ICCt (signatory), ICRM, IFRCS, IHO, IMO, IMSO, Interpol, IOC, IPU, ITSO, ITU, OIF, OPCW, OSCE, Schengen Convention, UN, UNCTAD, UNESCO, UNIDO, Union Latina, UNWTO, UPU, WFTU, WHO, WIPO, WMO

**Diplomatic representation in the US:**
*chief of mission:* Ambassador to the US and Representative to the UN Gilles NOGHES
*chancery:* 3400 International Drive NW, Suite 2K-100, Washington, DC 20008
*telephone:* (202) 234-1530
*FAX:* (202) 552-5778
*consulate(s) general:* New York

**Diplomatic representation from the US:** the US does not have an embassy in Monaco; the US Ambassador to France is accredited to Monaco; the US Consul General in Marseille (France), under the authority of the US ambassador to France, handles routine diplomatic and consular matters concerning Monaco

**Flag description:** two equal horizontal bands of red (top) and white; similar to the flag of Indonesia which is longer and the flag of Poland which is white (top) and red

## Economy

**Economy - overview:** Monaco, bordering France on the Mediterranean coast, is a popular resort, attracting tourists to its casino and pleasant climate. The principality also is a major banking center and has successfully sought to diversify into services and small, high-value-added, nonpolluting industries. The state has no income tax and low business taxes and thrives as a tax haven both for individuals who have established residence and for foreign companies that have set up businesses and offices. The state retains monopolies in a number of sectors, including tobacco, the telephone network, and the postal service. Living standards are high, roughly comparable to those in prosperous French metropolitan areas.

**GDP (purchasing power parity):**
$976.3 million (2006 est.)
*note:* Monaco does not publish national income figures; the estimates are extremely rough

**GDP (official exchange rate):** $NA

**GDP - real growth rate:** 0.9% (2000 est.)

**GDP - per capita (PPP):**
$30,000 (2006 est.)

**GDP - composition by sector:**
*agriculture:* 0%
*industry:* 4.9%
*services:* 95.1% (2005)

**Labor force:** 44,000
*note:* includes workers from all foreign countries (2005 est.)

**Unemployment rate:**
0% (2005)

**Population below poverty line:** NA%

**Household income or consumption by percentage share:**
*lowest 10%:* NA%
*highest 10%:* NA%

**Budget:**
*revenues:* $863 million
*expenditures:* $920.6 million (2005 est.)

**Inflation rate (consumer prices):**
1.9% (2000)

**Market value of publicly traded shares:** $NA

**Agriculture - products:** none

**Industries:** tourism, construction, small-scale industrial and consumer products

**Industrial production growth rate:** NA%

**Electricity - consumption:** NA kWh

**Electricity - imports:** NA kWh; note - electricity supplied by France

**Exports:** $716.3 million
*note:* full customs integration with France, which collects and rebates Monegasque trade duties; also participates in EU market system through customs union with France (2005)

**Imports:** $916.1 million f.o.b.
*note:* full customs integration with France, which collects and rebates Monegasque trade duties; also participates in EU market system through customs union with France (2005)

**Debt - external:** $18 billion (2000 est.)

**Exchange rates:** euros (EUR) per US dollar - 0.6827 (2008 est.), 0.7345 (2007), 0.7964 (2006), 0.8041 (2005), 0.8054 (2004)

## Communications

**Telephones - main lines in use:** 34,000 (2005)

**Telephones - mobile cellular:** 17,200 (2005)

**Telephone system:**
*general assessment:* modern automatic telephone system; the country's sole fixed line operator offers a full range of services to residential and business customers
*domestic:* combined fixed line and mobile telephone density exceeds 100%
*international:* country code - 377; no satellite earth stations; connected by cable into the French communications system

**Radio broadcast stations:** AM 1, FM 11, shortwave 1 (2008)

**Television broadcast stations:** 5 (1998)

**Internet country code:** .mc

**Internet hosts:** 21,058 (2008)

**Internet users:** 20,000 (2006)

## Transportation

**Heliports:** 1 (2007)

**Roadways:**
*total:* 50 km
*paved:* 50 km (2007)

**Merchant marine:**
*registered in other countries:* 70 (Bahamas 15, Georgia 4, Isle of Man 3, Liberia 8, Marshall Islands 13, Norway 5, Panama 16, Saint Vincent and the Grenadines 5, Vanuatu 1) (2008)

**Ports and terminals:** Monaco

## Military

**Military branches:** no regular military forces; the Palace Guard performs ceremonial duties

**Manpower available for military service:**
*males age 16-49:* 6,687 (2008 est.)

**Manpower fit for military service:**
*males age 16-49:* 5,495
*females age 16-49:* 5,406 (2009 est.)

**Manpower reaching militarily significant age annually:**
*male:* 190
*female:* 182 (2009 est.)

**Military - note:** defense is the responsibility of France

## Transnational Issues

**Disputes - international:** none

# Mongolia

## Introduction

**Background:** The Mongols gained fame in the 13th century when under Chinggis KHAN they established a huge Eurasian empire through conquest. After his death the empire was divided into several powerful Mongol states, but these broke apart in the 14th century. The Mongols eventually retired to their original steppe homelands and in the late 17th century came under Chinese rule. Mongolia won its independence in 1921 with Soviet backing and a Communist regime was installed in 1924. The modern country of Mongolia, however, represents only part of the Mongols' historical homeland; more Mongols live in the Inner Mongolia Autonomous Region in the People's Republic of China than in Mongolia. Following a peaceful democratic revolution, the ex-Communist Mongolian People's Revolutionary Party (MPRP) won elections in 1990 and 1992, but was defeated by the Democratic Union Coalition (DUC) in the 1996 parliamentary election. The MPRP won an overwhelming majority in the 2000 parliamentary election, but the party lost seats in the 2004 election and shared power with democratic coalition parties from 2004-08. The MPRP regained a solid majority in the 2008 parliamentary elections but nevertheless formed a coalition government with the Democratic Party. The prime minister and most cabinet members are MPRP members.

## Geography

**Location:** Northern Asia, between China and Russia
**Geographic coordinates:** 46 00 N, 105 00 E
**Map references:** Asia
**Area:**
*total:* 1,564,116 sq km
*land:* 1,554,731 sq km
*water:* 9,385 sq km

**Area - comparative:** slightly smaller than Alaska
**Land boundaries:**
*total:* 8,220 km
*border countries:* China 4,677 km, Russia 3,543 km
**Coastline:** 0 km (landlocked)
**Maritime claims:** none (landlocked)
**Climate:** desert; continental (large daily and seasonal temperature ranges)
**Terrain:** vast semidesert and desert plains, grassy steppe, mountains in west and southwest; Gobi Desert in south-central
**Elevation extremes:**
*lowest point:* Hoh Nuur 518 m
*highest point:* Nayramadlin Orgil (Huyten Orgil) 4,374 m
**Natural resources:** oil, coal, copper, molybdenum, tungsten, phosphates, tin, nickel, zinc, fluorspar, gold, silver, iron
**Land use:**
*arable land:* 0.76%
*permanent crops:* 0%
*other:* 99.24% (2005)
**Irrigated land:** 840 sq km (2003)
**Total renewable water resources:** 34.8 cu km (1999)
**Freshwater withdrawal (domestic/industrial/agricultural):**
*total:* 0.44 cu km/yr (20%/27%/52%)
*per capita:* 166 cu m/yr (2000)
**Natural hazards:** dust storms; grassland and forest fires; drought; "zud," which is harsh winter conditions
**Environment - current issues:** limited natural fresh water resources in some areas; the policies of former Communist regimes promoted rapid urbanization and industrial growth that had negative effects on the environment; the burning of soft coal in power plants and the lack of enforcement of environmental laws severely polluted the air in Ulaanbaatar; deforestation, overgrazing, and the converting of virgin land to agricultural production increased soil erosion from wind and rain; desertification and mining activities had a deleterious effect on the environment
**Environment - international agreements:**
*party to:* Biodiversity, Climate Change, Climate Change-Kyoto Protocol, Desertification, Endangered Species, Environmental Modification, Hazardous Wastes, Law of the Sea, Ozone Layer Protection, Ship Pollution, Wetlands, Whaling
*signed, but not ratified:* none of the selected agreements
**Geography - note:** landlocked; strategic location between China and Russia

## People

**Population:** 3,041,142 (July 2009 est.)
**Age structure:**
*0-14 years:* 28.1% (male 436,391/female 418,923)
*15-64 years:* 67.9% (male 1,031,819/female 1,033,806)
*65 years and over:* 4% (male 52,430/female 67,773) (2009 est.)
**Median age:**
*total:* 25.3 years
*male:* 24.9 years
*female:* 25.7 years (2009 est.)
**Population growth rate:** 1.493% (2009 est.)
**Birth rate:** 21.05 births/1,000 population (2009 est.)
**Death rate:** 6.16 deaths/1,000 population (2008 est.)
**Net migration rate:** NA
**Urbanization:**
*urban population:* 57% of total population (2008)
*rate of urbanization:* 1.2% annual rate of change (2005-10 est.)
**Sex ratio:**
*at birth:* 1.05 male(s)/female
*under 15 years:* 1.04 male(s)/female
*15-64 years:* 1 male(s)/female
*65 years and over:* 0.77 male(s)/female
*total population:* 1 male(s)/female (2009 est.)
**Infant mortality rate:**
*total:* 39.88 deaths/1,000 live births
*male:* 42.99 deaths/1,000 live births
*female:* 36.61 deaths/1,000 live births (2009 est.)
**Life expectancy at birth:**
*total population:* 67.65 years
*male:* 65.23 years
*female:* 70.19 years (2009 est.)
**Total fertility rate:** 2.23 children born/woman (2009 est.)
**HIV/AIDS - adult prevalence rate:** less than 0.1% (2007 est.)
**HIV/AIDS - people living with HIV/AIDS:** fewer than 500 (2007 est.)
**HIV/AIDS - deaths:** fewer than 200 (2003 est.)
**Nationality:**
*noun:* Mongolian(s)
*adjective:* Mongolian
**Ethnic groups:** Mongol (mostly Khalkha) 94.9%, Turkic (mostly Kazakh) 5%, other (including Chinese and Russian) 0.1% (2000)

# Mongolia (continued)

**Religions:** Buddhist Lamaist 50%, Shamanist and Christian 6%, Muslim 4%, none 40% (2004)
**Languages:** Khalkha Mongol 90%, Turkic, Russian (1999)
**Literacy:**
*definition:* age 15 and over can read and write
*total population:* 97.8%
*male:* 98%
*female:* 97.5% (2000 census)
**School life expectancy (primary to tertiary education):**
*total:* 13 years
*male:* 12 years
*female:* 14 years (2006)
**Education expenditures:** 5% of GDP (2004)

## Government

**Country name:**
*conventional long form:* none
*conventional short form:* Mongolia
*local long form:* none
*local short form:* Mongol Uls
*former:* Outer Mongolia
**Government type:** parliamentary
**Capital:**
*name:* Ulaanbaatar
*geographic coordinates:* 47 55 N, 106 55 E
*time difference:* UTC+8 (13 hours ahead of Washington, DC during Standard Time)
**Administrative divisions:** 21 provinces (aymguud, singular - aymag) and 1 municipality* (singular - hot); Arhangay, Bayanhongor, Bayan-Olgiy, Bulgan, Darhan-Uul, Dornod, Dornogovi, Dundgovi, Dzavhan (Zavkhan), Govi-Altay, Govisumber, Hentiy, Hovd, Hovsgol, Omnogovi, Orhon, Ovorhangay, Selenge, Suhbaatar, Tov, Ulaanbaatar*, Uvs
**Independence:** 11 July 1921 (from China)
**National holiday:** Independence Day/Revolution Day, 11 July (1921)
**Constitution:** 13 January 1992
**Legal system:** blend of Soviet and German systems that employ "continental" or "civil" code; case-precedent may be used to inform judges, but all decisions must refer to the law as written; constitution ambiguous on judicial review of legislative acts; has not accepted compulsory ICJ jurisdiction
**Suffrage:** 18 years of age; universal
**Executive branch:**
*chief of state:* President Tsakhia ELBEGDORJ (since 18 June 2009)
*head of government:* Prime Minister Sanjaa BAYAR (since 22 November 2007); First Deputy Prime Minister (Norov ALTANKHUYAG (since 20 September 2008); Vice Prime Minister Miegombyn ENKHBOLD (since 6 December 2007)
*cabinet:* Cabinet nominated by the prime minister in consultation with the president and confirmed by the State Great Hural (parliament)
*elections:* presidential candidates nominated by political parties represented in State Great Hural and elected by popular vote for a four-year term (eligible

for a second term); election last held 24 May 2009 (next to be held in May 2013); following legislative elections, leader of majority party or majority coalition is usually elected prime minister by State Great Hural
*election results:* in elections in May 2009, Tsakhia ELBEGDORJ elected president; percent of vote - Tsakhia ELBEGDORJ 51.24%, Nambaryn ENKHBAYAR 47.44%, others 1.32%
**Legislative branch:** unicameral State Great Hural 76 seats; members elected by popular vote to serve four-year terms
*elections:* last held 29 June 2008 (next to be held in June 2012)
*election results:* percent of vote by party - NA; seats by party - MPRP 45, DP 27, others 4; note - 1 seat disputed and unfilled
**Judicial branch:** Supreme Court (serves as appeals court for people's and provincial courts but rarely overturns verdicts of lower courts; judges are nominated by the General Council of Courts and approved by the president)
**Political parties and leaders:** Democratic Party or DP [Norov ALTANHUYAG]; Mongolian People's Revolutionary Party or MPRP [Sanjaa BAYAR]
**Political pressure groups and leaders:**
*other:* human rights groups; women's groups
**International organization participation:** ADB, ARF, CP, EBRD, FAO, G-77, IAEA, IBRD, ICAO, ICCt, ICRM, IDA, IFAD, IFC, IFRCS, ILO, IMF, IMO, Interpol, IOC, IOM, IPU, ISO, ITSO, ITU, ITUC, MIGA, MINURSO, MONUC, NAM, OPCW, OSCE (partner), SCO (observer), UN, UNCTAD, UNESCO, UNIDO, UNMIL, UNMIS, UNOMIG, UNWTO, UPU, WCO, WFTU, WHO, WIPO, WMO, WTO
**Diplomatic representation in the US:**
*chief of mission:* Ambassador Khasbazaryn BEKHBAT
*chancery:* 2833 M Street NW, Washington, DC 20007
*telephone:* [1] (202) 333-7117
*FAX:* [1] (202) 298-9227
*consulate(s) general:* New York
**Diplomatic representation from the US:**
*chief of mission:* Ambassador Mark C. MINTON
*embassy:* Big Ring Road, 11th Micro Region, Ulaanbaatar, 14171 Mongolia
*mailing address:* PSC 461, Box 300, FPO AP 96521-0002; P.O. Box 1021, Ulaanbaatar-13
*telephone:* [976] (11) 329-095
*FAX:* [976] (11) 320-776
**Flag description:** three equal, vertical bands of red (hoist side), blue, and red; centered on the hoist-side red band in yellow is the national emblem ("soyombo" -a columnar arrangement of abstract and geometric representation for fire, sun, moon, earth, water, and the yin-yang symbol)

## Economy

**Economy - overview:** Economic activity in Mongolia has traditionally been based on herding and agriculture. Mongolia has extensive mineral deposits. Copper, coal, gold, molybdenum, fluorspar, uranium, tin, and

tungsten account for a large part of industrial production and foreign direct investment. Soviet assistance, at its height one-third of GDP, disappeared almost overnight in 1990 and 1991 at the time of the dismantlement of the USSR. The following decade saw Mongolia endure both deep recession because of political inaction and natural disasters, as well as economic growth because of reform-embracing, free-market economics and extensive privatization of the formerly state-run economy. Severe winters and summer droughts in 2000-02 resulted in massive livestock die-off and zero or negative GDP growth. This was compounded by falling prices for Mongolia's primary sector exports and widespread opposition to privatization. Growth averaged nearly 9% per year in 2004-08, largely because of high copper prices and new gold production. Until late 2008 Mongolia experienced a soaring inflation rate, with year-to-year inflation reaching nearly 40% - the highest inflation rate in over a decade. In late 2008 falling commodity prices in this import-reliant country helped lower inflation, but by that time, the country had begun to feel the effects of the global financial crisis. Falling prices for copper and other mineral exports reduced government revenues and is forcing cuts in spending. The global credit crisis has stalled growth in key sectors, especially those that had been fueled by foreign investment. Mongolia's economy continues to be heavily influenced by its neighbors. Mongolia purchases 95% of its petroleum products and a substantial amount of electric power from Russia, leaving it vulnerable to price increases. Trade with China represents more than half of Mongolia's total external trade - China receives about 70% of Mongolia's exports. Remittances from Mongolians working abroad both legally and illegally are sizable, but have fallen due to the economic crisis; money laundering is a growing concern. Mongolia settled its $11 billion debt with Russia at the end of 2003 on favorable terms. Mongolia, which joined the World Trade Organization in 1997, seeks to expand its participation and integration into Asian regional economic and trade regimes.
**GDP (purchasing power parity):**
$9.557 billion (2008 est.)
$8.696 billion (2007)
$7.913 billion (2006)
*note:* data are in 2008 US dollars
**GDP (official exchange rate):** $4.991 billion (2008 est.)
**GDP - real growth rate:**
8.9% (2008 est.)
9.9% (2007 est.)
8.6% (2006 est.)
**GDP - per capita (PPP):**
$3,200 (2008 est.)
$2,900 (2007 est.)
$2,700 (2006 est.)
*note:* data are in 2008 US dollars
**GDP - composition by sector:**
*agriculture:* 18.8%
*industry:* 38.5%
*services:* 42.7% (2008)

# Mongolia *(continued)*

**Labor force:** 1.068 million (2008)
**Labor force - by occupation:**
*agriculture:* 34%
*industry:* 5%
*services:* 61% (2008)
**Unemployment rate:**
2.8% (2008)
3% (2007)
**Population below poverty line:** 36.1% (2004)
**Household income or consumption by percentage share:**
*lowest 10%:* 3%
*highest 10%:* 24.6% (2002)
**Distribution of family income - Gini index:** 32.8 (2002)
**Budget:**
*revenues:* $1.71 billion
*expenditures:* $1.95 billion (2008)
**Inflation rate (consumer prices):**
28% (2008 est.)
9% (2007 est.)
**Central bank discount rate:** 9.75% (31 December 2008)
**Commercial bank prime lending rate:** 17.54% (31 December 2007)
**Stock of money:** $521.2 million (31 December 2008)
**Stock of quasi money:** $1.326 billion (31 December 2008)
**Stock of domestic credit:** $2.07 billion (31 December 2008)
**Market value of publicly traded shares:** $412 million (31 December 2008)
**Agriculture - products:** wheat, barley, vegetables, forage crops; sheep, goats, cattle, camels, horses
**Industries:** construction and construction materials; mining (coal, copper, molybdenum, fluorspar, tin, tungsten, and gold); oil; food and beverages; processing of animal products, cashmere and natural fiber manufacturing
**Industrial production growth rate:** 3% (2006 est.)
**Electricity - production:** 3.979 billion kWh (2008)
**Electricity - consumption:** 3.491 billion kWh (2008)
**Electricity - exports:** 15.8 million kWh (2008)
**Electricity - imports:** 197.5 million kWh (2008)
**Oil - production:** 3,216 bbl/day (2008)
**Oil - consumption:** 12,780 bbl/day (2008)
**Oil - exports:** 2,902 bbl/day (2008)
**Oil - imports:** 17,680 bbl/day (2008)
**Oil - proved reserves:** NA bbl
**Natural gas - production:** 0 cu m (2007 est.)
**Natural gas - consumption:** 0 cu m (2007 est.)
**Natural gas - exports:** 0 cu m (2007 est.)
**Natural gas - imports:** 0 cu m (2007 est.)
**Natural gas - proved reserves:** 0 cu m (1 January 2006 est.)
**Current account balance:** -$1 billion (2008 est.)
**Exports:** $2.539 billion f.o.b. (2008)
**Exports - commodities:** copper, apparel, livestock, animal products, cashmere, wool, hides, fluorspar, other nonferrous metals, coal

**Exports - partners:** China 71.9%, Canada 10.7%, US 4.8% (2007)
**Imports:** $3.615 billion c.i.f. (2008)
**Imports - commodities:** machinery and equipment, fuel, cars, food products, industrial consumer goods, chemicals, building materials, sugar, tea
**Imports - partners:** China 32%, Russia 29.4%, South Korea 7.9%, Japan 7.2% (2007)
**Debt - external:** $1.6 billion (2008)
**Stock of direct foreign investment - at home:** $NA
**Stock of direct foreign investment - abroad:** $NA
**Exchange rates:** togrog/tugriks (MNT) per US dollar -1,267.51 (2008), 1,170 (2007), 1,165 (2006), 1,205 (2005), 1,185.3 (2004)

## Communications

**Telephones - main lines in use:** 148,200 (2008)
**Telephones - mobile cellular:** 1.796 million (2008)
**Telephone system:**
*general assessment:* network is improving with international direct dialing available in many areas
*domestic:* very low fixed-line density; there are multiple mobile cellular service providers and subscribership is increasing rapidly; a fiber-optic network has been installed that is improving broadband and communication services between major urban centers with multiple companies providing inter-city fiber-optic cable services
*international:* country code - 976; satellite earth stations - 7
**Radio broadcast stations:** AM 7, FM 115 (includes 20 national radio broadcaster repeaters), shortwave 4 (2006)
**Television broadcast stations:** 68 (2008)
**Internet country code:** .mn
**Internet hosts:** 356 (2008)
**Internet users:** 320,000 (2007)

## Transportation

**Airports:** 44 (2008)
**Airports - with paved runways:**
*total:* 12
*over 3,047 m:* 1
*2,438 to 3,047 m:* 10
*1,524 to 2,437 m:* 1 (2008)
**Airports - with unpaved runways:**
*total:* 32
*over 3,047 m:* 1
*2,438 to 3,047 m:* 5
*1,524 to 2,437 m:* 24
*914 to 1,523 m:* 1
*under 914 m:* 1 (2008)
**Heliports:** 1 (2007)
**Railways:**
*total:* 1,810 km
*broad gauge:* 1,810 km 1.520-m gauge (2008)
**Roadways:**
*total:* 49,249 km
*paved:* 2,671 km
*unpaved:* 46,578 km (2008)

**Waterways:** 580 km
*note:* only waterway in operation is Lake Hovsgol (135 km); Selenge River (270 km) and Orhon River (175 km) are navigable but carry little traffic; lakes and rivers freeze in winter, are open from May to September (2007)
**Merchant marine:**
*total:* 77
*by type:* bulk carrier 20, cargo 44, chemical tanker 2, liquefied gas 1, passenger/cargo 1, petroleum tanker 2, roll on/roll off 6, vehicle carrier 1
*foreign-owned:* 53 (China 1, Germany 4, Indonesia 1, North Korea 1, South Korea 1, Lebanon 2, Russia 9, Singapore 9, Thailand 1, Ukraine 1, Vietnam 23) (2008)

## Military

**Military branches:** Mongolian Armed Forces: Mongolian Army, Mongolian Air Force; there is no navy (2009)
**Military service age and obligation:** 18-25 years of age for compulsory military service; conscript service obligation - 12 months in land or air defense forces or police; a small portion of Mongolian land forces (2.5 percent) is comprised of contract soldiers; women cannot be deployed overseas for military operations (2006)
**Manpower available for military service:**
*males age 16-49:* 865,425
*females age 16-49:* 860,669 (2008 est.)
**Manpower fit for military service:**
*males age 16-49:* 706,774
*females age 16-49:* 740,550 (2009 est.)
**Manpower reaching militarily significant age annually:**
*male:* 28,251
*female:* 27,344 (2009 est.)
**Military expenditures:** 1.4% of GDP (2006)

## Transnational Issues

**Disputes - international:** none

# Montenegro

## Introduction

**Background:** The use of the name Montenegro began in the 15th century when the Crnojevic dynasty began to rule the Serbian principality of Zeta; over subsequent centuries Montenegro was able to maintain its independence from the Ottoman Empire. From the 16th to 19th centuries, Montenegro became a theocracy ruled by a series of bishop princes; in 1852, it was transformed into a secular principality. After World War I, Montenegro was absorbed by the Kingdom of Serbs, Croats, and Slovenes, which became the Kingdom of Yugoslavia in 1929; at the conclusion of World War II, it became a constituent republic of the Socialist Federal Republic of Yugoslavia. When the latter dissolved in 1992, Montenegro federated with Serbia, first as the Federal Republic of Yugoslavia and, after 2003, in a looser union of Serbia and Montenegro. In May 2006, Montenegro invoked its right under the Constitutional Charter of Serbia and Montenegro to hold a referendum on independence from the state union. The vote for severing ties with Serbia exceeded 55% - the threshold set by the EU - allowing Montenegro to formally declare its independence on 3 June 2006.

## Geography

**Location:** Southeastern Europe, between the Adriatic Sea and Serbia
**Geographic coordinates:** 42 30 N, 19 18 E
**Map references:** Europe
**Area:**
*total:* 14,026 sq km
*land:* 13,812 sq km
*water:* 214 sq km
**Area - comparative:** slightly smaller than Connecticut
**Land boundaries:**
*total:* 625 km
*border countries:* Albania 172 km, Bosnia and Herzegovina 225 km, Croatia 25 km, Kosovo 79 km, Serbia 124 km
**Coastline:** 293.5 km

**Maritime claims:**
*territorial sea:* 12 nm
*continental shelf:* defined by treaty
**Climate:** Mediterranean climate, hot dry summers and autumns and relatively cold winters with heavy snowfalls inland
**Terrain:** highly indented coastline with narrow coastal plain backed by rugged high limestone mountains and plateaus
**Elevation extremes:**
*lowest point:* Adriatic Sea 0 m
*highest point:* Bobotov Kuk 2,522 m
**Natural resources:** bauxite, hydroelectricity
**Land use:**
*arable land:* 13.7%
*permanent crops:* 1%
*other:* 85.3%
**Irrigated land:** NA
**Natural hazards:** destructive earthquakes
**Environment - current issues:** pollution of coastal waters from sewage outlets, especially in tourist-related areas such as Kotor
**Environment - international agreements:**
*party to:* Air Pollution, Biodiversity, Climate Change, Climate Change-Kyoto Protocol, Desertification, Hazardous Wastes, Law of the Sea, Marine Dumping, Marine Life Conservation, Ozone Layer Protection, Ship Pollution
*signed, but not ratified:* none of the selected agreements
**Geography - note:** strategic location along the Adriatic coast

## People

**Population:** 672,180 (July 2009 est.)
**Age structure:**
*0-14 years:* 16% (male 52,645/female 54,846)
*15-64 years:* 70.3% (male 244,949/female 227,794)
*65 years and over:* 13.7% (male 37,217/female 54,729) (2009 est.)
**Median age:**
*total:* 36.7 years
*male:* 35.2 years
*female:* 38.4 years (2009 est.)
**Population growth rate:** -0.851% (2009 est.)
**Birth rate:** 11.14 births/1,000 population (2009 est.)
**Death rate:** 8.51 deaths/1,000 population (2008 est.)
**Urbanization:**
*urban population:* 60% of total population (2008)
*rate of urbanization:* -0.8% annual rate of change (2005-10 est.)
**Sex ratio:**
*at birth:* 1.08 male(s)/female
*under 15 years:* 0.96 male(s)/female
*15-64 years:* 1.08 male(s)/female
*65 years and over:* 0.68 male(s)/female
*total population:* 0.99 male(s)/female (2009 est.)
**Major infectious diseases:**
*degree of risk:* intermediate
*food or waterborne diseases:* bacterial diarrhea
*vectorborne disease:* Crimean Congo hemorrhagic fever (2009)

**Nationality:**
*noun:* Montenegrin(s)
*adjective:* Montenegrin
**Ethnic groups:** Montenegrin 43%, Serbian 32%, Bosniak 8%, Albanian 5%, other (Muslims, Croats, Roma (Gypsy)) 12% (2003 census)
**Religions:** Orthodox 74.2%, Muslim 17.7%, Catholic 3.5%, other 0.6%, unspecified 3%, atheist 1% (2003 census)
**Languages:** Serbian 63.6%, Montenegrin (official) 22%, Bosnian 5.5%, Albanian 5.3%, unspecified 3.7% (2003 census)
**Education expenditures:** NA

## Government

**Country name:**
*conventional long form:* none
*conventional short form:* Montenegro
*local long form:* none
*local short form:* Crna Gora
*former:* People's Republic of Montenegro, Socialist Republic of Montenegro, Republic of Montenegro
**Government type:** republic
**Capital:**
*name:* Podgorica
*geographic coordinates:* 42 26 N, 19 16 E
*time difference:* UTC+1 (6 hours ahead of Washington, DC during Standard Time)
*daylight saving time:* +1 hr, begins last Sunday in March; ends last Sunday in October
**Administrative divisions:** 21 municipalities (opstine, singular - opstina); Andrijevica, Bar, Berana, Bijelo Polje, Budva, Cetinje, Danilovgrad, Herceg Novi, Kolasin, Kotor, Mojkovac, Niksic, Plav, Pljevlja, Pluzine, Podgorica, Rozaje, Savnik, Tivat, Ulcinj, Zabljak
**Independence:** 3 June 2006 (from Serbia and Montenegro)
**National holiday:** National Day, 13 July (1878)
**Constitution:** approved 19 October 2007 (by the Assembly)
**Legal system:** based on civil law system; has not accepted compulsory ICJ jurisdiction
**Suffrage:** 18 years of age; universal
**Executive branch:**
*chief of state:* President Filip VUJANOVIC (since 6 April 2008)
*head of government:* Prime Minister Milo DJUKANOVIC (since 29 February 2008)
*cabinet:* Ministries act as cabinet
*elections:* president elected by direct vote for five-year term (eligible for a second term); election last held 6 April 2008 (next to be held in 2013); prime minister proposed by president, accepted by Assembly
*election results:* Filip VUJANOVIC reelected president; Filip VUJANOVIC 51.89%, Andrija MANDIC 19.55%, Nebojsa MEDOJEVIC 16.64%, Srdan MILIC 11.92%

# Montenegro (continued)

**Legislative branch:** unicameral Assembly (81 seats; members elected by direct vote for four-year terms; changed from 74 seats in 2006)
*elections:* last held 29 March 2009 (next to be held in 2013)
*election results:* percent of vote by party - Coalition for European Montenegro 51.94%, SNP 16.83%, NSD 9.22%, PZP 6.03%, other (including Albanian minority parties) 15.98%; seats by party - Coalition for European Montenegro 48, SNP 16, NSD 8, PZP 5, Albanian minority parties 4
**Judicial branch:** Constitutional Court (five judges with nine-year terms); Supreme Court (judges have life tenure)
**Political parties and leaders:** Albanian Alternative or AA [Vesel SINISHTAJ]; Coalition for European Montenegro or DPS-SDP (bloc) [Milo DJUKANOVIC] (includes Democratic Party of Socialists or DPS [Milo DJUKANOVIC] and Social Democratic Party or SDP [Ranko KRIVOKAPIC]); Coalition SNP-NS-DSS (bloc) (includes Socialist People's Party or SNP [Srdjan MILIC], People's Party of Montenegro or NS [Predrag POPOVIC], and Democratic Serbian Party of Montenegro or DSS [Ranko KADIC]); Democratic League-Party of Democratic Prosperity or SPP [Mehmet BARDHIJ]; Democratic Union of Albanians or DUA [Ferhat DINOSA]; Liberals and the Bosniak Party (bloc) [Miodrag ZIVKOVIC (includes Liberal Party of Montenegro or LP [Miodrag ZIVKOVIC] and Bosniak Party or BS [Rafet HUSOVIC]); Movement for Changes or PZP [Nebojsa MEDOJEVIC]; New Serb Democracy or NSD [Andrija MANDIC]; Serbian List (bloc) [Andrija MANDIC] (includes Party of Serb Radicals or SSR [Dusko SEKULIC], People's Socialist Party or NSS [Emilo LABUDOVIC], and Serbian People's Party of Montenegro or SNS [Andrija MANDIC]); Socialist People's Party of Montenegro or SNP [Srdjan MILIC]
**International organization participation:** CE, CEI, EAPC, EBRD, FAO, IAEA, IBRD, ICAO, ICCt, ICRM, IDA, IFC, IFRCS, ILO, IMF, IMO, IMSO, Interpol, IOC, IOM, IPU, ISO (correspondent), ITU, ITUC, MIGA, OPCW, OSCE, PCA, PFP, SECI, UN, UNESCO, UNHCR, UNIDO, UNMIL, UNWTO, UPU, WCO, WFTU, WHO, WIPO, WMO, WTO (observer)
**Diplomatic representation in the US:**
*chief of mission:* Ambassador Miodrag VLAHOVIC
*chancery:* 1610 New Hampshire Avenue NW, Washington, DC, 20009
*telephone:* [1] (202) 234-6108
*FAX:* [1] (202) 234-6109
*consulate(s) general:* New York
**Diplomatic representation from the US:**
*chief of mission:* Ambassador Roderick W. MOORE
*embassy:* Ljubljanska bb, 81000 Podgorica, Montenegro
*mailing address:* use embassy street address
*telephone:* [382] 81 225 417
*FAX:* [382] 81 241 358
**Flag description:** a red field bordered by a narrow golden-yellow stripe with the Montenegrin coat of arms centered

## Economy

**Economy - overview:** Montenegro severed its economy from federal control and from Serbia during the MILOSEVIC era and maintained its own central bank, adopted the Deutchmark, then the euro - rather than the Yugoslav dinar - as official currency, collected customs tariffs, and managed its own budget. The dissolution of the loose political union between Serbia and Montenegro in 2006 led to separate membership in several international financial institutions, such as the European Bank for Reconstruction and Development. On 18 January 2007, Montenegro joined the World Bank and IMF. Montenegro is pursuing its own membership in the World Trade Organization and signed a Stabilization and Association agreement with the European Union in October 2007. On December 15, 2007, Montenegro submitted an EU membership application. Unemployment and regional disparities in development are key political and economic problems. Montenegro has privatized its large aluminum complex - the dominant industry - as well as most of its financial sector, and has begun to attract foreign direct investment in the tourism sector. The global financial crisis is likely to have a significant negative impact on the economy.
**GDP (purchasing power parity):**
$6.6 billion (2008 est.)
$6.198 billion (2007)
$5.792 billion (2006)
*note:* data are in 2008 US dollars
**GDP (official exchange rate):** $4.515 billion (2008 est.)
**GDP - real growth rate:**
6.5% (2008 est.)
7% (2007 est.)
8.6% (2006 est.)
**GDP - per capita (PPP):**
$9,700 (2008 est.)
$9,100 (2007 est.)
$8,400 (2006 est.)
*note:* data are in 2008 US dollars
**GDP - composition by sector:**
*agriculture:* NA%
*industry:* NA%
*services:* NA%
**Labor force:** 259,100 (2004)
**Labor force - by occupation:**
*agriculture:* 2%
*industry:* 30%
*services:* 68% (2004 est.)
**Unemployment rate:**
14.7% (2007 est.)
**Population below poverty line:** 7% (2007 est.)
**Distribution of family income - Gini index:** 30 (2003)
**Investment (gross fixed):** 30.5% of GDP (2006 est.)
**Budget:**
*revenues:* NA
*expenditures:* NA

**Public debt:** 38% of GDP (2006)
**Inflation rate (consumer prices):**
3.4% (2007)
**Commercial bank prime lending rate:** 9.09% (31 December 2007)
**Stock of money:** $1.172 billion (31 December 2007)
**Stock of quasi money:** $1.446 billion (31 December 2007)
**Stock of domestic credit:** $3.083 billion (31 December 2007)
**Market value of publicly traded shares:** $3.699 billion (31 December 2007)
**Agriculture - products:** grains, tobacco, potatoes, citrus fruits, olives, grapes; sheepherding; commercial fishing negligible
**Industries:** steelmaking, aluminum, agricultural processing, consumer goods, tourism
**Electricity - production:** 2.864 billion kWh (2005 est.)
**Electricity - consumption:** 18.6 million kWh (2005)
**Electricity - exports:** 0 kWh (2005)
**Electricity - imports:** 0 kWh (2005)
**Oil - production:** 0 bbl/day (2007 est.)
**Oil - consumption:** 450 bbl/day (2004)
**Oil - exports:** 313.6 bbl/day (2005)
**Oil - imports:** 6,093 bbl/day (2005)
**Oil - proved reserves:** 0 bbl (1 January 2006 est.)
**Natural gas - consumption:** NA cu m
**Current account balance:** -$1.102 billion.(2007 est.)
**Exports:** $171.3 million (2003)
**Imports:** $601.7 million f.o.b. (2003)
**Reserves of foreign exchange and gold:** $NA
**Debt - external:** $650 million (2006)
**Exchange rates:** euros (EUR) per US dollar - 0.6827 (2008 est.), 0.7345 (2007), 0.7964 (2006), 0.8041 (2005), 0.8054 (2004)

## Communications

**Telephones - main lines in use:** 353,300 (2006)
**Telephones - mobile cellular:** 643,700 (2006)
**Telephone system:**
*general assessment:* modern telecommunications system with access to European satellites
*domestic:* GSM wireless service, available through 3 providers with national coverage, is growing rapidly
*international:* country code - 382; 2 international switches connect the national system
**Radio broadcast stations:** 31 (station frequency types NA) (2004)
**Television broadcast stations:** 13 (2004)
**Internet country code:** .me
**Internet users:** 280,000 (2007)

## Transportation

**Airports:** 5 (2008)
**Airports - with paved runways:**
*total:* 3
*2,438 to 3,047 m:* 2
*1,524 to 2,437 m:* 1 (2008)

**Airports - with unpaved runways:**
*total:* 2
*914 to 1,523 m:* 1
*under 914 m:* 1 (2008)
**Heliports:** 1 (2007)
**Railways:**
*total:* 250 km
*standard gauge:* 250 km 1.435-m gauge (electrified 169 km) (2006)
**Roadways:**
*total:* 7,368 km
*paved:* 4,742 km
*unpaved:* 2,626 km (2006)
**Merchant marine:**
*total:* 6
*by type:* cargo 5, passenger/cargo 1
*registered in other countries:* 3 (Bahamas 2, Saint Vincent and the Grenadines 1) (2008)
**Ports and terminals:** Bar

### Military

**Military branches:** Armed Forces of the Republic of Montenegro: Army, Navy, Air Force (2009)
**Military service age and obligation:** compulsory national military service abolished August 2006
**Manpower fit for military service:**
*males age 16-49:* 154,029
*females age 16-49:* 136,847 (2009 est.)
**Manpower reaching militarily significant age annually:**
*male:* 3,945
*female:* 3,907 (2009 est.)
**Military - note:** Montenegrin plans call for the establishment of a fully professional armed forces

### Transnational Issues

**Disputes - international:** none
**Refugees and internally displaced persons:**
*refugees (country of origin):* 7,000 (Kosovo); note - mostly ethnic Serbs and Roma who fled Kosovo in 1999
*IDPs:* 16,192 (ethnic conflict in 1999 and riots in 2004) (2007)
**Trafficking in persons:**
*current situation:* Montenegro is primarily a transit country for the trafficking of women and girls to Western Europe for the purpose of commercial sexual exploitation; women and girls from the Balkans and Eastern Europe are trafficked across Montenegro to Western European countries
*tier rating:* Tier 2 Watch List - Montenegro is on the Tier 2 Watch List for its failure to provide evidence of increasing efforts to combat trafficking in persons in 2007; public attention to the issue of trafficking has diminished considerably in Montenegro in recent years (2008)

# Montserrat
*(overseas territory of the UK)*

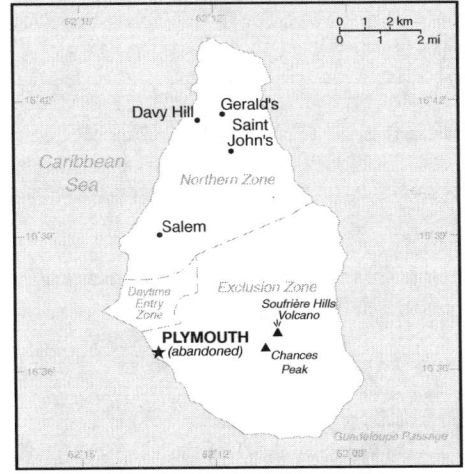

### Introduction

**Background:** English and Irish colonists from St. Kitts first settled on Montserrat in 1632; the first African slaves arrived three decades later. The British and French fought for possession of the island for most of the 18th century, but it finally was confirmed as a British possession in 1783. The island's sugar plantation economy was converted to small farm landholdings in the mid 19th century. Much of this island was devastated and two-thirds of the population fled abroad because of the eruption of the Soufriere Hills Volcano that began on 18 July 1995. Montserrat has endured volcanic activity since, with the last eruption occurring in July 2003.

### Geography

**Location:** Caribbean, island in the Caribbean Sea, southeast of Puerto Rico
**Geographic coordinates:** 16 45 N, 62 12 W
**Map references:** Central America and the Caribbean
**Area:**
*total:* 102 sq km
*land:* 102 sq km
*water:* 0 sq km
**Area - comparative:** about 0.6 times the size of Washington, DC
**Land boundaries:** 0 km
**Coastline:** 40 km
**Maritime claims:**
*territorial sea:* 3 nm
*exclusive fishing zone:* 200 nm
**Climate:** tropical; little daily or seasonal temperature variation
**Terrain:** volcanic island, mostly mountainous, with small coastal lowland
**Elevation extremes:**
*lowest point:* Caribbean Sea 0 m
*highest point:* lava dome in English's Crater (in the Soufriere Hills volcanic complex) estimated at over 930 m (2006)

**Natural resources:** NEGL
**Land use:**
*arable land:* 20%
*permanent crops:* 0%
*other:* 80% (2005)
**Irrigated land:** NA
**Natural hazards:** severe hurricanes (June to November); volcanic eruptions (Soufriere Hills volcano has erupted continuously since 1995)
**Environment - current issues:** land erosion occurs on slopes that have been cleared for cultivation
**Geography - note:** the island is entirely volcanic in origin and comprised of three major volcanic centers of differing ages

### People

**Population:** 5,097
*note:* an estimated 8,000 refugees left the island following the resumption of volcanic activity in July 1995; some have returned (July 2009 est.)
**Age structure:**
*0-14 years:* 27.6% (male 731/female 678)
*15-64 years:* 65.5% (male 1,599/female 1,738)
*65 years and over:* 6.9% (male 232/female 119) (2009 est.)
**Median age:**
*total:* 28.5 years
*male:* 28.2 years
*female:* 28.7 years (2009 est.)
**Population growth rate:** 0.392% (2009 est.)
**Birth rate:** 12.36 births/1,000 population (2009 est.)
**Death rate:** 8.86 deaths/1,000 population (2008 est.)
**Net migration rate:** NA
**Urbanization:**
*urban population:* 14% of total population (2008)
*rate of urbanization:* 2.2% annual rate of change (2005-10 est.)
**Sex ratio:**
*at birth:* 1.03 male(s)/female
*under 15 years:* 1.08 male(s)/female
*15-64 years:* 0.92 male(s)/female
*65 years and over:* 1.95 male(s)/female
*total population:* 1.01 male(s)/female (2009 est.)
**Infant mortality rate:**
*total:* 16.08 deaths/1,000 live births
*male:* 12.01 deaths/1,000 live births
*female:* 20.36 deaths/1,000 live births (2009 est.)
**Life expectancy at birth:**
*total population:* 72.76 years
*male:* 74.74 years
*female:* 70.68 years (2009 est.)
**Total fertility rate:** 1.23 children born/woman (2009 est.)
**HIV/AIDS - adult prevalence rate:** NA
**HIV/AIDS - people living with HIV/AIDS:** NA
**HIV/AIDS - deaths:** NA
**Nationality:**
*noun:* Montserratian(s)
*adjective:* Montserratian
**Ethnic groups:** black, white

# Montserrat *(continued)*

**Religions:** Anglican, Methodist, Roman Catholic, Pentecostal, Seventh-Day Adventist, other Christian denominations
**Languages:** English
**Literacy:**
*definition:* age 15 and over has ever attended school
*total population:* 97%
*male:* 97%
*female:* 97% (1970 est.)
**School life expectancy (primary to tertiary education):**
*total:* 16 years
*male:* 15 years
*female:* 16 years (2006)
**Education expenditures:** 3.3% of GDP (2004)

## Government

**Country name:**
*conventional long form:* none
*conventional short form:* Montserrat
**Dependency status:** overseas territory of the UK
**Government type:** NA
**Capital:**
*name:* Plymouth
*geographic coordinates:* 16 42 N, 62 13 W
*time difference:* UTC-4 (1 hour ahead of Washington, DC during Standard Time)
*note:* Plymouth was abandoned in 1997 because of volcanic activity; interim government buildings have been built at Brades Estate in the Carr's Bay/Little Bay vicinity at the northwest end of Montserrat
**Administrative divisions:** 3 parishes; Saint Anthony, Saint Georges, Saint Peter
**Independence:** none (overseas territory of the UK)
**National holiday:** Birthday of Queen ELIZABETH II, second Saturday in June (1926)
**Constitution:** effective 19 December 1989
**Legal system:** English common law and statutory law
**Suffrage:** 18 years of age; universal
**Executive branch:**
*chief of state:* Queen ELIZABETH II (since 6 February 1952); represented by Governor Peter A. WATERWORTH (since 27 July 2007)
*head of government:* Chief Minister Lowell LEWIS (since 2 June 2006)
*cabinet:* Executive Council consists of the governor, the chief minister, three other ministers, the attorney general, and the finance secretary
*elections:* the monarch is hereditary; governor appointed by the monarch; following legislative elections, the leader of the majority party usually becomes chief minister
**Legislative branch:** unicameral Legislative Council (11 seats, 9 popularly elected; members serve five-year terms)
*note:* expanded in 2001 from 7 to 9 elected members with attorney general and financial secretary sitting as ex-officio members
*elections:* last held 31 May 2006 (next to be held by 2011)

*election results:* percent of vote by party - MCAP 36.1%, NPLM 29.4%, MDP 24.4%, independents 10.1%; seats by party - MCAP 4, NPLM 3, MDP 1, independents 1
*note:* in 2001, the Elections Commission instituted a single constituency/voter-at-large system whereby all eligible voters cast ballots for all nine seats of the Legislative Council
**Judicial branch:** Eastern Caribbean Supreme Court (based in Saint Lucia, one judge of the Supreme Court is a resident of the islands and presides over the High Court)
**Political parties and leaders:** Montserrat Democratic Party or MDP [Lowell LEWIS]; Movement for Change and Prosperity or MCAP [Roselyn CASSELL-SEALY]; New People's Liberation Movement or NPLM [John A. OSBORNE]
**Political pressure groups and leaders:** NA
**International organization participation:** Caricom, CDB, Interpol (subbureau), OECS, UPU, WFTU
**Diplomatic representation in the US:** none (overseas territory of the UK)
**Diplomatic representation from the US:** none (overseas territory of the UK)
**Flag description:** blue, with the flag of the UK in the upper hoist-side quadrant and the Montserratian coat of arms centered in the outer half of the flag; the coat of arms features a woman standing beside a yellow harp with her arm around a black cross

## Economy

**Economy - overview:** Severe volcanic activity, which began in July 1995, has put a damper on this small, open economy. A catastrophic eruption in June 1997 closed the airports and seaports, causing further economic and social dislocation. Two-thirds of the 12,000 inhabitants fled the island. Some began to return in 1998 but lack of housing limited the number. The agriculture sector continued to be affected by the lack of suitable land for farming and the destruction of crops. Prospects for the economy depend largely on developments in relation to the volcanic activity and on public sector construction activity. The UK has launched a three-year $122.8 million aid program to help reconstruct the economy. Half of the island is expected to remain uninhabitable for another decade.
**GDP (purchasing power parity):**
$29 million (2002 est.)
**GDP (official exchange rate):** $NA
**GDP - real growth rate:**
-1% (2002 est.)
**GDP - per capita (PPP):**
$3,400 (2002 est.)
**GDP - composition by sector:**
*agriculture:* 1.2%
*industry:* 23.1%
*services:* 75.7% (1999 est.)
**Labor force:** 4,521
*note:* lowered by flight of people from volcanic activity (2000 est.)

**Unemployment rate:**
6% (1998 est.)
**Population below poverty line:** NA%
**Household income or consumption by percentage share:**
*lowest 10%:* NA%
*highest 10%:* NA%
**Budget:**
*revenues:* $31.4 million
*expenditures:* $31.6 million (1997 est.)
**Inflation rate (consumer prices):**
2.6% (2002 est.)
**Central bank discount rate:** 6.5% (31 December 2007)
**Commercial bank prime lending rate:** 10.4% (31 December 2007)
**Stock of money:** $17.9 million (31 December 2007)
**Stock of quasi money:** $43.9 million (31 December 2007)
**Stock of domestic credit:** $5.537 million (31 December 2007)
**Agriculture - products:** cabbages, carrots, cucumbers, tomatoes, onions, peppers; livestock products
**Industries:** tourism, rum, textiles, electronic appliances
**Industrial production growth rate:** NA%
**Electricity - production:** 22 million kWh (2006 est.)
**Electricity - consumption:** 20.46 million kWh (2006 est.)
**Electricity - exports:** 0 kWh (2007 est.)
**Electricity - imports:** 0 kWh (2007 est.)
**Oil - production:** 0 bbl/day (2007 est.)
**Oil - consumption:** 505.5 bbl/day (2006 est.)
**Oil - exports:** 0 bbl/day (2005)
**Oil - imports:** 482.6 bbl/day (2005)
**Oil - proved reserves:** 0 bbl (1 January 2006 est.)
**Natural gas - production:** 0 cu m (2007 est.)
**Natural gas - consumption:** 0 cu m (2007 est.)
**Natural gas - exports:** 0 cu m (2007 est.)
**Natural gas - imports:** 0 cu m (2007 est.)
**Natural gas - proved reserves:** 0 cu m (1 January 2006 est.)
**Exports:** $700,000 (2001)
**Exports - commodities:** electronic components, plastic bags, apparel; hot peppers, limes, live plants; cattle
**Imports:** $17 million (2001)
**Imports - commodities:** machinery and transportation equipment, foodstuffs, manufactured goods, fuels, lubricants, and related materials
**Debt - external:** $8.9 million (1997)
**Exchange rates:** East Caribbean dollars (XCD) per US dollar - 2.7 (2007), 2.7 (2006), 2.7 (2005), 2.7 (2004), 2.7 (2003)
*note:* fixed rate since 1976

**Telephones - main lines in use:** NA
**Telephones - mobile cellular:** NA
**Telephone system:**
*general assessment:* modern and fully digitalized
*domestic:* NA
*international:* country code - 1-664; landing point for the East Caribbean Fiber System (ECFS) optic submarine cable with links to 13 other islands in the eastern Caribbean extending from the British Virgin Islands to Trinidad
**Radio broadcast stations:** AM 1, FM 2, shortwave 0 (1998)
**Television broadcast stations:** 1 (1997)
**Internet country code:** .ms
**Internet hosts:** 409 (2008)
**Internet users:** NA

## Transportation

**Airports:** 2 (2008)
**Airports - with paved runways:**
*total:* 2
*under 914 m:* 2 (2008)
**Roadways:**
*note:* volcanic eruptions that began in 1995 destroyed most of the 227 km road system; a new road infrastructure has been built in the north end of the island (2008)
**Ports and terminals:** Little Bay, Plymouth

## Military

**Military branches:** no regular military forces; Royal Montserrat Police Force (2008)
**Manpower available for military service:**
*males age 16-49:* 2,528 (2008 est.)
**Manpower fit for military service:**
*males age 16-49:* 1,126
*females age 16-49:* 1,226 (2009 est.)
**Manpower reaching militarily significant age annually:**
*male:* 36
*female:* 33 (2009 est.)
**Military - note:** defense is the responsibility of the UK

## Transnational Issues

**Disputes - international:** none
**Illicit drugs:** transshipment point for South American narcotics destined for the US and Europe

# Morocco

## Introduction

**Background:** In 788, about a century after the Arab conquest of North Africa, successive Moorish dynasties began to rule in Morocco. In the 16th century, the Sa'adi monarchy, particularly under Ahmad AL-MANSUR (1578-1603), repelled foreign invaders and inaugurated a golden age. In 1860, Spain occupied northern Morocco and ushered in a half century of trade rivalry among European powers that saw Morocco's sovereignty steadily erode; in 1912, the French imposed a protectorate over the country. A protracted independence struggle with France ended successfully in 1956. The internationalized city of Tangier and most Spanish possessions were turned over to the new country that same year. Morocco virtually annexed Western Sahara during the late 1970s, but final resolution on the status of the territory remains unresolved. Gradual political reforms in the 1990s resulted in the establishment of a bicameral legislature, which first met in 1997. The country has made improvements in human rights under King MOHAMMED VI and its press is moderately free. Despite the continuing reforms, ultimate authority remains in the hands of the monarch.

## Geography

**Location:** Northern Africa, bordering the North Atlantic Ocean and the Mediterranean Sea, between Algeria and Western Sahara
**Geographic coordinates:** 32 00 N, 5 00 W
**Map references:** Africa
**Area:**
*total:* 446,550 sq km
*land:* 446,300 sq km
*water:* 250 sq km
**Area - comparative:** slightly larger than California
**Land boundaries:**
*total:* 2,017.9 km
*border countries:* Algeria 1,559 km, Western Sahara 443 km, Spain (Ceuta) 6.3 km, Spain (Melilla) 9.6 km

**Coastline:** 1,835 km
**Maritime claims:**
*territorial sea:* 12 nm
*contiguous zone:* 24 nm
*exclusive economic zone:* 200 nm
*continental shelf:* 200 m depth or to the depth of exploitation
**Climate:** Mediterranean, becoming more extreme in the interior
**Terrain:** northern coast and interior are mountainous with large areas of bordering plateaus, intermontane valleys, and rich coastal plains
**Elevation extremes:**
*lowest point:* Sebkha Tah -55 m
*highest point:* Jebel Toubkal 4,165 m
**Natural resources:** phosphates, iron ore, manganese, lead, zinc, fish, salt
**Land use:**
*arable land:* 19%
*permanent crops:* 2%
*other:* 79% (2005)
**Irrigated land:** 14,450 sq km (2003)
**Total renewable water resources:** 29 cu km (2003)
**Freshwater withdrawal (domestic/industrial/agricultural):**
*total:* 12.6 cu km/yr (10%/3%/87%)
*per capita:* 400 cu m/yr (2000)
**Natural hazards:** northern mountains geologically unstable and subject to earthquakes; periodic droughts
**Environment - current issues:** land degradation/desertification (soil erosion resulting from farming of marginal areas, overgrazing, destruction of vegetation); water supplies contaminated by raw sewage; siltation of reservoirs; oil pollution of coastal waters
**Environment - international agreements:**
*party to:* Biodiversity, Climate Change, Climate Change-Kyoto Protocol, Desertification, Endangered Species, Hazardous Wastes, Law of the Sea, Marine Dumping, Ozone Layer Protection, Ship Pollution, Wetlands, Whaling
*signed, but not ratified:* Environmental Modification
**Geography - note:** strategic location along Strait of Gibraltar

## People

**Population:** 34,859,364 (July 2009 est.)
**Age structure:**
*0-14 years:* 30% (male 5,333,396/female 5,131,886)
*15-64 years:* 64.7% (male 11,261,139/female 11,305,792)
*65 years and over:* 5.2% (male 781,089/female 1,046,062) (2009 est.)
**Median age:**
*total:* 25 years
*male:* 24.5 years
*female:* 25.6 years (2009 est.)
**Population growth rate:** 1.479% (2009 est.)
**Birth rate:** 20.96 births/1,000 population (2009 est.)
**Death rate:** 5.49 deaths/1,000 population (2008 est.)

# Morocco (continued)

**Net migration rate:** -0.72 migrant(s)/1,000 population (2009 est.)

**Urbanization:**

*urban population:* 56% of total population (2008)

*rate of urbanization:* 1.8% annual rate of change (2005-10 est.)

**Sex ratio:**

*at birth:* 1.05 male(s)/female

*under 15 years:* 1.04 male(s)/female

*15-64 years:* 1 male(s)/female

*65 years and over:* 0.75 male(s)/female

*total population:* 0.99 male(s)/female (2009 est.)

**Infant mortality rate:**

*total:* 36.88 deaths/1,000 live births

*male:* 40.35 deaths/1,000 live births

*female:* 33.24 deaths/1,000 live births (2009 est.)

**Life expectancy at birth:**

*total population:* 71.8 years

*male:* 69.42 years

*female:* 74.3 years (2009 est.)

**Total fertility rate:** 2.51 children born/woman (2009 est.)

**HIV/AIDS - adult prevalence rate:** 0.1% (2007 est.)

**HIV/AIDS - people living with HIV/AIDS:** 21,000 (2007 est.)

**HIV/AIDS - deaths:** fewer than 1,000 (2007 est.)

**Nationality:**

*noun:* Moroccan(s)

*adjective:* Moroccan

**Ethnic groups:** Arab-Berber 99.1%, other 0.7%, Jewish 0.2%

**Religions:** Muslim 98.7%, Christian 1.1%, Jewish 0.2%

**Languages:** Arabic (official), Berber dialects, French often the language of business, government, and diplomacy

**Literacy:**

*definition:* age 15 and over can read and write

*total population:* 52.3%

*male:* 65.7%

*female:* 39.6% (2004 census)

**School life expectancy (primary to tertiary education):**

*total:* 10 years

*male:* 11 years

*female:* 9 years (2005)

**Education expenditures:** NA

## Government

**Country name:**

*conventional long form:* Kingdom of Morocco

*conventional short form:* Morocco

*local long form:* Al Mamlakah al Maghribiyah

*local short form:* Al Maghrib

**Government type:** constitutional monarchy

**Capital:**

*name:* Rabat

*geographic coordinates:* 34 01 N, 6 49 W

*time difference:* UTC 0 (5 hours ahead of Washington, DC during Standard Time)

**Administrative divisions:** 15 regions; Grand Casablanca, Chaouia-Ouardigha, Doukkala-Abda, Fes-Boulemane, Gharb-Chrarda-Beni Hssen, Guelmim-Es Smara, Laayoune-Boujdour-Sakia El Hamra, Marrakech-Tensift-Al Haouz, Meknes-Tafilalet, Oriental, Rabat-Sale-Zemmour-Zaer, Souss-Massa-Draa, Tadla-Azilal, Tanger-Tetouan, Taza-Al Hoceima-Taounate

*note:* Morocco claims the territory of Western Sahara, the political status of which is considered undetermined by the US Government; portions of the regions Guelmim-Es Smara and Laayoune-Boujdour-Sakia El Hamra as claimed by Morocco lie within Western Sahara; Morocco also claims Oued Eddahab-Lagouira, another region which falls entirely within Western Sahara

**Independence:** 2 March 1956 (from France)

**National holiday:** Throne Day (accession of King MOHAMMED VI to the throne), 30 July (1999)

**Constitution:** 10 March 1972; revised 4 September 1992, amended September 1996

*note:* the amendment of September 1996 was to create a bicameral legislature

**Legal system:** based on Islamic law and French and Spanish civil law systems; judicial review of legislative acts in Constitutional Chamber of Supreme Court; has not accepted compulsory ICJ jurisdiction

**Suffrage:** 18 years of age; universal (as of January 2003)

**Executive branch:**

*chief of state:* King MOHAMMED VI (since 30 July 1999)

*head of government:* Prime Minister Abbas EL FASSI (since 19 September 2007)

*cabinet:* Council of Ministers appointed by the monarch

*elections:* the monarch is hereditary; prime minister appointed by the monarch following legislative elections

**Legislative branch:** bicameral Parliament consists of a Chamber of Counselors (or upper house) (270 seats; members elected indirectly by local councils, professional organizations, and labor syndicates for nine-year terms; one-third of the members are elected every three years) and Chamber of Representatives (or lower house) (325 seats; 295 members elected by multi-seat constituencies and 30 from national lists of women; members elected by popular vote for five-year terms)

*elections:* Chamber of Counselors - last held 8 September 2006 (next to be held in 2009); Chamber of Representatives - last held 7 September 2007 (next to be held in 2012)

*election results:* Chamber of Counselors - percent of vote by party - NA; seats by party - PI 17, MP 14, RNI 13, USFP 11, UC 6, PND 4, PPS 4, Al Ahd 4, other 17; Chamber of Representatives - percent of vote by party -NA; seats by party - PI 52, PJD 46, MP 41, RNI 39, USFP 38, UC 27, PPS 17, FFD 9, MDS 9, Al Ahd 8, other 39

**Judicial branch:** Supreme Court (judges are appointed on the recommendation of the Supreme Council of the Judiciary, presided over by the monarch)

**Political parties and leaders:** Action Party or PA [Mohammed EL IDRISSI]; Al Ahd (The Covenant) Party [Najib EL OUAZZANI]; Alliance des Libert'es (Alliance of Liberty) or ADL [Ali BELHAJ]; An-Nahj Ad-Dimocrati or An-Nahj [Abdellah EL HARIF]; Authenticity and Modernity Party or PAM [Mohamed Cheikh BIADILLAH]; Choura et Istiqlal (Consultation and Independence) Party or PCI [Abdelwahed MAACH]; Citizens' Forces or FC [Abderrahman LAHJOUJI]; Citizenship and Development Initiative or ICD [Mohamed BENHAMOU]; Constitutional Union Party or UC [Mohammed ABIED]; Democratic and Social Movement or MDS [Mahmoud ARCHANE]; Democratic Forces Front or FFD [Touhami EL KHIARI]; Democratic Socialist Vanguard Party or PADS [Ahmed BENJELLOUN]; Democratic Society Party or PSD [Zhor CHEKKAFI]; Democratic Union or UD [Bouazza IKKEN]; Environment and Development Party or PED [Ahmed EL ALAMI]; Istiqlal (Independence) Party or PI [Abbas EL FASSI]; Justice and Development Party or PJD [Abdelilah BENKIRANE]; Labor Party or PT [Abdelkrim BENATIK]; Moroccan Liberal Party or PML [Mohamed ZIANE]; National Democratic Party or PND [Abdallah KADIRI]; National Ittihadi Congress Party or CNI [Abdelmajid BOUZOUBAA]; National Popular Movement or MNP [Mahjoubi AHERDANE]; National Rally of Independents or RNI [Mustapha EL MANSOURI]; National Union of Popular Forces or UNFP [Abdellah IBRAHIM]; Popular Movement or MP [Mohamed LAENSER]; Progress and Socialism Party or PPS [Ismail ALAOUI]; Reform and Development Party or PRD [Abderrahmane EL KOUHEN]; Renaissance and Virtue Party or PRV [Mohamed KHALIDI]; Renewal and Equity Party or PRE [Chakir ACHABAR]; Social Center Party or PSC [Lahcen MADIH]; Socialist Democratic Party or PSD [Aissa OUARDIGHI]; Socialist Union of Popular Forces or USFP [Abdelwahed RADI]; Unified Socialist Left Party or PGSU [Mohamed Ben Said AIT IDDER]

**Political pressure groups and leaders:** Democratic Confederation of Labor or CDT [Noubir AMAOUI]; General Union of Moroccan Workers or UGTM [Abderrazzak AFILAL]; Moroccan Employers Association or CGEM [Hassan CHAMI]; National Labor Union of Morocco or UNMT [Abdelslam MAATI]; Union of Moroccan Workers or UMT [Mahjoub BENSEDDIK]

**International organization participation:** ABEDA, AfDB, AFESD, AMF, AMU, EBRD, FAO, G-77, IAEA, IBRD, ICAO, ICC, ICCt (signatory), ICRM, IDA, IDB, IFAD, IFC, IFRCS, IHO, ILO, IMF, IMO, IMSO, Interpol, IOC, IOM, IPU, ISO, ITSO, ITU, ITUC, LAS, MIGA, MONUC, NAM, OAS (observer), OIC, OIF, OPCW, OSCE (partner), PCA, UN, UNCTAD, UNESCO, UNHCR, UNIDO, UNOCI, UNWTO, UPU, WCL, WCO, WFTU, WHO, WIPO, WMO, WTO

# Morocco *(continued)*

## Diplomatic representation in the US:

*chief of mission:* Ambassador Aziz MEKOUAR

*chancery:* 1601 21st Street NW, Washington, DC 20009

*telephone:* [1] (202) 462-7979

*FAX:* [1] (202) 265-0161

*consulate(s) general:* New York

## Diplomatic representation from the US:

*chief of mission:* Ambassador (vacant); Charge d'Affaires Robert P. JACKSON

*embassy:* 2 Avenue de Mohamed El Fassi, Rabat

*mailing address:* PSC 74, Box 021, APO AE 09718

*telephone:* [212] (37) 76 22 65

*FAX:* [212] (37) 76 56 61

*consulate(s) general:* Casablanca

**Flag description:** red with a green pentacle (five-pointed, linear star) known as Sulayman's (Solomon's) seal in the center of the flag; red and green are traditional colors in Arab flags, although the use of red is more commonly associated with the Arab states of the Persian gulf; design dates to 1912

## Economy

**Economy - overview:** Moroccan economic policies brought macroeconomic stability to the country in the early 1990s but have not spurred growth sufficient to reduce unemployment - nearing 20% in urban areas - despite the Moroccan Government's ongoing efforts to diversify the economy. Morocco's GDP growth rose to 5.9% in 2008, with the economy recovering from a drought in 2007 that severely reduced agricultural output and necessitated wheat imports at rising world prices. Moroccan authorities understand that reducing poverty and providing jobs are key to domestic security and development. In 2005, Morocco launched the National Initiative for Human Development (INDH), a $2 billion social development plan to address poverty and unemployment and to improve the living conditions of the country's urban slums. Moroccan authorities are implementing reform efforts to open the economy to international investors. Despite structural adjustment programs supported by the IMF, the World Bank, and the Paris Club, the dirham is only fully convertible for current account transactions. In 2000, Morocco entered an Association Agreement with the EU and, in 2006, entered a Free Trade Agreement (FTA) with the US. Long-term challenges include improving education and job prospects for Morocco's youth, and closing the income gap between the rich and the poor, which the government hopes to achieve by increasing tourist arrivals and boosting competitiveness in textiles.

**GDP (purchasing power parity):**

$137.3 billion (2008 est.)

$129.7 billion (2007)

$125.7 billion (2006)

*note:* data are in 2008 US dollars

**GDP (official exchange rate):** $90.47 billion (2008 est.)

**GDP - real growth rate:**

5.9% (2008 est.)

3.2% (2007 est.)

7.8% (2006 est.)

**GDP - per capita (PPP):**

$4,000 (2008 est.)

$3,800 (2007 est.)

$3,800 (2006 est.)

*note:* data are in 2008 US dollars

**GDP - composition by sector:**

*agriculture:* 14.7%

*industry:* 38.9%

*services:* 46.5% (2008 est.)

**Labor force:** 11.5 million (2008 est.)

**Labor force - by occupation:**

*agriculture:* 44.6%

*industry:* 19.8%

*services:* 35.5% (2006 est.)

**Unemployment rate:**

10% (2008 est.)

9.8% (2007 est.)

**Population below poverty line:** 15% (2007 est.)

**Household income or consumption by percentage share:**

*lowest 10%:* 2.6%

*highest 10%:* 30.9% (1999)

**Distribution of family income - Gini index:** 40 (2005 est.)

**Investment (gross fixed):** 31.9% of GDP (2008 est.)

**Budget:**

*revenues:* $26.09 billion

*expenditures:* $28.41 billion (2008 est.)

**Public debt:** 60.2% of GDP (2008 est.)

**Inflation rate (consumer prices):**

4.6% (2008 est.)

2% (2007 est.)

**Central bank discount rate:** 3.25% (31 December 2007)

**Commercial bank prime lending rate:** NA

**Stock of money:** $67.42 billion (31 December 2007)

**Stock of quasi money:** $16.23 billion (31 December 2007)

**Stock of domestic credit:** $71.9 billion (31 December 2007)

**Market value of publicly traded shares:** $75.49 billion (31 December 2007)

**Agriculture - products:** barley, wheat, citrus, wine, vegetables, olives; livestock

**Industries:** phosphate rock mining and processing, food processing, leather goods, textiles, construction, tourism

**Industrial production growth rate:** 5.8% (2008 est.)

**Electricity - production:** 21.88 billion kWh (2006 est.)

**Electricity - consumption:** 19.58 billion kWh (2006 est.)

**Electricity - exports:** 0 kWh (2007 est.)

**Electricity - imports:** 1.998 billion kWh (2006 est.)

**Oil - production:** 3,746 bbl/day (2007 est.)

**Oil - consumption:** 179,700 bbl/day (2006 est.)

**Oil - exports:** 24,360 bbl/day (2005 est.)

**Oil - imports:** 192,500 bbl/day (2005 est.)

**Oil - proved reserves:** 836,000 bbl (1 January 2008 est.)

**Natural gas - production:** 60 million cu m (2006 est.)

**Natural gas - consumption:** 60 million cu m (2006 est.)

**Natural gas - exports:** 0 cu m (2007 est.)

**Natural gas - imports:** 0 cu m (2007 est.)

**Natural gas - proved reserves:** 1.557 billion cu m (1 January 2008 est.)

**Current account balance:** -$1.667 billion (2008 est.)

**Exports:** $16.14 billion f.o.b. (2008 est.)

**Exports - commodities:** clothing and textiles, electric components, inorganic chemicals, transistors, crude minerals, fertilizers (including phosphates), petroleum products, citrus fruits, vegetables, fish

**Exports - partners:** Spain 21.2%, France 19%, Italy 4.9%, UK 4.6%, India 4.2% (2007)

**Imports:** $34.44 billion f.o.b. (2008 est.)

**Imports - commodities:** crude petroleum, textile fabric, telecommunications equipment, wheat, gas and electricity, transistors, plastics

**Imports - partners:** France 16.1%, Spain 13.6%, China 7.3%, Italy 6.7%, Saudi Arabia 6.4%, Germany 5.9%, US 4.5%, Netherlands 4.1% (2007)

**Reserves of foreign exchange and gold:** $27.29 billion (31 December 2008 est.)

**Debt - external:** $21.11 billion (31 December 2008 est.)

**Stock of direct foreign investment - at home:** $35.36 billion (2008 est.)

**Stock of direct foreign investment - abroad:** $582 million (2008 est.)

**Exchange rates:** Moroccan dirhams (MAD) per US dollar - 7.526 (2008 est.), 8.3563 (2007), 8.7722 (2006), 8.865 (2005), 8.868 (2004)

## Communications

**Telephones - main lines in use:** 2.394 million (2007)

**Telephones - mobile cellular:** 20.029 million (2007)

**Telephone system:**

*general assessment:* modern system with all important capabilities; however, density is low with only 7 fixed lines available for each 100 persons; mobile-cellular subscribership reached 60 per 100 persons in 2007

*domestic:* good system composed of open-wire lines, cables, and microwave radio relay links; Internet available but expensive; principal switching centers are Casablanca and Rabat; national network nearly 100% digital using fiber-optic links; improved rural service employs microwave radio relay

*international:* country code - 212; landing point for the SEA-ME-WE-3 optical telecommunications submarine cable that provides connectivity to Asia, the Middle East, and Europe; satellite earth stations - 2 Intelsat (Atlantic Ocean) and 1 Arabsat; microwave

## Morocco (continued)

radio relay to Gibraltar, Spain, and Western Sahara; coaxial cable and microwave radio relay to Algeria; participant in Medarabtel; fiber-optic cable link from Agadir to Algeria and Tunisia (2007)
**Radio broadcast stations:** AM 27, FM 25, shortwave 6 (1998)
**Television broadcast stations:** 35 (plus 66 repeaters) (1995)
**Internet country code:** .ma
**Internet hosts:** 275,889 (2008)
**Internet users:** 7.3 million (2007)

### Transportation

**Airports:** 60 (2008)
**Airports - with paved runways:**
*total:* 31
*over 3,047 m:* 10
*2,438 to 3,047 m:* 8
*1,524 to 2,437 m:* 9
*914 to 1,523 m:* 2
*under 914 m:* 2 (2008)
**Airports - with unpaved runways:**
*total:* 29
*2,438 to 3,047 m:* 1
*1,524 to 2,437 m:* 8
*914 to 1,523 m:* 11
*under 914 m:* 9 (2008)
**Heliports:** 1 (2007)
**Pipelines:** gas 830 km; oil 439 km (2008)
**Railways:**
*total:* 1,907 km
*standard gauge:* 1,907 km 1.435-m gauge (1,003 km electrified) (2006)
**Roadways:**
*total:* 57,625 km
*paved:* 35,664 km (includes 639 km of expressways)
*unpaved:* 21,961 km (2006)
**Merchant marine:**
*total:* 35
*by type:* cargo 3, chemical tanker 6, container 8, passenger/cargo 13, petroleum tanker 1, roll on/roll off 4
*foreign-owned:* 16 (France 14, Germany 2)
*registered in other countries:* 4 (Gibraltar 4) (2008)
**Ports and terminals:** Agadir, Casablanca, Mohammedia, Safi

### Military

**Military branches:** Royal Armed Forces (Forces Armees Royales, FAR): Royal Moroccan Army (includes Air Defense), Navy (includes Marines), Royal Moroccan Air Force (Al Quwwat al Jawyiya al Malakiya Marakishiya; Force Aerienne Royale Marocaine) (2008)
**Military service age and obligation:** 18 years of age for compulsory and voluntary military service; conscript service obligation - 18 months (2004)
**Manpower available for military service:**
*males age 16-49:* 9,152,580
*females age 16-49:* 9,080,830 (2008 est.)

**Manpower fit for military service:**
*males age 16-49:* 7,779,589
*females age 16-49:* 7,881,024 (2009 est.)
**Manpower reaching militarily significant age annually:**
*male:* 356,014
*female:* 343,520 (2009 est.)
**Military expenditures:** 5% of GDP (2003 est.)

### Transnational Issues

**Disputes - international:** claims and administers Western Sahara whose sovereignty remains unresolved - UN-administered cease-fire has remained in effect since September 1991, but attempts to hold a referendum have failed and parties thus far have rejected all brokered proposals; Morocco protests Spain's control over the coastal enclaves of Ceuta, Melilla, and Penon de Velez de la Gomera, the islands of Penon de Alhucemas and Islas Chafarinas, and surrounding waters; discussions have not progressed on a comprehensive maritime delimitation, setting limits on resource exploration and refugee interdiction, since Morocco's 2002 rejection of Spain's unilateral designation of a median line from the Canary Islands; Morocco serves as one of the primary launching areas of illegal migration into Spain from North Africa
**Illicit drugs:** one of the world's largest producers of illicit hashish; shipments of hashish mostly directed to Western Europe; transit point for cocaine from South America destined for Western Europe; significant consumer of cannabis

# Mozambique

### Introduction

**Background:** Almost five centuries as a Portuguese colony came to a close with independence in 1975. Large-scale emigration, economic dependence on South Africa, a severe drought, and a prolonged civil war hindered the country's development until the mid 1990's. The ruling Front for the Liberation of Mozambique (FRELIMO) party formally abandoned Marxism in 1989, and a new constitution the following year provided for multiparty elections and a free market economy. A UN-negotiated peace agreement between FRELIMO and rebel Mozambique National Resistance (RENAMO) forces ended the fighting in 1992. In December 2004, Mozambique underwent a delicate transition as Joaquim CHISSANO stepped down after 18 years in office. His elected successor, Armando Emilio GUEBUZA, promised to continue the sound economic policies that have encouraged foreign investment. Mozambique has seen very strong economic growth since the end of the civil war largely due to post-conflict reconstruction.

# Mozambique (continued)

## Geography

**Location:** Southeastern Africa, bordering the Mozambique Channel, between South Africa and Tanzania

**Geographic coordinates:** 18 15 S, 35 00 E

**Map references:** Africa

**Area:**

*total:* 801,590 sq km

*land:* 784,090 sq km

*water:* 17,500 sq km

**Area - comparative:** slightly less than twice the size of California

**Land boundaries:**

*total:* 4,571 km

*border countries:* Malawi 1,569 km, South Africa 491 km, Swaziland 105 km, Tanzania 756 km, Zambia 419 km, Zimbabwe 1,231 km

**Coastline:** 2,470 km

**Maritime claims:**

*territorial sea:* 12 nm

*exclusive economic zone:* 200 nm

**Climate:** tropical to subtropical

**Terrain:** mostly coastal lowlands, uplands in center, high plateaus in northwest, mountains in west

**Elevation extremes:**

*lowest point:* Indian Ocean 0 m

*highest point:* Monte Binga 2,436 m

**Natural resources:** coal, titanium, natural gas, hydropower, tantalum, graphite

**Land use:**

*arable land:* 5.43%

*permanent crops:* 0.29%

*other:* 94.28% (2005)

**Irrigated land:** 1,180 sq km (2003)

**Total renewable water resources:** 216 cu km (1992)

**Freshwater withdrawal (domestic/industrial/agricultural):**

*total:* 0.63 cu km/yr (11%/2%/87%)

*per capita:* 32 cu m/yr (2000)

**Natural hazards:** severe droughts; devastating cyclones and floods in central and southern provinces

**Environment - current issues:** a long civil war and recurrent drought in the hinterlands have resulted in increased migration of the population to urban and coastal areas with adverse environmental consequences; desertification; pollution of surface and coastal waters; elephant poaching for ivory is a problem

**Environment - international agreements:**

*party to:* Biodiversity, Climate Change, Climate Change-Kyoto Protocol, Desertification, Endangered Species, Hazardous Wastes, Law of the Sea, Ozone Layer Protection, Ship Pollution, Wetlands

*signed, but not ratified:* none of the selected agreements

**Geography - note:** the Zambezi flows through the north-central and most fertile part of the country

## People

**Population:** 21,669,278

*note:* estimates for this country explicitly take into account the effects of excess mortality due to AIDS; this can result in lower life expectancy, higher infant mortality, higher death rates, lower population growth rates, and changes in the distribution of population by age and sex than would otherwise be expected; the 1997 Mozambican census reported a population of 16,099,246 (July 2009 est.)

**Age structure:**

*0-14 years:* 44.3% (male 4,829,272/female 4,773,209)

*15-64 years:* 52.8% (male 5,605,227/female 5,842,679)

*65 years and over:* 2.9% (male 257,119/female 361,772) (2009 est.)

**Median age:**

*total:* 17.4 years

*male:* 17 years

*female:* 17.8 years (2009 est.)

**Population growth rate:** 1.791% (2009 est.)

**Birth rate:** 37.98 births/1,000 population (2009 est.)

**Death rate:** 20.29 deaths/1,000 population (2008 est.)

**Net migration rate:** NA

**Urbanization:**

*urban population:* 37% of total population (2008)

*rate of urbanization:* 4.1% annual rate of change (2005-10 est.)

**Sex ratio:**

*at birth:* 1.02 male(s)/female

*under 15 years:* 1.01 male(s)/female

*15-64 years:* 0.96 male(s)/female

*65 years and over:* 0.71 male(s)/female

*total population:* 0.97 male(s)/female (2009 est.)

**Infant mortality rate:**

*total:* 105.8 deaths/1,000 live births

*male:* 108.57 deaths/1,000 live births

*female:* 103 deaths/1,000 live births (2009 est.)

**Life expectancy at birth:**

*total population:* 41.18 years

*male:* 41.83 years

*female:* 40.53 years (2009 est.)

**Total fertility rate:** 5.18 children born/woman (2009 est.)

**HIV/AIDS - adult prevalence rate:** 12.5% (2007 est.)

**HIV/AIDS - people living with HIV/AIDS:** 1.5 million (2007 est.)

**HIV/AIDS - deaths:** 81,000 (2007 est.)

**Major infectious diseases:**

*degree of risk:* very high

*food or waterborne diseases:* bacterial and protozoal diarrhea, hepatitis A, and typhoid fever

*vectorborne diseases:* malaria and plague

*water contact disease:* schistosomiasis

*animal contact disease:* rabies (2009)

**Nationality:**

*noun:* Mozambican(s)

*adjective:* Mozambican

**Ethnic groups:** African 99.66% (Makhuwa, Tsonga, Lomwe, Sena, and others), Europeans 0.06%, Euro-Africans 0.2%, Indians 0.08%

**Religions:** Catholic 23.8%, Muslim 17.8%, Zionist Christian 17.5%, other 17.8%, none 23.1% (1997 census)

**Languages:** Emakhuwa 26.1%, Xichangana 11.3%, Portuguese 8.8% (official; spoken by 27% of population as a second language), Elomwe 7.6%, Cisena 6.8%, Echuwabo 5.8%, other Mozambican languages 32%, other foreign languages 0.3%, unspecified 1.3% (1997 census)

**Literacy:**

*definition:* age 15 and over can read and write

*total population:* 47.8%

*male:* 63.5%

*female:* 32.7% (2003 est.)

**School life expectancy (primary to tertiary education):**

*total:* 8 years

*male:* 9 years

*female:* 7 years (2005)

**Education expenditures:** 5% of GDP (2005)

## Government

**Country name:**

*conventional long form:* Republic of Mozambique

*conventional short form:* Mozambique

*local long form:* Republica de Mocambique

*local short form:* Mocambique

*former:* Portuguese East Africa

**Government type:** republic

**Capital:**

*name:* Maputo

*geographic coordinates:* 25 57 S, 32 35 E

*time difference:* UTC+2 (7 hours ahead of Washington, DC during Standard Time)

**Administrative divisions:** 10 provinces (provincias, singular - provincia), 1 city (cidade)*; Cabo Delgado, Gaza, Inhambane, Manica, Maputo, Cidade de Maputo*, Nampula, Niassa, Sofala, Tete, Zambezia

**Independence:** 25 June 1975 (from Portugal)

**National holiday:** Independence Day, 25 June (1975)

**Constitution:** 30 November 1990

**Legal system:** based on Portuguese civil law system and customary law; has not accepted compulsory ICJ jurisdiction

**Suffrage:** 18 years of age; universal

**Executive branch:**

*chief of state:* President Armando GUEBUZA (since 2 February 2005)

*head of government:* Prime Minister Luisa DIOGO (since 17 February 2004)

*cabinet:* Cabinet

*elections:* president elected by popular vote for a five-year term (eligible for a second term); election last held 1-2 December 2004 (next to be held in December 2009); prime minister appointed by the president

*election results:* Armando GUEBUZA elected president; percent of vote - Armando GUEBUZA 63.7%, Afonso DHLAKAMA 31.7%

**Legislative branch:** unicameral Assembly of the Republic or Assembleia da Republica (250 seats; members are directly elected by popular vote to serve five-year terms)
*elections:* last held 1-2 December 2004 (next to be held in December 2009)
*election results:* percent of vote by party - FRELIMO 62%, RENAMO 29.7%, other 8.3%; seats by party - FRELIMO 160, RENAMO 90

**Judicial branch:** Supreme Court (the court of final appeal; some of its professional judges are appointed by the president, and some are elected by the Assembly); other courts include an Administrative Court, Constitutional Court, customs courts, maritime courts, courts marshal, labor courts

**Political parties and leaders:** Front for the Liberation of Mozambique (Frente de Liberatacao de Mocambique) or FRELIMO [Armando Emilio GUEBUZA]; Mozambique National Resistance (Resistencia Nacional Mocambicana) or RENAMO [Afonso DHLAKAMA]

**Political pressure groups and leaders:** Mozambican League of Human Rights (Liga Mocambicana dos Direitos Humanos) or LDH [Alice MABOTE, president]

**International organization participation:** ACP, AfDB, AU, C, CPLP, FAO, G-77, IAEA, IBRD, ICAO, ICCt (signatory), ICRM, IDA, IDB, IFAD, IFC, IFRCS, IHO, ILO, IMF, IMO, IMSO, Interpol, IOC, IOM (observer), IPU, ISO (correspondent), ITSO, ITU, ITUC, MIGA, MONUC, NAM, OIC, OIF (observer), OPCW, SADC, UN, UNCTAD, UNESCO, UNHCR, UNIDO, Union Latina, UNMIS, UNWTO, UPU, WCO, WFTU, WHO, WIPO, WMO, WTO

**Diplomatic representation in the US:**
*chief of mission:* Ambassador Armando PANGUENE
*chancery:* 1525 New Hampshire Avenue, Washington, DC 20036
*telephone:* [1] (202) 293-7146
*FAX:* [1] (202) 835-0245

**Diplomatic representation from the US:**
*chief of mission:* Ambassador (vacant); Charge d'Affaires Todd C. CHAPMAN
*embassy:* Avenida Kenneth Kuanda 193, Maputo
*mailing address:* P. O. Box 783, Maputo
*telephone:* [258] (21) 492797
*FAX:* [258] (21) 490114

**Flag description:** three equal horizontal bands of green (top), black, and yellow with a red isosceles triangle based on the hoist side; the black band is edged in white; centered in the triangle is a yellow five-pointed star bearing a crossed rifle and hoe in black superimposed on an open white book

## Economy

**Economy - overview:** At independence in 1975, Mozambique was one of the world's poorest countries. Socialist mismanagement and a brutal civil war from 1977-92 exacerbated the situation. In 1987, the government embarked on a series of macroeconomic reforms designed to stabilize the economy. These steps, combined with donor assistance and with political stability since the multi-party elections in 1994, have led to dramatic improvements in the country's growth rate. Inflation was reduced to single digits during the late 1990s, and although it returned to double digits in 2000-06, in 2007 inflation had slowed to 8%, while GDP growth reached 7.5%. Fiscal reforms, including the introduction of a value-added tax and reform of the customs service, have improved the government's revenue collection abilities. In spite of these gains, Mozambique remains dependent upon foreign assistance for much of its annual budget, and the majority of the population remains below the poverty line. Subsistence agriculture continues to employ the vast majority of the country's work force. A substantial trade imbalance persists although the opening of the Mozal aluminum smelter, the country's largest foreign investment project to date, has increased export earnings. At the end of 2007, and after years of negotiations, the government took over Portugal's majority share of the Cahora Bassa Hydroelectricity (HCB) company, a dam that was not transferred to Mozambique at independence because of the ensuing civil war and unpaid debts. More power is needed for additional investment projects in titanium extraction and processing and garment manufacturing that could further close the import/export gap. Mozambique's once substantial foreign debt has been reduced through forgiveness and rescheduling under the IMF's Heavily Indebted Poor Countries (HIPC) and Enhanced HIPC initiatives, and is now at a manageable level. In July 2007 the Millennium Challenge Corporation (MCC) signed a Compact with Mozambique; the Compact entered into force in September 2008 and will continue for five years. Compact projects will focus on improving sanitation, roads, agriculture, and the business regulation environment in an effort to spur economic growth in the four northern provinces of the country.

**GDP (purchasing power parity):**
$18.95 billion (2008 est.)
$17.79 billion (2007)
$16.63 billion (2006)
*note:* data are in 2008 US dollars

**GDP (official exchange rate):** $9.788 billion (2008 est.)

**GDP - real growth rate:**
6.5% (2008 est.)
7% (2007 est.)
8.5% (2006 est.)

**GDP - per capita (PPP):**
$900 (2008 est.)
$900 (2007 est.)
$800 (2006 est.)
*note:* data are in 2008 US dollars

**GDP - composition by sector:**
*agriculture:* 23.4%
*industry:* 30.7%
*services:* 45.9% (2008 est.)

**Labor force:** 10.04 million (2008 est.)

**Labor force - by occupation:**
*agriculture:* 81%
*industry:* 6%
*services:* 13% (1997 est.)

**Unemployment rate:**
21% (1997 est.)

**Population below poverty line:** 70% (2001 est.)

**Household income or consumption by percentage share:**
*lowest 10%:* 2.1%
*highest 10%:* 39.4% (2002)

**Distribution of family income - Gini index:** 47.3 (2002)

**Investment (gross fixed):** 24% of GDP (2008 est.)

**Budget:**
*revenues:* $2.786 billion
*expenditures:* $3.108 billion (2008 est.)

**Public debt:** 21.4% of GDP (2008 est.)

**Inflation rate (consumer prices):**
11.2% (2008 est.)
8.2% (2007 est.)

**Central bank discount rate:** 9.95% (31 December 2007)

**Commercial bank prime lending rate:** 19.52% (31 December 2007)

**Stock of money:** $1.261 billion (31 December 2007)

**Stock of quasi money:** $1.467 billion (31 December 2007)

**Stock of domestic credit:** $877.2 million (31 December 2007)

**Market value of publicly traded shares:** $NA

**Agriculture - products:** cotton, cashew nuts, sugarcane, tea, cassava (tapioca), corn, coconuts, sisal, citrus and tropical fruits, potatoes, sunflowers; beef, poultry

**Industries:** food, beverages, chemicals (fertilizer, soap, paints), aluminum, petroleum products, textiles, cement, glass, asbestos, tobacco

**Industrial production growth rate:** 9% (2008 est.)

**Electricity - production:** 14.62 billion kWh (2006 est.)

**Electricity - consumption:** 9.555 billion kWh (2006 est.)

**Electricity - exports:** 12.83 billion kWh (2006 est.)

**Electricity - imports:** 9.839 billion kWh (2006 est.)

**Oil - production:** 0 bbl/day (2007 est.)

**Oil - consumption:** 14,390 bbl/day (2006 est.)

**Oil - exports:** 0 bbl/day (2005)

**Oil - imports:** 13,240 bbl/day (2005)

**Oil - proved reserves:** 0 bbl (1 January 2006 est.)

**Natural gas - production:** 1.65 billion cu m (2006 est.)

**Natural gas - consumption:** 1.45 billion cu m (2006 est.)

**Natural gas - exports:** 0 cu m (2005 est.)

**Natural gas - imports:** 0 cu m (2007 est.)

**Natural gas - proved reserves:** 127.4 billion cu m (1 January 2008 est.)

**Current account balance:** -$981 million (2008 est.)

**Exports:** $2.693 billion f.o.b. (2008 est.)

**Exports - commodities:** aluminum, prawns, cashews, cotton, sugar, citrus, timber; bulk electricity

**Exports - partners:** Italy 19.4%, Belgium 18.4%, Spain 12.5%, South Africa 12.3%, UK 7.3%, China 4.1% (2007)

**Imports:** $3.292 billion f.o.b. (2008 est.)

## Mozambique (continued)

**Imports - commodities:** machinery and equipment, vehicles, fuel, chemicals, metal products, foodstuffs, textiles

**Imports - partners:** South Africa 36.7%, Australia 8.5%, China 4.6% (2007)

**Reserves of foreign exchange and gold:** $2.067 billion (31 December 2008 est.)

**Debt - external:** $4.316 billion (31 December 2008 est.)

**Exchange rates:** meticais (MZM) per US dollar - 24.125 (2008 est.), 26.264 (2007), 25.4 (2006), 23,061 (2005), 22,581 (2004)

*note:* in 2006 Mozambique revalued its currency, with 1000 old meticais equal to 1 new meticais

### Communications

**Telephones - main lines in use:** 67,000 (2006)

**Telephones - mobile cellular:** 3.3 million (2007)

**Telephone system:**

*general assessment:* fair system with an extremely low density of less than 1 fixed line per 100 persons

*domestic:* the telecommunications sector is shackled with a heavy state presence, lack of competition, and high operating costs and charges; stagnation in the fixed-line network contrasts with rapid growth in the mobile-cellular network; mobile-cellular coverage now includes all the main cities and key roads, including those from Maputo to the South African and Swaziland borders, the national highway through Gaza and Inhambane provinces, the Beira corridor, and from Nampula to Nacala

*international:* country code - 258; satellite earth stations - 5 Intelsat (2 Atlantic Ocean and 3 Indian Ocean)

**Radio broadcast stations:** AM 13, FM 17, shortwave 11 (2001)

**Television broadcast stations:** 4 (2008)

**Internet country code:** .mz

**Internet hosts:** 22,532 (2008)

**Internet users:** 200,000 (2007)

### Transportation

**Airports:** 111 (2008)

**Airports - with paved runways:**

*total:* 23

*over 3,047 m:* 1

*2,438 to 3,047 m:* 3

*1,524 to 2,437 m:* 10

*914 to 1,523 m:* 4

*under 914 m:* 5 (2008)

**Airports - with unpaved runways:**

*total:* 88

*2,438 to 3,047 m:* 1

*1,524 to 2,437 m:* 9

*914 to 1,523 m:* 32

*under 914 m:* 46 (2008)

**Pipelines:** gas 918 km; refined products 278 km (2008)

**Railways:**

*total:* 3,123 km

*narrow gauge:* 2,983 km 1.067-m gauge; 140 km 0.762-m gauge (2006)

**Roadways:**

*total:* 30,400 km

*paved:* 5,685 km

*unpaved:* 24,715 km (2000)

**Waterways:** 460 km (Zambezi River navigable to Tete and along Cahora Bassa Lake) (2008)

**Merchant marine:**

*total:* 2

*by type:* cargo 2

*foreign-owned:* 2 (Belgium 2) (2008)

**Ports and terminals:** Beira, Maputo, Nacala

### Military

**Military branches:** Mozambique Armed Defense Forces (FADM): Mozambique Army, Mozambique Navy (Marinha Mocambique, MM), Mozambique Air Force (Forca Aerea de Mocambique, FAM) (2006)

**Military service age and obligation:** 19-35 years of age for compulsory military service; 18 years of age for voluntary service; 2-year service obligation (2009)

**Manpower available for military service:**

*males age 16-49:* 4,545,975 (2008 est.)

**Manpower fit for military service:**

*males age 16-49:* 2,366,897

*females age 16-49:* 2,209,764 (2009 est.)

**Manpower reaching militarily significant age annually:**

*male:* 263,994

*female:* 265,058 (2009 est.)

**Military expenditures:** 0.8% of GDP (2006)

### Transnational Issues

**Disputes - international:** none

**Trafficking in persons:**

*current situation:* Mozambique is a source and, to a much lesser extent, a destination country for men, women, and children trafficked for the purposes of forced labor and sexual exploitation; the use of forced and bonded child laborers is a common practice in Mozambique's rural areas; women and girls are trafficked from rural to urban areas of Mozambique, as well as to South Africa, for domestic servitude and commercial sexual exploitation; young men and boys are trafficked to South Africa for farm work and mining

*tier rating:* Tier 2 Watch List - for the second consecutive year, Mozambique is on the Tier 2 Watch List for its failure to provide evidence of increasing efforts to combat human trafficking in 2007; while the government conducted investigations into cases of human trafficking, there were no prosecutions or convictions of traffickers; government efforts to protect victims of trafficking continued to suffer from limited resources and a lack of political commitment (2008)

**Illicit drugs:** southern African transit point for South Asian hashish and heroin, and South American cocaine probably destined for the European and South African markets; producer of cannabis (for local consumption) and methaqualone (for export to South Africa); corruption and poor regulatory capability makes the banking system vulnerable to money laundering, but the lack of a well-developed financial infrastructure limits the country's utility as a money-laundering center

## Namibia

### Introduction

**Background:** South Africa occupied the German colony of South-West Africa during World War I and administered it as a mandate until after World War II, when it annexed the territory. In 1966 the Marxist South-West Africa People's Organization (SWAPO) guerrilla group launched a war of independence for the area that became Namibia, but it was not until 1988 that South Africa agreed to end its administration in accordance with a UN peace plan for the entire region. Namibia has been governed by SWAPO since the country won independence in 1990. Hifikepunye POHAMBA was elected president in November 2004 in a landslide victory replacing Sam NUJOMA who led the country during its first 14 years of self rule.

### Geography

**Location:** Southern Africa, bordering the South Atlantic Ocean, between Angola and South Africa

**Geographic coordinates:** 22 00 S, 17 00 E

**Map references:** Africa

**Area:**

*total:* 825,418 sq km

*land:* 825,418 sq km

*water:* 0 sq km

**Area - comparative:** slightly more than half the size of Alaska

**Land boundaries:**

*total:* 3,936 km

*border countries:* Angola 1,376 km, Botswana 1,360 km, South Africa 967 km, Zambia 233 km

**Coastline:** 1,572 km

**Maritime claims:**

*territorial sea:* 12 nm

*contiguous zone:* 24 nm

*exclusive economic zone:* 200 nm

**Climate:** desert; hot, dry; rainfall sparse and erratic

**Terrain:** mostly high plateau; Namib Desert along coast; Kalahari Desert in east

# Namibia (continued)

**Elevation extremes:**
*lowest point:* Atlantic Ocean 0 m
*highest point:* Konigstein 2,606 m
**Natural resources:** diamonds, copper, uranium, gold, silver, lead, tin, lithium, cadmium, tungsten, zinc, salt, hydropower, fish
*note:* suspected deposits of oil, coal, and iron ore
**Land use:**
*arable land:* 0.99%
*permanent crops:* 0.01%
*other:* 99% (2005)
**Irrigated land:** 80 sq km (2003)
**Total renewable water resources:** 45.5 cu km (1991)
**Freshwater withdrawal (domestic/industrial/agricultural):**
*total:* 0.3 cu km/yr (24%/5%/71%)
*per capita:* 148 cu m/yr (2000)
**Natural hazards:** prolonged periods of drought
**Environment - current issues:** limited natural fresh water resources; desertification; wildlife poaching; land degradation has led to few conservation areas
**Environment - international agreements:**
*party to:* Antarctic-Marine Living Resources, Biodiversity, Climate Change, Climate Change-Kyoto Protocol, Desertification, Endangered Species, Hazardous Wastes, Law of the Sea, Ozone Layer Protection, Wetlands
*signed, but not ratified:* none of the selected agreements
**Geography - note:** first country in the world to incorporate the protection of the environment into its constitution; some 14% of the land is protected, including virtually the entire Namib Desert coastal strip

## People

**Population:** 2,108,665
*note:* estimates for this country explicitly take into account the effects of excess mortality due to AIDS; this can result in lower life expectancy, higher infant mortality, higher death rates, lower population growth rates, and changes in the distribution of population by age and sex than would otherwise be expected (July 2009 est.)
**Age structure:**
*0-14 years:* 35.9% (male 381,904/female 375,059)
*15-64 years:* 60.2% (male 641,995/female 627,146)
*65 years and over:* 3.9% (male 36,894/female 45,667) (2009 est.)
**Median age:**
*total:* 21 years
*male:* 20.9 years
*female:* 21.1 years (2009 est.)
**Population growth rate:** 0.95% (2009 est.)
**Birth rate:** 22.51 births/1,000 population (2009 est.)
**Death rate:** 14.07 deaths/1,000 population (2008 est.)
**Net migration rate:** 0.3 migrant(s)/1,000 population (2009 est.)

**Urbanization:**
*urban population:* 37% of total population (2008)
*rate of urbanization:* 2.9% annual rate of change (2005-10 est.)
**Sex ratio:**
*at birth:* 1.03 male(s)/female
*under 15 years:* 1.02 male(s)/female
*15-64 years:* 1.02 male(s)/female
*65 years and over:* 0.81 male(s)/female
*total population:* 1.01 male(s)/female (2009 est.)
**Infant mortality rate:**
*total:* 45.51 deaths/1,000 live births
*male:* 48.98 deaths/1,000 live births
*female:* 41.94 deaths/1,000 live births (2009 est.)
**Life expectancy at birth:**
*total population:* 51.24 years
*male:* 51.61 years
*female:* 50.86 years (2009 est.)
**Total fertility rate:** 2.69 children born/woman (2009 est.)
**HIV/AIDS - adult prevalence rate:** 15.3% (2007 est.)
**HIV/AIDS - people living with HIV/AIDS:** 200,000 (2007 est.)
**HIV/AIDS - deaths:** 5,100 (2007 est.)
**Major infectious diseases:**
*degree of risk:* high
*food or waterborne diseases:* bacterial diarrhea, hepatitis A, and typhoid fever
*vectorborne disease:* malaria
*water contact disease:* schistosomiasis (2009)
**Nationality:**
*noun:* Namibian(s)
*adjective:* Namibian
**Ethnic groups:** black 87.5%, white 6%, mixed 6.5%
*note:* about 50% of the population belong to the Ovambo tribe and 9% to the Kavangos tribe; other ethnic groups include Herero 7%, Damara 7%, Nama 5%, Caprivian 4%, Bushmen 3%, Baster 2%, Tswana 0.5%
**Religions:** Christian 80% to 90% (Lutheran 50% at least), indigenous beliefs 10% to 20%
**Languages:** English 7% (official), Afrikaans common language of most of the population and about 60% of the white population, German 32%, indigenous languages 1% (includes Oshivambo, Herero, Nama)
**Literacy:**
*definition:* age 15 and over can read and write
*total population:* 85%
*male:* 86.8%
*female:* 83.5% (2001 census)
**School life expectancy (primary to tertiary education):**
*total:* 11 years
*male:* 11 years
*female:* 11 years (2006)
**Education expenditures:** 6.9% of GDP (2003)

## Government

**Country name:**
*conventional long form:* Republic of Namibia
*conventional short form:* Namibia
*local long form:* Republic of Namibia
*local short form:* Namibia
*former:* German Southwest Africa, South-West Africa
**Government type:** republic
**Capital:**
*name:* Windhoek
*geographic coordinates:* 22 34 S, 17 05 E
*time difference:* UTC+1 (6 hours ahead of Washington, DC during Standard Time)
*daylight saving time:* +1hr, begins first Sunday in September; ends first Sunday in April
**Administrative divisions:** 13 regions; Caprivi, Erongo, Hardap, Karas, Khomas, Kunene, Ohangwena, Okavango, Omaheke, Omusati, Oshana, Oshikoto, Otjozondjupa
**Independence:** 21 March 1990 (from South African mandate)
**National holiday:** Independence Day, 21 March (1990)
**Constitution:** ratified 9 February 1990, effective 12 March 1990
**Legal system:** based on Roman-Dutch law and 1990 constitution; has not accepted compulsory ICJ jurisdiction
**Suffrage:** 18 years of age; universal
**Executive branch:**
*chief of state:* President Hifikepunye POHAMBA (since 21 March 2005)
*head of government:* Prime Minister Nahas ANGULA (since 21 March 2005)
*cabinet:* Cabinet appointed by the president from among the members of the National Assembly
*elections:* president elected by popular vote for a five-year term (eligible for a second term); election last held 15 November 2004 (next to be held in November 2009)
*election results:* Hifikepunye POHAMBA elected president; percent of vote - Hifikepunye POHAMBA 76.4%, Den ULENGA 7.3%, Katuutire KAURA 5.1%, Kuaima RIRUAKO 4.2%, Justus GAROEB 3.8%, other 3.2%
**Legislative branch:** bicameral legislature consists of the National Council (26 seats; two members are chosen from each regional council to serve six-year terms) and the National Assembly (72 seats; members are elected by popular vote to serve five-year terms)
*elections:* National Council - elections for regional councils to determine members of the National Council held 29-30 November 2004 (next to be held in November 2010); National Assembly - last held 15-16 November 2004 (next to be held in November 2009)
*election results:* National Council - percent of vote by party - SWAPO 89.7%, UDF 4.7%, NUDO 2.8%, DTA 1.9%, other 0.9%; seats by party - SWAPO 24, UDF 1, DTA 1; National Assembly - percent of vote by party -SWAPO 76.1%, COD 7.3%, DTA 5.1%,

NUDO 4.2%, UDF 3.6%, RP 1.9%, MAG 0.8%, other 1.0%; seats by party - SWAPO 55, COD 5, DTA 4, NUDO 3, UDF 3, RP 1, MAG 1

*note:* the National Council is primarily an advisory body

**Judicial branch:** Supreme Court (judges appointed by the president on the recommendation of the Judicial Service Commission)

**Political parties and leaders:** All People's Party or APP [Ignatius SHIXWAMENI]; Congress of Democrats or COD [Ben ULENGA]; Democratic Turnhalle Alliance of Namibia or DTA [Katuutire KAURA]; Monitor Action Group or MAG [Jurie VILJOEN]; National Democratic Movement for Change or NamDMC; National Unity Democratic Organization or NUDO [Kuaima RIRUAKO]; Rally for Democracy and Progress or RDP [Hidipo HAMUTENYA]; Republican Party or RP [Henk MUDGE]; South West Africa National Union or SWANU [Usutuaije MAAMBERUA]; South West Africa People's Organization or SWAPO [Hifikepunye POHAMBA]; United Democratic Front or UDF [Justus GAROEB]

**Political pressure groups and leaders:** Earthlife Namibia [Berthchen KOHRS] (environmentalist group); National Society for Human Rights or NSHR; The World Information Services of Energy or WISE (group against nuclear power)

**International organization participation:** ACP, AfDB, AU, C, FAO, G-77, IAEA, IBRD, ICAO, ICCt, ICRM, IDA, IFAD, IFC, IFRCS, ILO, IMF, IMO, Interpol, IOC, IOM (observer), IPU, ISO (correspondent), ITSO, ITU, MIGA, NAM, OPCW, SACU, SADC, UN, UNAMID, UNCTAD, UNESCO, UNHCR, UNIDO, UNMIL, UNMIS, UNOCI, UNWTO, UPU, WCL, WCO, WFTU, WHO, WIPO, WMO, WTO

**Diplomatic representation in the US:**
*chief of mission:* Ambassador Patrick NANDAGO
*chancery:* 1605 New Hampshire Avenue NW, Washington, DC 20009
*telephone:* [1] (202) 986-0540
*FAX:* [1] (202) 986-0443

**Diplomatic representation from the US:**
*chief of mission:* Ambassador G. Dennise MATHIEU
*embassy:* 14 Lossen Street, Windhoek
*mailing address:* Private Bag 12029 Ausspannplatz, Windhoek
*telephone:* [264] (61) 295-8500
*FAX:* [264] (61) 295-8603

**Flag description:** a wide red stripe edged by narrow white stripes divides the flag diagonally from lower hoist corner to upper fly corner; the upper hoist-side triangle is blue and charged with a yellow, 12-rayed sunburst; the lower fly-side triangle is green

## Economy

**Economy - overview:** The economy is heavily dependent on the extraction and processing of minerals for export. Mining accounts for 8% of GDP, but provides more than 50% of foreign exchange earnings. Rich alluvial diamond deposits make Namibia a primary source for gem-quality diamonds. Namibia is the fourth-largest exporter of nonfuel minerals in Africa, the world's fifth-largest producer of uranium, and the producer of large quantities of lead, zinc, tin, silver, and tungsten. The mining sector employs only about 3% of the population while about half of the population depends on subsistence agriculture for its livelihood. Namibia normally imports about 50% of its cereal requirements; in drought years food shortages are a major problem in rural areas. A high per capita GDP, relative to the region, hides one of the world's most unequal income distributions. The Namibian economy is closely linked to South Africa with the Namibian dollar pegged one-to-one to the South African rand. Increased payments from the Southern African Customs Union (SACU) put Namibia's budget into surplus in 2007 for the first time since independence, but SACU payments will decline after 2008 as part of a new revenue sharing formula. Increased fish production and mining of zinc, copper, uranium, and silver spurred growth in 2003-07, but growth in recent years was undercut by poor fish catches and high costs for metal inputs.

**GDP (purchasing power parity):**
$11.23 billion (2008 est.)
$10.87 billion (2007)
$10.45 billion (2006)
*note:* data are in 2008 US dollars

**GDP (official exchange rate):** $7.781 billion (2008 est.)

**GDP - real growth rate:**
3.3% (2008 est.)
4.1% (2007 est.)
7.1% (2006 est.)

**GDP - per capita (PPP):**
$5,400 (2008 est.)
$5,300 (2007 est.)
$5,100 (2006 est.)
*note:* data are in 2008 US dollars

**GDP - composition by sector:**
*agriculture:* 10.4%
*industry:* 36.2%
*services:* 53.4% (2008 est.)

**Labor force:** 667,000 (2008 est.)

**Labor force - by occupation:**
*agriculture:* 47%
*industry:* 20%
*services:* 33% (1999 est.)

**Unemployment rate:**
5% (2008 est.)

**Population below poverty line:** the UNDP's 2005 Human Development Report indicated that 34.9% of the population live on $1 per day and 55.8% live on $2 per day

**Household income or consumption by percentage share:**
*lowest 10%:* 0.5%
*highest 10%:* 64.5% (2003)

**Distribution of family income - Gini index:** 70.7 (2003)

**Investment (gross fixed):** 27.4% of GDP (2008 est.)

**Budget:**
*revenues:* $2.668 billion
*expenditures:* $2.896 billion (2008 est.)

**Public debt:** 24.8% of GDP (2008 est.)

**Inflation rate (consumer prices):**
10.3% (2008 est.)
6.7% (2007 est.)

**Central bank discount rate:** 10.5% (31 December 2007)

**Commercial bank prime lending rate:** 12.88% (31 December 2007)

**Stock of money:** $2.149 billion (31 December 2007)

**Stock of quasi money:** $1.493 billion (31 December 2007)

**Stock of domestic credit:** $4.446 billion (31 December 2007)

**Market value of publicly traded shares:** $702 million (31 December 2007)

**Agriculture - products:** millet, sorghum, peanuts, grapes; livestock; fish

**Industries:** meatpacking, fish processing, dairy products; mining (diamonds, lead, zinc, tin, silver, tungsten, uranium, copper)

**Industrial production growth rate:** 6.5% (2008 est.)

**Electricity - production:** 1.606 billion kWh (2007 est.)

**Electricity - consumption:** 3.194 billion kWh (2006 est.)

**Electricity - exports:** 40 million kWh (2007 est.)

**Electricity - imports:** 1.948 billion kWh; note - electricity supplied by South Africa (2006 est.)

**Oil - production:** 0 bbl/day (2007 est.)

**Oil - consumption:** 19,840 bbl/day (2006 est.)

**Oil - exports:** 0 bbl/day (2005)

**Oil - imports:** 17,750 bbl/day (2005)

**Oil - proved reserves:** 0 bbl (1 January 2006 est.)

**Natural gas - production:** 0 cu m (2007 est.)

**Natural gas - consumption:** 0 cu m (2007 est.)

**Natural gas - exports:** 0 cu m (2007 est.)

**Natural gas - imports:** 0 cu m (2007 est.)

**Natural gas - proved reserves:** 62.29 billion cu m (1 January 2008 est.)

**Current account balance:** $326 million (2008 est.)

**Exports:** $2.98 billion f.o.b. (2008 est.)

**Exports - commodities:** diamonds, copper, gold, zinc, lead, uranium; cattle, processed fish, karakul skins

**Imports:** $3.56 billion f.o.b. (2008 est.)

**Imports - commodities:** foodstuffs; petroleum products and fuel, machinery and equipment, chemicals

**Reserves of foreign exchange and gold:** $1.375 billion (31 December 2008 est.)

**Debt - external:** $1.151 billion (31 December 2008 est.)

**Stock of direct foreign investment - at home:** $NA

**Stock of direct foreign investment - abroad:** $NA

**Exchange rates:** Namibian dollars (NAD) per US dollar - 7.75 (2008 est.), 7.18 (2007), 6.7649 (2006), 6.3593 (2005), 6.4597 (2004)

## Namibia (continued)

### Communications

**Telephones - main lines in use:** 138,100 (2007)
**Telephones - mobile cellular:** 800,300 (2007)
**Telephone system:**
*general assessment:* good system with a combined fixed-line and mobile-cellular teledensity of about 45 per 100 persons
*domestic:* core fiber-optic network links most centers and connections are now digital; Namibia's first mobile-cellular network, launched in 1994, provides coverage to 86 percent of Namibia by area
*international:* country code - 264; fiber-optic cable to South Africa, microwave radio relay link to Botswana, direct links to other neighboring countries; connected to the South African Far East (SAFE) submarine cable through South Africa; satellite earth stations - 4 Intelsat (2007)
**Radio broadcast stations:** AM 2, FM 39, shortwave 4 (2001)
**Television broadcast stations:** 2 (2007)
**Internet country code:** .na
**Internet hosts:** 6,296 (2008)
**Internet users:** 101,000 (2007)

### Transportation

**Airports:** 132 (2008)
**Airports - with paved runways:**
*total:* 20
*over 3,047 m:* 3
*2,438 to 3,047 m:* 2
*1,524 to 2,437 m:* 12
*914 to 1,523 m:* 3 (2008)
**Airports - with unpaved runways:**
*total:* 112
*2,438 to 3,047 m:* 2
*1,524 to 2,437 m:* 23
*914 to 1,523 m:* 73
*under 914 m:* 14 (2008)
**Railways:**
*total:* 2,382 km
*narrow gauge:* 2,382 km 1.067-m gauge (2006)
**Roadways:**
*total:* 42,237 km
*paved:* 5,406 km
*unpaved:* 36,831 km (2002)
**Merchant marine:**
*total:* 1
*by type:* cargo 1
*registered in other countries:* 1 (Saint Vincent and the Grenadines 1) (2008)
**Ports and terminals:** Luderitz, Walvis Bay

### Military

**Military branches:** Namibian Defense Force: Army, Navy, Air Wing (2008)
**Military service age and obligation:** 18-25 years of age for voluntary military service; no conscription (2008)
**Manpower available for military service:**
*males age 16-49:* 527,948 (2008 est.)

**Manpower fit for military service:**
*males age 16-49:* 329,614
*females age 16-49:* 294,490 (2009 est.)
**Manpower reaching militarily significant age annually:**
*male:* 25,857
*female:* 25,505 (2009 est.)
**Military expenditures:** 3.7% of GDP (2006)

### Transnational Issues

**Disputes - international:** concerns from international experts and local populations over the Okavango Delta ecology in Botswana and human displacement scuttled Namibian plans to construct a hydroelectric dam on Popa Falls along the Angola-Namibia border; managed dispute with South Africa over the location of the boundary in the Orange River; Namibia has supported, and in 2004 Zimbabwe dropped objections to, plans between Botswana and Zambia to build a bridge over the Zambezi River, thereby de facto recognizing a short, but not clearly delimited, Botswana-Zambia boundary in the river
**Refugees and internally displaced persons:**
*refugees (country of origin):* 4,700 (Angola) (2007)

# Nauru

### Introduction

**Background:** The exact origins of the Nauruans are unclear since their language does not resemble any other in the Pacific. The island was annexed by Germany in 1888. Its phosphate deposits began to be mined early in the 20th century by a German-British consortium. Nauru was occupied by Australian forces in World War I and subsequently became a League of Nations mandate. After the Second World War - and a brutal occupation by Japan - Nauru became a UN trust territory. It achieved independence in 1968 and joined the UN in 1999 as the world's smallest independent republic.

### Geography

**Location:** Oceania, island in the South Pacific Ocean, south of the Marshall Islands
**Geographic coordinates:** 0 32 S, 166 55 E
**Map references:** Oceania
**Area:**
*total:* 21 sq km
*land:* 21 sq km
*water:* 0 sq km
**Area - comparative:** about 0.1 times the size of Washington, DC
**Land boundaries:** 0 km
**Coastline:** 30 km
**Maritime claims:**
*territorial sea:* 12 nm
*contiguous zone:* 24 nm
*exclusive economic zone:* 200 nm
**Climate:** tropical with a monsoonal pattern; rainy season (November to February)
**Terrain:** sandy beach rises to fertile ring around raised coral reefs with phosphate plateau in center
**Elevation extremes:**
*lowest point:* Pacific Ocean 0 m
*highest point:* unnamed location along plateau rim 61 m

# Nauru (continued)

**Natural resources:** phosphates, fish
**Land use:**
*arable land:* 0%
*permanent crops:* 0%
*other:* 100% (2005)
**Irrigated land:** NA
**Natural hazards:** periodic droughts
**Environment - current issues:** limited natural fresh water resources, roof storage tanks collect rainwater but mostly dependent on a single, aging desalination plant; intensive phosphate mining during the past 90 years - mainly by a UK, Australia, and NZ consortium - has left the central 90% of Nauru a wasteland and threatens limited remaining land resources
**Environment - international agreements:**
*party to:* Biodiversity, Climate Change, Climate Change-Kyoto Protocol, Desertification, Hazardous Wastes, Law of the Sea, Marine Dumping, Ozone Layer Protection, Whaling
*signed, but not ratified:* none of the selected agreements
**Geography - note:** Nauru is one of the three great phosphate rock islands in the Pacific Ocean - the others are Banaba (Ocean Island) in Kiribati and Makatea in French Polynesia; only 53 km south of Equator

## People

**Population:** 14,019 (July 2009 est.)
**Age structure:**
*0-14 years:* 34.7% (male 2,482/female 2,384)
*15-64 years:* 63.2% (male 4,362/female 4,495)
*65 years and over:* 2.1% (male 151/female 145) (2009 est.)
**Median age:**
*total:* 21.6 years
*male:* 21 years
*female:* 22.2 years (2009 est.)
**Population growth rate:** 1.748% (2009 est.)
**Birth rate:** 23.9 births/1,000 population (2009 est.)
**Death rate:** 6.54 deaths/1,000 population (2008 est.)
**Net migration rate:** NA
**Urbanization:**
*urban population:* 100% of total population (2008)
*rate of urbanization:* 0.3% annual rate of change (2005-10 est.)
**Sex ratio:**
*at birth:* 1.05 male(s)/female
*under 15 years:* 1.04 male(s)/female
*15-64 years:* 0.97 male(s)/female
*65 years and over:* 1.04 male(s)/female
*total population:* 1 male(s)/female (2009 est.)
**Infant mortality rate:**
*total:* 9.25 deaths/1,000 live births
*male:* 11.58 deaths/1,000 live births
*female:* 6.8 deaths/1,000 live births (2009 est.)
**Life expectancy at birth:**
*total population:* 64.2 years
*male:* 60.58 years
*female:* 68.01 years (2009 est.)

**Total fertility rate:** 2.85 children born/woman (2009 est.)
**HIV/AIDS - adult prevalence rate:** NA
**HIV/AIDS - people living with HIV/AIDS:** NA
**HIV/AIDS - deaths:** NA
**Nationality:**
*noun:* Nauruan(s)
*adjective:* Nauruan
**Ethnic groups:** Nauruan 58%, other Pacific Islander 26%, Chinese 8%, European 8%
**Religions:** Nauru Congregational 35.4%, Roman Catholic 33.2%, Nauru Independent Church 10.4%, other 14.1%, none 4.5%, unspecified 2.4% (2002 census)
**Languages:** Nauruan (official; a distinct Pacific Island language), English widely understood, spoken, and used for most government and commercial purposes
**Literacy:** NA
**School life expectancy (primary to tertiary education):**
*total:* 8 years
*male:* 8 years
*female:* 9 years (2006)
**Education expenditures:** NA

## Government

**Country name:**
*conventional long form:* Republic of Nauru
*conventional short form:* Nauru
*local long form:* Republic of Nauru
*local short form:* Nauru
*former:* Pleasant Island
**Government type:** republic
**Capital:** no official capital; government offices in Yaren District
*time difference:* UTC+12 (17 hours ahead of Washington, DC during Standard Time)
**Administrative divisions:** 14 districts; Aiwo, Anabar, Anetan, Anibare, Baiti, Boe, Buada, Denigomodu, Ewa, Ijuw, Meneng, Nibok, Uaboe, Yaren
**Independence:** 31 January 1968 (from the Australia-, NZ-, and UK-administered UN trusteeship)
**National holiday:** Independence Day, 31 January (1968)
**Constitution:** 29 January 1968; amended 17 May 1968
**Legal system:** acts of the Nauru Parliament and British common law; accepts compulsory ICJ jurisdiction with reservations
**Suffrage:** 20 years of age; universal and compulsory
**Executive branch:**
*chief of state:* President Marcus STEPHEN (since 19 December 2007); note - the president is both the chief of state and head of government
*head of government:* President Marcus STEPHEN (since 19 December 2007); note - President Ludwig SCOTTY defeated in a no confidence vote in parliament on 19 December 2007

*cabinet:* Cabinet appointed by the president from among the members of parliament
*elections:* president elected by parliament for a three-year term; election last held 19 December 2007 (next to be held in 2010)
*election results:* NA
**Legislative branch:** unicameral parliament (18 seats; members elected by popular vote to serve three-year terms)
*elections:* last held 26 April 2008 (next to be held in 2011)
*election results:* percent of vote - NA; seats - independents 18; note - President Marcus STEPHEN called a snap election to break a parliamentary stalemate blocking legislative action
**Judicial branch:** Supreme Court
**Political parties and leaders:** Democratic Party [Kennan ADEANG]; Nauru Party (informal); Nauru First (Naoero Amo) Party; note - loose multiparty system
**Political pressure groups and leaders:** Woman Information and News Agency (women's issues)
**International organization participation:** ACP, ADB, C, FAO, ICAO, ICCt, Interpol, IOC, ITU, OPCW, PIF, Sparteca, SPC, UN, UNCTAD, UNESCO, UPU, WHO
**Diplomatic representation in the US:**
*chief of mission:* Ambassador Marlene I. MOSES
*chancery:* 800 2nd Avenue, Suite 400 D, New York, NY 10017
*telephone:* [1] (212) 937-0074
*FAX:* [1] (212) 937-0079
*consulate(s):* Agana (Guam)
**Diplomatic representation from the US:** the US does not have an embassy in Nauru; the US Ambassador to Fiji is accredited to Nauru
**Flag description:** blue with a narrow, horizontal, yellow stripe across the center and a large white 12-pointed star below the stripe on the hoist side; the star indicates the country's location in relation to the Equator (the yellow stripe) and the 12 points symbolize the 12 original tribes of Nauru

## Economy

**Economy - overview:** Revenues of this tiny island have traditionally come from exports of phosphates now significantly depleted. An Australian company in 2005 entered into an agreement intended to exploit remaining supplies. Few other resources exist with most necessities being imported, mainly from Australia its former occupier and later major source of support. The rehabilitation of mined land and the replacement of income from phosphates are serious long-term problems. Reserves of phosphates may only last until 2010 at current mining rates. In anticipation of the exhaustion of Nauru's phosphate deposits, substantial amounts of phosphate income were invested in trust funds to help cushion the transition and provide for Nauru's economic future. As a result of heavy spending from the trust funds, the government faces virtual bankruptcy. To cut costs the government has frozen wages and reduced overstaffed public service departments. Nauru lost further revenue in 2008 with the closure of Australia's refugee processing center, making it almost totally dependent on food imports and foreign aid. Housing, hospitals, and other capital plant is deteriorating. The cost to Australia of keeping the government and economy afloat continues to climb. Few comprehensive statistics on the Nauru economy exist with estimates of Nauru's GDP varying widely.

**GDP (purchasing power parity):**
$60 million (2005 est.)

**GDP (official exchange rate):** $NA

**GDP - real growth rate:** NA%

**GDP - per capita (PPP):**
$5,000 (2005 est.)

**GDP - composition by sector:**
*agriculture:* NA%
*industry:* NA%
*services:* NA%

**Labor force - by occupation:**
*note:* employed in mining phosphates, public administration, education, and transportation (1992)

**Unemployment rate:**
90% (2004 est.)

**Population below poverty line:** NA%

**Household income or consumption by percentage share:**
*lowest 10%:* NA%
*highest 10%:* NA%

**Budget:**
*revenues:* $13.5 million
*expenditures:* $13.5 million (2005)

**Inflation rate (consumer prices):**
NA%

**Agriculture - products:** coconuts

**Industries:** phosphate mining, offshore banking, coconut products

**Industrial production growth rate:** NA%

**Electricity - production:** 31 million kWh (2006 est.)

**Electricity - consumption:** 28.83 million kWh (2006 est.)

**Electricity - exports:** 0 kWh (2007 est.)

**Electricity - imports:** 0 kWh (2007 est.)

**Oil - production:** 0 bbl/day (2007 est.)

**Oil - consumption:** 1,070 bbl/day (2006 est.)

**Oil - exports:** 0 bbl/day (2005)

**Oil - imports:** 1,049 bbl/day (2005)

**Oil - proved reserves:** 0 bbl (1 January 2006 est.)

**Natural gas - production:** 0 cu m (2007 est.)

**Natural gas - consumption:** 0 cu m (2007 est.)

**Natural gas - exports:** 0 cu m (2007 est.)

**Natural gas - imports:** 0 cu m (2007 est.)

**Natural gas - proved reserves:** 0 cu m (1 January 2006 est.)

**Exports:** $64,000 f.o.b. (2005 est.)

**Exports - commodities:** phosphates

**Imports:** $20 million c.i.f. (2004 est.)

**Imports - commodities:** food, fuel, manufactures, building materials, machinery

**Debt - external:** $33.3 million (2002)

**Exchange rates:** Australian dollars (AUD) per US dollar - 1.2059 (2008 est.), 1.2137 (2007), 1.3285 (2006), 1.3095 (2005), 1.3598 (2004)

## Communications

**Telephones - main lines in use:** 1,900 (2002)

**Telephones - mobile cellular:** 1,500 (2002)

**Telephone system:**
*general assessment:* adequate local and international radiotelephone communication provided via Australian facilities
*domestic:* NA
*international:* country code - 674; satellite earth station -1 Intelsat (Pacific Ocean)

**Radio broadcast stations:** AM 1, FM 0, shortwave 0 (1998)

**Television broadcast stations:** 1 (1997)

**Internet country code:** .nr

**Internet hosts:** 42 (2008)

**Internet users:** 300 (2002)

## Transportation

**Airports:** 1 (2008)

**Airports - with paved runways:**
*total:* 1
*1,524 to 2,437 m:* 1 (2008)

**Roadways:**
*total:* 24 km
*paved:* 24 km (2002)

**Ports and terminals:** Nauru

## Military

**Military branches:** no regular military forces; Nauru Police Force (2009)

**Manpower available for military service:**
*males age 16-49:* 3,470 (2008 est.)

**Manpower fit for military service:**
*males age 16-49:* 2,592
*females age 16-49:* 2,966 (2009 est.)

**Manpower reaching militarily significant age annually:**
*male:* 179
*female:* 174 (2009 est.)

**Military expenditures:** NA

**Military - note:** Nauru maintains no defense forces; under an informal agreement, defense is the responsibility of Australia

## Transnational Issues

**Disputes - international:** none

# Navassa Island
*(territory of the US)*

## Introduction

**Background:** This uninhabited island was claimed by the US in 1857 for its guano. Mining took place between 1865 and 1898. The lighthouse, built in 1917, was shut down in 1996 and administration of Navassa Island transferred from the Coast Guard to the Department of the Interior. A 1998 scientific expedition to the island described it as a unique preserve of Caribbean biodiversity; the following year it became a National Wildlife Refuge and annual scientific expeditions have continued.

## Geography

**Location:** Caribbean, island in the Caribbean Sea, 35 miles west of Tiburon Peninsula of Haiti

**Geographic coordinates:** 18 25 N, 75 02 W

**Map references:** Central America and the Caribbean

**Area:**
*total:* 5.4 sq km
*land:* 5.4 sq km
*water:* 0 sq km

**Area - comparative:** about nine times the size of The Mall in Washington, DC

**Land boundaries:** 0 km

**Coastline:** 8 km

**Maritime claims:**
*territorial sea:* 12 nm
*exclusive economic zone:* 200 nm

**Climate:** marine, tropical

**Terrain:** raised coral and limestone plateau, flat to undulating; ringed by vertical white cliffs (9 to 15 m high)

**Elevation extremes:**
*lowest point:* Caribbean Sea 0 m
*highest point:* unnamed location on southwest side 77 m

## Navassa Island (continued)

**Natural resources:** guano
**Land use:**
*arable land:* 0%
*permanent crops:* 0%
*other:* 100% (2005)
**Natural hazards:** hurricanes
**Environment - current issues:** NA
**Geography - note:** strategic location 160 km south of the US Naval Base at Guantanamo Bay, Cuba; mostly exposed rock with numerous solution holes but with enough grassland to support goat herds; dense stands of fig trees, scattered cactus

### People

**Population:** uninhabited
*note:* transient Haitian fishermen and others camp on the island

### Government

**Country name:**
*conventional long form:* none
*conventional short form:* Navassa Island
**Dependency status:** unorganized, unincorporated territory of the US; administered by the Fish and Wildlife Service, US Department of the Interior from the Caribbean Islands National Wildlife Refuge in Boqueron, Puerto Rico; in September 1996 the Coast Guard ceased operations and maintenance of Navassa Island Light a 46-meter-tall lighthouse on the southern side of the island; there has also been a private claim advanced against the island
**Legal system:** the laws of the US, where applicable, apply
**Diplomatic representation from the US:** none (territory of the US)
**Flag description:** the flag of the US is used

### Economy

**Economy - overview:** Subsistence fishing and commercial trawling occur within refuge waters.

### Transportation

**Ports and terminals:** none; offshore anchorage only

### Military

**Military - note:** defense is the responsibility of the US

### Transnational Issues

**Disputes - international:** claimed by Haiti, source of subsistence fishing

## Nepal

### Introduction

**Background:** In 1951, the Nepalese monarch ended the century-old system of rule by hereditary premiers and instituted a cabinet system of government. Reforms in 1990 established a multiparty democracy within the framework of a constitutional monarchy. An insurgency led by Maoist extremists broke out in 1996. The ensuing ten-year civil war between insurgents and government forces witnessed the dissolution of the cabinet and parliament and assumption of absolute power by the king. Several weeks of mass protests in April 2006 were followed by several months of peace negotiations between the Maoists and government officials, and culminated in a November 2006 peace accord and the promulgation of an interim constitution. Following a nation-wide election in April 2008, the newly formed Constituent Assembly declared Nepal a federal democratic republic and abolished the monarchy at its first meeting the following month. The Constituent Assembly elected the country's first president in July. The Maoists, who received a plurality of votes in the Constituent Assembly election, formed a coalition government in August 2008.

### Geography

**Location:** Southern Asia, between China and India
**Geographic coordinates:** 28 00 N, 84 00 E
**Map references:** Asia
**Area:**
*total:* 147,181 sq km
*land:* 143,181 sq km
*water:* 4,000 sq km
**Area - comparative:** slightly larger than Arkansas
**Land boundaries:**
*total:* 2,926 km
*border countries:* China 1,236 km, India 1,690 km
**Coastline:** 0 km (landlocked)

**Maritime claims:** none (landlocked)
**Climate:** varies from cool summers and severe winters in north to subtropical summers and mild winters in south
**Terrain:** Tarai or flat river plain of the Ganges in south, central hill region, rugged Himalayas in north
**Elevation extremes:**
*lowest point:* Kanchan Kalan 70 m
*highest point:* Mount Everest 8,850 m
**Natural resources:** quartz, water, timber, hydropower, scenic beauty, small deposits of lignite, copper, cobalt, iron ore
**Land use:**
*arable land:* 16.07%
*permanent crops:* 0.85%
*other:* 83.08% (2005)
**Irrigated land:** 11,700 sq km (2003)
**Total renewable water resources:** 210.2 cu km (1999)
**Freshwater withdrawal (domestic/industrial/agricultural):**
*total:* 10.18 cu km/yr (3%/1%/96%)
*per capita:* 375 cu m/yr (2000)
**Natural hazards:** severe thunderstorms; flooding; landslides; drought and famine depending on the timing, intensity, and duration of the summer monsoons
**Environment - current issues:** deforestation (overuse of wood for fuel and lack of alternatives); contaminated water (with human and animal wastes, agricultural runoff, and industrial effluents); wildlife conservation; vehicular emissions
**Environment - international agreements:**
*party to:* Biodiversity, Climate Change, Climate Change-Kyoto Protocol, Desertification, Endangered Species, Hazardous Wastes, Law of the Sea, Ozone Layer Protection, Tropical Timber 83, Tropical Timber 94, Wetlands
*signed, but not ratified:* Marine Life Conservation

# Nepal (continued)

**Geography - note:** landlocked; strategic location between China and India; contains eight of world's 10 highest peaks, including Mount Everest and Kanchenjunga - the world's tallest and third tallest - on the borders with China and India respectively

## People

**Population:** 28,563,377 (July 2009 est.)
**Age structure:**
*0-14 years:* 36.6% (male 5,327,484/female 5,127,178)
*15-64 years:* 59.2% (male 8,094,494/female 8,812,675)
*65 years and over:* 4.2% (male 566,666/female 634,880) (2009 est.)
**Median age:**
*total:* 20.8 years
*male:* 19.8 years
*female:* 21.7 years (2009 est.)
**Population growth rate:** 1.281% (2009 est.)
**Birth rate:** 23.18 births/1,000 population (2009 est.)
**Death rate:** 8.97 deaths/1,000 population (2008 est.)
**Net migration rate:** -3.39 migrant(s)/1,000 population (2009 est.)
**Urbanization:**
*urban population:* 17% of total population (2008)
*rate of urbanization:* 4.9% annual rate of change (2005-10 est.)
**Sex ratio:**
*at birth:* 1.04 male(s)/female
*under 15 years:* 1.04 male(s)/female
*15-64 years:* 0.92 male(s)/female
*65 years and over:* 0.89 male(s)/female
*total population:* 0.96 male(s)/female (2009 est.)
**Infant mortality rate:**
*total:* 47.46 deaths/1,000 live births
*male:* 47.4 deaths/1,000 live births
*female:* 47.52 deaths/1,000 live births (2009 est.)
**Life expectancy at birth:**
*total population:* 65.46 years
*male:* 64.3 years
*female:* 66.67 years (2009 est.)
**Total fertility rate:** 2.64 children born/woman (2009 est.)
**HIV/AIDS - adult prevalence rate:** 0.5% (2007 est.)
**HIV/AIDS - people living with HIV/AIDS:** 70,000 (2007 est.)
**HIV/AIDS - deaths:** 5,000 (2007 est.)
**Major infectious diseases:**
*degree of risk:* high
*food or waterborne diseases:* bacterial diarrhea, hepatitis A, and typhoid fever
*vectorborne disease:* Japanese encephalitis, malaria, and dengue fever (2009)
**Nationality:**
*noun:* Nepalese (singular and plural)
*adjective:* Nepalese
**Ethnic groups:** Chhettri 15.5%, Brahman-Hill

12.5%, Magar 7%, Tharu 6.6%, Tamang 5.5%, Newar 5.4%, Muslim 4.2%, Kami 3.9%, Yadav 3.9%, other 32.7%, unspecified 2.8% (2001 census)
**Religions:** Hindu 80.6%, Buddhist 10.7%, Muslim 4.2%, Kirant 3.6%, other 0.9% (2001 census)
*note:* only official Hindu state in the world
**Languages:** Nepali 47.8%, Maithali 12.1%, Bhojpuri 7.4%, Tharu (Dagaura/Rana) 5.8%, Tamang 5.1%, Newar 3.6%, Magar 3.3%, Awadhi 2.4%, other 10%, unspecified 2.5% (2001 census)
*note:* many in government and business also speak English (2001 est.)
**Literacy:**
*definition:* age 15 and over can read and write
*total population:* 48.6%
*male:* 62.7%
*female:* 34.9% (2001 census)
**School life expectancy (primary to tertiary education):**
*total:* 9 years
*male:* 10 years
*female:* 8 years (2003)
**Education expenditures:** 3.4% of GDP (2003)

## Government

**Country name:**
*conventional long form:* Federal Democratic Republic of Nepal
*conventional short form:* Nepal
*local long form:* Sanghiya Loktantrik Ganatantra Nepal
*local short form:* Nepal
**Government type:** federal democratic republic
**Capital:**
*name:* Kathmandu
*geographic coordinates:* 27 43 N, 85 19 E
*time difference:* UTC+5.75 (10.75 hours ahead of Washington, DC during Standard Time)
**Administrative divisions:** 14 zones (anchal, singular and plural); Bagmati, Bheri, Dhawalagiri, Gandaki, Janakpur, Karnali, Kosi, Lumbini, Mahakali, Mechi, Narayani, Rapti, Sagarmatha, Seti
**Independence:** 1768 (unified by Prithvi Narayan SHAH)
**National holiday:** Republic Day, 29 May; Democracy Day, 24 April
**Constitution:** 15 January 2007 (interim Constitution); note - in April 2008, a Constituent Assembly was elected to draft and promulgate a new constitution by May 2010
**Legal system:** based on Hindu legal concepts and English common law; has not accepted compulsory ICJ jurisdiction
**Suffrage:** 18 years of age; universal
**Executive branch:**
*chief of state:* President Ram Baran YADAV (as of 23July 2008); Vice President Paramananda JHA (as of 23 July 2008)
*head of government:* Prime Minister Madhav Kumar NEPAL (as of 25 May 2009); Deputy Prime Minister Bijay Kumar GACHHEDAR

*cabinet:* cabinet formed in August 2008 by a majority coalition made up of the Communist Party of Nepal (Maoist), Communist Party of Nepal-United Marxist-Leninist, Madhesi People's Rights Forum, and several smaller parties
*elections:* president elected by Parliament; term extends until the new constitution is promulgated; election last held 21 July 2008; date of next election NA
*election results:* Ram Baran YADAV elected president by the Constituent Assembly in a second round of voting on 21 July 2008; Ram Baran YADAV 308, Ram Jaja Prasad SINGH 282
**Legislative branch:** unicameral Constituent Assembly (601 seats; 240 seats decided by direct popular vote; 335 seats by proportional representation; 26 appointed by the Cabinet (Council of Ministers))
*elections:* last held 10 April 2008 (next to be held NA)
*election results:* percent of vote by party - CPN-M 38%, NC 19%, CPN-UML 19%, Madhesi People's Right Forum 9%, Terai-Madhes Democratic Party and Sadbhavana Party 5%, other 10%; seats by party - CPN-M 220, NC 110, CPN-UML 103, Madhesi People's Rights Forum 52, Terai-Madhes Democratic Party 20, Sadbhawana Party 9, other smaller parties 61; note - 26 seats filled by the new Cabinet
**Judicial branch:** Supreme Court or Sarbochha Adalat (the president appoints the chief justice is appointed by the monarch on recommendation of the Constitutional Council; the chief justice appoints other judges on the recommendation of the Judicial Council)
**Political parties and leaders:** Chure Bhawar Rastriya Ekata Party [Keshav Prasad MAINALI]; Communist Party of Nepal (ML) [C.P. MAINALI]; Communist Party of Nepal (Unified) [Raj Singh SHRIS]; Communist Party of Nepal (United) [Ganesh SHAH]; Communist Party of Nepal/United Marxist-Leninist or CPN/UML [Jhalanath KHANAL]; Dalit Janajati Party [Vishwendraman PASHWAN]; Madhesi People's Rights Forum [Upendra YADAV]; National Democratic Party or NDP [Pashupati Shumsher RANA] (also called Rastriya Prajatantra Party or RPP); Nepal Loktantrik Samajbadi Dal [Upendra GACHCHHADAR]; Nepal Pariwar Dal [Vinod DANGI]; Nepal Rastriya Party [Khushilal YADAV]; Nepal Sadbhavana Party (Anandi Devi) [Shyam Sundar GUPTA]; Nepal Workers and Peasants Party or NWPP [Narayan Man BIJUKCHHE]; Nepali Congress Party or NCP [Girija Prasad KOIRALA]; Nepali Janata Dal [Bharat Prasad MAHATO]; Rastriya Janamorcha [Chitra BAHADUR K.C.]; Rastriya Janamukti Party [Malwar Singh THAPA]; Rastriya Janashakti Party or RJP [Surya Bahadur THAPA]; Rastriya Prajatantra Party Nepal [Kamal THAPA]; Sadbhavana Party (Mahato) [Rajendra MAHATO]; Samajbadi Prajatantrik Janata Party Nepal [Prem Bahadur SINGH]; Sanghiya Loktantrik Rastriya Manch [Kamal CHHARAHANG]; Terai-Madhes Democratic Party [Mahantha THAKUR]; United Communist Party of Nepal (Maoist) [Pushpa Kamal DAHAL, also known as PRACHANDA, chairman]

# Nepal (continued)

**Political pressure groups and leaders:**
*other:* several small armed Madhesi groups along the southern border with India; a variety of groups advocating regional autonomy for individual ethnic groups

**International organization participation:** ADB, BIMSTEC, CP, FAO, G-77, IBRD, ICAO, ICC, ICRM, IDA, IFAD, IFC, IFRCS, ILO, IMF, IMO, Interpol, IOC, IOM, IPU, ISO (correspondent), ITSO, ITU, ITUC, MIGA, MINURCAT, MINUSTAH, MONUC, NAM, OPCW, SAARC, SACEP, UN, UNAMID, UNCTAD, UNESCO, UNIDO, UNIFIL, UNMIL, UNMIS, UNMIT, UNOCI, UNOMIG, UNTSO, UNWTO, UPU, WCL, WCO, WFTU, WHO, WIPO, WMO, WTO

**Diplomatic representation in the US:**
*chief of mission:* Ambassador (vacant); Charge d'Affaires Kali POKHREL
*chancery:* 2131 Leroy Place NW, Washington, DC 20008
*telephone:* [1] (202) 667-4550
*FAX:* [1] (202) 667-5534
*consulate(s) general:* New York

**Diplomatic representation from the US:**
*chief of mission:* Ambassador Nancy J. POWELL
*embassy:* Maharajgunj, Kathmandu
*mailing address:* use embassy street address
*telephone:* [977] (1) 400-7200
*FAX:* [977] (1) 400-7272

**Flag description:** red with a blue border around the unique shape of two overlapping right triangles; the smaller, upper triangle bears a white stylized moon and the larger, lower triangle bears a white 12-pointed sun

## Economy

**Economy - overview:** Nepal is among the poorest and least developed countries in the world with almost one-third of its population living below the poverty line. Agriculture is the mainstay of the economy, providing a livelihood for three-fourths of the population and accounting for about one-third of GDP. Industrial activity mainly involves the processing of agricultural products, including pulses, jute, sugarcane, tobacco, and grain. Bumper crops, better security, improved transportation, and increased tourism pushed growth past 5% in 2008, after growth had hovered around 3% -barely above the rate of population growth - for the previous three years. The deteriorating world economy in 2009 will challenge tourism and remittance growth, a key source of foreign exchange. Nepal has considerable scope for exploiting its potential in hydropower and tourism, areas of recent foreign investment interest. Prospects for foreign trade or investment in other sectors will remain poor, however, because of the small size of the economy, its technological backwardness, its remoteness and landlocked geographic location, its civil strife and labor unrest, and its susceptibility to natural disaster.

**GDP (purchasing power parity):**
$31.09 billion (2008 est.)
$29.69 billion (2007)
$28.77 billion (2006)
*note:* data are in 2008 US dollars
**GDP (official exchange rate):** $12.64 billion (2008 est.)
**GDP - real growth rate:**
5.6% (2008 est.)
3.2% (2007 est.)
3.7% (2006 est.)
**GDP - per capita (PPP):**
$1,100 (2008 est.)
$1,100 (2007 est.)
$1,000 (2006 est.)
*note:* data are in 2008 US dollars
**GDP - composition by sector:**
*agriculture:* 32.5%
*industry:* 16.6%
*services:* 50.9% (FY07 est.)
**Labor force:** 14.6 million
*note:* severe lack of skilled labor (2008 est.)
**Labor force - by occupation:**
*agriculture:* 76%
*industry:* 6%
*services:* 18% (2004 est.)
**Unemployment rate:**
46% (2008 est.)
42% (2004 est.)
**Population below poverty line:** 30.9% (2004)
**Household income or consumption by percentage share:**
*lowest 10%:* 2.6%
*highest 10%:* 40.6% (2006)
**Distribution of family income - Gini index:** 47.2 (2008)
**Budget:**
*revenues:* $1.7 billion
*expenditures:* $2.3 billion (FY08)
**Inflation rate (consumer prices):**
7.7% (2008 est.)
6.4% (2007 est.)
**Central bank discount rate:** 6.5% (31 December 2008)
**Commercial bank prime lending rate:** 7% (16 July 2008)
**Stock of money:** $2.204 billion (16 July 2008)
**Stock of quasi money:** $4.872 billion (16 July 2008)
**Stock of domestic credit:** $6.027 billion (16 July 2008)
**Market value of publicly traded shares:** $5.5 billion (31 December 2008)
**Agriculture - products:** pulses, rice, corn, wheat, sugarcane, jute, root crops; milk, water buffalo meat
**Industries:** tourism, carpets, textiles; small rice, jute, sugar, and oilseed mills; cigarettes, cement and brick production
**Industrial production growth rate:** 1.8% (FY08)
**Electricity - production:** 2.703 billion kWh (2007 est.)

**Electricity - consumption:** 2.276 billion kWh (2006 est.)
**Electricity - exports:** 165 million kWh (2007 est.)
**Electricity - imports:** 560 million kWh (2008 est.)
**Oil - production:** 0 bbl/day (2008 est.)
**Oil - consumption:** 12,500 bbl/day (2008 est.)
**Oil - exports:** 0 bbl/day (2008)
**Oil - imports:** 12,500 bbl/day (2008 est.)
**Oil - proved reserves:** 0 bbl (1 January 2006 est.)
**Natural gas - production:** 0 cu m (2008 est.)
**Natural gas - consumption:** 0 cu m (2008 est.)
**Natural gas - exports:** 0 cu m (2008 est.)
**Natural gas - imports:** 0 cu m (2008 est.)
**Natural gas - proved reserves:** 0 cu m (1 January 2008 est.)
**Current account balance:** $241 million (2008)
**Exports:** $868 million f.o.b.; note - does not include unrecorded border trade with India (2008)
**Exports - commodities:** clothing, carpets, leather goods, jute goods, pulses, grain
**Exports - partners:** India 69.3%, US 8.8%, Germany 4.1% (2007)
**Imports:** $3.229 billion f.o.b. (2008)
**Imports - commodities:** petroleum products, machinery and equipment, electrical goods
**Imports - partners:** India 58.9%, China 13.6%, Japan 1.6% (2007)
**Debt - external:** $3.285 billion (2008)
**Stock of direct foreign investment - at home:** $NA
**Stock of direct foreign investment - abroad:** $NA
**Exchange rates:** Nepalese rupees (NPR) per US dollar - 65.21 (2008), 70.35 (2007), 72.446 (2006), 72.16 (2005), 73.674 (2004)

## Communications

**Telephones - main lines in use:** 766,400 (2007)
**Telephones - mobile cellular:** 1.157 million (2006)
**Telephone system:**
*general assessment:* poor telephone and telegraph service; fair radiotelephone communication service and mobile-cellular telephone network
*domestic:* NA
*international:* country code - 977; radiotelephone communications; microwave landline to India; satellite earth station - 1 Intelsat (Indian Ocean)
**Radio broadcast stations:** AM 6, FM 80, shortwave 4 (2008)
**Television broadcast stations:** 9 (plus 9 repeaters) (2008)
**Internet country code:** .np
**Internet hosts:** 42,219 (2008)
**Internet users:** 337,100 (2007)

## Transportation

**Airports:** 47 (2008)
**Airports - with paved runways:**
*total:* 11
*over 3,047 m:* 1
*914 to 1,523 m:* 9
*under 914 m:* 1 (2008)

**Airports - with unpaved runways:**
*total:* 36
*1,524 to 2,437 m:* 1
*914 to 1,523 m:* 5
*under 914 m:* 30 (2008)
**Railways:**
*total:* 59 km
*narrow gauge:* 59 km 0.762-m gauge (2006)
**Roadways:**
*total:* 17,280 km
*paved:* 9,829 km
*unpaved:* 7,451 km (2004)

## Military

**Military branches:** Nepal Army (2009)
**Military service age and obligation:** 18 years of age for voluntary military service; 15 years of age for military training; no conscription (2008)
**Manpower available for military service:**
*males age 16-49:* 7,322,965
*females age 16-49:* 6,859,064 (2008 est.)
**Manpower fit for military service:**
*males age 16-49:* 4,886,103
*females age 16-49:* 5,525,764 (2009 est.)
**Manpower reaching militarily significant age annually:**
*male:* 365,567
*female:* 352,643 (2009 est.)
**Military expenditures:** 1.6% of GDP (2006)

## Transnational Issues

**Disputes - international:** joint border commission continues to work on contested sections of boundary with India, including the 400 square kilometer dispute over the source of the Kalapani River; India has instituted a stricter border regime to restrict transit of Maoist insurgents and illegal cross-border activities; approximately 106,000 Bhutanese Lhotshampas (Hindus) have been confined in refugee camps in southeastern Nepal since 1990
**Refugees and internally displaced persons:**
*refugees (country of origin):* 107,803 (Bhutan); 20,153 (Tibet/China)
*IDPs:* 50,000-70,000 (remaining from ten-year Maoist insurgency that officially ended in 2006; displacement spread across the country) (2007)
**Illicit drugs:** illicit producer of cannabis and hashish for the domestic and international drug markets; transit point for opiates from Southeast Asia to the West

# Netherlands

## Introduction

**Background:** The Dutch United Provinces declared their independence from Spain in 1579; during the 17th century, they became a leading seafaring and commercial power, with settlements and colonies around the world. After a 20-year French occupation, a Kingdom of the Netherlands was formed in 1815. In 1830 Belgium seceded and formed a separate kingdom. The Netherlands remained neutral in World War I, but suffered invasion and occupation by Germany in World War II. A modern, industrialized nation, the Netherlands is also a large exporter of agricultural products. The country was a founding member of NATO and the EEC (now the EU), and participated in the introduction of the euro in 1999.

## Geography

**Location:** Western Europe, bordering the North Sea, between Belgium and Germany
**Geographic coordinates:** 52 30 N, 5 45 E
**Map references:** Europe
**Area:**
*total:* 41,526 sq km
*land:* 33,883 sq km
*water:* 7,643 sq km
**Area - comparative:** slightly less than twice the size of New Jersey
**Land boundaries:**
*total:* 1,027 km
*border countries:* Belgium 450 km, Germany 577 km
**Coastline:** 451 km
**Maritime claims:**
*territorial sea:* 12 nm
*contiguous zone:* 24 nm
*exclusive fishing zone:* 200 nm
**Climate:** temperate; marine; cool summers and mild winters
**Terrain:** mostly coastal lowland and reclaimed land (polders); some hills in southeast

**Elevation extremes:**
*lowest point:* Zuidplaspolder -7 m
*highest point:* Vaalserberg 322 m
**Natural resources:** natural gas, petroleum, peat, limestone, salt, sand and gravel, arable land
**Land use:**
*arable land:* 21.96%
*permanent crops:* 0.77%
*other:* 77.27% (2005)
**Irrigated land:** 5,650 sq km (2003)
**Total renewable water resources:** 89.7 cu km (2005)
**Freshwater withdrawal (domestic/industrial/agricultural):**
*total:* 8.86 cu km/yr (6%/60%/34%)
*per capita:* 544 cu m/yr (2001)
**Natural hazards:** flooding
**Environment - current issues:** water pollution in the form of heavy metals, organic compounds, and nutrients such as nitrates and phosphates; air pollution from vehicles and refining activities; acid rain
**Environment - international agreements:**
*party to:* Air Pollution, Air Pollution-Nitrogen Oxides, Air Pollution-Persistent Organic Pollutants, Air Pollution-Sulfur 85, Air Pollution-Sulfur 94, Air Pollution-Volatile Organic Compounds, Antarctic-Environmental Protocol, Antarctic-Marine Living Resources, Antarctic Treaty, Biodiversity, Climate Change, Climate Change-Kyoto Protocol, Desertification, Endangered Species, Environmental Modification, Hazardous Wastes, Kyoto Protocol, Law of the Sea, Marine Dumping, Marine Life Conservation, Ozone Layer Protection, Ship Pollution, Tropical Timber 83, Tropical Timber 94, Wetlands, Whaling
*signed, but not ratified:* none of the selected agreements
**Geography - note:** located at mouths of three major European rivers (Rhine, Maas or Meuse, and Schelde)

## People

**Population:** 16,715,999 (July 2009 est.)
**Age structure:**
*0-14 years:* 17.4% (male 1,485,873/female 1,416,999)
*15-64 years:* 67.7% (male 5,720,387/female 5,604,014)
*65 years and over:* 14.9% (male 1,070,496/female 1,418,230) (2009 est.)
**Median age:**
*total:* 40.4 years
*male:* 39.6 years
*female:* 41.2 years (2009 est.)
**Population growth rate:** 0.412% (2009 est.)
**Birth rate:** 10.4 births/1,000 population (2009 est.)
**Death rate:** 8.71 deaths/1,000 population (2008 est.)
**Net migration rate:** 2.46 migrant(s)/1,000 population (2009 est.)

# Netherlands (continued)

**Urbanization:**

*urban population:* 82% of total population (2008)

*rate of urbanization:* 0.9% annual rate of change (2005-10 est.)

**Sex ratio:**

*at birth:* 1.05 male(s)/female

*under 15 years:* 1.05 male(s)/female

*15-64 years:* 1.02 male(s)/female

*65 years and over:* 0.76 male(s)/female

*total population:* 0.98 male(s)/female (2009 est.)

**Infant mortality rate:**

*total:* 4.73 deaths/1,000 live births

*male:* 5.25 deaths/1,000 live births

*female:* 4.19 deaths/1,000 live births (2009 est.)

**Life expectancy at birth:**

*total population:* 79.4 years

*male:* 76.8 years

*female:* 82.14 years (2009 est.)

**Total fertility rate:** 1.66 children born/woman (2009 est.)

**HIV/AIDS - adult prevalence rate:** 0.2% (2007 est.)

**HIV/AIDS - people living with HIV/AIDS:** 18,000 (2007 est.)

**HIV/AIDS - deaths:** fewer than 200 (2007 est.)

**Nationality:**

*noun:* Dutchman(men), Dutchwoman(women)

*adjective:* Dutch

**Ethnic groups:** Dutch 80.7%, EU 5%, Indonesian 2.4%, Turkish 2.2%, Surinamese 2%, Moroccan 2%, Netherlands Antilles & Aruba 0.8%, other 4.8% (2008 est.)

**Religions:** Roman Catholic 30%, Dutch Reformed 11%, Calvinist 6%, other Protestant 3%, Muslim 5.8%, other 2.2%, none 42% (2006)

**Languages:** Dutch (official), Frisian (official)

**Literacy:**

*definition:* age 15 and over can read and write

*total population:* 99%

*male:* 99%

*female:* 99% (2003 est.)

**School life expectancy (primary to tertiary education):**

*total:* 16 years

*male:* 17 years

*female:* 16 years (2006)

**Education expenditures:** 5.3% of GDP (2005)

## Government

**Country name:**

*conventional long form:* Kingdom of the Netherlands

*conventional short form:* Netherlands

*local long form:* Koninkrijk der Nederlanden

*local short form:* Nederland

**Government type:** constitutional monarchy

**Capital:**

*name:* Amsterdam

*geographic coordinates:* 52 23 N, 4 54 E

*time difference:* UTC+1 (6 hours ahead of Washington, DC during Standard Time)

*daylight saving time:* +1hr, begins last Sunday in March; ends last Sunday in October

*note:* The Hague is the seat of government; time descriptions apply to the continental Netherlands only, not to the Caribbean components

**Administrative divisions:** 12 provinces (provincies, singular - provincie); Drenthe, Flevoland, Friesland (Fryslan), Gelderland, Groningen, Limburg, Noord-Brabant (North Brabant), Noord-Holland (North Holland), Overijssel, Utrecht, Zeeland (Zealand), Zuid-Holland (South Holland)

**Dependent areas:** Aruba, Netherlands Antilles

**Independence:** 23 January 1579 (the northern provinces of the Low Countries conclude the Union of Utrecht breaking with Spain; on 26 July 1581 they formally declared their independence with an Act of Abjuration; however, it was not until 30 January 1648 and the Peace of Westphalia that Spain recognized this independence)

**National holiday:** Queen's Day (Birthday of Queen-Mother JULIANA and accession to the throne of her oldest daughter BEATRIX), 30 April (1909 and 1980)

**Constitution:** adopted 1815; amended many times, most recently in 2002

**Legal system:** based on civil law system incorporating French penal theory; constitution does not permit judicial review of acts of the States General; accepts compulsory ICJ jurisdiction with reservations

**Suffrage:** 18 years of age; universal

**Executive branch:**

*chief of state:* Queen BEATRIX (since 30 April 1980); Heir Apparent WILLEM-ALEXANDER (born 27 April 1967), son of the monarch

*head of government:* Prime Minister Jan Peter BALKENENDE (since 22 July 2002); Deputy Prime Ministers Wouter BOS (since 22 February 2007) and Andre ROUVOET (since 22 February 2007)

*cabinet:* Council of Ministers appointed by the monarch

*elections:* the monarchy is hereditary; following Second Chamber elections, the leader of the majority party or leader of a majority coalition is usually appointed prime minister by the monarch; deputy prime ministers appointed by the monarch

*note:* there is also a Council of State composed of the monarch, heir apparent, and councilors that provides consultations to the cabinet on legislative and administrative policy

**Legislative branch:** bicameral States General or Staten Generaal consists of the First Chamber or Eerste Kamer (75 seats; members indirectly elected by the country's 12 provincial councils to serve four-year terms) and the Second Chamber or Tweede Kamer (150 seats; members elected by popular vote to serve four-year terms)

*elections:* First Chamber - last held 29 May 2007 (next to be held in May 2011); Second Chamber - last held 22 November 2006 (next to be held by early 2011)

*election results:* First Chamber - percent of vote by party - NA%; seats by party - CDA 21, PvdA 14, VVD 14, Socialist Party 11, Christian Union 4, Green Left Party 4, D66 2, other 5; Second Chamber - percent of vote by party - CDA 26.5%, PvdA 21.2%, Socialist Party 16.6%, VVD 14.6%, Party for Freedom 5.9%, Green Party 4.6%, Christian Union 4.0%, other 6.6%; seats by party - CDA 41, PvdA 33, Socialist Party 25, VVD 22, Party for Freedom 9, Green Party 7, Christian Union 6, other 7

**Judicial branch:** Supreme Court or Hoge Raad (justices are nominated for life by the monarch)

**Political parties and leaders:** Christian Democratic Appeal or CDA [Pieter VAN GEEL]; Christian Union Party [Arie SLOB]; Democrats 66 or D66 [Alexander PECHTOLD]; Green Left Party [Femke HALSEMA]; Labor Party or PvdA [Mariette HAMER]; Party for Freedom or PVV [Geert WILDERS]; Party for the Animals or PvdD [Marianne THIEME]; People's Party for Freedom and Democracy (Liberal) or VVD [Mark RUTTE]; Reformed Political Party of SGP [Bas VAN DER VLIES]; Socialist Party [Agnes KANT]; plus a few minor parties

**Political pressure groups and leaders:** Christian Trade Union Federation or CNV [Rene PAAS]; Confederation of Netherlands Industry and Employers or VNO-NCW [Bernard WIENTJES]; Federation for Small and Medium-sized businesses or MKB [Loek HERMANS]; Netherlands Trade Union Federation or FNV [Agnes JONGERIUS]; Social Economic Council or SER [Alexander RINNOOY KAN]; Trade Union Federation of Middle and High Personnel or MHP [Ad VERHOEVEN]

**International organization participation:** ADB (nonregional member), AfDB (nonregional member), Arctic Council (observer), Australia Group, Benelux, BIS, CBSS (observer), CE, CERN, EAPC, EBRD, EIB, EMU, ESA, EU, FAO, G-10, IADB, IAEA, IBRD, ICAO, ICC, ICCt, ICRM, IDA, IEA, IFAD, IFC, IFRCS, IHO, ILO, IMF, IMO, IMSO, Interpol, IOC, IOM, IPU, ISO, ITSO, ITU, ITUC, MIGA, NAM (guest), NATO, NEA, NSG, OAS (observer), OECD, OPCW, OSCE, Paris Club, PCA, Schengen Convention, SECI (observer), UN, UNCTAD, UNESCO, UNHCR, UNIDO, UNMIS, UNRWA, UNTSO, UNWTO, UPU, WCL, WCO, WEU, WFTU, WHO, WIPO, WMO, WTO, ZC

**Diplomatic representation in the US:**

*chief of mission:* Ambassador Regina "Renee" JONES-BOS

*chancery:* 4200 Linnean Avenue NW, Washington, DC 20008

*telephone:* [1] (202) 244-5300, [1] 877-388-2443

*FAX:* [1] (202) 362-3430

*consulate(s) general:* Chicago, Los Angeles, Miami, New York

*consulate(s):* Boston

**Diplomatic representation from the US:**

*chief of mission:* Ambassador (vacant); Charge d'Affaires Michael GALLAGHER

*embassy:* Lange Voorhout 102, 2514 EJ, The Hague

*mailing address:* PSC 71, Box 1000, APO AE 09715

*telephone:* [31] (70) 310-2209

*FAX:* [31] (70) 361-4688

*consulate(s) general:* Amsterdam

**Flag description:** three equal horizontal bands of red (top), white, and blue; similar to the flag of Luxembourg, which uses a lighter blue and is longer; one of the oldest flags in constant use, originating with WILLIAM I, Prince of Orange, in the latter half of the 16th century

## Economy

**Economy - overview:** The Netherlands has a prosperous and open economy, which depends heavily on foreign trade. The economy is noted for stable industrial relations, moderate unemployment and inflation, a sizable current account surplus, and an important role as a European transportation hub. Industrial activity is predominantly in food processing, chemicals, petroleum refining, and electrical machinery. A highly mechanized agricultural sector employs no more than 3% of the labor force but provides large surpluses for the food-processing industry and for exports. The Netherlands, along with 11 of its EU partners, began circulating the euro currency on 1 January 2002. The country has been one of the leading European nations for attracting foreign direct investment and is one of the four largest investors in the US. The pace of job growth reached 10-year highs in 2007, but economic growth fell sharply in 2008 as fallout from the world financial crisis constricted demand and raised the specter of a recession in 2009.

**GDP (purchasing power parity):**
$670.2 billion (2008 est.)
$658.4 billion (2007)
$636.1 billion (2006)
*note:* data are in 2008 US dollars
**GDP (official exchange rate):** $909.5 billion (2008 est.)
**GDP - real growth rate:**
1.8% (2008 est.)
3.5% (2007 est.)
3.4% (2006 est.)
**GDP - per capita (PPP):**
$40,300 (2008 est.)
$39,700 (2007 est.)
$38,600 (2006 est.)
*note:* data are in 2008 US dollars
**GDP - composition by sector:**
*agriculture:* 2%
*industry:* 24.4%
*services:* 73.6% (2008 est.)
**Labor force:** 7.75 million (2008 est.)
**Labor force - by occupation:**
*agriculture:* 2%
*industry:* 18%
*services:* 80% (2005 est.)
**Unemployment rate:**
4.5% (2008 est.)
4.6% (2007 est.)
**Population below poverty line:** 10.5% (2005)
**Household income or consumption by percentage share:**
*lowest 10%:* 2.5%
*highest 10%:* 22.9% (1999)

**Distribution of family income - Gini index:** 30.9 (2007)
**Investment (gross fixed):** 20.3% of GDP (2008 est.)
**Budget:**
*revenues:* $408.5 billion
*expenditures:* $398.8 billion (2008 est.)
**Public debt:** 43% of GDP (2008 est.)
**Inflation rate (consumer prices):**
1.5% (2008 est.)
1.6% (2007 est.)
**Central bank discount rate:** 4%
*note:* this is the European Central Bank's rate on the marginal lending facility, which offers overnight credit to banks in the euro area
**Commercial bank prime lending rate:** 8.72% (31 December 2007)
**Stock of money:** NA
*note:* see entry for the European Union for money supply in the euro area; the European Central Bank (ECB) controls monetary policy for the 16 members of the Economic and Monetary Union (EMU); individual members of the EMU do not control the quantity of money and quasi money circulating within their own borders
**Stock of quasi money:** NA
**Stock of domestic credit:** $1.876 trillion (31 December 2007)
**Market value of publicly traded shares:** $456.2 billion (31 December 2008)
**Agriculture - products:** grains, potatoes, sugar beets, fruits, vegetables; livestock
**Industries:** agroindustries, metal and engineering products, electrical machinery and equipment, chemicals, petroleum, construction, microelectronics, fishing
**Industrial production growth rate:** 2.1% (2008 est.)
**Electricity - production:** 105.2 billion kWh (2007)
**Electricity - consumption:** 122.8 billion kWh (2007)
**Electricity - exports:** 5.48 billion kWh (2007)
**Electricity - imports:** 23.09 billion kWh (2007)
**Oil - production:** 88,950 bbl/day (2007 est.)
**Oil - consumption:** 984,200 bbl/day (2007 est.)
**Oil - exports:** 1.639 million bbl/day (2005)
**Oil - imports:** 2.648 million bbl/day (2005)
**Oil - proved reserves:** 100 million bbl (1 January 2008 est.)
**Natural gas - production:** 76.33 billion cu m (2007 est.)
**Natural gas - consumption:** 46.42 billion cu m (2007 est.)
**Natural gas - exports:** 55.66 billion cu m (2007 est.)
**Natural gas - imports:** 25.73 billion cu m (2007 est.)
**Natural gas - proved reserves:** 1.416 trillion cu m (1 January 2008 est.)
**Current account balance:** $47 billion (2008 est.)
**Exports:** $537.5 billion f.o.b. (2008 est.)
**Exports - commodities:** machinery and equipment, chemicals, fuels; foodstuffs

**Exports - partners:** Germany 24.4%, Belgium 13.6%, UK 9.1%, France 8.5%, Italy 5.1%, US 4.3% (2007)
**Imports:** $485.3 billion f.o.b. (2008 est.)
**Imports - commodities:** machinery and transport equipment, chemicals, fuels, foodstuffs, clothing
**Imports - partners:** Germany 17.7%, China 10.5%, Belgium 9.3%, US 7.3%, UK 5.8%, Russia 5.1%, France 4.4% (2007)
**Reserves of foreign exchange and gold:** $24.28 billion (31 December 2008 est.)
**Debt - external:** $2.277 trillion (30 June 2007)
**Stock of direct foreign investment - at home:** $726.9 billion (2008 est.)
**Stock of direct foreign investment - abroad:** $872.5 billion (2008 est.)
**Exchange rates:** euros (EUR) per US dollar - 0.6827 (2008 est.), 0.7345 (2007), 0.7964 (2006), 0.8041 (2005), 0.8054 (2004)

## Communications

**Telephones - main lines in use:** 7.334 million (2007)
**Telephones - mobile cellular:** 17.3 million (2006)
**Telephone system:**
*general assessment:* highly developed and well maintained
*domestic:* extensive fixed-line fiber-optic network; large cellular telephone system with 5 major operators utilizing the third generation of the Global System for Mobile Communications (GSM) technology; one in five households now use Voice over the Internet Protocol (VoIP) services
*international:* country code - 31; submarine cables provide links to the US and Europe; satellite earth stations - 5 (3 Intelsat - 1 Indian Ocean and 2 Atlantic Ocean, 1 Eutelsat, and 1 Inmarsat (2007)
**Radio broadcast stations:** AM 4, FM 567, shortwave 1 (2008)
**Television broadcast stations:** 342 (2008)
**Internet country code:** .nl
**Internet hosts:** 10.983 million (2008)
**Internet users:** 15 million (2007)

## Transportation

**Airports:** 27 (2008)
**Airports - with paved runways:**
*total:* 20
*over 3,047 m:* 2
*2,438 to 3,047 m:* 9
*1,524 to 2,437 m:* 3
*914 to 1,523 m:* 5
*under 914 m:* 1 (2008)
**Airports - with unpaved runways:**
*total:* 7
*914 to 1,523 m:* 3
*under 914 m:* 4 (2008)
**Heliports:** 1 (2007)
**Pipelines:** gas 3,816 km; oil 365 km; refined products 716 km (2008)

# Netherlands *(continued)*

**Railways:**
*total:* 2,801 km
*standard gauge:* 2,801 km 1.435-m gauge (2,064 km electrified) (2007)
**Roadways:**
*total:* 135,470 km (includes 2,582 km of expressways) (2007)
**Waterways:** 6,215 km (navigable for ships of 50 tons) (2007)
**Merchant marine:**
*total:* 622
*by type:* bulk carrier 9, cargo 381, carrier 19, chemical tanker 44, container 76, liquefied gas 15, passenger 16, passenger/cargo 15, petroleum tanker 11, refrigerated cargo 10, roll on/roll off 23, specialized tanker 3
*foreign-owned:* 203 (Belgium 2, Cyprus 8, Denmark 29, Finland 14, France 1, Germany 75, Ireland 10, Italy 1, South Korea 1, Norway 12, Sweden 28, Turkey 1, UAE 5, UK 2, US 14)
*registered in other countries:* 178 (Antigua and Barbuda 20, Australia 2, Austria 2, Bahamas 9, Cambodia 1, Canada 1, Cyprus 22, Germany 1, Gibraltar 21, Isle of Man 1, Liberia 6, Luxembourg 2, Marshall Islands 8, Netherlands Antilles 38, Panama 14, Paraguay 1, Philippines 23, Portugal 1, Saint Vincent and the Grenadines 3, US 1, unknown 1) (2008)
**Ports and terminals:** Amsterdam, IJmuiden, Rotterdam, Terneuzen, Vlissingen

## Military

**Military branches:** Royal Netherlands Army, Royal Netherlands Navy (includes Naval Air Service and Marine Corps), Royal Netherlands Air Force (Koninklijke Luchtmacht, KLu), Royal Military Police (2009)
**Military service age and obligation:** 20 years of age for an all-volunteer force (2004)
**Manpower available for military service:**
*males age 16-49:* 3,950,825
*females age 16-49:* 3,850,800 (2008 est.)
**Manpower fit for military service:**
*males age 16-49:* 3,224,790
*females age 16-49:* 3,143,096 (2009 est.)
**Manpower reaching militarily significant age annually:**
*male:* 105,194
*female:* 100,341 (2009 est.)
**Military expenditures:** 1.6% of GDP (2005 est.)

## Transnational Issues

**Disputes - international:** none
**Illicit drugs:** major European producer of synthetic drugs, including ecstasy, and cannabis cultivator; important gateway for cocaine, heroin, and hashish entering Europe; major source of US-bound ecstasy; large financial sector vulnerable to money laundering; significant consumer of ecstasy

# Netherlands Antilles
*(part of the Kingdom of the Netherlands)*

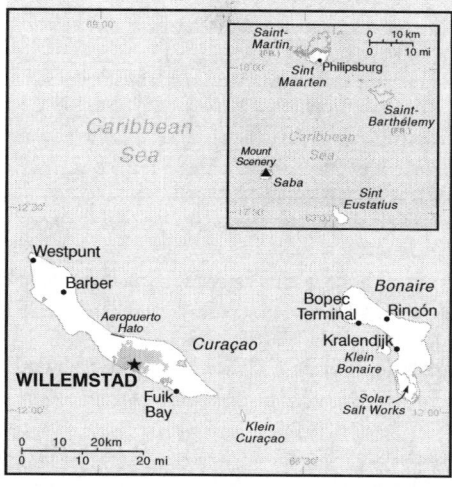

## Introduction

**Background:** Once the center of the Caribbean slave trade, the island of Curacao was hard hit by the abolition of slavery in 1863. Its prosperity (and that of neighboring Aruba) was restored in the early 20th century with the construction of oil refineries to service newly discovered Venezuelan oil fields. The island of Saint Martin is shared with France; its southern portion is named Sint Maarten and is part of the Netherlands Antilles; its northern portion, called Saint Martin, is an overseas collectivity of France.

## Geography

**Location:** Caribbean, two island groups in the Caribbean Sea - composed of five islands, Curacao and Bonaire located off the coast of Venezuela, and Sint Maarten, Saba, and Sint Eustatius lie east of the US Virgin Islands
**Geographic coordinates:**
*Bonaire:* 12 12 N, 68 15 W
*Curacao:* 12 10 N, 69 00 W
*Saba:* 17 38 N, 63 14 W
*Sint Eustatius:* 17 30 N, 62 58 W
*Sint Maarten:* 18 04 N, 63 04 W
**Map references:** Central America and the Caribbean
**Area:**
*total:* 960 sq km
*land:* 960 sq km
*water:* 0 sq km
*note:* includes Bonaire, Curacao, Saba, Sint Eustatius, and Sint Maarten (Dutch part of the island of Saint Martin)
**Area - comparative:** more than five times the size of Washington, DC
**Land boundaries:**
*total:* 15 km
*border countries:* Saint Martin 15 km
**Coastline:** 364 km

**Maritime claims:**
*territorial sea:* 12 nm
*exclusive fishing zone:* 12 nm
**Climate:** tropical; ameliorated by northeast trade winds
**Terrain:** generally hilly, volcanic interiors
**Elevation extremes:**
*lowest point:* Caribbean Sea 0 m
*highest point:* Mount Scenery 862 m
**Natural resources:** phosphates (Curacao only), salt (Bonaire only)
**Land use:**
*arable land:* 10%
*permanent crops:* 0%
*other:* 90% (2005)
**Irrigated land:** NA
**Natural hazards:** Sint Maarten, Saba, and Sint Eustatius are subject to hurricanes from July to October; Curacao and Bonaire are south of Caribbean hurricane belt and are rarely threatened
**Environment - current issues:** NA
**Geography - note:** the five islands of the Netherlands Antilles are divided geographically into the Leeward Islands (northern) group (Saba, Sint Eustatius, and Sint Maarten) and the Windward Islands (southern) group (Bonaire and Curacao); the island of Saint Martin is the smallest landmass in the world shared by two independent states, the French territory of Saint Martin and the Dutch territory of Sint Maarten

## People

**Population:** 227,049 (July 2009 est.)
**Age structure:**
*0-14 years:* 22.7% (male 26,429/female 25,162)
*15-64 years:* 67.7% (male 74,183/female 79,434)
*65 years and over:* 9.6% (male 8,875/female 12,966) (2009 est.)
**Median age:**
*total:* 33.7 years
*male:* 31.9 years
*female:* 35.5 years (2009 est.)
**Population growth rate:** 0.732% (2009 est.)
**Birth rate:** 14.19 births/1,000 population (2009 est.)
**Death rate:** 6.43 deaths/1,000 population (2008 est.)
**Net migration rate:** -0.39 migrant(s)/1,000 population (2009 est.)
**Urbanization:**
*urban population:* 93% of total population (2008)
*rate of urbanization:* 1.6% annual rate of change (2005-10 est.)
**Sex ratio:**
*at birth:* 1.05 male(s)/female
*under 15 years:* 1.05 male(s)/female
*15-64 years:* 0.93 male(s)/female
*65 years and over:* 0.68 male(s)/female
*total population:* 0.93 male(s)/female (2009 est.)
**Infant mortality rate:**
*total:* 9.09 deaths/1,000 live births
*male:* 9.76 deaths/1,000 live births
*female:* 8.39 deaths/1,000 live births (2009 est.)

# Netherlands Antilles (continued)

**Life expectancy at birth:**
*total population:* 76.65 years
*male:* 74.33 years
*female:* 79.09 years (2009 est.)
**Total fertility rate:** 1.97 children born/woman (2009 est.)
**HIV/AIDS - adult prevalence rate:** NA
**HIV/AIDS - people living with HIV/AIDS:** NA
**HIV/AIDS - deaths:** NA
**Nationality:**
*noun:* Dutch Antillean(s)
*adjective:* Dutch Antillean
**Ethnic groups:** mixed black 85%, other 15% (includes Carib Amerindian, white, East Asian)
**Religions:** Roman Catholic 72%, Pentecostal 4.9%, Protestant 3.5%, Seventh-Day Adventist 3.1%, Methodist 2.9%, Jehovah's Witnesses 1.7%, other Christian 4.2%, Jewish 1.3%, other or unspecified 1.2%, none 5.2% (2001 census)
**Languages:** Papiamento 65.4% (a Spanish-Portuguese-Dutch-English dialect), English 15.9% (widely spoken), Dutch 7.3% (official), Spanish 6.1%, Creole 1.6%, other 1.9%, unspecified 1.8% (2001 census)
**Literacy:**
*definition:* age 15 and over can read and write
*total population:* 96.7%
*male:* 96.7%
*female:* 96.8% (2003 est.)
**School life expectancy (primary to tertiary education):**
*total:* 14 years
*male:* 14 years
*female:* 15 years (2002)
**Education expenditures:** NA

## Government

**Country name:**
*conventional long form:* none
*conventional short form:* Netherlands Antilles
*local long form:* none
*local short form:* Nederlandse Antillen
*former:* Curacao and Dependencies
**Dependency status:** an autonomous country within the Kingdom of the Netherlands; full autonomy in internal affairs granted in 1954; Dutch Government responsible for defense and foreign affairs
**Government type:** parliamentary
**Capital:**
*name:* Willemstad (on Curacao)
*geographic coordinates:* 12 06 N, 68 56 W
*time difference:* UTC-4 (1 hour ahead of Washington, DC during Standard Time)
**Administrative divisions:** none (part of the Kingdom of the Netherlands)
*note:* each island has its own government
**Independence:** none (part of the Kingdom of the Netherlands)
**National holiday:** Queen's Day (Birthday of Queen-Mother JULIANA and accession to the throne of her oldest daughter BEATRIX), 30 April (1909 and 1980)

**Constitution:** 29 December 1954, Statute of the Realm of the Netherlands, as amended
**Legal system:** based on Dutch civil law system with some English common law influence
**Suffrage:** 18 years of age; universal
**Executive branch:**
*chief of state:* Queen BEATRIX of the Netherlands (since 30 April 1980); represented by Governor General Frits GOEDGEDRAG (since 1 July 2002)
*head of government:* Prime Minister Emily de JONGH-ELHAGE (since 26 March 2006)
*cabinet:* Council of Ministers elected by the Staten (legislature)
*elections:* the monarch is hereditary; governor general appointed by the monarch for a six-year term; following legislative elections, the leader of the majority party is usually elected prime minister by the Staten; election last held 27 January 2006 (next to be held by 2010)
*note:* government coalition - PAR, PNP, DP-St. M, UPB, WIPM Saba, DP-St. E
**Legislative branch:** unicameral States or Staten (22 seats, Curacao 14, Bonaire 3, St. Maarten 3, St. Eustatius 1, Saba 1; members are elected by popular vote to serve four-year terms)
*elections:* last held 27 January 2006 (next to be held in 2010)
*election results:* percent of vote by party - NA; seats by party - PAR 5, MAN 3, FOL 2, Forsa Korsou 2, National Alliance 2, PNP 2, UPB 2, DP-St. E 1, DP-St. M 1, PDB 1, WIPM 1
*note:* the government is a coalition of several parties
**Judicial branch:** Joint High Court of Justice (judges appointed by the monarch)
**Political parties and leaders:**
*Bonaire:* Democratic Party of Bonaire or PDB [Jopi ABRAHAM]; Patriotic Union of Bonaire or UPB [Ramonsito BOOI]
*Curacao:* Ban Vota [Norbert GEORGE]; C-93 [Stanley BROWN]; Democratic Party of Curacao or DP [Errol HERNANDEZ]; E Mayoria [Aurelio PEDRO]; Forsa Korsou [Nelson NAVARRO]; Liste Ni'un Paso Atras [Nelson PIERRE]; Movemiento Patriotiko Korsou [Reginald LAK]; New Antilles Movement or MAN [Charles COOPER]; Partido Akshon Pa Prosperidat I Seguridat [Sonja BERKEMEYER]; Partido Laboral Krusada Popular or PLKP [Errol COVA]; Party for the Restructured Antilles or PAR [Emily de JONGH-ELHAGE]; People's National Party or PNP [Ersilia DE LANNOOY]; Pidjin [Jasmin PINEDO]; Pueblo Soberano [Herman WIELS]; Workers' Liberation Front or FOL [Anthony GODETT]
*Saba:* Saba Labor Party [Akilah LEVENSTONE]; Windward Islands People's Movement or WIPM [Ray HASSELL]
*Sint Eustatius:* Democratic Party of Sint Eustatius or DP-St. E [Julian WOODLEY]; Progressive Labor Party [Clyde VAN PUTTEN]; St. Eustatius Alliance [Ingrid HOUTMAN-WHITFIELD]
*Sint Maarten:* Democratic Party of Sint Maarten or DP-St. M [Sarah WESCOTT-WILLIAMS]; Freedom Slate of National Democratic Party [Theophilus

PRIEST]; National Alliance or NA [William MARLIN]; People's Progressive Alliance or PPA [Gracita ARRINDELL]; St. Maarten People's Party [Johan LEONARD]; United People's Labor Party [Bienvenido RICHARDSON]
*note:* political parties are indigenous to each island
**Political pressure groups and leaders:** Employers Association (VBC); Unions (AVBO)
**International organization participation:** Caricom (observer), ILO, IMF, Interpol, IOC, UNESCO (associate), UNWTO (associate), UPU, WCL, WCO, WMO
**Diplomatic representation in the US:** none (represented by the Kingdom of the Netherlands); note - Mr. Jeffrey CORRION, Minister Plenipotentiary for Aruba at the Embassy of the Kingdom of the Netherlands
**Diplomatic representation from the US:**
*chief of mission:* Consul General Robert E. SORENSON
*consulate(s) general:* J. B. Gorsiraweg #1, Willemstad, Curacao
*mailing address:* P. O. Box 158, Willemstad, Curacao
*telephone:* [599] (9) 461-3066
*FAX:* [599] (9) 461-6489
**Flag description:** white, with a horizontal blue stripe in the center superimposed on a vertical red band, also centered; five white, five-pointed stars are arranged in an oval pattern in the center of the blue band; the five stars represent the five main islands of Bonaire, Curacao, Saba, Sint Eustatius, and Sint Maarten

## Economy

**Economy - overview:** Tourism, petroleum refining, and offshore finance are the mainstays of this small economy, which is closely tied to the outside world. Although GDP has declined or grown slightly in each of the past eight years, the islands enjoy a high per capita income and a well-developed infrastructure compared with other countries in the region. Most of the oil Netherlands Antilles imports for its refineries come from Venezuela. Almost all consumer and capital goods are imported, the US, Italy, and Mexico being the major suppliers. Poor soils and inadequate water supplies hamper the development of agriculture. Budgetary problems hamper reform of the health and pension systems of an aging population. The Netherlands provides financial aid to support the economy.
**GDP (purchasing power parity):**
$2.8 billion (2004 est.)
**GDP (official exchange rate):** $NA
**GDP - real growth rate:**
1% (2004 est.)
**GDP - per capita (PPP):**
$16,000 (2004 est.)
**GDP - composition by sector:**
*agriculture:* 1%
*industry:* 15%
*services:* 84% (2000 est.)

# Netherlands Antilles *(continued)*

**Labor force:** 83,600 (2005)
**Labor force - by occupation:**
*agriculture:* 1%
*industry:* 20%
*services:* 79% (2005 est.)
**Unemployment rate:**
17% (2002 est.)
**Population below poverty line:** NA%
**Household income or consumption by percentage share:**
*lowest 10%:* NA%
*highest 10%:* NA%
**Budget:**
*revenues:* $757.9 million
*expenditures:* $949.5 million (2004)
**Inflation rate (consumer prices):**
2.1% (2003 est.)
**Central bank discount rate:** %NA
**Commercial bank prime lending rate:** 9.21%
(31 December 2007)
**Stock of money:** $1.133 billion (31 December 2007)
**Stock of quasi money:** $2.309 billion (31 December 2007)
**Stock of domestic credit:** $2.927 billion
(31 December 2007)
**Market value of publicly traded shares:** $488.6
billion (2003)
**Agriculture - products:** aloes, sorghum, peanuts,
vegetables, tropical fruit
**Industries:** tourism (Curacao, Sint Maarten, and
Bonaire), petroleum refining (Curacao), petroleum
transshipment facilities (Curacao and Bonaire), light
manufacturing (Curacao)
**Industrial production growth rate:** NA%
**Electricity - production:** 1.195 billion kWh
(2006 est.)
**Electricity - consumption:** 992 million kWh
(2006 est.)
**Electricity - exports:** 0 kWh (2007 est.)
**Electricity - imports:** 0 kWh (2007 est.)
**Oil - production:** 0 bbl/day (2005 est.)
**Oil - consumption:** 67,450 bbl/day (2006 est.)
**Oil - exports:** 206,900 bbl/day (2005)
**Oil - imports:** 277,600 bbl/day (2005)
**Oil - proved reserves:** 0 bbl (1 January 2006 est.)
**Natural gas - production:** 0 cu m (2007 est.)
**Natural gas - consumption:** 0 cu m (2007 est.)
**Natural gas - exports:** 0 cu m (2007 est.)
**Natural gas - imports:** 0 cu m (2007 est.)
**Natural gas - proved reserves:** 0 cu m (1 January
2006 est.)
**Exports:** $3.71 billion f.o.b. (2006)
**Exports - commodities:** petroleum products
**Exports - partners:** US 18.9%, Mexico 13.3%,
Panama 11.4%, Singapore 6.9%, Haiti 6.6%, The
Bahamas 5.3% (2007)
**Imports:** $15.74 billion f.o.b. (2006)
**Imports - commodities:** crude petroleum, food,
manufactures
**Imports - partners:** Venezuela 59.1%, US 17.7%,
Brazil 7.1% (2007)

**Debt - external:** $2.68 billion (2004)
**Stock of direct foreign investment - at home:**
$NA
**Stock of direct foreign investment - abroad:** $NA
**Exchange rates:** Netherlands Antillean guilders
(ANG) per US dollar - NA (2007), 1.79 (2006), 1.79
(2005), 1.79 (2004), 1.79 (2003)

## Communications

**Telephones - main lines in use:** 81,000 (2001)
**Telephones - mobile cellular:** 200,000 (2004)
**Telephone system:**
*general assessment:* generally adequate facilities
*domestic:* extensive interisland microwave radio relay
links
*international:* country code - 599; the Americas
Region Caribbean Ring System (ARCOS-1) and the
Americas-2 submarine cable systems provide
connectivity to Central America, parts of South
America and the Caribbean, and the US; satellite
earth stations - 2 Intelsat (Atlantic Ocean)
**Radio broadcast stations:** AM 8, FM 19,
shortwave 0 (2003)
**Television broadcast stations:** 3 (there is also a
cable service that supplies programs received from
various US satellite networks and 4 Venezuelan
channels) (2003)
**Internet country code:** .an
**Internet hosts:** 47,597 (2008)
**Internet users:** 2,000 (2000)

## Transportation

**Airports:** 5 (2008)
**Airports - with paved runways:**
*total:* 5
*over 3,047 m:* 1
*2,438 to 3,047 m:* 1
*1,524 to 2,437 m:* 1
*914 to 1,523 m:* 1
*under 914 m:* 1 (2008)
**Roadways:**
*total:* 845
**Merchant marine:**
*total:* 147
*by type:* barge carrier 2, bulk carrier 2, cargo 72,
carrier 19, chemical tanker 2, container 8, liquefied
gas 1, passenger 2, petroleum tanker 3, refrigerated
cargo 27, roll on/roll off 6, specialized tanker 3
*foreign-owned:* 123 (Belgium 1, Cuba 1, Cyprus 21,
Denmark 2, Germany 43, Hong Kong 2, Netherlands
38, Norway 3, Sweden 1, Turkey 10, US 1) (2008)
**Ports and terminals:** Bopec Terminal, Willemstad

## Military

**Military branches:** no regular military forces;
National Guard (2008)
**Military service age and obligation:** 16 years of
age for National Guard recruitment; no conscription
(2004)

**Manpower available for military service:**
*males age 16-49:* 55,365
*females age 16-49:* 57,060 (2008 est.)
**Manpower fit for military service:**
*males age 16-49:* 46,461
*females age 16-49:* 47,325 (2009 est.)
**Manpower reaching militarily significant age
annually:**
*male:* 1,920
*female:* 1,827 (2009 est.)
**Military - note:** defense is the responsibility of the
Kingdom of the Netherlands

## Transnational Issues

**Disputes - international:** none
**Illicit drugs:** transshipment point for South American
drugs bound for the US and Europe;
money-laundering center

# New Caledonia
## (self-governing territory of France)

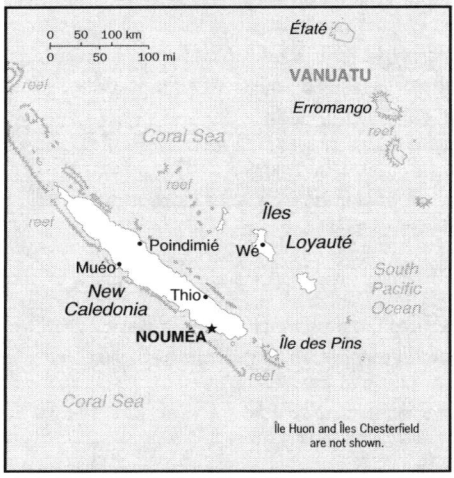

0 50 100 km
0 50 100 mi

VANUATU
*Éfaté*
*Erromango*
Coral Sea
*reef*
*Îles*
*Loyauté*
Poindimié Wé•
Muéo• *Wé*
New Thio•
Caledonia
South
Pacific
Ocean
NOUMÉA★
*Île des Pins*
*reef*
Coral Sea

Île Huon and Îles Chesterfield
are not shown.

## Introduction

**Background:** Settled by both Britain and France during the first half of the 19th century, the island was made a French possession in 1853. It served as a penal colony for four decades after 1864. Agitation for independence during the 1980s and early 1990s ended in the 1998 Noumea Accord, which over a period of 15 to 20 years will transfer an increasing amount of governing responsibility from France to New Caledonia. The agreement also commits France to conduct as many as three referenda between 2013 and 2018, to decide whether New Caledonia should assume full sovereignty and independence.

## Geography

**Location:** Oceania, islands in the South Pacific Ocean, east of Australia
**Geographic coordinates:** 21 30 S, 165 30 E
**Map references:** Oceania
**Area:**
*total:* 19,060 sq km
*land:* 18,575 sq km
*water:* 485 sq km
**Area - comparative:** slightly smaller than New Jersey
**Land boundaries:** 0 km
**Coastline:** 2,254 km
**Maritime claims:**
*territorial sea:* 12 nm
*exclusive economic zone:* 200 nm
**Climate:** tropical; modified by southeast trade winds; hot, humid
**Terrain:** coastal plains with interior mountains
**Elevation extremes:**
*lowest point:* Pacific Ocean 0 m
*highest point:* Mont Panie 1,628 m
**Natural resources:** nickel, chrome, iron, cobalt, manganese, silver, gold, lead, copper

**Land use:**
*arable land:* 0.32%
*permanent crops:* 0.22%
*other:* 99.46% (2005)
**Irrigated land:** 100 sq km (2003)
**Natural hazards:** cyclones, most frequent from November to March
**Environment - current issues:** erosion caused by mining exploitation and forest fires
**Geography - note:** consists of the main island of New Caledonia (one of the largest in the Pacific Ocean), the archipelago of Iles Loyaute, and numerous small, sparsely populated islands and atolls

## People

**Population:** 227,436 (July 2009 est.)
**Age structure:**
*0-14 years:* 26.8% (male 31,191/female 29,870)
*15-64 years:* 65.8% (male 75,189/female 74,552)
*65 years and over:* 7.3% (male 7,681/female 8,953) (2009 est.)
**Median age:**
*total:* 28.7 years
*male:* 28.2 years
*female:* 29.2 years (2009 est.)
**Population growth rate:** 1.136% (2009 est.)
**Birth rate:** 17.04 births/1,000 population (2009 est.)
**Death rate:** 5.64 deaths/1,000 population (2008 est.)
**Net migration rate:** NA
*note:* there has been steady emigration from Wallis and Futuna to New Caledonia (2009 est.)
**Urbanization:**
*urban population:* 65% of total population (2008)
*rate of urbanization:* 2.1% annual rate of change (2005-10 est.)
**Sex ratio:**
*at birth:* 1.05 male(s)/female
*under 15 years:* 1.04 male(s)/female
*15-64 years:* 1.01 male(s)/female
*65 years and over:* 0.86 male(s)/female
*total population:* 1.01 male(s)/female (2009 est.)
**Infant mortality rate:**
*total:* 7.05 deaths/1,000 live births
*male:* 7.7 deaths/1,000 live births
*female:* 6.36 deaths/1,000 live births (2009 est.)
**Life expectancy at birth:**
*total population:* 74.98 years
*male:* 71.99 years
*female:* 78.12 years (2009 est.)
**Total fertility rate:** 2.18 children born/woman (2009 est.)
**HIV/AIDS - adult prevalence rate:** NA
**HIV/AIDS - people living with HIV/AIDS:** NA
**HIV/AIDS - deaths:** NA
**Nationality:**
*noun:* New Caledonian(s)
*adjective:* New Caledonian
**Ethnic groups:** Melanesian 44.1%, European 34.1%, Wallisian & Futunian 9%, Tahitian 2.6%, Indonesian 2.5%, Vietnamese 1.4%, Ni-Vanuatu 1.1%, other 5.2% (1996 census)

**Religions:** Roman Catholic 60%, Protestant 30%, other 10%
**Languages:** French (official), 33 Melanesian-Polynesian dialects
**Literacy:**
*definition:* age 15 and over can read and write
*total population:* 96.2%
*male:* 96.8%
*female:* 95.5% (1996 census)

## Government

**Country name:**
*conventional long form:* Territory of New Caledonia and Dependencies
*conventional short form:* New Caledonia
*local long form:* Territoire des Nouvelle-Caledonie et Dependances
*local short form:* Nouvelle-Caledonie
**Dependency status:** territorial collectivity of France since 1998
**Government type:** NA
**Capital:**
*name:* Noumea
*geographic coordinates:* 22 16 S, 166 27 E
*time difference:* UTC+11 (16 hours ahead of Washington, DC during Standard Time)
**Administrative divisions:** none (overseas territory of France); there are no first-order administrative divisions as defined by the US Government, but there are 3 provinces named Province des Iles, Province Nord, and Province Sud
**Independence:** none (overseas territory of France); note - a referendum on independence was held in 1998 but did not pass; a new referendum is scheduled for 2014
**National holiday:** Bastille Day, 14 July (1789)
**Constitution:** 4 October 1958 (French Constitution)
**Legal system:** based on French civil law; the 1988 Matignon Accords grant substantial autonomy to the islands
**Suffrage:** 18 years of age; universal
**Executive branch:**
*chief of state:* President Nicolas SARKOZY (since 16 May 2007); represented by High Commissioner Yves DASSONVILLE (since 9 November 2007)
*head of government:* President of the Government Harold MARTIN (since 7 August 2007)
*cabinet:* Cabinet consisting of 11 members elected from and by the Territorial Congress
*elections:* French president elected by popular vote for a five-year term; high commissioner appointed by the French president on the advice of the French Ministry of Interior; president of the government elected by the members of the Territorial Congress for a five-year term (no term limits); note - last election held 7 August 2007 when Harold MARTIN was elected following the resignation of Marie-Noelle THEMEREAU as president on 24 July 2007 (next to be held in 2012)

**Legislative branch:**
*elections:* unicameral Territorial Congress or Congres du territoire (54 seats; members belong to the three Provincial Assemblies or Assemblees Provinciales elected by popular vote to serve five-year terms) last held 9 May 2009 (next to be held in 10 May 2014)
*election results:* percent of vote by party - NA; seats by party - UMP 13, Caledonia Together 10, UC 8, UNI 8, AE 6, FLNKS 3, Labor Party 3, other 3
*note:* New Caledonia holds two seats in the French Senate; elections last held 21 September 2008 (next to be held not later than September 2014); results - percent of vote by party - NA; seats by party - UMP 2; New Caledonia also elects two seats to the French National Assembly; elections last held 10 and 17 June 2007 (next to be held on June 2012); results - percent of vote by party - NA; seats by party - UMP 2
**Judicial branch:** Court of Appeal or Cour d'Appel; County Courts; Joint Commerce Tribunal Court; Children's Court
**Political parties and leaders:** Alliance pour la Caledonie or APLC [Didier LE ROUX]; Caledonia Together [Philippe GOMES]; Caledonian Union or UC [Charles PIDJOT]; Federation des Comites de Coordination des Independantistes or FCCI [Francois BURCK]; Front National or FN [Jean-Marie LE PEN]; Front Uni de Liberation Kanak or FULK [Ernest UNE]; Labor Party or PT [Louis Kora UREGEI]; Kanak Socialist Front for National Liberation or FLNKS (includes PALIKA, UNI, UC, and UPM); Parti de Liberation Kanak or PALIKA [Paul NEAOUTYINE]; Rally for Caledonia or RPC [Jacques LAFLEUR]; The Future Together or AE [Didier LEROUX]; The Rally or UMP [Pierre FROGIER]; Union Nationale pour l'Independance or UNI; Union Progressiste Melanesienne or UPM [Victor TUTUGORO]
**Political pressure groups and leaders:** NA
**International organization participation:** ITUC, PIF (associate member), SPC, UPU, WFTU, WMO
**Diplomatic representation in the US:** none (overseas territory of France)
**Diplomatic representation from the US:** none (overseas territory of France)
**Flag description:** the flag of France is used

## Economy

**Economy - overview:** New Caledonia has about 25% of the world's known nickel resources. Only a small amount of the land is suitable for cultivation, and food accounts for about 20% of imports. In addition to nickel, substantial financial support from France - equal to more than 15% of GDP - and tourism are keys to the health of the economy. Substantial new investment in the nickel industry, combined with the recovery of global nickel prices, brightens the economic outlook for the next several years.
**GDP (purchasing power parity):**
$3.158 billion (2003 est.)
**GDP (official exchange rate):** $3.3 billion (2003 est.)
**GDP - real growth rate:** NA%

**GDP - per capita (PPP):**
$15,000 (2003 est.)
**GDP - composition by sector:**
*agriculture:* 15%
*industry:* 8.8%
*services:* 76.2% (2003)
**Labor force:** 78,990 (2004)
**Labor force - by occupation:**
*agriculture:* 20%
*industry:* 20%
*services:* 60% (2002)
**Unemployment rate:**
17.1% (2004)
**Population below poverty line:** NA%
**Household income or consumption by percentage share:**
*lowest 10%:* NA%
*highest 10%:* NA%
**Budget:**
*revenues:* $996 million
*expenditures:* $1.072 billion (2001 est.)
**Inflation rate (consumer prices):**
1.4% (2000 est.)
**Market value of publicly traded shares:** $NA
**Agriculture - products:** vegetables; beef, deer, other livestock products; fish
**Industries:** nickel mining and smelting
**Electricity - production:** 1.602 billion kWh (2006 est.)
**Electricity - consumption:** 1.49 billion kWh (2006 est.)
**Electricity - exports:** 0 kWh (2007 est.)
**Electricity - imports:** 0 kWh (2007 est.)
**Oil - production:** 0 bbl/day (2007 est.)
**Oil - consumption:** 11,560 bbl/day (2006 est.)
**Oil - exports:** 356.2 bbl/day (2005)
**Oil - imports:** 11,780 bbl/day (2005)
**Oil - proved reserves:** 0 bbl (1 January 2006 est.)
**Natural gas - production:** 0 cu m (2007 est.)
**Natural gas - consumption:** 0 cu m (2007 est.)
**Natural gas - exports:** 0 cu m (2007 est.)
**Natural gas - imports:** 0 cu m (2007 est.)
**Natural gas - proved reserves:** 0 cu m (1 January 2006 est.)
**Exports:** $1.341 billion f.o.b. (2006)
**Exports - commodities:** ferronickels, nickel ore, fish
**Exports - partners:** Japan 20.1%, China 14.5%, Taiwan 14.2%, France 11.6%, Belgium 10.4%, Spain 8.6%, South Africa 6.9% (2007)
**Imports:** $1.998 billion f.o.b. (2006)
**Imports - commodities:** machinery and equipment, fuels, chemicals, foodstuffs
**Imports - partners:** France 36.7%, Singapore 14.7%, Australia 12.1%, NZ 5.2%, Germany 4.6% (2007)
**Debt - external:** $79 million (1998 est.)
**Exchange rates:** Comptoirs Francais du Pacifique francs (XPF) per US dollar - 87.59 (2007), 94.97 (2006), 95.89 (2005), 96.04 (2004), 105.66 (2003)

## Communications

**Telephones - main lines in use:** 60,200 (2007)
**Telephones - mobile cellular:** 176,400 (2007)
**Telephone system:**
*general assessment:* NA
*domestic:* a submarine cable network connection between New Caledonia and Australia, completed in 2007, is expected to significantly increase network capacity and improve high-speed connectivity and access to international networks
*international:* country code - 687; satellite earth station -1 Intelsat (Pacific Ocean) (2007)
**Radio broadcast stations:** AM 1, FM 5, shortwave 0 (1998)
**Television broadcast stations:** 6 (plus 25 repeaters) (1997)
**Internet country code:** .nc
**Internet hosts:** 15,487 (2008)
**Internet users:** 80,000 (2006)

## Transportation

**Airports:** 25 (2008)
**Airports - with paved runways:**
*total:* 12
*over 3,047 m:* 1
*914 to 1,523 m:* 10
*under 914 m:* 1 (2008)
**Airports - with unpaved runways:**
*total:* 13
*914 to 1,523 m:* 5
*under 914 m:* 8 (2008)
**Heliports:** 6 (2007)
**Roadways:**
*total:* 5,622 km (2006)
**Merchant marine:**
*total:* 2
*by type:* cargo 1, passenger/cargo 1 (2008)
**Ports and terminals:** Noumea

## Military

**Military branches:** no regular military forces (2009)
**Manpower available for military service:**
*males age 16-49:* 57,738 (2008 est.)
**Manpower fit for military service:**
*males age 16-49:* 48,288
*females age 16-49:* 48,959 (2009 est.)
**Manpower reaching militarily significant age annually:**
*male:* 2,160
*female:* 2,087 (2009 est.)
**Military expenditures:** NA
**Military - note:** defense is the responsibility of France

## Transnational Issues

**Disputes - international:** Matthew and Hunter Islands east of New Caledonia claimed by France and Vanuatu

# New Zealand

Chatham Islands and Kermadec Islands are not shown.

## Introduction

**Background:** The Polynesian Maori reached New Zealand in about A.D. 800. In 1840, their chieftains entered into a compact with Britain, the Treaty of Waitangi, in which they ceded sovereignty to Queen Victoria while retaining territorial rights. In that same year, the British began the first organized colonial settlement. A series of land wars between 1843 and 1872 ended with the defeat of the native peoples. The British colony of New Zealand became an independent dominion in 1907 and supported the UK militarily in both World Wars. New Zealand's full participation in a number of defense alliances lapsed by the 1980s. In recent years, the government has sought to address longstanding Maori grievances.

## Geography

**Location:** Oceania, islands in the South Pacific Ocean, southeast of Australia
**Geographic coordinates:** 41 00 S, 174 00 E
**Map references:** Oceania
**Area:**
*total:* 268,680 sq km
*land:* 268,021 sq km
*water:* NA
*note:* includes Antipodes Islands, Auckland Islands, Bounty Islands, Campbell Island, Chatham Islands, and Kermadec Islands
**Area - comparative:** about the size of Colorado
**Land boundaries:** 0 km
**Coastline:** 15,134 km
**Maritime claims:**
*territorial sea:* 12 nm
*contiguous zone:* 24 nm
*exclusive economic zone:* 200 nm
*continental shelf:* 200 nm or to the edge of the continental margin
**Climate:** temperate with sharp regional contrasts
**Terrain:** predominately mountainous with some large coastal plains
**Elevation extremes:**
*lowest point:* Pacific Ocean 0 m
*highest point:* Aoraki-Mount Cook 3,754 m
**Natural resources:** natural gas, iron ore, sand, coal, timber, hydropower, gold, limestone
**Land use:**
*arable land:* 5.54%
*permanent crops:* 6.92%
*other:* 87.54% (2005)
**Irrigated land:** 2,850 sq km (2003)
**Total renewable water resources:** 397 cu km (1995)
**Freshwater withdrawal (domestic/industrial/agricultural):**
*total:* 2.11 cu km/yr (48%/9%/42%)
*per capita:* 524 cu m/yr (2000)
**Natural hazards:** earthquakes are common, though usually not severe; volcanic activity
**Environment - current issues:** deforestation; soil erosion; native flora and fauna hard-hit by invasive species
**Environment - international agreements:**
*party to:* Antarctic-Environmental Protocol, Antarctic-Marine Living Resources, Antarctic Treaty, Biodiversity, Climate Change, Climate Change-Kyoto Protocol, Desertification, Endangered Species, Environmental Modification, Hazardous Wastes, Law of the Sea, Marine Dumping, Ozone Layer Protection, Ship Pollution, Tropical Timber 83, Tropical Timber 94, Wetlands, Whaling
*signed, but not ratified:* Antarctic Seals, Marine Life Conservation
**Geography - note:** about 80% of the population lives in cities; Wellington is the southernmost national capital in the world

## People

**Population:** 4,213,418 (July 2009 est.)
**Age structure:**
*0-14 years:* 20.7% (male 447,174/female 424,522)
*15-64 years:* 66.5% (male 1,404,143/female 1,399,530)
*65 years and over:* 12.8% (male 244,986/female 293,063) (2009 est.)
**Median age:**
*total:* 36.6 years
*male:* 35.8 years
*female:* 37.4 years (2009 est.)
**Population growth rate:** 0.935% (2009 est.)
**Birth rate:** 13.94 births/1,000 population (2009 est.)
**Death rate:** 7 deaths/1,000 population (2008 est.)
**Net migration rate:** 2.46 migrant(s)/1,000 population (2009 est.)
**Urbanization:**
*urban population:* 87% of total population (2008)
*rate of urbanization:* 1% annual rate of change (2005-10 est.)
**Sex ratio:**
*at birth:* 1.05 male(s)/female
*under 15 years:* 1.05 male(s)/female
*15-64 years:* 1 male(s)/female
*65 years and over:* 0.84 male(s)/female
*total population:* 0.99 male(s)/female (2009 est.)
**Infant mortality rate:**
*total:* 4.92 deaths/1,000 live births
*male:* 5.53 deaths/1,000 live births
*female:* 4.27 deaths/1,000 live births (2009 est.)
**Life expectancy at birth:**
*total population:* 80.36 years
*male:* 78.43 years
*female:* 82.39 years (2009 est.)
**Total fertility rate:** 2.1 children born/woman (2009 est.)
**HIV/AIDS - adult prevalence rate:** 0.1% (2007 est.)
**HIV/AIDS - people living with HIV/AIDS:** 1,400 (2007 est.)
**HIV/AIDS - deaths:** fewer than 200 (2003 est.)
**Nationality:**
*noun:* New Zealander(s)
*adjective:* New Zealand
**Ethnic groups:** European 69.8%, Maori 7.9%, Asian 5.7%, Pacific islander 4.4%, other 0.5%, mixed 7.8%, unspecified 3.8% (2001 census)
**Religions:** Anglican 14.9%, Roman Catholic 12.4%, Presbyterian 10.9%, Methodist 2.9%, Pentecostal 1.7%, Baptist 1.3%, other Christian 9.4%, other 3.3%, unspecified 17.2%, none 26% (2001 census)
**Languages:** English (official), Maori (official), Sign Language (official)
**Literacy:**
*definition:* age 15 and over can read and write
*total population:* 99%
*male:* 99%
*female:* 99% (2003 est.)

**School life expectancy (primary to tertiary education):**
*total:* 19 years
*male:* 19 years
*female:* 20 years (2006)
**Education expenditures:** 6.2% of GDP (2006)

## Government

**Country name:**
*conventional long form:* none
*conventional short form:* New Zealand
*abbreviation:* NZ
**Government type:** parliamentary democracy and a Commonwealth realm
**Capital:**
*name:* Wellington
*geographic coordinates:* 41 28 S, 174 51 E
*time difference:* UTC+12 (17 hours ahead of Washington, DC during Standard Time)
*daylight saving time:* +1hr, begins last Sunday in September; ends first Sunday in April
*note:* New Zealand is divided into two time zones - New Zealand standard time (12 hours in advance of UTC), and Chatham Islands time (45 minutes in advance of New Zealand standard time)
**Administrative divisions:** 16 regions and 1 territory*; Auckland, Bay of Plenty, Canterbury, Chatham Islands*, Gisborne, Hawke's Bay, Manawatu-Wanganui, Marlborough, Nelson, Northland, Otago, Southland, Taranaki, Tasman, Waikato, Wellington, West Coast
**Dependent areas:** Cook Islands, Niue, Tokelau
**Independence:** 26 September 1907 (from the UK)
**National holiday:** Waitangi Day (Treaty of Waitangi established British sovereignty over New Zealand), 6 February (1840); ANZAC Day (commemorated as the anniversary of the landing of troops of the Australian and New Zealand Army Corps during World War I at Gallipoli, Turkey, 25 April (1915)
**Constitution:** consists of a series of legal documents, including certain acts of the UK and New Zealand parliaments, as well as The Constitution Act 1986, which is the principal formal charter; adopted 1 January 1987, effective 1 January 1987
**Legal system:** based on English law, with special land legislation and land courts for the Maori; accepts compulsory ICJ jurisdiction with reservations
**Suffrage:** 18 years of age; universal
**Executive branch:**
*chief of state:* Queen ELIZABETH II (since 6 February 1952); represented by Governor General Anand SATYANAND (since 23 August 2006)
*head of government:* Prime Minister John KEY (since 19 November 2008); Deputy Prime Minister Bill ENGLISH (since 19 November 2008)
*cabinet:* Executive Council appointed by the governor general on the recommendation of the prime minister
*elections:* the monarch is hereditary; governor general appointed by the monarch; following legislative elections, the leader of the majority party or the leader of a majority coalition is usually appointed prime minister by the governor general; deputy prime minister appointed by the governor general

**Legislative branch:** unicameral House of Representatives - commonly called Parliament (usually 120 seats; 69 members elected by popular vote in single-member constituencies including 7 Maori constituencies, and 51 proportional seats chosen from party lists; serve three-year terms)
*elections:* last held 8 November 2008 (next to be held not later than 27 November 2011)
*election results:* percent of vote by party - NP 44.9%, NZLP 34%, Green Party 6.7%, NZ First 4%, ACT New Zealand 3.7%, Maori 2.4%, Progressive 0.9%, UF 0.9%, other 6.6%; seats by party - NP 58, NZLP 43, Green Party 9, ACT New Zealand 5, Maori 5, Progressive 1, UF 1
*note:* results of 2008 election saw the total number of seats increase to 122
**Judicial branch:** Supreme Court; Court of Appeal; High Court; note - judges appointed by the governor general
**Political parties and leaders:** ACT New Zealand [Rodney HIDE]; Green Party [Jeanette FITZSIMONS]; Maori Party [Tariana TURIA and Pita SHARPLES]; National Party or NP [John KEY]; New Zealand First Party or NZ First [Winston PETERS]; New Zealand Labor Party or NZLP [Phil GOFF]; Progressive Party [James (Jim) ANDERTON]; United Future or UF [Peter DUNNE]
**Political pressure groups and leaders:** Women's Electoral Lobby or WEL
*other:* apartheid groups; civil rights groups; farmers groups; Maori; nuclear weapons groups; women's rights groups
**International organization participation:** ADB, ANZUS (US suspended security obligations to NZ on 11 August 1986), APEC, ARF, ASEAN (dialogue partner), Australia Group, BIS, C, CP, EAS, EBRD, FAO, IAEA, IBRD, ICAO, ICC, ICCt, ICRM, IDA, IEA, IFAD, IFC, IFRCS, IHO, ILO, IMF, IMO, IMSO, Interpol, IOC, IOM, IPU, ISO, ITSO, ITU, ITUC, NAM (guest), NSG, OECD, OPCW, PCA, PIF, Sparteca, SPC, UN, UNCTAD, UNESCO, UNHCR, UNIDO, UNMIS, UNMIT, UNTSO, UPU, WCO, WFTU, WHO, WIPO, WMO, WTO
**Diplomatic representation in the US:**
*chief of mission:* Ambassador Roy N. FERGUSON
*chancery:* 37 Observatory Circle NW, Washington, DC 20008
*telephone:* [1] (202) 328-4800
*FAX:* [1] (202) 667-5227
*consulate(s) general:* New York, Santa Monica
**Diplomatic representation from the US:**
*chief of mission:* Ambassador William P. McCORMICK
*embassy:* 29 Fitzherbert Terrace, Thorndon, Wellington
*mailing address:* P. O. Box 1190, Wellington; PSC 467, Box 1, APO AP 96531-1034
*telephone:* [64] (4) 462-6000
*FAX:* [64] (4) 499-0490
*consulate(s) general:* Auckland

**Flag description:** blue with the flag of the UK in the upper hoist-side quadrant with four red five-pointed stars edged in white centered in the outer half of the flag; the stars represent the Southern Cross constellation
**Government - note:** while not an official symbol, the Kiwi, a small native flightless bird, represents New Zealand

## Economy

**Economy - overview:** Over the past 20 years the government has transformed New Zealand from an agrarian economy dependent on concessionary British market access to a more industrialized, free market economy that can compete globally. This dynamic growth has boosted real incomes - but left behind some at the bottom of the ladder - and broadened and deepened the technological capabilities of the industrial sector. Per capita income has risen for nine consecutive years and reached $27,900 in 2008 in purchasing power parity terms. Debt-driven consumer spending drove robust growth in the first half of the decade, helping fuel a large balance of payments deficit that posed a challenge for economic managers. Inflationary pressures caused the central bank to raise its key rate steadily from January 2004 until it was among the highest in the OECD in 2007-08; international capital inflows attracted to the high rates further strengthened the currency and housing market, however, aggravating the current account deficit. The economy fell into recession in 2008. In line with global peers, the central bank has cut interest rates aggressively; the new government is responding with plans to raise productivity growth and develop infrastructure.
**GDP (purchasing power parity):**
$116.6 billion (2008 est.)
$116.3 billion (2007)
$112.8 billion (2006)
*note:* data are in 2008 US dollars
**GDP (official exchange rate):** $135.7 billion (2008 est.)
**GDP - real growth rate:**
0.2% (2008 est.)
3.1% (2007 est.)
2% (2006 est.)
**GDP - per capita (PPP):**
$27,900 (2008 est.)
$28,200 (2007 est.)
$27,600 (2006 est.)
*note:* data are in 2008 US dollars
**GDP - composition by sector:**
*agriculture:* 4.4%
*industry:* 26%
*services:* 69.6% (2008 est.)
**Labor force:** 2.26 million (2008 est.)
**Labor force - by occupation:**
*agriculture:* 7%
*industry:* 19%
*services:* 74% (2006 est.)

**Unemployment rate:**
4% (2008 est.)
3.6% (2007 est.)
**Population below poverty line:** NA%
**Household income or consumption by percentage share:**
*lowest 10%:* %NA
*highest 10%:* %NA
**Distribution of family income - Gini index:** 36.2 (1997)
**Investment (gross fixed):** 23.6% of GDP (2008 est.)
**Budget:**
*revenues:* $55.1 billion
*expenditures:* $54.66 billion (2008 est.)
**Public debt:** 22.9% of GDP (2008 est.)
**Inflation rate (consumer prices):**
4.3% (2008 est.)
2.4% (2007 est.)
**Central bank discount rate:** 8.25% (31 December 2007)
**Commercial bank prime lending rate:** 12.83% (31 December 2007)
**Stock of money:** $24.2 billion (31 December 2007)
**Stock of quasi money:** $117.8 billion (31 December 2007)
**Stock of domestic credit:** $200.1 billion (31 December 2007)
**Market value of publicly traded shares:** $47.45 billion (31 December 2007)
**Agriculture - products:** dairy products, lamb and mutton; wheat, barley, potatoes, pulses, fruits, vegetables; wool, beef; fish
**Industries:** food processing, wood and paper products, textiles, machinery, transportation equipment, banking and insurance, tourism, mining
**Industrial production growth rate:** -1.2% (2008 est.)
**Electricity - production:** 42.41 billion kWh (2007 est.)
**Electricity - consumption:** 38.93 billion kWh (2006 est.)
**Electricity - exports:** 0 kWh (2007 est.)
**Electricity - imports:** 0 kWh (2007 est.)
**Oil - production:** 47,850 bbl/day (2007 est.)
**Oil - consumption:** 158,400 bbl/day (2007 est.)
**Oil - exports:** 14,570 bbl/day (2005)
**Oil - imports:** 137,300 bbl/day (2005)
**Oil - proved reserves:** 55 million bbl (1 January 2008 est.)
**Natural gas - production:** 4.573 billion cu m (2007 est.)
**Natural gas - consumption:** 4.572 billion cu m (2007 est.)
**Natural gas - exports:** 0 cu m (2007 est.)
**Natural gas - imports:** 0 cu m (2007 est.)
**Natural gas - proved reserves:** 29.67 billion cu m (1 January 2008 est.)
**Current account balance:** -$9.047 billion (2008 est.)
**Exports:** $29.53 billion (2008 est.)

**Exports - commodities:** dairy products, meat, wood and wood products, fish, machinery
**Exports - partners:** Australia 22%, US 11.5%, Japan 9.2%, China 5.3%, UK 4.6% (2007)
**Imports:** $31.11 billion f.o.b. (2008 est.)
**Imports - commodities:** machinery and equipment, vehicles and aircraft, petroleum, electronics, textiles, plastics
**Imports - partners:** Australia 20.7%, China 13.4%, US 9.7%, Japan 9.5%, Singapore 4.9%, Germany 4.7% (2007)
**Reserves of foreign exchange and gold:** $15.25 billion (31 December 2008 est.)
**Debt - external:** $59.08 billion (31 December 2008 est.)
**Stock of direct foreign investment - at home:** $72.41 billion (2008 est.)
**Stock of direct foreign investment - abroad:** $NA
**Exchange rates:** New Zealand dollars (NZD) per US dollar - 1.4151 (2008 est.), 1.3811 (2007), 1.5408 (2006), 1.4203 (2005), 1.5087 (2004)

## Communications

**Telephones - main lines in use:** 1.706 million (2007)
**Telephones - mobile cellular:** 4.245 million (2007)
**Telephone system:**
*general assessment:* excellent domestic and international systems
*domestic:* NA
*international:* country code - 64; the Southern Cross submarine cable system provides links to Australia, Fiji, and the US; satellite earth stations - 8 (1 Inmarsat -Pacific Ocean, 7 other)
**Radio broadcast stations:** AM 124, FM 290, shortwave 4 (1998)
**Television broadcast stations:** 41 (plus about 700 repeaters) (1997)
**Internet country code:** .nz
**Internet hosts:** 1.72 million (2008)
**Internet users:** 3.36 million (2007)

## Transportation

**Airports:** 121 (2008)
**Airports - with paved runways:**
*total:* 41
*over 3,047 m:* 2
*2,438 to 3,047 m:* 1
*1,524 to 2,437 m:* 12
*914 to 1,523 m:* 25
*under 914 m:* 1 (2008)
**Airports - with unpaved runways:**
*total:* 80
*1,524 to 2,437 m:* 3
*914 to 1,523 m:* 31
*under 914 m:* 46 (2008)
**Pipelines:** condensate 331 km; gas 1,838 km; liquid petroleum gas 172 km; oil 288 km; refined products 198 km (2008)

**Railways:**
*total:* 4,128 km
*narrow gauge:* 4,128 km 1.067-m gauge (506 km electrified) (2006)
**Roadways:**
*total:* 93,576 km
*paved:* 61,564 km (includes 172 km of expressways)
*unpaved:* 32,012 km (2006)
**Merchant marine:**
*total:* 13
*by type:* bulk carrier 3, cargo 2, chemical tanker 1, passenger/cargo 4, petroleum tanker 1, roll on/roll off 2
*foreign-owned:* 3 (Australia 1, Germany 1, South Africa 1)
*registered in other countries:* 5 (Antigua and Barbuda 2, Cook Islands 1, France 1, UK 1) (2008)
**Ports and terminals:** Auckland, Lyttelton, Marsden Point, Tauranga, Wellington, Whangarei

## Military

**Military branches:** New Zealand Defense Force (NZDF): New Zealand Army, Royal New Zealand Navy, Royal New Zealand Air Force (2009)
**Military service age and obligation:** 17 years of age for voluntary military service; soldiers cannot be deployed until the age of 18; no conscription (2008)
**Manpower available for military service:**
*males age 16-49:* 1,009,298
*females age 16-49:* 997,134 (2008 est.)
**Manpower fit for military service:**
*males age 16-49:* 837,553
*females age 16-49:* 825,981 (2009 est.)
**Manpower reaching militarily significant age annually:**
*male:* 31,461
*female:* 29,809 (2009 est.)
**Military expenditures:** 1% of GDP (2005 est.)

## Transnational Issues

**Disputes - international:** asserts a territorial claim in Antarctica (Ross Dependency)
**Illicit drugs:** significant consumer of amphetamines

# Nicaragua

## Introduction

**Background:** The Pacific coast of Nicaragua was settled as a Spanish colony from Panama in the early 16th century. Independence from Spain was declared in 1821 and the country became an independent republic in 1838. Britain occupied the Caribbean Coast in the first half of the 19th century, but gradually ceded control of the region in subsequent decades. Violent opposition to governmental manipulation and corruption spread to all classes by 1978 and resulted in a short-lived civil war that brought the Marxist Sandinista guerrillas to power in 1979. Nicaraguan aid to leftist rebels in El Salvador caused the US to sponsor anti-Sandinista contra guerrillas through much of the 1980s. Free elections in 1990, 1996, and 2001, saw the Sandinistas defeated, but voting in 2006 announced the return of former Sandinista President Daniel ORTEGA Saavedra. The 2008 municipal elections were characterized by widespread irregularities. Nicaragua's infrastructure and economy - hard hit by the earlier civil war and by Hurricane Mitch in 1998 - are slowly being rebuilt, but democratic institutions face new challenges under the ORTEGA administration.

## Geography

**Location:** Central America, bordering both the Caribbean Sea and the North Pacific Ocean, between Costa Rica and Honduras
**Geographic coordinates:** 13 00 N, 85 00 W
**Map references:** Central America and the Caribbean
**Area:**
*total:* 129,494 sq km
*land:* 120,254 sq km
*water:* 9,240 sq km
**Area - comparative:** slightly smaller than New York state

**Land boundaries:**
*total:* 1,231 km
*border countries:* Costa Rica 309 km, Honduras 922 km
**Coastline:** 910 km
**Maritime claims:**
*territorial sea:* 12 nm
*contiguous zone:* 24 nm
*continental shelf:* natural prolongation
**Climate:** tropical in lowlands, cooler in highlands
**Terrain:** extensive Atlantic coastal plains rising to central interior mountains; narrow Pacific coastal plain interrupted by volcanoes
**Elevation extremes:**
*lowest point:* Pacific Ocean 0 m
*highest point:* Mogoton 2,438 m
**Natural resources:** gold, silver, copper, tungsten, lead, zinc, timber, fish
**Land use:**
*arable land:* 14.81%
*permanent crops:* 1.82%
*other:* 83.37% (2005)
**Irrigated land:** 610 sq km (2003)
**Total renewable water resources:** 196.7 cu km (2000)
**Freshwater withdrawal (domestic/industrial/agricultural):**
*total:* 1.3 cu km/yr (15%/2%/83%)
*per capita:* 237 cu m/yr (2000)
**Natural hazards:** destructive earthquakes; volcanoes; landslides; extremely susceptible to hurricanes
**Environment - current issues:** deforestation; soil erosion; water pollution
**Environment - international agreements:**
*party to:* Biodiversity, Climate Change, Climate Change-Kyoto Protocol, Desertification, Endangered Species, Environmental Modification, Hazardous Wastes, Law of the Sea, Ozone Layer Protection, Ship Pollution, Wetlands, Whaling
*signed, but not ratified:* none of the selected agreements
**Geography - note:** largest country in Central America; contains the largest freshwater body in Central America, Lago de Nicaragua

## People

**Population:** 5,891,199 (July 2009 est.)
**Age structure:**
*0-14 years:* 33.8% (male 1,013,866/female 976,430)
*15-64 years:* 62.9% (male 1,847,756/female 1,857,264)
*65 years and over:* 3.3% (male 85,782/female 110,101) (2009 est.)
**Median age:**
*total:* 22.1 years
*male:* 21.7 years
*female:* 22.5 years (2009 est.)
**Population growth rate:** 1.784% (2009 est.)
**Birth rate:** 23.25 births/1,000 population (2009 est.)
**Death rate:** 4.33 deaths/1,000 population (2008 est.)

**Net migration rate:** -1.11 migrant(s)/1,000 population (2009 est.)
**Urbanization:**
*urban population:* 57% of total population (2008)
*rate of urbanization:* 1.8% annual rate of change (2005-10 est.)
**Sex ratio:**
*at birth:* 1.05 male(s)/female
*under 15 years:* 1.04 male(s)/female
*15-64 years:* 1 male(s)/female
*65 years and over:* 0.78 male(s)/female
*total population:* 1 male(s)/female (2009 est.)
**Infant mortality rate:**
*total:* 25.02 deaths/1,000 live births
*male:* 28.09 deaths/1,000 live births
*female:* 21.8 deaths/1,000 live births (2009 est.)
**Life expectancy at birth:**
*total population:* 71.5 years
*male:* 69.35 years
*female:* 73.75 years (2009 est.)
**Total fertility rate:** 2.57 children born/woman (2009 est.)
**HIV/AIDS - adult prevalence rate:** 0.2% (2007 est.)
**HIV/AIDS - people living with HIV/AIDS:** 7,700 (2007 est.)
**HIV/AIDS - deaths:** fewer than 500 (2007 est.)
**Major infectious diseases:**
*degree of risk:* high
*food or waterborne diseases:* bacterial diarrhea, hepatitis A, and typhoid fever
*vectorborne disease:* dengue fever and malaria
*water contact disease:* leptospirosis (2009)
**Nationality:**
*noun:* Nicaraguan(s)
*adjective:* Nicaraguan
**Ethnic groups:** mestizo (mixed Amerindian and white) 69%, white 17%, black 9%, Amerindian 5%
**Religions:** Roman Catholic 58.5%, Evangelical 21.6%, Moravian 1.6%, Jehovah's Witness 0.9%, other 1.7%, none 15.7% (2005 census)
**Languages:** Spanish 97.5% (official), Miskito 1.7%, other 0.8% (1995 census)
*note:* English and indigenous languages on Atlantic coast
**Literacy:**
*definition:* age 15 and over can read and write
*total population:* 67.5%
*male:* 67.2%
*female:* 67.8% (2003 est.)
**School life expectancy (primary to tertiary education):**
*total:* 11 years
*male:* 11 years
*female:* 11 years (2003)
**Education expenditures:** 3.1% of GDP (2003)

## Government

**Country name:**
*conventional long form:* Republic of Nicaragua
*conventional short form:* Nicaragua
*local long form:* Republica de Nicaragua
*local short form:* Nicaragua

# Nicaragua (continued)

**Government type:** republic

**Capital:**

*name:* Managua

*geographic coordinates:* 12 09 N, 86 17 W

*time difference:* UTC-6 (1 hour behind Washington, DC during Standard Time)

**Administrative divisions:** 15 departments (departamentos, singular - departamento) and 2 autonomous regions* (regiones autonomistas, singular - region autonoma); Atlantico Norte*, Atlantico Sur*, Boaco, Carazo, Chinandega, Chontales, Esteli, Granada, Jinotega, Leon, Madriz, Managua, Masaya, Matagalpa, Nueva Segovia, Rio San Juan, Rivas

**Independence:** 15 September 1821 (from Spain)

**National holiday:** Independence Day, 15 September (1821)

**Constitution:** 9 January 1987; revised in 1995, 2000, and 2005

**Legal system:** civil law system; Supreme Court may review administrative acts; accepts compulsory ICJ jurisdiction

**Suffrage:** 16 years of age; universal

**Executive branch:**

*chief of state:* President Daniel ORTEGA Saavedra (since 10 January 2007); Vice President Jaime MORALES Carazo (since 10 January 2007); note - the president is both chief of state and head of government

*head of government:* President Daniel ORTEGA Saavedra (since 10 January 2007); Vice President Jaime MORALES Carazo (since 10 January 2007)

*cabinet:* Council of Ministers appointed by the president

*elections:* president and vice president elected on the same ticket by popular vote for a five-year term (eligible for a second term so long as it is not consecutive); election last held 5 November 2006 (next to be held by November 2011)

*election results:* Daniel ORTEGA Saavedra elected president - 38.07%, Eduardo MONTEALEGRE 29%, Jose RIZO 26.21%, Edmundo JARQUIN 6.44%

**Legislative branch:** unicameral National Assembly or Asamblea Nacional (92 seats; 90 members are elected by proportional representation and party lists to serve five-year terms; 1 seat for the previous president, 1 seat for the runner-up in previous presidential election)

*elections:* last held 5 November 2006 (next to be held by November 2011)

*election results:* percent of vote by party - NA; seats by party - FSLN 38, PLC 25, ALN 23 (22 plus one for presidential candidate Eduardo MONTEALEGRE, runner-up in the 2006 presidential election), MRS 5, APRE 1 (outgoing President Enrique BOLANOS); note - as of 1 January 2009: seats by party - FSLN 38, PLC 25, BDN 15, ALN 6, MRS 3, APRE 1, Independent 4

**Judicial branch:** Supreme Court or Corte Suprema de Justicia (16 judges elected for five-year terms by the National Assembly)

**Political parties and leaders:** Conservative Party or PC [Azalia AVILES Salmeron]; Liberal Constitutionalist Party or PLC [Jorge CASTILLO Quant]; Nicaraguan Democratic Bloc or BDN [Eduardo MONTEALEGRE]; Nicaraguan Liberal Alliance or ALN [Eliseo NUNEZ Sr.]; Sandinista National Liberation Front or FSLN [Daniel ORTEGA Saavedra]; Sandinista Renovation Movement or MRS [Enrique SAENZ Navarrete]

**Political pressure groups and leaders:** National Workers Front or FNT (a Sandinista umbrella group of eight labor unions including: Farm Workers Association or ATC, Health Workers Federation or FETASALUD, Heroes and Martyrs Confederation of Professional Associations or CONAPRO, National Association of Educators of Nicaragua or ANDEN, National Union of Employees or UNE, National Union of Farmers and Ranchers or UNAG, Sandinista Workers Central or CST, and Union of Journalists of Nicaragua or UPN); Permanent Congress of Workers or CPT (an umbrella group of four non-Sandinista labor unions including: Autonomous Nicaraguan Workers Central or CTN-A, Confederation of Labor Unification or CUS, Independent General Confederation of Labor or CGT-I, and Labor Action and Unity Central or CAUS); Nicaraguan Workers' Central or CTN (an independent labor union); Superior Council of Private Enterprise or COSEP (a confederation of business groups)

**International organization participation:** BCIE, CACM, FAO, G-77, IADB, IAEA, IBRD, ICAO, ICRM, IDA, IFAD, IFC, IFRCS, ILO, IMF, IMO, Interpol, IOC, IOM, IPU, ITSO, ITU, ITUC, LAES, LAIA (observer), MIGA, NAM, OAS, OPANAL, OPCW, PCA, RG, SICA, UN, UNCTAD, UNESCO, UNHCR, UNIDO, Union Latina, UNWTO, UPU, WCL, WCO, WFTU, WHO, WIPO, WMO, WTO

**Diplomatic representation in the US:**

*chief of mission:* Ambassador Arturo CRUZ Sequeira, Jr.

*chancery:* 1627 New Hampshire Avenue NW, Washington, DC 20009

*telephone:* [1] (202) 939-6570, 6573

*FAX:* [1] (202) 939-6545

*consulate(s) general:* Houston, Los Angeles, Miami, New York, San Francisco

**Diplomatic representation from the US:**

*chief of mission:* Ambassador Robert J. CALLAHAN

*embassy:* Kilometer 5.5 Carretera Sur, Managua

*mailing address:* American Embassy Managua, APO AA 34021

*telephone:* [505] 252-7100, 252-7888; 252-7634 (after hours)

*FAX:* [505] 252-7304

**Flag description:** three equal horizontal bands of blue (top), white, and blue with the national coat of arms centered in the white band; the coat of arms features a triangle encircled by the words REPUBLICA DE NICARAGUA on the top and AMERICA CENTRAL on the bottom; similar to the flag of El Salvador, which features a round emblem encircled by the words REPUBLICA DE EL SALVADOR EN LA AMERICA CENTRAL centered in the white band; also similar to the flag of Honduras, which has five blue stars arranged in an X pattern centered in the white band

## Economy

**Economy - overview:** Nicaragua has widespread underemployment and the second lowest per capita income in the Western Hemisphere. The US-Central America Free Trade Agreement (CAFTA) has been in effect since April 2006 and has expanded export opportunities for many agricultural and manufactured goods. Textiles and apparel account for nearly 60% of Nicaragua's exports, but recent increases in the minimum wage will likely erode its comparative advantage in this industry. Nicaragua relies on international economic assistance to meet internal- and external-debt financing obligations. In early 2004, Nicaragua secured some $4.5 billion in foreign debt reduction under the Heavily Indebted Poor Countries (HIPC) initiative, and in October 2007, the IMF approved a new poverty reduction and growth facility (PRGF) program. However, severe budget shortfalls resulting from the suspension of large amounts of direct budget support from foreign donors concerned with recent political developments has caused a slowdown in PRGF disbursements. Similarly, private sector concerns surrounding ORTEGA's handling of economic issues have dampened investment. Economic growth has slowed in 2009, due to decreased export demand from the US and Central American markets, lower commodity prices for key agricultural exports, and low remittance growth - remittances are equivalent to almost 15% of GDP.

**GDP (purchasing power parity):**

$16.83 billion (2008 est.)

$16.37 billion (2007)

$15.77 billion (2006)

*note:* data are in 2008 US dollars

**GDP (official exchange rate):** $6.561 billion (2008 est.)

**GDP - real growth rate:**

2% (2008 est.)

3.8% (2007 est.)

3.9% (2006 est.)

**GDP - per capita (PPP):**

$2,900 (2008 est.)

$2,900 (2007 est.)

$2,800 (2006 est.)

*note:* data are in 2008 US dollars

**GDP - composition by sector:**

*agriculture:* 17%

*industry:* 26.1%

*services:* 56.9% (2008 est.)

**Labor force:** 2.322 million (2008 est.)

**Labor force - by occupation:**

*agriculture:* 29%

*industry:* 19%

*services:* 52% (2006 est.)

# Nicaragua *(continued)*

**Unemployment rate:**
3.9% (2008 est.)
4.9% (2007 est.)
*note:* underemployment was 46.5% in 2008
**Population below poverty line:** 48% (2005)
**Household income or consumption by percentage share:**
*lowest 10%:* 2.2%
*highest 10%:* 33.8% (2001)
**Distribution of family income - Gini index:** 43.1 (2001)
**Investment (gross fixed):** 32.1% of GDP (2008 est.)
**Budget:**
*revenues:* $1.271 billion
*expenditures:* $1.593 billion (2008 est.)
**Public debt:** 53.6% of GDP (2008 est.)
**Inflation rate (consumer prices):**
20.6% (2008 est.)
11.1% (2007 est.)
**Central bank discount rate:** NA
**Commercial bank prime lending rate:** 13.04% (31 December 2007)
**Stock of money:** $465.1 million (31 December 2007)
**Stock of quasi money:** $1.802 billion (31 December 2007)
**Stock of domestic credit:** $4.133 billion (31 December 2007)
**Market value of publicly traded shares:** $NA
**Agriculture - products:** coffee, bananas, sugarcane, cotton, rice, corn, tobacco, sesame, soya, beans; beef, veal, pork, poultry, dairy products; shrimp, lobsters
**Industries:** food processing, chemicals, machinery and metal products, textiles, clothing, petroleum refining and distribution, beverages, footwear, wood
**Industrial production growth rate:** 3% (2008 est.)
**Electricity - production:** 3.012 billion kWh (2006 est.)
**Electricity - consumption:** 2.413 billion kWh (2006 est.)
**Electricity - exports:** 0 kWh (2007 est.)
**Electricity - imports:** 63.95 million kWh (2007 est.)
**Oil - production:** 0 bbl/day (2005 est.)
**Oil - consumption:** 28,880 bbl/day (2006 est.)
**Oil - exports:** 808.5 bbl/day (2005)
**Oil - imports:** 29,700 bbl/day (2005 est.)
**Oil - proved reserves:** 0 bbl (1 January 2006 est.)
**Natural gas - production:** 0 cu m (2007 est.)
**Natural gas - consumption:** 0 cu m (2007 est.)
**Natural gas - exports:** 0 cu m (2007 est.)
**Natural gas - imports:** 0 cu m (2007 est.)
**Natural gas - proved reserves:** 0 cu m (1 January 2006 est.)
**Current account balance:** -$1.31 billion (2008 est.)
**Exports:** $3.183 billion f.o.b.; note - includes free trade zones (2008 est.)
**Exports - commodities:** coffee, beef, shrimp and lobster, tobacco, sugar, gold, peanuts

**Exports - partners:** US 31.7%, El Salvador 14%, Honduras 9.3%, Costa Rica 7.2%, Canada 5.8%, Guatemala 5.5%, Mexico 4.8% (2007)
**Imports:** $5.279 billion f.o.b. (2008 est.)
**Imports - commodities:** consumer goods, machinery and equipment, raw materials, petroleum products
**Imports - partners:** US 22.5%, Mexico 13.5%, Costa Rica 8.4%, Venezuela 6.4%, Guatemala 6.2%, El Salvador 4.8% (2007)
**Reserves of foreign exchange and gold:** $1.035 billion (31 December 2008 est.)
**Debt - external:** $3.214 billion (31 December 2008 est.)
**Exchange rates:** cordobas (NIO) per US dollar - 19.374 (2008 est.), 18.457 (2007), 17.582 (2006), 16.733 (2005), 15.937 (2004)

## Communications

**Telephones - main lines in use:** 247,900 (2006)
**Telephones - mobile cellular:** 2.123 million (2007)
**Telephone system:**
*general assessment:* system being upgraded by foreign investment; nearly all installed telecommunications capacity now uses digital technology, owing to investments since privatization of the formerly state-owned telecommunications company
*domestic:* since privatization, access to fixed-line and mobile-cellular services has improved but teledensity still lags behind other Central American countries; connected to Central American Microwave System
*international:* country code - 505; the Americas Region Caribbean Ring System (ARCOS-1) fiber optic submarine cable provides connectivity to South and Central America, parts of the Caribbean, and the US; satellite earth stations - 1 Intersputnik (Atlantic Ocean region) and 1 Intelsat (Atlantic Ocean) (2007)
**Radio broadcast stations:** AM 63, FM 32, shortwave 1 (1998)
**Television broadcast stations:** 3 (plus 7 repeaters) (1997)
**Internet country code:** .ni
**Internet hosts:** 58,157 (2008)
**Internet users:** 155,000 (2006)

## Transportation

**Airports:** 144 (2008)
**Airports - with paved runways:**
*total:* 11
*2,438 to 3,047 m:* 3
*1,524 to 2,437 m:* 2
*914 to 1,523 m:* 3
*under 914 m:* 3 (2008)
**Airports - with unpaved runways:**
*total:* 133
*1,524 to 2,437 m:* 1
*914 to 1,523 m:* 16
*under 914 m:* 116 (2008)
**Pipelines:** oil 54 km (2008)

**Railways:**
*total:* 6 km
*narrow gauge:* 6 km 1.067-m gauge (2006)
**Roadways:**
*total:* 19,036 km
*paved:* 2,299 km
*unpaved:* 16,737 km (2005)
**Waterways:** 2,220 km (including lakes Managua and Nicaragua) (2008)
**Ports and terminals:** Bluefields, Corinto, El Bluff

## Military

**Military branches:** National Army of Nicaragua (ENN; includes Navy, Air Force) (2008)
**Military service age and obligation:** 17 years of age for voluntary military service; tour of duty 18-36 months (2008)
**Manpower available for military service:**
*males age 16-49:* 1,513,312
*females age 16-49:* 1,507,999 (2008 est.)
**Manpower fit for military service:**
*males age 16-49:* 1,277,878
*females age 16-49:* 1,339,413 (2009 est.)
**Manpower reaching militarily significant age annually:**
*male:* 72,366
*female:* 70,118 (2009 est.)
**Military expenditures:** 0.6% of GDP (2006)

## Transnational Issues

**Disputes - international:** memorials and countermemorials were filed by the parties in Nicaragua's 1999 and 2001 proceedings against Honduras and Colombia at the ICJ over the maritime boundary and territorial claims in the western Caribbean Sea, final public hearings are scheduled for 2007; the 1992 ICJ ruling for El Salvador and Honduras advised a tripartite resolution to establish a maritime boundary in the Gulf of Fonseca, which considers Honduran access to the Pacific; legal dispute over navigational rights of San Juan River on border with Costa Rica
**Illicit drugs:** transshipment point for cocaine destined for the US and transshipment point for arms-for-drugs dealing

# Niger

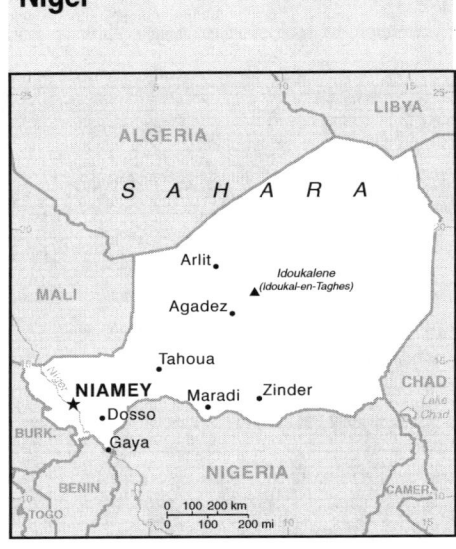

## Introduction

**Background:** Niger became independent from France in 1960 and experienced single-party and military rule until 1991, when Gen. Ali SAIBOU was forced by public pressure to allow multiparty elections, which resulted in a democratic government in 1993. Political infighting brought the government to a standstill and in 1996 led to a coup by Col. Ibrahim BARE. In 1999, BARE was killed in a coup by military officers who promptly restored democratic rule and held elections that brought Mamadou TANDJA to power in December of that year. TANDJA was reelected in 2004. Niger is one of the poorest countries in the world with minimal government services and insufficient funds to develop its resource base. The largely agrarian and subsistence-based economy is frequently disrupted by extended droughts common to the Sahel region of Africa. A predominately Tuareg ethnic group emerged in February 2007, the Nigerien Movement for Justice (MNJ), and attacked several military targets in Niger's northern region throughout 2007 and 2008. Events have since evolved into a fledging insurgency.

## Geography

**Location:** Western Africa, southeast of Algeria
**Geographic coordinates:** 16 00 N, 8 00 E
**Map references:** Africa
**Area:**
*total:* 1.267 million sq km
*land:* 1,266,700 sq km
*water:* 300 sq km
**Area - comparative:** slightly less than twice the size of Texas
**Land boundaries:**
*total:* 5,697 km
*border countries:* Algeria 956 km, Benin 266 km, Burkina Faso 628 km, Chad 1,175 km, Libya 354 km, Mali 821 km, Nigeria 1,497 km
**Coastline:** 0 km (landlocked)

**Maritime claims:** none (landlocked)
**Climate:** desert; mostly hot, dry, dusty; tropical in extreme south
**Terrain:** predominately desert plains and sand dunes; flat to rolling plains in south; hills in north
**Elevation extremes:**
*lowest point:* Niger River 200 m
*highest point:* Mont Bagzane 2,022 m
**Natural resources:** uranium, coal, iron ore, tin, phosphates, gold, molybdenum, gypsum, salt, petroleum
**Land use:**
*arable land:* 11.43%
*permanent crops:* 0.01%
*other:* 88.56% (2005)
**Irrigated land:** 730 sq km (2003)
**Total renewable water resources:** 33.7 cu km (2003)
**Freshwater withdrawal (domestic/industrial/ agricultural):**
*total:* 2.18 cu km/yr (4%/0%/95%)
*per capita:* 156 cu m/yr (2000)
**Natural hazards:** recurring droughts
**Environment - current issues:** overgrazing; soil erosion; deforestation; desertification; wildlife populations (such as elephant, hippopotamus, giraffe, and lion) threatened because of poaching and habitat destruction
**Environment - international agreements:**
*party to:* Biodiversity, Climate Change, Climate Change-Kyoto Protocol, Desertification, Endangered Species, Environmental Modification, Hazardous Wastes, Ozone Layer Protection, Wetlands
*signed, but not ratified:* Law of the Sea
**Geography - note:** landlocked; one of the hottest countries in the world; northern four-fifths is desert, southern one-fifth is savanna, suitable for livestock and limited agriculture

## People

**Population:** 15,306,252 (July 2009 est.)
**Age structure:**
*0-14 years:* 49.6% (male 3,840,379/female 3,758,674)
*15-64 years:* 48% (male 3,658,361/female 3,690,373)
*65 years and over:* 2.3% (male 159,984/female 198,481) (2009 est.)
**Median age:**
*total:* 15.2 years
*male:* 14.9 years
*female:* 15.4 years (2009 est.)
**Population growth rate:** 3.677% (2009 est.)
**Birth rate:** 51.6 births/1,000 population (2009 est.)
**Death rate:** 20.26 deaths/1,000 population (2008 est.)
**Net migration rate:** -0.57 migrant(s)/1,000 population (2009 est.)
**Urbanization:**
*urban population:* 16% of total population (2008)
*rate of urbanization:* 4% annual rate of change (2005-10 est.)

**Sex ratio:**
*at birth:* 1.03 male(s)/female
*under 15 years:* 1.02 male(s)/female
*15-64 years:* 0.99 male(s)/female
*65 years and over:* 0.81 male(s)/female
*total population:* 1 male(s)/female (2009 est.)
**Infant mortality rate:**
*total:* 116.66 deaths/1,000 live births
*male:* 121.72 deaths/1,000 live births
*female:* 111.45 deaths/1,000 live births (2009 est.)
**Life expectancy at birth:**
*total population:* 52.6 years
*male:* 51.39 years
*female:* 53.85 years (2009 est.)
**Total fertility rate:** 7.75 children born/woman (2009 est.)
**HIV/AIDS - adult prevalence rate:** 0.8% (2007 est.)
**HIV/AIDS - people living with HIV/AIDS:** 60,000 (2007 est.)
**HIV/AIDS - deaths:** 4,000 (2007 est.)
**Major infectious diseases:**
*degree of risk:* very high
*food or waterborne diseases:* bacterial and protozoal diarrhea, hepatitis A, and typhoid fever
*vectorborne disease:* malaria
*water contact disease:* schistosomiasis
*animal contact disease:* rabies
*respiratory disease:* meningococcal meningitis
*note:* highly pathogenic H5N1 avian influenza has been identified in this country; it poses a negligible risk with extremely rare cases possible among US citizens who have close contact with birds (2009)
**Nationality:**
*noun:* Nigerien(s)
*adjective:* Nigerien
**Ethnic groups:** Haoussa 55.4%, Djerma Sonrai 21%, Tuareg 9.3%, Peuhl 8.5%, Kanouri Manga 4.7%, other 1.2% (2001 census)
**Religions:** Muslim 80%, other (includes indigenous beliefs and Christian) 20%
**Languages:** French (official), Hausa, Djerma
**Literacy:**
*definition:* age 15 and over can read and write
*total population:* 28.7%
*male:* 42.9%
*female:* 15.1% (2005 est.)
**School life expectancy (primary to tertiary education):**
*total:* 4 years
*male:* 5 years
*female:* 3 years (2006)
**Education expenditures:** 3.4% of GDP (2006)

## Government

**Country name:**
*conventional long form:* Republic of Niger
*conventional short form:* Niger
*local long form:* Republique du Niger
*local short form:* Niger
**Government type:** republic

# Niger *(continued)*

**Capital:**
*name:* Niamey
*geographic coordinates:* 13 31 N, 2 07 E
*time difference:* UTC+1 (6 hours ahead of Washington, DC during Standard Time)
**Administrative divisions:** 8 regions (regions, singular - region) includes 1 capital district* (communite urbaine); Agadez, Diffa, Dosso, Maradi, Niamey*, Tahoua, Tillaberi, Zinder
**Independence:** 3 August 1960 (from France)
**National holiday:** Republic Day, 18 December (1958)
**Constitution:** adopted 18 July 1999
**Legal system:** based on French civil law system and customary law; has not accepted compulsory ICJ jurisdiction
**Suffrage:** 18 years of age; universal
**Executive branch:**
*chief of state:* President Mamadou TANDJA (since 22 December 1999)
*head of government:* Prime Minister Seyni OUMAROU (since 3 June 2007); appointed by the president and shares some executive responsibilities with the president
*cabinet:* 26-member Cabinet appointed by the president
*elections:* president elected by popular vote for a five-year term (eligible for a second term); second round of election last held 4 December 2004 (next to be held December 2009)
*election results:* Mamadou TANDJA reelected president; percent of vote - Mamadou TANDJA 65.5%, Mahamadou ISSOUFOU 34.5%
**Legislative branch:** unicameral National Assembly (113 seats; members elected by popular vote to serve five-year terms)
*elections:* last held 4 December 2004 (next to be held in December 2009)
*election results:* percent of vote by party - NA; seats by party - MNSD 47, PNDS 25, CDS 22, RSD 7, RDP 6, ANDP 5, PSDN 1
**Judicial branch:** State Court or Cour d'Etat; Court of Appeals or Cour d'Appel
**Political parties and leaders:** Democratic and Social Convention-Rahama or CDS-Rahama [Mahamane OUSMANE]; National Movement for a Developing Society-Nassara or MNSD-Nassara [Hama AMADOU]; Niger Social Democratic Party or PSDN; Nigerien Alliance for Democracy and Social Progress-Zaman Lahiya or ANDP-Zaman Lahiya [Moumouni DJERMAKOYE]; Nigerien Party for Autonomy or PNA-Alouma'a [Sanousi JACKOU]; Nigerien Party for Democracy and Socialism or PNDS-Tarrayya [Issifou MAHAMADOU]; Nigerien Progressive Party or PPN-RDA; Rally for Democracy and Progress or RDP-jama'a [Hamid ALGABID]; Social and Democratic Rally or RSD-Gaskiyya [Cheiffou AMADOU]
**Political pressure groups and leaders:** The Nigerien Movement for Justice or MNJ, a predominantly Tuareg rebel group

**International organization participation:** ACP, AfDB, AU, ECOWAS, Entente, FAO, FZ, G-77, IAEA, IBRD, ICAO, ICCt, ICRM, IDA, IDB, IFAD, IFC, IFRCS, ILO, IMF, Interpol, IOC, IOM, IPU, ITSO, ITU, ITUC, MONUC, NAM, OIC, OIF, OPCW, UN, UNCTAD, UNESCO, UNIDO, UNMIL, UNOCI, UNWTO, UPU, WADB (regional), WAEMU, WCL, WCO, WFTU, WHO, WIPO, WMO, WTO
**Diplomatic representation in the US:**
*chief of mission:* Ambassador Aminata Djibrilla Maiga TOURE
*chancery:* 2204 R Street NW, Washington, DC 20008
*telephone:* [1] (202) 483-4224 through 4227
*FAX:* [1] (202)483-3169
**Diplomatic representation from the US:**
*chief of mission:* Ambassador Bernadette M. ALLEN
*embassy:* Rue Des Ambassades, Niamey
*mailing address:* B. P. 11201, Niamey
*telephone:* [227] 20-72-26-61 thru 64
*FAX:* [227] 20-73-31-67
**Flag description:** three equal horizontal bands of orange (top), white, and green with a small orange disk (representing the sun) centered in the white band; similar to the flag of India, which has a blue spoked wheel centered in the white band

## Economy

**Economy - overview:** Niger is one of the poorest countries in the world, ranking near last on the United Nations Development Fund index of human development. It is a landlocked, Sub-Saharan nation, whose economy centers on subsistence crops, livestock, and some of the world's largest uranium deposits. Drought cycles, desertification, and strong population growth have undercut the economy. Niger shares a common currency, the CFA franc, and a common central bank, the Central Bank of West African States (BCEAO), with seven other members of the West African Monetary Union. In December 2000, Niger qualified for enhanced debt relief under the International Monetary Fund program for Highly Indebted Poor Countries (HIPC) and concluded an agreement with the Fund on a Poverty Reduction and Growth Facility (PRGF). Debt relief provided under the enhanced HIPC initiative significantly reduces Niger's annual debt service obligations, freeing funds for expenditures on basic health care, primary education, HIV/AIDS prevention, rural infrastructure, and other programs geared at poverty reduction. In December 2005, Niger received 100% multilateral debt relief from the IMF, which translates into the forgiveness of approximately US $86 million in debts to the IMF, excluding the remaining assistance under HIPC. Nearly half of the government's budget is derived from foreign donor resources. Future growth may be sustained by exploitation of oil, gold, coal, and other mineral resources. Uranium prices have increased sharply in the last few years. A drought and locust infestation in 2005 led to food shortages for as many as 2.5 million Nigeriens.

**GDP (purchasing power parity):**
$9.784 billion (2008 est.)
$9.239 billion (2007)
$8.944 billion (2006)
*note:* data are in 2008 US dollars
**GDP (official exchange rate):** $5.322 billion (2008 est.)
**GDP - real growth rate:**
5.9% (2008 est.)
3.3% (2007 est.)
5.2% (2006 est.)
**GDP - per capita (PPP):**
$700 (2008 est.)
$600 (2007 est.)
$700 (2006 est.)
*note:* data are in 2008 US dollars
**GDP - composition by sector:**
*agriculture:* 39%
*industry:* 17%
*services:* 44% (2001)
**Labor force:** 70,000 salaried workers, 60% of whom are employed in the public sector (1995)
**Labor force - by occupation:**
*agriculture:* 90%
*industry:* 6%
*services:* 4% (1995)
**Unemployment rate:**
NA%
**Population below poverty line:** 63% (1993 est.)
**Household income or consumption by percentage share:**
*lowest 10%:* 0.8%
*highest 10%:* 35.4% (1995)
**Distribution of family income - Gini index:** 50.5 (1995)
**Budget:**
*revenues:* $320 million (includes $134 million from foreign sources)
*expenditures:* $320 million (2002 est.)
**Inflation rate (consumer prices):**
0.1% (2007 est.)
**Central bank discount rate:** 4.25% (31 December 2007)
**Commercial bank prime lending rate:** NA
**Stock of money:** $604.5 million (31 December 2007)
**Stock of quasi money:** $193.7 million (31 December 2007)
**Stock of domestic credit:** $318.9 million (31 December 2007)
**Market value of publicly traded shares:** $NA
**Agriculture - products:** cowpeas, cotton, peanuts, millet, sorghum, cassava (tapioca), rice; cattle, sheep, goats, camels, donkeys, horses, poultry
**Industries:** uranium mining, cement, brick, soap, textiles, food processing, chemicals, slaughterhouses
**Industrial production growth rate:** 5.1% (2003 est.)
**Electricity - production:** 240 million kWh (2006 est.)
**Electricity - consumption:** 443.2 million kWh (2006 est.)

## Niger (continued)

**Electricity - exports:** 0 kWh (2007 est.)
**Electricity - imports:** 225 million kWh (2007 est.)
**Oil - production:** 0 bbl/day (2007 est.)
**Oil - consumption:** 5,550 bbl/day (2006 est.)
**Oil - exports:** 0 bbl/day (2005)
**Oil - imports:** 5,425 bbl/day (2005)
**Oil - proved reserves:** NA bbl
**Natural gas - production:** 0 cu m (2007 est.)
**Natural gas - consumption:** 0 cu m (2007 est.)
**Natural gas - exports:** 0 cu m (2007 est.)
**Natural gas - imports:** 0 cu m (2007 est.)
**Natural gas - proved reserves:** 0 cu m (1 January 2006 est.)
**Current account balance:** -$321 million (2007 est.)
**Exports:** $428 million f.o.b. (2006)
**Exports - commodities:** uranium ore, livestock, cowpeas, onions
**Exports - partners:** France 57%, Nigeria 26.4%, Ghana 4.1% (2007)
**Imports:** $800 million f.o.b. (2006)
**Imports - commodities:** foodstuffs, machinery, vehicles and parts, petroleum, cereals
**Imports - partners:** France 15.9%, French Polynesia 8.8%, Nigeria 8.6%, Belgium 8.6%, US 6.9%, Cote d'Ivoire 5.6% (2007)
**Debt - external:** $2.1 billion (2003 est.)
**Exchange rates:** Communaute Financiere Africaine francs (XOF) per US dollar - 447.81 (2008 est.), 493.51 (2007), 522.59 (2006), 527.47 (2005), 528.29 (2004)
*note:* since 1 January 1999, the West African CFA franc (XOF) has been pegged to the euro at a rate of 655.957 CFA francs per euro; West African CFA franc (XOF) coins and banknotes are not accepted in countries using Central African CFA francs (XAF), and vice versa, even though the two currencies trade at par

### Communications

**Telephones - main lines in use:** 24,000 (2005)
**Telephones - mobile cellular:** 900,000 (2007)
**Telephone system:**
*general assessment:* inadequate; small system of wire, radio telephone communications, and microwave radio relay links concentrated in the southwestern area of Niger
*domestic:* combined fixed-line and mobile-cellular teledensity only about 7 per 100 persons; domestic satellite system with 3 earth stations and 1 planned
*international:* country code - 227; satellite earth stations - 2 Intelsat (1 Atlantic Ocean and 1 Indian Ocean)
**Radio broadcast stations:** AM 5, FM 6, shortwave 4 (2001)
**Television broadcast stations:** 5 (2007)
**Internet country code:** .ne
**Internet hosts:** 216 (2008)
**Internet users:** 40,000 (2006)

### Transportation

**Airports:** 27 (2008)
**Airports - with paved runways:**
*total:* 9
*2,438 to 3,047 m:* 3
*1,524 to 2,437 m:* 5
*914 to 1,523 m:* 1 (2008)
**Airports - with unpaved runways:**
*total:* 18
*1,524 to 2,437 m:* 2
*914 to 1,523 m:* 13
*under 914 m:* 3 (2008)
**Roadways:**
*total:* 18,550 km
*paved:* 3,803 km
*unpaved:* 14,747 km (2006)
**Waterways:** 300 km (the Niger, the only major river, is navigable to Gaya between September and March) (2008)

### Military

**Military branches:** Nigerien Armed Forces (Forces Armees Nigeriennes, FAN): Army, Niger Air Force (Force Aerienne du Niger) (2008)
**Military service age and obligation:** 17-21 years of age for voluntary military service; 2-year service term; women may serve in health care (2008)
**Manpower available for military service:**
*males age 16-49:* 2,871,868
*females age 16-49:* 2,696,966 (2008 est.)
**Manpower fit for military service:**
*males age 16-49:* 2,019,553
*females age 16-49:* 2,046,906 (2009 est.)
**Manpower reaching militarily significant age annually:**
*male:* 170,060
*female:* 163,996 (2009 est.)
**Military expenditures:** 1.3% of GDP (2006)

### Transnational Issues

**Disputes - international:** Libya claims about 25,000 sq km in a currently dormant dispute in the Tommo region; much of Benin-Niger boundary, including tripoint with Nigeria, remains undemarcated; only Nigeria and Cameroon have heeded the Lake Chad Commission's admonition to ratify the delimitation treaty which also includes the Chad-Niger and Niger-Nigeria boundaries
**Trafficking in persons:**
*current situation:* Niger is a source, transit, and destination country for children and women trafficked for forced labor and sexual exploitation; caste-based slavery practices, rooted in ancestral master-slave relationships, continue in isolated areas of the country -an estimated 8,800 to 43,000 Nigeriens live under conditions of traditional slavery; children are trafficked within Niger for forced begging, forced labor in gold mines, domestic servitude, sexual exploitation, and possibly for forced labor in agriculture and stone quarries; women and children from neighboring states are trafficked to and through Niger for domestic servitude, sexual exploitation, forced labor in mines and on farms, and as mechanics and welders
*tier rating:* Tier 2 Watch List - Niger is on the Tier 2 Watch List for its failure to provide evidence of increasing efforts to eliminate trafficking in 2007; in particular, measures to combat and eliminate traditional slavery practices were weak; the government's overall law enforcement efforts have stalled from 2006; while efforts to protect child trafficking victims were steady, the government failed to provide services to or rescue adult victims subjected to traditional slavery practices, and made poor efforts to educate the public about traditional slavery practices in general (2008)

# Nigeria

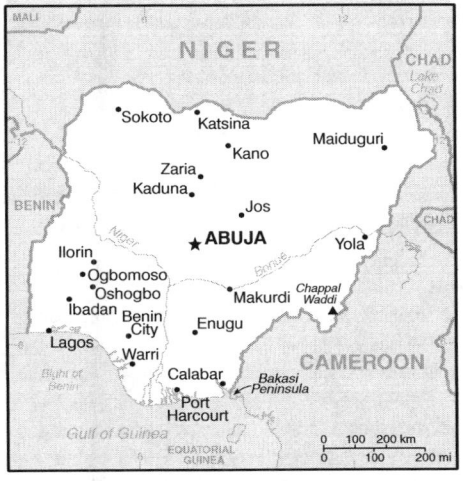

## Introduction

**Background:** British influence and control over what would become Nigeria and Africa's most populous country grew through the 19th century. A series of constitutions after World War II granted Nigeria greater autonomy; independence came in 1960. Following nearly 16 years of military rule, a new constitution was adopted in 1999, and a peaceful transition to civilian government was completed. The government continues to face the daunting task of reforming a petroleum-based economy, whose revenues have been squandered through corruption and mismanagement, and institutionalizing democracy. In addition, Nigeria continues to experience longstanding ethnic and religious tensions. Although both the 2003 and 2007 presidential elections were marred by significant irregularities and violence, Nigeria is currently experiencing its longest period of civilian rule since independence. The general elections of April 2007 marked the first civilian-to-civilian transfer of power in the country's history.

## Geography

**Location:** Western Africa, bordering the Gulf of Guinea, between Benin and Cameroon
**Geographic coordinates:** 10 00 N, 8 00 E
**Map references:** Africa
**Area:**
*total:* 923,768 sq km
*land:* 910,768 sq km
*water:* 13,000 sq km
**Area - comparative:** slightly more than twice the size of California
**Land boundaries:**
*total:* 4,047 km
*border countries:* Benin 773 km, Cameroon 1,690 km, Chad 87 km, Niger 1,497 km
**Coastline:** 853 km

**Maritime claims:**
*territorial sea:* 12 nm
*exclusive economic zone:* 200 nm
*continental shelf:* 200 m depth or to the depth of exploitation
**Climate:** varies; equatorial in south, tropical in center, arid in north
**Terrain:** southern lowlands merge into central hills and plateaus; mountains in southeast, plains in north
**Elevation extremes:**
*lowest point:* Atlantic Ocean 0 m
*highest point:* Chappal Waddi 2,419 m
**Natural resources:** natural gas, petroleum, tin, iron ore, coal, limestone, niobium, lead, zinc, arable land
**Land use:**
*arable land:* 33.02%
*permanent crops:* 3.14%
*other:* 63.84% (2005)
**Irrigated land:** 2,820 sq km (2003)
**Total renewable water resources:** 286.2 cu km (2003)
**Freshwater withdrawal (domestic/industrial/agricultural):**
*total:* 8.01 cu km/yr (21%/10%/69%)
*per capita:* 61 cu m/yr (2000)
**Natural hazards:** periodic droughts; flooding
**Environment - current issues:** soil degradation; rapid deforestation; urban air and water pollution; desertification; oil pollution - water, air, and soil; has suffered serious damage from oil spills; loss of arable land; rapid urbanization
**Environment - international agreements:**
*party to:* Biodiversity, Climate Change, Climate Change-Kyoto Protocol, Desertification, Endangered Species, Hazardous Wastes, Law of the Sea, Marine Dumping, Marine Life Conservation, Ozone Layer Protection, Ship Pollution, Wetlands
*signed, but not ratified:* none of the selected agreements
**Geography - note:** the Niger enters the country in the northwest and flows southward through tropical rain forests and swamps to its delta in the Gulf of Guinea

## People

**Population:** 149,229,090
*note:* estimates for this country explicitly take into account the effects of excess mortality due to AIDS; this can result in lower life expectancy, higher infant mortality, higher death rates, lower population growth rates, and changes in the distribution of population by age and sex than would otherwise be expected (July 2009 est.)
**Age structure:**
*0-14 years:* 41.5% (male 31,624,050/female 30,242,637)
*15-64 years:* 55.5% (male 42,240,641/female 40,566,672)
*65 years and over:* 3.1% (male 2,211,840/female 2,343,250) (2009 est.)

**Median age:**
*total:* 19 years
*male:* 18.9 years
*female:* 19.1 years (2009 est.)
**Population growth rate:** 1.999% (2009 est.)
**Birth rate:** 36.65 births/1,000 population (2009 est.)
**Death rate:** 16.88 deaths/1,000 population (2008 est.)
**Net migration rate:** -0.1 migrant(s)/1,000 population (2009 est.)
**Urbanization:**
*urban population:* 48% of total population (2008)
*rate of urbanization:* 3.8% annual rate of change (2005-10 est.)
**Sex ratio:**
*at birth:* 1.06 male(s)/female
*under 15 years:* 1.05 male(s)/female
*15-64 years:* 1.04 male(s)/female
*65 years and over:* 0.94 male(s)/female
*total population:* 1.04 male(s)/female (2009 est.)
**Infant mortality rate:**
*total:* 94.35 deaths/1,000 live births
*male:* 100.38 deaths/1,000 live births
*female:* 87.97 deaths/1,000 live births (2009 est.)
**Life expectancy at birth:**
*total population:* 46.94 years
*male:* 46.16 years
*female:* 47.76 years (2009 est.)
**Total fertility rate:** 4.91 children born/woman (2009 est.)
**HIV/AIDS - adult prevalence rate:** 3.1% (2007 est.)
**HIV/AIDS - people living with HIV/AIDS:** 2.6 million (2007 est.)
**HIV/AIDS - deaths:** 170,000 (2007 est.)
**Major infectious diseases:**
*degree of risk:* very high
*food or waterborne diseases:* bacterial and protozoal diarrhea, hepatitis A and E, and typhoid fever
*vectorborne disease:* malaria and yellow fever
*respiratory disease:* meningococcal meningitis
*aerosolized dust or soil contact disease:* one of the most highly endemic areas for Lassa fever
*water contact disease:* leptospirosis and shistosomiasis
*animal contact disease:* rabies
*note:* highly pathogenic H5N1 avian influenza has been identified in this country; it poses a negligible risk with extremely rare cases possible among US citizens who have close contact with birds (2009)
**Nationality:**
*noun:* Nigerian(s)
*adjective:* Nigerian
**Ethnic groups:** Nigeria, Africa's most populous country, is composed of more than 250 ethnic groups; the following are the most populous and politically influential: Hausa and Fulani 29%, Yoruba 21%, Igbo (Ibo) 18%, Ijaw 10%, Kanuri 4%, Ibibio 3.5%, Tiv 2.5%
**Religions:** Muslim 50%, Christian 40%, indigenous beliefs 10%
**Languages:** English (official), Hausa, Yoruba, Igbo (Ibo), Fulani

# Nigeria (continued)

**Literacy:**

*definition:* age 15 and over can read and write

*total population:* 68%

*male:* 75.7%

*female:* 60.6% (2003 est.)

**School life expectancy (primary to tertiary education):**

*total:* 8 years

*male:* 9 years

*female:* 7 years (2004)

**Education expenditures:** 0.9% of GDP (1991)

## Government

**Country name:**

*conventional long form:* Federal Republic of Nigeria

*conventional short form:* Nigeria

**Government type:** federal republic

**Capital:**

*name:* Abuja

*geographic coordinates:* 9 05 N, 7 32 E

*time difference:* UTC+1 (6 hours ahead of Washington, DC during Standard Time)

**Administrative divisions:** 36 states and 1 territory*; Abia, Adamawa, Akwa Ibom, Anambra, Bauchi, Bayelsa, Benue, Borno, Cross River, Delta, Ebonyi, Edo, Ekiti, Enugu, Federal Capital Territory*, Gombe, Imo, Jigawa, Kaduna, Kano, Katsina, Kebbi, Kogi, Kwara, Lagos, Nassarawa, Niger, Ogun, Ondo, Osun, Oyo, Plateau, Rivers, Sokoto, Taraba, Yobe, Zamfara

**Independence:** 1 October 1960 (from the UK)

**National holiday:** Independence Day (National Day), 1 October (1960)

**Constitution:** adopted 5 May 1999; effective 29 May 1999

**Legal system:** based on English common law, Islamic law (in 12 northern states), and traditional law; accepts compulsory ICJ jurisdiction with reservations

**Suffrage:** 18 years of age; universal

**Executive branch:**

*chief of state:* President Umaru Musa YAR'ADUA (since 29 May 2007); note - the president is both the chief of state and head of government

*head of government:* President Umaru Musa YAR'ADUA (since 29 May 2007)

*cabinet:* Federal Executive Council

*elections:* president is elected by popular vote for a four-year term (eligible for a second term); election last held 21 April 2007 (next to be held in April 2011)

*election results:* Umaru Musa YAR'ADUA elected president; percent of vote - Umaru Musa YAR'ADUA 69.8%, Muhammadu BUHARI 18.7%, Atiku ABUBAKAR 7.5%, Orji Uzor KALU 1.7%, other 2.3%

**Legislative branch:** bicameral National Assembly consists of the Senate (109 seats, 3 from each state plus 1 from Abuja; members elected by popular vote to serve four-year terms) and House of Representatives (360 seats; members elected by popular vote to serve four-year terms)

*elections:* Senate - last held 21 April 2007 (next to be held in April 2011); House of Representatives - last held 21 April 2007 (next to be held in April 2011)

*election results:* Senate - percent of vote by party - PDP 53.7%, ANPP 27.9%, AD 9.7%, other 8.7%; seats by party - PDP 76, ANPP 27, AD 6; House of Representatives - percent of vote by party - PDP 54.5%, ANPP 27.4%, AD 8.8%, UNPP 2.8%, NPD 1.9%, APGA 1.6%, PRP 0.8%; seats by party - PDP 76, ANPP 27, AD 6, UNPP 2, APGA 2, NPD 1, PRP 1, vacant 1

**Judicial branch:** Supreme Court (judges recommended by the National Judicial Council and appointed by the president); Federal Court of Appeal (judges are appointed by the federal government from a pool of judges recommended by the National Judicial Council)

**Political parties and leaders:** Accord Party [Ikra Aliyu BILBIS]; Action Congress or AC [Hassan ZUMI]; Alliance for Democracy or AD [Mojisoluwa AKINFENWA]; All Nigeria Peoples' Party or ANPP [Edwin UME-EZEOKE]; All Progressives Grand Alliance or APGA [Victor C. UMEH]; Democratic People's Party or DPP [Jeremiah USENI]; Fresh Democratic Party [Chris OKOTIE]; Labor Party [Dan NWANYANWU]; Movement for the Restoration and Defense of Democracy or MRDD [Mohammed Gambo JIMETA]; National Democratic Party or NDP [Aliyu Habu FARI]; Peoples Democratic Party or PDP [Vincent OGBULAFOR]; Peoples Progressive Alliance [Clement EBRI]; Peoples Redemption Party or PRP [Abdulkadir Balarabe MUSA]; Peoples Salvation Party or PSP [Lawal MAITURARE]; United Nigeria Peoples Party or UNPP [Mallam Selah JAMBO]

**Political pressure groups and leaders:** Academic Staff Union for Universities or ASUU; Campaign for Democracy or CD; Civil Liberties Organization or CLO; Committee for the Defense of Human Rights or CDHR; Constitutional Right Project or CRP; Human Right Africa; National Association of Democratic Lawyers or NADL; National Association of Nigerian Students or NANS; Nigerian Bar Association or NBA; Nigerian Labor Congress or NLC; Nigerian Medical Association or NMA; the Press; Universal Defenders of Democracy or UDD

**International organization participation:** ACP, AfDB, AU, C, ECOWAS, FAO, G-15, G-24, G-77, IAEA, IBRD, ICAO, ICC, ICCt, ICRM, IDA, IDB, IFAD, IFC, IFRCS, IHO, ILO, IMF, IMO, IMSO, Interpol, IOC, IOM, IPU, ISO, ITSO, ITU, ITUC, MIGA, MINURCAT, MINURSO, MONUC, NAM, OAS (observer), OIC, OPCW, OPEC, PCA, UN, UNAMID, UNCTAD, UNESCO, UNHCR, UNIDO, UNMIL, UNMIS, UNOCI, UNOMIG, UNWTO, UPU, WCO, WFTU, WHO, WIPO, WMO, WTO

**Diplomatic representation in the US:**

*chief of mission:* Ambassador (vacant); Charge d'Affaires Baba Gana WIKIL

*chancery:* 3519 International Court NW, Washington, DC 20008

*telephone:* [1] (202) 986-8400

*FAX:* [1] (202) 775-1385

*consulate(s) general:* Atlanta, New York

**Diplomatic representation from the US:**

*chief of mission:* Ambassador Robin SANDERS

*embassy:* 1075 Diplomatic Drive, Central District Area, Abuja

*mailing address:* P. O. Box 5760, Garki, Abuja

*telephone:* [234] (9) 461-4000

*FAX:* [234] (9) 461-4036

**Flag description:** three equal vertical bands of green (hoist side), white, and green

## Economy

**Economy - overview:** Oil-rich Nigeria, long hobbled by political instability, corruption, inadequate infrastructure, and poor macroeconomic management, has undertaken several reforms over the past decade. Nigeria's former military rulers failed to diversify the economy away from its overdependence on the capital-intensive oil sector, which provides 95% of foreign exchange earnings and about 80% of budgetary revenues. Following the signing of an IMF stand-by agreement in August 2000, Nigeria received a debt-restructuring deal from the Paris Club and a $1 billion credit from the IMF, both contingent on economic reforms. Nigeria pulled out of its IMF program in April 2002, after failing to meet spending and exchange rate targets, making it ineligible for additional debt forgiveness from the Paris Club. Since 2008 the government has begun showing the political will to implement the market-oriented reforms urged by the IMF, such as to modernize the banking system, to curb inflation by blocking excessive wage demands, and to resolve regional disputes over the distribution of earnings from the oil industry. In 2003, the government began deregulating fuel prices, announced the privatization of the country's four oil refineries, and instituted the National Economic Empowerment Development Strategy, a domestically designed and run program modeled on the IMF's Poverty Reduction and Growth Facility for fiscal and monetary management. In November 2005, Abuja won Paris Club approval for a debt-relief deal that eliminated $18 billion of debt in exchange for $12 billion in payments - a total package worth $30 billion of Nigeria's total $37 billion external debt. The deal requires Nigeria to be subject to stringent IMF reviews. Based largely on increased oil exports and high global crude prices, GDP rose strongly in 2007 and 2008. President YAR'ADUA has pledged to continue the economic reforms of his predecessor with emphasis on infrastructure improvements. Infrastructure is the main impediment to growth. The government is working toward developing stronger public-private partnerships for electricity and roads.

**GDP (purchasing power parity):**

$338.1 billion (2008 est.)

$318.7 billion (2007)

$299.5 billion (2006)

*note:* data are in 2008 US dollars

**GDP (official exchange rate):** $220.3 billion (2008 est.)

# Nigeria (continued)

**GDP - real growth rate:**
6.1% (2008 est.)
6.4% (2007 est.)
6.2% (2006 est.)
**GDP - per capita (PPP):**
$2,300 (2008 est.)
$2,200 (2007 est.)
$2,100 (2006 est.)
*note:* data are in 2008 US dollars
**GDP - composition by sector:**
*agriculture:* 18%
*industry:* 50.9%
*services:* 31.1% (2008 est.)
**Labor force:** 51.04 million (2008 est.)
**Labor force - by occupation:**
*agriculture:* 70%
*industry:* 10%
*services:* 20% (1999 est.)
**Unemployment rate:**
4.9% (2007 est.)
**Population below poverty line:** 70% (2007 est.)
**Household income or consumption by percentage share:**
*lowest 10%:* 1.9%
*highest 10%:* 33.2% (2003)
**Distribution of family income - Gini index:** 43.7 (2003)
**Investment (gross fixed):** 21.4% of GDP (2008 est.)
**Budget:**
*revenues:* $29.49 billion
*expenditures:* $30.61 billion (2008 est.)
**Public debt:** 12.2% of GDP (2008 est.)
**Inflation rate (consumer prices):**
10.6% (2008 est.)
5.4% (2007 est.)
**Central bank discount rate:** 9.5% (31 December 2007)
**Commercial bank prime lending rate:** 16.94% (31 December 2007)
**Stock of money:** $21.72 billion (31 December 2007)
**Stock of quasi money:** $19.07 billion (31 December 2007)
**Stock of domestic credit:** $16.15 billion (31 December 2007)
**Market value of publicly traded shares:** $86.35 billion (31 December 2007)
**Agriculture - products:** cocoa, peanuts, palm oil, corn, rice, sorghum, millet, cassava (tapioca), yams, rubber; cattle, sheep, goats, pigs; timber; fish
**Industries:** crude oil, coal, tin, columbite; palm oil, peanuts, cotton, rubber, wood; hides and skins, textiles, cement and other construction materials, food products, footwear, chemicals, fertilizer, printing, ceramics, steel, small commercial ship construction and repair
**Industrial production growth rate:** 2.8% (2008 est.)
**Electricity - production:** 22.11 billion kWh (2006 est.)

**Electricity - consumption:** 15.85 billion kWh (2006 est.)
**Electricity - exports:** 0 kWh (2007 est.)
**Electricity - imports:** 0 kWh (2007 est.)
**Oil - production:** 2.352 million bbl/day (2007 est.)
**Oil - consumption:** 312,000 bbl/day (2006 est.)
**Oil - exports:** 2.473 million bbl/day (2005)
**Oil - imports:** 154,300 bbl/day (2005)
**Oil - proved reserves:** 36.22 billion bbl (1 January 2008 est.)
**Natural gas - production:** 34.1 billion cu m (2007 est.)
**Natural gas - consumption:** 12.9 billion cu m (2007 est.)
**Natural gas - exports:** 21.2 billion cu m (2007 est.)
**Natural gas - imports:** 0 cu m (2007 est.)
**Natural gas - proved reserves:** 5.21 trillion cu m (1 January 2008 est.)
**Current account balance:** $7.722 billion (2008 est.)
**Exports:** $83.09 billion f.o.b. (2008 est.)
**Exports - commodities:** petroleum and petroleum products 95%, cocoa, rubber
**Exports - partners:** US 51.6%, Brazil 8.9%, Spain 7.7% (2007)
**Imports:** $46.36 billion f.o.b. (2008 est.)
**Imports - commodities:** machinery, chemicals, transport equipment, manufactured goods, food and live animals
**Imports - partners:** China 10.6%, Netherlands 7.9%, US 7.8%, South Korea 6.6%, UK 5.7%, France 4.3%, Brazil 4.2%, Germany 4.1% (2007)
**Reserves of foreign exchange and gold:** $72.04 billion (31 December 2008 est.)
**Debt - external:** $9.132 billion (31 December 2008 est.)
**Stock of direct foreign investment - at home:** $35.75 billion (2008 est.)
**Stock of direct foreign investment - abroad:** $12.83 billion (2008 est.)
**Exchange rates:** nairas (NGN) per US dollar - 117.8 (2008 est.), 127.46 (2007), 127.38 (2006), 132.59 (2005), 132.89 (2004)

## Communications

**Telephones - main lines in use:** 1.58 million (2007)
**Telephones - mobile cellular:** 40.395 million (2007)
**Telephone system:**
*general assessment:* further expansion and modernization of the fixed-line telephone network is needed
*domestic:* the addition of a second fixed-line provider in 2002 resulted in faster growth but subscribership remains only about 1 per 100 persons; wireless telephony has grown rapidly, in part responding to the shortcomings of the fixed-line network; multiple service providers operate nationally; mobile-cellular teledensity reached 30 per 100 persons in 2007
*international:* country code - 234; landing point for the SAT-3/WASC fiber-optic submarine cable that provides connectivity to Europe and Asia; satellite earth stations - 3 Intelsat (2 Atlantic Ocean and 1 Indian Ocean) (2007)

**Radio broadcast stations:** AM 83, FM 36, shortwave 11 (2001)
**Television broadcast stations:** 3 (the government controls 2 of the broadcasting stations and 15 repeater stations) (2001)
**Internet country code:** .ng
**Internet hosts:** 1,048 (2008)
**Internet users:** 10 million (2007)

## Transportation

**Airports:** 60 (2008)
**Airports - with paved runways:**
*total:* 38
*over 3,047 m:* 6
*2,438 to 3,047 m:* 12
*1,524 to 2,437 m:* 11
*914 to 1,523 m:* 7
*under 914 m:* 2 (2008)
**Airports - with unpaved runways:**
*total:* 22
*1,524 to 2,437 m:* 2
*914 to 1,523 m:* 13
*under 914 m:* 7 (2008)
**Heliports:** 2 (2007)
**Pipelines:** condensate 21 km; gas 2,560 km; liquid petroleum gas 97 km; oil 3,396 km; refined products 4,090 km (2008)
**Railways:**
*total:* 3,505 km
*narrow gauge:* 3,505 km 1.067-m gauge (2006)
**Roadways:**
*total:* 193,200 km
*paved:* 28,980 km
*unpaved:* 164,220 km (2004)
**Waterways:** 8,600 km (Niger and Benue rivers and smaller rivers and creeks) (2008)
**Merchant marine:**
*total:* 68
*by type:* cargo 4, chemical tanker 12, combination ore/oil 1, liquefied gas 2, passenger/cargo 1, petroleum tanker 46, specialized tanker 2
*foreign-owned:* 3 (Japan 1, South Africa 1, Spain 1)
*registered in other countries:* 34 (Bahamas 2, Bermuda 11, Cook Islands 1, Georgia 1, Italy 1, Liberia 2, Panama 10, Poland 1, Seychelles 1, Sierra Leone 1, unknown 3) (2008)
**Ports and terminals:** Bonny Inshore Terminal, Calabar, Lagos
**Transportation - note:** the International Maritime Bureau reports the territorial and offshore waters in the Niger Delta and Gulf of Guinea as high risk for piracy and armed robbery against ships; numerous commercial vessels have been attacked and hijacked both at anchor and while underway; crews have been robbed and stores or cargoes stolen

## Military

**Military branches:** Nigerian Armed Forces: Army, Navy, Air Force (2008)
**Military service age and obligation:** 18 years of age for voluntary military service (2007)

# Nigeria (continued)

**Manpower available for military service:**
*males age 16-49:* 31,929,204
*females age 16-49:* 30,638,979 (2008 est.)
**Manpower fit for military service:**
*males age 16-49:* 19,763,535
*females age 16-49:* 18,850,650 (2009 est.)
**Manpower reaching militarily significant age annually:**
*male:* 1,697,030
*female:* 1,618,561 (2009 est.)
**Military expenditures:** 1.5% of GDP (2006)

## Transnational Issues

**Disputes - international:** Joint Border Commission with Cameroon reviewed 2002 ICJ ruling on the entire boundary and bilaterally resolved differences, including June 2006 Greentree Agreement that immediately cedes sovereignty of the Bakassi Peninsula to Cameroon with a phase-out of Nigerian control within two years while resolving patriation issues; the ICJ ruled on an equidistance settlement of Cameroon-Equatorial Guinea-Nigeria maritime boundary in the Gulf of Guinea, but imprecisely defined coordinates in the ICJ decision and a sovereignty dispute between Equatorial Guinea and Cameroon over an island at the mouth of the Ntem River all contribute to the delay in implementation; only Nigeria and Cameroon have heeded the Lake Chad Commission's admonition to ratify the delimitation treaty which also includes the Chad-Niger and Niger-Nigeria boundaries
**Refugees and internally displaced persons:**
*refugees (country of origin):* 5,778 (Liberia)
*IDPs:* undetermined (communal violence between Christians and Muslims since President OBASANJO's election in 1999; displacement is mostly short-term) (2007)
**Illicit drugs:** a transit point for heroin and cocaine intended for European, East Asian, and North American markets; consumer of amphetamines; safe haven for Nigerian narcotraffickers operating worldwide; major money-laundering center; massive corruption and criminal activity; Nigeria has improved some anti-money-laundering controls, resulting in its removal from the Financial Action Task Force's (FATF's) Noncooperative Countries and Territories List in June 2006; Nigeria's anti-money-laundering regime continues to be monitored by FATF

# Niue
(self-governing in free association with New Zealand)

## Introduction

**Background:** Niue's remoteness, as well as cultural and linguistic differences between its Polynesian inhabitants and those of the rest of the Cook Islands, have caused it to be separately administered. The population of the island continues to drop (from a peak of 5,200 in 1966 to an estimated 1,398 in 2009) with substantial emigration to New Zealand 2,400 km to the southwest.

## Geography

**Location:** Oceania, island in the South Pacific Ocean, east of Tonga
**Geographic coordinates:** 19 02 S, 169 52 W
**Map references:** Oceania
**Area:**
*total:* 260 sq km
*land:* 260 sq km
*water:* 0 sq km
**Area - comparative:** 1.5 times the size of Washington, DC
**Land boundaries:** 0 km
**Coastline:** 64 km
**Maritime claims:**
*territorial sea:* 12 nm
*exclusive economic zone:* 200 nm
**Climate:** tropical; modified by southeast trade winds
**Terrain:** steep limestone cliffs along coast, central plateau
**Elevation extremes:**
*lowest point:* Pacific Ocean 0 m
*highest point:* unnamed location near Mutalau settlement 68 m
**Natural resources:** fish, arable land
**Land use:**
*arable land:* 11.54%
*permanent crops:* 15.38%
*other:* 73.08% (2005)
**Irrigated land:** NA
**Natural hazards:** typhoons

**Environment - current issues:** increasing attention to conservationist practices to counter loss of soil fertility from traditional slash and burn agriculture
**Environment - international agreements:**
*party to:* Biodiversity, Climate Change, Climate Change-Kyoto Protocol, Desertification, Law of the Sea, Ozone Layer Protection
**Geography - note:** one of world's largest coral islands

## People

**Population:** 1,398 (July 2009 est.)
**Age structure:**
*0-14 years:* NA
*15-64 years:* NA
*65 years and over:* NA
**Population growth rate:** -0.032% (2009 est.)
**Birth rate:** NA
**Death rate:** NA
**Net migration rate:** NA
**Urbanization:**
*urban population:* 39% of total population (2008)
*rate of urbanization:* -0.2% annual rate of change (2005-10 est.)
**Sex ratio:** NA
**Infant mortality rate:**
*total:* NA
*male:* NA
*female:* NA (2008 est.)
**Life expectancy at birth:**
*total population:* NA
*male:* NA
*female:* NA
**Total fertility rate:** NA (2008 est.)
**HIV/AIDS - adult prevalence rate:** NA
**HIV/AIDS - people living with HIV/AIDS:** NA
**HIV/AIDS - deaths:** NA
**Nationality:**
*noun:* Niuean(s)
*adjective:* Niuean
**Ethnic groups:** Niuen 78.2%, Pacific islander 10.2%, European 4.5%, mixed 3.9%, Asian 0.2%, unspecified 3% (2001 census)
**Religions:** Ekalesia Niue (Niuean Church - a Protestant church closely related to the London Missionary Society) 61.1%, Latter-Day Saints 8.8%, Roman Catholic 7.2%, Jehovah's Witnesses 2.4%, Seventh-Day Adventist 1.4%, other 8.4%, unspecified 8.7%, none 1.9% (2001 census)
**Languages:** Niuean, a Polynesian language closely related to Tongan and Samoan; English
**Literacy:**
*definition:* NA
*total population:* 95%
*male:* NA
*female:* NA
**School life expectancy (primary to tertiary education):**
*total:* 12 years
*male:* 12 years
*female:* 12 years (2005)
**Education expenditures:** NA

# Niue *(continued)*

## Government

**Country name:**
*conventional long form:* none
*conventional short form:* Niue
*note:* pronunciation falls between nyu-way and new-way, but not like new-wee
*former:* Savage Island

**Dependency status:** self-governing in free association with New Zealand since 1974; Niue fully responsible for internal affairs; New Zealand retains responsibility for external affairs and defense; however, these responsibilities confer no rights of control and are only exercised at the request of the Government of Niue

**Government type:** self-governing parliamentary democracy

**Capital:**
*name:* Alofi
*geographic coordinates:* 19 01 S, 169 55 W
*time difference:* UTC-11 (6 hours behind Washington, DC during Standard Time)

**Administrative divisions:** none; note - there are no first-order administrative divisions as defined by the US Government, but there are 14 villages at the second order

**Independence:** on 19 October 1974, Niue became a self-governing parliamentary government in free association with New Zealand

**National holiday:** Waitangi Day (Treaty of Waitangi established British sovereignty over New Zealand), 6 February (1840)

**Constitution:** 19 October 1974 (Niue Constitution Act)

**Legal system:** English common law; note - Niue is self-governing with the power to make its laws

**Suffrage:** 18 years of age; universal

**Executive branch:**
*chief of state:* Queen ELIZABETH II (since 6 February 1952); represented by Governor General of New Zealand Anand SATYANAND (since 23 August 2006); the UK and New Zealand are represented by New Zealand High Commissioner John BRYAN (since May 2000)
*head of government:* Premier Toke TALAGI (since 18 June 2008)
*cabinet:* Cabinet consists of the premier and three ministers
*elections:* the monarch is hereditary; premier elected by the Legislative Assembly for a three-year term; election last held 18 June 2008 (next to be held in 2011)
*election results:* Toke TALAGI defeats incumbent Young VIVIAN in Legislative Assembly vote; Toke TALAGI - 14, Young VIVIAN - 5

**Legislative branch:** unicameral Legislative Assembly (20 seats; members elected by popular vote to serve three-year terms; six elected from a common roll and 14 are village representatives)
*elections:* last held 7 June 2008 (next to be held in 2011)
*election results:* percent of vote by party - NA; seats by party - 20 independents

**Judicial branch:** Supreme Court of New Zealand; High Court of Niue

**Political parties and leaders:** Alliance of Independents or AI; Niue People's Action Party or NPP [Young VIVIAN]

**Political pressure groups and leaders:** NA

**International organization participation:** ACP, FAO, IFAD, OPCW, PIF, Sparteca, SPC, UNESCO, UPU, WHO, WMO

**Diplomatic representation in the US:** none (self-governing territory in free association with New Zealand)

**Diplomatic representation from the US:** none (self-governing territory in free association with New Zealand)

**Flag description:** yellow with the flag of the UK in the upper hoist-side quadrant; the flag of the UK bears five yellow five-pointed stars - a large star on a blue disk in the center and a smaller star on each arm of the bold red cross

## Economy

**Economy - overview:** The economy suffers from the typical Pacific island problems of geographic isolation, few resources, and a small population. Government expenditures regularly exceed revenues, and the shortfall is made up by critically needed grants from New Zealand that are used to pay wages to public employees. Niue has cut government expenditures by reducing the public service by almost half. The agricultural sector consists mainly of subsistence gardening, although some cash crops are grown for export. Industry consists primarily of small factories to process passion fruit, lime oil, honey, and coconut cream. The sale of postage stamps to foreign collectors is an important source of revenue. The island in recent years has suffered a serious loss of population because of emigration to New Zealand. Efforts to increase GDP include the promotion of tourism and a financial services industry, although the International Banking Repeal Act of 2002 resulted in the termination of all offshore banking licenses. Economic aid from New Zealand in 2002 was US$2.6 million. Niue suffered a devastating typhoon in January 2004, which decimated nascent economic programs. While in the process of rebuilding, Niue has been dependent on foreign aid.

**GDP (purchasing power parity):**
$10.01 million (2003 est.)

**GDP (official exchange rate):** $10.01 million (2003)

**GDP - real growth rate:**
6.2% (2003 est.)

**GDP - per capita (PPP):**
$5,800 (2003 est.)

**GDP - composition by sector:**
*agriculture:* 23.5%
*industry:* 26.9%
*services:* 49.5% (2003)

**Labor force:** 663 (2001)

**Labor force - by occupation:**
*note:* most work on family plantations; paid work exists only in government service, small industry, and the Niue Development Board

**Unemployment rate:**
12% (2001)

**Population below poverty line:** NA%

**Household income or consumption by percentage share:**
*lowest 10%:* NA%
*highest 10%:* NA%

**Budget:**
*revenues:* $15.07 million
*expenditures:* $16.33 million (FY0405)

**Inflation rate (consumer prices):**
4% (2005)

**Agriculture - products:** coconuts, passion fruit, honey, limes, taro, yams, cassava (tapioca), sweet potatoes; pigs, poultry, beef cattle

**Industries:** tourism, handicrafts, food processing

**Industrial production growth rate:** NA%

**Electricity - production:** 4 million kWh (2006 est.)

**Electricity - consumption:** 3.72 million kWh (2006 est.)

**Electricity - exports:** 0 kWh (2007 est.)

**Electricity - imports:** 0 kWh (2007 est.)

**Oil - production:** 0 bbl/day (2007 est.)

**Oil - consumption:** 20 bbl/day (2006 est.)

**Oil - exports:** 0 bbl/day (2005)

**Oil - imports:** 26.57 bbl/day (2005)

**Oil - proved reserves:** 0 bbl (1 January 2006 est.)

**Natural gas - production:** 0 cu m (2007 est.)

**Natural gas - consumption:** 0 cu m (2007 est.)

**Natural gas - exports:** 0 cu m (2007 est.)

**Natural gas - imports:** 0 cu m (2007 est.)

**Natural gas - proved reserves:** 0 cu m (1 January 2006 est.)

**Exports:** $201,400 (2004)

**Exports - commodities:** canned coconut cream, copra, honey, vanilla, passion fruit products, pawpaws, root crops, limes, footballs, stamps, handicrafts

**Imports:** $9.038 million f.o.b. (2004)

**Imports - commodities:** food, live animals, manufactured goods, machinery, fuels, lubricants, chemicals, drugs

**Debt - external:** $418,000 (2002 est.)

**Exchange rates:** New Zealand dollars (NZD) per US dollar - 1.4151 (2008 est.), 1.3811 (2007), 1.5408 (2006), 1.4203 (2005), 1.5087 (2004)

## Communications

**Telephones - main lines in use:** 1,100 (2002 est.)
**Telephones - mobile cellular:** 400 (2002)
**Telephone system:**
*domestic:* single-line telephone system connects all villages on island
*international:* country code - 683 (2001)
**Radio broadcast stations:** AM 1, FM 1, shortwave 0 (1998)
**Television broadcast stations:** 1 (1997)

## Niue (continued)

Internet country code: .nu
Internet hosts: 382,599 (2008)
Internet users: 900 (2002)

### Transportation

Airports: 1 (2008)
Airports - with paved runways:
*total:* 1
*1,524 to 2,437 m:* 1 (2008)
Roadways:
*total:* 120 km
*paved:* 120 km (2008)
Ports and terminals: none; offshore anchorage only

### Military

Military branches: no regular indigenous military forces; Police Force
Military - note: defense is the responsibility of New Zealand

### Transnational Issues

Disputes - international: none

# Norfolk Island
*(territory of Australia)*

### Introduction

Background: Two British attempts at establishing the island as a penal colony (1788-1814 and 1825-55) were ultimately abandoned. In 1856, the island was resettled by Pitcairn Islanders, descendants of the Bounty mutineers and their Tahitian companions.

### Geography

Location: Oceania, island in the South Pacific Ocean, east of Australia
Geographic coordinates: 29 02 S, 167 57 E
Map references: Oceania
Area:
*total:* 34.6 sq km
*land:* 34.6 sq km
*water:* 0 sq km
Area - comparative: about 0.2 times the size of Washington, DC
Land boundaries: 0 km
Coastline: 32 km
Maritime claims:
*territorial sea:* 12 nm
*exclusive fishing zone:* 200 nm
Climate: subtropical; mild, little seasonal temperature variation
Terrain: volcanic formation with mostly rolling plains
Elevation extremes:
*lowest point:* Pacific Ocean 0 m
*highest point:* Mount Bates 319 m
Natural resources: fish
Land use:
*arable land:* 0%
*permanent crops:* 0%
*other:* 100% (2005)
Irrigated land: NA
Natural hazards: typhoons (especially May to July)
Environment - current issues: NA

Geography - note: most of the 32 km coastline consists of almost inaccessible cliffs, but the land slopes down to the sea in one small southern area on Sydney Bay, where the capital of Kingston is situated

### People

Population: 2,141 (July 2009 est.)
Age structure:
*0-14 years:* 20.2%
*15-64 years:* 63.9%
*65 years and over:* 15.9% (2009 est.)
Population growth rate: 0.006% (2009 est.)
Birth rate: NA
Death rate: NA
Net migration rate: NA
Sex ratio: NA
Infant mortality rate:
*total:* NA
*male:* NA
*female:* NA (2008 est.)
Life expectancy at birth:
*total population:* NA
*male:* NA
*female:* NA
Total fertility rate: NA
HIV/AIDS - adult prevalence rate: NA
HIV/AIDS - people living with HIV/AIDS: NA
HIV/AIDS - deaths: NA
Nationality:
*noun:* Norfolk Islander(s)
*adjective:* Norfolk Islander(s)
Ethnic groups: descendants of the Bounty mutineers, Australian, New Zealander, Polynesian
Religions: Anglican 31.8%, Roman Catholic 11.5%, Uniting Church in Australia 10.6%, Seventh-Day Adventist 3.2%, other Christian 5.6%, none 19.9%, unspecified 16.6% (2006 census)
Languages: English (official), Norfolk - a mixture of 18th century English and ancient Tahitian
Literacy: NA
Education expenditures: NA

### Government

Country name:
*conventional long form:* Territory of Norfolk Island
*conventional short form:* Norfolk Island
Dependency status: self governing territory of Australia; administered from Canberra by the Australian Government Attorney-General's Department
Government type: NA
Capital:
*name:* Kingston
*geographic coordinates:* 29 03 S, 167 58 E
*time difference:* UTC+11.5 (16.5 hours ahead of Washington, DC during Standard Time)
Administrative divisions: none (territory of Australia)
Independence: none (territory of Australia)
National holiday: Bounty Day (commemorates the arrival of Pitcairn Islanders), 8 June (1856)

# Norfolk Island (continued)

**Constitution:** Norfolk Island Act of 1979 as amended in 2005

**Legal system:** based on the laws of Australia, local ordinances and acts; English common law applies in matters not covered by either Australian or Norfolk Island law

**Suffrage:** 18 years of age; universal

**Executive branch:**

*chief of state:* Queen ELIZABETH II (since 6 February 1952); represented by the Australian governor general

*head of government:* Acting Administrator Owen WALSH (since October 2007)

*cabinet:* Executive Council is made up of four of the nine members of the Legislative Assembly; the council devises government policy and acts as an advisor to the administrator

*elections:* the monarch is hereditary; administrator appointed by the governor general of Australia and represents the monarch and Australia

**Legislative branch:** unicameral Legislative Assembly (9 seats; members elected by electors who have nine equal votes each but only four votes can be given to any one candidate; to serve three-year terms)

*elections:* last held 21 March 2007 (next to be held by 28 March 2010)

*election results:* seats - independents 9 (note - no political parties)

**Judicial branch:** Supreme Court; Court of Petty Sessions

**Political parties and leaders:** none

**Political pressure groups and leaders:** none

**International organization participation:** UPU

**Diplomatic representation in the US:** none (territory of Australia)

**Diplomatic representation from the US:** none (territory of Australia)

**Flag description:** three vertical bands of green (hoist side), white, and green with a large green Norfolk Island pine tree centered in the slightly wider white band

## Economy

**Economy - overview:** Tourism, the primary economic activity, has steadily increased over the years and has brought a level of prosperity unusual among inhabitants of the Pacific islands. The agricultural sector has become self sufficient in the production of beef, poultry, and eggs.

**GDP (purchasing power parity):** $NA

**Labor force:** NA

**Labor force - by occupation:**

*agriculture:* 10%

*industry and services:* 90%

**Budget:**

*revenues:* $4.6 million

*expenditures:* $4.8 million (FY99/00)

**Agriculture - products:** Norfolk Island pine seed, Kentia palm seed, cereals, vegetables, fruit; cattle, poultry

**Industries:** tourism, light industry, ready mixed concrete

**Electricity - production:** NA kWh

**Electricity - consumption:** NA kWh

**Exports:** $1.5 million f.o.b. (FY91/92)

**Exports - commodities:** postage stamps, seeds of the Norfolk Island pine and Kentia palm, small quantities of avocados

**Imports:** $17.9 million c.i.f. (FY91/92)

**Imports - commodities:** NA

**Debt - external:** $NA

**Exchange rates:** Australian dollars (AUD) per US dollar - 1.2059 (2008 est.), 1.2137 (2007), 1.3285 (2006), 1.3095 (2005), 1.3598 (2004)

## Communications

**Telephones - main lines in use:** 2,532; note - a mix of analog (2,500) and digital (32) circuits (2004)

**Telephones - mobile cellular:** 0; note - proposed cellular service disallowed in August 2002 island referendum (2002)

**Telephone system:**

*general assessment:* adequate

*domestic:* free local calls

*international:* country code - 672; undersea coaxial cable links with Australia and New Zealand; satellite earth station - 1

**Radio broadcast stations:** AM 1, FM 3, shortwave 0 (2005)

**Television broadcast stations:** 1 (local programming station plus 2 repeaters that air Australian programs by satellite) (2005)

**Internet country code:** .nf

**Internet hosts:** 51 (2008)

**Internet users:** 700 (2002 est.)

## Transportation

**Airports:** 1 (2008)

**Airports - with paved runways:**

*total:* 1

*1,524 to 2,437 m:* 1 (2008)

**Roadways:**

*total:* 80 km

*paved:* 53 km

*unpaved:* 27 km (2008)

**Ports and terminals:** none; loading jetties at Kingston and Cascade

## Military

**Military - note:** defense is the responsibility of Australia

## Transnational Issues

**Disputes - international:** none

# Northern Mariana Islands
*(commonwealth in political union with the US)*

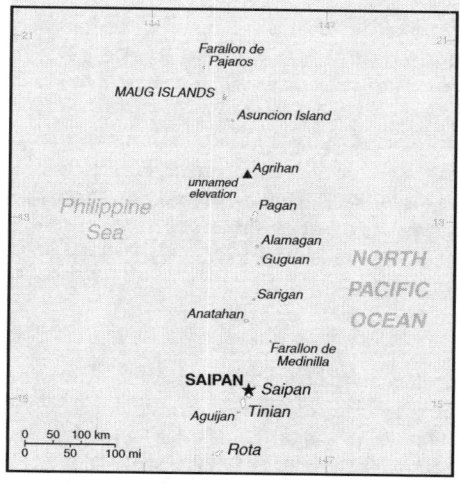

## Introduction

**Background:** Under US administration as part of the UN Trust Territory of the Pacific, the people of the Northern Mariana Islands decided in the 1970s not to seek independence but instead to forge closer links with the US. Negotiations for territorial status began in 1972. A covenant to establish a commonwealth in political union with the US was approved in 1975, and came into force on 24 March 1976. A new government and constitution went into effect in 1978.

## Geography

**Location:** Oceania, islands in the North Pacific Ocean, about three-quarters of the way from Hawaii to the Philippines

**Geographic coordinates:** 15 12 N, 145 45 E

**Map references:** Oceania

**Area:**

*total:* 477 sq km

*land:* 477 sq km

*water:* 0 sq km

*note:* consists of 14 islands including Saipan, Rota, and Tinian

**Area - comparative:** 2.5 times the size of Washington, DC

**Land boundaries:** 0 km

**Coastline:** 1,482 km

**Maritime claims:**

*territorial sea:* 12 nm

*exclusive economic zone:* 200 nm

**Climate:** tropical marine; moderated by northeast trade winds, little seasonal temperature variation; dry season December to June, rainy season July to October

**Terrain:** southern islands are limestone with level terraces and fringing coral reefs; northern islands are volcanic

**Elevation extremes:**

*lowest point:* Pacific Ocean 0 m

*highest point:* unnamed location on Agrihan 965 m

**Natural resources:** arable land, fish
**Land use:**
*arable land:* 13.04%
*permanent crops:* 4.35%
*other:* 82.61% (2005)
**Irrigated land:** NA
**Natural hazards:** active volcanoes on Pagan and Agrihan; typhoons (especially August to November)
**Environment - current issues:** contamination of groundwater on Saipan may contribute to disease; clean-up of landfill; protection of endangered species conflicts with development
**Geography - note:** strategic location in the North Pacific Ocean

## People

**Population:** 88,662 (July 2009 est.)
**Age structure:**
*0-14 years:* 18% (male 8,372/female 7,616)
*15-64 years:* 80.3% (male 28,602/female 42,557)
*65 years and over:* 1.7% (male 786/female 729) (2009 est.)
**Median age:**
*total:* 30.1 years
*male:* 32.1 years
*female:* 29.2 years (2009 est.)
**Population growth rate:** 2.292% (2009 est.)
**Birth rate:** 18.77 births/1,000 population (2009 est.)
**Death rate:** 2.31 deaths/1,000 population (2008 est.)
**Net migration rate:** 6.47 migrant(s)/1,000 population (2009 est.)
**Urbanization:**
*urban population:* 91% of total population (2008)
*rate of urbanization:* 2.1% annual rate of change (2005-10 est.)
**Sex ratio:**
*at birth:* 1.06 male(s)/female
*under 15 years:* 1.1 male(s)/female
*15-64 years:* 0.67 male(s)/female
*65 years and over:* 1.08 male(s)/female
*total population:* 0.74 male(s)/female (2009 est.)
**Infant mortality rate:**
*total:* 6.59 deaths/1,000 live births
*male:* 6.56 deaths/1,000 live births
*female:* 6.63 deaths/1,000 live births (2009 est.)
**Life expectancy at birth:**
*total population:* 76.7 years
*male:* 74.08 years
*female:* 79.47 years (2009 est.)
**Total fertility rate:** 1.15 children born/woman (2009 est.)
**HIV/AIDS - adult prevalence rate:** NA
**HIV/AIDS - people living with HIV/AIDS:** NA
**HIV/AIDS - deaths:** NA
**Nationality:**
*noun:* NA (US citizens)
*adjective:* NA
**Ethnic groups:** Asian 56.3%, Pacific islander 36.3%, Caucasian 1.8%, other 0.8%, mixed 4.8% (2000 census)

**Religions:** Christian (Roman Catholic majority, although traditional beliefs and taboos may still be found)
**Languages:** Philippine languages 24.4%, Chinese 23.4%, Chamorro 22.4%, English 10.8%, other Pacific island languages 9.5%, other 9.6% (2000 census)
**Literacy:**
*definition:* age 15 and over can read and write
*total population:* 97%
*male:* 97%
*female:* 96% (1980 est.)
**Education expenditures:** NA

## Government

**Country name:**
*conventional long form:* Commonwealth of the Northern Mariana Islands
*conventional short form:* Northern Mariana Islands
*abbreviation:* CNMI
*former:* Trust Territory of the Pacific Islands, Mariana Islands District
**Dependency status:** commonwealth in political union with the US; federal funds to the Commonwealth administered by the US Department of the Interior, Office of Insular Affairs
**Government type:** commonwealth; self-governing with locally elected governor, lieutenant governor, and legislature
**Capital:**
*name:* Saipan
*geographic coordinates:* 15 12 N, 145 45 E
*time difference:* UTC+10 (15 hours ahead of Washington, DC during Standard Time)
**Administrative divisions:** none (commonwealth in political union with the US); there are no first-order administrative divisions as defined by the US Government, but there are four municipalities at the second order: Northern Islands, Rota, Saipan, Tinian
**Independence:** none (commonwealth in political union with the US)
**National holiday:** Commonwealth Day, 8 January (1978)
**Constitution:** Constitution of the Commonwealth of the Northern Mariana Islands effective 1 January 1978; Covenant Agreement fully effective 4 November 1986
**Legal system:** based on US system, except for customs, wages, immigration laws, and taxation
**Suffrage:** 18 years of age; universal; indigenous inhabitants are US citizens but do not vote in US presidential elections
**Executive branch:**
*chief of state:* President Barack H. OBAMA (since 20 January 2009); Vice President Joseph R. BIDEN (since 20 January 2009)
*head of government:* Governor Benigno R. FITIAL (since 9 January 2006); Lieutenant Governor Eloy S. INOS (since 1 May 2009)
*cabinet:* the cabinet consists of the heads of the 10 principal departments under the executive branch who are appointed by the governor with the advice and

consent of the Senate; other members include Special Assistants to the governor and office heads appointed by and reporting directly to the governor
*elections:* under the US Constitution, residents of unincorporated territories, such as the Commonwealth of the Northern Mariana Islands, do not vote in elections for US president and vice president; however, they may vote in the Democratic and Republican party presidential primary elections; governor and lieutenant governor elected on the same ticket by popular vote for four-year terms (eligible for a second term); election last held 5 November 2005 (next to be held in November 2009)
*election results:* Benigno R. FITIAL elected governor; percent of vote - Benigno R. FITIAL 28.07%, Heinz HOFSCHNEIDER 27.34%, Juan BABAUTA 26.6%, Froilan TENORIO 17.99%
**Legislative branch:** bicameral legislature consists of the Senate (9 seats; members are elected by popular vote to serve four-year staggered terms) and the House of Representatives (20 seats; members are elected by popular vote to serve two-year terms)
*elections:* Senate - last held 3 November 2007 (next to be held in November 2009); House of Representatives - last held 3 November 2007 (next to be held in November 2009)
*election results:* Senate - percent of vote by party - NA; seats by party - Covenant Party 3, Republican Party 3, Democratic Party 1, independents 2; House of Representatives - percent of vote by party - NA; seats by party - Republican Party 12, Covenant Party 4, Democratic Party 1, independents 3
*note:* the Northern Mariana Islands elects one nonvoting delegate to the US House of Representatives; election last held 4 November 2008 (next to be held in November 2010); seats by party - independent 1
**Judicial branch:** Commonwealth Supreme Court; Superior Court; Federal District Court
**Political parties and leaders:** Covenant Party [Benigno R. FITIAL]; Democratic Party [Dr. Carlos S. CAMACHO]; Republican Party [Juan S. REYES]
**Political pressure groups and leaders:** NA
**International organization participation:** SPC, UPU
**Flag description:** blue, with a white, five-pointed star superimposed on the gray silhouette of a latte stone (a traditional foundation stone used in building) in the center, surrounded by a wreath

## Economy

**Economy - overview:** The economy benefits substantially from financial assistance from the US. The rate of funding has declined as locally generated government revenues have grown. The key tourist industry employs about 50% of the work force and accounts for roughly one-fourth of GDP. Japanese tourists predominate. Annual tourist entries have exceeded one-half million in recent years, but financial difficulties in Japan have caused a temporary slowdown. The agricultural sector is made up of cattle ranches and small farms producing coconuts, breadfruit, tomatoes, and melons. Garment production is by far the most important industry with the employment of 17,500 mostly Chinese workers and sizable shipments to the US under duty and quota exemptions.

**GDP (purchasing power parity):**
$900 million (2000 est.)
*note:* GDP estimate includes US subsidy

**GDP (official exchange rate):** $633.4 million (2000)

**GDP - real growth rate:** NA%

**GDP - per capita (PPP):**
$12,500 (2000 est.)

**GDP - composition by sector:**
*agriculture:* NA%
*industry:* NA%
*services:* NA%

**Labor force:** 38,450 total indigenous labor force; 2,699 unemployed; 28,717 foreign workers (2005 est.)

**Labor force - by occupation:**
*agriculture:* NA%
*industry:* NA%
*services:* NA%

**Unemployment rate:**
8% (2005 est.)
3.9% (2001)

**Population below poverty line:** NA%

**Household income or consumption by percentage share:**
*lowest 10%:* NA%
*highest 10%:* NA%

**Budget:**
*revenues:* $193 million
*expenditures:* $223 million (FY01/02 est.)

**Inflation rate (consumer prices):**
-0.8% (2000)

**Agriculture - products:** vegetables and melons, fruits and nuts, ornamental plants, livestock, poultry and eggs, fish and aquaculture products

**Industries:** banking, construction, fishing, garment, tourism, handicrafts

**Industrial production growth rate:** NA%

**Electricity - production:** 60,600 kWh (January 2009)

**Electricity - consumption:** 48,300 kWh (January 2009)

**Electricity - exports:** 0 kWh (January 2009 est.)

**Electricity - imports:** 0 kWh (January 2009 est.)

**Exports:** $98.2 million (2008)

**Exports - commodities:** garments

**Imports:** $214.4 million c.i.f. (2001)

**Imports - commodities:** food, construction equipment and materials, petroleum products

**Debt - external:** $NA

**Exchange rates:** the US dollar is used

**Telephones - main lines in use:** 21,000 (2000)

**Telephones - mobile cellular:** 20,500 (2004)

**Telephone system:**
*general assessment:* NA
*domestic:* NA
*international:* country code - 1-670; satellite earth stations - 2 Intelsat (Pacific Ocean)

**Radio broadcast stations:** AM 1, FM 6, shortwave 1 (2005)

**Television broadcast stations:** 1 (on Saipan; in addition, 2 cable services on Saipan provide varied programming from satellite networks) (2006)

**Internet country code:** .mp

**Internet hosts:** 6 (2008)

**Internet users:** 10,000 (2003)

**Airports:** 5 (2008)

**Airports - with paved runways:**
*total:* 3
*2,438 to 3,047 m:* 2
*1,524 to 2,437 m:* 1 (2008)

**Airports - with unpaved runways:**
*total:* 2
*2,438 to 3,047 m:* 1
*under 914 m:* 1 (2008)

**Heliports:** 1 (2007)

**Roadways:**
*total:* 536 km (2007)

**Ports and terminals:** Saipan, Tinian

**Manpower fit for military service:**
*males age 16-49:* 19,209
*females age 16-49:* 33,074 (2009 est.)

**Manpower reaching militarily significant age annually:**
*male:* 570
*female:* 587 (2009 est.)

**Military - note:** defense is the responsibility of the US

**Disputes - international:** none

# Norway

**Background:** Two centuries of Viking raids into Europe tapered off following the adoption of Christianity by King Olav TRYGGVASON in 994. Conversion of the Norwegian kingdom occurred over the next several decades. In 1397, Norway was absorbed into a union with Denmark that lasted more than four centuries. In 1814, Norwegians resisted the cession of their country to Sweden and adopted a new constitution. Sweden then invaded Norway but agreed to let Norway keep its constitution in return for accepting the union under a Swedish king. Rising nationalism throughout the 19th century led to a 1905 referendum granting Norway independence. Although Norway remained neutral in World War I, it suffered heavy losses to its shipping. Norway proclaimed its neutrality at the outset of World War II, but was nonetheless occupied for five years by Nazi Germany (1940-45). In 1949, neutrality was abandoned and Norway became a member of NATO. Discovery of oil and gas in adjacent waters in the late 1960s boosted Norway's economic fortunes. The current focus is on

## Norway *(continued)*

containing spending on the extensive welfare system and planning for the time when petroleum reserves are depleted. In referenda held in 1972 and 1994, Norway rejected joining the EU.

### Geography

**Location:** Northern Europe, bordering the North Sea and the North Atlantic Ocean, west of Sweden
**Geographic coordinates:** 62 00 N, 10 00 E
**Map references:** Europe
**Area:**
*total:* 323,802 sq km
*land:* 307,442 sq km
*water:* 16,360 sq km
**Area - comparative:** slightly larger than New Mexico
**Land boundaries:**
*total:* 2,542 km
*border countries:* Finland 727 km, Sweden 1,619 km, Russia 196 km
**Coastline:** 25,148 km (includes mainland 2,650 km, as well as long fjords, numerous small islands, and minor indentations 22,498 km; length of island coastlines 58,133 km)
**Maritime claims:**
*territorial sea:* 12 nm
*contiguous zone:* 10 nm
*exclusive economic zone:* 200 nm
*continental shelf:* 200 nm
**Climate:** temperate along coast, modified by North Atlantic Current; colder interior with increased precipitation and colder summers; rainy year-round on west coast
**Terrain:** glaciated; mostly high plateaus and rugged mountains broken by fertile valleys; small, scattered plains; coastline deeply indented by fjords; arctic tundra in north
**Elevation extremes:**
*lowest point:* Norwegian Sea 0 m
*highest point:* Galdhopiggen 2,469 m
**Natural resources:** petroleum, natural gas, iron ore, copper, lead, zinc, titanium, pyrites, nickel, fish, timber, hydropower
**Land use:**
*arable land:* 2.7%
*permanent crops:* 0%
*other:* 97.3% (2005)
**Irrigated land:** 1,270 sq km (2003)
**Total renewable water resources:** 381.4 cu km (2005)
**Freshwater withdrawal (domestic/industrial/agricultural):**
*total:* 2.4 cu km/yr (23%/67%/10%)
*per capita:* 519 cu m/yr (1996)
**Natural hazards:** rockslides, avalanches
**Environment - current issues:** water pollution; acid rain damaging forests and adversely affecting lakes, threatening fish stocks; air pollution from vehicle emissions

**Environment - international agreements:**
*party to:* Air Pollution, Air Pollution-Nitrogen Oxides, Air Pollution-Persistent Organic Pollutants, Air Pollution-Sulfur 85, Air Pollution-Sulfur 94, Air Pollution-Volatile Organic Compounds, Antarctic-Environmental Protocol, Antarctic-Marine Living Resources, Antarctic Seals, Antarctic Treaty, Biodiversity, Climate Change, Climate Change-Kyoto Protocol, Desertification, Endangered Species, Environmental Modification, Hazardous Wastes, Law of the Sea, Marine Dumping, Ozone Layer Protection, Ship Pollution, Tropical Timber 83, Tropical Timber 94, Wetlands, Whaling
*signed, but not ratified:* none of the selected agreements
**Geography - note:** about two-thirds mountains; some 50,000 islands off its much-indented coastline; strategic location adjacent to sea lanes and air routes in North Atlantic; one of the most rugged and longest coastlines in the world

### People

**Population:** 4,660,539 (July 2009 est.)
**Age structure:**
*0-14 years:* 18.5% (male 441,508/female 422,050)
*15-64 years:* 66.2% (male 1,564,482/female 1,522,519)
*65 years and over:* 15.2% (male 305,120/female 404,860) (2009 est.)
**Median age:**
*total:* 39.4 years
*male:* 38.5 years
*female:* 40.2 years (2009 est.)
**Population growth rate:** 0.341% (2009 est.)
**Birth rate:** 10.99 births/1,000 population (2009 est.)
**Death rate:** 9.33 deaths/1,000 population (2008 est.)
**Net migration rate:** 1.71 migrant(s)/1,000 population (2009 est.)
**Urbanization:**
*urban population:* 77% of total population (2008)
*rate of urbanization:* 0.7% annual rate of change (2005-10 est.)
**Sex ratio:**
*at birth:* 1.05 male(s)/female
*under 15 years:* 1.05 male(s)/female
*15-64 years:* 1.03 male(s)/female
*65 years and over:* 0.75 male(s)/female
*total population:* 0.98 male(s)/female (2009 est.)
**Infant mortality rate:**
*total:* 3.58 deaths/1,000 live births
*male:* 3.92 deaths/1,000 live births
*female:* 3.22 deaths/1,000 live births (2009 est.)
**Life expectancy at birth:**
*total population:* 79.95 years
*male:* 77.29 years
*female:* 82.74 years (2009 est.)
**Total fertility rate:** 1.78 children born/woman (2009 est.)
**HIV/AIDS - adult prevalence rate:** 0.1% (2007 est.)

**HIV/AIDS - people living with HIV/AIDS:** 3,000 (2007 est.)
**HIV/AIDS - deaths:** fewer than 100 (2003 est.)
**Nationality:**
*noun:* Norwegian(s)
*adjective:* Norwegian
**Ethnic groups:** Norwegian 94.4% (includes Sami, about 60,000), other European 3.6%, other 2% (2007 estimate)
**Religions:** Church of Norway 85.7%, Pentecostal 1%, Roman Catholic 1%, other Christian 2.4%, Muslim 1.8%, other 8.1% (2004)
**Languages:** Bokmal Norwegian (official), Nynorsk Norwegian (official), small Sami- and Finnish-speaking minorities; note - Sami is official in six municipalities
**Literacy:**
*definition:* age 15 and over can read and write
*total population:* 100%
*male:* 100%
*female:* 100%
**School life expectancy (primary to tertiary education):**
*total:* 17 years
*male:* 17 years
*female:* 18 years (2006)
**Education expenditures:** 7.2% of GDP (2005)

### Government

**Country name:**
*conventional long form:* Kingdom of Norway
*conventional short form:* Norway
*local long form:* Kongeriket Norge
*local short form:* Norge
**Government type:** constitutional monarchy
**Capital:**
*name:* Oslo
*geographic coordinates:* 59 55 N, 10 45 E
*time difference:* UTC+1 (6 hours ahead of Washington, DC during Standard Time)
*daylight saving time:* +1hr, begins last Sunday in March; ends last Sunday in October
**Administrative divisions:** 19 counties (fylker, singular - fylke); Akershus, Aust-Agder, Buskerud, Finnmark, Hedmark, Hordaland, More og Romsdal, Nordland, Nord-Trondelag, Oppland, Oslo, Ostfold, Rogaland, Sogn og Fjordane, Sor-Trondelag, Telemark, Troms, Vest-Agder, Vestfold
**Dependent areas:** Bouvet Island, Jan Mayen, Svalbard
**Independence:** 7 June 1905 (Norway declared the union with Sweden dissolved); 26 October 1905 (Sweden agreed to the repeal of the union)
**National holiday:** Constitution Day, 17 May (1814)
**Constitution:** 17 May 1814; amended many times
**Legal system:** mixture of customary law, civil law system, and common law traditions; Supreme Court renders advisory opinions to legislature when asked; accepts compulsory ICJ jurisdiction with reservations

# Norway (continued)

**Suffrage:** 18 years of age; universal

**Executive branch:**

*chief of state:* King HARALD V (since 17 January 1991); Heir Apparent Crown Prince HAAKON MAGNUS, son of the monarch (born 20 July 1973)

*head of government:* Prime Minister Jens STOLTENBERG (since 17 October 2005)

*cabinet:* State Council appointed by the monarch with the approval of parliament

*elections:* the monarch is hereditary; following parliamentary elections, the leader of the majority party or the leader of the majority coalition is usually appointed prime minister by the monarch with the approval of the parliament

**Legislative branch:** modified unicameral Parliament or Storting (169 seats; members are elected by popular vote by proportional representation to serve four-year terms); note - in 2009 the number of seats will change to 165

*elections:* last held 12 September 2005 (next to be held in September 2009)

*election results:* percent of vote by party - Labor Party 32.7%, Progress Party 22.1%, Conservative Party 14.1%, Socialist Left Party 8.8%, Christian People's Party 6.8%, Center Party 6.5%, Liberal Party 5.9%, other 3.1%; seats by party - Labor Party 61, Progress Party 38, Conservative Party 23, Socialist Left Party 15, Christian People's Party 11, Center Party 11, Liberal Party 10

*note:* for certain purposes, the parliament divides itself into two chambers and elects one-fourth of its membership in the Lagting and three-fourths of its membership in the Odelsting

**Judicial branch:** Supreme Court or Hoyesterett (justices appointed by the monarch)

**Political parties and leaders:** Center Party [Liv Signe NAVARSETE]; Christian People's Party [Dagfinn HOYBRATEN]; Conservative Party [Erna SOLBERG]; Labor Party [Jens STOLTENBERG]; Liberal Party [Lars SPONHEIM]; Progress Party [Siv JENSEN]; Socialist Left Party [Kristin HALVORSEN]

**Political pressure groups and leaders:** Norwegian Aid Committee or NORWAC; Norwegian Association of the Disabled; Pure Salmon Campaign; The Consumer Council (consumer advocacy group)

*other:* environmental groups; media; reform movements

**International organization participation:** ADB (nonregional member), AfDB (nonregional member), Arctic Council, Australia Group, BIS, CBSS, CE, CERN, EAPC, EBRD, EFTA, ESA, FAO, IADB, IAEA, IBRD, ICAO, ICC, ICCt, ICRM, IDA, IEA, IFAD, IFC, IFRCS, IHO, ILO, IMF, IMO, IMSO, Interpol, IOC, IOM, IPU, ISO, ITSO, ITU, ITUC, MIGA, NAM (guest), NATO, NC, NEA, NIB, NSG, OAS (observer), OECD, OPCW, OSCE, Paris Club, PCA, Schengen Convention, UN, UNCTAD, UNESCO, UNHCR, UNIDO, UNIFIL, UNITAR, UNMIS, UNRWA, UNTSO, UNWTO, UPU, WCO, WEU (associate), WFTU, WHO, WIPO, WMO, WTO, ZC

**Diplomatic representation in the US:**

*chief of mission:* Ambassador Wegger C. STROMMEN

*chancery:* 2720 34th Street NW, Washington, DC 20008

*telephone:* [1] (202) 333-6000

*FAX:* [1] (202) 337-0870

*consulate(s) general:* Houston, Minneapolis, New York, San Francisco

**Diplomatic representation from the US:**

*chief of mission:* Ambassador Benson K. WHITNEY

*embassy:* Henrik Ibsens gate 48, 0244 Oslo; note - the embassy will move to Huseby in the near future

*mailing address:* PSC 69, Box 1000, APO AE 09707

*telephone:* [47] (22) 44 85 50

*FAX:* [47] (22) 44 33 63, 56 27 51

**Flag description:** red with a blue cross outlined in white that extends to the edges of the flag; the vertical part of the cross is shifted to the hoist side in the style of the Dannebrog (Danish flag)

## Economy

**Economy - overview:** The Norwegian economy is a prosperous bastion of welfare capitalism, featuring a combination of free market activity and government intervention. The government controls key areas, such as the vital petroleum sector, through large-scale state enterprises. The country is richly endowed with natural resources - petroleum, hydropower, fish, forests, and minerals - and is highly dependent on the petroleum sector, which accounts for nearly half of exports and over 30% of state revenue. Norway is the world's third-largest gas exporter; its position as an oil exporter has slipped to seventh-largest as production has begun to decline. Norway opted to stay out of the EU during a referendum in November 1994; nonetheless, as a member of the European Economic Area, it contributes sizably to the EU budget. In anticipation of eventual declines in oil and gas production, Norway saves almost all state revenue from the petroleum sector in a sovereign wealth fund. After lackluster growth of less than 1.5% in 2002-03, GDP growth picked up to 2.5-6.2% in 2004-07, partly due to higher oil prices. Growth fell to 2.3% in 2008 as a result of the slowing world economy and the drop in oil prices.

**GDP (purchasing power parity):**
$256.5 billion (2008 est.)
$252 billion (2007)
$243 billion (2006)
*note:* data are in 2008 US dollars

**GDP (official exchange rate):** $481.1 billion (2008 est.)

**GDP - real growth rate:**
1.8% (2008 est.)
3.7% (2007 est.)
2.5% (2006 est.)

**GDP - per capita (PPP):**
$55,200 (2008 est.)
$54,400 (2007 est.)
$52,700 (2006 est.)
*note:* data are in 2008 US dollars

**GDP - composition by sector:**
*agriculture:* 2.4%
*industry:* 40.7%
*services:* 56.8% (2008 est.)

**Labor force:** 2.59 million (2008 est.)

**Labor force - by occupation:**
*agriculture:* 2.9%
*industry:* 21.1%
*services:* 76% (2008)

**Unemployment rate:**
2.6% (2008 est.)
2.5% (2007 est.)

**Population below poverty line:** NA%

**Household income or consumption by percentage share:**
*lowest 10%:* 3.9%
*highest 10%:* 23.4% (2000)

**Distribution of family income - Gini index:** 25 (2008)

**Investment (gross fixed):** 20.3% of GDP (2008 est.)

**Budget:**
*revenues:* $283.7 billion
*expenditures:* $197 billion (2008 est.)

**Public debt:** 52% of GDP (2007)

**Inflation rate (consumer prices):**
3.6% (2008 est.)
0.8% (2007 est.)

**Central bank discount rate:** 2.5% (1st quarter 2009)

**Commercial bank prime lending rate:** 3.5% (1st quarter 2009)

**Stock of money:** NA

**Stock of quasi money:** NA

**Stock of domestic credit:** NA

**Market value of publicly traded shares:** $142.5 billion (31 December 2008)

**Agriculture - products:** barley, wheat, potatoes; pork, beef, veal, milk; fish

**Industries:** petroleum and gas, food processing, shipbuilding, pulp and paper products, metals, chemicals, timber, mining, textiles, fishing

**Industrial production growth rate:** 0.2% (2008 est.)

**Electricity - production:** 142.7 billion kWh (2008 est.)

**Electricity - consumption:** 128.8 billion kWh (2008 est.)

**Electricity - exports:** 17.3 billion kWh (2008 est.)

**Electricity - imports:** 3.45 billion kWh (2008 est.)

**Oil - production:** 2.565 million bbl/day (2007 est.)

**Oil - consumption:** 224,500 bbl/day (2007 est.)

**Oil - exports:** 2.31 million bbl/day (2007)

**Oil - imports:** 92,650 bbl/day (2005)

**Oil - proved reserves:** 6.865 billion bbl (1 January 2008 est.)

**Natural gas - production:** 99.3 billion cu m (2008 est.)

**Natural gas - consumption:** 6.5 billion cu m (2007 est.)

**Natural gas - exports:** 85.7 billion cu m (2007 est.)

**Natural gas - imports:** 0 cu m (2007 est.)

**Natural gas - proved reserves:** 2.241 trillion cu m (1 January 2008 est.)

**Current account balance:** $84.35 billion (2008 est.)

**Exports:** $177.6 billion f.o.b. (2008 est.)

**Exports - commodities:** petroleum and petroleum products, machinery and equipment, metals, chemicals, ships, fish

**Exports - partners:** UK 26.3%, Germany 12.3%, Netherlands 10.2%, France 8%, Sweden 6.5%, US 6.2% (2007)

**Imports:** $93.21 billion f.o.b. (2008 est.)

**Imports - commodities:** machinery and equipment, chemicals, metals, foodstuffs

**Imports - partners:** Sweden 14.7%, Germany 13.6%, UK 6.9%, Denmark 6.4%, China 6.1%, US 4.8%, Canada 4.3% (2007)

**Reserves of foreign exchange and gold:** $60.84 billion (2006 est.)

**Debt - external:** $469.1 billion; note - Norway is a net external creditor (30 June 2007)

**Stock of direct foreign investment - at home:** $69.04 billion (2008 est.)

**Stock of direct foreign investment - abroad:** $142.3 billion (2008 est.)

**Exchange rates:** Norwegian kroner (NOK) per US dollar - 5.6361 (2008), 5.86 (2007), 6.418 (2006), 6.445 (2005), 6.7327 (2004)

## Communications

**Telephones - main lines in use:** 1.988 million (2007)

**Telephones - mobile cellular:** 5.192 million (2007)

**Telephone system:**

*general assessment:* modern in all respects; one of the most advanced telecommunications networks in Europe

*domestic:* Norway has a domestic satellite system; moreover, the prevalence of rural areas encourages the wide use of cellular-mobile systems instead of fixed-wire systems

*international:* country code - 47; 2 buried coaxial cable systems; submarine cables provide links to other Nordic countries and Europe; satellite earth stations - NA Eutelsat, NA Intelsat (Atlantic Ocean), and 1 Inmarsat (Atlantic and Indian Ocean regions); note - Norway shares the Inmarsat earth station with the other Nordic countries (Denmark, Finland, Iceland, and Sweden) (1999)

**Radio broadcast stations:** AM 5, FM 160, shortwave 1 (2008)

**Television broadcast stations:** 69 (2008)

**Internet country code:** .no

**Internet hosts:** 2.995 million (2008)

**Internet users:** 3.8 million (2007)

## Transportation

**Airports:** 98 (2008)

**Airports - with paved runways:**

*total:* 67

*2,438 to 3,047 m:* 13

*1,524 to 2,437 m:* 12

*914 to 1,523 m:* 15

*under 914 m:* 27 (2008)

**Airports - with unpaved runways:**

*total:* 31

*914 to 1,523 m:* 6

*under 914 m:* 25 (2008)

**Heliports:** 1 (2007)

**Pipelines:** condensate 31 km; gas 64 km (2008)

**Railways:**

*total:* 4,114 km

*standard gauge:* 4,114 km 1.435-m gauge (2,552 km electrified) (2008)

**Roadways:**

*total:* 92,946 km

*paved:* 72,033 km (includes 664 km of expressways)

*unpaved:* 20,913 km (2007)

**Waterways:** 1,577 km (2008)

**Merchant marine:**

*total:* 688

*by type:* bulk carrier 46, cargo 141, carrier 3, chemical tanker 137, combination ore/oil 12, container 4, liquefied gas 65, passenger/cargo 117, petroleum tanker 85, refrigerated cargo 14, roll on/roll off 13, specialized tanker 1, vehicle carrier 50

*foreign-owned:* 199 (Canada 10, Chile 2, China 36, Denmark 25, Estonia 1, Finland 1, France 3, Germany 1, Greece 3, Hong Kong 20, Iceland 3, Italy 4, Japan 29, Lithuania 1, Malaysia 1, Monaco 5, Poland 3, Saudi Arabia 3, Singapore 1, Sweden 34, UK 5, US 8)

*registered in other countries:* 923 (Antigua and Barbuda 8, Australia 1, Bahamas 189, Barbados 38, Belize 3, Bermuda 5, Brazil 5, Canada 3, Cayman Islands 1, China 1, Comoros 1, Cook Islands 5, Cyprus 18, Denmark 3, Dominica 1, Estonia 2, Faroe Islands 4, Finland 3, France 5, Gibraltar 33, Hong Kong 40, Indonesia 1, Isle of Man 20, Italy 2, South Korea 2, Liberia 40, Libya 1, Malta 93, Marshall Islands 66, Netherlands 12, Netherlands Antilles 3, Panama 89, Philippines 10, Russia 2, Saint Vincent and the Grenadines 13, Singapore 143, Spain 5, Sweden 7, Tuvalu 1, UK 31, US 9, unknown 4) (2008)

**Ports and terminals:** Bergen, Borg Havn, Haugesund, Maaloy, Mongstad, Narvik, Oslo, Sture

## Military

**Military branches:** Norwegian Army (Haeren), Royal Norwegian Navy (Kongelige Norske Sjoeforsvaret, RNoN; includes Coastal Rangers and Coast Guard (Kystvakt)), Royal Norwegian Air Force (Kongelige Norske Luftforsvaret, RNoAF), Home Guard (Heimevernet, HV) (2007)

**Military service age and obligation:** 18-44 years of age for male compulsory military service; 16 years of age in wartime; 17 years of age for male volunteers; 18 years of age for women; 12-month service obligation, in practice shortened to 8 to 9 months; although all males between ages of 18 and 44 are liable for service, in practice they are seldom called to duty after age 30; reserve obligation to age 35-60; 16 years of age for volunteers to the Home Guard, who serve 6-month duty tours (2009)

**Manpower available for military service:**

*males age 16-49:* 1,078,181

*females age 16-49:* 1,046,550 (2008 est.)

**Manpower fit for military service:**

*males age 16-49:* 888,219

*females age 16-49:* 863,255 (2009 est.)

**Manpower reaching militarily significant age annually:**

*male:* 31,980

*female:* 30,543 (2009 est.)

**Military expenditures:** 1.9% of GDP (2005 est.)

## Transnational Issues

**Disputes - international:** Norway asserts a territorial claim in Antarctica (Queen Maud Land and its continental shelf); despite dialogue, Russia and Norway continue to dispute their maritime limits in the Barents Sea and Russia's fishing rights beyond Svalbard's territorial limits within the Svalbard Treaty zone

# Oman

## Introduction

**Background:** The inhabitants of the area of Oman have long prospered on Indian Ocean trade. In the late 18th century, a newly established sultanate in Muscat signed the first in a series of friendship treaties with Britain. Over time, Oman's dependence on British political and military advisors increased, but it never became a British colony. In 1970, QABOOS bin Said al-Said overthrew the restrictive rule of his father; he has ruled as sultan ever since. His extensive modernization program has opened the country to the outside world while preserving the longstanding close ties with the UK. Oman's moderate, independent foreign policy has sought to maintain good relations with all Middle Eastern countries.

## Geography

**Location:** Middle East, bordering the Arabian Sea, Gulf of Oman, and Persian Gulf, between Yemen and UAE
**Geographic coordinates:** 21 00 N, 57 00 E
**Map references:** Middle East
**Area:**
*total:* 212,460 sq km
*land:* 212,460 sq km
*water:* 0 sq km
**Area - comparative:** slightly smaller than Kansas
**Land boundaries:**
*total:* 1,374 km
*border countries:* Saudi Arabia 676 km, UAE 410 km, Yemen 288 km
**Coastline:** 2,092 km
**Maritime claims:**
*territorial sea:* 12 nm
*contiguous zone:* 24 nm
*exclusive economic zone:* 200 nm
**Climate:** dry desert; hot, humid along coast; hot, dry interior; strong southwest summer monsoon (May to September) in far south

**Terrain:** central desert plain, rugged mountains in north and south
**Elevation extremes:**
*lowest point:* Arabian Sea 0 m
*highest point:* Jabal Shams 2,980 m
**Natural resources:** petroleum, copper, asbestos, some marble, limestone, chromium, gypsum, natural gas
**Land use:**
*arable land:* 0.12%
*permanent crops:* 0.14%
*other:* 99.74% (2005)
**Irrigated land:** 720 sq km (2003)
**Total renewable water resources:** 1 cu km (1997)
**Freshwater withdrawal (domestic/industrial/agricultural):**
*total:* 1.36 cu km/yr (7%/2%/90%)
*per capita:* 529 cu m/yr (2000)
**Natural hazards:** summer winds often raise large sandstorms and dust storms in interior; periodic droughts
**Environment - current issues:** rising soil salinity; beach pollution from oil spills; limited natural fresh water resources
**Environment - international agreements:**
*party to:* Biodiversity, Climate Change, Climate Change-Kyoto Protocol, Desertification, Hazardous Wastes, Law of the Sea, Marine Dumping, Ozone Layer Protection, Ship Pollution, Whaling
*signed, but not ratified:* none of the selected agreements
**Geography - note:** strategic location on Musandam Peninsula adjacent to Strait of Hormuz, a vital transit point for world crude oil

## People

**Population:** 3,418,085
*note:* includes 577,293 non-nationals (July 2009 est.)
**Age structure:**
*0-14 years:* 42.7% (male 744,265/female 714,116)
*15-64 years:* 54.5% (male 1,079,511/female 783,243)
*65 years and over:* 2.8% (male 55,180/female 41,770) (2009 est.)
**Median age:**
*total:* 18.8 years
*male:* 21.1 years
*female:* 16.7 years (2009 est.)
**Population growth rate:** 3.138% (2009 est.)
**Birth rate:** 34.79 births/1,000 population (2009 est.)
**Death rate:** 3.68 deaths/1,000 population (2008 est.)
**Net migration rate:** 0.24 migrant(s)/1,000 population (2009 est.)
**Urbanization:**
*urban population:* 72% of total population (2008)
*rate of urbanization:* 2% annual rate of change (2005-10 est.)
**Sex ratio:**
*at birth:* 1.05 male(s)/female
*under 15 years:* 1.04 male(s)/female
*15-64 years:* 1.38 male(s)/female
*65 years and over:* 1.32 male(s)/female
*total population:* 1.22 male(s)/female (2009 est.)

**Infant mortality rate:**
*total:* 16.88 deaths/1,000 live births
*male:* 19.29 deaths/1,000 live births
*female:* 14.35 deaths/1,000 live births (2009 est.)
**Life expectancy at birth:**
*total population:* 74.16 years
*male:* 71.87 years
*female:* 76.55 years (2009 est.)
**Total fertility rate:** 5.53 children born/woman (2009 est.)
**HIV/AIDS - adult prevalence rate:** 0.1% (2001 est.)
**HIV/AIDS - people living with HIV/AIDS:** 1,300 (2001 est.)
**HIV/AIDS - deaths:** fewer than 200 (2003 est.)
**Nationality:**
*noun:* Omani(s)
*adjective:* Omani
**Ethnic groups:** Arab, Baluchi, South Asian (Indian, Pakistani, Sri Lankan, Bangladeshi), African
**Religions:** Ibadhi Muslim 75%, other (includes Sunni Muslim, Shia Muslim, Hindu) 25%
**Languages:** Arabic (official), English, Baluchi, Urdu, Indian dialects
**Literacy:**
*definition:* NA
*total population:* 81.4%
*male:* 86.8%
*female:* 73.5% (2003 census)
**School life expectancy (primary to tertiary education):**
*total:* 12 years
*male:* 12 years
*female:* 11 years (2006)
**Education expenditures:** 4% of GDP (2006)

## Government

**Country name:**
*conventional long form:* Sultanate of Oman
*conventional short form:* Oman
*local long form:* Saltanat Uman
*local short form:* Uman
*former:* Muscat and Oman
**Government type:** monarchy
**Capital:**
*name:* Muscat
*geographic coordinates:* 23 37 N, 58 35 E
*time difference:* UTC+4 (9 hours ahead of Washington, DC during Standard Time)
**Administrative divisions:** 5 regions (manatiq, singular - mintaqat) and 4 governorates* (muhafazat, singular - muhafazat) Ad Dakhiliyah, Al Batinah, Al Buraymi*, Al Wusta, Ash Sharqiyah, Az Zahirah, Masqat (Muscat)*, Musandam*, Zufar (Dhofar)*
**Independence:** 1650 (expulsion of the Portuguese)
**National holiday:** Birthday of Sultan QABOOS, 18 November (1940)
**Constitution:** none; note - on 6 November 1996, Sultan QABOOS issued a royal decree promulgating a basic law considered by the government to be a constitution which, among other things, clarifies the royal succession, provides for a prime minister, bars

# Oman *(continued)*

ministers from holding interests in companies doing business with the government, establishes a bicameral legislature, and guarantees basic civil liberties for Omani citizens

**Legal system:** based on English common law and Islamic law; ultimate appeal to the monarch; has not accepted compulsory ICJ jurisdiction

**Suffrage:** 21 years of age; universal; note - members of the military and security forces are not allowed to vote

**Executive branch:**

*chief of state:* Sultan and Prime Minister QABOOS bin Said al-Said (sultan since 23 July 1970 and prime minister since 23 July 1972); note - the monarch is both the chief of state and head of government

*head of government:* Sultan and Prime Minister QABOOS bin Said al-Said (sultan since 23 July 1970 and prime minister since 23 July 1972)

*cabinet:* Cabinet appointed by the monarch

*elections:* the monarch is hereditary

**Legislative branch:** bicameral Majlis Oman consists of Majlis al-Dawla or upper chamber (71 seats; members appointed by the monarch; has advisory powers only) and Majlis al-Shura or lower chamber (84 seats; members elected by popular vote to serve four-year terms; body has only advisory powers)

*elections:* last held 27 October 2007 (next to be held in 2011)

*election results:* new candidates won 46 seats and 38 members of the outgoing Majlis kept their positions; none of the 20 female candidates were elected

**Judicial branch:** Supreme Court

*note:* the nascent civil court system, administered by region, has judges who practice secular and Sharia law

**Political parties and leaders:** none

**Political pressure groups and leaders:** none

**International organization participation:** ABEDA, AFESD, AMF, FAO, G-77, GCC, IBRD, ICAO, ICCt (signatory), IDA, IDB, IFAD, IFC, IHO, ILO, IMF, IMO, IMSO, Interpol, IOC, IPU, ISO, ITSO, ITU, LAS, MIGA, NAM, OIC, OPCW, UN, UNCTAD, UNESCO, UNIDO, UNWTO, UPU, WCO, WFTU, WHO, WIPO, WMO, WTO

**Diplomatic representation in the US:**

*chief of mission:* Ambassador Hunaina bint Sultan bin Ahmad al-MUGHAIRI

*chancery:* 2535 Belmont Road, NW, Washington, DC 20008

*telephone:* [1] (202) 387-1980

*FAX:* [1] (202) 745-4933

**Diplomatic representation from the US:**

*chief of mission:* Ambassador Gary A. GRAPPO

*embassy:* Jameat A'Duwal Al Arabiya Street, Al Khuwair area, Muscat

*mailing address:* P. O. Box 202, P.C. 115, Madinat Sultan Qaboos, Muscat

*telephone:* [968] 24-643-400

*FAX:* [968] 24-699771

**Flag description:** three horizontal bands of white, red, and green of equal width with a broad, vertical, red band on the hoist side; the national emblem (a khanjar dagger in its sheath superimposed on two crossed swords in scabbards) in white is centered near the top of the vertical band

## Economy

**Economy - overview:** Oman is a middle-income economy that is heavily dependent on dwindling oil resources, but sustained high oil prices in recent years have helped build Oman's budget and trade surpluses and foreign reserves. As a result of its dwindling oil resources, Oman is actively pursuing a development plan that focuses on diversification, industrialization, and privatization, with the objective of reducing the oil sector's contribution to GDP to 9% by 2020. Some of these projects may be in jeopardy, however, because Muscat overestimated its ability to produce or secure the natural gas needed to power them. Oman actively seeks private foreign investors, especially in the industrial, information technology, tourism, and higher education fields. Industrial development plans focus on gas resources, metal manufacturing, petrochemicals, and international transshipment ports. The drop in oil prices and the global financial crisis in 2008 will affect Oman's fiscal position and it may post a deficit in 2009 if oil prices stay low. In addition, the global credit crisis is slowing the pace of investment and development projects - a trend that probably will continue into 2009.

**GDP (purchasing power parity):**

$67 billion (2008 est.)

$62.97 billion (2007)

$59.51 billion (2006)

*note:* data are in 2008 US dollars

**GDP (official exchange rate):** $56.32 billion (2008 est.)

**GDP - real growth rate:**

6.7% (2008 est.)

5.8% (2007 est.)

7.5% (2006 est.)

**GDP - per capita (PPP):**

$20,200 (2008 est.)

$19,600 (2007 est.)

$19,200 (2006 est.)

*note:* data are in 2008 US dollars

**GDP - composition by sector:**

*agriculture:* 2.1%

*industry:* 37.2%

*services:* 60.7% (2008 est.)

**Labor force:** 920,000 (2002 est.)

**Labor force - by occupation:**

*agriculture:* NA%

*industry:* NA%

*services:* NA%

**Unemployment rate:**

15% (2004 est.)

**Population below poverty line:** NA%

**Household income or consumption by percentage share:**

*lowest 10%:* NA%

*highest 10%:* NA%

**Investment (gross fixed):** 17.9% of GDP (2008 est.)

**Budget:**

*revenues:* $14.6 billion

*expenditures:* $16.7 billion (2009 est.)

**Public debt:** 2.4% of GDP (2008 est.)

**Inflation rate (consumer prices):**

12.5% (2008 est.)

5.9% (2007 est.)

**Central bank discount rate:** 1.98% (31 December 2007)

**Commercial bank prime lending rate:** 7.29% (31 December 2007)

**Stock of money:** $4.984 billion (31 December 2007)

**Stock of quasi money:** $11.04 billion (31 December 2007)

**Stock of domestic credit:** $13.88 billion (31 December 2007)

**Market value of publicly traded shares:** $23.49 billion (31 December 2007)

**Agriculture - products:** dates, limes, bananas, alfalfa, vegetables; camels, cattle; fish

**Industries:** crude oil production and refining, natural and liquefied natural gas (LNG) production; construction, cement, copper, steel, chemicals, optic fiber

**Industrial production growth rate:** 3.4% (2008 est.)

**Electricity - production:** 14.43 billion kWh (2007)

**Electricity - consumption:** 11.19 billion kWh (2007)

**Electricity - exports:** 0 kWh (2007 est.)

**Electricity - imports:** 0 kWh (2007 est.)

**Oil - production:** 758,600 bbl/day (2008 est.)

**Oil - consumption:** 69,100 bbl/day (2006 est.)

**Oil - exports:** 593,700 bbl/day (2008 est.)

**Oil - imports:** 15,440 bbl/day (2005)

**Oil - proved reserves:** 5.5 billion bbl (1 January 2008 est.)

**Natural gas - production:** 24.1 billion cu m (2007 est.)

**Natural gas - consumption:** 11 billion cu m (2007 est.)

**Natural gas - exports:** 13.1 billion cu m (2007 est.)

**Natural gas - imports:** 0 cu m (2007 est.)

**Natural gas - proved reserves:** 849.5 billion cu m (1 January 2008 est.)

**Current account balance:** $5.669 billion (2008 est.)

**Exports:** $33.9 billion f.o.b. (2008 est.)

**Exports - commodities:** petroleum, reexports, fish, metals, textiles

**Exports - partners:** China 26.8%, South Korea 15.2%, Japan 14.3%, Thailand 10.4%, UAE 7.6%, US 4.3%, Iran 4.1% (2007)

**Imports:** $13.32 billion f.o.b. (2008 est.)

**Imports - commodities:** machinery and transport equipment, manufactured goods, food, livestock, lubricants

## Oman *(continued)*

**Imports - partners:** UAE 19.3%, Japan 17.6%, US 7.4%, Germany 5.2%, India 4.1% (2007)
**Reserves of foreign exchange and gold:** $11.11 billion (31 December 2008 est.)
**Debt - external:** $6.12 billion (31 December 2008 est.)
**Stock of direct foreign investment - at home:** $NA
**Stock of direct foreign investment - abroad:** $NA
**Exchange rates:** Omani rials (OMR) per US dollar - 0.3845 (2008 est.), 0.3845 (2007), 0.3845 (2006), 0.3845 (2005), 0.3845 (2004)

### Communications

**Telephones - main lines in use:** 268,100 (2007)
**Telephones - mobile cellular:** 2.5 million (2007)
**Telephone system:**
*general assessment:* modern system consisting of open-wire, microwave, and radiotelephone communication stations; limited coaxial cable
*domestic:* fixed-line phone service gradually being introduced to remote villages using wireless local loop systems; fixed-line and mobile-cellular subscribership both increasing; open-wire, microwave, radiotelephone communications, and a domestic satellite system with 8 earth stations
*international:* country code - 968; the Fiber-Optic Link Around the Globe (FLAG) and the SEA-ME-WE-3 submarine cable provide connectivity to Asia, the Middle East, and Europe; satellite earth stations - 2 Intelsat (Indian Ocean), 1 Arabsat (2007)
**Radio broadcast stations:** AM 3, FM 9, shortwave 2 (1999)
**Television broadcast stations:** 13 (plus 25 repeaters) (1999)
**Internet country code:** .om
**Internet hosts:** 4,785 (2008)
**Internet users:** 340,000 (2007)

### Transportation

**Airports:** 130 (2008)
**Airports - with paved runways:**
*total:* 10
*over 3,047 m:* 5
*2,438 to 3,047 m:* 4
*914 to 1,523 m:* 1 (2008)
**Airports - with unpaved runways:**
*total:* 120
*over 3,047 m:* 1
*2,438 to 3,047 m:* 7
*1,524 to 2,437 m:* 52
*914 to 1,523 m:* 33
*under 914 m:* 27 (2008)
**Heliports:** 2 (2007)
**Pipelines:** gas 4,126 km; oil 3,558 km; refined products 263 km (2008)
**Roadways:**
*total:* 42,300 km
*paved:* 16,500 km (includes 550 km of expressways)
*unpaved:* 25,800 km (2005)

**Merchant marine:**
*total:* 3
*by type:* chemical tanker 1, passenger 1, passenger/cargo 1
*registered in other countries:* 2 (Panama 2) (2008)
**Ports and terminals:** Mina' Qabus, Salalah

### Military

**Military branches:** Sultan's Armed Forces (SAF): Royal Army of Oman, Royal Navy of Oman, Royal Air Force of Oman (2008)
**Military service age and obligation:** 18-30 years of age for voluntary military service; no conscription (2008)
**Manpower available for military service:**
*males age 16-49:* 802,455
*females age 16-49:* 626,841 (2008 est.)
**Manpower fit for military service:**
*males age 16-49:* 675,454
*females age 16-49:* 563,890 (2009 est.)
**Manpower reaching militarily significant age annually:**
*male:* 35,647
*female:* 34,407 (2009 est.)
**Military expenditures:** 11.4% of GDP (2005 est.)

### Transnational Issues

**Disputes - international:** boundary agreement reportedly signed and ratified with UAE in 2003 for entire border, including Oman's Musandam Peninsula and Al Madhah exclave, but details of the alignment have not been made public
**Trafficking in persons:**
*current situation:* Oman is a destination country for men and women primarily from Bangladesh, India, Sri Lanka, and Pakistan who migrate willingly, but some of whom become victims of trafficking when subjected to conditions of involuntary servitude as domestic workers and laborers; mistreatment includes non-payment of wages, restrictions on movement and withholding of passports, threats, and physical or sexual abuse; Oman may also be a destination country for women from Asia, Eastern Europe, and North Africa for commercial sexual exploitation
*tier rating:* Tier 3 - Oman was rated as Tier 3 for the second consecutive year because it did not report any law enforcement efforts to prosecute and punish trafficking offenses in 2007 and continues to lack victim protection services or a systematic procedure to identify victims of trafficking (2008)

# Pacific Ocean

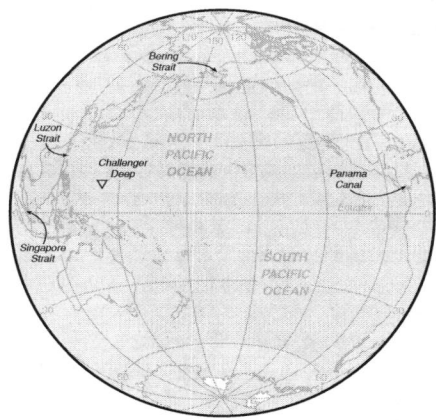

### Introduction

**Background:** The Pacific Ocean is the largest of the world's five oceans (followed by the Atlantic Ocean, Indian Ocean, Southern Ocean, and Arctic Ocean). Strategically important access waterways include the La Perouse, Tsugaru, Tsushima, Taiwan, Singapore, and Torres Straits. The decision by the International Hydrographic Organization in the spring of 2000 to delimit a fifth ocean, the Southern Ocean, removed the portion of the Pacific Ocean south of 60 degrees south.

### Geography

**Location:** body of water between the Southern Ocean, Asia, Australia, and the Western Hemisphere
**Geographic coordinates:** 0 00 N, 160 00 W
**Map references:** Political Map of the World
**Area:**
*total:* 155.557 million sq km
*note:* includes Bali Sea, Bering Sea, Bering Strait, Coral Sea, East China Sea, Gulf of Alaska, Gulf of Tonkin, Philippine Sea, Sea of Japan, Sea of Okhotsk, South China Sea, Tasman Sea, and other tributary water bodies
**Area - comparative:** about 15 times the size of the US; covers about 28% of the global surface; almost equal to the total land area of the world
**Coastline:** 135,663 km
**Climate:** planetary air pressure systems and resultant wind patterns exhibit remarkable uniformity in the south and east; trade winds and westerly winds are well-developed patterns, modified by seasonal fluctuations; tropical cyclones (hurricanes) may form south of Mexico from June to October and affect Mexico and Central America; continental influences cause climatic uniformity to be much less pronounced in the eastern and western regions at the same latitude in the North Pacific Ocean; the western Pacific is monsoonal - a rainy season occurs during the summer months, when moisture-laden winds blow

from the ocean over the land, and a dry season during the winter months, when dry winds blow from the Asian landmass back to the ocean; tropical cyclones (typhoons) may strike southeast and east Asia from May to December

**Terrain:** surface currents in the northern Pacific are dominated by a clockwise, warm-water gyre (broad circular system of currents) and in the southern Pacific by a counterclockwise, cool-water gyre; in the northern Pacific, sea ice forms in the Bering Sea and Sea of Okhotsk in winter; in the southern Pacific, sea ice from Antarctica reaches its northernmost extent in October; the ocean floor in the eastern Pacific is dominated by the East Pacific Rise, while the western Pacific is dissected by deep trenches, including the Mariana Trench, which is the world's deepest

**Elevation extremes:**

*lowest point:* Challenger Deep in the Mariana Trench -10,924 m

*highest point:* sea level 0 m

**Natural resources:** oil and gas fields, polymetallic nodules, sand and gravel aggregates, placer deposits, fish

**Natural hazards:** surrounded by a zone of violent volcanic and earthquake activity sometimes referred to as the "Pacific Ring of Fire"; subject to tropical cyclones (typhoons) in southeast and east Asia from May to December (most frequent from July to October); tropical cyclones (hurricanes) may form south of Mexico and strike Central America and Mexico from June to October (most common in August and September); cyclical El Nino/La Nina phenomenon occurs in the equatorial Pacific, influencing weather in the Western Hemisphere and the western Pacific; ships subject to superstructure icing in extreme north from October to May; persistent fog in the northern Pacific can be a maritime hazard from June to December

**Environment - current issues:** endangered marine species include the dugong, sea lion, sea otter, seals, turtles, and whales; oil pollution in Philippine Sea and South China Sea

**Geography - note:** the major chokepoints are the Bering Strait, Panama Canal, Luzon Strait, and the Singapore Strait; the Equator divides the Pacific Ocean into the North Pacific Ocean and the South Pacific Ocean; dotted with low coral islands and rugged volcanic islands in the southwestern Pacific Ocean

## Economy

**Economy - overview:** The Pacific Ocean is a major contributor to the world economy and particularly to those nations its waters directly touch. It provides low-cost sea transportation between East and West, extensive fishing grounds, offshore oil and gas fields, minerals, and sand and gravel for the construction industry. In 1996, over 60% of the world's fish catch came from the Pacific Ocean. Exploitation of offshore oil and gas reserves is playing an ever-increasing role in the energy supplies of the US, Australia, NZ, China,

and Peru. The high cost of recovering offshore oil and gas, combined with the wide swings in world prices for oil since 1985, has led to fluctuations in new drillings.

## Transportation

**Ports and terminals:** Bangkok (Thailand), Hong Kong (China), Kao-hsiung (Taiwan), Los Angeles (US), Manila (Philippines), Pusan (South Korea), San Francisco (US), Seattle (US), Shanghai (China), Singapore, Sydney (Australia), Vladivostok (Russia), Wellington (NZ), Yokohama (Japan)

**Transportation - note:** Inside Passage offers protected waters from southeast Alaska to Puget Sound (Washington state); the International Maritime Bureau reports the territorial waters of littoral states and offshore waters in the South China Sea as high risk for piracy and armed robbery against ships; numerous commercial vessels have been attacked and hijacked both at anchor and while underway; hijacked vessels are often disguised and cargoes stolen; crew and passengers are often held for ransom, murdered, or cast adrift

## Transnational Issues

**Disputes - international:** some maritime disputes (see littoral states)

# Pakistan

## Introduction

**Background:** The Indus Valley civilization, one of the oldest in the world and dating back at least 5,000 years, spread over much of what is presently Pakistan. During the second millennium B.C., remnants of this culture fused with the migrating Indo-Aryan peoples. The area underwent successive invasions in subsequent centuries from the Persians, Greeks, Scythians, Arabs (who brought Islam), Afghans, and Turks. The Mughal Empire flourished in the 16th and 17th centuries; the British came to dominate the region in the 18th century. The separation in 1947 of British India into the Muslim state of Pakistan (with West and East sections) and largely Hindu India was never satisfactorily resolved, and India and Pakistan fought two wars - in 1947-48 and 1965 - over the disputed Kashmir territory. A third war between these countries in 1971 - in which India capitalized on Islamabad's marginalization of Bengalis in Pakistani politics - resulted in East Pakistan becoming the separate nation of Bangladesh. In response to Indian nuclear weapons testing, Pakistan conducted its own tests in 1998. The dispute over the state of Kashmir is ongoing, but discussions and confidence-building measures have led to decreased tensions since 2002. Mounting public dissatisfaction with President MUSHARRAF, coupled with the assassination of the prominent and popular political leader, Benazir BHUTTO, in late 2007, and MUSHARRAF's resignation in August 2008, led to the September presidential election of Asif ZARDARI, BHUTTO's widower. Pakistani government and military leaders are struggling to control Islamist militants, many of whom are located in the tribal areas adjacent to the border with Afghanistan. The November 2008 Mumbai attacks again inflamed Indo-Pakistan relations. The Pakistani Government is also faced with a deteriorating economy as foreign exchange reserves decline, the currency depreciates, and the current account deficit widens.

# Pakistan *(continued)*

## Geography

**Location:** Southern Asia, bordering the Arabian Sea, between India on the east and Iran and Afghanistan on the west and China in the north

**Geographic coordinates:** 30 00 N, 70 00 E

**Map references:** Asia

**Area:**
*total:* 803,940 sq km
*land:* 778,720 sq km
*water:* 25,220 sq km

**Area - comparative:** slightly less than twice the size of California

**Land boundaries:**
*total:* 6,774 km
*border countries:* Afghanistan 2,430 km, China 523 km, India 2,912 km, Iran 909 km

**Coastline:** 1,046 km

**Maritime claims:**
*territorial sea:* 12 nm
*contiguous zone:* 24 nm
*exclusive economic zone:* 200 nm
*continental shelf:* 200 nm or to the edge of the continental margin

**Climate:** mostly hot, dry desert; temperate in northwest; arctic in north

**Terrain:** flat Indus plain in east; mountains in north and northwest; Balochistan plateau in west

**Elevation extremes:**
*lowest point:* Indian Ocean 0 m
*highest point:* K2 (Mt. Godwin-Austen) 8,611 m

**Natural resources:** land, extensive natural gas reserves, limited petroleum, poor quality coal, iron ore, copper, salt, limestone

**Land use:**
*arable land:* 24.44%
*permanent crops:* 0.84%
*other:* 74.72% (2005)

**Irrigated land:** 182,300 sq km (2003)

**Total renewable water resources:** 233.8 cu km (2003)

**Freshwater withdrawal (domestic/industrial/agricultural):**
*total:* 169.39 cu km/yr (2%/2%/96%)
*per capita:* 1,072 cu m/yr (2000)

**Natural hazards:** frequent earthquakes, occasionally severe especially in north and west; flooding along the Indus after heavy rains (July and August)

**Environment - current issues:** water pollution from raw sewage, industrial wastes, and agricultural runoff; limited natural fresh water resources; most of the population does not have access to potable water; deforestation; soil erosion; desertification

**Environment - international agreements:**
*party to:* Biodiversity, Climate Change, Climate Change-Kyoto Protocol, Desertification, Endangered Species, Environmental Modification, Hazardous Wastes, Law of the Sea, Marine Dumping, Ozone Layer Protection, Ship Pollution, Wetlands
*signed, but not ratified:* Marine Life Conservation

**Geography - note:** controls Khyber Pass and Bolan Pass, traditional invasion routes between Central Asia and the Indian Subcontinent

## People

**Population:** 176,242,949 (July 2009 est.)

**Age structure:**
*0-14 years:* 37.2% (male 33,739,547/female 31,868,065)
*15-64 years:* 58.6% (male 52,849,607/female 50,378,198)
*65 years and over:* 4.2% (male 3,475,927/female 3,931,605) (2009 est.)

**Median age:**
*total:* 20.8 years
*male:* 20.6 years
*female:* 21 years (2009 est.)

**Population growth rate:** 1.947% (2009 est.)

**Birth rate:** 27.62 births/1,000 population (2009 est.)

**Death rate:** 7.85 deaths/1,000 population (2008 est.)

**Net migration rate:** -0.48 migrant(s)/1,000 population (2009 est.)

**Urbanization:**
*urban population:* 36% of total population (2008)
*rate of urbanization:* 3% annual rate of change (2005-10 est.)

**Sex ratio:**
*at birth:* 1.05 male(s)/female
*under 15 years:* 1.06 male(s)/female
*15-64 years:* 1.05 male(s)/female
*65 years and over:* 0.88 male(s)/female
*total population:* 1.04 male(s)/female (2009 est.)

**Infant mortality rate:**
*total:* 65.14 deaths/1,000 live births
*male:* 65.24 deaths/1,000 live births
*female:* 65.05 deaths/1,000 live births (2009 est.)

**Life expectancy at birth:**
*total population:* 64.49 years
*male:* 63.4 years
*female:* 65.64 years (2009 est.)

**Total fertility rate:** 3.6 children born/woman (2009 est.)

**HIV/AIDS - adult prevalence rate:** 0.1% (2007 est.)

**HIV/AIDS - people living with HIV/AIDS:** 96,000 (2007 est.)

**HIV/AIDS - deaths:** 5,100 (2007 est.)

**Major infectious diseases:**
*degree of risk:* high
*food or waterborne diseases:* bacterial diarrhea, hepatitis A and E, and typhoid fever
*vectorborne diseases:* dengue fever and malaria
*animal contact disease:* rabies
*note:* highly pathogenic H5N1 avian influenza has been identified in this country; it poses a negligible risk with extremely rare cases possible among US citizens who have close contact with birds (2009)

**Nationality:**
*noun:* Pakistani(s)
*adjective:* Pakistani

**Ethnic groups:** Punjabi 44.68%, Pashtun (Pathan) 15.42%, Sindhi 14.1%, Sariaki 8.38%, Muhagirs 7.57%, Balochi 3.57%, other 6.28%

**Religions:** Muslim 95% (Sunni 75%, Shia 20%), other (includes Christian and Hindu) 5%

**Languages:** Punjabi 48%, Sindhi 12%, Siraiki (a Punjabi variant) 10%, Pashtu 8%, Urdu (official) 8%, Balochi 3%, Hindko 2%, Brahui 1%, English (official; lingua franca of Pakistani elite and most government ministries), Burushaski, and other 8%

**Literacy:**
*definition:* age 15 and over can read and write
*total population:* 49.9%
*male:* 63%
*female:* 36% (2005 est.)

**School life expectancy (primary to tertiary education):**
*total:* 7 years
*male:* 7 years
*female:* 6 years (2006)

**Education expenditures:** 2.6% of GDP (2006)

## Government

**Country name:**
*conventional long form:* Islamic Republic of Pakistan
*conventional short form:* Pakistan
*local long form:* Jamhuryat Islami Pakistan
*local short form:* Pakistan
*former:* West Pakistan

**Government type:** federal republic

**Capital:**
*name:* Islamabad
*geographic coordinates:* 33 42 N, 73 10 E
*time difference:* UTC+5 (10 hours ahead of Washington, DC during Standard Time)
*daylight saving time:* +1hr, in 2009 - begins third Wednesday in April; ends first Sunday in November; note - a new policy of daylight saving time was initiated by the government in 2008; the specific date of the start of DST has varied over the last two years

**Administrative divisions:** 4 provinces, 1 territory*, and 1 capital territory**; Balochistan, Federally Administered Tribal Areas*, Islamabad Capital Territory**, North-West Frontier Province, Punjab, Sindh
*note:* the Pakistani-administered portion of the disputed Jammu and Kashmir region consists of two administrative entities: Azad Kashmir and Northern Areas

**Independence:** 14 August 1947 (from British India)

**National holiday:** Republic Day, 23 March (1956)

**Constitution:** 12 April 1973; suspended 5 July 1977, restored 30 December 1985; suspended 15 October 1999, restored in stages in 2002; amended 31 December 2003; suspended 3 November 2007; restored on 15 December 2007

**Legal system:** based on English common law with provisions to accommodate Pakistan's status as an Islamic state; accepts compulsory ICJ jurisdiction with reservations

# Pakistan (continued)

**Suffrage:** 18 years of age; universal; joint electorates and reserved parliamentary seats for women and non-Muslims

**Executive branch:**

*chief of state:* President Asif Ali ZARDARI (since 9 September 2008)

*note:* following President Pervez MUSHARRAF's resignation on 18 August 2008, elections were held on 6 September in which Asif Ali ZARDARI won a clear majority; ZARDARI'S inauguration as president of Pakistan on 9 September solidified the country's return to civilian government after more than eight years of military rule

*head of government:* Prime Minister Syed Yousuf Raza GILANI (since 25 March 2008)

*cabinet:* Cabinet appointed by the president upon the advice of the prime minister

*elections:* the president is elected by secret ballot through an Electoral College comprising the members of the Senate, National Assembly, and the provincial assemblies for a five-year term; election last held on 6 September 2008 (next to be held not later than 2013); note - any person who is a Muslim and not less than 45 years of age and is qualified to be elected as a member of the National Assembly can contest the presidential election; the prime minister is selected by the National Assembly; election last held on 24 March 2008

*election results:* Asif Ali ZARDARI elected president; ZARDARI 481 votes, SIDDIQUE 153 votes, SYED 44 votes; Syed Yousuf Raza GILANI elected prime minister; GILANI 264 votes, Pervaiz ELAHI 42 votes; several abstentions

**Legislative branch:** bicameral parliament or Majlis-e-Shoora consists of the Senate (100 seats; members indirectly elected by provincial assemblies and the territories' representatives in the National Assembly to serve six-year terms; one half are elected every three years) and the National Assembly (342 seats; 272 members elected by popular vote; 60 seats reserved for women; 10 seats reserved for non-Muslims; serve five-year terms)

*elections:* Senate - last held on 3 March 2009 (next to be held in March 2012); National Assembly - last held on 18 February 2008 with by-elections on 26 June 2008 (next to be held in 2013)

*election results:* Senate - percent of vote by party - NA; seats by party - PPPP 27, PML-Q 21, MMA 9, PML-N 7, ANP 6, MQM 6, JUI-F 4, BNP-A 2, JWP 1, NPP 1, PKMAP 1, PML-F 1, PPP 1, independents 13; National Assembly - percent of votes by party - NA; seats by party - PPPP 124, PML-N 91, PML 54, MQM 25, ANP 13, MMA 7, PML-F 5, BNP-A 1, NPP 1, PPP-S 1, independents 17; note - 3 seats remain unfilled

**Judicial branch:** Supreme Court (justices appointed by the president); Federal Islamic or Sharia Court

**Political parties and leaders:** Awami National Party or ANP [Asfandyar Wali KHAN]; Balochistan National Party-Hayee Group or BNP-H [Dr. Hayee BALOCH]; Balochistan National Party-Awami or BNP-A [Moheem Khan BALOCH]; Balochistan National

Party-Mengal or BNP-M [Sardar Ataullah MENGAL]; Jamhoori Watan Party or JWP; Jamiat Ahle Hadith or JAH [Sajid MIR]; Jamaat-i Islami or JI [Qazi Hussain AHMED]; Jamiat Ulema-i Islam Fazlur Rehman or JUI-F [Fazlur REHMAN]; Jamiat Ulema-i Islam Sami-ul HAQ or JUI-S [Sami ul-HAQ]; Jamiat Ulema-i Pakistan or JUP [Shah Faridul HAQ]; Muttahida Majlis-e Amal or MMA [Qazi Hussain AHMED]; Muttahida Qaumi Movement or MQM [Altaf HUSSAIN]; National Alliance or NA [Ghulam Mustapha JATOI] (merged with PML); National Peoples Party or NPP; Pakhtun Khwa Milli Awami Party or PKMAP [Mahmood Khan ACHAKZAI]; Pakistan Awami Tehrik or PAT [Tahir ul QADRI]; Pakistan Muslim League-Functional or PML-F [Pir PAGARO]; Pakistan Muslim League-Nawaz Sharif or PML-N [Nawaz SHARIF]; Pakistan Muslim League or PML [Chaudhry Shujaat HUSSAIN]; Pakistan Peoples Party-SHERPAO or PPP-S [Aftab Ahmed Khan SHERPAO]; Pakistan Peoples Party Parliamentarians or PPPP [Bilawal Bhutto ZARDARI, chairman; Asif Ali ZARDARI, co-chairman]; Pakistan Tehrik-e Insaaf or PTI [Imran KHAN]; Tehrik-i Islami [Allama Sajid NAQVI]

*note:* political alliances in Pakistan can shift frequently

**Political pressure groups and leaders:**

*other:* military (most important political force); ulema (clergy); landowners; industrialists; small merchants

**International organization participation:** ADB, ARF, C, CP, ECO, FAO, G-24, G-77, IAEA, IBRD, ICAO, ICC, ICRM, IDA, IDB, IFAD, IFC, IFRCS, IHO, ILO, IMF, IMO, IMSO, Interpol, IOC, IOM, IPU, ISO, ITSO, ITU, ITUC, MIGA, MINURCAT, MINURSO, MONUC, NAM, OAS (observer), OIC, OPCW, PCA, SAARC, SACEP, SCO (observer), UN, UNAMID, UNCTAD, UNESCO, UNHCR, UNIDO, UNMIL, UNMIS, UNMIT, UNOCI, UNOMIG, UNWTO, UPU, WCL, WCO, WFTU, WHO, WIPO, WMO, WTO

**Diplomatic representation in the US:**

*chief of mission:* Ambassador Husain HAQQANI

*chancery:* 3517 International Court, Washington, DC 20008

*telephone:* [1] (202) 243-6500

*FAX:* [1] (202) 686-1544

*consulate(s) general:* Los Angeles, New York, Sunnyvale (California)

*consulate(s):* Chicago, Houston

**Diplomatic representation from the US:**

*chief of mission:* Ambassador Anne W. PATTERSON

*embassy:* Diplomatic Enclave, Ramna 5, Islamabad

*mailing address:* P. O. Box 1048, Unit 62200, APO AE 09812-2200

*telephone:* [92] (51) 208-0000

*FAX:* [92] (51) 2276427

*consulate(s) general:* Karachi

*consulate(s):* Lahore, Peshawar

**Flag description:** green with a vertical white band (symbolizing the role of religious minorities) on the hoist side; a large white crescent and star are centered in the green field; the crescent, star, and color green are traditional symbols of Islam

## Economy

**Economy - overview:** Pakistan, an impoverished and underdeveloped country, has suffered from decades of internal political disputes, low levels of foreign investment, and declining exports of manufactures. Faced with untenable budgetary deficits, high inflation, and hemorrhaging foreign exchange reserves, the government agreed to an International Monetary Fund Standby Arrangement in November 2008. Between 2004-07, GDP growth in the 6-8% range was spurred by gains in the industrial and service sectors, despite severe electricity shortfalls. Poverty levels decreased by 10% since 2001, and Islamabad steadily raised development spending in recent years. In 2008 the fiscal deficit - a result of chronically low tax collection and increased spending - exceeded Islamabad's target of 4% of GDP. Inflation remains the top concern among the public, jumping from 7.7% in 2007 to 20.8% in 2008, primarily because of rising world fuel and commodity prices. In addition, the Pakistani rupee has depreciated significantly as a result of political and economic instability.

**GDP (purchasing power parity):**

$452.7 billion (2008 est.)

$427.9 billion (2007)

$404.5 billion (2006)

*note:* data are in 2008 US dollars

**GDP (official exchange rate):** $160.9 billion (2008 est.)

**GDP - real growth rate:**

5.8% (2008 est.)

5.8% (2007 est.)

6.4% (2006 est.)

**GDP - per capita (PPP):**

$2,600 (2008 est.)

$2,500 (2007 est.)

$2,400 (2006 est.)

*note:* data are in 2008 US dollars

**GDP - composition by sector:**

*agriculture:* 20.4%

*industry:* 26.6%

*services:* 53% (2008 est.)

**Labor force:** 50.58 million

*note:* extensive export of labor, mostly to the Middle East, and use of child labor (2008 est.)

**Labor force - by occupation:**

*agriculture:* 43%

*industry:* 20.3%

*services:* 36.6% (2005 est.)

**Unemployment rate:**

7.4% (2008 est.)

5.6% (2007 est.)

*note:* substantial underemployment exists

**Population below poverty line:** 24% (FY05/06 est.)

**Household income or consumption by percentage share:**

*lowest 10%:* 4%

*highest 10%:* 26.3% (2002)

**Distribution of family income - Gini index:** 30.6 (FY07/08)

# Pakistan *(continued)*

**Investment (gross fixed):** 20% of GDP (2008 est.)
**Budget:**
*revenues:* $22.14 billion
*expenditures:* $32.09 billion (2008 est.)
**Public debt:** 49.8% of GDP (2008 est.)
**Inflation rate (consumer prices):**
20.8% (2008 est.)
7.6% (2007 est.)
**Central bank discount rate:** 15% (31 November 2008)
**Stock of money:** $52.76 billion (31 December 2007)
**Stock of quasi money:** $18.42 billion (31 December 2007)
**Stock of domestic credit:** $65.05 billion (31 December 2007)
**Market value of publicly traded shares:** $70.26 billion (31 December 2007)
**Agriculture - products:** cotton, wheat, rice, sugarcane, fruits, vegetables; milk, beef, mutton, eggs
**Industries:** textiles and apparel, food processing, pharmaceuticals, construction materials, paper products, fertilizer, shrimp
**Industrial production growth rate:** 4.6% (2008 est.)
**Electricity - production:** 93.26 billion kWh (2007 est.)
**Electricity - consumption:** 68.4 billion kWh (2006 est.)
**Electricity - exports:** 0 kWh (2007 est.)
**Electricity - imports:** 0 kWh (2007 est.)
**Oil - production:** 68,670 bbl/day (2007 est.)
**Oil - consumption:** 345,000 bbl/day (2006 est.)
**Oil - exports:** 28,060 bbl/day (2005)
**Oil - imports:** 290,600 bbl/day (2005)
**Oil - proved reserves:** 289.2 million bbl (1 January 2008 est.)
**Natural gas - production:** 30.8 billion cu m (2007 est.)
**Natural gas - consumption:** 30.8 billion cu m (2007 est.)
**Natural gas - exports:** 0 cu m (2007 est.)
**Natural gas - imports:** 0 cu m (2007 est.)
**Natural gas - proved reserves:** 792.8 billion cu m (1 January 2008 est.)
**Current account balance:** -$10.57 billion (2008 est.)
**Exports:** $20.62 billion f.o.b. (2008 est.)
**Exports - commodities:** textiles (garments, bed linen, cotton cloth, yarn), rice, leather goods, sports goods, chemicals, manufactures, carpets and rugs
**Exports - partners:** US 18%, UAE 10.4%, Afghanistan 8.4%, China 5.2%, UK 4.7% (2007)
**Imports:** $35.38 billion f.o.b. (2008 est.)
**Imports - commodities:** petroleum, petroleum products, machinery, plastics, transportation equipment, edible oils, paper and paperboard, iron and steel, tea
**Imports - partners:** China 16.2%, Saudi Arabia 10.9%, UAE 10.1%, US 5.7%, Kuwait 4.9%, Japan 4.4% (2007)

**Reserves of foreign exchange and gold:** $9.104 billion (31 December 2008 est.)
**Debt - external:** $43.23 billion (31 December 2008 est.)
**Stock of direct foreign investment - at home:** $25.31 billion (2008 est.)
**Stock of direct foreign investment - abroad:** $1.032 billion (2008 est.)
**Exchange rates:** Pakistani rupees (PKR) per US dollar - 70.64 (2008 est.), 60.6295 (2007), 60.35 (2006), 59.515 (2005), 58.258 (2004)

## Communications

**Telephones - main lines in use:** 4.546 million (2008)
**Telephones - mobile cellular:** 88.02 million (2008)
**Telephone system:**
*general assessment:* the telecommunications infrastructure is improving dramatically with foreign and domestic investments into fixed-line and mobile networks; mobile-cellular subscribership has skyrocketed, reaching some 88 million in 2008, up from only about 300,000 in 2000; fiber systems are being constructed throughout the country to aid in network growth; main line availability has risen only marginally over the same period and there are still difficulties getting main line service to rural areas
*domestic:* microwave radio relay, coaxial cable, fiber-optic cable, cellular, and satellite networks
*international:* country code - 92; landing point for the SEA-ME-WE-3 and SEA-ME-WE-4 submarine cable systems that provide links to Asia, the Middle East, and Europe; satellite earth stations - 3 Intelsat (1 Atlantic Ocean and 2 Indian Ocean); 3 operational international gateway exchanges (1 at Karachi and 2 at Islamabad); microwave radio relay to neighboring countries (2008)
**Radio broadcast stations:** AM 31, FM 68, shortwave NA (2006)
**Television broadcast stations:** 20 (5 state-run channels and 15 privately-owned satellite channels) (2006)
**Internet country code:** .pk
**Internet hosts:** 197,264 (2008)
**Internet users:** 17.5 million (2007)

## Transportation

**Airports:** 143 (2008)
**Airports - with paved runways:**
*total:* 95
*over 3,047 m:* 16
*2,438 to 3,047 m:* 20
*1,524 to 2,437 m:* 32
*914 to 1,523 m:* 16
*under 914 m:* 11 (2008)
**Airports - with unpaved runways:**
*total:* 48
*1,524 to 2,437 m:* 14
*914 to 1,523 m:* 14
*under 914 m:* 20 (2008)

**Heliports:** 18 (2007)
**Pipelines:** gas 10,402 km; oil 2,076 km; refined products 792 km (2008)
**Railways:**
*total:* 8,163 km
*broad gauge:* 7,718 km 1.676-m gauge (293 km electrified)
*narrow gauge:* 445 km 1.000-m gauge (2006)
**Roadways:**
*total:* 259,758 km
*paved:* 162,879 km (includes 711 km of expressways)
*unpaved:* 96,879 km (2005)
**Merchant marine:**
*total:* 15
*by type:* bulk carrier 1, cargo 10, petroleum tanker 4
*registered in other countries:* 19 (Comoros 4, Malta 2, Marshall Islands 1, Panama 9, Saint Kitts and Nevis 3) (2008)
**Ports and terminals:** Karachi, Port Muhammad Bin Qasim

## Military

**Military branches:** Army (includes National Guard), Navy (includes Marines and Maritime Security Agency), Pakistan Air Force (Pakistan Fiza'ya) (2008)
**Military service age and obligation:** 17-23 years of age for voluntary military service; soldiers cannot be deployed for combat until age 18; the Pakistani Air Force and Pakistani Navy have inducted their first female pilots and sailors (2009)
**Manpower available for military service:**
*males age 16-49:* 42,633,765
*females age 16-49:* 40,114,017 (2008 est.)
**Manpower fit for military service:**
*males age 16-49:* 33,690,322
*females age 16-49:* 32,602,910 (2009 est.)
**Manpower reaching militarily significant age annually:**
*male:* 2,089,936
*female:* 1,964,090 (2009 est.)
**Military expenditures:** 3% of GDP (2007 est.)

## Transnational Issues

**Disputes - international:** various talks and confidence-building measures cautiously have begun to defuse tensions over Kashmir, particularly since the October 2005 earthquake in the region; Kashmir nevertheless remains the site of the world's largest and most militarized territorial dispute with portions under the de facto administration of China (Aksai Chin), India (Jammu and Kashmir), and Pakistan (Azad Kashmir and Northern Areas); UN Military Observer Group in India and Pakistan (UNMOGIP) has maintained a small group of peacekeepers since 1949; India does not recognize Pakistan's ceding historic Kashmir lands to China in 1964; India and Pakistan have maintained their 2004 cease fire in Kashmir and initiated discussions on defusing the armed stand-off in the Siachen glacier region; Pakistan protests India's fencing the highly militarized Line of Control and construction of the Baglihar Dam on the Chenab River in Jammu and Kashmir, which is part of the larger dispute on water sharing of the Indus River and its tributaries; to defuse tensions and prepare for discussions on a maritime boundary, India and Pakistan seek technical resolution of the disputed boundary in Sir Creek estuary at the mouth of the Rann of Kutch in the Arabian Sea; Pakistani maps continue to show the Junagadh claim in India's Gujarat State; by 2005, Pakistan, with UN assistance, repatriated 2.3 million Afghan refugees leaving slightly more than a million, many of whom remain at their own choosing; Pakistan has proposed and Afghanistan protests construction of a fence and laying of mines along portions of their porous border; Pakistan has sent troops into remote tribal areas to monitor and control the border with Afghanistan and to stem terrorist or other illegal activities

**Refugees and internally displaced persons:**
*refugees (country of origin):* 1,043,984 (Afghanistan)
*IDPs:* undetermined (government strikes on Islamic militants in South Waziristan); 34,000 (October 2005 earthquake; most of those displaced returned to their home villages in the spring of 2006) (2007)

**Illicit drugs:** significant transit area for Afghan drugs, including heroin, opium, morphine, and hashish, bound for Iran, Western markets, the Gulf States, Africa, and Asia; financial crimes related to drug trafficking, terrorism, corruption, and smuggling remain problems; opium poppy cultivation estimated to be 2,300 hectares in 2007 with 600 of those hectares eradicated; federal and provincial authorities continue to conduct anti-poppy campaigns that utilizes forced eradication, fines, and arrests

# Palau

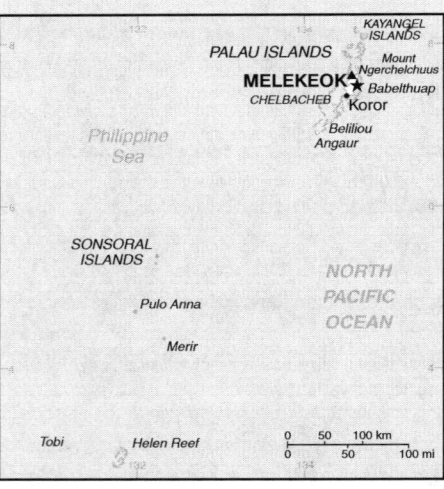

## Introduction

**Background:** After three decades as part of the UN Trust Territory of the Pacific under US administration, this westernmost cluster of the Caroline Islands opted for independence in 1978 rather than join the Federated States of Micronesia. A Compact of Free Association with the US was approved in 1986 but not ratified until 1993. It entered into force the following year when the islands gained independence.

## Geography

**Location:** Oceania, group of islands in the North Pacific Ocean, southeast of the Philippines
**Geographic coordinates:** 7 30 N, 134 30 E
**Map references:** Oceania
**Area:**
*total:* 458 sq km
*land:* 458 sq km
*water:* 0 sq km
**Area - comparative:** slightly more than 2.5 times the size of Washington, DC
**Land boundaries:** 0 km
**Coastline:** 1,519 km
**Maritime claims:**
*territorial sea:* 3 nm
*exclusive fishing zone:* 200 nm
**Climate:** tropical; hot and humid; wet season May to November
**Terrain:** varying geologically from the high, mountainous main island of Babelthuap to low, coral islands usually fringed by large barrier reefs
**Elevation extremes:**
*lowest point:* Pacific Ocean 0 m
*highest point:* Mount Ngerchelchuus 242 m
**Natural resources:** forests, minerals (especially gold), marine products, deep-seabed minerals
**Land use:**
*arable land:* 8.7%
*permanent crops:* 4.35%
*other:* 86.95% (2005)

**Irrigated land:** NA
**Natural hazards:** typhoons (June to December)
**Environment - current issues:** inadequate facilities for disposal of solid waste; threats to the marine ecosystem from sand and coral dredging, illegal fishing practices, and overfishing
**Environment - international agreements:**
*party to:* Biodiversity, Climate Change, Climate Change-Kyoto Protocol, Desertification, Law of the Sea, Ozone Layer Protection, Wetlands, Whaling
*signed, but not ratified:* none of the selected agreements
**Geography - note:** westernmost archipelago in the Caroline chain, consists of six island groups totaling more than 300 islands; includes World War II battleground of Beliliou (Peleliu) and world-famous rock islands

## People

**Population:** 20,796 (July 2009 est.)
**Age structure:**
*0-14 years:* 22.9% (male 2,458/female 2,314)
*15-64 years:* 70.8% (male 8,207/female 6,521)
*65 years and over:* 6.2% (male 401/female 895)
(2009 est.)
**Median age:**
*total:* 32.2 years
*male:* 32 years
*female:* 32.7 years (2009 est.)
**Population growth rate:** 0.428% (2009 est.)
**Birth rate:** 11.2 births/1,000 population (2009 est.)
**Death rate:** 6.73 deaths/1,000 population (2008 est.)
**Net migration rate:** 0.96 migrant(s)/1,000 population (2009 est.)
**Urbanization:**
*urban population:* 81% of total population (2008)
*rate of urbanization:* 1.8% annual rate of change (2005-10 est.)
**Sex ratio:**
*at birth:* 1.06 male(s)/female
*under 15 years:* 1.06 male(s)/female
*15-64 years:* 1.26 male(s)/female
*65 years and over:* 0.45 male(s)/female
*total population:* 1.14 male(s)/female (2009 est.)
**Infant mortality rate:**
*total:* 13.14 deaths/1,000 live births
*male:* 14.83 deaths/1,000 live births
*female:* 11.36 deaths/1,000 live births (2009 est.)
**Life expectancy at birth:**
*total population:* 71.22 years
*male:* 68.08 years
*female:* 74.54 years (2009 est.)
**Total fertility rate:** 1.82 children born/woman (2009 est.)
**HIV/AIDS - adult prevalence rate:** NA
**HIV/AIDS - people living with HIV/AIDS:** NA
**HIV/AIDS - deaths:** NA
**Nationality:**
*noun:* Palauan(s)
*adjective:* Palauan

# Palau (continued)

**Ethnic groups:** Palauan (Micronesian with Malayan and Melanesian admixtures) 69.9%, Filipino 15.3%, Chinese 4.9%, other Asian 2.4%, white 1.9%, Carolinian 1.4%, other Micronesian 1.1%, other or unspecified 3.2% (2000 census)

**Religions:** Roman Catholic 41.6%, Protestant 23.3%, Modekngei 8.8% (indigenous to Palau), Seventh-Day Adventist 5.3%, Jehovah's Witness 0.9%, Latter-Day Saints 0.6%, other 3.1%, unspecified or none 16.4% (2000 census)

**Languages:** Palauan 64.7% official in all islands except Sonsoral (Sonsoralese and English are official), Tobi (Tobi and English are official), and Angaur (Angaur, Japanese, and English are official), Filipino 13.5%, English 9.4%, Chinese 5.7%, Carolinian 1.5%, Japanese 1.5%, other Asian 2.3%, other languages 1.5% (2000 census)

**Literacy:**
*definition:* age 15 and over can read and write
*total population:* 92%
*male:* 93%
*female:* 90% (1980 est.)

**School life expectancy (primary to tertiary education):**
*total:* 15 years
*male:* 14 years
*female:* 15 years (2000)

**Education expenditures:** 10.3% of GDP (2002)

## Government

**Country name:**
*conventional long form:* Republic of Palau
*conventional short form:* Palau
*local long form:* Beluu er a Belau
*local short form:* Belau
*former:* Trust Territory of the Pacific Islands, Palau District

**Government type:** constitutional government in free association with the US; the Compact of Free Association entered into force 1 October 1994

**Capital:**
*name:* Melekeok
*geographic coordinates:* 7 29 N, 134 38 E
*time difference:* UTC+9 (14 hours ahead of Washington, DC during Standard Time)

**Administrative divisions:** 16 states; Aimeliik, Airai, Angaur, Hatohobei, Kayangel, Koror, Melekeok, Ngaraard, Ngarchelong, Ngardmau, Ngatpang, Ngchesar, Ngeremlengui, Ngiwal, Peleliu, Sonsorol

**Independence:** 1 October 1994 (from the US-administered UN trusteeship)

**National holiday:** Constitution Day, 9 July (1979)

**Constitution:** 1 January 1981

**Legal system:** based on Trust Territory laws, acts of the legislature, municipal, common, and customary laws; has not accepted compulsory ICJ jurisdiction

**Suffrage:** 18 years of age; universal

**Executive branch:**
*chief of state:* President Johnson TORIBIONG (since 15 January 2009); Vice President Kerai MARIUR (since 15 January 2009); note - the president is both

the chief of state and head of government
*head of government:* President Johnson TORIBIONG (since 15 January 2009); Vice President Kerai MARIUR (since 15 January 2009)
*cabinet:* NA
*elections:* president and vice president elected on separate tickets by popular vote for four-year terms (eligible for a second term); election last held 4 November 2008 (next to be held in November 2012)
*election results:* Johnson TORIBIONG (51%) defeats Elias Camsek CHIN (49%) for president; Kerai MARIUR elected vice president

**Legislative branch:** bicameral National Congress or Olbiil Era Kelulau (OEK) consists of the Senate (9 seats; members elected by popular vote on a population basis to serve four-year terms) and the House of Delegates (16 seats; members elected by popular vote to serve four-year terms)
*elections:* Senate - last held 4 November 2008 (next to be held in November 2012); House of Delegates - last held 4 November 2008 (next to be held in November 2012)
*election results:* Senate - percent of vote - NA; seats - independents 9; House of Delegates - percent of vote -NA; seats - independents 16

**Judicial branch:** Supreme Court; Court of Common Pleas; Land Court

**Political parties and leaders:** none

**Political pressure groups and leaders:** NA

**International organization participation:** ACP, ADB, FAO, IAEA, IBRD, ICAO, ICRM, IDA, IFC, IFRCS, IMF, IOC, IPU, MIGA, OPCW, PIF, Sparteca, SPC, UN, UNCTAD, UNESCO, WHO

**Diplomatic representation in the US:**
*chief of mission:* Ambassador Hersey KYOTA
*chancery:* 1700 Pennsylvania Avenue NW, Suite 400, Washington, DC 20006
*telephone:* [1] (202) 452-6814
*FAX:* [1] (202) 452-6281
*consulate(s):* Tamuning (Guam)

**Diplomatic representation from the US:**
*chief of mission:* Charge d'Affaires Mark BEZNER
*embassy:* Koror (no street address)
*mailing address:* P. O. Box 6028, Republic of Palau 96940
*telephone:* [680] 488-2920, 2990
*FAX:* [680] 488-2911

**Flag description:** light blue with a large yellow disk (representing the moon) shifted slightly to the hoist side

## Economy

**Economy - overview:** The economy consists primarily of tourism, subsistence agriculture, and fishing. The government is the major employer of the work force relying heavily on financial assistance from the US. The Compact of Free Association with the US, entered into after the end of the UN trusteeship on 1 October 1994, provided Palau with up to $700 million in US aid for the following 15 years in return for furnishing military facilities. Business and tourist

arrivals numbered 85,000 in 2007. The population enjoys a per capita income roughly 50% higher than that of the Philippines and much of Micronesia. Long-run prospects for the key tourist sector have been greatly bolstered by the expansion of air travel in the Pacific, the rising prosperity of leading East Asian countries, and the willingness of foreigners to finance infrastructure development.

**GDP (purchasing power parity):**
$164 million (2008 est.)
$124.5 million (2004)
*note:* data are in 2008 US dollars
GDP estimate includes US subsidy

**GDP (official exchange rate):** $164 million (2008)

**GDP - real growth rate:**
5.5% (2005 est.)

**GDP - per capita (PPP):**
$8,100 (2008 est.)
$7,600 (2005 est.)
*note:* data are in 2008 US dollars

**GDP - composition by sector:**
*agriculture:* 6.2%
*industry:* 12%
*services:* 81.8% (2003)

**Labor force:** 9,777 (2005)

**Labor force - by occupation:**
*agriculture:* 20%
*industry:* NA%
*services:* NA% (1990)

**Unemployment rate:**
4.2% (2005 est.)

**Population below poverty line:** NA%

**Household income or consumption by percentage share:**
*lowest 10%:* NA%
*highest 10%:* NA%

**Budget:**
*revenues:* $114.8 million
*expenditures:* $99.5 million (2008 est.)

**Inflation rate (consumer prices):**
2.7% (2005 est.)

**Market value of publicly traded shares:** $NA

**Agriculture - products:** coconuts, copra, cassava (tapioca), sweet potatoes; fish

**Industries:** tourism, craft items (from shell, wood, pearls), construction, garment making

**Industrial production growth rate:** NA%

**Current account balance:** $15.09 million (FY03/04)

**Exports:** $5.882 million f.o.b. (2004 est.)

**Exports - commodities:** shellfish, tuna, copra, garments

**Imports:** $107.3 million f.o.b. (2004 est.)

**Imports - commodities:** machinery and equipment, fuels, metals; foodstuffs

**Debt - external:** $0 (FY99/00)

**Exchange rates:** the US dollar is used

## Communications

**Telephones - main lines in use:** 6,700 (2002)
**Telephones - mobile cellular:** 1,000 (2002)
**Telephone system:**
*general assessment:* NA
*domestic:* NA
*international:* country code - 680; satellite earth station -1 Intelsat (Pacific Ocean)
**Radio broadcast stations:** AM 1, FM 4, shortwave 1 (2001)
**Television broadcast stations:** 1 (cable) (2005)
**Internet country code:** .pw
**Internet hosts:** 0 (2008)

## Transportation

**Airports:** 3 (2008)
**Airports - with paved runways:**
*total:* 1
*1,524 to 2,437 m:* 1 (2008)
**Airports - with unpaved runways:**
*total:* 2
*1,524 to 2,437 m:* 2 (2008)
**Roadways:**
*note:* estimated to have 60 km of roads as of 1996
**Ports and terminals:** Koror

## Military

**Military branches:** no regular military forces; Palau National Police (2009)
**Manpower available for military service:**
*males age 16-49:* 5,973 (2008 est.)
**Manpower fit for military service:**
*males age 16-49:* 5,177
*females age 16-49:* 3,936 (2009 est.)
**Manpower reaching militarily significant age annually:**
*male:* 207
*female:* 214 (2009 est.)
**Military expenditures:** NA
**Military - note:** defense is the responsibility of the US; under a Compact of Free Association between Palau and the US, the US military is granted access to the islands for 50 years, but it has not stationed any military forces there (2008)

## Transnational Issues

**Disputes - international:** maritime delineation negotiations continue with Philippines, Indonesia

# Palmyra Atoll
*(territory of the US)*

**Description under**

**United States**

**Pacific Island**

**Wildlife Refuges**

# Panama

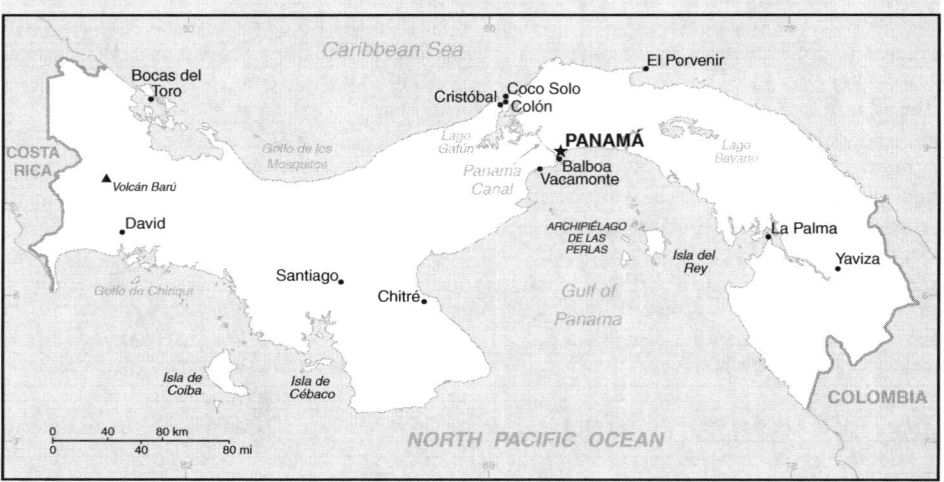

## Introduction

**Background:** Explored and settled by the Spanish in the 16th century, Panama broke with Spain in 1821 and joined a union of Colombia, Ecuador, and Venezuela - named the Republic of Gran Colombia. When the latter dissolved in 1830, Panama remained part of Colombia. With US backing, Panama seceded from Colombia in 1903 and promptly signed a treaty with the US allowing for the construction of a canal and US sovereignty over a strip of land on either side of the structure (the Panama Canal Zone). The Panama Canal was built by the US Army Corps of Engineers between 1904 and 1914. In 1977, an agreement was signed for the complete transfer of the Canal from the US to Panama by the end of the century. Certain portions of the Zone and increasing responsibility over the Canal were turned over in the subsequent decades. With US help, dictator Manuel NORIEGA was deposed in 1989. The entire Panama Canal, the area supporting the Canal, and remaining US military bases were transferred to Panama by the end of 1999. In October 2006, Panamanians approved an ambitious plan to expand the Canal. The project, which began in 2007 and could double the Canal's capacity, is expected to be completed in 2014-15.

## Geography

**Location:** Central America, bordering both the Caribbean Sea and the North Pacific Ocean, between Colombia and Costa Rica
**Geographic coordinates:** 9 00 N, 80 00 W
**Map references:** Central America and the Caribbean
**Area:**
*total:* 78,200 sq km
*land:* 75,990 sq km
*water:* 2,210 sq km

**Area - comparative:** slightly smaller than South Carolina
**Land boundaries:**
*total:* 555 km
*border countries:* Colombia 225 km, Costa Rica 330 km
**Coastline:** 2,490 km
**Maritime claims:**
*territorial sea:* 12 nm
*contiguous zone:* 24 nm
*exclusive economic zone:* 200 nm or edge of continental margin
**Climate:** tropical maritime; hot, humid, cloudy; prolonged rainy season (May to January), short dry season (January to May)
**Terrain:** interior mostly steep, rugged mountains and dissected, upland plains; coastal areas largely plains and rolling hills
**Elevation extremes:**
*lowest point:* Pacific Ocean 0 m
*highest point:* Volcan Baru 3,475 m
**Natural resources:** copper, mahogany forests, shrimp, hydropower
**Land use:**
*arable land:* 7.26%
*permanent crops:* 1.95%
*other:* 90.79% (2005)
**Irrigated land:** 430 sq km (2003)
**Total renewable water resources:** 148 cu km (2000)
**Freshwater withdrawal (domestic/industrial/agricultural):**
*total:* 0.82 cu km/yr (67%/5%/28%)
*per capita:* 254 cu m/yr (2000)
**Natural hazards:** occasional severe storms and forest fires in the Darien area

# Panama *(continued)*

**Environment - current issues:** water pollution from agricultural runoff threatens fishery resources; deforestation of tropical rain forest; land degradation and soil erosion threatens siltation of Panama Canal; air pollution in urban areas; mining threatens natural resources

**Environment - international agreements:**
*party to:* Biodiversity, Climate Change, Climate Change-Kyoto Protocol, Desertification, Endangered Species, Environmental Modification, Hazardous Wastes, Law of the Sea, Marine Dumping, Ozone Layer Protection, Ship Pollution, Tropical Timber 83, Tropical Timber 94, Wetlands, Whaling
*signed, but not ratified:* Marine Life Conservation

**Geography - note:** strategic location on eastern end of isthmus forming land bridge connecting North and South America; controls Panama Canal that links North Atlantic Ocean via Caribbean Sea with North Pacific Ocean

## People

**Population:** 3,360,474 (July 2009 est.)
**Age structure:**
*0-14 years:* 29.3% (male 501,950/female 481,750)
*15-64 years:* 63.9% (male 1,085,435/female 1,061,530)
*65 years and over:* 6.8% (male 106,934/female 122,875) (2009 est.)
**Median age:**
*total:* 27 years
*male:* 26.6 years
*female:* 27.3 years (2009 est.)
**Population growth rate:** 1.503% (2009 est.)
**Birth rate:** 20.18 births/1,000 population (2009 est.)
**Death rate:** 4.71 deaths/1,000 population (2008 est.)
**Net migration rate:** -0.49 migrant(s)/1,000 population (2009 est.)
**Urbanization:**
*urban population:* 73% of total population (2008)
*rate of urbanization:* 2.7% annual rate of change (2005-10 est.)
**Sex ratio:**
*at birth:* 1.04 male(s)/female
*under 15 years:* 1.04 male(s)/female
*15-64 years:* 1.02 male(s)/female
*65 years and over:* 0.87 male(s)/female
*total population:* 1.02 male(s)/female (2009 est.)
**Infant mortality rate:**
*total:* 12.67 deaths/1,000 live births
*male:* 13.53 deaths/1,000 live births
*female:* 11.77 deaths/1,000 live births (2009 est.)
**Life expectancy at birth:**
*total population:* 77.25 years
*male:* 74.47 years
*female:* 80.16 years (2009 est.)
**Total fertility rate:** 2.53 children born/woman (2009 est.)
**HIV/AIDS - adult prevalence rate:** 1% (2007 est.)
**HIV/AIDS - people living with HIV/AIDS:** 20,000 (2007 est.)
**HIV/AIDS - deaths:** fewer than 1,000 (2007 est.)

**Major infectious diseases:**
*degree of risk:* intermediate
*food or waterborne diseases:* bacterial diarrhea
*vectorborne disease:* dengue fever and malaria (2009)
**Nationality:**
*noun:* Panamanian(s)
*adjective:* Panamanian
**Ethnic groups:** mestizo (mixed Amerindian and white) 70%, Amerindian and mixed (West Indian) 14%, white 10%, Amerindian 6%
**Religions:** Roman Catholic 85%, Protestant 15%
**Languages:** Spanish (official), English 14%; note - many Panamanians bilingual
**Literacy:**
*definition:* age 15 and over can read and write
*total population:* 91.9%
*male:* 92.5%
*female:* 91.2% (2000 census)
**School life expectancy (primary to tertiary education):**
*total:* 13 years
*male:* 13 years
*female:* 14 years (2006)
**Education expenditures:** 3.8% of GDP (2004)

## Government

**Country name:**
*conventional long form:* Republic of Panama
*conventional short form:* Panama
*local long form:* Republica de Panama
*local short form:* Panama
**Government type:** constitutional democracy
**Capital:**
*name:* Panama
*geographic coordinates:* 8 58 N, 79 32 W
*time difference:* UTC-5 (same time as Washington, DC during Standard Time)
**Administrative divisions:** 11 provinces (provincias, singular - provincia) and 1 territory* (comarca); Bocas del Toro, Comarca Kuna Yala, Comarca Ngobe-Bugle, Chiriqui, Cocle, Colon, Darien, Herrera, Los Santos, Panama, San Blas*(Kuna Yala), and Veraguas
**Independence:** 3 November 1903 (from Colombia; became independent from Spain 28 November 1821)
**National holiday:** Independence Day, 3 November (1903)
**Constitution:** 11 October 1972; revised in 1978, 1983, 1994, and 2004
**Legal system:** based on civil law system; judicial review of legislative acts in the Supreme Court of Justice; accepts compulsory ICJ jurisdiction with reservations
**Suffrage:** 18 years of age; universal and compulsory
**Executive branch:**
*chief of state:* President Martin TORRIJOS Espino (since 1 September 2004); First Vice President Samuel LEWIS Navarro (since 1 September 2004); Second Vice President Ruben AROSEMENA Valdes (since 1 September 2004); note - the president is both

the chief of state and head of government
*head of government:* President Martin TORRIJOS Espino (since 1 September 2004); First Vice President Samuel LEWIS Navarro (since 1 September 2004); Second Vice President Ruben AROSEMENA Valdes (since 1 September 2004)
*cabinet:* Cabinet appointed by the president
*elections:* president and vice presidents elected on the same ticket by popular vote for five-year terms (not eligible for immediate reelection; president and vice presidents must sit out two additional terms (10 years) before becoming eligible for reelection); election last held 3 May 2009 (next to be held in 2014); note - beginning in 2009, Panama will have only one vice president
*election results:* Ricardo MARTINELLI elected president; percent of vote - Ricardo MARTINELLI 60%, Balbina HERRERA 38%, Guillermo ENDARA Galimany 2%; note - Ricardo MARTINELLI is to assume office 1 July 2009
*note:* government coalition - PRD (Democratic Revolutionary Party), PP (Popular Party)
**Legislative branch:** unicameral National Assembly or Asamblea Nacional (71 seats; members are elected by popular vote to serve five-year terms)
*elections:* last held 3 May 2009 (next to be held May 2014)
*election results:* percent of vote by party - NA; seats by party - PRD 26, Panamenista 22, CD 14, PU 4, Independent 2, MOLIRENA 2, PP 1
*note:* legislators from outlying rural districts are chosen on a plurality basis while districts located in more populous towns and cities elect multiple legislators by means of a proportion-based formula
**Judicial branch:** Supreme Court of Justice or Corte Suprema de Justicia (nine judges appointed for 10-year terms); five superior courts; three courts of appeal
**Political parties and leaders:** Democratic Change or CD [Ricardo MARTINELLI]; Democratic Revolutionary Party or PRD [Martin TORRIJOS Espino]; Nationalist Republican Liberal Movement or MOLIRENA [Sergio GONZALEZ-Ruiz]; Panamenista Party [Juan Carlos VARELA] (formerly the Arnulfista Party); Patriotic Union Party or UP (combination of the Liberal National Party or PLN and the Solidarity Party or PS) [Guillermo "Billy" FORD and Anibal GALINDO]; Popular Party or PP [Rene ORILLAC] (formerly Christian Democratic Party or PDC)
**Political pressure groups and leaders:** Chamber of Commerce; National Civic Crusade; National Council of Organized Workers or CONATO; National Council of Private Enterprise or CONEP; National Union of Construction and Similar Workers (SUNTRACS); Panamanian Association of Business Executives or APEDE; Panamanian Industrialists Society or SIP; Workers Confederation of the Republic of Panama or CTRP

# Panama (continued)

**International organization participation:** BCIE, CAN (observer), CSN (observer), FAO, G-77, IADB, IAEA, IBRD, ICAO, ICC, ICCt, ICRM, IDA, IFAD, IFC, IFRCS, ILO, IMF, IMO, IMSO, Interpol, IOC, IOM, IPU, ISO, ITSO, ITU, ITUC, LAES, LAIA (observer), MIGA, NAM, OAS, OPANAL, OPCW, PCA, RG, SICA, UN, UNASUR (observer), UNCTAD, UNESCO, UNIDO, Union Latina, UNWTO, UPU, WCL, WCO, WFTU, WHO, WIPO, WMO, WTO

**Diplomatic representation in the US:**
*chief of mission:* Ambassador Federico HUMBERT Arias
*chancery:* 2862 McGill Terrace NW, Washington, DC 20008
*telephone:* [1] (202) 483-1407
*FAX:* [1] (202) 483-8416
*consulate(s) general:* Atlanta, Houston, Miami, New Orleans, New York, Philadelphia, San Diego, San Francisco, Tampa

**Diplomatic representation from the US:**
*chief of mission:* Ambassador Barbara J. STEPHENSON
*embassy:* Edificio 783, Avenida Demetrio Basilio Lakas Panama, Apartado Postal 0816-02561, Zona 5, Panama City
*mailing address:* American Embassy Panama, Unit 0945, APO AA 34002
*telephone:* [507] 207-7000
*FAX:* [507] 317-5568

**Flag description:** divided into four, equal rectangles; the top quadrants are white (hoist side) with a blue five-pointed star in the center and plain red; the bottom quadrants are plain blue (hoist side) and white with a red five-pointed star in the center

## Economy

**Economy - overview:** Panama's dollarized economy rests primarily on a well-developed services sector that accounts for 80% of GDP. Services include operating the Panama Canal, banking, the Colon Free Zone, insurance, container ports, flagship registry, and tourism. Economic growth will be bolstered by the Panama Canal expansion project that began in 2007 and is scheduled to be completed by 2014 at a cost of $5.3 billion - about 25% of current GDP. The expansion project will more than double the Canal's capacity, enabling it to accommodate ships that are now too large to transverse the transoceanic crossway, and should help to reduce the high unemployment rate. Strong economic performance has reduced the national poverty level to 29% in 2008; however, Panama has the second most unequal income distribution in Latin America. The government has implemented tax reforms, as well as social security reforms, and backs regional trade agreements and development of tourism. Not a CAFTA signatory, Panama in December 2006 independently negotiated a free trade agreement with the US, which, when implemented, will help promote the country's economic growth.

**GDP (purchasing power parity):**
$38.49 billion (2008 est.)
$35.54 billion (2007)
$31.96 billion (2006)
*note:* data are in 2008 US dollars

**GDP (official exchange rate):** $23.42 billion (2008 est.)

**GDP - real growth rate:**
8.3% (2008)
11.2% (2007 est.)
8.7% (2006 est.)

**GDP - per capita (PPP):**
$11,600 (2008 est.)
$10,900 (2007 est.)
$10,000 (2006 est.)
*note:* data are in 2008 US dollars

**GDP - composition by sector:**
*agriculture:* 6.2%
*industry:* 16.1%
*services:* 77.6% (2008 est.)

**Labor force:** 1.392 million
*note:* shortage of skilled labor, but an oversupply of unskilled labor (2008 est.)

**Labor force - by occupation:**
*agriculture:* 15%
*industry:* 18%
*services:* 67% (2006)

**Unemployment rate:**
6.3% (2008 est.)
6.4% (2007 est.)

**Population below poverty line:** 28.6% (2006 est.)

**Household income or consumption by percentage share:**
*lowest 10%:* 0.7%
*highest 10%:* 43% (2003)

**Distribution of family income - Gini index:** 56.1 (2003)

**Investment (gross fixed):** 24.9% of GDP (2008 est.)

**Budget:**
*revenues:* $6.09 billion
*expenditures:* $6 billion (2008 est.)

**Public debt:** 46.4% of GDP (2008 est.)

**Inflation rate (consumer prices):**
10.6% (2008 est.)
4.2% (2007 est.)

**Commercial bank prime lending rate:** 8.25% (31 December 2007)

**Stock of money:** $3.054 billion (31 December 2007)

**Stock of quasi money:** $14.26 billion (31 December 2007)

**Stock of domestic credit:** $17.4 billion (31 December 2007)

**Market value of publicly traded shares:** $6.219 billion (31 December 2007)

**Agriculture - products:** bananas, rice, corn, coffee, sugarcane, vegetables; livestock; shrimp

**Industries:** construction, brewing, cement and other construction materials, sugar milling

**Industrial production growth rate:** 6.6% (2008 est.)

**Electricity - production:** 5.805 billion kWh (2006 est.)

**Electricity - consumption:** 4.768 billion kWh (2006 est.)

**Electricity - exports:** 124.9 million kWh (2007 est.)

**Electricity - imports:** 8.74 million kWh (2007 est.)

**Oil - production:** 0 bbl/day (2007 est.)

**Oil - consumption:** 92,790 bbl/day (2006 est.)

**Oil - exports:** 4,447 bbl/day (2005)

**Oil - imports:** 88,790 bbl/day (2005)

**Oil - proved reserves:** 0 bbl (1 January 2006 est.)

**Natural gas - production:** 0 cu m (2007 est.)

**Natural gas - consumption:** 0 cu m (2007 est.)

**Natural gas - exports:** 0 cu m (2007 est.)

**Natural gas - imports:** 0 cu m (2007 est.)

**Natural gas - proved reserves:** 0 cu m (1 January 2006 est.)

**Current account balance:** -$2.536 billion (2008 est.)

**Exports:** $10.37 billion f.o.b.; note - includes the Colon Free Zone (2008 est.)

**Exports - commodities:** bananas, shrimp, sugar, coffee, clothing

**Exports - partners:** US 35.6%, Netherlands 10.2%, China 6%, Sweden 5.5%, UK 5.4%, Costa Rica 5.1%, Spain 5% (2007)

**Imports:** $15.18 billion f.o.b.
*note:* includes the Colon Free Zone (2008 est.)

**Imports - commodities:** capital goods, foodstuffs, consumer goods, chemicals

**Imports - partners:** US 32.8%, Netherlands Antilles 7.6%, China 5.6%, Japan 5.1%, Costa Rica 5.1%, South Korea 4.1% (2007)

**Reserves of foreign exchange and gold:** $1.655 billion (31 December 2008 est.)

**Debt - external:** $10.89 billion (31 December 2008 est.)

**Stock of direct foreign investment - at home:** $NA

**Stock of direct foreign investment - abroad:** $NA

**Exchange rates:** balboas (PAB) per US dollar - 1 (2008 est.), 1 (2007), 1 (2006), 1 (2005), 1 (2004)
*note:* the US dollar is the legal currency

## Communications

**Telephones - main lines in use:** 491,900 (2007)

**Telephones - mobile cellular:** 2.392 million (2007)

**Telephone system:**
*general assessment:* domestic and international facilities well developed
*domestic:* combined fixed-line and mobile-cellular teledensity is approaching 90 per 100 persons
*international:* country code - 507; landing point for the Americas Region Caribbean Ring System (ARCOS-1), the MAYA-1, and PAN-AM submarine cable systems that together provide links to the US and parts of the Caribbean, Central America, and South America; satellite earth stations - 2 Intelsat (Atlantic Ocean); connected to the Central American Microwave System (2007)

**Radio broadcast stations:** AM 101, FM 134, shortwave 0 (1998)

# Panama (continued)

**Television broadcast stations:** 38 (including repeaters) (1998)
**Internet country code:** .pa
**Internet hosts:** 7,858 (2008)
**Internet users:** 525,200 (2007)

## Transportation

**Airports:** 117 (2008)
**Airports - with paved runways:**
*total:* 54
*over 3,047 m:* 1
*2,438 to 3,047 m:* 1
*1,524 to 2,437 m:* 5
*914 to 1,523 m:* 17
*under 914 m:* 30 (2008)
**Airports - with unpaved runways:**
*total:* 63
*1,524 to 2,437 m:* 1
*914 to 1,523 m:* 11
*under 914 m:* 51 (2008)
**Heliports:** 2 (2007)
**Railways:**
*total:* 355 km
*standard gauge:* 77 km 1.435-m gauge
*narrow gauge:* 278 km 0.914-m gauge (2006)
**Roadways:**
*total:* 11,978 km
*paved:* 4,300 km
*unpaved:* 7,678 km (2002)
**Waterways:** 800 km (includes 82 km Panama Canal) (2008)
**Merchant marine:**
*total:* 6,323
*by type:* barge carrier 2, bulk carrier 2,143, cargo 1,208, carrier 13, chemical tanker 565, combination ore/oil 6, container 790, liquefied gas 189, passenger 44, passenger/cargo 71, petroleum tanker 557, refrigerated cargo 265, roll on/roll off 128, specialized tanker 29, vehicle carrier 313
*foreign-owned:* 5,394 (Albania 2, Argentina 8, Australia 4, Azerbaijan 1, Bahamas 9, Bangladesh 2, Belgium 2, British Virgin Islands 1, Bulgaria 3, Burma 1, Canada 18, Chile 12, China 532, Colombia 4, Croatia 3, Cuba 10, Cyprus 19, Denmark 40, Dominican Republic 1, Ecuador 4, Egypt 17, Estonia 5, Finland 2, France 5, Gabon 1, Germany 44, Gibraltar 1, Greece 510, Hong Kong 130, India 27, Indonesia 31, Iran 7, Israel 3, Italy 28, Japan 2,335, Jordan 13, North Korea 1, South Korea 303, Kuwait 2, Latvia 8, Lebanon 5, Lithuania 7, Malaysia 12, Maldives 1, Malta 3, Mexico 2, Monaco 16, Netherlands 14, Nigeria 10, Norway 89, Oman 2, Pakistan 9, Peru 16, Philippines 7, Poland 11, Portugal 9, Qatar 1, Romania 7, Russia 18, Saudi Arabia 16, Singapore 100, Spain 50, Sri Lanka 1, Sweden 6, Switzerland 25, Syria 32, Taiwan 320, Thailand 10, Tunisia 1, Turkey 94, Turks and Caicos Islands 1, Ukraine 10, UAE 109, UK 59, US 126, Venezuela 10, Vietnam 30, Yemen 6)
*registered in other countries:* 3 (Marshall Islands 1, Sierra Leone 1, Venezuela 1) (2008)
**Ports and terminals:** Balboa, Colon, Cristobal

## Military

**Military branches:** no regular military forces; Panamanian public forces include: Panamanian National Police (PNP), National Air-Naval Service (SENAN), National Border Service (SENAFRONT) (2009)
**Manpower available for military service:**
*males age 16-49:* 851,044 (2008 est.)
**Manpower fit for military service:**
*males age 16-49:* 705,160
*females age 16-49:* 710,521 (2009 est.)
**Manpower reaching militarily significant age annually:**
*male:* 31,089
*female:* 29,939 (2009 est.)
**Military expenditures:** 1% of GDP (2006)
**Military - note:** on 10 February 1990, the government of then President ENDARA abolished Panama's military and reformed the security apparatus by creating the Panamanian Public Forces; in October 1994, Panama's Legislative Assembly approved a constitutional amendment prohibiting the creation of a standing military force but allowing the temporary establishment of special police units to counter acts of "external aggression"

## Transnational Issues

**Disputes - international:** organized illegal narcotics operations in Colombia operate within the remote border region with Panama
**Trafficking in persons:**
*current situation:* Panama is a source, transit, and destination country for women and children trafficked for the purpose of commercial sexual exploitation; the majority of victims are Panamanian women and children trafficked within the country into the sex trade; rural children in Panama may be trafficked internally to urban areas for labor exploitation
*tier rating:* Tier 2 Watch List - Panama is on the Tier 2 Watch List for failing to show evidence of increasing efforts to combat human trafficking, particularly with respect to prosecuting, convicting, and sentencing human traffickers for their crimes, and for failing to provide adequate victim assistance (2008)
**Illicit drugs:** major cocaine transshipment point and primary money-laundering center for narcotics revenue; money-laundering activity is especially heavy in the Colon Free Zone; offshore financial center; negligible signs of coca cultivation; monitoring of financial transactions is improving; official corruption remains a major problem

# Papua New Guinea

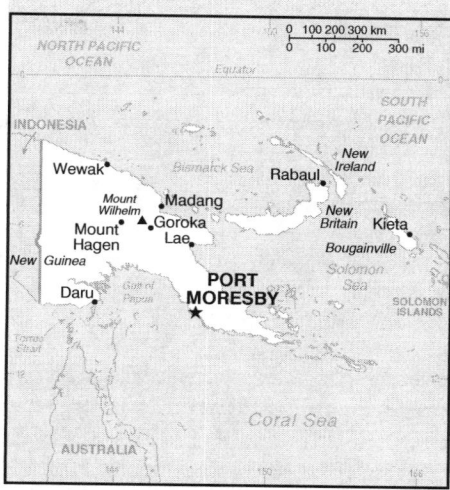

## Introduction

**Background:** The eastern half of the island of New Guinea - second largest in the world - was divided between Germany (north) and the UK (south) in 1885. The latter area was transferred to Australia in 1902, which occupied the northern portion during World War I and continued to administer the combined areas until independence in 1975. A nine-year secessionist revolt on the island of Bougainville ended in 1997 after claiming some 20,000 lives.

## Geography

**Location:** Oceania, group of islands including the eastern half of the island of New Guinea between the Coral Sea and the South Pacific Ocean, east of Indonesia
**Geographic coordinates:** 6 00 S, 147 00 E
**Map references:** Oceania
**Area:**
*total:* 462,840 sq km
*land:* 452,860 sq km
*water:* 9,980 sq km
**Area - comparative:** slightly larger than California
**Land boundaries:**
*total:* 820 km
*border countries:* Indonesia 820 km
**Coastline:** 5,152 km
**Maritime claims:** measured from claimed archipelagic baselines
*territorial sea:* 12 nm
*continental shelf:* 200 m depth or to the depth of exploitation
*exclusive fishing zone:* 200 nm
**Climate:** tropical; northwest monsoon (December to March), southeast monsoon (May to October); slight seasonal temperature variation
**Terrain:** mostly mountains with coastal lowlands and rolling foothills

# Papua New Guinea *(continued)*

**Elevation extremes:**
*lowest point:* Pacific Ocean 0 m
*highest point:* Mount Wilhelm 4,509 m
**Natural resources:** gold, copper, silver, natural gas, timber, oil, fisheries
**Land use:**
*arable land:* 0.49%
*permanent crops:* 1.4%
*other:* 98.11% (2005)
**Irrigated land:** NA
**Total renewable water resources:** 801 cu km (1987)
**Freshwater withdrawal (domestic/industrial/agricultural):**
*total:* 0.1 cu km/yr (56%/43%/1%)
*per capita:* 17 cu m/yr (1987)
**Natural hazards:** active volcanism; situated along the Pacific "Ring of Fire"; the country is subject to frequent and sometimes severe earthquakes; mud slides; tsunamis
**Environment - current issues:** rain forest subject to deforestation as a result of growing commercial demand for tropical timber; pollution from mining projects; severe drought
**Environment - international agreements:**
*party to:* Antarctic Treaty, Biodiversity, Climate Change, Climate Change-Kyoto Protocol, Desertification, Endangered Species, Environmental Modification, Hazardous Wastes, Law of the Sea, Marine Dumping, Ozone Layer Protection, Ship Pollution, Tropical Timber 83, Tropical Timber 94, Wetlands
*signed, but not ratified:* none of the selected agreements
**Geography - note:** shares island of New Guinea with Indonesia; one of world's largest swamps along southwest coast

## People

**Population:** 6,057,263 (July 2009 est.)
**Age structure:**
*0-14 years:* 36.9% (male 1,137,796/female 1,099,365)
*15-64 years:* 59% (male 1,836,272/female 1,735,298)
*65 years and over:* 4.1% (male 114,789/female 133,743) (2009 est.)
**Median age:**
*total:* 21.7 years
*male:* 21.8 years
*female:* 21.6 years (2009 est.)
**Population growth rate:** 2.069% (2009 est.)
**Birth rate:** 27.55 births/1,000 population (2009 est.)
**Death rate:** 6.96 deaths/1,000 population (2008 est.)
**Net migration rate:** NA
**Urbanization:**
*urban population:* 12% of total population (2008)
*rate of urbanization:* 1.9% annual rate of change (2005-10 est.)

**Sex ratio:**
*at birth:* 1.05 male(s)/female
*under 15 years:* 1.03 male(s)/female
*15-64 years:* 1.06 male(s)/female
*65 years and over:* 0.86 male(s)/female
*total population:* 1.04 male(s)/female (2009 est.)
**Infant mortality rate:**
*total:* 45.23 deaths/1,000 live births
*male:* 49.17 deaths/1,000 live births
*female:* 41.09 deaths/1,000 live births (2009 est.)
**Life expectancy at birth:**
*total population:* 66.34 years
*male:* 64.08 years
*female:* 68.72 years (2009 est.)
**Total fertility rate:** 3.62 children born/woman (2009 est.)
**HIV/AIDS - adult prevalence rate:** 1.5% (2007 est.)
**HIV/AIDS - people living with HIV/AIDS:** 54,000 (2007 est.)
**HIV/AIDS - deaths:** fewer than 1,000 (2007 est.)
**Major infectious diseases:**
*degree of risk:* very high
*food or waterborne diseases:* bacterial diarrhea, hepatitis A, and typhoid fever
*vectorborne diseases:* dengue fever and malaria (2009)
**Nationality:**
*noun:* Papua New Guinean(s)
*adjective:* Papua New Guinean
**Ethnic groups:** Melanesian, Papuan, Negrito, Micronesian, Polynesian
**Religions:** Roman Catholic 27%, Evangelical Lutheran 19.5%, United Church 11.5%, Seventh-Day Adventist 10%, Pentecostal 8.6%, Evangelical Alliance 5.2%, Anglican 3.2%, Baptist 2.5%, other Protestant 8.9%, Bahai 0.3%, indigenous beliefs and other 3.3% (2000 census)
**Languages:** Tok Pisin, English, and Hiri Motu are official languages; some 860 indigenous languages spoken (over one-tenth of the world's total)
*note:* Tok Pisin, a creole language, is widely used and understood; English is spoken by 1%-2%; Hiri Motu is spoken by less than 2%
**Literacy:**
*definition:* age 15 and over can read and write
*total population:* 57.3%
*male:* 63.4%
*female:* 50.9% (2000 census)
**Education expenditures:** NA
**People - note:** the indigenous population of Papua New Guinea is one of the most heterogeneous in the world; PNG has several thousand separate communities, most with only a few hundred people; divided by language, customs, and tradition, some of these communities have engaged in low-scale tribal conflict with their neighbors for millennia; the advent of modern weapons and modern migrants into urban areas has greatly magnified the impact of this lawlessness

## Government

**Country name:**
*conventional long form:* Independent State of Papua New Guinea
*conventional short form:* Papua New Guinea
*local short form:* Papuaniugini
*former:* Territory of Papua and New Guinea
*abbreviation:* PNG
**Government type:** constitutional parliamentary democracy and a Commonwealth realm
**Capital:**
*name:* Port Moresby
*geographic coordinates:* 9 30 S, 147 10 E
*time difference:* UTC+10 (15 hours ahead of Washington, DC during Standard Time)
**Administrative divisions:** 20 provinces; Bougainville (autonomous region), Central, Chimbu, Eastern Highlands, East New Britain, East Sepik, Enga, Gulf, Madang, Manus, Milne Bay, Morobe, National Capital, New Ireland, Northern, Sandaun, Southern Highlands, Western, Western Highlands, West New Britain
**Independence:** 16 September 1975 (from the Australian-administered UN trusteeship)
**National holiday:** Independence Day, 16 September (1975)
**Constitution:** 16 September 1975
**Legal system:** based on English common law; has not accepted compulsory ICJ jurisdiction
**Suffrage:** 18 years of age; universal
**Executive branch:**
*chief of state:* Queen ELIZABETH II (since 6 February 1952); represented by governor general Sir Paulius MATANE (since 29 June 2004)
*head of government:* Prime Minister Sir Michael SOMARE (since 2 August 2002); Deputy Prime Minister Puka TEMU (since 29 August 2007)
*cabinet:* National Executive Council appointed by the governor general on the recommendation of the prime minister
*elections:* the monarch is hereditary; the governor general is nominated by parliament and appointed by the chief of state; following legislative elections, the leader of the majority party or leader of the majority coalition usually is appointed prime minister by the governor general acting in accordance with a decision of the parliament
**Legislative branch:** unicameral National Parliament (109 seats, 89 filled from open electorates and 20 from provinces and national capital district; members elected by popular vote to serve five-year terms); constitution allows up to 126 seats
*elections:* last held from 30 June to 10 July 2007; next to be held in June 2012
*election results:* percent of vote by party - NA; seats by party - National Alliance 27, PNGP 8, PAP 6, URP 6, PANGU 5, PDM 5, independents 19, others 33; note - election to 1 seat was nullified
*note:* 15 other parties won 4 or fewer seats; association with political parties is fluid

# Papua New Guinea (continued)

**Judicial branch:** Supreme Court (the chief justice is appointed by the governor general on the proposal of the National Executive Council after consultation with the minister responsible for justice; other judges are appointed by the Judicial and Legal Services Commission)

**Political parties and leaders:** National Alliance Party or NA [Michael SOMARE]; Papua and Niugini Union Party or PANGU PATI [Andrew KUMBAKOR]; Papua New Guinea Party or PNGP [Sir Mekere MORAUTA]; People's Democratic Movement or PDM [Michael OGIO]; People's Action Party or PAP [Gabriel KAPRIS]; United Resources Party or URP [William DUMA] (2007)

**Political pressure groups and leaders:** Ahora [Andrew MAMOKO] (represents local tribes); Centre for Environment Law and Community Rights or Celcor [Damien ASE]; Community Coalition Against Corruption

**International organization participation:** ACP, ADB, APEC, ARF, ASEAN (observer), C, CP, FAO, G-77, IBRD, ICAO, ICRM, IDA, IFAD, IFC, IFRCS, IHO, ILO, IMF, IMO, Interpol, IOC, IOM (observer), IPU, ISO (correspondent), ITSO, ITU, MIGA, NAM, OPCW, PIF, Sparteca, SPC, UN, UNCTAD, UNESCO, UNIDO, UNWTO, UPU, WCO, WHO, WIPO, WMO, WTO

**Diplomatic representation in the US:**
*chief of mission:* Ambassador Evan Jeremy PAKI
*chancery:* 1779 Massachusetts Avenue NW, Suite 805, Washington, DC 20036
*telephone:* [1] (202) 745-3680
*FAX:* [1] (202) 745-3679

**Diplomatic representation from the US:**
*chief of mission:* Ambassador Leslie V. ROWE
*embassy:* Douglas Street, Port Moresby, N.C.D.
*mailing address:* 4240 Port Moresby Pl, US Department of State, Washington DC 20521-4240
*telephone:* [675] 321-1455
*FAX:* [675] 321-3423

**Flag description:** divided diagonally from upper hoist-side corner; the upper triangle is red with a soaring yellow bird of paradise centered; the lower triangle is black with five, white, five-pointed stars of the Southern Cross constellation centered

## Economy

**Economy - overview:** Papua New Guinea is richly endowed with natural resources, but exploitation has been hampered by rugged terrain and the high cost of developing infrastructure. Agriculture provides a subsistence livelihood for 75% of the population. Mineral deposits, including copper, gold, and oil, account for nearly two-thirds of export earnings. The government of Prime Minister SOMARE has expended much of its energy remaining in power. He was the first prime minister ever to serve a full five-year term. The government also brought stability to the national budget, largely through expenditure control; however, it relaxed spending constraints in 2006 and 2007 as elections approached. Numerous challenges still face the government including regaining investor confidence, restoring integrity to state institutions, promoting economic efficiency by privatizing moribund state institutions, and balancing relations with Australia, its former colonial ruler. Other socio-cultural challenges could upend the economy including a worsening HIV/AIDS epidemic, currently the highest rate in all of East Asia and the Pacific, and chronic law and order and land tenure issues. Australia supplied more than $300 million in aid in FY07/08, which accounts for nearly 20% of the national budget. A consortium led by a major American oil company hopes to begin the commercialization of the country's estimated 227 billion cubic meters of natural gas reserves through the construction of a liquefied natural gas (LNG) production facility by 2010. The project has the potential to double the GDP of Papua New Guinea.

**GDP (purchasing power parity):**
$13.29 billion (2008 est.)
$12.5 billion (2007)
$11.79 billion (2006)
*note:* data are in 2008 US dollars

**GDP (official exchange rate):** $6.363 billion (2008 est.)

**GDP - real growth rate:**
6.3% (2008 est.)
6% (2007 est.)
2.6% (2006 est.)

**GDP - per capita (PPP):**
$2,200 (2008 est.)
$2,200 (2007 est.)
$2,100 (2006 est.)
*note:* data are in 2008 US dollars

**GDP - composition by sector:**
*agriculture:* 32.8%
*industry:* 36.5%
*services:* 30.6% (2008 est.)

**Labor force:** 3.639 million (2008 est.)

**Labor force - by occupation:**
*agriculture:* 75%
*industry:* NA%
*services:* NA% (2005 est.)

**Unemployment rate:**
1.9% (2004)

**Population below poverty line:** 37% (2002 est.)

**Household income or consumption by percentage share:**
*lowest 10%:* 1.7%
*highest 10%:* 40.5% (1996)

**Distribution of family income - Gini index:** 50.9 (1996)

**Investment (gross fixed):** 19.9% of GDP (2008 est.)

**Budget:**
*revenues:* $3.098 billion
*expenditures:* $2.949 billion (2008 est.)

**Public debt:** 34% of GDP (2008 est.)

**Inflation rate (consumer prices):**
8.8% (2008 est.)
0.9% (2007 est.)

**Central bank discount rate:** 7.38% (31 December 2007)

**Commercial bank prime lending rate:** 9.78% (31 December 2007)

**Stock of money:** $1.685 billion (31 December 2007)

**Stock of quasi money:** $1.482 billion (31 December 2007)

**Stock of domestic credit:** $1.486 billion (31 December 2007)

**Market value of publicly traded shares:** $4.863 billion (2005)

**Agriculture - products:** coffee, cocoa, copra, palm kernels, tea, sugar, rubber, sweet potatoes, fruit, vegetables, vanilla; shell fish, poultry, pork

**Industries:** copra crushing, palm oil processing, plywood production, wood chip production; mining of gold, silver, and copper; crude oil production, petroleum refining; construction, tourism

**Industrial production growth rate:** 6.3% (2008 est.)

**Electricity - production:** 2.875 billion kWh (2006 est.)

**Electricity - consumption:** 2.674 billion kWh (2006 est.)

**Electricity - exports:** 0 kWh (2007 est.)

**Electricity - imports:** 0 kWh (2007 est.)

**Oil - production:** 42,100 bbl/day (2008 est.)

**Oil - consumption:** 29,050 bbl/day (2006 est.)

**Oil - exports:** 39,310 bbl/day (2005)

**Oil - imports:** 24,150 bbl/day (2005)

**Oil - proved reserves:** 88 million bbl (1 January 2008 est.)

**Natural gas - production:** 140 million cu m (2006 est.)

**Natural gas - consumption:** 140 million cu m (2006 est.)

**Natural gas - exports:** 0 cu m (2007 est.)

**Natural gas - imports:** 0 cu m (2007 est.)

**Natural gas - proved reserves:** 226.5 billion cu m (1 January 2008 est.)

**Current account balance:** $438 million (2008 est.)

**Exports:** $5.658 billion f.o.b. (2008 est.)

**Exports - commodities:** oil, gold, copper ore, logs, palm oil, coffee, cocoa, crayfish, prawns

**Exports - partners:** Australia 27.3%, Japan 9.5%, China 5.7% (2007)

**Imports:** $3.013 billion f.o.b. (2008 est.)

**Imports - commodities:** machinery and transport equipment, manufactured goods, food, fuels, chemicals

**Imports - partners:** Australia 51.3%, Singapore 11.6%, China 7.9%, Japan 5.7% (2007)

**Reserves of foreign exchange and gold:** $2.548 billion (31 December 2008 est.)

**Debt - external:** $1.582 billion (31 December 2008 est.)

**Stock of direct foreign investment - at home:** $NA

**Stock of direct foreign investment - abroad:** $NA

**Exchange rates:** kina (PGK) per US dollar - 2.6956 (2008 est.), 3.03 (2007), 3.0643 (2006), 3.08 (2005), 3.2225 (2004)

### Communications

**Telephones - main lines in use:** 60,000 (2007)
**Telephones - mobile cellular:** 300,000 (2007)
**Telephone system:**
*general assessment:* services are minimal; facilities provide radiotelephone and telegraph, coastal radio, aeronautical radio, and international radio communication services
*domestic:* access to telephone services is now widely available; combined fixed-line and mobile-cellular teledensity is 6 per 100 persons
*international:* country code - 675; submarine cables to Australia and Guam; satellite earth station - 1 Intelsat (Pacific Ocean); international radio communication service (2007)
**Radio broadcast stations:** AM 8, FM 19, shortwave 28 (1998)
**Television broadcast stations:** 3 (all in the Port Moresby area; stations at Mt. Hagen, Goroka, Lae, and Rabaul are planned) (2004)
**Internet country code:** .pg
**Internet hosts:** 3,422 (2008)
**Internet users:** 110,000 (2006)

### Transportation

**Airports:** 557 (2008)
**Airports - with paved runways:**
*total:* 21
*2,438 to 3,047 m:* 2
*1,524 to 2,437 m:* 14
*914 to 1,523 m:* 4
*under 914 m:* 1 (2008)
**Airports - with unpaved runways:**
*total:* 536
*1,524 to 2,437 m:* 8
*914 to 1,523 m:* 62
*under 914 m:* 466 (2008)
**Heliports:** 2 (2007)
**Pipelines:** oil 195 km (2008)
**Roadways:**
*total:* 19,600 km
*paved:* 686 km
*unpaved:* 18,914 km (2000)
**Waterways:** 11,000 km (2006)
**Merchant marine:**
*total:* 21
*by type:* bulk carrier 2, cargo 17, petroleum tanker 2
*foreign-owned:* 6 (UAE 6) (2008)
**Ports and terminals:** Kimbe, Lae, Madang, Rabaul, Wewak

### Military

**Military branches:** Papua New Guinea Defense Force (PNGDF; includes Maritime Operations Element, Air Operations Element) (2009)
**Military service age and obligation:** 16 years of age for voluntary military service (with parental consent); no conscription (2008)

**Manpower available for military service:**
*males age 16-49:* 1,481,417
*females age 16-49:* 1,385,040 (2008 est.)
**Manpower fit for military service:**
*males age 16-49:* 1,110,175
*females age 16-49:* 1,127,758 (2009 est.)
**Manpower reaching militarily significant age annually:**
*male:* 64,636
*female:* 62,803 (2009 est.)
**Military expenditures:** 1.4% of GDP (2005 est.)

### Transnational Issues

**Disputes - international:** relies on assistance from Australia to keep out illegal cross-border activities from primarily Indonesia, including goods smuggling, illegal narcotics trafficking, and squatters and secessionists
**Refugees and internally displaced persons:**
*refugees (country of origin):* 10,177 (Indonesia) (2007)
**Trafficking in persons:**
*current situation:* Papua New Guinea is a country of destination for women and children from Malaysia, the Philippines, Thailand, and China trafficked for the purpose of commercial sexual exploitation; internal trafficking of women and children for the purposes of sexual exploitation and involuntary domestic servitude occurs as well
*tier rating:* Tier 3 - Papua New Guinea does not fully comply with the minimum standards for the elimination of trafficking and is not making significant efforts to do so; the current legal framework does not contain elements of crimes that characterize trafficking; the government lacks victim protection services or a systematic procedure to identify victims of trafficking; the government did not prosecute anyone in 2007 for trafficking; Papua New Guinea has not ratified the 2000 UN TIP Protocol (2008)
**Illicit drugs:** major consumer of cannabis

# Paracel Islands

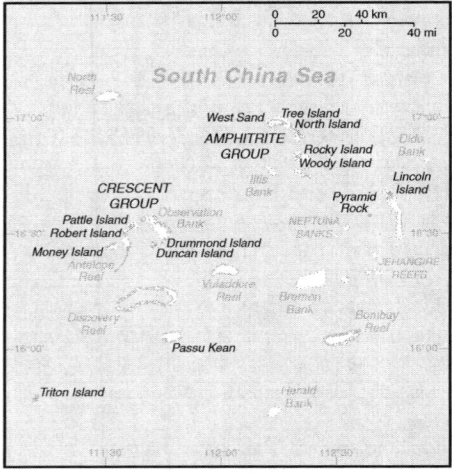

### Introduction

**Background:** The Paracel Islands are surrounded by productive fishing grounds and by potential oil and gas reserves. In 1932, French Indochina annexed the islands and set up a weather station on Pattle Island; maintenance was continued by its successor, Vietnam. China has occupied the Paracel Islands since 1974, when its troops seized a South Vietnamese garrison occupying the western islands. China built a military installation on Mischief Reef in 1999. The islands are claimed by Taiwan and Vietnam.

### Geography

**Location:** Southeastern Asia, group of small islands and reefs in the South China Sea, about one-third of the way from central Vietnam to the northern Philippines
**Geographic coordinates:** 16 30 N, 112 00 E
**Map references:** Southeast Asia
**Area:**
*total:* NA sq km
*land:* NA sq km
*water:* 0 sq km
**Area - comparative:** NA
**Land boundaries:** 0 km
**Coastline:** 518 km
**Maritime claims:** NA
**Climate:** tropical
**Terrain:** mostly low and flat
**Elevation extremes:**
*lowest point:* South China Sea 0 m
*highest point:* unnamed location on Rocky Island 14 m
**Natural resources:** none
**Land use:**
*arable land:* 0%
*permanent crops:* 0%
*other:* 100% (2005)
**Irrigated land:** 0 sq km
**Natural hazards:** typhoons

**Environment - current issues:** NA
**Geography - note:** composed of 130 small coral islands and reefs divided into the northeast Amphitrite Group and the western Crescent Group

## People

**Population:** no indigenous inhabitants
*note:* there are scattered Chinese garrisons

## Government

**Country name:**
*conventional long form:* none
*conventional short form:* Paracel Islands

## Economy

**Economy - overview:** China announced plans in 1997 to open the islands for tourism.

## Transportation

**Airports:** 1 (2008)
**Airports - with paved runways:**
*total:* 1
*1,524 to 2,437 m:* 1 (2008)
**Ports and terminals:** small Chinese port facilities on Woody Island and Duncan Island being expanded

## Military

**Military - note:** occupied by China

## Transnational Issues

**Disputes - international:** occupied by China, also claimed by Taiwan and Vietnam

# Paraguay

## Introduction

**Background:** Paraguay achieved its independence from Spain in 1811. In the disastrous War of the Triple Alliance (1865-70) - between Paraguay and Argentina, Brazil, and Uruguay - Paraguay lost two-thirds of all adult males and much of its territory. The country stagnated economically for the next half century. Following the Chaco War of 1932-35 with Bolivia, Paraguay gained a large part of the Chaco lowland region. The 35-year military dictatorship of Alfredo STROESSNER ended in 1989, and, despite a marked increase in political infighting in recent years, Paraguay has held relatively free and regular presidential elections since then.

## Geography

**Location:** Central South America, northeast of Argentina
**Geographic coordinates:** 23 00 S, 58 00 W
**Map references:** South America
**Area:**
*total:* 406,750 sq km
*land:* 397,300 sq km
*water:* 9,450 sq km
**Area - comparative:** slightly smaller than California
**Land boundaries:**
*total:* 3,995 km
*border countries:* Argentina 1,880 km, Bolivia 750 km, Brazil 1,365 km
**Coastline:** 0 km (landlocked)
**Maritime claims:** none (landlocked)
**Climate:** subtropical to temperate; substantial rainfall in the eastern portions, becoming semiarid in the far west
**Terrain:** grassy plains and wooded hills east of Rio Paraguay; Gran Chaco region west of Rio Paraguay mostly low, marshy plain near the river, and dry forest and thorny scrub elsewhere

**Elevation extremes:**
*lowest point:* junction of Rio Paraguay and Rio Parana 46 m
*highest point:* Cerro Pero (Cerro Tres Kandu) 842 m
**Natural resources:** hydropower, timber, iron ore, manganese, limestone
**Land use:**
*arable land:* 7.47%
*permanent crops:* 0.24%
*other:* 92.29% (2005)
**Irrigated land:** 670 sq km (2003)
**Total renewable water resources:** 336 cu km (2000)
**Freshwater withdrawal (domestic/industrial/agricultural):**
*total:* 0.49 cu km/yr (20%/8%/71%)
*per capita:* 80 cu m/yr (2000)
**Natural hazards:** local flooding in southeast (early September to June); poorly drained plains may become boggy (early October to June)
**Environment - current issues:** deforestation; water pollution; inadequate means for waste disposal pose health risks for many urban residents; loss of wetlands
**Environment - international agreements:**
*party to:* Biodiversity, Climate Change, Climate Change-Kyoto Protocol, Desertification, Endangered Species, Hazardous Wastes, Law of the Sea, Ozone Layer Protection, Wetlands
*signed, but not ratified:* none of the selected agreements
**Geography - note:** landlocked; lies between Argentina, Bolivia, and Brazil; population concentrated in southern part of country

## People

**Population:** 6,995,655 (July 2009 est.)
**Age structure:**
*0-14 years:* 36.7% (male 1,304,115/ female 1,260,560)
*15-64 years:* 58.1% (male 2,043,509/ female 2,023,317)
*65 years and over:* 5.2% (male 168,554/ female 195,600) (2009 est.)
**Median age:**
*total:* 21.9 years
*male:* 21.6 years
*female:* 22.2 years (2009 est.)
**Population growth rate:** 2.364% (2009 est.)
**Birth rate:** 28.17 births/1,000 population (2009 est.)
**Death rate:** 4.49 deaths/1,000 population (2008 est.)
**Net migration rate:** -0.07 migrant(s)/1,000 population (2009 est.)
**Urbanization:**
*urban population:* 60% of total population (2008)
*rate of urbanization:* 2.8% annual rate of change (2005-10 est.)
**Sex ratio:**
*at birth:* 1.05 male(s)/female
*under 15 years:* 1.03 male(s)/female
*15-64 years:* 1.01 male(s)/female
*65 years and over:* 0.86 male(s)/female
*total population:* 1.01 male(s)/female (2009 est.)

# Paraguay (continued)

**Infant mortality rate:**

*total:* 24.68 deaths/1,000 live births

*male:* 28.77 deaths/1,000 live births

*female:* 20.38 deaths/1,000 live births (2009 est.)

**Life expectancy at birth:**

*total population:* 75.77 years

*male:* 73.19 years

*female:* 78.49 years (2009 est.)

**Total fertility rate:** 3.75 children born/woman (2009 est.)

**HIV/AIDS - adult prevalence rate:** 0.6% (2007 est.)

**HIV/AIDS - people living with HIV/AIDS:** 21,000 (2007 est.)

**HIV/AIDS - deaths:** fewer than 1,000 (2007 est.)

**Major infectious diseases:**

*degree of risk:* intermediate

*food or waterborne diseases:* bacterial diarrhea, hepatitis A, and typhoid fever

*vectorborne disease:* dengue fever and malaria (2009)

**Nationality:**

*noun:* Paraguayan(s)

*adjective:* Paraguayan

**Ethnic groups:** mestizo (mixed Spanish and Amerindian) 95%, other 5%

**Religions:** Roman Catholic 89.6%, Protestant 6.2%, other Christian 1.1%, other or unspecified 1.9%, none 1.1% (2002 census)

**Languages:** Spanish (official), Guarani (official)

**Literacy:**

*definition:* age 15 and over can read and write

*total population:* 94%

*male:* 94.9%

*female:* 93% (2003 est.)

**School life expectancy (primary to tertiary education):**

*total:* 12 years

*male:* 12 years

*female:* 12 years (2005)

**Education expenditures:** 4% of GDP (2004)

## Government

**Country name:**

*conventional long form:* Republic of Paraguay

*conventional short form:* Paraguay

*local long form:* Republica del Paraguay

*local short form:* Paraguay

**Government type:** constitutional republic

**Capital:**

*name:* Asuncion

*geographic coordinates:* 25 16 S, 57 40 W

*time difference:* UTC-4 (1 hour ahead of Washington, DC during Standard Time)

**Administrative divisions:** 17 departments (departamentos, singular - departamento) and 1 capital city*; Alto Paraguay, Alto Parana, Amambay, Asuncion*, Boqueron, Caaguazu, Caazapa, Canindeyu, Central, Concepcion, Cordillera, Guaira, Itapua, Misiones, Neembucu, Paraguari, Presidente Hayes, San Pedro

**Independence:** 14 May 1811 (from Spain)

**National holiday:** Independence Day, 14 May 1811 (observed 15 May)

**Constitution:** promulgated 20 June 1992

**Legal system:** based on Argentine codes, Roman law, and French codes; judicial review of legislative acts in Supreme Court of Justice; accepts compulsory ICJ jurisdiction

**Suffrage:** 18 years of age; universal and compulsory up to age 75

**Executive branch:**

*chief of state:* President Fernando Armindo LUGO Mendez (since 15 August 2008); Vice President Federico FRANCO (since 15 August 2008); note - the president is both the chief of state and head of government

*head of government:* President Fernando Armindo LUGO Mendez (since 15 August 2008); Vice President Federico FRANCO (since 15 August 2008)

*cabinet:* Council of Ministers appointed by the president

*elections:* president and vice president elected on the same ticket by popular vote for a single five-year term; election last held 20 April 2008 (next to be held April 2013)

*election results:* Fernando Armindo LUGO Mendez elected president; percent of vote - Fernando Armindo LUGO Mendez 40.8%, Blanca OVELAR 30.6%, Lino OVIEDO 21.9%, Pedro FADUL 2.4%, other 4.3%

**Legislative branch:** bicameral National Congress or Congreso Nacional consists of the Chamber of Senators or Camara de Senadores (45 seats; members are elected by popular vote to serve five-year terms) and the Chamber of Deputies or Camara de Diputados (80 seats; members are elected by popular vote to serve five-year terms)

*elections:* Chamber of Senators - last held 20 April 2008 (next to be held in April 2013); Chamber of Deputies - last held 20 April 2008 (next to be held in April 2013)

*election results:* Chamber of Senators - percent of vote by party - NA; seats by party - ANR 15, PLRA 14, UNACE 9, PPQ 4, other 3; Chamber of Deputies - percent of vote by party - NA; seats by party - ANR 30, PLRA 27, UNACE 15, PPQ 3, APC 2, other 3

**Judicial branch:** Supreme Court of Justice or Corte Suprema de Justicia (nine judges appointed on the proposal of the Council of Magistrates or Consejo de la Magistratura)

**Political parties and leaders:** Alianza Patriotica por el Cambio (Patriotic Alliance for Change) or APC [Fernando LUGO]; Asociacion Nacional Republicana - Colorado Party or ANR [Lilian SAMANIEGO]; Movimiento Union Nacional de Ciudadanos Eticos or UNACE [Lino Cesar OVIEDO Silva]; Patria Querida (Beloved Fatherland Party) or PPQ [Pedro Nicolas Maraa FADUL Niella]; Partido del Movimiento al Socialismo or P-MAS; Partido Encuentro Nacional or PEN [Emilio CAMACHO Paredes]; Partido Liberal Radical Autentico or PLRA [Gustavo CARDOZO]; Partido Pais Solidario or PPS [Carlos Alberto FILIZZOLA Pallares]

**Political pressure groups and leaders:** Ahorristas Estafados or AE; National Coordinating Board of Campesino Organizations or MCNOC [Luis AGUAYO]; National Federation of Campesinos or FNC [Odilon ESPINOLA]; National Workers Central or CNT [Secretary General Juan TORRALES]; Paraguayan Workers Confederation or CPT; Roman Catholic Church; Unitary Workers Central or CUT [Jorge Guzman ALVARENGA Malgarejo]

**International organization participation:** CAN (associate), FAO, G-77, IADB, IAEA, IBRD, ICAO, ICCt, ICRM, IDA, IFAD, IFC, IFRCS, ILO, IMF, IMO, Interpol, IOC, IOM, IPU, ISO (correspondent), ITSO, ITU, ITUC, LAES, LAIA, Mercosur, MIGA, MINURSO, MINUSTAH, MONUC, NAM (observer), OAS, OPANAL, OPCW, PCA, RG, UN, UNASUR, UNCTAD, UNESCO, UNIDO, Union Latina, UNMIL, UNMIS, UNOCI, UNWTO, UPU, WCL, WCO, WFTU, WHO, WIPO, WMO, WTO

**Diplomatic representation in the US:**

*chief of mission:* Ambassador James SPALDING Hellmers

*chancery:* 2400 Massachusetts Avenue NW, Washington, DC 20008

*telephone:* [1] (202) 483-6960 through 6962

*FAX:* [1] (202) 234-4508

*consulate(s) general:* Kansas City (Kansas), Los Angeles, Miami, New York

**Diplomatic representation from the US:**

Ambassador Liliana AYALDE

*embassy:* 1776 Avenida Mariscal Lopez, Casilla Postal 402, Asuncion

*mailing address:* Unit 4711, APO AA 34036-0001

*telephone:* [595] (21) 213-715

*FAX:* [595] (21) 228-603

**Flag description:** three equal, horizontal bands of red (top), white, and blue with an emblem centered in the white band; unusual flag in that the emblem is different on each side; the obverse (hoist side at the left) bears the national coat of arms (a yellow five-pointed star within a green wreath capped by the words REPUBLICA DEL PARAGUAY, all within two circles); the reverse (hoist side at the right) bears the seal of the treasury (a yellow lion below a red Cap of Liberty and the words Paz y Justicia (Peace and Justice) capped by the words REPUBLICA DEL PARAGUAY, all within two circles)

## Economy

**Economy - overview:** Landlocked Paraguay has a market economy marked by a large informal sector, featuring reexport of imported consumer goods to neighboring countries, as well as the activities of thousands of microenterprises and urban street vendors. A large percentage of the population, especially in rural areas, derives its living from agricultural activity, often on a subsistence basis. Because of the importance of the informal sector, accurate economic measures are difficult to obtain. On a per capita basis, real income has stagnated at 1980 levels. Most observers attribute Paraguay's poor economic performance to political uncertainty, corruption, limited progress on structural reform, and deficient infrastructure. The economy rebounded between 2003 and 2008, however, as growing world demand for commodities combined with high prices and favorable weather to support Paraguay's commodity-based export expansion. Paraguay is the sixth largest soy producer in the world.

**GDP (purchasing power parity):**
$28.71 billion (2008 est.)
$27.21 billion (2007)
$25.57 billion (2006)
*note:* data are in 2008 US dollars

**GDP (official exchange rate):** $16.36 billion (2008 est.)

**GDP - real growth rate:**
5.5% (2008 est.)
6.4% (2007 est.)
4.3% (2006 est.)

**GDP - per capita (PPP):**
$4,200 (2008 est.)
$4,100 (2007 est.)
$3,900 (2006 est.)
*note:* data are in 2008 US dollars

**GDP - composition by sector:**
*agriculture:* 23.1%
*industry:* 17.2%
*services:* 59.6% (2008 est.)

**Labor force:** 2.839 million (2008 est.)

**Labor force - by occupation:**
*agriculture:* 31%
*industry:* 17%
*services:* 52% (2007)

**Unemployment rate:**
5.4% (2008 est.)
5.6% (2007 est.)

**Population below poverty line:** 32% (2005 est.)

**Household income or consumption by percentage share:**
*lowest 10%:* 0.7%
*highest 10%:* 46.1% (2003)

**Distribution of family income - Gini index:** 56.8 (2008)

**Investment (gross fixed):** 20.2% of GDP (2008 est.)

**Budget:**
*revenues:* $2.939 billion
*expenditures:* $2.866 billion (2008 est.)

**Public debt:** 22.2% of GDP (2008 est.)

**Inflation rate (consumer prices):**
11% (2008 est.)
8.1% (2007 est.)

**Central bank discount rate:** 20% (31 December 2007)

**Commercial bank prime lending rate:** 25.03% (31 December 2007)

**Stock of money:** $1.943 billion (31 December 2007)

**Stock of quasi money:** $1.368 billion (31 December 2007)

**Stock of domestic credit:** $2.457 billion (31 December 2007)

**Market value of publicly traded shares:** $233.8 million (2005)

**Agriculture - products:** cotton, sugarcane, soybeans, corn, wheat, tobacco, cassava (tapioca), fruits, vegetables; beef, pork, eggs, milk; timber

**Industries:** sugar, cement, textiles, beverages, wood products, steel, metallurgic, electric power

**Industrial production growth rate:** 2.5% (2008 est.)

**Electricity - production:** 70 billion kWh (2007)

**Electricity - consumption:** 6 billion kWh (2007)

**Electricity - exports:** 64 billion kWh (2007)

**Electricity - imports:** 0 kWh (2007)

**Oil - production:** 0 bbl/day (2007 est.)

**Oil - consumption:** 27,410 bbl/day (2006 est.)

**Oil - exports:** 0 bbl/day (2007)

**Oil - imports:** 25,940 bbl/day (2007)

**Oil - proved reserves:** 0 bbl (1 January 2006 est.)

**Natural gas - production:** 0 cu m (2007 est.)

**Natural gas - consumption:** 0 cu m (2007 est.)

**Natural gas - exports:** 0 cu m (2007 est.)

**Natural gas - imports:** 0 cu m (2007 est.)

**Natural gas - proved reserves:** 0 cu m (1 January 2007 est.)

**Current account balance:** $178 million (2008 est.)

**Exports:** $6.901 billion f.o.b. (2008 est.)

**Exports - commodities:** soybeans, feed, cotton, meat, edible oils, electricity, wood, leather

**Exports - partners:** Argentina 28.1%, Uruguay 15.2%, Brazil 12.7%, Chile 5.9%, Germany 4.9%, Russia 4.5% (2007)

**Imports:** $7.351 billion f.o.b. (2008 est.)

**Imports - commodities:** road vehicles, consumer goods, tobacco, petroleum products, electrical machinery, tractors, chemicals, vehicle parts

**Imports - partners:** Brazil 30.4%, US 22.8%, Argentina 14.4%, China 8.6% (2007)

**Reserves of foreign exchange and gold:** $2.629 billion (31 December 2008 est.)

**Debt - external:** $3.487 billion (31 December 2008 est.)

**Stock of direct foreign investment - at home:** $2.057 million (2007)

**Stock of direct foreign investment - abroad:** $NA

**Exchange rates:** guarani (PYG) per US dollar - 4,337.7 (2008 est.), 5,031 (2007), 5,672.8 (2006), 6,178 (2005), 5,974.6 (2004)

## Communications

**Telephones - main lines in use:** 453,800 (2007)

**Telephones - mobile cellular:** 4.33 million (2007)

**Telephone system:**
*general assessment:* meager telephone service; principal switching center is in Asuncion
*domestic:* the fixed-line market is a state monopoly; deficiencies in provision of fixed-line service have resulted in a rapid expansion of mobile-cellular services fostered by competition among multiple providers
*international:* country code - 595; satellite earth station -1 Intelsat (Atlantic Ocean)

**Radio broadcast stations:** AM 41, FM 121, shortwave 6 (2006)

**Television broadcast stations:** 5 (2007)

**Internet country code:** .py

**Internet hosts:** 19,691 (2008)

**Internet users:** 280,000 (2007)

## Transportation

**Airports:** 797 (2008)

**Airports - with paved runways:**
*total:* 13
*over 3,047 m:* 3
*1,524 to 2,437 m:* 5
*914 to 1,523 m:* 5 (2008)

**Airports - with unpaved runways:**
*total:* 784
*1,524 to 2,437 m:* 26
*914 to 1,523 m:* 288
*under 914 m:* 470 (2008)

**Railways:**
*total:* 36 km
*standard gauge:* 36 km 1.435-m gauge (2006)

**Roadways:**
*total:* 29,500 km
*paved:* 14,986 km
*unpaved:* 14,514 km (2000)

**Waterways:** 3,100 km (2008)

**Merchant marine:**
*total:* 23
*by type:* cargo 18, carrier 1, passenger 1, petroleum tanker 2, roll on/roll off 1
*foreign-owned:* 6 (Argentina 5, Netherlands 1) (2008)

**Ports and terminals:** Asuncion, Villeta, San Antonio, Encarnacion

## Military

**Military branches:** Army, National Navy (Armada Nacional, includes Naval Aviation, Marine Corps, General Naval Prefecture), Air Force (Fuerza Aerea Paraguay, FAP) (2008)

**Military service age and obligation:** 18 years of age for compulsory and voluntary military service; conscript service obligation - 12 months for Army, 24 months for Navy (2007)

**Manpower available for military service:**
*males age 16-49:* 1,589,873
*females age 16-49:* 1,585,573 (2008 est.)

**Manpower fit for military service:**
*males age 16-49:* 1,363,746
*females age 16-49:* 1,390,799 (2009 est.)

**Manpower reaching militarily significant age annually:**
*male:* 73,660
*female:* 72,046 (2009 est.)

**Military expenditures:** 1% of GDP (2006 est.)

# Paraguay (continued)

## Transnational Issues

**Disputes - international:** unruly region at convergence of Argentina-Brazil-Paraguay borders is locus of money laundering, smuggling, arms and illegal narcotics trafficking, and fundraising for extremist organizations

**Illicit drugs:** major illicit producer of cannabis, most or all of which is consumed in Brazil, Argentina, and Chile; transshipment country for Andean cocaine headed for Brazil, other Southern Cone markets, and Europe; weak border controls, extensive corruption and money-laundering activity, especially in the Tri-Border Area; weak anti-money-laundering laws and enforcement

# Peru

## Introduction

**Background:** Ancient Peru was the seat of several prominent Andean civilizations, most notably that of the Incas whose empire was captured by the Spanish conquistadors in 1533. Peruvian independence was declared in 1821, and remaining Spanish forces defeated in 1824. After a dozen years of military rule, Peru returned to democratic leadership in 1980, but experienced economic problems and the growth of a violent insurgency. President Alberto FUJIMORI's election in 1990 ushered in a decade that saw a dramatic turnaround in the economy and significant progress in curtailing guerrilla activity. Nevertheless, the president's increasing reliance on authoritarian measures and an economic slump in the late 1990s generated mounting dissatisfaction with his regime, which led to his ouster in 2000. A caretaker government oversaw new elections in the spring of 2001, which ushered in Alejandro TOLEDO Manrique as the new head of government - Peru's first democratically elected president of Native American ethnicity. The presidential election of 2006 saw the return of Alan GARCIA Perez who, after a disappointing presidential term from 1985 to 1990, has overseen a robust macroeconomic performance.

## Geography

**Location:** Western South America, bordering the South Pacific Ocean, between Chile and Ecuador
**Geographic coordinates:** 10 00 S, 76 00 W
**Map references:** South America
**Area:**
*total:* 1,285,220 sq km
*land:* 1.28 million sq km
*water:* 5,220 sq km
**Area - comparative:** slightly smaller than Alaska
**Land boundaries:**
*total:* 7,461 km
*border countries:* Bolivia 1,075 km, Brazil 2,995 km, Chile 171 km, Colombia 1,800 km, Ecuador 1,420 km

**Coastline:** 2,414 km
**Maritime claims:**
*territorial sea:* 200 nm
*continental shelf:* 200 nm
**Climate:** varies from tropical in east to dry desert in west; temperate to frigid in Andes
**Terrain:** western coastal plain (costa), high and rugged Andes in center (sierra), eastern lowland jungle of Amazon Basin (selva)
**Elevation extremes:**
*lowest point:* Pacific Ocean 0 m
*highest point:* Nevado Huascaran 6,768 m
**Natural resources:** copper, silver, gold, petroleum, timber, fish, iron ore, coal, phosphate, potash, hydropower, natural gas
**Land use:**
*arable land:* 2.88%
*permanent crops:* 0.47%
*other:* 96.65% (2005)
**Irrigated land:** 12,000 sq km (2003)
**Total renewable water resources:** 1,913 cu km (2000)
**Freshwater withdrawal (domestic/industrial/agricultural):**
*total:* 20.13 cu km/yr (8%/10%/82%)
*per capita:* 720 cu m/yr (2000)
**Natural hazards:** earthquakes, tsunamis, flooding, landslides, mild volcanic activity
**Environment - current issues:** deforestation (some the result of illegal logging); overgrazing of the slopes of the costa and sierra leading to soil erosion; desertification; air pollution in Lima; pollution of rivers and coastal waters from municipal and mining wastes
**Environment - international agreements:**
*party to:* Antarctic-Environmental Protocol, Antarctic-Marine Living Resources, Antarctic Treaty, Biodiversity, Climate Change, Climate Change-Kyoto Protocol, Desertification, Endangered Species, Hazardous Wastes, Marine Dumping, Ozone Layer Protection, Ship Pollution, Tropical Timber 83, Tropical Timber 94, Wetlands, Whaling
*signed, but not ratified:* none of the selected agreements
**Geography - note:** shares control of Lago Titicaca, world's highest navigable lake, with Bolivia; a remote slope of Nevado Mismi, a 5,316 m peak, is the ultimate source of the Amazon River

## People

**Population:** 29,546,963 (July 2009 est.)
**Age structure:**
*0-14 years:* 29.1% (male 4,370,923/female 4,216,364)
*15-64 years:* 65.2% (male 9,695,270/female 9,574,018)
*65 years and over:* 5.7% (male 796,631/female 893,757) (2009 est.)
**Median age:**
*total:* 26.1 years
*male:* 25.8 years
*female:* 26.4 years (2009 est.)

# Peru *(continued)*

**Population growth rate:** 1.229% (2009 est.)
**Birth rate:** 19.38 births/1,000 population (2009 est.)
**Death rate:** 6.16 deaths/1,000 population (2008 est.)
**Net migration rate:** -0.95 migrant(s)/1,000 population (2009 est.)
**Urbanization:**
*urban population:* 71% of total population (2008)
*rate of urbanization:* 1.3% annual rate of change (2005-10 est.)
**Sex ratio:**
*at birth:* 1.05 male(s)/female
*under 15 years:* 1.04 male(s)/female
*15-64 years:* 1.01 male(s)/female
*65 years and over:* 0.89 male(s)/female
*total population:* 1.01 male(s)/female (2009 est.)
**Infant mortality rate:**
*total:* 28.62 deaths/1,000 live births
*male:* 31.07 deaths/1,000 live births
*female:* 26.06 deaths/1,000 live births (2009 est.)
**Life expectancy at birth:**
*total population:* 70.74 years
*male:* 68.88 years
*female:* 72.69 years (2009 est.)
**Total fertility rate:** 2.37 children born/woman (2009 est.)
**HIV/AIDS - adult prevalence rate:** 0.5% (2007 est.)
**HIV/AIDS - people living with HIV/AIDS:** 76,000 (2007 est.)
**HIV/AIDS - deaths:** 3,300 (2007 est.)
**Major infectious diseases:**
*degree of risk:* very high
*food or waterborne diseases:* bacterial, hepatitis A, and typhoid fever
*vectorborne disease:* dengue fever, malaria, and yellow fever
*water contact disease:* leptospirosis (2009)
**Nationality:**
*noun:* Peruvian(s)
*adjective:* Peruvian
**Ethnic groups:** Amerindian 45%, mestizo (mixed Amerindian and white) 37%, white 15%, black, Japanese, Chinese, and other 3%
**Religions:** Roman Catholic 81.3%, Evangelical 12.5%, other 3.3%, unspecified or none 2.9% (2007 Census)
**Languages:** Spanish (official), Quechua (official), Aymara, and a large number of minor Amazonian languages
**Literacy:**
*definition:* age 15 and over can read and write
*total population:* 92.9%
*male:* 96.4%
*female:* 89.4% (2007 Census)
**School life expectancy (primary to tertiary education):**
*total:* 14 years
*male:* 14 years
*female:* 14 years (2006)
**Education expenditures:** 2.5% of GDP (2006)

## Government

**Country name:**
*conventional long form:* Republic of Peru
*conventional short form:* Peru
*local long form:* Republica del Peru
*local short form:* Peru
**Government type:** constitutional republic
**Capital:**
*name:* Lima
*geographic coordinates:* 12 03 S, 77 03 W
*time difference:* UTC-5 (same time as Washington, DC during Standard Time)
**Administrative divisions:** 25 regions (regiones, singular - region) and 1 province* (provincia); Amazonas, Ancash, Apurimac, Arequipa, Ayacucho, Cajamarca, Callao, Cusco, Huancavelica, Huanuco, Ica, Junin, La Libertad, Lambayeque, Lima, Lima*, Loreto, Madre de Dios, Moquegua, Pasco, Piura, Puno, San Martin, Tacna, Tumbes, Ucayali
**Independence:** 28 July 1821 (from Spain)
**National holiday:** Independence Day, 28 July (1821)
**Constitution:** 29 December 1993
**Legal system:** based on civil law system; accepts compulsory ICJ jurisdiction with reservations
**Suffrage:** 18 years of age; universal and compulsory until the age of 70; note - for the first time in recent elections, members of the military and national police were eligible to vote in the 2006 elections
**Executive branch:**
*chief of state:* President Alan GARCIA Perez (since 28 July 2006); First Vice President Luis GIAMPIETRI Rojas (since 28 July 2006); Second Vice President Lourdes MENDOZA del Solar (since 28 July 2006); note - the president is both the chief of state and head of government
*head of government:* President Alan GARCIA Perez (since 28 July 2006); First Vice President Luis GIAMPIETRI Rojas (since 28 July 2006); Second Vice President Lourdes MENDOZA del Solar (since 28 July 2006)
*note:* Prime Minister Yehude SIMON Munaro (since 14 October 2008) does not exercise executive power; this power is in the hands of the president
*cabinet:* Council of Ministers appointed by the president
*elections:* president elected by popular vote for a five-year term (eligible for a nonconsecutive reelection); presidential and congressional elections held 9 April 2006 with runoff election held 4 June 2006; next to be held in April 2011
*election results:* Alan GARCIA Perez elected president in runoff election; percent of vote - Alan GARCIA Perez 52.5%, Ollanta HUMALA Tasso 47.5%

**Legislative branch:** unicameral Congress of the Republic of Peru or Congreso de la Republica del Peru (120 seats; members are elected by popular vote to serve five-year terms)
*elections:* last held 9 April 2006 (next to be held in April 2011)
*election results:* percent of vote by party - UPP 21.2%, PAP 20.6%, UN 15.3%, AF 13.1%, FC 7.1%, PP 4.1%, RN 4.0%, other 14.6%; seats by party - UPP 45, PAP 36, UN 17, AF 13, FC 5, PP 2, RN 2
**Judicial branch:** Supreme Court of Justice or Corte Suprema de Justicia (judges are appointed by the National Council of the Judiciary)
**Political parties and leaders:** Alliance For Progress (Alianza Para El Progreso) [Cesar ACUNA Peralta]; Alliance For The Future (Alianza Por El Futuro) or AF (a coalition of pro-FUJIMORI parties including Cambio 90, Nueva Mayoria, and Si Cumple); Central Front (Frente Del Centro) or FC (a coalition of Accion Popular, Somos Peru, and Coordinadora Nacional de Independientes) [Victor Andres GARCIA Belaunde]; National Renovation Party (Partido Renovacion Nacional) [Rafael REY]; National Restoration Party (Restauracion Nacional) or RN [Humberto LAY Sun]; National Solidarity Party (Partido Solidaridad Nacional) or SN [Luis CASTANEDA Lossio]; Peru Possible (Peru Posible) or PP [Alejandro TOLEDO Manrique]; Peruvian Aprista Party (Partido Aprista Peruano) or PAP [Alan GARCIA Perez] (also referred to by its original name Alianza Popular Revolucionaria Americana or APRA); Peruvian Nationalist Party (Partido Nacionalista Peruano) or PNP [Ollanta HUMALA Tasso]; Popular Christian Party (Partido Popular Cristiano) or PPC [Lourdes FLORES Nano]; Union for Peru (Union por el Peru) or UPP [Aldo ESTRADA Choque]
**Political pressure groups and leaders:** General Workers Confederation of Peru (Confederacion General de Trabajadores del Peru) or CGTP [Mario HUAMAN]; Shining Path (Sendero Luminoso) or SL [Abimael GUZMAN Reynoso (imprisoned), Victor QUISPE Palomino (top leader at-large)] (leftist guerrilla group)
**International organization participation:** APEC, CAN, FAO, G-15, G-24, G-77, IADB, IAEA, IBRD, ICAO, ICCt, ICRM, IDA, IFAD, IFC, IFRCS, IHO, ILO, IMF, IMO, IMSO, Interpol, IOC, IOM, IPU, ISO, ITSO, ITU, ITUC, LAES, LAIA, Mercosur (associate), MIGA, MINUSTAH, MONUC, NAM, OAS, OPANAL, OPCW, PCA, RG, UN, UNASUR, UNCTAD, UNESCO, UNIDO, Union Latina, UNMIL, UNMIS, UNOCI, UNWTO, UPU, WCL, WCO, WFTU, WHO, WIPO, WMO, WTO
**Diplomatic representation in the US:**
*chief of mission:* Ambassador Luis VALDIVIESO Montano
*chancery:* 1700 Massachusetts Avenue NW, Washington, DC 20036
*telephone:* [1] (202) 833-9860 through 9869
*FAX:* [1] (202) 659-8124
*consulate(s) general:* Atlanta, Boston, Chicago, Dallas, Denver, Hartford, Houston, Los Angeles, Miami, New York, Paterson (New Jersey), San Francisco

# Peru *(continued)*

**Diplomatic representation from the US:**

*chief of mission:* Ambassador P. Michael MCKINLEY

*embassy:* Avenida La Encalada, Cuadra 17s/n, Surco, Lima 33

*mailing address:* P. O. Box 1995, Lima 1; American Embassy (Lima), APO AA 34031-5000

*telephone:* [51] (1) 434-3000

*FAX:* [51] (1) 618-2397

**Flag description:** three equal, vertical bands of red (hoist side), white, and red with the coat of arms centered in the white band; the coat of arms features a shield bearing a vicuna, cinchona tree (the source of quinine), and a yellow cornucopia spilling out gold coins, all framed by a green wreath

## Economy

**Economy - overview:** Peru's economy reflects its varied geography - an arid coastal region, the Andes further inland, and tropical lands bordering Colombia and Brazil. Abundant mineral resources are found in the mountainous areas, and Peru's coastal waters provide excellent fishing grounds. The Peruvian economy grew by more than 4% per year during the period 2002-06, with a stable exchange rate and low inflation. Growth jumped to 9% per year in 2007 and 2008, driven by higher world prices for minerals and metals and the government's aggressive trade liberalization strategies. Peru's rapid expansion has helped to reduce the national poverty rate by about 15% since 2002, though underemployment and inflation remain high. Despite Peru's strong macroeconomic performance, overdependence on minerals and metals subjects the economy to fluctuations in world prices, and poor infrastructure precludes the spread of growth to Peru's non-coastal areas. Not all Peruvians therefore have shared in the benefits of growth. President GARCIA's pursuit of sound trade and macroeconomic policies has cost him political support since his election. Nevertheless, he remains committed to Peru's free-trade path. The United States and Peru completed negotiations on the implementation of the US-Peru Trade Promotion Agreement (PTPA), and the agreement entered into force February 1, 2009, opening the way to greater trade and investment between the two economies.

**GDP (purchasing power parity):**

$238.9 billion (2008 est.)

$218.8 billion (2007)

$206.6 billion (2006)

*note:* data are in 2008 US dollars

**GDP (official exchange rate):** $131.4 billion (2008 est.)

**GDP - real growth rate:**

9.2% (2008 est.)

9% (2007 est.)

7.6% (2006 est.)

**GDP - per capita (PPP):**

$8,400 (2008 est.)

$7,800 (2007 est.)

$7,300 (2006 est.)

*note:* data are in 2008 US dollars

**GDP - composition by sector:**

*agriculture:* 8.5%

*industry:* 21.2%

*services:* 70.3% (2008 est.)

**Labor force:** 10.2 million (2008 est.)

**Labor force - by occupation:**

*agriculture:* 0.7%

*industry:* 23.8%

*services:* 75.5% (2005)

**Unemployment rate:**

8.4% (2008 est.)

6.9% (2007 est.)

*note:* data are for metropolitan Lima; widespread underemployment

**Population below poverty line:** 44.5% (2006)

**Household income or consumption by percentage share:**

*lowest 10%:* 1.3%

*highest 10%:* 40.9% (2003)

**Distribution of family income - Gini index:** 49.8 (2005)

**Investment (gross fixed):** 24.4% of GDP (2008 est.)

**Budget:**

*revenues:* $38.83 billion

*expenditures:* $35.5 billion (2008 est.)

**Public debt:** 24.1% of GDP (2008 est.)

**Inflation rate (consumer prices):**

6.7% (2008 est.)

1.8% (2007 est.)

**Central bank discount rate:** 6.5% (December 2008)

**Commercial bank prime lending rate:** 24.1% (December 2008)

**Stock of money:** $14.66 billion (31 December 2007)

**Stock of quasi money:** $19.95 billion (31 December 2007)

**Stock of domestic credit:** $17.88 billion (31 December 2007)

**Market value of publicly traded shares:** $57.23 billion (31 July 2008)

**Agriculture - products:** asparagus, coffee, cocoa, cotton, sugarcane, rice, potatoes, corn, plantains, grapes, oranges, pineapples, guavas, bananas, apples, lemons, pears, coca, tomatoes, mango, barley, medicinal plants, palm oil, marigold, onion, wheat, dry beans; poultry, beef, dairy products; fish, guinea pigs

**Industries:** mining and refining of minerals; steel, metal fabrication; petroleum extraction and refining, natural gas; fishing and fish processing, textiles, clothing, food processing

**Industrial production growth rate:** 4.5% (2008 est.)

**Electricity - production:** 30.57 billion kWh (2008 est.)

**Electricity - consumption:** 28.97 billion kWh (2008 est.)

**Electricity - exports:** 0 kWh (2008 est.)

**Electricity - imports:** 0 kWh (2008 est.)

**Oil - production:** 110,800 bbl/day (2008 est.)

**Oil - consumption:** 170,000 bbl/day (2007 est.)

**Oil - exports:** 27,390 bbl/day (2007 est.)

**Oil - imports:** 109,000 bbl/day (2007 est.)

**Oil - proved reserves:** 930 million bbl (1 January 2008 est.)

**Natural gas - production:** 3.4 billion cu m (2008 est.)

**Natural gas - consumption:** 3.4 billion cu m (2008 est.)

**Natural gas - exports:** 0 cu m (2008 est.)

**Natural gas - imports:** 0 cu m (2008 est.)

**Natural gas - proved reserves:** 334.7 billion cu m (1 January 2008 est.)

**Current account balance:** -$3.631 billion (2008 est.)

**Exports:** $33.27 billion f.o.b. (2008 est.)

**Exports - commodities:** copper, gold, zinc, crude petroleum and petroleum products, coffee, potatoes, asparagus, textiles, fishmeal

**Exports - partners:** US 19.5%, China 12.7%, Canada 7.6%, Japan 7.5%, Chile 5.9%, Switzerland 4.2%, Spain 4.1% (2007)

**Imports:** $29.08 billion f.o.b. (2008 est.)

**Imports - commodities:** petroleum and petroleum products, plastics, machinery, vehicles, iron and steel, wheat, paper

**Imports - partners:** US 20.5%, China 10.8%, Brazil 9%, Ecuador 6.1%, Argentina 5.6%, Chile 5%, Colombia 4.8% (2007)

**Reserves of foreign exchange and gold:** $31.79 billion (31 December 2008 est.)

**Debt - external:** $35.46 billion (31 December 2008 est.)

**Stock of direct foreign investment - at home:** $32.14 billion (2008 est.)

**Stock of direct foreign investment - abroad:** $1.476 billion (2008 est.)

**Exchange rates:** nuevo sol (PEN) per US dollar - 2.91 (2008 est.), 3.1731 (2007), 3.2742 (2006), 3.2958 (2005), 3.4132 (2004)

## Communications

**Telephones - main lines in use:** 2.673 million (2007)

**Telephones - mobile cellular:** 15.417 million (2007)

**Telephone system:**

*general assessment:* adequate for most requirements

*domestic:* fixed-line teledensity is only about 9 per 100 persons; mobile-cellular teledensity, spurred by competition among multiple providers, has increased to roughly 55 telephones per 100 persons; nationwide microwave radio relay system and a domestic satellite system with 12 earth stations

*international:* country code - 51; the South America-1 (SAM-1) and Pan American (PAN-AM) submarine cable systems provide links to parts of Central and South America, the Caribbean, and US; satellite earth stations - 2 Intelsat (Atlantic Ocean)

**Radio broadcast stations:** AM 472, FM 198, shortwave 189 (1999)

# Peru (continued)

**Television broadcast stations:** 13 (plus 112 repeaters) (1997)
**Internet country code:** .pe
**Internet hosts:** 271,745 (2008)
**Internet users:** 7.636 million (2007)

## Transportation

**Airports:** 202 (2008)
**Airports - with paved runways:**
*total:* 56
*over 3,047 m:* 6
*2,438 to 3,047 m:* 20
*1,524 to 2,437 m:* 15
*914 to 1,523 m:* 11
*under 914 m:* 4 (2008)
**Airports - with unpaved runways:**
*total:* 146
*2,438 to 3,047 m:* 2
*1,524 to 2,437 m:* 24
*914 to 1,523 m:* 39
*under 914 m:* 81 (2008)
**Heliports:** 1 (2007)
**Pipelines:** extra heavy crude 533 km; gas 1,078 km; liquid petroleum gas 654 km; oil 1,018 km; refined products 15 km (2008)
**Railways:**
*total:* 1,989 km
*standard gauge:* 1,726 km 1.435-m gauge
*narrow gauge:* 263 km 0.914-m gauge (2006)
**Roadways:**
*total:* 78,829 km
*paved:* 11,351 km (includes 276 km of expressways)
*unpaved:* 67,478 km (2004)
**Waterways:** 8,808 km
*note:* 8,600 km of navigable tributaries of Amazon system and 208 km of Lago Titicaca (2008)
**Merchant marine:**
*total:* 8
*by type:* cargo 3, chemical tanker 1, petroleum tanker 4
*foreign-owned:* 1 (Bahamas 1)
*registered in other countries:* 17 (Belize 1, Panama 16) (2008)
**Ports and terminals:** Callao, Iquitos, Matarani, Paita, Pucallpa, Yurimaguas; note - Iquitos, Pucallpa, and Yurimaguas are on the upper reaches of the Amazon and its tributaries

## Military

**Military branches:** Army of Peru (Ejercito Peruano), Navy of Peru (Marina de Guerra del Peru, MGP (includes naval air, naval infantry, and Coast Guard)), Air Force of Peru (Fuerza Aerea del Peru, FAP) (2008)
**Military service age and obligation:** 18-30 years of age for voluntary male and female military service; no conscription (2008)
**Manpower available for military service:**
*males age 16-49:* 7,653,898
*females age 16-49:* 7,531,329 (2008 est.)

**Manpower fit for military service:**
*males age 16-49:* 5,920,716
*females age 16-49:* 6,359,803 (2009 est.)
**Manpower reaching militarily significant age annually:**
*male:* 310,575
*female:* 300,838 (2009 est.)
**Military expenditures:** 1.5% of GDP (2006)

## Transnational Issues

**Disputes - international:** Chile and Ecuador rejected Peru's November 2005 unilateral legislation to shift the axis of their joint treaty-defined maritime boundaries along the parallels of latitude to equidistance lines which favor Peru; organized illegal narcotics operations in Colombia have penetrated Peru's shared border; Peru rejects Bolivia's claim to restore maritime access through a sovereign corridor through Chile along the Peruvian border
**Refugees and internally displaced persons:**
*IDPs:* 60,000-150,000 (civil war from 1980-2000; most IDPs are indigenous peasants in Andean and Amazonian regions) (2007)
**Illicit drugs:** until 1996 the world's largest coca leaf producer, Peru is now the world's second largest producer of coca leaf, though it lags far behind Colombia; cultivation of coca in Peru declined to 36,000 hectares in 2007; second largest producer of cocaine, estimated at 210 metric tons of potential pure cocaine in 2007; finished cocaine is shipped out from Pacific ports to the international drug market; increasing amounts of base and finished cocaine, however, are being moved to Brazil, Chile, Argentina, and Bolivia for use in the Southern Cone or transshipment to Europe and Africa; increasing domestic drug consumption

# Philippines

## Introduction

**Background:** The Philippine Islands became a Spanish colony during the 16th century; they were ceded to the US in 1898 following the Spanish-American War. In 1935 the Philippines became a self-governing commonwealth. Manuel QUEZON was elected president and was tasked with preparing the country for independence after a 10-year transition. In 1942 the islands fell under Japanese occupation during World War II, and US forces and Filipinos fought together during 1944-45 to regain control. On 4 July 1946 the Republic of the Philippines attained its independence. The 20-year rule of Ferdinand MARCOS ended in 1986, when a "people power" movement in Manila ("EDSA 1") forced him into exile and installed Corazon AQUINO as president. Her presidency was hampered by several coup attempts, which prevented a return to full political stability and economic development. Fidel RAMOS was elected president in 1992 and his administration was marked by greater stability and progress on economic reforms. In 1992, the US

# Philippines (continued)

closed its last military bases on the islands. Joseph ESTRADA was elected president in 1998, but was succeeded by his vice-president, Gloria MACAPAGAL-ARROYO, in January 2001 after ESTRADA's stormy impeachment trial on corruption charges broke down and another "people power" movement ("EDSA 2") demanded his resignation. MACAPAGAL-ARROYO was elected to a six-year term as president in May 2004. The Philippine Government faces threats from three terrorist groups on the US Government's Foreign Terrorist Organization list, but in 2006 and 2007 scored some major successes in capturing or killing key wanted terrorists. Decades of Muslim insurgency in the southern Philippines have led to a peace accord with one group and on-again/off-again peace talks with another.

## Geography

**Location:** Southeastern Asia, archipelago between the Philippine Sea and the South China Sea, east of Vietnam
**Geographic coordinates:** 13 00 N, 122 00 E
**Map references:** Southeast Asia
**Area:**
*total:* 300,000 sq km
*land:* 298,170 sq km
*water:* 1,830 sq km
**Area - comparative:** slightly larger than Arizona
**Land boundaries:** 0 km
**Coastline:** 36,289 km
**Maritime claims:**
*territorial sea:* irregular polygon extending up to 100 nm from coastline as defined by 1898 treaty; since late 1970s has also claimed polygonal-shaped area in South China Sea up to 285 nm in breadth
*exclusive economic zone:* 200 nm
*continental shelf:* to depth of exploitation
**Climate:** tropical marine; northeast monsoon (November to April); southwest monsoon (May to October)
**Terrain:** mostly mountains with narrow to extensive coastal lowlands
**Elevation extremes:**
*lowest point:* Philippine Sea 0 m
*highest point:* Mount Apo 2,954 m
**Natural resources:** timber, petroleum, nickel, cobalt, silver, gold, salt, copper
**Land use:**
*arable land:* 19%
*permanent crops:* 16.67%
*other:* 64.33% (2005)
**Irrigated land:** 15,500 sq km (2003)
**Total renewable water resources:** 479 cu km (1999)
**Freshwater withdrawal (domestic/industrial/agricultural):**
*total:* 28.52 cu km/yr (17%/9%/74%)
*per capita:* 343 cu m/yr (2000)

**Natural hazards:** astride typhoon belt, usually affected by 15 and struck by five to six cyclonic storms per year; landslides; active volcanoes; destructive earthquakes; tsunamis
**Environment - current issues:** uncontrolled deforestation especially in watershed areas; soil erosion; air and water pollution in major urban centers; coral reef degradation; increasing pollution of coastal mangrove swamps that are important fish breeding grounds
**Environment - international agreements:**
*party to:* Biodiversity, Climate Change, Climate Change-Kyoto Protocol, Desertification, Endangered Species, Hazardous Wastes, Law of the Sea, Marine Dumping, Ozone Layer Protection, Ship Pollution, Tropical Timber 83, Tropical Timber 94, Wetlands, Whaling
*signed, but not ratified:* Air Pollution-Persistent Organic Pollutants
**Geography - note:** the Philippine archipelago is made up of 7,107 islands; favorably located in relation to many of Southeast Asia's main water bodies: the South China Sea, Philippine Sea, Sulu Sea, Celebes Sea, and Luzon Strait

## People

**Population:** 97,976,603 (July 2009 est.)
**Age structure:**
*0-14 years:* 35.2% (male 17,606,352/female 16,911,376)
*15-64 years:* 60.6% (male 29,679,327/female 29,737,919)
*65 years and over:* 4.1% (male 1,744,248/female 2,297,381) (2009 est.)
**Median age:**
*total:* 22.5 years
*male:* 22 years
*female:* 23 years (2009 est.)
**Population growth rate:** 1.957% (2009 est.)
**Birth rate:** 26.01 births/1,000 population (2009 est.)
**Death rate:** 5.15 deaths/1,000 population (2008 est.)
**Net migration rate:** -1.34 migrant(s)/1,000 population (2009 est.)
**Urbanization:**
*urban population:* 65% of total population (2008)
*rate of urbanization:* 3% annual rate of change (2005-10 est.)
**Sex ratio:**
*at birth:* 1.05 male(s)/female
*under 15 years:* 1.04 male(s)/female
*15-64 years:* 1 male(s)/female
*65 years and over:* 0.76 male(s)/female
*total population:* 1 male(s)/female (2009 est.)
**Infant mortality rate:**
*total:* 20.56 deaths/1,000 live births
*male:* 23.17 deaths/1,000 live births
*female:* 17.83 deaths/1,000 live births (2009 est.)
**Life expectancy at birth:**
*total population:* 71.09 years
*male:* 68.17 years
*female:* 74.15 years (2009 est.)

**Total fertility rate:** 3.27 children born/woman (2009 est.)
**HIV/AIDS - adult prevalence rate:** less than 0.1% (2003 est.)
**HIV/AIDS - people living with HIV/AIDS:** 8,300 (2007 est.)
**HIV/AIDS - deaths:** fewer than 200 (2007 est.)
**Major infectious diseases:**
*degree of risk:* high
*food or waterborne diseases:* bacterial diarrhea, hepatitis A, and typhoid fever
*vectorborne diseases:* dengue fever, malaria, and Japanese encephalitis
*water contact disease:* leptospirosis (2009)
**Nationality:**
*noun:* Filipino(s)
*adjective:* Philippine
**Ethnic groups:** Tagalog 28.1%, Cebuano 13.1%, Ilocano 9%, Bisaya/Binisaya 7.6%, Hiligaynon Ilonggo 7.5%, Bikol 6%, Waray 3.4%, other 25.3% (2000 census)
**Religions:** Roman Catholic 80.9%, Muslim 5%, Evangelical 2.8%, Iglesia ni Kristo 2.3%, Aglipayan 2%, other Christian 4.5%, other 1.8%, unspecified 0.6%, none 0.1% (2000 census)
**Languages:** Filipino (official; based on Tagalog) and English (official); eight major dialects - Tagalog, Cebuano, Ilocano, Hiligaynon or Ilonggo, Bicol, Waray, Pampango, and Pangasinan
**Literacy:**
*definition:* age 15 and over can read and write
*total population:* 92.6%
*male:* 92.5%
*female:* 92.7% (2000 census)
**School life expectancy (primary to tertiary education):**
*total:* 12 years
*male:* 11 years
*female:* 12 years (2006)
**Education expenditures:** 2.5% of GDP (2005)

## Government

**Country name:**
*conventional long form:* Republic of the Philippines
*conventional short form:* Philippines
*local long form:* Republika ng Pilipinas
*local short form:* Pilipinas
**Government type:** republic
**Capital:**
*name:* Manila
*geographic coordinates:* 14 35 N, 121 00 E
*time difference:* UTC+8 (13 hours ahead of Washington, DC during Standard Time)
**Administrative divisions:** 80 provinces and 120 chartered cities
*provinces:* Abra, Agusan del Norte, Agusan del Sur, Aklan, Albay, Antique, Apayao, Aurora, Basilan, Bataan, Batanes, Batangas, Biliran, Benguet, Bohol, Bukidnon, Bulacan, Cagayan, Camarines Norte, Camarines Sur, Camiguin, Capiz, Catanduanes, Cavite, Cebu, Compostela, Davao del Norte, Davao del Sur, Davao

Oriental, Dinagat Islands, Eastern Samar, Guimaras, Ifugao, Ilocos Norte, Ilocos Sur, Iloilo, Isabela, Kalinga, Laguna, Lanao del Norte, Lanao del Sur, La Union, Leyte, Maguindanao, Marinduque, Masbate, Mindoro Occidental, Mindoro Oriental, Misamis Occidental, Misamis Oriental, Mountain Province, Negros Occidental, Negros Oriental, North Cotabato, Northern Samar, Nueva Ecija, Nueva Vizcaya, Palawan, Pampanga, Pangasinan, Quezon, Quirino, Rizal, Romblon, Samar, Sarangani, Siquijor, Sorsogon, South Cotabato, Southern Leyte, Sultan Kudarat, Sulu, Surigao del Norte, Surigao del Sur, Tarlac, Tawi-Tawi, Zambales, Zamboanga del Norte, Zamboanga del Sur, Zamboanga Sibugay

chartered cities: Alaminos, Angeles, Antipolo, Bacolod, Bago, Baguio, Bais, Balanga, Batac, Batangas, Bayawan, Bislig, Butuan, Cabadbaran, Cabanatuan, Cadiz, Cagayan de Oro, Calamba, Calapan, Calbayog, Candon, Canlaon, Cauayan, Cavite, Cebu, Cotabato, Dagupan, Danao, Dapitan, Davao, Digos, Dipolog, Dumaguete, Escalante, Gapan, General Santos, Gingoog, Himamaylan, Iligan, Iloilo, Isabela, Iriga, Kabankalan, Kalookan, Kidapawan, Koronadal, La Carlota, Laoag, Lapu-Lapu, Las Pinas, Legazpi, Ligao, Lipa, Lucena, Maasin, Makati, Malabon, Malaybalay, Malolos, Mandaluyong, Mandaue, Manila, Marawi, Marikina, Masbate, Mati, Meycauayan, Muntinlupa, Munoz, Naga, Navotas, Olongapo, Ormoc, Oroquieta, Ozamis, Pagadian, Palayan, Panabo, Paranaque, Pasay, Pasig, Passi, Puerto Princesa, Quezon, Roxas, Sagay, Samal, San Carlos (in Negros Occidental), San Carlos (in Pangasinan), San Fernando (in La Union), San Fernando (in Pampanga), San Jose, San Jose del Monte, San Juan, San Pablo, Santa Rosa, Santiago, Silay, Sipalay, Sorsogon, Surigao, Tabaco, Tacloban, Tacurong, Tagaytay, Tagbilaran, Taguig, Tagum, Talisay (in Cebu), Talisay (in Negros Occidental), Tanauan, Tangub, Tanjay, Tarlac, Toledo, Tuguegarao, Trece Martires, Urdaneta, Valencia, Valenzuela, Victorias, Vigan, Zamboanga (2009)

**Independence:** 12 June 1898 (independence proclaimed from Spain); 4 July 1946 (from the US)

**National holiday:** Independence Day, 12 June (1898); note - 12 June 1898 was date of declaration of independence from Spain; 4 July 1946 was date of independence from US

**Constitution:** 2 February 1987, effective 11 February 1987

**Legal system:** based on Spanish and Anglo-American law; accepts compulsory ICJ jurisdiction with reservations

**Suffrage:** 18 years of age; universal

**Executive branch:**

chief of state: President Gloria MACAPAGAL-ARROYO (since 20 January 2001); Vice President (Manuel "Noli" DE CASTRO (since 10 May 2004); note - president is both chief of state and head of government

head of government: President Gloria MACAPAGAL-ARROYO (since 20 January 2001)

cabinet: Cabinet appointed by the president with consent of Commission of Appointments

elections: president and vice president elected on separate tickets by popular vote for a single six-year term; election last held on 10 May 2004 (next to be held in May 2010)

election results: Gloria MACAPAGAL-ARROYO elected president; percent of vote - Gloria MACAPAGAL-ARROYO 40%, Fernando POE 37%, three others 23%

**Legislative branch:** bicameral Congress or Kongreso consists of the Senate or Senado (24 seats -one-half elected every three years; members elected at large by popular vote to serve six-year terms) and the House of Representatives or Kapulungan Ng Nga Kinatawan (as a result of May 2007 election it has 240 seats including 218 members representing districts and 22 sectoral party-list members representing special minorities elected on the basis of 1 seat for every 2% of the total vote but limited to 3 seats; members elected by popular vote to serve three-year terms; note - the Constitution prohibits the House of Representatives from having more than 250 members)

elections: Senate - last held on 14 May 2007 (next to be held in May 2010); House of Representatives - elections last held on 14 May 2007 (next to be held in May 2010)

election results: Senate - percent of vote by party - NA; seats by party - Lakas 4, LP 4, Nacionalista 3, NPC 2, PDP-Laban 2, PMP 2, Kampi 1, LDP 1, PRP 1, independents 3; note - there are 23 rather than 24 sitting senators because one senator was elected mayor of Manila; House of Representatives - percent of vote by party - NA; seats by party - Lakas 92, Kampi 54, NPC 25, LP 21, Party-list 22, independents 3, others 26; there are 238 rather than 240 sitting representatives because two died in office

**Judicial branch:** Supreme Court (15 justices are appointed by the president on the recommendation of the Judicial and Bar Council and serve until 70 years of age); Court of Appeals; Sandigan-bayan (special court for hearing corruption cases of government officials)

**Political parties and leaders:** Kabalikat ng Malayang Pilipino or Kampi [Luis VILLAFUERTE]; Laban ng Demokratikong Pilipino (Struggle of Filipino Democrats) or LDP [Edgardo ANGARA]; Lakas ng EDSA-Christian Muslim Democrats or Lakas-CMD [Prospero NOGRALES]; Liberal Party or LP [Manuel ROXAS]; Nacionalista Party or NP [Manuel VILLAR]; Nationalist People's Coalition or NPC [Frisco SAN JUAN]; PDP-Laban [Aquilino PIMENTEL]; People's Reform Party [Miriam Defensor SANTIAGO]; Puwersa ng Masang Pilipino (Force of the Philippine Masses) or PMP [Joseph ESTRADA]; United Opposition or UNO [Jejomar BINAY]

note: Lakas-CMD and Kampi merged on 29 May 2009 to form Lakas-Kampi CMD

**Political pressure groups and leaders:** ABONO [Robert ESTRELLA]; AKBAYAN [Anna Theresia BARAQUIEL]; An Waray [Florencio NOEL]; Anak Mindanao [Mujiv HATAMIN]; ANAKPAWIS [Rafael MARIANO]; ARC [Narciso SANTIAGO III]; Association of Philippine Electric Cooperatives (APEC) [Ernesto PABLO and Edgar VALDEZ]; A TEACHER [Mariano PIAMONTE]; Bayan Muna [Satur OCAMPO and

Teodoro CASINO, Jr.]; Black and White Movement [Vicente ROMANO]; BUHAY [Rene VELARDE, Carissa COSCOLLUELLA, and William TIENG]; BUTIL [Leonila CHAVEZ]; CIBAC [Emmanuel Joel VILLANUEVA]; COOP-NATCO [Jose PING-AY]; GABRIELA [Liza MAZA and Luzviminda ILAGAN]; Kilosbayan [Jovito SALONGA]; YACAP [Carol LOPEZ]

**International organization participation:** ADB, APEC, APT, ARF, ASEAN, BIS, CP, EAS, FAO, G-24, G-77, IAEA, IBRD, ICAO, ICC, ICCt (signatory), ICRM, IDA, IFAD, IFC, IFRCS, IHO, ILO, IMF, IMO, IMSO, Interpol, IOC, IOM, IPU, ISO, ITSO, ITU, ITUC, MIGA, MINUSTAH, NAM, OAS (observer), OPCW, PIF (partner), UN, UNCTAD, UNESCO, UNHCR, UNIDO, Union Latina, UNMIL, UNMIS, UNMIT, UNOCI, UNWTO, UPU, WCL, WCO, WFTU, WHO, WIPO, WMO, WTO

**Diplomatic representation in the US:**

chief of mission: Ambassador Willy C. GAA

chancery: 1600 Massachusetts Avenue NW, Washington, DC 20036

telephone: [1] (202) 467-9300

FAX: [1] (202) 467-9417

consulate(s) general: Chicago, Honolulu, Los Angeles, New York, Saipan (Northern Mariana Islands), San Francisco, Tamuning (Guam)

**Diplomatic representation from the US:**

chief of mission: Ambassador Kristie A. KENNEY

embassy: 1201 Roxas Boulevard, Ermita 1000, Manila

mailing address: PSC 500, FPO AP 96515-1000

telephone: [63] (2) 301-2000

FAX: [63] (2) 301-2399

**Flag description:** two equal horizontal bands of blue (top; representing peace and justice) and red (representing courage); a white equilateral triangle based on the hoist side represents equality; the center of the triangle displays a yellow sun with eight primary rays, each representing one of the first eight provinces that sought independence from Spain; each corner of the triangle contains a small, yellow, five-pointed star representing the three major geographical divisions of the country: Luzon, Visayas, and Mindanao; the design of the flag dates to 1897; in wartime the flag is flown upside down with the red band at the top

## Economy

**Economy - overview:** Economic growth has averaged 5% since President MACAPAGAL-ARROYO took office in 2001. MACAPAGAL-ARROYO averted a fiscal crisis by pushing for new revenue measures and, until recently, tightening expenditures. Declining fiscal deficits, tapering debt and debt service ratios, and increased spending on infrastructure and social services bolstered optimism over Philippine economic prospects. Although the general macroeconomic outlook improved significantly in recent years, the economy still faces several long term challenges. The Philippines must maintain the reform momentum in order to catch up with regional competitors, improve employment opportunities, and alleviate poverty. The Philippines will need still higher, sustained growth to make progress in alleviating poverty, given its high population growth and unequal distribution of income. The Philippine economy grew at its fastest pace in three decades in 2007 with real GDP growth exceeding 7%, but growth slowed to 4.6% in 2008 as a result of the world financial crisis. High government spending, a relatively small trade sector, a resilient service sector, and large remittances from the four- to five-million Filipinos who work abroad have helped cushion the economy from the current financial crisis.

**GDP (purchasing power parity):**
$320.6 billion (2008 est.)
$306.5 billion (2007)
$285.9 billion (2006)
*note:* data are in 2008 US dollars

**GDP (official exchange rate):** $168.6 billion (2008 est.)

**GDP - real growth rate:**
4.6% (2008 est.)
7.2% (2007 est.)
5.4% (2006 est.)

**GDP - per capita (PPP):**
$3,300 (2008 est.)
$3,300 (2007 est.)
$3,100 (2006 est.)
*note:* data are in 2008 US dollars

**GDP - composition by sector:**
*agriculture:* 14.7%
*industry:* 31.6%
*services:* 53.7% (2008 est.)

**Labor force:** 36.81 million (2008 est.)

**Labor force - by occupation:**
*agriculture:* 35%
*industry:* 15%
*services:* 50% (2008 est.)

**Unemployment rate:**
7.4% (2008 est.)
7.3% (2007 est.)

**Population below poverty line:** 30% (2003 est.)

**Household income or consumption by percentage share:**
*lowest 10%:* 2.4%
*highest 10%:* 31.2% (2006)

**Distribution of family income - Gini index:** 45.8 (2006)

**Investment (gross fixed):** 16.8% of GDP (2008 est.)

**Budget:**
*revenues:* $26.75 billion
*expenditures:* $28.2 billion (2008 est.)

**Public debt:** 56.5% of GDP (2008 est.)

**Inflation rate (consumer prices):**
9.3% (2008 est.)
2.8% (2007 est.)

**Central bank discount rate:** 6% (31 December 2008)

**Commercial bank prime lending rate:** 8.69% (31 December 2007)

**Stock of money:** $22.53 billion (31 December 2008)
**Stock of quasi money:** $65.85 billion (31 December 2007)

**Stock of domestic credit:** $65.66 billion (31 December 2007)

**Market value of publicly traded shares:** $85.6 billion (31 December 2008)

**Agriculture - products:** sugarcane, coconuts, rice, corn, bananas, cassavas, pineapples, mangoes; pork, eggs, beef; fish

**Industries:** electronics assembly, garments, footwear, pharmaceuticals, chemicals, wood products, food processing, petroleum refining, fishing

**Industrial production growth rate:** 5% (2008 est.)

**Electricity - production:** 56.51 billion kWh (2007 est.)

**Electricity - consumption:** 47.04 billion kWh (2006 est.)

**Electricity - exports:** 0 kWh (2007)

**Electricity - imports:** 0 kWh (2007)

**Oil - production:** 23,930 bbl/day (2007 est.)

**Oil - consumption:** 340,100 bbl/day (2006 est.)

**Oil - exports:** 41,160 bbl/day (2005)

**Oil - imports:** 355,800 bbl/day (2005)

**Oil - proved reserves:** 138.5 million bbl (1 January 2008 est.)

**Natural gas - production:** 2.2 billion cu m (2006 est.)

**Natural gas - consumption:** 2.2 billion cu m (2006 est.)

**Natural gas - exports:** 0 cu m (2007 est.)

**Natural gas - imports:** 0 cu m (2007 est.)

**Natural gas - proved reserves:** 98.54 billion cu m (1 January 2008 est.)

**Current account balance:** $2.687 billion (2008 est.)

**Exports:** $49 billion f.o.b. (2008 est.)

**Exports - commodities:** semiconductors and electronic products, transport equipment, garments, copper products, petroleum products, coconut oil, fruits

**Exports - partners:** US 17%, Japan 14.5%, Hong Kong 11.5%, China 11.4%, Netherlands 8.2%, Singapore 6.2%, Malaysia 5%, Germany 4.3% (2007)

**Imports:** $58 billion f.o.b. (2008 est.)

**Imports - commodities:** electronic products, mineral fuels, machinery and transport equipment, iron and steel, textile fabrics, grains, chemicals, plastic

**Imports - partners:** US 14.1%, Japan 12.3%, Singapore 11.2%, Taiwan 7.3%, China 7.2%, Saudi Arabia 6.4%, South Korea 5.9%, Malaysia 4.1%, Thailand 4.1% (2007)

**Reserves of foreign exchange and gold:** $36.15 billion (31 December 2008 est.)

**Debt - external:** $53.48 billion (31 September 2008 est.)

**Stock of direct foreign investment - at home:** $20.78 billion (2008 est.)

**Stock of direct foreign investment - abroad:** $5.564 billion (2008 est.)

**Exchange rates:** Philippine pesos (PHP) per US dollar - 44.439 (2008 est.), 46.148 (2007), 51.246 (2006), 55.086 (2005), 56.04 (2004)

## Communications

**Telephones - main lines in use:** 3.633 million (2006)
**Telephones - mobile cellular:** 51.795 million (2007)
**Telephone system:**
*general assessment:* good international radiotelephone and submarine cable services; domestic and interisland service adequate
*domestic:* domestic satellite system with 11 earth stations; cellular communications now dominate the industry; combined fixed-line and mobile-cellular telephone density about 60 telephones per 100 persons
*international:* country code - 63; a series of submarine cables together provide connectivity to Asia, US, the Middle East, and Europe; multiple international gateways (2007)

**Radio broadcast stations:** AM 381, FM 628, shortwave 4 (2007)

**Television broadcast stations:** 250 (plus 1,501 CATV networks) (2007)

**Internet country code:** .ph

**Internet hosts:** 283,579 (2008)

**Internet users:** 5.3 million (2007)

## Transportation

**Airports:** 254 (2008)
**Airports - with paved runways:**
*total:* 85
*over 3,047 m:* 4
*2,438 to 3,047 m:* 7
*1,524 to 2,437 m:* 28
*914 to 1,523 m:* 36
*under 914 m:* 10 (2008)

**Airports - with unpaved runways:**
*total:* 169
*1,524 to 2,437 m:* 4
*914 to 1,523 m:* 66
*under 914 m:* 99 (2008)

**Heliports:** 2 (2007)

**Pipelines:** oil 107 km; refined products 112 km (2008)

**Railways:**
*total:* 897 km
*narrow gauge:* 897 km 1.067-m gauge (492 km are in operation) (2006)

**Roadways:**
*total:* 200,037 km
*paved:* 19,804 km
*unpaved:* 180,233 km (2003)

**Waterways:** 3,219 km (limited to vessels with draft less than 1.5 m) (2008)

**Merchant marine:**
*total:* 391
*by type:* bulk carrier 75, cargo 125, carrier 16, chemical tanker 17, container 6, liquefied gas 5, passenger 6, passenger/cargo 68, petroleum tanker 36, refrigerated cargo 15, roll on/roll off 11, vehicle carrier 11
*foreign-owned:* 161 (Bermuda 34, China 4, Greece 4, Hong Kong 1, Japan 81, Malaysia 1, Netherlands 23, Norway 10, Singapore 1, Taiwan 1, UAE 1)
*registered in other countries:* 11 (Comoros 1, Cyprus 1, Hong Kong 1, Indonesia 1, Panama 7) (2008)

# Philippines (continued)

**Ports and terminals:** Cagayan de Oro, Cebu, Davao, Liman, Manila, Nasipit Harbor

**Transportation - note:** the International Maritime Bureau reports the territorial and offshore waters in the South China Sea as high risk for piracy and armed robbery against ships; numerous commercial vessels have been attacked and hijacked both at anchor and while underway; hijacked vessels are often disguised and cargo diverted to ports in East Asia; crews have been murdered or cast adrift

## Military

**Military branches:** Armed Forces of the Philippines (AFP): Army, Navy (includes Marine Corps and Coast Guard), Air Force (2009)

**Military service age and obligation:** 18-25 years of age (officers 21-29) for compulsory and voluntary military service; applicants must be single male or female Philippine citizens (2007)

**Manpower available for military service:**
*males age 16-49:* 23,547,252
*females age 16-49:* 23,177,487 (2008 est.)

**Manpower fit for military service:**
*males age 16-49:* 19,169,298
*females age 16-49:* 20,636,853 (2009 est.)

**Manpower reaching militarily significant age annually:**
*male:* 1,023,431
*female:* 986,434 (2009 est.)

**Military expenditures:** 0.9% of GDP (2005 est.)

## Transnational Issues

**Disputes - international:** Philippines claims sovereignty over certain of the Spratly Islands, known locally as the Kalayaan (Freedom) Islands, also claimed by China, Malaysia, Taiwan, and Vietnam; the 2002 "Declaration on the Conduct of Parties in the South China Sea," has eased tensions in the Spratly Islands but falls short of a legally binding "code of conduct" desired by several of the disputants; in March 2005, the national oil companies of China, the Philippines, and Vietnam signed a joint accord to conduct marine seismic activities in the Spratly Islands; Philippines retains a dormant claim to Malaysia's Sabah State in northern Borneo based on the Sultanate of Sulu's granting the Philippines Government power of attorney to pursue a sovereignty claim on his behalf; maritime delimitation negotiations continue with Palau

**Refugees and internally displaced persons:**
*IDPs:* 300,000 (fighting between government troops and MILF and Abu Sayyaf groups) (2007)

**Illicit drugs:** domestic methamphetamine production has been a growing problem in recent years despite government crackdowns; major consumer of amphetamines; longstanding marijuana producer mainly in rural areas where Manila's control is limited

# Pitcairn Islands
*(overseas territory of the UK)*

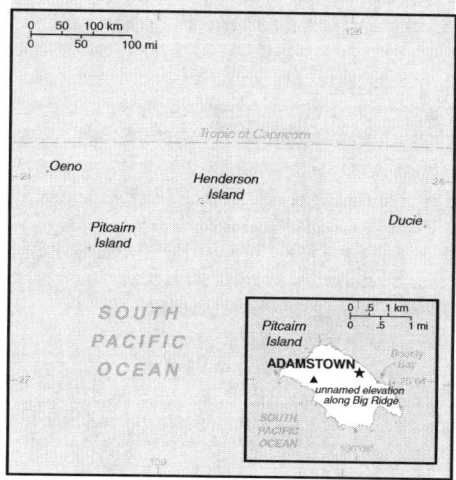

## Introduction

**Background:** Pitcairn Island was discovered in 1767 by the British and settled in 1790 by the Bounty mutineers and their Tahitian companions. Pitcairn was the first Pacific island to become a British colony (in 1838) and today remains the last vestige of that empire in the South Pacific. Outmigration, primarily to New Zealand, has thinned the population from a peak of 233 in 1937 to less than 50 today.

## Geography

**Location:** Oceania, islands in the South Pacific Ocean, about midway between Peru and New Zealand

**Geographic coordinates:** 25 04 S, 130 06 W

**Map references:** Oceania

**Area:**
*total:* 47 sq km
*land:* 47 sq km
*water:* 0 sq km

**Area - comparative:** about 0.3 times the size of Washington, DC

**Land boundaries:** 0 km

**Coastline:** 51 km

**Maritime claims:**
*territorial sea:* 3 nm
*exclusive economic zone:* 200 nm

**Climate:** tropical; hot and humid; modified by southeast trade winds; rainy season (November to March)

**Terrain:** rugged volcanic formation; rocky coastline with cliffs

**Elevation extremes:**
*lowest point:* Pacific Ocean 0 m
*highest point:* Pawala Valley Ridge 347 m

**Natural resources:** miro trees (used for handicrafts), fish
*note:* manganese, iron, copper, gold, silver, and zinc have been discovered offshore

**Land use:**
*arable land:* NA
*permanent crops:* NA
*other:* NA

**Irrigated land:** NA

**Natural hazards:** typhoons (especially November to March)

**Environment - current issues:** deforestation (only a small portion of the original forest remains because of burning and clearing for settlement)

**Geography - note:** Britain's most isolated dependency; only the larger island of Pitcairn is inhabited but it has no port or natural harbor; supplies must be transported by rowed longboat from larger ships stationed offshore

## People

**Population:** 48 (July 2009 est.)

**Age structure:**
*0-14 years:* NA
*15-64 years:* NA
*65 years and over:* NA

**Population growth rate:** 0% (2009 est.)

**Birth rate:** NA

**Death rate:** NA

**Net migration rate:** NA

**Urbanization:**
*urban population:* 0% of total population (2008)
*rate of urbanization:* 0% annual rate of change (2005-10 est.)

**Sex ratio:** NA

**Infant mortality rate:**
*total:* NA
*male:* NA
*female:* NA (2008 est.)

**Life expectancy at birth:**
*total population:* NA
*male:* NA
*female:* NA

**Total fertility rate:** NA (2008 est.)

**HIV/AIDS - adult prevalence rate:** NA

**HIV/AIDS - people living with HIV/AIDS:** NA

**HIV/AIDS - deaths:** NA

**Nationality:**
*noun:* Pitcairn Islander(s)
*adjective:* Pitcairn Islander

**Ethnic groups:** descendants of the Bounty mutineers and their Tahitian wives

**Religions:** Seventh-Day Adventist 100%

**Languages:** English (official), Pitkern (mixture of an 18th century English dialect and a Tahitian dialect)

**Literacy:** NA

## Government

**Country name:**
*conventional long form:* Pitcairn, Henderson, Ducie, and Oeno Islands
*conventional short form:* Pitcairn Islands

**Dependency status:** overseas territory of the UK

**Government type:** NA

## Pitcairn Islands *(continued)*

**Capital:**

*name:* Adamstown

*geographic coordinates:* 25 04 S, 130 05 W

*time difference:* UTC-9 (4 hours behind Washington, DC during Standard Time)

**Administrative divisions:** none (overseas territory of the UK)

**Independence:** none (overseas territory of the UK)

**National holiday:** Birthday of Queen ELIZABETH II, second Saturday in June (1926)

**Constitution:** 30 November 1838; reformed 1904 with additional reforms in 1940; further refined by the Local Government Ordinance of 1964

**Legal system:** local island by-laws

**Suffrage:** 18 years of age; universal with three years residency

**Executive branch:**

*chief of state:* Queen ELIZABETH II (since 6 February 1952); represented by UK High Commissioner to New Zealand and Governor (nonresident) of the Pitcairn Islands George FERGUSSON (since April 2006); Commissioner (nonresident) Leslie JAQUES (since September 2003) serves as liaison between the governor and the Island Council

*head of government:* Governor George FERGUSSON (since April 2006); Mayor and Chairman of the Island Council Mike WARREN (since 1 January 2008)

*cabinet:* NA

*elections:* the monarchy is hereditary; governor and commissioner appointed by the monarch; island mayor elected by popular vote for a three-year term; election last held December 2007 (next to be held in December 2010)

*election results:* Mike WARREN elected mayor and chairman of the Island Council

**Legislative branch:** unicameral Island Council (10 seats; 5 members elected by popular vote, 1 nominated by the 5 elected members, 2 appointed by the governor including 1 seat for the Island Secretary, the Island Mayor, and a commissioner liaising between the governor and council; elected members serve one-year terms)

*elections:* last held 24 December 2008 (next to be held in 24 December 2009)

*election results:* percent of vote - NA; seats - all independents

**Judicial branch:** Magistrate's Court; Supreme Court; Court of Appeal; judicial officers are appointed by the governor

**Political parties and leaders:** none

**Political pressure groups and leaders:** none

**International organization participation:** SPC, UPU

**Diplomatic representation in the US:** none (overseas territory of the UK)

**Diplomatic representation from the US:** none (overseas territory of the UK)

**Flag description:** blue with the flag of the UK in the upper hoist-side quadrant and the Pitcairn Islander coat of arms centered on the outer half of the flag; the coat of arms is yellow, green, and light blue with a shield featuring a yellow anchor

## Economy

**Economy - overview:** The inhabitants of this tiny isolated economy exist on fishing, subsistence farming, handicrafts, and postage stamps. The fertile soil of the valleys produces a wide variety of fruits and vegetables, including citrus, sugarcane, watermelons, bananas, yams, and beans. Bartering is an important part of the economy. The major sources of revenue are the sale of postage stamps to collectors and the sale of handicrafts to passing ships. In October 2004, more than one-quarter of Pitcairn's small labor force was arrested, putting the economy in a bind, since their services were required as lighter crew to load or unload passing ships.

**GDP (purchasing power parity):** $NA

**Labor force:** 15 able-bodied men (2004)

**Labor force - by occupation:**

*note:* no business community in the usual sense; some public works; subsistence farming and fishing

**Budget:**

*revenues:* $746,000

*expenditures:* $1.028 million (FY04/05)

**Agriculture - products:** honey; wide variety of fruits and vegetables; goats, chickens, fish

**Industries:** postage stamps, handicrafts, beekeeping, honey

**Electricity - production:** NA kWh; note - electric power is provided by a small diesel-powered generator

**Exports:** $NA

**Exports - commodities:** fruits, vegetables, curios, stamps

**Imports:** $NA

**Imports - commodities:** fuel oil, machinery, building materials, flour, sugar, other foodstuffs

**Exchange rates:** New Zealand dollars (NZD) per US dollar - 1.4151 (2008 est.), 1.3811 (2007), 1.5408 (2006), 1.4203 (2005), 1.5087 (2004)

## Communications

**Telephones - main lines in use:** 1 (there are 17 telephones on one party line); (2004)

**Telephone system:**

*general assessment:* satellite phone services

*domestic:* domestic communication via radio (CB)

*international:* country code - 872; satellite earth station -1 (Inmarsat)

**Radio broadcast stations:** AM 1, FM 0, shortwave 0 (15 ham radio operators (VP6)) (2004)

**Internet country code:** .pn

**Internet hosts:** 12 (2008)

**Internet users:** NA

## Transportation

**Ports and terminals:** Adamstown (on Bounty Bay)

## Military

**Military - note:** defense is the responsibility of the UK

## Transnational Issues

**Disputes - international:** none

# Poland

## Introduction

**Background:** Poland is an ancient nation that was conceived near the middle of the 10th century. Its golden age occurred in the 16th century. During the following century, the strengthening of the gentry and internal disorders weakened the nation. In a series of agreements between 1772 and 1795, Russia, Prussia, and Austria partitioned Poland amongst themselves. Poland regained its independence in 1918 only to be overrun by Germany and the Soviet Union in World War II. It became a Soviet satellite state following the war, but its government was comparatively tolerant and progressive. Labor turmoil in 1980 led to the formation of the independent trade union "Solidarity" that over time became a political force and by 1990 had swept parliamentary elections and the presidency. A "shock therapy" program during the early 1990s enabled the country to transform its economy into one of the most robust in Central Europe, but Poland still faces the lingering challenges of high unemployment, underdeveloped and dilapidated infrastructure, and a poor rural underclass. Solidarity suffered a major defeat in the 2001 parliamentary elections when it failed to elect a single deputy to the lower house of Parliament, and the new leaders of the Solidarity Trade Union subsequently pledged to reduce the Trade Union's political role. Poland joined NATO in 1999 and the European Union in 2004. With its transformation to a democratic, market-oriented country largely completed, Poland is an increasingly active member of Euro-Atlantic organizations.

## Geography

**Location:** Central Europe, east of Germany

**Geographic coordinates:** 52 00 N, 20 00 E

**Map references:** Europe

**Area:**

*total:* 312,679 sq km

*land:* 304,459 sq km

*water:* 8,220 sq km

# Poland (continued)

**Area - comparative:** slightly smaller than New Mexico

**Land boundaries:**

*total:* 3,047 km

*border countries:* Belarus 605 km, Czech Republic 615 km, Germany 456 km, Lithuania 91 km, Russia (Kaliningrad Oblast) 432 km, Slovakia 420 km, Ukraine 428 km

**Coastline:** 440 km

**Maritime claims:**

*territorial sea:* 12 nm

*exclusive economic zone:* defined by international treaties

**Climate:** temperate with cold, cloudy, moderately severe winters with frequent precipitation; mild summers with frequent showers and thundershowers

**Terrain:** mostly flat plain; mountains along southern border

**Elevation extremes:**

*lowest point:* near Raczki Elblaskie -2 m

*highest point:* Rysy 2,499 m

**Natural resources:** coal, sulfur, copper, natural gas, silver, lead, salt, amber, arable land

**Land use:**

*arable land:* 40.25%

*permanent crops:* 1%

*other:* 58.75% (2005)

**Irrigated land:** 1,000 sq km (2003)

**Total renewable water resources:** 63.1 cu km (2005)

**Freshwater withdrawal (domestic/industrial/agricultural):**

*total:* 11.73 cu km/yr (13%/79%/8%)

*per capita:* 304 cu m/yr (2002)

**Natural hazards:** flooding

**Environment - current issues:** situation has improved since 1989 due to decline in heavy industry and increased environmental concern by post-Communist governments; air pollution nonetheless remains serious because of sulfur dioxide emissions from coal-fired power plants, and the resulting acid rain has caused forest damage; water pollution from industrial and municipal sources is also a problem, as is disposal of hazardous wastes; pollution levels should continue to decrease as industrial establishments bring their facilities up to EU code, but at substantial cost to business and the government

**Environment - international agreements:**

*party to:* Air Pollution, Antarctic-Environmental Protocol, Antarctic-Marine Living Resources, Antarctic Seals, Antarctic Treaty, Biodiversity, Climate Change, Climate Change-Kyoto Protocol, Desertification, Endangered Species, Environmental Modification, Hazardous Wastes, Kyoto Protocol, Law of the Sea, Marine Dumping, Ozone Layer Protection, Ship Pollution, Wetlands

*signed, but not ratified:* Air Pollution-Nitrogen Oxides, Air Pollution-Persistent Organic Pollutants, Air Pollution-Sulfur 94

**Geography - note:** historically, an area of conflict because of flat terrain and the lack of natural barriers on the North European Plain

## People

**Population:** 38,482,919 (July 2009 est.)

**Age structure:**

*0-14 years:* 15% (male 2,964,995/female 2,802,278)

*15-64 years:* 71.6% (male 13,713,078/female 13,845,251)

*65 years and over:* 13.4% (male 1,966,406/female 3,190,911) (2009 est.)

**Median age:**

*total:* 37.9 years

*male:* 36.1 years

*female:* 39.7 years (2009 est.)

**Population growth rate:** -0.047% (2009 est.)

**Birth rate:** 10.04 births/1,000 population (2009 est.)

**Death rate:** 9.99 deaths/1,000 population (2008 est.)

**Net migration rate:** -0.47 migrant(s)/1,000 population (2009 est.)

**Urbanization:**

*urban population:* 61% of total population (2008)

*rate of urbanization:* -0.3% annual rate of change (2005-10 est.)

**Sex ratio:**

*at birth:* 1.06 male(s)/female

*under 15 years:* 1.06 male(s)/female

*15-64 years:* 0.99 male(s)/female

*65 years and over:* 0.62 male(s)/female

*total population:* 0.94 male(s)/female (2009 est.)

**Infant mortality rate:**

*total:* 6.8 deaths/1,000 live births

*male:* 7.52 deaths/1,000 live births

*female:* 6.03 deaths/1,000 live births (2009 est.)

**Life expectancy at birth:**

*total population:* 75.63 years

*male:* 71.65 years

*female:* 79.85 years (2009 est.)

**Total fertility rate:** 1.28 children born/woman (2009 est.)

**HIV/AIDS - adult prevalence rate:** 0.1%; note - no country specific models provided (2007 est.)

**HIV/AIDS - people living with HIV/AIDS:** 20,000 (2007 est.)

**HIV/AIDS - deaths:** fewer than 200 (2007 est.)

**Major infectious diseases:**

*degree of risk:* intermediate

*food or waterborne diseases:* bacterial diarrhea

*vectorborne disease:* tickborne encephalitis

*note:* highly pathogenic H5N1 avian influenza has been identified in this country; it poses a negligible risk with extremely rare cases possible among US citizens who have close contact with birds (2009)

**Nationality:**

*noun:* Pole(s)

*adjective:* Polish

**Ethnic groups:** Polish 96.7%, German 0.4%, Belarusian 0.1%, Ukrainian 0.1%, other and unspecified 2.7% (2002 census)

**Religions:** Roman Catholic 89.8% (about 75% practicing), Eastern Orthodox 1.3%, Protestant 0.3%, other 0.3%, unspecified 8.3% (2002)

**Languages:** Polish 97.8%, other and unspecified 2.2% (2002 census)

**Literacy:**

*definition:* age 15 and over can read and write

*total population:* 99.8%

*male:* 99.8%

*female:* 99.7% (2003 est.)

**School life expectancy (primary to tertiary education):**

*total:* 15 years

*male:* 15 years

*female:* 16 years (2006)

**Education expenditures:** 5.5% of GDP (2005)

## Government

**Country name:**

*conventional long form:* Republic of Poland

*conventional short form:* Poland

*local long form:* Rzeczpospolita Polska

*local short form:* Polska

**Government type:** republic

**Capital:**

*name:* Warsaw

*geographic coordinates:* 52 15 N, 21 00 E

*time difference:* UTC+1 (6 hours ahead of Washington, DC during Standard Time)

*daylight saving time:* +1hr, begins last Sunday in March; ends last Sunday in October

**Administrative divisions:** 16 provinces (wojewodztwa, singular - wojewodztwo); Dolnoslaskie (Lower Silesia), Kujawsko-Pomorskie (Kuyavia-Pomerania), Lodzkie, Lubelskie (Lublin), Lubuskie (Lubusz), Malopolskie (Lesser Poland), Mazowieckie (Masovia), Opolskie, Podkarpackie (Subcarpathia), Podlaskie, Pomorskie (Pomerania), Slaskie (Silesia), Swietokrzyskie, Warminsko-Mazurskie (Warmia-Masuria), Wielkopolskie (Greater Poland), Zachodniopomorskie (West Pomerania)

**Independence:** 11 November 1918 (republic proclaimed)

**National holiday:** Constitution Day, 3 May (1791)

**Constitution:** adopted by the National Assembly 2 April 1997; passed by national referendum 25 May 1997; effective 17 October 1997

**Legal system:** based on a mixture of Continental (Napoleonic) civil law and holdover Communist legal theory; changes being gradually introduced as part of broader democratization process; limited judicial review of legislative acts, but rulings of the Constitutional Tribunal are final; court decisions can be appealed to the European Court of Justice in Strasbourg; accepts compulsory ICJ jurisdiction with reservations

**Suffrage:** 18 years of age; universal

**Executive branch:**

*chief of state:* President Lech KACZYNSKI (since 23 December 2005)

# Poland (continued)

*head of government:* Prime Minister Donald TUSK (since 16 November 2007); Deputy Prime Ministers Waldemar PAWLAK (since 16 November 2007) and Grzegorz SCHETYNA (since 16 November 2007)
*cabinet:* Council of Ministers responsible to the prime minister and the Sejm; the prime minister proposes, the president appoints, and the Sejm approves the Council of Ministers
*elections:* president elected by popular vote for a five-year term (eligible for a second term); election last held 9 and 23 October 2005 (next to be held in the fall 2010); prime minister and deputy prime ministers appointed by the president and confirmed by the Sejm
*election results:* Lech KACZYNSKI elected president; percent of popular vote - Lech KACZYNSKI 54%, Donald Tusk 46%

**Legislative branch:** bicameral legislature consists of an upper house, the Senate or Senat (100 seats; members are elected by a majority vote on a provincial basis to serve four-year terms), and a lower house, the Sejm (460 seats; members are elected under a complex system of proportional representation to serve four-year terms); the designation of National Assembly or Zgromadzenie Narodowe is only used on those rare occasions when the two houses meet jointly
*elections:* Senate - last held 21 October 2007 (next to be held by October 2011); Sejm elections last held 21 October 2007 (next to be held by October 2011)
*election results:* Senate - percent of vote by party - NA; seats by party - PO 60, PiS 39, independents 1; Sejm - percent of vote by party - PO 41.5%, PiS 32.1%, LiD 13.2%, PSL 8.9%, other 4.3%; seats by party - PO 209, PiS 166, LiD 53, PSL 31, German minorities 1; note - seats by parliamentary grouping as of February 2009 - PO 208, PiS 156, Left 42, PSL 31, SDPL-New Left 5, Polska XXI 6, Democratic Caucus 3, German minorities 1, nonaffiliated 8
*note:* one seat is assigned to ethnic minority parties in the Sejm only

**Judicial branch:** Supreme Court (judges are appointed by the president on the recommendation of the National Council of the Judiciary for an indefinite period); Constitutional Tribunal (judges are chosen by the Sejm for nine-year terms)

**Political parties and leaders:** Civic Platform or PO [chairman Donald TUSK; parliamentary caucus leader Zbigniew CHLEBOWSKI]; Democratic Caucus (Democratic Party and independents) [Bogdan LIS]; Democratic Left Alliance or SLD [Grzegorz NAPIERALSKI]; Democratic Party or PD [Brygida KUZNIAK]; German Minority of Lower Silesia or MNSO [Henryk KROLL]; Law and Justice or PiS [Przemyslaw GOSIEWSKI]; League of Polish Families or LPR [Miroslaw ORZECHOWSKI]; Left (Democratic Left Alliance and independents) [Wojciech OLEJNICZAK]; Polish People's Party or PSL [Stanislaw ZELICHOWSKI]; Polska XXI (political grouping of former PiS members; not officially registered) [Jaroslaw SELLIN]; Samoobrona or SO [Andrzej LEPPER]; Social Democratic Party of Poland or SDPL [chairman Wojciech FILEMONOWICZ];

Social Democratic Party of Poland-New Left (SDPL-New Left) [parliamentary caucus leader Marek BOROWSKI]; Union of Labor or UP [Waldemar WITKOWSKI]

**Political pressure groups and leaders:** All Poland Trade Union Alliance or OPZZ (trade union) [Jan GUZ]; Roman Catholic Church [Cardinal Stanislaw DZIWISZ, Archbishop Jozef MICHALIK]; Solidarity Trade Union [Janusz SNIADEK]

**International organization participation:** Arctic Council (observer), Australia Group, BIS, BSEC (observer), CBSS, CE, CEI, CERN, EAPC, EBRD, EIB, ESA (cooperating state), EU, FAO, IAEA, IBRD, ICAO, ICC, ICCt, ICRM, IDA, IEA, IFC, IFRCS, IHO, ILO, IMF, IMO, IMSO, Interpol, IOC, IOM, IPU, ISO, ITSO, ITU, ITUC, MIGA, MINURCAT, MINURSO, MONUC, NAM (guest), NATO, NSG, OAS (observer), OECD, OIF (observer), OPCW, OSCE, PCA, Schengen Convention, SECI (observer), UN, UNCTAD, UNDOF, UNESCO, UNHCR, UNIDO, UNIFIL, UNMIL, UNMIS, UNOCI, UNOMIG, UNWTO, UPU, WCL, WCO, WEU (associate), WFTU, WHO, WIPO, WMO, WTO, ZC

**Diplomatic representation in the US:**
*chief of mission:* Ambassador Robert KUPIECKI
*chancery:* 2640 16th Street NW, Washington, DC 20009
*telephone:* [1] (202) 234-3800 through 3802
*FAX:* [1] (202) 328-6271
*consulate(s) general:* Chicago, Los Angeles, New York

**Diplomatic representation from the US:**
*chief of mission:* Ambassador Victor ASHE
*embassy:* Aleje Ujazdowskie 29/31 00-540 Warsaw
*mailing address:* American Embassy Warsaw, US Department of State, Washington, DC 20521-5010 (pouch)
*telephone:* [48] (22) 504-2000
*FAX:* [48] (22) 504-2688
*consulate(s) general:* Krakow

**Flag description:** two equal horizontal bands of white (top) and red; similar to the flags of Indonesia and Monaco which are red (top) and white

## Economy

**Economy - overview:** Poland has pursued a policy of economic liberalization since 1990 and today stands out as a success story among transition economies. In 2008, GDP grew an estimated 4.8%, based on rising private consumption, a jump in corporate investment, and EU funds inflows. GDP per capita is still much below the EU average, but is similar to that of the three Baltic states. Since 2004, EU membership and access to EU structural funds have provided a major boost to the economy. Unemployment is falling rapidly, though at roughly 9.7% in 2008, it remains above the EU average. In 2008 inflation reached 4.3%, more than the upper limit of the National Bank of Poland's target range, but has been falling due to global economic slowdown. Poland's economic performance could improve further

if the country addresses some of the remaining deficiencies in its business environment. An inefficient commercial court system, a rigid labor code, bureaucratic red tape, and persistent low-level corruption keep the private sector from performing up to its full potential. Rising demands to fund health care, education, and the state pension system present a challenge to the Polish Government's effort to hold the consolidated public sector budget deficit under 3.0% of GDP, a target which was achieved in 2007-08. The PO/PSL coalition government which came to power in November 2007 plans to further reduce the budget deficit with the aim of eventually adopting the euro by 2012. The new government has also announced its intention to enact business-friendly reforms, reduce public sector spending growth, lower taxes, and accelerate privatization. The government, however, has moved slowly on major reforms. Pension and health-care bills passed through the legislature, but the legislature failed to overturn a presidential veto.

**GDP (purchasing power parity):**
$667.4 billion (2008 est.)
$636.9 billion (2007)
$596.9 billion (2006)
*note:* data are in 2008 US dollars

**GDP (official exchange rate):** $567.4 billion (2008 est.)

**GDP - real growth rate:**
4.8% (2008 est.)
6.7% (2007 est.)
6.2% (2006 est.)

**GDP - per capita (PPP):**
$17,300 (2008 est.)
$16,500 (2007 est.)
$15,500 (2006 est.)
*note:* data are in 2008 US dollars

**GDP - composition by sector:**
*agriculture:* 4%
*industry:* 31.3%
*services:* 64.7% (2008 est.)

**Labor force:** 16.95 million (2008 est.)

**Labor force - by occupation:**
*agriculture:* 17.4%
*industry:* 29.2%
*services:* 53.4% (2005)

**Unemployment rate:**
9.7% (2008 est.)
12.8% (2007 est.)

**Population below poverty line:** 17% (2003 est.)

**Household income or consumption by percentage share:**
*lowest 10%:* 3.1%
*highest 10%:* 27% (2002)

**Distribution of family income - Gini index:** 34.9 (2005)

**Investment (gross fixed):** 22.7% of GDP (2008 est.)

**Budget:**
*revenues:* $117 billion
*expenditures:* $127.3 billion (2008 est.)

# Poland *(continued)*

**Public debt:** 41.6% of GDP (2008 est.)

**Inflation rate (consumer prices):**
4.3% (2008 est.)
2.5% (2007 est.)

**Central bank discount rate:** 5% (31 December 2007)

**Commercial bank prime lending rate:** 5.48% (31 December 2006)

**Stock of money:** $137.4 billion (31 December 2007)

**Stock of quasi money:** $93.99 billion (31 December 2007)

**Stock of domestic credit:** $223.2 billion (31 December 2007)

**Market value of publicly traded shares:** $207.3 billion (31 December 2007)

**Agriculture - products:** potatoes, fruits, vegetables, wheat; poultry, eggs, pork, dairy

**Industries:** machine building, iron and steel, coal mining, chemicals, shipbuilding, food processing, glass, beverages, textiles

**Industrial production growth rate:** 6% (2008 est.)

**Electricity - production:** 149.3 billion kWh (2007 est.)

**Electricity - consumption:** 126.2 billion kWh (2006 est.)

**Electricity - exports:** 13.11 billion kWh (2007)

**Electricity - imports:** 7.761 billion kWh (2007 est.)

**Oil - production:** 37,670 bbl/day (2007 est.)

**Oil - consumption:** 524,000 bbl/day (2007 est.)

**Oil - exports:** 57,920 bbl/day (2005)

**Oil - imports:** 499,200 bbl/day (2005)

**Oil - proved reserves:** 96.38 million bbl (1 January 2008 est.)

**Natural gas - production:** 6.025 billion cu m (2007 est.)

**Natural gas - consumption:** 16.38 billion cu m (2007 est.)

**Natural gas - exports:** 45 million cu m (2007 est.)

**Natural gas - imports:** 10.12 billion cu m (2007 est.)

**Natural gas - proved reserves:** 164.8 billion cu m (1 January 2008 est.)

**Current account balance:** -$29.51 billion (2008 est.)

**Exports:** $190.5 billion f.o.b. (2008 est.)

**Exports - commodities:** machinery and transport equipment 37.8%, intermediate manufactured goods 23.7%, miscellaneous manufactured goods 17.1%, food and live animals 7.6% (2003)

**Exports - partners:** Germany 25.9%, Italy 6.6%, France 6.1%, UK 5.9%, Czech Republic 5.5%, Russia 4.6% (2007)

**Imports:** $213.9 billion f.o.b. (2008 est.)

**Imports - commodities:** machinery and transport equipment 38%, intermediate manufactured goods 21%, chemicals 14.8%, minerals, fuels, lubricants, and related materials 9.1% (2003)

**Imports - partners:** Germany 29%, Russia 8.7%, Italy 6.6%, Netherlands 5.7%, France 5.1%, China 4.2% (2007)

**Reserves of foreign exchange and gold:** $84.48 billion (31 December 2008 est.)

**Debt - external:** $227.5 billion (31 December 2008 est.)

**Stock of direct foreign investment - at home:** $196.1 billion (2008 est.)

**Stock of direct foreign investment - abroad:** $24.59 billion (2008 est.)

**Exchange rates:** zlotych (PLN) per US dollar - 2.3 (2008 est.), 2.81 (2007), 3.1032 (2006), 3.2355 (2005), 3.6576 (2004)
*note:* zlotych is the plural form of zloty

## Communications

**Telephones - main lines in use:** 10.336 million (2007)

**Telephones - mobile cellular:** 41.389 million (2007)

**Telephone system:**
*general assessment:* modernization of the telecommunications network has accelerated with market based competition finalized in 2003; fixed-line service, dominated by the former state-owned company, is dwarfed by the growth in wireless telephony
*domestic:* mobile-cellular service available since 1993 and provided by three nation-wide networks with a fourth provider beginning operations in late 2006; cellular coverage is generally good with some gaps in the east; fixed-line service is growing slowly and still lags in rural areas
*international:* country code - 48; international direct dialing with automated exchanges; satellite earth station - 1 with access to Intelsat, Eutelsat, Inmarsat, and Intersputnik (2007)

**Radio broadcast stations:** AM 14, FM 63, shortwave 2 (2008)

**Television broadcast stations:** 75 (2008)

**Internet country code:** .pl

**Internet hosts:** 7.808 million (2008)

**Internet users:** 16 million (2007)

## Transportation

**Airports:** 126 (2008)

**Airports - with paved runways:**
*total:* 84
*over 3,047 m:* 4
*2,438 to 3,047 m:* 30
*1,524 to 2,437 m:* 39
*914 to 1,523 m:* 7
*under 914 m:* 4 (2008)

**Airports - with unpaved runways:**
*total:* 42
*2,438 to 3,047 m:* 1
*1,524 to 2,437 m:* 5
*914 to 1,523 m:* 14
*under 914 m:* 22 (2008)

**Heliports:** 7 (2007)

**Pipelines:** gas 13,631 km; oil 1,384 km; refined products 777 km (2008)

**Railways:**
*total:* 23,072 km
*broad gauge:* 629 km 1.524-m gauge
*standard gauge:* 22,443 km 1.435-m gauge
(20,555 km operational; 11,910 km electrified) (2006)

**Roadways:**
*total:* 423,997 km
*paved:* 295,356 km (includes 662 km of expressways)
*unpaved:* 128,641 km (2006)

**Waterways:** 3,997 km (navigable rivers and canals) (2007)

**Merchant marine:**
*total:* 15
*by type:* cargo 8, chemical tanker 4, passenger/cargo 1, roll on/roll off 1, vehicle carrier 1
*foreign-owned:* 2 (Cyprus 1, Nigeria 1)
*registered in other countries:* 98 (Antigua and Barbuda 2, Bahamas 17, Cyprus 18, Liberia 13, Malta 24, Norway 3, Panama 11, Saint Vincent and the Grenadines 1, Slovakia 2, Vanuatu 7) (2008)

**Ports and terminals:** Gdansk, Gdynia, Swinoujscie, Szczecin

## Military

**Military branches:** Polish Armed Forces: Land Forces, Navy, Air and Air Defense Aviation Forces, Special Forces (2008)

**Military service age and obligation:** 18-28 years of age for male voluntary or compulsory military service; service obligation shortened from 12 to 9 months in 2005; conscription is to end in 2012; only soldiers who have completed their conscript service are allowed to volunteer for professional service; as of April 2004, women are only allowed to serve as officers and noncommissioned officers; reserve obligation to age 50 (2009)

**Manpower available for military service:**
*males age 16-49:* 9,741,508
*females age 16-49:* 9,514,843 (2008 est.)

**Manpower fit for military service:**
*males age 16-49:* 7,898,892
*females age 16-49:* 7,888,035 (2009 est.)

**Manpower reaching militarily significant age annually:**
*male:* 246,667
*female:* 235,698 (2009 est.)

**Military expenditures:** 1.71% of GDP (2005 est.)

## Transnational Issues

**Disputes - international:** as a member state that forms part of the EU's external border, Poland has implemented the strict Schengen border rules to restrict illegal immigration and trade along its eastern borders with Belarus and Ukraine

**Illicit drugs:** despite diligent counternarcotics measures and international information sharing on cross-border crimes, a major illicit producer of synthetic drugs for the international market; minor transshipment point for Southwest Asian heroin and Latin American cocaine to Western Europe

# Portugal

## Introduction

**Background:** Following its heyday as a global maritime power during the 15th and 16th centuries, Portugal lost much of its wealth and status with the destruction of Lisbon in a 1755 earthquake, occupation during the Napoleonic Wars, and the independence of its wealthiest colony of Brazil in 1822. A 1910 revolution deposed the monarchy; for most of the next six decades, repressive governments ran the country. In 1974, a left-wing military coup installed broad democratic reforms. The following year, Portugal granted independence to all of its African colonies. Portugal is a founding member of NATO and entered the EC (now the EU) in 1986.

## Geography

**Location:** Southwestern Europe, bordering the North Atlantic Ocean, west of Spain
**Geographic coordinates:** 39 30 N, 8 00 W

**Map references:** Europe
**Area:**
*total:* 92,391 sq km
*land:* 91,951 sq km
*water:* 440 sq km
*note:* includes Azores and Madeira Islands
**Area - comparative:** slightly smaller than Indiana
**Land boundaries:**
*total:* 1,214 km
*border countries:* Spain 1,214 km
**Coastline:** 1,793 km
**Maritime claims:**
*territorial sea:* 12 nm
*contiguous zone:* 24 nm
*exclusive economic zone:* 200 nm
*continental shelf:* 200 m depth or to the depth of exploitation
**Climate:** maritime temperate; cool and rainy in north, warmer and drier in south
**Terrain:** mountainous north of the Tagus River, rolling plains in south
**Elevation extremes:**
*lowest point:* Atlantic Ocean 0 m
*highest point:* Ponta do Pico (Pico or Pico Alto) on Ilha do Pico in the Azores 2,351 m
**Natural resources:** fish, forests (cork), iron ore, copper, zinc, tin, tungsten, silver, gold, uranium, marble, clay, gypsum, salt, arable land, hydropower
**Land use:**
*arable land:* 17.29%
*permanent crops:* 7.84%
*other:* 74.87% (2005)
**Irrigated land:** 6,500 sq km (2003)
**Total renewable water resources:** 73.6 cu km (2005)
**Freshwater withdrawal (domestic/industrial/agricultural):**
*total:* 11.09 cu km/yr (10%/12%/78%)
*per capita:* 1,056 cu m/yr (1998)
**Natural hazards:** Azores subject to severe earthquakes
**Environment - current issues:** soil erosion; air pollution caused by industrial and vehicle emissions; water pollution, especially in coastal areas
**Environment - international agreements:**
*party to:* Air Pollution, Biodiversity, Climate Change, Climate Change-Kyoto Protocol, Desertification, Endangered Species, Hazardous Wastes, Law of the Sea, Marine Dumping, Marine Life Conservation, Ozone Layer Protection, Ship Pollution, Tropical Timber 83, Tropical Timber 94, Wetlands, Whaling
*signed, but not ratified:* Air Pollution-Persistent Organic Pollutants, Air Pollution-Volatile Organic Compounds, Environmental Modification
**Geography - note:** Azores and Madeira Islands occupy strategic locations along western sea approaches to Strait of Gibraltar

## People

**Population:** 10,707,924 (July 2009 est.)
**Age structure:**
*0-14 years:* 16.3% (male 912,147/female 834,941)
*15-64 years:* 66.1% (male 3,525,717/female 3,554,513)
*65 years and over:* 17.6% (male 772,413/female 1,108,193) (2009 est.)
**Median age:**
*total:* 39.4 years
*male:* 37.3 years
*female:* 41.6 years (2009 est.)
**Population growth rate:** 0.275% (2009 est.)
**Birth rate:** 10.29 births/1,000 population (2009 est.)
**Death rate:** 10.62 deaths/1,000 population (2008 est.)
**Net migration rate:** 3.14 migrant(s)/1,000 population (2009 est.)
**Urbanization:**
*urban population:* 59% of total population (2008)
*rate of urbanization:* 1.4% annual rate of change (2005-10 est.)
**Sex ratio:**
*at birth:* 1.07 male(s)/female
*under 15 years:* 1.09 male(s)/female
*15-64 years:* 0.99 male(s)/female
*65 years and over:* 0.7 male(s)/female
*total population:* 0.95 male(s)/female (2009 est.)
**Infant mortality rate:**
*total:* 4.78 deaths/1,000 live births
*male:* 5.24 deaths/1,000 live births
*female:* 4.29 deaths/1,000 live births (2009 est.)
**Life expectancy at birth:**
*total population:* 78.21 years
*male:* 74.95 years
*female:* 81.69 years (2009 est.)
**Total fertility rate:** 1.49 children born/woman (2009 est.)
**HIV/AIDS - adult prevalence rate:** 0.5% (2007 est.)
**HIV/AIDS - people living with HIV/AIDS:** 34,000 (2007 est.)
**HIV/AIDS - deaths:** fewer than 500 (2007 est.)
**Nationality:**
*noun:* Portuguese (singular and plural)
*adjective:* Portuguese
**Ethnic groups:** homogeneous Mediterranean stock; citizens of black African descent who immigrated to mainland during decolonization number less than 100,000; since 1990 East Europeans have entered Portugal
**Religions:** Roman Catholic 84.5%, other Christian 2.2%, other 0.3%, unknown 9%, none 3.9% (2001 census)
**Languages:** Portuguese (official), Mirandese (official -but locally used)
**Literacy:**
*definition:* age 15 and over can read and write
*total population:* 93.3%
*male:* 95.5%
*female:* 91.3% (2003 est.)

# Portugal (continued)

**School life expectancy (primary to tertiary education):**
*total:* 15 years
*male:* 15 years
*female:* 16 years (2006)
**Education expenditures:** 5.5% of GDP (2005)

## Government

**Country name:**
*conventional long form:* Portuguese Republic
*conventional short form:* Portugal
*local long form:* Republica Portuguesa
*local short form:* Portugal
**Government type:** republic; parliamentary democracy
**Capital:**
*name:* Lisbon
*geographic coordinates:* 38 43 N, 9 08 W
*time difference:* UTC 0 (5 hours ahead of Washington, DC during Standard Time)
*daylight saving time:* +1hr, begins last Sunday in March; ends last Sunday in October
**Administrative divisions:** 18 districts (distritos, singular - distrito) and 2 autonomous regions* (regioes autonomas, singular - regiao autonoma); Aveiro, Acores (Azores)*, Beja, Braga, Braganca, Castelo Branco, Coimbra, Evora, Faro, Guarda, Leiria, Lisboa (Lisbon), Madeira*, Portalegre, Porto, Santarem, Setubal, Viana do Castelo, Vila Real, Viseu
**Independence:** 1143 (Kingdom of Portugal recognized); 5 October 1910 (republic proclaimed)
**National holiday:** Portugal Day (Dia de Portugal), 10 June (1580); note - also called Camoes Day, the day that revered national poet Luis de Camoes (1524-80) died
**Constitution:** adopted 2 April 1976; subsequently revised
*note:* the revisions placed the military under strict civilian control, trimmed the powers of the president, and laid the groundwork for a stable, pluralistic liberal democracy; and they allowed for the privatization of nationalized firms and the government-owned communications media
**Legal system:** based on civil law system; the Constitutional Tribunal reviews the constitutionality of legislation; accepts compulsory ICJ jurisdiction with reservations
**Suffrage:** 18 years of age; universal
**Executive branch:**
*chief of state:* President Anibal CAVACO SILVA (since 9 March 2006)
*head of government:* Prime Minister Jose SOCRATES Carvalho Pinto de Sousa (since 12 March 2005)
*cabinet:* Council of Ministers appointed by the president on the recommendation of the prime minister
*note:* there is also a Council of State that acts as a consultative body to the president

*elections:* president elected by popular vote for a five-year term (eligible for a second term); election last held 22 January 2006 (next to be held in January 2011); following legislative elections, the leader of the majority party or leader of a majority coalition is usually appointed prime minister by the president
*election results:* Anibal CAVACO SILVA elected president; percent of vote - Anibal CAVACO SILVA 50.6%, Manuel ALEGRE 20.7%, Mario Alberto Nobre Lopes SOARES 14.3%, Jeronimo DE SOUSA 8.5%, Franciso LOUCA 5.3%
**Legislative branch:** unicameral Assembly of the Republic or Assembleia da Republica (230 seats; members are elected by popular vote to serve four-year terms)
*elections:* last held 20 February 2005 (next to be held in fall 2009)
*election results:* percent of vote by party - PS 45.1%, PSD 28.7%, CDU 7.6%, CDS/PP 7.3%, BE 6.4%, other 4.9%; seats by party - PS 121, PSD 75, CDU 14, CDS/PP 12, BE 8
**Judicial branch:** Supreme Court (Supremo Tribunal de Justica); judges appointed for life by the Conselho Superior da Magistratura
**Political parties and leaders:** Democratic and Social Center/Popular Party or CDS/PP [Paulo PORTAS]; Green Ecologist Party (The Greens) or PEV [leadership commission elected by members]; Portuguese Communist Party or PCP [Jeronimo DE SOUSA]; Portuguese Socialist Party or PS [Jose SOCRATES Carvalho Pinto de Sousa]; Social Democratic Party or PSD [Manuela FERREIRA LEITE]; The Left Bloc or BE [Franciso Anacleto LOUCA]; Unitarian Democratic Coalition or CDU [Jeronimo DE SOUSA] (includes PCP and PEV)
**Political pressure groups and leaders:** the media; labor unions
**International organization participation:** ADB (nonregional member), AfDB (nonregional member), Australia Group, BIS, CE, CERN, CPLP, EAPC, EBRD, EIB, EMU, ESA, EU, FAO, IADB, IAEA, IBRD, ICAO, ICC, ICCt, ICRM, IDA, IEA, IFAD, IFC, IFRCS, IHO, ILO, IMF, IMO, IMSO, Interpol, IOC, IOM, IPU, ISO, ITSO, ITU, ITUC, LAIA (observer), MIGA, MINURCAT, NAM (guest), NATO, NEA, NSG, OAS (observer), OECD, OPCW, OSCE, PCA, Schengen Convention, SECI (observer), UN, UNCTAD, UNESCO, UNHCR, UNIDO, UNIFIL, Union Latina, UNMIT, UNWTO, UPU, WCL, WCO, WEU, WFTU, WHO, WIPO, WMO, WTO, ZC
**Diplomatic representation in the US:**
*chief of mission:* Ambassador Joao DE VALLERA
*chancery:* 2012 Massachusetts Avenue NW, Washington, DC 20036
*telephone:* [1] (202) 350-5400
*FAX:* [1] (202) 462-3726
*consulate(s) general:* Boston, New York, Newark (New Jersey), San Francisco
*consulate(s):* New Bedford (Massachusetts), Providence (Rhode Island)

**Diplomatic representation from the US:**
*chief of mission:* Ambassador Thomas F. STEPHENSON
*embassy:* Avenida das Forcas Armadas, 1600-081 Lisbon
*mailing address:* Apartado 43033, 1601-301 Lisboa; PSC 83, APO AE 09726
*telephone:* [351] (21) 727-3300
*FAX:* [351] (21) 726-9109
*consulate(s):* Ponta Delgada (Azores)
**Flag description:** two vertical bands of green (hoist side, two-fifths) and red (three-fifths) with the Portuguese coat of arms centered on the dividing line

## Economy

**Economy - overview:** Portugal has become a diversified and increasingly service-based economy since joining the European Community in 1986. Over the past two decades, successive governments have privatized many state-controlled firms and liberalized key areas of the economy, including the financial and telecommunications sectors. The country qualified for the European Monetary Union (EMU) in 1998 and began circulating the euro on 1 January 2002 along with 11 other EU member economies. Economic growth had been above the EU average for much of the 1990s, but fell back in 2001-08. GDP per capita stands at roughly two-thirds of the EU-27 average. A poor educational system, in particular, has been an obstacle to greater productivity and growth. Portugal has been increasingly overshadowed by lower-cost producers in Central Europe and Asia as a target for foreign direct investment. The budget deficit surged to an all-time high of 6% of GDP in 2005, but the government reduced the deficit to 2.6% in 2007 - a year ahead of Portugal's targeted schedule. Nonetheless, the government faces tough choices in its attempts to boost the economy, which grew by 0.9% in 2008, while keeping the budget deficit within the euro-zone 3%-of-GDP ceiling.
**GDP (purchasing power parity):**
$237.3 billion (2008 est.)
$236.8 billion (2007)
$232.4 billion (2006)
*note:* data are in 2008 US dollars
**GDP (official exchange rate):** $255.5 billion (2008 est.)
**GDP - real growth rate:**
0.2% (2008 est.)
1.9% (2007 est.)
1.4% (2006 est.)
**GDP - per capita (PPP):**
$22,000 (2008 est.)
$22,300 (2007 est.)
$21,900 (2006 est.)
*note:* data are in 2008 US dollars
**GDP - composition by sector:**
*agriculture:* 3%
*industry:* 25.6%
*services:* 71.5% (2008 est.)
**Labor force:** 5.64 million (2008 est.)

# Portugal (continued)

**Labor force - by occupation:**
*agriculture:* 10%
*industry:* 30%
*services:* 60% (2007 est.)
**Unemployment rate:**
7.6% (2008 est.)
8% (2007 est.)
**Population below poverty line:** 18% (2006)
**Household income or consumption by percentage share:**
*lowest 10%:* 3.1%
*highest 10%:* 28.4% (1995 est.)
**Distribution of family income - Gini index:** 38.5 (2007)
**Investment (gross fixed):** 21.9% of GDP (2008 est.)
**Budget:**
*revenues:* $108.6 billion
*expenditures:* $114.7 billion (2008 est.)
**Public debt:** 64.2% of GDP (2008 est.)
**Inflation rate (consumer prices):**
2.9% (2008 est.)
2.4% (2007 est.)
**Central bank discount rate:** 4%
*note:* this is the European Central Bank's rate on the marginal lending facility, which offers overnight credit to banks in the euro area
**Commercial bank prime lending rate:** 7.92% (31 December 2007)
**Stock of money:** NA
*note:* see entry for the European Union for money supply in the euro area; the European Central Bank (ECB) controls monetary policy for the 16 members of the Economic and Monetary Union (EMU); individual members of the EMU do not control the quantity of money and quasi money circulating within their own borders
**Stock of quasi money:** NA
**Stock of domestic credit:** $451.9 billion (31 December 2007)
**Market value of publicly traded shares:** $132.3 billion (31 December 2007)
**Agriculture - products:** grain, potatoes, tomatoes, olives, grapes; sheep, cattle, goats, swine, poultry, dairy products; fish
**Industries:** textiles, clothing, footwear, wood and cork, paper, chemicals, auto-parts manufacturing, base metals, diary products, wine and other foods, porcelain and ceramics, glassware, technology, telecommunications; ship construction and refurbishment; tourism
**Industrial production growth rate:** 1% (2008 est.)
**Electricity - production:** 44.83 billion kWh (2007 est.)
**Electricity - consumption:** 48.02 billion kWh (2006 est.)
**Electricity - exports:** 1.906 billion kWh (2007 est.)
**Electricity - imports:** 8,371 kWh (2007 est.)
**Oil - production:** 6,281 bbl/day (2007 est.)
**Oil - consumption:** 301,000 bbl/day (2007 est.)
**Oil - exports:** 50,490 bbl/day (2005)

**Oil - imports:** 390,300 bbl/day (2005)
**Oil - proved reserves:** NA bbl
**Natural gas - production:** 0 cu m (2007 est.)
**Natural gas - consumption:** 4.112 billion cu m (2007 est.)
**Natural gas - exports:** 0 cu m (2007 est.)
**Natural gas - imports:** 4.095 billion cu m (2007 est.)
**Natural gas - proved reserves:** 0 cu m (1 January 2006 est.)
**Current account balance:** -$23.97 billion (2008 est.)
**Exports:** $57.8 billion f.o.b. (2008 est.)
**Exports - commodities:** agricultural products, food products, oil products, chemical products, plastics and rubber, skins and leather, wood and cork, wood pulp and paper, textile materials, clothing, footwear, minerals and mineral products, base metals, machinery and tools, vehicles and other transport material, and optical and precision instruments
**Exports - partners:** Spain 27.1%, Germany 12.9%, France 12.3%, UK 5.9%, US 4.8%, Angola 4.5%, Italy 4% (2007)
**Imports:** $87.92 billion f.o.b. (2008 est.)
**Imports - commodities:** agricultural products, food products, oil products, chemical products, plastics and rubber, skins and leather, wood and cork, wood pulp and paper, textile materials, clothing, footwear, minerals and mineral products, base metals, machinery and tools, vehicles and other transport material, and optical and precision instruments, computer accessories and parts, semi-conductors and related devices, household goods, passenger cars new and used, and wine products
**Imports - partners:** Spain 29.5%, Germany 12.9%, France 8.4%, Italy 5.2%, Netherlands 4.6% (2007)
**Reserves of foreign exchange and gold:** $11.55 billion (31 December 2007 est.)
**Debt - external:** $461.2 billion (31 December 2007)
**Stock of direct foreign investment - at home:** $118.1 billion (2008 est.)
**Stock of direct foreign investment - abroad:** $69.24 billion (2008 est.)
**Exchange rates:** euros (EUR) per US dollar - 0.6827 (2008 est.), 0.7345 (2007), 0.7964 (2006), 0.8041 (2005), 0.8054 (2004)

## Communications

**Telephones - main lines in use:** 4.139 million (2007)
**Telephones - mobile cellular:** 13.413 million (2007)
**Telephone system:**
*general assessment:* Portugal's telephone system has achieved a state-of-the-art network with broadband, high-speed capabilities
*domestic:* integrated network of coaxial cables, open-wire, microwave radio relay, and domestic satellite earth stations
*international:* country code - 351; a combination of submarine cables provide connectivity to Europe, North and East Africa, South Africa, the Middle East, Asia, and the US; satellite earth stations - 3 Intelsat (2 Atlantic Ocean and 1 Indian Ocean), NA Eutelsat; tropospheric scatter to Azores (1998)

**Radio broadcast stations:** AM 2, FM 63, shortwave 1 (2008)
**Television broadcast stations:** 42 (2008)
**Internet country code:** .pt
**Internet hosts:** 1.858 million (2008)
**Internet users:** 3.549 million (2007)

## Transportation

**Airports:** 65 (2008)
**Airports - with paved runways:**
*total:* 43
*over 3,047 m:* 5
*2,438 to 3,047 m:* 9
*1,524 to 2,437 m:* 5
*914 to 1,523 m:* 13
*under 914 m:* 11 (2008)
**Airports - with unpaved runways:**
*total:* 22
*914 to 1,523 m:* 1
*under 914 m:* 21 (2008)
**Pipelines:** gas 1,098 km; oil 11 km; refined products 188 km (2008)
**Railways:**
*total:* 2,786 km
*broad gauge:* 2,603 km 1.668-m gauge (1,351 km electrified)
*narrow gauge:* 183 km 1.000-m gauge (2006)
**Roadways:**
*total:* 82,900 km
*paved:* 71,294 km (includes 2,300 km of expressways)
*unpaved:* 11,606 km (2005)
**Waterways:** 210 km (on Douro River from Porto) (2008)
**Merchant marine:**
*total:* 117
*by type:* bulk carrier 10, cargo 36, carrier 1, chemical tanker 15, container 6, liquefied gas 9, passenger 10, passenger/cargo 9, petroleum tanker 4, roll on/roll off 1, specialized tanker 1, vehicle carrier 15
*foreign-owned:* 84 (Bahamas 1, Belgium 8, Denmark 3, Germany 20, Greece 4, Hong Kong 2, Italy 12, Japan 15, Mexico 1, Netherlands 1, Spain 11, Sweden 3, Switzerland 2, US 1)
*registered in other countries:* 15 (Cyprus 1, Hong Kong 1, Italy 1, Malta 3, Panama 9) (2008)
**Ports and terminals:** Leixoes, Lisbon, Setubal, Sines

## Military

**Military branches:** Portuguese Army (Exercito Portugues), Portuguese Navy (Marinha Portuguesa; includes Marine Corps), Portuguese Air Force (Forca Aerea Portuguesa, FAP) (2009)
**Military service age and obligation:** 18 years of age for voluntary military service; compulsory military service ended in 2004; women serve in the armed forces, on naval ships since 1993, but are prohibited from serving in some combatant specialties; reserve obligation to age 35 (2007)

## Portugal *(continued)*

**Manpower available for military service:**
*males age 16-49:* 2,573,913
*females age 16-49:* 2,498,262 (2008 est.)
**Manpower fit for military service:**
*males age 16-49:* 2,103,558
*females age 16-49:* 2,049,032 (2009 est.)
**Manpower reaching militarily significant age annually:**
*male:* 64,047
*female:* 57,630 (2009 est.)
**Military expenditures:** 2.3% of GDP (2005 est.)

### Transnational Issues

**Disputes - international:** Portugal does not recognize Spanish sovereignty over the territory of Olivenza based on a difference of interpretation of the 1815 Congress of Vienna and the 1801 Treaty of Badajoz
**Illicit drugs:** seizing record amounts of Latin American cocaine destined for Europe; a European gateway for Southwest Asian heroin; transshipment point for hashish from North Africa to Europe; consumer of Southwest Asian heroin

# Puerto Rico
*(territory of the US with commonwealth status)*

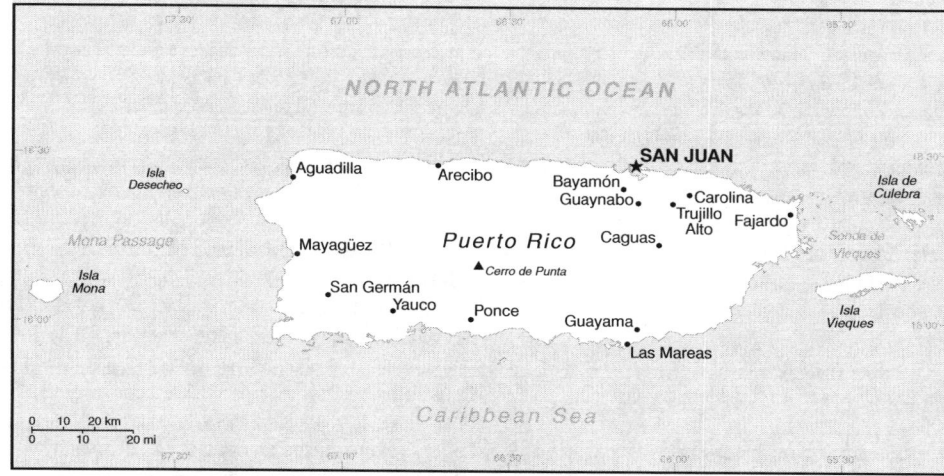

### Introduction

**Background:** Populated for centuries by aboriginal peoples, the island was claimed by the Spanish Crown in 1493 following COLUMBUS' second voyage to the Americas. In 1898, after 400 years of colonial rule that saw the indigenous population nearly exterminated and African slave labor introduced, Puerto Rico was ceded to the US as a result of the Spanish-American War. Puerto Ricans were granted US citizenship in 1917. Popularly-elected governors have served since 1948. In 1952, a constitution was enacted providing for internal self government. In plebiscites held in 1967, 1993, and 1998, voters chose not to alter the existing political status.

### Geography

**Location:** Caribbean, island between the Caribbean Sea and the North Atlantic Ocean, east of the Dominican Republic
**Geographic coordinates:** 18 15 N, 66 30 W
**Map references:** Central America and the Caribbean
**Area:**
*total:* 13,790 sq km
*land:* 8,870 sq km
*water:* 4,921 sq km
**Area - comparative:** slightly less than three times the size of Rhode Island
**Land boundaries:** 0 km
**Coastline:** 501 km
**Maritime claims:**
*territorial sea:* 12 nm
*exclusive economic zone:* 200 nm
**Climate:** tropical marine, mild; little seasonal temperature variation
**Terrain:** mostly mountains with coastal plain belt in north; mountains precipitous to sea on west coast; sandy beaches along most coastal areas

**Elevation extremes:**
*lowest point:* Caribbean Sea 0 m
*highest point:* Cerro de Punta 1,339 m
**Natural resources:** some copper and nickel; potential for onshore and offshore oil
**Land use:**
*arable land:* 3.69%
*permanent crops:* 5.59%
*other:* 90.72% (2005)
**Irrigated land:** 400 sq km (2003)
**Natural hazards:** periodic droughts; hurricanes
**Environment - current issues:** erosion; occasional drought causing water shortages
**Geography - note:** important location along the Mona Passage - a key shipping lane to the Panama Canal; San Juan is one of the biggest and best natural harbors in the Caribbean; many small rivers and high central mountains ensure land is well watered; south coast relatively dry; fertile coastal plain belt in north

### People

**Population:** 3,971,020 (July 2009 est.)
**Age structure:**
*0-14 years:* 19.9% (male 404,635/female 386,733)
*15-64 years:* 66% (male 1,260,114/female 1,361,193)
*65 years and over:* 14.1% (male 240,318/female 318,027) (2009 est.)
**Median age:**
*total:* 36.2 years
*male:* 34.5 years
*female:* 37.9 years (2009 est.)
**Population growth rate:** 0.34% (2009 est.)
**Birth rate:** 12.12 births/1,000 population (2009 est.)
**Death rate:** 7.88 deaths/1,000 population (2008 est.)
**Net migration rate:** -0.96 migrant(s)/1,000 population (2009 est.)

# Puerto Rico *(continued)*

## Urbanization:

*urban population:* 98% of total population (2008)
*rate of urbanization:* 0.8% annual rate of change
(2005-10 est.)

## Sex ratio:

*at birth:* 1.05 male(s)/female
*under 15 years:* 1.05 male(s)/female
*15-64 years:* 0.93 male(s)/female
*65 years and over:* 0.76 male(s)/female
*total population:* 0.92 male(s)/female (2009 est.)

## Infant mortality rate:

*total:* 8.42 deaths/1,000 live births
*male:* 9.69 deaths/1,000 live births
*female:* 7.1 deaths/1,000 live births (2009 est.)

## Life expectancy at birth:

*total population:* 78.53 years
*male:* 74.85 years
*female:* 82.39 years (2009 est.)

**Total fertility rate:** 1.71 children born/woman
(2009 est.)

**HIV/AIDS - adult prevalence rate:** NA
**HIV/AIDS - people living with HIV/AIDS:** 7,397
(1997)
**HIV/AIDS - deaths:** NA

## Nationality:

*noun:* Puerto Rican(s) (US citizens)
*adjective:* Puerto Rican

**Ethnic groups:** white (mostly Spanish origin) 76.2%,
black 6.9%, Asian 0.3%, Amerindian 0.2%, mixed
4.4%, other 12% (2007)

**Religions:** Roman Catholic 85%, Protestant and
other 15%

**Languages:** Spanish, English

## Literacy:

*definition:* age 15 and over can read and write
*total population:* 94.1%
*male:* 93.9%
*female:* 94.4% (2002 est.)

**Education expenditures:** NA

### Government

## Country name:

*conventional long form:* Commonwealth of Puerto
Rico
*conventional short form:* Puerto Rico

**Dependency status:** unincorporated, organized
territory of the US with commonwealth status; policy
relations between Puerto Rico and the US conducted
under the jurisdiction of the Office of the President

**Government type:** commonwealth

## Capital:

*name:* San Juan
*geographic coordinates:* 18 28 N, 66 07 W
*time difference:* UTC-4 (1 hour ahead of Washington,
DC during Standard Time)

**Administrative divisions:** none (territory of the US
with commonwealth status); there are no first-order
administrative divisions as defined by the US
Government, but there are 78 municipalities (municipios,
singular - municipio) at the second order; Adjuntas,
Aguada, Aguadilla, Aguas Buenas, Aibonito, Anasco,

Arecibo, Arroyo, Barceloneta, Barranquitas, Bayamon,
Cabo Rojo, Caguas, Camuy, Canovanas, Carolina,
Catano, Cayey, Ceiba, Ciales, Cidra, Coamo, Comerio,
Corozal, Culebra, Dorado, Fajardo, Florida, Guanica,
Guayama, Guayanilla, Guaynabo, Gurabo, Hatillo,
Hormigueros, Humacao, Isabela, Jayuya, Juana Diaz,
Juncos, Lajas, Lares, Las Marias, Las Piedras, Loiza,
Luquillo, Manati, Maricao, Maunabo, Mayaguez, Moca,
Morovis, Naguabo, Naranjito, Orocovis, Patillas,
Penuelas, Ponce, Quebradillas, Rincon, Rio Grande,
Sabana Grande, Salinas, San German, San Juan, San
Lorenzo, San Sebastian, Santa Isabel, Toa Alta, Toa
Baja, Trujillo Alto, Utuado, Vega Alta, Vega Baja,
Vieques, Villalba, Yabucoa, Yauco

**Independence:** none (territory of the US with
commonwealth status)

**National holiday:** US Independence Day, 4 July
(1776); Puerto Rico Constitution Day, 25 July (1952)

**Constitution:** ratified 3 March 1952; approved by US
Congress 3 July 1952; effective 25 July 1952

**Legal system:** based on Spanish civil code and
within the US Federal system of justice

**Suffrage:** 18 years of age; universal; island residents
are US citizens but do not vote in US presidential
elections

## Executive branch:

*chief of state:* President Barack H. OBAMA (since
20 January 2009); Vice President Joseph R. BIDEN
(since 20 January 2009)
*head of government:* Governor Luis FORTUNO
(since 2 January 2009)
*cabinet:* Cabinet appointed by the governor with the
consent of the legislature
*elections:* under the US Constitution, residents of
unincorporated territories, such as Puerto Rico, do not
vote in elections for US president and vice president;
however, they may vote in Democratic and
Republican party presidential primary elections;
governor elected by popular vote for a four-year term
(no term limits); election last held 4 November 2008
(next to be held in November 2012)
*election results:* Luis FORTUNO elected governor
with 52.8% of the vote

**Legislative branch:** bicameral Legislative Assembly
consists of the Senate (at least 27 seats; members are
directly elected by popular vote to serve four-year
terms) and the House of Representatives (51 seats;
members are elected by popular vote to serve
four-year terms)
*elections:* Senate - last held 4 November 2008 (next to
be held November 2012); House of Representatives -
last held 4 November 2008 (next to be held
in November 2012)
*election results:* Senate - percent of vote by party -
PNP 81.5%, PPD 18.5%; seats by party - PNP 22,
PPD 5; House of Representatives - percent of vote by
party - PNP 72.5%, PPD 27.5%; seats by party - PNP
37, PPD 14
*note:* Puerto Rico elects, by popular vote, a resident
commissioner to serve a four-year term as a
nonvoting representative in the US House of
Representatives; aside from not voting on the House

floor, he enjoys all the rights of a member of Congress;
elections last held 4 November 2008 (next to be held
in November 2012); results - percent of vote by
party -NA; seats by party - PNP 1

**Judicial branch:** Supreme Court; Appellate Court;
Court of First Instance composed of two sections: a
Superior Court and a Municipal Court (justices for all
these courts appointed by the governor with the
consent of the Senate)

**Political parties and leaders:** National Democratic
Party [Roberto PRATS]; National Republican Party of
Puerto Rico [Dr. Tiody FERRE]; New Progressive
Party or PNP [Pedro ROSSELLO] (pro-US
statehood); Popular Democratic Party or PPD [Anibal
ACEVEDO-VILA] (pro-commonwealth); Puerto Rican
Independence Party or PIP [Ruben BERRIOS
Martinez] (pro-independence)

**Political pressure groups and leaders:** Boricua
Popular Army or EPB (a revolutionary group also
known as Los Macheteros); note - the following radical
groups are considered dormant by Federal law
enforcement: Armed Forces for National Liberation or
FALN, Armed Forces of Popular Resistance,
Volunteers of the Puerto Rican Revolution

**International organization participation:** Caricom
(observer), Interpol (subbureau), IOC, ITUC, UNWTO
(associate), UPU, WCL, WFTU

**Diplomatic representation in the US:** none
(territory of the US with commonwealth status)

**Diplomatic representation from the US:** none
(territory of the US with commonwealth status)

**Flag description:** five equal horizontal bands of red
(top and bottom) alternating with white; a blue
isosceles triangle based on the hoist side bears a
large, white, five-pointed star in the center; design
initially influenced by the US flag, but similar to the
Cuban flag, with the colors of the bands and triangle
reversed

### Economy

**Economy - overview:** Puerto Rico has one of the
most dynamic economies in the Caribbean region. A
diverse industrial sector has far surpassed agriculture as
the primary locus of economic activity and income.
Encouraged by duty-free access to the US and by tax
incentives, US firms have invested heavily in Puerto Rico
since the 1950s. US minimum wage laws apply. Sugar
production has lost out to dairy production and other
livestock products as the main source of income in the
agricultural sector. Tourism has traditionally been an
important source of income with estimated arrivals of
nearly 5 million tourists in 2004. Growth fell off in 2001-03,
largely due to the slowdown in the US economy,
recovered in 2004-05, but declined again in 2006-07.

## GDP (purchasing power parity):

$70.59 billion (2008 est.)
$72.03 billion (2007)
$73.35 billion (2006)
*note:* data are in 2008 US dollars

**GDP (official exchange rate):** $88 billion
(2008 est.)

**GDP - real growth rate:**
-2% (2008 est.)
-1.8% (2007 est.)
0.5% (2006 est.)
**GDP - per capita (PPP):**
$17,800 (2008 est.)
$18,300 (2007 est.)
$18,700 (2006 est.)
*note:* data are in 2008 US dollars
**GDP - composition by sector:**
*agriculture:* 1%
*industry:* 45%
*services:* 54% (2002 est.)
**Labor force:** 1.3 million (2000)
**Labor force - by occupation:**
*agriculture:* 2.1%
*industry:* 19%
*services:* 79% (2005)
**Unemployment rate:**
12% (2002)
**Population below poverty line:** NA%
**Household income or consumption by percentage share:**
*lowest 10%:* NA%
*highest 10%:* NA%
**Budget:**
*revenues:* $6.7 billion
*expenditures:* $9.6 billion (FY99/00)
**Inflation rate (consumer prices):**
6.5% (2003 est.)
**Market value of publicly traded shares:** $NA
**Agriculture - products:** sugarcane, coffee, pineapples, plantains, bananas; livestock products, chickens
**Industries:** pharmaceuticals, electronics, apparel, food products, tourism
**Industrial production growth rate:** NA%
**Electricity - production:** 23.84 billion kWh (2006 est.)
**Electricity - consumption:** 22.17 billion kWh (2006 est.)
**Electricity - exports:** 0 kWh (2007 est.)
**Electricity - imports:** 0 kWh (2007 est.)
**Oil - production:** 1,354 bbl/day (2007 est.)
**Oil - consumption:** 215,000 bbl/day (2007 est.)
**Oil - exports:** 10,610 bbl/day (2005)
**Oil - imports:** 230,700 bbl/day (2005)
**Oil - proved reserves:** 0 bbl (1 January 2006 est.)
**Natural gas - production:** 0 cu m (2007 est.)
**Natural gas - consumption:** 736.2 million cu m (2007 est.)
**Natural gas - exports:** 0 cu m (2007 est.)
**Natural gas - imports:** 736.2 million cu m (2007 est.)
**Natural gas - proved reserves:** 0 cu m (1 January 2006 est.)
**Exports:** $46.9 billion f.o.b. (2001)
**Exports - commodities:** chemicals, electronics, apparel, canned tuna, rum, beverage concentrates, medical equipment

**Imports:** $29.1 billion c.i.f. (2001)
**Imports - commodities:** chemicals, machinery and equipment, clothing, food, fish, petroleum products
**Debt - external:** $NA
**Exchange rates:** the US dollar is used

## Communications

**Telephones - main lines in use:** 1.038 million (2005)
**Telephones - mobile cellular:** 3.354 million (2005)
**Telephone system:**
*general assessment:* modern system integrated with that of the US by high-capacity submarine cable and Intelsat with high-speed data capability
*domestic:* digital telephone system; cellular telephone service
*international:* country code - 1-787, 939; submarine cables provide connectivity to the US, Caribbean, Central and South America; satellite earth station - 1 Intelsat
**Radio broadcast stations:** AM 74, FM 53, shortwave 0 (2008)
**Television broadcast stations:** 34 (2008)
**Internet country code:** .pr
**Internet hosts:** 404 (2008)
**Internet users:** 1 million (2007)

## Transportation

**Airports:** 29 (2008)
**Airports - with paved runways:**
*total:* 17
*over 3,047 m:* 3
*1,524 to 2,437 m:* 2
*914 to 1,523 m:* 7
*under 914 m:* 5 (2008)
**Airports - with unpaved runways:**
*total:* 12
*1,524 to 2,437 m:* 1
*914 to 1,523 m:* 1
*under 914 m:* 10 (2008)
**Railways:**
*total:* 96 km
*narrow gauge:* 96 km 1.000-m gauge (2006)
**Roadways:**
*total:* 26,186 km
*paved:* 24,877 km (includes 427 km of expressways)
*unpaved:* 1,309 km (2007)
**Merchant marine:**
*total:* 3
*by type:* roll on/roll off 3
*foreign-owned:* 3 (US 3)
*registered in other countries:* 1 (Saint Vincent and the Grenadines 1) (2008)
**Ports and terminals:** Guayanilla, Mayaguez, San Juan

## Military

**Military branches:** no regular indigenous military forces; paramilitary National Guard, Police Force
**Manpower fit for military service:**
*males age 16-49:* 699,784
*females age 16-49:* 790,482 (2009 est.)
**Manpower reaching militarily significant age annually:**
*male:* 30,422
*female:* 29,396 (2009 est.)
**Military - note:** defense is the responsibility of the US

## Transnational Issues

**Disputes - international:** increasing numbers of illegal migrants from the Dominican Republic cross the Mona Passage to Puerto Rico each year looking for work

# Qatar

The island of Ḥālūl is not shown.

## Introduction

**Background:** Ruled by the al-Thani family since the mid-1800s, Qatar transformed itself from a poor British protectorate noted mainly for pearling into an independent state with significant oil and natural gas revenues. During the late 1980s and early 1990s, the Qatari economy was crippled by a continuous siphoning off of petroleum revenues by the Amir, who had ruled the country since 1972. His son, the current Amir HAMAD bin Khalifa al-Thani, overthrew him in a bloodless coup in 1995. In 2001, Qatar resolved its longstanding border disputes with both Bahrain and Saudi Arabia. As of 2007, oil and natural gas revenues had enabled Qatar to attain the second-highest per capita income in the world.

## Geography

**Location:** Middle East, peninsula bordering the Persian Gulf and Saudi Arabia
**Geographic coordinates:** 25 30 N, 51 15 E
**Map references:** Middle East

**Area:**
*total:* 11,437 sq km
*land:* 11,437 sq km
*water:* 0 sq km
**Area - comparative:** slightly smaller than Connecticut
**Land boundaries:**
*total:* 60 km
*border countries:* Saudi Arabia 60 km
**Coastline:** 563 km
**Maritime claims:**
*territorial sea:* 12 nm
*contiguous zone:* 24 nm
*exclusive economic zone:* as determined by bilateral agreements or the median line
**Climate:** arid; mild, pleasant winters; very hot, humid summers
**Terrain:** mostly flat and barren desert covered with loose sand and gravel
**Elevation extremes:**
*lowest point:* Persian Gulf 0 m
*highest point:* Qurayn Abu al Bawl 103 m
**Natural resources:** petroleum, natural gas, fish
**Land use:**
*arable land:* 1.64%
*permanent crops:* 0.27%
*other:* 98.09% (2005)
**Irrigated land:** 130 sq km (2002)
**Total renewable water resources:** 0.1 cu km (1997)
**Freshwater withdrawal (domestic/industrial/ agricultural):**
*total:* 0.29 cu km/yr (24%/3%/72%)
*per capita:* 358 cu m/yr (2000)
**Natural hazards:** haze, dust storms, sandstorms common
**Environment - current issues:** limited natural fresh water resources are increasing dependence on large-scale desalination facilities
**Environment - international agreements:**
*party to:* Biodiversity, Climate Change, Climate Change-Kyoto Protocol, Desertification, Endangered Species, Hazardous Wastes, Law of the Sea, Ozone Layer Protection, Ship Pollution
*signed, but not ratified:* none of the selected agreements
**Geography - note:** strategic location in central Persian Gulf near major petroleum deposits

## People

**Population:** 833,285 (July 2009 est.)
**Age structure:**
*0-14 years:* 21.8% (male 93,805/female 88,040)
*15-64 years:* 76.8% (male 454,714/female 185,004)
*65 years and over:* 1.4% (male 6,792/female 4,930) (2009 est.)
**Median age:**
*total:* 30.8 years
*male:* 32.8 years
*female:* 25.4 years (2009 est.)

**Population growth rate:** 0.957% (2009 est.)
**Birth rate:** 15.61 births/1,000 population (2009 est.)
**Death rate:** 2.47 deaths/1,000 population (2008 est.)
**Net migration rate:** -3.58 migrant(s)/1,000 population (2009 est.)
**Urbanization:**
*urban population:* 96% of total population (2008)
*rate of urbanization:* 2.2% annual rate of change (2005-10 est.)
**Sex ratio:**
*at birth:* 1.06 male(s)/female
*under 15 years:* 1.06 male(s)/female
*15-64 years:* 2.46 male(s)/female
*65 years and over:* 1.38 male(s)/female
*total population:* 2 male(s)/female (2009 est.)
**Infant mortality rate:**
*total:* 12.66 deaths/1,000 live births
*male:* 13.51 deaths/1,000 live births
*female:* 11.77 deaths/1,000 live births (2009 est.)
**Life expectancy at birth:**
*total population:* 75.35 years
*male:* 73.66 years
*female:* 77.14 years (2009 est.)
**Total fertility rate:** 2.45 children born/woman (2009 est.)
**HIV/AIDS - adult prevalence rate:** 0.09% (2001 est.)
**HIV/AIDS - people living with HIV/AIDS:** NA
**HIV/AIDS - deaths:** NA
**Nationality:**
*noun:* Qatari(s)
*adjective:* Qatari
**Ethnic groups:** Arab 40%, Indian 18%, Pakistani 18%, Iranian 10%, other 14%
**Religions:** Muslim 77.5%, Christian 8.5%, other 14% (2004 census)
**Languages:** Arabic (official), English commonly used as a second language
**Literacy:**
*definition:* age 15 and over can read and write
*total population:* 89%
*male:* 89.1%
*female:* 88.6% (2004 census)
**School life expectancy (primary to tertiary education):**
*total:* 13 years
*male:* 13 years
*female:* 14 years (2006)
**Education expenditures:** 3.3% of GDP (2005)

## Government

**Country name:**
*conventional long form:* State of Qatar
*conventional short form:* Qatar
*local long form:* Dawlat Qatar
*local short form:* Qatar
*note:* closest approximation of the native pronunciation falls between cutter and gutter, but not like guitar

# Qatar *(continued)*

**Government type:** emirate
**Capital:**
*name:* Doha
*geographic coordinates:* 25 17 N, 51 32 E
*time difference:* UTC+3 (8 hours ahead of Washington, DC during Standard Time)
**Administrative divisions:** 10 municipalities (baladiyat, singular - baladiyah); Ad Dawhah, Al Ghuwayriyah, Al Jumayliyah, Al Khawr, Al Wakrah, Ar Rayyan, Jarayan al Batinah, Madinat ash Shamal, Umm Sa'id, Umm Salal
**Independence:** 3 September 1971 (from the UK)
**National holiday:** Independence Day, 3 September (1971); also observed is National Day, 18 December
**Constitution:** ratified by public referendum on 29 April 2003, endorsed by the Amir on 8 June 2004, effective on 9 June 2005
**Legal system:** based on Islamic and civil law codes; discretionary system of law controlled by the Amir, although civil codes are being implemented; Islamic law dominates family and personal matters; has not accepted compulsory ICJ jurisdiction
**Suffrage:** 18 years of age; universal
**Executive branch:**
*chief of state:* Amir HAMAD bin Khalifa al-Thani (since 27 June 1995 when, as heir apparent, he ousted his father, Amir KHALIFA bin Hamad al-Thani, in a bloodless coup); Heir Apparent TAMIM bin Hamad bin Khalifa al-Thani, fourth son of the monarch (selected Heir Apparent by the monarch on 5 August 2003); note - Amir HAMAD also holds the positions of Minister of Defense and Commander-in-Chief of the Armed Forces
*head of government:* Prime Minister HAMAD bin Jasim bin Jabir al-Thani (since 3 April 2007); Deputy Prime Minister Abdallah bin Hamad al-ATIYAH (since 3 April 2007)
*cabinet:* Council of Ministers appointed by the monarch
*elections:* the monarch is hereditary
*note:* in April 2007, Qatar held nationwide elections for a 29-member Central Municipal Council (CMC), which has limited consultative powers aimed at improving the provision of municipal services; the first election for the CMC was held in March 1999
**Legislative branch:** unicameral Advisory Council or Majlis al-Shura (35 seats; members appointed)
*note:* no legislative elections have been held since 1970 when there were partial elections to the body; Council members have had their terms extended every year since the new constitution came into force on 9 June 2005; the constitution provides for a new 45-member Advisory Council or Majlis al-Shura; the public would elect two-thirds of the Majlis al-Shura; the Amir would appoint the remaining members; preparations are underway to conduct elections to the Majlis al-Shura
**Judicial branch:** Courts of First Instance, Appeal, and Cassation; an Administrative Court and a Constitutional Court were established in 2007; note - all judges are appointed by Amiri Decree based on the recommendation of the Supreme Judiciary Council for renewable three-year terms

**Political parties and leaders:** none
**Political pressure groups and leaders:** none
**International organization participation:** ABEDA, ACC, AFESD, AMF, FAO, G-77, GCC, IAEA, IBRD, ICAO, ICC, ICRM, IDA, IDB, IFAD, IFC, IFRCS, IHO, ILO, IMF, IMO, IMSO, Interpol, IOC, IPU, ISO, ITSO, ITU, LAS, MIGA, NAM, OAPEC, OAS (observer), OIC, OPCW, OPEC, PCA, UN, UNCTAD, UNESCO, UNIDO, UNIFIL, UNWTO, UPU, WCO, WFTU, WHO, WIPO, WMO, WTO
**Diplomatic representation in the US:**
*chief of mission:* Ambassador Ali Fahad al-Shahwany al-HAJRI
*chancery:* 2555 M Street NW, Washington, DC 20037
*telephone:* [1] (202) 274-1600 and 274-1603
*FAX:* [1] (202) 237-0061
*consulate(s) general:* Houston
**Diplomatic representation from the US:**
*chief of mission:* Ambassador Joseph E. LEBARON
*embassy:* Al-Luqta District, 22 February Road, Doha
*mailing address:* P. O. Box 2399, Doha
*telephone:* [974] 488 4161
*FAX:* [974] 488 4150
**Flag description:** maroon with a broad white serrated band (nine white points) on the hoist side

## Economy

**Economy - overview:** Qatar has experienced rapid economic growth over the last several years on the back of high oil prices, and in 2008 posted its eighth consecutive budget surplus. Economic policy is focused on developing Qatar's nonassociated natural gas reserves and increasing private and foreign investment in non-energy sectors, but oil and gas still account for more than 50% of GDP, roughly 85% of export earnings, and 70% of government revenues. Oil and gas have made Qatar the second highest per-capita income country - following Liechtenstein - and one of the world's fastest growing. Proved oil reserves of 15 billion barrels should enable continued output at current levels for 37 years. Qatar's proved reserves of natural gas are nearly 26 trillion cubic meters, about 14% of the world total and third largest in the world. The drop in oil prices in late 2008 and the global financial crisis will reduce Qatar's budget surplus and may slow the pace of investment and development projects in 2009.
**GDP (purchasing power parity):**
$85.35 billion (2008 est.)
$76.75 billion (2007)
$68.84 billion (2006)
*note:* data are in 2008 US dollars
**GDP (official exchange rate):** $116.9 billion (2008 est.)
**GDP - real growth rate:**
11.2% (2008 est.)
11.5% (2007 est.)
12.8% (2006 est.)
**GDP - per capita (PPP):**
$103,500 (2008 est.)
$94,200 (2007 est.)
$85,800 (2006 est.)
*note:* data are in 2008 US dollars

**GDP - composition by sector:**
*agriculture:* 0.1%
*industry:* 79.4%
*services:* 20.5% (2008 est.)
**Labor force:** 1.124 million (2008 est.)
**Unemployment rate:**
0.6% (2008 est.)
0.7% (2007 est.)
**Population below poverty line:** NA%
**Household income or consumption by percentage share:**
*lowest 10%:* NA%
*highest 10%:* NA%
**Investment (gross fixed):** 41.4% of GDP (2008 est.)
**Budget:**
*revenues:* $40.36 billion
*expenditures:* $28.08 billion (2008 est.)
**Public debt:** 6% of GDP (2008 est.)
**Inflation rate (consumer prices):**
15.2% (2008 est.)
13.7% (2007 est.)
**Central bank discount rate:** NA
**Commercial bank prime lending rate:** 7.43% (31 December 2007)
**Stock of money:** $9.718 billion (31 December 2007)
**Stock of quasi money:** $22.6 billion (31 December 2007)
**Stock of domestic credit:** $30.52 billion (31 December 2007)
**Market value of publicly traded shares:** $95.49 billion (31 December 2007)
**Agriculture - products:** fruits, vegetables; poultry, dairy products, beef; fish
**Industries:** crude oil production and refining, ammonia, fertilizers, petrochemicals, steel reinforcing bars, cement, commercial ship repair
**Industrial production growth rate:** 12.6% (2008 est.)
**Electricity - production:** 14.41 billion kWh (2006 est.)
**Electricity - consumption:** 13.19 billion kWh (2006 est.)
**Electricity - exports:** 0 kWh (2007 est.)
**Electricity - imports:** 0 kWh (2007 est.)
**Oil - production:** 1.125 million bbl/day (2007 est.)
**Oil - consumption:** 108,900 bbl/day (2006 est.)
**Oil - exports:** 1.026 million bbl/day (2005)
**Oil - imports:** 0 bbl/day (2005)
**Oil - proved reserves:** 15.21 billion bbl (1 January 2008 est.)
**Natural gas - production:** 59.8 billion cu m (2007 est.)
**Natural gas - consumption:** 20.5 billion cu m (2007 est.)
**Natural gas - exports:** 39.3 billion cu m (2007 est.)
**Natural gas - imports:** 0 cu m (2007 est.)
**Natural gas - proved reserves:** 25.63 trillion cu m (1 January 2008 est.)
**Current account balance:** $22.71 billion (2008 est.)
**Exports:** $62.44 billion f.o.b. (2008 est.)

## Qatar *(continued)*

**Exports - commodities:** liquefied natural gas (LNG), petroleum products, fertilizers, steel
**Exports - partners:** Japan 39.9%, South Korea 19.9%, Singapore 9.9%, India 5.1%, Thailand 4.9%, UAE 4% (2007)
**Imports:** $24.96 billion f.o.b. (2008 est.)
**Imports - commodities:** machinery and transport equipment, food, chemicals
**Imports - partners:** US 13.3%, Italy 10.8%, Japan 8.9%, France 7.9%, Germany 7.3%, UK 5.7%, South Korea 5.6%, UAE 5.1%, Saudi Arabia 4.3% (2007)
**Reserves of foreign exchange and gold:** $16.81 billion (31 December 2008 est.)
**Debt - external:** $48.91 billion (31 December 2008 est.)
**Stock of direct foreign investment - at home:** $3.627 billion (2008 est.)
**Stock of direct foreign investment - abroad:** $9.143 billion (2008 est.)
**Exchange rates:** Qatari rials (QAR) per US dollar - 3.64 (2008 est.), 3.64 (2007), 3.64 (2006), 3.64 (2005), 3.64 (2004)

### Communications

**Telephones - main lines in use:** 237,400 (2007)
**Telephones - mobile cellular:** 1.264 million (2007)
**Telephone system:**
*general assessment:* modern system centered in Doha
*domestic:* combined fixed-line and mobile-cellular telephone density is roughly 165 telephones per 100 persons
*international:* country code - 974; landing point for the Fiber-Optic Link Around the Globe (FLAG) submarine cable network that provides links to Asia, Middle East, Europe, and the US; tropospheric scatter to Bahrain; microwave radio relay to Saudi Arabia and the UAE; satellite earth stations - 2 Intelsat (1 Atlantic Ocean and 1 Indian Ocean) and 1 Arabsat
**Radio broadcast stations:** AM 6, FM 5, shortwave 1 (1998)
**Television broadcast stations:** 1 (plus 3 repeaters) (2001)
**Internet country code:** .qa
**Internet hosts:** 563 (2008)
**Internet users:** 351,000 (2007)

### Transportation

**Airports:** 5 (2008)
**Airports - with paved runways:**
*total:* 3
*over 3,047 m:* 2
*1,524 to 2,437 m:* 1 (2008)
**Airports - with unpaved runways:**
*total:* 2
*914 to 1,523 m:* 1
*under 914 m:* 1 (2008)
**Heliports:** 1 (2007)
**Pipelines:** condensate 145 km; condensate/gas 132 km; gas 978 km; liquid petroleum gas 90 km; oil 382 km(2008)

**Roadways:**
*total:* 7,790 km (2006)
**Merchant marine:**
*total:* 22
*by type:* bulk carrier 2, cargo 2, chemical tanker 2, container 8, liquefied gas 4, petroleum tanker 4
*foreign-owned:* 7 (Kuwait 7)
*registered in other countries:* 5 (Liberia 4, Panama 1) (2008)
**Ports and terminals:** Doha, Ra's Laffan

### Military

**Military branches:** Qatari Amiri Land Force (QALF), Qatari Amiri Navy (QAN), Qatari Amiri Air Force (QAAF) (2007)
**Military service age and obligation:** 18 years of age for voluntary military service; no conscription (2008)
**Manpower available for military service:**
*males age 16-49:* 320,383
*females age 16-49:* 167,475 (2008 est.)
**Manpower fit for military service:**
*males age 16-49:* 318,388
*females age 16-49:* 136,841 (2009 est.)
**Manpower reaching militarily significant age annually:**
*male:* 6,337
*female:* 5,059 (2009 est.)
**Military expenditures:** 10% of GDP (2005 est.)

### Transnational Issues

**Disputes - international:** none
**Trafficking in persons:**
*current situation:* Qatar is a destination country for men and women from South and Southeast Asia who migrate willingly, but are subsequently trafficked into involuntary servitude as domestic workers and laborers, and, to a lesser extent, commercial sexual exploitation; the most common offense was forcing workers to accept worse contract terms than those under which they were recruited; other conditions include bonded labor, withholding of pay, restrictions on movement, arbitrary detention, and physical, mental, and sexual abuse
*tier rating:* Tier 3 - Qatar failed, for the second consecutive year, to enforce criminal laws against traffickers, or to provide an effective mechanism to identify and protect victims; it continues to detain and deport victims rather than providing them protection; the government made little progress to increase prosecutions for trafficking in a meaningful way in 2007; workers complaining of working conditions or non-payment of wages were sometimes penalized (2008)

# Romania

### Introduction

**Background:** The principalities of Wallachia and Moldavia - for centuries under the suzerainty of the Turkish Ottoman Empire - secured their autonomy in 1856; they united in 1859 and a few years later adopted the new name of Romania. The country gained recognition of its independence in 1878. It joined the Allied Powers in World War I and acquired new territories - most notably Transylvania - following the conflict. In 1940, Romania allied with the Axis powers and participated in the 1941 German invasion of the USSR. Three years later, overrun by the Soviets, Romania signed an armistice. The post-war Soviet occupation led to the formation of a Communist "people's republic" in 1947 and the abdication of the king. The decades-long rule of dictator Nicolae CEAUSESCU, who took power in 1965, and his Securitate police state became increasingly oppressive and draconian through the 1980s. CEAUSESCU was overthrown and executed in late 1989. Former Communists dominated the government until 1996 when they were swept from power. Romania joined NATO in 2004 and the EU in 2007.

### Geography

**Location:** Southeastern Europe, bordering the Black Sea, between Bulgaria and Ukraine
**Geographic coordinates:** 46 00 N, 25 00 E
**Map references:** Europe
**Area:**
*total:* 237,500 sq km
*land:* 230,340 sq km
*water:* 7,160 sq km
**Area - comparative:** slightly smaller than Oregon
**Land boundaries:**
*total:* 2,508 km
*border countries:* Bulgaria 608 km, Hungary 443 km, Moldova 450 km, Serbia 476 km, Ukraine (north) 362 km, Ukraine (east) 169 km

# Romania *(continued)*

**Coastline:** 225 km
**Maritime claims:**
*territorial sea:* 12 nm
*contiguous zone:* 24 nm
*exclusive economic zone:* 200 nm
*continental shelf:* 200 m depth or to the depth of exploitation
**Climate:** temperate; cold, cloudy winters with frequent snow and fog; sunny summers with frequent showers and thunderstorms
**Terrain:** central Transylvanian Basin is separated from the Moldavian Plateau on the east by the Eastern Carpathian Mountains and separated from the Walachian Plain on the south by the Transylvanian Alps
**Elevation extremes:**
*lowest point:* Black Sea 0 m
*highest point:* Moldoveanu 2,544 m
**Natural resources:** petroleum (reserves declining), timber, natural gas, coal, iron ore, salt, arable land, hydropower
**Land use:**
*arable land:* 39.49%
*permanent crops:* 1.92%
*other:* 58.59% (2005)
**Irrigated land:** 30,770 sq km (2003)
**Total renewable water resources:** 42.3 cu km (2003)
**Freshwater withdrawal (domestic/industrial/agricultural):**
*total:* 6.5 cu km/yr (9%/34%/57%)
*per capita:* 299 cu m/yr (2003)
**Natural hazards:** earthquakes, most severe in south and southwest; geologic structure and climate promote landslides
**Environment - current issues:** soil erosion and degradation; water pollution; air pollution in south from industrial effluents; contamination of Danube delta wetlands
**Environment - international agreements:**
*party to:* Air Pollution, Air Pollution-Persistent Organic Pollutants, Antarctic-Environmental Protocol, Antarctic Treaty, Biodiversity, Climate Change, Climate Change-Kyoto Protocol, Desertification, Endangered Species, Environmental Modification, Hazardous Wastes, Law of the Sea, Ozone Layer Protection, Ship Pollution, Wetlands
*signed, but not ratified:* none of the selected agreements
**Geography - note:** controls most easily traversable land route between the Balkans, Moldova, and Ukraine

## People

**Population:** 22,215,421 (July 2009 est.)
**Age structure:**
*0-14 years:* 15.5% (male 1,772,583/ female 1,681,539)
*15-64 years:* 69.7% (male 7,711,062/ female 7,784,041)
*65 years and over:* 14.7% (male 1,332,120/female 1,934,076) (2009 est.)

**Median age:**
*total:* 37.7 years
*male:* 36.3 years
*female:* 39.2 years (2009 est.)
**Population growth rate:** -0.147% (2009 est.)
**Birth rate:** 10.53 births/1,000 population (2009 est.)
**Death rate:** 11.84 deaths/1,000 population (2008 est.)
**Net migration rate:** -0.13 migrant(s)/1,000 population (2009 est.)
**Urbanization:**
*urban population:* 54% of total population (2008)
*rate of urbanization:* -0.1% annual rate of change (2005-10 est.)
**Sex ratio:**
*at birth:* 1.06 male(s)/female
*under 15 years:* 1.05 male(s)/female
*15-64 years:* 0.99 male(s)/female
*65 years and over:* 0.69 male(s)/female
*total population:* 0.95 male(s)/female (2009 est.)
**Infant mortality rate:**
*total:* 22.9 deaths/1,000 live births
*male:* 25.94 deaths/1,000 live births
*female:* 19.66 deaths/1,000 live births (2009 est.)
**Life expectancy at birth:**
*total population:* 72.45 years
*male:* 68.95 years
*female:* 76.16 years (2009 est.)
**Total fertility rate:** 1.39 children born/woman (2009 est.)
**HIV/AIDS - adult prevalence rate:** less than 0.1% (2007 est.)
**HIV/AIDS - people living with HIV/AIDS:** 15,000 (2007 est.)
**HIV/AIDS - deaths:** 350 (2001 est.)
**Nationality:**
*noun:* Romanian(s)
*adjective:* Romanian
**Ethnic groups:** Romanian 89.5%, Hungarian 6.6%, Roma 2.5%, Ukrainian 0.3%, German 0.3%, Russian 0.2%, Turkish 0.2%, other 0.4% (2002 census)
**Religions:** Eastern Orthodox (including all sub-denominations) 86.8%, Protestant (various denominations including Reformate and Pentecostal) 7.5%, Roman Catholic 4.7%, other (mostly Muslim) and unspecified 0.9%, none 0.1% (2002 census)
**Languages:** Romanian 91% (official), Hungarian 6.7%, Romany (Gypsy) 1.1%, other 1.2%
**Literacy:**
*definition:* age 15 and over can read and write
*total population:* 97.3%
*male:* 98.4%
*female:* 96.3% (2002 census)
**School life expectancy (primary to tertiary education):**
*total:* 14 years
*male:* 14 years
*female:* 14 years (2006)
**Education expenditures:** 3.5% of GDP (2005)

## Government

**Country name:**
*conventional long form:* none
*conventional short form:* Romania
*local long form:* none
*local short form:* Romania
**Government type:** republic
**Capital:**
*name:* Bucharest
*geographic coordinates:* 44 26 N, 26 06 E
*time difference:* UTC+2 (7 hours ahead of Washington, DC during Standard Time)
*daylight saving time:* +1hr, begins last Sunday in March; ends last Sunday in October
**Administrative divisions:** 41 counties (judete, singular - judet) and 1 municipality* (municipiu); Alba, Arad, Arges, Bacau, Bihor, Bistrita-Nasaud, Botosani, Braila, Brasov, Bucuresti (Bucharest)*, Buzau, Calarasi, Caras-Severin, Cluj, Constanta, Covasna, Dimbovita, Dolj, Galati, Gorj, Giurgiu, Harghita, Hunedoara, Ialomita, Iasi, Ilfov, Maramures, Mehedinti, Mures, Neamt, Olt, Prahova, Salaj, Satu Mare, Sibiu, Suceava, Teleorman, Timis, Tulcea, Vaslui, Vilcea, Vrancea
**Independence:** 9 May 1877 (independence proclaimed from the Ottoman Empire; independence recognized 13 July 1878 by the Treaty of Berlin); 26 March 1881 (kingdom proclaimed); 30 December 1947 (republic proclaimed)
**National holiday:** Unification Day (of Romania and Transylvania), 1 December (1918)
**Constitution:** 8 December 1991; revised 29 October 2003
**Legal system:** based on civil law system; has not accepted compulsory ICJ jurisdiction
**Suffrage:** 18 years of age; universal
**Executive branch:**
*chief of state:* President Traian BASESCU (since 20 December 2004); note - President Traian BASESCU was suspended by vote of parliament on 19 April 2007, but resumed his duties on 23 May 2007 after a popular referendum confirmed that his impeachment should not stand
*head of government:* Prime Minister Emil BOC (since 22 December 2008)
*cabinet:* Council of Ministers appointed by the prime minister
*elections:* president elected by popular vote for a five-year term (eligible for a second term); election last held 28 November 2004 with runoff between the top two candidates held 12 December 2004 (next to be held in November-December 2009); prime minister appointed by the president with the consent of the Parliament
*election results:* percent of vote - Traian BASESCU 51.23%, Adrian NASTASE 48.77%
**Legislative branch:** bicameral Parliament or Parlament consists of the Senate or Senat (137 seats; members are elected by popular vote in a mixed electoral system to serve four-year terms) and the Chamber of Deputies or Camera Deputatilor (334 seats; members are elected by popular vote in a mixed electoral system to serve four-year terms)

# Romania (continued)

elections: Senate - last held 30 November 2008 (next expected to be held in November 2012); Chamber of Deputies - last held 30 November 2008 (next expected to be held November 2012)

election results: Senate - percent of vote by alliance/party - PSD-PC 34.2%, PDL 33.6%, PNL 18.7%, UDMR 6.4%, other 7.1%; seats by alliance/party - PSD-PC 49, PDL 51, PNL 28, UDMR 9; Chamber of Deputies - percent of vote by alliance/party - PSD-PC 33.1%, PDL 32.4%, PNL 18.6%, UDMR 6.2%, ethnic minorities 3.6%, other 6.1%; seats by alliance/party - PSD-PC 114, PDL 115, PNL 65, UDMR 22, ethnic minorities 18

**Judicial branch:** Supreme Court of Justice (comprised of 11 judges appointed for three-year terms by the president in consultation with the Superior Council of Magistrates, which is comprised of the minister of justice, the prosecutor general, two civil society representatives appointed by the Senate, and 14 judges and prosecutors elected by their peers); a separate body, the Constitutional Court, validates elections and makes decisions regarding the constitutionality of laws, treaties, ordinances, and internal rules of the Parliament; it is comprised of nine members serving nine-year terms, with three members each appointed by the president, the Senate, and the Chamber of Deputies

**Political parties and leaders:** Conservative Party or PC [Daniela POPA] (formerly Humanist Party or PUR); Democratic Liberal Party or PDL [Emil BOC]; Democratic Union of Hungarians in Romania or UDMR [Bela MARKO]; National Liberal Party or PNL [Calin Popescu-TARICEANU]; Social Democratic Party or PSD [Mircea Dan GEOANA] (formerly Party of Social Democracy in Romania or PDSR)

**Political pressure groups and leaders:**
other: various human rights and professional associations

**International organization participation:** Australia Group, BIS, BSEC, CE, CEI, EAPC, EBRD, EIB, ESA (cooperating state), EU, FAO, G-9, IAEA, IBRD, ICAO, ICC, ICCt, ICRM, IDA, IFAD, IFC, IFRCS, IHO, ILO, IMF, IMO, IMSO, Interpol, IOC, IOM, IPU, ISO, ITSO, ITU, ITUC, LAIA (observer), MIGA, MONUC, NAM (guest), NATO, NSG, OAS (observer), OIF, OPCW, OSCE, PCA, SECI, UN, UNCTAD, UNESCO, UNHCR, UNIDO, Union Latina, UNMIL, UNMIS, UNOCI, UNOMIG, UNWTO, UPU, WCL, WCO, WEU (associate partner), WFTU, WHO, WIPO, WMO, WTO, ZC

**Diplomatic representation in the US:**
chief of mission: Ambassador Adrian Cosmin VIERITA
chancery: 1607 23rd Street NW, Washington, DC 20008
telephone: [1] (202) 332-4846, 4848, 4851, 4852
FAX: [1] (202) 232-4748
consulate(s) general: Chicago, Los Angeles, New York

**Diplomatic representation from the US:**
chief of mission: Ambassador (vacant); Charge D'Affaires Jeri GUTHRIE-CORN
embassy: Strada Tudor Arghezi 7-9, Bucharest
mailing address: pouch: American Embassy Bucharest, US Department of State, 5260 Bucharest Place, Washington, DC 20521-5260 (pouch)
telephone: [40] (21) 200-3300
FAX: [40] (21) 200-3442

**Flag description:** three equal vertical bands of blue (hoist side), yellow, and red; the national coat of arms that used to be centered in the yellow band has been removed; now similar to the flag of Chad, also resembles the flags of Andorra and Moldova

## Economy

**Economy - overview:** Romania, which joined the European Union on 1 January 2007, began the transition from Communism in 1989 with a largely obsolete industrial base and a pattern of output unsuited to the country's needs. The country emerged in 2000 from a punishing three-year recession thanks to strong demand in EU export markets. Domestic consumption and investment have fueled strong GDP growth in recent years, but have led to large current account imbalances. Romania's macroeconomic gains have only recently started to spur creation of a middle class and address Romania's widespread poverty. Corruption and red tape continue to handicap its business environment. Inflation rose in 2007-08, driven in part by strong consumer demand and high wage growth, rising energy costs, a nation-wide drought affecting food prices, and a relaxation of fiscal discipline. Romania's strong GDP growth moderated markedly in the last quarter of 2008 as the country began to feel the effects of a global downturn in financial markets and trade, and growth is expected to be much weaker in 2009. Romania hopes to adopt the euro by 2014.

**GDP (purchasing power parity):**
$271.2 billion (2008 est.)
$252.1 billion (2007)
$237.8 billion (2006)
note: data are in 2008 US dollars

**GDP (official exchange rate):** $213.9 billion (2008 est.)

**GDP - real growth rate:**
7.6% (2008 est.)
6% (2007 est.)
7.9% (2006 est.)

**GDP - per capita (PPP):**
$12,200 (2008 est.)
$11,300 (2007 est.)
$10,700 (2006 est.)
note: data are in 2008 US dollars

**GDP - composition by sector:**
agriculture: 8.1%
industry: 36%
services: 55.9% (2008 est.)

**Labor force:** 9.32 million (2008 est.)

**Labor force - by occupation:**
agriculture: 29.7%
industry: 23.2%
services: 47.1% (2006)

**Unemployment rate:**
3.6% (2008 est.)
4.1% (2007 est.)

**Population below poverty line:** 25% (2005 est.)

**Household income or consumption by percentage share:**
lowest 10%: 1.2%
highest 10%: 20.8% (2006)

**Distribution of family income - Gini index:** 32 (2008)

**Investment (gross fixed):** 31.5% of GDP (2008 est.)

**Budget:**
revenues: $64.44 billion
expenditures: $71.16 billion (2008 est.)

**Public debt:** 14.1% of GDP (2008 est.)

**Inflation rate (consumer prices):**
7.8% (2008 est.)
4.8% (2007 est.)

**Central bank discount rate:** NA

**Commercial bank prime lending rate:** 13.35% (31 December 2007)

**Stock of money:** $25.17 billion (31 December 2007)

**Stock of quasi money:** $34.96 billion (31 December 2007)

**Stock of domestic credit:** $58.76 billion (31 December 2007)

**Market value of publicly traded shares:** $44.93 billion (31 December 2007)

**Agriculture - products:** wheat, corn, barley, sugar beets, sunflower seed, potatoes, grapes; eggs, sheep

**Industries:** electric machinery and equipment, textiles and footwear, light machinery and auto assembly, mining, timber, construction materials, metallurgy, chemicals, food processing, petroleum refining

**Industrial production growth rate:** 8% (2008 est.)

**Electricity - production:** 58.25 billion kWh (2007 est.)

**Electricity - consumption:** 48.43 billion kWh (2006 est.)

**Electricity - exports:** 3.362 billion kWh (2007 est.)

**Electricity - imports:** 1.277 billion kWh (2007 est.)

**Oil - production:** 112,400 bbl/day (2007 est.)

**Oil - consumption:** 238,200 bbl/day (2006 est.)

**Oil - exports:** 125,200 bbl/day (2005)

**Oil - imports:** 219,000 bbl/day (2005)

**Oil - proved reserves:** 600 million bbl (1 January 2008 est.)

**Natural gas - production:** 12.5 billion cu m (2006 est.)

**Natural gas - consumption:** 17.09 billion cu m (2007)

**Natural gas - exports:** 0 cu m (2007 est.)

**Natural gas - imports:** 4.8 billion cu m (2007 est.)

**Natural gas - proved reserves:** 63 billion cu m (1 January 2008 est.)

**Current account balance:** -$28.03 billion (2008 est.)

**Exports:** $59.75 billion f.o.b. (2008 est.)

**Exports - commodities:** machinery and equipment, textiles and footwear, metals and metal products, machinery and equipment, minerals and fuels, chemicals, agricultural products

**Exports - partners:** Italy 17.2%, Germany 16.9%, France 7.7%, Turkey 7%, Hungary 5.6%, UK 4.1% (2007)

**Imports:** $92.09 billion f.o.b. (2008 est.)

**Imports - commodities:** machinery and equipment, fuels and minerals, chemicals, textile and products, metals, agricultural products

**Imports - partners:** Germany 17.2%, Italy 12.8%, Hungary 6.9%, Russia 6.3%, France 6.2%, Turkey 5.4%, Austria 4.8% (2007)
**Reserves of foreign exchange and gold:** $44.47 billion (31 December 2008 est.)
**Debt - external:** $92.76 billion (31 December 2008 est.)
**Stock of direct foreign investment - at home:** $72.82 billion (2008 est.)
**Stock of direct foreign investment - abroad:** $1.015 billion (2008 est.)
**Exchange rates:** lei (RON) per US dollar - 2.5 (2008 est.), 2.43 (2007), 2.809 (2006), 3 (2005), 3 (2004)

## Communications

**Telephones - main lines in use:** 4.3 million (2007)
**Telephones - mobile cellular:** 22.875 million (2007)
**Telephone system:**
*general assessment:* the telecommunications sector is being expanded and modernized; domestic and international service improving rapidly, especially in wireless telephony
*domestic:* more than 90 percent of telephone network is automatic; fixed-line teledensity is roughly 20 telephones per 100 persons; mobile-cellular teledensity, expanding rapidly, now slightly exceeds 100 telephones per 100 persons
*international:* country code - 40; the Black Sea Fiber Optic System provides connectivity to Bulgaria and Turkey; satellite earth stations - 10; digital, international, direct-dial exchanges operate in Bucharest (2007)
**Radio broadcast stations:** 698 (station frequency type NA) (2006)
**Television broadcast stations:** 623 (plus 200 repeaters) (2006)
**Internet country code:** .ro
**Internet hosts:** 2.195 million (2008)
**Internet users:** 12 million (2007)

## Transportation

**Airports:** 53 (2008)
**Airports - with paved runways:**
*total:* 25
*over 3,047 m:* 4
*2,438 to 3,047 m:* 10
*1,524 to 2,437 m:* 11 (2008)
**Airports - with unpaved runways:**
*total:* 28
*914 to 1,523 m:* 7
*under 914 m:* 21 (2008)
**Heliports:** 2 (2007)
**Pipelines:** gas 3,588 km; oil 2,424 km (2008)
**Railways:**
*total:* 10,789 km
*broad gauge:* 57 km 1.524-m gauge
*standard gauge:* 10,731 km 1.435-m gauge (3,965 km electrified)
*narrow gauge:* 1 km 0.760-m gauge (2007)

**Roadw: ays:**
*total:* 198,817 km
*paved:* 60,043 km (includes 228 km of expressways)
*unpaved:* 138,774 km (2004)
**Waterways:** 1,731 km
*note:* includes 1,075 km on Danube River, 524 km on secondary branches, and 132 km on canals (2006)
**Merchant marine:**
*total:* 17
*by type:* cargo 11, passenger 1, passenger/cargo 2, petroleum tanker 2, roll on/roll off 1
*registered in other countries:* 49 (Cambodia 1, Georgia 16, North Korea 4, Liberia 2, Malta 8, Marshall Islands 1, Moldova 3, Panama 7, Saint Kitts and Nevis 1, Saint Vincent and the Grenadines 1, Sierra Leone 3, Syria 2) (2008)
**Ports and terminals:** Braila, Constanta, Galati, Tulcea

## Military

**Military branches:** Land Forces, Naval Forces, Romanian Air Force (Fortele Aeriene Romane, FAR), Special Operations (2009)
**Military service age and obligation:** 18-35 years of age for male and female voluntary military service; conscription officially ended October 2006; all military inductees (including women) contract for an initial 5-year term of service, with subsequent successive contracts for 3-year terms until age 36 (2009)
**Manpower available for military service:**
*males age 16-49:* 5,682,299
*females age 16-49:* 5,557,098 (2008 est.)
**Manpower fit for military service:**
*males age 16-49:* 4,542,720
*females age 16-49:* 4,604,484 (2009 est.)
**Manpower reaching militarily significant age annually:**
*male:* 124,356
*female:* 118,430 (2009 est.)
**Military expenditures:** 1.9% of GDP (2007 est.)

## Transnational Issues

**Disputes - international:** the ICJ gave Ukraine until December 2006 to reply, and Romania until June 2007 to issue a rejoinder, in their dispute submitted in 2004 over Ukrainian-administered Zmiyinyy/Serpilor (Snake) Island and Black Sea maritime boundary delimitation; Romania also opposes Ukraine's reopening of a navigation canal from the Danube border through Ukraine to the Black Sea
**Illicit drugs:** major transshipment point for Southwest Asian heroin transiting the Balkan route and small amounts of Latin American cocaine bound for Western Europe; although not a significant financial center, role as a narcotics conduit leaves it vulnerable to laundering, which occurs via the banking system, currency exchange houses, and casinos

# Russia

## Introduction

**Background:** Founded in the 12th century, the Principality of Muscovy, was able to emerge from over 200 years of Mongol domination (13th-15th centuries) and to gradually conquer and absorb surrounding principalities. In the early 17th century, a new Romanov Dynasty continued this policy of expansion across Siberia to the Pacific. Under PETER I (ruled 1682-1725), hegemony was extended to the Baltic Sea and the country was renamed the Russian Empire. During the 19th century, more territorial acquisitions were made in Europe and Asia. Defeat in the Russo-Japanese War of 1904-05 contributed to the Revolution of 1905, which resulted in the formation of a parliament and other reforms. Repeated devastating defeats of the Russian army in World War I led to widespread rioting in the major cities of the Russian Empire and to the overthrow in 1917 of the imperial household. The Communists under Vladimir LENIN seized power soon after and formed the USSR. The brutal rule of Iosif STALIN (1928-53) strengthened Communist rule and Russian dominance of the Soviet Union at a cost of tens of millions of lives. The Soviet economy and society stagnated in the following decades until General Secretary Mikhail GORBACHEV (1985-91) introduced glasnost (openness) and perestroika (restructuring) in an attempt to modernize Communism, but his initiatives inadvertently released forces that by December 1991 splintered the USSR into Russia and 14 other independent republics. Since then, Russia has shifted its post-Soviet democratic ambitions in favor of a centralized semi-authoritarian state whose legitimacy is buttressed, in part, by carefully managed national elections, former President PUTIN's genuine popularity, and the prudent management of Russia's windfall energy wealth. Russia has severely disabled a Chechen rebel movement, although violence still occurs throughout the North Caucasus.

## Geography

**Location:** Northern Asia (the area west of the Urals is considered part of Europe), bordering the Arctic Ocean, between Europe and the North Pacific Ocean

**Geographic coordinates:** 60 00 N, 100 00 E

**Map references:** Asia

**Area:**

*total:* 17,075,200 sq km

*land:* 16,995,800 sq km

*water:* 79,400 sq km

**Area - comparative:** approximately 1.8 times the size of the US

**Land boundaries:**

*total:* 20,241.5 km

*border countries:* Azerbaijan 284 km, Belarus 959 km, China (southeast) 3,605 km, China (south) 40 km, Estonia 290 km, Finland 1,313 km, Georgia 723 km, Kazakhstan 6,846 km, North Korea 17.5 km, Latvia 292 km, Lithuania (Kaliningrad Oblast) 227 km, Mongolia 3,441 km, Norway 196 km, Poland (Kaliningrad Oblast) 432 km, Ukraine 1,576 km

**Coastline:** 37,653 km

**Maritime claims:**

*territorial sea:* 12 nm

*contiguous zone:* 24 nm

*exclusive economic zone:* 200 nm

*continental shelf:* 200 m depth or to the depth of exploitation

**Climate:** ranges from steppes in the south through humid continental in much of European Russia; subarctic in Siberia to tundra climate in the polar north; winters vary from cool along Black Sea coast to frigid in Siberia; summers vary from warm in the steppes to cool along Arctic coast

**Terrain:** broad plain with low hills west of Urals; vast coniferous forest and tundra in Siberia; uplands and mountains along southern border regions

**Elevation extremes:**

*lowest point:* Caspian Sea -28 m

*highest point:* Gora El'brus 5,633 m

**Natural resources:** wide natural resource base including major deposits of oil, natural gas, coal, and many strategic minerals, timber

*note:* formidable obstacles of climate, terrain, and distance hinder exploitation of natural resources

**Land use:**

*arable land:* 7.17%

*permanent crops:* 0.11%

*other:* 92.72% (2005)

**Irrigated land:** 46,000 sq km (2003)

**Total renewable water resources:** 4,498 cu km (1997)

**Freshwater withdrawal (domestic/industrial/agricultural):**

*total:* 76.68 cu km/yr (19%/63%/18%)

*per capita:* 535 cu m/yr (2000)

**Natural hazards:** permafrost over much of Siberia is a major impediment to development; volcanic activity in the Kuril Islands; volcanoes and earthquakes on the Kamchatka Peninsula; spring floods and summer/autumn forest fires throughout Siberia and parts of European Russia

**Environment - current issues:** air pollution from heavy industry, emissions of coal-fired electric plants, and transportation in major cities; industrial, municipal, and agricultural pollution of inland waterways and seacoasts; deforestation; soil erosion; soil contamination from improper application of agricultural chemicals; scattered areas of sometimes intense radioactive contamination; groundwater contamination from toxic waste; urban solid waste management; abandoned stocks of obsolete pesticides

**Environment - international agreements:**

*party to:* Air Pollution, Air Pollution-Nitrogen Oxides, Air Pollution-Sulfur 85, Antarctic-Environmental Protocol, Antarctic-Marine Living Resources, Antarctic Seals, Antarctic Treaty, Biodiversity, Climate Change, Climate Change-Kyoto Protocol, Desertification, Endangered Species, Environmental Modification, Hazardous Wastes, Law of the Sea, Marine Dumping, Ozone Layer Protection, Ship Pollution, Tropical Timber 83, Wetlands, Whaling

*signed, but not ratified:* Air Pollution-Sulfur 94

**Geography - note:** largest country in the world in terms of area but unfavorably located in relation to major sea lanes of the world; despite its size, much of the country lacks proper soils and climates (either too cold or too dry) for agriculture; Mount El'brus is Europe's tallest peak

## People

**Population:** 140,041,247 (July 2009 est.)

**Age structure:**

*0-14 years:* 14.8% (male 10,644,833/female 10,095,011)

*15-64 years:* 71.5% (male 48,004,040/female 52,142,313)

*65 years and over:* 13.7% (male 5,880,877/female 13,274,173) (2009 est.)

# Russia (continued)

**Median age:**

*total:* 38.4 years

*male:* 35.2 years

*female:* 41.6 years (2009 est.)

**Population growth rate:** -0.467% (2009 est.)

**Birth rate:** 11.1 births/1,000 population (2009 est.)

**Death rate:** 16.06 deaths/1,000 population (2008 est.)

**Net migration rate:** 0.28 migrant(s)/1,000 population (2009 est.)

**Urbanization:**

*urban population:* 73% of total population (2008)

*rate of urbanization:* -0.5% annual rate of change (2005-10 est.)

**Sex ratio:**

*at birth:* 1.06 male(s)/female

*under 15 years:* 1.05 male(s)/female

*15-64 years:* 0.92 male(s)/female

*65 years and over:* 0.44 male(s)/female

*total population:* 0.86 male(s)/female (2009 est.)

**Infant mortality rate:**

*total:* 10.56 deaths/1,000 live births

*male:* 12.08 deaths/1,000 live births

*female:* 8.94 deaths/1,000 live births (2009 est.)

**Life expectancy at birth:**

*total population:* 66.03 years

*male:* 59.33 years

*female:* 73.14 years (2009 est.)

**Total fertility rate:** 1.41 children born/woman (2009 est.)

**HIV/AIDS - adult prevalence rate:** 1.1% (2007 est.)

**HIV/AIDS - people living with HIV/AIDS:** 940,000 (2007 est.)

**HIV/AIDS - deaths:** 40,000 (2007 est.)

**Major infectious diseases:**

*degree of risk:* intermediate

*food or waterborne diseases:* bacterial diarrhea

*vectorborne disease:* tickborne encephalitis

*note:* highly pathogenic H5N1 avian influenza has been identified in this country; it poses a negligible risk with extremely rare cases possible among US citizens who have close contact with birds (2009)

**Nationality:**

*noun:* Russian(s)

*adjective:* Russian

**Ethnic groups:** Russian 79.8%, Tatar 3.8%, Ukrainian 2%, Bashkir 1.2%, Chuvash 1.1%, other or unspecified 12.1% (2002 census)

**Religions:** Russian Orthodox 15-20%, Muslim 10-15%, other Christian 2% (2006 est.)

*note:* estimates are of practicing worshipers; Russia has large populations of non-practicing believers and non-believers, a legacy of over seven decades of Soviet rule

**Languages:** Russian, many minority languages

**Literacy:**

*definition:* age 15 and over can read and write

*total population:* 99.4%

*male:* 99.7%

*female:* 99.2% (2002 census)

**School life expectancy (primary to tertiary education):**

*total:* 14 years

*male:* 13 years

*female:* 14 years (2006)

**Education expenditures:** 3.8% of GDP (2005)

## Government

**Country name:**

*conventional long form:* Russian Federation

*conventional short form:* Russia

*local long form:* Rossiyskaya Federatsiya

*local short form:* Rossiya

*former:* Russian Empire, Russian Soviet Federative Socialist Republic

**Government type:** federation

**Capital:**

*name:* Moscow

*geographic coordinates:* 55 45 N, 37 35 E

*time difference:* UTC+3 (8 hours ahead of Washington, DC during Standard Time)

*daylight saving time:* +1hr, begins last Sunday in March; ends last Sunday in October

*note:* Russia is divided into 11 time zones

**Administrative divisions:** 46 oblasts (oblastey, singular - oblast), 21 republics (respublik, singular - respublika), 4 autonomous okrugs (avtonomnykh okrugov, singular - avtonomnyy okrug), 9 krays (krayev, singular - kray), 2 federal cities (goroda, singular - gorod), and 1 autonomous oblast (avtonomnaya oblast')

*oblasts:* Amur (Blagoveshchensk), Arkhangel'sk, Astrakhan', Belgorod, Bryansk, Chelyabinsk, Irkutsk, Ivanovo, Kaliningrad, Kaluga, Kemerovo, Kirov, Kostroma, Kurgan, Kursk, Leningrad, Lipetsk, Magadan, Moscow, Murmansk, Nizhniy Novgorod, Novgorod, Novosibirsk, Omsk, Orenburg, Orel, Penza, Pskov, Rostov, Ryazan', Sakhalin (Yuzhno-Sakhalinsk), Samara, Saratov, Smolensk, Sverdlovsk (Yekaterinburg), Tambov, Tomsk, Tula, Tver', Tyumen', Ul'yanovsk, Vladimir, Volgograd, Vologda, Voronezh, Yaroslavl'

*republics:* Adygeya (Maykop), Altay (Gorno-Altaysk), Bashkortostan (Ufa), Buryatiya (Ulan-Ude), Chechnya (Groznyy), Chuvashiya (Cheboksary), Dagestan (Makhachkala), Ingushetiya (Magas), Kabardino-Balkariya (Nal'chik), Kalmykiya (Elista), Karachayevo-Cherkesiya (Cherkessk), Kareliya (Petrozavodsk), Khakasiya (Abakan), Komi (Syktyvkar), Mariy-El (Yoshkar-Ola), Mordoviya (Saransk), North Ossetia (Vladikavkaz), Sakha [Yakutiya] (Yakutsk), Tatarstan (Kazan'), Tyva (Kyzyl), Udmurtiya (Izhevsk)

*autonomous okrugs:* Chukotka (Anadyr'), Khanty-Mansi (Khanty-Mansiysk), Nenets (Nar'yan-Mar), Yamalo-Nenets (Salekhard)

*krays:* Altay (Barnaul), Kamchatka (Petropavlovsk-Kamchatskiy), Khabarovsk, Krasnodar, Krasnoyarsk, Perm', Primorskiy [Maritime] (Vladivostok), Stavropol', Zabaykal'sk (Chita)

*federal cities:* Moscow (Moskva), Saint Petersburg (Sankt-Peterburg)

*autonomous oblast:* Yevrey [Jewish] (Birobidzhan)

*note:* administrative divisions have the same names as their administrative centers (exceptions have the administrative center name following in parentheses)

**Independence:** 24 August 1991 (from the Soviet Union)

**National holiday:** Russia Day, 12 June (1990)

**Constitution:** adopted 12 December 1993

**Legal system:** based on civil law system; judicial review of legislative acts; has not accepted compulsory ICJ jurisdiction

**Suffrage:** 18 years of age; universal

**Executive branch:**

*chief of state:* President Dmitriy Anatolyevich MEDVEDEV (since 7 May 2008)

*head of government:* Premier Vladimir Vladimirovich PUTIN (since 8 May 2008); First Deputy Premiers Igor Ivanovich SHUVALOV and Viktor Alekseyevich ZUBKOV (since 12 May 2008); Deputy Premiers Sergey Borisovich IVANOV (since 12 May 2008), Dmitriy Nikolayevich KOZAK (since 14 October 2008), Aleksey Leonidovich KUDRIN (since 24 September 2007), Igor Ivanovich SECHIN (since 12 May 2008), Sergey Semenovich SOBYANIN (since 12 May 2008), Aleksandr Dmitriyevich ZHUKOV (since 9 March 2004), and Dmitry Nikolayevich KOZAK (since 14 October 2008)

*cabinet:* Ministries of the Government or "Government" composed of the premier and his deputies, ministers, and selected other individuals; all are appointed by the president

*note:* there is also a Presidential Administration (PA) that provides staff and policy support to the president, drafts presidential decrees, and coordinates policy among government agencies; a Security Council also reports directly to the president

*elections:* president elected by popular vote for a four-year term (eligible for a second term); election last held 2 March 2008 (next to be held in March 2012); note - no vice president; if the president dies in office, cannot exercise his powers because of ill health, is impeached, or resigns, the premier serves as acting president until a new presidential election is held, which must be within three months; premier appointed by the president with the approval of the Duma

*election results:* Dmitriy MEDVEDEV elected president; percent of vote - Dmitry MEDVEDEV 70.2%, Gennady ZYUGANOV 17.7%, Vladimir ZHIRINOVSKY 9.4%, Andrey BOGDANOV 1.3%

**Legislative branch:** bicameral Federal Assembly or Federalnoye Sobraniye consists of an upper house, the Federation Council or Sovet Federatsii (168 seats; as of July 2000, members appointed by the top executive and legislative officials in each of the 84 federal administrative units - oblasts, krays, republics, autonomous okrugs and oblasts, and the federal cities of Moscow and Saint Petersburg; serve four-year terms) and a lower house, the State Duma or Gosudarstvennaya Duma (450 seats; as of 2007, all members elected by proportional representation from party lists winning at least 7% of the vote; members elected by popular vote to serve four-year terms) *elections:* State Duma - last held 2 December 2007 (next to be held in December 2011)

*election results:* State Duma - United Russia 64.3%, CPRF 11.5%, LDPR 8.1%, Just Russia 7.7%, other 8.4%; total seats by party - United Russia 315, CPRF 57, LDPR 40, Just Russia 38

**Judicial branch:** Constitutional Court; Supreme Court; Supreme Arbitration Court; judges for all courts are appointed for life by the Federation Council on the recommendation of the president

**Political parties and leaders:** A Just Russia [Sergey MIRONOV]; Communist Party of the Russian Federation or CPRF [Gennadiy Andreyevich ZYUGANOV]; Liberal Democratic Party of Russia or LDPR [Vladimir Volfovich ZHIRINOVSKIY]; Patriots of Russia [Gennadiy SEMIGIN]; People's Union [Sergey BABURIN]; Right Cause [Leonid Yakovlevich GOZMAN, Boris Yuriyevich TITOV, and Georgiy Georgiyevich BOVT] (registration pending; formed from merger of Union of Right Forces, Democratic Party of Russia, and Civic Force); United Russia [Vladimir Vladimirovich PUTIN]; Yabloko Party [Sergey Sergeyevich MITROKHIN]

**Political pressure groups and leaders:** All-Russian Confederation of Labor; Baikal Environmental Wave; Federation of Independent Labor Unions of Russia; Freedom of Choice Interregional Organization of Automobilists; Glasnost Defense Foundation; Golos Association in Defense of Voters' Rights; Greenpeace Russia; Human Rights Watch (Russian chapter); Institute for Collective Action; Memorial (human rights group); Movement Against Illegal Migration; Pamjat (preservation of historical monuments and recording of history); Russian Orthodox Church; Russian-Chechen Friendship Society; SOVA Analytical-Information Center; Union of the Committees of Soldiers' Mothers; World Wildlife Fund (Russian chapter)

**International organization participation:** APEC, Arctic Council, ARF, ASEAN (dialogue partner), BIS, BSEC, CBSS, CE, CERN (observer), CIS, CSTO, EAEC, EAPC, EBRD, G-20, G-8, GCTU, IAEA, IBRD, ICAO, ICC, ICCt (signatory), ICRM, IDA, IFC, IFRCS, IHO, ILO, IMF, IMO, IMSO, Interpol, IOC, IOM (observer), IPU, ISO, ITSO, ITU, ITUC, LAIA (observer), MIGA, MINURSO, MONUC, NAM (guest), NSG, OAS (observer), OECD (accession state), OIC (observer), OPCW, OSCE, Paris Club, PCA, PFP, SCO, UN, UN Security Council, UNCTAD, UNESCO, UNHCR, UNIDO, UNITAR, UNMIL, UNMIS, UNOCI, UNOMIG, UNTSO, UNWTO, UPU, WCO, WFTU, WHO, WIPO, WMO, WTO (observer), ZC

**Diplomatic representation in the US:**
*chief of mission:* Ambassador Sergey Ivanovich KISLYAK
*chancery:* 2650 Wisconsin Avenue NW, Washington, DC 20007
*telephone:* [1] (202) 298-5700, 5701, 5704, 5708
*FAX:* [1] (202) 298-5735
*consulate(s) general:* Houston, New York, San Francisco, Seattle

**Diplomatic representation from the US:**
*chief of mission:* Ambassador John R. BEYRLE
*embassy:* Bolshoy Deviatinskiy Pereulok No. 8, 121099 Moscow
*mailing address:* PSC-77, APO AE 09721
*telephone:* [7] (495) 728-5000
*FAX:* [7] (495) 728-5090
*consulate(s) general:* Saint Petersburg, Vladivostok, Yekaterinburg

**Flag description:** three equal horizontal bands of white (top), blue, and red

## Economy

**Economy - overview:** Russia ended 2008 with GDP growth of 6.0%, following 10 straight years of growth averaging 7% annually since the financial crisis of 1998. Over the last six years, fixed capital investment growth and personal income growth have averaged above 10%, but both grew at slower rates in 2008. Growth in 2008 was driven largely by non-tradable services and domestic manufacturing, rather than exports. During the past decade, poverty and unemployment declined steadily and the middle class continued to expand. Russia also improved its international financial position, running balance of payments surpluses since 2000. Foreign exchange reserves grew from $12 billion in 1999 to almost $600 billion by end July 2008, which include $200 billion in two sovereign wealth funds: a reserve fund to support budgetary expenditures in case of a fall in the price of oil and a national welfare fund to help fund pensions and infrastructure development. Total foreign debt is almost one-third of GDP. The state component of foreign debt has declined, but commercial short-term debt to foreigners has risen strongly. These positive trends began to reverse in the second half of 2008. Investor concerns over the Russia-Georgia conflict, corporate governance issues, and the global credit crunch in September caused the Russian stock market to fall by roughly 70%, primarily due to margin calls that were difficult for many Russian companies to meet. The global crisis also affected Russia's banking system, which faced liquidity problems. Moscow responded quickly in early October 2008, initiating a rescue plan of over $200 billion that was designed to increase liquidity in the financial sector, to help firms refinance foreign debt, and to support the stock market. The government also unveiled a $20 billion tax cut plan and other safety nets for society and industry. Meanwhile, a 70% drop in the price of oil since mid-July further exacerbated imbalances in external accounts and the federal budget. In mid-November, mini-devaluations of the currency by the Central Bank caused increased capital flight and froze domestic credit markets, resulting in growing unemployment, wage arrears, and a severe drop in production. Foreign exchange reserves dropped to around $435 billion by end 2008, as the Central Bank defended an overvalued ruble. In the first year of his term, President MEDVEDEV outlined a number of economic priorities for Russia including improving infrastructure, innovation, investment, and institutions; reducing the

state's role in the economy; reforming the tax system and banking sector; developing one of the biggest financial centers in the world, combating corruption, and improving the judiciary. The Russian government needs to diversify the economy further, as energy and other raw materials still dominate Russian export earnings and federal budget receipts. Russia's infrastructure requires large investments and must be replaced or modernized if the country is to achieve broad-based economic growth. Corruption, lack of trust in institutions, and more recently, exchange rate uncertainty and the global economic crisis continue to dampen domestic and foreign investor sentiment. Russia has made some progress in building the rule of law, the bedrock of a modern market economy, but much work remains on judicial reform. Moscow continues to seek accession to the WTO and has made some progress, but its timeline for entry into the organization continues to slip, and the negotiating atmosphere has soured in the wake of the Georgia and global economic crises.

**GDP (purchasing power parity):**
$2.225 trillion (2008 est.)
$2.146 trillion (2007)
$1.985 trillion (2006)
*note:* data are in 2008 US dollars

**GDP (official exchange rate):** $1.757 trillion (2008 est.)

**GDP - real growth rate:**
6% (2008 est.)
8.1% (2007 est.)
7.7% (2006 est.)

**GDP - per capita (PPP):**
$15,800 (2008 est.)
$15,200 (2007 est.)
$14,000 (2006 est.)
*note:* data are in 2008 US dollars

**GDP - composition by sector:**
*agriculture:* 4.1%
*industry:* 41.1%
*services:* 54.8% (2007 est.)

**Labor force:** 75.7 million (2008 est.)

**Labor force - by occupation:**
*agriculture:* 10.2%
*industry:* 27.4%
*services:* 62.4% (2007 est.)

**Unemployment rate:**
6.2% (2008 est.)
6.2% (2007 est.)

**Population below poverty line:** 15.8% (November 2007)

**Household income or consumption by percentage share:**
*lowest 10%:* 1.9%
*highest 10%:* 30.4% (September 2007)

**Distribution of family income - Gini index:** 41.5 (September 2008)

**Investment (gross fixed):** 24.7% of GDP (2007 est.)

**Budget:**
*revenues:* $383.5 billion
*expenditures:* $273.5 billion (2008 est.)

# Russia (continued)

**Public debt:** 6.8% of GDP (2008 est.)

**Inflation rate (consumer prices):**
13.9% (2008 est.)
9% (2007 est.)

**Central bank discount rate:** 13% (31 December 2008)

**Commercial bank prime lending rate:** 13% (31 December 2008)

**Stock of money:** $166.4 billion (October 2008)

**Stock of quasi money:** $343 billion (October 2008)

**Stock of domestic credit:** $503.7 billion (1 October 2008)

**Market value of publicly traded shares:** $450 billion (15 December 2008 est.)

**Agriculture - products:** grain, sugar beets, sunflower seed, vegetables, fruits; beef, milk

**Industries:** complete range of mining and extractive industries producing coal, oil, gas, chemicals, and metals; all forms of machine building from rolling mills to high-performance aircraft and space vehicles; defense industries including radar, missile production, and advanced electronic components, shipbuilding; road and rail transportation equipment; communications equipment; agricultural machinery, tractors, and construction equipment; electric power generating and transmitting equipment; medical and scientific instruments; consumer durables, textiles, foodstuffs, handicrafts

**Industrial production growth rate:** 1.9% (2008 est.)

**Electricity - production:** 1.016 trillion kWh (2007 est.)

**Electricity - consumption:** 1.003 trillion kWh (2006 est.)

**Electricity - exports:** 18.6 billion kWh (2007 est.)

**Electricity - imports:** 6 billion kWh (2007 est.)

**Oil - production:** 9.98 million bbl/day (2007 est.)

**Oil - consumption:** 2.699 million bbl/day (2007 est.)

**Oil - exports:** 5.17 million bbl/day (2007)

**Oil - imports:** 54,000 bbl/day (2005)

**Oil - proved reserves:** 79 billion bbl (1 January 2008 est.)

**Natural gas - production:** 654 billion cu m (2007 est.)

**Natural gas - consumption:** 481 billion cu m (2007 est.)

**Natural gas - exports:** 173 billion cu m (2007 est.)

**Natural gas - imports:** 68.2 billion cu m (2007 est.)

**Natural gas - proved reserves:** 44.65 trillion cu m (1 January 2008 est.)

**Current account balance:** $97.6 billion (2008 est.)

**Exports:** $476 billion (2008 est.)

**Exports - commodities:** petroleum and petroleum products, natural gas, wood and wood products, metals, chemicals, and a wide variety of civilian and military manufactures

**Exports - partners:** Netherlands 12.2%, Italy 7.8%, Germany 7.5%, Turkey 5.2%, Belarus 5%, Ukraine 4.7%, China 4.5% (2007)

**Imports:** $302 billion f.o.b. (2008 est.)

**Imports - commodities:** vehicles, machinery and equipment, plastics, medicines, iron and steel, consumer goods, meat, fruits and nuts, semifinished metal products

**Imports - partners:** Germany 13.3%, China 12.2%, Ukraine 6.7%, Japan 6.4%, US 4.8%, Belarus 4.4%, South Korea 4.4%, Italy 4.3% (2007)

**Reserves of foreign exchange and gold:** $435.4 billion (12 December 2008)

**Debt - external:** $527.1 billion (June 2008 est.)

**Stock of direct foreign investment - at home:** $491.2 billion (2007)

**Stock of direct foreign investment - abroad:** $370.2 billion (2007)

**Exchange rates:** Russian rubles (RUB) per US dollar - 24.3 (2008 est.), 25.659 (2007), 27.19 (2006), 28.284 (2005), 28.814 (2004)

## Communications

**Telephones - main lines in use:** 43.9 million (2006)

**Telephones - mobile cellular:** 170 million (2007)

**Telephone system:**

*general assessment:* the telephone system is experiencing significant changes; there are more than 1,000 companies licensed to offer communication services; access to digital lines has improved, particularly in urban centers; Internet and e-mail services are improving; Russia has made progress toward building the telecommunications infrastructure necessary for a market economy; the estimated number of mobile subscribers jumped from fewer than 1 million in 1998 to 170 million in 2007; a large demand for main line service remains unsatisfied, but fixed-line operators continue to grow their services

*domestic:* cross-country digital trunk lines run from Saint Petersburg to Khabarovsk, and from Moscow to Novorossiysk; the telephone systems in 60 regional capitals have modern digital infrastructures; cellular services, both analog and digital, are available in many areas; in rural areas, the telephone services are still outdated, inadequate, and low density

*international:* country code - 7; Russia is connected internationally by undersea fiber optic cables; digital switches in several cities provide more than 50,000 lines for international calls; satellite earth stations provide access to Intelsat, Intersputnik, Eutelsat, Inmarsat, and Orbita systems

**Radio broadcast stations:** AM 323, FM 1,500 est., shortwave 62 (2004)

**Television broadcast stations:** 7,306 (1998)

**Internet country code:** .ru; note - Russia also has responsibility for a legacy domain ".su" that was allocated to the Soviet Union and is being phased out

**Internet hosts:** 4.822 million (2008)

**Internet users:** 30 million (2007)

## Transportation

**Airports:** 1,232 (2008)

**Airports - with paved runways:**
*total:* 596
*over 3,047 m:* 52
*2,438 to 3,047 m:* 197
*1,524 to 2,437 m:* 129
*914 to 1,523 m:* 100
*under 914 m:* 118 (2008)

**Airports - with unpaved runways:**
*total:* 636
*over 3,047 m:* 3
*2,438 to 3,047 m:* 12
*1,524 to 2,437 m:* 68
*914 to 1,523 m:* 87
*under 914 m:* 466 (2008)

**Heliports:** 47 (2007)

**Pipelines:** condensate 122 km; gas 158,767 km; liquid petroleum gas 127 km; oil 74,285 km; refined products 13,658 km; water 23 km (2008)

**Railways:**
*total:* 87,157 km
*broad gauge:* 86,200 km 1.520-m gauge (40,300 km electrified)
*narrow gauge:* 957 km 1.067-m gauge (on Sakhalin Island)
*note:* an additional 30,000 km of non-common carrier lines serve industries (2006)

**Roadways:**
*total:* 933,000 km
*paved:* 754,984 km (includes 30,000 km of expressways)
*unpaved:* 178,016 km
*note:* includes public, local, and departmental roads (2006)

**Waterways:** 102,000 km (including 33,000 km with guaranteed depth)
*note:* 72,000 km system in European Russia links Baltic Sea, White Sea, Caspian Sea, Sea of Azov, and Black Sea (2007)

**Merchant marine:**
*total:* 1,074
*by type:* bulk carrier 25, cargo 663, carrier 2, chemical tanker 27, combination ore/oil 34, container 11, passenger 14, passenger/cargo 7, petroleum tanker 217, refrigerated cargo 59, roll on/roll off 10, specialized tanker 5
*foreign-owned:* 112 (Belgium 4, Cyprus 2, Germany 1, Greece 1, Italy 4, South Korea 1, Latvia 2, Norway 2, Switzerland 3, Turkey 80, Ukraine 11, US 1)
*registered in other countries:* 486 (Antigua and Barbuda 4, Bahamas 4, Belize 31, Bulgaria 1, Cambodia 83, Comoros 12, Cyprus 50, Dominica 3, Georgia 12, Hong Kong 2, Jamaica 3, Liberia 94, Malaysia 2, Malta 58, Marshall Islands 9, Moldova 3, Mongolia 9, Panama 18, Saint Kitts and Nevis 19, Saint Vincent and the Grenadines 21, Sierra Leone 11, Slovakia 1, Tuvalu 2, Ukraine 1, Vanuatu 2, unknown 31) (2008)

**Ports and terminals:** Azov, Kaliningrad, Kavkaz, Nakhodka, Novorossiysk, Primorsk, Saint Petersburg, Vostochnyy

## Russia *(continued)*

### Military

**Military branches:** Ground Forces (Sukhoputnyye Voyskia, SV), Navy (Voyenno-Morskoy Flot, VMF), Air Forces (Voyenno-Vozdushniye Sily, VVS); Airborne Troops (VDV), Strategic Rocket Forces (Raketnyye Voyska Strategicheskogo Naznacheniya, RVSN), and Space Troops (Kosmicheskiye Voyska, KV) are independent "combat arms," not subordinate to any of the three branches; Russian Ground Forces include the following combat arms: motorized-rifle troops, tank troops, missile and artillery troops, air defense of ground troops (2009)

**Military service age and obligation:** 18-27 years of age for compulsory or voluntary military service; males are registered for the draft at 17 years of age; service obligation - 1 year; reserve obligation to age 50; as of July 2008, a draft military strategy called for the draft to continue up to the year 2030 (2009)

**Manpower available for military service:**
*males age 16-49:* 36,219,908
*females age 16-49:* 37,019,853 (2008 est.)

**Manpower fit for military service:**
*males age 16-49:* 21,098,306
*females age 16-49:* 27,968,883 (2009 est.)

**Manpower reaching militarily significant age annually:**
*male:* 741,692
*female:* 706,081 (2009 est.)

**Military expenditures:** 3.9% of GDP (2005)

### Transnational Issues

**Disputes - international:** China and Russia have demarcated the once disputed islands at the Amur and Ussuri confluence and in the Argun River in accordance with the 2004 Agreement, ending their centuries-long border disputes; the sovereignty dispute over the islands of Etorofu, Kunashiri, Shikotan, and the Habomai group, known in Japan as the "Northern Territories" and in Russia as the "Southern Kurils," occupied by the Soviet Union in 1945, now administered by Russia, and claimed by Japan, remains the primary sticking point to signing a peace treaty formally ending World War II hostilities; Russia and Georgia agree on delimiting all but small, strategic segments of the land boundary and the maritime boundary; OSCE observers monitor volatile areas such as the Pankisi Gorge in the Akhmeti region and the Kodori Gorge in Abkhazia; Azerbaijan, Kazakhstan, and Russia signed equidistance boundaries in the Caspian seabed but the littoral states have no consensus on dividing the water column; Russia and Norway dispute their maritime limits in the Barents Sea and Russia's fishing rights beyond Svalbard's territorial limits within the Svalbard Treaty zone; various groups in Finland advocate restoration of Karelia (Kareliya) and other areas ceded to the Soviet Union following the Second World War but the Finnish Government asserts no territorial demands; in May 2005, Russia recalled its signatures to the 1996 border agreements with Estonia (1996) and Latvia (1997), when the two Baltic states announced issuance of unilateral declarations referencing Soviet occupation and ensuing

territorial losses; Russia demands better treatment of ethnic Russians in Estonia and Latvia; Estonian citizen groups continue to press for realignment of the boundary based on the 1920 Tartu Peace Treaty that would bring the now divided ethnic Setu people and parts of the Narva region within Estonia; Lithuania and Russia committed to demarcating their boundary in 2006 in accordance with the land and maritime treaty ratified by Russia in May 2003 and by Lithuania in 1999; Lithuania operates a simplified transit regime for Russian nationals traveling from the Kaliningrad coastal exclave into Russia, while still conforming, as an EU member state with an EU external border, where strict Schengen border rules apply; preparations for the demarcation delimitation of land boundary with Ukraine have commenced; the dispute over the boundary between Russia and Ukraine through the Kerch Strait and Sea of Azov remains unresolved despite a December 2003 framework agreement and on-going expert-level discussions; Kazakhstan and Russia boundary delimitation was ratified on November 2005 and field demarcation should commence in 2007; Russian Duma has not yet ratified 1990 Bering Sea Maritime Boundary Agreement with the US

**Refugees and internally displaced persons:**
*IDPs:* 18,000-160,000 (displacement from Chechnya and North Ossetia) (2007)

**Trafficking in persons:**
*current situation:* Russia is a source, transit, and destination country for men, women, and children trafficked for various purposes; it remains a significant source of women trafficked to over 50 countries for commercial sexual exploitation; Russia is also a transit and destination country for men and women trafficked from Central Asia, Eastern Europe, and North Korea to Central and Western Europe and the Middle East for purposes of forced labor and sexual exploitation; internal trafficking remains a problem in Russia with women trafficked from rural areas to urban centers for commercial sexual exploitation, and men trafficked internally and from Central Asia for forced labor in the construction and agricultural industries; debt bondage is common among trafficking victims, and child sex tourism remains a concern
*tier rating:* Tier 2 Watch List - Russia is on the Tier 2 Watch List for a fifth consecutive year for its failure to show evidence of increasing efforts to combat trafficking over the previous year, particularly in providing assistance to victims of trafficking; comprehensive trafficking victim assistance legislation, which would address key deficiencies, has been pending before the Duma since 2003 and was neither passed nor enacted in 2007 (2008)

**Illicit drugs:** limited cultivation of illicit cannabis and opium poppy and producer of methamphetamine, mostly for domestic consumption; government has active illicit crop eradication program; used as transshipment point for Asian opiates, cannabis, and Latin American cocaine bound for growing domestic markets, to a lesser extent Western and Central Europe, and occasionally to the US; major source of heroin precursor chemicals; corruption and organized crime are key concerns; major consumer of opiates

## Rwanda

### Introduction

**Background:** In 1959, three years before independence from Belgium, the majority ethnic group, the Hutus, overthrew the ruling Tutsi king. Over the next several years, thousands of Tutsis were killed, and some 150,000 driven into exile in neighboring countries. The children of these exiles later formed a rebel group, the Rwandan Patriotic Front (RPF), and began a civil war in 1990. The war, along with several political and economic upheavals, exacerbated ethnic tensions, culminating in April 1994 in the genocide of roughly 800,000 Tutsis and moderate Hutus. The Tutsi rebels defeated the Hutu regime and ended the killing in July 1994, but approximately 2 million Hutu refugees - many fearing Tutsi retribution - fled to neighboring Burundi, Tanzania, Uganda, and Zaire. Since then, most of the refugees have returned to Rwanda, but several thousand remained in the neighboring Democratic Republic of the Congo (DRC; the former Zaire) and formed an extremist insurgency bent on retaking Rwanda, much as the RPF tried in 1990. Despite substantial international assistance and political reforms - including Rwanda's first local elections in March 1999 and its first post-genocide presidential and legislative elections in August and September 2003 - the country continues to struggle to boost investment and agricultural output, and ethnic reconciliation is complicated by the real and perceived Tutsi political dominance. Kigali's increasing centralization and intolerance of dissent, the nagging Hutu extremist insurgency across the border, and Rwandan involvement in two wars in recent years in the neighboring DRC continue to hinder Rwanda's efforts to escape its bloody legacy.

### Geography

**Location:** Central Africa, east of Democratic Republic of the Congo
**Geographic coordinates:** 2 00 S, 30 00 E

# Rwanda (continued)

**Map references:** Africa

**Area:**

*total:* 26,338 sq km

*land:* 24,948 sq km

*water:* 1,390 sq km

**Area - comparative:** slightly smaller than Maryland

**Land boundaries:**

*total:* 893 km

*border countries:* Burundi 290 km, Democratic Republic of the Congo 217 km, Tanzania 217 km, Uganda 169 km

**Coastline:** 0 km (landlocked)

**Maritime claims:** none (landlocked)

**Climate:** temperate; two rainy seasons (February to April, November to January); mild in mountains with frost and snow possible

**Terrain:** mostly grassy uplands and hills; relief is mountainous with altitude declining from west to east

**Elevation extremes:**

*lowest point:* Rusizi River 950 m

*highest point:* Volcan Karisimbi 4,519 m

**Natural resources:** gold, cassiterite (tin ore), wolframite (tungsten ore), methane, hydropower, arable land

**Land use:**

*arable land:* 45.56%

*permanent crops:* 10.25%

*other:* 44.19% (2005)

**Irrigated land:** 90 sq km (2003)

**Total renewable water resources:** 5.2 cu km (2003)

**Freshwater withdrawal (domestic/industrial/agricultural):**

*total:* 0.15 cu km/yr (24%/8%/68%)

*per capita:* 17 cu m/yr (2000)

**Natural hazards:** periodic droughts; the volcanic Virunga mountains are in the northwest along the border with Democratic Republic of the Congo

**Environment - current issues:** deforestation results from uncontrolled cutting of trees for fuel; overgrazing; soil exhaustion; soil erosion; widespread poaching

**Environment - international agreements:**

*party to:* Biodiversity, Climate Change, Climate Change-Kyoto Protocol, Desertification, Endangered Species, Hazardous Wastes, Ozone Layer Protection, Wetlands

*signed, but not ratified:* Law of the Sea

**Geography - note:** landlocked; most of the country is savanna grassland with the population predominantly rural

## People

**Population:** 10,473,282

*note:* estimates for this country explicitly take into account the effects of excess mortality due to AIDS; this can result in lower life expectancy, higher infant mortality, higher death rates, lower population growth rates, and changes in the distribution of population by age and sex than would otherwise be expected (July 2009 est.)

**Age structure:**

*0-14 years:* 42.1% (male 2,216,352/ female 2,196,327)

*15-64 years:* 55.4% (male 2,897,003/ female 2,909,994)

*65 years and over:* 2.4% (male 100,920/ female 152,686) (2009 est.)

**Median age:**

*total:* 18.7 years

*male:* 18.5 years

*female:* 18.9 years (2009 est.)

**Population growth rate:** 2.782% (2009 est.)

**Birth rate:** 39.67 births/1,000 population (2009 est.)

**Death rate:** 14.46 deaths/1,000 population (2008 est.)

**Net migration rate:** 2.17 migrant(s)/1,000 population (2009 est.)

**Urbanization:**

*urban population:* 18% of total population (2008)

*rate of urbanization:* 4.2% annual rate of change (2005-10 est.)

**Sex ratio:**

*at birth:* 1.03 male(s)/female

*under 15 years:* 1.01 male(s)/female

*15-64 years:* 1 male(s)/female

*65 years and over:* 0.66 male(s)/female

*total population:* 0.99 male(s)/female (2009 est.)

**Infant mortality rate:**

*total:* 81.61 deaths/1,000 live births

*male:* 86.68 deaths/1,000 live births

*female:* 76.38 deaths/1,000 live births (2009 est.)

**Life expectancy at birth:**

*total population:* 50.52 years

*male:* 49.25 years

*female:* 51.83 years (2009 est.)

**Total fertility rate:** 5.25 children born/woman (2009 est.)

**HIV/AIDS - adult prevalence rate:** 2.8% (2007 est.)

**HIV/AIDS - people living with HIV/AIDS:** 150,000 (2007 est.)

**HIV/AIDS - deaths:** 7,800 (2007 est.)

**Major infectious diseases:**

*degree of risk:* very high

*food or waterborne diseases:* bacterial diarrhea, hepatitis A, and typhoid fever

*vectorborne disease:* malaria

*animal contact disease:* rabies (2009)

**Nationality:**

*noun:* Rwandan(s)

*adjective:* Rwandan

**Ethnic groups:** Hutu (Bantu) 84%, Tutsi (Hamitic) 15%, Twa (Pygmy) 1%

**Religions:** Roman Catholic 56.5%, Protestant 26%, Adventist 11.1%, Muslim 4.6%, indigenous beliefs 0.1%, none 1.7% (2001)

**Languages:** Kinyarwanda (official) universal Bantu vernacular, French (official), English (official), Kiswahili (Swahili) used in commercial centers

**Literacy:**

*definition:* age 15 and over can read and write

*total population:* 70.4%

*male:* 76.3%

*female:* 64.7% (2003 est.)

**School life expectancy (primary to tertiary education):**

*total:* 9 years

*male:* 8 years

*female:* 9 years (2005)

**Education expenditures:** 3.8% of GDP (2005)

**People - note:** Rwanda is the most densely populated country in Africa

## Government

**Country name:**

*conventional long form:* Republic of Rwanda

*conventional short form:* Rwanda

*local long form:* Republika y'u Rwanda

*local short form:* Rwanda

*former:* Ruanda, German East Africa

**Government type:** republic; presidential, multiparty system

**Capital:**

*name:* Kigali

*geographic coordinates:* 1 57 S, 30 04 E

*time difference:* UTC+2 (7 hours ahead of Washington, DC during Standard Time)

**Administrative divisions:** 4 provinces (in French - provinces, singular - province; in Kinyarwanda - intara for singular and plural) and 1 city* (in French - ville; in Kinyarwanda - umujyi); Est (Eastern), Kigali*, Nord (Northern), Ouest (Western), Sud (Southern)

**Independence:** 1 July 1962 (from Belgium-administered UN trusteeship)

**National holiday:** Independence Day, 1 July (1962)

**Constitution:** new constitution passed by referendum 26 May 2003

**Legal system:** based on German and Belgian civil law systems and customary law; judicial review of legislative acts in the Supreme Court; has not accepted compulsory ICJ jurisdiction

**Suffrage:** 18 years of age; universal

**Executive branch:**

*chief of state:* President Paul KAGAME (since 22 April 2000)

*head of government:* Prime Minister Bernard MAKUZA (since 8 March 2000)

*cabinet:* Council of Ministers appointed by the president

*elections:* President elected by popular vote for a seven-year term (eligible for a second term); elections last held 25 August 2003 (next to be held in 2010)

*election results:* Paul KAGAME elected president in first direct popular vote; Paul KAGAME 95.05%, Faustin TWAGIRAMUNGU 3.62%, Jean-Nepomuscene NAYINZIRA 1.33%

**Legislative branch:** bicameral Parliament consists of Senate (26 seats; 12 members elected by local councils, 8 appointed by the president, 4 by the Political Organizations Forum, 2 represent institutions of higher learning; to serve eight-year terms) and Chamber of Deputies (80 seats; 53 members elected by popular vote, 24 women elected by local bodies, 3 selected by youth and disability organizations; serve five-year terms)

# Rwanda *(continued)*

*elections:* Senate - members appointed as part of the transitional government (next to be held in 2011); Chamber of Deputies - last held 15 September 2008 (next to be held September 2013)

*election results:* percent of vote by party - RPF 78.8%, PSD 13.1%, PL 7.5%; seats by party - RPF 42, PSD 7, PL 4, additional 27 members indirectly elected

**Judicial branch:** Supreme Court; High Courts of the Republic; Provincial Courts; District Courts; mediation committees

**Political parties and leaders:** Centrist Democratic Party or PDC [Alfred MUKEZAMFURA]; Democratic Popular Union of Rwanda or UDPR [Adrien RANGIRA]; Democratic Republican Movement or MDR [Celestin KABANDA] (officially banned); Islamic Democratic Party or PDI [Andre BUMAYA]; Liberal Party or PL [Protais MITALI]; Party for Democratic Renewal (officially banned); Rwandan Patriotic Front or RPF [Paul KAGAME]; Social Democratic Party or PSD [Vincent BIRUTA]

**Political pressure groups and leaders:** IBUKA (association of genocide survivors)

**International organization participation:** ACP, AfDB, AU, CEPGL, COMESA, EAC, EADB, FAO, G-77, IBRD, ICAO, ICRM, IDA, IFAD, IFC, IFRCS, ILO, IMF, Interpol, IOC, IOM, IPU, ISO (correspondent), ITSO, ITU, ITUC, MIGA, MINURCAT, NAM, OIF, OPCW, UN, UNAMID, UNCTAD, UNESCO, UNIDO, UNMIS, UNWTO, UPU, WCL, WCO, WFTU, WHO, WIPO, WMO, WTO

**Diplomatic representation in the US:**
*chief of mission:* Ambassador James KOMONYO
*chancery:* 1714 New Hampshire Avenue NW, Washington, DC 20009
*telephone:* [1] (202) 232-2882
*FAX:* [1] (202) 232-4544

**Diplomatic representation from the US:**
*chief of mission:* Ambassador W. Stuart SYMINGTON
*embassy:* 2657 Avenue de la Gendarmerie, Kigali
*mailing address:* B. P. 28, Kigali
*telephone:* [250] 596-400
*FAX:* [250] 596-591

**Flag description:** three horizontal bands of sky blue (top, double width), yellow, and green, with a golden sun with 24 rays near the fly end of the blue band

## Economy

**Economy - overview:** Rwanda is a poor rural country with about 90% of the population engaged in (mainly subsistence) agriculture. It is the most densely populated country in Africa and is landlocked with few natural resources and minimal industry. Primary foreign exchange earners are coffee and tea. The 1994 genocide decimated Rwanda's fragile economic base, severely impoverished the population, particularly women, and eroded the country's ability to attract private and external investment. However, Rwanda has made substantial progress in stabilizing and rehabilitating its economy to pre-1994 levels, although poverty levels are higher now. GDP has rebounded and inflation has been curbed. Despite Rwanda's fertile ecosystem, food production often does not keep pace with population growth, requiring food imports. Rwanda continues to receive substantial aid money and obtained IMF-World Bank Heavily Indebted Poor Country (HIPC) initiative debt relief in 2005-06. Rwanda also received Millennium Challenge Account Threshold status in 2006. The government has embraced an expansionary fiscal policy to reduce poverty by improving education, infrastructure, and foreign and domestic investment and pursuing market-oriented reforms, although energy shortages, instability in neighboring states, and lack of adequate transportation linkages to other countries continue to handicap growth.

**GDP (purchasing power parity):**
$9.061 billion (2008 est.)
$8.429 billion (2007)
$7.952 billion (2006)
*note:* data are in 2008 US dollars

**GDP (official exchange rate):** $4.027 billion (2008 est.)

**GDP - real growth rate:**
7.5% (2008 est.)
6% (2007 est.)
5.5% (2006 est.)

**GDP - per capita (PPP):**
$900 (2008 est.)
$900 (2007 est.)
$800 (2006 est.)
*note:* data are in 2008 US dollars

**GDP - composition by sector:**
*agriculture:* 35%
*industry:* 22.1%
*services:* 42.9% (2008 est.)

**Labor force:** 4.6 million (2000)

**Labor force - by occupation:**
*agriculture:* 90%
*industry and services:* 10% (2000)

**Unemployment rate:**
NA%

**Population below poverty line:** 60% (2001 est.)

**Household income or consumption by percentage share:**
*lowest 10%:* 2.1%
*highest 10%:* 38.2% (2000)

**Distribution of family income - Gini index:** 46.8 (2000)

**Investment (gross fixed):** 22.5% of GDP (2008 est.)

**Budget:**
*revenues:* $902.2 million
*expenditures:* $1.032 billion; including capital expenditures of $NA (2008 est.)

**Inflation rate (consumer prices):**
9.5% (2008 est.)
9.1% (2007 est.)

**Central bank discount rate:** 12.5% (31 December 2007)

**Commercial bank prime lending rate:** 15.84% (31 December 2007)

**Stock of money:** $233.6 million (31 December 2005)

**Stock of quasi money:** $227.4 million (31 December 2005)

**Stock of domestic credit:** $209.2 million (31 December 2005)

**Market value of publicly traded shares:** $NA

**Agriculture - products:** coffee, tea, pyrethrum (insecticide made from chrysanthemums), bananas, beans, sorghum, potatoes; livestock

**Industries:** cement, agricultural products, small-scale beverages, soap, furniture, shoes, plastic goods, textiles, cigarettes

**Industrial production growth rate:** 8% (2008 est.)

**Electricity - production:** 134 million kWh (2006 est.)

**Electricity - consumption:** 234.6 million kWh (2006 est.)

**Electricity - exports:** 10 million kWh (2007 est.)

**Electricity - imports:** 130 million kWh (2007 est.)

**Oil - production:** 0 bbl/day (2007 est.)

**Oil - consumption:** 5,320 bbl/day (2006 est.)

**Oil - exports:** 0 bbl/day (2005)

**Oil - imports:** 5,597 bbl/day (2005)

**Oil - proved reserves:** 0 bbl (1 January 2006 est.)

**Natural gas - production:** 0 cu m (2007 est.)

**Natural gas - consumption:** 0 cu m (2007 est.)

**Natural gas - exports:** 0 cu m (2007 est.)

**Natural gas - imports:** 0 cu m (2007 est.)

**Natural gas - proved reserves:** 56.63 billion cu m (1 January 2008 est.)

**Current account balance:** -$220 million (2008 est.)

**Exports:** $219 million f.o.b. (2008 est.)

**Exports - commodities:** coffee, tea, hides, tin ore

**Exports - partners:** China 8.9%, Germany 6.8%, US 4.9%, Hong Kong 4.8% (2007)

**Imports:** $759 million f.o.b. (2008 est.)

**Imports - commodities:** foodstuffs, machinery and equipment, steel, petroleum products, cement and construction material

**Imports - partners:** Kenya 19.6%, Uganda 6.9%, Germany 6.2%, Belgium 5.9%, China 5% (2007)

**Reserves of foreign exchange and gold:** $657 million (31 December 2008 est.)

**Debt - external:** $1.4 billion (2004 est.)

**Exchange rates:** Rwandan francs (RWF) per US dollar - 550 (2008 est.), 585 (2007), 560 (2006), 610 (2005), 574.62 (2004)

## Communications

**Telephones - main lines in use:** 23,100 (2007)

**Telephones - mobile cellular:** 635,100 (2007)

**Telephone system:**
*general assessment:* small, inadequate telephone system primarily serves business and government
*domestic:* the capital, Kigali, is connected to the centers of the provinces by microwave radio relay and, recently, by cellular telephone service; much of the network depends on wire and HF radiotelephone; combined fixed-line and mobile-cellular telephone density is only about 7 telephones per 100 persons

# Rwanda *(continued)*

*international:* country code - 250; international connections employ microwave radio relay to neighboring countries and satellite communications to more distant countries; satellite earth stations - 1 Intelsat (Indian Ocean) in Kigali (includes telex and telefax service)

**Radio broadcast stations:** AM 0, FM 10 (two main FM programs are broadcast through a system of repeaters; international FM programming includes the BBC, VOA, and Deutchewelle) (2007)

**Television broadcast stations:** 2 (2004)

**Internet country code:** .rw

**Internet hosts:** 2,363 (2008)

**Internet users:** 100,000 (2007)

## Transportation

**Airports:** 9 (2008)

**Airports - with paved runways:**
*total:* 4
*over 3,047 m:* 1
*914 to 1,523 m:* 2
*under 914 m:* 1 (2008)

**Airports - with unpaved runways:**
*total:* 5
*914 to 1,523 m:* 2
*under 914 m:* 3 (2008)

**Roadways:**
*total:* 14,008 km
*paved:* 2,662 km
*unpaved:* 11,346 km (2004)

**Waterways:** Lac Kivu navigable by shallow-draft barges and native craft (2008)

**Ports and terminals:** Cyangugu, Gisenyi, Kibuye

## Military

**Military branches:** Rwandan Defense Forces: Army, Air Force

**Military service age and obligation:** 18 years of age for voluntary military service; no conscription (2008)

**Manpower available for military service:**
*males age 16-49:* 2,430,469
*females age 16-49:* 2,392,933 (2008 est.)

**Manpower fit for military service:**
*males age 16-49:* 1,452,768
*females age 16-49:* 1,456,207 (2009 est.)

**Manpower reaching militarily significant age annually:**
*male:* 106,741
*female:* 106,935 (2009 est.)

**Military expenditures:** 2.9% of GDP (2006 est.)

## Transnational Issues

**Disputes - international:** fighting among ethnic groups - loosely associated political rebels, armed gangs, and various government forces in Great Lakes region transcending the boundaries of Burundi, Democratic Republic of the Congo, Rwanda, and Uganda - abated substantially from a decade ago due largely to UN peacekeeping, international mediation, and efforts by local governments to create civil societies; nonetheless, 57,000 Rwandan refugees still reside in 21 African states, including Zambia, Gabon, and 20,000 who fled to Burundi in 2005 and 2006 to escape drought and recriminations from traditional courts investigating the 1994 massacres; the 2005 DROC and Rwanda border verification mechanism to stem rebel actions on both sides of the border remains in place

**Refugees and internally displaced persons:**
*refugees (country of origin):* 46,272 (Democratic Republic of the Congo); 4,400 (Burundi) (2007)

# Saint Barthelemy
*(overseas collectivity of France)*

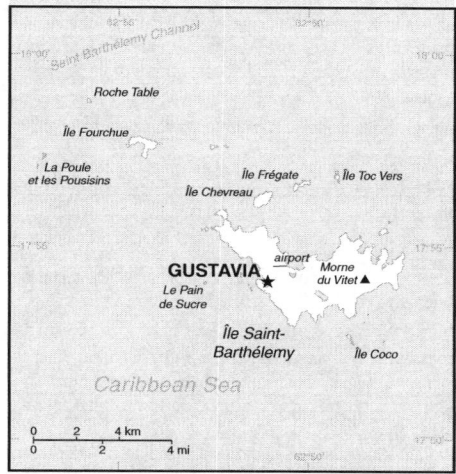

## Introduction

**Background:** Discovered in 1493 by Christopher COLUMBUS who named it for his brother Bartolomeo, St. Barthelemy was first settled by the French in 1648. In 1784, the French sold the island to Sweden, who renamed the largest town Gustavia, after the Swedish King GUSTAV III, and made it a free port; the island prospered as a trade and supply center during the colonial wars of the 18th century. France repurchased the island in 1878 and placed it under the administration of Guadeloupe. St. Barthelemy retained its free port status along with various Swedish appellations such as Swedish street and town names, and the three-crown symbol on the coat of arms. In 2003, the populace of the island voted to secede from Guadeloupe and in 2007, the island became a French overseas collectivity.

## Geography

**Location:** located approximately 125 miles northwest of Guadeloupe

**Geographic coordinates:** 17 90 N, 62 85 W

**Map references:** Central America and the Caribbean

**Area:** 21 sq km

**Area - comparative:** less than an eighth of the size of Washington, DC

**Land boundaries:** 0 km

**Climate:** tropical, with practically no variation in temperature; has two seasons (dry and humid)

**Terrain:** hilly, almost completely surrounded by shallow-water reefs, with 20 beaches

**Elevation extremes:**
*lowest point:* Caribbean Ocean 0 m
*highest point:* Morne du Vitet 286 m

**Natural resources:** has few natural resources, its beaches being the most important

**Environment - current issues:** with no natural rivers or streams, fresh water is in short supply, especially in summer, and provided by desalinization of sea water, collection of rain water, or imported via water tanker

# Saint Barthelemy *(continued)*

## People

**Population:** 7,448 (July 2009 est.)
**Age structure:**
*0-14 years:* 19.2% (male 734/female 696)
*15-64 years:* 70.6% (male 2,855/female 2,402)
*65 years and over:* 10.2% (male 378/female 383)
(2009 est.)
**Median age:**
*total:* 39.1 years
*male:* 39.3 years
*female:* 38.9 years (2009 est.)
**Sex ratio:**
*at birth:* 1.05 male(s)/female
*under 15 years:* 1.06 male(s)/female
*15-64 years:* 1.19 male(s)/female
*65 years and over:* 0.99 male(s)/female
*total population:* 1.14 male(s)/female (2009 est.)
**Ethnic groups:** white, Creole (mulatto), black, Guadeloupe Mestizo (French-East Asia)
**Religions:** Roman Catholic, Protestant, Jehovah's Witness
**Languages:** French (primary), English

## Government

**Country name:**
*conventional long form:* Overseas Collectivity of Saint Barthelemy
*conventional short form:* Saint Barthelemy
*local long form:* Collectivite d'outre mer de Saint-Barthelemy
*local short form:* Saint-Barthelemy
**Dependency status:** overseas collectivity of France
**Capital:**
*name:* Gustavia
*geographic coordinates:* 17 53 N, 62 51 W
*time difference:* UTC-4 (1 hour ahead of Washington, DC, during Standard Time)
**Independence:** none (overseas collectivity of France)
**National holiday:** Bastille Day, 14 July (1789); note -local holiday is St. Barthelemy Day, 24 August
**Constitution:** 4 October 1958 (French Constitution)
**Legal system:** the laws of France, where applicable, apply
**Suffrage:** 18 years of age, universal
**Executive branch:**
*chief of state:* President Nicolas SARKOZY (since 16 May 2007), represented by Prefect Dominique LACROIX (since 21 March 2007)
*head of government:* President of the Territorial Council Bruno MAGRAS (since 16 July 2007)
*cabinet:* Executive Council; note - there is also an advisory, economic, social, and cultural council
*elections:* French president elected by popular vote for a five-year term; prefect appointed by the French president on the advice of the French Ministry of Interior; president of the Territorial Council is elected by the members of the Council for a five-year term
*election results:* Bruno MAGRAS unanimously elected president by the Territorial Council on 16 July 2007

**Legislative branch:** unicameral Territorial Council (19 seats; members are elected by popular vote to serve five-year terms)
*elections:* last held 1 and 8 July 2007 (next to be held in July 2012)
*election results:* percent of vote by party - SBA 72.2%, Action-Equilibre-Transparence 9.9%, Ensemble pour Saint-Barthelemy 7.9%, Tous Unis pour Saint-Barthelemy 9.9%; seats by party - SBA 16, Action-Equilibre-Transparence 1, Ensemble pour Saint-Barthelemy 1, Tous Unis pour Saint-Barthelemy 1
*note:* Saint Barthelemy elects one seat to the French Senate; elections last held 21 September 2008 (next to be held in September 2014); results - percent of vote by party - NA; seats by party - UMP 1
**Political parties and leaders:**
Action-Equilibre-Transparence [Maxime DESOUCHES]; Ensemble pour Saint-Barthelemy [Benoit CHAUVIN]; Saint-Barth d'Abord! or SBA [Bruno MAGRAS]; Tous Unis pour Saint-Barthelemy [Karine MIOT-RICHARD]
**Political pressure groups and leaders:** The Marine Reserve (protection of fish); Rotary Club
**International organization participation:** UPU, WFTU
**Diplomatic representation in the US:** none (overseas collectivity of France)
**Diplomatic representation from the US:** none (overseas collectivity of France)
**Flag description:** the flag of France is used

## Economy

**Economy - overview:** The economy of Saint Barthelemy is based upon high-end tourism and duty-free luxury commerce, serving visitors primarily from North America. The luxury hotels and villas host 70,000 visitors each year with another 130,000 arriving by boat. The relative isolation and high cost of living inhibits mass tourism. The construction and public sectors also enjoy significant investment in support of tourism. With limited fresh water resources, all food must be imported, as must all energy resources and most manufactured goods. Employment is strong and attracts labor from Brazil and Portugal.
**Exchange rates:** euros (EUR) per US dollar - 0.7345 (2007), 0.7964 (2006), 0.8041 (2005), 0.8054 (2004), 0.886 (2003)

## Communications

**Telephone system:**
*general assessment:* fully integrated access
*domestic:* direct dial capability with both fixed and wireless systems
*international:* country code - 590; undersea fiber-optic cable provides voice and data connectivity to Puerto Rico and Guadeloupe
**Internet country code:** .bl; note - .gp, the internet country code for Guadeloupe, and .fr, the internet country code for France, might also be encountered

## Transportation

**Airports:** 1 (2008)
**Airports - with paved runways:**
*total:* 1
*under 914 m:* 1 (2008)
**Transportation - note:** nearest airport for international flights is Princess Juliana International Airport (SXM) located in Sint Maarten (Netherlands Antilles)

## Military

**Manpower fit for military service:**
*males age 16-49:* 1,594
*females age 16-49:* 1,340 (2009 est.)
**Manpower reaching militarily significant age annually:**
*male:* 21
*female:* 20 (2009 est.)
**Military - note:** defense is the responsibility of France

# Saint Helena
*(overseas territory of the UK)*

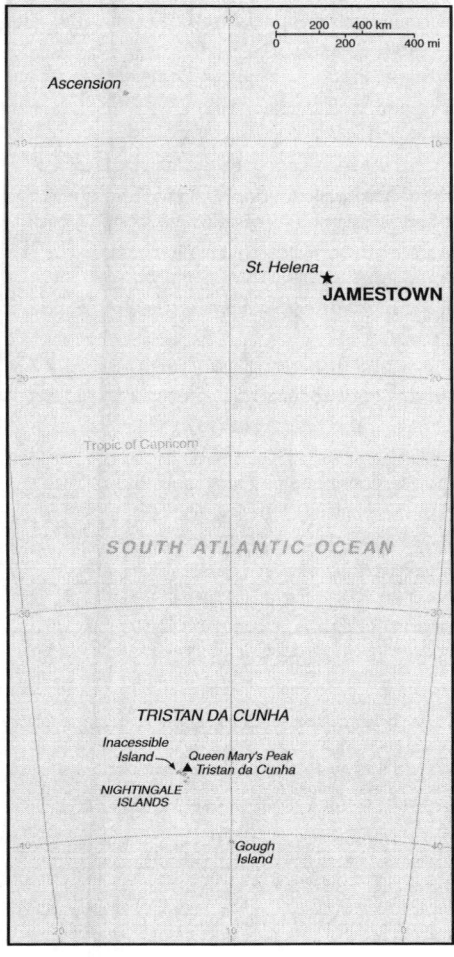

## Introduction

**Background:** Saint Helena is a British Overseas Territory consisting of Saint Helena and Ascension Islands, and the island group of Tristan da Cunha. *Saint Helena:* Uninhabited when first discovered by the Portuguese in 1502, Saint Helena was garrisoned by the British during the 17th century. It acquired fame as the place of Napoleon BONAPARTE's exile from 1815 until his death in 1821, but its importance as a port of call declined after the opening of the Suez Canal in 1869. During the Anglo-Boer War in South Africa, several thousand Boer prisoners were confined on the island between 1900 and 1903. *Ascension Island:* This barren and uninhabited island was discovered and named by the Portuguese in 1503. The British garrisoned the island in 1815 to prevent a rescue of Napoleon from Saint Helena. It served as a provisioning station for the Royal Navy's West Africa Squadron on anti-slavery patrol. The island remained under Admiralty control until 1922, when it became a dependency of Saint Helena. During World War II, the UK permitted the US to construct an airfield on Ascension in support of trans-Atlantic flights to Africa and anti-submarine operations in the South Atlantic. In the 1960s the island became an important space tracking station for the US. In 1982, Ascension was an essential staging area for British forces during the Falklands War. It remains a critical refueling point in the air-bridge from the UK to the South Atlantic. *Tristan da Cunha:* The island group consists of the islands of Tristan da Cunha, Nightingale, Inaccessible, and Gough. Tristan da Cunha is named after its Portuguese discoverer (1506); it was garrisoned by the British in 1816 to prevent any attempt to rescue Napoleon from Saint Helena. Gough and Inaccessible Islands have been designated World Heritage Sites. South Africa leases a site for a meteorological station on Gough Island.

## Geography

**Location:** islands in the South Atlantic Ocean, about midway between South America and Africa; Ascension Island lies 700 nm northwest of Saint Helena; Tristan da Cunha lies 2,300 nm southwest of Saint Helena

**Geographic coordinates:**
*Saint Helena:* 15 57 S, 5 42 W
*Ascension Island:* 7 57 S, 14 22 W
*Tristan da Cunha island group:* 37 15 S, 12 30 W

**Map references:** Africa

**Area:**
*total:* 413 sq km
*land:* Saint Helena Island 122 sq km; Ascension Island 90 sq km; Tristan da Cunha island group 201 sq km
*water:* 0 sq km

**Area - comparative:** slightly more than twice the size of Washington, DC

**Land boundaries:** 0 km

**Coastline:**
*Saint Helena:* 60 km
*Ascension Island:* NA
*Tristan da Cunha:* 40 km

**Maritime claims:**
*territorial sea:* 12 nm
*exclusive fishing zone:* 200 nm

**Climate:**
*Saint Helena:* tropical marine; mild, tempered by trade winds
*Ascension Island:* tropical marine; mild, semi-arid
*Tristan da Cunha:* temperate marine; mild, tempered by trade winds (tends to be cooler than Saint Helena)

**Terrain:** the islands of this group result from volcanic activity associated with the Atlantic Mid-Ocean Ridge
*Saint Helena:* rugged, volcanic; small scattered plateaus and plains
*Ascension:* surface covered by lava flows and cinder cones of 44 dormant volcanoes; ground rises to the east
*Tristan da Cunha:* sheer cliffs line the coastline of the nearly circular island; the flanks of the central volcanic peak are deeply dissected; narrow coastal plain lies between The Peak and the coastal cliffs

**Elevation extremes:**
*lowest point:* Atlantic Ocean 0 m
*highest point:* Queen Mary's Peak on Tristan da Cunha 2,062 m; Green Mountain on Ascension Island 859 m; Mount Actaeon on Saint Helena Island 818 m

**Natural resources:** fish, lobster

**Land use:**
*arable land:* 12.9%
*permanent crops:* 0%
*other:* 87.1% (2005)

**Irrigated land:** NA

**Natural hazards:** active volcanism on Tristan da Cunha, last eruption in 1961

**Environment - current issues:** NA

**Geography - note:** Saint Helena harbors at least 40 species of plants unknown anywhere else in the world; Ascension is a breeding ground for sea turtles and sooty terns; Queen Mary's Peak on Tristan da Cunha is the highest island mountain in the South Atlantic and a prominent landmark on the sea lanes around southern Africa

## People

**Population:** 7,637
*note:* only Saint Helena, Ascension, and Tristan da Cunha islands are inhabited (July 2009 est.)

**Age structure:**
*0-14 years:* 18.3% (male 712/female 685)
*15-64 years:* 70.4% (male 2,744/female 2,629)
*65 years and over:* 11.4% (male 412/female 455)
(2009 est.)

**Median age:**
*total:* 37.6 years
*male:* 37.7 years
*female:* 37.5 years (2009 est.)

**Population growth rate:** 0.445% (2009 est.)

**Birth rate:** 11.13 births/1,000 population (2009 est.)

**Death rate:** 6.58 deaths/1,000 population (2008 est.)

**Net migration rate:** NA

**Urbanization:**
*urban population:* 39% of total population (2008)
*rate of urbanization:* 1.5% annual rate of change (2005-10 est.)

**Sex ratio:**
*at birth:* 1.05 male(s)/female
*under 15 years:* 1.04 male(s)/female
*15-64 years:* 1.04 male(s)/female
*65 years and over:* 0.9 male(s)/female
*total population:* 1.03 male(s)/female (2009 est.)

**Infant mortality rate:**
*total:* 17.63 deaths/1,000 live births
*male:* 20.71 deaths/1,000 live births
*female:* 14.4 deaths/1,000 live births (2009 est.)

**Life expectancy at birth:**
*total population:* 78.44 years
*male:* 75.52 years
*female:* 81.5 years (2009 est.)

**Total fertility rate:** 1.56 children born/woman (2009 est.)

**HIV/AIDS - adult prevalence rate:** NA

**HIV/AIDS - people living with HIV/AIDS:** NA

**HIV/AIDS - deaths:** NA
**Nationality:**
*noun:* Saint Helenian(s)
*adjective:* Saint Helenian
*note:* referred to locally as "Saints"
**Ethnic groups:** African descent 50%, white 25%, Chinese 25%
**Religions:** Anglican (majority), Baptist, Seventh-Day Adventist, Roman Catholic
**Languages:** English
**Literacy:**
*definition:* age 20 and over can read and write
*total population:* 97%
*male:* 97%
*female:* 98% (1987 est.)
**Education expenditures:** NA

## Government

**Country name:**
*conventional long form:* none
*conventional short form:* Saint Helena
**Dependency status:** overseas territory of the UK
**Government type:** NA
**Capital:**
*name:* Jamestown
*geographic coordinates:* 15 56 S, 5 44 W
*time difference:* UTC 0 (5 hours ahead of Washington, DC during Standard Time)
**Administrative divisions:** 1 administrative area and 2 dependencies*; Ascension*, Saint Helena, Tristan da Cunha*
**Independence:** none (overseas territory of the UK)
**National holiday:** Birthday of Queen ELIZABETH II, second Saturday in June (1926)
**Constitution:** 1 January 1989
**Legal system:** English common law and statutes supplemented by local statutes
**Suffrage:** NA
**Executive branch:**
*chief of state:* Queen ELIZABETH II (since 6 February 1952)
*head of government:* Governor and Commander in Chief Andrew GURR (since 11 November 2007)
*cabinet:* Executive Council consists of the governor, three ex-officio officers, and five elected members of the Legislative Council
*elections:* the monarch is hereditary; governor is appointed by the monarch
**Legislative branch:** unicameral Legislative Council (16 seats, including the speaker, three ex officio and 12 elected members; members are elected by popular vote to serve four-year terms)
*elections:* last held 31 August 2005 (next to be held in 2009)
*election results:* percent of vote - NA; seats - independents 12
**Judicial branch:** Magistrate's Court; Supreme Court; Court of Appeal
**Political parties and leaders:** none
**Political pressure groups and leaders:**
*other:* private sector; unions

**International organization participation:** UPU, WFTU
**Diplomatic representation in the US:** none (overseas territory of the UK)
**Diplomatic representation from the US:** none (overseas territory of the UK)
**Flag description:** blue with the flag of the UK in the upper hoist-side quadrant and the Saint Helenian shield centered on the outer half of the flag; the shield features a rocky coastline and three-masted sailing ship

## Economy

**Economy - overview:** The economy depends largely on financial assistance from the UK, which amounted to about $27 million in FY06/07 or more than twice the level of annual budgetary revenues. The local population earns income from fishing, raising livestock, and sales of handicrafts. Because there are few jobs, 25% of the work force has left to seek employment on Ascension Island, on the Falklands, and in the UK.
**GDP (purchasing power parity):**
$18 million (1998 est.)
**GDP (official exchange rate):** $NA
**GDP - real growth rate:** NA%
**GDP - per capita (PPP):**
$2,500 (1998 est.)
**GDP - composition by sector:**
*agriculture:* NA%
*industry:* NA%
*services:* NA%
**Labor force:** 2,486
*note:* 1,200 work offshore (1998 est.)
**Labor force - by occupation:**
*agriculture:* 6%
*industry:* 48%
*services:* 46% (1987 est.)
**Unemployment rate:**
14% (1998 est.)
**Population below poverty line:** NA%
**Household income or consumption by percentage share:**
*lowest 10%:* NA%
*highest 10%:* NA%
**Budget:**
*revenues:* $12.33 million
*expenditures:* $30.28 million
*note:* revenue data reflect locally raised revenues only; the budget deficit is resolved by grant aid from the United Kingdom (FY06/07 est.)
**Inflation rate (consumer prices):**
3.2% (1997 est.)
3.2% (1997 est.)
**Agriculture - products:** coffee, corn, potatoes, vegetables; timber; fish, lobster (on Tristan da Cunha); livestock
**Industries:** construction, crafts (furniture, lacework, fancy woodwork), fishing, philatelic sales
**Industrial production growth rate:** NA%

**Electricity - production:** 8 million kWh (2006 est.)
**Electricity - consumption:** 7.44 million kWh (2006 est.)
**Electricity - exports:** 0 kWh (2007 est.)
**Electricity - imports:** 0 kWh (2007 est.)
**Oil - production:** 0 bbl/day (2007 est.)
**Oil - consumption:** 60 bbl/day (2006 est.)
**Oil - exports:** 0 bbl/day (2005)
**Oil - imports:** 85.42 bbl/day (2005)
**Oil - proved reserves:** 0 bbl (1 January 2006 est.)
**Natural gas - production:** 0 cu m (2007 est.)
**Natural gas - consumption:** 0 cu m (2007 est.)
**Natural gas - exports:** 0 cu m (2007 est.)
**Natural gas - imports:** 0 cu m (2007 est.)
**Natural gas - proved reserves:** 0 cu m (1 January 2006 est.)
**Exports:** $19 million f.o.b. (2004 est.)
**Exports - commodities:** fish (frozen, canned, and salt-dried skipjack, tuna), coffee, handicrafts
**Imports:** $45 million c.i.f. (2004 est.)
**Imports - commodities:** food, beverages, tobacco, fuel oils, animal feed, building materials, motor vehicles and parts, machinery and parts
**Debt - external:** $NA
**Exchange rates:** Saint Helenian pounds (SHP) per US dollar - 0.5302 (2008), 0.4993 (2007), 0.5418 (2006), 0.5493 (2005), 0.5462 (2004)
*note:* the Saint Helenian pound is on par with the British pound

## Communications

**Telephones - main lines in use:** 2,200 (2002)
**Telephone system:**
*general assessment:* can communicate worldwide
*domestic:* automatic digital network
*international:* country code (Saint Helena) - 290, (Ascension Island) - 247; international direct dialing; satellite voice and data communications; satellite earth stations - 5 (Ascension Island - 4, Saint Helena -1)
**Radio broadcast stations:**
*Saint Helena:* AM 1, FM 1, shortwave 0
*Ascension:* AM 1, FM 1, shortwave 1 (2005)
**Television broadcast stations:** 0 (3 television channels are received via satellite and distributed by UHF) (2005)
**Internet country code:** .sh; note - Ascension Island assigned .ac
**Internet hosts:** 306 (2008)
**Internet users:** 1,000; note - includes Ascension Island (2003)
**Communications - note:** South Africa maintains a meteorological station on Gough Island

## Transportation

**Airports:** 1 (2008)
**Airports - with paved runways:**
*total:* 1
*over 3,047 m:* 1 (2008)

# Saint Helena *(continued)*

**Roadways:**

*total:* 198 km (Saint Helena 138 km, Ascension 40 km, Tristan da Cunha 20 km)

*paved:* 168 km (Saint Helena 118 km, Ascension 40 km, Tristan da Cunha 10 km)

*unpaved:* 30 km (Saint Helena 20 km, Ascension 0 km, Tristan da Cunha 10 km) (2002)

**Ports and terminals:**

*Saint Helena:* Jamestown

*Ascension Island:* Georgetown

*Tristan da Cunha:* Calshot Harbor

**Transportation - note:** there is no air connection to Saint Helena or Tristan da Cunha; an international airport for Saint Helena is in development for 2010

## Military

**Manpower fit for military service:**

*males age 16-49:* 1,586

*females age 16-49:* 1,600 (2009 est.)

**Manpower reaching militarily significant age annually:**

*male:* 47

*female:* 45 (2009 est.)

**Military - note:** defense is the responsibility of the UK

## Transnational Issues

**Disputes - international:** none

---

# Saint Kitts and Nevis

## Introduction

**Background:** Carib Indians occupied the islands for hundreds of years before the British began settlement in 1623. The islands became an associated state of the UK with full internal autonomy in 1967. The island of Anguilla rebelled and was allowed to secede in 1971. Saint Kitts and Nevis achieved independence in 1983. In 1998, a vote in Nevis on a referendum to separate from Saint Kitts fell short of the two-thirds majority needed. Nevis continues in its efforts to separate from Saint Kitts.

## Geography

**Location:** Caribbean, islands in the Caribbean Sea, about one-third of the way from Puerto Rico to Trinidad and Tobago

**Geographic coordinates:** 17 20 N, 62 45 W

**Map references:** Central America and the Caribbean

**Area:**

*total:* 261 sq km (Saint Kitts 168 sq km; Nevis 93 sq km)

*land:* 261 sq km

*water:* 0 sq km

**Area - comparative:** 1.5 times the size of Washington, DC

**Land boundaries:** 0 km

**Coastline:** 135 km

**Maritime claims:**

*territorial sea:* 12 nm

*contiguous zone:* 24 nm

*exclusive economic zone:* 200 nm

*continental shelf:* 200 nm or to the edge of the continental margin

**Climate:** tropical, tempered by constant sea breezes; little seasonal temperature variation; rainy season (May to November)

**Terrain:** volcanic with mountainous interiors

**Elevation extremes:**

*lowest point:* Caribbean Sea 0 m

*highest point:* Mount Liamuiga 1,156 m

**Natural resources:** arable land

**Land use:**

*arable land:* 19.44%

*permanent crops:* 2.78%

*other:* 77.78% (2005)

**Irrigated land:** NA

**Total renewable water resources:** 0.02 cu km (2000)

**Natural hazards:** hurricanes (July to October)

**Environment - current issues:** NA

**Environment - international agreements:**

*party to:* Biodiversity, Climate Change, Climate Change-Kyoto Protocol, Desertification, Endangered Species, Hazardous Wastes, Law of the Sea, Marine Dumping, Ozone Layer Protection, Ship Pollution, Whaling

*signed, but not ratified:* none of the selected agreements

**Geography - note:** with coastlines in the shape of a baseball bat and ball, the two volcanic islands are separated by a 3-km-wide channel called The Narrows; on the southern tip of long, baseball bat-shaped Saint Kitts lies the Great Salt Pond; Nevis Peak sits in the center of its almost circular namesake island and its ball shape complements that of its sister island

## People

**Population:** 40,131 (July 2009 est.)

**Age structure:**

*0-14 years:* 26.3% (male 5,397/female 5,138)

*15-64 years:* 65.9% (male 13,231/female 13,196)

*65 years and over:* 7.9% (male 1,326/female 1,843) (2009 est.)

**Median age:**

*total:* 28.6 years

*male:* 27.9 years

*female:* 29.3 years (2009 est.)

**Population growth rate:** 0.847% (2009 est.)

**Birth rate:** 17.67 births/1,000 population (2009 est.)

**Death rate:** 8.19 deaths/1,000 population (2008 est.)

**Net migration rate:** -1.15 migrant(s)/1,000 population (2009 est.)

**Urbanization:**

*urban population:* 32% of total population (2008)

*rate of urbanization:* 1.4% annual rate of change (2005-10 est.)

**Sex ratio:**

*at birth:* 1.06 male(s)/female

*under 15 years:* 1.05 male(s)/female

*15-64 years:* 1 male(s)/female

*65 years and over:* 0.72 male(s)/female

*total population:* 0.99 male(s)/female (2009 est.)

**Infant mortality rate:**

*total:* 13.94 deaths/1,000 live births

*male:* 15.66 deaths/1,000 live births

*female:* 12.11 deaths/1,000 live births (2009 est.)

**Life expectancy at birth:**

*total population:* 73.2 years

*male:* 70.33 years

*female:* 76.25 years (2009 est.)

**Total fertility rate:** 2.26 children born/woman (2009 est.)

**HIV/AIDS - adult prevalence rate:** NA

**HIV/AIDS - people living with HIV/AIDS:** NA

**HIV/AIDS - deaths:** NA

**Nationality:**

*noun:* Kittitian(s), Nevisian(s)

*adjective:* Kittitian, Nevisian

**Ethnic groups:** predominantly black; some British, Portuguese, and Lebanese

**Religions:** Anglican, other Protestant, Roman Catholic

**Languages:** English

**Literacy:**

*definition:* age 15 and over has ever attended school

*total population:* 97.8%

*male:* NA

*female:* NA (2003 est.)

**School life expectancy (primary to tertiary education):**

*total:* 12 years

*male:* 12 years

*female:* 13 years (2005)

**Education expenditures:** 9.3% of GDP (2005)

## Government

**Country name:**

*conventional long form:* Federation of Saint Kitts and Nevis

*conventional short form:* Saint Kitts and Nevis

*former:* Federation of Saint Christopher and Nevis

**Government type:** parliamentary democracy and a Commonwealth realm

**Capital:**

*name:* Basseterre

*geographic coordinates:* 17 18 N, 62 43 W

*time difference:* UTC-4 (1 hour ahead of Washington, DC during Standard Time)

**Administrative divisions:** 14 parishes; Christ Church Nichola Town, Saint Anne Sandy Point, Saint George Basseterre, Saint George Gingerland, Saint James Windward, Saint John Capesterre, Saint John Figtree, Saint Mary Cayon, Saint Paul Capesterre, Saint Paul Charlestown, Saint Peter Basseterre, Saint Thomas Lowland, Saint Thomas Middle Island, Trinity Palmetto Point

**Independence:** 19 September 1983 (from the UK)

**National holiday:** Independence Day, 19 September (1983)

**Constitution:** 19 September 1983

**Legal system:** based on English common law; has not accepted compulsory ICJ jurisdiction

**Suffrage:** 18 years of age; universal

**Executive branch:**

*chief of state:* Queen ELIZABETH II (since 6 February 1952); represented by Governor General Cuthbert Montraville SEBASTIAN (since 1 January 1996)

*head of government:* Prime Minister Dr. Denzil DOUGLAS (since 6 July 1995); Deputy Prime Minister Sam CONDOR (since 6 July 1995)

*cabinet:* Cabinet appointed by the governor general in consultation with the prime minister

*elections:* the monarch is hereditary; the governor general is appointed by the monarch; following legislative elections, the leader of the majority party or leader of a majority coalition is usually appointed prime minister by the governor general; deputy prime minister appointed by the governor general

**Legislative branch:** unicameral National Assembly (14 seats, 3 appointed and 11 popularly elected from single-member constituencies; members serve five-year terms)

*elections:* last held 25 October 2004 (next to be held by 2009)

*election results:* percent of vote by party - NA; seats by party - SKNLP 7, CCM 2, NRP 1, PAM 1

**Judicial branch:** Eastern Caribbean Supreme Court (consisting of a Court of Appeal and a High Court; based on Saint Lucia; two judges of the Supreme Court reside in Saint Kitts and Nevis); member of the Caribbean Court of Justice (CCJ)

**Political parties and leaders:** Concerned Citizens Movement or CCM [Vance AMORY]; Nevis Reformation Party or NRP [Joseph PARRY]; People's Action Movement or PAM [Lindsay GRANT]; Saint Kitts and Nevis Labor Party or SKNLP [Dr. Denzil DOUGLAS]

**Political pressure groups and leaders:** NA

**International organization participation:** ACP, C, Caricom, CDB, FAO, G-77, IBRD, ICAO, ICCt, ICRM, IDA, IFAD, IFC, IFRCS, ILO, IMF, IMO, Interpol, IOC, ITU, MIGA, NAM, OAS, OECS, OPANAL, OPCW, UN, UNCTAD, UNESCO, UNIDO, UPU, WFTU, WHO, WIPO, WTO

**Diplomatic representation in the US:**

*chief of mission:* Ambassador Izben Cordinal WILLIAMS

*chancery:* 3216 New Mexico Avenue NW, Washington, DC 20016

*telephone:* [1] (202) 686-2636

*FAX:* [1] (202) 686-5740

*consulate(s) general:* New York

**Diplomatic representation from the US:** the US does not have an embassy in Saint Kitts and Nevis; the US Ambassador to Barbados is accredited to Saint Kitts and Nevis

**Flag description:** divided diagonally from the lower hoist side by a broad black band bearing two white, five-pointed stars; the black band is edged in yellow; the upper triangle is green, the lower triangle is red

## Economy

**Economy - overview:** The economy of Saint Kitts and Nevis is heavily dependent upon tourism revenues, which has replaced sugar, the traditional mainstay of the economy until the 1970s. Following the 2005 harvest, the government closed the sugar industry after decades of losses of 3-4% of GDP annually. To compensate for employment losses, the government has embarked on a program to diversify the agricultural sector and to stimulate other sectors of the economy, such as tourism, export-oriented manufacturing, and offshore banking. Economic growth was above average for Latin America from 2004 to 2006, but has since slowed. Like other tourist destinations in the Caribbean, the St. Kitts and Nevis is vulnerable to damage from natural disasters and shifts in tourism demand. The current government is constrained by a high public debt burden equivalent to nearly 185% of GDP by the end of 2006, largely attributable to public enterprise losses.

**GDP (purchasing power parity):**

$784.9 million (2008 est.)

$758.5 million (2007)

$735.6 million (2006)

*note:* data are in 2008 US dollars

**GDP (official exchange rate):** $559 million (2008 est.)

**GDP - real growth rate:**

3.5% (2008 est.)

3.1% (2007 est.)

6.4% (2006 est.)

**GDP - per capita (PPP):**

$19,700 (2008 est.)

$19,200 (2007 est.)

$18,700 (2006 est.)

*note:* data are in 2008 US dollars

**GDP - composition by sector:**

*agriculture:* 3.5%

*industry:* 25.8%

*services:* 70.7% (2001)

**Labor force:** 18,170 (June 1995)

**Unemployment rate:**

4.5% (1997)

**Population below poverty line:** NA%

**Household income or consumption by percentage share:**

*lowest 10%:* NA%

*highest 10%:* NA%

**Budget:**

*revenues:* $89.7 million

*expenditures:* $128.2 million (2003 est.)

**Inflation rate (consumer prices):**

4.5% (2007 est.)

**Central bank discount rate:** 6.5% (31 December 2007)

**Commercial bank prime lending rate:** 9.28% (31 December 2007)

**Stock of money:** $97.31 million (31 December 2007)

**Stock of quasi money:** $688.6 million (31 December 2007)

**Stock of domestic credit:** $782.4 million (31 December 2007)

**Market value of publicly traded shares:** $439.7 million (31 December 2007)

**Agriculture - products:** sugarcane, rice, yams, vegetables, bananas; fish

**Industries:** tourism, cotton, salt, copra, clothing, footwear, beverages

**Industrial production growth rate:** NA%

**Electricity - production:** 130 million kWh (2006 est.)

**Electricity - consumption:** 120.9 million kWh (2006 est.)
**Electricity - exports:** 0 kWh (2007 est.)
**Electricity - imports:** 0 kWh (2007 est.)
**Oil - production:** 0 bbl/day (2007 est.)
**Oil - consumption:** 950 bbl/day (2006 est.)
**Oil - exports:** 0 bbl/day (2005)
**Oil - imports:** 917.8 bbl/day (2005)
**Oil - proved reserves:** 0 bbl (1 January 2006 est.)
**Natural gas - production:** 0 cu m (2007 est.)
**Natural gas - consumption:** 0 cu m (2007 est.)
**Natural gas - exports:** 0 cu m (2007 est.)
**Natural gas - imports:** 0 cu m (2007 est.)
**Natural gas - proved reserves:** 0 cu m (1 January 2006 est.)
**Current account balance:** -$163 million (2007 est.)
**Exports:** $84 million (2006)
**Exports - commodities:** machinery, food, electronics, beverages, tobacco
**Exports - partners:** US 66.3%, Canada 4.9%, Turkey 3.3% (2007)
**Imports:** $383 million (2006)
**Imports - commodities:** machinery, manufactures, food, fuels
**Imports - partners:** US 47.7%, Trinidad and Tobago 13.3%, UK 5.6% (2007)
**Debt - external:** $314 million (2004)
**Exchange rates:** East Caribbean dollars (XCD) per US dollar - 2.7 (2007), 2.7 (2006), 2.7 (2005), 2.7 (2004), 2.7 (2003)

## Communications

**Telephones - main lines in use:** 25,000 (2004)
**Telephones - mobile cellular:** 10,000 (2004)
**Telephone system:**
*general assessment:* good interisland and international connections
*domestic:* interisland links via Eastern Caribbean Fiber Optic cable; construction of enhanced wireless infrastructure launched in November 2004
*international:* country code - 1-869; connected internationally by the East Caribbean Fiber Optic System (ECFS) and Southern Caribbean fiber optic system (SCF) submarine cables
**Radio broadcast stations:** AM 3, FM 3, shortwave 0 (2003)
**Television broadcast stations:** 1 (plus 3 repeaters) (2003)
**Internet country code:** .kn
**Internet hosts:** 45 (2008)
**Internet users:** 10,000 (2002)

## Transportation

**Airports:** 2 (2008)
**Airports - with paved runways:**
*total:* 2
*1,524 to 2,437 m:* 1
*914 to 1,523 m:* 1 (2008)

**Railways:**
*total:* 50 km
*narrow gauge:* 50 km 0.762-m gauge on Saint Kitts for tourists (2006)
**Roadways:**
*total:* 383 km
*paved:* 163 km
*unpaved:* 220 km (2002)
**Merchant marine:**
*total:* 159
*by type:* bulk carrier 10, cargo 109, chemical tanker 7, container 1, liquefied gas 1, passenger 1, passenger/cargo 2, petroleum tanker 19, refrigerated cargo 7, roll on/roll off 1, specialized tanker 1
*foreign-owned:* 121 (Belgium 1, Cyprus 1, Egypt 2, Estonia 3, Finland 1, Greece 3, India 1, Italy 1, Japan 3, Kuwait 1, Latvia 5, Malaysia 1, Pakistan 3, Romania 1, Russia 19, Singapore 1, Spain 1, Syria 7, Turkey 35, Ukraine 9, UAE 18, UK 3, Yemen 1) (2008)
**Ports and terminals:** Basseterre

## Military

**Military branches:** Royal Saint Kitts and Nevis Defense Force (includes Coast Guard), Royal Saint Kitts and Nevis Police Force (2009)
**Military service age and obligation:** 18 years of age for voluntary military service; no conscription (2008)
**Manpower available for military service:**
*males age 16-49:* 10,095
*females age 16-49:* 10,081 (2008 est.)
**Manpower fit for military service:**
*males age 16-49:* 8,159
*females age 16-49:* 8,517 (2009 est.)
**Manpower reaching militarily significant age annually:**
*male:* 376
*female:* 362 (2009 est.)
**Military expenditures:** NA

## Transnational Issues

**Disputes - international:** joins other Caribbean states to counter Venezuela's claim that Aves Island sustains human habitation, a criterion under UNCLOS, which permits Venezuela to extend its EEZ/continental shelf over a large portion of the eastern Caribbean Sea
**Illicit drugs:** transshipment point for South American drugs destined for the US and Europe; some money-laundering activity

# Saint Lucia

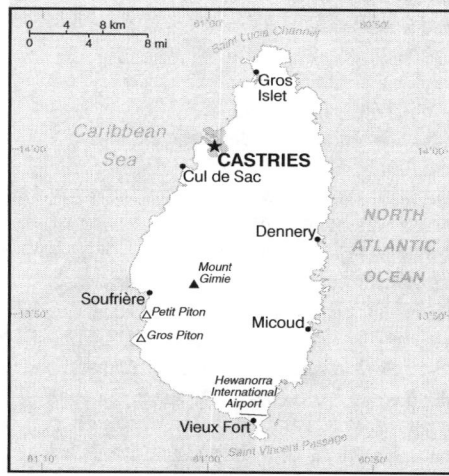

## Introduction

**Background:** The island, with its fine natural harbor at Castries, was contested between England and France throughout the 17th and early 18th centuries (changing possession 14 times); it was finally ceded to the UK in 1814. Even after the abolition of slavery on its plantations in 1834, Saint Lucia remained an agricultural island, dedicated to producing tropical commodity crops. Self-government was granted in 1967 and independence in 1979.

## Geography

**Location:** Caribbean, island between the Caribbean Sea and North Atlantic Ocean, north of Trinidad and Tobago
**Geographic coordinates:** 13 53 N, 60 58 W
**Map references:** Central America and the Caribbean
**Area:**
*total:* 616 sq km
*land:* 606 sq km
*water:* 10 sq km
**Area - comparative:** 3.5 times the size of Washington, DC
**Land boundaries:** 0 km
**Coastline:** 158 km
**Maritime claims:**
*territorial sea:* 12 nm
*contiguous zone:* 24 nm
*exclusive economic zone:* 200 nm
*continental shelf:* 200 nm or to the edge of the continental margin
**Climate:** tropical, moderated by northeast trade winds; dry season January to April, rainy season May to August
**Terrain:** volcanic and mountainous with some broad, fertile valleys
**Elevation extremes:**
*lowest point:* Caribbean Sea 0 m
*highest point:* Mount Gimie 950 m

# Saint Lucia *(continued)*

## Natural resources, Land use, etc.

**Natural resources:** forests, sandy beaches, minerals (pumice), mineral springs, geothermal potential

**Land use:**
*arable land:* 6.45%
*permanent crops:* 22.58%
*other:* 70.97% (2005)

**Irrigated land:** 30 sq km (2003)

**Freshwater withdrawal (domestic/industrial/agricultural):**
*total:* 0.01
*per capita:* 81 cu m/yr (1997)

**Natural hazards:** hurricanes; volcanic activity

**Environment - current issues:** deforestation; soil erosion, particularly in the northern region

**Environment - international agreements:**
*party to:* Biodiversity, Climate Change, Climate Change-Kyoto Protocol, Desertification, Endangered Species, Environmental Modification, Hazardous Wastes, Law of the Sea, Marine Dumping, Ozone Layer Protection, Ship Pollution, Wetlands, Whaling
*signed, but not ratified:* none of the selected agreements

**Geography - note:** the twin Pitons (Gros Piton and Petit Piton), striking cone-shaped peaks south of Soufriere, are one of the scenic natural highlights of the Caribbean

## People

**Population:** 160,267 (July 2009 est.)

**Age structure:**
*0-14 years:* 24.4% (male 20,035/female 19,021)
*15-64 years:* 66.4% (male 51,593/female 54,843)
*65 years and over:* 9.2% (male 6,668/female 8,107)
(2009 est.)

**Median age:**
*total:* 29.8 years
*male:* 28.7 years
*female:* 30.8 years (2009 est.)

**Population growth rate:** 0.416% (2009 est.)

**Birth rate:** 15.1 births/1,000 population (2009 est.)

**Death rate:** 6.71 deaths/1,000 population (2008 est.)

**Net migration rate:** -4.14 migrant(s)/1,000 population (2009 est.)

**Urbanization:**
*urban population:* 28% of total population (2008)
*rate of urbanization:* 1.4% annual rate of change (2005-10 est.)

**Sex ratio:**
*at birth:* 1.06 male(s)/female
*under 15 years:* 1.05 male(s)/female
*15-64 years:* 0.94 male(s)/female
*65 years and over:* 0.82 male(s)/female
*total population:* 0.96 male(s)/female (2009 est.)

**Infant mortality rate:**
*total:* 13.43 deaths/1,000 live births
*male:* 12.47 deaths/1,000 live births
*female:* 14.44 deaths/1,000 live births (2009 est.)

**Life expectancy at birth:**
*total population:* 76.45 years
*male:* 73.78 years
*female:* 79.27 years (2009 est.)

**Total fertility rate:** 1.84 children born/woman (2009 est.)

**HIV/AIDS - adult prevalence rate:** NA

**HIV/AIDS - people living with HIV/AIDS:** NA

**HIV/AIDS - deaths:** NA

**Nationality:**
*noun:* Saint Lucian(s)
*adjective:* Saint Lucian

**Ethnic groups:** black 82.5%, mixed 11.9%, East Indian 2.4%, other or unspecified 3.1% (2001 census)

**Religions:** Roman Catholic 67.5%, Seventh Day Adventist 8.5%, Pentecostal 5.7%, Rastafarian 2.1%, Anglican 2%, Evangelical 2%, other Christian 5.1%, other 1.1%, unspecified 1.5%, none 4.5% (2001 census)

**Languages:** English (official), French patois

**Literacy:**
*definition:* age 15 and over has ever attended school
*total population:* 90.1%
*male:* 89.5%
*female:* 90.6% (2001 est.)

**School life expectancy (primary to tertiary education):**
*total:* 14 years
*male:* 13 years
*female:* 14 years (2006)

**Education expenditures:** 6.6% of GDP (2006)

## Government

**Country name:**
*conventional long form:* none
*conventional short form:* Saint Lucia

**Government type:** parliamentary democracy and a Commonwealth realm

**Capital:**
*name:* Castries
*geographic coordinates:* 14 01 N, 61 00 W
*time difference:* UTC-4 (1 hour ahead of Washington, DC during Standard Time)

**Administrative divisions:** 11 quarters; Anse-la-Raye, Castries, Choiseul, Dauphin, Dennery, Gros-Islet, Laborie, Micoud, Praslin, Soufriere, Vieux-Fort

**Independence:** 22 February 1979 (from the UK)

**National holiday:** Independence Day, 22 February (1979)

**Constitution:** 22 February 1979

**Legal system:** based on English common law; has not accepted compulsory ICJ jurisdiction

**Suffrage:** 18 years of age; universal

**Executive branch:**
*chief of state:* Queen ELIZABETH II (since 6 February 1952); represented by Governor General Dame Pearlette LOUISY (since September 1997)
*head of government:* Prime Minister Stephenson KING (since 9 September 2007); note - Sir John COMPTON died in office 7 September 2007
*cabinet:* Cabinet appointed by the governor general on the advice of the prime minister
*elections:* the monarch is hereditary; the governor general is appointed by the monarch; following legislative elections, the leader of the majority party or the leader of a majority coalition is usually appointed prime minister by the governor general; deputy prime minister appointed by the governor general

**Legislative branch:** bicameral Parliament consists of the Senate (11 seats; six members appointed on the advice of the prime minister, three on the advice of the leader of the opposition, and two after consultation with religious, economic, and social groups) and the House of Assembly (17 seats; members are elected by popular vote to serve five-year terms)
*elections:* House of Assembly - last held 11 December 2006 (next to be held in December 2011)
*election results:* House of Assembly - percent of vote by party - UWP 50%, SLP 46.9%, other 3.1%; seats by party - UWP 11, SLP 6

**Judicial branch:** Eastern Caribbean Supreme Court (consists of a High Court and a Court of Appeals; based on Saint Lucia; three judges of the Supreme Court reside in Saint Lucia); member of the Caribbean Court of Justice (CCJ)

**Political parties and leaders:** National Alliance or NA [George ODLUM]; Saint Lucia Freedom Party or SFP [Martinus FRANCOIS]; Saint Lucia Labor Party or SLP [Kenneth ANTHONY]; Sou Tout Apwe Fete Fini or STAFF [Christopher HUNTE]; United Workers Party or UWP [Stephenson KING]

**Political pressure groups and leaders:** NA

**International organization participation:** ACP, C, Caricom, CDB, FAO, G-77, IBRD, ICAO, ICCt (signatory), ICRM, IDA, IFAD, IFC, IFRCS, ILO, IMF, IMO, Interpol, IOC, ISO, ITU, ITUC, MIGA, NAM, OAS, OECS, OIF, OPANAL, OPCW, UN, UNCTAD, UNESCO, UNIDO, UPU, WCL, WCO, WFTU, WHO, WIPO, WMO, WTO

**Diplomatic representation in the US:**
*chief of mission:* Ambassador Michael LOUIS
*chancery:* 3216 New Mexico Avenue NW, Washington, DC 20016
*telephone:* [1] (202) 364-6792 through 6795
*FAX:* [1] (202) 364-6723
*consulate(s) general:* Miami, New York

**Diplomatic representation from the US:** the US does not have an embassy in Saint Lucia; the US Ambassador to Barbados is accredited to Saint Lucia

**Flag description:** blue, with a gold isosceles triangle below a black arrowhead; the upper edges of the arrowhead have a white border

## Economy

**Economy - overview:** The island nation has been able to attract foreign business and investment, especially in its offshore banking and tourism industries, with a surge in foreign direct investment in 2006, attributed to the construction of several tourism projects. Although crops such as bananas, mangos, and avocados continue to be grown for export, tourism provides Saint Lucia's main source of income and the

# Saint Lucia *(continued)*

industry is the island's biggest employer. The tourism sector is likely to face declining revenues with the global economic downturn as US and European travel declines. The manufacturing sector is the most diverse in the Eastern Caribbean area, and the government is trying to revitalize the banana industry, although recent hurricanes have caused exports to contract. Saint Lucia is vulnerable to a variety of external shocks including volatile tourism receipts, natural disasters, and dependence on foreign oil. The public debt-to-GDP ratio is about 70% and high debt servicing obligations constrain the KING administration's ability to respond to adverse external shocks. Economic fundamentals remain solid, even though unemployment needs to be reduced.

**GDP (purchasing power parity):**
$1.801 billion (2008 est.)
$1.761 billion (2007)
$1.732 billion (2006)
*note:* data are in 2008 US dollars

**GDP (official exchange rate):** $1.031 billion (2008 est.)

**GDP - real growth rate:**
2.3% (2008 est.)
1.7% (2007 est.)
4.9% (2006 est.)

**GDP - per capita (PPP):**
$11,300 (2008 est.)
$11,100 (2007 est.)
$11,000 (2006 est.)
*note:* data are in 2008 US dollars

**GDP - composition by sector:**
*agriculture:* 5%
*industry:* 15%
*services:* 80% (2005 est.)

**Labor force:** 43,800 (2001 est.)

**Labor force - by occupation:**
*agriculture:* 21.7%
*industry:* 24.7%
*services:* 53.6% (2002 est.)

**Unemployment rate:**
20% (2003 est.)

**Population below poverty line:** NA%

**Household income or consumption by percentage share:**
*lowest 10%:* NA%
*highest 10%:* NA%

**Budget:**
*revenues:* $141.2 million
*expenditures:* $146.7 million (2000 est.)

**Inflation rate (consumer prices):**
1.9% (2007 est.)

**Central bank discount rate:** 6.5% (31 December 2007)

**Commercial bank prime lending rate:** 10.12% (31 December 2007)

**Stock of money:** $264.7 million (31 December 2007)

**Stock of quasi money:** $720.9 million (31 December 2007)

**Stock of domestic credit:** $1.217 billion (31 December 2007)

**Agriculture - products:** bananas, coconuts, vegetables, citrus, root crops, cocoa

**Industries:** clothing, assembly of electronic components, beverages, corrugated cardboard boxes, tourism; lime processing, coconut processing

**Industrial production growth rate:** NA

**Electricity - production:** 325 million kWh (2007 est.)

**Electricity - consumption:** 289.2 million kWh (2006 est.)

**Electricity - exports:** 0 kWh (2007 est.)

**Electricity - imports:** 0 kWh (2007 est.)

**Oil - production:** 0 bbl/day (2007 est.)

**Oil - consumption:** 2,780 bbl/day (2006 est.)

**Oil - exports:** 0 bbl/day (2005)

**Oil - imports:** 2,631 bbl/day (2005)

**Oil - proved reserves:** 0 bbl (1 January 2006 est.)

**Natural gas - production:** 0 cu m (2007 est.)

**Natural gas - consumption:** 0 cu m (2007 est.)

**Natural gas - exports:** 0 cu m (2007 est.)

**Natural gas - imports:** 0 cu m (2007 est.)

**Natural gas - proved reserves:** 0 cu m (1 January 2006 est.)

**Current account balance:** -$199 million (2007 est.)

**Exports:** $288 million (2006)

**Exports - commodities:** bananas 41%, clothing, cocoa, vegetables, fruits, coconut oil

**Exports - partners:** US 24.5%, France 23.2%, UK 19.3%, Antigua and Barbuda 5%, Dominica 4.9%, Barbados 4.4%, Trinidad and Tobago 4.1% (2007)

**Imports:** $791 million (2006)

**Imports - commodities:** food 23%, manufactured goods 21%, machinery and transportation equipment 19%, chemicals, fuels

**Imports - partners:** Brazil 63.6%, US 10.2%, Trinidad and Tobago 8.2% (2007)

**Debt - external:** $257 million (2004)

**Exchange rates:** East Caribbean dollars (XCD) per US dollar - 2.7 (2007), 2.7 (2006), 2.7 (2005), 2.7 (2004), 2.7 (2003)

## Communications

**Telephones - main lines in use:** 51,100 (2002)

**Telephones - mobile cellular:** 105,700 (2005)

**Telephone system:**
*general assessment:* adequate system
*domestic:* system is automatically switched
*international:* country code - 1-758; the East Caribbean Fiber Optic System (ECFS) and Southern Caribbean fiber optic system (SCF) submarine cables, along with Intelsat from Martinique, carry calls internationally; direct microwave radio relay link with Martinique and Saint Vincent and the Grenadines; tropospheric scatter to Barbados

**Radio broadcast stations:** AM 2, FM 7, shortwave 0 (2003)

**Television broadcast stations:** 2 (1 commercial broadcast station and 1 community antenna television or CATV channel) (2003)

**Internet country code:** .lc

**Internet hosts:** 17 (2008)

**Internet users:** 110,000 (2007)

## Transportation

**Airports:** 2 (2008)

**Airports - with paved runways:**
*total:* 2
*2,438 to 3,047 m:* 1
*1,524 to 2,437 m:* 1 (2008)

**Roadways:**
*total:* 1,210 km (2002)

**Ports and terminals:** Castries, Cul-de-Sac, Vieux-Fort

## Military

**Military branches:** no regular military forces; Royal Saint Lucia Police Force (includes Special Service Unit and Coast Guard) (2007)

**Manpower available for military service:**
*males age 16-49:* 48,358 (2008 est.)

**Manpower fit for military service:**
*males age 16-49:* 32,094
*females age 16-49:* 36,110 (2009 est.)

**Manpower reaching militarily significant age annually:**
*male:* 1,607
*female:* 1,511 (2009 est.)

**Military expenditures:** NA

## Transnational Issues

**Disputes - international:** joins other Caribbean states to counter Venezuela's claim that Aves Island sustains human habitation, a criterion under UNCLOS, which permits Venezuela to extend its EEZ/continental shelf over a large portion of the eastern Caribbean Sea

**Illicit drugs:** transit point for South American drugs destined for the US and Europe

# Saint Martin
*(overseas collectivity of France)*

## Introduction

**Background:** Although sighted by Christopher COLUMBUS in 1493 and claimed for Spain, it was the Dutch who occupied the island in 1631 and set about exploiting its salt deposits. The Spanish retook the island in 1633, but continued to be harassed by the Dutch. The Spanish finally relinquished St. Martin to the French and Dutch, who divided it amongst themselves in 1648. The cultivation of sugar cane introduced slavery to the island in the late 18th century; the practice was not abolished until 1848. The island became a free port in 1939; the tourism industry was dramatically expanded during the 1970s and 1980s. In 2003, the populace of St. Martin voted to secede from Guadeloupe and in 2007, the northern portion of the island became a French overseas collectivity.

## Geography

**Location:** island 300 km southeast of Puerto Rico
**Geographic coordinates:** 18 05 N, 63 57 W
**Map references:** Central America and the Caribbean
**Area:**
*total:* 54.4 sq km
*land:* 54.4 sq km
*water:* NEGL
**Area - comparative:** more than one-third the size of Washington, DC
**Land boundaries:**
*total:* 15 km
*border countries:* Netherlands Antilles (Sint Maarten) 15 km
**Coastline:** 58.9 km (for entire island)
**Climate:** temperature averages 80-85 degrees all year long; low humidity, gentle trade winds, brief, intense rain showers; July-November is the hurricane season

**Elevation extremes:**
*lowest point:* Caribbean Ocean 0 m
*highest point:* Pic du Paradis 424 m
**Natural resources:** salt
**Environment - current issues:** fresh water supply is dependent on desalinization of sea water
**Geography - note:** the island of Saint Martin is the smallest landmass in the world shared by two independent states, the French territory of Saint Martin and the Dutch territory of Sint Maarten

## People

**Population:** 29,820 (July 2009 est.)
**Age structure:**
*0-14 years:* 27% (male 3,991/female 4,048)
*15-64 years:* 67.5% (male 9,596/female 10,532)
*65 years and over:* 5.5% (male 742/female 911) (2009 est.)
**Median age:**
*total:* 30.5 years
*male:* 29.5 years
*female:* 31.3 years (2009 est.)
**Sex ratio:**
*at birth:* 1.04 male(s)/female
*under 15 years:* 0.99 male(s)/female
*15-64 years:* 0.91 male(s)/female
*65 years and over:* 0.81 male(s)/female
*total population:* 0.92 male(s)/female (2009 est.)
**Ethnic groups:** creole (mulatto), black, Guadeloupe Mestizo (French-East Asia), white, East Indian
**Religions:** Roman Catholic, Jehovah's Witness, Protestant, Hindu
**Languages:** French (official language), English, Dutch, French Patois, Spanish, Papiamento (dialect of Netherlands Antilles)

## Government

**Country name:**
*conventional long form:* Overseas Collectivity of Saint Martin
*conventional short form:* Saint Martin
*local long form:* Collectivity d'outre mer de Saint-Martin
*local short form:* Saint-Martin
**Dependency status:** overseas collectivity of France
**Capital:**
*name:* Marigot
*geographical coordinates:* 18 04 N, 63 05 W
*time difference:* UTC-4 (1 hour behind Washington, DC, during Standard Time)
*daylight savings:* +1 hour
**Independence:** none (overseas collectivity of France)
**National holiday:** Bastille Day, 14 July (1789); note -local holiday is Schoalcher Day (Slavery Abolition Day) 12 July (1848)
**Constitution:** 4 October 1958 (French Constitution)
**Legal system:** the laws of France, where applicable, apply
**Suffrage:** 18 years of age, universal

**Executive branch:**
*chief of state:* President Nicolas SARKOZY (since 16 May 2007), represented by Prefect Dominique LACROIX (since 21 March 2007)
*head of government:* President of the Territorial Council Frantz GUMBS (since 5 May 2009)
*cabinet:* Executive Council; note - there is also an advisory economic, social, and cultural council
*election:* French president elected by popular vote to a five-year term; prefect appointed by the French president on the advice of the French Ministry of Interior; president of the Territorial Council is elected by the members of the Council for a five-year term
*election results:* Frantz GUMBS elected president by the Territorial Council on 7 August 2008 but election was declared invalid on 10 April 2009
**Legislative branch:** unicameral Territorial Council (23 seats; members are elected by popular vote to serve five-year terms)
*elections:* last held 1 and 8 July 2007 (next to be held in July 2012)
*election results:* percent of seats by party - UPP 49%, RRR 42.2%, Reussir Saint-Martin 8.9%; seats by party - UPP 16, RRR 6, Reussir Saint-Martin 1
*note:* Saint Martin elects one seat to the French Senate; election last held 21 September 2008 (next to be held in September 2014); results - percent of vote by party - NA; seats by party - UMP 1
**Political parties and leaders:** Union Pour le Progres or UPP [Louis-Constant FLEMING]; Rassemblement Responsabilite Reussite or RRR [Alain RICHARDSON]; Reussir Saint-Martin [Jean-Luc HAMLET]
**Political pressure groups and leaders:** NA
**International organization participation:** UPU, WFTU
**Diplomatic representation in the US:** none (overseas collectivity of France)
**Diplomatic representation from the US:** none (overseas collectivity of France)
**Flag description:** the flag of France is used

## Economy

**Economy - overview:** The economy of Saint Martin centers around tourism with 85% of the labor force engaged in this sector. Over one million visitors come to the island each year with most arriving through the Princess Juliana International Airport in Sint Maarten. No significant agriculture and limited local fishing means that almost all food must be imported. Energy resources and manufactured goods are also imported, primarily from Mexico and the United States. Saint Martin is reported to have the highest per capita income in the Caribbean.
**GDP - composition by sector:**
*agriculture:* 1%
*industry:* 15%
*services:* 84% (2000)
**Labor force - by occupation:** 85% directly or indirectly employed in tourist industry

# Saint Martin *(continued)*

**Industries:** tourism, light industry and manufacturing, heavy industry
**Imports - commodities:** crude petroleum, food, manufactured items
**Exchange rates:** euros (EUR) per US dollar - 0.6827 (2008), 0.7345 (2007), 0.7964 (2006), 0.8041 (2005), 0.8054 (2004)

## Communications

**Telephone system:**
*general assessment:* fully integrated access
*domestic:* direct dial capability with both fixed and wireless systems
*international:* country code - 590; undersea fiber-optic cable provides voice and data connectivity to Puerto Rico and Guadeloupe
**Radio broadcast stations:** AM 0, FM 3, shortwave 0 (2007)
**Internet country code:** .mf; note - .gp, the internet country code for Guadeloupe, and .fr, the internet country code for France, might also be encountered

## Transportation

**Airports:** 1 (2008)
**Airports - with paved runways:**
*total:* 1
*914 to 1,523 m:* 1 (2008)
**Transportation - note:** nearest airport for international flights is Princess Juliana International Airport (SXM) located in Sint Maarten

## Military

**Manpower fit for military service:**
*males age 16-49:* 6,336
*females age 16-49:* 6,925 (2009 est.)
**Manpower reaching militarily significant age annually:**
*male:* 177
*female:* 162 (2009 est.)
**Military - note:** defense is the responsibility of France

# Saint Pierre and Miquelon
*(territorial overseas collectivity of France)*

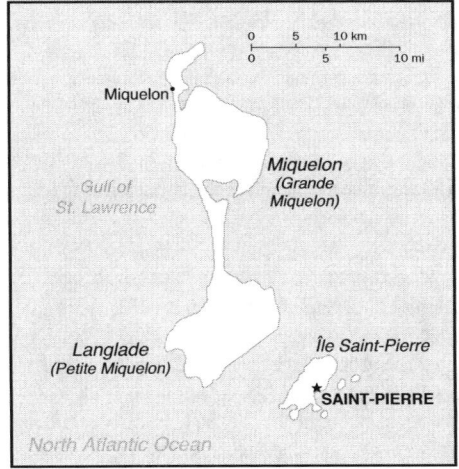

## Introduction

**Background:** First settled by the French in the early 17th century, the islands represent the sole remaining vestige of France's once vast North American possessions.

## Geography

**Location:** Northern North America, islands in the North Atlantic Ocean, south of Newfoundland (Canada)
**Geographic coordinates:** 46 50 N, 56 20 W
**Map references:** North America
**Area:**
*total:* 242 sq km
*land:* 242 sq km
*water:* 0 sq km
*note:* includes eight small islands in the Saint Pierre and the Miquelon groups
**Area - comparative:** 1.5 times the size of Washington, DC
**Land boundaries:** 0 km
**Coastline:** 120 km
**Maritime claims:**
*territorial sea:* 12 nm
*exclusive economic zone:* 200 nm
**Climate:** cold and wet, with much mist and fog; spring and autumn are windy
**Terrain:** mostly barren rock
**Elevation extremes:**
*lowest point:* Atlantic Ocean 0 m
*highest point:* Morne de la Grande Montagne 240 m
**Natural resources:** fish, deepwater ports
**Land use:**
*arable land:* 12.5%
*permanent crops:* 0%
*other:* 87.5% (2005)
**Irrigated land:** NA
**Natural hazards:** persistent fog throughout the year can be a maritime hazard

**Environment - current issues:** recent test drilling for oil in waters around Saint Pierre and Miquelon may bring future development that would impact the environment
**Geography - note:** vegetation scanty

## People

**Population:** 7,051 (July 2009 est.)
**Age structure:**
*0-14 years:* 21.9% (male 788/female 756)
*15-64 years:* 66.5% (male 2,378/female 2,312)
*65 years and over:* 11.6% (male 379/female 438) (2009 est.)
**Median age:**
*total:* 35.2 years
*male:* 34.6 years
*female:* 35.7 years (2009 est.)
**Population growth rate:** 0.085% (2009 est.)
**Birth rate:** 12.76 births/1,000 population (2009 est.)
**Death rate:** 6.81 deaths/1,000 population (2008 est.)
**Net migration rate:** -4.96 migrant(s)/1,000 population (2009 est.)
**Urbanization:**
*urban population:* 89% of total population (2008)
*rate of urbanization:* 0.1% annual rate of change (2005-10 est.)
**Sex ratio:**
*at birth:* 1.05 male(s)/female
*under 15 years:* 1.04 male(s)/female
*15-64 years:* 1.03 male(s)/female
*65 years and over:* 0.86 male(s)/female
*total population:* 1.01 male(s)/female (2009 est.)
**Infant mortality rate:**
*total:* 6.87 deaths/1,000 live births
*male:* 7.86 deaths/1,000 live births
*female:* 5.82 deaths/1,000 live births (2009 est.)
**Life expectancy at birth:**
*total population:* 79.07 years
*male:* 76.69 years
*female:* 81.57 years (2009 est.)
**Total fertility rate:** 1.97 children born/woman (2009 est.)
**HIV/AIDS - adult prevalence rate:** NA
**HIV/AIDS - people living with HIV/AIDS:** NA
**HIV/AIDS - deaths:** NA
**Nationality:**
*noun:* Frenchman(men), Frenchwoman(women)
*adjective:* French
**Ethnic groups:** Basques and Bretons (French fishermen)
**Religions:** Roman Catholic 99%, other 1%
**Languages:** French (official)
**Literacy:**
*definition:* age 15 and over can read and write
*total population:* 99%
*male:* 99%
*female:* 99% (1982 est.)
**Education expenditures:** NA

# Saint Pierre and Miquelon (continued)

## Government

**Country name:**
*conventional long form:* Territorial Collectivity of Saint Pierre and Miquelon
*conventional short form:* Saint Pierre and Miquelon
*local long form:* Departement de Saint-Pierre et Miquelon
*local short form:* Saint-Pierre et Miquelon
**Dependency status:** self-governing territorial overseas collectivity of France
**Government type:** NA
**Capital:**
*name:* Saint-Pierre
*geographic coordinates:* 46 46 N, 56 11 W
*time difference:* UTC-3 (2 hours ahead of Washington, DC during Standard Time)
*daylight saving time:* +1hr, begins second Sunday in March; ends first Sunday in November
**Administrative divisions:** none (territorial overseas collectivity of France); note - there are no first-order administrative divisions as defined by the US Government, but there are two communes - Saint Pierre, Miquelon at the second order
**Independence:** none (territorial collectivity of France; has been under French control since 1763)
**National holiday:** Bastille Day, 14 July (1789)
**Constitution:** 4 October 1958 (French Constitution)
**Legal system:** the laws of France, where applicable, apply
**Suffrage:** 18 years of age; universal
**Executive branch:**
*chief of state:* President Nicolas SARKOZY (since 16 May 2007); represented by Prefect Jean-Pierre BERCOT (since 28 July 2008)
*head of government:* President of the Territorial Council Stephane ARTANO (since 21 February 2007)
*cabinet:* NA
*elections:* French president elected by popular vote for a five-year term; election last held 6 May 2007 (next to be held in 2012); prefect appointed by the French president on the advice of the French Ministry of Interior; president of the Territorial Council is elected by the members of the council
**Legislative branch:** unicameral Territorial Council or Conseil Territorial (19 seats, 15 from Saint Pierre and four from Miquelon; members are elected by popular vote to serve six-year terms)
*elections:* elections last held 19 and 26 in March 2006 (next to be held in March 2012)
*election results:* percent of vote by party - NA; seats by party - AD 16, Cap sur l'Avenir 2, SPM 2000/AM 1
*note:* Saint Pierre and Miquelon elect one seat to the French Senate; elections last held 21 September 2008 (next to be held in September 2014); results - percent of vote by party - NA; seats by party - UMP 1; Saint Pierre and Miquelon also elects one seat to the French National Assembly; elections last held, first round - 10 June 2007, second round - 17 June 2007 (next to be held in 2012); results - percent of vote by party - NA; seats by party - Left Radical Party 1

**Judicial branch:** Superior Tribunal of Appeals or Tribunal Superieur d'Appel
**Political parties and leaders:** Archipelago Tomorrow or AD affiliated with UDF/RPR list; Cap sur l'Avenir affiliated with PRG; Left Radical Party or PRG; Rassemblement pour la Republique or RPR (now UMP); Saint Pierre and Miquelon 2000/Avenir Miquelon or SPM 2000/AM; Socialist Party or PS; Union pour la Democratie Francaise or UDF
**Political pressure groups and leaders:** NA
**International organization participation:** UPU, WFTU
**Diplomatic representation in the US:** none (territorial overseas collectivity of France)
**Diplomatic representation from the US:** none (territorial overseas collectivity of France)
**Flag description:** a yellow sailing ship facing the hoist side rides on a dark blue background with yellow wavy lines under the ship; on the hoist side, a vertical band is divided into three parts: the top part (called ikkurina) is red with a green diagonal cross extending to the corners overlaid by a white cross dividing the rectangle into four sections; the middle part has a white background with an ermine pattern; the third part has a red background with two stylized yellow lions outlined in black, one above the other; these three heraldic arms represent settlement by colonists from the Basque Country (top), Brittany, and Normandy; the flag of France is used for official occasions

## Economy

**Economy - overview:** The inhabitants have traditionally earned their livelihood by fishing and by servicing fishing fleets operating off the coast of Newfoundland. The economy has been declining, however, because of disputes with Canada over fishing quotas and a steady decline in the number of ships stopping at Saint Pierre. In 1992, an arbitration panel awarded the islands an exclusive economic zone of 12,348 sq km to settle a longstanding territorial dispute with Canada, although it represents only 25% of what France had sought. France heavily subsidizes the islands to the great betterment of living standards. The government hopes an expansion of tourism will boost economic prospects. Fish farming, crab fishing, and agriculture are being developed to diversify the local economy. Recent test drilling for oil may pave the way for development of the energy sector.
**GDP (purchasing power parity):**
$48.3 million (2003 est.)
*note:* supplemented by annual payments from France of about $60 million
**GDP (official exchange rate):** $NA
**GDP - real growth rate:** NA%
**GDP - per capita (PPP):**
$7,000 (2001 est.)
**GDP - composition by sector:**
*agriculture:* NA%
*industry:* NA%
*services:* NA%

**Labor force:** 3,450 (2005)
**Labor force - by occupation:**
*agriculture:* 18%
*industry:* 41%
*services:* 41% (1996 est.)
**Unemployment rate:**
10.3% (1999)
**Population below poverty line:** NA%
**Household income or consumption by percentage share:**
*lowest 10%:* NA%
*highest 10%:* NA%
**Budget:**
*revenues:* $70 million
*expenditures:* $60 million (1996 est.)
**Inflation rate (consumer prices):**
8.1% (2005)
**Agriculture - products:** vegetables; poultry, cattle, sheep, pigs; fish
**Industries:** fish processing and supply base for fishing fleets; tourism
**Industrial production growth rate:** NA%
**Electricity - production:** 53 million kWh (2006 est.)
**Electricity - consumption:** 49.29 million kWh (2006 est.)
**Electricity - exports:** 0 kWh (2007 est.)
**Electricity - imports:** 0 kWh (2007 est.)
**Oil - production:** 0 bbl/day (2007 est.)
**Oil - consumption:** 560 bbl/day (2006 est.)
**Oil - exports:** 0 bbl/day (2005)
**Oil - imports:** 556.8 bbl/day (2005)
**Oil - proved reserves:** 0 bbl (1 January 2006 est.)
**Natural gas - production:** 0 cu m (2007 est.)
**Natural gas - consumption:** 0 cu m (2007 est.)
**Natural gas - exports:** 0 cu m (2007 est.)
**Natural gas - imports:** 0 cu m (2007 est.)
**Natural gas - proved reserves:** 0 cu m (1 January 2006 est.)
**Exports:** $5.5 million f.o.b. (2005 est.)
**Exports - commodities:** fish and fish products, soybeans, animal feed, mollusks and crustaceans, fox and mink pelts
**Imports:** $68.2 million f.o.b. (2005 est.)
**Imports - commodities:** meat, clothing, fuel, electrical equipment, machinery, building materials
**Debt - external:** $NA
**Exchange rates:** euros (EUR) per US dollar - 0.6734 (2008 est.), 0.7345 (2007), 0.7964 (2006), 0.8041 (2005), 0.8054 (2004)

## Communications

**Telephones - main lines in use:** 4,800 (2002)
**Telephone system:**
*general assessment:* adequate
*domestic:* NA
*international:* country code - 508; radiotelephone communication with most countries in the world; satellite earth station - 1 in French domestic satellite system

**Radio broadcast stations:** AM 1, FM 4, shortwave 0 (1998)

**Television broadcast stations:** 0 (2 repeaters rebroadcast programs from France, Canada, and the US) (1997)

**Internet country code:** .pm

**Internet hosts:** 0 (2008)

**Internet users:** NA

## Transportation

**Airports:** 2 (2008)

**Airports - with paved runways:**

*total:* 2

*1,524 to 2,437 m:* 1

*914 to 1,523 m:* 1 (2008)

**Roadways:**

*total:* 117 km

*paved:* 80 km

*unpaved:* 37 km (2000)

**Ports and terminals:** Saint-Pierre

## Military

**Manpower fit for military service:**

*males age 16-49:* 1,427

*females age 16-49:* 1,406 (2009 est.)

**Manpower reaching militarily significant age annually:**

*male:* 61

*female:* 57 (2009 est.)

**Military - note:** defense is the responsibility of France

## Transnational Issues

**Disputes - international:** none

# Saint Vincent and the Grenadines

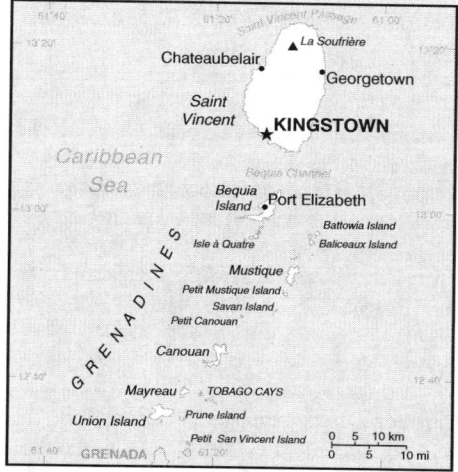

## Introduction

**Background:** Resistance by native Caribs prevented colonization on St. Vincent until 1719. Disputed between France and the United Kingdom for most of the 18th century, the island was ceded to the latter in 1783. Between 1960 and 1962, Saint Vincent and the Grenadines was a separate administrative unit of the Federation of the West Indies. Autonomy was granted in 1969 and independence in 1979.

## Geography

**Location:** Caribbean, islands between the Caribbean Sea and North Atlantic Ocean, north of Trinidad and Tobago

**Geographic coordinates:** 13 15 N, 61 12 W

**Map references:** Central America and the Caribbean

**Area:**

*total:* 389 sq km (Saint Vincent 344 sq km)

*land:* 389 sq km

*water:* 0 sq km

**Area - comparative:** twice the size of Washington, DC

**Land boundaries:** 0 km

**Coastline:** 84 km

**Maritime claims:**

*territorial sea:* 12 nm

*contiguous zone:* 24 nm

*exclusive economic zone:* 200 nm

*continental shelf:* 200 nm

**Climate:** tropical; little seasonal temperature variation; rainy season (May to November)

**Terrain:** volcanic, mountainous

**Elevation extremes:**

*lowest point:* Caribbean Sea 0 m

*highest point:* La Soufriere 1,234 m

**Natural resources:** hydropower, cropland

**Land use:**

*arable land:* 17.95%

*permanent crops:* 17.95%

*other:* 64.1% (2005)

**Irrigated land:** 10 sq km (2003)

**Freshwater withdrawal (domestic/industrial/agricultural):**

*total:* 0.01

*per capita:* 83 cu m/yr (1995)

**Natural hazards:** hurricanes; Soufriere volcano on the island of Saint Vincent is a constant threat

**Environment - current issues:** pollution of coastal waters and shorelines from discharges by pleasure yachts and other effluents; in some areas, pollution is severe enough to make swimming prohibitive

**Environment - international agreements:**

*party to:* Biodiversity, Climate Change, Climate Change-Kyoto Protocol, Desertification, Endangered Species, Environmental Modification, Hazardous Wastes, Law of the Sea, Marine Dumping, Ozone Layer Protection, Ship Pollution, Whaling

*signed, but not ratified:* none of the selected agreements

**Geography - note:** the administration of the islands of the Grenadines group is divided between Saint Vincent and the Grenadines and Grenada; Saint Vincent and the Grenadines is comprised of 32 islands and cays

## People

**Population:** 104,574 (July 2009 est.)

**Age structure:**

*0-14 years:* 25.9% (male 13,637/female 13,425)

*15-64 years:* 66.4% (male 35,693/female 33,701)

*65 years and over:* 7.8% (male 3,659/female 4,459) (2009 est.)

**Median age:**

*total:* 28.9 years

*male:* 29 years

*female:* 28.9 years (2009 est.)

**Population growth rate:** -0.344% (2009 est.)

**Birth rate:** 15.27 births/1,000 population (2009 est.)

**Death rate:** 5.96 deaths/1,000 population (2008 est.)

**Net migration rate:** -11.8 migrant(s)/1,000 population (2009 est.)

**Urbanization:**

*urban population:* 47% of total population (2008)

*rate of urbanization:* 1.3% annual rate of change (2005-10 est.)

**Sex ratio:**

*at birth:* 1.03 male(s)/female

*under 15 years:* 1.02 male(s)/female

*15-64 years:* 1.06 male(s)/female

*65 years and over:* 0.82 male(s)/female

*total population:* 1.03 male(s)/female (2009 est.)

**Infant mortality rate:**

*total:* 15.14 deaths/1,000 live births

*male:* 16.48 deaths/1,000 live births

*female:* 13.76 deaths/1,000 live births (2009 est.)

**Life expectancy at birth:**

*total population:* 73.65 years

*male:* 71.82 years

*female:* 75.54 years (2009 est.)

**Total fertility rate:** 1.98 children born/woman (2009 est.)

# Saint Vincent and the Grenadines (continued)

**HIV/AIDS - adult prevalence rate:** NA
**HIV/AIDS - people living with HIV/AIDS:** NA
**HIV/AIDS - deaths:** NA
**Nationality:**
*noun:* Saint Vincentian(s) or Vincentian(s)
*adjective:* Saint Vincentian or Vincentian
**Ethnic groups:** black 66%, mixed 19%, East Indian 6%, European 4%, Carib Amerindian 2%, other 3%
**Religions:** Anglican 47%, Methodist 28%, Roman Catholic 13%, other (includes Hindu, Seventh-Day Adventist, other Protestant) 12%
**Languages:** English, French patois
**Literacy:**
*definition:* age 15 and over has ever attended school
*total population:* 96%
*male:* 96%
*female:* 96% (1970 est.)
**School life expectancy (primary to tertiary education):**
*total:* 12 years
*male:* 12 years
*female:* 12 years (2005)
**Education expenditures:** 8.1% of GDP (2005)

## Government

**Country name:**
*conventional long form:* none
*conventional short form:* Saint Vincent and the Grenadines
**Government type:** parliamentary democracy and a Commonwealth realm
**Capital:**
*name:* Kingstown
*geographic coordinates:* 13 09 N, 61 14 W
*time difference:* UTC-4 (1 hour ahead of Washington, DC during Standard Time)
**Administrative divisions:** 6 parishes; Charlotte, Grenadines, Saint Andrew, Saint David, Saint George, Saint Patrick
**Independence:** 27 October 1979 (from the UK)
**National holiday:** Independence Day, 27 October (1979)
**Constitution:** 27 October 1979
**Legal system:** based on English common law; has not accepted compulsory ICJ jurisdiction
**Suffrage:** 18 years of age; universal
**Executive branch:**
*chief of state:* Queen ELIZABETH II (since 6 February 1952); represented by Governor General Sir Fredrick Nathaniel BALLANTYNE (since 2 September 2002)
*head of government:* Prime Minister Ralph E. GONSALVES (since 29 March 2001)
*cabinet:* Cabinet appointed by the governor general on the advice of the prime minister
*elections:* the monarch is hereditary; the governor general is appointed by the monarch; following legislative elections, the leader of the majority party is usually appointed prime minister by the governor general; deputy prime minister appointed by the governor general on the advice of the prime minister

**Legislative branch:** unicameral House of Assembly (21 seats, 15 elected representatives and six appointed senators; representatives are elected by popular vote to serve five-year terms)
*elections:* last held 7 December 2005 (next to be held in 2010)
*election results:* percent of vote by party - ULP 55.3%, NDP 44.7%; seats by party - ULP 12, NDP 3
**Judicial branch:** Eastern Caribbean Supreme Court (consisting of a High Court and Court of Appeals; based on Saint Lucia; two judges of the Supreme Court reside in Saint Vincent and the Grenadines)
**Political parties and leaders:** New Democratic Party or NDP [Arnhim EUSTACE]; Unity Labor Party or ULP [Ralph GONSALVES] (formed by the coalition of Saint Vincent Labor Party or SVLP and the Movement for National Unity or MNU)
**Political pressure groups and leaders:** NA
**International organization participation:** ACP, C, Caricom, CDB, FAO, G-77, IBRD, ICAO, ICCt, ICRM, IDA, IFAD, IFRCS, ILO, IMF, IMO, Interpol, IOC, ISO (subscriber), ITU, ITUC, MIGA, NAM, OAS, OECS, OPANAL, OPCW, UN, UNCTAD, UNESCO, UNIDO, UPU, WCL, WFTU, WHO, WIPO, WTO
**Diplomatic representation in the US:**
*chief of mission:* Ambassador La Celia A. PRINCE
*chancery:* 3216 New Mexico Avenue NW, Washington, DC 20016
*telephone:* [1] (202) 364-6730
*FAX:* [1] (202) 364-6736
*consulate(s) general:* New York
**Diplomatic representation from the US:** the US does not have an embassy in Saint Vincent and the Grenadines; the US Ambassador to Barbados is accredited to Saint Vincent and the Grenadines
**Flag description:** three vertical bands of blue (hoist side), gold (double width), and green; the gold band bears three green diamonds arranged in a V pattern

## Economy

**Economy - overview:** Economic growth slowed in 2008 after reaching a 10-year high of nearly 7% in 2006, and will likely slow in 2009 with the global economic downturn, though it will be above average for Latin America. Success of the economy hinges upon seasonal variations in agriculture, tourism, and construction activity as well as remittance inflows. Much of the workforce is employed in banana production and tourism, but persistent high unemployment has prompted many to leave the islands. This lower-middle-income country is vulnerable to natural disasters - tropical storms wiped out substantial portions of crops in 1994, 1995, and 2002. In 2007, the islands had more than 200,000 tourist arrivals, mostly to the Grenadines. Saint Vincent is home to a small offshore banking sector and has moved to adopt international regulatory

standards. The government's ability to invest in social programs and respond to external shocks is constrained by its high debt burden - 25% of current revenues are directed towards debt servicing. An agreement with Italy to write-off debt reduced the public debt-to-GDP ratio to about 70%. The GONSALVES administration is directing government resources to infrastructure projects, including a new international airport that is expected to be completed in 2011.
**GDP (purchasing power parity):**
$1.103 billion (2008 est.)
$1.05 billion (2007)
$984.9 million (2006)
*note:* data are in 2008 US dollars
**GDP (official exchange rate):** $597 million (2008 est.)
**GDP - real growth rate:**
5% (2008 est.)
6.6% (2007 est.)
6.9% (2006 est.)
**GDP - per capita (PPP):**
$10,500 (2008 est.)
$10,000 (2007 est.)
$9,300 (2006 est.)
*note:* data are in 2008 US dollars
**GDP - composition by sector:**
*agriculture:* 10%
*industry:* 26%
*services:* 64% (2001 est.)
**Labor force:** 41,680 (1991 est.)
**Labor force - by occupation:**
*agriculture:* 26%
*industry:* 17%
*services:* 57% (1980 est.)
**Unemployment rate:**
15% (2001 est.)
**Population below poverty line:** NA%
**Household income or consumption by percentage share:**
*lowest 10%:* NA%
*highest 10%:* NA%
**Budget:**
*revenues:* $94.6 million
*expenditures:* $85.8 million (2000 est.)
**Inflation rate (consumer prices):**
6.1% (2007 est.)
**Central bank discount rate:** 6.5% (31 December 2007)
**Commercial bank prime lending rate:** 9.61% (31 December 2007)
**Stock of money:** $155.5 million (31 December 2007)
**Stock of quasi money:** $280.2 million (31 December 2007)
**Stock of domestic credit:** $387.8 million (31 December 2007)
**Agriculture - products:** bananas, coconuts, sweet potatoes, spices; small numbers of cattle, sheep, pigs, goats; fish
**Industries:** food processing, cement, furniture, clothing, starch

# Saint Vincent and the Grenadines (continued)

**Electricity - production:** 129 million kWh (2006 est.)
**Electricity - consumption:** 120 million kWh (2006 est.)
**Electricity - exports:** 0 kWh (2007 est.)
**Electricity - imports:** 0 kWh (2007 est.)
**Oil - production:** 0 bbl/day (2007 est.)
**Oil - consumption:** 1,570 bbl/day (2006 est.)
**Oil - exports:** 0 bbl/day (2005)
**Oil - imports:** 1,460 bbl/day (2005)
**Oil - proved reserves:** 0 bbl (1 January 2006 est.)
**Natural gas - production:** 0 cu m (2007 est.)
**Natural gas - consumption:** 0 cu m (2007 est.)
**Natural gas - exports:** 0 cu m (2007 est.)
**Natural gas - imports:** 0 cu m (2007 est.)
**Natural gas - proved reserves:** 0 cu m (1 January 2006 est.)
**Current account balance:** -$149 million (2007 est.)
**Exports:** $193 million (2006)
**Exports - commodities:** bananas, eddoes and dasheen (taro), arrowroot starch; tennis racquets
**Exports - partners:** Greece 28.4%, Italy 14.6%, France 12%, UK 7.5%, Trinidad and Tobago 4.8%, Spain 4.6%, Germany 4.3%, Saint Lucia 4.2% (2007)
**Imports:** $578 million (2006)
**Imports - commodities:** foodstuffs, machinery and equipment, chemicals and fertilizers, minerals and fuels
**Imports - partners:** Singapore 15.9%, Trinidad and Tobago 14.9%, Italy 13.3%, US 13%, China 5% (2007)
**Debt - external:** $223 million (2004)
**Exchange rates:** East Caribbean dollars (XCD) per US dollar - 2.7 (2007), 2.7 (2006), 2.7 (2005), 2.7 (2004), 2.7 (2003)

## Communications

**Telephones - main lines in use:** 22,800 (2007)
**Telephones - mobile cellular:** 104,000 (2007)
**Telephone system:**
*general assessment:* adequate system
*domestic:* islandwide, fully automatic telephone system; VHF/UHF radiotelephone from Saint Vincent to the other islands of the Grenadines; mobile-cellular teledensity roughly 100 telephones per 100 persons
*international:* country code - 1-784; the East Caribbean Fiber Optic System (ECFS) and Southern Caribbean fiber optic system (SCF) submarine cables carry international calls; connectivity also provided by VHF/UHF radiotelephone from Saint Vincent to Barbados; SHF radiotelephone to Grenada and Saint Lucia; access to Intelsat earth station in Martinique through Saint Lucia
**Radio broadcast stations:** AM 1, FM 6, shortwave 0 (2004)
**Television broadcast stations:** 1 (plus 3 repeaters) (2004)
**Internet country code:** .vc
**Internet hosts:** 124 (2008)
**Internet users:** 57,000 (2007)

## Transportation

**Airports:** 6 (2008)
**Airports - with paved runways:**
*total:* 5
*914 to 1,523 m:* 4
*under 914 m:* 1 (2008)
**Airports - with unpaved runways:**
*total:* 1
*under 914 m:* 1 (2008)
**Roadways:**
*total:* 829 km
*paved:* 580 km
*unpaved:* 249 km (2003)
**Merchant marine:**
*total:* 525
*by type:* barge carrier 1, bulk carrier 83, cargo 315, carrier 20, chemical tanker 2, liquefied gas 6, passenger 3, passenger/cargo 17, petroleum tanker 17, refrigerated cargo 20, roll on/roll off 18, specialized tanker 2, container 21
*foreign-owned:* 476 (Austria 2, Barbados 1, Belgium 8, Bulgaria 15, Canada 1, China 94, Croatia 7, Cyprus 1, Czech Republic 1, Denmark 16, Egypt 3, Estonia 16, France 6, Germany 3, Gibraltar 1, Greece 71, Guyana 2, Hong Kong 6, Iceland 7, India 7, Iran 1, Israel 2, Italy 17, Japan 3, Kenya 2, Latvia 17, Lebanon 6, Lithuania 9, Monaco 5, Montenegro 1, Namibia 1, Netherlands 3, Norway 13, Poland 1, Puerto Rico 1, Romania 1, Russia 21, Singapore 4, Slovenia 5, South Africa 1, Sweden 2, Switzerland 6, Syria 13, Turkey 20, Ukraine 11, UAE 9, UK 14, US 18, Venezuela 1) (2008)
**Ports and terminals:** Kingstown

## Military

**Military branches:** no regular military forces; Royal Saint Vincent and the Grenadines Police Force, Coast Guard (2007)
**Manpower available for military service:**
*males age 16-49:* 34,373 (2008 est.)
**Manpower fit for military service:**
*males age 16-49:* 22,975
*females age 16-49:* 22,250 (2009 est.)
**Manpower reaching militarily significant age annually:**
*male:* 1,020
*female:* 1,009 (2009 est.)
**Military expenditures:** NA

## Transnational Issues

**Disputes - international:** joins other Caribbean states to counter Venezuela's claim that Aves Island sustains human habitation, a criterion under UNCLOS, which permits Venezuela to extend its EEZ/continental shelf over a large portion of the eastern Caribbean Sea
**Illicit drugs:** transshipment point for South American drugs destined for the US and Europe; small-scale cannabis cultivation

# Samoa

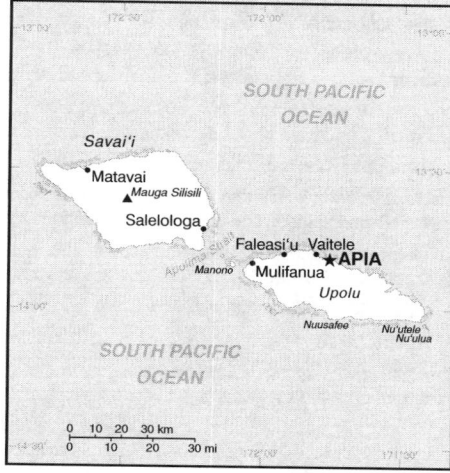

## Introduction

**Background:** New Zealand occupied the German protectorate of Western Samoa at the outbreak of World War I in 1914. It continued to administer the islands as a mandate and then as a trust territory until 1962, when the islands became the first Polynesian nation to reestablish independence in the 20th century. The country dropped the "Western" from its name in 1997.

## Geography

**Location:** Oceania, group of islands in the South Pacific Ocean, about half way between Hawaii and New Zealand
**Geographic coordinates:** 13 35 S, 172 20 W
**Map references:** Oceania
**Area:**
*total:* 2,944 sq km
*land:* 2,934 sq km
*water:* 10 sq km
**Area - comparative:** slightly smaller than Rhode Island
**Land boundaries:** 0 km
**Coastline:** 403 km
**Maritime claims:**
*territorial sea:* 12 nm
*contiguous zone:* 24 nm
*exclusive economic zone:* 200 nm
**Climate:** tropical; rainy season (November to April), dry season (May to October)
**Terrain:** two main islands (Savaii, Upolu) and several smaller islands and uninhabited islets; narrow coastal plain with volcanic, rocky, rugged mountains in interior
**Elevation extremes:**
*lowest point:* Pacific Ocean 0 m
*highest point:* Mauga Silisili (Savaii) 1,857 m
**Natural resources:** hardwood forests, fish, hydropower

# Samoa (continued)

**Land use:**
*arable land:* 21.13%
*permanent crops:* 24.3%
*other:* 54.57% (2005)
**Irrigated land:** NA
**Natural hazards:** occasional typhoons; active volcanism
**Environment - current issues:** soil erosion, deforestation, invasive species, overfishing
**Environment - international agreements:**
*party to:* Biodiversity, Climate Change, Climate Change-Kyoto Protocol, Desertification, Hazardous Wastes, Law of the Sea, Ozone Layer Protection, Ship Pollution, Wetlands
*signed, but not ratified:* none of the selected agreements
**Geography - note:** occupies an almost central position within Polynesia

## People

**Population:** 219,998
*note:* prior estimates used official net migration data by sex, but a highly unusual pattern for 1993 lead to a significant imbalance in the sex ratios (more men and fewer women) and a seeming reduction in the female population; the revised total was calculated using a 1993 number that was an average of the 1992 and 1994 migration figures (July 2009 est.)
**Age structure:**
*0-14 years:* 37.6% (male 42,117/female 40,603)
*15-64 years:* 56.7% (male 65,541/female 59,292)
*65 years and over:* 5.7% (male 5,538/female 6,907) (2009 est.)
**Median age:**
*total:* 20.8 years
*male:* 21 years
*female:* 20.5 years (2009 est.)
**Population growth rate:** 1.346% (2009 est.)
**Birth rate:** 28.06 births/1,000 population (2009 est.)
**Death rate:** 5.84 deaths/1,000 population (2008 est.)
**Net migration rate:** -8.81 migrant(s)/1,000 population (2009 est.)
**Urbanization:**
*urban population:* 23% of total population (2008)
*rate of urbanization:* 1.7% annual rate of change (2005-10 est.)
**Sex ratio:**
*at birth:* 1.05 male(s)/female
*under 15 years:* 1.04 male(s)/female
*15-64 years:* 1.1 male(s)/female
*65 years and over:* 0.8 male(s)/female
*total population:* 1.06 male(s)/female (2009 est.)
**Infant mortality rate:**
*total:* 24.22 deaths/1,000 live births
*male:* 28.61 deaths/1,000 live births
*female:* 19.6 deaths/1,000 live births (2009 est.)
**Life expectancy at birth:**
*total population:* 71.86 years
*male:* 69.03 years
*female:* 74.84 years (2009 est.)

**Total fertility rate:** 4.16 children born/woman (2009 est.)
**HIV/AIDS - adult prevalence rate:** NA
**HIV/AIDS - people living with HIV/AIDS:** NA
**HIV/AIDS - deaths:** NA
**Nationality:**
*noun:* Samoan(s)
*adjective:* Samoan
**Ethnic groups:** Samoan 92.6%, Euronesians (persons of European and Polynesian blood) 7%, Europeans 0.4% (2001 census)
**Religions:** Congregationalist 34.8%, Roman Catholic 19.6%, Methodist 15%, Latter-Day Saints 12.7%, Assembly of God 6.6%, Seventh-Day Adventist 3.5%, Worship Centre 1.3%, other Christian 4.5%, other 1.9%, unspecified 0.1% (2001 census)
**Languages:** Samoan (Polynesian), English
**Literacy:**
*definition:* age 15 and over can read and write
*total population:* 99.7%
*male:* 99.6%
*female:* 99.7% (2003 est.)
**School life expectancy (primary to tertiary education):**
*total:* 12 years
*male:* 12 years
*female:* 12 years (2001)
**Education expenditures:** 4.3% of GDP (2002)

## Government

**Country name:**
*conventional long form:* Independent State of Samoa
*conventional short form:* Samoa
*local long form:* Malo Sa'oloto Tuto'atasi o Samoa
*local short form:* Samoa
*former:* Western Samoa
**Government type:** parliamentary democracy
**Capital:**
*name:* Apia
*geographic coordinates:* 13 50 S, 171 44 W
*time difference:* UTC-11 (6 hours behind Washington, DC during Standard Time)
**Administrative divisions:** 11 districts; A'ana, Aiga-i-le-Tai, Atua, Fa'asaleleaga, Gaga'emauga, Gagaifomauga, Palauli, Satupa'itea, Tuamasaga, Va'a-o-Fonoti, Vaisigano
**Independence:** 1 January 1962 (from New Zealand-administered UN trusteeship)
**National holiday:** Independence Day Celebration, 1 June (1962); note - 1 January 1962 is the date of independence from the New Zealand-administered UN trusteeship; it is observed in June
**Constitution:** 1 January 1962
**Legal system:** based on English common law and local customs; judicial review of legislative acts with respect to fundamental rights of the citizen; has not accepted compulsory ICJ jurisdiction
**Suffrage:** 21 years of age; universal
**Executive branch:**
*chief of state:* TUIATUA Tupua Tamasese Efi (since 20 June 2007)

*head of government:* Prime Minister Sailele Malielegaoi TUILA'EPA (since 1998); Deputy Prime Minister MISA Telefoni (since 2001)
*cabinet:* Cabinet consists of 12 members appointed by the chief of state on the prime minister's advice
*elections:* chief of state is elected by the Legislative Assembly to serve a five-year term (no term limits); election last held 15 June 2007 (next to be held in 2012); following legislative elections, the leader of the majority party is usually appointed prime minister by the chief of state with the approval of the Legislative Assembly
*election results:* TUIATUA Tupua Tamasese Efi unanimously elected by the Legislative Assembly
**Legislative branch:** unicameral Legislative Assembly or Fono (49 seats, 47 elected by voters affiliated with traditional village-based electoral districts, 2 elected by independent, mostly non-Samoan or part-Samoan, voters who cannot, (or choose not to) establish a village affiliation; only chiefs (matai) may stand for election to the Fono from the 47 village-based electorates; members serve five-year terms)
*elections:* election last held 31 March 2006 (next election to be held not later than March 2011)
*election results:* percent of vote by party - NA; seats by party - HRPP 35, SDUP 10, independents 4
**Judicial branch:** Court of Appeal; Supreme Court; District Court; Land and Titles Court
**Political parties and leaders:** Human Rights Protection Party or HRPP [Sailele Malielegaoi TUILA'EPA]; Samoa Christian Party or TCP [Tuala Tiresa MALIETOA]; Samoa Democratic United Party or SDUP [LE MAMEA Ropati]; Samoa Party or SP [Su'a Rimoni Ah CHONG]; Samoa Progressive Political Party or SPPP [Toeolesulusulu SIUEVA]
**Political pressure groups and leaders:** NA
**International organization participation:** ACP, ADB, C, FAO, G-77, IBRD, ICAO, ICCt, ICRM, IDA, IFAD, IFC, IFRCS, ILO, IMF, IMO, IOC, IPU, ITU, ITUC, MIGA, OPCW, PIF, Sparteca, SPC, UN, UNCTAD, UNESCO, UPU, WCO, WHO, WIPO, WMO, WTO (observer)
**Diplomatic representation in the US:**
*chief of mission:* Ambassador Aliioaiga Feturi ELISAIA
*chancery:* 800 Second Avenue, Suite 400D, New York, NY 10017
*telephone:* [1] (212) 599-6196 through 6197
*FAX:* [1] (212) 599-0797
*consulate(s) general:* Pago Pago (American Samoa)
**Diplomatic representation from the US:**
*chief of mission:* none; US Ambassador to New Zealand is accredited to Samoa
*embassy:* Accident Corporation Building, 5th Floor, Matafele, Apia
*mailing address:* P. O. Box 3430, Matafele, Apia
*telephone:* [685] 21436/21631/21452/22696
*FAX:* [685] 22030
**Flag description:** red with a blue rectangle in the upper hoist-side quadrant bearing five white five-pointed stars representing the Southern Cross constellation

# Samoa (continued)

## Economy

**Economy - overview:** The economy of Samoa has traditionally been dependent on development aid, family remittances from overseas, agriculture, and fishing. The country is vulnerable to devastating storms. Agriculture employs two-thirds of the labor force and furnishes 90% of exports, featuring coconut cream, coconut oil, and copra. The fish catch declined during the El Nino of 2002-03 but returned to normal by mid-2005. The manufacturing sector mainly processes agricultural products. One factory in the Foreign Trade Zone employs 3,000 people to make automobile electrical harnesses for an assembly plant in Australia. Tourism is an expanding sector accounting for 25% of GDP; 122,000 tourists visited the islands in 2007. The Samoan Government has called for deregulation of the financial sector, encouragement of investment, and continued fiscal discipline, while at the same time protecting the environment. Observers point to the flexibility of the labor market as a basic strength for future economic advances. Foreign reserves are in a relatively healthy state, the external debt is stable, and inflation is low.

**GDP (purchasing power parity):**
$1.057 billion (2008 est.)
$1.024 billion (2007)
$992.7 million (2006)
*note:* data are in 2008 US dollars

**GDP (official exchange rate):** $537 million (2008 est.)

**GDP - real growth rate:**
3.3% (2008 est.)
3.1% (2007 est.)
2.2% (2006 est.)

**GDP - per capita (PPP):**
$4,900 (2008 est.)
$4,800 (2007 est.)
$4,700 (2006 est.)
*note:* data are in 2008 US dollars

**GDP - composition by sector:**
*agriculture:* 11.6%
*industry:* 13.1%
*services:* 75.3% (2004 est.)

**Labor force:** 90,000 (2000 est.)

**Labor force - by occupation:**
*agriculture:* NA%
*industry:* NA%
*services:* NA%

**Unemployment rate:**
NA%

**Population below poverty line:** NA%

**Household income or consumption by percentage share:**
*lowest 10%:* NA%
*highest 10%:* NA%

**Budget:**
*revenues:* $171.3 million
*expenditures:* $78.1 million (FY04/05 est.)

**Inflation rate (consumer prices):**
6% (2007 est.)

**Commercial bank prime lending rate:** 12.65% (31 December 2007)

**Stock of money:** $69.97 million (31 December 2007)

**Stock of quasi money:** $168.7 million (31 December 2007)

**Stock of domestic credit:** $215.1 million (31 December 2007)

**Market value of publicly traded shares:** $NA

**Agriculture - products:** coconuts, bananas, taro, yams, coffee, cocoa

**Industries:** food processing, building materials, auto parts

**Industrial production growth rate:** 2.8% (2000)

**Electricity - production:** 109 million kWh (2006 est.)

**Electricity - consumption:** 101.4 million kWh (2006 est.)

**Electricity - exports:** 0 kWh (2007 est.)

**Electricity - imports:** 0 kWh (2007 est.)

**Oil - production:** 0 bbl/day (2007 est.)

**Oil - consumption:** 1,130 bbl/day (2006 est.)

**Oil - exports:** 0 bbl/day (2005)

**Oil - imports:** 1,128 bbl/day (2005)

**Oil - proved reserves:** 0 bbl (1 January 2006 est.)

**Natural gas - production:** 0 cu m (2007 est.)

**Natural gas - consumption:** 0 cu m (2007 est.)

**Natural gas - exports:** 0 cu m (2007 est.)

**Natural gas - imports:** 0 cu m (2007 est.)

**Natural gas - proved reserves:** 0 cu m (1 January 2006 est.)

**Current account balance:** -$24 million (2007 est.)

**Exports:** $131 million f.o.b. (2006)

**Exports - commodities:** fish, coconut oil and cream, copra, taro, automotive parts, garments, beer

**Exports - partners:** Australia 48.1%, American Samoa 30%, Taiwan 8% (2007)

**Imports:** $324 million f.o.b. (2006)

**Imports - commodities:** machinery and equipment, industrial supplies, foodstuffs

**Imports - partners:** NZ 22.1%, Fiji 17.2%, Singapore 16.1%, Australia 7.9%, Japan 6.8%, Indonesia 5.4%, US 5.3% (2007)

**Reserves of foreign exchange and gold:** $70.15 million (FY03/04)

**Debt - external:** $177 million (2004)

**Exchange rates:** tala (SAT) per US dollar - NA (2007), 2.7594 (2006), 2.7103 (2005), 2.7807 (2004), 2.9732 (2003)

## Communications

**Telephones - main lines in use:** 19,500 (2005)

**Telephones - mobile cellular:** 86,000 (2007)

**Telephone system:**
*general assessment:* adequate
*domestic:* combined fixed-line and mobile-cellular teledensity roughly 50 telephones per 100 persons
*international:* country code - 685; satellite earth station -1 Intelsat (Pacific Ocean)

**Radio broadcast stations:** AM 2, FM 5, shortwave 0 (2004)

**Television broadcast stations:** 2 (2002)

**Internet country code:** .ws

**Internet hosts:** 11,307 (2008)

**Internet users:** 8,000 (2006)

## Transportation

**Airports:** 4 (2008)

**Airports - with paved runways:**
*total:* 3
*2,438 to 3,047 m:* 1
*under 914 m:* 2 (2008)

**Airports - with unpaved runways:**
*total:* 1
*under 914 m:* 1 (2008)

**Roadways:**
*total:* 2,337 km
*paved:* 332 km
*unpaved:* 2,005 km (2001)

**Merchant marine:**
*total:* 1
*by type:* cargo 1
*foreign-owned:* 1 (Cyprus 1) (2008)

**Ports and terminals:** Apia

## Military

**Military branches:** no regular military forces; Samoa Police Force (2008)

**Manpower available for military service:**
*males age 16-49:* 53,417 (2008 est.)

**Manpower fit for military service:**
*males age 16-49:* 43,169
*females age 16-49:* 40,957 (2009 est.)

**Manpower reaching militarily significant age annually:**
*male:* 2,597
*female:* 2,477 (2009 est.)

**Military expenditures:** NA

**Military - note:** Samoa has no formal defense structure or regular armed forces; informal defense ties exist with NZ, which is required to consider any Samoan request for assistance under the 1962 Treaty of Friendship

## Transnational Issues

**Disputes - international:** none

# San Marino

## Introduction

**Background:** The third smallest state in Europe (after the Holy See and Monaco), San Marino also claims to be the world's oldest republic. According to tradition, it was founded by a Christian stonemason named Marinus in A.D. 301. San Marino's foreign policy is aligned with that of Italy; social and political trends in the republic also track closely with those of its larger neighbor.

## Geography

**Location:** Southern Europe, an enclave in central Italy
**Geographic coordinates:** 43 46 N, 12 25 E
**Map references:** Europe
**Area:**
*total:* 61.2 sq km
*land:* 61.2 sq km
*water:* 0 sq km
**Area - comparative:** about one third times the size of Washington, DC
**Land boundaries:**
*total:* 39 km
*border countries:* Italy 39 km
**Coastline:** 0 km (landlocked)
**Maritime claims:** none (landlocked)
**Climate:** Mediterranean; mild to cool winters; warm, sunny summers
**Terrain:** rugged mountains
**Elevation extremes:**
*lowest point:* Torrente Ausa 55 m
*highest point:* Monte Titano 755 m
**Natural resources:** building stone
**Land use:**
*arable land:* 16.67%
*permanent crops:* 0%
*other:* 83.33% (2005)
**Irrigated land:** NA
**Natural hazards:** NA

**Environment - current issues:** NA
**Environment - international agreements:**
*party to:* Biodiversity, Climate Change, Desertification, Whaling
*signed, but not ratified:* Air Pollution
**Geography - note:** landlocked; smallest independent state in Europe after the Holy See and Monaco; dominated by the Apennines

## People

**Population:** 30,324 (July 2009 est.)
**Age structure:**
*0-14 years:* 16.8% (male 2,636/female 2,451)
*15-64 years:* 65.8% (male 9,539/female 10,428)
*65 years and over:* 17.4% (male 2,273/female 2,997) (2009 est.)
**Median age:**
*total:* 41.5 years
*male:* 41.1 years
*female:* 41.9 years (2009 est.)
**Population growth rate:** 1.148% (2009 est.)
**Birth rate:** 9.63 births/1,000 population (2009 est.)
**Death rate:** 8.37 deaths/1,000 population (2008 est.)
**Net migration rate:** 10.32 migrant(s)/1,000 population (2009 est.)
**Urbanization:**
*urban population:* 94% of total population (2008)
*rate of urbanization:* 0.9% annual rate of change (2005-10 est.)
**Sex ratio:**
*at birth:* 1.09 male(s)/female
*under 15 years:* 1.08 male(s)/female
*15-64 years:* 0.92 male(s)/female
*65 years and over:* 0.76 male(s)/female
*total population:* 0.91 male(s)/female (2009 est.)
**Infant mortality rate:**
*total:* 5.34 deaths/1,000 live births
*male:* 5.76 deaths/1,000 live births
*female:* 4.88 deaths/1,000 live births (2009 est.)
**Life expectancy at birth:**
*total population:* 81.97 years
*male:* 78.53 years
*female:* 85.72 years (2009 est.)
**Total fertility rate:** 1.36 children born/woman (2009 est.)
**HIV/AIDS - adult prevalence rate:** NA
**HIV/AIDS - people living with HIV/AIDS:** NA
**HIV/AIDS - deaths:** NA
**Nationality:**
*noun:* Sammarinese (singular and plural)
*adjective:* Sammarinese
**Ethnic groups:** Sammarinese, Italian
**Religions:** Roman Catholic
**Languages:** Italian
**Literacy:**
*definition:* age 10 and over can read and write
*total population:* 96%
*male:* 97%
*female:* 95%
**Education expenditures:** NA

## Government

**Country name:**
*conventional long form:* Republic of San Marino
*conventional short form:* San Marino
*local long form:* Repubblica di San Marino
*local short form:* San Marino
**Government type:** republic
**Capital:**
*name:* San Marino
*geographic coordinates:* 43 56 N, 12 25 E
*time difference:* UTC+1 (6 hours ahead of Washington, DC during Standard Time)
*daylight saving time:* +1hr, begins last Sunday in March; ends last Sunday in October
**Administrative divisions:** 9 municipalities (castelli, singular - castello); Acquaviva, Borgo Maggiore, Chiesanuova, Domagnano, Faetano, Fiorentino, Montegiardino, San Marino Citta, Serravalle
**Independence:** 3 September 301
**National holiday:** Founding of the Republic, 3 September (AD 301)
**Constitution:** 8 October 1600; electoral law of 1926 serves some of the functions of a constitution
**Legal system:** based on civil law system with Italian law influences; has not accepted compulsory ICJ jurisdiction
**Suffrage:** 18 years of age; universal
**Executive branch:**
*chief of state:* Co-chiefs of State Captain Regent Massimo CENCI and Captain Regent Oscar MINA (for the period 1 April-30 September 2009)
*head of government:* Secretary of State for Foreign and Political Affairs Antonella MULARONI (since 3 December 2008)
*cabinet:* Congress of State elected by the Great and General Council for a five-year term
*elections:* co-chiefs of state (captains regent) elected by the Great and General Council for a six-month term; election last held in March 2009 (next to be held in September 2009); secretary of state for foreign and political affairs elected by the Great and General Council for a five-year term; election last held 9 November 2008 (next to be held by 2013)
*election results:* Massimo CENCI and Oscar MINA elected captains regent; percent of legislative vote - NA; Antonella MULARONI elected secretary of state for foreign and political affairs; percent of legislative vote - NA
*note:* the popularly elected parliament (Grand and General Council) selects two of its members to serve as the Captains Regent (co-chiefs of state) for a six-month period; they preside over meetings of the Grand and General Council and its cabinet (Congress of State), which has 10 other members, all selected by the Grand and General Council; assisting the captains regent are 10 secretaries of state; the secretary of state for Foreign Affairs has assumed some prime ministerial roles
**Legislative branch:** unicameral Grand and General Council or Consiglio Grande e Generale (60 seats; members are elected by popular vote to serve five-year terms)

*elections:* last held 9 November 2008 (next to be held by June 2013)

*election results:* percent of vote by party - Pact for San Marino coalition 54.2%: PDCS 31.9%, AP 11.5%, Freedom List 6.3%, San Marino Union of Moderates 4.2%; Reforms and Freedom coalition 45.8%: Party of Socialists and Democrats 32%, United Left 8.6%, Democrats of the Center 4.9%; seats by party - Pact for San Marino coalition 35: PDCS 22, AP 7, the Freedom List 4, San Marino Union of Moderates 2; Reforms and Freedom coalition 25: Party of Socialists and Democrats 18, United Left 5, Democrats of the Center 2

**Judicial branch:** Council of Twelve or Consiglio dei XII

**Political parties and leaders:** Christian Democrats or PDCS [Pasquale VALENTINI]; Communist Refoundation or RC [Ivan FOSHI]; Democrats of the Center or DdC [Giovanni LONGERNINI]; Freedom List (including NPS and We Sammarinesi or NS [Gabriele GATTEI]; New Socialist Party or NPS [Augusto CASALI]; Party of Socialists and Democrats or PDS [Paride ANDREOLI]; Popular Alliance or AP [Carlo FRANCIOSI]; Union of Moderates (including National Alliance or ANS [Glcuco SANSOVINI] and San Marino Populars or pop [Romeo MORRI and Angela VENTURINI]; United Left of SU [Alessandro ROSSI]

**Political pressure groups and leaders:** NA

**International organization participation:** CE, FAO, IBRD, ICAO, ICCt, ICRM, IFRCS, ILO, IMF, IMO, Interpol, IOC, IOM (observer), IPU, ITU, ITUC, OPCW, OSCE, UN, UNCTAD, UNESCO, Union Latina, UNWTO, UPU, WFTU, WHO, WIPO

**Diplomatic representation in the US:**
*chief of mission:* Ambassador Paolo RONDELLI
*chancery:* 888 27th Street NW, Suite 900, Washington, DC 20006
*telephone:* 202-337-2260

**Diplomatic representation from the US:** the US does not have an embassy in San Marino; the ambassador to Italy is accredited to San Marino

**Flag description:** two equal horizontal bands of white (top) and light blue with the national coat of arms superimposed in the center; the coat of arms has a shield (featuring three towers on three peaks) flanked by a wreath, below a crown and above a scroll bearing the word LIBERTAS (Liberty)

## Economy

**Economy - overview:** San Marino's economy relies heavily on its tourism and banking industries, as well as from the manufacture and export of ceramics, clothing, fabrics, furniture, paints, spirits, tiles, and wine. The economy also benefits from foreign investment due to its relatively low corporate taxes and low taxes on interest earnings. The San Marino government, sworn in on 3 December 2008, will continue to work towards an economic cooperation agreement with Italy - a longstanding priority - as well as harmonizing its fiscal laws with EU members. The per capita level of output and standard of living are comparable to those of the most prosperous regions of Italy, which supplies much of its food.

**GDP (purchasing power parity):**
$1.662 billion (2007)
$850 million (2004)

**GDP (official exchange rate):** $850 million (2004)

**GDP - real growth rate:**
4.3% (2007 est.)

**GDP - per capita (PPP):**
$41,900 (2007)

**GDP - composition by sector:**
*agriculture:* 0.1%
*industry:* 46.5%
*services:* 53.4% (2007)

**Labor force:** 22,660 (2008)

**Labor force - by occupation:**
*agriculture:* 0.1%
*industry:* 37.7%
*services:* 62.2% (2008 est.)

**Unemployment rate:**
3.1% (2008)

**Population below poverty line:** NA%

**Household income or consumption by percentage share:**
*lowest 10%:* NA%
*highest 10%:* NA%

**Budget:**
*revenues:* $690.6 million
*expenditures:* $652.9 million (2006)

**Inflation rate (consumer prices):**
-3.5% (2008)
-1.5% (2006)

**Commercial bank prime lending rate:** 7.58% (31 December 2007)

**Stock of money:** $1.326 billion (31 December 2007)

**Stock of quasi money:** $4.584 billion (31 December 2007)

**Stock of domestic credit:** $7.513 billion (31 December 2007)

**Market value of publicly traded shares:** $NA

**Agriculture - products:** wheat, grapes, corn, olives; cattle, pigs, horses, beef, cheese, hides

**Industries:** tourism, banking, textiles, electronics, ceramics, cement, wine

**Industrial production growth rate:** 3.1% (2007)

**Exports:** $4.628 billion (2007)

**Exports - commodities:** building stone, lime, wood, chestnuts, wheat, wine, baked goods, hides, ceramics

**Imports:** $3.744 billion (2007)

**Imports - commodities:** wide variety of consumer manufactures, food

**Debt - external:** $NA

**Exchange rates:** euros (EUR) per US dollar - 0.6734 (2008 est.), 0.7345 (2007), 0.7964 (2006), 0.8041 (2005), 0.8054 (2004)

## Communications

**Telephones - main lines in use:** 21,000 (2006)

**Telephones - mobile cellular:** 17,390 (2006)

**Telephone system:**

*general assessment:* adequate connections

*domestic:* automatic telephone system completely integrated into Italian system; combined fixed-line and mobile-cellular teledensity exceeds 130 telephones per 100 persons

*international:* country code - 378; connected to Italian international network

**Radio broadcast stations:** AM 0, FM 2, shortwave 0 (2008)

**Television broadcast stations:** 1 (San Marino residents also receive broadcasts from Italy) (1997)

**Internet country code:** .sm

**Internet hosts:** 6,665 (2008)

**Internet users:** 15,400 (2006)

## Transportation

**Roadways:**
*total:* 292 km
*paved:* 292 km (2006)

## Military

**Military branches:** no regular military forces; Voluntary Military Force (Corpi Militari Voluntar) performs ceremonial duties and limited police support functions (2008)

**Military service age and obligation:** 16-55 for voluntary service in Voluntary Military Force (2006)

**Manpower available for military service:**
*males age 16-49:* 6,613 (2008 est.)

**Manpower fit for military service:**
*males age 16-49:* 5,343
*females age 16-49:* 6,048 (2009 est.)

**Manpower reaching militarily significant age annually:**
*male:* 161
*female:* 160 (2009 est.)

**Military expenditures:** NA

**Military - note:** defense is the responsibility of Italy

## Transnational Issues

**Disputes - international:** none

# Sao Tome and Principe

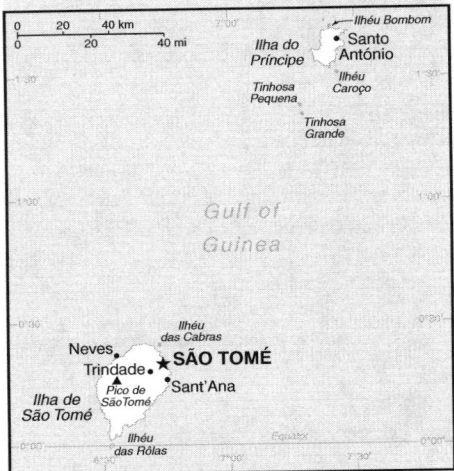

## Introduction

**Background:** Discovered and claimed by Portugal in the late 15th century, the islands' sugar-based economy gave way to coffee and cocoa in the 19th century - all grown with plantation slave labor, a form of which lingered into the 20th century. While independence was achieved in 1975, democratic reforms were not instituted until the late 1980s. The country held its first free elections in 1991, but frequent internal wrangling between the various political party's precipitated repeated changes in leadership and two failed coup attempts in 1995 and 2003. The recent discovery of oil in the Gulf of Guinea promises to attract increased attention to the small island nation.

## Geography

**Location:** Western Africa, islands in the Gulf of Guinea, straddling the Equator, west of Gabon
**Geographic coordinates:** 1 00 N, 7 00 E
**Map references:** Africa
**Area:**
*total:* 1,001 sq km
*land:* 1,001 sq km
*water:* 0 sq km
**Area - comparative:** more than five times the size of Washington, DC
**Land boundaries:** 0 km
**Coastline:** 209 km
**Maritime claims:** measured from claimed archipelagic baselines
*territorial sea:* 12 nm
*exclusive economic zone:* 200 nm
**Climate:** tropical; hot, humid; one rainy season (October to May)
**Terrain:** volcanic, mountainous
**Elevation extremes:**
*lowest point:* Atlantic Ocean 0 m
*highest point:* Pico de Sao Tome 2,024 m

**Natural resources:** fish, hydropower
**Land use:**
*arable land:* 8.33%
*permanent crops:* 48.96%
*other:* 42.71% (2005)
**Irrigated land:** 100 sq km (2003)
**Natural hazards:** NA
**Environment - current issues:** deforestation; soil erosion and exhaustion
**Environment - international agreements:**
*party to:* Biodiversity, Climate Change, Climate Change-Kyoto Protocol, Desertification, Endangered Species, Environmental Modification, Law of the Sea, Ozone Layer Protection, Ship Pollution, Wetlands
*signed, but not ratified:* none of the selected agreements
**Geography - note:** the smallest country in Africa; the two main islands form part of a chain of extinct volcanoes and both are mountainous

## People

**Population:** 212,679 (July 2009 est.)
**Age structure:**
*0-14 years:* 46.9% (male 50,475/female 49,188)
*15-64 years:* 49.7% (male 51,325/female 54,289)
*65 years and over:* 3.5% (male 3,335/female 4,067) (2009 est.)
**Median age:**
*total:* 16.4 years
*male:* 15.9 years
*female:* 17 years (2009 est.)
**Population growth rate:** 3.093% (2009 est.)
**Birth rate:** 38.54 births/1,000 population (2009 est.)
**Death rate:** 5.98 deaths/1,000 population (2008 est.)
**Net migration rate:** -1.81 migrant(s)/1,000 population (2009 est.)
**Urbanization:**
*urban population:* 61% of total population (2008)
*rate of urbanization:* 3% annual rate of change (2005-10 est.)
**Sex ratio:**
*at birth:* 1.03 male(s)/female
*under 15 years:* 1.03 male(s)/female
*15-64 years:* 0.94 male(s)/female
*65 years and over:* 0.82 male(s)/female
*total population:* 0.98 male(s)/female (2009 est.)
**Infant mortality rate:**
*total:* 37.12 deaths/1,000 live births
*male:* 38.84 deaths/1,000 live births
*female:* 35.35 deaths/1,000 live births (2009 est.)
**Life expectancy at birth:**
*total population:* 68.32 years
*male:* 66.65 years
*female:* 70.04 years (2009 est.)
**Total fertility rate:** 5.33 children born/woman (2009 est.)
**HIV/AIDS - adult prevalence rate:** NA
**HIV/AIDS - people living with HIV/AIDS:** NA
**HIV/AIDS - deaths:** NA

**Major infectious diseases:**
*degree of risk:* high
*food or waterborne diseases:* bacterial diarrhea, hepatitis A, and typhoid fever
*vectorborne disease:* malaria
*animal contact disease:* rabies (2009)
**Nationality:**
*noun:* Sao Tomean(s)
*adjective:* Sao Tomean
**Ethnic groups:** mestico, angolares (descendants of Angolan slaves), forros (descendants of freed slaves), servicais (contract laborers from Angola, Mozambique, and Cape Verde), tongas (children of servicais born on the islands), Europeans (primarily Portuguese)
**Religions:** Catholic 70.3%, Evangelical 3.4%, New Apostolic 2%, Adventist 1.8%, other 3.1%, none 19.4% (2001 census)
**Languages:** Portuguese (official)
**Literacy:**
*definition:* age 15 and over can read and write
*total population:* 84.9%
*male:* 92.2%
*female:* 77.9% (2001 census)
**School life expectancy (primary to tertiary education):**
*total:* 10 years
*male:* 10 years
*female:* 10 years (2006)
**Education expenditures:** NA

## Government

**Country name:**
*conventional long form:* Democratic Republic of Sao Tome and Principe
*conventional short form:* Sao Tome and Principe
*local long form:* Republica Democratica de Sao Tome e Principe
*local short form:* Sao Tome e Principe
**Government type:** republic
**Capital:**
*name:* Sao Tome
*geographic coordinates:* 0 12 N, 6 39 E
*time difference:* UTC 0 (5 hours ahead of Washington, DC during Standard Time)
**Administrative divisions:** 2 provinces; Principe, Sao Tome
*note:* Principe has had self government since 29 April 1995
**Independence:** 12 July 1975 (from Portugal)
**National holiday:** Independence Day, 12 July (1975)
**Constitution:** approved March 1990, effective 10 September 1990
**Legal system:** based on Portuguese legal system and customary law; has not accepted compulsory ICJ jurisdiction
**Suffrage:** 18 years of age; universal

# Sao Tome and Principe (continued)

**Executive branch:**

*chief of state:* President Fradique DE MENEZES (since 3 September 2001)

*head of government:* Prime Minister Joachim Rafael BRANCO (since 22 June 2008)

*cabinet:* Council of Ministers appointed by the president on the proposal of the prime minister

*elections:* president elected by popular vote for a five-year term (eligible for a second term); election last held 30 July 2006 (next to be held July 2011); prime minister chosen by the National Assembly and approved by the president

*election results:* Fradique DE MENEZES elected president; percent of vote - Fradique DE MENEZES 60%, Patrice TROVOADA 38.5%

**Legislative branch:** unicameral National Assembly or Assembleia Nacional (55 seats; members are elected by popular vote to serve four-year terms)

*elections:* last held on 26 March 2006 (next to be held in March 2010)

*election results:* percent of vote by party - MDFM-PCD 37.2%, MLSTP 28.9%, ADI 20.0%, NR 4.7%, others 9.2%; seats by party - MDFM-PCD 23, MLSTP 19, ADI 12, NR 1

**Judicial branch:** Supreme Court (judges are appointed by the National Assembly)

**Political parties and leaders:** Force for Change Democratic Movement or MDFM [Tome Soares da VERA CRUZ]; Independent Democratic Action or ADI [[Patrice TROVOADA]; Movement for the Liberation of Sao Tome and Principe-Social Democratic Party or MLSTP-PSD [Rafael BRANCO]; New Way Movement or NR; Party for Democratic Convergence or PCD [Delfim NEVES]; Ue-Kedadji coalition; other small parties

**Political pressure groups and leaders:** Association of Sao Tome and Principe NGOs or FONG

*other:* the media

**International organization participation:** ACP, AfDB, AU, CPLP, FAO, G-77, IBRD, ICAO, ICCt (signatory), ICRM, IDA, IFAD, IFC, IFRCS, ILO, IMF, IMO, Interpol, IOC, IOM (observer), IPU, ITU, ITUC, NAM, OIF, OPCW, UN, UNCTAD, UNESCO, UNIDO, Union Latina, UNWTO, UPU, WCL, WFTU, WHO, WIPO, WMO, WTO (observer)

**Diplomatic representation in the US:**

*chief of mission:* Ambassador (vacant)

*chancery:* 400 Park Avenue, 7th Floor, New York, NY 10022

*telephone:* [1] (212) 317-0580

*FAX:* [1] (212) 935-7348

**Diplomatic representation from the US:** the US does not have an embassy in Sao Tome and Principe; the Ambassador to Gabon is accredited to Sao Tome and Principe on a nonresident basis and makes periodic visits to the islands

**Flag description:** three horizontal bands of green (top), yellow (double width), and green with two black five-pointed stars placed side by side in the center of the yellow band and a red isosceles triangle based on the hoist side; uses the popular pan-African colors of Ethiopia

## Economy

**Economy - overview:** This small, poor island economy has become increasingly dependent on cocoa since independence in 1975. Cocoa production has substantially declined in recent years because of drought and mismanagement. Sao Tome has to import all fuels, most manufactured goods, consumer goods, and a substantial amount of food. Over the years, it has had difficulty servicing its external debt and has relied heavily on concessional aid and debt rescheduling. Sao Tome benefited from $200 million in debt relief in December 2000 under the Highly Indebted Poor Countries (HIPC) program, which helped bring down the country's $300 million debt burden. In August 2005, Sao Tome signed on to a new 3-year IMF Poverty Reduction and Growth Facility (PRGF) program worth $4.3 million. Considerable potential exists for development of a tourist industry, and the government has taken steps to expand facilities in recent years. The government also has attempted to reduce price controls and subsidies. Potential exists for the development of petroleum resources in Sao Tome's territorial waters in the oil-rich Gulf of Guinea, which are being jointly developed in a 60-40 split with Nigeria, but any actual production is at least several years off. The first production licenses were sold in 2004, though a dispute over licensing with Nigeria delayed Sao Tome's receipt of more than $20 million in signing bonuses for almost a year. Real GDP growth averaged about 6% in 2006-08, as a result of increases in public expenditures and oil-related capital investment.

**GDP (purchasing power parity):**
$276.6 million (2008 est.)
$262.1 million (2007)
$247.3 million (2006)
*note:* data are in 2008 US dollars

**GDP (official exchange rate):** $160 million (2008 est.)

**GDP - real growth rate:**
5.5% (2008 est.)
6% (2007 est.)
6.7% (2006 est.)

**GDP - per capita (PPP):**
$1,300 (2008 est.)
$1,300 (2007 est.)
$1,300 (2006 est.)
*note:* data are in 2008 US dollars

**GDP - composition by sector:**
*agriculture:* 14.6%
*industry:* 14.6%
*services:* 70.8% (2008 est.)

**Labor force:** 35,050 (1991)

**Labor force - by occupation:**
*note:* population mainly engaged in subsistence agriculture and fishing; shortages of skilled workers

**Unemployment rate:**
NA%

**Population below poverty line:** 54% (2004 est.)

**Household income or consumption by percentage share:**
*lowest 10%:* NA%
*highest 10%:* NA%

**Investment (gross fixed):** 36.7% of GDP (2008 est.)

**Budget:**
*revenues:* $47.65 million
*expenditures:* $51.48 million (2008 est.)

**Inflation rate (consumer prices):**
27% (2008 est.)
18% (2007 est.)

**Central bank discount rate:** 28% (31 December 2007)

**Commercial bank prime lending rate:** 32.4% (31 December 2007)

**Stock of money:** $19.99 million (31 December 2007)

**Stock of quasi money:** $33.5 million (31 December 2007)

**Stock of domestic credit:** $31.84 million (31 December 2007)

**Market value of publicly traded shares:** $NA

**Agriculture - products:** cocoa, coconuts, palm kernels, copra, cinnamon, pepper, coffee, bananas, papayas, beans; poultry; fish

**Industries:** light construction, textiles, soap, beer, fish processing, timber

**Industrial production growth rate:** 9.5% (2008 est.)

**Electricity - production:** 18 million kWh (2006 est.)

**Electricity - consumption:** 16.74 million kWh (2006 est.)

**Electricity - exports:** 0 kWh (2007)

**Electricity - imports:** 0 kWh (2007 est.)

**Oil - production:** 0 bbl/day (2007 est.)

**Oil - consumption:** 660 bbl/day (2006 est.)

**Oil - exports:** 0 bbl/day (2005)

**Oil - imports:** 659.5 bbl/day (2005)

**Oil - proved reserves:** 0 bbl (1 January 2006 est.)

**Natural gas - production:** 0 cu m (2007 est.)

**Natural gas - consumption:** 0 cu m (2007 est.)

**Natural gas - exports:** 0 cu m (2007 est.)

**Natural gas - imports:** 0 cu m (2007 est.)

**Natural gas - proved reserves:** 0 cu m (1 January 2006 est.)

**Current account balance:** -$71 million (2008 est.)

**Exports:** $9 million f.o.b. (2008 est.)

**Exports - commodities:** cocoa 80%, copra, coffee, palm oil

**Exports - partners:** Netherlands 23.7%, Belgium 23.7%, France 12.9%, US 5.9%, Portugal 4.1% (2007)

**Imports:** $91 million f.o.b. (2008 est.)

**Imports - commodities:** machinery and electrical equipment, food products, petroleum products

**Imports - partners:** Portugal 62.2%, US 11.6%, Gabon 4.5% (2007)

**Reserves of foreign exchange and gold:** $45 million (31 December 2008 est.)

**Debt - external:** $318 million (2002)
**Exchange rates:** dobras (STD) per US dollar - 14,900 (2008 est.), 13,700 (2007), 12,050 (2006), 9,900.4 (2005), 9,902.3 (2004)

## Communications

**Telephones - main lines in use:** 7,700 (2007)
**Telephones - mobile cellular:** 30,100 (2007)
**Telephone system:**
*general assessment:* local telephone network of adequate quality with most lines connected to digital switches
*domestic:* combined fixed-line and mobile-cellular teledensity approaching 20 telephones per 100 persons
*international:* country code - 239; satellite earth station -1 Intelsat (Atlantic Ocean)
**Radio broadcast stations:** AM 1, FM 5, shortwave 1 (2001)
**Television broadcast stations:** 2 (2001)
**Internet country code:** .st
**Internet hosts:** 1,355 (2008)
**Internet users:** 23,000 (2007)

## Transportation

**Airports:** 2 (2008)
**Airports - with paved runways:**
*total:* 2
*1,524 to 2,437 m:* 1
*914 to 1,523 m:* 1 (2008)
**Roadways:**
*total:* 320 km
*paved:* 218 km
*unpaved:* 102 km (2000)
**Merchant marine:**
*total:* 6
*by type:* bulk carrier 1, cargo 5
*foreign-owned:* 1 (Greece 1) (2008)
**Ports and terminals:** Sao Tome

## Military

**Military branches:** Armed Forces of Sao Tome and Principe (FASTP): Army, Coast Guard of Sao Tome e Principe (Guarda Costeira de Sao Tome e Principe, GCSTP), Presidential Guard (2007)
**Military service age and obligation:** 18 years of age (est.) (2004)
**Manpower available for military service:**
*males age 16-49:* 42,340
*females age 16-49:* 43,781 (2008 est.)
**Manpower fit for military service:**
*males age 16-49:* 35,216
*females age 16-49:* 38,329 (2009 est.)
**Manpower reaching militarily significant age annually:**
*male:* 2,534
*female:* 2,485 (2009 est.)
**Military expenditures:** 0.8% of GDP (2006)

**Military - note:** Sao Tome and Principe's army is a tiny force with almost no resources at its disposal and would be wholly ineffective operating unilaterally; infantry equipment is considered simple to operate and maintain but may require refurbishment or replacement after 25 years in tropical climates; poor pay, working conditions, and alleged nepotism in the promotion of officers have been problems in the past, as reflected in the 1995 and 2003 coups; these issues are being addressed with foreign assistance aimed at improving the army and its focus on realistic security concerns; command is exercised from the president, through the Minister of Defense, to the Chief of the Armed Forces staff (2005)

## Transnational Issues

**Disputes - international:** none

# Saudi Arabia

## Introduction

**Background:** Saudi Arabia is the birthplace of Islam and home to Islam's two holiest shrines in Mecca and Medina. The king's official title is the Custodian of the Two Holy Mosques. The modern Saudi state was founded in 1932 by ABD AL-AZIZ bin Abd al-Rahman AL SAUD (Ibn Saud) after a 30-year campaign to unify most of the Arabian Peninsula. A male descendent of Ibn Saud, his son ABDALLAH bin Abd al-Aziz, rules the country today as required by the country's 1992 Basic Law. Following Iraq's invasion of Kuwait in 1990, Saudi Arabia accepted the Kuwaiti royal family and 400,000 refugees while allowing Western and Arab troops to deploy on its soil for the liberation of Kuwait the following year. The continuing presence of foreign troops on Saudi soil after the liberation of Kuwait became a source of tension between the royal family and the public until all operational US troops left the country in 2003. Major terrorist attacks in May and November 2003 spurred a strong on-going campaign against domestic terrorism and extremism. King ABDALLAH has continued the cautious reform program begun when he was crown prince. To promote increased political participation, the government held elections nationwide from February through April 2005 for half the members of 179 municipal councils. In December 2005, King ABDALLAH completed the process by appointing the remaining members of the advisory municipal councils. The king instituted an Inter-Faith Dialogue initiative in 2008 to encourage religious tolerance on a global level; in February 2009, he reshuffled the cabinet, which led to more moderates holding ministerial and judicial positions, and appointed the first female to the cabinet. The country remains a leading producer of oil and natural gas and holds more than 20% of the world's proven oil reserves. The government continues to pursue economic reform and diversification, particularly since Saudi Arabia's accession to the WTO in

December 2005, and promotes foreign investment in the kingdom. A burgeoning population, aquifer depletion, and an economy largely dependent on petroleum output and prices are all ongoing governmental concerns.

## Geography

**Location:** Middle East, bordering the Persian Gulf and the Red Sea, north of Yemen

**Geographic coordinates:** 25 00 N, 45 00 E

**Map references:** Middle East

**Area:**
*total:* 2,149,690 sq km
*land:* 2,149,690 sq km
*water:* 0 sq km

**Area - comparative:** slightly more than one-fifth the size of the US

**Land boundaries:**
*total:* 4,431 km
*border countries:* Iraq 814 km, Jordan 744 km, Kuwait 222 km, Oman 676 km, Qatar 60 km, UAE 457 km, Yemen 1,458 km

**Coastline:** 2,640 km

**Maritime claims:**
*territorial sea:* 12 nm
*contiguous zone:* 18 nm
*continental shelf:* not specified

**Climate:** harsh, dry desert with great temperature extremes

**Terrain:** mostly uninhabited, sandy desert

**Elevation extremes:**
*lowest point:* Persian Gulf 0 m
*highest point:* Jabal Sawda' 3,133 m

**Natural resources:** petroleum, natural gas, iron ore, gold, copper

**Land use:**
*arable land:* 1.67%
*permanent crops:* 0.09%
*other:* 98.24% (2005)

**Irrigated land:** 16,200 sq km (2003)

**Total renewable water resources:** 2.4 cu km (1997)

**Freshwater withdrawal (domestic/industrial/agricultural):**
*total:* 17.32 cu km/yr (10%/1%/89%)
*per capita:* 705 cu m/yr (2000)

**Natural hazards:** frequent sand and dust storms

**Environment - current issues:** desertification; depletion of underground water resources; the lack of perennial rivers or permanent water bodies has prompted the development of extensive seawater desalination facilities; coastal pollution from oil spills

**Environment - international agreements:**
*party to:* Biodiversity, Climate Change, Climate Change-Kyoto Protocol, Desertification, Endangered Species, Hazardous Wastes, Law of the Sea, Marine Dumping, Ozone Layer Protection, Ship Pollution
*signed, but not ratified:* none of the selected agreements

**Geography - note:** extensive coastlines on Persian Gulf and Red Sea provide great leverage on shipping (especially crude oil) through Persian Gulf and Suez Canal

## People

**Population:** 28,686,633
*note:* includes 5,576,076 non-nationals (July 2009 est.)

**Age structure:**
*0-14 years:* 38% (male 5,557,453/female 5,340,614)
*15-64 years:* 59.5% (male 9,608,032/female 7,473,543)
*65 years and over:* 2.5% (male 363,241/female 343,750) (2009 est.)

**Median age:**
*total:* 21.6 years
*male:* 22.9 years
*female:* 19.9 years (2009 est.)

**Population growth rate:** 1.848% (2009 est.)

**Birth rate:** 28.55 births/1,000 population (2009 est.)

**Death rate:** 2.49 deaths/1,000 population (2008 est.)

**Net migration rate:** -7.6 migrant(s)/1,000 population (2009 est.)

**Urbanization:**
*urban population:* 82% of total population (2008)
*rate of urbanization:* 2.5% annual rate of change (2005-10 est.)

**Sex ratio:**
*at birth:* 1.05 male(s)/female
*under 15 years:* 1.04 male(s)/female
*15-64 years:* 1.29 male(s)/female
*65 years and over:* 1.06 male(s)/female
*total population:* 1.18 male(s)/female (2009 est.)

**Infant mortality rate:**
*total:* 11.57 deaths/1,000 live births
*male:* 13.15 deaths/1,000 live births
*female:* 9.91 deaths/1,000 live births (2009 est.)

**Life expectancy at birth:**
*total population:* 76.3 years
*male:* 74.23 years
*female:* 78.48 years (2009 est.)

**Total fertility rate:** 3.83 children born/woman (2009 est.)

**HIV/AIDS - adult prevalence rate:** 0.01% (2001 est.)

**HIV/AIDS - people living with HIV/AIDS:** NA

**HIV/AIDS - deaths:** NA

**Nationality:**
*noun:* Saudi(s)
*adjective:* Saudi or Saudi Arabian

**Ethnic groups:** Arab 90%, Afro-Asian 10%

**Religions:** Muslim 100%

**Languages:** Arabic

**Literacy:**
*definition:* age 15 and over can read and write
*total population:* 78.8%
*male:* 84.7%
*female:* 70.8% (2003 est.)

**Education expenditures:** 6.8% of GDP (2004)

## Government

**Country name:**
*conventional long form:* Kingdom of Saudi Arabia
*conventional short form:* Saudi Arabia

*local long form:* Al Mamlakah al Arabiyah as Suudiyah
*local short form:* Al Arabiyah as Suudiyah

**Government type:** monarchy

**Capital:**
*name:* Riyadh
*geographic coordinates:* 24 38 N, 46 43 E
*time difference:* UTC+3 (8 hours ahead of Washington, DC during Standard Time)

**Administrative divisions:** 13 provinces (mintaqat, singular - mintaqah); Al Bahah, Al Hudud ash Shamaliyah, Al Jawf, Al Madinah, Al Qasim, Ar Riyad, Ash Sharqiyah (Eastern Province), 'Asir, Ha'il, Jizan, Makkah, Najran, Tabuk

**Independence:** 23 September 1932 (unification of the kingdom)

**National holiday:** Unification of the Kingdom, 23 September (1932)

**Constitution:** governed according to Islamic law; the Basic Law that articulates the government's rights and responsibilities was promulgated by royal decree in 1992

**Legal system:** based on Sharia law, several secular codes have been introduced; commercial disputes handled by special committees; has not accepted compulsory ICJ jurisdiction

**Suffrage:** 21 years of age; male

**Executive branch:**
*chief of state:* King and Prime Minister ABDALLAH bin Abd al-Aziz Al Saud (since 1 August 2005); Heir Apparent Crown Prince SULTAN bin Abd al- Aziz Al Saud (half brother of the monarch); note - the monarch is both the chief of state and head of government
*head of government:* King and Prime Minister ABDALLAH bin Abd al-Aziz Al Saud (since 1 August 2005); Deputy Prime Minister SULTAN bin Abd al-Aziz Al Saud; Second Deputy Prime Minister NAYIF bin Abd Al-Aziz Al Saud
*cabinet:* Council of Ministers is appointed by the monarch every four years and includes many royal family members
*elections:* none; the monarchy is hereditary; note - a new Allegiance Commission created by royal decree in October 2006 established a committee of Saudi princes that will play a role in selecting future Saudi kings, but the new system will not take effect until after Crown Prince Sultan becomes king

**Legislative branch:** Consultative Council or Majlis al-Shura (150 members and a chairman appointed by the monarch for four-year terms); note - though the Council of Ministers announced in October 2003 its intent to introduce elections for half of the members of local and provincial assemblies and a third of the members of the national Consultative Council or Majlis al-Shura incrementally over a period of four to five years, to date no such elections have been held or announced

**Judicial branch:** Supreme Council of Justice

**Political parties and leaders:** none

**Political pressure groups and leaders:** Ansar Al Marah (supports women's rights)
*other:* gas companies; religious groups

# Saudi Arabia *(continued)*

**International organization participation:** ABEDA, AfDB (nonregional member), AFESD, AMF, BIS, FAO, G-20, G-77, GCC, IAEA, IBRD, ICAO, ICC, ICRM, IDB, IFAD, IFC, IFRCS, IHO, ILO, IMF, IMO, IMSO, Interpol, IOC, IPU, ISO, ITSO, ITU, LAS, MIGA, NAM, OAPEC, OAS (observer), OIC, OPCW, OPEC, PCA, UN, UNCTAD, UNESCO, UNIDO, UNRWA, UNWTO, UPU, WCO, WFTU, WHO, WIPO, WMO, WTO

**Diplomatic representation in the US:**
*chief of mission:* Ambassador Adil al-Ahmad al-JUBAYR
*chancery:* 601 New Hampshire Avenue NW, Washington, DC 20037
*telephone:* [1] (202) 342-3800
*FAX:* [1] (202) 944-3113
*consulate(s) general:* Houston, Los Angeles, New York

**Diplomatic representation from the US:**
*chief of mission:* Ambassador Ford M. FRAKER
*embassy:* Collector Road M, Diplomatic Quarter, Riyadh
*mailing address:* American Embassy, Unit 61307, APO AE 09803-1307; International Mail: P. O. Box 94309, Riyadh 11693
*telephone:* [966] (1) 488-3800
*FAX:* [966] (1) 488-7360
*consulate(s) general:* Dhahran, Jiddah (Jeddah)

**Flag description:** green, a traditional color in Islamic flags, with the Shahada or Muslim creed in large white Arabic script (translated as "There is no god but God; Muhammad is the Messenger of God") above a white horizontal saber (the tip points to the hoist side); design dates to the early twentieth century and is closely associated with the Al Saud family which established the kingdom in 1932

## Economy

**Economy - overview:** Saudi Arabia has an oil-based economy with strong government controls over major economic activities. It possesses more than 20% of the world's proven petroleum reserves, ranks as the largest exporter of petroleum, and plays a leading role in OPEC. The petroleum sector accounts for roughly 80% of budget revenues, 45% of GDP, and 90% of export earnings. About 40% of GDP comes from the private sector. Roughly 6.4 million foreign workers play an important role in the Saudi economy, particularly in the oil and service sectors. High oil prices through mid-2008 have boosted growth, government revenues, and Saudi ownership of foreign assets, while enabling Riyadh to pay down domestic debt. The government is encouraging private sector growth - especially in power generation, telecommunications, natural gas exploration, and petrochemicals - to lessen the kingdom's dependence on oil exports and to increase employment opportunities for the swelling Saudi population, nearly 40% of which are youths under 15 years old. Unemployment is high, and the large youth population generally lacks the education and technical skills the private sector needs. Riyadh has substantially boosted spending on job training and education, infrastructure development, and government salaries. As part of its effort to attract foreign investment and diversify the economy, Saudi Arabia acceded to the WTO in December 2005 after many years of negotiations. The government has announced plans to establish six "economic cities" in different regions of the country to promote development and diversification. The last five years of high oil prices have given the Kingdom ample financial reserves to manage the impact of the global financial crisis, but tight international credit, falling oil prices, and the global economic slowdown will reduce Saudi economic growth in 2009.

**GDP (purchasing power parity):**
$582.8 billion (2008 est.)
$553.5 billion (2007)
$535.3 billion (2006)
*note:* data are in 2008 US dollars

**GDP (official exchange rate):** $467.7 billion (2008 est.)

**GDP - real growth rate:**
4.2% (2008 est.)
3.4% (2007 est.)
3.2% (2006 est.)

**GDP - per capita (PPP):**
$20,700 (2008 est.)
$20,100 (2007 est.)
$19,800 (2006 est.)
*note:* data are in 2008 US dollars

**GDP - composition by sector:**
*agriculture:* 3.1%
*industry:* 61.6%
*services:* 35.4% (2008 est.)

**Labor force:** 6.74 million
*note:* about one-third of the population in the 15-64 age group is non-national (2008 est.)

**Labor force - by occupation:**
*agriculture:* 6.7%
*industry:* 21.4%
*services:* 71.9% (2005 est.)

**Unemployment rate:**
8.8% (2008 est.)
13% (2004 est.)
*note:* data are for Saudi males only (local bank estimates; some estimates range as high as 25%)

**Population below poverty line:** NA%

**Household income or consumption by percentage share:**
*lowest 10%:* NA%
*highest 10%:* NA%

**Investment (gross fixed):** 19.5% of GDP (2008 est.)

**Budget:**
*revenues:* $293 billion
*expenditures:* $136 billion (2008 est.)

**Public debt:** 13.5% of GDP (2008 est.)

**Inflation rate (consumer prices):**
10.3% (2008 est.)
4.1% (2007 est.)

**Central bank discount rate:** 2.5% (31 December 2008)

**Commercial bank prime lending rate:** NA

**Stock of money:** $113.2 billion (31 December 2008)

**Stock of quasi money:** $134.3 billion (31 December 2008)

**Stock of domestic credit:** $66.94 billion (31 December 2007)

**Market value of publicly traded shares:** $246.4 billion (31 December 2008)

**Agriculture - products:** wheat, barley, tomatoes, melons, dates, citrus; mutton, chickens, eggs, milk

**Industries:** crude oil production, petroleum refining, basic petrochemicals, ammonia, industrial gases, sodium hydroxide (caustic soda), cement, fertilizer, plastics, metals, commercial ship repair, commercial aircraft repair, construction

**Industrial production growth rate:** 4.5% (2008 est.)

**Electricity - production:** 179.1 billion kWh (2007 est.)

**Electricity - consumption:** 156.8 billion kWh (2006 est.)

**Electricity - exports:** 0 kWh (2007 est.)

**Electricity - imports:** 0 kWh (2007 est.)

**Oil - production:** 9.2 million bbl/day (2008 est.)

**Oil - consumption:** 1 million bbl/day (2008 est.)

**Oil - exports:** 8.2 million bbl/day (2007 est.)

**Oil - imports:** 41,680 bbl/day (2005)

**Oil - proved reserves:** 266.8 billion bbl (1 January 2008 est.)

**Natural gas - production:** 75.9 billion cu m (2007 est.)

**Natural gas - consumption:** 75.9 billion cu m (2007 est.)

**Natural gas - exports:** 0 cu m (2007 est.)

**Natural gas - imports:** 0 cu m (2007 est.)

**Natural gas - proved reserves:** 7.167 trillion cu m (1 January 2008 est.)

**Current account balance:** $151 billion (2008 est.)

**Exports:** $311.1 billion f.o.b. (2008 est.)

**Exports - commodities:** petroleum and petroleum products 90%

**Exports - partners:** US 17.1%, Japan 16.3%, South Korea 9.7%, China 8.1%, Taiwan 4.7%, Singapore 4% (2007)

**Imports:** $92.4 billion f.o.b. (2008 est.)

**Imports - commodities:** machinery and equipment, foodstuffs, chemicals, motor vehicles, textiles

**Imports - partners:** US 12.6%, China 9.4%, Germany 8.8%, Japan 8.1%, Italy 5%, South Korea 4.9%, UK 4.5% (2007)

# Saudi Arabia *(continued)*

**Reserves of foreign exchange and gold:** $28.5 billion (31 December 2008 est.)

**Debt - external:** $63.2 billion (31 December 2008 est.)

**Stock of direct foreign investment - at home:** $NA

**Stock of direct foreign investment - abroad:** $NA

**Exchange rates:** Saudi riyals (SAR) per US dollar - 3.75 (2008 est.), 3.745 (2007), 3.745 (2006), 3.747 (2005), 3.75 (2004)

## Communications

**Telephones - main lines in use:** 3.996 million (2007)

**Telephones - mobile cellular:** 28.381 million (2007)

**Telephone system:**

*general assessment:* modern system

*domestic:* extensive microwave radio relay, coaxial cable, and fiber-optic cable systems; mobile-cellular subscribership has been increasing rapidly

*international:* country code - 966; landing point for the international submarine cable Fiber-Optic Link Around the Globe (FLAG) and for both the SEA-ME-WE-3 and SEA-ME-WE-4 submarine cable networks providing connectivity to Asia, Middle East, Europe, and US; microwave radio relay to Bahrain, Jordan, Kuwait, Qatar, UAE, Yemen, and Sudan; coaxial cable to Kuwait and Jordan; satellite earth stations - 5 Intelsat (3 Atlantic Ocean and 2 Indian Ocean), 1 Arabsat, and 1 Inmarsat (Indian Ocean region)

**Radio broadcast stations:** AM 43, FM 31, shortwave 2 (1998)

**Television broadcast stations:** 117 (1997)

**Internet country code:** .sa

**Internet hosts:** 141,232 (2008)

**Internet users:** 6.2 million (2007)

## Transportation

**Airports:** 215 (2008)

**Airports - with paved runways:**

*total:* 79

*over 3,047 m:* 31

*2,438 to 3,047 m:* 16

*1,524 to 2,437 m:* 27

*914 to 1,523 m:* 2

*under 914 m:* 3 (2008)

**Airports - with unpaved runways:**

*total:* 136

*2,438 to 3,047 m:* 8

*1,524 to 2,437 m:* 71

*914 to 1,523 m:* 41

*under 914 m:* 16 (2008)

**Heliports:** 8 (2007)

**Pipelines:** condensate 212 km; gas 1,880 km; liquid petroleum gas 1,183 km; oil 4,239 km; refined products 1,148 km (2008)

**Railways:**

*total:* 1,392 km

*standard gauge:* 1,392 km 1.435-m gauge (with branch lines and sidings) (2006)

**Roadways:**

*total:* 221,372 km

*paved:* 47,529 km (includes 3,891 km of expressways)

*unpaved:* 173,843 km (2006)

**Merchant marine:**

*total:* 62

*by type:* cargo 5, chemical tanker 13, container 5, passenger/cargo 8, petroleum tanker 20, refrigerated cargo 3, roll on/roll off 8

*foreign-owned:* 12 (Egypt 1, Greece 3, Kuwait 7, UAE 1)

*registered in other countries:* 71 (Bahamas 16, Comoros 1, Dominica 2, France 1, Liberia 27, Marshall Islands 5, Norway 3, Panama 16) (2008)

**Ports and terminals:** Ad Dammam, Al Jubayl, Jiddah, Yanbu' al Sinaiyah

## Military

**Military branches:** Land Forces (Army), Navy, Air Force, Air Defense Force, National Guard, Ministry of Interior Forces (paramilitary)

**Military service age and obligation:** 18 years of age (est.); no conscription (2004)

**Manpower available for military service:**

*males age 16-49:* 8,547,441

*females age 16-49:* 6,381,098 (2008 est.)

**Manpower fit for military service:**

*males age 16-49:* 7,486,622

*females age 16-49:* 5,652,819 (2009 est.)

**Manpower reaching militarily significant age annually:**

*male:* 278,179

*female:* 267,905 (2009 est.)

**Military expenditures:** 10% of GDP (2005 est.)

## Transnational Issues

**Disputes - international:** Saudi Arabia has reinforced its concrete-filled security barrier along sections of the now fully demarcated border with Yemen to stem illegal cross-border activities; Kuwait and Saudi Arabia continue discussions on a maritime boundary with Iran

**Refugees and internally displaced persons:**

*refugees (country of origin):* 240,015 (Palestinian Territories) (2007)

**Trafficking in persons:**

*current situation:* Saudi Arabia is a destination country for workers from South and Southeast Asia who are subjected to conditions that constitute involuntary servitude including being subjected to physical and sexual abuse, non-payment of wages, confinement, and withholding of passports as a restriction on their movement; domestic workers are particularly vulnerable because some are confined to the house in which they work unable to seek help; Saudi Arabia is also a destination country for Nigerian, Yemeni, Pakistani, Afghan, Somali, Malian, and Sudanese children trafficked for forced begging and involuntary servitude as street vendors; some Nigerian women were reportedly trafficked into Saudi Arabia for commercial sexual exploitation

*tier rating:* Tier 3 - Saudi Arabia does not fully comply with the minimum standards for the elimination of trafficking and is not making significant efforts to do so; the government continues to lack adequate anti-trafficking laws and, despite evidence of widespread trafficking abuses, did not report any criminal prosecutions, convictions, or prison sentences for trafficking crimes committed against foreign domestic workers (2008)

**Illicit drugs:** death penalty for traffickers; improving anti-money-laundering legislation and enforcement

# Senegal

## Introduction

**Background:** The French colonies of Senegal and the French Sudan were merged in 1959 and granted their independence as the Mali Federation in 1960. The union broke up after only a few months. Senegal joined with The Gambia to form the nominal confederation of Senegambia in 1982, but the envisaged integration of the two countries was never carried out, and the union was dissolved in 1989. The Movement of Democratic Forces in the Casamance (MFDC) has led a low-level separatist insurgency in southern Senegal since the 1980s, and several peace deals have failed to resolve the conflict. Nevertheless, Senegal remains one of the most stable democracies in Africa. Senegal was ruled by a Socialist Party for 40 years until current President Abdoulaye WADE was elected in 2000. He was reelected in February 2007, but complaints of fraud led opposition parties to boycott June 2007 legislative polls. Senegal has a long history of participating in international peacekeeping.

## Geography

**Location:** Western Africa, bordering the North Atlantic Ocean, between Guinea-Bissau and Mauritania
**Geographic coordinates:** 14 00 N, 14 00 W
**Map references:** Africa
**Area:**
*total:* 196,190 sq km
*land:* 192,000 sq km
*water:* 4,190 sq km
**Area - comparative:** slightly smaller than South Dakota
**Land boundaries:**
*total:* 2,640 km
*border countries:* The Gambia 740 km, Guinea 330 km, Guinea-Bissau 338 km, Mali 419 km, Mauritania 813 km

**Coastline:** 531 km
**Maritime claims:**
*territorial sea:* 12 nm
*contiguous zone:* 24 nm
*exclusive economic zone:* 200 nm
*continental shelf:* 200 nm or to the edge of the continental margin
**Climate:** tropical; hot, humid; rainy season (May to November) has strong southeast winds; dry season (December to April) dominated by hot, dry, harmattan wind
**Terrain:** generally low, rolling, plains rising to foothills in southeast
**Elevation extremes:**
*lowest point:* Atlantic Ocean 0 m
*highest point:* unnamed feature near Nepen Diakha 581 m
**Natural resources:** fish, phosphates, iron ore
**Land use:**
*arable land:* 12.51%
*permanent crops:* 0.24%
*other:* 87.25% (2005)
**Irrigated land:** 1,200 sq km (2003)
**Total renewable water resources:** 39.4 cu km (1987)
**Freshwater withdrawal (domestic/industrial/agricultural):**
*total:* 2.22 cu km/yr (4%/3%/93%)
*per capita:* 190 cu m/yr (2002)
**Natural hazards:** lowlands seasonally flooded; periodic droughts
**Environment - current issues:** wildlife populations threatened by poaching; deforestation; overgrazing; soil erosion; desertification; overfishing
**Environment - international agreements:**
*party to:* Biodiversity, Climate Change, Climate Change-Kyoto Protocol, Desertification, Endangered Species, Hazardous Wastes, Law of the Sea, Marine Life Conservation, Ozone Layer Protection, Ship Pollution, Wetlands, Whaling
*signed, but not ratified:* none of the selected agreements
**Geography - note:** westernmost country on the African continent; The Gambia is almost an enclave within Senegal

## People

**Population:** 13,711,597 (July 2009 est.)
**Age structure:**
*0-14 years:* 42.2% (male 2,911,324/female 2,877,804)
*15-64 years:* 54.8% (male 3,728,664/female 3,786,000)
*65 years and over:* 3% (male 190,343/female 217,462) (2009 est.)
**Median age:**
*total:* 18.6 years
*male:* 18.4 years
*female:* 18.8 years (2009 est.)
**Population growth rate:** 2.709% (2009 est.)
**Birth rate:** 36.84 births/1,000 population (2009 est.)

**Death rate:** 10.72 deaths/1,000 population (2008 est.)
**Net migration rate:** 0 migrant(s)/1,000 population (2009 est.)
**Urbanization:**
*urban population:* 42% of total population (2008)
*rate of urbanization:* 3.1% annual rate of change (2005-10 est.)
**Sex ratio:**
*at birth:* 1.03 male(s)/female
*under 15 years:* 1.01 male(s)/female
*15-64 years:* 0.98 male(s)/female
*65 years and over:* 0.88 male(s)/female
*total population:* 0.99 male(s)/female (2009 est.)
**Infant mortality rate:**
*total:* 58.94 deaths/1,000 live births
*male:* 65.7 deaths/1,000 live births
*female:* 51.98 deaths/1,000 live births (2009 est.)
**Life expectancy at birth:**
*total population:* 59 years
*male:* 57.12 years
*female:* 60.93 years (2009 est.)
**Total fertility rate:** 4.95 children born/woman (2009 est.)
**HIV/AIDS - adult prevalence rate:** 1% (2007 est.)
**HIV/AIDS - people living with HIV/AIDS:** 67,000 (2007 est.)
**HIV/AIDS - deaths:** 1,800 (2007 est.)
**Major infectious diseases:**
*degree of risk:* very high
*food or waterborne diseases:* bacterial and protozoal diarrhea, hepatitis A, and typhoid fever
*vectorborne diseases:* Crimean-Congo hemorrhagic fever, dengue fever, malaria, Rift Valley fever, and yellow fever
*water contact disease:* schistosomiasis
*respiratory disease:* meningococcal meningitis
*animal contact disease:* rabies (2009)
**Nationality:**
*noun:* Senegalese (singular and plural)
*adjective:* Senegalese
**Ethnic groups:** Wolof 43.3%, Pular 23.8%, Serer 14.7%, Jola 3.7%, Mandinka 3%, Soninke 1.1%, European and Lebanese 1%, other 9.4%
**Religions:** Muslim 94%, Christian 5% (mostly Roman Catholic), indigenous beliefs 1%
**Languages:** French (official), Wolof, Pulaar, Jola, Mandinka
**Literacy:**
*definition:* age 15 and over can read and write
*total population:* 39.3%
*male:* 51.1%
*female:* 29.2% (2002 est.)
**Education expenditures:** 5% of GDP (2006)

## Government

**Country name:**
*conventional long form:* Republic of Senegal
*conventional short form:* Senegal
*local long form:* Republique du Senegal
*local short form:* Senegal
*former:* Senegambia (along with The Gambia), Mali Federation

# Senegal (continued)

**Government type:** republic
**Capital:**
*name:* Dakar
*geographic coordinates:* 14 40 N, 17 26 W
*time difference:* UTC 0 (5 hours ahead of Washington, DC during Standard Time)
**Administrative divisions:** 11 regions (regions, singular - region); Dakar, Diourbel, Fatick, Kaolack, Kolda, Louga, Matam, Saint-Louis, Tambacounda, Thies, Ziguinchor
**Independence:** 4 April 1960 (from France); note - complete independence achieved upon dissolution of federation with Mali on 20 August 1960
**National holiday:** Independence Day, 4 April (1960)
**Constitution:** adopted 7 January 2001
**Legal system:** based on French civil law system; judicial review of legislative acts in Constitutional Court; the Council of State audits the government's accounting office; accepts compulsory ICJ jurisdiction with reservations
**Suffrage:** 18 years of age; universal
**Executive branch:**
*chief of state:* President Abdoulaye WADE (since 1 April 2000)
*head of government:* Prime Minister Soulayemane Ndene NDIAYE (since 1 May 2009)
*cabinet:* Council of Ministers appointed by the prime minister in consultation with the president
*elections:* president elected by popular vote for a five-year term (eligible for a second term) under new constitution; election last held on 25 February 2007 (next to be held in 2012); prime minister appointed by the president
*election results:* Abdoulaye WADE reelected president; percent of vote - Abdoulaye WADE 55.9%, Idrissa SECK 14.9%, Ousmane Tanor DIENG 13.6%, Moustapha NIASSE 5.9%, other 9.7%
**Legislative branch:** bicameral Parliament consisting of the Senate, reinstituted in 2007, (100 seats; 35 indirectly elected with the remaining 65 members to be appointed by the president) and the National Assembly or Assemblee Nationale (150 seats; 90 members elected by direct popular vote with the remaining members elected by proportional representation from party lists to serve five-year terms)
*elections:* Senate - last held 19 August 2007 (next to be held - NA); National Assembly - last held on 3 June 2007 (next to be held 2012); note - the National Assembly in December 2005 voted to postpone legislative elections originally scheduled for 2006; legislative elections were first rescheduled to coincide with the 25 February 2007 presidential elections and later rescheduled for 3 June 2007; the June election was boycotted by 12 opposition parties, including the former ruling Socialist Party, which resulted in a record-low 35% voter turnout
*election results:* Senate results - percent of vote by party - NA; seats by party - PDS 34, AJ/PADS 1, 65 appointed by the president; National Assembly results -percent of vote by party - NA; seats by party - SOPI Coalition 131, other 19

**Judicial branch:** Constitutional Court; Council of State; Court of Final Appeals or Cour de Cassation; Court of Appeals
**Political parties and leaders:** African Party of Independence [Majhemout DIOP]; Alliance for the Republic-Yakaar [Macky Sall]; And-Jef/African Party for Democracy and Socialism or AJ/PADS [Landing SAVANE]; Alliance of Forces of Progress or AFP [Moustapha NIASSE]; Democratic League-Labor Party Movement or LD-MPT [Dr. Abdoulaye BATHILY]; Front for Socialism and Democracy/Benno Jubel or FSD/BJ [Cheikh Abdoulaye Bamba DIEYE]; Gainde Centrist Bloc or BGC [Jean-Paul DIAS]; Independence and Labor Party or PIT [Amath DANSOKHO]; Jef-Jel [Talla SYLLA]; National Democratic Rally or RND [Madior DIOUF]; People's Labor Party or PTP [El Hadji DIOUF]; Reform Party or PR [Abdourahim AGNE]; Rewmi Party [Idrissa Seck]; Senegalese Democratic Party or PDS [Abdoulaye WADE]; Socialist Party or PS [Ousmane Tanor DIENG]; SOPI Coalition [Abdoulaye WADE] (a coalition led by the PDS); Union for Democratic Renewal or URD [Djibo Leyti KA]
**Political pressure groups and leaders:**
*other:* labor; students; Sufi brotherhoods, including the Mourides and Tidjanes; teachers
**International organization participation:** ACP, AfDB, AU, CPLP (associate), ECOWAS, FAO, FZ, G-15, G-77, IAEA, IBRD, ICAO, ICC, ICCt, ICRM, IDA, IDB, IFAD, IFC, IFRCS, ILO, IMF, IMO, IMSO, Interpol, IOC, IOM, IPU, ISO (correspondent), ITSO, ITU, ITUC, MIGA, MINURCAT, MONUC, NAM, OIC, OIF, OPCW, PCA, UN, UNAMID, UNCTAD, UNESCO, UNIDO, Union Latina, UNMIL, UNOCI, UNWTO, UPU, WADB (regional), WAEMU, WCL, WCO, WFTU, WHO, WIPO, WMO, WTO
**Diplomatic representation in the US:**
*chief of mission:* Ambassador Amadou Lamine BA
*chancery:* 2112 Wyoming Avenue NW, Washington, DC 20008
*telephone:* [1] (202) 234-0540
*FAX:* [1] (202) 332-6315
*consulate(s) general:* Houston, New York
**Diplomatic representation from the US:**
*chief of mission:* Ambassador Marcia S. BERNICAT
*embassy:* Avenue Jean XXIII at the corner of Rue Kleber, Dakar
*mailing address:* B. P. 49, Dakar
*telephone:* [221] 33-829-2100
*FAX:* [221] 33-822-2991
**Flag description:** three equal vertical bands of green (hoist side), yellow, and red with a small green five-pointed star centered in the yellow band; uses the popular pan-African colors of Ethiopia

## Economy

**Economy - overview:** In January 1994, Senegal undertook a bold and ambitious economic reform program with the support of the international donor community. This reform began with a 50% devaluation of Senegal's currency, the CFA franc, which was linked at a fixed rate to the French franc. Government price controls and subsidies have been steadily dismantled. After seeing its economy contract by 2.1% in 1993, Senegal made an important turnaround, thanks to the reform program, with real growth in GDP averaging over 5% annually during 1995-2008. Annual inflation had been pushed down to the single digits. As a member of the West African Economic and Monetary Union (WAEMU), Senegal is working toward greater regional integration with a unified external tariff and a more stable monetary policy. High unemployment, however, continues to prompt illegal migrants to flee Senegal in search of better job opportunities in Europe. Senegal was also beset by an energy crisis that caused widespread blackouts in 2006 and 2007. The phosphate industry has struggled for two years to secure capital, and reduced output has directly impacted GDP. In 2007, Senegal signed agreements for major new mining concessions for iron, zircon, and gold with foreign companies. Firms from Dubai have agreed to manage and modernize Dakar's maritime port, and create a new special economic zone. Senegal still relies heavily upon outside donor assistance. Under the IMF's Highly Indebted Poor Countries (HIPC) debt relief program, Senegal has benefited from eradication of two-thirds of its bilateral, multilateral, and private-sector debt. In 2007, Senegal and the IMF agreed to a new, non-disbursing, Policy Support Initiative program.
**GDP (purchasing power parity):**
$21.9 billion (2008 est.)
$20.92 billion (2007)
$20.08 billion (2006)
*note:* data are in 2008 US dollars
**GDP (official exchange rate):** $13.9 billion (2008 est.)
**GDP - real growth rate:**
4.7% (2008 est.)
4.2% (2007 est.)
2% (2006 est.)
**GDP - per capita (PPP):**
$1,600 (2008 est.)
$1,600 (2007 est.)
$1,600 (2006 est.)
*note:* data are in 2008 US dollars
**GDP - composition by sector:**
*agriculture:* 16%
*industry:* 19.4%
*services:* 64.6% (2008 est.)
**Labor force:** 4.973 million (2008 est.)
**Labor force - by occupation:**
*agriculture:* 77.5%
*industry and services:* 22.5% (2007 est.)
**Unemployment rate:**
48% (2007 est.)
**Population below poverty line:** 54% (2001 est.)
**Household income or consumption by percentage share:**
*lowest 10%:* 2.7%
*highest 10%:* 33.4% (2001)
**Distribution of family income - Gini index:** 41.3 (2001)

# Senegal (continued)

**Investment (gross fixed):** 25.4% of GDP (2008 est.)

**Budget:**
*revenues:* $3.141 billion
*expenditures:* $3.799 billion (2008 est.)

**Public debt:** 21.4% of GDP (2008 est.)

**Inflation rate (consumer prices):**
6.6% (2008 est.)
5.9% (2007 est.)

**Central bank discount rate:** 4.25% (31 December 2007)

**Commercial bank prime lending rate:** NA

**Stock of money:** $2.842 billion (31 December 2007)

**Stock of quasi money:** $1.579 billion (31 December 2007)

**Stock of domestic credit:** $2.97 billion (31 December 2007)

**Market value of publicly traded shares:** $NA

**Agriculture - products:** peanuts, millet, corn, sorghum, rice, cotton, tomatoes, green vegetables; cattle, poultry, pigs; fish

**Industries:** agricultural and fish processing, phosphate mining, fertilizer production, petroleum refining; iron ore, zircon, and gold mining, construction materials, ship construction and repair

**Industrial production growth rate:** 5% (2008 est.)

**Electricity - production:** 2.28 billion kWh (2006 est.)

**Electricity - consumption:** 1.657 billion kWh (2006 est.)

**Electricity - exports:** 0 kWh (2007 est.)

**Electricity - imports:** 0 kWh (2007 est.)

**Oil - production:** 0 bbl/day (2005 est.)

**Oil - consumption:** 36,200 bbl/day (2006 est.)

**Oil - exports:** 4,298 bbl/day (2005)

**Oil - imports:** 40,450 bbl/day (2005)

**Oil - proved reserves:** 0 bbl (1 January 2006 est.)

**Natural gas - production:** 50 million cu m (2006 est.)

**Natural gas - consumption:** 50 million cu m (2006 est.)

**Natural gas - exports:** 0 cu m (2007 est.)

**Natural gas - imports:** 0 cu m (2007 est.)

**Natural gas - proved reserves:** NA cu m

**Current account balance:** -$2.078 billion (2008 est.)

**Exports:** $1.904 billion f.o.b. (2008 est.)

**Exports - commodities:** fish, groundnuts (peanuts), petroleum products, phosphates, cotton

**Exports - partners:** Mali 18.9%, France 9.1%, Italy 5.9%, India 5.7%, The Gambia 5.2% (2007)

**Imports:** $4.654 billion f.o.b. (2008 est.)

**Imports - commodities:** food and beverages, capital goods, fuels

**Imports - partners:** France 22.2%, Netherlands 10%, China 7.4%, UK 6.2%, Thailand 5.2%, Belgium 4.5% (2007)

**Reserves of foreign exchange and gold:** $1.765 billion (31 December 2008 est.)

**Debt - external:** $2.528 billion (31 December 2008 est.)

**Exchange rates:** Communaute Financiere Africaine francs (XOF) per US dollar - 447.81 (2008 est.), 481.83 (2007), 522.89 (2006), 527.47 (2005), 528.29 (2004)

*note:* since 1 January 1999, the West African CFA franc (XOF) has been pegged to the euro at a rate of 655.957 CFA francs per euro; West African CFA franc (XOF) coins and banknotes are not accepted in countries using Central African CFA francs (XAF), and vice versa, even though the two currencies trade at par

## Communications

**Telephones - main lines in use:** 269,100 (2007)

**Telephones - mobile cellular:** 4.123 million (2007)

**Telephone system:**
*general assessment:* good system
*domestic:* above-average urban system with a fiber-optic network; nearly two-thirds of all fixed-line connections are in Dakar where a call-center industry is emerging; expansion of fixed-line services in rural areas needed; mobile-cellular service is expanding rapidly; microwave radio relay, coaxial cable and fiber-optic cable in trunk system
*international:* country code - 221; the SAT-3/WASC fiber optic cable provides connectivity to Europe and Asia while Atlantis-2 provides connectivity to South America; satellite earth station - 1 Intelsat (Atlantic Ocean) (2007)

**Radio broadcast stations:** AM 8, FM 20, shortwave 1 (2001)

**Television broadcast stations:** 4 (2007)

**Internet country code:** .sn

**Internet hosts:** 217 (2008)

**Internet users:** 820,000 (2007)

## Transportation

**Airports:** 17 (2008)

**Airports - with paved runways:**
*total:* 9
*over 3,047 m:* 1
*1,524 to 2,437 m:* 7
*914 to 1,523 m:* 1 (2008)

**Airports - with unpaved runways:**
*total:* 8
*1,524 to 2,437 m:* 6
*914 to 1,523 m:* 2 (2008)

**Pipelines:** gas 43 km; refined products 8 km (2008)

**Railways:**
*total:* 906 km
*narrow gauge:* 906 km 1.000 meter gauge (2006)

**Roadways:**
*total:* 13,576 km
*paved:* 3,972 km (includes 7 km of expressways)
*unpaved:* 9,604 km (2003)

**Waterways:** 1,000 km (primarily on Senegal, Saloum, and Casamance rivers) (2008)

**Ports and terminals:** Dakar

## Military

**Military branches:** Army, Senegalese Navy (Marine Senegalaise), Senegalese Air Force (Armee de l'Air du Senegal) (2008)

**Military service age and obligation:** 18 years of age for compulsory and voluntary military service; conscript service obligation - 2 years (2004)

**Manpower available for military service:**
*males age 16-49:* 2,943,619
*females age 16-49:* 2,955,179 (2008 est.)

**Manpower fit for military service:**
*males age 16-49:* 2,038,508
*females age 16-49:* 2,207,510 (2009 est.)

**Manpower reaching militarily significant age annually:**
*male:* 154,249
*female:* 153,679 (2009 est.)

**Military expenditures:** 1.4% of GDP (2005 est.)

## Transnational Issues

**Disputes - international:** The Gambia and Guinea-Bissau attempt to stem separatist violence, cross border raids, and arms smuggling into their countries from Senegal's Casamance region, and in 2006, respectively accepted 6,000 and 10,000 Casamance residents fleeing the conflict; 2,500 Guinea-Bissau residents fled into Senegal in 2006 to escape armed confrontations along the border

**Refugees and internally displaced persons:**
*refugees (country of origin):* 19,630 (Mauritania)
*IDPs:* 22,400 (approximately 65% of the IDP population returned in 2005, but new displacement is occurring due to clashes between government troops and separatists in Casamance region) (2007)

**Illicit drugs:** transshipment point for Southwest and Southeast Asian heroin and South American cocaine moving to Europe and North America; illicit cultivator of cannabis

# Serbia

## Introduction

**Background:** The Kingdom of Serbs, Croats, and Slovenes was formed in 1918; its name was changed to Yugoslavia in 1929. Various paramilitary bands resisted Nazi Germany's occupation and division of Yugoslavia from 1941 to 1945, but fought each other and ethnic opponents as much as the invaders. The military and political movement headed by Josip TITO (Partisans) took full control of Yugoslavia when German and Croatian separatist forces were defeated in 1945. Although Communist, TITO's new government and his successors (he died in 1980) managed to steer their own path between the Warsaw Pact nations and the West for the next four and a half decades. In 1989, Slobodan MILOSEVIC became president of the Serbian Republic and his ultranationalist calls for Serbian domination led to the violent breakup of Yugoslavia along ethnic lines. In 1991, Croatia, Slovenia, and Macedonia declared independence, followed by Bosnia in 1992. The remaining republics of Serbia and Montenegro declared a new Federal Republic of Yugoslavia (FRY) in April 1992 and under MILOSEVIC's leadership, Serbia led various military campaigns to unite ethnic Serbs in neighboring republics into a "Greater Serbia." These actions led to Yugoslavia being ousted from the UN in 1992, but Serbia continued its - ultimately unsuccessful - campaign until signing the Dayton Peace Accords in 1995. MILOSEVIC kept tight control over Serbia and eventually became president of the FRY in 1997. In 1998, an ethnic Albanian insurgency in the formerly autonomous Serbian province of Kosovo provoked a Serbian counterinsurgency campaign that resulted in massacres and massive expulsions of ethnic Albanians living in Kosovo. The MILOSEVIC government's rejection of a proposed international settlement led to NATO's bombing of Serbia in the spring of 1999 and to the eventual withdrawal of Serbian military and police forces from Kosovo in June 1999. UNSC Resolution 1244 in June

1999 authorized the stationing of a NATO-led force (KFOR) in Kosovo to provide a safe and secure environment for the region's ethnic communities, created a UN interim Administration Mission in Kosovo (UNMIK) to foster self-governing institutions, and reserved the issue of Kosovo's final status for an unspecified date in the future. In 2001, UNMIK promulgated a constitutional framework that allowed Kosovo to establish institutions of self-government and led to Kosovo's first parliamentary election. FRY elections in September 2000 led to the ouster of MILOSEVIC and installed Vojislav KOSTUNICA as president. A broad coalition of democratic reformist parties known as DOS (the Democratic Opposition of Serbia) was subsequently elected to parliament in December 2000 and took control of the government. DOS arrested MILOSEVIC in 2001 and allowed for him to be tried in The Hague for crimes against humanity. (MILOSEVIC died in March 2006 before the completion of his trial.) In 2001, the country's suspension from the UN was lifted. In 2003, the FRY became Serbia and Montenegro, a loose federation of the two republics with a federal level parliament. Widespread violence predominantly targeting ethnic Serbs in Kosovo in March 2004 caused the international community to open negotiations on the future status of Kosovo in January 2006. In May 2006, Montenegro invoked its right to secede from the federation and - following a successful referendum - it declared itself an independent nation on 3 June 2006. Two days later, Serbia declared that it was the successor state to the union of Serbia and Montenegro. A new Serbian constitution was approved in October 2006 and adopted the following month. After 15 months of inconclusive negotiations mediated by the UN and four months of further inconclusive negotiations mediated by the US, EU, and Russia, on 17 February 2008, the UNMIK-administered province of Kosovo declared itself independent of Serbia.

## Geography

**Location:** Southeastern Europe, between Macedonia and Hungary
**Geographic coordinates:** 44 00 N, 21 00 E
**Map references:** Europe
**Area:**
*total:* 77,474 sq km
*land:* 77,474 sq km
*water:* 0 sq km
**Area - comparative:** slightly smaller than South Carolina
**Land boundaries:**
*total:* 2,026 km
*border countries:* Bosnia and Herzegovina 302 km, Bulgaria 318 km, Croatia 241 km, Hungary 151 km, Kosovo 352 km, Macedonia 62 km, Montenegro 124 km, Romania 476 km
**Coastline:** 0 km (landlocked)
**Maritime claims:** none (landlocked)

**Climate:** in the north, continental climate (cold winters and hot, humid summers with well distributed rainfall); in other parts, continental and Mediterranean climate (relatively cold winters with heavy snowfall and hot, dry summers and autumns)
**Terrain:** extremely varied; to the north, rich fertile plains; to the east, limestone ranges and basins; to the southeast, ancient mountains and hills
**Elevation extremes:**
*lowest point:* NA
*highest point:* Midzor 2,169 m
**Natural resources:** oil, gas, coal, iron ore, copper, zinc, antimony, chromite, gold, silver, magnesium, pyrite, limestone, marble, salt, arable land
**Land use:**
*arable land:* NA
*permanent crops:* NA
*other:* NA
**Irrigated land:** NA
**Total renewable water resources:** 208.5 cu km (note - includes Kosovo) (2003)
**Natural hazards:** destructive earthquakes
**Environment - current issues:** air pollution around Belgrade and other industrial cities; water pollution from industrial wastes dumped into the Sava which flows into the Danube
**Environment - international agreements:**
*party to:* Air Pollution, Biodiversity, Climate Change, Climate Change-Kyoto Protocol, Desertification, Endangered Species, Hazardous Wastes, Law of the Sea, Marine Dumping, Marine Life Conservation, Ozone Layer Protection, Ship Pollution, Wetlands
*signed, but not ratified:* none of the selected agreements
**Geography - note:** controls one of the major land routes from Western Europe to Turkey and the Near East

## People

**Population:** 7,379,339 (July 2009 est.)
**Age structure:**
*0-14 years:* 15.4% (male 586,806/female 549,900)
*15-64 years:* 67.8% (male 2,503,194/female 2,502,807)
*65 years and over:* 16.8% (male 508,606/female 728,026) (2009 est.)
**Median age:**
*total:* 41 years
*male:* 39.3 years
*female:* 42.7 years (2009 est.)
**Population growth rate:** -0.468% (2009 est.)
**Birth rate:** 9.19 births/1,000 population (2009 est.)
**Death rate:** 13.86 deaths/1,000 population (2009 est.)
**Net migration rate:** 0 migrant(s)/1,000 population (2008 est.)
**Urbanization:**
*urban population:* 52% of total population (2008)
*rate of urbanization:* 0.5% annual rate of change (2005-10 est.)

# Serbia *(continued)*

**Sex ratio:**
*at birth:* 1.07 male(s)/female
*under 15 years:* 1.07 male(s)/female
*15-64 years:* 1 male(s)/female
*65 years and above:* 0.7 male(s)/female
*total population:* 0.95 male(s)/female (2009 est.)

**Infant mortality rate:**
*total:* 6.75 deaths/1,000 live births
*male:* 7.79 deaths/1,000 live births
*female:* 5.64 deaths/1,000 live births (2009 est.)

**Life expectancy at birth:**
*total population:* 73.9 years
*male:* 71.09 years
*female:* 76.89 years (2009 est.)

**Total fertility rate:** 1.38 children born/woman (2009 est.)

**HIV/AIDS - adult prevalence rate:** 0.1% (2009 est.)

**HIV/AIDS - people living with HIV/AIDS:** 6,400 (2009 est.)

**HIV/AIDS - deaths:** fewer than 100 (2009 est.)

**Major infectious diseases:**
*degree of risk:* intermediate
*food or waterborne diseases:* bacterial diarrhea
*vectorborne disease:* Crimean Congo hemorrhagic fever
*note:* highly pathogenic H5N1 avian influenza has been identified in this country; it poses a negligible risk with extremely rare cases possible among US citizens who have close contact with birds (2009)

**Nationality:**
*noun:* Serb(s)
*adjective:* Serbian

**Ethnic groups:** Serb 82.9%, Hungarian 3.9%, Romany (Gypsy) 1.4%, Yugoslavs 1.1%, Bosniaks 1.8%, Montenegrin 0.9%, other 8% (2002 census)

**Religions:** Serbian Orthodox 85%, Catholic 5.5%, Protestant 1.1%, Muslim 3.2%, unspecified 2.6%, other, unknown, or atheist 2.6% (2002 census)

**Languages:** Serbian 88.3% (official), Hungarian 3.8%, Bosniak 1.8%, Romany (Gypsy) 1.1%, other 4.1%, unknown 0.9% (2002 census)
*note:* Romanian, Hungarian, Slovak, Ukrainian, and Croatian all official in Vojvodina

**Literacy:**
*definition:* age 15 and over can read and write
*total population:* 96.4%
*male:* 98.9%
*female:* 94.1% (2003 census)
*note:* includes Montenegro

**Education expenditures:** NA

## Government

**Country name:**
*conventional long form:* Republic of Serbia
*conventional short form:* Serbia
*local long form:* Republika Srbija
*local short form:* Srbija
*former:* People's Republic of Serbia, Socialist Republic of Serbia

**Government type:** republic

**Capital:**
*name:* Belgrade (Beograd)
*geographic coordinates:* 44 50 N, 20 30 E
*time difference:* UTC+1 (6 hours ahead of Washington, DC during Standard Time)
*daylight saving time:* +1hr, begins last Sunday in March; ends last Sunday in October

**Administrative divisions:** 167 municipalities (opcstine, singular - opcstina)
*Serbia Proper:* Belgrade City (Beograd): Barajevo, Cukarica, Grocka, Lazarevac, Mladenovac, Novi Beograd, Obrenovac, Palilula, Rakovica, Savski Venac, Sopot, Stari Grad, Surcin, Vozdovac, Vracar, Zemun, Zvezdara; Bor: Bor, Kladovo, Majdanpek, Negotin; Branicevo: Golubac, Kucevo, Malo Crnice, Petrovac, Pozarevac, Veliko Gradiste, Zabari, Zagubica; Grad Nis: Crveni Krst, Mediana, Niska Banja, Palilula, Pantelej Jablanica: Bojnik, Crna Trava, Lebane, Leskovac, Medveda, Vlasotince; Kolubara: Lajkovac, Ljig, Mionica, Osecina, Ub, Valjevo; Macva: Bogatic, Koceljeva, Krupanj, Ljubovija, Loznica, Mali Zvornik, Sabac, Vladimirci; Moravica: Cacak, Gornkji Milanovac, Ivanjica, Lucani; Nisava: Aleksinac, Doljevac, Gadzin Han, Merosina, Nis, Razanj, Svrljig; Pcinja: Bosilegrad, Bujanovac, Presevo, Surdulica, Trgoviste, Vladicin Han, Vranje; Pirot: Babusnica, Bela Palanka, Dimitrovgrad, Pirot; Podunavlje: Smederevo, Smederevskia Palanka, Velika Plana; Pomoravlje: Cuprija, Despotovac, Jagodina, Paracin, Rekovac, Svilajnac; Rasina: Aleksandrovac, Brus, Cicevac, Krusevac, Trstenik, Varvarin; Raska: Kraljevo, Novi Pazar, Raska, Tutin, Vrnjacka Banja; Sumadija: Arandelovac, Batocina, Knic, Kragujevac, Lapovo, Raca, Topola; Toplica: Blace, Kursumlija, Prokuplje, Zitorada; Zajecar: Boljevac, Knjazevac, Sokobanja, Zajecar; Zlatibor: Arilje, Bajina Basta, Cajetina, Kosjeric, Nova Varos, Pozega, Priboj, Prijepolje, Sjenica, Uzice
*Vojvodina Autonomous Province:* South Backa: Bac, Backa Palanka, Backi Petrovac, Becej, Beocin, Novi Sad, Sremski Karlovci, Srobobran, Temerin, Titel, Vrbas, Zabalj; South Banat: Alibunar, Bela Crkva, Kovacica, Kovin, Opovo, Pancevo, Plandiste, Vrsac; North Backa: Backa Topola, Mali Idjos, Subotica; North Banat: Ada, Coka, Kanjiza, Kikinda, Novi Knezevac, Senta; Central Banat: Nova Crnja, Novi Becej, Secanj, Zitiste, Zrenjanin; Srem: Indija, Irig, Pecinci, Ruma, Sid, Sremska Mitrovica, Stara Pazova; West Backa: Apatin, Kula, Odzaci, Sombor

**Independence:** 5 June 2006 (from Serbia and Montenegro)

**National holiday:** National Day, 15 February

**Constitution:** adopted 8 November 2006; effective 10 November 2006

**Legal system:** based on civil law system

**Suffrage:** 18 years of age; universal

**Executive branch:**
*chief of state:* President Boris TADIC (since 11 July 2004)
*head of government:* Prime Minister Mirko CVETKOVIC (since 7 July 2008)
*cabinet:* Federal Ministries act as cabinet
*elections:* president elected by direct vote for a five-year term (eligible for a second term); election last held 3 February 2008 (next to be held in 2013); prime minister elected by the National Assembly
*election results:* Boris TADIC elected president in the second round of voting; Boris TADIC received 51.2% of the vote and Tomislav NIKOLIC 48.8%

**Legislative branch:** unicameral National Assembly (250 seats; deputies elected according to party lists to serve four-year terms)
*elections:* last held on 11 May 2008 (next to be held in May 2012)
*election results:* percent of vote by party - For a European Serbia coalition 38.4%, SRS 29.5%, DSS-NS 11.6%, SPS-led coalition 7.6%, LPD 5.2%, other 7.7%; seats by party - For a European Serbia coalition 102, SRS 77, DSS-NS 30, SNS 21, SPS-led coalition 20, LDP 13, other 7; note - the seat allocation for the SNS and SRS is uncertain because of an ongoing dispute with the SRS

**Judicial branch:** Constitutional Court, Supreme Court (to become court of cassation under new constitution), appellate courts, district courts, municipal courts

**Political parties and leaders:** Coalition of Albanians of the Presevo Valley or KAPD [Riza HALIMI]; Coalition for Sandzak or KZS [Sulejman UGLJANIN]; Democratic Party of Albanians or PDSh [Ragmi MUSTAFA]; Democratic Party of Serbia or DSS [Vojislav KOSTUNICA]; Democratic Party or DS [Boris TADIC]; Democratic Union of the Valley or BDL [Skender DESTANI]; For a European Serbia [Boris TADIC]; Force of Serbia Movement or PSS [Bogoljub KARIC]; G17 Plus [Mladjan DINKIC]; League of Vojvodina Hungarians or SVM [Istvan PASTOR]; Liberal Democratic Party or LDP [Cedomir JOVANOVIC]; Movement for Democratic Progress or LPD [Jonuz MUSLIU]; New Serbia or NS [Velimir ILIC]; Party of Democratic Action or PVD [Riza HALIMI]; People's Party or NS [Maja GOJKOVIC]; Roma Party or RP [Srdjan SAJN]; Serbian Progressive Party or SNS [Tomislav NIKOLIC]; Serbian Radical Party or SRS [Vojislav SESELJ (currently on trial at The Hague), with Dragan TODOROVIC as acting leader]; Socialist Party of Serbia or SPS [Ivica DACIC]; Union of Roma of Serbia or URS [Rajko DJURIC]

**Political pressure groups and leaders:** NA

**International organization participation:** BSEC, CE, CEI, EAPC, EBRD, FAO, G-9, IAEA, IBRD, ICAO, ICC, ICCt, ICRM, IDA, IFAD (suspended), IFC, IFRCS, IHO, ILO, IMF, IMO, IMSO, Interpol, IOC, IOM, IPU, ISO, ITSO, ITU, ITUC, MIGA, MONUC, NAM (observer), OAS (observer), OIF (observer), OPCW, OSCE, PCA, PFP, SECI, UN, UNCTAD, UNESCO, UNHCR, UNIDO, UNMIL, UNOCI, UNWTO, UPU, WCL, WCO, WFTU, WHO, WIPO, WMO, WTO (observer)

# Serbia (continued)

## Diplomatic representation in the US:

*chief of mission:* Ambassador Vladimir PETROVIC (since 14 April 2009)

*chancery:* 2134 Kalorama Road NW, Washington, DC 20008

*telephone:* [1] (202) 332-0333

*FAX:* [1] (202) 332-3933

*consulate(s) general:* Chicago, New York

## Diplomatic representation from the US:

*chief of mission:* Ambassador Cameron MUNTER

*embassy:* Kneza Milosa 50, 11000 Belgrade

*mailing address:* 5070 Belgrade Place, Washington, DC 20521-5070

*telephone:* [381] (11) 361-9344

*FAX:* [381] (11) 361-8230

**Flag description:** three equal horizontal stripes of red (top), blue, and white; charged with the coat of arms of Serbia shifted slightly to the hoist side

## Economy

**Economy - overview:** MILOSEVIC-era mismanagement of the economy, an extended period of international economic sanctions, and the damage to Yugoslavia's infrastructure and industry during the NATO airstrikes in 1999 left the economy only half the size it was in 1990. After the ousting of former Federal Yugoslav President MILOSEVIC in September 2000, the Democratic Opposition of Serbia (DOS) coalition government implemented stabilization measures and embarked on a market reform program. After renewing its membership in the IMF in December 2000, Yugoslavia continued to reintegrate into the international community by rejoining the World Bank (IBRD) and the European Bank for Reconstruction and Development (EBRD). A World Bank-European Commission sponsored Donors' Conference held in June 2001 raised $1.3 billion for economic restructuring. In November 2001, the Paris Club agreed to reschedule the country's $4.5 billion public debt and wrote off 66% of the debt. In July 2004, the London Club of private creditors forgave $1.7 billion of debt just over half the total owed. Belgrade has made progress in trade liberalization and enterprise restructuring and privatization, including telecommunications and small- and medium-size firms. It has made halting progress towards EU membership despite signing a Stabilization and Association Agreement with Brussels in May 2008. Serbia is also pursuing membership in the World Trade Organization. Unemployment and the large current account deficit remain ongoing political and economic problems.

**GDP (purchasing power parity):**
$80.74 billion (2008 est.)
$76.46 billion (2007)
$71.39 billion (2006)
*note:* data are in 2008 US dollars

**GDP (official exchange rate):** $52.18 billion (2008 est.)

**GDP - real growth rate:**
5.6% (2008 est.)
7.1% (2007 est.)
5.6% (2006 est.)

**GDP - per capita (PPP):**
$10,900 (2008 est.)
$10,300 (2007 est.)
$9,500 (2006 est.)
*note:* data are in 2008 US dollars

**GDP - composition by sector:**
*agriculture:* 12.3%
*industry:* 24.2%
*services:* 63.5% (2007 est.)

**Labor force:** 2.961 million (2002 est.)

**Labor force - by occupation:**
*agriculture:* 30%
*industry:* 46%
*services:* 24% (2002)

**Unemployment rate:**
18.8% (2007 est.)

**Population below poverty line:** 6.5% (2007 est.)

**Distribution of family income - Gini index:** 30 (2003)

**Investment (gross fixed):** 20.1% of GDP (2007 est.)

**Budget:**
*revenues:* $9.6 billion
*expenditures:* $9.8 billion (2007 est.)

**Public debt:** 37% of GDP (2007 est.)

**Inflation rate (consumer prices):**
6.8% (2007)

**Central bank discount rate:** 9.57% (31 December 2007)

**Commercial bank prime lending rate:** 11.13% (31 December 2007)

**Stock of money:** $4.632 billion (31 December 2007)

**Stock of quasi money:** $12.19 billion (31 December 2007)

**Stock of domestic credit:** $13.44 billion (31 December 2007)

**Market value of publicly traded shares:** $23.93 billion (31 December 2007)

**Agriculture - products:** wheat, maize, sugar beets, sunflower, raspberries, beef, pork, milk

**Industries:** sugar, agricultural machinery, electrical and communication equipment, paper and pulp, lead, transportation equipment

**Industrial production growth rate:** 1.8% (2007 est.)

**Electricity - production:** 33.87 billion kWh (2004)

**Electricity - consumption:** NA kWh

**Electricity - exports:** 12.05 billion kWh (2004 est.)

**Electricity - imports:** 11.23 billion kWh (2004)

**Oil - production:** 11,410 bbl/day (2007 est.)

**Oil - consumption:** 85,000 bbl/day (2003 est.)

**Oil - exports:** 3,641 bbl/day (2005)

**Oil - imports:** 70,760 bbl/day (2005 est.)

**Oil - proved reserves:** 77.5 million bbl (1 January 2008 est.)

**Natural gas - production:** 650 million cu m (2005 est.)

**Natural gas - consumption:** 2.55 billion cu m (2005 est.)

**Natural gas - exports:** 0 cu m (2005 est.)

**Natural gas - imports:** 2.1 billion cu m (2004 est.)

**Natural gas - proved reserves:** 48.14 billion cu m (1 January 2008 est.)

**Current account balance:** -$6.889 billion (2007 est.)

**Exports:** $8.824 billion (2007 est.)

**Exports - commodities:** manufactured goods, food and live animals, machinery and transport equipment

**Imports:** $18.35 billion f.o.b. (2007 est.)

**Reserves of foreign exchange and gold:** $14.22 billion (2007 est.)

**Debt - external:** $26.24 billion (includes debt for Montenegro and Kosovo) (2007 est.)

**Stock of direct foreign investment - at home:** $11.95 billion (2006 est.)

**Stock of direct foreign investment - abroad:** $NA

**Exchange rates:** Serbian dinars (RSD) per US dollar -54.5 (2007), 59.98 (2006)

## Communications

**Telephones - main lines in use:** 2.993 million (2007)

**Telephones - mobile cellular:** 8.453 million (2007)

**Telephone system:**
*general assessment:* modernization of the telecommunications network has been slow as a result of damage stemming from the 1999 war and transition to a competitive market-based system; network was 90% digitalized in 2006
*domestic:* teledensity remains below the average for neighboring states; GSM wireless service, available through multiple providers with national coverage, is growing very rapidly; best telecommunications service limited to urban centers
*international:* country code - 381

**Radio broadcast stations:** 153 (station types NA) (2001)

**Internet country code:** .rs

**Internet hosts:** NA

**Internet users:** 1.5 million (2007)

## Transportation

**Airports:** 39 (2007)

**Airports - with paved runways:**
*total:* 14
*over 3,047 m:* 2
*2,438 to 3,047 m:* 4
*1,524 to 2,437 m:* 4
*914 to 1,523 m:* 2
*under 914 m:* 2 (2008)

**Airports - with unpaved runways:**
*total:* 23
*1,524 to 2,437 m:* 2
*914 to 1,523 m:* 9
*under 914 m:* 12 (2008)

**Heliports:** 2 (2007)
**Pipelines:** gas 1,921 km; oil 323 km (2008)
**Railways:**
*total:* 3,379 km
*standard gauge:* 3,379 km 1.435-m gauge (electrified 1,254 km) (2006)
**Roadways:**
*total:* 36,875 km
*paved:* 31,392 km
*unpaved:* 5,483 km (2006)
**Waterways:** 587 km (primarily on Danube and Sava rivers) (2008)

## Military

**Military branches:** Serbian Armed Forces (Vojska Srbije, VS): Land Forces Command (includes Riverine Component, consisting of a river flotilla on the Danube), Joint Operations Command, Air and Air Defense Forces Command (2009)
**Military service age and obligation:** 19-35 years of age for male compulsory military service; under a state of war or impending war, conscription can begin at age 16; conscription is to be abolished in 2010; 6-month service obligation, with a reserve obligation to age 60 for men and 50 for women (2007)
**Manpower fit for military service:**
*males age 16-49:* 1,415,007
*females age 16-49:* 1,379,541 (2009 est.)
**Manpower reaching militarily significant age annually:**
*male:* 44,601
*female:* 41,845 (2009 est.)

## Transnational Issues

**Disputes - international:** Serbia with several other states protest the U.S. and other states' recognition of Kosovo's declaring itself as a sovereign and independent state in February 2008; ethnic Serbian municipalities along Kosovo's northern border challenge final status of Kosovo-Serbia boundary; several thousand NATO-led KFOR peacekeepers under UNMIK authority continue to keep the peace within Kosovo between the ethnic Albanian majority and the Serb minority in Kosovo; Serbia delimited about half of the boundary with Bosnia and Herzegovina, but sections along the Drina River remain in dispute
**Refugees and internally displaced persons:**
*refugees (country of origin):* 71,111 (Croatia); 27,414 (Bosnia and Herzegovina); 206,000 (Kosovo), note - mostly ethnic Serbs and Roma who fled Kosovo in 1999 (2007)
**Illicit drugs:** transshipment point for Southwest Asian heroin moving to Western Europe on the Balkan route; economy vulnerable to money laundering

# Seychelles

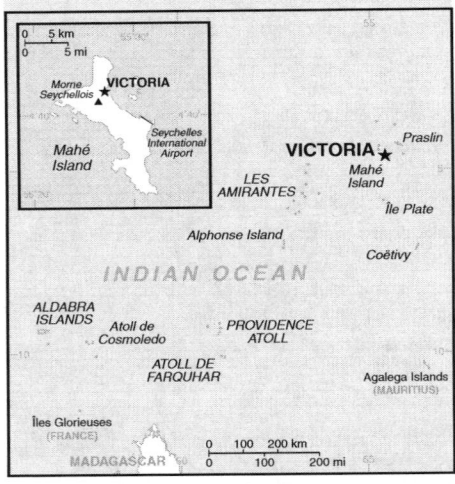

## Introduction

**Background:** A lengthy struggle between France and Great Britain for the islands ended in 1814, when they were ceded to the latter. Independence came in 1976. Socialist rule was brought to a close with a new constitution and free elections in 1993. President France-Albert RENE, who had served since 1977, was re-elected in 2001, but stepped down in 2004. Vice President James MICHEL took over the presidency and in July 2006 was elected to a new five-year term.

## Geography

**Location:** archipelago in the Indian Ocean, northeast of Madagascar
**Geographic coordinates:** 4 35 S, 55 40 E
**Map references:** Africa
**Area:**
*total:* 455 sq km
*land:* 455 sq km
*water:* 0 sq km
**Area - comparative:** 2.5 times the size of Washington, DC
**Land boundaries:** 0 km
**Coastline:** 491 km
**Maritime claims:**
*territorial sea:* 12 nm
*contiguous zone:* 24 nm
*exclusive economic zone:* 200 nm
*continental shelf:* 200 nm or to the edge of the continental margin
**Climate:** tropical marine; humid; cooler season during southeast monsoon (late May to September); warmer season during northwest monsoon (March to May)
**Terrain:** Mahe Group is granitic, narrow coastal strip, rocky, hilly; others are coral, flat, elevated reefs

**Elevation extremes:**
*lowest point:* Indian Ocean 0 m
*highest point:* Morne Seychellois 905 m
**Natural resources:** fish, copra, cinnamon trees
**Land use:**
*arable land:* 2.17%
*permanent crops:* 13.04%
*other:* 84.79% (2005)
**Irrigated land:** NA
**Natural hazards:** lies outside the cyclone belt, so severe storms are rare; short droughts possible
**Environment - current issues:** water supply depends on catchments to collect rainwater
**Environment - international agreements:**
*party to:* Biodiversity, Climate Change, Climate Change-Kyoto Protocol, Desertification, Endangered Species, Hazardous Wastes, Law of the Sea, Marine Dumping, Ozone Layer Protection, Ship Pollution, Wetlands
*signed, but not ratified:* none of the selected agreements
**Geography - note:** 41 granitic and about 75 coralline islands

## People

**Population:** 87,476 (July 2009 est.)
**Age structure:**
*0-14 years:* 22.8% (male 10,201/female 9,732)
*15-64 years:* 70.1% (male 31,870/female 29,439)
*65 years and over:* 7.1% (male 2,321/female 3,913) (2009 est.)
**Median age:**
*total:* 31.4 years
*male:* 30.9 years
*female:* 32 years (2009 est.)
**Population growth rate:** 0.999% (2009 est.)
**Birth rate:** 15.87 births/1,000 population (2009 est.)
**Death rate:** 6.21 deaths/1,000 population (2008 est.)
**Net migration rate:** 1.05 migrant(s)/1,000 population (2009 est.)
**Urbanization:**
*urban population:* 54% of total population (2008)
*rate of urbanization:* 1.4% annual rate of change (2005-10 est.)
**Sex ratio:**
*at birth:* 1.03 male(s)/female
*under 15 years:* 1.05 male(s)/female
*15-64 years:* 1.08 male(s)/female
*65 years and over:* 0.59 male(s)/female
*total population:* 1.03 male(s)/female (2009 est.)
**Infant mortality rate:**
*total:* 12.3 deaths/1,000 live births
*male:* 15.44 deaths/1,000 live births
*female:* 9.06 deaths/1,000 live births (2009 est.)
**Life expectancy at birth:**
*total population:* 73.02 years
*male:* 68.33 years
*female:* 77.85 years (2009 est.)
**Total fertility rate:** 1.93 children born/woman (2009 est.)
**HIV/AIDS - adult prevalence rate:** NA

# Seychelles (continued)

**HIV/AIDS - people living with HIV/AIDS:** NA
**HIV/AIDS - deaths:** NA
**Nationality:**
*noun:* Seychellois (singular and plural)
*adjective:* Seychellois
**Ethnic groups:** mixed French, African, Indian, Chinese, and Arab
**Religions:** Roman Catholic 82.3%, Anglican 6.4%, Seventh Day Adventist 1.1%, other Christian 3.4%, Hindu 2.1%, Muslim 1.1%, other non-Christian 1.5%, unspecified 1.5%, none 0.6% (2002 census)
**Languages:** Creole 91.8%, English 4.9% (official), other 3.1%, unspecified 0.2% (2002 census)
**Literacy:**
*definition:* age 15 and over can read and write
*total population:* 91.8%
*male:* 91.4%
*female:* 92.3% (2002 census)
**School life expectancy (primary to tertiary education):**
*total:* 15 years
*male:* 14 years
*female:* 15 years (2007)
**Education expenditures:** 6.5% of GDP (2006)

## Government

**Country name:**
*conventional long form:* Republic of Seychelles
*conventional short form:* Seychelles
*local long form:* Republic of Seychelles
*local short form:* Seychelles
**Government type:** republic
**Capital:**
*name:* Victoria
*geographic coordinates:* 4 38 S, 55 27 E
*time difference:* UTC+4 (9 hours ahead of Washington, DC during Standard Time)
**Administrative divisions:** 23 administrative districts; Anse aux Pins, Anse Boileau, Anse Etoile, Anse Louis, Anse Royale, Baie Lazare, Baie Sainte Anne, Beau Vallon, Bel Air, Bel Ombre, Cascade, Glacis, Grand' Anse (on Mahe), Grand' Anse (on Praslin), La Digue, La Riviere Anglaise, Mont Buxton, Mont Fleuri, Plaisance, Pointe La Rue, Port Glaud, Saint Louis, Takamaka
**Independence:** 29 June 1976 (from the UK)
**National holiday:** Constitution Day (National Day), 18 June (1993)
**Constitution:** 18 June 1993
**Legal system:** based on English common law, French civil law, and customary law; has not accepted compulsory ICJ jurisdiction
**Suffrage:** 17 years of age; universal
**Executive branch:**
*chief of state:* President James Alix MICHEL (since 14 April 2004); note - the president is both the chief of state and head of government
*head of government:* President James MICHEL (since 14 April 2004)
*cabinet:* Council of Ministers appointed by the president

*elections:* president elected by popular vote for a five-year term (eligible for two more terms); election last held 28-30 July 2006 (next to be held in 2011)
*election results:* President James MICHEL elected president; percent of vote - James MICHEL 53.73%, Wavel RAMKALAWAN 45.71%, Philippe BOULLE 0.56%; note - this was the first election in which President James MICHEL participated; he was originally sworn in as president after former president France Albert RENE stepped down in April 2004
**Legislative branch:** unicameral National Assembly or Assemblee Nationale (34 seats; 25 members elected by popular vote, 9 allocated on a proportional basis to parties winning at least 10% of the vote; to serve five-year terms)
*elections:* last held 10-12 May 2007 (next to be held in 2012)
*election results:* percent of vote by party - SPPF 56.2%, SNP 43.8%; seats by party - SPPF 23, SNP 11
**Judicial branch:** Court of Appeal; Supreme Court; judges for both courts are appointed by the president
**Political parties and leaders:** Democratic Party or DP [James MANCHAM, Paul CHOW]; Seychelles National Party or SNP [Wavel RAMKALAWAN] (formerly the United Opposition or UO); People's Party (Parti Lepep) or LP [France Albert RENE, James MICHEL] (the governing party)
**Political pressure groups and leaders:** Roman Catholic Church
*other:* trade unions
**International organization participation:** ACP, AfDB, AU, C, COMESA, FAO, G-77, IAEA, IBRD, ICAO, ICCt (signatory), ICRM, IFAD, IFC, IFRCS, ILO, IMF, IMO, InOC, Interpol, IOC, ISO (correspondent), ITU, ITUC, MIGA, NAM, OIF, OPCW, SADC, UN, UNCTAD, UNESCO, UNIDO, UNWTO, UPU, WCO, WFTU, WHO, WIPO, WMO, WTO (observer)
**Diplomatic representation in the US:**
*chief of mission:* Ambassador Jean Ronald JUMEAU
*chancery:* 800 Second Avenue, Suite 400C, New York, NY 10017
*telephone:* [1] (212) 972-1785
*FAX:* [1] (212) 972-1786
**Diplomatic representation from the US:** the US does not have an embassy in Seychelles; the ambassador to Mauritius is accredited to Seychelles
**Flag description:** five oblique bands of blue (hoist side), yellow, red, white, and green (bottom) radiating from the bottom of the hoist side

## Economy

**Economy - overview:** Since independence in 1976, per capita output in this Indian Ocean archipelago has expanded to roughly seven times the pre-independence, near-subsistence level, moving the island into the upper-middle income group of countries. Growth has been led by the tourist sector, which employs about 30% of the labor force and provides more than 70% of hard currency earnings, and by tuna fishing. In recent years, the government

has encouraged foreign investment to upgrade hotels and other services. At the same time, the government has moved to reduce the dependence on tourism by promoting the development of farming, fishing, and small-scale manufacturing. GDP grew about 7-8% per year in 2006-07, driven by tourism and a boom in tourism-related construction. The Seychelles rupee was allowed to depreciate in 2006 after being overvalued for years and fell by 10% in the first 9 months of 2007. Despite these actions, the Seychelles economy has struggled to maintain its gains and in 2008 suffered from food and oil price shocks, a foreign exchange shortage, high inflation and large financing gaps, with GDP growth reduced to about 3% in 2008. In July 2008 the government defaulted on a Euro amortizing note worth roughly US$80 million, leading to a downgrading of Seychelles credit rating. Seychelles requested an IMF Stand-By Agreement in December 2008.
**GDP (purchasing power parity):**
$1.473 billion (2008 est.)
$1.429 billion (2007)
$1.332 billion (2006)
*note:* data are in 2008 US dollars
**GDP (official exchange rate):** $779 million (2008 est.)
**GDP - real growth rate:**
3.1% (2008 est.)
7.3% (2007 est.)
8.3% (2006 est.)
**GDP - per capita (PPP):**
$17,000 (2008 est.)
$16,700 (2007 est.)
$15,700 (2006 est.)
*note:* data are in 2008 US dollars
**GDP - composition by sector:**
*agriculture:* 1.9%
*industry:* 28.3%
*services:* 69.9% (2008 est.)
**Labor force:** 39,560 (2006)
**Labor force - by occupation:**
*agriculture:* 3%
*industry:* 23%
*services:* 74% (2006)
**Unemployment rate:**
2% (2006 est.)
**Population below poverty line:** NA%
**Household income or consumption by percentage share:**
*lowest 10%:* NA%
*highest 10%:* NA%
**Investment (gross fixed):** 10.1% of GDP (2008 est.)
**Budget:**
*revenues:* $318.1 million
*expenditures:* $324.6 million (2008 est.)
**Public debt:** 92.6% of GDP (2008 est.)
**Inflation rate (consumer prices):**
25.8% (2008 est.)
5.3% (2007 est.)
**Central bank discount rate:** 5.13% (31 December 2007)

## Seychelles (continued)

**Commercial bank prime lending rate:** 10.89% (31 December 2007)

**Stock of money:** $330.8 million (31 December 2007)

**Stock of quasi money:** $249 million (31 December 2007)

**Stock of domestic credit:** $660.2 million (31 December 2007)

**Market value of publicly traded shares:** $NA

**Agriculture - products:** coconuts, cinnamon, vanilla, sweet potatoes, cassava (tapioca), bananas; poultry; tuna

**Industries:** fishing, tourism, processing of coconuts and vanilla, coir (coconut fiber) rope, boat building, printing, furniture; beverages

**Industrial production growth rate:** 4% (2008 est.)

**Electricity - production:** 208 million kWh (2006 est.)

**Electricity - consumption:** 193.4 million kWh (2006 est.)

**Electricity - exports:** 0 kWh (2007 est.)

**Electricity - imports:** 0 kWh (2007 est.)

**Oil - production:** 0 bbl/day (2007 est.)

**Oil - consumption:** 6,560 bbl/day (2006 est.)

**Oil - exports:** 0 bbl/day (2006)

**Oil - imports:** 5,722 bbl/day (2005)

**Oil - proved reserves:** 0 bbl (1 January 2006)

**Natural gas - production:** 0 cu m (2007 est.)

**Natural gas - consumption:** 0 cu m (2007 est.)

**Natural gas - exports:** 0 cu m (2007 est.)

**Natural gas - imports:** 0 cu m (2007 est.)

**Natural gas - proved reserves:** 0 cu m (1 January 2006 est.)

**Current account balance:** -$307 million (2008 est.)

**Exports:** $425 million f.o.b. (2008 est.)

**Exports - commodities:** canned tuna, frozen fish, cinnamon bark, copra, petroleum products (reexports)

**Exports - partners:** UK 23.7%, France 19.8%, Mauritius 10%, Japan 8.3%, Italy 5.7%, Spain 5.1% (2007)

**Imports:** $952 million f.o.b. (2008 est.)

**Imports - commodities:** machinery and equipment, foodstuffs, petroleum products, chemicals

**Imports - partners:** Saudi Arabia 17.6%, Germany 10.8%, France 8.1%, Spain 7.6%, South Africa 6.4%, Singapore 5.8% (2007)

**Reserves of foreign exchange and gold:** $59 million (31 December 2008 est.)

**Debt - external:** $1.161 billion (31 December 2008 est.)

**Exchange rates:** Seychelles rupees (SCR) per US dollar - 8 (2008 est.), 6.5 (2007), 5.5 (2006), 5.5 (2005), 5.5 (2004)

### Communications

**Telephones - main lines in use:** 22,700 (2007)

**Telephones - mobile cellular:** 77,300 (2007)

**Telephone system:**
*general assessment:* effective system
*domestic:* combined fixed-line and mobile-cellular teledensity is nearly 125 telephones per 100 persons; radiotelephone communications between islands in the archipelago
*international:* country code - 248; direct radiotelephone communications with adjacent island countries and African coastal countries; satellite earth station - 1 Intelsat (Indian Ocean)

**Radio broadcast stations:** AM 1, FM 1, shortwave 2 (2001)

**Television broadcast stations:** 2 (plus 9 repeaters) (1997)

**Internet country code:** .sc

**Internet hosts:** 284 (2008)

**Internet users:** 32,000 (2007)

### Transportation

**Airports:** 15 (2008)

**Airports - with paved runways:**
*total:* 9
*2,438 to 3,047 m:* 1
*914 to 1,523 m:* 6
*under 914 m:* 2 (2008)

**Airports - with unpaved runways:**
*total:* 6
*914 to 1,523 m:* 2
*under 914 m:* 4 (2008)

**Roadways:**
*total:* 458 km
*paved:* 440 km
*unpaved:* 18 km (2003)

**Merchant marine:**
*total:* 8
*by type:* cargo 1, carrier 1, chemical tanker 6
*foreign-owned:* 3 (Hong Kong 1, Nigeria 1, South Africa 1) (2008)

**Ports and terminals:** Victoria

### Military

**Military branches:** Seychelles Defense Force: Army, Coast Guard (includes Naval Wing, Air Wing), National Guard (2005)

**Military service age and obligation:** 18 years of age for voluntary military service (younger with parental consent); no conscription (2008)

**Manpower available for military service:**
*males age 16-49:* 23,598
*females age 16-49:* 24,424 (2008 est.)

**Manpower fit for military service:**
*males age 16-49:* 19,702
*females age 16-49:* 19,780 (2009 est.)

**Manpower reaching militarily significant age annually:**
*male:* 714
*female:* 685 (2009 est.)

**Military expenditures:** 2% of GDP (2006 est.)

### Transnational Issues

**Disputes - international:** together with Mauritius, Seychelles claims the Chagos Archipelago (UK-administered British Indian Ocean Territory)

# Sierra Leone

### Introduction

**Background:** Democracy is slowly being reestablished after the civil war from 1991 to 2002 that resulted in tens of thousands of deaths and the displacement of more than 2 million people (about one-third of the population). The military, which took over full responsibility for security following the departure of UN peacekeepers at the end of 2005, is increasingly developing as a guarantor of the country's stability. The armed forces remained on the sideline during the 2007 presidential election, but still look to the UN Integrated Office in Sierra Leone (UNIOSIL) - a civilian UN mission - to support efforts to consolidate peace. The new government's priorities include furthering development, creating jobs, and stamping out endemic corruption.

### Geography

**Location:** Western Africa, bordering the North Atlantic Ocean, between Guinea and Liberia

**Geographic coordinates:** 8 30 N, 11 30 W

**Map references:** Africa

**Area:**
*total:* 71,740 sq km
*land:* 71,620 sq km
*water:* 120 sq km

**Area - comparative:** slightly smaller than South Carolina

**Land boundaries:**
*total:* 958 km
*border countries:* Guinea 652 km, Liberia 306 km

**Coastline:** 402 km

**Maritime claims:**
*territorial sea:* 12 nm
*contiguous zone:* 24 nm
*exclusive economic zone:* 200 nm
*continental shelf:* 200 nm

**Climate:** tropical; hot, humid; summer rainy season (May to December); winter dry season (December to April)

# Sierra Leone *(continued)*

**Terrain:** coastal belt of mangrove swamps, wooded hill country, upland plateau, mountains in east

**Elevation extremes:**

*lowest point:* Atlantic Ocean 0 m

*highest point:* Loma Mansa (Bintimani) 1,948 m

**Natural resources:** diamonds, titanium ore, bauxite, iron ore, gold, chromite

**Land use:**

*arable land:* 7.95%

*permanent crops:* 1.05%

*other:* 91% (2005)

**Irrigated land:** 300 sq km (2003)

**Total renewable water resources:** 160 cu km (1987)

**Freshwater withdrawal (domestic/industrial/agricultural):**

*total:* 0.38 cu km/yr (5%/3%/92%)

*per capita:* 69 cu m/yr (2000)

**Natural hazards:** dry, sand-laden harmattan winds blow from the Sahara (December to February); sandstorms, dust storms

**Environment - current issues:** rapid population growth pressuring the environment; overharvesting of timber, expansion of cattle grazing, and slash-and-burn agriculture have resulted in deforestation and soil exhaustion; civil war depleted natural resources; overfishing

**Environment - international agreements:**

*party to:* Biodiversity, Climate Change, Climate Change-Kyoto Protocol, Desertification, Endangered Species, Law of the Sea, Marine Life Conservation, Ozone Layer Protection, Ship Pollution, Wetlands

*signed, but not ratified:* Environmental Modification

**Geography - note:** rainfall along the coast can reach 495 cm (195 inches) a year, making it one of the wettest places along coastal, western Africa

## People

**Population:** 6,440,053 (July 2009 est.)

**Age structure:**

*0-14 years:* 44.5% (male 1,407,226/female 1,460,366)

*15-64 years:* 52.2% (male 1,613,554/female 1,750,250)

*65 years and over:* 3.2% (male 95,533/female 113,124) (2009 est.)

**Median age:**

*total:* 17.5 years

*male:* 17.2 years

*female:* 17.8 years (2009 est.)

**Population growth rate:** 2.282% (2009 est.)

**Birth rate:** 44.73 births/1,000 population (2009 est.)

**Death rate:** 22.26 deaths/1,000 population (2008 est.)

**Net migration rate:** 0 migrant(s)/1,000 population

*note:* refugees currently in surrounding countries are slowly returning (2009 est.)

**Urbanization:**

*urban population:* 38% of total population (2008)

*rate of urbanization:* 2.9% annual rate of change (2005-10 est.)

**Sex ratio:**

*at birth:* 1.03 male(s)/female

*under 15 years:* 0.96 male(s)/female

*15-64 years:* 0.92 male(s)/female

*65 years and over:* 0.84 male(s)/female

*total population:* 0.94 male(s)/female (2009 est.)

**Infant mortality rate:**

*total:* 154.43 deaths/1,000 live births

*male:* 171.57 deaths/1,000 live births

*female:* 136.78 deaths/1,000 live births (2009 est.)

**Life expectancy at birth:**

*total population:* 41.24 years

*male:* 38.92 years

*female:* 43.64 years (2009 est.)

**Total fertility rate:** 5.88 children born/woman (2009 est.)

**HIV/AIDS - adult prevalence rate:** 1.7% (2007 est.)

**HIV/AIDS - people living with HIV/AIDS:** 55,000 (2007 est.)

**HIV/AIDS - deaths:** 3,300 (2007 est.)

**Major infectious diseases:**

*degree of risk:* very high

*food or waterborne diseases:* bacterial and protozoal diarrhea, hepatitis A, and typhoid fever

*vectorborne diseases:* malaria and yellow fever

*water contact disease:* schistosomiasis

*aerosolized dust or soil contact disease:* Lassa fever (2009)

**Nationality:**

*noun:* Sierra Leonean(s)

*adjective:* Sierra Leonean

**Ethnic groups:** 20 African ethnic groups 90% (Temne 30%, Mende 30%, other 30%), Creole (Krio) 10% (descendants of freed Jamaican slaves who were settled in the Freetown area in the late-18th century), refugees from Liberia's recent civil war, small numbers of Europeans, Lebanese, Pakistanis, and Indians

**Religions:** Muslim 60%, Christian 10%, indigenous beliefs 30%

**Languages:** English (official, regular use limited to literate minority), Mende (principal vernacular in the south), Temne (principal vernacular in the north), Krio (English-based Creole, spoken by the descendants of freed Jamaican slaves who were settled in the Freetown area, a lingua franca and a first language for 10% of the population but understood by 95%)

**Literacy:**

*definition:* age 15 and over can read and write English, Mende, Temne, or Arabic

*total population:* 35.1%

*male:* 46.9%

*female:* 24.4% (2004 est.)

**School life expectancy (primary to tertiary education):**

*total:* 7 years

*male:* 8 years

*female:* 6 years (2001)

**Education expenditures:** 3.8% of GDP (2005)

## Government

**Country name:**

*conventional long form:* Republic of Sierra Leone

*conventional short form:* Sierra Leone

*local long form:* Republic of Sierra Leone

*local short form:* Sierra Leone

**Government type:** constitutional democracy

**Capital:**

*name:* Freetown

*geographic coordinates:* 8 30 N, 13 15 W

*time difference:* UTC 0 (5 hours ahead of Washington, DC during Standard Time)

**Administrative divisions:** 3 provinces and 1 area*; Eastern, Northern, Southern, Western*

**Independence:** 27 April 1961 (from the UK)

**National holiday:** Independence Day, 27 April (1961)

**Constitution:** 1 October 1991; amended several times

**Legal system:** based on English law and customary laws indigenous to local tribes; has not accepted compulsory ICJ jurisdiction

**Suffrage:** 18 years of age; universal

**Executive branch:**

*chief of state:* President Ernest Bai KOROMA (since 17 September 2007); note - the president is both the chief of state and head of government

*head of government:* President Ernest Bai KOROMA (since 17 September 2007)

*cabinet:* Ministers of State appointed by the president with the approval of the House of Representatives; the cabinet is responsible to the president

*elections:* president elected by popular vote for a five-year term (eligible for a second term); election last held 11 August 2007 and 8 September 2007 (next to be held in 2012)

*election results:* second round results; percent of vote - Ernest Bai KOROMA 54.6%, Solomon BEREWA 45.4%

**Legislative branch:** unicameral Parliament (124 seats; 112 members elected by popular vote, 12 filled by paramount chiefs elected in separate elections; serve five-year terms)

*elections:* last held on 11 August 2007 (next to be held in 2012)

*election results:* percent of vote by party - NA; seats by party - APC 59, SLPP 43, PMDC 10

**Judicial branch:** Supreme Court; Appeals Court; High Court

**Political parties and leaders:** All People's Congress or APC [Ernest Bai KOROMA]; Peace and Liberation Party or PLP [Darlington MORRISON]; People's Movement for Democratic Change or PMDC [Charles MARGAI]; Sierra Leone People's Party or SLPP [Solomon BEREWA]; numerous others

**Political pressure groups and leaders:**

*other:* student unions; trade unions

**International organization participation:** ACP, AfDB, AU, C, ECOWAS, FAO, G-77, IAEA, IBRD, ICAO, ICCt, ICRM, IDA, IDB, IFAD, IFC, IFRCS, ILO, IMF, IMO, Interpol, IOC, IOM, IPU, ITU, ITUC, MIGA,

# Sierra Leone (continued)

NAM, OIC, OPCW, UN, UNCTAD, UNESCO, UNIDO, UNMIT, UNWTO, UPU, WCL, WCO, WFTU, WHO, WIPO, WMO, WTO

**Diplomatic representation in the US:**
*chief of mission:* Ambassador Bockari Kortu STEVENS
*chancery:* 1701 19th Street NW, Washington, DC 20009
*telephone:* [1] (202) 939-9261 through 9263
*FAX:* [1] (202) 483-1793

**Diplomatic representation from the US:**
*chief of mission:* Ambassador June Carter PERRY
*embassy:* Southridge-Hill Station, Freetown
*mailing address:* use embassy street address
*telephone:* [232] (22) 515 000 or (76) 515 000
*FAX:* [232] (22) 515 355

**Flag description:** three equal horizontal bands of light green (top), white, and light blue

## Economy

**Economy - overview:** Sierra Leone is an extremely poor nation with tremendous inequality in income distribution. While it possesses substantial mineral, agricultural, and fishery resources, its physical and social infrastructure is not well developed, and serious social disorders continue to hamper economic development. Nearly half of the working-age population engages in subsistence agriculture. Manufacturing consists mainly of the processing of raw materials and of light manufacturing for the domestic market. Alluvial diamond mining remains the major source of hard currency earnings accounting for nearly half of Sierra Leone's exports. The fate of the economy depends upon the maintenance of domestic peace and the continued receipt of substantial aid from abroad, which is essential to offset the severe trade imbalance and supplement government revenues. The IMF has completed a Poverty Reduction and Growth Facility program that helped stabilize economic growth and reduce inflation. A recent increase in political stability has led to a revival of economic activity such as the rehabilitation of bauxite and rutile mining.

**GDP (purchasing power parity):**
$4.307 billion (2008 est.)
$4.063 billion (2007)
$3.819 billion (2006)
*note:* data are in 2008 US dollars

**GDP (official exchange rate):** $1.971 billion (2008 est.)

**GDP - real growth rate:**
6% (2008 est.)
6.4% (2007 est.)
7.4% (2006 est.)

**GDP - per capita (PPP):**
$700 (2008 est.)
$700 (2007 est.)
$600 (2006 est.)
*note:* data are in 2008 US dollars

**GDP - composition by sector:**
*agriculture:* 49%
*industry:* 31%
*services:* 21% (2001 est.)

**Labor force:** 1.369 million (1981 est.)

**Labor force - by occupation:**
*agriculture:* NA%
*industry:* NA%
*services:* NA%

**Unemployment rate:**
NA%

**Population below poverty line:** 70.2% (2004)

**Household income or consumption by percentage share:**
*lowest 10%:* 0.5%
*highest 10%:* 43.6% (1989)

**Distribution of family income - Gini index:** 62.9 (1989)

**Budget:**
*revenues:* $96 million
*expenditures:* $351 million (2000 est.)

**Inflation rate (consumer prices):**
11.7% (2007 est.)

**Central bank discount rate:** NA

**Commercial bank prime lending rate:** 25% (31 December 2007)

**Stock of money:** $184.6 million (31 December 2007)

**Stock of quasi money:** $177.7 million (31 December 2007)

**Stock of domestic credit:** $162.9 million (31 December 2007)

**Market value of publicly traded shares:** $NA

**Agriculture - products:** rice, coffee, cocoa, palm kernels, palm oil, peanuts; poultry, cattle, sheep, pigs; fish

**Industries:** diamond mining; small-scale manufacturing (beverages, textiles, cigarettes, footwear); petroleum refining, small commercial ship repair

**Industrial production growth rate:** NA%

**Electricity - production:** 250 million kWh (2006 est.)

**Electricity - consumption:** 232.5 million kWh (2006 est.)

**Electricity - exports:** 0 kWh (2007 est.)

**Electricity - imports:** 0 kWh (2007 est.)

**Oil - production:** 0.7008 bbl/day (2007 est.)

**Oil - consumption:** 8,430 bbl/day (2006 est.)

**Oil - exports:** 432.3 bbl/day (2005)

**Oil - imports:** 8,271 bbl/day (2005)

**Oil - proved reserves:** 0 bbl (1 January 2006 est.)

**Natural gas - production:** 0 cu m (2007 est.)

**Natural gas - consumption:** 0 cu m (2007 est.)

**Natural gas - exports:** 0 cu m (2007 est.)

**Natural gas - imports:** 0 cu m (2007 est.)

**Natural gas - proved reserves:** 0 cu m (1 January 2006 est.)

**Current account balance:** -$63 million (2007 est.)

**Exports:** $216 million f.o.b. (2006)

**Exports - commodities:** diamonds, rutile, cocoa, coffee, fish

**Exports - partners:** Belgium 49.3%, US 20.5%, Netherlands 4.5%, Canada 4.1% (2007)

**Imports:** $560 million f.o.b. (2006)

**Imports - commodities:** foodstuffs, machinery and equipment, fuels and lubricants, chemicals

**Imports - partners:** Cote d'Ivoire 10%, China 10%, US 9.5%, UK 6.2%, Netherlands 5.1%, India 4.7% (2007)

**Debt - external:** $1.61 billion (2003 est.)

**Exchange rates:** leones (SLL) per US dollar - NA (2007), 2,961.7 (2006), 2,889.6 (2005), 2,701.3 (2004), 2,347.9 (2003)

## Communications

**Telephones - main lines in use:** 24,000 (2002)

**Telephones - mobile cellular:** 776,000 (2007)

**Telephone system:**
*general assessment:* marginal telephone service
*domestic:* the national microwave radio relay trunk system connects Freetown to Bo and Kenema; mobile-cellular service is growing rapidly from a small base
*international:* country code - 232; satellite earth station -1 Intelsat (Atlantic Ocean)

**Radio broadcast stations:** AM 1, FM 9, shortwave 1 (2001)

**Television broadcast stations:** 2 (1999)

**Internet country code:** .sl

**Internet hosts:** 8 (2008)

**Internet users:** 13,000 (2007)

## Transportation

**Airports:** 10 (2008)

**Airports - with paved runways:**
*total:* 1
*over 3,047 m:* 1 (2008)

**Airports - with unpaved runways:**
*total:* 9
*914 to 1,523 m:* 7
*under 914 m:* 2 (2008)

**Heliports:** 2 (2007)

**Roadways:**
*total:* 11,300 km
*paved:* 904 km
*unpaved:* 10,396 km (2002)

**Waterways:** 800 km (600 km year round) (2007)

**Merchant marine:**
*total:* 182
*by type:* bulk carrier 4, cargo 143, carrier 2, chemical tanker 3, container 6, liquefied gas 2, passenger 1, passenger/cargo 6, petroleum tanker 10, roll on/roll off 3, specialized tanker 2
*foreign-owned:* 95 (Belgium 1, China 15, Egypt 3, Greece 1, Hong Kong 1, Lebanon 1, Nigeria 1, Panama 1, Romania 3, Russia 11, Syria 18, Taiwan 1, Turkey 15, Ukraine 10, UAE 8, UK 2, US 1, Yemen 2) (2008)

**Ports and terminals:** Freetown, Pepel, Sherbro Islands

# Sierra Leone (continued)

## Military

**Military branches:** Republic of Sierra Leone Armed Forces (RSLAF): Army (includes Maritime Wing and Air Wing) (2008)
**Military service age and obligation:** 17 years 6 months of age for voluntary military service (younger with parental consent); no conscription (2008)
**Manpower available for military service:**
*males age 16-49:* 1,315,561 (2008 est.)
**Manpower fit for military service:**
*males age 16-49:* 692,469
*females age 16-49:* 762,239 (2009 est.)
**Manpower reaching militarily significant age annually:**
*male:* 71,524
*female:* 75,491 (2009 est.)
**Military expenditures:** 2.3% of GDP (2006)

## Transnational Issues

**Disputes - international:** as domestic fighting among disparate ethnic groups, rebel groups, warlords, and youth gangs in Cote d'Ivoire, Guinea, Liberia, and Sierra Leone gradually abate, the number of refugees in border areas has begun to slowly dwindle; UN Mission in Sierra Leone (UNAMSIL) has maintained over 4,000 peacekeepers in Sierra Leone since 1999; Sierra Leone considers excessive Guinea's definition of the flood plain limits to define the left bank boundary of the Makona and Moa rivers and protests Guinea's continued occupation of these lands including the hamlet of Yenga occupied since 1998
**Refugees and internally displaced persons:**
*refugees (country of origin):* 27,311 (Liberia) (2007)

# Singapore

## Introduction

**Background:** Singapore was founded as a British trading colony in 1819. It joined the Malaysian Federation in 1963 but separated two years later and became independent. Singapore subsequently became one of the world's most prosperous countries with strong international trading links (its port is one of the world's busiest in terms of tonnage handled) and with per capita GDP equal to that of the leading nations of Western Europe.

## Geography

**Location:** Southeastern Asia, islands between Malaysia and Indonesia
**Geographic coordinates:** 1 22 N, 103 48 E
**Map references:** Southeast Asia
**Area:**
*total:* 692.7 sq km
*land:* 682.7 sq km
*water:* 10 sq km
**Area - comparative:** slightly more than 3.5 times the size of Washington, DC
**Land boundaries:** 0 km
**Coastline:** 193 km
**Maritime claims:**
*territorial sea:* 3 nm
*exclusive fishing zone:* within and beyond territorial sea, as defined in treaties and practice
**Climate:** tropical; hot, humid, rainy; two distinct monsoon seasons - Northeastern monsoon (December to March) and Southwestern monsoon (June to September); inter-monsoon - frequent afternoon and early evening thunderstorms
**Terrain:** lowland; gently undulating central plateau contains water catchment area and nature preserve
**Elevation extremes:**
*lowest point:* Singapore Strait 0 m
*highest point:* Bukit Timah 166 m

**Natural resources:** fish, deepwater ports
**Land use:**
*arable land:* 1.47%
*permanent crops:* 1.47%
*other:* 97.06% (2005)
**Irrigated land:** NA
**Total renewable water resources:** 0.6 cu km (1975)
**Freshwater withdrawal (domestic/industrial/agricultural):**
*total:* 0.19 cu km/yr (45%/51%/4%)
*per capita:* 44 cu m/yr (1975)
**Natural hazards:** NA
**Environment - current issues:** industrial pollution; limited natural fresh water resources; limited land availability presents waste disposal problems; seasonal smoke/haze resulting from forest fires in Indonesia
**Environment - international agreements:**
*party to:* Biodiversity, Climate Change, Climate Change-Kyoto Protocol, Desertification, Endangered Species, Hazardous Wastes, Law of the Sea, Ozone Layer Protection, Ship Pollution
*signed, but not ratified:* none of the selected agreements
**Geography - note:** focal point for Southeast Asian sea routes

## People

**Population:** 4,657,542 (July 2009 est.)
**Age structure:**
*0-14 years:* 14.4% (male 348,382/female 324,050)
*15-64 years:* 76.7% (male 1,737,972/female 1,833,415)
*65 years and over:* 8.9% (male 184,393/female 229,330) (2009 est.)
**Median age:**
*total:* 39 years
*male:* 38.5 years
*female:* 39.4 years (2009 est.)
**Population growth rate:** 0.998% (2009 est.)
**Birth rate:** 8.82 births/1,000 population (2009 est.)
**Death rate:** 4.53 deaths/1,000 population (2008 est.)
**Net migration rate:** 5.82 migrant(s)/1,000 population (2009 est.)
**Urbanization:**
*urban population:* 100% of total population (2008)
*rate of urbanization:* 1.2% annual rate of change (2005-10 est.)
**Sex ratio:**
*at birth:* 1.08 male(s)/female
*under 15 years:* 1.08 male(s)/female
*15-64 years:* 0.95 male(s)/female
*65 years and over:* 0.8 male(s)/female
*total population:* 0.95 male(s)/female (2009 est.)

**Infant mortality rate:**
*total:* 2.31 deaths/1,000 live births
*male:* 2.51 deaths/1,000 live births
*female:* 2.09 deaths/1,000 live births (2009 est.)
**Life expectancy at birth:**
*total population:* 81.98 years
*male:* 79.37 years
*female:* 84.78 years (2009 est.)
**Total fertility rate:** 1.09 children born/woman
(2009 est.)
**HIV/AIDS - adult prevalence rate:** 0.2% (2007 est.)
**HIV/AIDS - people living with HIV/AIDS:** 4,200
(2007 est.)
**HIV/AIDS - deaths:** fewer than 200 (2007 est.)
**Nationality:**
*noun:* Singaporean(s)
*adjective:* Singapore
**Ethnic groups:** Chinese 76.8%, Malay 13.9%,
Indian 7.9%, other 1.4% (2000 census)
**Religions:** Buddhist 42.5%, Muslim 14.9%, Taoist
8.5%, Hindu 4%, Catholic 4.8%, other Christian 9.8%,
other 0.7%, none 14.8% (2000 census)
**Languages:** Mandarin 35%, English 23%, Malay
14.1%, Hokkien 11.4%, Cantonese 5.7%, Teochew
4.9%, Tamil 3.2%, other Chinese dialects 1.8%, other
0.9% (2000 census)
**Literacy:**
*definition:* age 15 and over can read and write
*total population:* 92.5%
*male:* 96.6%
*female:* 88.6% (2000 census)
**Education expenditures:** 3.7% of GDP (2001)

## Government

**Country name:**
*conventional long form:* Republic of Singapore
*conventional short form:* Singapore
*local long form:* Republic of Singapore
*local short form:* Singapore
**Government type:** parliamentary republic
**Capital:**
*name:* Singapore
*geographic coordinates:* 1 17 N, 103 51 E
*time difference:* UTC+8 (13 hours ahead of
Washington, DC during Standard Time)
**Administrative divisions:** none
**Independence:** 9 August 1965 (from Malaysian
Federation)
**National holiday:** National Day, 9 August (1965)
**Constitution:** 3 June 1959; amended 1965 (based
on pre-independence State of Singapore Constitution)
**Legal system:** based on English common law; has
not accepted compulsory ICJ jurisdiction
**Suffrage:** 21 years of age; universal and compulsory
**Executive branch:**
*chief of state:* President S R NATHAN (since
1 September 1999)
*note:* uses S R NATHAN but his full name and the one
used in formal communications is Sellapan
RAMANATHAN

*head of government:* Prime Minister LEE Hsien
Loong (since 12 August 2004); Senior Minister GOH
Chok Tong (since 12 August 2004); Senior Minister
Shunmugam JAYAKUMAR (since 1 April 2009);
Minister Mentor LEE Kuan Yew (since 12 August
2004); Deputy Prime Minister TEO Chee Huan (since
1 April 2009) and Deputy Prime Minister WONG Kan
Seng (since 1 September 2005)
*cabinet:* appointed by president, responsible to
parliament
*elections:* president elected by popular vote for
six-year term; appointed on 17 August 2005 (next
election to be held by August 2011); following
legislative elections, leader of majority party or leader
of majority coalition is usually appointed prime
minister by president; deputy prime ministers
appointed by president
*election results:* Sellapan Rama (S R) NATHAN
appointed president in August 2005 after Presidential
Elections Committee disqualified three other would-be
candidates; scheduled election not held
**Legislative branch:** unicameral Parliament (84
seats; members elected by popular vote to serve
five-year terms); note - in addition, there are up to nine
nominated members; up to three losing opposition
candidates who came closest to winning seats may be
appointed as "nonconstituency" members
*elections:* last held on 6 May 2006 (next to be held by
2011)
*election results:* percent of vote by party - PAP 66.6%,
WP 16.3%, SDA 13%, SDP 4.1%; seats by party -
PAP 82, WP 1, SDA 1
**Judicial branch:** Supreme Court (chief justice is
appointed by the president with the advice of the
prime minister, other judges are appointed by the
president with the advice of the chief justice); Court of
Appeals
**Political parties and leaders:** People's Action Party
or PAP [LEE Hsien Loong]; Reform Party [NG Teck
Siong]; Singapore Democratic Alliance or SDA
[CHIAM See Tong]; Singapore Democratic Party or
SDP [CHEE Soon Juan]; Workers' Party or WP [Sylvia
LIM Swee Lian]
*note:* SDA includes Singapore Justice Party or SJP,
Singapore National Malay Organization or PKMS,
Singapore People's Party or SPP
**Political pressure groups and leaders:** none
**International organization participation:** ADB,
APEC, APT, ARF, ASEAN, BIS, C, CP, EAS, G-77,
IAEA, IBRD, ICAO, ICC, ICRM, IDA, IFC, IFRCS,
IHO, ILO, IMF, IMO, IMSO, Interpol, IOC, IPU, ISO,
ITSO, ITU, ITUC, MIGA, NAM, OPCW, PCA, UN,
UNCTAD, UNESCO, UNMIT, UPU, WCL, WCO,
WFTU, WHO, WIPO, WMO, WTO
**Diplomatic representation in the US:**
*chief of mission:* Ambassador CHAN Heng Chee
*chancery:* 3501 International Place NW, Washington,
DC 20008
*telephone:* [1] (202) 537-3100
*FAX:* [1] (202) 537-0876
*consulate(s) general:* San Francisco
*consulate(s):* New York

**Diplomatic representation from the US:**
*chief of mission:* Ambassador (vacant); Charge
d'Affaires Daniel L. SHIELDS III
*embassy:* 27 Napier Road, Singapore 258508
*mailing address:* FPO AP 96507-0001
*telephone:* [65] 6476-9100
*FAX:* [65] 6476-9340
**Flag description:** two equal horizontal bands of red
(top) and white; near the hoist side of the red band,
there is a vertical, white crescent (closed portion is
toward the hoist side) partially enclosing five white
five-pointed stars arranged in a circle

## Economy

**Economy - overview:** Singapore has a highly
developed and successful free-market economy. It
enjoys a remarkably open and corruption-free
environment, stable prices, and a per capita GDP
higher than that of most developed countries. The
economy depends heavily on exports, particularly in
consumer electronics, information technology
products, pharmaceuticals, and on a growing service
sector. Real GDP growth averaged 7% between 2004
and 2007, but dropped to 1.2% in 2008 as a result of
the global financial crisis. The economy contracted in
the last three quarters of 2008, and Prime Minister
LEE and other senior officials have dampened
expectations for a quick rebound in 2009. Over the
longer term, the government hopes to establish a new
growth path that will be less vulnerable to global
demand cycles, especially for information technology
products - it has attracted major investments in
pharmaceuticals and medical technology production -
and will continue efforts to establish Singapore as
Southeast Asia's financial and high-tech hub.
**GDP (purchasing power parity):**
$240 billion (2008 est.)
$237.2 billion (2007)
$216.4 billion (2006)
*note:* data are in 2008 US dollars
**GDP (official exchange rate):** $154.5 billion
(2008 est.)
**GDP - real growth rate:**
1.2% (2008 est.)
7.7% (2007 est.)
8.2% (2006 est.)
**GDP - per capita (PPP):**
$52,000 (2008 est.)
$51,200 (2007 est.)
$48,200 (2006 est.)
*note:* data are in 2008 US dollars
**GDP - composition by sector:**
*agriculture:* 0%
*industry:* 33.2%
*services:* 66.8% (2008 est.)
**Labor force:** 2.96 million (2008 est.)
**Labor force - by occupation:** agriculture 0%,
industry 22.6%, services 77.4% (2007)
**Unemployment rate:**
2.3% (2008 est.)
2.1% (2007 est.)

**Population below poverty line:** NA%
**Household income or consumption by percentage share:**
*lowest 10%:* 4.4%
*highest 10%:* 23.2% (2008)
**Distribution of family income - Gini index:** 48.1 (2008)
**Investment (gross fixed):** 45% of GDP (2008 est.)
**Budget:**
*revenues:* $28.6 billion
*expenditures:* $27.5 billion (2008 est.)
**Public debt:** 113.7% of GDP (2008 est.)
**Inflation rate (consumer prices):**
4.3% (2008 est.)
2.1% (2007 est.)
**Commercial bank prime lending rate:** 5.38% (31 December 2008)
**Stock of money:** $52.6 billion (31 December 2008)
**Stock of quasi money:** $234.5 billion (31 December 2008)
**Stock of domestic credit:** $171.3 billion (31 December 2008)
**Market value of publicly traded shares:** $268.6 billion (31 December 2008)
**Agriculture - products:** orchids, vegetables; poultry, eggs; fish, ornamental fish
**Industries:** electronics, chemicals, financial services, oil drilling equipment, petroleum refining, rubber processing and rubber products, processed food and beverages, ship repair, offshore platform construction, life sciences, entrepot trade
**Industrial production growth rate:** -4.1% (2008 est.)
**Electricity - production:** 41.14 billion kWh (2007)
**Electricity - consumption:** 37.42 billion kWh (2007)
**Electricity - exports:** 0 kWh (2007 est.)
**Electricity - imports:** 0 kWh (2007 est.)
**Oil - production:** 8,550 bbl/day (2007)
**Oil - consumption:** 916,000 bbl/day (2007)
**Oil - exports:** 1.27 million bbl/day (2007)
**Oil - imports:** 2.44 million bbl/day (2007)
**Oil - proved reserves:** 0 bbl (1 January 2006 est.)
**Natural gas - production:** 0 cu m (2007 est.)
**Natural gas - consumption:** 6.6 billion cu m (2008 est.)
**Natural gas - exports:** 0 cu m (2007 est.)
**Natural gas - imports:** 6.6 billion cu m
*note:* from Indonesia and Malaysia (2008 est.)
**Natural gas - proved reserves:** 0 cu m (1 January 2006 est.)
**Current account balance:** $28.42 billion (2008 est.)
**Exports:** $235.8 billion f.o.b. (2008 est.)
**Exports - commodities:** machinery and equipment (including electronics), consumer goods, pharmaceuticals and other chemicals, mineral fuels
**Exports - partners:** Malaysia 12.9%, Hong Kong 10.5%, Indonesia 9.8%, China 9.7%, US 8.9%, Japan 4.8%, Thailand 4.1% (2007)
**Imports:** $219.5 billion (2008 est.)
**Imports - commodities:** machinery and equipment, mineral fuels, chemicals, foodstuffs, consumer goods

**Imports - partners:** Malaysia 13.1%, US 12.5%, China 12.1%, Japan 8.2%, Taiwan 5.9%, Indonesia 5.6%, South Korea 4.9% (2007)
**Reserves of foreign exchange and gold:** $168.8 billion (31 December 2008 est.)
**Debt - external:** $25.54 billion (31 December 2008 est.)
**Stock of direct foreign investment - at home:** $225.7 billion (2008 est.)
**Stock of direct foreign investment - abroad:** $142.4 billion (2006)
**Exchange rates:** Singapore dollars (SGD) per US dollar - 1.415 (2008 est.), 1.507 (2007), 1.5889 (2006), 1.6644 (2005), 1.6902 (2004)

## Communications

**Telephones - main lines in use:** 1.859 million (2007)
**Telephones - mobile cellular:** 5.619 million (2007)
**Telephone system:**
*general assessment:* excellent service
*domestic:* excellent domestic facilities; launched 3G wireless service in February 2005; combined fixed-line and mobile-cellular teledensity is about 165 telephones per 100 persons
*international:* country code - 65; numerous submarine cables provide links throughout Asia, Australia, the Middle East, Europe, and US; satellite earth stations -4; supplemented by VSAT coverage (2007)
**Radio broadcast stations:** AM 0, FM 19, shortwave 1 (2008)
**Television broadcast stations:** 1 (broadcasting on 8 channels); additional reception of numerous UHF and VHF signals originating in Malaysia and Indonesia (2008)
**Internet country code:** .sg
**Internet hosts:** 837,559 (2008)
**Internet users:** 3.105 million (2007)

## Transportation

**Airports:** 8 (2008)
**Airports - with paved runways:**
*total:* 8
*over 3,047 m:* 2
*2,438 to 3,047 m:* 1
*1,524 to 2,437 m:* 4
*914 to 1,523 m:* 1 (2008)
**Pipelines:** gas 106 km (2008)
**Roadways:**
*total:* 3,262 km
*paved:* 3,262 km (includes 150 km of expressways) (2006)
**Merchant marine:**
*total:* 1,292
*by type:* bulk carrier 167, cargo 87, carrier 5, chemical tanker 209, container 273, liquefied gas 96, petroleum tanker 386, refrigerated cargo 5, roll on/roll off 4, specialized tanker 7, vehicle carrier 53
*foreign-owned:* 774 (Australia 12, Bangladesh 2, Belgium 8, Chile 6, China 14, Cyprus 1, Denmark 87, France 1, Germany 24, Greece 15, Hong Kong 47,

India 13, Indonesia 66, Italy 5, Japan 131, South Korea 3, Malaysia 27, Norway 143, Slovenia 1, Sweden 20, Switzerland 2, Taiwan 72, Thailand 23, UAE 12, UK 17, US 22)
*registered in other countries:* 331 (Australia 1, Bahamas 17, Belize 2, Bolivia 1, Cambodia 4, Cayman Islands 10, Comoros 1, Cyprus 3, Dominica 7, France 2, Honduras 12, Hong Kong 18, Indonesia 27, Isle of Man 1, Kiribati 4, Liberia 32, Malaysia 16, Marshall Islands 18, Mongolia 9, Norway 1, Panama 100, Philippines 1, Saint Kitts and Nevis 1, Saint Vincent and the Grenadines 4, Thailand 2, Tuvalu 23, US 12, unknown 2) (2008)
**Ports and terminals:** Singapore
**Transportation - note:** the International Maritime Bureau reports the territorial and offshore waters in the South China Sea as high risk for piracy and armed robbery against ships; numerous commercial vessels have been attacked and hijacked both at anchor and while underway; hijacked vessels are often disguised and cargo diverted to ports in East Asia; crews have been murdered or cast adrift

## Military

**Military branches:** Singapore Armed Forces: Army, Navy, Air Force (includes Air Defense) (2009)
**Military service age and obligation:** 18-21 years of age for male compulsory military service; 16 years of age for volunteers; 2-year conscript service obligation, with a reserve obligation to age 40 (enlisted) or age 50 (officers) (2008)
**Manpower available for military service:**
*males age 16-49:* 1,277,862 (2008 est.)
**Manpower fit for military service:**
*males age 16-49:* 1,033,961
*females age 16-49:* 1,104,952 (2009 est.)
**Manpower reaching militarily significant age annually:**
*male:* 27,715
*female:* 26,290 (2009 est.)
**Military expenditures:** 4.9% of GDP (2005 est.)

## Transnational Issues

**Disputes - international:** disputes persist with Malaysia over deliveries of fresh water to Singapore, Singapore's extensive land reclamation works, bridge construction, and maritime boundaries in the Johor and Singapore Straits; in November 2007, the ICJ will hold public hearings as a consequence of the Memorials and Countermemorials filed by the parties in 2003 and 2005 over sovereignty of Pedra Branca Island/Pulau Batu Puteh, Middle Rocks and South Ledge; Indonesia and Singapore continue to work on finalization of their 1973 maritime boundary agreement by defining unresolved areas north of Indonesia's Batam Island; piracy remains a problem in the Malacca Strait
**Illicit drugs:** drug abuse limited because of aggressive law enforcement efforts; as a transportation and financial services hub, Singapore is vulnerable, despite strict laws and enforcement, as a venue for money laundering

# Slovakia

**Population:** 5,463,046 (July 2009 est.)
**Age structure:**
*0-14 years:* 15.8% (male 442,168/female 422,055)
*15-64 years:* 71.7% (male 1,952,527/female 1,965,646)
*65 years and over:* 12.5% (male 254,510/female 426,140) (2009 est.)
**Median age:**
*total:* 36.9 years
*male:* 35.2 years
*female:* 38.6 years (2009 est.)
**Population growth rate:** 0.137% (2009 est.)
**Birth rate:** 10.6 births/1,000 population (2009 est.)
**Death rate:** 9.5 deaths/1,000 population (2008 est.)
**Net migration rate:** 0.3 migrant(s)/1,000 population (2009 est.)
**Urbanization:**
*urban population:* 56% of total population (2008)
*rate of urbanization:* 0.2% annual rate of change (2005-10 est.)
**Sex ratio:**
*at birth:* 1.05 male(s)/female
*under 15 years:* 1.05 male(s)/female
*15-64 years:* 0.99 male(s)/female
*65 years and over:* 0.6 male(s)/female
*total population:* 0.94 male(s)/female (2009 est.)
**Infant mortality rate:**
*total:* 6.84 deaths/1,000 live births
*male:* 7.99 deaths/1,000 live births
*female:* 5.64 deaths/1,000 live births (2009 est.)
**Life expectancy at birth:**
*total population:* 75.4 years
*male:* 71.47 years
*female:* 79.53 years (2009 est.)
**Total fertility rate:** 1.35 children born/woman (2009 est.)
**HIV/AIDS - adult prevalence rate:** less than 0.1% (2007 est.)
**HIV/AIDS - people living with HIV/AIDS:** fewer than 200 (2007 est.)
**HIV/AIDS - deaths:** fewer than 100 (2001 est.)
**Nationality:**
*noun:* Slovak(s)
*adjective:* Slovak
**Ethnic groups:** Slovak 85.8%, Hungarian 9.7%, Roma 1.7%, Ruthenian/Ukrainian 1%, other and unspecified 1.8% (2001 census)
**Religions:** Roman Catholic 68.9%, Protestant 10.8%, Greek Catholic 4.1%, other or unspecified 3.2%, none 13% (2001 census)
**Languages:** Slovak (official) 83.9%, Hungarian 10.7%, Roma 1.8%, Ukrainian 1%, other or unspecified 2.6% (2001 census)
**Literacy:**
*definition:* age 15 and over can read and write
*total population:* 99.6%
*male:* 99.7%
*female:* 99.6% (2004)

## Introduction

**Background:** The dissolution of the Austro-Hungarian Empire at the close of World War I allowed the Slovaks to join the closely related Czechs to form Czechoslovakia. Following the chaos of World War II, Czechoslovakia became a Communist nation within Soviet-dominated Eastern Europe. Soviet influence collapsed in 1989 and Czechoslovakia once more became free. The Slovaks and the Czechs agreed to separate peacefully on 1 January 1993. Slovakia joined both NATO and the EU in the spring of 2004 and the euro area on 1 January 2009.

## Geography

**Location:** Central Europe, south of Poland
**Geographic coordinates:** 48 40 N, 19 30 E
**Map references:** Europe
**Area:**
*total:* 48,845 sq km
*land:* 48,800 sq km
*water:* 45 sq km
**Area - comparative:** about twice the size of New Hampshire
**Land boundaries:**
*total:* 1,474 km
*border countries:* Austria 91 km, Czech Republic 197 km, Hungary 676 km, Poland 420 km, Ukraine 90 km
**Coastline:** 0 km (landlocked)
**Maritime claims:** none (landlocked)
**Climate:** temperate; cool summers; cold, cloudy, humid winters
**Terrain:** rugged mountains in the central and northern part and lowlands in the south
**Elevation extremes:**
*lowest point:* Bodrok River 94 m
*highest point:* Gerlachovsky Stit 2,655 m

**Natural resources:** brown coal and lignite; small amounts of iron ore, copper and manganese ore; salt; arable land
**Land use:**
*arable land:* 29.23%
*permanent crops:* 2.67%
*other:* 68.1% (2005)
**Irrigated land:** 1,830 sq km (2003)
**Total renewable water resources:** 50.1 cu km (2003)
**Freshwater withdrawal (domestic/industrial/agricultural):**
*total:* 1.04
*per capita:* 193 cu m/yr (2003)
**Natural hazards:** NA
**Environment - current issues:** air pollution from metallurgical plants presents human health risks; acid rain damaging forests
**Environment - international agreements:**
*party to:* Air Pollution, Air Pollution-Nitrogen Oxides, Air Pollution-Persistent Organic Pollutants, Air Pollution-Sulfur 85, Air Pollution-Sulfur 94, Air Pollution-Volatile Organic Compounds, Antarctic Treaty, Biodiversity, Climate Change, Climate Change-Kyoto Protocol, Desertification, Endangered Species, Environmental Modification, Hazardous Wastes, Law of the Sea, Ozone Layer Protection, Ship Pollution, Wetlands, Whaling
*signed, but not ratified:* none of the selected agreements
**Geography - note:** landlocked; most of the country is rugged and mountainous; the Tatra Mountains in the north are interspersed with many scenic lakes and valleys

# Slovakia (continued)

**School life expectancy (primary to tertiary education):**
*total:* 15 years
*male:* 14 years
*female:* 15 years (2006)
**Education expenditures:** 3.9% of GDP (2005)

## Government

**Country name:**
*conventional long form:* Slovak Republic
*conventional short form:* Slovakia
*local long form:* Slovenska Republika
*local short form:* Slovensko
**Government type:** parliamentary democracy
**Capital:**
*name:* Bratislava
*geographic coordinates:* 48 09 N, 17 07 E
*time difference:* UTC+1 (6 hours ahead of Washington, DC during Standard Time)
*daylight saving time:* +1hr, begins last Sunday in March; ends last Sunday in October
**Administrative divisions:** 8 regions (kraje, singular -kraj); Banskobystricky, Bratislavsky, Kosicky, Nitriansky, Presovsky, Trenciansky, Trnavsky, Zilinsky
**Independence:** 1 January 1993 (Czechoslovakia split into the Czech Republic and Slovakia)
**National holiday:** Constitution Day, 1 September (1992)
**Constitution:** ratified 1 September 1992, effective 1 January 1993; changed in September 1998; amended February 2001
*note:* the change in September 1998 allowed direct election of the president; the amendment of February 2001 allowed Slovakia to apply for NATO and EU membership
**Legal system:** civil law system based on Austro-Hungarian codes; accepts compulsory ICJ jurisdiction with reservations; legal code modified to comply with the obligations of Organization on Security and Cooperation in Europe (OSCE) and to expunge Marxist-Leninist legal theory
**Suffrage:** 18 years of age; universal
**Executive branch:**
*chief of state:* President Ivan GASPAROVIC (since 15 June 2004)
*head of government:* Prime Minister Robert FICO (since 4 July 2006); Deputy Prime Ministers Dusan CAPLOVIC, Robert KALINAK, Stefan HARABIN, Jan MIKOLAJ (since 4 July 2006)
*cabinet:* Cabinet appointed by the president on the recommendation of the prime minister
*elections:* president elected by popular vote for a five-year term (eligible for a second term); election last held 21 March and 4 April 2009 (next to be held no later than April 2014); following National Council elections, the leader of the majority party or the leader of a majority coalition is usually appointed prime minister by the president
*election results:* Ivan GASPAROVIC reelected president in runoff; percent of vote - Ivan GASPAROVIC 55.5%, Iveta RADICOVA 44.5%

**Legislative branch:** unicameral National Council of the Slovak Republic or Narodna Rada Slovenskej Republiky (150 seats; members are elected on the basis of proportional representation to serve four-year terms)
*elections:* last held 17 June 2006 (next to be held in 2010)
*election results:* percent of vote by party - Smer 29.1%, SDKU 18.4%, SMK 11.7%, SNS 11.7%, LS-HZDS 8.8%, KDH 8.3%, other 12%; seats by party -Smer 50, SDKU-DS 31, SMK 20, SNS 19, LS-HZDS 16, KDH 14; note - seats by party as of December 2008 - Smer 50, SDKU-DS 28, SMK 20, SNS 19, LS-HZDS 15, KDH 9, nonaffiliated 9
**Judicial branch:** Supreme Court (judges are elected by the National Council); Constitutional Court (judges appointed by president from group of nominees approved by the National Council); Special Court (judges elected by a council of judges and appointed by president)
**Political parties and leaders:**
*parties in the Parliament:* Christian Democratic Movement or KDH [Pavol HRUSOVSKY]; Direction-Social Democracy or Smer-SD [Robert FICO]; Party of the Hungarian Coalition or SMK [Pal CSAKY]; People's Party - Movement for a Democratic Slovakia or LS-HZDS [Vladimir MECIAR]; Slovak Democratic and Christian Union-Democratic Party or SDKU-DS [Mikulas DZURINDA]; Slovak National Party or SNS [Jan SLOTA]
*selected parties outside the Parliament:* Agrarian Party of the Provinces or ASV [Vladimir GOZORA]; Alliance of the New Citizen or ANO [Pavol RUSKO]; Civic Conservative Party or OKS [Peter ZAJAC]; Free Forum [Zuzana MARTINAKOVA]; Mission 21 - New Christian Democracy or MISIA 21 [Ivan SIMKO]; Movement for Democracy or HZD [Jozef GRAPA]; Party of the Democratic Left or SDL [Ladislav KOZMON]; Prosperita Slovenska or PS [Frantisek A. ZVRSKOVEC]; Slovak Communist Party or KSS [Jozef HRDLICKA]; Slovak People's Party or SLS [Jozef SASIK]; Union of the Workers of Slovakia or ZRS [Jan LUPTAK]
**Political pressure groups and leaders:** Association of Towns and Villages or ZMOS; Confederation of Trade Unions or KOZ; Entrepreneurs Association of Slovakia or ZPS; Federation of Employers' Associations of the Slovak Republic; National Union of Employers or RUZ; Slovak Chamber of Commerce and Industry or SOPK; The Business Alliance of Slovakia or PAS
**International organization participation:** Australia Group, BIS, BSEC (observer), CBSS (observer), CE, CEI, CERN, EAPC, EBRD, EIB, EU, FAO, IAEA, IBRD, ICAO, ICC, ICCt, ICRM, IDA, IEA, IFC, IFRCS, ILO, IMF, IMO, IMSO, Interpol, IOC, IOM, IPU, ISO, ITU, ITUC, MIGA, NAM (guest), NATO, NEA, NSG, OAS (observer), OECD, OIF (observer), OPCW, OSCE, PCA, Schengen Convention, SECI (observer), UN, UNCTAD, UNESCO, UNFICYP, UNIDO, UNTSO, UNWTO, UPU, WCL, WCO, WEU (associate partner), WFTU, WHO, WIPO, WMO, WTO, ZC

**Diplomatic representation in the US:**
*chief of mission:* Ambassador Peter BURIAN
*chancery:* 3523 International Court NW, Washington, DC 20008
*telephone:* [1] (202) 237-1054
*FAX:* [1] (202) 237-6438
*consulate(s) general:* Los Angeles, New York
**Diplomatic representation from the US:**
*chief of mission:* Ambassador (vacant); Charge d'Affaires Keith EDDINS
*embassy:* Hviezdoslavovo Namestie 4, 81102 Bratislava
*mailing address:* P.O. Box 309, 814 99 Bratislava
*telephone:* [421] (2) 5443-3338
*FAX:* [421] (2) 5441-8861
**Flag description:** three equal horizontal bands of white (top), blue, and red superimposed with the coat of arms of Slovakia (consisting of a red shield bordered in white and bearing a white Cross of Lorraine surmounting three blue hills); the coat of arms is centered vertically and offset slightly to the hoist side

## Economy

**Economy - overview:** Slovakia has made significant economic reforms since its separation from the Czech Republic in 1993. Reforms to the taxation, healthcare, pension, and social welfare systems helped Slovakia to consolidate its budget and get on track to join the EU in 2004 and to adopt the euro in January 2009. Major privatizations are nearly complete, the banking sector is almost entirely in foreign hands, and the government has helped facilitate a foreign investment boom with business friendly policies such as labor market liberalization and a 19% flat tax. Foreign investment in the automotive and electronic sectors has been strong. Slovakia's economic growth exceeded expectations in 2001-08 despite the general European slowdown. Unemployment, at an unacceptable 18% in 2003-04, dropped to 8.4% in 2008 but remains the economy's Achilles heel. Despite its 2006 pre-election promises to loosen fiscal policy and reverse the previous DZURINDA government's pro-market reforms, FICO's cabinet has thus far been careful to keep a lid on spending in order to meet euro adoption criteria and has focused on regulating energy and food prices instead. The OECD expects Slovakia's GDP growth to be positive in 2009.
**GDP (purchasing power parity):**
$119.5 billion (2008 est.)
$112.3 billion (2007)
$101.7 billion (2006)
*note:* data are in 2008 US dollars
**GDP (official exchange rate):** $100.6 billion (2008 est.)
**GDP - real growth rate:**
6.4% (2008 est.)
10.4% (2007 est.)
8.5% (2006 est.)

# Slovakia (continued)

**GDP - per capita (PPP):**
$21,900 (2008 est.)
$20,600 (2007 est.)
$18,700 (2006 est.)
*note:* data are in 2008 US dollars
**GDP - composition by sector:**
*agriculture:* 2.6%
*industry:* 33.4%
*services:* 64% (2008 est.)
**Labor force:** 2.254 million (2008 est.)
**Labor force - by occupation:** agriculture 4%, industry 39%, services 56.9% (30 September 2008)
**Unemployment rate:**
8.4% (2008)
8.4% (2007 est.)
**Population below poverty line:** 21% (2002)
**Household income or consumption by percentage share:**
*lowest 10%:* 3.1%
*highest 10%:* 20.9% (1996)
**Distribution of family income - Gini index:** 26 (2005)
**Investment (gross fixed):** 25.9% of GDP (2008 est.)
**Budget:**
*revenues:* $44.86 billion
*expenditures:* $46.96 billion (2008 est.)
**Public debt:** 35% of GDP (2008 est.)
**Inflation rate (consumer prices):**
4.6% (2008))
2.8% (2007 est.)
**Central bank discount rate:** 4%
*note:* this is the European Central Bank's rate on the marginal lending facility, which offers overnight credit to banks from the euro area; as of 1 January 2009 Slovakia became a member of the Economic and Monetary Union (EMU) (February 2009)
**Commercial bank prime lending rate:** 6.42% (31 December 2008)
**Stock of money:** $26.93 billion
*note:* this figure represents the US dollar value of Slovak koruny in circulation prior to Slovakia joining the Economic and Monetary Union (EMU); see entry for the European Union for money supply in the euro area; the European Central Bank (ECB) controls monetary policy for the 16 members of the Economic and Monetary Union (EMU); individual members of the EMU do not control the quantity of money and quasi money circulating within their own borders (31 December 2007)
**Stock of quasi money:** $23.16 billion (31 December 2008)
**Stock of domestic credit:** $55.1 billion (31 December 2008)
**Market value of publicly traded shares:** $6.971 billion (31 December 2007)
**Agriculture - products:** grains, potatoes, sugar beets, hops, fruit; pigs, cattle, poultry; forest products

**Industries:** metal and metal products; food and beverages; electricity, gas, coke, oil, nuclear fuel; chemicals and manmade fibers; machinery; paper and printing; earthenware and ceramics; transport vehicles; textiles; electrical and optical apparatus; rubber products
**Industrial production growth rate:** 6.5% (2008 est.)
**Electricity - production:** 26.17 billion kWh (2007 est.)
**Electricity - consumption:** 26 billion kWh (2006 est.)
**Electricity - exports:** 11.85 billion kWh (2007 est.)
**Electricity - imports:** 12.73 billion kWh (2007 est.)
**Oil - production:** 12,770 bbl/day (2007 est.)
**Oil - consumption:** 82,860 bbl/day (2007 est.)
**Oil - exports:** 72,240 bbl/day (2005)
**Oil - imports:** 134,100 bbl/day (2005)
**Oil - proved reserves:** 9 million bbl (1 January 2008 est.)
**Natural gas - production:** 128 million cu m (2007 est.)
**Natural gas - consumption:** 6.216 billion cu m (2007 est.)
**Natural gas - exports:** 180 million cu m (2007 est.)
**Natural gas - imports:** 6.268 billion cu m (2007 est.)
**Natural gas - proved reserves:** 14.16 billion cu m (1 January 2008 est.)
**Current account balance:** -$5.359 billion (2008 est.)
**Exports:** $79.12 billion f.o.b. (2008 est.)
**Exports - commodities:** vehicles 25.9%, machinery and electrical equipment 21.3%, base metals 14.6%, chemicals and minerals 10.1%, plastics 5.4% (2004)
**Exports - partners:** Germany 21.4%, Czech Republic 12.6%, France 6.7%, Italy 6.4%, Poland 6.2%, Hungary 6%, Austria 5.8%, UK 4.8% (2007)
**Imports:** $79.76 billion f.o.b. (2008 est.)
**Imports - commodities:** machinery and transport equipment 41.1%, intermediate manufactured goods 19.3%, fuels 12.3%, chemicals 9.8%, miscellaneous manufactured goods 10.2% (2003)
**Imports - partners:** Germany 22.1%, Czech Republic 17.3%, Russia 9.2%, Hungary 6.7%, Austria 5.1%, Poland 4.9%, South Korea 4.7% (2007)
**Reserves of foreign exchange and gold:** $19.47 billion (31 December 2008 est.)
**Debt - external:** $53.04 billion (30 September 2008 est.)
**Stock of direct foreign investment - at home:** $47.68 billion (2008 est.)
**Stock of direct foreign investment - abroad:** $1.564 billion (2008 est.)
**Exchange rates:** Slovak koruny (SKK) per US dollar - 21.05 (2008 est.), 24.919 (2007), 29.611 (2006), 31.018 (2005), 32.257 (2004)
*note:* on 1 January 2009 Slovakia adopted the euro as legal tender

**Telephones - main lines in use:** 1.151 million (2007)
**Telephones - mobile cellular:** 6.068 million (2007)
**Telephone system:**
*general assessment:* Slovakia has a modern telecommunications system that has expanded dramatically in recent years with the growth in cellular services
*domestic:* analog system is now receiving digital equipment and is being enlarged with fiber-optic cable, especially in the larger cities; 3 companies provide nationwide cellular services
*international:* country code - 421; 3 international exchanges (1 in Bratislava and 2 in Banska Bystrica) are available; Slovakia is participating in several international telecommunications projects that will increase the availability of external services
**Radio broadcast stations:** AM 1, FM 22, shortwave 1 (2008)
**Television broadcast stations:** 37 (2008)
**Internet country code:** .sk
**Internet hosts:** 717,744 (2008)
**Internet users:** 2.35 million (2007)

**Airports:** 35 (2008)
**Airports - with paved runways:**
*total:* 20
*over 3,047 m:* 2
*2,438 to 3,047 m:* 2
*1,524 to 2,437 m:* 3
*914 to 1,523 m:* 3
*under 914 m:* 10 (2008)
**Airports - with unpaved runways:**
*total:* 15
*914 to 1,523 m:* 8
*under 914 m:* 7 (2008)
**Heliports:** 1 (2007)
**Pipelines:** gas 6,769 km; oil 416 km (2008)
**Railways:**
*total:* 3,662 km
*broad gauge:* 100 km 1.520-m gauge
*standard gauge:* 3,512 km 1.435-m gauge (1,588 km electrified)
*narrow gauge:* 50 km (1.000-m or 0.750-m gauge) (2006)
**Roadways:**
*total:* 43,761 km
*paved:* 38,085 km (includes 316 km of expressways)
*unpaved:* 5,676 km (2006)
**Waterways:** 172 km (on Danube River) (2008)
**Merchant marine:**
*total:* 51
*by type:* bulk carrier 5, cargo 42, refrigerated cargo 4
*foreign-owned:* 47 (Bulgaria 6, Germany 3, Greece 2, Ireland 1, Israel 4, Italy 2, Poland 2, Russia 1, Slovenia 1, Syria 2, Turkey 10, Ukraine 12, UK 1) (2008)
**Ports and terminals:** Bratislava, Komarno

## Military

**Military branches:** Armed Forces of the Slovak Republic (Ozbrojene Sily Slovenskej Republiky): Land Forces (Pozemne Sily), Air Forces (Vzdusne Sily) (2009)

**Military service age and obligation:** 17-30 years of age for voluntary military service; conscription abolished in 2006; women are eligible to serve (2007)

**Manpower available for military service:**
*males age 16-49:* 1,420,966
*females age 16-49:* 1,386,259 (2008 est.)

**Manpower fit for military service:**
*males age 16-49:* 1,165,470
*females age 16-49:* 1,152,941 (2009 est.)

**Manpower reaching militarily significant age annually:**
*male:* 36,552
*female:* 34,783 (2009 est.)

**Military expenditures:** 1.87% of GDP (2005 est.)

## Transnational Issues

**Disputes - international:** bilateral government, legal, technical and economic working group negotiations continued in 2006 between Slovakia and Hungary over Hungary's completion of its portion of the Gabcikovo-Nagymaros hydroelectric dam project along the Danube; as a member state that forms part of the EU's external border, Slovakia has implemented the strict Schengen border rules

**Illicit drugs:** transshipment point for Southwest Asian heroin bound for Western Europe; producer of synthetic drugs for regional market; consumer of ecstasy

# Slovenia

## Introduction

**Background:** The Slovene lands were part of the Austro-Hungarian Empire until the latter's dissolution at the end of World War I. In 1918, the Slovenes joined the Serbs and Croats in forming a new multinational state, which was named Yugoslavia in 1929. After World War II, Slovenia became a republic of the renewed Yugoslavia, which though Communist, distanced itself from Moscow's rule. Dissatisfied with the exercise of power by the majority Serbs, the Slovenes succeeded in establishing their independence in 1991 after a short 10-day war. Historical ties to Western Europe, a strong economy, and a stable democracy have assisted in Slovenia's transformation to a modern state. Slovenia acceded to both NATO and the EU in the spring of 2004.

## Geography

**Location:** Central Europe, eastern Alps bordering the Adriatic Sea, between Austria and Croatia

**Geographic coordinates:** 46 07 N, 14 49 E

**Map references:** Europe

**Area:**
*total:* 20,273 sq km
*land:* 20,151 sq km
*water:* 122 sq km

**Area - comparative:** slightly smaller than New Jersey

**Land boundaries:**
*total:* 1,086 km
*border countries:* Austria 330 km, Croatia 455 km, Hungary 102 km, Italy 199 km

**Coastline:** 46.6 km

**Maritime claims:**
*territorial sea:* 12 nm

**Climate:** Mediterranean climate on the coast, continental climate with mild to hot summers and cold winters in the plateaus and valleys to the east

**Terrain:** a short coastal strip on the Adriatic, an alpine mountain region adjacent to Italy and Austria, mixed mountains and valleys with numerous rivers to the east

**Elevation extremes:**
*lowest point:* Adriatic Sea 0 m
*highest point:* Triglav 2,864 m

**Natural resources:** lignite coal, lead, zinc, building stone, hydropower, forests

**Land use:**
*arable land:* 8.53%
*permanent crops:* 1.43%
*other:* 90.04% (2005)

**Irrigated land:** 30 sq km (2003)

**Total renewable water resources:** 32.1 cu km (2005)

**Freshwater withdrawal (domestic/industrial/agricultural):**
*total:* 0.9
*per capita:* 457 cu m/yr (2002)

**Natural hazards:** flooding; earthquakes

**Environment - current issues:** Sava River polluted with domestic and industrial waste; pollution of coastal waters with heavy metals and toxic chemicals; forest damage near Koper from air pollution (originating at metallurgical and chemical plants) and resulting acid rain

**Environment - international agreements:**
*party to:* Air Pollution, Air Pollution-Nitrogen Oxides, Air Pollution-Persistent Organic Pollutants, Air Pollution-Sulfur 94, Biodiversity, Climate Change, Climate Change-Kyoto Protocol, Desertification, Endangered Species, Environmental Modification, Hazardous Wastes, Law of the Sea, Marine Dumping, Ozone Layer Protection, Ship Pollution, Wetlands, Whaling
*signed, but not ratified:* none of the selected agreements

**Geography - note:** despite its small size, this eastern Alpine country controls some of Europe's major transit routes

## People

**Population:** 2,005,692 (July 2009 est.)

**Age structure:**
*0-14 years:* 13.5% (male 139,880/female 131,826)
*15-64 years:* 69.9% (male 707,219/female 695,470)
*65 years and over:* 16.5% (male 129,662/female 201,635) (2009 est.)

**Median age:**
*total:* 41.7 years
*male:* 40.1 years
*female:* 43.3 years (2009 est.)

**Population growth rate:** -0.113% (2009 est.)

**Birth rate:** 8.97 births/1,000 population (2009 est.)

**Death rate:** 10.51 deaths/1,000 population (2008 est.)

**Net migration rate:** 0.52 migrant(s)/1,000 population (2009 est.)

## Slovenia (continued)

**Urbanization:**

*urban population:* 48% of total population (2008)
*rate of urbanization:* -0.6% annual rate of change
(2005-10 est.)

**Sex ratio:**

*at birth:* 1.07 male(s)/female
*under 15 years:* 1.06 male(s)/female
*15-64 years:* 1.02 male(s)/female
*65 years and over:* 0.64 male(s)/female
*total population:* 0.95 male(s)/female (2009 est.)

**Infant mortality rate:**

*total:* 4.25 deaths/1,000 live births
*male:* 4.82 deaths/1,000 live births
*female:* 3.65 deaths/1,000 live births (2009 est.)

**Life expectancy at birth:**

*total population:* 76.92 years
*male:* 73.25 years
*female:* 80.84 years (2009 est.)

**Total fertility rate:** 1.28 children born/woman
(2009 est.)

**HIV/AIDS - adult prevalence rate:** less than 0.1%
(2007 est.)

**HIV/AIDS - people living with HIV/AIDS:** 280
(2007 est.)

**HIV/AIDS - deaths:** fewer than 100 (2007 est.)

**Nationality:**

*noun:* Slovene(s)
*adjective:* Slovenian

**Ethnic groups:** Slovene 83.1%, Serb 2%, Croat
1.8%, Bosniak 1.1%, other or unspecified 12% (2002
census)

**Religions:** Catholic 57.8%, Muslim 2.4%, Orthodox
2.3%, other Christian 0.9%, unaffiliated 3.5%, other or
unspecified 23%, none 10.1% (2002 census)

**Languages:** Slovenian 91.1%, Serbo-Croatian
4.5%, other or unspecified 4.4% (2002 census)

**Literacy:**

*definition:* NA
*total population:* 99.7%
*male:* 99.7%
*female:* 99.6%

**School life expectancy (primary to tertiary
education):**

*total:* 17 years
*male:* 16 years
*female:* 17 years (2006)

**Education expenditures:** 6% of GDP (2005)

### Government

**Country name:**

*conventional long form:* Republic of Slovenia
*conventional short form:* Slovenia
*local long form:* Republika Slovenija
*local short form:* Slovenija
*former:* People's Republic of Slovenia, Socialist
Republic of Slovenia

**Government type:** parliamentary republic

**Capital:**

*name:* Ljubljana
*geographic coordinates:* 46 03 N, 14 31 E
*time difference:* UTC+1 (6 hours ahead of
Washington, DC during Standard Time)
*daylight saving time:* +1hr, begins last Sunday
in March; ends last Sunday in October

**Administrative divisions:** 182 municipalities
(obcine, singular - obcina) and 11 urban
municipalities* (mestne obcine , singular - mestna
obcina ) Ajdovscina, Beltinci, Benedikt, Bistrica ob
Sotli, Bled, Bloke, Bohinj, Borovnica, Bovec,
Braslovce, Brda, Brezice, Brezovica, Cankova, Celje*,
Cerklje na Gorenjskem, Cerknica, Cerkno,
Cerkvenjak, Crensovci, Crna na Koroskem, Crnomelj,
Destrnik, Divaca, Dobje, Dobrepolje, Dobrna,
Dobrova-Horjul-Polhov Gradec, Dobrovnik-Dobronak,
Dolenjske Toplice, Dol pri Ljubljani, Domzale,
Dornava, Dravograd, Duplek, Gorenja Vas-Poljane,
Gorisnica, Gornja Radgona, Gornji Grad, Gornji
Petrovci, Grad, Grosuplje, Hajdina, Hoce-Slivnica,
Hodos-Hodos, Horjul, Hrastnik, Hrpelje-Kozina, Idrija,
Ig, Ilirska Bistrica, Ivancna Gorica, Izola-Isola,
Jesenice, Jezersko, Jursinci, Kamnik, Kanal,
Kidricevo, Kobarid, Kobilje, Kocevje, Komen,
Komenda, Koper-Capodistria*, Kostel, Kozje, Kranj*,
Kranjska Gora, Krizevci, Krsko, Kungota, Kuzma,
Lasko, Lenart, Lendava-Lendva, Litija, Ljubljana*,
Ljubno, Ljutomer, Logatec, Loska Dolina, Loski Potok,
Lovrenc na Pohorju, Luce, Lukovica, Majsperk,
Maribor*, Markovci, Medvode, Menges, Metlika,
Mezica, Miklavz na Dravskem Polju,
Miren-Kostanjevica, Mirna Pec, Mislinja, Moravce,
Moravske Toplice, Mozirje, Murska Sobota*, Muta,
Naklo, Nazarje, Nova Gorica*, Novo Mesto*, Odranci,
Oplotnica, Ormoz, Osilnica, Pesnica, Piran-Pirano,
Pivka, Podcetrtek, Podlehnik, Podvelka, Polzela,
Postojna, Prebold, Preddvor, Prevalje, Ptuj*, Puconci,
Race-Fram, Radece, Radenci, Radlje ob Dravi,
Radovljica, Ravne na Koroskem, Razkrizje, Ribnica,
Ribnica na Pohorju, Rogasovci, Rogaska Slatina,
Rogatec, Ruse, Salovci, Selnica ob Dravi, Semic,
Sempeter-Vrtojba, Sencur, Sentilj, Sentjernej, Sentjur
pri Celju, Sevnica, Sezana, Skocjan, Skofja Loka,
Skofljica, Slovenj Gradec*, Slovenska Bistrica,
Slovenske Konjice, Smarje pri Jelsah, Smartno ob
Paki, Smartno pri Litiji, Sodrazica, Solcava, Sostanj,
Starse, Store, Sveta Ana, Sveti Andraz v Slovenskih
Goricah, Sveti Jurij, Tabor, Tisina, Tolmin, Trbovlje,
Trebnje, Trnovska Vas, Trzic, Trzin, Turnisce,
Velenje*, Velika Polana, Velike Lasce, Verzej, Videm,
Vipava, Vitanje, Vodice, Vojnik, Vransko, Vrhnika,
Vuzenica, Zagorje ob Savi, Zalec, Zavrc, Zelezniki,
Zetale, Ziri, Zirovnica, Zuzemberk, Zrece

*note:* the Government of Slovenia has reported 210
municipalities

**Independence:** 25 June 1991 (from Yugoslavia)

**National holiday:** Independence Day/Statehood
Day, 25 June (1991)

**Constitution:** adopted 23 December 1991,
amended 14 July 1997 and 25 July 2000

**Legal system:** based on civil law system; has not
accepted compulsory ICJ jurisdiction

**Suffrage:** 18 years of age; universal (16 years of
age, if employed)

**Executive branch:**

*chief of state:* President Danilo TURK (since
22 December 2007)
*head of government:* Prime Minister Borut PAHOR
(since 7 November 2008)
*cabinet:* Council of Ministers nominated by the prime
minister and elected by the National Assembly
*elections:* president elected by popular vote for a
five-year term (eligible for a second term); election last
held 21 October and 11 November 2007 (next to be
held in the 8 October 2012); following National
Assembly elections, the leader of the majority party or
the leader of a majority coalition is usually nominated
to become prime minister by the president and elected
by the National Assembly; election last held on
21 September 2008 (next National Assembly
elections to be held in 8 October 2012)
*election results:* Danilo TURK elected president;
percent of vote - Danilo TURK 68.2%, Alojze
PETERLE 31.8%; Borut PAHOR elected prime
minister by National Assembly vote

**Legislative branch:** bicameral Parliament consists
of a National Council or Drzavni Svet (40 seats;
members indirectly elected by an electoral college to
serve five-year terms; note - this is primarily an
advisory body with limited legislative powers; it may
propose laws, ask to review any National Assembly
decision, and call national referenda) and the National
Assembly or Drzavni Zbor (90 seats; 40 members are
directly elected and 50 are elected on a proportional
basis; note - the number of directly elected and
proportionally elected seats varies with each election;
the constitution mandates 1 seat each for Slovenia's
Hungarian and Italian minorities; members are elected
by popular vote to serve four-year terms)
*elections:* National Assembly - last held 21 September
2008 (next to be held 8 October 2012)
*election results:* percent of vote by party - SD 30.5%,
SDS 29.3%, ZARES 9.4%, DeSUS 7.5%, SNS 5.5%,
SLS+SMS 5.2%, LDS 5.2%, other 7.4%; seats by
party - SD 29, SDS 28, ZARES 9, DeSUS 7, SNS 5,
SLS+SMS 5, LDS 5, Hungarian minority 1, Italian
minority 1

**Judicial branch:** Supreme Court (judges are elected
by the National Assembly on the recommendation of
the Judicial Council); Constitutional Court (judges
elected for nine-year terms by the National Assembly
and nominated by the president)

**Political parties and leaders:** Liberal Democracy of
Slovenia or LDS [Katarina KRESAL]; New Slovenia or
NSi [Ljudmila NOVAK (acting)]; Slovenian Democratic
Party or SDS [Janez JANSA]; Democratic Party of
Pensioners of Slovenia or DeSUS [Karl ERJAVEC];
Slovene National Party or SNS [Zmago JELINCIC];
Slovene People's Party or SLS [Bojan SROT];
Slovene Youth Party or SMS [Darko KRANJC]; Social
Democrats or SD [Borut PAHOR] (formerly ZLSD);
ZARES [Gregor Golobic]

# Slovenia (continued)

**Political pressure groups and leaders:**
Democratic Party of Slovenian Pensioners or DeSUS (protecting the rights of the older generation); Slovenian Roma Association [Jozek Horvat MUC]
*other:* Catholic Church

**International organization participation:** Australia Group, BIS, CE, CEI, EAPC, EBRD, EIB, EMU, EU, FAO, IADB, IAEA, IBRD, ICAO, ICC, ICCt, ICRM, IDA, IFC, IFRCS, IHO, ILO, IMF, IMO, Interpol, IOC, IOM, IPU, ISO, ITU, MIGA, NAM (guest), NATO, NSG, OAS (observer), OECD (accession state), OIF (observer), OPCW, OSCE, PCA, Schengen Convention, SECI, UN, UNCTAD, UNESCO, UNIDO, UNIFIL, UNTSO, UNWTO, UPU, WCO, WEU (associate partner), WFTU, WHO, WIPO, WMO, WTO, ZC

**Diplomatic representation in the US:**
*chief of mission:* Ambassador (vacant); Charge d'Affaires Mariam MOZGAN
*chancery:* 2410 California Street N.W., Washington, DC 20008
*telephone:* [1] (202) 386-6601
*FAX:* [1] (202) 386-6633
*consulate(s) general:* Cleveland, New York

**Diplomatic representation from the US:**
*chief of mission:* Ambassador (vacant); Charge d'Affaires Brad FREDEN
*embassy:* Presernova 31, 1000 Ljubljana
*mailing address:* American Embassy Ljubljana, US Department of State, 7140 Ljubljana Place, Washington, DC 20521-7140
*telephone:* [386] (1) 200-5500
*FAX:* [386] (1) 200-5555

**Flag description:** three equal horizontal bands of white (top), blue, and red, with the Slovenian seal (a shield with the image of Triglav, Slovenia's highest peak, in white against a blue background at the center; beneath it are two wavy blue lines depicting seas and rivers, and above it are three six-pointed stars arranged in an inverted triangle, which are taken from the coat of arms of the Counts of Celje, the great Slovene dynastic house of the late 14th and early 15th centuries); the seal is in the upper hoist side of the flag centered on the white and blue bands

## Economy

**Economy - overview:** Slovenia, which on 1 January 2007 became the first 2004 European Union entrant to adopt the euro, is a model of economic success and stability for the region. With the highest per capita GDP in Central Europe, Slovenia has excellent infrastructure, a well-educated work force, and a strategic location between the Balkans and Western Europe. Privatization has lagged since 2002, and the economy has one of highest levels of state control in the EU. Structural reforms to improve the business environment have allowed for somewhat greater foreign participation in Slovenia's economy and have helped to lower unemployment. In March 2004, Slovenia became the first transition country to graduate from borrower status to donor partner at the World Bank. In December 2007, Slovenia was invited to begin the accession process for joining the OECD. Despite its economic success, foreign direct investment (FDI) in Slovenia has lagged behind the region average, and taxes remain relatively high. Furthermore, the labor market is often seen as inflexible, and legacy industries are losing sales to more competitive firms in China, India, and elsewhere.

**GDP (purchasing power parity):**
$59.14 billion (2008 est.)
$56.7 billion (2007)
$53.09 billion (2006)
*note:* data are in 2008 US dollars

**GDP (official exchange rate):** $57.01 billion (2008 est.)

**GDP - real growth rate:**
4.3% (2008 est.)
6.8% (2007 est.)
5.9% (2006 est.)

**GDP - per capita (PPP):**
$29,500 (2008 est.)
$28,200 (2007 est.)
$26,400 (2006 est.)
*note:* data are in 2008 US dollars

**GDP - composition by sector:**
*agriculture:* 2.2%
*industry:* 34.2%
*services:* 63.6% (2008 est.)

**Labor force:** 920,000 (2008 est.)

**Labor force - by occupation:**
*agriculture:* 2.5%
*industry:* 36%
*services:* 61.5% (2007)

**Unemployment rate:**
6.7% (2008 est.)
7.7% (2007 est.)

**Population below poverty line:** 12.9% (2004)

**Household income or consumption by percentage share:**
*lowest 10%:* 3.6%
*highest 10%:* 21.4% (1998)

**Distribution of family income - Gini index:** 24 (2005)

**Investment (gross fixed):** 27.8% of GDP (2008 est.)

**Budget:**
*revenues:* $23.16 billion
*expenditures:* $22.93 billion (2008 est.)

**Public debt:** 22% of GDP (2008 est.)

**Inflation rate (consumer prices):**
6% (2008 est.)
3.6% (2007 est.)

**Central bank discount rate:** 4%
*note:* this is the European Central Bank's rate on the marginal lending facility, which offers overnight credit to banks in the euro area

**Commercial bank prime lending rate:** 6.82% (31 December 2007)

**Stock of money:** $9.347 billion
*note:* this figure represents the US dollar value of tolars in circulation prior to Slovenia joining the Economic and Monetary Union (EMU); see entry for the European Union for money supply in the euro area; the European Central Bank (ECB) controls monetary policy for the 16 members of the Economic and Monetary Union (EMU); individual members of the EMU do not control the quantity of money and quasi money circulating within their own borders (31 December 2006)

**Stock of quasi money:** $12.69 billion (31 December 2006)

**Stock of domestic credit:** NA

**Market value of publicly traded shares:** $28.96 billion (31 December 2007)

**Agriculture - products:** potatoes, hops, wheat, sugar beets, corn, grapes; cattle, sheep, poultry

**Industries:** ferrous metallurgy and aluminum products, lead and zinc smelting; electronics (including military electronics), trucks, automobiles, electric power equipment, wood products, textiles, chemicals, machine tools

**Industrial production growth rate:** 4.5% (2008 est.)

**Electricity - production:** 14.13 billion kWh (2007 est.)

**Electricity - consumption:** 13.4 billion kWh (2006 est.)

**Electricity - exports:** 5.894 billion kWh (2007 est.)

**Electricity - imports:** 6.14 billion kWh (2007 est.)

**Oil - production:** 5 bbl/day (2007 est.)

**Oil - consumption:** 54,310 bbl/day (2006 est.)

**Oil - exports:** 4,535 bbl/day (2005)

**Oil - imports:** 59,110 bbl/day (2005)

**Oil - proved reserves:** 0 bbl (1 January 2006 est.)

**Natural gas - production:** 4 million cu m (2006 est.)

**Natural gas - consumption:** 1.105 billion cu m (2006 est.)

**Natural gas - exports:** 0 cu m (2007 est.)

**Natural gas - imports:** 1.073 billion cu m (2005)

**Natural gas - proved reserves:** 0 cu m (1 January 2006 est.)

**Current account balance:** -$3.706 billion (2008 est.)

**Exports:** $34.27 billion f.o.b. (2008 est.)

**Exports - commodities:** manufactured goods, machinery and transport equipment, chemicals, food

**Exports - partners:** Germany 18.7%, Italy 12.5%, Croatia 8%, Austria 7.5%, France 5.9%, Russia 4.4% (2007)

**Imports:** $38.12 billion f.o.b. (2008 est.)

**Imports - commodities:** machinery and transport equipment, manufactured goods, chemicals, fuels and lubricants, food

**Imports - partners:** Germany 18.1%, Italy 17.1%, Austria 11.7%, France 5%, Croatia 4.6% (2007)

**Reserves of foreign exchange and gold:** $8.912 billion (31 December 2008 est.)

**Debt - external:** $40.42 billion (30 June 2007)

**Stock of direct foreign investment - at home:** $11.51 billion (2008 est.)

## Slovenia (continued)

**Stock of direct foreign investment - abroad:**
$7.527 billion (2008 est.)
**Exchange rates:** euros (EUR) per US dollar - 0.6827
(2008 est.), 0.7345 (2007)
*note:* Slovenia adopted the euro as its currency on
1 January 2007

### Communications

**Telephones - main lines in use:** 857,100 (2007)
**Telephones - mobile cellular:** 1.928 million (2007)
**Telephone system:**
*general assessment:* well-developed
telecommunications infrastructure
*domestic:* combined fixed-line and mobile-cellular
teledensity roughly 140 telephones per 100 persons
*international:* country code - 386
**Radio broadcast stations:** AM 10, FM 230,
shortwave 0 (2006)
**Television broadcast stations:** 31 (2006)
**Internet country code:** .si
**Internet hosts:** 75,984 (2008)
**Internet users:** 1.3 million (2007)

### Transportation

**Airports:** 14 (2008)
**Airports - with paved runways:**
*total:* 6
*over 3,047 m:* 1
*2,438 to 3,047 m:* 1
*1,524 to 2,437 m:* 1
*914 to 1,523 m:* 2
*under 914 m:* 1 (2008)
**Airports - with unpaved runways:**
*total:* 8
*1,524 to 2,437 m:* 2
*914 to 1,523 m:* 2
*under 914 m:* 4 (2008)
**Pipelines:** gas 840 km; oil 11 km (2008)
**Railways:**
*total:* 1,229 km
*standard gauge:* 1,229 km 1.435-m gauge (504 km
electrified) (2006)
**Roadways:**
*total:* 38,562 km
*paved:* 38,562 km (includes 579 km of expressways)
(2006)
**Waterways:** some transport on Danube River (2008)
**Merchant marine:**
*registered in other countries:* 29 (Antigua and
Barbuda 6, Bahamas 1, Cyprus 4, Liberia 3, Malta 4,
Marshall Islands 4, Saint Vincent and the Grenadines
5, Singapore 1, Slovakia 1) (2008)
**Ports and terminals:** Koper

### Military

**Military branches:** Slovenian Army (includes air and
naval forces)
**Military service age and obligation:** 17 years of
age for voluntary military service; conscription
abolished in 2003 (2007)

**Manpower available for military service:**
*males age 16-49:* 494,496
*females age 16-49:* 481,180 (2008 est.)
**Manpower fit for military service:**
*males age 16-49:* 402,484
*females age 16-49:* 390,559 (2009 est.)
**Manpower reaching militarily significant age
annually:**
*male:* 10,192
*female:* 9,717 (2009 est.)
**Military expenditures:** 1.7% of GDP (2005 est.)

### Transnational Issues

**Disputes - international:** the Croatia-Slovenia land
and maritime boundary agreement, which would have
ceded most of Piran Bay and maritime access to
Slovenia and several villages to Croatia, remains
unratified and in dispute; Slovenia also protests
Croatia's 2003 claim to an exclusive economic zone in
the Adriatic; as a member state that forms part of the
EU's external border, Slovenia has implemented the
strict Schengen border rules to curb illegal migration
and commerce through southeastern Europe while
encouraging close cross-border ties with Croatia
**Illicit drugs:** minor transit point for cocaine and
Southwest Asian heroin bound for Western Europe,
and for precursor chemicals

# Solomon Islands

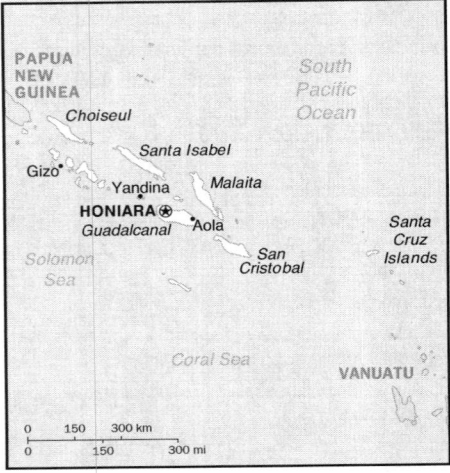

### Introduction

**Background:** The UK established a protectorate
over the Solomon Islands in the 1890s. Some of the
most bitter fighting of World War II occurred on this
archipelago. Self-government was achieved in 1976
and independence two years later. Ethnic violence,
government malfeasance, and endemic crime have
undermined stability and civil society. In June 2003,
then Prime Minister Sir Allan KEMAKEZA sought the
assistance of Australia in reestablishing law and
order; the following month, an Australian-led
multinational force arrived to restore peace and
disarm ethnic militias. The Regional Assistance
Mission to the Solomon Islands (RAMSI) has
generally been effective in restoring law and order and
rebuilding government institutions.

### Geography

**Location:** Oceania, group of islands in the South
Pacific Ocean, east of Papua New Guinea
**Geographic coordinates:** 8 00 S, 159 00 E
**Map references:** Oceania
**Area:**
*total:* 28,450 sq km
*land:* 27,540 sq km
*water:* 910 sq km
**Area - comparative:** slightly smaller than Maryland
**Land boundaries:** 0 km
**Coastline:** 5,313 km
**Maritime claims:** measured from claimed
archipelagic baselines
*territorial sea:* 12 nm
*exclusive economic zone:* 200 nm
*continental shelf:* 200 nm
**Climate:** tropical monsoon; few extremes of
temperature and weather
**Terrain:** mostly rugged mountains with some low
coral atolls

# Solomon Islands (continued)

**Elevation extremes:**

*lowest point:* Pacific Ocean 0 m

*highest point:* Mount Makarakomburu 2,447 m

**Natural resources:** fish, forests, gold, bauxite, phosphates, lead, zinc, nickel

**Land use:**

*arable land:* 0.62%

*permanent crops:* 2.04%

*other:* 97.34% (2005)

**Irrigated land:** NA

**Total renewable water resources:** 44.7 cu km (1987)

**Natural hazards:** typhoons, but rarely destructive; geologically active region with frequent earthquakes, tremors, and volcanic activity; tsunamis

**Environment - current issues:** deforestation; soil erosion; many of the surrounding coral reefs are dead or dying

**Environment - international agreements:**

*party to:* Biodiversity, Climate Change, Climate Change-Kyoto Protocol, Desertification, Environmental Modification, Law of the Sea, Marine Dumping, Marine Life Conservation, Ozone Layer Protection, Whaling

*signed, but not ratified:* none of the selected agreements

**Geography - note:** strategic location on sea routes between the South Pacific Ocean, the Solomon Sea, and the Coral Sea; on 2 April 2007 an undersea earthquake measuring 8.1 on the Richter scale occurred 345 km WNW of the capital Honiara; the resulting tsunami devastated coastal areas of Western and Choiseul provinces with dozens of deaths and thousands dislocated; the provincial capital of Gizo was especially hard hit

## People

**Population:** 595,613 (July 2009 est.)

**Age structure:**

*0-14 years:* 39.5% (male 119,875/female 115,127)

*15-64 years:* 57.1% (male 171,792/female 168,023)

*65 years and over:* 3.5% (male 9,849/female 10,947) (2009 est.)

**Median age:**

*total:* 19.7 years

*male:* 19.5 years

*female:* 19.8 years (2009 est.)

**Population growth rate:** 2.392% (2009 est.)

**Birth rate:** 27.69 births/1,000 population (2009 est.)

**Death rate:** 3.81 deaths/1,000 population (2008 est.)

**Net migration rate:** NA

**Urbanization:**

*urban population:* 18% of total population (2008)

*rate of urbanization:* 4.1% annual rate of change (2005-10 est.)

**Sex ratio:**

*at birth:* 1.05 male(s)/female

*under 15 years:* 1.04 male(s)/female

*15-64 years:* 1.02 male(s)/female

*65 years and over:* 0.9 male(s)/female

*total population:* 1.02 male(s)/female (2009 est.)

**Infant mortality rate:**

*total:* 19.03 deaths/1,000 live births

*male:* 21.65 deaths/1,000 live births

*female:* 16.28 deaths/1,000 live births (2009 est.)

**Life expectancy at birth:**

*total population:* 73.69 years

*male:* 71.14 years

*female:* 76.37 years (2009 est.)

**Total fertility rate:** 3.52 children born/woman (2009 est.)

**HIV/AIDS - adult prevalence rate:** NA

**HIV/AIDS - people living with HIV/AIDS:** NA

**HIV/AIDS - deaths:** NA

**Nationality:**

*noun:* Solomon Islander(s)

*adjective:* Solomon Islander

**Ethnic groups:** Melanesian 94.5%, Polynesian 3%, Micronesian 1.2%, other 1.1%, unspecified 0.2% (1999 census)

**Religions:** Church of Melanesia 32.8%, Roman Catholic 19%, South Seas Evangelical 17%, Seventh-Day Adventist 11.2%, United Church 10.3%, Christian Fellowship Church 2.4%, other Christian 4.4%, other 2.4%, unspecified 0.3%, none 0.2% (1999 census)

**Languages:** Melanesian pidgin in much of the country is lingua franca; English (official but spoken by only 1%-2% of the population); 120 indigenous languages

**Literacy:** NA

**School life expectancy (primary to tertiary education):**

*total:* 8 years

*male:* 9 years

*female:* 8 years (2005)

**Education expenditures:** 3.3% of GDP (1999)

## Government

**Country name:**

*conventional long form:* none

*conventional short form:* Solomon Islands

*local long form:* none

*local short form:* Solomon Islands

*former:* British Solomon Islands

**Government type:** parliamentary democracy and a Commonwealth realm

**Capital:**

*name:* Honiara

*geographic coordinates:* 9 26 S, 159 57 E

*time difference:* UTC+11 (16 hours ahead of Washington, DC during Standard Time)

**Administrative divisions:** 9 provinces and 1 capital territory*; Central, Choiseul, Guadalcanal, Honiara*, Isabel, Makira, Malaita, Rennell and Bellona, Temotu, Western

**Independence:** 7 July 1978 (from the UK)

**National holiday:** Independence Day, 7 July (1978)

**Constitution:** 7 July 1978

**Legal system:** English common law, which is widely disregarded; has not accepted compulsory ICJ jurisdiction

**Suffrage:** 21 years of age; universal

**Executive branch:**

*chief of state:* Queen ELIZABETH II (since 6 February 1952); represented by Governor General Nathaniel WAENA (since 7 July 2004)

*head of government:* Prime Minister Derek SIKUA (since 20 December 2007); note - Prime Minister Manasseh SOGAVARE defeated in a no confidence vote in parliament on 13 December 2007; SIKUA elected on 20 December 2007

*cabinet:* Cabinet consists of 20 members appointed by the governor general on the advice of the prime minister from among the members of Parliament

*elections:* the monarch is hereditary; governor general appointed by the monarch on the advice of parliament for up to five years (eligible for a second term); following legislative elections, the leader of the majority party or the leader of a majority coalition is usually elected prime minister by parliament; deputy prime minister appointed by the governor general on the advice of the prime minister from among the members of parliament

**Legislative branch:** unicameral National Parliament (50 seats; members elected from single-member constituencies by popular vote to serve four-year terms)

*elections:* last held on 5 April 2006 (next to be held in 2010)

*election results:* percent of vote by party - National Party 6.9%, PAP 6.3%, SIPRA 6.3%, Liberal 5%, Democratic 4.9%, SOCRED 4.3%, LAFARI 2.8%, independents 60.3%; seats by party - National Party 4, SIPRA 4, Democratic 3, PAP 3, LAFARI 2, Liberal 2, SOCRED 2, independents 30

**Judicial branch:** Court of Appeal

**Political parties and leaders:** Association of Independent Members or AIM [Thomas CHAN]; Christian Alliance Solomon Islands or CASI [Edward RONIA]; LAFARI Party [John GARO]; National Party [Francis HILLY]; People's Alliance Party or PAP [Sir Allan KEMAKEZA]; Social Credit Party or SOCRED [Manasseh Damukana SOGAVARE]; Solomon First Party [David QUAN]; Solomon Islands Democratic Party [Gabriel SURI]; Solomon Islands Labor Party or SILP [Joses TUHANUKU]; Solomon Islands Liberal Party [Bartholomew ULUFA'ALU]; Solomon Islands Party for Rural Advancement or SIPRA [Job D. TAUSINGA]; United Party [Sir Peter KENILOREA]

*note:* in general, Solomon Islands politics is characterized by fluid coalitions

**Political pressure groups and leaders:** Isatabu Freedom Movement (IFM); Malaita Eagle Force (MEF); note - these rival armed ethnic factions crippled the Solomon Islands in a wave of violence from 1999 to 2003

**International organization participation:** ACP, ADB, C, ESCAP, FAO, G-77, IBRD, ICAO, ICCt (signatory), ICRM, IDA, IFAD, IFC, IFRCS, ILO, IMF, IMO, IOC, ITU, MIGA, OPCW, PIF, Sparteca, SPC, UN, UNCTAD, UNESCO, UPU, WHO, WMO, WTO

# Solomon Islands (continued)

**Diplomatic representation in the US:**
*chief of mission:* Ambassador Collin David BECK
*chancery:* 800 Second Avenue, Suite 400L, New York, NY 10017
*telephone:* [1] (212) 599-6192, 6193
*FAX:* [1] (212) 661-8925
**Diplomatic representation from the US:** the US does not have an embassy in Solomon Islands (embassy closed July 1993); the ambassador to Papua New Guinea is accredited to the Solomon Islands
**Flag description:** divided diagonally by a thin yellow stripe from the lower hoist-side corner; the upper triangle (hoist side) is blue with five white five-pointed stars arranged in an X pattern; the lower triangle is green
**Government - note:** by the end of 2007, the Regional Assistance Mission to the Solomon Islands (RAMSI) - originally made up of police and troops from Australia, NZ, Fiji, Papua New Guinea, and Tonga - had been scaled back to 303 police officers, 197 civilian technical advisers, and 72 military advisers from 15 countries across the region

## Economy

**Economy - overview:** The bulk of the population depends on agriculture, fishing, and forestry for at least part of its livelihood. Most manufactured goods and petroleum products must be imported. The islands are rich in undeveloped mineral resources such as lead, zinc, nickel, and gold. Prior to the arrival of RAMSI, severe ethnic violence, the closing of key businesses, and an empty government treasury culminated in economic collapse. RAMSI's efforts to restore law and order and economic stability have led to modest growth as the economy rebuilds.
**GDP (purchasing power parity):**
$1.078 billion (2008 est.)
$1.005 billion (2007)
$911.1 million (2006)
*note:* data are in 2008 US dollars
**GDP (official exchange rate):** $460 million (2008 est.)
**GDP - real growth rate:**
7.3% (2008 est.)
10.3% (2007 est.)
6.1% (2006 est.)
**GDP - per capita (PPP):**
$1,900 (2008 est.)
$1,800 (2007 est.)
$1,600 (2006 est.)
*note:* data are in 2008 US dollars
**GDP - composition by sector:**
*agriculture:* 42%
*industry:* 11%
*services:* 47% (2000 est.)
**Labor force:** 249,200 (1999)
**Labor force - by occupation:**
*agriculture:* 75%
*industry:* 5%
*services:* 20% (2000 est.)

**Unemployment rate:**
NA%
**Population below poverty line:** NA%
**Household income or consumption by percentage share:**
*lowest 10%:* NA%
*highest 10%:* NA%
**Budget:**
*revenues:* $49.7 million
*expenditures:* $75.1 million (2003)
**Inflation rate (consumer prices):**
6.3% (2007 est.)
**Commercial bank prime lending rate:** 14.12% (31 December 2007)
**Stock of money:** $118.3 million (31 December 2007)
**Stock of quasi money:** $57.89 million (31 December 2007)
**Stock of domestic credit:** $126.9 million (31 December 2007)
**Agriculture - products:** cocoa beans, coconuts, palm kernels, rice, potatoes, vegetables, fruit; timber; cattle, pigs; fish
**Industries:** fish (tuna), mining, timber
**Industrial production growth rate:** NA%
**Electricity - production:** 70 million kWh (2007 est.)
**Electricity - consumption:** 70 million kWh (2007 est.)
**Electricity - exports:** 0 kWh (2007 est.)
**Electricity - imports:** 0 kWh (2007 est.)
**Oil - production:** 0 bbl/day (2007 est.)
**Oil - consumption:** 1,320 bbl/day (2006 est.)
**Oil - exports:** 0 bbl/day (2005)
**Oil - imports:** 1,426 bbl/day (2005)
**Oil - proved reserves:** 0 bbl (1 January 2006 est.)
**Natural gas - production:** 0 cu m (2007 est.)
**Natural gas - consumption:** 0 cu m (2007 est.)
**Natural gas - exports:** 0 cu m (2007 est.)
**Natural gas - imports:** 0 cu m (2007 est.)
**Natural gas - proved reserves:** 0 cu m (1 January 2006 est.)
**Current account balance:** -$143 million (2007 est.)
**Exports:** $237 million f.o.b. (2006)
**Exports - commodities:** timber, fish, copra, palm oil, cocoa
**Exports - partners:** China 50.8%, South Korea 7%, Thailand 6.5%, Japan 5.7%, Philippines 4.3% (2007)
**Imports:** $256 million f.o.b. (2006)
**Imports - commodities:** food, plant and equipment, manufactured goods, fuels, chemicals
**Imports - partners:** Singapore 28.2%, Australia 25.4%, Japan 4.6%, NZ 4.5%, Fiji 4% (2007)
**Debt - external:** $166 million (2004)
**Exchange rates:** Solomon Islands dollars (SBD) per US dollar - NA (2007), 7.3447 (2006), 7.5299 (2005), 7.4847 (2004), 7.5059 (2003)

## Communications

**Telephones - main lines in use:** 7,600 (2006)
**Telephones - mobile cellular:** 10,900 (2007)
**Telephone system:**
*general assessment:* NA
*domestic:* NA
*international:* country code - 677; satellite earth station -1 Intelsat (Pacific Ocean)
**Radio broadcast stations:** AM 1, FM 1, shortwave 1 (2004)
**Internet country code:** .sb
**Internet hosts:** 3,804 (2008)
**Internet users:** 8,000 (2006)

## Transportation

**Airports:** 35 (2008)
**Airports - with paved runways:**
*total:* 2
*1,524 to 2,437 m:* 1
*914 to 1,523 m:* 1 (2008)
**Airports - with unpaved runways:**
*total:* 33
*1,524 to 2,437 m:* 1
*914 to 1,523 m:* 8
*under 914 m:* 24 (2008)
**Heliports:** 3 (2007)
**Roadways:**
*total:* 1,360 km
*paved:* 33 km
*unpaved:* 1,327 km
*note:* includes 800 km of private plantation roads (2002)
**Ports and terminals:** Honiara, Malloco Bay, Viru Harbor

## Military

**Military branches:** no regular military forces; Solomon Islands Police Force (2009)
**Manpower available for military service:**
*males age 16-49:* 141,051 (2008 est.)
**Manpower fit for military service:**
*males age 16-49:* 121,368
*females age 16-49:* 122,821 (2009 est.)
**Manpower reaching militarily significant age annually:**
*male:* 7,091
*female:* 6,837 (2009 est.)
**Military expenditures:** 3% of GDP (2006)

## Transnational Issues

**Disputes - international:** since 2003, RAMSI, consisting of police, military, and civilian advisors drawn from 15 countries, has assisted in reestablishing and maintaining civil and political order while reinforcing regional stability and security
**Refugees and internally displaced persons:**
*IDPs:* 5,400 (displaced by tsunami on 2 April 2007) (2007)

# Somalia

## Introduction

**Background:** Britain withdrew from British Somaliland in 1960 to allow its protectorate to join with Italian Somaliland and form the new nation of Somalia. In 1969, a coup headed by Mohamed SIAD Barre ushered in an authoritarian socialist rule that managed to impose a degree of stability in the country for a couple of decades. After the regime's collapse early in 1991, Somalia descended into turmoil, factional fighting, and anarchy. In May 1991, northern clans declared an independent Republic of Somaliland that now includes the administrative regions of Awdal, Woqooyi Galbeed, Togdheer, Sanaag, and Sool. Although not recognized by any government, this entity has maintained a stable existence and continues efforts to establish a constitutional democracy, including holding municipal, parliamentary, and presidential elections. The regions of Bari, Nugaal, and northern Mudug comprise a neighboring self-declared autonomous state of Puntland, which has been self-governing since 1998 but does not aim at independence; it has also made strides toward reconstructing a legitimate, representative government but has suffered some civil strife. Puntland disputes its border with Somaliland as it also claims portions of eastern Sool and Sanaag. Beginning in 1993, a two-year UN humanitarian effort (primarily in the south) was able to alleviate famine conditions, but when the UN withdrew in 1995, having suffered significant casualties, order still had not been restored. A two-year peace process, led by the Government of Kenya under the auspices of the Intergovernmental Authority on Development (IGAD), concluded in October 2004 with the election of Abdullahi YUSUF Ahmed as President of the Transitional Federal Government (TFG) of Somalia and the formation of an interim government, known as the Somalia Transitional Federal Institutions (TFIs). The TFIs included a 275-member parliamentary body, known as the Transitional Federal Assembly (TFA).

President YUSUF resigned late in 2008 while United Nations-sponsored talks between the TFG and the opposition Alliance for the Re-Liberation of Somalia (ARS) were underway in Djibouti. In January 2009, following the creation of a TFG-ARS unity government, Ethiopian military forces, which had entered Somalia in December 2006 to support the TFG in the face of advances by the opposition Council of Islamic Courts (CIC), withdrew from the country. The TFA was increased to 550 seats with the addition of 275 ARS members of parliament. The expanded parliament elected Sheikh SHARIF Sheikh Ahmed, the former CIC and ARS chairman as president on 31 January 2009, in Djibouti. Subsequently, President SHARIF appointed Omar Abdirashid ali SHARMARKE, son of a former president of Somalia, as prime minister on 13 February 2009. The TFIs are based on the Transitional Federal Charter (TFC), which outlines a five-year mandate leading to the establishment of a new Somali constitution and a transition to a representative government following national elections. However, in January 2009 the TFA amended the TFC to extend TFG's mandate until 2011. While its institutions remain weak, the TFG continues to reach out to Somali stakeholders and work with international donors to help build the governance capacity of the TFIs and work toward national elections in 2011.

## Geography

**Location:** Eastern Africa, bordering the Gulf of Aden and the Indian Ocean, east of Ethiopia

**Geographic coordinates:** 10 00 N, 49 00 E

**Map references:** Africa

**Area:**
*total:* 637,657 sq km
*land:* 627,337 sq km
*water:* 10,320 sq km

**Area - comparative:** slightly smaller than Texas

**Land boundaries:**
*total:* 2,340 km
*border countries:* Djibouti 58 km, Ethiopia 1,600 km, Kenya 682 km

**Coastline:** 3,025 km

**Maritime claims:**
*territorial sea:* 200 nm

**Climate:** principally desert; northeast monsoon (December to February), moderate temperatures in north and hot in south; southwest monsoon (May to October), torrid in the north and hot in the south, irregular rainfall, hot and humid periods (tangambili) between monsoons

**Terrain:** mostly flat to undulating plateau rising to hills in north

**Elevation extremes:**
*lowest point:* Indian Ocean 0 m
*highest point:* Shimbiris 2,416 m

**Natural resources:** uranium and largely unexploited reserves of iron ore, tin, gypsum, bauxite, copper, salt, natural gas, likely oil reserves

**Land use:**
*arable land:* 1.64%
*permanent crops:* 0.04%
*other:* 98.32% (2005)

**Irrigated land:** 2,000 sq km (2003)

**Total renewable water resources:** 15.7 cu km (1997)

**Freshwater withdrawal (domestic/industrial/agricultural):**
*total:* 3.29 cu km/yr (0%/0%/100%)
*per capita:* 400 cu m/yr (2000)

**Natural hazards:** recurring droughts; frequent dust storms over eastern plains in summer; floods during rainy season

**Environment - current issues:** famine; use of contaminated water contributes to human health problems; deforestation; overgrazing; soil erosion; desertification

**Environment - international agreements:**
*party to:* Biodiversity, Desertification, Endangered Species, Law of the Sea, Ozone Layer Protection
*signed, but not ratified:* none of the selected agreements

**Geography - note:** strategic location on Horn of Africa along southern approaches to Bab el Mandeb and route through Red Sea and Suez Canal

## People

**Population:** 9,832,017
*note:* this estimate was derived from an official census taken in 1975 by the Somali Government; population counting in Somalia is complicated by the large number of nomads and by refugee movements in response to famine and clan warfare (July 2009 est.)

**Age structure:**
*0-14 years:* 45% (male 2,215,331/female 2,204,503)
*15-64 years:* 52.6% (male 2,588,356/female 2,579,737)
*65 years and over:* 2.5% (male 101,764/female 142,326) (2009 est.)

**Median age:**
*total:* 17.5 years
*male:* 17.4 years
*female:* 17.6 years (2009 est.)

**Population growth rate:** 2.815% (2009 est.)

**Birth rate:** 43.7 births/1,000 population (2009 est.)

**Death rate:** 15.89 deaths/1,000 population (2008 est.)

**Net migration rate:** 0 migrant(s)/1,000 population (2009 est.)

**Urbanization:**
*urban population:* 37% of total population (2008)
*rate of urbanization:* 4.2% annual rate of change (2005-10 est.)

**Sex ratio:**
*at birth:* 1.03 male(s)/female
*under 15 years:* 1 male(s)/female
*15-64 years:* 1 male(s)/female
*65 years and over:* 0.72 male(s)/female
*total population:* 1 male(s)/female (2009 est.)

# Somalia (continued)

**Infant mortality rate:**
*total:* 109.19 deaths/1,000 live births
*male:* 118.31 deaths/1,000 live births
*female:* 99.79 deaths/1,000 live births (2009 est.)
**Life expectancy at birth:**
*total population:* 49.63 years
*male:* 47.78 years
*female:* 51.53 years (2009 est.)
**Total fertility rate:** 6.52 children born/woman
(2009 est.)
**HIV/AIDS - adult prevalence rate:** 0.5% (2007 est.)
**HIV/AIDS - people living with HIV/AIDS:** 24,000
(2007 est.)
**HIV/AIDS - deaths:** 1,600 (2007 est.)
**Major infectious diseases:**
*degree of risk:* high
*food or waterborne diseases:* bacterial and protozoal
diarrhea, hepatitis A and E, and typhoid fever
*vectorborne diseases:* dengue fever, malaria, and Rift
Valley fever
*water contact disease:* schistosomiasis
*animal contact disease:* rabies (2009)
**Nationality:**
*noun:* Somali(s)
*adjective:* Somali
**Ethnic groups:** Somali 85%, Bantu and other
non-Somali 15% (including Arabs 30,000)
**Religions:** Sunni Muslim
**Languages:** Somali (official), Arabic, Italian, English
**Literacy:**
*definition:* age 15 and over can read and write
*total population:* 37.8%
*male:* 49.7%
*female:* 25.8% (2001 est.)
**Education expenditures:** NA

## Government

**Country name:**
*conventional long form:* none
*conventional short form:* Somalia
*local long form:* Jamhuuriyada Demuqraadiga
Soomaaliyeed
*local short form:* Soomaaliya
*former:* Somali Republic, Somali Democratic Republic
**Government type:** no permanent national
government; transitional, parliamentary federal
government
**Capital:**
*name:* Mogadishu
*geographic coordinates:* 2 04 N, 45 22 E
*time difference:* UTC+3 (8 hours ahead of
Washington, DC during Standard Time)
**Administrative divisions:** 18 regions (plural - NA,
singular - gobolka); Awdal, Bakool, Banaadir, Bari,
Bay, Galguduud, Gedo, Hiiraan, Jubbada Dhexe,
Jubbada Hoose, Mudug, Nugaal, Sanaag,
Shabeellaha Dhexe, Shabeellaha Hoose, Sool,
Togdheer, Woqooyi Galbeed

**Independence:** 1 July 1960 (from a merger of British
Somaliland, which became independent from the UK
on 26 June 1960, and Italian Somaliland, which
became independent from the Italian-administered
UN trusteeship on 1 July 1960, to form the Somali
Republic)
**National holiday:** Foundation of the Somali
Republic, 1 July (1960); note - 26 June (1960) in
Somaliland
**Constitution:** 25 August 1979, presidential approval
23 September 1979
*note:* the formation of transitional governing
institutions, known as the Transitional Federal
Government, is currently ongoing
**Legal system:** no national system; a mixture of
English common law, Italian law, Islamic Sharia, and
Somali customary law; accepts compulsory ICJ
jurisdiction with reservations
**Suffrage:** 18 years of age; universal
**Executive branch:**
*chief of state:* Transitional Federal President Sheikh
SHARIF Sheikh Ahmed (since 31 January 2009);
note -a transitional governing entity with a five-year
mandate, known as the Transitional Federal
Institutions (TFIs), was established in October 2004;
the TFIs relocated to Somalia in June 2004
*head of government:* Prime Minister Omar Abdirashid
Ali SHARMARKE (since 13 February 2009)
*cabinet:* Cabinet appointed by the prime minister and
approved by the Transitional Federal Assembly
*election results:* Sheikh SHARIF Sheikh Ahmed was
elected president by the expanded Transitional
Federal Assembly in Djibouti
**Legislative branch:** unicameral National Assembly
*note:* unicameral Transitional Federal Assembly
(TFA) (550 seats; 475 members appointed according
to the 4.5 clan formula, with the remaining 75 seats
reserved for civil society and business persons)
**Judicial branch:** following the breakdown of the
central government, most regions have reverted to
local forms of conflict resolution, either secular,
traditional Somali customary law, or Sharia (Islamic)
law with a provision for appeal of all sentences
**Political parties and leaders:** none
**Political pressure groups and leaders:**
*other:* numerous clan and sub-clan factions exist both
in support and in opposition to the transitional
government
**International organization participation:** ACP,
AfDB, AFESD, AMF, AU, CAEU, FAO, G-77, IBRD,
ICAO, ICRM, IDA, IDB, IFAD, IFC, IFRCS, IGAD, ILO,
IMF, IMO, Interpol, IOC, IOM, IPU, ITSO, ITU, LAS,
NAM, OIC, UN, UNCTAD, UNESCO, UNHCR,
UNIDO, UPU, WFTU, WHO, WIPO, WMO
**Diplomatic representation in the US:** Somalia
does not have an embassy in the US (ceased
operations on 8 May 1991); note - the Transitional
Federal Government is represented in the United
States through its Permanent Mission to the United
Nations

**Diplomatic representation from the US:** the US
does not have an embassy in Somalia; US interests
are represented by the US Embassy in Nairobi, Kenya
at United Nations Avenue, Nairobi; mailing address:
Unit 64100, Nairobi; APO AE 09831; telephone: [254]
(20) 363-6000; FAX [254] (20) 363-6157
**Flag description:** light blue with a large white
five-pointed star in the center; blue field influenced by
the flag of the UN
**Government - note:** although an interim
government was created in 2004, other regional and
local governing bodies continue to exist and control
various regions of the country, including the
self-declared Republic of Somaliland in northwestern
Somalia and the semi-autonomous State of Puntland
in northeastern Somalia

## Economy

**Economy - overview:** Despite the lack of effective
national governance, Somalia has maintained a
healthy informal economy, largely based on livestock,
remittance/money transfer companies, and
telecommunications. Agriculture is the most important
sector, with livestock normally accounting for about
40% of GDP and about 65% of export earnings.
Nomads and semi-pastoralists, who are dependent
upon livestock for their livelihood, make up a large
portion of the population. Livestock, hides, fish,
charcoal, and bananas are Somalia's principal
exports, while sugar, sorghum, corn, qat, and
machined goods are the principal imports. Somalia's
small industrial sector, based on the processing of
agricultural products, has largely been looted and sold
as scrap metal. Somalia's service sector also has
grown. Telecommunication firms provide wireless
services in most major cities and offer the lowest
international call rates on the continent. In the
absence of a formal banking sector, money transfer/
remittance services have sprouted throughout the
country, handling roughly $2 billion in remittances
annually. Mogadishu's main market offers a variety of
goods from food to the newest electronic gadgets.
Hotels continue to operate and are supported with
private-security militias. Somalia's arrears to the IMF
continued to grow in 2008. Statistics on Somalia's
GDP, growth, per capita income, and inflation should
be viewed skeptically.
**GDP (purchasing power parity):**
$5.524 billion (2008 est.)
$5.387 billion (2007)
$5.252 billion (2006)
*note:* data are in 2008 US dollars
**GDP (official exchange rate):** $2.6 billion
(2008 est.)
**GDP - real growth rate:**
2.6% (2008 est.)
2.6% (2007 est.)
2.6% (2006 est.)

# Somalia (continued)

**GDP - per capita (PPP):**
$600 (2008 est.)
$600 (2007 est.)
$600 (2006 est.)
*note:* data are in 2008 US dollars
**GDP - composition by sector:**
*agriculture:* 65%
*industry:* 10%
*services:* 25% (2000 est.)
**Labor force:** 3.7 million (few skilled laborers) (1975)
**Labor force - by occupation:**
*agriculture:* 71%
*industry and services:* 29% (1975)
**Unemployment rate:**
NA%
**Population below poverty line:** NA%
**Household income or consumption by percentage share:**
*lowest 10%:* NA%
*highest 10%:* NA%
**Budget:**
*revenues:* $NA
*expenditures:* $NA
**Inflation rate (consumer prices):**
NA%
*note:* businesses print their own money, so inflation rates cannot be easily determined
**Agriculture - products:** bananas, sorghum, corn, coconuts, rice, sugarcane, mangoes, sesame seeds, beans; cattle, sheep, goats; fish
**Industries:** a few light industries, including sugar refining, textiles, wireless communication
**Industrial production growth rate:** NA%
**Electricity - production:** 280 million kWh (2006 est.)
**Electricity - consumption:** 260.4 million kWh (2006 est.)
**Electricity - exports:** 0 kWh (2007 est.)
**Electricity - imports:** 0 kWh (2007 est.)
**Oil - production:** 0 bbl/day (2007 est.)
**Oil - consumption:** 5,040 bbl/day (2006 est.)
**Oil - exports:** 0 bbl/day (2005)
**Oil - imports:** 4,772 bbl/day (2005)
**Oil - proved reserves:** 0 bbl (1 January 2006 est.)
**Natural gas - production:** 0 cu m (2007 est.)
**Natural gas - consumption:** 0 cu m (2007 est.)
**Natural gas - exports:** 0 cu m (2007 est.)
**Natural gas - imports:** 0 cu m (2007 est.)
**Natural gas - proved reserves:** 5.663 billion cu m (1 January 2008 est.)
**Exports:** $300 million f.o.b. (2006)
**Exports - commodities:** livestock, bananas, hides, fish, charcoal, scrap metal
**Exports - partners:** UAE 50.7%, Yemen 21%, Oman 6.1% (2007)
**Imports:** $798 million f.o.b. (2006)
**Imports - commodities:** manufactures, petroleum products, foodstuffs, construction materials, qat
**Imports - partners:** Djibouti 34.4%, India 9.1%, Kenya 9%, Oman 6%, UAE 5.6%, Yemen 5.5% (2007)

**Debt - external:** $3 billion (2001 est.)
**Exchange rates:** Somali shillings (SOS) per US dollar - NA (2007-08), 1,438.3 (2006) official rate; the unofficial black market rate was about 23,000 shillings per dollar as of February 2007
*note:* the Republic of Somaliland, a self-declared independent country not recognized by any foreign government, issues its own currency, the Somaliland shilling

## Communications

**Telephones - main lines in use:** 100,000 (2007)
**Telephones - mobile cellular:** 600,000 (2007)
**Telephone system:**
*general assessment:* the public telecommunications system was almost completely destroyed or dismantled during the civil war; private companies offer limited local fixed-line service and private wireless companies offer service in most major cities while charging the lowest international rates on the continent
*domestic:* local cellular telephone systems have been established in Mogadishu and in several other population centers
*international:* country code - 252; international connections are available from Mogadishu by satellite (2001)
**Radio broadcast stations:** AM 0, FM 11 (also 1 station each in Puntland and Somaliland), shortwave 1 (in Mogadishu) (2001)
**Television broadcast stations:** 4 (2 in Mogadishu and 2 in Hargeisa) (2001)
**Internet country code:** .so
**Internet hosts:** 1 (2008)
**Internet users:** 98,000 (2007)

## Transportation

**Airports:** 59 (2008)
**Airports - with paved runways:**
*total:* 7
*over 3,047 m:* 4
*2,438 to 3,047 m:* 2
*1,524 to 2,437 m:* 1 (2008)
**Airports - with unpaved runways:**
*total:* 52
*2,438 to 3,047 m:* 4
*1,524 to 2,437 m:* 19
*914 to 1,523 m:* 23
*under 914 m:* 6 (2008)
**Roadways:**
*total:* 22,100 km
*paved:* 2,608 km
*unpaved:* 19,492 km (2000)
**Merchant marine:**
*total:* 1
*by type:* cargo 1
*foreign-owned:* 1 (UAE 1) (2008)
**Ports and terminals:** Berbera, Kismaayo

**Transportation - note:** the International Maritime Bureau reports the territorial and offshore waters in the Gulf of Aden and Indian Ocean are high risk for piracy and armed robbery against ships; numerous vessels, including commercial shipping and pleasure craft, have been attacked and hijacked both at anchor and while underway; crew, passengers, and cargo are held for ransom

## Military

**Military branches:** no national-level armed forces (2008)
**Manpower available for military service:**
*males age 16-49:* 2,181,050
*females age 16-49:* 2,125,558 (2008 est.)
**Manpower fit for military service:**
*males age 16-49:* 1,301,026
*females age 16-49:* 1,351,649 (2009 est.)
**Manpower reaching militarily significant age annually:**
*male:* 93,763
*female:* 93,738 (2009 est.)
**Military expenditures:** 0.9% of GDP (2005 est.)

## Transnational Issues

**Disputes - international:** Ethiopian forces invaded southern Somalia and routed Islamist Courts from Mogadishu in January 2007; "Somaliland" secessionists provide port facilities in Berbera to landlocked Ethiopia and have established commercial ties with other regional states; "Puntland" and "Somaliland" "governments" seek international support in their secessionist aspirations and overlapping border claims; the undemarcated former British administrative line has little meaning as a political separation to rival clans within Ethiopia's Ogaden and southern Somalia's Oromo region; Kenya works hard to prevent the clan and militia fighting in Somalia from spreading south across the border, which has long been open to nomadic pastoralists
**Refugees and internally displaced persons:**
*IDPs:* 1.1 million (civil war since 1988, clan-based competition for resources) (2007)

# South Africa

## Introduction

**Background:** Dutch traders landed at the southern tip of modern day South Africa in 1652 and established a stopover point on the spice route between the Netherlands and the East, founding the city of Cape Town. After the British seized the Cape of Good Hope area in 1806, many of the Dutch settlers (the Boers) trekked north to found their own republics. The discovery of diamonds (1867) and gold (1886) spurred wealth and immigration and intensified the subjugation of the native inhabitants. The Boers resisted British encroachments but were defeated in the Boer War (1899-1902); however, the British and the Afrikaners, as the Boers became known, ruled together under the Union of South Africa. In 1948, the National Party was voted into power and instituted a policy of apartheid - the separate development of the races. The first multi-racial elections in 1994 brought an end to apartheid and ushered in black majority rule under the African National Congress (ANC). ANC infighting, which has grown in recent years, came to a head in September 2008 after President Thabo MBEKI resigned. Kgalema MOTLANTHE, the party's General-Secretary, succeeded as interim president until general elections scheduled for 2009.

## Geography

**Location:** Southern Africa, at the southern tip of the continent of Africa
**Geographic coordinates:** 29 00 S, 24 00 E
**Map references:** Africa
**Area:**
*total:* 1,219,912 sq km
*land:* 1,219,912 sq km
*water:* 0 sq km
*note:* includes Prince Edward Islands (Marion Island and Prince Edward Island)
**Area - comparative:** slightly less than twice the size of Texas

**Land boundaries:**
*total:* 4,862 km
*border countries:* Botswana 1,840 km, Lesotho 909 km, Mozambique 491 km, Namibia 967 km, Swaziland 430 km, Zimbabwe 225 km
**Coastline:** 2,798 km
**Maritime claims:**
*territorial sea:* 12 nm
*contiguous zone:* 24 nm
*exclusive economic zone:* 200 nm
*continental shelf:* 200 nm or to edge of the continental margin
**Climate:** mostly semiarid; subtropical along east coast; sunny days, cool nights
**Terrain:** vast interior plateau rimmed by rugged hills and narrow coastal plain
**Elevation extremes:**
*lowest point:* Atlantic Ocean 0 m
*highest point:* Njesuthi 3,408 m
**Natural resources:** gold, chromium, antimony, coal, iron ore, manganese, nickel, phosphates, tin, uranium, gem diamonds, platinum, copper, vanadium, salt, natural gas
**Land use:**
*arable land:* 12.1%
*permanent crops:* 0.79%
*other:* 87.11% (2005)
**Irrigated land:** 14,980 sq km (2003)
**Total renewable water resources:** 50 cu km (1990)
**Freshwater withdrawal (domestic/industrial/agricultural):**
*total:* 12.5 cu km/yr (31%/6%/63%)
*per capita:* 264 cu m/yr (2000)
**Natural hazards:** prolonged droughts
**Environment - current issues:** lack of important arterial rivers or lakes requires extensive water conservation and control measures; growth in water usage outpacing supply; pollution of rivers from agricultural runoff and urban discharge; air pollution resulting in acid rain; soil erosion; desertification
**Environment - international agreements:**
*party to:* Antarctic-Environmental Protocol, Antarctic-Marine Living Resources, Antarctic Seals, Antarctic Treaty, Biodiversity, Climate Change, Climate Change-Kyoto Protocol, Desertification, Endangered Species, Hazardous Wastes, Law of the Sea, Marine Dumping, Marine Life Conservation, Ozone Layer Protection, Ship Pollution, Wetlands, Whaling
*signed, but not ratified:* none of the selected agreements
**Geography - note:** South Africa completely surrounds Lesotho and almost completely surrounds Swaziland

## People

**Population:** 49,052,489
*note:* estimates for this country explicitly take into account the effects of excess mortality due to AIDS; this can result in lower life expectancy, higher infant mortality, higher death rates, lower population growth rates, and changes in the distribution of population by age and sex than would otherwise be expected (July 2009 est.)
**Age structure:**
*0-14 years:* 28.9% (male 7,093,328/female 7,061,579)
*15-64 years:* 65.8% (male 16,275,424/female 15,984,181)
*65 years and over:* 5.4% (male 1,075,117/female 1,562,860) (2009 est.)
**Median age:**
*total:* 24.4 years
*male:* 24.1 years
*female:* 24.8 years (2009 est.)
**Population growth rate:** 0.281% (2009 est.)
**Birth rate:** 19.93 births/1,000 population (2009 est.)
**Death rate:** 16.94 deaths/1,000 population (2008 est.)
**Net migration rate:** -0.13 migrant(s)/1,000 population
*note:* there is an increasing flow of Zimbabweans into South Africa and Botswana in search of better economic opportunities (2009 est.)
**Urbanization:**
*urban population:* 61% of total population (2008)
*rate of urbanization:* 1.4% annual rate of change (2005-10 est.)
**Sex ratio:**
*at birth:* 1.02 male(s)/female
*under 15 years:* 1 male(s)/female
*15-64 years:* 1.02 male(s)/female
*65 years and over:* 0.69 male(s)/female
*total population:* 0.99 male(s)/female (2009 est.)
**Infant mortality rate:**
*total:* 44.42 deaths/1,000 live births
*male:* 48.66 deaths/1,000 live births
*female:* 40.1 deaths/1,000 live births (2009 est.)
**Life expectancy at birth:**
*total population:* 48.98 years
*male:* 49.81 years
*female:* 48.13 years (2009 est.)
**Total fertility rate:** 2.38 children born/woman (2009 est.)
**HIV/AIDS - adult prevalence rate:** 18.1% (2007 est.)
**HIV/AIDS - people living with HIV/AIDS:** 5.7 million (2007 est.)
**HIV/AIDS - deaths:** 350,000 (2007 est.)
**Major infectious diseases:**
*degree of risk:* intermediate
*food or waterborne diseases:* bacterial diarrhea, hepatitis A, and typhoid fever
*water contact disease:* schistosomiasis (2009)

# South Africa (continued)

## Nationality:
*noun:* South African(s)
*adjective:* South African

**Ethnic groups:** black African 79%, white 9.6%, colored 8.9%, Indian/Asian 2.5% (2001 census)

**Religions:** Zion Christian 11.1%, Pentecostal/Charismatic 8.2%, Catholic 7.1%, Methodist 6.8%, Dutch Reformed 6.7%, Anglican 3.8%, Muslim 1.5%, other Christian 36%, other 2.3%, unspecified 1.4%, none 15.1% (2001 census)

**Languages:** IsiZulu 23.8%, IsiXhosa 17.6%, Afrikaans 13.3%, Sepedi 9.4%, English 8.2%, Setswana 8.2%, Sesotho 7.9%, Xitsonga 4.4%, other 7.2% (2001 census)

## Literacy:
*definition:* age 15 and over can read and write
*total population:* 86.4%
*male:* 87%
*female:* 85.7% (2003 est.)

**School life expectancy (primary to tertiary education):**
*total:* 13 years
*male:* 13 years
*female:* 13 years (2004)

**Education expenditures:** 5.4% of GDP (2006)

## Government

**Country name:**
*conventional long form:* Republic of South Africa
*conventional short form:* South Africa
*former:* Union of South Africa
*abbreviation:* RSA

**Government type:** republic

**Capital:**
*name:* Pretoria (administrative capital)
*geographic coordinates:* 25 42 S, 28 13 E
*time difference:* UTC+2 (7 hours ahead of Washington, DC during Standard Time)
*note:* Cape Town (legislative capital); Bloemfontein (judicial capital)

**Administrative divisions:** 9 provinces; Eastern Cape, Free State, Gauteng, KwaZulu-Natal, Limpopo, Mpumalanga, Northern Cape, North-West, Western Cape

**Independence:** 31 May 1910 (Union of South Africa formed from four British colonies: Cape Colony, Natal, Transvaal, and Orange Free State); 31 May 1961 (republic declared) 27 April 1994 (majority rule)

**National holiday:** Freedom Day, 27 April (1994)

**Constitution:** 10 December 1996; note - certified by the Constitutional Court on 4 December 1996; was signed by then President MANDELA on 10 December 1996; and entered into effect on 4 February 1997

**Legal system:** based on Roman-Dutch law and English common law; has not accepted compulsory ICJ jurisdiction

**Suffrage:** 18 years of age; universal

**Executive branch:**
*chief of state:* President Jacob ZUMA (since 9 May 2009); Executive Deputy President Kgalema MOTLANTHE (since 11 May 2009); note - the president is both the chief of state and head of government
*head of government:* President Jacob ZUMA (since 9 May 2009); Executive Deputy President Kgalema MOTLANTHE (since 11 May 2009)
*cabinet:* Cabinet appointed by the president
*elections:* president elected by the National Assembly for a five-year term (eligible for a second term); election last held on 6 May 2009 (next to be held in 2014)
*election results:* Jacob ZUMA elected president; National Assembly vote - Jacob ZUMA 277, Mvume DANDALA 47, other 76

**Legislative branch:** bicameral Parliament consisting of the National Council of Provinces (90 seats, 10 members elected by each of the nine provincial legislatures for five-year terms; has special powers to protect regional interests, including the safeguarding of cultural and linguistic traditions among ethnic minorities) and the National Assembly (400 seats; members are elected by popular vote under a system of proportional representation to serve five-year terms); note - following the implementation of the new constitution on 4 February 1997, the former Senate was disbanded and replaced by the National Council of Provinces with essentially no change in membership and party affiliations, although the new institution's responsibilities have been changed somewhat by the new constitution
*elections:* National Assembly and National Council of Provinces - last held on 22 April 2009 (next to be held in April 2014)
*election results:* National Council of Provinces - percent of vote by party - NA; seats by party - NA; National Assembly - percent of vote by party - ANC 65.9%, DA 16.7%, COPE 7.4%, IFP 4.6%, other 5.4%; seats by party - ANC 264, DA 67, COPE 30, IFP 18, other 21

**Judicial branch:** Constitutional Court; Supreme Court of Appeals; High Courts; Magistrate Courts

**Political parties and leaders:** African Christian Democratic Party or ACDP [Kenneth MESHOE]; African National Congress or ANC [Jacob ZUMA]; Congress of the People or COPE [Mosiuoa LEKOTA]; Democratic Alliance or DA [Helen ZILLE]; Freedom Front Plus or FF+ [Pieter MULDER]; Independent Democrats or ID [Patricia DE LILLE]; Inkatha Freedom Party or IFP [Mangosuthu BUTHELEZI]; Pan-Africanist Congress or PAC [Motsoko PHEKO]; United Christian Democratic Party or UCDP [Lucas MANGOPE]; United Democratic Movement or UDM [Bantu HOLOMISA]

**Political pressure groups and leaders:** Congress of South African Trade Unions or COSATU [Zwelinzima VAVI, general secretary]; South African Communist Party or SACP [Blade NZIMANDE, general secretary]; South African National Civics Organization or SANCO [Mlungisi HLONGWANE, national president]
*note:* note - COSATU and SACP are in a formal alliance with the ANC

**International organization participation:** ACP, AfDB, AU, BIS, C, FAO, G-20, G-24, G-77, IAEA, IBRD, ICAO, ICC, ICCt, ICRM, IDA, IFAD, IFC, IFRCS, IHO, ILO, IMF, IMO, IMSO, Interpol, IOC, IOM, IPU, ISO, ITSO, ITU, ITUC, MIGA, MONUC, NAM, NSG, OPCW, PCA, SACU, SADC, UN, UNAMID, UNCTAD, UNESCO, UNHCR, UNIDO, UNITAR, UNWTO, UPU, WCL, WCO, WFTU, WHO, WIPO, WMO, WTO, ZC

**Diplomatic representation in the US:**
*chief of mission:* Ambassador Welile Augustine NHLAPO
*chancery:* 3051 Massachusetts Avenue NW, Washington, DC 20008
*telephone:* [1] (202) 232-4400
*FAX:* [1] (202) 265-1607
*consulate(s) general:* Chicago, Los Angeles, New York

**Diplomatic representation from the US:**
*chief of mission:* Ambassador Eric BOST
*embassy:* 877 Pretorius Street, Pretoria
*mailing address:* P. O. Box 9536, Pretoria 0001
*telephone:* [27] (12) 431-4000
*FAX:* [27] (12) 342-2299
*consulate(s) general:* Cape Town, Durban, Johannesburg

**Flag description:** two equal width horizontal bands of red (top) and blue separated by a central green band that splits into a horizontal Y, the arms of which end at the corners of the hoist side; the Y embraces a black isosceles triangle from which the arms are separated by narrow yellow bands; the red and blue bands are separated from the green band and its arms by narrow white stripes

## Economy

**Economy - overview:** South Africa is a middle-income, emerging market with an abundant supply of natural resources; well-developed financial, legal, communications, energy, and transport sectors; a stock exchange that is 17th largest in the world; and modern infrastructure supporting an efficient distribution of goods to major urban centers throughout the region. Growth was robust from 2004 to 2008 as South Africa reaped the benefits of macroeconomic stability and a global commodities boom, but began to slow in the second half of 2008 due to the global financial crisis' impact on commodity prices and demand. However, unemployment remains high and outdated infrastructure has constrained growth. At the end of 2007, South Africa began to experience an electricity crisis because state power

# South Africa *(continued)*

supplier Eskom suffered supply problems with aged plants, necessitating "load-shedding" cuts to residents and businesses in the major cities. Daunting economic problems remain from the apartheid era - especially poverty, lack of economic empowerment among the disadvantaged groups, and a shortage of public transportation. South African economic policy is fiscally conservative but pragmatic, focusing on controlling inflation, maintaining a budget surplus, and using state-owned enterprises to deliver basic services to low-income areas as a means to increase job growth and household income.

**GDP (purchasing power parity):**
$489.7 billion (2008 est.)
$476.4 billion (2007)
$453.3 billion (2006)
*note:* data are in 2008 US dollars

**GDP (official exchange rate):** $300.4 billion (2008 est.)

**GDP - real growth rate:**
2.8% (2008 est.)
5.1% (2007 est.)
5.3% (2006 est.)

**GDP - per capita (PPP):**
$10,000 (2008 est.)
$9,800 (2007 est.)
$9,500 (2006 est.)
*note:* data are in 2008 US dollars

**GDP - composition by sector:**
*agriculture:* 3.4%
*industry:* 31.3%
*services:* 65.3% (2008 est.)

**Labor force:** 18.22 million economically active (2008 est.)

**Labor force - by occupation:**
*agriculture:* 9%
*industry:* 26%
*services:* 65% (2007 est.)

**Unemployment rate:**
21.7% (2008 est.)
24.3% (2007 est.)

**Population below poverty line:** 50% (2000 est.)

**Household income or consumption by percentage share:**
*lowest 10%:* 1.4%
*highest 10%:* 44.7% (2000)

**Distribution of family income - Gini index:** 65 (2005)

**Investment (gross fixed):** 20.1% of GDP (2008 est.)

**Budget:**
*revenues:* $83.85 billion
*expenditures:* $83.3 billion (2008 est.)

**Public debt:** 29.9% of GDP (2008 est.)

**Inflation rate (consumer prices):**
11.3% (2008 est.)
6.5% (2007 est.)

**Central bank discount rate:** 11% (31 December 2007)

**Commercial bank prime lending rate:** 13.17% (31 December 2007)

**Stock of money:** $58.49 billion (31 December 2007)

**Stock of quasi money:** $141.9 billion (31 December 2007)

**Stock of domestic credit:** $254.9 billion (31 December 2007)

**Market value of publicly traded shares:** $842 billion (January 2008)

**Agriculture - products:** corn, wheat, sugarcane, fruits, vegetables; beef, poultry, mutton, wool, dairy products

**Industries:** mining (world's largest producer of platinum, gold, chromium), automobile assembly, metalworking, machinery, textiles, iron and steel, chemicals, fertilizer, foodstuffs, commercial ship repair

**Industrial production growth rate:** 3.8% (2008 est.)

**Electricity - production:** 264 billion kWh (2007)
**Electricity - consumption:** 241.4 billion kWh (2007)
**Electricity - exports:** 13.77 billion kWh (2006 est.)
**Electricity - imports:** 11.32 billion kWh (2007)
**Oil - production:** 199,100 bbl/day (2007 est.)
**Oil - consumption:** 504,900 bbl/day (2006 est.)
**Oil - exports:** 267,700 bbl/day (2005)
**Oil - imports:** 319,000 bbl/day (2006 est.)
**Oil - proved reserves:** 15 million bbl (1 January 2008 est.)
**Natural gas - production:** 2.9 billion cu m (2006 est.)
**Natural gas - consumption:** 3.1 billion cu m (2006 est.)
**Natural gas - exports:** 0 cu m (2007 est.)
**Natural gas - imports:** 0 cu m (2005)
**Natural gas - proved reserves:** 27.16 million cu m (1 January 2006 est.)

**Current account balance:** -$21.67 billion (2008 est.)

**Exports:** $81.47 billion f.o.b. (2008 est.)

**Exports - commodities:** gold, diamonds, platinum, other metals and minerals, machinery and equipment

**Exports - partners:** US 11.9%, Japan 11.1%, Germany 8%, UK 7.7%, China 6.6%, Netherlands 4.5% (2007)

**Imports:** $87.3 billion f.o.b. (2008 est.)

**Imports - commodities:** machinery and equipment, chemicals, petroleum products, scientific instruments, foodstuffs

**Imports - partners:** Germany 10.9%, China 10%, Spain 8.2%, US 7.2%, Japan 6.1%, UK 4.5%, Saudi Arabia 4.2% (2007)

**Reserves of foreign exchange and gold:** $33.59 billion (31 December 2008 est.)

**Debt - external:** $39.69 billion (31 December 2008 est.)

**Stock of direct foreign investment - at home:** $99.61 billion (2008 est.)

**Stock of direct foreign investment - abroad:** $57.08 billion (2008 est.)

**Exchange rates:** rand (ZAR) per US dollar - 7.9576 (2008 est.), 7.05 (2007), 6.7649 (2006), 6.3593 (2005), 6.4597 (2004)

**Telephones - main lines in use:** 4.642 million (2007)
**Telephones - mobile cellular:** 42.3 million (2007)
**Telephone system:**
*general assessment:* the system is the best developed and most modern in Africa
*domestic:* combined fixed-line and mobile-cellular teledensity is nearly 110 telephones per 100 persons; consists of carrier-equipped open-wire lines, coaxial cables, microwave radio relay links, fiber-optic cable, radiotelephone communication stations, and wireless local loops; key centers are Bloemfontein, Cape Town, Durban, Johannesburg, Port Elizabeth, and Pretoria
*international:* country code - 27; the SAT-3/WASC and SAFE fiber optic cable systems connect South Africa to Europe and Asia; satellite earth stations - 3 Intelsat (1 Indian Ocean and 2 Atlantic Ocean)

**Radio broadcast stations:** AM 14, FM 347 (plus 243 repeaters), shortwave 1 (1998)
**Television broadcast stations:** 556 (plus 144 network repeaters) (1997)
**Internet country code:** .za
**Internet hosts:** 1.297 million (2008)
**Internet users:** 5.1 million (2005)

**Airports:** 636 (2008)
**Airports - with paved runways:**
*total:* 146
*over 3,047 m:* 10
*2,438 to 3,047 m:* 5
*1,524 to 2,437 m:* 52
*914 to 1,523 m:* 66
*under 914 m:* 13 (2008)

**Airports - with unpaved runways:**
*total:* 490
*over 3,047 m:* 1
*2,438 to 3,047 m:* 1
*1,524 to 2,437 m:* 31
*914 to 1,523 m:* 312
*under 914 m:* 145 (2008)

**Heliports:** 1 (2007)

**Pipelines:** condensate 11 km; gas 908 km; oil 980 km; refined products 1,379 km (2008)

**Railways:**
*total:* 20,872 km
*narrow gauge:* 20,436 km 1.065-m gauge (8,931 km electrified); 436 km 0.610-m gauge (2006)

**Roadways:**
*total:* 362,099 km
*paved:* 73,506 km (includes 239 km of expressways)
*unpaved:* 288,593 km (2002)

**Merchant marine:**

*total:* 3

*by type:* container 1, petroleum tanker 2

*foreign-owned:* 1 (Denmark 1)

*registered in other countries:* 8 (Bahamas 1, Nigeria 1, NZ 1, Saint Vincent and the Grenadines 1, Seychelles 1, UK 3) (2008)

**Ports and terminals:** Cape Town, Durban, Port Elizabeth, Richards Bay, Saldanha Bay

## Military

**Military branches:** South African National Defense Force (SANDF): South African Army, South African Navy (SAN), South African Air Force (SAAF), Joint Operations Command, Military Intelligence, South African Military Health Services (2009)

**Military service age and obligation:** 18 years of age for voluntary military service; women are eligible to serve in noncombat roles; 2-year service obligation (2007)

**Manpower available for military service:**

*males age 16-49:* 11,622,507

*females age 16-49:* 11,501,537 (2008 est.)

**Manpower fit for military service:**

*males age 16-49:* 7,641,557

*females age 16-49:* 6,518,793 (2009 est.)

**Manpower reaching militarily significant age annually:**

*male:* 511,616

*female:* 510,540 (2009 est.)

**Military expenditures:** 1.7% of GDP (2006)

**Military - note:** with the end of apartheid and the establishment of majority rule, former military, black homelands forces, and ex-opposition forces were integrated into the South African National Defense Force (SANDF); as of 2003 the integration process was considered complete

## Transnational Issues

**Disputes - international:** South Africa has placed military along the border to apprehend the thousands of Zimbabweans fleeing economic dysfunction and political persecution; as of January 2007, South Africa also supports large numbers of refugees and asylum seekers from the Democratic Republic of the Congo (33,000), Somalia (20,000), Burundi (6,500), and other states in Africa (26,000); managed dispute with Namibia over the location of the boundary in the Orange River; in 2006, Swazi king advocates resort to ICJ to claim parts of Mpumalanga and KwaZulu-Natal from South Africa

**Refugees and internally displaced persons:**

*refugees (country of origin):* 10,772 (Democratic Republic of Congo); 7,818 (Somalia); 5,759 (Angola) (2007)

**Trafficking in persons:**

*current situation:* South Africa is a source, transit, and destination country for men, women, and children trafficked for forced labor and sexual exploitation; women and girls are trafficked internally - and occasionally to European and Asian countries - for sexual exploitation; women from other African countries are trafficked to South Africa and, less frequently, onward to Europe for sexual exploitation; men and boys are trafficked from neighboring countries for forced agricultural labor; Asian and Eastern European women are trafficked to South Africa for debt-bonded sexual exploitation

*tier rating:* Tier 2 Watch List - South Africa is on the Tier 2 Watch List for a fourth consecutive year for its failure to show increasing efforts to address trafficking; the government provided inadequate data in 2007 on trafficking crimes investigated or prosecuted, or on resulting convictions or sentences; it also did not provide information on its efforts to protect victims of trafficking; the country continues to deport and/or prosecute suspected foreign victims without providing appropriate protective services (2008)

**Illicit drugs:** transshipment center for heroin, hashish, and cocaine, as well as a major cultivator of marijuana in its own right; cocaine and heroin consumption on the rise; world's largest market for illicit methaqualone, usually imported illegally from India through various east African countries, but increasingly producing its own synthetic drugs for domestic consumption; attractive venue for money launderers given the increasing level of organized criminal and narcotics activity in the region and the size of the South African economy

# South Georgia and South Sandwich Islands

*(overseas territory of the UK, also claimed by Argentina)*

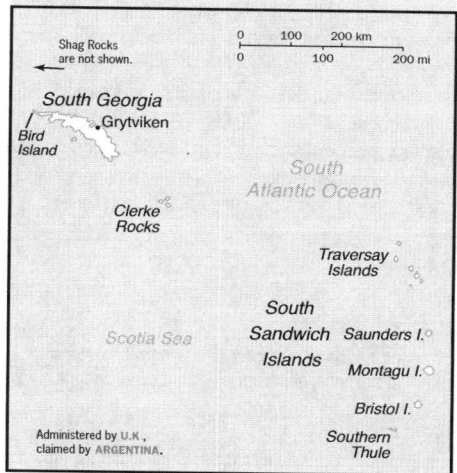

## Introduction

**Background:** The islands, which have large bird and seal populations, lie approximately 1,000 km east of the Falkland Islands and have been under British administration since 1908 - except for a brief period in 1982 when Argentina occupied them. Grytviken, on South Georgia, was a 19th and early 20th century whaling station. Famed explorer Ernest SHACKLETON stopped there in 1914 en route to his ill-fated attempt to cross Antarctica on foot. He returned some 20 months later with a few companions in a small boat and arranged a successful rescue for the rest of his crew, stranded off the Antarctic Peninsula. He died in 1922 on a subsequent expedition and is buried in Grytviken. Today, the station houses scientists from the British Antarctic Survey. Recognizing the importance of preserving the marine stocks in adjacent waters, the UK, in 1993, extended the exclusive fishing zone from 12 nm to 200 nm around each island.

## Geography

**Location:** Southern South America, islands in the South Atlantic Ocean, east of the tip of South America

**Geographic coordinates:** 54 30 S, 37 00 W

**Map references:** Antarctic Region

**Area:**

*total:* 3,903 sq km

*land:* 3,903 sq km

*water:* 0 sq km

*note:* includes Shag Rocks, Black Rock, Clerke Rocks, South Georgia Island, Bird Island, and the South Sandwich Islands, which consist of 11 islands

**Area - comparative:** slightly larger than Rhode Island

**Land boundaries:** 0 km

**Coastline:** NA

**Maritime claims:**

# South Georgia and South Sandwich Islands *(continued)*

*territorial sea:* 12 nm
*exclusive fishing zone:* 200 nm
**Climate:** variable, with mostly westerly winds throughout the year interspersed with periods of calm; nearly all precipitation falls as snow
**Terrain:** most of the islands, rising steeply from the sea, are rugged and mountainous; South Georgia is largely barren and has steep, glacier-covered mountains; the South Sandwich Islands are of volcanic origin with some active volcanoes
**Elevation extremes:**
*lowest point:* Atlantic Ocean 0 m
*highest point:* Mount Paget (South Georgia) 2,934 m
**Natural resources:** fish
**Land use:**
*arable land:* 0%
*permanent crops:* 0%
*other:* 100% (largely covered by permanent ice and snow with some sparse vegetation consisting of grass, moss, and lichen) (2005)
**Irrigated land:** 0 sq km
**Natural hazards:** the South Sandwich Islands have prevailing weather conditions that generally make them difficult to approach by ship; they are also subject to active volcanism
**Environment - current issues:** NA
**Geography - note:** the north coast of South Georgia has several large bays, which provide good anchorage; reindeer, introduced early in the 20th century, live on South Georgia

## People

**Population:** no indigenous inhabitants
*note:* the small military garrison on South Georgia withdrew in March 2001 replaced by a permanent group of scientists of the British Antarctic Survey, which also has a biological station on Bird Island; the South Sandwich Islands are uninhabited

## Government

**Country name:**
*conventional long form:* South Georgia and the South Sandwich Islands
*conventional short form:* South Georgia and South Sandwich Islands
*abbreviation:* SGSSI
**Dependency status:** overseas territory of the UK, also claimed by Argentina; administered from the Falkland Islands by a commissioner, who is concurrently governor of the Falkland Islands, representing Queen ELIZABETH II
**Legal system:** the laws of the UK, where applicable, apply; the senior magistrate from the Falkland Islands presides over the Magistrates Court
**Diplomatic representation in the US:** none (overseas territory of the UK, also claimed by Argentina)
**Diplomatic representation from the US:** none (overseas territory of the UK, also claimed by Argentina)
**Flag description:** blue, with the flag of the UK in the upper hoist-side quadrant and the South Georgia and South Sandwich Islands coat of arms centered on the outer half of the flag; the coat of arms features a shield with a golden lion centered; the shield is supported by a fur seal on the left and a penguin on the right; a reindeer appears above the shield, and below it on a scroll is the motto LEO TERRAM PROPRIAM PROTEGAT (Let the Lion Protect its Own Land)

## Economy

**Economy - overview:** Some fishing takes place in adjacent waters. There is a potential source of income from harvesting finfish and krill. The islands receive income from postage stamps produced in the UK, sale of fishing licenses, and harbor and landing fees from tourist vessels. Tourism from specialized cruise ships is increasing rapidly.

## Communications

**Telephone system:**
*general assessment:* NA
*domestic:* NA
*international:* coastal radiotelephone station at Grytviken
**Radio broadcast stations:** 0 (2003)
**Television broadcast stations:** 0 (2003)
**Internet country code:** .gs
**Internet hosts:** 196 (2008)

## Transportation

**Ports and terminals:** Grytviken

## Military

**Military - note:** defense is the responsibility of the UK

## Transnational Issues

**Disputes - international:** Argentina, which claims the islands in its constitution and briefly occupied them by force in 1982, agreed in 1995 to no longer seek settlement by force

# Southern Ocean

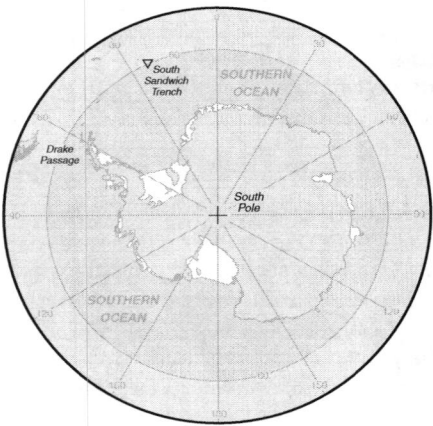

## Introduction

**Background:** A large body of recent oceanographic research has shown that the Antarctic Circumpolar Current (ACC), an ocean current that flows from west to east around Antarctica, plays a crucial role in global ocean circulation. The region where the cold waters of the ACC meet and mingle with the warmer waters of the north defines a distinct border - the Antarctic Convergence - which fluctuates with the seasons, but which encompasses a discrete body of water and a unique ecologic region. The Convergence concentrates nutrients, which promotes marine plant life, and which in turn allows for a greater abundance of animal life. In the spring of 2000, the International Hydrographic Organization decided to delimit the waters within the Convergence as a fifth world ocean - the Southern Ocean - by combining the southern portions of the Atlantic Ocean, Indian Ocean, and Pacific Ocean. The Southern Ocean extends from the coast of Antarctica north to 60 degrees south latitude, which coincides with the Antarctic Treaty Limit and which approximates the extent of the Antarctic Convergence. As such, the Southern Ocean is now the fourth largest of the world's five oceans (after the Pacific Ocean, Atlantic Ocean, and Indian Ocean, but larger than the Arctic Ocean). It should be noted that inclusion of the Southern Ocean does not imply recognition of this feature as one of the world's primary oceans by the US Government.

## Geography

**Location:** body of water between 60 degrees south latitude and Antarctica
**Geographic coordinates:** 60 00 S, 90 00 E (nominally), but the Southern Ocean has the unique distinction of being a large circumpolar body of water totally encircling the continent of Antarctica; this ring of water lies between 60 degrees south latitude and the coast of Antarctica and encompasses 360 degrees of longitude

# Southern Ocean (continued)

**Map references:** Antarctic Region

**Area:**

*total:* 20.327 million sq km

*note:* includes Amundsen Sea, Bellingshausen Sea, part of the Drake Passage, Ross Sea, a small part of the Scotia Sea, Weddell Sea, and other tributary water bodies

**Area - comparative:** slightly more than twice the size of the US

**Coastline:** 17,968 km

**Climate:** sea temperatures vary from about 10 degrees Celsius to -2 degrees Celsius; cyclonic storms travel eastward around the continent and frequently are intense because of the temperature contrast between ice and open ocean; the ocean area from about latitude 40 south to the Antarctic Circle has the strongest average winds found anywhere on Earth; in winter the ocean freezes outward to 65 degrees south latitude in the Pacific sector and 55 degrees south latitude in the Atlantic sector, lowering surface temperatures well below 0 degrees Celsius; at some coastal points intense persistent drainage winds from the interior keep the shoreline ice-free throughout the winter

**Terrain:** the Southern Ocean is deep, 4,000 to 5,000 mover most of its extent with only limited areas of shallow water; the Antarctic continental shelf is generally narrow and unusually deep, its edge lying at depths of 400 to 800 m (the global mean is 133 m); the Antarctic icepack grows from an average minimum of 2.6 million sq km in March to about 18.8 million sq km in September, better than a sixfold increase in area; the Antarctic Circumpolar Current (21,000 km in length) moves perpetually eastward; it is the world's largest ocean current, transporting 130 million cubic meters of water per second - 100 times the flow of all the world's rivers

**Elevation extremes:**

*lowest point:* -7,235 m at the southern end of the South Sandwich Trench

*highest point:* sea level 0 m

**Natural resources:** probable large and possible giant oil and gas fields on the continental margin; manganese nodules, possible placer deposits, sand and gravel, fresh water as icebergs; squid, whales, and seals - none exploited; krill, fish

**Natural hazards:** huge icebergs with drafts up to several hundred meters; smaller bergs and iceberg fragments; sea ice (generally 0.5 to 1 m thick) with sometimes dynamic short-term variations and with large annual and interannual variations; deep continental shelf floored by glacial deposits varying widely over short distances; high winds and large waves much of the year; ship icing, especially May-October; most of region is remote from sources of search and rescue

**Environment - current issues:** increased solar ultraviolet radiation resulting from the Antarctic ozone hole in recent years, reducing marine primary productivity (phytoplankton) by as much as 15% and damaging the DNA of some fish; illegal, unreported, and unregulated fishing in recent years, especially the landing of an estimated five to six times more Patagonian toothfish than the regulated fishery, which is likely to affect the sustainability of the stock; large amount of incidental mortality of seabirds resulting from long-line fishing for toothfish

*note:* the now-protected fur seal population is making a strong comeback after severe overexploitation in the 18th and 19th centuries

**Environment - international agreements:** the Southern Ocean is subject to all international agreements regarding the world's oceans; in addition, it is subject to these agreements specific to the Antarctic region: International Whaling Commission (prohibits commercial whaling south of 40 degrees south [south of 60 degrees south between 50 degrees and 130 degrees west]); Convention on the Conservation of Antarctic Seals (limits sealing); Convention on the Conservation of Antarctic Marine Living Resources (regulates fishing)

*note:* many nations (including the US) prohibit mineral resource exploration and exploitation south of the fluctuating Polar Front (Antarctic Convergence), which is in the middle of the Antarctic Circumpolar Current and serves as the dividing line between the cold polar surface waters to the south and the warmer waters to the north

**Geography - note:** the major chokepoint is the Drake Passage between South America and Antarctica; the Polar Front (Antarctic Convergence) is the best natural definition of the northern extent of the Southern Ocean; it is a distinct region at the middle of the Antarctic Circumpolar Current that separates the cold polar surface waters to the south from the warmer waters to the north; the Front and the Current extend entirely around Antarctica, reaching south of 60 degrees south near New Zealand and near 48 degrees south in the far South Atlantic coinciding with the path of the maximum westerly winds

## Economy

**Economy - overview:** Fisheries in 2006-07 landed 126,976 metric tons, of which 82% (104,586 tons) was krill (*Euphausia superba*) and 9.5% (12,027 tons) Patagonian toothfish (*Dissostichus eleginoides* - also known as Chilean sea bass), compared to 127,910 tons in 2005-06 of which 83% (106,591 tons) was krill and 9.7% (12,396 tons) Patagonian toothfish (estimated fishing from the area covered by the Convention of the Conservation of Antarctic Marine Living Resources (CCAMLR), which extends slightly beyond the Southern Ocean area). International agreements were adopted in late 1999 to reduce illegal, unreported, and unregulated fishing, which in the 2000-01 season landed, by one estimate, 8,376 metric tons of Patagonian and Antarctic toothfish. In the 2007-08 Antarctic summer, 45,213 tourists visited the Southern Ocean, compared to 35,552 in 2006-2007, and 29,799 in 2005-2006 (estimates provided to the Antarctic Treaty by the International Association of Antarctica Tour Operators (IAATO), and does not include passengers on overflights and those flying directly in and out of Antarctica).

## Transportation

**Ports and terminals:** McMurdo, Palmer, and offshore anchorages in Antarctica

*note:* few ports or harbors exist on southern side of Southern Ocean; ice conditions limit use of most to short periods in midsummer; even then some cannot be entered without icebreaker escort; most Antarctic ports are operated by government research stations and, except in an emergency, are not open to commercial or private vessels (2007)

**Transportation - note:** Drake Passage offers alternative to transit through the Panama Canal

## Transnational Issues

**Disputes - international:** Antarctic Treaty defers claims (see Antarctica entry), but Argentina, Australia, Chile, France, NZ, Norway, and UK assert claims (some overlapping), including the continental shelf in the Southern Ocean; several states have expressed an interest in extending those continental shelf claims under the United Nations Convention on the Law of the Sea (UNCLOS) to include undersea ridges; the US and most other states do not recognize the land or maritime claims of other states and have made no claims themselves (the US and Russia have reserved the right to do so); no formal claims exist in the waters in the sector between 90 degrees west and 150 degrees west

# Spain

*Canary Islands are not shown.*

## Introduction

**Background:** Spain's powerful world empire of the 16th and 17th centuries ultimately yielded command of the seas to England. Subsequent failure to embrace the mercantile and industrial revolutions caused the country to fall behind Britain, France, and Germany in economic and political power. Spain remained neutral in World Wars I and II but suffered through a devastating civil war (1936-39). A peaceful transition to democracy following the death of dictator Francisco FRANCO in 1975, and rapid economic modernization (Spain joined the EU in 1986) gave Spain a dynamic and rapidly growing economy and made it a global champion of freedom and human rights. The government continues to battle the Basque Fatherland and Liberty (ETA) terrorist organization, but its major focus for the immediate future will be on measures to reverse the severe economic recession that started in mid-2008.

## Geography

**Location:** Southwestern Europe, bordering the Bay of Biscay, Mediterranean Sea, North Atlantic Ocean, and Pyrenees Mountains, southwest of France
**Geographic coordinates:** 40 00 N, 4 00 W
**Map references:** Europe
**Area:**
*total:* 504,782 sq km
*land:* 499,542 sq km
*water:* 5,240 sq km
*note:* there are two autonomous cities - Ceuta and Melilla - and 17 autonomous communities including Balearic Islands and Canary Islands, and three small Spanish possessions off the coast of Morocco - Islas Chafarinas, Penon de Alhucemas, and Penon de Velez de la Gomera
**Area - comparative:** slightly more than twice the size of Oregon

**Land boundaries:**
*total:* 1,917.8 km
*border countries:* Andorra 63.7 km, France 623 km, Gibraltar 1.2 km, Portugal 1,214 km, Morocco (Ceuta) 6.3 km, Morocco (Melilla) 9.6 km
**Coastline:** 4,964 km
**Maritime claims:**
*territorial sea:* 12 nm
*contiguous zone:* 24 nm
*exclusive economic zone:* 200 nm (applies only to the Atlantic Ocean)
**Climate:** temperate; clear, hot summers in interior, more moderate and cloudy along coast; cloudy, cold winters in interior, partly cloudy and cool along coast
**Terrain:** large, flat to dissected plateau surrounded by rugged hills; Pyrenees in north
**Elevation extremes:**
*lowest point:* Atlantic Ocean 0 m
*highest point:* Pico de Teide (Tenerife) on Canary Islands 3,718 m
**Natural resources:** coal, lignite, iron ore, copper, lead, zinc, uranium, tungsten, mercury, pyrites, magnesite, fluorspar, gypsum, sepiolite, kaolin, potash, hydropower, arable land
**Land use:**
*arable land:* 27.18%
*permanent crops:* 9.85%
*other:* 62.97% (2005)
**Irrigated land:** 37,800 sq km (2003)
**Total renewable water resources:** 111.1 cu km (2005)
**Freshwater withdrawal (domestic/industrial/agricultural):**
*total:* 37.22 cu km/yr (13%/19%/68%)
*per capita:* 864 cu m/yr (2002)
**Natural hazards:** periodic droughts
**Environment - current issues:** pollution of the Mediterranean Sea from raw sewage and effluents from the offshore production of oil and gas; water quality and quantity nationwide; air pollution; deforestation; desertification
**Environment - international agreements:**
*party to:* Air Pollution, Air Pollution-Nitrogen Oxides, Air Pollution-Sulfur 94, Air Pollution-Volatile Organic Compounds, Antarctic-Environmental Protocol, Antarctic-Marine Living Resources, Antarctic Treaty, Biodiversity, Climate Change, Climate Change-Kyoto Protocol, Desertification, Endangered Species, Environmental Modification, Hazardous Wastes, Law of the Sea, Marine Dumping, Marine Life Conservation, Ozone Layer Protection, Ship Pollution, Tropical Timber 83, Tropical Timber 94, Wetlands, Whaling
*signed, but not ratified:* Air Pollution-Persistent Organic Pollutants
**Geography - note:** strategic location along approaches to Strait of Gibraltar; Spain controls a number of territories in northern Morocco including the enclaves of Ceuta and Melilla, and the islands of Penon de Velez de la Gomera, Penon de Alhucemas, and Islas Chafarinas

## People

**Population:** 40,525,002 (July 2009 est.)
**Age structure:**
*0-14 years:* 14.5% (male 3,021,822/female 2,842,597)
*15-64 years:* 67.4% (male 13,705,107/female 13,601,399)
*65 years and over:* 18.1% (male 3,071,394/female 4,282,683) (2009 est.)
**Median age:**
*total:* 41.1 years
*male:* 39.7 years
*female:* 42.5 years (2009 est.)
**Population growth rate:** 0.072% (2009 est.)
**Birth rate:** 9.72 births/1,000 population (2009 est.)
**Death rate:** 9.9 deaths/1,000 population (2008 est.)
**Net migration rate:** 0.99 migrant(s)/1,000 population (2009 est.)
**Urbanization:**
*urban population:* 77% of total population (2008)
*rate of urbanization:* 0.9% annual rate of change (2005-10 est.)
**Sex ratio:**
*at birth:* 1.07 male(s)/female
*under 15 years:* 1.06 male(s)/female
*15-64 years:* 1.01 male(s)/female
*65 years and over:* 0.72 male(s)/female
*total population:* 0.96 male(s)/female (2009 est.)
**Infant mortality rate:**
*total:* 4.21 deaths/1,000 live births
*male:* 4.59 deaths/1,000 live births
*female:* 3.8 deaths/1,000 live births (2009 est.)
**Life expectancy at birth:**
*total population:* 80.05 years
*male:* 76.74 years
*female:* 83.57 years (2009 est.)
**Total fertility rate:** 1.31 children born/woman (2009 est.)
**HIV/AIDS - adult prevalence rate:** 0.5% (2007 est.)
**HIV/AIDS - people living with HIV/AIDS:** 140,000 (2007 est.)
**HIV/AIDS - deaths:** 2,300 (2007 est.)
**Nationality:**
*noun:* Spaniard(s)
*adjective:* Spanish
**Ethnic groups:** composite of Mediterranean and Nordic types
**Religions:** Roman Catholic 94%, other 6%
**Languages:** Castilian Spanish (official) 74%, Catalan 17%, Galician 7%, Basque 2%, are official regionally
**Literacy:**
*definition:* age 15 and over can read and write
*total population:* 97.9%
*male:* 98.7%
*female:* 97.2% (2003 est.)
**School life expectancy (primary to tertiary education):**
*total:* 16 years
*male:* 16 years
*female:* 17 years (2006)
**Education expenditures:** 4.2% of GDP (2005)

# Spain (continued)

## Government

**Country name:**
*conventional long form:* Kingdom of Spain
*conventional short form:* Spain
*local long form:* Reino de Espana
*local short form:* Espana
**Government type:** parliamentary monarchy
**Capital:**
*name:* Madrid
*geographic coordinates:* 40 24 N, 3 41 W
*time difference:* UTC+1 (6 hours ahead of Washington, DC during Standard Time)
*daylight saving time:* +1hr, begins last Sunday in March; ends last Sunday in October
*note:* Spain is divided into two time zones including the Canary Islands

**Administrative divisions:** 17 autonomous communities (comunidades autonomas, singular - comunidad autonoma) and 2 autonomous cities* (ciudades autonomas, singular - ciudad autonoma); Andalucia, Aragon, Asturias, Baleares (Balearic Islands), Ceuta*, Canarias (Canary Islands), Cantabria, Castilla-La Mancha, Castilla y Leon, Cataluna (Catalonia), Comunidad Valenciana (Valencian Community), Extremadura, Galicia, La Rioja, Madrid, Melilla*, Murcia, Navarra, Pais Vasco (Basque Country)
*note:* the autonomous cities of Ceuta and Melilla plus three small islands of Islas Chafarinas, Penon de Alhucemas, and Penon de Velez de la Gomera, administered directly by the Spanish central government, are all along the coast of Morocco and are collectively referred to as Places of Sovereignty (Plazas de Soberania)

**Independence:** 1492; the Iberian peninsula was characterized by a variety of independent kingdoms prior to the Muslim occupation that began in the early 8th century A.D. and lasted nearly seven centuries; the small Christian redoubts of the north began the reconquest almost immediately, culminating in the seizure of Granada in 1492; this event completed the unification of several kingdoms and is traditionally considered the forging of present-day Spain

**National holiday:** National Day, 12 October (1492); year when Columbus first set foot in the Americas

**Constitution:** approved by legislature 31 October 1978; passed by referendum 6 December 1978; effective 29 December 1978

**Legal system:** civil law system, with regional applications; accepts compulsory ICJ jurisdiction with reservations

**Suffrage:** 18 years of age; universal

**Executive branch:**
*chief of state:* King JUAN CARLOS I (since 22 November 1975); Heir Apparent Prince FELIPE, son of the monarch, born 30 January 1968
*head of government:* President of the Government (Prime Minister equivalent) Jose Luis Rodriguez ZAPATERO (since 17 April 2004); First Vice President (and Minister of the Presidency) Maria Teresa FERNANDEZ DE LA VEGA (since 18 April 2004),

Second Vice President (and Minister of Economy and Finance) Elena SALGADO Mendez (since 8 April 2009), and Third Vice President (and Minister of Regional Affairs) Manuel CHAVES Gonzalez (since 8 April 2009)
*cabinet:* Council of Ministers designated by the president
*note:* there is also a Council of State that is the supreme consultative organ of the government, but its recommendations are non-binding
*elections:* the monarchy is hereditary; following legislative elections, the leader of the majority party or the leader of the majority coalition is usually proposed president by the monarch and elected by the National Assembly; election last held on 9 and 11 April 2008 (next to be held in March 2012); vice presidents appointed by the monarch on the proposal of the president
*election results:* Jose Luis Rodriguez ZAPATERO reelected President of the Government; percent of National Assembly vote - 46.94%

**Legislative branch:** bicameral; General Courts or Las Cortes Generales (National Assembly) consists of the Senate or Senado (264 seats as of 2008; 208 members directly elected by popular vote and the other 56 - as of 2008 - appointed by the regional legislatures; to serve four-year terms) and the Congress of Deputies or Congreso de los Diputados (350 seats; each of the 50 electoral provinces fills a minimum of two seats and the North African enclaves of Ceuta and Melilla fill one seat each with members serving a four-year term; the other 248 members are determined by proportional representation based on popular vote on block lists who serve four-year terms)
*elections:* Senate - last held on 9 March 2008 (next to be held not later than March 2012); Congress of Deputies - last held on 9 March 2008 (next to be held not later than March 2012)
*election results:* Senate - percent of vote by party - NA; seats by party - PP 101, PSOE 88, Entesa Catalona de Progress 12, CiU 4, PNV 2, CC 1, members appointed by regional legislatures 56; Congress of Deputies - percent of vote by party - PSOE 43.6%, PP 40.1%, CiU 3.1%, PNV 1.2%, ERC 1.2%, other 10.8%; seats by party - PSOE 169, PP 154, CiU 10, PNV 6, ERC 3, other 8

**Judicial branch:** Supreme Court or Tribunal Supremo

**Political parties and leaders:** Aragonese Party or CHA [Bizen FUSTER]; Basque Nationalist Party or PNV or EAJ [Inigo URKULLU]; Basque Solidarity or EA [Begona ERRAZTI]; Canarian Coalition or CC [Jose Torres STINGA] (a coalition of five parties); Convergence and Union or CiU [Artur MAS i Gavarro] (a coalition of the Democratic Convergence of Catalonia or CDC [Artur MAS i Gavarro] and the Democratic Union of Catalonia or UDC [Josep Antoni DURAN i LLEIDA]); Entesa Catalonia de Progress (a Senate coalition grouping four Catalan parties - PSC, ERC, ICV, EUA); Galician Nationalist Bloc or BNG [Anxo Manuel QUINTANA Gonzalez]; Initiative for Catalonia Greens or ICV [Joan SAURA i Laporta];

Navarra yes or Na Bai [Uxue BARKOS Berruezo] (a coalition of four Navarran parties); Popular Party or PP [Mariano RAJOY Brey]; Republican Left of Catalonia or ERC [Joan RIDAO]; Spanish Socialist Workers Party or PSOE [Jose Luis Rodriguez ZAPATERO]; United Left or IU [Cayo LARA] (a coalition of parties including the Communist Party of Spain or PCE and other small parties)

**Political pressure groups and leaders:** Association for Victims of Terrorism or AVT (grassroots organization devoted primarily to opposing ETA terrorist attacks and supporting its victims); Basta Ya (Spanish for "Enough is Enough"; grassroots organization devoted primarily to opposing ETA terrorist attacks and supporting its victims); Nunca Mais (Galician for "Never Again"; formed in response to the oil Tanker Prestige oil spill); Socialist General Union of Workers or UGT and the smaller independent Workers Syndical Union or USO; Trade Union Confederation of Workers' Commissions or CC.OO.
*other:* business and landowning interests; Catholic Church; free labor unions (authorized in April 1977); university students

**International organization participation:** ADB (nonregional member), AfDB (nonregional member), Arctic Council (observer), Australia Group, BCIE, BIS, CE, CERN, EAPC, EBRD, EIB, EMU, ESA, EU, FAO, IADB, IAEA, IBRD, ICAO, ICC, ICCt, ICRM, IDA, IEA, IFAD, IFC, IFRCS, IHO, ILO, IMF, IMO, IMSO, Interpol, IOC, IOM, IPU, ISO, ITSO, ITU, ITUC, LAIA (observer), MIGA, MINURCAT, MONUC, NAM (guest), NATO, NEA, NSG, OAS (observer), OECD, OPCW, OSCE, Paris Club, PCA, Schengen Convention, SECI (observer), SICA (observer), UN, UNCTAD, UNESCO, UNHCR, UNIDO, UNIFIL, Union Latina, UNRWA, UNWTO, UPU, WCL, WCO, WEU, WFTU, WHO, WIPO, WMO, WTO, ZC

**Diplomatic representation in the US:**
*chief of mission:* Ambassador Jorge DEZCALLAR de Mazarredo
*chancery:* 2375 Pennsylvania Avenue NW, Washington, DC 20037
*telephone:* [1] (202) 452-0100, 728-2340
*FAX:* [1] (202) 833-5670
*consulate(s) general:* Boston, Chicago, Houston, Los Angeles, Miami, New Orleans, New York, San Francisco, San Juan (Puerto Rico)

**Diplomatic representation from the US:**
*chief of mission:* Ambassador (vacant); Charge d'Affaires Arnold A. CHACON
*embassy:* Serrano 75, 28006 Madrid
*mailing address:* PSC 61, APO AE 09642
*telephone:* [34] (91) 587-2200
*FAX:* [34] (91) 587-2303
*consulate(s) general:* Barcelona

**Flag description:** three horizontal bands of red (top), yellow (double width), and red with the national coat of arms on the hoist side of the yellow band; the coat of arms is quartered to display the emblems of the traditional kingdoms of Spain (clockwise from upper left, Castile, Leon, Navarre, and Aragon) while

# Spain (continued)

Granada is represented by the stylized pomegranate at the bottom of the shield; the arms are framed by two columns representing the Pillars of Hercules, which are the two promontories (Gibraltar and Ceuta) on either side of the eastern end of the Strait of Gibraltar; the red scroll across the two columns bears the imperial motto of "Plus Ultra" (further beyond) referring to Spanish lands beyond Europe

## Economy

**Economy - overview:** The Spanish economy grew every year from 1994 through 2008 before entering a recession that started in the third quarter of 2008. Spain's mixed capitalist economy supports a GDP that on a per capita basis is approaching that of the largest West European economies. The Socialist president, Jose Luis Rodriguez ZAPATERO, in office since 2004, has made mixed progress in carrying out key structural reforms. The economy was greatly affected, especially after Zapatero's second term began in April 2008, by the bursting of the housing bubble and construction boom that had fueled much of the economic growth between 2001 and 2007. The global financial crisis exacerbated the economic downturn. GDP growth in 2008 was 1.1%, well below the 3% or higher growth the country enjoyed from 1997 through 2007. The Spanish banking system is considered solid, thanks in part to conservative oversight by the European Central Bank, and government intervention to rescue banks on the scale seen elsewhere in Europe in 2008 was not necessary. After considerable success since the mid-1990s in reducing unemployment to a 2007 low of 8%, Spain suffered a major spike in unemployment in the last few months of 2008, finishing the year with an unemployment rate over 13%.

**GDP (purchasing power parity):**
$1.378 trillion (2008 est.)
$1.36 trillion (2007)
$1.337 trillion (2006)
*note:* data are in 2008 US dollars

**GDP (official exchange rate):** $1.683 trillion (2008 est.)

**GDP - real growth rate:**
1.1% (2008 est.)
3.7% (2007 est.)
3.9% (2006 est.)

**GDP - per capita (PPP):**
$34,600 (2008 est.)
$34,300 (2007 est.)
$33,100 (2006 est.)
*note:* data are in 2008 US dollars

**GDP - composition by sector:**
*agriculture:* 3.6%
*industry:* 28.9%
*services:* 67.5% (2008 est.)

**Labor force:** 23.1 million (2008 est.)

**Labor force - by occupation:**
*agriculture:* 4%
*industry:* 26.4%
*services:* 69.5% (2008 est.)

**Unemployment rate:**
13.9% (2008 est.)
8.3% (2007 est.)

**Population below poverty line:** 19.8% (2005)

**Household income or consumption by percentage share:**
*lowest 10%:* 2.6%
*highest 10%:* 26.6% (2000)

**Distribution of family income - Gini index:** 32 (2005)

**Investment (gross fixed):** 30.1% of GDP (2008 est.)

**Budget:**
*revenues:* $443.3 billion
*expenditures:* $535.6 billion (2008 est.)

**Public debt:** 37.5% of GDP (2008)

**Inflation rate (consumer prices):**
1.4% (2008 est.)
2.8% (2007 est.)

**Central bank discount rate:** 4%
*note:* this is the European Central Bank's rate on the marginal lending facility, which offers overnight credit to banks in the euro area

**Commercial bank prime lending rate:** 9.54% (31 December 2008)

**Stock of money:** NA
*note:* see entry for the European Union for money supply in the euro area; the European Central Bank (ECB) controls monetary policy for the 16 members of the Economic and Monetary Union (EMU); individual members of the EMU do not control the quantity of money and quasi money circulating within their own borders

**Stock of quasi money:** NA

**Stock of domestic credit:** $3.724 trillion (30 November 2008)

**Market value of publicly traded shares:** $1.132 trillion (31 December 2008)

**Agriculture - products:** grain, vegetables, olives, wine grapes, sugar beets, citrus; beef, pork, poultry, dairy products; fish

**Industries:** textiles and apparel (including footwear), food and beverages, metals and metal manufactures, chemicals, shipbuilding, automobiles, machine tools, tourism, clay and refractory products, footwear, pharmaceuticals, medical equipment

**Industrial production growth rate:** -6.5% (2008)

**Electricity - production:** 294.3 billion kWh (2008 est.)

**Electricity - consumption:** 276.1 billion kWh (2008 est.)

**Electricity - exports:** 14.52 billion kWh (2007 est.)

**Electricity - imports:** 8.773 billion kWh (2007 est.)

**Oil - production:** 29,000 bbl/day (2007 est.)

**Oil - consumption:** 1.611 million bbl/day (2007 est.)

**Oil - exports:** 181,800 bbl/day (2005)

**Oil - imports:** 1.777 million bbl/day (2005)

**Oil - proved reserves:** 150 million bbl (1 January 2008 est.)

**Natural gas - production:** 88 million cu m (2007 est.)

**Natural gas - consumption:** 34.43 billion cu m (2007 est.)

**Natural gas - exports:** 0 cu m (2007 est.)

**Natural gas - imports:** 34.47 billion cu m (2007 est.)

**Natural gas - proved reserves:** 2.548 billion cu m (1 January 2008 est.)

**Current account balance:** -$152.5 billion (2008 est.)

**Exports:** $292.8 billion f.o.b. (2008 est.)

**Exports - commodities:** machinery, motor vehicles; foodstuffs, pharmaceuticals, medicines, other consumer goods

**Exports - partners:** France 18.8%, Germany 10.8%, Portugal 8.6%, Italy 8.5%, UK 7.6%, US 4.2% (2007)

**Imports:** $444.9 billion f.o.b. (2008 est.)

**Imports - commodities:** machinery and equipment, fuels, chemicals, semifinished goods, foodstuffs, consumer goods, measuring and medical control instruments

**Imports - partners:** Germany 15.7%, France 12.7%, Italy 8.4%, China 5.8%, UK 4.8%, Netherlands 4.6% (2007)

**Reserves of foreign exchange and gold:** $21.38 billion (31 December 2008 est.)

**Debt - external:** $2.478 trillion (30 September 2008 est.)

**Stock of direct foreign investment - at home:** $606.8 billion (2008 est.)

**Stock of direct foreign investment - abroad:** $738.5 billion (2008 est.)

**Exchange rates:** euros (EUR) per US dollar - 0.6827 (2008 est.), 0.7345 (2007), 0.7964 (2006), 0.8041 (2005), 0.8054 (2004)

## Communications

**Telephones - main lines in use:** 18.583 million (2007)

**Telephones - mobile cellular:** 48.813 million (2007)

**Telephone system:**
*general assessment:* well developed, modern facilities; fixed-line teledensity is about 45 per 100 persons
*domestic:* combined fixed-line and mobile-cellular teledensity is nearly 170 telephones per 100 persons
*international:* country code - 34; submarine cables provide connectivity to Europe, Middle East, Asia, and US; satellite earth stations - 2 Intelsat (1 Atlantic Ocean and 1 Indian Ocean), NA Eutelsat; tropospheric scatter to adjacent countries

**Radio broadcast stations:** AM 18, FM 250, shortwave 2 (2008)

**Television broadcast stations:** 379 (2008)

**Internet country code:** .es

**Internet hosts:** 3.264 million (2008)

**Internet users:** 19.69 million (2007)

## Spain (continued)

### Transportation

**Airports:** 154 (2008)
**Airports - with paved runways:**
*total:* 96
*over 3,047 m:* 18
*2,438 to 3,047 m:* 12
*1,524 to 2,437 m:* 18
*914 to 1,523 m:* 24
*under 914 m:* 24 (2008)
**Airports - with unpaved runways:**
*total:* 58
*1,524 to 2,437 m:* 2
*914 to 1,523 m:* 17
*under 914 m:* 39 (2008)
**Heliports:** 8 (2007)
**Pipelines:** gas 7,738 km; oil 560 km; refined products 3,445 km (2008)
**Railways:**
*total:* 14,974 km
*broad gauge:* 11,919 km 1.668-m gauge (6,950 km electrified)
*standard gauge:* 1,099 km 1.435-m gauge (1,054 km electrified)
*narrow gauge:* 1,928 km 1.000-m gauge (815 km electrified); 28 km 0.914-m gauge (28 km electrified) (2006)
**Roadways:**
*total:* 681,224 km
*paved:* 681,224 km (includes 13,872 km of expressways) (2006)
**Waterways:** 1,000 km (2008)
**Merchant marine:**
*total:* 158
*by type:* bulk carrier 9, cargo 14, chemical tanker 11, container 22, liquefied gas 11, passenger 1, passenger/cargo 47, petroleum tanker 16, refrigerated cargo 5, roll on/roll off 15, specialized tanker 2, vehicle carrier 5
*foreign-owned:* 26 (Canada 4, Denmark 2, Germany 5, Italy 2, Mexico 3, Norway 5, UK 5)
*registered in other countries:* 110 (Angola 1, Argentina 2, Bahamas 14, Belize 1, Brazil 9, Cape Verde 1, Cuba 1, Cyprus 6, Malta 3, Marshall Islands 1, Nigeria 1, Panama 50, Portugal 11, Saint Kitts and Nevis 1, UK 1, Uruguay 6, Venezuela 1) (2008)
**Ports and terminals:** Algeciras, Barcelona, Bilbao, Cartagena, Huelva, Tarragona, Valencia

### Military

**Military branches:** Spanish Armed Forces: Army (Ejercito de Tierra), Spanish Navy (Armada Espanola, AE; includes Marine Corps), Spanish Air Force (Ejercito del Aire Espanola, EdA) (2009)
**Military service age and obligation:** 20 years of age (2004)
**Manpower available for military service:**
*males age 16-49:* 10,033,069
*females age 16-49:* 9,764,937 (2008 est.)

**Manpower fit for military service:**
*males age 16-49:* 8,139,020
*females age 16-49:* 7,899,157 (2009 est.)
**Manpower reaching militarily significant age annually:**
*male:* 199,124
*female:* 187,224 (2009 est.)
**Military expenditures:** 1.2% of GDP (2005 est.)

### Transnational Issues

**Disputes - international:** in 2002, Gibraltar residents voted overwhelmingly by referendum to remain a British colony and against a "total shared sovereignty" arrangement while demanding participation in talks between the UK and Spain; Spain disapproves of UK plans to grant Gibraltar greater autonomy; Morocco protests Spain's control over the coastal enclaves of Ceuta, Melilla, and the islands of Penon de Velez de la Gomera, Penon de Alhucemas, and Islas Chafarinas, and surrounding waters; Morocco serves as the primary launching site of illegal migration into Spain from North Africa; Portugal does not recognize Spanish sovereignty over the territory of Olivenza based on a difference of interpretation of the 1815 Congress of Vienna and the 1801 Treaty of Badajoz
**Illicit drugs:** despite rigorous law enforcement efforts, North African, Latin American, Galician, and other European traffickers take advantage of Spain's long coastline to land large shipments of cocaine and hashish for distribution to the European market; consumer for Latin American cocaine and North African hashish; destination and minor transshipment point for Southwest Asian heroin; money-laundering site for Colombian narcotics trafficking organizations and organized crime

## Spratly Islands

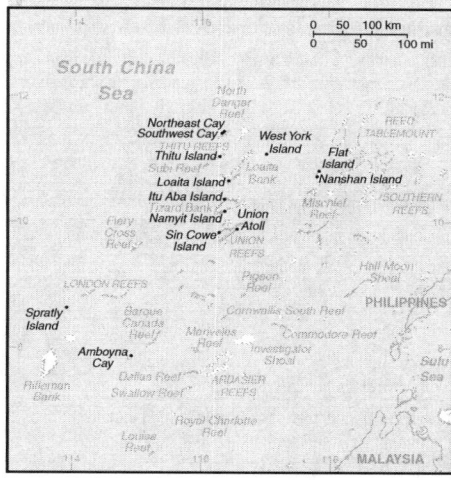

### Introduction

**Background:** The Spratly Islands consist of more than 100 small islands or reefs. They are surrounded by rich fishing grounds and potentially by gas and oil deposits. They are claimed in their entirety by China, Taiwan, and Vietnam, while portions are claimed by Malaysia and the Philippines. About 45 islands are occupied by relatively small numbers of military forces from China, Malaysia, the Philippines, Taiwan, and Vietnam. Brunei has established a fishing zone that overlaps a southern reef but has not made any formal claim.

### Geography

**Location:** Southeastern Asia, group of reefs and islands in the South China Sea, about two-thirds of the way from southern Vietnam to the southern Philippines
**Geographic coordinates:** 8 38 N, 111 55 E
**Map references:** Southeast Asia
**Area:**
*total:* less than 5 sq km
*land:* less than 5 sq km
*water:* 0 sq km
*note:* includes 100 or so islets, coral reefs, and sea mounts scattered over an area of nearly 410,000 sq kmof the central South China Sea
**Area - comparative:** NA
**Land boundaries:** 0 km
**Coastline:** 926 km
**Maritime claims:** NA
**Climate:** tropical
**Terrain:** flat
**Elevation extremes:**
*lowest point:* South China Sea 0 m
*highest point:* unnamed location on Southwest Cay 4 m
**Natural resources:** fish, guano, undetermined oil and natural gas potential
**Land use:**
*arable land:* 0%
*permanent crops:* 0%
*other:* 100% (2005)

**Irrigated land:** 0 sq km
**Natural hazards:** typhoons; numerous reefs and shoals pose a serious maritime hazard
**Environment - current issues:** NA
**Geography - note:** strategically located near several primary shipping lanes in the central South China Sea; includes numerous small islands, atolls, shoals, and coral reefs

### People

**Population:** no indigenous inhabitants
*note:* there are scattered garrisons occupied by personnel of several claimant states

### Government

**Country name:**
*conventional long form:* none
*conventional short form:* Spratly Islands

### Economy

**Economy - overview:** Economic activity is limited to commercial fishing. The proximity to nearby oil- and gas-producing sedimentary basins suggests the potential for oil and gas deposits, but the region is largely unexplored. There are no reliable estimates of potential reserves. Commercial exploitation has yet to be developed.

### Transportation

**Airports:** 4 (2008)
**Airports - with paved runways:**
*total:* 3
*914 to 1,523 m:* 2
*under 914 m:* 1 (2008)
**Airports - with unpaved runways:**
*total:* 1
*914 to 1,523 m:* 1 (2008)
**Heliports:** 3 (2007)
**Ports and terminals:** none; offshore anchorage only

### Military

**Military - note:** Spratly Islands consist of more than 100 small islands or reefs of which about 45 are claimed and occupied by China, Malaysia, the Philippines, Taiwan, and Vietnam

### Transnational Issues

**Disputes - international:** all of the Spratly Islands are claimed by China, Taiwan, and Vietnam; parts of them are claimed by Malaysia and the Philippines; in 1984, Brunei established an exclusive fishing zone that encompasses Louisa Reef in the southern Spratly Islands but has not publicly claimed the reef; claimants in November 2002 signed the "Declaration on the Conduct of Parties in the South China Sea," which has eased tensions but falls short of a legally binding "code of conduct"; in March 2005, the national oil companies of China, the Philippines, and Vietnam signed a joint accord to conduct marine seismic activities in the Spratly Islands

# Sri Lanka

### Introduction

**Background:** The first Sinhalese arrived in Sri Lanka late in the 6th century B.C. probably from northern India. Buddhism was introduced in about the mid-third century B.C., and a great civilization developed at the cities of Anuradhapura (kingdom from circa 200 B.C. to circa A.D. 1000) and Polonnaruwa (from about 1070 to 1200). In the 14th century, a south Indian dynasty established a Tamil kingdom in northern Sri Lanka. The coastal areas of the island were controlled by the Portuguese in the 16th century and by the Dutch in the 17th century. The island was ceded to the British in 1796, became a crown colony in 1802, and was united under British rule by 1815. As Ceylon, it became independent in 1948; its name was changed to Sri Lanka in 1972. Tensions between the Sinhalese majority and Tamil separatists erupted into war in 1983. Tens of thousands have died in the ethnic conflict that continues to fester. After two decades of fighting, the government and Liberation Tigers of Tamil Eelam (LTTE) formalized a cease-fire in February 2002 with Norway brokering peace negotiations. Violence between the LTTE and government forces intensified in 2006 and the government regained control of the Eastern Province in 2007. In January 2008, the government officially withdrew from the cease-fire, and by late January 2009, the LTTE remained in control of a small and shrinking area of Mullaitivu district in the North.

### Geography

**Location:** Southern Asia, island in the Indian Ocean, south of India
**Geographic coordinates:** 7 00 N, 81 00 E
**Map references:** Asia
**Area:**
*total:* 65,610 sq km
*land:* 64,740 sq km
*water:* 870 sq km
**Area - comparative:** slightly larger than West Virginia

**Land boundaries:** 0 km
**Coastline:** 1,340 km
**Maritime claims:**
*territorial sea:* 12 nm
*contiguous zone:* 24 nm
*exclusive economic zone:* 200 nm
*continental shelf:* 200 nm or to the edge of the continental margin
**Climate:** tropical monsoon; northeast monsoon (December to March); southwest monsoon (June to October)
**Terrain:** mostly low, flat to rolling plain; mountains in south-central interior
**Elevation extremes:**
*lowest point:* Indian Ocean 0 m
*highest point:* Pidurutalagala 2,524 m
**Natural resources:** limestone, graphite, mineral sands, gems, phosphates, clay, hydropower
**Land use:**
*arable land:* 13.96%
*permanent crops:* 15.24%
*other:* 70.8% (2005)
**Irrigated land:** 7,430 sq km (2003)
**Total renewable water resources:** 50 cu km (1999)
**Freshwater withdrawal (domestic/industrial/agricultural):**
*total:* 12.61 cu km/yr (2%/2%/95%)
*per capita:* 608 cu m/yr (2000)
**Natural hazards:** occasional cyclones and tornadoes
**Environment - current issues:** deforestation; soil erosion; wildlife populations threatened by poaching and urbanization; coastal degradation from mining activities and increased pollution; freshwater resources being polluted by industrial wastes and sewage runoff; waste disposal; air pollution in Colombo
**Environment - international agreements:**
*party to:* Biodiversity, Climate Change, Climate Change-Kyoto Protocol, Desertification, Endangered Species, Environmental Modification, Hazardous Wastes, Law of the Sea, Ozone Layer Protection, Ship Pollution, Wetlands
*signed, but not ratified:* Marine Life Conservation
**Geography - note:** strategic location near major Indian Ocean sea lanes

### People

**Population:** 21,324,791
*note:* since the outbreak of hostilities between the government and armed Tamil separatists in the mid-1980s, several hundred thousand Tamil civilians have fled the island and more than 200,000 Tamils have sought refuge in the West (July 2009 est.)
**Age structure:**
*0-14 years:* 23.9% (male 2,594,815/female 2,493,002)
*15-64 years:* 68% (male 7,089,307/female 7,418,123)
*65 years and over:* 8.1% (male 803,172/female 926,372) (2009 est.)

# Sri Lanka *(continued)*

**Median age:**

*total:* 30.9 years

*male:* 29.9 years

*female:* 31.8 years (2009 est.)

**Population growth rate:** 0.904% (2009 est.)

**Birth rate:** 16.26 births/1,000 population (2009 est.)

**Death rate:** 6.07 deaths/1,000 population (2008 est.)

**Net migration rate:** -1.09 migrant(s)/1,000 population (2009 est.)

**Urbanization:**

*urban population:* 15% of total population (2008)

*rate of urbanization:* 0.5% annual rate of change (2005-10 est.)

**Sex ratio:**

*at birth:* 1.04 male(s)/female

*under 15 years:* 1.04 male(s)/female

*15-64 years:* 0.96 male(s)/female

*65 years and over:* 0.87 male(s)/female

*total population:* 0.97 male(s)/female (2009 est.)

**Infant mortality rate:**

*total:* 18.57 deaths/1,000 live births

*male:* 20.33 deaths/1,000 live births

*female:* 16.73 deaths/1,000 live births (2009 est.)

**Life expectancy at birth:**

*total population:* 75.14 years

*male:* 73.08 years

*female:* 77.28 years (2009 est.)

**Total fertility rate:** 1.99 children born/woman (2009 est.)

**HIV/AIDS - adult prevalence rate:** less than 0.1% (2001 est.)

**HIV/AIDS - people living with HIV/AIDS:** 3,800 (2007 est.)

**HIV/AIDS - deaths:** fewer than 200 (2003 est.)

**Major infectious diseases:**

*degree of risk:* high

*food or waterborne diseases:* bacterial diarrhea and hepatitis A

*vectorborne disease:* dengue fever and chikungunya

*water contact disease:* leptospirosis

*animal contact disease:* rabies (2009)

**Nationality:**

*noun:* Sri Lankan(s)

*adjective:* Sri Lankan

**Ethnic groups:** Sinhalese 73.8%, Sri Lankan Moors 7.2%, Indian Tamil 4.6%, Sri Lankan Tamil 3.9%, other 0.5%, unspecified 10% (2001 census provisional data)

**Religions:** Buddhist 69.1%, Muslim 7.6%, Hindu 7.1%, Christian 6.2%, unspecified 10% (2001 census provisional data)

**Languages:** Sinhala (official and national language) 74%, Tamil (national language) 18%, other 8%

*note:* English is commonly used in government and is spoken competently by about 10% of the population

**Literacy:**

*definition:* age 15 and over can read and write

*total population:* 90.7%

*male:* 92.3%

*female:* 89.1% (2001 census)

**Education expenditures:** NA

## Government

**Country name:**

*conventional long form:* Democratic Socialist Republic of Sri Lanka

*conventional short form:* Sri Lanka

*local long form:* Shri Lamka Prajatantrika Samajaya di Janarajaya/Ilankai Jananayaka Choshalichak Kutiyarachu

*local short form:* Shri Lamka/Ilankai

*former:* Serendib, Ceylon

**Government type:** republic

**Capital:**

*name:* Colombo

*geographic coordinates:* 6 56 N, 79 51 E

*time difference:* UTC+5.5 (10.5 hours ahead of Washington, DC during Standard Time)

*note:* Sri Jayewardenepura Kotte (legislative capital)

**Administrative divisions:** 8 provinces; Central, North Central, North Eastern, North Western, Sabaragamuwa, Southern, Uva, Western

*note:* in October 2006, a Sri Lankan Supreme Court ruling voided a presidential directive merging the North and Eastern Provinces; many have defended the merger as a prerequisite for a negotiated settlement to the ethnic conflict; a parliamentary decision on the issue is pending

**Independence:** 4 February 1948 (from the UK)

**National holiday:** Independence Day, 4 February (1948)

**Constitution:** adopted 16 August 1978, certified 31 August 1978; amended 20 December 2000

**Legal system:** a highly complex mixture of English common law, Roman-Dutch, Kandyan, and Jaffna Tamil law; has not accepted compulsory ICJ jurisdiction

**Suffrage:** 18 years of age; universal

**Executive branch:**

*chief of state:* President Mahinda Percy RAJAPAKSA (since 19 November 2005); note - the president is both the chief of state and head of government; Ratnasiri WICKREMANAYAKE (since 21 November 2005) holds the largely ceremonial title of prime minister

*head of government:* President Mahinda Percy RAJAPAKSA (since 19 November 2005)

*cabinet:* Cabinet appointed by the president in consultation with the prime minister

*elections:* president elected by popular vote for a six-year term (eligible for a second term); election last held on 17 November 2005 (next to be held in 2011)

*election results:* Mahinda RAJAPAKSA elected president; percent of vote - Mahinda RAJAPAKSA 50.3%, Ranil WICKREMESINGHE 48.4%, other 1.3%

**Legislative branch:** unicameral Parliament (225 seats; members elected by popular vote on the basis of an open-list, proportional representation system by electoral district to serve six-year terms)

*elections:* last held on 2 April 2004 (next to be held by 2010)

*election results:* percent of vote by party or electoral alliance - SLFP and JVP (no longer in formal UPFA alliance) 45.6%, UNP 37.8%, TNA 6.8%, JHU 6%, SLMC 2%, UPF 0.5%, EPDP 0.3%, other 1%; seats by party - UNP 68, SLFP 57, JVP 39, TNA 22, CWC 8, JHU 7, SLMC 6, SLMC dissidents 4, Communist Party 2, JHU dissidents 2, LSSP 2, MEP 2, NUA 2, UPF 2, EPDP 1, UNP dissident 1

**Judicial branch:** Supreme Court; Court of Appeals; judges for both courts are appointed by the president

**Political parties and leaders:** All Ceylon Tamil Congress or ACTC [G.PONNAMBALAM]; Ceylon Workers Congress or CWC [Arumugam THONDAMAN]; Communist Party or CP [D. GUNASEKERA]; Eelam People's Democratic Party or EPDP [Douglas DEVANANDA]; Eelam People's Revolutionary Liberation Front or EPRLF [Suresh PREMACHANDRAN]; Janatha Vimukthi Peramuna or JVP [Somawansa AMARASINGHE]; Lanka Sama Samaja Party or LSSP [Tissa VITHARANA]; Mahajana Eksath Peramuna (People's United Front) or MEP [D. GUNAWARDENE]; National Heritage Party or JHU [Ellawala METHANANDA]; National Unity Alliance or NUA [Ferial ASHRAFF]; People's Liberation Organization of Tamil Eelam or PLOTE [D. SIDHARTHAN]; Sri Lanka Freedom Party or SLFP [Mahinda RAJAPAKSA]; Sri Lanka Muslim Congress or SLMC [Rauff HAKEEM]; Tamil Eelam Liberation Organization or TELO [Selvam ADAIKALANATHAN]; Tamil National Alliance or TNA [R. SAMPANTHAN]; Tamil United Liberation Front or TULF [V. ANANDASANGAREE]; United National Party or UNP [Ranil WICKREMASINGHE]; Up-country People's Front or UPF [P. CHANDRASEKARAN]

**Political pressure groups and leaders:** Liberation Tigers of Tamil Eelam or LTTE [Velupillai PRABHAKARAN](insurgent group fighting for a separate state); Tamil Makkal Viduthalai Pulikal (TMVP) or Karuna Faction [Vinayagamurthi MURALITHARAN] (paramilitary breakaway from LTTE and fighting LTTE)

*other:* Buddhist clergy; labor unions; radical chauvinist Sinhalese groups such as the National Movement Against Terrorism; Sinhalese Buddhist lay groups

**International organization participation:** ADB, BIMSTEC, C, CP, FAO, G-15, G-24, G-77, IAEA, IBRD, ICAO, ICC, ICRM, IDA, IFAD, IFC, IFRCS, IHO, ILO, IMF, IMO, IMSO, Interpol, IOC, IOM, IPU, ISO, ITSO, ITU, ITUC, MIGA, MINURSO, MINUSTAH, MONUC, NAM, OAS (observer), OPCW, PCA, SAARC, SACEP, UN, UNCTAD, UNESCO, UNIDO, UNMIS, UNWTO, UPU, WCL, WCO, WFTU, WHO, WIPO, WMO, WTO

**Diplomatic representation in the US:**

*chief of mission:* Ambassador Jaliya Chitran WICKRAMASURIYA

*chancery:* 2148 Wyoming Avenue NW, Washington, DC 20008

*telephone:* [1] (202) 483-4025 through 4028

*FAX:* [1] (202) 232-7181

*consulate(s) general:* Los Angeles

*consulate(s):* New York

# Sri Lanka (continued)

**Diplomatic representation from the US:**
*chief of mission:* Ambassador Robert O. BLAKE, Jr.
*embassy:* 210 Galle Road, Colombo 3
*mailing address:* P. O. Box 106, Colombo
*telephone:* [94] (11) 249-8500
*FAX:* [94] (11) 243-7345
**Flag description:** yellow with two panels; the smaller hoist-side panel has two equal vertical bands of green (hoist side) and orange; the other panel is a large dark red rectangle with a yellow lion holding a sword, and there is a yellow bo leaf in each corner; the yellow field appears as a border around the entire flag and extends between the two panels

## Economy

**Economy - overview:** In 1977, Colombo abandoned statist economic policies and its import substitution trade policy for more market-oriented policies, export-oriented trade, and encouragement of foreign investment. Recent changes in government, however, have brought some policy reversals. Currently, the ruling Sri Lanka Freedom Party has a more statist economic approach, which seeks to reduce poverty by steering investment to disadvantaged areas, developing small and medium enterprises, promoting agriculture, and expanding the already enormous civil service. The government has halted privatizations. Although suffering a brutal civil war that began in 1983, Sri Lanka saw GDP growth average 4.5% in the last 10 years with the exception of a recession in 2001. In late December 2004, a major tsunami took about 31,000 lives, left more than 6,300 missing and 443,000 displaced, and destroyed an estimated $1.5 billion worth of property. Government spending on development and fighting the LTTE drove GDP growth to about 7% per year in 2006-07 before the global recession slow growth in 2008, but high government spending and high oil and commodity prices also raised inflation to around 15% in 2008. Sri Lanka's most dynamic sectors now are food processing, textiles and apparel, food and beverages, port construction, telecommunications, and insurance and banking. In 2008, plantation crops made up only about 20% of exports (compared with more than 90% in 1970), while textiles and garments accounted for more than 40%. About 1.5 million Sri Lankans work abroad, 90% of them in the Middle East. They send home more than $2.5 billion a year. The 25-year civil conflict between LTTE and the government of Sri Lanka has been a serious impediment to economic activities. By mid February 2009, the LTTE remained in control of small and shrinking area in the North. The conflict continues to cast a shadow over the economy.
**GDP (purchasing power parity):**
$91.9 billion (2008 est.)
$86.7 billion (2007)
$81.18 billion (2006)
*note:* data are in 2008 US dollars
**GDP (official exchange rate):** $38 billion (2008 est.)

**GDP - real growth rate:**
6% (2008 est.)
6.8% (2007 est.)
7.7% (2006 est.)
**GDP - per capita (PPP):**
$4,300 (2008 est.)
$4,100 (2007 est.)
$3,900 (2006 est.)
*note:* data are in 2008 US dollars
**GDP - composition by sector:**
*agriculture:* 15.5%
*industry:* 27%
*services:* 57.5% (2008 est.)
**Labor force:** 7.588 million
*note:* excludes northern and eastern provinces (2008 est.)
**Labor force - by occupation:**
*agriculture:* 34.7%
*industry:* 26.1%
*services:* 39.2% (30 September 2008 est.)
**Unemployment rate:**
5.2% (30 September 2008 est.)
6% (2007 est.)
**Population below poverty line:** 22% (2002 est.)
**Household income or consumption by percentage share:**
*lowest 10%:* 1.1%
*highest 10%:* 39.7% (2004)
**Distribution of family income - Gini index:** 49 (2007)
**Investment (gross fixed):** 30% of GDP (2008 est.)
**Budget:**
*revenues:* $7.8 billion
*expenditures:* $11 billion (2009 est.)
**Public debt:** 78% of GDP (2008 est.)
**Inflation rate (consumer prices):**
14.4% (2008 est.)
15.8% (2007 est.)
**Central bank discount rate:** 11.75% (12 February 2009)
**Commercial bank prime lending rate:** 18.5% (31 December 2008)
**Stock of money:** $2.55 billion (30 September 2008)
**Stock of quasi money:** $9.01 billion (30 September 2008)
**Stock of domestic credit:** $15.92 billion (30 September 2008)
**Market value of publicly traded shares:** $4.32 billion (31 December 2008)
**Agriculture - products:** rice, sugarcane, grains, pulses, oilseed, spices, tea, rubber, coconuts; milk, eggs, hides, beef; fish
**Industries:** processing of rubber, tea, coconuts, tobacco and other agricultural commodities; telecommunications, insurance, banking; clothing, textiles; cement, petroleum refining, information technology services
**Industrial production growth rate:** 6.2% (2008 est.)
**Electricity - production:** 9.814 billion kWh (2007 est.)

**Electricity - consumption:** 8.276 billion kWh (2007 est.)
**Electricity - exports:** 0 kWh (2008 est.)
**Electricity - imports:** 0 kWh (2008 est.)
**Oil - production:** 0 bbl/day (2008 est.)
**Oil - consumption:** 86,030 bbl/day (2006 est.)
**Oil - exports:** 291.9 bbl/day (2005)
**Oil - imports:** 87,090 bbl/day (2005)
**Oil - proved reserves:** 0 bbl (1 January 2008 est.)
**Natural gas - production:** 0 cu m (2008 est.)
**Natural gas - consumption:** 0 cu m (2008 est.)
**Natural gas - exports:** 0 cu m (2008 est.)
**Natural gas - proved reserves:** 0 cu m (1 January 2008 est.)
**Current account balance:** -$1.981 billion (2008 est.)
**Exports:** $8.1 billion f.o.b. (2008 est.)
**Exports - commodities:** textiles and apparel, tea and spices; diamonds, emeralds, rubies; coconut products, rubber manufactures, fish
**Exports - partners:** US 25.5%, UK 13.2%, India 6.7%, Germany 5.7%, Italy 5.1% (2007)
**Imports:** $14.05 billion f.o.b. (2008 est.)
**Imports - commodities:** textile fabrics, mineral products, petroleum, foodstuffs, machinery and transportation equipment
**Imports - partners:** India 23.1%, Singapore 9.9%, China 8.2%, Iran 7.5%, Hong Kong 6.4% (2007)
**Reserves of foreign exchange and gold:** $3.364 billion (31 December 2008 est.)
**Debt - external:** $12.99 billion (31 December 2008 est.)
**Stock of direct foreign investment - at home:** $NA
**Stock of direct foreign investment - abroad:** $NA
**Exchange rates:** Sri Lankan rupees (LKR) per US dollar - 108.33 (2008), 110.78 (2007), 103.99 (2006), 100.498 (2005), 101.194 (2004)

## Communications

**Telephones - main lines in use:** 2.742 million (2007)
**Telephones - mobile cellular:** 7.983 million (2007)
**Telephone system:**
*general assessment:* telephone services have improved significantly and are available in most parts of the country
*domestic:* national trunk network consists mostly of digital microwave radio relay; fiber-optic links now in use in Colombo area and fixed wireless local loops have been installed; competition is strong in mobile cellular systems and mobile cellular subscribership is increasing
*international:* country code - 94; the SEA-ME-WE-3 and SEA-ME-WE-4 submarine cables provide connectivity to Asia, Australia, Middle East, Europe, US; satellite earth stations - 2 Intelsat (Indian Ocean)
**Radio broadcast stations:** AM 15, FM 52, shortwave 4 (2007)

# Sri Lanka *(continued)*

**Television broadcast stations:** 14 (2006)
**Internet country code:** .lk
**Internet hosts:** 4,940 (2008)
**Internet users:** 771,700 (2007)

## Transportation

**Airports:** 18 (2008)
**Airports - with paved runways:**
*total:* 14
*over 3,047 m:* 1
*1,524 to 2,437 m:* 6
*914 to 1,523 m:* 7 (2008)
**Airports - with unpaved runways:**
*total:* 4
*914 to 1,523 m:* 1
*under 914 m:* 3 (2008)
**Railways:**
*total:* 1,449 km
*broad gauge:* 1,449 km 1.676-m gauge (2006)
**Roadways:**
*total:* 97,286 km
*paved:* 78,802 km
*unpaved:* 18,484 km (2003)
**Waterways:** 160 km (primarily on rivers in southwest) (2008)
**Merchant marine:**
*total:* 26
*by type:* bulk carrier 4, cargo 18, chemical tanker 1, container 1, petroleum tanker 2
*foreign-owned:* 5 (Germany 5)
*registered in other countries:* 1 (Panama 1) (2008)
**Ports and terminals:** Colombo

## Military

**Military branches:** Sri Lanka Army, Sri Lanka Navy, Sri Lanka Air Force (2009)
**Military service age and obligation:** 18 years of age for voluntary military service; 5-year service obligation (2007)
**Manpower available for military service:**
*males age 16-49:* 5,458,720
*females age 16-49:* 5,594,006 (2008 est.)
**Manpower fit for military service:**
*males age 16-49:* 4,498,667
*females age 16-49:* 4,693,895 (2009 est.)
**Manpower reaching militarily significant age annually:**
*male:* 173,256
*female:* 167,645 (2009 est.)
**Military expenditures:** 2.6% of GDP (2006)

## Transnational Issues

**Disputes - international:** none
**Refugees and internally displaced persons:**
*IDPs:* 460,000 (both Tamils and non-Tamils displaced due to long-term civil war between the government and the separatist Liberation Tigers of Tamil Eelam (LTTE)) (2007)

**Trafficking in persons:**
*current situation:* Sri Lanka is a source and destination country for men and women trafficked for the purposes of involuntary servitude and commercial sexual exploitation; Sri Lankan men and women migrate willingly to the Persian Gulf, Middle East, and East Asia to work as construction workers, domestic servants, or garment factory workers, where some find themselves in situations of involuntary servitude when faced with restrictions on movement, withholding of passports, threats, physical or sexual abuse, and debt bondage; children are trafficked internally for commercial sexual exploitation and, less frequently, for forced labor
*tier rating:* Tier 2 Watch List - for a second consecutive year, Sri Lanka is on the Tier 2 Watch List for failing to provide evidence of increasing efforts to combat severe forms of human trafficking, particularly in the area of law enforcement; the government failed to arrest, prosecute, or convict any person for trafficking offenses and continued to punish some victims of trafficking for crimes committed as a result of being trafficked; Sri Lanka has not ratified the 2000 UN TIP Protocol (2008)

# Sudan

## Introduction

**Background:** Military regimes favoring Islamic-oriented governments have dominated national politics since independence from the UK in 1956. Sudan was embroiled in two prolonged civil wars during most of the remainder of the 20th century. These conflicts were rooted in northern economic, political, and social domination of largely non-Muslim, non-Arab southern Sudanese. The first civil war ended in 1972 but broke out again in 1983. The second war and famine-related effects resulted in more than four million people displaced and, according to rebel estimates, more than two million deaths over a period of two decades. Peace talks gained momentum in 2002-04 with the signing of several accords. The final North/South Comprehensive Peace Agreement (CPA), signed in January 2005, granted the southern rebels autonomy for six years. After which, a referendum for independence is scheduled to be held. A separate conflict, which broke out in the western region of Darfur in 2003, has displaced nearly two million people and caused an estimated 200,000 to 400,000 deaths. The UN took command of the Darfur peacekeeping operation from the African Union on 31 December 2007. As of early 2009, peacekeeping troops were struggling to stabilize the situation, which has become increasingly regional in scope, and has brought instability to eastern Chad, and Sudanese incursions into the Central African Republic. Sudan also has faced large refugee influxes from neighboring countries, primarily Ethiopia and Chad. Armed conflict, poor transport infrastructure, and lack of government support have chronically obstructed the provision of humanitarian assistance to affected populations.

# Sudan (continued)

## Geography

**Location:** Northern Africa, bordering the Red Sea, between Egypt and Eritrea
**Geographic coordinates:** 15 00 N, 30 00 E
**Map references:** Africa
**Area:**
*total:* 2,505,810 sq km
*land:* 2.376 million sq km
*water:* 129,810 sq km
**Area - comparative:** slightly more than one-quarter the size of the US
**Land boundaries:**
*total:* 7,687 km
*border countries:* Central African Republic 1,165 km, Chad 1,360 km, Democratic Republic of the Congo 628 km, Egypt 1,273 km, Eritrea 605 km, Ethiopia 1,606 km, Kenya 232 km, Libya 383 km, Uganda 435 km
**Coastline:** 853 km
**Maritime claims:**
*territorial sea:* 12 nm
*contiguous zone:* 18 nm
*continental shelf:* 200 m depth or to the depth of exploitation
**Climate:** tropical in south; arid desert in north; rainy season varies by region (April to November)
**Terrain:** generally flat, featureless plain; mountains in far south, northeast and west; desert dominates the north
**Elevation extremes:**
*lowest point:* Red Sea 0 m
*highest point:* Kinyeti 3,187 m
**Natural resources:** petroleum; small reserves of iron ore, copper, chromium ore, zinc, tungsten, mica, silver, gold, hydropower
**Land use:**
*arable land:* 6.78%
*permanent crops:* 0.17%
*other:* 93.05% (2005)
**Irrigated land:** 18,630 sq km (2003)
**Total renewable water resources:** 154 cu km (1997)
**Freshwater withdrawal (domestic/industrial/agricultural):**
*total:* 37.32 cu km/yr (3%/1%/97%)
*per capita:* 1,030 cu m/yr (2000)
**Natural hazards:** dust storms and periodic persistent droughts
**Environment - current issues:** inadequate supplies of potable water; wildlife populations threatened by excessive hunting; soil erosion; desertification; periodic drought
**Environment - international agreements:**
*party to:* Biodiversity, Climate Change, Climate Change-Kyoto Protocol, Desertification, Endangered Species, Hazardous Wastes, Law of the Sea, Ozone Layer Protection, Wetlands
*signed, but not ratified:* none of the selected agreements
**Geography - note:** largest country in Africa; dominated by the Nile and its tributaries

## People

**Population:** 41,087,825 (July 2009 est.)
**Age structure:**
*0-14 years:* 40.7% (male 8,535,551/female 8,173,616)
*15-64 years:* 56.8% (male 11,745,683/female 11,603,906)
*65 years and over:* 2.5% (male 532,968/female 496,101) (2009 est.)
**Median age:**
*total:* 19.1 years
*male:* 18.9 years
*female:* 19.2 years (2009 est.)
**Population growth rate:** 2.143% (2009 est.)
**Birth rate:** 33.74 births/1,000 population (2009 est.)
**Death rate:** 13.64 deaths/1,000 population (2008 est.)
**Net migration rate:** 0.63 migrant(s)/1,000 population (2009 est.)
**Urbanization:**
*urban population:* 43% of total population (2008)
*rate of urbanization:* 4.3% annual rate of change (2005-10 est.)
**Sex ratio:**
*at birth:* 1.05 male(s)/female
*under 15 years:* 1.04 male(s)/female
*15-64 years:* 1.01 male(s)/female
*65 years and over:* 1.07 male(s)/female
*total population:* 1.03 male(s)/female (2009 est.)
**Infant mortality rate:**
*total:* 82.43 deaths/1,000 live births
*male:* 82.48 deaths/1,000 live births
*female:* 82.37 deaths/1,000 live births (2009 est.)
**Life expectancy at birth:**
*total population:* 51.42 years
*male:* 50.49 years
*female:* 52.4 years (2009 est.)
**Total fertility rate:** 4.48 children born/woman (2009 est.)
**HIV/AIDS - adult prevalence rate:** 1.4% (2007 est.)
**HIV/AIDS - people living with HIV/AIDS:** 320,000 (2007 est.)
**HIV/AIDS - deaths:** 25,000 (2007 est.)
**Major infectious diseases:**
*degree of risk:* very high
*food or waterborne diseases:* bacterial and protozoal diarrhea, hepatitis A and E, and typhoid fever
*vectorborne diseases:* malaria, dengue fever, African trypanosomiasis (sleeping sickness)
*water contact disease:* schistosomiasis
*respiratory disease:* meningococcal meningitis
*animal contact disease:* rabies
*note:* highly pathogenic H5N1 avian influenza has been identified in this country; it poses a negligible risk with extremely rare cases possible among US citizens who have close contact with birds (2009)
**Nationality:**
*noun:* Sudanese (singular and plural)
*adjective:* Sudanese

**Ethnic groups:** black 52%, Arab 39%, Beja 6%, foreigners 2%, other 1%
**Religions:** Sunni Muslim 70% (in north), Christian 5% (mostly in south and Khartoum), indigenous beliefs 25%
**Languages:** Arabic (official), English (official), Nubian, Ta Bedawie, diverse dialects of Nilotic, Nilo-Hamitic, Sudanic languages
*note:* program of "Arabization" in process
**Literacy:**
*definition:* age 15 and over can read and write
*total population:* 61.1%
*male:* 71.8%
*female:* 50.5% (2003 est.)
**Education expenditures:** 6% of GDP (1991)

## Government

**Country name:**
*conventional long form:* Republic of the Sudan
*conventional short form:* Sudan
*local long form:* Jumhuriyat as-Sudan
*local short form:* As-Sudan
*former:* Anglo-Egyptian Sudan
**Government type:** Government of National Unity (GNU) - the National Congress Party (NCP) and Sudan People's Liberation Movement (SPLM) formed a power-sharing government under the 2005 Comprehensive Peace Agreement (CPA); the NCP, which came to power by military coup in 1989, is the majority partner; the agreement stipulates national elections in 2009
**Capital:**
*name:* Khartoum
*geographic coordinates:* 15 36 N, 32 32 E
*time difference:* UTC+3 (8 hours ahead of Washington, DC during Standard Time)
**Administrative divisions:** 25 states (wilayat, singular - wilayah); A'ali an Nil (Upper Nile), Al Bahr al Ahmar (Red Sea), Al Buhayrat (Lakes), Al Jazirah (El Gezira), Al Khartum (Khartoum), Al Qadarif (Gedaref), Al Wahdah (Unity), An Nil al Abyad (White Nile), An Nil al Azraq (Blue Nile), Ash Shamaliyah (Northern), Bahr al Jabal (Bahr al Jebel), Gharb al Istiwa'iyah (Western Equatoria), Gharb Bahr al Ghazal (Western Bahr al Ghazal), Gharb Darfur (Western Darfur), Janub Darfur (Southern Darfur), Janub Kurdufan (Southern Kordofan), Junqali (Jonglei), Kassala (Kassala), Nahr an Nil (River Nile), Shamal Bahr al Ghazal (Northern Bahr al Ghazal), Shamal Darfur (Northern Darfur), Shamal Kurdufan (Northern Kordofan), Sharq al Istiwa'iyah (Eastern Equatoria), Sinnar (Sinnar), Warab (Warab)
**Independence:** 1 January 1956 (from Egypt and the UK)
**National holiday:** Independence Day, 1 January (1956)
**Constitution:** Interim National Constitution ratified 5 July 2005
*note:* under the Comprehensive Peace Agreement, the Interim National Constitution was ratified 5 July 2005; Constitution of Southern Sudan was signed December 2005

# Sudan *(continued)*

**Legal system:** based on English common law and Islamic law; as of 20 January 1991, the now defunct Revolutionary Command Council imposed Islamic law in the northern states; Islamic law applies to all residents of the northern states regardless of their religion; however, the CPA establishes some protections for non-Muslims in Khartoum; some separate religious courts; accepts compulsory ICJ jurisdiction with reservations; the southern legal system is still developing under the CPA following the civil war; Islamic law will not apply to the southern states

**Suffrage:** 17 years of age; universal

**Executive branch:**

*chief of state:* President Umar Hassan Ahmad al-BASHIR (since 16 October 1993); First Vice President Salva KIIR (since 4 August 2005), Vice President Ali Osman TAHA (since 20 September 2005); note - the president is both the chief of state and head of government

*head of government:* President Umar Hassan Ahmad al-BASHIR (since 16 October 1993); First Vice President Salva KIIR (since 4 August 2005), Vice President Ali Osman TAHA (since 20 September 2005)

*cabinet:* Council of Ministers appointed by the president; note - the National Congress Party or NCP (formerly the National Islamic Front or NIF) dominates al-BASHIR's cabinet

*elections:* election last held 13-23 December 2000; next to be held February 2010

*election results:* Umar Hassan Ahmad al-BASHIR reelected president; percent of vote - Umar Hassan Ahmad al-BASHIR 86.5%, Ja'afar Muhammed NUMAYRI 9.6%, three other candidates received a combined vote of 3.9%; election widely viewed as rigged; all popular opposition parties boycotted elections because of a lack of guarantees for a free and fair election

*note:* al-BASHIR assumed power as chairman of Sudan's Revolutionary Command Council for National Salvation (RCC) in June 1989 and served concurrently as chief of state, chairman of the RCC, prime minister, and minister of defense until mid-October 1993 when he was appointed president by the RCC; he was elected president by popular vote for the first time in March 1996

**Legislative branch:** bicameral National Legislature consists of a Council of States (50 seats; members indirectly elected by state legislatures to serve six-year terms) and a National Assembly (450 seats; members presently appointed, but in the future 60% from geographic constituencies, 25% from a women's list, and 15% from party lists; to serve six-year terms)

*elections:* last held 13-22 December 2000 (next to be held February 2010)

*election results:* NCP 355, others 5; note - replaced by appointments under the 2005 Comprehensive Peace Agreement

**Judicial branch:** Constitutional Court of nine justices; National Supreme Court; National Courts of Appeal; other national courts; National Judicial Service Commission will undertake overall management of the National Judiciary

**Political parties and leaders:** National Congress Party or NCP [Umar Hassan al-BASHIR]; Sudan People's Liberation Movement or SPLM [Salva KIIR]; and elements of the National Democratic Alliance or NDA including factions of the Democratic Union Party [Muhammad Uthman al-MIRGHANI] and Umma Party; Popular Congress Party or PCP [Hassan al-TURABI]

**Political pressure groups and leaders:** Umma Party [SADIQ Siddiq al-Mahdi]; Popular Congress Party or PCP [Hassan al-TURABI]; Darfur rebel groups including the Justice and Equality Movement or JEM [Khalil IBRAHIM] and the Sudan Liberation Movement or SLM [various factional leaders]

**International organization participation:** ABEDA, ACP, AfDB, AFESD, AMF, AU, CAEU, COMESA, FAO, G-77, IAEA, IBRD, ICAO, ICCt (signatory), ICRM, IDA, IDB, IFAD, IFC, IFRCS, IGAD, ILO, IMF, IMO, Interpol, IOC, IOM, IPU, ISO, ITSO, ITU, LAS, MIGA, NAM, OIC, OPCW, PCA, UN, UNCTAD, UNESCO, UNHCR, UNIDO, UNWTO, UPU, WCO, WFTU, WHO, WIPO, WMO, WTO (observer)

**Diplomatic representation in the US:**

*chief of mission:* Ambassador (vacant); Charge d'Affaires Akec Khoc ACIEW Khoc

*chancery:* 2210 Massachusetts Avenue NW, Washington, DC 20008

*telephone:* [1] (202) 338-8565

*FAX:* [1] (202) 667-2406

**Diplomatic representation from the US:**

*chief of mission:* Ambassador (vacant); Charge d'Affaires Alberto M. FERNANDEZ

*embassy:* Sharia Ali Abdul Latif Street, Khartoum

*mailing address:* P. O. Box 699, Khartoum; APO AE 09829

*telephone:* [249] (183) 774700 through 704

*FAX:* [249] (183) 774137

**Flag description:** three equal horizontal bands of red (top), white, and black with a green isosceles triangle based on the hoist side

## Economy

**Economy - overview:** Until the second half of 2008, Sudan's economy boomed on the back of increases in oil production, high oil prices, and large inflows of foreign direct investment. GDP growth registered more than 10% per year in 2006 and 2007. From 1997 to date, Sudan has been working with the IMF to implement macroeconomic reforms, including a managed float of the exchange rate. Sudan began exporting crude oil in the last quarter of 1999. Agricultural production remains important, because it employs 80% of the work force and contributes a third of GDP. The Darfur conflict, the aftermath of two decades of civil war in the south, the lack of basic infrastructure in large areas, and a reliance by much of the population on subsistence agriculture ensure much of the population will remain at or below the poverty line for years despite rapid rises in average per capita income. In January 2007, the government introduced a new currency, the Sudanese Pound, at an initial exchange rate of $1.00 equals 2 Sudanese Pounds.

**GDP (purchasing power parity):**
$87.27 billion (2008 est.)
$82.72 billion (2007)
$75.06 billion (2006)
*note:* data are in 2008 US dollars

**GDP (official exchange rate):** $62.19 billion (2008 est.)

**GDP - real growth rate:**
5.5% (2008 est.)
10.2% (2007 est.)
11.3% (2006 est.)

**GDP - per capita (PPP):**
$2,200 (2008 est.)
$2,100 (2007 est.)
$1,900 (2006 est.)
*note:* data are in 2008 US dollars

**GDP - composition by sector:**
*agriculture:* 32.9%
*industry:* 31.2%
*services:* 36% (2008 est.)

**Labor force:** 7.415 million (1996 est.)

**Labor force - by occupation:**
*agriculture:* 80%
*industry:* 7%
*services:* 13% (1998 est.)

**Unemployment rate:**
18.7% (2002 est.)

**Population below poverty line:** 40% (2004 est.)

**Household income or consumption by percentage share:**
*lowest 10%:* NA%
*highest 10%:* NA%

**Investment (gross fixed):** 18.1% of GDP (2008 est.)

**Budget:**
*revenues:* $11.84 billion
*expenditures:* $12.95 billion (2008 est.)

**Public debt:** 86.1% of GDP (2008 est.)

**Inflation rate (consumer prices):**
16.5% (2008 est.)
8% (2007 est.)

**Stock of money:** $5.549 billion (31 December 2007)

**Stock of quasi money:** $4.068 billion (31 December 2007)

**Stock of domestic credit:** $8.659 billion (31 December 2007)

**Market value of publicly traded shares:** $NA

**Agriculture - products:** cotton, groundnuts (peanuts), sorghum, millet, wheat, gum arabic, sugarcane, cassava (tapioca), mangos, papaya, bananas, sweet potatoes, sesame; sheep, livestock

**Industries:** oil, cotton ginning, textiles, cement, edible oils, sugar, soap distilling, shoes, petroleum refining, pharmaceuticals, armaments, automobile/light truck assembly

**Industrial production growth rate:** -4% (2008 est.)

**Electricity - production:** 4.037 billion kWh (2006 est.)

**Electricity - consumption:** 3.398 billion kWh (2006 est.)

**Electricity - exports:** 0 kWh (2007 est.)

# Sudan (continued)

**Electricity - imports:** 0 kWh (2007 est.)
**Oil - production:** 466,100 bbl/day (2007 est.)
**Oil - consumption:** 79,760 bbl/day (2006 est.)
**Oil - exports:** 282,100 bbl/day (2005)
**Oil - imports:** 7,558 bbl/day (2005)
**Oil - proved reserves:** 5 billion bbl (1 January 2008 est.)
**Natural gas - production:** 0 cu m (2007 est.)
**Natural gas - consumption:** 0 cu m (2007 est.)
**Natural gas - exports:** 0 cu m (2007 est.)
**Natural gas - imports:** 0 cu m (2007 est.)
**Natural gas - proved reserves:** 84.95 billion cu m (1 January 2008 est.)
**Current account balance:** -$952 million (2008 est.)
**Exports:** $13.62 billion f.o.b. (2008 est.)
**Exports - commodities:** oil and petroleum products; cotton, sesame, livestock, groundnuts, gum arabic, sugar
**Exports - partners:** China 82.1%, Japan 8.4%, UAE 2.5% (2007)
**Imports:** $7.757 billion f.o.b. (2008 est.)
**Imports - commodities:** foodstuffs, manufactured goods, refinery and transport equipment, medicines and chemicals, textiles, wheat
**Imports - partners:** China 27.9%, Saudi Arabia 7.5%, India 6.3%, Egypt 5.6%, UAE 5.5%, Japan 4.2% (2007)
**Reserves of foreign exchange and gold:** $2.329 billion (31 December 2008 est.)
**Debt - external:** $30.48 billion (31 December 2008 est.)
**Exchange rates:** Sudanese pounds (SDG) per US dollar - 2.1 (2008 est.), 2.06 (2007), 2.172 (2006), 2.4361 (2005), 2.5791 (2004)
*note:* in October 2007 Sudan redenominated its currency by transforming 100 units of Sudanese dinar into one unit of Sudanese pound

## Communications

**Telephones - main lines in use:** 345,200 (2007)
**Telephones - mobile cellular:** 7.464 million (2007)
**Telephone system:**
*general assessment:* well-equipped system by regional standards and being upgraded; cellular communications started in 1996 and have expanded substantially with wide coverage of most major cities
*domestic:* consists of microwave radio relay, cable, fiber optic, radiotelephone communications, tropospheric scatter, and a domestic satellite system with 14 earth stations
*international:* country code - 249; linked to international submarine cable Fiber-Optic Link Around the Globe (FLAG); satellite earth stations - 1 Intelsat (Atlantic Ocean), 1 Arabsat (2000)
**Radio broadcast stations:** AM 12, FM 1, shortwave 1 (1998)
**Television broadcast stations:** 3 (1997)
**Internet country code:** .sd
**Internet hosts:** 33 (2008)
**Internet users:** 1.5 million (2007)

## Transportation

**Airports:** 109 (2008)
**Airports - with paved runways:**
*total:* 17
*over 3,047 m:* 3
*2,438 to 3,047 m:* 9
*1,524 to 2,437 m:* 4
*under 914 m:* 1 (2008)
**Airports - with unpaved runways:**
*total:* 92
*1,524 to 2,437 m:* 18
*914 to 1,523 m:* 43
*under 914 m:* 31 (2008)
**Heliports:** 4 (2007)
**Pipelines:** gas 156 km; oil 4,070 km; refined products 1,613 km (2008)
**Railways:**
*total:* 5,978 km
*narrow gauge:* 4,578 km 1.067-m gauge; 1,400 km 0.600-m gauge for cotton plantations (2006)
**Roadways:**
*total:* 11,900 km
*paved:* 4,320 km
*unpaved:* 7,580 km (2000)
**Waterways:** 4,068 km (1,723 km open year round on White and Blue Nile rivers) (2008)
**Merchant marine:**
*total:* 3
*by type:* cargo 2, carrier 1 (2008)
**Ports and terminals:** Port Sudan

## Military

**Military branches:** Sudanese Armed Forces (SAF): Land Forces, Navy, Sudanese Air Force (Sikakh al-Jawwiya as-Sudaniya), Popular Defense Forces; Sudan People's Liberation Army (SPLA): Land Forces (2009)
**Military service age and obligation:** 18-33 years of age for compulsory and voluntary military service; 12-24 month service obligation (2009)
**Manpower available for military service:**
*males age 16-49:* 9,639,923
*females age 16-49:* 9,321,106 (2008 est.)
**Manpower fit for military service:**
*males age 16-49:* 5,836,971
*females age 16-49:* 5,942,043 (2009 est.)
**Manpower reaching militarily significant age annually:**
*male:* 498,376
*female:* 479,005 (2009 est.)
**Military expenditures:** 3% of GDP (2005 est.)

## Transnational Issues

**Disputes - international:** the effects of Sudan's almost constant ethnic and rebel militia fighting since the mid-20th century have penetrated all of the neighboring states; as of 2006, Chad, Ethiopia, Kenya, Central African Republic, Democratic Republic of the Congo, and Uganda provided shelter for over half a million Sudanese refugees, which includes 240,000 Darfur residents driven from their homes by Janjawid armed militia and the Sudanese military forces; Sudan, in turn, hosted about 116,000 Eritreans, 20,000 Chadians, and smaller numbers of Ethiopians, Ugandans, Central Africans, and Congolese as refugees; in February 2006, Sudan and DROC signed an agreement to repatriate 13,300 Sudanese and 6,800 Congolese; Sudan accuses Eritrea of supporting Sudanese rebel groups; efforts to demarcate the porous boundary with Ethiopia proceed slowly due to civil and ethnic fighting in eastern Sudan; the boundary that separates Kenya and Sudan's sovereignty is unclear in the "Ilemi Triangle," which Kenya has administered since colonial times; Sudan claims to administer the Hala'ib Triangle north of the 1899 Treaty boundary with Egypt along the 22nd Parallel; both states withdrew their military presence in the 1990s, but Egypt has invested in and effectively administers the area; periodic violent skirmishes with Sudanese residents over water and grazing rights persist among related pastoral populations along the border with the Central African Republic
**Refugees and internally displaced persons:**
*refugees (country of origin):* 157,220 (Eritrea); 25,023 (Chad); 11,009 (Ethiopia); 7,895 (Uganda); 5,023 (Central African Republic)
*IDPs:* 5.3 - 6.2 million (civil war 1983-2005; ongoing conflict in Darfur region) (2007)
**Trafficking in persons:**
*current situation:* Sudan is a source country for men, women, and children trafficked internally for the purposes of forced labor and sexual exploitation; Sudan is also a transit and destination country for Ethiopian women trafficked abroad for domestic servitude; Sudanese women and girls are trafficked within the country, as well as possibly to Middle Eastern countries for domestic servitude; the terrorist rebel organization, Lord's Resistance Army, continues to harbor small numbers of Sudanese and Ugandan children in the southern part of the country for use as cooks, porters, and combatants; some of these children are also trafficked across borders into Uganda or the Democratic Republic of the Congo; militia groups in Darfur, some of which are linked to the government, abduct women for short periods of forced labor and to perpetrate sexual violence; during the two decades-long north-south civil war, thousands of Dinka women and children were abducted and subsequently enslaved by members of the Missiriya and Rezeigat tribes; while there have been no known new abductions of Dinka by members of Baggara tribes in the last few years, inter-tribal abductions continue in southern Sudan
*tier rating:* Tier 3 - Sudan does not fully comply with the minimum standards for the elimination of trafficking and is not making significant efforts to do so; combating human trafficking through law enforcement or prevention measures was not a priority for the government in 2007 (2008)

# Suriname

## Introduction

**Background:** First explored by the Spaniards in the 16th century and then settled by the English in the mid-17th century, Suriname became a Dutch colony in 1667. With the abolition of slavery in 1863, workers were brought in from India and Java. Independence from the Netherlands was granted in 1975. Five years later the civilian government was replaced by a military regime that soon declared a socialist republic. It continued to exert control through a succession of nominally civilian administrations until 1987, when international pressure finally forced a democratic election. In 1990, the military overthrew the civilian leadership, but a democratically elected government - a four-party New Front coalition - returned to power in 1991 and has ruled since; the coalition expanded to eight parties in 2005.

## Geography

**Location:** Northern South America, bordering the North Atlantic Ocean, between French Guiana and Guyana
**Geographic coordinates:** 4 00 N, 56 00 W
**Map references:** South America
**Area:**
*total:* 163,270 sq km
*land:* 161,470 sq km
*water:* 1,800 sq km
**Area - comparative:** slightly larger than Georgia
**Land boundaries:**
*total:* 1,703 km
*border countries:* Brazil 593 km, French Guiana 510 km, Guyana 600 km
**Coastline:** 386 km
**Maritime claims:**
*territorial sea:* 12 nm
*exclusive economic zone:* 200 nm
**Climate:** tropical; moderated by trade winds
**Terrain:** mostly rolling hills; narrow coastal plain with swamps

**Elevation extremes:**
*lowest point:* unnamed location in the coastal plain -2 m
*highest point:* Juliana Top 1,230 m
**Natural resources:** timber, hydropower, fish, kaolin, shrimp, bauxite, gold, and small amounts of nickel, copper, platinum, iron ore
**Land use:**
*arable land:* 0.36%
*permanent crops:* 0.06%
*other:* 99.58% (2005)
**Irrigated land:** 510 sq km (2003)
**Total renewable water resources:** 122 cu km (2003)
**Freshwater withdrawal (domestic/industrial/agricultural):**
*total:* 0.67 cu km/yr (4%/3%/93%)
*per capita:* 1,489 cu m/yr (2000)
**Natural hazards:** NA
**Environment - current issues:** deforestation as timber is cut for export; pollution of inland waterways by small-scale mining activities
**Environment - international agreements:**
*party to:* Biodiversity, Climate Change, Climate Change-Kyoto Protocol, Desertification, Endangered Species, Law of the Sea, Marine Dumping, Ozone Layer Protection, Ship Pollution, Tropical Timber 94, Wetlands, Whaling
*signed, but not ratified:* none of the selected agreements
**Geography - note:** smallest independent country on South American continent; mostly tropical rain forest; great diversity of flora and fauna that, for the most part, is increasingly threatened by new development; relatively small population, mostly along the coast

## People

**Population:** 481,267 (July 2009 est.)
**Age structure:**
*0-14 years:* 27.1% (male 66,603/female 64,035)
*15-64 years:* 66.6% (male 159,525/female 160,871)
*65 years and over:* 6.3% (male 13,004/female 17,229) (2009 est.)
**Median age:**
*total:* 27.9 years
*male:* 27.5 years
*female:* 28.3 years (2009 est.)
**Population growth rate:** 1.103% (2009 est.)
**Birth rate:** 16.8 births/1,000 population (2009 est.)
**Death rate:** 5.51 deaths/1,000 population (2008 est.)
**Net migration rate:** -0.26 migrant(s)/1,000 population (2009 est.)
**Urbanization:**
*urban population:* 75% of total population (2008)
*rate of urbanization:* 1% annual rate of change (2005-10 est.)
**Sex ratio:**
*at birth:* 1.07 male(s)/female
*under 15 years:* 1.04 male(s)/female
*15-64 years:* 0.99 male(s)/female
*65 years and over:* 0.76 male(s)/female
*total population:* 0.99 male(s)/female (2009 est.)

**Infant mortality rate:**
*total:* 18.81 deaths/1,000 live births
*male:* 22.21 deaths/1,000 live births
*female:* 15.18 deaths/1,000 live births (2009 est.)
**Life expectancy at birth:**
*total population:* 73.73 years
*male:* 71 years
*female:* 76.65 years (2009 est.)
**Total fertility rate:** 1.99 children born/woman (2009 est.)
**HIV/AIDS - adult prevalence rate:** 2.4% (2007 est.)
**HIV/AIDS - people living with HIV/AIDS:** 6,800 (2007 est.)
**HIV/AIDS - deaths:** fewer than 500 (2003 est.)
**Major infectious diseases:**
*degree of risk:* high
*food or waterborne diseases:* bacterial and protozoal diarrhea, hepatitis A, and typhoid fever
*vectorborne disease:* dengue fever, Mayaro virus, and malaria
*water contact disease:* leptospirosis (2009)
**Nationality:**
*noun:* Surinamer(s)
*adjective:* Surinamese
**Ethnic groups:** Hindustani (also known locally as "East Indians"; their ancestors emigrated from northern India in the latter part of the 19th century) 37%, Creole (mixed white and black) 31%, Javanese 15%, "Maroons" (their African ancestors were brought to the country in the 17th and 18th centuries as slaves and escaped to the interior) 10%, Amerindian 2%, Chinese 2%, white 1%, other 2%
**Religions:** Hindu 27.4%, Protestant 25.2% (predominantly Moravian), Roman Catholic 22.8%, Muslim 19.6%, indigenous beliefs 5%
**Languages:** Dutch (official), English (widely spoken), Sranang Tongo (Surinamese, sometimes called Taki-Taki, is native language of Creoles and much of the younger population and is lingua franca among others), Caribbean Hindustani (a dialect of Hindi), Javanese
**Literacy:**
*definition:* age 15 and over can read and write
*total population:* 89.6%
*male:* 92%
*female:* 87.2% (2004 census)
**School life expectancy (primary to tertiary education):**
*total:* 12 years
*male:* 11 years
*female:* 13 years (2002)
**Education expenditures:** NA

## Government

**Country name:**
*conventional long form:* Republic of Suriname
*conventional short form:* Suriname
*local long form:* Republiek Suriname
*local short form:* Suriname
*former:* Netherlands Guiana, Dutch Guiana

## Suriname (continued)

**Government type:** constitutional democracy
**Capital:**
*name:* Paramaribo
*geographic coordinates:* 5 50 N, 55 10 W
*time difference:* UTC-3 (2 hours ahead of Washington, DC during Standard Time)
**Administrative divisions:** 10 districts (distrikten, singular - distrikt); Brokopondo, Commewijne, Coronie, Marowijne, Nickerie, Para, Paramaribo, Saramacca, Sipaliwini, Wanica
**Independence:** 25 November 1975 (from the Netherlands)
**National holiday:** Independence Day, 25 November (1975)
**Constitution:** ratified 30 September 1987; effective 30 October 1987
**Legal system:** based on Dutch legal system incorporating French penal theory; accepts compulsory ICJ jurisdiction with reservations
**Suffrage:** 18 years of age; universal
**Executive branch:**
*chief of state:* President Runaldo Ronald VENETIAAN (since 12 August 2000); Vice President Ramdien SARDJOE (since 3 August 2005); note - the president is both the chief of state and head of government
*head of government:* President Runaldo Ronald VENETIAAN (since 12 August 2000); Vice President Ram SARDJOE (since 3 August 2005)
*cabinet:* Cabinet of Ministers appointed by the president
*elections:* president and vice president elected by the National Assembly or, if no presidential or vice presidential candidate receives a two-thirds constitutional majority in the National Assembly after two votes, by a simple majority in the larger United People's Assembly (893 representatives from the national, local, and regional councils), for five-year terms (no term limits); election last held on 25 May 2005 (next to be held in 2010)
*election results:* Runaldo Ronald VENETIAAN reelected president; percent of vote - Runaldo Ronald VENETIAAN 62.9%, Rabin PARMESSAR 35.4%, other 1.7%; note - after two votes in the parliament failed to secure a two-thirds majority for a candidate, the vote then went to a special session of the United People's Assembly on 3 August 2005
**Legislative branch:** unicameral National Assembly or Nationale Assemblee (51 seats; members are elected by popular vote to serve five-year terms)
*elections:* last held on 25 May 2005 (next to be held in 2010)
*election results:* percent of vote by party - NF 39.7%, NDP 22.2%, VVV 13.8%, A-Com 7.2%, A-1 5.9%, other 11.2%; seats by party - NF 23, NDP 15, VVV 5, A-Com 5, A-1 3
**Judicial branch:** Cantonal Courts and a Court of Justice as an appellate court (justices are nominated for life); member of the Caribbean Court of Justice (CCJ)

**Political parties and leaders:** Alternative-1 or A-1 (a coalition of Amazone Party of Suriname or APS [Kenneth VAN GENDEREN], Democrats of the 21st Century or D-21 [Soewarto MOESTADJA], Nieuw Suriname or NS [Radjen Nanan PANDAY], Political Wing of the FAL or PVF [Jiwan SITAL], Trefpunt 2000 or T-2000 [Arti JESSURUN]); General Interior Development Party or ABOP [Ronnie BRUNSWIJK]; National Democratic Party or NDP [Desire BOUTERSE]; New Front for Democracy and Development or NF (a coalition that includes A-Combination or A-Com, Democratic Alternative 1991 or DA-91, an independent, business-oriented party [Winston JESSURUN], National Party Suriname or NPS [Ronald VENETIAAN], United Reform Party or VHP [Ramdien SARDJOE], Pertjaja Luhur or PL [Salam Paul SOMOHARDJO], Surinamese Labor Party or SPA [Siegfried GILDS]); Party for Democracy and Development in Unity or DOE [Marten SCHALKWIJK]; People's Alliance for Progress or VVV (a coalition of Democratic National Platform 2000 or DNP-2000 [Jules WIJDENBOSCH], Grassroots Party for Renewal and Democracy or BVD [Tjan GOBARDHAN], Party for National Unity and Solidarity of the Highest Order or KTPI [Willy SOEMITA], Party for Progression, Justice, and Perseverance or PPRS [Renee KAIMAN], Pendawalima or PL [Raymond SAPOEN]); Progressive Laborers and Farmers Union or PALU [Jim HOK]; Progressive Political Party or PPP [Surinder MUNGRA]; Seeka [Paul ABENA]; Union of Progressive Surinamers or UPS [Sheoradj PANDAY]
**Political pressure groups and leaders:**
Association of Indigenous Village Chiefs [Ricardo PANE]; Association of Saramaccan Authorities or Maroon [Head Captain WASE]; Women's Parliament Forum or PVF [Iris GILLIAD]
**International organization participation:** ACP, Caricom, FAO, G-77, IADB, IBRD, ICAO, ICCt, ICRM, IDB, IFAD, IFRCS, IHO (suspended), ILO, IMF, IMO, Interpol, IOC, IPU, ISO (subscriber), ITU, ITUC, LAES, MIGA, NAM, OAS, OIC, OPANAL, OPCW, PCA, UN, UNASUR, UNCTAD, UNESCO, UNIDO, UPU, WCL, WFTU, WHO, WIPO, WMO, WTO
**Diplomatic representation in the US:**
*chief of mission:* Ambassador Jacques Ruben Constantijn KROSS
*chancery:* Suite 460, 4301 Connecticut Avenue NW, Washington, DC 20008
*telephone:* [1] (202) 244-7488
*FAX:* [1] (202) 244-5878
*consulate(s) general:* Miami
**Diplomatic representation from the US:**
*chief of mission:* Ambassador Lisa Bobbie SCHREIBER HUGHES
*embassy:* Dr. Sophie Redmondstraat 129, Paramaribo
*mailing address:* US Department of State, PO Box 1821, Paramaribo
*telephone:* [597] 472-900
*FAX:* [597] 410-025
**Flag description:** five horizontal bands of green (top, double width), white, red (quadruple width), white, and green (double width); there is a large, yellow, five-pointed star centered in the red band

**Economy - overview:** The economy is dominated by the mining industry, with exports of alumina, gold, and oil accounting for about 85% of exports and 25% of government revenues, making the economy highly vulnerable to mineral price volatility. Prospects for local onshore oil production are good, and a drilling program is underway. Offshore oil drilling was given a boost in 2004 when the State Oil Company (Staatsolie) signed exploration agreements with several Western oil companies. Bidding on these new offshore blocks was completed in July 2006. The short-term economic outlook depends on the government's ability to control inflation and on the development of projects in the bauxite and gold mining sectors, though investment in these projects may slow with the tightening of global credit markets. Suriname has received aid for these projects from Netherlands, Belgium, and the European Development Fund. Suriname's economic prospects for the medium term will depend on continued commitment to responsible monetary and fiscal policies and to the introduction of structural reforms to liberalize markets and promote competition. In 2000, the government of Ronald VENETIAAN, returned to office and inherited an economy with inflation of over 100% and a growing fiscal deficit. He quickly implemented an austerity program, raised taxes, attempted to control spending, and tamed inflation. The VENETIAAN administration also has created a stabilization fund to insulate future revenue from commodity shocks. These economic policies are likely to remain in effect during VENETIAAN's third term.
**GDP (purchasing power parity):**
$4.256 billion (2008 est.)
$4.015 billion (2007)
$3.805 billion (2006)
*note:* data are in 2008 US dollars
**GDP (official exchange rate):** $2.984 billion (2008 est.)
**GDP - real growth rate:**
6% (2008 est.)
5.5% (2007 est.)
4.8% (2006 est.)
**GDP - per capita (PPP):**
$8,900 (2008 est.)
$8,500 (2007 est.)
$8,200 (2006 est.)
*note:* data are in 2008 US dollars
**GDP - composition by sector:**
*agriculture:* 10.8%
*industry:* 24.4%
*services:* 64.8% (2005 est.)
**Labor force:** 156,700 (2004)
**Labor force - by occupation:**
*agriculture:* 8%
*industry:* 14%
*services:* 78% (2004)
**Unemployment rate:**
9.5% (2004)

# Suriname (continued)

**Population below poverty line:** 70% (2002 est.)
**Household income or consumption by percentage share:**
*lowest 10%:* NA%
*highest 10%:* NA%
**Budget:**
*revenues:* $392.6 million
*expenditures:* $425.9 million (2004)
**Inflation rate (consumer prices):**
6.4% (2007 est.)
**Commercial bank prime lending rate:** 13.77%
(31 December 2007)
**Stock of money:** $416.6 million (31 December 2007)
**Stock of quasi money:** $824.4 million
(31 December 2007)
**Stock of domestic credit:** $651 million
(31 December 2007)
**Market value of publicly traded shares:** $NA
**Agriculture - products:** paddy rice, bananas, palm kernels, coconuts, plantains, peanuts; beef, chickens; shrimp; forest products
**Industries:** bauxite and gold mining, alumina production; oil, lumbering, food processing, fishing
**Industrial production growth rate:** 6.5%
(1994 est.)
**Electricity - production:** 1.595 billion kWh
(2006 est.)
**Electricity - consumption:** 1.457 billion kWh
(2006 est.)
**Electricity - exports:** 0 kWh (2007 est.)
**Electricity - imports:** 0 kWh (2007 est.)
**Oil - production:** 13,000 bbl/day (2007 est.)
**Oil - consumption:** 12,370 bbl/day (2006 est.)
**Oil - exports:** 2,899 bbl/day (2005)
**Oil - imports:** 6,369 bbl/day (2005)
**Oil - proved reserves:** 88 million bbl (1 January 2008 est.)
**Natural gas - production:** 0 cu m (2007 est.)
**Natural gas - consumption:** 0 cu m (2007 est.)
**Natural gas - exports:** 0 cu m (2007 est.)
**Natural gas - imports:** 0 cu m (2007 est.)
**Natural gas - proved reserves:** 0 cu m (1 January 2006 est.)
**Current account balance:** $24 million (2007 est.)
**Exports:** $1.391 billion f.o.b. (2006 est.)
**Exports - commodities:** alumina, gold, crude oil, lumber, shrimp and fish, rice, bananas
**Exports - partners:** Canada 26.8%, Norway 20.2%, Belgium 9.2%, US 8.9%, UAE 7.9%, France 7.2%
(2007)
**Imports:** $1.297 billion f.o.b. (2006 est.)
**Imports - commodities:** capital equipment, petroleum, foodstuffs, cotton, consumer goods
**Imports - partners:** US 27%, Netherlands 17.3%, Trinidad and Tobago 14.3%, China 5.9%, Japan 5.1%
(2007)
**Reserves of foreign exchange and gold:** $263.3 million (2006)
**Debt - external:** $504.3 million (2005 est.)

**Exchange rates:** Surinamese dollars (SRD) per US dollar - 2.745 (2007), 2.745 (2006), 2.7317 (2005), 2.7336 (2004), 2.6013 (2003)
*note:* in January 2004, the government replaced the guilder with the Surinamese dollar, tied to a US dollar-dominated currency basket

## Communications

**Telephones - main lines in use:** 81,500 (2006)
**Telephones - mobile cellular:** 320,000 (2006)
**Telephone system:**
*general assessment:* international facilities are good
*domestic:* combined fixed-line and mobile-cellular teledensity about 90 telephones per 100 persons; microwave radio relay network
*international:* country code - 597; satellite earth stations - 2 Intelsat (Atlantic Ocean)
**Radio broadcast stations:** AM 4, FM 13, shortwave 1 (1998)
**Television broadcast stations:** 3 (plus 7 repeaters) (2000)
**Internet country code:** .sr
**Internet hosts:** 33 (2008)
**Internet users:** 44,000 (2007)

## Transportation

**Airports:** 50 (2008)
**Airports - with paved runways:**
*total:* 5
*over 3,047 m:* 1
*under 914 m:* 4 (2008)
**Airports - with unpaved runways:**
*total:* 45
*914 to 1,523 m:* 5
*under 914 m:* 40 (2008)
**Pipelines:** oil 50 km (2008)
**Roadways:**
*total:* 4,304 km
*paved:* 1,130 km
*unpaved:* 3,174 km (2003)
**Waterways:** 1,200 km (most navigable by ships with drafts up to 7 m) (2008)
**Merchant marine:**
*total:* 1
*by type:* cargo 1 (2008)
**Ports and terminals:** Paramaribo, Wageningen

## Military

**Military branches:** National Army (Nationaal Leger, NL; includes Naval Wing, Air Wing) (2007)
**Military service age and obligation:** 18 years of age (est.); recruitment is voluntary, with personnel drawn almost exclusively from the Creole community (2007)
**Manpower available for military service:**
*males age 16-49:* 130,534
*females age 16-49:* 130,243 (2008 est.)
**Manpower fit for military service:**
*males age 16-49:* 107,367
*females age 16-49:* 111,000 (2009 est.)

**Manpower reaching militarily significant age annually:**
*male:* 4,251
*female:* 4,265 (2009 est.)
**Military expenditures:** 0.6% of GDP (2006 est.)

## Transnational Issues

**Disputes - international:** area claimed by French Guiana between Riviere Litani and Riviere Marouini (both headwaters of the Lawa); Suriname claims a triangle of land between the New and Kutari/Koetari rivers in a historic dispute over the headwaters of the Courantyne; Guyana seeks United Nations Convention on the Law of the Sea (UNCLOS) arbitration to resolve the long-standing dispute with Suriname over the axis of the territorial sea boundary in potentially oil-rich waters
**Illicit drugs:** growing transshipment point for South American drugs destined for Europe via the Netherlands and Brazil; transshipment point for arms-for-drugs dealing

# Svalbard
*(territory of Norway)*

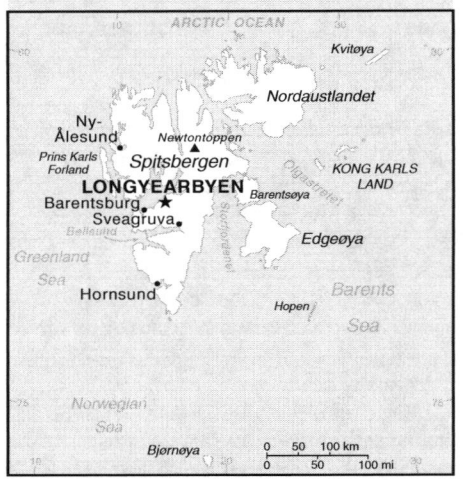

## Introduction

**Background:** First discovered by the Norwegians in the 12th century, the islands served as an international whaling base during the 17th and 18th centuries. Norway's sovereignty was recognized in 1920; five years later it officially took over the territory.

## Geography

**Location:** Northern Europe, islands between the Arctic Ocean, Barents Sea, Greenland Sea, and Norwegian Sea, north of Norway

**Geographic coordinates:** 78 00 N, 20 00 E

**Map references:** Arctic Region

**Area:**
*total:* 61,020 sq km
*land:* 61,020 sq km
*water:* 0 sq km
*note:* includes Spitsbergen and Bjornoya (Bear Island)

**Area - comparative:** slightly smaller than West Virginia

**Land boundaries:** 0 km

**Coastline:** 3,587 km

**Maritime claims:**
*territorial sea:* 4 nm
*exclusive fishing zone:* 200 nm unilaterally claimed by Norway but not recognized by Russia

**Climate:** arctic, tempered by warm North Atlantic Current; cool summers, cold winters; North Atlantic Current flows along west and north coasts of Spitsbergen, keeping water open and navigable most of the year

**Terrain:** wild, rugged mountains; much of high land ice covered; west coast clear of ice about one-half of the year; fjords along west and north coasts

**Elevation extremes:**
*lowest point:* Arctic Ocean 0 m
*highest point:* Newtontoppen 1,717 m

**Natural resources:** coal, iron ore, copper, zinc, phosphate, wildlife, fish

**Land use:**
*arable land:* 0%
*permanent crops:* 0%
*other:* 100% (no trees; the only bushes are crowberry and cloudberry) (2005)

**Irrigated land:** NA

**Natural hazards:** ice floes often block the entrance to Bellsund (a transit point for coal export) on the west coast and occasionally make parts of the northeastern coast inaccessible to maritime traffic

**Environment - current issues:** NA

**Geography - note:** northernmost part of the Kingdom of Norway; consists of nine main islands; glaciers and snowfields cover 60% of the total area; Spitsbergen Island is the site of the Svalbard Global Seed Vault, a seed repository established by the Global Crop Diversity Trust and the Norwegian Government

## People

**Population:** 2,116 (July 2009 est.)

**Age structure:**
*0-14 years:* NA
*15-64 years:* NA
*65 years and over:* NA

**Population growth rate:** -0.023% (2009 est.)

**Birth rate:** NA

**Death rate:** NA

**Net migration rate:** NA

**Sex ratio:** NA

**Infant mortality rate:**
*total:* NA
*male:* NA
*female:* NA (2008 est.)

**Life expectancy at birth:**
*total population:* NA
*male:* NA
*female:* NA

**Total fertility rate:** NA (2008 est.)

**HIV/AIDS - adult prevalence rate:** 0% (2001)

**HIV/AIDS - people living with HIV/AIDS:** 0 (2001)

**HIV/AIDS - deaths:** 0 (2001)

**Ethnic groups:** Norwegian 55.4%, Russian and Ukrainian 44.3%, other 0.3% (1998)

**Languages:** Norwegian, Russian

**Literacy:** NA

## Government

**Country name:**
*conventional long form:* none
*conventional short form:* Svalbard (sometimes referred to as Spitzbergen)

**Dependency status:** territory of Norway; administered by the Polar Department of the Ministry of Justice, through a governor (sysselmann) residing in Longyearbyen, Spitsbergen; by treaty (9 February 1920) sovereignty was awarded to Norway

**Government type:** NA

**Capital:**
*name:* Longyearbyen
*geographic coordinates:* 78 13 N, 15 33 E
*time difference:* UTC+1 (6 hours ahead of Washington, DC during Standard Time)
*daylight saving time:* +1hr, begins last Sunday in March; ends last Sunday in October

**Independence:** none (territory of Norway)

**Legal system:** the laws of Norway, where applicable, apply

**Executive branch:**
*chief of state:* King HARALD V of Norway (since 17 January 1991)
*head of government:* Governor Per SEFLAND (since 1 October 2005); Assistant Governor Rune Baard HANSEN (since 2003)
*elections:* none; the monarch is hereditary; governor and assistant governor responsible to the Polar Department of the Ministry of Justice

**Political pressure groups and leaders:** NA

**International organization participation:** none

**Flag description:** the flag of Norway is used

## Economy

**Economy - overview:** Coal mining is the major economic activity on Svalbard. The treaty of 9 February 1920 gave the 41 signatories equal rights to exploit mineral deposits, subject to Norwegian regulation. Although US, UK, Dutch, and Swedish coal companies have mined in the past, the only companies still mining are Norwegian and Russian. The settlements on Svalbard are essentially company towns. The Norwegian state-owned coal company employs nearly 60% of the Norwegian population on the island, runs many of the local services, and provides most of the local infrastructure. There is also some hunting of seal, reindeer, and fox.

**GDP (purchasing power parity):** $NA

**GDP - real growth rate:** NA%

**Labor force:** NA

**Budget:**
*revenues:* $25.07 million
*expenditures:* $NA (2004 est.)

**Exports:** $197.6 million (2004)

**Imports:** $NA

**Exchange rates:** Norwegian kroner (NOK) per US dollar - 5.6361 (2008), 5.86 (2007), 6.418 (2006), 6.445 (2005), 6.7327 (2004)

## Communications

**Telephones - main lines in use:** NA

**Telephone system:**
*general assessment:* probably adequate
*domestic:* local telephone service
*international:* country code - 47-790; satellite earth station - 1 of unknown type (for communication with Norwegian mainland only)

**Radio broadcast stations:** AM 1, FM 1 (plus 2 repeaters), shortwave 0 (1998)

**Television broadcast stations:** NA

**Internet country code:** .sj

**Internet users:** NA

# Svalbard *(continued)*

## Transportation

**Airports:** 4 (2008)
**Airports - with paved runways:**
*total:* 1
*2,438 to 3,047 m:* 1 (2008)
**Airports - with unpaved runways:**
*total:* 3
*under 914 m:* 3 (2008)
**Heliports:** 1 (2007)
**Ports and terminals:** Barentsburg, Longyearbyen, Ny-Alesund, Pyramiden

## Military

**Military branches:** no regular military forces
**Military - note:** Svalbard is a territory of Norway, demilitarized by treaty on 9 February 1920

## Transnational Issues

**Disputes - international:** despite recent discussions, Russia and Norway dispute their maritime limits in the Barents Sea and Russia's fishing rights beyond Svalbard's territorial limits within the Svalbard Treaty zone

# Swaziland

## Introduction

**Background:** Autonomy for the Swazis of southern Africa was guaranteed by the British in the late 19th century; independence was granted in 1968. Student and labor unrest during the 1990s pressured King MSWATI III, the world's last absolute monarch, to grudgingly allow political reform and greater democracy, although he has backslid on these promises in recent years. A constitution came into effect in 2006, but political parties remain banned. The African United Democratic Party tried unsuccessfully to register as an official political party in mid 2006. Talks over the constitution broke down between the government and progressive groups in 2007. Swaziland recently surpassed Botswana as the country with the world's highest known HIV/AIDS prevalence rate.

## Geography

**Location:** Southern Africa, between Mozambique and South Africa
**Geographic coordinates:** 26 30 S, 31 30 E
**Map references:** Africa
**Area:**
*total:* 17,363 sq km
*land:* 17,203 sq km
*water:* 160 sq km
**Area - comparative:** slightly smaller than New Jersey
**Land boundaries:**
*total:* 535 km
*border countries:* Mozambique 105 km, South Africa 430 km
**Coastline:** 0 km (landlocked)
**Maritime claims:** none (landlocked)
**Climate:** varies from tropical to near temperate
**Terrain:** mostly mountains and hills; some moderately sloping plains
**Elevation extremes:**
*lowest point:* Great Usutu River 21 m
*highest point:* Emlembe 1,862 m

**Natural resources:** asbestos, coal, clay, cassiterite, hydropower, forests, small gold and diamond deposits, quarry stone, and talc
**Land use:**
*arable land:* 10.25%
*permanent crops:* 0.81%
*other:* 88.94% (2005)
**Irrigated land:** 500 sq km (2003)
**Total renewable water resources:** 4.5 cu km (1987)
**Freshwater withdrawal (domestic/industrial/agricultural):**
*total:* 1.04 cu km/yr (2%/1%/97%)
*per capita:* 1,010 cu m/yr (2000)
**Natural hazards:** drought
**Environment - current issues:** limited supplies of potable water; wildlife populations being depleted because of excessive hunting; overgrazing; soil degradation; soil erosion
**Environment - international agreements:**
*party to:* Biodiversity, Climate Change, Climate Change-Kyoto Protocol, Desertification, Endangered Species, Hazardous Wastes, Ozone Layer Protection
*signed, but not ratified:* Law of the Sea
**Geography - note:** landlocked; almost completely surrounded by South Africa

## People

**Population:** 1,123,913
*note:* estimates for this country explicitly take into account the effects of excess mortality due to AIDS; this can result in lower life expectancy, higher infant mortality, higher death rates, lower population growth rates, and changes in the distribution of population by age and sex than would otherwise be expected (July 2009 est.)
**Age structure:**
*0-14 years:* 39.4% (male 223,420/female 219,420)
*15-64 years:* 56.9% (male 308,251/female 331,623)
*65 years and over:* 3.7% (male 15,261/female 25,938) (2009 est.)
**Median age:**
*total:* 18.8 years
*male:* 18.2 years
*female:* 19.5 years (2009 est.)
**Population growth rate:** -0.459% (2009 est.)
**Birth rate:** 26.25 births/1,000 population (2009 est.)
**Death rate:** 30.7 deaths/1,000 population (2008 est.)
**Net migration rate:** NA
**Urbanization:**
*urban population:* 25% of total population (2008)
*rate of urbanization:* 1.7% annual rate of change (2005-10 est.)
**Sex ratio:**
*at birth:* 1.03 male(s)/female
*under 15 years:* 1.02 male(s)/female
*15-64 years:* 0.93 male(s)/female
*65 years and over:* 0.59 male(s)/female
*total population:* 0.95 male(s)/female (2009 est.)

# Swaziland (continued)

**Infant mortality rate:**
*total:* 68.63 deaths/1,000 live births
*male:* 71.87 deaths/1,000 live births
*female:* 65.29 deaths/1,000 live births (2009 est.)
**Life expectancy at birth:**
*total population:* 31.88 years
*male:* 31.62 years
*female:* 32.15 years (2009 est.)
**Total fertility rate:** 3.24 children born/woman
(2009 est.)
**HIV/AIDS - adult prevalence rate:** 26.1%
(2007 est.)
**HIV/AIDS - people living with HIV/AIDS:** 190,000
(2007 est.)
**HIV/AIDS - deaths:** 10,000 (2007 est.)
**Major infectious diseases:**
*degree of risk:* high
*food or waterborne diseases:* bacterial diarrhea,
hepatitis A, and typhoid fever
*vectorborne disease:* malaria
*water contact disease:* schistosomiasis (2009)
**Nationality:**
*noun:* Swazi(s)
*adjective:* Swazi
**Ethnic groups:** African 97%, European 3%
**Religions:** Zionist 40% (a blend of Christianity and
indigenous ancestral worship), Roman Catholic 20%,
Muslim 10%, other (includes Anglican, Bahai,
Methodist, Mormon, Jewish) 30%
**Languages:** English (official, government business
conducted in English), siSwati (official)
**Literacy:**
*definition:* age 15 and over can read and write
*total population:* 81.6%
*male:* 82.6%
*female:* 80.8% (2003 est.)
**School life expectancy (primary to tertiary
education):**
*total:* 10 years
*male:* 10 years
*female:* 10 years (2005)
**Education expenditures:** 7% of GDP (2005)

## Government

**Country name:**
*conventional long form:* Kingdom of Swaziland
*conventional short form:* Swaziland
*local long form:* Umbuso weSwatini
*local short form:* eSwatini
**Government type:** monarchy
**Capital:**
*name:* Mbabane
*geographic coordinates:* 26 18 S, 31 06 E
*time difference:* UTC+2 (7 hours ahead of
Washington, DC during Standard Time)
*note:* Lobamba (royal and legislative capital)
**Administrative divisions:** 4 districts; Hhohho,
Lubombo, Manzini, Shiselweni
**Independence:** 6 September 1968 (from the UK)
**National holiday:** Independence Day, 6 September
(1968)

**Constitution:** signed by the King in July 2005 went
into effect on 8 February 2006
**Legal system:** based on South African
Roman-Dutch law in statutory courts and Swazi
traditional law and custom in traditional courts;
accepts compulsory ICJ jurisdiction with reservations
**Suffrage:** 18 years of age
**Executive branch:**
*chief of state:* King MSWATI III (since 25 April 1986)
*head of government:* Prime Minister Barnabas
Sibusiso DLAMINI (since 16 October 2008)
*cabinet:* Cabinet recommended by the prime minister
and confirmed by the monarch
*elections:* the monarch is hereditary; prime minister
appointed by the monarch from among the elected
members of the House of Assembly
**Legislative branch:** bicameral Parliament or
Libandla consists of the Senate (30 seats; 10
members appointed by the House of Assembly and 20
appointed by the monarch; to serve five-year terms)
and the House of Assembly (65 seats; 10 members
appointed by the monarch and 55 elected by popular
vote; serve five-year terms)
*elections:* House of Assembly - last held
19 September 2008 (next to be held in 2013)
*election results:* House of Assembly - balloting is done
on a nonparty basis; candidates for election are
nominated by the local council of each constituency
and for each constituency the three candidates with
the most votes in the first round of voting are narrowed
to a single winner by a second round
**Judicial branch:** High Court; Supreme Court;
judges for both courts are appointed by the monarch
**Political parties and leaders:** the status of political
parties, previously banned, is unclear under the new
(2006) Constitution and currently being debated - the
following are considered political associations; African
United Democratic Party or AUDP [Stanley
MAUNDZISA, president]; Imbokodvo National
Movement or INM; Ngwane National Liberatory
Congress or NNLC [Obed DLAMINI, president];
People's United Democratic Movement or PUDEMO
[Mario MASUKU, president]
**Political pressure groups and leaders:** Swaziland
Federation of Trade Unions; Swaziland and Solidarity
Network or SSN
**International organization participation:** ACP,
AfDB, AU, C, COMESA, FAO, G-77, IBRD, ICAO,
ICRM, IDA, IFAD, IFC, IFRCS, ILO, IMF, Interpol,
IOC, ISO (correspondent), ITSO, ITU, ITUC, MIGA,
NAM, OPCW, PCA, SACU, SADC, UN, UNCTAD,
UNESCO, UNIDO, UNWTO, UPU, WCO, WFTU,
WHO, WIPO, WMO, WTO
**Diplomatic representation in the US:**
*chief of mission:* Ambassador Ephraim Mandla
HLOPHE
*chancery:* 1712 New Hampshire Avenue, NW,
Washington, DC 20009
*telephone:* [1] (202) 234-5002
*FAX:* [1] (202) 234-8254

**Diplomatic representation from the US:**
*chief of mission:* Ambassador Maurice S. PARKER
*embassy:* 2350 Mbabane Place, Mbabane
*mailing address:* P. O. Box 199, Mbabane
*telephone:* [268] 404-2445
*FAX:* [268] 404-2059
**Flag description:** three horizontal bands of blue
(top), red (triple width), and blue; the red band is
edged in yellow; centered in the red band is a large
black and white shield covering two spears and a staff
decorated with feather tassels, all placed horizontally

## Economy

**Economy - overview:** In this small, landlocked
economy, subsistence agriculture occupies
approximately 70% of the population. The
manufacturing sector has diversified since the
mid-1980s. Sugar and wood pulp remain important
foreign exchange earners. In 2007, the sugar industry
increased efficiency and diversification efforts, in
response to a 17% decline in EU sugar prices. Mining
has declined in importance in recent years with only
coal and quarry stone mines remaining active.
Surrounded by South Africa, except for a short border
with Mozambique, Swaziland is heavily dependent on
South Africa from which it receives more than
nine-tenths of its imports and to which it sends 60% of
its exports. Swaziland's currency is pegged to the
South African rand, subsuming Swaziland's monetary
policy to South Africa. Customs duties from the
Southern African Customs Union, which may equal as
much as 70% of government revenue this year, and
worker remittances from South Africa substantially
supplement domestically earned income. Swaziland is
not poor enough to merit an IMF program; however,
the country is struggling to reduce the size of the civil
service and control costs at public enterprises. The
government is trying to improve the atmosphere for
foreign investment. With an estimated 40%
unemployment rate, Swaziland's need to increase the
number and size of small and medium enterprises and
attract foreign direct investment is acute. Overgrazing,
soil depletion, drought, and sometimes floods persist
as problems for the future. More than one-fourth of the
population needed emergency food aid in 2006-07
because of drought, and nearly two-fifths of the adult
population has been infected by HIV/AIDS.
**GDP (purchasing power parity):**
$5.703 billion (2008 est.)
$5.553 billion (2007)
$5.366 billion (2006)
*note:* data are in 2008 US dollars
**GDP (official exchange rate):** $2.968 billion
(2008 est.)
**GDP - real growth rate:**
2.7% (2008 est.)
3.5% (2007 est.)
2.8% (2006 est.)

**GDP - per capita (PPP):**
$5,100 (2008 est.)
$4,900 (2007 est.)
$4,700 (2006 est.)
*note:* data are in 2008 US dollars
**GDP - composition by sector:**
*agriculture:* 11.9%
*industry:* 45.1%
*services:* 43% (2008 est.)
**Labor force:** 300,000 (2006)
**Labor force - by occupation:**
*agriculture:* NA%
*industry:* NA%
*services:* NA%
**Unemployment rate:**
40% (2006 est.)
**Population below poverty line:** 69% (2006)
**Household income or consumption by percentage share:**
*lowest 10%:* 1.6%
*highest 10%:* 40.7% (2001)
**Distribution of family income - Gini index:** 50.4 (2001)
**Investment (gross fixed):** 19.7% of GDP (2008 est.)
**Budget:**
*revenues:* $1.215 billion
*expenditures:* $1.155 billion (2008 est.)
**Inflation rate (consumer prices):**
12.7% (2008 est.)
8.1% (2007 est.)
**Central bank discount rate:** 11% (31 December 2007)
**Commercial bank prime lending rate:** 13.17% (31 December 2007)
**Stock of money:** $244.8 million (31 December 2007)
**Stock of quasi money:** $529.4 million (31 December 2007)
**Stock of domestic credit:** $204.1 million (31 December 2007)
**Market value of publicly traded shares:** $203.1 million (31 December 2007)
**Agriculture - products:** sugarcane, cotton, corn, tobacco, rice, citrus, pineapples, sorghum, peanuts; cattle, goats, sheep
**Industries:** coal, wood pulp, sugar, soft drink concentrates, textiles and apparel
**Industrial production growth rate:** 1.1% (2008 est.)
**Electricity - production:** 460 million kWh (2007)
**Electricity - consumption:** 1.2 billion kWh (2007)
**Electricity - exports:** 0 kWh (2007)
**Electricity - imports:** 872 million kWh; note - electricity supplied by South Africa (2007)
**Oil - production:** 0 bbl/day (2007 est.)
**Oil - consumption:** 3,490 bbl/day (2006 est.)
**Oil - exports:** 0 bbl/day (2005)
**Oil - imports:** 3,530 bbl/day (2005)
**Oil - proved reserves:** 0 bbl (1 January 2006 est.)

**Natural gas - production:** 0 cu m (2007 est.)
**Natural gas - consumption:** 0 cu m (2007 est.)
**Natural gas - exports:** 0 cu m (2007 est.)
**Natural gas - imports:** 0 cu m (2007 est.)
**Natural gas - proved reserves:** 0 cu m (1 January 2006 est.)
**Current account balance:** -$10 million (2008 est.)
**Exports:** $1.83 billion f.o.b. (2008 est.)
**Exports - commodities:** soft drink concentrates, sugar, wood pulp, cotton yarn, refrigerators, citrus and canned fruit
**Imports:** $1.978 billion f.o.b. (2008 est.)
**Imports - commodities:** motor vehicles, machinery, transport equipment, foodstuffs, petroleum products, chemicals
**Reserves of foreign exchange and gold:** $997 million (31 December 2008 est.)
**Debt - external:** $548 million (31 December 2008 est.)
**Stock of direct foreign investment - at home:** $NA
**Stock of direct foreign investment - abroad:** $NA
**Exchange rates:** emalangeni per US dollar - 7.75 (2008 est.), 7.4 (2007), 6.85 (2006), 6.3593 (2005), 6.4597 (2004)

## Communications

**Telephones - main lines in use:** 44,000 (2006)
**Telephones - mobile cellular:** 380,000 (2007)
**Telephone system:**
*general assessment:* a somewhat modern but not an advanced system
*domestic:* mobile-cellular subscribership is increasing; combined fixed-line and mobile cellular teledensity approaching 40 telephones per 100 persons; telephone system consists of carrier-equipped, open-wire lines and low-capacity, microwave radio relay
*international:* country code - 268; satellite earth station -1 Intelsat (Atlantic Ocean) (2007)
**Radio broadcast stations:** AM 3, FM 2 (plus 4 repeaters), shortwave 3 (2004)
**Television broadcast stations:** 12 (includes 7 relay stations) (2004)
**Internet country code:** .sz
**Internet hosts:** 2,582 (2008)
**Internet users:** 42,000 (2006)

## Transportation

**Airports:** 16 (2008)
**Airports - with paved runways:**
*total:* 1
*2,438 to 3,047 m:* 1 (2008)
**Airports - with unpaved runways:**
*total:* 15
*914 to 1,523 m:* 7
*under 914 m:* 8 (2008)
**Railways:**
*total:* 301 km
*narrow gauge:* 301 km 1.067-m gauge (2006)

**Roadways:**
*total:* 3,594 km
*paved:* 1,078 km
*unpaved:* 2,516 km (2002)

## Military

**Military branches:** Umbutfo Swaziland Defense Force (USDF): Ground Force (includes air wing) (2008)
**Military service age and obligation:** 18-30 years of age for male and female voluntary military service; no conscription (2008)
**Manpower available for military service:**
*males age 16-49:* 266,311 (2008 est.)
**Manpower fit for military service:**
*males age 16-49:* 124,132
*females age 16-49:* 118,570 (2009 est.)
**Manpower reaching militarily significant age annually:**
*male:* 15,985
*female:* 15,754 (2009 est.)
**Military expenditures:** 4.7% of GDP (2006)

## Transnational Issues

**Disputes - international:** in 2006, Swazi king advocates resort to ICJ to claim parts of Mpumalanga and KwaZulu-Natal from South Africa

# Sweden

## Introduction

**Background:** A military power during the 17th century, Sweden has not participated in any war in almost two centuries. An armed neutrality was preserved in both World Wars. Sweden's long-successful economic formula of a capitalist system interlarded with substantial welfare elements was challenged in the 1990s by high unemployment and in 2000-02 by the global economic downturn, but fiscal discipline over the past several years has allowed the country to weather economic vagaries. Sweden joined the EU in 1995, but the public rejected the introduction of the euro in a 2003 referendum.

## Geography

**Location:** Northern Europe, bordering the Baltic Sea, Gulf of Bothnia, Kattegat, and Skagerrak, between Finland and Norway
**Geographic coordinates:** 62 00 N, 15 00 E
**Map references:** Europe

**Area:**
*total:* 449,964 sq km
*land:* 410,934 sq km
*water:* 39,030 sq km
**Area - comparative:** slightly larger than California
**Land boundaries:**
*total:* 2,233 km
*border countries:* Finland 614 km, Norway 1,619 km
**Coastline:** 3,218 km
**Maritime claims:**
*territorial sea:* 12 nm (adjustments made to return a portion of straits to high seas)
*exclusive economic zone:* agreed boundaries or midlines
*continental shelf:* 200 m depth or to the depth of exploitation
**Climate:** temperate in south with cold, cloudy winters and cool, partly cloudy summers; subarctic in north
**Terrain:** mostly flat or gently rolling lowlands; mountains in west
**Elevation extremes:**
*lowest point:* reclaimed bay of Lake Hammarsjon, near Kristianstad -2.4 m
*highest point:* Kebnekaise 2,111 m
**Natural resources:** iron ore, copper, lead, zinc, gold, silver, tungsten, uranium, arsenic, feldspar, timber, hydropower
**Land use:**
*arable land:* 5.93%
*permanent crops:* 0.01%
*other:* 94.06% (2005)
**Irrigated land:** 1,150 sq km (2003)
**Total renewable water resources:** 179 cu km (2005)
**Freshwater withdrawal (domestic/industrial/agricultural):**
*total:* 2.68 cu km/yr (37%/54%/9%)
*per capita:* 296 cu m/yr (2002)
**Natural hazards:** ice floes in the surrounding waters, especially in the Gulf of Bothnia, can interfere with maritime traffic
**Environment - current issues:** acid rain damage to soils and lakes; pollution of the North Sea and the Baltic Sea
**Environment - international agreements:**
*party to:* Air Pollution, Air Pollution-Nitrogen Oxides, Air Pollution-Persistent Organic Pollutants, Air Pollution-Sulfur 85, Air Pollution-Sulfur 94, Air Pollution-Volatile Organic Compounds, Antarctic-Environmental Protocol, Antarctic-Marine Living Resources, Antarctic Treaty, Biodiversity, Climate Change, Climate Change-Kyoto Protocol, Desertification, Endangered Species, Environmental Modification, Hazardous Wastes, Law of the Sea, Marine Dumping, Ozone Layer Protection, Ship Pollution, Tropical Timber 83, Tropical Timber 94, Wetlands, Whaling
*signed, but not ratified:* none of the selected agreements
**Geography - note:** strategic location along Danish Straits linking Baltic and North Seas

## People

**Population:** 9,059,651 (July 2009 est.)
**Age structure:**
*0-14 years:* 15.7% (male 733,597/female 692,194)
*15-64 years:* 65.5% (male 3,003,358/female 2,927,038)
*65 years and over:* 18.8% (male 753,293/female 950,171) (2009 est.)
**Median age:**
*total:* 41.5 years
*male:* 40.4 years
*female:* 42.6 years (2009 est.)
**Population growth rate:** 0.158% (2009 est.)
**Birth rate:** 10.13 births/1,000 population (2009 est.)
**Death rate:** 10.24 deaths/1,000 population (2008 est.)
**Net migration rate:** 1.66 migrant(s)/1,000 population (2009 est.)
**Urbanization:**
*urban population:* 85% of total population (2008)
*rate of urbanization:* 0.5% annual rate of change (2005-10 est.)
**Sex ratio:**
*at birth:* 1.06 male(s)/female
*under 15 years:* 1.06 male(s)/female
*15-64 years:* 1.03 male(s)/female
*65 years and over:* 0.79 male(s)/female
*total population:* 0.98 male(s)/female (2009 est.)
**Infant mortality rate:**
*total:* 2.75 deaths/1,000 live births
*male:* 2.91 deaths/1,000 live births
*female:* 2.58 deaths/1,000 live births (2009 est.)
**Life expectancy at birth:**
*total population:* 80.86 years
*male:* 78.59 years
*female:* 83.26 years (2009 est.)
**Total fertility rate:** 1.67 children born/woman (2009 est.)
**HIV/AIDS - adult prevalence rate:** 0.1% (2007 est.)
**HIV/AIDS - people living with HIV/AIDS:** 6,200 (2007 est.)
**HIV/AIDS - deaths:** fewer than 100 (2007 est.)
**Nationality:**
*noun:* Swede(s)
*adjective:* Swedish
**Ethnic groups:** indigenous population: Swedes with Finnish and Sami minorities; foreign-born or first-generation immigrants: Finns, Yugoslavs, Danes, Norwegians, Greeks, Turks
**Religions:** Lutheran 87%, other (includes Roman Catholic, Orthodox, Baptist, Muslim, Jewish, and Buddhist) 13%
**Languages:** Swedish, small Sami- and Finnish-speaking minorities
**Literacy:**
*definition:* age 15 and over can read and write
*total population:* 99%
*male:* 99%
*female:* 99% (2003 est.)

# Sweden *(continued)*

**School life expectancy (primary to tertiary education):**
*total:* 16 years
*male:* 15 years
*female:* 17 years (2006)
**Education expenditures:** 7.1% of GDP (2005)

## Government

**Country name:**
*conventional long form:* Kingdom of Sweden
*conventional short form:* Sweden
*local long form:* Konungariket Sverige
*local short form:* Sverige
**Government type:** constitutional monarchy
**Capital:**
*name:* Stockholm
*geographic coordinates:* 59 20 N, 18 03 E
*time difference:* UTC+1 (6 hours ahead of Washington, DC during Standard Time)
*daylight saving time:* +1hr, begins last Sunday in March; ends last Sunday in October
**Administrative divisions:** 21 counties (lan, singular and plural); Blekinge, Dalarnas, Gavleborgs, Gotlands, Hallands, Jamtlands, Jonkopings, Kalmar, Kronobergs, Norrbottens, Orebro, Ostergotlands, Skane, Sodermanlands, Stockholm, Uppsala, Varmlands, Vasterbottens, Vasternorrlands, Vastmanlands, Vastra Gotalands
**Independence:** 6 June 1523 (Gustav VASA elected king)
**National holiday:** Swedish Flag Day, 6 June (1916); National Day, 6 June (1983)
**Constitution:** 1 January 1975
**Legal system:** civil law system influenced by customary law; accepts compulsory ICJ jurisdiction with reservations
**Suffrage:** 18 years of age; universal
**Executive branch:**
*chief of state:* King CARL XVI GUSTAF (since 19 September 1973); Heir Apparent Princess VICTORIA Ingrid Alice Desiree, daughter of the monarch (born 14July 1977)
*head of government:* Prime Minister Fredrik REINFELDT (since 5 October 2006)
*cabinet:* Cabinet appointed by the prime minister
*elections:* the monarchy is hereditary; following legislative elections, the prime minister is elected by the parliament; election last held on 17 September 2006 (next to be held in September 2010)
*election results:* Center-right coalition of Moderate, Center, Liberal, and Christian Democrats parties win 175 out of 349 votes; Fredrik REINFELDT becomes prime minister
**Legislative branch:** unicameral Parliament or Riksdag (349 seats; members are elected by popular vote on a proportional representation basis to serve four-year terms)
*elections:* last held on 17 September 2006 (next to be held in September 2010)

*election results:* percent of vote by party - Social Democrats 37.2%, Moderates 27.8%, Center Party 8.3%, Liberal People's Party 8.0%, Christian Democrats 6.9%, Left Party 6.3%, Greens 5.4%; seats by party - Social Democrats 130, Moderates 97, Center Party 29, Liberal People's Party 28, Christian Democrats 24, Left Party 22, Greens 19
**Judicial branch:** Supreme Court or Hogsta Domstolen (judges are appointed by the prime minister and the cabinet)
**Political parties and leaders:** Center Party [Maud OLOFSSON]; Christian Democratic Party [Goran HAGGLUND]; Environment Party the Greens [no formal leader but party spokespersons are Maria WETTERSTRAND and Peter ERIKSSON]; Left Party or V (formerly Communist) [Lars OHLY]; Liberal People's Party [Jan BJORKLUND]; Moderate Party (conservative) [Fredrik REINFELDT]; Social Democratic Party [Mona SAHLIN]
**Political pressure groups and leaders:** Children's Rights in Society; Central Association of Salaried Employees or TCO; Swedish Federation of Trade Unions or LO
*other:* media
**International organization participation:** ADB (nonregional member), AfDB (nonregional member), Arctic Council, Australia Group, BIS, CBSS, CE, CERN, EAPC, EBRD, EIB, ESA, EU, FAO, G-9, G-10, IADB, IAEA, IBRD, ICAO, ICC, ICCt, ICRM, IDA, IEA, IFAD, IFC, IFRCS, IHO, ILO, IMF, IMO, IMSO, Interpol, IOC, IOM, IPU, ISO, ITSO, ITU, ITUC, MIGA, MINURCAT, MONUC, NAM (guest), NC, NEA, NIB, NSG, OAS (observer), OECD, OPCW, OSCE, Paris Club, PCA, PFP, Schengen Convention, UN, UNCTAD, UNESCO, UNHCR, UNIDO, UNMIL, UNMIS, UNMOGIP, UNOMIG, UNRWA, UNTSO, UPU, WCO, WEU (observer), WFTU, WHO, WIPO, WMO, WTO, ZC
**Diplomatic representation in the US:**
*chief of mission:* Ambassador Jonas HAFSTROM
*chancery:* 2900 K Street NW, Washington, DC 20007
*telephone:* [1] (202) 467-2600
*FAX:* [1] (202) 467-2699
*consulate(s) general:* Los Angeles, New York
**Diplomatic representation from the US:**
*chief of mission:* Ambassador (vacant); Charge d'Affaires Robert J. SILVERMAN
*embassy:* Dag Hammarskjolds Vag 31, SE-11589 Stockholm
*mailing address:* American Embassy Stockholm, US Department of State, 5750 Stockholm Place, Washington, DC 20521-5750
*telephone:* [46] (08) 783 53 00
*FAX:* [46] (08) 661 19 64
**Flag description:** blue with a golden yellow cross extending to the edges of the flag; the vertical part of the cross is shifted to the hoist side in the style of the Dannebrog (Danish flag)

## Economy

**Economy - overview:** Aided by peace and neutrality for the whole of the 20th century, Sweden has achieved an enviable standard of living under a mixed system of high-tech capitalism and extensive welfare benefits. It has a modern distribution system, excellent internal and external communications, and a skilled labor force. In September 2003, Swedish voters turned down entry into the euro system concerned about the impact on the economy and sovereignty. Timber, hydropower, and iron ore constitute the resource base of an economy heavily oriented toward foreign trade. Privately owned firms account for about 90% of industrial output, of which the engineering sector accounts for 50% of output and exports. Agriculture accounts for only 1% of GDP and of employment. Until 2008, Sweden was in the midst of a sustained economic upswing, boosted by increased domestic demand and strong exports. This and robust finances offered the center-right government considerable scope to implement its reform program aimed at increasing employment, reducing welfare dependence, and streamlining the state's role in the economy. Despite strong finances and underlying fundamentals, the Swedish economy slid into recession in the third quarter of 2008 and growth continued downward in the fourth as deteriorating global conditions reduced export demand and consumption. On 3 February 2009, the Swedish Government announced a $6 billon rescue package for the banking sector.
**GDP (purchasing power parity):**
$348.6 billion (2008 est.)
$346.2 billion (2007)
$337.1 billion (2006)
*note:* data are in 2008 US dollars
**GDP (official exchange rate):** $512.9 billion (2008 est.)
**GDP - real growth rate:**
0.7% (2008 est.)
2.7% (2007 est.)
4.6% (2006 est.)
**GDP - per capita (PPP):**
$38,500 (2008 est.)
$38,300 (2007 est.)
$37,400 (2006 est.)
*note:* data are in 2008 US dollars
**GDP - composition by sector:**
*agriculture:* 1.5%
*industry:* 28.9%
*services:* 69.6% (2008 est.)
**Labor force:** 4.9 million (2008 est.)
**Labor force - by occupation:**
*agriculture:* 1.1%
*industry:* 28.2%
*services:* 70.7% (2008 est.)
**Unemployment rate:**
6.4% (2008 est.)
6.1% (2007 est.)
**Population below poverty line:** NA%

**Household income or consumption by percentage share:**
*lowest 10%:* 3.6%
*highest 10%:* 22.2% (2000)
**Distribution of family income - Gini index:** 23 (2005)
**Investment (gross fixed):** 19.6% of GDP (2008 est.)
**Budget:**
*revenues:* $270.5 billion
*expenditures:* $258.6 billion (2008 est.)
**Public debt:** 36.5% of GDP (2008 est.)
**Inflation rate (consumer prices):**
1.6% (November 2008 est.)
2.2% (2007 est.)
**Central bank discount rate:** 3.5% (31 December 2007)
**Commercial bank prime lending rate:** 4% (2004)
**Stock of money:** $217.1 billion (31 December 2007)
**Stock of quasi money:** $48.49 billion (31 December 2007)
**Stock of domestic credit:** $630.8 billion (31 December 2007)
**Market value of publicly traded shares:** $612.5 billion (31 December 2007)
**Agriculture - products:** barley, wheat, sugar beets; meat, milk
**Industries:** iron and steel, precision equipment (bearings, radio and telephone parts, armaments), wood pulp and paper products, processed foods, motor vehicles
**Industrial production growth rate:** 1.1% (2008 est.)
**Electricity - production:** 143.8 billion kWh (2007 est.)
**Electricity - consumption:** 133.6 billion kWh (2006 est.)
**Electricity - exports:** 14.74 billion kWh (2007)
**Electricity - imports:** 16.61 billion kWh (2007 est.)
**Oil - production:** 2,350 bbl/day (2007 est.)
**Oil - consumption:** 353,700 bbl/day (2007 est.)
**Oil - exports:** 219,200 bbl/day (2005)
**Oil - imports:** 581,000 bbl/day (2005)
**Oil - proved reserves:** 0 bbl (1 January 2006 est.)
**Natural gas - production:** 0 cu m (2007 est.)
**Natural gas - consumption:** 1.006 billion cu m (2007 est.)
**Natural gas - exports:** 0 cu m (2007 est.)
**Natural gas - imports:** 1.006 billion cu m (2007 est.)
**Natural gas - proved reserves:** 0 cu m (1 January 2006 est.)
**Current account balance:** $35.22 billion (2008 est.)
**Exports:** $185.1 billion f.o.b. (2008 est.)
**Exports - commodities:** machinery 35%, motor vehicles, paper products, pulp and wood, iron and steel products, chemicals
**Exports - partners:** Germany 10.4%, Norway 9.4%, US 7.6%, Denmark 7.4%, UK 7.1%, Finland 6.4%, Netherlands 5.1%, France 5%, Belgium 4.6% (2007)
**Imports:** $166.6 billion f.o.b. (2008 est.)

**Imports - commodities:** machinery, petroleum and petroleum products, chemicals, motor vehicles, iron and steel; foodstuffs, clothing
**Imports - partners:** Germany 18.4%, Denmark 9.2%, Norway 8.3%, UK 6.8%, Finland 6.1%, Netherlands 5.8%, France 5%, China 4.3%, Belgium 4.1% (2007)
**Reserves of foreign exchange and gold:** $31.04 billion (2006 est.)
**Debt - external:** $598.2 billion (30 June 2006)
**Stock of direct foreign investment - at home:** $225.9 billion (2008 est.)
**Stock of direct foreign investment - abroad:** $289.6 billion (2008 est.)
**Exchange rates:** Swedish kronor (SEK) per US dollar - 6.4074 (2008 est.), 6.7629 (2007), 7.3731 (2006), 7.4731 (2005), 7.3489 (2004)

## Communications

**Telephones - main lines in use:** 5.506 million (2007)
**Telephones - mobile cellular:** 10.371 million (2007)
**Telephone system:**
*general assessment:* highly developed telecommunications infrastructure; ranked among leading countries for fixed-line, mobile-cellular, Internet and broadband penetration
*domestic:* coaxial and multiconductor cables carry most of the voice traffic; parallel microwave radio relay systems carry some additional telephone channels
*international:* country code - 46; submarine cables provide links to other Nordic countries and Europe; satellite earth stations - 1 Intelsat (Atlantic Ocean), 1 Eutelsat, and 1 Inmarsat (Atlantic and Indian Ocean regions); note - Sweden shares the Inmarsat earth station with the other Nordic countries (Denmark, Finland, Iceland, and Norway)
**Radio broadcast stations:** AM 1, FM 124, shortwave 0 (2008)
**Television broadcast stations:** 252 (2008)
**Internet country code:** .se
**Internet hosts:** 3.579 million (2008)
**Internet users:** 7 million (2007)

## Transportation

**Airports:** 249 (2008)
**Airports - with paved runways:**
*total:* 152
*over 3,047 m:* 3
*2,438 to 3,047 m:* 12
*1,524 to 2,437 m:* 76
*914 to 1,523 m:* 25
*under 914 m:* 36 (2008)
**Airports - with unpaved runways:**
*total:* 97
*914 to 1,523 m:* 5
*under 914 m:* 92 (2008)
**Heliports:** 2 (2007)
**Pipelines:** gas 786 km (2008)

**Railways:**
*total:* 11,528 km
*standard gauge:* 11,528 km 1.435-m gauge (7,527 km electrified) (2006)
**Roadways:**
*total:* 425,300 km
*paved:* 139,300 km (includes 1,740 km of expressways)
*unpaved:* 286,000 km (2008)
**Waterways:** 2,052 km (2007)
**Merchant marine:**
*total:* 195
*by type:* bulk carrier 6, cargo 23, carrier 1, chemical tanker 45, passenger 4, passenger/cargo 36, petroleum tanker 15, roll on/roll off 37, specialized tanker 3, vehicle carrier 25
*foreign-owned:* 41 (Denmark 4, Estonia 2, Finland 12, Germany 5, Italy 9, Norway 7, UK 2)
*registered in other countries:* 207 (Antigua and Barbuda 1, Bahamas 4, Barbados 7, Bermuda 20, Cook Islands 8, Cyprus 2, Denmark 6, Finland 2, France 9, Germany 1, Gibraltar 13, Isle of Man 1, Italy 1, Liberia 10, Malaysia 3, Malta 2, Marshall Islands 1, Netherlands 28, Netherlands Antilles 1, Norway 34, Panama 6, Portugal 3, Saint Vincent and the Grenadines 2, Singapore 20, UK 17, US 5) (2008)
**Ports and terminals:** Brofjorden, Goteborg, Helsingborg, Lulea, Malmo, Stenungsund, Stockholm, Trelleborg, Visby

## Military

**Military branches:** Swedish Armed Forces (Forsvarsmakten): Army (Armen), Royal Swedish Navy (Marinen), Swedish Air Force (Svenska Flygvapnet) (2008)
**Military service age and obligation:** 18-47 years of age for male compulsory or voluntary military service; conscript service obligation: 7.5 months (Army), 7-15 months (Navy), 8-12 months (Air Force); after completing initial service, soldiers have a reserve commitment until age 47; women are eligible for voluntary military service (2009)
**Manpower available for military service:**
*males age 16-49:* 2,052,890
*females age 16-49:* 1,980,550 (2008 est.)
**Manpower fit for military service:**
*males age 16-49:* 1,705,746
*females age 16-49:* 1,645,070 (2009 est.)
**Manpower reaching militarily significant age annually:**
*male:* 62,262
*female:* 59,340 (2009 est.)
**Military expenditures:** 1.5% of GDP (2005 est.)

## Transnational Issues

**Disputes - international:** none

# Switzerland

## Introduction

**Background:** The Swiss Confederation was founded in 1291 as a defensive alliance among three cantons. In succeeding years, other localities joined the original three. The Swiss Confederation secured its independence from the Holy Roman Empire in 1499. A constitution of 1848, subsequently modified in 1874, replaced the confederation with a centralized federal government. Switzerland's sovereignty and neutrality have long been honored by the major European powers, and the country was not involved in either of the two World Wars. The political and economic integration of Europe over the past half century, as well as Switzerland's role in many UN and international organizations, has strengthened Switzerland's ties with its neighbors. However, the country did not officially become a UN member until 2002. Switzerland remains active in many UN and international organizations but retains a strong commitment to neutrality.

## Geography

**Location:** Central Europe, east of France, north of Italy

**Geographic coordinates:** 47 00 N, 8 00 E

**Map references:** Europe

**Area:**
*total:* 41,290 sq km
*land:* 39,770 sq km
*water:* 1,520 sq km

**Area - comparative:** slightly less than twice the size of New Jersey

**Land boundaries:**
*total:* 1,852 km
*border countries:* Austria 164 km, France 573 km, Italy 740 km, Liechtenstein 41 km, Germany 334 km

**Coastline:** 0 km (landlocked)

**Maritime claims:** none (landlocked)

**Climate:** temperate, but varies with altitude; cold, cloudy, rainy/snowy winters; cool to warm, cloudy, humid summers with occasional showers

**Terrain:** mostly mountains (Alps in south, Jura in northwest) with a central plateau of rolling hills, plains, and large lakes

**Elevation extremes:**
*lowest point:* Lake Maggiore 195 m
*highest point:* Dufourspitze 4,634 m

**Natural resources:** hydropower potential, timber, salt

**Land use:**
*arable land:* 9.91%
*permanent crops:* 0.58%
*other:* 89.51% (2005)

**Irrigated land:** 250 sq km (2003)

**Total renewable water resources:** 53.3 cu km (2005)

**Freshwater withdrawal (domestic/industrial/agricultural):**
*total:* 2.52 cu km/yr (24%/74%/2%)
*per capita:* 348 cu m/yr (2002)

**Natural hazards:** avalanches, landslides; flash floods

**Environment - current issues:** air pollution from vehicle emissions and open-air burning; acid rain; water pollution from increased use of agricultural fertilizers; loss of biodiversity

**Environment - international agreements:**
*party to:* Air Pollution, Air Pollution-Nitrogen Oxides, Air Pollution-Persistent Organic Pollutants, Air Pollution-Sulfur 85, Air Pollution-Sulfur 94, Air Pollution-Volatile Organic Compounds, Antarctic Treaty, Biodiversity, Climate Change, Climate Change-Kyoto Protocol, Desertification, Endangered Species, Environmental Modification, Hazardous Wastes, Marine Dumping, Marine Life Conservation, Ozone Layer Protection, Ship Pollution, Tropical Timber 83, Tropical Timber 94, Wetlands, Whaling
*signed, but not ratified:* Law of the Sea

## People

**Population:** 7,604,467 (July 2009 est.)

**Age structure:**
*0-14 years:* 15.6% (male 616,561/female 571,610)
*15-64 years:* 68.1% (male 2,609,673/female 2,567,245)
*65 years and over:* 16.3% (male 514,761/female 724,617) (2009 est.)

**Median age:**
*total:* 41 years
*male:* 40 years
*female:* 42 years (2009 est.)

**Population growth rate:** 0.276% (2009 est.)

**Birth rate:** 9.59 births/1,000 population (2009 est.)

**Death rate:** 8.54 deaths/1,000 population (2008 est.)

**Net migration rate:** 1.76 migrant(s)/1,000 population (2009 est.)

**Urbanization:**
*urban population:* 73% of total population (2008)
*rate of urbanization:* 0.5% annual rate of change (2005-10 est.)

**Sex ratio:**
*at birth:* 1.05 male(s)/female
*under 15 years:* 1.08 male(s)/female
*15-64 years:* 1.02 male(s)/female
*65 years and over:* 0.71 male(s)/female
*total population:* 0.97 male(s)/female (2009 est.)

**Infant mortality rate:**
*total:* 4.18 deaths/1,000 live births
*male:* 4.64 deaths/1,000 live births
*female:* 3.68 deaths/1,000 live births (2009 est.)

**Life expectancy at birth:**
*total population:* 80.85 years
*male:* 78.03 years
*female:* 83.83 years (2009 est.)

**Total fertility rate:** 1.45 children born/woman (2009 est.)

**HIV/AIDS - adult prevalence rate:** 0.6% (2007 est.)

**HIV/AIDS - people living with HIV/AIDS:** 25,000 (2007 est.)

**HIV/AIDS - deaths:** fewer than 500 (2007 est.)

**Nationality:**
*noun:* Swiss (singular and plural)
*adjective:* Swiss

**Ethnic groups:** German 65%, French 18%, Italian 10%, Romansch 1%, other 6%

**Religions:** Roman Catholic 41.8%, Protestant 35.3%, Muslim 4.3%, Orthodox 1.8%, other Christian 0.4%, other 1%, unspecified 4.3%, none 11.1% (2000 census)

**Languages:** German (official) 63.7%, French (official) 20.4%, Italian (official) 6.5%, Serbo-Croatian 1.5%, Albanian 1.3%, Portuguese 1.2%, Spanish 1.1%, English 1%, Romansch (official) 0.5%, other 2.8% (2000 census)
*note:* German, French, Italian, and Romansch are all national and official languages

# Switzerland (continued)

**Literacy:**
*definition:* age 15 and over can read and write
*total population:* 99%
*male:* 99%
*female:* 99% (2003 est.)
**School life expectancy (primary to tertiary education):**
*total:* 15 years
*male:* 15 years
*female:* 15 years (2006)
**Education expenditures:** 5.8% of GDP (2005)

## Government

**Country name:**
*conventional long form:* Swiss Confederation
*conventional short form:* Switzerland
*local long form:* Schweizerische Eidgenossenschaft (German); Confederation Suisse (French); Confederazione Svizzera (Italian); Confederaziun Svizra (Romansh)
*local short form:* Schweiz (German); Suisse (French); Svizzera (Italian); Svizra (Romansh)
**Government type:** formally a confederation but similar in structure to a federal republic
**Capital:**
*name:* Bern
*geographic coordinates:* 46 57 N, 7 26 E
*time difference:* UTC+1 (6 hours ahead of Washington, DC during Standard Time)
*daylight saving time:* +1hr, begins last Sunday in March; ends last Sunday in October
**Administrative divisions:** 26 cantons, singular - canton in French; cantoni, singular - cantone in Italian; Kantone, singular - Kanton in German); Aargau, Appenzell Ausser-Rhoden, Appenzell Inner-Rhoden, Basel-Landschaft, Basel-Stadt, Bern, Fribourg, Geneve, Glarus, Graubunden, Jura, Luzern, Neuchatel, Nidwalden, Obwalden, Sankt Gallen, Schaffhausen, Schwyz, Solothurn, Thurgau, Ticino, Uri, Valais, Vaud, Zug, Zurich
*note:* 6 of the cantons - Appenzell Ausser-Rhoden, Appenzell-Inner-Rhoden, Basel-Landschaft, Basel-Stadt, Nidwalden, Obwalden - are styled half cantons because they elect only one member to the Council of States and, in popular referendums where a majority of popular votes and a majority of cantonal votes are required, these six cantons only have a half vote
**Independence:** 1 August 1291 (founding of the Swiss Confederation)
**National holiday:** Founding of the Swiss Confederation, 1 August (1291)
**Constitution:** revision of Constitution of 1874 approved by the Federal Parliament 18 December 1998, adopted by referendum 18 April 1999, officially entered into force 1 January 2000
**Legal system:** civil law system influenced by customary law; judicial review of legislative acts, except with respect to federal decrees of general obligatory character; accepts compulsory ICJ jurisdiction with reservations

**Suffrage:** 18 years of age; universal
**Executive branch:**
*chief of state:* President Hans-Rudolf MERZ (since 1 January 2009); Vice President Doris LEUTHARD (since 1 January 2009); note - the president is both the chief of state and head of government representing the Federal Council; the Federal Council is the formal chief of state and head of government whose council members, rotating in one-year terms as federal president, represent the Council
*head of government:* President Hans-Rudolf MERZ (since 1 January 2009); Vice President Doris LEUTHARD (since 1 January 2009);
*cabinet:* Federal Council or Bundesrat (in German), Conseil Federal (in French), Consiglio Federale (in Italian) elected by the Federal Assembly usually from among its members for a four-year term
*elections:* president and vice president elected by the Federal Assembly from among the members of the Federal Council for a one-year term (they may not serve consecutive terms); election last held on 10 December 2008 (next to be held in December 2009)
*election results:* Hans-Rudolf MERZ elected president; percent of Federal Assembly vote - 88.5%; Doris LEUTHARD elected vice president; percent of Federal Assembly vote - 87.4%
**Legislative branch:** bicameral Federal Assembly or Bundesversammlung (in German), Assemblee Federale (in French), Assemblea Federale (in Italian) consists of the Council of States or Standerat (in German), Conseil des Etats (in French), Consiglio degli Stati (in Italian) (46 seats; membership consists of 2 representatives from each canton and 1 from each half canton; to serve four-year terms) and the National Council or Nationalrat (in German), Conseil National (in French), Consiglio Nazionale (in Italian) (200 seats; members are elected by popular vote on the basis of proportional representation to serve four-year terms)
*elections:* Council of States - last held in most cantons in October 2007 (each canton determines when the next election will be held); National Council - last held on 21 October 2007 (next to be held in October 2011)
*election results:* Council of States - percent of vote by party - NA; seats by party - CVP 15, FDP 12, SVP 7, SPS 9, other 3; National Council - percent of vote by party - SVP 29%, SPS 19.5%, FDP 15.6%, CVP 14.6%, Greens 9.6%, other 11.7%; seats by party - SVP 62, SPS 43, FDP 31, CVP 31, Green Party 20, other small parties 13
**Judicial branch:** Federal Supreme Court (judges elected for six-year terms by the Federal Assembly)
**Political parties and leaders:** Green Party (Gruene Partei der Schweiz or Gruene, Parti Ecologiste Suisse or Les Verts, Partito Ecologista Svizzero or I Verdi, Partida Ecologica Svizra or La Verda) [Ueli LEUENBERGER]; Christian Democratic People's Party (Christlichdemokratische Volkspartei der Schweiz or CVP, Parti Democrate-Chretien Suisse or PDC, Partito Democratico-Cristiano Popolare Svizzero or PDC, Partida Cristiandemocratica dalla

Svizra or PCD) [Christophe DARBELLAY]; Radical Free Democratic Party (Freisinnig-Demokratische Partei der Schweiz or FDP, Parti Radical-Democratique Suisse or PRD, Partitio Liberal-Radicale Svizzero or PLR) [Fulvio PELLI]; Social Democratic Party (Sozialdemokratische Partei der Schweiz or SPS, Parti Socialist Suisse or PSS, Partito Socialista Svizzero or PSS, Partida Socialdemocratica de la Svizra or PSS) [Christian LEVRAT]; Swiss People's Party (Schweizerische Volkspartei or SVP, Union Democratique du Centre or UDC, Unione Democratica de Centro or UDC, Uniun Democratica dal Center or UDC) [Toni BRUNNER]; and other minor parties
**Political pressure groups and leaders:** NA
**International organization participation:** ADB (nonregional member), AfDB (nonregional member), Australia Group, BIS, CE, CERN, EAPC, EBRD, EFTA, ESA, FAO, G-10, IADB, IAEA, IBRD, ICAO, ICC, ICCt, ICRM, IDA, IEA, IFAD, IFC, IFRCS, ILO, IMF, IMO, IMSO, Interpol, IOC, IOM, IPU, ISO, ITSO, ITU, ITUC, LAIA (observer), MIGA, MONUC, NAM (guest), NEA, NSG, OAS (observer), OECD, OIF, OPCW, OSCE, Paris Club, PCA, PFP, UN, UNCTAD, UNESCO, UNHCR, UNIDO, UNITAR, UNOMIG, UNRWA, UNTSO, UNWTO, UPU, WCL, WCO, WFTU, WHO, WIPO, WMO, WTO, ZC
**Diplomatic representation in the US:**
*chief of mission:* Ambassador Urs ZISWILER
*chancery:* 2900 Cathedral Avenue NW, Washington, DC 20008
*telephone:* [1] (202) 745-7900
*FAX:* [1] (202) 387-2564
*consulate(s) general:* Atlanta, Chicago, Los Angeles, New York, San Francisco
*consulate(s):* Boston
**Diplomatic representation from the US:**
*chief of mission:* Ambassador (vacant); Charge d'Affaires Leigh CARTER
*embassy:* Sulgeneckstrasse 19, CH-3007 Bern
*mailing address:* use embassy street address
*telephone:* [41] (031) 357 70 11
*FAX:* [41] (031) 357 73 44
**Flag description:** red square with a bold, equilateral white cross in the center that does not extend to the edges of the flag

## Economy

**Economy - overview:** Switzerland is a peaceful, prosperous, and stable modern market economy with low unemployment, a highly skilled labor force, and a per capita GDP among the highest in the world. Switzerland's economy benefits from a highly developed service sector led by financial services and a manufacturing industry that specializes in high-technology, knowledge-based production. The Swiss in recent years have brought their economic practices largely into conformity with the EU's to enhance their international competitiveness, but some trade protectionism remains, particularly for its small agricultural sector. Switzerland remains a safehaven for investors, because it has maintained a degree of bank secrecy and has kept up the franc's long-term external value. The global financial crisis and resulting economic downturn could, however, put Switzerland in a recession in 2009, particularly as global export demand stalls. Switzerland's largest banks suffered significant losses in 2008 and the country's largest bank accepted a government rescue deal in late 2008. The Swiss National Bank, beginning in October 2008, cut interest rates on several consecutive occasions, effectively instituting a zero-rate policy in a bid to boost the economy.

**GDP (purchasing power parity):**
$309.9 billion (2008 est.)
$310 billion (2007)
$300.1 billion (2006)
*note:* data are in 2008 US dollars

**GDP (official exchange rate):** $492.6 billion (2008 est.)

**GDP - real growth rate:**
1.9% (2008 est.)
3.3% (2007 est.)
3.4% (2006 est.)

**GDP - per capita (PPP):**
$40,900 (2008 est.)
$41,000 (2007 est.)
$39,900 (2006 est.)
*note:* data are in 2008 US dollars

**GDP - composition by sector:**
*agriculture:* 1.5%
*industry:* 34%
*services:* 64.5% (2003 est.)

**Labor force:** 4.04 million (2008 est.)

**Labor force - by occupation:**
*agriculture:* 3.9%
*industry:* 22.8%
*services:* 73.2% (2005)

**Unemployment rate:**
3% (December 2008)
2.8% (2007 est.)

**Population below poverty line:** NA%

**Household income or consumption by percentage share:**
*lowest 10%:* 2.9%
*highest 10%:* 25.9% (2000)

**Distribution of family income - Gini index:** 33.7 (2008)

**Investment (gross fixed):** 21.5% of GDP (2008 est.)

**Budget:**
*revenues:* $173.6 billion
*expenditures:* $168.2 billion (2008 est.)

**Public debt:** 44% of GDP (2008 est.)

**Inflation rate (consumer prices):**
2.4% (2008 est.)
0.7% (2007 est.)

**Central bank discount rate:** 2.05% (31 December 2007)

**Commercial bank prime lending rate:** 3.15% (31 December 2007)

**Stock of money:** $207 billion (31 December 2008 est.)

**Stock of quasi money:** $477.6 billion (31 December 2008 est.)

**Stock of domestic credit:** $864.4 billion (31 December 2008 est.)

**Market value of publicly traded shares:** $1.275 trillion (31 December 2007)

**Agriculture - products:** grains, fruits, vegetables; meat, eggs

**Industries:** machinery, chemicals, watches, textiles, precision instruments, tourism, banking, and insurance

**Industrial production growth rate:** 6.5% (2006 est.)

**Electricity - production:** 64.56 billion kWh (2007 est.)

**Electricity - consumption:** 58.77 billion kWh (2006 est.)

**Electricity - exports:** 50.2 billion kWh (2007 est.)

**Electricity - imports:** 48.4 billion kWh (2007 est.)

**Oil - production:** 3,202 bbl/day (2007 est.)

**Oil - consumption:** 244,900 bbl/day (2007 est.)

**Oil - exports:** 9,370 bbl/day (2005)

**Oil - imports:** 274,900 bbl/day (2005)

**Oil - proved reserves:** NA

**Natural gas - production:** 0 cu m (2007 est.)

**Natural gas - consumption:** 3.232 billion cu m (2007 est.)

**Natural gas - exports:** 0 cu m (2007 est.)

**Natural gas - imports:** 3.232 billion cu m (2007 est.)

**Natural gas - proved reserves:** 0 cu m (1 January 2006 est.)

**Current account balance:** $40.81 billion (2008 est.)

**Exports:** $172.7 billion f.o.b. (2008 est.)

**Exports - commodities:** machinery, chemicals, metals, watches, agricultural products

**Exports - partners:** Germany 20.3%, US 9.7%, Italy 8.7%, France 8.4%, UK 5.1% (2007)

**Imports:** $212.8 billion f.o.b. (2008 est.)

**Imports - commodities:** machinery, chemicals, vehicles, metals; agricultural products, textiles

**Imports - partners:** Germany 32.6%, Italy 10.8%, France 9.5%, US 5.8%, Netherlands 4.6%, Austria 4.2%, UK 4.2% (2007)

**Reserves of foreign exchange and gold:** $75.37 billion (2008 est.)

**Debt - external:** $1.34 trillion (30 June 2007)

**Stock of direct foreign investment - at home:** $333.8 billion (2008 est.)

**Stock of direct foreign investment - abroad:** $621.7 billion (2008 est.)

**Exchange rates:** Swiss francs (CHF) per US dollar - 1.0774 (2008 est.), 1.1973 (2007), 1.2539 (2006), 1.2452 (2005), 1.2435 (2004)

## Communications

**Telephones - main lines in use:** 5 million (2007)

**Telephones - mobile cellular:** 8.096 million (2007)

**Telephone system:**
*general assessment:* highly developed telecommunications infrastructure with excellent domestic and international services
*domestic:* ranked among leading countries for fixed-line teledensity and infrastructure; mobile-cellular subscribership roughly 100 per 100 persons; extensive cable and microwave radio relay networks
*international:* country code - 41; satellite earth stations -2 Intelsat (Atlantic Ocean and Indian Ocean)

**Radio broadcast stations:** AM 3, FM 106 (plus many low-power stations), shortwave 3 (2008)

**Television broadcast stations:** 106 (2007)

**Internet country code:** .ch

**Internet hosts:** 3.437 million (2008)

**Internet users:** 4.61 million (2007)

## Transportation

**Airports:** 66 (2008)

**Airports - with paved runways:**
*total:* 43
*over 3,047 m:* 3
*2,438 to 3,047 m:* 4
*1,524 to 2,437 m:* 14
*914 to 1,523 m:* 5
*under 914 m:* 17 (2008)

**Airports - with unpaved runways:**
*total:* 23
*under 914 m:* 23 (2008)

**Heliports:** 2 (2007)

**Pipelines:** gas 1,662 km; oil 94 km; refined products 7 km (2008)

**Railways:**
*total:* 4,839 km
*standard gauge:* 3,561 km 1.435-m gauge (3,195 km electrified)
*narrow gauge:* 1,268 km 1.000-m gauge (1,274 km electrified); 10 km 0.800-m gauge (10 km electrified) (2006)

**Roadways:**
*total:* 71,298 km
*paved:* 71,298 km (includes 1,758 of expressways) (2006)

**Waterways:** 65 km (Rhine River between Basel-Rheinfelden and Schaffhausen-Bodensee) (2008)

**Merchant marine:**
*total:* 35
*by type:* bulk carrier 13, cargo 9, chemical tanker 6, container 6, specialized tanker 1
*registered in other countries:* 106 (Antigua and Barbuda 8, Bahamas 1, France 3, Italy 8, Liberia 13, Malta 20, Marshall Islands 12, Panama 25, Portugal 2, Russia 3, Saint Vincent and the Grenadines 6, Singapore 2, Tonga 1, UK 1, Vanuatu 1) (2008)

**Ports and terminals:** Basel

## Military

**Military branches:** Swiss Armed Forces: Land Forces, Swiss Air Force (Schweizer Luftwaffe) (2009)

**Military service age and obligation:** 19 years of age for male compulsory military service; 18 years of age for voluntary male and female military service; the

Swiss Constitution states that "every Swiss male is obliged to do military service"; every Swiss male has to serve at least 260 days in the armed forces; conscripts receive 18 weeks of mandatory training, followed by seven 3-week intermittent recalls for training during the next 10 years (2008)

**Manpower available for military service:**
*males age 16-49:* 1,852,580
*females age 16-49:* 1,807,667 (2008 est.)
**Manpower fit for military service:**
*males age 16-49:* 1,510,259
*females age 16-49:* 1,475,993 (2009 est.)
**Manpower reaching militarily significant age annually:**
*male:* 48,076
*female:* 44,049 (2009 est.)
**Military expenditures:** 1% of GDP (2005 est.)

### Transnational Issues

**Disputes - international:** none
**Illicit drugs:** a major international financial center vulnerable to the layering and integration stages of money laundering; despite significant legislation and reporting requirements, secrecy rules persist and nonresidents are permitted to conduct business through offshore entities and various intermediaries; transit country for and consumer of South American cocaine, Southwest Asian heroin, and Western European synthetics; domestic cannabis cultivation and limited ecstasy production

# Syria

### Introduction

**Background:** Following the breakup of the Ottoman Empire during World War I, France administered Syria until its independence in 1946. The country lacked political stability, however, and experienced a series of military coups during its first decades. Syria united with Egypt in February 1958 to form the United Arab Republic. In September 1961, the two entities separated, and the Syrian Arab Republic was reestablished. In November 1970, Hafiz al-ASAD, a member of the Socialist Ba'th Party and the minority Alawite sect, seized power in a bloodless coup and brought political stability to the country. In the 1967 Arab-Israeli War, Syria lost the Golan Heights to Israel. During the 1990s, Syria and Israel held occasional peace talks over its return. Following the death of President al-ASAD, his son, Bashar al-ASAD, was approved as president by popular referendum in July 2000. Syrian troops - stationed in Lebanon since 1976 in an ostensible peacekeeping role - were withdrawn in April 2005. During the July-August 2006 conflict between Israel and Hizballah, Syria placed its military forces on alert but did not intervene directly on behalf of its ally Hizballah.

### Geography

**Location:** Middle East, bordering the Mediterranean Sea, between Lebanon and Turkey
**Geographic coordinates:** 35 00 N, 38 00 E
**Map references:** Middle East
**Area:**
*total:* 185,180 sq km
*land:* 184,050 sq km
*water:* 1,130 sq km
*note:* includes 1,295 sq km of Israeli-occupied territory
**Area - comparative:** slightly larger than North Dakota
**Land boundaries:**
*total:* 2,253 km
*border countries:* Iraq 605 km, Israel 76 km, Jordan 375 km, Lebanon 375 km, Turkey 822 km

**Coastline:** 193 km
**Maritime claims:**
*territorial sea:* 12 nm
*contiguous zone:* 24 nm
**Climate:** mostly desert; hot, dry, sunny summers (June to August) and mild, rainy winters (December to February) along coast; cold weather with snow or sleet periodically in Damascus
**Terrain:** primarily semiarid and desert plateau; narrow coastal plain; mountains in west
**Elevation extremes:**
*lowest point:* unnamed location near Lake Tiberias -200 m
*highest point:* Mount Hermon 2,814 m
**Natural resources:** petroleum, phosphates, chrome and manganese ores, asphalt, iron ore, rock salt, marble, gypsum, hydropower
**Land use:**
*arable land:* 24.8%
*permanent crops:* 4.47%
*other:* 70.73% (2005)
**Irrigated land:** 13,330 sq km (2003)
**Total renewable water resources:** 46.1 cu km (1997)
**Freshwater withdrawal (domestic/industrial/agricultural):**
*total:* 19.95 cu km/yr (3%/2%/95%)
*per capita:* 1,048 cu m/yr (2000)
**Natural hazards:** dust storms, sandstorms
**Environment - current issues:** deforestation; overgrazing; soil erosion; desertification; water pollution from raw sewage and petroleum refining wastes; inadequate potable water
**Environment - international agreements:**
*party to:* Biodiversity, Climate Change, Climate Change-Kyoto Protocol, Desertification, Endangered Species, Hazardous Wastes, Ozone Layer Protection, Ship Pollution, Wetlands
*signed, but not ratified:* Environmental Modification
**Geography - note:** there are 42 Israeli settlements and civilian land use sites in the Israeli-occupied Golan Heights (August 2005 est.)

### People

**Population:** 20,178,485
*note:* in addition, about 40,000 people live in the Israeli-occupied Golan Heights - 20,000 Arabs (18,000 Druze and 2,000 Alawites) and about 20,000 Israeli settlers (July 2009 est.)
**Age structure:**
*0-14 years:* 35.9% (male 3,724,770/female 3,510,182)
*15-64 years:* 60.8% (male 6,285,866/female 5,980,029)
*65 years and over:* 3.4% (male 318,646/female 358,992) (2009 est.)
**Median age:**
*total:* 21.7 years
*male:* 21.6 years
*female:* 21.9 years (2009 est.)
**Population growth rate:** 2.129% (2009 est.)
**Birth rate:** 25.9 births/1,000 population (2009 est.)
**Death rate:** 4.68 deaths/1,000 population (2008 est.)

**Net migration rate:** NA

**Urbanization:**

*urban population:* 54% of total population (2008)

*rate of urbanization:* 3.1% annual rate of change (2005-10 est.)

**Sex ratio:**

*at birth:* 1.06 male(s)/female

*under 15 years:* 1.06 male(s)/female

*15-64 years:* 1.05 male(s)/female

*65 years and over:* 0.89 male(s)/female

*total population:* 1.05 male(s)/female (2009 est.)

**Infant mortality rate:**

*total:* 25.87 deaths/1,000 live births

*male:* 26.13 deaths/1,000 live births

*female:* 25.59 deaths/1,000 live births (2009 est.)

**Life expectancy at birth:**

*total population:* 71.19 years

*male:* 69.8 years

*female:* 72.68 years (2009 est.)

**Total fertility rate:** 3.12 children born/woman (2009 est.)

**HIV/AIDS - adult prevalence rate:** less than 0.1% (2001 est.)

**HIV/AIDS - people living with HIV/AIDS:** fewer than 500 (2003 est.)

**HIV/AIDS - deaths:** fewer than 200 (2003 est.)

**Nationality:**

*noun:* Syrian(s)

*adjective:* Syrian

**Ethnic groups:** Arab 90.3%, Kurds, Armenians, and other 9.7%

**Religions:** Sunni Muslim 74%, other Muslim (includes Alawite, Druze) 16%, Christian (various denominations) 10%, Jewish (tiny communities in Damascus, Al Qamishli, and Aleppo)

**Languages:** Arabic (official); Kurdish, Armenian, Aramaic, Circassian widely understood; French, English somewhat understood

**Literacy:**

*definition:* age 15 and over can read and write

*total population:* 79.6%

*male:* 86%

*female:* 73.6% (2004 census)

**Education expenditures:** 3.9% of GDP (1999)

## Government

**Country name:**

*conventional long form:* Syrian Arab Republic

*conventional short form:* Syria

*local long form:* Al Jumhuriyah al Arabiyah as Suriyah

*local short form:* Suriyah

*former:* United Arab Republic (with Egypt)

**Government type:** republic under an authoritarian military-dominated regime

**Capital:**

*name:* Damascus

*geographic coordinates:* 33 30 N, 36 18 E

*time difference:* UTC+2 (7 hours ahead of Washington, DC during Standard Time)

*daylight saving time:* +1hr, begins 1 April; ends 30 September

**Administrative divisions:** 14 provinces (muhafazat, singular - muhafazah); Al Hasakah, Al Ladhiqiyah, Al Qunaytirah, Ar Raqqah, As Suwayda', Dar'a, Dayr az Zawr, Dimashq, Halab, Hamah, Hims, Idlib, Rif Dimashq, Tartus

**Independence:** 17 April 1946 (from League of Nations mandate under French administration)

**National holiday:** Independence Day, 17 April (1946)

**Constitution:** 13 March 1973

**Legal system:** based on a combination of French and Ottoman civil law; Islamic law is used in the family court system; has not accepted compulsory ICJ jurisdiction

**Suffrage:** 18 years of age; universal

**Executive branch:**

*chief of state:* President Bashar al-ASAD (since 17 July 2000); Vice President Farouk al-SHARA (since 11 February 2006) oversees foreign policy; Vice President Najah al-ATTAR (since 23 March 2006) oversees cultural policy

*head of government:* Prime Minister Muhammad Naji al-UTRI (since 10 September 2003); Deputy Prime Minister for Economic Affairs Abdallah al-DARDARI (since 14 June 2005)

*cabinet:* Council of Ministers appointed by the president

*elections:* president approved by popular referendum for a second seven-year term (no term limits); referendum last held on 27 May 2007 (next to be held in May 2014); the president appoints the vice presidents, prime minister, and deputy prime ministers

*election results:* Bashar al-ASAD approved as president; percent of vote - Bashar al-ASAD 97.6%

**Legislative branch:** unicameral People's Council or Majlis al-Shaab (250 seats; members elected by popular vote to serve four-year terms)

*elections:* last held on 22-23 April 2007 (next to be held in 2011)

*election results:* percent of vote by party - NA; seats by party - NPF 172, independents 78

**Judicial branch:** Supreme Judicial Council (appoints and dismisses judges; headed by the president); national level - Supreme Constitutional Court (adjudicates electoral disputes and rules on constitutionality of laws and decrees; justices appointed for four-year terms by the president); Court of Cassation; Appeals Courts (Appeals Courts represent an intermediate level between the Court of Cassation and local level courts); local level - Magistrate Courts; Courts of First Instance; Juvenile Courts; Customs Courts; specialized courts - Economic Security Courts (hear cases related to economic crimes); Supreme State Security Court (hear cases related to national security); Personal Status Courts (religious; hear cases related to marriage and divorce)

**Political parties and leaders:**

*legal parties:* National Progressive Front or NPF [President Bashar al-ASAD, Dr. Suleiman QADDAH] (includes Arab Socialist Renaissance (Ba'th) Party [President Bashar al-ASAD]; Socialist Unionist

Democratic Party [Fadlallah Nasr Al-DIN]; Syrian Arab Socialist Union or ASU [Safwan QUDSI]; Syrian Communist Party (two branches) [Wissal Farha BAKDASH, Yusuf Rashid FAYSAL]; Syrian Social Nationalist Party [Ali QANSU]; Unionist Socialist Party [Fayez ISMAIL])

*opposition parties not legally recognized:* Arab Democratic Socialist Union Party [Hasan Abdul AZIM]; Arab Socialist Movement; Democratic Ba'th Party [Ibrahim MAHKOS]; National Democratic Front [Hasan Abdul AZIM, spokesman] (includes five parties - Arab Democratic Socialist Union Party [Hasan Abdul AZIM], Arab Socialist Movement, Democratic Ba'th Party [Ibrahim MAHKOS], People's Democratic Party [Riad al TURK], Revolutionary Workers' Party [Abdul Hafeez al HAFEZ]); People's Democratic Party; Revolutionary Workers' Party [Abdul Hafeez al HAFEZ]

*Kurdish parties (considered illegal):* Azadi Party [Kheirudin MURAD]; Future Party [Masha'l TAMMO]; Kurdish Democratic Alliance (includes four parties); Kurdish Democratic Front (includes three parties); Yekiti Party [Hasan SALEH, Fu'ad ALEYKO]

*other parties:* Nahda Party [Abdul Aziz al MISLET]; Syrian Democratic Party [Mustafa QALAAJI]

**Political pressure groups and leaders:** Damascus Declaration National Council [Riyad SEIF, secretary general] (a broad alliance of opposition groups and individuals including: Committee for Revival of Civil Society [Michel KILO, Riyad SEIF]; Communist Action Party [Fateh JAMOUS]; Kurdish Democratic Alliance; Kurdish Democratic Front; Liberal Nationalists' Movement; National Democratic Rally; and Syrian Human Rights Society or HRAS [Fawed FAWUZ]); National Salvation Front (alliance between former Vice President Abd al-Halim KHADDAM, the SMB, and other small opposition groups); Syrian Muslim Brotherhood or SMB [Sadr al-Din al-BAYANUNI] (operates in exile in London; endorsed the Damascus Declaration, but is not an official member)

**International organization participation:** ABEDA, AFESD, AMF, CAEU, FAO, G-24, G-77, IAEA, IBRD, ICAO, ICC, ICCt (signatory), ICRM, IDA, IDB, IFAD, IFC, IFRCS, IHO, ILO, IMF, IMO, Interpol, IOC, IPU, ISO, ITSO, ITU, LAS, MIGA, NAM, OAPEC, OIC, UN, UNCTAD, UNESCO, UNIDO, UNRWA, UNWTO, UPU, WCO, WFTU, WHO, WIPO, WMO

**Diplomatic representation in the US:**

*chief of mission:* Ambassador Imad MOUSTAPHA

*chancery:* 2215 Wyoming Avenue NW, Washington, DC 20008

*telephone:* [1] (202) 232-6313

*FAX:* [1] (202) 265-4585

**Diplomatic representation from the US:**

*chief of mission:* Ambassador (vacant); Charge d'Affaires Maura CONNELLY

*embassy:* Abou Roumaneh, Al-Mansour Street, No. 2, Damascus

*mailing address:* P. O. Box 29, Damascus

*telephone:* [963] (11) 3391-4444

*FAX:* [963] (11) 3391-3999

# Syria (continued)

**Flag description:** three equal horizontal bands of red (top), white, and black, colors associated with the Arab Liberation flag; two small, green, five-pointed stars in a horizontal line centered in the white band; former flag of the United Arab Republic where the two stars represented the constituent states of Syria and Egypt; similar to the flag of Yemen, which has a plain white band, Iraq, which has an Arabic inscription centered in the white band, and that of Egypt, which has a gold Eagle of Saladin centered in the white band; the current design dates to 1980

## Economy

**Economy - overview:** The Syrian economy grew by an estimated 2.4% in real terms in 2008 led by the petroleum and agricultural sectors, which together account for about one-half of GDP. Higher crude oil prices countered declining oil production and led to higher budgetary and export receipts. Damascus has implemented modest economic reforms in the past few years, including cutting lending interest rates, opening private banks, consolidating all of the multiple exchange rates, raising prices on some subsidized items, most notably gasoline and cement, and establishing the Damascus Stock Exchange - which is set to begin operations in 2009. In October 2007, for example, Damascus raised the price of subsidized gasoline by 20%, then instituted a rationing system in 2008. In addition, President ASAD signed legislative decrees to encourage corporate ownership reform, and to allow the Central Bank to issue Treasury bills and bonds for government debt. Nevertheless, the economy remains highly controlled by the government. Long-run economic constraints include declining oil production, high unemployment and inflation, rising budget deficits, and increasing pressure on water supplies caused by heavy use in agriculture, rapid population growth, industrial expansion, and water pollution.

**GDP (purchasing power parity):**
$95.36 billion (2008 est.)
$90.99 billion (2007)
$87.15 billion (2006)
*note:* data are in 2008 US dollars

**GDP (official exchange rate):** $44.49 billion (2008 est.)

**GDP - real growth rate:**
4.8% (2008 est.)
4.4% (2007 est.)
5.1% (2006 est.)

**GDP - per capita (PPP):**
$4,800 (2008 est.)
$4,700 (2007 est.)
$4,600 (2006 est.)
*note:* data are in 2008 US dollars

**GDP - composition by sector:**
*agriculture:* 22.5%
*industry:* 27.9%
*services:* 49.6% (2008 est.)

**Labor force:** 5.547 million (2008 est.)

**Labor force - by occupation:**
*agriculture:* 19.2%
*industry:* 14.5%
*services:* 66.3% (2006 est.)

**Unemployment rate:**
9% (2008 est.)
9% (2007 est.)

**Population below poverty line:** 11.9% (2006 est.)

**Household income or consumption by percentage share:**
*lowest 10%:* NA%
*highest 10%:* NA%

**Investment (gross fixed):** 22.6% of GDP (2008 est.)

**Budget:**
*revenues:* $10.9 billion
*expenditures:* $13.77 billion (2008 est.)

**Public debt:** 41.2% of GDP (2008 est.)

**Inflation rate (consumer prices):**
14.9% (2008 est.)
12.2% (2007 est.)

**Commercial bank prime lending rate:** 7% (6 November 2008)

**Stock of money:** $14.29 billion (30 September 2008)

**Stock of quasi money:** $25.67 billion (30 September 2008)

**Stock of domestic credit:** $50.92 billion (31 December 2006)

**Market value of publicly traded shares:** $NA

**Agriculture - products:** wheat, barley, cotton, lentils, chickpeas, olives, sugar beets; beef, mutton, eggs, poultry, milk

**Industries:** petroleum, textiles, food processing, beverages, tobacco, phosphate rock mining, cement, oil seeds crushing, car assembly

**Industrial production growth rate:** 3.2% (2008 est.)

**Electricity - production:** 40.5 billion kWh (2007)
**Electricity - consumption:** 39.5 billion kWh (2007)
**Electricity - exports:** 991 million kWh (2007 est.)
**Electricity - imports:** 1.4 billion kWh (2007)

**Oil - production:** 381,600 bbl/day (2008 est.)
**Oil - consumption:** 229,000 bbl/day (2007 est.)
**Oil - exports:** 155,000 bbl/day (2008 est.)
**Oil - imports:** 160,000 bbl/day (2007 est.)
**Oil - proved reserves:** 2.5 billion bbl (1 January 2008 est.)

**Natural gas - production:** 6.5 billion cu m (2008 est.)
**Natural gas - consumption:** 4.4 billion cu m (2008 est.)
**Natural gas - exports:** NA cu m
**Natural gas - imports:** 0 cu m (2007 est.)
**Natural gas - proved reserves:** 240.7 billion cu m (1 January 2008 est.)

**Current account balance:** -$192 million (2008 est.)

**Exports:** $13.12 billion f.o.b. (2008 est.)

**Exports - commodities:** crude oil, minerals, petroleum products, fruits and vegetables, cotton fiber, textiles, clothing, meat and live animals, wheat

**Exports - partners:** Iraq 30%, Lebanon 10%, Germany 9.7%, Italy 8%, Egypt 5.5%, Saudi Arabia 5.2%, France 4.9% (2007)

**Imports:** $14.32 billion f.o.b. (2008 est.)

**Imports - commodities:** machinery and transport equipment, electric power machinery, food and livestock, metal and metal products, chemicals and chemical products, plastics, yarn, paper

**Imports - partners:** Saudi Arabia 12%, China 8.7%, Egypt 6.2%, Italy 6%, UAE 5.9%, Ukraine 4.8%, Russia 4.8%, Germany 4.7%, Iran 4.3% (2007)

**Reserves of foreign exchange and gold:** $6.104 billion (31 December 2008 est.)

**Debt - external:** $6.72 billion (31 December 2008 est.)

**Exchange rates:** Syrian pounds (SYP) per US dollar - 46.5281 (2008 est.), 50.0085 (2007), 51.689 (2006), 50 (2005), 48.5 (2004)
*note:* data for 2004-06 are the public sector rate; data for 2002-03 are the parallel market rate in 'Amman and Beirut; the official rate for repaying loans was 11.25 Syrian pounds per US dollars during 2004-06,

## Communications

**Telephones - main lines in use:** 3.452 million (2007)

**Telephones - mobile cellular:** 6.7 million (2007)

**Telephone system:**
*general assessment:* fair system currently undergoing significant improvement and digital upgrades, including fiber-optic technology
*domestic:* the number of fixed-line connections has increased markedly since 2000; mobile-cellular service growing rapidly with teledensity reaching 35 wireless telephones per 100 persons in 2007; coaxial cable and microwave radio relay network still in use
*international:* country code - 963; submarine cable connection to Egypt, Lebanon, and Cyprus; satellite earth stations - 1 Intelsat (Indian Ocean) and 1 Intersputnik (Atlantic Ocean region); coaxial cable and microwave radio relay to Iraq, Jordan, Lebanon, and Turkey; participant in Medarabtel

**Radio broadcast stations:** AM 14, FM 2, shortwave 1 (1998)

**Television broadcast stations:** 44 (plus 17 repeaters) (1995)

**Internet country code:** .sy
**Internet hosts:** 7,857 (2008)
**Internet users:** 3.47 million (2007)

## Transportation

**Airports:** 101 (2008)
**Airports - with paved runways:**
*total:* 28
*over 3,047 m:* 6
*2,438 to 3,047 m:* 15
*914 to 1,523 m:* 2
*under 914 m:* 5 (2008)

## Syria (continued)

**Airports - with unpaved runways:**
*total:* 73
*1,524 to 2,437 m:* 1
*914 to 1,523 m:* 14
*under 914 m:* 58 (2008)
**Heliports:** 7 (2007)
**Pipelines:** gas 2,900 km; oil 2,000 km (2008)
**Railways:**
*total:* 2,711 km
*standard gauge:* 2,460 km 1.435-m gauge
*narrow gauge:* 251 km 1.050-m gauge (2006)
**Roadways:**
*total:* 97,401 km
*paved:* 19,490 km (includes 1,103 km of expressways)
*unpaved:* 77,911 km (2006)
**Waterways:** 900 km (not economically significant) (2008)
**Merchant marine:**
*total:* 77
*by type:* bulk carrier 5, cargo 65, carrier 4, container 1, petroleum tanker 1, roll on/roll off 1
*foreign-owned:* 7 (Jordan 2, Lebanon 3, Romania 2)
*registered in other countries:* 196 (Barbados 1, Bolivia 2, Cambodia 48, Comoros 4, Cyprus 2, Dominica 2, Georgia 49, Hong Kong 1, North Korea 1, Lebanon 2, Libya 2, Malta 6, Moldova 1, Panama 32, Saint Kitts and Nevis 7, Saint Vincent and the Grenadines 13, Sierra Leone 18, Slovakia 2, Togo 2, unknown 1) (2008)
**Ports and terminals:** Latakia, Tartus

### Military

**Military branches:** Syrian Armed Forces: Syrian Arab Army, Syrian Arab Navy, Syrian Arab Air and Air Defense Forces (includes Air Defense Command) (2008)
**Military service age and obligation:** 18 years of age for compulsory military service; conscript service obligation - 30 months (18 months in the Syrian Arab Navy); women are not conscripted but may volunteer to serve (2004)
**Manpower available for military service:**
*males age 16-49:* 5,251,875
*females age 16-49:* 4,966,367 (2008 est.)
**Manpower fit for military service:**
*males age 16-49:* 4,360,934
*females age 16-49:* 4,344,895 (2009 est.)
**Manpower reaching militarily significant age annually:**
*male:* 213,513
*female:* 201,055 (2009 est.)
**Military expenditures:** 5.9% of GDP (2005 est.)

### Transnational Issues

**Disputes - international:** Golan Heights is Israeli-occupied with the almost 1,000-strong UN Disengagement Observer Force (UNDOF) patrolling a buffer zone since 1964; lacking a treaty or other documentation describing the boundary, portions of the Lebanon-Syria boundary are unclear with several sections in dispute; since 2000, Lebanon has claimed Shabaa farms in the Golan Heights; 2004 Agreement and pending demarcation settles border dispute with Jordan; approximately two million Iraqis have fled the conflict in Iraq with the majority taking refuge in Syria and Jordan
**Refugees and internally displaced persons:**
*refugees (country of origin):* 1-1.4 million (Iraq); 522,100 (Palestinian Refugees (UNRWA))
*IDPs:* 305,000 (most displaced from Golan Heights during 1967 Arab-Israeli War) (2007)
**Trafficking in persons:**
*current situation:* Syria is a destination and transit country for women and children trafficked for commercial sexual exploitation and forced labor; a significant number of women and children in the large and expanding Iraqi refugee community in Syria are reportedly forced into commercial sexual exploitation by Iraqi gangs or, in some cases, their families; women from Indonesia, Sri Lanka, the Philippines, Ethiopia, and Sierra Leone are recruited for work in Syria as domestic servants, but some face conditions of involuntary servitude, including long hours, non-payment of wages, withholding of passports, restrictions on movement, threats, and physical or sexual abuse
*tier rating:* Tier 3 - Syria again failed to report any law enforcement efforts to punish trafficking offenses in 2007; in addition, the government did not offer protection services to victims of trafficking and may have arrested, prosecuted, or deported some victims for prostitution or immigration violations; Syria has not ratified the 2000 UN TIP Protocol (2008)
**Illicit drugs:** a transit point for opiates, hashish, and cocaine bound for regional and Western markets; weak anti-money-laundering controls and bank privatization may leave it vulnerable to money laundering

# Taiwan

Entry

follows

Zimbabwe

# Tajikistan

## Introduction

**Background:** The Tajik people came under Russian rule in the 1860s and 1870s, but Russia's hold on Central Asia weakened following the Revolution of 1917. Bolshevik control of the area was fiercely contested and not fully reestablished until 1925. Much of present-day Sughd province was transferred from the Uzbek SSR to the newly formed Tajik SSR in 1929. Ethnic Uzbeks form a substantial minority in Sughd province. Tajikistan became independent in 1991 following the breakup of the Soviet Union, and experienced a civil war between regional factions from 1992-97. There have been no major security incidents in recent years, although the country remains the poorest in the former Soviet sphere. Attention by the international community since the beginning of the NATO intervention in Afghanistan has brought increased economic development and security assistance, which could create jobs and strengthen stability in the long term. Tajikistan is in the early stages of seeking World Trade Organization membership and has joined NATO's Partnership for Peace.

## Geography

**Location:** Central Asia, west of China
**Geographic coordinates:** 39 00 N, 71 00 E
**Map references:** Asia
**Area:**
*total:* 143,100 sq km
*land:* 142,700 sq km
*water:* 400 sq km
**Area - comparative:** slightly smaller than Wisconsin
**Land boundaries:**
*total:* 3,651 km
*border countries:* Afghanistan 1,206 km, China 414 km, Kyrgyzstan 870 km, Uzbekistan 1,161 km
**Coastline:** 0 km (landlocked)

**Maritime claims:** none (landlocked)
**Climate:** midlatitude continental, hot summers, mild winters; semiarid to polar in Pamir Mountains
**Terrain:** Pamir and Alay Mountains dominate landscape; western Fergana Valley in north, Kofarnihon and Vakhsh Valleys in southwest
**Elevation extremes:**
*lowest point:* Syr Darya (Sirdaryo) 300 m
*highest point:* Qullai Ismoili Somoni 7,495 m
**Natural resources:** hydropower, some petroleum, uranium, mercury, brown coal, lead, zinc, antimony, tungsten, silver, gold
**Land use:**
*arable land:* 6.52%
*permanent crops:* 0.89%
*other:* 92.59% (2005)
**Irrigated land:** 7,220 sq km (2003)
**Total renewable water resources:** 99.7 cu km (1997)
**Freshwater withdrawal (domestic/industrial/agricultural):**
*total:* 11.96 cu km/yr (4%/5%/92%)
*per capita:* 1,837 cu m/yr (2000)
**Natural hazards:** earthquakes; floods
**Environment - current issues:** inadequate sanitation facilities; increasing levels of soil salinity; industrial pollution; excessive pesticides
**Environment - international agreements:**
*party to:* Biodiversity, Climate Change, Climate Change-Kyoto Protocol, Desertification, Environmental Modification, Ozone Layer Protection, Wetlands
*signed, but not ratified:* none of the selected agreements
**Geography - note:** landlocked; mountainous region dominated by the Trans-Alay Range in the north and the Pamirs in the southeast; highest point, Qullai Ismoili Somoni (formerly Communism Peak), was the tallest mountain in the former USSR

**Population:** 7,349,145 (July 2009 est.)
**Age structure:**
*0-14 years:* 34.3% (male 1,282,681/female 1,238,607)
*15-64 years:* 62.1% (male 2,260,552/female 2,303,034)
*65 years and over:* 3.6% (male 112,334/female 151,937) (2009 est.)
**Median age:**
*total:* 21.9 years
*male:* 21.5 years
*female:* 22.4 years (2009 est.)
**Population growth rate:** 1.878% (2009 est.)
**Birth rate:** 26.9 births/1,000 population (2009 est.)
**Death rate:** 6.94 deaths/1,000 population (2008 est.)
**Net migration rate:** -1.28 migrant(s)/1,000 population (2009 est.)
**Urbanization:**
*urban population:* 26% of total population (2008)
*rate of urbanization:* 1.6% annual rate of change (2005-10 est.)
**Sex ratio:**
*at birth:* 1.05 male(s)/female
*under 15 years:* 1.04 male(s)/female
*15-64 years:* 0.98 male(s)/female
*65 years and over:* 0.74 male(s)/female
*total population:* 0.99 male(s)/female (2009 est.)
**Infant mortality rate:**
*total:* 41.03 deaths/1,000 live births
*male:* 45.9 deaths/1,000 live births
*female:* 35.91 deaths/1,000 live births (2009 est.)
**Life expectancy at birth:**
*total population:* 65.33 years
*male:* 62.29 years
*female:* 68.52 years (2009 est.)
**Total fertility rate:** 2.99 children born/woman (2009 est.)
**HIV/AIDS - adult prevalence rate:** less than 0.3% (2007 est.)
**HIV/AIDS - people living with HIV/AIDS:** 10,000 (2007 est.)
**HIV/AIDS - deaths:** fewer than 500 (2007 est.)
**Major infectious diseases:**
*degree of risk:* high
*food or waterborne diseases:* bacterial diarrhea, hepatitis A, and typhoid fever
*vectorborne disease:* malaria (2009)
**Nationality:**
*noun:* Tajikistani(s)
*adjective:* Tajikistani
**Ethnic groups:** Tajik 79.9%, Uzbek 15.3%, Russian 1.1%, Kyrgyz 1.1%, other 2.6% (2000 census)
**Religions:** Sunni Muslim 85%, Shia Muslim 5%, other 10% (2003 est.)
**Languages:** Tajik (official), Russian widely used in government and business
**Literacy:**
*definition:* age 15 and over can read and write
*total population:* 99.5%
*male:* 99.7%
*female:* 99.2% (2000 census)

# Tajikistan (continued)

**School life expectancy (primary to tertiary education):**
*total:* 11 years
*male:* 12 years
*female:* 10 years (2006)
**Education expenditures:** 3.4% of GDP (2006)

## Government

**Country name:**
*conventional long form:* Republic of Tajikistan
*conventional short form:* Tajikistan
*local long form:* Jumhurii Tojikiston
*local short form:* Tojikiston
*former:* Tajik Soviet Socialist Republic
**Government type:** republic
**Capital:**
*name:* Dushanbe
*geographic coordinates:* 38 35 N, 68 48 E
*time difference:* UTC+5 (10 hours ahead of Washington, DC during Standard Time)
**Administrative divisions:** 2 provinces (viloyatho, singular - viloyat) and 1 autonomous province* (viloyati mukhtor); Viloyati Khatlon (Qurghonteppa), Viloyati Mukhtori Kuhistoni Badakhshon* [Gorno-Badakhshan] (Khorugh), Viloyati Sughd (Khujand)
*note:* the administrative center name follows in parentheses
**Independence:** 9 September 1991 (from the Soviet Union)
**National holiday:** Independence Day (or National Day), 9 September (1991)
**Constitution:** 6 November 1994
**Legal system:** based on civil law system; no judicial review of legislative acts; has not accepted compulsory ICJ jurisdiction
**Suffrage:** 18 years of age; universal
**Executive branch:**
*chief of state:* President Emomali RAHMON (since 6 November 1994; head of state and Supreme Assembly chairman since 19 November 1992)
*head of government:* Prime Minister Oqil OQILOV (since 20 January 1999)
*cabinet:* Council of Ministers appointed by the president, approved by the Supreme Assembly
*elections:* president elected by popular vote for a seven-year term (eligible for a second term); election last held 6 November 2006 (next to be held in November 2013); prime minister appointed by the president
*election results:* Emomali RAHMON reelected president; percent of vote - Emomali RAHMON 79.3%, Olimjon BOBOEV 6.2%, other 14.5%
**Legislative branch:** bicameral Supreme Assembly or Majlisi Oli consists of the National Assembly (upper chamber) or Majlisi Milliy (34 seats; 25 members selected by local deputies, 8 appointed by the president; 1 seat reserved for the former president; to serve five-year terms) and the Assembly of Representatives (lower chamber) or Majlisi Namoyandagon (63 seats; members are elected by

popular vote to serve five-year terms)
*elections:* National Assembly - last held 25 March 2005 (next to be held in February 2010); Assembly of Representatives 27 February and 13 March 2005 (next to be held in February 2010)
*election results:* National Assembly - percent of vote by party - NA; seats by party - PDPT 29, CPT 2, independents 3; Assembly of Representatives - percent of vote by party - PDPT 74.9%, CPT 13.6%, Islamic Revival Party 8.9%, other 2.5%; seats by party -PDPT 51, CPT 5, Islamic Revival Party 2, independents 5
**Judicial branch:** Supreme Court (judges are appointed by the president)
**Political parties and leaders:** Agrarian Party of Tajikistan or APT [Amir QARAQULOV]; Democratic Party or DPT [Mahmadruzi ISKANDAROV (imprisoned October 2005); Rahmatullo VALIYEV, deputy]; Islamic Revival Party [Muhiddin KABIRI]; Party of Economic Reform or PER [Olimjon BOBOEV]; People's Democratic Party of Tajikistan or PDPT [Emomali RAHMON]; Social Democratic Party or SDPT [Rahmatullo ZOYIROV]; Socialist Party or SPT [Mirhuseyn NARZIEV]; Tajik Communist Party or CPT [Shodi SHABDOLOV]
**Political pressure groups and leaders:**
*splinter parties recognized by the government but not by the base of the party:* Democratic Party or DPT [Masud SOBIROV] (splintered from ISKANDAROV's DPT); Socialist Party or SPT [Abduhalim GHAFFOROV] (splintered from NARZIEV's SPT)
*unregistered political parties:* Agrarian Party [Hikmatullo NASREDDINOV]; Progressive Party [Sulton QUVVATOV]; Unity Party [Hikmatullo SAIDOV]
**International organization participation:** ADB, CIS, CSTO, EAEC, EAPC, EBRD, ECO, FAO, GCTU, IAEA, IBRD, ICAO, ICCt, ICRM, IDA, IDB, IFAD, IFC, IFRCS, ILO, IMF, Interpol, IOC, IOM, IPU, ISO (correspondent), ITSO, ITU, MIGA, OIC, OPCW, OSCE, PFP, SCO, UN, UNCTAD, UNESCO, UNIDO, UNWTO, UPU, WCO, WFTU, WHO, WIPO, WMO, WTO (observer)
**Diplomatic representation in the US:**
*chief of mission:* Ambassador Abdujabbor SHIRINOV
*chancery:* 1005 New Hampshire Avenue NW, Washington, DC 20037
*telephone:* [1] (202) 223-6090
*FAX:* [1] (202) 223-6091
**Diplomatic representation from the US:**
*chief of mission:* Ambassador Tracey Ann JACOBSON
*embassy:* 109-A Ismoili Somoni Avenue, Dushanbe 734019
*mailing address:* 7090 Dushanbe Place, Dulles, VA 20189
*telephone:* [992] (37) 229-20-00
*FAX:* [992] (37) 229-20-50
**Flag description:** three horizontal stripes of red (top), a wider stripe of white, and green; a gold crown surmounted by seven gold, five-pointed stars is located in the center of the white stripe

## Economy

**Economy - overview:** Tajikistan has one of the lowest per capita GDPs among the 15 former Soviet republics. Because of a lack of employment opportunities in Tajikistan, nearly half of the labor force works abroad, primarily in Russia, supporting families in Tajikistan through remittances. The exact number of labor migrants is unknown, but estimated at around 1 million. Less than 7% of the land area is arable. Cotton is the most important crop, but this sector is burdened with debt and obsolete infrastructure. Mineral resources include silver, gold, uranium, and tungsten. Industry consists only of a large aluminum plant, hydropower facilities, and small obsolete factories mostly in light industry and food processing. The civil war (1992-97) severely damaged the already weak economic infrastructure and caused a sharp decline in industrial and agricultural production. Tajikistan's economic situation remains fragile due to uneven implementation of structural reforms, corruption, weak governance, widespread unemployment, seasonal power shortages, and the external debt burden. A debt restructuring agreement was reached with Russia in December 2002 including a $250 million write-off of Tajikistan's $300 million debt. Completion of the Sangtuda I hydropower dam - built with Russian investment - and the Sangtuda II and Rogun dams will add substantially to electricity output. If finished according to Tajik plans, Rogun will be the world's tallest dam. Tajikistan has also received substantial infrastructure development loans from the Chinese government to improve roads and an electricity transmission network. To help increase north-south trade, the US funded a $36 million bridge which opened in August 2007 and links Tajikistan and Afghanistan. While, Tajikistan has experienced steady economic growth since 1997, nearly two-thirds of the population continues to live in poverty. Economic growth reached 10.6% in 2004, but dropped to below 8% in 2005-08, as the effects of higher oil prices and then the international financial crisis began to register - mainly in the form of lower prices for key commodities and lower remittances from Tajiks working in Russia, due to the declining economic conditions in that country.
**GDP (purchasing power parity):**
$15.4 billion (2008 est.)
$14.27 billion (2007)
$11.32 billion (2006)
*note:* data are in 2008 US dollars
**GDP (official exchange rate):** $4.788 billion (2008 est.)
**GDP - real growth rate:**
7.9% (2008 est.)
7.8% (2007 est.)
7% (2006 est.)
**GDP - per capita (PPP):**
$2,100 (2008 est.)
$1,700 (2007 est.)
$1,600 (2006 est.)
*note:* data are in 2008 US dollars

# Tajikistan (continued)

**GDP - composition by sector:**
*agriculture:* 23%
*industry:* 29.4%
*services:* 47.6% (2008 est.)
**Labor force:** 2.1 million (2008)
**Labor force - by occupation:**
*agriculture:* 67.2%
*industry:* 7.5%
*services:* 25.3% (2000 est.)
**Unemployment rate:**
2.3% (2008 est.)
2.4% (2007 est.)
*note:* official rates; actual unemployment is higher
**Population below poverty line:** 60% (2007 est.)
**Household income or consumption by percentage share:**
*lowest 10%:* 3.3%
*highest 10%:* 25.6% (2007 est.)
**Distribution of family income - Gini index:** 32.6 (2006)
**Investment (gross fixed):** 20% of GDP (2008 est.)
**Budget:**
*revenues:* $1.28 billion
*expenditures:* $1.3 billion (2008 est.)
**Inflation rate (consumer prices):**
11.8% (2008)
13.1% (2007 est.)
**Central bank discount rate:** 13.5% (30 September 2008)
**Commercial bank prime lending rate:** 23.1% (31 December 2008)
**Stock of money:** $330 million (31 December 2007)
**Stock of quasi money:** $544 million (31 December 2008)
**Stock of domestic credit:** $889 million (31 December 2008)
**Market value of publicly traded shares:** $NA
**Agriculture - products:** cotton, grain, fruits, grapes, vegetables; cattle, sheep, goats
**Industries:** aluminum, zinc, lead; chemicals and fertilizers, cement, vegetable oil, metal-cutting machine tools, refrigerators and freezers
**Industrial production growth rate:** 4% (2008)
**Electricity - production:** 14.8 billion kWh (2008)
**Electricity - consumption:** 17.8 billion kWh (2008)
**Electricity - exports:** 1 billion kWh (2008 est.)
**Electricity - imports:** 3 billion kWh (2008 est.)
**Oil - production:** 503 bbl/day (2008)
**Oil - consumption:** 10,600 bbl/day (2008)
**Oil - exports:** NA bbl/day
**Oil - imports:** 10,100 bbl/day (2008)
**Oil - proved reserves:** 12 million bbl (1 January 2008 est.)
**Natural gas - production:** 16 million cu m (2008)
**Natural gas - consumption:** 542.7 million cu m (2008)
**Natural gas - exports:** 0 cu m (2008)
**Natural gas - imports:** 512.7 million cu m (2008)
**Natural gas - proved reserves:** 5.663 billion cu m (1 January 2008 est.)
**Current account balance:** -$1.8 billion (2008)

**Exports:** $1.4 billion f.o.b. (2008)
**Exports - commodities:** aluminum, electricity, cotton, fruits, vegetable oil, textiles
**Exports - partners:** Netherlands 38.9%, Turkey 32.5%, Russia 6.6%, Uzbekistan 5.9%, Iran 5.1% (2007)
**Imports:** $3.2 billion f.o.b. (2008)
**Imports - commodities:** electricity, petroleum products, aluminum oxide, machinery and equipment, foodstuffs
**Imports - partners:** Russia 32.1%, Kazakhstan 13.1%, China 10.8%, Uzbekistan 8.4% (2007)
**Reserves of foreign exchange and gold:** $220 million (31 December 2008)
**Debt - external:** $1.37 billion (31 December 2008)
**Stock of direct foreign investment - at home:** $88 million (2008 est.)
**Stock of direct foreign investment - abroad:** NA
**Exchange rates:** Tajikistani somoni (TJS) per US dollar - 3.4563 (2008 est.), 3.4418 (2007), 3.3 (2006), 3.1166 (2005), 2.9705 (2004)

**Telephones - main lines in use:** 340,000 (2007)
**Telephones - mobile cellular:** 3.5 million (2007)
**Telephone system:**
*general assessment:* foreign investment in the telephone system has resulted in major improvements
*domestic:* the domestic telecommunications network has historically been under funded and poorly maintained; main line availability has not changed significantly since 1998; mobile cellular use, aided by competition among multiple operators, has expanded rapidly; coverage now extends to all major cities and towns
*international:* country code - 992; linked by cable and microwave radio relay to other CIS republics and by leased connections to the Moscow international gateway switch; Dushanbe linked by Intelsat to international gateway switch in Ankara (Turkey); satellite earth stations - 3 (2 Intelsat and 1 Orbita) (2008)
**Radio broadcast stations:** 16 (number of licensed stations with only about 10 broadcasting) (2009)
**Television broadcast stations:** 24 (number of licensed stations with only about 15 active) (2009)
**Internet country code:** .tj
**Internet hosts:** 1,158 (2008)
**Internet users:** 19,500 (2005)

**Airports:** 26 (2008)
**Airports - with paved runways:**
*total:* 18
*over 3,047 m:* 2
*2,438 to 3,047 m:* 4
*1,524 to 2,437 m:* 6
*914 to 1,523 m:* 3
*under 914 m:* 3 (2008)
**Airports - with unpaved runways:**
*total:* 8
*914 to 1,523 m:* 1
*under 914 m:* 7 (2008)

**Pipelines:** gas 549 km; oil 38 km (2008)
**Railways:**
*total:* 482 km
*broad gauge:* 482 km 1.520-m gauge (2006)
**Roadways:**
*total:* 27,767 km (2000)
**Waterways:** 200 km (along Vakhsh River) (2008)

**Military branches:** Ground Forces, Air and Air Defense Forces, Mobile Forces (2008)
**Military service age and obligation:** 18 years of age for compulsory military service; 2-year conscript service obligation (2007)
**Manpower available for military service:**
*males age 16-49:* 1,897,356
*females age 16-49:* 1,911,594 (2008 est.)
**Manpower fit for military service:**
*males age 16-49:* 1,428,218
*females age 16-49:* 1,603,779 (2009 est.)
**Manpower reaching militarily significant age annually:**
*male:* 80,819
*female:* 78,460 (2009 est.)
**Military expenditures:** 3.9% of GDP (2005 est.)

**Disputes - international:** in 2006, China and Tajikistan pledged to commence demarcation of the revised boundary agreed to in the delimitation of 2002; talks continue with Uzbekistan to delimit border and remove minefields; disputes in Isfara Valley delay delimitation with Kyrgyzstan
**Trafficking in persons:**
*current situation:* Tajikistan is a source country for women trafficked through Kyrgyzstan and Russia to the UAE, Turkey, and Russia for the purpose of commercial sexual exploitation; men are trafficked to Russia and Kazakhstan for the purpose of forced labor, primarily in the construction and agricultural industries; boys and girls are trafficked internally for various purposes, including forced labor and forced begging
*tier rating:* Tier 2 Watch List - Tajikistan is on the Tier 2 Watch List for its failure to provide evidence of increasing efforts to combat human trafficking, especially efforts to investigate, prosecute, convict, and sentence traffickers; despite evidence of low- and mid-level officials' complicity in trafficking, the government did not punish any public officials for trafficking complicity during 2007; lack of capacity and poor coordination between government institutions remained key obstacles to effective anti-trafficking efforts (2008)
**Illicit drugs:** major transit country for Afghan narcotics bound for Russian and, to a lesser extent, Western European markets; limited illicit cultivation of opium poppy for domestic consumption; Tajikistan seizes roughly 80% of all drugs captured in Central Asia and stands third worldwide in seizures of opiates (heroin and raw opium); significant consumer of opiates

# Tanzania

## Introduction

**Background:** Shortly after achieving independence from Britain in the early 1960s, Tanganyika and Zanzibar merged to form the nation of Tanzania in 1964. One-party rule came to an end in 1995 with the first democratic elections held in the country since the 1970s. Zanzibar's semi-autonomous status and popular opposition have led to two contentious elections since 1995, which the ruling party won despite international observers' claims of voting irregularities.

## Geography

**Location:** Eastern Africa, bordering the Indian Ocean, between Kenya and Mozambique
**Geographic coordinates:** 6 00 S, 35 00 E
**Map references:** Africa
**Area:**
*total:* 945,087 sq km
*land:* 886,037 sq km
*water:* 59,050 sq km
*note:* includes the islands of Mafia, Pemba, and Zanzibar
**Area - comparative:** slightly larger than twice the size of California
**Land boundaries:**
*total:* 3,861 km
*border countries:* Burundi 451 km, Democratic Republic of the Congo 459 km, Kenya 769 km, Malawi 475 km, Mozambique 756 km, Rwanda 217 km, Uganda 396 km, Zambia 338 km
**Coastline:** 1,424 km
**Maritime claims:**
*territorial sea:* 12 nm
*exclusive economic zone:* 200 nm
**Climate:** varies from tropical along coast to temperate in highlands
**Terrain:** plains along coast; central plateau; highlands in north, south

**Elevation extremes:**
*lowest point:* Indian Ocean 0 m
*highest point:* Kilimanjaro 5,895 m
**Natural resources:** hydropower, tin, phosphates, iron ore, coal, diamonds, gemstones, gold, natural gas, nickel
**Land use:**
*arable land:* 4.23%
*permanent crops:* 1.16%
*other:* 94.61% (2005)
**Irrigated land:** 1,840 sq km (2003)
**Total renewable water resources:** 91 cu km (2001)
**Freshwater withdrawal (domestic/industrial/agricultural):**
*total:* 5.18 cu km/yr (10%/0%/89%)
*per capita:* 135 cu m/yr (2000)
**Natural hazards:** flooding on the central plateau during the rainy season; drought
**Environment - current issues:** soil degradation; deforestation; desertification; destruction of coral reefs threatens marine habitats; recent droughts affected marginal agriculture; wildlife threatened by illegal hunting and trade, especially for ivory
**Environment - international agreements:**
*party to:* Biodiversity, Climate Change, Climate Change-Kyoto Protocol, Desertification, Endangered Species, Hazardous Wastes, Law of the Sea, Ozone Layer Protection, Wetlands
*signed, but not ratified:* none of the selected agreements
**Geography - note:** Kilimanjaro is highest point in Africa; bordered by three of the largest lakes on the continent: Lake Victoria (the world's second-largest freshwater lake) in the north, Lake Tanganyika (the world's second deepest) in the west, and Lake Nyasa in the southwest

## People

**Population:** 41,048,532
*note:* estimates for this country explicitly take into account the effects of excess mortality due to AIDS; this can result in lower life expectancy, higher infant mortality, higher death rates, lower population growth rates, and changes in the distribution of population by age and sex than would otherwise be expected (July 2009 est.)
**Age structure:**
*0-14 years:* 43% (male 8,853,529/female 8,805,810)
*15-64 years:* 54.1% (male 10,956,133/female 11,255,868)
*65 years and over:* 2.9% (male 513,959/female 663,233) (2009 est.)
**Median age:**
*total:* 18 years
*male:* 17.8 years
*female:* 18.3 years (2009 est.)
**Population growth rate:** 2.04% (2009 est.)
**Birth rate:** 34.29 births/1,000 population (2009 est.)
**Death rate:** 12.92 deaths/1,000 population (2008 est.)

**Net migration rate:** -1.3 migrant(s)/1,000 population (2009 est.)
**Urbanization:**
*urban population:* 25% of total population (2008)
*rate of urbanization:* 4.2% annual rate of change (2005-10 est.)
**Sex ratio:**
*at birth:* 1.03 male(s)/female
*under 15 years:* 1 male(s)/female
*15-64 years:* 0.97 male(s)/female
*65 years and over:* 0.78 male(s)/female
*total population:* 0.98 male(s)/female (2009 est.)
**Infant mortality rate:**
*total:* 69.28 deaths/1,000 live births
*male:* 76.24 deaths/1,000 live births
*female:* 62.1 deaths/1,000 live births (2009 est.)
**Life expectancy at birth:**
*total population:* 52.01 years
*male:* 50.56 years
*female:* 53.51 years (2009 est.)
**Total fertility rate:** 4.46 children born/woman (2009 est.)
**HIV/AIDS - adult prevalence rate:** 6.2% (2007 est.)
**HIV/AIDS - people living with HIV/AIDS:** 1.4 million (2007 est.)
**HIV/AIDS - deaths:** 96,000 (2007 est.)
**Major infectious diseases:**
*degree of risk:* very high
*food or waterborne diseases:* bacterial diarrhea, hepatitis A, and typhoid fever
*vectorborne diseases:* malaria and plague
*water contact disease:* schistosomiasis
*animal contact disease:* rabies (2009)
**Nationality:**
*noun:* Tanzanian(s)
*adjective:* Tanzanian
**Ethnic groups:** mainland - African 99% (of which 95% are Bantu consisting of more than 130 tribes), other 1% (consisting of Asian, European, and Arab); Zanzibar - Arab, African, mixed Arab and African
**Religions:** mainland - Christian 30%, Muslim 35%, indigenous beliefs 35%; Zanzibar - more than 99% Muslim
**Languages:** Kiswahili or Swahili (official), Kiunguja (name for Swahili in Zanzibar), English (official, primary language of commerce, administration, and higher education), Arabic (widely spoken in Zanzibar), many local languages
*note:* Kiswahili (Swahili) is the mother tongue of the Bantu people living in Zanzibar and nearby coastal Tanzania; although Kiswahili is Bantu in structure and origin, its vocabulary draws on a variety of sources including Arabic and English; it has become the lingua franca of central and eastern Africa; the first language of most people is one of the local languages
**Literacy:**
*definition:* age 15 and over can read and write Kiswahili (Swahili), English, or Arabic
*total population:* 69.4%
*male:* 77.5%
*female:* 62.2% (2002 census)
**Education expenditures:** 2.2% of GDP (1999)

# Tanzania (continued)

## Government

**Country name:**
*conventional long form:* United Republic of Tanzania
*conventional short form:* Tanzania
*local long form:* Jamhuri ya Muungano wa Tanzania
*local short form:* Tanzania
*former:* United Republic of Tanganyika and Zanzibar
**Government type:** republic
**Capital:**
*name:* Dar es Salaam
*geographic coordinates:* 6 48 S, 39 17 E
*time difference:* UTC+3 (8 hours ahead of Washington, DC during Standard Time)
*note:* legislative offices have been transferred to Dodoma, which is planned as the new national capital; the National Assembly now meets there on a regular basis
**Administrative divisions:** 26 regions; Arusha, Dar es Salaam, Dodoma, Iringa, Kagera, Kigoma, Kilimanjaro, Lindi, Manyara, Mara, Mbeya, Morogoro, Mtwara, Mwanza, Pemba North, Pemba South, Pwani, Rukwa, Ruvuma, Shinyanga, Singida, Tabora, Tanga, Zanzibar Central/South, Zanzibar North, Zanzibar Urban/West
**Independence:** 26 April 1964; Tanganyika became independent 9 December 1961 (from UK-administered UN trusteeship); Zanzibar became independent 19 December 1963 (from UK); Tanganyika united with Zanzibar 26 April 1964 to form the United Republic of Tanganyika and Zanzibar; renamed United Republic of Tanzania 29 October 1964
**National holiday:** Union Day (Tanganyika and Zanzibar), 26 April (1964)
**Constitution:** 25 April 1977; major revisions October 1984
**Legal system:** based on English common law; judicial review of legislative acts limited to matters of interpretation; has not accepted compulsory ICJ jurisdiction
**Suffrage:** 18 years of age; universal
**Executive branch:**
*chief of state:* President Jakaya KIKWETE (since 21 December 2005); Vice President Dr. Ali Mohammed SHEIN (since 5 July 2001); note - the president is both chief of state and head of government
*head of government:* President Jakaya KIKWETE (since 21 December 2005); Vice President Dr. Ali Mohammed SHEIN (since 5 July 2001)
*note:* Zanzibar elects a president who is head of government for matters internal to Zanzibar; Amani Abeid KARUME was reelected to that office on 30 October 2005

*cabinet:* Cabinet appointed by the president from among the members of the National Assembly
*elections:* president and vice president elected on the same ballot by popular vote for five-year terms (eligible for a second term); election last held 14 December 2005 (next to be held in December 2010); prime minister appointed by the president
*election results:* Jakaya KIKWETE elected president; percent of vote - Jakaya KIKWETE 80.3%, Ibrahim LIPUMBA 11.7%, Freeman MBOWE 5.9%
**Legislative branch:** unicameral National Assembly or Bunge (274 seats; 232 members elected by popular vote, 37 allocated to women nominated by the president, 5 to members of the Zanzibar House of Representatives; to serve five-year terms); note - in addition to enacting laws that apply to the entire United Republic of Tanzania, the Assembly enacts laws that apply only to the mainland; Zanzibar has its own House of Representatives to make laws especially for Zanzibar (the Zanzibar House of Representatives has 50 seats elected by universal suffrage to serve five-year terms)
*elections:* last held 14 December 2005 (next to be held in December 2010)
*election results:* National Assembly - percent of vote by party - NA; seats by party - CCM 206, CUF 19, CHADEMA 5, other 2, women appointed by the president 37, Zanzibar representatives 5 Zanzibar House of Representatives - percent of vote by party - NA; seats by party - CCM 30, CUF 19; 1 seat was nullified with a rerun to take place soon
**Judicial branch:** Permanent Commission of Enquiry (official ombudsman); Court of Appeal (consists of a chief justice and four judges); High Court (consists of a Jaji Kiongozi and 29 judges appointed by the president; holds regular sessions in all regions); District Courts; Primary Courts (limited jurisdiction and appeals can be made to the higher courts)
**Political parties and leaders:** Chama Cha Demokrasia na Maendeleo (Party of Democracy and Development) or CHADEMA [Bob MAKANI]; Chama Cha Mapinduzi or CCM (Revolutionary Party) [Jakaya Mrisho KIKWETE]; Civic United Front or CUF [Ibrahim LIPUMBA]; Democratic Party [Christopher MTIKLA] (unregistered); Tanzania Labor Party or TLP [Augustine Lyatonga MREME]; United Democratic Party or UDP [John CHEYO]
**Political pressure groups and leaders:** Economic and Social Research Foundation or ESRF; Free Zanzibar; Tanzania Media Women's Association or TAMWA
**International organization participation:** ACP, AfDB, AU, C, EAC, EADB, FAO, G-6, G-77, IAEA, IBRD, ICAO, ICC, ICCt, ICRM, IDA, IFAD, IFC, IFRCS, ILO, IMF, IMO, IMSO, Interpol, IOC, IOM, IPU, ISO, ITSO, ITU, ITUC, MIGA, NAM, OPCW, SADC, UN, UNAMID, UNCTAD, UNESCO, UNHCR, UNIDO, UNIFIL, UNMIS, UNOCI, UNWTO, UPU, WCO, WFTU, WHO, WIPO, WMO, WTO

**Diplomatic representation in the US:**
*chief of mission:* Ambassador Ombeni Yohana SEFUE
*chancery:* 2139 R Street NW, Washington, DC 20008
*telephone:* [1] (202) 939-6125
*FAX:* [1] (202) 797-7408
**Diplomatic representation from the US:**
*chief of mission:* Ambassador Mark GREEN
*embassy:* 686 Old Bagamoyo Road, Msasani, Dar es Salaam
*mailing address:* P. O. Box 9123, Dar es Salaam
*telephone:* [255] (22) 266-8001
*FAX:* [255] (22) 266-8238, 266-8373
**Flag description:** divided diagonally by a yellow-edged black band from the lower hoist-side corner; the upper triangle (hoist side) is green and the lower triangle is blue

## Economy

**Economy - overview:** Tanzania is in the bottom ten percent of the world's economies in terms of per capita income. The economy depends heavily on agriculture, which accounts for more than 40% of GDP, provides 85% of exports, and employs 80% of the work force. Topography and climatic conditions, however, limit cultivated crops to only 4% of the land area. Industry traditionally featured the processing of agricultural products and light consumer goods. The World Bank, the IMF, and bilateral donors have provided funds to rehabilitate Tanzania's out-of-date economic infrastructure and to alleviate poverty. Long-term growth through 2005 featured a pickup in industrial production and a substantial increase in output of minerals led by gold. Recent banking reforms have helped increase private-sector growth and investment. Continued donor assistance and solid macroeconomic policies supported real GDP growth of 7.1% in 2008.
**GDP (purchasing power parity):**
$54.26 billion (2008 est.)
$50.67 billion (2007)
$47.29 billion (2006)
*note:* data are in 2008 US dollars
**GDP (official exchange rate):** $20.63 billion (2008 est.)
**GDP - real growth rate:**
7.1% (2008 est.)
7.1% (2007 est.)
6.7% (2006 est.)
**GDP - per capita (PPP):**
$1,300 (2008 est.)
$1,300 (2007 est.)
$1,200 (2006 est.)
*note:* data are in 2008 US dollars
**GDP - composition by sector:**
*agriculture:* 27%
*industry:* 22.7%
*services:* 50.3% (2008 est.)
**Labor force:** 20.38 million (2008 est.)
**Labor force - by occupation:**
*agriculture:* 80%
*industry and services:* 20% (2002 est.)

**Unemployment rate:**
NA%

**Population below poverty line:** 36% (2002 est.)

**Household income or consumption by percentage share:**
*lowest 10%:* 2.9%
*highest 10%:* 26.9% (2000)

**Distribution of family income - Gini index:** 34.6 (2000)

**Investment (gross fixed):** 24.2% of GDP (2008 est.)

**Budget:**
*revenues:* $4.216 billion
*expenditures:* $4.658 billion (2008 est.)

**Public debt:** 22% of GDP (2008 est.)

**Inflation rate (consumer prices):**
9.3% (2008 est.)
7% (2007 est.)

**Central bank discount rate:** 16.4% (31 December 2007)

**Commercial bank prime lending rate:** 16.03% (31 December 2007)

**Stock of money:** $2.263 billion (31 December 2007)

**Stock of quasi money:** $2.885 billion (31 December 2007)

**Stock of domestic credit:** $2.25 billion (31 December 2007)

**Market value of publicly traded shares:** $587.9 million (2005)

**Agriculture - products:** coffee, sisal, tea, cotton, pyrethrum (insecticide made from chrysanthemums), cashew nuts, tobacco, cloves, corn, wheat, cassava (tapioca), bananas, fruits, vegetables; cattle, sheep, goats

**Industries:** agricultural processing (sugar, beer, cigarettes, sisal twine); diamond, gold, and iron mining, salt, soda ash; cement, oil refining, shoes, apparel, wood products, fertilizer

**Industrial production growth rate:** 10% (2008 est.)

**Electricity - production:** 2.682 billion kWh (2006 est.)

**Electricity - consumption:** 2.225 billion kWh (2006 est.)

**Electricity - exports:** 0 kWh (2007 est.)

**Electricity - imports:** 123 million kWh (2006 est.)

**Oil - production:** 0 bbl/day (2007 est.)

**Oil - consumption:** 27,270 bbl/day (2006 est.)

**Oil - exports:** 0 bbl/day (2005)

**Oil - imports:** 26,760 bbl/day (2005)

**Oil - proved reserves:** 0 bbl (1 January 2006 est.)

**Natural gas - production:** 146 million cu m (2006 est.)

**Natural gas - consumption:** 146 million cu m (2006 est.)

**Natural gas - exports:** 0 cu m (2007 est.)

**Natural gas - imports:** 0 cu m (2007 est.)

**Natural gas - proved reserves:** 6.513 billion cu m (1 January 2008 est.)

**Current account balance:** -$2.275 billion (2008 est.)

**Exports:** $2.49 billion f.o.b. (2008 est.)

**Exports - commodities:** gold, coffee, cashew nuts, manufactures, cotton

**Exports - partners:** China 10.3%, India 9.7%, Netherlands 6.5%, Germany 6.3%, UAE 4.9% (2007)

**Imports:** $5.901 billion f.o.b. (2008 est.)

**Imports - commodities:** consumer goods, machinery and transportation equipment, industrial raw materials, crude oil

**Imports - partners:** China 12%, Kenya 8%, South Africa 7.7%, India 6.9%, UAE 5.9% (2007)

**Reserves of foreign exchange and gold:** $2.624 billion (31 December 2008 est.)

**Debt - external:** $5.311 billion (31 December 2008 est.)

**Stock of direct foreign investment - at home:** $NA

**Stock of direct foreign investment - abroad:** $NA

**Exchange rates:** Tanzanian shillings (TZS) per US dollar - 1,178.1 (2008 est.), 1,255 (2007), 1,251.9 (2006), 1,128.93 (2005), 1,089.33 (2004)

## Communications

**Telephones - main lines in use:** 165,013 (2008)

**Telephones - mobile cellular:** 9.358 million (2008)

**Telephone system:**
*general assessment:* telecommunications services are inadequate; system operating below capacity and being modernized for better service; small aperture terminal (VSAT) system under construction
*domestic:* fixed-line telephone network inadequate with less than 1 connection per 100 persons; mobile-cellular service, aided by multiple providers, is increasing; trunk service provided by open-wire, microwave radio relay, tropospheric scatter, and fiber-optic cable; some links being made digital
*international:* country code - 255; satellite earth stations - 2 Intelsat (1 Indian Ocean, 1 Atlantic Ocean)

**Radio broadcast stations:** AM 12, FM 11, shortwave 2 (1998)

**Television broadcast stations:** 3 (1999)

**Internet country code:** .tz

**Internet hosts:** 24,271 (2008)

**Internet users:** 400,000 (2007)

## Transportation

**Airports:** 124 (2008)

**Airports - with paved runways:**
*total:* 9
*over 3,047 m:* 2
*2,438 to 3,047 m:* 2
*1,524 to 2,437 m:* 4
*914 to 1,523 m:* 1 (2008)

**Airports - with unpaved runways:**
*total:* 115
*1,524 to 2,437 m:* 18
*914 to 1,523 m:* 63
*under 914 m:* 34 (2008)

**Pipelines:** gas 253 km; oil 888 km; refined products 8 km (2008)

**Railways:**
*total:* 3,690 km
*narrow gauge:* 969 km 1.067-m gauge; 2,721 km 1.000-m gauge (2006)

**Roadways:**
*total:* 78,891 km
*paved:* 6,808 km
*unpaved:* 72,083 km (2003)

**Waterways:** Lake Tanganyika, Lake Victoria, and Lake Nyasa principal avenues of commerce with neighboring countries; rivers not navigable (2007)

**Merchant marine:**
*total:* 9
*by type:* cargo 1, passenger/cargo 4, petroleum tanker 4
*registered in other countries:* 1 (Honduras 1) (2008)

**Ports and terminals:** Dar es Salaam

**Transportation - note:** the International Maritime Bureau reports the territorial and offshore waters in the Indian Ocean are high risk for piracy and armed robbery against ships; numerous commercial vessels have been attacked and hijacked both at anchor and while underway; crews have been robbed and stores or cargoes stolen

## Military

**Military branches:** Tanzanian People's Defense Force (Jeshi la Wananchi la Tanzania, JWTZ): Army, Naval Wing (includes Coast Guard), Air Defense Command (includes Air Wing), National Service (2007)

**Military service age and obligation:** 18 years of age for voluntary military service (2007)

**Manpower available for military service:**
*males age 16-49:* 9,108,177 (2008 est.)

**Manpower fit for military service:**
*males age 16-49:* 5,473,552
*females age 16-49:* 5,493,188 (2009 est.)

**Manpower reaching militarily significant age annually:**
*male:* 487,742
*female:* 489,462 (2009 est.)

**Military expenditures:** 0.2% of GDP (2005 est.)

## Transnational Issues

**Disputes - international:** Tanzania still hosts more than a half-million refugees, more than any other African country, mainly from Burundi and the Democratic Republic of the Congo, despite the international community's efforts at repatriation; disputes with Malawi over the boundary in Lake Nyasa (Lake Malawi) and the meandering Songwe River remain dormant

**Refugees and internally displaced persons:**
*refugees (country of origin):* 352,640 (Burundi); 127,973 (Democratic Republic of the Congo) (2007)

**Illicit drugs:** growing role in transshipment of Southwest and Southeast Asian heroin and South American cocaine destined for South African, European, and US markets and of South Asian methaqualone bound for southern Africa; money laundering remains a problem

# Thailand

## Introduction

**Background:** A unified Thai kingdom was established in the mid-14th century. Known as Siam until 1939, Thailand is the only Southeast Asian country never to have been taken over by a European power. A bloodless revolution in 1932 led to a constitutional monarchy. In alliance with Japan during World War II, Thailand became a US treaty ally following the conflict. A military coup in September 2006 ousted then Prime Minister THAKSIN Chinnawat. The interim government held elections in December 2007 that saw the former pro-THAKSIN People's Power Party (PPP) emerge at the head of a coalition government. The anti-THAKSIN People's Alliance for Democracy (PAD) in May 2008 began street demonstrations against the new government, eventually occupying the prime minister's office in August. Clashes in October 2008 between PAD protesters blocking parliament and police resulted in the death of at least two people. The PAD occupied Bangkok's international airports briefly, ending their protests in early December 2008 following a court ruling that dissolved the ruling PPP and two other coalition parties for election violations. The Democrat Party then formed a new coalition government with the support of some of THAKSIN's former political allies, and ABHISIT Wetchachiwa became prime minister. Since January 2004, thousands have been killed as separatists in Thailand's southern ethnic Malay-Muslim provinces increased the violence associated with their cause.

## Geography

**Location:** Southeastern Asia, bordering the Andaman Sea and the Gulf of Thailand, southeast of Burma

**Geographic coordinates:** 15 00 N, 100 00 E

**Map references:** Southeast Asia

**Area:**
*total:* 514,000 sq km
*land:* 511,770 sq km
*water:* 2,230 sq km

**Area - comparative:** slightly more than twice the size of Wyoming

**Land boundaries:**
*total:* 4,863 km
*border countries:* Burma 1,800 km, Cambodia 803 km, Laos 1,754 km, Malaysia 506 km

**Coastline:** 3,219 km

**Maritime claims:**
*territorial sea:* 12 nm
*exclusive economic zone:* 200 nm
*continental shelf:* 200 m depth or to the depth of exploitation

**Climate:** tropical; rainy, warm, cloudy southwest monsoon (mid-May to September); dry, cool northeast monsoon (November to mid-March); southern isthmus always hot and humid

**Terrain:** central plain; Khorat Plateau in the east; mountains elsewhere

**Elevation extremes:**
*lowest point:* Gulf of Thailand 0 m
*highest point:* Doi Inthanon 2,576 m

**Natural resources:** tin, rubber, natural gas, tungsten, tantalum, timber, lead, fish, gypsum, lignite, fluorite, arable land

**Land use:**
*arable land:* 27.54%
*permanent crops:* 6.93%
*other:* 65.53% (2005)

**Irrigated land:** 49,860 sq km (2003)

**Total renewable water resources:** 409.9 cu km (1999)

**Freshwater withdrawal (domestic/industrial/agricultural):**
*total:* 82.75 cu km/yr (2%/2%/95%)
*per capita:* 1,288 cu m/yr (2000)

**Natural hazards:** land subsidence in Bangkok area resulting from the depletion of the water table; droughts

**Environment - current issues:** air pollution from vehicle emissions; water pollution from organic and factory wastes; deforestation; soil erosion; wildlife populations threatened by illegal hunting

**Environment - international agreements:**
*party to:* Biodiversity, Climate Change, Climate Change-Kyoto Protocol, Desertification, Endangered Species, Hazardous Wastes, Marine Life Conservation, Ozone Layer Protection, Tropical Timber 83, Tropical Timber 94, Wetlands
*signed, but not ratified:* Law of the Sea

**Geography - note:** controls only land route from Asia to Malaysia and Singapore

## People

**Population:** 65,905,410
*note:* estimates for this country explicitly take into account the effects of excess mortality due to AIDS; this can result in lower life expectancy, higher infant mortality, higher death rates, lower population growth rates, and changes in the distribution of population by age and sex than would otherwise be expected (July 2009 est.)

**Age structure:**
*0-14 years:* 20.8% (male 7,009,845/female 6,691,470)
*15-64 years:* 70.5% (male 22,977,945/female 23,512,538)
*65 years and over:* 8.7% (male 2,594,387/female 3,119,225) (2009 est.)

**Median age:**
*total:* 33.3 years
*male:* 32.4 years
*female:* 34.2 years (2009 est.)

**Population growth rate:** 0.615% (2009 est.)

**Birth rate:** 13.4 births/1,000 population (2009 est.)

**Death rate:** 7.17 deaths/1,000 population (2008 est.)

**Net migration rate:** NA

**Urbanization:**
*urban population:* 33% of total population (2008)
*rate of urbanization:* 1.7% annual rate of change (2005-10 est.)

**Sex ratio:**
*at birth:* 1.05 male(s)/female
*under 15 years:* 1.05 male(s)/female
*15-64 years:* 0.98 male(s)/female
*65 years and over:* 0.83 male(s)/female
*total population:* 0.98 male(s)/female (2009 est.)

**Infant mortality rate:**
*total:* 17.63 deaths/1,000 live births
*male:* 18.9 deaths/1,000 live births
*female:* 16.3 deaths/1,000 live births (2009 est.)

**Life expectancy at birth:**
*total population:* 73.1 years
*male:* 70.77 years
*female:* 75.55 years (2009 est.)

**Total fertility rate:** 1.65 children born/woman (2009 est.)

**HIV/AIDS - adult prevalence rate:** 1.4% (2007 est.)

**HIV/AIDS - people living with HIV/AIDS:** 610,000 (2007 est.)

**HIV/AIDS - deaths:** 30,000 (2007 est.)

# Thailand (continued)

**Major infectious diseases:**

*degree of risk:* high

*food or waterborne diseases:* bacterial diarrhea

*vectorborne diseases:* dengue fever, Japanese encephalitis, and malaria

*animal contact disease:* rabies

*water contact disease:* leptospirosis

*note:* highly pathogenic H5N1 avian influenza has been identified in this country; it poses a negligible risk with extremely rare cases possible among US citizens who have close contact with birds (2009)

**Nationality:**

*noun:* Thai (singular and plural)

*adjective:* Thai

**Ethnic groups:** Thai 75%, Chinese 14%, other 11%

**Religions:** Buddhist 94.6%, Muslim 4.6%, Christian 0.7%, other 0.1% (2000 census)

**Languages:** Thai, English (secondary language of the elite), ethnic and regional dialects

**Literacy:**

*definition:* age 15 and over can read and write

*total population:* 92.6%

*male:* 94.9%

*female:* 90.5% (2000 census)

**School life expectancy (primary to tertiary education):**

*total:* 14 years

*male:* 13 years

*female:* 14 years (2006)

**Education expenditures:** 4.2% of GDP (2005)

## Government

**Country name:**

*conventional long form:* Kingdom of Thailand

*conventional short form:* Thailand

*local long form:* Ratcha Anachak Thai

*local short form:* Prathet Thai

*former:* Siam

**Government type:** constitutional monarchy

**Capital:**

*name:* Bangkok

*geographic coordinates:* 13 45 N, 100 31 E

*time difference:* UTC+7 (12 hours ahead of Washington, DC during Standard Time)

**Administrative divisions:** 76 provinces (changwat, singular and plural); Amnat Charoen, Ang Thong, Buriram, Chachoengsao, Chai Nat, Chaiyaphum, Chanthaburi, Chiang Mai, Chiang Rai, Chon Buri, Chumphon, Kalasin, Kamphaeng Phet, Kanchanaburi, Khon Kaen, Krabi, Krung Thep Mahanakhon (Bangkok), Lampang, Lamphun, Loei, Lop Buri, Mae Hong Son, Maha Sarakham, Mukdahan, Nakhon Nayok, Nakhon Pathom, Nakhon Phanom, Nakhon Ratchasima, Nakhon Sawan, Nakhon Si Thammarat, Nan, Narathiwat, Nong Bua Lamphu, Nong Khai, Nonthaburi, Pathum Thani, Pattani, Phangnga, Phatthalung, Phayao, Phetchabun, Phetchaburi, Phichit, Phitsanulok, Phra Nakhon Si Ayutthaya, Phrae, Phuket, Prachin Buri, Prachuap Khiri Khan, Ranong, Ratchaburi, Rayong, Roi Et, Sa Kaeo, Sakon Nakhon, Samut Prakan, Samut Sakhon, Samut Songkhram, Sara Buri, Satun, Sing Buri, Sisaket, Songkhla, Sukhothai, Suphan Buri, Surat Thani, Surin, Tak, Trang, Trat, Ubon Ratchathani, Udon Thani, Uthai Thani, Uttaradit, Yala, Yasothon

**Independence:** 1238 (traditional founding date; never colonized)

**National holiday:** Birthday of King PHUMIPHON (BHUMIBOL), 5 December (1927)

**Constitution:** 24 August 2007

**Legal system:** based on civil law system with influences of common law; has not accepted compulsory ICJ jurisdiction

**Suffrage:** 18 years of age; universal and compulsory

**Executive branch:**

*chief of state:* King PHUMIPHON Adunyadet, also spelled BHUMIBOL Adulyadej (since 9 June 1946)

*head of government:* Prime Minister ABHISIT Wetchachiwa, also spelled ABHISIT Vejjajiva (since 17 December 2008); Deputy Prime Minister KORBSAK Saphawasu, also spelled KORBSAK Sabhavasu (since 22 December 2008); Deputy Prime Minister SANAN Kachornprasat, also spelled SANAN Kachornparsart (since 7 February 2008); Deputy Prime Minister SUTHEP Thueaksuban, also spelled SUTHEP Thaugsuban (since 22 December 2008)

*cabinet:* Council of Ministers

*note:* there is also a Privy Council advising the king

*elections:* monarch is hereditary; according to 2007 constitution, prime minister is elected from among members of House of Representatives; following national elections for House of Representatives, leader of party that could organize a majority coalition usually was appointed prime minister by king; prime minister is limited to two 4-year terms

**Legislative branch:** bicameral National Assembly or Rathasapha consisted of the Senate or Wuthisapha (150 seats; 76 members elected by popular vote representing 76 provinces, 74 appointed by judges and independent government bodies; all serve six-year terms) and the House of Representatives or Sapha Phuthaen Ratsadon (480 seats; 400 members elected from 157 multi-seat constituencies and 80 elected on proportional party-list basis of 10 per eight zones or groupings of provinces; all serve four-year terms)

*elections:* Senate - last held on 2 March 2008 (next to be held in March 2014); House of Representatives - last election held on 23 December 2007 (next to be held by December 2011)

*election results:* Senate - percent of vote by party - NA; seats by party - NA; House of Representatives - percent of vote by party - NA; seats by party - PPP 233, DP 164, TNP 34, Motherland 24, Middle Way 11, Unity 9, Royalist People's 5

*note:* 74 senators were appointed on 19 February 2008 by a seven-member committee headed by the chief of the Constitutional Court; 76 senators were elected on 2 March 2008; elections to the Senate are non-partisan; registered political party members are disqualified from being senators

**Judicial branch:** Supreme Court or Sandika (judges appointed by the monarch)

**Political parties and leaders:** Chat Thai Phattana Party or CP (Thai Nation Development Party) [CHUMPON Silpa-archa]; Democrat Party or DP (Prachathipat Party) [ABHISIT Wetchachiwa, also spelled ABHISIT Vejjajiva]; Motherland Party (Phuea Phaendin Party) [CHANCHAI Chairungrueang]; Phuea Thai Party (For Thais Party) or PTP [YONGYUT Wichaidit]; Phumchai (Bhumjai) Thai Party or PCT (Thai Pride) [CHAVARAT Charnvirakul]; Royalist People's Party (Pracharaj) [SANOH Thienthong]; Ruam Jai Thai Party (Thai Unity Party) [WANNARAT Channukul]

**Political pressure groups and leaders:** People's Alliance for Democracy or PAD; United Front for Democracy Against Dictatorship

**International organization participation:** ADB, APEC, APT, ARF, ASEAN, BIMSTEC, BIS, CP, EAS, FAO, G-77, IAEA, IBRD, ICAO, ICC, ICCt (signatory), ICRM, IDA, IFAD, IFC, IFRCS, IHO, ILO, IMF, IMO, IMSO, Interpol, IOC, IOM, IPU, ISO, ITSO, ITU, ITUC, MIGA, NAM, OAS (observer), OIC (observer), OIF (observer), OPCW, OSCE (partner), PCA, PIF (partner), UN, UNAMID, UNCTAD, UNESCO, UNHCR, UNIDO, UNITAR, UNMIS, UNWTO, UPU, WCL, WCO, WFTU, WHO, WIPO, WMO, WTO

**Diplomatic representation in the US:**

*chief of mission:* Ambassador (vacant); Charge d'Affaires DAMRONG Kraikruan

*chancery:* 1024 Wisconsin Avenue NW, Suite 401, Washington, DC 20007

*telephone:* [1] (202) 944-3600

*FAX:* [1] (202) 944-3611

*consulate(s) general:* Chicago, Los Angeles, New York

**Diplomatic representation from the US:**

*chief of mission:* Ambassador Eric G. JOHN

*embassy:* 120-122 Wireless Road, Bangkok 10330

*mailing address:* APO AP 96546

*telephone:* [66] (2) 205-4000

*FAX:* [66] (2) 254-2990, 205-4131

*consulate(s) general:* Chiang Mai

**Flag description:** five horizontal bands of red (top), white, blue (double width), white, and red

## Economy

**Economy - overview:** With a well-developed infrastructure, a free-enterprise economy, and generally pro-investment policies, Thailand was one of East Asia's best performers from 2002-04, averaging more than 6% annual real GDP growth. However, overall economic growth has fallen sharply - averaging 4.9% from 2005 to 2007 - as persistent political crisis stalled infrastructure mega-projects, eroded investor and consumer confidence, and damaged the country's international image. Exports were the key economic driver as foreign investment and consumer demand stalled. Export growth from January 2005 to November 2008 averaged 17.5% annually. Business uncertainty escalated, however,

# Thailand (continued)

following the September 2006 coup when the military-installed government imposed capital controls and considered far-reaching changes to foreign investment rules and other business legislation. Although controversial capital controls have since been lifted and business rules largely remain unchanged, investor sentiment has not recovered. Moreover, the 2008 global financial crisis further darkened Thailand's economic horizon. Continued political uncertainty will hamper resumption of infrastructure mega-projects.

**GDP (purchasing power parity):**
$553.4 billion (2008 est.)
$533.7 billion (2007)
$508.8 billion (2006)
*note:* data are in 2008 US dollars

**GDP (official exchange rate):** $272.1 billion (2008 est.)

**GDP - real growth rate:**
3.6% (2008 est.)
4.9% (2007 est.)
5.2% (2006 est.)

**GDP - per capita (PPP):**
$8,500 (2008 est.)
$8,200 (2007 est.)
$7,900 (2006 est.)
*note:* data are in 2008 US dollars

**GDP - composition by sector:**
*agriculture:* 11.4%
*industry:* 44.5%
*services:* 44.1% (2008 est.)

**Labor force:** 37.78 million (2008 est.)

**Labor force - by occupation:**
*agriculture:* 42.6%
*industry:* 20.2%
*services:* 37.1% (2005 est.)

**Unemployment rate:**
1.2% (2008 est.)
1.4% (2007 est.)

**Population below poverty line:** 10% (2004 est.)

**Household income or consumption by percentage share:**
*lowest 10%:* 2.7%
*highest 10%:* 33.4% (2002)

**Distribution of family income - Gini index:** 42 (2002)

**Investment (gross fixed):** 22.2% of GDP (2008 est.)

**Budget:**
*revenues:* $45.3 billion
*expenditures:* $55.76 billion (2008 est.)

**Public debt:** 42% of GDP (2008 est.)

**Inflation rate (consumer prices):**
5.5% (2008 est.)
2.2% (2007 est.)

**Central bank discount rate:** 2% (14 January 2009)

**Commercial bank prime lending rate:** 7.25% (31 December 2007)

**Stock of money:** $28.62 billion (31 December 2007)

**Stock of quasi money:** $216.6 billion (31 December 2007)

**Stock of domestic credit:** $241.8 billion (31 December 2007)

**Market value of publicly traded shares:** $196 billion (31 December 2007)

**Agriculture - products:** rice, cassava (tapioca), rubber, corn, sugarcane, coconuts, soybeans

**Industries:** tourism, textiles and garments, agricultural processing, beverages, tobacco, cement, light manufacturing such as jewelry and electric appliances, computers and parts, integrated circuits, furniture, plastics, automobiles and automotive parts; world's second-largest tungsten producer and third-largest tin producer

**Industrial production growth rate:** 8% (2008 est.)

**Electricity - production:** 148.4 billion kWh (2007 est.)

**Electricity - consumption:** 138.6 billion kWh (2007 est.)

**Electricity - exports:** 731 million kWh (2007 est.)

**Electricity - imports:** 4.488 billion kWh (2007 est.)

**Oil - production:** 348,600 bbl/day (2007 est.)

**Oil - consumption:** 928,600 bbl/day (2006 est.)

**Oil - exports:** 207,400 bbl/day (2005)

**Oil - imports:** 832,900 bbl/day (2005)

**Oil - proved reserves:** 176 million bbl (1 January 2008 est.)

**Natural gas - production:** 25.4 billion cu m (2007 est.)

**Natural gas - consumption:** 35.3 billion cu m (2007 est.)

**Natural gas - exports:** 0 cu m (2007 est.)

**Natural gas - imports:** 9.8 billion cu m (2007 est.)

**Natural gas - proved reserves:** 331.2 billion cu m (1 January 2008 est.)

**Current account balance:** -$1.049 billion (2008 est.)

**Exports:** $178.4 billion f.o.b. (2008 est.)

**Exports - commodities:** textiles and footwear, fishery products, rice, rubber, jewelry, automobiles, computers and electrical appliances

**Exports - partners:** US 12.6%, Japan 11.9%, China 9.7%, Singapore 6.3%, Hong Kong 5.7%, Malaysia 5.1% (2007)

**Imports:** $179 billion f.o.b. (2008 est.)

**Imports - commodities:** capital goods, intermediate goods and raw materials, consumer goods, fuels

**Imports - partners:** Japan 20.3%, China 11.6%, US 6.8%, Malaysia 6.2%, UAE 4.9%, Singapore 4.5%, Taiwan 4.1% (2007)

**Reserves of foreign exchange and gold:** $106.3 billion (31 December 2008 est.)

**Debt - external:** $64.8 billion (September 2008 est.)

**Stock of direct foreign investment - at home:** $80.83 billion (2007 est.)

**Stock of direct foreign investment - abroad:** $7.013 billion (2007 est.)

**Exchange rates:** baht per US dollar - 33.37 (2008 est.), 34.52 (2007), 37.882 (2006), 40.22 (2005), 40.222 (2004)

**Telephones - main lines in use:** 7.024 million (2007)
**Telephones - mobile cellular:** 51.377 million (2007)
**Telephone system:**
*general assessment:* high quality system, especially in urban areas like Bangkok
*domestic:* fixed line system provided by both a government owned and commercial provider; wireless service expanding rapidly and outpacing fixed lines
*international:* country code - 66; connected to major submarine cable systems providing links throughout Asia, Australia, Middle East, Europe, and US; satellite earth stations - 2 Intelsat (1 Indian Ocean, 1 Pacific Ocean)

**Radio broadcast stations:** AM 238, FM 351, shortwave 6 (2007)

**Television broadcast stations:** 111 (2006)

**Internet country code:** .th

**Internet hosts:** 1.116 million (2008)

**Internet users:** 13.416 million (2007)

**Airports:** 104 (2008)
**Airports - with paved runways:**
*total:* 64
*over 3,047 m:* 8
*2,438 to 3,047 m:* 11
*1,524 to 2,437 m:* 24
*914 to 1,523 m:* 15
*under 914 m:* 6 (2008)

**Airports - with unpaved runways:**
*total:* 40
*1,524 to 2,437 m:* 1
*914 to 1,523 m:* 13
*under 914 m:* 26 (2008)

**Heliports:** 3 (2007)

**Pipelines:** gas 1,348 km; refined products 323 km (2008)

**Railways:**
*total:* 4,071 km
*narrow gauge:* 4,071 km 1.000-m gauge (2006)

**Roadways:**
*total:* 180,053 km (includes 450 km of expressways) (2006)

**Waterways:** 4,000 km
*note:* 3,701 km navigable by boats with drafts up to 0.9 m (2008)

**Merchant marine:**
*total:* 398
*by type:* bulk carrier 53, cargo 135, chemical tanker 15, container 22, liquefied gas 28, passenger/cargo 10, petroleum tanker 100, refrigerated cargo 32, specialized tanker 2, vehicle carrier 1
*foreign-owned:* 16 (China 1, Japan 4, Malaysia 3, Singapore 2, Taiwan 1, UK 5)
*registered in other countries:* 40 (Bahamas 5, Mongolia 1, Panama 10, Singapore 23, Tuvalu 1) (2008)

**Ports and terminals:** Bangkok, Laem Chabang, Prachuap Port, Si Racha

# Thailand (continued)

**Military branches:** Royal Thai Army (Kongthap Bok Thai, RTA), Royal Thai Navy (Kongthap Ruea Thai, RTN, includes Royal Thai Marine Corps), Royal Thai Air Force (Kongtap Agard Thai, RTAF) (2009)

**Military service age and obligation:** 21 years of age for compulsory military service; 18 years of age for voluntary military service; males are registered at 18 years of age; 2-year conscript service obligation (2007)

**Manpower available for military service:**
*males age 16-49:* 17,553,410
*females age 16-49:* 17,751,268 (2008 est.)

**Manpower fit for military service:**
*males age 16-49:* 13,086,106
*females age 16-49:* 14,126,398 (2009 est.)

**Manpower reaching militarily significant age annually:**
*male:* 532,977
*female:* 510,737 (2009 est.)

**Military expenditures:** 1.8% of GDP (2005 est.)

## Transnational Issues

**Disputes - international:** separatist violence in Thailand's predominantly Muslim southern provinces prompt border closures and controls with Malaysia to stem terrorist activities; Southeast Asian states have enhanced border surveillance to check the spread of avian flu; talks continue on completion of demarcation with Laos but disputes remain over several islands in the Mekong River; despite continuing border committee talks, Thailand must deal with Karen and other ethnic rebels, refugees, and illegal cross-border activities, and as of 2006, over 116,000 Karen, Hmong, and other refugees and asylum seekers from Burma; Cambodia and Thailand dispute sections of historic boundary with missing boundary markers; Cambodia claims Thai encroachments into Cambodian territory and obstructing access to Preah Vihear temple ruins awarded to Cambodia by ICJ decision in 1962; Thailand is studying the feasibility of jointly constructing the Hatgyi Dam on the Salween river near the border with Burma; in 2004, international environmentalist pressure prompted China to halt construction of 13 dams on the Salween River that flows through China, Burma, and Thailand

**Refugees and internally displaced persons:**
*refugees (country of origin):* 132,241 (Burma) (2007)

**Illicit drugs:** a minor producer of opium, heroin, and marijuana; transit point for illicit heroin en route to the international drug market from Burma and Laos; eradication efforts have reduced the area of cannabis cultivation and shifted some production to neighboring countries; opium poppy cultivation has been reduced by eradication efforts; also a drug money-laundering center; minor role in methamphetamine production for regional consumption; major consumer of methamphetamine since the 1990s despite a series of government crackdowns

# Timor-Leste

## Introduction

**Background:** The Portuguese began to trade with the island of Timor in the early 16th century and colonized it in mid-century. Skirmishing with the Dutch in the region eventually resulted in an 1859 treaty in which Portugal ceded the western portion of the island. Imperial Japan occupied Portuguese Timor from 1942 to 1945, but Portugal resumed colonial authority after the Japanese defeat in World War II. East Timor declared itself independent from Portugal on 28 November 1975 and was invaded and occupied by Indonesian forces nine days later. It was incorporated into Indonesia in July 1976 as the province of Timor Timur (East Timor). An unsuccessful campaign of pacification followed over the next two decades, during which an estimated 100,000 to 250,000 individuals lost their lives. On 30 August 1999, in a UN-supervised popular referendum, an overwhelming majority of the people of Timor-Leste voted for independence from Indonesia. Between the referendum and the arrival of a multinational peacekeeping force in late September 1999, anti-independence Timorese militias - organized and supported by the Indonesian military - commenced a large-scale, scorched-earth campaign of retribution. The militias killed approximately 1,400 Timorese and forcibly pushed 300,000 people into western Timor as refugees. The majority of the country's infrastructure, including homes, irrigation systems, water supply systems, and schools, and nearly 100% of the country's electrical grid were destroyed. On 20 September 1999, the Australian-led peacekeeping troops of the International Force for East Timor (INTERFET) deployed to the country and brought the violence to an end. On 20 May 2002, Timor-Leste was internationally recognized as an independent state. In late April 2006, internal tensions threatened the new nation's security when a military strike led to violence and a near breakdown of law and order in Dili. At the request of the Government of Timor-Leste, an Australian-led International Stabilization Force (ISF) deployed to Timor-Leste in late May. In August, the UN Security Council established the UN Integrated Mission in Timor-Leste (UNMIT), which included an authorized police presence of over 1,600 personnel. The ISF and UNMIT restored stability, allowing the Government of Timor-Leste to hold presidential and parliamentary elections in April and June 2007 in a largely peaceful atmosphere. In February 2008, a rebel group staged an unsuccessful attack against the president and prime minister. The ringleader was killed in the attack and the majority of the rebels surrendered to the government in April 2008.

## Geography

**Location:** Southeastern Asia, northwest of Australia in the Lesser Sunda Islands at the eastern end of the Indonesian archipelago; note - Timor-Leste includes the eastern half of the island of Timor, the Oecussi (Ambeno) region on the northwest portion of the island of Timor, and the islands of Pulau Atauro and Pulau Jaco

**Geographic coordinates:** 8 50 S, 125 55 E

**Map references:** Southeast Asia

**Area:**
*total:* 15,007 sq km
*land:* NA sq km
*water:* NA sq km

**Area - comparative:** slightly larger than Connecticut

**Land boundaries:**
*total:* 228 km
*border countries:* Indonesia 228 km

**Coastline:** 706 km

**Maritime claims:**
*territorial sea:* 12 nm
*contiguous zone:* 24 nm
*exclusive fishing zone:* 200 nm

**Climate:** tropical; hot, humid; distinct rainy and dry seasons

**Terrain:** mountainous

**Elevation extremes:**
*lowest point:* Timor Sea, Savu Sea, and Banda Sea 0 m
*highest point:* Foho Tatamailau 2,963 m

**Natural resources:** gold, petroleum, natural gas, manganese, marble

**Land use:**
*arable land:* 8.2%
*permanent crops:* 4.57%
*other:* 87.23% (2005)

**Irrigated land:** 1,065 sq km (2003)

**Natural hazards:** floods and landslides are common; earthquakes; tsunamis; tropical cyclones

**Environment - current issues:** widespread use of slash and burn agriculture has led to deforestation and soil erosion

**Environment - international agreements:**
*party to:* Biodiversity, Climate Change, Climate Change-Kyoto Protocol, Desertification
*signed, but not ratified:* none of the selected agreements
**Geography - note:** Timor comes from the Malay word for "East"; the island of Timor is part of the Malay Archipelago and is the largest and easternmost of the Lesser Sunda Islands

## People

**Population:** 1,131,612
*note:* other estimates range as low as 800,000 (July 2009 est.)
**Age structure:**
*0-14 years:* 34.7% (male 199,237/female 192,900)
*15-64 years:* 61.9% (male 356,772/female 344,103)
*65 years and over:* 3.4% (male 18,403/female 20,197) (2009 est.)
**Median age:**
*total:* 21.8 years
*male:* 21.8 years
*female:* 21.8 years (2009 est.)
**Population growth rate:** 2.027% (2009 est.)
**Birth rate:** 26.25 births/1,000 population (2009 est.)
**Death rate:** 6.02 deaths/1,000 population (2008 est.)
**Net migration rate:** NA
**Urbanization:**
*urban population:* 27% of total population (2008)
*rate of urbanization:* 5% annual rate of change (2005-10 est.)
**Sex ratio:**
*at birth:* 1.05 male(s)/female
*under 15 years:* 1.03 male(s)/female
*15-64 years:* 1.04 male(s)/female
*65 years and over:* 0.91 male(s)/female
*total population:* 1.03 male(s)/female (2009 est.)
**Infant mortality rate:**
*total:* 40.65 deaths/1,000 live births
*male:* 46.72 deaths/1,000 live births
*female:* 34.28 deaths/1,000 live births (2009 est.)
**Life expectancy at birth:**
*total population:* 67.27 years
*male:* 64.92 years
*female:* 69.75 years (2009 est.)
**Total fertility rate:** 3.28 children born/woman (2009 est.)
**HIV/AIDS - adult prevalence rate:** NA
**HIV/AIDS - people living with HIV/AIDS:** NA
**HIV/AIDS - deaths:** NA
**Major infectious diseases:**
*degree of risk:* very high
*food or waterborne diseases:* bacterial and protozoal diarrhea, hepatitis A, and typhoid fever
*vectorborne diseases:* chikungunya, dengue fever and malaria (2009)
**Nationality:**
*noun:* Timorese
*adjective:* Timorese
**Ethnic groups:** Austronesian (Malayo-Polynesian), Papuan, small Chinese minority

**Religions:** Roman Catholic 98%, Muslim 1%, Protestant 1% (2005)
**Languages:** Tetum (official), Portuguese (official), Indonesian, English
*note:* there are about 16 indigenous languages; Tetum, Galole, Mambae, and Kemak are spoken by significant numbers of people
**Literacy:**
*definition:* age 15 and over can read and write
*total population:* 58.6%
*male:* NA
*female:* NA (2002)
**Education expenditures:** NA

## Government

**Country name:**
*conventional long form:* Democratic Republic of Timor-Leste (pronounced TEE-mor LESS-tay)
*conventional short form:* Timor-Leste
*local long form:* Republika Demokratika Timor Lorosa'e [Tetum]; Republica Democratica de Timor-Leste [Portuguese]
*local short form:* Timor Lorosa'e [Tetum]; Timor-Leste [Portuguese]
*former:* East Timor, Portuguese Timor
**Government type:** republic
**Capital:**
*name:* Dili
*geographic coordinates:* 8 35 S, 125 36 E
*time difference:* UTC+9 (14 hours ahead of Washington, DC during Standard Time)
**Administrative divisions:** 13 administrative districts; Aileu, Ainaro, Baucau, Bobonaro (Maliana), Cova-Lima (Suai), Dili, Ermera, Lautem (Los Palos), Liquica, Manatuto, Manufahi (Same), Oecussi (Ambeno), Viqueque
**Independence:** 28 November 1975 (independence proclaimed from Portugal); note - 20 May 2002 is the official date of international recognition of Timor-Leste's independence from Indonesia
**National holiday:** Independence Day, 28 November (1975)
**Constitution:** 22 March 2002 (based on the Portuguese model)
**Legal system:** UN-drafted legal system based on Indonesian law remains in place but is to be replaced by civil and penal codes based on Portuguese law; these have passed but have not been promulgated; has not accepted compulsory ICJ jurisdiction
**Suffrage:** 17 years of age; universal
**Executive branch:**
*chief of state:* President Jose RAMOS-HORTA (since 20 May 2007); note - the president plays a largely symbolic role but is able to veto legislation, dissolve parliament, and call national elections
*head of government:* Prime Minister Kay Rala Xanana GUSMAO (since 8 August 2007), note - he formerly used the name Jose Alexandre GUSMAO; Vice Prime Minister Mario Viegas CARRASCALAO (since 5 March 2009); Vice Prime Minister Jose Luis GUTERRES (since 8 August 2007)

*cabinet:* Council of Ministers
*elections:* president elected by popular vote for a five-year term (eligible for a second term); election last held on 9 April 2007 with run-off on 8 May 2007 (next to be held in May 2012); following elections, president appoints leader of majority party or majority coalition as prime minister
*election results:* Jose RAMOS-HORTA elected president; percent of vote - Jose RAMOS-HORTA 69.2%, Francisco GUTTERES 30.8%
**Legislative branch:** unicameral National Parliament (number of seats can vary from 52 to 65; members elected by popular vote to serve five-year terms)
*elections:* last held on 30 June 2007 (next elections due by June 2012)
*election results:* percent of vote by party - FRETILIN 29%, CNRT 24.1%, ASDT-PSD 15.8%, PD 11.3%, PUN 4.5%, KOTA-PPT (Democratic Alliance) 3.2%, UNDERTIM 3.2%, others 8.9%; seats by party - FRETILIN 21, CNRT 18, ASDT-PSD 11, PD 8, PUN 3, KOTA-PPT 2, UNDERTIM 2
**Judicial branch:** Supreme Court of Justice - constitution calls for one judge to be appointed by National Parliament and rest appointed by Superior Council for Judiciary; note - until Supreme Court is established, Court of Appeals is highest court
**Political parties and leaders:** Democratic Party or PD [Fernando de ARAUJO]; National Congress for Timorese Reconstruction or CNRT [Xanana GUSMAO]; National Democratic Union of Timorese Resistance or UNDERTIM [Cornelio DA Conceicao GAMA]; National Unity Party or PUN [Fernanda BORGES]; People's Party of Timor or PPT [Jacob XAVIER]; Revolutionary Front of Independent Timor-Leste or FRETILIN [Mari ALKATIRI]; Social Democratic Association of Timor or ASDT [Francisco Xavier do AMARAL]; Social Democratic Party or PSD [Zacarias Albano da COSTA]; Sons of the Mountain Warriors or KOTA [Manuel TILMAN] (also known as Association of Timorese Heroes)
**Political pressure groups and leaders:** NA
**International organization participation:** ACP, ADB, ARF, CPLP, FAO, G-77, IBRD, ICAO, ICCt, IDA, IFAD, IFC, IFRCS, ILO, IMF, IMO, Interpol, IOC, IPU, MIGA, NAM, OPCW, PIF (observer), UN, UNCTAD, UNESCO, UNIDO, Union Latina, UNWTO, UPU, WCO, WFTU, WHO
**Diplomatic representation in the US:**
*chief of mission:* Ambassador (vacant); Charge d'Affaires Jorge CAMEO
*chancery:* 4201 Connecticut Avenue NW, Suite 504, Washington, DC 20008
*telephone:* [1] (202) 966-3202
*FAX:* [1] (202) 966-3205
**Diplomatic representation from the US:**
*chief of mission:* Ambassador Hans G. KLEMM
*embassy:* Avenida de Portugal, Praia dos Conqueiros, Dili
*mailing address:* US Department of State, 8250 Dili Place, Washington, DC 20521-8250
*telephone:* (670) 332-4684
*FAX:* (670) 331-3206

# Timor-Leste (continued)

**Flag description:** red, with a black isosceles triangle (based on the hoist side) superimposed on a slightly longer yellow arrowhead that extends to the center of the flag; a white star is in the center of the black triangle

## Economy

**Economy - overview:** In late 1999, about 70% of the economic infrastructure of Timor-Leste was laid waste by Indonesian troops and anti-independence militias. Three hundred thousand people fled westward. Over the next three years a massive international program, manned by 5,000 peacekeepers (8,000 at peak) and 1,300 police officers, led to substantial reconstruction in both urban and rural areas. By the end of 2005, refugees had returned or had settled in Indonesia. The country continues to face great challenges in rebuilding its infrastructure, strengthening the civil administration, and generating jobs for young people entering the work force. The development of oil and gas resources in offshore waters has begun to supplement government revenues ahead of schedule and above expectations. The technology-intensive industry, however, has done little to create jobs for the unemployed because there are no production facilities in Timor. Gas is piped to Australia. In June 2005, the National Parliament unanimously approved the creation of a Petroleum Fund to serve as a repository for all petroleum revenues and preserve the value of Timor-Leste's petroleum wealth for future generations. The Fund held assets of US$3.9 billion as of October 2008. The economy is recovering from the mid-2006 outbreak of violence and civil unrest, which disrupted both private and public sector economic activity. The government in 2008 resettled tens of thousands of an estimated 100,000 internally displaced persons. The underlying economic policy challenge the country faces remains how best to use oil-and-gas wealth to lift the non-oil economy onto a higher growth path and to reduce poverty.

**GDP (purchasing power parity):**
$2.713 billion (2008 est.)
$2.591 billion (2007)
$2.23 billion (2006)
*note:* data are in 2008 US dollars

**GDP (official exchange rate):** $489 million (2008 est.)

**GDP - real growth rate:**
4.7% (2008 est.)
16.2% (2007 est.)
-3.4% (2006 est.)

**GDP - per capita (PPP):**
$2,400 (2008 est.)
$2,400 (2007 est.)
$2,100 (2006 est.)
*note:* data are in 2008 US dollars

**GDP - composition by sector:**
*agriculture:* 32.2%
*industry:* 12.8%
*services:* 55% (2005)

**Labor force:** NA

**Labor force - by occupation:**
*agriculture:* 90%
*industry:* NA%
*services:* NA% (2006 est.)

**Unemployment rate:**
20% (2006 est.)
*note:* data are for rural areas, unemployment rises to more than 40% among urban youth

**Population below poverty line:** 42% (2003 est.)

**Household income or consumption by percentage share:**
*lowest 10%:* NA%
*highest 10%:* NA%

**Distribution of family income - Gini index:** 38 (2002 est.)

**Budget:**
*revenues:* $733 million
*expenditures:* $309 million
*note:* the government in 2008 moved to a fiscal year calendar; it passed a supplementary spending package to cover the latter half of 2008 (FY06/07 est.)

**Inflation rate (consumer prices):**
7.8% (2007 est.)

**Commercial bank prime lending rate:** 15.05% (31 December 2007)

**Stock of money:** $74.94 million (31 December 2007)

**Stock of quasi money:** $68.78 million (31 December 2007)

**Stock of domestic credit:** NA

**Market value of publicly traded shares:** $NA

**Agriculture - products:** coffee, rice, corn, cassava, sweet potatoes, soybeans, cabbage, mangoes, bananas, vanilla

**Industries:** printing, soap manufacturing, handicrafts, woven cloth

**Industrial production growth rate:** 8.5% (2004 est.)

**Electricity - production:** NA kWh

**Electricity - consumption:** NA kWh

**Electricity - exports:** 0 kWh (2007 est.)

**Electricity - imports:** 0 kWh (2007 est.)

**Oil - production:** 78,480 bbl/day (2007 est.)

**Oil - consumption:** NA bbl/day

**Oil - proved reserves:** 553.8 million bbl (1 January 2008)

**Natural gas - production:** 0 cu m (2007 est.)

**Natural gas - consumption:** 0 cu m (2007 est.)

**Natural gas - exports:** 0 cu m (2007 est.)

**Natural gas - imports:** 0 cu m (2007 est.)

**Natural gas - proved reserves:** 200 billion cu m (1 January 2006 est.)

**Current account balance:** $1.161 billion (2007 est.)

**Exports:** $10 million; note - excludes oil (2005 est.)

**Exports - commodities:** coffee, sandalwood, marble; note - potential for oil and vanilla exports

**Imports:** $202 million (2004 est.)

**Imports - commodities:** food, gasoline, kerosene, machinery

**Exchange rates:** the US dollar is used

## Communications

**Telephones - main lines in use:** 2,400 (2006)

**Telephones - mobile cellular:** 69,000 (2007)

**Telephone system:**
*general assessment:* rudimentary service limited to urban areas
*domestic:* system suffered significant damage during the violence associated with independence; extremely limited fixed-line services; mobile-cellular services and coverage limited primarily to urban areas
*international:* country code - 670; international service is available in major urban centers

**Radio broadcast stations:** at least 21 (Timor-Leste has one national public broadcaster and 20 community and church radio stations - station frequency types NA) (2007)

**Television broadcast stations:** 1 (Timor-Leste has one national public broadcaster)

**Internet country code:** .tl

**Internet hosts:** 285 (2008)

**Internet users:** 1,200 (2006)

## Transportation

**Airports:** 6 (2008)

**Airports - with paved runways:**
*total:* 2
*2,438 to 3,047 m:* 1
*1,524 to 2,437 m:* 1 (2008)

**Airports - with unpaved runways:**
*total:* 4
*914 to 1,523 m:* 2
*under 914 m:* 2 (2008)

**Heliports:** 9 (2007)

**Roadways:**
*total:* 6,040 km
*paved:* 2,600 km
*unpaved:* 3,440 km (2005)

**Merchant marine:**
*total:* 1
*by type:* passenger/cargo 1 (2008)

**Ports and terminals:** Dili

## Military

**Military branches:** Timor-Leste Defense Force (Forcas de Defesa de Timor-L'este, Falintil (F-FDTL)): Army, Navy (Armada) (2009)

**Military service age and obligation:** 18 years of age for voluntary military service; no conscription (2008)

**Manpower available for military service:**
*males age 16-49:* 284,903
*females age 16-49:* 272,212 (2008 est.)

**Manpower fit for military service:**
*males age 16-49:* 230,534
*females age 16-49:* 238,610 (2009 est.)

**Manpower reaching militarily significant age annually:**
*male:* 12,887
*female:* 12,529 (2009 est.)

**Military expenditures:** NA

# Timor-Leste *(continued)*

**Disputes - international:** Timor-Leste-Indonesia Boundary Committee has resolved all but a small portion of the land boundary, but discussions on maritime boundaries are stalemated over sovereignty of the uninhabited coral island of Pulau Batek/Fatu Sinai in the north and alignment with Australian claims in the south; many refugees who left Timor-Leste in 2003 still reside in Indonesia and refuse repatriation; Australia and Timor-Leste agreed in 2005 to defer the disputed portion of the boundary for 50 years and to split hydrocarbon revenues evenly outside the Joint Petroleum Development Area covered by the 2002 Timor Sea Treaty

**Refugees and internally displaced persons:**
*IDPs:* 100,000 (2007)

**Illicit drugs:** NA

# Togo

## Introduction

**Background:** French Togoland became Togo in 1960. Gen. Gnassingbe EYADEMA, installed as military ruler in 1967, ruled Togo with a heavy hand for almost four decades. Despite the facade of multiparty elections instituted in the early 1990s, the government was largely dominated by President EYADEMA, whose Rally of the Togolese People (RPT) party has maintained power almost continually since 1967 and maintains a majority of seats in today's legislature. Upon EYADEMA's death in February 2005, the military installed the president's son, Faure GNASSINGBE, and then engineered his formal election two months later. Democratic gains since then allowed Togo to hold its first relatively free and fair legislative elections in October 2007. After years of political unrest and fire from international organizations for human rights abuses, Togo is finally being re-welcomed into the international community.

## Geography

**Location:** Western Africa, bordering the Bight of Benin, between Benin and Ghana

**Geographic coordinates:** 8 00 N, 1 10 E

**Map references:** Africa

**Area:**
*total:* 56,785 sq km
*land:* 54,385 sq km
*water:* 2,400 sq km

**Area - comparative:** slightly smaller than West Virginia

**Land boundaries:**
*total:* 1,647 km
*border countries:* Benin 644 km, Burkina Faso 126 km, Ghana 877 km

**Coastline:** 56 km

**Maritime claims:**
*territorial sea:* 30 nm
*exclusive economic zone:* 200 nm

**Climate:** tropical; hot, humid in south; semiarid in north

**Terrain:** gently rolling savanna in north; central hills; southern plateau; low coastal plain with extensive lagoons and marshes

**Elevation extremes:**
*lowest point:* Atlantic Ocean 0 m
*highest point:* Mont Agou 986 m

**Natural resources:** phosphates, limestone, marble, arable land

**Land use:**
*arable land:* 44.2%
*permanent crops:* 2.11%
*other:* 53.69% (2005)

**Irrigated land:** 70 sq km (2003)

**Total renewable water resources:** 14.7 cu km (2001)

**Freshwater withdrawal (domestic/industrial/ agricultural):**
*total:* 0.17 cu km/yr (53%/2%/45%)
*per capita:* 28 cu m/yr (2000)

**Natural hazards:** hot, dry harmattan wind can reduce visibility in north during winter; periodic droughts

**Environment - current issues:** deforestation attributable to slash-and-burn agriculture and the use of wood for fuel; water pollution presents health hazards and hinders the fishing industry; air pollution increasing in urban areas

**Environment - international agreements:**
*party to:* Biodiversity, Climate Change, Climate Change-Kyoto Protocol, Desertification, Endangered Species, Law of the Sea, Ozone Layer Protection, Ship Pollution, Tropical Timber 83, Tropical Timber 94, Wetlands, Whaling
*signed, but not ratified:* none of the selected agreements

**Geography - note:** the country's length allows it to stretch through six distinct geographic regions; climate varies from tropical to savanna

## People

**Population:** 6,019,877
*note:* estimates for this country explicitly take into account the effects of excess mortality due to AIDS; this can result in lower life expectancy, higher infant mortality, higher death rates, lower population growth rates, and changes in the distribution of population by age and sex than would otherwise be expected (July 2009 est.)

**Age structure:**
*0-14 years:* 41.5% (male 1,252,662/female 1,245,379)
*15-64 years:* 55.7% (male 1,640,982/female 1,714,278)
*65 years and over:* 2.8% (male 65,427/female 101,149) (2009 est.)

**Median age:**
*total:* 18.7 years
*male:* 18.3 years
*female:* 19.2 years (2009 est.)

**Population growth rate:** 2.711% (2009 est.)

**Birth rate:** 36.44 births/1,000 population (2009 est.)

# Togo (continued)

**Death rate:** 9.48 deaths/1,000 population (2008 est.)

**Net migration rate:** NA

**Urbanization:**

*urban population:* 42% of total population (2008)

*rate of urbanization:* 4.3% annual rate of change (2005-10 est.)

**Sex ratio:**

*at birth:* 1.03 male(s)/female

*under 15 years:* 1.01 male(s)/female

*15-64 years:* 0.96 male(s)/female

*65 years and over:* 0.65 male(s)/female

*total population:* 0.97 male(s)/female (2009 est.)

**Infant mortality rate:**

*total:* 56.24 deaths/1,000 live births

*male:* 63.5 deaths/1,000 live births

*female:* 48.77 deaths/1,000 live births (2009 est.)

**Life expectancy at birth:**

*total population:* 58.69 years

*male:* 56.56 years

*female:* 60.88 years (2009 est.)

**Total fertility rate:** 4.79 children born/woman (2009 est.)

**HIV/AIDS - adult prevalence rate:** 3.3% (2007 est.)

**HIV/AIDS - people living with HIV/AIDS:** 130,000 (2007 est.)

**HIV/AIDS - deaths:** 9,100 (2007 est.)

**Major infectious diseases:**

*degree of risk:* very high

*food or waterborne diseases:* bacterial and protozoal diarrhea, hepatitis A, and typhoid fever

*vectorborne diseases:* malaria and yellow fever

*water contact disease:* schistosomiasis

*respiratory disease:* meningococcal meningitis

*animal contact disease:* rabies

*note:* highly pathogenic H5N1 avian influenza has been identified in this country; it poses a negligible risk with extremely rare cases possible among US citizens who have close contact with birds (2009)

**Nationality:**

*noun:* Togolese (singular and plural)

*adjective:* Togolese

**Ethnic groups:** African (37 tribes; largest and most important are Ewe, Mina, and Kabre) 99%, European and Syrian-Lebanese less than 1%

**Religions:** Christian 29%, Muslim 20%, indigenous beliefs 51%

**Languages:** French (official and the language of commerce), Ewe and Mina (the two major African languages in the south), Kabye (sometimes spelled Kabiye) and Dagomba (the two major African languages in the north)

**Literacy:**

*definition:* age 15 and over can read and write

*total population:* 60.9%

*male:* 75.4%

*female:* 46.9% (2003 est.)

**School life expectancy (primary to tertiary education):**

*total:* 9 years

*male:* 11 years

*female:* 7 years (2000)

**Education expenditures:** 2.6% of GDP (2002)

## Government

**Country name:**

*conventional long form:* Togolese Republic

*conventional short form:* Togo

*local long form:* Republique togolaise

*local short form:* none

*former:* French Togoland

**Government type:** republic under transition to multiparty democratic rule

**Capital:**

*name:* Lome

*geographic coordinates:* 6 08 N, 1 13 E

*time difference:* UTC 0 (5 hours ahead of Washington, DC during Standard Time)

**Administrative divisions:** 5 regions (regions, singular - region); Centrale, Kara, Maritime, Plateaux, Savanes

**Independence:** 27 April 1960 (from French-administered UN trusteeship)

**National holiday:** Independence Day, 27 April (1960)

**Constitution:** adopted by public referendum 27 September 1992

**Legal system:** French-based court system; accepts compulsory ICJ jurisdiction with reservations

**Suffrage:** 18 years of age; universal (adult)

**Executive branch:**

*chief of state:* President Faure GNASSINGBE (since 4 May 2005); note - Gnassingbe EYADEMA died on 5 February 2005 and was succeeded by his son, Faure GNASSINGBE, with the support of the military; following international condemnation for the unconstitutional move he then stepped aside pending elections, and Abass BONFOH served as interim president; Faure GNASSINGBE later won popular elections in April 2005

*head of government:* Prime Minister Gilbert HOUNGBO (since 7 September 2008)

*cabinet:* Council of Ministers appointed by the president and the prime minister

*elections:* president elected by popular vote for a five-year term (no term limits); election last held 24 April 2005 (next to be held by 2010); prime minister appointed by the president

*election results:* Faure GNASSINGBE elected president; percent of vote - Faure GNASSINGBE 60.2%, Emmanuel Akitani BOB 38.3%, Nicolas LAWSON 1%, Harry OLYMPIO 0.5%

**Legislative branch:** unicameral National Assembly (81 seats; members are elected by popular vote to serve five-year terms)

*elections:* last held on 14 October 2007 (next to be held in 2012)

*election results:* percent of vote by party - RPT 39.4%, UFC 37.0%, CAR 8.2%, independents 2.5%, other 12.9%; seats by party - RPT 50, UFC 27, CAR 4

**Judicial branch:** Court of Appeal or Cour d'Appel; Supreme Court or Cour Supreme

**Political parties and leaders:** Action Committee for Renewal or CAR [Yawovi AGBOYIBO]; Democratic Convention of African Peoples or CDPA; Democratic Party for Renewal or PDR; Juvento [Monsilia DJATO]; Movement of the Believers of Peace and Equality or MOCEP; Pan-African Patriotic Convergence or CPP; Rally for the Support for Development and Democracy or RSDD [Harry OLYMPIO]; Rally of the Togolese People or RPT [Faure GNASSINGBE]; Socialist Pact for Renewal or PSR; Union for Democracy and Social Progress or UDPS [Gagou KOKOU]; Union of Forces for a Change or UFC [Gilchrist OLYMPIO]

**Political pressure groups and leaders:** NA

**International organization participation:** ACP, AfDB, AU, ECOWAS, Entente, FAO, FZ, G-77, IAEA, IBRD, ICAO, ICC, ICRM, IDA, IDB, IFAD, IFC, IFRCS, ILO, IMF, IMO, Interpol, IOC, IOM, IPU, ISO (correspondent), ITSO, ITU, ITUC, MIGA, NAM, OIC, OIF, OPCW, PCA, UN, UNAMID, UNCTAD, UNESCO, UNIDO, UNMIL, UNOCI, UNWTO, UPU, WADB (regional), WAEMU, WCL, WCO, WFTU, WHO, WIPO, WMO, WTO

**Diplomatic representation in the US:**

*chief of mission:* Ambassador (vacant); Charge d'Affaires Lorempo LANDJERGUE

*chancery:* 2208 Massachusetts Avenue NW, Washington, DC 20008

*telephone:* [1] (202) 234-4212

*FAX:* [1] (202) 232-3190

**Diplomatic representation from the US:**

*chief of mission:* Ambassador Patricia McMahon HAWKINS

*embassy:* 4332 Blvd. Gnassingbe Eyadema, Cite OUA, Lome

*mailing address:* B. P. 852, Lome; 2300 Lome Place, Washington, DC 20512-2300

*telephone:* [228] 261-5470

*FAX:* [228] 261-5501

**Flag description:** five equal horizontal bands of green (top and bottom) alternating with yellow; a white five-pointed star on a red square is in the upper hoist-side corner; uses the popular pan-African colors of Ethiopia

## Economy

**Economy - overview:** This small, sub-Saharan economy is heavily dependent on both commercial and subsistence agriculture, which provides employment for 65% of the labor force. Some basic foodstuffs must still be imported. Cocoa, coffee, and cotton generate about 40% of export earnings with cotton being the most important cash crop. Togo is the world's fourth-largest producer of phosphate. The government's decade-long effort, supported by the World Bank and the IMF, to implement economic reform measures, encourage foreign investment, and bring revenues in line with expenditures has moved slowly. Progress depends on follow through on privatization, increased openness in government financial operations, progress toward legislative elections, and continued support from foreign donors. Togo is working with donors to write a Poverty Reduction and Growth Facility (PRGF) that could eventually lead to a debt reduction plan. Economic

# Togo (continued)

growth remains marginal due to declining cotton production, underinvestment in phosphate mining, and strained relations with donors.

**GDP (purchasing power parity):**
$5.105 billion (2008 est.)
$5.064 billion (2007)
$4.97 billion (2006)
*note:* data are in 2008 US dollars

**GDP (official exchange rate):** $3.009 billion (2008 est.)

**GDP - real growth rate:**
0.8% (2008 est.)
1.9% (2007 est.)
3.9% (2006 est.)

**GDP - per capita (PPP):**
$900 (2008 est.)
$900 (2007 est.)
$900 (2006 est.)
*note:* data are in 2008 US dollars

**GDP - composition by sector:**
*agriculture:* 40%
*industry:* 25%
*services:* 35% (2008 est.)

**Labor force:** 1.302 million (1998)

**Labor force - by occupation:**
*agriculture:* 65%
*industry:* 5%
*services:* 30% (1998 est.)

**Unemployment rate:**
NA%

**Population below poverty line:** 32% (1989 est.)

**Household income or consumption by percentage share:**
*lowest 10%:* NA%
*highest 10%:* NA%

**Investment (gross fixed):** 18.4% of GDP (2008 est.)

**Budget:**
*revenues:* $551.5 million
*expenditures:* $620.1 million (2008 est.)

**Inflation rate (consumer prices):**
9.8% (2008 est.)
1% (2007 est.)

**Central bank discount rate:** 4.25% (31 December 2007)

**Commercial bank prime lending rate:** NA

**Stock of money:** $624.9 million (31 December 2007)

**Stock of quasi money:** $383.9 million (31 December 2007)

**Stock of domestic credit:** $590.7 million (31 December 2007)

**Market value of publicly traded shares:** $NA

**Agriculture - products:** coffee, cocoa, cotton, yams, cassava (tapioca), corn, beans, rice, millet, sorghum; livestock; fish

**Industries:** phosphate mining, agricultural processing, cement, handicrafts, textiles, beverages

**Industrial production growth rate:** 3% (2008 est.)

**Electricity - production:** 203 million kWh (2006 est.)

**Electricity - consumption:** 607 million kWh (2006 est.)

**Electricity - exports:** 0 kWh (2007 est.)

**Electricity - imports:** 505 million kWh; note - electricity supplied by Ghana (2006 est.)

**Oil - production:** 0 bbl/day (2007 est.)

**Oil - consumption:** 17,770 bbl/day (2006 est.)

**Oil - exports:** 1,547 bbl/day (2005)

**Oil - imports:** 16,650 bbl/day (2005)

**Oil - proved reserves:** 0 bbl (1 January 2006 est.)

**Natural gas - production:** 0 cu m (2007 est.)

**Natural gas - consumption:** 0 cu m (2007 est.)

**Natural gas - exports:** 0 cu m (2007 est.)

**Natural gas - imports:** 0 cu m (2007 est.)

**Natural gas - proved reserves:** 0 cu m (1 January 2006 est.)

**Current account balance:** -$433 million (2008 est.)

**Exports:** $1.001 billion f.o.b. (2008 est.)

**Exports - commodities:** reexports, cotton, phosphates, coffee, cocoa

**Exports - partners:** Ghana 16.8%, Burkina Faso 14.5%, Germany 9.2%, Benin 9.1%, Netherlands 5.9%, Mali 5.8%, India 4.7% (2007)

**Imports:** $1.725 billion f.o.b. (2008 est.)

**Imports - commodities:** machinery and equipment, foodstuffs, petroleum products

**Imports - partners:** China 36.3%, Estonia 9.6%, US 7.6%, Netherlands 7.3%, France 7% (2007)

**Reserves of foreign exchange and gold:** $502 million (31 December 2008 est.)

**Debt - external:** $2 billion (2005)

**Exchange rates:** Communaute Financiere Africaine francs (XOF) per US dollar - 447.81 (2008 est.), 482.71 (2007), 522.59 (2006), 527.47 (2005), 528.29 (2004)
*note:* since 1 January 1999, the West African CFA franc (XOF) has been pegged to the euro at a rate of 655.957 CFA francs per euro; West African CFA franc (XOF) coins and banknotes are not accepted in countries using Central African CFA francs (XAF), and vice versa, even though the two currencies trade at par

## Communications

**Telephones - main lines in use:** 82,100 (2006)

**Telephones - mobile cellular:** 1.19 million (2007)

**Telephone system:**
*general assessment:* fair system based on a network of microwave radio relay routes supplemented by open-wire lines and a mobile-cellular system
*domestic:* microwave radio relay and open-wire lines for conventional system; combined fixed-line and mobile-cellular teledensity roughly 15 telephones per 100 persons
*international:* country code - 228; satellite earth stations - 1 Intelsat (Atlantic Ocean), 1 Symphonie

**Radio broadcast stations:** AM 2, FM 9, shortwave 4 (1998)

**Television broadcast stations:** 3 (plus 2 repeaters) (1997)

**Internet country code:** .tg

**Internet hosts:** 769 (2008)

**Internet users:** 320,000 (2006)

## Transportation

**Airports:** 8 (2008)

**Airports - with paved runways:**
*total:* 2
*2,438 to 3,047 m:* 2 (2008)

**Airports - with unpaved runways:**
*total:* 6
*914 to 1,523 m:* 4
*under 914 m:* 2 (2008)

**Railways:**
*total:* 568 km
*narrow gauge:* 568 km 1.000-m gauge (2006)

**Roadways:**
*total:* 7,520 km
*paved:* 2,376 km
*unpaved:* 5,144 km (2000)

**Waterways:** 50 km (seasonally on Mono River depending on rainfall) (2008)

**Merchant marine:**
*total:* 10
*by type:* cargo 9, refrigerated cargo 1
*foreign-owned:* 6 (Bangladesh 1, Denmark 1, Egypt 1, Lebanon 1, Syria 2) (2008)

**Ports and terminals:** Kpeme, Lome

## Military

**Military branches:** Togolese Armed Forces (Forces Armees Togolaise, FAT): Ground Forces, Togolese Navy (Marine du Togo), Togolese Air Force (Force Aerienne Togolaise, FAT), National Gendarmerie (2009)

**Military service age and obligation:** 18 years of age for selective compulsory and voluntary military service; 2-year service obligation (2006)

**Manpower available for military service:**
*males age 16-49:* 1,365,505
*females age 16-49:* 1,374,993 (2008 est.)

**Manpower fit for military service:**
*males age 16-49:* 929,395
*females age 16-49:* 943,967 (2009 est.)

**Manpower reaching militarily significant age annually:**
*male:* 70,775
*female:* 70,051 (2009 est.)

**Military expenditures:** 1.6% of GDP (2005 est.)

## Transnational Issues

**Disputes - international:** in 2001, Benin claimed Togo moved boundary monuments - joint commission continues to resurvey the boundary; in 2006, 14,000 Togolese refugees remain in Benin and Ghana out of the 40,000 who fled there in 2005

**Refugees and internally displaced persons:**
*refugees (country of origin):* 5,000 (Ghana)
*IDPs:* 1,500 (2007)

**Illicit drugs:** transit hub for Nigerian heroin and cocaine traffickers; money laundering not a significant problem

# Tokelau
*(territory of New Zealand)*

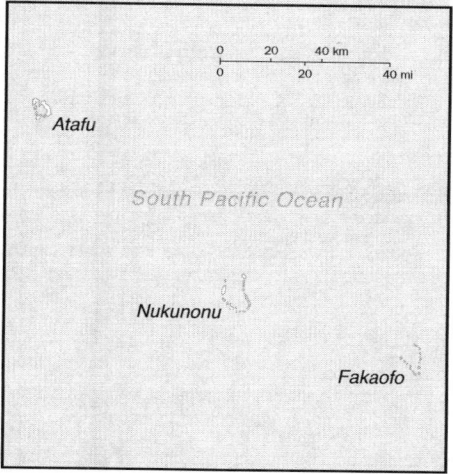

## Introduction

**Background:** Originally settled by Polynesian emigrants from surrounding island groups, the Tokelau Islands were made a British protectorate in 1889. They were transferred to New Zealand administration in 1925. Referenda held in 2006 and 2007 to change the status of the islands from that of a New Zealand territory to one of free association with New Zealand did not meet the needed threshold for approval.

## Geography

**Location:** Oceania, group of three atolls in the South Pacific Ocean, about one-half of the way from Hawaii to New Zealand
**Geographic coordinates:** 9 00 S, 172 00 W
**Map references:** Oceania
**Area:**
*total:* 10 sq km
*land:* 10 sq km
*water:* 0 sq km
**Area - comparative:** about 17 times the size of The Mall in Washington, DC
**Land boundaries:** 0 km
**Coastline:** 101 km
**Maritime claims:**
*territorial sea:* 12 nm
*exclusive economic zone:* 200 nm
**Climate:** tropical; moderated by trade winds (April to November)
**Terrain:** low-lying coral atolls enclosing large lagoons
**Elevation extremes:**
*lowest point:* Pacific Ocean 0 m
*highest point:* unnamed location 5 m
**Natural resources:** NEGL
**Land use:**
*arable land:* 0% (soil is thin and infertile)
*permanent crops:* 0%
*other:* 100% (2005)

**Irrigated land:** NA
**Natural hazards:** lies in Pacific typhoon belt
**Environment - current issues:** limited natural resources and overcrowding are contributing to emigration to New Zealand
**Geography - note:** consists of three atolls (Atafu, Fakaofo, Nukunonu), each with a lagoon surrounded by a number of reef-bound islets of varying length and rising to over 3 m above sea level

## People

**Population:** 1,416 (July 2009 est.)
**Age structure:**
*0-14 years:* 42%
*15-64 years:* 53%
*65 years and over:* 5% (2009 est.)
**Population growth rate:** -0.011% (2009 est.)
**Birth rate:** NA
**Death rate:** NA
**Net migration rate:** NA
**Urbanization:**
*urban population:* 0% of total population (2008)
*rate of urbanization:* 0% annual rate of change (2005-10 est.)
**Sex ratio:** NA
**Infant mortality rate:**
*total:* NA
*male:* NA
*female:* NA (2008 est.)
**Life expectancy at birth:**
*total population:* NA
*male:* NA
*female:* NA
**Total fertility rate:** NA (2008 est.)
**HIV/AIDS - adult prevalence rate:** NA
**HIV/AIDS - people living with HIV/AIDS:** NA
**HIV/AIDS - deaths:** NA
**Nationality:**
*noun:* Tokelauan(s)
*adjective:* Tokelauan
**Ethnic groups:** Polynesian
**Religions:** Congregational Christian Church 70%, Roman Catholic 28%, other 2%
*note:* on Atafu, all Congregational Christian Church of Samoa; on Nukunonu, all Roman Catholic; on Fakaofo, both denominations, with the Congregational Christian Church predominant
**Languages:** Tokelauan (a Polynesian language), English
**Literacy:** NA
**School life expectancy (primary to tertiary education):**
*total:* 11 years
*male:* 10 years
*female:* 11 years (2004)
**Education expenditures:** NA

## Government

**Country name:**
*conventional long form:* none
*conventional short form:* Tokelau
**Dependency status:** self-administering territory of New Zealand; note - Tokelau and New Zealand have agreed to a draft constitution as Tokelau moves toward free association with New Zealand; a UN-sponsored referendum on self governance in October 2007 did not produce the two-thirds majority vote necessary for changing the political status
**Government type:** NA
**Capital:** none; each atoll has its own administrative center
*time difference:* UTC-11 (6 hours behind Washington, DC during Standard Time)
**Administrative divisions:** none (territory of New Zealand)
**Independence:** none (territory of New Zealand)
**National holiday:** Waitangi Day (Treaty of Waitangi established British sovereignty over New Zealand), 6 February (1840)
**Constitution:** administered under the Tokelau Islands Act of 1948; amended in 1970
**Legal system:** New Zealand and local statutes
**Suffrage:** 21 years of age; universal
**Executive branch:**
*chief of state:* Queen ELIZABETH II (since 6 February 1952); represented by Governor General of New Zealand Anand SATYANAND (since 23 August 2006); New Zealand is represented by Administrator David PAYTON (since 17 October 2006)
*head of government:* Pio TUIA (since 23 February 2008); note - position rotates annually among the three Faipule (village leaders)
*cabinet:* the Council for the Ongoing Government of Tokelau, consisting of three Faipule (village leaders) and three Pulenuku (village mayors), functions as a cabinet
*elections:* the monarch is hereditary; administrator appointed by the Minister of Foreign Affairs and Trade in New Zealand; the head of government is chosen from the Council of Faipule and serves a one-year term
**Legislative branch:** unicameral General Fono (20 seats; based upon proportional representation from the three islands elected by popular vote to serve three-year terms; Atafu has seven seats, Fakaofo has seven seats, Nukunonu has six seats); note - the Tokelau Amendment Act of 1996 confers limited legislative power to the General Fono
*elections:* last held 17-19 January 2008 (next to be held in 2011)
*election results:* independents 20
**Judicial branch:** Supreme Court in New Zealand exercises civil and criminal jurisdiction in Tokelau
**Political parties and leaders:** none
**Political pressure groups and leaders:** none
**International organization participation:** PIF (observer), SPC, UNESCO (associate), UPU

**Diplomatic representation in the US:** none (territory of New Zealand)
**Diplomatic representation from the US:** none (territory of New Zealand)
**Flag description:** the flag of New Zealand is used

## Economy

**Economy - overview:** Tokelau's small size (three villages), isolation, and lack of resources greatly restrain economic development and confine agriculture to the subsistence level. The people rely heavily on aid from New Zealand - about $4 million annually - to maintain public services with annual aid being substantially greater than GDP. The principal sources of revenue come from sales of copra, postage stamps, souvenir coins, and handicrafts. Money is also remitted to families from relatives in New Zealand.
**GDP (purchasing power parity):**
$1.5 million (1993 est.)
**GDP (official exchange rate):** $NA
**GDP - real growth rate:** NA%
**GDP - per capita (PPP):**
$1,000 (1993 est.)
**GDP - composition by sector:**
*agriculture:* NA%
*industry:* NA%
*services:* NA%
**Labor force:** 440 (2001)
**Unemployment rate:**
NA%
**Population below poverty line:** NA%
**Budget:**
*revenues:* $430,800
*expenditures:* $2.8 million (1987 est.)
**Inflation rate (consumer prices):**
NA%
**Agriculture - products:** coconuts, copra, breadfruit, papayas, bananas; pigs, poultry, goats; fish
**Industries:** small-scale enterprises for copra production, woodworking, plaited craft goods; stamps, coins; fishing
**Electricity - production:** NA kWh
**Electricity - consumption:** NA kWh
**Exports:** $0 (2002)
**Exports - commodities:** stamps, copra, handicrafts
**Imports:** $969,200 c.i.f. (2002)
**Imports - commodities:** foodstuffs, building materials, fuel
**Exchange rates:** New Zealand dollars (NZD) per US dollar - 1.4151 (2008 est.), 1.3811 (2007), 1.5408 (2006), 1.4203 (2005), 1.5087 (2004)

## Communications

**Telephones - main lines in use:** 300 (2002)
**Telephone system:**
*general assessment:* modern satellite-based communications system
*domestic:* radiotelephone service between islands
*international:* country code - 690; radiotelephone service to Samoa; government-regulated telephone service (TeleTok); satellite earth stations - 3

**Radio broadcast stations:** AM NA, FM NA, shortwave NA (one radio station provides service to all islands) (2002)
**Internet country code:** .tk
**Internet hosts:** 273 (2008)
**Internet users:** NA

## Transportation

**Ports and terminals:** none; offshore anchorage only

## Military

**Military - note:** defense is the responsibility of New Zealand

## Transnational Issues

**Disputes - international:** Tokelau included American Samoa's Swains Island (Olohega) in its 2006 draft constitution

# Tonga

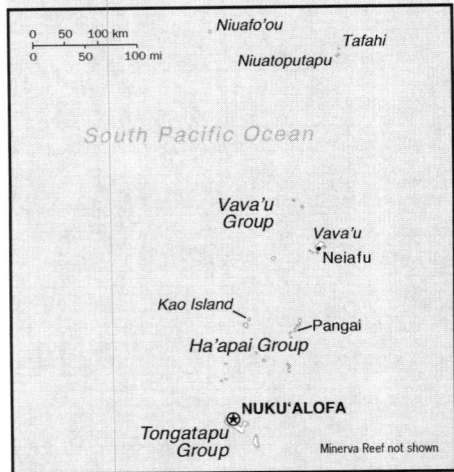

## Introduction

**Background:** Tonga - unique among Pacific nations - never completely lost its indigenous governance. The archipelagos of "The Friendly Islands" were united into a Polynesian kingdom in 1845. Tonga became a constitutional monarchy in 1875 and a British protectorate in 1900; it withdrew from the protectorate and joined the Commonwealth of Nations in 1970. Tonga remains the only monarchy in the Pacific.

## Geography

**Location:** Oceania, archipelago in the South Pacific Ocean, about two-thirds of the way from Hawaii to New Zealand
**Geographic coordinates:** 20 00 S, 175 00 W
**Map references:** Oceania
**Area:**
*total:* 748 sq km
*land:* 718 sq km
*water:* 30 sq km
**Area - comparative:** four times the size of Washington, DC
**Land boundaries:** 0 km
**Coastline:** 419 km
**Maritime claims:**
*territorial sea:* 12 nm
*exclusive economic zone:* 200 nm
*continental shelf:* 200 m depth or to the depth of exploitation
**Climate:** tropical; modified by trade winds; warm season (December to May), cool season (May to December)
**Terrain:** most islands have limestone base formed from uplifted coral formation; others have limestone overlying volcanic base
**Elevation extremes:**
*lowest point:* Pacific Ocean 0 m
*highest point:* unnamed location on Kao Island 1,033 m

# Tonga *(continued)*

**Natural resources:** fish, fertile soil
**Land use:**
*arable land:* 20%
*permanent crops:* 14.67%
*other:* 65.33% (2005)
**Irrigated land:** NA
**Natural hazards:** cyclones (October to April); earthquakes and volcanic activity on Fonuafo'ou
**Environment - current issues:** deforestation results as more and more land is being cleared for agriculture and settlement; some damage to coral reefs from starfish and indiscriminate coral and shell collectors; overhunting threatens native sea turtle populations
**Environment - international agreements:**
*party to:* Biodiversity, Climate Change, Climate Change-Kyoto Protocol, Desertification, Law of the Sea, Marine Dumping, Marine Life Conservation, Ozone Layer Protection, Ship Pollution
*signed, but not ratified:* none of the selected agreements
**Geography - note:** archipelago of 169 islands (36 inhabited)

## People

**Population:** 120,898 (July 2009 est.)
**Age structure:**
*0-14 years:* 32.8% (male 20,270/female 19,428)
*15-64 years:* 62.9% (male 37,837/female 38,166)
*65 years and over:* 4.3% (male 2,163/female 3,034) (2009 est.)
**Median age:**
*total:* 22.3 years
*male:* 21.8 years
*female:* 22.8 years (2009 est.)
**Population growth rate:** 1.482% (2009 est.)
**Birth rate:** 19.84 births/1,000 population (2009 est.)
**Death rate:** 5.12 deaths/1,000 population (2008 est.)
**Net migration rate:** NA
**Urbanization:**
*urban population:* 25% of total population (2008)
*rate of urbanization:* 1.6% annual rate of change (2005-10 est.)
**Sex ratio:**
*at birth:* 1.05 male(s)/female
*under 15 years:* 1.04 male(s)/female
*15-64 years:* 0.99 male(s)/female
*65 years and over:* 0.71 male(s)/female
*total population:* 0.99 male(s)/female (2009 est.)
**Infant mortality rate:**
*total:* 11.58 deaths/1,000 live births
*male:* 12.74 deaths/1,000 live births
*female:* 10.35 deaths/1,000 live births (2009 est.)
**Life expectancy at birth:**
*total population:* 70.73 years
*male:* 68.18 years
*female:* 73.41 years (2009 est.)
**Total fertility rate:** 2.25 children born/woman (2009 est.)

**HIV/AIDS - adult prevalence rate:** NA
**HIV/AIDS - people living with HIV/AIDS:** NA
**HIV/AIDS - deaths:** NA
**Nationality:**
*noun:* Tongan(s)
*adjective:* Tongan
**Ethnic groups:** Polynesian, Europeans
**Religions:** Christian (Free Wesleyan Church claims over 30,000 adherents)
**Languages:** Tongan, English
**Literacy:**
*definition:* can read and write Tongan and/or English
*total population:* 98.9%
*male:* 98.8%
*female:* 99% (1999 est.)
**School life expectancy (primary to tertiary education):**
*total:* 13 years
*male:* 13 years
*female:* 13 years (2004)
**Education expenditures:** 5% of GDP (2004)

## Government

**Country name:**
*conventional long form:* Kingdom of Tonga
*conventional short form:* Tonga
*local long form:* Pule'anga Tonga
*local short form:* Tonga
*former:* Friendly Islands
**Government type:** constitutional monarchy
**Capital:**
*name:* Nuku'alofa
*geographic coordinates:* 21 08 S, 175 12 W
*time difference:* UTC+13 (18 hours ahead of Washington, DC during Standard Time)
**Administrative divisions:** 3 island groups; Ha'apai, Tongatapu, Vava'u
**Independence:** 4 June 1970 (from UK protectorate)
**National holiday:** Emancipation Day, 4 June (1970)
**Constitution:** 4 November 1875; revised 1 January 1967
**Legal system:** based on English common law; has not accepted compulsory ICJ jurisdiction
**Suffrage:** 21 years of age; universal
**Executive branch:**
*chief of state:* King George TUPOU V (since 11 September 2006)
*head of government:* Prime Minister Dr. Feleti SEVELE (since 11 February 2006); Deputy Prime Minister Dr. Viliami TANGI (since 16 May 2006)
*cabinet:* Cabinet consists of 14 members, 10 appointed by the monarch for life; four appointed from among the elected members of the Legislative Assembly, including two each from the nobles' and peoples' representatives serving three-year terms
*note:* there is also a Privy Council that consists of the monarch, the cabinet, and two governors
*elections:* the monarch is hereditary; prime minister and deputy prime minister appointed by the monarch

**Legislative branch:** unicameral Legislative Assembly or Fale Alea (32 seats - 14 reserved for cabinet ministers sitting ex officio, nine for nobles selected by the country's 33 nobles, and nine elected by popular vote; members serve three-year terms)
*elections:* last held on 23-24 April 2008 (next to be held in 2011)
*election results:* Peoples Representatives: percent of vote - independents 54%, THRDM 28%, PDP 14%; seats - THRDM 4, independents 3, PDP 2
**Judicial branch:** Supreme Court (judges are appointed by the monarch); Court of Appeal (Chief Justice and high court justices from overseas chosen and approved by Privy Council)
**Political parties and leaders:** Tonga Human Rights and Democracy Movement or THRDM [Uliti UATA]; People's Democratic Party or PDP [Tesina FUKO]
**Political pressure groups and leaders:** Human Rights and Democracy Movement Tonga or HRDMT [Rev. Simote VEA, chairman]; Public Servant's Association [Finau TUTONE]
**International organization participation:** ACP, ADB, C, FAO, G-77, IBRD, ICAO, ICRM, IDA, IFAD, IFC, IFRCS, IHO, IMF, IMO, IMSO, Interpol, IOC, ITU, ITUC, OPCW, PIF, Sparteca, SPC, UN, UNCTAD, UNESCO, UNIDO, UPU, WCO, WFTU, WHO, WIPO, WMO, WTO
**Diplomatic representation in the US:**
*chief of mission:* Ambassador Fekitamoeloa 'UTOIKAMANU
*chancery:* 250 East 51st Street, New York, NY 10022
*telephone:* [1] (917) 369-1025
*FAX:* [1] (917) 369-1024
*consulate(s) general:* San Francisco
**Diplomatic representation from the US:** the US does not have an embassy in Tonga; the ambassador to Fiji is accredited to Tonga
**Flag description:** red with a bold red cross on a white rectangle in the upper hoist-side corner

## Economy

**Economy - overview:** Tonga has a small, open, South Pacific island economy. It has a narrow export base in agricultural goods. Squash, vanilla beans, and yams are the main crops. Agricultural exports, including fish, make up two-thirds of total exports. The country must import a high proportion of its food, mainly from New Zealand. The country remains dependent on external aid and remittances from Tongan communities overseas to offset its trade deficit. Tourism is the second-largest source of hard currency earnings following remittances. Tonga had 41,000 visitors in 2004. The government is emphasizing the development of the private sector, especially the encouragement of investment, and is committing increased funds for health and education. Tonga has a reasonably sound basic infrastructure and well developed social services. High unemployment among the young, a continuing upturn in inflation, pressures for democratic reform, and rising civil service expenditures are major issues facing the government.

## Tonga *(continued)*

**GDP (purchasing power parity):**
$549.1 million (2008 est.)
$542.6 million (2007)
$544.2 million (2006)
*note:* data are in 2008 US dollars
**GDP (official exchange rate):** $258 million
(2008 est.)
**GDP - real growth rate:**
1.2% (2008 est.)
-0.3% (2007 est.)
3.2% (2006 est.)
**GDP - per capita (PPP):**
$4,600 (2008 est.)
$4,600 (2007 est.)
$4,700 (2006 est.)
*note:* data are in 2008 US dollars
**GDP - composition by sector:**
*agriculture:* 25%
*industry:* 17%
*services:* 57% (FY05/06 est.)
**Labor force:** 33,910 (2003)
**Labor force - by occupation:**
*agriculture:* 31.8%
*industry:* 30.6%
*services:* 2,003% (2003 est.)
**Unemployment rate:**
13% (FY03/04 est.)
**Population below poverty line:** 24% (FY03/04)
**Household income or consumption by
percentage share:**
*lowest 10%:* NA%
*highest 10%:* NA%
**Budget:**
*revenues:* $80.48 million
*expenditures:* $109.8 million (FY07/08)
**Inflation rate (consumer prices):**
5.9% (2007 est.)
**Commercial bank prime lending rate:** 12.16%
(31 December 2007)
**Stock of money:** $46.38 million (31 December
2007)
**Stock of quasi money:** $106.8 million
(31 December 2007)
**Stock of domestic credit:** $163.1 million
(31 December 2007)
**Market value of publicly traded shares:** $NA
**Agriculture - products:** squash, coconuts, copra,
bananas, vanilla beans, cocoa, coffee, ginger, black
pepper; fish
**Industries:** tourism, construction, fishing
**Industrial production growth rate:** 1% (2003 est.)
**Electricity - production:** 43 million kWh (2007 est.)
**Electricity - consumption:** 39.99 million kWh
(2006 est.)
**Electricity - exports:** 0 kWh (2007)
**Electricity - imports:** 0 kWh (2007 est.)
**Oil - production:** 0 bbl/day (2007 est.)
**Oil - consumption:** 870 bbl/day (2006 est.)
**Oil - exports:** 0 bbl/day (2007 est.)
**Oil - imports:** 1,035 bbl/day (2005)
**Oil - proved reserves:** 0 bbl (1 January 2007 est.)

**Natural gas - production:** 0 cu m (2007 est.)
**Natural gas - consumption:** 0 cu m (2007 est.)
**Natural gas - exports:** 0 cu m (2007 est.)
**Natural gas - imports:** 0 cu m (2007 est.)
**Natural gas - proved reserves:** 0 cu m (1 January
2007 est.)
**Current account balance:** -$23 million (2007 est.)
**Exports:** $22 million f.o.b. (2006)
**Exports - commodities:** squash, fish, vanilla beans,
root crops
**Exports - partners:** US 36.7%, Japan 21.6%, NZ
10.1%, Fiji 5.8%, Samoa 4.9% (2007)
**Imports:** $139 million f.o.b. (2006)
**Imports - commodities:** foodstuffs, machinery and
transport equipment, fuels, chemicals
**Imports - partners:** Fiji 32.5%, NZ 27.5%, US 9%,
Australia 7.4%, China 5% (2007)
**Reserves of foreign exchange and gold:** $40.83
million (yearend, FY04/05)
**Debt - external:** $80.7 million (2004)
**Exchange rates:** pa'anga (TOP) per US dollar - NA
(2007), 2.0277 (2006), 1.96 (2005), 1.9716 (2004),
2.142 (2003)

### Communications

**Telephones - main lines in use:** 21,000 (2007)
**Telephones - mobile cellular:** 46,500 (2007)
**Telephone system:**
*general assessment:* competition between Tonga
Telecommunications Corporation (TCC) and
Shoreline Communications Tonga (SCT) is
accelerating expansion of telecommunications; SCT
granted approval to introduce high-speed digital
service for telephone, Internet, and television while
TCC has exclusive rights to operate the mobile-phone
network; international telecom services are provided
by government-owned Tonga Telecommunications
International (TTI)
*domestic:* combined fixed-line and mobile-cellular
teledensity roughly 40 telephones per 100 persons;
fully automatic switched network
*international:* country code - 676; satellite earth
station -1 Intelsat (Pacific Ocean) (2007)
**Radio broadcast stations:** AM 1, FM 4, shortwave
1 (2001)
**Television broadcast stations:** 3 (2004)
**Internet country code:** .to
**Internet hosts:** 19,231 (2008)
**Internet users:** 8,400 (2007)

### Transportation

**Airports:** 6 (2008)
**Airports - with paved runways:**
*total:* 1
*2,438 to 3,047 m:* 1 (2008)
**Airports - with unpaved runways:**
*total:* 5
*1,524 to 2,437 m:* 1
*914 to 1,523 m:* 3
*under 914 m:* 1 (2008)

**Roadways:**
*total:* 680 km
*paved:* 184 km
*unpaved:* 496 km (2000)
**Merchant marine:**
*total:* 13
*by type:* bulk carrier 1, cargo 8, carrier 1, liquefied gas
1, passenger/cargo 1, refrigerated cargo 1
*foreign-owned:* 4 (Australia 1, Cyprus 1, Switzerland
1, UK 1) (2008)
**Ports and terminals:** Nuku'alofa

### Military

**Military branches:** Tonga Defense Services (TDS):
Land Force (Royal Guard), Naval Force (includes
Royal Marines, Air Wing) (2009)
**Military service age and obligation:** 18 years of
age (est.); no conscription (2008)
**Manpower available for military service:**
*males age 16-49:* 32,053
*females age 16-49:* 30,981 (2008 est.)
**Manpower fit for military service:**
*males age 16-49:* 26,471
*females age 16-49:* 27,715 (2009 est.)
**Manpower reaching militarily significant age
annually:**
*male:* 1,458
*female:* 1,403 (2009 est.)
**Military expenditures:** 0.9% of GDP (2006 est.)

### Transnational Issues

**Disputes - international:** none

# Trinidad and Tobago

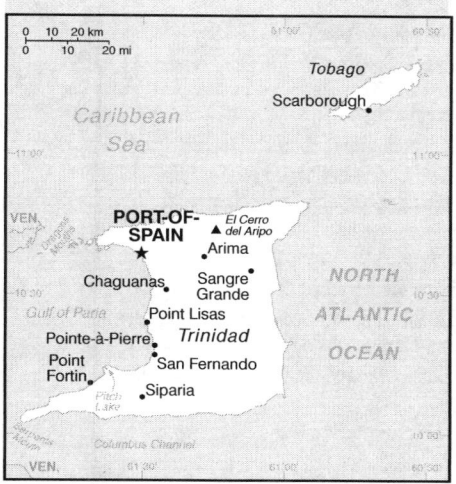

## Introduction

**Background:** First colonized by the Spanish, the islands came under British control in the early 19th century. The islands' sugar industry was hurt by the emancipation of the slaves in 1834. Manpower was replaced with the importation of contract laborers from India between 1845 and 1917, which boosted sugar production as well as the cocoa industry. The discovery of oil on Trinidad in 1910 added another important export. Independence was attained in 1962. The country is one of the most prosperous in the Caribbean thanks largely to petroleum and natural gas production and processing. Tourism, mostly in Tobago, is targeted for expansion and is growing. The government is coping with a rise in violent crime.

## Geography

**Location:** Caribbean, islands between the Caribbean Sea and the North Atlantic Ocean, northeast of Venezuela
**Geographic coordinates:** 11 00 N, 61 00 W
**Map references:** Central America and the Caribbean
**Area:**
*total:* 5,128 sq km
*land:* 5,128 sq km
*water:* 0 sq km
**Area - comparative:** slightly smaller than Delaware
**Land boundaries:** 0 km
**Coastline:** 362 km
**Maritime claims:** measured from claimed archipelagic baselines
*territorial sea:* 12 nm
*contiguous zone:* 24 nm
*exclusive economic zone:* 200 nm
*continental shelf:* 200 nm or to the outer edge of the continental margin
**Climate:** tropical; rainy season (June to December)
**Terrain:** mostly plains with some hills and low mountains

**Elevation extremes:**
*lowest point:* Caribbean Sea 0 m
*highest point:* El Cerro del Aripo 940 m
**Natural resources:** petroleum, natural gas, asphalt
**Land use:**
*arable land:* 14.62%
*permanent crops:* 9.16%
*other:* 76.22% (2005)
**Irrigated land:** 40 sq km (2003)
**Total renewable water resources:** 3.8 cu km (2000)
**Freshwater withdrawal (domestic/industrial/agricultural):**
*total:* 0.31 cu km/yr (68%/26%/6%)
*per capita:* 237 cu m/yr (2000)
**Natural hazards:** outside usual path of hurricanes and other tropical storms
**Environment - current issues:** water pollution from agricultural chemicals, industrial wastes, and raw sewage; oil pollution of beaches; deforestation; soil erosion
**Environment - international agreements:**
*party to:* Biodiversity, Climate Change, Climate Change-Kyoto Protocol, Desertification, Endangered Species, Hazardous Wastes, Law of the Sea, Marine Dumping, Marine Life Conservation, Ozone Layer Protection, Ship Pollution, Tropical Timber 83, Tropical Timber 94, Wetlands
*signed, but not ratified:* none of the selected agreements
**Geography - note:** Pitch Lake, on Trinidad's southwestern coast, is the world's largest natural reservoir of asphalt

## People

**Population:** 1,229,953 (July 2009 est.)
**Age structure:**
*0-14 years:* 19.6% (male 123,214/female 117,584)
*15-64 years:* 72.6% (male 457,868/female 434,486)
*65 years and over:* 7.9% (male 41,467/female 55,334) (2009 est.)
**Median age:**
*total:* 32.1 years
*male:* 31.6 years
*female:* 32.7 years (2009 est.)
**Population growth rate:** -0.102% (2009 est.)
**Birth rate:** 14.36 births/1,000 population (2009 est.)
**Death rate:** 7.99 deaths/1,000 population (2008 est.)
**Net migration rate:** -7.28 migrant(s)/1,000 population (2009 est.)
**Urbanization:**
*urban population:* 13% of total population (2008)
*rate of urbanization:* 2.9% annual rate of change (2005-10 est.)
**Sex ratio:**
*at birth:* 1.03 male(s)/female
*under 15 years:* 1.05 male(s)/female
*15-64 years:* 1.05 male(s)/female
*65 years and over:* 0.75 male(s)/female
*total population:* 1.02 male(s)/female (2009 est.)

**Infant mortality rate:**
*total:* 29.93 deaths/1,000 live births
*male:* 31.14 deaths/1,000 live births
*female:* 28.7 deaths/1,000 live births (2009 est.)
**Life expectancy at birth:**
*total population:* 70.86 years
*male:* 67.98 years
*female:* 73.82 years (2009 est.)
**Total fertility rate:** 1.72 children born/woman (2009 est.)
**HIV/AIDS - adult prevalence rate:** 1.5% (2007 est.)
**HIV/AIDS - people living with HIV/AIDS:** 14,000 (2007 est.)
**HIV/AIDS - deaths:** 1,900 (2003 est.)
**Nationality:**
*noun:* Trinidadian(s), Tobagonian(s)
*adjective:* Trinidadian, Tobagonian
**Ethnic groups:** Indian (South Asian) 40%, African 37.5%, mixed 20.5%, other 1.2%, unspecified 0.8% (2000 census)
**Religions:** Roman Catholic 26%, Hindu 22.5%, Anglican 7.8%, Baptist 7.2%, Pentecostal 6.8%, Muslim 5.8%, Seventh Day Adventist 4%, other Christian 5.8%, other 10.8%, unspecified 1.4%, none 1.9% (2000 census)
**Languages:** English (official), Caribbean Hindustani (a dialect of Hindi), French, Spanish, Chinese
**Literacy:**
*definition:* age 15 and over can read and write
*total population:* 98.6%
*male:* 99.1%
*female:* 98% (2003 est.)
**School life expectancy (primary to tertiary education):**
*total:* 11 years
*male:* 11 years
*female:* 11 years (2005)
**Education expenditures:** 4.2% of GDP (2002)
**People - note:** in 2007, the government of Trinidad and Tobago estimated the population to be 1.3 million

## Government

**Country name:**
*conventional long form:* Republic of Trinidad and Tobago
*conventional short form:* Trinidad and Tobago
**Government type:** parliamentary democracy
**Capital:**
*name:* Port-of-Spain
*geographic coordinates:* 10 39 N, 61 31 W
*time difference:* UTC-4 (1 hour ahead of Washington, DC during Standard Time)
**Administrative divisions:** 9 regional corporations, 2 city corporations, 3 borough corporations, 1 ward
*regional corporations:* Couva/Tabaquite/Talparo, Diego Martin, Mayaro/Rio Claro, Penal/Debe, Princes Town, Sangre Grande, San Juan/Laventille, Siparia, Tunapuna/Piarco
*city corporations:* Port-of-Spain, San Fernando
*borough corporations:* Arima, Chaguanas, Point Fortin
*ward:* Tobago

# Trinidad and Tobago (continued)

**Independence:** 31 August 1962 (from the UK)
**National holiday:** Independence Day, 31 August (1962)
**Constitution:** 1 August 1976
**Legal system:** based on English common law; judicial review of legislative acts in the Supreme Court; has not accepted compulsory ICJ jurisdiction
**Suffrage:** 18 years of age; universal
**Executive branch:**
*chief of state:* President George Maxwell RICHARDS (since 17 March 2003)
*head of government:* Prime Minister Patrick MANNING (since 24 December 2001)
*cabinet:* Cabinet appointed from among the members of Parliament
*elections:* president elected by an electoral college, which consists of the members of the Senate and House of Representatives, for a five-year term (eligible for a second term); election last held on 11 February 2008 (next to be held by February 2013); the president usually appoints as prime minister the leader of the majority party in the House of Representatives
*election results:* George Maxwell RICHARDS reelected president; percent of electoral college vote - NA
**Legislative branch:** bicameral Parliament consists of the Senate (31 seats; 16 members appointed by the ruling party, nine by the President, six by the opposition party to serve a maximum term of five years) and the House of Representatives (41 seats; members are elected by popular vote to serve five-year terms)
*elections:* House of Representatives - last held on 5 November 2007 (next to be held in 2012)
*election results:* House of Representatives - percent of vote - PNM 46%, UNC 29.7%; seats by party - PNM 26, UNC 15
*note:* Tobago has a unicameral House of Assembly with 12 members serving four-year terms; last election held in January 2005; seats by party - PNM 11, DAC 1
**Judicial branch:** Supreme Court of Judicature (comprised of the High Court of Justice and the Court of Appeals; the chief justice is appointed by the president after consultation with the prime minister and the leader of the opposition; other justices are appointed by the president on the advice of the Judicial and Legal Service Commission); the highest court of appeal is the Privy Council in London; member of the Caribbean Court of Justice (CCJ)
**Political parties and leaders:** Congress of the People [Winston DOOKERAN]; Democratic Action Congress or DAC [Hochoy CHARLES] (only active in Tobago); Democratic National Alliance or DNA [Gerald YETMING] (coalition of NAR, DDPT, MND); Movement for National Development or MND [Garvin NICHOLAS]; National Alliance for Reconstruction or NAR [Dr. Carson CHARLES]; People's National Movement or PNM [Patrick MANNING]; United National Congress or UNC [Basdeo PANDAY]
**Political pressure groups and leaders:** Jamaat-al Muslimeen [Yasin BAKR]

**International organization participation:** ACP, C, Caricom, CDB, FAO, G-24, G-77, IADB, IBRD, ICAO, ICCt, ICRM, IDA, IFAD, IFC, IFRCS, IHO, ILO, IMF, IMO, Interpol, IOC, ISO, ITSO, ITU, ITUC, LAES, MIGA, NAM, OAS, OPANAL, OPCW, UN, UNCTAD, UNESCO, UNIDO, UPU, WCL, WCO, WFTU, WHO, WIPO, WMO, WTO
**Diplomatic representation in the US:**
*chief of mission:* Ambassador Glenda MOREAN-PHILLIP
*chancery:* 1708 Massachusetts Avenue NW, Washington, DC 20036
*telephone:* [1] (202) 467-6490
*FAX:* [1] (202) 785-3130
*consulate(s) general:* Miami, New York
**Diplomatic representation from the US:**
*chief of mission:* Ambassador Roy L. AUSTIN
*embassy:* 15 Queen's Park West, Port-of-Spain
*mailing address:* P. O. Box 752, Port-of-Spain
*telephone:* [1] (868) 622-6371 through 6376
*FAX:* [1] (868) 822-5905
**Flag description:** red with a white-edged black diagonal band from the upper hoist side to the lower fly side

## Economy

**Economy - overview:** Trinidad and Tobago has earned a reputation as an excellent investment site for international businesses and has one of the highest growth rates and per capita incomes in Latin America. Economic growth for the past seven years has averaged slightly over 8%, significantly above the regional average of about 3.7% for that same period; however, it has slowed down this year to about 5% and is expected to slow further with the global downturn. Growth has been fueled by investments in liquefied natural gas (LNG), petrochemicals, and steel. Additional petrochemical, aluminum, and plastics projects are in various stages of planning. Trinidad and Tobago is the leading Caribbean producer of oil and gas, and its economy is heavily dependent upon these resources but it also supplies manufactured goods, notably food and beverages, as well as cement to the Caribbean region. Oil and gas account for about 40% of GDP and 80% of exports, but only 5% of employment. The country is also a regional financial center, and tourism is a growing sector, although it is not proportionately as important as in many other Caribbean islands. The economy benefits from a growing trade surplus. The MANNING administration has benefited from fiscal surpluses fueled by the dynamic export sector; however, declines in oil and gas prices have reduced government revenues which will challenge his government's commitment to maintaining high levels of public investment.
**GDP (purchasing power parity):**
$24.19 billion (2008 est.)
$23.37 billion (2007)
$26.57 billion (2006)
*note:* data are in 2008 US dollars
**GDP (official exchange rate):** $24.16 billion (2008 est.)

**GDP - real growth rate:**
3.5% (2008 est.)
5.5% (2007 est.)
12.2% (2006 est.)
**GDP - per capita (PPP):**
$18,600 (2008 est.)
$22,700 (2007 est.)
$21,500 (2006 est.)
*note:* data are in 2008 US dollars
**GDP - composition by sector:**
*agriculture:* 0.5%
*industry:* 47.9%
*services:* 51.6% (2008 est.)
**Labor force:** 620,800 (2008 est.)
**Labor force - by occupation:** agriculture 3.8%, manufacturing, mining, and quarrying 12.8%, construction and utilities 20.4%, services 62.9% (2007 est.)
**Unemployment rate:**
5.3% (2008 est.)
4.5% (2007 est.)
**Population below poverty line:** 17% (2007 est.)
**Household income or consumption by percentage share:**
*lowest 10%:* NA%
*highest 10%:* NA%
**Investment (gross fixed):** 17.1% of GDP (2008 est.)
**Budget:**
*revenues:* $8.317 billion
*expenditures:* $8.311 billion (2008 est.)
**Public debt:** 28% of GDP (2008 est.)
**Inflation rate (consumer prices):**
14.5% (2008 est.)
7.9% (2007 est.)
**Central bank discount rate:** 6.94% (31 December 2008)
**Commercial bank prime lending rate:** 11.75% (31 December 2007)
**Stock of money:** $2.39 billion (31 December 2008)
**Stock of quasi money:** $3.506 billion (31 December 2008)
**Stock of domestic credit:** $3.423 billion (31 December 2008)
**Market value of publicly traded shares:** $15.61 billion (31 December 2007)
**Agriculture - products:** cocoa, rice, citrus, coffee, vegetables; poultry
**Industries:** petroleum, chemicals, tourism, food processing, cement, beverage, cotton textiles
**Industrial production growth rate:** 4.4% (2008 est.)
**Electricity - production:** 7.704 billion kWh (2007)
**Electricity - consumption:** 7.083 billion kWh (2007)
**Electricity - exports:** 0 kWh (2007 est.)
**Electricity - imports:** 0 kWh (2007 est.)
**Oil - production:** 163,300 bbl/day (2007 est.)
**Oil - consumption:** 28,730 bbl/day (2006 est.)
**Oil - exports:** 38,990 bbl/day (2007)
**Oil - imports:** 72,780 bbl/day (2005)
**Oil - proved reserves:** 728.3 million bbl (1 January 2008 est.)
**Natural gas - production:** 39 billion cu m (2007 est.)

# Trinidad and Tobago *(continued)*

**Natural gas - consumption:** 20.8 billion cu m (2007 est.)

**Natural gas - exports:** 18.1 billion cu m (2007 est.)

**Natural gas - imports:** 0 cu m (2007 est.)

**Natural gas - proved reserves:** 481.3 billion cu m (1 January 2008 est.)

**Current account balance:** $5.721 billion (2008 est.)

**Exports:** $16.73 billion f.o.b. (2008 est.)

**Exports - commodities:** petroleum and petroleum products, liquefied natural gas (LNG), methanol, ammonia, urea, steel products, beverages, cereal and cereal products, sugar, cocoa, coffee, citrus fruit, vegetables, flowers

**Exports - partners:** US 57.5%, Jamaica 6.5%, Spain 3.9% (2007)

**Imports:** $10.26 billion f.o.b. (2008 est.)

**Imports - commodities:** mineral fuels, lubricants, machinery, transportation equipment, manufactured goods, food, chemicals, live animals

**Imports - partners:** US 28.2%, Brazil 11%, Venezuela 8.2%, Colombia 5.4%, Gabon 4.9%, China 4.2% (2007)

**Reserves of foreign exchange and gold:** $8.765 billion (31 December 2008 est.)

**Debt - external:** $3.4 billion (31 December 2008 est.)

**Stock of direct foreign investment - at home:** $12.44 billion (2007)

**Stock of direct foreign investment - abroad:** $3.829 billion (2007)

**Exchange rates:** Trinidad and Tobago dollars (TTD) per US dollar - 6.2896 (2008 est.), 6.3275 (2007), 6.3107 (2006), 6.2842 (2005), 6.299 (2004)

## Communications

**Telephones - main lines in use:** 323,800 (2007)

**Telephones - mobile cellular:** 1.008 million (2007)

**Telephone system:**
*general assessment:* excellent international service; good local service
*domestic:* mobile-cellular teledensity exceeds 125 telephones per 100 persons
*international:* country code - 1-868; submarine cable systems provide connectivity to US and parts of the Caribbean and South America; satellite earth station - 1 Intelsat (Atlantic Ocean); tropospheric scatter to Barbados and Guyana

**Radio broadcast stations:** AM 4, FM 18, shortwave 0 (2001)

**Television broadcast stations:** 6 (2005)

**Internet country code:** .tt

**Internet hosts:** 155,722 (2008)

**Internet users:** 430,800 (2007)

## Transportation

**Airports:** 6 (2008)

**Airports - with paved runways:**
*total:* 3
*over 3,047 m:* 1
*2,438 to 3,047 m:* 1
*1,524 to 2,437 m:* 1 (2008)

**Airports - with unpaved runways:**
*total:* 3
*914 to 1,523 m:* 1
*under 914 m:* 2 (2008)

**Pipelines:** gas 659 km; oil 336 km (2008)

**Roadways:**
*total:* 8,320 km
*paved:* 4,252 km
*unpaved:* 4,068 km (2000)

**Merchant marine:**
*total:* 9
*by type:* passenger 2, passenger/cargo 5, petroleum tanker 2
*foreign-owned:* 1 (US 1)
*registered in other countries:* 2 (Bahamas 1, unknown 1) (2008)

**Ports and terminals:** Point Fortin, Point Lisas, Port-of-Spain

## Military

**Military branches:** Trinidad and Tobago Defense Force (TTDF): Trinidad and Tobago Army, Coast Guard, Air Guard, Trinidad and Tobago Police Service (2008)

**Military service age and obligation:** 18 years of age for voluntary military service (16 years of age with parental consent); no conscription (2008)

**Manpower available for military service:**
*males age 16-49:* 301,561
*females age 16-49:* 264,225 (2008 est.)

**Manpower fit for military service:**
*males age 16-49:* 276,224
*females age 16-49:* 271,677 (2009 est.)

**Manpower reaching militarily significant age annually:**
*male:* 9,183
*female:* 8,662 (2009 est.)

**Military expenditures:** 0.3% of GDP (2006)

## Transnational Issues

**Disputes - international:** in April 2006, the Permanent Court of Arbitration issued a decision that delimited a maritime boundary with Trinidad and Tobago and compelled Barbados to enter a fishing agreement that limited Barbadian fishermen's catches of flying fish in Trinidad and Tobago's exclusive economic zone; in 2005, Barbados and Trinidad and Tobago agreed to compulsory international arbitration under UNCLOS challenging whether the northern limit of Trinidad and Tobago's and Venezuela's maritime boundary extends into Barbadian waters; Guyana has also expressed its intention to include itself in the arbitration as the Trinidad and Tobago-Venezuela maritime boundary may extend into its waters as well

**Illicit drugs:** transshipment point for South American drugs destined for the US and Europe; producer of cannabis

# Tunisia

## Introduction

**Background:** Rivalry between French and Italian interests in Tunisia culminated in a French invasion in 1881 and the creation of a protectorate. Agitation for independence in the decades following World War I was finally successful in getting the French to recognize Tunisia as an independent state in 1956. The country's first president, Habib BOURGUIBA, established a strict one-party state. He dominated the country for 31 years, repressing Islamic fundamentalism and establishing rights for women unmatched by any other Arab nation. In November 1987, BOURGUIBA was removed from office and replaced by Zine el Abidine BEN ALI in a bloodless coup. BEN ALI is currently serving his fourth consecutive five-year term as president; the next elections are scheduled for October 2009. Tunisia has long taken a moderate, non-aligned stance in its foreign relations. Domestically, it has sought to defuse rising pressure for a more open political society.

# Tunisia (continued)

## Geography

**Location:** Northern Africa, bordering the Mediterranean Sea, between Algeria and Libya
**Geographic coordinates:** 34 00 N, 9 00 E
**Map references:** Africa
**Area:**
*total:* 163,610 sq km
*land:* 155,360 sq km
*water:* 8,250 sq km
**Area - comparative:** slightly larger than Georgia
**Land boundaries:**
*total:* 1,424 km
*border countries:* Algeria 965 km, Libya 459 km
**Coastline:** 1,148 km
**Maritime claims:**
*territorial sea:* 12 nm
*contiguous zone:* 24 nm
*exclusive economic zone:* 12 nm
**Climate:** temperate in north with mild, rainy winters and hot, dry summers; desert in south
**Terrain:** mountains in north; hot, dry central plain; semiarid south merges into the Sahara
**Elevation extremes:**
*lowest point:* Shatt al Gharsah -17 m
*highest point:* Jebel ech Chambi 1,544 m
**Natural resources:** petroleum, phosphates, iron ore, lead, zinc, salt
**Land use:**
*arable land:* 17.05%
*permanent crops:* 13.08%
*other:* 69.87% (2005)
**Irrigated land:** 3,940 sq km (2003)
**Total renewable water resources:** 4.6 cu km (2003)
**Freshwater withdrawal (domestic/industrial/agricultural):**
*total:* 2.64 cu km/yr (14%/4%/82%)
*per capita:* 261 cu m/yr (2000)
**Natural hazards:** NA
**Environment - current issues:** toxic and hazardous waste disposal is ineffective and poses health risks; water pollution from raw sewage; limited natural fresh water resources; deforestation; overgrazing; soil erosion; desertification
**Environment - international agreements:**
*party to:* Biodiversity, Climate Change, Climate Change-Kyoto Protocol, Desertification, Endangered Species, Environmental Modification, Hazardous Wastes, Law of the Sea, Marine Dumping, Ozone Layer Protection, Ship Pollution, Wetlands
*signed, but not ratified:* Marine Life Conservation
**Geography - note:** strategic location in central Mediterranean; Malta and Tunisia are discussing the commercial exploitation of the continental shelf between their countries, particularly for oil exploration

## People

**Population:** 10,486,339 (July 2009 est.)
**Age structure:**
*0-14 years:* 22.7% (male 1,227,238/ female 1,149,796)
*15-64 years:* 70.1% (male 3,701,661/ female 3,652,322)
*65 years and over:* 7.2% (male 352,003/ female 403,319) (2009 est.)
**Median age:**
*total:* 29.2 years
*male:* 28.7 years
*female:* 29.8 years (2009 est.)
**Population growth rate:** 0.98% (2009 est.)
**Birth rate:** 15.42 births/1,000 population (2009 est.)
**Death rate:** 5.17 deaths/1,000 population (2008 est.)
**Net migration rate:** -0.41 migrant(s)/1,000 population (2009 est.)
**Urbanization:**
*urban population:* 67% of total population (2008)
*rate of urbanization:* 1.7% annual rate of change (2005-10 est.)
**Sex ratio:**
*at birth:* 1.07 male(s)/female
*under 15 years:* 1.07 male(s)/female
*15-64 years:* 1.01 male(s)/female
*65 years and over:* 0.87 male(s)/female
*total population:* 1.01 male(s)/female (2009 est.)
**Infant mortality rate:**
*total:* 22.57 deaths/1,000 live births
*male:* 24.81 deaths/1,000 live births
*female:* 20.17 deaths/1,000 live births (2009 est.)
**Life expectancy at birth:**
*total population:* 75.78 years
*male:* 73.98 years
*female:* 77.7 years (2009 est.)
**Total fertility rate:** 1.72 children born/woman (2009 est.)
**HIV/AIDS - adult prevalence rate:** less than 0.1% (2007 est.)
**HIV/AIDS - people living with HIV/AIDS:** 3,700 (2007 est.)
**HIV/AIDS - deaths:** fewer than 200 (2007 est.)
**Nationality:**
*noun:* Tunisian(s)
*adjective:* Tunisian
**Ethnic groups:** Arab 98%, European 1%, Jewish and other 1%
**Religions:** Muslim 98%, Christian 1%, Jewish and other 1%
**Languages:** Arabic (official and one of the languages of commerce), French (commerce)
**Literacy:**
*definition:* age 15 and over can read and write
*total population:* 74.3%
*male:* 83.4%
*female:* 65.3% (2004 census)
**School life expectancy (primary to tertiary education):**
*total:* 14 years
*male:* 13 years
*female:* 14 years (2006)
**Education expenditures:** 7.3% of GDP (2005)

## Government

**Country name:**
*conventional long form:* Tunisian Republic
*conventional short form:* Tunisia
*local long form:* Al Jumhuriyah at Tunisiyah
*local short form:* Tunis
**Government type:** republic
**Capital:**
*name:* Tunis
*geographic coordinates:* 36 48 N, 10 11 E
*time difference:* UTC+1 (6 hours ahead of Washington, DC during Standard Time)
*daylight saving time:* +1hr, begins last Sunday in March; ends last Sunday in October
**Administrative divisions:** 24 governorates; Ariana (Aryanah), Beja (Bajah), Ben Arous (Bin 'Arus), Bizerte (Banzart), Gabes (Qabis), Gafsa (Qafsah), Jendouba (Jundubah), Kairouan (Al Qayrawan), Kasserine (Al Qasrayn), Kebili (Qibili), Kef (Al Kaf), Mahdia (Al Mahdiyah), Manouba (Manubah), Medenine (Madanin), Monastir (Al Munastir), Nabeul (Nabul), Sfax (Safaqis), Sidi Bou Zid (Sidi Bu Zayd), Siliana (Silyanah), Sousse (Susah), Tataouine (Tatawin), Tozeur (Tawzar), Tunis, Zaghouan (Zaghwan)
**Independence:** 20 March 1956 (from France)
**National holiday:** Independence Day, 20 March (1956); also the anniversary of BEN ALI's assumption of the presidency, 7 November (1987)
**Constitution:** 1 June 1959; amended 1988, 2002
**Legal system:** based on French civil law system and Islamic law; some judicial review of legislative acts in the Supreme Court in joint session; has not accepted compulsory ICJ jurisdiction
**Suffrage:** 18 years of age; universal except for active government security forces (including the police and the military), people with mental disabilities, people who have served more than three months in prison (criminal cases only), and people given a suspended sentence of more than six months
**Executive branch:**
*chief of state:* President Zine el Abidine BEN ALI (since 7 November 1987)
*head of government:* Prime Minister Mohamed GHANNOUCHI (since 17 November 1999)
*cabinet:* Council of Ministers appointed by the president
*elections:* president elected by popular vote for a five-year term (no term limits); election last held on 24 October 2004 (next to be held in October 2009); prime minister appointed by the president
*election results:* President Zine El Abidine BEN ALI reelected for a fourth term; percent of vote - Zine El Abidine BEN ALI 94.5%, Mohamed BOUCHIHA 3.8%, Mohamed Ali HALOUANI 1%
**Legislative branch:** bicameral system consists of the Chamber of Deputies or Majlis al-Nuwaab (189 seats; members elected by popular vote to serve five-year terms) and the Chamber of Advisors (126 seats; 85 members elected by municipal counselors, deputies, mayors, and professional associations and trade unions; 41 members are presidential appointees; members serve six-year terms)

# Tunisia (continued)

elections: Chamber of Deputies - last held on 24 October 2004 (next to be held in October 2009); Chamber of Advisors - last held on 3 July 2005 (next to be held in July 2011)

election results: Chamber of Deputies - percent of vote by party - NA; seats by party - RCD 152, MDS 14, PUP 11, UDU 7, Al-Tajdid 3, PSL 2; Chamber of Advisors - percent of vote by party - NA; seats by party - RCD 71 (14 trade union seats vacant (due to boycott))

**Judicial branch:** Court of Cassation or Cour de Cassation

**Political parties and leaders:** Al-Tajdid Movement [Ahmed IBRAHIM]; Constitutional Democratic Rally Party (Rassemblement Constitutionnel Democratique) or RCD (official ruling party) [President Zine El Abidine BEN ALI]; Democratic Forum for Labor and Liberties or FDTL [Mustapha Ben JAFAAR]; Green Party for Progress or PVP [Mongi KHAMASSI]; Liberal Social Party or PSL [Mondher THABET]; Movement of Socialist Democrats or MDS [Ismail BOULAHYA]; Popular Unity Party or PUP [Mohamed BOUCHIHA]; Progressive Democratic Party [Maya JERIBI]; Unionist Democratic Union or UDU [Ahmed INOUBLI]; note - the Islamist party, Al Nahda (Renaissance), is outlawed

**Political pressure groups and leaders:** 18 October Group [collective leadership]; Tunisian League for Human Rights or LTDH [Mokhtar TRIFI]

**International organization participation:** ABEDA, AfDB, AFESD, AMF, AMU, AU, BSEC (observer), FAO, G-77, IAEA, IBRD, ICAO, ICC, ICRM, IDA, IDB, IFAD, IFC, IFRCS, IHO, ILO, IMF, IMO, IMSO, Interpol, IOC, IOM, IPU, ISO, ITSO, ITU, ITUC, LAS, MIGA, MONUC, NAM, OAPEC (suspended), OAS (observer), OIC, OIF, OPCW, OSCE (partner), UN, UNCTAD, UNESCO, UNHCR, UNIDO, UNOCI, UNWTO, UPU, WCO, WFTU, WHO, WIPO, WMO, WTO

**Diplomatic representation in the US:**
chief of mission: Ambassador Habib MANSOUR
chancery: 1515 Massachusetts Avenue NW, Washington, DC 20005
telephone: [1] (202) 862-1850
FAX: [1] (202) 862-1858

**Diplomatic representation from the US:**
chief of mission: Ambassador Robert F. GODEC
embassy: Zone Nord-Est des Berges du Lac Nord de Tunis 1053
mailing address: use embassy street address
telephone: [216] 71 107-000
FAX: [216] 71 963-263

**Flag description:** red with a white disk in the center bearing a red crescent nearly encircling a red five-pointed star; the crescent and star are traditional symbols of Islam

## Economy

**Economy - overview:** Tunisia has a diverse economy, with important agricultural, mining, tourism, and manufacturing sectors. Governmental control of economic affairs while still heavy has gradually lessened over the past decade with increasing privatization, simplification of the tax structure, and a prudent approach to debt. Progressive social policies also have helped raise living conditions in Tunisia relative to the region. Real growth, which averaged almost 5% over the past decade, declined to 4.7% in 2008 and probably will decline further in 2009 because of economic contraction and slowing of import demand in Europe - Tunisia's largest export market. However, development of non-textile manufacturing, a recovery in agricultural production, and strong growth in the services sector somewhat mitigated the economic effect of slowing exports. Tunisia will need to reach even higher growth levels to create sufficient employment opportunities for an already large number of unemployed as well as the growing population of university graduates. The challenges ahead include: privatizing industry, liberalizing the investment code to increase foreign investment, improving government efficiency, reducing the trade deficit, and reducing socioeconomic disparities in the impoverished south and west.

**GDP (purchasing power parity):**
$81.88 billion (2008 est.)
$78.21 billion (2007)
$73.56 billion (2006)
note: data are in 2008 US dollars

**GDP (official exchange rate):** $41.77 billion (2008 est.)

**GDP - real growth rate:**
4.7% (2008 est.)
6.3% (2007 est.)
5.4% (2006 est.)

**GDP - per capita (PPP):**
$7,900 (2008 est.)
$7,600 (2007 est.)
$7,200 (2006 est.)
note: data are in 2008 US dollars

**GDP - composition by sector:**
agriculture: 10.8%
industry: 28.3%
services: 61% (2008 est.)

**Labor force:** 3.676 million (2008 est.)

**Labor force - by occupation:**
agriculture: 55%
industry: 23%
services: 22% (1995 est.)

**Unemployment rate:**
14% (2008 est.)
14.1% (2007 est.)

**Population below poverty line:** 7.4% (2005 est.)

**Household income or consumption by percentage share:**
lowest 10%: 2.3%
highest 10%: 31.5% (2000)

**Distribution of family income - Gini index:** 40 (2005 est.)

**Investment (gross fixed):** 24.4% of GDP (2008 est.)

**Budget:**
revenues: $9.652 billion
expenditures: $11.03 billion (2008 est.)

**Public debt:** 53.1% of GDP (2008 est.)

**Inflation rate (consumer prices):**
5% (2008 est.)
3.1% (2007 est.)

**Stock of money:** $9.491 billion (31 December 2007)

**Stock of quasi money:** $13.56 billion (31 December 2007)

**Stock of domestic credit:** $25.23 billion (31 December 2007)

**Market value of publicly traded shares:** $5.355 billion (31 December 2007)

**Agriculture - products:** olives, olive oil, grain, tomatoes, citrus fruit, sugar beets, dates, almonds; beef, dairy products

**Industries:** petroleum, mining (particularly phosphate and iron ore), tourism, textiles, footwear, agribusiness, beverages

**Industrial production growth rate:** 4.5% (2008 est.)

**Electricity - production:** 12.65 billion kWh (2006 est.)

**Electricity - consumption:** 10.75 billion kWh (2006 est.)

**Electricity - exports:** 135 million kWh (2006 est.)

**Electricity - imports:** 0 kWh (2007 est.)

**Oil - production:** 86,210 bbl/day (2007 est.)

**Oil - consumption:** 91,110 bbl/day (2006 est.)

**Oil - exports:** 73,790 bbl/day (2005)

**Oil - imports:** 89,130 bbl/day (2005)

**Oil - proved reserves:** 400 million bbl (1 January 2008 est.)

**Natural gas - production:** 2.55 billion cu m (2006 est.)

**Natural gas - consumption:** 3.85 billion cu m (2006 est.)

**Natural gas - exports:** 0 cu m (2007 est.)

**Natural gas - imports:** 0 cu m (2005)

**Natural gas - proved reserves:** 65.13 billion cu m (1 January 2008 est.)

**Current account balance:** -$993 million (2008 est.)

**Exports:** $19.7 billion f.o.b. (2008 est.)

**Exports - commodities:** clothing, semi-finished goods and textiles, agricultural products, mechanical goods, phosphates and chemicals, hydrocarbons, electrical equipment

**Exports - partners:** France 31.3%, Italy 21%, Germany 8.5%, Spain 5.5%, Libya 5.5% (2007)

**Imports:** $23 billion f.o.b. (2008 est.)

**Imports - commodities:** textiles, machinery and equipment, hydrocarbons, chemicals, foodstuffs

**Imports - partners:** France 23.8%, Italy 21.9%, Germany 9.7%, Spain 5%, Libya 4.4% (2007)

**Reserves of foreign exchange and gold:** $8.875 billion (31 December 2008 est.)

# Tunisia *(continued)*

**Debt - external:** $19.33 billion (31 December 2008 est.)
**Stock of direct foreign investment - at home:** $28.51 billion (2008 est.)
**Stock of direct foreign investment - abroad:** $130 million (2008 est.)
**Exchange rates:** Tunisian dinars (TND) per US dollar - 1.211 (2008 est.), 1.2776 (2007), 1.331 (2006), 1.2974 (2005), 1.2455 (2004)

## Communications

**Telephones - main lines in use:** 1.273 million (2007)
**Telephones - mobile cellular:** 7.842 million (2007)
**Telephone system:**
*general assessment:* above the African average and continuing to be upgraded; key centers are Sfax, Sousse, Bizerte, and Tunis; Internet access available
*domestic:* in an effort jumpstart expansion of the fixed-line network, the government has awarded a concession to build and operate a VSAT network with international connectivity; competition between the two mobile-cellular service providers has resulted in lower activation and usage charges and a strong surge in subscribership; expansion of mobile-cellular services to include multimedia messaging and e-mail and Internet to mobile phone services also leading to a surge in subscribership; overall fixed-line and mobile-cellular teledensity is about 90 telephones per 100 persons
*international:* country code - 216; a landing point for the SEA-ME-WE-4 submarine cable system that provides links to Europe, Middle East, and Asia; satellite earth stations - 1 Intelsat (Atlantic Ocean) and 1 Arabsat; coaxial cable and microwave radio relay to Algeria and Libya; participant in Medarabtel; 2 international gateway digital switches
**Radio broadcast stations:** AM 7, FM 38, shortwave 2 (2007)
**Television broadcast stations:** 26 (plus 76 repeaters) (1995)
**Internet country code:** .tn
**Internet hosts:** 376 (2008)
**Internet users:** 1.722 million (2007)

## Transportation

**Airports:** 30 (2008)
**Airports - with paved runways:**
*total:* 14
*over 3,047 m:* 3
*2,438 to 3,047 m:* 6
*1,524 to 2,437 m:* 2
*914 to 1,523 m:* 3 (2008)
**Airports - with unpaved runways:**
*total:* 16
*1,524 to 2,437 m:* 2
*914 to 1,523 m:* 7
*under 914 m:* 7 (2008)
**Pipelines:** gas 2,102 km; oil 1,195 km; refined products 372 km (2008)

**Railways:**
*total:* 2,153 km
*standard gauge:* 471 km 1.435-m gauge
*narrow gauge:* 1,674 km 1.000-m gauge (65 km electrified)
*dual gauge:* 8 km 1.435 m and 1.000-m gauges (three rails) (2006)
**Roadways:**
*total:* 19,232 km
*paved:* 12,655 km (includes 262 km of expressways)
*unpaved:* 6,577 km (2004)
**Merchant marine:**
*total:* 7
*by type:* bulk carrier 1, cargo 1, chemical tanker 1, passenger/cargo 4
*registered in other countries:* 1 (Panama 1) (2008)
**Ports and terminals:** Bizerte, Gabes, La Goulette, Rades, Sfax, Skhira

## Military

**Military branches:** Army, Navy, Republic of Tunisia Air Force (Al-Quwwat al-Jawwiya al-Jamahiriyah At'tunisia) (2008)
**Military service age and obligation:** 20 years of age for compulsory military service, 18 years of age for voluntary military service; 1-year conscript service obligation (2007)
**Manpower available for military service:**
*males age 16-49:* 2,992,249
*females age 16-49:* 2,912,819 (2008 est.)
**Manpower fit for military service:**
*males age 16-49:* 2,569,403
*females age 16-49:* 2,489,651 (2009 est.)
**Manpower reaching militarily significant age annually:**
*male:* 100,478
*female:* 94,055 (2009 est.)
**Military expenditures:** 1.4% of GDP (2006)

## Transnational Issues

**Disputes - international:** none

# Turkey

## Introduction

**Background:** Modern Turkey was founded in 1923 from the Anatolian remnants of the defeated Ottoman Empire by national hero Mustafa KEMAL, who was later honored with the title Ataturk or "Father of the Turks." Under his authoritarian leadership, the country adopted wide-ranging social, legal, and political reforms. After a period of one-party rule, an experiment with multi-party politics led to the 1950 election victory of the opposition Democratic Party and the peaceful transfer of power. Since then, Turkish political parties have multiplied, but democracy has been fractured by periods of instability and intermittent military coups (1960, 1971, 1980), which in each case eventually resulted in a return of political power to civilians. In 1997, the military again helped engineer the ouster - popularly dubbed a "post-modern coup" - of the then Islamic-oriented government. Turkey intervened militarily on Cyprus in 1974 to prevent a Greek takeover of the island and has since acted as patron state to the "Turkish Republic of Northern Cyprus," which only Turkey recognizes. A separatist insurgency begun in 1984 by the Kurdistan Workers' Party (PKK) - now known as the People's Congress of Kurdistan or Kongra-Gel (KGK) - has dominated the Turkish military's attention and claimed more than 30,000 lives. After the capture of the group's leader in 1999, the insurgents largely withdrew from Turkey mainly to northern Iraq. In 2004, KGK announced an end to its ceasefire and attacks attributed to the KGK increased. Turkey joined the UN in 1945 and in 1952 it became a member of NATO; it holds a non-permanent seat on the UN Security Council from 2009-10. In 1964, Turkey became an associate member of the European Community. Over the past decade, it has undertaken many reforms to strengthen its democracy and economy; it began accession membership talks with the European Union in 2005.

## Geography

**Location:** Southeastern Europe and Southwestern Asia (that portion of Turkey west of the Bosporus is geographically part of Europe), bordering the Black Sea, between Bulgaria and Georgia, and bordering the Aegean Sea and the Mediterranean Sea, between Greece and Syria

**Geographic coordinates:** 39 00 N, 35 00 E

**Map references:** Middle East

**Area:**

*total:* 780,580 sq km

*land:* 770,760 sq km

*water:* 9,820 sq km

**Area - comparative:** slightly larger than Texas

**Land boundaries:**

*total:* 2,648 km

*border countries:* Armenia 268 km, Azerbaijan 9 km, Bulgaria 240 km, Georgia 252 km, Greece 206 km, Iran 499 km, Iraq 352 km, Syria 822 km

**Coastline:** 7,200 km

**Maritime claims:**

*territorial sea:* 6 nm in the Aegean Sea; 12 nm in Black Sea and in Mediterranean Sea

*exclusive economic zone:* in Black Sea only: to the maritime boundary agreed upon with the former USSR

**Climate:** temperate; hot, dry summers with mild, wet winters; harsher in interior

**Terrain:** high central plateau (Anatolia); narrow coastal plain; several mountain ranges

**Elevation extremes:**

*lowest point:* Mediterranean Sea 0 m

*highest point:* Mount Ararat 5,166 m

**Natural resources:** coal, iron ore, copper, chromium, antimony, mercury, gold, barite, borate, celestite (strontium), emery, feldspar, limestone, magnesite, marble, perlite, pumice, pyrites (sulfur), clay, arable land, hydropower

**Land use:**

*arable land:* 29.81%

*permanent crops:* 3.39%

*other:* 66.8% (2005)

**Irrigated land:** 52,150 sq km (2003)

**Total renewable water resources:** 234 cu km (2003)

**Freshwater withdrawal (domestic/industrial/agricultural):**

*total:* 39.78 cu km/yr (15%/11%/74%)

*per capita:* 544 cu m/yr (2001)

**Natural hazards:** severe earthquakes, especially in northern Turkey, along an arc extending from the Sea of Marmara to Lake Van

**Environment - current issues:** water pollution from dumping of chemicals and detergents; air pollution, particularly in urban areas; deforestation; concern for oil spills from increasing Bosporus ship traffic

**Environment - international agreements:**

*party to:* Air Pollution, Antarctic Treaty, Biodiversity, Climate Change, Desertification, Endangered Species, Hazardous Wastes, Ozone Layer Protection, Ship Pollution, Wetlands

*signed, but not ratified:* Environmental Modification

**Geography - note:** strategic location controlling the Turkish Straits (Bosporus, Sea of Marmara, Dardanelles) that link Black and Aegean Seas; Mount Ararat, the legendary landing place of Noah's ark, is in the far eastern portion of the country

## People

**Population:** 76,805,524 (July 2009 est.)

**Age structure:**

*0-14 years:* 27.2% (male 10,701,631/female 10,223,260)

*15-64 years:* 66.7% (male 25,896,326/female 25,327,403)

*65 years and over:* 6.1% (male 2,130,360/female 2,526,544) (2009 est.)

**Median age:**

*total:* 27.7 years

*male:* 27.4 years

*female:* 28.1 years (2009 est.)

**Population growth rate:** 1.312% (2009 est.)

**Birth rate:** 18.66 births/1,000 population (2009 est.)

**Death rate:** 6.02 deaths/1,000 population (2008 est.)

**Net migration rate:** 0.56 migrant(s)/1,000 population (2009 est.)

**Urbanization:**

*urban population:* 69% of total population (2008)

*rate of urbanization:* 1.9% annual rate of change (2005-10 est.)

**Sex ratio:**

*at birth:* 1.05 male(s)/female

*under 15 years:* 1.05 male(s)/female

*15-64 years:* 1.02 male(s)/female

*65 years and over:* 0.84 male(s)/female

*total population:* 1.02 male(s)/female (2009 est.)

**Infant mortality rate:**

*total:* 25.78 deaths/1,000 live births

*male:* 26.84 deaths/1,000 live births

*female:* 24.67 deaths/1,000 live births (2009 est.)

## Turkey *(continued)*

**Life expectancy at birth:**
*total population:* 71.96 years
*male:* 70.12 years
*female:* 73.89 years (2009 est.)
**Total fertility rate:** 2.21 children born/woman (2009 est.)
**HIV/AIDS - adult prevalence rate:** less than 0.1%; note - no country specific models provided (2001 est.)
**HIV/AIDS - people living with HIV/AIDS:** NA (2007 est.)
**HIV/AIDS - deaths:** NA
**Nationality:**
*noun:* Turk(s)
*adjective:* Turkish
**Ethnic groups:** Turkish 70-75%, Kurdish 18%, other minorities 7-12% (2008 est.)
**Religions:** Muslim 99.8% (mostly Sunni), other 0.2% (mostly Christians and Jews)
**Languages:** Turkish (official), Kurdish, other minority languages
**Literacy:**
*definition:* age 15 and over can read and write
*total population:* 87.4%
*male:* 95.3%
*female:* 79.6% (2004 est.)
**School life expectancy (primary to tertiary education):**
*total:* 11 years
*male:* 12 years
*female:* 11 years (2006)
**Education expenditures:** 4% of GDP (2004)

### Government

**Country name:**
*conventional long form:* Republic of Turkey
*conventional short form:* Turkey
*local long form:* Turkiye Cumhuriyeti
*local short form:* Turkiye
**Government type:** republican parliamentary democracy
**Capital:**
*name:* Ankara
*geographic coordinates:* 39 56 N, 32 52 E
*time difference:* UTC+2 (7 hours ahead of Washington, DC during Standard Time)
*daylight saving time:* +1hr, begins last Sunday in March; ends last Sunday in October
**Administrative divisions:** 81 provinces (iller, singular - ili); Adana, Adiyaman, Afyonkarahisar, Agri, Aksaray, Amasya, Ankara, Antalya, Ardahan, Artvin, Aydin, Balikesir, Bartin, Batman, Bayburt, Bilecik, Bingol, Bitlis, Bolu, Burdur, Bursa, Canakkale, Cankiri, Corum, Denizli, Diyarbakir, Duzce, Edirne, Elazig, Erzincan, Erzurum, Eskisehir, Gaziantep, Giresun, Gumushane, Hakkari, Hatay, Icel (Mersin), Igdir, Isparta, Istanbul, Izmir (Smyrna), Kahramanmaras, Karabuk, Karaman, Kars, Kastamonu, Kayseri, Kilis, Kirikkale, Kirklareli, Kirsehir, Kocaeli, Konya, Kutahya, Malatya, Manisa, Mardin, Mugla, Mus, Nevsehir, Nigde, Ordu, Osmaniye, Rize, Sakarya, Samsun, Sanliurfa, Siirt, Sinop, Sirnak, Sivas, Tekirdag, Tokat, Trabzon (Trebizond), Tunceli, Usak, Van, Yalova, Yozgat, Zonguldak

**Independence:** 29 October 1923 (successor state to the Ottoman Empire)
**National holiday:** Republic Day, 29 October (1923)
**Constitution:** 7 November 1982; amended 17 May 1987, 1995, 2001, and 2007; note - amendment passed by referendum concerning presidential elections on 21 October 2007
**Legal system:** civil law system derived from various European continental legal systems; note - member of the European Court of Human Rights (ECHR), although Turkey claims limited derogations on the ratified European Convention on Human Rights; has not accepted compulsory ICJ jurisdiction
**Suffrage:** 18 years of age; universal
**Executive branch:**
*chief of state:* President Abdullah GUL (since 28August 2007)
*head of government:* Prime Minister Recep Tayyip ERDOGAN (since 14 March 2003); Deputy Prime Minister Cemil CICEK (since 29 August 2007); Deputy Prime Minister Ali BABACAN (since 1 May 2009); Deputy Prime Minister Bulent ARINC (since 1 May 2009)
*cabinet:* Council of Ministers appointed by the president on the nomination of the prime minister
*elections:* president elected directly for a five-year term (eligible for a second term); prime minister appointed by the president from among members of parliament
*election results:* on 28 August 2007 the National Assembly elected Abdullah GUL president on the third ballot; National Assembly vote - 339
*note:* in October 2007 Turkish voters approved a referendum package of constitutional amendments including a provision for direct presidential elections
**Legislative branch:** unicameral Grand National Assembly of Turkey or Turkiye Buyuk Millet Meclisi (550 seats; members are elected by popular vote to serve five-year terms)
*elections:* last held on 22 July 2007 (next to be held in November 2012)
*election results:* percent of vote by party - AKP 46.7%, CHP 20.8%, MHP 14.3%, independents 5.2%, and other 13.0%; seats by party - AKP 341, CHP 112, MHP 71, independents 26; note - seats by party as of 31 January 2009 - AKP 340, CHP 97, MHP 70, DTP 21, DSP 13, ODP 1, BBP 1, independents 5, vacant 2 (DTP entered parliament as independents; DSP entered parliament on CHP's party list); only parties surpassing the 10% threshold are entitled to parliamentary seats
**Judicial branch:** Constitutional Court; High Court of Appeals (Yargitay); Council of State (Danistay); Court of Accounts (Sayistay); Military High Court of Appeals; Military High Administrative Court
**Political parties and leaders:** Anavatan Partisi (Motherland Party) or Anavatan [Erkan MUMCU]; note -True Path Party or DYP has merged with the Motherland Party; Democratic Party or DP [Husamettin CINDORUK]; Democratic Left Party or DSP [Masum TURKER]; Democratic Society Party or DTP [Ahmet TURK]; Felicity Party or SP [Numan KURTULMUS]

(sometimes translated as Contentment Party); Freedom and Solidarity Party or ODP [Hayri KOZANOGLU]; Grand Unity Party or BBP; note - Mushin YAZICIOGLU, former leader of the Grand Unity Party was killed in an March 2009 helicopter crash; Justice and Development Party or AKP [Recep Tayyip ERDOGAN]; Nationalist Movement Party or MHP [Devlet BAHCELI] (sometimes translated as Nationalist Action Party); People's Rise Party (Halkin Yukselisi Partisi) or HYP [Yasar Nuri OZTURK]; Republican People's Party or CHP [Deniz BAYKAL]; Social Democratic People's Party or SHP [Ugur CILASUN (acting)]; Young Party or GP [Cem Cengiz UZAN]
*note:* the parties listed above are some of the more significant of the 49 parties that Turkey had as of 31 January 2009
**Political pressure groups and leaders:** Confederation of Public Sector Unions or KESK [Sami EVREN]; Confederation of Revolutionary Workers Unions or DISK [Suleyman CELEBI]; Independent Industrialists' and Businessmen's Association or MUSIAD [Omer Cihad VARDAN]; Moral Rights Workers Union or Hak-Is [Salim USLU]; Turkish Confederation of Employers' Unions or TISK [Tugurl KUDATGOBILIK]; Turkish Confederation of Labor or Turk-Is [Mustafa KUMLU]; Turkish Confederation of Tradesmen and Craftsmen or TESK [Dervis GUNDAY]; Turkish Industrialists' and Businessmen's Association or TUSIAD [Arzuhan Dogan YALCINDAG]; Turkish Union of Chambers of Commerce and Commodity Exchanges or TOBB [M. Rifat HISARCIKLIOGLU]
**International organization participation:** ADB (nonregional member), Australia Group, BIS, BSEC, CE, CERN (observer), EAPC, EBRD, ECO, EU (applicant), FAO, G-20, IAEA, IBRD, ICAO, ICC, ICRM, IDA, IDB, IEA, IFAD, IFC, IFRCS, IHO, ILO, IMF, IMO, IMSO, Interpol, IOC, IOM, IPU, ISO, ITSO, ITU, ITUC, MIGA, NATO, NEA, NSG, OAS (observer), OECD, OIC, OPCW, OSCE, PCA, SECI, UN, UNCTAD, UNESCO, UNHCR, UNIDO, UNIFIL, UNMIS, UNOCI, UNOMIG, UNRWA, UNWTO, UPU, WCO, WEU (associate), WFTU, WHO, WIPO, WMO, WTO, ZC
**Diplomatic representation in the US:**
*chief of mission:* Ambassador Nabi SENSOY
*chancery:* 2525 Massachusetts Avenue NW, Washington, DC 20008
*telephone:* [1] (202) 612-6700
*FAX:* [1] (202) 612-6744
*consulate(s) general:* Chicago, Houston, Los Angeles, New York
**Diplomatic representation from the US:**
*chief of mission:* Ambassador James F. JEFFREY
*embassy:* 110 Ataturk Boulevard, Kavaklidere, 06100 Ankara
*mailing address:* PSC 93, Box 5000, APO AE 09823
*telephone:* [90] (312) 455-5555
*FAX:* [90] (312) 467-0019
*consulate(s) general:* Istanbul
*consulate(s):* Adana; note - there is a Consular Agent in Izmir

# Turkey (continued)

**Flag description:** red with a vertical white crescent (the closed portion is toward the hoist side) and white five-pointed star centered just outside the crescent opening

## E c o n o m y

**Economy - overview:** Turkey's dynamic economy is a complex mix of modern industry and commerce along with a traditional agriculture sector that still accounts for about 30% of employment. It has a strong and rapidly growing private sector, yet the state remains a major participant in basic industry, banking, transport, and communication. The largest industrial sector is textiles and clothing, which accounts for one-third of industrial employment; it faces stiff competition in international markets with the end of the global quota system. However, other sectors, notably the automotive and electronics industries, are rising in importance within Turkey's export mix. Real GNP growth has exceeded 6% in many years, but this strong expansion has been interrupted by sharp declines in output in 1994, 1999, and 2001. The economy turned around with the implementation of economic reforms, and 2004 GDP growth reached 9%, followed by roughly 5% annual growth from 2005-07. Due to global contractions, annual growth is estimated to have fallen to 1.5% in 2008. Inflation fell to 7.7% in 2005 - a 30-year low - but climbed to over 10% in 2008. Despite the strong economic gains from 2002-07, which were largely due to renewed investor interest in emerging markets, IMF backing, and tighter fiscal policy, the economy is still burdened by a high current account deficit and high external debt. Further economic and judicial reforms and prospective EU membership are expected to boost foreign direct investment. The stock value of FDI currently stands at about $85 billion. Privatization sales are currently approaching $21 billion. Oil began to flow through the Baku-Tblisi-Ceyhan pipeline in May 2006, marking a major milestone that will bring up to 1 million barrels per day from the Caspian to market. In 2007 and 2008, Turkish financial markets weathered significant domestic political turmoil, including turbulence sparked by controversy over the selection of former Foreign Minister Abdullah GUL as Turkey's 11th president and the possible closure of the Justice and Development Party (AKP). Economic fundamentals are sound, marked by moderate economic growth and foreign direct investment. Nevertheless, the Turkish economy may be faced with more negative economic indicators in 2009 as a result of the global economic slowdown. In addition, Turkey's high current account deficit leaves the economy vulnerable to destabilizing shifts in investor confidence.

**GDP (purchasing power parity):**
$906.5 billion (2008 est.)
$893.1 billion (2007)
$853.8 billion (2006)
*note:* data are in 2008 US dollars
**GDP (official exchange rate):** $798.9 billion (2008 est.)

**GDP - real growth rate:**
1.5% (2008 est.)
4.6% (2007 est.)
6.9% (2006 est.)
**GDP - per capita (PPP):**
$12,000 (2008 est.)
$11,900 (2007 est.)
$11,600 (2006 est.)
*note:* data are in 2008 US dollars
**GDP - composition by sector:**
*agriculture:* 8.5%
*industry:* 28.6%
*services:* 62.9% (2008 est.)
**Labor force:** 23.21 million
*note:* about 1.2 million Turks work abroad (2008 est.)
**Labor force - by occupation:**
*agriculture:* 29.5%
*industry:* 24.7%
*services:* 45.8% (2005)
**Unemployment rate:**
7.9% (2008 est.)
9.9% (2007 est.)
*note:* underemployment amounted to 4% in 2008
**Population below poverty line:** 20% (2002)
**Household income or consumption by percentage share:**
*lowest 10%:* 2%
*highest 10%:* 34.1% (2003)
**Distribution of family income - Gini index:** 43.6 (2003)
**Investment (gross fixed):** 21% of GDP (2008 est.)
**Budget:**
*revenues:* $164.6 billion
*expenditures:* $176.3 billion (2008 est.)
**Public debt:** 37.1% of GDP (2008 est.)
**Inflation rate (consumer prices):**
10.2% (2008 est.)
8.7% (2007 est.)
**Central bank discount rate:** 25% (31 December 2007)
**Stock of money:** $64.43 billion (31 December 2007)
**Stock of quasi money:** $254.3 billion (31 December 2007)
**Stock of domestic credit:** $358.1 billion (31 December 2007)
**Market value of publicly traded shares:** $286.6 billion (31 December 2007)
**Agriculture - products:** tobacco, cotton, grain, olives, sugar beets, hazelnuts, pulse, citrus; livestock
**Industries:** textiles, food processing, autos, electronics, mining (coal, chromite, copper, boron), steel, petroleum, construction, lumber, paper
**Industrial production growth rate:** 4% (2008 est.)
**Electricity - production:** 181.6 billion kWh (2007 est.)
**Electricity - consumption:** 141.5 billion kWh (2006 est.)
**Electricity - exports:** 2.576 billion kWh (2007 est.)
**Electricity - imports:** 863 million kWh (2007 est.)
**Oil - production:** 42,800 bbl/day (2007 est.)
**Oil - consumption:** 676,600 bbl/day (2007 est.)

**Oil - exports:** 114,600 bbl/day (2005)
**Oil - imports:** 714,100 bbl/day (2005)
**Oil - proved reserves:** 300 million bbl (1 January 2008 est.)
**Natural gas - production:** 893 million cu m (2007 est.)
**Natural gas - consumption:** 36.6 billion cu m (2007 est.)
**Natural gas - exports:** 31 million cu m (2007 est.)
**Natural gas - imports:** 35.83 billion cu m (2007 est.)
**Natural gas - proved reserves:** 8.495 billion cu m (1 January 2008 est.)
**Current account balance:** -$51.68 billion (2008 est.)
**Exports:** $141.8 billion f.o.b. (2008 est.)
**Exports - commodities:** apparel, foodstuffs, textiles, metal manufactures, transport equipment
**Exports - partners:** Germany 11.2%, UK 8.1%, Italy 7%, France 5.6%, Russia 4.4%, Spain 4.3% (2007)
**Imports:** $204.8 billion f.o.b. (2008 est.)
**Imports - commodities:** machinery, chemicals, semi-finished goods, fuels, transport equipment
**Imports - partners:** Russia 13.8%, Germany 10.3%, China 7.8%, Italy 5.9%, US 4.8%, France 4.6% (2007)
**Reserves of foreign exchange and gold:** $82.82 billion (31 December 2008 est.)
**Debt - external:** $294.3 billion (31 December 2008 est.)
**Stock of direct foreign investment - at home:** $124.8 billion (2008 est.)
**Stock of direct foreign investment - abroad:** $13.97 billion (2008 est.)
**Exchange rates:** Turkish liras (TRY) per US dollar - 1.3179 (2008 est.), 1.319 (2007), 1.4286 (2006), 1.3436 (2005), 1.4255 (2004)
*note:* on 1 January 2005, the old Turkish lira (TRL) was converted to new Turkish lira (TRY) at a rate of 1,000,000 old to 1 new Turkish lira; on 1 January 2009, the Turkish government dropped the word "new" and the currency is now called simply the Turkish lira

## C o m m u n i c a t i o n s

**Telephones - main lines in use:** 18.413 million (2007)
**Telephones - mobile cellular:** 61.976 million (2007)
**Telephone system:**
*general assessment:* comprehensive telecommunications network undergoing rapid modernization and expansion especially in mobile-cellular services
*domestic:* additional digital exchanges are permitting a rapid increase in subscribers; the construction of a network of technologically advanced intercity trunk lines, using both fiber-optic cable and digital microwave radio relay, is facilitating communication between urban centers; remote areas are reached by a domestic satellite system; the number of subscribers to mobile-cellular telephone service is growing rapidly
*international:* country code - 90; international service is provided by the SEA-ME-WE-3 submarine cable and by submarine fiber-optic cables in the Mediterranean and

# Turkey (continued)

Black Seas that link Turkey with Italy, Greece, Israel, Bulgaria, Romania, and Russia; satellite earth stations - 12 Intelsat; mobile satellite terminals - 328 in the Inmarsat and Eutelsat systems (2002)
**Radio broadcast stations:** AM 16, FM 107, shortwave 6 (2001)
**Television broadcast stations:** 635 (plus 2,934 repeaters) (1995)
**Internet country code:** .tr
**Internet hosts:** 2.667 million (2008)
**Internet users:** 13.15 million (2006)

## Transportation

**Airports:** 103 (2008)
**Airports - with paved runways:**
*total:* 90
*over 3,047 m:* 16
*2,438 to 3,047 m:* 33
*1,524 to 2,437 m:* 19
*914 to 1,523 m:* 19
*under 914 m:* 3 (2008)
**Airports - with unpaved runways:**
*total:* 13
*1,524 to 2,437 m:* 2
*914 to 1,523 m:* 7
*under 914 m:* 4 (2008)
**Heliports:** 18 (2007)
**Pipelines:** gas 7,555 km; oil 3,636 km (2008)
**Railways:**
*total:* 8,697 km
*standard gauge:* 8,697 km 1.435-m gauge (1,920 km electrified) (2006)
**Roadways:**
*total:* 426,951 km (includes 1,987 km of expressways) (2006)
**Waterways:** 1,200 km (2008)
**Merchant marine:**
*total:* 612
*by type:* bulk carrier 101, cargo 281, chemical tanker 70, combination ore/oil 1, container 35, liquefied gas 7, passenger 4, passenger/cargo 51, petroleum tanker 31, refrigerated cargo 1, roll on/roll off 28, specialized tanker 2
*foreign-owned:* 8 (Cyprus 2, Germany 1, Greece 1, Italy 3, UAE 1)
*registered in other countries:* 595 (Albania 1, Antigua and Barbuda 6, Bahamas 8, Belize 15, Cambodia 26, Comoros 8, Dominica 5, Georgia 14, Greece 1, Isle of Man 2, Italy 1, Kiribati 1, Liberia 7, Malta 176, Marshall Islands 50, Moldova 3, Netherlands 1, Netherlands Antilles 10, Panama 94, Russia 80, Saint Kitts and Nevis 35, Saint Vincent and the Grenadines 20, Sierra Leone 15, Slovakia 10, Tuvalu 2, UK 2, unknown 2) (2008)
**Ports and terminals:** Aliaga, Diliskelesi, Izmir, Kocaeli (Izmit), Mercin Limani, Nemrut Limani

## Military

**Military branches:** Turkish Armed Forces (TSK): Turkish Land Forces (Turk Kara Kuvvetleri), Turkish Naval Forces (Turk Deniz Kuvvetleri; includes naval air and naval infantry), Turkish Air Force (Turk Hava Kuvvetleri) (2009)
**Military service age and obligation:** 20 years of age (2004)
**Manpower available for military service:**
*males age 16-49:* 20,213,205
*females age 16-49:* 19,432,688 (2008 est.)
**Manpower fit for military service:**
*males age 16-49:* 17,223,506
*females age 16-49:* 16,995,299 (2009 est.)
**Manpower reaching militarily significant age annually:**
*male:* 692,592
*female:* 663,689 (2009 est.)
**Military expenditures:** 5.3% of GDP (2005 est.)
**Military - note:** a "National Security Policy Document" adopted in October 2005 increases the Turkish Armed Forces (TSK) role in internal security, augmenting the General Directorate of Security and Gendarmerie General Command (Jandarma); the TSK leadership continues to play a key role in politics and considers itself guardian of Turkey's secular state; in April 2007, it warned the ruling party about any pro-Islamic appointments; despite on-going negotiations on EU accession since October 2005, progress has been limited in establishing required civilian supremacy over the military; primary domestic threats are listed as fundamentalism (with the definition in some dispute with the civilian government), separatism (the Kurdish problem), and the extreme left wing; Ankara strongly opposed establishment of an autonomous Kurdish region; an overhaul of the Turkish Land Forces Command (TLFC) taking place under the "Force 2014" program is to produce 20-30% smaller, more highly trained forces characterized by greater mobility and firepower and capable of joint and combined operations; the TLFC has taken on increasing international peacekeeping responsibilities, and took charge of a NATO International Security Assistance Force (ISAF) command in Afghanistan in April 2007; the Turkish Navy is a regional naval power that wants to develop the capability to project power beyond Turkey's coastal waters; the Navy is heavily involved in NATO, multinational, and UN operations; its roles include control of territorial waters and security for sea lines of communications; the Turkish Air Force adopted an "Aerospace and Missile Defense Concept" in 2002 and has initiated project work on an integrated missile defense system; Air Force priorities include attaining a modern deployable, survivable, and sustainable force structure, and establishing a sustainable command and control system (2008)

## Transnational Issues

**Disputes - international:** complex maritime, air, and territorial disputes with Greece in the Aegean Sea; status of north Cyprus question remains; Syria and Iraq protest Turkish hydrological projects to control upper Euphrates waters; Turkey has expressed concern over the status of Kurds in Iraq; border with Armenia remains closed over Nagorno-Karabakh

**Refugees and internally displaced persons:**
*IDPs:* 1-1.2 million (fighting 1984-99 between Kurdish PKK and Turkish military; most IDPs in southeastern provinces) (2007)
**Illicit drugs:** key transit route for Southwest Asian heroin to Western Europe and, to a lesser extent, the US - via air, land, and sea routes; major Turkish and other international trafficking organizations operate out of Istanbul; laboratories to convert imported morphine base into heroin exist in remote regions of Turkey and near Istanbul; government maintains strict controls over areas of legal opium poppy cultivation and over output of poppy straw concentrate; lax enforcement of money-laundering controls

# Turkmenistan

## Introduction

**Background:** Eastern Turkmenistan for centuries formed part of the Persian province of Khurasan; in medieval times Merv (today known as Mary) was one of the great cities of the Islamic world and an important stop on the Silk Road. Annexed by Russia between 1865 and 1885, Turkmenistan became a Soviet republic in 1924. It achieved independence upon the dissolution of the USSR in 1991. Extensive hydrocarbon/natural gas reserves could prove a boon to this underdeveloped country if extraction and delivery projects were to be expanded. The Turkmenistan Government is actively seeking to develop alternative petroleum transportation routes to break Russia's pipeline monopoly. President for Life Saparmurat NYYAZOW died in December 2006, and Turkmenistan held its first multi-candidate presidential electoral process in February 2007. Gurbanguly BERDIMUHAMEDOW, a vice premier under NYYAZOW, emerged as the country's new president.

## Geography

**Location:** Central Asia, bordering the Caspian Sea, between Iran and Kazakhstan
**Geographic coordinates:** 40 00 N, 60 00 E
**Map references:** Asia
**Area:**
*total:* 488,100 sq km
*land:* 488,100 sq km
*water:* NEGL
**Area - comparative:** slightly larger than California
**Land boundaries:**
*total:* 3,736 km
*border countries:* Afghanistan 744 km, Iran 992 km, Kazakhstan 379 km, Uzbekistan 1,621 km
**Coastline:** 0 km; note - Turkmenistan borders the Caspian Sea (1,768 km)

**Maritime claims:** none (landlocked)
**Climate:** subtropical desert
**Terrain:** flat-to-rolling sandy desert with dunes rising to mountains in the south; low mountains along border with Iran; borders Caspian Sea in west
**Elevation extremes:**
*lowest point:* Vpadina Akchanaya -81 m; note - Sarygamysh Koli is a lake in northern Turkmenistan with a water level that fluctuates above and below the elevation of Vpadina Akchanaya (the lake has dropped as low as -110 m)
*highest point:* Gora Ayribaba 3,139 m
**Natural resources:** petroleum, natural gas, sulfur, salt
**Land use:**
*arable land:* 4.51%
*permanent crops:* 0.14%
*other:* 95.35% (2005)
**Irrigated land:** 18,000 sq km (2003)
**Total renewable water resources:** 60.9 cu km (1997)
**Freshwater withdrawal (domestic/industrial/agricultural):**
*total:* 24.65 cu km/yr (2%/1%/98%)
*per capita:* 5,104 cu m/yr (2000)
**Natural hazards:** NA
**Environment - current issues:** contamination of soil and groundwater with agricultural chemicals, pesticides; salination, water logging of soil due to poor irrigation methods; Caspian Sea pollution; diversion of a large share of the flow of the Amu Darya into irrigation contributes to that river's inability to replenish the Aral Sea; desertification
**Environment - international agreements:**
*party to:* Biodiversity, Climate Change, Climate Change-Kyoto Protocol, Desertification, Hazardous Wastes, Ozone Layer Protection
*signed, but not ratified:* none of the selected agreements

**Geography - note:** landlocked; the western and central low-lying desolate portions of the country make up the great Garagum (Kara-Kum) desert, which occupies over 80% of the country; eastern part is plateau

## People

**Population:** 4,884,887 (July 2009 est.)
**Age structure:**
*0-14 years:* 28.9% (male 713,698/female 697,222)
*15-64 years:* 66.9% (male 1,618,678/female 1,646,992)
*65 years and over:* 4.3% (male 90,352/female 117,945) (2009 est.)
**Median age:**
*total:* 24.4 years
*male:* 24.1 years
*female:* 24.8 years (2009 est.)
**Population growth rate:** 1.141% (2009 est.)
**Birth rate:** 19.69 births/1,000 population (2009 est.)
**Death rate:** 6.11 deaths/1,000 population (2008 est.)
**Net migration rate:** -1.97 migrant(s)/1,000 population (2009 est.)
**Urbanization:**
*urban population:* 49% of total population (2008)
*rate of urbanization:* 2.2% annual rate of change (2005-10 est.)
**Sex ratio:**
*at birth:* 1.05 male(s)/female
*under 15 years:* 1.02 male(s)/female
*15-64 years:* 0.98 male(s)/female
*65 years and over:* 0.77 male(s)/female
*total population:* 0.98 male(s)/female (2009 est.)
**Infant mortality rate:**
*total:* 45.36 deaths/1,000 live births
*male:* 53.85 deaths/1,000 live births
*female:* 36.46 deaths/1,000 live births (2009 est.)
**Life expectancy at birth:**
*total population:* 67.87 years
*male:* 64.94 years
*female:* 70.95 years (2009 est.)
**Total fertility rate:** 2.22 children born/woman (2009 est.)
**HIV/AIDS - adult prevalence rate:** less than 0.1% (2007 est.)
**HIV/AIDS - people living with HIV/AIDS:** fewer than 200 (2007 est.)
**HIV/AIDS - deaths:** fewer than 100 (2004 est.)
**Nationality:**
*noun:* Turkmen(s)
*adjective:* Turkmen
**Ethnic groups:** Turkmen 85%, Uzbek 5%, Russian 4%, other 6% (2003)
**Religions:** Muslim 89%, Eastern Orthodox 9%, unknown 2%
**Languages:** Turkmen 72%, Russian 12%, Uzbek 9%, other 7%
**Literacy:**
*definition:* age 15 and over can read and write
*total population:* 98.8%
*male:* 99.3%
*female:* 98.3% (1999 est.)
**Education expenditures:** 3.9% of GDP (1991)

# Turkmenistan *(continued)*

## Government

**Country name:**
*conventional long form:* none
*conventional short form:* Turkmenistan
*local long form:* none
*local short form:* Turkmenistan
*former:* Turkmen Soviet Socialist Republic
**Government type:** republic; authoritarian presidential rule, with little power outside the executive branch
**Capital:**
*name:* Ashgabat (Ashkhabad)
*geographic coordinates:* 37 57 N, 58 23 E
*time difference:* UTC+5 (10 hours ahead of Washington, DC during Standard Time)
**Administrative divisions:** 5 provinces (welayatlar, singular - welayat) and 1 independent city*: Ahal Welayaty (Anew), Ashgabat*, Balkan Welayaty (Balkanabat), Dashoguz Welayaty, Lebap Welayaty (Turkmenabat), Mary Welayaty
*note:* administrative divisions have the same names as their administrative centers (exceptions have the administrative center name following in parentheses)
**Independence:** 27 October 1991 (from the Soviet Union)
**National holiday:** Independence Day, 27 October (1991)
**Constitution:** adopted 18 May 1992
**Legal system:** based on civil law system and Islamic law; has not accepted compulsory ICJ jurisdiction
**Suffrage:** 18 years of age; universal
**Executive branch:**
*chief of state:* President Gurbanguly BERDIMUHAMEDOW (since 14 February 2007); note -the president is both the chief of state and head of government
*head of government:* President Gurbanguly BERDIMUHAMEDOW (since 14 February 2007)
*cabinet:* Cabinet of Ministers appointed by the president
*elections:* president elected by popular vote for a five-year term; election last held on 11 February 2007 (next to be held in February 2012)
*election results:* Gurbanguly BERDIMUHAMEDOW elected president; percent of vote - Gurbanguly BERDIMUHAMEDOW 89.2%, Amanyaz ATAJYKOW 3.2%, other candidates 7.6%
**Legislative branch:** unicameral parliament known as the National Assembly (Mejlis) (125 seats; members are elected by popular vote to serve five-year terms)
*elections:* last held 14 December 2008 (next to be held December 2013)
*election results:* 100% of elected officials are members of either the Democratic Party of Turkmenistan or its pseudo-civil society parent organization, the Revival Movement, and are preapproved by the president
*note:* in autumn 2008, the constitution of Turkmenistan was revised to abolish the 2,507-member legislative body known as the People's Council and to expand the number of deputies in the National Assembly from 65 to 125; the powers formerly held by the People's Council were divided up between the president and the National Assembly
**Judicial branch:** Supreme Court (judges are appointed by the president)
**Political parties and leaders:** Democratic Party of Turkmenistan or DPT [Gurbanguly BERDIMUHAMEDOW]
*note:* formal opposition parties are outlawed; unofficial, small opposition movements exist abroad; the three most prominent opposition groups-in-exile are the National Democratic Movement of Turkmenistan (NDMT), the Republican Party of Turkmenistan, and the Watan (Fatherland) Party; the NDMT was led by former Foreign Minister Boris SHIKHMURADOV until his arrest and imprisonment in the wake of the 25 November 2002 attack on President NYYAZOW's motorcade
**Political pressure groups and leaders:** NA
**International organization participation:** ADB, CIS, EAPC, EBRD, ECO, FAO, G-77, IBRD, ICAO, ICRM, IDA, IDB, IFC, IFRCS, ILO, IMF, IMO, Interpol, IOC, IOM (observer), ISO (correspondent), ITU, MIGA, NAM, OIC, OPCW, OSCE, PFP, SCO (guest), UN, UNCTAD, UNESCO, UNIDO, UNWTO, UPU, WCO, WFTU, WHO, WIPO, WMO
**Diplomatic representation in the US:**
*chief of mission:* Ambassador Meret Bairamovich ORAZOW
*chancery:* 2207 Massachusetts Avenue NW, Washington, DC 20008
*telephone:* [1] (202) 588-1500
*FAX:* [1] (202) 588-0697
**Diplomatic representation from the US:**
*chief of mission:* Ambassador (vacant); Charge d'Affaires Richard M. MILES
*embassy:* No. 9 1984 Street (formerly Pushkin Street), Ashgabat, Turkmenistan 744000
*mailing address:* 7070 Ashgabat Place, Washington, DC 20521-7070
*telephone:* [993] (12) 35-00-45
*FAX:* [993] (12) 39-26-14
**Flag description:** green field with a vertical red stripe near the hoist side, containing five tribal guls (designs used in producing carpets) stacked above two crossed olive branches; a white crescent moon representing Islam with five white stars representing the regions or welayats of Turkmenistan appear in the upper corner of the field just to the fly side of the red stripe

## Economy

**Economy - overview:** Turkmenistan is largely a desert country with intensive agriculture in irrigated oases and sizeable gas and oil resources. One-half of its irrigated land is planted in cotton; formerly it was the world's 10th-largest producer. Poor harvests in recent years have led to an almost 50% decline in cotton exports. With an authoritarian ex-Communist regime in power and a tribally based social structure, Turkmenistan has taken a cautious approach to economic reform, hoping to use gas and cotton sales to sustain its inefficient economy. Privatization goals remain limited. From 1998-2005, Turkmenistan suffered from the continued lack of adequate export routes for natural gas and from obligations on extensive short-term external debt. At the same time, however, total exports rose by an average of roughly 15% per year from 2003-08, largely because of higher international oil and gas prices. A new pipeline to China, set to come online in late 2009 or early 2010, will give Turkmenistan an additional export route for its gas. Overall prospects in the near future are discouraging because of widespread internal poverty, a poor educational system, government misuse of oil and gas revenues, and Ashgabat's reluctance to adopt market-oriented reforms. In the past, Turkmenistan's economic statistics were state secrets. The new government has established a State Agency for Statistics, but GDP numbers and other figures are subject to wide margins of error. In particular, the rate of GDP growth is uncertain. Since his election, President BERDIMUHAMEDOW has sought to improve the health and education systems, unified the country's dual currency exchange rate, ordered the redenomination of the manat, reduced state subsidies for gasoline, increased Internet access both in schools and Internet cafes, ordered an independent audit of Turkmenistan's gas resources, and created a special tourism zone on the Caspian Sea. Although foreign investment is encouraged, numerous bureaucratic obstacles from the NYYZOW-era remain.
**GDP (purchasing power parity):**
$29.65 billion (2008 est.)
$26.96 billion (2007)
$24.18 billion (2006)
*note:* data are in 2008 US dollars
**GDP (official exchange rate):** $28.82 billion (2008 est.)
**GDP - real growth rate:**
10% (2008 est.)
11.5% (2007 est.)
9% (2006 est.)
**GDP - per capita (PPP):**
$6,100 (2008 est.)
$5,600 (2007 est.)
$5,100 (2006 est.)
*note:* data are in 2008 US dollars
**GDP - composition by sector:**
*agriculture:* 10.7%
*industry:* 38.8%
*services:* 50.4% (2008 est.)
**Labor force:** 2.089 million (2004 est.)
**Labor force - by occupation:**
*agriculture:* 48.2%
*industry:* 14%
*services:* 37.8% (2004 est.)
**Unemployment rate:**
60% (2004 est.)
**Population below poverty line:** 30% (2004 est.)

**Household income or consumption by percentage share:**
*lowest 10%:* 2.6%
*highest 10%:* 31.7% (1998)
**Distribution of family income - Gini index:** 40.8 (1998)
**Investment (gross fixed):** 11.6% of GDP (2008 est.)
**Budget:**
*revenues:* $1.393 billion
*expenditures:* $1.42 billion (2008 est.)
**Inflation rate (consumer prices):**
18% (2008 est.)
11.3% (2007 est.)
**Market value of publicly traded shares:** $NA
**Agriculture - products:** cotton, grain; livestock
**Industries:** natural gas, oil, petroleum products, textiles, food processing
**Industrial production growth rate:** -0.1% (2008 est.)
**Electricity - production:** 12.83 billion kWh (2006 est.)
**Electricity - consumption:** 9.584 billion kWh (2006 est.)
**Electricity - exports:** 1.34 billion kWh (2006 est.)
**Electricity - imports:** 0 kWh (2007 est.)
**Oil - production:** 180,400 bbl/day (2007est.)
**Oil - consumption:** 107,400 bbl/day (2006 est.)
**Oil - exports:** 40,000 bbl/day (2007 est.)
**Oil - imports:** 5,283 bbl/day (2005)
**Oil - proved reserves:** 600 million bbl (1 January 2008 est.)
**Natural gas - production:** 68.88 billion cu m (2007 est.)
**Natural gas - consumption:** 19.48 billion cu m (2007 est.)
**Natural gas - exports:** 49.4 billion cu m (2007 est.)
**Natural gas - imports:** 0 cu m (2007 est.)
**Natural gas - proved reserves:** 2.832 trillion cu m (1 January 2008 est.)
**Current account balance:** $2.897 billion (2008 est.)
**Exports:** $9.887 billion f.o.b. (2008 est.)
**Exports - commodities:** gas, crude oil, petrochemicals, textiles, cotton fiber
**Exports - partners:** Ukraine 51.3%, Iran 18.5%, Turkey 5% (2007)
**Imports:** $5.291 billion f.o.b. (2008 est.)
**Imports - commodities:** machinery and equipment, chemicals, foodstuffs
**Imports - partners:** UAE 14.3%, Russia 11.6%, Turkey 10.3%, China 9.1%, Ukraine 8.7%, Iran 7%, Germany 6.5%, US 5.6% (2007)
**Reserves of foreign exchange and gold:** $5.501 billion (31 December 2008 est.)
**Debt - external:** $1.4 billion
*note:* some estimates put this figure as high as $5 billion (2004 est.)
**Exchange rates:** Turkmen manat (TMM) per US dollar - 14,250 (as of 1 May 2008 est.)

## Communications

**Telephones - main lines in use:** 457,900 (2007)
**Telephones - mobile cellular:** 810,000 (2008)
**Telephone system:**
*general assessment:* telecommunications network remains underdeveloped and progress toward improvement is slow; strict government control and censorship inhibits liberalization and modernization
*domestic:* Turkmentelekom, in cooperation with foreign partners, has installed high speed fiber-optic lines and has upgraded most of the country's telephone exchanges and switching centers with new digital technology; mobile telephone usage is expanding with Russia's Mobile Telesystems (MTS) the primary service provider
*international:* country code - 993; linked by fiber-optic cable and microwave radio relay to other CIS republics and to other countries by leased connections to the Moscow international gateway switch; an exchange in Ashgabat switches international traffic through Turkey via Intelsat; satellite earth stations - 1 Orbita and 1 Intelsat (2008)
**Radio broadcast stations:** AM 16, FM 8, shortwave 2 (1998)
**Television broadcast stations:** 4 (government-owned and programmed) (2004)
**Internet country code:** .tm
**Internet hosts:** 640 (2008)
**Internet users:** 70,000 (2007)

## Transportation

**Airports:** 28 (2008)
**Airports - with paved runways:**
*total:* 22
*over 3,047 m:* 1
*2,438 to 3,047 m:* 11
*1,524 to 2,437 m:* 8
*914 to 1,523 m:* 2 (2008)
**Airports - with unpaved runways:**
*total:* 6
*1,524 to 2,437 m:* 2
*under 914 m:* 4 (2008)
**Heliports:** 1 (2007)
**Pipelines:** gas 6,417 km; oil 1,457 km (2008)
**Railways:**
*total:* 2,440 km
*broad gauge:* 2,440 km 1.520-m gauge (2006)
**Roadways:**
*total:* 58,592 km
*paved:* 47,577 km
*unpaved:* 11,015 km (2002)
**Waterways:** 1,300 km (Amu Darya and Kara Kum canal are important inland waterways) (2008)
**Merchant marine:**
*total:* 7
*by type:* cargo 4, petroleum tanker 2, refrigerated cargo 1 (2008)
**Ports and terminals:** Turkmenbasy

## Military

**Military branches:** Army, Navy, Air and Air Defense Forces (2009)
**Military service age and obligation:** 18-30 years of age for compulsory military service; 2-year conscript service obligation (2007)
**Manpower available for military service:**
*males age 16-49:* 1,316,698
*females age 16-49:* 1,331,005 (2008 est.)
**Manpower fit for military service:**
*males age 16-49:* 1,024,884
*females age 16-49:* 1,147,714 (2009 est.)
**Manpower reaching militarily significant age annually:**
*male:* 57,021
*female:* 56,064 (2009 est.)
**Military expenditures:** 3.4% of GDP (2005 est.)

## Transnational Issues

**Disputes - international:** cotton monoculture in Uzbekistan and Turkmenistan creates water-sharing difficulties for Amu Darya river states; field demarcation of the boundaries with Kazakhstan commenced in 2005, but Caspian seabed delimitation remains stalled with Azerbaijan, Iran, and Kazakhstan due to Turkmenistan's indecision over how to allocate the sea's waters and seabed
**Refugees and internally displaced persons:**
*refugees (country of origin):* 11,173 (Tajikistan); less than 1,000 (Afghanistan) (2007)
**Illicit drugs:** transit country for Afghan narcotics bound for Russian and Western European markets; transit point for heroin precursor chemicals bound for Afghanistan

# Turks and Caicos Islands
*(overseas territory of the UK)*

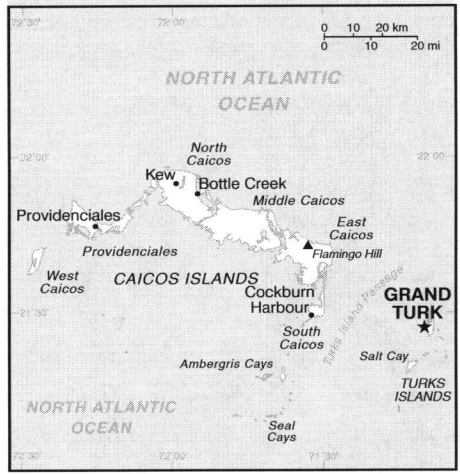

## Introduction

**Background:** The islands were part of the UK's Jamaican colony until 1962, when they assumed the status of a separate crown colony upon Jamaica's independence. The governor of The Bahamas oversaw affairs from 1965 to 1973. With Bahamian independence, the islands received a separate governor in 1973. Although independence was agreed upon for 1982, the policy was reversed and the islands remain a British overseas territory.

## Geography

**Location:** Caribbean, two island groups in the North Atlantic Ocean, southeast of The Bahamas, north of Haiti
**Geographic coordinates:** 21 45 N, 71 35 W
**Map references:** Central America and the Caribbean
**Area:**
*total:* 430 sq km
*land:* 430 sq km
*water:* 0 sq km
**Area - comparative:** 2.5 times the size of Washington, DC
**Land boundaries:** 0 km
**Coastline:** 389 km
**Maritime claims:**
*territorial sea:* 12 nm
*exclusive fishing zone:* 200 nm
**Climate:** tropical; marine; moderated by trade winds; sunny and relatively dry
**Terrain:** low, flat limestone; extensive marshes and mangrove swamps
**Elevation extremes:**
*lowest point:* Caribbean Sea 0 m
*highest point:* Blue Hills 49 m
**Natural resources:** spiny lobster, conch
**Land use:**
*arable land:* 2.33%
*permanent crops:* 0%
*other:* 97.67% (2005)

**Irrigated land:** NA
**Natural hazards:** frequent hurricanes
**Environment - current issues:** limited natural fresh water resources, private cisterns collect rainwater
**Geography - note:** about 40 islands (eight inhabited)

## People

**Population:** 22,942 (July 2009 est.)
**Age structure:**
*0-14 years:* 30.2% (male 3,528/female 3,401)
*15-64 years:* 65.6% (male 7,875/female 7,164)
*65 years and over:* 4.2% (male 475/female 499) (2009 est.)
**Median age:**
*total:* 27.9 years
*male:* 28.7 years
*female:* 27.2 years (2009 est.)
**Population growth rate:** 2.563% (2009 est.)
**Birth rate:** 20.79 births/1,000 population (2009 est.)
**Death rate:** 4.16 deaths/1,000 population (2008 est.)
**Net migration rate:** 9.02 migrant(s)/1,000 population (2009 est.)
**Urbanization:**
*urban population:* 92% of total population (2008)
*rate of urbanization:* 2.2% annual rate of change (2005-10 est.)
**Sex ratio:**
*at birth:* 1.05 male(s)/female
*under 15 years:* 1.04 male(s)/female
*15-64 years:* 1.1 male(s)/female
*65 years and over:* 0.95 male(s)/female
*total population:* 1.07 male(s)/female (2009 est.)
**Infant mortality rate:**
*total:* 13.89 deaths/1,000 live births
*male:* 16.02 deaths/1,000 live births
*female:* 11.64 deaths/1,000 live births (2009 est.)
**Life expectancy at birth:**
*total population:* 75.42 years
*male:* 73.12 years
*female:* 77.83 years (2009 est.)
**Total fertility rate:** 2.95 children born/woman (2009 est.)
**HIV/AIDS - adult prevalence rate:** NA
**HIV/AIDS - people living with HIV/AIDS:** NA
**HIV/AIDS - deaths:** NA
**Nationality:**
*noun:* none
*adjective:* none
**Ethnic groups:** black 90%, mixed, European, or North American 10%
**Religions:** Baptist 40%, Anglican 18%, Methodist 16%, Church of God 12%, other 14% (1990)
**Languages:** English (official)
**Literacy:**
*definition:* age 15 and over has ever attended school
*total population:* 98%
*male:* 99%
*female:* 98% (1970 est.)

**School life expectancy (primary to tertiary education):**
*total:* 11 years
*male:* 11 years
*female:* 12 years (2005)
**Education expenditures:** NA
**People - note:** destination and transit point for illegal Haitian immigrants bound for the Turks and Caicos Islands, The Bahamas, and the US

## Government

**Country name:**
*conventional long form:* none
*conventional short form:* Turks and Caicos Islands
*abbreviation:* TCI
**Dependency status:** overseas territory of the UK
**Government type:** NA
**Capital:**
*name:* Grand Turk (Cockburn Town)
*geographic coordinates:* 21 28 N, 71 08 W
*time difference:* UTC-5 (same time as Washington, DC during Standard Time)
*daylight saving time:* +1hr, begins first Sunday in April; ends last Sunday in October
**Administrative divisions:** none (overseas territory of the UK)
**Independence:** none (overseas territory of the UK)
**National holiday:** Constitution Day, 30 August (1976)
**Constitution:** Turks and Caicos Islands Constitution Order 2006 effective 9 August 2006
**Legal system:** based on laws of England and Wales with a few adopted from Jamaica and The Bahamas
**Suffrage:** 18 years of age; universal
**Executive branch:**
*chief of state:* Queen ELIZABETH II (since 6 February 1952); represented by Governor Gordon WETHERELL (since 5 August 2008)
*head of government:* Premier Galmore WILLIAMS (since 24 March 2009)
*cabinet:* Cabinet consists of the governor, the premier, six ministers appointed by the governor from among the members of the House of Assembly, and the attorney general
*elections:* the monarch is hereditary; governor appointed by the monarch; following legislative elections, the leader of the majority party is appointed premier by the governor
**Legislative branch:** unicameral House of Assembly (21 seats of which 15 are popularly elected; members serve four-year terms)
*elections:* last held 9 February 2007 (next to be held in 2011)
*election results:* percent of vote by party - PNP 60%, PDM 40%; seats by party - PNP 13, PDM 2
**Judicial branch:** Supreme Court; Court of Appeal
**Political parties and leaders:** People's Democratic Movement or PDM [Floyd SEYMOUR]; Progressive National Party or PNP [Michael Eugene MISICK]

# Turks and Caicos Islands *(continued)*

**Political pressure groups and leaders:** NA
**International organization participation:** Caricom (associate), CDB, Interpol (subbureau), UPU
**Diplomatic representation in the US:** none (overseas territory of the UK)
**Diplomatic representation from the US:** none (overseas territory of the UK)
**Flag description:** blue, with the flag of the UK in the upper hoist-side quadrant and the colonial shield centered on the outer half of the flag; the shield is yellow and contains a conch shell, lobster, and cactus

## Economy

**Economy - overview:** The Turks and Caicos economy is based on tourism, offshore financial services, and fishing. Most capital goods and food for domestic consumption are imported. The US is the leading source of tourists, accounting for more than three-quarters of the 175,000 visitors that arrived in 2004. Major sources of government revenue also include fees from offshore financial activities and customs receipts.
**GDP (purchasing power parity):**
$216 million (2002 est.)
**GDP (official exchange rate):** $NA
**GDP - real growth rate:**
4.9% (2000 est.)
**GDP - per capita (PPP):**
$11,500 (2002 est.)
**GDP - composition by sector:**
*agriculture:* NA%
*industry:* NA%
*services:* NA%
**Labor force:** 4,848 (1990 est.)
**Labor force - by occupation:**
*note:* about 33% in government and 20% in agriculture and fishing; significant numbers in tourism, financial, and other services
**Unemployment rate:**
10% (1997 est.)
**Population below poverty line:** NA%
**Household income or consumption by percentage share:**
*lowest 10%:* NA%
*highest 10%:* NA%
**Budget:**
*revenues:* $47 million
*expenditures:* $33.6 million (1997-98 est.)
**Inflation rate (consumer prices):**
4% (1995)
**Agriculture - products:** corn, beans, cassava (tapioca), citrus fruits; fish
**Industries:** tourism, offshore financial services
**Industrial production growth rate:** NA%
**Electricity - production:** 10 million kWh (2006 est.)
**Electricity - consumption:** 9.3 million kWh (2006 est.)
**Electricity - exports:** 0 kWh (2007 est.)
**Electricity - imports:** 0 kWh (2007 est.)
**Oil - production:** 0 bbl/day (2007 est.)
**Oil - consumption:** 80 bbl/day (2006 est.)

**Oil - exports:** 0 bbl/day (2005)
**Oil - imports:** 83.78 bbl/day (2005)
**Oil - proved reserves:** 0 bbl (1 January 2006 est.)
**Natural gas - production:** 0 cu m (2007 est.)
**Natural gas - consumption:** 0 cu m (2007 est.)
**Natural gas - exports:** 0 cu m (2007 est.)
**Natural gas - imports:** 0 cu m (2007 est.)
**Natural gas - proved reserves:** 0 cu m (1 January 2006 est.)
**Exports:** $169.2 million (2000)
**Exports - commodities:** lobster, dried and fresh conch, conch shells
**Imports:** $175.6 million (2000)
**Imports - commodities:** food and beverages, tobacco, clothing, manufactures, construction materials
**Debt - external:** $NA
**Exchange rates:** the US dollar is used

## Communications

**Telephones - main lines in use:** 5,700 (2002)
**Telephones - mobile cellular:** 1,700 (1999)
**Telephone system:**
*general assessment:* fully digital system with international direct dialing
*domestic:* full range of services available; GSM wireless service available
*international:* country code - 1-649; the Americas Region Caribbean Ring System (ARCOS-1) fiber optic telecommunications submarine cable provides connectivity to South and Central America, parts of the Caribbean, and the US; satellite earth station - 1 Intelsat (Atlantic Ocean)
**Radio broadcast stations:** AM 2, FM 7, shortwave 0 (2003)
**Television broadcast stations:** 0 (broadcasts received from The Bahamas; 2 cable television networks) (2003)
**Internet country code:** .tc
**Internet hosts:** 2,352 (2008)
**Internet users:** NA

## Transportation

**Airports:** 8 (2008)
**Airports - with paved runways:**
*total:* 6
*1,524 to 2,437 m:* 3
*914 to 1,523 m:* 1
*under 914 m:* 2 (2008)
**Airports - with unpaved runways:**
*total:* 2
*914 to 1,523 m:* 1
*under 914 m:* 1 (2008)
**Roadways:**
*total:* 121 km
*paved:* 24 km
*unpaved:* 97 km (2003)
**Merchant marine:**
*registered in other countries:* 1 (Panama 1) (2008)
**Ports and terminals:** Grand Turk, Providenciales

## Military

**Manpower fit for military service:**
*males age 16-49:* 4,937
*females age 16-49:* 4,648 (2009 est.)
**Manpower reaching militarily significant age annually:**
*male:* 226
*female:* 218 (2009 est.)
**Military - note:** defense is the responsibility of the UK

## Transnational Issues

**Disputes - international:** have received Haitians fleeing economic and civil disorder
**Illicit drugs:** transshipment point for South American narcotics destined for the US and Europe

# Tuvalu

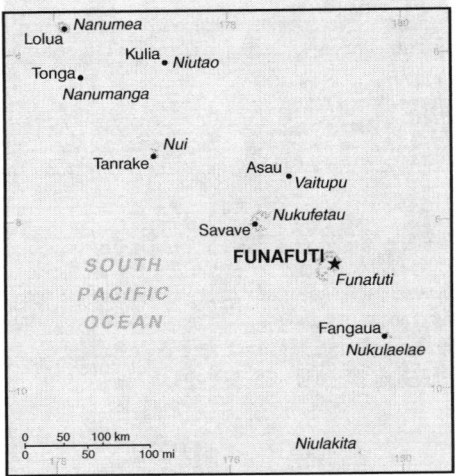

## Introduction

**Background:** In 1974, ethnic differences within the British colony of the Gilbert and Ellice Islands caused the Polynesians of the Ellice Islands to vote for separation from the Micronesians of the Gilbert Islands. The following year, the Ellice Islands became the separate British colony of Tuvalu. Independence was granted in 1978. In 2000, Tuvalu negotiated a contract leasing its Internet domain name ".tv" for $50 million in royalties over a 12-year period.

## Geography

**Location:** Oceania, island group consisting of nine coral atolls in the South Pacific Ocean, about one-half of the way from Hawaii to Australia
**Geographic coordinates:** 8 00 S, 178 00 E
**Map references:** Oceania
**Area:**
*total:* 26 sq km
*land:* 26 sq km
*water:* 0 sq km
**Area - comparative:** 0.1 times the size of Washington, DC
**Land boundaries:** 0 km
**Coastline:** 24 km
**Maritime claims:**
*territorial sea:* 12 nm
*contiguous zone:* 24 nm
*exclusive economic zone:* 200 nm
**Climate:** tropical; moderated by easterly trade winds (March to November); westerly gales and heavy rain (November to March)
**Terrain:** low-lying and narrow coral atolls
**Elevation extremes:**
*lowest point:* Pacific Ocean 0 m
*highest point:* unnamed location 5 m
**Natural resources:** fish

**Land use:**
*arable land:* 0%
*permanent crops:* 66.67%
*other:* 33.33% (2005)
**Irrigated land:** NA
**Natural hazards:** severe tropical storms are usually rare, but in 1997 there were three cyclones; low level of islands make them sensitive to changes in sea level
**Environment - current issues:** since there are no streams or rivers and groundwater is not potable, most water needs must be met by catchment systems with storage facilities (the Japanese Government has built one desalination plant and plans to build one other); beachhead erosion because of the use of sand for building materials; excessive clearance of forest undergrowth for use as fuel; damage to coral reefs from the spread of the Crown of Thorns starfish; Tuvalu is concerned about global increases in greenhouse gas emissions and their effect on rising sea levels, which threaten the country's underground water table; in 2000, the government appealed to Australia and New Zealand to take in Tuvaluans if rising sea levels should make evacuation necessary
**Environment - international agreements:**
*party to:* Biodiversity, Climate Change, Climate Change-Kyoto Protocol, Desertification, Law of the Sea, Ozone Layer Protection, Ship Pollution, Whaling
*signed, but not ratified:* none of the selected agreements
**Geography - note:** one of the smallest and most remote countries on Earth; six of the nine coral atolls - Nanumea, Nui, Vaitupu, Nukufetau, Funafuti, and Nukulaelae - have lagoons open to the ocean; Nanumaya and Niutao have landlocked lagoons; Niulakita does not have a lagoon

## People

**Population:** 12,373 (July 2009 est.)
**Age structure:**
*0-14 years:* 29.2% (male 1,841/female 1,770)
*15-64 years:* 65.6% (male 3,973/female 4,141)
*65 years and over:* 5.2% (male 240/female 408) (2009 est.)
**Median age:**
*total:* 25.4 years
*male:* 24.4 years
*female:* 26.6 years (2009 est.)
**Population growth rate:** 1.616% (2009 est.)
**Birth rate:** 23.11 births/1,000 population (2009 est.)
**Death rate:** 6.98 deaths/1,000 population (2008 est.)
**Net migration rate:** NA
**Urbanization:**
*urban population:* 49% of total population (2008)
*rate of urbanization:* 1.3% annual rate of change (2005-10 est.)
**Sex ratio:**
*at birth:* 1.05 male(s)/female
*under 15 years:* 1.04 male(s)/female
*15-64 years:* 0.96 male(s)/female
*65 years and over:* 0.59 male(s)/female
*total population:* 0.96 male(s)/female (2009 est.)

**Infant mortality rate:**
*total:* 18.43 deaths/1,000 live births
*male:* 20.95 deaths/1,000 live births
*female:* 15.77 deaths/1,000 live births (2009 est.)
**Life expectancy at birth:**
*total population:* 69.29 years
*male:* 66.99 years
*female:* 71.7 years (2009 est.)
**Total fertility rate:** 2.91 children born/woman (2009 est.)
**HIV/AIDS - adult prevalence rate:** NA
**HIV/AIDS - people living with HIV/AIDS:** NA
**HIV/AIDS - deaths:** NA
**Nationality:**
*noun:* Tuvaluan(s)
*adjective:* Tuvaluan
**Ethnic groups:** Polynesian 96%, Micronesian 4%
**Religions:** Church of Tuvalu (Congregationalist) 97%, Seventh-Day Adventist 1.4%, Baha'i 1%, other 0.6%
**Languages:** Tuvaluan, English, Samoan, Kiribati (on the island of Nui)
**Literacy:** NA
**School life expectancy (primary to tertiary education):**
*total:* 11 years
*male:* 11 years
*female:* 11 years (2001)
**Education expenditures:** NA

## Government

**Country name:**
*conventional long form:* none
*conventional short form:* Tuvalu
*local long form:* none
*local short form:* Tuvalu
*former:* Ellice Islands
*note:* "Tuvalu" means "group of eight" referring to the country's eight traditionally inhabited islands
**Government type:** a parliamentary democracy and a Commonwealth realm
**Capital:**
*name:* Funafuti
*geographic coordinates:* 8 30 S, 179 12 E
*time difference:* UTC+12 (17 hours ahead of Washington, DC during Standard Time)
*note:* administrative offices are in Vaiaku Village on Fongafale Islet
**Administrative divisions:** none
**Independence:** 1 October 1978 (from the UK)
**National holiday:** Independence Day, 1 October (1978)
**Constitution:** 1 October 1978
**Legal system:** English common law supplemented by local customary law
**Suffrage:** 18 years of age; universal
**Executive branch:**
*chief of state:* Queen ELIZABETH II (since 6 February 1952); represented by Governor General Filoimea TELITO (since 15 April 2005)
*head of government:* Prime Minister Apisai IELEMIA (since 14 August 2006)

# Tuvalu (continued)

*cabinet:* Cabinet appointed by the governor general on the recommendation of the prime minister
*elections:* the monarch is hereditary; governor general appointed by the monarch on the recommendation of the prime minister; prime minister and deputy prime minister elected by and from the members of parliament; election last held 14 August 2006 (next to be held following parliamentary elections in 2010)
*election results:* Apisai IELEMIA elected prime minister in a parliamentary election on 14 August 2006
**Legislative branch:** unicameral Parliament or Fale I Fono, also called House of Assembly (15 seats; members elected by popular vote to serve four-year terms)
*elections:* last held 3 August 2006 (next to be held in 2010)
*election results:* percent of vote - NA; seats - independents 15
**Judicial branch:** High Court (a chief justice visits twice a year to preside over its sessions; its rulings can be appealed to the Court of Appeal in Fiji); eight Island Courts (with limited jurisdiction)
**Political parties and leaders:** there are no political parties but members of parliament usually align themselves in informal groupings
**Political pressure groups and leaders:** none
**International organization participation:** ACP, ADB, C, FAO, IFRCS (observer), IMO, IOC, ITU, OPCW, PIF, Sparteca, SPC, UN, UNCTAD, UNESCO, UPU, WHO
**Diplomatic representation in the US:** Tuvalu does not have an embassy in the US - the country's only diplomatic post is in Fiji - Tuvalu does, however, have a UN office located at 800 2nd Avenue, Suite 400D, New York, NY 10017, telephone: [1] (212) 490-0534
**Diplomatic representation from the US:** the US does not have an embassy in Tuvalu; the US ambassador to Fiji is accredited to Tuvalu
**Flag description:** light blue with the flag of the UK in the upper hoist-side quadrant; the outer half of the flag represents a map of the country with nine yellow five-pointed stars symbolizing the nine islands

## Economy

**Economy - overview:** Tuvalu consists of a densely populated, scattered group of nine coral atolls with poor soil. The country has no known mineral resources and few exports and is almost entirely dependent upon imported food and fuel. Subsistence farming and fishing are the primary economic activities. Fewer than 1,000 tourists, on average, visit Tuvalu annually. Job opportunities are scarce and public sector workers make up most of those employed. About 15% of the adult male population work as seamen on merchant ships abroad, and remittances are a vital source of income contributing around $4 million in 2006. Substantial income is received annually from the Tuvalu Trust Fund (TTF) an international trust fund established in 1987 by Australia, NZ, and the UK and supported also by Japan and South Korea. Thanks to wise investments and conservative withdrawals, this fund grew from an initial $17 million to an estimated value of $77 million in 2006. The TFF contributed nearly $9 million towards the government budget in 2006 and is an important cushion for meeting shortfalls in the government's budget. The US Government is also a major revenue source for Tuvalu because of payments from a 1988 treaty on fisheries. In an effort to ensure financial stability and sustainability, the government is pursuing public sector reforms, including privatization of some government functions and personnel cuts. Tuvalu also derives royalties from the lease of its ".tv" Internet domain name with revenue of more than $2 million in 2006. A minor source of government revenue comes from the sale of stamps and coins. With merchandise exports only a fraction of merchandise imports, continued reliance must be placed on fishing and telecommunications license fees, remittances from overseas workers, official transfers, and income from overseas investments. Growing income disparities and the vulnerability of the country to climatic change are among leading concerns for the nation.

**GDP (purchasing power parity):**
$14.94 million (2002 est.)
**GDP (official exchange rate):** $14.94 million (2002)
**GDP - real growth rate:**
3% (2006 est.)
**GDP - per capita (PPP):**
$1,600 (2002 est.)
**GDP - composition by sector:**
*agriculture:* 16.6%
*industry:* 27.2%
*services:* 56.2% (2002)
**Labor force:** 3,615 (2004 est.)
**Labor force - by occupation:**
*note:* people make a living mainly through exploitation of the sea, reefs, and atolls and from wages sent home by those abroad (mostly workers in the phosphate industry and sailors)
**Unemployment rate:**
NA%
**Population below poverty line:** NA%
**Household income or consumption by percentage share:**
*lowest 10%:* NA%
*highest 10%:* NA%
**Budget:**
*revenues:* $21.54 million
*expenditures:* $23.05 million (2006)
**Inflation rate (consumer prices):**
3.8% (2006 est.)
**Agriculture - products:** coconuts; fish
**Industries:** fishing, tourism, copra
**Industrial production growth rate:** NA%
**Current account balance:** -$11.68 million (2003)
**Exports:** $1 million f.o.b. (2004 est.)
**Exports - commodities:** copra, fish
**Imports:** $12.91 million c.i.f. (2005)
**Imports - commodities:** food, animals, mineral fuels, machinery, manufactured goods

**Debt - external:** $NA
**Exchange rates:** Tuvaluan dollars or Australian dollars (AUD) per U 1.2059 (2008 est.), 1.2137 (2007), 1.3285 (2006), 1.3095 (2005), 1.3598 (2004)

## Communications

**Telephones - main lines in use:** 900 (2005)
**Telephones - mobile cellular:** 1,300 (2005)
**Telephone system:**
*general assessment:* serves particular needs for internal communications
*domestic:* radiotelephone communications between islands
*international:* country code - 688; international calls can be made by satellite
**Radio broadcast stations:** AM 1, FM 1, shortwave 0 (2004)
**Television broadcast stations:** 0 (2004)
**Internet country code:** .tv
**Internet hosts:** 56,209 (2008)
**Internet users:** 1,300 (2002)

## Transportation

**Airports:** 1 (2008)
**Airports - with unpaved runways:**
*total:* 1
*1,524 to 2,437 m:* 1 (2008)
**Roadways:**
*total:* 8 km
*paved:* 8 km (2002)
**Merchant marine:**
*total:* 80
*by type:* bulk carrier 7, cargo 30, chemical tanker 14, container 2, passenger 2, passenger/cargo 1, petroleum tanker 22, refrigerated cargo 1, specialized tanker 1
*foreign-owned:* 63 (China 16, Hong Kong 7, Kenya 1, South Korea 1, Malaysia 1, Maldives 1, Norway 1, Russia 2, Singapore 23, Thailand 1, Turkey 2, Ukraine 1, US 1, Vietnam 5) (2008)
**Ports and terminals:** Funafuti

## Military

**Military branches:** no regular military forces; Tuvalu Police Force (2008)
**Manpower fit for military service:**
*males age 16-49:* 2,462
*females age 16-49:* 2,631 (2009 est.)
**Manpower reaching militarily significant age annually:**
*male:* 125
*female:* 121 (2009 est.)
**Military expenditures:** NA

## Transnational Issues

**Disputes - international:** none

# Uganda

## Introduction

**Background:** The colonial boundaries created by Britain to delimit Uganda grouped together a wide range of ethnic groups with different political systems and cultures. These differences prevented the establishment of a working political community after independence was achieved in 1962. The dictatorial regime of Idi AMIN (1971-79) was responsible for the deaths of some 300,000 opponents; guerrilla war and human rights abuses under Milton OBOTE (1980-85) claimed at least another 100,000 lives. The rule of Yoweri MUSEVENI since 1986 has brought relative stability and economic growth to Uganda. During the 1990s, the government promulgated non-party presidential and legislative elections. In January 2009, Uganda assumed a nonpermanent seat on the UN Security Council for the 2009-10 term.

## Geography

**Location:** Eastern Africa, west of Kenya
**Geographic coordinates:** 1 00 N, 32 00 E
**Map references:** Africa
**Area:**
*total:* 236,040 sq km
*land:* 199,710 sq km
*water:* 36,330 sq km
**Area - comparative:** slightly smaller than Oregon
**Land boundaries:**
*total:* 2,698 km
*border countries:* Democratic Republic of the Congo 765 km, Kenya 933 km, Rwanda 169 km, Sudan 435 km, Tanzania 396 km
**Coastline:** 0 km (landlocked)
**Maritime claims:** none (landlocked)
**Climate:** tropical; generally rainy with two dry seasons (December to February, June to August); semiarid in northeast
**Terrain:** mostly plateau with rim of mountains

**Elevation extremes:**
*lowest point:* Lake Albert 621 m
*highest point:* Margherita Peak on Mount Stanley 5,110 m
**Natural resources:** copper, cobalt, hydropower, limestone, salt, arable land
**Land use:**
*arable land:* 21.57%
*permanent crops:* 8.92%
*other:* 69.51% (2005)
**Irrigated land:** 90 sq km (2003)
**Total renewable water resources:** 66 cu km (1970)
**Freshwater withdrawal (domestic/industrial/agricultural):**
*total:* 0.3 cu km/yr (43%/17%/40%)
*per capita:* 10 cu m/yr (2002)
**Natural hazards:** NA
**Environment - current issues:** draining of wetlands for agricultural use; deforestation; overgrazing; soil erosion; water hyacinth infestation in Lake Victoria; widespread poaching
**Environment - international agreements:**
*party to:* Biodiversity, Climate Change, Climate Change-Kyoto Protocol, Desertification, Endangered Species, Hazardous Wastes, Law of the Sea, Marine Life Conservation, Ozone Layer Protection, Wetlands
*signed, but not ratified:* Environmental Modification
**Geography - note:** landlocked; fertile, well-watered country with many lakes and rivers

## People

**Population:** 32,369,558
*note:* estimates for this country explicitly take into account the effects of excess mortality due to AIDS; this can result in lower life expectancy, higher infant mortality, higher death rates, lower population growth rates, and changes in the distribution of population by age and sex than would otherwise be expected (July 2009 est.)
**Age structure:**
*0-14 years:* 50% (male 8,152,830/female 8,034,366)
*15-64 years:* 47.9% (male 7,789,209/female 7,703,143)
*65 years and over:* 2.1% (male 286,693/female 403,317) (2009 est.)
**Median age:**
*total:* 15 years
*male:* 14.9 years
*female:* 15.1 years (2009 est.)
**Population growth rate:** 2.692% (2009 est.)
**Birth rate:** 47.84 births/1,000 population (2009 est.)
**Death rate:** 12.32 deaths/1,000 population (2008 est.)
**Net migration rate:** -8.83 migrant(s)/1,000 population (2009 est.)
**Urbanization:**
*urban population:* 13% of total population (2008)
*rate of urbanization:* 4.4% annual rate of change (2005-10 est.)

**Sex ratio:**
*at birth:* 1.03 male(s)/female
*under 15 years:* 1.01 male(s)/female
*15-64 years:* 1.01 male(s)/female
*65 years and over:* 0.71 male(s)/female
*total population:* 1 male(s)/female (2009 est.)
**Infant mortality rate:**
*total:* 64.82 deaths/1,000 live births
*male:* 68.46 deaths/1,000 live births
*female:* 61.07 deaths/1,000 live births (2009 est.)
**Life expectancy at birth:**
*total population:* 52.72 years
*male:* 51.66 years
*female:* 53.81 years (2009 est.)
**Total fertility rate:** 6.77 children born/woman (2009 est.)
**HIV/AIDS - adult prevalence rate:** 5.4% (2007 est.)
**HIV/AIDS - people living with HIV/AIDS:** 940,000 (2007 est.)
**HIV/AIDS - deaths:** 77,000 (2007 est.)
**Major infectious diseases:**
*degree of risk:* very high
*food or waterborne diseases:* bacterial diarrhea, hepatitis A, and typhoid fever
*vectorborne diseases:* malaria, plague, and African trypanosomiasis (sleeping sickness)
*water contact disease:* schistosomiasis
*animal contact disease:* rabies (2009)
**Nationality:**
*noun:* Ugandan(s)
*adjective:* Ugandan
**Ethnic groups:** Baganda 16.9%, Banyakole 9.5%, Basoga 8.4%, Bakiga 6.9%, Iteso 6.4%, Langi 6.1%, Acholi 4.7%, Bagisu 4.6%, Lugbara 4.2%, Bunyoro 2.7%, other 29.6% (2002 census)
**Religions:** Roman Catholic 41.9%, Protestant 42% (Anglican 35.9%, Pentecostal 4.6%, Seventh Day Adventist 1.5%), Muslim 12.1%, other 3.1%, none 0.9% (2002 census)
**Languages:** English (official national language, taught in grade schools, used in courts of law and by most newspapers and some radio broadcasts), Ganda or Luganda (most widely used of the Niger-Congo languages, preferred for native language publications in the capital and may be taught in school), other Niger-Congo languages, Nilo-Saharan languages, Swahili, Arabic
**Literacy:**
*definition:* age 15 and over can read and write
*total population:* 66.8%
*male:* 76.8%
*female:* 57.7% (2002 census)
**School life expectancy (primary to tertiary education):**
*total:* 10 years
*male:* 11 years
*female:* 10 years (2004)
**Education expenditures:** 5.2% of GDP (2004)

# Uganda (continued)

## Government

**Country name:**
*conventional long form:* Republic of Uganda
*conventional short form:* Uganda
**Government type:** republic
**Capital:**
*name:* Kampala
*geographic coordinates:* 0 19 N, 32 25 E
*time difference:* UTC+3 (8 hours ahead of Washington, DC during Standard Time)
**Administrative divisions:** 80 districts; Abim, Adjumani, Amolatar, Amuria, Amuru, Apac, Arua, Budaka, Bududa, Bugiri, Bukedea, Bukwa, Bulisa, Bundibugyo, Bushenyi, Busia, Butaleja, Dokolo, Gulu, Hoima, Ibanda, Iganga, Isingiro, Jinja, Kaabong, Kabale, Kabarole, Kaberamaido, Kalangala, Kaliro, Kampala, Kamuli, Kamwenge, Kanungu, Kapchorwa, Kasese, Katakwi, Kayunga, Kibale, Kiboga, Kiruhara, Kisoro, Kitgum, Koboko, Kotido, Kumi, Kyenjojo, Lira, Luwero, Lyantonde, Manafwa, Maracha, Masaka, Masindi, Mayuge, Mbale, Mbarara, Mityana, Moroto, Moyo, Mpigi, Mubende, Mukono, Nakapiripirit, Nakaseke, Nakasongola, Namutumba, Nebbi, Ntungamo, Oyam, Pader, Pallisa, Rakai, Rukungiri, Sembabule, Sironko, Soroti, Tororo, Wakiso, Yumbe
**Independence:** 9 October 1962 (from the UK)
**National holiday:** Independence Day, 9 October (1962)
**Constitution:** 8 October 1995; amended in 2005
*note:* the amendments in 2005 removed presidential term limits and legalized a multiparty political system
**Legal system:** in 1995, the government restored the legal system to one based on English common law and customary law; accepts compulsory ICJ jurisdiction with reservations
**Suffrage:** 18 years of age; universal
**Executive branch:**
*chief of state:* President Lt. Gen. Yoweri Kaguta MUSEVENI (since seizing power 26 January 1986); note - the president is both chief of state and head of government
*head of government:* President Lt. Gen. Yoweri Kaguta MUSEVENI (since seizing power 26 January 1986); Prime Minister Apolo NSIBAMBI (since 5 April 1999); note - the prime minister assists the president in the supervision of the cabinet
*cabinet:* Cabinet appointed by the president from among elected legislators
*elections:* president reelected by popular vote for a five-year term; election last held 23 February 2006 (next to be held in 2011)
*election results:* Lt. Gen. Yoweri Kaguta MUSEVENI elected president; percent of vote - Lt. Gen. Yoweri Kaguta MUSEVENI 59.3%, Kizza BESIGYE 37.4%, other 3.3%
**Legislative branch:** unicameral National Assembly (332 seats; 215 members elected by popular vote, 104 nominated by legally established special interest groups [women 79, army 10, disabled 5, youth 5, labor 5], 13 ex officio members; serve five-year terms)
*elections:* last held 23 February 2006 (next to be held in 2011)

*election results:* percent of vote by party - NA; seats by party - NRM 191, FDC 37, UPC 9, DP 8, CP 1, JEEMA 1, independents 36, other 49
**Judicial branch:** Court of Appeal (judges are appointed by the president and approved by the legislature); High Court (judges are appointed by the president)
**Political parties and leaders:** Conservative Party or CP [Ken LUKYAMUZI]; Democratic Party or DP [Kizito SSEBAANA]; Forum for Democratic Change or FDC [Kizza BESIGYE]; Justice Forum or JEEMA [Muhammad Kibirige MAYANJA]; National Resistance Movement or NRM [Yoweri MUSEVENI]; Peoples Progressive Party or PPP [Bidandi SSALI]; Ugandan People's Congress or UPC [Miria OBOTE]
*note:* a national referendum in July 2005 opened the way for Uganda's transition to a multi-party political system
**Political pressure groups and leaders:** Lord's Resistance Army or LRA [Joseph KONY]; Young Parliamentary Association [Henry BANYENZAKI]; Parliamentary Advocacy Forum or PAFO; National Association of Women Organizations in Uganda or NAWOU [Florence NEKYON]; The Ugandan Coalition for Political Accountability to Women or COPAW
**International organization participation:** ACP, AfDB, AU, C, COMESA, EAC, EADB, FAO, G-77, IAEA, IBRD, ICAO, ICCt, ICRM, IDA, IDB, IFAD, IFC, IFRCS, IGAD, ILO, IMF, Interpol, IOC, IOM, IPU, ISO (correspondent), ITSO, ITU, ITUC, MIGA, MINURCAT, NAM, OIC, OPCW, PCA, UN, UNAMID, UNCTAD, UNESCO, UNHCR, UNIDO, UNMIS, UNOCI, UNWTO, UPU, WCO, WFTU, WHO, WIPO, WMO, WTO
**Diplomatic representation in the US:**
*chief of mission:* Ambassador Perezi Karukubiro KAMUNANWIRE
*chancery:* 5911 16th Street NW, Washington, DC 20011
*telephone:* [1] (202) 726-7100 through 7102, 0416
*FAX:* [1] (202) 726-1727
**Diplomatic representation from the US:**
*chief of mission:* Ambassador Steven BROWNING
*embassy:* 1577 Ggaba Road, Kampala
*mailing address:* P. O. Box 7007, Kampala
*telephone:* [256] (414) 259 791 through 93, 95
*FAX:* [256] (414) 258-794
**Flag description:** six equal horizontal bands of black (top), yellow, red, black, yellow, and red; a white disk is superimposed at the center and depicts a red-crested crane (the national symbol) facing the hoist side

## Economy

**Economy - overview:** Uganda has substantial natural resources, including fertile soils, regular rainfall, and sizable mineral deposits of copper, cobalt, gold, and other minerals. Agriculture is the most important sector of the economy, employing over 80% of the work force. Coffee accounts for the bulk of export revenues. Since 1986, the government - with the support of foreign countries and international

agencies - has acted to rehabilitate and stabilize the economy by undertaking currency reform, raising producer prices on export crops, increasing prices of petroleum products, and improving civil service wages. The policy changes are especially aimed at dampening inflation and boosting production and export earnings. During 1990-2001, the economy turned in a solid performance based on continued investment in the rehabilitation of infrastructure, improved incentives for production and exports, reduced inflation, gradually improved domestic security, and the return of exiled Indian-Ugandan entrepreneurs. Growth continues to be solid, despite variability in the price of coffee, Uganda's principal export, and a consistent upturn in Uganda's export markets. In 2000, Uganda qualified for enhanced Highly Indebted Poor Countries (HIPC) debt relief worth $1.3 billion and Paris Club debt relief worth $145 million. These amounts combined with the original HIPC debt relief added up to about $2 billion.
**GDP (purchasing power parity):**
$35.88 billion (2008 est.)
$33.57 billion (2007)
$30.9 billion (2006)
*note:* data are in 2008 US dollars
**GDP (official exchange rate):** $15.04 billion (2008 est.)
**GDP - real growth rate:**
6.9% (2008 est.)
8.6% (2007 est.)
6.6% (2006 est.)
**GDP - per capita (PPP):**
$1,100 (2008 est.)
$1,100 (2007 est.)
$1,100 (2006 est.)
*note:* data are in 2008 US dollars
**GDP - composition by sector:**
*agriculture:* 29%
*industry:* 24.8%
*services:* 46.2% (2008 est.)
**Labor force:** 14.48 million (2008 est.)
**Labor force - by occupation:**
*agriculture:* 82%
*industry:* 5%
*services:* 13% (1999 est.)
**Unemployment rate:**
NA%
**Population below poverty line:** 35% (2001 est.)
**Household income or consumption by percentage share:**
*lowest 10%:* 2.3%
*highest 10%:* 37.7% (2002)
**Distribution of family income - Gini index:** 45.7 (2002)
**Investment (gross fixed):** 26.5% of GDP (2008 est.)
**Budget:**
*revenues:* $2.72 billion
*expenditures:* $3.05 billion; including capital expenditures of $NA (2008 est.)
**Public debt:** 19.5% of GDP (2008 est.)

# Uganda (continued)

**Inflation rate (consumer prices):**
10.5% (2008 est.)
6.1% (2007 est.)
**Central bank discount rate:** 14.68% (31 December 2007)
**Commercial bank prime lending rate:** 19.11% (31 December 2007)
**Stock of money:** $1.363 billion (31 December 2007)
**Stock of quasi money:** $1.302 billion (31 December 2007)
**Stock of domestic credit:** $907.3 million (31 December 2007)
**Market value of publicly traded shares:** $103.4 million (2005)
**Agriculture - products:** coffee, tea, cotton, tobacco, cassava (tapioca), potatoes, corn, millet, pulses, cut flowers; beef, goat meat, milk, poultry
**Industries:** sugar, brewing, tobacco, cotton textiles; cement, steel production
**Industrial production growth rate:** 7% (2008 est.)
**Electricity - production:** 1.161 billion kWh (2006 est.)
**Electricity - consumption:** 899.7 million kWh (2006 est.)
**Electricity - exports:** 180 million kWh (2006)
**Electricity - imports:** 0 kWh (2007 est.)
**Oil - production:** 0 bbl/day (2007 est.)
**Oil - consumption:** 11,570 bbl/day (2006 est.)
**Oil - exports:** 115.2 bbl/day (2005)
**Oil - imports:** 11,540 bbl/day (2005)
**Oil - proved reserves:** 0 bbl (1 January 2006 est.)
**Natural gas - production:** 0 cu m (2007 est.)
**Natural gas - consumption:** 0 cu m (2007 est.)
**Natural gas - exports:** 0 cu m (2007 est.)
**Natural gas - imports:** 0 cu m (2007 est.)
**Natural gas - proved reserves:** 0 cu m (1 January 2006 est.)
**Current account balance:** -$933 million (2008 est.)
**Exports:** $2.03 billion f.o.b. (2008 est.)
**Exports - commodities:** coffee, fish and fish products, tea, cotton, flowers, horticultural products; gold
**Exports - partners:** Netherlands 10.2%, Belgium 9.8%, Germany 7.9%, France 7.2%, Rwanda 5.6% (2007)
**Imports:** $3.579 billion f.o.b. (2008 est.)
**Imports - commodities:** capital equipment, vehicles, petroleum, medical supplies; cereals
**Imports - partners:** Kenya 31.8%, China 7.8%, UAE 7.7%, South Africa 5.9%, India 5.2%, Japan 4.8% (2007)

**Reserves of foreign exchange and gold:** $2.8 billion (31 December 2008 est.)
**Debt - external:** $1.705 billion (31 December 2008 est.)
**Stock of direct foreign investment - at home:** $NA
**Stock of direct foreign investment - abroad:** $NA
**Exchange rates:** Ugandan shillings (UGX) per US dollar - 1,658.1 (2008 est.), 1,685.8 (2007), 1,834.9 (2006), 1,780.7 (2005), 1,810.3 (2004)

## Communications

**Telephones - main lines in use:** 162,300 (2007)
**Telephones - mobile cellular:** 4.195 million (2007)
**Telephone system:**
*general assessment:* seriously inadequate; mobile cellular service is increasing rapidly, but the number of main lines is still deficient; e-mail and Internet services are available
*domestic:* intercity traffic by wire, microwave radio relay, and radiotelephone communication stations, fixed and mobile-cellular systems for short-range traffic
*international:* country code - 256; satellite earth stations - 1 Intelsat (Atlantic Ocean) and 1 Inmarsat; analog links to Kenya and Tanzania
**Radio broadcast stations:** AM 7, FM 33, shortwave 2 (2001)
**Television broadcast stations:** 8 (plus 1 repeater) (2001)
**Internet country code:** .ug
**Internet hosts:** 1,090 (2008)
**Internet users:** 2 million (2007)

## Transportation

**Airports:** 33 (2008)
**Airports - with paved runways:**
*total:* 5
*over 3,047 m:* 3
*1,524 to 2,437 m:* 1
*914 to 1,523 m:* 1 (2008)
**Airports - with unpaved runways:**
*total:* 28
*2,438 to 3,047 m:* 1
*1,524 to 2,437 m:* 6
*914 to 1,523 m:* 13
*under 914 m:* 8 (2008)
**Railways:**
*total:* 1,244 km
*narrow gauge:* 1,244 km 1.000-m gauge (2006)
**Roadways:**
*total:* 70,746 km
*paved:* 16,272 km
*unpaved:* 54,474 km (2003)
**Waterways:** on Lake Victoria, 200 km on Lake Albert, Lake Kyoga, and parts of Albert Nile (2008)
**Ports and terminals:** Entebbe, Jinja, Port Bell

## Military

**Military branches:** Uganda Peoples Defense Force (UPDF): Army (includes Marine Unit), Air Force (2007)
**Military service age and obligation:** 18-26 years of age for compulsory and voluntary military duty; 18-30 years of age for professionals; 9-year service obligation; the government has stated that recruitment below 18 years of age could occur with proper consent and that "no person under the apparent age of 13 years shall be enrolled in the armed forces"; Ugandan citizenship and secondary education required (2008)
**Manpower available for military service:**
*males age 16-49:* 6,532,894
*females age 16-49:* 6,352,416 (2008 est.)
**Manpower fit for military service:**
*males age 16-49:* 3,996,597
*females age 16-49:* 3,899,717 (2009 est.)
**Manpower reaching militarily significant age annually:**
*male:* 399,134
*female:* 395,505 (2009 est.)
**Military expenditures:** 2.2% of GDP (2006)

## Transnational Issues

**Disputes - international:** Uganda is subject to armed fighting among hostile ethnic groups, rebels, armed gangs, militias, and various government forces that extend across its borders; Uganda hosts 209,860 Sudanese, 27,560 Congolese, and 19,710 Rwandan refugees, while Ugandan refugees as well as members of the Lord's Resistance Army (LRA) seek shelter in southern Sudan and the Democratic Republic of the Congo's Garamba National Park; LRA forces have also attacked Kenyan villages across the border
**Refugees and internally displaced persons:**
*refugees (country of origin):* 215,700 (Sudan); 28,880 (Democratic Republic of Congo); 24,900 (Rwanda)
*IDPs:* 1.27 million (350,000 IDPs returned in 2006 following ongoing peace talks between the Lord's Resistance Army (LRA) and the Government of Uganda) (2007)

# Ukraine

## Introduction

**Background:** Ukraine was the center of the first eastern Slavic state, Kyivan Rus, which during the 10th and 11th centuries was the largest and most powerful state in Europe. Weakened by internecine quarrels and Mongol invasions, Kyivan Rus was incorporated into the Grand Duchy of Lithuania and eventually into the Polish-Lithuanian Commonwealth. The cultural and religious legacy of Kyivan Rus laid the foundation for Ukrainian nationalism through subsequent centuries. A new Ukrainian state, the Cossack Hetmanate, was established during the mid-17th century after an uprising against the Poles. Despite continuous Muscovite pressure, the Hetmanate managed to remain autonomous for well over 100 years. During the latter part of the 18th century, most Ukrainian ethnographic territory was absorbed by the Russian Empire. Following the collapse of czarist Russia in 1917, Ukraine was able to bring about a short-lived period of independence (1917-20), but was reconquered and forced to endure a brutal Soviet rule that engineered two artificial famines (1921-22 and 1932-33) in which over 8 million died. In World War II, German and Soviet armies were responsible for some 7 to 8 million more deaths. Although final independence for Ukraine was achieved in 1991 with the dissolution of the USSR, democracy remained elusive as the legacy of state control and endemic corruption stalled efforts at economic reform, privatization, and civil liberties. A peaceful mass protest "Orange Revolution" in the closing months of 2004 forced the authorities to overturn a rigged presidential election and to allow a new internationally monitored vote that swept into power a reformist slate under Viktor YUSHCHENKO. Subsequent internal squabbles in the YUSHCHENKO camp allowed his rival Viktor YANUKOVYCH to stage a comeback in parliamentary elections and become prime minister in August of 2006. An early legislative election, brought on by a political crisis in the spring of 2007, saw Yuliya TYMOSHENKO, as head of an "Orange" coalition, installed as a new prime minister in December 2007.

## Geography

**Location:** Eastern Europe, bordering the Black Sea, between Poland, Romania, and Moldova in the west and Russia in the east

**Geographic coordinates:** 49 00 N, 32 00 E

**Map references:** Asia, Europe

**Area:**
*total:* 603,700 sq km
*land:* 603,700 sq km
*water:* 0 sq km

**Area - comparative:** slightly smaller than Texas

**Land boundaries:**
*total:* 4,566 km
*border countries:* Belarus 891 km, Hungary 103 km, Moldova 940 km, Poland 428 km, Romania (south) 176 km, Romania (southwest) 362 km, Russia 1,576 km, Slovakia 90 km

**Coastline:** 2,782 km

**Maritime claims:**
*territorial sea:* 12 nm
*exclusive economic zone:* 200 nm
*continental shelf:* 200 m or to the depth of exploitation

**Climate:** temperate continental; Mediterranean only on the southern Crimean coast; precipitation disproportionately distributed, highest in west and north, lesser in east and southeast; winters vary from cool along the Black Sea to cold farther inland; summers are warm across the greater part of the country, hot in the south

**Terrain:** most of Ukraine consists of fertile plains (steppes) and plateaus, mountains being found only in the west (the Carpathians), and in the Crimean Peninsula in the extreme south

**Elevation extremes:**
*lowest point:* Black Sea 0 m
*highest point:* Hora Hoverla 2,061 m

**Natural resources:** iron ore, coal, manganese, natural gas, oil, salt, sulfur, graphite, titanium, magnesium, kaolin, nickel, mercury, timber, arable land

**Land use:**
*arable land:* 53.8%
*permanent crops:* 1.5%
*other:* 44.7% (2005)

**Irrigated land:** 22,080 sq km (2003)

**Total renewable water resources:** 139.5 cu km (1997)

**Freshwater withdrawal (domestic/industrial/agricultural):**
*total:* 37.53 cu km/yr (12%/35%/52%)
*per capita:* 807 cu m/yr (2000)

**Natural hazards:** NA

**Environment - current issues:** inadequate supplies of potable water; air and water pollution; deforestation; radiation contamination in the northeast from 1986 accident at Chornobyl' Nuclear Power Plant

**Environment - international agreements:**
*party to:* Air Pollution, Air Pollution-Nitrogen Oxides, Air Pollution-Sulfur 85, Antarctic-Environmental Protocol, Antarctic-Marine Living Resources, Antarctic Treaty, Biodiversity, Climate Change, Climate Change-Kyoto Protocol, Desertification, Endangered Species, Environmental Modification, Hazardous Wastes, Law of the Sea, Marine Dumping, Ozone Layer Protection, Ship Pollution, Wetlands
*signed, but not ratified:* Air Pollution-Persistent Organic Pollutants, Air Pollution-Sulfur 94, Air Pollution-Volatile Organic Compounds

**Geography - note:** strategic position at the crossroads between Europe and Asia; second-largest country in Europe

## People

**Population:** 45,700,395 (July 2009 est.)

**Age structure:**
*0-14 years:* 13.8% (male 3,238,280/female 3,066,594)
*15-64 years:* 70.3% (male 15,399,488/female 16,742,612)
*65 years and over:* 15.9% (male 2,422,311/female 4,831,110) (2009 est.)

**Median age:**
*total:* 39.5 years
*male:* 36.3 years
*female:* 42.7 years (2009 est.)

**Population growth rate:** -0.632% (2009 est.)

**Birth rate:** 9.6 births/1,000 population (2009 est.)

**Death rate:** 15.93 deaths/1,000 population (2008 est.)

**Net migration rate:** -0.11 migrant(s)/1,000 population (2009 est.)

# Ukraine (continued)

**Urbanization:**

*urban population:* 68% of total population (2008)

*rate of urbanization:* -0.7% annual rate of change (2005-10 est.)

**Sex ratio:**

*at birth:* 1.06 male(s)/female

*under 15 years:* 1.06 male(s)/female

*15-64 years:* 0.92 male(s)/female

*65 years and over:* 0.5 male(s)/female

*total population:* 0.86 male(s)/female (2009 est.)

**Infant mortality rate:**

*total:* 8.98 deaths/1,000 live births

*male:* 11.2 deaths/1,000 live births

*female:* 6.61 deaths/1,000 live births (2009 est.)

**Life expectancy at birth:**

*total population:* 68.25 years

*male:* 62.37 years

*female:* 74.5 years (2009 est.)

**Total fertility rate:** 1.26 children born/woman (2009 est.)

**HIV/AIDS - adult prevalence rate:** 1.6% (2007 est.)

**HIV/AIDS - people living with HIV/AIDS:** 440,000 (2007 est.)

**HIV/AIDS - deaths:** 19,000 (2007 est.)

**Nationality:**

*noun:* Ukrainian(s)

*adjective:* Ukrainian

**Ethnic groups:** Ukrainian 77.8%, Russian 17.3%, Belarusian 0.6%, Moldovan 0.5%, Crimean Tatar 0.5%, Bulgarian 0.4%, Hungarian 0.3%, Romanian 0.3%, Polish 0.3%, Jewish 0.2%, other 1.8% (2001 census)

**Religions:** Ukrainian Orthodox - Kyiv Patriarchate 50.4%, Ukrainian Orthodox - Moscow Patriarchate 26.1%, Ukrainian Greek Catholic 8%, Ukrainian Autocephalous Orthodox 7.2%, Roman Catholic 2.2%, Protestant 2.2%, Jewish 0.6%, other 3.2% (2006 est.)

**Languages:** Ukrainian (official) 67%, Russian 24%, other 9% (includes small Romanian-, Polish-, and Hungarian-speaking minorities)

**Literacy:**

*definition:* age 15 and over can read and write

*total population:* 99.4%

*male:* 99.7%

*female:* 99.2% (2001 census)

**School life expectancy (primary to tertiary education):**

*total:* 14 years

*male:* 14 years

*female:* 15 years (2006)

**Education expenditures:** 6.3% of GDP (2006)

## Government

**Country name:**

*conventional long form:* none

*conventional short form:* Ukraine

*local long form:* none

*local short form:* Ukrayina

*former:* Ukrainian National Republic, Ukrainian State, Ukrainian Soviet Socialist Republic

**Government type:** republic

**Capital:**

*name:* Kyiv (Kiev)

*geographic coordinates:* 50 26 N, 30 31 E

*time difference:* UTC+2 (7 hours ahead of Washington, DC during Standard Time)

*daylight saving time:* +1hr, begins last Sunday in March; ends last Sunday in October

**Administrative divisions:** 24 provinces (oblasti, singular - oblast'), 1 autonomous republic* (avtonomna respublika), and 2 municipalities (mista, singular - misto) with oblast status**; Cherkasy, Chernihiv, Chernivtsi, Crimea or Avtonomna Respublika Krym* (Simferopol'), Dnipropetrovs'k, Donets'k, Ivano-Frankivs'k, Kharkiv, Kherson, Khmel'nyts'kyy, Kirovohrad, Kyiv**, Kyiv, Luhans'k, L'viv, Mykolayiv, Odesa, Poltava, Rivne, Sevastopol'**, Sumy, Ternopil', Vinnytsya, Volyn' (Luts'k), Zakarpattya (Uzhhorod), Zaporizhzhya, Zhytomyr

*note:* administrative divisions have the same names as their administrative centers (exceptions have the administrative center name following in parentheses)

**Independence:** 24 August 1991 (from the Soviet Union)

**National holiday:** Independence Day, 24 August (1991); note - 22 January 1918, the day Ukraine first declared its independence (from Soviet Russia) and the day the short-lived Western and Central Ukrainian republics united (1919), is now celebrated as Unity Day

**Constitution:** adopted 28 June 1996

**Legal system:** based on civil law system; judicial review of legislative acts; has not accepted compulsory ICJ jurisdiction

**Suffrage:** 18 years of age; universal

**Executive branch:**

*chief of state:* President Viktor A. YUSHCHENKO (since 23 January 2005)

*head of government:* Prime Minister Yuliya TYMOSHENKO (since 18 December 2007); First Deputy Prime Minister Oleksandr TURCHYNOV (since 18 December 2007); Deputy Prime Ministers Hryhoriy NEMYRYA and Ivan VASYUNYK (since 18 December 2007)

*cabinet:* Cabinet of Ministers selected by the prime minister; the only exceptions are the foreign and defense ministers, who are chosen by the president

*note:* there is also a National Security and Defense Council or NSDC originally created in 1992 as the National Security Council; the NSDC staff is tasked with developing national security policy on domestic and international matters and advising the president; a Presidential Secretariat helps draft presidential edicts and provides policy support to the president

*elections:* president elected by popular vote for a five-year term (eligible for a second term); note - a special repeat runoff presidential election between Viktor YUSHCHENKO and Viktor YANUKOVYCH took place on 26 December 2004 after the earlier 21 November 2004 contest - won by YANUKOVYCH - was invalidated by the Ukrainian Supreme Court because of widespread and significant violations; under constitutional reforms that went into effect 1 January 2006, the majority in parliament takes the lead in naming the prime minister

*election results:* Viktor YUSHCHENKO elected president; percent of vote - Viktor YUSHCHENKO 52%, Viktor YANUKOVYCH 44.2%

**Legislative branch:** unicameral Supreme Council or Verkhovna Rada (450 seats; members allocated on a proportional basis to those parties that gain 3% or more of the national electoral vote; serve five-year terms)

*elections:* last held 30 September 2007 (next to be held in 2012)

*election results:* percent of vote by party/bloc - Party of Regions 34.4%, Yuliya Tymoshenko Bloc 30.7%, Our Ukraine-People's Self Defense 14.2%, CPU 5.4%, Lytvyn bloc 4%, other parties 11.3%; seats by party/bloc - Party of Regions 175, Yuliya Tymoshenko Bloc 156, Our Ukraine-People's Self Defense 72, CPU 27, Lytvyn bloc 20

**Judicial branch:** Supreme Court; Constitutional Court

**Political parties and leaders:** Christian Democratic Union [Volodymyr STRETOVYCH]; Communist Party of Ukraine or CPU [Petro SYMONENKO]; European Party of Ukraine [Mykola KATERYNCHUK]; Fatherland Party (Batkivshchyna) [Yuliya TYMOSHENKO]; Forward Ukraine! [Viktor MUSIYAKA]; Labor Party of Ukraine [Mykola SYROTA]; People's Union Our Ukraine [Viktor YUSHCHENKO]; Party of Industrialists and Entrepreneurs [Anatoliy KINAKH]; Party of the Defenders of the Fatherland [Yuriy Karmazin]; People's Movement of Ukraine (Rukh) [Borys TARASYUK]; People's Party [Volodymyr LYTVYN]; Peoples' Self-Defense [Yuriy LUTSENKO]; PORA! (It's Time!) party [Vladyslav KASKIV]; Progressive Socialist Party [Natalya VITRENKO]; Reforms and Order Party [Viktor PYNZENYK]; Party of Regions [Viktor YANUKOVYCH]; Sobor [Anatoliy MATVIYENKO]; Social Democratic Party [Yevhen KORNICHUK]; Social Democratic Party (United) or SDPU(o) [Yuriy ZAHORODNIY]; Socialist Party of Ukraine or SPU [Oleksandr MOROZ]; Ukrainian People's Party [Yuriy KOSTENKO]; United Center [Ihor Krill]; Viche [Inna BOHOSLOVSKA]

**Political pressure groups and leaders:** Committee of Voters of Ukraine [Ihor POPOV]

**International organization participation:** Australia Group, BSEC, CBSS (observer), CE, CEI, CIS, EAEC (observer), EAPC, EBRD, FAO, GCTU, GUAM, IAEA, IBRD, ICAO, ICC, ICCt (signatory), ICRM, IDA, IFC, IFRCS, IHO, ILO, IMF, IMO, IMSO, Interpol, IOC, IOM, IPU, ISO, ITU, ITUC, LAIA (observer), MIGA, MONUC, NAM (observer), NSG, OAS (observer), OIF (observer), OPCW, OSCE, PCA, PFP, SECI (observer), UN, UNCTAD, UNESCO, UNIDO, UNMIL, UNMIS, UNOMIG, UNWTO, UPU, WCL, WCO, WFTU, WHO, WIPO, WMO, WTO, ZC

# Ukraine (continued)

**Diplomatic representation in the US:**
*chief of mission:* Ambassador Oleh V. SHAMSHUR
*chancery:* 3350 M Street NW, Washington, DC 20007
*telephone:* [1] (202) 333-0606
*FAX:* [1] (202) 333-0817
*consulate(s) general:* Chicago, New York, San Francisco

**Diplomatic representation from the US:**
*chief of mission:* Ambassador William B. TAYLOR Jr.
*embassy:* 10 Yurii Kotsiubynsky Street, 01901 Kyiv
*mailing address:* 5850 Kiev Place, Washington, DC 20521-5850
*telephone:* [380] (44) 490-4000
*FAX:* [380] (44) 490-4085

**Flag description:** two equal horizontal bands of azure (top) and golden yellow represent grain fields under a blue sky

## Economy

**Economy - overview:** After Russia, the Ukrainian republic was far and away the most important economic component of the former Soviet Union, producing about four times the output of the next-ranking republic. Its fertile black soil generated more than one-fourth of Soviet agricultural output, and its farms provided substantial quantities of meat, milk, grain, and vegetables to other republics. Likewise, its diversified heavy industry supplied the unique equipment (for example, large diameter pipes) and raw materials to industrial and mining sites (vertical drilling apparatus) in other regions of the former USSR. Shortly after independence was ratified in December 1991, the Ukrainian Government liberalized most prices and erected a legal framework for privatization, but widespread resistance to reform within the government and the legislature soon stalled reform efforts and led to some backtracking. Output by 1999 had fallen to less than 40% of the 1991 level. Ukraine's dependence on Russia for energy supplies and the lack of significant structural reform have made the Ukrainian economy vulnerable to external shocks. Ukraine depends on imports to meet about three-fourths of its annual oil and natural gas requirements. Ukraine concluded a deal with Russia in January 2006 that almost doubled the price Ukraine pays for Russian gas. Disputes with Russia over pricing have led to periodic gas cut-offs. Outside institutions - particularly the IMF - have encouraged Ukraine to quicken the pace and scope of reforms. Ukrainian Government officials eliminated most tax and customs privileges in a March 2005 budget law, bringing more economic activity out of Ukraine's large shadow economy, but more improvements are needed, including fighting corruption, developing capital markets, and improving the legislative framework. Ukraine's economy was buoyant despite political turmoil between the prime minister and president until mid-2008. Real GDP growth reached roughly 7% in 2006-07, fueled by high global prices for steel - Ukraine's top export - and by strong domestic consumption, spurred by rising pensions and wages.

The drop in steel prices and Ukraine's exposure to the global financial crisis due to aggressive foreign borrowing has lowered growth in 2008 and the economy probably will contract in 2009. Ukraine reached an agreement with the IMF for a $16.5 billion standby arrangement in November 2008 to deal with the economic crisis. However, political turmoil in Ukraine as well as deteriorating external conditions are likely to hamper efforts for economic recovery.

**GDP (purchasing power parity):**
$337 billion (2008 est.)
$330 billion (2007)
$306.7 billion (2006)
*note:* data are in 2008 US dollars

**GDP (official exchange rate):** $198 billion (2008 est.)

**GDP - real growth rate:**
2.1% (2008 est.)
7.6% (2007 est.)
7.3% (2006 est.)

**GDP - per capita (PPP):**
$6,900 (2008 est.)
$7,100 (2007 est.)
$6,600 (2006 est.)
*note:* data are in 2008 US dollars

**GDP - composition by sector:**
*agriculture:* 9.3%
*industry:* 31.7%
*services:* 58.9% (2008 est.)

**Labor force:** 21.71 million (2008 est.)

**Labor force - by occupation:**
*agriculture:* 19.4%
*industry:* 24.2%
*services:* 56.4% (2005)

**Unemployment rate:**
3% (2008 est.)
2.3% (2007 est.)
*note:* officially registered; large number of unregistered or underemployed workers

**Population below poverty line:** 37.7% (2003)

**Household income or consumption by percentage share:**
*lowest 10%:* 3.4%
*highest 10%:* 25.7% (2006)

**Distribution of family income - Gini index:** 31 (2006)

**Investment (gross fixed):** 23.4% of GDP (2008 est.)

**Budget:**
*revenues:* $65.02 billion
*expenditures:* $68.48 billion; note - this is the planned, consolidated budget (2008 est.)

**Public debt:** 10% of GDP (2008 est.)

**Inflation rate (consumer prices):**
25% (2008 est.)
12.8% (2007 est.)

**Central bank discount rate:** 8% (31 December 2007)

**Commercial bank prime lending rate:** 13.9% (31 December 2007)

**Stock of money:** $35.97 billion (31 December 2007)

**Stock of quasi money:** $41.51 billion (31 December 2007)

**Stock of domestic credit:** $87.13 billion (31 December 2007)

**Market value of publicly traded shares:** $111.8 billion (31 December 2007)

**Agriculture - products:** grain, sugar beets, sunflower seeds, vegetables; beef, milk

**Industries:** coal, electric power, ferrous and nonferrous metals, machinery and transport equipment, chemicals, food processing (especially sugar)

**Industrial production growth rate:** 5% (2008 est.)

**Electricity - production:** 182.4 billion kWh (2006 est.)

**Electricity - consumption:** 148.1 billion kWh (2006 est.)

**Electricity - exports:** 12.52 billion kWh (2006 est.)

**Electricity - imports:** 2.082 billion kWh (2006 est.)

**Oil - production:** 102,400 bbl/day (2007 est.)

**Oil - consumption:** 344,000 bbl/day (2006 est.)

**Oil - exports:** 190,500 bbl/day (2005)

**Oil - imports:** 441,200 bbl/day (2005)

**Oil - proved reserves:** 395 million bbl (1 January 2008 est.)

**Natural gas - production:** 21.05 billion cu m (2008 est.)

**Natural gas - consumption:** 66.32 billion cu m (2008 est.)

**Natural gas - exports:** 4 billion cu m (2006 est.)

**Natural gas - imports:** 65.4 billion cu m (2007 est.)

**Natural gas - proved reserves:** 1.104 trillion cu m (1 January 2008 est.)

**Current account balance:** -$14.22 billion (2008 est.)

**Exports:** $64.89 billion (2008 est.)

**Exports - commodities:** ferrous and nonferrous metals, fuel and petroleum products, chemicals, machinery and transport equipment, food products

**Exports - partners:** Russia 23.3%, Turkey 7.9%, Italy 5.8% (2007)

**Imports:** $82.52 billion (2008 est.)

**Imports - commodities:** energy, machinery and equipment, chemicals

**Imports - partners:** Russia 23.9%, Germany 11.8%, China 8.5%, Poland 8.1%, Turkmenistan 5.4% (2007)

**Reserves of foreign exchange and gold:** $31.92 billion (1 November 2008)

**Debt - external:** $82.07 billion (31 December 2008 est.)

**Stock of direct foreign investment - at home:** $44.08 billion (2008 est.)

**Stock of direct foreign investment - abroad:** $1.13 billion (2008 est.)

**Exchange rates:** hryvnia (UAH) per US dollar - 4.9523 (2008 est.), 5.05 (2007), 5.05 (2006), 5.1247 (2005), 5.3192 (2004)

## Communications

**Telephones - main lines in use:** 12.858 million (2007)

**Telephones - mobile cellular:** 55.24 million (2007)

**Telephone system:**

*general assessment:* Ukraine's telecommunication development plan emphasizes improving domestic trunk lines, international connections, and the mobile-cellular system

*domestic:* at independence in December 1991, Ukraine inherited a telephone system that was antiquated, inefficient, and in disrepair; more than 3.5 million applications for telephones could not be satisfied; telephone density is rising and the domestic trunk system is being improved; about one-third of Ukraine's networks are digital and a majority of regional centers now have digital switching stations; improvements in local networks and local exchanges continue to lag; the mobile-cellular telephone system's expansion has slowed, largely due to saturation of the market which had reached 100 mobile phones per 100 people by early 2007

*international:* country code - 380; 2 new domestic trunk lines are a part of the fiber-optic Trans-Asia-Europe (TAE) system and 3 Ukrainian links have been installed in the fiber-optic Trans-European Lines (TEL) project that connects 18 countries; additional international service is provided by the Italy-Turkey-Ukraine-Russia (ITUR) fiber-optic submarine cable and by an unknown number of earth stations in the Intelsat, Inmarsat, and Intersputnik satellite systems

**Radio broadcast stations:** 524 (station frequency types NA) (2006)

**Television broadcast stations:** 647 (2006)

**Internet country code:** .ua

**Internet hosts:** 524,202 (2008)

**Internet users:** 10 million (2007)

## Transportation

**Airports:** 434 (2008)

**Airports - with paved runways:**

*total:* 193

*over 3,047 m:* 12

*2,438 to 3,047 m:* 53

*1,524 to 2,437 m:* 26

*914 to 1,523 m:* 6

*under 914 m:* 96 (2008)

**Airports - with unpaved runways:**

*total:* 241

*2,438 to 3,047 m:* 2

*1,524 to 2,437 m:* 8

*914 to 1,523 m:* 14

*under 914 m:* 217 (2008)

**Heliports:** 10 (2007)

**Pipelines:** gas 33,327 km; oil 4,514 km; refined products 4,211 km (2008)

**Railways:**

*total:* 21,852 km

*broad gauge:* 21,852 km 1.524-m gauge (9,648 km electrified) (2007)

**Roadways:**

*total:* 169,422 km

*paved:* 165,611 km (includes 15 km of expressways)

*unpaved:* 3,811 km (2007)

**Waterways:** 2,176 km (most on Dnieper River) (2007)

**Merchant marine:**

*total:* 189

*by type:* bulk carrier 6, cargo 141, chemical tanker 1, container 3, passenger 6, passenger/cargo 3, petroleum tanker 9, refrigerated cargo 11, roll on/roll off 7, specialized tanker 2

*foreign-owned:* 2 (Luxembourg 1, Russia 1)

*registered in other countries:* 204 (Belize 7, Cambodia 34, Comoros 8, Cyprus 4, Dominica 4, Georgia 18, Liberia 25, Lithuania 1, Malta 30, Moldova 5, Mongolia 1, Panama 10, Russia 11, Saint Kitts and Nevis 9, Saint Vincent and the Grenadines 11, Sierra Leone 10, Slovakia 12, Tuvalu 1, unknown 3) (2008)

**Ports and terminals:** Feodosiya, Kerch, Kherson, Mariupol', Mykolayiv, Odesa, Yuzhnyy

## Military

**Military branches:** Ground Forces, Naval Forces, Air and Air Defense Forces (Viyskovo-Povitryani Syly, VPS) (2009)

**Military service age and obligation:** 18-25 years of age for compulsory and voluntary military service; conscript service obligation - 18 months for Army and Air Force, 24 months for Navy (2004)

**Manpower available for military service:**

*males age 16-49:* 11,457,562

*females age 16-49:* 11,767,357 (2008 est.)

**Manpower fit for military service:**

*males age 16-49:* 7,056,742

*females age 16-49:* 9,234,591 (2009 est.)

**Manpower reaching militarily significant age annually:**

*male:* 269,311

*female:* 257,656 (2009 est.)

**Military expenditures:** 1.4% of GDP (2005 est.)

## Transnational Issues

**Disputes - international:** 1997 boundary delimitation treaty with Belarus remains un-ratified due to unresolved financial claims, stalling demarcation and reducing border security; delimitation of land boundary with Russia is complete with preparations for demarcation underway; the dispute over the boundary between Russia and Ukraine through the Kerch Strait and Sea of Azov remains unresolved despite a December 2003 framework agreement and ongoing expert-level discussions; Moldova and Ukraine operate joint customs posts to monitor transit of people and commodities through Moldova's break-away Transnistria Region, which remains under OSCE supervision; the ICJ gave Ukraine until December 2006 to reply, and Romania until June 2007 to rejoin, in their dispute submitted in 2004 over Ukrainian-administered Zmiyinyy/Serpilor (Snake) Island and Black Sea maritime boundary; Romania opposes Ukraine's reopening of a navigation canal from the Danube border through Ukraine to the Black Sea

**Illicit drugs:** limited cultivation of cannabis and opium poppy, mostly for CIS consumption; some synthetic drug production for export to the West; limited government eradication program; used as transshipment point for opiates and other illicit drugs from Africa, Latin America, and Turkey to Europe and Russia; Ukraine has improved anti-money-laundering controls, resulting in its removal from the Financial Action Task Force's (FATF's) Noncooperative Countries and Territories List in February 2004; Ukraine's anti-money-laundering regime continues to be monitored by FATF

# United Arab Emirates

## Introduction

**Background:** The Trucial States of the Persian Gulf coast granted the UK control of their defense and foreign affairs in 19th century treaties. In 1971, six of these states - Abu Zaby, 'Ajman, Al Fujayrah, Ash Shariqah, Dubayy, and Umm al Qaywayn - merged to form the United Arab Emirates (UAE). They were joined in 1972 by Ra's al Khaymah. The UAE's per capita GDP is on par with those of leading West European nations. Its generosity with oil revenues and its moderate foreign policy stance have allowed the UAE to play a vital role in the affairs of the region.

## Geography

**Location:** Middle East, bordering the Gulf of Oman and the Persian Gulf, between Oman and Saudi Arabia

**Geographic coordinates:** 24 00 N, 54 00 E

**Map references:** Middle East

**Area:**
*total:* 83,600 sq km
*land:* 83,600 sq km
*water:* 0 sq km

**Area - comparative:** slightly smaller than Maine

**Land boundaries:**
*total:* 867 km
*border countries:* Oman 410 km, Saudi Arabia 457 km

**Coastline:** 1,318 km

**Maritime claims:**
*territorial sea:* 12 nm
*contiguous zone:* 24 nm
*exclusive economic zone:* 200 nm
*continental shelf:* 200 nm or to the edge of the continental margin

**Climate:** desert; cooler in eastern mountains

**Terrain:** flat, barren coastal plain merging into rolling sand dunes of vast desert wasteland; mountains in east

**Elevation extremes:**
*lowest point:* Persian Gulf 0 m
*highest point:* Jabal Yibir 1,527 m

**Natural resources:** petroleum, natural gas

**Land use:**
*arable land:* 0.77%
*permanent crops:* 2.27%
*other:* 96.96% (2005)

**Irrigated land:** 760 sq km (2003)

**Total renewable water resources:** 0.2 cu km (1997)

**Freshwater withdrawal (domestic/industrial/agricultural):**
*total:* 2.3 cu km/yr (23%/9%/68%)
*per capita:* 511 cu m/yr (2000)

**Natural hazards:** frequent sand and dust storms

**Environment - current issues:** lack of natural freshwater resources compensated by desalination plants; desertification; beach pollution from oil spills

**Environment - international agreements:**
*party to:* Biodiversity, Climate Change, Climate Change-Kyoto Protocol, Desertification, Endangered Species, Hazardous Wastes, Marine Dumping, Ozone Layer Protection
*signed, but not ratified:* Law of the Sea

**Geography - note:** strategic location along southern approaches to Strait of Hormuz, a vital transit point for world crude oil

## People

**Population:** 4,798,491
*note:* estimate is based on the results of the 2005 census that included a significantly higher estimate of net inmigration of non-citizens than previous estimates (July 2009 est.)

**Age structure:**
*0-14 years:* 20.4% (male 500,928/female 478,388)
*15-64 years:* 78.7% (male 2,768,030/female 1,008,404)
*65 years and over:* 0.9% (male 27,601/female 15,140)
*note:* 73.9% of the population in the 15-64 age group is non-national (2009 est.)

**Median age:**
*total:* 30.1 years
*male:* 32 years
*female:* 24.7 years (2009 est.)

**Population growth rate:** 3.689% (2009 est.)

**Birth rate:** 16.02 births/1,000 population (2009 est.)

**Death rate:** 2.13 deaths/1,000 population (2008 est.)

**Net migration rate:** 22.98 migrant(s)/1,000 population (2009 est.)

**Urbanization:**
*urban population:* 78% of total population (2008)
*rate of urbanization:* 2.9% annual rate of change (2005-10 est.)

**Sex ratio:**
*at birth:* 1.05 male(s)/female
*under 15 years:* 1.05 male(s)/female
*15-64 years:* 2.74 male(s)/female
*65 years and over:* 1.82 male(s)/female
*total population:* 2.19 male(s)/female (2009 est.)

**Infant mortality rate:**
*total:* 12.7 deaths/1,000 live births
*male:* 14.86 deaths/1,000 live births
*female:* 10.44 deaths/1,000 live births (2009 est.)

**Life expectancy at birth:**
*total population:* 76.11 years
*male:* 73.56 years
*female:* 78.78 years (2009 est.)

**Total fertility rate:** 2.42 children born/woman (2009 est.)

**HIV/AIDS - adult prevalence rate:** 0.18% (2001 est.)

**HIV/AIDS - people living with HIV/AIDS:** NA

**HIV/AIDS - deaths:** NA

**Nationality:**
*noun:* Emirati(s)
*adjective:* Emirati

**Ethnic groups:** Emirati 19%, other Arab and Iranian 23%, South Asian 50%, other expatriates (includes Westerners and East Asians) 8% (1982)
*note:* less than 20% are UAE citizens (1982)

**Religions:** Muslim 96% (Shia 16%), other (includes Christian, Hindu) 4%

**Languages:** Arabic (official), Persian, English, Hindi, Urdu

**Literacy:**
*definition:* age 15 and over can read and write
*total population:* 77.9%
*male:* 76.1%
*female:* 81.7% (2003 est.)

**School life expectancy (primary to tertiary education):**
*total:* 11 years
*male:* 11 years
*female:* 12 years (2003)

**Education expenditures:** 1.3% of GDP (2005)

# United Arab Emirates *(continued)*

## Government

**Country name:**
*conventional long form:* United Arab Emirates
*conventional short form:* none
*local long form:* Al Imarat al Arabiyah al Muttahidah
*local short form:* none
*former:* Trucial Oman, Trucial States
*abbreviation:* UAE
**Government type:** federation with specified powers delegated to the UAE federal government and other powers reserved to member emirates
**Capital:**
*name:* Abu Dhabi
*geographic coordinates:* 24 28 N, 54 22 E
*time difference:* UTC+4 (9 hours ahead of Washington, DC during Standard Time)
**Administrative divisions:** 7 emirates (imarat, singular - imarah); Abu Zaby (Abu Dhabi), 'Ajman, Al Fujayrah, Ash Shariqah (Sharjah), Dubayy (Dubai), Ra's al Khaymah, Umm al Qaywayn (Quwayn)
**Independence:** 2 December 1971 (from the UK)
**National holiday:** Independence Day, 2 December (1971)
**Constitution:** 2 December 1971; made permanent in 1996
**Legal system:** based on a dual system of Sharia and civil courts; has not accepted compulsory ICJ jurisdiction
**Suffrage:** none
**Executive branch:**
*chief of state:* President KHALIFA bin Zayid al-Nuhayyan (since 3 November 2004), ruler of Abu Zaby (Abu Dhabi) (since 4 November 2004); Vice President and Prime Minister MUHAMMAD BIN RASHID al-Maktum (since 5 January 2006)
*head of government:* Prime Minister and Vice President MUHAMMAD bin Rashid al-Maktum (since 5 January 2006); Deputy Prime Ministers SULTAN bin Zayid al-Nuhayyan (since 20 November 1990) and HAMDAN bin Zayid al-Nuhayyan (since 20 October 2003)
*cabinet:* Council of Ministers appointed by the president
*note:* there is also a Federal Supreme Council (FSC) composed of the seven emirate rulers; the FSC is the highest constitutional authority in the UAE; establishes general policies and sanctions federal legislation; meets four times a year; Abu Zaby (Abu Dhabi) and Dubayy (Dubai) rulers have effective veto power
*elections:* president and vice president elected by the FSC for five-year terms (no term limits) from among the seven FSC members; election last held 3 November 2004 upon the death of the UAE's Founding Father and first President ZAYID bin Sultan al Nuhayyan (next to be held in 2009); prime minister and deputy prime minister appointed by the president
*election results:* KHALIFA bin Zayid al-Nuhayyan elected president by a unanimous vote of the FSC; MUHAMMAD bin Rashid al-Maktum unanimously affirmed vice president after the 2006 death of his brother Sheikh Maktum bin Rashid al-Maktum

**Legislative branch:** unicameral Federal National Council (FNC) or Majlis al-Ittihad al-Watani (40 seats; 20 members appointed by the rulers of the constituent states, 20 members elected to serve two-year terms)
*elections:* elections for one half of the FNC (the other half remains appointed) held in the UAE on 18-20 December 2006; the new electoral college - a body of 6,689 Emiratis (including 1,189 women) appointed by the rulers of the seven emirates - were the only eligible voters and candidates; 456 candidates including 65 women ran for 20 contested FNC seats; one female from the Emirate of Abu Dhabi won a seat and 8 women were among the 20 appointed members
*note:* reviews legislation but cannot change or veto
**Judicial branch:** Union Supreme Court (judges are appointed by the president)
**Political parties and leaders:** none; political parties are not allowed
**Political pressure groups and leaders:** NA
**International organization participation:** ABEDA, AFESD, AMF, FAO, G-77, GCC, IAEA, IBRD, ICAO, ICC, ICCt (signatory), ICRM, IDA, IDB, IFAD, IFC, IFRCS, IHO, ILO, IMF, IMO, IMSO, Interpol, IOC, IPU, ISO, ITSO, ITU, LAS, MIGA, NAM, OAPEC, OIC, OPCW, OPEC, UN, UNCTAD, UNESCO, UNIDO, UPU, WCO, WFTU, WHO, WIPO, WMO, WTO
**Diplomatic representation in the US:**
*chief of mission:* Ambassador Yousef bin Mani Saeed al-OTAIBA
*chancery:* 3522 International Court NW, Suite 400, Washington, DC 20008
*telephone:* [1] (202) 243-2400
*FAX:* [1] (202) 243-2432
**Diplomatic representation from the US:**
*chief of mission:* Ambassador Richard G. OLSON, Jr.
*embassy:* Embassies District, Plot 38 Sector W59-02, Street No. 4, Abu Dhabi
*mailing address:* P. O. Box 4009, Abu Dhabi
*telephone:* [971] (2) 414-2200
*FAX:* [971] (2) 414-2603
*consulate(s) general:* Dubai
**Flag description:** three equal horizontal bands of green (top), white, and black with a wider vertical red band on the hoist side

## Economy

**Economy - overview:** The UAE has an open economy with a high per capita income and a sizable annual trade surplus. Successful efforts at economic diversification have reduced the portion of GDP based on oil and gas output to 25%. Since the discovery of oil in the UAE more than 30 years ago, the UAE has undergone a profound transformation from an impoverished region of small desert principalities to a modern state with a high standard of living. The government has increased spending on job creation and infrastructure expansion and is opening up utilities to greater private sector involvement. In April 2004, the UAE signed a Trade and Investment Framework Agreement with Washington and

in November 2004 agreed to undertake negotiations toward a Free Trade Agreement with the US. The country's Free Trade Zones - offering 100% foreign ownership and zero taxes - are helping to attract foreign investors. Higher oil revenue, strong liquidity, housing shortages, and cheap credit in 2005-07 led to a surge in asset prices (shares and real estate) and consumer inflation. The global financial crisis and the resulting tight international credit market and falling oil prices have already begun to deflate asset prices and will result in slower economic growth for 2009. Dependence on oil and a large expatriate workforce are significant long-term challenges. The UAE's strategic plan for the next few years focuses on diversification and creating more opportunities for nationals through improved education and increased private sector employment.
**GDP (purchasing power parity):**
$184.6 billion (2008 est.)
$171.4 billion (2007)
$159.3 billion (2006)
*note:* data are in 2008 US dollars
**GDP (official exchange rate):** $270 billion (2008 est.)
**GDP - real growth rate:**
7.7% (2008 est.)
7.6% (2007 est.)
9.4% (2006 est.)
**GDP - per capita (PPP):**
$40,000 (2008 est.)
$38,600 (2007 est.)
$37,300 (2006 est.)
*note:* data are in 2008 US dollars
**GDP - composition by sector:**
*agriculture:* 1.6%
*industry:* 61.8%
*services:* 36.6% (2008 est.)
**Labor force:** 3.266 million
*note:* expatriates account for about 85% of the work force (2008 est.)
**Labor force - by occupation:**
*agriculture:* 7%
*industry:* 15%
*services:* 78% (2000 est.)
**Unemployment rate:**
2.4% (2001)
**Population below poverty line:** 19.5% (2003)
**Household income or consumption by percentage share:**
*lowest 10%:* NA%
*highest 10%:* NA%
**Investment (gross fixed):** 20.8% of GDP (2008 est.)
**Budget:**
*revenues:* $83.15 billion
*expenditures:* $48.3 billion (2008 est.)
**Public debt:** 22.4% of GDP (2008 est.)
**Inflation rate (consumer prices):**
14.4% (2008 est.)
14% (2007 est.)
**Central bank discount rate:** NA
**Stock of money:** $49.5 billion (31 December 2007)

# United Arab Emirates *(continued)*

**Stock of quasi money:** $104.6 billion (31 December 2007)

**Stock of domestic credit:** $155.4 billion (31 December 2007)

**Market value of publicly traded shares:** $224.7 billion (31 December 2007)

**Agriculture - products:** dates, vegetables, watermelons; poultry, eggs, dairy products; fish

**Industries:** petroleum and petrochemicals; fishing, aluminum, cement, fertilizers, commercial ship repair, construction materials, some boat building, handicrafts, textiles

**Industrial production growth rate:** 7.7% (2008 est.)

**Electricity - production:** 62.76 billion kWh (2006 est.)

**Electricity - consumption:** 57.88 billion kWh (2006 est.)

**Electricity - exports:** 0 kWh (2007 est.)

**Electricity - imports:** 0 kWh (2007 est.)

**Oil - production:** 2.948 million bbl/day (2007 est.)

**Oil - consumption:** 381,000 bbl/day (2006 est.)

**Oil - exports:** 2.703 million bbl/day (2005 est.)

**Oil - imports:** 232,300 bbl/day (2005)

**Oil - proved reserves:** 97.8 billion bbl (1 January 2008 est.)

**Natural gas - production:** 48.79 billion cu m (2006 est.)

**Natural gas - consumption:** 43.11 billion cu m (2006 est.)

**Natural gas - exports:** 6.848 billion cu m (2005 est.)

**Natural gas - imports:** 1.343 billion cu m (2005)

**Natural gas - proved reserves:** 6.071 trillion cu m (1 January 2008 est.)

**Current account balance:** $36.41 billion (2008 est.)

**Exports:** $207.7 billion f.o.b. (2008 est.)

**Exports - commodities:** crude oil 45%, natural gas, reexports, dried fish, dates

**Exports - partners:** Japan 23.6%, South Korea 9.2%, Thailand 5%, India 4.8% (2007)

**Imports:** $141.1 billion f.o.b. (2008 est.)

**Imports - commodities:** machinery and transport equipment, chemicals, food

**Imports - partners:** China 12.8%, India 10%, US 8.7%, Japan 6.1%, Germany 5.9%, UK 5.3%, Italy 4.6% (2007)

**Reserves of foreign exchange and gold:** $67.24 billion (31 December 2008 est.)

**Debt - external:** $73.71 billion (31 December 2008 est.)

**Stock of direct foreign investment - at home:** $62.69 billion (2008 est.)

**Stock of direct foreign investment - abroad:** $28.95 billion (2008 est.)

**Exchange rates:** Emirati dirhams (AED) per US dollar - 3.6725 (2008 est.), 3.6725 (2007), 3.6725 (2006), 3.6725 (2005), 3.6725 (2004)
*note:* officially pegged to the US dollar since February 2002

## Communications

**Telephones - main lines in use:** 1.385 million (2007)

**Telephones - mobile cellular:** 7.595 million (2007)

**Telephone system:**
*general assessment:* modern fiber-optic integrated services; digital network with rapidly growing use of mobile-cellular telephones; key centers are Abu Dhabi and Dubai
*domestic:* microwave radio relay, fiber optic and coaxial cable
*international:* country code - 971; linked to the international submarine cable FLAG (Fiber-Optic Link Around the Globe); landing point for both the SEA-ME-WE-3 and SEA-ME-WE-4 submarine cable networks; satellite earth stations - 3 Intelsat (1 Atlantic Ocean and 2 Indian Ocean) and 1 Arabsat; tropospheric scatter to Bahrain; microwave radio relay to Saudi Arabia

**Radio broadcast stations:** AM 13, FM 8, shortwave 2 (2004)

**Television broadcast stations:** 15 (2004)

**Internet country code:** .ae

**Internet hosts:** 381,915 (2008)

**Internet users:** 2.3 million (2007)

## Transportation

**Airports:** 39 (2008)

**Airports - with paved runways:**
*total:* 22
*over 3,047 m:* 10
*2,438 to 3,047 m:* 3
*1,524 to 2,437 m:* 3
*914 to 1,523 m:* 4
*under 914 m:* 2 (2008)

**Airports - with unpaved runways:**
*total:* 17
*over 3,047 m:* 2
*2,438 to 3,047 m:* 1
*1,524 to 2,437 m:* 4
*914 to 1,523 m:* 5
*under 914 m:* 5 (2008)

**Heliports:** 5 (2007)

**Pipelines:** condensate 458 km; gas 2,129 km; liquid petroleum gas 220 km; oil 1,310 km; refined products 212 km; water 90 km (2008)

**Roadways:**
*total:* 4,080 km
*paved:* 4,080 km (includes 253 km of expressways) (2008)

**Merchant marine:**
*total:* 58
*by type:* bulk carrier 6, cargo 9, chemical tanker 4, container 8, liquefied gas 1, passenger/cargo 1, petroleum tanker 24, roll on/roll off 4, specialized tanker 1
*foreign-owned:* 14 (Denmark 1, Greece 3, Kuwait 10)
*registered in other countries:* 313 (Bahamas 23, Bahrain 1, Belize 5, Cambodia 2, Comoros 7, Cyprus 9, Dominica 1, Georgia 1, Gibraltar 3, Hong Kong 1, India 6, Indonesia 2, Iran 1, Jordan 13, North Korea 8, Liberia 23, Malta 5, Marshall Islands 15, Mexico 1, Netherlands 5, Panama 109, Papua New Guinea 6, Philippines 1, Saint Kitts and Nevis 18, Saint Vincent and the Grenadines 9, Saudi Arabia 1, Sierra Leone 8, Singapore 12, Somalia 1, Turkey 1, UK 9, unknown 6) (2008)

**Ports and terminals:** Mina' Zayid (Abu Dhabi), Al Fujayrah, Mina' Jabal 'Ali (Dubai), Mina' Rashid (Dubai), Mina' Saqr (Ra's al Khaymah), Khawr Fakkan (Sharjah)

## Military

**Military branches:** United Arab Emirates Armed Forces: Army, Navy (includes Marines), Air Force and Air Defense, National Coast Guard (2008)

**Military service age and obligation:** 18 years of age (est.) for voluntary military service; 18 years of age for officers and women; no conscription (2008)

**Manpower available for military service:**
*males age 16-49:* 2,405,884 (includes non-nationals)
*females age 16-49:* 884,853 (2008 est.)

**Manpower fit for military service:**
*males age 16-49:* 2,081,491
*females age 16-49:* 788,632 (2009 est.)

**Manpower reaching militarily significant age annually:**
*male:* 26,659
*female:* 23,793 (2009 est.)

**Military expenditures:** 3.1% of GDP (2005 est.)

## Transnational Issues

**Disputes - international:** boundary agreement was signed and ratified with Oman in 2003 for entire border, including Oman's Musandam Peninsula and Al Madhah enclaves, but contents of the agreement and detailed maps showing the alignment have not been published; Iran and UAE dispute Tunb Islands and Abu Musa Island, which Iran occupies

**Illicit drugs:** the UAE is a drug transshipment point for traffickers given its proximity to Southwest Asian drug-producing countries; the UAE's position as a major financial center makes it vulnerable to money laundering; anti-money-laundering controls improving, but informal banking remains unregulated

# United Kingdom

The island of Rockall is not shown.

## Introduction

**Background:** As the dominant industrial and maritime power of the 19th century, the United Kingdom of Great Britain and Ireland played a leading role in developing parliamentary democracy and in advancing literature and science. At its zenith, the British Empire stretched over one-fourth of the earth's surface. The first half of the 20th century saw the UK's strength seriously depleted in two World Wars and the Irish republic withdraw from the union. The second half witnessed the dismantling of the Empire and the UK rebuilding itself into a modern and prosperous European nation. As one of five permanent members of the UN Security Council, a founding member of NATO, and of the Commonwealth, the UK pursues a global approach to foreign policy; it currently is weighing the degree of its integration with continental Europe. A member of the EU, it chose to remain outside the Economic and Monetary Union for the time being. Constitutional reform is also a significant issue in the UK. The Scottish Parliament, the National Assembly for Wales, and the Northern Ireland Assembly were established in 1999, but the latter was suspended until May 2007 due to wrangling over the peace process.

## Geography

**Location:** Western Europe, islands including the northern one-sixth of the island of Ireland between the North Atlantic Ocean and the North Sea, northwest of France
**Geographic coordinates:** 54 00 N, 2 00 W
**Map references:** Europe
**Area:**
*total:* 244,820 sq km
*land:* 241,590 sq km
*water:* 3,230 sq km
*note:* includes Rockall and Shetland Islands
**Area - comparative:** slightly smaller than Oregon
**Land boundaries:**
*total:* 360 km
*border countries:* Ireland 360 km
**Coastline:** 12,429 km
**Maritime claims:**
*territorial sea:* 12 nm
*exclusive fishing zone:* 200 nm
*continental shelf:* as defined in continental shelf orders or in accordance with agreed upon boundaries
**Climate:** temperate; moderated by prevailing southwest winds over the North Atlantic Current; more than one-half of the days are overcast
**Terrain:** mostly rugged hills and low mountains; level to rolling plains in east and southeast
**Elevation extremes:**
*lowest point:* The Fens -4 m
*highest point:* Ben Nevis 1,343 m
**Natural resources:** coal, petroleum, natural gas, iron ore, lead, zinc, gold, tin, limestone, salt, clay, chalk, gypsum, potash, silica sand, slate, arable land
**Land use:**
*arable land:* 23.23%
*permanent crops:* 0.2%
*other:* 76.57% (2005)
**Irrigated land:** 1,700 sq km (2003)
**Total renewable water resources:** 160.6 cu km (2005)
**Freshwater withdrawal (domestic/industrial/agricultural):**
*total:* 11.75 cu km/yr (22%/75%/3%)
*per capita:* 197 cu m/yr (1994)
**Natural hazards:** winter windstorms; floods
**Environment - current issues:** continues to reduce greenhouse gas emissions (has met Kyoto Protocol target of a 12.5% reduction from 1990 levels and intends to meet the legally binding target and move toward a domestic goal of a 20% cut in emissions by 2010); by 2005 the government reduced the amount of industrial and commercial waste disposed of in landfill sites to 85% of 1998 levels and recycled or composted at least 25% of household waste, increasing to 33% by 2015

**Environment - international agreements:**
*party to:* Air Pollution, Air Pollution-Nitrogen Oxides, Air Pollution-Persistent Organic Pollutants, Air Pollution-Sulfur 94, Air Pollution-Volatile Organic Compounds, Antarctic-Environmental Protocol, Antarctic-Marine Living Resources, Antarctic Seals, Antarctic Treaty, Biodiversity, Climate Change, Climate Change-Kyoto Protocol, Desertification, Endangered Species, Environmental Modification, Hazardous Wastes, Law of the Sea, Marine Dumping, Marine Life Conservation, Ozone Layer Protection, Ship Pollution, Tropical Timber 83, Tropical Timber 94, Wetlands, Whaling
*signed, but not ratified:* none of the selected agreements
**Geography - note:** lies near vital North Atlantic sea lanes; only 35 km from France and linked by tunnel under the English Channel; because of heavily indented coastline, no location is more than 125 km from tidal waters

## People

**Population:** 61,113,205 (July 2009 est.)
**Age structure:**
*0-14 years:* 16.7% (male 5,233,756/female 4,986,131)
*15-64 years:* 67.1% (male 20,774,192/female 20,246,519)
*65 years and over:* 16.2% (male 4,259,654/female 5,612,953) (2009 est.)
**Median age:**
*total:* 40.2 years
*male:* 39.1 years
*female:* 41.3 years (2009 est.)
**Population growth rate:** 0.279% (2009 est.)
**Birth rate:** 10.65 births/1,000 population (2009 est.)
**Death rate:** 10.05 deaths/1,000 population (2008 est.)
**Net migration rate:** 2.16 migrant(s)/1,000 population (2009 est.)
**Urbanization:**
*urban population:* 90% of total population (2008)
*rate of urbanization:* 0.5% annual rate of change (2005-10 est.)
**Sex ratio:**
*at birth:* 1.05 male(s)/female
*under 15 years:* 1.05 male(s)/female
*15-64 years:* 1.03 male(s)/female
*65 years and over:* 0.76 male(s)/female
*total population:* 0.98 male(s)/female (2009 est.)
**Infant mortality rate:**
*total:* 4.85 deaths/1,000 live births
*male:* 5.4 deaths/1,000 live births
*female:* 4.28 deaths/1,000 live births (2009 est.)
**Life expectancy at birth:**
*total population:* 79.01 years
*male:* 76.52 years
*female:* 81.63 years (2009 est.)
**Total fertility rate:** 1.66 children born/woman (2009 est.)
**HIV/AIDS - adult prevalence rate:** 0.2% (2007 est.)

# United Kingdom (continued)

**HIV/AIDS - people living with HIV/AIDS:** 77,000 (2007 est.)

**HIV/AIDS - deaths:** fewer than 500 (2007 est.)

**Nationality:**

*noun:* Briton(s), British (collective plural)

*adjective:* British

**Ethnic groups:** white (of which English 83.6%, Scottish 8.6%, Welsh 4.9%, Northern Irish 2.9%) 92.1%, black 2%, Indian 1.8%, Pakistani 1.3%, mixed 1.2%, other 1.6% (2001 census)

**Religions:** Christian (Anglican, Roman Catholic, Presbyterian, Methodist) 71.6%, Muslim 2.7%, Hindu 1%, other 1.6%, unspecified or none 23.1% (2001 census)

**Languages:** English, Welsh (about 26% of the population of Wales), Scottish form of Gaelic (about 60,000 in Scotland)

**Literacy:**

*definition:* age 15 and over has completed five or more years of schooling

*total population:* 99%

*male:* 99%

*female:* 99% (2003 est.)

**School life expectancy (primary to tertiary education):**

*total:* 16 years

*male:* 16 years

*female:* 17 years (2006)

**Education expenditures:** 5.6% of GDP (2005)

## Government

**Country name:**

*conventional long form:* United Kingdom of Great Britain and Northern Ireland; note - Great Britain includes England, Scotland, and Wales

*conventional short form:* United Kingdom

*abbreviation:* UK

**Government type:** constitutional monarchy and Commonwealth realm

**Capital:**

*name:* London

*geographic coordinates:* 51 30 N, 0 10 W

*time difference:* UTC 0 (5 hours ahead of Washington, DC during Standard Time)

*daylight saving time:* +1hr, begins last Sunday in March; ends last Sunday in October

*note:* applies to the United Kingdom proper, not to its overseas dependencies or territories

**Administrative divisions:**

*England:* 34 two-tier counties, 32 London boroughs and 1 City of London or Greater London, 36 metropolitan counties, 46 unitary authorities

*two-tier counties:* Bedfordshire, Buckinghamshire, Cambridgeshire, Cheshire, Cornwall and Isles of Scilly, Cumbria, Derbyshire, Devon, Dorset, Durham, East Sussex, Essex, Gloucestershire, Hampshire, Hertfordshire, Kent, Lancashire, Leicestershire, Lincolnshire, Norfolk, North Yorkshire, Northamptonshire, Northumberland, Nottinghamshire, Oxfordshire, Shropshire, Somerset, Staffordshire, Suffolk, Surrey, Warwickshire, West Sussex, Wiltshire, Worcestershire

*London boroughs and City of London or Greater London:* Barking and Dagenham, Barnet, Bexley, Brent, Bromley, Camden, Croydon, Ealing, Enfield, Greenwich, Hackney, Hammersmith and Fulham, Haringey, Harrow, Havering, Hillingdon, Hounslow, Islington, Kensington and Chelsea, Kingston upon Thames, Lambeth, Lewisham, City of London, Merton, Newham, Redbridge, Richmond upon Thames, Southwark, Sutton, Tower Hamlets, Waltham Forest, Wandsworth, Westminster

*metropolitan counties:* Barnsley, Birmingham, Bolton, Bradford, Bury, Calderdale, Coventry, Doncaster, Dudley, Gateshead, Kirklees, Knowlsey, Leeds, Liverpool, Manchester, Newcastle upon Tyne, North Tyneside, Oldham, Rochdale, Rotherham, Salford, Sandwell, Sefton, Sheffield, Solihull, South Tyneside, St. Helens, Stockport, Sunderland, Tameside, Trafford, Wakefield, Walsall, Wigan, Wirral, Wolverhampton

*unitary authorities:* Bath and North East Somerset, Blackburn with Darwen, Blackpool, Bournemouth, Bracknell Forest, Brighton and Hove, City of Bristol, Darlington, Derby, East Riding of Yorkshire, Halton, Hartlepool, County of Herefordshire, Isle of Wight, City of Kingston upon Hull, Leicester, Luton, Medway, Middlesbrough, Milton Keynes, North East Lincolnshire, North Lincolnshire, North Somerset, Nottingham, Peterborough, Plymouth, Poole, Portsmouth, Reading, Redcar and Cleveland, Rutland, Slough, South Gloucestershire, Southampton, Southend-on-Sea, Stockton-on-Tees, Stoke-on-Trent, Swindon, Telford and Wrekin, Thurrock, Torbay, Warrington, West Berkshire, Windsor and Maidenhead, Wokingham, York

*Northern Ireland:* 26 district council areas

*district council areas:* Antrim, Ards, Armagh, Ballymena, Ballymoney, Banbridge, Belfast, Carrickfergus, Castlereagh, Coleraine, Cookstown, Craigavon, Derry, Down, Dungannon, Fermanagh, Larne, Limavady, Lisburn, Magherafelt, Moyle, Newry and Mourne, Newtownabbey, North Down, Omagh, Strabane

*Scotland:* 32 unitary authorities

*unitary authorities:* Aberdeen City, Aberdeenshire, Angus, Argyll and Bute, Clackmannanshire, Dumfries and Galloway, Dundee City, East Ayrshire, East Dunbartonshire, East Lothian, East Renfrewshire, City of Edinburgh, Eilean Siar (Western Isles), Falkirk, Fife, Glasgow City, Highland, Inverclyde, Midlothian, Moray, North Ayrshire, North Lanarkshire, Orkney Islands, Perth and Kinross, Renfrewshire, Shetland Islands, South Ayrshire, South Lanarkshire, Stirling, The Scottish Borders, West Dunbartonshire, West Lothian

*Wales:* 22 unitary authorities

*unitary authorities:* Blaenau Gwent; Bridgend; Caerphilly; Cardiff; Carmarthenshire; Ceredigion; Conwy; Denbighshire; Flintshire; Gwynedd; Isle of Anglesey; Merthyr Tydfil; Monmouthshire; Neath Port Talbot; Newport; Pembrokeshire; Powys; Rhondda, Cynon, Taff; Swansea; The Vale of Glamorgan; Torfaen; Wrexham

**Dependent areas:** Anguilla, Bermuda, British Indian Ocean Territory, British Virgin Islands, Cayman Islands, Falkland Islands, Gibraltar, Montserrat, Pitcairn Islands, Saint Helena, South Georgia and the South Sandwich Islands, Turks and Caicos Islands

**Independence:** 1927; England has existed as a unified entity since the 10th century; the union between England and Wales, begun in 1284 with the Statute of Rhuddlan, was not formalized until 1536 with an Act of Union; in another Act of Union in 1707, England and Scotland agreed to permanently join as Great Britain; the legislative union of Great Britain and Ireland was implemented in 1801, with the adoption of the name the United Kingdom of Great Britain and Ireland; the Anglo-Irish treaty of 1921 formalized a partition of Ireland; six northern Irish counties remained part of the United Kingdom as Northern Ireland and the current name of the country, the United Kingdom of Great Britain and Northern Ireland, was adopted in 1927

**National holiday:** the UK does not celebrate one particular national holiday

**Constitution:** unwritten; partly statutes, partly common law and practice

**Legal system:** based on common law tradition with early Roman and modern continental influences; has nonbinding judicial review of Acts of Parliament under the Human Rights Act of 1998; accepts compulsory ICJ jurisdiction with reservations

**Suffrage:** 18 years of age; universal

**Executive branch:**

*chief of state:* Queen ELIZABETH II (since 6 February 1952); Heir Apparent Prince CHARLES (son of the queen, born 14 November 1948)

*head of government:* Prime Minister James Gordon BROWN (since 27 June 2007)

*cabinet:* Cabinet of Ministers appointed by the prime minister

*elections:* the monarchy is hereditary; following legislative elections, the leader of the majority party or the leader of the majority coalition is usually the prime minister

**Legislative branch:** bicameral Parliament consists of House of Lords (618 seats; consisting of approximately 500 life peers, 92 hereditary peers, and 26 clergy) and House of Commons (646 seats since 2005 elections; members are elected by popular vote to serve five-year terms unless the House is dissolved earlier)

*elections:* House of Lords - no elections (note - in 1999, as provided by the House of Lords Act, elections were held in the House of Lords to determine the 92 hereditary peers who would remain there; elections are held only as vacancies in the hereditary peerage arise); House of Commons - last held 5 May 2005 (next to be held by June 2010)

*election results:* House of Commons - percent of vote by party - Labor 35.2%, Conservative 32.3%, Liberal Democrats 22%, other 10.5%; seats by party - Labor 355, Conservative 198, Liberal Democrat 62, other 31; seats by party in the House of Commons as of 21 November 2008 - Labor 350,

Conservative 192, Liberal Democrat 63, Scottish National Party/Plaid Cymru 10, Democratic Unionist 9, Sinn Fein 5, other 17
*note:* in 1998 elections were held for a Northern Ireland Assembly (because of unresolved disputes among existing parties, the transfer of power from London to Northern Ireland came only at the end of 1999 and has been suspended four times, the latest occurring in October 2002 and lasting until 8 May 2007); in 1999, the UK held the first elections for a Scottish Parliament and a Welsh Assembly, the most recent of which were held in May 2007
**Judicial branch:** House of Lords (highest court of appeal; several Lords of Appeal in Ordinary are appointed by the monarch for life); Supreme Courts of England, Wales, and Northern Ireland (comprising the Courts of Appeal, the High Courts of Justice, and the Crown Courts); Scotland's Court of Session and Court of the Justiciary
**Political parties and leaders:** Conservative [David CAMERON]; Democratic Unionist Party (Northern Ireland) [Peter ROBINSON]; Labor Party [Gordon BROWN]; Liberal Democrats [Nick CLEGG]; Party of Wales (Plaid Cymru) [Ieuan Wyn JONES]; Scottish National Party or SNP [Alex SALMOND]; Sinn Fein (Northern Ireland) [Gerry ADAMS]; Social Democratic and Labor Party or SDLP (Northern Ireland) [Mark DURKAN]; Ulster Unionist Party (Northern Ireland) [Sir Reg EMPEY]
**Political pressure groups and leaders:** Campaign for Nuclear Disarmament; Confederation of British Industry; National Farmers' Union; Trades Union Congress
**International organization participation:** ADB (nonregional member), AfDB (nonregional member), Arctic Council (observer), Australia Group, BIS, C, CBSS (observer), CDB, CE, CERN, EAPC, EBRD, EIB, ESA, EU, FAO, G-20, G-5, G-7, G-8, G-10, IADB, IAEA, IBRD, ICAO, ICC, ICCt, ICRM, IDA, IEA, IFAD, IFC, IFRCS, IHO, ILO, IMF, IMO, IMSO, Interpol, IOC, IOM, IPU, ISO, ITSO, ITU, ITUC, MIGA, NATO, NEA, NSG, OAS (observer), OECD, OPCW, OSCE, Paris Club, PCA, PIF (partner), SECI (observer), UN, UN Security Council, UNAMID, UNCTAD, UNESCO, UNFICYP, UNHCR, UNIDO, UNMIL, UNMIS, UNOMIG, UNRWA, UNWTO, UPU, WCO, WEU, WFTU, WHO, WIPO, WMO, WTO, ZC
**Diplomatic representation in the US:**
*chief of mission:* Ambassador Sir Nigel E. SHEINWALD
*chancery:* 3100 Massachusetts Avenue NW, Washington, DC 20008
*telephone:* [1] (202) 588-6500
*FAX:* [1] (202) 588-7870
*consulate(s) general:* Atlanta, Boston, Chicago, Houston, Los Angeles, Miami, New York, San Francisco
*consulate(s):* Dallas, Denver, Orlando

**Diplomatic representation from the US:**
*chief of mission:* Ambassador Robert Holmes TUTTLE
*embassy:* 24 Grosvenor Square, London, W1A 1AE
*mailing address:* PSC 801, Box 40, FPO AE 09498-4040
*telephone:* [44] (0) 20 7499-9000
*FAX:* [44] (0) 20 7629-9124
*consulate(s) general:* Belfast, Edinburgh
**Flag description:** blue field with the red cross of Saint George (patron saint of England) edged in white superimposed on the diagonal red cross of Saint Patrick (patron saint of Ireland), which is superimposed on the diagonal white cross of Saint Andrew (patron saint of Scotland); properly known as the Union Flag, but commonly called the Union Jack; the design and colors (especially the Blue Ensign) have been the basis for a number of other flags including other Commonwealth countries and their constituent states or provinces, and British overseas territories

## Economy

**Economy - overview:** The UK, a leading trading power and financial center, is one of the quintet of trillion dollar economies of Western Europe. Over the past two decades, the government has greatly reduced public ownership and contained the growth of social welfare programs. Agriculture is intensive, highly mechanized, and efficient by European standards, producing about 60% of food needs with less than 2% of the labor force. The UK has large coal, natural gas, and oil resources, but its oil and natural gas reserves are declining and the UK became a net importer of energy in 2005; energy industries now contribute about 4% to GDP. Services, particularly banking, insurance, and business services, account by far for the largest proportion of GDP while industry continues to decline in importance. Since emerging from recession in 1992, Britain's economy enjoyed the longest period of expansion on record during which time growth outpaced most of Western Europe. The global economic slowdown, tight credit, and falling home prices, however, pushed Britain back into recession in the latter half of 2008 and prompted the BROWN government to implement a number of new measures to stimulate the economy and stabilize the financial markets; these include part-nationalizing the banking system, cutting taxes, suspending public sector borrowing rules, and bringing forward public spending on capital projects. The Bank of England periodically coordinates interest rate moves with the European Central Bank, but Britain remains outside the European Economic and Monetary Union (EMU), and opinion polls show a majority of Britons oppose joining the euro.
**GDP (purchasing power parity):**
$2.231 trillion (2008 est.)
$2.215 trillion (2007)
$2.151 trillion (2006)
*note:* data are in 2008 US dollars

**GDP (official exchange rate):** $2.787 trillion (2008 est.)
**GDP - real growth rate:**
0.7% (2008 est.)
3% (2007 est.)
2.8% (2006 est.)
**GDP - per capita (PPP):**
$36,600 (2008 est.)
$36,500 (2007 est.)
$35,500 (2006 est.)
*note:* data are in 2008 US dollars
**GDP - composition by sector:**
*agriculture:* 0.9%
*industry:* 22.8%
*services:* 76.2% (2008 est.)
**Labor force:** 31.2 million (2008 est.)
**Labor force - by occupation:**
*agriculture:* 1.4%
*industry:* 18.2%
*services:* 80.4% (2006 est.)
**Unemployment rate:**
5.5% (2008 est.)
5.3% (2007 est.)
**Population below poverty line:** 14% (2006 est.)
**Household income or consumption by percentage share:**
*lowest 10%:* 2.1%
*highest 10%:* 28.5% (1999)
**Distribution of family income - Gini index:** 34 (2005)
**Investment (gross fixed):** 16.7% of GDP (2008 est.)
**Budget:**
*revenues:* $1.107 trillion
*expenditures:* $1.242 trillion (2008 est.)
**Public debt:** 47.2% of GDP (2008 est.)
**Inflation rate (consumer prices):**
3.8% (2008 est.)
2.3% (2007 est.)
**Central bank discount rate:** NA
**Commercial bank prime lending rate:** 5.52% (31 December 2007)
**Stock of money:** NA
**Stock of quasi money:** NA
**Stock of domestic credit:** $5.278 trillion (31 December 2007)
**Market value of publicly traded shares:** $3.859 trillion (31 December 2007)
**Agriculture - products:** cereals, oilseed, potatoes, vegetables; cattle, sheep, poultry; fish
**Industries:** machine tools, electric power equipment, automation equipment, railroad equipment, shipbuilding, aircraft, motor vehicles and parts, electronics and communications equipment, metals, chemicals, coal, petroleum, paper and paper products, food processing, textiles, clothing, other consumer goods
**Industrial production growth rate:** -0.1% (2008 est.)

# United Kingdom (continued)

**Electricity - production:** 371 billion kWh (2007 est.)
**Electricity - consumption:** 348.5 billion kWh (2006 est.)
**Electricity - exports:** 3.398 billion kWh (2007 est.)
**Electricity - imports:** 8.613 billion kWh (2007 est.)
**Oil - production:** 1.69 million bbl/day (2007est.)
**Oil - consumption:** 1.763 million bbl/day (2007 est.)
**Oil - exports:** 1.749 million bbl/day (2005)
**Oil - imports:** 1.673 million bbl/day (2005)
**Oil - proved reserves:** 3.6 billion bbl (1 January 2008 est.)
**Natural gas - production:** 72.3 billion cu m (2007 est.)
**Natural gas - consumption:** 91.1 billion cu m (2007 est.)
**Natural gas - exports:** 10.4 billion cu m (2007 est.)
**Natural gas - imports:** 29.2 billion cu m (2007 est.)
**Natural gas - proved reserves:** 412 billion cu m (1 January 2008 est.)
**Current account balance:** -$72.54 billion (2008 est.)
**Exports:** $468.7 billion f.o.b. (2008 est.)
**Exports - commodities:** manufactured goods, fuels, chemicals; food, beverages, tobacco
**Exports - partners:** US 14.2%, Germany 11.1%, France 8.1%, Ireland 8%, Netherlands 6.8%, Belgium 5.3%, Spain 4.5%, Italy 4.1% (2007)
**Imports:** $645.7 billion f.o.b. (2008 est.)
**Imports - commodities:** manufactured goods, machinery, fuels; foodstuffs
**Imports - partners:** Germany 14.2%, US 8.6%, China 7.3%, Netherlands 7.3%, France 6.9%, Belgium 4.7%, Norway 4.7%, Italy 4.2% (2007)
**Reserves of foreign exchange and gold:** $57.3 billion (31 December 2007 est.)
**Debt - external:** $10.45 trillion (30 June 2007)
**Stock of direct foreign investment - at home:** $1.409 trillion (2008 est.)
**Stock of direct foreign investment - abroad:** $1.841 trillion (2008 est.)
**Exchange rates:** British pounds (GBP) per US dollar - 0.5302 (2008 est.), 0.4993 (2007), 0.5418 (2006), 0.5493 (2005), 0.5462 (2004)

## Communications

**Telephones - main lines in use:** 33.682 million (2007)
**Telephones - mobile cellular:** 71.992 million (2007)
**Telephone system:**
*general assessment:* technologically advanced domestic and international system
*domestic:* equal mix of buried cables, microwave radio relay, and fiber-optic systems
*international:* country code - 44; numerous submarine cables provide links throughout Europe, Asia, Australia, the Middle East, and US; satellite earth stations - 10 Intelsat (7 Atlantic Ocean and 3 Indian Ocean), 1 Inmarsat (Atlantic Ocean region), and 1 Eutelsat; at least 8 large international switching centers

**Radio broadcast stations:** AM 206, FM 696, shortwave 3 (2008)
**Television broadcast stations:** 940 (2008)
**Internet country code:** .uk
**Internet hosts:** 8.269 million (2008)
**Internet users:** 40.2 million (2007)

## Transportation

**Airports:** 510 (2008)
**Airports - with paved runways:**
*total:* 312
*over 3,047 m:* 9
*2,438 to 3,047 m:* 32
*1,524 to 2,437 m:* 127
*914 to 1,523 m:* 79
*under 914 m:* 65 (2008)
**Airports - with unpaved runways:**
*total:* 198
*over 3,047 m:* 1
*1,524 to 2,437 m:* 3
*914 to 1,523 m:* 21
*under 914 m:* 173 (2008)
**Heliports:** 11 (2007)
**Pipelines:** condensate 43 km; gas 7,541 km; liquid petroleum gas 59 km; oil 699 km; refined products 4,417 km (2008)
**Railways:**
*total:* 16,567 km
*broad gauge:* 303 km 1.600-m gauge (in Northern Ireland)
*standard gauge:* 16,264 km 1.435-m gauge (5,361 km electrified) (2006)
**Roadways:**
*total:* 398,366 km
*paved:* 398,366 km (includes 3,520 km of expressways) (2006)
**Waterways:** 3,200 km (620 km used for commerce) (2008)
**Merchant marine:**
*total:* 518
*by type:* bulk carrier 33, cargo 67, carrier 5, chemical tanker 61, container 180, liquefied gas 18, passenger 10, passenger/cargo 67, petroleum tanker 23, refrigerated cargo 12, roll on/roll off 24, vehicle carrier 18
*foreign-owned:* 264 (Cyprus 2, Denmark 62, Finland 1, France 23, Germany 76, Hong Kong 2, Ireland 1, Italy 5, Japan 4, NZ 1, Norway 31, South Africa 3, Spain 1, Sweden 17, Switzerland 1, Taiwan 11, Turkey 2, UAE 9, US 12)
*registered in other countries:* 391 (Algeria 11, Antigua and Barbuda 9, Argentina 4, Australia 5, Bahamas 56, Barbados 9, Belize 5, Bermuda 3, Brunei 1, Cape Verde 1, Cayman Islands 3, Cyprus 19, Gibraltar 2, Greece 32, Hong Kong 39, India 2, Italy 7, South Korea 1, Liberia 20, Luxembourg 8, Malta 19, Marshall Islands 18, Netherlands 2, Norway 5, Panama 59, Saint Kitts and Nevis 3, Saint Vincent and the Grenadines 14, Sierra Leone 2, Singapore 17, Slovakia 1, Spain 5, Sweden 2, Thailand 5, Tonga 1, US 1) (2008)

**Ports and terminals:** Dover, Felixstowe, Immingham, Liverpool, London, Southampton, Teesport (England); Forth Ports, Hound Point (Scotland); Milford Haven (Wales)

## Military

**Military branches:** Army, Royal Navy (includes Royal Marines), Royal Air Force (2009)
**Military service age and obligation:** 16-33 years of age (officers 17-28) for voluntary military service (with parental consent under 18); women serve in military services, but are excluded from ground combat positions and some naval postings; must be citizen of the UK, Commonwealth, or Republic of Ireland; reservists serve a minimum of 3 years, to age 45 or 55; 16 years of age for voluntary military service by Nepalese citizens in the Brigade of the Gurkhas; 16-34 years of age for voluntary military service by Papua New Guinean citizens (2008)
**Manpower available for military service:**
*males age 16-49:* 14,729,500
*females age 16-49:* 14,125,600 (2008 est.)
**Manpower fit for military service:**
*males age 16-49:* 12,123,900
*females age 16-49:* 11,616,769 (2009 est.)
**Manpower reaching militarily significant age annually:**
*male:* 393,892
*female:* 376,351 (2009 est.)
**Military expenditures:** 2.4% of GDP (2005 est.)

## Transnational Issues

**Disputes - international:** in 2002, Gibraltar residents voted overwhelmingly by referendum to reject any "shared sovereignty" arrangement between the UK and Spain; the Government of Gibraltar insists on equal participation in talks between the two countries; Spain disapproves of UK plans to grant Gibraltar greater autonomy; Mauritius and Seychelles claim the Chagos Archipelago (British Indian Ocean Territory), and its former inhabitants since their eviction in 1965; most Chagossians reside in Mauritius, and in 2001 were granted UK citizenship, where some have since resettled; in May 2006, the High Court of London reversed the UK Government's 2004 orders of council that banned habitation on the islands; UK rejects sovereignty talks requested by Argentina, which still claims the Falkland Islands (Islas Malvinas) and South Georgia and the South Sandwich Islands; territorial claim in Antarctica (British Antarctic Territory) overlaps Argentine claim and partially overlaps Chilean claim; Iceland, the UK, and Ireland dispute Denmark's claim that the Faroe Islands' continental shelf extends beyond 200 nm
**Illicit drugs:** producer of limited amounts of synthetic drugs and synthetic precursor chemicals; major consumer of Southwest Asian heroin, Latin American cocaine, and synthetic drugs; money-laundering center

# United States

## Introduction

**Background:** Britain's American colonies broke with the mother country in 1776 and were recognized as the new nation of the United States of America following the Treaty of Paris in 1783. During the 19th and 20th centuries, 37 new states were added to the original 13 as the nation expanded across the North American continent and acquired a number of overseas possessions. The two most traumatic experiences in the nation's history were the Civil War (1861-65), in which a northern Union of states defeated a secessionist Confederacy of 11 southern slave states, and the Great Depression of the 1930s, an economic downturn during which about a quarter of the labor force lost its jobs. Buoyed by victories in World Wars I and II and the end of the Cold War in 1991, the US remains the world's most powerful nation state. The economy is marked by steady growth, low unemployment and inflation, and rapid advances in technology.

## Geography

**Location:** North America, bordering both the North Atlantic Ocean and the North Pacific Ocean, between Canada and Mexico
**Geographic coordinates:** 38 00 N, 97 00 W
**Map references:** North America
**Area:**
*total:* 9,826,630 sq km
*land:* 9,161,923 sq km
*water:* 664,707 sq km
*note:* includes only the 50 states and District of Columbia
**Area - comparative:** about half the size of Russia; about three-tenths the size of Africa; about half the size of South America (or slightly larger than Brazil); slightly larger than China; more than twice the size of the European Union

**Land boundaries:**
*total:* 12,034 km
*border countries:* Canada 8,893 km (including 2,477 kmwith Alaska), Mexico 3,141 km
*note:* US Naval Base at Guantanamo Bay, Cuba is leased by the US and is part of Cuba; the base boundary is 28 km
**Coastline:** 19,924 km
**Maritime claims:**
*territorial sea:* 12 nm
*contiguous zone:* 24 nm
*exclusive economic zone:* 200 nm
*continental shelf:* not specified
**Climate:** mostly temperate, but tropical in Hawaii and Florida, arctic in Alaska, semiarid in the great plains west of the Mississippi River, and arid in the Great Basin of the southwest; low winter temperatures in the northwest are ameliorated occasionally in January and February by warm chinook winds from the eastern slopes of the Rocky Mountains
**Terrain:** vast central plain, mountains in west, hills and low mountains in east; rugged mountains and broad river valleys in Alaska; rugged, volcanic topography in Hawaii
**Elevation extremes:**
*lowest point:* Death Valley -86 m
*highest point:* Mount McKinley 6,198 m
**Natural resources:** coal, copper, lead, molybdenum, phosphates, uranium, bauxite, gold, iron, mercury, nickel, potash, silver, tungsten, zinc, petroleum, natural gas, timber
*note:* the US has the world's largest coal reserves with 491 billion short tons accounting for 27% of the world's total
**Land use:**
*arable land:* 18.01%
*permanent crops:* 0.21%
*other:* 81.78% (2005)

**Irrigated land:** 223,850 sq km (2003)
**Total renewable water resources:** 3,069 cu km (1985)
**Freshwater withdrawal (domestic/industrial/agricultural):**
*total:* 477 cu km/yr (13%/46%/41%)
*per capita:* 1,600 cu m/yr (2000)
**Natural hazards:** tsunamis; volcanoes; earthquake activity around Pacific Basin; hurricanes along the Atlantic and Gulf of Mexico coasts; tornadoes in the midwest and southeast; mud slides in California; forest fires in the west; flooding; permafrost in northern Alaska, a major impediment to development
**Environment - current issues:** air pollution resulting in acid rain in both the US and Canada; the US is the largest single emitter of carbon dioxide from the burning of fossil fuels; water pollution from runoff of pesticides and fertilizers; limited natural fresh water resources in much of the western part of the country require careful management; desertification
**Environment - international agreements:**
*party to:* Air Pollution, Air Pollution-Nitrogen Oxides, Antarctic-Environmental Protocol, Antarctic-Marine Living Resources, Antarctic Seals, Antarctic Treaty, Climate Change, Desertification, Endangered Species, Environmental Modification, Marine Dumping, Marine Life Conservation, Ozone Layer Protection, Ship Pollution, Tropical Timber 83, Tropical Timber 94, Wetlands, Whaling
*signed, but not ratified:* Air Pollution-Persistent Organic Pollutants, Air Pollution-Volatile Organic Compounds, Biodiversity, Climate Change-Kyoto Protocol, Hazardous Wastes
**Geography - note:** world's third-largest country by size (after Russia and Canada) and by population (after China and India); Mt. McKinley is highest point in North America and Death Valley the lowest point on the continent

## People

**Population:** 307,212,123 (July 2009 est.)
**Age structure:**
*0-14 years:* 20.2% (male 31,639,127/female 30,305,704)
*15-64 years:* 67% (male 102,665,043/female 103,129,321)
*65 years and over:* 12.8% (male 16,901,232/female 22,571,696) (2009 est.)
**Median age:**
*total:* 36.7 years
*male:* 35.4 years
*female:* 38 years (2009 est.)
**Population growth rate:** 0.975% (2009 est.)
**Birth rate:** 13.82 births/1,000 population (2009 est.)
**Death rate:** 8.27 deaths/1,000 population (2008 est.)
**Net migration rate:** 4.31 migrant(s)/1,000 population (2009 est.)
**Urbanization:**
*urban population:* 82% of total population (2008)
*rate of urbanization:* 1.3% annual rate of change (2005-10 est.)

**Sex ratio:**
*at birth:* 1.05 male(s)/female
*under 15 years:* 1.04 male(s)/female
*15-64 years:* 1 male(s)/female
*65 years and over:* 0.75 male(s)/female
*total population:* 0.97 male(s)/female (2009 est.)

**Infant mortality rate:**
*total:* 6.26 deaths/1,000 live births
*male:* 6.94 deaths/1,000 live births
*female:* 5.55 deaths/1,000 live births (2009 est.)

**Life expectancy at birth:**
*total population:* 78.11 years
*male:* 75.65 years
*female:* 80.69 years (2009 est.)

**Total fertility rate:** 2.05 children born/woman (2009 est.)

**HIV/AIDS - adult prevalence rate:** 0.6% (2007 est.)

**HIV/AIDS - people living with HIV/AIDS:** 1.2 million (2007 est.)

**HIV/AIDS - deaths:** 22,000 (2007 est.)

**Nationality:**
*noun:* American(s)
*adjective:* American

**Ethnic groups:** white 79.96%, black 12.85%, Asian 4.43%, Amerindian and Alaska native 0.97%, native Hawaiian and other Pacific islander 0.18%, two or more races 1.61% (July 2007 estimate)
*note:* a separate listing for Hispanic is not included because the US Census Bureau considers Hispanic to mean a person of Latin American descent (including persons of Cuban, Mexican, or Puerto Rican origin) living in the US who may be of any race or ethnic group (white, black, Asian, etc.); about 15.1% of the total US population is Hispanic

**Religions:** Protestant 51.3%, Roman Catholic 23.9%, Mormon 1.7%, other Christian 1.6%, Jewish 1.7%, Buddhist 0.7%, Muslim 0.6%, other or unspecified 2.5%, unaffiliated 12.1%, none 4% (2007 est.)

**Languages:** English 82.1%, Spanish 10.7%, other Indo-European 3.8%, Asian and Pacific island 2.7%, other 0.7% (2000 census)
*note:* Hawaiian is an official language in the state of Hawaii

**Literacy:**
*definition:* age 15 and over can read and write
*total population:* 99%
*male:* 99%
*female:* 99% (2003 est.)

**School life expectancy (primary to tertiary education):**
*total:* 16 years
*male:* 15 years
*female:* 16 years (2006)

**Education expenditures:** 5.3% of GDP (2005)

## Government

**Country name:**
*conventional long form:* United States of America
*conventional short form:* United States
*abbreviation:* US or USA

**Government type:** Constitution-based federal republic; strong democratic tradition

**Capital:**
*name:* Washington, DC
*geographic coordinates:* 38 53 N, 77 02 W
*time difference:* UTC-5 (during Standard Time)
*daylight saving time:* +1hr, begins second Sunday in March; ends first Sunday in November
*note:* the 50 United States cover six time zones

**Administrative divisions:** 50 states and 1 district*; Alabama, Alaska, Arizona, Arkansas, California, Colorado, Connecticut, Delaware, District of Columbia*, Florida, Georgia, Hawaii, Idaho, Illinois, Indiana, Iowa, Kansas, Kentucky, Louisiana, Maine, Maryland, Massachusetts, Michigan, Minnesota, Mississippi, Missouri, Montana, Nebraska, Nevada, New Hampshire, New Jersey, New Mexico, New York, North Carolina, North Dakota, Ohio, Oklahoma, Oregon, Pennsylvania, Rhode Island, South Carolina, South Dakota, Tennessee, Texas, Utah, Vermont, Virginia, Washington, West Virginia, Wisconsin, Wyoming

**Dependent areas:** American Samoa, Baker Island, Guam, Howland Island, Jarvis Island, Johnston Atoll, Kingman Reef, Midway Islands, Navassa Island, Northern Mariana Islands, Palmyra Atoll, Puerto Rico, Virgin Islands, Wake Island
*note:* from 18 July 1947 until 1 October 1994, the US administered the Trust Territory of the Pacific Islands; it entered into a political relationship with all four political units: the Northern Mariana Islands is a commonwealth in political union with the US (effective 3 November 1986); the Republic of the Marshall Islands signed a Compact of Free Association with the US (effective 21 October 1986); the Federated States of Micronesia signed a Compact of Free Association with the US (effective 3 November 1986); Palau concluded a Compact of Free Association with the US (effective 1 October 1994)

**Independence:** 4 July 1776 (from Great Britain)

**National holiday:** Independence Day, 4 July (1776)

**Constitution:** 17 September 1787, effective 4 March 1789

**Legal system:** federal court system based on English common law; each state has its own unique legal system, of which all but one (Louisiana, which is still influenced by the Napoleonic Code) is based on English common law; judicial review of legislative acts; has not accepted compulsory ICJ jurisdiction

**Suffrage:** 18 years of age; universal

**Executive branch:**
*chief of state:* President Barack H. OBAMA (since 20 January 2009); Vice President Joseph R. BIDEN (since 20 January 2009); note - the president is both the chief of state and head of government
*head of government:* President Barack H. OBAMA (since 20 January 2009); Vice President Joseph BIDEN (since 20 January 2009)
*cabinet:* Cabinet appointed by the president with Senate approval
*elections:* president and vice president elected on the same ticket by a college of representatives who are elected directly from each state; president and vice

president serve four-year terms (eligible for a second term); election last held 4 November 2008 (next to be held on 6 November 2012)
*election results:* Barack H. OBAMA elected president; percent of popular vote - Barack H. OBAMA 52.4%, John MCCAIN 46.3%, other 1.3%;

**Legislative branch:** bicameral Congress consists of the Senate (100 seats, 2 members are elected from each state by popular vote to serve six-year terms; one-third are elected every two years) and the House of Representatives (435 seats; members are directly elected by popular vote to serve two-year terms)
*elections:* Senate - last held 4 November 2008 (next to be held November 2010); House of Representatives - last held 4 November 2008 (next to be held in November 2010)
*election results:* Senate - percent of vote by party - NA; seats by party - Democratic Party 57, Republican Party 41, independent 2; House of Representatives - percent of vote by party - NA; seats by party - Democratic Party 257, Republican Party 178

**Judicial branch:** Supreme Court (nine justices; nominated by the president and confirmed with the advice and consent of the Senate; appointed to serve for life); United States Courts of Appeal; United States District Courts; State and County Courts

**Political parties and leaders:** Democratic Party [Timothy KAINE]; Green Party; Libertarian Party [William (Bill) REDPATH]; Republican Party [Michael STEELE]

**Political pressure groups and leaders:** environmentalists; business groups; labor unions; churches; ethnic groups; political action committees or PAC; health groups; education groups; civic groups; youth groups; transportation groups; agricultural groups; veterans groups; women's groups; reform lobbies

**International organization participation:** ADB (nonregional member), AfDB (nonregional member), ANZUS, APEC, Arctic Council, ARF, ASEAN (dialogue partner), Australia Group, BIS, BSEC (observer), CBSS (observer), CE (observer), CERN (observer), CP, EAPC, EBRD, FAO, G-20, G-5, G-7, G-8, G-10, IADB, IAEA, IBRD, ICAO, ICC, ICCt (signatory), ICRM, IDA, IEA, IFAD, IFC, IFRCS, IHO, ILO, IMF, IMO, IMSO, Interpol, IOC, IOM, ISO, ITSO, ITU, ITUC, MIGA, MINUSTAH, NAFTA, NATO, NEA, NSG, OAS, OECD, OPCW, OSCE, Paris Club, PCA, PIF (partner), SAARC (observer), SECI (observer), SPC, UN, UN Security Council, UNCTAD, UNESCO, UNHCR, UNITAR, UNMIL, UNOMIG, UNRWA, UNTSO, UPU, WCL, WCO, WFTU, WHO, WIPO, WMO, WTO, ZC

**Flag description:** 13 equal horizontal stripes of red (top and bottom) alternating with white; there is a blue rectangle in the upper hoist-side corner bearing 50 small, white, five-pointed stars arranged in nine offset horizontal rows of six stars (top and bottom) alternating with rows of five stars; the 50 stars represent the 50 states, the 13 stripes represent the 13 original colonies; known as Old Glory; the design and colors have been the basis for a number of other flags, including Chile, Liberia, Malaysia, and Puerto Rico

## Economy

**Economy - overview:** The US has the largest and most technologically powerful economy in the world, with a per capita GDP of $48,000. In this market-oriented economy, private individuals and business firms make most of the decisions, and the federal and state governments buy needed goods and services predominantly in the private marketplace. US business firms enjoy greater flexibility than their counterparts in Western Europe and Japan in decisions to expand capital plant, to lay off surplus workers, and to develop new products. At the same time, they face higher barriers to enter their rivals' home markets than foreign firms face entering US markets. US firms are at or near the forefront in technological advances, especially in computers and in medical, aerospace, and military equipment; their advantage has narrowed since the end of World War II. The onrush of technology largely explains the gradual development of a "two-tier labor market" in which those at the bottom lack the education and the professional/technical skills of those at the top and, more and more, fail to get comparable pay raises, health insurance coverage, and other benefits. Since 1975, practically all the gains in household income have gone to the top 20% of households. The war in March-April 2003 between a US-led coalition and Iraq, and the subsequent occupation of Iraq, required major shifts in national resources to the military. Hurricane Katrina caused extensive damage in the Gulf Coast region in August 2005, but had a small impact on overall GDP growth for the year. Soaring oil prices between 2005 and the first half of 2008 threatened inflation and unemployment, as higher gasoline prices ate into consumers' budgets. Imported oil accounts for about two-thirds of US consumption. Long-term problems include inadequate investment in economic infrastructure, rapidly rising medical and pension costs of an aging population, sizable trade and budget deficits, and stagnation of family income in the lower economic groups. The merchandise trade deficit reached a record $847 billion in 2007, but declined to $810 billion in 2008, as a depreciating exchange rate for the dollar against most major currencies discouraged US imports and made US exports more competitive abroad. The global economic downturn, the sub-prime mortgage crisis, investment bank failures, falling home prices, and tight credit pushed the United States into a recession by mid-2008. To help stabilize financial markets, the US Congress established a $700 billion Troubled Asset Relief Program (TARP) in October 2008. The government used some of these funds to purchase equity in US banks and other industrial corporations. In January 2009 the US Congress passed and President Barack OBAMA signed a bill providing an additional $787 billion fiscal stimulus - two-thirds on additional spending and one-third on tax cuts - to create jobs and to help the economy recover.

**GDP (purchasing power parity):**
$14.29 trillion (2008 est.)
$14.11 trillion (2007)
$13.83 trillion (2006)
*note:* data are in 2008 US dollars
**GDP (official exchange rate):** $14.33 trillion (2008 est.)
**GDP - real growth rate:**
1.3% (2008 est.)
2% (2007 est.)
2.8% (2006 est.)
**GDP - per capita (PPP):**
$47,000 (2008 est.)
$46,800 (2007 est.)
$46,300 (2006 est.)
*note:* data are in 2008 US dollars
**GDP - composition by sector:**
*agriculture:* 1.2%
*industry:* 19.6%
*services:* 79.2% (2008 est.)
**Labor force:** 155.2 million (includes unemployed) (2008 est.)
**Labor force - by occupation:** farming, forestry, and fishing 0.6%, manufacturing, extraction, transportation, and crafts 22.6%, managerial, professional, and technical 35.5%, sales and office 24.8%, other services 16.5%
*note:* figures exclude the unemployed (2007)
**Unemployment rate:**
7.2% (December 2008 est.)
4.6% (2007 est.)
**Population below poverty line:** 12% (2004 est.)
**Household income or consumption by percentage share:**
*lowest 10%:* 2%
*highest 10%:* 30% (2007 est.)
**Distribution of family income - Gini index:** 45 (2007)
**Investment (gross fixed):** 14.6% of GDP (2008 est.)
**Budget:**
*revenues:* $2.524 trillion
*expenditures:* $2.979 trillion (2008 est.)
**Public debt:** 60.8% of GDP (2007 est.)
**Inflation rate (consumer prices):**
4.2% (2008 est.)
2.9% (2007 est.)
**Central bank discount rate:** 0.5% (31 March 2009)
**Commercial bank prime lending rate:** 3.25% (31 March 2009)
**Stock of money:** $1.596 trillion (31 December 2007)
**Stock of quasi money:** $8.154 trillion (31 December 2007)
**Stock of domestic credit:** $14.15 trillion (31 December 2007)
**Market value of publicly traded shares:** $19.95 trillion (31 December 2007)
**Agriculture - products:** wheat, corn, other grains, fruits, vegetables, cotton; beef, pork, poultry, dairy products; fish; forest products

**Industries:** leading industrial power in the world, highly diversified and technologically advanced; petroleum, steel, motor vehicles, aerospace, telecommunications, chemicals, electronics, food processing, consumer goods, lumber, mining
**Industrial production growth rate:** 0.2% (2008 est.)
**Electricity - production:** 4.167 trillion kWh (2007 est.)
**Electricity - consumption:** 3.892 trillion kWh (2007 est.)
**Electricity - exports:** 20.14 billion kWh (2007 est.)
**Electricity - imports:** 51.4 billion kWh (2007 est.)
**Oil - production:** 8.457 million bbl/day (2007 est.)
**Oil - consumption:** 20.68 million bbl/day (2007 est.)
**Oil - exports:** 1.165 million bbl/day (2005)
**Oil - imports:** 13.71 million bbl/day (2005)
**Oil - proved reserves:** 20.97 billion bbl (1 January 2008 est.)
**Natural gas - production:** 545.9 billion cu m (2007 est.)
**Natural gas - consumption:** 652.9 billion cu m (2007 est.)
**Natural gas - exports:** 23.28 billion cu m (2007 est.)
**Natural gas - imports:** 130.3 billion cu m (2007 est.)
**Natural gas - proved reserves:** 5.977 trillion cu m (1 January 2008 est.)
**Current account balance:** -$568.8 billion (2008 est.)
**Exports:** $1.377 trillion f.o.b. (2008 est.)
**Exports - commodities:** agricultural products (soybeans, fruit, corn) 9.2%, industrial supplies (organic chemicals) 26.8%, capital goods (transistors, aircraft, motor vehicle parts, computers, telecommunications equipment) 49.0%, consumer goods (automobiles, medicines) 15.0% (2003)
**Exports - partners:** Canada 21.4%, Mexico 11.7%, China 5.6%, Japan 5.4%, UK 4.3%, Germany 4.3% (2007)
**Imports:** $2.19 trillion f.o.b. (2008 est.)
**Imports - commodities:** agricultural products 4.9%, industrial supplies 32.9% (crude oil 8.2%), capital goods 30.4% (computers, telecommunications equipment, motor vehicle parts, office machines, electric power machinery), consumer goods 31.8% (automobiles, clothing, medicines, furniture, toys) (2003)
**Imports - partners:** China 16.9%, Canada 15.7%, Mexico 10.6%, Japan 7.4%, Germany 4.8% (2007)
**Reserves of foreign exchange and gold:** $70.57 billion (31 December 2007 est.)
**Debt - external:** $12.25 trillion (30 June 2007)
**Stock of direct foreign investment - at home:** $2.22 trillion (2008 est.)
**Stock of direct foreign investment - abroad:** $2.751 trillion (2008 est.)

# United States *(continued)*

**Exchange rates:**
*British pounds per US dollar:* 0.5302 (2008), 0.4993 (2007), 0.5418 (2006), 0.5493 (2005), 0.5462 (2004)
*Canadian dollars per US dollar:* 1.0364 (2008), 1.0724 (2007), 1.1334 (2006), 1.2118 (2005), 1.3010 (2004)
*Chinese yuan per US dollar:* 6.9385 (2008), 7.61 (2007), 7.97 (2006), 8.1943 (2005), 8.2768 (2004)
*euros per US dollar:* 0.6827 (2008), 0.7345 (2007), 0.7964 (2006), 0.8041 (2005), 0.8054 (2004)
*Japanese yen per US dollar:* 103.58 (2008), 117.99 (2007), 116.18 (2006) 110.22 (2005), 108.19 (2004)

## Communications

**Telephones - main lines in use:** 163.2 million (2007)
**Telephones - mobile cellular:** 255 million (2007)
**Telephone system:**
*general assessment:* a large, technologically advanced, multipurpose communications system
*domestic:* a large system of fiber-optic cable, microwave radio relay, coaxial cable, and domestic satellites carries every form of telephone traffic; a rapidly growing cellular system carries mobile telephone traffic throughout the country
*international:* country code - 1; multiple ocean cable systems provide international connectivity; satellite earth stations - 61 Intelsat (45 Atlantic Ocean and 16 Pacific Ocean), 5 Intersputnik (Atlantic Ocean region), and 4 Inmarsat (Pacific and Atlantic Ocean regions) (2000)
**Radio broadcast stations:** AM 4,789, FM 8,961, shortwave 19 (2006)
**Television broadcast stations:** 2,218 (2006)
**Internet country code:** .us
**Internet hosts:** 316 million (2008); note - the US Internet total host count includes the following top level domain host addresses: .us, .com, .edu, .gov, .mil, .net, and .org
**Internet users:** 223 million (2008)

## Transportation

**Airports:** 14,951 (2008)
**Airports - with paved runways:**
*total:* 5,146
*over 3,047 m:* 190
*2,438 to 3,047 m:* 227
*1,524 to 2,437 m:* 1,464
*914 to 1,523 m:* 2,307
*under 914 m:* 958 (2008)
**Airports - with unpaved runways:**
*total:* 9,805
*2,438 to 3,047 m:* 6
*1,524 to 2,437 m:* 156
*914 to 1,523 m:* 1,734
*under 914 m:* 7,909 (2008)
**Heliports:** 146 (2007)
**Pipelines:** petroleum products 244,620 km; natural gas 548,665 km (2006)

**Railways:**
*total:* 226,612 km
*standard gauge:* 226,612 km 1.435-m gauge (2005)
**Roadways:**
*total:* 6,465,799 km
*paved:* 4,209,835 km (includes 75,040 km of expressways)
*unpaved:* 2,255,964 km (2007)
**Waterways:** 41,009 km (19,312 km used for commerce)
*note:* Saint Lawrence Seaway of 3,769 km, including the Saint Lawrence River of 3,058 km, shared with Canada (2008)
**Merchant marine:**
*total:* 422
*by type:* barge carrier 6, bulk carrier 61, cargo 69, carrier 2, chemical tanker 22, container 81, passenger 19, passenger/cargo 59, petroleum tanker 53, refrigerated cargo 3, roll on/roll off 25, vehicle carrier 22
*foreign-owned:* 74 (Australia 1, Denmark 31, Germany 5, Japan 7, Malaysia 2, Netherlands 1, Norway 9, Singapore 12, Sweden 5, UK 1)
*registered in other countries:* 732 (Antigua and Barbuda 8, Australia 2, Bahamas 106, Bermuda 23, Cambodia 6, Canada 10, Cayman Islands 42, Comoros 2, Cyprus 5, Ecuador 1, Greece 8, Hong Kong 29, Ireland 2, Isle of Man 4, Italy 17, South Korea 7, Liberia 98, Luxembourg 4, Malta 23, Marshall Islands 123, Netherlands 14, Netherlands Antilles 1, Norway 8, Panama 126, Portugal 1, Puerto Rico 3, Russia 1, Saint Vincent and the Grenadines 18, Sierra Leone 1, Singapore 22, Trinidad and Tobago 1, Tuvalu 1, UK 12, Vanuatu 1, unknown 2) (2008)
**Ports and terminals:** Corpus Christi, Duluth, Hampton Roads, Houston, Long Beach, Los Angeles, New York, Philadelphia, Tampa, Texas City

## Military

**Military branches:** United States Armed Forces: US Army, US Navy (includes Marine Corps), US Air Force, US Coast Guard; note - Coast Guard administered in peacetime by the Department of Homeland Security, but in wartime reports to the Department of the Navy (2009)
**Military service age and obligation:** 18 years of age (17 years of age with parental consent) for male and female voluntary service; maximum enlistment age 42 (Army), 27 (Air Force), 34 (Navy), 28 (Marines); service obligation 8 years, including 2-5 years active duty (Army), 2 years active (Navy), 4 years active (Air Force, Marines) (2008)
**Manpower available for military service:**
*males age 16-49:* 72,715,332
*females age 16-49:* 71,638,785 (2008 est.)
**Manpower fit for military service:**
*males age 16-49:* 59,764,677
*females age 16-49:* 59,437,663 (2009 est.)

**Manpower reaching militarily significant age annually:**
*male:* 2,196,124
*female:* 2,085,085 (2009 est.)
**Military expenditures:** 4.06% of GDP (2005 est.)

## Transnational Issues

**Disputes - international:** the U.S. has intensified domestic security measures and is collaborating closely with its neighbors, Canada and Mexico, to monitor and control legal and illegal personnel, transport, and commodities across the international borders; abundant rainfall in recent years along much of the Mexico-US border region has ameliorated periodically strained water-sharing arrangements; 1990 Maritime Boundary Agreement in the Bering Sea still awaits Russian Duma ratification; managed maritime boundary disputes with Canada at Dixon Entrance, Beaufort Sea, Strait of Juan de Fuca, and around the disputed Machias Seal Island and North Rock; The Bahamas and US have not been able to agree on a maritime boundary; US Naval Base at Guantanamo Bay is leased from Cuba and only mutual agreement or US abandonment of the area can terminate the lease; Haiti claims US-administered Navassa Island; US has made no territorial claim in Antarctica (but has reserved the right to do so) and does not recognize the claims of any other states; Marshall Islands claims Wake Island; Tokelau included American Samoa's Swains Island among the islands listed in its 2006 draft constitution
**Refugees and internally displaced persons:**
*refugees (country of origin):* the US admitted 62,643 refugees during FY04/05 including; 10,586 (Somalia); 8,549 (Laos); 6,666 (Russia); 6,479 (Cuba); 3,100 (Haiti); 2,136 (Iran) (2006)
**Illicit drugs:** world's largest consumer of cocaine (shipped from Colombia through Mexico and the Caribbean), Colombian heroin, and Mexican heroin and marijuana; major consumer of ecstasy and Mexican methamphetamine; minor consumer of high-quality Southeast Asian heroin; illicit producer of cannabis, marijuana, depressants, stimulants, hallucinogens, and methamphetamine; money-laundering center

# United States Pacific Island Wildlife Refuges
*(territories of the US)*

## Introduction

**Background:** All of the following US Pacific island territories except Midway Atoll constitute the Pacific Remote Islands National Wildlife Refuge (NWR) Complex and as such are managed by the Fish and Wildlife Service of the US Department of the Interior. Midway Atoll NWR has been included in a Refuge Complex with the Hawaiian Islands NWR and also designated as part of Papahanaumokuakea Marine National Monument. These remote refuges are the most widespread collection of marine- and terrestrial-life protected areas on the planet under a single country's jurisdiction. They sustain many endemic species including corals, fish, shellfish, marine mammals, seabirds, water birds, land birds, insects, and vegetation not found elsewhere.

*Baker Island:* The US took possession of the island in 1857. Its guano deposits were mined by US and British companies during the second half of the 19th century. In 1935, a short-lived attempt at colonization began on this island but was disrupted by World War II and thereafter abandoned. The island was established as a NWR in 1974.

*Howland Island:* Discovered by the US early in the 19th century, the uninhabited atoll was officially claimed by the US in 1857. Both US and British companies mined for guano deposits until about 1890. In 1935, a short-lived attempt at colonization began on this island, similar to the effort on nearby Baker Island, but was disrupted by World War II and thereafter abandoned. The famed American aviatrix Amelia EARHART disappeared while seeking out Howland Island as a refueling stop during her 1937 round-the-world flight; Earhart Light, a day beacon near the middle of the west coast, was named in her memory. The island was established as a NWR in 1974.

*Jarvis Island:* First discovered by the British in 1821, the uninhabited island was annexed by the US in 1858 but abandoned in 1879 after tons of guano had been removed. The UK annexed the island in 1889 but never carried out plans for further exploitation. The US occupied and reclaimed the island in 1935. It was abandoned in 1942 during World War II. The island was established as a NWR in 1974.

*Johnston Atoll:* Both the US and the Kingdom of Hawaii annexed Johnston Atoll in 1858, but it was the US that mined the guano deposits until the late 1880s. Johnston and Sand Islands were designated wildlife refuges in 1926. The US Navy took over the atoll in 1934. Subsequently, the US Air Force assumed control in 1948. The site was used for high-altitude nuclear tests in the 1950s and 1960s. Until late in 2000 the atoll was maintained as a storage and disposal site for chemical weapons. Munitions destruction, cleanup, and closure of the facility were completed by May 2005. The Fish and Wildlife Service and the US Air Force are currently discussing future management options; in the interim, Johnston Atoll and the three-mile Naval Defensive Sea around it remain under the jurisdiction and administrative control of the US Air Force.

*Kingman Reef:* The US annexed the reef in 1922. Its sheltered lagoon served as a way station for flying boats on Hawaii-to-American Samoa flights during the late 1930s. There are no terrestrial plants on the reef, which is frequently awash, but it does support abundant and diverse marine fauna and flora. In 2001, the waters surrounding the reef out to 12 nm were designated a US NWR.

*Midway Islands:* The US took formal possession of the islands in 1867. The laying of the trans-Pacific cable, which passed through the islands, brought the first residents in 1903. Between 1935 and 1947, Midway was used as a refueling stop for trans-Pacific flights. The US naval victory over a Japanese fleet off Midway in 1942 was one of the turning points of World War II. The islands continued to serve as a naval station until closed in 1993. Today the islands are a NWR and are the site of the world's largest Laysan albatross colony.

*Palmyra Atoll:* The Kingdom of Hawaii claimed the atoll in 1862, and the US included it among the Hawaiian Islands when it annexed the archipelago in 1898. The Hawaii Statehood Act of 1959 did not include Palmyra Atoll, which is now partly privately owned by the Nature Conservancy with the rest owned by the Federal government and managed by the US Fish and Wildlife Service. These organizations are managing the atoll as a wildlife refuge. The lagoons and surrounding waters within the 12 nm US territorial seas were transferred to the US Fish and Wildlife Service and designated as a NWR in January 2001.

## Geography

**Location:** Oceania
*Baker Island:* atoll in the North Pacific Ocean 1,830 nm (3,389 km) southwest of Honolulu, about half way between Hawaii and Australia
*Howland Island:* island in the North Pacific Ocean 1,815 nm (3,361 km) southwest of Honolulu, about half way between Hawaii and Australia
*Jarvis Island:* island in the South Pacific Ocean 1,305 nm (2,417 km) south of Honolulu, about half way between Hawaii and Cook Islands
*Johnston Atoll:* atoll in the North Pacific Ocean 717 nm (1,328 km) southwest of Honolulu, about one-third of the way from Hawaii to the Marshall Islands
*Kingman Reef:* reef in the North Pacific Ocean 930 nm (1,722 km) south of Honolulu, about half way between Hawaii and American Samoa
*Midway Islands:* atoll in the North Pacific Ocean 1,260 nm (2,334 km) northwest of Honolulu near the end of the Hawaiian Archipelago, about one-third of the way from Honolulu to Tokyo
*Palmyra Atoll:* atoll in the North Pacific Ocean 960 nm (1,778 km) south of Honolulu, about half way between Hawaii and American Samoa

**Geographic coordinates:**
*Baker Island:* 0 13 N, 176 28 W
*Howland Island:* 0 48 N, 176 38 W
*Jarvis Island:* 0 23 S, 160 01 W
*Johnston Atoll:* 16 45 N, 169 31 W
*Kingman Reef:* 6 23 N, 162 25 W
*Midway Islands:* 28 12 N, 177 22 W
*Palmyra Atoll:* 5 53 N, 162 05 W

**Map references:** Oceania

**Area:** total - 6,959.41 sq km; emergent land - 22.41 sq km; submerged - 6,937 sq km
*Baker Island:* total - 129.1 sq km; emergent land - 2.1 sq km; submerged - 127 sq km
*Howland Island:* total - 138.6 sq km; emergent land - 2.6 sq km; submerged - 136 sq km
*Jarvis Island:* total - 152 sq km; emergent land - 5 sq km; submerged - 147 sq km
*Johnston Atoll:* total - 276.6 sq km; emergent land - 2.6 sq km; submerged - 274 sq km
*Kingman Reef:* total - 1,958.01 sq km; emergent land -0.01 sq km; submerged - 1,958 sq km
*Midway Islands:* total - 2,355.2 sq km; emergent land -6.2 sq km; submerged - 2,349 sq km
*Palmyra Atoll:* total - 1,949.9 sq km; emergent land - 3.9 sq km; submerged - 1,946 sq km

**Area - comparative:**
*Baker Island:* about two and a half times the size of The Mall in Washington, DC
*Howland Island:* about three times the size of The Mall in Washington, DC
*Jarvis Island:* about eight times the size of The Mall in Washington, DC
*Johnston Atoll:* about four and a half times the size of The Mall in Washington, DC
*Kingman Reef:* a little more than one and a half times the size of The Mall in Washington, DC
*Midway Islands:* about nine times the size of The Mall in Washington, DC
*Palmyra Atoll:* about 20 times the size of The Mall in Washington, DC

**Land boundaries:** none

**Coastline:**
*Baker Island:* 4.8 km
*Howland Island:* 6.4 km
*Jarvis Island:* 8 km
*Johnston Atoll:* 34 km
*Kingman Reef:* 3 km
*Midway Islands:* 15 km
*Palmyra Atoll:* 14.5 km

**Maritime claims:**
*territorial sea:* 12 nm
*exclusive economic zone:* 200 nm

**Climate:**
*Baker, Howland, and Jarvis Islands:* equatorial; scant rainfall, constant wind, burning sun
*Johnston Atoll and Kingman Reef:* tropical, but generally dry; consistent northeast trade winds with little seasonal temperature variation
*Midway Islands:* subtropical with cool, moist winters (December to February) and warm, dry summers (May to October); moderated by prevailing easterly winds; most of the 1,067 mm (42 in) of annual rainfall occurs during the winter

# United States Pacific Island Wildlife Refuges *(continued)*

**Midway Islands**

NORTH PACIFIC OCEAN

Sand Islet

Sand Island
airfield
Spit Island
Eastern Island
airfield
reef

**Johnston Atoll**

NORTH PACIFIC OCEAN

reef

Akau Island
Hikina Island
Sand Island
airstrip
Johnston Island
reef

**Howland Island**

reef

Earhart Light (day beacon)

NORTH PACIFIC OCEAN

reef

**Baker Island**

day beacon

NORTH PACIFIC OCEAN

**Kingman Reef**

reef

NORTH PACIFIC OCEAN

reef          reef

**Palmyra Atoll**

reef

airstrip

NORTH PACIFIC OCEAN

reef

**Jarvis Island**

reef

reef          Millersville
(usually uninhabited)

reef

SOUTH PACIFIC OCEAN

Midway Islands
(U.S.)

UNITED STATES

Tropic of Cancer

HAWAIIAN ISLANDS

Hawaii

Johnston Atoll
(U.S.)

NORTH PACIFIC OCEAN

Kingman Reef
(U.S.)

Palmyra Atoll
(U.S.)

Howland Island
(U.S.)

Baker Island
(U.S.)

Equator

Jarvis Island
(U.S.)

K I R I B A T I

SOUTH PACIFIC OCEAN

Tokelau
(N.Z.)

TUVALU

Wallis and Futuna
(FRANCE)

SAMOA

American Samoa
(U.S.)

Cook Islands
(N.Z.)

# United States Pacific Island Wildlife Refuges *(continued)*

*Palmyra Atoll:* equatorial, hot; located within the low pressure area of the Intertropical Convergence Zone (ITCZ) where the northeast and southeast trade winds meet, it is extremely wet with between 4,000-5,000 mm (160-200 in) of rainfall each year

**Terrain:** low and nearly level sandy coral islands with narrow fringing reefs that have developed at the top of submerged volcanic mountains, which in most cases rise steeply from the ocean floor

**Elevation extremes:**

*lowest point:* Pacific Ocean 0 m

*highest point:* Baker Island, unnamed location - 8 m; Howland Island, unnamed location - 3 m; Jarvis Island, unnamed location - 7 m; Johnston Atoll, Sand Island - 10 m; Kingman Reef, unnamed location - less than 2 m; Midway Islands, unnamed location - 13 m; Palmyra Atoll, unnamed location - 3 m

**Natural resources:** terrestrial and aquatic wildlife

**Land use:**

*arable land:* 0%

*permanent crops:* 0%

*other:* 100% (2008)

**Natural hazards:**

*Baker, Howland, and Jarvis Islands:* the narrow fringing reef surrounding the island can be a maritime hazard

*Kingman Reef:* wet or awash most of the time, maximum elevation of less than 2 m makes Kingman Reef a maritime hazard

*Midway Islands, Johnston, and Palmyra Atolls:* NA

**Environment - current issues:**

*Baker, Howland, and Jarvis Islands, and Johnston Atoll:* no natural fresh water resources

*Kingman Reef:* none

*Midway Islands and Palmyra Atoll:* NA

**Geography - note:**

*Baker, Howland, and Jarvis Islands:* scattered vegetation consisting of grasses, prostrate vines, and low growing shrubs; primarily a nesting, roosting, and foraging habitat for seabirds, shorebirds, and marine wildlife; closed to the public

*Johnston Atoll:* Johnston Island and Sand Island are natural islands, which have been expanded by coral dredging; North Island (Akau) and East Island (Hikina) are manmade islands formed from coral dredging; the egg-shaped reef is 34 km in circumference; closed to the public

*Kingman Reef:* barren coral atoll with deep interior lagoon; closed to the public

*Midway Islands:* a coral atoll managed as a NWR and open to the public for wildlife-related recreation in the form of wildlife observation and photography

*Palmyra Atoll:* the high rainfall and resulting lush vegetation make the environment of this atoll unique among the US Pacific Island territories; supports a large undisturbed stand of Pisonia beach forest

## People

**Population:** no indigenous inhabitants

*note:* public entry is by special-use permit from US Fish and Wildlife Service only and generally restricted to scientists and educators; visited annually by US Fish and Wildlife Service

*Johnston Atoll:* in previous years, an average of 1,100 US military and civilian contractor personnel were present; as of May 2005, all US government personnel had left the island

*Midway Islands:* approximately 40 people make up the staff of US Fish and Wildlife Service and their services contractor living at the atoll

*Palmyra Atoll:* four to 20 Nature Conservancy, US Fish and Wildlife staff, and researchers

## Government

**Country name:**

*conventional long form:* none

*conventional short form:* Baker Island; Howland Island; Jarvis Island; Johnston Atoll; Kingman Reef; Midway Islands; Palmyra Atoll

**Dependency status:** unincorporated territories of the US; administered from Washington, DC by the Fish and Wildlife Service of the US Department of the Interior as part of the National Wildlife Refuge system

*note on Palmyra Atoll:* incorporated Territory of the US; partly privately owned and partly federally owned; administered from Washington, DC by the Fish and Wildlife Service of the US Department of the Interior; the Office of Insular Affairs of the US Department of the Interior continues to administer nine excluded areas comprising certain tidal and submerged lands within the 12 nm territorial sea or within the lagoon

**Legal system:** the laws of the US, where applicable, apply

**Diplomatic representation from the US:** none (territories of the US)

**Flag description:** the flag of the US is used

## Economy

**Economy - overview:** no economic activity

## Transportation

**Airports:**

*Baker Island:* one abandoned World War II runway of 1,665 m covered with vegetation and unusable

*Howland Island:* airstrip constructed in 1937 for scheduled refueling stop on the round-the-world flight of Amelia EARHART and Fred NOONAN; the aviators left Lae, New Guinea, for Howland Island but were never seen again; the airstrip is no longer serviceable

*Johnston Atoll:* one closed and not maintained

*Kingman Reef:* lagoon was used as a halfway station between Hawaii and American Samoa by Pan American Airways for flying boats in 1937 and 1938

*Midway Islands:* 3 - one operational (2,409 m paved); no fuel for sale except emergencies

*Palmyra Atoll:* 1 - 1,846 m unpaved runway; privately owned (2008)

**Ports and terminals:**

*Baker, Howland, and Jarvis Islands, and Kingman Reef:* none; offshore anchorage only

*Johnston Atoll:* Johnston Island

*Midway Islands:* Sand Island

*Palmyra Atoll:* West Lagoon

## Military

**Military - note:** defense is the responsibility of the US

## Transnational Issues

**Disputes - international:** none

# Uruguay

## Introduction

**Background:** Montevideo, founded by the Spanish in 1726 as a military stronghold, soon took advantage of its natural harbor to become an important commercial center. Claimed by Argentina but annexed by Brazil in 1821, Uruguay declared its independence four years later and secured its freedom in 1828 after a three-year struggle. The administrations of President Jose BATLLE in the early 20th century established widespread political, social, and economic reforms that established a statist tradition. A violent Marxist urban guerrilla movement named the Tupamaros, launched in the late 1960s, led Uruguay's president to cede control of the government to the military in 1973. By yearend, the rebels had been crushed, but the military continued to expand its hold over the government. Civilian rule was not restored until 1985. In 2004, the left-of-center Frente Amplio Coalition won national elections that effectively ended 170 years of political control previously held by the Colorado and Blanco parties. Uruguay's political and labor conditions are among the freest on the continent.

## Geography

**Location:** Southern South America, bordering the South Atlantic Ocean, between Argentina and Brazil
**Geographic coordinates:** 33 00 S, 56 00 W
**Map references:** South America
**Area:**
*total:* 176,220 sq km
*land:* 173,620 sq km
*water:* 2,600 sq km
**Area - comparative:** slightly smaller than the state of Washington
**Land boundaries:**
*total:* 1,648 km
*border countries:* Argentina 580 km, Brazil 1,068 km
**Coastline:** 660 km

**Maritime claims:**
*territorial sea:* 12 nm
*contiguous zone:* 24 nm
*exclusive economic zone:* 200 nm
*continental shelf:* 200 nm or edge of continental margin
**Climate:** warm temperate; freezing temperatures almost unknown
**Terrain:** mostly rolling plains and low hills; fertile coastal lowland
**Elevation extremes:**
*lowest point:* Atlantic Ocean 0 m
*highest point:* Cerro Catedral 514 m
**Natural resources:** arable land, hydropower, minor minerals, fisheries
**Land use:**
*arable land:* 7.77%
*permanent crops:* 0.24%
*other:* 91.99% (2005)
**Irrigated land:** 2,100 sq km (2003)
**Total renewable water resources:** 139 cu km (2000)
**Freshwater withdrawal (domestic/industrial/agricultural):**
*total:* 3.15 cu km/yr (2%/1%/96%)
*per capita:* 910 cu m/yr (2000)
**Natural hazards:** seasonally high winds (the pampero is a chilly and occasional violent wind that blows north from the Argentine pampas), droughts, floods; because of the absence of mountains, which act as weather barriers, all locations are particularly vulnerable to rapid changes from weather fronts
**Environment - current issues:** water pollution from meat packing/tannery industry; inadequate solid/hazardous waste disposal
**Environment - international agreements:**
*party to:* Antarctic-Environmental Protocol, Antarctic-Marine Living Resources, Antarctic Treaty, Biodiversity, Climate Change, Climate Change-Kyoto Protocol, Desertification, Endangered Species, Environmental Modification, Hazardous Wastes, Law of the Sea, Ozone Layer Protection, Ship Pollution, Wetlands
*signed, but not ratified:* Marine Dumping, Marine Life Conservation
**Geography - note:** second-smallest South American country (after Suriname); most of the low-lying landscape (three-quarters of the country) is grassland, ideal for cattle and sheep raising

## People

**Population:** 3,494,382 (July 2009 est.)
**Age structure:**
*0-14 years:* 22.4% (male 397,942/female 385,253)
*15-64 years:* 64.3% (male 1,115,963/female 1,129,478)
*65 years and over:* 13.3% (male 187,176/female 278,570) (2009 est.)
**Median age:**
*total:* 33.4 years
*male:* 32 years
*female:* 34.8 years (2009 est.)

**Population growth rate:** 0.466% (2009 est.)
**Birth rate:** 13.91 births/1,000 population (2009 est.)
**Death rate:** 9.12 deaths/1,000 population (2008 est.)
**Net migration rate:** -0.16 migrant(s)/1,000 population (2009 est.)
**Urbanization:**
*urban population:* 92% of total population (2008)
*rate of urbanization:* 0.4% annual rate of change (2005-10 est.)
**Sex ratio:**
*at birth:* 1.04 male(s)/female
*under 15 years:* 1.03 male(s)/female
*15-64 years:* 0.99 male(s)/female
*65 years and over:* 0.67 male(s)/female
*total population:* 0.95 male(s)/female (2009 est.)
**Infant mortality rate:**
*total:* 11.32 deaths/1,000 live births
*male:* 12.73 deaths/1,000 live births
*female:* 9.87 deaths/1,000 live births (2009 est.)
**Life expectancy at birth:**
*total population:* 76.35 years
*male:* 73.1 years
*female:* 79.72 years (2009 est.)
**Total fertility rate:** 1.92 children born/woman (2009 est.)
**HIV/AIDS - adult prevalence rate:** 0.6% (2007 est.)
**HIV/AIDS - people living with HIV/AIDS:** 10,000 (2007 est.)
**HIV/AIDS - deaths:** fewer than 500 (2007 est.)
**Nationality:**
*noun:* Uruguayan(s)
*adjective:* Uruguayan
**Ethnic groups:** white 88%, mestizo 8%, black 4%, Amerindian (practically nonexistent)
**Religions:** Roman Catholic 47.1%, non-Catholic Christians 11.1%, nondenominational 23.2%, Jewish 0.3%, atheist or agnostic 17.2%, other 1.1% (2006)
**Languages:** Spanish, Portunol, or Brazilero (Portuguese-Spanish mix on the Brazilian frontier)
**Literacy:**
*definition:* age 15 and over can read and write
*total population:* 98%
*male:* 97.6%
*female:* 98.4% (2003 est.)
**School life expectancy (primary to tertiary education):**
*total:* 15 years
*male:* 14 years
*female:* 16 years (2006)
**Education expenditures:** 2.9% of GDP (2006)

## Government

**Country name:**
*conventional long form:* Oriental Republic of Uruguay
*conventional short form:* Uruguay
*local long form:* Republica Oriental del Uruguay
*local short form:* Uruguay
*former:* Banda Oriental, Cisplatine Province
**Government type:** constitutional republic

# Uruguay (continued)

**Capital:**

*name:* Montevideo

*geographic coordinates:* 34 53 S, 56 11 W

*time difference:* UTC-3 (2 hours ahead of Washington, DC during Standard Time)

*daylight saving time:* +1hr, begins second Sunday in October; ends second Sunday in March

**Administrative divisions:** 19 departments (departamentos, singular - departamento); Artigas, Canelones, Cerro Largo, Colonia, Durazno, Flores, Florida, Lavalleja, Maldonado, Montevideo, Paysandu, Rio Negro, Rivera, Rocha, Salto, San Jose, Soriano, Tacuarembo, Treinta y Tres

**Independence:** 25 August 1825 (from Brazil)

**National holiday:** Independence Day, 25 August (1825)

**Constitution:** 27 November 1966; effective 15 February 1967; suspended 27 June 1973; revised 26 November 1989 and 7 January 1997

**Legal system:** based on Spanish civil law system; accepts compulsory ICJ jurisdiction

**Suffrage:** 18 years of age; universal and compulsory

**Executive branch:**

*chief of state:* President Tabare VAZQUEZ Rosas (since 1 March 2005); Vice President Rodolfo NIN NOVOA (since 1 March 2005); note - the president is both the chief of state and head of government

*head of government:* President Tabare VAZQUEZ Rosas (since 1 March 2005); Vice President Rodolfo NIN NOVOA (since 1 March 2005)

*cabinet:* Council of Ministers appointed by the president with parliamentary approval

*elections:* president and vice president elected on the same ticket by popular vote for five-year terms (may not serve consecutive terms); election last held 31 October 2004 (next to be held in October 2009)

*election results:* Tabare VAZQUEZ elected president; percent of vote - Tabare VAZQUEZ 50.5%, Jorge LARRANAGA 35.1%, Guillermo STIRLING 10.3%; other 4.1%

**Legislative branch:** bicameral General Assembly or Asamblea General consists of Chamber of Senators or Camara de Senadores (30 seats; members are elected by popular vote to serve five-year terms; vice president has one vote in the Senate) and Chamber of Representatives or Camara de Representantes (99 seats; members are elected by popular vote to serve five-year terms)

*elections:* Chamber of Senators - last held 31 October 2004 (next to be held in October 2009); Chamber of Representatives - last held 31 October 2004 (next to be held in October 2009)

*election results:* Chamber of Senators - percent of vote by party - NA; seats by party - EP-FA 16, Blanco 11, Colorado Party 3; Chamber of Representatives - percent of vote by party - NA; seats by party - EP-FA 52, Blanco 36, Colorado Party 10, Independent Party 1

**Judicial branch:** Supreme Court (judges are nominated by the president and elected for 10-year terms by the General Assembly)

**Political parties and leaders:** Broad Front (Frente Amplio) - formerly known as the Progressive Encounter/Broad Front Coalition or EP-FA [Jorge BROVETTO] (a broad governing coalition that includes Movement of the Popular Participation or MPP [Jose MUJICA], New Space Party (Nuevo Espacio) [Rafael MICHELINI], Progressive Alliance (Alianza Progresista) [Rodolfo NIN NOVOA], Socialist Party [Eduardo FERNANDEZ], the Communist Party [Marina ARISMENDI], Uruguayan Assembly (Asamblea Uruguay) [Danilo ASTORI], and Vertiente Artiguista [Mariano ARANA]); Colorado Party (Foro Batllista) [Julio Maria SANGUINETTI]; National Party or Blanco [Luis Alberto LACALLE and Jorge LARRANAGA]

**Political pressure groups and leaders:** Architect's Society of Uruguay (professional organization); Chamber of Uruguayan Industries (manufacturer's association); Chemist and Pharmaceutical Association (professional organization); PIT/CNT (powerful federation of Uruguayan Unions - umbrella labor organization); Rural Association of Uruguay (rancher's association); Uruguayan Construction League; Uruguayan Network of Political Women

*other:* Catholic Church; students

**International organization participation:** CAN (associate), FAO, G-77, IADB, IAEA, IBRD, ICAO, ICC, ICCt, ICRM, IDA, IFAD, IFC, IFRCS, IHO, ILO, IMF, IMO, Interpol, IOC, IOM, IPU, ISO, ITSO, ITU, LAES, LAIA, Mercosur, MIGA, MINURSO, MINUSTAH, MONUC, NAM (observer), OAS, OPANAL, OPCW, PCA, RG, UN, UNASUR, UNCTAD, UNESCO, UNIDO, Union Latina, UNMIS, UNMOGIP, UNOCI, UNOMIG, UNWTO, UPU, WCL, WCO, WFTU, WHO, WIPO, WMO, WTO

**Diplomatic representation in the US:**

*chief of mission:* Ambassador Carlos Alberto GIANELLI Derois

*chancery:* 1913 I Street NW, Washington, DC 20006

*telephone:* [1] (202) 331-1313 through 1316

*FAX:* [1] (202) 331-8142

*consulate(s) general:* Chicago, Los Angeles, Miami, New York

*consulate(s):* San Juan (Puerto Rico)

**Diplomatic representation from the US:**

*chief of mission:* Ambassador (vacant); Charge d'Affaires Robin H. MATTHEWMAN

*embassy:* Lauro Muller 1776, Montevideo 11200

*mailing address:* APO AA 34035

*telephone:* [598] (2) 418-7777

*FAX:* [598] (2) 418-8611

**Flag description:** nine equal horizontal stripes of white (top and bottom) alternating with blue; a white square in the upper hoist-side corner with a yellow sun bearing a human face known as the Sun of May with 16 rays that alternate between triangular and wavy

## Economy

**Economy - overview:** Uruguay's economy is characterized by an export-oriented agricultural sector, a well-educated work force, and high levels of social spending. After averaging growth of 5% annually during 1996-98, in 1999-2002 the economy suffered a major downturn, stemming largely from the spillover effects of the economic problems of its large neighbors, Argentina and Brazil. In 2001-02, Argentine citizens made massive withdrawals of dollars deposited in Uruguayan banks after bank deposits in Argentina were frozen, which led to a plunge in the Uruguayan peso, a banking crisis, and a sharp economic contraction. Real GDP fell in four years by nearly 20%, with 2002 the worst year. The unemployment rate rose, inflation surged, and the burden of external debt doubled. Financial assistance from the IMF helped stem the damage. Uruguay restructured its external debt in 2003 without asking creditors to accept a reduction on the principal. Economic growth for Uruguay resumed, and averaged 8% annually during the period 2004-08.

**GDP (purchasing power parity):**

$42.46 billion (2008 est.)

$38.29 billion (2007)

$35.65 billion (2006)

*note:* data are in 2008 US dollars

**GDP (official exchange rate):** $31.3 billion (2008 est.)

**GDP - real growth rate:**

8.5% (2008 est.)

7.4% (2007 est.)

7% (2006 est.)

**GDP - per capita (PPP):**

$12,200 (2008 est.)

$11,100 (2007 est.)

$10,400 (2006 est.)

*note:* data are in 2008 US dollars

**GDP - composition by sector:**

*agriculture:* 9.8%

*industry:* 32.8%

*services:* 57.4% (2008 est.)

**Labor force:** 1.641 million (2008 est.)

**Labor force - by occupation:**

*agriculture:* 9%

*industry:* 15%

*services:* 76% (2007 est.)

**Unemployment rate:**

7.6% (2008 est.)

9.2% (2007 est.)

**Population below poverty line:** 27.4% of households (2006)

**Household income or consumption by percentage share:**

*lowest 10%:* 1.9%

*highest 10%:* 34% (2003)

**Distribution of family income - Gini index:** 45.2 (2006)

# Uruguay (continued)

**Investment (gross fixed):** 15.1% of GDP (2008 est.)

**Budget:**

*revenues:* $8.204 billion

*expenditures:* $8.526 billion (2008 est.)

**Public debt:** 57% of GDP (September 2008)

**Inflation rate (consumer prices):**

9.2% (2008)

8.1% (2007 est.)

**Central bank discount rate:** 10% (February 2009)

**Commercial bank prime lending rate:** 7% (February 2009)

**Stock of money:** $2.5 billion (31 November 2008)

**Stock of quasi money:** $7.919 billion (31 December 2007)

**Stock of domestic credit:** $7.8 billion (31 December 2008)

**Market value of publicly traded shares:** $159 million (31 December 2007)

**Agriculture - products:** rice, wheat, soybeans, barley; livestock, beef; fish; forestry

**Industries:** food processing, electrical machinery, transportation equipment, petroleum products, textiles, chemicals, beverages

**Industrial production growth rate:** 14.1% (2008 est.)

**Electricity - production:** 9.2 billion kWh (2007)

**Electricity - consumption:** 7.03 billion kWh (2007)

**Electricity - exports:** 995.4 million kWh (2007 est.)

**Electricity - imports:** 788.4 million kWh (2007 est.)

**Oil - production:** 935.7 bbl/day (2007 est.)

**Oil - consumption:** 33,400 bbl/day (2007 est.)

**Oil - exports:** 4,410 bbl/day (2007)

**Oil - imports:** 43,670 bbl/day (2007)

**Oil - proved reserves:** NA bbl

**Natural gas - production:** 0 cu m (2007 est.)

**Natural gas - consumption:** 102.8 million cu m (2007 est.)

**Natural gas - exports:** 0 cu m (2007 est.)

**Natural gas - imports:** 116.9 million cu m (2007)

**Natural gas - proved reserves:** 0 cu m (1 January 2006 est.)

**Current account balance:** -$1 billion (2008 est.)

**Exports:** $6 billion f.o.b. (2008 est.)

**Exports - commodities:** meat, rice, leather products, wool, fish, dairy products

**Exports - partners:** Brazil 15.5%, US 9.4%, Argentina 8.4%, Mexico 6.6%, China 6.1%, Germany 4.8% (2007)

**Imports:** $7 billion f.o.b. (2008 est.)

**Imports - commodities:** crude petroleum and petroleum products, machinery, chemicals, road vehicles, paper, plastics

**Imports - partners:** Brazil 19.1%, Argentina 17.9%, US 9.5%, China 9.1%, Paraguay 7.7%, Nigeria 4.7% (2007)

**Reserves of foreign exchange and gold:** $6.3 billion (31 December 2008 est.)

**Debt - external:** $11.48 billion (31 December 2008 est.)

**Stock of direct foreign investment - at home:** $4.19 billion (2007)

**Stock of direct foreign investment - abroad:** $156 million (2007)

**Exchange rates:** Uruguayan pesos (UYU) per US dollar - 20.936 (2008 est.), 23.947 (2007), 24.048 (2006), 24.479 (2005), 28.704 (2004)

## Communications

**Telephones - main lines in use:** 965,200 (2007)

**Telephones - mobile cellular:** 3.004 million (2007)

**Telephone system:**

*general assessment:* fully digitalized

*domestic:* most modern facilities concentrated in Montevideo; new nationwide microwave radio relay network; overall fixed-line and mobile-cellular teledensity is 115 telephones per 100 persons

*international:* country code - 598; the UNISOR submarine cable system provides direct connectivity to Brazil and Argentina; satellite earth stations - 2 Intelsat (Atlantic Ocean) (2002)

**Radio broadcast stations:** AM 93, FM 191, shortwave 7 (2005)

**Television broadcast stations:** 62 (2005)

**Internet country code:** .uy

**Internet hosts:** 480,593 (2008)

**Internet users:** 968,000 (2007)

## Transportation

**Airports:** 56 (2008)

**Airports - with paved runways:**

*total:* 9

*over 3,047 m:* 1

*1,524 to 2,437 m:* 4

*914 to 1,523 m:* 2

*under 914 m:* 2 (2008)

**Airports - with unpaved runways:**

*total:* 47

*1,524 to 2,437 m:* 3

*914 to 1,523 m:* 19

*under 914 m:* 25 (2008)

**Pipelines:** gas 226 km; oil 155 km (2008)

**Railways:**

*total:* 2,073 km

*standard gauge:* 2,073 km 1.435-m gauge

*note:* 461 km have been taken out of service and 460 kmare in partial use (2006)

**Roadways:**

*total:* 77,732 km

*paved:* 7,743 km

*unpaved:* 69,989 km (2004)

**Waterways:** 1,600 km (2008)

**Merchant marine:**

*total:* 17

*by type:* cargo 3, chemical tanker 2, passenger/cargo 9, petroleum tanker 2, roll on/roll off 1

*foreign-owned:* 10 (Argentina 3, Greece 1, Spain 6)

*registered in other countries:* 3 (Liberia 3) (2008)

**Ports and terminals:** Montevideo

## Military

**Military branches:** Uruguayan Armed Forces: Army (Ejercito), National Navy (Armada Nacional; includes naval air arm, Marine Corps (Cuerpo de Fusileros Navales, FUSNA), Maritime Prefecture in wartime), Air Force (Fuerza Aerea Uruguaya, FAU) (2008)

**Military service age and obligation:** 18 years of age for voluntary and compulsory military service; enlistment is voluntary in peacetime, but the government has the authority to conscript in emergencies (2007)

**Manpower available for military service:**

*males age 16-49:* 837,252

*females age 16-49:* 824,096 (2008 est.)

**Manpower fit for military service:**

*males age 16-49:* 708,545

*females age 16-49:* 693,622 (2009 est.)

**Manpower reaching militarily significant age annually:**

*male:* 27,452

*female:* 26,479 (2009 est.)

**Military expenditures:** 1.6% of GDP (2006)

## Transnational Issues

**Disputes - international:** in Jan 2007, ICJ provisionally ruled Uruguay may begin construction of two paper mills on the Uruguay River, which forms the border with Argentina, while the court examines further whether Argentina has the legal right to stop such construction with potential environmental implications to both countries; uncontested dispute with Brazil over certain islands in the Quarai/Cuareim and Invernada streams and the resulting tripoint with Argentina

**Illicit drugs:** small-scale transit country for drugs mainly bound for Europe, often through sea-borne containers; law enforcement corruption; money laundering because of strict banking secrecy laws; weak border control along Brazilian frontier; increasing consumption of cocaine base and synthetic drugs

# Uzbekistan

## Introduction

**Background:** Russia conquered Uzbekistan in the late 19th century. Stiff resistance to the Red Army after World War I was eventually suppressed and a socialist republic set up in 1924. During the Soviet era, intensive production of "white gold" (cotton) and grain led to overuse of agrochemicals and the depletion of water supplies, which have left the land poisoned and the Aral Sea and certain rivers half dry. Independent since 1991, the country seeks to gradually lessen its dependence on agriculture while developing its mineral and petroleum reserves. Current concerns include terrorism by Islamic militants, economic stagnation, and the curtailment of human rights and democratization.

## Geography

**Location:** Central Asia, north of Afghanistan
**Geographic coordinates:** 41 00 N, 64 00 E
**Map references:** Asia
**Area:**
*total:* 447,400 sq km
*land:* 425,400 sq km
*water:* 22,000 sq km
**Area - comparative:** slightly larger than California
**Land boundaries:**
*total:* 6,221 km
*border countries:* Afghanistan 137 km, Kazakhstan 2,203 km, Kyrgyzstan 1,099 km, Tajikistan 1,161 km, Turkmenistan 1,621 km
**Coastline:** 0 km (doubly landlocked); note - Uzbekistan includes the southern portion of the Aral Sea with a 420 km shoreline
**Maritime claims:** none (doubly landlocked)
**Climate:** mostly midlatitude desert, long, hot summers, mild winters; semiarid grassland in east

**Terrain:** mostly flat-to-rolling sandy desert with dunes; broad, flat intensely irrigated river valleys along course of Amu Darya, Syr Darya (Sirdaryo), and Zarafshon; Fergana Valley in east surrounded by mountainous Tajikistan and Kyrgyzstan; shrinking Aral Sea in west
**Elevation extremes:**
*lowest point:* Sariqarnish Kuli -12 m
*highest point:* Adelunga Toghi 4,301 m
**Natural resources:** natural gas, petroleum, coal, gold, uranium, silver, copper, lead and zinc, tungsten, molybdenum
**Land use:**
*arable land:* 10.51%
*permanent crops:* 0.76%
*other:* 88.73% (2005)
**Irrigated land:** 42,810 sq km (2003)
**Total renewable water resources:** 72.2 cu km (2003)
**Freshwater withdrawal (domestic/industrial/ agricultural):**
*total:* 58.34 cu km/yr (5%/2%/93%)
*per capita:* 2,194 cu m/yr (2000)
**Natural hazards:** NA
**Environment - current issues:** shrinkage of the Aral Sea is resulting in growing concentrations of chemical pesticides and natural salts; these substances are then blown from the increasingly exposed lake bed and contribute to desertification; water pollution from industrial wastes and the heavy use of fertilizers and pesticides is the cause of many human health disorders; increasing soil salination; soil contamination from buried nuclear processing and agricultural chemicals, including DDT
**Environment - international agreements:**
*party to:* Biodiversity, Climate Change, Climate Change-Kyoto Protocol, Desertification, Endangered Species, Environmental Modification, Hazardous Wastes, Ozone Layer Protection, Wetlands
*signed, but not ratified:* none of the selected agreements

## People

**Population:** 27,606,007 (July 2009 est.)
**Age structure:**
*0-14 years:* 28.1% (male 3,970,386/female 3,787,371)
*15-64 years:* 67% (male 9,191,439/female 9,309,791)
*65 years and over:* 4.9% (male 576,191/female 770,829) (2009 est.)
**Median age:**
*total:* 24.7 years
*male:* 24.2 years
*female:* 25.2 years (2009 est.)
**Population growth rate:** 0.935% (2009 est.)
**Birth rate:** 17.58 births/1,000 population (2009 est.)
**Death rate:** 5.3 deaths/1,000 population (2008 est.)
**Net migration rate:** -2.94 migrant(s)/1,000 population (2009 est.)
**Urbanization:**
*urban population:* 37% of total population (2008)
*rate of urbanization:* 1.6% annual rate of change (2005-10 est.)
**Sex ratio:**
*at birth:* 1.06 male(s)/female
*under 15 years:* 1.05 male(s)/female
*15-64 years:* 0.99 male(s)/female
*65 years and over:* 0.75 male(s)/female
*total population:* 0.99 male(s)/female (2009 est.)
**Infant mortality rate:**
*total:* 23.43 deaths/1,000 live births
*male:* 27.7 deaths/1,000 live births
*female:* 18.9 deaths/1,000 live births (2009 est.)
**Life expectancy at birth:**
*total population:* 71.96 years
*male:* 68.95 years
*female:* 75.15 years (2009 est.)
**Total fertility rate:** 1.95 children born/woman (2009 est.)
**HIV/AIDS - adult prevalence rate:** less than 0.1% (2007 est.)
**HIV/AIDS - people living with HIV/AIDS:** 16,000 (2007 est.)
**HIV/AIDS - deaths:** fewer than 500 (2007 est.)
**Nationality:**
*noun:* Uzbekistani
*adjective:* Uzbekistani
**Ethnic groups:** Uzbek 80%, Russian 5.5%, Tajik 5%, Kazakh 3%, Karakalpak 2.5%, Tatar 1.5%, other 2.5% (1996 est.)
**Religions:** Muslim 88% (mostly Sunnis), Eastern Orthodox 9%, other 3%
**Languages:** Uzbek 74.3%, Russian 14.2%, Tajik 4.4%, other 7.1%
**Literacy:**
*definition:* age 15 and over can read and write
*total population:* 99.3%
*male:* 99.6%
*female:* 99% (2003 est.)

# Uzbekistan (continued)

**School life expectancy (primary to tertiary education):**
*total:* 11 years
*male:* 12 years
*female:* 11 years (2007)
**Education expenditures:** 9.4% of GDP (1991)

## Government

**Country name:**
*conventional long form:* Republic of Uzbekistan
*conventional short form:* Uzbekistan
*local long form:* Ozbekiston Respublikasi
*local short form:* Ozbekiston
*former:* Uzbek Soviet Socialist Republic
**Government type:** republic; authoritarian presidential rule, with little power outside the executive branch
**Capital:**
*name:* Tashkent (Toshkent)
*geographic coordinates:* 41 20 N, 69 18 E
*time difference:* UTC+5 (10 hours ahead of Washington, DC during Standard Time)
**Administrative divisions:** 12 provinces (viloyatlar, singular - viloyat), 1 autonomous republic* (respublika), and 1 city** (shahar); Andijon Viloyati, Buxoro Viloyati, Farg'ona Viloyati, Jizzax Viloyati, Namangan Viloyati, Navoiy Viloyati, Qashqadaryo Viloyati (Qarshi), Qoraqalpog'iston Respublikasi [Karakalpakstan]* (Nukus), Samarqand Viloyati, Sirdaryo Viloyati (Guliston), Surxondaryo Viloyati (Termiz), Toshkent Shahri**, Toshkent Viloyati, Xorazm Viloyati (Urganch)
*note:* administrative divisions have the same names as their administrative centers (exceptions have the administrative center name following in parentheses)
**Independence:** 1 September 1991 (from the Soviet Union)
**National holiday:** Independence Day, 1 September (1991)
**Constitution:** adopted 8 December 1992
**Legal system:** based on civil law system; has not accepted compulsory ICJ jurisdiction
**Suffrage:** 18 years of age; universal
**Executive branch:**
*chief of state:* President Islom KARIMOV (since 24 March 1990, when he was elected president by the then Supreme Soviet)
*head of government:* Prime Minister Shavkat MIRZIYOYEV (since 11 December 2003); First Deputy Prime Minister Rustam AZIMOV (since 2 January 2008)
*cabinet:* Cabinet of Ministers appointed by the president with approval of the Supreme Assembly
*elections:* president elected by popular vote for a seven-year term (eligible for a second term; previously was a five-year term, extended by constitutional amendment in 2002; election last held 23 December 2007 (next to be held in 2014); prime minister, ministers, and deputy ministers appointed by the president

*election results:* Islom KARIMOV reelected president; percent of vote - Islom KARIMOV 88.1%, Asliddin RUSTAMOV 3.2%, Dilorom TOSHMUHAMEDOVA 2.9%, Akmal SAIDOV 2.6%
**Legislative branch:** bicameral Supreme Assembly or Oliy Majlis consists of an upper house or Senate (100 seats; 84 members are elected by regional governing councils and 16 appointed by the president; to serve five-year terms) and a lower house or Legislative Chamber (120 seats; members elected by popular vote to serve five-year terms)
*elections:* last held 26 December 2004 and 9 January 2005 (next to be held in December 2009)
*election results:* Senate - percent of vote by party - NA; seats by party - NA; Legislative Chamber - percent of vote by party - NA; seats by party - LDPU 41, NDP 32, Fidokorlar 17, MTP 11, Adolat 9, unaffiliated 10
*note:* all parties in the Supreme Assembly support President KARIMOV
**Judicial branch:** Supreme Court (judges are nominated by the president and confirmed by the Supreme Assembly)
**Political parties and leaders:** Adolat (Justice) Social Democratic Party [Dilorom TOSHMUHAMEDOVA]; Democratic National Rebirth Party (Milliy Tiklanish) or MTP [Hurshid DOSMUHAMMEDOV]; Fidokorlar National Democratic Party (Self-Sacrificers) [Ahtam TURSUNOV]; Liberal Democratic Party of Uzbekistan or LDPU [Adham SHADMANOV; People's Democratic Party or NDP (formerly Communist Party) [Asliddin RUSTAMOV]
**Political pressure groups and leaders:** Agrarian and Entrepreneurs' Party [Marat ZAHIDOV]; Birlik (Unity) Movement [Abdurahim POLAT, chairman]; Committee for the Protection of Human Rights [Marat ZAHIDOV]; Erk (Freedom) Democratic Party [Muhammad SOLIH, chairman] (was banned 9 December 1992); Ezgulik Human Rights Society [Vasila INOYATOVA]; Free Farmers' Party or Ozod Dehqonlar [Nigora HIDOYATOVA]; Human Rights Society of Uzbekistan [Talib YAKUBOV, chairman]; Independent Human Rights Organization of Uzbekistan [Mikhail ARDZINOV, chairman]; Mazlum; Sunshine Coalition [Sanjar UMAROV, chairman]
**International organization participation:** ADB, CIS, CSTO, EAEC, EAPC, EBRD, ECO, FAO, GCTU, IAEA, IBRD, ICAO, ICCt (signatory), ICRM, IDA, IDB, IFC, IFRCS, ILO, IMF, Interpol, IOC, ISO, ITSO, ITU, MIGA, NAM, OIC, OPCW, OSCE, PFP, SCO, UN, UNCTAD, UNESCO, UNIDO, UNWTO, UPU, WCO, WFTU, WHO, WIPO, WMO, WTO (observer)
**Diplomatic representation in the US:**
*chief of mission:* Ambassador Abdulaziz KAMILOV
*chancery:* 1746 Massachusetts Avenue NW, Washington, DC 20036
*telephone:* [1] (202) 887-5300
*FAX:* [1] (202) 293-6804
*consulate(s) general:* New York

**Diplomatic representation from the US:**
*chief of mission:* Ambassador Richard B. NORLAND
*embassy:* 3 Moyqo'rq'on, 5th Block, Yunusobod District, Tashkent 100093
*mailing address:* use embassy street address
*telephone:* [998] (71) 120-5450
*FAX:* [998] (71) 120-6335
**Flag description:** three equal horizontal bands of blue (top), white, and green separated by red fimbriations with a white crescent moon and 12 white stars in the upper hoist-side quadrant

## Economy

**Economy - overview:** Uzbekistan is a dry, landlocked country of which 11% consists of intensely cultivated, irrigated river valleys. More than 60% of its population lives in densely populated rural communities. Uzbekistan is now the world's second-largest cotton exporter and fifth largest producer; it relies heavily on cotton production as the major source of export earnings and has come under increasing international criticism for the use of child labor in its annual cotton harvest. Other major export earners include gold, natural gas, and oil. Following independence in September 1991, the government sought to prop up its Soviet-style command economy with subsidies and tight controls on production and prices. While aware of the need to improve the investment climate, the government still sponsors measures that often increase, not decrease, its control over business decisions. A sharp increase in the inequality of income distribution has hurt the lower ranks of society since independence. In 2003, the government accepted Article VIII obligations under the IMF, providing for full currency convertibility. However, strict currency controls and tightening of borders have lessened the effects of convertibility and have also led to some shortages that have further stifled economic activity. The Central Bank often delays or restricts convertibility, especially for consumer goods. Potential investment by Russia and China in Uzbekistan's gas and oil industry, as well as increased cooperation with South Korea in the realm of civil aviation, may boost growth prospects. In November 2005, Russian President Vladimir PUTIN and Uzbekistan President KARIMOV signed an "alliance," which included provisions for economic and business cooperation. Russian businesses have shown increased interest in Uzbekistan, especially in mining, telecom, and oil and gas. In 2006, Uzbekistan took steps to rejoin the Collective Security Treaty Organization (CSTO) and the Eurasian Economic Community (EurASEC), which it subsequently left in 2008, both organizations dominated by Russia. Uzbek authorities have accused US and other foreign companies operating in Uzbekistan of violating Uzbek tax laws and have frozen their assets.
**GDP (purchasing power parity):**
$71.63 billion (2008 est.)
$65.77 billion (2007)
$60.07 billion (2006)
*note:* data are in 2008 US dollars
**GDP (official exchange rate):** $26.62 billion (2008 est.)

# Uzbekistan (continued)

**GDP - real growth rate:**
8.9% (2008 est.)
9.5% (2007 est.)
7.3% (2006 est.)
**GDP - per capita (PPP):**
$2,600 (2008 est.)
$2,400 (2007 est.)
$2,200 (2006 est.)
*note:* data are in 2008 US dollars
**GDP - composition by sector:**
*agriculture:* 28.2%
*industry:* 33.9%
*services:* 37.9% (2008 est.)
**Labor force:** 15.28 million (2008 est.)
**Labor force - by occupation:**
*agriculture:* 44%
*industry:* 20%
*services:* 36% (1995)
**Unemployment rate:**
0.9% (2008 est.)
0.8% (2007 est.)
*note:* officially measured by the Ministry of Labor, plus another 20% underemployed
**Population below poverty line:** 33% (2004 est.)
**Household income or consumption by percentage share:**
*lowest 10%:* 2.8%
*highest 10%:* 29.6% (2003)
**Distribution of family income - Gini index:** 36.8 (2003)
**Budget:**
*revenues:* $8.005 billion
*expenditures:* $8.127 billion (2008 est.)
**Public debt:** 13.6% of GDP (2008 est.)
**Inflation rate (consumer prices):**
13.5% (2008 est.)
12% (2007 est.)
*note:* official data; based on independent analysis of consumer prices, inflation reached 38% in 2008
**Market value of publicly traded shares:** $36.89 million (2005)
**Agriculture - products:** cotton, vegetables, fruits, grain; livestock
**Industries:** textiles, food processing, machine building, metallurgy, gold, petroleum, natural gas, chemicals
**Industrial production growth rate:** 11.2% (2008 est.)
**Electricity - production:** 48.79 billion kWh (2007 est.)
**Electricity - consumption:** 42.23 billion kWh (2006 est.)
**Electricity - exports:** 11.52 billion kWh (2006 est.)
**Electricity - imports:** 11.44 billion kWh (2006 est.)
**Oil - production:** 99,260 bbl/day (2007 est.)
**Oil - consumption:** 157,100 bbl/day (2006 est.)
**Oil - exports:** 11,940 bbl/day (2005)
**Oil - imports:** 31,440 bbl/day (2005)
**Oil - proved reserves:** 594 million bbl (1 January 2008 est.)

**Natural gas - production:** 65.19 billion cu m (2007 est.)
**Natural gas - consumption:** 51.18 billion cu m (2007 est.)
**Natural gas - exports:** 14.01 billion cu m (2007 est.)
**Natural gas - imports:** 0 cu m (2007 est.)
**Natural gas - proved reserves:** 1.841 trillion cu m (1 January 2008 est.)
**Current account balance:** $5.726 billion (2008 est.)
**Exports:** $9.96 billion f.o.b. (2008 est.)
**Exports - commodities:** cotton, gold, energy products, mineral fertilizers, ferrous and non-ferrous metals, textiles, food products, machinery, automobiles
**Exports - partners:** Russia 22.4%, Poland 10.4%, Turkey 9.4%, Kazakhstan 6.1%, Hungary 6%, China 5.6%, Ukraine 4.8%, Bangladesh 4.3% (2007)
**Imports:** $6.5 billion f.o.b. (2008 est.)
**Imports - commodities:** machinery and equipment, foodstuffs, chemicals, ferrous and non-ferrous metals
**Imports - partners:** Russia 30.1%, China 13.3%, South Korea 13%, Germany 6.3%, Kazakhstan 6.2%, Ukraine 4% (2007)
**Reserves of foreign exchange and gold:** $10.15 billion (31 December 2008 est.)
**Debt - external:** $4.052 billion (31 December 2008 est.)
**Stock of direct foreign investment - at home:** $NA
**Stock of direct foreign investment - abroad:** $NA
**Exchange rates:** Uzbekistani soum (UZS) per US dollar - 1,317 (2008 est.), 1,263.8 (2007), 1,219.8 (2006), 1,020 (2005), 971.265 (2004)

## Communications

**Telephones - main lines in use:** 1.821 million (2007)
**Telephones - mobile cellular:** 10.4 million (2008)
**Telephone system:**
*general assessment:* antiquated and inadequate; in serious need of modernization
*domestic:* the main line telecommunications system is dilapidated and telephone density is low; the state-owned telecommunications company, Uzbektelecom, is using loans from the Japanese government and the China Development Bank to improve mainline services; completion of conversion to digital exchanges planned for 2010; mobile services are growing rapidly, with the subscriber base reaching 10.4 million in 2008
*international:* country code - 998; linked by fiber-optic cable or microwave radio relay with CIS member states and to other countries by leased connection via the Moscow international gateway switch; after the completion of the Uzbek link to the Trans-Asia-Europe (TAE) fiber-optic cable, Uzbekistan plans to establish a fiber-optic connection to Afghanistan (2008)

**Radio broadcast stations:** AM 4, FM 12, shortwave 3 (2008)
**Television broadcast stations:** 28 (includes 1 cable rebroadcaster in Tashkent and approximately 20 stations in regional capitals) (2006)
**Internet country code:** .uz
**Internet hosts:** 38,183 (2008)
**Internet users:** 2.1 million (2008)

## Transportation

**Airports:** 54 (2008)
**Airports - with paved runways:**
*total:* 33
*over 3,047 m:* 6
*2,438 to 3,047 m:* 13
*1,524 to 2,437 m:* 6
*914 to 1,523 m:* 4
*under 914 m:* 4 (2008)
**Airports - with unpaved runways:**
*total:* 21
*2,438 to 3,047 m:* 2
*under 914 m:* 19 (2008)
**Pipelines:** gas 9,706 km; oil 868 km (2008)
**Railways:**
*total:* 3,950 km
*broad gauge:* 3,950 km 1.520-m gauge (620 km electrified) (2006)
**Roadways:**
*total:* 86,496 km
*paved:* 75,511 km
*unpaved:* 10,985 km (2000)
**Waterways:** 1,100 km (2008)
**Ports and terminals:** Termiz (Amu Darya)

## Military

**Military branches:** Army, Air and Air Defense Forces, National Guard
**Military service age and obligation:** 18 years of age for compulsory military service; 1-year conscript service obligation; moving toward a professional military, but conscription will continue; the military cannot accommodate everyone who wishes to enlist, and competition for entrance into the military is similar to the competition for admission to universities (2007)
**Manpower available for military service:**
*males age 16-49:* 7,480,484
*females age 16-49:* 7,542,017 (2008 est.)
**Manpower fit for military service:**
*males age 16-49:* 6,340,446
*females age 16-49:* 6,559,769 (2009 est.)
**Manpower reaching militarily significant age annually:**
*male:* 313,131
*female:* 310,442 (2009 est.)
**Military expenditures:** 2% of GDP (2005 est.)

# Uzbekistan *(continued)*

## Transnational Issues

**Disputes - international:** prolonged drought and cotton monoculture in Uzbekistan and Turkmenistan creates water-sharing difficulties for Amu Darya river states; field demarcation of the boundaries with Kazakhstan commenced in 2004; border delimitation of 130 km of border with Kyrgyzstan is hampered by serious disputes around enclaves and other areas

**Refugees and internally displaced persons:**
*refugees (country of origin):* 39,202 (Tajikistan); 1,060 (Afghanistan)
*IDPs:* 3,400 (forced population transfers by government from villages near Tajikistan border) (2007)

**Trafficking in persons:**
*current situation:* Uzbekistan is a source country for women and girls trafficked to Kazakhstan, Russia, Middle East, and Asia for the purpose of commercial sexual exploitation; men are trafficked to Kazakhstan and Russia for purposes of forced labor in the construction, cotton, and tobacco industries; men and women are also trafficked internally for the purposes of domestic servitude, forced labor in the agricultural and construction industries, and for commercial sexual exploitation
*tier rating:* Tier 2 Watch List - Uzbekistan is on the Tier 2 Watch List for its failure to provide evidence of increasing efforts to combat severe forms of trafficking in 2007; the government did not amend its criminal code to increase penalties for convicted traffickers; in March 2008, Uzbekistan adopted ILO Conventions on minimum age of employment and on the elimination of the worst forms of child labor and is working with the ILO on implementation; the government also demonstrated its increasing commitment to combat trafficking in March 2008 by adopting a comprehensive anti-trafficking law; Uzbekistan has not ratified the 2000 UN TIP Protocol (2008)

**Illicit drugs:** transit country for Afghan narcotics bound for Russian and, to a lesser extent, Western European markets; limited illicit cultivation of cannabis and small amounts of opium poppy for domestic consumption; poppy cultivation almost wiped out by government crop eradication program; transit point for heroin precursor chemicals bound for Afghanistan

# Vanuatu

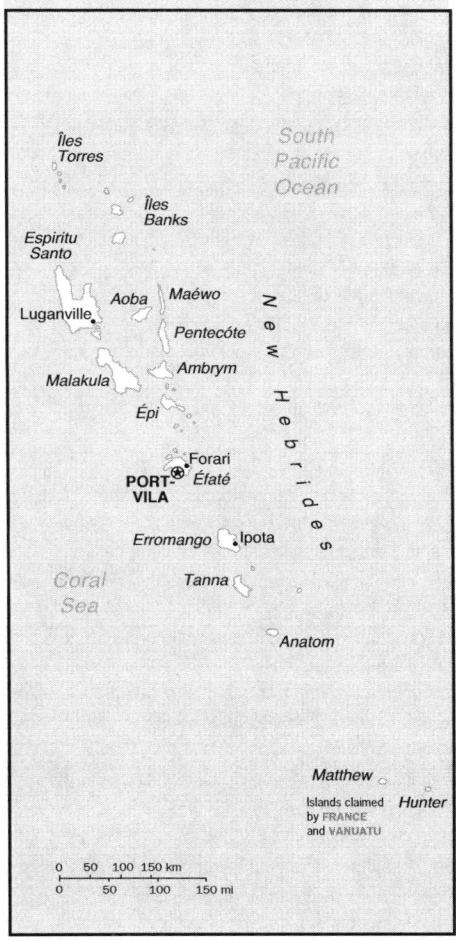

## Introduction

**Background:** Multiple waves of colonizers, each speaking a distinct language, migrated to the New Hebrides in the millennia preceding European exploration in the 18th century. This settlement pattern accounts for the complex linguistic diversity found on the archipelago to this day. The British and French, who settled the New Hebrides in the 19th century, agreed in 1906 to an Anglo-French Condominium, which administered the islands until independence in 1980, when the new name of Vanuatu was adopted.

## Geography

**Location:** Oceania, group of islands in the South Pacific Ocean, about three-quarters of the way from Hawaii to Australia
**Geographic coordinates:** 16 00 S, 167 00 E
**Map references:** Oceania

**Area:**
*total:* 12,200 sq km
*land:* 12,200 sq km
*water:* 0 sq km
*note:* includes more than 80 islands, about 65 of which are inhabited
**Area - comparative:** slightly larger than Connecticut
**Land boundaries:** 0 km
**Coastline:** 2,528 km
**Maritime claims:** measured from claimed archipelagic baselines
*territorial sea:* 12 nm
*contiguous zone:* 24 nm
*exclusive economic zone:* 200 nm
*continental shelf:* 200 nm or to the edge of the continental margin
**Climate:** tropical; moderated by southeast trade winds from May to October; moderate rainfall from November to April; may be affected by cyclones from December to April
**Terrain:** mostly mountainous islands of volcanic origin; narrow coastal plains
**Elevation extremes:**
*lowest point:* Pacific Ocean 0 m
*highest point:* Tabwemasana 1,877 m
**Natural resources:** manganese, hardwood forests, fish
**Land use:**
*arable land:* 1.64%
*permanent crops:* 6.97%
*other:* 91.39% (2005)
**Irrigated land:** NA
**Natural hazards:** tropical cyclones or typhoons (January to April); volcanic eruption on Aoba (Ambae) island began 27 November 2005, volcanism also causes minor earthquakes; tsunamis
**Environment - current issues:** most of the population does not have access to a reliable supply of potable water; deforestation
**Environment - international agreements:**
*party to:* Antarctic-Marine Living Resources, Biodiversity, Climate Change, Climate Change-Kyoto Protocol, Desertification, Endangered Species, Law of the Sea, Marine Dumping, Ozone Layer Protection, Ship Pollution, Tropical Timber 94
*signed, but not ratified:* none of the selected agreements
**Geography - note:** a Y-shaped chain of four main islands and 80 smaller islands; several of the islands have active volcanoes

## People

**Population:** 218,519 (July 2009 est.)
**Age structure:**
*0-14 years:* 30.7% (male 34,263/female 32,833)
*15-64 years:* 65.3% (male 72,670/female 69,970)
*65 years and over:* 4% (male 4,516/female 4,267) (2009 est.)

# Vanuatu (continued)

**Median age:**
*total:* 24.2 years
*male:* 24.2 years
*female:* 24.2 years (2009 est.)
**Population growth rate:** 1.398% (2009 est.)
**Birth rate:** 21.53 births/1,000 population (2009 est.)
**Death rate:** 7.61 deaths/1,000 population (2008 est.)
**Net migration rate:** NA
**Urbanization:**
*urban population:* 25% of total population (2008)
*rate of urbanization:* 4.1% annual rate of change
(2005-10 est.)
**Sex ratio:**
*at birth:* 1.05 male(s)/female
*under 15 years:* 1.04 male(s)/female
*15-64 years:* 1.04 male(s)/female
*65 years and over:* 1.06 male(s)/female
*total population:* 1.04 male(s)/female (2009 est.)
**Infant mortality rate:**
*total:* 49.45 deaths/1,000 live births
*male:* 51.97 deaths/1,000 live births
*female:* 46.81 deaths/1,000 live births (2009 est.)
**Life expectancy at birth:**
*total population:* 63.98 years
*male:* 62.37 years
*female:* 65.66 years (2009 est.)
**Total fertility rate:** 2.5 children born/woman
(2009 est.)
**HIV/AIDS - adult prevalence rate:** NA
**HIV/AIDS - people living with HIV/AIDS:** NA
**HIV/AIDS - deaths:** NA
**Nationality:**
*noun:* Ni-Vanuatu (singular and plural)
*adjective:* Ni-Vanuatu
**Ethnic groups:** Ni-Vanuatu 98.5%, other 1.5%
(1999 Census)
**Religions:** Presbyterian 31.4%, Anglican 13.4%,
Roman Catholic 13.1%, Seventh-Day Adventist
10.8%, other Christian 13.8%, indigenous beliefs
5.6% (including Jon Frum cargo cult), other 9.6%,
none 1%, unspecified 1.3% (1999 Census)
**Languages:** local languages (more than 100) 72.6%,
pidgin (known as Bislama or Bichelama) 23.1%,
English 1.9%, French 1.4%, other 0.3%, unspecified
0.7% (1999 Census)
**Literacy:**
*definition:* age 15 and over can read and write
*total population:* 74%
*male:* NA
*female:* NA (1999 census)
**School life expectancy (primary to tertiary
education):**
*total:* 10 years
*male:* 11 years
*female:* 10 years (2004)
**Education expenditures:** 9.5% of GDP (2003)

## Government

**Country name:**
*conventional long form:* Republic of Vanuatu
*conventional short form:* Vanuatu
*local long form:* Ripablik blong Vanuatu
*local short form:* Vanuatu
*former:* New Hebrides
**Government type:** parliamentary republic
**Capital:**
*name:* Port-Vila (on Efate)
*geographic coordinates:* 17 44 S, 168 19 E
*time difference:* UTC+11 (16 hours ahead of
Washington, DC during Standard Time)
**Administrative divisions:** 6 provinces; Malampa,
Penama, Sanma, Shefa, Tafea, Torba
**Independence:** 30 July 1980 (from France and the
UK)
**National holiday:** Independence Day, 30 July
(1980)
**Constitution:** 30 July 1980
**Legal system:** unified system being created from
former dual French and British systems; has not
accepted compulsory ICJ jurisdiction
**Suffrage:** 18 years of age; universal
**Executive branch:**
*chief of state:* President Kalkot Matas KELEKELE
(since 16 August 2004)
*head of government:* Prime Minister Edward
NATAPEI (since 22 September 2008); Deputy Prime
Minister Ham LINI (since 22 September 2008)
*cabinet:* Council of Ministers appointed by the prime
minister, responsible to parliament
*elections:* president elected for a five-year term by an
electoral college consisting of parliament and the
presidents of the regional councils; election for president
last held 16 August 2004 (next to be held in 2009);
following legislative elections, the leader of the majority
party or majority coalition is usually elected prime minister
by parliament from among its members; election for
prime minister last held 22 September 2008 (next to be
held following general elections in 2012)
*election results:* Kalkot Matas KELEKELE elected
president, with 49 votes out of 56, after several ballots
on 16 August 2004
**Legislative branch:** unicameral Parliament (52
seats; members elected by popular vote to serve
four-year terms)
*elections:* last held 2 September 2008 (next to be held
in 2012)
*election results:* percent of vote by party - NA; seats
by party - VP 11, NUP 8, UMP 7, VRP 7, PPP 4, GC
2, MPP 1, NA 1, NAG 1, PAP 1, Shepherds Alliance 1,
VFFP 1, VLP 1, VNP 1, VPRFP 1, and independent 4;
note - political party associations are fluid
*note:* the National Council of Chiefs advises on
matters of culture and language
**Judicial branch:** Supreme Court (chief justice is
appointed by the president after consultation with the
prime minister and the leader of the opposition, three
other justices are appointed by the president on the
advice of the Judicial Service Commission)

**Political parties and leaders:** Greens
Confederation or GC [Moana CARCASSES]; Jon
Frum Movement or JF [Song KEASPAI]; Melanesian
Progressive Party or MPP [Barak SOPE]; Nagriamel
movement or NAG [Havo MOLI]; Namangi Aute or NA
[Paul TELUKLUK]; National United Party or NUP
[Ham LINI]; People's Action Party or PAP [Peter
VUTA]; People's Progressive Party or PPP [Sato
KILMAN]; Shepherds Alliance Party [leader NA];
Union of Moderate Parties or UMP [Serge VOHOR];
Vanuatu Family First Party or VFFP [Eta RORI];
Vanuatu Labor Party or VLP [Joshua KALSAKAU];
Vanuatu National Party or VNP [Issac HAMARILIU];
Vanua'aku Pati (Our Land Party) or VP [Edward
NATAPEI]; Vanuatu Republican Party or VRP
[Maxime Carlot KORMAN]; Vanuatu Republican
Farmers Party or VPRFP [Jean RAVOU]
**Political pressure groups and leaders:** NA
**International organization participation:** ACCT,
ACP, ADB, C, FAO, G-77, IBRD, ICAO, ICRM, IDA,
IFC, IFRCS, ILO, IMF, IMO, IOC, ITU, ITUC, MIGA,
NAM, OAS (observer), OIF, OPCW, PIF, Sparteca,
SPC, UN, UNCTAD, UNESCO, UNIDO, UPU, WHO,
WMO, WTO (observer)
**Diplomatic representation in the US:** Vanuatu
does not have an embassy in the US; it does,
however, have a Permanent Mission to the UN
**Diplomatic representation from the US:** the US
does not have an embassy in Vanuatu; the
ambassador to Papua New Guinea is accredited to
Vanuatu
**Flag description:** two equal horizontal bands of red
(top) and green with a black isosceles triangle (based
on the hoist side) all separated by a black-edged
yellow stripe in the shape of a horizontal Y (the two
points of the Y face the hoist side and enclose the
triangle); centered in the triangle is a boar's tusk
encircling two crossed namele leaves, all in yellow

## Economy

**Economy - overview:** This South Pacific island
economy is based primarily on small-scale agriculture,
which provides a living for over 70% of the population.
Fishing, offshore financial services, and tourism, with
more than 167,000 visitors in 2007 are other
mainstays of the economy. Mineral deposits are
negligible; the country has no known petroleum
deposits. A small light industry sector caters to the
local market. Tax revenues come mainly from import
duties. Economic development is hindered by
dependence on relatively few commodity exports,
vulnerability to natural disasters, and long distances
from main markets and between constituent islands.
In response to foreign concerns, the government has
promised to tighten regulation of its offshore financial
center. In mid-2002, the government stepped up
efforts to boost tourism through improved air
connections, resort development, and cruise ship
facilities. Agriculture, especially livestock farming, is a
second target for growth. Australia and New Zealand
are the main suppliers of tourists and foreign aid.

# Vanuatu *(continued)*

**GDP (purchasing power parity):**
$983.2 million (2008 est.)
$925 million (2007)
$868.5 million (2006)
*note:* data are in 2008 US dollars
**GDP (official exchange rate):** $560 million (2008 est.)
**GDP - real growth rate:**
6.3% (2008 est.)
6.5% (2007 est.)
7.2% (2006 est.)
**GDP - per capita (PPP):**
$4,600 (2008 est.)
$4,400 (2007 est.)
$4,200 (2006 est.)
*note:* data are in 2008 US dollars
**GDP - composition by sector:**
*agriculture:* 26%
*industry:* 12%
*services:* 62% (2000 est.)
**Labor force:** 76,410 (1999)
**Labor force - by occupation:**
*agriculture:* 65%
*industry:* 5%
*services:* 30% (2000 est.)
**Unemployment rate:**
1.7% (1999)
**Population below poverty line:** NA%
**Household income or consumption by percentage share:**
*lowest 10%:* NA%
*highest 10%:* NA%
**Budget:**
*revenues:* $78.7 million
*expenditures:* $72.23 million (2005)
**Inflation rate (consumer prices):**
3.9% (2007 est.)
**Central bank discount rate:** 6% (31 December 2007)
**Commercial bank prime lending rate:** 8.16% (31 December 2007)
**Stock of money:** $107.1 million (31 December 2007)
**Stock of quasi money:** $421.8 million (31 December 2007)
**Stock of domestic credit:** $229.5 million (31 December 2007)
**Market value of publicly traded shares:** $NA
**Agriculture - products:** copra, coconuts, cocoa, coffee, taro, yams, fruits, vegetables; beef; fish
**Industries:** food and fish freezing, wood processing, meat canning
**Electricity - production:** 46 million kWh (2007 est.)
**Electricity - consumption:** 39.99 million kWh (2006 est.)
**Electricity - exports:** 0 kWh (2007 est.)
**Electricity - imports:** 0 kWh (2007 est.)

**Oil - production:** 0 bbl/day (2007 est.)
**Oil - consumption:** 660 bbl/day (2006 est.)
**Oil - exports:** 0 bbl/day (2005)
**Oil - imports:** 671.1 bbl/day (2005)
**Oil - proved reserves:** 0 bbl (1 January 2006 est.)
**Natural gas - production:** 0 cu m (2007 est.)
**Natural gas - consumption:** 0 cu m (2007 est.)
**Natural gas - exports:** 0 cu m (2007 est.)
**Natural gas - imports:** 0 cu m (2007 est.)
**Natural gas - proved reserves:** 0 cu m (1 January 2006 est.)
**Current account balance:** -$60 million (2007 est.)
**Exports:** $40 million f.o.b. (2006)
**Exports - commodities:** copra, beef, cocoa, timber, kava, coffee
**Exports - partners:** Thailand 58.3%, India 18.5%, Japan 11.3% (2007)
**Imports:** $156 million c.i.f. (2006)
**Imports - commodities:** machinery and equipment, foodstuffs, fuels
**Imports - partners:** Australia 20.7%, Singapore 11.8%, NZ 11.2%, Norway 8.5%, US 8.3%, Fiji 8.1%, China 7.2%, New Caledonia 4.5% (2007)
**Reserves of foreign exchange and gold:** $40.54 million (2003)
**Debt - external:** $81.2 million (2004)
**Exchange rates:** vatu (VUV) per US dollar - NA (2007), 111.93 (2006), NA (2005), 111.79 (2004), 122.19 (2003)

## Communications

**Telephones - main lines in use:** 8,800 (2007)
**Telephones - mobile cellular:** 26,000 (2007)
**Telephone system:**
*general assessment:* NA
*domestic:* NA
*international:* country code - 678; satellite earth station -1 Intelsat (Pacific Ocean)
**Radio broadcast stations:** AM 2, FM 4, shortwave 1 (2001)
**Television broadcast stations:** 1 (2004)
**Internet country code:** .vu
**Internet hosts:** 990 (2008)
**Internet users:** 17,000 (2007)

## Transportation

**Airports:** 31 (2008)
**Airports - with paved runways:**
*total:* 3
*2,438 to 3,047 m:* 1
*1,524 to 2,437 m:* 1
*914 to 1,523 m:* 1 (2008)
**Airports - with unpaved runways:**
*total:* 28
*914 to 1,523 m:* 5
*under 914 m:* 23 (2008)
**Roadways:**
*total:* 1,070 km
*paved:* 256 km
*unpaved:* 814 km (1999)

**Merchant marine:**
*total:* 54
*by type:* bulk carrier 32, cargo 8, container 1, liquefied gas 2, passenger 1, petroleum tanker 1, refrigerated cargo 4, vehicle carrier 5
*foreign-owned:* 54 (Australia 2, Belgium 4, Canada 5, Estonia 1, Greece 1, Japan 29, Monaco 1, Poland 7, Russia 2, Switzerland 1, US 1) (2008)
**Ports and terminals:** Forari, Port-Vila, Santo (Espiritu Santo)

## Military

**Military branches:** no regular military forces; Vanuatu Police Force (VPF), Vanuatu Mobile Force (VMF; includes Police Maritime Wing (PMW)) (2009)
**Manpower available for military service:**
*males age 16-49:* 58,900 (2008 est.)
**Manpower fit for military service:**
*males age 16-49:* 41,533
*females age 16-49:* 42,837 (2009 est.)
**Manpower reaching militarily significant age annually:**
*male:* 2,368
*female:* 2,272 (2009 est.)
**Military expenditures:** NA

## Transnational Issues

**Disputes - international:** Matthew and Hunter Islands east of New Caledonia claimed by Vanuatu and France

# Venezuela

## Introduction

**Background:** Venezuela was one of three countries that emerged from the collapse of Gran Colombia in 1830 (the others being Ecuador and New Granada, which became Colombia). For most of the first half of the 20th century, Venezuela was ruled by generally benevolent military strongmen, who promoted the oil industry and allowed for some social reforms. Democratically elected governments have held sway since 1959. Hugo CHAVEZ, president since 1999, seeks to implement his "21st Century Socialism," which purports to alleviate social ills while at the same time attacking globalization and undermining regional stability. Current concerns include: a weakening of democratic institutions, political polarization, a politicized military, drug-related violence along the Colombian border, increasing internal drug consumption, overdependence on the petroleum industry with its price fluctuations, and irresponsible mining operations that are endangering the rain forest and indigenous peoples.

## Geography

**Location:** Northern South America, bordering the Caribbean Sea and the North Atlantic Ocean, between Colombia and Guyana

**Geographic coordinates:** 8 00 N, 66 00 W

**Map references:** South America

**Area:**
*total:* 912,050 sq km
*land:* 882,050 sq km
*water:* 30,000 sq km

**Area - comparative:** slightly more than twice the size of California

**Land boundaries:**
*total:* 4,993 km
*border countries:* Brazil 2,200 km, Colombia 2,050 km, Guyana 743 km

**Coastline:** 2,800 km

**Maritime claims:**
*territorial sea:* 12 nm
*contiguous zone:* 15 nm
*exclusive economic zone:* 200 nm
*continental shelf:* 200 m depth or to the depth of exploitation

**Climate:** tropical; hot, humid; more moderate in highlands

**Terrain:** Andes Mountains and Maracaibo Lowlands in northwest; central plains (llanos); Guiana Highlands in southeast

**Elevation extremes:**
*lowest point:* Caribbean Sea 0 m
*highest point:* Pico Bolivar (La Columna) 5,007 m

**Natural resources:** petroleum, natural gas, iron ore, gold, bauxite, other minerals, hydropower, diamonds

**Land use:**
*arable land:* 2.85%
*permanent crops:* 0.88%
*other:* 96.27% (2005)

**Irrigated land:** 5,750 sq km (2003)

**Total renewable water resources:** 1,233.2 cu km (2000)

**Freshwater withdrawal (domestic/industrial/agricultural):**
*total:* 8.37 cu km/yr (6%/7%/47%)
*per capita:* 313 cu m/yr (2000)

**Natural hazards:** subject to floods, rockslides, mudslides; periodic droughts

**Environment - current issues:** sewage pollution of Lago de Valencia; oil and urban pollution of Lago de Maracaibo; deforestation; soil degradation; urban and industrial pollution, especially along the Caribbean coast; threat to the rainforest ecosystem from irresponsible mining operations

**Environment - international agreements:**
*party to:* Antarctic Treaty, Biodiversity, Climate Change, Climate Change-Kyoto Protocol, Desertification, Endangered Species, Hazardous Wastes, Marine Life Conservation, Ozone Layer Protection, Ship Pollution, Tropical Timber 83, Tropical Timber 94, Wetlands
*signed but not ratified:* none of the selected agreements

**Geography - note:** on major sea and air routes linking North and South America; Angel Falls in the Guiana Highlands is the world's highest waterfall

## People

**Population:** 26,814,843 (July 2009 est.)

**Age structure:**
*0-14 years:* 30.5% (male 4,157,194/female 4,022,595)
*15-64 years:* 64.3% (male 8,480,872/female 8,754,620)
*65 years and over:* 5.2% (male 620,657/female 778,905) (2009 est.)

**Median age:**
*total:* 25.5 years
*male:* 24.8 years
*female:* 26.2 years (2009 est.)

**Population growth rate:** 1.508% (2009 est.)

**Birth rate:** 20.61 births/1,000 population (2009 est.)

**Death rate:** 5.1 deaths/1,000 population (2008 est.)

**Net migration rate:** -0.42 migrant(s)/1,000 population (2009 est.)

**Urbanization:**
*urban population:* 93% of total population (2008)
*rate of urbanization:* 2% annual rate of change (2005-10 est.)

**Sex ratio:**
*at birth:* 1.05 male(s)/female
*under 15 years:* 1.03 male(s)/female
*15-64 years:* 0.97 male(s)/female
*65 years and over:* 0.8 male(s)/female
*total population:* 0.98 male(s)/female (2009 est.)

**Infant mortality rate:**
*total:* 21.54 deaths/1,000 live births
*male:* 25.1 deaths/1,000 live births
*female:* 17.81 deaths/1,000 live births (2009 est.)

**Life expectancy at birth:**
*total population:* 73.61 years
*male:* 70.54 years
*female:* 76.83 years (2009 est.)

**Total fertility rate:** 2.48 children born/woman (2009 est.)

**HIV/AIDS - adult prevalence rate:** 0.7%; note - no country specific models provided (2001 est.)

**HIV/AIDS - people living with HIV/AIDS:** 110,000 (1999 est.)

**HIV/AIDS - deaths:** 4,100 (2003 est.)

**Major infectious diseases:**
*degree of risk:* high
*food or waterborne diseases:* bacterial diarrhea
*vectorborne disease:* dengue fever and malaria (2009)

**Nationality:**
*noun:* Venezuelan(s)
*adjective:* Venezuelan

**Ethnic groups:** Spanish, Italian, Portuguese, Arab, German, African, indigenous people

**Religions:** nominally Roman Catholic 96%, Protestant 2%, other 2%

**Languages:** Spanish (official), numerous indigenous dialects

**Literacy:**
*definition:* age 15 and over can read and write
*total population:* 93%
*male:* 93.3%
*female:* 92.7% (2001 census)

**School life expectancy (primary to tertiary education):**
*total:* 12 years
*male:* 11 years
*female:* 12 years (2003)

**Education expenditures:** 3.7% of GDP (2006)

# Venezuela (continued)

## Government

**Country name:**
*conventional long form:* Bolivarian Republic of Venezuela
*conventional short form:* Venezuela
*local long form:* Republica Bolivariana de Venezuela
*local short form:* Venezuela
**Government type:** federal republic
**Capital:**
*name:* Caracas
*geographic coordinates:* 10 30 N, 66 56 W
*time difference:* UTC-4.5 (half an hour ahead of Washington, DC during Standard Time)
**Administrative divisions:** 23 states (estados, singular - estado), 1 capital district* (distrito capital), and 1 federal dependency** (dependencia federal); Amazonas, Anzoategui, Apure, Aragua, Barinas, Bolivar, Carabobo, Cojedes, Delta Amacuro, Dependencias Federales**, Distrito Federal*, Falcon, Guarico, Lara, Merida, Miranda, Monagas, Nueva Esparta, Portuguesa, Sucre, Tachira, Trujillo, Vargas, Yaracuy, Zulia
*note:* the federal dependency consists of 11 federally controlled island groups with a total of 72 individual islands
**Independence:** 5 July 1811 (from Spain)
**National holiday:** Independence Day, 5 July (1811)
**Constitution:** 30 December 1999
**Legal system:** open, adversarial court system; has not accepted compulsory ICJ jurisdiction
**Suffrage:** 18 years of age; universal
**Executive branch:**
*chief of state:* President Hugo CHAVEZ Frias (since 3 February 1999); Executive Vice President Ramon Alonzo CARRIZALEZ Rengifo (since 4 January 2008); note - the president is both the chief of state and head of government
*head of government:* President Hugo CHAVEZ Frias (since 3 February 1999); Executive Vice President Ramon Alonzo CARRIZALEZ Rengifo (since 4 January 2008)
*cabinet:* Council of Ministers appointed by the president
*elections:* president elected by popular vote for a six-year term (eligible for a second term); election last held 3 December 2006 (next to be held in December 2012)
*note:* in 1999, a National Constituent Assembly drafted a new constitution that increased the presidential term to six years; an election was subsequently held on 30 July 2000 under the terms of this constitution
*election results:* Hugo CHAVEZ Frias reelected president; percent of vote - Hugo CHAVEZ Frias 62.9%, Manuel ROSALES 36.9%
**Legislative branch:** unicameral National Assembly or Asamblea Nacional (167 seats; members elected by popular vote to serve five-year terms; three seats reserved for the indigenous peoples of Venezuela)
*elections:* last held 4 December 2005 (next to be held in 2010)

*election results:* percent of vote by party - NA; seats by party - pro-government 167 (MVR 114, PODEMOS 15, PPT 11, indigenous 2, other 25), opposition 0; total seats by party as of 1 January 2008 - pro-government 152 (PSUV 114, PPT 11, indigenous 2, other 25), PODEMOS 15
**Judicial branch:** Supreme Tribunal of Justice or Tribuna Suprema de Justicia (magistrates are elected by the National Assembly for a single 12-year term)
**Political parties and leaders:** A New Time or UNT [Manuel ROSALES]; Christian Democrats or COPEI [Cesar PEREZ Vivas]; Communist Party of Venezuela or PCV [Jeronimo CARRERA]; Democratic Action or AD [Henry RAMOS Allup]; Fatherland for All or PPT [Jose ALBORNOZ]; Justice First [Julio BORGES]; Movement Toward Socialism or MAS [Hector MUJICA]; United Socialist Party of Venezuela or PSUV [Hugo CHAVEZ]; Venezuela Project or PV [Henrique SALAS Romer]; We Can or PODEMOS [Ismael GARCIA]
**Political pressure groups and leaders:** FEDECAMARAS, a conservative business group; VECINOS groups; Venezuelan Confederation of Workers or CTV (labor organization dominated by the Democratic Action)
**International organization participation:** Caricom (observer), CDB, FAO, G-15, G-24, G-77, IADB, IAEA, IBRD, ICAO, ICC, ICCt, ICRM, IDA, IFAD, IFC, IFRCS, IHO, ILO, IMF, IMO, IMSO, Interpol, IOC, IOM, IPU, ISO, ITSO, ITU, ITUC, LAES, LAIA, LAS (observer), Mercosur (associate), MIGA, NAM, OAS, OPANAL, OPCW, OPEC, PCA, RG, UN, UNASUR, UNCTAD, UNESCO, UNHCR, UNIDO, Union Latina, UNWTO, UPU, WCL, WCO, WFTU, WHO, WIPO, WMO, WTO
**Diplomatic representation in the US:**
*chief of mission:* Ambassador (vacant); Charge d'Affaires Angelo Rivero SANTOS
*chancery:* 1099 30th Street NW, Washington, DC 20007
*telephone:* [1] (202) 342-2214
*FAX:* [1] (202) 342-6820
*consulate(s) general:* Boston, Chicago, Houston, Miami, New Orleans, New York, San Francisco, San Juan (Puerto Rico)
*note:* as of September 2008, the US has expelled the Venezuelan ambassador to the US
**Diplomatic representation from the US:**
*chief of mission:* Ambassador (vacant); Charge d'Affaires John CAULFIELD
*embassy:* Calle F con Calle Suapure, Urbanizacion Colinas de Valle Arriba, Caracas 1080
*mailing address:* P. O. Box 62291, Caracas 1060-A; APO AA 34037
*telephone:* [58] (212) 975-6411, 907-8400 (after hours)
*FAX:* [58] (212) 907-8199
*note:* as of September 2008, the Venezuelan Government has expelled the US Ambassador to Venezuela

**Flag description:** three equal horizontal bands of yellow (top), blue, and red with the coat of arms on the hoist side of the yellow band and an arc of eight white five-pointed stars centered in the blue band

## Economy

**Economy - overview:** Venezuela remains highly dependent on oil revenues, which account for roughly 90% of export earnings, about 50% of the federal budget revenues, and around 30% of GDP. A nationwide strike between December 2002 and February 2003 had far-reaching economic consequences - real GDP declined by around 9% in 2002 and 8% in 2003 - but economic output since then has recovered strongly. Fueled by high oil prices, record government spending helped to boost GDP by about 9% in 2006, 8% in 2007, and nearly 6% in 2008. This spending, combined with recent minimum wage hikes and improved access to domestic credit, has created a consumption boom but has come at the cost of higher inflation - roughly 20% in 2007 and more than 30% in 2008. Imports also have jumped significantly. Declining oil prices in the latter part of 2008 are expected to undermine the govenment's ability to continue the high rate of spending. President Hugo CHAVEZ in 2008 continued efforts to increase the government's contol of the economy by nationalizing firms in the cement and steel sectors. In 2007, he nationalized firms in the petroleum, communications, and electricity sectors. In July 2008, CHAVEZ implemented by decree a number of laws that further consolidate and centralize authority over the economy through his plan for "21st Century Socialism."
**GDP (purchasing power parity):**
$357.9 billion (2008 est.)
$341.2 billion (2007)
$314.7 billion (2006)
*note:* data are in 2008 US dollars
**GDP (official exchange rate):** $331.8 billion (2008 est.)
**GDP - real growth rate:**
4.9% (2008 est.)
8.4% (2007 est.)
10.3% (2006 est.)
**GDP - per capita (PPP):**
$13,500 (2008 est.)
$13,100 (2007 est.)
$12,300 (2006 est.)
*note:* data are in 2008 US dollars
**GDP - composition by sector:**
*agriculture:* 3.6%
*industry:* 35.3%
*services:* 61.1% (2008 est.)
**Labor force:** 12.49 million (2008 est.)
**Labor force - by occupation:**
*agriculture:* 13%
*industry:* 23%
*services:* 64% (1997 est.)
**Unemployment rate:**
8.5% (2008 est.)
8.5% (2007 est.)

# Venezuela (continued)

**Population below poverty line:** 37.9% (end 2005 est.)

**Household income or consumption by percentage share:**
*lowest 10%:* 0.7%
*highest 10%:* 35.2% (2003)

**Distribution of family income - Gini index:** 48.2 (2003)

**Investment (gross fixed):** 20.5% of GDP (2008 est.)

**Budget:**
*revenues:* $106.2 billion
*expenditures:* $100.8 billion (2008 est.)

**Public debt:** 17.4% of GDP (2008 est.)

**Inflation rate (consumer prices):**
31% (2008 est.)
18.7% (2007 est.)

**Central bank discount rate:** 28.5% (31 December 2007)

**Commercial bank prime lending rate:** 17.11% (31 December 2007)

**Stock of money:** $63.18 billion (31 December 2007)

**Stock of quasi money:** $8.889 billion (31 December 2007)

**Stock of domestic credit:** $50.24 billion (31 December 2007)

**Market value of publicly traded shares:** $8.251 billion (2006)

**Agriculture - products:** corn, sorghum, sugarcane, rice, bananas, vegetables, coffee; beef, pork, milk, eggs; fish

**Industries:** petroleum, construction materials, food processing, textiles; iron ore mining, steel, aluminum; motor vehicle assembly

**Industrial production growth rate:** -3.3% (2008 est.)

**Electricity - production:** 110.7 billion kWh (2007 est.)

**Electricity - consumption:** 83.84 billion kWh (2006 est.)

**Electricity - exports:** 542 million kWh (2006 est.)

**Electricity - imports:** 0 kWh (2007 est.)

**Oil - production:** 2.667 million bbl/day (2007 est.)

**Oil - consumption:** 738,300 bbl/day (2007 est.)

**Oil - exports:** 2.203 million bbl/day (2006 est.)

**Oil - imports:** 0 bbl/day (2006 est.)

**Oil - proved reserves:** 87.04 billion bbl (1 January 2008 est.)

**Natural gas - production:** 26.5 billion cu m (2007 est.)

**Natural gas - consumption:** 26.5 billion cu m (2007 est.)

**Natural gas - exports:** 0 cu m (2007 est.)

**Natural gas - imports:** 0 cu m (2007 est.)

**Natural gas - proved reserves:** 4.708 trillion cu m (1 January 2008 est.)

**Current account balance:** $48.44 billion (2008 est.)

**Exports:** $103.5 billion f.o.b. (2008 est.)

**Exports - commodities:** petroleum, bauxite and aluminum, steel, chemicals, agricultural products, basic manufactures

**Exports - partners:** US 42.7%, Netherlands Antilles 8%, China 3.1% (2007)

**Imports:** $53.44 billion f.o.b. (2008 est.)

**Imports - commodities:** raw materials, machinery and equipment, transport equipment, construction materials

**Imports - partners:** US 26.6%, Colombia 13.5%, Brazil 9.5%, China 6.7%, Mexico 5.2%, Panama 5% (2007)

**Reserves of foreign exchange and gold:** $36.36 billion (31 December 2008 est.)

**Debt - external:** $47.99 billion (31 December 2008 est.)

**Stock of direct foreign investment - at home:** $44.31 billion (2008 est.)

**Stock of direct foreign investment - abroad:** $15.81 billion (2008 est.)

**Exchange rates:** bolivars (VEB) per US dollar - 2.147 (2008 est.), 2,147 (2007), 2,147 (2006), 2,089.8 (2005), 1,891.3 (2004)
*note:* on 1 January 2008 Venezuela revalued its currency with 1000 old bolivares equal to 1 new bolivar

## Communications

**Telephones - main lines in use:** 5.082 million (2007)

**Telephones - mobile cellular:** 23.82 million (2007)

**Telephone system:**
*general assessment:* modern and expanding
*domestic:* domestic satellite system with 3 earth stations; recent substantial improvement in telephone service in rural areas; substantial increase in digitalization of exchanges and trunk lines; installation of a national interurban fiber-optic network capable of digital multimedia services; fixed-line teledensity 20 per 100 persons; mobile-cellular teledensity more than 90 per 100 persons
*international:* country code - 58; submarine cable systems provide connectivity to the Caribbean, Central and South America, and US; satellite earth stations - 1 Intelsat (Atlantic Ocean) and 1 PanAmSat; participating with Colombia, Ecuador, Peru, and Bolivia in the construction of an international fiber-optic network (2007)

**Radio broadcast stations:** AM 201, FM unknown, but at least 25 in Caracas, shortwave 11 (1998)

**Television broadcast stations:** 66 (plus 45 repeaters) (1997)

**Internet country code:** .ve

**Internet hosts:** 145,394 (2008)

**Internet users:** 5.72 million (2007)

## Transportation

**Airports:** 402 (2008)

**Airports - with paved runways:**
*total:* 131
*over 3,047 m:* 5
*2,438 to 3,047 m:* 9
*1,524 to 2,437 m:* 35
*914 to 1,523 m:* 64
*under 914 m:* 18 (2008)

**Airports - with unpaved runways:**
*total:* 271
*2,438 to 3,047 m:* 1
*1,524 to 2,437 m:* 16
*914 to 1,523 m:* 102
*under 914 m:* 152 (2008)

**Heliports:** 2 (2007)

**Pipelines:** extra heavy crude 980 km; gas 5,036 km; oil 6,695 km; refined products 1,484 km; unknown 141 km(2008)

**Railways:**
*total:* 682 km
*standard gauge:* 682 km 1.435-m gauge (2006)

**Roadways:**
*total:* 96,155 km
*paved:* 32,308 km
*unpaved:* 63,847 km (2002)

**Waterways:** 7,100 km
*note:* Orinoco River (400 km) and Lake de Maracaibo navigable by oceangoing vessels (2008)

**Merchant marine:**
*total:* 62
*by type:* bulk carrier 9, cargo 16, chemical tanker 3, liquefied gas 5, passenger/cargo 10, petroleum tanker 17, refrigerated cargo 2
*foreign-owned:* 12 (Chile 1, Denmark 1, Greece 3, Mexico 5, Panama 1, Spain 1)
*registered in other countries:* 12 (Bahamas 1, Panama 10, Saint Vincent and the Grenadines 1) (2008)

**Ports and terminals:** La Guaira, Maracaibo, Puerto Cabello, Punta Cardon

**Transportation - note:** the International Maritime Bureau reports the territorial and offshore waters in the Caribbean Sea as a significant risk for piracy and armed robbery against ships; numerous vessels, including commercial shipping and pleasure craft, have been attacked and hijacked both at anchor and while underway; crews have been robbed and stores or cargoes stolen

## Military

**Military branches:** National Bolivarian Armed Forces (Fuerza Armada Nacional Bolivariana, FANB): National Bolivarian Army (Ejercito Nacional Bolivariano, ENB), Bolivarian Navy (Fuerza Armada Bolivariana (FAB); includes Naval Infantry, Coast Guard, Naval Aviation), Bolivarian National Military Aviation (Aviacion Militar Nacional Bolivariana, AMNB), Bolivarian National Guard (Guardia Nacional Bolivaria, GNB) (2009)

**Military service age and obligation:** 18-30 years of age for compulsory and voluntary military service; 30-month conscript service obligation; all citizens 18-50 years old are obligated to register for military service (2008)

**Manpower available for military service:**
*males age 16-49:* 6,647,124
*females age 16-49:* 6,801,133 (2008 est.)

**Manpower fit for military service:**
*males age 16-49:* 5,391,582
*females age 16-49:* 5,873,563 (2009 est.)

# Venezuela (continued)

**Manpower reaching militarily significant age annually:**
*male:* 276,051
*female:* 274,162 (2009 est.)
**Military expenditures:** 1.2% of GDP (2005 est.)

## Transnational Issues

**Disputes - international:** claims all of the area west of the Essequibo River in Guyana, preventing any discussion of a maritime boundary; Guyana has expressed its intention to join Barbados in asserting claims before the United Nations Convention on the Law of the Sea (UNCLOS) that Trinidad and Tobago's maritime boundary with Venezuela extends into their waters; dispute with Colombia over maritime boundary and Venezuelan-administered Los Monjes islands near the Gulf of Venezuela; Colombian-organized illegal narcotics and paramilitary activities penetrate Venezuela's shared border region; in 2006, an estimated 139,000 Colombians sought protection in 150 communities along the border in Venezuela; US, France, and the Netherlands recognize Venezuela's granting full effect to Aves Island, thereby claiming a Venezuelan EEZ/continental shelf extending over a large portion of the eastern Caribbean Sea; Dominica, Saint Kitts and Nevis, Saint Lucia, and Saint Vincent and the Grenadines protest Venezuela's full effect claim

**Trafficking in persons:**
*current situation:* Venezuela is a source, transit, and destination country for men, women, and children trafficked for the purposes of commercial sexual exploitation and forced labor; Venezuelan women and girls are trafficked within the country for sexual exploitation, lured from the nation's interior to urban and tourist areas; child prostitution in urban areas and child sex tourism in resort destinations appear to be growing; Venezuelan women and girls are trafficked for commercial sexual exploitation to Western Europe, Mexico, and Caribbean destinations
*tier rating:* Tier 2 Watch List - Venezuela is placed on the Tier 2 Watch List, up from Tier 3, as it showed greater resolve to address trafficking through law enforcement measures and prevention efforts in 2007, although stringent punishment of offenders and victim assistance remain lacking (2008)

**Illicit drugs:** small-scale illicit producer of opium and coca for the processing of opiates and coca derivatives; however, large quantities of cocaine, heroin, and marijuana transit the country from Colombia bound for US and Europe; significant narcotics-related money-laundering activity, especially along the border with Colombia and on Margarita Island; active eradication program primarily targeting opium; increasing signs of drug-related activities by Colombian insurgents on border

# Vietnam

## Introduction

**Background:** The conquest of Vietnam by France began in 1858 and was completed by 1884. It became part of French Indochina in 1887. Vietnam declared independence after World War II, but France continued to rule until its 1954 defeat by Communist forces under Ho Chi MINH. Under the Geneva Accords of 1954, Vietnam was divided into the Communist North and anti-Communist South. US economic and military aid to South Vietnam grew through the 1960s in an attempt to bolster the government, but US armed forces were withdrawn following a cease-fire agreement in 1973. Two years later, North Vietnamese forces overran the South reuniting the country under Communist rule. Despite the return of peace, for over a decade the country experienced little economic growth because of conservative leadership policies, the persecution and mass exodus of individuals - many of them successful South Vietnamese merchants - and growing international isolation. However, since the enactment of Vietnam's "doi moi" (renovation) policy in 1986, Vietnamese authorities have committed to increased economic liberalization and enacted structural reforms needed to modernize the economy and to produce more competitive, export-driven industries. The country continues to experience small-scale protests from various groups, the vast majority connected to land-use issues and the lack of equitable mechanisms for resolving disputes. Various ethnic minorities, such as the Montagnards of the Central Highlands and the Khmer Krom in the southern delta region, have also held protests. In January 2008, Vietnam assumed a nonpermanent seat on the UN Security Council for the 2008-09 term.

## Geography

**Location:** Southeastern Asia, bordering the Gulf of Thailand, Gulf of Tonkin, and South China Sea, alongside China, Laos, and Cambodia
**Geographic coordinates:** 16 10 N, 107 50 E
**Map references:** Southeast Asia
**Area:**
*total:* 329,560 sq km
*land:* 325,360 sq km
*water:* 4,200 sq km
**Area - comparative:** slightly larger than New Mexico
**Land boundaries:**
*total:* 4,639 km
*border countries:* Cambodia 1,228 km, China 1,281 km, Laos 2,130 km
**Coastline:** 3,444 km (excludes islands)
**Maritime claims:**
*territorial sea:* 12 nm
*contiguous zone:* 24 nm
*exclusive economic zone:* 200 nm
*continental shelf:* 200 nm or to the edge of the continental margin
**Climate:** tropical in south; monsoonal in north with hot, rainy season (May to September) and warm, dry season (October to March)
**Terrain:** low, flat delta in south and north; central highlands; hilly, mountainous in far north and northwest
**Elevation extremes:**
*lowest point:* South China Sea 0 m
*highest point:* Fan Si Pan 3,144 m
**Natural resources:** phosphates, coal, manganese, bauxite, chromate, offshore oil and gas deposits, forests, hydropower
**Land use:**
*arable land:* 20.14%
*permanent crops:* 6.93%
*other:* 72.93% (2005)
**Irrigated land:** 30,000 sq km (2003)
**Total renewable water resources:** 891.2 cu km (1999)
**Freshwater withdrawal (domestic/industrial/agricultural):**
*total:* 71.39 cu km/yr (8%/24%/68%)
*per capita:* 847 cu m/yr (2000)

# Vietnam (continued)

**Natural hazards:** occasional typhoons (May to January) with extensive flooding, especially in the Mekong River delta

**Environment - current issues:** logging and slash-and-burn agricultural practices contribute to deforestation and soil degradation; water pollution and overfishing threaten marine life populations; groundwater contamination limits potable water supply; growing urban industrialization and population migration are rapidly degrading environment in Hanoi and Ho Chi Minh City

**Environment - international agreements:**
*party to:* Biodiversity, Climate Change, Climate Change-Kyoto Protocol, Desertification, Endangered Species, Environmental Modification, Hazardous Wastes, Law of the Sea, Ozone Layer Protection, Ship Pollution, Wetlands
*signed, but not ratified:* none of the selected agreements

**Geography - note:** extending 1,650 km north to south, the country is only 50 km across at its narrowest point

## People

**Population:** 86,967,524 (July 2009 est.)
**Age structure:**
*0-14 years:* 24.9% (male 11,230,402/female 10,423,901)
*15-64 years:* 69.4% (male 29,971,088/female 30,356,393)
*65 years and over:* 5.7% (male 1,920,043/female 3,065,697) (2009 est.)
**Median age:**
*total:* 27.4 years
*male:* 26.4 years
*female:* 28.5 years (2009 est.)
**Population growth rate:** 0.977% (2009 est.)
**Birth rate:** 16.31 births/1,000 population (2009 est.)
**Death rate:** 6.18 deaths/1,000 population (2008 est.)
**Net migration rate:** -0.38 migrant(s)/1,000 population (2009 est.)
**Urbanization:**
*urban population:* 28% of total population (2008)
*rate of urbanization:* 3.1% annual rate of change (2005-10 est.)
**Sex ratio:**
*at birth:* 1.07 male(s)/female
*under 15 years:* 1.08 male(s)/female
*15-64 years:* 0.99 male(s)/female
*65 years and over:* 0.63 male(s)/female
*total population:* 0.98 male(s)/female (2009 est.)
**Infant mortality rate:**
*total:* 22.88 deaths/1,000 live births
*male:* 23.27 deaths/1,000 live births
*female:* 22.46 deaths/1,000 live births (2009 est.)
**Life expectancy at birth:**
*total population:* 71.58 years
*male:* 68.78 years
*female:* 74.57 years (2009 est.)
**Total fertility rate:** 1.83 children born/woman (2009 est.)

**HIV/AIDS - adult prevalence rate:** 0.5% (2007 est.)
**HIV/AIDS - people living with HIV/AIDS:** 290,000 (2007 est.)
**HIV/AIDS - deaths:** 24,000 (2007 est.)
**Major infectious diseases:**
*degree of risk:* high
*food or waterborne diseases:* bacterial diarrhea, hepatitis A, and typhoid fever
*vectorborne diseases:* dengue fever, malaria, Japanese encephalitis, and plague
*water contact disease:* leptospirosis
*note:* highly pathogenic H5N1 avian influenza has been identified in this country; it poses a negligible risk with extremely rare cases possible among US citizens who have close contact with birds (2009)
**Nationality:**
*noun:* Vietnamese (singular and plural)
*adjective:* Vietnamese
**Ethnic groups:** Kinh (Viet) 86.2%, Tay 1.9%, Thai 1.7%, Muong 1.5%, Khome 1.4%, Hoa 1.1%, Nun 1.1%, Hmong 1%, others 4.1% (1999 census)
**Religions:** Buddhist 9.3%, Catholic 6.7%, Hoa Hao 1.5%, Cao Dai 1.1%, Protestant 0.5%, Muslim 0.1%, none 80.8% (1999 census)
**Languages:** Vietnamese (official), English (increasingly favored as a second language), some French, Chinese, and Khmer; mountain area languages (Mon-Khmer and Malayo-Polynesian)
**Literacy:**
*definition:* age 15 and over can read and write
*total population:* 90.3%
*male:* 93.9%
*female:* 86.9% (2002 est.)
**School life expectancy (primary to tertiary education):**
*total:* 10 years
*male:* 11 years
*female:* 10 years (2000)
**Education expenditures:** 1.8% of GDP (1991)

## Government

**Country name:**
*conventional long form:* Socialist Republic of Vietnam
*conventional short form:* Vietnam
*local long form:* Cong Hoa Xa Hoi Chu Nghia Viet Nam
*local short form:* Viet Nam
*abbreviation:* SRV
**Government type:** Communist state
**Capital:**
*name:* Hanoi (Ha Noi)
*geographic coordinates:* 21 02 N, 105 51 E
*time difference:* UTC+7 (12 hours ahead of Washington, DC during Standard Time)
**Administrative divisions:** 59 provinces (tinh, singular and plural) and 5 municipalities (thanh pho, singular and plural)
*provinces:* An Giang, Bac Giang, Bac Kan, Bac Lieu, Bac Ninh, Ba Ria-Vung Tau, Ben Tre, Binh Dinh, Binh Duong, Binh Phuoc, Binh Thuan, Ca Mau, Cao Bang, Da Nang*, Dac Lak, Dac Nong, Dien Bien, Dong Nai,

Dong Thap, Gia Lai, Ha Giang, Ha Nam, Ha Tay, Ha Tinh, Hai Duong, Hau Giang, Hoa Binh, Hung Yen, Khanh Hoa, Kien Giang, Kon Tum, Lai Chau, Lam Dong, Lang Son, Lao Cai, Long An, Nam Dinh, Nghe An, Ninh Binh, Ninh Thuan, Phu Tho, Phu Yen, Quang Binh, Quang Nam, Quang Ngai, Quang Ninh, Quang Tri, Soc Trang, Son La, Tay Ninh, Thai Binh, Thai Nguyen, Thanh Hoa, Thua Thien-Hue, Tien Giang, Tra Vinh, Tuyen Quang, Vinh Long, Vinh Phuc, Yen Bai
*municipalities:* Can Tho, Da Nang, Ha Noi, Ho Chi Minh,
**Independence:** 2 September 1945 (from France)
**National holiday:** Independence Day, 2 September (1945)
**Constitution:** 15 April 1992
**Legal system:** based on communist legal theory and French civil law system; has not accepted compulsory ICJ jurisdiction
**Suffrage:** 18 years of age; universal
**Executive branch:**
*chief of state:* President Nguyen Minh TRIET (since 27 June 2006); Vice President Nguyen Thi DOAN (since 25 July 2007)
*head of government:* Prime Minister Nguyen Tan DUNG (since 27 June 2006); Permanent Deputy Prime Minister Nguyen Sinh HUNG (since 28 June 2006), Deputy Prime Minister Hoang Trung HAI (since 2 August 2007), Deputy Prime Minister Nguyen Thien NHAN (since 2 August 2007), Deputy Prime Minister Pham Gia KHIEM (since 28 June 2006), and Deputy Prime Minister Truong Vinh TRONG (since 28 June 2006)
*cabinet:* Cabinet appointed by president based on proposal of prime minister and confirmed by National Assembly
*elections:* president elected by the National Assembly from among its members for five-year term; last held 27 June 2006 (next to be held in 2011); prime minister appointed by the president from among the members of the National Assembly; deputy prime ministers appointed by the prime minister; appointment of prime minister and deputy prime ministers confirmed by National Assembly
*election results:* Nguyen Minh TRIET elected president; percent of National Assembly vote - 94%; Nguyen Tan DUNG elected prime minister; percent of National Assembly vote - 92%
**Legislative branch:** unicameral National Assembly or Quoc Hoi (500 seats; members elected by popular vote to serve five-year terms)
*elections:* last held 20 May 2007 (next to be held in May 2012)
*election results:* percent of vote by party - NA; seats by party - CPV 450, non-party CPV-approved 42, self-nominated 1; note - 493 candidates were elected; CPV and non-party CPV-approved delegates were members of the Vietnamese Fatherland Front
**Judicial branch:** Supreme People's Court (chief justice is elected for a five-year term by the National Assembly on the recommendation of the president)
**Political parties and leaders:** Communist Party of Vietnam or CPV [Nong Duc MANH]; other parties proscribed

# Vietnam (continued)

**Political pressure groups and leaders:** 8406 Bloc; Democratic Party of Vietnam or DPV; People's Democratic Party Vietnam or PDP-VN; Alliance for Democracy

*note:* these groups advocate democracy but are not recognized by the government

**International organization participation:** ADB, APEC, APT, ARF, ASEAN, CP, EAS, FAO, G-77, IAEA, IBRD, ICAO, ICRM, IDA, IFAD, IFC, IFRCS, ILO, IMF, IMO, IMSO, Interpol, IOC, IOM, IPU, ISO, ITSO, ITU, MIGA, NAM, OIF, OPCW, UN, UNCTAD, UNESCO, UNIDO, UNWTO, UPU, WCL, WCO, WFTU, WHO, WIPO, WMO, WTO

**Diplomatic representation in the US:**
*chief of mission:* Ambassador Le Cong PHUNG
*chancery:* 1233 20th Street NW, Suite 400, Washington, DC 20036
*telephone:* [1] (202) 861-0737
*FAX:* [1] (202) 861-0917
*consulate(s) general:* San Francisco

**Diplomatic representation from the US:**
*chief of mission:* Ambassador Michael W. MICHALAK
*embassy:* 7 Lang Ha Street, Ba Dinh District, Hanoi
*mailing address:* PSC 461, Box 400, FPO AP 96521-0002
*telephone:* [84] (4) 3850-5000
*FAX:* [84] (4) 3850-5010
*consulate(s) general:* Ho Chi Minh City

**Flag description:** red field with a large yellow five-pointed star in the center

## Economy

**Economy - overview:** Vietnam is a densely-populated developing country that in the last 30 years has had to recover from the ravages of war, the loss of financial support from the old Soviet Bloc, and the rigidities of a centrally-planned economy. Since 2001, Vietnamese authorities have reaffirmed their commitment to economic liberalization and international integration. They have moved to implement the structural reforms needed to modernize the economy and to produce more competitive export-driven industries. Vietnam's membership in the ASEAN Free Trade Area (AFTA) and entry into force of the US-Vietnam Bilateral Trade Agreement in December 2001 have led to even more rapid changes in Vietnam's trade and economic regime. Vietnam's exports to the US increased 900% from 2001 to 2007. Vietnam joined the WTO in January 2007 following over a decade long negotiation process. WTO membership has provided Vietnam an anchor to the global market and reinforced the domestic economic reform process. Among other benefits, accession allows Vietnam to take advantage of the phase-out of the Agreement on Textiles and Clothing, which eliminated quotas on textiles and clothing for WTO partners on 1 January 2005. Agriculture's share of economic output has continued to shrink from about 25% in 2000 to less than 20% in 2008. Deep poverty has declined significantly and is now smaller than that of China, India, and the

Philippines. Vietnam is working to create jobs to meet the challenge of a labor force that is growing by more than one-and-a-half million people every year. The global financial crisis, however, will constrain Vietnam's ability to create jobs and further reduce poverty. As global growth sharply drops in 2009, Vietnam's export-oriented economy - exports were 68% of GDP in 2007 - will suffer from lower exports, higher unemployment and corporate bankruptcies, and decreased foreign investment. Real GDP growth for 2009 could fall between 4% and 5%. Inflation, which reached nearly 25% in 2008, will likely moderate to single digits in 2009.

**GDP (purchasing power parity):**
$241.8 billion (2008 est.)
$227.7 billion (2007)
$209.8 billion (2006)
*note:* data are in 2008 US dollars

**GDP (official exchange rate):** $90.88 billion (2008 est.)

**GDP - real growth rate:**
6.2% (2008 est.)
8.5% (2007 est.)
8.2% (2006 est.)

**GDP - per capita (PPP):**
$2,800 (2008 est.)
$2,700 (2007 est.)
$2,500 (2006 est.)
*note:* data are in 2008 US dollars

**GDP - composition by sector:**
*agriculture:* 19%
*industry:* 42.7%
*services:* 38.4% (2008 est.)

**Labor force:** 47.41 million (2008 est.)

**Labor force - by occupation:**
*agriculture:* 55.6%
*industry:* 18.9%
*services:* 25.5% (July 2005)

**Unemployment rate:**
4.9% (2008 est.)
4.3% (2007 est.)

**Population below poverty line:** 14.8% (2007 est.)

**Household income or consumption by percentage share:**
*lowest 10%:* 2.9%
*highest 10%:* 28.9% (2004)

**Distribution of family income - Gini index:** 37 (2004)

**Investment (gross fixed):** 44.5% of GDP (2008 est.)

**Budget:**
*revenues:* $22.39 billion
*expenditures:* $24.19 billion (2008 est.)

**Public debt:** 38.6% of GDP (2008 est.)

**Inflation rate (consumer prices):**
24.5% (2008 est.)
8.3% (2007 est.)

**Central bank discount rate:** 6.5% (31 December 2007)

**Commercial bank prime lending rate:** 11.18% (31 December 2007)

**Stock of money:** $27.15 billion (31 December 2007)

**Stock of quasi money:** $51.08 billion (31 December 2007)

**Stock of domestic credit:** $68.63 billion (31 December 2007)

**Market value of publicly traded shares:** $19.54 billion (31 December 2007)

**Agriculture - products:** paddy rice, coffee, rubber, cotton, tea, pepper, soybeans, cashews, sugar cane, peanuts, bananas; poultry; fish, seafood

**Industries:** food processing, garments, shoes, machine-building; mining, coal, steel; cement, chemical fertilizer, glass, tires, oil, paper

**Industrial production growth rate:** 7% (2008 est.)

**Electricity - production:** 61.02 billion kWh (2007 est.)

**Electricity - consumption:** 48.08 billion kWh (2006 est.)

**Electricity - exports:** 0 kWh (2007 est.)

**Electricity - imports:** 0 kWh (2007 est.)

**Oil - production:** 350,700 bbl/day (2007 est.)

**Oil - consumption:** 271,100 bbl/day (2007 est.)

**Oil - exports:** 394,400 bbl/day (2005)

**Oil - imports:** 271,100 bbl/day (2007)

**Oil - proved reserves:** 600 million bbl (1 January 2008 est.)

**Natural gas - production:** 6.86 billion cu m (2007 est.)

**Natural gas - consumption:** 6.86 billion cu m (2007 est.)

**Natural gas - exports:** 0 cu m (2007 est.)

**Natural gas - imports:** 0 cu m (2007 est.)

**Natural gas - proved reserves:** 192.5 billion cu m (1 January 2008 est.)

**Current account balance:** -$12.74 billion (2008 est.)

**Exports:** $63.73 billion f.o.b. (2008 est.)

**Exports - commodities:** crude oil, marine products, rice, coffee, rubber, tea, garments, shoes

**Exports - partners:** US 20.8%, Japan 12.5%, Australia 7.3%, China 6.9%, Singapore 4.5% (2007)

**Imports:** $79.37 billion f.o.b. (2008 est.)

**Imports - commodities:** machinery and equipment, petroleum products, fertilizer, steel products, raw cotton, grain, cement, motorcycles

**Imports - partners:** China 19.9%, Singapore 12.1%, Taiwan 11%, Japan 9.9%, South Korea 8.5%, Thailand 6% (2007)

**Reserves of foreign exchange and gold:** $22.78 billion (31 December 2008 est.)

**Debt - external:** $23.72 billion (31 December 2008 est.)

**Stock of direct foreign investment - at home:** $43.06 billion (2008 est.)

**Stock of direct foreign investment - abroad:** $NA

**Exchange rates:** dong (VND) per US dollar - 16,548.3 (2008 est.), 16,119 (2007), 15,983 (2006), 15,746 (2005), NA (2004)

## Communications

**Telephones - main lines in use:** 10.8 million (2007)
**Telephones - mobile cellular:** 33.2 million (2007)
**Telephone system:** ⸌

*general assessment:* Vietnam is putting considerable effort into modernization and expansion of its telecommunication system, but its performance continues to lag behind that of its more modern neighbors

*domestic:* all provincial exchanges are digitalized and connected to Hanoi, Da Nang, and Ho Chi Minh City by fiber-optic cable or microwave radio relay networks; main lines have been substantially increased, and the use of mobile telephones is growing rapidly

*international:* country code - 84; a landing point for the SEA-ME-WE-3, the C2C, and Thailand-Vietnam-Hong Kong submarine cable systems; the Asia-America Gateway submarine cable system, scheduled for completion by the end of 2008, will provide new access links to Asia and the US; satellite earth stations - 2 Intersputnik (Indian Ocean region)

**Radio broadcast stations:** AM 65, FM 7, shortwave 29 (1999)

**Television broadcast stations:** 67 (includes 61 relay, provincial, and city TV stations) (2006)

**Internet country code:** .vn
**Internet hosts:** 84,151 (2008)
**Internet users:** 17.87 million (2007)

## Transportation

**Airports:** 44 (2008)
**Airports - with paved runways:**
*total:* 37
*over 3,047 m:* 9
*2,438 to 3,047 m:* 5
*1,524 to 2,437 m:* 14
*914 to 1,523 m:* 9 (2008)
**Airports - with unpaved runways:**
*total:* 7
*1,524 to 2,437 m:* 1
*914 to 1,523 m:* 3
*under 914 m:* 3 (2008)
**Heliports:** 1 (2007)
**Pipelines:** condensate/gas 42 km; gas 66 km; refined products 206 km (2008)
**Railways:**
*total:* 2,600 km
*standard gauge:* 178 km 1.435-m gauge
*narrow gauge:* 2,169 km 1.000-m gauge
*dual gauge:* 253 km three-rail track combining 1.435 m and 1.000-m gauges (2006)
**Roadways:**
*total:* 222,179 km
*paved:* 42,167 km
*unpaved:* 180,012 km (2004)
**Waterways:** 17,702 km (5,000 km navigable by vessels up to 1.8 m draft) (2008)

**Merchant marine:**
*total:* 387
*by type:* barge carrier 1, bulk carrier 36, cargo 280, chemical tanker 12, container 14, liquefied gas 6, passenger 1, passenger/cargo 1, petroleum tanker 32, refrigerated cargo 2, roll on/roll off 1, specialized tanker 1
*foreign-owned:* 2 (Hong Kong 1, Japan 1)
*registered in other countries:* 64 (Honduras 1, Liberia 4, Mongolia 23, Panama 30, Tuvalu 5, unknown 1) (2008)
**Ports and terminals:** Da Nang, Hai Phong, Ho Chi Minh City
**Transportation - note:** the International Maritime Bureau reports the territorial and offshore waters in the South China Sea as high risk for piracy and armed robbery against ships; numerous commercial vessels have been attacked and hijacked both at anchor and while underway; hijacked vessels are often disguised and cargo diverted to ports in East Asia; crews have been murdered or cast adrift

## Military

**Military branches:** People's Armed Forces: People's Army of Vietnam (PAVN) (includes People's Navy Command (with naval infantry, coast guard), Air and Air Defense Force (Kon Quan Nhan Dan), Border Defense Command), People's Public Security Forces, Militia Force, Self-Defense Forces (2005)

**Military service age and obligation:** 18 years of age (male) for compulsory military service; females may volunteer for active duty military service; conscript service obligation - 2 years (3 to 4 years in the navy); 18-45 years of age (male) or 18-40 years of age (female) for Militia Force or Self Defense Forces (2006)

**Manpower available for military service:**
*males age 16-49:* 24,586,328
*females age 16-49:* 24,335,132 (2008 est.)
**Manpower fit for military service:**
*males age 16-49:* 19,190,676
*females age 16-49:* 20,768,508 (2009 est.)
**Manpower reaching militarily significant age annually:**
*male:* 893,726
*female:* 834,279 (2009 est.)
**Military expenditures:** 2.5% of GDP (2005 est.)

## Transnational Issues

**Disputes - international:** southeast Asian states have enhanced border surveillance to check the spread of avian flu; Cambodia and Laos protest Vietnamese squatters and armed encroachments along border; an estimated 300,000 Vietnamese refugees reside in China; establishment of a maritime boundary with Cambodia is hampered by unresolved dispute over the sovereignty of offshore islands; demarcation of the China-Vietnam boundary proceeds slowly and although the maritime boundary delimitation and fisheries agreements were ratified in June 2004, implementation has been delayed; China occupies the Paracel Islands also claimed by Vietnam and Taiwan; involved in complex dispute with China, Malaysia, Philippines, Taiwan, and possibly Brunei over the Spratly Islands; the 2002 "Declaration on the Conduct of Parties in the South China Sea" has eased tensions but falls short of a legally binding "code of conduct" desired by several of the disputants; Vietnam continues to expand construction of facilities in the Spratly Islands; in March 2005, the national oil companies of China, the Philippines, and Vietnam signed a joint accord to conduct marine seismic activities in the Spratly Islands

**Illicit drugs:** minor producer of opium poppy; probable minor transit point for Southeast Asian heroin; government continues to face domestic opium/heroin/methamphetamine addiction problems despite longstanding crackdowns

# Virgin Islands
*(territory of the US)*

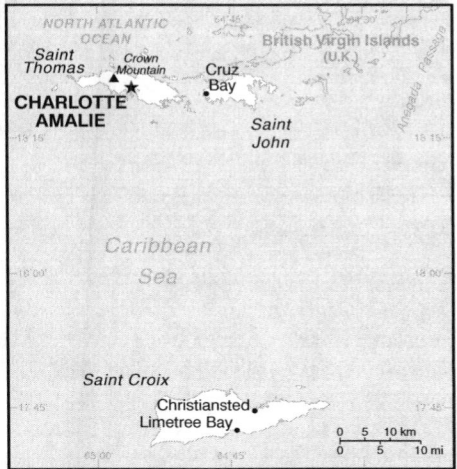

## Introduction

**Background:** During the 17th century, the archipelago was divided into two territorial units, one English and the other Danish. Sugarcane, produced by slave labor, drove the islands' economy during the 18th and early 19th centuries. In 1917, the US purchased the Danish portion, which had been in economic decline since the abolition of slavery in 1848.

## Geography

**Location:** Caribbean, islands between the Caribbean Sea and the North Atlantic Ocean, east of Puerto Rico
**Geographic coordinates:** 18 20 N, 64 50 W
**Map references:** Central America and the Caribbean
**Area:**
*total:* 1,910 sq km
*land:* 346 sq km
*water:* 1,564 sq km
**Area - comparative:** twice the size of Washington, DC
**Land boundaries:** 0 km
**Coastline:** 188 km
**Maritime claims:**
*territorial sea:* 12 nm
*exclusive economic zone:* 200 nm
**Climate:** subtropical, tempered by easterly trade winds, relatively low humidity, little seasonal temperature variation; rainy season September to November
**Terrain:** mostly hilly to rugged and mountainous with little level land
**Elevation extremes:**
*lowest point:* Caribbean Sea 0 m
*highest point:* Crown Mountain 475 m
**Natural resources:** sun, sand, sea, surf
**Land use:**
*arable land:* 5.71%
*permanent crops:* 2.86%
*other:* 91.43% (2005)

**Irrigated land:** NA
**Natural hazards:** several hurricanes in recent years; frequent and severe droughts and floods; occasional earthquakes
**Environment - current issues:** lack of natural freshwater resources
**Geography - note:** important location along the Anegada Passage - a key shipping lane for the Panama Canal; Saint Thomas has one of the best natural deepwater harbors in the Caribbean

## People

**Population:** 109,825 (July 2009 est.)
**Age structure:**
*0-14 years:* 20.4% (male 11,394/female 11,048)
*15-64 years:* 65.9% (male 33,843/female 38,574)
*65 years and over:* 13.6% (male 6,747/female 8,219) (2009 est.)
**Median age:**
*total:* 39.1 years
*male:* 38.6 years
*female:* 39.6 years (2009 est.)
**Population growth rate:** -0.029% (2009 est.)
**Birth rate:** 11.95 births/1,000 population (2009 est.)
**Death rate:** 6.55 deaths/1,000 population (2008 est.)
**Net migration rate:** -5.49 migrant(s)/1,000 population (2009 est.)
**Urbanization:**
*urban population:* 95% of total population (2008)
*rate of urbanization:* 0.2% annual rate of change (2005-10 est.)
**Sex ratio:**
*at birth:* 1.06 male(s)/female
*under 15 years:* 1.03 male(s)/female
*15-64 years:* 0.88 male(s)/female
*65 years and over:* 0.82 male(s)/female
*total population:* 0.9 male(s)/female (2009 est.)
**Infant mortality rate:**
*total:* 7.56 deaths/1,000 live births
*male:* 8.28 deaths/1,000 live births
*female:* 6.79 deaths/1,000 live births (2009 est.)
**Life expectancy at birth:**
*total population:* 79.05 years
*male:* 76.02 years
*female:* 82.26 years (2009 est.)
**Total fertility rate:** 1.85 children born/woman (2009 est.)
**HIV/AIDS - adult prevalence rate:** NA
**HIV/AIDS - people living with HIV/AIDS:** NA
**HIV/AIDS - deaths:** NA
**Nationality:**
*noun:* Virgin Islander(s) (US citizens)
*adjective:* Virgin Islander
**Ethnic groups:** black 76.2%, white 13.1%, Asian 1.1%, other 6.1%, mixed 3.5% (2000 census)
**Religions:** Baptist 42%, Roman Catholic 34%, Episcopalian 17%, other 7%
**Languages:** English 74.7%, Spanish or Spanish Creole 16.8%, French or French Creole 6.6%, other 1.9% (2000 census)

**Literacy:**
*definition:* age 15 and over can read and write
*total population:* 90-95% est.
*male:* NA
*female:* NA (2005 est.)
**Education expenditures:** NA

## Government

**Country name:**
*conventional long form:* United States Virgin Islands
*conventional short form:* Virgin Islands
*former:* Danish West Indies
*abbreviation:* USVI
**Dependency status:** organized, unincorporated territory of the US with policy relations between the Virgin Islands and the US under the jurisdiction of the Office of Insular Affairs, US Department of the Interior
**Government type:** NA
**Capital:**
*name:* Charlotte Amalie
*geographic coordinates:* 18 21 N, 64 56 W
*time difference:* UTC-4 (1 hour ahead of Washington, DC during Standard Time)
**Administrative divisions:** none (territory of the US); there are no first-order administrative divisions as defined by the US Government, but there are three islands at the second order; Saint Croix, Saint John, Saint Thomas
**Independence:** none (territory of the US)
**National holiday:** Transfer Day (from Denmark to the US), 31 March (1917)
**Constitution:** Revised Organic Act of 22 July 1954
**Legal system:** based on US laws
**Suffrage:** 18 years of age; universal; island residents are US citizens but do not vote in US presidential elections
**Executive branch:**
*chief of state:* President Barack H. OBAMA (since 20 January 2009); Vice President Joseph R. BIDEN (since 20 January 2009)
*head of government:* Governor John DeJONGH (since 1 January 2007)
*cabinet:* NA
*elections:* under the US Constitution, residents of unincorporated territories, such as the Virgin Islands, do not vote in elections for US president and vice president; however, they may vote in the Democratic and Republican presidential primary elections; governor and lieutenant governor elected on the same ticket by popular vote for four-year terms (eligible for a second term); election last held 7 and 21 November 2006 (next to be held November 2010)
*election results:* John DeJONGH elected governor; percent of vote - John DeJONGH 57.3%, Kenneth MAPP 42.7%
**Legislative branch:** unicameral Senate (15 seats; members are elected by popular vote to serve two-year terms)
*elections:* last held 7 November 2006 (next to be held in November 2008)
*election results:* percent of vote by party - NA; seats by party - Democratic Party 8, ICM 4, independent 3

# Virgin Islands *(continued)*

*note:* the Virgin Islands elects one non-voting representative to the US House of Representatives; election last held 7 November 2006 (next to be held in November 2008)

**Judicial branch:** US District Court of the Virgin Islands (under Third Circuit jurisdiction); Superior Court of the Virgin Islands (judges appointed by the governor for 10-year terms)

**Political parties and leaders:** Democratic Party [Arturo WATLINGTON]; Independent Citizens' Movement or ICM [Usie RICHARDS]; Republican Party [Gary SPRAUVE]

**Political pressure groups and leaders:** NA

**International organization participation:** IOC, UPU, WFTU

**Diplomatic representation in the US:** none (territory of the US)

**Diplomatic representation from the US:** none (territory of the US)

**Flag description:** white field with a modified US coat of arms in the center between the large blue initials V and I; the coat of arms shows a yellow eagle holding an olive branch in one talon and three arrows in the other with a superimposed shield of vertical red and white stripes below a blue panel

## Economy

**Economy - overview:** Tourism is the primary economic activity, accounting for 80% of GDP and employment. The islands hosted 2.6 million visitors in 2005. The manufacturing sector consists of petroleum refining, rum distilling, textiles, electronics, pharmaceuticals, and watch assembly. One of the world's largest petroleum refineries is at Saint Croix. The agricultural sector is small, with most food being imported. International business and financial services are small but growing components of the economy. The islands are vulnerable to substantial damage from storms. The government is working to improve fiscal discipline, to support construction projects in the private sector, to expand tourist facilities, to reduce crime, and to protect the environment.

**GDP (purchasing power parity):** $1.577 billion (2004 est.)

**GDP (official exchange rate):** $NA

**GDP - real growth rate:** 2% (2002 est.)

**GDP - per capita (PPP):** $14,500 (2004 est.)

**GDP - composition by sector:**
*agriculture:* 1%
*industry:* 19%
*services:* 80% (2003 est.)

**Labor force:** 43,980 (2004 est.)

**Labor force - by occupation:**
*agriculture:* 1%
*industry:* 19%
*services:* 80% (2003 est.)

**Unemployment rate:**
6.2% (2004)

**Population below poverty line:** 28.9% (2002)

**Household income or consumption by percentage share:**
*lowest 10%:* NA%
*highest 10%:* NA%

**Budget:**
*revenues:* $837 million
*expenditures:* $837 million (FY08/09)

**Inflation rate (consumer prices):**
2.2% (2003)

**Agriculture - products:** fruit, vegetables, sorghum; Senepol cattle

**Industries:** tourism, petroleum refining, watch assembly, rum distilling, construction, pharmaceuticals, textiles, electronics

**Industrial production growth rate:** NA%

**Electricity - production:** 960 million kWh (2006 est.)

**Electricity - consumption:** 892.8 million kWh (2006 est.)

**Electricity - exports:** 0 kWh (2007 est.)

**Electricity - imports:** 0 kWh (2007 est.)

**Oil - production:** 17,620 bbl/day (2007 est.)

**Oil - consumption:** 91,680 bbl/day (2007 est.)

**Oil - exports:** 398,500 bbl/day (2005)

**Oil - imports:** 492,300 bbl/day (2005)

**Oil - proved reserves:** NA bbl

**Natural gas - production:** 0 cu m (2007 est.)

**Natural gas - consumption:** 0 cu m (2007 est.)

**Natural gas - exports:** 0 cu m (2007 est.)

**Natural gas - imports:** 0 cu m (2007 est.)

**Natural gas - proved reserves:** 0 cu m (1 January 2006 est.)

**Exports:** $4.234 billion (2001)

**Exports - commodities:** refined petroleum products

**Imports:** $4.609 billion f.o.b. (2001)

**Imports - commodities:** crude oil, foodstuffs, consumer goods, building materials

**Debt - external:** $NA

**Exchange rates:** the US dollar is used

## Communications

**Telephones - main lines in use:** 71,700 (2005)

**Telephones - mobile cellular:** 80,300 (2005)

**Telephone system:**
*general assessment:* modern system with total digital switching, uses fiber-optic cable and microwave radio relay
*domestic:* full range of services available
*international:* country code - 1-340; submarine cable connections to US, the Caribbean, Central and South America; satellite earth stations - NA

**Radio broadcast stations:** AM 6, FM 16, shortwave 0 (2005)

**Television broadcast stations:** 5 (2006)

**Internet country code:** .vi

**Internet hosts:** 4,610 (2008)

**Internet users:** 30,000 (2007)

## Transportation

**Airports:** 2 (2008)

**Airports - with paved runways:**
*total:* 2
*over 3,047 m:* 1
*1,524 to 2,437 m:* 1 (2008)

**Roadways:**
*total:* 1,257 km (2007)

**Ports and terminals:** Charlotte Amalie, Limetree Bay

## Military

**Manpower fit for military service:**
*males age 16-49:* 17,820
*females age 16-49:* 21,193 (2009 est.)

**Manpower reaching militarily significant age annually:**
*male:* 831
*female:* 873 (2009 est.)

**Military - note:** defense is the responsibility of the US

## Transnational Issues

**Disputes - international:** none

# Wake Island
*(territory of the US)*

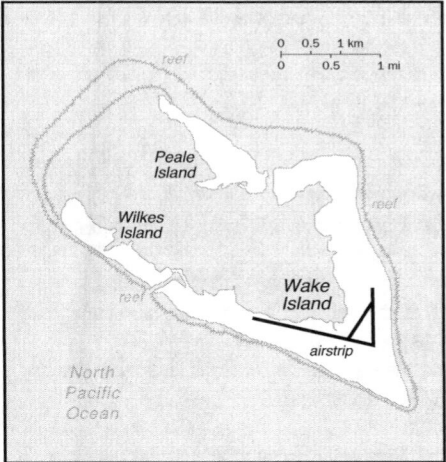

## Introduction

**Background:** The US annexed Wake Island in 1899 for a cable station. An important air and naval base was constructed in 1940-41. In December 1941, the island was captured by the Japanese and held until the end of World War II. In subsequent years, Wake was developed as a stopover and refueling site for military and commercial aircraft transiting the Pacific. Since 1974, the island's airstrip has been used by the US military, as well as for emergency landings. All operations on the island were suspended and all personnel evacuated in August 2006 with the approach of super typhoon IOKE (category 5), which struck the island with sustained winds of 250 kph and a 6 m storm surge inflicting major damage. A US Air Force assessment and repair team returned to the island in September and restored limited function to the airfield and facilities. The future status of activities on the island will be determined upon completion of the survey and assessment.

## Geography

**Location:** Oceania, atoll in the North Pacific Ocean, about two-thirds of the way from Hawaii to the Northern Mariana Islands
**Geographic coordinates:** 19 17 N, 166 39 E
**Map references:** Oceania
**Area:**
*total:* 6.5 sq km
*land:* 6.5 sq km
*water:* 0 sq km
**Area - comparative:** about 11 times the size of The Mall in Washington, DC
**Land boundaries:** 0 km
**Coastline:** 19.3 km
**Maritime claims:**
*territorial sea:* 12 nm
*exclusive economic zone:* 200 nm

**Climate:** tropical
**Terrain:** atoll of three low coral islands, Peale, Wake, and Wilkes, built up on an underwater volcano; central lagoon is former crater, islands are part of the rim
**Elevation extremes:**
*lowest point:* Pacific Ocean 0 m
*highest point:* unnamed location 6 m
**Natural resources:** none
**Land use:**
*arable land:* 0%
*permanent crops:* 0%
*other:* 100% (2005)
**Irrigated land:** 0 sq km
**Natural hazards:** occasional typhoons
**Environment - current issues:** NA
**Geography - note:** strategic location in the North Pacific Ocean; emergency landing location for transpacific flights

## People

**Population:** no indigenous inhabitants
*note:* since super typhoon IOKE, a small military contingent along with 75 contractor personnel have returned to the island to conduct clean-up and restore basic operations on the island (July 2008 est.)

## Government

**Country name:**
*conventional long form:* none
*conventional short form:* Wake Island
**Dependency status:** unorganized, unincorporated territory of the US; administered from Washington, DC, by the Department of the Interior; activities in the atoll are currently conducted by the US Air Force
**Legal system:** the laws of the US, where applicable, apply
**Flag description:** the flag of the US is used

## Economy

**Economy - overview:** Economic activity is limited to providing services to military personnel and contractors located on the island. All food and manufactured goods must be imported.
**Electricity - production:** NA kWh

## Communications

**Telephone system:**
*general assessment:* satellite communications; 2 DSN circuits off the Overseas Telephone System (OTS)
*domestic:* NA
*international:* NA
**Radio broadcast stations:** AM 0, FM 0, shortwave 0 (American Armed Forces Radio and Television Service (AFRTS)) provides satellite radio service (2005)
**Television broadcast stations:** 0 (2005)

## Transportation

**Airports:** 1 (2008)
**Airports - with paved runways:**
*total:* 1
*2,438 to 3,047 m:* 1 (2008)
**Ports and terminals:** none; two offshore anchorages for large ships
**Transportation - note:** there are no commercial or civilian flights to and from Wake Island, except in direct support of island missions; emergency landing is available

## Military

**Military - note:** defense is the responsibility of the US; the US Air Force is responsible for overall administration and operation of the island; the launch support facility is administered by the US Missile Defense Agency (MDA)

## Transnational Issues

**Disputes - international:** claimed by Marshall Islands

# Wallis and Futuna
*(overseas collectivity of France)*

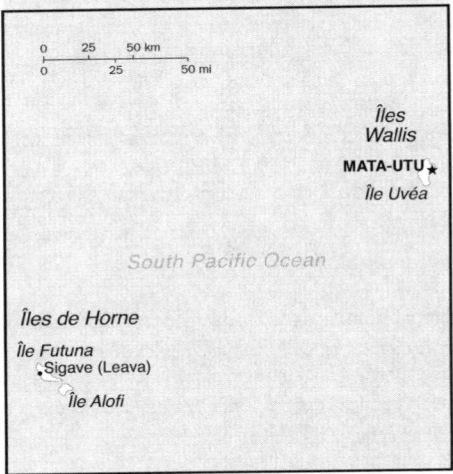

## Introduction

**Background:** The Futuna island group was discovered by the Dutch in 1616 and Wallis by the British in 1767, but it was the French who declared a protectorate over the islands in 1842. In 1959, the inhabitants of the islands voted to become a French overseas territory.

## Geography

**Location:** Oceania, islands in the South Pacific Ocean, about two-thirds of the way from Hawaii to New Zealand
**Geographic coordinates:** 13 18 S, 176 12 W
**Map references:** Oceania
**Area:**
*total:* 274 sq km
*land:* 274 sq km
*water:* 0 sq km
*note:* includes Ile Uvea (Wallis Island), Ile Futuna (Futuna Island), Ile Alofi, and 20 islets
**Area - comparative:** 1.5 times the size of Washington, DC
**Land boundaries:** 0 km
**Coastline:** 129 km
**Maritime claims:**
*territorial sea:* 12 nm
*exclusive economic zone:* 200 nm
**Climate:** tropical; hot, rainy season (November to April); cool, dry season (May to October); rains 2,500-3,000 mm per year (80% humidity); average temperature 26.6 degrees C
**Terrain:** volcanic origin; low hills
**Elevation extremes:**
*lowest point:* Pacific Ocean 0 m
*highest point:* Mont Singavi (on Futuna) 765 m
**Natural resources:** NEGL
**Land use:**
*arable land:* 7.14%
*permanent crops:* 35.71%
*other:* 57.15% (2005)

**Irrigated land:** NA
**Natural hazards:** NA
**Environment - current issues:** deforestation (only small portions of the original forests remain) largely as a result of the continued use of wood as the main fuel source; as a consequence of cutting down the forests, the mountainous terrain of Futuna is particularly prone to erosion; there are no permanent settlements on Alofi because of the lack of natural fresh water resources
**Geography - note:** both island groups have fringing reefs

## People

**Population:** 15,289 (July 2009 est.)
**Age structure:**
*0-14 years:* 26.7% (male 2,141/female 1,935)
*15-64 years:* 66.3% (male 5,069/female 5,065)
*65 years and over:* 7.1% (male 488/female 591) (2009 est.)
**Median age:**
*total:* 27.2 years
*male:* 26.1 years
*female:* 28.5 years (2009 est.)
**Population growth rate:** 0.347% (2009 est.)
**Birth rate:** NA
**Death rate:** NA
**Net migration rate:** -6.08 migrant(s)/1,000 population
*note:* there has been steady emigration from Wallis and Futuna to New Caledonia (2009 est.)
**Urbanization:**
*urban population:* 0% of total population (2008)
*rate of urbanization:* 0% annual rate of change (2005-10 est.)
**Sex ratio:**
*at birth:* 1.05 male(s)/female
*under 15 years:* 1.11 male(s)/female
*15-64 years:* 1 male(s)/female
*65 years and over:* 0.83 male(s)/female
*total population:* 1.01 male(s)/female (2009 est.)
**Infant mortality rate:**
*total:* 5.02 deaths/1,000 live births
*male:* 5.27 deaths/1,000 live births
*female:* 4.75 deaths/1,000 live births (2009 est.)
**Life expectancy at birth:**
*total population:* 78.2 years
*male:* 75.22 years
*female:* 81.32 years (2009 est.)
**Total fertility rate:** 1.87 children born/woman (2009 est.)
**HIV/AIDS - adult prevalence rate:** NA
**HIV/AIDS - people living with HIV/AIDS:** NA
**HIV/AIDS - deaths:** NA
**Nationality:**
*noun:* Wallisian(s), Futunan(s), or Wallis and Futuna Islanders
*adjective:* Wallisian, Futunan, or Wallis and Futuna Islander
**Ethnic groups:** Polynesian
**Religions:** Roman Catholic 99%, other 1%

**Languages:** Wallisian 58.9% (indigenous Polynesian language), Futunian 30.1%, French 10.8%, other 0.2% (2003 census)
**Literacy:**
*definition:* age 15 and over can read and write
*total population:* 50%
*male:* 50%
*female:* 50% (1969 est.)

## Government

**Country name:**
*conventional long form:* Territory of the Wallis and Futuna Islands
*conventional short form:* Wallis and Futuna
*local long form:* Territoire des Iles Wallis et Futuna
*local short form:* Wallis et Futuna
**Dependency status:** overseas territory of France
**Government type:** NA
**Capital:**
*name:* Mata-Utu (on Ile Uvea)
*geographic coordinates:* 13 57 S, 171 56 W
*time difference:* UTC+12 (17 hours ahead of Washington, DC during Standard Time)
**Administrative divisions:** none (overseas territory of France); there are no first-order administrative divisions as defined by the US Government, but there are three kingdoms at the second order named Alo, Sigave, Wallis
**Independence:** none (overseas territory of France)
**National holiday:** Bastille Day, 14 July (1789)
**Constitution:** 4 October 1958 (French Constitution)
**Legal system:** the laws of France, where applicable, apply
**Suffrage:** 18 years of age; universal
**Executive branch:**
*chief of state:* President Nicolas SARKOZY (since 16 May 2007); represented by High Administrator Philippe PAOLANTONI (since 28 July 2008)
*head of government:* President of the Territorial Assembly Pesamino TAPUTAI (since 11 April 2007)
*cabinet:* Council of the Territory consists of three kings and three members appointed by the high administrator on the advice of the Territorial Assembly
*note:* there are three traditional kings with limited powers
*elections:* French president elected by popular vote for a five-year term; high administrator appointed by the French president on the advice of the French Ministry of the Interior; the presidents of the Territorial Government and the Territorial Assembly are elected by the members of the assembly
**Legislative branch:** unicameral Territorial Assembly or Assemblee Territoriale (20 seats; members are elected by popular vote to serve five-year terms)
*elections:* last held 1 April 2007 (next to be held April 2012)
*election results:* percent of vote by party - NA; seats by party - UMP 13, other 7
*note:* Wallis and Futuna elects one senator to the French Senate and one deputy to the French National Assembly; French Senate - elections last held

21 September 2008 (next to be held by September 2014); results - percent of vote by party - NA; seats - UMP 1; French National Assembly - elections last held 17 June 2007 (next to be held by 2012); results - percent of vote by party - NA; seats - PS 1

**Judicial branch:** justice generally administered under French law by the high administrator, but the three traditional kings administer customary law and there is a magistrate in Mata-Utu; a court of appeal is located in Noumea, New Caledonia

**Political parties and leaders:** Lua Kae Tahi (Giscardians); Mouvement des Radicaux de Gauche or MRG; Rally for the Republic or RPR (UMP) [Clovis LOGOLOGOFOLAU]; Socialist Party or PS; Taumu'a Lelei [Soane Muni UHILA]; Union Populaire Locale or UPL [Falakiko GATA]; Union Pour la Democratie Francaise or UDF

**Political pressure groups and leaders:** NA

**International organization participation:** PIF (observer), SPC, UPU, WFTU

**Diplomatic representation in the US:** none (overseas territory of France)

**Diplomatic representation from the US:** none (overseas territory of France)

**Flag description:** unofficial, local flag has a red field with four white isosceles triangles in the middle, representing the three native kings of the islands and the French administrator; the apexes of the triangles are oriented inward and at right angles to each other; the flag of France, outlined in white on two sides, is in the upper hoist quadrant; the flag of France is the only official flag

## Economy

**Economy - overview:** The economy is limited to traditional subsistence agriculture, with about 80% of labor force earnings from agriculture (coconuts and vegetables), livestock (mostly pigs), and fishing. About 4% of the population is employed in government. Revenues come from French Government subsidies, licensing of fishing rights to Japan and South Korea, import taxes, and remittances from expatriate workers in New Caledonia.

**GDP (purchasing power parity):** $60 million (2004 est.)

**GDP (official exchange rate):** $NA

**GDP - real growth rate:** NA%

**GDP - per capita (PPP):** $3,800 (2004 est.)

**GDP - composition by sector:**
*agriculture:* NA%
*industry:* NA%
*services:* NA%

**Labor force:** 3,104 (2003)

**Labor force - by occupation:**
*agriculture:* 80%
*industry:* 4%
*services:* 16% (2001 est.)

**Unemployment rate:** 15.2% (2003)

**Population below poverty line:** NA%

**Household income or consumption by percentage share:**
*lowest 10%:* NA%
*highest 10%:* NA%

**Budget:**
*revenues:* $29,730
*expenditures:* $31,330 (2004)

**Public debt:** 5.6% of GDP (2004 est.)

**Inflation rate (consumer prices):** 2.8% (2005)

**Agriculture - products:** breadfruit, yams, taro, bananas; pigs, goats; fish

**Industries:** copra, handicrafts, fishing, lumber

**Industrial production growth rate:** NA%

**Electricity - production:** NA kWh

**Electricity - consumption:** NA kWh

**Electricity - exports:** 0 kWh (2002)

**Electricity - imports:** 0 kWh (2002)

**Exports:** $47,450 f.o.b. (2004)

**Exports - commodities:** copra, chemicals, construction materials

**Imports:** $61.17 million f.o.b. (2004)

**Imports - commodities:** chemicals, machinery, passenger ships, consumer goods

**Debt - external:** $3.67 million (2004)

**Exchange rates:** Comptoirs Francais du Pacifique francs (XPF) per US dollar - 87.59 (2007), 94.97 (2006), 95.89 (2005), 96.04 (2004), 105.66 (2003)

## Communications

**Telephones - main lines in use:** 1,900 (2002)

**Telephones - mobile cellular:** NA

**Telephone system:**
*general assessment:* NA
*domestic:* NA
*international:* country code - 681

**Radio broadcast stations:** AM 1, FM 0, shortwave 0 (2000)

**Television broadcast stations:** 2 (2000)

**Internet country code:** .wf

**Internet hosts:** 1 (2008)

**Internet users:** 900 (2002)

## Transportation

**Airports:** 2 (2008)

**Airports - with paved runways:**
*total:* 1
*1,524 to 2,437 m:* 1 (2008)

**Airports - with unpaved runways:**
*total:* 1
*914 to 1,523 m:* 1 (2008)

**Merchant marine:**
*total:* 8
*by type:* chemical tanker 2, passenger 6
*foreign-owned:* 8 (France 6, French Polynesia 2) (2008)

**Ports and terminals:** Leava, Mata-Utu

## Military

**Manpower fit for military service:**
*males age 16-49:* 3,273
*females age 16-49:* 3,297 (2009 est.)

**Manpower reaching militarily significant age annually:**
*male:* 175
*female:* 164 (2009 est.)

**Military - note:** defense is the responsibility of France

## Transnational Issues

**Disputes - international:** none

# West Bank

West Bank is Israeli-occupied with current status subject to the Israeli-Palestinian Interim Agreement; permanent status to be determined through further negotiation.

## Introduction

**Background:** The September 1993 Israel-PLO Declaration of Principles on Interim Self-Government Arrangements provided for a transitional period of Palestinian self-rule in the West Bank and Gaza Strip. Under a series of agreements signed between May 1994 and September 1999, Israel transferred to the Palestinian Authority (PA) security and civilian responsibility for Palestinian-populated areas of the West Bank and Gaza. Negotiations to determine the permanent status of the West Bank and Gaza stalled following the outbreak of an intifada in September 2000, as Israeli forces reoccupied most Palestinian-controlled areas. In April 2003, the Quartet (US, EU, UN, and Russia) presented a roadmap to a final settlement of the conflict by 2005 based on reciprocal steps by the two parties leading to two states, Israel and a democratic Palestine. The proposed date for a permanent status agreement was postponed indefinitely due to violence and

accusations that both sides had not followed through on their commitments. Following Palestinian leader Yasir ARAFAT's death in late 2004, Mahmud ABBAS was elected PA president in January 2005. A month later, Israel and the PA agreed to the Sharm el-Sheikh Commitments in an effort to move the peace process forward. In September 2005, Israel unilaterally withdrew all its settlers and soldiers and dismantled its military facilities in the Gaza Strip and withdrew settlers and redeployed soldiers from four small northern West Bank settlements. Nonetheless, Israel controls maritime, airspace, and most access to the Gaza Strip. A November 2005 PA-Israeli agreement authorized the reopening of the Rafah border crossing between the Gaza Strip and Egypt under joint PA and Egyptian control. In January 2006, the Islamic Resistance Movement, HAMAS, won control of the Palestinian Legislative Council (PLC). The international community refused to accept the HAMAS-led government because it did not recognize Israel, would not renounce violence, and refused to honor previous peace agreements between Israel and the PA. HAMAS took control of the PA government in March 2006, but President ABBAS had little success negotiating with HAMAS to present a political platform acceptable to the international community so as to lift economic sanctions on Palestinians. The PLC was unable to convene throughout most of 2006 as a result of Israel's detention of many HAMAS PLC members and Israeli-imposed travel restrictions on other PLC members. Violent clashes took place between Fatah and HAMAS supporters in the Gaza Strip in 2006 and early 2007, resulting in numerous Palestinian deaths and injuries. ABBAS and HAMAS Political Bureau Chief MISHAL in February 2007 signed the Mecca Agreement in Saudi Arabia that resulted in the formation of a Palestinian National Unity Government (NUG) headed by HAMAS member Ismail HANIYA. However, fighting continued in the Gaza Strip, and in June 2007, HAMAS militants succeeded in a violent takeover of all military and governmental institutions in the Gaza Strip. ABBAS dismissed the NUG and through a series of presidential decrees formed a PA government in the West Bank led by independent Salam FAYYAD. HAMAS rejected the NUG's dismissal and has called for resuming talks with Fatah, but ABBAS has ruled out negotiations until HAMAS agrees to a return of PA control over the Gaza Strip and recognizes the FAYYAD-led government. FAYYAD and his PA government initiated a series of security and economic reforms to improve conditions in the West Bank. ABBAS participated in talks with Israel's Prime Minister OLMERT and secured the release of some Palestinian prisoners and previously withheld customs revenue. During a November 2007 international meeting in Annapolis Maryland, ABBAS and OLMERT agreed to resume peace negotiations with the goal of reaching a final peace settlement.

## Geography

**Location:** Middle East, west of Jordan
**Geographic coordinates:** 32 00 N, 35 15 E
**Map references:** Middle East
**Area:**
*total:* 5,860 sq km
*land:* 5,640 sq km
*water:* 220 sq km
*note:* includes West Bank, Latrun Salient, and the northwest quarter of the Dead Sea, but excludes Mt. Scopus; East Jerusalem and Jerusalem No Man's Land are also included only as a means of depicting the entire area occupied by Israel in 1967
**Area - comparative:** slightly smaller than Delaware
**Land boundaries:**
*total:* 404 km
*border countries:* Israel 307 km, Jordan 97 km
**Coastline:** 0 km (landlocked)
**Maritime claims:** none (landlocked)
**Climate:** temperate; temperature and precipitation vary with altitude, warm to hot summers, cool to mild winters
**Terrain:** mostly rugged dissected upland, some vegetation in west, but barren in east
**Elevation extremes:**
*lowest point:* Dead Sea -408 m
*highest point:* Tall Asur 1,022 m
**Natural resources:** arable land
**Land use:**
*arable land:* 16.9%
*permanent crops:* 18.97%
*other:* 64.13% (2001)
**Irrigated land:** 150 sq km; note - includes Gaza Strip (2003)
**Natural hazards:** droughts
**Environment - current issues:** adequacy of fresh water supply; sewage treatment
**Geography - note:** landlocked; highlands are main recharge area for Israel's coastal aquifers; there are about 340 Israeli civilian sites – including 100 small outpost communities in the West Bank and 29 sites in East Jerusalem (July 2008 est.)

## People

**Population:** 2,461,267
*note:* in addition, there are about 187,000 Israeli settlers in the West Bank and fewer than 177,000 in East Jerusalem (July 2009 est.)
**Age structure:**
*0-14 years:* 37.3% (male 470,735/female 446,878)
*15-64 years:* 59.1% (male 744,822/female 708,695)
*65 years and over:* 3.7% (male 37,471/female 52,666) (2009 est.)
**Median age:**
*total:* 20.5 years
*male:* 20.4 years
*female:* 20.8 years (2009 est.)
**Population growth rate:** 2.178% (2009 est.)
**Birth rate:** 25.44 births/1,000 population (2009 est.)
**Death rate:** 3.7 deaths/1,000 population (2008 est.)

# West Bank (continued)

**Net migration rate:** 0 migrant(s)/1,000 population (2009 est.)

**Urbanization:**

*urban population:* 72% of total population (2008)

*rate of urbanization:* 3.3% annual rate of change (2005-10 est.)

**Sex ratio:**

*at birth:* 1.06 male(s)/female

*under 15 years:* 1.05 male(s)/female

*15-64 years:* 1.05 male(s)/female

*65 years and over:* 0.71 male(s)/female

*total population:* 1.04 male(s)/female (2009 est.)

**Infant mortality rate:**

*total:* 15.96 deaths/1,000 live births

*male:* 17.87 deaths/1,000 live births

*female:* 13.93 deaths/1,000 live births (2009 est.)

**Life expectancy at birth:**

*total population:* 74.54 years

*male:* 72.54 years

*female:* 76.65 years (2009 est.)

**Total fertility rate:** 3.22 children born/woman (2009 est.)

**HIV/AIDS - adult prevalence rate:** NA

**HIV/AIDS - people living with HIV/AIDS:** NA

**HIV/AIDS - deaths:** NA

**Nationality:**

*noun:* NA

*adjective:* NA

**Ethnic groups:** Palestinian Arab and other 83%, Jewish 17%

**Religions:** Muslim 75% (predominantly Sunni), Jewish 17%, Christian and other 8%

**Languages:** Arabic, Hebrew (spoken by Israeli settlers and many Palestinians), English (widely understood)

**Literacy:**

*definition:* age 15 and over can read and write

*total population:* 92.4%

*male:* 96.7%

*female:* 88% (2004 est.)

**School life expectancy (primary to tertiary education):**

*total:* 14 years

*male:* 13 years

*female:* 14 years (2006)

**Education expenditures:** NA

## Government

**Country name:**

*conventional long form:* none

*conventional short form:* West Bank

## Economy

**Economy - overview:** The West Bank - the larger of the two areas comprising the Palestinian Authority (PA) - has experienced a general decline in economic conditions since the second intifada began in September 2000. The downturn has been largely a result of Israeli closure policies - the imposition of closures and access restrictions in response to security concerns in Israel - which disrupted labor and trading relationships. In 2001, and even more severely in 2002, Israeli military measures in PA areas resulted in the destruction of capital, the disruption of administrative structures, and widespread business closures. International aid of at least $1.14 billion to the West Bank and Gaza Strip in 2004 prevented the complete collapse of the economy and allowed some reforms in the government's financial operations. In 2005, high unemployment and limited trade opportunities - due to continued closures both within the West Bank and externally - stymied growth. Israel's and the international community's financial embargo of the PA when HAMAS ran the PA during March 2006 - June 2007 interrupted the provision of PA social services and the payment of PA salaries. Since then the FAYYAD government in the West Bank has restarted salary payments and the provision of services but would be unable to operate absent high levels of international assistance.

**GDP (purchasing power parity):**

$11.95 billion (2008 est.)

*note:* data are in 2008 US dollars

**GDP (official exchange rate):** $6.641 billion (includes Gaza Strip) (2008 est.)

**GDP - real growth rate:**

0.8% (2008 est.)

**GDP - per capita (PPP):**

$2,900 (2008 est.)

*note:* data are in 2008 US dollars

**GDP - composition by sector:**

*agriculture:* 8%

*industry:* 13%

*services:* 79% (includes Gaza Strip) (2007 est.)

**Labor force:** 605,000 (2006)

**Labor force - by occupation:**

*agriculture:* 17%

*industry:* 15%

*services:* 68% (June 2008)

**Unemployment rate:**

16.3% (2008 est.)

18.6% (2006)

**Population below poverty line:** 46% (2007 est.)

**Household income or consumption by percentage share:**

*lowest 10%:* NA%

*highest 10%:* NA%

**Budget:**

*revenues:* $1.149 billion

*expenditures:* $2.31 billion

*note:* includes Gaza Strip (2006)

**Inflation rate (consumer prices):**

11.5% (2008)

3.6% (2006)

*note:* data in include Gaza Strip

**Commercial bank prime lending rate:** 7.73% (31 December 2006)

**Stock of money:** $1.574 billion (31 December 2007)

**Stock of quasi money:** $3.048 billion (31 December 2007)

**Stock of domestic credit:** $1.455 billion (31 December 2007)

**Market value of publicly traded shares:** $2.475 billion (31 December 2007)

**Agriculture - products:** olives, citrus, vegetables; beef, dairy products

**Industries:** cement, quarrying, textiles, soap, olive-wood carvings, and mother-of-pearl souvenirs; the Israelis have established some small-scale, modern industries in the settlements and industrial centers

**Industrial production growth rate:** 2.4% (includes Gaza Strip) (2005)

**Electricity - production:** NA kWh; note - most electricity imported from Israel; East Jerusalem Electric Company buys and distributes electricity to Palestinians in East Jerusalem and its concession in the West Bank; the Israel Electric Company directly supplies electricity to most Jewish residents and military facilities; some Palestinian municipalities, such as Nablus and Janin, generate their own electricity from small power plants

**Electricity - consumption:** NA kWh

**Electricity - imports:** NA kWh

**Exports:** $339 million f.o.b.

*note:* includes Gaza Strip (2006)

**Exports - commodities:** olives, fruit, vegetables, limestone

**Imports:** $1.3 billion c.i.f.; (includes Gaza Strip) (2006)

**Imports - commodities:** food, consumer goods, construction materials

**Debt - external:** $1.3 billion (2007 est.)

**Exchange rates:** new Israeli shekels (ILS) per US dollar - 3.56 (2008 est.), 4.14 (2007), 4.4565 (2006), 4.4877 (2005), 4.482 (2004)

## Communications

**Telephones - main lines in use:** 350,400 (includes Gaza Strip) (2007)

**Telephones - mobile cellular:** 1.026 million (includes Gaza Strip) (2007)

**Telephone system:**

*general assessment:* NA

*domestic:* Israeli company BEZEK and the Palestinian company PALTEL are responsible for fixed line services; the Palestinian JAWAL company provides cellular services

*international:* country code - 970 (2004)

**Radio broadcast stations:** AM 0, FM 25, shortwave 0 (2008)

**Television broadcast stations:** 30 (2008)

**Internet country code:** .ps; note - same as Gaza Strip

**Internet users:** 355,500 (includes Gaza Strip) (2007)

## Transportation

**Airports:** 2 (2008)

**Airports - with paved runways:**

*total:* 2

*1,524 to 2,437 m:* 1

*under 914 m:* 1 (2008)

**Roadways:**
*total:* 5,147 km
*paved:* 5,147 km
*note:* includes Gaza Strip (2006)

## Military

**Manpower fit for military service:**
*males age 16-49:* 545,653
*females age 16-49:* 515,102 (2009 est.)
**Manpower reaching militarily significant age annually:**
*male:* 30,233
*female:* 28,745 (2009 est.)
**Military expenditures:** NA

## Transnational Issues

**Disputes - international:** West Bank and Gaza Strip are Israeli-occupied with current status subject to the Israeli-Palestinian Interim Agreement - permanent status to be determined through further negotiation; Israel continues construction of a "seam line" separation barrier along parts of the Green Line and within the West Bank; Israel withdrew from four settlements in the northern West Bank in August 2005; since 1948, about 350 peacekeepers from the UN Truce Supervision Organization (UNTSO), headquartered in Jerusalem, monitor ceasefires, supervise armistice agreements, prevent isolated incidents from escalating, and assist other UN personnel in the region
**Refugees and internally displaced persons:**
*refugees (country of origin):* 722,000 (Palestinian Refugees (UNRWA)) (2007)

# Western Sahara

## Introduction

**Background:** Morocco virtually annexed the northern two-thirds of Western Sahara (formerly Spanish Sahara) in 1976, and claimed the rest of the territory in 1979, following Mauritania's withdrawal. A guerrilla war with the Polisario Front contesting Rabat's sovereignty ended in a 1991 UN-brokered cease-fire; a UN-organized referendum on the territory's final status has been repeatedly postponed. In April 2007, Morocco presented an autonomy plan for the territory to the UN, which the U.S. considers serious and credible. The Polisario also presented a plan to the UN in 2007 that called for independence. Representatives from the Government of Morocco and the Polisario Front have met four times since June 2007 to negotiate the status of Western Sahara, but talks have stalled since the UN envoy to the territory stated in April 2008 that independence is unrealistic.

## Geography

**Location:** Northern Africa, bordering the North Atlantic Ocean, between Mauritania and Morocco
**Geographic coordinates:** 24 30 N, 13 00 W
**Map references:** Africa
**Area:**
*total:* 266,000 sq km
*land:* 266,000 sq km
*water:* 0 sq km
**Area - comparative:** about the size of Colorado
**Land boundaries:**
*total:* 2,046 km
*border countries:* Algeria 42 km, Mauritania 1,561 km, Morocco 443 km
**Coastline:** 1,110 km
**Maritime claims:** contingent upon resolution of sovereignty issue
**Climate:** hot, dry desert; rain is rare; cold offshore air currents produce fog and heavy dew

**Terrain:** mostly low, flat desert with large areas of rocky or sandy surfaces rising to small mountains in south and northeast
**Elevation extremes:**
*lowest point:* Sebjet Tah -55 m
*highest point:* unnamed elevation 805 m
**Natural resources:** phosphates, iron ore
**Land use:**
*arable land:* 0.02%
*permanent crops:* 0%
*other:* 99.98% (2005)
**Irrigated land:** NA
**Natural hazards:** hot, dry, dust/sand-laden sirocco wind can occur during winter and spring; widespread harmattan haze exists 60% of time, often severely restricting visibility
**Environment - current issues:** sparse water and lack of arable land
**Environment - international agreements:**
*party to:* none of the selected agreements
**Geography - note:** the waters off the coast are particularly rich fishing areas

## People

**Population:** 405,210
*note:* estimate is based on projections by age, sex, fertility, mortality, and migration; fertility and mortality are based on data from neighboring countries (July 2009 est.)
**Age structure:**
*0-14 years:* 44.9% (male 92,428/female 89,570)
*15-64 years:* 52.8% (male 105,191/female 108,803)
*65 years and over:* 2.3% (male 3,881/female 5,337) (2009 est.)
**Median age:**
*total:* 17.3 years
*male:* 16.8 years
*female:* 17.8 years (2009 est.)
**Population growth rate:** 2.829% NA
**Birth rate:** 39.54 births/1,000 population (2009 est.)
**Death rate:** 11.74 deaths/1,000 population (2008 est.)
**Urbanization:**
*urban population:* 81% of total population (2008)
*rate of urbanization:* 4% annual rate of change (2005-10 est.)
**Sex ratio:**
*at birth:* 1.04 male(s)/female
*under 15 years:* 1.03 male(s)/female
*15-64 years:* 0.97 male(s)/female
*65 years and over:* 0.73 male(s)/female
*total population:* 0.99 male(s)/female (2009 est.)
**Infant mortality rate:**
*total:* 69.66 deaths/1,000 live births
*male:* 69.84 deaths/1,000 live births
*female:* 69.47 deaths/1,000 live births (2009 est.)
**Life expectancy at birth:**
*total population:* 54.32 years
*male:* 52 years
*female:* 56.73 years (2009 est.)

# Western Sahara *(continued)*

**Total fertility rate:** NA 5.61 children born/woman (2009 est.)
**HIV/AIDS - adult prevalence rate:** NA
**HIV/AIDS - people living with HIV/AIDS:** NA
**HIV/AIDS - deaths:** NA
**Nationality:**
*noun:* Sahrawi(s), Sahraoui(s)
*adjective:* Sahrawi, Sahrawian, Sahraouian
**Ethnic groups:** Arab, Berber
**Religions:** Muslim
**Languages:** Hassaniya Arabic, Moroccan Arabic
**Literacy:** NA

## Government

**Country name:**
*conventional long form:* none
*conventional short form:* Western Sahara
*former:* Spanish Sahara
**Government type:** legal status of territory and issue of sovereignty unresolved; territory contested by Morocco and Polisario Front (Popular Front for the Liberation of the Saguia el Hamra and Rio de Oro), which in February 1976 formally proclaimed a government-in-exile of the Sahrawi Arab Democratic Republic (SADR), led by President Mohamed ABDELAZIZ; territory partitioned between Morocco and Mauritania in April 1976 when Spain withdrew, with Morocco acquiring northern two-thirds; Mauritania, under pressure from Polisario guerrillas, abandoned all claims to its portion in August 1979; Morocco moved to occupy that sector shortly thereafter and has since asserted administrative control; the Polisario's government-in-exile was seated as an Organization of African Unity (OAU) member in 1984; guerrilla activities continued sporadically until a UN-monitored cease-fire was implemented on 6 September 1991 (Security Council Resolution 690) by the United Nations Mission for the Referendum in Western Sahara or MINURSO
**Capital:** none
*time difference:* UTC 0 (5 hours ahead of Washington, DC during Standard Time)
**Administrative divisions:** none (under de facto control of Morocco)
**Suffrage:** none; a UN-sponsored voter identification campaign not yet completed
**Executive branch:** none
**Political pressure groups and leaders:** none
**International organization participation:** WFTU
**Diplomatic representation in the US:** none
**Diplomatic representation from the US:** none

## Economy

**Economy - overview:** Western Sahara depends on pastoral nomadism, fishing, and phosphate mining as the principal sources of income for the population. The territory lacks sufficient rainfall for sustainable agricultural production, and most of the food for the urban population must be imported. Incomes in Western Sahara are substantially below the Moroccan level. The Moroccan Government controls all trade and other economic activities in Western Sahara. Morocco and the EU signed a four-year agreement in July 2006 allowing European vessels to fish off the coast of Morocco, including the disputed waters off the coast of Western Sahara. Moroccan energy interests in 2001 signed contracts to explore for oil off the coast of Western Sahara, which has angered the Polisario. However, in 2006 the Polisario awarded similar exploration licenses in the disputed territory, which would come into force if Morocco and the Polisario resolve their dispute over Western Sahara.
**GDP (purchasing power parity):** $900 million (2007 est.)
**GDP (official exchange rate):** $NA
**GDP - real growth rate:** NA%
**GDP - per capita (PPP):** $2,500 (2007 est.)
**GDP - composition by sector:**
*agriculture:* NA%
*industry:* NA%
*services:* 40% (2007 est.)
**Labor force:** 12,000 (2005 est.)
**Labor force - by occupation:**
*agriculture:* 50%
*industry and services:* 50% (2005 est.)
**Unemployment rate:** NA%
**Population below poverty line:** NA%
**Household income or consumption by percentage share:**
*lowest 10%:* NA%
*highest 10%:* NA%
**Budget:**
*revenues:* $NA
*expenditures:* $NA
**Inflation rate (consumer prices):** NA%
**Agriculture - products:** fruits and vegetables (grown in the few oases); camels, sheep, goats (kept by nomads); fish
**Industries:** phosphate mining, handicrafts
**Industrial production growth rate:** NA%
**Electricity - production:** 90 million kWh (2006 est.)
**Electricity - consumption:** 83.7 million kWh (2006 est.)
**Electricity - exports:** 0 kWh (2007)
**Electricity - imports:** 0 kWh (2007 est.)
**Oil - production:** 0 bbl/day (2007 est.)
**Oil - consumption:** 1,760 bbl/day (2006 est.)
**Oil - exports:** 0 bbl/day (2005)
**Oil - imports:** 1,925 bbl/day (2005)
**Oil - proved reserves:** 0 bbl (1 January 2006 est.)
**Natural gas - production:** 0 cu m (2007 est.)
**Natural gas - consumption:** 0 cu m (2007 est.)
**Natural gas - exports:** 0 cu m (2007 est.)
**Natural gas - imports:** 0 cu m (2007 est.)
**Natural gas - proved reserves:** 0 cu m (1 January 2006 est.)
**Exports:** $NA
**Exports - commodities:** phosphates 62%
**Imports:** $NA
**Imports - commodities:** fuel for fishing fleet, foodstuffs
**Debt - external:** $NA
**Exchange rates:** Moroccan dirhams (MAD) per US dollar - 7.526 (2008 est.), 8.3563 (2007), 8.7722 (2006), 8.865 (2005), 8.868 (2004)

## Communications

**Telephones - main lines in use:** about 2,000 (1999 est.)
**Telephones - mobile cellular:** 0 (1999)
**Telephone system:**
*general assessment:* sparse and limited system
*domestic:* NA
*international:* country code - 212; tied into Morocco's system by microwave radio relay, tropospheric scatter, and satellite; satellite earth stations - 2 Intelsat (Atlantic Ocean) linked to Rabat, Morocco
**Radio broadcast stations:** AM 2, FM 0, shortwave 0 (1998)
**Television broadcast stations:** NA
**Internet country code:** .eh
**Internet users:** NA

## Transportation

**Airports:** 9 (2008)
**Airports - with paved runways:**
*total:* 3
*2,438 to 3,047 m:* 3 (2008)
**Airports - with unpaved runways:**
*total:* 6
*1,524 to 2,437 m:* 1
*914 to 1,523 m:* 3
*under 914 m:* 2 (2008)
**Ports and terminals:** Ad Dakhla, Cabo Bojador, Laayoune (El Aaiun)

## Military

**Manpower fit for military service:**
*males age 16-49:* 52,267
*females age 16-49:* 59,221 (2009 est.)
**Manpower reaching militarily significant age annually:**
*male:* 4,796
*female:* 4,679 (2009 est.)

## Transnational Issues

**Disputes - international:** Morocco claims and administers Western Sahara, whose sovereignty remains unresolved; UN-administered cease-fire has remained in effect since September 1991, administered by the UN Mission for the Referendum in Western Sahara (MINURSO), but attempts to hold a referendum have failed and parties thus far have rejected all brokered proposals; several states have extended diplomatic relations to the "Sahrawi Arab Democratic Republic" represented by the Polisario Front in exile in Algeria, while others recognize Moroccan sovereignty over Western Sahara; most of the approximately 102,000 Sahrawi refugees are sheltered in camps in Tindouf, Algeria

# Yemen

## Introduction

**Background:** North Yemen became independent of the Ottoman Empire in 1918. The British, who had set up a protectorate area around the southern port of Aden in the 19th century, withdrew in 1967 from what became South Yemen. Three years later, the southern government adopted a Marxist orientation. The massive exodus of hundreds of thousands of Yemenis from the south to the north contributed to two decades of hostility between the states. The two countries were formally unified as the Republic of Yemen in 1990. A southern secessionist movement in 1994 was quickly subdued. In 2000, Saudi Arabia and Yemen agreed to a delimitation of their border.

## Geography

**Location:** Middle East, bordering the Arabian Sea, Gulf of Aden, and Red Sea, between Oman and Saudi Arabia

**Geographic coordinates:** 15 00 N, 48 00 E

**Map references:** Middle East

**Area:**
*total:* 527,970 sq km
*land:* 527,970 sq km
*water:* 0 sq km
*note:* includes Perim, Socotra, the former Yemen Arab Republic (YAR or North Yemen), and the former People's Democratic Republic of Yemen (PDRY or South Yemen)

**Area - comparative:** slightly larger than twice the size of Wyoming

**Land boundaries:**
*total:* 1,746 km
*border countries:* Oman 288 km, Saudi Arabia 1,458 km

**Coastline:** 1,906 km

**Maritime claims:**
*territorial sea:* 12 nm
*contiguous zone:* 24 nm
*exclusive economic zone:* 200 nm
*continental shelf:* 200 nm or to the edge of the continental margin

**Climate:** mostly desert; hot and humid along west coast; temperate in western mountains affected by seasonal monsoon; extraordinarily hot, dry, harsh desert in east

**Terrain:** narrow coastal plain backed by flat-topped hills and rugged mountains; dissected upland desert plains in center slope into the desert interior of the Arabian Peninsula

**Elevation extremes:**
*lowest point:* Arabian Sea 0 m
*highest point:* Jabal an Nabi Shu'ayb 3,760 m

**Natural resources:** petroleum, fish, rock salt, marble; small deposits of coal, gold, lead, nickel, and copper; fertile soil in west

**Land use:**
*arable land:* 2.91%
*permanent crops:* 0.25%
*other:* 96.84% (2005)

**Irrigated land:** 5,500 sq km (2003)

**Total renewable water resources:** 4.1 cu km (1997)

**Freshwater withdrawal (domestic/industrial/agricultural):**
*total:* 6.63 cu km/yr (4%/1%/95%)
*per capita:* 316 cu m/yr (2000)

**Natural hazards:** sandstorms and dust storms in summer

**Environment - current issues:** limited natural fresh water resources; inadequate supplies of potable water; overgrazing; soil erosion; desertification

**Environment - international agreements:**
*party to:* Biodiversity, Climate Change, Climate Change-Kyoto Protocol, Desertification, Endangered Species, Environmental Modification, Hazardous Wastes, Law of the Sea, Ozone Layer Protection
*signed, but not ratified:* none of the selected agreements

**Geography - note:** strategic location on Bab el Mandeb, the strait linking the Red Sea and the Gulf of Aden, one of world's most active shipping lanes

## People

**Population:** 23,822,783 (July 2009 est.)

**Age structure:**
*0-14 years:* 46.2% (male 5,602,590/female 5,398,103)
*15-64 years:* 51.3% (male 6,212,378/female 6,009,401)
*65 years and over:* 2.5% (male 288,501/female 311,810) (2009 est.)

**Median age:**
*total:* 16.8 years
*male:* 16.7 years
*female:* 16.8 years (2009 est.)

**Population growth rate:** 3.453% (2009 est.)

**Birth rate:** 42.14 births/1,000 population (2009 est.)

**Death rate:** 7.83 deaths/1,000 population (2008 est.)

**Net migration rate:** NA

**Urbanization:**
*urban population:* 31% of total population (2008)
*rate of urbanization:* 4.9% annual rate of change (2005-10 est.)

**Sex ratio:**
*at birth:* 1.05 male(s)/female
*under 15 years:* 1.04 male(s)/female
*15-64 years:* 1.03 male(s)/female
*65 years and over:* 0.92 male(s)/female
*total population:* 1.03 male(s)/female (2009 est.)

**Infant mortality rate:**
*total:* 54.7 deaths/1,000 live births
*male:* 59.12 deaths/1,000 live births
*female:* 50.07 deaths/1,000 live births (2009 est.)

**Life expectancy at birth:**
*total population:* 63.27 years
*male:* 61.3 years
*female:* 65.33 years (2009 est.)

**Total fertility rate:** 6.32 children born/woman (2009 est.)

**HIV/AIDS - adult prevalence rate:** 0.1% (2001 est.)

**HIV/AIDS - people living with HIV/AIDS:** 12,000 (2001 est.)

**HIV/AIDS - deaths:** NA

**Major infectious diseases:**
*degree of risk:* high
*food or waterborne diseases:* bacterial diarrhea, hepatitis A, and typhoid fever
*vectorborne diseases:* dengue fever and malaria
*water contact disease:* schistosomiasis (2009)

**Nationality:**
*noun:* Yemeni(s)
*adjective:* Yemeni

**Ethnic groups:** predominantly Arab; but also Afro-Arab, South Asians, Europeans

**Religions:** Muslim including Shaf'i (Sunni) and Zaydi (Shia), small numbers of Jewish, Christian, and Hindu

**Languages:** Arabic

**Literacy:**
*definition:* age 15 and over can read and write
*total population:* 50.2%
*male:* 70.5%
*female:* 30% (2003 est.)

**School life expectancy (primary to tertiary education):**
*total:* 9 years
*male:* 11 years
*female:* 7 years (2005)

**Education expenditures:** 9.6% of GDP (2001)

# Yemen *(continued)*

## Government

**Country name:**

*conventional long form:* Republic of Yemen
*conventional short form:* Yemen
*local long form:* Al Jumhuriyah al Yamaniyah
*local short form:* Al Yaman
*former:* Yemen Arab Republic [Yemen (Sanaa) or North Yemen] and People's Democratic Republic of Yemen [Yemen (Aden) or South Yemen]

**Government type:** republic

**Capital:**

*name:* Sanaa
*geographic coordinates:* 15 21 N, 44 12 E
*time difference:* UTC+3 (8 hours ahead of Washington, DC during Standard Time)

**Administrative divisions:** 19 governorates (muhafazat, singular - muhafazah); Abyan, 'Adan, Ad Dali', Al Bayda', Al Hudaydah, Al Jawf, Al Mahrah, Al Mahwit, 'Amran, Dhamar, Hadramawt, Hajjah, Ibb, Lahij, Ma'rib, Sa'dah, San'a', Shabwah, Ta'izz
*note:* for electoral and administrative purposes, the capital city of Sanaa is treated as an additional governorate

**Independence:** 22 May 1990 (Republic of Yemen was established with the merger of the Yemen Arab Republic [Yemen (Sanaa) or North Yemen] and the Marxist-dominated People's Democratic Republic of Yemen [Yemen (Aden) or South Yemen]); note - previously North Yemen became independent in November 1918 (from the Ottoman Empire) and became a republic with the overthrow of the theocratic Imamate in 1962; South Yemen became independent on 30 November 1967 (from the UK)

**National holiday:** Unification Day, 22 May (1990)

**Constitution:** 16 May 1991; amended 29 September 1994 and February 2001

**Legal system:** based on Islamic law, Turkish law, English common law, and local tribal customary law; has not accepted compulsory ICJ jurisdiction

**Suffrage:** 18 years of age; universal

**Executive branch:**

*chief of state:* President Ali Abdallah SALIH (since 22 May 1990, the former president of North Yemen, assumed office upon the merger of North and South Yemen); Vice President Maj. Gen. Abd al-Rab Mansur al-HADI (since 3 October 1994)
*head of government:* Prime Minister Ali Muhammad MUJAWWAR (since 31 March 2007)
*cabinet:* Council of Ministers appointed by the president on the advice of the prime minister
*elections:* president elected by popular vote for a seven-year term; election last held 20 September 2006 (next to be held in September 2013); vice president appointed by the president; prime minister and deputy prime ministers appointed by the president
*election results:* Ali Abdallah SALIH elected president; percent of vote - Ali Abdallah SALIH 77.2%, Faysal BIN SHAMLAN 21.8%

**Legislative branch:** a bicameral legislature consisting of a Shura Council (111 seats; members appointed by the president) and a House of Representatives (301 seats; members elected by popular vote to serve six-year terms)
*elections:* last held on 27 April 2003 (next to be held in April 2009)
*election results:* percent of vote by party - NA; seats by party - GPC 228, Islah 47, YSP 7, Nasserite Unionist Party 3, National Arab Socialist Ba'th Party 2, independents 14

**Judicial branch:** Supreme Court

**Political parties and leaders:** General People's Congress or GPC [Abdul-Kader BAJAMMAL]; Islamic Reform Grouping or Islah [Mohammed Abdullah AL-YADOUMI (acting)]; Nasserite Unionist Party [Abdal Malik al-MAKHLAFI]; National Arab Socialist Ba'th Party [Dr. Qasim SALAM]; Yemeni Socialist Party or YSP [Ali Salih MUQBIL]; note - there are at least seven more active political parties

**Political pressure groups and leaders:** Muslim Brotherhood; Women National Committee
*other:* conservative tribal groups

**International organization participation:** AFESD, AMF, CAEU, FAO, G-77, IAEA, IBRD, ICAO, ICCt (signatory), ICRM, IDA, IDB, IFAD, IFC, IFRCS, ILO, IMF, IMO, Interpol, IOC, IOM, IPU, ISO (correspondent), ITSO, ITU, ITUC, LAS, MIGA, MINURCAT, MINURSO, MONUC, NAM, OAS (observer), OIC, OPCW, UN, UNAMID, UNCTAD, UNESCO, UNHCR, UNIDO, UNMIL, UNMIS, UNOCI, UNOMIG, UNWTO, UPU, WCO, WFTU, WHO, WIPO, WMO, WTO (observer)

**Diplomatic representation in the US:**

*chief of mission:* Ambassador Abd al-Wahab Abdallah al-HAJRI
*chancery:* 2319 Wyoming Avenue NW, Washington, DC 20008
*telephone:* [1] (202) 965-4760
*FAX:* [1] (202) 337-2017

**Diplomatic representation from the US:**

*chief of mission:* Ambassador Stephen A. SECHE
*embassy:* Sa'awan Street, Sanaa
*mailing address:* P. O. Box 22347, Sanaa
*telephone:* [967] (1) 755-2000 ext. 2153 or 2266
*FAX:* [967] (1) 303-182

**Flag description:** three equal horizontal bands of red (top), white, and black; similar to the flag of Syria, which has two green stars in the white band, and of Iraq, which has an Arabic inscription centered in the white band; also similar to the flag of Egypt, which has a heraldic eagle centered in the white band

## Economy

**Economy - overview:** Yemen, one of the poorest countries in the Arab world, reported average annual growth in the range of 3-4% from 2000 through 2007. In 2008, growth declined slightly as the price of oil dropped and the slowing global economy reduced demand for oil. Yemen's economic fortunes depend mostly on declining oil resources, but the country is trying to diversify its earnings. In 2006, Yemen began an economic reform program designed to bolster non-oil sectors of the economy and foreign investment. As a result of the program, international donors pledged about $5 billion for development projects. A liquefied natural gas facility is scheduled to open in 2009. Yemen has limited exposure to the international financial system and no capital markets, however, the global financial crisis probably will reduce international aid in 2009.

**GDP (purchasing power parity):**
$55.29 billion (2008 est.)
$53.58 billion (2007)
$51.77 billion (2006)
*note:* data are in 2008 US dollars

**GDP (official exchange rate):** $27.56 billion (2008 est.)

**GDP - real growth rate:**
3.2% (2008 est.)
3.5% (2007 est.)
3.2% (2006 est.)

**GDP - per capita (PPP):**
$2,400 (2008 est.)
$2,400 (2007 est.)
$2,400 (2006 est.)
*note:* data are in 2008 US dollars

**GDP - composition by sector:**
*agriculture:* 9.4%
*industry:* 52.4%
*services:* 38.1% (2008 est.)

**Labor force:** 6.494 million (2008 est.)

**Labor force - by occupation:**
*note:* most people are employed in agriculture and herding; services, construction, industry, and commerce account for less than one-fourth of the labor force

**Unemployment rate:**
35% (2003 est.)

**Population below poverty line:** 45.2% (2003)

**Household income or consumption by percentage share:**
*lowest 10%:* 3%
*highest 10%:* 25.9% (2003)

**Distribution of family income - Gini index:** 37.7 (2005)

**Investment (gross fixed):** 26.3% of GDP (2008 est.)

**Budget:**
*revenues:* $9.097 billion
*expenditures:* $10.55 billion (2008 est.)

**Public debt:** 31.8% of GDP (2008 est.)

**Inflation rate (consumer prices):**
18% (2008 est.)
10% (2007 est.)

**Central bank discount rate:** NA

**Commercial bank prime lending rate:** 18% (31 December 2007)

**Stock of money:** $3.076 billion (31 December 2007)

**Stock of quasi money:** $4.526 billion (31 December 2007)

**Stock of domestic credit:** $2.224 billion (31 December 2007)

**Market value of publicly traded shares:** $NA

**Agriculture - products:** grain, fruits, vegetables, pulses, qat, coffee, cotton; dairy products, livestock (sheep, goats, cattle, camels), poultry; fish

**Industries:** crude oil production and petroleum refining; small-scale production of cotton textiles and leather goods; food processing; handicrafts; small aluminum products factory; cement; commercial ship repair

**Industrial production growth rate:** 2.5% (2008 est.)

**Electricity - production:** 5.017 billion kWh (2006 est.)

**Electricity - consumption:** 3.804 billion kWh (2006 est.)

**Electricity - exports:** 0 kWh (2007 est.)

**Electricity - imports:** 0 kWh (2007 est.)

**Oil - production:** 320,600 bbl/day (2007 est.)

**Oil - consumption:** 135,400 bbl/day (2006 est.)

**Oil - exports:** 336,600 bbl/day (2005)

**Oil - imports:** 62,850 bbl/day (2005)

**Oil - proved reserves:** 3 billion bbl (1 January 2008 est.)

**Natural gas - production:** 0 cu m (2007 est.)

**Natural gas - consumption:** 0 cu m (2007 est.)

**Natural gas - exports:** 0 cu m (2007 est.)

**Natural gas - imports:** 0 cu m (2007 est.)

**Natural gas - proved reserves:** 478.5 billion cu m (1 January 2008 est.)

**Current account balance:** -$2.175 billion (2008 est.)

**Exports:** $9.234 billion f.o.b. (2008 est.)

**Exports - commodities:** crude oil, coffee, dried and salted fish

**Exports - partners:** China 23.3%, India 20.4%, Thailand 19.1%, Japan 7.2%, UAE 5%, US 4.2% (2007)

**Imports:** $9.215 billion f.o.b. (2008 est.)

**Imports - commodities:** food and live animals, machinery and equipment, chemicals

**Imports - partners:** UAE 15.1%, China 11.6%, US 7.8%, Saudi Arabia 7.1%, Kuwait 5.3%, Germany 4.8% (2007)

**Reserves of foreign exchange and gold:** $8.306 billion (31 December 2008 est.)

**Debt - external:** $6.472 billion (31 December 2008 est.)

**Exchange rates:** Yemeni rials (YER) per US dollar - 199.76 (2008 est.), 199.14 (2007), 197.18 (2006), 192.67 (2005), 184.78 (2004)

## Communications

**Telephones - main lines in use:** 968,300 (2006)

**Telephones - mobile cellular:** 2.978 million (2006)

**Telephone system:**

*general assessment:* since unification in 1990, efforts have been made to create a national telecommunications network

*domestic:* the national network consists of microwave radio relay, cable, tropospheric scatter, GSM and CDMA mobile-cellular telephone systems; fixed-line and mobile-cellular teledensity remains low by regional standards

*international:* country code - 967; landing point for the international submarine cable Fiber-Optic Link Around the Globe (FLAG); satellite earth stations - 3 Intelsat (2 Indian Ocean and 1 Atlantic Ocean), 1 Intersputnik (Atlantic Ocean region), and 2 Arabsat; microwave radio relay to Saudi Arabia and Djibouti

**Radio broadcast stations:** AM 6, FM 1, shortwave 2 (1998)

**Television broadcast stations:** 3 (including one Egypt-based station that broadcasts in Yemen); plus several repeaters (2007)

**Internet country code:** .ye

**Internet hosts:** 167 (2008)

**Internet users:** 320,000 (2007)

## Transportation

**Airports:** 54 (2008)

**Airports - with paved runways:**

*total:* 17

*over 3,047 m:* 4

*2,438 to 3,047 m:* 8

*1,524 to 2,437 m:* 3

*914 to 1,523 m:* 1

*under 914 m:* 1 (2008)

**Airports - with unpaved runways:**

*total:* 37

*over 3,047 m:* 3

*2,438 to 3,047 m:* 7

*1,524 to 2,437 m:* 5

*914 to 1,523 m:* 14

*under 914 m:* 8 (2008)

**Pipelines:** gas 96 km; liquid petroleum gas 22 km; oil 1,367 km (2008)

**Roadways:**

*total:* 71,300 km

*paved:* 6,200 km

*unpaved:* 65,100 km (2005)

**Merchant marine:**

*total:* 4

*by type:* cargo 1, chemical tanker 1, petroleum tanker 1, roll on/roll off 1

*registered in other countries:* 13 (North Korea 2, Moldova 1, Panama 6, Saint Kitts and Nevis 1, Sierra Leone 2, unknown 1) (2008)

**Ports and terminals:** Aden, Hudaydah, Mukalla

**Transportation - note:** the International Maritime Bureau reports offshore waters in the Gulf of Aden are high risk for piracy; numerous vessels, including commercial shipping and pleasure craft, have been attacked and hijacked both at anchor and while underway; crew, passengers, and cargo are held for ransom

## Military

**Military branches:** Army (includes Republican Guard), Navy (includes Marines), Yemen Air Force (Al Quwwat al Jawwiya al Jamahiriya al Yemeniya; includes Air Defense Force) (2009)

**Military service age and obligation:** voluntary military service program authorized in 2001; 2-year service obligation (2006)

**Manpower available for military service:**

*males age 16-49:* 5,080,038

*females age 16-49:* 4,852,555 (2008 est.)

**Manpower fit for military service:**

*males age 16-49:* 3,733,704

*females age 16-49:* 3,773,626 (2009 est.)

**Manpower reaching militarily significant age annually:**

*male:* 273,624

*female:* 263,402 (2009 est.)

**Military expenditures:** 6.6% of GDP (2006)

**Military - note:** a Coast Guard was established in 2002

## Transnational Issues

**Disputes - international:** Saudi Arabia has reinforced its concrete-filled security barrier along sections of the fully demarcated border with Yemen to stem illegal cross-border activities

**Refugees and internally displaced persons:**

*refugees (country of origin):* 91,587 (Somalia) (2007)

# Zambia

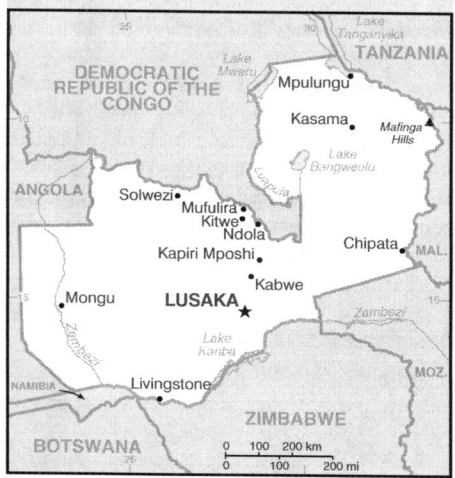

## Introduction

**Background:** The territory of Northern Rhodesia was administered by the [British] South Africa Company from 1891 until it was taken over by the UK in 1923. During the 1920s and 1930s, advances in mining spurred development and immigration. The name was changed to Zambia upon independence in 1964. In the 1980s and 1990s, declining copper prices and a prolonged drought hurt the economy. Elections in 1991 brought an end to one-party rule, but the subsequent vote in 1996 saw blatant harassment of opposition parties. The election in 2001 was marked by administrative problems with three parties filing a legal petition challenging the election of ruling party candidate Levy MWANAWASA. The new president launched an anticorruption investigation in 2002 to probe high-level corruption during the previous administration. In 2006-07, this task force successfully prosecuted four cases, including a landmark civil case in the UK in which former President CHILUBA and numerous others were found liable for USD 41 million. MWANAWASA was reelected in 2006 in an election that was deemed free and fair. Upon his abrupt death in August 2008, he was succeeded by his Vice-president Rupiah BANDA, who subsequently won a special presidential election in October 2008.

## Geography

**Location:** Southern Africa, east of Angola
**Geographic coordinates:** 15 00 S, 30 00 E
**Map references:** Africa
**Area:**
*total:* 752,614 sq km
*land:* 740,724 sq km
*water:* 11,890 sq km
**Area - comparative:** slightly larger than Texas
**Land boundaries:**
*total:* 5,664 km
*border countries:* Angola 1,110 km, Democratic Republic of the Congo 1,930 km, Malawi 837 km, Mozambique 419 km, Namibia 233 km, Tanzania 338 km, Zimbabwe 797 km
**Coastline:** 0 km (landlocked)
**Maritime claims:** none (landlocked)
**Climate:** tropical; modified by altitude; rainy season (October to April)
**Terrain:** mostly high plateau with some hills and mountains
**Elevation extremes:**
*lowest point:* Zambezi river 329 m
*highest point:* unnamed location in Mafinga Hills 2,301 m
**Natural resources:** copper, cobalt, zinc, lead, coal, emeralds, gold, silver, uranium, hydropower
**Land use:**
*arable land:* 6.99%
*permanent crops:* 0.04%
*other:* 92.97% (2005)
**Irrigated land:** 1,560 sq km (2003)
**Total renewable water resources:** 105.2 cu km (2001)
**Freshwater withdrawal (domestic/industrial/agricultural):**
*total:* 1.74 cu km/yr (17%/7%/76%)
*per capita:* 149 cu m/yr (2000)
**Natural hazards:** periodic drought; tropical storms (November to April)
**Environment - current issues:** air pollution and resulting acid rain in the mineral extraction and refining region; chemical runoff into watersheds; poaching seriously threatens rhinoceros, elephant, antelope, and large cat populations; deforestation; soil erosion; desertification; lack of adequate water treatment presents human health risks
**Environment - international agreements:**
*party to:* Biodiversity, Climate Change, Climate Change-Kyoto Protocol, Desertification, Endangered Species, Hazardous Wastes, Law of the Sea, Ozone Layer Protection, Wetlands
*signed, but not ratified:* none of the selected agreements
**Geography - note:** landlocked; the Zambezi forms a natural riverine boundary with Zimbabwe

## People

**Population:** 11,862,740
*note:* estimates for this country explicitly take into account the effects of excess mortality due to AIDS; this can result in lower life expectancy, higher infant mortality, higher death rates, lower population growth rates, and changes in the distribution of population by age and sex than would otherwise be expected (July 2009 est.)
**Age structure:**
*0-14 years:* 45.1% (male 2,685,142/ female 2,659,771)
*15-64 years:* 52.6% (male 3,122,305/ female 3,116,846)
*65 years and over:* 2.3% (male 114,477/ female 164,199) (2009 est.)
**Median age:**
*total:* 17 years
*male:* 16.9 years
*female:* 17.2 years (2009 est.)
**Population growth rate:** 1.631% (2009 est.)
**Birth rate:** 40.24 births/1,000 population (2009 est.)
**Death rate:** 21.35 deaths/1,000 population (2008 est.)
**Net migration rate:** -2.59 migrant(s)/1,000 population (2009 est.)
**Urbanization:**
*urban population:* 35% of total population (2008)
*rate of urbanization:* 2.3% annual rate of change (2005-10 est.)
**Sex ratio:**
*at birth:* 1.03 male(s)/female
*under 15 years:* 1.01 male(s)/female
*15-64 years:* 1 male(s)/female
*65 years and over:* 0.7 male(s)/female
*total population:* 1 male(s)/female (2009 est.)
**Infant mortality rate:**
*total:* 101.2 deaths/1,000 live births
*male:* 105.97 deaths/1,000 live births
*female:* 96.28 deaths/1,000 live births (2009 est.)
**Life expectancy at birth:**
*total population:* 38.63 years
*male:* 38.53 years
*female:* 38.73 years (2009 est.)
**Total fertility rate:** 5.15 children born/woman (2009 est.)
**HIV/AIDS - adult prevalence rate:** 15.2% (2007 est.)
**HIV/AIDS - people living with HIV/AIDS:** 1.1 million (2007 est.)
**HIV/AIDS - deaths:** 56,000 (2007 est.)
**Major infectious diseases:**
*degree of risk:* very high
*food or waterborne diseases:* bacterial and protozoal diarrhea, hepatitis A, and typhoid fever
*vectorborne diseases:* malaria and plague are high risks in some locations
*water contact disease:* schistosomiasis
*animal contact disease:* rabies (2009)
**Nationality:**
*noun:* Zambian(s)
*adjective:* Zambian
**Ethnic groups:** African 99.5% (includes Bemba, Tonga, Chewa, Lozi, Nsenga, Tumbuka, Ngoni, Lala, Kaonde, Lunda, and other African groups), other 0.5% (includes Europeans, Asians, and Americans) (2000 Census)
**Religions:** Christian 50%-75%, Muslim and Hindu 24%-49%, indigenous beliefs 1%
**Languages:** English (official), major vernaculars - Bemba, Kaonda, Lozi, Lunda, Luvale, Nyanja, Tonga, and about 70 other indigenous languages
**Literacy:**
*definition:* age 15 and over can read and write English
*total population:* 80.6%
*male:* 86.8%
*female:* 74.8% (2003 est.)

# Zambia (continued)

**School life expectancy (primary to tertiary education):**
*total:* 7 years
*male:* 7 years
*female:* 7 years (2000)
**Education expenditures:** 2% of GDP (2005)

## Government

**Country name:**
*conventional long form:* Republic of Zambia
*conventional short form:* Zambia
*former:* Northern Rhodesia
**Government type:** republic
**Capital:**
*name:* Lusaka
*geographic coordinates:* 15 25 S, 28 17 E
*time difference:* UTC+2 (7 hours ahead of Washington, DC during Standard Time)
**Administrative divisions:** 9 provinces; Central, Copperbelt, Eastern, Luapula, Lusaka, Northern, North-Western, Southern, Western
**Independence:** 24 October 1964 (from the UK)
**National holiday:** Independence Day, 24 October (1964)
**Constitution:** 24 August 1991; amended in 1996 to establish presidential term limits
**Legal system:** based on English common law and customary law; judicial review of legislative acts in an ad hoc constitutional council; has not accepted compulsory ICJ jurisdiction
**Suffrage:** 18 years of age; universal
**Executive branch:**
*chief of state:* President Rupiah BANDA (since 19August 2008); Vice President George KUNDA (since 14 November 2008); note - President BANDA was acting president since the illness and eventual death of President Levy MWANAWASA on 18 August 2008, he was then elected president on 30 October 2008 to serve out the remainder of MWANAWASA's term; the president is both the chief of state and head of government
*head of government:* President Rupiah BANDA (since 19 August 2008); Vice President George KUNDA (since 14 November 2008)
*cabinet:* Cabinet appointed by the president from among the members of the National Assembly
*elections:* president elected by popular vote for a five-year term (eligible for a second term); election last held 30 October 2008 (next to be held in 2011); vice president appointed by the president; note - due to the death of former President Levy MWANAWASA, early elections were held to identify a replacement to serve out the remainder of his term
*election results:* Rupiah BANDA elected president; percent of vote - Rupiah BANDA 40.1%, Michael SATA 38.1%, Hakainde HICHILEMA 19.7%, Godfrey MIYANDA 0.8%, other 1.3%
**Legislative branch:** unicameral National Assembly (158 seats; 150 members are elected by popular vote, 8 members are appointed by the president, to serve five-year terms)

*elections:* last held 28 September 2006 (next to be held in 2011)
*election results:* percent of vote by party - NA; seats by party - MMD 72, PF 44, UDA 27, ULP 2, NDF 1, independents 2; seats not determined 2
**Judicial branch:** Supreme Court (the final court of appeal; justices are appointed by the president); High Court (has unlimited jurisdiction to hear civil and criminal cases)
**Political parties and leaders:** Forum for Democracy and Development or FDD [Edith NAWAKWI]; Heritage Party or HP [Godfrey MIYANDA]; Movement for Multiparty Democracy or MMD [vacant]; Patriotic Front or PF [Michael SATA]; Party of Unity for Democracy and Development or PUDD [Dan PULE]; Reform Party [Nevers MUMBA]; United Democratic Alliance or UDA (a coalition of RP, ZADECO, PUDD, and ZRP); United Liberal Party or ULP [Sakwiba SIKOTA]; United National Independence Party or UNIP [Tilyenji KAUNDA]; United Party for National Development or UPND [Hakainde HICHILEMA]; Zambia Democratic Congress or ZADECO [Langton SICHONE]; Zambian Republican Party or ZRP [Benjamin MWILA]
**Political pressure groups and leaders:** NA
**International organization participation:** ACP, AfDB, AU, C, COMESA, FAO, G-77, IAEA, IBRD, ICAO, ICCt, ICRM, IDA, IFAD, IFC, IFRCS, ILO, IMF, Interpol, IOC, IOM, IPU, ISO (correspondent), ITSO, ITU, ITUC, MIGA, MINURCAT, MONUC, NAM, OPCW, PCA, SADC, UN, UNAMID, UNCTAD, UNESCO, UNHCR, UNIDO, UNMIL, UNMIS, UNOCI, UNWTO, UPU, WCL, WCO, WFTU, WHO, WIPO, WMO, WTO
**Diplomatic representation in the US:**
*chief of mission:* Ambassador Inonge MBIKUSITA-LEWANIKA
*chancery:* 2419 Massachusetts Avenue NW, Washington, DC 20008
*telephone:* [1] (202) 265-9717 through 9719
*FAX:* [1] (202) 332-0826
**Diplomatic representation from the US:**
*chief of mission:* Ambassador Donald E. BOOTH
*embassy:* corner of Independence and United Nations Avenues, Lusaka
*mailing address:* P. O. Box 31617, Lusaka
*telephone:* [260] (211) 250-955
*FAX:* [260] (211) 252-225
**Flag description:** green field with a panel of three vertical bands of red (hoist side), black, and orange below a soaring orange eagle, on the outer edge of the flag

## Economy

**Economy - overview:** Zambia's economy has experienced strong growth in recent years, with real GDP growth in 2005-08 about 6% per year. Privatization of government-owned copper mines in the 1990s relieved the government from covering mammoth losses generated by the industry and greatly improved the chances for copper mining to

return to profitability and spur economic growth. Copper output has increased steadily since 2004, due to higher copper prices and foreign investment. In 2005, Zambia qualified for debt relief under the Highly Indebted Poor Country Initiative, consisting of approximately USD 6 billion in debt relief. Zambia experienced a bumper harvest in 2007, which helped to boost GDP and agricultural exports and contain inflation. Although poverty continues to be significant problem in Zambia, its economy has strengthened, featuring single-digit inflation, a relatively stable currency, decreasing interest rates, and increasing levels of trade. The decline in world commodity prices and demand will hurt GDP growth in 2009, and elections and campaign promises are likely to weaken Zambia's improved fiscal stance.
**GDP (purchasing power parity):**
$17.39 billion (2008 est.)
$16.43 billion (2007)
$15.55 billion (2006)
*note:* data are in 2008 US dollars
**GDP (official exchange rate):** $15.23 billion (2008 est.)
**GDP - real growth rate:**
5.8% (2008 est.)
5.7% (2007 est.)
6.2% (2006 est.)
**GDP - per capita (PPP):**
$1,500 (2008 est.)
$1,400 (2007 est.)
$1,400 (2006 est.)
*note:* data are in 2008 US dollars
**GDP - composition by sector:**
*agriculture:* 16.7%
*industry:* 26%
*services:* 57.3% (2008 est.)
**Labor force:** 5.093 million (2008 est.)
**Labor force - by occupation:**
*agriculture:* 85%
*industry:* 6%
*services:* 9% (2004)
**Unemployment rate:**
50% (2000 est.)
**Population below poverty line:** 86% (1993)
**Household income or consumption by percentage share:**
*lowest 10%:* 1.2%
*highest 10%:* 38.8% (2004)
**Distribution of family income - Gini index:** 50.8 (2004)
**Investment (gross fixed):** 26% of GDP (2008 est.)
**Budget:**
*revenues:* $3.777 billion
*expenditures:* $4.104 billion (2008 est.)
**Public debt:** 25.7% of GDP (2008 est.)
**Inflation rate (consumer prices):**
11.8% (2008 est.)
10.6% (2007 est.)
**Central bank discount rate:** 11.73% (31 December 2007)

# Zambia (continued)

**Commercial bank prime lending rate:** 18.89% (31 December 2007)

**Stock of money:** $995.8 million (31 December 2007)

**Stock of quasi money:** $1.709 billion (31 December 2007)

**Stock of domestic credit:** $1.968 billion (31 December 2007)

**Market value of publicly traded shares:** $2.346 billion (31 December 2007)

**Agriculture - products:** corn, sorghum, rice, peanuts, sunflower seed, vegetables, flowers, tobacco, cotton, sugarcane, cassava (tapioca), coffee; cattle, goats, pigs, poultry, milk, eggs, hides

**Industries:** copper mining and processing, construction, foodstuffs, beverages, chemicals, textiles, fertilizer, horticulture

**Industrial production growth rate:** 7% (2008 est.)

**Electricity - production:** 9.289 billion kWh (2006 est.)

**Electricity - consumption:** 8.625 billion kWh (2006 est.)

**Electricity - exports:** 255 million kWh (2006)

**Electricity - imports:** 68 million kWh (2007 est.)

**Oil - production:** 150 bbl/day (2007 est.)

**Oil - consumption:** 14,760 bbl/day (2006 est.)

**Oil - exports:** 190.6 bbl/day (2005)

**Oil - imports:** 13,810 bbl/day (2005)

**Oil - proved reserves:** NA bbl

**Natural gas - production:** 0 cu m (2007 est.)

**Natural gas - consumption:** 0 cu m (2007 est.)

**Natural gas - exports:** 0 cu m (2007 est.)

**Natural gas - imports:** 0 cu m (2007 est.)

**Natural gas - proved reserves:** 0 cu m (1 January 2006 est.)

**Current account balance:** -$478 million (2008 est.)

**Exports:** $5.632 billion f.o.b. (2008 est.)

**Exports - commodities:** copper/cobalt 64%, cobalt, electricity; tobacco, flowers, cotton

**Exports - partners:** Switzerland 41.8%, South Africa 12%, Thailand 5.9%, Democratic Republic of the Congo 5.3%, Egypt 5%, Saudi Arabia 4.7%, China 4.1% (2007)

**Imports:** $4.423 billion f.o.b. (2008 est.)

**Imports - commodities:** machinery, transportation equipment, petroleum products, electricity, fertilizer; foodstuffs, clothing

**Imports - partners:** South Africa 47.4%, UAE 6.3%, China 6%, India 4.1%, UK 4% (2007)

**Reserves of foreign exchange and gold:** $1.35 billion (31 December 2008 est.)

**Debt - external:** $2.913 billion (31 December 2008 est.)

**Stock of direct foreign investment - at home:** $NA

**Stock of direct foreign investment - abroad:** $NA

**Exchange rates:** Zambian kwacha (ZMK) per US dollar - 3,512.9 (2008 est.), 3,990.2 (2007), 3,601.5 (2006), 4,463.5 (2005), 4,778.9 (2004)

## Communications

**Telephones - main lines in use:** 91,800 (2007)

**Telephones - mobile cellular:** 2.639 million (2007)

**Telephone system:**

*general assessment:* facilities are aging but still among the best in Sub-Saharan Africa

*domestic:* high-capacity microwave radio relay connects most larger towns and cities; several cellular telephone services in operation and network coverage is improving; Internet service is widely available; very small aperture terminal (VSAT) networks are operated by private firms

*international:* country code - 260; satellite earth stations - 2 Intelsat (1 Indian Ocean and 1 Atlantic Ocean)

**Radio broadcast stations:** AM 19, FM 5, shortwave 4 (2001)

**Television broadcast stations:** 9 (2001)

**Internet country code:** .zm

**Internet hosts:** 7,610 (2008)

**Internet users:** 500,000 (2007)

## Transportation

**Airports:** 101 (2008)

**Airports - with paved runways:**

*total:* 9

*over 3,047 m:* 1

*2,438 to 3,047 m:* 2

*1,524 to 2,437 m:* 4

*914 to 1,523 m:* 2 (2008)

**Airports - with unpaved runways:**

*total:* 92

*2,438 to 3,047 m:* 1

*1,524 to 2,437 m:* 4

*914 to 1,523 m:* 65

*under 914 m:* 22 (2008)

**Pipelines:** oil 771 km (2008)

**Railways:**

*total:* 2,157 km

*narrow gauge:* 2,157 km 1.067-m gauge

*note:* includes 891 km of the Tanzania-Zambia Railway Authority (TAZARA) (2006)

**Roadways:**

*total:* 91,440 km

*paved:* 20,117 km

*unpaved:* 71,323 km (2001)

**Waterways:** 2,250 km (includes Lake Tanganyika and the Zambezi and Luapula rivers) (2008)

**Ports and terminals:** Mpulungu

## Military

**Military branches:** Zambian National Defense Force (ZNDF): Zambian Army, Zambian Air Force, National Service (2009)

**Military service age and obligation:** 18 years of age for voluntary military service (16 years of age with parental consent); mandatory HIV testing on enlistment; no conscription (2009)

**Manpower available for military service:**

*males age 16-49:* 2,678,668

*females age 16-49:* 2,567,433 (2008 est.)

**Manpower fit for military service:**

*males age 16-49:* 1,364,173

*females age 16-49:* 1,245,220 (2009 est.)

**Manpower reaching militarily significant age annually:**

*male:* 149,567

*female:* 148,889 (2009 est.)

**Military expenditures:** 1.8% of GDP (2005 est.)

## Transnational Issues

**Disputes - international:** in 2004, Zimbabwe dropped objections to plans between Botswana and Zambia to build a bridge over the Zambezi River, thereby de facto recognizing a short, but not clearly delimited, Botswana-Zambia boundary in the river

**Refugees and internally displaced persons:**

*refugees (country of origin):* 42,565 (Angola); 60,874 (Democratic Republic of the Congo); 4,100 (Rwanda) (2007)

**Trafficking in persons:**

*current situation:* Zambia is a source, transit, and destination country for women and children trafficked for the purposes of forced labor and sexual exploitation; many Zambian child laborers, particularly those in the agriculture, domestic service, and fishing sectors, are also victims of human trafficking; Zambian women, lured by false employment or marriage offers abroad, are trafficked to South Africa via Zimbabwe and to Europe via Malawi for sexual exploitation; Zambia is a transit point for regional trafficking of women and children, particularly from Angola to Namibia and from the Democratic Republic of the Congo to South Africa for agricultural labor

*tier rating:* Tier 2 Watch List - Zambia is on the Tier 2 Watch List for failing to provide evidence of increasing efforts to combat severe forms of trafficking, particularly in regard to its inability to bring alleged traffickers to justice through prosecutions and convictions; unlike 2006, there were no new prosecutions or convictions of alleged traffickers in 2007; government efforts to protect victims of trafficking remained extremely limited throughout the year (2008)

**Illicit drugs:** transshipment point for moderate amounts of methaqualone, small amounts of heroin, and cocaine bound for southern Africa and possibly Europe; a poorly developed financial infrastructure coupled with a government commitment to combating money laundering make it an unattractive venue for money launderers; major consumer of cannabis

# Zimbabwe

## Introduction

**Background:** The UK annexed Southern Rhodesia from the [British] South Africa Company in 1923. A 1961 constitution was formulated that favored whites in power. In 1965 the government unilaterally declared its independence, but the UK did not recognize the act and demanded more complete voting rights for the black African majority in the country (then called Rhodesia). UN sanctions and a guerrilla uprising finally led to free elections in 1979 and independence (as Zimbabwe) in 1980. Robert MUGABE, the nation's first prime minister, has been the country's only ruler (as president since 1987) and has dominated the country's political system since independence. His chaotic land redistribution campaign, which began in 2000, caused an exodus of white farmers, crippled the economy, and ushered in widespread shortages of basic commodities. Ignoring international condemnation, MUGABE rigged the 2002 presidential election to ensure his reelection. The ruling ZANU-PF party used fraud and intimidation to win a two-thirds majority in the March 2005 parliamentary election, allowing it to amend the constitution at will and recreate the Senate, which had been abolished in the late 1980s. In April 2005, Harare embarked on Operation Restore Order, ostensibly an urban rationalization program, which resulted in the destruction of the homes or businesses of 700,000 mostly poor supporters of the opposition. President MUGABE in June 2007 instituted price controls on all basic commodities causing panic buying and leaving store shelves empty for months. General elections held in March 2008 contained irregularities but still amounted to a censure of the ZANU-PF-led government with significant gains in opposition seats in parliament. MDC opposition leader Morgan TSVANGIRAI won the presidential polls, and may have won an out right majority, but official results posted by the Zimbabwe Electoral Committee did not reflect this. In the lead up to a run-off election in late June 2008, considerable violence enacted against opposition party members led to the withdrawal of TSVANGIRAI from the ballot. Extensive evidence of vote tampering and ballot-box stuffing resulted in international condemnation of the process. Difficult negotiations over a power sharing agreement, allowing MUGABE to remain as president and creating the new position of prime minister for TSVANGIRAI, were finally settled in February 2009.

## Geography

**Location:** Southern Africa, between South Africa and Zambia

**Geographic coordinates:** 20 00 S, 30 00 E

**Map references:** Africa

**Area:**
*total:* 390,580 sq km
*land:* 386,670 sq km
*water:* 3,910 sq km

**Area - comparative:** slightly larger than Montana

**Land boundaries:**
*total:* 3,066 km
*border countries:* Botswana 813 km, Mozambique 1,231 km, South Africa 225 km, Zambia 797 km

**Coastline:** 0 km (landlocked)

**Maritime claims:** none (landlocked)

**Climate:** tropical; moderated by altitude; rainy season (November to March)

**Terrain:** mostly high plateau with higher central plateau (high veld); mountains in east

**Elevation extremes:**
*lowest point:* junction of the Runde and Save rivers 162 m
*highest point:* Inyangani 2,592 m

**Natural resources:** coal, chromium ore, asbestos, gold, nickel, copper, iron ore, vanadium, lithium, tin, platinum group metals

**Land use:**
*arable land:* 8.24%
*permanent crops:* 0.33%
*other:* 91.43% (2005)

**Irrigated land:** 1,740 sq km (2003)

**Total renewable water resources:** 20 cu km (1987)

**Freshwater withdrawal (domestic/industrial/agricultural):**
*total:* 4.21 cu km/yr (14%/7%/79%)
*per capita:* 324 cu m/yr (2002)

**Natural hazards:** recurring droughts; floods and severe storms are rare

**Environment - current issues:** deforestation; soil erosion; land degradation; air and water pollution; the black rhinoceros herd - once the largest concentration of the species in the world - has been significantly reduced by poaching; poor mining practices have led to toxic waste and heavy metal pollution

**Environment - international agreements:**
*party to:* Biodiversity, Climate Change, Desertification, Endangered Species, Law of the Sea, Ozone Layer Protection
*signed, but not ratified:* none of the selected agreements

**Geography - note:** landlocked; the Zambezi forms a natural riverine boundary with Zambia; in full flood (February-April) the massive Victoria Falls on the river forms the world's largest curtain of falling water

## People

**Population:** 11,392,629
*note:* estimates for this country explicitly take into account the effects of excess mortality due to AIDS; this can result in lower life expectancy, higher infant mortality, higher death rates, lower population growth rates, and changes in the distribution of population by age and sex than would otherwise be expected (July 2009 est.)

**Age structure:**
*0-14 years:* 43.9% (male 2,523,119/female 2,473,928)
*15-64 years:* 52.2% (male 2,666,928/female 3,283,474)
*65 years and over:* 3.9% (male 194,360/female 250,820) (2009 est.)

**Median age:**
*total:* 17.6 years
*male:* 16.3 years
*female:* 18.8 years (2009 est.)

**Population growth rate:** 1.53% (2009 est.)

**Birth rate:** 31.49 births/1,000 population (2009 est.)

**Death rate:** 17.29 deaths/1,000 population (2008 est.)

**Net migration rate:** NA
*note:* there is an increasing flow of Zimbabweans into South Africa and Botswana in search of better economic opportunities (2009 est.)

**Urbanization:**
*urban population:* 37% of total population (2008)
*rate of urbanization:* 2.2% annual rate of change (2005-10 est.)

**Sex ratio:**
*at birth:* 1.03 male(s)/female
*under 15 years:* 1.02 male(s)/female
*15-64 years:* 0.81 male(s)/female
*65 years and over:* 0.78 male(s)/female
*total population:* 0.9 male(s)/female (2009 est.)

**Infant mortality rate:**
*total:* 32.31 deaths/1,000 live births
*male:* 34.9 deaths/1,000 live births
*female:* 29.64 deaths/1,000 live births (2009 est.)

**Life expectancy at birth:**
*total population:* 45.77 years
*male:* 46.36 years
*female:* 45.16 years (2009 est.)

**Total fertility rate:** 3.69 children born/woman (2009 est.)

**HIV/AIDS - adult prevalence rate:** 15.3% (2007 est.)

**HIV/AIDS - people living with HIV/AIDS:** 1.3 million (2007 est.)

**HIV/AIDS - deaths:** 140,000 (2007 est.)

# Zimbabwe (continued)

**Major infectious diseases:**

*degree of risk:* high

*food or waterborne diseases:* bacterial and protozoal diarrhea, hepatitis A, and typhoid fever

*vectorborne disease:* malaria

*water contact disease:* schistosomiasis

*animal contact disease:* rabies (2009)

**Nationality:**

*noun:* Zimbabwean(s)

*adjective:* Zimbabwean

**Ethnic groups:** African 98% (Shona 82%, Ndebele 14%, other 2%), mixed and Asian 1%, white less than 1%

**Religions:** syncretic (part Christian, part indigenous beliefs) 50%, Christian 25%, indigenous beliefs 24%, Muslim and other 1%

**Languages:** English (official), Shona, Sindebele (the language of the Ndebele, sometimes called Ndebele), numerous but minor tribal dialects

**Literacy:**

*definition:* age 15 and over can read and write English

*total population:* 90.7%

*male:* 94.2%

*female:* 87.2% (2003 est.)

**School life expectancy (primary to tertiary education):**

*total:* 9 years

*male:* 9 years

*female:* 9 years (2003)

**Education expenditures:** 4.6% of GDP (2000)

## Government

**Country name:**

*conventional long form:* Republic of Zimbabwe

*conventional short form:* Zimbabwe

*former:* Southern Rhodesia, Rhodesia

**Government type:** parliamentary democracy

**Capital:**

*name:* Harare

*geographic coordinates:* 17 50 S, 31 03 E

*time difference:* UTC+2 (7 hours ahead of Washington, DC during Standard Time)

**Administrative divisions:** 8 provinces and 2 cities* with provincial status; Bulawayo*, Harare*, Manicaland, Mashonaland Central, Mashonaland East, Mashonaland West, Masvingo, Matabeleland North, Matabeleland South, Midlands

**Independence:** 18 April 1980 (from the UK)

**National holiday:** Independence Day, 18 April (1980)

**Constitution:** 21 December 1979

**Legal system:** mixture of Roman-Dutch and English common law; has not accepted compulsory ICJ jurisdiction

**Suffrage:** 18 years of age; universal

**Executive branch:**

*chief of state:* Executive President Robert Gabriel MUGABE (since 31 December 1987); Vice President Joseph MSIKA (since December 1999) and Vice President Joyce MUJURU (since 6 December 2004)

*head of government:* Prime Minister Morgan TSVANGIRAI (since 11 February 2009); Deputy Prime Minister Arthur MUTAMBARA

*cabinet:* Cabinet appointed by the president; responsible to the House of Assembly

*elections:* presidential candidates nominated with a nomination paper signed by at least 10 registered voters (at least one from each province) and elected by popular vote for a five-year term (no term limits); elections last held 28 March 2008 followed by a run-off on 27 June 2008 (next to be held in 2013); co-vice presidents appointed by the president

*election results:* Robert Gabriel MUGABE reelected president; percent of vote - Robert Gabriel MUGABE 85.5%, Morgan TSVANGIRAI 9.3%, other 5.2%; note -first round voting results - Morgan TSVANGIRAI 47.9%, Robert Gabriel MUGABE 43.2%, Simba MAKONI 8.3%, other 0.6%; first-round round polls were deemed to be flawed suppressing TSVANGIRAI's results; the 27 June 2008 run-off between MUGABE and TSVANGIRAI were severely flawed and internationally condemned

**Legislative branch:** bicameral Parliament consists of a Senate (93 seats - 60 elected by popular vote for a five-year term, 10 provincial governors nominated by the president, 16 traditional chiefs elected by the Council of Chiefs, 2 held by the president and deputy president of the Council of Chiefs, and 5 appointed by the president) and a House of Assembly (210 seats - all elected by popular vote for five-year terms)

*elections:* last held 28 March 2008 (next to be held in 2013)

*election results:* Senate - percent of vote by party - MDC 51.6%, ZANU-PF 45.8%, other 2.6%; seats by party - MDC 30, ZANU-PF 30; House of Assembly - percent of vote by party - MDC 51.3%, ZANU-PF 45.8%, other 2.9%; seats by party - MDC 109, ZANU-PF 97, other 4

**Judicial branch:** Supreme Court; High Court

**Political parties and leaders:** African National Party or ANP [Egypt DZINEMUNHENZVA]; Movement for Democratic Change or MDC [Morgan TSVANGIRAI, Arthur MUTAMBARA, splinter faction]; Peace Action is Freedom for All or PAFA; United Parties [Abel MUZOREWA]; United People's Party or UPP [Daniel SHUMBA]; Zimbabwe African National Union-Ndonga or ZANU-Ndonga [Wilson KUMBULA]; Zimbabwe African National Union-Patriotic Front or ZANU-PF [Robert Gabriel MUGABE]; Zimbabwe African Peoples Union or ZAPU [Agrippa MADLELA]; Zimbabwe Youth in Alliance or ZIYA

**Political pressure groups and leaders:** Crisis in Zimbabwe Coalition [Xolani ZITHA]; National Constitutional Assembly or NCA [Lovemore MADHUKU]; Women of Zimbabwe Arise or WOZA [Jenny WILLIAMS]; Zimbabwe Congress of Trade Unions or ZCTU [Wellington CHIBEBE]

**International organization participation:** ACP, AfDB, AU, COMESA, FAO, G-15, G-77, IAEA, IBRD, ICAO, ICCt (signatory), ICRM, IDA, IFAD, IFC, IFRCS, ILO, IMF, IMO, Interpol, IOC, IOM, IPU, ISO, ITSO, ITU, ITUC, MIGA, NAM, OPCW, PCA, SADC, UN, UNCTAD, UNESCO, UNIDO, UNMIL, UNMIS, UNOCI, UNWTO, UPU, WCL, WCO, WFTU, WHO, WIPO, WMO, WTO

**Diplomatic representation in the US:**

*chief of mission:* Ambassador Machivenyika MAPURANGA

*chancery:* 1608 New Hampshire Avenue NW, Washington, DC 20009

*telephone:* [1] (202) 332-7100

*FAX:* [1] (202) 483-9326

**Diplomatic representation from the US:**

*chief of mission:* Ambassador James D. MCGEE

*embassy:* 172 Herbert Chitepo Avenue, Harare

*mailing address:* P. O. Box 3340, Harare

*telephone:* [263] (4) 250-593 through 250-594

*FAX:* [263] (4) 796-488, or 722-618

**Flag description:** seven equal horizontal bands of green, yellow, red, black, red, yellow, and green with a white isosceles triangle edged in black with its base on the hoist side; a yellow Zimbabwe bird representing the long history of the country is superimposed on a red five-pointed star in the center of the triangle, which symbolizes peace; green symbolizes agriculture, yellow - mineral wealth, red - blood shed to achieve independence, and black stands for the native people

## Economy

**Economy - overview:** The government of Zimbabwe faces a wide variety of difficult economic problems as it struggles with an unsustainable fiscal deficit, an overvalued official exchange rate, hyperinflation, and bare store shelves. Its 1998-2002 involvement in the war in the Democratic Republic of the Congo drained hundreds of millions of dollars from the economy. The government's land reform program, characterized by chaos and violence, has badly damaged the commercial farming sector, the traditional source of exports and foreign exchange and the provider of 400,000 jobs, turning Zimbabwe into a net importer of food products. The EU and the US provide food aid on humanitarian grounds. Badly needed support from the IMF has been suspended because of the government's arrears on past loans and the government's unwillingness to enact reforms that would stabilize the economy. The Reserve Bank of Zimbabwe routinely prints money to fund the budget deficit, causing the official annual inflation rate to rise from 32% in 1998, to 133% in 2004, 585% in 2005, past 1,000% in 2006, and 26,000% in November 2007, and to 11.2 million percent in 2008. Meanwhile, the official exchange rate fell from approximately 1 (revalued) Zimbabwean dollar per US dollar in 2003 to 30,000 per US dollar in September 2007.

**GDP (purchasing power parity):**

$1.959 billion (2008 est.)

$2.242 billion (2007)

$2.372 billion (2006)

*note:* data are in 2008 US dollars

**GDP (official exchange rate):** $4.548 billion

*note:* hyperinflation and the plunging value of the Zimbabwean dollar makes Zimbabwe's GDP at the official exchange rate a highly inaccurate statistic (2008 est.)

# Zimbabwe *(continued)*

**GDP - real growth rate:**
-12.6% (2008 est.)
-5.5% (2007 est.)
-4.6% (2006 est.)
**GDP - per capita (PPP):**
$200 (2008 est.)
$200 (2007 est.)
$200 (2006 est.)
*note:* data are in 2008 US dollars
**GDP - composition by sector:**
*agriculture:* 18.1%
*industry:* 22.6%
*services:* 59.3% (2008 est.)
**Labor force:** 4.039 million (2008 est.)
**Labor force - by occupation:**
*agriculture:* 66%
*industry:* 10%
*services:* 24% (1996)
**Unemployment rate:**
80% (2005 est.)
**Population below poverty line:** 68% (2004)
**Household income or consumption by percentage share:**
*lowest 10%:* 2%
*highest 10%:* 40.4% (1995)
**Distribution of family income - Gini index:** 50.1 (2006)
**Investment (gross fixed):** 17.5% of GDP (2008 est.)
**Budget:**
*revenues:* $153,700
*expenditures:* $179,300 (2008 est.)
**Public debt:** 241.2% of GDP (2008 est.)
**Inflation rate (consumer prices):**
11.2 million% (2008 est.)
12,563% (2007 est.)
**Central bank discount rate:** 975% (31 December 2007)
**Commercial bank prime lending rate:** 578.96% (31 December 2007)
**Stock of money:** $14.18 billion
*note:* this number reflects the vastly overvalued official exchange rate of 30,000 Zimbabwe dollars per US dollar; at an unofficial rate of 800,000 Zimbabwe dollars per US dollar, the stock of Zimbabwe dollars would equal only about US$500 million and Zimbabwe's velocity of money (the number of times money turns over in the course of a year) would be nine, in line with the velocity of money for other countries in the region (31 December 2007)
**Stock of quasi money:** $5.349 billion (31 December 2007)
**Stock of domestic credit:** $24.91 billion (31 December 2007)
**Market value of publicly traded shares:** $5.333 billion (31 December 2007)
**Agriculture - products:** corn, cotton, tobacco, wheat, coffee, sugarcane, peanuts; sheep, goats, pigs
**Industries:** mining (coal, gold, platinum, copper, nickel, tin, clay, numerous metallic and nonmetallic ores), steel; wood products, cement, chemicals, fertilizer, clothing and footwear, foodstuffs, beverages

**Industrial production growth rate:** -6% (2008 est.)
**Electricity - production:** 9.467 billion kWh (2006 est.)
**Electricity - consumption:** 11.59 billion kWh (2006 est.)
**Electricity - exports:** 34 million kWh (2006 est.)
**Electricity - imports:** 2.867 billion kWh (2006 est.)
**Oil - production:** 0 bbl/day (2007 est.)
**Oil - consumption:** 14,590 bbl/day (2006 est.)
**Oil - exports:** 0 bbl/day (2005 est.)
**Oil - imports:** 15,800 bbl/day (2005 est.)
**Oil - proved reserves:** 0 bbl (1 January 2006 est.)
**Natural gas - production:** 0 cu m (2007 est.)
**Natural gas - consumption:** 0 cu m (2007 est.)
**Natural gas - exports:** 0 cu m (2007 est.)
**Natural gas - imports:** 0 cu m (2007 est.)
**Natural gas - proved reserves:** 0 cu m (1 January 2006 est.)
**Current account balance:** -$597 million (2008 est.)
**Exports:** $1.806 billion f.o.b. (2008 est.)
**Exports - commodities:** platinum, cotton, tobacco, gold, ferroalloys, textiles/clothing
**Exports - partners:** South Africa 33.8%, Democratic Republic of the Congo 8.3%, Japan 8.1%, Botswana 7.4%, Netherlands 5.2%, China 5.2%, Italy 4.1%, Zambia 4.1% (2007)
**Imports:** $2.337 billion f.o.b. (2008 est.)
**Imports - commodities:** machinery and transport equipment, other manufactures, chemicals, fuels
**Imports - partners:** South Africa 50.7%, China 8.4%, US 4.5%, Botswana 4.3% (2007)
**Reserves of foreign exchange and gold:** $100 million (31 December 2008 est.)
**Debt - external:** $5.255 billion (31 December 2008 est.)
**Stock of direct foreign investment - at home:** $NA
**Stock of direct foreign investment - abroad:** $NA
**Exchange rates:** Zimbabwean dollars (ZWD) per US dollar - NA (2008 est.), 30,000 (2007), 162.07 (2006), 77.965 (2005), 5.729 (2004)
*note:* these are official exchange rates; non-official rates vary significantly

## Communications

**Telephones - main lines in use:** 344,500 (2007)
**Telephones - mobile cellular:** 1.226 million (2007)
**Telephone system:**
*general assessment:* system was once one of the best in Africa, but now suffers from poor maintenance; more than 100,000 outstanding requests for connection despite an equally large number of installed but unused main lines
*domestic:* consists of microwave radio relay links, open-wire lines, radiotelephone communication stations, fixed wireless local loop installations, and a substantial mobile-cellular network; Internet connection is available in Harare and planned for all major towns and for some of the smaller ones
*international:* country code - 263; satellite earth stations - 2 Intelsat; 2 international digital gateway exchanges (in Harare and Gweru)

**Radio broadcast stations:** AM 7, FM 20 (plus 17 repeater stations), shortwave 1 (1998)
**Television broadcast stations:** 16 (1997)
**Internet country code:** .zw
**Internet hosts:** 19,157 (2008)
**Internet users:** 1.351 million (2007)

## Transportation

**Airports:** 227 (2008)
**Airports - with paved runways:**
*total:* 20
*over 3,047 m:* 3
*2,438 to 3,047 m:* 2
*1,524 to 2,437 m:* 5
*914 to 1,523 m:* 10 (2008)
**Airports - with unpaved runways:**
*total:* 207
*1,524 to 2,437 m:* 3
*914 to 1,523 m:* 126
*under 914 m:* 78 (2008)
**Pipelines:** refined products 270 km (2008)
**Railways:**
*total:* 3,077 km
*narrow gauge:* 3,077 km 1.067-m gauge (313 km electrified) (2006)
**Roadways:**
*total:* 97,267 km
*paved:* 18,481 km
*unpaved:* 78,786 km (2002)
**Waterways:** on Lake Kariba (2008)
**Ports and terminals:** Binga, Kariba

## Military

**Military branches:** Zimbabwe Defense Forces (ZDF): Zimbabwe National Army (ZNA), Air Force of Zimbabwe (AFZ), Zimbabwe Republic Police (ZRP) (2009)
**Military service age and obligation:** 18-24 years of age for compulsory military service; women are eligible to serve (2007)
**Manpower available for military service:**
*males age 16-49:* 3,264,258
*females age 16-49:* 3,048,049 (2008 est.)
**Manpower fit for military service:**
*males age 16-49:* 1,198,727
*females age 16-49:* 1,436,232 (2009 est.)
**Manpower reaching militarily significant age annually:**
*male:* 149,592
*female:* 149,717 (2009 est.)
**Military expenditures:** 3.8% of GDP (2006)

## Transnational Issues

**Disputes - international:** Botswana built electric fences and South Africa has placed military along the border to stem the flow of thousands of Zimbabweans fleeing to find work and escape political persecution; Namibia has supported, and in 2004 Zimbabwe dropped objections to, plans between Botswana and Zambia to build a bridge over the Zambezi River, thereby de facto recognizing a short, but not clearly delimited, Botswana-Zambia boundary in the river

## Zimbabwe (continued)

**Refugees and internally displaced persons:**
*refugees (country of origin):* 2,500 (Democratic Republic of Congo)
*IDPs:* 569,685 (MUGABE-led political violence, human rights violations, land reform, and economic collapse) (2007)

**Trafficking in persons:**
*current situation:* Zimbabwe is a source, transit, and destination country for men, women, and children trafficked for the purposes of forced labor and sexual exploitation; large scale migration of Zimbabweans to surrounding countries - as they flee a progressively more desperate situation at home - has increased; rural Zimbabwean men, women, and children are trafficked internally to farms for agricultural labor and domestic servitude and to cities for domestic labor and commercial sexual exploitation; young men and boys are trafficked to South Africa for farm work, often laboring for months in South Africa without pay before "employers" have them arrested and deported as illegal immigrants; young women and girls are lured abroad with false employment offers that result in involuntary domestic servitude or commercial sexual exploitation; men, women, and children from neighboring states are trafficked through Zimbabwe en route to South Africa
*tier rating:* Tier 2 Watch List - Zimbabwe is on the Tier 2 Watch List for its failure to provide evidence of increasing efforts to combat severe forms of human trafficking, and because the absolute number of victims of severe forms of trafficking is significantly increasing; the trafficking situation in the country is worsening as more of the population is made vulnerable by declining socio-economic conditions (2008)

**Illicit drugs:** transit point for cannabis and South Asian heroin, mandrax, and methamphetamines en route to South Africa

# Taiwan

## Introduction

**Background:** In 1895, military defeat forced China to cede Taiwan to Japan. Taiwan reverted to Chinese control after World War II. Following the Communist victory on the mainland in 1949, 2 million Nationalists fled to Taiwan and established a government using the 1946 constitution drawn up for all of China. Over the next five decades, the ruling authorities gradually democratized and incorporated the local population within the governing structure. In 2000, Taiwan underwent its first peaceful transfer of power from the Nationalist to the Democratic Progressive Party. Throughout this period, the island prospered and became one of East Asia's economic "Tigers." The dominant political issues continue to be the relationship between Taiwan and China - specifically the question of Taiwan's eventual status - as well as domestic political and economic reform.

## Geography

**Location:** Eastern Asia, islands bordering the East China Sea, Philippine Sea, South China Sea, and Taiwan Strait, north of the Philippines, off the southeastern coast of China
**Geographic coordinates:** 23 30 N, 121 00 E
**Map references:** Southeast Asia
**Area:**
*total:* 35,980 sq km
*land:* 32,260 sq km
*water:* 3,720 sq km
*note:* includes the Pescadores, Matsu, and Quemoy islands
**Area - comparative:** slightly smaller than Maryland and Delaware combined
**Land boundaries:** 0 km
**Coastline:** 1,566.3 km
**Maritime claims:**
*territorial sea:* 12 nm
*exclusive economic zone:* 200 nm

**Climate:** tropical; marine; rainy season during southwest monsoon (June to August); cloudiness is persistent and extensive all year
**Terrain:** eastern two-thirds mostly rugged mountains; flat to gently rolling plains in west
**Elevation extremes:**
*lowest point:* South China Sea 0 m
*highest point:* Yu Shan 3,952 m
**Natural resources:** small deposits of coal, natural gas, limestone, marble, and asbestos
**Land use:**
*arable land:* 24%
*permanent crops:* 1%
*other:* 75% (2001)
**Irrigated land:** NA
**Total renewable water resources:** 67 cu km (2000)
**Natural hazards:** earthquakes; typhoons
**Environment - current issues:** air pollution; water pollution from industrial emissions, raw sewage; contamination of drinking water supplies; trade in endangered species; low-level radioactive waste disposal
**Environment - international agreements:**
*party to:* none of the selected agreements because of Taiwan's international status
**Geography - note:** strategic location adjacent to both the Taiwan Strait and the Luzon Strait

## People

**Population:** 22,974,347 (July 2009 est.)
**Age structure:**
*0-14 years:* 16.7% (male 1,996,905/female 1,844,611)
*15-64 years:* 72.6% (male 8,416,300/female 8,267,675)
*65 years and over:* 10.7% (male 1,183,382/female 1,265,474) (2009 est.)
**Median age:**
*total:* 36.5 years
*male:* 35.9 years
*female:* 37.1 years (2009 est.)
**Population growth rate:** 0.227% (2009 est.)
**Birth rate:** 8.99 births/1,000 population (2009 est.)
**Death rate:** 6.65 deaths/1,000 population (2008 est.)
**Net migration rate:** 0.03 migrant(s)/1,000 population (2009 est.)
**Sex ratio:**
*at birth:* 1.09 male(s)/female
*under 15 years:* 1.08 male(s)/female
*15-64 years:* 1.02 male(s)/female
*65 years and over:* 0.94 male(s)/female
*total population:* 1.02 male(s)/female (2009 est.)
**Infant mortality rate:**
*total:* 5.35 deaths/1,000 live births
*male:* 5.64 deaths/1,000 live births
*female:* 5.04 deaths/1,000 live births (2009 est.)
**Life expectancy at birth:**
*total population:* 77.96 years
*male:* 75.12 years
*female:* 81.05 years (2009 est.)

# Taiwan (continued)

**Total fertility rate:** 1.14 children born/woman (2009 est.)
**HIV/AIDS - adult prevalence rate:** NA
**HIV/AIDS - people living with HIV/AIDS:** NA
**HIV/AIDS - deaths:** NA
**Nationality:**
*noun:* Taiwan (singular and plural)
*note:* example - he or she is from Taiwan; they are from Taiwan
*adjective:* Taiwan
**Ethnic groups:** Taiwanese (including Hakka) 84%, mainland Chinese 14%, indigenous 2%
**Religions:** mixture of Buddhist and Taoist 93%, Christian 4.5%, other 2.5%
**Languages:** Mandarin Chinese (official), Taiwanese (Min), Hakka dialects
**Literacy:**
*definition:* age 15 and over can read and write
*total population:* 96.1%
*male:* NA
*female:* NA (2003)
**Education expenditures:** NA

## Government

**Country name:**
*conventional long form:* none
*conventional short form:* Taiwan
*local long form:* none
*local short form:* T'ai-wan
*former:* Formosa
**Government type:** multiparty democracy
**Capital:**
*name:* Taipei
*geographic coordinates:* 25 03 N, 121 30 E
*time difference:* UTC+8 (13 hours ahead of Washington, DC during Standard Time)
**Administrative divisions:** includes main island of Taiwan plus smaller islands nearby and off coast of China's Fujian Province; Taiwan is divided into 18 counties (hsien, singular and plural), 5 municipalities (shih, singular and plural), and 2 special municipalities (chih-hsia-shih, singular and plural)
*note:* Taiwan uses a variety of romanization systems; while a modified Wade-Giles system still dominates, the city of Taipei has adopted a Pinyin romanization for street and place names within its boundaries; other local authorities use different romanization systems; names for administrative divisions that follow are taken from the Taiwan Yearbook 2007 published by the Government Information Office in Taipei.
*counties:* Changhua, Chiayi [county], Hsinchu [county], Hualien, Kaohsiung [county], Kinmen, Lienchiang, Miaoli, Nantou, Penghu, Pingtung, Taichung [county], Tainan [county], Taipei [county], Taitung, Taoyuan, Yilan, and Yunlin
*municipalities:* Chiayi [city], Hsinchu [city], Keelung, Taichung [city], Tainan [city]
*special municipalities:* Kaohsiung [city], Taipei [city]
**National holiday:** Republic Day (Anniversary of the Chinese Revolution), 10 October (1911)

**Constitution:** adopted on 25 December 1946; effective 25 December 1947; amended in 1991, 1992, 1994, 1997, 1999, 2000, 2005
**Legal system:** based on civil law system; has not accepted compulsory ICJ jurisdiction
**Suffrage:** 20 years of age; universal
**Executive branch:**
*chief of state:* President MA Ying-jeou (since 20 May 2008); Vice President Vincent SIEW (since 20 May 2008)
*head of government:* Premier (President of the Executive Yuan) LIU Chao-shiuan (since 20 May 2008); Vice Premier (Vice President of Executive Yuan) Paul CHIU (CHANG-hsiung) (since 20 May 2008)
*cabinet:* Executive Yuan - (ministers appointed by president on recommendation of premier)
*elections:* president and vice president elected on the same ticket by popular vote for four-year terms (eligible for a second term); election last held 22 March 2008 (next to be held in March 2012); premier appointed by the president; vice premiers appointed by the president on the recommendation of the premier
*election results:* MA Ying-jeou elected president; percent of vote - MA Ying-jeou 58.45%, Frank HSIEH 41.55%
**Legislative branch:** unicameral Legislative Yuan (113 seats - 73 district members elected by popular vote, 34 at-large members elected on basis of proportion of islandwide votes received by participating political parties, 6 elected by popular vote among aboriginal populations; to serve four-year terms); parties must receive 5% of vote to qualify for at-large seats
*elections:* Legislative Yuan - last held 12 January 2008 (next to be held in December 2011 or January 2012)
*election results:* Legislative Yuan - percent of vote by party - KMT 53.5%, DPP 38.2%, NPSU 2.4%, PFP 0.3%, others 1.6%, independents 4%; seats by party - KMT 81, DPP 27, NPSU 3, PFP 1, independent 1
**Judicial branch:** Judicial Yuan (justices appointed by the president with consent of the Legislative Yuan)
**Political parties and leaders:** Democratic Progressive Party or DPP [TSAI Ing-wen]; Kuomintang or KMT (Nationalist Party) [WU Po-hsiung]; Non-Partisan Solidarity Union or NPSU [LIN Pin-kuan]; People First Party or PFP [James SOONG]
**Political pressure groups and leaders:**
Organization for Taiwan Nation Building; World United Formosans for Independence
*other:* environmental groups; independence movement; various business groups
*note:* debate on Taiwan independence has become acceptable within the mainstream of domestic politics on Taiwan; political liberalization and the increased representation of opposition parties in Taiwan's legislature have opened public debate on the island's national identity; a broad public consensus has developed that the government enjoys popular

sovereignty and - whatever the ultimate outcome regarding unification or independence - that Taiwan's people must have the deciding voice; public opinion polls consistently show a substantial majority of Taiwan people supports maintaining Taiwan's status quo for the foreseeable future; advocates of Taiwan independence oppose the stand that the island will eventually unify with mainland China; goals of the Taiwan independence movement include establishing a sovereign nation on Taiwan and entering the UN; advocates of eventual unification predicate their goal on the democratic transformation of the mainland
**International organization participation:** ADB, APEC, BCIE, ICC, IOC, ITUC, WCL, WFTU, WTO
**Diplomatic representation in the US:**
*consulate(s):* New York
**Diplomatic representation from the US:** none; unofficial commercial and cultural relations with the people on Taiwan are maintained through an unofficial instrumentality - the American Institute in Taiwan (AIT) - which has offices in the US and Taiwan; US office at 1700 N. Moore St., Suite 1700, Arlington, VA 22209-1996, telephone: [1] (703) 525-8474, FAX: [1] (703) 841-1385); Taiwan offices at #7 Lane 134, Hsin Yi Road, Section 3, Taipei, Taiwan, telephone: [886] (2) 2162-2000, FAX: [886] (2) 2162-2251; #2 Chung Cheng 3rd Road, 5th Floor, Kaohsiung, Taiwan, telephone: [886] (7) 238-7744, FAX: [886] (7) 238-5237; and the American Trade Center, Room 3208 International Trade Building, Taipei World Trade Center, 333 Keelung Road Section 1, Taipei, Taiwan 10548, telephone: [886] (2) 2720-1550, FAX: [886] (2) 2757-7162
**Flag description:** red field with a dark blue rectangle in the upper hoist-side corner bearing a white sun with 12 triangular rays

## Economy

**Economy - overview:** Taiwan has a dynamic capitalist economy with gradually decreasing government guidance of investment and foreign trade. In keeping with this trend, some large, state-owned banks and industrial firms have been privatized. Exports have provided the primary impetus for industrialization. The island runs a large trade surplus, and its foreign reserves are among the world's largest. Recently opened cross-strait travel, transportation, and tourism links are likely to increase Taiwan and China's economic interdependence. In 2008 China overtook the US to become Taiwan's second-largest source of imports, after Japan. China is also the island's number one destination for foreign direct investment. Growth fell below 2% in 2008 because of the global slowdown.
**GDP (purchasing power parity):**
$738.8 billion (2008 est.)
$725 billion (2007)
$673.1 billion (2006)
*note:* data are in 2008 US dollars
**GDP (official exchange rate):** $401.6 billion (2008 est.)

# Taiwan (continued)

**GDP - real growth rate:**
1.9% (2008 est.)
5.7% (2007 est.)
4.8% (2006 est.)
**GDP - per capita (PPP):**
$31,900 (2008 est.)
$31,100 (2007 est.)
$29,500 (2006 est.)
*note:* data are in 2008 US dollars
**GDP - composition by sector:**
*agriculture:* 1.5%
*industry:* 27.8%
*services:* 70.7% (2008 est.)
**Labor force:** 10.85 million (2008 est.)
**Labor force - by occupation:**
*agriculture:* 5.1%
*industry:* 36.8%
*services:* 58% (2008 est.)
**Unemployment rate:**
4.1% (2008 est.)
3.9% (2007 est.)
**Population below poverty line:** 0.95% (2007 est.)
**Household income or consumption by percentage share:**
*lowest 10%:* 6.7%
*highest 10%:* 41.1% (2002 est.)
**Investment (gross fixed):** 20.9% of GDP (2008 est.)
**Budget:**
*revenues:* $50.91 billion
*expenditures:* $54.7 billion (2008 est.)
**Public debt:** 30.9% of GDP (2008 est.)
**Inflation rate (consumer prices):**
3.7% (2008 est.)
1.8% (2007 est.)
**Central bank discount rate:** 1.5% (January 2009)
**Commercial bank prime lending rate:** 4.06% (2008 est.)
**Stock of money:** $225.3 billion (November 2008)
**Stock of quasi money:** $618 billion (November 2008)
**Stock of domestic credit:** $677.8 billion (November 2008)
**Market value of publicly traded shares:** $654 billion (28 December 2007)
**Agriculture - products:** rice, corn, vegetables, fruit, tea; pigs, poultry, beef, milk; fish
**Industries:** electronics, petroleum refining, armaments, chemicals, textiles, iron and steel, machinery, cement, food processing, vehicles, consumer products, pharmaceuticals
**Industrial production growth rate:** -2% (2008 est.)
**Electricity - production:** 225.3 billion kWh (2008 est.)
**Electricity - consumption:** 233 billion kWh (2008 est.)
**Electricity - exports:** 0 kWh (2008)
**Electricity - imports:** 0 kWh (2008 est.)
**Oil - production:** 1,306 bbl/day (2007 est.)
**Oil - consumption:** 935,600 bbl/day (2007 est.)
**Oil - exports:** 340,200 bbl/day (2007)

**Oil - imports:** 660,400 bbl/day (2007)
**Oil - proved reserves:** 1.88 million bbl (2008 est.)
**Natural gas - production:** 416 million cu m (2007)
**Natural gas - consumption:** 13.6 billion cu m (2007)
**Natural gas - exports:** 0 cu m (2008 est.)
**Natural gas - imports:** 10.9 billion cu m (2007)
**Natural gas - proved reserves:** 6.229 billion cu m (1 January 2008)
**Current account balance:** $25 billion (2008 est.)
**Exports:** $255.7 billion f.o.b. (2008 est.)
**Exports - commodities:** electronics, flat panels, machinery, metals, textiles, plastics, chemicals, auto parts (2008)
**Exports - partners:** China 29.2%, US 12%, Hong Kong 9.8%, Japan 6.9%, Singapore 4.6% (2008)
**Imports:** $236 billion f.o.b. (2008 est.)
**Imports - commodities:** electronics, machinery, petroleum, precision instruments, organic chemicals, metals (2008)
**Imports - partners:** Japan 19.3%, China 13%, US 10.9%, Saudi Arabia 6.3%, South Korea 5.5% (2008)
**Reserves of foreign exchange and gold:** $296.4 billion (31 December 2008)
**Debt - external:** $109.6 billion (31 December 2008)
**Stock of direct foreign investment - at home:** $102.3 billion (2008)
**Stock of direct foreign investment - abroad:** $135.3 billion (2008)
**Exchange rates:** New Taiwan dollars (TWD) per US dollar - 31.53 (2008 est.), 32.84 (2007), 32.534 (2006), 31.71 (2005), 34.418 (2004)

## Communications

**Telephones - main lines in use:** 14.313 million (2007)
**Telephones - mobile cellular:** 24.302 million (2007)
**Telephone system:**
*general assessment:* provides telecommunications service for every business and private need
*domestic:* thoroughly modern; completely digitalized
*international:* country code - 886; numerous submarine cables provide links throughout Asia, Australia, the Middle East, Europe, and the US; satellite earth stations - 2
**Radio broadcast stations:** AM 21, FM 143, shortwave 1 (2008)
**Television broadcast stations:** 76 (5 television networks with 46 digital and 30 analog stations) (2007)
**Internet country code:** .tw
**Internet hosts:** 5.225 million (2008)
**Internet users:** 14.76 million (2007)

## Transportation

**Airports:** 41 (2008)
**Airports - with paved runways:**
*total:* 37
*over 3,047 m:* 8
*2,438 to 3,047 m:* 8
*1,524 to 2,437 m:* 11
*914 to 1,523 m:* 7
*under 914 m:* 3 (2008)

**Airports - with unpaved runways:**
*total:* 4
*1,524 to 2,437 m:* 2
*under 914 m:* 2 (2008)
**Heliports:** 4 (2007)
**Pipelines:** gas 406 km (2008)
**Railways:**
*total:* 1,588 km
*standard gauge:* 345 km 1.435-m gauge
*narrow gauge:* 1,093 km 1.067-m gauge; 150 km .762-m gauge
*note:* the 150 km of .762 gauge track belongs primarily to Taiwan Sugar Corporation and Taiwan Forestry Bureau; some to other entities (2007)
**Roadways:**
*total:* 40,262 km
*paved:* 38,171 km (includes 976 km of expressways)
*unpaved:* 2,091 km (2007)
**Merchant marine:**
*total:* 102
*by type:* bulk carrier 32, cargo 19, chemical tanker 1, container 24, passenger/cargo 3, petroleum tanker 14, refrigerated cargo 7, roll on/roll off 2
*foreign-owned:* 3 (Canada 2, France 1)
*registered in other countries:* 536 (Bolivia 1, Cambodia 1, Honduras 2, Hong Kong 11, Indonesia 2, Italy 13, Kiribati 5, Liberia 91, Marshall Islands 1, Panama 320, Philippines 1, Sierra Leone 1, Singapore 72, Thailand 1, UK 11, unknown 3) (2008)
**Ports and terminals:** Chilung (Keelung), Kaohsiung, Taichung

## Military

**Military branches:** Army, Navy (includes Marine Corps), Air Force, Coast Guard Administration, Armed Forces Reserve Command, Combined Service Forces Command, Armed Forces Police Command
**Military service age and obligation:** 19-35 years of age for male compulsory military service; service obligation 14 months (reducing to 1 year in 2009); women may enlist; women in Air Force service are restricted to noncombat roles; reserve obligation to age 30 (Army); the Ministry of Defense has announced plans to implement an incremental voluntary enlistment system beginning 2010, with 10% fewer conscripts each year thereafter, although nonvolunteers will still be required to perform alternative service or go through 3-4 months of military training (2009)
**Manpower available for military service:**
*males age 16-49:* 6,283,134
*females age 16-49:* 6,098,599 (2008 est.)
**Manpower fit for military service:**
*males age 16-49:* 5,106,730
*females age 16-49:* 5,008,563 (2009 est.)
**Manpower reaching militarily significant age annually:**
*male:* 165,738
*female:* 154,123 (2009 est.)
**Military expenditures:** 2.2% of GDP (2006)

# Taiwan (continued)

**Disputes - international:** involved in complex dispute with China, Malaysia, Philippines, Vietnam, and possibly Brunei over the Spratly Islands; the 2002 "Declaration on the Conduct of Parties in the South China Sea" has eased tensions but falls short of a legally binding "code of conduct" desired by several of the disputants; Paracel Islands are occupied by China, but claimed by Taiwan and Vietnam; in 2003, China and Taiwan became more vocal in rejecting both Japan's claims to the uninhabited islands of the Senkaku-shoto (Diaoyu Tai) and Japan's unilaterally declared exclusive economic zone in the East China Sea where all parties engage in hydrocarbon prospecting

**Illicit drugs:** regional transit point for heroin, methamphetamine, and precursor chemicals; transshipment point for drugs to Japan; major problem with domestic consumption of methamphetamine and heroin; rising problems with use of ketamine and club drugs

# European Union

## Introduction

**Preliminary statement:** The evolution of the European Union (EU) from a regional economic agreement among six neighboring states in 1951 to today's supranational organization of 27 countries across the European continent stands as an unprecedented phenomenon in the annals of history. Dynastic unions for territorial consolidation were long the norm in Europe. On a few occasions even country-level unions were arranged - the Polish-Lithuanian Commonwealth and the Austro-Hungarian Empire were examples - but for such a large number of nation-states to cede some of their sovereignty to an overarching entity is truly unique. Although the EU is not a federation in the strict sense, it is far more than a free-trade association such as ASEAN, NAFTA, or Mercosur, and it has many of the attributes associated with independent nations: its own flag, anthem, founding date, and currency, as well as an incipient common foreign and security policy in its dealings with other nations.

In the future, many of these nation-like characteristics are likely to be expanded. Thus, inclusion of basic intelligence on the EU has been deemed appropriate as a new, separate entity in The World Factbook. However, because of the EU's special status, this description is placed after the regular country entries.

**Background:** Following the two devastating World Wars in the first half of the 20th century, a number of European leaders in the late 1940s became convinced that the only way to establish a lasting peace was to unite the two chief belligerent nations - France and Germany - both economically and politically. In 1950, the French Foreign Minister Robert SCHUMAN proposed an eventual union of all Europe, the first step of which would be the integration of the coal and steel industries of Western Europe. The following year the European Coal and Steel Community (ECSC) was set up when six members, Belgium, France, West Germany, Italy, Luxembourg, and the Netherlands, signed the Treaty of Paris. The ECSC was so successful that within a few years the decision was made to integrate other parts of the

# European Union *(continued)*

countries' economies. In 1957, the Treaties of Rome created the European Economic Community (EEC) and the European Atomic Energy Community (Euratom), and the six member states undertook to eliminate trade barriers among themselves by forming a common market. In 1967, the institutions of all three communities were formally merged into the European Community (EC), creating a single Commission, a single Council of Ministers, and the European Parliament. Members of the European Parliament were initially selected by national parliaments, but in 1979 the first direct elections were undertaken and they have been held every five years since.

In 1973, the first enlargement of the EC took place with the addition of Denmark, Ireland, and the United Kingdom. The 1980s saw further membership expansion with Greece joining in 1981 and Spain and Portugal in 1986. The 1992 Treaty of Maastricht laid the basis for further forms of cooperation in foreign and defense policy, in judicial and internal affairs, and in the creation of an economic and monetary union - including a common currency. This further integration created the European Union (EU). In 1995, Austria, Finland, and Sweden joined the EU, raising the membership total to 15.

A new currency, the euro, was launched in world money markets on 1 January 1999; it became the unit of exchange for all of the EU states except the United Kingdom, Sweden, and Denmark. In 2002, citizens of the 12 euro-area countries began using the euro banknotes and coins. Ten new countries joined the EU in 2004 - Cyprus, the Czech Republic, Estonia, Hungary, Latvia, Lithuania, Malta, Poland, Slovakia, and Slovenia - and in 2007 Bulgaria and Romania joined, bringing the current membership to 27. In order to ensure that the EU can continue to function efficiently with an expanded membership, the Treaty of Nice (in force as of 1 February 2003) set forth rules streamlining the size and procedures of EU institutions. An effort to establish an EU constitution, begun in October 2004, failed to attain unanimous ratification. A new effort, undertaken in June 2007, calls for the creation of an Intergovernmental Conference to form a political agreement, known as the Reform Treaty, which is to serve as a constitution. Unlike the constitution, however, the Reform Treaty would amend existing treaties rather than replace them. In June 2008, the Irish rejected the Reform Treaty in a referendum.

## Geography

**Location:** Europe between the North Atlantic Ocean in the west and Russia, Belarus, and Ukraine to the east

**Map references:** Europe

**Area:**

*total:* 4,324,782 sq km

**Area - comparative:** less than one-half the size of the US

**Land boundaries:**

*total:* 12,440.8 km

*border countries:* Albania 282 km, Andorra 120.3 km, Belarus 1,050 km, Croatia 999 km, Holy See 3.2 km, Liechtenstein 34.9 km, Macedonia 394 km, Moldova 450 km, Monaco 4.4 km, Norway 2,348 km, Russia 2,257 km, San Marino 39 km, Serbia 945 km, Switzerland 1,811 km, Turkey 446 km, Ukraine 1,257 km

*note:* data for European Continent only

**Coastline:** 65,992.9 km

**Maritime claims:** NA

**Climate:** cold temperate; potentially subarctic in the north to temperate; mild wet winters; hot dry summers in the south

**Terrain:** fairly flat along the Baltic and Atlantic coast; mountainous in the central and southern areas

**Elevation extremes:**

*lowest point:* Lammefjord, Denmark -7 m; Zuidplaspolder, Netherlands -7 m

*highest point:* Mont Blanc 4,807 m; note - situated on the border between France and Italy

**Natural resources:** iron ore, natural gas, petroleum, coal, copper, lead, zinc, bauxite, uranium, potash, salt, hydropower, arable land, timber, fish

**Land use:**

*arable land:* NA

*permanent crops:* NA

*other:* NA

**Irrigated land:** 168,050 sq km (2003 est.)

**Natural hazards:** flooding along coasts; avalanches in mountainous area; earthquakes in the south; volcanic eruptions in Italy; periodic droughts in Spain; ice floes in the Baltic

**Environment - current issues:** NA

**Environment - international agreements:**

*party to:* Air Pollution, Air Pollution-Nitrogen Oxides, Air Pollution-Persistent Organic Pollutants, Air Pollution-Sulphur 94, Antarctic-Marine Living Resources, Biodiversity, Climate Change, Climate Change-Kyoto Protocol, Desertification, Hazardous Wastes, Law of the Sea, Ozone Layer Protection, Tropical Timber 83, Tropical Timber 94

*signed but not ratified:* Air Pollution-Volatile Organic Compounds

## People

**Population:** 491,582,852 (July 2009 est.)

**Age structure:**

*0-14 years:* 15.44% (male 38,975,981/female 36,925,704)

*15-64 years:* 67.22% (male 166,277,341/female 164,183,829)

*65 years and over:* 17.34% (male 35,372,684/female 49,847,313) (2009 est.)

**Median age:** note - see individual country entries of member states (2009 est.)

**Population growth rate:** 0.108% (2009 est.)

**Birth rate:** 9.9 births/1,000 population (2009 est.)

**Death rate:** 10.28 deaths/1,000 population (2009 est.)

**Net migration rate:** 1.46 migrant(s)/1,000 population (2009 est.)

**Sex ratio:**

*at birth:* 1.06 male(s)/female

*under 15 years:* 1.06 male(s)/female

*15-64 years:* 1 male(s)/female

*65 years and over:* 0.68 male(s)/female

*total population:* 0.92 male(s)/female (2009 est.)

**Infant mortality rate:**

*total:* 5.72 deaths/1,000 live births

*male:* 6.38 deaths/1,000 live births

*female:* 5.02 deaths/1,000 live births (2009 est.)

**Life expectancy at birth:**

*total population:* 78.67 years

*male:* 75.54 years

*female:* 81.97 years (2009 est.)

**Total fertility rate:** 1.51 children born/woman (2009 est.)

**HIV/AIDS - adult prevalence rate:** note - see individual country entries of member states

**HIV/AIDS - people living with HIV/AIDS:** note - see individual country entries of member states

**HIV/AIDS - deaths:** note - see individual country entries of member states

**Religions:** Roman Catholic, Protestant, Orthodox, Muslim, Jewish

**Languages:** Bulgarian, Czech, Danish, Dutch, English, Estonian, Finnish, French, Gaelic, German, Greek, Hungarian, Italian, Latvian, Lithuanian, Maltese, Polish, Portuguese, Romanian, Slovak, Slovene, Spanish, Swedish

*note:* only official languages are listed; German, the major language of Germany, Austria, and Switzerland, is the most widely spoken mother tongue - over 19% of the EU population; English is the most widely spoken language - about 49% of the EU population is conversant with it (2007)

## Government

**Union name:**

*conventional long form:* European Union

*abbreviation:* EU

**Political structure:** a hybrid intergovernmental and supranational organization

**Capital:**

*name:* Brussels (Belgium), Strasbourg (France), Luxembourg

*geographic coordinates:* 50 50 N, 4 20 E

*time difference:* UTC+1 (6 hours ahead of Washington, DC during Standard Time)

*daylight saving time:* +1hr, begins last Sunday in March; ends last Sunday in October

*note:* the Council of the European Union meets in Brussels, Belgium; the European Parliament meets in Brussels and Strasbourg, France; the Court of Justice of the European Communities meets in Luxembourg

**Member states:** 27 countries: Austria, Belgium, Bulgaria, Cyprus, Czech Republic, Denmark, Estonia, Finland, France, Germany, Greece, Hungary, Ireland, Italy, Latvia, Lithuania, Luxembourg, Malta, Netherlands, Poland, Portugal, Romania, Slovakia,

Slovenia, Spain, Sweden, UK; note - Canary Islands (Spain), Azores and Madeira (Portugal), French Guiana, Guadeloupe, Martinique, and Reunion (France) are sometimes listed separately even though they are legally a part of Spain, Portugal, and France; candidate countries: Croatia, Macedonia, Turkey

**Independence:** 7 February 1992 (Maastricht Treaty signed establishing the EU); 1 November 1993 (Maastricht Treaty entered into force)

**National holiday:** Europe Day 9 May (1950); note - a Union-wide holiday, the day that Robert SCHUMAN proposed the creation of the European Coal and Steel Community to achieve an organized Europe

**Constitution:** none

*note:* based on a series of treaties: the Treaty of Paris, which set up the European Coal and Steel Community (ECSC) in 1951; the Treaties of Rome, which set up the European Economic Community (EEC) and the European Atomic Energy Community (Euratom) in 1957; the Single European Act in 1986; the Treaty on European Union (Maastricht) in 1992; the Treaty of Amsterdam in 1997; and the Treaty of Nice in 2003; note - a new draft Constitutional Treaty, signed on 29 October 2004 in Rome, gave member states two years for ratification either by parliamentary vote or national referendum before it was scheduled to take effect on 1 November 2006; defeat in French and Dutch referenda in May-June 2005 dealt a severe setback to the ratification process; in June 2007, the European Council agreed on a clear and concise mandate for an Intergovernmental Conference to form a political agreement and put it into legal form; this agreement, known as the Reform Treaty, would have served as a constitution and was presented to the European Council in October 2007 for individual country ratification; it was rejected by Irish voters in June 2008, again stalling the ratification process

**Legal system:** comparable to the legal systems of member states; first supranational law system

**Suffrage:** 18 years of age; universal

**Executive branch:**

*chief of union:* President of the European Commission Jose Manuel DURAO BARROSO (since 22 November 2004)

*cabinet:* European Commission (composed of 27 members, one from each member country; each commissioner responsible for one or more policy areas)

*elections:* the president of the European Commission is designated by member governments and is confirmed by the European Parliament; working from member state recommendations, the Commission president then assembles a "college" of Commission members; the European Parliament confirms the entire Commission for a five-year term; the last confirmation process was held 18 November 2004 (next to be held in 2009)

*election results:* European Parliament approved the European Commission by a vote of 449 to 149 with 82 abstentions

*note:* the European Council brings together heads of state and government and the president of the European Commission and meets at least four times a year; its aim is to provide the impetus for the major political issues relating to European integration and to issue general policy guidelines

**Legislative branch:** two legislative bodies consisting of the Council of the European Union (27 member-state ministers having 345 votes; the number of votes is roughly proportional to member-states' population; note - the Council is the main decision-making body of the EU) and the European Parliament (736 seats; seats allocated among member states in proportion to population; members elected by direct universal suffrage for a five-year term)

*elections:* last held 4-7 June 2009 (next to be held in June 2014)

*election results:* percent of vote - EPP 35.9%, PES 21.9%, ALDE 10.9%, Greens/EFA 7.2%, UEN 4.8%, GUE/NGL 4.3%, IND/DEM 2.4%, others 12.6%; seats by party - EPP 266, PES 161, ALDE 80, Greens/EFA 53, UEN 35, GUE/NGL 32, IND/DEM 18, others 93

**Judicial branch:** Court of Justice of the European Communities (ensures that the treaties are interpreted and applied uniformly throughout the EU; resolve constitutional issues among the EU institutions) - 27 justices (one from each member state) appointed for a six-year term; note - for the sake of efficiency, the court can sit with 13 justices known as the "Grand Chamber"; Court of First Instance - 27 justices appointed for a six-year term

**Political parties and leaders:** Confederal Group of the European United Left-Nordic Green Left or GUE/NGL [Francis WURTZ]; European People's Party-European Democrats or EPP-ED [Joseph DAUL]; Group of the Alliance of Liberals and Democrats for Europe or ALDE [Graham R. WATSON]; Group of Greens/European Free Alliance or Greens/EFA [Monica FRASSONI and Daniel Marc COHN-BENDIT]; Identity, Tradition, Sovereignty Group or ITS [Bruno GOLLNISCH]; Independence/Democracy Group or IND/DEM [Hanne DAHL and Nigel FARAGE]; Socialist Group in the European Parliament or PES [Martin SCHULZ]; Union for Europe of the Nations Group or UEN [Brian CROWLEY and Cristiana MUSCARDINI]

**International organization participation:**

*European Union:* ARF (dialogue member), ASEAN (dialogue member), IDA, OAS (observer), PIF (partner), SAARC (observer), UN (observer)

*European Community:* Australian Group, CBSS, CERN, FAO, EBRD, G-10, LAIA, NSG (observer), OECD, UNRWA, WCO, WTO, ZC (observer)

*European Central Bank:* BIS

*European Investment Bank:* EBRD, WADB (nonregional member)

**Diplomatic representation in the US:**

*chief of mission:* Ambassador John BRUTON

*chancery:* 2300 M Street, NW, Washington, DC 20037

*telephone:* [1] (202) 862-9500

*FAX:* [1] (202) 429-1766

**Diplomatic representation from the US:**

*chief of mission:* Ambassador (vacant); Charge d'Affaires Christopher MURRAY

*embassy:* 13 Zinnerstraat/Rue Zinner, B-1000 Brussels

*mailing address:* same as above

*telephone:* [32] (2) 508-2111

*FAX:* [32] (2) 508-2063

**Flag description:** blue field with 12 five-pointed gold stars arranged in a circle in the center, representing the union of the peoples of Europe; the number of stars is fixed

## Economy

**Economy - overview:** Internally, the EU is attempting to lower trade barriers, adopt a common currency, and move toward convergence of living standards. Internationally, the EU aims to bolster Europe's trade position and its political and economic power. Because of the great differences in per capita income among member states (from $7,000 to $69,000) and historic national animosities, the EU faces difficulties in devising and enforcing common policies. For example, since 2003 Germany and France have flouted the member states' treaty obligation to prevent their national budgets from running more than a 3% deficit. Between 2004 and 2007, the EU admitted 12 countries that are, in general, less advanced technologically and economically than the other 15. Eleven established EU member states introduced the euro as their common currency on 1 January 1999 (Greece did so two years later), but the UK, Sweden, and Denmark chose not to participate. Of the 12 most recent member states, only Slovenia (1 January 2007) and Cyprus and Malta (1 January 2008) have adopted the euro; the remaining nine are legally required to adopt the currency upon meeting EU's fiscal and monetary convergence criteria.

**GDP (purchasing power parity):**

$14.82 trillion (2008 est.)

$14.66 trillion (2007)

$14.34 trillion (2006)

*note:* data are in 2008 US dollars

**GDP (official exchange rate):** $18.85 trillion (2008 est.)

**GDP - real growth rate:**

1% (2008 est.)

3% (2007 est.)

3.3% (2006 est.)

**GDP - per capita (PPP):**

$33,400 (2008 est.)

$33,400 (2007 est.)

$32,600 (2006 est.)

*note:* data are in 2008 US dollars

**GDP - composition by sector:**

*agriculture:* 2%

*industry:* 26.8%

*services:* 71.1% (2008 est.)

**Labor force:** 224.8 million (2008 est.)

# European Union *(continued)*

**Labor force - by occupation:**
*agriculture:* 5.6%
*industry:* 27.7%
*services:* 66.7%
*note:* the remainder is in miscellaneous public and private sector industries and services (2007 est.)
**Unemployment rate:**
7.5% (2008 est.)
8.5% (2006 est.)
**Population below poverty line:** note - see individual country entries of member states
**Household income or consumption by percentage share:**
*lowest 10%:* 2.8%
*highest 10%:* 25.2% (2001 est.)
**Distribution of family income - Gini index:** 31 (2005 est.)
**Investment (gross fixed):** 21% of GDP (2008 est.)
**Inflation rate (consumer prices):**
3% (2008 est.)
1.8% (2006 est.)
**Central bank discount rate:** 4%
*note:* this is the European Central Bank's rate on the marginal lending facility, which offers overnight credit to banks in the euro area (31 December 2008)
**Commercial bank prime lending rate:** 8.03% (31 December 2007)
**Stock of money:** $5.679 trillion
*note:* this is the quantity of money, M1, for the euro area, converted into US dollars at the exchange rate for the date indicated; it excludes the stock of money carried by non-euro-area members of the European Union (31 December 2008)
**Stock of quasi money:** $11.38 trillion
*note:* this is the quantity of quasi money, M2, for the euro area, converted into US dollars at the exchange rate for the date indicated; it excludes the stock of quasi money carried by non-euro-area members of the European Union (31 December 2008)
**Stock of domestic credit:** $20.94 trillion
*note:* this figure refers to the euro area only; it excludes credit data for non-euro-area members of the EU (31 December 2007)
**Market value of publicly traded shares:** $14.37 trillion (31 December 2008 est.)
**Agriculture - products:** wheat, barley, oilseeds, sugar beets, wine, grapes; dairy products, cattle, sheep, pigs, poultry; fish
**Industries:** among the world's largest and most technologically advanced, the EU industrial base includes: ferrous and non-ferrous metal production and processing, metal products, petroleum, coal, cement, chemicals, pharmaceuticals, aerospace, rail transportation equipment, passenger and commercial vehicles, construction equipment, industrial equipment, shipbuilding, electrical power equipment, machine tools and automated manufacturing systems, electronics and telecommunications equipment, fishing, food and beverage processing, furniture, paper, textiles, tourism

**Industrial production growth rate:** -0.4% (2008 est.)
**Electricity - production:** 3.103 trillion kWh (2007 est.)
**Electricity - consumption:** 2.926 trillion kWh (2007 est.)
**Electricity - exports:** NA kWh
**Electricity - imports:** NA kWh
**Oil - production:** 2.676 million bbl/day (2007 est.)
**Oil - consumption:** 14.38 million bbl/day (2007 est.)
**Oil - exports:** 2.196 million bbl/day (2007 est.)
**Oil - imports:** 8.613 million bbl/day (2007 est.)
**Oil - proved reserves:** 6.146 billion bbl (1 January 2008)
**Natural gas - production:** 197.8 billion cu m (2007 est.)
**Natural gas - consumption:** 497.3 billion cu m (2007 est.)
**Natural gas - exports:** NA cu m
**Natural gas - imports:** NA cu m
**Natural gas - proved reserves:** 2.476 trillion cu m (1 January 2008 est.)
**Current account balance:** $51.4 billion (2008 est.)
**Exports:** $1.952 trillion; note - external exports, excluding intra-EU trade (2007)
**Exports - commodities:** machinery, motor vehicles, aircraft, plastics, pharmaceuticals and other chemicals, fuels, iron and steel, nonferrous metals, wood pulp and paper products, textiles, meat, dairy products, fish, alcoholic beverages.
**Imports:** $1.69 trillion f.o.b.; note - external imports, excluding intra-EU trade (2007)
**Imports - commodities:** machinery, vehicles, aircraft, plastics, crude oil, chemicals, textiles, metals, foodstuffs, clothing
**Reserves of foreign exchange and gold:** $NA
**Exchange rates:** euros per US dollar - 0.6827 (2008 est.), 0.7345 (2007), 0.7964 (2006), 0.8041 (2005), 0.8054 (2004)

## Communications

**Telephones - main lines in use:** 238 million (2005)
**Telephones - mobile cellular:** 466 million (2005)
**Telephone system:** note - see individual country entries of member states
**Radio broadcast stations:** AM 930, FM 13,655, shortwave 71 (1998); note - sum of individual country radio broadcast stations; there is also a European-wide station (Euroradio)
**Television broadcast stations:** 2,700 (1995); note - sum of individual country television broadcast stations excluding repeaters; there is also a European-wide station (Eurovision)
**Internet country code:** .eu; note - see country entries of member states for individual country codes
**Internet hosts:** 31,693 (2008); note - this sum reflects the number of internet hosts assigned the .eu internet country code
**Internet users:** 247 million (2006)

## Transportation

**Airports:** 3,127 3,393 (2008)
**Airports - with paved runways:**
*total:* 1,642
*over 3,047 m:* 107
*2,438 to 3,047 m:* 316
*1,524 to 2,437 m:* 518
*914 to 1,523 m:* 424
*under 914 m:* 277 (2008)
**Airports - with unpaved runways:**
*total:* 1,285
*over 3,047 m:* 3
*2,438 to 3,047 m:* 3
*1,524 to 2,437 m:* 27
*914 to 1,523 m:* 243
*under 914 m:* 1,009 (2008)
**Heliports:** 100 (2007)
**Railways:**
*total:* 236,436 km
*broad gauge:* 28,250 km
*standard gauge:* 200,401 km
*narrow gauge:* 7,771 km
*other:* 23 km (2007)
**Roadways:**
*total:* 5,454,446 km (2008)
**Waterways:** 52,332 km (2006)
**Ports and terminals:** Antwerp (Belgium), Barcelona (Spain), Braila (Romania), Bremen (Germany), Burgas (Bulgaria), Constanta (Romania), Copenhagen (Denmark), Galati (Romania), Gdansk (Poland), Hamburg (Germany), Helsinki (Finland), Las Palmas (Canary Islands, Spain), Le Havre (France), Lisbon (Portugal), London (UK), Marseille (France), Naples (Italy), Peiraiefs or Piraeus (Greece), Riga (Latvia), Rotterdam (Netherlands), Stockholm (Sweden), Talinn (Estonia), Tulcea (Romania), Varna (Bulgaria)

## Military

**Military - note:** the five-nation Eurocorps - created in 1992 by France, Germany, Belgium, Spain, and Luxembourg - has deployed troops and police on peacekeeping missions to Bosnia-Herzegovina, Macedonia, and the Democratic Republic of the Congo and assumed command of the ISAF in Afghanistan in August 2004; Eurocorps directly commands the 5,000-man Franco-German Brigade, the Multinational Command Support Brigade, and EUFOR in Bosnia and Herzegovina; in November 2004, the EU Council of Ministers formally committed to creating 13 1,500-man battle groups by the end of 2007, to respond to international crises on a rotating basis; 22 of the EU's 27 nations have agreed to supply troops; France, Italy, and the UK formed the first of three battle groups in 2005; Norway, Sweden, Estonia, and Finland established the Nordic Battle Group effective 1 January 2008; nine other groups are to be formed; a rapid-reaction naval EU Maritime Task Group was stood up in March 2007 (2007)

## Transnational Issues

**Disputes - international:** as a political union, the EU has no border disputes with neighboring countries, but Estonia has no land boundary agreements with Russia, Slovenia disputes its land and maritime boundaries with Croatia, and Spain has territorial and maritime disputes with Morocco and with the UK over Gibraltar; the EU has set up a Schengen area - consisting of 22 EU member states that have signed the convention implementing the Schengen agreements or "acquis" (1985 and 1990) on the free movement of persons and the harmonization of border controls in Europe; these agreements became incorporated into EU law with the implementation of the 1997 Treaty of Amsterdam on 1 May 1999; in addition, non-EU states Iceland and Norway (as part of the Nordic Union) have been included in the Schengen area since 1996 (full members in 2001), and Switzerland since 2008 bringing the total current membership to 25; the UK (since 2000) and Ireland (since 2002) take part in only some aspects of the Schengen area, especially with respect to police and criminal matters; nine of the 12 new member states that joined the EU since 2004 joined Schengen on 21 December 2007; of the three remaining EU states, Cyprus is expected to join by 2009, while Romania and Bulgaria continue to enhance their border security systems

# Appendix A:

## Abbreviations

## Appendix A: Abbreviations *(continued)*

| | | |
|---|---|---|
| | BGN | United States Board on Geographic Names |
| | BIS | Bank for International Settlements |
| | BSEC | Black Sea Economic Cooperation Zone |
| **C** | C | Commonwealth |
| | c.i.f. | cost, insurance, and freight |
| | CACM | Central American Common Market |
| | CAEU | Council of Arab Economic Unity |
| | CAN | Andean Community of Nations |
| | Caricom | Caribbean Community and Common Market |
| | CB | citizen's band mobile radio communications |
| | CBSS | Council of the Baltic Sea States |
| | CCC | Customs Cooperation Council |
| | CDB | Caribbean Development Bank |
| | CE | Council of Europe |
| | CEI | Central European Initiative |
| | CEMAC | Economic and Monetary Community of Central Africa |
| | CEPGL | Economic Community of the Great Lakes Countries |
| | CERN | European Organization for Nuclear Research |
| | CEPT | Conference Europeanne des Poste et Telecommunications |
| | CIS | Commonwealth of Independent States |
| | CITES | see Endangered Species |
| | Climate Change | United Nations Framework Convention on Climate Change |
| | Climate Change-Kyoto Protocol | Kyoto Protocol to the United Nations Framework Convention on Climate Change |
| | COCOM | Coordinating Committee on Export Controls |
| | Comsat | Communications Satellite Corporation |
| | COMESA | Common Market for Eastern and Southern Africa |
| | CTBTO | Preparation commission for the Nuclear-Ban-Treaty Operation |
| | CY | calendar year |
| | CP | Colombo Plan |
| **D** | DC | developed country |
| | Desertification | United Nations Convention to Combat Desertification in Those Countries Experiencing Serious Drought and/or Desertification, Particularly in Africa |
| | DDT | dichloro-diphenyl-trichloro-ethane |
| | DIA | United States Defense Intelligence Agency |
| | DSN | Defense Switched Network |
| | DST | daylight savings time |
| | DWT | deadweight ton |
| **E** | EADB | East African Development Bank |
| | EAEC | Eurasian Economic Community |
| | EAPC | Euro-Atlantic Partnership Council |
| | EBRD | European Bank for Reconstruction and Development |
| | EC | European Community |

| | |
|---|---|
| ECA | Economic Commission for Africa |
| ECE | Economic Commission for Europe |
| ECLAC | Economic Commission for Latin America and the Caribbean |
| ECO | Economic Cooperation Organization |
| ECOSOC | Economic and Social Council |
| ECOWAS | Economic Community of West African States |
| ECSC | European Coal and Steel Community |
| EEC | European Economic Community |
| EFTA | European Free Trade Association |
| EEZ | exclusive economic zone |
| EIB | European Investment Bank |
| EMU | European Monetary Union |
| Endangered Species | Convention on the International Trade in Endangered Species of Wild Flora and Fauna (CITES) |
| Entente | Council of the Entente |
| Environmental Modification | Convention on the Prohibition of Military or Any Other Hostile Use of Environmental Modification Techniques |
| ESA | European Space Agency |
| ESCAP | Economic and Social Commission for Asia and the Pacific |
| ESCWA | Economic and Social Commission for Western Asia |
| est. | estimate |
| EU | European Union |
| Euratom | European Atomic Energy Community |
| Eutelsat | European Telecommunications Satellite Organization |
| Ex-Im | Export-Import Bank of the United States |
| f.o.b. | free on board |
| FAO | Food and Agriculture Organization |
| FAX | facsimile |
| FLS | Front Line States |
| FOC | flags of convenience |
| FSU | former Soviet Union |
| FY | fiscal year |
| FZ | Franc Zone |
| G-2 | Group of 2 |
| G-3 | Group of 3 |
| G-5 | Group of 5 |
| G-6 | Group of 6 |
| G-7 | Group of 7 |
| G-8 | Group of 8 |
| G-9 | Group of 9 |
| G-10 | Group of 10 |
| G-15 | Group of 15 |
| G-11 | Group of 11 |
| G-24 | Group of 24 |
| G-77 | Group of 77 |

F

G

## Appendix A: Abbreviations *(continued)*

| | |
|---|---|
| GATT | General Agreement on Tariffs and Trade; now WTO |
| GCC | Gulf Cooperation Council |
| GDP | gross domestic product |
| GMT | Greenwich Mean Time |
| GNP | gross national product |
| GRT | gross register ton |
| GSM | global system for mobile cellular communications |
| GUAM | Organization for Democracy and Economic Development; acronym for member states - Georgia, Ukraine, Azerbaijan, Moldova |
| GWP | gross world product |
| Hazardous Wastes | Basel Convention on the Control of Transboundary Movements of Hazardous Wastes and Their Disposal |
| HF | high-frequency |
| HIV/AIDS | human immunodeficiency virus/acquired immune deficiency syndrome |
| IADB | Inter-American Development Bank |
| IAEA | International Atomic Energy Agency |
| IANA | Internet Assigned Numbers Authority |
| IBRD | International Bank for Reconstruction and Development (World Bank) |
| ICAO | International Civil Aviation Organization |
| ICC | International Chamber of Commerce |
| ICCt | International Criminal Court |
| ICJ | International Court of Justice (World Court) |
| ICRC | International Committee of the Red Cross |
| ICRM | International Red Cross and Red Crescent Movement |
| ICSID | International Center for Secretariat of Investment Disputes |
| ICTR | International Criminal Tribunal for Rwanda |
| ICTY | International Criminal Tribunal for the former Yugoslavia |
| IDA | International Development Association |
| IDB | Islamic Development Bank |
| IDP | Internally Displaced Person |
| IEA | International Energy Agency |
| IFAD | International Fund for Agricultural Development |
| IFC | International Finance Corporation |
| IFRCS | International Federation of Red Cross and Red Crescent Societies |
| IGAD | Inter-Governmental Authority on Development |
| IHO | International Hydrographic Organization |
| ILO | International Labor Organization |
| IMF | International Monetary Fund |
| IMO | International Maritime Organization |
| Inmarsat | International Maritime Satellite Organization |
| InOC | Indian Ocean Commission |
| INSTRAW | International Research and Training Institute for the Advancement of Women |
| Intelsat | International Telecommunications Satellite Organization |

H

I

## Appendix A: Abbreviations *(continued)*

| | | |
|---|---|---|
| | Interpol | International Criminal Police Organization |
| | Intersputnik | International Organization of Space Communications |
| | IOC | International Olympic Committee |
| | IOM | International Organization for Migration |
| | IPU | Inter-parliamentary Union |
| | ISO | International Organization for Standardization |
| | ISP | Internet Service Provider |
| | ITU | International Telecommunication Union |
| | ITUC | International Trade Union Confederation, the successor to ICFTU (International Confederation of Free Trade Unions) and the WCL (World Confederation of Labor) |
| K | kHz | kilohertz |
| | km | kilometer |
| | kW | kilowatt |
| | kWh | kilowatt-hour |
| L | LAES | Latin American Economic System |
| | LAIA | Latin American Integration Association |
| | LAS | League of Arab States |
| | Law of the Sea | United Nations Convention on the Law of the Sea (LOS) |
| | LDC | less developed country |
| | LLDC | least developed country |
| | London Convention | see Marine Dumping |
| | LOS | see Law of the Sea |
| M | m | meter |
| | Marecs | Maritime European Communications Satellite |
| | Marine Dumping | Convention on the Prevention of Marine Pollution by Dumping Wastes and Other Matter |
| | Marine Life Conservation | Convention on Fishing and Conservation of Living Resources of the High Seas |
| | MARPOL | see Ship Pollution |
| | Medarabtel | Middle East Telecommunications Project of the International Telecommunications Union |
| | Mercosur | Southern Cone Common Market |
| | MHz | megahertz |
| | MICAH | International Civilian Support Mission in Haiti |
| | MINURSO | United Nations Mission for the Referendum in Western Sahara |
| | MIGA | Multilateral Investment Geographic Agency |
| | MINUSTAH | United Nations Stabilization Mission in Haiti |
| | MONUC | United Nations Organization Mission in the Democratic Republic of the Congo |
| N | NA | not available |
| | NAFTA | North American Free Trade Agreement |
| | NAM | Nonaligned Movement |
| | NATO | North Atlantic Treaty Organization |
| | NC | Nordic Council |
| | NEA | Nuclear Energy Agency |
| | NEGL | negligible |

| | |
|---|---|
| NGA | National Geospatial-Intelligence Agency |
| NIB | Nordic Investment Bank |
| NIC | newly industrializing country |
| NIE | newly industrializing economy |
| NIS | new independent states |
| nm | nautical mile |
| NMT | Nordic Mobile Telephone |
| NSG | Nuclear Suppliers Group |
| Nuclear Test Ban | Treaty Banning Nuclear Weapons Tests in the Atmosphere, in Outer Space, and Under Water |
| NZ | New Zealand |

**O**

| | |
|---|---|
| OAPEC | Organization of Arab Petroleum Exporting Countries |
| OAS | Organization of American States |
| OAU | Organization of African Unity; see African Union |
| ODA | official development assistance |
| OECD | Organization for Economic Cooperation and Development |
| OECS | Organization of Eastern Caribbean States |
| OHCHR | Office of the United Nations High Commissioner for Human Rights |
| OIC | Organization of the Islamic Conference |
| OIF | International Organization of the French-speaking World |
| ONUB | United Nations Operation in Burundi |
| OOF | other official flows |
| OPANAL | Agency for the Prohibition of Nuclear Weapons in Latin America and the Caribbean |
| OPCW | Organization for the Prohibition of Chemical Weapons |
| OPEC | Organization of Petroleum Exporting Countries |
| OSCE | Organization for Security and Cooperation in Europe |
| Ozone Layer Protection | Montreal Protocol on Substances That Deplete the Ozone Layer |

**P**

| | |
|---|---|
| PCA | Permanent Court of Arbitration |
| PFP | Partnership for Peace |
| PIF | Pacific Islands Forum |
| PPP | purchasing power parity |

**R**

| | |
|---|---|
| Ramsar | see Wetlands |
| RG | Rio Group |

**S**

| | |
|---|---|
| SAARC | South Asian Association for Regional Cooperation |
| SACU | Southern African Customs Union |
| SACEP | South Asia Co-operative Environment Programme |
| SADC | Southern African Development Community |
| SCO | Shanghai Cooperation Organization |
| SAFE | South African Far East Cable |
| SECI | Southeast European Cooperative Initiative |
| SHF | super-high-frequency |
| Ship Pollution | Protocol of 1978 Relating to the International Convention for the Prevention of Pollution From Ships, 1973 (MARPOL) |

## Appendix A: Abbreviations *(continued)*

|  |  |
|---|---|
| Sparteca | South Pacific Regional Trade and Economic Cooperation Agreement |
| SPC | Secretariat of the Pacific Communities |
| SPF | South Pacific Forum |
| sq km | square kilometer |
| sq mi | square mile |
| TAT | Trans-Atlantic Telephone |
| Tropical Timber 83 | International Tropical Timber Agreement, 1983 |
| Tropical Timber 94 | International Tropical Timber Agreement, 1994 |
| UAE | United Arab Emirates |
| UDEAC | Central African Customs and Economic Union |
| UHF | ultra-high-frequency |
| UK | United Kingdom |
| UN | United Nations |
| UNAMSIL | United Nations Mission in Sierra Leone |
| UNCLOS | United Nations Convention on the Law of the Sea, also known as LOS |
| UNCTAD | United Nations Conference on Trade and Development |
| UNDCP | United Nations Drug Control Program |
| UNDOF | United Nations Disengagement Observer Force |
| UNDP | United Nations Development Program |
| UNEP | United Nations Environment Program |
| UNESCO | United Nations Educational, Scientific, and Cultural Organization |
| UNFICYP | United Nations Peacekeeping Force in Cyprus |
| UNFPA | United Nations Population Fund |
| UNHCR | United Nations High Commissioner for Refugees |
| UNICEF | United Nations Children's Fund |
| UNICRI | United Nations Interregional Crime and Justice Research Institute |
| UNIDIR | United Nations Institute for Disarmament Research |
| UNIDO | United Nations Industrial Development Organization |
| UNIFIL | United Nations Interim Force in Lebanon |
| UNITAR | United Nations Institute for Training and Research |
| UNMEE | United Nations Mission in Ethiopia and Eritrea |
| UNMIK | United Nations Interim Administration Mission in Kosovo |
| UNMIL | United Nations Mission in Liberia |
| UNMIT | United Nations Integrated Mission in Timor-Leste |
| UNMOGIP | United Nations Military Observer Group in India and Pakistan |
| UNMOVIC | United Nations Monitoring, Verification, and Inspection Commission |
| UNOCI | United Nations Operation in Cote d'Ivoire |
| UNOMIG | United Nations Observer Mission in Georgia |
| UNOPS | United Nations Office of Project Services |
| UNRISD | United Nations Research Institute for Social Development |
| UNRWA | United Nations Relief and Works Agency for Palestine Refugees in the Near East |
| UNSC | United Nations Security Council |
| UNSSC | Untied Nations System Staff College |
| UNTSO | United Nations Truce Supervision Organization |

The letters **T** and **U** appear in the left margin marking the alphabetical sections.

| | | |
|---|---|---|
| | UNU | United Nations University |
| | UNWTO | World Tourism Organization |
| | UPU | Universal Postal Union |
| | US | United States |
| | USSR | Union of Soviet Socialist Republics (Soviet Union); used for information dated before 25 December 1991 |
| | UTC | Coordinated Universal Time |
| | UV | ultra violet |
| V | VHF | very-high-frequency |
| | VSAT | very small aperture terminal |
| W | WADB | West African Development Bank |
| | WAEMU | West African Economic and Monetary Union |
| | WCL | World Confederation of Labor |
| | WCO | World Customs Organization |
| | Wetlands | Convention on Wetlands of International Importance Especially As Waterfowl Habitat |
| | WEU | Western European Union |
| | WFP | World Food Program |
| | WFTU | World Federation of Trade Unions |
| | Whaling | International Convention for the Regulation of Whaling |
| | WHO | World Health Organization |
| | WIPO | World Intellectual Property Organization |
| | WMO | World Meteorological Organization |
| | WP | Warsaw Pact |
| | WTO | World Trade Organization |
| Z | ZC | Zangger Committee |

# Appendix B:

## International Organizations and Groups

Complete descriptions of all the international organizations and groups listed below may now be found in the online Factbook at: (**https://www.cia.gov/library/publications/the-world-factbook/appendix/appendix-b.html**). These descriptions include information on the aim(s) of the various organizations, the date they were established, when they became effective, and a list of the member nations, as well as any possible observer countries or organizations.

| Organization/Group | Organization/Group | Organization/Group |
| --- | --- | --- |
| advanced developing countries | Bay of Bengal Iniative for Multisectoral Technical and Economic Cooperation (BIMSTEC) | Communist countries |
| advanced economies | Bank for International Settlements (BIS) | Coordinating Committee on Export Controls (COCOM) |
| African Development Bank (AfDB) | Benelux Economic Union (Benelux) | Council for Mutual Economic Assistance (CEMA) |
| African Union (AU) | Big Seven | Council of Arab Economic Unity (CAEU) |
| African, Caribbean, and Pacific Group of States (ACP Group) | Black Sea Economic Cooperation Zone (BSEC) | Council of Europe (CE) |
| Agency for the Prohibition of Nuclear Weapons in Latin America (OPANAL) | Caribbean Community and Common Market (Caricom) | Council of the Baltic Sea States (CBSS) |
| Andean Community of Nations (CAN) | Caribbean Development Bank (CDB) | Council of the Entente (Entente) |
| Arab Bank for Economic Development in Africa (ABEDA) | Central African Customs and Economic Union (UDEAC) | countries in transition |
| Arab Fund for Economic and Social Development (AFESD) | Central African States Development Bank (BDEAC) | Customs Cooperation Council (CCC) |
| Arab Maghreb Union (AMU) | Central American Bank for Economic Integration (BCIE) | developed countries (DCs) |
| Arab Monetary Fund (AMF) | Central American Common Market (CACM) | developing countries |
| Arctic Council | Central European Initiative (CEI) | East African Development Bank (EADB) |
| ASEAN Regional Forum (ARF) | centrally planned economies | East Asia Summit (EAS) |
| Asian Development Bank (ADB) | Colombo Plan (CP) | Economic and Monetary Community of Central Africa (CEMAC) |
| Asia-Pacific Economic Cooperation (APEC) | Common Market for Eastern and Southern Africa (COMESA) | Economic and Monetary Union (EMU) |
| Association of Southeast Asian Nations (ASEAN) | Commonwealth (C) | Economic and Social Council (ECOSOC) |
| Australia Group (AG) | Commonwealth of Independent States (CIS) | Economic Community of the Great Lakes Countries (CEPGL) |
| Australia-New Zealand-United States Security Treaty (ANZUS) | | Economic Community of West African States (ECOWAS) |
| Baltic Assembly (BA) | | Economic Cooperation Organization (ECO) |
| | | Euro-Atlantic Partnership Council (EAPC) |

| Organization/Group | Organization/Group | Organization/Group |
|---|---|---|
| Eurasian Economic Community (EAEC) | Group of 11 (G-11) | International Energy Agency (IEA) |
| European Bank for Reconstruction and Development (EBRD) | Group of 15 (G-15) | International Federation of Red Cross and Red Crescent Societies (IFRCS) |
| European Community (or European Communities, EC) | Group of 24 (G-24) | International Finance Corporation (IFC) |
| European Free Trade Association (EFTA) | Group of 77 (G-77) | International Fund for Agricultural Development (IFAD) |
| European Investment Bank (EIB) | Gulf Cooperation Council (GCC) | International Hydrographic Organization (IHO) |
| European Organization for Nuclear Research (CERN) | Organization for Democracy and Economic Development (GUAM) | International Labor Organization (ILO) |
| European Space Agency (ESA) | high income countries | International Maritime Organization (IMO) |
| European Union (EU) | Indian Ocean Commission (InOC) | International Monetary Fund (IMF) |
| First World | industrial countries | International Olympic Committee (IOC) |
| Food and Agriculture Organization (FAO) | Inter-American Development Bank (IADB) | International Organization for Migration (IOM) |
| former Soviet Union (FSU) | Inter-Governmental Authority on Development (IGAD) | International Organization for Standardization (ISO) |
| former USSR/Eastern Europe (former USSR/EE) | Inter-Parliamentary Union (IPU) | International Organization of the French-speaking World (OIF) |
| Four Dragons | International Atomic Energy Agency (IAEA) | International Red Cross and Red Crescent Movement (ICRM) |
| Franc Zone (FZ) | International Bank for Reconstruction and Development (IBRD) | International Telecommunication Union (ITU) |
| Front Line States (FLS) | International Chamber of Commerce (ICC) | International Trade Union Confederation (ITUC) |
| General Agreement on Tariffs and Trade (GATT) | International Civil Aviation Organization (ICAO) | Islamic Development Bank (IDB) |
| Group of 2 (G-2) | International Civilian Support Mission in Haiti (MICAH) | Latin American Economic System (LAES) |
| Group of 3 (G-3) | International Committee of the Red Cross (ICRC) | Latin American Integration Association (LAIA) |
| Group of 5 (G-5) | International Court of Justice (ICJ) | League of Arab States (LAS) |
| Group of 6 (G-6) | International Criminal Court (ICCt) | least developed countries (LLDCs) |
| Group of 7 (G-7) | International Criminal Police Organization (Interpol) | less developed countries (LDCs) |
| Group of 8 (G-8) | International Development Association (IDA) | |
| Group of 9 (G-9) | | |
| Group of 10 (G-10) | | |

| Organization/Group | Organization/Group | Organization/Group |
|---|---|---|
| low-income countries | Organization of the Islamic Conference (OIC) | Third World |
| middle-income countries | Pacific Community (SPC) | underdeveloped countries |
| Multilateral Investment Guarantee Agency (MIGA) | Pacific Islands Forum (PIF) | undeveloped countries |
| Near Abroad | Paris Club | United Nations (UN) |
| new independent states (NIS) | Partnership for Peace (PFP) | United Nations Children's Fund (UNICEF) |
| newly industrializing countries (NICs) | Permanent Court of Arbitration (PCA) | United Nations Conference on Trade and Development (UNCTAD) |
| newly industrializing economies (NIEs) | Rio Group (RG) | United Nations Development Program (UNDP) |
| Nonaligned Movement (NAM) | Second World | United Nations Disengagement Observer Force (UNDOF) |
| Nordic Council (NC) | Secretariat of the Pacific Communities (SPC) | United Nations Educational, Scientific, and Cultural Organization (UNESCO) |
| Nordic Investment Bank (NIB) | Shanghai Cooperation Organization (SCO) | United Nations Environment Program (UNEP) |
| North | socialist countries | United Nations General Assembly |
| North American Free Trade Agreement (NAFTA) | South | United Nations High Commissioner for Refugees (UNHCR) |
| North Atlantic Treaty Organization (NATO) | South American Community of Nations (CSN) | United Nations Industrial Development Organization (UNIDO) |
| Nuclear Energy Agency (NEA) | South Asia Co-operative Environment Program (SACEP) | United Nations Institute for Training and Research (UNITAR) |
| Nuclear Suppliers Group (NSG) | South Asian Association for Regional Cooperation (SAARC) | United Nations Interim Administration Mission in Kosovo (UNMIK) |
| Organization for Economic Cooperation and Development (OECD) | South Pacific Forum (SPF) | United Nations Interim Force in Lebanon (UNIFIL) |
| Organization for Security and Cooperation in Europe (OSCE) | South Pacific Regional Trade and Economic Cooperation Agreement (Sparteca) | United Nations Military Observer Group in India and Pakistan (UNMOGIP) |
| Organization for the Prohibition of Chemical Weapons (OPCW) | Southeast European Cooperative Initiative (SECI) | United Nations Mission for the Referendum in Western Sahara (MINURSO) |
| Organization of African Unity (OAU) | Southern African Customs Union (SACU) | United Nations Mission in Ethiopia and Eritrea (UNMEE) |
| Organization of American States (OAS) | Southern African Development Community (SADC) | |
| Organization of Arab Petroleum Exporting Countries (OAPEC) | Southern Cone Common Market (Mercosur) or Southern Common Market | |
| Organization of Eastern Caribbean States (OECS) | | |
| Organization of Petroleum Exporting Countries (OPEC) | | |

## Appendix B: International Organizations and Groups *(continued)*

| Organization/Group | Organization/Group | Organization/Group |
|---|---|---|
| United Nations Mission in Liberia (UNMIL) | United Nations Population Fund (UNFPA) | West African Economic and Monetary Union (WAEMU) |
| United Nations Mission in Sierra Leone (UNAMSIL) | United Nations Relief and Works Agency for Palestine Refugees in the Near East (UNRWA) | Western European Union (WEU) |
| United Nations Mission in the Sudan (UNMIS) | United Nations Research Institute for Social Development (UNRISD) | World Bank Group |
| United Nations Mission of Support in East Timor (UNMISET) | United Nations Secretariat | World Confederation of Labor (WCL) |
| United Nations Monitoring, Verification, and Inspection Commission (UNMOVIC) | United Nations Security Council (UNSC) | World Customs Organization (WCO) |
| United Nations Operation in Burundi (ONUB) | United Nations Stabilization Mission in Haiti (MINUSTAH) | World Federation of Trade Unions (WFTU) |
| United Nations Observer Mission in Georgia (UNOMIG) | United Nations Truce Supervision Organization (UNTSO) | World Food Program (WFP) |
| United Nations Organization Mission in the Democratic Republic of the Congo (MONUC) | United Nations Trusteeship Council | World Health Organization (WHO) |
| United Nations Operation in Cote d'Ivoire (UNOCI) | United Nations University (UNU) | World Intellectual Property Organization (WIPO) |
| United Nations Peace-keeping Force in Cyprus (UNFICYP) | Universal Postal Union (UPU) | World Meteorological Organization (WMO) |
| | Warsaw Pact (WP) | World Tourism Organization (UNWTO) |
| | West African Development Bank (WADB) | World Trade Organization (WTO) |
| | | Zangger Committee (ZC) |

# Appendix C:

## Selected International Environmental Agreements

Complete descriptions of all the major international environmental agreements listed below may now be found in the online Factbook at: (**https://www.cia.gov/cia/publications/factbook/appendix/appendix-c.html**). These descriptions include information on the objective(s) of the various agreements, when they were opened for signature, the date they went into force, and a list of the countries party to the agreements, as well as those that have signed but not yet ratified them.

| Agreement | Short Form Designation |
| --- | --- |
| **Antarctic Treaty** | |
| **Basel Convention on the Control of Transboundary Movements of Hazardous Wastes and Their Disposal** | Hazardous Wastes |
| **Convention for the Conservation of Antarctic Seals** | Antarctic Seals |
| **Convention on Biological Diversity** | Biodiversity |
| **Convention on Fishing and Conservation of Living Resources of the High Seas** | Marine Life Conservation |
| **Convention on Long-Range Transboundary Air Pollution** | Air Pollution |
| **Convention on the Conservation of Antarctic Marine Living Resources** | Antarctic-Marine Living Resources |
| **Convention on the International Trade in Endangered Species of Wild Flora and Fauna (CITES)** | Endangered Species |
| **Convention on the Prevention of Marine Pollution by Dumping Wastes and Other Matter (London Convention)** | Marine Dumping |
| **Convention on the Prohibition of Military or Any Other Hostile Use of Environmental Modification Techniques** | Environmental Modification |
| **Convention on Wetlands of International Importance Especially as Waterfowl Habitat (Ramsar)** | Wetlands |
| **International Convention for the Regulation of Whaling** | Whaling |
| **International Tropical Timber Agreement, 1983** | Tropical Timber 83 |
| **International Tropical Timber Agreement, 1994** | Tropical Timber 94 |
| **Kyoto Protocol to the United Nations Framework Convention on Climate Change** | Climate Change-Kyoto Protocol |
| **Montreal Protocol on Substances That Deplete the Ozone Layer** | Ozone Layer Protection |
| **Protocol of 1978 Relating to the International Convention for the Prevention of Pollution From Ships, 1973 (MARPOL)** | Ship Pollution |
| **Protocol on Environmental Protection to the Antarctic Treaty** | Antarctic-Environmental Protocol |
| **Protocol to the 1979 Convention on Long-Range Transboundary Air Pollution Concerning the Control of Emissions of Nitrogen Oxides or Their Transboundary Fluxes** | Air Pollution-Nitrogen Oxides |
| **Protocol to the 1979 Convention on Long-Range Transboundary Air Pollution Concerning the Control of Emissions of Volatile Organic Compounds or Their Transboundary Fluxes** | Air Pollution-Volatile Organic Compounds |

# Appendix C: Selected International Environmental Agreements *(continued)*

| Agreement (Continued) | Short Form Designation |
|---|---|
| Protocol to the 1979 Convention on Long-Range Transboundary Air Pollution on Further Reduction of Sulphur Emissions | Air Pollution-Sulphur 94 |
| Protocol to the 1979 Convention on Long-Range Transboundary Air Pollution on Persistent Organic Pollutants | Air Pollution-Persistent Organic Pollutants |
| Protocol to the 1979 Convention on Long-Range Transboundary Air Pollution on the Reduction of Sulphur Emissions or Their Transboundary Fluxes by at Least 30% | Air Pollution-Sulphur 85 |
| Treaty Banning Nuclear Weapon Tests in the Atmosphere, in Outer Space, and Under Water | Nuclear Test Ban |
| United Nations Convention on the Law of the Sea (LOS) | Law of the Sea |
| United Nations Convention to Combat Desertification in Those Countries Experiencing Serious Drought and/or Desertification, Particularly in Africa | Desertification |
| United Nations Framework Convention on Climate Change | Climate Change |

# Appendix D:

## Cross-Reference List of Country Data Codes

| FIPS 10: | Countries, Dependencies, Areas of Special Sovereignty, and Their Principal Administrative Divisions (FIPS 10) is maintained by the Office of Targeting and Transnational Issues, National Geospatial-Intelligence Agency, and published by the National Institute of Standards and Technology (Department of Commerce). FIPS 10 codes are intended for general use throughout the US Government, especially in activities associated with the mission of the Department of State and national defense programs. |
|---|---|
| ISO 3166: | Codes for the Representation of Names of Countries (ISO 3166) is prepared by the International Organization for Standardization. ISO 3166 includes two- and three-character alphabetic codes and three-digit numeric codes that may be needed for activities involving exchange of data with international organizations that have adopted that standard. |
| Internet: | The Internet country code is the two-letter digraph maintained by the International Organization for Standardization (ISO) in the ISO 3166 Alpha-2 list and used by the Internet Assigned Numbers Authority (IANA) to establish country-coded top-level domains (ccTLDs). |

| Entity | FIPS 10-4 | ISO 3166 | | | Internet | Comments |
|---|---|---|---|---|---|---|
| Afghanistan | AF | AF | AFG | 004 | .af | |
| Albania | AL | AL | ALB | 008 | .al | |
| Algeria | AG | DZ | DZA | 012 | .dz | |
| American Samoa | AQ | AS | ASM | 016 | .as | |
| Andorra | AN | AD | AND | 020 | .ad | |
| Angola | AO | AO | AG | 024 | .ao | |
| Anguilla | AV | AI | AIA | 660 | .ai | |
| Antarctica | AY | AQ | ATA | 010 | .aq | ISO defines as the territory south of 60 degrees south latitude |
| Antigua and Barbuda | AC | AG | ATG | 028 | .ag | |
| Argentina | AR | AR | ARG | 032 | .ar | |
| Armenia | AM | AM | ARM | 051 | .am | |
| Aruba | AA | AW | AB | 533 | .aw | |
| Ashmore and Cartier Islands | AT | — | — | — | — | ISO includes with Australia |
| Australia | AS | AU | AUS | 036 | .au | ISO includes Ashmore and Cartier Islands, Coral Sea Islands |
| Austria | AU | AT | AUT | 040 | .at | |
| Azerbaijan | AJ | AZ | AZE | 031 | .az | |
| Bahamas, The | BF | BS | BHS | 044 | .bs | |
| Bahrain | BA | BH | BHR | 048 | .bh | |
| Baker Island | FQ | — | — | — | — | ISO includes with the US Minor Outlying Islands |
| Bangladesh | BG | BD | BGD | 050 | .bd | |
| Barbados | BB | BB | BRB | 052 | .bb | |
| Bassas da India | BS | — | — | — | — | administered as part of French Southern and Antarctic Lands; no ISO codes assigned |
| Belarus | BO | BY | BLR | 112 | .by | |
| Belgium | BE | BE | BEL | 056 | .be | |
| Belize | BH | BZ | BLZ | 084 | .bz | |
| Benin | BN | BJ | BEN | 204 | .bj | |
| Bermuda | BD | BM | BMU | 060 | .bm | |

# Appendix D: Cross-Reference List of Country Data Codes *(continued)*

| Entity | FIPS 10-4 | ISO 3166 | | | Internet | Comment |
|---|---|---|---|---|---|---|
| Bhutan | BT | BT | BTN | 064 | .bt | |
| Bolivia | BL | BO | BOL | 068 | .bo | |
| Bosnia and Herzegovina | BK | BA | BIH | 070 | .ba | |
| Botswana | BC | BW | BW | 072 | .bw | |
| Bouvet Island | BV | BV | BVT | 074 | .bv | |
| Brazil | BR | BR | BRA | 076 | .br | |
| British Indian Ocean Territory | IO | IO | IOT | 086 | .io | |
| British Virgin Islands | VI | VG | VGB | 092 | .vg | |
| Brunei | BX | BN | BRN | 096 | .bn | |
| Bulgaria | BU | BG | BGR | 100 | .bg | |
| Burkina Faso | UV | BF | BFA | 854 | .bf | |
| Burma | BM | MM | MMR | 104 | .mm | ISO uses the name Myanmar |
| Burundi | BY | BI | BDI | 108 | .bi | |
| Cambodia | CB | KH | KHM | 116 | .kh | |
| Cameroon | CM | CM | CMR | 120 | .cm | |
| Canada | CA | CA | CAN | 124 | .ca | |
| Cape Verde | CV | CV | CPV | 132 | .cv | |
| Cayman Islands | CJ | KY | CYM | 136 | .ky | |
| Central African Republic | CT | CF | CAF | 140 | .cf | |
| Chad | CD | TD | TCD | 148 | .td | |
| Chile | CI | CL | CHL | 152 | .cl | |
| China | CH | CN | CHN | 156 | .cn | see also Taiwan |
| Christmas Island | KT | CX | CXR | 162 | .cx | |
| Clipperton Island | IP | — | — | — | — | ISO includes with French Polynesia |
| Cocos (Keeling) Islands | CK | CC | CCK | 166 | .cc | |
| Colombia | CO | CO | COL | 170 | .co | |
| Comoros | CN | KM | COM | 174 | .km | |
| Congo, Democratic Republic of the | CG | CD | COD | 180 | .cd | formerly Zaire |
| Congo, Republic of the | CF | CG | COG | 178 | .cg | |
| Cook Islands | CW | CK | COK | 184 | .ck | |
| Coral Sea Islands | CR | — | — | — | — | ISO includes with Australia |
| Costa Rica | CS | CR | CRI | 188 | .cr | |
| Cote d'Ivoire | IV | CI | CIV | 384 | .ci | |
| Croatia | HR | HR | HRV | 191 | .hr | |
| Cuba | CU | CU | CUB | 192 | .cu | |
| Cyprus | CY | CY | CYP | 196 | .cy | |
| Czech Republic | EZ | CZ | CZE | 203 | .cz | |
| Denmark | DA | DK | DNK | 208 | .dk | |
| Djibouti | DJ | DJ | DJI | 262 | .dj | |
| Dominica | DO | DM | DMA | 212 | .dm | |
| Dominican Republic | DR | DO | DOM | 214 | .do | |

# Appendix D: Cross-Reference List of Country Data Codes *(continued)*

| Entity | FIPS 10-4 | ISO 3166 | | | Internet | Comment |
|---|---|---|---|---|---|---|
| East Timor | TT | TL | TLS | 626 | .tl | |
| Ecuador | EC | EC | ECU | 218 | .ec | |
| Egypt | EG | EG | EGY | 818 | .eg | |
| El Salvador | ES | SV | SLV | 222 | .sv | |
| Equatorial Guinea | EK | GQ | GNQ | 226 | .gq | |
| Eritrea | ER | ER | ERI | 232 | .er | |
| Estonia | EN | EE | EST | 233 | .ee | |
| Ethiopia | ET | ET | ETH | 231 | .et | |
| Europa Island | EU | — | — | — | — | administered as part of French Southern and Antarctic Lands; no ISO codes assigned |
| Falkland Islands (Islas Malvinas) | FK | FK | FLK | 238 | .fk | |
| Faroe Islands | FO | FO | FRO | 234 | .fo | |
| Fiji | FJ | FJ | FJI | 242 | .fj | |
| Finland | FI | FI | FIN | 246 | .fi | |
| France | FR | FR | FRA | 250 | .fr | |
| France, Metropolitan | — | FX | FXX | 249 | .fx | ISO limits to the European part of France, excluding French Guiana, French Polynesia, French Southern and Antarctic Lands, Guadeloupe, Martinique, Mayotte, New Caledonia, Reunion, Saint Pierre and Miquelon, Wallis and Futuna |
| French Guiana | FG | GF | GUF | 254 | .gf | |
| French Polynesia | FP | PF | PYF | 258 | .pf | ISO includes Clipperton Island |
| French Southern and Antarctic Lands | FS | TF | ATF | 260 | .tf | FIPS 10-4 does not include the French-claimed portion of Antarctica (Terre Adelie) |
| Gabon | GB | GA | GAB | 266 | .ga | |
| Gambia, The | GA | GM | GMB | 270 | .gm | |
| Gaza Strip | GZ | PS | PSE | 275 | .ps | ISO identifies as Occupied Palestinian Territory |
| Georgia | GG | GE | GEO | 268 | .ge | |
| Germany | GM | DE | DEU | 276 | .de | |
| Ghana | GH | GH | GHA | 288 | .gh | |
| Gibraltar | GI | GI | GIB | 292 | .gi | |
| Glorioso Islands | GO | — | — | — | — | administered as part of French Southern and Antarctic Lands; no ISO codes assigned |
| Greece | GR | GR | GRC | 300 | .gr | |
| Greenland | GL | GL | GRL | 304 | .gl | |
| Grenada | GJ | GD | GRD | 308 | .gd | |
| Guadeloupe | GP | GP | GLP | 312 | .gp | |
| Guam | GQ | GU | GUM | 316 | .gu | |
| Guatemala | GT | GT | GTM | 320 | .gt | |
| Guernsey | GK | GG | GG | 831 | .gg | |

## Appendix D: Cross-Reference List of Country Data Codes *(continued)*

| Entity | FIPS 10-4 | ISO 3166 | | | Internet | Comment |
|---|---|---|---|---|---|---|
| Guinea | GV | GN | GIN | 324 | .gn | |
| Guinea-Bissau | PU | GW | GNB | 624 | .gw | |
| Guyana | GY | GY | GUY | 328 | .gy | |
| Haiti | HA | HT | HTI | 332 | .ht | |
| Heard Island and McDonald Islands | HM | HM | HMD | 334 | .hm | |
| Holy See (Vatican City) | VT | VA | VAT | 336 | .va | |
| Honduras | HO | HN | HND | 340 | .hn | |
| Hong Kong | HK | HK | HKG | 344 | .hk | |
| Howland Island | HQ | — | — | — | — | ISO includes with the US Minor Outlying Islands |
| Hungary | HU | HU | HUN | 348 | .hu | |
| Iceland | IC | IS | ISL | 352 | .is | |
| India | IN | IN | IND | 356 | .in | |
| Indonesia | ID | ID | IDN | 360 | .id | |
| Iran | IR | IR | IRN | 364 | .ir | |
| Iraq | IZ | IQ | IRQ | 368 | .iq | |
| Ireland | EI | IE | IRL | 372 | .ie | |
| Isle of Man | IM | IM | IMN | 833 | .im | |
| Israel | IS | IL | ISR | 376 | .il | |
| Italy | IT | IT | ITA | 380 | .it | |
| Jamaica | JM | JM | JAM | 388 | .jm | |
| Jan Mayen | JN | — | — | — | — | ISO includes with Svalbard |
| Japan | JA | JP | JPN | 392 | .jp | |
| Jarvis Island | DQ | — | — | — | — | ISO includes with the US Minor Outlying Islands |
| Jersey | JE | JE | JEY | 832 | .je | |
| Johnston Atoll | JQ | — | — | — | — | ISO includes with the US Minor Outlying Islands |
| Jordan | JO | JO | JOR | 400 | .jo | |
| Juan de Nova Island | JU | — | — | — | — | administered as part of French Southern and Antarctic Lands; no ISO codes assigned |
| Kazakhstan | KZ | KZ | KAZ | 398 | .kz | |
| Kenya | KE | KE | KEN | 404 | .ke | |
| Kingman Reef | KQ | — | — | — | — | ISO includes with the US Minor Outlying Islands |
| Kiribati | KR | KI | KIR | 296 | .ki | |
| Korea, North | KN | KP | PRK | 408 | .kp | |
| Korea, South | KS | KR | KOR | 410 | .kr | |
| Kuwait | KU | KW | KWT | 414 | .kw | |
| Kyrgyzstan | KG | KG | KGZ | 417 | .kg | |
| Laos | LA | LA | LAO | 418 | .la | |
| Latvia | LG | LV | LVA | 428 | .lv | |
| Lebanon | LE | LB | LBN | 422 | .lb | |

# Appendix D: Cross-Reference List of Country Data Codes *(continued)*

| Entity | FIPS 10-4 | ISO 3166 | | | Internet | Comment |
|---|---|---|---|---|---|---|
| Lesotho | LT | LS | LSO | 426 | .ls | |
| Liberia | LI | LR | LBR | 430 | .lr | |
| Libya | LY | LY | LBY | 434 | .ly | |
| Liechtenstein | LS | LI | LIE | 438 | .li | |
| Lithuania | LH | LT | LTU | 440 | .lt | |
| Luxembourg | LU | LU | LUX | 442 | .lu | |
| Macau | MC | MO | MAC | 446 | .mo | |
| Macedonia | MK | MK | MKD | 807 | .mk | |
| Madagascar | MA | MG | MDG | 450 | .mg | |
| Malawi | MI | MW | MWI | 454 | .mw | |
| Malaysia | MY | MY | MYS | 458 | .my | |
| Maldives | MV | MV | MDV | 462 | .mv | |
| Mali | ML | ML | MLI | 466 | .ml | |
| Malta | MT | MT | MLT | 470 | .mt | |
| Marshall Islands | RM | MH | MHL | 584 | .mh | |
| Martinique | MB | MQ | MTQ | 474 | .mq | |
| Mauritania | MR | MR | MRT | 478 | .mr | |
| Mauritius | MP | MU | MUS | 480 | .mu | |
| Mayotte | MF | YT | MYT | 175 | .yt | |
| Mexico | MX | MX | MEX | 484 | .mx | |
| Micronesia, Federated States of | FM | FM | FSM | 583 | .fm | |
| Midway Islands | MQ | — | — | — | — | ISO includes with the US Minor Outlying Islands |
| Moldova | MD | MD | MDA | 498 | .md | |
| Monaco | MN | MC | MCO | 492 | .mc | |
| Mongolia | MG | MN | MNG | 496 | .mn | |
| Montenegro | MJ | ME | MNE | 499 | .me | |
| Montserrat | MH | MS | MSR | 500 | .ms | |
| Morocco | MO | MA | MAR | 504 | .ma | |
| Mozambique | MZ | MZ | MOZ | 508 | .mz | |
| Myanmar | — | — | — | — | — | see Burma |
| Namibia | WA | NA | NAM | 516 | .na | |
| Nauru | NR | NR | NRU | 520 | .nr | |
| Navassa Island | BQ | — | — | — | — | ISO includes with the US Minor Outlying Islands |
| Nepal | NP | NP | NPL | 524 | .np | |
| Netherlands | NL | NL | NLD | 528 | .nl | |
| Netherlands Antilles | NT | AN | ANT | 530 | .an | |
| New Caledonia | NC | NC | NCL | 540 | .nc | |
| New Zealand | NZ | NZ | NZL | 554 | .nz | |
| Nicaragua | NU | NI | NIC | 558 | .ni | |
| Niger | NG | NE | NER | 562 | .ne | |

# Appendix D: Cross-Reference List of Country Data Codes *(continued)*

| Entity | FIPS 10-4 | ISO 3166 | | | Internet | Comment |
|--------|-----------|------|------|------|----------|---------|
| Nigeria | NI | NG | NGA | 566 | .ng | |
| Niue | NE | NU | NIU | 570 | .nu | |
| Norfolk Island | NF | NF | NFK | 574 | .nf | |
| Northern Mariana Islands | CQ | MP | MNP | 580 | .mp | |
| Norway | NO | NO | NOR | 578 | .no | |
| Oman | MU | OM | OMN | 512 | .om | |
| Pakistan | PK | PK | PAK | 586 | .pk | |
| Palau | PS | PW | PLW | 585 | .pw | |
| Palmyra Atoll | LQ | — | — | — | — | ISO includes with the US Minor Outlying Islands |
| Panama | PM | PA | PAN | 591 | .pa | |
| Papua New Guinea | PP | PG | PNG | 598 | .pg | |
| Paracel Islands | PF | — | — | — | — | |
| Paraguay | PA | PY | PRY | 600 | .py | |
| Peru | PE | PE | PER | 604 | .pe | |
| Philippines | RP | PH | PHL | 608 | .ph | |
| Pitcairn Islands | PC | PN | PCN | 612 | .pn | |
| Poland | PL | PL | POL | 616 | .pl | |
| Portugal | PO | PT | PRT | 620 | .pt | |
| Puerto Rico | RQ | PR | PRI | 630 | .pr | |
| Qatar | QA | QA | QAT | 634 | .qa | |
| Reunion | RE | RE | REU | 638 | .re | |
| Romania | RO | RO | ROU | 642 | .ro | |
| Russia | RS | RU | RUS | 643 | .ru | |
| Rwanda | RW | RW | RW | 646 | .rw | |
| Saint Helena | SH | SH | SHN | 654 | .sh | |
| Saint Kitts and Nevis | SC | KN | KNA | 659 | .kn | |
| Saint Lucia | ST | LC | LCA | 662 | .lc | |
| Saint Pierre and Miquelon | SB | PM | SPM | 666 | .pm | |
| Saint Vincent and the Grenadines | VC | VC | VCT | 670 | .vc | |
| Samoa | WS | WS | WS | 882 | .ws | |
| San Marino | SM | SM | SMR | 674 | .sm | |
| Sao Tome and Principe | TP | ST | STP | 678 | .st | |
| Saudi Arabia | SA | SA | SAU | 682 | .sa | |
| Senegal | SG | SN | SEN | 686 | .sn | |
| Serbia | RB | RS | SRB | 688 | .rs | |
| Seychelles | SE | SC | SYC | 690 | .sc | |
| Sierra Leone | SL | SL | SLE | 694 | .sl | |
| Singapore | SN | SG | SGP | 702 | .sg | |
| Slovakia | LO | SK | SVK | 703 | .sk | |
| Slovenia | SI | SI | SVN | 705 | .si | |
| Solomon Islands | BP | SB | SLB | 090 | .sb | |

# Appendix D: Cross-Reference List of Country Data Codes *(continued)*

| Entity | FIPS 10-4 | ISO 3166 | | | Internet | Comment |
|---|---|---|---|---|---|---|
| Somalia | SO | SO | SOM | 706 | .so | |
| South Africa | SF | ZA | ZAF | 710 | .za | |
| South Georgia and the Islands | SX | GS | SGS | 239 | .gs | |
| Spain | SP | ES | ESP | 724 | .es | |
| Spratly Islands | PG | — | — | — | — | |
| Sri Lanka | CE | LK | LKA | 144 | .lk | |
| Sudan | SU | SD | SDN | 736 | .sd | |
| Suriname | NS | SR | SUR | 740 | .sr | |
| Svalbard | SV | SJ | SJM | 744 | .sj | ISO includes Jan Mayen |
| Swaziland | WZ | SZ | SW | 748 | .sz | |
| Sweden | SW | SE | SWE | 752 | .se | |
| Switzerland | SZ | CH | CHE | 756 | .ch | |
| Syria | SY | SY | SYR | 760 | .sy | |
| Taiwan | TW | TW | TWN | 158 | .tw | |
| Tajikistan | TI | TJ | TJK | 762 | .tj | |
| Tanzania | TZ | TZ | TZA | 834 | .tz | |
| Thailand | TH | TH | THA | 764 | .th | |
| Togo | TO | TG | TGO | 768 | .tg | |
| Tokelau | TL | TK | TKL | 772 | .tk | |
| Tonga | TN | TO | TON | 776 | .to | |
| Trinidad and Tobago | TD | TT | TTO | 780 | .tt | |
| Tromelin Island | TE | — | — | — | — | administered as part of French Southern and Antarctic Lands; no ISO codes assigned |
| Tunisia | TS | TN | TUN | 788 | .tn | |
| Turkey | TU | TR | TUR | 792 | .tr | |
| Turkmenistan | TX | TM | TKM | 795 | .tm | |
| Turks and Caicos Islands | TK | TC | TCA | 796 | .tc | |
| Tuvalu | TV | TV | TUV | 798 | .tv | |
| Uganda | UG | UG | UGA | 800 | .ug | |
| Ukraine | UP | UA | UKR | 804 | .ua | |
| United Arab Emirates | AE | AE | ARE | 784 | .ae | |
| United Kingdom | UK | GB | GBR | 826 | .uk | |
| United States | US | US | USA | 840 | .us | |
| United States Minor Outlying Islands | — | UM | UMI | 581 | .um | ISO includes Baker Island, Howland Island, Jarvis Island, Johnston Atoll, Kingman Reef, Midway Islands, Navassa Island, Palmyra Atoll, Wake Island |
| Uruguay | UY | UY | URY | 858 | .uy | |
| Uzbekistan | UZ | UZ | UZB | 860 | .uz | |
| Vanuatu | NH | VU | VUT | 548 | .vu | |
| Venezuela | VE | VE | VEN | 862 | .ve | |
| Vietnam | VM | VN | VNM | 704 | .vn | |

# Appendix D: Cross-Reference List of Country Data Codes *(continued)*

| Entity | FIPS 10-4 | ISO 3166 | | | Internet | Comment |
|---|---|---|---|---|---|---|
| Virgin Islands | VQ | VI | VIR | 850 | .vi | |
| Virgin Islands (UK) | — | — | — | — | .vg | see British Virgin Islands |
| Virgin Islands (US) | — | — | — | — | .vi | see Virgin Islands |
| Wake Island | WQ | — | — | — | — | ISO includes with the US Minor Outlying Islands |
| Wallis and Futuna | WF | WF | WLF | 876 | .wf | |
| West Bank | WE | PS | PSE | 275 | .ps | ISO identifies as Occupied Palestinian Territory |
| Western Sahara | WI | EH | ESH | 732 | .eh | |
| Western Samoa | — | — | — | — | ws | see Samoa |
| World | — | — | — | — | — | the *Factbook* uses the W data code from *DIAM 65-18 Geopolitical Data Elements and Related Features, Data Standard No. 3*, December 1994, published by the Defense Intelligence Agency |
| Yemen | YM | YE | YEM | 887 | .ye | |
| Zaire | — | — | — | — | — | see Democratic Republic of the Congo |
| Zambia | ZA | ZM | ZMB | 894 | .zm | |
| Zimbabwe | ZI | ZW | ZWE | 716 | .zw | |

# Appendix E:

## Cross-Reference List of Hydrographic Data Codes

| | |
|---|---|
| **IHO 23 4TH:** | *Limits of Oceans and Seas*, Special Publication 23, Draft 4th Edition 1986, published by the International Hydrographic Bureau of the International Hydrographic Organization; note - this document has not yet been ratified and only the 3rd Edition (1953) remains in force |
| **IHO 23 3RD:** | *Limits of Oceans and Seas*, Special Publication 23, 3rd Edition 1953, published by the International Hydrographic Organization |
| **ACIC M 49 1:** | *Chart of Limits of Seas and Oceans*, revised January 1958, published by the Aeronautical Chart and Information Center (ACIC), United States Air Force; note - ACIC is now part of the National Geospatial-Intelligence Agency (NGA) |
| **DIAM 65 18:** | *Geopolitical Data Elements and Related Features*, Data Standard No.4, Defense Ingtelligence Agency Manual 65-18, December 1994, published by the Defense Intellegence Agency |
| | The US Government has not yet adopted a standard for hydrographic codes similar to the Federal Information Processing Standards (FIPS) 10-4 country codes. The names and limits of the following oceans and seas are not always directly comparable because of differences in the customers, needs, and requirements of the individual organizations. Even the number of principal water bodies varies from organization to organization. *Factbook* users, for example, find the Atlantic Ocean and Pacific Ocean entries useful, but none of the following standards include those oceans in their entirety. Nor is there any provision for combining codes or overcodes to aggregate water bodies. The recently delimited Southern Ocean is not included. |

**Principal Oceans and Seas of the World**
**With Hydrographic Codes by Institution**

| | IHO 23-4th | IHO* 23-3rd | ACIC M 49-1 | DIAM |
|---|---|---|---|---|
| Arctic Ocean | 9 | 17 | A | 5A |
| Atlantic Ocean | — | — | — | — |
| North Atlantic Ocean | 1 | 23 | B | 1A |
| South Atlantic Ocean | 4 | 32 | C | 2A |
| Baltic Sea | 2 | 1 | B26 | 7B |
| Indian Ocean | 5 | 45 | F | 6A |
| Mediterranean Sea | 3.1 | 28 | B11 | — |
| Eastern Mediterranean | 3.1.2 | 28 B | — | 8E |
| Western Mediterranean | 3.1.1 | 28 A | — | 8W |
| Pacific Ocean | — | — | — | — |
| North Pacific Ocean | 7 | 57 | D | 3A |
| South Pacific Ocean | 8 | 61 | E | 4A |
| South China and Eastern Archipelagic Seas | 6 | 49, 48 | D18 plus others | 3U plus others |

* The letters after the numbers are subdivisions, not footnotes.

# Appendix F:

## Cross-Reference List of Geographic Names

---

The Cross-Reference List of Geographic Names may now be found in the online *Factbook* at: (**https://www.cia.gov/library/publications/the-world-factbook/appendix/appendix-f.html**). This appendix cross-references a wide variety of geographic names to the appropriate *Factbook* "country" entry and also includes additional geographic information in parentheses.

---

# Appendix G:

## Weights and Measures

The comprehensive listing of weights, measures, and conversions that ran as an appendix in *The World Factbook* from 1983 to 2000 has been restored in the online *Factbook* at: (**https://www.cia.gov/library/publications/the-world-factbook/appendix/appendix-g.html**). The appendix includes information on mathematical notation and metric interrelationships, as well as over 400 examples of conversion factors. Included in the latter are not only instances of common conversions such as how to determine meters from feet or gallons from liters, but also obscure conversions such as grains to pennyweights or cables to fathoms.